ROUTES IN UPPER BURMA

ROUTES

IN

UPPER BURMA

INCLUDING

THE CHIN HILLS AND SHAN STATES,

TO WHICH ARB ADDED

A NUMBER OF ROUTES LEADING FROM LOWER BURMA

AND SIAM INTO THOSE DISTRICTS.

COMPILED FOR

THE QUARTERMASTER·GENERAL OF THE MADRAS ARMY

BY

MAJOR A. B. FENTON,

COMMA NDANT, 2 ND MADRAS LANCERS (LATE DEPUTY ASSISTA.NT
QUARTERMASTER-GENERAL FOB INTELLIGENCE) BURMA).

(IN TWO VOLUMES)

VOLUME I

GYAN

ISBN : 978-81-212-1474-2(Set)

ISBN : 978-81-212-1475-9

Published, 2018

Published by

Gyan Publishing House
5, Ansari Road
Daryaganj, New Delhi-110002
Phone: 011-47034999, 9811692060
www.gyanbooks.com
E-mail: books@gyanbooks.com

Printed at: G. Print Process, Delhi.

PREFACE.

Eight years having elapsed since the occupation of Upper Burma, it has been considered desirable to collate the large mass of route material that has been collecting in the Burma Intelligence Office during that period into book form, both to prevent the loss of material already collected and to ensure its proper correction up to date, from time to time, as opportunity offers.

In the compilation of this work every available source of information has been taken advantage of up to the date each section has gone to press, and further information received subsequently has been added up to the latest possible date in the appendices.

Owing to the fact that for a long time there was no very special form adhered to in the transliteration of Burmese, and especially of Shan, names, so much so that even now the same name, though apparently a simple one, is found spelt in several different ways in the same route, even by the most practised officers of the Intelligence Department, it is evident that there must be many instances of incorrect spelling and accentuation in this work, but every endeavour has been made to adopt a uniform and, as nearly as possible, the Hunterian method of spelling. This issue of the work must, however, necessarily be considered merely a preliminary one, and it is hoped that its publication even in this imperfect form is the surest way to the production of a reliable and useful book of reference.

Communications are therefore invited from all officers and others in a position to point out mistakes or to supply additional information.

Quartermaster-General's Office,
Ootacamund, 1*st June* 1894.

CONTENTS.

VOLUME-I

PART I.

ROUTES IN THE NORTHERN (CIVIL) DIVISION.

PART II.

ROUTES IN THE CENTRAL (CIVIL) DIVISION.

PART III.

ROUTES IN THE CHIN HILLS DIVISION.

PART IV.

ROUTES IN THE EASTERN (CIVIL) DIVISION.

PART V.

ROUTES IN THE SOUTHERN (CIVIL) DIVISION.

VOLUME–II

PART VI.

ROUTES IN THE SHAN HILLS DIVISION.

PART VII.

ROUTES IN THE LOWER BURMA DIVISION.

APPENDIX I.

ADDITIONAL ROUTES IN NORTHERN DIVISION.

APPENDIX II.

ADDITIONAL ROUTES IN THE SHAN HILLS DIVISION.

APPENDIX III.

ROUTES IN SIAM.

APPENDIX IV.

ADDITIONAL ROUTES IN SOUTHERN (CIVIL) DIVISION.

APPENDIX V.

ADDITIONAL ROUTES IN CENTRAL (CIVIL) DIVISION.

PART I.

ROUTES IN THE NORTHERN (CIVIL) DIVISION.

No. 1.

From ATAN (KAUKKWÉ VALLEY) to BHAMO viâ NAMSHA and KAUNGSIN.

BY E. P. CLONEY, ESQ., BURMA COMMISSION, 1891-92.

Authorities.		Number and Names of Stages, Rivers and Streams.	Distances.		Remarks.
Military.	Civil.		Intermediate.	Total.	
			M. F.	M. F.	
G.O.C. Mandalay District and O.C. Bhamo.	Commissioner, Northern Division and Deputy Commissioner, Bhamo.	**1. Namsha** ... Sanpyeng, Singgat, Kwaikong, and Namsan Kong streams.	**14 0**	14 0	Road goes from Atan in the Kaukkwé valley in an easterly direction, rising gradually for ¼ mile and then along the level jungle ; open road along old taungya site. Leaving Pau ché (½ mile) the road runs to the south-east along almost a level hillside for a ¼ mile, passes well of the village of Pau ché, then turns east and ascends a bit, goes on for about ¾ mile along fairly level ridge—jungle on both sides thick—then commences a long descent about ¾ mile in an eastern direction, crosses the stream (about 1 foot good running water) and goes on for another ¼ mile. Here road branches ; the one to the right leads to Man-aw, the other to the left leads to Naung or Nong-aw. Taking the road to the right one ascends for about ½ mile in a south-west direction, then along level for ¼ mile in an eastern direction. Jungle open, and after crossing a few taungya sites road runs through a little jungle and comes out on the village graveyard. Road is good all the way. Distance 3½ miles. Man-aw itself has not a sufficient water-supply for more than a few men. Later on one would be obliged to encamp somewhere near the Sanpyeng Ka or in some other site in a ravine wherever water is to be found. Road leaving village goes west a short distance, then gradually descends in a south-west direction for about 1 mile and crosses the bed of the chaung ; a little muddy ; no water. Road then goes on the edge of the hill in same direction for about another mile, and gradually descending for a ¼ mile crosses at the junction of the two streams—Sanpyeng Ka and Kwaikong Ka. Up to here jungle dense ; goes west through bed of stream for about 100 feet and then turns south and ascends the hill. Ascent for ½ mile ; pretty stiff jungle bush and large tree. Path narrow and runs along a level ridge for about 2 miles ; jungle open ; bamboos and big trees. Descends gradually for ½ mile and

No. 1.

FROM ATAN (KAUKKWÉ VALLEY) TO BHAMO *viâ* NAMSHA, &c.—*continued.*

Authorities.		Number and Names of Stages, Rivers and Streams.	Distances.		Remarks.
Military.	Civil.		Intermediate.	Total.	
G.O.C. Mandalay District and O.C. Bhamo.	Commissioner, Northern Division and Deputy Commissioner, Bhamo.	**1. Namsha**—*cont.*			crosses the Namsan Kong; plenty of good water. Turning to the right again path goes through bed of stream a short way and again ascends another hill. Ascent is about ¼ mile only, but it is stiffer than the pass. Thick jungle on both sides of the path while ascending. On reaching the top of the hill path runs along a level ridge with open jungle for about 1 mile. Here road branches. The path to the right leads to the small village of Kushé (under Man-aw Sawbwa). The village cannot be seen, but it is only ¼ mile off. The path going straight ahead leads to Kushé, the Lakun village. This road runs along the edge of the hill for about a ¼ mile, then over the level ridge for about 1¾ miles; jungle open. Here sacrificial altars (not sins) of the village of Kushé (Lakun ¼ off) are seen. If the path straight ahead is followed it leads to the village. The path that turns right round and goes down the hill (west) is the road to the Nampaung stream. Kushé itself has a scanty supply of water. The path to the left east runs along the edge of the hill. It is quite level for ¼ mile; the path again branches. The one to the left leads to the Lakun south side village Kong-ra. Following the main path for about ½ mile the path from Kong-ra village meets it again. The path here turns a bit south and runs along a ridge for about ¼ mile. It comes out again on a level ridge—an old taungya site—runs along this level the whole way for about 1¼ miles in an easterly direction. Near Namsha village itself there is a short ascent; jungle all the way; fairly open; water about ½ mile off. Namsha has a small well, but this suffices for the inhabitants only. Distance 14 miles.
		2. Mosit chaung camp. Namsa Kong, Leiksin and a few smaller streams.	M. F. **11 4**	M. F. 25 4	Leaving Namsha road runs in a south-east direction along the ridge and, descending gradually, comes into the plains after 2¾ miles. About ½ mile further path divides, the one to the right leading to Mosit Going on still in same direction for 1 mile crosses a hillock; ground rutty. Then after 1 mile in a north-east direction road crosses the Namsa Kong chaung. After crossing stream goes on for ½ mile, and here the disused road from Pawpon meets the main road. About 400 yards on Leiksin chaung is crossed. Road then continues through teak, bamboos and grass jungle. Road again takes a south-east direction and crosses bed of a small stream after ½ mile. For another ½ mile road goes in a north-east direction; jungle, teak; open; goes on in a south-east direction for 1 mile and crosses the dry bed of a stream. In this ¼ mile road ascends and descends over rising ground and frequently crosses another small stream (shallow) after 1½ miles going. After 1½ miles nearly this stream is met again and is crossed. A ¾ mile further a path to the left is seen, this leads to Pomshi; going on still in a south-east direction about ¾ mile the Mosit chaung is struck and here we camped; jungle open; road fair the whole way. Distance 11½ miles.

FROM ATAN (KAUKKWÉ VALLEY) TO BHAMO *viâ* NAMSHA, &c.—*continued.*

Authorities. Military.	Authorities. Civil.	Number and Names of Stages, Rivers and Streams.	Distances. Inter-mediate.	Distances. Total.	Remarks.
G.O.C. Mandalay District and O.C. Bhamo.	Commissioner, Northern Division and Deputy Commissioner, Bhamo.	**3. Sinténgpôn** ... Mosit chaung, Séngsông, Singgat, Indaung, Lakat, Namténg or Lwaiténg and Lakra streams.	M. F. **10 6**	M. F. 36 2	Crossing the stream at the spot where the depth is about 1 foot, road runs out in a southerly direction, and after ¾ mile crosses bed of a dry stream. From this stream to the Séngsông Ka road goes for ¾ mile over broken ground, crosses this, and continuing in the same south direction, after 2 miles crosses the dry bed of a pretty big stream. Quarter mile further on a small stream with very little water is crossed; going on in the same direction for 1¼ miles the Indaung chaung (with plenty of water) is crossed. Road goes through this stream for about 200 yards, and continuing in same south direction for 1¾ miles the Lakat Ka (with plenty of water) is crossed. Here an ascent of ¼ mile over a low hill commences and the deserted village of Lakat-pôn is reached. From here runs along ridge and descends for ½ mile and crosses the Namténg or Lwaiténg Ka (plenty of water). From here a gradual ascent for 1 mile in a north-east direction, a small descent for about ¼ mile crosses a small hollow, goes up again through bamboo jungle for about ¾ mile descends a bit, crosses a trickling stream, and ascends gradually about ¼ mile and the village of Sinténgpôn is reached. Goes out of village in a north-east direction for about ¼ mile and gradually descending through high grass for ½ mile in east direction reaches the village taungya where camp was pitched near the stream called the Lakra Ka. Up to the Namténg Ka jungle teak bamboo, Zinbyun, and other large trees near the streams; pretty thick undergrowth, otherwise open. From this stream up to hill, jungle bamboo and grass.
		4. Kaungsin ... Lakra, Thabyudan, Alémyaung, Magyidôk, and Naunkam streams.	**11 0**	47 2	Road runs out from taungya in a north-east direction for about 300 yards and crosses the Lakra Ka and goes through the bed for about 200 yards; ascends banks and goes on in an east direction for about 1 mile and crosses the Namkam Ka; continues in same direction for about another mile and crosses the Mokya Ka near the deserted village of Kanna. Up to here jungle on both sides pretty thick with dense undergrowth. Leaving village jungle is more open, road through overgrown taungya sites, pass site of another deserted village (Thôngwa), near which are fields overgrown with kaing: up to here is about 1 mile. Crosses a little mud and goes on in the same direction for 2 miles: jungle open; teak, bamboo and Zinbyun, and comes out on the *mayin* fields worked by the Kaungsin villagers; about ¼ mile further on a few taungya huts and one Kachin hut are passed. Leaving this the Thabyudan chaung is crossed (crossing muddy) and path goes through heavy kaing jungle for about ½ mile, and crosses the Alémyaung chaung. This crossing, too, is muddy; goes on for another mile and crosses the Magyidôk chaung. Road now continues through heavy kaing jungle, and the usual cotton, wood and other large trees seen in places that are subject to inundation for about 1 to 3 miles and nearing the village the road turns directly east and then south and Kaungsin is reached. Roughly calculated from Sinténgpôn to the *mayin* fields is about 6 miles; thence on to Kaungsin about 5 miles only. Kaungsin is situated on the right bank of the Irrawaddy, a short distance above Bhamo (which is of course on the opposite bank of the river)

No. 2.

From ATAN (KAUKKWÉ VALLEY) to THAYETTA.

BY E. P. CLONEY, ESQ., CIVIL OFFICER WITH KAUKKWÉ COLUMN, 1891-92.

Authorities.		Number and Names of Stages, Rivers and Streams.	Distances.				Remarks.
Military.	Civil.		Inter-mediate.		Total.		
			M.	F.	M.	F.	
G.O.C. Mandalay District and O. C. Bhamo.	Commissioner, Northern Division and Deputy Commissioner, Bhamo.	**1. Panbôn** ... Dry bed of a small chaung, Namphai chaung, and Panbôn chaung.	7	0	...		Leaving camp road goes back to the village of Atan nearly ½ mile north of camp. From village turns slightly north-west and goes down-hill for nearly 1¾ miles and passes through the village of Maisakyan, where there is now only one house occupied, the road leading down-hill to the left (west) goes on to Mamhsongtam camp and Mígé, &c. The road to the north right ahead descends ¼ mile and crosses the dry bed of a stream and runs through bamboo and tree jungle with open undergrowth and goes on thus for about 2 miles, then ascends for about ½ mile, gradually descends ¾ mile and crosses the Kamphai chaung, ascends gradually for about ½ mile, descends again, and crosses the Panbôn chaung. Gradually ascending passes over a ridge overgrown with high grass, evidently an old taungya site, and goes on along level ridge or taungya sites for a mile. The village lies hidden from sight by rising ground. The road to the right (east) leads to a small well. The water-supply for the column had to be got from the Panbôn chaung, which flows down in the ravine below the village, about ½ mile by road to it.
		2. Nanko	4	0	11	0	Road leaves village in northerly direction; very good along ridge; ascends gradually for about 1 mile, then along level ridge for about ¾ mile, and descends and passes Panbôn boundary ¾ mile in a westerly direction, then ascending in a northerly direction runs along level ridge covered with heavy kaing, and that kaing jungle which has been cut for 1 mile, then descending for about 1 mile in a westerly direction meets the village road to the Nanko chaung. Ascending in a northerly direction for about 100 yards Nanko is reached; camp on high ground commanding houses of the village; water plentiful, drawn from Nanko chaung.
		3. Lwai Paw ...	4	6	15	6	Road from camp descends in south-west direction to the chaung; ascends from chaung; ascent very slippery; turns north, ascending gradually for about a mile; but for the fallen bamboos across path road very good; undergrowth short, when short ascents and descents for a mile, then along the level ridge for another mile, then descends for a short distance and passes through big tree jungle with dense undergrowth. Road runs along level base of hill through some kind of jungle and ascends about a 100 yards and Lwai Paw is reached. In two or three places fences are thrown across the road with openings left at the places where the road passes through them. These are likely to be mistaken for stockades. They are simply fences or cattle-pens into which the Kachins are obliged to drive their cattle when they wish to catch any.

FROM ATAN (KAUKKWÉ VALLEY) TO THAYETTA, &c.—*continued.*

Authorities. Military.	Authorities. Civil.	Number and Names of Stages, Rivers and Streams.	Distances. Inter-mediate. M. F.	Distances. Total. M. F.	Remarks.
G.O.C. Mandalay District and O.C. Bhamo.	Commissioner, Northern Division and Deputy Commissioner, Bhamo.	**4. Lôngpha chaung camp** ...	**5 0**	20 6	Leaving Lwai Paw road goes through village in a westerly direction, and turning north skirts hill and goes down for a short distance. Road ahead leads through the village Kaitu, but on coming out of this village to join the road that leads to the Lôngtha camp, it is swampy. It is best to take the first road which leads to the left. This road meets the road that runs through Kaitu after 1 mile of descent. Road then level for about 2 miles, gradually turning south-west; jungle bamboo, and tree jungle with dense undergrowth. Still going south-westerly direction road descends open jungle. Path is rather stony for about ½ mile, comes out on a small plain, evidently old paddy-fields, goes on through plain, then through jungle and another small plain, turns south through jungle and comes out and joins road running north to Misho camp. Up Lo Lôngpha stream about 1 mile.
		5. Thayetta ... Lôngpha chaung, Kaukkwé chaung.	**6 4**	27 2	Leaving camp road crosses Lôngpha chaung (shallow stream), runs through the jungle for a short distance, then comes out on the old paddy-fields of Tamaing, goes on south-west direction, then enters jungle of bamboo and large trees with high undergrowth, continuing through thin jungle for about 5½ miles until the left bank of the Kaukkwé (opposite Thayetta), is reached. *See* Route No. 108.

BRANCH I.

FROM NANKO (NAMKU), STAGE 2, TO KA PÔK.

Authorities. Military.	Authorities. Civil.	Number and Names of Stages, Rivers and Streams.	Distances. Inter-mediate. M. F.	Distances. Total. M. F.	Remarks.
G.O.C. Mandalay District and O.C. Bhamo.	Commissioner, Northern Division and Deputy Commissioner, Bhamo.	**1. Ka Pôk** ... Kapra Ka and Kara Ka (Ka=stream).	**3 0**	3 0	Leaving Nanko road runs down about 100 feet, then goes through bamboo jungle into level about ¼ mile. Large Kachin tomb, road good, general direction easterly. Road goes on through open bamboo jungle on the level in a slightly north-east direction for 1 mile and near the stream descends a little, crosses the stream which is almost dry, and ascends to village of Kara Yang (1½ miles), which looks a rather wretched one. Has eight houses and plenty of grass and water to the south-west. Road in the same direction through the village clearing and descends rather sharply for about 200 yards; descent always rather slippery; crosses the Kara Ka; shallow with plenty of good running water and ascends gradually, reached level, and goes on into the village of Namun (2 miles), eight houses, and plenty of grass at this time of the year. Leave the village by the northern road and go out on the level ridge for almost 200 or 300 yards, road then turns to the left slightly, descends and crosses the Kara Ka, and ascending going on through open bamboo jungle nearly all the way till the village of Ka Pôk is seen. Village on open site. Water and grass plentiful. Distance 3 miles.

No. 2.

FROM ATAN (KAUKKWÉ VALLEY) TO THAYETTA, &c.—*continued.*

BRANCH II.

FROM NANKO, STAGE 2, TO MANLWAI.

Authorities. Military.	Authorities. Civil.	Number and Names of Stages, Rivers and Streams.	Distances. Inter-mediate.		Distances. Total.		Remarks.
			M.	F.	M.	F.	
G.O.C. Mandalay District and O.C. Bhamo.	Commissioner, Northern Division and Deputy Commissioner, Bhamo.	**1. Manlwai** ... Kapra Ka Kara Ka, Ukrut Ka, two smaller streams, and the Mong Kong Ka.	**6**	**4**	6	4	Road already described in Branch as far as village of Namun, 2 mile Leaving village of Namun road go in an east direction through thicki grass growth and descends a sho distance and crosses the Kara K Ascent from the stream rather sli pery : goes on through open bamb jungle for about ½ mile and comes o on the Namun taungya sites, pass through the taungya in the same direction and goes o through small patch of bamboos. Here the road branch to the right (south) ; the roads lead to Kapra and Ukr Ka villages to the left (north). The road goes to Kochan Road goes on for a short distance through the bamb jungle, then turning north-east descends a cleared taung site ; commands splendid view : descends for about ½ mi and ascends on the other side for another ½ mile ; continu through bamboo jungle, open with short undergrowth goes on the level for about 1 mile and then gradual descends and crosses the Ukrut Ka, the muddy beds of tw smaller strean s. Goes on again along the level throug open bamboo j ngle, comes out on the Manlwai taung sites, descendi g for about ½ mile, and crosses the Mon Kong Ka stream, about 20 feet broad, but water shallow goes on again along the level for about ½ mile and Man wai is reach d. On the road to the village there a numerous fe es thrown across the path which, even b experienced officers, are likely to be mistaken for stockade These are simply fences with gates to keep the cattle fro straying into the taungya from the village, a road to the le leads down to the water. The village has no stockade, b has bamboo jungle surrounding it.

No. 3.

From BAW to KADOZEIK (on Irrawaddy River).

BY LIEUT. McSWINEY AND RESSALDAR SYED AHMED, 3RD CAVALRY HYDERABAD CONTINGENT, JUNE 1887.

Military	Civil	Stages	Inter. M.	Inter. F.	Total M.	Total F.	Remarks
G.O.C. Mandalay District.	Commissioner, Northern Division and Deputy Commissioner, Shwébo.	**1. Lepandaw** ... Small streams.	**9**	**6**	9	6	Baw, a village in north-eastern corn of Shwébo district, formerly a daco refuge. Several kyaungs and zaya and water good from wells in strea bed. Good cart road over hard soil. Several small strean crossing, or close to the road ; at 1 mile Lekogôn ; 5 mil Katta ; 7½ Zim. Country generally level.
		2. Yôgôn ... ... Large streams.	**10**	**0**	19	6	Cart road up to the end of this stag Dense jungle throughout until th Irrawaddy is reached. The roa follows generally the course of a larg stream, whence the villages of Nawgô (5¼ miles), Hinthaw (7¾ miles) and Yôgôn draw the water-supply. The village of Thambingôn is also passed 2 miles. There are also wells at Hinthaw and Yôgôn an a tank at Nawgôn.

FROM BAW TO KADOZEIK (ON IRRAWADDY RIVER)—*continued.*

Authorities. Military.	Authorities. Civil.	Number and Names of Stages, Rivers and Streams.	Distances. Intermediate.	Distances. Total.	Remarks.
G.O.C. Mandalay District.	Commr., Northern Division and Dy. Commr., Shwébo.	**3. Kadozeik** ... Large stream, Irrawaddy River.	M. F. **13 6**	M. F. 33 4	On leaving Yôgôn the road enters the hills and is in parts very steep and difficult, the final descent to the river being very rapid.

No. 4.

From BAW to KYANZABIN or TAMOWA (Irrawaddy River).

BY LIEUT. J. R. DYAS, HANTS REGIMENT, APRIL 1887.

Military	Civil	Stages	Intermediate	Total	Remarks
G.O.C. Mandalay District.	Commissioner, Northern Division and Deputy Commissioner, Shwébo.	**1. Kyanzabin or Tamowa.** Zin chaung and numerous other smaller streams.	M. F. **14 0**	M. F. 14 0	The best road from Baw to the Irrawaddy river is that leading to Kyanzabin, the site of a former village on the right bank of the river about a mile above Kyanhnyat, where there is a good landing place, deep water close up to the bank, which is in terraces. General direction easterly. Cart takes 2 to 3 days over the journey, the last 3 or 4 miles being very difficult indeed, steep descents and road rocky and rough. Elsewhere the road is generally good. Bamboo jungle throughout, a little teak in places, very little undergrowth. Water in pools, or obtainable by digging to a slight depth, in the beds of several streams. For the first 5 miles the track follows the course of a large stream (the Zin chaung) 40 yards broad and said to be from 4 to 5 feet deep from July to November, crossing it several times. At 11 miles track diverges to the right to Tamowa, exactly opposite Kyanhnyat, also distant from Baw about 14 miles; last 3 miles very steep descent, at present ('87) impracticable for carts.

No. 5.

From BERNARDMYO to MOMEIK.

BY LIEUT. STEVENS, R.A., NOVEMBER 1887.

Military	Civil	Stages	Intermediate	Total	Remarks
G.O.C. Mandalay District.	Commissioner, Northern Division and Deputy Commissioner, Ruby Mines.	**1. Kyetnapa** ... Wabo stream.	M. F. **11 0**	M. F. 11 0	Leaving Bernardmyo the road after a small ascent out of the station descends all the way to Mom Pein village (6 miles) being very steep most of the way. It is a narrow jungle path, much cut up by traffic and would be very difficult in the rains. Thick jungle, mostly bamboo on both sides. Mom Pein is a Palaung village; there are good but small pôngyi kyaungs and one small zayat. Accommodation for 50 men. Good water. No supplies. From Mom Pein road runs along a steep khud, descending slightly to Kyaukdwin; small (Palaung) village at 7½ miles then down a very steep long hill to the village of Kyetnapa (Palaung) 11 miles, crossing first a rapid mountain stream with steep

FROM BERNARDMYO TO MOMEIK—*continued.*

Authorities.		Number and Names of Stages, Rivers and Streams.	Distances.		Remarks.
Military.	Civil.		Intermediate.	Total.	
G.O.C. Mandalay District.	Commissioner, Northern Division and Deputy Commissioner, Ruby Mines.	**1. Kyetnapa**—*cont.*			banks, which was just fordable at the end of November 1887, but the villagers said it was very low that year, then across some paddy-fields over another easily fordable stream into the village. Kyetnapa is a Palaung village of about 15 houses; kyaung; accommodation for 50 men. Good water. No supplies.
			M. F.	M. F.	
		2. Magyibin ... Wabomyein Taung-gyi streams.	11 0	22 0	First mile of road very much cut up by buffaloes and would be difficult in the rains. Road descends slightly through jungle to a small fordable stream to the village of Maingngwé (small jungle village, no accommodation or supplies 2 miles). Road still descends slightly and becomes better to Taungbo (2½ miles) village like Maingngwé with no accommodation. From here the road is very good. It rises for about 2 miles, then descends rapidly about 1,000 feet to a small fordable stream at foot of hill (7½ miles). Road down this hill is good. The road now runs level for about 3 miles through teak forest, no undergrowth. Road good. At end of teak forest large and good encamping ground. Road here meets the Sagadaung-Momeik cart road. About ½ a mile along the cart road is the large village of Magyibin, one small zayat only; no other accommodation. Paddy cultivation here begins.
		3. Momeik ... Nami, Tagaungma. Namaung and Nameit rivers.	10 0	32 0	For the first mile the road runs level through jungle to Mogaung-u, small village, 15 or 20 houses. No accommodation or supplies. Here road leaves cart road and becomes a path running level through paddy-fields to Nami village (3½ miles) large, but without accommodation. Just outside village is the Nami river, barely fordable for mules at end of November 1887, then about 20 yards broad with tree felled for foot-bridge difficult to cross. Soon after Nami the cart road is again struck. The road is sandy and runs through bamboo jungle and looks as if it was under water in the rains. No water at present between Nami and next river. At end of bamboo jungle road leaves cart road and crosses large patches of paddy-fields divided by small belts of jungle, arriving at Tagaungma river, easily fordable in November. The road is still continues through paddy-fields and must be here very muddy in the rains. At 6½ miles Lekopin village with kyaungs and 2 zayats with good well water. Leaving Lekopin the path (here very bad) runs through paddy-fields and belts of jungle to Momeik. Just before coming to the town the Namaung river has to be crossed. At the end of November 1887 this river was very low and easily fordable. About 35 yards of water, then not more than 2 feet deep. Momeik is a town of about 300 bamboo houses, standing in a tongue of jungle, hiding it entirely between two rivers, the Namaung and Nameit rivers on the west and east respectively, both flowing into the Shwéli river. Small boats, 12 feet long, are said to work between Momeik and the Shwéli, which is said to be 80 miles distant. Larger boats are said to work on the Shwéli. The Nameit is about 1½ miles east of the town. Momeik consists chiefly of one long street forming the bazaar. This street is 350 or 400 yards long and

FROM BERNARDMYO TO MOMEIK—*continued.*

Authorities. Military.	Authorities. Civil.	Number and Names of Stages, Rivers and Streams.	Distances. Intermediate.	Distances. Total.	Remarks.
G.O.C. Mandalay District.	Commr., Northern Divn., &c.	**3. Momeik**—*cont.*			about 25 yards broad and is very straight and well kept. Large convoys of bullocks work between Sagadaung and Kyanhnyat. There are supplies of bullocks and rice. There are a few kyaungs, and a small zayat by a bridge over a small nullah about ¾ of a mile from the town.

No. 6.

From BHAMO to AYEINDAMA (Irrawaddy left bank below Hokat) viâ THEINLÔN.

BY G. W. SHAW, ESQ., DEPUTY COMMISSIONER, BHAMO, JANUARY 1889.

Military	Civil	Stages	Intermediate	Total	Remarks
G.O.C. Mandalay District and O.C. Bhamo.	Commissioner, Northern Division and Deputy Commissioner, Bhamo.		M. F.	M. F.	
		1. Mannaung ... Tapin river.	**16 0**	16 0	Road good. North for first 2 miles, then north-east. Smaller streams bridged. At about 7 miles Môpein where the Tapin has to be crossed; never fordable. At about 7½ miles Hélôn crosses Mannaung branch of Tapin to Mannaung, Burman Shan village with Chinese and Kachin quarters adjoining. These quarters or villages are situated, the Shan on an island in the Mannaung branch of the Tapin, the Chinese where the roads to the Môlé chaung and to China start, the Kachin at a point where the road from Bhamo abuts.
		2. Ngagadaung ...	**13 0**	29 0	Recross branch of Tapin. Road thence level and good all the way. At about 4 miles the road to China branches off to the right. At about 10 miles pass Pinthet, Kachin village, on level ground near foot of hills. Ngagadaung is a small Kachin village. No accommodation.
		3. Theinlôn ... Môlé chaung.	**13 0**	42 0	Road in parts very narrow, hardly wide enough for baggage animals. Steep ascent for about a mile at starting and descent on the other side of the hill of about 2 miles and numerous smaller ascents and descents; also four muddy streams and swamps to be crossed, which delay baggage animals. Another small Kachin village a short distance before reaching the summit of the first hill. From the summit of this hill a good view would be obtained both on the Tapin and Môlé sides if the jungle were cleared. Several Kachin taungyas passed. Rice nearly ripe early in November. Theinlôn is a Shan village of 16 houses (left bank Môlé chaung). At present the largest village in the Môlé chaung district. There are four or five Kachin houses in the village, and the Laka Kachin Sawbwa, who "protects" the village, lives there. Traders come up here by boat with salt. It takes them about four days to get to Yeinthaw, which is in the lower part of the river and within easy distance of Bhamo. Up to Theinlôn the road from Bhamo presents few difficulties to pack animals in the dry weather and, with a little bridging of the small muddy places, a very easy matter, and a little jungle cutting in the narrow places, could be made a really good pack track.

FROM BHAMO TO AYEINDAMA (IRRAWADDY, &c.) *viâ* THEINLÔN—*continued.*

Authorities. Military.	Authorities. Civil.	Number and Names of Stages, Rivers and Streams.	Distances. Intermediate. M.	F.	Total. M.	F.	Remarks.
G.O.C. Mandalay District and O.C. Bhamo.	Commissioner, Northern Division and Deputy Commissioner, Bhamo.	**4. Camp in jungle.** Small stream.	**15**	**0**	57	0	From Theinlôn there is a direct road to Mannaw, a day's journey distant. Cross the Môlé chaung at starting; not fordable. At about 7 miles small stream. No water from here until camp at 15 miles is reached. Path easy for pack animals.
		5. Camp on Nantaung chaung. Namsan and Nantaung chaungs.	**19**	**0**	76	0	For many miles in this and the previous march road runs through open grass plain, under cultivation near the villages of Manpin and Kauksin, which are passed at about 5½ miles and 11¼ miles respectively, but elsewhere waste and cut up by the tracks of wild elephants. At about 15¾ miles cross Namsan chaung. Water is scarce, and there is no population to speak of. A couple of muddy places between last camp and Manpin require to be bridged—an easy matter.
		6. Ayeindama ... Irrawaddy river.	**13**	**0**	89	0	A few miles from Ayeindama similar wide plain, cultivated only in one corner by the people of that village. Ayeindama is a Shan village of houses, with several "protecting" Kachin houses adjoining on the left bank of the Irrawaddy. It has a pôngyi kyaung; no other accommodation. Hôkat is about 7 miles higher up the river and on the opposite bank. Country boats (laungs) do the distance in about three hours upwards and half that time downwards in January. A good deal of gold-washing appears to be carried on by Kachins and Chinese at Lônsôn on the upper part of the Môlé chaung, about a day's march above Theinlôn.

No. 7.

From BHAMO to AYEINDAMA viâ TÁLÍ.

BY CAPT. COUCHMAN, D.S.O., SOMERSETSHIRE LIGHT INFANTRY, COLD SEASON, 1891-92, AND OTHERS.

Military	Civil	Stages	M.	F.	M.	F.	Remarks
G.O.C. Mandalay Dist., &c.	Commr., Northern Divn., &c.	**1. Malula** ...	**13**	**4**	13	4	For details of these stages, *see* Route No. 11 and Alternative IV.
		2. Myothit ...	**10**	**2**	23	6	
		3. Tálí	**7**	**4**	31	2	
		4. Tálí Uma ...	**6**	**2**	37	4	

FROM BHAMO TO AYEINDAMA *viâ* TÁLÍ—*continued.*

Authorities. Military.	Authorities. Civil.	Number and Names of Stages, Rivers and Streams.	Distances. Intermediate. (M. F.)	Distances. Total. (M. F.)	Remarks.
G.O.C. Mandalay District and O.C. Bhamo.	Commissioner, Northern Division and Deputy Commissioner, Bhamo.	**5. Lagat** ... Sumpi Ka jheel; two streams.	**5 2**	42 6	The road now descends and crosses the Sumpi Ka which flows in a southerly direction. The right bank is very stony and a bad descent. From here the road ascends steeply for ¾ mile through good fodder grass. General direction north-east. From here there is a road which leads to Wasik and Lôngu. It then descends and crosses a muddy jheel, 40 yards broad; water and mud 2 feet deep; and 200 yards further on a rocky stream (probably Kachong Ka), 5 yards broad, 18 inches deep, flowing west. For 300 yards it then follows up the right bank of the stream, along some terraced paddy-fields, which are too damp to camp in. From here there is a steep ascent to Marawtawng of 23 minutes. Distance 2 miles from Tálí Uma, crossing one small stream twice 2 feet wide, 2 inches deep. Country fodder and kaing grass and small trees. From here there is road to Talang. The ascent is now very steep up to Kanlang (3¼ miles) (40 minutes from Marawtawng). This road is in very good condition, except when leaving Marawtawng where it is rather rutty. Jungle as before. Water scarce. From here to Lagat (5¼ miles) 1 hour, up two steep ascents, over taungyas (old) and past a large bare white patch of decomposed felspar (distinctly visible from Bhamo) along the bottom of Alawpum hill. The road here for 20 minutes is exceedingly bad, passing through several deep cuttings, which are full of slippery boulders. Tree jungle. From here to Lagat is a very good road, passing through good fodder and big trees. A road leaves Kanlang for Wédu, which is immediately down the spur to the west, about 1 mile distant. There are two supplies of water at Lagat, but not sufficient for animals. The water along the watershed is not at all plentiful.
		6. Warra ... Tálí Ka and numerous small streams.	**12 4**	55 2	General direction north. The road leaves Lagat and descends through grass and bamboos into some taungyas. At 2½ miles there is a road to the right (east) 'Nbao. From here there is a steep ascent for 200 yards. The road then descends steeply at first and then more gradually into some more taungyas (2¾ miles). From here to 3 miles it has a gradual ascent and then descends into Nawku village 3½ miles. There is a good site for a camp here. Two small streams are brought down from the hill by bamboos and supply the village. Two hundred yards below and north of the village are some paddy-fields. A small artificial stream, brought down from the hills above, runs through these; stream 2 feet wide, 1 foot deep. This can be dammed up to water animals. Fodder good and plentiful. The road from here has a north-westerly direction. It first descends and crosses a small stream, 3 feet wide, and stony bottom, 1 foot of water. It then ascends steeply for a ¼ mile and then descends to cross a small muddy stream 2 feet wide and with a few inches of water in it, and 100 yards further on another stream 3 feet wide. From here the road is fairly level, and a road runs west to Teingram. (?) The road now passes through some swampy ground and crosses another small swampy stream and then ascends steeply for a ¼ mile. From this point it descends very steeply to the Tálí Ka, just above which are some

FROM BHAMO TO AYEINDAMA *viâ* TÁLÍ—*continued.*

Authorities.		Number and Names of Stages, Rivers and Streams.	Distances.		Remarks.
Military.	Civil.		Inter-mediate.	Total.	
G.O.C. Mandalay District and O.C. Bhamo.	Commissioner, Northern Division and Deputy Commissioner, Bhamo.	**6. Warra**—*cont.*			taungyas. All this road from the swampy ground is much overgrown and runs through grass and bamboo jungle; at the top of the hill are a few big trees; road otherwise good; Tálí Ka 5 yards broad, 1 foot deep; boulders; bad crossing; then up into the village of Meunglai 6½ miles. From here the road runs north-east and is very good. It crosses a small stream, 4 yards broad and passes through some terraced paddy-fields over three small streams. These fields are fairly dry and would camp 250 men. From these fields the road ascends steeply through kaing grass and bamboos and is much overgrown. At 9½ miles the village of Letsao* is reached, and from here the road is excellent and 6 feet broad, having been recently cleared. It crosses two more very tiny streams and then descends rather steeply into Letsao* (Pumkatong) 9¾ miles. The road after leaving Letsao runs generally north, descending through big tree jungle. After ¼ mile two roads branch off to the right to ? ? ? . The road now becomes overgrown and descends steeply along the side of hill After 11 miles the road becomes very bad for transport, as it is cut into the side of hill with steep sides and has not been cut wide enough, the result being that laden animals are pushed over the khud. At 12 miles reach Warra Pumkatang and descend very steeply to Lower Warra 12½ miles by a zigzag road and crossing two small streams, only one of which would be of any use for watering animals. A dam should be constructed. This part of the road is not good at present, but would not require much labour to make good, as the ground is very soft. Camping ground in the village. Fodder plentiful.
		7. Manmaw ... Numerous small streams and Môlé chaung.	M. F. **11 2**	M. F. 66 4	The road now descends very steeply over stony ground and through tree jungle and is here very good, but at the bottom of the hill (2 miles), it passes through kaing grass and is overgrown. It again descends steeply and then ascends past some Kachin huts steeply into Unkaw Ningaw village 3 miles. Four small streams, each 3 feet wide, are crossed. Unkaw. Good camp. Fodder excellent. Water from a bamboo spring north-east of village (200 yards) along a level path; very slow supply. From Unkaw the road descends over stony ground for ½ mile and then passes along the side of a hill along grass and bamboo jungle, gradually ascends at first, and then very steeply over stony ground, and in zigzags through first kaing grass and then tree jungle, into Pumpien 4½ miles. One small nullah, 3 feet wide, is crossed. The road from Pumpien to the plain is very steep, but good. It varies from 6 feet to 15 feet broad, is very smooth and good, and descends in zigzags through tree jungle and taungyas to the plains below. From here it passes through alternate paddy-fields and kaing grass to Nepeudaw 8¼ miles, a small village on the Môlé chaung called in Kachin language Nam Li. Good fodder and camping ground. A little paddy to be got here. The road now follows along the left bank of the Môlé chaung through kaing grass, which has overgrown the path in many places. Occasional Kachin paddy-fields are crossed. Manmaw is on the right bank of the Môlé chaung, which is 45 yards broad

* Captain Couchman states later on that "Pumkatawng" infers "on top of the hill," therefore apparently these names should be transposed.

FROM BHAMO TO AYEINDAMA *viâ* TÁLÍ—*continued.*

Authorities.		Number and Names of Stages, Rivers and Streams.	Distances.		Remarks.
Military.	Civil.		Inter-mediate.	Total.	
		7. Manmaw—*cont.*			here, hip deep, with sandy bottom, and current 1 mile an hour. Water clear and good and full of fish. Banks: kaing grass on sand. A small village, with eight to ten boats, most of which have come from Bhamo trading. There is a small bamboo pôngyi kyaung here which would hold a dozen men. Good ground for camping on both sides of the river. Manmaw is "two nights" (*i.e.*, three days') journey from Bahmo by road and four "nights" (*i.e.*, five days) by the river which is very tortuous. Very large Burman boats can come up to here and Manmaw would form a very good base for a column operating in these parts.
G.O.C. Mandalay District and O.C. Bhamo.	Commissioner, Northern Division and Deputy Commissioner, Bhamo.	**8. Ka-u** ... Môlé, Namsang and Namkhan chaungs, and numerous smaller streams.	M. F. 14 0	M. F. 80 4	The road has a general direction of north-west from Manmaw. For ½ a mile it goes along a kaing grass plain. It then enters thick bamboo jungle and goes west along the edge of the plain. After 1½ miles it turns more north and passes through fine teak jungle to the Nan Ngaw Ka (3 miles). This is 10 yards broad and has steep sheer banks 8 feet high and has a muddy bottom, with 2 feet of water. There is a single plank foot-bridge here and timber at hand to make a larger bridge. Water bad. From here the road has a gradual ascent of 2 miles over a small ridge of 200 feet height through tree, cane, and kaing grass jungle with occasional small descents. From the top of this ridge the road descents to a small sakhán ½ a mile further on. From here for another 2 miles the road is comparatively level, having a few slight ascents and descents, and crossing and re-crossing several small rocky streams, which form no obstacle, but contain good water. It now ascends 400 to 500 feet steeply and over some stony bits in the next mile to the village of Tutap (deserted and overgrown with good fodder grass), and thence descends steeply 1 mile to the village of Kao-sin (Kaukchan), down a slippery clay bit of soil. Distance 9½ miles. All this road is much overgrown, but has no obstacles and could be made very good in two days. Kao-sin is a Burma-Shan village; it has some Kachin houses in it and the Kachin village of Karpaung (Wapaung) overlooks it from the neighbouring hill. There is plenty of fodder grass on this part of the march. There is another village of Kao-sin about a mile north-west in the paddy-fields, which is an off-shoot of this village. From here the road passes for 1½ miles along a paddy and grass plain. Road good at 1 mile cross a tributary of the Nan Ngaw Ka stream which is 6 yards broad, has 2 feet of water and a bad muddy bottom which is likely to cause trouble to transport. A few bamboos are thrown across to form a foot-bridge, but there are no materials very near for making a longer bridge. From 1½ miles into Ka-u (14 miles) is through trees and kaing grass. Road good; crosses 2 small streams with very little water, over one of which is a plank bridge, to the Namsang chaung, 40 yards broad, 2 feet deep, sluggish current, gravelly and sandy bottom. Timber on both banks; right bank steep ascent which can easily be dug out into a more convenient approach. Ka-u village is on the left bank. The Namkhan chaung joins the Namsang just above the village; Ka-u is a Lapai village.

No. 7.

FROM BHAMO TO AYEINDAMA *viâ* TÁLÍ—*continued.*

Authorities.		Number and Names of Stages, Rivers and Streams.	Distances.		Remarks
Military.	Civil.		Inter-mediate.	Total.	
			M. F.	M. F.	
G.O.C. Mandalay District and O.C. Bhamo.	Commissioner, Northern Division and Deputy Commissioner, Bhamo.	**9. Ayeindama** ... Irrawaddy and smaller streams.	**15 0**	95 4	The road from Ka-u is level, for the first mile through dense, matted jungle. Beyond this the track is clearer through jungle and crosses six long glades of rumnah. The last 3 or 4 miles, on approaching Ayeindama, are over a broad open track, 6 feet broad. Two streams, at 3 miles and 12½ miles from Ka-u, are crossed, neither form any obstacle to mule transport. No. 2, 25 feet in breadth, 2¼ feet deep; No. 1, 10 feet in breadth only, 1 foot of water at present. Three other dry nullahs are crossed; no obstacle. Troops can camp on small open space south of village and on the bank of the Irrawaddy, 600 yards broad here. The village is divided into two halves, north and south. North half Kachins, south Burmans. Supplies from Bhamo by large boats. Launches at this time of year (January) cannot approach nearer than the bend of river, ½ mile below.

ALTERNATIVE I.

FROM TÁLÍ UMA, STAGE 4, TO KA-U, STAGE 8.

BY LIEUT. H. C. SANDFORD, 3RD BURMA BATTALION, JANUARY 1892.

Military	Civil	Stages	Intermediate	Total	Remarks
G.O.C. Mandalay District and O.C. Bhamo.	Commissioner, Northern Division and Deputy Commissioner, Bhamo.	**1. Legrakatawng.** Two small streams and Môlé chaung.	**12 6**	12 6	Road returns towards Tálí for about ¾ mile, then proceeds north-east by north for 12¾ miles to Legrakatawng. On the way we pass Kateng (?) five houses at 3½ miles; Inchong (?) three houses, at 5th mile; Theinlôn, nine houses, at the 8th mile; Maraw, 11 houses, at the 9th mile. Road very hilly, passing over two spurs about 600 feet high and two insignificant streams. Good for mules, about 6½ hours' journey. The village of Legrakatawng is built on two sides of a large stretch of paddy-field, enough to camp 1,000 men. Good water close by. Contains about 13 houses. At Theinlôn, 13 houses cross the Môlé chaung, about 60 yards broad just fordable now (1st January) for loaded mules, but dug-outs are available.
		2. Camp (4 miles short of Manpang).	**14 0**	26 6	After leaving camp, first 6 miles north-west by west thence for 8 miles due north through a dark and evil-smelling forest, just beyond which is a stretch of open country, very good for camping, with good water just beyond. Four miles beyond forest stands Manpang, 10 houses camping ground for 500 animals, and a large pôngyi kyaung, beneath which 100 men could sleep, is in the village. Road very bad the last 2 miles. About 10 hours' journey. Road, very bad for last 4 miles, being very muddy and wet. About 4 miles due north to Ka-u very good road.
		3. Ka-u	**8 0**	34 6	
					Note 1 *by Captain Couchman.*—This route is evidently by Kasukeng, Kukum, and Lana to Theinlôn. The village of Lagrakatawng, where they camped, is, I imagine, below Lana to the west in the Lana paddy-fields.
					Note 2.—This is evidently the shortest way from Tálí to Ayeindama, the road previously described (No. 7) evidently taking a circle into the hills between Tálí and Ka-u.—A. F.

FROM BHAMO TO AYEINDAMA *viâ* TÁLÍ—*continued.*

ALTERNATIVE II.

FROM TÁLÍ UMA, STAGE 4, TO LAGAT, STAGE 5, *viâ* LÔNGU.

BY CAPT. COUCHMAN AND SURVEYOR SULTAN SUKHREE, DECEMBER 1891.

Authorities.		Number and Names of Stages, Rivers and Streams.	Distances.		Remarks.
Military.	Civil.		Inter-mediate.	Total.	
			M. F.	M. F.	
G.O.C. Mandalay District and O.C. Bhamo.	Commissioner, Northern Division and Deputy Commissioner, Bhamo.	**1. Lagat** ... ... Sumpi Ka.	**10 0**	10 0	General direction east-north-east to Lôngu (? miles), thence north. Cross the Sumpi Ka and proceed up to 2 miles as by Route 2. Thence to Achang (1) (2 miles) through kaing grass and tree jungle up a steep ascent. Just above Achang (2) (3 miles) a road branches off to the south to Wasik. The road here is very steep through tree jungle, but is good. Thence the road turns north and passes along the top of the watershed to Achang (3), a small hamlet of three houses at 5 miles. Water scarce. Thence the road by a series of small ascents and descents goes along the watershed to Lagat (10 miles). This is the best route to Lagat, although it is the longest, as there are no bad places for transport. At 1 mile before Lagat the road passes Kanghphang. From here a road passes along the watershed to Maın and thence along the frontier line to Taolung, and then to Manwyne.

BRANCH I.

FROM TÁLÍ UMA, STAGE 4, TO WÉDU UMA.

BY CAPT. COUCHMAN, DECEMBER 1891.

Military.	Civil.	Number and Names of Stages, Rivers and Streams.	Inter-mediate.	Total.	Remarks.
G.O.C. Mandalay District and O.C. Bhamo.	Commissioner, Northern Division and Deputy Commissioner, Bhamo.	**1. Wédu Uma—** **(a) viâ Kukam** ... **(b) „ Sumpra**... Tumpi, Nakut and several smaller streams.	**6 4** **7 0**	6 4 7 0	General direction north-east. From Tálí Uma the road descends into some taungyas and crosses a small stream, 3 feet wide, muddy and bad crossing, but very easily bridged. From here the road ascends into Talang (1 mile). Road much overgrown with grass. Branch road to Marawtatang from Talang. From here the road descends into some taungyas and then ascends into Lawpum (2¼ miles). Road as before. Branch route to Tálí (21 minutes). From Lawpum road passes through taungyas and descends steeply to the Tumpi Ka; 4 yards broad; stony bottom; 1 foot deep; and ascends steeply to Wédu Lagatan along the right bank of the stream and high above it (4¼ miles) (39 minutes). From here there are two routes to Wédu Uma *viâ* Kukam as follows, and *viâ* Sumpra. Road now ascends steeply and over good smooth ground into Kukam (17 minutes) (15 miles). From Kukam road descends steeply and crosses the Nakut Ka; 3 yards broad; 1 foot deep; muddy bottom, and passes along some paddy-fields. It then ascends steeply into the straggling village of Wédu Uma (6½ miles), crossing one other small stream (31 minutes). All this route is good and there is plenty of good fodder all along the route. The Sumpra route on leaving Wédu Lagatan turns east-north-east and again crosses the Tumpi Ka, 6 feet wide, 1 foot deep; rocky; and ascends steeply through tree jungle to Sumpra (17 minutes). It then descends and joins road from Kukam to Wédu Uma, about

No. 7.

FROM BHAMO TO AYEINDAMA *viâ* TÁLÍ—*continued.*

BRANCH I—*continued.*

Authorities. Military.	Authorities. Civil.	Number and Names of Stages, Rivers and Streams.	Distances. Intermediate. M.	F.	Distances. Total. M.	F.	Remarks.
G.O.C. Mandalay, &c.	Commr., Northern Divn., &c.	**1. Wédu Uma**—*cont.*					a ½ mile from Sumpra. It crosses two small muddy streams before it reaches the other road. Wédu Uma is immediately under and to the west of Alawpum. A road is reported up to it. If so, it must be very steep.

BRANCH II.

FROM MANMAW, STAGE 7, TO WÉDU UMA.

BY CAPT. COUCHMAN, JANUARY 1892.

Authorities. Military.	Authorities. Civil.	Number and Names of Stages, Rivers and Streams.	Distances. Intermediate. M.	F.	Distances. Total. M.	F.	Remarks.
G.O.C. Mandalay District and O.C. Bhamo.	Commissioner, Northern Division and Deputy Commissioner, Bhamo.	**1. Laimôk** ... ... Môlé chaung, Asin Ka and six small streams.	**6**	**0**	6	0	Crossing the Môlé chaung the road goes along paddy-fields and kaing grass for about 1¾ miles along the route to Nepeodaw. It then turns south-east and at 2¼ miles crosses the Asin Ka, 10 yards broad, 2 feet deep, and muddy bottom with kaing grass banks. The crossing is easy and good. At 2½ miles the road leaves the plain and turns south going a few feet above the plain through bamboo jungle and grass and fairly level till at 3 miles it again crosses the Asin Ka, here 5 yards broad with firm level bottom and easy crossing. It now continues through tree and grass jungle over four small boggy streams with steep ascents and descents of 6 feet each, and crossed by a single pole for a foot-bridge. These are from 3 to 5 feet broad at bottom, and if much traffic went across would form impediments. They could easily be made passable in half-an-hour by cutting down a few trees and kaing grass. Just after crossing the Asin Ka there is a road to the right to Pakaw. The road now passes through some open paddy-fields (damp) and then ascends steeply through taungyas and bamboo jungle up to Laimôk crossing two small streams, each 1 foot broad and with very little water. Just before reaching Laimôk there is a road to the right to Pakaw. All this road is good and smooth (distance estimated by time, which was 2½ hours *actual* marching). At Laimôk camping place is in the village. No supplies, water scanty, from a spring (below the village) which is carried off by a bamboo. Grass and bamboo plentiful. Laimôk is about 1,200 feet above Manmaw. For the last part of the march, the Asin Ka is below the road some 300 to 500 feet on the left-hand side, and is a small rocky torrent.
		2. Lana ... ... U La Ka and many smaller streams.	**9**	**0**	15	0	From Laimôk the road has an easy descent through taungyas and bamboo jungle for a mile, when it crosses the site of old Laimôk. It then descends through taungyas very steeply and with occasional strong bits into kaing grass and tree jungle, where it is very steep and slippery, but otherwise good. At 2 miles it becomes overgrown, and crosses a small stream 2 feet broad. It continues descending and crosses five more small streams. To one of these the descent is very steep indeed, and two others have boggy edges, which are at present a slight impediment, which could easily be remedied. At 3¼ miles cross the U La Ka, 2 feet deep, 15 yards broad, sand and mud bottom banks kaing grass. The road is now boggy and about 50 yards further a boggy

FROM BHAMO TO AYEINDAMA *viâ* TÁLÍ—*continued.*

BRANCH II—*continued.*

Authorities.		Number and Names of Stages, Rivers and Streams.	Distances.		Remarks.
Military.	Civil.		Intermediate.	Total.	
G.O.C. Mandalay District and O.C. Bhamo.	Commissioner, Northern Division and Deputy Commissioner, Bhamo.	**2. Lana**—*cont.*			tributary of the U La Ka, 6 yards broad and 2 feet deep is crossed. This would have to be taken in hand if much traffic crossed it. At 3½ miles the road enters some paddy-fields. Good fodder all the way. General direction from Laimôk south-south-east. From here to Teingár the road is very good and kept in good condition, as it is evidently used for conveying paddy up to Teingár. Leaving the paddy-fields it enters kaing grass and gradually ascends for 1½ miles, when it passes four Kachins huts belonging to Teingár. It is 4 to 6 feet broad and very smooth. Just after leaving these huts the U La Ka is again crossed. The stream is here 7 to 8 yards broad, 1 foot deep, with gravelly and stony bed. From here it ascends steeply up to Teingár (4¼ miles), winding up the side of the hill and crossing four small streams. It is a little stony at first, but afterwards is good. It passes through taungyas and at the top enters some fine large tree forest. To here the direction is east-south-east. The road now goes south, and gradually descends to the village of Laryang (5¼ miles), crossing one small stream, and thence to Lana village across a small taungya. Just before reaching Lana there is a road east to Teingram. At Lana (9 miles), water scarce, and has to be collected by a dam for animals. Camp in the village. Fodder plentiful. No supplies. Duration of march for transport 4½ hours. Distance estimated by time.
		3. Wédu Uma ...	M. F. 3 4	M. F. 18 4	The road now continues south-south-west along top of range and is fairly level with a few easy ascents and descents to Kukam. After leaving Lana it is rather overgrown, but otherwise smooth. Jungle, tree, bamboo, and kaing grass. It joins a fine open and well-kept road, 6 feet broad, about ¼ mile from Kukam. This road comes from Teingram. From here there is a road west to Pakayan and Lônsôn. Kukam is on the same level as Lana by barometer. Distance, estimated by time, 40 minutes for Mounted Infantry. This is a good road from Manmaw and has few obstacles for transport. Forage and water plentiful all along. From here to Wédu Uma *see* Branch No. 1 (*a*).—From Wédu to Tálí Uma, *see* Branch I.

BRANCH III.

FROM TEINGÁR, *see* BRANCH II, STAGE 2, TO LETSAO (*see* ROUTE NO. 7, STAGE 6).

BY CAPT. COUCHMAN, JANUARY 1891.

Military	Civil	Stages	Intermediate	Total	Remarks
G.O.C. Mandalay Dist., and O.C. Bhamo.	Commr., Northern Divn. and Deputy Commr., Bhamo.	**1. Letsao** ... Six small streams.	5 0	5 0	Direction of road north-east. A road branches off from this to Meunglai or M'lai (2 miles) on the eastward, and goes over taungyas and ascending and descending to cross six small streams, ranging in size from 3 to 6 feet in breadth. At 2 miles it comes on to some terraced paddy-fields, and then joins the road from Meunglai to Letsao (*see* Route 7, Stage 6). There are no obstacles on this road, and it is easy going, and only goes to a height of 200 feet above Teingár. It passes about ¼ mile to the north of Meunglai.

FROM BHAMO TO AYEINDAMA *viâ* TÁLÍ—*continued.*

BRANCH IV.

FROM KUKAM, *see* BRANCH I-A, TO LANA (BRANCH II, STAGE 2), *viâ* MATYANG AND TEINGRAM.

BY CAPT. COUCHMAN, JANUARY 1892.

Authorities. Military.	Authorities. Civil.	Number and Names of Stages, Rivers and Streams.	Distances. Intermediate. M. F.	Distances. Total. M. F.	Remarks.
G.O.C. Mandalay District and O.C. Bhamo.	Commissioner, Northern Division and Deputy Commissioner, Bhamo.	**1. Lana** ... Tálí Ka and Rítu Ka, and numerous smaller streams.	5 4	5 4	Matyang is nearly due east from Kukam. The road descends steeply through grass and bamboo for ½ mile and down 250 feet and crosses the Tálí Ka, which is 7 yards broad, stony bottom, 1 foot deep, and easy crossing. Just before the Tálí Ka are two small boggy streams 3 and 6 yards broad, which are, however, no obstacle and have only 6 inches of mud and water. It now ascends steeply into some taungyas crossing one small stream 3 yards wide and after a small level piece, ascends steeply into Matyang (1½ miles). Branch roads from here to Wédu and N'bao, Lagat, and Nawku. The road follows the route to N'bao for 300 yards, and then turns north towards Teingram. It ascends at first steeply into some taungyas, and is then fairly level, with some ascents and descents over six small streams, none of which exceed 6 feet in width, and have good water and stony beds. From Teingram at 4 miles are branch roads to Kukam and Nawku and Meunglai. Road up to here good, smooth, but narrow. The road is now very good, 6 feet broad and well kept. It gradually descends at first, and then goes more steeply through tree jungle down to the Rítu Ka, which has a rough foot-bridge, and is 9 feet broad, stony bed, with rather difficult crossing. Two hundred yards further on it crosses the Tálí Ka (as above) which has a rough foot-bridge, and then ascends steeply over some taungyas and joins the road from Teingár to Lana (Branch II, Stage 2) about 300 yards short of Lana which is reached at 5½ miles.

BRANCH V.

FROM WARRA UMA, STAGE 6, TO WAJAO.

BY CAPT. COUCHMAN, JANUARY 1892.

Authorities. Military.	Authorities. Civil.	Number and Names of Stages, Rivers and Streams.	Distances. Intermediate. M. F.	Distances. Total. M. F.	Remarks.
G.O.C. Mandalay District and O.C. Bhamo.	Commissioner, Northern Division and Deputy Commissioner, Bhamo.	**1. Wajao** ... ... Two small streams near Warra Uma and 'Ntum Ka.	5 4	5 4	General direction east. The road goes towards Warra-Legra-katawng for ¼ mile (*see* Route 7). It then goes east through tree jungle, and ascends on to the ridge on which Warra-Legra-katawng stands and joins a road from the village to its paddy-field. Up to here the road is very rough and steep. It follows along the road to paddy-fields for 200 or 300 yards and then goes down very steeply through kaing grass to the 'Ntum Ka, 12 feet broad, 1 foot deep, stony bottom, and good water. It then ascends still more steeply through kaing grass, into tree jungle, and joins a fine open path 6 feet broad from Letsao and 200 yards further on reaches the small village of Laja (3 miles). Up to this junction the road is much overgrown and very steep and slippery. From Laja the road ascends

FROM BHAMO TO AYEINDAMA *viâ* TÂLÎ—*continued.*

BRANCH V—*continued.*

Authorities. Military.	Authorities. Civil.	Number and Names of Stages, Rivers and Streams.	Distances. Intermediate.	Distances. Total.	Remarks.
G.O.C. Mandalay District, &c.	Commr., Northern Division, &c.	**1. Wajao**—*cont.*			gradually through tree jungle into Wajao. There is a fine open road 9 feet broad to the Wajao paddy-fields to the east. Time to Wajao from Warra Uma for Mounted Infantry 1¼ hours. Distance estimated by time at 5½ miles. *Note.*—For transport it would be far better to go round by Warra-Pum-katawng, which is about ½ mile longer, but a better road.

BRANCH VI.

FROM PUMPIEN, *see* STAGE 7, TO MANMAW (STAGE 7).

BY CAPT. COUCHMAN, JANUARY 1892.

Military	Civil	Stages	Intermediate M.	Intermediate F.	Total M.	Total F.	Remarks
G.O.C. Mandalay District, &c.	Commissioner, Northern Division and Deputy Commissioner, Bhamo.	**1. Manmaw** ... Molé chaung and ten streams.	**6**	**4**	6	4	General direction west-north-west. This road goes along the spur west of Pumpien. Leaving the Pumpien Sawbwa's house it descends through tree jungle. This part is rather rough and stony for ¼ mile. It then descends more gradually with occasional ascents and descents first through tree jungle, and then through kaing grass and bamboo jungle. There are two very steep descents, but the road is good throughout, and, though not as broad as the road in Route 7, is, I think, preferable for ascent, as there are occasional level pieces, while in the other it is against the collar all the way. Ten streams in all are crossed, nine of which are merely little springs conducted out of the hill side by bamboo pipes. The tenth and last stream is about 6 feet broad and has muddy banks, which are boggy. From here the road goes west-south-west along damp paddy-fields, leaving the small Shan village of Loileng on the left about ¼ mile distant. It joins Route 6 at Nepeodaw. (From here *see* Route 7.) It is but little shorter than the other route (No. 7). Distance estimated by time 1½ hours for a small party of Mounted Infantry.

BRANCH VII.

FROM PUMPIEN, *see* STAGE 7, TO NINGKAW *viâ* HTINGCHU.

BY H. F. HERTZ, ESQ., CIVIL OFFICER, NORTH-EASTERN COLUMN, JANUARY 1882.

Military	Civil	Stages	Intermediate M.	Intermediate F.	Total M.	Total F.	Remarks
G.O.C. Mandalay District, &c.	Commr., Northern division, &c.	**1. Ningkaw** ... Four small streams.	**2**	**6**	2	6	General direction south-west. Road goes round the south side of the Pumpien hill, and crosses two small streams. It is pretty level throughout, and a good road for transport animals. A ¼ of a mile from Pumpien a branch road leads off to the Teingár paddy plain, south-east of Laimôk. Jungle, small trees. At 1¼ miles Htingchu.

FROM BHAMO TO AYEINDAMA *viâ* TÁLÍ—*continued.*

BRANCH VII—*continued.*

Authorities.		Number and Names of Stages, Rivers and Streams.	Distances.		Remarks.
Military.	Civil.		Inter-mediate.	Total.	
			M. F.	M. F.	
G.O.C. Mandalay District and O.C. Bhamo.	Commissioner, Northern Division and Deputy Commissioner, Bhamo.	**1. Ningkaw**—*cont.*			General direction from Htingchu, south-south-east. Road returns about 400 yards along Pumpien route and then branches off to the right. It descends gradually for about ½ mile and is fairly good. The descent then becomes very steep and crosses two small streams with rocky beds within the next ½ mile. The road about here is very narrow and along the steep hill side, and when it crosses the streams, it is bad for transport animals. At ¾ mile it joins the Pumpien-Ningkaw road. Jungle at first, grass and then tree jungle. Distance estimated by time.

No. 8.

From BHAMO to KÁNTI (up the Irrawaddy River).

FROM BHAMO TO NAWNAW (OR LAWNAW) RAPID ON MALÍKA RIVER (*i.e.*, WESTERN BRANCH OF IRRAWADDY RIVER ABOVE THE BIFURCATION) AND THENCE TO KÁNTI.

BY MAJOR FENTON, DEPUTY ASSISTANT QUARTERMASTER-GENERAL, INTELLIGENCE BRANCH, BURMAH, JUNE 1890.

Small steamers of the *Pathfinder* and *Mary* class are the only ones utilised at present for plying on the river from Bhamo upwards. Unfortunately in the low river season, say, from the end of October to the end of May, the river *above* Senbo is cut up into short lengths by sand and gravel banks, or reefs of rock over which there is not water enough for even the lightest draught steamers to pass upwards for any long distance.* In the flood season, on the other hand (from the end of May to the end of October), the river rushes with such violence through the defile *below* Senbo that it is only with the very greatest difficulty and with considerable danger that a steamer of either of the above classes could be got up under the most advantageous circumstances. To bring a steamer down at this season is almost out of the question. Nothing but the most urgent necessity could justify the attempt now that the danger of the proceeding has been practically tested.†

It is therefore at present impossible to run steamers the whole way between Bhamo and the Upper Irrawaddy (*i.e.*, above Senbo) throughout the year, and under those circumstances all that can be done is to use them between Bhamo and Senbo in the low-river season and above Senbo in the high-river. The annual rise of the river may be expected at the end of May or early in June, so any steamers that are wanted to work above Senbo in the high-river have to be sent up to that place by the end of May at the latest, or must at all events be prepared to start up at short notice for fully a week before then in case the river should show a steady rising tendency earlier than usual. There is a river-gauge at Bhamo. Roughly speaking, until this marks 13 feet of water in the river, steamers *can* get up the defile, but *cannot* get above Senbo; over 13 feet it is exactly the reverse.

Fuel.

Unless orders are issued beforehand for its collection, little or no wood for fuel can be obtained from the villages along the river, even the larger ones: but with a few days' notice any quantity that may be named up to 15 or 20 tons could be collected at Senbo, Hôkát, Tálawgyi, Kaungpu, Kátkyo, Zígyun, Waingmaw, Myitkyina, Maingna, and, with a week or two's notice, probably also at Wátu and Lapé. The longer the notice

* I understand that dredging operations are being carried on above Senbo, with a view to enabling small launches to pass up even in the dry season.—A. F. 18-2-93.

† Captain Black of H.M.'s Indian Marine brought the *Pirate* down safely in July 1888, but was several times in imminent danger of being wrecked.—A. F.

FROM BHAMO TO KÁNTI (UP THE IRRAWADDY RIVER)—*continued.*

the drier and better the fuel. As much coal as can conveniently be stowed should also be taken for use with the wood fuel in case this should be fresh and damp. If it is intended to go on far up the river axes and a cross-cut saw should be taken as there is a great deal of taungya cultivation up river and from the half-burnt logs on these clearings, it would be easy to replenish the stock of fuel, provided means of cutting it up are handy.

Country traversed.

Roughly speaking for the first 10 miles from Bhamo the river passes through low-lying jungle-covered country with numerous villages along the banks. It then enters the hills gradually and passes through them until just before reaching Senbo (about 50 miles from Bhamo). The country now opens out again, and, with the exception of a low and occasionally broken range of hills, which extends up the right bank from the river side below Hátha as far as Akyé, generally not further than 2½ to 3 miles from it and much nearer in parts, the country on both sides as far north as Wátu is flat and covered with low tree jungle or kaing grass. Except where cleared for cultivation near the villages, a little north of Wátu, the hills commence again and the river runs through them so far as it has been traversed up to the present. Those on the right bank are high and but little cleared of the thick jungle that covers them, but those on the left bank are lower and taungya clearings are numerous and extensive, especially from Lapé upwards on both branches, though few villages are in sight.

River.

The river varies in width from 600 to 1,000 yards and even more, except in the defile between Bhamo and Senbo and from the Mawkan rapid above Wátu onwards. In the former case it is about 300 yards at the widest, and 40 at the narrowest. In the latter case it narrows from Mawkan upwards to a general width of about 400 yards, a little less than that in some places, and a little more in others. At Lapé it is at about its narrowest (below the bifurcation), about 350 yards, and at the Manthémaw and the bend of the Tangpé rapids, and also just below the bifurcation it is at its widest, which is certainly under 500 yards.

At the junction the eastern branch (Méka, the Burmanized form of Nmaika, which is Kachin and means "a river that has bad, *i.e.*, turbulent water") is rather wider than the western branch or Malíka (Kachin, meaning "a large river" *). The former is about 400 yards wide and the latter about 300.

As you ascend the Malíka it narrows gradually to about 150 yards at Nawnaw (or Lawnaw) rapid. There is one narrow place before that, about 60 yards wide, but the current is now strong, probably about 3½ to 4 miles an hour at this season.

Above Nawnaw (or Lawnaw) as far as one can see it is still about the same width. *Boats* can get up as far as a place called Santa (about 3 days' journey up stream from the bifurcation), but never go any higher. Small bamboo rafts, however, come down from Nhúmnágá in the high-river season, which is a day's journey (with the stream) above Santa, whence they can get down to Sakáp in a day at the same season.

Current.

The current, generally speaking, must be about 3½ to 4½ miles an hour in the high-river season; in the defile often 6 or 7, and probably as much as 9 or 10 in the strongest parts of any very narrow places. From Bhamo to Senbo generally occupies about seven hours by steamer, the return journey about four.

Boats in the flood season take five days to ten days going up and come down easily in a day.

Boats ascending in the dry season from Senbo to Nawnaw would take about 17 days; longer than that if in large parties owing to delays that would occur at rapids, increasing in proportion to the number of boats. Steamers descending in the flood season from above Senbo take about half the time noted in the following route. Boats descending in the dry season would take probably about a quarter the time they take to get up.

Tributaries.

The only tributaries navigable by small steamers during high-river season are—

Right bank.—Mogaung chaung. *Left bank.*—Nantabet chaung.

Other smaller tributaries navigable by small boats for a day or two days' journey at the same season are—

Right bank.—Mawpaung, Nansan, and Sinkan chaungs and Pungin Ka.

Left bank.—Nammali, Nantabet, Natmyin and Namfu (Kwétu) chaungs.

---

* The name Malíka is given to any large river, *e.g.*, the Chindwin.—A. F.

No. 8.

FROM BHAMO TO KÁNTI—*continued.*

Authorities. Military.	Authorities. Civil.	Number and Names of Stages, Rivers and Streams.	Time. Intermediate. H. M.	Time. Total. H. M.	Remarks.
G.O.C. Mandalay District and O.C. Bhamo.	Commissioner, Northern Division and Deputy Commissioner, Bhamo.	**1. Senbo**	7 30	7 30	Right bank large Shan village. Plentiful supply of wood can be collected at short notice.
		Shwé-in	4 0	4 0	Left bank small mixed Shan-Kachin village, opposite mouth of Mogaung chaung. Wood obtainable on short notice.
		Kátha	1 15	5 15	Right bank small Shan village of five or six houses.
		Ayeindama ...	1 0	6 15	Left bank mixed Shan-Kachin village. From here a trade route leads to Thama and China (Maingla and Sanda districts), five or six mule marches.
		Kayôn	1 0	7 15	Small Kachin villages right bank.
		Manhwé	0 15	7 30	
		2. Hôkát	0 15	7 45	Right bank large mixed Shan-Kachin village. Police post. Plentiful supply of wood on short notice. Two days' march hence to Mogaung.
		Tálawgyi and Kaungpu.	2 45	10 30	Tálawgyi, 48 Shan houses, two Seinma Kayá Kachin, left bank, Kaungpu about 30 Shan houses, right bank. Plentiful supply of wood at both places on short notice. The chief local civil official (Atetléywa Kayaing-ôk) lives at Kaungpu. His district, extending from here to Maingna, belongs to the Mogaung sub-division. The most frequented trade route from here to China runs up the Nantabet chaung to Kázu, where it joins the routes from Maingmaw, Kátkyo, and Waingmaw and runs east over the hills to Thama on the highest range (two marches from Kázu). Here the Ayeindama route joins and it is two marches hence to the first villages of the Maingla and Sanda districts.
		Nantabet chaung.	1 30	11 0	This river is navigable by *Pathfinder* class as far as Nanpaung; 23 Shan and two Seinma Kaya Kachin houses right bank, about 14 miles up, and probably to Kázu (four Latawng Kachin houses, and formerly some Shan also) as far again beyond. It enters the Irrawaddy by the left bank opposite the island of Ngawnhohawk, on either side of which there is plenty of water.
		Tazaing	2 15	13 15	Small Salaung-Latawng-Kachin village; five houses; right bank.

FROM BHAMO TO KÁNTI—*continued.*

Authorities.		Number and Names of Stages, Rivers and Streams.	Time.		Remarks.
Military.	Civil.		Intermediate.	Total.	
			H. M.	H. M.	
G.O.C. Mandalay District and O.C. Bhamo.	Commissioner, Northern Division and Deputy Commissioner, Bhamo.	**Nátsé Kyauktán.**	0 45	14 0	Reef of rocks. Shallow near right bank, but plenty of water on the other side towards mid-stream and left bank.
		3. Ulauk	1 0	15 0	Mixed village (Shan, five houses, and Lepé Kachin, 10 houses). Firewood could be obtained with a few days' notice, but it is easier to get sufficient at Tâlawgyi and Káungpu to carry the steamer on to Kátkyo or Ligyun, both big villages. From here on a clear day the Shwedaungyi hills (Loi Kham), north and north-east of Mogaung, are visible; 20 miles or more away to the north-west are two conspicuous sugar-loaf peaks close together called Loi Ngu (snake hill) and Loi Ngo (bullock's hump hill) stand out clearly to the north-east, 20 to 30 miles off.
		Kaingtaung ...	1 15	16 15	Kaingtaung, Kachin village of two or three houses on island of same name, on which considerable opium was grown (and probably still *is*, though they say *not* during last season) by local Kachins, as well as others who come down from far north for the cultivating season (November to March).
		Maingma. ...	0 45	17 0	Maingmaw is a Marip Kachin village of about a dozen houses left bank. This and Sanka appear to be the only villages of this tribe on the river bank. The ruins of the ancient Shan town of the same name are in the jungle about a mile inland. Maingmaw is just opposite the upper end of the Kaingtaung Island and is one of the crossing places used by Caravans passing between China and Mogaung.
		Páraw	0 15	17 15	Small Latawng Kachin village of six houses, right bank.
		Akyé	0 15	17 30	Right bank Latawng Kachin village of about a dozen houses. This is the southernmost village under the Wátu Kachin Sawbwa, his northernmost village being Lapé just below the bifurcation.
		Sanka	1 30	19 0	Left bank Marip Kachin village of 11 houses, some Maru families also living there. Gold-washing carried on by these villagers, but the return seems very small. The Maru says he is *not* a Kachin, but in appearance there is little difference between them. They (Maru) have a language of their own, which is said to resemble Burmese rather than Kachin, but can all speak Kachin.

No. 8.

FROM BHAMO TO KÁNTI—*continued.*

Authorities. Military.	Authorities. Civil.	Number and Names of Stages, Rivers and Streams.	Time. Inter-mediate. H. M.	Time. Total. H. M.	Remarks.
G.O.C. Mandalay District and O.C. Bhamo.	Commissioner, Northern Division and Deputy Commissioner, Bhamo.	**Naunghé, Héchein and Utong.**	1 30	20 30	Naunghé, left bank, Maru village of six houses, clean and well-to-do. Héchein, right bank, Kachin village of half a dozen houses. Utông, right bank, another small Kachin village a few hundred yards higher up.
		4. Zígyun and Katkyo.	1 15	21 45	Kâtkyo, left bank, large Shan village of 30 houses with half a dozen Chinese-Shan houses at the eastern end. Plenty of wood procurable here and at Zígyun, a large Shan village of 40 houses, on an island opposite, channel on both sides of which has plenty of water at this season (June to October). The best place to bank at Zígyun Island is up the western channel, the narrower of the two. These two are almost the only Shan villages on the river above Senbo that have not their resident "protecting" Kachins. A trade route leads hence to Kázu on the Nantabet chaung and China (Maingla and Sanda districts).
		Thágaya and Pukaw.	0 30	22 15	Small Shan villages of a dozen huts each; former, on left bank of Irrawaddy, has also a few resident Matu-Sadan Kachins; latter on north-east corner of Zígyun Island just about opposite.
		Waingmaw ...	0 15	22 30	Left bank, Shan village of 40 houses and five Sadan Kachin and one or two Chinese or Shan-Chinese houses adjoining, but outside the stockade. Plenty of wood obtainable at short notice. Caravans from China *viâ* Kázu on the Nantabet chaung reach the Irrawaddy here and cross over to the right bank, making for Tháyágôn, whence they get over to Mogaung in three or four marches by the Nanti-chaung route.
		Nátmyin chaung and Ywadaw.	0 30	23 0	Ywadaw, left bank, small mixed village, five Shan houses, one Masang (or Mashang) Sadan Kachin. There were also a few Chinese-Shan houses here, but they were recently burnt by a raiding party of Sadan Kachins, who came from the other (*i.e.*, Chinese) side of the frontier some five or six days' journey eastward. The Nátmyin chaung is a small stream which enters the Irrawaddy by the left bank, a short distance below Ywadaw. Two days' journey by small boat (*peingaw*) up this stream (one day by land) there is a Chinese-Shan village called Lwésaw protected by Sadan Kachins, whence the people

FROM BHAMO TO KÁNTI—*continued.*

Authorities. Military.	Authorities. Civil.	Number and Names of Stages, Rivers and Streams.	Time. Intermediate. H. M.	Time. Total. H. M.	Remarks.
G.O.C. Mandalay District and O.C. Bhamo.	Commissioner, Northern Division and Deputy Commissioner, Bhamo.	**Nátmyin chaung and Ywadaw**—*cont.*			of Waingmaw obtain their rice as they themselves do no cultivating, living entirely by their profits as "middlemen" between the traders from down country and the Kachins, as indeed do most of the inhabitants of the Shan villages from Hôkát upwards. Only the smallest sized boats can get up the Nátmyin chaung, and their buoyancy is increased by lashing bamboos along each side.
		Tháyágôn ...	1 15	24 15	Right bank, mixed villages of about 12 Shan, four Chinese or Chinese-Shan, and two or three Lataung (Peinglán Sána) Kachin houses. Saya Kyaw Dôn, who accompanied the explorer "Maung Alaga" in his journey to the upper waters of the Irrawaddy 10 years ago, now lives here. Current between this and Ywadaw very strong.
		Myitkyina and Naungtálaw.	0 15	24 30	Myitkyina, right bank, mixed village of about Shan and Lataung (Lakun) Kachin; two Kyaungs. From here there is a route to Mogaung *viâ* the Nanti chaung, three or four marches, easy going in dry weather. Plenty of wood at short notice. Naungtálaw is on an island just opposite and consists of 20 Shan houses under the protection of Sadan Kachins of Loi Ngu, none of whom, however, live in the village. This is one of the few Shan villages on the Upper Irrawaddy that goes in at all extensively for cultivation.
		5. Maingna ...	0 45	25 15	Left bank, Shan village of 30 houses, with three or four houses of resident Kachins belonging to the Maran tribe, who "protect" the village. This is the furthest village on the Upper Irrawaddy, from which revenue was collected in the Burmese time. Plenty of wood procurable on a few days' notice.
		Aré	0 30	25 45	Right bank, Kachins, about 10 houses, probably belonging to the 'Nkum tribe and a few Maru houses too, perhaps, the villages along the river between Maingna and the bifurcation, with the exception of Wátu, Sakáp, and Lapé, belonging exclusively to 'Nkum Kachins or to Marus. Just beyond Aré, a high sugar-loaf peak called Loi Long shows up over the nearer ranges at the end of a long reach of the river, bearing about north-north-east. The Loi Ngu peaks bear about east-north-east from here, distant about 15 miles.

FROM BHAMO TO KÁNTI—*continued.*

Authorities.		Number and Names of Stages, Rivers and Streams.	Time.		Remarks.
Military	Civil.		Inter-mediate.	Total.	
			H. M	H. M.	
G.O.C. Mandalay District and O.C. Bhamo.	Commissioner, Northern Division and Deputy Commissioner, Bhamo.	**Naunglau and Wátu.**	1 0	26 45	Wátu (Lawkum-Latawng Kachin village), 10 or 12 houses, right bank; Sawbwa Sauktwémaw. Just below it on the same bank is a Chinese-Shan village of 15 or more houses called, I think, Naunglau. A few miles above Wátu, the Thetké Taung (Loi Ka), a high range of hills running east and west for about 8 miles about on the right bank of the river. Long high spurs run northwards from this range near the river up to and beyond the bifurcation west of the Malíka. On the left bank, nearly opposite, low hills, commencing with the Maingsôn Taung run parallel to and never more than a mile from that bank up to and beyond the bifurcation, south of the Méka which runs east from the bifurcation, the Malíka running north. From here, therefore, the Irrawaddy enters another defile which may probably be correctly called the first defile, as from all accounts its course now is entirely amongst hills up to its source above Kánti. Small streams break through the low hills on the left bank here and there, but the only right bank tributaries are streams that take their rise in the Loi Ka.
		Sakáp or Sakráp.	1 30	28 15	Right bank (Lawkum-Latawng Kachin village, 10 or 12 houses). About 15 minutes' run above this village; the course of the river is almost due north and south, and at the end of a very long reach on that bearing a high pointed topped hill shows up straight ahead, apparently not more than 15 miles off. From its summit broad easy sloping spurs, mostly cleared of trees, run down southwards. This hill is called Loi Lom in Shan, Pu.n Nen in Kachin, and is between the Malíka and the Méka near the former.
		Namfu stream ...	0 45	29 0	Stream entering by left bank, probably same as Kwétu chaung.
		'Nkum and Mawmé.	0 15	29 15	'Nkum Kachin village, 15 houses of tribe of same name, left bank; Mawmé, right bank a little higher up, about the same size and probably same tribe or Marâ.
		Mawkan rapid ...	0 15	29 30	Not very difficult rapid; best course up right bank close round the point.
		Manthémaw rapid.	0 45	30 15	Difficult rapid except when river is very full; best course near right bank up to a projecting point, then a little way towards mid-stream in slack water below a rock that crops up there, then back again slanting upwards to the right bank. This appears to have been the point up to which Captain Rimmer of the Irrawaddy Flotilla Company's service succeeded in bringing his boat in December 1887, as there is said to be no other rapid in the lowest state of the river (and there certainly is not in flood time) between this and Tángpé rapid close to the bifurcation.

FROM BHAMO TO KÁNTI—*continued.*

Authorities. Military.	Authorities. Civil.	Number and Names of Stages, Rivers and Streams.	Time. Intermediate. H. M.	Time. Total. H. M.	Remarks.
G.O.C. Mandalay District and O.C. Bhamo.	Commissioner, Northern Division and Deputy Commissioner, Bhamo.	**Lapé**	**0 45**	31 0	Small Lawkum-Latawng Kachin village of six or eight houses, right bank. This is one of the Wátu Sawbwa's villages and would be a good place for a steamer wishing to proceed up the Malíka to replenish its stock of wood, as the Sawbwa is on good terms with Government and would no doubt be able to arrange for the collection of several tons with due notice beforehand.
		Tángpé rapid ...	**1 0**	32 0	Difficult rapid, very strong water. Best course up left bank under shelter of large rock just above water at high-flood season, which forms a strong backwater (just above this same rock there is a well defined, but not dangerous, whirlpool), skirt round the mid-stream side of the rock, keeping as near to it as possible, then skirt the whirlpool as near as possible and get in again to the left bank above it as soon as you can. The difficult part is now over and you can cross gradually over to the right bank, where the current is slacker. The bifurcation is in sight directly you turn the rapid, but not before, as the river takes such a sharp turn there, considerably less than a right angle.
		Bifurcation of Irrawaddy river.	**0 30**	32 30	From above Tángpé rapid course is due east and this is the direction up the 'Nmaika (or Méka). The Malíka runs in at the junction from almost due north apparently, varying but little from that course for a long distance, 20 to 30 miles at least, and probably it runs almost due south all the way from where Colonel Woodthorpe saw it in about latitude 27°. At the junction the 'Nmaika is slightly wider than the Malíka, but even in high-flood a steamer cannot get more than 2½ to 3 miles up it in consequence of a reef which extends right across the stream, the channel between being nowhere clear of broken water.
		Tángpu and Mara.	**0 15**	32 45	Latawng Kachin village of five or six houses just over the crest of the hills bordering left bank. Taungya clearing extends almost to the river bank and path runs up across it to the villages, passing another small village of the same tribe called Mara; neither village is in sight from the river, but a few houses belonging to the latter have settled on the right bank of the 'Nmaika, a little above the junction.

FROM BHAMO TO KÁNTI—*continued.*

Authorities. Military.	Authorities. Civil.	Number and Names of Stages, Rivers and Streams.	Time. Inter-mediate.	Time. Total.	Remarks.
G.O.C. Mandalay District and O.C. Bhamo.	Commissioner, Northern Division and Deputy Commissioner, Bhamo.		H. M.	H. M.	
		Kwitan	0 15	33 0	Left bank, two or three Kachin houses a little way up the hill side; taungya clearing all round. There is a ferry here, the route being much used by Kachins going down to the Lémyo district for salt or right away down to Mogaung, Mohnyin, and Mawlu even to buy buffaloes.
		Pungin Ka ...	1 0	34 0	A stream which joins by the left bank about 60 feet wide at its mouth; slow current, probably partly due to the Malika being in flood and damming it up. It comes from the west-south-east, and is said to rise in the Loi Ka range.
		Nawnaw or (Lawnaw rapid).	0 15	34 15	Does not look difficult; best course probably up right bank. At the rapid the river takes a bit of a bend, but it is only a short one and one can see up the course for a couple of miles, it then disappears behind a hill running down from the east.

The following description of the route onwards INTO KÁNTI was furnished by SAN MAUNG PWA OF MAINGNA:—

Authorities. Military.	Authorities. Civil.	Number and Names of Stages, Rivers and Streams.	Distances. Inter-mediate.	Distances. Total.	Remarks.
Beyond the sphere of Civil and Military authority at present.			M. F.	M. F.	There are no villages, other than Kachin throughout this route until Kánti Shan country is reached. Meungyaka is apparently the chief place in the southern part of Kánti.
		1. Wunnan ...	...	...	Village on left bank.
		2. Alun	...	...	At about one-third of the way past village of Nunglan, left bank, just south of which a small stream enters river by same bank. Alun is a village on left bank.
		3. Sawan	...	...	At about one-third of the way pass village of Santá, left bank, just above which the Namsáng chaung, a good big stream (as large as the Nátmyin below Ywadaw) enters by the same bank. At two-thirds pass village of Namsókatawng at the mouth of a small stream that enters by the left bank. Sawan is a village on the right bank. "*Launga*" (medium size country

FROM BHAMO TO KÁNTI—*continued.*

Authorities. Military.	Authorities. Civil.	Number and Names of Stages, Rivers and Streams.	Distances. Intermediate. M. F.	Distances. Total. M. F.	Remarks.
Beyond the sphere of Civil and Military authority at present.		**3. Sawan**—*cont.*			boats) can get up so far, but no further, and apparently very few go up during the year even so far, the Shans trusting to the Kachins to come down themselves and fetch what they want. From Santá upwards there are numerous Kachin villages on the hills on either side of the river. Only "*peingaws*" (small "dug-outs") and bamboo rafts can be used on the river above Sawan.
		4. Tamáng sakhán.	...	...	Halting place on left bank. No village near.
		5. Kassa sakhán.	...	...	Halting place on left bank. No village near.
		6. Tarátsup ...	...	...	At about two-thirds of the way village of Keungsungyáng, left bank. Tarátsup is just below the mouth of a stream that enters by the left bank. Doubtful whether this is a village or merely a halting place.
		7. Wulaw ...	...	...	Matkyikatawng village on left bank is passed midway. Wulaw is a village also on left bank.
		8. Lapaung and Pungleng.	...	...	Lapaung and Pungleng are villages on the river bank opposite each other, the former on the right bank, the latter on the left. No boats, however small, can get higher up than this, and travellers must take to the road which follows the right bank.
		9. 'Ntingnoi ...	...	...	A long day's march passing the villages of Maraw-Sitta (just beyond which a stream is crossed), Sanáyáng and Lôpla, all on the right bank.
		10. Kacheing ...	...	...	Passing the villages of Ngankán, Pomyáng, and Sakám, all right bank.
		11. Masi chaung.	...	...	Just north of Kácheing, a large stream called the Pungin Ka enters by the right bank. It comes from the west and some little distance up it forks, the southern branch being called the Pungin and the northern the Pungsán Ka (Ka = river in Kachin). After crossing the Pungin pass the villages of Lashulatáp, Salékyet, Pási, Kátsu, and Taungmatsa and camp at halting place on Masi chaung, a short distance beyond the last-named village. This stream comes in from the north-west or west by the right bank.
		12. 'Ntawng ...	...	...	Village on right bank. Here the path apparently bears away to the west of the Malíka, and it is two days' march to Meungyaka.

No. 8.

FROM BHAMO TO KÁNTI—*continued.*

Authorities. Military.	Authorities. Civil.	Number and Names of Stages, Rivers and Streams.	Distances. Intermediate.	Distances. Total.	Remarks.
			M. F.	M. F.	
Beyond the sphere of Civil and Military authority at present.		**13. Meungyaka or Meungyeuka.**	...	...	This is a large village or town in Kánti, probably situated in the valley of the Namyuk, which is shown in the 2nd edition of sheet No. 22 N. W.; N. E. T. F. Series as joining the Namlung just above *its* junction with the Namkiu or Malíka in about latitude 27° 15′. From Lapaung upwards the country is thickly populated by Káku Kachin tribes. It is said to be eight days' journey from Kacheing into Assam, but they must be very long marches and even so would scarcely land one more than on the borders of that country. If, however, the high range forming the watershed between the Brahmaputra and the Irrawaddy be taken as bounding Assam on the east then eight days' journey from Kacheing or thereabouts *viâ* the Chaukan pass would just about land one in Assam, and very likely this is what they mean. The first eight stages from Nawnaw are by water, probably about 8 miles each, if so much, as there are numerous rapids and progress would be slow. The remaining stages are each a day's march. The distance from Nawnaw to Meungyaka as the crow flies must be about 80 miles, not more, and as travelled by water and road would not be as much as 120. Probably the land stages cannot therefore be long, and 14 days must be a very liberal estimate of the time required to perform the whole journey. Transport animals do not appear to be used, the Kachins carrying their loads on the back, with a band passing round the forehead and a yoke resting on the shoulders to steady the load just like the Manipur, Kuki, or Tonkul coolies carry theirs. A path runs northwards from Lapé below the bifurcation to Kwitau ferry, whence there must certainly be a path up the left bank to Santá, and there is probably another path up the right bank as there is another ferry at a place called 'Npáng about a day's journey above Nawnaw. The path crossing here may, however, go direct west to the Amber Mines District and not come down the river bank towards Lapé. From Nawnaw upwards the river is shut in on both sides by hills, and numerous rapids are met with.

No. 9.

From BHAMO to MANWEIN viâ KARWÁN.

BY CAPT. SLADEN, 1868.

G.O.C. Mandalay Dist. and O.C. Bhamo.	Commr., N. Divn. and Dy. Commr., Bhamo.	Stages	Intermediate M. F.	Total M. F.	Remarks
Doubtful.		**1. Mansi** ...	**14 0**	14 0	*See* No. 13 Bhamo to Namkham *viâ* Karwán.
		2. Camp ...	**8 0**	22 0	
		3. Karwán, Great Pônkan.	**9 0**	31 0	
		4. Camp ...	**17 0**	48 0	One zayat. Road descends slightly all the way.
		5. Naungin ...	**22 0**	70 0	A Shan village of 75 houses.
		6. Lompa ...	**17 0**	87 0	A Shan village of 60 houses.
		7. Mantap ...	**10 0**	97 0	A Shan village of 30 houses.
		8. Lakom ...	**21 0**	118 0	A Shan village of 50 houses. Maingtha Shans.
		9. Hôtha ...	**3 0**	121 0	

FROM BHAMO TO MANWEIN *viâ* KARWÂN—*continued.*

Authorities. Military.	Authorities. Civil.	Number and Names of Stages, Rivers and Streams.	Distances. Intermediate.	Distances. Total.	Remarks.
China.		**10 & 11. Manwein.**	M. F. **20 0**	M. F. 141 0	*Note* 1.—Lompa and Mantap are believed to be in the Mainwan State, the town of Mainwan lying a short distance east of them. This is the regular Sawadi route to Momein. *Note* 2.—This is a very old account and should be superseded.—A. F.

No. 10.

From BHAMO to MÁTIN viâ HÁNGTÔN.

BY LIEUT. H. G. BURTON, MOGAUNG LEVY, MARCH 1891.

Authorities. Military.	Authorities. Civil.	Number and Names of Stages, Rivers and Streams.	Distances. Intermediate.	Distances. Total.	Remarks.
G.O.C. Mandalay District and O.C. Bhamo.	Commissioner, Northern Division and Deputy Commissioner, Bhamo.	**1. Namsiri chaung, sakhán.**	M. F. **12 0**	M. F. 12 0	Road runs east-north-east to Mômauk-sakhán through thin jungle as far as Mômauk; is fit for native wheeled carts, but is under water in rains. At Mômauk, 9 miles, there is camping ground east to Namsiri sakhán at foot of Lawtan hill. Distance 12 miles. Road good, running through *kaing* grass over flat country, but is under water in rains. Camp large and water good. Is best first halting place from Bhamo.
		2. Patsa Ka camp, 2 miles beyond Lawtan. Patsa Ka.	**7 0**	19 0	Road runs ½ mile east through taungya clearing to foot of hill. Then ascends east-north-east 2,800 feet to camping ground (4 miles). Camp small and water scanty. Half mile south-west from here is village of Palaung; 5 houses; (Cowri-Lepai). From camp ascent of 500 feet in ¾ mile to Lawtan; 32 houses (Cowri-Lepai). No camping ground in village. Height of Lawtan 3,600 feet. Road very steep. Road ascends ½ mile east-south-east to top of Lawtan hill, then descends through tree jungle 1,000 feet by steep gradients to Patsa Ka stream and camping ground 2 miles from Lawtan. This is best second halting place from Bhamo.
		3. Hángtôn ... Wara Ka.	**10 0**	29 0	From here road ascends east 500 feet to Lawmun, 3 miles; ascent stiff over grass-covered spurs and taungya sites; Lawmun, a marán village of 16 houses. Camping ground is ¾ mile from village, is small, but has good water-supply. Road descends about 500 feet in ¾ mile to camping ground in Wara Ka, then ascends east-north-east, 1,000 feet through grass jungle to Seinlumgyi, 6 miles; Cowri-Lepai; 50 houses; room in the village for 100 men to camp; good water. From Sinlun road runs east, descends 300 feet in ¼ mile to the Kaya Ka stream which is crossed by a foot-bridge; mules have to ford stream; crossing difficult, owing to the rocky nature of the bed, then ascends 1,200 feet through taungya sites to Pônka 8½ miles. Camp and water in village; Cowri-Lepai; 10 houses. Road descends 500 feet through grass and taungya to Nantabet valley, crosses Nantabet (20 yards × 18 inches deep), 800 yards below site of village, then runs through taungya ½ mile along right bank and ascends east-north-east 500 feet to Hángtôn (5,500 feet high). Camp on site of village; water good. Distance 10 miles.

FROM BHAMO TO MÁTIN *viâ* HÁNGTÔN—*continued*.

Authorities. Military.	Authorities. Civil.	Number and Names of Stages, Rivers and Streams.	Distances. Inter-mediate.	Distances. Total.	Remarks.
G.O.C. Mandalay District and O.C. Bhamo.	Commr., Northern Division and Dy. Commissioner, Bhamo.	**4. Mátin** ...	M. F. **11 0**	M. F. 40 0	Road ascends hill to north 100 yards (500 feet), then descends north-east for 1½ miles to bottom of valley (1,000 feet). Road fairly good. Crosses a stream at bottom of valley and ascends through taungya 1,200 feet to Sinmakôn 3 miles. Ascent steep. From Sinmakôn road to Walaung descends hill ¼ mile to east. Waloung is also reached by a branch road ½ mile south on Hángtôn-Sinmakôn road. Both villages since burnt. From Waloung road runs north descending hill through dense kaing grass 800 feet in 1½ miles to taungya sites on stream at foot of hill. Path then crosses to right bank of stream and runs east 1 mile to Manglwai valley. Valley is 2 miles long, ¾ mile broad. All under cultivation; good camping ground and water. Village of Manglwai (Cowri-Lepai; 30 houses); 800 yards north-east of camping ground. Distance 6 miles. Road from Manglwai ascends by easy gradients 2½ miles (500 feet) to Lwéyin; Cowri-Lepai; 25 houses. Lwéyin also reached by road direct from Sinmakôn, running north 1½ miles to bottom of hill, crossing stream and then ascending through cultivation 1½ miles to village of Lwéyin, reducing the length of the stage to 11 miles. From Lwéyin road runs west-north-west 1 mile along spurs, then branches off north 4 miles down easy gradients to Mátin, 13½ miles. From Lwéyin there is also a direct road to Chikai; fairly good; runs north-west nearly parallel with Mátin road.

BRANCH I.

FROM HÁNGTÔN, STAGE 3, TO LETPATKÔM.

Military	Civil	Stage	Intermediate	Total	Remarks
G.O.C. Mandalay District and O.C. Bhamo.	Commissioner, Northern Division and Dy. Commissioner, Bhamo.	**1. Letpatkôm** ...	**6 4**	6 4	Road follows Nantabet chaung for 1 mile, then ascends hills to north-east through grass and bamboo jungle. Follows ridge of hills to east for 4 miles to foot of Letpatkôm hill. No water after leaving Nantabet. Road ascends Letpatkôm hill 1½ miles; large bare hill. Village (Lakuns); 12 houses at top in clump of trees, 7,000 feet; 300 feet down hill ¼ mile east of Letpatkôm is village of Yawyins; 25 houses. Camping ground is on rising ground 300 yards north of Upper Letpatkôm. Water good.

BRANCH II.

FROM HÁNGTÔN TO NEIGHBOURING VILLAGES.

Military	Civil	Stage	Intermediate	Total	Remarks
G.O.C. Mandalay district and O.C. Bhamo.	Commr., Northern Division and Dy. Commr., Bhamo.	**Sinlungalé** ...	**1 4**	...	Road ascends hill to north-west 600 feet in ¾ mile through taungyas, then runs north-north-west ¾ mile over spurs to Sinlungalé (Cowri-Lepai); 20 houses; road good. From here there is also a road to Sinmakôn. It runs round to north of Sinmakôn hill meeting the Sinmakôn-Lwéyin road ½ mile north of Sinmakôn.

FROM BHAMO TO MÁTIN *viâ* HÁNGTÔN—*continued.*

BRANCH II—*continued.*

Authorities. Military.	Authorities. Civil.	Number and Names of Stages, Rivers and Streams.	Distances. Intermediate.	Distances. Total.	Remarks.
			M. F.	M. F.	
G.O.C. Mandalay Dist. and O.C. Bhamo.	Commr., Northern Divn. and Dy. Commr., Bhamo.	**Hángtônpum** ...	1 4	...	Road from Hángtôn ascends wooded hill to east 800 feet in ½ mile, then runs east along narrow ridge ¾ mile to Hángtônpum; Lakuns; 4 houses; since burnt. One mile east of Hángtônpum this road runs into the Letpatkôm road.

No. 11.

From BHAMO to MÔMIEN viâ NAMPAUNG CHAUNG FORT.

BY E. P. CLONEY, ESQ., CIVIL OFFICER WITH EASTERN KACHIN COLUMN, DECEMBER 1890, AND CAPT. COUCHMAN, D.S.O., SOMERSETSHIRE REGIMENT, DECEMBER 1891.

Military	Civil	Stages	Intermediate	Total	Remarks
G.O.C. Mandalay District and O.C. Bhamo.	Commissioner, Northern Division and Deputy Commissioner, Bhamo.	**1. Malula** .. ... Tapin and Nampa-Chaungwa.	13 4	13 4	Leaving Bhamo the road goes north to Fort A, then takes a north-easterly direction for about 2 miles and crosses two little streams, over which the Public Works Department have spanned substantial wooden bridges. Road good all the way and passes through high wooded ground; not much undergrowth. Near the village of Nampa-Chaungwa, about 4 miles from Fort A, a large Public Works Department wooden bridge is crossed. The road becomes more open and broader after leaving Nampa till Môpeing, a Shan-Talôk village of 60 houses, is reached. Môpeing has a very large camping ground outside village towards south, just before entering. Water from the Tapin. From Môpeing the road strikes east; though the road itself is good the jungle on the both sides is very thick with thick undergrowth. Two or three small chaungs are crossed. These are generally bridged by the villagers, but the water is never deep in the cold weather. About 1 mile south of Malula is a deep chaung with very steep banks. This the villagers had temporarily bridged. After crossing this the road goes north again. The road on both sides of the chaung is through kaing grass and is, during the rains, under water. It would therefore be useless to have a permanent bridge over the chaung. A quarter of a mile before entering Malula the road leads through paddy-fields. Malula, a Shan-Burman village of 30 houses, has a good camping ground and a pôngyi kyaung for officers to stay in. Malula is situated on the left bank of the Tapin river, whence its water-supply is obtained.
		2. Myothit ... Tapin.	10 2	23 6	The road runs through paddy-fields, passing after 1½ miles the village of Kywégyo to the left, still running through paddy-fields. After another mile and-a-half two Shan-Burman villages of Maubin and Manyé to the right, then the road runs along the bank of the Tapin for a mile over sandy ground till the Shan-Burman village of Naungpaung is reached. The road runs close to the village stockade, leaving the village to the left, taking a slightly north-easterly direction, for about half a mile through open ground and about ¼ of a mile through kaing jungle before the Shan-Talôk village of Kanni or Naung

FROM BHAMO TO MÖMIEN *viâ* NAMPAUNG CHAUNG FORT—*continued.*

Authorities. Military.	Authorities. Civil.	Number and Names of Stages, Rivers and Streams.	Distances. Intermediate.	Distances. Total.	Remarks.
G.O.C. Mandalay District and O.C. Bhamo.	Commissioner, Northern Division and Deputy Commissioner, Bhamo.	**2. Myothit**—*cont.*			Paung is reached. The road runs along in front of the village stockade and beyond it for a few hundred yards and crosses a small stream; continues through kaing jungle for a mile and-a-half and goes into the dry bed of the Tapin. Through dry bed of the river great care should be taken in following the tracks of the villagers as there are treacherous quicksands off the track. The waters of the Tapin are confined to the right bank. The crossing is by boat between the two Shan-Burman villages of Hintha. The breadth of the stream here is abont 200 yards. The road runs through the upper village of Hintha and turns east running through kaing grass and keeping along the right bank of the Tapin all the way for 2¼ miles. A quarter of a mile from the village the road runs through low, sandy ground, commanded on the left by low hilly ground thickly wooded. Myothit, called by the Shans Möngmai, has abont 25 houses and is a good camping ground, but has only kaing grass as forage. There is an abundant supply of water, being on the Tapin. The Lawku Sawbwa has a large house here and looks after the welfare of the village. At Myothit after the rainy season of 1891 a bridge (temporary) was constructed over the Tapin 180 yards long, 5 feet broad, 4 feet over the water; built on piles with a hand-rail 3 feet high. Roadway is formed of poles laid longitudinally along bridge; these are covered with split bamboos and kaing grass, on the top of which is a layer of sand. It is rather shaky, but passable for mounted men and laden mules: it would be washed away in the rains. Bridge 5 feet above the water. Banks sandy and covered with kaing grass and only (except where the village stands) 8 feet above the water. Left bank shelves gradually, but right is steeper. Bottom of river sandy. Current 2 miles an hour. Water clear, good, and full of fish. The river flows out of a defile in a northerly direction at Myothit. The right bank commands the left. [*N.B.*—Breadth of river 172 yards.] Good camping ground to the north of village, which would hold over 1,000 men, but would require clearing. Myothit has 15 Burman houses, 3 Kachin, and 2 Chinese. Myothit is on the right bank of the Taping. There are three small dug-outs.
		3. Nampaung Chaung Fort. Namsong Ka, Panma Ka, Nampaung Ka, and numerous smaller streams.	M. 13 F. 0	M. 36 F. 6	General direction east-north-east. Road passes through the camping ground into thick kaing grass. After ½ mile it follows up the banks of the Numsong Ka, crossing and recrossing it seven times, occasionally going along its bed. At 3½ miles it leaves the stream and ascends a very steep stony hill. Road here very bad and slippery. It then follows up a ridge, crossing some small streams, the ascents and descents of which are generally a little difficult. The country about here consists of heavy tree jungle alternating with kaing grass and taungyas (cultivated clearings). At 4½ miles reach Lar-chong, a La-htaw (? Latawng) Kachin hamlet of three huts. Time 2¾ hours. The Namsong is a rocky torrent with no depth of water except in small pools. It is 5 to 6 yards broad. Lar-chong B.P. thermometer 208·4 at 11 A.M., or 1,885 feet elevation. It is a very poor-looking village and has no cattle or paddy. This village is grouped with Ten-

FROM BHAMO TO MÔMIEN *viâ* NAMPAUNG CHAUNG FORT—*continued.*

Authorities.		Number and Names of Stages, Rivers and Streams.	Distances.				Remarks.
Military.	Civil.		Intermediate.		Total.		
G.O.C. Mandalay District and O.C. Bhamo.	Commissioner, Northern Division and Deputy Commissioner, Bhamo.	**3. Nampaung Chaung Fort**—*cont.*					griyaw and Panma. There is a road from here to La-htaw, Sinyu, and Htingchu, the latter is about ¾ mile to the north-west over a steep ridge. From Lar-chong there is a steep descent for a mile to the Panma Ka, 10 to 15 yards broad, a torrent in a deep gorge easily fordable (1 foot deep). There is an open maidan on each side of this stream capable of camping over 2,000 men. Water good and plentiful. Numerous small streams are crossed, one of them four times. To the south, 2 miles away, perched on a high hill, is the Kowri-Kachin village of Latong. From here there is a very steep ascent to the Kachin ('Nkum) village of Panma (8¼ miles). The path here is in better order. B.P. thermometer 206·8 or 2,730 feet elevation above the sea. The road now descends to the 'Nkum-Kachin village of Nawku (9 miles) and then again descends very steeply through old overgrown clearings till at 11 miles it crosses a stream with good water. It is a torrent 1 foot deep and about 10 yards broad. On the other side is an open space which would camp 500 men. After a rise of 300 feet the road passes the police post of Sumpráya; from here the direction of the road is north; from here there is a good view of the Tapin, which is a rocky torrent to the east. From the police post there is a sharp descent of ¾ mile, when the Nampaung chaung is reached, a rocky torrent, easily fordable, good water full of mahseer, and 30 to 40 yards broad. The road runs northerly now along its right bank along some paddy-fields, and at 13 miles the crossing is reached. This is commanded by the Chinese outpost about 100 feet above and 100 yards distant on the left bank. The British fort is 750 yards distant on the right bank and 525 feet above it. B.P. thermometer 210·2 — 940 feet elevation at crossing. The B.P. thermometer showed 209·2 at the fort, which is reached by a very steep ascent (1,465 feet). The road up to this point is, though rough in places, perfectly passable for men and loaded animals, but always in single file. In the rains a few caravans go down as far as Mannaung, from which place merchandize goes down to Bhamo in boats. I should not have thought it possible to march mules from Nampaung chaung to Myothit in the rains. *Note.*—There is a road from Sumpráya to Manwein *viâ* Pônsi. The description of the remainder of this route is from native information.
China.			M.	F.	M.	F.	
		4. Saré-gyi ...	**13**	**0**	49	6	Up a steep hill past Yawyong and Yangkwé stockades (visible from Nampaung chaung) and then down to Yangkwé Ka. Pass Kauntong and two villages of Manyaung and Maru. Up an ascent to Kunchi (15 houses, 'Nkum Kachin, stockaded); then down to Kumpár Ka and up to Saré and Sarégyi (Salégyi) on the Saré Ka. Before reaching Kunchi the road passes along the north side of the Lakampum. Road and jungle as in Route No. 7, Stage 5.
		Yangkwé Ka (6 feet broad), Cheti Ka (6 feet broad), Kúm-pár Ka (12 feet broad, Saré Ka (12 feet broad).					

FROM BHAMO TO MÔMIEN *viâ* NAMPAUNG CHAUNG FORT—*continued.*

Authorities. Military.	Authorities. Civil.	Number and Names of Stages, Rivers and Streams.	Distances. Intermediate. M.	F.	Distances. Total. M.	F.	Remarks.
China.		**5. Manwein** ... Nam-hpyit Ka (Devil's river) 15 feet broad, Kadu Ka (25 yards broad).	10	2	60	0	Road descends to the south of Wachaung hill, and then to Nam-hpyit Ka. It then ascends to between Pomwa stockade and village (20 houses, Lapai Kachins). From here the road is at no great distance from the right bank of the Taping. It now descends into a level paddy plain and, after crossing the Kadu Ka, reaches Manwyne (400 to 500 Shan houses, surrounded by a brick wall 7 feet high). Boats can now ply for two hours' journey down the Tapin, and also up stream. There is a daily bazaar held.
		6. Sánda ... ... Several small streams.	12	0	72	0	The road follows a paddy plain and is level. There are, however, no carts in this country at all. Sánda, Shan town, surrounded by a brick wall about 7 feet high. Has 500 or 600 houses. Ten years ago there were 20 to 25 dug-outs here. The road has an easterly direction in this march and passes the village of Naunmu (Shan).
		7. Meungla ... Nanting Ka.	12	0	84	0	Road as in No. 6 stage. Meungla has 400 houses, is Shan, and is stockaded. Boats can ply up the Tapin as far as here. There is a bazaar held every five days. There is a ferry on the Nanting chaung.
		8. Mainti ... Tapin river.	20	0	104	0	The road crosses one small hill and the Tapin river by a chain and plank bridge at Chetao Cheng. This bridge is 90 yards long and 12 feet broad. Mainti is on the west side of a hill. It has 200 Shan houses and is stockaded.
		9. Hsiao-to-hi ... One stream.	13	0	117	0	Good road over a paddy plain. Hsiao-to-hi has 15 Chinese houses and is not stockaded.
		10. Mômien ...	14	0	131	0	Road crosses one hill about 400 feet high. Mômien has a brick wall round it as "high as that round Mandalay," but has no moat. All the above route and stages are as performed by laden mules. *N.B.*—From Myothit to Nampaung chaung the distance was paced. From Nampaung chaung to Mômien each march was described as being as far as from so and so to so and so, two places being named which were known to the parties conversing.

FROM BHAMO TO MÔMIEN *viâ* NAMPAUNG CHAUNG FORT—*continued.*

ALTERNATIVE I.

FROM MYOTHIT, STAGE 2, TO NAMPAUNG CHAUNG FORT, STAGE 3.

BY CAPT. COUCHMAN, D.S.O., DECEMBER 1891.

Authorities.		Number and Names of Stages, Rivers and Streams.	Distances.		Remarks.
Military.	Civil.		Inter-mediate.	Total.	
			M. F.	M. F.	
G.O.C. Mandalay District and O.C. Bhamo.	Commissioner, Northern Division, and Deputy Commissioner, Bhamo.	**1. Nampaung Chaung Fort.** Several small streams.	**13 0**	13 0	There is another and a better route from Myothit to Nampaung Fort as follows: For the first 2 miles the road is the same as that described above. It then branches off in a northerly direction. General direction east-north-east. There is a very steep ascent through kaing grass up to the village of Sinyu Htingnong (3 miles). The road is much overgrown here; thence the road has a very gradual ascent and is very good for about a mile, when it again ascends steeply over stony ground to Sinyu (1) (5 miles). Sinyu is a double village number (2), being a ¼ of a mile further on down a steep stony piece of road. From here there is a road to the west (left) to Sihet. Between here and Peto three streams are crossed. All are small and have very little but good water. The ascent to Peto (Peshito, 6 miles) is very steep and stony, the latter part being along the right bank of a small rocky stream. From Peto the road has a gradual ascent and two small descents to Liya (7½ miles) and thence to Pônlein (8½ miles), crossing one small stream. This road is very good and smooth; indeed all the way up from Sinyu Htingnong one has occasional views of the Bhamo plain. From Pônlein the road gradually descends for ½ a mile and then gradually ascends for 1 mile. The road here is along the side of a steep hill and in some places passes over large slabs of rock. On reaching a halting place about 1½ miles from Pônlein, where there is room for 100 men to encamp, the road ascends steeply over rocky ground to Ungaw 11 miles. There are several bad places here and the road winds a good deal up the hill. There are six streams on this portion of road, all small. Ungaw is 3,000 feet above sea level (two observations B. P. thermometer). From here the road descends steeply for ½ a mile to Lower Ungaw, whence there are two roads down to the Nampaung chaung— (1) *Viâ the fort.*—Road ascends for ¼ mile and then descends very steeply at an angle of 22½° to the fort; thence to the ford on the Nampaung chaung ⅛ mile, very steep, and crossing a small stream which has been temporarily bridged. Jungle kaing grass. (2) *Viâ the spur to the south of the fort.*—Level for a mile and then down steeply to the ford. This road is a better one than the other *viâ* the fort as it is not so steep.

ALTERNATIVE II.

FROM MYOTHIT, STAGE 2, TO NAMPAUNG, STAGE 3, *viâ* NAMSANGYA SAKHÁN.

BY E. P. CLONEY, ESQ., DECEMBER 1890.

Military	Civil	Stages	Intermediate	Total	Remarks
G.O.C. Mandalay District and O.C. Bhamo.	Commr., Northern Divn., and Deputy Commr., Bhamo.	**1. Namsangya sakhán.** Namsangya.	**10 0**	10 0	The road for the first few hundred yards or so runs north by the Lawku Sawbwa's house and turns to the right. Here the ooze from the foot of the hills has formed a small marsh. From here we commence ascending. Road fairly good, but narrow; ascent long but gradual, and general direction

From BHAMO to MÔMIEN *viâ* NAMPAUNG CHAUNG FORT—*continued*.

ALTERNATIVE II—*continued*.

Authorities. Military.	Authorities. Civil.	Number and Names of Stages, Rivers and Streams.	Distances. Intermediate.	Distances. Total.	Remarks.
G.O.C. Mandalay District and O.C. Bhamo.	Commissioner, Northern Division, and Deputy Commissioner, Bhamo.	**1. Namsangya sakhán**—*cont.*			easterly. On the lower slopes coarse grass and small trees. The upper slopes open, with larger trees, commanding a good view of the Tapin. No water met with on the road. Within ½ a mile of Salégalé to the left, off the road, is Lawku, about 3,000 feet high. Lawku has 40 houses and is a Lawkum village. Half a mile further north is Salégalé, 3,000 feet high, with 20 houses (tribe Lakum). No good camping ground for a large number of men. Water and grass sufficient for a small number of animals, but not plentiful (distance 5½ miles). The road good and easy; mostly down hill, though here and there are small ascents from 50 to 100 yards. First passes near the village of Panma (1), 10 houses (left of road); through Panma (2), 10 houses; near Panma (3), seven houses (right of road); through Panma (4) seven houses; through Lawkulat, six houses; then a mile of descent all the way brings us to the first crossing of the Namsangya chaung, where the alternating direct caravan route from Myothit is met. The stream has plenty of very good water. It is not deep. The general direction of the road is northerly. The descent is above 2,000 feet in 4½ miles; then turning to the right crossing the Namsangya thrice the caravan camp is reached at 16 miles; not capable of containing more than a couple of hundred men with transport. Camping ground good; grass and water good and plentiful.
		2. Nampaung Chaung Fort. Tumpônya chaung.	M. F. **6 4**	M. F. 16 4	The road runs south-east through camp and turns east and goes up north-east. From camp the general direction northerly. Ascent gradual, but continuing the whole way till within a ¼ of a mile of Panma (5), eight houses. Road very good; no water to cross. Good camping ground; water-supply from village; fair, forage, but some distance off. To the south lies Panma (6) or Wakow. The road runs along north-east on the level saddle of the hill for ¼ of a mile till Lawkugyi (five houses) is passed; another of a ¼ mile in the same direction along the saddle, then a slight ascent commences. Road passes through open taungya-sites for ½ a mile, then going east commences to descend for about a mile to the camp of Sumprâya. A ¼ of a mile further is Tumpônya sakhán. Tumpônya chaung is close below and has to be crossed. This is a large camping ground with a plentiful supply of water and grass. On crossing the stream the road to the left is the proper caravan route. The one straight ahead leads to the Nompaung chaung for about 2 miles. It is very rough and stony with obstacles of fallen trunks of trees. Then about ½ a mile of gradual descent brings us to the Nampaung chaung.

ALTERNATIVE III.

From MYOTHIT, Stage 2, to NAMSANGYA SAKHÁN (Stage 3, Alt. II) as follows :—

By E. P. CLONEY, Esq., December 1890.

Military	Civil	Stages	Intermediate	Total	Remarks
G.O.C. Mandalay District and O.C. Bhamo.	Commr., Northern Divn., and Dy. Cr., Bhamo.	**1. Namsangya sakhán.** Nanmaw chaung.	**8 0**	8 0	There is another route from Myothit to Namsangya. The road on leaving Myothit follows the Salégalé route, but instead of going on to the right the path to the front is followed 300

FROM BHAMO TO MÔMIEN *viâ* NAMPAUNG CHAUNG FORT—*continued.*

ALTERNATIVE III—*continued.*

Authorities. Military.	Authorities. Civil.	Number and Names of Stages, Rivers and Streams.	Distances. Intermediate.	Distances. Total.	Remarks.
G.O.C. Mandalay District and O.C. Bhamo.	Commissioner, Northern Division, and Deputy Commissioner, Bhamo.	**1. Namsangya sakhán**—*cont.*			yards when it crosses the Nanmaw chaung. General direction northerly. Both sides of the road thickly wooded. The road crosses the bed of the stream some eight or ten times and gradually ascends. Crossing is very stony and slippery. After 4 miles the road in two or three places in detached bits becomes very bad. After 6 miles passes a single large Kachin house under one of the Panma Sawbwas. Two miles more of descent the Namsangya camp is reached after crossing the stream three times as described in the previous alternative route.

ALTERNATIVE IV.

FROM MYOTHIT, STAGE 2, TO MANWEIN, STAGE 5, *viâ* TÁLI.

BY CAPT. COUCHMAN, D.S.O., DECEMBER 1891.

Authorities. Military.	Authorities. Civil.	Number and Names of Stages, Rivers and Streams.	Distances. Intermediate.	Distances. Total.	Remarks.
			M. F.	M. F.	
G.O.C. Mandalay District and O.C. Bhamo.	Commissioner, Northern Division, and Deputy Commissioner, Bhamo.	**1. Táli** ... ... Numsong Ka, Liya Ka, and several swamps and streams.	7 4	7 4	General direction north. The road passes down the right bank of the Taping, and after ¼ mile turns to the north. It crosses two swamps 2½ feet deep (muddy bottom), which are offshoots of the Numsong Ka. Up to here is through kaing grass. It then passes along paddy-fields and again crosses an offshoot of the Numsong Ka, and thence into Syhet. Leaving Syhet the road after 100 yards passes the Chinese Shan village of Thégôn and after 300 yards crosses the Liya Ka, which is here 15 yards broad with sandy bottom and good water. Approaches easy. Banks, kaing grass. It then passes through high kaing grass for 2 miles, when it crosses a swamp (similar to the before-mentioned ones) and 2 feet deep. A ¼ mile further on the road again crosses a swamp (as before) and goes along up to high ground leaving some paddy-fields on the left. From here there is a road to Karwun. Two-and-a-half miles from Syhet it crosses a small stream which flows west; and gets on to rising ground with tree jungle and fine grass. Three miles from Syhet it crosses another swamp 2 feet deep (as before), and ¼ mile further on a small nullah, 4 feet broad, 1½ feet deep, and then through paddy-fields into Táli. The road itself is good, except that it is much overground. There is also a nullah which is passed close by the last paddy-fields. Other roads to Karwun from miles 6¾ and 7¼. In the event of rain this road would be impassable. There is another and longer road to the west, which crosses the Liya Ka as before and two small streams and avoids all the swamps. It joins a road from Táli to Mannaung about a mile from Táli. Time for transport three hours from Syhet. The latter part is through fine tree jungle, and there is very good fodder grass all along. *Táli village.*—Good water and camping ground throughout the village. A large maidan to east, but is low-lying and damp. Very good fodder here. Roads to Punsak, Jawma, Mannaung, and Táli.

FROM BHAMO TO MÔMIEN *viâ* NAMPAUNG CHAUNG FORT—*continued.*

ALTERNATIVE IV—*continued.*

Authorities. Military.	Authorities. Civil.	Number and Names of Stages, Rivers and Streams.	Distances. Intermediate. M. F.	Distances. Total. M. F.	Remarks.
G.O.C. Mandalay District and O.C. Bhamo.	Commissioner, Northern Division, and Deputy Commissioner, Bhamo.	**2. Tálí Uma** ... Tálí Ka; five small streams.	6 2	13 6	The road crosses the Tálí Ka by a ford 3½ feet deep, 45 feet broad; sandy bottom and easy approaches. There is an old bamboo bridge which is barely passable and very ricketty. General direction of road north-east. Very good going for 1 mile, when again cross the Tálí Ka (as before). Descent from right bank very bad and steep. The road now crosses a very bad piece of bog, about 150 yards long. There is only 2 feet of water, but the mud is shoulder-deep for mules. Only material for repair near is kaing grass. Would require timber bridging. Two small streams cross the bog joining the Tálí Ka a little higher up stream than the ford. From here the road is very good, but steep (2,000 feet) to Tálí Uma. Jungle tree and kaing grass. Passes through several taungyas. Fodder grass good and abundant.
		3. Acháng (3) ...	5 0	18 6	March to Lôngu and Acháng (3) as per Route No. 7, Alternative II.
China.		**4. Loiyin** ... Fusong and Katu; 15 streams.	9 0	27 6	March to Loiyin, about 9 miles. Good road. Steep descent. Cross about 15 streams and two rivers. Fusong river, 15 yards broad, waist-deep, and Katu river, 5 yards broad and 2 feet deep.
		5. Manwein ...	9 0	37 2	Good road past Palônkôn, Katu, Pyonkahtôn, Sawpatsyé, and Tônlôn (Taolung), all Chinese villages.

ALTERNATIVE V.

FROM MYOTHIT, STAGE 2, TO MANWEIN, STAGE 5, *viâ* KARWUN.

BY CAPT. COUCHMAN, D.S.O., DECEMBER 1891.

Authorities. Military.	Authorities. Civil.	Number and Names of Stages, Rivers and Streams.	Distances. Intermediate. M. F.	Distances. Total. M. F.	Remarks.
G.O.C. Mandalay District and O.C. Bhamo.	Commissioner, Northern Division, and Deputy Commissioner, Bhamo.	**1. Karwun** ... Namsong Ka, two small streams. One stream, Liya Ka.	10 0	10 0	General direction of road north-east. The route first passes along the Larchong road for ½ mile. It then turns to the left and descends to the Namsong Ka (rocky bed, 10 feet broad, 1½ feet deep, flowing from east to west) which it crosses. It then winds up a very steep and stony track, through dense kaing grass and occasional clumps of trees, till it reaches an altitude of 1,000 feet above Myothit when it joins the Ungaw-Peto route (*see* Alternative No. 1). It follows this descending to the village of Kadaw Kong (3½ miles). It again descends to a small stream 500 yards further on from the north-west, 3 feet wide; little water; rocky bed. It follows up this stream for 50 yards leaving the Ungaw-Peto route in a north-west direction, and then ascends steeply for ½ mile, over a rough and stony track which ascends to an elevation of 400 feet. It then descends 600 feet into the paddy and kaing grass plain in which Syhet is situated. It crosses one small stream flowing from south-west to north-east. On the plain it passes through kaing grass and past one or two swampy bits of ground, over which there is one small ricketty foot-bridge (which is unserviceable) into

FROM BHAMO TO MÔMIEN *viâ* NAMPAUNG CHAUNG FORT—*continued.*

ALTERNATIVE V—*continued.*

Authorities. Military.	Authorities. Civil.	Number and Names of Stages, Rivers and Streams.	Distances. Intermediate.	Distances. Total.	Remarks.
G.O.C. Mandalay District and O.C. Bhamo.	Commissioner, Northern Division, and Deputy Commissioner, Bhamo.	**1. Karwun**—*cont.*			Syhet, 5 miles. Time $1\frac{3}{4}$ hours for transport. Syhet is a Burman-Shan village with 50 houses and headman. There is a very good pôngyi kyaung here made of bamboo and wood which would easily house 150 to 200 men. There is good grazing ground here. It has 40 buffaloes and can supply paddy, eggs, and fowls. Water from stream good. There are roads from here to Myothit (direct) Sinyu, Tálí, and Karwun. The road now goes north passing the small village of Thégôn; no supplies; 15 houses; from here it crosses the plain through alternate kaing grass and cultivation in a north-east direction. At $6\frac{1}{4}$ miles it crosses a small chaung, 10 yards broad, knee-deep; course from south-east to north-west; water good; rapid current; sand and gravel bottom, kaing grass banks. At $6\frac{1}{2}$ miles the village of Nam Yow (three houses, mixed Burma-Shan and Kachin village; no supplies) is passed. It is about $\frac{1}{4}$ mile to the left of the road. The route now ascends a steep, tortuous, rough road to Lapang (1,000 feet above Syhet), 8 miles. From here there is a path to Peto. The road now ascends gradually by several small ascents to Karwun, 10 miles. Time $2\frac{1}{2}$ hours. From Nam Yow to Lapang is mostly through tree jungle, but beyond this it is kaing grass. It is overgrown and not much used all the way from Myothit, especially the latter part. There is a track to Pônlein from here. Good grass and bamboo here for forage. Water good, but not very plentiful; no supplies. Height above sea 1,570 feet.
		2. Táli Uma ...	M. F. **6 6**	M. F. 16 6	From Lower Karwun the road ascends steeply for 200 feet to Upper Karwun. From here there is a road north-west to Tálí. The road descends to Tiya. From here the road is fair and up an easy ascent to Jawma (Tatlôn) village. There is good grass along this part of the route. Just before Jawma (Tatlôn) there is a good road to Tálí Kabor (big) and Numkaw. From here the road is very good and smooth, but steep up to Jawma (Tatlôn), passing through kaing grass and tree jungle. Just before Jawma (Tatlôn) there is a magnificent view to the north, and the Shwédaungyi range near Mogaung is distinctly visible. Beyond Jawma (Tatlôn), after descending to a spring, the road ascends steeply to Saré, passing several taungyas on the left. The road is still excellent. There is a road to Tálí from here. The road now descends steeply over bad ground to 'Mpong through good grass, joining the Taliachang road just before reaching the village. All this road from Karwun is very practicable. The road leaves 'Mpong and goes west crossing a small stream after $\frac{1}{4}$ mile. This is about 1 yard broad and only a few inches deep. Just beyond this it is joined by a road Saré (Shiré), after $\frac{1}{2}$ mile a road branches off to the west to Tálí, and the road itself runs north over some taungyas, and into thick bamboo and tree jungle, and thence into Tálí Uma, a good road throughout. Good camp at Tálí Uma. For particulars of route from Tálí Uma to Manwein, *see* Alt. No. IV. *Note.*—The best route is to proceed *viâ* the plains to Syhet ($2\frac{3}{4}$ miles), thence to Karwun ($7\frac{3}{4}$ miles), Saré ($11\frac{3}{4}$ miles), and Tálí Uma (14 miles). This is far better than the plain route *viâ* Tálí, as the gradients are easier and the bad bogs between Syhet and Tálí, and between Tálí and Tálí Uma are avoided.

No. 11.

From BHAMO to MÔMIEN *viâ* NAMPAUNG CHAUNG FORT—*continued.*

ALTERNATIVE VI.

From SYHET, *see* Stage 3, to KARWUN, Stage 3.

Authorities.		Number and Names of Stages, Rivers and Streams.	Distances.		Remarks.
Military.	Civil.		Inter-mediate.	Total.	
			M. F.	M. F.	
G.O.C. Mandalay District and O.C. Bhamo.	Commissioner, Northern Division, and Deputy Commissioner, Bhamo.	**1. Karwun** ... One stream. Five small streams. One jheel.	*	*	There is an alternative route between Syhet and Karwun as follows: General direction north-east. To 6½ miles follow the Lapang route to Karwun, Alt. V, Stage 3. The road then follows along the paddy-fields for 300 yards and ascends through tree jungle to Namyow (three houses, no supplies). Thence the road turns north crossing two small streams, up one of which there is a track to Lapang, and at ½ mile passes a Kachin hut in a taungya. It then gradually ascends through tree jungle for ½ a mile. It then divides into two, the left road going to Tálí. The right road descends to a jheel which is a very bad obstacle. It is 70 yards broad and has a muddy bottom covered with water, the whole being over 3 feet deep. The water is almost stagnant. From here the bearing to Karwun is 49°. The road has now a gradual ascent for ¾ mile, when it becomes very steep and tortuous, right up to the junction with the Lapang route. It is also very stony. From the jheel the road passes through kaing grass and after that through taungyas belonging to Karwun. This is a bad road and not to be compared with the Lapang route.

ALTERNATIVE VII.

From TÁLÍ UMA, Alt. IV, Stage 4, to LÔNGU (*see* Route No. 7, Alt. II).

Military.	Civil.	Number and Names of Stages, Rivers and Streams.	Inter-mediate.	Total.	Remarks.
G.O.C. Mandalay District and O.C. Bhamo.	Commissioner, Northern Division, and Deputy Commissioner, Bhamo.	**1. Lôngu** ... ... Kachong Ka.	†	†	There is another alternative route between Tálí Uma and Lôngu as follows: *See* Route No. 7 up to Acháng (1) 2 miles. The road goes north-east from Acháng (1), descending and crossing the Kachong Ka, 9 feet wide, 1 foot deep. Good water. Crossing bad and approaches stony, bad and steep. The road then ascends very steeply through small tree, kaing grass, and fern jungle to the old site of Acháng village, which is now overgrown with grass. From here it ascends still more steeply by zigzags over occasional stony pieces and joins the road from Acháng (2) to Lôngu (*see* Route No. 7) and Acháng (3). This, though shorter, not such a good route as No. 7 for transport. Time of descent for Mounted Infantry, 40 minutes.

* *N.B.*—Distance not given, but it must be longer than the Lapang route.—A. F.
† *N.B.*—Distance not given, but must be under 5 miles.

FROM BHAMO TO MÔMIEN *viâ* NAMPAUNG CHAUNG FORT—*continued.*

BRANCH I.

FROM KANNI, *see* STAGE 2, TO MAICHU AND MANKÔN KA.

BY E. P. CLONEY, ESQ., CIVIL OFFICER WITH EASTERN KACHIN COLUMN, JANUARY 1891.

Authorities.		Number and Names of Stages, Rivers and Streams.	Distances.		Remarks.
Military.	Civil.		Intermediate.	Total.	
			M. F.	M. F.	
G.O.C. Mandalay District and O.C. Bhamo.	Commissioner, Northern Division and Deputy Commissioner, Bhamo.	**1. Nantabet Sakhân.** Nantabet chaung.	**5 4**	5 4	Road good and easy across a more or less level plain for about for 2 miles; *eng* forest with very little undergrowth. General direction east; comes out on fields worked by the Pompya Kachins; skirts them and turns south-west; crosses small stream and turning east and west at the foot of Shinlômpum hill for about 2½ miles, turns north-east and descends to the Nantabet chaung. This chaung at ford is about 100 yards wide from bank to bank. In the cold weather water confined to a bed of 40 feet depth; at ford 6 inches to 1 foot; continues east through dry, stony bed and ascends right bank and runs along in an easterly direction over high ground at the foot of the Kinchangpum hill, then runs through dense kaing jungle for nearly a mile and comes out on a taungya-site worked by the Pakwan Kachins. It is a regular camping ground with plenty of grass and water from the Nantabet.
		2. Namsang Ka... Namsang Ka.	**5 0**	10 4	Road first runs north-east and is good for a ¼ mile; crosses small stream two or three times, then runs through bamboo jungles and through patches of muddy ground; continues fair up to sakhân, which is a good camping ground with plenty of water and grass. (At this sakhân two roads meet, the one going straight ahead up the village is the proper caravan route). It runs with the Tapin through the valley, ascending and descending low hills occasionally until Möngwai (2), a Lakum village, with 13 houses, is reached. Open bamboo jungle all the way. Road is good up to ascent to Mantow (old village).
		3. Mantow ... Namkyinli chaung.	**5 0**	15 4	From camp road ascends in an easterly direction for about 3½ miles. Road good, but ascent nearly all the way stiff, then the Namkyinli chaung is crossed. Half a mile of gradual ascent, then another mile along the saddle, then a short descent into camping ground, 200 yards south of village. Water and grass plentiful, but camping ground very damp, uneven, and shut in. Much better to go on another mile over, and then down, the hill of Mantow and get into the paddy-fields. Beyond Mantow is a Kowri-Lepé village with 30 houses.

FROM BHAMO TO MÔMIEN *viâ* NAMPAUNG CHAUNG FORT—*continued.*

BRANCH I—*continued.*

Authorities.		Number and Names of Stages, Rivers and Streams.	Distances.				Remarks.
Military.	Civil.		Intermediate.		Total.		
			M.	F.	M.	F.	
G.O.C. Mandalay District and O.C. Bhamo.	Commissioner, Northern Division and Deputy Commissioner, Bhamo.	**4. Chikai**	5	0	20	4	The road is good all the way and open till Chikai is reached. At first goes round hill from camp in an easterly direction, then turns north and continuing in an easterly direction for ½ a mile passes through Ching Swai, a Hotôn village of eight or 10 houses; descends gradually and then through paddy-fields in the basin formed by the hills for about 2½ miles; then crosses a fairly large stream; goes up a stiffish ascent for a little over ½ a mile, then passing through first part of Chikai, it gradually descends on to the saddle of the hill near the second part of Chikai. Chikai is a Kowri-Lepé village of 52 houses.
		5. Maichu and Mankôn Ka. Kalông Ka.	5	4	26	0	Road fair all the way; passes through upper village of Chikai; descends for 1¼ miles, crosses the Kalông Ka stream which is about 30 to 40 feet wide. Owing to the swift current and boulders this will be impassable for loaded animals unless temporarily bridged from year to year. The Kachins could be got to do it for about Rs. 40. For another ¼ mile through rough road another small stream has to be crossed, and road comes out on the fields of Kumkow and the ascent commences. First half of ascent gradual and fairly open; second half steep; tree jungle on sides, then the lower village of Kumkow is reached. General direction up to lower village north, then turns east passes along saddle between the two parts of the village and passes through the upper village. Kumkow is a Lakum village with 24 houses in both. Continues along saddle and after a short, easy ascent of ½ a mile turns round base of hill continuing east and north-east for about 1 mile. Descending gradually a small stream is crossed, and descending still farther runs along for another 1½ miles through open taungya and field sites; then a short ascent in a southerly direction another stream, with plenty of water, though not deep, is crossed; then skirting the base of the hill gradually turning east for about ¼ mile, the village of Maichu, an important Lakum village of 40 houses, is reached. The road still leading east goes down-hill for ½ mile; the paddy-fields of Maichu to the left and open jungle to the right and the Mankôn Ka (about 30 or 40 feet wide and 2 feet deep) is reached at 6¼ miles.

BRANCH II.

FROM KANNI, *see* STAGE 2, TO MOMÂUK SAKHÁN (*see* ROUTE No. 10, STAGE 1).

BY E. P. CLONEY, ESQ., CIVIL OFFICER WITH EASTERN KACHIN COLUMN, FEBRUARY 1891.

Military	Civil	Stage	Inter. M.	Inter. F.	Total M.	Total F.	Remarks
G.O.C. Mandalay District and O.C. Bhamo.	Commr., Northern Divn. and Deputy Commr., Bhamo.	**1. Nantabet sakhán.** Nantabet chaung.	5	4	5	4	*See* Branch I, Stage 1.
		2. Kyetin or Kyetyang.	5	0	10	4	Starting from the Nantabet sakhán the road is good and takes a south-easterly direction; runs through kaing grass, then crosses the Nantabet chaung at the upper ford, by which all caravans from Bhamo that travel through Mantow or along the Tapin valley cross.

FROM BHAMO TO MÔMIEN *viâ* NAMPAUNG CHAUNG FORT—*continued.*

BRANCH II—*continued.*

Authorities.		Number and Names of Stages, Rivers and Streams.	Distances.		Remarks.
Military.	Civil.		Intermediate.	Total.	
G.O.C. Mandalay District and O.C. Bhamo.	Commissioner, Northern Division and Deputy Commissioner, Bhamo.	**2. Kyetyin or Kyetyang**—*cont.*			They do not go on from Môpeing by the road along the river, but branch off from Môpeing to the right and following a fairly good road for about 8 or 10 miles they come out here and cross; then continuing in the same direction the road winds along foot of a hill for about 2 miles; takes an easterly direction gradually ascending through open tree jungle for another 1¼ miles, the lower part of Pompya, about 2,000 feet high, is reached. The villages of Pompya at 3¼ miles are Kowri-Lepé villages; total 40 houses. Road very good and leads north of Pompya, then turns west and continues for ½ a mile along taungya-sites of lower village and down a lower hill, winding around its almost level base for another ½ mile, then turns east and after going about 300 yards the camp (which lies in a grove between the upper and lower villages of Kyetyin) is reached. Camp very good for 100 men and transport. Water and grass plentiful. Kyetyin is a Kowri-Lepé village of 20 houses.
		3. Mômauk sakhán. Namsari chaung.	M. F. 7 0	M. F. 17 4	Leaving camp the road goes east and turns and goes down a bit, passes through the village of Lônsa, a Kowri-Lepé village of 20 houses. Quarter of a mile from Kampáng the houses extend along the village for ¼ mile. Until the village of Lônsa is passed the road is very good; then it takes a westerly direction skirting the base of the hill and after another 1¼ miles comes out at the village of Kampáng. The last 1¼ miles may be said to be fair, but on two or three places very narrow and decidedly bad; view shut in on all sides. Kampáng is a Kowri-Lepé village of 10 houses. View all round open. The road leads down-hill in a south-westerly direction for 2 miles and is very good. Care must be taken *not* to follow the good, *broad road* leading ahead as it is apt to lead one astray, but to turn off to the left on a much narrower path about a mile from the village, then through a bit of kaing jungle crosses a stream (crossing nasty) near the Kampáng paddy-fields, then through the bamboo jungle for a mile and through a large open *eng* or *in* forest for another mile or so, and comes out on the road to Bhamo near the deserted village of Mômauk. Grass plentiful, but good water-supply has to be got from the chaung a little further east.

No. 12.

From BHAMO to NAMKHAM viâ MÁNSI and WARABÔN.

BY LIEUT. E. W. M. NORIE, OFFICIATING DEPUTY ASSISTANT QUARTERMASTER-GENERAL, INTELLIGENCE BRANCH, APRIL 1889.

Military.	Civil.	Number and Names of Stages, Rivers and Streams.	Intermediate.	Total.	Remarks.
G.O.C. Mandalay District and O.C. Bhamo.	Commr., Northern Divn. and Dy. Commr., Bhamo.	**1. Mánsi** ... ... Namsalé and Thenglin chaungs.	14 0	14 0	Road leaves the fort by a road running south-east and crosses the broken ground on that side for about ¾ mile, when it enters in jungle through which it runs almost all the way to Mánsi. At 1¾ miles it crosses a low-lying strip of paddy land by a wooden bridge

FROM BHAMO TO NAMKHAM *viâ* MÁNSI AND WARABÔN—*continued.*

Authorities.		Number and Names of Stages, Rivers and Streams.	Distances.		Remarks.
Military.	Civil.		Intermediate.	Total.	
G.O.C. Mandalay District and O.C. Bhamo.	Commissioner, Northern Division and Deputy Commissioner, Bhamo.	**1. Mánsi**—*cont.*			passable for carts, approached by an embankment from each end. At 4 miles the road descends to another broad tract of of low-lying land, impassable in the wet weather. On the further edge of this strip it crosses the Namsalé, a muddy stream with 1½ feet of water in it in the hot weather, by a good wooden bridge for carts, and beyond this passes the small village of Kabani of about 15 houses. At 7½ miles the road crosses another strip of low-lying ground similar to the last and also impassable in the rains. On the further edge of this the Thenglin river is crossed. It is a shallow stream with a gravelly bottom, about 20 yards broad, and easily fordable by carts in the dry season, when it is about 1 foot deep. The banks are low and easy. Before reaching the Thenglin, the village of Manyut is passed on the right, and beyond the stream the village of Namapui on the left. From here the road runs on high ground all the way to Mansi police post. The road is a good cart road in the dry weather. The police post is situated on a small spur and is a small fort, 50 yards square, surrounded by a ditch, parapet, and spicked stockade. Water from wells close by. Below the post is the site of the village of Mánsi, lately burnt, situated on the site of the Mânsi stream, from which a plentiful supply of water is always procurable. To the south of the post is a paddy plain, where camp could be pitched in dry weather. Mánsi is not healthy for troops, being feverish. From here there is a direct track to Sáwadi, distance 11 miles. *See* Branch I of Route No. 13.
		2. Pita	M. F. **15 0**	M. F. 29 0	The road after leaving Mánsi runs up the valley of the stream and is level going for about 2 miles, when it passes the village of Kyawgaung of Ponkan Kachins and leads up the side of the Lônsa hill. Here the road is steep and the jungle dense on both sides of the road. On reaching the top of the ridge the direct road to Karwán branches off, running down the opposite side, while the Pita road runs along the top of the ridge, and is steep and difficult for pack animals in places, but could be greatly improved with a little labour. At 5 miles pass the small village of Malu on the ridge, about 10 houses. Immediately beyond this the road is very bad and very rough and broken. It then runs along again pretty level to 7 miles, when it begins to ascend and becomes very steep and rough and trying for pack animals until the top of the Pita ridge is reached. Beyond this it improves again and at 14 miles Pita is reached, a good-sized village of about 20 houses of the Kara tribe of Kachins. The halting place is about a mile beyond the village on a bare neck of land near a small muddy spring. The camping ground is badly situated and the water-supply from the spring on the right of the road very inferior. There is plenty of water obtainable from a stream ¼ mile down the hill to the left. This is a bad and trying march, as there is no water along the road with the exception of one place, where a very small supply is obtainable, about 12 miles. The road is also very bad, but could be very greatly improved with a little labour, being worn away by weather and traffic and never repaired.

FROM BHAMO TO NAMKHAM *viâ* MÂNSI AND WARABÔN—*continued.*

Authorities.		Number and Names of Stages, Rivers and Streams.	Distances.				Remarks.
Military.	Civil.		Intermediate.		Total.		
			M.	F.	M.	F.	
G.O.C. Mandalay District and O.C. Bhamo.	Commissioner, Northern Division, and Deputy Commissioner, Bhamo.	**3. Kwina** ... ... One small stream.	**6**	**0**	35	0	Leaving camp the road runs east and immediately leads up a steep ascent for a short distance, then down to a small nullah, which it crosses, and again ascends; going is fairly easy. At 1 mile pass the small village of Mamayaung of six or seven houses, and at 2 miles Kanwé of six or seven houses. A short distance beyond the latter a very steep ascent commences and leads up to the top of the ridge about ¾ of a mile. Near the top a small rill of water is passed, but the supply is very scanty. The road is now much easier, and at 4 miles the large village of Warabôn is reached containing about 40 houses. Warabôn is beautifully situated on the top of the ridge among fine timber. Water is plentiful from springs below. Passing through Warabôn the road is still easy without any steep ascent; follows generally the watershed. At 5½ miles it descends to a stream of good water about 6 feet broad and 6 inches deep. There is a good ground for camping here in some fields for a considerable force. About ½ mile beyond the village of Kwina is reached, and here too there is space for a camp and water close to two Kachin houses, in which troops could find shelter in case of rain. The village proper is about ¼ of a mile further on. There is a small and clean zayát between the first two houses and the village.
		4. Nawkham ... Some small streams.	**8**	**0**	43	0	The road runs south-east and passes through the village and is fairly good the whole way, though there are some steep ascents and descents in places, which are trying to transport animals and would be very difficult after rain. Pass several small villages. The country is the same as before in character, consisting of rugged ridges, with deep valleys between, everywhere covered with trees and jungle except where cleared for "taungya" cultivation. Nawkham is a good-sized village of about 20 houses. There is camping room in the village and accommodation for troops in the long houses. Water is plentiful from wells. About ½ mile before reaching the village there is a good place for a camp on a bare spur with a stream running below. Altitude of Nawkham is approximately 4,600 feet.
		5. Namkhai ... Small streams.	**5**	**0**	48	0	Direction south-east. Road generally followed the watershed and led downhill until within a short distance of Namkhai, when it again rises towards the village. The country is the same in character as before, and on this march fine views are obtained across the Shwéli valley to the hills beyond in the north of Theinni, Shan States. The ground for camping on is very cramped, but accommodation can be got in the houses of the village.

FROM BHAMO TO NAMKHAM *viâ* MÁNSI AND WARABÔN—*continued.*

Authorities. Military.	Authorities. Civil.	Number and Names of Stages, Rivers and Streams.	Distances. Inter-mediate. M. F.	Distances. Total. M. F.	Remarks.
G.O.C. Mandalay District and O.C. Bhamo.	Commr., Northern Divn., and D.C., Bhamo.	**5. Namkhai**—*cont.*			Water in limited quantities is plentiful from springs, &c., below the ridge, but large supplies for transport animals, &c., can only be got from a stream about ¾ of a mile off. Namkhai contains about 30 houses. Below Namkhai on the north-east, at the bottom of a deep valley, flows the Namwan, which forms the boundary between the Chinese State of Maingmaw and the Kachin country.
	Superintendent, Northern Shan States.	**6. Namkham** ... Namwan and Shwéli rivers.	12 0	60 0	Leaving Namkhai the road runs in a south-easterly direction and passes along the ridge through fine trees for ¾ of a mile to a point from which a magnificent view can be obtained across the valley to Namkham and the Shan Hills. From here there is a very steep descent for 700 feet down to the bed of a small stream. Here water is plentiful and there is room for a good-sized camp. This descent would be trying for animals in wet weather. Crossing the stream the path ascends steeply for about 300 yards and then more gradually for ½ a mile, after which it leads downhill the whole way to the ford over the Namwan at about 7 miles. From there the road is over level grass land to the Shwéli river, which is deep, rapid, and 200 yards broad. It is crossed by a ferry of two boats. Namkham is about 1½ miles from the ferry. It is a large unstockaded village containing over 100 houses and a large bazaar. Supplies of all kinds and water plentiful. A good site for a camp on the east of the village. For description *see* Route No. 49, Shan Division, Namsan to Namkham. *Note.*—This appears to be the most direct and most practicable road beween Bhamo and Namkham. It would only be practicable for baggage animals, but could be made a very good mule road with proper labour. At present it is much worn by traffic and weather and is never repaired, but most of the bad bits could be easily improved and some of the worst gradients could be avoided. From the nature of the soil, which is a red clay, it would become impassable in wet weather for loaded animals. Supplies of paddy, rice, and fowls in small quantities can be got at all the villages. Water is plentiful in limited quantities all along the road, except between Mansi and Pita.

BRANCH I.

FROM KWINA, STAGE 3, TO PALAUNGTU.

TAKEN FROM DIARY OF THE COMMANDANT, MOGAUNG LEVY, MAY 1891.

Military	Civil	Stage	Inter-mediate	Total	Remarks
G.O.C. Mandalay Dist. and O.C. Bhamo.	Commr., Northern Divn., and Dy. Commissioner, Bhamo.	**1. Palaungtu** ... Branch of Namya chaung.	7 0	7 0	Road runs south-east for 5 miles passing through village (Lana) of Kapra. At 6 miles main road to Namwan is left, the road to Palaungtu to the right, south-west through Taungya and descending to a branch of the Namya chaung. The road then ascends a slight hill for ¾ of a mile to Palaungtu. There are two villages of Palaungtu; The lower or south village (five houses) is the head Sawbwa's place. For direct routes from Bhamo to Palaungtu *see* Route No. 16.

No. 13.

From BHAMO to NAMKHAM *viâ* KARWÁN.

By Lieut. E. W. M. NORIE, Officiating Deputy Assistant Quartermaster-General, Intelligence Branch, May 1889.

Authorities. Military.	Authorities. Civil.	Number and Names of Stages, Rivers and Streams.	Distances. Intermediate. M.	Distances. Intermediate. F.	Distances. Total. M.	Distances. Total. F.	Remarks.
G.O.C. Mandalay District and O.C. Bhamo.	Commissioner, Northern Division and Deputy Commissioner, Bhamo.	**1. Mánsi**	14	0	14	0	*Vide* Route No. 12, Stage 1.
		2. Camp ... ... Thenglin and Tansa chaungs; one small stream.	8	0	22	0	Direction east. The road runs as in the above route until the top of the Lônsa ridge is reached. From here it leaves the Warabôn road and runs down the opposite side of the ridge and is rather steep and very stony. At 3 miles it reaches the bottom of the ridge and from here is level and easy all the way to the Tansa chaung at 5 miles. At 3½ miles it reaches the Thenglin river and runs up the left bank of this stream. Jungle dense. There is a camping ground on the Tansa chaung, which joins the Thenglin river just below the point where the road crosses it. The road crosses the Tansa chaung by a ford about 10 yards broad and 1½ feet deep, stony bottom; water clear and good. Immediately after crossing the chaung the road leads up a very steep and difficult ascent for 300 or 400 yards, and beyond this continues to ascend more or less steeply all the way until the camp is reached at about 8 miles. The road is very stony in places and the soil is clay, which becomes very slippery after rain. The road runs near a small stream of good water for the last 2 miles. Camp is on a clear space on both sides of the stream. This place was found to be very feverish for troops staying in it for a few days.
		3. Karwán ...	9	0	31	0	Direction east-south-east. The road continues to ascend, and at 1½ miles reaches Shwényaungbin, a camp named after the large banyan tree which is passed there. There are two or three houses on a small hill above the camp. From here the road is pretty level and easy for 3 miles and then becomes pretty steep again till Ka-u is reached at 6¼ miles. Ka-u is on the top of the ridge and contains about 20 houses. Water from wells near, on the side of the ridge. From here the road is level and runs along the ridge through tree jungle. At 6¾ miles reach Pantát, a village of 30 houses which nearly joins on to Ka-u The road runs on as before and is easy going till the entrance of Karwán village is reached. This was found to be a very large village of about 130 long houses and more than a mile in length. Water is obtainable from numerous springs and wells below the ridge. The height of Karwán is about 4,000 feet, and a view can be obtained right down to the Irrawaddy and Bhamo. There is plenty of ground for camping on, and troops could always be accommodated in the houses.
		4. Loilaw ... ... Three or four small streams.	11	0	42	0	General direction south-east. The road runs out of Karwán along the ridge in an easterly direction for about a mile. It then branches off across a small rocky stream and runs south-east with one or two pretty steep descents and ascents to Neinsin village, which is

FROM BHAMO TO NAMKHAM *viâ* KARWÁN—*continued.*

Authorities. Military.	Authorities. Civil.	Number and Names of Stages, Rivers and Streams.	Distances. Intermediate. M.	F.	Distances. Total. M.	F.	Remarks.
G.O.C. Mandalay District and O.C. Bhamo.	Commissioner, Northern Division and Deputy Commissioner, Bhamo.	**4. Loilaw**—*cont.*					reached at about 3½ miles. Neinsin is a Pônkan village of about 30 houses. From here the road runs over pretty level ground, with no difficult gradients, but gradually rising until the Loilaw ridge is crossed at a height of about 5,000 feet above the sea. No villages are passed beyond Neinsin, though several are seen at some distance to the north. Immediately below the ridge is the uppermost village of Loilaw, where a camping ground can be found, and water obtained.
		5. Camp ... ... One stream and the Namwán.	6	0	48	0	Direction south-east. Road runs downhill and is very steep and difficult for baggage animals, &c. It passes two lower villages of Loilaw and at 4½ miles reaches a rocky stream which it crosses. From here it is very rough up and down short steep ascents and descents till it strikes the bank of the Namwán at about 5½ miles. It runs down the bank of this stream for about ½ a mile to the camping ground. The Namwán flowing from the north makes a sudden bend to the south-east at the point where the road meets it. It is a fine clear stream about 40 yards broad and 4 or 5 feet deep in the dry weather. It forms the boundary between the Chinese State of Maingmaw (Meungmow) and the Burma Kachin country. The camping ground is on a level, cleared space on the right bank of the river and is sufficient for a considerable force.
	Superintendent, Northern Shan States.	**6. Namkham** ... Namwán and Shwéli rivers.	12	0	60	0	The road runs on as before down the bank of the river until it crosses a small stream, the same stream which is crossed after leaving Namkhai in Route No. 12. From this point it runs south-south-east and is steep and rough and would be difficult for baggage animals. At 2½ miles it joins Route No. 12.

Note.—This road, though not longer than the one *viâ* Warabôn, is certainly more difficult, and the part between Loilaw and the point where it joins the other road is very steep indeed, and would be particularly difficult for loaded animals going from Namkham to Bhamo, as in 4 miles it rises nearly 2,000 feet. The march between the Tansa chaung and Ka-u is also difficult. Karwán is the capital of the Pônkan tribe. Water is plentiful all along this route, and supplies of fowls, paddy, &c., would be procurable in limited quantities.

The road would be impassable for loaded animals during wet weather, as they could not stand on the slippery clay soil.

No. 14.

From BHAMO to NAMKHAM viâ MANYA and HÔMA.

By Lieut. DAVIES, Attaché, Intelligence Branch, January 1892.

Authorities. Military.	Authorities. Civil.	Number and Names of Stages, Rivers and Streams.	Distances. Intermediate. M. F.	Distances. Total. M. F.	Remarks.
G.O.C. Mandalay District and O.C. Bhamo.	Commissioner, Northern Division and Deputy Commissioner, Bhamo.	**1. Sáwadi** ... Namsiri, Namapwé or Thinlin and one other stream.	9 0	9 0	General direction south-south-west. Good mule road. Leave the fort by the west gate down the left bank of the Irrawaddy the whole way. For 1½ miles through streets. At 1¼ miles cross the Namsiri chaung from the left, 35 yards wide; wooden cart bridge. At 3 miles cross the Namapwé or Thinlin chaung from the left, 30 yards wide; wooden cart bridge. Cross five more small streams by bridges. At 7 miles Kachin village of Mankôn or Kônywagyi; 17 houses. At 7½ miles cross a chaung from the left, 20 yards wide; wooden mule bridge; too narrow for carts. Sáwadi, a large village of 50 houses; large pôngyi kyaung and zayat in middle of village with room to camp round it. From here there is a branch route to Mánsi, Stage 1, of the other two routes to Namkham (Nos. 12 and 13), for full details of which *see* below (Branch 1).
		2. Manya ... ... Moyu chaung.	12 0	21 0	General direction south. Good mule road. Along the left bank of Irrawaddy crossing the Moyu chaung at 1 mile from the left 18 yards wide; wooden mule bridge 6 feet wide; also a ford 150 yards higher up knee-deep. As far as Moyu at 1¼ miles, 16 houses and pôngyi kyaung at the junction of the Moyu chaung and Irrawaddy. Here a road goes on west to Sinkán and the route turns south. At 9 miles a road goes straight on to Mankin and the route turns eastward till it meets the Hantet Manya road at 11 miles, thence south to Manya; 12 houses and one zayat in the middle of the village on right bank of the Naunghu chaung. Good camping ground in paddy-fields, ¼ mile to the east.
		3. Namlôn camp.	10 4	31 4	General direction south-east. Good mule road. Follows up the right bank of the Naunghu chaung for 6 miles. At 1¼ miles road to the right across the Naunghu chaung to Khappan. At 6 miles the Maingkhaung or Möngkhaung bullock camp. Just beyond the camp is an open space 250 and 150 yards not used by bullocks and consequently clean. This would be the best place to camp here. The Naunghu chaung is close by on the right. Here the route leaves the Naunghu chaung, another road going on up the chaung to Chusai eventually to Pangtán, where it joins the Sikaw-Namkham road. At 7 miles the ascent of the hills begins. At 8½ miles is the Kachin village of Makyen ½ mile off on the left. At 10 miles a road to the left at Tanankatawng

FROM BHAMO TO NAMKHAM *viâ* MANYA AND HÔMA—*continued.*

Authorities. Military.	Authorities. Civil.	Number and Names of Stages, Rivers and Streams.	Distances. Intermediate. M.	F.	Distances. Total. M.	F.	Remarks.
G.O.C. Mandalay District and O.C. Bhamo.	Commissioner, Northern Division and Deputy Commissioner, Bhamo.	**3. Namlôn camp** —*cont.*					and Walu rejoining the route in the next stage near Sarikatawng. Then steep descent to Namlôn camp, 150 × 80 yards on the Namlôn chaung 5 yards broad and ankle-deep; also more room to camp in a taungya on the opposite side of the stream. Not much grass, but bamboo leaves can be got. The camp is shut in by the hills which overlook it on all sides.
		4. Kailé ... ... Namlôn chaung crossed twice on leaving the camp, from the left. At 3 miles from the right 5 yards wide; ankle-deep; easy fords.	9	6	41	2	General direction south-east. Good mule road. All over hills. At 2¾ miles road to the right to Kashôt (*k*)* ¼ mile off the road. Here there is an alternative route to the south of the present one, rejoining it at Wazigôn (*k*)*; 30 houses. From here a road to the right to Pumsang 5 or 6 miles off. At 7½ miles road to the right to Pumsang. At 8 miles Wabawgap (*k*). At 8½ miles is a road straight to Kailé, but difficult. The route goes round by Kasankhu (*k*),* 40 houses, thence descent to Kailé camp (200 × 40 yards). There are two streams, 1 yard × 3 inches, the other 2 yards × 6 inches, one on each side of the camp, each about ¼ mile off. The village of Kailé is ¼ mile further on.
		5. Pengkaw or Warátabaung. Mawswé chaung.	8	6	50	0	General direction south-east. Good mule road all over hills. Steep ascent for 2 miles over Loipang Lan, thence easy road. At 4½ miles Mansôk camp, 100 × 40 yards. Good water from a chaung 3 yards wide, ½ mile to the south on the Kasháng road. The jungle is thin here and could be cleared for a large camp. From here is a road to the right to Kasháng and eventually to Pángtáng, where it joins the Sikaw-Namkham road. At 4½ miles Mansôk (*k*)*; 50 houses. From here a road to the left to Soma where it joins the Mánsi-Namkham road. At 6 miles village of Homakatawng (*k*)*; seven houses. At 6½ miles road to the left to Manlep and to the right to Saikhow; both small villages under Pengkaw. At 7¾ miles Pengkaw (*k*)*; 24 houses. There is very little water in the village itself. The best place to camp is the Waratabaung camp at 8¾ miles (200 × 25 yards) on the Mawswé chaung, 7 yards wide and knee-deep; easy ford. One hundred yards to the left of the road are paddy-fields to camp in.
China (doubtful).		**6. Nammaw** ... Nammák.	9	6	59	6	General direction east. Good mule road over hills; some steep bits of up and down hill. At ¼ mile road to the left to Sowpôn. At 1¾ miles cross the Nammák from the left; 7 yards wide; knee-deep; easy ford; after passing along a paddy plain for a mile. Here is a road to the right to Mawswé and roads to the left (1) to Sowpôn (2) to Mansán. At the Nammák the route enters territory claimed by the Chinese.

* (*k*) = Kachin village.

FROM BHAMO TO NAMKHAM *viâ* MANYA AND HÔMA—*continued.*

Authorities. Military.	Authorities. Civil.	Number and Names of Stages, Rivers and Streams.	Distances. Inter-mediate.	Distances. Total.	Remarks.
China (doubtful).		**6. Nammaw**—*cont.*			Hence steep ascent for ½ mile of Loi Namkha, thence descent all the way. At 4 miles small village of Namkha (*k*) *; 14 houses. At 5¼ miles big village of Namkha (*k*) *; 14 houses. Here there is a camping ground in paddy-fields ½ mile to the left down a steep hill on the Namkha chaung; 3 yards wide; ankle-deep. At 6½ miles the main Namkham road goes straight on meeting the present route in the next stage at Pasang; but avoiding the territory claimed by the Chinese as much as possible, follow a road to the right leading down steep hill to Manpong (*k*) *, two houses, at 7¾ miles. Here the road reaches the plains and is joined by the S'Kaw road from the right. At 8½ miles pass village of Manhwe; 24 houses. From here there are no more Kachin villages. At 9½ miles cross the Mammak again here from the right; 15 yards wide; knee-deep; easy ford; stony bottom, leaving the territory claimed by the Chinese. At 9¾ miles village of Nammaw, large camping grounds in paddy-fields everywhere.
G.O.C. Mandalay District and O.C. Bhamo.	Superintendent, Northern Shan States.	**7. Namkham** ... Nammák, Shwéli or Nammaw.	M. 3 F. 6	M. 67 F. 4	General direction north-east by east. Good mule road, down the Nammak village for 3½ miles, passing the valley of Hinlôn, Pasang, Manmyang, and Sopkham. At Sopkham the road turns north, crossing the Nammak at its junction with Shwéli from the left 15 yards wide; knee-deep; easy ford; stony bottom. Hence up the right bank of the Shwéli, here 300 yards wide, passing through Kunkyem to the ferry opposite Maungkong, where the Shwéli is crossed. From the left 200 yards wide at the ferry, as the width is lessened by the spit of land running out; unfordable. Animals swam across. Men and baggage crossed by five canoes with bamboos tied on to the sides to prevent them upsetting easily. Thence by good road through paddy plain to Namkham; kyaung and zayats and open space 250 and 150 yards for camping in the middle of the town; also large camping grounds in surrounding paddy land. Water from wells and stream; grass rather scarce, having to be brought from the hills 2 miles off; bamboo leaves can be got. Large supplies of beet, paddy, and rice obtainable. The town measures about ½ mile each way and is not fortified.

BRANCH I.

FROM SÁWADI TO MÁNSI.

BY LIEUT. G. H. H. COUCHMAN, SOMERSETSHIRE REGIMENT, MOUNTED INFANTRY, JUNE 1886.

Authorities. Military.	Authorities. Civil.	Number and Names of Stages, Rivers and Streams.	Distances. Inter-mediate.	Distances. Total.	Remarks.
G.O.C. Mandalay Dist. and O.C. Bhamo.	Commr., Northern Division and Deputy Commr., Bhamo.	**1. Mánsi** ... ... Moyu chaung.	11 0	11 0	Road leaves Sáwadi by south gate and goes nearly due east. An open maidan is crossed, which is about 600 yards broad. Some low hills are on the right of this maidan. The road then ascends a bank of about 40 feet and passes through thick tree jungle. Three-quarters of a mile further on reached a clearing and then passed through heavy jungle. Three

* (*k*) = Kachin village.

FROM BHAMO TO NAMKHAM *viâ* MANYA AND HÔMA—*continued.*

BRANCH I—*continued.*

Authorities.		Number and Names of Stages, Rivers and Streams.	Distances.		Remarks.
Military.	Civil.		Inter-mediate.	Total.	
G.O.C. Mandalay District and O.C. Bhamo.	Commissioner, Northern Division and Deputy Commissioner, Bhamo.	**1. Mánsi**—*cont.*			miles from Sáwadi a road branches off to the right and south-west to Moyu. It then passes through alternate grass and tree jungle. Seven miles from Sáwadi is a large caravan camp. There is plenty of good grass, and there is sufficient space to camp 300 men. There is evidently some water close by, or the caravans would not stay here. The road up to this point is over high ground of a sandy nature and is passable for wheel traffic at all seasons of the year. A few hundred yards beyond this the ground again rises, and this part of the road is very bad and rutty, but could easily be repaired. There is some hill cultivation here, and the village (Kachin) of Hantet is near here. After 2 miles of this hilly country a broad open maidan is reached and the road descends into it, crossing a small stream. A little beyond this the Moyu chaung is met with and runs nearly parallel to the road as far as Mánsi, which is two miles further on over the plain. Mánsi is under the protection of the Lana Kachins.

No. 15.

From BHAMO to NGWANSAI viâ TÔNHÔN.

BY MAJOR HOBDAY, B.S.C., SURVEY OF INDIA AND INTELLIGENCE OFFICER, TÔNHÔN FORCE, DECEMBER 1889.

Military	Civil	Stages	Inter-mediate	Total	Remarks
G.O.C. Mandalay District and O.C. Bhamo.	Commissioner, Northern Division and Deputy Commissioner, Bhamo.	**1. Moyu** ... Namsiri chaung, Theinlin chaung, Moyu chaung.	M. F. 9 4	M. F. 9 4	*Loilet Road.* Road runs south-west throughout along left bank of Irrawaddy, passes through villages of Tátgalé and Paukkôn within suburbs of Bhamo and within a mile of it, then crosses Namsiri chaung at 1½ miles by a bridge constructed by Public Works Department, passable for all arms. At 2½ miles the Theinlin chaung is crossed by a temporary bridge. At 8 miles pass village of Sáwadi, where there is a police post. Road from Namsiri chaung to Sáwadi passes through thick forest and high kaing grass. Numerous short but steep ascents and descents are encountered on account of the banks of the Irrawaddy being cut up by ravines. The Moyu chaung is crossed close to and on the near side of the village of that name by a temporary bridge. Camping ground in jungle 300 or 400 yards beyond village. Water plentiful from Irrawaddy or Moyu chaung. A few Kachin huts beyond camping ground. Inhabitants Shan-Burmese and a few Kachins. Number of houses 20. [*N. B.*—This road is impassable in the rains.]
		2. Mankin ... Nahu chaung	9 4	19 0	Road runs south on the flat through thick forest. A small stream forded at 6 miles. At 7 miles a road branches off to the left towards village of Mankaong, distant about 10 miles. Village of Mankin on north bank of Nahu chaung, which is crossed by a temporary bridge. Camping ground on south bank, rather confined and dirty; more room in paddy-fields on north bank. Number of houses 10. Inhabitants Shan-Burmese. Water plentiful from Nahu chaung.

FROM BHAMO TO NGWANSAI *via* TÔNHÔN—*continued.*

Authorities.		Number and Names of Stages, Rivers and Streams.	Distances.		Remarks.
Military.	Civil.		Intermediate.	Total.	
			M. F.	M. F.	
G.O.C. Mandalay District and O.C. Bhamo.	Commissioner, Northern Division and Deputy Commissioner, Bhamo.	**3. Sikaw** (*Shan*, **Sékao**). Chaungmagyi or Sinkán chaung, Manna chaung.	**14 0**	33 0	Road continues along the plain in a south-south-west direction through thick tree forest. The Manna chaung is forded at 2¼ miles. At 7 miles a cross road is met, leading to village of Wégyi on the right, distant about ¾ mile, and to Mankaong on the left, distant about 8 miles. A mile beyond the road approaches the Chaungmagyi or Sinkán chaung and follows down its right bank to the village of Malin (15 houses) at 11 miles, where the Sinkán chaung is easily forded. Malin is on the left bank and the small village of Seiktu on the opposite bank. The road continues along the left bank. Village of Kônka (15 houses) passed at 12½ miles. Small village of Kombaung on opposite bank. Extensive camping ground in paddy-fields at Sikaw. Water plentiful from Sinkán chaung. Stockaded police post built on opposite (right) bank, about ¼ mile distant. A new village has been built adjoining stockade. Space cleared for camping ground between old Sikaw and stockade. Good ford across Sinkan chaung. Sikaw is the residence of a Myo-ôk. Inhabitants Shan-Burmese and Kachins. Number of houses 30. A shorter road to the stockade crosses the Sinkán chaung at Kônka and runs along its right bank.
		4. Puntukatawng. Lapé chaung.	**8 4**	41 4	Road runs south along right bank of Sinkan chaung, crosses small stream at ¾ mile. At 2 miles passes through village of Sakhángalé (10 houses), then over some paddy-fields and crosses the Lapé chaung (foot-bridge, animals ford), on the opposite bank of which is the village of Sakhángyi (10 houses). From Sakhángyi the track runs south-east on the flat through thick forest to the village of Puntukatawng, which is at the foot of the hills. At 6 miles a road branches off to the left to the village of Tántabin, distant ½ mile. At 7 miles a road branches off to the right to Manlu, Nampalaung, and Saga. Number of houses at Puntukatawng 6; inhabitants Kachins; camping ground in village and very confined. Water plentiful from hill stream south of village.
		5. Nampu chaung. Nampu chaung.	**9 0**	50 4	Track is taken up along spur to near the crest of Loilet hill. The ascent commences shortly after leaving Puntukatawng; is steep for about 1½ miles. At 2½ miles Kachin village of Pinpien or Pangving (10 houses) and close to it Pinket (5 houses) is reached; elevation above sea-level 2,300 feet. From Pinpien the track proceeds by zigzags and is very steep to Loilet village at 5 miles (Kachin, 10 houses); elevation 3,700 feet. From Loilet the track descends slightly, skirting the hill of that name on its left to the village of Yama (Kachin, 10 houses) at 6 miles, where you are again on the summit of the ridge. The track continues along the ridge in an easterly direction to the Kachin village of Man Ngwan (15 houses) at 7 miles. Just before entering this village the path turns off south down a spur to the Nampu chaung. Camping ground in some paddy-fields, somewhat confined and boggy. Water plentiful. Elevation 2,700 feet.

FROM BHAMO TO NGWANSAI *viâ* TÔNHÔN—*continued.*

Authorities. Military.	Authorities. Civil.	Number and Names of Stages, Rivers and Streams.	Distances. Intermediate. M.	Intermediate. F.	Total. M.	Total. F.	Remarks.
G.O.C. Mandalay District and O.C. Bhamo.	Commissioner, Northern Division and Deputy Commissioner, Bhamo.	**6. Tônhôn** ... Nampu and Namla chaungs.	**10**	**4**	61	0	Small track runs for about a mile in a south-easterly direction along Nampu chaung, crossing and recrossing it some half-a-dozen times; very boggy in places; then path suddenly turns south up a steep ascent on to the ridge on which the Kachin village of Teinkat is situated. Elevation 2,800 feet. Water in hill streams. From Teinkat the track descends some 1,300 feet in a south-westerly direction to the Namla chaung, which is easily forded at about 4 miles. A few paddy-fields are then crossed and a short but steep ascent for about ½ mile brings one to the Kachin village of Kindaung (11 houses). The path continues up a long spur to Lwésaing 7½ miles (in Shan language, Lwoi Seng). A few hundred yards beyond Kindaung a track branches off to Sarikatawng on the left and Tatmanan on the right, distant 1 mile and 2 miles, respectively. The last mile of the road to Lwésaing is fairly level. Number of houses 45. Elevation 3,400 feet. Water in hill streams not very plentiful. Track descends south-west some 800 feet along side of hill to Wábo Sakhân at 9 miles, where road branches off to the right to Si-u, distant about 7 miles. From Wábo Sakhân the road runs first south-east and then south to Tônhôn ascending slightly, distance 10½ miles. The village of Tônhôn contains about 47 houses and is built on a small spur running down in a south-easterly direction from a prominent peak. Elevation 2,800 feet. Water plentiful in hill stream to the west below village.
		7. Ngwansai ... Shwéli (Nammow).	**5**	**4**	66	4	Path leads south-east down a spur of the hills to the Shwéli river passing site of old village of Namtwé 2½ miles and reaching the river at about 4 miles. Road narrow and very steep in places. No village of Namtwé in existence now, a few plantains and trees indicate former site. There is a small stretch of sand on right bank of Shwéli river, which serves as a camping ground. Elevation 650 feet. From Namkham, which is at an elevation of 2,500 feet, the Shwéli flows through this hilly country by a succession of rapids in a sort of gorge as far as Molo, some 25 miles down the river, from which point it is said to be navigable for small boats. At Namtwé there is a pool, about ¼ mile long, and the ferry is across this pool just below the rapid. Bamboo rafts have to be constructed and swung across by ropes, as no boats or dug-outs exist. The water is very deep in the pool and the current strong in the rapids. The hills are steep on the opposite bank, sloping down to the water's edge. There are two other known ferries near Namtwé, that of Supla above and Ngwadé below Namtwé, about 5 or 6 miles distant. The path is very steep and narrow at first until it crosses a small stream running into the Shwéli at 1 mile. From this point the ascent and road is fairly easy. Ngwansai at 5½ miles is a Palaung village of 15 houses, situated on a low ridge above the Shwéli. Water from small streams a short distance down the sides of the hill, but not very plentiful. Elevation 1,600 feet. At Ngwansai you are on the high road between Namkham and Momeik. *See* Routes Nos. 77 and 78.

FROM BHAMO TO NGWANSAI *viâ* TÔNHÔN—*continued.*

ALTERNATIVE I.

FROM SIKAW, STAGE 3, TO TÔNHÔN, STAGE 6, *viâ* SI-U AND LWÉPAN.

Authorities. Military.	Authorities. Civil.	Number and Names of Stages, Rivers and Streams.	Distances. Intermediate. M.	Distances. Intermediate. F.	Distances. Total. M.	Distances. Total. F.	Remarks.
G.O.C. Mandalay District and O.C. Bhamo.	Commissioner, Northern Division, and Deputy Commissioner, Bhamo.	**1. Si-u**	**15**	**0**	15	0	From Sikaw to Sakhángyi as in Stage 4 above. At 3 miles road runs through village of Munsin (10 houses), and at 4 miles through village of Kagyin (10 houses). A mile beyond it leaves the right bank of Sinkán chaung and at 5 miles crosses a stream rising from Saga hill, recrossing it again at 7 miles. The road then runs south-west for 1 mile and then south until the village of Manphon (8 houses) is reached at 14 miles, where another stream is crossed and again another close to Si-u. Si-u is a Shan-Burmese village, formerly contained about 45 houses, now burnt. Water plentiful.
		2. Tônhôn ...	**9**	**4**	24	4	From Si-u the road runs south-east along the flat to the village of Kamut, 2½ miles deserted, where the ascent commences up a long spur of the hills, portions of the road being somewhat steep. The Kachin village of Lwépan (26 houses) is reached at 6½ miles; elevation 2,800 feet; the road then descends for a short distance and ascends up a steep gradient to Panlun (25 houses) at 8 miles. From Panlun the road descends to Tônhôn. A small hill stream is crossed about ½ mile from Tônhôn, the descent to it being rather slippery for pack animals.

ALTERNATIVE II.

FROM SIKAW, STAGE 3, TO LWÉSAING, *see* STAGE 6, *viâ* NAMPALAUNG.

Military.	Civil.	Stages.	Inter. M.	Inter. F.	Total M.	Total F.	Remarks.
G.O.C. Mandalay District and O.C. Bhamo.	Commissioner, Northern Division, and Deputy Commissioner, Bhamo.	**1. Tántabin** ...	**6**	**4**	6	4	*Vide* Stage 4 above.
		2. Nampalaung ...	**6**	**0**	12	4	Track runs south along the flat for 1½ miles and then ascends the hills. At 4 miles passes through Kachin village of Manlu and then descends slightly to Nampalaung, which is on a saddle of the ridge.
		3. Lwésaing ...	**6**	**0**	18	4	Road continues south-south-east, ascends to Kachin village of Saga at 2 miles, then descends slightly to Tatmanan, (19 houses) at 4 miles. From this the road ascends to near the summit of Thôngwa hill, a conspicuous conical peak, by narrow and steep path to an elevation of about 4,300 feet and then descends to Lwésaing some 900 feet, the first portion being steep, then flat for a short distance where you pass an old pagoda, and then a slight ascent to Lwésaing. *N.B.*—This road is a difficult one for pack animals, the path being narrow and very steep in places.

No. 15.

From BHAMO to NGWANSAI *viâ* TONHÔN—*continued.*

BRANCH I.

From TEINKAT, *see* Stage 6, to TEINMAKAUK, SUPPLA, NAMTWÉ and NGWADÉ FERRIES.

By Capt. O'DONNELL, D.S.O., January 1890.

Authorities. Military.	Authorities. Civil.	Number and Names of Stages, Rivers and Streams.	Distances. Intermediate.	Distances. Total.	Remarks.
G.O.C. Mandalay District and O.C. Bhamo.	Commissioner, Northern Division, and Deputy Commissioner, Bhamo.	**1. Ngwadé ferry.**	M. 11 F. 2	M. 11 F. 2	Good road; steep descent to Lwébin at 1¼ miles; 40 houses in two divisions on ridge of hill. Good road; steep descent of 1½ miles to Teinmakauk 2¾ miles. Road in many places very bad; village consists of 30 houses; small supply of water. Ferry crosses the Shwéli river, 2½ miles distant. Pôngyi kyaung in the village. Good road, in many places overgrown with jungle at 5¾ miles; Suppla, 20 houses. Very small supply of water. Ferry over Shwéli river, 2 miles distant. Road now almost impassable, overgrown with jungle, evidently never used, hardly traceable. Easy ascents and descents at 8¾ miles site of village Namtwé destroyed; 1½ miles from here to ferry over the Shwéli river on the Ngwansai roads. No road; along river bank over sands and rocks; gentle ascents and descents 2½ miles. The village of Ngwadé is distant from the ferry 2 miles on the south, *i.e.*, left bank of the Shwéli river.

BRANCH II.

From LWÉSAING, *see* Stage 6, to KINDAUNG, *see* Stage 6, *viâ* TATMANAN.

By Lieut. OZZARD, 1st Hampshire Regiment, January 1890.

Military	Civil	Stage	Intermediate	Total	Remarks
G.O.C. Mandalay District and O.C. Bhamo.	Commissioner, Northern Division, and Deputy Commissioner, Bhamo.	**1. Kindaung** ...	3 6	3 6	Road runs due north of ½ mile, then branches off to the west for 1 mile. Road good, gradual ascents, passes round Thôngwa. Hill to north of it level ½ mile; descends ½ mile; very steep, almost impassable for animals. (This agrees with the information received from the villagers at Teinkat on 22nd December 1889 that the road from Teinkat to Lwésain *viâ* Tatmanan is impassable for animals.) Twenty houses. Water plentiful; no camping ground. Thick jungle close around village. Track from Tatmanan to Kindaung, distance 2 miles. Total 3¾.

BRANCH III.

From WABO SAKHÂN, *see* Stage 6, to SI-U (*see* Alternative I, Stage 4).

By Lieut. BLOSSE, King's Own Scottish Borderers, January 1890.

Military	Civil	Stage	Intermediate	Total	Remarks
G.O.C. Mandalay District and O.C. Bhamo.	Commissioner, Northern Division, and Deputy Commissioner, Bhamo.	**1. Si-u**	4 0	4 0	Jungle; camping ground 1½ miles from Lwésaing, 40 yards × 30 yards. Good road running west. Gentle ascents and descents for 1 mile. Very steep descents 1½ miles. Road evidently not used for some time. Much overgrown with jungle and cut up to form obstacles to troops advancing from Si-u. Road impassable for animals 1½ miles on to foot of hill in Si-u plain.

No. 16.

From BHAMO to PALAUNGTU.

By Capt. O'DONNELL, Commandant, Mogaung Levy, 31st May 1891.

Authorities. Military.	Authorities. Civil.	Number and Names of Stages, Rivers and Streams.	Distances. Intermediate. M.	F.	Distances. Total. M.	F.	Remarks.
G.O.C. Mandalay District and O.C. Bhamo.	Commissioner, Northern Division and Deputy Commissioner, Bhamo.	**1. Mánsi** ... ... Namsalé chaung, Thenglinchaung chaung.	**14**	**0**	14	0	*See* No. 12, Stage 1. The road from Bhamo to Mánsi is in a fairly good State, but has evidently not been used by carts for some time
		2. Camp, 2 miles from Ku Tu.	**13**	**0**	27	0	From Mánsi the road bears south for 8 miles along a valley to the Namyu chaung crossing this 2 miles further on a small village, four houses, Kara Kachins, is reached. From this village the road continues south and by gentle gradients gradually ascends to within 2 miles of Ku Tu, where there is an excellent camping ground in some paddy-fields. Water good and plentiful. A long, hot march.
		3. Palaungtu ... Manti chaung.	**9**	**2**	36	2	From camp the road gradually ascends for 2 miles to Ku Tu. General direction south-east. At Ku Tu there is a very good and large camping ground. Leaving Ku Tu, the road, still bearing in a south-easterly direction, ascends for 2 miles to Lama; 45 houses. From Lama the road turns to the east and descends ¾ of a mile to the Manti chaung. From the Manti chaung it ascends 1½ miles to Namyu; 40 houses; Lana tribe. From Namyu to Palaungtu it is 3 miles; road good all the way. *General Remarks.*—There is an alternative route from Mánsi to Palaungtu *viâ* Wazigôn, Hôpôn, and Hôma along the Hôpôn-Hôma range, and it can also be reached from the Bhamo-Namkham road, *see* Route No. 12, Branch I, but the Ku Tu route is the one most commonly used. *Note—Supplies.*—All the villages literally swarn with cattle, the result probably of blackmail on the Shan trade routes.

No. 17.

From BHAMO to SADÔN (Bhamo Sub-Division*) viâ MEUNGWAI.

By D. L. RICHARDSON, Esq., Civil Officer with Eastern Kachin Column, April and May 1891, and Lieut. G. MORRIS, Intelligence Branch, February 1892.

Military	Civil	Stage	Inter. M.	F.	Total M.	F.	Remarks
G.O.C. Mandalay District and O.C. B[illegible]	Commr., Northern Divn. and Deputy Commr., Bhamo.	**1. Mômauk** ... Namsari chaung.	**11**	**0**	11	0	*See* Route No. 10, Stage 1, as far as Mômauk Sakhán 9 miles, whence the direct road takes a southerly direction and the first half is through tall kaing jungle and then through open bamboo jungle till the village, which is about 300 feet above the plains, is reached. There is an alternative route from about ½ mile before Khatut Sakhán is reached. From Mômauk Sakhán the

* As distinguished from the place of the same name in the Myitkyina Sub-Division, now called Fort Harrison.

No. 17.

From BHAMO to SADÔN (Bhamo Sub-Division) *viâ* MEUNGWAI—*continued.*

Authorities.		Number and Names of Stages, Rivers and Streams.	Distances.		Remarks.
Military.	Civil.		Intermediate.	Total.	
G.O.C. Mandalay District and O.C. Bhamo.	Commissioner, Northern Division and Deputy Commissioner, Bhamo.	**1. Mômauk**—*cont.*			same route as described in Route No. 10, but instead of going right on to the foot of Lawtán hill ¼ mile, before the sakhán is reached a pathway leads to the right through sandy soil and shut in on both sides by tall kaing jungle, open here and there. A dry stony bed of a feeder of the Namsari is crossed about 400 yards from the cross road. The same kind of ground has to be gone over for another 500 yards when the Namsari has to be forded. The water in it is 1 foot to 18 inches deep and is about 30 yards wide with a stony bed. The road then becomes open for 800 yards; soil sandy till the foot of Mômauk hill is reached. Here a narrow streamlet, with about 2 feet of water, has to be followed for 20 feet. This track is overhung by tall kaing grass. The ascent to Mômauk is very gradual and in some parts imperceptible. The road is through open bamboo jungle. A trickling stream is crossed after ascending half way up the hill. Mômauk is a Kowri-Lepé village of five houses. Fair camping ground in the village, but water is scarce and has to be obtained from the foot of the hill a little over ¾ of a mile away.
		2. Meungwai ...	M. F. 11 2	M. F. 22 2	The road is steep and undulating with little or no water-supply on the way and is wooded the whole way. A mile before the Lower Chiri (1), a Kaw-Lepé village of nine houses, is reached, the road leads us over an open taungya site. At the village a fair supply of water can be obtained. Direction of road south-south-east. The upper or Chiri south (2) is 4,000 feet high and about ¾ mile from lower village. The road to it is fairly good and goes along the saddle of the hill. Chiri south at 4¾ miles is the seat of the Sawbwa and has 15 houses. Water-supply at village insufficient. On leaving Chiri (2) the road is very steep and rugged and is on the east side of the village, but runs south-south-east. It is not bad for any length. The route was formerly the caravan route, but as the bit near Chiri (2) was badly cut up and rugged, the caravans pass through Sama which is towards the right. There is no water on the way. After going for about a mile of a fairly good road on the saddle of the hill Kampán (1) or Kumpa (1) is reached. It is a Kowri-Lepé village of four houses. Kampán (2) is ½ mile further (6¼ miles), the road to it open and fairly level along the ridge of the hill. There is a good camping ground here. Forage plentiful; water-supply is sufficient and fairly good, but a short distance from the camp; six houses. Road continues south-south-east. Road very good, but no water-supply on the way. It runs along the ridge of the hill, but descends gradually till Lakya, a Marán village of 25 houses, is reached (8¾ miles). Water-supply at village fairly good. There is a good camping ground in the village, as well as about 300 yards further out of the village. The road still continues in a south-south-easterly direction and is fairly good. A slight ascent till the first part of Meungwai is reached at 11¼ miles. Meungwai is a Marán village with 24 houses, scattered over those hills a couple of furlongs from each other. There is a very scanty supply of water in the village, but there is a good camping ground ¼ mile further from the village at an altitude of about 4,200 feet, where there is an ample supply of water and grass.

FROM BHAMO TO SADÔN (BHAMO SUB-DIVISION) *viâ* MEUNGWAI—*continued.*

Authorities. Military.	Authorities. Civil.	Number and Names of Stages, Rivers and Streams.	Distances. Intermediate. M. F.	Distances. Total. M. F.	Remarks.
G.O.C. Mandalay District and O.C. Bhamo.	Commissioner, Northern Division and Deputy Commissioner, Bhamo.	**3. Léka**	**7 0**	29 2	General direction south for the first 4 miles. The road is an easy descent passing through Upper and Lower Sama* at 2 miles. After leaving Sama the road continues west for 2 miles and is fairly good, then turning slightly south descends the hill to Pônkyun (4½ miles), this portion is rather steep. Pônkyun, a village of the Marán tribe, 20 houses, 51 inhabitants, 8 buffaloes, a fair camping ground and moderate supply of water. Leaving Pônkyun the road ascends abruptly for ½ a mile and is narrow; the descent then becomes easier and the direction more southerly till Léka (7 miles) is reached on the crest of the hill; a village of the Marán tribe ruled by a Sawbwa named Sao Tang who is the most influential man in this district. From a point 100 yards south of Léka, a good signalling post for communication with Bhamo is obtainable (bearing 310°).
		4. Karwán ... Thiring chaung.	**10 0**	39 2	Leaving Léka the road turns south descending the hill to Pakwán, rather rocky in places but not very steep. Pakwán consists of a few houses scattered on the east slope of the hill under the Sawbwa of Léka (½ mile from Léka) in thick jungle; no camping ground; good water; fair camp ground at Léka. Leaving Pakwán the road runs in an easterly direction through Tum Tu Mowun (½ mile) descending to the Thiring chaung (4 miles), the last mile of the descent is abrupt; no bridge; stony bottom; current rapid, but no difficulty in crossing at this season. The road then ascends gradually to Karwán (6 miles from river) and is fairly good; water plentiful. Supplies: paddy, fowls, eggs and a few green vegetables are obtainable at most of the villages. Camping ground with sufficient supply of water for small force at Sama, Léka and Karwán. Surrounding country mountains with extensive taungyas; the valleys mostly cultivated. Karwán is a village built on the saddle of three hills, inhabited by the Marán tribe with an excellent supply of water and good camping ground for a considerable force. At the present season (February) the temperature ranges between 60° and 70°. This village well defended would be a commanding position.
		5. Warabôn ... Kapra and Kumkáng chaungs, tributaries of the Thiring chaung.	**6 4**	45 6	General direction south-east. Road leaves Karwán in westerly direction turning south-west after ½ a mile and winding through tall pine grass at a general slope of 30° to the Kapra chaung (2 miles), a mountain torrent with a rocky bed, swift current, but only a few inches deep in February. The road then ascends in a more westerly direction to the village of Lapailawkum

* There is a direct road hence to Bhamo, *see* Route No. 20.

FROM BHAMO TO SADÔN (BHAMO SUB-DIVISION) *viâ* MEUNGWAI—*continued.*

Authorities.		Number and Names of Stages, Rivers and Streams.	Distances.		Remarks.
Military.	Civil.		Intermediate.	Total.	
G.O.C. Mandalay District and O.C. Bhamo.	Commissioner, Northern Division and Deputy Commissioner, Bhamo.	**5. Warabôn**—*cont.*			and is rather steep and rocky. Lapailawkum (3½ miles) is situated on the crest of a spur running out from Neinsin, inhabited by the Lepé tribe, a small village with a bad supply of water. The road then descends in a southerly direction to the Kumkáng chaung (1 mile) similar in all respects to the Kapra chaung, and is still narrow, mostly through bamboo jungle, but not so steep as the first part. After crossing the Kumkáng chaung the road winds over minor spurs and hills gradually ascending to Warabôn (6½ miles), a village of the Marán tribe situated on the crest of the Lanaka range of hills; 24 houses; 102 inhabitants very scattered; bad camping ground and fair supply of water ½ mile distant. Supplies: paddy, fowls, rice, and eggs obtainable. (Rate of marching 2 miles an hour.)
		6. Tuku (Kacháng chaung). Enkong, Lamyu, and Kachang chaungs.	M. F. **8 0**	M. F. 53 6	The road leaves Warabôn in a south-westerly direction winding through tall kaing grass for 2 miles. This part of the road is very much overgrown, and also steep and rocky descending to the valley of the Enkong chaung. The last ½ mile of the descent is very difficult and dangerous for animals. The Enkong chaung (2½ miles), a mountain torrent with a rocky bed and swift current. The crossing is difficult for animals owing to the nature of the bottom. The road then ascends abruptly a small spur and for 2½ miles winds over minor hills and crosses a few small mountain streams. It then becomes very difficult descending to the Lamyu chaung (5½ miles). The crossing here is easy. Here the road turns south-east and ascends for 2 miles to the village of Matet, the last ½ mile being very steep. Matet (7½ miles), inhabited by the Kura tribe, is built on the crest of the hill, consists of 16 houses with 54 inhabitants. There is very little open ground, and no good water within ½ a mile. Half mile further on in an easterly direction the valley of the Kacháng is reached, which is an excellent camping ground. This valley, 800 yards long × 200 yards broad, lying at an elevation of over 3,000 feet, watered by the Kacháng chaung, is a succession of paddy-fields. There is a second valley, also cultivated, of about the same size, watered by the same stream, lying at right angles. Tuku, a village of 30 houses, inhabited by the Kara tribe, is situated along the crest of a low range on the south side of the valley.
		7. Loilaw (Pumkatawng).	**13 0**	66 6	The road crosses the Kacháng chaung, tributary of Namyu, stony bed, 15 feet wide 2 feet deep in February at the angle, and ascends the hill in a south-east direction to the village of Sama (1 mile), a Marán village of 21 houses, 82 inhabitants, situated on the crest of the hill with a fair camping ground and good supply of water. Leaving Sama the road turns due east descending easily for 1 mile, where it crosses the Kayun chaung, and 1 mile further on in the same direction the Namyu chaung. Here the road ascends to Namyu (4½ miles,) a Marán village of 47 houses and 214 inhabitants, situated on the summit of a hill overlooking the Namyu chaung. Here there is good water and a small camping ground. The latter part of the ascent to Namyu is steep; average rate of marching from Tuku 2½ miles an

FROM BHAMO TO SADÔN (BHAMO SUB-DIVISION) *viâ* MEUNGWAI—*continued.*

Authorities.		Number and Names of Stages, Rivers and Streams.	Distances.				Remarks.
Military.	Civil.		Intermediate.		Total.		
			M.	F.	M.	F.	
G.O.C. Mandalay District and O.C. Bhamo.	Commissioner, Northern Division and Deputy Commissioner, Bhamo.	**7. Loilaw (Pumkatawng)**—*cont.*					hour. Leaving Namyu the road improves considerably turning north by east, and is fairly level for 5 miles, passing through the villages of Lasé and Warákatawng (5¼ miles), two villages of the Marán tribe, ½ a mile apart, scattered along the crest of the range. The road still continues north-east for 3 miles and is good; crosses two small streams, and leaving Paiton on the left, turns east, ascending gradually to the village of Pumkatawng (12¼ miles from Tuku), situated near the summit of Loilaw hill (5,460 feet high). Here there is good water and a fair camping ground. The village consists of five houses under the Sawbwa of Loilaw, which is situated ¼ mile down the east slope of the hill towards the valley of the Namwan; water is plentiful along the whole route. Paddy, fowls and eggs are obtainable in small quantities in most of the villages. The road is good generally speaking. The surrounding country is hilly with extensive taungyas; very much broken with numerous water courses. Average rate of marching, 2½ to 3 miles an hour.
		8. Letaw Kapra or Palawngatawng. Kawa and Wégyo chaungs, the former of which flows into the Namwan.	6	0	72	6	General direction north by east. Road leaves Loilaw in a northerly direction following the trade route to Neinsin for 2 miles. This part is rough and very much cut up by the passage of bullocks. Leaving the trade route it descends through tall kaing grass and crosses the Kawa chaung (¼ mile) 1 foot to 2 feet of water in February; a narrow path very much grown over. One mile further on it crosses a small mountain stream (Wégyo chaung 2 feet of water in February and joins Kawa chaung), and then ascends a spur of the Saiprompôn range rather abruptly to Kapra Letaw or Palaungatawng, 2½ miles further on. Kapra Letaw is a name applied to the district inhabited chiefly by the Letaw (? Latawng) tribe, extending from the Namwan river on the east to Neinsin and Pakom on the west, comprising the villages situated on the Saiprompôn range. Palaungatawng, which is marked on the maps as Letaw, is a straggling village of 22 houses and 75 inhabitants scattered along the crest of the hill, with a fair supply of water, but no good camping ground. There are 30 buffaloes, 9 bullocks, and a few ponies; also a good supply of rice and paddy. Surrounding country, looking west, the hills are closely wooded, here and there taungyas cultivated with paddy, rice, and rarely opium. Turning east and south stretch the valleys of the Shwéli and Namwan rivers, with a distant view of the valley of the Nammak river. In contrast to the other side the country is open, appears thickly populated and well cultivated in the valleys.
		9. Walakong ...	7	0	79	6	Leaving Letaw Kapra in a north-easterly direction, the road is fairly level, though narrow in places, to Mong-ba (3 miles), a large well-to-do Lenar village extending for a mile along the crest of the hill, consisting of 31 houses and 100 inhabitants, 18 bullocks, 16 buffaloes, a few ponies, and an ample supply of paddy and rice. Quarter of a mile after leaving Mong-ba the route leaves a well-used road (which runs along the Namwan valley to Sadôn) striking in

FROM BHAMO TO SADÛN (BHAMO SUB-DIVISION) *viâ* MEUNGWAI—*continued.*

Authorities. Military.	Authorities. Civil.	Number and Names of Stages, Rivers and Streams.	Distances. Intermediate.	Distances. Total.	Remarks.
G.O.C. Mandalay District and O.C. Bhamo.	Commissioner, Northern Division and Deputy Commissioner, Bhamo.	**9. Walakong**—*cont.*			an easterly direction by a narrow path through thick bamboo jungle. For 2 miles the road is difficult running over minor spurs and crossing two small rocky mountain streams. The last mile to Walakong is good. Rate of marching 2½ miles an hour. For the most part the road runs through thick jungle; very scanty supply of water. Walakong (7 miles), a large village of 46 houses, 126 inhabitants, 28 buffaloes, 9 bullocks, is situated on the crest of a spur which divides the Namwan and Mong-ba streams. There is a fair supply of water 1 mile distant, but the road to it is bad; ½ mile down a good road on the west slope there is a rather scanty supply which can be used for drinking purposes.
			M. F.	M. F.	
		10. Letaw Krán. Mong-ba chaung, 15 yards broad, from 4 to 6 feet deep; crossed by a ford, 2 feet deep; flows into the Namwan chaung close below the village of Palen from the hills behind Pansum in the form of an "S" and gives its name to the valley which it waters.	**7 0**	86 6	There is no good camping ground, as the ridge is narrow and the ground broken: it is better to push on to the end of the village, where there is a small piece of open ground. Road leaves Walakong in a northerly direction winding down the west slope of the spur into the Mong-ba valley. The descent is easy, the road 4 yards broad and well kept as far as the Mong-ba chaung (3 miles). After crossing the above chaung there is a fairly level road for 1 mile in a westerly direction, then turning north ascends the face of the spur upon which Letaw Kran is situated. The ascent is about 2½ miles and is not very steep. Letaw Krán, at 7 miles, a small village of the Letaw tribe of 14 houses and 60 inhabitants, situated at the end of a spur jutting south-west, overlooking the valley. There is a good supply of water. The camping ground is bad, and the village seems poor in the extreme. This and Manseng (2½ miles further up-hill) are both noted for thieving; it is advisable to keep a sharp look-out on mules and ponies while in this neighbourhood.
		11. Panlun or Panlwin.	**6 4**	93 2	Road leaves Letaw Krán in westerly direction for 1 mile down the face of the spur, crosses the Mong-ba chaung (1½ miles), gradually turning towards the north as it ascends the valley of a small tributary of the Mong-ba chaung; the road is good and the ascent easy. It then turns north-east winding round the hill upon which Panlun is situated (6½ miles); good supply of water; a fair camping ground ½ mile before reaching the village on a saddle between two hills. Panlun, a large village of the Lapai tribe of 26 houses, 80 inhabitants, 21 bullocks, and 5 buffaloes, with a good supply of water and an influential Sawbwa; situated on the trade route between Maik ng and Kowri Tum.
		12. Pansum ... Mong-ba chaung.	5 0	98 2	Road leaves Panlun in a north-east direction, crosses two small chaungs, tributaries of the Mong-ba chaung, and ascends a steepish hill to Kowri Tum or Wagwasi (3 miles). An Asi-Lapai village of 9 houses and 39 inhabitants, with a scanty supply of water and no camping ground. Leaving Kowri Tum the road ascends for ¼ mile, then gradually descends to Pansum (2 miles), which consists of 5

FROM BHAMO TO SADÔN (BHAMO SUB-DIVISION) *viâ* MEUNGWAI—*continued.*

Authorities. Military.	Authorities. Civil.	Number and Names of Stages, Rivers and Streams.	Distances. Intermediate. M.	F.	Distances. Total. M.	F.	Remarks.
G.O.C. Mandalay District and O.C. Bhamo.	Commissioner, Northern Division, and Deputy Commissioner, Bhamo.	**12. Pansum**—*cont.*					houses and 24 inhabitants. One mile down the valley on the banks of the Mong-ba chaung, there is a fair camping ground with good supply of water, but cold at night and hot by day (difference of temperature 26°). General rate of marching from Panlun 2½ to 3 miles an hour.
		13. Sadôn ... Sawthen Ka, 5 or 6 yards broad, 18 inches to 2 feet of water; rocky bed swift current; flows into the Namwan.	7	0	105	2	Road leaves camping ground after crossing the Mong-ba chaung in an easterly direction ascending a steep hill to Pakôm (1½ miles), an Asi-Lapai village of 20 houses, 79 inhabitants, 10 buffaloes, 7 bullocks, and 1 pony. Leaving Pakôm the road descends fairly easily for, ½ miles to a tributary of the Sawthen Ka chaung. Here the road turns slightly north, passing over a small spur, and descends abruptly to the valley of the Sawthen Ka which it follows for ½ of a mile crossing the river three times. Then turning east ascends abruptly to Sadôn (4½ miles). Just before reaching Sadôn the road crosses a small valley about 250 yards wide watered by a small stream. This would make a good camping ground with regard to size and is level, but there is ample room in the village above for a considerable force. Sadôn is the name given to the spur and minor hills which run towards the Namwan, between the Sawthen Ka and Mantein Ka. The principal village is called Sadôn and is situated along the crest of the hill extending for 1½ miles, inhabited by the Asi-Lapai tribe, 50 houses, 186 inhabitants, 40 bullocks, 11 buffaloes, and a few ponies. Paddy, rice, fowls and eggs are obtainable. Water is good and plentiful. From the top of the hill a fine view is obtained of the valley of the Namwan. The Mantein Ka which passes close under Sadôn hill is considered at present as the Chinese frontier. Two miles from Sadôn is the large Asi-Lapai village of Mawshwé reached by a good road elevation about 4,000 feet; 50 houses; from here roads lead into the Mowun valley to the Asi-Lapai villages of Sagán (nine houses) and Latawng; 50 houses, both within one boundary.

BRANCH I.

FROM KOWRI TUM OR WAGWAAI, *see* STAGE 12, TO HÁNGTÓN *viâ* SINGMAI AND PANYAO.

BY LIEUT. GODFREY MORRIS, ATTACHÉ, INTELLIGENCE BRANCH, EASTERN COLUMN, MARCH 1892.

Military	Civil	Stages	Inter. M.	F.	Total M.	F.	Remarks
G.O.C. Mandalay District and O.C. Bhamo.	Commissioner, Northern Division, and Deputy Commissioner, Bhamo.	**1. Singmai** ... Mongba Ka, 20 feet broad; 2 to 3 feet of water; rocky bed and swift current. Mongpé Ka; 20 feet broad; 1 to 2 feet water; rocky bed and swift current.	6	4	6	4	Panlun to Kowri Tum (3 miles) *vide* stage 12 above. General direction north-east. Road gradually descends in northerly direction through bamboo jungle and tall kaing grass to the Mongba Ka (8 miles); rather narrow and over-grown, but fairly good; then turning north-east undulates over two minor spurs with nullahs between to the Mongpé Ka (3 miles). On the top of the last spur a road leads off on the right to Pakôm, and another 100

No. 17.

FROM BHAMO TO SADÔN (BHAMO SUB-DIVISION) *viâ* MEUNGWAI—*continued.*

BRANCH I—*continued.*

Authorities. Military.	Authorities. Civil.	Number and Names of Stages, Rivers and Streams.	Distances. Intermediate.	Distances. Total.	Remarks.
G.O.C. Mandalay District and O.C. Bhamo.	Commissioner, Northern Division, and Deputy Commissioner, Bhamo.	**1. Singmai**—*cont.*			yards further on, on the left, to Bhamo *viâ* Watáng; both are said to be good and fit for animal transport. After crossing the Mongpé Ka the road ascends at a fairly easy gradient for 2½ miles to Singmai, an Asi-Lapai village of 10 houses and 32 inhabitants, built on the crest of the hill at an altitude of 6,000 feet. Here there is a good camping ground, but a scarcity of water, which is obtained from the Mantein Ka, 2 miles down the north slope of the hill. On the right bank of this stream there is also a good camping ground.
			M. F.	M. F.	
		2. Panyao ... Mantein Ka, 30 feet broad; 2 to 3 feet of water; rocky bed; swift current.	7 0	13 4	General direction north. Leaving Singmai the road descends abruptly to the Mantein Ka (2 miles), then ascends the opposite spur at a steep gradient to Maokun (½ mile). An Asi-Lapai village of six houses and 22 inhabitants, built on a small spur jutting out from the Phaláng range. Continuing to ascend the road passes through the top end of the village of Phaláng (2 miles). A large Marán village of over 100 houses and 160 inhabitants extending along the crest line of the Phaláng range for 2 miles with large pieces of open ground and good water. Though the houses are large and well built, the people do not appear to possess any cattle and are dirtier and worse clad than the ordinary run. The road leaves Phaláng in a northerly direction ascending gradually for 1 mile till it reaches the Shaintan range. Here the ascent becomes steep and difficult for 1½ miles. The side of the hill is clothed with short grass, cultivated here and there with opium. Half a mile from the top of the hill along a level road Panyao is reached; a village of the Asi-Lapai tribe of 16 houses and 86 inhabitants, built on a spur jutting out in a north-west direction from the main range which constitutes the watershed of the Namwan (on the east) and the Nantabet stream (on the west). The village is built at an altitude of about 7,000 feet very much exposed. The camping ground is fair, but water is some distance off. Rate of marching 1½ miles an hour.
		3. Hángtôn ... Lapai Ka, 15 feet broad; 1 foot of water; stony bed; flows into the Nantabet chaung.	8 6	22 2	General direction north-west. Road leaves Panyao in north direction descending easily for 1 mile through thick young bamboos to the Lapai-kayet then turns west and follows the valley passing through taungyas and open country for 4 miles crossing and re-crossing the stream four or five times. With the exception of 20 or 30 yards of road, here and there where it is rocky and sometimes deep mud, the greater portion is level and good. Passing over the spur upon which Lekatpôn is situated without entering the village, there is a steepish descent to the Nantabet chaung (2 miles). The Lapai Ka is again crossed at its junction with the Nantabet chaung, and the road then follows the left bank of the latter stream to the side of the old village of Hángtôn. Here and there is an excellent camping ground with a good supply of water.

From BHAMO to SENBO (Up left bank, Irrawaddy).

BY LIEUT. MOUL, CHESHIRE REGIMENT, JANUARY 1888.

The march from Bhamo to Senbo along the left bank of the river is excessively difficult, especially when accompanied by a large number of baggage animals. An enormous quantity of nullahs have to be crossed and a large amount of labour is required to render these practicable for transport; the ascents of many are too steep for a loaded animal, and ramps and winding paths have to be constructed. There are also two rivers to be crossed (Tapin river and Môlé chaung). By the expenditure of some labour the road could be rendered better and a good many of the steep ascents avoided, but it would always remain a very arduous march when accompanied by loaded animals, and impassable in the rains. The march could be accomplished in 5 or 6 days, if the baggage went by river. The following might then be the stages:—

Bhamo.—Thapánbin, 9 miles.*
Thamángyi, 20 miles; camping ground could be cleared near village.
Nanti, 31½ miles.
Nanhé, 44 miles.
Senbo, 52½ miles.

The road from Bhamo ends at Nanhé; it used to end at Léma, but a path has been recently cut. At Nanhé the Irrawaddy is 250 yards wide, current about 4 miles an hour. From Nanhé to Senbo the road is excellent. The road mostly runs close to the Irrawaddy through grass and tree jungle.

Numerous small villages are passed on or near the route; most of them miserably poor; no supplies, except a few fowls and eggs are obtainable. The inhabitants are chiefly Shan-Burmese and Pwun. There are usually one or two Kachin houses in every village. Only one or two are stockaded and that weekly. Supplies are obtainable at Pinlôn and Senbo (paddy, rice, salt, fowls).

Authorities.		Number and Names of Stages, Rivers and Streams.	Distances.				Remarks.
Military.	Civil.		Intermediate.		Total.		
			M.	F.	M.	F.	
G.O.C. Mandalay District and O.C. Bhamo.	Commissioner, Northern Division, and Deputy Commissioner, Bhamo.	**1. Tapin River (right bank).** Tapin.	3	0	...		First mile north through bazaar then leads along bed of river to the mouth of the Tapin river which is reached at 3 miles. At this point the Tapin is joined by the Kado chaung, which diverged some 9 miles up. The Tapin is about 350 yards broad and the Kado chaung about 40 yards. The two are divided by a narrow islet of sand. The descent to the river is very bad and muddy, the bed of the river is shifting sand, it is only deep for 20 yards from left bank. The Kado chaung is easily fordable. The baggage and men were conveyed across in boats, the transport animals swum. Camping ground right bank of Kado chaung cramped (for large force); water from Irrawaddy.
		2. Thapánbin ... Môlé chaung, Lewut chaung (small stream).	6	0	9	0	First mile runs north-west through a grass jungle close to the Irrawaddy, passing the village of Sinkin at ⅛ mile, thence north-west through jungle close to Irrawaddy. At 3⅛ miles Môlé chaung, 60 yards wide, 3 feet deep; a bridge of rice boats was constructed and the baggage carried across; the animals were led. Half a mile later pass village of Ngapiedaw on the left. Next two miles road runs west to Thapánbin through tree jungle close to Irrawaddy. Camping ground good; water from Irrawaddy.
		3. Camp on river bank.	6	6	15	6	First mile runs north-west level through jungle (patches of cultivation) about 200 yards from the Irrawaddy. Next two miles north-west through a thick tree jungle, road good and level. At 3

* For a more recent account of the first two stages of this route *see* Route No. 23.

From BHAMO to SENBO (Up left bank, Irrawaddy)—*continued.*

Authorities. Military.	Authorities. Civil.	Number and Names of Stages, Rivers and Streams.	Distances. Intermediate.	Distances. Total.	Remarks.
G.O.C. Mandalay District and O.C. Bhamo.	Commissioner, Northern Division, and Deputy Commissioner, Bhamo.	**3. Camp on river bank**—*cont.*			miles road becomes much intersected by nullahs, some of which require ramping; the bottoms of some are marshy, and grass has to be laid down. Road follows the river through thick jungle, nullahs every 100 yards, occasional paddy clearings. At 6¾ miles camp. Camping ground (paddy clearing) fair; water from Irrawaddy (50 yards). A very difficult march owing to the numerous nullahs which rendered it very trying for transport.
		4. Camp near Thamángyi. Wura chaung.	M. F. 5 0	M. F. 20 6	The road goes north for about ⅛ mile close to Irrawaddy, some of the spurs on the right are cleared for paddy. The road then goes inland over one or two small streams through a large paddy clearing; ascends a hill, through a paddy clearing down to the Irrawaddy. Road then runs north close to the Irrawaddy over a large number of nullahs to Thabiyébin which is reached at 3 miles. Before reaching Thabiyébin the road bifurcates—the road to the left must be taken, the other is a grass-cutters' road. Next mile road follows river about 100 yards inland over several nullahs crossing the Wura chaung, small stream. At 4¼ miles Thamángyi, thence over fair road to camp at 5 miles. Camping ground (in paddy clearing), water from Irrawaddy fair (50 yards). A good road which, however, was intersected by a large number of nullahs.
		5. Nansao ... Kómni chaung. Kyaupsu chaung. Nungo chaung (18 inches deep).	5 6	26 4	Road goes north-east down steep descent to Nungo chaung, rocky bed 15 feet wide; it then runs west along right bank of the stream for 300 yards. Road good, 27 feet wide. At ⅛ mile road runs north-west and continues level. At ¾ mile road comes in from Tamin, a small Kachin village on the right. At 1 mile cross Kômni chaung, banks very steep, require ramping. The road now passes over three hills in a north-west direction. At 1¾ miles road ascends the first hill, ascent and descent very steep, at the bottom cross the Kyaupsu chaung (small stream) and then north-west up a steep winding path to the top of the second hill called Sheitsabu, 700 feet high; round the hill and down over a ravine up to the top of the third hill, this ascent is very steep and requires ramping. Road then runs north-west through jungle over hills and nullahs down to the Irrawaddy which is reached at 4¾ miles, thence north along good road for 1 mile to camp. Camp (on road east of Namsán) good. Water from Irrawaddy (100 yards). Fair road, one or two nullahs require ramping.
		6. Nanti ... ... Taminsha stream.	5 0	31 4	The road leads north along a good path crossing 2 nullahs. At 450 yards it turns north-west and ascends a hill for 200 yards and then along a ridge up to the top of the hill, the Irrawaddy being here about a mile distant, the ground on the right consists of high hills covered with jungle on the left of spurs and ravines running down to the Irrawaddy. The road then goes 300 yards along a ridge and down a ravine, the banks of which are very steep. The road then goes north-west over a ravine and down a ridge to the

FROM BHAMO TO SENBO (UP LEFT BANK, IRRAWADDY)—*continued.*

Authorities.		Number and Names of Stages, Rivers and Streams.	Distances.		Remarks.
Military.	Civil.		Intermediate.	Total.	
G.O.C. Mandalay District and O.C. Bhamo.	Commissioner, Northern Division, and Deputy Commissioner, Bhamo.	**6. Nanti**—*cont.*			Taminsha stream which is here about 20 feet wide, rocky bed, both the descent and ascent were almost impassable to loaded animals, and a winding path had to be constructed up the ascent and firmly revetted. The road then goes north-west cut in the side of the hill, and bad. At 3 miles it comes down to the river and goes north, still bad, crossing a large number of nullahs and spurs, the ascents of which are very trying for transport animals and require ramping. At 5 miles Nanti. Camping ground in village good; water from Irrawaddy (50 yards). This was a very trying march, by far the worst of the whole distance. A large amount of manual labour was required to make the road practicable, and the very steep ascents and descents together with a long time the mules were under their loads rendered it a very bad march for transport.
			M. F.	M. F.	
		7. Laungpu ... Nanti chaung.	5 4	37 0	The first mile is along a good road north-west about 250 yards from the river, 40 feet above it. Occasional patches of cultivation, mostly high grass and tree jungle. At 1¼ miles cross Nanti chaung, a stream about 15 feet wide, steep sandy sides. Next two miles north over a series of hills and nullahs, the sides of which are steep and require ramping for transport animals; bad road. At 4 miles road passes pagoda on an island in the Irrawaddy; the road then runs north, good, level and through jungle to Laungpu. Camping ground (in village) good; water from Irrawaddy. A hard march for transport.
		8. Nanhé	7 0	44 0	Road follows the course of the river north-west crossing a bad nullah just out of camp; road narrow and bad. At 1 mile a very steep nullah, a bad place for transport animals. At 1¾ miles pass Léma on the left; the path after Léma has only been recently cut; the road is now good and level, passing through tree jungle with occasional cultivated patches. At 3½ miles the road bifurcates—the path being to the left up the rocky bed of the river, 400 yards later it leaves the river and goes up-hill over a bad track cut in the side of the hill, and then over a series of hills and ravines, still bad. At 5 miles the road comes down to the bed of the river, which it follows for about 2 miles into camp; road very bad and rocky. Camp on bed of river fair; water from Irrawaddy. Road from Bhamo ends here.
		Nethagôn ...	...	...	Crossed river from Nanhé to Nethagôn; small village just opposite. River about 250 yards wide; current about 4 miles an hour. Commenced 8-30, finished 2-30. Two launches and a large number of native boats.
		9. Senbo ... Nankát stream.	8 4	52 4	The road leads north out of camp along up sandy river bed for 1¾ miles, then leaves the river and turns west crossing two hills. Fourth mile through bamboo jungle in a south-west direction. At 4 miles the road debouches on a large open plain and runs north-west. A quarter of a mile later a road from the village of Papywa meets it. The road then runs north-

No. 18.

FROM BHAMO TO SENBO (UP LEFT BANK, IRRAWADDY)—*continued.*

Authorities. Military.	Authorities. Civil.	Number and Names of Stages, Rivers and Streams.	Distances. Inter-mediate.	Distances. Total.	Remarks.
G.O.C. Mandalay District and O.C. Bhamo.	Commissioner, Northern Division, and Deputy Commissioner, Bhamo.	**9. Senbo**—*cont.*			west through the plain till at 5¾ miles it again enters jungle crossing the Nankát stream (24 feet wide, 1 foot deep) ¼ mile later. At 6½ miles the bank of the Irrawaddy is reached. The road then follows the bank of the Irrawaddy north-north-west through villages of Myintha, Mantin and Pinlôn for two miles. At 8¾ miles Senbo. Camping ground good; water from Irrawaddy. Supplies in abundance. An excellent road during this march. There is another route up the right bank (*see* Route No. 90) equally, if not more difficult than this, and it is probable that a better trace could be found for a road between Bhamo and Senbo by keeping well away from the river side to the east, in fact more or less on the line of the Bhamo-Ayeindama route *viâ* Theinlôn. *See* Route No. 6.

No. 19.

From BHAMO to SI-U.

BY LIEUT. DAVIES, OXFORD LIGHT INFANTRY, DECEMBER 1891.

Military	Civil	Stages	Intermediate	Total	Remarks
G.O.C. Mandalay District and O.C. Bhamo.	Commissioner, Northern Division, and Deputy Commissioner, Bhamo.		M. F.	M. F.	
		1. Sáwadi ... Namsari chaung, Thinlin or Namápwé chaung, and smaller streams.	9 0	9 0	General direction south-south-west. Leave the fort by the west gate. Along left bank of Irrawaddy the whole way. First 1½ miles through streets. At 1¾ miles, cross Namsari chaung; 35 yards wide and wooden pile-bridge fit for carts. Road then passes through high kaing grass for the rest of the way, with tree jungle as well as kaing grass after 3½ miles. At 3 miles cross Thinlin chaung; bridge 10 spans of 3 yards each. At 3½ miles bridge 30 yards long over small nullah. Five more wooden bridges over small nullahs. At 7 miles the Kachin village of Nankôn, called Kônywagyi by the Burmese; 17 houses. At 7½ miles cross a chaung: wooden bridge 7 spans, 3 yards each, too narrow for carts. Thence mule path to Sáwadi. Carts could go as far as Mankôn, and right up to Sáwadi, if the bridge at 7½ miles were widened; though probably the road would be impassable in the rains. Carts are scarce in the district, and this road does not appear to be used by carts to any extent. Large kyaung and sayát at Sáwadi. Good grass.
		2. Mankin ... Moyu chaung, back-water of Naunghu chaung.	12 2	21 2	General direction south-west to Moyu; thence south. Good mule road. At 1 mile cross the Moyu chaung flowing from the left, 20 yards wide, steep banks 12 feet high. Wooden bridge and easy knee-deep ford, 150 yards above it. Rather rapid current and sandy bottom. At 1¼ miles village of Moyu, 16 houses, in bamboo stockade; a small kyaung, at the junction of the Moyu chaung and Irrawaddy. Thence through tree jungle, pass no villages or streams till Mankin. At 4 miles a road from the right from Kaungtôn. At 6¾ miles a muddy well, called Nát-yé-dwin, 150 yards on the left of the road. At 9¼ miles road to left to Manya. At 11¼ miles road to left to Thayetkôn and

FROM BHAMO TO SI-U—*continued.*

Authorities. Military.	Authorities. Civil.	Number and Names of Stages, Rivers and Streams.	Distances. Intermediate.	Distances. Total.	Remarks.
G.O.C. Mandalay District and O.C. Bhamo.	Commissioner, Northern Division, and Deputy Commissioner, Bhamo.	**2. Mankin**—*cont.*			Manya. Just before reaching Mankin, cross a backwater of the Naunghu chaung, 10 yards wide, 4 feet 6 inches deep, at first crossing by mule bridge, ankle-deep at second crossing by ford, twice. Mankin on right bank of Naunghu chaung, 10 houses; rest-house for 50 men; camping ground in paddy-fields.
		3. Sikaw ... ... Naunghu, Manna, Namma, Sinkán and Nankhwin chaungs.	M. F. **16 0**	M. F. 37 2	The next two stages can, if desired, be converted into three, the halts being made at Malin 12¼ miles, Kyunbintha 8½ and Si-u 10½. General direction south. Good mule road, crossing the Naunghu chaung, 15 yards wide, 4 feet deep, rapid current, sandy bottom crossed by mule bridge, flowing from the left at Mankin. Thence through tree jungle all the way except some paddy round the villages. At ½ mile, road to right to Kángyi. At 3¼ miles cross the Manna chaung, from the left 5 yards wide, easy, ankle-deep ford. Just beyond this a road to the right to Khappan. At 6½ miles road to the right to Naungwin, and to the left to Uzu. At 7¾ miles road to right to Wégyi, and to left to Uzu and Khappan. At 8 miles road to left to Makawyin and Makawkha (both deserted). At 8½ miles cross the Namma chaung from the left, 5 yards wide, nearly stagnant, muddy, and might be difficult to cross in a wetter year. At 12 miles road to the left to Seiktu. At 12¼ miles cross the Sinkán chaung, 30 yards wide, easy knee-deep ford, gentle current and reach Malin, a village on its left bank, pôngyi kyaung, and good camping ground. From here there is a fairly good road leading north-north-west to Simaw, Namu (or Nanu) and Kashin; distance to Namu 4 miles and Kashin 10 miles. The first 4 miles is through open country, paddy plain and open forest, the remainder through dense bamboo, cane, and evergreen bush jungle. The Namlaw is crossed close to Simaw, and the Namu and the Namugalé between Namu and Kashin. Opposite Malin on right bank is Seiktu. At 13¾ miles village of Kônkha, 36 houses, kyaung and zayát on left bank of Sinkán chaung. Opposite it on right bank of stream is Kônbaung, five houses. At 14¼ miles cross the Sinkán chaung again ford as before. Here another path goes straight on up the left bank and crosses the stream at Sikaw. At 15 miles cross the Nankhwin chaung from the left, 5 yards wide, nearly dry, but muddy, and would be difficult for mules in a wetter year. If this stream is deep in mud, the road up the left bank of the Sinkán chaung is the best. Sikaw on right bank of Sinkán chaung, 40 houses. Military police post, circuit house, and camping ground. Two marches can be made of this stage by halting at Wégyi, ½ mile to the right of the road, on Sinkán chaung, military police post and camping ground in paddy-fields. No zayát or kyaung. For another description of these three first stages, *see* Route No. 15.
		4. Si-u ... ... Lapé, Namsán, Namkow, Nankha and Si-u chaungs.	**15 4**	52 6	General direction south. Good mule road. At 2 miles village of Sakhángalé 10 houses. At 2¼ miles Sakhángyi (after crossing the Lapé chaung from the left 15 yards wide, sandy bottom; foot-bridge and easy knee-deep ford), 20 houses, one zayát in middle of village. Main road goes through Munsin. But at 3¼

Authorities. Military.	Authorities. Civil.	Number and Names of Stages, Rivers and Streams.	Distances. Intermediate.	Distances. Total.	Remarks.
G.O.C. Mandalay District and O.C. Bhamo.	Commissioner, Northern Division, and Deputy Commissioner, Bhamo.	**4. Si-u**—*cont.*			miles a short cut, practicable for mules, turns to the left and meets main road again just short of Khágyin at 4½ miles, 14 houses on right bank of Sinkán chaung. At 5 miles just before reaching Kyunbintha road turns off to the left front. The next 2½ miles of road not traversed, but mules have gone by it and there are said to be no difficulties. The Namsán chaung from the left, 7 yards wide, ankle-deep, easy ford, is crossed close to Kyunbintha. In this 2½ miles two roads go off to the left to Nanaik. At 7½ miles road to left to Nanaik. Cross the Namkow chaung from the left, 5 yards wide, 1 foot deep, easy sandy ford, and 200 yards further on the Nankha chaung from the left, 3 yards wide, stagnant, easy ford. At 9 miles road to right to Gwégyi. At 10½ miles enter grass plain ¾ mile wide, 1¾ miles long. At 11 miiles road to right front to Namkán (the Mômeik road). At'21¼ miles road to right to Namkán and to left to Nankha. At 12¾ miles road to right to Namkán. At 14 miles enter the Si-u paddy plain. At 15¼ miles cross Si-u chaung twice first from left, then from right within 150 yards; 7 yards wide, ankle-deep, easy fords, twice first from left and then from right. Si-u contains 30 houses and small kyaung. Good water and fair grass. Large camping grounds.

ALTERNATIVE I.

FROM BHAMO TO MANKIN *viâ* MÁNSI.

BY LIEUT. DAVIES, JANUARY 1892.

Military.	Civil.	Stages, Rivers and Streams.	Intermediate. M. F.	Total. M. F.	Remarks.
G.O.C. Mandalay District and O.C. Bhamo.	Commissioner, Northern Division, and Deputy Commissioner, Bhamo.	**1. Mánsi** ... ... Namsari, and Namápwé, or Thinlin chaungs.	12 4	12 4	General direction south-south-east. Good mule road through tree jungle. Leave the fort by the east gate. At 1¼ miles bridge over a paddy valley, 4 spans of 3 yards each, 9 feet wide. At 4 miles cross the Namsari chaung from the left, 18 yards wide, 2 feet 6 inches deep. Wooden cart bridge, 7 spans 3 yards each, 9 feet wide. On the further bank village of Kabbani, 20 houses. At 7½ miles village of Manyát, 25 houses, on right bank of Namápwé chaung, from the left 40 yards wide, easy sandy ford, over knee-deep. Up the chaung for ¼ mile, then cross it. On further bank village of Namápwé to left of road, 10 houses. At 12½ miles, Mánsi, 13 houses, on right bank of Moyu chaung; large camping grounds. (Lieut. Norie makes it 14 miles. *See* Route No. 12.)
		2. Hántet ... Kyaungán, Mankham, Naunghi, Moyu and several smaller streams.	7 0	19 4	General direction south-west, good mule road. Follows the right bank of the Moyu chaung the whole way. Through the Mánsi paddy plain (600 yards wide) for ¾ mile. At ½ mile cross the Kyaungán chaung from right, 2 yards wide, dry, mule bridge, at the Kyaungán bullock camp 30 and 50 yards. At 1¾ miles cross a chaung from right, 2 yards wide, stagnant, mule bridge. At 2 miies cross a chaung from right, 8 yards wide, ankle-deep, muddy, passable now, but might be difficult in a wetter year. At 2¼ miles cross a chaung. At 2½ miles cross Mankham chaung from right, dry and easy. At 5 miles cross Naunghi chaung, from right, 3 yards wide, stagnant mule bridge. Just before this stream a road to the left to Maungwé, 300 yards to left of the road across the Moyu, which is crossed by a ford

FROM BHAMO TO SI-U—*continued.*

ALTERNATIVE I—*continued.*

Authorities. Military.	Authorities. Civil.	Number and Names of Stages, Rivers and Streams.	Distances. Intermediate.	Distances. Total.	Remarks.
G.O.C. Mandalay District and O.C. Bhamo.	Commissioner, Northern Division, and Deputy Commissioner, Bhamo.	**2. Hántet**—*cont.*			3 feet deep. Village contains 30 houses, small kyaung and zayát. Below the village a foot-bridge and ford, 3 feet 6 inches deep leads back into the Mánsi-Hántet road at 5⅛ miles. At 5¾ miles village of Kôndein, 19 houses. Hence through paddy plain ½ to ¾ mile wide to Hántet. Before entering Hántet the Moyu chaung is crossed from left, 20 yards wide, foot-bridge and knee-deep, ford 10 yards below the bridge. Sandy bottom and gentle current; easy ford. Hántet contains 45 houses and large kyaung. Large camping grounds in paddy-fields.
		3. Mankin ... Nampi chaung, Naung Pôn En, and Naunghu chaung.	M. 10 F. 2	M. 29 F. 6	General direction south-west, all through tree jungle, not much bamboo, good mule road. At ⅛ mile cross the Nampi chaung, 10 yards wide, 1 foot deep, sandy bottom, gentle current from left, easy approaches to ford. Just beyond a dry swamp, easily passable now, but waist-deep in the rains, thus rendering the road impassable then for bullocks, though foot-bridges are made. At 1¼ miles cross Naung Pôn En, a marsh, yards 20 wide, now nearly dry. In the rains knee-deep, with a stream from the right running into Nampi chaung. Hpwihôk chaung from left, 5 yards wide, now dry, knee-deep in the rains. At 1¾ miles road from Gwegyé from right rear. At 1¼ miles cross the Hpwihôk chaung. At 4⅛ miles a swamp, now nearly dry and easily passable, measures 12 yards + 400 yards; said to be more than knee-deep in the rains. At 6⅛ miles road to left to Hôma, to right to Moyu. At 6¾ miles there is a short cut to the right front, which joins the rain road again at Thayetkôn, but impassable for loaded mules owing to a swamp close to Thayetkôn. At 7⅛ miles village of Manyán (or Manya) on right bank of Naunghu chaung, 12 houses and 1 zayát in middle of village. Room to camp round the village. At 9¼ miles village of Thayetkôn, 8 houses. At 10 miles cross a backwater of the Naunghu chaung, 4 feet 6 inches deep, 10 yards wide, mule bridge. At 10¼ miles cross the same backwater again ankle-deep, easy, and enter Mankin, 16 houses, on right of Naunghu chaung, rest-house for 50 men; camping ground in paddy-fields.

ALTERNATIVE II.

FROM SÁWADI, STAGE 1, TO MANKIN, STAGE 2, *viâ* SINKÁN.

BY LIEUT. DAVIES, DECEMBER 1891.

Military.	Civil.	Number and Names of Stages, Rivers and Streams.	Intermediate.	Total.	Remarks.
G.O.C. Mandalay District and O.C. Bhamo.	Commissioner, Northern Division, and Deputy Commissioner, Bhamo.	**1. Sinkán** ... Moyu, Mayen, Yé-ó, Bôngwin and Sinkán chaungs.	10 2	10 2	General direction west. A fair mule road, but at present much overgrown with kaing grass, and several steep nullahs, to cross which might make it impassable till later in a wetter year. The road follows the telegraph line and left bank of the Irrawaddy the whole way. At 1 mile cross Moyu chaung from the left, 15 to 20 yards wide, steep banks 10 or 12 feet high. Crossed by wooden foot-bridge and easy knee-deep ford 150 yards above the

FROM BHAMO TO SI-U—*continued.*

ALTERNATIVE II—*continued.*

Authorities. Military.	Authorities. Civil.	Number and Names of Stages, Rivers and Streams.	Distances. Inter-mediate.	Distances. Total.	Remarks.
G.O.C. Mandalay District and O.C. Bhamo.	Commissioner, Northern Division, and Deputy Commissioner, Bhamo.	**1. Sinkán**—*cont.*			bridge. At $1\frac{1}{4}$ miles village of Moyu on left bank of Moyu chaung at its junction with the Irrawaddy; 16 houses; small kyaung. At 4 miles village of Kaungtôn, 18 houses and kyaung; not stockaded. Surrounded by a backwater of the Irrawaddy (dry in low water season) which is crossed on entering and on leaving the village; before entering village steep banks, but passable for mules. On leaving the village crossed by wooden mule bridge, 6 spans of 3 yards each, 8 feet broad. At $4\frac{1}{4}$ miles Burmese village of Peinegôn, 10 houses. At $5\frac{1}{4}$ miles cross Mayen chaung from the left 5 yards wide, steep banks. At 6 miles village of Myalé, 15 houses. From here a road to the left to Kachin village of Pingyein. At $6\frac{3}{4}$ miles cross the Yé-6 chaung from the left 15 yards wide, steep banks, 1 yard width of water, 6 inches deep. At $9\frac{1}{4}$ miles cross the Bôngwin chaung from left, 1 yard wide 6 inches deep, easily crossed. At $10\frac{1}{4}$ miles cross the Sinkán chaung from left, 30 yards, rapid current, waist-deep, crossed by boat, swimming the mules over and enter Sinkán. Police fort 50 yards square. The part of Sinkán at the mouth of the ford is called Chaungwa, Sinkán proper being further south. Chaungwa contains 25 houses and Sinkán 20 houses. Room for camp round the fort.
		2. Mankin ... Kyauk-ku, Kyauk-pôt, Nawtáng, Minking, Sinkán, Naunghu and three smaller chaungs.	M. F. 15 0	M. F. 25 2	General direction south-south-east till the Sinkán chaung is crossed; thence east to Mankin, a difficult road for mules, badly overgrown with jungle, and several nullahs near Sinkán so muddy that the mules had to be unloaded to cross them; this was partly due to 6 hours' rain the day before. Mules started at 9 A.M. and arrived at 6 P.M. At $\frac{1}{4}$ mile crossed the Kyauk-ku chaung from right, 8 yards wide, 6 inches width of water, wooden mule bridge 4 feet wide. At $\frac{1}{2}$ mile village of Kyauk-pôt, six houses. Just beyond it cross Kyauk-pôt chaung from right, 3 yards wide, easy ford. At $1\frac{3}{4}$ miles cross Nawtáng chaung from right, 3 yards wide; deep mud, mules had to be unloaded. Then cross three more muddy chaungs and enter Kachin village of Hinsein, five houses, from the right, muddy and difficult for mules, on left bank of Sinkán chaung. At $5\frac{3}{4}$ miles cross Minking chaung from right, 5 yards wide, 6 inches deep, easily crossed. At 6 miles village of Kyauktôn on left bank of Sinkán chaung, six houses. At $9\frac{2}{3}$ miles crossed the Sinkán chaung from the left to the right bank, where the path to the ford turns off to the left, the main road goes on to Wégyi. The chaung is crossed at a ford called Nammun with no village near it from the right, 35 yards wide, nearly waist-deep, sandy bottom, gentle current, easy approaches, landing 60 yards above the entrance to the ford. At $13\frac{1}{2}$ miles village of Kángyi, 20 houses, on left bank of Naunghu chaung. At 15 miles cross the Naunghu chaung from the right, 20 yards wide, good mule bridge and enter Mankin, 10 houses, rest-house for 50 men; camping grounds in paddy-field.

FROM BHAMO TO SI-U—*continued.*

ALTERNATIVE III.

FROM SÁWADI, STAGE 1, TO SIKAW, STAGE 3, *viâ* SINKÁN.

BY LIEUT. DAVIES, JANUARY 1892.

Authorities. Military.	Authorities. Civil.	Number and Names of Stages, Rivers and Streams.	Distances. Intermediate. M.	F.	Distances. Total. M.	F.	Remarks.
G.O.C. Mandalay District and O.C. Bhamo.	Commissioner, Northern Division, and Deputy Commissioner, Bhamo.	**1. Sinkán** ...	**10**	**2**	10	2	*See* Alternative II, Stage 1.
		2. Nanthé ...	**13**	**0**	23	2	General direction south-south-east. Fair mule road, but somewhat overgrown with jungle, and some muddy nullahs to cross. Along the Sinkán-Mankin route for $9\frac{1}{4}$ miles till the Mankin road turns east to the **Nammun** ford. At $10\frac{1}{4}$ miles cross a muddy ditch from the right, 3 yards wide, muddy; might be difficult in a wetter year. At $11\frac{1}{4}$ miles cross another ditch, 5 yards wide, muddy; might be difficult for mules. At 13 miles Nanthé, 10 houses (two inhabited), empty kyaung on left bank of Sinkán chaung. Large camping grounds. From Nanthé is a road to the west to Nahangyi, a deserted village.
		3. Sikaw ... ... Nanthé, Pabo, Sinkán and Namma chaungs.	**15**	**0**	38	2	General direction south-east to Naungyin; thence south to Sikaw. Fair mule road to Wégyi, but somewhat overgrown; some muddy ditches to cross; thence good mule road to Sikaw. At $\frac{1}{2}$ mile cross the Nanthé chaung from the right, 2 yards wide, ankle-deep, easy sandy ford. At 1 mile deserted village of Kyaunglain on Sinkán chaung. At $1\frac{1}{2}$ miles road turns to the east another road going straight on to Ngathin, a Kachin village. At $2\frac{1}{4}$ miles cross the Pabo chaung from the right, 5 yards wide, ankle-deep, muddy; easy now, but might be difficult. At $2\frac{3}{4}$ miles cross a ditch from the right, 2 yards wide, muddy. At $3\frac{1}{4}$ miles deserted village of Hna-u on Sinkán chaung. At $4\frac{3}{4}$ miles at the deserted village of Naungyin cross the Sinkán chaung from the right, 25 yards wide, knee-deep, easy sandy ford, and follow up its right bank in the water for 500 yards. At $5\frac{1}{4}$ miles deserted village of Mankôn on Sinkán chaung. At $5\frac{1}{2}$ miles cross Namma chaung from the left, 5 yards wide, stagnant, muddy. Is crossed at present by a plank laid on the mud strong enough to bear mules. At 6 miles village of Wégyi, 12 houses, Military police post, on Sinkán chaung, good camping ground in paddy-fields. At $5\frac{3}{4}$ miles meet the Mankin-Sikaw road. *See* Main-route, Stage 3 above.

ALTERNATIVE IV.

FROM MALIN, *see* STAGE 3, TO SI-U, STAGE 4, *viâ* KANNI.

BY D. W. RAE, ESQ., BURMA POLICE, JANUARY 1892.

Military	Civil	Stages	Intermediate M.	F.	Total M.	F.	Remarks
G.O.C. Mandalay District and O.C. Bhamo.	Commissioner, Northern Division, and Deputy Commissioner, Bhamo.	**1. Sumshin camp.** Namlaw chaung.	**6**	**0**	6	0	Road follows the Sinkán stream till Kônka is reached, turns to the right from here, crosses a paddy plain and enters some dense bamboo and other small jungle, which had to be cut for the greater portion of the road, especially near the crossings of the Namlaw stream; at short intervals it also passes through some very good young teak forests. Time taken over this march 6 hours.

FROM BHAMO TO SI-U—*continued.*

ALTERNATIVE IV—*continued.*

Authorities. Military.	Authorities. Civil.	Number and Names of Stages, Rivers and Streams.	Distances. Intermediate. M.	Distances. Intermediate. F.	Distances. Total. M.	Distances. Total. F.	Remarks.
G.O.C. Mandalay District and O.C. Bhamo.	Commissioner, Northern Division, and Deputy Commissioner, Bhamo.	**2. Walu** ... ... Malinmi and Sama streams.	**4**	**0**	10	0	7-45 A.M. Left Sumshin camp for Walu. The road as far as Thin Tu village is fairly good, after this it passes through dense bamboo jungle and ascends gradually to Atetwalu, impossible to encamp here owing to water being scarce; camp at Auk Walu, which is only ½ mile from the upper village and down-hill. Camping ground small, but fairly level; water-supply ample and is about 300 yards down-hill from camp.
		3. Nyaungôn ... Sama, Lawkai and Sinkán streams.	**4**	**0**	14	0	Road after leaving camp descends into the Sama stream, crosses some undulating country and drops into the Namlaw stream near Nyaungôn. The road is a well-defined foot-path and is free from jungle overhead. Water-supply ample; direction travelled south-east.
		4. Sikaw ...	**8**	**0**	22	0	Road takes a south-east direction and passes close to Kônmaik village, then goes due east to the deserted village of Nawkôn, crosses the Lawkai stream hard by, and continues due east through open forest to Sikaw (Stage 3 of main-route above).
		5. Kanni ... ... Lapai Namsán.	**7**	**4**	29	4	Road is very good all the way; it is portion of the trade route and passes through the villages of Sakhángalé, Sakhángyi, Nyaungbintha, and Mansin. The Lapai stream is crossed between Sakhángalé and Sakhángyi, and about 2 miles further on crosses the Namsán stream and 1½ miles further the Sinkán stream, on the right bank of which Kanni is situated. There is also a rather nasty ditch about 2½ miles from Sikaw; there is a small plank bridge across, but only sufficient to allow pedestrians across. At the present time pack animals are able to get down the hollow without difficulty, but in the rains probably impassable. The ditch is about 8 feet broad and might be spanned by a good bridge.
		6. Si-u ... ... Sinkán, Namkao, Namkha, Namthin, Nampôn, Namtao and Si-u streams.	**11**	**0**	40	4	The road cuts across portion of Kanni paddy-fields and drops into Sinkán stream, short distance from camp: follows a south-easterly course for about 2 miles and then crosses the Namkao and Namkha streams, after which it goes due south for about 5 or 6 miles and again south-east till Si-u is reached.

FROM BHAMO TO SI-U—*continued.*

ALTERNATIVE IV—*continued.*

Authorities. Military.	Authorities. Civil.	Number and Names of Stages, Rivers and Streams.	Distances. Intermediate.	Distances. Total.	Remarks.
G.O.C. Mandalay District and O.C. Bhamo.	Commissioner, Northern Division, &c.	**6. Si-u**—*cont.*			The Namthin, Nampôn, Namtao, and Si-u streams are also crossed; they are all very small and have about 6 inches of water. *Note.*—There is apparently no reason for making such short marches in the first three stages and probably the whole distance might easily be covered in four marches.

BRANCH I.

FROM SÁWADI, STAGE 1, TO HÁNTET.

BY LIEUT. DAVIES, DECEMBER 1891.

Military	Civil	Stage	Intermediate M. F.	Total M. F.	Remarks
G.O.C. Mandalay District and O.C. Bhamo.	Commissioner, Northern Division, and Deputy Commissioner, Bhamo.	**1. Hántet** ... ... Ngápedôn, Thányinsi, Nanthékao, Moyu and Nampé chaungs.	8 0	8 0	General direction south-south-east to Sithôn, then south-east to Hántet. Good mule road all the way, but said to be impassable in the rains. The road used in the rains follows the Mánsi road part of the way and joins the present route at Manthé. Road passes near paddy-fields at first, then through kaing grass, and teak jungle to Shwégyaung. At 1¼ miles cross Ngápedôn chaung flowing from left, 12 yards wide, water stagnant. Mule bridge, 5 feet wide, made of wood and grass, supported by short posts and earth on top. At 2 miles Thányinsi chaung from left, 5 yards wide, water stagnant; bridge as before. Two hundred yards further or. Nanthékao chaung from left, 10 yards wide; bridge as before. At 3¼ and 3¾ miles roads to left front (south) to Mánsi. At 4 miles village of Shwégyaung on the Moyu chaung, 13 houses, 80 yards square, bamboo stockade. Cross Moyu chaung from left, 20 to 25 yards wide, sandy bottom. No bridge, good ford just over knee-deep, easy approaches to ford. Two boats by which to cross in the rains. Banks steep except at ford, gentle current at this time of year. Hence the road turns to the left and follows the left bank of the Moyu chaung to Hántet, skirting paddy-fields nearly continuously all the way. At 4¾ miles village of Thitsôn, 200 × 100 yards, bamboo stockade, 25 houses, one kyaung, two zayáts, three or four boats, and a few buffaloes. At 5¾ miles village of Manmakauk, bamboo stockade, 30 houses, three or four boats and some buffaloes. At 6½ miles cross Nampé chaung from right, 15 yards wide, runs into Moyu chaung close to road. Wooden foot-bridge 2 feet 6 inches broad. Ford 30 yards above knee-deep, good approaches, sandy bottom, gentle stream. At 6¾ miles village of Gwégyi on left bank of Moyu chaung and Manthé opposite it on right bank. Connected by bridge, 17 spans of 4 yards each, strong posts, but roadway only of bamboo hurdles. Ford at the bridge knee-deep. Manthé contains 35 houses and kyaung. Gwégyi 20 houses and kyaung. Both with bamboo stockade. At 7½ miles road to right front to Hôpôn. Hántet has 45 houses and large kyaung. Foot-bridge and knee-deep ford across Moyu chaung.

FROM BHAMO TO SI-U—*continued.*

BRANCH II.

FROM SÁWADI, STAGE 1, TO MÁNSI.

BY LIEUT. DAVIES, JANUARY 1892.

Authorities. Military.	Authorities. Civil.	Number and Names of Stages, Rivers and Streams.	Distances. Intermediate. M.	F.	Distances. Total. M.	F.	Remarks.
G.O.C. Mandalay District and O.C. Bhamo.	Commissioner, Northern Division, and Deputy Commissioner, Bhamo.	**1. Mánsi** ... ... Mankham, Khôtám and Kyaungán chaungs.	**10**	**0**	10	0	General direction south-east by east, good mule road through tree jungle past the old police fort at Sáwadi, 300 yards from the village. At 2¾ miles road to the right to Manthé and Hántet. At 6½ miles bullock camp of of Pangkha 150 × 50 yards. A pool of water there earlier in the season; no water now. At 7½ miles cross Mankham chaung from the left, 3 yards wide, dry, no mud. At 7¾ miles cross a small chaung from left, 1 yard, stagnant water, easy. At 8¼ miles Khôtám chaung from left, 2 yards wide, stagnant, easy. Here a road to the left front to Mánsi; this road is used in the rains, the present one then being impassable. A road from the right rear from Kôndein and Hántet. Hence the road follows up the right bank of the Moyu chaung, though not always close to it. At 8½ miles cross the Kyaungán channg from left, 2 yards wide, dry; crossed by mule bridge. Here is the Kyanngán bullock camp on right bank of Moyu chaung, 50 × 30 yards. At 9½ reach the Mánsi paddy plain, ¾ mile long by 600 yards broad. Through paddy-fields to Mánsi, 13 houses on right bank of Moyu chaung, large camping ground. *See* Route No. 12.

BRANCH III.

FROM MANKIN, STAGE 2, TO KHAPPAN.

BY LIEUT. DAVIES, DECEMBER 1891.

Authorities. Military.	Authorities. Civil.	Number and Names of Stages, Rivers and Streams.	Distances. Intermediate. M.	F.	Distances. Total. M.	F.	Remarks.
G.O.C. Mandalay District and O.C. Bhamo.	Commissioner, Northern Division, and Deputy Commissioner, Bhamo.	**1. Khappan** ... Manna and Naunghu chaungs.	**7** or **9**	**4** **4**	7 9	4 4	There are two routes (1) *viâ* Kyaungzôn, (2) *viâ* Manya. (1) is the shortest and best, but is at present so overgrown with jungle that mules could not get along it unless it was cleared. *Route* (1).—General direction south for 3 miles, thence east. Along the Sikaw road (*see* Route No. 19, Stage 3 above) for 3 miles till past the Manna chaung, then turn to the right through kaing grass. At 4½ miles deserted village of Kyaungzôn, then cross the Manna chaung steep descent to ford which is ample deep. At 5¾ miles cross the Manna chaung again, ford easy and only ample deep. At 7 miles down an open valley 600 yards broad to Khappan, five houses (only one inhabited) on left bank of Manna chaung, here 5 yards wide and ankle-deep. The rest-house, where the troops used to be, has been burnt down. *Route* (2).—General direction east to Manya, thence south. Along Hántet road to Manya (or Manyán) at 3 miles (*see* Alternative No. 1, Stage 3); thence good mule road. At 4¼ miles road turns to the right to the ford, a road going straight on to Hôma. At 4½ miles cross the Naunghu chaung from the left, 20 yards wide, 2 feet 4 inches deep, sandy bottom,

FROM BHAMO TO SI-U—*continued.*

BRANCH III—*continued.*

Authorities. Military.	Authorities. Civil.	Number and Names of Stages, Rivers and Streams.	Distances. Intermediate.	Distances. Total.	Remarks.
G.O.C. Mandalay District and O.C. Bhamo.	Commr., Northern Division, &c.	**1. Khappan**—*cont.*			steep banks, which ought to be ramped to allow loaded mules to cross. This could be done with tools in half an hour. At $5\frac{3}{4}$ miles cross small chaung with a woodcutter's hut called Wábo on its further bank. At $7\frac{1}{2}$ miles cross the Manna chaung, a bullock camp on its further bank. At $7\frac{3}{4}$ miles cross a muddy ditch from right, 5 yards wide; easy now, but might be difficult in a wetter year. At 8 miles Route No. (1) joins from the right.

BRANCH IV.

FROM SIKAW, STAGE 3, TO AUKAINGKAUNG.

BY LIEUT. DAVIES, JANUARY 1892.

Military	Civil	Stages	Intermediate M. F.	Total M. F.	Remarks
G.O.C. Mandalay District and O.C. Bhamo.	Commissioner, Northern Division, and Deputy Commissioner, Bhamo.	**1. Aukaingkaung.** Lapé and Nanlit chaungs.	**12 0**	12 0	General direction south to Sakhángyi, thence east to Aukaingkaung. Good mule road to Khamôt; thence fair mule road somewhat overgrown with jungle. Along the Si-u road (*see* Route No. 19, Stage 4) to Sakhángyi at $2\frac{1}{4}$ miles. At $6\frac{3}{4}$ miles pass the Kachin village of Tántabin, $\frac{1}{2}$ mile to the left of the road, nine houses on left of Lapé chaung. From here to Nanlit at 8 miles road not traversed, but the natives say it is easy for mules. Nanlit, six houses, on left bank of Lapé chaung. Cross Lapé chaung at Nanlit 10 yards wide, $2\frac{1}{2}$ deep, easy ford. At $8\frac{1}{2}$ miles Kachin village of Makyaingkatawng, three houses, at the junction of the Nanlit and Lapé chaungs. At $9\frac{1}{2}$ miles Kachin village of Khamôt, eight houses, on right bank of Nanlit chaung, 3 yards wide, ankle-deep. At $10\frac{1}{2}$ miles road to right to Loi Lom and Loi Kham; then cross the Nanlit chaung three times within 300 yards: first from left, then from right, then from left; 3 yards wide, ankle-deep, easy fords. Hence a steepish ascent with occasional level bits to Aukaingkaung, Kachin village, five houses; the road goes on to Loi Lom and Loi Kham. Only well water here; no stream.

BRANCH V.

FROM SIKAW, STAGE 3, TO KHAPPAN.

BY LIEUT. DAVIES, DECEMBER 1891.

Military	Civil	Stages	Intermediate M. F.	Total M. F.	Remarks
G.O.C. Mandalay District and O.C. Bhamo.	Commissioner, Northern Division, and Deputy Commissioner, Bhamo.	**1. Khappan** ... Myogu or Uzu chaung.	**15 6**	15 6	General direction north for 8 miles, thence east good mule road. Along the Mankin road (*see* Route No. 19, Stage 3) for 8 miles till the turning to Wégyi, then turn to the right. At $11\frac{1}{4}$ miles cross the Myogu or Uzu chaung from the right, 4 yards wide, ankle-deep, easy ford. At $13\frac{1}{2}$ miles a road to the right to Uzu $\frac{1}{4}$ mile off, six houses and small zayát on left bank of Myogu or Uzu chaung. Khappan contains only five inhabited houses, on right bank of Manna

FROM BHAMO TO SI-U—*continued.*

BRANCH V—*continued.*

Authorities. Military.	Authorities. Civil.	Number and Names of Stages, Rivers and Streams.	Distances. Intermediate. M.	F.	Distances. Total. M.	F.	Remarks.
G.O.C. Mandalay District, &c.	Commissioner, Northern Division, &c.	**1. Khappan**—*cont.*					chaung, 5 yards wide and ankle-deep. The rest-house formerly occupied by troops has been burnt down. In the early part of 1891 a road was cleared from Khappan to Seiktu. At present it is said to be much overgrown with jungle, but ordered to be cleared again. By this route the distance from Sikaw to Khappan would be about 13 or 13½ miles.

BRANCH VI.

FROM SIKAW, STAGE 3, TO NANAIK.

BY LIEUT. DAVIES, JANUARY 1892.

Authorities. Military.	Authorities. Civil.	Number and Names of Stages, Rivers and Streams.	Intermediate. M.	F.	Total. M.	F.	Remarks.
G.O.C. Mandalay District and O.C. Bhamo.	Commissioner, Northern Division, and Deputy Commissioner, Bhamo.	**1. Nanaik** ... ... Nanaik chaung.	**10**	**0**	10	0	From Sikaw there are two roads to Nanaik, one is a good mule road, but the other is only a foot-path impassable for mules. The description of the routes is as follows :— *Route* (1).—General direction south to Kyunbintha ; thence south-east to Nanaik. Good mule road. For 7 miles along Si-u road (*see* main-route, Stage 4 above) ; thence to the south-east crossing a plain. At 9 miles cross the Nanaik chaung from the left, 6 yards wide, ankle-deep, easy ford. At 10 miles the Shan village of Nanaik on left of Nanaik chaung, 11 houses. At 1½ miles south-east is the Kachin village of the same name, 10 houses.
		1. Nanaik	**10**	**4**	10	4	*Route* (2).—From Sikaw to Nankhauktaik (*see* Branch Route No. VII below); thence by foot-path for 2 miles across small spur of the hills. Path too narrow and overgrown for mules, and some steep and muddy nullahs to cross. This foot-path might be easily made practicable for mules by making rough bridges over the chaungs and cutting the path broader in places.

BRANCH VII.

FROM SIKAW, STAGE 3, TO NANKHAUKTAIK.

BY LIEUT. DAVIES, JANUARY 1892.

Authorities. Military.	Authorities. Civil.	Number and Names of Stages, Rivers and Streams.	Intermediate. M.	F.	Total. M.	F.	Remarks.
G.O.C. Mandalay District and O.C. Bhamo.	Commissioner, Northern Division, and Deputy Commissioner, Bhamo.	**1. Nankhauktaik.** Namsán chaung.	**8**	**2**	8	2	General direction south to Sikangyi, thence east to Tantabin, thence south to Nankhauktaik. Good mule road. As far as where the road passes Tantabin at 6¾ miles along the Aukaingkaung road (*see* Branch Route No. IV). At 7¼ miles road to left to Pakyé, Yama, and Namkham 300 feet yards ; along this road another road branches off from it to the left to Nanlit). At 7¾ miles cross the Namsán chaung, first from left, then from right, then from left. Six yards wide, ankle-deep, easy fords, and enter Kachin village of Nankhauktaik, seven houses. Here a road to the left to Namalu, Nampalán, and Lwé Saing. Cross the Namsán chaung again twice. At 8¼ miles the Shan village of Nankhauktaik on left bank of Namsán chaung, seven houses.

FROM BHAMO TO SI-U—*continued.*

BRANCH VIII.

FROM SIKAW, STAGE 3, TO SIENG *viâ* PÉSWÉ.

BY LIEUT. DAVIES, DECEMBER 1891.

Authorities. Military.	Authorities. Civil.	Number and Names of Stages, Rivers and Streams.	Distances. Intermediate. M.	Distances. Intermediate. F.	Distances. Total. M.	Distances. Total. F.	Remarks.
G.O.C. Mandalay District and O.C. Bhamo.	Commissioner, Northern Division and Deputy Commissioner, Bhamo.	**1. Péswé** ... ... Namsán and Sinkán chaungs.	**9**	**2**	9	2	General direction south-west beyond Kanni, thence west; good mule road. Along the Si-u road as far as Khágyin (4½ miles) (*see* Main-route, Stage 4 above). At 5 miles village of Kyunbintha, 14 houses; kyaung, one zayát in middle of village. At the other end of the village cross the Namsán chaung. From left 7 yards wide, ankle-deep, foot-bridge and easy ford. At 6 miles cross the Sinkán chaung. From left 18 yards wide, easy knee-deep ford, and enter Kanni, 30 houses; kyaung, zayát, in middle of village. Thence through paddy and open ground till 7½ miles where the village of Gwégyi is left ¼ mile off on the left. Thence through jungle to Péswé, 13 houses, and small kyaung, on left bank of the Mana chaung, which is nearly stagnant, 10 yards wide, steep banks. From Péswé there are roads (1) to Nampahôt and Mainseingtaung to the west; (2) to Yenbo a little further south; (3) to Pingyaing and Mabein to the south-west; (4) to Loi Maw and Loi Hpauk to the north-west.
		2. Sieng ... ... Sinkán, Sepu, Namkán, Nanyán, Namhun and Môhlaing chaungs.	**13**	**4**	22	6	Sieng is now deserted and the Bhamo-Mômeik road does not pass through it, but turns off south-west, 3 miles short of it, to Sipein. General direction west for 3 miles to the junction of the Sikaw-Si-u road, thence south, good mule road except the last 3 miles which is much overgrown by jungle, though passable for mules. At ½ mile road to left front to Kanni and Sikaw. At 1½ miles village of Gwégyi, eight houses, on left bank of Sinkán chaung, from the right, channel 20 yards wide, water 10 yards wide, knee-deep, easy ford, which is crossed beyond the village. At 1¾ miles cross the Sepu chaung from right, 5 yards wide, hair knee-deep, easy ford. At 2¼ miles pass through an open plain, 1 mile long, ½ mile wide. At the other side of this, road from Kyunbintha-Sikaw from the left. At 4½ miles through another grass plain, 2 miles long by ¾ mile broad. At 5 miles road to Si-u to the left. At 6½ miles village of Namkán, 13 houses, and one zayát in middle of village on right bank of Namkán chaung from left, 5 yards wide, easy ankle-deep ford, and foot-bridge which is crossed before entering village. Before crossing the chaung a road to the left to Si-u. At 6¼ miles another road to the left to Si-u. At 6¾ miles through a plain ¾ mile long. At other end of the plain road to left to Si-u and Sitha, and to right to deserted village of Mankyaing, 8¼ miles cross Nanyán chaung from left, 3 yards wide, 6 inches deep, easy ford. Hence across plain for 1¼ miles. At 10 miles road from left from Si-u. At 10¼ miles deserted village of Nahaw. At 10½ miles cross Namhun chaung from left, 3 yards wide, dry, muddy, but easy now. Here road to right to Sipein and Mômeik, the main Bhamo-Mômeik road. Hence skirt a large plain on the right for 1½ miles, thence through jungle to Sieng, a deserted village on left of Môhlaing chaung from left, 5 yards wide, ankle-deep, easy ford, which is crossed there.

FROM BHAMO TO SI-U—*continued.*

BRANCH IX.

FROM SI-U, STAGE 4, TO NAMKÁN.

BY LIEUT. DAVIES, DECEMBER 1891.

Authorities. Military.	Authorities. Civil.	Number and Names of Stages, Rivers and Streams.	Distances. Intermediate. M. F.	Distances. Total. M. F.	Remarks.
G.O.C. Mandalay District and O.C. Bhamo.	Commissioner, Northern Division, and Deputy Commissioner, Bhamo.	**1. Namkán** ... Namkán chaung.	3 6	3 6	There are two roads, almost exactly the same distance and equally good. General direction north-west; good mule roads. *Route* (1).—Along Sikaw road for 2¾ miles (*see* Main-route, Stage 4 above). At 3¼ miles road to the right of Nankha. At 3¼ miles join the Péswé Sieng road (Branch No. VII), 200 yards short of Namkán. Cross the Namkán chaung from left, 5 yards wide, easy ankle-deep ford and foot-bridge, and enter village, 13 houses and one zayát in middle of village. *Route* (2).—Further south than (1); through paddy for 1½ miles. At 2 miles cross Namkán chaung from left, 7 yards wide, easy ankle-deep ford. Beyond this a road to the left to Sieng and Sipein; thence through jungle to the south end of Namkán village.

BRANCH X.

FROM SI-U, STAGE 4, TO NANAIK.

BY LIEUT. DAVIES, JANUARY 1892.

Authorities. Military.	Authorities. Civil.	Number and Names of Stages, Rivers and Streams.	Intermediate. M. F.	Total. M. F.	Remarks.
G.O.C. Mandalay District and O.C. Bhamo.	Commissioner, Northern Division, and Deputy Commissioner, Bhamo.	**1. Nanaik** ... Nanaik chaung.	11 0	11 0	General direction north for 8 miles thence east; good mule road. Along the Si-u-Sikaw road for 8 miles (*see* Main-route, Stage 4 above). At 3¼ miles road to right to Nankha, which lies 1½ miles off the road; ¼ mile along this road is a marsh 10 yards wide, passable now, but might be difficult in a wetter year. Nankha contains seven Shan and two Kachin houses and kyaung, on left bank of Nankha chaung, 3 yards wide, almost stagnant. At 8½ miles two roads within 100 yards of each other join in from Khágyin and Sikaw. At 10 miles cross the Nanaik chaung from left, 6 yards wide, easy ankle-deep ford; thence through bamboo jungle to Nanaik, 11 houses. On left of Nanaik chaung 1½ miles south-east is the Kachin village of Nanaik, 10 houses.

BRANCH XI.

FROM SI-U, STAGE 4, TO SIENG.

BY LIEUT. DAVIES, DECEMBER 1891.

Authorities. Military.	Authorities. Civil.	Number and Names of Stages, Rivers and Streams.	Intermediate. M. F.	Total. M. F.	Remarks.
G.O.C. Mandalay Dist., &c.	Commr., Northern Dist., &c.	**1. Sieng** ... ... Si-u, Sitha, Namkán, Nanyán and Môhlaing chaungs.	6 2	6 2	General direction south-south-west to Nanyán; thence west to Sieng. Fair mule road, but the jungle wants clearing in places beyond Sitha, the road from there to Sieng being very little used, as Sieng is deserted and the Mômeik road does not now pass through it. Cross the Si-u chaung

FROM BHAMO TO SI-U—*continued.*

BRANCH XI—*continued.*

Authorities. Military.	Authorities. Civil.	Number and Names of Stages, Rivers and Streams.	Distances. Intermediate.	Distances. Total.	Remarks.
G.O.C. Mandalay District and O.C. Bhamo.	Commissioner, Northern Division, and Deputy Commissioner, Bhamo.	**1. Sieng**—*cont.*			first from left, then from right, 7 yards wide, easy ankle deep ford, twice. At ½ mile road to right to Sipein and Mômeik. At 1 mile cross Sitha chaung, from left, 2 yards wide, easy ford and foot-bridge, 6 inches deep; thence through paddy to Sitha at 1¼ miles, 10 houses. Beyond the village cross the Namkán chaung, from the left, 5 yards wide, ankle-deep, easy ford. At 2¾ miles cross the Nanyán chaung crossed seven times, first from left, channel 4 to 7 yards wide, water 1 to 3 yards wide, easy fords, 6 inches deep. Continue up the stream crossing it seven times, to Nanyán, Kachin village, three houses, at 4¾ miles; ¼ mile before reaching the village a road to the left to Hinkhat, a Kachin village; 100 yards beyond Nanyán, road to left to Mana, Loi Hpai, Pônkin. At 5¾ miles cross the Môhlaing chaung, and continue down it, crossing it seven times in the next ½ mile, all easy fords, only ankle-deep, to Sieng, a deserted village on the left bank.

No. 20.

From BHAMO to SAMA (see Route No. 17, Stage 3).

BY D. L. RICHARDSON, ESQ., CIVIL OFFICER WITH EASTERN KACHIN COLUMN, APRIL AND MAY 1891.

Military	Civil	Stages	Intermediate M.	Intermediate F.	Total M.	Total F.	Remarks
G.O.C. Mandalay District and O.C. Bhamo.	Commissioner, Northern Division, and Deputy Commissioner, Bhamo.	**1. Nampansán sakhán.** Namsari and Nampansán chaungs.	11	0	11	0	The road leads out by the Theindawgyi-paya road along the military police lines and past Fort C. It then takes an easterly route, first through open country and crosses a stream bridged by the Public Works Department. It then goes through open *eng* forest; road good and level all the way to Kabani (5 miles). On leaving Kabani the road goes over a bridge crossing the Namsari and then leads south-easterly through a plain over taungya sites. Ground very damp and must be impracticable during the rains. After going 1½ miles or so a streamlet of Namsari is crossed and there is a slight ascent of 50 feet, the road leading again through fairly level ground through open *eng* forest and Nampansán sakhán is reached. The stream from which the sakhán derives its name passes through the camp. It is 6 inches to 18 inches deep at the ford. Fish can be obtained lower down the stream; camp very good. Water and grass plentiful. There is also a road from Mômauk to the sakhán. The road is fairly good, but would be impracticable during the rains, as there are streams and marshes on the way. The road also is rather covered with overhanging bamboo jungle.
		2. Sama ... ... Theinlun chaung.	10	0	21	0	On leaving camp the road is very good and level and fairly open, running through big tree jungle till the foot of Wábaung hill is reached. At first the ascent is slight and gets steeper by degrees till a height of 2,800 feet is ascended and Wábaung is reached at 4 miles. The nature of jungle passed through is chiefly bamboo; road fairly good except one or two bits on nearing the village. Wábaung is a Marán village of 21 houses, and Kyetyin or Kyetyáng, 15 houses adjoins.

No. 20.

FROM BHAMO TO SUMA (SEE ROUTE NO. 17, STAGE 3)—*continued.*

Authorities.		Number and Names of Stages, Rivers and Streams.	Distances.		Remarks.
Military.	Civil.		Intermediate.	Total.	
G.O.C. Mandalay Dist. and O.C. Bhamo.	Commr., Northern Divn., &c.	**2. Sama**—*cont.*			Good camping ground; grass sufficient; water scarce. Tl road on leaving Kyetyin is rather steep and bad, but improves gradually and goes along the saddle of the hill aı through fairly open country, chiefly *taungya* sites, aı Sama, a Marán village of 18 houses, is reached at 10 mil. The road along the ridge is the caravan route and go along to Meungwai and Chiri (*see* Route No. 17, Stages and 3).

No. 21.

From BHAMO to TÁLAWGYI viâ MYOTHIT, MANMAW, &c.

BY CAPT. G. H. H. COUCHMAN, D.S.O., SOMERSETSHIRE LIGHT INFANTRY, JANUARY 1892.

Military	Civil	Stages	M.	F.	M.	F.	Remarks
G.O.C. Mandalay District and O.C. Bhamo.	Commissioner, Northern Division, and Deputy Commissioner, Bhamo.	**1. Malula**	**13**	**4**	13	4	For details *see* Route No. 11, Stage and 2 and Alternative IV of sa route.
		2. Myothit ...	**10**	**2**	23	6	
		3. Tálí	**7**	**4**	31	2	
		4. Tálí Uma ...	**6**	**2**	37	4	
		5. Lagat	**5**	**2**	42	6	For details *see* Route No. 7, Stage to 7.
		6. Warra	**12**	**4**	55	2	
		7. Manmaw ...	**11**	**2**	66	4	
		8. Kaichi chaung. Pakha, Kaichi, and two smaller streams.	**8**	**4**	75	0	General direction of march north-ea The road passes along the right ba of the Môlé chaung in an easte direction through kaing grass a occasional clearings and is much ov grown; after 1⅛ miles it crosses small muddy stream 6 feet broad with muddy approac which has been temporarily bridged. It would form obstacle unbridged. Shortly after this the road turns nor east and enters some paddy-fields in which there are t Kachin houses and some granaries. At 1⅜ miles it ent small tree and rumnah grass jungle, and is very good goi there are some small teak trees about here. At 2¼ m there is a road on the right from the Chinese-Shan vill of Meungseng. Road open and good. At 2¾ miles a r goes to the north-west to Ningtáp. At 3¾ miles cros stream which has now three beds, each respectively 1 f 4 feet and 8 feet broad, and which is no obstacle. At miles is a shorter and smaller road to Kaichi. At miles cross the Pakha Ka, 18 feet wide, with stony bot and which has an easy crossing. From here the r ascends steeply for about 2,000 feet to Kaiya, pass through old taungyas and bamboo and kaing grass jur with small trees, till at the top it passes into some taung now under cultivation. Here it is joined by the road m tioned above, and after 200 yards reaches Kaiya (7½ mil There is a branch road to Ningtáp from Kaiya. From l the road ascends and descends gently and finally pa through tree jungle into some taungyas which form a g camp. One stream is crossed close to camp. Water, w and bamboo plentiful. This road is very good, but rat steep, and there are occasional stony pieces in the asc Camp just below Kaichi at 8½ miles.

From BHAMO to TÁLAWGYI *viâ* MYOTHIT, MANMAW, &c.—*continued.*

Authorities. Military.	Authorities. Civil.	Number and Names of Stages, Rivers and Streams.	Distances. Inter-mediate. M.	F.	Distances. Total. M.	F.	Remarks.
G.O.C. Mandalay District and O.C. Bhamo.	Commissioner, Northern Division, and Deputy Commissioner, Bhamo.	**9. Namsángyáng.** Namsángyáng and two smaller streams.	7	4	82	4	The road now ascends easily into Kaichi, crossing a small stream. It then passes village and descends, very steep in parts and slippery on account of the red clay the path is cut in. Jungle trees on the plain. Two streams 2½ feet deep are crossed, the stream nearest Namsángyáng being the chaung of that name 12 yards broad; sandy bottom; no obstacle; approaches good. Camp on some extensive paddy-plains between the chaung and village. Namsángyáng is a Chinese-Shan village and consists of six houses; supplies, paddy and good fodder; water good from chaung. Time of march 3 hours.
		10. Kantaoyáng... Saláp and several smaller streams.	10	4	93	0	The track leaves Namsángyáng in north-westerly direction; country flat; thick kaing grass for 1½ miles, then slight ascent to the village of Tumpáng 2½ miles; small village; 10 houses; north-north-east from Namsángyáng. The path continues in a gradual ascent from the paddy land near Tumpáng through thick jungle to Drong 4 miles, where there is a drop to a small stream 1 mile north. The track ascends easy slope to Ningpwon 6½ miles; large village of 20 houses; no paddy; a few cattle. From Ningpwon the track turns north-north-west descending into valley along which it winds to Kantaoyáng 10½ miles after passing through Yán Lôn Kao at 8½ miles, crossing and recrossing the Saláp Ka. The path from Namsángyáng is good and the gradients easy, but the crossings to streams are bad. All the streams have firm, sandy, and stony bottoms, but clay banks 2 to 3 feet in height, which soon work into quagmires from traffic.
		11. Namsáng ... Saláp, Lômwai and several smaller streams.	11	4	104	4	General direction north-west. Leaving Kantaoyáng village the road crosses the Saláp Ka, 6 feet broad, stiff clay soil on either approach, and passes through bamboo and tree jungle, gradually ascending at first and then steeply into Kuma village (1 mile). Two small muddy and unimportant streams, 3 feet and 1 foot broad, are crossed. From here the road ascends rather steeply into Kuma-Uma village (2 miles) through bamboo and tree jungle. From here the road descends gradually for ½ mile to a small and nearly dry stream, 2 feet broad. To here it is through bamboo and tree jungle, but after this it is a little overgrown with bamboo and coarse grass. It passes along a ridge with occasional small ascents and descents into Nkongkong village (4 miles). Camping ground in village. Fodder plentiful. Water from a spring and not very plentiful. This is about 300 feet above Kantaoyáng. The road is good throughout, but

No. 21.

FROM BHAMO TO TÁLAWGYI *viâ* MYOTHIT, MANMAW, &c.—*continued.*

Authorities. Military.	Authorities. Civil.	Number and Names of Stages, Rivers and Streams.	Distances. Inter-mediate.	Distances. Total.	Remarks.
G.C.C. Mandalay District and O.C. Bhamo.	Commissioner, Northern Division, and Deputy Commissioner, Bhamo.	**11. Namsáng**—*cont.*			on account of the clayey soil, would be very slippery in wet weather. There is a road from Ninglaw, which joins the above just before Kuma-Uma. From Nkongkong the road descends gradually and smoothly about 300 feet to a level plain covered with dense bamboo and small tree jungle. Three small streams with muddy bottoms (9 feet broad 1½ feet deep, 6 feet broad 1 foot deep, and 3 feet broad and 6 inches deep) are crossed. They are no obstacles. The Pumwai Ka (properly Lômwai Ka) is crossed at 7 miles. This has steep banks of clay and sand of at least 25 feet in height. It is now 10 yards broad and about 2 feet deep, with muddy bottom and at present not a bad obstacle, but in the rains there would be a great deal of water and it would be impassable without rafts or boats. From here the road ascends gradually with occasional descends to the village of Siyáng (9 miles), road good, but there are two steep ascents. Jungle, small trees, bamboo, and cane. One small muddy stream is crossed, which is now nearly dry. From here the road ascends through tree jungle, at first gradually and then very steeply over hard and stony ground to some taungyas. There is a road to the left to the village of Htingnu which is visible from here about ½ mile distant. It then ascends rather steeply to the village of Wunya (11 miles), passing along the top of the ridge. From here to Namsáng the road is fairly level through tree jungle and is good going. From the Lammai Ka the ascent is one of about 1,500 feet. This road though overgrown and rough in parts could be easily repaired. The Lammai Ka is quite 50 yards broad from bank top to bank top, and would require a very good bridge. Namsáng at 11½ miles camp in village. Fodder plentiful. Water from two places, a well on the north of the village and a spring on the south. Water good and sufficient for transport if dammed up. This march was in a westerly direction from Nkongkong.
		12. Tálawgyi ... Irrawaddy.	M. 12 F. 0	M. 116 F. 4	General direction north-west. The road is now very good through tree jungle and nearly level with occasional ascents and descents to the village of Kraokra, 2 miles. Thence it descends through small tree, grass, and bamboo jungle, at first gently and then very steeply. This part is very stony and steep, but is not much of an obstacle. It is a descent of about 1,500 feet and 2 miles in length. At the bottom an almost dry stream is crossed, and also a muddy stream (dry), and the road passes through dense undergrowth on to the plain, which here is covered with kaing grass. About a quarter mile into the plain is a boggy bit of ground 150 yards long, but it is not much of an obstacle. From here the road crosses the plain (which is very little cultivated) through grass jungle and a few patches of tree jungle into Tálawgyi, the last part being through small tree jungle. Distance 12 miles. The road is used by carts, and the traces of carts were seen right up to the bog at the foot of the hills; all this is good going. Tálawgyi is on the Irrawaddy. Water from the river good. Bamboo fodder. Camp north of village. There is a police post here and launches run up to here.

No. 21.

FROM BHAMO TO TÁLAWGYI *viâ* MYOTHIT, MANMAW, &c.—*continued.*

BRANCH I.

FROM KAIYA, *see* STAGE 8, TO NAMSÁNGYÁNG, STAGE 9, *viâ* LAISA AND KHWI-KHAW.

Authorities.		Number and Names of Stages, Rivers and Streams.	Distances.		Remarks.
Military.	Civil.		Inter-mediate.	Total.	
			M. F.	M. F.	
G.O.C. Mandalay [illegible] and O.C. Bhamo.	Commissioner, Northern Division, and Deputy Commissioner, Bhamo.	**1. Kadôn** ... Môlé chaung (Namli Ka) and numerous smaller streams.	**10 0**	10 0	*N.B.*—Kaiya being only 8½ miles from Namsángyáng by the direct route, this route which is a circular "*daur*" can be more appropriately called a branch than an alternative route. General direction south. The road descends steeply through tree jungle into some taungyas, crossing two small streams each 3 feet broad, the latter having steep approaches. It then further descends till at ¾ mile it crosses a rocky stream, 6 feet broad with 1 foot of water. From here there is a branch road south-west to Manmaw. It then ascends steeply for ¼ mile to where there is a single Kachin house belonging to Kaiya. It then crosses a small stream 3 feet broad and goes through kaing grass, over alternate ascents and descents along a hillside, and over three small streams with very little water. It is much overgrown here. At 2¼ miles it joins a good track from Ninglum through tree and bamboo jungle and gradually ascends to Lakra (or Legra) (1) 3¾ miles; from here there is a road west to Manmaw. The road then goes easterly and descends steeply into Lakra (2) 4 miles, crossing a small stream which rises from a bamboo. It then descends steeply by a broad track to Lakra (3). All this road from the junction with the Ninglum road is very good and has no obstacles. The last part is much worn by bullock traffic. Fodder, grass and bamboos plentiful. The road now descends at first gradually and then very steeply indeed first through tree jungle, then tree jungle and bamboos, and then grass and bamboos into a paddy plain on the right bank of the Môlé chaung nearly due north of Pumpien. At first it is 6 to 9 feet broad and very good and smooth, but lower it is narrower and very steep and tortuous with loose soil and stones. Just before the plain is reached there are branch roads to Manmaw and Pumpien. The road then turns east along some paddy and grass land and keeping up the right bank of the Môlé chaung after 200 yards, a small pebbly stream is crossed which is 5 yards broad, and has good water, and 200 yards further on a bad bit of bog, 20 yards broad and over the mules' tracks; this would require a lot of filling in with kaing grass. The road then ascends about 50 feet and goes through teak, grass, bamboo, and other tree jungle along the right bank of the Môlé. At 7 miles there is a crossing which leads to Pumpien. The river is here 40 yards broad, a little over knee-deep, pebbly bottom, and current of 1½ miles an hour. It has beautiful, clear water. Two small streams are crossed, and then a larger one 7 yards broad 1 foot deep, with pebbly bottom. The road now ascends very steeply to Kadôn, leaving the Molé chaung and passing through grass, bamboo, and tree jungle. It is in good order, but very steep indeed. Just before the village is a branch road south to Pumpien. Camp in the village (lately burnt); grass and bamboos; water from a small spring close by. **Animals have to be watered at a stream to the east and about 500 feet down.**

No. 21.

From BHAMO to TÁLAWGYI *viâ* MYOTHIT, MANMAW, &c.—*continued*.

BRANCH I—*continued*.

Authorities. Military.	Authorities. Civil.	Number and Names of Stages, Rivers and Streams.	Distances. Intermediate. M. F.	Distances. Total. M. F.	Remarks.
G.O.C. Mandalay District and O.C. Bhamo.	Commissioner, Northern Division, and Deputy Commissioner, Bhamo.	**2. Laisa** ... Laisa, Kyungni and several smaller streams.	7 0	17 0	From Kadôn the road descends steeply for 1 mile and crosses 2 streams each 12 feet broad and 1 foot deep with good water and one small stream. Road good and through mixed bamboo, kaing grass, and tree jungle. It now ascends steeply into some taungyas where there is a very good camping ground and then descends through grass and plantain trees to the Laisa Ka, passing three small streams. Laisa Ka, 25 yards broad 2 feet deep, with large stones and good water. It joins the Môlé chaung about 200 yards to the south. This is but a small obstacle. From here the road is very good and ascends through old overgrown taungyas for 300 feet and then goes fairly level with occasional small ascents and descents till at 4 miles reach the Kyungni Ka, 10 yards broad and rocky bottom. From here the road ascends very steeply and by zigzags to Laisa. The road is good : jungle, bamboos and grass with a few trees. Just at the top is a branch road to 'Nkum. Camp in the village. Water from small spring east of camp.
		3. Khwi-khaw (Kaban). Small streams.	9 0	26 0	General direction north-east. Leaving Laisa road descends out of the village for 200 yards. It then ascends through tree jungle into taungyas and thence along a spur to Wachôn 1½ miles. This part is zigzag and very steep indeed, having occasional stony bits and places where the soil is loose under foot. From here the road is very good and nearly level through tree jungle to Wachôn (Kaban) 2¾ miles. The road still continues through tree jungle and one small taungya for half a mile when it ascends steeply along a hillside by zigzags and with occasional cuttings into small tree jungle. At 4 miles there is a road to the left (north) to Nawkhum which is visible on the opposite spur. The road now passes up along a very narrow spur which is barely wide enough to allow two loaded mules to pass. The sides of this spur are nearly sheer and quite impassable. The path here is very narrow. At 6 miles the road ascends steeply over a grass hill by zigzags and is very stony; grass 6 to 8 feet high. At 7½ miles it begins to descend, and there is a road to Khwi-khaw (Kasi). At 8 miles cross a stream 9 feet broad with stony bottom and rough stony approaches. Good water. It now ascends steeply and passes just below Khwi-khaw (Kasi) village along a narrow path cut in tree jungle. It then descends steeply by zigzags over a stony and loose-soiled bit of ground to a stream 15 feet broad with stony bottom and good water, and thence ascends steeply to Khwi-khaw (Kaban), crossing two very small streams. There is no serious obstacle on this march at all, but it is over a steep rise of about 3,500 feet. About 4 hours' march, and for baggage animals about 6 hours. Camp in village. Very good site; water as above; bamboos and grass plentiful.

FROM BHAMO TO TÁLAWGYI *viâ* MYOTHIT, MANMAW, &c.—*continued.*

BRANCH I—*continued.*

Authorities. Military.	Authorities. Civil.	Number and Names of Stages, Rivers and Streams.	Distances. Intermediate. M.	F.	Distances. Total. M.	F.	Remarks.
G.O.C. Mandalay District and O.C. Bhamo.	Commissioner, Northern Division, and Deputy Commissioner, Bhamo.	**4. Camp in Namsáng taungyas.** Namsáng Ka.	**5**	**0**	31	0	General direction north-north-west: From Khwi-khaw (Kaban) the road ascends very steeply (after passing through a small belt of trees) through grass up 1,400 feet. There are some very bad bits of road here which are steep and sunken into cuttings which are very stony and full of roots and loose soil and pebbles. This road is not much used and would require a great deal of repair which, however, would not take long. At 1¾ miles a road goes to the left to Nawkhum (*see* Branch II below). The road then goes along the side of a hill through small tree jungle over stones along a narrow ledge to the highest point, which is 100 feet immediately below, and to the west of Kuntong hill. It then descends very steeply with one or two steep ascents for 2¾ miles down to the Namsáng Ka, passing small, dry, stony nullah about 3 feet broad. The whole of this is very steep, stony and bad, with loose soil and pebbles, and blocked by roots and fallen trees. The first part is through small tree jungle and the latter through grass. The descent is over 2,200 feet. Namsáng Ka, 12 feet broad; stony bed with good water and about 1 foot deep; crossed by a rough bridge of two poles. General direction north-north-west. The road then ascends into some taungyas which form a good camp; grass plentiful.*
		5. Chingnakong Möngsi. Two boggy streams.	**6**	**0**	37	0	The road now ascends very steeply, but in good condition through taungyas into Náhpaw, 1½ miles. A good road forward from here. Náhpaw camp in the village. Water from a stream 200 yards north and below the village. Height of village above sea level 5,000 feet. Fodder plentiful; water not plentiful. From here there is a good broad road descending gradually through tree jungle to Htingsa, 2 miles, passing through Wáhtángkong and 'Nkongkatawng at ½ mile and 1 mile respectively. After leaving Náhpaw the road is very good and well kept, and descends fairly steeply for 1,500 feet with occasional level bits for about 3¼ miles mostly through grass jungle with few trees, but not too steep for mounted infantry to ride down. At 3¼ miles there is a road to the west (left) to Ninglum, and the road now enters into taungyas and then ascends fairly steeply for 300 feet through small tree jungle, crossing two small boggy streams, which are a small obstacle but not much, till it reaches a fine broad track, and then a ¼ of a mile further on reaches the village of Chingnakong Möngsi on the top of the open of that name (Möngsi); grass and fodder plentiful; water from a spring; good but not very plentiful. Camp in village.

* This, though so short a distance, took the north-east column (91-92) 4 hours to march. The transport did not arrive till some 4 hours later, several mules having fallen over the steep khuds on the descent. It would require a great deal of repair and is the worst hill road I have ever seen.—G.H.H.C.

No. 21.

FROM BHAMO TO TÁLAWGYI *viâ* MYOTHIT, MANMAW, &c.—*continued.*

BRANCH I—*continued.*

Authorities. Military.	Authorities. Civil.	Number and Names of Stages, Rivers and Streams.	Distances. Intermediate.	Distances. Total.	Remarks.
G.O.C. Mandalay District and O.C. Bhamo.	Commissioner, Northern Division, and Deputy Commissioner, Bhamo.	**6. Namsáng-yáng.** Three small streams, one larger stream.	M. F. 7 4	M. F. 44 4	The road to Namsángyáng is fairly good, but very steep indeed; jungle similar to that between Náhpaw and Chingnakong. It is, however, in good order. First ascend a little and then descend steeply passing the village of Wurawkong which is on the west face of the hill at 3 miles. From here the road descends very steeply indeed through tree jungle into the plains, but it is in good order; soil, red clay. Cross two or three small streams and one larger one ¾ mile beyond Wuraw which is 1½ feet deep and 4 or 5 yards broad; stony bottom and no obstacle. Namsángyáng camp is a very good one indeed in paddy-fields, but is low-lying. Forage and water plentiful. There are two good camping grounds there. There are about 12 houses. Inhabitants, Chinese-Shans, very well to do. Fowls and paddy obtainable. Three miles east-north-east from here is another village of about six houses, also Chinese-Shan, where they make bamboo baskets.

BRANCH II.

FROM KHWI-KHAW (KABAN) (BRANCH I, STAGE 3) TO NAWKHUM.

BY LIEUT. RUSTON, DEVONSHIRE REGIMENT, JANUARY 1892.

Authorities. Military.	Authorities. Civil.	Number and Names of Stages, Rivers and Streams.	Distances. Intermediate.	Distances. Total.	Remarks.
G.O.C. Mandalay District and O.C. Bhamo.	Commissioner, Northern Division, and Deputy Commissioner, Bhamo.	**1. Nawkhum** ...	8 0	8 0	General direction north-west. The road ascends through tree jungle and is good and smooth. It then is a bit stony and at the top (1,000 feet above camp) it goes down zigzag and good and over an easy descent. Then a small level stretch of 50 yards through grass. It then descends by a gentle slope through tree jungle and is much blocked by fallen trees. It then becomes level and is covered with tree roots and loose soil. It then goes along the bed of a very stony nullah and after 100 yards crosses it. Then up and down, being narrow, soft and stony, down a steep slope; loose soil. It then, after 20 yards level going, descends again as before very steeply and is more stony. It then crosses a nullah (stony) with very little water. It then ascends very steeply over moist, stony, and loose soil gradually getting less steep, after which it is zigzag through a cutting through dead tree jungle and tree jungle. Then level through bamboo jungle (overgrown). The road now descends through kaing grass and tree jungle, steep khud on the left, then on to open and down a slight descent through young bamboo jungle. Road good after ¼ mile down a zigzag, stony descent for 100 yards, then level through tree and bamboo jungle. The road then descends through a rocky cutting. This road is very bad indeed, but not quite so bad as the latter part of Branch I above. From 6 miles Nawkhum was visible across a deep valley and quite 2½ miles away, the road being very circuitous to it, and in its present condition more than can be managed in one day.

FROM BHAMO TO TÁLAWGYI *viâ* MYOTHIT, MANMAW, &c.—*continued.*

BRANCH III.

FROM NÁHPAW (BRANCH I, STAGE 5) TO NAWKHUM-PUMKATAWNG.

BY CAPT. COUCHMAN, JANUARY 1892.

Authorities. Military.	Authorities. Civil.	Number and Names of Stages, Rivers and Streams.	Distances. Intermediate. M. F.	Distances. Total. M. F.	Remarks.
G.O.C. Mandalay District and O.C. Bhamo.	Commissioner, Northern Division, and Deputy Commissioner, Bhamo.	**1. Nawkhum-Pumkatawng.** Namsáng and three smaller streams.	...	...	General direction south-south-west. Road descends towards Namsáng taungya camp (*see* Branch I, Stage 5 above). After ½ mile the road turns westerly and descends over taungyas to the Namsáng Ka. The last descent is very steep and quite impassable for transport. The stream is 30 feet broad, full of large boulders, and with water 1½ feet deep. This also is impassable for transport. It then ascends steeply for 500 feet through old taungyas covered with grass 6 to 8 feet high. It is then fairly level, but overgrown for ¾ mile, when it descends very steeply along the side of a soft soiled hill to two streams, each about 5 feet broad; stony; and good water. The first is impassable for transport, as it has a steep descent and very bad rocky bed with big boulders. It then crosses some poppy cultivation ascending for 100 feet, descending again to a stream 5 feet broad and stony bed. From here the road ascends very steeply indeed and quite straight up about 400 feet into Marao village (5 miles) through grass and small tree jungle. This bit is impassable. The road from Khwi-khaw joins on here for transport. From here to Nawkhum-Pumkatawng is 1 mile over good road with easy ascents and descents. Time for infantry 3 hours. This is a very bad road, and would require much repair and alteration. The soil is soft and easily workable.

BRANCH IV.

FROM CHINGNUKONG MÖNGSI (BRANCH I, STAGE 5) there are three short branch routes TO NAMSÁNGYÁNG, NINGLUM AND KANTAOYÁNG, *viâ* NINGPWOT AND NINGRONG, as follows:—

BY LIEUT. CAMPBELL, 18TH MADRAS INFANTRY, JANUARY 1892.

(1) TO NAMSÁNGYÁNG.

Authorities. Military.	Authorities. Civil.	Number and Names of Stages, Rivers and Streams.	Distances. Intermediate. M. F.	Distances. Total. M. F.	Remarks.
G.O.C. Mandalay District and O.C. Bhamo.	Commissioner, Northern Division, and Deputy Commissioner, Bhamo.	**1. Namsángyáng.** Nambáng Ka and two other small streams.	7 0	7 0	The road from Chingnukong Möngsi leads down a very steep descent for 3 miles to Nambáng Ka, 1½ feet deep and 15 feet broad; stony bottom; no obstacle for mule transport. The track is fairly good, 6 feet in breadth, but stony and full of boulders in parts; soil is dark-coloured; hard clay with sand. Half a mile before reaching the Nambáng Ka is the village of Htingsa, about eight houses; a small brook east of this village; no paddy; six head of cattle (buffalo). From the Nambáng Ka the track ascends very abruptly for ⅛ mile to the village of Nambáng; 25 houses; about 300 inhabitants (3½ miles); soil red, clay, hard, dry and sandy; a few cuttings along track jungle thick. From Nambáng the track descends very steeply to within a mile of Namsángyáng; soil, yellowish clay; stony in parts. The last mile before Namsángyáng is through kaing grass. One small stream ⅛ mile from Namsángyáng; 6 feet broad 1 foot deep; stony and sandy bottom. Two large clearings; stretches of paddy land south of the village. Namsángyáng

No. 21.

FROM BHAMO TO TÁLAWGYI *viâ* MYOTHIT, MANMAW, &c.—*continued.*

BRANCH IV—*continued.*

Authorities. Military.	Authorities. Civil.	Number and Names of Stages, Rivers and Streams.	Distances. Intermediate. M. F.	Distances. Total. M. F.	Remarks.
G.O.C. Mandalay District, &c.	Commissioner, Northern Divn., &c.	**1. Namsángyáng** —*cont.*			enclosed with stockade; 20 houses. Tiger, panther, sambhur and pig in surrounding jungle north-east and west. To the south, flat country with tall kaing grass and thick scrub jungle.
		(2) To NINGLUM.			
G.O.C. Mandalay District and O.C. Bhamo.	Commr., Northern Division, and Deputy Commr., Bhamo.	**Ninglum** ...	1 2	1 2	General direction south-south-west. The road passes back along Branch Route No. I, Stage 5, for about 500 yards when it ascends to the village of Lashi at ½ a mile. From here it descends passing a Kachin grave on the right and a branch road to Náhpaw on the left into Ninglum at 1¼ miles. Road good through tree jungle and along a ridge. There is a road southward from Ninglum towards Nawkhum.
		(3) To KANTAOYÁNG.			
G.O.C. Mandalay District and O.C. Bhamo.	Commissioner, Northern Division, and Deputy Commissioner, Bhamo.	**1. Ningrong-Uma** Pasi Ka.	8 0	8 0	The road goes north for ¾ mile along the top of a ridge, and is very good indeed, passing an old taungya which would make a good camp, and then into tree jungle. At ¾ mile there is a road to the right to Sama. It now turns north-west and at 1¼ miles descends into Ukoi village, eight houses. It still further descends, but there is no bad bit in all of it, though it is a little stony at times. It now ascends a little steeply and passes along a hillside and then gradually ascends into Ningpwot at 3 miles. Just before this there are two branch roads to the west to Namsángyáng. All this road is very good. From Ningpwot there is a well-cut road to Hpáneng and an overgrown grassy one to Warra, which is visible from about ½ mile beyond the village and appears to be a mile distant, first descending steeply, then rising into Warra village. There is a good view of the country towards Mali. Just outside Ningpwot there is a road to the left to Hpáneng. The road leaves this and ascends steeply for about 60 yards into some tree jungle, and is level for about 300 yards when it begins to descend first through grass jungle where it is rather overgrown, then through taungyas and finally through tree jungle again. There are one or two fairly steep descents, but not too great for transport. Road good throughout to Ningrong Ningnum (new) through which it passes (5 miles). Just before reaching the village there is a road east to Kumsai. From here the road is very good, gradually descending the whole way through tree jungle with occasional small ascents along a spur. At 7 miles a road goes east to Wuláng village which is only a ¼ mile off. Two streams, one crossed just after leaving Ningrong Ningnum, namely, a small one 3 feet broad and good water, and the Pasi Ka 9 feet broad; stony bottom and good water, the latter having rather steep approaches but no obstacle. Camp in Ningrong-Uma village, rather confined. Water scarce from a small spring 200 feet below on east side; fodder plentiful; distance 8 miles; easy march. No difficulties except in first mile or so after leaving Ningpwot and even there the descents are nothing very bad.

FROM BHAMO TO TÁLAWGYI *viâ* MYOTHIT, MANMAW, &c.—*continued.*

BRANCH IV—*continued.*

Authorities. Military.	Authorities. Civil.	Number and Names of Stages, Rivers and Streams.	Distances. Intermediate. M. F.	Distances. Total. M. F.	Remarks.
G.O.C. Mandalay District and O.C. Bhamo.	Commissioner, Northern Division, and Deputy Commissioner, Bhamo.	**2. Kantaoyáng** ... Lemu, Wutsa, Pasi, Hôna, and one other stream.	**6 0**	14 0	General direction north-west. The road is very good for the first mile gradually descending and passing through tree jungle and then through old overgrown taungyas. It then descends very steeply indeed for ¾ mile and is rough and stony and rather difficult for transport. At 1¼ miles is a road to the right (north) to Kukam. The path is narrow over this last steep bit. It then continues by small descents and occasional ascents through grass, bamboo, and small tree jungle to the Lemu Ka (3¼ miles and 1,200 feet below Ningrong); 8 to 10 yards broad, 6 inches deep; stony bottom and no obstacle. It continues through bamboo jungle, crossing and recrossing the Wutsa Ka in the next ½ mile. Jungle bamboos. Wutsa Ka 10 to 12 yards broad 6 inches deep; stony bottom. From here it descends gradually by occasional ascents and descents to Kantaoyáng plain through grass, bamboo, and small tree jungle, crossing the Pasi Ka; 4 yards broad and 1 foot deep, and the Hôna Ka, 9 feet broad and 2 feet deep, muddy bottom, and also a small stream in the plain. Road good; camping ground enough for a brigade. Fodder and water good and plentiful. This is an easy march. Camp at 6 miles.

There is another route FROM NINGPWOT TO KANTAOYÁNG, passing through HPÁNENG and SHILLAP, as follows:—

BY LIEUT. RUSTON, DEVONSHIRE REGIMENT, FEBRUARY 1892.

Military	Civil	Stage	Intermediate M. F.	Total M. F.	Remarks
G.O.C. Mandalay District and O.C. Bhamo.	Commissioner, Northern Division, and Deputy Commissioner, Bhamo.	**Kantaoyáng** ... Three streams.	**8 0**	8 0	Road very good and level for ½ mile; it then descends and is rather stony. It then rises up to Hpáneng, through which it passes at 2 miles. It then descends continuously down to a narrow paddy plain. It then goes level along it for ½ mile. It then crosses two boggy streams, and rises over a taungya through tree jungle with small ascents and descents to another stream, and then rises steeply to Saláp (*see* Stage 10 above) close to Kantaoyáng. This is a very good road throughout and has no obstacles at all. Time of march from Ningpwot to Kantaoyáng 6 hours for transport.

BRANCH V.

FROM KANTAOYÁNG (STAGE 10) TO KÁZU.

BY LIEUT. CAMPBELL, 15TH MADRAS INFANTRY, FEBRUARY 1892.

Military	Civil	Stage	Intermediate M. F.	Total M. F.	Remarks
G.O.C. Mandalay District and O.C. Bhamo.	Commissioner, Northern Division, and Deputy Commissioner, Bhamo.	**1. Beinbin** ... Saláp Ka, two small streams, and the Mali Ka.	**9 4**	9 4	General direction north cross the Saláp Ka and then over short and steep ascents and descents through thick bamboo and tree jungle over red clay soil to Kuma (2½ miles). From here the jungle is very thick, and two small stony streams are crossed. The path is very narrow and like the above, only not so steep. Pass village of Ninglaw (stockaded) at 4½ miles, which is surrounded by bamboo jungle. From here the road passes high up above the left bank of the Mali Ka, through bamboo

No. 21.

FROM BHAMO TO TÁLAWGYI *viâ* MYOTHIT, MANMAW, &c.—*continued.*

BRANCH V—*continued.*

Authorities. Military.	Authorities. Civil.	Number and Names of Stages, Rivers and Streams.	Distances. Intermediate.		Distances. Total.		Remarks.
G.O.C. Mandalay District and O.C. Bhamo.	Commr., Northern Divn., and Deputy Commr., Bhamo.	**1. Beinbin**—*cont.*					and tree jungle, and down a gradual descent to the village of Beinbin, which is reached at 9¼ miles after crossing the Mali Ka; 80 yards broad; ford 2 to 3 feet deep; sandy bottom; good crossing and left bank kaing grass. The latter part of the road is broader and good going. Beinbin is a Chinese-Shan village in paddy-fields and has a stockade round it.
			M.	F.	M.	F.	
		2. Kázu	**8**	**0**	17	4	*See* Route No. 100.

No. 22.

From BHAMO to TÔNHÔN viâ KYUSAING (KYUSAI) and KAPRAW.

BY E. P. CLONEY, ESQ., EXTRA ASSISTANT COMMISSIONER, BHAMO, MAY 1890.

Military	Civil	Stages	M.	F.	M.	F.	Remarks
G.O.C. Mandalay District and O.C. Bhamo.	Commissioner, Northern Division, and Deputy Commissioner, Bhamo.	**1. Moyu**	**9**	**4**	9	4	*See* Route No. 15, Bhamo to Ngwansai *viâ* Tônhôn, Stages 1 and 2, which is the direct route to Tônhôn and thence to Namkham or Mômeik.
		2. Mankin ...	**9**	**4**	19	0	
		3. Laika sakhán... Naunghu chaung (tributary of Sinkán chaung), Laika chaung.	**12**	**0**	31	0	Leaving Mankin road runs in a generally easterly direction, parallel to the Naunghu chaung, and through taungya sites. At about 1 mile pass Thayetgôn, five houses, to the left of the road; thence follows the right bank of the stream, sometimes actually on it, never far from it. Road very boggy, even after only one or two showers, and quite impassable for pack animals in the rainy season. At about 3½ miles Manya (Shan-Burmese), nine or 10 houses, on right bank of stream. From here there is a direct road to Sáwadi, said to be longer than that *viâ* Mankin, but it cannot possibly be so. Road runs still east and very slightly north-east through tree jungle; shady, but very muddy in places. About 9½ miles path branches to the right, leading to Maingkaung, two Kachin houses, about 1¼ miles distant. At 12 miles reach Laika sakhán; the last couple of miles through tree jungle, bamboo, and kaing here and there. This is a regular camping ground for caravans on the right bank of the Laika chaung and at foot of hills. From here there is direct path to Bhamo *viâ* Mathi.
		4. Kyusaing (Palaung, Kyusai; elevation 2,350 feet). Laika and Kawán chaungs.	**10**	**0**	41	0	Cross Laika chaung; descent to stream over rough rocky ground. At about 1¼ miles cross small stream (Kawán chaung), and at 1½ miles Kashut (Kachin); two houses. From here the road gets on to higher ground, and on the east and west running a little south and south-east are the Hôma and Táli hills. The Naunghu chaung is again met with

FROM BHAMO TO TÔNHÔN *viâ* KYUSAING (KYUSAI) AND KAPRAW—*continued.*

Authorities. Military.	Authorities. Civil.	Number and Names of Stages, Rivers and Streams.	Distances. Intermediate.	Distances. Total.	Remarks.
G.O.C. Mandalay District and O.C. Bhamo.	Commissioner, Northern Division, and Deputy Commissioner, Bhamo.	**4. Kyusaing (Palaung, Kyusai; elevation 2,350 feet)**—*cont.*			and the path follows its banks and crosses it at about 6 miles; crossing bad and slippery after any rain. Road through fairly level ground in the valley, not yet on hills. At about 8½ miles there is a Kachin village abont ¼ mile to the right of the road, called Mankyagatawng, whence there is a road (the only one) to Táli and Pônkaw. At about 9¾ miles commence the ascent of some low hills; path rather steep. At 10 miles Palaung village of Kyusaing (or Kyusai), 16 houses; small pôngyi kyaung and zayát. Roads in and about village nicely made and, judging from the jack and tamarind trees growing around it, it must have been established here for 12 or 15 years. Good camping ground to the south of the village for a force of 200 rifles with transport animals and followers. Plenty of grass and water. On the ranges running north and south, situated to the west of Kyusaing, are the Kachin villages of Táli, Pônkaw, and Lathein. On the long range of hills north and south of Kyusaing (Palaung) are the villages of Hôpôn, Huma, Kyusaing (Kachin), and Kapraw. One spur running south-west leads to Tônhôn, &c., the other running south-east or east leads into Namkham and Maingmau (Möngmao). In the valley are Kyusaing (Palaung) and Singteingatawng and south of this on a high spur Lungpwán.
		5. Kapraw (elevation 3,625 feet). Naunghu chaung.	M. F. **5 2**	M. F. 46 2	From Kyusaing (Palaung) to Kyusaing (Kachin) there are two routes,—the caravan route which runs round the low hill on which the former village is situated and passes through Singteingatawng, and the direct route which keeps more to the north. The former is a fairly good path, descending southwards and winding about. At about ¾ mile cross the Naunghu by foot-bridge, but ponies can get round, then ascend, and meet the other road near Singteingatawng, 1¾ miles, Kachin village of 10 houses (elevation 2,550 feet). From here the road runs east up-hill nearly all the way; very fair path, but slippery after rains. At 4¼ miles reach Kyusaing (Kachin), the direct route from Kyusaing (Palaung) joining in just below the village is reached. Village consists of six houses (two deserted); jungle all round; elevation 3,470 feet. The direct route reduces the distance to 2½ miles, but is not good for pack animals. It at first descends slightly, then ascends nearly all the rest of the way, joining the longer route as described above. Pômsáng (Kara) and Magyigôn on the range north-east can be seen from the path below Kyusaing (Kachin). From Kyusaing (Kachin) path runs south to Kapraw; 5¼ miles, Kachin village of 10 houses. The greater part of stages 3 and 4 are very bad marching in wet weather; streams up to and over the pack animals' saddles and the path terribly muddy. Just beyond Kapraw the routes to Tônhôn and Möngmao or Namkham separate, the former passing through Pánglwi, Pinkyeingyi, Pinkyeingalé, Pángtán, Lwékam, and Papángyi, the latter through Hinpôk (or Kinpôk), Namsa, Lwépang, Kakán, Manswé, Manhwi, Manhôm, and Manwaing.
		6. Pinkyein chaung. Pinkyein chaung.	**5 0**	51 2	**Passing Panglwi 30 houses at 4 miles. The Pinkyein chaung has water in March for a large number of transport animals.**

No. 22.

FROM BHAMO TO TÔNHÔN *viâ* KYUSAING (KYUSAI) AND KAPRAW—*continued.*

Authorities.		Number and Names of Stages, Rivers and Streams.	Distances.				Remarks.
Military.	Civil.		Inter-mediate.		Total.		
			M.	F.	M.	F.	
G.O.C. Mandalay Dist. and O.C. Bhamo.	Commr., Northern Division, and Deputy Commr., Bhamo.	**7. Katán chaung.** Katán chaung.	8	4	59	6	Pass Pinkyeingalé at ½ a mile and touch Pinkyein chaung again at ½ mile. Makawpum 20 houses at 2 miles and Páugtán 30 houses at 8 miles. Plenty of water in Katán chaung.
		8. Nanpu chaung. Sikat and Nanpu chaungs.	10	0	69	6	At ¼ mile Lwékán 10 houses (Lapai Kachin), Mankyát (Lakun) at 2 miles. At 3 miles Sikat stream, very little water after March until rainy season. At 3½ miles Papán and at 10 miles Nanpu chaung.
		9. Tônhôn ...	10	4	80	2	*See* Stage 6 of Route No. 15.

No. 23.

From BHAMO to WÉGYI viâ SINKIN, &c.

BY LIEUT. GODFREY MORRIS, INTELLIGENCE OFFICER, EASTERN COLUMN, JANUARY 1892.

Military	Civil	Stages	M.	F.	M.	F.	Remarks
G.O.C. Mandalay District and O.C. Bhamo.	Commissioner, Northern Division, and Deputy Commissioner, Bhamo.	**1. Sinkin** ... ... Tapin river flows in the Irrawaddy ¾ of a mile below Shwékina, current swift, depth about 6 feet, breadth 350 feet, navigable for large country boats to Myothit.	5	0	5	0	General direction north-west. By boat, or mule track over low ground, along the left bank of the Irrawaddy, crossing the Tapin river by the Shwékyina gold pagoda in country boats at 3½ miles. Very fair mule track. Shwékyina, a Shan village of 60 houses, situated on the left bank of the Tapin river a ¼ of a mile down towards the Irrawaddy. On a few small hills are the Shwékyina pagodas, consisting of one large central gilded pagoda and over 100 smaller stone ones. This gold pagoda is a good landmark and can be seen from most parts of the hills to the north, marking the junction of the Tapin and Irrawaddy. Road leads on through swampy ground to Sinkin, 5 miles. The village is divided into Upper and Lower Sinkin, Upper Sinkin consists of 28 houses; a Shan village; 140 inhabitants. Lower Sinkin, 105 houses; 500 inhabitants; very clean and well kept. There is a good water-supply and good shelter for considerable force. *Note.*—As far as Thapánbin (Stage 2,) this is the same road as is described in Route No. 18.
		2. Thapánbin ... Môlé chaung flows south-west joining the Irrawaddy ½ mile below Ngapiedaw ford.	5	4	10	4	By boat or mule track, leaving Sinkin in a north-west direction, leads over the spurs of small hills for 3 miles; would become very difficult after any rain. The tract between the road and the Irrawaddy is very swampy and cultivated in places. There are the remnants of a few bamboo bridges, but they are practically useless. At 3 miles on the left bank of the Môlé chaung, 80 yards wide, chest deep, no bridge. Country boats can go 2 miles beyond Thainthaw. Current sluggish at crossing. A Shan stockaded village of 50 houses and 200 inhabitants. Plenty of water and 1 mile square of open ground. At 5½ miles Thapánbin stockaded; 52 houses; 300 inhabitants; eggs and vegetables, good water-supply, camping plenty of ground for 100 men at most.

FROM BHAMO TO WÉGYI *viâ* SINKIN, &c.—*continued.*

Authorities. Military.	Authorities. Civil.	Number and Names of Stages, Rivers and Streams.	Distances. Intermediate. M.	F.	Total. M.	F.	Remarks.
G.O.C. Mandalay District and O.C. Bhamo.	Commissioner, Northern Division, and Deputy Commissioner, Bhamo.	**3. Kaulein** ... A small stream at foot of Kaulein hill almost dry; runs into Irrawaddy ½ mile below Thapánbin.	**8**	**6**	19	2	The track skirts the bank of the Irrawaddy for 2 miles, then turns north-east up the valley at a gentle slope for 3½ miles. Here the foot of Kaulein hill is reached crossing the small stream mentioned. The track then becomes steep and difficult (ankle 30°) for 1½ miles, and from there fairly good to Kaulein, a small scattered Kachin village on the east slope of the hill 2,340 feet high. Water scarce; no good camping ground and very dirty.
		4. Shé-u	**6**	**4**	25	6	Mule track in north-east direction, fairly good; gradual ascent. Teinpaung (2 miles) on east slope just below the crest of the hill; a Kachin village of 30 houses, 65 inhabitants; water good, but a long way off. Cleaner than the ordinary Kachin village. Bhamo plainly visible. Would be a good signalling post. A small jungle path passable only by coolies, leads down to Irrawaddy north of Thapánbin. The air is very fine. Track leaves Teinpaung in north direction; steep and narrow at 3 miles. Lowpôn. A few Kachin houses scattered on the side of the hill; 45 inhabitants; no good camping ground; houses badly built and water very scarce. It is better to halt at the last village. Track north-west direction; gradual descent for 2 miles good. The last 1½ miles to Shé-u are steep and difficult. Shé-u (6½ miles) Kachin village, six houses; bad halting place; water scarce; no open ground on west slope of the hill. There is an alternative route for coolies *viâ* Kaunán.
		5. Lipôn ... ... Nampaung and two smaller streams.	**8**	**0**	33	6	Track leaves Shé-u in a northerly direction for the first 2 miles; is rather steep for mules. It then descends and crosses two small streams, both tributaries of the Nampaung chaung. At about 6 miles from Shé-u, at the foot of the hill upon which Lipôn is situated, the Nampaung chaung is crossed; 14 feet broad 1 foot deep, no current to speak of at this time of year; road here turns north and ascends at a general slope of 35° for 2 miles. Lipôn at 8 miles is a Kachin village of 22 houses and 60 inhabitants, situated on the crest of the hill and a good signalling station for Mannaung on the Tapin, and Seinpaung. This village would make the best halting place of any visited, though water is rather difficult to get.

FROM BHAMO TO WÉGYI *viâ* SINKIN, &c.—*continued.*

Authorities. Military.	Authorities. Civil.	Number and Names of Stages, Rivers and Streams.	Distances. Intermediate. M. F.	Distances. Total. M. F.	Remarks.
G.O.C. Mandalay District and O.C. Bhamo.	Commissioner, Northern Division, and Deputy Commissioner, Bhamo.	**6. Pamna** ... Káchaing chaung.	9 4	43 2	Road runs from Lipôn in northerly direction; very difficult and narrow; much overgrown with bamboo and grass. Teinkaw (1) at 2 miles a Kachin village, five houses, 24 inhabitants, bad halting place built on a slope; water scarce, open ground none. For the next 3 miles the road continues in the same direction, then turns west. For the next 3 miles the road continues in same direction, then turns west and is very steep, crossing the Káchaing stream, 10 yards broad 1 foot deep, flows north and ultimately into Moló chaung, then ascends for 2 miles to Kánrong (8 miles), small Kachin village of 10 houses, inhabited by Maku tribe, 63 inhabitants, near the top of the hill, would serve as a local signalling post. Water scarce. General direction from here south-west. Path fair over the crest of the hill at 9½ miles. Pamna, Kachin village of the Maku tribe, 19 houses, 100 inhabitants, and fair camping ground with good water from a spring, 100 feet down the hill. A track just passable by mules runs west to Irrawaddy river about 5½ miles. The headman of this village is also headman of five subordinate neighbouring ones, namely, Kánrong, Kumpánpôn, Shwépu,-Wakaai, and Htáyán.
		7. Lwé ... ... Namhé chaung.	8 0	51 2	General direction north, fairly level to Warásaing (3 miles) jungle not quite so thick as during last stage. Warásaing, Kachin village, with a bamboo stockade, five houses, 20 inhabitants. Water very scarce; subordinate to Lwésaing. Path runs north-west till it reaches the Namhé chaung, 10 feet broad 6 inches deep, flows south into Irrawaddy, then turns south-west and ascends the hill; ascent and descent very steep and jungle very thick. There is an alternative route running west, which is 2 miles shorter, but steeper and impassable by laden mules in its present state. Munkatawng at 7 miles, small Kachin village, seven houses, 20 inhabitants, subordinate to Lwésaing. Water scarce, 1 mile distant. Path still runs north-west, fairly good. Lwésaing at 8 miles, Kachin village, 10 houses, 40 inhabitants; water good, but scarce, ½ mile down the valley. The village is situated in a crescent-shaped valley on a small spur and is scattered. Looking in south-westerly direction towards the Irrawaddy there is a high point from which the Lenoipum hill is visible; this point 1 mile south-west of this village would be a good signalling post.
		8. Kengkong ... Nampin chaung.	5 0	56 2	Path leaves Lwésaing in a westerly direction running along the crest of a spur for 2 miles; this part is good. It then turns north, descending the valley of the Nampin chaung, 20 feet broad 1 foot deep at this season and becomes very steep. Kengkong at 5 miles, a Kachin village, 42 inhabitants,

FROM BHAMO TO WÉGYI *viâ* SINKIN, &c.—*continued.*

Authorities. Military.	Authorities. Civil.	Number and Names of Stages, Rivers and Streams.	Distances. Intermediate. M.	Distances. Intermediate. F.	Distances. Total. M.	Distances. Total. F.	Remarks.
G.O.C. Mandalay District and O.C. Bhamo.	Commissioner, Northern Division, and Deputy Commissioner, Bhamo.	**8. Kengkong**—*cont.*					14 houses. Water very scarce. The headman also rules Namsein, a small village of four houses and 16 inhabitants, south-west about 2 miles. The track to Namsein is very bad, it leads on to Nanhé on the Irrawaddy.
		9. Teinkaw (2) ... Punlaung chaung.	**9**	**4**	65	6	The track leaves Kenkong in a northerly direction leading along a spur for 6 miles; this part is good going. It then turns east, crosses the Punlaung chaung, 5 yards broad 8 feet deep, and is very steep to the top of the hill for 2 miles; it then turns south-east skirting the hill to Teinkaw (2), 9½ miles, a Kachin village of eight houses, situated on the east slope of the range, is a good open place, but water is far away.
		10. Manpin ... Tsein Tsa chaung, 20 feet broad 2 feet deep, runs into Nansán chaung.	**10**	**0**	75	6	General direction north-east, road fairly level, but rocky and damp, through thick bamboo jungle. Teintin at 4½ miles, a small Shan village, four houses, well situated, but some way from water. From here direction east, fairly level road, a gentle slope to the plain. At 10 miles Manpin, a Shan village, 22 houses, 60 inhabitants, good camping ground with plenty of water. Care should be taken in camping in these Kachin villages, as small-pox is often prevalent.
		11. Punkán ... Tsein Tsa chaung.	**5**	**4**	81	2	From Manpin general direction west until 1 mile beyond Punkán; this portion is fairly level. It then turns south-west along the stream called Pánlaung chaung. This portion is very bad, and would be utterly impassable after the slightest rain. Punkán at 5½ miles is a small Kachin village, three or four houses, scattered on a small hill and four more at the base. There is plenty of water, but no good camping ground.
		12. Manségalé ... Pánlaung chaung, 30 feet broad 2 feet deep, flows into Irrawaddy.	**6**	**0**	87	2	Manségalé, Kachin village, three houses, one of which is being built for the headman on the summit of the hill, lower down four scattered huts. Water is a long way off about ½ mile. This village is a bad halting place.
		13. Wégyi ... Sumpsai chaung, 20 feet broad 1 foot deep, flows into Irrawaddy.	**6**	**4**	93	6	Road leaves Manségalé in south-west direction and runs along a cliff for 2 miles, then crossing a small range gently descends to Wégyi.

No. 24.

From KÁMAING to LONTÔN (Indawgyi Lake).

BY LIEUT. BURTON, 4TH SIKHS (ATTACHED MOGAUNG LEVY), MAY 1890.

Authorities. Military.	Authorities. Civil.	Number and Names of Stages, Rivers and Streams.	Distances. Intermediate. M.	F.	Total. M.	F.	Remarks.
G.O.C. Mandalay District and O.C. Bhamo.	Commissioner, Northern Division, and Deputy Commissioner, Bhamo.	**1. Camp on Indaw chaung.** Indaw chaung, breadth 30 yards, depth 5 feet, current 2 miles.	12	0	12	0	The shorter route from Môgaung to Lôntôn is up the valley of the Namyin-chaung (Mohnyin river), *vide* Route No. 65. Marched 4 A. M., halted 11 A.M. Good path south-west to Sákaw, 7 miles on left bank of Indaw chaung, but would be impassable in rains, being entirely through plain of kaing grass. River has to be crossed 6¼ miles from Kámaing and is never fordable. Troops should send boats from Kámaing to cross river. From Sákaw path runs south-west for 2 miles, then south through thick jungle over low hills till halting place is reached on bank of Indaw chaung 12 miles from Kámaing. From Sákaw onwards the path keeps on left bank of Indaw chaung. Sákaw is a Marip Kachin village. Sawbwa Letchinawng, an influential chief, resides here.
G.O.C. Mandalay District and O.C. Bhamo.	Commissioner, Northern Division, and Deputy Commissioner, Bhamo.	**2. Camp ... ...** Several small water-courses and streams *en route*, all left bank tributaries of Indaw chaung.	10	0	22	0	5 A.M. to 11-45 A.M. Road very bad. Runs along eastern lower slopes of a range of hills over spurs which are very trying for baggage animals. Dense jungle all the way. Passed Paulu (Kachins) at 3rd mile; water from several small streams *en route*; camping ground on large plain 2 miles from Indaw chaung on bank of small streams; water good. Shan village of Hôka ¼ mile off. Inhabited by Shans, Burmans, and a few Kachins.
G.O.C. Mandalay District and O.C. Bhamo.	Commissioner, Northern Division, and Deputy Commissioner, Bhamo.	**3. Camp ... ...** Several small streams, left bank tributaries of Indaw chaung.	8	0	30	0	5 A.M. to 11-30 A.M. Road good for 2 miles, then very bad crossing Manwé hill, about 1,200 feet high. Transport ponies only got up with difficulty. Halted on edge of plain at foot of hill by small stream. Indaw chaung about 3 miles off.
G.O.C. Mandalay District and O.C. Bhamo.	Commissioner, Northern Division, and Deputy Commissioner, Bhamo.	**4. Camp on Nantein chaung.**	10	0	40	0	3-30 A. M. to 8-45 A. M. Road fairly good, first 5 miles over low ground, one swamp which would be bad in rains. Next 4 miles over low hills and last mile through valley cultivated by villagers of Makawlwé (?). Halted by Nantein chaung, which runs into Indaw chaung near Lawsun.
G.O.C. Mandalay District and O.C. Bhamo.	Commissioner, Northern Division, and Deputy Commissioner, Bhamo.	**5. Camp by village of Kônmamôn (20 houses).** One small stream and Nansanti chaung.	12	0	52	0	3-30 A. M. to 10 A.M. Road good in dry weather. Path runs for 5 miles south-east through low-lying plain, which would become a swamp in rains, then crosses a small spur of Shwédaungyi hill south-west and skirts north-west corner of Indawgyi lake for 3 miles. Path for last 2 miles good through light jungle. Halting place at Kônmamôn, 20 houses.

FROM KÁMAING TO LÔNTÔN (INDAWGYI LAKE)—*continued.*

Authorities.		Number and Names of Stages, Rivers and Streams.	Distances.				Remarks.
Military.	Civil.		Intermediate.		Total.		
			M.	F.	M.	F.	
G.O.C. Mandalay District and O.C. Bhamo.	Commissioner, Northern Divn., and Deputy Commissioner, Bhamo.	**6. Lôntôn** ... Nawángwé chaung and one other stream.	**11**	**0**	63	0	4 A. M. to 10 A. M. Road good. First 2 miles on shore of lake. Thence bearing away westward across large plains it passes the villages of Nankát and Nanpadéchaungbya, the two first deserted owing to raids of Kachins (Sana Sawbwa) two months previously. Road after passing Nanpadéchaungbya returns through plains to Lôntôn (24 houses) on bank of Indawgyi lake, distance 11 miles.

There is another route FROM SÁKAW (*see* Stage 1 above) TO LÔNTÔN. It seems in every respect inferior to that above described and would probably never be used in preference except for the purpose of visiting the villages lying along or near it. The stages are :—

Military.	Civil.	Stages.	Inter. M.	Inter. F.	Total M.	Total F.	Remarks.
G.O.C. Mandalay District and O.C. Bhamo.	Commr., Northern Divn., and Deputy Commr., Bhamo.	**1. Kákaw.**	**11**	**0**	11	0	Kákaw, small Latawng Kachin village.
		2. Po Sánkong ...	**13**	**0**	24	0	
		3. Lawsun ...	**9**	**0**	33	0	Lawsun (Shan), 32 houses.
		4. Nansôngta chaung.	**8**	**0**	41	0	
		5. Lôntôn ...	**11**	**0**	52	0	Military post, &c.

In the 3rd stage the following Latawng Kachin villages are passed :—Mangwé (10 houses); Sakito (15); Kaiyông Kyôngyi (5); Lataw (7); Phonu (12); Lataung(?) (8); and in the 4th stage, Mapin (25) and Panla (35), both Shan.

Troops moving FROM KÁMAING TO LÔNTÔN or *vice versâ* by boat, can proceed as follows :—

BY LIEUT. W. V. MOUL, CHESHIRE REGIMENT, FEBRUARY 1888.

Military.	Civil.	Stages.	Inter. M.	Inter. F.	Total M.	Total F.	Remarks.
G.O.C. Mandalay District and O.C. Bhamo.	Commissioner, Northern Division, and Deputy Commissioner, Bhamo.	**1. Camp near Sákaw.**	**10**	**0**	10	0	By boat. The boats used were the big covered-in boats called *talé*, (smaller size *laung*; dug-out, *pengaw*) by the natives; they have a crew of five, of whom four pole and one steers. These boats should not be laden with more than 7,000 lbs. or 25 men and 2,000 lbs; not more than 12 men could sleep on board. Ropes should be provided for each boat to haul them over the rapids above Sákaw and care should be taken to ascertain that each boat is supplied with spare poles to avoid delay. There are no good camping grounds along the river side and camp usually has to be pitched in dense kaing grass. In the wet weather (from June onwards) hardly a dry spot can be found affording space sufficient even for 30 men to cook, except at the rapids above Sákaw and on the Shwédaung hill at the entrance to the lake. The mouth of the Nanya

FROM KÁMAING TO LÔNTÔN (INDAWGYI LAKE)—*continued.*

Authorities.		Number and Names of Stages, Rivers and Streams.	Distances.				Remarks.
Military.	Civil.		Intermediate.		Total.		
			M.	F.	M.	F.	
G.O.C. Mandalay District and O.C. Bhamo.	Commissioner, Northern Division, and Deputy Commissioner, Bhamo.	**1. Camp near Sákaw**—*cont.*					chaung, down which most of the jade comes, is passed on the left bank. The river winds through a level plain covered with kaing grass. Sákaw is a Kachin village about a mile from the river on the west. Small supplies obtainable.
		2. Camp	**6**	**0**	16	0	The only rapids on the river are passed about 2 miles above Sákaw. They are about 400 yards long, but are not difficult. River winds through low hills covered with forest.
		3. Camp on Nanso chaung.	**10**	**0**	26	0	Through level plain covered with kaing grass. On the left the Ithi or Issi hills about 2 miles distant, on the right a range of hills, on which Kachin villages and "taungyas" can be seen. At 19½ miles from Kámaing a road goes off on the left bank to Lepun, a Kachin village. This road also goes to Lake Indawgyi, distant 2 days. On the right bank a road goes off to Môhnyin across the hills.
		4. Camp near Nantein chaung.	**12**	**0**	38	0	The whole way through plain covered with kaing grass. There is an excellent place for a camp here about 600 yards above the Nantein chaung on the left bank. A road goes from here to Lawsun, Kachin village. Small supplies obtainable.
		5. Camp Kônmamôn, Lake Endawgyi.	**11**	**4**	49	4	River becomes very deep and sluggish through low swampy ground covered with kaing grass. At the entrance to the lake there is a low barren range of hills called the Shwédaung which runs down to the left bank of the river. Kônmamôn is a small village on the west shore of the lake about 2 miles from the entrance. Good camping ground. Small supplies obtainable. The return journey from Kônmamôn to Kámaing was accomplished in three days. The working hours on the boats were from 6-30 A. M. to 5 P. M. with an hour's halt at 10 o'clock to allow the boats to close up and to enable the boatmen to have their food. Launches of the "Pathfinder" class can get up from Kámaing to Kônmamôn in two to two and-a-half days, and about the same time on the return journey when the river is in full flood. The delay caused by the stronger current on the up-journey being equalized on the return journey by the numerous "stickings" at turning the sharp corners.

No. 25.

From KATHA to MÁNSI (KAYINGÔN).

BY MAJOR J. H. SEWELL, NORFOLK REGIMENT, ASSISTANT ADJUTANT-GENERAL, MANDALAY DISTRICT, JANUARY 1892.

Authorities. Military	Authorities. Civil	Number and Names of Stages, Rivers and Streams.	Distances. Intermediate. M.	F.	Distances. Total. M.	F.	Remarks.
G.O.C. Mandalay District and O.C. Bhamo	Commissioner, Northern Division, and Deputy Commissioner, Katha.	**1. Lébwé ... ...**	**8**	**0**	8	0	I. If going easy with carts.
		2. Nahákaung ...	**8**	**0**	16	0	
		3. Mawteik ...	**15**	**0**	31	0	
		4. Kywégawgyi or Pehinga (14).	**11**	**0**	42	0	
		5. Bamauk ...	**5**	**0**	47	0	
		6. Pimbôn ...	**16**	**0**	63	0	
		7. Mánsi	**13**	**0**	76	0	
		1. Nahákaung ...	**16**	**0**	16	0	II. If going steady with mules or hard with carts.
		2. Mawteik ...	**15**	**0**	31	0	
		3. Bamauk ...	**16**	**0**	47	0	
		4. Pimbôn ...	**16**	**0**	63	0	
		5. Mánsi	**13**	**0**	76	0	
		1. Indaw	**19**	**0**	19	0	III. Going hard.
		2. Kywégawgyi ...	**23**	**0**	42	0	
		3. Pehinga ...	**14**	**0**	56	0	
		4. Mánsi	**20**	**0**	76	0	

From Katha to Mánsi, a distance of 76 miles, there is an easy cart track throughout, with the steep parts run to a gradient of 1 in 20, and the low ground causewayed in earth. In the northern part between Bamauk and Mánsi all nullahs and streams are ramped and bridged. Between Bamauk and Mawteik the Méza river at Kywégawgyi and a chaung at Mawteik are ramped, but not bridged. The former is 50 yards wide with a depth (now) from 40 to 2 feet of water, with high banks. The latter is 40 yards broad and 1 foot deep, with low banks. At Nantha, the chaung, which is 40 yards wide with high banks, has been dammed for irrigation. The road runs below the dam, the banks being ramped in and out.

There are good Public Works Department bungalows at Mawteik, Kywégawgyi, Bamauk, and Mánsi and fair at Kya-in. There is a fair house inside the stockade at Pimbôn. Zayáts are fair at Indaw, Nantha, Mauka, Sagadaung, and Sakhán. There are small rest camp-houses at Pehinga, Kya-in and Seyadaung. Between Nantha and Indaw the temporary bridges or culverts are in a bad condition, and three boggy places exist on the road where it runs along the east side of the Indaw lake. A bridge is in process of construction over the Indaw chaung, where the road crosses it 1 mile north of Indaw village. From Indaw to Katha the road follows and crosses the line now under construction, and nothing has been done to the road in the way of cutting or bridging. It is a somewhat rough, bnt easy cart track, and crosses the Indaw stream seven times, and a stream which runs into the Irrawaddy 1 mile south of Katha, some four times. Both are insignificant and would probably be at no time unfordable.

From Mánsi there are doubtless routes on into the Chindwin, but no reconnoitred route has been recorded so far, though a route from native information gives one of 7 marches to Maingkaing on the Uru river, the stages being from Kya-in 1. Hwésôtgyi (10 miles); 2. Payintaung (9); 3. Magyigôn (7); 4. Kyauksé (12); 5. Sindaing (18); 6. Pinthet (9); 7. Maingkaing (10).

FROM KATHA TO MÁNSI (KAYINGÔN)—*continued.*

The following is a more detailed account of the same route :—

BY LIEUT. TANCRED, R.A., ATTACHÉ, INTELLIGENCE DEPARTMENT, MAY 1890.

Authorities. Military.	Authorities. Civil.	Number and Names of Stages, Rivers and Streams.	Distances. Intermediate. M. F.	Distances. Total. M. F.	Remarks.
G.O.C. Mandalay District and O.C. Bhamo.	Commissioner, Northern Division, and Deputy Commissioner, Katha.	**1. Petsut** ...	**10 0**	10 0	Direction north-west. The track is a good cart road through scrub and forest jungle. At 2½ miles a stream is crossed three times, always passable for carts. At 6 miles the village of Langwa, 30 houses, 1 zayát (15 men), and a large pôngyi kyaung; water from stream east of village; stockaded. Cultivated ground round the village. At 6½ miles village Pyinmalut, 10 houses, stockaded; water from stream. At 7½ miles village Lébwé, 10 houses, stockaded; water from stream. At 10 miles village Petsut, situated in the pass, 15 houses, stockaded; soap-stone quarries; taungya cultivation.
		2. Indaw ... ... Indaw stream.	**9 0**	10 0	Direction south-west by west. Cart road continues through thick bamboo jungle crossing the Indaw stream continually. At 2 miles the Mawlu road branches off to the north-west, a good cart road. At 6 miles the village of Nabakaung, 10 houses, police post, accommodation, one large barrack for 60 men, 1 officer's quarter, good water, cultivation south-west of village. Cart road continues through bamboo jungle crossing the stream several times. At 7 miles road to Mawlu branches off to the north-west, a good cart road. At about 7½ miles village Si haung, 15 houses, 1 kyaung. At about 7¾ miles village Kyindapya, 15 houses, 1 zayát. There is a good camping ground before reaching this village. At 9 miles village Indaw, 40 houses, 3 zayáts, 1 pôngyi kyaung (300 men); water from stream and wells.
		3. Mawteik (Kyaungbauk). Indawgyi lake, Ledán chaung.	**15 0**	31 0	Cart road continues through paddy-fields and bamboo jungle. At 1¾ miles the Indaw lake is reached. The road here turns northward skirting the lake for 2 miles; this part is one continuous marsh in the rains. At 5 miles the road turns to the westward and passes through *eng* jungle for 2 miles, then through open ground, very marshy in rains. At 8¾ miles, the Ledán chaung is crossed, 30 feet wide 2 feet deep. During the rains it is not fordable even for elephants. The road continues through grass and thick jungle to Mawteik at 15 miles. This part is also much flooded in the rainy season. During the rains the route *viâ* Mánlé is used in preference. Mawteik is situated on left bank of the Méza; 40 houses, military police post of 50 men; paddy plentiful; 200 coolies obtainable. The following small villages are passed:—Nankin, Thekégyin, Ing-u, and Nantba.
		4. Kywégaw ... Méza river, Namé chaung.	**11 0**	42 0	From here routes lead to Mánlé and Mawlu, distant 8 and 19 miles respectively. Good cart tracks except in rains. Direction at first north-west, then north. The road is jungle path. Carts can go no further than Mawteik. The Namé chaung (not fordable in rains) is crossed and path follows the

FROM KATHA TO MÁNSI (KAYINGÔN)—*continued.*

Authorities. Military.	Authorities. Civil.	Number and Names of Stages, Rivers and Streams.	Distances. Inter-mediate. M.	F.	Total. M.	F.	Remarks.
G.O.C. Mandalay District and O.C. Bhamo.	Commissioner, Northern Division, and Deputy Commissioner, Katha.						left bank (east bank) of Méza through tree jungle. At about $1\frac{1}{2}$ miles pass Kyundaung and $\frac{1}{2}$ a mile further Nansin. At about 8 miles site of old village of Baingbin and about 1 mile further Pathé. At 10 miles the road crosses the Méza to Kywégaw. Kywégaw is a village in Wuntho.
		5. Bamauk ...	**5**	**0**	47	0	Good road through jungle to Singán at $2\frac{3}{4}$ miles ($\frac{3}{4}$ mile off the road, about 30 houses). Shortly after cross rocky bit of hill and descend into paddy cultivation around Bamauk, which is situated in the open and consisted of about 60 houses before it was shelled and partially destroyed in the early part of 1891.
		6. Pimbôn ...	**16**	**0**	63	0	Easy cart track. At 9 miles village of Pehinga, 20 houses, 1 kyaung, and 16 Pimbôn where there is a stockaded post.
		7. Mánsi ...	**13**	**0**	76	0	Road as before. Jungle very thick.

ALTERNATIVE I.

FROM BAMAUK (STAGE 5) TO KAYINGÔN (MÁNSI CIRCLE) *viâ* SIAKÔN AND TOMBÔN.

BY CAPT. W. HUSSEY-WALSH, INTELLIGENCE BRANCH, MARCH 1891.

Authorities. Military.	Authorities. Civil.	Number and Names of Stages, Rivers and Streams.	Inter-mediate. M.	F.	Total.	Remarks.
G.O.C. Mandalay District and O.C. Bhamo.	Commissioner, Northern Division, and Deputy Commissioner, Katha.	**1. Siakôn** ... ... Méza chaung and several smaller streams.	**14**	**0**	...	For the first two miles the road goes in a north-east by north direction; perfectly level through thin forest jungles. At the second mile a stream is crossed about 20 feet wide and 8 inches deep, flowing in an easterly direction; no perceptible current. Three-quarters of a mile further on in the same direction another smaller stream is crossed flowing in the same direction. About 100 yards after crossing this stream there is a small zayát or hut; the track takes north-east direction for a mile or so, then almost due north for about 2 miles more through teak forest with thin undergrowth; road very good. About 1 mile beyond this there is another very small stream. The track then leads through bamboo jungle and continues for several miles, 2 to 3, in a north-east by north direction through jungle and through a few open places. There were several tracks we passed which led to the villages of Kyungôn and O Kínu; the direction again became north through teak forest; $1\frac{1}{2}$ miles led to a small stream of the same description as the other ones. About 2 miles from this stream we came across two tracks, one on the right from Pandaw and 100 yards beyond one from Môtsi on the left; about 1 mile beyond we crossed the Méza chaung flowing from a west-north-west direction, about 40 yards wide 1 foot deep; current about 3 miles an hour. On the left bank of the stream is the village of Siakôn; 13 houses; stockaded with a large kyaung capable of accommodating 100 men.

No. 25.

FROM KATHA TO MÁNSI (KAYINGÔN)—*continued.*

ALTERNATIVE I—*continued.*

Authorities. Military.	Authorities. Civil.	Number and Names of Stages, Rivers and Streams.	Distances. Intermediate. M.	F.	Distances. Total. M.	F.	Remarks.
G.O.C. Mandalay District and O.C. Bhamo.	Commissioner, Northern Division, and Deputy Commissioner, Katha.	**2. Tombôn** ... Kalát chaung.	**15**	**4**	29	4	Leaving Siakôn the road takes a north-west direction for the first 1½ miles skirting the Kalát chaung, then crosses and recrosses that stream constantly. We left the village of Kamdángya on the left-hand side; eight houses but only two occupied. A mile beyond is the village of Zidawgai, deserted; 10 houses; stockaded; paddy-fields on the right, jungle and stream on the left. The road now continues in a north-north-west direction for about 5½ miles constantly recrossing the Kalát chaung as also along the bed of the stream. Most of these 5 miles the track may be said to have ceased entirely. At about 8 miles from Siakôn the road ascends a hill, very steep for the first 150 feet, then gradual for the next 400 to 500 feet through dense jungle; the final 300 to 400 feet towards the top of the hill the road was very bad, stony, and rocky. The descent of this hill was very steep at first, then gradual and finally easy, when we reached a stockade. From the foot of this hill, on the other side to the stockade, the distance is about 6 miles. One and-a-half miles beyond, direction west-north-west, we came to the village of Tombôn; stockaded; 10 houses.
		3. Kayingôn ... Nansayit chaung and another small stream.	**12**	**0**	41	4	From Tombôn to Kayingôn the track starts in a north-west direction through paddy-fields along the valley of the Nansayit chaung. The village of Nansayit is passed in the left about ¾ of a mile from Tombôn; partly stockaded; 10 houses. About 1½ miles, direction west-north-west, is the village of Tándánpaya; nine houses; the road is undulating, then crosses a hill about 200 feet high and continues undulating; road good through jungle for the next 2 miles where there is a stream. The track enters paddy-fields, and for the first 1½ miles direction west, for the next 1½ miles north-north-west still through paddy-fields; on leaving these fields the track continues for a couple of miles in a westerly direction. We entered the large village of Mankwin, leaving the village of Nwagôn on the right abont ½ a mile off. Mankwin has 13 large houses besides many small ones and huts; large pôngyi kyaung capable of accommodating 100 men; many pagodas; a flourishing being looking village. Two miles beyond, in a westerly direction, through thin jungle, road good, is the village of Kayingôn (Mánsi Circle).

ALTERNATIVE II.

FROM PEHINGA (*see* STAGE 6) TO KAYINGÔN.

BY LIEUT. W. J. STERLING, ASSISTANT COMMANDANT, KATHA POLICE, 3RD MARCH 1891.

Military	Civil	Stage	Inter. M.	F.	Total	Remarks
G.O.C. Mandalay District and O.C. Bhamo.	Commr., Northern Divn., and Dy. Commr., Katha.	**1. Mánbin** ...	**7**	**0**	...	Road round to west over hills, teak forest and bamboo, joining main road at Kyauktôntôn where there is no village. The village of Mánbin is about 2 miles to the west of the road and 7 miles from Pehinga. Number of houses nine.

FROM KATHA TO MÁNSI (KAYINGÔN)—*continued.*

ALTERNATIVE II—*continued.*

Authorities. Military.	Authorities. Civil.	Number and Names of Stages, Rivers and Streams.	Distances. Intermediate. M.	F.	Distances. Total. M.	F.	Remarks.
G.O.C. Mandalay District and O.C. Bhamo.	Commissioner, Northern Division, and Deputy Commissioner, Katha.	**2. Leni**	7	0	14	0	Leni, small village on the west of the road 7 miles from Mánbin.
		3. Nanthaung ...	11	0	25	0	At 2 miles Thayetgôn and Pinkôn two villages about 100 yards apart; good accommodation for 100 men in kyaung; good water from stream; paddy cultivation; would do very well for a post if necessary to place one there; the road from Pehinga to Pinkôn is good, being fairly level, but in the rains would be bad, owing to the number of chaungs to be crossed. Number of houses 45. Road good and level. Kya-in at 8 miles has about 16 houses; plenty of water from tank in vicinity. At 11 miles Nanthaung, 20 houses; good pôngyi kyaung; accommodation for 60 men; water plentiful; good place for a post.
		4. Kayingôn ...	6	0	31	0	Twenty-five houses; water good; good place for a post; paddy cultivation. At Saungnoketu, 2 miles from Kayingôn, was situated the Wuntho Sawbwa's father's camp, unsuitable for a post, being in the hills; water scarce; no cultivation of any sort.

BRANCH I.

FROM KYWÉGAW (STAGE 4) TO KALÁT.

BY LIEUT. TANCRED, R.A., ATTACHÉ, INTELLIGENCE DEPARTMENT, MAY 1890.

Authorities. Military.	Authorities. Civil.	Number and Names of Stages, Rivers and Streams.	Distances. Intermediate. M.	F.	Distances. Total. M.	F.	Remarks.
G.O.C. Mandalay District and O.C. Bhamo.	Commissioner, Northern Division, and Deputy Commissioner, Katha.	**1. Kaingyi** ...	7	0	7	0	Recross the Méza chaung and take path to left up course of stream. At 7 miles the village of Kaingyi. A military police post of 100 men; good water from well; Méza river 100 yards away. The following small villages are passed: Kyundaw, Nansin, Thôka, and the deserted villages of Baingbin and Kyetléthit. The track crosses many nullahs, some very steep, and is said to be impassable for animals in the rains.
		2. Kalát	10	4	17	4	Direction north. The road crosses the Méza and follows right bank for 5½ miles, crossing several nullahs (bridged for men). The Méza is there recrossed and the road continues along the left bank to Mantôn at 9 miles. Mantôn is a small village with pôngyi kyaung (40 men). The following villages are passed: Tônlai, Pinlun, Kyaungôn, Ôngbin, Sangyawin (eight houses), and Pándaw. The first four are on right (west) bank of river and are deserted. Sangyawin

FROM KATHA TO MÁNSI (KAYINGÔN)—*continued.*

BRANCH I—*continued.*

Authorities. Military.	Authorities. Civil.	Number and Names of Stages, Rivers and Streams.	Distances. Intermediate.		Distances. Total.		Remarks.
G.O.C. Mandalay District.	Commissioner, Northern Division, and Deputy Commissioner, Katha.	**2. Kalát**—*cont.*					is on left (east) bank, Pándaw is on right (west) bank and is in Wuntho. From Ôngbin (5 miles) a road goes westward to Nauktaw at foot of Kalát hill and Mánsi in Wuntho. This road is a good track. From Mantôn a road goes eastwards to Mawlu, crossing the Namíchaung and meeting the main road between Mawlu and Môhnyin at Pinlôn. At 1 mile from Mantôn it ascends a steep hill and then descends; after which there are no more hills of any size. From Mantôn a road goes through Kalát, 1½ miles further north or south-east of Méza and thence westward to Mánsi, crossing the hills north of Kalát hill. The villagers state that this is a good track and that the distance from Mantôn to Mánsi is about 20 miles. The path up the Méza valley after Mantôn continues on the left (east) bank through paddy-fields to Naungmé at 10 miles. There are two small villages, both called Naungmé. The path then crosses Méza to Kalát ½ mile further on. After this there is no path on left bank, but the path on right bank continues up the stream.

No. 26.

From KATHA to MÔGAUNG viâ MÔHNYIN.

I. B. COMPILATION, 1888.

Authorities. Military.	Authorities. Civil.	Number and Names of Stages, Rivers and Streams.	Distances. Intermediate.		Distances. Total.		Remarks.
G.O.C. Mandalay District.	Commissioner, Northern Division, and Deputy Commissioner, Katha.	**1. Petsut**	**10**	**0**	10	0	*See* Route No. 25, Katha to Mánsi, Stage 1.
		2. Pinwé	**9**	**4**	19	4	Cart road through thick bamboo jungle frequently crossing the Indaw chaung. At about 3½ miles pass ends. Here Mánlé road goes to left and south-west; Mawlu road to right; at 6 miles cross Simaw chaung; 8½ miles Pintin; six houses; 9½ miles Pinwé seven houses; camp to right of village. Two zayáts; good water. All this road through jungle.
		3. Mawlu	**10**	**0**	29	4	Just before Pinwé road divides, main road to east, path formerly used west, both go to Mawlu, latter is about 1½ miles shorter and passes Pônhôn. Eastern road; 1 mile from Pinwé, is Tônlôn, eight houses; at 9 miles Simaw; 20 houses, stockaded. Shallow stream between it and Mawlu. Mawlu at 10 miles is surrounded by large paddy plain about 3 miles by 5. Strongly stockaded. Police post 150 men. Kyaungs, zayáts, &c., numerous; water plentiful and good. Western road, Pinwé to Myaungbin 1 mile, eight houses; at 7 miles Pônhôn; 14 houses, stockaded. On to Simaw and Mawlu about 1½ miles.

FROM KATHA TO MÔGAUNG *viâ* MÔHNYIN—*continued.*

Authorities. Military.	Authorities. Civil.	Number and Names of Stages, Rivers and Streams.	Distances. Intermediate. M.	F.	Total. M.	F.	Remarks.
G.O.C. Mandalay District.	Commissioner, Northern Division, and Deputy Commissioner, Katha.	**4. Mawhun or Hngetpyaw-daw.** Ledán chaung.	13	4	43	0	From Mawhu road crosses paddy-fields to Hénu (1 mile), crosses Hénu chaung and proceeds along fairly level ground to Mauhé and the Manhé chaung (4½ miles), thence to Paket (6 miles), Pontôn (7¼ miles), Mawhé (8¾ miles), crosses to west bank of Ledán chaung (12¼ miles), and then goes on to Mawhun 13½ miles, last part through paddy-fields. Mawhun is situated on the Ledán chaung and contains an unoccupied wooden kyaung capable of holding 100 men at a pinch. The road is passable for carts the whole way.
		5. Môhnyin ... Nanyin chaung.	14	6	57	6	Leaving the kyaung at Mawhun the road crosses the Ledán chaung and runs eastwards across paddy-fields for 1¼ miles to foot of the Lwékandaung hills; at 1½ miles the top of the hill is reached. The ascent is for the most part gradual and easy, but near the top is a steep part. A road passable for carts will shortly be made up the hill. The hill is covered with bamboo jungle. At the top a broad open road is reached which leads on all the way to Môhnyin, and except at one or two points where repairs will shortly be carried out is a good cart road, almost level throughout. A stream is passed at 3¼ miles, and at 4 miles the Nanyin chaung is reached lying in a deep hollow on the right. This stream runs on to Môgaung, at 5 miles Ywathit, a small village with no accommodation, but a very small kyaung. The Nanyin chaung runs at no great distance from the village. The road runs for a mile from the village through an open plain partly under cultivation and enters the jungle again. At 9¼ miles the Nanyin chaung is crossed (to the east bank). The banks need ramping, also those of two steep nullahs, before reaching the Nanyin crossing. In the next ½ mile a small swamp and a steep nullah are crossed; at 10 miles the road forks left hand branch leading into the village of Nyaungaing ¼ mile off; right branch running direct to Môhnyin along high ground and leaving Nyaungaing paddy plain to the left. Nyaungaing is a village of houses containing no accommodation, but a small bamboo kyaung. From Nyaungaing the road runs on to Môhnyin (14¾ miles) and with the exception of one or two places, where ramping is required, is a good level road of similar character to that south of Nyaungaing. On approaching Môhnyin it opens into a plain on the bank of the Nanyin; Môhnyin lies on the west bank. The banks are high and steep, but the river is fordable in dry weather. The village is surrounded by a stockade. The late Sawbwa's "*Haw*" (*i.e.*, palace) is a large bamboo building in good preservation, affording accommodation to about 100 men. It is situated in the middle of the village in a confined space surrounded by a stockade with houses close outside. The village is crowded and full of intricate paths blocked by quagmires. There is a look-out tower at the Haw, which commands a view of the surrounding country. The village contains houses. In former times boats of 300 baskets capacity used to go up the Nanyin from

FROM KATHA TO MOGAUNG *viâ* MÔHNYIN—*continued.*

Authorities. Military.	Authorities. Civil.	Number and Names of Stages, Rivers and Streams.	Distances. Intermediate. M.	F.	Distances. Total. M.	F.	Remarks.
G.O.C. Mandalay District.	Commissioner, Northern Division, and Deputy Commissioner, Katha.	**5. Môhnyin**—*cont.*					Môgaung to Môhnyin for paddy in the rain season. The road from the Lwékandaung hill to Môhnyin and onwards to Môgaung follows the valley of the Nanyin chaung. The hills on the right are called the Gangaw range, and are a continuation of the Pannyo range, or Môda hills, which separate Mawlu from Môda. There is said to be only one road across the Shwédaungyi which leads from Môhnyin to Thayetta on the Kaukkwé chaung, a two days' journey (probably 20 to 30 miles). The range of hills on the left beginning with the Mawhuntaung near Mawhun run northwards to within a short distance of Môgaung. They are called the Namanklé (or Namaklaing) hills and are crossed by the road from Môhnyin (or Môgaung) to Indaw, and by a road south of this from Môhnyin to the Saikmu-letmaing country. The railway line follows more or less the line of this route and there are or will be stations at or near each stage. Nahákaung which lies 3 miles west of stage 1, on the road to Mánsi (*See* Route No. 25, Stage 2) is the junction of the Katha branch with the main line from Wuntho (*viâ* Mánlé) to Môgaung.
G.O.C. Mandalay District.	Commissioner, Northern Division, and Deputy Commissioner, Bhamo.	**6. Maingnaung** ...	**6**	**2**	64	0	
		7. Camp near Hôpin.	**13**	**2**	77	2	
		8. Nansánkwin chaung.	**16**	**2**	93	4	For details of these stages *see* Route No. 67.
		9. Nampadaung.	**13**	**2**	106	6	
		10. Môgaung ...	**18**	**0**	124	6	

BRANCH I.

FROM MAWLU (STAGE 3) TO MANTÔN (*vide* ROUTE NO. 25, BRANCH I, STAGE 2).

BY DEPUTY COMMISSIONER, KATHA.

Military.	Civil.	Number and Names of Stages, Rivers and Streams.	Intermediate. M.	F.	Total. M.	F.	Remarks.
G.O.C. Mandalay District.	Commissioner, Northern Division, and Deputy Commissioner, Katha.	**1. Nammi** ...	**11**	**0**	11	0	Road (direction westerly) almost practicable for carts throughout and easily made so. Nammi is situated on the Nammi stream; kyaung and zayát; accommodation for 70 men.
		2. Mantôn ... **Méza chaung.**	**10**	**0**	21	0	Crosses a range almost throughout the stage. Passable for pack cattle or coolies; could be made a good pack cattle road, but not a cart road. Mantôn is a village on the Méza and has accommodation in one kyaung and one zayát for 30 men.

FROM KATHA TO MÔGAUNG *viâ* MÔHNYIN—*continued.*

BRANCH I—*continued.*

Authorities. Military.	Authorities. Civil.	Number and Names of Stages, Rivers and Streams.	Distances. Intermediate.	Distances. Total.	Remarks.
G.O.C. Mandalay Dist., &c.	Commr., Northern Divn., &c., Katha.	**2. Mantôn**—*cont.*	Another route runs north from Mawlu, to Pinlôn 7 or 8 miles on the road to Môhnyin, thence west to Mantôn, crossing a steep range 1 mile before reaching that place.		

BRANCH II.

FROM MÔHNYIN (STAGE 5) TO HÉDAUNG (INDAWGYI LAKE).

Military	Civil	Stages	M. F.	M. F.	Remarks
G.O.C. Mandalay District.	Commissioner, Northern Division, and Deputy Commissioner, Katha.	**1. Nankun** ...	16 0	...	From Môhnyin the road to Indaw runs west and north-west, reaches Bilumyo at 6 miles. Bilumyo is now a place of only houses. It is situated on the north bank of the Nankinha chaung. The road crosses this and, at 8 miles from Môhnyin, reaches the foot of the Namanklé hills. From there it is another 8 miles to the top, a gradual ascent. At the top there is a small Kachin village of nine or 10 houses. The road is good and level from Môhnyin to foot of hills, that up the hills passable for pack animals and ponies.
G.O.C. Mandalay District.	Commissioner, Northern Division, and Deputy Commissioner, Katha.	**2. Camp on Nanyinkán chaung.** Nanyinkán chaung.	16 0	32 0	The roads descend the hills for a distance equal to that between Nankun and Môhnyin. It is similar in character to that on the east slope. The country is inhabited by Kachins. Jungle camp on Nanyinkán chaung at foot of hills, there is also an alternative halting place at small Shan hamlet of Nanmôn, 2 miles before reaching Nanyinkán.
G.O.C. Mandalay District.	Commissioner, Northern Division, and Deputy Commissioner, Bhamo.	**3. Hédaung (on the Indawgyi Lake).**	16 0	48 0	The hills are covered with rather thick jungle. From the foot of the hills the road runs for a distance equal to that to Nankun across a *lwin* (plain), muddy in the rains, but dry by February. It is covered with kaing grass, otherwise open. A few small spurs are covered at intervals. The villages of Lôntôn, Lônkyo and Hédaung are close to each other, and on small knolls of rising ground. The roads pass by them successively. Lônkyo and Hédaung are now deserted. They stand a short distance from the shore of the lake, but boats can be obtained at Lôntôn (30 houses), the usual landing place at the west bank of the lake.

No. 27.

From KATHA to SENBO viâ MÔDA and KAUKKWÉ VALLEY.

By Capt. E. S. HASTINGS, M.S.C., 1886–87 and Deputy Commissioner, Bhamo, 1887.

Authorities. Military.	Authorities. Civil.	Number and Names of Stages, Rivers and Streams.	Intermediate. M.	Intermediate. F.	Total. M.	Total. F.	Remarks.
G.O.C. Mandalay District.	Commissioner, Northern Division, and Deputy Commissioner, Katha.	**1. Minlé** ... ... Stream.	**12**	**0**	12	0	First 3 miles along the river bank northwards passing through the villages of Panlôngwé, Kyaukhmaw and Myitthalin. The road now bears away from the river, and at 5 miles pass Bawma, a little to the south of the road. Between 7 and 8 miles pass the villages of Komingyaung, Pungona and Méhé. At 10 miles Naungwé and at 11 miles Naungku. Thence for a mile over low-lying ground and cross a stream to Minlé (Minlí on map).
		2. Kyaungbin ... Mézalu chaung.	**11**	**0**	23	0	Road through teak forest. Some easy ascents and descents. Cross Mézalu chaung twice just before reaching Kyaungbin.
		3. Môda ... ... Irrawaddy river.	**8**	**0**	31	0	Cross the Mézalu again twice directly after leaving Kyaungbin. At 2½ miles Héywa and branch road to Wéko. Moda is a large village on the right bank of the Irrawaddy.
		4. Imma Forest (Camp).	**7**	**0**	38	0	Road throughout this and the remaining stages practicable for elephants.
		5. Maung Taw ...	**8**	**0**	46	0	
G.O.C. Mandalay District and O.C. Bhamo.	Commissioner, Northern Division, and Deputy Commissioner, Bhamo.	**6. Máttát** ...	**8**	**0**	54	0	Cross the Kaukkwé stream, stage 1 of Route No. 108.
		7. Camp (Nansa stream).	**11**	**0**	65	0	At 5 miles pass the village of Ségyi; road good.
		8. Káku-Kachin village.	**12**	**0**	77	0	
		9. Camp at Nansaya stream.	**8**	**0**	85	0	
		10. Camp at eastern foot of Makan hills.	**8**	**0**	93	0	Cross steep hills ; difficult march.
		11. Camp at Mankin rice field.	**7**	**0**	100	0	
		12. Senbo ...	**6**	**0**	106	0	Pass Pinlun village at 3 miles. *Note.*—The above route is from information supplied by men who travelled over it with a party of 72 elephants, the elephants being, according to the Indian scale, very lightly laden. The marches, short as they are, usually occupy six hours, namely, 6 A.M. to 12 noon. There is little or no house accommodation, the villages passed being small. The last two or three stages seem to be the same road as is described in No. 87, Senbo to Makan and Pinzun. There is a somewhat short route from Katha to Môda describing a smaller arc than that given in stages 1 to 3 above, but being nearer the river bank is liable to be flooded, and could only be used in the very dry season (March and April).

No. 28.

From KATHA to WUNTHO viâ MÁNLÉ.

By Lieut. TANCRED, R.A., May 1890 and others.

Authorities.		Number and Names of Stages, Rivers and Streams.	Distances.				Remarks.
Military.	Civil.		Intermediate.		Total.		
			M.	F.	M.	F.	
G.O.C. Mandalay District.	Commissioner, Northern Division, and Deputy Commissioner, Katha.	**1. Petsut** ...	**10**	**0**	10	0	*See* Route No. 25.
		2. Indaw ...	**9**	**0**	19	0	*See* Route No. 25.
		3. Mánlé, Kyunbintha, Konitywa. Môwa and Méza chaungs.	**7**	**0**	26	0	Direction south-west-west. Cart road continues for 3 miles through paddy-fields and then crosses the Môwa twice. The road then passes over low hills through In and bamboo jungle, and reaches Mánlé at 7 miles. This road is impassable for carts in the rains. The Môwa is very deep and rapid (60 feet wide), and no rafts or boats are procurable; and there is no bridge for footmen. The foot track *viâ* Namahôk and Séywa is used during the rains. There is a foot-bridge over the Môwa at Séywa, but ponies have to be swum across. Mánlé consists of two villages ½ mile apart, situated on the Méza; 250 houses, three pôngyi kyaungs, many zayâts (600 men).
		4. Tátlwin ... Méza chaung.	**11**	**0**	37	0	There is a good cart track from here to Mawteik on Route No. 25 up the left bank of the Méza chaung, distance 8 miles. Méza river crossed at 2 miles from Mánlé 1½ feet deep; 3 miles on to Ingun marshy and cultivated ground, 3 miles open jungle to Bainbin, then up hills to Tátlwin. This is on top of Minwun hills; the gradient is easy and the road free from stones; the pass is reported easier than Petsut pass. At Tátlwin there are about 25 houses, kyaung and zayâts.
		5. Mawkán ... Seiktha chaung.	**13**	**2**	50	2	Road between Tátlwin and Wuntho runs mostly in a south-south-westerly direction and passes through undulating ground and open forest, formerly a fairly good cart road, but, owing to its having been unused for a long time, rather out of repair, and grown over with trees and creepers in parts. It could, however, be very soon made good enough for cart traffic in the dry season throughout. The road runs south, fairly good for carts, for 2¼ miles up to Payadaw, deserted, with an old broken down double stockade. About five tumble-down houses. Water obtained by digging in beds of small hill streams. Jungle round about not very thick. Road good for cart traffic and very fairly level. At 5¾ miles Kyauk-in. Water obtained as at Payadaw. Village, 10 houses, one kyaung. The road now crosses more open country. At 6¼ miles village of Tántabin, one well, five or six houses, water as above. At 11¼ miles Ka-u. Road skirts low spurs and is fairly good; water obtained as above, open jungle. At 12¼ miles Seiktha; water obtained from the Seiktha chaung, which runs west of village. Large camping ground to south of village. At 13¼ miles Mawkán village, situated on slight rising ground. After leaving Seiktha the Seiktha chaung is crossed, about 40 feet broad and 1 foot deep. Water rapid and very good for drinking purposes. Small stream close to Mawkán. There is a kyaung and zayât here in fairly good order, also a well. Good camping ground.

FROM KATHA TO WUNTHO *viâ* MÁNLÉ—*continued.*

Authorities. Military.	Authorities. Civil.	Number and Names of Stages, Rivers and Streams.	Distances. Intermediate. M. F.	Distances. Total. M. F.	Remarks.
G.O.C. Mandalay District.	Commissioner, Northern Division, and Deputy Commissioner, Katha.	**6. Mawnaing** ...	6 6	57 0	At 3½ miles Maka. There is a tank here, about 100 yards long by 50 yards broad. Water low in the dry season year, January to June. Road continues fairly good. Good camping ground and a stream. There is a fairly thick bamboo jungle through which the road passes before it gets into the Mawnaing paddy-fields. This open ground is entered upon about ¾ of a mile before Mawnaing is reached. Village situated in the centre of large paddy-fields with rising ground on north, east and west.
		7. Wuntho ...	12 0	69 0	Five or six wells. Between Mawnaing and Wuntho the road is good (only wanting repairs in a few places) and passes along paddy-fields nearly the whole way. The following villages are passed in the first 4 or 5 miles: Engbin, Khayauzát, Panyu, and Thindaw, and in the next 3 or 4 Gwégyo, Kyaingkaung and Kinywa. At the last-named place there are two wells situated on rising ground. Wuntho is a prettily situated place, in open ground with hills close round and good water from stream running close by. It can be seen about 1 mile before it is reached. There are a great number of kyaungs and zayáts, capable of accommodating a large force. Plenty of cattle and paddy. Wuntho has proved to be extremely unhealthy, as indeed seems the whole of this district.

No. 29.

From KÁZU to KAO-I (on Sánsi Route).

BY CAPT. G. H. H. COUCHMAN, D.S.O., SOMERSETSHIRE LIGHT INFANTRY, MARCH 1892.

Military.	Civil.	Stages.	Intermediate. M. F.	Total. M. F.	Remarks.
G.O.C. Mandalay District and O.C. Bhamo.	Commissioner, Northern Division, and Deputy Commissioner, Bhamo.	**1. Laipong** ... Nantabet chaung (Tabak Ka) and numerous other smaller streams, all fordable.	10 6	10 6	General direction east. Road is level and good for 1½ miles through bamboo and small tree jungle. At ¼ mile road to left to Makawng. After 1½ miles road begins to ascend with occasional small descents and then steeply up along a spur. It is again undulating, and at 2½ miles crosses a small rocky stream. Jungle as before, but with high grass. From here it has a slight descent into a taungya, where there is a good place for a camp, there being a good stream here which is crossed (5 yards broad and 1 foot deep). The road now for about ½ mile follows the bed of a boggy stream, but this is no obstacle. It then ascends steeply up for 200 yards and then goes down and crosses a stream 6 feet wide and 6 inches deep. From here it ascends steeply along a spur till it meets the cross roads on the top from Shantin to Pakong (on left), and then descends steeply and tortuously to the Lima Ka, at 6 miles a rocky stream with deep pools, 8 yards broad and 1 foot deep and easy crossing; water good. The last mile is steep, and in some places the road is worn into cuttings and is a little stony. From here the road ascends through high grass along a spur fairly steeply and after ½ mile along the top of the ridge in moderate undulations. At 7 miles there is a road from the left from Pakaw,

FROM KÁZU TO KAO-I (ON SÁNSI ROUTE)—*continued.*

Authorities. Military.	Authorities. Civil.	Number and Names of Stages, Rivers and Streams.	Distances. Inter-mediate.	Distances. Total.	Remarks.
G.O.C. Mandalay District and O.C. Bhamo.	Commissioner, Northern Division, and Deputy Commissioner, Bhamo.	**1. Laipong**—*cont.*			and the road passes along an easy descent, crossing and passing along the bed of a muddy stream for 50 yards, then fairly level to another stream 3 to 6 feet broad 6 inches deep, with good water. It then ascends through grass and small tree jungle for 200 yards, and then descends to a small muddy stream 9 feet broad. It follows along the right bank of this stream and above it for 200 yards and then recrosses it. Another road from Paseng now joins it, and the road passes through high kaing grass into a small paddy plain at about 9 miles; good camp for 300 men; water and forage plentiful. This latter part of the road is a little overgrown, but it has no obstacles. The road then crosses the 'Ndun Ka, 6 yards broad 1 foot deep, good water, and ascends some newly cleared ground rather steeply, and then undulates along the ridge for ½ mile, again ascending rather steeply through tree jungle into Laipong 10¾ miles. Camp on east side of village; water scarce from three small springs, and for animals from a small stream on Nawkhum road. Road all good. A road, steep but passable for pony transport, runs from Laipong to Uka through the village of Nawkum. 20 houses at 3 miles, and crossing the Saga Ka twice, at 1½ and 4½ miles, rocky bed, about 3 feet of water in the middle of March, crossing difficult steep ascents and descents. Total distance from Laipong to Uka 8 miles.
		2. Nacháng ... Numerous hill streams.	M. F. 7 2	M. F. 18 0	From Laipong the general direction is south-east and the road descends steadily along a ridge through tree jungle for ¼ mile, when it becomes steeper, passing through grass to a small muddy stream and thence to the Kazar Ka 15 yards broad 1 foot deep, bed of large stones, good water, and no obstacles. It then goes through kaing grass for 250 yards, crossing a small muddy stream and the Tazar Ka, which joins the Kazar Ka ¼ mile down and is a stream similar to Kazar in all respects. The road then crosses two small boggy streams. The road then ascends first easily and then steeply through grass and small tree jungle into Uka* 13¾ miles, road from Nawkhum joining it from the north at 13¼ miles. The road still continues to ascend from Uka fairly steeply through old over-grown taungyas for ½ mile, when it ascends by easy undulations to Paotaw 15¾ miles, crossing a small stream and also the Kashi and Paotaw streams; both small, rocky streams here with very little water. The last part into Paotaw is fairly steep; from here the road descends at first easily through tree and bamboo jungle into some old taungyas and then steeply down to the Sama Ka, 15 to 20 yards broad 1 foot deep; bottom large stones. The last part to the stream is tortuous, steep, and in some parts has big stones in the path and is very dusty. From the Sama Ka it is a steady ascent into Nachang, through first high grass, then a clump of trees, then taungyas, and finally tree jungle, two small streams being crossed. At 17¼ miles is a road from the north from Ninglum. All this road is good and presents no obstacles. Camp in Nachang village very good; grass fodder here. Water from two small streams and difficult to collect for transport.

* A report of the same route by Lieut. Campbell, 15th Madras Infantry, makes the distance to Laipong 11½ and Uka 16.

FROM KÁZU TO KAO-I (ON SÁNSI ROUTE)—*continued.*

Authorities. Military.	Authorities. Civil.	Number and Names of Stages, Rivers and Streams.	Distances. Intermediate.	Distances. Total.	Remarks.
			M. F.	M. F.	
G.O.C. Mandalay District and O.C. Bhamo.	Commissioner, Northern Division, and Deputy Commissioner, Bhamo.	**3. Kao-i** ... Nantabet chaung (Tabak Ka) and numerous hill streams.	10 4	28 4	From here the general direction is east and the road descends to the Tabak Ka (Nantabet chaung) by an easy gradient along the hillside, with one easy ascent of ½ mile through small tree and high grass jungle and, crossing three small rocky and unimportant streams, approaches easy to Tabak Ka. Bamboo plentiful for bridging purposes, but not many large trees. Over the Tabak is a small temporary bamboo bridge made up in a single day and passable for transport. Its length is 36 yards, which is the present breadth of the stream. The whole bed is 75 yards broad and full of large boulders. The stream at crossing has a gentle current with maximum depth of 4 feet. There are numerous deep pools and in the rains it would be impassable as the water rises from 20 to 25 feet, which would require a bridge very high up above the present bed and at least 100 yards long. From here is a steady ascent through high grass into Lumiáng 3¼ miles, crossing three small, rocky, and unimportant streams. Road good. The road now descends through clumps of large trees and taungyas and crosses a cól, then ascending steadily to a small stream, which is apparently used as a halting place by caravans. It still ascends through high grass, and at 2 miles from Lumiáng the road to Wátung branches off up a steep bit of hill to the right. Wátung is ½ mile distant from the road and has about eight houses. Road now has a steady ascent through high grass and then, after meeting a road from Watung, ascends very steeply for ½ mile through small tree jungle. This part is rather stony. It then follows along the ridge rising gradually with occasional undulations through tree jungle and, after crossing a small stony stream, rises into the Yawyin village of Siba, 7½ miles. The road then ascends steadily with occasional undulations through high grass and old taungyas and then newly cleared taungyas to the side of Siba Pum, crossing a col which connects the latter with Mata Pum (26½ miles). From here there is a road south to Kaiya visible about a mile down towards the Möngka Ka. After a short ascent the road commences to descend and curves round first in a northerly and then easterly direction across a horse-shoe shaped valley all through grass jungle into Kao-i 10½ miles. Parts of this road are rocky and a little overgrown. Two small boggy streams and one stony one with good water are crossed. Kao-i is above the Möngka Ka, which is the boundary. It is a Yawyin village. All this road is good throughout from Kázu, having no bad obstacle except the Tabak Ka. Most of the ascents and descents are easy. Kao-i is not on the Seden (*sic ?*) route, but there is a road north from it which joins it, the Seden route branching off to the left about 1 mile short of Kao-i.

BRANCH I.

FROM NACHÁNG (STAGE 2) TO NINGLUM.

BY LIEUT. RUSTON, DEVONSHIRE REGIMENT, MARCH 1892.

Military	Civil	Stage	Intermediate	Total	Remarks
G.O.C. Mandalay Dist. and O.C. Bhamo.	Commr., Northern Divn., and Dy. Commr., Bhamo.	**1. Ninglum** ... Sama Ka and other small streams.	5 0	5 0	General direction north-north-west. Follow back on main road for 15 minutes, then turn to right, continuing down-hill for 5 minutes, cross small stream, then up 5 minutes, then level for 5 minutes winding

FROM KÁZU TO KAO-I (ON SÁNSI ROUTE)—*continued.*

Authorities. Military.	Authorities. Civil.	Number and Names of Stages, Rivers and Streams.	Distances. Inter-mediate.	Distances. Total.	Remarks.
G.O.C. Mandalay District and O.C. Bhamo.	Commissioner, Northern Division, and Deputy Commissioner, Bhamo.	**1. Ninglum**—*cont.*			round spur, cross another small stream gradually up for 5 minutes, and cross another small stream, and then level 5 minutes, cross a fourth small stream, then at 40 minutes cross the Sama Ka, then level for 100 yards, then winding up a steep hill for 20 minutes, then less steep to the top of the hill 10 minutes over to the west side of the range, cross a taungya in a northerly direction, slightly ascending through tree jungle for 200 yards to Ninglum village, 80 minutes. Road generally good and through grass and fern jungle; distance estimated at 5 miles.

BRANCH II.

FROM LUMIÁNG (*see* STAGE 3) TO TINGRONG.

BY LIEUT. C. MAYNARD, DEVONSHIRE REGIMENT, MARCH 1892.

Military	Civil	Stages	Intermediate M. F.	Total M. F.	Remarks
G.O.C. Mandalay District and O.C. Bhamo.	Commissioner, Northern Division, and Deputy Commissioner, Bhamo.	**1. Tingrong** ... 'Nlao Ka, Tabak Ka and another small stream.	6 0	6 0	From Lumiáng track descends down an open taungya for 1 mile down to the 'Nlao Ka, 40 yards broad 2½ feet to 4½ feet deep, rocky and swift, but just passable for transport. From river ascend gently ¼ mile, then ½ mile flat and ¼ descent to small stream, 5 yards broad 9 inches deep. Road from river through thick grass, but from this last stream ascends through dense bamboo and dry kaing grass up a slippery track for 1¾ miles to village of Samakhet (3¾ miles). From here, turning westwards, road descends sharply for 1 mile through bamboo jungle to Nantabet chaung (Tabak Ka), this portion of the road being in better condition than the last 3 miles. River 35 yards broad and in shallowest place near the path 4 feet deep. No loaded mule could cross. From the river track ascends steeply for 1¼ miles to Tingrong (15 houses), road in places being rough and rocky. Distance 6 miles. The road is not good for transport. General direction of road north to Samakhet, and then west-south-west to Tingrong.

BRANCH III.

FROM LUMIÁNG (*see* STAGE 3) TO WAROR.

BY CAPT. G. H. H. COUCHMAN, MARCH 1892.

Military	Civil	Stages	Intermediate M. F.	Total M. F.	Remarks
G.O.C. Mandalay District and O.C. Bhamo.	Commissioner, Northern Division, and Deputy Commissioner, Bhamo.	**1. Waror** ... ... Möngka, Wayup, Simin, Hpáng, Yamaw, Yataw, Waror and several other smaller hill streams.	9 0	9 0	General direction south. The road descends through alternate tree jungle, bamboo jungle, and high grass and crossing four small streams for 1 mile. At first gentle descent and then steeper with occasional level pieces and a few stony places to the Möngka Ka at 1½ miles. This road is very dusty, which would be bad mud in the rains. It then goes level along the right bank of the Möngka Ka for ¼ mile, crossing on to an island over a small arm of the stream 15 yards broad.

No. 29.

FROM KÁZU TO KAO-I (ON SÁNSI ROUTE)—*continued.*

BRANCH III—*continued.*

Authorities.		Number and Names of Stages, Rivers and Streams.	Distances.		Remarks.
Military.	Civil.		Intermediate.	Total.	
G.O.C. Mandalay District and O.C. Bhamo.	Commissioner, Northern Division, and Deputy Commissioner, Bhamo.	**1. Waror**—*cont.*			It then crosses; at the crossing stream is 30 yards broad 3 feet deep, stony bottom, strong current, good water, and easy approaches. Timber and bamboos for bridge-making on either bank. The river would be quite 200 yards broad in the rains and quite impassable, except for a floating bridge attached at each end and probably not for that. The road then ascends into some terraced paddy-fields (good camping ground for 200 men and good fodder), previously crossing a small rocky stream. From here the road ascends easily through grass and small tree jungle and then high grass, crossing the Wayup Ka, 10 yards broad, rocky bed, and now temporarily bridged (bamboo bridge passable for mules), at 2 miles and going into some more terraced paddy-fields. It then descends through small trees to the Simin Ka (similar to Wayup Ka), with stony approaches, and then passes through tree jungle down to some open taungyas. From here there is a road to the right to Pôntu. The road then continues through the taungyas by an easy ascent to Mawun, just below which it recrosses the Simin Ka. Good camp here. Water and fodder good and plentiful. From Mawun general direction east. The road now descends through tree jungle for ¼ mile, when it crosses a small stream and then the Kayup Ka (3½ miles), 4 yards broad and 6 inches deep, and then ascends into some old taungyas, descending at 3¾ miles to the Hpáng Ka, 5 yards broad and 1 foot deep, with good water. From here there is a steady very steep ascent of 1,700 feet to the top of the range through high grass ferns and small trees. In places the road is stony and half-way up is on a very narrow ledge. The whole of it is very dusty and slippery from dead grass and is a little overgrown. At the top it is fairly level for ¼ mile, passing the 'Szi village of Hpao-kong at 5¼ miles, which has only three houses. The road then descends steeply first through high grass and then taungyas to the Yamaw Ka, a rocky stream, 8 yards broad and 1 foot deep (5¾ miles). It then passes over undulating ground, gradually ascending through high grass and crossing two boggy streams, 8 and 6 yards broad with 1 foot of mud and water, but not bad obstacles, to the Yataw Ka, 6 yards broad 6 inches deep, rocky bed, and good water (6¾ miles). It then ascends through open taungyas rather steeply into Kaiya village at 7½ miles. From Hpao-kong the road has occasionally very large stones on it, but is fairly good, though dusty and slippery from dead grass. From here there is a road north to Kao-i and Siba. From Kaiya the road descends steeply for ½ a mile through high grass and larch-like trees, crossing two small streams, down to the Waror Ka, parts of the road being stony and dusty and slippery as before. Waror Ka, 10 yards broad, stony bottom, good water, and easy approaches. It then ascends very steeply through first high grass and then larches and high grass to the top of the spur and then descends easily into some small terraced paddy-fields, ascending through tree jungle and rather stony ground into Waror; camp in the village at 9 miles where there is a regular kind of "village green." Fodder plentiful. Water not plentiful, coming from a spring on the east of the village. From here there is a road east to Möngkata, a Chinese village. All this road is good and has no bad obstacles, but some of the ascents and descents from Mawun are very steep. The road east appears to be good and not very steep.

FROM KÁZU TO KAO-I (ON SÁNSI ROUTE)—*continued.*

BRANCH IV.

FROM MAWUN (*see* BRANCH III) TO UPRA.

BY CAPT. G. H. H. COUCHMAN, MARCH 1892.

Authorities. Military.	Authorities. Civil.	Number and Names of Stages, Rivers and Streams.	Distances. Intermediate.	Distances. Total.	Remarks.
G.O.C. Mandalay District and O.C. Bhamo.	Commissioner, Northern Division, and Deputy Commissioner, Bhamo.	**1. Upra** ... ... Hpáng, Hláng, Shámting, Kaonar, Pumpyit, Shíjit, Moiláng, Kuntai and numerous smaller streams.	M. F. **12 0**	M. F. 12 0	General direction south. For the first ½ mile road goes down open taungyas in a direction east (*see* Branch Route No. III) and descends to the Hpáng and Hláng streams, each 5 yards broad 1 foot deep with stony bottom and good water 1 mile. It then ascends steeply through grass and fern jungle into Nawla 1½ miles. From here the road turns south-east and follows up the ridge by a gentle ascent with occasional descents and level bits. It is in parts stony and rather narrow. Jungle grass and small trees. Five small streams are crossed and Pôntu is reached at 3 miles. From Pôntu the road goes south, gradually descending to the Shámting Ka at 5 miles, the boundary between the Maráns and Sadáns. At first the road is broad, but gets more narrow lower down the spur. One small stream is crossed. Part of this road is rather stony. Jungle small trees and grass. Shámting Ka, 10 yards broad 1 foot deep, stony bottom, good water, and easy approaches. The road from here now passes through taungyas and paddy-fields, with occasional bits of small tree and grass jungle and undulating up the right bank of the Kaonar Ka, taking a south-east direction at 6 miles, which at 8 miles it crosses. All the road is good, but has stony bits on it. Between the crossings of the Shamting and Kaonar streams the road crosses the Pumpyit Ka, 10 yards broad 6 inches deep, pebbly bottom, and nine small streams, some of which are a little boggy, but form no obstacles. The road continues along the left bank of the Kownar Ka (50 yards broad 1½ feet deep, stony bottom, rapid current, good water, and no obstacle at this time of year; there is a ricketty bamboo bridge over the stream), passing a hot spring and then ascending a bare lately cleared spur in a southerly direction; at first steeply and over some stony bits and level at the top, descending at 11½ miles into some small paddy-fields and then rising for ½ a mile into Upra. The Shíjit Ka, Moiláng Ka and Kuntai Ka (all small), and six other small streams are crossed. At 6, 10 and 12¾ miles are branch roads to the left of Pumpyit, at 8½ miles a road right to Tingrakong, and at 6 miles a road right to Khumlao. Road all passable for transport. Good camp below village. Fodder and water plentiful.

BRANCH V.

FROM UPRA (*see* BRANCH IV) TO KHUNRU *viâ* MAITONG AND PUMPYIT.

BY LIEUT. J. S. DALLAS, MARCH 1892.

Military	Civil	Stages	Intermediate	Total	Remarks
G.O.C. Mandalay District and O.C. Bhamo.	Commr., Northern Divn., and Dy. Commr., Bhamo.	**1. Khunru** ... Kaonar Ka and several smaller streams.	About **8 0**	8 0	From Upra to Kownar Ka (*see* Branch IV), cannot be more than 3 miles. The road from there goes almost due north ascending up a very steep hill. After ascending the hill for half an hour the road runs west-north-west along the side of the hill for 10 minutes, when winding round north-

FROM KÁZU TO KAO-I (ON SÁNSI ROUTE)—*continued.*

BRANCH V—*continued.*

Authorities. Military.	Authorities. Civil.	Number and Names of Stages, Rivers and Streams.	Distances. Intermediate.	Distances. Total.	Remarks.
G.O.C. Mandalay District and O.C. Bhamo.	Commissioner, Northern Division, and Deputy Commissioner, Bhamo.	**1. Khunru**—*cont.*			wards it enters the village of Maitong (40 minutes). The hill from the river up to within 400 yards is covered with grass from 3 to 4 feet high with only a few trees and shrubs here and there. The village is surrounded by a thick jungle. Three small streams are crossed between the river and the village. Descending from this village the road goes south-east with an easy descent along a spur and crossing two streams on the way after 25 minutes the road suddenly turns north-east for 20 minutes along the top of a spur with only a very slight fall, when the road again turns south-east down the side of the spur and after descending for 10 minutes the road crosses a small stream about 20 feet wide and 2 feet deep running northwards, and then again ascends with a fairly easy gradient in a south-easterly direction to the village of Pumpyit (1 hour and 10 minutes). The road, as far as the last stream passes through grass of about 4 feet high, but after crossing the stream enters a jungle which grows thicker as it meets the village. From this village the road turns south-south-west and after descending for 10 minutes the road crosses a small stream and turning east for about 200 yards along the side of the hill again turns south-south-west and ascends the hill for 15 minutes and enters the village of Khunru. This road is exceptionally good, the gradient being very slight and the road about 6 or 7 feet wide passing through a jungle. The distance from the river Kaonar to the village of Khunru being about 6½ miles. From Khunru to Upra direct, *see* Branch VI-*b*. Distance 3 miles.

BRANCH VI-*a*.

FROM UPRA (*see* BRANCH IV) TO MAI-MAI *viâ* SHALAOKRÁN.

BY CAPT. G. H. H. COUCHMAN, MARCH 1892.

Authorities. Military.	Authorities. Civil.	Number and Names of Stages, Rivers and Streams.	Distances. Intermediate. M. F.	Distances. Total. M. F.	Remarks.
G.O.C. Mandalay District and O.C. Bhamo.	Commissioner, Northern Division, and Deputy Commissioner, Bhamo.	**1. Mai-mai** ... Kunlong, Mönglun, Kaonar and many smaller streams.	10 0	10 0	General direction north-east. Road descends easily and winds through grass and small tree jungle to the Kunlong Ka at 1¼ miles, passing steeply into some small paddy-fields, the last part of the hill; seven small streams are also crossed. Kunlong Ka bed, 35 yards broad, has a small island in centre, the two side streams being each about 8 yards broad and 1 foot deep, and neither an obstacle. Road then ascends over a bare hill side a little steeply, then passes through small bare hills fairly level, when it descends easily to the Kaonar Ka, travelling up along the left bank in easy undulations till it reaches the Mönglun Ka at 3½ miles, 15 yards broad 1 foot deep, and gravel bottom, and the ascent on the right bank being rather boggy. Three small streams and a bog 3 yards long but 1½ feet deep in mud and water are also crossed, and above the Mönglun Ka the road is rather stony. From the latter stream the road ascends steeply and stonily through tree jungle for ½ mile, when it is level for ¼ mile and then descends rather steeply through bare burnt hills into some paddy-fields down to the Kaonar Ka 4¾ miles, 35 yards broad 2 feet deep, large boulders in bed and a rather difficult crossing, three other small streams are crossed. There are branch roads at 3½ miles left to Khunru, 4¼ miles right to

FROM KÁZU TO KAO-I (ON SÁNSI ROUTE)—*continued.*

BRANCH VI-*a*—*continued.*

Authorities. Military.	Authorities. Civil.	Number and Names of Stages, Rivers and Streams.	Distances. Intermediate.	Distances. Total.	Remarks.
G.O.C. Mandalay District and O.C. Bhamo.	Commissioner, Northern Division, and Deputy Commissioner, Bhamo.	**1. Mai-mai**—*cont.*			Lashi-Chingkong and right from Kalyen. The road then goes through paddy-fields and then up a bare hill rather steeply, passing some small springs. At 6 miles is a road right from Lashi-Chingkong, and the road then enters tree and bamboo jungle and ascends easily into Shalaokrán. At 6¾ miles is a road left to Mai-mai. Shalaokrán is at 7 miles. From here follow the road left to Mai-mai in a north-west direction through tree jungle and bamboos and thence into cultivated fields and bare hills undulating, but gradually ascending through alternate fields and high grass and crossing two small streams, one of which has an enormous tree 5 feet in diameter for a foot-bridge up to between two knolls, when the road descends easily and, after crossing a small stream ascends easily into Mai-mai through large tree and bamboo jungle. All this road is good for transport and has no bad obstacles. Distance 10 miles.

There is a shorter route FROM UPRA TO MAI-MAI *viâ* KHUNRU as follows:—

BRANCH VI-*b*.

FROM MAI-MAI (*see* BRANCH VI-*a*) TO UPRA *viâ* KHUNRU.

BY CAPT. G. H. H. COUCHMAN, MARCH 1892.

Military.	Civil.	Stages, Rivers and Streams.	Intermediate. M.	F.	Total. M.	F.	Remarks.
G.O.C. Mandalay District and O.C. Bhamo.	Commissioner, Northern Division, and Deputy Commissioner, Bhamo.	**1. Upra** ... ... Wélán, Kaonar and numerous smaller streams.	**6**	**0**	6	0	General direction south. Road descends easily at first through tree and bamboo jungle, passing through the lower village, from which it enters taungyas and descends more steeply to the Wélán Ka, 7 yards broad 1 foot deep, stony bottom, and crossing another small stream. It then descends easily between small hills covered with burnt grass undulating over them till it gets to some taungyas from which it ascends through tree jungle into Khunru at 3 miles. Eleven small streams are crossed. From here the road descends a spur first easily through tree jungle and then steeply through taungyas to the Kaonar Ka, 50 to 60 yards broad 2 feet deep, pebbly bed, and an easy crossing with rapid current at 3¾ miles. It then passes along paddy-fields and after ½ mile begins to ascend fairly steeply along a spur up to Upra hill through grass and small tree jungle. At the top of the hill (5¼ miles) it goes nearly level into Upra 6 miles. All the road is good and no obstacles. Five small streams are crossed between Kaonar Ka and Upra.

BRANCH VII.

FROM UPRA (*see* BRANCH IV) TO PASAO (PAJAO) AND NGATONG.

BY LIEUT. RUSTON, MARCH 1892.

Military.	Civil.	Stages, Rivers and Streams.	Intermediate. M.	F.	Total. M.	F.	Remarks.
G.O.C. Mandalay Dist. and O.C. Bhamo.	Commr., Northern Divn., and Deputy Commr., Bhamo.	**1. Camp on Pasao Ka.** Kuntai, Paknoi, Pasao and numerous small streams.	**10**	**0**	10	0	General direction south-west. Left camp 7-25 A.M. The road descends for ¼ mile then over Kuntai Ka up through tree jungle for 150 yards and taungya at 300 yards, over two small streams then up gently for 4 minutes, then undulating over a small stream and up a short, stony ascent; road

FROM KÁZU TO KAO-I (ON SÁNSI ROUTE)—*continued.*

BRANCH VII—*continued.*

Authorities. Military.	Authorities. Civil.	Number and Names of Stages, Rivers and Streams.	Distances. Intermediate.	Distances. Total.	Remarks.
G.O.C. Mandalay District and O.C. Bhamo.	Commissioner, Northern Division, and Deputy Commissioner, Bhamo.	**1. Camp on Pasao Ka**—*cont.*			bad, stony, and steep, then gentle slope, good. At 7-48 road descends till 7-53 over small stream, then up through small tree jungle for 150 yards, then level for 150 yards, then ascends through bamboo and tree jungle; road here rocky and bad for 50 yards, over a small stream up for 250 yards to Teingra at 8 A.M. (1¼ miles), then down through bamboo and tree jungle for 100 yards over small stream, then up for 50 yards and down for 50 yards, over small stream through grass jungle and raspberry canes undulating, then small tree jungle till 8-12 A.M. over a small stream down gradually till 8-18 over small stream, then descends steeply for 50 yards over small stream up steeply for 20 yards over a stream 3 yards broad 6 inches deep, rocky bottom, easy approaches, up then till 8-23 steep, rocky, stony and loose soil, very bad for 20 yards, then less steep and undulating till 8-28 over small stream. Now road ascends gradually till 8-35 over a stream 3 yards broad 6 inches deep; rocky bottom, easy approaches, then up and down gently over small stream, then up steeply till 8-42 over small stream, then level for 100 yards, then up steeply for 100 yards, then gradually up till 8-48 over stream, rocky bed, through bamboo jungle. Halt for 35 minutes till 9-23, then up through taungya over small stream and through small tree jungle till 9-42, then down for 50 yards, then level for 100 yards, then down for 30 yards through cutting, level for 200 yards, then gently down to Lôngprawyán at 9-54 probably about 4 miles. Halt here till 10-48, then down over stream 4 yards broad 6 inches deep, rocky bottom, easy approaches, then level and open for 200 yards over a small stream as before, gravelly bottom, then level for 50 yards, over stream 3 yards broad 1 foot deep, then up gently through small tree jungle, then through a taungya level for 100 yards, then down to two streams 11-5, then up gently through small tree jungle for 150 yards, then level to Yawyin village of Krawyán at 11-13 6 miles, then down over small stream, then undulating small tree jungle till 11-20 over stream 2 yards broad 8 inches deep, marshy approaches, then up over a taungya gently, then down over small stream and up again till 11-35 through small tree jungle, down over small stream and up again then down over small stream up rocky ascent for 100 yards through bamboo jungle, level, then up through winding cutting, steep and rocky for 100 yards, then level for 150 yards, then down gently for 150 yards through lemon grass, at 11-48 over small stream, then up for 50 yards through grass jungle, then down for 50 yards over small stream, up gently over old taungya for ¼ mile, then down gently through bamboo jungle for 30 yards, then generally level through big tree and bamboo jungle till 12-18 over stream, 6 feet broad 8 inches deep, marshy approaches, then through open tree jungle for 150 yards, over stream 12 feet broad 8 inches deep, easy approaches, then up over taungya undulating for 200 yards, through bamboo jungle over two small streams up a steep ascent for 50 yards till 12-30, over Paknoi Ka about 8¼ miles, 25 yards broad 1 foot deep, easy approaches, stony bottom, then gently ascends over old taungya into bamboo jungle, and then up and down over a small stream, through a taungya and down to camp at 1 P.M. on Pasao Ka, 15 yards broad 8 inches deep, easy approaches, stony bottom. Distance 10 miles. Here the roads to Pasao and Ngatong divide.

FROM KÁZU TO KAO-I (ON SÁNSI ROUTE)—*continued.*

BRANCH VII—*continued.*

Authorities. Military.	Authorities. Civil.	Number and Names of Stages, Rivers and Streams.	Distances. Intermediate. M. F.	Distances. Total. M. F.	Remarks.
G.O.C. Mandalay District and O.C. Bhamo.	Commissioner, Northern Division, and Deputy Commissioner, Bhamo.	**2. Pasao** ... ... Several small streams.	2 2	12 2	General direction south. Left camp on Pasao Ka 7-30. Road level at first for 100 yards and good, then down over a small stream. It runs generally along left bank of Pasao Ka through grass and bamboo jungle. After 300 yards road is undulating crossing two small streams. Then at 7-40 over a stream, 6 yards broad and 1 foot deep, muddy bottom, boggy approaches. Then at 20 yards over small stream and at 50 yards it gently ascends for 100 yards, then level for 100 yards over boggy bit, 2 yards wide, then undulating, but gradually rising over two small streams. The road now ascends for ¼ mile and is stony, after that down for 300 yards through bamboo jungle, road good and undulating, at 7-55 through big tree and bamboo jungle over two boggy pieces 10 and 6 yards broad, then over two small streams and then ascends for 100 yards, then level for 50 yards over a small stream up for 50 yards, then level and good. After 200 yards over boggy stream, 2 yards broad, then up stony ascent for 50 yards, steep, level for 30 yards, then down steep, stony descent for 100 yards over two small streams, then up steep, winding, stony ascent, bad road for 150 yards, then less steep and good; road through open ground for ½ mile to top of hill, then level for 200 yards over a small stream to village of Pasao at 8-15, 2¼ miles.
		or **2. Ngatong** ... Several small streams.	2 0	12 0	Leaving the camp which was on the right bank of the Pasao Ka, the road crosses the river and proceeds in a south-westerly direction, rising gradually for 5 minutes and then turns west rising to a height of about 200 feet above the camp, then descends about 50 feet, and turns gradually northwards for about 200 yards along the side of the hill, then descends with an easy gradient for 5 minutes, almost due north, when the road becomes steep for another 5 minutes and, crossing a small stream, turns north-west and after 150 yards crosses another small stream. The road so far passes through male bamboo and scrub with but few trees which now become more plentiful. The road now continues north-west through thick jungle for 8 minutes, still ascending, and after going 150 yards along a fairly good road it descends in the same direction for 8 minutes. The road is very bad from here, being much cut up and rocky. The road now turns west for 6 minutes and enters the village of Ngatong. Distance by time 50 minutes or about 2 miles.

BRANCH VIII-*a*.

FROM UPRA (*see* BRANCH IV) TO SEINTONG *viâ* LASHI-CHINGKONG.

BY CAPT. G. H. H. COUCHMAN, MARCH 1892.

Military	Civil	Stage	Inter. M. F.	Total M. F.	Remarks
G.O.C. Mandalay Dist., and O.C. Bhamo.	Commr., Northern Divn., and Deputy Commr., Bhamo.	**1. Seintong** ... Kumlong, Nlong, Mönglum, Punti and many smaller streams.	11 0	11 0	General direction east. Road passes through village of Upra, descending and passing over two small boggy streams; goes through small tree jungle and new-cleared taungyas to the Kumlong Ka (½ a mile), 4 yards broad,

FROM KÁZU TO KAO-I (ON SÁNSI ROUTE)—*continued.*

BRANCH VIII-*a*—*continued.*

Authorities. Military.	Authorities. Civil.	Number and Names of Stages, Rivers and Streams.	Distances. Inter-mediate.	Distances. Total.	Remarks.
G.O.C. Mandalay District and O.C. Bhamo.	Commissioner, Northern Division, and Deputy Commissioner, Bhamo.	**1. Seintong**—*cont.*			stony bottom, and good water. From here it is fairly level, passing between small bare hills and then down to the Nlong Ka (1¼ miles), 8 yards broad 2 feet deep, stony bed. It then ascends fairly steeply through grass and small tree jungle and there are occasional stony bits for ½ mile, descending easily to Kalyen (2¼ miles) through which a small boggy stream flows. It still continues to descend easily through taungyas and between small hills, stony in places, down to the Mönglum Ka (3¼ miles), stony bed, 1½ feet deep, 25 yards broad, with ricketty bamboo foot-bridge. The stones are fairly large in the crossing, but it is not a bad obstacle. Road then ascends by easy gradients to Tung-fut (5 miles) over bare, newly cleared hills, there being a little tree jungle on the top. From here the road descends into some paddy-fields which lie in a regular basin, through which runs a small boggy stream. Then easy ascent between small bare hills into tree jungle and into Kachang (6¼ miles) in which is a small muddy stream, and then, after crossing Punti Ka, 7 yards wide 1 foot deep (at 7¼ miles) and a small stream ascending fairly steeply through tree jungle into Lashi-Chingkong. The road now goes south-east and descends easily through grass for ¼ mile to a small stream. It then ascends steeply and stonily for ¼ mile through small hills and then easily for ⅛ mile, the latter over bare hill-tops. It then descends easily through small bare hills, crossing two small streams. At 8¾ miles is a branch road right to Kacháng (2 miles), an offshoot of the village mentioned before which is situated in a hollow among the hill-tops, and then descends into some open poppy-fields at about 9 miles after crossing a small stream. From here the road descends fairly steeply to the Mönglum Ka and then ascends very steeply through small tree jungle to the frontier village of Seintong 11 miles. All this road is good and has no bad obstacles. Forage is scarce, as all the country has been burnt to make taungyas, but water is plentiful.

There is an alternative route between Upra and Seintong *viâ* Upai and Tingya which joins the above route at poppy-fields between 2 and 3 miles beyond Kacháng as follows:—

BRANCH VIII-*b*.

FROM POPPY-FIELDS NEAR KACHÁNG (*see* BRANCH VIII-*a*) TO UPRA.

BY CAPT. G. H. H. COUCHMAN, MARCH 1892.

Military	Civil	Stages	Intermediate	Total	Remarks
			M. F.	M. F.	
G.O.C. Mandalay District and O.C. Bhamo.	Commissioner, Northern Division, and Deputy Commissioner, Bhamo.	**1. Upra** ... ... Mönglum, Shingnum and other small streams.	8 0	8 0	Road goes west and descends through open cultivation and bare hills to the Mönglum Ka at 1 mile, 20 yards broad and 1½ feet deep; stony bottom; then west through paddy-fields, after which ascend a bare hill crossing a small stream. Ascent steep, then level along hillside, then descending steeply and stonily to Shingnum Ka (2¼ miles) 10 yards broad 1 foot deep, stony bottom, having previously crossed a small bog, 10 yards broad and 1 foot deep; then up easily a bare hill into Tingya 3¼ miles. Descend from here down a stony bit steeply and then easily crossing a small stream to

FROM KÁZU TO KAO-I (ON SÁNSI ROUTE)—*continued.*

BRANCH VIII-*b*—*continued.*

Authorities.		Number and Names of Stages, Rivers and Streams.	Distances.		Remarks.
Military.	Civil.		Intermediate.	Total.	
G.O.C. Mandalay District and O.C. Bhamo.	Commissioner, Northern Division, and Deputy Commissioner, Bhamo.	**1. Upra**—*cont.*			another stream at 4 miles; rocky bed; 8 yards broad and 1 foot deep; then easy ascent through grass and small tree jungle through undulating hills, crossing three small streams to Upai 5½ miles. The road ascends steeply through village, and then descends at first easily and then steeply through grass and small tree crossing a small stream. It then ascends and crosses a ridge by an easy ascent, descending through paddy-fields and bare hillsides to the Kunlang Ka and then up a bare hill to Upra. All road good. Distance 8 miles.

BRANCH IX.

FROM UPRA TO TINGRAKONG *viâ* KUMLAO, WURRAKRÁNG AND SHIRAWKONG.

BY LIEUT. J. S. DALLAS, 23RD MARCH 1892.

Military.	Civil.	Number and Names of Stages, Rivers and Streams.	Intermediate.	Total.	Remarks.
			M. F.	M. F.	
G.O.C. Mandalay District and O.C. Bhamo.	Commissioner, Northern Division, and Deputy Commissioner, Bhamo.	**1. Tingrakong** ... Kaonar Ka and ten other streams, mostly small.	About **12 0**	12 0	From Upra to Kaonar Ka about 3 miles, *see* Branches IV and V. The road turns due west from the river along paddy beds and after 20 minutes crosses a large stream, about 18 yards wide and from 2 to 3 feet deep, running north into the Kaonar Ka; there is a swamp on both sides of this river. Ten minutes further on the road begins an easy ascent, turning north-west for 15 minutes. Leaving the paddy beds the road enters a jungle with thick undergrowth, but not very thick with trees; the road now turns west for 10 minutes, when trees became scarcer, the road now descends for about 50 feet and crossing a stream, about 10 yards wide and 2 feet deep running north-east, again rises northwards for 10 minutes and, winding round the base of a large knoll eastwards, enters a cutting in solid rocks about 150 yards long and 3 feet wide, the rocks on either side being about 18 or 20 feet high, with thick jungle. Passing through this cutting the road passes over a stream of about 8 feet wide which supplies the village of Kumlao with water (1 hour 25 minutes). From this village the road ascends for quarter of an hour up a steep knoll, almost due west, and then turns south down a very steep and difficult gradient, the road also being bad and very rocky. After descending for 20 minutes the road crosses a stream running west, and then turns south-west for 10 minutes, and crossing another small stream passes through some paddy-fields, and after continuing south-west for another 10 minutes turns south ascending the hill for 15 minutes into the village of Wurrawkráng (2 hours 35 minutes). With the exception of the paddy-fields the road is entirely through a thick jungle. From this village the road runs almost due east to Shirawkong. For the first 25 minutes the road ascends through the jungle and winding round for about 200 yards round the brow of the hill descends for 30 minutes, crossing a small stream about half way down and a larger one at this point. The road now ascends still eastward for 10 minutes into the village of Shirawkong, 3 hours 40 minutes. From here the road ascends with a very steep gradient along a base of a hill for 10 minutes, when the road crosses a stream 20 yards wide and 3 feet deep, running north (crossed before on way

FROM KÁZU TO KAO-I (ON SÁNSI ROUTE)—*continued.*

BRANCH IX—*continued.*

Authorities. Military.	Authorities. Civil.	Number and Names of Stages, Rivers and Streams.	Distances. Intermediate.	Distances. Total.	Remarks.
G.O.C. Mandalay Dist. and O.C. Bhamo.	Commr., Northern Division, and Deputy Commr., Bhamo.	**1. Tingrakong**—*cont.*			to Kumlao). Still continuing south-east the road ascends for half an hour up a steep side of the hill and turning south-south-east for 10 minutes crosses a small stream and descends for 15 minutes in the same direction, crosses another small stream and ascends for 20 minutes south-east into the village of Tingrakong. The road after crossing the large stream is through jungle. Total 5 hours 5 minutes or about 9 miles from Kaonar Ka, 13 miles from Upra.

No. 30.

From KÁZU to SADÔN (FORT HARRISON), (Myitkyina Sub-Division).

BY CAPT. G. H. H. COUCHMAN, D.S.O. SOMERSETSHIRE LIGHT INFANTRY, FEBRUARY 1892.

Military	Civil	Stages	Intermediate	Total	Remarks
G.O.C. Mandalay District and O.C. Bhamo.	Commissioner, Northern Division and Deputy Commissioner, Bhamo.	**1. Makawng Camp.** 'Nkum Ka, Pumwai Ka and many smaller streams.	M. F. 10 4	M. F. 10 4	General direction north-east. Up to the village of Loilaw the road passes through bamboo and tree jungle and one taungya for 5 miles, then through kaing grass for a mile and the remainder through paddy-fields. At ¼ mile from Kázu there is a road left to Laiphong. All the road is good throughout, but through the latter part the tree jungle is rather narrow and a little overgrown; 19 dry nullahs, two streams, and four bogs are crossed besides the Pumwai Ka twice. The dry nullahs and streams are none of them obstacles nor are the bogs, except one about 2 miles short of the second crossing of the Pumwai. This is 25 yards broad and 1½ feet deep in mud and water. The Pumwai is 10 yards broad (8 at second crossing), with gravel bottom, 2 feet deep, and easy approaches. The second crossing has a sort of plank bridge composed of a felled tree with planed top and also a bamboo bridge. From here to Sampai is a long ½ mile, total 8 miles. The Pumwai is crossed as again (as before but only 4 yards broad). Road across paddy plain; two dry nullahs are crossed. From here the road is good and broad through a belt of kaing grass and bamboos on to some paddy plains, crossing muddy stream of 9 feet broad and 1 foot deep which is no obstacle, and also a dry nullah, and Kachaung is reached at 9½ miles. The road now crosses the 'Nkum Ka, 7 yards broad 1 foot deep, good water and easy approaches, through a little bamboo jungle into paddy-fields for ½ a mile and then into grass, and at 10½ miles reach the Makawng paddy-fields; camp good; grass and water very plentiful, the latter from two streams one on each side of the plain. Makawng village is at the northern end of the plain ½ a mile off. From Makawng camp, Stage 1, there are alternative routes to Kanjiyong, Stage 2, and Wabong, Stage 3, *vide* Alternatives I and II. Good grazing here and room for 2,000 men.
		2. Kanjiyong ... Pumwai, Manwai, Shikum, Lamien and several smaller streams.	13 0	23 4	From here the road continues along the paddy-fields still going in a north-east direction, and then enters kaing grass and crosses a small stream twice, and then the Pumwai Ka, which is 12 yards

FROM KÂZU TO SADÔN (FORT HARRISON), (MYITKYINA SUB-DIVISION)—*continued.*

Authorities.		Number and Names of Stages, Rivers and Streams.	Distances.		Remarks.
Military.	Civil.		Intermediate.	Total.	
G.O.C. Mandalay District and O.C. Bhamo.	Commissioner, Northern Division, and Deputy Commissioner, Bhamo.	**2. Kanjiyong**—*cont.*			broad 6 inches deep, and stony bottom, with easy crossing. From here the road ascends very steeply for 1,200 feet over slippery, red clay through kaing grass and fern and small tree jungle on to the top of the ridge on which is the Kachin village of 'Nsingkong (3½ miles). About ½ a mile from the top it is joined by a good broad road from the left (from ?); and from here to the village is an easy ascent along the ridge through tree jungle. The road passes through the village and then descends easily for ¼ mile and is good and broad. At 4½ miles there is a road left to Lajing which is visible from here about 300 yards below. A road here branches off to the right and the track now becomes very steep and narrow, descending through dense grass and bamboo along a spur, and it is much overgrown with slippery, red clay soil and occasional stony bits. It descends 1,100 feet down to the Manwai Ka (15 yards broad 2 feet deep, stony bottom, and good water), having just before crossed a small, stony stream, 2 feet broad (no obstacle). From here the road ascends steeply for 300 feet on to the top of the small ridge, jungle as before, till at 3½ miles from Lajing it meets a good road from the left (from ?) and goes fairly level into Kanzé village (7½ miles) passing through tree and bamboo jungle. From here it descends and after ½ mile the good road goes to the right and the track becomes overgrown and bad again through high grass along a hillside, and is very steep down to the Shikum Ka, 9 feet broad 6 inches deep, and good water. Fodder: grass plentiful here. It now descends along the valley easily down to the Lamien Ka, having previously crossed a small unimportant stream. The road crosses the Lamien Ka twice going across an island; about 250 yards broad. The first crossing is 20 yards broad 1 foot deep, with rocky bed, and is no obstacle; the second crossing is 15 yards broad 2½ feet deep, with rapid stream and huge boulders, and is difficult crossing for transport. There is a very good water here. After crossing a small stream the road ascends easily through taungyas for ½ mile and it is here very good. It then enters tree and bamboo jungle and descends gently for ¼ mile into high grass, crossing five small streams. It here joins good broad open road from the left (from ?) and then enters a small paddy plain belonging to the Chinese-Shan village of Kanjiyong, and in which are two small streams. Good water here and grass and room for 500 men to camp. Distance 13 miles.
			M. F.	M. F.	
		3. Wabong ... 'Ntong Ka.	3 4	27 0	From here the road is good through grass and small tree jungle, except at the crossing of the 'Ntong Ka to which there is a steep and slippery descent of 30 yards. The stream is 12 yards broad and 6 inches deep and no obstacle in itself. The course is rough, tortuous and stony. The road then is good, undulating along old overgrown taungyas, after which it ascends very steeply indeed to the village of Wabong Uma (2½ miles), passing through high grass and clump of trees at the top. From here the road ascends still more steeply and is rough and stony in places through tree jungle into Wabong. This makes a fair camp; bamboo fodder; camp in village. Water from two springs below and to the east of the village.

FROM KÁZU TO SADÔN (FORT HARRISON), (MYITKYINA SUB-DIVISION)—*continued.*

Authorities. Military.	Authorities. Civil.	Number and Names of Stages, Rivers and Streams.	Distances. Intermediate. M. F.	Distances. Total. M. F.	Remarks.
G.O.C. Mandalay District and O.C. Bhamo.	Commissioner, Northern Division, and Deputy Commissioner, Bhamo.	**4. Pôkwán** ... 'Nwán, Mangna, Segwai and other smaller streams.	**6 0**	33 0	From here the road still continues north-east and descends steeply through grass and bamboo jungle with small trees, and through some old taungyas to 'Nwán Ka, crossing two small unimportant streams. From here the road ascends very steeply indeed through taungyas passing two nearly dry streams into tree jungle and then on to the top of the ridge on which is Lapum village (3 miles) through which it passes. It then descends through tree jungle into grass through which the road is very steep and slippery and narrow down to the Mangna Ka, 10 yards broad 1 foot deep and stony bottom. From here the road goes into paddy-fields which are too damp for a camp and then after crossing two small streams ascends steeply up through high, feathery grass, and small tree jungle up to the village of Pôkwán at 6 miles. Camping ground. Water from springs and scarce bamboo fodder.
		5. Sadôn Post (Fort Harrison). Namli Ka.	**11 2**	44 2	From here the road still continues in a north-east direction and descends from the village down a steep and slippery piece down to the Segwai Ka, 3 feet deep 20 yards broad and rocky bed; 200 yards further on it crosses a small rocky stream. The first is rather a bad obstacle for transport. From here the road ascends steeply through grass and bamboos for 1½ miles and then is level into 'Mbukong village through tree jungle. It ascends through the village and passes through high grass between two hills into bamboo and small tree jungle, descending very steeply indeed over open taungyas to the Namli Ka, which is 40 yards broad 3 feet deep, with very rapid stream. This is a very difficult crossing indeed. There are two bamboo suspension bridges here, but neither are fit for mules. The stream bed is full of big boulders. From here the road ascends steeply for 1 mile through grass into some tree jungle, beyond which is Sadôn village, a very large Kachin village. The post, which is now named Fort Harrison,* is ½ a mile further up on the top of the hill. The last three marches are very hard ones on account of the steep hills and numerous broad and rapid torrents to be crossed. It would be much improved by cutting the overgrown portions. It would probably be impassable in the rains unless well bridged.

ALTERNATIVE I.

FROM KANJIYONG (STAGE 2) TO MAKAWNG (STAGE 1) *viâ* LOISAW.

BY LIEUT. MAYNARD, DEVONSHIRE REGIMENT, MARCH 1892.

Military	Civil	Stages	Intermediate	Total	Remarks
G.O.C. Mandalay Dist. and O.C. Bhamo.	Commr., Northern Divn., and Deputy Commr., Bhamo.	**1. Loisaw** ... Pungyi, Endaw, Upai, Myen and Namion streams.	**15 0**	15 0	General direction west-north-west. Road ascends gently out of paddy-fields for ¾ mile, then descends ⅛ mile to Pungyi Ka, 6 yards broad and 1½ feet deep. Is flat for next ⅛ mile, then cross Endaw Ka (similar to Pungyi Ka), and then ascends for 1 mile through bamboo jungle and ½ mile through kaing grass and then still ascending reaches Waradut at 3½ miles. Road throughout very good.

* After Captain T. Harrison, D.S.O., R.E., who defended the post successfully against very overwhelming numbers of the Kachyins in February 1892.

FROM KÂZU TO SADÔN (FORT HARRISON), (MYITKYINA SUB-DIVISION)—*continued.*

ALTERNATIVE I—*continued.*

Authorities. Military.	Authorities. Civil.	Number and Names of Stages, Rivers and Streams.	Distances. Intermediate.	Distances. Total.	Remarks.
G.O.C. Mandalay District and O.C. Bhamo.	Commissioner, Northern Division, and Deputy Commissioner, Bhamo.	**1. Loisaw**—*cont.*			The road now descends for ¾ mile over large open taungyas and then enters tree jungle still descending for ¼ mile, the next 1¼ miles being undulating through bamboo jungle, the next ¼ mile being a gentle slope down and then a drop of ½ mile through thick dark jungle, with bamboos interlacing overhead, to the Upai Ka bed, 15 yards broad; 1 foot of water, 10 yards broad; rocky bed. Road all along good and much used by transport animals. Road then ascends up hill through jungle as before, then ¼ mile down through taungyas to the plain to the Myen Ka, 25 yards broad, 1½ feet deep; jungle thinner. Road for the next mile crosses several small hills and then for ½ mile ascends gently, then 1 mile steep ascent to Mai-li-katawng, 9½ miles, 13 houses. From here the road is level for ½ mile, and then descends for ½ mile, the last part being rough and stony, to the Namien Ka, 6 yards broad, 1 foot deep, and then level for 1 mile, then through a cleared track, 60 yards broad, for ½ mile into paddy-fields with large open tree jungle on right of road into Loisaw 15 miles. All road very good. Camp in paddy-fields. Water from Namien forage good and plentiful.
		2. Makawng ... Pumwai Ka and three small streams.	M. F. **14 4**	M. F. 29 4	General direction south-east. Back along road in last stage as far as Mai-li-katawng 5½ miles, the road descends ¾ mile, first through bamboo jungle and then taungyas down to a small stream, then ascending to Maisenkong (six houses) at 7½ miles, some parts of the road being very steep, but in good order. From Maisenkong the road is level for ½ mile, then descends gently through kaing grass for 1 mile to small stream, after which it ascends for ¼ mile and is then level for ½ mile to Kunkao village (10 houses); at 10¼ miles road good all along. Road from here rises suddenly for 300 yards, and then a long easy descent for nearly 2 miles; road good through bamboo and kaing grass, after which it is level for a short distance and then rises gently for 1 mile to Kumtáng (13 miles), this part of the road not being so good for transport as it is overgrown with bamboos and kaing grass. Kumtáng, six houses. From here the road descends rapidly for ¾ mile through kaing grass and bamboos down to a small stream, then up a steep knoll and then down again ½ mile to another stream (Pumwai Ka) and on to the Makawng paddy-fields reached at 14½ miles.

ALTERNATIVE II.

FROM WABONG (STAGE 3) TO MAKAWNG (SHAN), (STAGE 1).

BY CAPT. G. H. H. COUCHMAN, D.S.O., MARCH 1892.

Military	Civil	Stage	Intermediate	Total	Remarks
G.O.C. Mandalay District and O.C. Bhamo.	Commr., Northern Divn., and Deputy Commr., Bhamo.	**1. Pônkán** ... Namien Ka and small streams.	**9 0**	9 0	General direction south. The road ascends along the spur with occasional descents up fairly easy through small tree and bamboo jungle to the village of Lashi (1½ miles), just before which it crosses a small muddy stream and

FROM KÁZU TO SADÔN (FORT HARRISON), (MYITKYINA SUB-DIVISION)—*continued.*

ALTERNATIVE II—*continued.*

Authorities. Military.	Authorities. Civil.	Number and Names of Stages, Rivers and Streams.	Distances. Intermediate.	Distances. Total.	Remarks.
G.O.C. Mandalay District and O.C. Bhamo.	Commissioner, Northern Division, and Deputy Commissioner, Bhamo.	**1. Pônkán**—*cont.*			is good for transport throughout. After passing through the village it ascends still more steeply into some taungyas and afterwards is fairly level through high grass. At 2½ miles a road branches off to the left and east to the Yawyin village of Numlao ('Nlao) which is said to be two-day journey distant. The road now goes south-west through bamboos and grass on a hill side, with one rather steep descent and ascent, and is here very narrow. At 2¾ miles it meets a branch road from the east from Numlao, and then descends very steeply and over loose stones and soil through high grass for a mile when it enters tree and bamboo jungle, after ½ a mile of which it reaches Ningtáp village (4 miles). Fodder plentiful here and water from several small streams. Camp in village. All this road is easy for transport. From here the road goes nearly due south and then descends through tree jungle and bamboos and high grass down to the Namien Ka at 6 miles, passing a large Kachin house belonging to Ningtáp at 4¾ miles. Road good and an easy descent except the last ½ mile, which is very steep, and the descent into the stream a little stony. Namien Ka is 20 yards broad; a rocky torrent with large boulders, 1½ feet deep at crossing, which is no obstacle, with deep pools here and there. Road ascends very steeply for ¼ mile, the first 10 yards being stony, through high grass, and then easier ascent with occasional small descents along a spur crossing a small muddy stream at 7 miles, and then through old taungyas and then up very steeply for ¾ mile into Pônkán, 9 miles. Good camp in village here. Grass and water plentiful.
		2. Makawng ... Pumwé Ka and several small streams.	M. 10 F. 4	M. 19 F. 4	From here the road still continues south and rises steadily, first through bamboo and tree jungle, and then small tree and grass, still up the ridge, till at 1½ miles it descends a little out of some old taungyas and then goes up a slight ascent to the top of the range. It then follows the top of the range in a westerly direction through high grass, descending at first steeply and then more easily to 3 miles when, after meeting a road from the right from Makôk, it turns south-west passing a small spring at 3¼ miles and thence into Shirikong village 3½ miles. From here the road is comparatively level, descending a little through tree jungle into Foknoi 4½ miles. From here the road turns north-west and follows the ridge down to Makawng (Kachin) 7 miles, descending all the way, with the exception of a few easy ascents. Jungle alternately, trees, bamboos, and grass. In places the the road is cut into a hillside, and is here often very narrow. Half-a-mile before one reaches Makawng the road joins one from Makôk, which is visible ½ mile before about ¾ mile to right of the road, and then is good and broad down to Makawng (Kachin) 10½ miles. Camp ¼ mile beyond village. Water and fodder good and plentiful, the former from a stream 5 feet wide. All this road is good and easy for transport, though from the dry grass and leaves it is very slippery for men, but not animals, to walk on. Time from Ningtáp to Makawng, 4½ hours for troops and 6 hours

FROM KÁZU TO SADÔN (FORT HARRISON), (MYITKYINA SUB-DIVISION)—*continued.*

ALTERNATIVE II—*continued.*

Authorities. Military.	Authorities. Civil.	Number and Names of Stages, Rivers and Streams.	Distances. Inter-mediate.	Distances. Total.	Remarks.
G.O.C. Mandalay Dist., and O.C. Bhamo.	Commr., Northern Divn., and Dy. Commr., Bhamo.	**2. Makawng**—*cont.*			for transport. From here the road goes west descending a well made and kept track through alternate grass and tree jungle and a few taungyas. It crosses four small streams and the Pumwé Ka at 19 miles; a rocky stream 1 foot deep and 10 yards broad. The approaches to this are steep, but not difficult otherwise and the crossing easy. After a steep ascent of about 200 yards the road descends fairly steeply to Makawng (Shan). At 8¼ miles a road enters this one from Tingra from the right or north. All this latter portion is good-going. Distance estimated by time.

FROM NINGTÁP (*vide* Stage 1 of this Branch Route) there is a road TO SÁNSI, six stages as follow:—

Military	Civil	Stages	Inter-mediate M. F.	Total M. F.	Remarks
G.O.C. Mandalay District and O.C. Bhamo.	Commissioner, Northern Division, and Deputy Commissioner, Bhamo.	**1. Tainpwot** ...	...	...	An old village; no houses; fair road.
		2. Nan Lao ...	...	...	Yawyin village; 50 houses; road good; water plentiful.
		3. Séden	...	...	Yawyin village; 100 houses; on the plain; fair road.
		4. Hponkaw ...	...	...	Szi village; 15 houses on a hill; road good.
		5. Htwan Hpaw.	...	...	Shan and Chinese village on plain; 80 houses; road good.
		6. Sánsi	...	...	About 400 houses; brick walls 7 cubits high, 2 cubits thick. Soldiers here last year. No cannon; has a fair every five days.

BRANCH I.

FROM 'MBUKONG (*vide* STAGE 5) TO PUMKATAWNG.

BY CAPT. G. H. H. COUCHMAN, D.S.O., MARCH 1892.

Military	Civil	Stages	Inter-mediate M. F.	Total M. F.	Remarks
G.O.C. Mandalay District and O.C. Bhamo.	Commissioner, Northern Division, and Deputy Commissioner, Bhamo.	**1. Pumkatawng**... Kwimaw Ka and small stream.	2 4	2 4	General direction south-south-east. Road descends easily down to the Kwimaw Ka through grass and ferns and over one small stream and is in good order. Distance ¾ mile. There are some small terraced paddy-fields to the left at the bottom. The crossing of the stream is bad, there being a steep and stony drop into it, whilst the stream has large boulders and a strong current. It is 15 or 20 yards broad and has a small temporary bamboo bridge over it. Water good and 1 foot deep. The road now goes for 250 yards through some more paddy-fields and then crosses a small stream. From here it ascends steeply with two short bits nearly level to Pyángpraw (1½ miles), passing through grass and small tree jungle. There are only two small houses here. The road now ascends very steeply into Pumkatawng (2½ miles), the last part being not so very steep. Jungle as before. Road good. There is a branch road west from here to Pakwán (Seninkong). Fodder and grass plentiful all along this route. There is a very small stream running through the village of Pumkatawng which has only eight houses.

No. 31.

From KÁZU to WAINGMAW.

By Lieut. J. F. DALLAS, April 1892.

Authorities. Military.	Authorities. Civil.	Number and Names of Stages, Rivers and Streams.	Distances. Intermediate. M.	Distances. Intermediate. F.	Distances. Total. M.	Distances. Total. F.	Remarks.
G.O.C. Mandalay District and O.C. Bhamo.	Commissioner, Northern Division, and Deputy Commissioner, Bhamo.	**1. Namlum Ka** ... Nampumwé, Namlum and another stream.	**12**	**4**	12	4	General direction north-north-west. From Kázu the road goes west for a short distance through tree jungle, then passing through a cotton field enters a bamboo jungle crossing the Nampumwé Ka about ¾ of a mile from Kázu, and following the course of the Nantabet chaung for 3¼ miles turns north-west and crossing a small stream enters tree jungle and continues in a northward direction for 1½ miles and then enters an open plain and turning west skirts the jungle for 500 yards and again enters the jungle for a mile, then turning north-west winds along the open plain for 3 miles when the Maipanktum well is reached (about 9 miles), the water of which is good and appears to be plentiful, but there is no signs of water between this and the river in either direction. From the well the road turns north 1½ miles and then north-west to the Namlum Ka 2 miles further on. Total distance 12½ miles.
		2. Waingmaw ... A large stream.	**8**	**6**	21	2	The road now follows the course of the river for ½ mile eastward and then crossing it turns almost due north for 4½ miles, then turning north-north-west enters the village of Thágaya at 7¼ miles. From here the road again turns north and crossing a large stream enters the village of Waingmaw about 1½ miles further on. The road, the whole way from Kázu, is good and level, there being only one slight incline about 6 miles from Kázu. The Namlum Ka is almost dry in April and what water there is is dirty, and consequently the whole distance may have to be done in one march, which is possible, though of course a long march.

No. 32.

From KYAUKMYAUNG (Irrawaddy) to KABWET (Irrawaddy).

By Lieut. HUGHES, 2nd Oxfordshire Light Infantry, March 1888.

Authorities. Military.	Authorities. Civil.	Number and Names of Stages, Rivers and Streams.	Distances. Intermediate. M.	Distances. Intermediate. F.	Distances. Total. M.	Distances. Total. F.	Remarks.
G.O.C. Mandalay District.	Commissioner, Northern Division, and Deputy Commissioner, Shwébo.	**1. Ma-u** ...	**12**	**0**	12	0	General direction north, for the most part along the bank of the Irrawaddy. Fair cart road in dry season. Pass Sitha at 6 miles. Accommodation for 50 men.
		2. Kabwet ...	**8**	**4**	20	4	Road on is very rough and difficult for carts even in dry season *viâ* Tônbin and Kyibun. Between Tônbin and Kyibun there is a creek impassable for carts, which have to make a long detour inland. Kabwet is on the river, just north of the point where it takes a large bend eastward to Thingadaw. It used to be a large trading village. Roads lead from here through the jungle to Tántabin, and to Kinu (on the Shwébo-Tántabin road). There is good anchorage for steamers throughout the year, and the trade is consequently expected to increase.

No. 33.

From KYAUKMYAUNG (Irrawaddy) to THAMBAUK and MAUKADAW (Chindwin) viâ SHWÉBO and YÉ-U.

By Lieut. T. F. B. RENNY TAILYOUR, R.E., and others, 1887 and 1888.

Authorities.		Number and Names of Stages, Rivers and Streams.	Distances.				Remarks.
Military.	Civil.		Intermediate.		Total.		
			M.	F.	M.	F.	
G.O.C. Mandalay District.	Commissioner, Northern Division, and Deputy Commissioner, Shwébo.	**1. Ombôk** ...	7	4	7	4	A road from Kyaukmyaung to Yé-u *viâ* Shwébo is being made by the Public Works Department. All bridges have been completed except that over the Mu river. The piles average 1 foot in diameter, the roadway is about 10 feet broad, and they are strong enough to bear guns and heavy wagons. Where the road passes through jungle the jungle has been cleared to a breadth of 40 yards, and it is raised wherever it passes through paddy or low ground. Breadth of roadway 15 to 18 feet, breadth between ditches 18 yards. Streams and nullahs are all dry during the dry season, with exception of the Mu river. The moat at Shwébo contains water throughout the year, the road crossing on a bund. Kyaukmyaung has 200 houses extending 500 yards along the river bank. Good water can be obtained from the midstream of the Irrawaddy. Accommodation can be obtained for 200 men in the stockade north of the village on the river bank. There is good anchorage at the stockade for two steamers. Further accommodation could be obtained for 200 men in a kyaung ¼ mile north of the stockade. One zayát at the south end of the village would hold 30 men. At Naungaing, about a mile further down the bank, there are three zayáts that would hold 40 men. All the Flotilla Company's steamers passing up or down the river call here, and there is a daily ferry steamer to and from Mandalay. The general direction of the road to Shwébo is west, rising gradually as far as Ombôk through jungle for 6¼ miles, the first 2 miles thick and impenetrable, afterwards penetrable with smaller trees ; the soil is sandy and in some places hard. At 1¼ miles cross bridge over stream (dry in February). At 4 miles pass former site of village named Odwin, where there is a tank (dry in February). Here there is plenty of sandstone rock available for road-mending. At 6¼ miles paddy cultivation is reached. At 7½ miles the village of Ombôk with 50 houses. The police post is just east of the village, on the south side of the road, enclosed by parapet and stockade about 40 yards square. Good water can be obtained in the rains from a stream ¼ mile south-east of the village. There are three wells with good water, one being inside the police post. Accommodation in Public Works Department bungalow and sheds just north of the road for 40 men. Kyaung opposite (40 men) and one zayát (10 men). No accommodation at police post for more than 28 police now occupying it. (From Ombôk there is a road south to Heléngyi, 11 miles, practicable for carts at all seasons). Also a road north to Tama, 10 miles, and on northwards to Baw, which was formerly much used by dacoits.

No. 33.

FROM KYAUKMYAUNG (IRRAWADDY) TO THAMBAUK AND MAUKADAW (CHINDWIN) *viâ* SHWÉBO AND YÉ-U—*continued.*

Authorities. Military.	Authorities. Civil.	Number and Names of Stages, Rivers and Streams.	Distances. Intermediate. M.	Distances. Intermediate. F.	Distances. Total. M.	Distances. Total. F.	Remarks.
G.O.C. Mandalay District.	Commissioner, Northern Division, and Deputy Commissioner, Shwébo.	**2. Shwébo** ... Mugalé river, 20 yards broad, dry in dry season.	8	4	16	0	Road continues rising slightly through paddy ½ mile, then through thin jungle for 2 miles to Táong, from Táong to Shwébo over flat country, paddy cultivation, except a little thin jungle at 3 miles. Táong has 50 houses. Cross bridge over a small nullah just beyond. At 5 miles cross bridge over a small nullah and ½ mile further pass the village of Minyaung, north of the road; 10 houses. At 6½ miles pass Pagôgôn, north of road; 20 houses. At 8 miles cross Mugalé river. At 8½ miles reach Shwébo stockade. In the stockade about 1,200 men could be accommodated and 250 horses. About 500 more in kyaungs in the city. Good water is abundant from wells at all times of the year. The moat north of the stockade is always full of water and there are several good wells inside the stockade. The Shwébo cantonment lies to the right (north) of the road, on high ground, between the 7th and 8th milestones.
		3. Nyaungbintha. Nullah; no water in dry season, clay bottom, bank about 12 feet high.	12	4	28	4	Leave Shwébo stockade by the north gate and proceed westward. The road crosses the eastern moat and skirts the north side of the inner city wall; at ¾ mile it turns north-west through paddy-fields; at 1½ miles the western moat is crossed. The road continues in a north-westerly direction through paddy and here and there scrub jungle, passing Zígôn at 4½ miles, a village of 30 houses on the west side of the road. At 7½ miles reach Phayán; 60 houses and surrounded by a thorn fence. About 100 yards south is a tank enclosed by a bund and palings with water (March). No accommodation. After Phayán the road crosses a bridge 10 yards long over a nullah dry in March. At 8¼ miles bridge over nullah 18 yards long. Thick jungle along the banks of this nullah. From here the road passes through paddy to 10 miles, where light jungle begins. This jungle gradually becomes thicker till at 11 miles a deep nullah is crossed by a bridge 20 yards long. From here to Nyaungbintha the road is through paddy. Nyaungbintha has 140 houses enclosed by a dead thorn fence, situated 100 yards east of the road, surrounded by paddy-fields. The police post is about ½ mile south of the village, occupied by 25 police; might accommodate 40 in all. Two kyaungs (one north, the other south) would accommodate 100 men; one zayát and kyaung (north) 10 men. A well is being dug in the police post. There is good water to be got from one well between the road and the village (March); three tanks dry (March). From Nyaungbintha there is a road north-east to Lópanhla; good for carts in dry season; 2½ daings.
		4. Yé-u ... ... Large nullah; no water in dry season; banks about 10 feet high; clay bottom. Mu River.	13	4	42	0	Leaving Nyaungbintha the road passes through forest of young In trees over sandy soil and has been only raised 1 foot for 1½ miles. This portion is much cut up. Road on through penetrable jungle. At 3½ miles a bridge, 30 yards long, over a deep nullah which runs at the bottom of some low-lying ground. This bridge is approached along an embankment, 150 yards long and about 15 feet high where it joins the bridge, so that in heavy

FROM KYAUKMYAUNG (IRRAWADDY) TO THAMBAUK AND MAUKADAW (CHINDWIN) *viâ* SHWÉBO AND YÉ-U—*continued.*

Authorities. Military.	Authorities. Civil.	Number and Names of Stages, Rivers and Streams.	Distances. Inter-mediate.	Distances. Total.	Remarks.
G.O.C. Mandalay District.	Commissioner, Northern Division, and Deputy Commissioner, Shwébo.	**4. Yé-u**—*cont.*			rains there would be a defile 180 yards long at this point. The jungle is cleared about 40 yards on either side. Road on over two small nullahs (bridged) to 4½ miles, where another large nullah is crossed by a bridge 30 yards long. From here to Wumbuyen, at 9½ miles, the road passes through open country (mostly paddy), over two small bridges over nullahs passing Yônzu at 5 miles; Sepé at 6 miles, ¼ mile west of the road; Mutha at 7 miles, ¼ mile west of road. At 8 miles there is a kyaung, 300 yards west of road, for 50 men with good water. A small village. Ywathit (about 1 mile west of this kyaung) and Wumbuyen, two groups of 10 huts in each, 200 yards west of road at 9½ miles. From here till the Mu River is reached the road is for the most part through jungle with dry cultivation here and there. At 10 miles a cart track branches west to Magyidaw about ¾ mile away; at 11½ miles Indian (15 huts) is passed on the east of the road and just beyond a bridge, 8 yards long, over nullah. At 12½ miles the Mu is reached. Depth in March 18 inches. It is fordable for carts from December to May; the remaining months of the year a ferry is used In March the river at the ford is broad with about 150 yards of deep sand on either side. Yé-u is on the right bank of the river; has about 300 houses well laid out with broad streets. The stockades are about 1 mile west of the village. There are three stockades—that east occupied by the police, the next by the cavalry, and that west by the infantry. They would accommodate 800 men. There are in the vicinity of the village eight kyaungs; would accommodate 400 men; nine zayâts to accommodate 150 men There are wells at all the kyaungs and three inside the village.
G.O.C. Myingyân District.	Commissioner, Central Division, and Deputy Commissioner, Yé-u.	**5. Kunôn** ... ... Sawmé chaung.	M. 9 F. 4	M. 51 F. 4	The road passes over paddy-fields with patches of scrub jungle here and there. A number of palm trees are dotted about the country. At 1¾ miles Panthéywa (20 houses); can supply seven carts; one fair set of kyaungs (occupied by pôngyis), which would accommodate 75 men. Water from three wells and a large tank. Road as before. At 1½ miles a small tank is passed on the right of the road, which has water in it all the year round for men and animals. At 4 miles Lélántawywa, an old set of kyaungs (occupied) for 100 men. Water from one well. Road as before. At 5½ miles Mei-o, a bad set of kyaungs (occupied) for 50 men. Road as before. At 1½ miles the small dry bed of the Paozu chaung is crossed; at 8 miles Chaungzôn, 40 houses, 10 carts. Water from five wells. Road as before. At 9½ miles reach Kunôn; 92 houses, 20 carts, three good sets of kyaungs (occupied by pôngyis and part of one by military police) for 300 men. Plenty of water from one large tank and from shallow wells in the bed of the Sawmé chaung which runs past Kunôn. There is plenty of paddy and grass. The villagers round here trade a great deal in jaggery.
		6. Uyin ... ... One small stream and Uyin chaung.	9 4	61 0	The road now runs through paddy-fields with a large number of palm trees along the bunds. At 1¼ miles reach Nyaungzauk, 12 houses, six carts. Water from shallow wells in dry bed of a small stream running past the village.

FROM KYAUKMYAUNG (IRRAWADDY) TO THAMBAUK AND MAUKADAW (CHINDWIN) *viâ* SHWEBO AND YE-U—*continued.*

Authorities. Military.	Authorities. Civil.	Number and Names of Stages, Rivers and Streams.	Distances. Intermediate.	Distances. Total.	Remarks.
G.O.C. Myingyan District.	Commissioner, Central Division, and Deputy Commissioner, Yé-u.	**6. Uyin**—*cont.*			Road as before. At 2½ miles Pyindaung; 20 houses, six carts, one set of kyaungs (occupied) for 100 men. Water from two wells. Road as before. At 3¾ miles Sigyi, 22 houses, seven carts. Water from five or six wells. Road as before. At 4½ miles Kinmungyôu; 20 houses, 405 carts, one inferior set of kyaungs (occupied) for 50 men. Water from a large tank. Road as before. At 5½ miles Sandaung; a set of thatched kyaungs (occupied) for 50 men. Water from one well. Road as before. At 6¼ miles Shwégu; two fairly good set of kyaungs (occupied) for 300 men. Water from one large tank. There is a direct road from Yé-u to Shwégu kyaungs, said to be only about 14 miles. Road as before. At 7 miles Nakun, six houses. Water from two wells. Road now passes through fairly open scrub jungle. At 9½ miles reach Uyin; 25 houses, eight carts, two good sets of thatched kyaungs (occupied) for 150 men. Plenty of water obtained all the year round from numerous shallow wells in the dry bed of the small Uyin chaung, which runs about ¼ mile to the north of the village. Plenty of grass and 20 to 30 baskets of paddy can be supplied at 3 or 4 hours' notice.
		7. Ywangé ... Tawmé and Ywangé chaungs.	M. 14 F. 4	M. 75 F. 4	Road as before. At 2½ miles the scrub jungle changes into open "*in*" jungle. At 8¾ miles the left bank of the Tawmé chaung is reached. There is a small stream of water running here. The road goes up the bed for ¼ mile and up along the left bank of the stream. At 9½ miles the stream is crossed. There is no water running at the crossing, but running water is again found just above here. At 10¾ miles the road recrosses to the left bank. At 11½ miles Kimbin; 10 houses, two carts, one inferior set of deserted kyaungs for 60 men. Water from streams running into the Tawmé chaung, which above Kimbin is called the Ywangé chaung. At 14½ miles reach Ywangé; eight houses, one cart, one good set of thatched kyaungs (occupied) for 75 men. Water from one well and from stream in which water commences to flow here and flows all the year round, but gets very short in the dry season. Plenty of grass, but no paddy can be obtained.
	Commr., Central Divn., and Deputy Commr., Upper Chindwin.	**8. Saga** ... ... Nyaungthabyégyi, Paw and Dobin chaungs.	16 0	91 4	Road now runs through "*in*" and bamboo jungle. At 1½ miles the road strikes away from the right bank of the Ywangé chaung, gets into slightly higher ground, and passes through a very fine open "*in*" forest. At 7½ miles there is a small tank on the left bank of the road; there is always water in this tank, but it is only fit for men to drink during the rains. At the end of the dry season it gets very small and very dirty even for animals to drink. At 9 miles the road descends into the bed of the Nyaungthabyégyi chaung and runs down it. The banks are covered with a fairly thick bamboo and small tree jungle and are very hilly and steep in places. At 9¾ miles water commences to flow down the stream and is to be found running from this point all the way down to the Chindwin throughout the year. At 13 miles the stream is joined by the Paw chaung, and the combination is called the Dobin

FROM KYAUKMYAUNG (IRRAWADDY) TO THAMBAUK AND MAUKADAW (CHINDWIN) *vià* SHWEBO AND YÉ-U—*continued*.

Authorities. Military.	Authorities. Civil.	Number and Names of Stages, Rivers and Streams.	Distances. Intermediate. M. F.	Distances. Total. M. F.	Remarks.
G.O.C. Myingyán District.	Commissioner, Central Division, and Deputy Commissioner, Upper Chindwin.	**8. Saga**—*cont.*			chaung. The road continues down the valley of this stream until at $14\frac{1}{2}$ miles it flows into the Thambauk chaung, down whose valley the road then runs. At 16 miles reach Saga, seven huts on right bank, three carts, one very dilapidated kyaung (deserted) for 15 men. Water from the stream. No paddy procurable, but plenty of grass. Road as before.
		9. Thambauk ... Wetpo and Medán chaungs; Chindwin river.	7 0	98 4	At $1\frac{1}{2}$ miles the Wetpo chaung, a little water running in March, joins the Thambauk chaung by the right bank. At $2\frac{3}{4}$ miles Zídalôk on the right bank; three huts. Water from the stream. Road as before. At 1 mile the dry Medán chaung joins the Thambauk chaung also by the right bank. At 2 miles the road leaves the bed and runs along the right bank of the stream. At 7 miles reaches Thambauk near the left bank of the Chindwin river and about $\frac{1}{4}$ mile above where the Thambauk chaung flows in; seven houses, one cart, one good set of kyaungs (occupied) for 100 men. Water from one good well and from the river. Plenty of water, but paddy is rather scarce. There appears to be a good landing place here for steamers. From Yé-u to Thambauk the road is for the first few miles over clayey soil, but afterwards it is always more or less sandy and is excellent for baggage animals. Except in the beds of the streams the sand is rather heavy going. The average rate taken each march by the baggage animals was never under $2\frac{1}{2}$ miles an hour and generally 3 miles an hour. There also appears to be a very good cart road. The villagers all along the route state that the road is open and very fairly good all the year round even for carts. There is no cart road beyond here.
		10. Maukadaw ... Sanyingyi, East Myaungyin, West Myaungyin, Thayetaw, Kyauktaga, and Maukadaw chaungs.	11 0	109 4	The road now goes over very hilly ground and through thickish In and other jungle. At $1\frac{1}{4}$ miles it enters the bed of the Sanyingyi chaung just before it runs into the Chindwin river and goes up its dry bed. At $2\frac{1}{2}$ miles the road leaves the stream, crosses over a steep ridge, and at $2\frac{3}{4}$ miles enters and runs down the dry bed of the Sanyingyi chaung (which it leaves at $4\frac{1}{4}$ miles just before the Chindwin river is reached), and passes by the deserted village Sanyingyiywa. The road now passes over hilly ground until at $5\frac{1}{2}$ miles it strikes and crosses the East Myaungyin chaung, which has a small stream running down it. At $5\frac{3}{4}$ miles Myaungyin on the left bank of the Chindwin river; six houses, one zayát for six men. The road here gets into and then runs up the valley of the West Myaungyin chaung, which here has a small stream running down it. At 1 mile the road leaves the stream and goes over a high and very steep hill only just passable for loaded animals. At $1\frac{1}{2}$ miles further the road enters the bed of the Thayetaw chaung and runs down it. At $8\frac{3}{4}$ miles a small stream of water starts to flow in the stream, and the road here leaves it and passes over hilly ground, until at 9 miles it gets into and runs down the dry bed of the Kyauktaga chaung which it leaves at $9\frac{1}{2}$ miles. At $9\frac{3}{4}$ miles Shé on the left bank of

FROM KYAUKMYAUNG (IRRAWADDY) TO THAMBAUK AND MAUKADAW (CHINDWIN) *viâ* SHWÉBO AND YÉ-U—*continued.*

Authorities. Military.	Civil.	Number and Names of Stages, Rivers and Streams.	Distances. Intermediate.	Total.	Remarks.
G.O.C. Myingyán District.	Commissioner, Central Division, and Deputy Commissioner, Upper Chindwin.	**10. Maukadaw**—*cont.*			the Chindwin river; seven houses, one bad set of kyaungs (occupied) for 25 men. Road now goes over paddy-fields and across the Maukadaw chaung. At 11 miles reaches Maukadaw on the left bank of the Chindwin river; 60 houses, 20 carts, four sets of kyaungs (occupied) for 500 men. Water from one well and the river. Plenty of paddy and grass. The road from Thambauk to Maukadaw is open all the year round, but is in many places very hilly and rather bad going for loaded animals. The road is not very much used, as the villagers prefer going by the river. There has never been a cart road from Thambauk to Maukadaw, and the country presents considerable difficulty for any cart road being made. The column taken between Yé-u and Maukadaw comprised about 100 men, two elephants, and 175 mules and ponies. Plenty of water and grass was procurable at each stage, but paddy was very scarce at the last three stages. From Maukadaw there is a road up the stream of the same name to Pékyundaw (8½ miles), the sixth stage on the Yé-u-Kindat road *viâ* Yamôntaung. *See* Route No. 25, Central Division. *Note from Captain Poynder's Report.*—The route from Yé-u through Uyin and Saga to Thambauk on the Chindwin is direct and quite practicable for carts, and at Thambauk there is sufficient water for light draught steamers throughout the year. The 10 miles from here to Maukadaw embrace a very difficult piece of country with five small ranges of sandstone hills, but, if sufficient money could be allotted to make the track practicable for carts to Maukadaw, this last place would become an important base and the terminus of three good inland trade routes: (1) North-west to Balet and Kindát; (2) North-east to Sénan, a rich portion of Northern Yé-u district and the valley of the Maukadaw chaung; (3) East to Yé-u, much used before dacoity made it dangerous for caravans. This would then become the main road from Yé-u to Kindát (total 148 miles) and, as will be seen from reports, 4 miles shorter than the present cart road through Yamôntaung and Sénan (total 152 miles); also this tract of country being less wild and mountainous than the northern districts, it would be more easily brought under cultivation and protection, and this would doubtless bring back the population.

BRANCH I.

FROM MUTHA (*see* STAGE 4) TO TABAYEN *viâ* SINAIN.

Military	Civil	Stage	Intermediate M.	F.	Total M.	F.	Remarks
G.O.C. Myingyán District.	Commissioner, Central Division, and Deputy Commissioner, Yé-u.	**1. Tabayen** ... River Mu crossed.	8	0	8	0	Mutha is a large village (1,000 inhabitants) about 500 yards from the river Mu 6½ miles from Yé-u. From Mutha the road runs through elephant grass to the bank of the river, where there is an excellent ford. Depth between December and May about 2½ feet, with a very firm, sandy bottom. West of the Mu the road runs through cultivation, only small belts of jungle being left at all in this part of the country. Tabayenmyo is a village situated within an ancient wall. The wall is now

From KYAUKMYAUNG (Irrawaddy) to THAMBAUK and MAUKADAW (Chindwin) *viâ* SHWÉBO and YÉ-U—*continued.*

BRANCH I—*continued.*

Authorities.		Number and Names of Stages, Rivers and Streams.	Distances.		Remarks.
Military.	Civil.		Inter-mediate.	Total.	
G.O.C. Myingyán District.	Commissioner, Central Division, and Deputy Commissioner, Yé-u.	**1. Tabayen**—*cont.*			little more than an earthen parapet, overgrown in many parts by bushes and breached in many places. The wall is a square of about ¼ mile side. Outside are the remains of a moat in which, however, there is little water, excepting on the southern half of the western side. On the west side of the town and separated from the moat by a bund is an extensive jheel, with a depth of water of 3 to 4 feet. At the north-eastern and south-eastern corners, outside the walls, are pagodas. The road from Tabayenmyo to Sinain branches from the previous road near the village of Leyaka, runs through cultivation to the village of Onetgyi or Beitgyi, then runs along the river bank for about 1,000 yards, when it crosses through the village of Naniya to a point lower down in the river, which it follows for about 1 mile to the ford near Míyawgaung. This ford is about 3 feet deep in January, with a firm bottom; but the left bank is difficult of ascent, and would require to be ramped if wheeled transport were brought across. From the ford the road runs 1 mile through cultivation to the village of Sinain, as already reported on.

No. 34.

From KYAUKMYAUNG to YWATHIT (Route No. 91, Branch I).

By Lieut. J. W. B. MEADE, 3rd Cavalry Hyderabad Contingent, 1887.

Military.	Civil.	Number and Names of Stages, Rivers and Streams.	Inter-mediate. M. F.	Total. M. F.	Remarks.
G.O.C. Mandalay District.	Commissioner, Northern Division, and Deputy Commissioner, Shwébo.	**1. Ywathit** ... Water plentiful from Irrawaddy river.	**14 0**	14 0	**Good cart track not far from the bank of the river (Irrawaddy), bad crossing over a creek just outside Kyaukmyaung. At 2 miles, Naungyain, Shwégwé and Shwédaik three villages adjoining one another in the order named, about 30 houses each. Large manufacture of glazed pottery. Good cart track, road more open, and country clearer; at 2½ miles Makan large open space in front of village between it and river; about 40 houses. Good cart track for a short distance, then pathway to the left towards river bank through very high grass jungle. After 2 miles good cart road, again for 3 miles through wood. Then 1⅝ miles more open country near river bank to Shágé (11 miles) village, about 60 houses; very good kyaung, capable of lodging 150 men. Road very good. Country open and fit for cavalry to move as far as one can see from the river. At 13 miles Yegamo village of about 20 houses, which is practically joined to Ywathit. Ywathit is only 500 yards from Yegamo. There is a large kyaung between the two villages and close to it is the village of Thissengyi consisting chiefly of a number of large kyaungs along the river bank and up the small hills behind. Jungle appears thicker to south of Thissengyi. From here there is a road connecting with Route No. 91, from Sheinmaga to Shwébo.**

No. 35.

From KYWETNAPA to KAINGYI (up Myitngé Valley).

By Lieut. TANCRED, R.A., Intelligence Department, Burma, 21st February 1890.

Authorities. Military.	Authorities. Civil.	Number and Names of Stages, Rivers and Streams.	Distances. Intermediate. M. F.	Distances. Total. M. F.	Remarks.
G.O.C. Mandalay District.	Commissioner, Northern Division, and Deputy Commissioner, Mandalay.	**1. Gwébin** ...	17 0	17 0	The road follows the north (right) bank of the Myitngé river. It is a narrow jungle path crossing numerous nullahs, but presenting no difficulties to pack animals. At 4 miles path crosses stream easily fordable. There are no inhabited villages near the river, though many old village sites are passed. At 10 miles village and kyaung of Hngetgyiteik completely deserted, but kyaung still stands. At 13 miles the village of Thayetpin on south side of river; houses standing, but no inhabitants. From here there is a steep hill path to Pyintha (*see* Route No. 53) *viâ* Yébin, 10 miles, passable for pony transport. At 17 miles the village of Gwébin with 15 houses and a pôngyi kyaung. This village and the much larger one of Yé immediately opposite on the south (left) bank of the river are the only inhabited villages on the river between Kywetnapa and the Kaingyi. From Yé or Yé-u there is a route to Myogyi, Ywangán, &c., *see* Route No. 3, Eastern Division.
		2. Yégyán ...	10 0	27 0	Road still follows the right bank of Myitngé river. After Gwébin the current of the river becomes much more rapid and all traffic in boats ceases above this point. Up to Gwébin the navigation in boats is easy. At 3 miles the path becomes very difficult for pack animals, as it is overgrown with jungle and steep nullahs are very numerous. Occasional old village sites are passed between Gwébin and Yégyán, but no houses standing. At 10 miles the Yégyán stream runs into the Myitngé from the east, but there are no signs of a village.
		3. Sasaing (Léma chaung).	6 0	33 0	Track as before, nearly obliterated. There are two very steep hills at this stage which run right down to the water's edge, and track goes down on to the rocks at river's edge. It would be almost, if not quite, impossible for pack animals to go along at this stage. At 6 miles the Léma chaung runs into the Myitngé from the north. No villages passed during this stage. Léma village lies about 1 mile up the valley of the Léma chaung and a fairly good hill path leads to it from Yégyán up the left bank of the Myitngé for 6 miles, then cross the river by raft and follow the right bank to the Léma chaung.
		4. Payaseik ...	11 0	44 0	Track as before. The hills run down straight into the river. Numerous nullahs to be crossed; country seemingly entirely deserted.

FROM KYWETNAPA TO KAINGYI (UP MYITNGÉ VALLEY)—*continued.*

Authorities. Military.	Authorities. Civil.	Number and Names of Stages, Rivers and Streams.	Distances. Inter-mediate. M. F.	Distances. Total. M. F.	Remarks.
G.O.C. Mandalay District.	Commissioner, Northern Division, and Deputy Commissioner, Mandalay.	**5. Kaingyi** ...	**15 0**	59 0	Track exceedingly difficult, even coolies take 7½ hours to go 3 miles. At two places the only means of taking a pony along is to swim it up the river. The river here is very winding and rapid. At 15 miles the small village of Kaingyi, four or five houses. For 2 or 3 miles each side of Kaingyi the track is fairly good as the hills recede a little from the river. No ford was observed in this part of the river (*i.e.*, Gwébin to Kaingyi), which appears to be fairly deep. Its general width is about 400 feet. A large stream runs in near Kaingyi from the north, width about 200 feet. From Payazeik, a track runs up to Nalin; very difficult and steep. From Nalin path continues to Maymyo (*see* Route No. 53) a distance of 11 miles, through thick jungle. This part of the road is easily traversed by bullocks. All observations were taken from the north bank of the river, as the river was never crossed. The hills were so steep and close to the river on both sides that no observation of the country could be taken. The path all through was in thick jungle shaded by trees, except when it descended on to the bed of the river. From Kaingyi a good pack track leads to Wetwin on the Mandalay-Theinni road (Route No. 53, Stage 5), two easy marches or one long march with lightly laden cooly transport.

No. 36.

From LÔNTÔN (Indawgyi Lake) to MÁNSI (KAYINGÔN) viâ PAYANI and MANSAIN.

BY LIEUT. C. A. WILDING, INTELLIGENCE BRANCH, MARCH 1891.

Authorities. Military.	Authorities. Civil.	Number and Names of Stages, Rivers and Streams.	Inter-mediate. M. F.	Total. M. F.	Remarks.
G.O.C. Mandalay District and O.C. Bhamo.	Commissioner, Northern Division, and Deputy Commissioner, Bhamo.	**1. Nampanam chaung (1,875 feet).** Small streams.	**12 0**	12 0	General direction west. The road goes across a paddy plain for about 2 miles, it then leads over a small range of hills covered with bamboo jungle, it then descends into plains of bamboo jungle. There are a considerable number of small streams to be crossed, but none of them afford any difficulty. The bamboos were lying in huge clumps across the road and much cutting was required. The road otherwise is very good and plenty of good water is to be obtained all the way along. Camp at Nampanam chaung is good and is the site of an old village. The stream is small, but there is sufficient water for a small force.
		2. Nansong chaung (1,900 feet).	**13 0**	25 0	The first 2 miles of the road are very good. Leading over a small range of hills the road enters a marsh which is nearly a mile across, but fortunately only about 18 inches deep in mud. Just before reaching this marsh the road runs through the site of an old village called Mainpôk. The camp at

FROM LÛNTÔN (INDAWGYI LAKE) TO MÁNSI (KAYINGÔN) *viâ* PAYANI AND MANSAIN—*continued.*

Authorities.		Number and Names of Stages, Rivers and Streams.	Distances.		Remarks.
Military.	Civil.		Intermediate.	Total.	
G.O.C. Mandalay District and O.C. Bhamo.	Commissioner, Northern Division, and Deputy Commissioner, Bhamo.	**2. Nansong chaung (1,900 feet)**—*cont.*			Nansong chaung is a fair one at the edge of the stream; the water is very good. The Nansong chaung is a tributary of the Uru river; it flows due north and joins the Uru above Shwédwin. After this marsh the road leads through plains, chiefly long kaing grass, and eventually crosses another small range from which there is a good view of Taungthônlôn, again into the valley where the road leads into another marsh, small but almost impassable; about 300 yards in length. There is a road now cut into the jungle so as to avoid the marsh.
			M. F.	M. F.	
		3. Mansain (1,825 feet).	9 0	34 0	Two hundred yards below the camp there is a good ford only knee deep and a firm, sandy bottom. After crossing the Nansong chaung the road leads generally in a northerly direction crossing many streams; two large ones with swift currents. The fords across these streams are very difficult, the banks being very steep. In all other respects the road is an excellent one, showing signs of having at one time been very much used. It passes the sites of three deserted villages said to have been destroyed by the Sana Kachins some 20 years ago. About then this part of the country was thickly populated, but the Kachins and the Haw Saing rebellion of 1245 Burmese era (about A.D. 1884) have reduced it to the present state. Mansain has 20 houses and is heavily stockaded, and the jungle round it is clear for 70 yards. It is situated on the banks of the Nansong chaung; the bank on which the village stands is 50 feet high forming a complete natural fort, reaching the camp at 4,000 feet. Thick jungle all the way and no grass or bamboo available for the animals. The last three marches there has been very little or almost no fodder for the animals. At this camp there is none whatever, otherwise the camp is very good, and plenty of water from the Namai chaung, which the natives say is the same as the Méza chaung flowing into the Irrawaddy at Tigyaing. The road crosses the three southern spurs of Taungthônlôn at right angles which makes it very difficult going for the animals.
		4. Piépyu (2,100 feet). Nankathen chaung.	12 0	46 0	Road from Mansain starts for 1 mile through paddy-fields through which a small stream runs which, owing to its depth, had to be bridged. Three miles further on crosses Nankathen chaung which is 10 yards broad and 2 feet deep with a firm bottom. One mile further on the road joins the Shwédwin and Maingkaing trade route, which is a very good road, and runs on to the Jade Mines and is evidently much used. After two miles more this road is left on the right and the Taungthônlôn road leads through bamboo jungle where much cutting had to be done, and two small, bad nullahs had to be crossed, otherwise the road is good. Two small pieces of marsh had to be crossed which afford no difficulty. Camp on the Piépyu chaung. No hills are crossed on this marsh. The camp is good and there is plenty of water, but fodder scanty.

FROM LÔNTÔN (INDAWGYI LAKE) TO MÁNSI (KAYINGÔN) *viâ* PAYANI AND MANSAIN—*continued.*

Authorities.		Number and Names of Stages, Rivers and Streams.	Distances.				Remarks.
Military.	Civil.		Intermediate.		Total.		
			M.	F.	M.	F.	
G.O.C. Mandalay District and O.C. Bhamo.	Commissioner, Northern Division, and Deputy Commissioner, Bhamo.	**5. Pángsen (2,700 feet).** Nankathen chaung.	**12**	**0**	58	0	Road good for 3 miles out of camp and then crosses the Nankathen chaung to sites of two old villages, namely, on the right bank Kumlángyi, on the left bank Namthôn. After this the road leads for ¼ mile up stream; very difficult going. This is the cold weather road; the rainy season road leads to the left on the right bank and through thick jungle and meets the other road some 3 miles further on. After leaving this river the road leads up a long ridge of very gradual ascent, in all about 700 feet, right into camp. Camp not good and water very scarce from a very small stream down ridge on each side. Road throughout very good; has evidently been at one time very much used, but not now. No grass or other fodder was obtainable.
		6. Nankhopin chaung (3,550 feet).	**5**	**4**	63	4	Road ascends a hill to about 3,550 feet passing close under a peak called Loi Sinkaw, and a little further on another peak, Loi Paisaw, is passed. Road is very good throughout; passes through a camping ground called Panghok with a very small stream. Nankhopin chaung affords a very good camping ground. It takes its name from the stream which flows into the Nansong chaung near Manthein. The road throughout is a very good one and the ascents and descents are nowhere difficult. Almost no fodder available for the animals at this camp. A short march owing to the difficulty of the next one.
	Commissioner, Northern Division, and Deputy Commissioner, Katha.	**7. Namai chaung (4,000 feet).**	**6**	**0**	69	4	Road is much up and down hill and leads across two or three small streams, it then goes up a very steep ascent, so difficult that many of the mules rolled backwards down the hill. The march consequently a short one. Directly after leaving camp the road ascends to 4,725 feet, then down to a small stream 3,400 feet, then up again to 4,200 feet. No fodder. This Namai chaung appears to be the same stream as is called lower down the Méza chaung. Taungthônlôn lies to the north-east of this camp.
		8. Penling (2,950 feet).	**6**	**0**	75	4	The road crosses two or three of the southern spurs of Taungthônlôn, at right angles and goes generally in a westerly direction. The ascents and descents are many and very steep and difficult for transport. After 5 miles arrive at the small village of Penling; seven houses; heavily stockaded. Camp on the tributary of the Namai stream which was about 700 yards beyond the village.
		9. Payani ...	**13**	**0**	88	4	Road very good but crosses many spurs, one over 1,200 feet, and very steep and evidently not much used, for in many places cutting had to be done,

FROM LÔNTÔN (INDAWGYI LAKE) TO MÁNSI (KAYINGÔN) *viâ* PAYANI AND MANSAIN—*continued.*

Authorities. Military.	Authorities. Civil.	Number and Names of Stages, Rivers and Streams.	Distances. Intermediate. M.	F.	Distances. Total. M.	F.	Remarks.
G.O.C. Mandalay District and O.C. Bhamo.	Commissioner, Northern Division, and Deputy Commissioner, Katha.	**9. Payani**—*cont.*					but on arrival at the top of this ridge road leads into the Payani-Mánsi road which is a splendid one. From here into camp there is no difficulty. The Namai chaung is crossed twice before reaching Payani. This is the same stream as in Stage 7.
		10. Kônganuk ...	12	0	100	4	*See* No. 57 for full details of these two stages.
		11. Mánsi (Kayingôn).	12	0	112	4	The first three stages of this route are evidently the same as No. 39, in which, however, the distances are made slightly longer.

No. 37.

From LÔNTÔN to MATTAIN.

BY MAJOR T. H. SEWELL, NORFOLK REGIMENT, ASSISTANT ADJUTANT-GENERAL, JANUARY 1892.

Military	Civil	Stages	Inter. M.	F.	Total M.	F.	Remarks
G.O.C. Mandalay District and O.C. Bhamo.	Commissioner, Northern Division, and Deputy Commissioner, Bhamo.	**1. Nam Sai** ...	12	0	12	0	Eight houses; Kachin. Water good. Road fair but hilly.
		2. Meinthin ...	13	0	25	0	Road good and level. Pass Nampo (deserted) at 6 miles. Water distant; good grass. The village deserted is on the bank of Namsáng chaung.
		3. Lamai ...	10	0	35	0	Road is passable for mules. Three Kachin villages on road.
		4. Mattain ...	14	0	49	0	From Lawai there is a road to Maingthain (*see* Alt. No. I, Stage 2, below) *viâ* the Eila chaung. Distance 30 miles.

There are three other routes to MATTAIN as under :--

ALTERNATIVE I.

FROM LÔNTÔN TO MATTAIN.

BY MAJOR T. H. SEWELL, NORFOLK REGIMENT, ASSISTANT ADJUTANT-GENERAL, JANUARY 1892.

Military	Civil	Stages	Inter. M.	F.	Total M.	F.	Remarks
G.O.C. Mandalay Dist. and O.C. Bhamo.	Commr., Northern Divn., and Deputy Commr., Bhamo.	**1. Nantônmé** ...	12	0	12	0	Good road with water and grass plentiful.
		2. Maingthain ...	15	0	27	0	Road good except for a swamp.
		3. Hwéleik ...	13	0	40	0	Alternative camp on Wetaung chaung 9½ miles; water and grass plentiful.
		4. Mattain ...	16	0	56	0	

FROM LÔNTÔN TO MATTAIN—*continued.*

ALTERNATIVE II.

FROM LÔNTÔN TO MATTAIN.

BY MAJOR T. H. SEWELL, NORFOLK REGIMENT, ASSISTANT ADJUTANT-GENERAL, JANUARY 1892.

Authorities. Military.	Authorities. Civil.	Number and Names of Stages, Rivers and Streams.	Distances. Intermediate. M.	F.	Distances. Total. M.	F.	Remarks.
G.O.C. Mandalay Dist. and O.C. Bhamo.	Commr., Northern Divn., and Deputy Commr., Bhamo.	1. **Nantônmé** ...	**12**	**0**	12	0	
		2. **Saingmaing** ...	**13**	**0**	25	0	On Namsáng chaung.
		3. **Mansain** ...	**8**	**0**	33	0	Twenty houses, 12 miles from Shwédwin.
		4. **Môlé** ...	**13**	**0**	46	0	Road good on Namkata chaung.
		5. **Nankopin** ...	**14**	**0**	60	0	Water good.
		6. **Pinaing** ...	**11**	**0**	71	0	On the Nahlaman chaung; road very stiff.
		7. **Mattain** ...	**14**	**0**	85	0	Road better, but stiff.

ALTERNATIVE III.

FROM LÔNTÔN TO MATTAIN.

BY MAJOR T. H. SEWELL, NORFOLK REGIMENT, ASSISTANT ADJUTANT-GENERAL, JANUARY 1892.

Military	Civil	Stages	Int. M.	F.	Total M.	F.	Remarks
G.O.C. Mandalay District and O.C. Bhamo.	Commissioner, Northern Division, and Deputy Commissioner, Bhamo.	1. **Nantônmé** ...	**12**	**0**	12	0	
		2. **Saingmaing** ...	**13**	**0**	25	0	
		3. **Mansain** ...	**8**	**0**	33	0	
		4. **Péphen** ...	**10**	**0**	43	0	
		5. **Pansong** ...	**4**	**2**	54	2	Very hilly.
		6. **Nankopin** ...	**5**	**2**	59	4	(Very hilly.)
		7. **Namai** ...	**5**	**6**	65	2	(Very hilly.)
		8. **Pinaing** ...	**4**	**4**	69	6	(Very hilly.)
		9. **Mattain** ...	**14**	**0**	83	6	

No. 38.

From LÔNTÔN to SEIKMU (or SEIKMAW).

BY MAJOR FENTON, DEPUTY ASSISTANT QUARTERMASTER-GENERAL, FROM NATIVE INFORMATION, MÔGAUNG 1890.

Military	Civil	Stages	Int. M.	F.	Total M.	F.	Remarks
G.O.C. Mandalay District and O.C. Bhamo.	Commissioner, Northern Division, and Deputy Commissioner, Bhamo.	1. **Kônmamôn** ...	**11**	**0**	11	0	*Note.*—This route should have been, but is not yet superseded by one compiled from later information.—A.F.
		2. **Lawsun** ...	**12**	**0**	23	0	*See* Route No. 24, Stage 4, Kámaing to Lôntôn.
		3. **Mapu** ...	...		...		Mapu is a Kachin village on the right bank of the Nantein chaung (or north-west).
		Nantein chaung.					
		4. **Khaimanaw sakhán.**	...		...		Path runs westwards crossing a high hill to Khaimanaw sakhán, a jungle halting place.

FROM LÔNTÔN TO SEIKMU (OR SEIKMAW)—*continued.*

Authorities. Military.	Authorities. Civil.	Number and Names of Stages, Rivers and Streams.	Distances. Intermediate. M. F.	Distances. Total. M. F.	Remarks.
G.O.C. Mandalay District and O.C. Bhamo.	Commissioner, Northern Division, and Deputy Commissioner, Bhamo.	**5. Sápiya Chaung sakhán.** Sápiya chaung.	...	...	Path leads first over low hills, then crosses the Kawapum (pum = hill in Kachin), a very high hill.
		6. Seikmu (Seikmaw). Seikmu chaung.	...	...	At Seikmu there are jade pits along the banks of a small stream which runs into the Uyu (Uru) river. It is too small for navigation even by the smallest kind of boats (*peingaw*) at any time of year and jade from these mines is carried either to Haungpa on the Uyu river (one or two marches) or else to Mapu, or thereabouts, on the Nantein chaung, whence it is floated down to Lawsun and on to Kámaing on bamboo rafts. The Nantein chaung is about 15 yards wide at its junction with the Indaw chaung, but even when in flood it is not more than 3½ to 4 feet deep at Lawsun. It holds quantities of big fish, called by natives of India "saur," a fine sort of carp, excellent eating. The natives chase them in the shallow water and cut them down with their das. A charge of dynamite in a well-selected spot is certain to secure a large supply of fish, most acceptable to troops passing through this district, where little is to be got in the way of fresh rations. Of the above stages the first three are full day's marches for loaded coolies, the fourth only 2 or 3 hours. These are evidently the same mines as were visited by Bayfield in 1836-37, and he appears to have followed Route No. 24 up to the Nantein chaung, whence his route branches north up the valley of that stream.

The following is his account of the route :—

Military.	Civil.	Number and Names of Stages, Rivers and Streams.	Intermediate. M. F.	Total. M. F.	Remarks.
G.O.C. Mandalay District and O.C. Bhamo.	Commissioner, Northern Division, and Deputy Commissioner, Bhamo.	**1. Kámaing** ... Môgaung, Sí-eng chaung.	...	...	Road leaves Kámaing and crosses some low irregular forest-covered hills in rear of the village, and then passes along an extensively cultivated rice plain belonging to the villages of Kámaing and Piran, the former being inhabited by Shans and the latter by Lapai Kachyins. This latter is to the left of the road. Two hours from Kámaing it crosses the Si-eng chaung, at the source of which are some unworked salt-springs. It now continues over low bamboo-covered hills, and crosses the Indaw chaung, which is 50 yards broad, knee-deep, and with a strong current. Camp here. Direction of march S. 40 W.
		2. Camp ... Indaw chaung.	8 0	8 0	From here the road goes first over low hills and afterwards along the right side of a narrow hill-bound plain for about an hour, and then over alternate low hills and patches of plain. The camp is in a grassy and here-and-there cultivated plain called Ta-pha, and about 2 miles broad, with Indaw chaung running down the centre.

FROM LÔNTÔN TO SEIKMU (OR SEIKMAW)—*continued.*

Authorities. Military.	Authorities. Civil.	Number and Names of Stages, Rivers and Streams.	Distances. Intermediate. M. F.	Distances. Total. M. F.	Remarks.
G.O.C. Mandalay District and O.C. Bhamo.	Commissioner, Northern Division, and Deputy Commissioner, Bhamo.	**3. Ta-pha** ... Indaw and Namlék chaungs, and Mantein stream.	12 0	20 0	From here the road crosses a hill called Namseik-taung, which is covered with wild plantain jungle and a few teak trees. Elephant tracks numerous. At 1½ hours from camp and at the bottom of the hill is the Namlék chaung, a small stream. It now continues over low bamboo-covered hills with a red soil and serpentine base, and 2¼ hours from Namlék chaung it reaches a plain, and here bifurcates, one branch of the road running south to the village of Kyaukseik, and the other north to the mines. Follow the latter, which goes over a plain of high reeds and wild plantain jungle for a few furlongs, when a stream is crossed knee-deep and 30 yards broad. The road now ascends a low range of forest hills and then winds over a succession of low mounds between two ranges of hills called Nan-tein-taung, which are from 200 to 600 feet high.
		4. Camp ... ... Namsanta and Sápiya chaungs.	16 0	36 0	From here it descends to another hill-bound plain about 1½ miles broad, and then after a few minutes strikes into the jungle, where it crosses the Namsanta. Camp here. General directions as far as bifurcation south-west and afterwards north-west. The camp is on the edge of a narrow plain bounded on the west by a high range of mountains called Kawapum and on the east by the Namlék. From the nullah the road goes north-west obliquely across the plain, and then through large open forest to the foot of the mountain. It now ascends and the summit of the pass is reached in 80 minutes. Height above sea-level 2,799 feet. The ascent is by a tortuous, steep, and rugged footpath, through bamboo forest, and from here the great lake of Indawgyi can be seen due south 18 to 20 miles. The road now descends the western side of the mountain and in 40 minutes the Sápiya chaung (soap stream) is reached. Still descending 20 minutes further on is the alkaline spring from which it takes its name. Height above sea-level 1,535 feet.
		5. Jade Mines ... Seikmu chaung.	9 0	45 0	An hour from here over a very tortuous, rocky, and uneven road the serpentine mines are reached. These are in a valley bounded by the Kawapum on the east and on the west by the Kathem-taung. Through the valley runs the Seikmu chaung, which one day's journey from here empties itself into the Uru river.

No. 39.

From LÔNTÔN (Indawgyi Lake) to SHWÉDWIN (Uru River).

BY LIEUT. BURTON, 4TH SIKHS, ATTACHED MÔGAUNG LEVY, MAY 1890.

Military	Civil	Stage	Intermediate M. F.	Total M. F.	Remarks
G.O.C. Mandalay District and O.C. Bhamo.	Commr., Northern Divn., and Dy. Commr., Bhamo.	**1. Camp on site of deserted village.** Two small streams and a stream at halt.	14 0	14 0	Road west-north-west very good. First 4 miles across plain to range of hills running north and south. Then along a valley through this range between low hills till 10th or 11th mile. Jungle entirely bamboo and not dense.

FROM LÔNTÔN (INDAWGYI LAKE) TO SHWÉDWIN (URU RIVER)—*continued.*

Authorities.		Number and Names of Stages, Rivers and Streams.	Distances.				Remarks.
Military.	Civil.		Inter-mediate.		Total.		
			M.	F.	M.	F.	
G.O.C. Mandalay District and O.C. Bhamo.	Commissioner, Northern Division, and Deputy Commissioner, Bhamo.	**1. Camp on site of deserted village** —*cont.*					At 6 miles small stream. At 9 miles larger stream crossed by a wooden bridge. At 14 miles halt by the Nanpôk stream. Water *en route* and at halting place bad, being full of decaying bamboo leaves.
		2. Camp ... ... Small stream running through a large swamp and a stream at halting place.	10	0	24	0	Road good west-north-west for 3 miles through bamboo jungle, then a plain 1 mile broad. At 5 miles reach a swamp, 1 foot of water; swamp about ½ mile broad; transport ponies got through without much difficulty, but swamp is probably impassable in rains; from 6th to 8th mile road is along valley between low hills; 8th to 9th mile through a plain; at 10 miles camp by the Nanpôkgalé stream in bamboo jungle; water very bad, full of decaying leaves and almost stagnant. From here the Taungthonlôn peak is in sight 20 to 30 miles to the west well above every other hill anywhere around. It is also visible from here onwards to Shwédwin, whence it bears nearly due south.
		3. Camp on Nansáng (or Nansong) chaung. Nansáng and Nansalaung chaungs.	8	0	32	0	Road good west-north-west 3 miles to swamp, ½ mile broad. Some difficulty in crossing even in driest time of year. Path rendered almost impassable by elephants, which are very numerous. At 4 miles Nansáng chaung; breadth 30 yards, depth 2½ feet (dry weather). From 4 miles path changes direction due north and follows the course of the Nansáng along its left bank. At 5 miles Nansalaung chaung 15 yards by 1½ feet deep; also three small nullahs between this stream and halting place, which is on left bank of Nansáng chaung.
		4. Mansain ... Nansalaung and Nansáng chaungs.	7	0	39	0	Road good north. Crosses Nansalaung chaung twice and minor streams *en route*. At 5th mile crosses Nansáng chaung, 40 yards by 3 feet deep; at 6th mile recrosses to left bank. Road runs all way through thin tree jungle. Halt at Mansain, 18 houses (Shan), on bank of Nansáng chaung. For another account of these four stages *see* stages 1 to 3 inclusive of Route No. 36; the route is evidently the same, but the distances differ somewhat.
		5. Shwédwin ... Uru river.	12	0	51	0	Road good north for first 5 miles parallel with river and crosses four nullahs through tree jungle. For the next 6 miles path crosses an extensive level plain on left bank of the Uru river running west-north-west. The last mile is through thin tree jungle to village of Shwédwin, 20 houses, on Uru river. *Note.*—Throughout this march the highest hill crossed is not more than 150 feet high. The streams all run north-west into the Uru river. The country is entirely deserted.

FROM LÔNTÔN (INDAWGYI LAKE) TO SHWÉDWIN (URU RIVER)—*continued.*

Authorities. Military.	Authorities. Civil.	Number and Names of Stages, Rivers and Streams.	Distances. Inter-mediate.	Distances. Total.	Remarks.
G.O.C. Mandalay District and O.C. Bhamo.	Commissioner, Northern Division, and Deputy Commissioner, Bhamo.	**5. Shwédwin—** *cont.*			The above were the stages made in May 1890. A better division of marches would, on account of the badness of the water, be—

	Inter-mediate.	Total.
	M.	M
1. Same as above	14	14
2. To Nansáng chaung	14	28
3. Nansáng chaung to Mansain	11	39
4. Mansain to Shwédwin	12	51

The following deserted villages are passed :—
1st march, Hépán.
3rd march, Nantônmet.
3rd march, Maingpôk.
4th march, Nannit.
4th march, Mawiti at camping place.
5th march, Hômi.

No. 40.

From MÁBEIN to MÔMEIK viâ MYITZÔN.

I. B. COMPILATION, 1888.

Military	Civil	Stages	Inter. M.	Inter. F.	Total M.	Total F.	Remarks
G.O.C. Mandalay District and O.C. Bhamo.	Commissioner, Northern Division, and Deputy Commissioner, Katha and Ruby Mines.	**1. Malaingôn or Bahé.**	About 12	0	12	0	Not reported on at present, but apparently from the map two marches of 10 to 15 miles each. At Myitzôn cross the Shwéli river.
		Shwéli and Nameit rivers.					
		2. Myitzôn ...	12	0	24	0	
		3. Thayetchaung camp.	8		32	0	From Myitzôn the road runs almost due south along the right bank of the Nameit chaung. First 4 miles through forest good. Thence 2 miles swampy, through elephant grass. At 8 miles Thayet chaung sakhán. No houses, but open ground with mango trees.
		4. Limbángya chaung camp.	11	0	43	0	Thence to Limbángya chaung south-east still following Nameit chaung. First 2 miles through bamboo jungle, then forest again crossing two low spurs. Camping ground here, no houses.
		5. Letkokpin ...	6	0	49	0	From Limbángya sakhán road runs south-east through teak forest, at 6 miles village of Letkokpin 30 houses, water from wells. Here the Nameit is crossed, usually by rafts, but in the driest season it is fordable, being only about 1½ feet deep.

FROM MÁBEIN TO MÔMEIK *viâ* MYITZÔN—*continued.*

Authorities. Military.	Authorities. Civil.	Number and Names of Stages, Rivers and Streams.	Distances. Intermediate.	Distances. Total.	Remarks.
			M. F.	M. F.	
G.O.C. Mandalay District, &c.	Commissioner, Northern Division, &c.	**6. Mômeik** ...	5 0	54 0	From here through paddy cultivation to Mômeik 5 miles, passing through the villages of Tagaungma and Taungvain in the 1st mile. The general direction in the last stage is almost due east.

No. 41.

From MAINKHWAN to ASSAM.

Note.—No account of Mr. Needham's route (1891-92) received up to date of going to press.

A. F.
7-7-93.

No. 42.

From MAINGKHWAN to FORT O'DONNELL (SANKA-JADE MINES) viâ TAIFA, KANTAO and TARO.

BY LIEUT. T. H. E. DAUNCEY, 21ST HUSSARS, FEBRUARY 1892.

Military	Civil	Stages	Intermediate	Total	Remarks
G.O.C. Mandalay District and O.C. Bhamo.	Commissioner, Northern Division, and Deputy Commissioner, Bhamo.	**1. Taifa** ... ... Namkhwan, Summat, and Tanai chaungs.	**16 6**	16 6	Path leads out of Maingkhwan west-north-west across paddy-fields and thence into kaing grass. At ½ mile path bifurcates, route right very narrow and boggy. Two hundred yards further on across boggy nullah. At ¾ mile path enters forest and becomes less boggy, crosses boggy nullah at 2¼ miles, and at 6 miles turns to right and crosses the Namkhwan chaung (15 yards by 1 foot; clear; swift) and then turns to left up a dry water-course for 300 yards, when it leadsup a steep bank into forest. Here path bifurcates—route right. At 6½ miles reaches 'Ndong on Namkhwan chaung turning half-right through the village. At 6¾ miles through kaing grass again and across a small boggy nullah soon leads into forest and at 9 miles crosses small, steep, boggy nullah. At 9½ miles cross Summat chaung (47 yards by 6 inches; clear; swift) and up very steep bank. Through large village of Lákyen at 10 miles in a westerly direction and ½ mile further on across a deep, boggy nullah (foot-bridge). From here the path is very narrow for about a mile and at 11½ miles crosses two very steep nullahs. At 12¼ miles touches south bank of large jheel along which it runs for 3 miles. At 12¾ miles crosses a small clear rivulet and at 13¼ miles a steep nullah and leads through lemon trees, &c., until reaching the left bank of the Tanai river opposite Taifa at 16¾ miles. The Tanai river is here (150 yards and unfordable; right bank 40 feet high; loose sand). Camping space on left bank for 300 men. Path throughout narrow, but easy. Across the Tanai by boat, 250 yards above the village where the perpendicular right bank is made accessible, though still very steep. Mules started 9-30 A.M.; arrived opposite Taifa at 6-20 P.M. Good camping ground for small column in village.

FROM MAINGKHWAN TO FORT O'DONNELL (SANKA-JADE MINES) *viâ* TAIFA KANTAO AND TARO—*continued.*

<table>
<tr><th colspan="2">Authorities.</th><th rowspan="2">Number and Names of Stages, Rivers and Streams.</th><th colspan="2">Distances.</th><th rowspan="2">Remarks.</th></tr>
<tr><th>Military.</th><th>Civil.</th><th>Inter-mediate.</th><th>Total.</th></tr>
<tr><td rowspan="2">G.O.C. Mandalay District and O.C. Bhamo.</td><td rowspan="2">Commissioner, Northern Division, and Deputy Commissioner, Bhamo.</td><td>2. Sagôn ... ...
Bang-bra and Tarong chaungs.</td><td>M. F.
8 6</td><td>M. F.
25 4</td><td>Path leads out of Taifa north-west down a broad lane of green turf gradually narrowing until at ¼ mile path bifurcates—route left—and at ¾ mile leads north-west across a couple of paddy-fields for nearly ½ mile when it enters forest; fine broad path. At 1¾ miles through a small clearing and path becomes narrow but easy going and ¼ mile further on leads across the Bangbra chaung, 30 yards by 3 feet; clear, with firm bottom). Now the path broadens again through high forest, reaching the small village of 'Nkankôn at 3¾ miles and turning low down a steep bank and north-north-west along sand and shingle across the dry bed of an arm of the Tarong chaung turns south-west after nearly ½ mile in order to reach the ford over the Tarong chaung 300 yards further on. Cross the Tarong (150 yards by 3 feet; clear; swift; pebble bottom; bed 300 yards broad), and north-west along sand and shingle turning west-south-west after somewhat more than ¼ mile down the left of a creek of the Tarong chaung; dry at places, at others full of water and deep. Across this (dry) at 4¾ miles and along the right edge of it crossing it again (dry) a few hundred yards further on then leads along the left edge of it turning with the bend of the creek to the west-north-west at 5½ miles. At 5¾ miles leads west-south-west into high kaing grass along left bank of creek crossing it (40 yards by 2 feet; firm bottom) at 6¼ miles and leads south-west along river edge for 150 yards when it ascends the bank into high kaing grass running close to creek. Across a corner of the creek 10 yards by 4 feet, steep slippery landing, and on west-north-west still along right bank through high kaing grass emerging at 7½ miles and crosses creek here in the form of a swift rivulet 4 yards by 3 inches. Now north-west along a dry water course and up along right bank through forest until crossing creek again in form of an arm of water 8 yards by 2 feet just in front of village of Sagôn (15 good-sized houses) at 8¾ miles. Mules started at 11-50 A.M.; arrived at 3-30 P.M.; path good.</td></tr>
<tr><td>3. Kantao ...
Boggy jheel.</td><td>6 2</td><td>31 6</td><td>Path leads out of Sagôn north-north-west and then north-west across a paddy-field; west-south-west across another and into kaing grass. Path narrow and slippery until at 1½ miles it becomes good and reaches a very boggy jheel (15 yards by 3 feet) at 2 miles, a very difficult crossing necessitating the cutting and laying down of a great quantity of kaing grass. On through alternate high forest and kaing grass; path good. At 3½ miles leads into a cross path—route right—and 100 yards further on west-north-west across a paddy-field debouching on to a broad, well-cleared path, bifurcating at 5 miles—route left. Three hundred yards further on across a large paddy-field for ½ mile thence into kaing grass west-north-west; beautiful path through two more paddy-fields separated by kaing grass and into Kantao (five large houses) on Chindwin river at 6¼ miles. Good camping ground in paddy-fields or on sandy beach of river. Mules started at 8 A.M.; arrived at 11 A.M. (One hour spent in making the jheel passable).</td></tr>
</table>

FROM MAINGKHWAN TO FORT O'DONNELL (SANKA-JADE MINES) *viâ* TAIFA, KANTAO AND TARO—*continued.*

Authorities. Military.	Authorities. Civil.	Number and Names of Stages, Rivers and Streams.	Distances. Intermediate.	Distances. Total.	Remarks.
G.O.C. Mandalay District and O.C. Bhamo.	Commissioner, Northern Division, and Deputy Commissioner, Bhamo.	**4. Camp at Maitong-kyut** (*i.e.*, mouth of Maitong chaung). Chindwin river, Takan and Maitong chaungs.	M. 9 F. 0	M. 40 F. 6	Path leads out of Kantao west across the Chindwin river by a ford opposite the village (150 yards by 3½ feet, strong current. dangerous; boats available); and after crossing leads west-north-west along the sandy beach under the left bank. Unlimited camping ground bending round with the river from west-north-west to south-west by south. At 2½ miles from Kantao the path turns left off sandy beach up on to the left bank and leads on along the bank close to the water's edge. At 3½ miles the path leads inland up the right bank of a small, clear stream, the Takan chaung (4 yards by 4 inches, clear, firm bottom), which here flows into the Chindwin, follows it up for 100 yards and then crosses it and leads up a steep bank into high forest. From this point until reaching the Chindwin again at the mouth of a small stream named the Maitong chaung, the general direction is south-west and the path extremely difficult for mule transport and unpleasant for marching as it leads up and down short steep banks continually crossing and leading through shallow, pebbly streams, following up one stream for about 2½ miles and then down the Maitong chaung about 2½ miles until reaching the Chindwin where there is a tiny bit of dry sand large enough for only a dozen men. For further camping space the thick, damp jungle must be cleared. Mules started from left bank of Chindwin river opposite Kantao at 8-15 A.M; arrived at 4-45 P.M.
		5. Camp at Maru-kyut. Chindwin river and Maru chaung.	2 4	43 2	Path leads off south by east along under left bank of the Chindwin and is extremely boggy. (Our 100 mules took 3½ hours getting over the first ½ mile). The path leads along the river bank at one time near the water's edge at another time up the bank and through high forest, up and down precipitous hills and across boggy nullahs and is all but impassable by mule transport. This last 2 miles took those mules which managed to arrive at all 5 hours, the loads having had to be taken off and carried up several hills and over nullahs. General direction south. Camping space 6 yards broad on dry patches of sand and pebble up the bed and on either side of a rivulet called the Maru chaung. Mules started at 9-40 A.M., some managed to get in by 6-15 P.M.
		6. Camp at Padi-kyut. Chindwin river, Maru and Padi chaungs.	4 0	47 2	Path leads off in a south-easterly direction up the bed of the tiny Maru chaung, turning south-south-west after a couple of hundred yards up the bed of another small stream which here flows into it. On up through this stream (3 yards by 1 foot) for ½ mile between high banks when the path leads to the left up the bank. From here the path runs up and down low hills continually crossing and recrossing small rivulets and is not difficult. At 2 miles path ascends a long hill, very steep at first, and then

FROM MAINGKHWAN TO FORT O'DONNELL (SANKA-JADE MINES) *viâ* TAIFA, KANTAO AND TARO—*continued.*

Authorities. Military.	Authorities. Civil.	Number and Names of Stages, Rivers and Streams.	Distances. Intermediate.	Distances. Total.	Remarks.
G.O.C. Mandalay District and O.C. Bhamo.	Commissioner, Northern Division, and Deputy Commissioner, Bhamo.	**6. Camp at Padi-kyut**—*cont.*			descends and ascends repeatedly. At 2½ miles leads down a difficult descent and leads along the bed of a rivulet for a short distance and then ascends a hill reaching top at 3¼ miles and reaches top of another hill at 3½ miles and arrives at the mouth of the Padi chaung flowing into the Chindwin river at a little over 4 miles. Path good on the whole with the exception of the first ¾ mile through water. Mules started at 11-40 A.M.; arrived at 2 P.M. Good camping space on sand for 100 men and followers.
			M. F.	M. F.	
		7. Taro ... ... Ahauk chaung, Chindwin river.	**8 0**	55 2	Path leads from the mouth of the Padi chaung south-east by south up on to the top and along the left bank of the Chindwin river through high forest up and down hill; fairly easy path. At 1 mile up a very steep long hill and at 3 and 3¼ miles leads down to the edge of the river from which latter place the ford can be seen about ½ mile down the river. At nearly 4 miles the ford is reached at the mouth of the Ahauk chaung (6 yards by 6 inches; clear; swift; pebbly). Here there is camping space for 50 men. At the ford the Chindwin is 200 yards by 4¾ feet; too deep for troops, and boats must be sent for from Taro. After crossing the river, the path runs south west down under the right bank of the river, boggy at places, and leads up on to the top of the bank ¾ mile further on, descending to the water's edge again after ¼ mile. At 5¼ miles from the crossing the path becomes firm and good and continues so until arriving opposite Taro at 8 miles. Across the Chindwin by boat (200 yards by 5 feet) and up the high bank into Taro. Mules started from Padi-kyut at 7-30 A.M., arriving at crossing at 10-30 A.M. Started from crossing at (?) 2-15 P.M.; arriving opposite Taro at 4 P.M. Camping space unlimited on right bank of Chindwin (on sand) opposite Taro. Camping space unlimited in Taro paddy-fields.
		8. Camp at Panep-kyut. Chindwin river and Pan chaung.	**10 0**	65 2	Path leads out of Taro south-west by west across large paddy-fields for ¼ mile and then turns west into forest; good path. Veering round to south-west at 1 mile it reaches the river bank and leads west by north following the course of the river ¼ mile further on leading down and winding along under the left bank; very fair path and at 5¾ miles crosses the mouth of the Pan chaung (15 yards by 2 feet) and continues easy going until at 7 miles it ascends the bank a bit and here the path commences to be broken, irregular, and very boggy, becoming worse and worse and quite impassable for laden mules unless much time be spent in cutting and laying down a great quantity of kaing grass, &c. At 9¼ miles the path arrives opposite the north point of a large island in the middle of the river and at 9½ miles becomes good going again and reaches a good camping place on a sandy beach at 10 miles. Some 10 mules managed to arrive in camp by 10-30 P.M. The remaining loads had to be carried by the men for the last ½ mile. Camping space for 500 men.

No. 42.

From MAINGKHWAN to FORT O'DONNELL (SANKA-JADE MINES) *viâ* TAIFA, KANTAO and TARO—*continued.*

Authorities. Military.	Authorities. Civil.	Number and Names of Stages, Rivers and Streams.	Distances. Intermediate. M. F.	Distances. Total. M. F.	Remarks.
G.O.C. Mandalay District and O.C. Bhamo.	Commissioner, Northern Division, and Deputy Commissioner, Bhamo.	**9. Tagum** ... ... Panep chaung (a rivulet). Tawlé and Tagum chaungs.	5 4	70 6	Path leads off sand bank west by south under the left bank crossing the mouth of a small swift rivulet (Panep chaung) and after ¼ mile leads south-east by south up the bank into the forest; an excellent path. At 3 miles leads across a dry water-course 12 yards broad; general direction south, and at 4¾ miles turns west-north-west across the Tawlé chaung (12 yards by 1 foot; clear and swift). Camping space on sand here for 100 men and further down stream more space. After crossing path leads down under left bank for 100 yards, crosses again and along under right bank south-south-west for 200 yards and crosses again for the third time. After another 100 yards the path crosses the Tagum chaung (40 yards by 2 feet; clear and swift; pebbly bottom; 100 yards broad), which the Tawlé chaung joins here and then leads up under the left bank for 200 yards and crosses again and on up right bank for 300 yards and crosses for the third time following up the river till reaching Tagum at 5½ miles. Mules started at 2-20 P.M.; arrived at 5 P.M. Good camping ground just outside the village for 200 men.
		10. Camp on Taba chaung. Tagum and Taba chaungs.	9 2	80 0	Path leads out of Tagum south-south-east, good path through high forest bifurcating after ¼ mile (route right). Path bifurcates again at 1½ miles, both paths reaching the Tagum chaung 150 yards further on. The right path is too steep for animals, but the ford here is shallower so is better for the men. At the point where the left path reaches the river the ford is 50 yards by 4 feet. On again through forest, good path, descending a steep hill at 2¼ miles, across a rivulet and up an easy hill crossing another rivulet at 2¾ miles and leading paralleled to the Tagum chaung descending the bank at 4 miles to cross the mouth of a small rivulet, but ascending again immediately by a short, steep ascent. At nearly 5 miles path reaches the Tagum chaung again and crosses it (30 yards by 1 foot) and leads on under left bank, mostly through water for nearly ½ mile; crosses again and leads along shingle, &c., under river bank, crossing again at 5½ miles and on along sand and shingle and left bank crossing again at 5¾ miles. On again under right bank crossing again at 6 miles, and again 60 yards further on and on up under right bank crossing again at nearly 6½ miles and again 50 yards further on (20 yards by 4½ feet). This last crossing is deep for pack animals and they must be unloaded. After crossing the path turns to the right up under righ bank for 40 yards and then leads up into and through bamboo jungle, good path, crossing the Taba chaung (35 yards by 9 inches, clear and swift) at 9½ miles. Camping space *nil*, except by clearing the thick undergrowth of the high forest. Mules started at 9 A.M.; arrived at 4-15 P.M., of which time 2¾ hours were spent in effecting the two deep crossings where the loads had to be carried by the men.

FROM MAINGKHWAN TO FORT O'DONNELL (SANKA-JADE MINES) *viâ* TAIFA, KANTAO AND TARO—*continued.*

Authorities.		Number and Names of Stages, Rivers and Streams.	Distances.				Remarks.
Military.	Civil.		Intermediate.		Total.		
			M.	F.	M.	F.	
G.O.C. Mandalay District and O.C. Bhamo.	Commissioner, Northern Division, and Deputy Commissioner, Bhamo.	**11. Lunkun-kyun (2,800 feet).** Taba chaung.	8	6	88	6	Path leads from the Taba chaung south-east through high forest turning south-south-east at nearly 1 mile across the Taba chaung, again across rivulet at 3¼ miles and the Taba chaung again at a 4¼ miles crossing on to an island, round which the stream divides and leading up the further side of the island for 30 yards, then turns to the left across the other small arm into high forest again up a very steep bank. At 5¾ miles across a small rivulet and 200 yards further on leads up the pebbly bed of a rivulet, south-east, for 200 yards and then commences a long but easy ascent of 1,700 feet up to a small halting place in the Lunkun forest about 3 miles from the bottom of the hill and 8¾ miles from camp on the Taba chaung. No camping space except by clearing the forest. Clear water from a small, swift rivulet. Mules started at 8-50 A.M.; arrived 2-30 P.M. No bamboo or other fodder for the mules.
		12. Camp on Shé-et chaung (a small torrent). Shé-et chaung.	10	0	98	6	Path leads generally south-east crossing three rivulets in the first 200 yards. Path very hilly throughout with a few steep ascents and descents, reaching water again at nearly 8 miles in the form of a couple of small rivulets. At 10 miles reaches the Shé-et chaung, a bigger mountain stream than the others, where there is a small halting place. Only a very limited space, level enough for camping, and this must be cleared, barely accommodating 50 men. No bamboo or other fodder for the mules. Mules started at 9-30 A.M.; arrived at 4-30 P.M.
		13. Kora (3,000 feet). Tagum chaung.	7	0	105	6	Path leads out of camp at Shé-et chaung up a very steep, long hill reaching a short plateau at a little over ½ mile, then ascends again, but not so steeply, until 1¼ miles. It then leads up, and down low hills, mostly through bamboo forest until reaching Tingraw, two large and four small houses, at 3 miles. Path leads out of Tingraw south-east down a long hill until crossing a rivulet ½ mile further on then up a short, steep hill and a long an almost level path leading gradually down hill until at 2¾ miles from Tingraw it reaches the Tagum chaung (20 yards by 1½ feet) up the bed of which it leads, mostly through the water for ½ mile, and then leads up into forest up a steep hill reaching Kora at 7 miles eight houses—two large and six small. Mules started at 9-30 A.M.; arrived at 2 P.M.
		14. Mamsum (3,500 feet). Uru chaung.	8	0	113	6	Path leads out of Kora down the south side of the ravine below it crossing a small rivulet at the bottom then leads on down a steep but easy incline till crossing another rivulet at 1¼ miles and 30 yards further on across the Uru chaung (30 yards by 2 feet; swift; clear; pebbly; elevation 1,500 feet). Path now leads up opposite

No. 42.

From MAINGKHWAN to FORT O'DONNELL (SANKA-JADE MINES) *viâ* TAIFA, KANTAO and TARO—*continued*.

Authorities. Military.	Authorities. Civil.	Number and Names of Stages, Rivers and Streams.	Distances. Inter-mediate.	Distances. Total.	Remarks.
G.O.C. Mandalay District and O.C. Bhamo.	Commissioner, Northern Division, and Deputy Commissioner, Bhamo.	**14. Mamsum (3,500 feet)**—*cont.*			side of ravine by a steep, slippery ascent, reaching a plateau at $2\frac{1}{4}$ miles (2,050), gradually ascending again, easy riding-path, reaching 2,640 feet at 3 miles. From here the path leads up and down easy inclines until reaching the village of Pala (two large and nine small houses) at $3\frac{3}{4}$ miles (2,700 feet). Path leads out of Pala up an easy ascent and up and down easy inclines gradually ascending with one steep ascent of a couple of 100 yards $2\frac{1}{2}$ miles from Pala when it reaches a height of 3,360 feet. Leads on easily up and down and finally along a beautiful path reaching Mamsum at 8 miles, one large and eight small houses. Mules started at 11-30 A.M.; arrived at 3-45 P.M. Good camping space for 200 men. Water at bottom of hill 250 yards distant.
		15. Fort O'Donnell (Sanka). Sanka chaung, 15 yards by 9 inches; clear; swift; pebbly.	M. F. **15 0**	M. F. 128 6	Path leads out of Mamsum in a south direction down a short, steep hill across a muddy rivulet and up another short, steep hill with short steep descent and a good level path commences gradually descending until $2\frac{1}{4}$ miles. At 3 miles a steep hill with gradual descent at the bottom of which is a good clear rivulet and a small clearing used as a halting place. At $3\frac{3}{4}$ miles a very steep and difficult ascent for baggage animals with very steep descent and another steep climb at $4\frac{1}{2}$ miles (3,500), the highest point during the march, with gradual descent. There are two very steep descents after this, one at 5 miles with a rivulet at the bottom and another at nearly 6 miles. From here until reaching Tawmaw (Jade mines) the route is a perfect riding path. Path leads north-east out of Tawmaw and after $\frac{1}{4}$ mile turns east by south; level and good the whole way with the exception of about $\frac{1}{2}$ mile of hilly, broken ground covered with large stones at about half way to Sanka. A few hundred yards before reaching this village the path crosses the Sanka chaung twice, and once more before entering the fort which is only separated from the village by this stream. Mules started at 8 A.M.; arrived at 5-45 P.M.

No. 43.

From MAINGKHWAN to 'NTUP'NTSA.

By Lieut. T. H. E. DAUNCEY, 21st Hussars, January 1892.

Military	Civil	Stages	Intermediate	Total	Remarks
G.O.C. Mandalay District and O.C. Bhamo.	Commissioner, Northern Division, and Deputy Commissioner, Bhamo.	**1. Silaw** ... ... Edi and Nampyu chaungs; Tanai river (Chindwin).	**16 2**	16 2	Maingkhwan to Nangku 7 miles (*see* Route No. 66, Môgaung to Maingkhwan). A good path leads out of Nangku in an east by north-east direction down the left bank of the Nampyu chaung, and at $\frac{1}{2}$ mile passes through the small village of 'Nnam where there is a bamboo bridge for foot-passengers across the river. General direction from here north-north-west for about $4\frac{1}{2}$ miles. At 1 mile the route passes through the village of Khatu and $\frac{1}{2}$ mile further on is inclined to be narrow and boggy till at $1\frac{3}{4}$ miles it crosses twice a sluggish arm of the river (10 yards by 3 feet) within a couple of hundred

FROM MAINGKHWAN TO 'NTUP'NTSA—*continued.*

Authorities. Military.	Authorities. Civil.	Number and Names of Stages, Rivers and Streams.	Distances. Intermediate.	Distances. Total.	Remarks.
G.O.C. Mandalay District and O.C. Bhamo.	Commissioner, Northern Division, and Deputy Commissioner, Bhamo.	**1. Silaw**—*cont.*			yards. Between these crossings is a stretch of dry sand, useful for camping (400 by 50 yards). After this a splendid path leads off north-west through high bamboo and light forest. At 3¾ miles the path leads across the Nampyu chaung (50 yards by 3 feet) with a bridge for foot-passengers 50 yards down stream. Here there is another fine stretch of dry sand and on the bank above a splendid little spot to encamp 50 men. Now through Ninglep (100 yards from river) and north-north-east along a splendid path through bamboo and light forest, across a boggy stream 1 mile further on, 100 yards from which path meets a cross-path (route right). At 7¾ miles path leads into a broad cross-path (route right) and continues broad and straight until reaching the large village of Silaw situated high up on the left bank of the Tanai river (80 yards by 9 feet) unfordable; 4 dug-outs for ferry boats, mules started 9-30 A.M.; arrived 4-15 P.M.
		2. Makaw ... Tanai River, Lammaun and Tawan chaungs.	M. F. **8 6**	M. F. 25 0	Across the Tanai river by ferry and started north-west by west along a splendid path at ⅛ mile along east edge of a paddy-field north-east. At 1¼ miles direction changes north-west and north-north-west. At 2⅛ miles across a deep water nullah (20 yards by 4 feet) bridged for pack animals 100 yards beyond the foot-bridge, path then wheels right and crosses this nullah again, bridged as before and leads north-west to Lammaun chaung, 600 yards further on (40 yards by 4 feet); swift; high banks. Now north-north-west along a narrow path for 2 miles through low bamboo jungle till at 2½ miles from the Lammaun chaung the path leads north-west along the wedge of a very long narrow stretch of paddy for about ½ mile and then turns sharp to the left west close to a small shed. Now along a splendid path again. At ¾ mile from the paddy-field the path bifurcates (route left) and 6 minutes later leads through the village of Ningran on the left bank of the Tawan chaung. Descends into the river and turns north-north-east up the bed of the stream for ¾ mile and arrives opposite the village of Makaw. Tawan chaung here 100 yards by 3 feet; bed 300 yards; swift; clear; pebbly bottom. Unlimited camping space on the shingle or sandy bed of the river. Mules started 11-30 A.M.; arrived 3-30 P.M.
		3. 'Ntámaja ... Tawan and Tabat chaungs.	**11 2**	36 2	Route leads out of Makaw east-north-east into another portion of same village 100 yards on across a small stream, then north-east along a fine broad path of the left bank of the river. At ¾ mile through the village of Aikong. At 1¼ miles, the path turns off right from river through large opium garden at 1½ miles, through village of Pushi at 2½ miles, 100 yards from which path bifurcates (route left) at 3 miles through small village of Sana. At 4⅞ miles touches the river, turns left and crosses it twice (100 yards by 3 feet) and leads north-east up the pebbly beach under the left bank (unlimited camping ground) for 1½ miles and here leads across it again—rapids 2 feet deep—and turns north-north-west along the beach under the river bank for ½ an hour (difficult marching over large cobble stones) and then leads up on to river bank. At 8¾ miles across small, sluggish stream, Tabat chaung, into a plantation and

FROM MAINGKHWAN TO 'NTUP'NTSA—*continued.*

Authorities. Military.	Authorities. Civil.	Number and Names of Stages, Rivers and Streams.	Distances. Intermediate.	Distances. Total.	Remarks.
G.O.C. Mandalay District and O.C. Bhamo.	Commissioner, Northern Division, and Deputy Commissioner, Bhamo.	**3. 'Ntámaja**—*cont.*			across a boggy nullah and through a large paddy clearing. At 9½ miles through village of Tounjah and at 10¾ miles across the same sluggish stream (8 yards by 2 feet) on to large village of 'Ntámaja on Tabat chaung. Camping ground very limited and damp. Splendid path whole way. Mules started 9-10 A.M.; arrived 2-10 P.M.
		4. 'Ntup'ntsa ... Bang-bang, and Nampraw chaungs.	M. 9 F. 0	M. 45 F. 2	Path leads off north-west through light forest. At ¼ mile north through a paddy-field, debouching at north-east crosses east through three more small paddy-fields and then turns to right north-east along top of a paddy-field and then north by north-west to village of Séngléng at 1 mile out of Séngléng north-north-west through bamboo and light forest along a fine broad path. At 600 yards from village path bifurcates (route right) north-north-west across a small paddy-field into high forest. At 2¼ miles across small boggy stream and ¼ mile farther on across another small stream (6 yards by 6 inches; sluggish) into village of 'Njaw. Out of village east-north-east. At 4 miles through village of Kadôn north-east out of village, 100 yards from which the path bifurcates (route left). At 6¼ miles the path touches a chaung on the left and 100 yards further on leads along east side of a paddy-field at the end of which the path bifurcates (route left). At 6¾ miles the path crosses the above chaung, Bang-bang chaung (15 yards by 2 feet). At 7 miles through paddy-fields north-east, then through another north-north-east entering forest between a clump of bamboos and a sago palm. At 8¾ miles across a stream, a branch of the Nampraw chaung (10 yards by 6 inches; swift and clear) with bridge for foot-passengers and 9 minutes later across Nampraw chaung (15 yards by 2 feet) over a bund of cobble stones and a couple of hundred yards on to 'Ntup'ntsa on Nampraw chaung (15 yards by 2 feet), bridged for pack mules; splendid path the whole way. Good dry camping ground for 400 men on left bank. Mules started 9-22 A.M.; arrived 1-22 P.M. Distance between camps measured by rope.

BRANCH I.

FROM 'NTUP'NTSA (STAGE 4) TO SARAW (ROUTE No. 44).

BY LIEUT. T. H. E. DAUNCEY, 21ST HUSSARS, JANUARY 1892.

Military.	Civil.	Stages.	Intermediate.	Total.	Remarks.
G.O.C. Mandalay District and O.C. Bhamo.	Commissioner, Northern Division, and Deputy Commissioner, Bhamo.	**1. Kum** ... ... Nampraw and Sinwa chaungs.	12 6	12 6	Path leads out of 'Ntup'ntsa in a west direction along a fine broad path. At ½ mile path bifurcates at the entrance to a paddy-field and the well defined one is the wrong one (route right) This path enters forest at the west-north-west corner of the field and after 40 yards runs along the north side of another small paddy-field and again through another entering forest half way along north side of the field and runs south-west through another. At 1½ miles across a rivulet and along a splendid broad avenue across the Nampraw chaung, 200 yards farther on, with stone bund and bridge. At 2 miles through village of 'Ndong (on Nampraw chaung), south-west, following down the left bank of the river till reaching village of Sarengkyet at ¾ mile. Splendid camping ground here on dry turf (500 yards by 40 yards). At 4 miles the path bifurcates (route right) and 20 yards on

FROM MAINGKHWAN TO 'NTUP'NTSA—*continued.*

BRANCH I—*continued.*

Authorities.		Number and Names of Stages, Rivers and Streams.	Distances.		Remarks.
Military.	Civil.		Intermediate.	Total.	
G.O.C. Mandalay District and O.C. Bhamo.	Commissioner, Northern Division, and Deputy Commissioner, Bhamo.	**1. Kum**—*cont.*			leads across the Nampraw chaung and 200 yards further on across another branch of this stream; easy shallow crossings. At 4¾ miles through another small village of Sarengkyet west-south-west; here the path narrows and soon commences to be very tortuous and a mere elephant track for about 5 miles (9 miles required). At 6¾ miles through open space of kaing grass west-south-west for ¼ mile, then into forest for 20 yards and down into Sinwa chaung (1 foot deep; pebbly bottom) and along the bed of the stream for 150 yards, when the route goes round up the right bank, and for 100 yards is dangerous for pack animals, as the narrow path almost overhangs the stream 20 feet below. At 8½ miles across the Nampraw chaung again (25 yards by 3 feet). At 9¾ miles the path touches the left bank of this river and leads west-south-west. At 10 miles across small boggy crossing. At 10¼ miles along the top of an open grass field south-west by west. At 10½ miles path becomes wide again and leads into Kum at 12 miles, situated on the left bank of the Nampraw chaung (30 yards by 2 feet; clear; pebbly). Mules started 8-45 A.M., arrived 3-30 P.M. Measured distance, 12¾ miles.
			M. F.	M. F.	
		2. Saraw ... ... Saksai and Tarong chaungs.	**13 2**	26 0	Path leads out of Kum south-south-west along fine broad route through high forest. At 1 mile south-west by west across a small paddy-field and then across a small, boggy stream (4 yards by 6 inches), after which it leads west-north-west. At 2⅛ miles direction changes south-south-west. At 3⅛ miles across boggy stream (4 yards by 1 foot) and through the village of 'Ngukun. Out of village west-south-west along a good path for ½ mile, the path commences to be narrow through low bamboo jungle obstructed by fallen trees, &c., until reaching the Saksai chaung. At 5¾ miles (120 yards by 2 feet; swift; clear; pebbly). Path leads down under the left bank along shingle for ½ mile, thence on to the bank again and continues good easy going up to the village of Tabaung at 6¾ miles. Out of Tabaung north-north-west up the shingle under the left bank of the Tarong chaung (200 yards by 2 feet; swift; clear; pebbly)—(the Saksai chaung joins it at this village) for ¾ mile west-north-west crossing 3 arms of it, then across the Tarong chaung itself (200 yards by 2 feet) and up the shingle under the right bank for ⅛ mile when the route turns west by south-west and ¼ mile farther on leads up into the bank, good path, through a clearing and then through 10 acres of opium west-north-west on 2 miles to Ningpyen at 10¼ miles. Mules started 8-10 A.M., arrived 12-45 P.M. Path leads out of Ningpyen north-north-west through a couple of paddy-fields, then north-north-east through a bit of forest and two more paddy-fields. At 11¼ miles through more forest (good path throughout) for rather more than ½ mile when the path debouches into a long, narrow paddy-field and leads north by north-east along east side of it for a few hundred yards when it enters low kaing grass. On almost due north until reaching the small village of Malup at 12¾ miles turns round the further end of the village west-north-west and 200 yards farther on enters a large paddy-field, when Saraw, situated on a small hill in a most commanding position, comes into sight on the right front, and from the base

FROM MAINGKHWAM TO 'NTUP'NTSA—*continued.*

BRANCH I—*continued.*

Authorities. Military.	Authorities. Civil.	Number and Names of Stages, Rivers and Streams.	Distances. Inter-mediate.	Distances. Total.	Remarks.
G.O.C. Mandalay Dist., &c.	Commr., Northern Divn., &c., Bhamo.	**2. Saraw**—*cont.*			of the hill a fine broad path cleared for 30 yards on each side leads up to the stockaded village of Saraw which commands 3 miles of the river down stream. Distances between camps measured by rope.

No. 44.

From MAINGKHWAN to SARAW viâ TARING.

BY LIEUT. T. H. E. DAUNCEY, 21ST HUSSARS, JANUARY 1892.

Military	Civil	Stages	Intermediate	Total	Remarks
G.O.C. Mandalay District and O.C. Bhamo.	Commissioner, Northern Division, and Deputy Commissioner, Bhamo.	**1. From Saraw to 'Ntaumaja** ... Tarong, Takôn and Bangbang chaungs.	M. F. **18 0**	M. F. 18 0	*N.B.*—This and Route No. 43 and its branch form three sides of an inverted isosceles triangle, Maingkhwan, the apex, being at the south, 'Ntup'ntsa and Saraw at the eastern and western ends of the base respectively. Under ordinary circumstances this route should be reversed, but it is scarcely worth while to undertake the labour of doing this at present. From Saraw to Ningpyen (3 miles) *see* Route No. 43, Branch I. Path leads out of Ningpyen south-south-west down right bank of Tarong chaung. At 2 miles path bifurcates (route right). At ¼ mile farther on path bifurcates again (route left) and direction changes to east-south-east across a paddy-field, then across a small stream bridged for foot-passengers and south-east along a broad avenue through forest. At 3 miles the route leaves this broad avenue (which leads to Tabaung) and strikes off into a narrow path south and at ¾ mile south-west along the left of a paddy-field into forest for 200 yards and then south-west by south along the left edge of another paddy-field entering forest again in the centre of the south side of the field. Now 30 yards through forest and south-south-west across two small fields entering the forest at the south-west corner of the field along a broad path until reaching the river Tarong at 4½ miles. Unlimited camping ground on shingle bed. The path leads down the bank and under the river bank along the shingle, &c., for ½ mile and then leads up the bank through small village of Yôpang south by south-west along broad path reaching big village of Yôpang nearly ½ mile farther on. Here descends the river bank again leads along shingle for 300 yards crosses an arm of the river (80 yards by 2 feet) across 300 yards more shingle and across the Tarong itself at a ford (150 yards by 3 feet) and turns back north-north-east under the left bank for 300 yards and ascends the bank at the village of 'Ndong, then south by south-east along broad path through forest crossing a small, muddy stream ½ mile from this village; ¾ mile farther on a well defined path leads through paddy-fields entering forest again at east corner of the field. At 8½ miles small village of Ningchi 100 yards to left of path and 100 yards on across the Takôn chaung (10 yards by 6 inches). At 9½ miles east-south-east across grass field ¼ mile from which path leads down a steep descent into a chaung (8

FROM MAINGKHWAN TO SARAW *viâ* TARING—*continued.*

Authorities.		Number and Names of Stages, Rivers and Streams.	Distances.		Remarks.
Military.	Civil.		Inter-mediate.	Total.	
G.O.C. Mandalay District and O.C. Bhamo.	Commissioner, Northern Division, and Deputy Commissioner, Bhamo.	**1. From Saraw to 'Ntaumaja**—*cont.*			yards by 6 inches). At 11 miles through large village of Kadu-Makôn on the Bang-bang chaung (35 yards by 3 feet) Out of village south-east along river bank of chaung crossing it 100 yards on (30 yards by 6 inches) and turns south by south-west. At 12¾ miles path bifurcates at the end of a grass field (route right) south-south-east. Here the path becomes somewhat narrow and boggy until 14 miles when there is a very bad boggy crossing. Good path on to village of 'Ntaumaja at 18 miles. Mules started from Ningpyen 8-15 A.M.; arrived 2-30 P.M.
			M. F.	M. F.	
		2. Taring ... ... Moning, Namlap and Kunswé chaungs, and Tawan River.	9 0	27 0	Route leads out of 'Ntaumaja south-south-east along a well-cleared path; ¼ mile farther on turns south-south-west and leads across the Moning chaung (30 yards by 3 feet). At ½ mile passes through the village of Kashan. Out of village south-south-east and 200 yards farther on path bifurcates (route right) south-south-west. At 2 miles path becomes somewhat narrow through low bamboo jungle, but is dry and easy going. At 3½ miles a bad boggy crossing, easily made passable by throwing down kaing grass. At 4¼ miles a broad path from the south-south-east cuts in and route leads east-north-east; broad and well cleared. At 4½ miles another boggy crossing, ¼ mile farther on across a muddy stream, Namlap chaung (4 yards by 3 feet), 200 yards from which is the village of Dinkai. Route turns off to right south-south-east a hundred yards before reaching the village and a couple of hundred yards farther on the path bifurcates (route left) and commences to be narrow again. At 6 miles enters a paddy-field leaving it at the south-south-west corner, ½ mile on and then runs down the centre of another one east-south-east for several hundred yards and then turns south-south-west and out of the paddy-field at the south corner, now along broad well-cleared path south through forest. Nearly ½ mile farther on across a sluggish muddy stream, Kunswé chaung (4 yards by 6 inches), and reaches the village of Taring situated on the bank of the Tawan river (200 yards; unfordable). Mules started at 8-20 A.M.; arrived 12-40 P.M.
		3. Maingkhwan. Kunswé, Mantôn and Tanaiku chaungs.	9 4	36 4	Path leads out of Taring south-south-west and at 300 yards from village crosses a small, boggy stream (4 yards by 3 feet) the Kunswé chaung; 50 yards further on the path bifurcates (route left). Very narrow and slippery through high kaing grass. At 1¼ miles the path touches the bank of the Tawan chaung; path narrow, but here it is dry and good, south-west along the bank of the river. At 1¾ miles through about 3 acres of opium. At 2¼ miles through the village of Mashi (two small houses) and 200 yards further on the path débouches on the sandy bed of the Tanaiku river (100 yards by 15 feet; bed 300 yards broad). Here there is a fine stretch of dry sand (¾ mile by 200 yards) across the Tanaiku chaung by ferry and then the path leads in a southern direction—path good—and at 1½ miles from the river crosses the Mantôn chaung a very boggy crossing (4 yards by 3 feet). At 2 miles from the river, path becomes very narrow and tortuous and 3 miles farther on crosses another boggy stream and soon enters the Maingkhwan paddy-fields and Maingkhwan 6½ miles from the Tanaiku river and 9½ from Taring. Mules started 8-30 A.M.; arrived 4 P.M. Distances between camps measured by rope.

No. 45.

From MAINGNA to HÔKÁT (Upper Irrawaddy).

By Lieut. KELLY, R.E., 1886.

Authorities. Military.	Authorities. Civil.	Number and Names of Stages, Rivers and Streams.	Distances. Intermediate. M.	F.	Distances. Total. M.	F.	Remarks.
G.O.C. Mandalay District and O.C. Bhamo.	Commissioner, Northern Division, and Deputy Commissioner, Bhamo.	**1. Camp**	**15**	**0**	15	0	Maingna is about a mile up stream from Naungtálaw which is situated on an island opposite Myitkyina on the left bank of the Irrawaddy. Course south. Had to march east-north-east for a mile to avoid a bad crossing. First 4 miles along river, then across a vast paddy plain. A fair road. There is probably a better one running due south from Thágaya and coming in about the 62nd mile. Pass the village of Ywadaw at 3 miles, 12 houses, stockaded. The Ywadaw nullah at 3½ miles, 50 yards wide, 2 feet of water in March, banks steep and 6 feet high. Inhabitants of Ywadaw are Shan-Burmese. At 4½ miles the village of Wainmaw, 20 houses, stockaded. At 8 miles the Nawlun stream, 10 yards wide, 1½ feet of water in March, banks rather steep. The camping ground here is very cramped and is situated on a small stream.
		2. Camp	**10**	**0**	25	0	At 5½ miles a path turns off westward to the small Kachin village of Maingmaw on the Irrawaddy. Road good, but undefined towards the end.
		3. Tálawgyi ...	**8**	**0**	33	0	Road good as far as the Nantabet stream, unfordable. Detachment descended to Tálaw in boats. Transport marched down the banks unloaded.
		4. Hôkát	**9**	**0**	42	0	Detachment descended river in boats. Transport crossed the Irrawaddy and marched down the left bank along a bad road.

No. 46.

From MAINGNA to KÁNTI viâ LEKANNOI and TINGSA-PUMLUMPUM.

By Lieut. BLEWITT, King's Royal Rifles, January 1891.

Military	Civil	Stages	Intermediate M.	F.	Total M.	F.	Remarks
* G.O.C. Mandalay District and O.C. Bhamo.	* Commr., Northern Divn., and Deputy Commr., Bhamo.	**1. Kwitu chaung.** Kwitu chaung.	**12**	**4**	12	4	The road from Maingna to Lekannoi is simply a forest track which improves in the neighbourhood of the different villages met with along the road. It is quite passable for mule transport, but in places the jungle requires a little clearing. Maingna is an important village (Shan) on the left bank of the Irrawaddy; it numbers about 36 houses, and there are a good many Chinese traders living in boats and rafts on the river. The village is well stockaded. The Kachins are of the Marán tribe and they "protect" the village, that is to say,

* So far as any authority, Civil and Military, exists to the north of Maingna.—A.F.

From MAINGNA to KÂNTI *viâ* LEKANNOI and TINGSA-PUMLUMPUM—*continued.*

Authorities. Military.	Authorities. Civil.	Number and Names of Stages, Rivers and Streams.	Distances. Intermediate.	Distances. Total.	Remarks.
G.O.C. Mandalay District and O.C. Bhamo.	Commissioner, Northern Division, and Deputy Commissioner, Bhamo.	**1. Kwitu chaung** —*cont.*			they guarantee as far as they can that it will not be raided by other Kachins, and in return for which they tax the Shans. Supplies of rice and poultry can be obtained at Maingna and Kangpu. At Lekannoi ferry there is one "dug-out" capable of holding 12 men. The river is about 180 yards wide, very deep, and no stream. From Maingna the forest path bears north and continues along the left bank of the Irrawaddy through loose jungle for 10 miles. Then turning north-east for 2¼ miles, the Kwitu chaung is reached. It is 35 yards wide, 18 inches deep, with steep high banks; firm bottom. No camping ground for troops, but jungle can easily be cleared.
		2. Mailompum ... Namfu chaung.	M. F. 8 2	M. F. 20 6	Crossing the Kwitu chaung (dimensions as above) the road continues north for 1½ miles to the village of Kaichaung (Sampaung Lapai tribe); 15 houses. At 3 miles is Lawkyun (Sampaung Lapai); eight houses; and after crossing a small stream at 4 miles 4 furlongs Saré is reached ('Nkum tribe); six houses. Leaving Saré the forest track continues north through the jungle and at 5 miles 2 furlongs the Namfu river is met. It is 30 yards wide, 2 feet deep, with steep banks about 20 feet high, and the bottom is muddy. Between Lawkyum and Saré a road joins in from Layáng, Kwitu and Loisaw, *see* Branch I. From the Namfu to Kángpu is 6 furlongs. It is a Shan Talôk village surrounded by a bamboo stockade, and is situated in the middle of a well cultivated paddy plain. Supplies of rice and poultry can be obtained at the village. From Kángpu the road leaves the plains and by a steep ascent rises to Mailompum (Nawkhum-Latawng tribe); 15 houses.
		3. Lekannoi Ferry. 'Nsum Ka, 'Nsot Ka and 'Nmai Ka.	8 2	29 0	From Mailompum the road, which is a very fair forest track, descends into the valley of the 'Nsum Ka, about 5 yards wide and 1 foot deep with a rocky bottom. Crossing this and still bearing north the road ascends to the village of Taolangkong (Nawkhum-Latawng tribe); 10 houses. Passing through the village the path descends to the 'Nsot Ka, which is a narrow stream similar to the 'Nsum Ka and flows into the 'Nmai Ka quite close. From the 'Nsot Ka the path along the left bank of the 'Nmai Ka to Lekannoi is very bad, through thick jungle, and in many places the track is quite overgrown. No supplies procura[illegible]le at Lekannoi; one Kachin hut.
		4. Sei[illegible] ...	4 4	33 4	Cross the 'Nmai Ka (eastern branch of Irrawaddy river) by ferry, one "laung" available which will contain 12 men. River about 180 yards broad in January, very deep, little current. Thence broad road runs north through the villages of Kaitwé, Wagár and Wasát (Malei-Latawng of about eight houses each, all close together, whence a little rice and poultry can be obtained; leading up out of the 'Nmai Ka valley by a spur, steep slope at first, but becoming easier as the top is reached at Wallaw 4¼ miles (Malei-Latawng, 12 houses). Seinma is ½ mile further on (same tribe of Kachins, 10 houses). Sufficient poultry and p[illegible]dy procurable for the native followers of a small force.

FROM MAINGNA TO KÁNTI *viâ* LEKANNOI AND TINGSA-PUMLUMPUM—*continued.*

Authorities.		Number and Names of Stages, Rivers and Streams.	Distances.				Remarks.
Military.	Civil.		Intermediate.		Total.		
			M.	F.	M.	F.	
G.O.C. Mandalay District and O.C. Bhamo.	Commissioner, Northern Division, and Deputy Commissioner, Bhamo.	**5. Kwitu Ferry**... Indaw Ka and Malí Ka.	9	6	43	2	General direction west for first 6 miles, then west-south-west. Road descends and crosses valley to Tángpu (Malei-Latawng, 20 houses), thence descend to Indaw Ka, tributary of the 'Nmai Ka, 12 yards broad, 1 foot deep, stony bottom, low banks. Having crossed this stream road rises on to a spur of the Pun Nen mountain and runs down it west-south-west to Kwitu Ferry, through forest, crossing a stream just before reaching that place. At Kwitu there is one hut, in which live two or three men, who work the two small bamboo rafts which constitute the ferry. The passage is a difficult one, as the current is very swift. In midstream there is a large rock and, by constructing a "swing bridge" with the rafts, loads can be placed on to the rock and then again across on to the left bank. For troops crossing big bamboos must be collected and proper rafts constructed, for which good stout ropes are necessary.
		6. Warain ... ... Pungin Ka and Insôp Ka.	14	2	57	4	Cross the river and thence forest track for 5½ miles along the river bank to the mouth of the Pungin Ka, very bad and difficult for mule transport. The Pungin Ka is about 35 yards wide and 3 feet deep, rocky bottom, steep banks, and swift current. From the Pungin Ka the road continues north along the right bank of the Malí Ka for 4½ miles to the mouth of the Insôp Ka, the passage of which is in every respect very similar to that of the Pungin Ka. Here the path turns to the north-west and, leaving the valley of the Malí Ka, ascends a high hill, on which is situated the village of Warain (2,000 feet) (Latawng), 10 houses. Rather a long march, as the forest path is so bad, but it could be divided by camping at the crossings of the Pungin or Insôp streams.
		7. Sabaw	8	4	66	0	The forest track, which is much better than that along the river bank, leaving Warain at once, descends for 2 miles, where a small stream is crossed, 8 yards wide and 6 inches deep. From the stream the road ascends a high hill and Paokong village is reached (Sana-Latawng tribe), six houses. From Paokong the road passes over a spur and then descends into a valley with some boggy ground at the bottom. Ascending again through some taungya Túpum is reached (Wa-wang-Lapai tribe), five houses. From Túpum to Sabaw it is 2½ miles by a fair hill track through the jungle; steady descent all the way, the road bearing east. Sabaw is a small Kachin village situated on rising ground on the right bank of the Malí Ka (Sana-Latawng tribe), eight houses; a little paddy and poultry procurable. The Malí Ka is here about 140 yards broad with a swift current, and rapids above and below the village. Laungs, however, can reach Sabaw with difficulty all the year round. There is another ferry here, the road crossing some of the lower spurs of Pum Nen and cutting into the northern road between the Malí Ka and the 'Nmai Ka. Supplies *nil*, except small quantity of rice and poultry at the Kachin villages.

FROM MAINGNA TO KÁNTI *viâ* LEKANNOI AND TINGSA-PUMLUMPUM—*continued.*

Authorities. Military.	Authorities. Civil.	Number and Names of Stages, Rivers and Streams.	Distances. Intermediate. M.	F.	Total. M.	F.	Remarks.
G.O.C. Mandalay District and O.C. Bhamo.	Commissioner, Northern Division, and Deputy Commissioner, Bhamo.	**8. Pumwai (1)** ...	9	0	75	0	Back as far as Túpum 2½ miles, thence north-west through Pumwai (2), and joining the road from Myitkyina, No. 85, 2 miles before reaching camp at Pumwai (1), Wawang-Lapai village of six houses.
		9. Sup Ka	8	0	83	0	For details of Stages 9 to 12 *see* Route No. 85.
		10. Warra ...	8	0	91	0	
		11. Siyángkong ...	6	4	97	4	
		12. Tingsa-pumlumpum.	6	4	104	0	

BRANCH I.

FROM LEKANNOI FERRY (STAGE 3) TO LOISAW (STAGE 2 OF ROUTE NO. 79).

BY LIEUT. PEEBLES, FEBRUARY 1892.

Military	Civil	Stage	Int. M.	F.	Total M.	F.	Remarks
G.O.C. Mandalay District and O.C. Bhamo.	Commissioner, Northern Division, and Deputy Commissioner, Bhamo.	**1. 'Nsum Ka camp.** 'Nmrai Ka, 'Nsot Ka and 'Nsum Ka.	9	0	9	0	General direction south-west. Leaving the ferry the road runs due west following the stream 3 miles to the Kátup rapid, and crossing the 'Nmrai Ka and 'Nsot Ka the road then runs south up to the village of Taolangkong (Nawkhum Latawng), 12 houses, situated on the summit of small line of hills, and then down to the 'Nsum Ka, leaving the village of Inchunkong (Nawkhum Latawng) on the right. The camping ground is situated beside the 'Nsum Ka. This is an alternative route to that described in Stage 3 of the main route. The road for the first 3 miles is very bad passing through thick bamboo jungle, much overgrown, and over several small, deep nullahs. The remainder of road is through ordinary jungle and in good order. The 'Nmrai Ka is a small mountain stream. The 'Nsot Ka and 'Nsum Ka are two small streams about 5 yards wide and 12 inches deep with stony bottom; approaches good.
		2. Layáng ... Namfu Ka.	9	4	18	4	Leaving the 'Nsum Ka the road, which is a fine forest path, leads up a gradual incline to the village of Mailompum (Nawkhum Latawng), 20 houses; the road then runs down hill to the Shan Talôk village of Kángpu, 6 miles, which is surrounded by a bamboo stockade. Passing south through the paddy-fields which surrounded this village, the road crosses the Namfu Ka and leads on to the villages of Saré (Numkum), 7½ miles, and Layáng (Nawkhum Latawng), 9 miles 6 furlongs, the camp being situated on a small stream to the north of Layáng. The first 7½ miles or so of this stage is the same as Stage 3 of the main route, the road then bears away more to the east, evidently for Layáng and Kwitu. The Namfu is a small stream running into the Irrawaddy and is of a winding nature, being crossed by the road four times within ½ of mile. The stream is about 10 yards wide and 18 inches deep with gravelly bottom. The banks are not good, but can easily be made passable when required.

FROM MAINGNA TO KÁNTI *viâ* LEKANNOI AND TINGSA-PUMLUMPUM—*continued.*

BRANCH I—*continued.*

Authorities. Military.	Authorities. Civil.	Number and Names of Stages, Rivers and Streams.	Distances. Intermediate. M. F.	Distances. Total. M. F.	Remarks.
G.O.C. Mandalay District and O.C. Bhamo.	Commissioner, Northern Division, and Deputy Commissioner, Bhamo.	**3. Kwitu** ... ... Kwitu chaung.	9 0	27 4	After leaving the village of Layáng the road runs south and 1¼ miles further on passes through second village of Layáng and continues south. The road runs through the plain to Kwitu south crossing the Kwitu chaung ½ mile from Kwitu. The road throughout is good and can be easily marched in 3 hours. The Kwitu chaung runs into Irrawaddy and at the crossing is 20 yards wide and 1 foot deep; good banks and gravelly bottom.
		4. Loisaw ... ... Natmyin chaung.	9 4	37 0	Leaving Kwitu the road runs south through paddy-fields for ½ mile and then runs through jungle with occasional clearings. The road throughout is in very good order. Loisaw is a Shan-Talôk village on left bank of Natmyin chaung, which at the ford is 30 yards wide and 2 feet deep in the centre of the channel with good sloping banks and gravelly bottom. The village is situated in large paddy-fields.

No. 47.

From MALÉ to HLUTTAIK.

BY LIEUT. HUGHES, OXFORDSHIRE LIGHT INFANTRY, 1888.

Military	Civil	Stages	Intermediate	Total	Remarks
G.O.C. Mandalay District.	Commissioner, Northern Division, and Deputy Commissioner, Shwébo.	**1. Thándaw** ...	8 0	...	Follow the Tántabin road for 3 miles. Here the road branches off north-west to Thándaw through open forest: fair for carts throughout the year. Thándaw has zayát accommodation for 20 men. Good water can be obtained by digging in chaung.
		2. Paga	15 0	23 0	The road from Thándaw to Paga continues in a north-westerly direction through thick forest (15 miles). On approaching Paga the forest becomes more open with large trees. This part of the road is good for carts in dry season; practicable during the rains. Fair water can be obtained by digging in a chaung near. Accommodation none.
		3. Sabénetha ...	10 0	33 0	The road continues in a north-westerly direction to Sabénetha (10 miles). Water from nullah west of village. (From Sabénetha there is a road south-south-west to Tántabin 26 miles. This road is now being cleared of jungle by villagers. It passes through Kángyi at 11 miles, where there is water and accommodation in kyaung for 50 men).

FROM MALÉ TO HLUTTAIK—*continued.*

Authorities: Military.	Authorities: Civil.	Number and Names of Stages, Rivers and Streams.	Distances: Intermediate. M. F.	Distances: Total. M. F.	Remarks.
G.O.C. Mardalay District.	Commissioner, Northern Division, and Deputy Commissioner, Shwébo.	**4. Gáda**	**6 0**	39 0	The road from Sabénetha to Gáda can be traversed by carts in the dry season, but is a very bad road. Cross the creek to Sindilingo, south (1 mile). From Sindilingo the road runs north-west to Gáda (6 miles). At 2 miles the road descends into the Sabénetha creek and follows its course for 50 yards, when it again emerges on the same side. The banks of the creek here are from 50 to 60 feet high with thick jungle and undergrowth on the top. Road continues to Gáda through thick jungle and undergrowth crossing three creeks, all of which have water. The whole way from Sabénetha to Gáda the jungle is too thick for flanking parties. The road is little used and, in some places, the track is hardly perceptible. Accommodation at Gáda in one large kyaung. Water good from creek and wells.
		5. Ingyinzu ...	**12 0**	51 0	Road west to Ségyi (3 miles); a fair cart road through open country (2 miles), then 1 mile through jungle. From Ségyi there is said to be a cart track to Ingyinzu (9 miles). It is almost certain that this cart track exists or could easily be made, as the country in the vicinity is reported open with small teak trees suitable for carts, if not carts would have to go south-west to Kamballu (7 miles); fair cart road through open country and from Kambalu to Ingyinzu on the Tôkoshát-Pégôn road (6 miles) (Route No. 93): total 16 miles from Gáda. This would add 4 miles to the road. Ingyinzu has accommodation in one good kyaung.
		6. Pégôn	**7 0**	58 0	Road same as Tôkoshát to Pégôn. Pégôn has accommodation for 150 men in one kyaung and two zayáts. From Pégôn cross the creek to West Pégôn and on westward through varnish and teak tree forest to Léla, a small village to which the people have just returned. It has one somewhat dilapidated kyaung, capable, however, of affording shelter to 50 or 60 men. There is open paddy cultivation to the north and west of the village. Very little water. Road through forest as before. Direction north-west. At 5 miles the Madôn road branches northwards, the direct road leading to Kôkôgôn, distance about 4 miles, and situated on the left bank (east) of the Mu below Hluttaik. Remainder of march through forest as before up to Madôn, which is a village on the left (east) bank of the Mu, opposite Hluttaik. Carts cannot cross at Madôn, owing to the steepness of the river banks, but can do so a little higher up. There are, however, plenty of boats and, during the dry season, the river is fordable; bottom sandy; water 1 to 3 feet in January. This road, as also the branch leading to Kôkôgôn, is good and easy for carts. The forest abounds in deer, and there are also wild elephants. Grass plentiful, but water scarce. *Note.*—Lieutenant-Colonel Senior says: "No water excepting within a mile of Madôn."

No. 47.

FROM MALÉ TO HLUTTAIK—*continued.*

Authorities. Military.	Authorities. Civil.	Number and Names of Stages, Rivers and Streams.	Distances. Intermediate. M.	Distances. Intermediate. F.	Distances. Total. M.	Distances. Total. F.	Remarks.
G.O.C. Mandalay District.	Commissioner, Northern Division, and Deputy Commissioner, Shwébo.	**7. Hluttaik** ... Mu River.	13	0	71	0	This road at present would be difficult on account of bad accommodation. The part from Sabénetha to Gáda is probably impracticable in the rainy season for carts. It is, however, the the direct route from Malé to Hluttaik and will probably be much used when the country becomes settled down. At present (1888) the country is nearly deserted by the people from fear of dacoits; and carts go from Malé to Tántabin and Tántabin northwards, a route 13 miles longer.

No. 48.

From MALÉ to KAWLIN.

BY LIEUT. HUGHES, 2ND OXFORDSHIRE LIGHT INFANTRY, MARCH 1888.

Military.	Civil.	Stages.	Int. M.	Int. F.	Total M.	Total F.	Remarks.
G.O.C. Mandalay District.	Commissioner, Northern Division, and Deputy Commissioner, Shwébo.	**1. Thándaw** ...	8	0	8	0	Cross the hills by the Malé-Tántabin road, 3 miles. (*See* Route No. 49). Here the road turns north-west to Thándaw at 8 miles; a good road for carts through open forest. Thándaw has accommodation for 20 men, and good water by digging in chaung.
		2. Paga	14	0	22	0	Road continues north-west to Paga, 14 miles, through thick forest. On nearing Paga the forest becomes more open with large trees. Paga is deserted (March 1888) and has no accommodation, but fair water can be obtained by digging in chaung.
		3. Hlwéseik ...	8	0	30	0	Road on north-north-west to Hlwéseik, 8 miles. Hlwéseik has 30 houses; accommodation in zayáts for 30 men. Road crosses the Hlwéseik chaung close to the village (only a small chaung, impassable for a few hours after heavy rain). Road good and through dense jungle (both teak and bamboo) across a small chaung to Tabetlôn at 6 miles. No water in chaung, except for a few hours after heavy rain. Tabetlôn has about 50 houses. Water got from wells and from chaung. Has one kyaung and two zayáts.
		4. Baw	9	0	39	0	Road good and through thick jungle. Road crosses the Baw chaung. This is a broad shallow chaung. Carts can cross even in rainy weather. Village of about 20 houses. Water from chaung not good. Has one kyaung and one zayát for 50 men.

FROM MALÉ TO KAWLIN—*continued.*

Authorities. Military.	Authorities. Civil.	Number and Names of Stages, Rivers and Streams.	Distances. Intermediate. M.	F.	Total. M.	F.	Remarks.
G.O.C. Mandalay District.	Commr., Northern Divn., and Deputy Commr., Katha.	**5. Ukingyi** ...	**20**	**0**	59	0	Road on good for carts in dry season as far as Zin at 7½ miles, passing Katta at 5 miles, then north-west *viâ* Sinyán and Zígôn to Ukingyi at 20 miles.
		6. Kyungôn ...	**12**	**2**	71	2	For remainder *see* Route No. 93.
		7. Kawlin ...	**8**	**4**	79	6	

There is an alternative route, BAW TO KAWLIN, as follows (Native information):—

Military	Civil	Stage	Int. M.	F.	Total M.	F.	Remarks
G.O.C. Mandalay District.	Commissioner, Northern Division, and Deputy Commissioner, Katha.	**1. Baw**	**1**	**4**	1	4	Good kyaungs.
		2. Katta	**1**	**0**	2	4	No kyaungs.
		3. Zinyama ...	**1**	**0**	3	4	Good kyaungs.
		4. Letpándaw ...	**1**	**4**	5	0	Good kyaungs.
		5. Kudônbin ...	**4**	**0**	9	0	No kyaungs.
		6. Shawbyugôn ...	**1**	**4**	10	4	No kyaungs.
		7. Zibyugôn ...	**1**	**0**	11	4	Good kyaungs.
		8. Thôngdindut ...	**2**	**0**	13	0	Good kyaungs.
		9. Kyaukpintha ...	**4**	**0**	17	0	Good kyaungs. *Note.*—This road is described as through the heaviest possible cane jungle and scarcely ever used for fear of dacoits.

No. 49.

From MALÉ to YÉ-U viâ TÁNTABIN.

I. B. COMPILATION, MARCH 1888.

Military	Civil	Stage	Int. M.	F.	Total M.	F.	Remarks
G.O.C. Mandalay District.	Commissioner, Northern Division, and Deputy Commissioner, Shwébo.	**1. Kyátyé and Myémôn.** Chaungyi and four smaller nullahs.	**15**	**0**	15	0	Malé is a village on the right bank of the Irrawaddy, about 25 miles north of Kyaukmyaung. It extends 1,000 yards along the bank of the river, including the small village of Dahagôn (north) and is about 400 yards broad from east to west. There are about 300 houses in all. The stockade is in the centre overlooking the river from the bank, which is here rocky and steep, about 35 feet high. South of the stockade the bank of the river is not so steep and less rocky. Here the principal part of the village is situated and all boats are anchored; steamers anchor near the south end of the village in the dry season, but the anchorage is not good on account of rocks. When the river is high there is very good anchorage 200 yards lower down at the south end of the village, where there would be room for four steamers alongside the bank. Here, too, there is

No. 49.

From MALÉ to YÉ-U *viâ* TÁNTABIN—*continued.*

Authorities. Military.	Authorities. Civil.	Number and Names of Stages, Rivers and Streams.	Distances. Inter-mediate.	Distances. Total.	Remarks.
G.O.C. Mandalay District.	Commissioner, Northern Division, and Deputy Commissioner, Shwébo.	**1. Kyátyé and Myémôn**—*cont.*			good camping ground extending for 300 yards along the bank, 100 yards broad. The stockade is now occupied by 30 police; could hold 200 men and 40 horses. There are six kyaungs and eight zayáts in the vicinity. The kyaungs would accommodate 300 men and the zayáts, 150. Good water can be obtained from midstream of the Irrawaddy. The general direction of the road from Malé to Tántabin is west-south-west. All jungle has been cleared to a breadth of 40 yards, but the road has not been made yet, except near Malé and for a short distance west of Pazi. It is, however, a good road for carts in dry season and would be practicable for carts the whole year, except for some hours after heavy rain at 2½ miles, where it crosses Chaungyi creek twice; at 9½ miles where it crosses Chaungyi creek a third time; at 3, 4, 5 and 6 miles, where it crosses nullahs. In dry season, after leaving Pazi at 5 miles till reaching Kyauksakhán at 25 miles, water can only be obtained at one place (15 miles), where a temporary well has been dug in the bed of a small nullah between Kyátyé and Myémôn. These two villages were both deserted (March 1888). Kyátyé, south of the road at 15 miles, has no accommodation, but good camping ground north-east of the village Myémôn, which is about ½ mile north of road, reached by a track branching north just after passing the above-mentioned well, has two deserted kyaungs which would hold 30 men, and water can be obtained from well north-east of the village. The whole way from Pazi to Kyauksakhán is through forest and jungle. The old trade route used to pass through Myémôn. From Pazi a road branches south to Mézataw, and when the road is cut from Mézataw to Saingaung there will be an alternative route to Yé-u by that village. Maungyaukdaw, Alésha, Pindin, across the Shwébo-Tántabin road, about 2 miles north of Kinu, to Sibautya, and on to the Mu river about 48 miles. This road is at least as along as that *viâ* Tántabin, but might be found more convenient in the dry season on account of the scarcity of water at Kyátyé and Myémôn. It has also better accommodation for short marches. The stages would be Mézataw, 8 miles; Saingaung, 14 miles; Pindín or Kinu, 12 miles; Yé-u, 15 miles. The road from Malé to Pazi for the first 2½ miles, though very hilly and passing through open jungle, is quite practicable for carts. At three places, for about 40 yards, the road is very steep and very rough from action of the water in the rains, greatest slope $\frac{1}{12}$. At 2½ miles cross Chaungyi creek, 20 yards broad, sandy bottom, banks 12 feet high. Some water standing in places in March. A zayát on either side, 12 men in each. The road continues over flat ground ½ mile, when it again crosses Chaungyi creek. Road on over flat ground, through open jungle, across two nullahs to Pazi at 5 miles. North Pazi has 50 houses; South Pazi, ¼ mile south, has 20 houses, both surrounded by paddy and enclosed by dead thorn fences. Two zayáts; would hold 20 men, one pôngyi kyaung at South Pazi, 30 men. Water good from two wells; water from tank in the rains. The road from Pazi here is level and on the whole good; the soil being of a sandy nature soon dries. Chaungyi creek is again crossed about 6 miles from Pazi (this nullah forms the western boundary of Malé). About 1 mile from Kyátyé in a north-easterly direction, is the deserted village of Myémôn, where there are two kyaungs and a shed; 30 men could be housed for the night. There are two wells (in one of which is good drinking water), also plenty of grass.

FROM MALÉ TO YÉ-U *viâ* TÁNTABIN—*continued.*

Authorities. Military.	Authorities. Civil.	Number and Names of Stages, Rivers and Streams.	Distances. Intermediate. M. F.	Distances. Total. M. F.	Remarks.
G.O.C. Mandalay District.	Commissioner, Central Division, and Deputy Commissioner, Shwébo.	**2. Tántabin** ...	14 0	29 0	The road from Kyátyé for about 9 miles is through jungle, principally bamboo. The road to this point is fairly good to Kyauk sakhân at 11 miles. Accommodation for 50 men in kyaung and two zayáts, good water. The road from Kyauk sakhán is principally through paddy-fields, but is passable for carts at all seasons. For description of Tántabin *see* Route No. 93.
		3. Maunghla ...	11 0	40 0	Road on runs south-west and is for the most part very good in dry season through more or less open country and paddy-fields for the first 10 miles, when the river Mu is reached. The road then follows the left bank of the Mu to Maunghla. From Tántabin to Maunghla is very difficult for carts during the rains. Maunghla has one kyaung for 30 men, one zayát for 20 men. Water good.
	Commr., Northern Divn., and Deputy Commr., Yé-u.	**4. Yé-u** ... ... Mu river.	6 0	46 0	Road on along the left bank of the Mu through forest over firm ground, practicable for carts at all seasons. Cross the Mu opposite Yé-u; about 1 foot of water in March; stream 50 yards broad; deep sand ¼ mile on either side. The Mu river is impassable for carts from May to December. There is a ferry during the rainy season. The three stockades are about ½ mile west of the right bank on the further side of the village. Accommodation in stockades for 800 men; in kyaungs in vicinity for 400 men; nine zayáts for 150 men; good water from several wells and from river.

No. 50.

From MANDALAY to MÔGÔK *viâ* MAINGLÔN.

I. B. COMPILATION, NOVEMBER 1888.

Military	Civil	Stages	Intermediate	Total	Remarks
G.O.C. Mandalay District.	Commissioner, Northern Division, and Deputy Commissioner, Mandalay.	**1. Lamaing** ... Five or six sluices from Nánda lake; canal, Yedana (all bridged).	17 0	17 0	Leave Mandalay by east gate. Road runs north, leaving Mandalay hill on left and skirts Nánda lake for 4 miles. At 7 miles road to Kaingyi leads to east. At 8 miles cross canal and leave Shwédaung on the right. From this to Lamaing road follows west bank of Yedana river, passing numerous villages. Cross Yedana river at Lamaing. Police post in kyaung on east side of village. Water from well and river.

No. 50.

FROM MANDALAY TO MÔGÔK *viâ* MAINGLÔN—*continued.*

Authorities. Military.	Authorities. Civil.	Number and Names of Stages, Rivers and Streams.	Distances. Intermediate. M. F.	Distances. Total. M. F.	Remarks.
G.O.C. Mandalay District.	Commissioner, Northern Division, and Deputy Commissioner, Mandalay.	**2. Zagabin** ... Yedana river, Ômnin river (both bridged).	11 0	28 0	Recross Yedana river and follow west bank through thick jungle. At ¼ mile pass Shazíseik. At 6 miles pass Ômnin (kyaung) and at 6½ miles Tadán (several kyaungs) after crossing stream. At 9½ miles pass Ôkpo and follow east bank of Madaya river. Jungle thin with cultivation here and there. Post on hill with river on both sides. Several kyaungs. Water from river.
		3. Kaingyi (along right bank of Madaya river). Madaya river twice, crossed by rafts or boats; fords about 3 to 3½ feet deep.	8 4	36 4	Cross river to Salé on west bank; course east. Pass Pyinagwé at 1 mile, Sittaung at 2½ miles, chiefly through paddy country. At 4 miles pass camp ground on river bank, road turning north through thick jungle. Pass Taungzeik at 6 miles, Shwéthamin at 7 miles, Pandauk at 7½ miles, Nyaungbintha at 8 miles. Troops can either encamp here or cross the river to Kaingyi. Water from river. Cart road ceases here. There are two very good fords at this place, but the approach to the lower of the two, exactly opposite the encamping ground, on the left bank is abrupt and steep; this, however, could easily be ramped and made easy. Neither ford is at present more than 3 feet deep and the current slight. (11th January 1887.) The camping ground here (Kaingyi right bank of the river) is a very good one close to the river and about 20 feet above it. It has a fair command over the opposite bank and a good view both up and down the river; a capital place for a post. Kaingyi is a large village, with bazaar, on the left bank of Madaya river. Zayát in bad repair. Water and wood abundant. From Zagabin to Kaingyi along the left bank of the Madaya the road, though it does not cross the river, is 2 miles longer and not practicable for carts.
		4. Taungdeik ... Numerous small streams, all easily forded.	9 0	45 4	Road runs generally north-east to foot of hills, but winds a great deal and crosses the stream nine times. At 1½ miles pass Lepándaw, 12 houses; one zayát on left of road. After this the road enters the lower hills and follows the stream, of which the fall from the hills is visible at Mandalay. At 4½ miles pass Kyaukmyo, a large camping ground, but with no shelter. Water and wood abundant. After this the ascent begins at first towards north for 1 mile, then east up the hill. The path is very steep in parts, but passable for elephants and mule transport, if not very heavily laden. At 8½ miles the top is reached. Half a mile further Taungdeik, a small village, 10 houses; elevation about 2,700 feet. Camping ground had to be cleared of jungle. Water from small spring about 200 yards below camp to west. No supplies.
	Superintendent, Northern Shan States.	**5. Kalagwé** ... Three streams crossed, all fordable and provided with foot-bridges.	10 4	56 0	Road runs north-east and is very good as far as Kalagwé, though not cleared for carts. It is, however, easily made fit for them. Country undulating, with a gradual ascent towards Kalagwé; thin jungle, with small camping grounds cleared by caravans every

FROM MANDALAY TO MÔGÔK *viâ* MAINGLÔN—*continued.*

Authorities. Military.	Authorities. Civil.	Number and Names of Stages, Rivers and Streams.	Distances. Intermediate.	Distances. Total.	Remarks.
G.O.C. Mandalay District.	Superintendent, Northern Shan States.	**5. Kalagwé**—*cont.*			mile or so. At 4 miles pass Pinpya, and at 5 miles Kyaukkyi, small village of 10 or 12 huts, at present deserted. At 9½ miles cross large stream by a foot-bridge, but passable for transport. At 10½ miles reach Kalagwé; pass through village across stream ½ mile further to camp ground. Large village, deserted. Camping ground on slope of hills towards stream. Site good and space ample. Water and wood aburdant. Road to Thônzé branches to south-east; two marches.
		6. Pasi ... ... Streams crossed and recrossed continually; all fordable.	M. F. 15 4	M. F. 71 4	Road runs north, good for 3 miles; at 2 miles pass Thawmagôn, 20 houses. At 2½ miles cross stream and enter hills. From this for 3 miles the path runs principally along the bed of a small stream, constantly crossed by, and sometimes actually serving as, the road; hills precipitous on both sides and covered with jungle. At 5¾ miles an open space is reached, used by caravans as a camping ground, where the small stream joins a larger one running south. The road then turns north-east and follows the latter stream, crossing it frequently. At 11 miles a camping ground is reached and the ascent begins. As water is abundant here and scarce at the top of the pass, it might be advisable for a large force of men, or a considerable train of animals, to halt here in preference. The camping ground is large and wood abundant. The road here runs east following a spur and is very steep in parts, but always passable for elephants and mules not too heavily laden. The ascent is about 4 miles. Previous to reaching the foot of the hills, streams are crossed on this march nearly a hundred times. Pasi is a small village on summit of ridge; elevation about 4,500 feet; 20 houses; wood obtainable, but no supplies and water very scarce, obtained from a spring about 300 yards below village to north on Mainglôn road. Animals can drink at a pool immediately below, where the approaches make the water too muddy for men.
		7. Mainglôn (Mainlung). Three streams crossed, all fordable; two provided with foot-bridges.	14 4	86 0	Road runs north descending gradually, but always following the same spur close to the top; small ascents occur at intervals, and the descent is steep in many parts, but passable as above for animals. At 9½ miles cross large stream; this is the only water seen from the road after leaving Pasi. Although off the road, there must have been streams higher up. A few villages were passed on adjoining spurs. Road now undulates over lower spurs, crossing a few small streams. At 10½ miles pass Pinkaw on left; at 11½ miles Pinpaun, each about 40 houses, latter with zayáts and kyaung. A large basin is then passed mostly under paddy cultivation and traversed by a large stream. The camp was pitched in the centre of this. At 14½ miles pass Myohaung, 50 houses. This village with Pinpaun and others close by form old Mainglôn. At 14½ miles reach Mainglôn. A road runs west from old Mainglôn to Môgôk. Mainglôn lies in a valley at an elevation of about 3,000 feet, among trees and bush jungle, and to the south and west extends a broad cultivated plain laid out in paddy-fields, which is again bounded by low, grassy hills on the west and higher wooded ones on the south. To

FROM MANDALAY TO MÔGÔK *viâ* MAINGLÔN—*continued.*

Authorities. Military.	Authorities. Civil.	Number and Names of Stages, Rivers and Streams.	Distances. Intermediate. M. F.	Distances. Total. M. F.	Remarks.
G.O.C. Mandalay District.	Supdt., Northern Shan States.	**7. Mainglôn (Mainlung)**—*cont.*			the north and east of the town there are rolling hills covered with grass and jungle. To the north-east runs a road to Maingaung; to the south-east a road over the hills to Palaung villages; to the south a road to old Mainglôn and thence to Mandalay; and the north-west a road to Môgôk. There is plenty of rice straw made into neat ricks in the paddy-fields. There are no habitable kyaungs in Mainglôn proper, but there are said to be two good ones in the old town.

ALTERNATIVE HALTING PLACES (if the last two stages are considered too long) between Kalagwé and Mainglôn.

Military.	Civil.	Stage	Intermediate M.	Intermediate F.	Total M.	Total F.	Remarks.
	Supdt., Northern Shan States.	**6. Camp ground.**	12	4	68	4	The camp ground cleared for 300 by by 150 yards is at the foot of the steep part of the hills, at the top of which is Pazi.
		7. Ditto. ...	12	4	81	0	At foot of hill on north side of Pazi. Clearing small. Water abundant. Half a mile further is Pinpaw, where there is ample room and water.
		8. Mainglôn ...	5	0	86	0	
G.O.C. Mandalay District.	Commissioner, Northern Division, and Deputy Commissioner, Ruby Mines.	**8. Kyauktalôn** ... Nampé and Namyut.	8	4	94	4	Road runs north-north-west through grass and scrub jungle, passing Shan village of Namping at ½ mile. At 1⅛ miles road crosses Nampé river (30 yards broad, 2½ feet deep; rapid current rising apparently 3 or 4 feet in rains), leaving Mainglôn territory. Small Shan village of Kaungywa on south bank. Road then turns north over rolling, grass-covered hills to 3 miles. At 4½ miles good camping ground in paddy-fields. At 6½ miles large camping ground of paddy-fields and deserted village of Légyi, with inhabited Shan village of Namywa (20 houses), on opposite bank of Nampé river. Thence west along right bank of the river through thick jungle over undulating ground. At 7¾ miles turn north-east along the left bank of the Namyut stream, which here flows into the Nampé. Road follows the valley of this stream for ¾ mile, rising rapidly. At 8¼ miles cross the river, which is here a rapid torrent, 20 yards broad, 2 feet deep; island in centre; appears to rise 2 feet more in rains. At 8½ miles Kyauktalôn, a deserted Palaung village lying in a cultivated valley, with plenty of water and grass, at a height of 3,200 feet.
		9. Môgôk ... ... Streams, good water.	9	4	104	0	General direction north-west, up-hill through thick jungle, crossing many streams to small camp ground at 3¼ miles. Small Palaung village of Nyaungaung visible ½ mile to right of road. At 4½ miles a path leads to this village. At 6 miles the road crosses the top of the Mwin sakhén hill, 4,900 feet; thence north-north-west to Môgôk, crossing a small valley half way. At 7½ miles a path leads to small Palaung village of Pama. At 7¾ miles, another path (north-north-east) to same village, visible ⅛ mile off the road. At 9½ miles Môgôk.

FROM MANDALAY TO MÔGÔK *viâ* MAINGLÔN—*continued.*

BRANCH I.

FROM KAINGYI (STAGE 3) TO NUNG-É AND ON UP THE MADDAYA RIVER.

I. B. COMPILATION, AUGUST 1888.

Authorities. Military.	Authorities. Civil.	Number and Names of Stages, Rivers and Streams.	Distances. Intermediate. M. F.	Distances. Total. M. F.	Remarks.
G.O.C. Mandalay District.	Commissioner, Northern Division, and Deputy Commissioner, Mandalay.	**1. Nung-é** ... ... Maddaya river.	**11 6**	11 6	At 1 mile pôngyi kyaung to the east. At 1¼ miles Letpadaung (20 houses), but deserted. At 1½ miles cross a nullah. At 3¼ miles Kimadaung, 20 houses. Water from Maddaya river. At 3½ miles cross the Maddaya river 100 yards wide, bed stony, banks high, difficult for loaded animals. Fordable except after heavy rain. At present (end of May) water 2½ feet. At 4¾ miles Gwégyaung, deserted village, except one pôngyi kyaung. Water from Maddaya river. At 6¾ miles road followed a nullah for about 1 mile, and subsequently crossed the same nullah several times up to 10 miles, where the Ledaung chaung is crossed, 20 yards wide, bed stony, banks easy, fordable two days after heavy rain. At 10¼ miles road branches west to Dandin, 3¼ miles. At about 10¾ miles cross the same nullah twice again and ¼ mile further reach Ledaung. From Kaingyi to Letpadaung good cart road on level ground. From Letpadaung to Gwégyaung good path through thick jungle, practicable for animals. From Gwégyaung to Ledaung road through hills with occasional ascents and descents, rather difficult for loaded animals. River Maddaya is along the road up to Gwégyaung, then to the east of it Ledaung is a deserted village. Good encamping ground to the west in fields. At 11¼ miles cross a nullah 20 yards wide. Bed sandy and stony, banks difficult for loaded animals. Fordable three days after heavy rain. At 11¾ miles deserted Shan village of Nung-é on the Maddaya river. Here road from Singu joins (*see* Route No. 96). At 1¼ miles cross a nullah 30 yards wide. Bed stony, banks easy. Fordable two days after heavy rain. Country thick jungle. Ascent and descent difficult for loaded animals. From Nung-é the road runs along the left bank of the Maddaya river for 3 miles, when the course of the river turns to the right into the hills. No village. No camping ground. A small party of military police made their way easily in June before the rains had commenced from Nung-é up the valley of the Maddaya for about 10 miles, at which point a chaung, called by them the Kin chaung, runs in from the north-west. Bed of Maddaya river sandy with pebbles. Water at outside 4 feet deep and fordable anywhere until the rains. Party marched in the river bed almost all the way, apparently no path. Following generally the course of the Kin chaung, apparently nearly west, they came to a small village called Taungdeik at about 12 miles from the junction of the Kin chaung with the Maddaya river. The track was rough chiefly up the bed of the stream, and bad for naked feet, but not difficult. In the rains, however, it would be impossible to follow the stream bed, and to force a way through the dense jungle on either side of it would be most arduous, if not impracticable. This Taungdeik is probably the Ma-ubin of Route No. 95. From Taungdeik the party marched through rough hilly country to Malégyi, said to be 12 miles distant, and Singu. They took only cooly carriage, and the path according to these accounts is quite impracticable for

FROM MANDALAY TO MÔGÔK *viâ* MAINGLÔN—*continued.*

BRANCH I—*continued.*

Authorities. Military.	Authorities. Civil.	Number and Names of Stages, Rivers and Streams.	Distances. Intermediate.	Distances. Total.	Remarks.
G.O.C. Mandalay District.	Commissioner, Northern Division, &c., Mandalay.	**1. Nung-é**—*cont.*			pack animals at any season. From the traces of old encamping grounds along the Kin chaung this route from the Shan hills into the Singu district was evidently much used by dacoits at that time.

No. 51.

From MANDALAY to MYINGYÁN viâ MYOTHA.

I. B. COMPILATION, FEBRUARY 1888.

Military	Civil	Stages	Intermediate	Total	Remarks
G.O.C. Mandalay District. / G.O.C. Myingyán District.	Commissioner, Northern Division, and Deputy Commissioner, Mandalay. / Commissioner, Central Division, and Deputy Commissioner, Sagaing.	**1. Ava** ... ... Thagyin chaung (25 yards broad, February); Myitngé river (Namtu); and Irrawaddy.	M. F. **14 0**	M. F. 14 0	Leave the city by 84th street. At 3 miles cross broad deep nullah by a bridge. At 3½ miles pass Arakan pagoda on the left of road. At 5 miles cross the bund and, passing through north-west corner of Amarapura, leave it on the left. Road good and practicable for carts but unmetalled. At 8 miles pass through village of Taungyi (good bazaar) and over wooden bridge, 300 yards long, which spans the Thagyin chaung. Bridge not practicable for carts, which pass by ford 100 yards lower down. All carts have to be unloaded at the ford and contents taken across in boats, as the water is 4 feet 6 inches deep. One and-a-half miles to the east is another wooden bridge 1 mile long leading to Pabeik. Thagyin chaung runs into the Irrawaddy ½ mile below the ford. Pass through large village of Nyaungaung on opposite bank to Taungyi. Road runs west-south-west. At 10¾ miles pass village of Sinywé, strong wooden bridge, 30 yards long over nullah, practicable for carts and artillery.* At 11½ miles pass village of Thabyadin. Earth redoubt 100 yards to right of road. Telegraph wire runs along road from Myaungaung to Letheya. At 12 miles reach small village of Letheya on right bank of Myitngé river, where the ferry crosses to Ava. There is only one ferry boat which holds two carts, four horses or six ponies (one squadron of cavalry, strength 115 men, 118 horses, 48 ponies and 27 carts took ten hours to cross the river). Carts have to be unloaded and their contents taken across in boats. River 120 yards broad in February (when in full flood about 200 yards from bank to bank). There are four ordinary boats besides the ferry raft, and at 24 hours' notice a very large number could be collected from Sagaing, Ava, &c., to use as ferry boats or for the construction of rafts. At 13¾ miles reach Ava pagoda. Good road running through ruins of old city, well shaded by high trees. Accommodation for a large number of troops in pagoda, &c. At 14 miles reach Ava fort. Ava is the head-quarters of an Assistant Commissioner and occupied by 150 police, of which 35 are mounted. Head-quarters of the district are at Sagaing on the opposite side of the river. Accommodation for a regiment of cavalry or infantry in fort. A daily bazaar is held, but it is small, and better supplies can be obtained from Tada-u, 3½ miles east. Gram and grass for horses can be obtained. The pagoda and fort are 600 yards apart and

* Large parties might halt at Sinywé (10¾ miles) if accompanied by much baggage, the two crossings at Taungyi and the Myitngé river making it a long march to Ava.

FROM MANDALAY TO MYINGYÁN *viâ* MYOTHA—*continued.*

Authorities.		Number and Names of Stages, Rivers and Streams.	Distances.		Remarks.
Military	Civil.		Intermediate.	Total.	
G.O.C. Myingyán District.	Commissioner, Central Division, and Deputy Commissioner, Sagaing.	**1. Ava**—*cont.*			contain quarters for 800 men. The pagoda is large and partly ruined and is enclosed by a high brick wall with loop-holed flanking defences built out from it. Signalling to Sagaing, Kyauksé, and Chaungwa can be carried on from the top of the pagoda. The fort was built by King Thibaw and is 100 yards square with a masonry faced ditch all round it, 20 feet broad and 15 feet deep. Entrance over a fixed wooden bridge on the east side. There is no flanking defence for the fort or ditch. There is telegraph wire to Mandalay and a cable has been laid to Sagaing. The buildings in the fort are wood and matting. Earthen parapet 4 feet 6 inches high revetted with stone. The fort overlooks the river 30 feet below it, and is not commanded except from the top of the pagoda.
		2. Minthé ... Myitha chaung.	M. F. **9 0**	M. F. 23 0	Leave Ava pagoda, road runs east; open and cultivated ground on the right. At 1 mile road turns south and continues south for 2 miles, when the Mandalay-Myingyan telegraph wire is met at the village of Yatan. Road good, newly made, and well shaded by trees on each side. The road then turns west for ¼ mile and then meets the old King's road, a brick causeway in bad repair. At 3 miles cross Myitha chaung by a long wooden bridge and a few hundred yards further a second chaung also bridged. Both these bridges are in good repair and fit for carts. There is a military police post (10 men) at the first bridge. At 3½ miles reach Tada-u, large village, good bazaar. All the surrounding villages get their supplies here. To the north of Tada-u is a fine camping ground for over 1,000 men, but it would be swampy during the rains. There are five wells and a stream close at hand. At 4¼ miles pass small village of Nwégyawdát, a good road in dry weather, but impassable in the rains. The roads all about this part of the country are impassable during the rains, and at that season there is little or no communication between villages in consequence. At 4 miles pass small village of Thimbán. At 6 miles pass Gaungwé. The road along this bit is very bad, leading through wet cultivation. The telegraph wire to Myingyán runs through this village. It is only 2 miles in a straight line from here to Ava, but owing to the Myitha stream a detour has to be made to Tada-u to get here. There is an alternative route ½ mile shorter from Ava to Gaungwé through Kyibin and across the Myitha ferry, but except in the case of small parties without baggage no saving of time would be effected owing to the time taken in crossing the ferry. This route runs south-east after crossing the Myitha ferry, through Kadoseik to Gaungwé. Leaving Gaungwé the road turns south-south-west and runs through low-lying country covered with thin scrub jungle. At 9 miles reach Minthé, large village with kyaung and zayáts. Good wells. Cattle, Indian corn (in Burmese, *pyaung*), and fire-wood can be procured. The telegraph wire runs within 100 yards of the village and thence follows the road to Paukseín.
		3. Myotha ...	**13 0**	36 0	The road on leaving Minthé runs south-west and is a lane with hedges and then a hollow road and afterwards ascends till Sagadé is reached. At 3 miles passing at 1½ miles the small

FROM MANDALAY TO MYINGYÁN *viâ* MYOTHA—*continued.*

Authorities. Military.	Authorities. Civil.	Number and Names of Stages, Rivers and Streams.	Distances. Intermediate.	Distances. Total.	Remarks.
G.O.C. Myingyán District.	Commissioner, Central Division, and Deputy Commissioner, Sagaing.	**3. Myotha**—*cont.*			village of Auktaw, situated on rising ground surrounded by jungle and a little cultivation. The road now descends into a slight hollow, then rises and again dips by a lane through maize and paddy fields to the dry bed of a stream, and at 3½ miles reach large village of Tenaungaung. The village is on the bank of the stream just mentioned. There is plenty of water to be obtained at the village from wells. The road is heavy with sand and rough in places. The road now runs south-south-west and ascends on to high ground, and the telegraph wire is again seen; the road now descends to the dry bed of a stream, crosses it, and rises abruptly till at 5 miles Gwégôn is reached, a small village, two wells; the one nearest the village being the best. There are several places on rising ground suitable for a small encampment, and in dry weather a good camp could be made in the cholum fields close to the village. There is another route from Minthé to Gwégôn, but it is longer than the above. Leaving Gwégôn the road goes round the rear of the village along rising ground, with hedges on each side of it. The country consists of jungle and cultivation. At 1 mile a small village with a zayát and two wells of water is reached, and the wire seen. The road now runs parallel to the wire, and on each side of it the jungle has been cleared leaving on open space 50 yards broad. Soon after this a small clump of pagodas and a kyaung on a knoll to the right of the road is passed; the road dips slightly and then again rises, and further on makes a deep dip and rises into the village of Yamathit. It is a mere resting place for travellers; there are two zayáts and a well, village consisting of a few huts surrounded by the usual thorn hedge; it is situated on high ground. After this the road descends by a fairly easily gradient for about a mile, then ascends and again dips and passes through some cultivation by a lane. A zayát with a good well is then reached, and just past it is the village of Kônywa, only separated from Myotha by a stream. To the west of Kônywa are two pagodas in ruins, square in shape, some kyaungs, numerous zayáts, and a well. Four hundred yards on the Ava side of the village is a good camping ground in dry weather and a well. The water in the stream can be used for watering cattle, but is not good for drinking purposes. At 3 miles reach Myotha, a military police post. Fort 90 yards square, earthen parapet; good bazaar in village. Chenna and grass obtainable. Telegraph office in fort. Country fairly open all round, low thin scrub jungle, and patches of cultivation. Camping ground on west of village. All water here bad. Good water from a well beyond the stream ¼ mile off, where there is also a camping ground which it is considered advisable not to use, as cholera broke out on it when used before. Carts, &c., are obtainable in fair quantity. Leaving Myotha fort, road runs west.
	Commr., Southern Divn., and Dy. Commr., Myingyán.	**4. Pauksein** ... Two nullahs.	M. F. 9 0	M. F. 45 0	Cross bed of stream through cultivation to jungle. At 2½ miles pass village of Kywésein; near here is a pool of water. Then past a few huts surrounded by Indian corn, the country passed through being mostly scrub jungle. The telegraph line is in view nearly all the way. At 4 miles pass Nwadát, a small village with pagoda and zayát. The road here branches off to the right, leading up a slight incline: a tank

FROM MANDALAY TO MYINGYÁN *viâ* MYOTHA—*continued.*

Authorities.		Number and Names of Stages, Rivers and Streams.	Distances.		Remarks.
Military.	Civil.		Intermediate.	Total.	
G.O.C. Myingyán District.	Commissioner, Southern Division, and Deputy Commissioner, Myingyán.	**4. Pauksein**—*cont.*			in a re-entering angle of the hill is reached. The road lies along the bund of this tank and continues rising through open jungle for ½ mile, then descends. From here a red brick pagoda can be seen. This marks the road to Pauksein. The road descends again to the right, and a tank is reached fit for watering animals. Up again ¼ mile further on and on the other side of the dry sandy bed of a stream is Pauksein. The latter part of the road is rocky and in some places very heavy with sand. There is a good camping ground inside, a large kyaung enclosure ½ mile from the village. The kyaung is surrounded by a thorn hedge; there is a tank in it and one well. There is another well outside on the north. There are two villages north and south of Pauksein, and there are kyaungs fit for the accommodation of troops between them. There is plenty of good drinking water obtainable from wells. Chaff, Indian corn, firewood, carts, &c., obtainable.
		5. Koké ... ... One nullah.	M. F. **10 4**	M. F. 55 4	Road passes of out of Pauksein on the south of the village and goes through Indian-corn fields with hedges on each side and enters scrub jungle. The road crosses the spur of a hill; down again, at about 2 miles, a mango tree is passed on the right of the road, and a small depression holding water on the left. At 2¼ miles pass Kanhla. There is a kyaung here surrounded by a thorn hedge. Passing through Kanhla the road debouches on the same green fields. There is ample space to encamp a large force near Kanhla. Entering the the jungle again the road becomes sandy and heavy in places. At 3½ miles the village of Thekégyin, which is long and straggling. Then the road passes an enclosure on the left, containing five pagodas and a kyaung. Skirting this it enters a hollow cart track, heavy and rocky in places. At 4½ miles Sônywa is reached. Road fair, but sandy in places. Telegraph wire in view most of the way. The road now descends into the sandy bed of a stream, crosses it diagonally, rises and crosses a bend of the stream on firm soil, dips again into the stream, follows it for some way and leaves it by a hollow road till the general level of the country is attained. At 6 miles pass small village of Thengôn, consisting of only 10 houses with several pagodas and kyaungs. The road passes through fields, low scrub jungle, and over the edge of a hill, when cultivation is again met near the village of Kyinpyatin, which is reached at 9½ miles. This village is situated on a small knoll forming the termination of a high range of hills running away due south. The village is a very small one, surrounded by a thorn hedge. The road on leaving this village ascends to a ridge and following it some way the Koké hills are reached. This last bit of road is very bad with deep ruts and big rocks on it. The road then descends by a steep path into the plain, and passing through some Indian-corn fields, the village of Koké is reached at 10½ miles. This is a fair-sized village surrounded by a thorn fence. Firewood and Indian corn abundant, other supplies scarce. Outside the village is a tank fit for watering cattle, also a well. Some shady trees near would shelter a camp, but the ground appears to be damp. The best camping ground is ½ mile beyond the village in a kyaung with two zayâts, surrounded by a bamboo and thorn fence, and would

No. 51.

FROM MANDALAY TO MYINGYÁN *viâ* MYOTHA—*continued.*

Authorities. Military.	Authorities. Civil.	Number and Names of Stages, Rivers and Streams.	Distances. Intermediate.	Distances. Total.	Remarks.
G.O.C. Myingyán District.	Commissioner, Southern Division, and Deputy Commissioner, Myingyán.	**5. Koké**—*cont.*			accommodate a regiment. Outside the kyaung is room for another regiment to encamp. At the edge of it is a well of good water just beyond a brick kiln. In the pôngyi's garden is a tank fit for watering cattle. Very nearly all ordinary supplies and transport are procurable. The nullah mentioned above is always fordable.
		6. Myingyán ...	M. 12 F. 0	M. 67 F. 4	Road passes south-west through cultivation following the line of wire to the village of Nabíywa, which is passed at 4 miles. It is only a small village in a ring fence on the left of the road with a small zayát. Water from two wells, but not good. A small white pagoda on the right is passed. Here the road bifurcates: the one to the left hand is the proper one; it passes through some deep sand to a small tank with a bund on the left of the road. The telegraph line, which left the road 3 miles back, is again met here and runs parallel with it. The road is good, but during the rains is reported to be much cut up. At 8½ miles reach Lethit, which is a large village strongly stockaded with thorn hedges. There is a good camping ground here for a small force inside a kyaung with two deep wells of good water. The road from here to Myingyán adheres to the telegraph line and passes along bullock tracks and broad foot-paths, passing through several small hamlets. The ground is cultivated with Indian corn nearly all the way. At 10 miles pass some kyaungs 200 yards to the left of the road, and a tank and two good zayáts. The road continues through cultivation till Myingyán is reached. On north-east of the town is a fortified post held by British troops, the main town stretching away some 2 miles along the left bank of the Irrawaddy. There is a large trade carried on here with the villages of the interior. Myingyán is the chief town of the district and head-quarters of a brigade and has increased considerably during the last two years. It is situated on the left bank of the Irrawaddy, and steamers can come up to the landing place now, though there is said to be great probability of the river channel altering when steamers will be unable to approach within ½ mile of the town. There are a large number of transport animals and carts available at the transport lines, and the town is probably good for 300 more carts, while 500 carts could be shortly collected from the adjacent villages. The population of Myingyán is probably 6,000. There is a telegraph and post office and also a signal station. The roads are cart tracks on which carts can ply all the year round. Fodder is obtainable in fair quantity in all villages. There is a large bazaar in the town, and a large jail is in course of construction. It is the head-quarters of a Deputy Commissioner and possesses a treasury and court-house. The main road runs north and south through the military post and the outskirts of the town, crossing two large nullahs by strong wooden bridges erected by the Public Works Department. Water is obtained from the river. The country round is pretty open, covered by scrub jungle and cultivation alternately.

FROM MANDALAY TO MYINGYÁN *viâ* MYOTHA—*continued.*

BRANCH I.

FROM MYOTHA (STAGE 3) TO CHAUNGWA (STAGE 2 OF ROUTE NO. 56).

I. B. COMPILATION, FEBRUARY 1888.

Authorities. Military.	Authorities. Civil.	Number and Names of Stages, Rivers and Streams.	Distances. Inter-mediate. M.	F.	Total. M.	F.	Remarks.
G.O.C. Myingyán District.	Commissioner, Central Division, and Deputy Commissioner, Sagaing.	**1. Chaungwa** ...	**14**	**4**	14	4	Leaving Myotha post the road runs east and up-hill. At 2 miles small village of Yungaung. Road now runs east-north-east through undulating jungle about 6 feet high. This is a new road and has lately been cut through the rock. At 4 miles it is very rough and rocky and bad for carts. A high wooded range of hills runs parallel to the road for 4 miles, about 1 mile to the right. At 5 miles reach Shwé-daung. Small village. No supplies. Water from tank in hollow of the hill. At 6 miles pass a pagoda. The road still runs east-north-east through high jungle, but is better for carts. At 7 miles cross nullah, 15 feet broad, steep banks. No bridge. At 9 miles Tiyé-bin. Two small villages. No supplies. Large kyaung between the two villages, which are about 500 yards apart. Road now runs north-east through thin scrub jungle. At 11 miles small village of Chaungwa. Road now turns south-south-east and crosses chaung. Dry, sandy bed and fordable in rains. After 200 yards road turns east. At 13½ miles large pôngyi kyaung. At 14½ miles Chaungwa.

BRANCH II-*a*.

FROM MYOTHA TO NÁZUN *viâ* KYAUKTALÔN.

BY LIEUT. CAMPBELL, 25TH MADRAS INFANTRY, 1886.

Authorities. Military.	Authorities. Civil.	Number and Names of Stages, Rivers and Streams.	Distances. Inter-mediate. M.	F.	Total. M.	F.	Remarks.
G.O.C. Myingyán District.	Commissioner, Central Division, and Deputy Commissioner, Sagaing.	**1. Názun**	**13**	**0**	13	0	From Tabé the road runs in a north-west direction through fairly open country, mostly cultivated, for about a mile, until it reaches Tawyé, which is, however, of little importance, as it is almost deserted and the country immediately around is covered with jungle (scrub). Water can be obtained from two wells close to the villages, but supplies could not be got, save a few cattle and grass. There is a prominent pagoda on the top of a small hill near the village, which makes a good landmark. The road continues to run in a north-west direction, the country being, however, close and enclosed by long elephant grass and prickly evergreen jungle. It is, however, in the hot weather passable for cavalry and infantry, though during the rains progress with carts would be slow. The road now reaches the Irrawaddy river and turns almost due east, and after running in this direction to about 300 yards reaches Lepánzin, which is a large village

FROM MANDALAY TO MYINGYÁN *viá* MYOTHA—*continued.*

BRANCH II-*a*—*continued.*

Authorities.		Number and Names of Stages, Rivers and Streams.	Distances.		Remarks.
Military.	Civil.		Inter-mediate.	Total.	
G.O.C. Myingyán District.	Commissioner, Central Division, and Deputy Commissioner, Sagaing.	**1. Názun**—*cont.*			containing some 180 houses. Water is, of course, plentiful, as it is on the river; but there are also wells in considerable numbers. There is a considerable number of good cattle (draught and milch cows). Grass, paddy, and rice can be obtained, also fish. There are many good kyaungs and zayáts capable of containing 400 men. The road makes a semi-circular sweep southwards after leaving this village, to avoid the swampy paddy ground towards the river, and passes under some low jungle-covered hills on the north. The country is flat and swampy, but the road here is fair, although the kaing grass is thick in some places. Cavalry and infantry and carts would probably find it difficult in the rains. After about 2 miles the road again turns towards the river Irrawaddy and touches it at the village of Tyémenain, a small village of about 20 houses; rice, water, and grass are the only supplies procurable. There is no suitable place for the accommodation of troops. On leaving Tyémenain the road runs due east and is fairly good and open, but elephant grass is still somewhat prevalent. No special features recommend themselves to notice till we come to the small deserted village of Ywadaw. No supplies could be obtained here, for only three houses are occupied and there is no suitable place to encamp on. The aspect of the country now somewhat changes. The road runs still to the eastward, but with a southerly direction and winds about some low jungle-covered hills and is very bad indeed. Cavalry, infantry, and carts could, however, utilize it in all weathers. After running in this direction for rather less than a mile it enters the village of Kyauktalôn. Kyauktalôn is a large and prosperous village, pluckily defended by the inhabitants during the disturbed times of 1885, 1886 and 1887, and carrying on a considerable trade in cotton, hides, and paddy; grass and local commodities can be procured in considerable quantities. There are kyaungs sufficient for 600 men. There is a suitable place for a signalling station on west of village. On leaving Kyauktalôn the village crosses a nullah, dry in the hot weather, but with some 3 feet of water in the rains. This is spanned by a good wooden bridge, which, however, is not passable for carts, being too narrow; horses and ponies can cross it however. On crossing it thenext few hundred yards are very swampy, the road passing among paddy-fields. The road then becomes a little better and drier, and after about 2 miles reaches Pyetu, a small village of about 40 houses. Water, grass, and paddy is obtainable, also many cattle. The character of road remains unaltered and still continues in an easterly direction and, after passing a swampy piece of ground passable by ford in all weathers, reaches Péobin, a very small village with about six houses. Accommodation for 20 men, a few cattle in village; water got from two wells, but no supplies. The road then continues to run in an easterly direction through paddy-fields, passable for cavalry and infantry in dry weather, but almost impracticable in rains; crosses a nullah, dry in hot weather; in rains water about 6 inches to 1 foot deep. Crossing this and proceeding about 400 yards we reach Názun. Názun is a very large village with large bazaar. Accommodation for 800 men in kyaungs. Grass, cattle, rice, and paddy procurable in any quantities, also ghee and milk.

FROM MANDALAY TO MYINGYÁN *viâ* MYOTHA—*continued.*

BRANCH II-*b*.

FROM MYOTHA TO NÁZUN *viâ* GYO.

BY LIEUT. CREALOCK, SOMERSETSHIRE LIGHT INFANTRY, 1886.

Authorities. Military.	Authorities. Civil.	Number and Names of Stages, Rivers and Streams.	Distances. Intermediate. M.	F.	Distances. Total. M.	F.	Remarks.
G.O.C. Myingyán District.	Commissioner, Central Division, and Deputy Commissioner, Sagaing.	**1. Názun**	**13**	**0**	13	0	The road on leaving the fort goes N. by 15 W. as far as Gyo. A clearing of 50 yards has been made all the way on either side. The country is cultivated with cholum; in the valley with paddy. The village of Natwin is passed at 2 miles and is about ¼ mile off the road to the right. Ywatha is ¾ mile further on, about 200 yards from the right side of the road. At 4½ miles pass road going east to Taunghládaw, about ½ mile away and west to Taungbyin about ½ mile. Good camping ground in dry weather on flat; plenty of water and good road from Taunghládaw. Road inclines and declines continually, but straight, small jungle at long intervals at a short distance from road. Accommodation at Gyo in kyaungs for 300 men. Good camping ground on north-east and south side, river on west. Water from wells and river good and plenty. Plenty of cattle. Road goes due north from here and crosses river six times, always fordable; country flat and cultivated. At 10¼ miles pass Latwin village; water from wells good, not two plentiful. At 11½ miles pass Nyaungaing (small village). Water from wells good and plentiful. The road is at present in a very good condition.

No. 52.

From MANDALAY to THAYETMYO viâ MYOTHA, TAUNGDWINGYI and KADINMATHA.

BY LIEUT. E. W. M. NORIE, 2ND MIDDLESEX REGIMENT, FEBRUARY 1888.

Military.	Civil.	Stages.	Intermediate M.	F.	Total M.	F.	Remarks.
G.O.C. Mandalay District.	Commr., Northern Divn., &c., Mandalay.	**1. Ava**	**14**	**0**	14	0	Route No. 51, Mandalay to Myingyán.
G.O.C. Myingyán District.	Commissioner, Central Division, and Deputy Commissioner, Sagaing.	**2. Minthé** ...	**9**	**0**	23	0	
		3. Myotha ...	**36**	**4**	36	4	
		4. Subyagôn ...	**8**	**4**	45	0	From Myotha road runs due south through open and cultivated country. At 2 miles cross nullah fordable in rains. No bridge. At 2¼ miles pass small village of Tanaungbin on left of road. At 3¾ miles cross nullah fordable in rains. No bridge. At 4 miles pass village of Kôntha. One kyaung. Good well. No bazaar. At 4¼ miles cross nullah fordable in rains. Road good running due south through track 100 feet wide cleared through jungle. Low scrub jungle on each side of road with patches of cultivation. At 6 miles pass large village of Kángyi. Two kyaungs on left of road and good wells. No bazaar. At 8½ miles large village of Subyagôn. Kyaung and sayáts.

FROM MANDALAY TO THAYETMYO *viâ* MYOTHA, TAUNGDWINGYI AND KADINMATHA—*continued.*

Authorities. Military.	Authorities. Civil.	Number and Names of Stages, Rivers and Streams.	Distances. Intermediate. M.	F.	Total. M.	F.	Remarks.
G.O.C. Myingyán District.	Commissioner, Central Division, and Deputy Commissioner, Sagaing.	**5. Natôgyi** ...	8	0	53	0	Road runs due south. At 2 miles small village of Nabudaw. Kyaung. At 4½ miles small village of Myiyengyi. No kyaungs or supplies. At 6 miles large village of Kadaung. At 8 miles Natôgyi police post. Supplies and water good. One kyaung.
		6. Thekégyin ...	12	0	65	0	General direction of road south. A hard sandy cart track. First 2 miles passes through low cultivated country, afterwards through thin scrub jungle perfectly practicable for cavalry. One place at about 6 miles, where the road crosses a deep dip, is probably very bad in the rains. Pass small villages at 3, 5, and 7 miles. Good water from wells at all the villages. Country generally sandy and undulating with narrow strips of paddy in the villages. Cultivation cotton, jowari, and paddy. Thekégyin is a large village. Accommodation for 100 men in kyaungs on west of village. Large tank close to kyaungs and very good water from numerous wells (in kyaung enclosure). Supplies procurable from thugyi.
G.O.C. Rangoon District.	Commissioner, Eastern Division, and Deputy Commissioner, Meiktila.	**7. Máhlaing** ...	14	0	79	0	Road the same as before. Cotton more plentiful and a good number of toddy trees about. At 3½ miles pass the large village of Gwégyán, which appears to have a flourishing trade in cotton carried on by a Chinaman. Several kyaungs on south side of village. Plenty of excellent water from several wells. Supplies plentiful. At 6 miles pass a small village on left of road. Water from a well ¼ mile to right of road. No accommodation. About ½ mile on the road passes over some paddy and is very bad in rains. Two miles further on pass a village on right of road. Kyaungs. Before reaching the village, a large tank ½ mile to east of road. Plenty of good water from wells. About 1 mile further on the road passes over some paddy, probably very bad in the rains. At 11 miles reach Pánain and join main road from Myingyán. At 14 miles Máhlaing (*see* Route No. 17, Southern Division).
		8. Sédaw ... ... One nullah.	13	0	92	0	A hard sandy cart track through thin scrub jungle. At 8 miles pass big village of Sukingyi where there is plenty of good water from wells. At 12 miles cross a nullah 60 yards wide with very steep banks. This nullah is impassable after heavy rains, but in hot weather is dry with sandy bed. Sédaw is a large village under a Myoôk. There is a police post here. Accommodation for a large force in kyaungs south of village. Small tank in kyaung enclosure. Plenty of good water from wells. Usual supplies can be obtained. Cotton is grown about here in large quantities. There is a road from here to Meiktila, but it is not practicable for carts in wet weather, as it passes through a lot of paddy.
		9. Shánmangé ...	9	0	101	0	Broad hard sandy road through thin jungle. Very little cultivation and no water along the road. Shánmangé is a large village. There is a military

FROM MANDALAY TO THAYETMYO *viâ* MYOTHA, TAUNGDWINGYI AND KADINMATHA—*continued.*

Authorities. Military.	Authorities. Civil.	Number and Names of Stages, Rivers and Streams.	Distances. Intermediate. M.	Distances. Intermediate. F.	Distances. Total. M.	Distances. Total. F.	Remarks.
G.O.C. Rangoon District.	Commissioner, Eastern Division, and Deputy Commissioner, Meiktila.	**9. Shánmangé** —*cont.*					police post with accommodation for 200 men in post and for 200 more in kyaungs, about 500 yards to north of post. Water good and plentiful from a well in kyaung enclosure and for animals in nullah close by. There is an Assistant Superintendent of police and a telegraph office. The headman is the thugyi, and there is a bazaar every five days. Ordinary supplies plentiful, and about 100 carts procurable from surrounding villages.
		10. Kyetpyet ...	**9**	**0**	110	0	A good cart road through scrub jungle. At 2 miles pass the village of Inga and at 7 miles another village on a hill about 1 mile off the road. Kyetpyet is a village of about 40 houses. Accommodation for about 150 men in kyaungs and zayáts. Camping ground all round. Water from a large pond 150 yards south-east good. Supplies plentiful and probably a few carts could be obtained.
G.O.C. Myingyán District.	Commissioner, Southern Division, and Deputy Commissioner, Magwé.	**11. Sulégôn** ... One rocky stream.	**8**	**0**	118	0	Road, same as before, at about 2 miles passes a kyaung about 300 yards to west of road. At 4½ miles it crosses the Myinmana hills which are a steep rocky range about 500 feet above surrounding country. At about 6 miles pass Ségyi, a good-sized village with a large kyaung ¼ mile west. Myinmana hills run ½ mile east of road. Sulégôn is a small village. Accommodation for about 130 men in kyaungs and zayáts which are rather out of repair. Water from a well about ½ mile from the kyaung good. Supplies obtainable in small quantities.
		12. Shwébandaw. Myo chaung.	**12**	**4**	130	4	At 3½ miles road passes Kyauktaga, a small village with one small kyaung. At 7½ miles pass Kyaukwet, a village of about 40 houses with accommodation for 150 men in kyaungs and zayáts. Water from a large tank and supplies plentiful. The country is undulating, sandy and rocky covered with grass and thin scrub. Cultivation dry crop and only in small spaces round the villages. About 1 mile from Shwébandaw road descends and runs through paddy land.
		13. Ywamôn ... Myo chaung twice and small stream.	**8**	**0**	138	4	Road a good cart track cleared of jungle, fairly open for last few miles. Country same as before. Pass the village of Pin with a high thorn hedge. It is the head town of the district and contains a post. All supplies obtainable and a large number of carts. Ywamôn is a fair-sized village. Accommodation is good in kyaungs. Water good. Ordinary supplies obtainable and probably about 30 carts.

FROM MANDALAY TO THAYETMYO *viâ* MYOTHA, TAUNGDWINGYI AND KADINMATHA—*continued*.

Authorities. Military.	Authorities. Civil.	Number and Names of Stages, Rivers and Streams.	Distances. Intermediate. M. F.	Distances. Total. M. F.	Remarks.
G.O.C. Myingyán District.	Commissioner, Southern Division, and Deputy Commissioner, Magwé.	**14. Natmauk** ... One small stream.	14 0	152 4	Road and country are the same as before. At 4 miles pass the village of Zalôk-gyi, where the water is bad. At 8 and 10 miles pass Lé-aing and Nuang-yaung, at both of which places there is good water; at the latter accommodation for 50 men in two kyaungs. The road here crosses a dry sandy chaung. Natmauk is a strong, large thorn-fenced village and is really composed of four villages. It stands on the high bank of the Yen river. Accommodation for 50 men in police post and for 100 more in two kyaungs and zayáts. Good camping ground to north-west and south. Supplies of all sorts procurable from the Myoôk. Water good and plentiful from wells and chaung. About 50 carts can be obtained.
		15. Myothit ... Yen river.	12 0	164 4	The dry weather road runs along the bed of the Yen for about a mile. That used in the wet weather follows the river bank as far as Nakángyi, where it crosses and thence runs along the lower bank to Myothit. The Yen river is here about 500 yards broad and is dry in the hot weather, though impassable after rain. Water from the chaung. Road passes several fair-sized villages. Myothit is a large village with a military police post for 50 men. Accommodation for 150 more in kyaungs. Camping ground to east. Water good, though not very clear, from two or three wells and from chaung. It is the centre of a sub-division; and all supplies and a good many carts are obtainable from the thugyi.
		16. Taungdwingyi. Three streams.	17 0	181 4	As far as Myolin the road is good, running through thin jungle and crossing the Sûn and Palin chaungs, both of which are always fordable. From here it runs through paddy interspersed with patches of jungle the whole way to Taungdwingyi and is in dry weather very good, but in the rains is impassable for carts, which go by a road further to the west. There are a great many cart tracks and it is hard to say which is the regular road. Cross the Sidôn chaung at 12 miles, which is dry most of the year. Taungdwingyi is a large walled town with a stockaded military post for 400 men. There is also a large bazaar and supplies are plentiful. There is a Deputy Commissioner's court-house and treasury.
		17. Zebinwaing...	10 0	191 4	The road throughout from Taungdwingyi to the Kadinmatha is a fair one over undulating country, covered for the most part with jungle. Villages passed are Nyaungbinhla (1 mile), Kalagán (5 miles), Thaingôn (7½ miles). At all of these villages there are kyaungs and good water. At Zebinwaing there are five kyaungs and zayáts and good water.

FROM MANDALAY TO THAYETMYO *viâ* MYOTHA, TAUNGDWINGYI AND KADINMATHA—*continued.*

Authorities. Military.	Authorities. Civil.	Number and Names of Stages, Rivers and Streams.	Distances. Intermediate. M. F.		Distances. Total. M. F.		Remarks.
G.O.C. Myingyán District.	Commissioner, Lower Burmah, and Deputy Commissioner, Thayetmyo.	**18. Kadinmatha.**	**18**	**0**	209	4	Six villages passed. The principal ones are Pyingyaung, good water, two kyaungs, and two zayáts; Pelé (16 miles), good water, three kyaungs. Kadinmatha is a village of about 40 houses with three kyaungs. The water is good.
		19 20 21 } **Allanmyo** ...	**36**	**0**	245	4	From Kadinmatha to Allanmyo is a distance of about 36 miles south-west and west. The route is said to be a good cart road, but has not yet been reported on. Allanmyo is situated on the left bank of the Irrawaddy river, opposite to Thayetmyo.

No. 53.

From MANDALAY to THEINNI MYOMA viâ LÁSHIO (new post).

COMPILED FROM LATEST INFORMATION BY LIEUT. G. W. T. PROWSE, ATTACHÉ, INTELLIGENCE BRANCH, AUGUST 1891.

Military	Civil	Stages	Intermediate M.	F.	Total M.	F.	Remarks
G.O.C. Mandalay District	Commissioner, Northern Division, and Deputy Commissioner, Mandalay.	**1. Taungbo** ... Several outlets from Aungbinlé lake and small streams, all bridged for carts. Sé stream 6 to 10 feet wide, 3 to 4 feet deep; bridged for carts by Public Works Department.	**13**	**0**	13	0	General direction south-east. Leaving the city by the east gate the Yankintaung road is followed for 2 miles. Turn south along the bund of the Aungbinlé lake. The whole portion of the road to Taungbo is metalled 20 feet wide throughout, and sufficiently good for carts to do full marches throughout the year. After the first 2 miles cross frequent sluices regulating water-supply from Aungbinlé lake to low-lying country on west of road; reach southern end of lake at 6½ miles; country, however, continues swampy as far as 7½ miles. From 7½ miles to 10 miles the Sé stream runs parallel to road; village of Kyaukmé at 10 miles, where the stream runs between the road and the village. From Kyaukmé road follows the Sé stream, the country becoming drier and covered with thorn jungle until reaching Taungbo, 12 miles. Villages passed: 5 miles Aungbinlé village and zayáts; a good dry-weather cart track runs from here to the Arakan pagoda, distant 2½ miles. Seven-and-a-half miles Letkaung; 1,000 yards west of this village is the large one of Tasingôn; 10 miles Kyaukmé; kyaungs on south-east of village for 500 men; 12 miles Taungbo police guard and block-house. Public Works bungalow of three rooms, which would accommodate 50 men. Water from the Sé stream and few supplies. There is a telegraph line (single wire) from Mandalay to Láshio.
		2. Naungbaw ...	**10**	**0**	23	0	General direction south-east. After leaving Taungbo the road continues level and metalled up to the 15th mile. From 15 to 17½ miles the road averages 17 feet in width with ruling gradient 1 in 19 and 1 in 20, and metalled in the worst places. A bridge 40 feet wide is crossed, which spans a deep ravine

FROM MANDALAY TO THEINNI MYOMA *viâ* LÁSHIO (NEW POST)—*continued.*

Authorities. Military.	Authorities. Civil.	Number and Names of Stages, Rivers and Streams.	Distances. Intermediate.	Distances. Total.	Remarks.
G.O.C. Mandalay District.	Commissioner, Northern Division, and Deputy Commissioner, Mandalay.	**2. Naungbaw**—*cont.*			with perpendicular sides, filled with water all the year round. About ¾ mile beyond this bridge stands the village of Kywetnapa, 15 houses. Thence for ½ mile the road is fairly level and 15 feet wide, metalled in the worst portions. From here to 20th mile it is 18 feet wide, ruling gradient 1 in 19, rising steadily till the village of Naungbaw is reached. Naungbaw consists of only a few houses, and supplies are very scarce. There is a new pôngyi kyaung on the left of the road, also a new wooden inspection bungalow capable of holding 50 men. Water is very scarce during the dry weather and is to be obtained some 400 yards to the left of the bungalow. Paddy-field near pôngyi kyaung no longer under cultivation, which would make a camping ground for 500 men.
		3. Thôndaung ...	M. F. 8 0	M. F. 31 0	General direction north-east. Leaving Naungbaw the road rises at a gradient of about 1 in 40. It is not yet metalled and is a bad piece of road up to the 23rd mile and very slippery in rainy weather. Carts, however, can get through all the year round. From the 23rd to the 24th mile the road rises rapidly in zigzags, gradient 1 in 18. Thence into Pintha the road is fairly level, the steepest gradient being not more than 1 in 25. The village of Pintha consists of two parts, about 25 houses in all, half being on one side of the road and half on the other. On a small hill on the east side of the road and about 250 yards from it are several zayáts capable of holding 200 men. On the top of the hill is a small breast-work, with ditch and parapet of about 3 feet command, thrown up by troops who were recently quartered there. The trace is a square of about 40 yards; good water is plentiful from the village on the west of the road throughout the year, and during the rains can also be procured from a nullah crossing the road at the Maymyo end of the village. During the rains, transport animals can be watered from a small hollow in the ravine below the fort, but the water is unfit for drinking purposes. The road from Pintha to Thôndaung is very fairly level, and only metalled in a few places.* At Thôndaung there is a stream of water and a three-roomed Public Works bungalow.
		4. Maymyo † (Pyinulwin).	11 4	42 4	General direction north. From Thôndaung to Maymyo the road is only metalled in a few places, passing over undulating and wooded country almost throughout. Villages passed: Singaung or Wetnen, 6½ miles. Five-day bazaar held here. The barracks at Maymyo, which at present are built of bamboo matting, are situated on rising ground to the west of the village, which is itself situated in an open valley. A good dâk bungalow has been built in the village, consisting of three rooms with large verandah, also godowns, &c. It is the second house on the right coming from Mandalay. A large five-day bazaar is held here.

* There is another road from Pintha to Maymyo further east, distance about 16 daings. A very hilly road, steep gradients, passable but difficult for pack animals. The villages of Nyaungni, Phésut, Pénégôn and Miyébôn are passed *en route*.

† So called after Colonel James May, Bengal Infantry, who commanded the troops that first occupied the station permanently in 1887, with a view to its becoming a sanitarium for Mandalay.

FROM MANDALAY TO THEINNI MYOMA *viâ* LÁSHIO (NEW POST)—*continued.*

Authorities. Military.	Authorities. Civil.	Number and Names of Stages, Rivers and Streams.	Distances. Intermediate. M.	F.	Distances. Total. M.	F.	Remarks.
G.O.C. Mandalay District.	Commissioner, Northern Division, and Deputy Commissioner, Mandalay.	**5. Wetwin** ... Kélaung chaung or Yengé river, bridged for carts.	**12**	**0**	54	4	General direction north-east. Road bridged throughout. Ruling gradient 1 in 19. The road runs over the Maymyo plateau, the country on each side being fairly open and covered with thin scrub jungle. At 9 miles the descent to the Kélaung chaung commences. This is the only difficult portion of the stage for carts in wet weather, and in the present unmetalled state of the road they cannot surmount the hill after much rain. Villages passed: 3 miles Yégyán-o; 5 miles Yengé, kyaung; 7½ miles Kôngpaw; 8½ miles Tônbu; 9 miles Naunglôn. At Wetwin there is a small police post, small mat houses with a bamboo stockade. A Public Works bungalow with three rooms and stabling for four ponies, cook-house and godowns here. There is a large pôngyi kyaung which would accommodate at least 200 men. Water is good and plentiful, and a well-attended five-day bazaar is held in the village. December 1891, road in good condition for carts. A Public Works Department bungalow is built 100 yards to left of road, three rooms; paddy Rs. 1-4-0 per large basket.
	Superintendent, Northern Shan States.	**6. Omathi** ...	**12**	**4**	67	0	General direction north-east. The road is not metalled and is liable in consequence to cut up in wet weather. Ruling gradient 1 in 19. The road is bridged throughout. Villages passed: Péngmôn at 6 miles; Bámbwé 9 miles, kyaung and zayáts. After leaving Bámbwé the road descends by an easy gradient into the Thônzé valley, crossing several small streams. The road after mile 66 is very bad after rain. In November 1892, after 10 days, fine weather, mules could only do about 1 mile an hour, and carts moved with the greatest difficulty. At Omathi there is a small two-roomed Public Works Department bungalow with godown. The bungalow stands by the side of the road, the village being ½ mile to the south. Supplies consist of paddy, grass, and a few vegetables. If possible it is best to avoid this stage and push on to Thábiyé, as there is no accommodation for troops except the bungalow, and supplies are scanty. Good camping ground for small force by road side at bungalow and for 4,500 men in paddy-fields adjoining, which, however, were hardly dry in December. Water good and plentiful from stream 150 yards east of bungalow. Paddy, As. 8 per small basket.
		7. Thábiyé ... Numerous small streams almost dry in the dry season, but 3 to 5 feet deep in the rains.	**13**	**0**	80	0	General direction north-east. The road, which is bridged throughout, crosses the Thônzé valley which is intersected by numerous small but deep streams. First mile or more, very bad going, across a swamp. After crossing the valley it ascends the Kyaukkyan plateau; ruling gradient 1 in 19. Thence it crosses undulating country until Thábiyé is reached. At about 9 miles road to right to Ngôkgalé and at about 12 miles road to right to Thábiyé village and bungalow. Road to left is main road to Thibaw (Sipaw). The bungalow is situated a short distance from the right-hand side of the road, and is at present (January 1892) occupied by the Superintending Engineer of the section. It is built of wood

FROM MANDALAY TO THEINNI MYOMA *viâ* LÁSHIO (NEW POST)—*continued*.

Authorities. Military.	Authorities. Civil.	Number and Names of Stages, Rivers and Streams.	Distances. Intermediate.	Distances. Total.	Remarks.
G.O.C. Mandalay District.	Superintendent, Northern Shan States.	**7. Thábiyé**—*cont.*			and has three rooms with large godowns and stabling. Drinking water 100 yards west of bungalow from small marshy stream. Ponies, &c., can be watered lower down the same stream. Thábiyé is a small village of about 10 houses; supplies being chiefly obtainable from Ngôkgalé village, where there is a large bazaar and kyaung, distant about 3½ miles to the east. Carts can generally be obtained at Gnôkgalé. Village Nongkyeo, about six houses, passed at 12¼ miles. No paddy at Thábiyé; must be got from Ngôkgalé at Rs. 1-4-0 per basket. *Note on Maymyo-Thabéyé section.*—The road, as a rule, runs over hard red soil which does not cut up very much after rain; but in certain places it has been necessary to raise banks, and here after rain the going is very heavy. These portions will have to be metalled, but sanction has not yet been given. From the end of October the section of road Maymyo to Thábiyé will be sufficiently dry for carts to do regular marches, but until it is matalled over the Thônzé valley, they will only be able to get along very slowly up to the end of November.
		8. Chaungzôn[1] ... Chaungzôn stream at the bottom of the pass.	M. 7 F. 0	M. 87 F. 0	General direction north-east. There is a short cut from the rest-house bungalow through Thábiyé village which ends in a very steep descent into the main road near mile 82. By this road 4 miles are saved, but it is only practicable in dry weather. In wet weather in leaving Thabéyé retrace previous stage for a mile as far as junction with main road at mile 79. The road is fairly level for about 2 miles and then begins to descend to the Nampán stream at the bottom of the gorge. The hill on the western side is very precipitous, and three zigzags have had to be made in the trace of the new cart road. Three of the turning points of these zigzags are on very steep side-long ground, and will probably prove very awkward turns for loaded carts going down-hill. The ruling gradient is 1 in 19 throughout, with the exception of one short portion on the eastern side, which is graded 1 in 17. The total length of road on the pass itself is about 10 miles, the section being mostly heavy hill-side cutting, and the total rise and fall about 1,000 feet each way. From mile 82 to the river the road was, in November 1892, steep in stiff red mud through which carts were barely moving. Mules and bullocks only got along by taking short cuts, which are also deep and slippery, but infinitely easier than the road. The stream is temporarily bridged for carts and foot-passengers by an 80 feet iron bridge on masonry pier; road in good condition, but shows signs of cracking in places. The Public Works Department bungalow at Chaungzôn is built about a mile on the Nyaungpein side of the bridge; road up to it is good.
		9. Nyaungpein (Pyinsaw).	8 4	95 4	On the eastern side all bridging has been done and the road taken ont to its full width. The zigzags on this side are much easier and after the fourth turn the trace runs direct along the hill side for over a mile. Road in very good condition. A little beyond Chaungzôn mules can in dry weather go up a steep path which leads up the cliffs to the right and joins

FROM MANDALAY TO THEINNI MYOMA *viâ* LÁSHIO (NEW POST)—*continued.*

Authorities. Military.	Authorities. Civil.	Number and Names of Stages, Rivers and Streams.	Distances. Intermediate.	Distances. Total.	Remarks.
G.O.C. Mandalay District.	Superintendent, Northern Shan States.	**9. Nyaungpein (Pyinsaw)**—*cont.*			the main road at mile 89 just above a small village. By taking all short cuts between Thábiyé and Nyaungpein mulés can manage the distance in one march. Carts can go through at present during the dry weather; no metalling has been done or is yet sanctioned, but there are no places likely to be very bad on this length. The road has been opened out to its full breadth to Nyaungpein (Pyinsaw), where there is a three-roomed bungalow. At the village of Pyinsaw itself there is a small kyaung and of small bamboo zayáts for 40 men. Paddy Rs. 1-4-0 per basket. Ngôkteik village, which lies ½ mile to the south-west, has a good-sized five-day bazaar, large kyaung, but no zayáts. Good camping ground in the kyaung enclosure. Ngôkteik on the old bullock road lies to the south of the road at about 6½ miles.
			M. F.	M. F.	
		10. Pyaungyaung. Pyaungyaung river and several small streams, bridged.	9 4	105 0	General direction north. The road is in very good condition up to Kwégon (Kywégôn). Superintending Engineer's bungalow at Kwégon; zayáts also for about 50 men. Paddy scarce at Kwégon. The country is undulating and wooded at intervals. Villages passed: 1 mile Ponaw on right, 1 mile Pankin on left, 4½ miles Mantyet and Loinöp on right and left bank of river, 6½ miles Nyaungtaw (kyaung), 7 miles Pweingôn (kyaung). At Pyaungyaung there is a Public Works Department bungalow (three rooms) at north end of village, and a large wooden kyaung at the south-west end to accommodate 300 men. A large five-day bazaar is held and water is good and plentiful.
		11. Loikaw ...	11 0	116 0	General direction north. Gradual ascent most of the way. The old track is followed as far as Kwégôn, after which the new trace turns more to the north. The road is opened out to its full width and cleared, and the bridges are finished throughout. A short cut between miles 115 and 116, which leads to main road ¼ mile beyond the bungalow, should be avoided. At Loikaw there is a wooden Public Works Department bungalow, three rooms, each 16′ by 16′, two godowns and stabling for six ponies. No accommodation for troops at Loikaw, small camping ground for 40-50 men in south side of Public Works Department bungalow. Good camping ground for large force in paddy-fields 1 mile before reaching bungalow, water plentiful and close at hand. There are two Shan houses to accommodate 25 men close to the bungalow. Water is plentiful from a stream 100 yards below the bungalow; but no supplies are obtainable except a few vegetables.
		12. Namsim (or Kyinthé). Few nullahs. River Namsim.	10 0	126 0	General direction east. Descent the whole way to the Namsim. The road is bridged throughout except the Namsim bridge, of which the masonry piers only are at present (November 1892) ready. Cross the river ¼ mile above the bridge leaving main road and going over paddy-fields. Crossing 50 yards wide mules can cross from November until the rains without wetting loads. Road good and passable for carts up to Thîbaw.

FROM MANDALAY TO THEINNI MYOMA *viâ* LÁSHIO (NEW POST)—*continued.*

Authorities.		Number and Names of Stages, Rivers and Streams.	Distances.		Remarks.
Military.	Civil.		Inter-mediate.	Total.	
G.O.C. Mandalay District.	Superintendent, Northern Shan States.	**12. Namsim (or Kyinthé)**—*cont.*			Villages passed: Thôngyap ½ mile; Hongheng 5 miles, nine houses, whence there is a road to Môgôk, *see* Route No. 74. This is the head of a small circle. Many of the houses have been deserted, the water-supply being very scanty. Sunoi, 12 houses. Public Works Department bungalow at Namsim built on the left bank of the Namsim river at the point of its junction with the Myitngé. It contains three rooms with godowns and stables attached. Supplies chiefly from Bawgyo.
			M. F.	M. F.	
		13. Thíbaw (Myitngé).	8 0	134 0	General direction north-east. Road ascends the valley of the Myitngé river. At present carts cannot go through, the Namsim river being unbridged, and the road has not yet been taken out to its full breadth. Villages passed: at 2 miles Bawgyo, 40 houses and large wooden kyaung; at 4 miles Tikaunpo, eight houses; at 4¼ miles Manhai, 10 houses; at 6½ miles Tanpaw, 10 houses. Public Works Department bungalow (three rooms) on the left bank of the Myitngé river, close to the present ferry. The town of Thíbaw consists of two parts. Old Thíbaw, which contains the Sawbwa's palace, is situated on slightly rising ground on the right bank of the Myitngé river. There is a permanent bazaar here, several wooden kyaungs, and 50 to 60 houses, also mat rest-house on north-west side of old town. New Thíbaw, which lies across a valley ½ mile to the south, contains 200 or more houses and the site of the Sawbwa's new palace. As yet (August 1891) only four main posts have been erected and the work seems at a standstill. New Thíbaw is also situated on the right bank of the river. A bamboo raft worked by a wire rope across the Myitngé river to carry one cart or five pack ponies with loads. Ferry over the Myitngé at Thíbaw. Breadth 130 yards; current 2½ to 3 miles per hour. Flood rise 16 to 18 feet during the rainy season. Pebbly and muddy bottom. Two dug-outs only are regularly employed on the ferry, but 20 to 30 more could be obtained in the neighbourhood. A wire rope has been stretched across from bank to bank.
		14. Kôntha (Kôngsa).	9 0	143 0	General direction east. From Thíbaw to Kôntha the road is good for mules and bullocks and it is also fit for cart traffic all the way to Láshio, though the gradients are in places very steep. The present track follows the left bank of the Myitngé as far as the village of Suplán, thence to Kôntha it strikes inland. Villages passed on old route Kopat 1 mile, four houses and one rest-house, which would accommodate 15 men; Suplán 2½ miles, four houses; Pángyôk 5½ miles, 10 houses; Ngahôk, 8½ miles, six houses. Bridges on old route nine in all, varying in span from 25 feet to 43 feet and all in bad repair. At Kôntha a Public Works Department bungalow of three rooms is to be built, but in May 1891 there was absolutely no accommodation in the village except such as was to be obtained in the Shan houses. There is no kyaung here. During the cold weather there is camping ground for a large force in the paddy-fields below the village; water being good and plentiful. In the rainy season these fields are flooded. Public Works Department bungalow (three rooms) on right of road close to Kôntha (mile 143).

FROM MANDALAY TO THEINNI MYOMA *viâ* LÁSHIO (NEW POST)—*continued.*

Authorities.		Number and Names of Stages, Rivers and Streams.	Distances.				Remarks.
Military.	Civil.		Intermediate.		Total.		
			M.	F.	M.	F.	
G.O.C. Mandalay District.	Superintendent, Northern Shan States.	**15. Sé-in** ... Namma river.	**11**	**0**	154	0	General direction north-east. The path, which is broad and good throughout, runs over undulating country covered with thin jungle. No villages passed *en route*, but at mile 152½ road to right leads to Ta Ti and ¾ a mile further on another road from same place joins in. The ferry at Sé-in is composed of bamboo raft worked by a wire rope to carry, one loaded cart or five pack ponies with loads. Sé-in, which is situated on the right bank of the Namma river, is a Shan village of 15 houses, small kyaung. There is also a Public Works Department bungalow (three rooms) on right bank to the right of the road after crossing river. Good camping ground in paddy-fields on north side of village for 700 to 800 men. The site chosen for the permanent bridge is 100 yards above the present ferry. As a temporary measure a wire rope has been stretched from bank to bank; a bamboo raft is pulled backwards and forwards across the stream by means of it. There are also two or three dug-outs; width of river about 200 feet, depth 30 feet; flood rise 15 to 20 feet. During the dry season pack animals use a ford which exists about ¼ mile below the ferry. Width about 100 yards, depth 3½ feet; sound gravel bottom; swift current, running about 6 miles per hour. Flood rise is 12 to 15 feet. At present loads have to be ferried over and animals use the ford during the dry weather.
		16. Naungmôn (Naungmwon).	**10**	**0**	164	0	General direction north-east. The present road, which is a good one for pack animals, passes over undulating jungle country with patches of paddy cultivation round the villages. Villages passed: Nongkwai, 9 miles, eight houses. At Naungmôn there is a Public Works Department bungalow (three rooms) to the right of the road, and path branches off to it at mile 163¼. At present the village consists of 30 houses, large wooden kyaung and zayáts, with good camping ground in kyaung enclosure. Supplies in small quantities obtainable by giving notice, otherwise only a little paddy to be got. Water good from shallow wells.
		17. Láshio (new post).	**14**	**0**	178	0	General direction north-north-east. Road good for pack animals, some bad bridges, but all avoidable. Villages passed: at 2 miles Tinlwoi (deserted); at 8¾ miles Pánghai, 30 houses, a Palaung village; at 10 miles Maihan, 25 houses, Shan village. At Láshio (new post) it is proposed to build a regular dâk bungalow, or circuit-house, but there is at present no spare accommodation, and the existing houses and barracks are in very bad repair. Sanction has been accorded for the construction of permanent barracks. A small earthwork is being constructed, otherwise no defences. From Láshio the following roads diverge— (1) to Theinni north-north-east; (2) to Namkham, Pangkham, and Möngmao, north-north-west; (3) to Kunlôn and Kôkáng ferries, *viâ* Theinni, north-east; (4) to Möngyaw and thence to Kunlôn and other ferries over the Salween, east and east-north-east;

FROM MANDALAY TO THEINNI MYOMA *viâ* LÁSHIO (NEW POST)—*continued.*

Authorities. Military.	Authorities. Civil.	Number and Names of Stages, Rivers and Streams.	Distances. Intermediate.	Distances. Total.	Remarks.
G.O.C. Mandalay District.	Superintendent, Northern Shan States.	**17. Láshio (new post)**—*cont.*			(5) to Möngyin, north-east; (6) to Naungmwon and Möngma, south-south-east; (7) to Mansé, Hôya, and Möngyai, south-south-east.
		18. Pángtongmôn. Namshio and Namyaw rivers.	M. F. 13 6	M. F. 191 6	General direction north by east. There are two roads from Lashio towards The'nni which meet at a point about 2 miles from Lashio. From that point onward the road is one and the same. The best road of the two is the westerly, which crosses the Namyaw river (about 2 miles from Láshio bazaar) at the Ta Könka ferry, the other road crosses the Namyaw by the Ta Hatka ferry, 2 miles from the Láshio bazaar. The road to Möngyaw branches off to right (north-east), just after crossing the Namyaw river. Both these fords are easy. Depth of water 2 feet. Bottom firm and pebbly. Current moderate. The easterly road, which is the more difficult of the two for transport on account of the cultivated fields and irrigation channels (the latter not being bridged), passes in the first 4¼ miles the hamlets of Hatka, Tapông, Manpenglön, Namôn, and Phélong. After that no other villages or cultivation are passed except two, Mankáng and Lwéngö, Kachin hamlets perched on high ridges, and their taungyas. The road from the 5th mile onward passes through nothing but thin tree jungle. The hills are entered at the 6th mile. The pass, however, is unusually easy. There are very few steep gradients. The pass is called Kyushaw. At 7¼ miles is Pánghát. Camp and water for small body of troops. At 8¾ miles reach crest of pass. This place is very difficult for pack transport, the path being rocky, narrow, and steep. It could be easily improved by blasting away the rock and levelling the road. From Theinni to Láshio Shan daing posts are placed. The 7th from Theinni is at Pángkapôk. At 11 miles Pángkapôk. Camp and water for 50 to 100 men. Here path from Kônsa comes in from right (east). At 13 miles reach bank of Namti stream. At 13¾ reach Pángtongmôn. Good camp for 200 to 300 men. Plenty of good water for any force. No village.
		19. Theinni town Nampáng and Namtu rivers.	14 4	206 2	Good road all the way, mostly through sparse tree jungle, here and there taungyas. All the small streams are bridged for bullocks. Formerly there were *daing* posts from Theinni to Láshio, but they are now mostly destroyed. At 2¼ miles pass village of Möngli, ½ mile to right of road; 10 houses, kyaung. Water from Namti stream. At 5 miles path to right to Shan village of Nápung, eight houses, 1 mile distant. At 5¼ miles path to right to Shan village of Nakham, distant 1 mile, five houses. At 8 miles path to left to Shan village of Manmaw, five houses. At 8¼ miles path to right to village of Paimông, distant 1 to 2 miles, and then east or south-east over the hills to the village of Hôtong (30 houses and kyaung), on the easterly road from Láshio to Theinni. The village of Paimông is on the eastern bank of the Nampáng, which flows from Nángön and Hôtong and falls into the Namtu opposite Theinni. The Namti flows, into the Nampáng near Paimông. At 9 miles road to left to Shan village of Namsángsök, 16 houses. At 10¼ miles

FROM MANDALAY TO THEINNI MYOMA *viâ* LÁSHIO (NEW POST)—*continued.*

Authorities. Military.	Authorities. Civil.	Number and Names of Stages, Rivers and Streams.	Distances. Inter-mediate.	Distances. Total.	Remarks.
G.O.C. Mandalay District.	Superintendent, Northern Shan States.	**19. Theinni town** —*cont.*			Kônna village, 10 houses, lies ½ mile to right of road on the left bank of Nampáng. At 11¾ miles cross Nampáng stream; easy ford. From this point (near which the easterly road from Láshio to Theinni comes in) to the Namtu there are several roads. The Namtu is fordable in many places. The town of Theinni lies close under the hills that bound the valley to the north and about 1 to 1½ miles north of the river. The land between the river and the town is intersected by irrigation channels and flooded hollows, which troops cannot cross without inconvenience. By making a detour of 2 miles or so to the east, Theinni Myoma is approached by a good dry road and the Namtu crossed by a good ford. Water 2½ feet deep. Good, sound bottom. Current moderate. The Theinni valley is 4 to 5 miles by 15 to 20 miles, and appears to be mostly under rice cultivation. It is hemmed in by high hills. Grass is plentiful, but fuel rather scarce. The valley is almost destitute of trees. Theinni at present does not contain more than 100 houses, including the Chief's house, the bazaar, kyaung, &c. There are several villages situated east and west of the central village. Behind the town to the north the hills rise abruptly. There is a (for these parts) large bazaar here, fruit, vegetables, fish, cotton cloths, sugar, rice, salt, &c., procurable. Bullocks can be obtained. From Theinni there are roads—west down the Namtu valley to Möngyin; east up the Namtu valley to Kunlôn; north over the hills to Namkham, Hôpyet, Pangkam, &c.; north-east to Möngsi. There is an alternative easterly route from Láshio to Theinni as under— (1) Hantao, 3 daings; (2) Na-ngun, 2 daings; (3) Hôtong (mentioned above), 3 daings; (4) Theinni, 3 daings. The village of Kônsa (mentioned above, stage 5) lies a mile or two west of Kantam, and from there to Pángkapôk, on the western route, there is a road practicable for bullocks.

ALTERNATIVE I-*a*.

FROM MANDALAY (STAGE 1) TO MAYMYO (STAGE 4) *viâ* YANKINTAUNG.

BY LIEUT. DYAS, HANTS REGIMENT, JULY 1887.

Military	Civil	Stage	Inter-mediate M. F.	Total M. F.	Remarks
G.O.C. Mandalay District.	Commissioner, Northern Division, and Deputy Commissioner, Mandalay.	**1. Yankintaung.**	5 0	5 0	Leaving the east gate of the city the road runs due east, metalled throughout, in good repair. Houses on both sides of road, chiefly kyaungs. A few small shops. At 1 mile a large bridge built on piles, 50 yards long, 4½ yards wide, strong enough to bear artillery, crosses a canal, metalled throughout. Road metalled and raised on a bund above the general level of the ground. Ground on the right low. No houses, but numerous trees surrounded by a palisade fence. Ground on left low also, but houses built all alongside of the road. A few small shops. Road meets a bund running north and south with cart tracks on east side. Road metalled, raised on a bund. On right side a canal with a small bund, running parallel to road; beyond, canal water and swamp. On left of road water and swamp. Cultivation seen in distance on both sides of the road. Bridge over canal very strongly built on piles. Village of Yankintaung about 70 houses. Cattle and supplies plentiful. Road

FROM MANDALAY TO THEINNI MYOMA *viâ* LÁSHIO (NEW POST)—*continued.*

ALTERNATIVE I-*a*—*continued.*

Authorities. Military.	Authorities. Civil.	Number and Names of Stages, Rivers and Streams.	Distances. Inter-mediate.	Distances. Total.	Remarks.
G.O.C. Mandalay District.	Commissioner, Northern Division, and Deputy Commissioner, Mandalay.	**1. Yankintaung** —*cont.*			metalled. Hill about 300 feet high with a small fort on an eastern spur. Two pagodas on south. Bridge built on piles and strong enough to bear artillery. The Yankintaung post is situated at the northern end of the hill. At the south end there is a good camping ground under trees with water close by. Kyaungs and village also at south side of hill.
		2. Taungkyun ..	M. F. 13 4	M. F. 18 4	Road nearly new, due east, difficult even for mule transport. From south end of Yankintaung hill pass for 3 miles over level country partly along a bund between paddy-fields, partly through low jungle, chiefly bamboo. Road thus far practicable for carts. Enter a broad, stony bed of a mountain stream, water flowing under the stones unless stream is actually in flood. Then ascend a rocky and precipitous hill-side path, very narrow and difficult. Reach a small stream flowing into the stream mentioned above. The course of the main nullah or one of its large branches is generally followed for the last ascent, the road occasionally leaving it. At 1¼ miles from the foot of the hill there is a small but deep water-hole in the rocks, 7 yards to the right of the path. When the first ascent has been completed (height about 1,300 feet) cross comparatively easy ground, slightly descending for about 3 miles, crossing the stony beds of two streams, the latter of which had some running water in June 1887 and some pools; also a *sakhán* with a few shelters made of sticks with teak leaves. Then ascend a steep stony slope by a difficult and zigzag path, slope about 20° to top of the Wédaung range, about 3,000 feet above the level of Mandalay, which can be seen from here through a break in the first range. Road then fairly level for about ½ a mile to a point from which Pintha, Singaung, Taungkyun, and much of the country to the south-east can be seen. The path then suddenly makes a drop of 730 feet in about 600 yards into the valley of a small stream, which is followed for about a mile; then over gently undulating ground through open jungle to Taungkyun, which lies about ½ mile to the south of the direct Yankintaung-Maymyo road. Taungkyun consists of 15 huts and a small kyaung on rising ground, 5 yards north of the village; trees cut down and the trunks piled up into a low fence making a cleared space about 50 yards square. Water from bed of stream which flows round three sides of the village at a distance of 200 to 600 yards, standing in stagnant pools in July 1887, but good water can be got by digging. From Taungkyun a path goes north through Bayaw-Taungkyaung to Nyaungbintha. From Bayaw and Nyaungbintha paths lead westward to Bôk and Lamaing. The path described above is used by the villages of Taungkyun, Sakhángyi, and Thayetpin. It has been traversed by pack bullocks and elephants.
		3. Maymyo ...	10 4	29 0	From Taungkyun in east direction through open teak tree jungle, through which it is possible to see from 50 to 100 yards across the stream which supplies Taungkyun with water and shortly after joins the Yankintaung-Maymyo direct road. Reach a large tree and a small *sakhán* and ascend a rocky ravine.

From MANDALAY to THEINNI MYOMA *viâ* LÁSHIO (new post)—*continued.*

ALTERNATIVE I-*a*—*continued.*

Authorities. Military.	Authorities. Civil.	Number and Names of Stages, Rivers and Streams.	Distances. Intermediate.	Distances. Total.	Remarks.
G.O.C. Mandalay District.	Commissioner, Northern Division, and Deputy Commissioner, Mandalay.	**3. Maymyo**—*cont.*			Barring the road two breastworks of logs and stones facing west were found; jungle cleared for a view down the ravine. Then along a level saddle between two hills, after which there is a steep descent down another rocky ravine. At 3 miles pass a hut and patch of taungya cultivation, then reach a stream and follow the bed for 200 yards (water flowing under the surface). Crossing the stream afterwards twice, reach the village of Sakhángyi at 4 miles; 30 huts, shut in by hills. No camping ground. One old kyaung in ruins. Water from a fine stream. The path then crosses the stream and follows the right bank in a deep and rocky ravine, crossing it altogether four times. Then through thick bamboo jungle commence ascent of a steep rocky slope covered with teak trees towards the top. Ascent of 500 feet, then wind among the hills for about ½ mile after which the country opens out and the road becomes practicable for carts running over a grass-covered plain. Soon a group of kyaungs is passed and at 18½ miles reach Thayetpin, a village of about 40 houses, surrounded by trees. Thence cross a small stream, road running east-north-east over level country through light jungle and long grass to Maymyo.

ALTERNATIVE I-*b*.

From MANDALAY to MAYMYO (Stage 4) *viâ* YANKINTAUNG and SENBO.

I. B. Compilation, November 1888.

Military.	Civil.	Stages.	Intermediate. M. F.	Total. M. F.	Remarks.
[illegible] Mandalay District.	Commissioner, Northern Division, and Deputy Commissioner, Mandalay.	**1. Yankintaung...**	**5 0**	5 0	*See* Alternative Route No. I-*a* Mandalay to Maymyo *viâ* Yankintaung. From Yankintaung a road goes east by south, through the village of Sainbin, and ascends the hills to the hill village of Kwénadauk, south of the Yetagôn peak. It then descends again to the valley of the stream, which issues from the hills at Sádaw and passes the Taungbo outpost. It joins the Zíbingyi road at Pwédaung. It is said to be an easier road than any of those which lie north of the Yetagôn peak. *Note.*—The Nánda lake can be crossed almost anywhere from the Yankintaung road northwards after the month of February until the rains, end of May.
		2. Thibaing ...	**10 2**	15 2	From Yankintaung north-east road good, through mixed cultivation and scrub jungle. At 2¼ miles Thadíbin. At 4½ miles Senbo, a small village with one or two zayáts. At Senbo, on the Mandalay plain, a path practicable only for footmen, and called the "Thieves' path," ascends the hill due east. Continue north-east through thick thorn jungle. At 5 miles the village of Tawtsu. Turn east and ascend the hills to Thibaing. Thibaing is a small village with one zayát.

From MANDALAY to THEINNI MYOMA *viâ* LÁSHIO (New Post)—*continued.*

ALTERNATIVE I-*b*—*continued.*

Authorities. Military.	Authorities. Civil.	Number and Names of Stages, Rivers and Streams.	Distances. Intermediate. M.	F.	Total. M.	F.	Remarks.
G.O.C. Mandalay District.	Commissioner, Northern Division, and Deputy Commissioner, Mandalay.	**3. Naungthakaw.**	16	0	31	2	From Thibaing the steep ascent of the hills commences, very difficult for laden animals, and passing through jungle the whole way. Naungthakaw is a collection of small villages. Accommodation is to be obtained.
		4. Maymyo ...	4	0	35	2	This is a direct road to Maymyo, but very difficult. Two ranges have to be crossed, and the fall and rise between the first and second being allowed for, there is little or no advantage gained in time over the longer route and it would seldom be used.

ALTERNATIVE II.

From NGÔKTEIK (*see* Stage 9) to NAMSIM (Stage 12) *viâ* HAIKWI.

By Capt. A. C. YATE, 1st Belooche[illegible], December 1887.

Military.	Civil.	Stages.	Inter. M.	F.	Total M.	F.	Remarks.
G.O.C. Mandalay District.	Superintendent, Northern Shan States.	**1. Nammawpilu.**	7	6	7	6	The village of Ngôkteik lies 300 yards south-east of the kyaung, round which is the best camping ground for troops. Some half dozen villages (Lônkyein, Kei, Naungpin, Laungpa, Pinthôn, Nammawpithi, Nampawket) are grouped round Ngôkteik, and fuel for troops and grass for transport animals, &c.,* can be collected without much difficulty for a small force (say 100 European and 100 Native soldiers, 100 followers and 500 mules and ponies). Two hundred yards east of Ngôkteik village the road forms three branches, one north-east (50°) to Nammawpithi and thence on to Pyaungaung is the cart road. From Nammawpithi there is also a foot-path across the hills to Pinsán, a village said to be 4 daings (8 to 12 miles east or north-east of Haikwi). The second goes (90°) to Kei (¼ mile) and Laungpa (1½ miles) and then rejoins Ngôkteik-Namkôk road about 1½ miles from Ngôkteik. The third branch (140°) is the road to Nammawpilu. Road good throughout for pack bullocks, and appears also to be used for carts. It could be made a very good road for wheeled traffic with great ease. It has no steep gradients. Country overgrown with jungle, thickest from 4th to 7th mile where the Lwénamkôk is crossed. Taungyas here and there. This district has evidently suffered from the recent disturbances. At ⅝ mile path to right (south) to Pinthôn (1 mile), and at 1 mile path to left to Laungpa (30°, ⅙ mile). At 1¼ miles cart road comes in from Laungpa (north). At 1⅞ miles path to right (190°) to Pinthôn, ⅓ mile distant. At 3 miles path to right (150°) to Kônônyaung. At 3⅝ miles reach Namkôk sakhán and spring (water-supply very limited, enough for 200 men or so). Here path to right (170°) to Kôn-nyaung, distant ¾ mile; village of 10 houses. Taungya cultivation. From Namkôk sakhán commences the easy ascent and descent over the hill range called at this point Lwé-Namkôk. From this point to Nammawpilu jungle rather dense. Little

* *N.B.*—The Thibaw officials were unable to collect sufficient wood and grass for the Northern Shan Column at Pyaungaung, but did so at Kwégôn in the winter of 1887–88.

FROM MANDALAY TO THEINNI MYOMA *viâ* LÁSHIO (NEW POST)—*continued.*

ALTERNATIVE II—*continued.*

Authorities. Military.	Authorities. Civil.	Number and Names of Stages, Rivers and Streams.	Distances. Intermediate.	Distances. Total.	Remarks.
G.O.C. Mandalay District.	Superintendent, Northern Shan States.	**1. Nammawpilu** —*cont.*			or no sign of cultivation, and no habitations. At 7¾ miles reach Nammawpilu; 6 months ago a hamlet of 10 houses with a small bazaar, now, it is said, reduced to one house. There is a camping ground here sufficient for 50 men or so. Excellent water from spring and well. Fuel plentiful, grass less so. From here there is a road to Kyethi-Bansán regularly used by caravans trading between that place and Mandalay.
		2. Naungkwán ... **(Naungkaung).** Two largish streams near Naungkwan, both bridged for pack animals.	M. 11 F. 0	M. 18 F. 6	General direction north-east by north. From Nammawpilu to Haikwi road is level, from Haikwi to Naungkwán across a succession of low hills, but in no place are the gradients very steep; good road for pack animals, at any rate in the dry weather. The last 2 miles between Namwa and Naungkwán are the worst. A cart road could easily be made. The country traversed is all overgrown with forest cleared near villages and here and there for taungyas. There is a good deal of cultivation at Haikwi, but Naungkwán is at present much more populous and prosperous. Just after leaving Nammawpilu sakhán pass village to left of road. At 1⅛ miles road to left (140°) to Lôngyum (2 daings) and thence turning more eastward to Taungdeik (about 6 daings). This on the Ngôkteik-Kyethi-Bansán road. The roads from Nammawpilu, Namkángkön and Haikwi to Kyethi-Bansán all meet at or near Taungdeik. This is a route much used by bullock caravans. There are said to be about 100 Panthé and Chinese Shan traders at Kyethi-Bansán. At 2⅜ miles pass village of Nankángkön (10 or 12 houses) to left. Rice, thanapet, plantains, vegetables. Have seen not a single bullock since Maymyo; buffaloes, however, seen or heard near every village. Road from here to Lôngyun (Loigyán) and Taungdeik (Toughtek) (140°). At 4⅞ miles reach Haikwi, good-sized village, resident Hein, extensive cultivation, pôngyi kyaung ½ mile east of village. No zayáts. Road from Haikwi to Pyaungaung (4 daings) and to Kwégôn (5 daings) direction to north-north-east, same road for 1½ daings, then bifurcates; passes villages of Hôpai (½ daing) and Namnumpök (2 daings) on Pyaungaung road. At 5⅛ miles road to Nammaw and Naungkwán and to Pongwo and Taungdeik separates. The latter direction (115°) passes close by Haikwi pagoda and kyaung. At 5⅜ miles road to left to Hôpai (½ daing) and then on to Pyaungaung and Kwégôn, and road to right to Haikwi kyaung, Pongwo, &c. At 6⅛ miles path to left to Hôpai (?) and to right to Ngasôn (?) and Pongwo (?). At 6¾ miles path to Hôpai (?). At 7¼ miles road to left (330°) to Kwégôn, (4½ daings), and to right (120°) to Pongwo (3 daings). (This is the direct route from Kwégôn *viâ* Namwa to Pongwo). At 7½ miles pass hamlet of Namwa on eminence to right of road. At 9⅛ miles road to right east-south-east to Semôn Ferry (over the Myitngé) and to Thibaw direct. After this Naungkwán road takes a more northerly direction. At 10 miles path to right (120°) to Namwa-Semôn road. At 10½ miles enter village of Payi. At 10⅝ miles cross large stream (Namsihöng) by wooden bridge 40 feet long by 5 broad. At 10¾ miles cross a smaller stream by wooden bridge; then through north Naungkwán, and at 11 miles reach

No. 53.

FROM MANDALAY TO THEINNI MYOMA *viâ* LÁSHIO (NEW POST)—*continued.*

ALTERNATIVE II—*continued.*

Authorities. Military.	Authorities. Civil.	Number and Names of Stages, Rivers and Streams.	Distances. Intermediate.	Distances. Total.	Remarks.
G.C.C. Mandalay District.	Superintendent, Northern Shan States.	**2. Naungkwan (Naungkaung)** —*cont.*			kyaung, where is a good but limited camping ground. No zayáts, 50 houses. Some supplies. Resident Hein. Abundance of excellent water. This is at present one of the best camping places for troops hereabouts. Extensive rice cultivation. Water abundant for irrigation. Into the Namsihöng stream flow most of the smaller streams that flow eastward or south-east between Namwa and Konnyu. These streams irrigate a large area of rice fields, irrespective of taungyas. The Namsihöng falls into the Namtu (Myitngé) river just below the hamlet of Lômleng. From Naungkwán there is a road to Kwégôn, passing at 1¼ daings the village of Líkwolam. There is a foot-path over the hills to Pángwo south-east, distance 4-5 miles *viâ* Kôngpán (a village 1¼ miles east of Naungkwán). The Palaung village of Nánöm is about 1⅜ miles west of Naungkwan.
		3. Konnyu ... Numerous small streams, most of which are bridged for bullocks.	M. 7 F. 2	M. 26 F. 0	The road is practicable for pack transport, but not good. The gradients are in places steep, the path narrow and rough, the streams unbridged and difficult to cross for laden mules and ponies. The country traversed is more populous and highly cultivated than any other portion yet seen, and has evidently suffered less from the late disturbances. Rice is largely cultivated both in the valleys and hollows and on taungyas. Much of the jungle is bamboo. This road would be very bad indeed in the rains. At ¼ mile road to right (90°) to village of Manhohan (five houses), distant ¼ mile. At 1 mile cross wooden bridge (60 feet long by 6 feet broad) and just beyond pass Möngnwai (10 houses). At 1⅝ miles Palaung village of Lökwolam (distant 2 miles) situated on crest of hill range (308°). The Naungkwán-Kwégôn crosses this hill-range a little south of Lökwolam. At 1¾ miles path to left (285°) to Nampamung (village of Shans and Palaungs), distant 1⅛ miles. At 2⅛ miles path right (60°) to hamlet of Tongkyáng ¼ mile distant. At 2⅜ miles path to right to Tongkyáng. At 2⅞ miles path to left (305°) to Nammawkun (three or four houses, Shans), distant 1 mile. At 3 miles path to right (70°) to Lwé-un (three or four houses, Shans), distant 1 mile. At 3⅜ miles path (100°) to Lwé-un. At 4⅛ miles path to left (5°) to Namun (10 houses, Shans), distant 2 miles. At 5 miles cross Namtam stream, a tributary of Namsihöng at 5¾ miles. At 6⅛ miles path to left to Panlang (three or four houses), distant ¼ mile. The village of Namun lies 2 miles north-west of this, and of Banthalé 3 miles north-west on the crest of the range of hills which lies between the Kwégôn-Bawgyo and Naungkwán-Bawgyo roads. At 6⅜ miles path to right (45°) to Kaihyo village, distant 1 mile. At 7 miles cross Nam-namun stream. At 7⅛ miles cross Nam-nyu stream. At 7¼ miles reach village of Konnyu, 10 or 12 houses, small kyaung and zayát (housing for 50 men). Good water, some fuel and grass. No supplies. The village of Namun, a little further on to the right of the road to Bawgyo, may be found preferable as a camping place. Very little trade on this road. From Namun (mentioned just above) there is a road north-east to Nahai (1 daing) and thence 1 daing further north-north-east to the ferry over the Namtu at Ta Tingkun. From this point there is a foot-

FROM MANDALAY TO THEINNI MYOMA *viâ* LÁSHIO (NEW POST)—*continued.*

ALTERNATIVE II—*continued.*

Authorities. Military.	Authorities. Civil.	Number and Names of Stages, Rivers and Streams.	Distances. Intermediate.	Distances. Total.	Remarks.
G.O.C. Mandalay District.	Superintendent, Northern Shan States.	**3. Konnyu**—*cont.*			path north-east over the hills to Thibaw, distance 4 to 5 daings. From Ta Tingkun people and goods descend the Namtu in boats to Semôn.
		4. Namsim (Kyinsi). Many small streams, mostly bridged for bullock caravans.	M. F. 8 0	M. F. 34 0	Road practicable, but not good for pack transport; hilly and with steepish gradients, bad in rainy season. The last 2 miles into Namsim are better than the rest. In 1st mile three paths branch off to right leading to Namun and thence to Nahai and Ta Tingkun. The jungle traversed from Konnyu to Namsim is to a great extent teak which grows in profusion and round the valley of the Namtu (Myitngé). Teak is worked largely near Namsim. At 2⅛ miles cross stream called Namkohák by wooden bridge. At 5 miles path to right (160°) to I-haw, distant 2 daings, and so on to Nahai and the Namtu river. At 5¼ miles path to left (300°) to Nampyen, ¼ mile distant. At 5⅜ miles cross Nampyen stream by wooden bridge. At 6 miles pass stream by bridge. *Sakhán* on bank of stream. At 7 miles meet southern road from Kwégôn. (The road from Kwégôn to Bawgyo bifurcates a mile or so west of Namsim and re-unites about a mile east of it.) At 7⅜ path to right 120° to pôngyi kyaung and village of Byengkön, and to left (300°) to North Namsim and then on to the village of Nangôn (1 mile distant) on the northern Kwégôn-Bawgyo road. At 8 miles reach village of South Namsim. The Namsim river flows into the Namtu, ¼ mile east of South Namsim. There is a road due south from here *viâ* Byengkön to Ta Tingkun (1¾ miles) and Nahai (3 miles). Accommodation here for troops indifferent. Good water. Camping ground in dry weather in paddy-fields. Some supplies; grass and fuel plentiful.

ALTERNATIVE III.

FROM NAUNGMÔN (STAGE 16) TO THIBAW (MÖNGSIPAW), (STAGE 13) *viâ* TA SÉÁN (OR TÁSÉÁN), TA PHALAI (OR TÁPHALAI) AND TA TI (OR TÁTI).

BY CAPT. A. C. YATE, 1ST BELOOCHEES, MARCH 1888.

Authorities. Military.	Authorities. Civil.	Number and Names of Stages, Rivers and Streams.	Distances. Intermediate.	Distances. Total.	Remarks.
G.O.C. Mandalay District.	Superintendent, Northern Shan States.	**1. Manpángkáng.** Namma river fordable from January to May, at other times crossed by ferry; ford 2¾ feet deep; firm pebbly bottom; moderate current.	16 2	...	General direction south-east. Road good for pack transport. Traverses undulating and in places hill country overgrown with teak and other tree jungle. The high road between Láshio and Thibaw passes through or close to the actual village of Naungmôn, leaving the bazaar, kyaung, and Lwéwyeng to the east. Starting from the bazaar the road follows the left edge of the Naungmôn marsh. At ⅛ mile path from Lwéwyeng from left and at ¼ mile from Naungmôn from right. At ⅜ mile village of Konghung to left. At 1⅛ miles road from Konghung from left. At 1⅜ miles cross rice fields by causeway. At 1⅝ miles village of Nonglong to left. At 2 miles pass Namnonglong stream. At 2¼ miles village of Nongkwai-Manhong to right, and at

No. 53.

FROM MANDALAY TO THEINNI MYOMA *viâ* LÁSHIO (NEW POST)—*continued.*

ALTERNATIVE III—*continued.*

Authorities.		Number and Names of Stages, Rivers and Streams.	Distances.		Remarks.
Military.	Civil.		Inter-mediate.	Total.	
G.O.C. Mandalay District.	Superintendent, Northern Shan States.	**1. Manpángkáng**—*cont.*			2¼ miles to left Nongkwai-Mansán. Here kyaung, pagodas. Good camping ground for large force. Water abundant. At 2¾ miles cross rice fields and Nongkwai stream. At 3 miles road to left (south-south-east) to Katamöng ferry (about 6 miles distant) over the Namma and thence south-south-west to Pánghyo and Kônsa. At 3¼ miles village of Pánghai to left. At 4⅜ miles Nonguáng hamlet to right. At 5⅛ miles road to left. At 5⅝ miles Nonghwai village to left. At 7¼ miles road to Táti ferry to left, distant about 1 mile. Good ferry there, but no ford in dry season. At 8¾ miles reach Táséán ford and ferry over Namma. From here and Táti boats go down the river to Thibaw carrying rice and other produce for sale River at Táséán; ford about 70 yards broad and deep. The ford is about 200 yards below the ferry. Here is a kyaung. Good camping ground for large force and abundance of water. Leaving Táséán at ¾ mile meet road from Táti. At 1¾ miles village of Kômöng to left. At 2½ miles path from left from Kômöng. At 3½ miles village of Nampalám (here water from spring) to right. At 7½ miles reach Manpángkáng. There is great scarcity of water between the Namma river and Kônsa. The road from here onward to Thibaw passes through either Kônsa or Hônong. The direct route to Táphalai is by the Hônong road, branching off to the right some distance north of Hônong. The water-supply at Manpángkáng is limited. There are two small springs about ¼ mile east of village, and there is said to be a small stream about a mile to south-east of the village and east of the road to Kônsa. There is believed to be no good camping ground at Manpángkáng or near the sources of water-supply enumerated above, though shift may be made with such space as there is. In a march from Naungmôn to or towards Thibaw the natural stages are:—(1) Táti or Táséán, (2) Kônsa or Hônong, (3) Thibaw. These are, however, short stages, as barring the difficulty about camp and water half-way, the distance can be easily covered in two marches. The advantage of the Táséán route is that the river Namma can be forded there. The ferry plant on these rivers is very limited, consequently even a few hundred men and animals take one to two days to cross the Shan ferries. The transformation of the boats into rafts alone takes several hours even if the material for bridging and planking is ready to hand. There is yet another alternative, but somewhat longer route from Naungmôn to Thibaw, namely, *viâ* the Katamung ferry and Pánghyo. Natives of Mansé recommend the following routes and stages from Mansé to Thibaw:— A (1) Nakun, about 10 miles, crossing Namma river near village of Namma. (2) Pánghyo, 10 to 12 miles. Road more or less parallel to left bank of Namma. (3) Kônsa, about 8 miles. (4) Thibaw. B (1) Nasaw, about 8 miles. (2) Nongkwai, about 15 miles, passing Naungmôn at 12th or 13th mile. (3) Kônsa, 17 miles. (4) Thibaw. If the third stage is too long, then from Nongkwai go *viâ* Katamung ferry to Pánghyo, and so to Kônsa. It is important to note that Naungmôn and the country northward from

FROM MANDALAY TO THEINNI MYOMA *viâ* LÁSHIO (NEW POST)—*continued.*

ALTERNATIVE III—*continued.*

Authorities. Military.	Authorities. Civil.	Number and Names of Stages, Rivers and Streams.	Distances. Intermediate.	Distances. Total.	Remarks.
G.O.C. Mandalay District.	Superintendent, Northern Shan States.	**1. Manpángkáng** —*cont.*			it to Inai and Páugkyem, and southward from it to Kônsa and Hônong is entirely severed from Sisôn, Pánglôn and Mansám by a difficult pathless tract, and by the Namyaw river. From Kônsa and Hônong there are good bullock roads to Sisôn and Pánglôn *viâ* the Ta Phalai ferry over the Namma. The road from Pánglôn to Sisôn and Pánglôn to Pángkyem and Inai have been reported on elsewhere. From Sisôn to Naungmôn direct only men on foot can go. It appears, however, that a road practicable for pack transport could be made by bridging the deep nullahs and by making careful arrangements for fording the Namyaw. The ford is reported dangerous.
		2. Táphalai ...	M. 9 F. 0	M. 25 F. 2	General direction for 3 miles west, for 6 miles north, *i.e.*, on the whole course about north-north-west. Road fairly good. Country hilly and covered with teak and other jungle. At 3 miles is the junction of roads from Kônsa, Hônong, Manpángkáng, and Táphalai. From this point road to Kônsa runs south, and to Hônong south-east, that to Táphalai turns north. At 3¼ miles cross nullah by wooden bridge, then till end of 8th mile road follows the east of the low hills in a northerly direction. It then descends north-west for ½ mile to left bank of Namma, then ascends left bank for ½ mile to ferry near Phalai village. Only two or three boats at present available. Good camp, good water, fuel and fodder. No supplies. Abundant material for forming rafts obtainable from surrounding jungle. Few or no bamboos. Width of Namma 80 or 90 yards; depth considerable. From here as also from Táti and Táséán laden native boats descend Namma and Namtu to Thibaw. From here there are good roads west to Táti (about 7 miles) and north to Sisôn (about 6 miles). It is possible, as stated above, to descend by boats from here to Thibaw. A considerable number of boats, say 20 to 30, can be collected from the villages and ferries on the Namma from Táphalai to Katamung. Each boat can carry six to eight men, or from 500 to 1,000 lbs. of kit. The Namma from Táphalai to its junction with the Namtu, a distance of about 5 miles, is a succession of rapids over which the boats have to be dragged in the dry season. When the river is in flood the descent is easier. *Note.*—The following is an alternative route from Naungmôn to Thibaw *viâ* Pánglôn. General direction as far as Pánglôn due west, thence due south. The road for the first 4 miles is practicable for pack animals, and thence for another 4 miles to the banks of the Naungán impracticable. So far the road follows the course of a nullah, repeatedly crossing and recrossing it. No bridges. The banks of the Naungán are 5 feet high and very steep: must be ramped. The ford itself is crossed by men stepping from boulder to boulder. Laden animals cannot ford it because between each boulder the water is as much as 3½ or 4 feet deep. The current is rapid and the bottom composed of large loose shifting stones; and the boulders just mentioned. The road throughout traverses thick jungle. The following villages are passed east of the Namyaw river and north of the road:—villages of Kongpán, Kaiyu, and Mawpai. On

FROM MANDALAY TO THEINNI MYOMA *viâ* LÁSHIO (NEW POST)—*continued.*

ALTERNATIVE III—*continued.*

Authorities. Military.	Authorities. Civil.	Number and Names of Stages, Rivers and Streams.	Distances. Inter-mediate.	Distances. Total.	Remarks.
G.O.C. Mandalay District.	Superintendent, Northern Shan States.	**2. Táphalai**—*cont.*			the banks of the Namyaw there is camping room for a small party. From the Namyaw river to Sisôn is 7 miles. This part of the road is practicable for pack transport. Thick jungle. Pass villages of Mansáng and Mankángpáng, about 2 miles east of Sisôn. Camp and water at Mansáng. Good camp and water at Sisôn. From Sisôn is direct road to Táti and Táphalai. From Sisôn to Pánglôn is 9 miles, first 3 miles good road, but next 3 miles to Nammi river are impracticable for pack transport. From Hathai on left bank of Nammi to Pánglôn good road. From Pánglôn there is a good road to Táti (? Mote, of map), where Namtu has to be crossed by a ferry. Táti is on right or south bank of Namtu. No village on north bank. From Táti to Thibaw is about 7 miles.

BRANCH I.

FROM PINTHA (*see* STAGE 3) TO LÉMA.

BY LIEUT. H. B. H. WRIGHT, R.E., NOVEMBER 1888.

Military	Civil	Stages	Intermediate	Total	Remarks
G.O.C. Mandalay District.	Commissioner, Northern Division, and Deputy Commissioner, Mandalay.	**1. Thándaung** ...	Miles. **8 to 9**	Miles. 8 to 9	From Pintha post east and then south-east along good track fit for any pack transport passing Shwédaung and several villages through thin jungle with patches of cultivation to Thándaung, a small village with good water. Accommodation for about 100 men in kyaungs near.
		2. Léma ... ... Myitngé river, Léma chaung.	**9 to 10**	17 to 19	From Thándaung there are two roads. One along the stream from Thándaung right down to Léma; in places difficult, but passable for pack transport. There are some old stockades along this path, which strikes the Léma chaung about ½ mile west of Léma probably coming down close to Mézataung and then crossing the Léma chaung two or four times reaches Léma. The other path leads from Thándaung, in an easterly direction, over and along several spurs, until it descends by a steep zigzag path into a valley tributary to the Myitngé. The path along the valley is easy in the dry weather and almost perfectly level. No water is found from Thándaung until the Myitngé is reached at about 6 to 7 miles unless there is water in the stream along the valley (none in May 1887). The path then follows the right bank of the Myitngé up stream for 2 miles, almost impassable for mules or ponies, over sharp pointed rocks close to the river. A detachment of Mounted infantry with 20 mules went by this route in May 1887, and some of the mules fell into the river when climbing over the rocks. Léma lies about ¾ mile up the next valley, which flows into the Myitngé. Léma lies among mango and tamarind trees in a narrow valley with Taungma hill to the north-east and Mézataung hill to the west. There are some old paddy-fields to the south of the village where a camp could be formed. The village is completely surrounded by jungle except on this side, but as troops can move along the jungle skirting the paddy-fields, the village could probably be best surprised from this side, as there is a look-out post on the Maymyo road. The former road was found passable in July 1887 during heavy rains. The latter road would probably be quite impassable if the Myitngé were in flood.

No. 54.

From MANDALAY to THÔNZÉ viâ LAMAING.

I. B. Compilation, November 1888.

Authorities. Military.	Authorities. Civil.	Number and Names of Stages, Rivers and Streams.	Distances. Intermediate. M.	Intermediate. F.	Total. M.	Total. F.	Remarks.
G.O.C. Mandalay District.	Commissioner, Northern Division, and Deputy Commissioner, Mandalay.	**1. Lamaing** ...	**17**	**0**	17	0	*See* Route No. 50, Mandalay to Môgôk.
		2. Ônglut	**11**	**4**	28	4	Road level along a valley. General direction east. At 2 miles cross a stream. At 3¼ miles pass Kinywa on right (deserted) with a small kyaung in bad repair. Country up to this is open, principally paddy cultivation. From this on thick jungle, principally bamboo. At 3¾ miles pass to left (west) of lowest spurs of main range of hills, and reach Nyaungbintha at 8 miles. Cart road all the way. From this place the road to Ônglut runs north crossing the Laygi river at ¼ mile. Here the cart road stops. Thence through thick and thin jungle to Kyábin (10 miles). The road is not very good in the rains. Kyábin is a village of 25 houses. Population increasing fast. Position unhealthy, being in a cultivated basin where three or four villages meet. Kyaung burnt. Supplies of rice and vegetables to be obtained. Water got from stream close by. There is a road east to Letkawgyi, a road also runs to Taungdeik (top of hill), a difficult path. A road runs to Hmánzidaing (9½ miles) passing through a camp called Ywé (2½ miles). There is no village at Ywé, but camping ground and water procurable. From Kyábin to Ywé the ascent is difficult. Ywé to Hmánzidaing not difficult. On leaving Kyábin the path improves, crosses a rapid stream twice. Jungle on either side, very thick and reaches Ônglut at 11½ miles. Village burnt and deserted. Water can be got from stream. Just before reaching Ônglut the road curves to the east and passes through paddy-fields, crossing a small stream.
		3. Hmánzidaing. Thirty-two streams.	**6**	**4**	35	0	From Ônglut the road to Hmánzidaing is very bad, fairly level, but the path crosses a stream thirty-two times in 8 miles. This is only a camping ground. No kyaung or accommodation. At 1½ miles is a small knoll for a force of 50 men. Good water from stream close by. Half a mile further on the foot of the hill is reached; the ascent is very steep; mules just manage to ascend with the greatest difficulty. Twelve pack animals once took 3 hours ascending and 1½ descending. At 3 miles the summit is reached. Good grass obtainable on summit. At ½ mile on there is a good camping ground for a large force. Water near. At 2 miles pass Taungdaik, a deserted place.
	Superintendent, Northern Shan States.	**4. Kawpôksain** ...	**13**	**0**	48	0	Road rather more difficult, passes through tree jungle with frequent ascents and descents. A small village of 10 huts with a strong stockade. No supplies. Three-quarter mile from Kawpôksain is Sizôn, a large kyaung, which would accommodate 200 men or more.
		5. Thônsé ... Three streams.	**6**	**0**	54	0	Road good through long grass. Cross three streams. The first stream has no name. It is bridged for laden ponies and bullocks. The second, the Panlaung stream, bridged, but bridge not fit for elephants. The third, the Kingôngyi stream, bridged and fit for laden cattle of every description.

From MANDALAY to THÔNZÉ *viâ* LAMAING—*continued*.

ALTERNATIVE I.

From LAMAING (Stage 1) to ÔNGLUT (Stage 2).

I. B. Compilation, February 1888.

Authorities. Military.	Authorities. Civil.	Number and Names of Stages, Rivers and Streams.	Distances. Intermediate.	Distances. Total.	Remarks.
G.O.C. Mandalay District.	Commissioner, Northern Division, and Deputy Commissioner, Mandalay.	**1. Ônglut**	M. F. **12 6**	M. F. 12 6	A second route runs from Lamaing to Ônglut. Road runs north-east. Pass Tamagôn and Mazigôn at ¼ mile and ¾ mile. Thin jungle and paddy-fields till Kinywa is passed on right at 3¼ miles. This village is burnt. Road now turns north and enters thick bamboo jungle: it is cleared to 10 feet. Pass a small stream near Kinywa and two streams before entering Thapángain, 6¾ miles. Water and camping ground good. A large kyaung with stockade to accommodate 200 men at a pinch. Supplies of rice and vegetables. Water from stream close by. The road runs from here to Kyábin, first 2 miles swampy ground, with much elephant grass, crossing the same stream three times; it then goes through heavy jungle with undergrowth. A road also goes from here to Ôkpo (4 miles) and is fairly good till close to Ôkpo, when the swamp makes it difficult. Road on through thick jungle, but elevated and hard. At 12¾ miles reach Ônglut.

No. 55.

From MANDALAY to WÁPYUDAUNG viâ MADEYA and SINGU.

I. B. Compilation, 1888.

Authorities. Military.	Authorities. Civil.	Number and Names of Stages, Rivers and Streams.	Distances. Intermediate.	Distances. Total.	Remarks.
G.O.C. Mandalay District.	Commissioner, Northern Division, and Deputy Commissioner, Mandalay.	**1. Madeya** ... Shwétachaung canal.	**15 0**	15 0	Madeya, a large village of 800 houses, good bazaars, &c., is 15 miles north of Mandalay Palace on the Bhamo road. The latter runs along a bund on the west of Shwétachaung. It is a fairly good cutcha road, the only bad creek being 300 yards north of Mandalay embankment, which ought to be bridged at once. The ground east of the road is covered with villages and scrub. It seems fairly dry now, but it is doubtful if troops could move across it except on the roads. There are numerous good bridges over the chaung. The country west of road is cultivated with paddy; it is wet, has no roads, and is quite unsuitable for the movements of any troops. One mile from Madeya there is a ford over the chaung, the ground on the east becomes suitable for the movements of infantry in extended order, and in places cavalry could manœuvre at a steady pace and with caution. From here there is a branch route to Zagabin, distant about 6 miles east.
		2. Yenatha ... Shwétachaung and Chaungmagyi.	**12 0**	27 0	The road is a fairly good cart road and runs north to Pinya, 2 miles. Here it crosses the Shwéta chaung by a bridge and runs in a north-easterly direction to the village of Thángazé (6 miles) on the left bank of the Chaungmagyi, which is crossed by a permanently established ferry. On

FROM MANDALAY TO WÁPYUDAUNG *viâ* MADEYA AND SINGU—*continued.*

Authorities.		Number and Names of Stages, Rivers and Streams.	Distances.		Remarks.
Military.	Civil.		Inter-mediate.	Total.	
G.O.C. Mandalay District.	Commissioner, Northern Division, and Deputy Commissioner, Mandalay.	**2. Yenatha**—*cont.*			the opposite bank is a village of the same name Thángazé. The road now runs north to Yenatha and passes no more villages on the way. Carts can be obtained at Mádéya, Pinya, and Yenatha. Water-supply is plentiful and good. Food to be had in the shape of rice and vegetables. Road bad during the rains, especially between Thángazé and Yenatha, which is mostly paddy-fields. Yenatha contains 200 houses. Accommodation in zayáts and pôngyi kyaungs. There is a police post (one non-commissioned officer and 50 rifles) stockaded and capable of containing about 300 men. Good encamping ground outside post. From here there is a road to Zagabin, 9 miles, passable by carts throughout crossing the Madeya river at Salé just opposite Zagabin.
		3. Shwégôndainzu.	M. F. 13 0	M. F. 40 0	The whole road from Yenatha to Pinlé-eng is a continuous string of villages, all apparently in well-to-do circumstances, supporting one or more kyaungs, and all maintaining a considerable amount of ground in cultivation. Paddy was all cut, but each village seemed to have a fair amount of cattle, poultry, &c. On the march to Singu the longer road had to be taken to visit each village, but on the return the shorter line was taken. Road runs north-west through thin jungle. At 1 mile jungle becomes thick, principally consisting of bamboo; the general direction of the lower spurs of the range is followed, but at a greater distance (2 miles or more). At 5½ miles pass a hill on the left. At 6 miles Pinlé-eng, village of 50 or 60 houses; kyaung in good repair, but small, with zayáts. Would give cover to 100 men. To the west of the village is a large area partly under cultivation. It is about 2 miles square and appears to be mostly under water in the wet season. Two roads run from Pinlé-eng to Shwégôndainzu, the cart road being 1 mile longer; the latter runs north for 4 miles, then north-west always on the level; the shorter road runs generally north-west and crosses low hills— (i) The cart road runs north for 2 miles from Pinlé-eng through thin jungle. The jungle then becomes thick and continues so for 4 miles. At 6 miles from Pinlé-eng, 12½ to 13 from Yenatha the road runs through paddy cultivation up to village of Shwégôndainzu. (ii) The shorter road runs north-west 2 miles through thin jungle. At 2½ miles pass Magwédaya, a small village of 15 to 20 houses; road then crosses the neck between two hills by a gradual ascent. The path which up to Magwédaya was a cart track here becomes a mere path, rough in parts, but everywhere passable for transport animals. The descent is also gradual, the road running through thin jungle. At 5 miles pass village of Shwémyindin, small and only six or seven huts. From this 1 mile through paddy-fields to Shwégôndainzu. Total 12 miles. Large village, 100 houses, three kyaungs, each in a separate enclosure with numerous zayáts. Kyaungs are not in very good repair. Water is obtained from wells, of which there are one or more at each kyaung. Shwégôndainzu is the most southern of a cluster of villages known as Kyunzi, Thabôgôn, Taungyinzayátgôn, Lepángôn, &c.

FROM MANDALAY TO WÁPYUDAUNG *viâ* MADEYA AND SINGU—*continued.*

Authorities. Military.	Authorities. Civil.	Number and Names of Stages, Rivers and Streams.	Distances. Intermediate. M.	F.	Total. M.	F.	Remarks.
G.O.C. Mandalay District.	Commissioner, Northern Division, and Deputy Commissioner, Mandalay.	**4. Singu (Nga Singu).** Irrawaddy river.	12	4	52	4	From Shwégôndainzu the road runs north-east to Shwébyi, ½ mile. It then crosses the Kadetkyin creek, now dry, about 60 yards broad. On the other bank is Thabogôn; the road then runs north for 2½ miles. At 3 miles Nyaungwun, 60 houses, two pôngyi kyaungs, inhabited but in bad repair. One mile further north is Ngwédaung, about 50 houses and one kyaung (in bad repair). There is one thugyi of this circle, which consists of Myaungwun, Ngwédaung, and another village. The spurs of the hills are now approached again and the road passes through thin jungle and cultivation for 3 miles to Minywa. (The above is the longer road, a shorter one runs along a "bund" which divides the Maungma lake into two and runs more directly north-west.) By this road, which branches to the left at Nyaungwun, about 1 mile is saved, and it can be traversed by carts, although the last ½ mile, before reaching Minywa, after leaving the bund is heavy going. At 7 miles Minywa, 40 houses, one kyaung, and zayáts capable of accommodating 100 men. Water from two wells. At 7¾ miles north-west pass Kôko, a village burnt some time ago, and only containing some five or six huts at present. From Kôko road runs past Kampa to Lepánhla, reported to be a short distance north. After leaving Kôko a river running north-east to south-west is crossed but nearly dry. Reach Kampa at 9 miles; 20 houses, kyaung and zayáts; small accommodation. At 10 miles pass Ywa Sindaw, with kyaung; about 20 houses. The road now circles to the west and bending south-west reaches Singu, chiefly passing through cultivation and long grass, the country being low and evidently considerably flooded in the rainy season. A shorter path cuts off this bend, but is said to cross an unfordable creek crossed by a foot-bridge; only this path takes a straight line from Kampa to Singu. Singu, a large village on Irrawaddy. Myoôk, Maung Thé. Numerous kyaungs and zayáts. About 5 miles north, and on opposite bank is Kyaukmyaung.
		5. Nwégôn ...	11	0	63	4	A deserted village, distant about 11 miles. No difficulties were experienced on the road, it being a fair one for carts. This place is not suitable for a halting place, the water being indifferent and the camping ground small and confined and surrounded by dense jungle.
	Commr., Northern Divn., and Deputy Commr., Ruby Mines.	**6. Wápyudaung**...	20	0	83	4	This march was long and difficult, being through bamboo jungles and over rocky ground and, except in three places, no water could be procured on the road, which a short distance from Nwegôn becomes a mere path. There are no villages *en route*, Taungyi (5 miles) and Hlawzin (16 miles) being both deserted. The Singu district ends about 6 miles from Nwegôn, and a strip of the Thingadaw runs up from the west about 3 miles in breadth. The camping ground is open and large enough for a force of about 300 men. Water, from a stream, is good. Supplies of rice and paddy obtainable from the village, but grass is scarce and bamboo leaves are the only substitute for fodder.

FROM MANDALAY TO WÁPYUDAUNG *viâ* MADEYA AND SINGU—*continued.*

BRANCH I.

FROM YENATHA TO NUNG-É.

I. B. COMPILATION, 1888.

Authorities. Military.	Authorities. Civil.	Number and Names of Stages, Rivers and Streams.	Distances. Inter-mediate. M. F.	Distances. Total. M. F.	Remarks.
G.O.C. Mandalay District.	Commissioner, Northern Division, and Deputy Commissioner, Mandalay.	**1. Kadetkyin** ...	**9 0**	9 0	Country open and covered with thin jungle. Road practicable for carts. Cross six small nullahs in this stage. At 1½ miles a road branches off to Legulḗywa. At 2 miles the deserted village of Ulambaw is passed, lying about ½ a mile to the west of the road. Three-quarters of a mile beyond pass the village of Tamlu, 30 houses. At 4¼ miles a road branches off eastward, running to Zagabin, and at 5 miles one running northwards towards Singu. Kadetkyin is a village of 70 houses. There is one pôngyi kyaung capable of containing two companies, and good ground for encamping on to north of village. Water from stream.
		2. Ubiyégalé ...	**12 0**	21 0	For the first 6 miles the road runs across the open plain and is the same in character as the last stage. The Dandin chaung is crossed several times, also several other small nullahs. For the last 6 miles the path lies over hilly country and through thick jungle, the ascents and descents being steep and difficult for loaded animals. The Dandin chaung is nearly always fordable, except immediately after very heavy rain; bed sandy; banks easy. At 9¼ miles reach a *sakhán* or halting place. No village. Water from a small spring. At 10 miles cross a nullah with a little water in it. At 11 miles pass a small spring. Ubiyégalé is a deserted village. Camping ground to the north of the village. Water from a chaung. From here a road runs westward to Ngwéôbaw (*see* Route No. 96).
		3. Nung-é ...	**7 0**	28 0	At 1 mile pass the village of Ubiyégyi and at 4 miles reach Dandin, a small Shan village of five houses. The Ubyé chaung is crossed several times. Country thick jungle. Path through the hills steep and very difficult for loaded animals. From Dandin path runs west to Ledaung (Ledawywa) 3¼ miles where the road from Zagabin joins in (*see* Route No. 50, Branch I) and crosses the Ledaung chaung several times. At 7 miles reach the deserted Shan village of Nung-é.

No. 56.

From MANDALAY to WUNDWIN viâ PYINZI.

I. B. COMPILATION, MARCH 1888.

Military	Civil	Stages	Inter. M. F.	Total M. F.	Remarks
G.O.C. Myingyán District.	Commr., Central Divn., &c., Sagaing.	**1. Ava** ... ... Myitngé river.	**14 0**	14 0	*Vide* Route No. 51, Mandalay to Myingyán.

FROM MANDALAY TO WUNDWIN *viâ* PYINZI—*continued.*

Authorities.		Number and Names of Stages, Rivers and Streams.	Distances.				Remarks.
Military.	Civil.		Intermediate.		Total.		
			M.	F.	M.	F.	
G.O.C. Myingyán District.	Commissioner, Central Division, and Deputy Commissioner, Sagaing.	**2. Chaungwa** ...	**14**	**0**	28	0	*Vide* Route No. 4, Central Division, as far as Sagayin (7 miles from Ava). Leaving Sagayin road runs south for ½ a mile, where it meets the Ava-Wundwin road. The road now turns south-south-west past large ruined pagoda, and runs through low cultivated ground and then through low jungle. This portion of the road would be impracticable during the rains. At 9½ miles reach small village of Nazinyain. From Nazinyain road passes through low-lying ground impassable during rains the whole distance from Sagayin to Chaungwa. The road through clearing 100 feet wide through the jungle. At 14 miles reach Chaungwa. There is an alternative route from Sagayin to Chaungwa, which is the only route practicable in the rains. It branches off from the Ava-Wundwin road at Kinywa ¾ mile south of Sagayin, *vide* Ava-Wundwin road south, and runs west-south-west through Yégyi to Chaungwa. This route is 2 miles longer. Chaungwa: Large village; 130 houses; no bazaar Fort in which there is accommodation for 200 men, 120 by 80 yards earthern parapet revetted with iron band and wicket gabions, two bastions, ditch 6 feet deep. Water-supply rather scarce in dry season.
		3. Thindein ...	**9**	**2**	37	2	Leaving Chaungwa Fort the road runs due south, leaving the village of Chaungwa on the left. Scrub jungle on each side of road which is good and fit for carts at all seasons. At 2 miles cross dry nullah (no bridge but fordable in rains) and enter village of Ingán. One pôngyi kyaung (new) holding 50 men. Village of Aléywa on other side of nullah. Village of Kyonpu ¼ mile on right of road. All these three are small villages; no bazaar. From Ingán road runs through cultivation for 2 miles and then through thick jungle to Buyôk (5¼ miles). Large village. No kyaungs or zayáts. Thirty houses. Road still runs due south through 100 feet clearing. At 7⅛ miles village of Thetpán (deserted 2nd March 1888). Open country for 1 mile after leaving Thetpán. At 8¼ miles cross dry nullah. No bridge; 20 feet broad and steep banks, but practicable for carts and fordable in rains. Road now runs through thick jungle. At 9¼ miles reach Thindain. Big village. One kyaung, five zayáts, 60 houses, all deserted.
	Commissioner, Southern Division, and Deputy Commissioner, Myingyán.	**4. Pyinzi**	**11**	**6**	49	0	Road good through jungle, ½ mile south of Thindain, cross dry nullahs passable in rains. At 2 miles reach Gwézôn. Small village. Leaving Gwézôn road runs due south through very thick jungle. At 6¾ miles reach Kanna. There are two villages between which a chaung runs. One kyaung on south side of village; 200 houses in the two villages. Road continues south through very thick jungle, and at 11⅝ miles reaches Pyinzi; large village; 300 houses; bazaar; two kyaungs. Chenna and grass obtainable and water good. Much cultivation round village. Land very fertile. Chief crops paddy, cholum, sessamum, cotton, and chenna.

FROM MANDALAY TO WUNDWIN *viâ* PYINZI—*continued.*

Authorities. Military.	Authorities. Civil.	Number and Names of Stages, Rivers and Streams.	Distances. Inter-mediate.	Distances. Total.	Remarks.
			M. F.	M. F.	
G.O.C. Mandalay District.	Commissioner, Southern Divn., and Deputy Commissioner, Myingyán.	**5. Taungbo** ... Two nullahs.	12 2	61 2	Direction of road south-east through cultivation and jungle; fairly open and road in good condition and level. At 5 miles pass Paungtha village (60 houses) and cross sandy bed of nullah. Water good. At 7¼ miles pass Yògán road through cultivation. Beyond Yògán a good road has been cleared through thick jungle. Immediately before reaching Taungbo cross the sandy bed of a nullah. Village of 100 houses. Accommodation in kyaungs and zayáts bad. Well water good and plentiful. A large number of cattle here. Big pagoda ½ mile before Taungbo. Good camping ground for 300 men with a built reservoir and tank of good water.
G.O.C. Rangoon District.	Commissioner, Eastern Divn., and Deputy Commissioner, Meiktila.	**6. Wundwin** ... Two nullahs and several small ravines.	12 0	73 2	From Taungbo the road, bad in wet weather, runs through cultivation to Káugyi, a small village of 40 houses with a few cattle and good water. Passing Kángyi, the road crosses a dry nullah and passes the village of Kánswé, about ¼ mile to the left of the road. From here the road has been cleared through jungle and at 6 miles from Taungbo passes the small deserted village of Nbagôn, situated on rising ground surrounded by jungle. From here the road is level to Pyazu and crosses a dry sandy nullah just before reaching that village. From here a good level road runs to Wundwin. *See* Route No. 6, Lower Burma Division.

No. 57.

From MÁNSI (KAYINGÔN) to PAYANI.

BY CAPT. W. HUSSEY-WALSH, INTELLIGENCE BRANCH, 16TH MARCH 1891.

Military	Civil	Stages	Inter-mediate	Total	Remarks
G.O.C. Mandalay District.	Commissioner, Northern Division, and Deputy Commissioner, Katha.	**1. Kônganuk** ... Namma chaung about 15 yards wide and 2 feet deep, firm bed.	12 0	...	General direction for the first day's march north-east. We passed the village of Taungyi within the 1st mile about ¾ of a mile from Mánsi. The track is at first through paddy-fields, then jungle. About 1½ miles from Mánsi the road goes through the village of Nawgôn; three or four houses. We crossed the Namma chaung about 1½ miles further on; bed of stream firm; the track continues through jungle and recrosses this stream about 1 mile further on. Half a mile beyond is the village of Sanyasdain; five houses; crosses the same stream about ¼ of a mile beyond; slight ascent and 1 mile from stream left the village of Makyodaw on the left of the road, about ¼ of a mile off. Three-quarters of a mile beyond is the deserted village Hwédain; about 15 houses. The road for the last 2 miles is undulating and good; continues undulating for the next 2 miles or so; Jungle at first dense and high then thinner crosses a chaung; bamboo jungle. On the other side passes the village of Kyetkyát. After crossing the chaung at Kyetkyát a very muddy bit near the stream, and bridge. Enters paddy-fields leaving the villages of Natawgalé (eight houses)

FROM MÁNSI (KAYINGÔN) TO PAYANI—*continued.*

Authorities. Military.	Authorities. Civil.	Number and Names of Stages, Rivers and Streams.	Distances. Intermediate.	Distances. Total.	Remarks.
G.O.C. Mandalay District.	Commissioner, Northern Division, and Deputy Commissioner, Katha.	**1. Kôngauk**—*cont.*			on the right, and Kômbutaw (17 houses) on the left. Kôngauk kyaung about ¼ of a mile beyond; two zayáts and kyaung; accommodation for 100 men.
		2. Payani ... Méza chaung.	M. F. **12 0**	M. F. 24 0	Leaving the kyaung we pass through the village of Kôngauk; 9 hours. General direction to Payani north-east. Track is at first through paddy-fields across a chaung about 20 feet wide. The track continues after a slight ascent crossing and recrossing this chaung (the Nawa chaung) for the next 5 miles, as also along the bed of the stream. (Care should be taken at a place where a very large tree has fallen across this stream to keep *close* to the right bank when going underneath.) The road continues very indifferent, stony, and rocky. Tômôlwa, about 6 miles from Kôngauk, is completely burnt. Leaving Tômôlwa the ascent of a hill commences, at first gradual for about 500 feet, then very steep for about 200 feet; level for a short way, then a further rise of about 300 feet; after a short descent a small chaung is crossed and another hill is ascended for about 200 feet followed by a gradual ascent the whole way to the plains; one or two open places, the rest dense jungle. On reaching the foot of the hill we came to the Méza chaung, passed the village of Mangyaung (deserted) on the right. About 1½ miles north of this is the village of Payani; 21 houses; strongly stockaded.

No. 58.

From MÁNSI to TAUNGTHÔNLÔN PEAK.

BY LIEUT. C. R. OWEN, 2ND OXFORDSHIRE LIGHT INFANTRY, MARCH 1891.

Military	Civil	Stages	Intermediate (M. F.)	Total (M. F.)	Remarks
G.O.C. Mandalay District.	Commissioner, Northern Division, and Deputy Commissioner, Katha.	**1. Magyigôn** ...	**9 2**	9 2	Deserted village; country open and uncultivated between Tônthôn (2½ miles) and Ma-in (6½ miles). Road good, crossing three or four nullahs (dry). Main is a village of 20 houses; situated on stream. Accommodation in kyaung and zayát for 80 men. Partly destroyed stockade on west side overlooking river. Paddy plentiful; cattle and rice obtainable. At 9¼ miles Magyigôn six houses.
		2. Komokán ...	**13 4**	23 6	Good road to Komokán. At 7½ miles Nanantôn, 15 houses. Paddy and water available; at 13½ miles Komokán.
		3. Nánsakhán ...	**6 4**	29 2	Road very bad; small bridle path. Nánsakhán has six houses.

FROM MÁNSI TO TAUNGTHÔNLÔN PEAK—*continued.*

Authorities. Military.	Authorities. Civil.	Number and Names of Stages, Rivers and Streams.	Distances. Intermediate. M.	F.	Total. M.	F.	Remarks.
G.O.C. Mandalay District.	Commissioner, Northern Division, and Deputy Commissioner, Katha.	**4. Môté**	10	0	39	2	No village, only small camping ground close to river; water excellent. Road from Nánsakhán through almost impassable jungle; path had to be cut.
		5. Kyaukgôn (Camping ground).	11	0	50	2	Road steep and hilly but good when cleared; partly along narrow ridge or saddle, in some places narrowing to only 6 or 8 feet.
		6. Camping ground.	10	0	60	2	Road very hilly and almost impassable for mule transport; nearest water from hill-top.
		7. Hill-top, Taungthônlôn.	5	0	65	2	Road fair till 1 mile from top, then very steep and impassable for mule transport.

The following route is also given on the same authority as above. It appears to be in all respects preferable to the above being shorter and easier, besides passing through a country whence more supplies are forthcoming:—

FROM TAUNGTHÔNLÔN PEAK TO MÁNSI.

Military.	Civil.	Stages.	Intermediate. M.	F.	Total. M.	F.	Remarks.
G.O.C. Mandalay District.	Commissioner, Northern Division, and Deputy Commissioner, Katha.	**1. Pansinkyauk camp.**	10	0	...		Old ruined kyaung on top of hill; level plateau 300 yards in circumference covered with thin jungle easily cleared. Excellent view obtainable. Only camping ground near water. Road from top of hill very bad for mule transport.
		2. Camping ground.	12	0	22	0	Road level and passable for mule transport, but for jungle (dense) which had to be cleared the whole way. Good water in stream.
		3. Samôt	6	0	28	0	Road much improved, passing through dense jungle; passable for mule transport. Ten houses (poor); good water; paddy and provisions plentiful.
		4. Taungôn ...	7	4	35	4	Road good; 15 houses; provisions plentiful; ducks and chickens obtainable; also paddy and good water.
		5. Mánsi	12	0	47	4	Road very good, chiefly through young teak forest.

No. 59.

From MÁNSI to WUNTHO viâ MANYU.

BY MAJOR J. H. SEWELL, NORFOLK REGIMENT, ASSISTANT-ADJUTANT-GENERAL, JANUARY 1892.

Military.	Civil.	Stages.	Intermediate. M.	F.	Total. M.	F.	Remarks.
G.O.C. Mandalay District.	Commr., Northern Divn., and Dy. Commr., Katha.	**1. Kya-in**	8	0	8	0	Road across paddy-fields ¾ mile to village of Ké-u. Bamboo jungle with one small hill cut for cart road. Road through bamboo and tree jungle at 6

FROM MÁNSI TO WUNTHO *viâ* MANYU—*continued.*

Authorities. Military.	Authorities. Civil.	Number and Names of Stages, Rivers and Streams.	Distances. Intermediate. M.	F.	Distances. Total. M.	F.	Remarks.
G.O.C. Mandalay District.	Commissioner, Northern Division, and Deputy Commissioner, Katha.	**1. Kya-in**—*cont.*					miles, the road (foot with bridges) in a south-east direction to Pyébin, 2 miles. Village west of road and ¼ of a mile south of a large tank bridged for foot-passenger on and off. There is a tank with a large pagoda. The cart road runs round west end of tank. There is small bungalow, Public Works Department, and sheds for 50 men.
		2. Sagadaung ...	13	0	21	0	At ¼ mile a road comes in from Pyébin, a good wide foot track, bridged, through thin tree jungle, distant 1½ miles. At 2 miles the Pimbôn-Bamauk east road turns off south. From this point in the road is a foot track well cleared and easy. At Lé-u 5 miles a road from Pimbôn, 3 miles off, joins from the east. At 7 miles Manka, here a road runs west to Mankágalé, a large village west of road with a smaller one ¼ mile south and east of road. Road from Mankágalé joins in ½ mile north of village. There is here a large kyaung and three zayáts. Road continues a good foot track; level except for a short distance at 9½ miles where the (deserted) village of Sidôngán is passed. At 11 and 12 miles are deep nullahs bridged for foot-passengers, and at 12½ miles a road to Pehinga (Bamauk-Pimbôn road) runs in from north-north-east by Letwin and Pinnayu. Sagadaung is a small village (30 houses) fenced with three others within a radius of ¾ mile along the edge of an extensive paddy clearing. Water from stream and wells. North of the village is a kyaung and a Public Works Department hut for troops (100 men); also a zayát and a grassy clearing which would camp a battalion. There are fine trees east of the village.
		3. Manyu	7	4	28	4	This section of the road runs through more undulating country. At 1 mile it passes a kyaung on a hill and Pathet village on the west, it then crosses paddy-fields and the stream running north, past Maungaw village and rises slightly (4°) along a ridge to 2 miles and descends at 3 miles, crosses a small stream and ascends another easy ridge to 4 miles, then descends on to level ground to Sakhan, passing the branch road to Bamauk *viâ* Tabundain. At 4¾ miles there is a village on the west of the side of a small hill, 25 houses and two other villages at ¼ mile south and west respectively. There are three small zayáts and a kyaung ¼ of a mile on. The road crosses paddy-fields to kyaung and village noted above then runs along a level spur through thin tree jungle with one or two slight undulations to Manyu, a large stockaded village, with a large paddy clearing. The post is just north of the village consisting of a kyaung and one zayát and two bamboo houses, one for two officers and one for men of police. The post is strongly stockaded. There are roads south to Wuntho and west 23 miles over hilly country to Hawyán. Water from well in villages good. The whole road is an excellent one and quite practicable throughout for Burmese carts, and with a small amount of ramping, bridging, and cutting, would be fit for a tonga. The greater part can be ridden at a canter; the general direction throughout is south-south-west. From here the road to Wuntho (distant 48 miles) has been tra-

FROM MÁNSI TO WUNTHO *viâ* MANYU—*continued.*

Authorities. Military.	Authorities. Civil.	Number and Names of Stages, Rivers and Streams.	Distances. Intermediate.	Distances. Total.	Remarks.
G.O.C. Mandalay District.	Commr., Northern Divn., and Deputy Commr., Katha.	**3. Manyu**—*cont.*			versed, but not yet fully reported on. The onward stages would probably be as follows:— 4 Myindaukta. 5. Mankin. 6. Kyáhumaw. 7. Aungbin. 8. Satwégyin. 9. Wuntho. But as the road is in places evidently very difficult except for foot-passengers, parties with pack transport might take longer; the whole journey would thus be from 9 to 12 marches.

BRANCH I.

FROM SAGADAUNG (STAGE 2) TO PEHINGA (*see* ROUTE No. 25).

BY MAJOR J. H. SEWELL, NORFOLK REGIMENT, ASSISTANT-ADJUTANT-GENERAL, JANUARY 1892.

Military.	Civil.	Stages.	Intermediate. M. F.	Total. M. F.	Remarks.
G.O.C. Mandalay District.	Commr., Northern Divn., and Dy. Commr., Katha.	**1. Haipi**	**6 0**	6 0	Road turns off the Mánsi road ¼ mile north of Sagadaung and runs north-east part the villages of Mawkadaw, Pennigán, Okshitgôn, Letdwin (4 miles) to Haipi.
		2. Pehinga ...	**12 0**	18 0	Thence to Pehinga is 12 miles over a hill range.

BRANCH II.

FROM SAKHÁN (*see* STAGE 3) TO BAMAUK (*see* ROUTE No. 25).

BY MAJOR J. H. SEWELL, NORFOLK REGIMENT, ASSISTANT-ADJUTANT-GENERAL, JANUARY 1892.

Military.	Civil.	Stages.	Intermediate.	Total.	Remarks.
G.O.C. Mandalay District.	Commissioner, Northern Division, and Deputy Commissioner, Katha.	**1. Namundain** ...	**12 4**	12 4	Road runs east leaving the Sakhán-Sagadaung road 200 yards north of village and runs across paddy-fields to Natôngán ¾ mile, then for another ¾ mile east-south-east through tree jungle and then north to 2 miles along a low ridge when the road turns east-north-east to Ya Yu 2¼ miles. It is bridged for foot-passengers. There is a pôngyi chaung on hill ¼ mile west of village, village of some 20 houses fenced. Road runs out of the village north and runs along a bridge for ¾ mile and then descends to a stream running north-west at 3⅓ miles. Here are two tracts, the right one being kept and on over the same ridge and through thickish bamboo jungle which wants clearing in places in north-north-east direction to 4¼ miles when the village of Myingán, six houses on a small ridge overlooking paddy-fields, is passed through, the road descends to a stream at 4¾ miles and passes site for new village, then across paddy-fields, on north side of which a track to Sagadaung (said to be 2 miles) turns off west. Then north-east along left banks of stream to Kyunbintha (*see* notes below), eight houses with taungya of paddy, at 5⅓ miles. Track then turns east by south and runs along a hill side rising steadily, passing Kyauktaw, six houses, at 6 miles and turns north-east through cleared jungle bending to east by north to 7½ miles when the road runs on to Tabundain village 200 yards on, and bears to the left to Sahé. The

FROM MÁNSI TO WUNTHO *viâ* MANYU—*continued.*

BRANCH II—*continued.*

Authorities. Military.	Authorities. Civil.	Number and Names of Stages, Rivers and Streams.	Distances. Inter-mediate.	Distances. Total.	Remarks.
G.O.C. Mandalay District.	Commissioner, Northern Division, and Deputy Commissioner, Katha.	**1. Namundain** —*cont.*			last 2¼ miles a steady rise, a good foot-track, but somewhat stiff in parts. Tabundain, a fenced village of 10 houses; water good from wells. Hills all round. Road for a mile very steep and then on alongside of a high hill, road steep in places and somewhat narrow. At 10 miles track direct to Pehinga (said to be 6 miles) turns off north-east and is reported as leading direct into the plain. This would undoubtedly be the best cross road from Manyu to Bamauk, as only one hill is crossed. Road running east and east by north to 11 miles, where it descends. Bamauk is visible from here lying east-south-east. The road continues to descend in a east-south-east and east direction to 12 miles where there is a very steep descent for ¼ mile and then ¼ mile fairly level to a stream on the right bank of which is a kyaung and Namundain (upper), a village of 10 houses. The lower village is 200 yards down the stream, which runs east by north and north out of the valley.
		2. Bamauk ...	M. F. 9 0	M. F. 21 4	Descending the valley, crossing the stream twice, the road then ascends a steep, woody hill to 1 mile and descends again to a similar valley at 1¾ miles, through bamboo jungle. At 2 miles is the village of Sahé, 10 houses, in a valley surrounded by hills. The road follows and crosses a stream running north for ¼ mile and climbs a hill similar to the last to 2¾ miles and descends to the Bamauk valley, reaching Mawteik at 3¼ miles. This consists of three villages spread over ¾ mile. Road runs across paddy-fields north-east till it strikes the Bamauk-Mánsi road 5 miles west of the latter place. *Note* 1.—If marching from Manyu to Bamauk— First stage ... Kyunbintha ... 8 miles. Second stage ... Mawteik ... ... 13 „ or Kônyo ... ... 15 „ Third stage ... Mawteik *en route* to Katha ... ... 19 „ *Note* 2.—If marching from Manyu to Katha— First stage ... Kyunbintha ... 8 miles. Second stage ... Pehinga ... ... 11 „ Third stage ... Bamauk ... ... 8 „ This is a better road, as it avoids two hills, though possibly 3 miles longer.

No. 60.

From MANTÔN to MANPUN.

BY MAJOR J. H. SEWELL, NORFOLK REGIMENT, ASSISTANT-ADJUTANT-GENERAL, JANUARY 1890.

Military	Civil	Stages	Intermediate	Total	Remarks
G.O.C. Mandalay District.	Commr., Northern Divn., and Dy. Commr., Ruby Mines.	**1. Manpun (Dasit).** Five streams.	12 0	12 0	Follow the Gammaw road as far as Manpángyi, 2 miles. Here the two roads to Gammaw divide. The south one is taken. Pass Manpángalé at 2¼ miles, Kachin village of nine

FROM MANTÔN TO MANPUN—*continued.*

Authorities. Military.	Authorities. Civil.	Number and Names of Stages, Rivers and Streams.	Distances. Intermediate.	Distances. Total.	Remarks.
G.O.C. Mandalay District.	Commissioner, Northern Division, and Deputy Commissioner, Ruby Mines.	**1. Manpun (Dasit)**—*cont.*			houses. Here road to Laughain turns off to south. Road on level through taungya to $2\frac{3}{4}$ miles. Road furcates right to Gammaw. Follow left-hand road, which descends, steep and bad, to a stream at $3\frac{3}{4}$ miles; cross another stream 100 yards further on, and then ascend through thin jungle, steep, to $4\frac{1}{4}$ miles. Here a road comes in from north-east. Road on level to village, Kachin, 10 houses. Water on south, scanty. Road leaves the village in southerly direction and runs from end to end at 205°, distance as the crow flies $4\frac{1}{2}$ miles. Descend steep hill to $\frac{1}{2}$ mile. Here cross a small stream 500 feet below Pángpé. Ascend 1 furlong and run through taungya, descending steadily to a stream at $1\frac{5}{8}$ miles, 20 feet wide and 1 foot deep. Road now ascends steadily to $2\frac{1}{8}$ miles. Here a road joins from the east. Continue through bamboo jungle, level to $3\frac{3}{8}$ miles, Kachin village of Rôbáng, 20 large houses. Road then descends and is rather rough to $4\frac{7}{8}$ miles. Cross paddy-clearing and a stream 30 feet wide and 1 foot deep. From this point the road ascends steadily to Manpun, a Palaung village of 30 houses and a kyaung, at $6\frac{1}{4}$ miles. The road from the stream runs through low jungle. Road on to Dasit, level and broad, except at $7\frac{3}{8}$ miles, where it descends to a good stream, and ascend immediately after to kyaung and Palaung village of nine houses. Here is a group of pagodas; $\frac{1}{4}$ mile further on is an old red brick pagoda, which is a great land-mark, the ground all round being cleared. From here are visible Mômeik, Bernardmyo signal station, Yébôn, Pwa-án, Taungyi, Heinlôn, Loiya, and Mantôn signal hill. Accommodation for 100 men in kyaung and zayáts. Water good from stream and springs. Grass plentiful from valley lying west.

MANPUN can also be reached FROM MANTÔN *viâ* MANMAUK AND HUMÖNG, as follows:—

FROM MANPUN TO MANTÔN *viâ* MANMAUK.

BY H. F. HERTZ, ESQ., BURMA POLICE, FEBRUARY 1890.

Military.	Civil.	Stages.	Intermediate. M.	Intermediate. F.	Total. M.	Total. F.	Remarks.
G.O.C. Mandalay District.	Commissioner, Northern Division, and Deputy Commissioner, Ruby Mines.	**1. Humöng** ... One stream.	**10**	**0**	10	0	General direction of road east by south. The road leaves Manpun past the old pagoda and runs down a spur, being narrow and indifferent, to 2 miles. Here a small stream and boggy bit of ground is crossed. This would probably be impassable in the rains. Road still indifferent rises to Pángsu, 4 miles, a Palaung village of 10 houses. Accommodation in a kyaung for 20 men. Good water from a spring. The road on is good and undulating and well kept. Two springs are crossed and the Taungbaing border is crossed *en route*. The jungle is pretty light. Humöng is a Palaung village of 10 houses and one kyaung to hold 50 men. Several small Kachin villages are close by, one of four houses being within 200 yards. Water good, but scanty, from spring.
		2. Manmauk ...	**8**	**0**	18	0	General direction north by west. The road is good, except between the 3rd and 5th miles, where it is narrow and bad for transport. It is fairly level throughout. A Kachin (Maru tribe) village of 30 houses. Water from a spring good and plentiful.

FROM MONTÔN TO MANPUN—*continued.*

Authorities.		Number and Names of Stages, Rivers and Streams.	Distances.				Remarks.
Military.	Civil.		Intermediate.		Total.		
			M.	F.	M.	F.	
G.O.C. Mandalay District.	Commr., Northern Divn., and Deputy Commr., Ruby Mines.	**3. Mantôn** ... One stream.	**8**	**0**	26	0	Road fair and undulating, passing through thick jungle as far as Kao-ting, 5 miles (burnt), a Kachin (Lakun) village. It then passes through paddy-fields and is after that a fair road to 7 miles. Here cross paddy-fields and stream and ascend to Mantôn.

No. 61.

From MAYMYO (PYINULWIN) to KALAGWÉ.

BY LIEUT. H. B. WRIGHT, R.E., 1887.

Military.	Civil.	Number and Names of Stages, Rivers and Streams.	Intermediate M.	F.	Total M.	F.	Remarks.
G.O.C. Mandalay District.	Commr., N. Divn., &c., Mandalay.	**1. Naungthakaw.**	**10**	**4**	10	4	*See* Route No. 63, Alternative No. I.
	Superintendent, Northern Shan States.	**2. Sízôn**	**11**	**0**	21	4	From Naungthakaw there are two roads. One leads through Médaw, which is 5 miles distant, and thence to Lôntwé and runs as follows: Through low hills within places steep gradients, but nowhere very difficult. Good except near Médaw, where rain water does not drain off, and so makes the road very heavy and rough. It is also bad at a point where it crosses some paddy-fields below Médaw. Médaw contains one good kyaung and three zayáts, which could accommodate about 60 men, and about 30 houses. It is situated on a spur of the hills. Hence the road is fair, but in places swampy in the wet weather, to Lôntwé, distance about 19 miles. The other better road leads as follows: An easy road for pack transport over undulating country passing through Tanga-baing, Ingu, Thayetkôn, Nyabin, and Chaungyi to Sízôn, a deserted village. Some five kyaungs which were inhabited by pôngyis in July 1887.
		3. Lôntwé ...	**10**	**0**	31	4	Road over undulating country fairly open through Kôngyi to Lôntwé crossing numerous small streams, most of which are bridged. Thônzé can be seen from several points along this road. Lôntwé lies in an open plain slightly undulating, with some marshy ground on the north and east.
		4. Kalagwé ...	**9**	**0**	40	4	Water from spring. An easy road through open undulating country, crossing two or three small streams. This portion could easily be made practicable for carts. Kalagwé is now deserted, but once was a fine village with large kyaungs and some zayáts. Stream supplying good water runs near the village. The whole district round Kalagwé has been devastated and is now almost depopulated. There is another route to Kalagwé through Thônzé.

FROM MAYMYO (PYINULWIN) TO KALAGWÉ—*continued.*

ALTERNATIVE I.

FROM MAYMYO TO KALAGWÉ *vià* MÉDAW.

BY LIEUT. J. A. S. TULLOCH, R.E., 1887.

Authorities. Military.	Authorities. Civil.	Number and Names of Stages, Rivers and Streams.	Distances. Intermediate. M.	F.	Distances. Total. M.	F.	Remarks.
G.O.C. Mandalay District.	Superintendent, Northern Shan States.	**1. Médaw** ... ... Small stream, fordable.	**7**	**4**	7	4	Direction north. Direct but difficult pony track across hills. Steep gradients. Pass village of Naukángyi (1½ miles) and Sésébin (3½ miles). An alternative route is by a good pony road to Naungthakaw (10½ miles). (*See* Route No. 63, Alternative I, and then by easy pony road to Médaw (4½ miles), total 15 miles). The latter road is much the best. At Médaw small village, one kyaung, and two zayáts. Water from stream and some supplies.
		2. Lôntwé ...	**16**	**0**	23	4	As above.
		3. Kalagwé ...	**9**	**0**	32	4	As above.

No. 62.

From MAYMYO (Stage 4) to LÉMA and PINSÔK.

BY LIEUT. H. B. H. WRIGHT, R.E., NOVEMBER 1888.

Military	Civil	Stages	Int. M.	F.	Total M.	F.	Remarks
G.C.C. Mandalay District.	Commissioner, Northern Division, and Deputy Commissioner, Mandalay.	**1. Pongôn** ...	**12**	**4**	12	4	Road from Maymyo leads in a south-south-east direction crossing the ends of two marshes in the first 4 miles, then over a gentle spur; to Pathein, a village of about 40 houses, situated on the end of a small spur running north and south. The roads up the spur are steep. A small patch of ground on the spur is available for a camp for about 100 to 150 men and a small space in the valley which is marshy. Distance to Pathein 6 miles, road passable for carts thus far. Pack transport only can be used further on. As far as Pathein there are two alternative routes, one branches off from the above road at about the 3rd mile and leads south to Naungyi, a village wit' some fine kyaungs. From Naungyi gentle descent to Pathein. Naungyi can also be reached from Singaung on the Pintha-Maymyo road, from which it is about 4 miles distant. The other road to Pathein leads from Maymyo fort and through the village and across the long bridge to the north-east, and thence skirts the marshy ground and joins the road first described at about a mile from Pathein. The country passed through by all three roads is for the most part covered with light jungle, ground undulating. From Pathein the road leads over some small steep spurs and is a mere bridle path through thin jungle crossing two or three small streams. Reach Engbôk, at 9½ miles, passing Pawpyin, which lies in a fertile valley about 1 mile to the left of the road. Engbôk is a village of about 30 houses with some paddy, sugar-cane, and Indian-corn cultivation near it. At 12½ miles reach Pongôn, a small village on

From MAYMO (Stage 4) to LÉMA and PINSÔK—*continued.*

Authorities. Military.	Authorities. Civil.	Number and Names of Stages, Rivers and Streams.	Distances. Intermediate. M.	Distances. Intermediate. F.	Distances. Total. M.	Distances. Total. F.	Remarks.
G.O.C. Mandalay District.	Commissioner, Northern Division, and Deputy Commissioner, Mandalay.	**1. Pongôn** —*cont.*					high ground, whence a good view of the surrounding country can be obtained. A little open ground for camp or bivouac. The village houses have several times been used for the accommodation of 100 to 150 men. Forage plentiful. Water good from a small stream to the east of the village. Indian corn and garden cultivation.
		2. Léma ... ... Léma chaung.	**10**	**0**	22	4	Road as before descending to the site of Baw village at 1 mile which was burnt with a fine kyaung and some zayáts in May 1887 by order of the then Assistant Commissioner, when found occupied by dacoits. There are some inhabited villages close by. Hence the road leads south-south-west for about 4 miles over easy ground with gentle descent through bamboo and tree jungle. Many mango trees in the jungle. Then a very steep descent for about a mile to the Léma chaung. The road then leads for the remainder of the way about 4 miles along the valley through large forest trees crossing the Léma chaung (20 yards wide and about 1 foot deep, except during or after heavy rain), three times before reaching Léma. The stream is bunded at Léma, forded just below the bund, and Léma village entered by a gate in a thorn hedge. A small water channel runs through the village, the remainder of the stream runs to the west of the village. For description of Léma *see* Route No. 53, Branch I. A mile before reaching Léma a path leads off to the right along a tributary valley to Mézataung, a strong position occupied by the dacoits in June 1887. A path leads on beyond Léma to the Myitngé and along its right bank up stream to Shwégadaungwé, a whirlpool in the Myitngé about 5 miles from Léma. Opposite the mouth of the Léma chaung the Myitngé is very rapid and cannot be crossed. About a mile above or ¾ mile below the river could be crossed on rafts made of bamboo and transport could be swum across.
		3. Pinsôk	**3**	**0**	25	4	From Pongôn to Pinsôk pass through Baw and then continue for about 2 miles in east-south-east direction to Pinsôk from which village the dacoit position on Tawma was attacked in May 1887. There is a path connecting Pinsôk and Léma passable for pack transport, but difficult. There is also said to be another path passing through Tawma impassable for transport or ponies.

No. 63.

From MAYMYO to THÔNZÉ.

BY LIEUT. S. WILLCOCK, 2ND GLOUCESTERSHIRE REGIMENT, MAY 1889.

Military	Civil	Stage	Inter. M.	Inter. F.	Total M.	Total F.	Remarks
G.O.C. Mandalay District.	Commr., Northern Divn., &c., Mandalay.	**1. Wetwin** ...	**12**	**0**	12	0	*See* Route No. 53, Stage 5.

FROM MAYMYO TO THÔNZÉ—*continued.*

Authorities. Military.	Authorities. Civil.	Number and Names of Stages, Rivers and Streams.	Distances. Intermediate.		Distances. Total.		Remarks.
			M.	F.	M.	F.	
G.O.C. Mandalay District.	Commissioner, Northern Division, and Deputy Commissioner, Mandalay.	**2. Bámbwé** ...	9	0	21	0	Course north. Good cart road bridged throughout, but not metalled, over undulating hills. At ½ mile pass Wetwin east. At 4½ miles a camp ground with two sheds, but little water. At 6 miles Pángmôn. Camp ground with good water. Kyaung and zayáts ¼ mile south of Bámbwé, with accommodation for 100 men. Up to this point route is same as No. 53.
	Superintendent, Northern Shan States.	**3. Thônzé** ... Many small streams, nearly all bridged for carts; remainder no obstacle.	10	0	31	0	Direction north. Fairly good cart road. Thin jungle. Thônzé has been burnt twice lately and there are not more than 20 houses at present. There are ruins of a very large village. There are several large deserted pôngyi kyaungs in the immediate neighbourhood of the village, and two inhabited ones about ½ mile before reaching the village on north of road, and one on rising ground east of the bazaar; would accommodate 400 men. Small bazaar; supplies very hard to get; very little paddy. Water from stream good and plentiful.

ALTERNATIVE I.

FROM MAYMYO (PYINULWIN) TO THÔNZÉ *viâ* NAUNGTHAKAW AND BÁMBWÉ.

BY CAPT. A. C. YATE, 1ST BELUCH LIGHT INFANTRY, DECEMBER 1887.

Military	Civil	Stages	Intermediate M.	Intermediate F.	Total	Remarks
G.O.C. Mandalay District.	Commissioner, Northern Division, and Deputy Commissioner, Mandalay.	**1. Naungthakaw.** Several small streams, all bridged for ponies and bullocks.	10	4	...	*N.B.*—This is not the best but merely an alternative route to that usually taken (No. 63). Thônzé can be reached in two stages *viâ* Naungthakaw, or in three stages *viâ* Wetwin and Bambwé. The last is the best route being passable for carts. There is also a direct cart road from Wetwin to Thônzé. Direction N. 20° E. Road fit throughout for pack transport. Approaches to bridges in some places difficult and apt to dislodge loads. The road to Wetwin *viâ* Pinlein is identical with this one as far as a point about ½ mile beyond the village of Môgyobyit. After leaving village of Pyinulwin, road, which is a raised cart road, passes over marshy ground and among paddy-fields for about ½ mile; then crosses a bridge 80 yards long and 10 feet broad, passable for wheeled artillery. Beyond bridge is the hamlet of Tada-u, and here the road bifurcates, that to right being the southerly route to

FROM MAYMYO TO THÔNZÉ—*continued.*

ALTERNATIVE I—*continued.*

Authorities.		Number and Names of Stages, Rivers and Streams.	Distances.		Remarks.
Military.	Civil.		Inter-mediate.	Total.	
G.O.C. Mandalay District.	Commissioner, Northern Division, and Deputy Commissioner, Mandalay.	**1. Naungthakaw** —*cont.*			Wetwin, that to left the Naungthakaw road. Beyond this country gently undulating, marshy in hollows ; sparse jungle. Land suitable for dry crops, maize, jowari, cotton, sugar-cane. Rainfall lasts for five months (Jure to October), but is not very heavy. Rice grows well in hollows and on taungyas. The people of the villages appear to be mostly mixed Shan and Danus. Several hundreds of villagers flock to Pyinulwin with food and other supplies from the villages north-north-east and east of that place on bazaar days. Garlic, onions, a kind of cabbage or spinach, thanapet (leaf used as roller for cheroots), tomatoes, bark for paper, and coarse paper are among the articles brought in for sale. At $1\frac{3}{4}$ cross stream by wooden bridge for pack animals. Stream flows from west to east to Wetwin. Beyond this jungle thicker. At $2\frac{1}{4}$ miles path to left to small village of Naungkangalé, direction 290°, distance 1 mile, and to right to paddy-fields. At $2\frac{1}{3}$ miles cross pony bridge over stream and marshy ground. At 3 miles cross stream by bridge. Here road draws close to the range of hills that bounds the Pyinulwin basin on the north. From here the southern road to Wetwin may be traced winding along the northern slope of a low hill range 1 or $1\frac{1}{2}$ miles distant. At $4\frac{1}{3}$ miles reach Môgyobyit, village of 15 or 20 houses in the Pyinulwin district, situated on the eastern slope of the hill range that borders the road to the west. About $\frac{1}{4}$ mile east of and below village empty kyaung and a zayát, holding 50 to 100 men. A mile before Môgyobyit is reached the road bifurcates, that to left being a foot-path up to the village, while that to the right is a cart road skirting the foot of the spur. The cart road is heavy in the rains. These two roads meet $\frac{1}{4}$ mile north of the village. Excellent water from stream at Mogyobyit. Rice, garlic, onions, cabbage, tomatoes, sugar-cane, thanapet produced there. Inhabitants of Mogyobyit all Shans. From Mogyobyit there is a foot-path south-east to Yé-ngé, a village on the southerly road to Wetwin, distance 2 miles. Half a mile beyond Mogyobyit road to right (15°) to Penlein (30 houses, Shans and Danus) and so on to Wetwin. Country still undulating and overgrown with jungle. At $2\frac{1}{4}$ miles cart road to left winding round to Myawdaw, village of 40 houses with kyaung and zayát, distant 2 to $2\frac{1}{2}$ miles. At $3\frac{3}{4}$ miles cross stream by bridge. This stream flows east by south to Wetwin ; $\frac{1}{2}$ to $\frac{3}{4}$ mile up stream village of Thékán (15 houses). At $4\frac{3}{4}$ miles path to left to Thékán ($\frac{3}{4}$ mile) and Myawdaw (3 miles). At $5\frac{1}{2}$ miles reach Naungthakaw rice cultivation which is extensive. At 6 miles cross stream by bridge and enter village. At $6\frac{1}{4}$ miles reach pôngyi kyaung and zayáts situated on high ground north of village. Bazaar close to kyaung. Cabbage, tomatoes, onions, thanapet, grown in village which lies in a grove of fine bamboos. Kyaung, five zayáts and bazaar buildings amply sufficient for housing half battalion native troops. People of Naungthakaw, originally all Burmese and Danus ; but now many Shans come here. Hoing appointed from Thônzé. Good road from here to Thônzé *viâ* Zibyubin, 12 miles, to Médaw 5 miles, and to Bámbwé by pony path. Six or seven villages under Heing of Naungthakaw, viz., Taungtalôn (north-west), Baná (north), Theyakôn (north-east), Taunganaing (north-east), Zadi (north-east on road to Thônzé), Panyúyé (north-east), and Eng-u. The boundary between Pyinulwin and Naungthakaw is the stream just south of Naung-

FROM MAYMYO TO THÔNZÉ—*continued.*

ALTERNATIVE I—*continued.*

Authorities.		Number and Names of Stages, Rivers and Streams.	Distances.		Remarks.
Military.	Civil.		Intermediate.	Total.	
G.O.C. Mandalay District.	Commr., Northern Division, and Deputy Commr., Mandalay.	**1. Naungthakaw** —*cont.*			thakaw. Thékán and Myawdaw are in Pyinulwin district. All this neighbourhood is largely populated with Danus, who seem to extend all over that border portion of the Shan States known to the Burmese as "Myelát." The Dánu is more of a Burman than a Shan. He speaks Burmese and dresses like a Shan. The Danus are not found in the pure Shan States. From Naungthakaw kyaung angle to Lôntwé 353°, to Thônzé 40°, Ngôkteik 50°, Bámbwé 80°.
	Superintendent, Northern Shan States.	**2. Bámbwé** ... Small streams bridged for ponies.	M. F. **9 4**	M. F. 20 0	General direction nearly due east, for first half south of, and for second half of distance north of, east. Road throughout good for pack transport; was formerly a cart road and is so used now in places. Starting eastward from pôngyi kyaung at 300 yards road to left (355°) to village of Kyauktaw, 1½ miles distant. Just beyond meet main road from village of Nyaungthakaw to Bawhlaing and Bámbwé. Country traversed undulating covered with sparse jungle, cleared here and there for taungyas. Further on jungle grows thicker and the path from disuse is overgrown with grass. At 3⅛ miles cart road from Kyauktaw comes in from left (325°). Distance from Kyauktaw to the point, 2¼ miles. At 3¼ miles cart road to left to Bawhlaing kyaung. At 3¾ miles road to right (255°) to Pinlein, distant 3½ to 4 miles. A few paces further on enter village of Bawhlaing (Western) 12 houses. Eastern Bawhlaing (20 houses) lies to east of the kyaung.* At 3¾ miles main road from Môgyobyit by north to Bámbwé comes in from right (270°). From here road descends at first by gentle, then by steep gradient, and at 4¾ miles crosses small stream by pony bridge. Camping ground close by. At 5⅜ miles village of Letpángôn, 15 houses to left of road. At 5½ cart road from Wetwin comes in from right (195°). (Distance from here to Wetwin 3½ to 4 miles.) Fifty yards further cart road to left (25°) to Kyenganaing (2½ miles, 20 houses, kyaung and zayáts) and Thônzé (about 10 miles). This is probably the most direct road from Wetwin to Thônzé, distance about 15 miles. At 6 miles meet main cart road from Wetwin to Bámbwé. Village of east Letpángôn ¼ north-east of point of junction.
		3. Thônzé ... Numerous small streams, and one good-sized stream, 3 miles south of Thônzé. All bridged for carts, and failing bridges all fordable.	**8 2**	28 2	Direction nearly due north. Road passable throughout for carts, crosses a number of small streams which would greatly delay any transport had they not been recently bridged. The beds are of deep clinging mud. Surrounding country level, overgrown with thinnish tree jungle and undergrowth. Villages and cultivation few and far between. The ample supply of water from streams and the excellence of the soil suggest that the district might become a highly productive one. At 2¼ miles small village of Gángaw with kyaung and paddy-fields. From here path to right (east) to Thékaw, distance 2 miles, and to left to

* People of Bawhlaing are all Danus.

FROM MAYMYO TO THÔNZÉ—*continued.*

ALTERNATIVE I—*continued.*

Authorities. Military.	Authorities. Civil.	Number and Names of Stages, Rivers and Streams.	Distances. Intermediate.	Distances. Total.	Remarks.
G.O.C. Mandalay District.	Superintendent, Northern Shan States.	**3. Thônzé**—*cont.*			Kyenganaing (2½ miles) on the Wetwin-Thônzé road. At 5 miles road to right to village of Taungkaungbwaw, distant about 1¼ miles, east by north, and thence on to the village of Shwéleikôn, the Bámbwé-Nammaw road. At 5½ miles pass hills called Kalamadaung and Pudaung to right; at 5¾ miles cross largish stream (20′ to 25′ broad and 4′ deep flowing south by east, falls into the Myitngé). At 6¾ miles pass Myinkadaung (Pony-saddle Hill) to left. White pagoda on top, kyaung below to west of hill. This hill can be seen from any high ground for 15 or 20 miles round, and would make a good signalling station. It is only 1¼ miles from Thônzé. At 7 miles cart road to right (S.-E. 140°) to Taungkaungbwaw (2¼ to 3 miles), and on to the Bámbwé-Nammaw road. The Sawbwa lives in a stockaded house on rising ground with the bazaar and what remains of the village to the north and east. A mile west of Sawbwa's house are several kyaungs inhabited by pôngyis, around which a small force can encamp comfortably. Water good and plentiful, grass and fuel and a little paddy obtainable. Other supplies at present very scarce. Weekly bazaar. In the rains 200 men could be accommodated in the kyaungs and zayáts. *N.B.*—The natives report that the more direct road from Wetwin, *viâ* Kyenganaing to Thônzé, would be preferable to the detour *viâ* Bámbwé if the streams on the former were probably bridged. The bridges have fallen into disrepair. The stages would be Wetwin, Kyenganaing and Thônzé.

No. 64.

From MÔGAUNG to HÔKÁT.

BY CAPT. D. S. LEWIS, JANUARY 1890.

Military	Civil	Stages	Intermediate M.	Intermediate F.	Total M.	Total F.	Remarks
G.O.C. Mandalay District and O.C. Bhamo.	Commissioner, Northern Division, and Deputy Commissioner, Bhamo.	**1. Tápaw** ... ... One small Stream half-way.	**14**	**0**	...		Tápaw is a large village of 40 to 50 houses, lying east of Môgaung, on the right bank of the Môgaung river. The road from Môgaung is very bad, particularly the last half, which is a swamp during nine months of the year. At 5 miles from Môgaung a range of hills, 1,000 feet high, running north and south, is crossed. The road is impassable for carts, but passable for pack transport.
		2. Vinbát Sakhán.	**15**	**0**	29	0	The road from Tápaw to Vinbát after crossing the Môgaung river at Tápaw lies along the telegraph line and is a fairly good bridle path, passable for pack transport. It is very hilly and in parts steep and intersected by nullahs, at two of which animals have to be unladen. These nullahs could be bridged, as large quantities of felled trees are available close at hand. Vinbát lies south of Tápaw, and is the name given to a recognized halting place at the head of the Vinbát rapids on the Môgaung river. No village. From here there is a direct path to Hôkát which, however, is not so good as that *viâ* Namyát. Road bad, intersected with three small streams, which require bridging. Namyát is a small village of about five houses on the left bank of the Môgaung river.

FROM MÔGAUNG TO HÔKÁT—*continued.*

Authorities. Military.	Authorities. Civil.	Number and Names of Stages, Rivers and Streams.	Distances. Intermediate. M.	F.	Distances. Total. M.	F.	Remarks.
G.O.C. Mandalay District and O.C. Bhamo.	Commr., Northern Divn., and Deputy Commissioner, Bhamo.	**3. Hôkát**	**13**	**0**	42	0	From Namyát the road lies across a plain with paddy here and there. The road is good, and during the dry weather would admit of cart carriage being used. At 3 miles from Hôkát lies a stream with steep banks and muddy bottom, 3 feet deep and 15 feet wide. This should be bridged.

No. 65.

From MÔGAUNG to LÔNTÔN (Indawgyi Lake).

BY CAPT. D. S. LEWIS, M.S.C., ATTACHED MOGAUNG LEVY, APRIL 1890.

Military	Civil	Stages	M.	F.	M.	F.	Remarks
G.O.C. Mandalay District and O.C. Bhamo.	Commissioner, Northern Division, and Deputy Commissioner, Bhamo.	**1. Taungni** ... First the Nanyin chaung, 1 mile from Môgaung, and two other streams.	**18**	**0**	...		The village of Taungni is situate 18 miles south-west of Môgaung. The road is a 12-foot track recently made by contract and in the dry weather is passable for carts. Three streams between Môgaung and Taungni: first the Nanyin chaung at 1 mile, and two other small streams at 7 and 13 miles respectively.
		2. Camp on bank of stream. Several small streams.	**11**	**0**	29	0	General direction of road south-west along the new cutting referred to above, running through a plain. Five small streams to be crossed. Camping ground on the bank of a good stream.
		3. Camp on bank of stream. Several small streams.	**15**	**0**	44	0	General direction of road south-west through a plain; not many trees. A good stream of water is met with at 9 miles from last camp. Camping ground on the bank of a stream.
		4. Camp on stream.	**9**	**0**	53	0	Three miles south-west of camp is a hill running north and south. The road ascends the southern spur after following the bed of a dry stream. The hill is about 1,200 feet high. The road then runs along the summit for 1½ miles, then descends to camp on bank of a stream.
		5. Camp on Namwan stream.	**8**	**0**	61	0	General direction of road south-west. The first 2½ miles run through teak forest and then through undulating country. The road very narrow here and a deal of ramping necessary to make it fit for transport animals. At 6 miles the road ascends a hill 2,500 feet high, from the summit of which a glimpse of Indawgyi is obtainable. Half-way down the northern slope of this hill camp on small trickling stream called the Namwan lies close to it. The road in this stage is merely a footpath through virgin jungle, tree ferns, bamboos, and unworked teak forests.

FROM MÔGAUNG TO LÔNTÔN (INDAWGYI LAKE)—*continued.*

Authorities. Military.	Authorities. Civil.	Number and Names of Stages, Rivers and Streams.	Distances. Intermediate. M.	F.	Total. M.	F.	Remarks.
G.O.C. Mandalay District and O.C. Bhamo.	Commissioner, Northern Division, and Deputy Commissioner, Bhamo.	**6. Camp**	**9**	**0**	70	0	General direction west. At 5 miles about 200 yards of swamp, the remainder of the march through open teak forest. The camp is a fine open one, capable of holding 3,000 men. It is interspersed with gigantic teak trees and is half encircled by an excellent stream of water. The camp is situate 6 miles south of Indawgyi lake.
		7. Lôntôn	**7**	**0**	77	0	The road to Lôntôn village runs parallel to the southern shore of the lake, a mile distant from it, and then on reaching the west side, follows the shore of the lake till the village is reached. The village consists of 45 houses. No supplies are obtainable beyond fowls and a small quantity of rice. The Indawgyi military police post is on a knoll on the shore of the lake, about 600 yards north of Lôntôn village.

Capt. O'Donnell describes a route traversed by him FROM MÔGAUNG TO INDAWGYI LAKE in February 1891, as follows:—*

Authorities. Military.	Authorities. Civil.	Number and Names of Stages, Rivers and Streams.	Distances. Intermediate. M.	F.	Total. M.	F.	Remarks.
G.O.C. Mandalay District and O.C. Bhamo.	Commissioner, Northern Division, and Deputy Commissioner, Bhamo.	**1. Taungni** ...	**17**	**0**	17	0	Direction south-west. At 3 miles come to village of Lwélaw in paddy plains and on banks of the Nanyinchaung which is here crossed by a good ford knee-deep; sandy bottom and firm. The first 3 miles pass along good many small villages a little distance from the road. From all these camps paddy can be procured. After crossing Nanyinchaung road leads through kaing grass jungle some 4 miles and then comes on to the railway survey track. The remainder of the road is along this track which is very hard going, owing to its swampy state during the rains, and that elephants have been along it and cut it up to a great extent. Four small chaungs with steep banks and three of them with muddy bottoms have to be crossed causing much delay and trouble. Taungni, a Shan-Burman village, 2 miles from the military police post of Nyaungbintha, can provide much paddy. It is under the Waranlöng Sawbwa, an Ithi Kachin. On the hills east and west of this are the remaining Ithi villages, in all about 12 small ones.
		2. Sangin chaung.	**8**	**0**	25	0	From Taungni the railway track should not be followed (it leads through much swampy country), but the road along foot of hills on west of the valley. Three miles from Taungni it meets the railway track again and goes on along it, crossing five streams *en route*, namely— 1. Manna chaung. 2. Mulei chaung. 3. Tinkôk chaung. 4. Laikonaw chaung. 5. Sangin chaung.

* The route seems to be the same as that used by Capt. Lewis the year previous, but it is so impossible to combine the two that both are printed here separately.

FROM MÔGAUNG TO LÔNTÔN (INDAWGYI LAKE)—*continued.*

Authorities. Military.	Authorities. Civil.	Number and Names of Stages, Rivers and Streams.	Distances. Intermediate. M.	F.	Distances. Total. M.	F.	Remarks.
G.O.C. Mandalay District and O.C. Bhamo.	Commissioner, Northern Division, and Deputy Commissioner, Bhamo.	**2. Sangin chaung** —*cont.*					The Tinkôk is a bad crossing with much swampy ground about it also in the bed of the stream, and much ramping had to be done for the transport. The remainder are good streams, shingle bottoms, and about 1 foot deep. Good camping ground near all of them, except No. 3 where the water is nearly stagnant and consequently bad. The country along the march, which is still in the plain of the Nanyin chaung, is quite open, and the hills on both sides are visible throughout.
		3. Tákôn chaung. Namngam chaung, 4 yards broad and 1 foot deep; stony and sandy bottom. Firm and easy for transport. Small streams; sufficient water to supply a large force. Running and good water; sandy bottom.	**15**	**0**	40	0	The road runs roughly south-west along railway track as in the previous stage; is a good road and requires little description. It is entirely in the plains and during the day is a very hot march. Above half way crosses the Namngamchaung; a fine stream, sandy and shingle bottom with a most excellent camp on its banks. About 4 miles beyond this it crosses a small stream, and after that the Indawgyi road strikes off to the right, leaving the Môhnyin road and railway track on its left. After 3 miles along this road which runs in a north-west direction arrives at Tákôn chaung; a good stream some 4 yards broad and 12 inches deep; sandy and firm bottom. The banks need to be repaired to make it easy going for the transport animals; good camp available here by clearing kaing grass jungle. The proper march should be from Taungni to Namngam chaung and then on further than this camp.
		4. Sanhli chaung.	**9**	**0**	49	0	This road takes a great detour, and the camp in a direct line form Tákôn chaung is not more than 14 miles. The road is a very bad one; leading through much swampy land and also across small spurs of hills at right angles; much clearing of the road had to be done. The Sanhli chaung is almost dry. The camp is nearly at its source, and just below the pass which leads out of the Nanyin chaung into the Indawgyi valley. This pass is as far as can now be seen a low one. The road from Tákôn goes up the stream for some miles through very thick elephant grass jungle and boggy land. After leaving the Tákôn chaung it passes over small spurs of hills and through many dry beds of small streams, leading for a short time up one of them for a mile, The third march from Môgaung should be from the Namngam chaung to the head of the Tákôn chaung some 4 miles beyond where there is ground available for a camp. Sanhli is a good camping ground, but water is very scarce and for that reason would never do for these purposes.
		5. Sankai chaung.	**11**	**0**	60	0	Road leads almost directly over the pass which is south-east of the lake. Highest point of the pass by aneroid is 2,575 feet. My camp was 1,825 feet. This is not actual height, but barometer height, and gives the difference between camps, &c. Road is good

FROM MÔGAUNG TO LÔNTÔN (INDAWGYI LAKE)—*continued.*

Authorities. Military.	Authorities. Civil.	Number and Names of Stages, Rivers and Streams.	Distances. Intermediate.	Distances. Total.	Remarks.
G.O.C. Mandalay District and O.C. Bhamo.	Comr., Northern Dn., and Deputy Comr., Bhamo.	**5. Sankai chaung** —*cont.*			and after crossing the pass leads into the plain and over much boggy country. Camp Sankai.* The last portion of the road very bad indeed after rain. As the marshy ground would not be sufficiently dry for transport about June, it would be dangerous, as the streams swell up in a single night and become utterly impassable.

No. 66.

From MÔGAUNG to MAINGKHWAN.

BY LIEUT T. H. E. DAUNCEY, 21ST HUSSARS, JANUARY 1892.

Military	Civil	Stages	Intermediate M.	Intermediate F.	Total M.	Total F.	Remarks
G.O.C. Mandalay District and O.C. Bhamo.	Commissioner, Northern Division, and Deputy Commissioner, Bhamo.	**1. Jungle Camp (Nwénigyi chaung).** Nwénigyi chaung.	4	6	4	6	The Namkong (or Môgaung) chaung at Môgaung is about 100 yards broad and generally shallow. At the ford it is 3 feet at the deepest parts. Broad sandy beach here on both sides of the river. After crossing the river, the path leads north-west for a mile and then bends round to the south-west for ½ mile, all the way along the brink of the river, brushing through thick and high kaing grass. Path dangerous for pack animals owing to the precipitous and rotten banks. At 1½ miles the path leaves the river, striking off in a north-west direction; for next 3 miles good going, and at 4½ miles reach a small stream of good water, 3 yards broad, and at this point only a few inches deep. Good small camp. This little chaung, named Nwéni, flows south-west into the Namkong chaung, meeting it at Nampaung, 3½ miles above Môgaung.
		2. Jungle Camp (Nwénigyi chaung).	6	4	11	2	Path leads off in a north by north-west direction and after ½ mile comes to a bend of the Nwénigyi chaung, which, after flowing from the north by north-west for about 6 miles, turns off at this point sharp to the east. At the 3rd mile the path is wet and stony leading down into a valley, and the Nwénigyi is crossed for the first time at 3½ miles. Here it is 25 yards broad and shallow. A couple of furlongs farther on a small stream with slippery banks is crossed. At 5½ miles down a wet and stony slope and across another small clear stream 5 yards broad flowing west into the Nwénigyi. At 6¼ miles the path crosses the Nwénigyi for the second time; 25 yards broad and clear and shallow, gravelly bottom, and arrives at a good camping ground on the right bank. Path good; tree jungle.
		3. Jungle Camp (Nampaung chaung). Nampaung chaung.	5	0	16	2	At 2¼ miles the path leads across the Nampaung chaung, 8 yards, clear, and shallow, gravelly bottom, and then a furlong on, across a boggy little stream. At 4 miles across the Nampaung chaung again. At 5 miles across another river flowing from north-east to south-west, *i.e.*, in the same direction as the Nam-

* This camp appears to be the same as the sixth camp in the previous report by Capt. Lewis.

FROM MÔGAUNG TO MAINGKHWAN—*continued*.

Authorities. Military.	Authorities. Civil.	Number and Names of Stages, Rivers and Streams.	Distances. Intermediate.	Distances. Total.	Remarks.
G.O.C. Mandalay District and O.C. Bhamo.	Commissioner, Northern Division, and Deputy Commissioner, Bhamo.	**3. Jungle Camp (Nampaung chaung)**—*cont.*			paung chaung at the last crossing. Could not find out the name of it, so have written it Nampaung chaung; 25 yards broad, clear and shallow, gravelly bottom, good camping ground on the opposite bank. Good path the whole way. General direction north-west; tree jungle.
		4. Kámaing ... Kaché chaung, Namkong (or Môgaung) chaung.	M. F. **15 2**	M. F. 31 2	Path leads off west by north-west. At ½ mile crosses two boggy streams which flow into the Kaché chaung westward, and at 1 mile a path branches off west to this chaung. At 2½ miles across another small stream. At 6¼ miles across the Kaché chaung, 8 yards broad and shallow sandy bed. There is a small dry camping ground here on the high bank of this chaung. Half a mile further on a paddy clearing on the right of the path, which can also be used as a camping ground. Path up to this point through tree jungle with occasional open spaces. Path good except for the few tiresome boggy crossings. From this point until reaching the turning to Kámaing west at 12¼ miles, the route lies west by north-west, nearly the whole way through high kaing grass with a couple of boggy crossings. At the turning to Kámaing, at 12¼ miles, the route to Labán strikes in from the north. At 12 miles the path crosses the Swa chaung, 6 yards broad and muddy at the crossing. Here there is a small dry camping place. From the point where the Labán and Kámaing paths meet, the route to Kámaing leads west and then south-west. At 13½ miles a bend of the Namkong chaung is reached, where there is unlimited camping ground by clearing the kaing grass. Along the left bank for 1½ miles, on the very brink of the river which lies 20 feet below, dangerous for pack animals or even for unladen animals, as the banks seem rather rotten. At 15¼ miles the path arrives opposite Kámaing, which is situated high up above the right bank of the river. The Namkong is about 80 yards broad at the crossing and about 3 feet deep. Kámaing has about 50 houses and is situated at the junction of the Indaw and Namkong chaungs. Path generally good; a few boggy places.*
		5. Mampin Namkong and [illegible]ama chaungs.	**13 4**	44 6	The path from Kámaing to Maingkhwan leads out of Kámaing for 200 yards along the right bank of the river Namkong and then crosses it. Breadth at crossing 100 yards; depth 3 feet. Small camping ground at the crossing on the left bank. The path then leads off in a west direction following the left bank of the river for about a mile; a very dangerous narrow path along the high overhanging bank and shut in on the right by impenetrable kaing grass. At 1½ miles it reaches a small camping ground, and here the path leaves the river striking off in a north-east direction for 1½ miles where the path from Mogaung joins it from the east. The path now runs north-north-east for nearly 5 miles through a large valley of kaing grass with a view of distant hills on the other side of the Namkong chaung to the west and low ranges of hills running north about 4 miles distant on the right, on which are visible a great many old clearings and a few fresh ones and a small hut here and there. At 4½

* The distance from Môgaung to Kámaing can easily be done in three marches; in fact this was done by the Môgaung-Jade Mines column in 1887-89, *vide* Route No. 72.

FROM MÔGAUNG TO MAINGKHWAN—*continued.*

Authorities. Military.	Authorities. Civil.	Number and Names of Stages, Rivers and Streams.	Distances. Intermediate.	Distances. Total.	Remarks.
G.O.C. Mandalay District and O.C. Bhamo.	Commissioner, Northern Division, and Deputy Commissioner, Bhamo.	**5. Mampin**—*cont.*			miles from Kámaing a muddy, sticky jheel has to be crossed and ½ mile further on a bad swamp 30 yards broad. At 12¼ miles the Pama chaung is reached; 25 yards by 2 feet deep; a swift beautiful stream with a gravelly bed flowing south-west into the Namkong chaung. On the further side is the village of Mampin, 30 feet above the river; eight houses (Marip), the east side of which would be a good camping place for a small column (200 men). Path easy all the way.
		6. Hwélôn ... Pama and Tarôn chaungs.	M. F. 5 0	M. F. 49 6	Path leads out of the village of Mampin along the right bank of the river for 200 yards in and east by north-east direction and then turns off into tree jungle in a north-west direction for ¼ mile, when it changes almost due west, until the Tarôn chaung is reached at 1 mile. This chaung is about 10 yards broad, clear, shallow, and swift; gravelly bottom. A small damp camping ground here. Bamboo jungle; good path up to this point. The path leads from the Tarôn chaung, up-hill in a north-west direction and ½ mile from the chaung passes through the village of Tarôn, seven houses situated on the summit of a small hill. It then descends and leads close under hills on the right through kaing grass, path difficult, crossed by several deep muddy nullahs, very narrow and steep. At about 3 miles the path leads into tree jungle and soon commences to be most difficult going for pack mules and elephants, up and down almost perpendicular slopes, slippery, and obstructed by overhanging trees and great roots forming steps of 3 feet high or more, up or down which the mules have to jump. In the middle of these hills, the path, for about ¾ mile, leads through a deep, boggy stream between almost perpendicular banks; no path except in the stream. Then, after leading over another steep hill, the path crosses two more boggy streams and arrives at a small clearing in the midst of the hills with three small Kachin houses named Hwélôn, B. 860. Pack mules would have taken about 3 hours traversing this latter 4 miles from the Tarôn chaung. Hwélôn clearing makes a good camping ground for 150 men in dry season. Small shallow stream.
		7. Labán ... ... Naongmi, 'Nkúm, and Namkong chaungs.	15 0	64 6	Path leads out of Hwélôn clearing in a north direction up a steep hill through tree jungle over six more fairly steep hills and through several small jungle streams. In two places the path is under water for a few hundred yards. At 2¼ miles reaches the Naongmi chaung (8 yards by 1 foot, clear, swift, sandy bed) along the bed of which it leads for 150 yards, then turns off to the right through the small Kachin village of Naongmi, 200 yards further on; then on north-west through high kaing grass and tree jungle; crosses the Naongmi chaung for the second time at 3¾ miles; on through tree jungle and a clearing of about 8 acres and crosses to Naongmi chaung for the third time at 4¾ miles. At 5¼ miles a small stream and camping ground and the path commences to lead over a high range of hills and is boggy at places and a path from a large Kachin village named 'Nkúm (situated on a hill 1,500 feet high about 2 miles

FROM MÔGAUNG TO MAINGKHWAN—*continued.*

Authorities. Military.	Authorities. Civil.	Number and Names of Stages, Rivers and Streams.	Distances. Intermediate. M.	F.	Distances. Total. M.	F.	Remarks.
G.O.C. Mandalay District and O.C. Bhamo.	Commissioner, Northern Division, and Deputy Commissioner, Bhamo.	**7. Labán**—*cont.*					to east-north-east cuts in. At 6½ miles the path reaches an altitude of 1,100 feet, but is not difficult, and descends again until at 8 miles it crosses the 'Nkúm chaung (2 yards by 6 inches, swift, clear, good water). Now through kaing grass and across several boggy crossings, path generally boggy and narrow until at 9 miles it reaches a large paddy clearing of about 60 acres belonging to the village of Tinring 1½ miles further on. From this clearing to Tinring there is a fine broad path cleared for several yards on each side. Tinring is reached at 11 miles; a large and prosperous Kachin village situated high up on the left bank of the Namna chaung (30 yards by 2 feet, clear, swift, sandy bed). After passing through this village where a small, dry camping ground could be found, the path, as broad as before, runs along the left bank of the chaung, until at 11½ miles it leads down into the bed of the stream, and now for 3 miles the path leads west-south-west along the bed of the Namkong chaung (into which the Namna chaung flows here) crossing it thirteen times (general breadth 60 yards, depth 6 inches to 3 feet; swift and clear; hard, sandy bed) and at 15 miles arrives opposite the two-housed village of Labán, where the river bends to the south-west and narrows to 50 yards by 4 feet at the crossing. Good camping ground for 300 men on the left bank of the river opposite Labán.
		8. 'Nlamkatawng Namsáng and Namkong chaungs.	**10**	**0**	74	6	Path leads out of Labán along the bank of the Namkong chaung for ¼ mile and then strikes off north through low kaing grass jungle for 2 miles when it turns east and crosses a muddy stream, and 200 yards farther on crosses the Namsáng chaung (flowing south-east into the Namkong); 15 yards by 3 feet, clear, swift, sandy bed; then through the small Kachin village of Krup, due north for 1 mile, then north-east for 2 miles, until at 5 miles it touches the river bank of the Namkong chaung again, which is here 80 yards broad and fairly deep. Small village of 'Njúm perched high up on opposite bank 100 feet high; on through high tree jungle; good path following the river until at 10 miles it crosses the river (40 yards by 3 feet bed; 80 yards) and about 200 yards up stream on the left bank there is a large paddy clearing near the village of 'Nlamkatawng; a good camp in dry weather. Path good the whole way. Mules started 9 A.M., arrived in camp at 1-30 P.M. Difficult for elephants.
		9. Tinkauk chaung. Kaunglaw chaung.	**14**	**2**	89	0	Path leads off in a north direction through the small village of 'Nlam, across low hills, until at 3½ miles it crosses the Kaunglaw chaung (10 yards by 1 foot, clear, swift; pebbly bed), then on through fine tree jungle, light undergrowth, north by north-east across many small jungle streams. At 8 miles across the Kaunglaw chaung again (4 yards by 6 inches) across several more tiny streams over low hills through grand tree jungle and at 14¾ miles path reaches the Tinkauk chaung, where there is a small camping ground used by rubber merchants.

FROM MÔGAUNG TO MAINGKHWAN—*continued.*

Authorities. Military.	Authorities. Civil.	Number and Names of Stages, Rivers and Streams.	Distances. Intermediate.	Distances. Total.	Remarks.
G.O.C. Mandalay District and O.C. Bhamo.	Commissioner, Northern Division, and Deputy Commissioner, Bhamo.	**10. Palanpum (? Malawpum).** Tinkauk and Nampyet chaungs.	M. F. **14 4**	M. F. 103 4	Path leads across the Tinkauk chaung (15 yards by 2 feet, clear, swift, pebbly bed) north-north-west through tree jungle. At 2 miles it crosses two small jungle streams and at 4½ miles crosses the Tinkauk chaung again (15 yards by 2 feet) up a hill and along the left bank of the river, crossing the Nampyet chaung (15 yards by 2 feet) at 6 miles. The path then follows more or less the course of the Nampyet chaung north-north-west until reaching the large Marip Kachin village of Palanpum * at 14½ miles, having crossed *en route* several small jungle streams flowing east into the Nampyet chaung. Path good throughout through tree jungle, difficult for elephants owing to overhanging branches. Camping ground close to river limited, but unlimited space in dry weather in the paddy-fields ¼ mile distant. Nampyet chaung at Palanpum 25 yards by 3½ feet.
		11. Maingkhwan. Nampyu and Edi chaungs.	**12 4**	116 0	Path broad and well cleared; leads out of Palanpum in a north-west direction through paddy-fields and at 2 miles passes small village of Ra and crosses the Nampyu chaung (60 yards by 3 feet, clear, swift, gravelly bed), then through small village of Sat on along a broad path north-west following the course of the Nampyu through bamboo jungle, 1 mile to Waga. Path here strikes off in a north-east direction through high kaing grass still following the river to large Kachin village of Nangku at 5 miles. From here the path leaves the river and leads north-north-west for 1½ miles through paddy-fields and high kaing grass; path narrows here and becomes rather boggy. At 8 miles across small stream, very boggy; difficult crossing, through bamboo jungle and kaing grass; very narrow path and boggy until reaching the Edi chaung at 12 miles (6 yards by 2 feet, sluggish, muddy bed) on which Maingkhwan is situated, then across paddy-fields ½ mile to the Shan village of Maingkhwan. Good camping ground; water indifferent. Distances between camp measured and accurate. Intermediate distances between camps reckoned by time and approximate. There are no bridges over the rivers, but they are all shallow. Wading through water every day necessary. Camping places all more or less damp even in the driest season. During the rainy season (from June to November) the easiest way of reaching Maingkhwan from Môgaung would be by river as far as Labán (*certainly*, perhaps a stage further, 'Nlamkatawng); thence by land 4 (or 3) marches.

* I think the correct name of this village is Malawpum.

FROM MÔGAUNG TO MAINGKHWAN—*continued.*

WATER ROUTE.

FROM MÔGAUNG TO MAINGKHWAN (AMBER MINES) BY RIVER AS FAR AS LABÁN, THENCE BY ROAD.

BY MAJOR FENTON, DEPUTY ASSISTANT QUARTERMASTER-GENERAL, INTELLIGENCE BRANCH, JUNE 1890.

Authorities.		Number and Names of Stages, Rivers and Streams.	Distances.		Remarks.
Military.	Civil.		Intermediate.	Total.	
			M. F.	M. F.	
G.O.C. Mandalay District and O.C. Bhamo.	Commissioner, Northern Division, and Deputy Commissioner, Bhamo.	**1. Kámaing (three days' march by road).** **Môgaung (or Namkong) and Indaw chaungs.**	...	...	This portion of the Môgaung chaung is well known and has been constantly traversed by steamers of the *Pathfinder* class. When the river is full, that is to say, from about the middle of June to the middle of October, a steamer of this class can get up without difficulty in one day (about 10 hours' steaming) and can come down in from 4 to 5 hours. Country boats only can be used in the cold weather. Of these there are three kinds called "*talé*," "*laung*," and "*peingaw*" respectively. The former are large boats well suited for conveyance of rations requiring to be kept dry, which it is not so easy to do in *laungs* or *peingaws*, owing to their want of depth not admitting of a double bottom to keep the cargo out of the water which finds its away into the boat by leakage or drippings from the punting poles, &c. The *talé* is capable of carrying up to 10,000 lbs. of cargo in addition to its crew of five men, but 7,000 lbs. is quite enough to load in most of them, and if a guard is also to travel on board, the load must be still further reduced according to the number of soldiers taken. Twenty-five men is the outside number that could be carried in one boat, and if the men are to sleep on board not more than 12. The *laungs* are very handy boats for a shallow river, as they draw little water and are light enough to be hawled over or through rapids without great difficulty. Their crew consists of three men, two to row and pole, one to steer. There would be room for eight to 10 men on board, but not more than half that number could sleep on board under the covered portion of the boat. By putting in temporary bamboo false bottoms, certain amount of rations (certainly 15 to 20 60-lb. bags) could also go in each boat, but it would be impossible to load them to anything like their actual carrying capacity for fear of making them top heavy. Country boats can get up in three to four days at any season of the year, and come down in one to two days. A light *peingaw* can come down in 9 or 10 hours even in the very lowest water. From Môgaung to Kámaing there are no difficulties in the way of rapids to be encountered, and the current even in flood time probably seldom exceeds 4 miles an hour anywhere. Country on either side generally speaking level for some distance from the river, sometimes long grass and few trees, at others thick jungle. Hills run down nearly to the river (*quite* in parts) about midway, but bear away again as one approaches Kámaing. Since the establishment of the military post at Kámaing in the winter of 1888-89 the village has increased to about 40 houses, and from its position on the roads to the Jade and Amber mines is likely to still further increase as trade improves. The population is almost entirely Shan, the only other race represented being Chinese, who have two or three houses here and trade, as do several of the leading Shans, with the Kachins in rubber, amber, &c. The police post here, which is at present our most northern one, is built

FROM MÔGAUNG TO MAINGKHWAN—*continued.*

WATER ROUTE—*continued.*

Authorities. Military.	Authorities. Civil.	Number and Names of Stages, Rivers and Streams.	Distances. Intermediate.	Distances. Total.	Remarks.
G.O.C. Mandalay District and O.C. Bhamo.	Commissioner, Northern Division, and Deputy Commissioner, Bhamo.	**1. Kámaing (three days' march by road)** *—cont.*			on high ground and should be healthy. The main post is in and round a kyaung connected by a stockaded covered way with an outwork on high ground above, whence there is a good look-out in all directions. A good view is also obtainable from a small pagoda-topped ridge, the end of which overlooks the river south of the post. A path leads to it past the water-supply, which is in a ravine about midway. Jack-fruit, limes, plantains, and pine-apples appear to grow well here, and so no doubt would vegetables. Cattle and goats very scarce, but plenty of fowls. The village occupies rather a cramped position on the right bank of the western channel of the Môgaung river which is here divided into two channels by an island evidently formed by the silt brought down by the Indaw chaung which joins the Môgaung immediately above the village by the same bank. At the time of our visit both the Môgaung and the Indaw chaungs were in flood and part of the village was under water. The direct road from Môgaung to Maingkhwan keeps to the east or left bank of the Môgaung chaung and some 3 miles to the east of Kámaing, running straight on up the valley until it comes out on the river bank some miles above the junction of the Nampan chaung which comes in from the Shwédaungyi range eastward. It then follows the river, crossing it frequently, up to Labán, about two marches from Kámaing, five from Môgaung. The country on either side of the Môgaung above Kámaing is level, in many parts almost clear of jungle, but covered with long grass, in others dense tree jungle, and high kaing grass along the river banks. There should be little difficulty in taking transport animals of any kind all up the valley in the cold season, and as the road can never be far from the Môgaung chaung, or Namkong as it is generally called above Kámaing, there would never be any difficulty about camping grounds and water and grass supplies for the animals. In the event of an expedition visiting the Amber mines from the Môgaung side, it would effect a great economy in transport animals if the greater part of the stores could be brought up to Kámaing by steamer, whilst the river is high enough for this or even on up to Labán, if arrangements could be made for their storage there.
		2. Labán (six days' march by road from Môgaung). Namkong or Môgaung chaung.	M. F. ...	M. F. ...	When the Namkong is full there is no difficulty whatever in getting a steamer, even of the comparatively large *Pathfinder* class, up to Labán in a day (about 9 or 10 hours' steaming) and down again in about 4 hours. The river bends about a great deal, but the bends are not sharp, like those in the Indaw chaung, and the river is wider; 80 to 100 yards in the lower part and not less than 40 yards anywhere up to Labán, where it is about at its narrowest. Country boats of which laungs would probably be most useful in the low water season, get up to Labán in five or six days when the river is in flood and come down in one or two. In the dry season they get up quicker, but take longer coming down, the upward journey taking a day or two less and the downward a day or two more than in the wet weather, when the current is

FROM MÔGAUNG TO MAINGKHWAN—*continued.*

WATER ROUTE—*continued.*

Authorities.		Number and Names of Stages, Rivers and Streams.	Distances.		Remarks.
Military.	Civil.		Intermediate.	Total.	
G.O.C. Mandalay District and O.C. Bhamo.	Commissioner, Northern Division, and Deputy Commissioner, Bhamo.	**2. Labán (six days' march by road from Môgaung)**—*cont.*			strong. There are numbers of good places for camping all up the river even in the flood season as the banks are high and sound, and though in parts there are thick belts of kaing grass, in plenty of places there is none. In the low water season the sand banks would be in every way most suitable for boat parties to camp on. The river is full of fish. The valley is bounded on the east by the Kumunpum, a continuation northward of the Shwédaungyi, and on the west by the Kángpum. To the north-west showing up over the Kángpum, which is by no means a high range (1,000 to 1,500 feet above the plain at the outside), is the very conspicuous Mawmiyé taung * towering high above all the surrounding hills and visible probably from Kámaing in clear weather. This mountain is said to be situated on the left bank of the Uyu river between the jade mines and the amber mines. The Namkong rises in it, flowing first in an easterly direction, evidently round the northern end of the Kángpum, unless that range also bears round to the west and is connected with the Mawmiyé taung. The Kumunpum range must be connected with the Mawmiyé taung by the low ridge called (by Hannay) the Sanpu taung, which forms part of the watershed between the Môgaung and the Chindwin rivers, and is crossed on leaving the valley of the former river on the way to Maingkhwan. There is another very low part in this watershed further south, that is to say, nearer the Shwédaungyi mountains across which you can look from the pagoda hill at Kámaing and see a low range of hills stretching away between north and north-east, which no doubt divides the Tanaiku chaung from the Edi chaung on which the town of Maingkhwan is situated, or some other feeders of the Chindwin that join it below the Tanaiku, which is one of its chief sources. Labán is a Marip-Kachin village of about a dozen houses, and a few houses of Marus living with them situated on the right bank of the river. Usually these Kachin houses have only two entrances, one at each end. A Chinese firm (Lawlawka and Co.) who trade in rubber, &c., have houses at the northern end of the village on the river bank lightly stockaded on three sides but open towards the river. Labán is shut in by jungle and would not afford camping room, but the ground on the opposite side of the river has been cleared for cultivation and would do if the river is high. In the dry weather there would certainly be a sand bank at a bend of the river about ½ mile further up, which would be a much better place. Labán does not look as if it would be at all a healthy place to put a police post in, it is so jungly and shut in. The only village passed on the way from Kámaing is Pákyun and that is scarcely visible from the river. It is situated on the north-east corner of a low range of the same name running east and west, the eastern end terminating on the right bank of the river about 4 hours' steam from Kámaing, and here is the landing place for the village. The Namkong soon splits up into small streams above Kámaing, only one of which is to any extent navigable. This is the Nampama which rises in the Shwédaungyi and joins the Namkong by the left bank about 1½

* This must, I think, be the hill spoken of by Capt. Hannay at page 105 of "Selection of Papers regarding the Hill Tracts between Assam and Burma" (I. B. Library, heading D, Lib. No. 51, section I), as bearing south 35° west from Maingkhwan and about 25 miles distant.

No. 66.

From MÔGAUNG to MAINGKHWAN—*continued.*

WATER ROUTE—*continued.*

Authorities.		Number and Names of Stages, Rivers and Streams.	Distances.		Remarks.
Military.	Civil.		Intermediate.	Total.	
G.O.C. Mandalay District and O.C. Bhamo.	Commissioner, Northern Division, and Deputy Commissioner, Bhamo.	**2. Labén (six days' march by road (from Mógaung)**—*cont.*			miles below the landing place for Pákyun. Small peingaws can get up this stream a day's journey to a village called Manpen. The stream is 15 yards wide, where it joins the Namkong.* Just about opposite Pakyun landing place, another stream called the Tarung Ka or Naunmiyé chaung, 10 yards wide, comes in by the left bank. The only other stream we saw of any size coming in by that bank between this and Labán is the Pwélaw chaung, 5 yards wide at the mouth, but there was said to be another close by, which we missed. This stream comes in opposite where a former Labán was situated, some miles south of the present village, and just here is about the worst bit on the river; channel much split up by sand banks and snags. The only streams of any size joining by the right bank are the Máté chaung (= dead-dog creek) and the Wara chaung. The former is 15 yards wide at its junction with the Namkong, which is about a mile (by water) above Pákyun landing place. It is said to issue from a small lake close to the source of the Nanya chaung, a stream crossed on the way from Kámaing to Tawmaw jade mines, and down which from a place called Nanyaseik most of the jade from those mines is floated into the Indaw chaung and thence to Mógaung.† From close to the mouth of the Máté chaung a conical hill showed up over the Kángpum, bearing about west, and called Nanyaseik taung. The Wara chaung is about 15 yards wide at its mouth, but is only a shallow stream even at this time of year. It comes in about 2 miles below Labán.
		3. 'Nlamkatawng or Saduzup (7 or 8 marches from Mógaung). Namkong, Sadu chaung.	M. F. ...	M. F. ...	The word "zup" (pronounced rather short) means "junction of." The name Saduzup therefore means junction of the Sadu chaung. This is only a halting place (sakhán). There is no village there now, nor apparently has there ever been one for the last 50 years, but the Kachin village of Ngakatawng (? Nlamkatawng) is about midway between Labán and Saduzup. The Shans, who came up with us on the *Pathfinder*, said we should have no difficulty in taking that steamer on up to Saduzup, and could get there and back easily in a day in the present condition of the river. It is probably one long day's march by land and two by boat in high water season. In the dry season only the smallest peingaws can ascend so far. A short distance above Labán two streams of about the same size of the Nampama chaung join by the right and left bank called, respectively, the Namsán and the Namna. The former is navigable for a day's journey in peingaws up to a village of the same name as the stream. It is evidently at Saduzup or close to it that the Namkong quits its easterly course and turns south, and the Namsán

* The southernmost low gap in the Kumunpum is, I think, at the head of the valley of this stream.

† In the latest survey map, compiled from work executed in the cold season 1888-89, a continuous range of hills is shown to run close along the right bank of the Namkong, but this is incorrect. There are actually two ranges—one is the Pákyunpum running east and west, the other the Kángpum, to the north of the first and running north and south. They are divided by the Máté chaung, which flows past the southern end of, the latter and about parallel to the former, up to its junction with the Namkong.

FROM MÔGAUNG TO MAINGKHWAN—*continued.*

WATER ROUTE—*continued.*

Authorities. Military.	Authorities. Civil.	Number and Names of Stages, Rivers and Streams.	Distances. Intermediate.	Distances. Total.	Remarks.
G.O.C. Mandalay District and O.C. Bhamo.	Commissioner, Northern Division, and Deputy Commissioner, Bhamo.	**3. 'Nlamkatawng or Saduzup (7 or 8 marches from Môgaung)** —*cont.*			probably comes in from the south-west. The Sadu chaung comes in from the north or north-east.* Opposite Labán the hills (extension of Kumunpum) on the left bank rise to about 2,500 feet above the plain, and are only about 4 miles from the river, which higher up in its course must flow even nearer to them than this, from the direction it comes from above Labán and that in which the hills run. The most northern point bears 74° from Labán. Here the range drops suddenly or more probably turns away suddenly towards the east, but one cannot see from Labán, as the front peaks run up so steep. The hills are covered with jungle from foot to summit and do not appear to be inhab[illegible]ed on this side at any rate. From Saduzup there are t[illegible] routes: either quit the Namkong there and ascend the [illegible] valley or else keep on up the Namkong a little further t[illegible] [illegible]ere the Kawnglaw chaung (Bayfield's "Hounglo") join[illegible] (by the left bank) and ascend the valley of that stream. The former route is the one most used, and is the route a[illegible]dy described.
			M. F.	M. F.	
		1. Tinkauk chaung sakhán (one march from Saduzup). Small stream.	14 2	14 2	*See* last three stages of land route described above.
		2. Palanpum (? Malawpum) (one march from Tinkauk sakhán). Nampyet chaung.	14 4	28 6	
		3 Maingkhwan. Nampyu and Edi chaungs.	12 4	41 2	

No. 67.

From MÔGAUNG to MÔHNYIN.

BY LIEUT. W. V. MOU[illegible], CHESHIRE REGIMENT, MARCH 1888.

G.O.C. Mandalay District and O.C. Bhamo.	Commr., Northern Divn., and Deputy Commr., Bhamo.	**1. Nampadaung chaung.** Nanyin, Nampaung, Mawséhôn, and Nampadaung chaungs.	18 0	...	The road leaves Môgaung on the south and runs over a level pad[illegible] plain to Lwéli on the Nanyin chaung, d[illegible]stant 3¾ miles from Môgaung; this par[illegible] is a level cart road. Road crosses the Nanyin chaung at Lwéli. The river is here about 40 yards wide and 18 inches deep; hard sandy bottom. L[illegible]éli is a weekly stockaded village on the right bank of the Nanyin chaung, about 20 houses. As Moknaung, a

* I think Dr. Bayfield must have been mis-informed as to the name of the stream he calls the Tsa-doo-tshop, and that the stream he calls the Namthet was really the Sadu chaung. Shans with us could not identify the Nanthet stream at all.

FROM MÔGAUNG TO MÔHNYIN—*continued.*

Authorities. Military.	Authorities. Civil.	Number and Names of Stages, Rivers and Streams.	Distances. Intermediate.	Distances. Total.	Remarks.
G.O.C. Mandalay District and O.C. Bhamo.	Commissioner, Northern Division, and Deputy Commissioner, Bhamo.	**1. Nampadaung chaung**—*cont.*			village ½ a mile to the east of Lwéli, there is a pôngyi kyaung and a zayát for 40 men. After crossing the river the road runs south-west over a plain level and free from mud, passing some low hills, "Tapu hills," covered with forest on the left; the road is narrow and runs through short grass. At 10½ miles road crosses the Nanpaw or Nanpaung chaung, which rises in the Tapu hills on the left. This stream is about 5 yards broad and 2 feet deep, with a soft muddy bottom. A bridge had to be built of small trees, of which there are plenty on the bank of the river (time 1½ hours). Next 4 miles in a westerly direction over plain, road level and excellent. At 14½ miles road bifurcates, that to the right leading up to the salt mines, ¾ mile; later road crosses Mawséhôn chaung, a big stream rising in the Issé hills on the right and flowing into the Nanyin chaung. Excellent water. Camping ground available on left bank. Next 600 yards high kaing grass, then open plain again. The road now reaches the foot of the western hills and goes over undulating ground, crossing several small streams through short grass and small woods to the Nampadaung chaung, a small stream flowing into the Nanyin chaung. Camping ground on left bank of Nampadaung chaung very cramped. Water from Nampadaung chaung good, any quantity. Supplies, fuel and coarse grass. Excellent level road on this march, the only obstruction being the Nampaung chaung, across which a temporary bridge must be thrown for transport.
		2. Nansankwin chaung. Kyettaik and Nansankwin chaungs.	M. 13 F. 2	M. 31 F. 2	First 400 yards through kaing grass. Road then comes to the hills and goes south, then south-west over several spurs through tree jungle. Several paths going off on the right to Kachin villages. There are a few marshy places, but no difficult ones. At 4½ miles road passes through cultivation (poppy), the Kachin village of Taungni being visible about 500 yards up the hill on the right. There is a small stream here, Kyettaik chaung. The road continues along the foot of the hills through tree jungle, several paths going off to the right. At 5¾ miles road leaves the hills passing close to Shan village of Taungni, which lies to the left of the road and consists of seven or eight houses. There is some paddy cultivation here. After passing village of Taungni there is a bad piece of swamp which extends for 50 yards causing some delay. Next 2 miles alternately through short grass and tree jungle; road level and good. Remainder of the road south-west across level plain crossing several streams to the Nansankwin chaung, 13¼ miles. The Nansankwin chaung is a big stream, hard gravelly bottom, flowing into Nanyin chaung. Camping ground on right bank, in kaing grass, fair. Water from Nansankwin chaung excellent and abundant. Supplies, fuel and coarse grass.
		3. Camp near Hôpin. Nankwin chaung.	16 2	47 4	First ½ mile south-west through kaing grass to the foot of the western hills, just before reaching which there is a swampy place. Next 1½ miles through tree jungle at the foot of the hills, crossing two swampy places which had to be prepared for transport. At 1¾ miles road goes through

FROM MÔGAUNG TO MÔHNYIN—*continued.*

Authorities. Military.	Authorities. Civil.	Number and Names of Stages, Rivers and Streams.	Distances. Inter-mediate.	Distances. Total.	Remarks.
G.O.C. Mandalay District and O.C. Bhamo.	Commissioner, Northern Division, and Deputy Commissioner, Bhamo.	**3. Camp near Hôpin**—*cont.*			¼ mile of very dense kaing grass, following bed of small stream. Next 4 miles road up and down in a south-west direction along the foot of the hills, through forest and tree jungle which is very dense in parts; however, it does not obstruct the road which is in excellent order; it crosses several swampy water-courses which require ramping for transport. There is a good stream at 5 miles, the right bank of which is sufficiently clear for a camp. At 6 miles road finally leaves the foot of the western hills and goes south-west across a plain covered with short grass; road level and excellent. At 6½ miles there is a deep swampy pool. This can be avoided by going some 200 yards to the right. At 8 miles road passes through a belt of forest, down the middle of which runs the Nankwin chaung which is 7 yards wide, 1 foot deep, hard sandy bottom, excellent water. Remainder of the march in a south-west direction over a large plain of old paddy land. Occasional belts of forest and small streams. There are one or two swampy places, but they can mostly be avoided. Road level and excellent. Camping ground on small stream, about 1¼ miles from the Nanyin chaung, in kaing grass fair. Water from stream good, any quantity. Supplies, fuel and coarse grass. This march was mostly level road in good order.
	Commissioner, Northern Division, and Deputy Commissioner, Katha.	**4. Maingnaung** ... Nanyin and Nansalaw chaungs.	M. F. **13 2**	M. F. 60 6	Road runs south to Nanyin chaung, first ¼ mile through high kaing grass, crossing a small deep stream which had to be bridged for transport (35 men), then across plain to Nanyin chaung which is crossed. The river is here 30 yards wide, 18 inches deep, with a hard sandy bottom, dense kaing grass on both banks; ¾ mile after crossing road passes through remains of village of Hôpin. There is a small Shan-Burmese village some distance off the road consisting of eight or nine houses. After passing through Hôpin there is a bad marshy place about 40 yards long. Next mile through forest, good level road, to the foot of the eastern hills. Next 4 miles the road skirts the base of the hills through tree jungle crossing several marshy places, the path is very narrow in parts, cut into the side of the hill and encumbered with jungle; this is the worst part of the whole march. At 7 miles road leaves the hills and crosses a level plain free from mud and covered with short grass for a mile, it then runs through forest to the Nansalaw chaung, 8¾ miles. The Nansalaw chaung flows into the Nanyin, and is about 8 yards wide, 1 foot deep, sandy bottom, excellent water. A camp could be cleared on right bank. After crossing Nansalaw chaung, the road runs south-east through forest and tree jungle crossing one swampy place, passing at 9¼ miles the remains of the village of Nansalaw and coming to the hills ¼ mile later. The road now goes over a hill about 350 feet high through dense bamboo jungle, ascent steep at first, afterwards more gentle, gradual descent the other side, it then runs up and down through bamboo jungle. At 10 miles cross a spur cleared for paddy, 400 yards later road goes over a hill, after crossing which there is a bad piece of swamp 50 yards long. The road then leaves the hills and runs south-west through bamboo and tree jungle to Maingnaung on the right bank of the Nanyin chaung. Road good and level. Maingnaung was formerly a fair-sized village, but was burnt about three years ago.

FROM MÔGAUNG TO MÔHNYIN—*continued.*

Authorities. Military.	Authorities. Civil.	Number and Names of Stages, Rivers and Streams.	Distances. Inter-mediate.	Distances. Total.	Remarks.
G.O.C. Mandalay District and O.C. Bhamo.	Commissioner, Northern Division, and Deputy Commissioner, Katha.	**4. Maingnaung**—*cont.*			Camping ground on right bank of river fair. Water from Nanyin chaung. Supplies, fuel and bamboo leaves.
		5. Môhnyin ... Nanyin chaung.	M. F. 6 2	M. F. 67 0	Road follows right bank of Nanyin chaung for ½ a mile through bamboo jungle. At 1 mile there is a swampy place which requires a small bridge. Remainder of the march south-west through forest and tree jungle to Môhnyin. Camping ground on right bank of Nanyin chaung good. Water from Nanyin chaung good and abundant. Supplies but little obtainable in Môhnyin, which is a small weakly stockaded village on the left bank of the Nanyin chaung. This road was used as a cart road before Maingnaung was destroyed, and is practically the line that will be eventually taken by the railway. *Note.*—Capt. O'Donnell, "D.S.O.," gives a description of the first two stages at least of this same route. *See* Route No. 65.

No. 68.

From MÔGAUNG to MYITKYINA.

BY LIEUT. T. H. E. DAUNCEY, 1ST HUSSARS, MARCH 1892.

Military.	Civil.	Stages, Rivers and Streams.	Inter-mediate.	Total.	Remarks.
G.O.C. Mandalay District and O.C. Bhamo.	Commissioner, Northern Division, and Deputy Commissioner, Bhamo.	**1. Camp on Nanti chaung.** Môgaung chaung, Nwéni, Tengwa, Namkham } small streams. Nanti chaung.	13 0	13 0	Across the Môgaung chaung (120 yards by 3 feet), opposite the village and the path leads along the left bank of the river through high kaing grass and at about ½ mile turns north away from the river following up the Nanti chaung which, however, is not visible from the path, and crosses several small rivulets named in column 3. After about 9½ miles the path leads under the welcome shade of high forest and passes the small village of Nanti (Sawbwa's name, Sanpa) sometimes called Sanpa at 10 miles, then across two other rivulets named Nanti and Namkham and on in a north-north-east direction until crossing the Nanti chaung (25 yards by 2 feet, clear, swift, and pebbly) at 13 miles, where there is a good camping ground.
		2. Camp on Yamlam chaung. Tingwat, Pídum, and Yamlam chaungs.	11 2	24 4	Path leads off in a north-east direction through high forest, and after ¾ mile leads over about ½ mile of easy hills. At 1¼ miles the path is rather obstructed by stumps and fallen trees and leads down a steep incline into the bed of a rivulet which it follows up for about 100 yards and then leads up a steep bank and over another hill and becomes easy again. This latter ½ mile is the only uncomfortable bit of road to traverse between Môgaung and Myitkyina, the remainder being a perfect riding path. At 4½ miles across the Tingwat chaung, a small rivulet forming a stagnant pool at the crossing and on east-north-east * through a beautiful open country of short grass dotted with light forest at about 7 miles across a clear, swift rivulet

* From the Tingwat chaung to Myitkyina there is *unlimited* camping space wherever water is met, as the country is perfectly open.

FROM MÔGAUNG TO MYITKYINA—*continued.*

Authorities. Military.	Authorities. Civil.	Number and Names of Stages, Rivers and Streams.	Distances. Intermediate.	Distances. Total.	Remarks.
G.O.C. Mandalay District and O.C. Bhamo.	Commissioner, Northern Division, and Deputy Commissioner, Bhamo.	**2. Yamlam chaung, 4 yards and 9 inches; clear and swift** —*cont.*			where there is a large halting place and good water and now across the foot of low undulating hills soon turning north-north-east and across the head of the Pídum chaung (10 yards broad with precipitous banks and a very varying depth from 6 inches to 6 feet; shallow at the crossings). Keeping the same general direction the path reaches the Yamlam chaung at 11½ miles. Perfect camping place with a beautiful pool of water (4 yards broad, 9 inches deep, clear and swift) formed by this little chaung at the crossing.
		3. Myitkyina ... Wutalé, Pidum and Namkwi chaungs.	M. F. **14 0**	M. F. 38 2	Path leads from the Yamlam chaung in a north-north-east direction over high flat open country, bounded by high hills on the left about 7 miles to the north-west and by low hills on the right about 5 miles south-west, crossing a small rivulet at ¾ mile and turning east after another ¾ mile crosses the Wutalé chaung (4 yards by 6 inches; clear and swift) at 4 miles, and at 5¾ miles crosses the Pídum chaung again here, 10 yards broad and 1 foot deep. From here the path leads over low undulating hills with a beautiful view of a broad open valley of short grass and high forest lying beneath on the left until reaching the Namkwi chaung (35 yards by 3 feet; sluggish) at 9 miles. After crossing this stream the path soon leads south-south-east, across a perfectly level and open plain crossing two narrow strips of what in wet weather would be very boggy ground (paddy cultivation) about half-way between the Namkwi and the Irrawaddy (at about 12 miles); from here a well-defined path leads south-west towards Akyé, a village on the river bank below Kátkyo. At 14 miles reach Myitkyina. *

* In a previous description of the route by E. C. George, Esq., Burma Commission, it is stated that this road enters Myitkyina through Tháyagôn which is on the river bank about ½ a mile lower down, possibly this is an alternative.

No. 69.

From MÔGAUNG to NYAUNGBINTHA.

BY LIEUT. W. H. MANNING, XII KHELAT-I-GHILZAI REGIMENT, MARCH 1889.

Military	Civil	Stage	Intermediate	Total	Remarks
G.O.C. Mandalay District and O.C. Bhamo.	Commissioner, Northern Division, and Deputy Commissioner, Bhamo.	**1. Nyaungbintha.** Kyetteik and Nanyin chaungs.	**19 6**	19 6	Road, as in route No. 65, as far as Taungni, 17 miles. Road runs in a south-east direction from the village of Taungni and enters long kaing grass at 17¾ miles and passes through kaing grass to river Nanyin. At 18¾ miles crossing one nullah with sandy bottom and about 2 feet of water. The Nanyin is here about 40 yards wide; left bank very steep and a ramp had to be cut down to the water's edge. About 3 feet 6 inches of water in stream. Road then follows the right bank for ¼ mile through kaing grass and thin tree jungle, crossing one bad swampy nullah. It then leaves the river and at 19½ miles enters the paddy plains below Nyaungbintha and runs on into camp at 19¾ miles. Camp in paddy-fields about 300 yards from right bank of Nanyin. Coarse grass obtainable for transport.

FROM MÔGAUNG TO NYAUNGBINTHA—*continued.*

Authorities. Military.	Authorities. Civil.	Number and Names of Stages, Rivers and Streams.	Distances. Intermediate.	Distances. Total.	Remarks.
G.O.C. Mandalay District and O.C. Bhamo.	Commr., Northern Divn., and Deputy Commr., Bhamo.	1. **Nyaungbintha** —*cont.*			Water from Nanyin chaung. There were two villages of Nyaungbintha, one a Kachin village situated at the foot of the hills and the other Shan, in the paddy-fields between the hills and the Nanyin. The Kachin village consisted of about 15 houses and was unstockaded. The Shan village consisted of about 20 houses with a bamboo stockade round it. In this village enormous quantities of paddy were found. This is the best way from Môgaung to Nyaungbintha. It is too long for a single stage under ordinary circumstances, but a halt might be made at 14½ miles on the left bank of the Mawséhôn chaung (*see* Route No. 67, Stage 1).

BRANCH I.

FROM NYAUNGBINTHA CAMP TO LAUNGPU (ITHI TRIBE).

BY LIEUT. W. H. MANNING, XII KHELAT-I-GHILZAI REGIMENT, MARCH 1889.

Authorities. Military.	Authorities. Civil.	Number and Names of Stages, Rivers and Streams.	Intermediate. M.	Intermediate. F.	Total. M.	Total. F.	Remarks.
G.O.C. Mandalay District and O.C. Bhamo.	Commissioner, Northern Division, and Deputy Commissioner, Bhamo.	1. **Laungpu** ...	6	2	6	2	The road out of camp runs across the paddy plain in a south-easterly direction towards the village of Nyaungbintha (Kachin), passes through the village, and commences the ascent of the hills at ¾ mile. Ascent for 1st mile exceedingly steep and road bad. At 1¾ miles descend into a rocky nullah with a small stream in the bed, then ascend from the stream to the lower village of Sumaut at 2 miles. Road passes over paddy clearings the whole way up. This village consists of 10 houses and is not stockaded. Road passes through village and ascends to the upper village of Sumaut at 2¾ miles. This village consists of 10 houses and is not stockaded. A great number of roads leave Sumaut in all directions. The Laungpu road runs east out of the village, turning out just above the road from Nyaungbintha. Road passes through thin jungle and descends for a short distance down to a small stream, then ascends and passes over a level paddy clearing for 200 yards, then exceedingly steep descent through thin jungle down to a nullah with a small stream in its bed. At 3½ miles the road ascends from this nullah and, passing over a spur, descends again for a short distance. At 3¾ miles it ascends through kaing grass by a very stiff ascent to the Môgaung-Laungpu main road at 4¼ miles. The road enters main road from Laungpu to Môgaung at right angles. The road turns to the right up the main road and ascends along the summit of the ridge up to Laungpu at 6¼ miles. Latter part of road very good. Laungpu consists of 15 houses and was unstockaded.

BRANCH II.

FROM NYAUNGBINTHA CAMP TO LWÉTOM.

BY LIEUT. W. H. MANNING, XII KHELAT-I-GHILZAI REGIMENT, MARCH 1889.

Authorities. Military.	Authorities. Civil.	Number and Names of Stages, Rivers and Streams.	Intermediate. M.	Intermediate. F.	Total. M.	Total. F.	Remarks.
G.O.C. Mandalay District and O.C. Bhamo.	Commr., Northern Divn., and Deputy Commr., Bhamo.	1. **Lwétom** ... Lwétom chaung.	6	0	6	0	Road from camp runs east through paddy plains and, striking the Nanyin chaung at ¾ mile, follows the right bank for a short distance and at 1 mile passes over an awkward nullah with

FROM MÔGAUNG TO NYAUNGBINTHA—*continued.*

BRANCH II—*continued.*

Authorities. Military.	Authorities. Civil.	Number and Names of Stages, Rivers and Streams.	Distances. Intermediate.	Distances. Total.	Remarks.
G.O.C. Mandalay District and O.C. Bhamo.	Commissioner, Northern Division, and Deputy Commissioner, Bhamo.	**1. Lwétom**—*cont.*			steep sides and muddy bottom, which would require bridging for transport. The road then leaves the river and for the next ⅜ mile runs south through tree jungle and kaing grass. At 1⅜ miles the road turns east again and ascends slightly passing over a saddle between two small hills through thick jungle. The road is rocky and bad and descends from the saddle to level kaing grass plain at 2¼ miles, passing over a small stream with rocky bed as it enters the plain. It enters thick jungle again ¼ mile further on and winds round the foot of the hills past low spurs, crossing numerous swampy places, which would be almost impassable for transport. The road is also in many places almost entirely overgown with jungle. Just before reaching the village cross the Lwétom chaung, a small stream with stony bottom and excellent water. Lwétom is reached at the 6th mile. It is built on a small eminence at the foot of the hills. The Nanyin chaung is about ½ mile from the village across paddy plains. There were 20 houses in the village, which was unstockaded. The road for the last 3 miles of this march was excessively bad and would require an immense amount of labour to render it passable for transport.

BRANCH III.

FROM NYAUNGBINTHA CAMP TO MANSIN (ITHI TRIBE).

BY LIEUT. W. H. MANNING, XII KHELAT-I-GHILZAI REGIMENT, MARCH 1889.

Military	Civil	Stage	Intermediate M. F.	Total M. F.	Remarks
G.O.C. Mandalay District and O.C. Bhamo.	Commissioner, Northern Division, and Deputy Commissioner, Bhamo.	**1. Mansin** ...	5 4	5 4	Road as far as junction of Nyaungbintha and Môgaung-Laungpu main road as per Branch Route No. I. From the junction of the two roads the road to Mansin turns off to the left along the Môgaung main road and descends slightly for first ⅜ mile through old paddy clearings, now overgrown with kaing grass. It then passes through thin tree jungle to a paddy clearing at 5th mile. The road then turns off to the right and descends the hill side, very steep descent, for 600 yards down to a stream with a rocky bottom, passing through thick jungle. It then ascends out of the stream to the village of Mansin at 5½ miles. Ascent at first steep, then slight. Village, not stockaded, consisted of 11 houses. From Mansin a road runs in a north-easterly direction out of the village and ascends a hill just out of village and then descends along a spur down to the village of Lwé Tôn 3 miles distant in the plains at the foot of the hills.

BRANCH IV.

FROM NYAUNGBINTHA CAMP TO PANGA HILL.

BY LIEUT. W. H. MANNING, XII KHELAT-I-GHILZAI REGIMENT, MARCH 1889.

Military	Civil	Stage	Intermediate	Total	Remarks
G.O.C. Mandalay District and O.C. Bhamo.	Commr., Northern Divn., and Deputy Commr., Bhamo.	**1. Panga Hill** ... Nanyin chaung.	7 0	7 0	From camp to the Môgaung-Môhnyin road 3⅜ miles, thence along that road towards Môgaung for next ¼ of a mile, it then turns off to the left running in a north-westerly direction through short grass for the next ½ mile. At this point

FROM MÔGAUNG TO NYAUNGBINTHA—*continued.*

BRANCH III—*continued.*

Authorities. Military.	Authorities. Civil.	Number and Names of Stages, Rivers and Streams.	Distances. Intermediate.	Distances. Total.	Remarks.
G.O.C. Mandalay District and O.C. Bhamo.	Commissioner, Northern Division, and Deputy Commissioner, Bhamo.	**1. Panga Hill**—*cont.*			(4th mile) the road bifurcates and the right-hand road must be taken, which turns in a northerly direction and ascends a hill by a gentle ascent. At 5 miles cross a deep ravine with very steep rocky sides. A small stream in the bed of the ravine. The road then turns northwest and, the ascent becoming steeper, at 6 miles enters bamboo jungle for a short distance and then kaing grass. For the next ½ mile the ascent becomes very steep into the village of Marao at 6½ miles. This village consisted of 16 houses and was unstockaded. Road passes out of the upper end of the village and, crossing a nullah with a small stream in its bed just out of the village, leads up to the village of Tensé 100 yards off. This village consisted of six houses and was not stockaded. The main road continues the ascent of the hill through jungle and reaches the village of Panga at the 7th mile. The village consisted of eight houses and a portion of it was surrounded by a bamboo stockade.

No. 70.

From MÔGAUNG to PÁNLÁNG.

BY LIEUT. W. H. MANNING, XII KHELAT-I-GHILZAI REGIMENT, APRIL 1889.

Military.	Civil.	Number and Names of Stages, Rivers and Streams.	Intermediate. M. F.	Total. M. F.	Remarks.
G.O.C. Mandalay District and O.C. Bhamo.	Commissioner, Northern Division, and Deputy Commissioner, Bhamo.	**1. Nanti** ... ... Nanti chaung.	11 4	...	Force crossed the Môgaung river about ¼ mile above the police stockade. River shallow till within 10 yards of left bank, where it is about 5 feet in depth. Road runs in a north-easterly direction. First mile level through kaing grass. After 1st mile the road passes through thin tree jungle. At 3rd mile it crosses a small spur from the main range and then runs over several small dried-up nullahs. Road follows the right bank of the Nanti chaung through thin tree jungle up to the 9th mile, where it crosses a stream with muddy bottom, across which a bridge had to be made. At 10½ miles pass the village of Nanti, unstockaded; 17 houses. At 11½ miles cross a small nullah with rocky bottom, excellent water, about 18 inches deep. Camp in kaing grass on left bank in a space which has evidently been cleared by Shans and other trading caravans. Grass for transport animals in abundance. The nullahs passed on this march would require bridging earlier in the year.
		2. Camp in jungle on a small stream.	12 0	23 4	The road still follows the course of the Nanti chaung through kaing grass passing over several small dried-up nullahs, and passes through the village of Demala at 3 miles. It crosses the Zefán chaung at 7½ miles; about 2½ feet of water; rocky bottom; excellent water. The road then passes over old paddy plains and crosses a small spur at the 9th mile, then over small

FROM MÔGAUNG TO PÁNLÁNG—*continued.*

Authorities. Military.	Authorities. Civil.	Number and Names of Stages, Rivers and Streams.	Distances. Intermediate.	Distances. Total.	Remarks.
G.O.C. Mandalay District and O.C. Bhamo.	Commissioner, Northern Division, and Deputy Commissioner, Bhamo.	**2. Camp in jungle on a small stream**—*cont.*			hills covered with thin jungle to camp at 12 miles. Camp on banks of a stream, about 18 inches deep; water excellent; rocky bottom. Camp situated in a paddy clearing and was cramped. Grass for transport animals in abundance.
		3. Camp on Sana chaung. Sesan and Sana chaungs.	M. F. **15 4**	M. F. 39 0	Road enters thick jungle immediately out of camp and passes ever a large number of nullahs. As far as the 4th mile the road was fair: the road then ascends a steep hill and becomes bad, descending to the Sesan chaung at 6 miles; rocky bottom; water excellent; about 3 feet in depth. The road then passes over small hills and is narrow and bad, entering a small stream at 9½ miles and passing up the bed of it for 2½ miles; rocky bottom; water 1 foot to 6 inches in depth. The road leaves the stream at the 12th mile and ascends a small hill and ascends and descends over small ridges as far as Sana chaung at 15½ miles. Road very rough and bad through very thick jungle. Camp on Sana chaung on both sides of the stream is a very small and cramped camp in thick jungle. Small quantities of grass and bamboo leaves for transport animals were obtainable.
		4. Pánláng ... Sana chaung.	**5 4**	44 4	From camp the road passes up the bed of the Sana chaung for 3½ miles; rough rocky bed; it then leaves the stream, ascends a small hill and descends again to a small stream, then ascends again up a steep hill by a broad road through bamboo jungle to the village of Pánláng (Sana Latawng) at 5½ miles; eight houses; unstockaded. From Pánláng a road runs through the big Sana-Latawng valley to Nawkhum and cuts into the Senbo-Kánti road (Route No. 85 at Shángyáng, 4 miles from Paokaw, Stage 12). This is the route commonly used by Káku Kachins travelling to and fro between their country and Môgaung.

No. 71.

From MÔGAUNG to KHUAGÔN viâ PÔNTU.

BY LIEUT. W. H. MANNING, XII KHELAT-I-GHILZAI REGIMENT, MARCH 1889.

Military	Civil	Stages	Intermediate	Total	Remarks
G.O.C. Mandalay District and O.C. Bhamo.	Commissioner, Northern Divn., and Deputy Commissioner, Bhamo.	**1. Khuagôn** ...	**5 0**	5 0	From Môgaung to camp on the river bank below Pôntu, two days' journey up stream in country boats, a few hours only by launch when sufficient water in the river for launches to ply. The road from the landing place, left bank Môgaung river, runs north-east through kaing grass and occasional jungle, crossing one swampy place at 1st mile, and debouches on to a paddy plain at 1½ miles. It crosses the paddy plain and commences the ascent of Pôntu hill at 2 miles. At the foot of the hill there are about 10 small houses. Road up-hill is steep, but broad and excellent, the breadth throughout

FROM MÔGAUNG TO KHUAGÔN *viâ* PÔNTU—*continued.*

Authorities. Military.	Authorities. Civil.	Number and Names of Stages, Rivers and Streams.	Distances. Intermediate.	Distances. Total.	Remarks.
G.O.C. Mandalay District and O.C. Bhamo.	Commissioner, Northern Divn., and Deputy Commissioner, Bhamo.	**1. Khuagôn**—*cont.*			being about 20 feet. At 2¼ miles the road bifurcates; the left-hand road must be taken, which leads up to the village of Pôntu at 3¾ miles. The village consisted of six houses and was unstockaded. No water was found near the village. The road leaves the village by the same path as it enters, passing immediately outside the village a broad road to the right. At 200 yards from the village the Khuagôn road turns off sharp to the right down a narrow path and descends down to a small stream at 1¼ miles; muddy bottom; very little water. There is a little tobacco cultivation on the banks of this stream. The road then ascends slightly through a paddy clearing. At 1¾ miles the ascent becomes steeper and the road passes up a spur of a hill and reaches the village of Khuagôn at 2½ miles. Road up the spur runs through a large paddy clearing. Village consisted of six houses; not stockaded.

ALTERNATIVE ROUTE (DIRECT).

Military	Civil	Stages	Intermediate M. F.	Total M. F.	Remarks
G.O.C. Mandalay District and O.C. Bhamo.	Commissioner, Northern Divn., and Deputy Commissioner, Bhamo.	**1. Khuagôn** ...	3 4	3 4	Road for first 2 miles as per route from Môgaung river to Khuagôn *viâ* Pôntu. About 250 yards north of main road to Pôntu a narrow path leaves the paddy plains and runs north through bamboo jungle and ascends first up the side and then along the summit of a ridge. Some portions of this road were exceedingly steep. Last mile along summit of ridge to village of Khuagôn at 3½ miles. The village consisted of six houses; not stockaded. There must also be paths leading from these villages to the Môgaung-Kámaing road (Route No. 66) and onwards to Thama.

No. 72.

From MÔGAUNG to TAWMAW KYAUKSEINDWIN (JADE MINES) viâ FORT O'DONNELL (SANKA).

BY LIEUT. W. V. MOUL, CHESHIRE REGIMENT, JANUARY 1888 (ROUTE OF MÔGAUANG COLUMN, COLD SEASON 1887-88), AND BY LIEUT. H. C. HOLMAN, DEVONSHIRE REGIMENT, APRIL 1891.

Military	Civil	Stages	Intermediate	Total	Remarks
G.O.C. Mandalay District and O.C. Bhamo.	Commissioner, Northern Division, and Deputy Commissioner, Bhamo.	**1. Nwéni Sakhán.** Nwéni chaung.	11 4	...	For the 1st mile the path is a mere track through dense kaing grass on the edge of the river bank, it then joins the main road to Kámein, the road to the left going down to the ford on the river. Next 2 miles good level road through grass and tree jungle to Naungkyidauk, a halting place, where the road bifurcates, the road to right running up to Kachin hills; 100 yards later cross the Nwéni-chaungalé, small stream, then through forest coming down to right bank of Nwéni chaung at 5 miles. Road now follows right bank of Nwéni chaung through grass and tree jungle. At 6 miles the main path goes over a small hill. This is at present impassable for mules, numerous big trees having fallen across the path, which is narrow, cut out of the side of the hill. There is another small path which crosses the river (15 yards wide, 18 inches deep), and follows left bank for a

FROM MÔGAUNG TO TAWMAW KYAUKSEINDWIN (JADE MINES) *viâ* FORT O'DONNELL (SANKA)—*continued.*

Authorities. Military.	Authorities. Civil.	Number and Names of Stages, Rivers and Streams.	Distances. Intermediate.	Distances. Total.	Remarks.
G.O.C. Mandalay District and O.C. Bhamo.	Commissioner, Northern Division, and Deputy Commissioner, Bhamo.	**1. Nwéni Sakhán** —*cont.*			¼ of a mile through kaing grass, recrossing river and rejoining the proper path at a small Kachin garden, two houses. Next mile north-west through tree jungle over one or two swampy water-courses, across which small bridges have to be built. At 7¼ miles road crosses Nwéni chaung, which is here about 20 yards wide and 18 inches deep, gravelly bottom. Next 2 miles along left bank of river through forest and tree jungle, crossing one or two small streams; road level. At 9¼ miles road ascends a low hill, "Nonontaung," along the top of which it runs for ¾ mile descending a rocky nullah, the top of which is crowned by an old stockade, to a small stream. At 11¼ miles road crosses Nwéni chaung again, coming 400 yards later to Nwéni sakhán, a halting place on the right bank of the river; camping ground good but some clearing required. Water from Nwéni chaung excellent and abundant. Supplies, coarse grass and fuel.
		2. Nanseilong Sakhán. Kautaung, Nampôn (or Nampaung), Wébun and Nanseilöng chaungs.	M. F. **12 0**	M. F. 23 4	Road bifurcates just out of camp, that to right leads up to the territory of the Thama Sawbwa and is an excellent road; there are the remains of some old stockades at 3 miles. The proper road is to the left. For the first 2 miles it is a mere tract and runs north-west through dense grass and tree jungle crossing two small marshy places. At 2¾ miles cross large stream, Kautaung chaung, gravelly bottom, excellent water. Next mile over bad road through dense jungle crossing Kautaung chaung twice. At 4 miles pass through small clearing; here the proper path is almost impossible to follow without a guide, owing to numerous bifurcations; 200 yards later come down to left bank of Nampôn chaung, crossing it 400 yards later. The Nampôn chaung is here about 15 yards wide and 18 inches deep, excellent water. Next mile through grass jungle and forest. At 6 miles the proper road turns off sharp to right, the other road, which leads straight on, is impassable for transport. Next 3 miles through forest, path tortuous and obstructed by jungle. At 9 miles a road goes off to the right to India-rubber forests. Next 2 miles through clearings and high grass to the Nanseilöng chaung, 10 yards wide, 1 foot deep, gravelly bottom. Path then runs through kaing grass and paddy clearing to Nanseilöng Sakhán, one house in fair repair. Camping ground excellent in large paddy-field surrounded by low ranges of hills. Water from Nanseilöng chaung (distant 200 yards) good and abundant. Supplies, fuel and coarse grass. A guide is necessary on this march, the path being very ill-defined and blocked by jungle. The road is fairly level and the few small swampy places present no difficulty.
		3. Kámaing, ... Namping, Namkong (or Môgaung river), and Indaw chaungs.	**9 4**	33 0	First 2 miles alternately through grass jungle and forest in a north-west direction crossing one or two swampy pools. The road then debouches on a large open plain covered with short grass, through which it winds in a westerly direction till the Namping chaung is reached at 5¼ miles. The Namping is about 8 yards wide and 3 feet 6 inches deep,

From MÔGAUNG to TAWMAW KYAUKSEINDWIN (JADE MINES) *viâ* FORT O'DONNELL (SANKA)—*continued.*

Authorities. Military.	Authorities. Civil.	Number and Names of Stages, Rivers and Streams.	Distances. Intermediate.	Distances. Total.	Remarks.
G.O.C. Mandalay District and O.C. Bhamo.	Commissioner, Northern Division, and Deputy Commissioner, Bhamo.	**3. Kámaing**—*cont.*			muddy bottom. Some teak trees were cut across the stream and a temporary bridge built for the transport (time 1½ hours). The road now re-enters forest turning south-west across a marshy stream and reaching the Namkong or Môgaung river at 7½ miles. Next 1½ miles along the left bank of Môgaung river, through dense kaing grass, coming down to junction of Indaw chaung with the Môgaung river at 9 miles. The river here divides into two branches, both of which are usually fordable. The transport animals were unloaded, but crossed with their saddles on. Kámáing is situated on the right bank of the right branch about 400 yards from where the river divides. Camping ground outside stockade good. Water from Môgaung river excellent and abundant. Supplies, fowls, eggs, fish in small quantities, fuel and coarse grass. Easy level march, the only obstacle being the Namping chaung, which must be bridged. For another account of the road thus far, *see* Route No. 66, stages 1 to 4 inclusive.
		4. Sákaw ... ... Indaw river: at this time of year 30 yards broad at Sákaw ford; depth in middle 4 to 5 feet; water discoloured; rate of flow 2 miles an hour; banks steep and covered with kaing grass; rise of river in time of flood 10 feet; bottom firm. A small stream of clear running water flows past east side of village down to the Indaw river.	M. F. **8 0**	M. F. 41 0	Good mule track; nearly level the whole way, passing through tall kaing grass in many places. Half a mile from Sákaw the Indaw river has to be crossed. This entails a great delay upon a baggage train, as the mules have to be unloaded and unsaddled and taken across, whilst the loads and saddles are transported on rafts. Sakaw is composed of two distinct parts, a Kachin village and a Burmese settlement, the former situated on the highest part of a salient running out from the range of hills to the west, and the latter on the lowest part of the same, just above the extensive paddy plain to the north. The Kachin village consists of four fair-sized houses and four or five huts, the highest ground being stockaded with strong tiger-claw work (30 yards by 50 yards). The Burman village consists of 13 houses. There is a semi-circle of densely wooded hills to the west. There is a distillery of Shan beer here worked by two Chinamen. Paddy, rice, cows, and fowls are obtainable. Camping ground on paddy plain.
		5. Kala Sakhán (Foreigner's Camp). * Nansipu chaung: small hill stream of good, clear, running water; bottom stony; depth 4 to 6 inches at this time. It flows into the Indaw river several miles below Sákáw.	**8 0**	49 0	Good mule track on the whole, but a quantity of shallow water has to be passed through, as the track is defined, for a distance of several miles, by the bed of a stream, said by the natives to be practicable all the year round. Two small hills are acrossed between the 2nd and 5th miles from Sákaw, and 5 miles out the Nansipu chaung flows across the track in an easterly direction. With the exception of the first 2 miles of the road, which lead through the paddy plain of Sákaw

* The Jade Mines column, winter 1887-88, halted there, hence the name, which is quite modern.

FROM MÔGAUNG TO TAWMAW KYAUKSEINDWIN (JADE MINES) *viâ* FORT O'DONNELL (SANKA)—*continued.*

Authorities.		Number and Names of Stages, Rivers and Streams.	Distances.		Remarks.
Military.	Civil.		Intermediate.	Total.	
G.O.C. Mandalay District and O.C. Bhamo.	Commissioner, Northern Division, and Deputy Commissioner, Bhamo.	**5. Kala Sakhán (Foreigner's Camp)**—*cont.*			the track passes through dense, luxuriant jungle. Camping ground small and surrounded by dense jungle; would be useless for a large force. Good and sufficient supply of water from a stream close at hand.
			M. F.	M. F.	
		6. Nantein chaung. Nantein chaung flows here from east-north-east to west-south-west; water good; current slow; bottom muddy in places, stony in others; depth 6 inches to 3 feet. Where it crosses road few inches deep. Crossing stones.	**12 4**	61 4	Track for first 2 miles not good, passing along the bed of a stream; remainder very good indeed, though hilly and trying for transport animals. The bad bits are boggy places in the hollows between hills: could easily be made good. Camping ground on east and west banks of river; ample space for small column, but surrounded by dense jungle. Two miles from Kala Sakhán passed Nanuyán village. It is a small Kachin village, the houses composing which are scattered about among the trees on a slight rise of ground east of a large paddy plain. Considerable quantities of good paddy obtainable in this village; good water from clear, running stream. The road passes the Kachin village of Nanyaseik on the Nanya chaung leaving it a mile on the right.
		7. Fort O'Donnell (Sanka). Namsán chaung: stream of clear, running water; current rapid; bottom stony; width 30 to 40 feet at places where road crosses it; depth 18 inches; probable rise in rains 4 to 5 feet. Runs into Uru river ½ mile from Sanka. Uru chaung, ford 3 feet deep; indications of rise during rains 10 to 12 feet. River at Sanka is 40 yards broad, 5 feet deep in centre; current rapid; bottom stony; water clear and good. It is not navigable up to Sanka for a launch. Right bank steep; both banks thickly wooded. Sanka chaung: stream of good, clear, fast, running water; bottom stony. Left bank at this point steep and thickly wooded.	**11 4**	73 0	Road excellent, very few bad bits: jungle dense as usual. Opening out a little as the river Uru is approached. Crosses Namsán chaung several times. Passes village of Nanyôn (Kachin) on east side of extensive paddy plain, 3 miles from last camp. Stream of clear water flows by the village and across the paddy plain in westerly direction. Houses stored very good paddy. Sanka is reached ½ a mile beyond the crossing of the Uru river. Sanka is a prosperous Kachin village of from 12 to 16 substantial houses (very dirty), one of which measures 80 yards in length and two others 75 yards each. It is situated just below the junction of the Uru river and the Sanka chaung on the right bank of the former. Village surrounded by dense jungle. It is rich in supplies: mython, goats, fowls, paddy, and rice being obtainable. Camping ground limited, on west side of village, on the right bank of the Sanka chaung. Military Police Post established here in 1890-91 by Capt. O'Donnell, "D.S.O.," Commanding Môgaung Battalion, whence the name.

From MÔGAUNG to TAWMAW KYAUKSEINDWIN (JADE MINES) *viâ* FORT O'DONNELL (SANKA)—*continued.*

Authorities.		Number and Names of Stages, Rivers and Streams.	Distances.		Remarks.
Military.	Civil.		Inter-mediate.	Total.	
			M. F.	M. F.	
G.O.C. Mandalay District and O.C. Bhamo.	Commissioner, Northern Division, and Deputy Commissioner, Bhamo.	**8. Tawmaw Kyaukseindwin (Upper Jade Mines).**	8 0	*81 0	Good though trying mule track, leading upwards in a westerly direction to a height of 1,600 feet above river at Sanka, through dense jungle, containing a large number of kanyin trees; large mining village of 3,000 inhabitants in the working season; situated on a plateau in a clearing surrounded by dense jungle. There is no ground in the neighbourhood of the village suitable for camping, and water has to be brought from a spring 2 miles distant. Some English stores are procurable in the Chinese shops. *General remarks on road from Sákaw to Sanka.*—The road is a very good mule track on the whole, bearing evidence of being much used by traders. Two-thirds of the road are level, though, as above described, broken by streams, &c., the other third is hilly; the greater part of the climbing and descending has to be done during the second march. With very little difficulty and expense the track could be made excellent for mule transport throughout its length. All the rivers and streams met with are easily fordable during the dry season, and the road is said by the natives to be practicable all the year round, but during rains the camps would be very unhealthy owing to the dense, rank jungle. The alternative route by water to Nanyaseik is then far preferable. The distance from Sákaw to Sanka could be accomplished by a small column in two days, and by Mounted Infantry in one.

No. 73.

From MÔGAUNG to TKAMA *viâ* TANAIKU CHAUNG.

BY LIEUT. W. H. MANNING, XII KHELAT-I-GHILZAI REGIMENT, FEBRUARY 1889.

Military.	Civil.	Stages.	Inter-mediate.	Total.	Remarks.
G.O.C. Mandalay District and O.C. Bhamo.	Commissioner, Northern Division, and Deputy Commissioner, Bhamo.	**1. Nampaung (or Nampôn chaung).** Môgaung river, Nwéni, Nampaung chaungs.	15 0	...	*See* Route No. 72, Stages 1 and 2.
		2. Kumôngyi ... Nampaung chaung.	8 2	23 6	The road leaves camp in a north-easterly direction and follows the bank of the Nampaung chaung for the first ⅛ mile, then crosses the stream and passes through thick jungle on to the paddy plains at 1¼ miles. Winding across the plains it enters bamboo and kaing grass at 1¾ miles, and passes on the next mile through grass, passing a few paddy huts and crossing a stream several times. At 3 miles it ascends a small hill dropping down to a stream again on the opposite side; it then ascends again through scrub jungle passing over several low hills. Ascent nowhere very marked, the road being fair, and entering paddy clearings below Naikungyi at 6¼ miles, which it runs through up to the village at 6¾ miles,

* Lieut. Dauncey makes the distance from Môgaung to Kámaing 1¾ miles shorter than Lieut. Moul, so that according to him the total distance would be 79¼ miles.

FROM MÔGAUNG TO THAMA *viâ* TANAIKU CHAUNG—*continued.*

Authorities. Military.	Authorities. Civil.	Number and Names of Stages, Rivers and Streams.	Distances. Intermediate.	Distances. Total.	Remarks.
G.O.C. Mandalay District and O C. Bhamo.	Commissioner, Northern Division, and Deputy Commissioner, Bhamo.	**2. Kumôngyi**—*cont.*			consisting of 20 houses not stockaded. Naikungalé lies to the north-west, about 800 yards below Naikungyi; it consisted of eight houses and was unstockaded. The road runs north out of Naikungyi and descends into a ravine (1¼ miles in length); at the foot of the descent out of the village a road turns off to the left, which leads up a nullah to the village of Naikungalé. The main road is here broad and good. Passing over two small streams with rocky beds, excellent water, it ascends, slightly at first, through thick jungle and then through kaing grass. The road now begins to narrow and passes round the side of a hill for a short distance, and is narrow and dangerous. It then ascends again more steeply up to a saddle, between two ridges, at 1 mile. From this point it descends down to a ravine through thick jungle, very steep descent. There is a stream with rocky bed at the bottom of the ravine. The road ascends from this ravine up a very steep ascent, and at 1¼ miles turns off sharp to the right and passes up the spur of a hill through scrub jungle to the village of Kumôngyi at 1½ miles. The village is situated on the spur. It consisted of 25 houses and was unstockaded. Water about 400 yards distant down the side of the spur. Coarse grass obtainable for the transport animals. This is an easy march.
		3. Tanaiku chaung or Thama Tanaiku chaung.	M. F. **9 4** **2 0**	M. F. 33 2 35 2	The road leaves the upper end of the the village and turns north and passes round the hill side, fairly level and broad for the first ¾ of a mile; then narrower, passing at 1 mile a nullah with steep sides and a muddy bottom, which requires bridging for transport. Immediately afterwards a path is seen turning off to the left and descending the hill side to the valley. The main road passes round the hill side through kaing grass and bamboo jungle, crossing three bad nullahs with very steep rocky sides, excessively difficult for transport animals. At 2½ miles the village of Kumôngalé is passed, situated on the left, below the road and consisting of five houses and being unstockaded. From Kumôngalé a road runs south-east and passes round the opposite side of the hill to the Kumôngyi road. From Kumôngalé the road ascends a hill side and for ½ mile is cut out of the hill and is narrow and dangerous, but level for the next ½ mile. It commences to descend at 3¾ miles, very steep descent, down to the main road from the Tanaiku chaung, to Maklôn at 5 miles. The village of Maklôn is situated 200 yards to the right up the main road, and consisted of 20 houses unstockaded. Turning to the left down the Tanaiku valley the main road, which runs north-west and is level and broad through thick jungle, passes round a low hill on the left and crosses the Tanaiku chaung at 5½ miles. The river is here about 50 feet broad and varies from 3 feet to 6 inches in depth. The left bank being in one place, just opposite the crossing about 60 feet in height and overhanging the river. From the river the road passes through bamboo jungle to the village of Wawáng, then through the village into bamboo jungle again. This village consisted of nine houses and was unstockaded. The road enters a paddy clearing at 7¼ miles and passes on over undulating clearings, crossing a small stream with rocky bottom, at 7½ miles. The road then passes through

From MÔGAUNG to THAMA *viâ* TANAIKU CHAUNG—*continued.*

Authorities. Military.	Authorities. Civil.	Number and Names of Stages, Rivers and Streams.	Distances. Intermediate.	Distances. Total.	Remarks.
G.O.C. Mandalay District and O.C. Bhamo.	Commr., Northern Divn., and Deputy Commr., Bhamo.	**3. Tanaiku chaung, &c.—** *cont.*			clearings and follows the course of the Tanaiku chaung. At 8 miles a road runs south-east and goes up to the village of Tanaiku, which is situated on the summit of a ridge. From the 8th mile the river is crossed three times into camp at 9¼ miles; camp on the Tanaiku chaung sufficient for a large force. Water from Tanaiku; grass for transport animals in abundance. The road on the earlier part of this march is trying, the latter part is easy. The hill on which Thama is situated is distant about 2 miles to the east, in a direct line from camp.

ALTERNATIVE I.

From MÔGAUNG to NAMPAUNG CHAUNG (Stage 2) *viâ* WANÉYAUNG and KHADÔM.

By Lieut. W. H. MANNING, XII Khelat-i-Ghilzai Regiment, February 1889.

Military	Civil	Stages	Intermediate (M. F.)	Total (M. F.)	Remarks
G.O.C. Mandalay District and O.C. Bhamo.	Commissioner, Northern Division, and Deputy Commissioner, Bhamo.	**1. Nwéni Sakhán.** Môgaung river; Nwéni chaung.	11 4	...	*See* Route No. 72, Stage 1.
		2. Nampaung chaung. Khadôm and Nampaung chaungs.	8 0	19 4	From Nwéni Sakhán road leaves main road to Kámaing and turns off to the right through kaing grass and bamboo jungle for 1st mile. Road up to this point level, broad, and excellent; next mile road narrows and passes for some distance up a ravine. At 2nd mile the road passes over a low saddle between two hills and drops down by a gradual descent to Khadôm chaung at 2½ miles. From stream road ascends up the hill side through short grass by a steep ascent to the village of Wanéyaung. About 400 yards below the village a broad road runs off to the right to the village of Lalein about 5 miles distant. Wanéyaung consisted of about 20 houses and was unstockaded. From Wanéyaung the village of Khadôm was visible across a valley in a northerly direction. Road leaves the village opposite to where it enters and descends for 500 yards, then passes along the summit of a ridge, and ascends gradually into Khadôm at 4½ miles. Village consisted of 30 houses on the summits of two small hills and was unstockaded. Road between the two villages broad and excellent. Road leaves the village in a north-westerly direction and passes along the summit of a ridge with thick jungle on either side and descends gradually to 5th mile, where the road bifurcates. Left-hand road leads to paddy clearing and small village of Khadômgalé; 10 houses; unstockaded. The right-hand road passes round the hill side and is cut out. It descends for a short distance into a gorge (path here very narrow and dangerous): it then ascends out of the gorge by a very steep ascent and passes over the end of the ridge at 5½ miles, and then descends (first portion of descent very steep) and reaches the direct road from Môgaung to Tanaiku chaung at 6½ miles; last ¾ mile very steep descent across paddy plains to camp at 8 miles on Nampaung (Nampôn) chaung, *see* Route No. 72, Stage 2.

FROM MÔGAUNG TO THAMA *viâ* TANAIKU CHAUNG—*continued.*

ALTERNATIVE II.

FROM NAMPAUNG CHAUNG (STAGE 1) TO TANAIKU CHAUNG.

BY LIEUT. W. H. MANNING, KHELAT-I-GHILZAI REGIMENT, FEBRUARY 1889.

Authorities. Military.	Authorities. Civil.	Number and Names of Stages, Rivers and Streams.	Distances. Intermediate.	Distances. Total.	Remarks.
G.O.C. Mandalay District and O.C. Bhamo.	Commissioner, Northern Division, and Deputy Commissioner, Bhamo.		M. F.	M. F.	
		1. Cross roads, 2 miles short of Nanseilông.	6 4	6 4	For details of this stage, *see* Route No. 72, Stage 2.
		2. Pawkaw ...	7 0	13 4	At this point there are four cross-roads, one to Kámaing, one to Môgaung, one leading in the direction of the Môgaung river, and the fourth turning east and leading up to the village of Kanru and on to Tanaiku chaung. The Kanru road descends slightly for the first 300 yards, ascends for the next 800 yards, descends for 200 yards, level for 400 yards, and then is one continual ascent. At 4th mile from Nanseilông (2nd mile from turning of Môgaung-Kámaing main road) the road bifurcates; the left-hand road must be taken, which leads up to village of Kanru at 4½ miles. Kanru, 15 fair-sized houses on summit of low hill; village unstockaded. Water-supply on east of village scarce, about 300 yards below village. Paddy in quantities found in village. To the north of Kanru on the hill side, about ½ mile beyond and considerably lower down, was the village of Pawlam consisting of 11 houses. In this village considerable numbers of cattle were seen. Three roads run north-east out of Kanru—the first, a broad road, leads straight down to the valley and stream; the second cut out of and passing round the hill side is a narrow path; the third ascends to some outlying houses on the hill north of Kanru. The second road must be taken, which winds round the hill side and is narrow and dangerous for transport animals, descending into the valley for first 2 miles out of the village of Kanru; gradual descent. At 6¼ miles the road crosses a small stream with rocky bottom (no hindrance to transport), then level for 200 yards, crossing another small stream with rocky bed; excellent water in both streams. One hundred yards further on the road crosses another stream; rocky bed. It then turns north at 6 miles for 900 yards. Up to this point it passes through bamboo and light tree and thorn jungle. Road now enters plain with high kaing grass and occasional bamboo clumbs as far as 7th mile; it then ascends a hill covered with short grass (very steep ascent for first 600 yards), and turns north-west still ascending; stiff for next 500 yards; it then descends slightly for 300 yards along the hill side; a path cut out of hill side. At 8th mile road turns north and ascends again, passing through a cleared level space for 300 yards. The next 200 yards is a stiff ascent up a broad excellent road, next 300 yards gentle ascent, then 150 yards level to the village of Pawkaw at 9th mile; village on right of road and about 300 yards below it. The road here passes along the crest of a ridge. Pawkaw consisted of 13 houses, one of which was 70 yards in length and two 50 yards in length. The village is situated on the hill side and consists of two parts joined together by a broad road. The village was unstockaded and would be untenable, as it is commanded by hills in rear. Enormous quantities of paddy found in this village. Water-supply

FROM MÔGAUNG TO THAMA *viâ* TANAIKU CHAUNG—*continued.*

ALTERNATIVE II—*continued.*

Authorities. Military.	Authorities. Civil.	Number and Names of Stages, Rivers and Streams.	Distances. Intermediate. M.	Distances. Intermediate. F.	Distances. Total. M.	Distances. Total. F.	Remarks.
G.O.C. Mandalay District and O.C. Bhamo.	Commissioner, Northern Division, and Deputy Commissioner, Bhamo.	**2. Pawkaw**—*cont.*					some distance down the hill side below the village; scanty, but good. Force camped in the village, which was rather a cramped site. No grass for the animals, but small quantities of bamboo leaves procurable. The road on this march was excellent and broad throughout, except first ¼ mile out of Kanru. The stiff ascents and the length of time they were under their loads made this march trying to the transport animals.
		3. Paowéla ...	2	6	16	2	Road from Pawkaw to Paowéla runs along the crest of the ridge above the village of Pawkaw and ascends for 1st mile (an excellent road for first 500 yards), then cut out of hill side and dangerous to transport animals; the road is here very narrow and the hill side almost perpendicular. At 1 mile road descends slightly for 500 yards, then ascends for 600 yards, then up to 2nd mile fairly level, though very narrow and dangerous. From 2nd mile road passes over summit of ridge on to the hill-top and ascends slightly into the village of Paowéla at 2¾ miles. Last ¾ mile road broad and excellent; village unstockaded; 30 houses. Water 200 yards below village; scarce, but excellent on eastern side. Very little grass for transport animals, but bamboo leaves in abundance. Large quantities of paddy found in this village. Sufficient room for the force after burning the village. The road on this march was difficult and in many places was very narrow and dangerous to transport animals.
		4. Camp on Tanaiku chaung. Tanaiku chaung (one of the main sources of the Chindwin river).	6	0	22	2	First 200 yards runs along the same road as enters the village, the path then turns off sharp to the left through bamboo jungle, and ascends for 200 yards, passing over summit of a small hill, which is covered with short coarse grass. Road runs in a north-easterly direction along a ridge and rises and falls, ascents and descents nowhere very marked. At 2 miles there is a very precipitous ravine, the sides of which are excessively steep. The road passes over rocks and is rendered very difficult by the rocky nature of sides of ravine. There is a small stream at the bottom; bed rocky; the road is excessively trying to transport. Two hundred yards further on another similar ravine. The road on the opposite bank of this ravine is not so steep, but is very narrow. It ascends for 1¼ miles, nowhere very steep, and is good, passing through thin tree jungle; the road then passes round the side of a hill from which it has been cut out and becomes dangerous for transport animals for 250 yards; it then descends down to the village of Tangorbum at 4½ miles, passing through bamboo and tree jungle for last 300 yards. Village unstockaded; contains seven houses, none of any size; too small for camp. Village would be untenable as it is commanded by heights in rear. The road runs east out of the village of Tangorbum and descends and is a broad and excellent road. It descends in several places very steep, especially on nearing the plain, and passes over a small stream with a rocky bed as it debouches on the plain at 5⅞ miles, then on over a swampy stream, which

FROM MÔGAUNG TO THAMA *viâ* TANAIKU CHAUNG—*continued.*

ALTERNATIVE II—*continued.*

Authorities.		Number and Names of Stages, Rivers and Streams.	Distances.		Remarks.
Military.	Civil.		Intermediate.	Total.	
G.O.C. Mandalay District and O.C. Bhamo.	Commr., Northern Divn., and Deputy Commr., Bhamo.	**4. Camp on Tanaiku chaung**—*cont.*			required bridging, to camp at 6 miles on banks of Tanaiku chaung. Camp among short grass sufficient for any force. Tanaiku is here about 40 yards broad and varies in depth from 3 feet to 6 inches; excellent water; stony bottom; current very strong; banks low. This camp was 2,400 feet above sea-level. Excellent grass obtainable; water from Tanaiku. Road very trying to transport animals in several places.

No. 74.

From MÔGÔK to THÍBAW viâ KYAUNGYAUK (HONGHENG).

BY CAPT. H. R. B. DUNNE, NORFOLK REGIMENT, DECEMBER 1888.

Military	Civil	Stage	Intermediate M. F.	Total M. F.	Remarks
G.O.C. Mandalay District.	Commissioner, Northern Division, and Deputy Commissioner, Ruby Mines.	**1. Nyaungôn** ...	5 2	5 2	General direction south-east. For the first 300 yards the path runs along the level, after which it travels across some small spurs and is rather steep and rough in two or three places. From 3½ miles the rest of the way is fairly level. At 200 yards path crosses Môgôk stream by covered wooden bridge, passable for animals, 20 yards long, 9 feet wide; stream 3 yards wide, 1 foot deep (2 miles per hour). Water unfit for drinking, being discoloured by small streams used for washing the earth for rubies. Taungywa village on the left bank contains one kyaung, one zayát. Accommodation for 18 men. About 20 houses and a guard of police. At 300 yards a path leads off to Kyâtpin on the right, 7 miles distant. At ¼ mile good site for camp on left to accommodate 500 men. Good water close by. At 1½ miles path divides into two for 100 yards; both tracks rough, but the left is the better. At 2 miles rather a rough bit of up-hill path. At 2½ miles track ascends through defile for 50 yards. At 3 miles a path on right to Puyôn village, said to be 2 miles. At 3½ miles path becomes very rough, descending to stream. At 4½ miles small patch of open ground sufficient to camp 50 men. Water close by. At 5¼ miles halting place close to a large banyan tree and cluster of pagodas, sufficient to camp 250 men. Good water from stream close by. The small village of Nyaungôn, surrounded by a slight stockade, is 200 yards to the south and consists of five huts, one kyaung. No accommodation or supplies. Throughout this march water is plentiful, small streams crossing the track at about every ¾ mile. The country is open for the first 2 miles and for the rest of the march the track leads through jungle.
	Supt., Northern Shan States.	**2. Nyaungdauk (2,500 feet).** Namkyinko.	9 6	15 0	General direction of path south-east for first 3 miles, after that east for 7¼ miles through jungle, the remainder of march being over open ground. The track leads over low spurs and is good throughout, except at 2½ miles where the descent is rather rough and steep. Several small streams of good water cross the path up to 3½ miles, but after that the track

FROM MÔGÔK TO THÍBAW *viâ* KYAUNGYAUK (HONGHENG)—*continued.*

Authorities. Military.	Authorities. Civil.	Number and Names of Stages, Rivers and Streams.	Distances. Intermediate. M.	F.	Distances. Total. M.	F.	Remarks.
G.O.C. Mandalay District.	Superintendent, Northern Shan States.	**2. Nyaungdauk (2,500 feet)**—*cont.*					leads too near the watershed lines to strike any water until a small stream is reached 1 mile from Nyaungdauk. There is a small spring 100 yards beyond Kyunpanza. At 1¼ miles a path to right to village of Nyaungôn. At 2⅛ miles the path becomes rather rough, descending to the Namkyinko at 3⅛ miles, which is crossed by a ford 10 yards wide, 18 inches deep (3 miles per hour). Water good. This stream is spanned 100 yards lower down by a rough wooden foot-bridge. One hundred and fifty yards further path crosses small stream, the ground on the left bank being fairly level and sufficient to encamp 500 men, and in dry weather the paddy-fields on the right would accommodate 800 men. At 5⅛ miles the path passes close to the stockaded Palaung village of Yôngpansa, which consists of about 30 houses. No accommodation. Water from stream. At 7¾ miles the track commences to descend until the village of Nyaungdauk is reached at 9⅝ miles. It consists of two villages close together, situated on the western side of the Nampai valley, which is 1,200 yards across, containing 30 houses, four large kyaungs on hill to north, two zayáts. Accommodation for 40 men. Camping ground on paddy-fields sufficient for 2,000 men in dry weather. Water good from stream. Paddy plentiful.
		3. Loikham (3,400 feet). Nampai, Namkaw.	5	4	20	4	General direction for 1st mile south-west and for remainder of march south-east. The path travels at first along the level across paddy-fields, until at 1,000 yards the Nampai is crossed by a ford 25 yards wide, 18 inches deep (2½ miles per hour). Bottom hard, banks low, covered with long grass; would be impassable in the rains. At 200 yards and again at ⅛ mile beyond this river two small streams cross the track; the ground near them is soft. At ⅞ mile road ascends a terrace about 30 feet above plain running through long grass. At 1¼ miles the path begins to ascend gradually and continues winding up and down low hills through scattered bushes, until Loikham is reached. At 2½ miles path crosses stream by ford 3 yards wide, 9 inches deep. Water good. Path down to stream a little rough for 300 yards. Track then enters jungle. At 3 miles path crosses the Namkaw by a ford 6 yards wide, 1 foot deep (2½ miles per hour). Water good; hard bottom. On right bank site to camp 100 men. At 4 miles a path to the left leads to Mainglôn, 2½ miles distant. (This track is rough for transport animals and crosses the Namkaw and Nampai). At 5⅛ miles camping ground on small spur very cramped. The Palaung village of Loikham, which is open, lies at 300 yards to the north, 100 feet higher up, and contains one kyaung, two zayáts. Accommodation for 20 men, and 12 huts. The lower village is 300 yards to the south-west of it, containing one kyaung (uninhabited). Accommodation for 20, and 10 huts. It is inhabited by Shans, both villages being under the Myoza of Mainglôn. Good water from small stream.
		4. Kángkáng (3,050 feet). Namkaw.	5	6	26	2	General direction south-east. The path leads along the watershed line the whole way, and therefore no water is met with until end of March. It leads through jungle and is good throughout. At 2 miles a path on right leads to village of Páng-

Authorities. Military.	Authorities. Civil.	Number and Names of Stages, Rivers and Streams.	Distances. Intermediate.	Distances. Total.	Remarks.
G.O.C. Mandalay District.	Superintendent, Northern Shan States.	**4. Kángkáng (3,050 feet)**—*cont.*			yukut. At $3\frac{1}{4}$ miles a patch of fairly level ground, sufficient to encamp 300 men; but water would have to be brought up from about 200 to 300 feet below. At $3\frac{3}{4}$ miles path on right leads to village of Tournoyé (?), $\frac{1}{2}$ mile distant to south-west, consisting of six huts; no accommodation. At $5\frac{3}{4}$ miles path crosses Namkaw by ford 3 yards wide, 1 foot deep (3 miles per hour). Camping ground on paddy-fields on right bank, where there is room for 1,000 men in dry weather. The Shan village of Kángkáng is situate 300 yards to the west, 20 feet above stream, on the left bank. It is an open village, consisting of 32 houses, one kyaung, one zayát; accommodation for 30 men; lies 300 yards to south-west. It is under the Myoza of Mainglôn. Water good from stream. Paddy plentiful. The valley is here about 200 yards wide. No bazaar, but villagers go to Mankum for supplies. There is a route from here to Namsán.
		5. Longlaw stream (2,750 feet). Longlaw.	M. F. **6 6**	M. F. 33 0	General direction south-east. Path through jungle and long grass. There are two places where the track is rough for animals. The road first enters a gully south-west of the village and then turns up to the left at a gradient of one-third for 50 yards, rather rough. At $1\frac{3}{4}$ miles taungya clearing on right. Similar patches are met with from time to time along the route. At $3\frac{1}{2}$ miles the path winds round a steep hill, where it is very narrow and slippery (two mules slipped down the khud at this point for 100 feet). At $3\frac{3}{4}$ miles small stream. Water good but limited. Two hundred yards beyond this the path, having reached its highest point, commences to descend. At $4\frac{1}{2}$ miles small stream. Water good. Path rather rough for 60 yards leading down to it. At $4\frac{3}{4}$ miles path on left leads to village of Toigya and about here the track crosses another small stream. Water good. At 5 miles pagoda on left and village of Mankáng on right, through which route leads. It consists of one kyaung; no accommodation; 21 huts. Water brought from stream by means of bamboo aqueduct. Vegetables and paddy plentiful. At $6\frac{3}{4}$ miles camping ground on paddy on left bank of the Longlaw stream, which is 10 feet wide, 9 inches deep ($3\frac{1}{2}$ miles per hour). Water good. The valley at this point is 120 yards broad, sufficient to camp 800 men in dry weather.
		6. Pángkyeng ...	**8 0**	41 0	General direction south-east. The path at first travels north-east, crossing the Longlaw three times in 200 yards. It then ascends the right bank at an approximate gradient of $\frac{1}{3}$ for 100 yards, where the track is rough and slippery for animals, winding through long grass and thin jungle and gradually turning in a south-easterly direction. The route continues to ascend until at $3\frac{1}{4}$ miles it reaches the top of the ridge, whence it continues fairly level for 3 miles. From a point at $3\frac{1}{2}$ miles the villages of Hôkwo, Old Khön, and New Khön are visible at a distance on the left. They are halting places on the way to Namsán from Mainglôn *viâ* Kángkáng. At $3\frac{3}{4}$ miles small stream. Water good. At 4 miles the path is very narrow, the ground sloping down on the left at an angle of 45°, a little awkward for animals. At 4 miles path crosses small stream; water good; and a similar one 100 yards

FROM MÔGÔK TO THÍBAW *viâ* KYAUNGYAUK (HONGHENG)—*continued.*

Authorities. Military.	Authorities. Civil.	Number and Names of Stages, Rivers and Streams.	Distances. Intermediate.	Distances. Total.	Remarks.
G.O.C. Mandalay District.	Superintendent, Northern Shan States.	**6. Pángkyeng**—*cont.*			further on. At 4¼ miles track crosses small stream. At 4½ miles narrow bit of path as at 4 miles. At 4¾ miles fairly level piece of ground, sufficient to encamp 400 men. Water close by. At 5 miles small stream of water. At 7½ miles path crosses ridge (highest point in march), whence it descends to the small Palaung village of Pángkyeng, which is open and consists of one kyaung; no accommodation; eight huts. Water from small stream, but supply limited. A path leads in a north-easterly direction to Pángnôk village. Pángkyeng is under the Myoza of Mainglôn. Paddy plentiful.
		7. Kyuseo (3,800 feet).	M. F. **10 0**	M. F. 51 0	General direction east-south-east. At first the path travels in an easterly direction down the hill through long grass and shrubs, gradually entering thin jungle. Throughout this march the track traverses patches of jungle and open grass-covered ground alternately. At 2½ miles the small village of Hakwat lies along 500 yards to the right, 200 feet below. It contains one kyaung and about 14 houses. Accommodation not known. Just after this the road runs along the watershed line, from which two large valleys on the right and left spring, and then ascends until the highest elevation for the march is attained (5,400 feet) at 4¾ miles. At 6¼ miles the small village of Nongpyet is visible, situated on a ridge about 1,000 yards to the right. At 7 miles path crosses 20 yards of bare limestone rock. At 8½ miles track descends at a gradient of ⅓ for 40 yards, where it is rather rough. Quarter of a mile further another rough bit occurs. With the exception of these two places the road is good throughout. At about 10 miles small stream is crossed, brought down by bamboo aqueduct. Water good and plentiful. Small spring on the right, 6 yards further, and the village of Kyuseo lies close by on left. It is open and straggling and consists of 40 houses, one kyaung, one zayát. Accommodation for 20 men. Water good from small stream. This village is under the Sawbwa of Thíbaw. The camping ground is cramped, being on a small ridge (on the path) about ⅛ mile beyond the village. Paddy plentiful.
		8. Kyaukmé (2,800 feet).	**6 0**	57 0	General direction east-south-east. For the first 2½ miles the path descends through long grass and low jungle, being practically level for the rest of the way. It is good throughout. At 3 miles path crosses small stream which apparently rises in a swamp. Quality of water clear, but doubtful. From 2½ miles the ground affords sites for camps, sufficient for 2,000 or 3,000 men at any point up to Kyaukmé. Kyaukmé consists of two straggling villages situated to the south of a conspicuous white pagoda, ½ mile off. The combined villages contained about 60 houses, one kyaung 60 by 50 yards. No accommodation. Water good from small streams. A considerable amount of letpet is carried through this place by bullock transport (there were 200 there when passing through). Camping ground ¾ mile south-west of pagoda, sufficient for 600 men. Good water from stream. In rainy weather the higher ground north of pagoda would be more suitable. There is a bazaar every five days.

FROM MÔGÔK TO THÌBAW *viâ* KYAUNGYAUK (HONGHENG)—*continued.*

Authorities. Military.	Authorities. Civil.	Number and Names of Stages, Rivers and Streams.	Distances. Intermediate. M.	F.	Distances. Total. M.	F.	Remarks.
G O.C. Mandalay District.	Superintendent, Northern Shan States.	**9. Kyaungyauk. (Hongheng).** Namsim.	**8**	**2**	65	0	General direction east. Path runs along the level throughout this march and is easy for transport animals, except at one place just beyond 5¼ miles, where the right bank of the stream is rather slippery and steep. The country is generally wooded, but at 2¾ miles and again at 3¼ miles there is an open space where 500 men might camp. After passing through Kyaukmé the kyaung is passed on the right at ¾ mile. At 4 miles small spring of good water immediately on right of path. At 4½ miles the village of Heimán is on the left; consists of 26 houses. Paddy plentiful. At 4¾ miles path crosses stream 8 feet wide, 18 inches deep (3 miles per hour) by wooden bridge. At 5¼ miles path crosses stream by ford 4 yards wide, 1 foot deep (2½ miles per hour). Twenty yards above ford there is a rough log laid across the water as a foot-bridge. Fifty yards beyond another branch of the Namsim is crossed by ford of similar dimensions. No foot-bridge. Further on, right bank slippery. At 5¾ miles village of Loikaw on right; seven houses; no accommodation. At 6 miles the track strikes the main route between Mandalay and Thíbaw. At 8 miles small village of Kyaungyauk or Hongheng, consisting of eight huts. No accommodation. Paddy plentiful. Fair camping ground sufficient for 500 men. Water good.
		10. Namsim ...	**5**	**0**	70	0	*See* Route No. 53, Stages 12 and 13.
		11. Thíbaw ...	**8**	**0**	78	0	

No. 75.

From MÔMEIK to LWÉWAIN viâ YÉBÔN and MÔLO (or WÉGYI).

BY CAPT. SEWELL, NORFOLK REGIMENT, JANUARY 1890, AND MAJOR GREENAWAY, 6TH MADRAS INFANTRY, JANUARY 1890.

Military	Civil	Stages	Inter. M.	F.	Total M.	F.	Remarks
G.O.C. Mandalay District.	Commissioner, Northern Division, and Deputy Commissioner, Ruby Mines.	**1. Sinkán**	**6**	**1**	6	1	*See* Route No. 77, Stages 1 to 4.
		2. Heinlôn ...	**12**	**3**	18	4	
		3. Taungyi ...	**6**	**4**	25	0	
		4. Yébôn	**5**	**2**	30	2	
		5. Loikaw ... ... Seven streams.	**10**	**2**	40	4	Road leaves Yébôn (Palaung) in a north-westerly direction, and passes through Yébôn (Kachin) at ¼ mile, and another small Kachin village in the next 200 yards and follows a ridge through tree jungle to 1 mile. Here it crosses a small stream and runs through grass jungle to 1½ miles and descends steeply to 2½ miles. Here is a good camping ground. The road then ascends a hill, runs along a level spur, and descends slightly to a stream at 4 miles. Here is a camping ground in paddy-fields. To 5 miles the road runs over low hills and is indifferent. Here are more paddy-fields, and a stream is crossed. After

From MÔMEIK to LWÉWAIN *viâ* YÉBÔN and MÔLO (or WÉGYI)—*continued.*

Authorities. Military.	Authorities. Civil.	Number and Names of Stages, Rivers and Streams.	Distances. Intermediate.	Distances. Total.	Remarks.
G.O.C. Mandalay District.	Commissioner, Northern Division, and Deputy Commissioner, Ruby Mines.	**5. Loikaw**—*cont.*			this there is a steady ascent to Loiva village, at 7¼ miles, (Kachin) of 30 houses, covering a large area of ground. After leaving the village the roads divide. The right-hand one descends to 2 miles, crossing in this part of the road three small streams. Parts of the road here are steep and bad. It then runs level to 9⅜ miles and ascends to Loikaw, which is reached at 10¼ miles, a Kachin village of 20 houses. Camping ground good. Water from wells.
		6. Wégyi or Môlo Three streams.	M. 8 F. 0	M. 48 F. 4	Road runs north by west broad and good to 2 miles. At 1½ miles the road (left-hand one) that separates at Loiva rejoins. This road is a better one than that above described and is of the same length. There a good jungle. Camping ground ⅛ mile north of Loiva, with water from a stream. Road descends to a small stream at 3 miles, after which there is a sharp ascent to 3⅜ miles, where the road runs along a ridge to 4 miles. At 4¼ miles a road branches off to the north to Lwékyé. From this point the road descends to 4⅜ miles and is then level to 6 miles. Here it descends to a small stream, and immediately after a larger one is crossed; this is crossed again five times in the next mile. At 7 miles enter paddy-fields, which are crossed until Wégyi is reached. A large Burman village on the left bank of the Shwéli river and opposite to Môlo island. Wégyi is partly stockaded, and there is a good pôngyi kyaung. Môlo village (Burmese) lies on an island 200 yards wide and 600 yards long. It is stockaded and has 200 houses. The left branch of the river is fordable, but to pass from Môlo to the right bank boats are required. The Shwéli is navigable for boats carrying 2 tons, as Môlo all the year round is not navigable above this point. There are 10 large boats which can carry 20 men each belonging to the village, but these would seldom be available at one time, as regular trade is carried on with Mandalay. Dug-outs to carry six men are always to be had. *Ferries.* (1) Half-a-mile up-stream from Wégyi to Naungpaung deserted. River 70 yards wide, crossing easy, owing to sand bank in the river. Room on both banks. (2) Opposite Ekkyi 1¾ miles up-stream. This is a better ferry for a large force, as there is more room on either bank. River 100 yards wide, banks easy and shelving. (3) One mile down stream from Wégyi is a ferry similar to (2).
		7. Lwéwain ... Shwéli river.	4 2	52 6	* Crossing by ferry (1) or (2). There are roads running along both banks between these ferries, that on the left bank being the most open. Road runs north for ¾ mile through jungle, other ascends to 2 miles to Kawlain, Kachin village of 10 houses, with one well on east. This ascent is stiff and rises 2,100 feet from the river. From here the road runs on the level in a north-easterly direction to Lwéwain, a Kachin village of 20 houses. Water from two wells.

* This last stage requires explanation. In its present form it is not at all clear.

No. 76.

From MÔMEIK to MÔGÔK (the Kyauktada Road).

By Major HOBDAY, Survey of India, February 1890.

Authorities. Military.	Authorities. Civil.	Number and Names of Stages, Rivers and Streams.	Distances. Intermediate. M. F.	Distances. Total. M. F.	Remarks.
G.O.C. Mandalay District.	Commissioner, Northern Division, and Deputy Commissioner, Ruby Mines.	**1. Kunwat** ... Several mountain streams.	**12 0**	12 0	The road is fair throughout and runs at first south-east along the left bank of the South chaung and then turns south passing Athán at 1½ and Légyi at 3 miles, road level to this point. From here it commences to ascend bending gradually from south to south-south-west to Pángmo, 7 miles; it then winds up-hill a rather steep zigzag to Kyauktada (stone bridge), crossing a short distance from the village along a short stone ridge. Thence it winds up-hill south and then west to Kunwat, a Palaung village. Three mountain streams are crossed up to this point.
		2. Môgôk	**14 0**	26 0	The road continues to rise and fall, running south-west fairly on the level past Kônsa, 1 mile, and after crossing a stream at 2 miles turns south to 3 miles and again west to Pángkyit village, 4½ miles; from here it turns south to the pass, the highest point of which is reached at 6 miles, and thence runs south-west by a steady decline to Môgôk. *Note.*—All the hill villages are Palaung and the road is much used by traders.

No. 77.

From MÔMEIK to NAMKHAM viâ MANTÔN.

By Capt. SEWELL, Norfolk Regiment, Intelligence Officer, Mômeik Column, Tônhôn Force, January 1890.

Authorities. Military.	Authorities. Civil.	Number and Names of Stages, Rivers and Streams.	Distances. Intermediate. M. F.	Distances. Total. M. F.	Remarks.
G.O.C. Mandalay District.	Commissioner, Northern Division, and Deputy Commissioner, Ruby Mines.	**1. Sinkán (Sinkin), (Singém).** Nameit chaung and nullahs (now dry).	**6 1**	6 1	Cross Nameit chaung at 500 yards from the town by ford 2 feet deep. River 30 yards wide. Left bank steep. Then follow general line of river by a bridle track through tree jungle. Direction north-east. At 1 mile out is a road to the golden pagoda standing on a spur ¼ mile off. Road then winds east and passes Yaunglebin (banian tree) at 2¾ miles; 12 houses. Near river bank cross nullah by plank bridge at 3¼ miles. Here road to Matein turns off north. Forward direction east. Winding road through bamboo jungle. Cross bridged nullah at 3½ miles and dry nullah at 3¾, 4½, 5¼, and 6 miles. Pass Khyaur (sweet mango) village at 5¼ miles; 30 houses. Cotton grown in valley of river. Cross a small spur at 5½ miles and at 6 miles turn east; up to a small slope to village Sinkán, 30 houses, Palaung and Shan. Room in two huts for 100 men. River 350 yards south, 30 feet wide, 2 feet deep, running under low hills. Room for camp on low ground cultivated near river.

FROM MÔMEIK TO NAMKHAM *viâ* MANTÔN—*continued.*

Authorities. Military.	Authorities. Civil.	Number and Names of Stages, Rivers and Streams.	Distances. Intermediate. M.	Distances. Intermediate. F.	Distances. Total. M.	Distances. Total. F.	Remarks.
G.O.C. Mandalay District.	Commissioner, Northern Division, and Deputy Commissioner, Ruby Mines.	**2. Heinlôn** ... Sukôngyi stream and two small ones.	**12**	**3**	18	4	Direction throughout north-east. Road fairly level for $5\frac{3}{4}$ miles to Sukôngyi, a halting place only. Runs through bamboo and tree jungle. Fairly easy. One bad nullah (dry at $3\frac{1}{3}$ miles) and the track between 4 and $5\frac{5}{8}$ miles runs over stony ravine with several bad bits. Road begins to ascend at $5\frac{3}{4}$ miles and continues to do so to the end. The steepest slope is 10° and in several places it is 8°. It is however fair in the way of width, and there are few places awkward for mules on this account. It winds up spurs and along cols, and at $11\frac{1}{3}$ miles turns east to Heinlôn. This is the site of old village on spur 300 yards by 20 yards. Water from a spring 200 yards east, 50 yards down-hill. A stream from this runs north and should be improved for watering cattle. New Heinlôn is on a spur 1 mile off, 12 houses, Palaung. To reach it follow the road inwards for $\frac{3}{4}$ mile and turn down-hill to left of road 600 yards. Grass good about Heinlôn. Signal station for Bernardmyo visible. Height 2,350 feet above Mômeik.
		3. Taungyi ... Several small hill streams.	**6**	**4**	25	0	General direction of road is east-north-east. Road a narrow hill track fairly level for the first $1\frac{1}{2}$ miles, but dangerously narrow in places. It runs along ridges for the first 4 miles. In this portion there are four steep bits. Then a very steep winding descent through bamboo jungle, and the next $1\frac{1}{2}$ miles the road winds up and down in a south-east direction crossing numerous hills, running down from the hills on the left of the road. At $5\frac{3}{4}$ miles is a small clearing which would serve as an alternative camp. The next $\frac{1}{4}$ mile is a steep climb to a col, here level for 100 yards and then a gentle descent to Taungyi village. This is a Kachin village of 28 houses standing on a clearing running east. The houses stand on four different levels and are long barrack-looking buildings of bamboo. Water from a stream $\frac{1}{4}$ mile south-east, good and plentiful. Pass Paka, Palaung village at 2 miles, $\frac{1}{2}$ mile south of road.
		4. Yébôn ... ... Two streams.	**5**	**2**	30	2	General direction east-south-east, which is fairly maintained throughout. The road descends a good deal; cross a stream at $\frac{1}{4}$ mile after descending over a bad stony bit; then winds along hill side to $\frac{3}{4}$ mile. At 1 mile follow a gentle sloping ridge, a steep bit, at $1\frac{1}{4}$ miles* and again at $1\frac{3}{4}$ miles. Here is water in a stream down the hill. Road again descends to 2 miles. At $2\frac{1}{8}$ and $2\frac{1}{4}$ are narrow bits bad for laden mules. At $2\frac{1}{3}$ miles water from a spring on left of road. Road here turns north for $\frac{1}{4}$ mile and then resumes the original direction at $2\frac{3}{4}$. Strike a good stream on right of road; this is followed to $4\frac{1}{8}$ miles. Road rising over spur and descending into cultivated (old) ground, cross and recross stream in the valley. Here are four old pagodas and several cultivated huts. At 4 miles cross stream again. Here is a good place for a small camp. Road then turns south-east, rises over a bad bit round corner of the hill side, descends and ascends,

* After which pass through village of Taungyi, Kachin, four houses, Minhlin on map.

FROM MÔMEIK TO NAMKHAM *viâ* MANTÔN—*continued.*

Authorities. Military.	Authorities. Civil.	Number and Names of Stages, Rivers and Streams.	Distances. Intermediate.	Distances. Total.	Remarks.
G.O.C. Mandalay District.	Commissioner, Northern Division, and Deputy Commissioner, Ruby Mines.	**4. Yébôn**—*cont.*			all rather bad road to 5 miles. Here a track runs to pôngyi kyaung and four houses 120 yards off the road to south. Road turns east to Yébôn, a Palaung village of 20 houses, and a large kyaung and zayát. Water from a spring and stream 300 yards down-hill on north of village.
			M. F.	M. F.	
		5. Pwa-án (Pa-shata). One stream and Nameit chaung, 10 yards wide, 1 foot deep, and 1 mile an hour.	5 4	35 6	The track turns east out of centre of village and runs north-east and subsequently north along the hill side descending and level by turns to ¾ mile, descent not over 6°. At ¾ mile is a pool and stream. A road runs in from west at 1 mile. Road then runs north-east and north-north-east. Mostly level and good along ridges and spurs to 2 miles. Pass a big clearing at 1¾ miles. Road then descends, being rather rough and narrow for loaded mules 2¼ miles.* Then good to 2¾ miles. Here direction changes to north to 3 miles with one steep descent for 60 yards. Here is a big banian tree and a village, name not ascertained. Road turns east and winds after east and north-east to 3⅓ miles, mostly level. Then east down a spur with average slope of 4° to 3½ miles. Direction here changes to north-east down a spur to 4 miles, slope 6°. Then east down the same spur to Nameit stream at 4⅝ miles. The last 5 furlongs is steep and rough for mules. Ascent from stream stony and very difficult; mules must go up singly. The road then runs up a spur stiff the whole way to within 300 yards of village. It rises 200 feet in the first 350 yards and most of the rest is 8°. Village (Palaung) of 11 houses and kyaung in a small spur 300 yards long running south. Height 300 feet below Yébôn. Water from stream 300 yards south of village in valley; plentiful. Road to Gummaw turns off 100 yards short of village.
		6. Gummaw ... One large stream 5¼ inches and three small ones between 3 and 4 inches.	6 6	42 4	General direction east. At starting road runs north-north-east and east over steep ascents and descents for the first ⅓ mile, then pretty level to 1⅓ miles. After this a steady rise for ¼ mile to the Kachin village of Kunlôn, 15 houses. Road passes through the village and is level to 2⅓ miles, when it descends gradually and becomes very narrow, running along a steep hill side cleared to 3 miles. A road runs off to the left front at 2⅝ miles. Here cross two small streams. Road on still narrow along the north side of a gorge. At 3⅜ miles the road divides, the left one running north-east is followed, and at 3⅝ miles a stream and level bit of ground is passed. Here is a room for a small camp. Then ascend a steep spur and afterwards follows a col to 3⅞ miles. Here ¼ mile on the left of the road is the Palaung village of Manloi-i. Here the road turns round the head of a valley and runs south-east to 4 miles. Here is a bamboo and banian tree round a nat house. From here the road runs down to a valley and then winds down the hill side at about 10° slope to 5¼ miles. Here cross a stream 20 yards wide below, where two join rocky bottom 1 foot deep. Then ascend a spur at a similar slope to that descended previously to 6 miles. Road very sound. It then follows the head of

* A road runs in near here from a Kachin village called Manthé.

FROM MÔMEIK TO NAMKHAM *viâ* MANTÔN—*continued*.

Authorities: Military.	Authorities: Civil.	Number and Names of Stages, Rivers and Streams.	Distances: Intermediate.	Distances: Total.	Remarks.
G.O.C. Mandalay District.	Commissioner, Northern Division, and Deputy Commissioner, Ruby Mines.	**6. Gummaw**—*cont.*			a valley and winds round the end of a small spur to the scattered village of Gummaw, nine houses. Water from stream to east of village.
		7. Mantôn (Manpun), (Mapun), (Malôn).	M. 7 F. 4	M. 50 F. 0	Height 2,900 feet above Mômeik. Road runs fairly east throughout, bending south-east and north-east at intervals. At 500 yards, after leaving Gummaw, the road divides, left-hand one is followed, a narrow not much used track. It rises to 1 mile, descends and then follows a hill side over a col and then along another hill side. At 1¾ miles Manloi-i and Manchan are visible bearing W.N.W. Follow a short valley and then along a spur and round the head of a valley at 2¼ miles. Descend and cross a muddy stream at 2¾ miles and then rise through long grass to 3¼ miles. Road improves, at 3½ miles runs between low hills. At 3¾ miles a road comes in from south-west, and at 4 miles pass Kachin village of Ma Paung, 200 yards to north. Road then runs through taungya clearing to 4½ miles, turns north and then bending east descends a valley of dense jungle with muddy stream running along it to 5¼ miles. The road then bends north and again east, rising at first and then descends into paddy-fields at about 6¾ miles. Cross these for 100 yards and a small stream, then up a steep slope through thin tree jungle at 7¼ miles, six Kachin houses (burnt), 300 yards south. The road to Manlun turns north for ¼ mile. Village of about 20 Palaung houses and a pôngyi kyaung scattered along an uneven ridge running north and south. Water from a stream to west 300 yards. Height 350 feet above Gummaw.
		8. Kaukkyaing ... Namkhôn and other small streams.	12 0	62 0	Path good. Direction east for first ¾ of a mile, then north for the rest of the way. The Namkhôn stream is crossed frequently between Mantôn and Wámáng (7 miles), banks sometimes steep, but no serious difficulty. Small Kachin village of Laungshé lies up the hill to the left, about ½ a mile off the road at 3 miles. At 7 miles the Palaung village of Wámang is passed, built on a small bare knoll. A Kachin village of the same name (10 houses) stands on the hill above on the left of the road about ¾ mile distant. Beyond this there are a few hill clearings on the left. The road is now very narrow, ascending the valley of the Namkhôn in a north-easterly direction. At 12 miles Kaukkyaing, a halting place, no village. Camping ground on slope of hill, rather confined; water from hill stream to the west, which can be best reached by following the back track for a few hundred yards. Elevation of camp 5,200 feet.
		9. Nampao chaung. Nampao and other smaller streams.	7 0	69 0	Leaving camp road ascends 700 feet in a northerly direction to the summit of a high forest-clad ridge, along which it descends north-east to Sasaw (or Sasôkkatawng) village at 3 miles. Thence it runs generally north, crossing several tributaries of the Nampao chaung. At the

FROM MÔMEIK TO NAMKHAM *viâ* MANTÔN—*continued.*

Authorities.		Number and Names of Stages, Rivers and Streams.	Distances.		Remarks.
Military.	Civil.		Intermediate.	Total.	
G.O.C. Mandalay District.	Commissioner, Northern Division, and Deputy Commissioner, Ruby Mines.	**9. Nampao chaung** —*cont.*			crossings there is a good deal of boggy ground which has to be crossed carefully when travelling with pack animals, especially in the last mile. Camp at 7 miles in paddy-fields on the bank Nampao river, which is here easily fordable. Water plentiful. Elevation 4,300 feet; 2° or 3° of frost experienced here during the night in January.
		10. Lwékáng (Loikáng). Namkit and smaller streams.	M. 11 F. 4	M. 80 F. 4	Cross the Nampao and ascend 300 feet, passing through the Palaung village of Sekao (25 houses). Road then descends, very narrow and steep in places, to a new village (name not ascertained) at 5½ miles. For the next mile the path is mostly paved throughout with stones. At 6¼ miles Hômôn or Manna (15 houses) the principal village of the Maingkwáng circle, lying about ½ a mile to the left of the road. From here there is a good road to Kyusa, the principal village of the Maumauk circle of Mômeik state, *viâ* Môkadu and Mankán. Road runs on across some paddy cultivation crossing a couple of small streams, with slight ascents and descents. At 7½ miles ford the Namkit, follow the opposite bank for a mile, then ascend north-east through some hill clearings to Lwékáng (11½ miles). Palaung village of 30 houses. Camping ground on a cleared knoll north-east of the village. Water from hill streams. Elevation 4,000 feet.
		11. Maingkát (Möngkák). Namkák.	13 0	93 4	At first, short steep descent, then across a few boggy hill streams round the face of a hill and then descending gradually in a northerly direction along the ridge of a spur to Loiving. Palaung village at 3 miles. Road still descending along same spur to 6 miles, where a stream is crossed. Crossing some paddy cultivation, road now ascends north-east up to 7 miles. Here a branch road to the right leads to Mankao ½ a mile distant, whence there is a good road to Möngwi; two stages; village of Lawliao half way. At 8½ miles reach the top of the ascent, the village of Loichom (14 houses) lying ½ a mile to the left on the summit of the hill. Thence for next 4½ miles road good through steep in parts. Direction at first north-east, then north descending along a long spur to 12 miles where the Namkák is reached, and the road following its course for the next mile crosses and recrosses it half-a-dozen times. At 13 miles Maingkát, 20 houses. Shan, Palaung and a few Kachins; chief village of the Húmai circle of Mômeik state. Camping ground extensive in paddy-fields, water plentiful. Elevation 850 feet. Hsaileng, the chief village of one of the Mômeik circles (of the same name), lies 5 miles to the east.
		12. Sheolán ...	12 0	105 4	*See* Route No. 78.
		13. Möngwi ...	...	...	
		14. Manpu ...	...	...	
		15. Namkham ...	...	...	

FROM MÔMEIK TO NAMKHAM *viâ* MANTÔN—*continued.*

ALTERNATIVE I.

FROM YÉBÔN (STAGE 4) TO PWA-ÁN (STAGE 5) *viâ* MANPUN.

BY LIEUT. SOLBÉ, FEBRUARY 1890.

Authorities. Military.	Authorities. Civil.	Number and Names of Stages, Rivers and Streams.	Distances. Intermediate. M.	F.	Distances. Total. M.	F.	Remarks.
G.O.C. Mandalay District.	Commissioner, Northern Division, and Deputy Commissioner, Ruby Mines.	**1. Manpun** ... Nameit chaung and two streams.	**10**	**0**	10	0	The general direction of the road from the point where it quits the Yébôn-Pwa-án road to the point where it meets the Pwa-án-Manpun road is south-south-east. The Pwa-án road is followed for 700 yards. Here the track turns off to south and descends winding south and east to 1 mile through tree jungle. Then kaing grass to 1¼ miles. For next ¼ mile it ascends slightly and then descends steeply to 2¾ miles, the road winding considerably. Here cross a small stream and then descend to the Nameit chaung at 3 miles. The last 300 yards through paddy-fields. Chaung 30 feet wide and 2½ feet deep, bottom shingly. The road to this point is good and fit for pack animals though steep in places. After crossing the chaung the old road is overgrown and bad from disuse. It ascends at first steeply over a ridge to 3¾ miles and then descends to 4 miles. For the next 4 miles it winds east and south continuing to ascend over rough undulations till it meets the Pwa-án-Manpun road at 8 miles, and at a point 2 miles from Manpun. From the chaung at 3 miles onwards the road is unfit for pack animals.
		2. Pwa-án ... Nameit chaung.	**6**	**0**	16	0	General direction north-north-west. Road descends rather steeply for the first ¼ mile, but is fairly easy, through thin jungle. A small stream is crossed and the road is level to ¾ mile and then runs down-hill in a northerly direction and crosses the Dasit stream at 1 mile. A gradual ascent to 1½ miles and then a steady descent to 4¼ miles. This part of the road runs along a spur through thin jungle and grass. Here cross the Dasit stream again and ascend a slight rise and then descend and cross the Nameit chaung at 4½ miles, 30 yards wide and 1½ feet deep. The road then runs up a steep ascent to 5½ miles, rough and rather difficult. Descend to small stream, the water-supply of Pwa-án, and ascend to the village.

BRANCH I.

FROM MANTÔN (STAGE 7) TO KATHÔN (STAGE 5 OF ROUTE No. 78).

BY MAJOR KELSALL, 2ND DEVONSHIRE REGIMENT, JANUARY 1891.

Authorities. Military.	Authorities. Civil.	Number and Names of Stages, Rivers and Streams.	Distances. Intermediate. M.	F.	Distances. Total. M.	F.	Remarks.
G.O.C. Mandalay District.	Commissioner, Northern Division, and Deputy Commissioner, Ruby Mines.	**1. Sinkángyi** ... Three streams about 15 feet wide; fordable. River fordable; gravelly bottom.	**11**	**4**	11	4	From Mantôn the road runs in a northern direction; descends for about ¾ of a mile; crosses a small stream and passes for some distance through swampy ground (small village). At about 2 miles cross another stream 15 yards wide and 1 foot deep. A road here branches off to the eastward to Seku. The road then ascends for about 3 miles through tree jungle, village of Pungka is passed about 9th mile, some distance to the east of the road. Rather a steep descent to Sinkángyi. Camping ground; good stream of water; no village; road fairly good all through.

FROM MÔMEIK TO NAMKHAM *viâ* MANTÔN—*continued.*

BRANCH I—*continued.*

Authorities. Military.	Authorities. Civil.	Number and Names of Stages, Rivers and Streams.	Distances. Intermediate.	Distances. Total.	Remarks.
			M. F.	M. F.	
G.O.C. Mandalay District.	Commissioner, Northern Division, and Deputy Commissioner, Ruby Mines.	**2. Manmauk** ... Two streams rocky bottom; fordable. Rocky bottom; fordable except during the rain.	**6 0**	17 4	From Sinkángyi the road runs north and ascends for about 1½ miles through tree jungle; road then descends to a stream 2½ miles and passes through a village about a mile further. At 5th mile a stream 30 yards wide and 2 feet deep has to be forded; from here steep ascent of 1 mile to Manmauk, Palaung village situated on a spur about 4,000 feet above the sea. Good water from a spring. Road from here to Kyusa, 9 miles distant on bank of Shwéli fair road, but very steep. Another road branches off to the east.
		3. Kathôn ... Two streams rocky bottom; fordable. Rocky bottom; fordable except during the rain.	**5 4**	23 0	From Manmauk the road runs north through grass jungle and cultivated ground to village of Loimun (Palaung) 2 miles; good spring of water near village; road nearly level. From here very steep descent for 1½ miles through grass jungle to a small stream. Road then ascends for about 1 mile; remainder of the road fairly level, last 2½ miles through tree jungle. No village at Kathôn; camping ground on a hill about 4,000 feet above the sea; water about 400 yards distant. Two small Palaung villages about 1 mile south-east and south-west from Kathôn. (*See* Route No. 78, Stage 5.)

BRANCH II.

FROM MAINGKÂT (STAGE 11) TO NGWANSAI (*see* ROUTE No. 15).

BY CAPT. SEWELL, NORFOLK REGIMENT, INTELLIGENCE OFFICER, MÔMEIK COLUMN,

TÔNHÔN FORCE, JANUARY 1890.

Military	Civil	Stages	Intermediate	Total	Remarks
G.O.C. Mandalay District.	Commissioner, Northern Division, and Deputy Commissioner, Ruby Mines.	**1. Ngwansai** ... Shwéli and other smaller hill streams.	**9 0**	9 0	Leaving the village, path runs north-west skirting some paddy-fields to the Namkák which is crossed at 1½ miles, easily fordable. Thence ascending spur pass through village of Myenmun or Vingmun (10 houses) at 3 miles, and at 4 miles the Palaung village of Hakôk or Kôhôk (10 houses). At 5 miles Vingshé (12 houses) lies ¼ mile to the right of the road. At 6 miles Palaung village of Tantao (12 houses). From here the path ascends for a short distance, then descends for 2 miles to a small stream, tributary of the Shwéli river, whence it ascends south-west to Ngwansai. At 9 miles, Palaung village of 15 houses situated on a low ridge above the Shwéli. Water from small streams a short distance down the side of the hill, but not very plentiful. Elevation 1,600 feet. For route from here to Bhamo *see* No. 15.

No. 78.

From MÔMEIK to NAMKHAM (up Shwéli Valley).

BY MAJOR HOBDAY, SURVEY OF INDIA, FEBRUARY 1890, AND MAJOR YULE, DEVONSHIRE REGIMENT, FEBRUARY 1891.

Authorities. Military.	Authorities. Civil.	Number and Names of Stages, Rivers and Streams.	Distances. Intermediate. M.	Distances. Intermediate. F.	Distances. Total. M.	Distances. Total. F.	Remarks.
G.O.C. Mandalay District.	Commissioner, Northern Division, and Deputy Commissioner, Ruby Mines.	**1. Paungadaw camp.** Nameit chaung and small streams.	13	4	13	4	Immediately on leaving Mômeik cross the Nameit stream, 50 yards wide, 2 feet deep. Thence for 2 miles through open grass jungle, road level and good. For the rest of the stages through bamboo jungle, road as before. At $5\frac{1}{3}$ and $11\frac{1}{3}$ miles two hill ridges are crossed 700 feet and 600 feet high respectively, ascents and descents in both cases easy. Camp in forest clearing. Water from hill streams.
		2. Nayôk ... Hill streams and Shwéli river.	12	0	25	4	Road good and level throughout running through bamboo jungle. Water plentiful throughout from hill streams. Nayôk is a Shan-Burmese village of 12 houses, on the left bank of the Shwéli river. No boats available here.
		3. Wégyi or Môlo. Shwéli river.	6	4	32	0	Road level and good in dry weather, first through bamboo jungle, then through paddy cultivation. Wégyi is a large Burman village on the left bank of the Shwéli, and has a good kyaung. Môlo is on an island opposite Wégyi (*see* Route No. 75).
		4. Kyusa ... ... Shwéli and small streams.	14	0	46	0	Road level and good along left bank of Shwéli, except at one or two places, where it is very narrow on edge of river, and mules are apt to fall over through teak and bamboo jungle. At 7 miles Môlaw, Kachin village; eight houses. Good camping ground just beyond village by stream on some paddy-fields. Stream 12 yards wide, $1\frac{1}{2}$ feet deep. At 13 miles cross small stream, then some paddy-fields to Kynsa (burnt) village on bank of Shwéli river. Good camping ground and water from small stream.
		5. Kathôn ... ... Shwéli and small streams.	8	0	54	0	Road along left bank of river. At 1 mile turn eastward and ascend a long spur, steep in places through bamboo and grass jungle. At 5 miles pass Loikôn (burnt). At 7 miles road divides, right road going to a Palaung village, left to Kathôn camping ground on clearing on crest of hill to left of road. Small stockade here in 1891, 2,000 feet above Kyusa. Water-supply from spring 500 yards on Kyusa road. Village of Kathôn (burnt). From here there is a road to Mantôn, *see* Branch I of Route No. 77.
		6. Hptib (Hpatip) Shwéli and small streams.	8	4	62	4	Road as before through tree jungle up to Loilôn, thence bamboo jungle except last mile which is through grass, very steep descent for 4 miles, then slight ascents and descents through village of Loilôn (burnt) at about 5 miles. At 7 miles cross stream 20 yards wide, $2\frac{1}{4}$ feet deep. At $8\frac{1}{3}$ miles Hptib, old kyaung (no village) on banks on Shwéli. Accommodation for 50 men. River

FROM MÔMEIK TO NAMKHAM (UP SHWÉLI VALLEY)—*continued.*

Authorities. Military.	Authorities. Civil.	Number and Names of Stages, Rivers and Streams.	Distances. Intermediate. M.	Distances. Intermediate. F.	Distances. Total. M.	Distances. Total. F.	Remarks.
G.O.C. Mandalay District.	Commissioner, Northern Division, and Deputy Commissioner, Ruby Mines.	**6. Hptib (Hpatip)** —*cont.*					here 100 to 120 yards wide; no boats; but river can be crossed by means of bamboo rafts. A small Palaung village built recently 2 miles north-east and ½ a mile from the river. (There is no direct road along river from Kyusa to Hptib owing to rocks and precipices.)
		7. Ngwansai ... Shwéli and small streams.	9	0	71	4	Road leaves river bank again through jungle. At 1¼ miles cross stream 20 yards wide, 2½ feet deep, and at 2 miles Chitsaung, Palaung village, 12 houses; accommodation in and under huts. Water from stream 500 yards. Road improves; several ascents and descents, but gradually rising, passing through Palaung village at 4 miles. At about 6 miles Loilem, Palaung village, about 15 houses; accommodation in kyaung, zayát, and under houses. Water from wells, scarce. Road ascends to Ngawdé; 12 houses (8 miles). Road to river and ferry by bamboo rafts for Lwépân, turns off to left at entrance of village. At 9 miles Ngwansai, 12 houses; road to river and ferry by bamboo rafts for Tônhôn turns off to left beyond village. Water from stream ½ mile from village on road; steep descent.
		8. Maingkát (Möngkák). Small streams.	*10	0	81	4	Road very good and well made in parts, ascents and descents, but gradually descending, passing through several Palaung villages. At 9 miles cross small stream and skirt paddy-fields to Maingkát 10 miles, chief village in Humai; 30 houses; market every week; accommodation in kyaung and zayáts (two) for 200 men. Good stream of water close by. Supplies obtainable at most of these villages.
		9. Sheolán (Sailong).	12	0	93	4	Direction easterly. At 2 miles commence ascents, very steep in places, short descent. At 6 miles cross stream 15 yards wide, 1½ feet deep. Pass through small village and a number of paddy-fields, then steep ascent nearly all the way to Sheolán 4,500 feet. Large village, 30 houses. Kyaung and zayát for 100 men; water plentiful from springs below village. Height of hill behind village 5,300 feet.
	Superintendent, Northern Shan States.	**10. Möngwi** ...	...		...		The next stages are said to be Möngwi, Manpu and Namkham. There is also said to be an alternative route from Maingkát, the stages of which are— 9. Tunsôn. 10. Pángyôk. 11. Patma. 12. Namkham.
		11. Manpu ...	...		...		
		12. Namkham ...	...		...		

* Major Hobday makes the distance from Ngwansai to Maingkát 9 miles, Major Yule, 11, so I have split the difference and called it 10.—A. F.

No. 79.

From MYITKYINA to SADÔN.

By Lieut. PEEBLES, 1st Norfolk Regiment, December 1891.

Authorities.		Number and Names of Stages, Rivers and Streams.	Distances.		Remarks.
Military.	Civil.		Intermediate.	Total.	
			M. F.	M. F.	
G.O.C. Mandalay District and O.C. Bhamo.	Commissioner, Northern Division, and Deputy Commissioner, Bhamo.	**1. Waingmaw** ... Irrawaddy.	**3 0**	3 0	Cross the Irrawaddy to Naungtâlaw opposite Myitkyina, passing over shingle on the bank of the river for 2 miles, till the village of Ywadaw, on the Nâtmyin chaung, is reached, and then through cultivation to Waingmaw, a Kachin village of 30 houses, surrounded by a double stockade. The Irrawaddy at the point of crossing is 150 yards wide and 18 feet deep in the middle of the stream, current 2¼ miles per hour. The Nátmyin chaung is 20 yards wide, 2 feet 6 inches deep, with steep bank, and rapid current.
		2. Loisaw ... Natmyin chaung.	**12 6**	15 6	From Waingmaw the road leads north-east till the village of Loisaw (Shan Talôk) is reached; the road is level throughout and marching is good. For the first 5 miles the road passes through an open plain covered with high kaing grass, then for 6 miles through jungle, after which a large open plain is reached, which is under paddy cultivation, the village of Loisaw being situated at the further end of this plain. The camping ground is south-east of the village, which is situated on the left bank of the Nátmyin chaung. From here there is a road to Lekaunoi Ferry *viâ* Kwitu, *see* Route No. 46, Branch I.
		3. Hpong ... ... Nátmyin, Namlao, and Namtong chaungs.	**11 6**	27 4	Leaving Loisaw the road leads east following the Natmyin chaung for 1½ miles, at which point the river is crossed. Half-a-mile further the road runs beside the Namlao chaung, crossing it at 3½ miles from Loisaw. Up to this point the road is level and in good order, but from the crossing of the Namlao chaung, the road leads up a steep hill to an elevation of 1,500 feet. The remainder of the road to Hpong leads alternately up and down steep inclines of from 2 to 300 feet in height. The road which is a forest track is in good order, but not being much used is overgrown with vegetation. Hpong is a Marán Kachin village of 30 houses. The Nátmyin chaung drains this part of the country, and at the point of crossing is 30 yards wide and 3 feet deep with pebbly bottom and good banks, current 2 miles per hour. The Namlao is a tributary of the Natmyin and drains the country north of Loisaw, running into the main stream a few miles east of Loisaw, and at the point where the road crosses is 20 yards wide and 2 feet deep. The Namtong is a small stream which runs into the Namlao and is crossed by the road about 200 yards beyond where it crosses the Namlao.
		4. Kritu ... ... Namli Ka.	**9 0**	36 4	The village of Singtum is passed 2 miles from Hpong. The road to Kritu runs due east from Hpong; the 1st mile is up-hill and steep, the road then for 2½ miles leads along the side of the hill crossing several small nullahs, the rest of the road to the river is down-hill and very steep in parts. The Namli is crossed at (?) miles by a ford, * the river at this point

* It was bridged in May 1892, but the bridge was washed away again a few months later.—A. F.

FROM MYITKYINA TO SADÔN—*continued.*

Authorities. Military.	Authorities. Civil.	Number and Names of Stages, Rivers and Streams.	Distances. Intermediate.	Distances. Total.	Remarks.
G.O.C. Mandalay District and O.C. Bhamo.	Commissioner, Northern Division, and Deputy Commissioner, Bhamo.	**4. Kritu**—*cont.*			being about 60 yards wide and 3 feet deep, current rapid with stony bottom, making the crossing a tedious business, especially for pack animals. Here there is a military police post and telegraph office, and a halt can be made here instead of at Hpong. Kritu is situated on the summit of a hill, the road to which is 2½ miles long and very steep in parts. The villages of Seku, Singtum and Singrum were passed at 1, 2 and 3 miles respectively from Hpong, of which place the first and last are off-shoots. Kritu is a Maru-Kachin village of 30 houses.
		5. Nawláng ... Tingri Ka.	M. F. 9 6	M. F. 46 2	The road to Nawlang leads due north along a spur gradually rising from 2,500 feet at Kritu to a height of 4,500 feet, it then gradually drops down to the Tingri Ka, which it crosses near its source and then leads due east over the summit of another spur down to Nawláng, a small village of 30 houses. The village of Pungán was passed 2 miles from Kritu; it consists of 100 houses divided into four quarters. At 7½ miles from Kritu the road branches off to the right to Sadôn *viâ* Sana. *See* Alternative I. The Tingri is a small stream running into the Namli east of Kritu.
		6. Sadôn ... ... Sadôn Ka.	3 4	49 6	Sadôn lies upon a spur to the south of Nawláng; the road for the first 1½ miles runs south-east and down-hill, crossing some paddy-fields at the bottom of the valley across the Sadôn Ka, and then to the south-west up a steep incline to the village of Sadôn which consists of 100 Kachin houses. The road for the first 2 miles is good, but the latter part is very steep and rocky in parts. The Sadôn Ka is a small stream which rises to the north-east of Sadôn, running into the Namli, south of Kritu, it is about 25 yards wide and 2 feet 6 inches deep, with good banks, current moderate, and stony bottom, bridged. *N.B.*—The distance between stages 1 and 6 is now done in three marches, the stages being Loisaw, Namli River Police Post, and Sadôn. Helio communication can be maintained between Myitkyina and Sadôn in favourable weather.

ALTERNATIVE I.

FROM KRITU (STAGE 4) TO SADÔN (STAGE 6).

BY LIEUT. PEEBLES, 1ST NORFOLK REGIMENT, DECEMBER 1891.

Military	Civil	Stage	Intermediate	Total	Remarks
G.O.C. Mandalay District and O.C. Bhamo.	Commissioner, Northern Division, and Deputy Commissioner, Bhamo.	**1. Sadôn** ... ... Sadôn Ka.	...	...	The first part of the route is as to Nawlang for 7½ miles, at which point the road branches off to the south-east, leading through Sana, the site of which alone remains, which is situated on the summit of a small hill and then down-hill till the Sadôn Ka is reached, after which it runs south-west up a moderate incline to Sadôn. The Sadôn Ka is a small stream which rises to the north-east of Sadôn, running into the Namli south of Kritu. At the point of fording, the stream is 30 yards wide and 2 feet 6 inches deep with pebbly bottom. (The distance by this route is not mentioned, but it is presumably longer than that first described, though probably only slightly so.)

No. 80.

From SADÔN to KAOLÁNG-PUM.

By Lieut. PEEBLES, 1st Norfolk Regiment, Attaché, Intelligence Branch, January 1892.

Authorities. Military.	Authorities. Civil.	Number and Names of Stages, Rivers and Streams.	Distances. Intermediate. M.	F.	Distances. Total. M.	F.	Remarks.
G.O.C. Mandalay District and O.C. Bhamo.	Commissioner, Northern Division, and Deputy Commissioner, Bhamo.	**1. Rukri** ... ... Sadôn Ka.	8	4	8	4	Rukri lies to the east-north-east of Sadôn. The road for the first 2½ miles is down-hill and very good, being about 10 feet wide and cut out of the side of the hill. At 1 mile from Sadôn the road bifurcates to the left, leading north to 'Nsentaru and that to the right to Nawláng. At 2½ miles the Sadôn Ka is reached, the road running for ¾ mile through paddy-fields, the village of Sadôn-pa being passed on the left. The road then leads up-hill at a steep gradient and at 1½ miles from the river the village of Nawláng is reached. This village is inhabited by Marán Kachins and consists of 40 houses. The summit of the hill (Lepai-pum) is reached at 6¼ miles from Sadôn. The road then leads down to Rukri at a steep incline, passing several small mountain streams. The road is good throughout and passes through jungle, except near the villages of Sadôn Ka and Nawláng, where the jungle is cleared for paddy cultivation. The Sadôn Ka is a small stream running into the Namli south of Sadôn, and at the ford is 12 yards wide and 1½ feet deep; current moderate. Rukri is a small village of eight houses, the camping ground being in a taungya beside a small stream.
		2. Nawchôn ... Tumpaing Ka.	6	0	14	4	The road continues to lead east-north-east and down-hill. At 2 miles from Rukri the village of Lepai (Lashi) is reached; this village consists of 40 houses. At 4½ miles the Tumpaing Ka is reached; crossing the river the road leads up a steep hill for 1 mile, till the village of Nawchôn (Szi), 80 houses, is reached. The camp lies ½ mile beyond the village in a taungya. Water-supply good. The Tumpaing Ka is a large stream rising between Chingai and Sabu Pum, and at the point of crossing is 20 yards wide and 3 feet deep, bottom being big boulders; current rapid. The crossing is difficult owing to rapidity of stream and badness of bottom.
		3. Kumbaiti Sakhán. Rutong Ka.	9	0	23	4	The road leads due east through taungyas till the Rutong Ka is reached at 1¾ miles. The road then leads through the village of Rutong (Lashi) 30 houses, along the side of a hill, crossing the Rutong Ka at 6½ miles and again at 7 miles from Nawchôn. The village of Lônkán (Lashi) is passed at 6 miles from Nawchôn, the camping ground being 3 miles further on on the hill side near a good spring. The road from Rutong runs up-hill till the camp is reached; it is in good condition and the slope gradual. The Rutong Ka rises between Warong-pum and Kaoláng-pum, and at the first ford is 20 yards wide and 1 foot deep; current very rapid. At the second and third crossings the stream is narrow and easily forded. The approaches, however, are bad in each case, causing delay to the transport. This stream falls 2,350 feet in 10 miles.

FROM SADÔN TO KAOLÁNG-PUM—*continued.*

Authorities. Military.	Authorities. Civil.	Number and Names of Stages, Rivers and Streams.	Distances. Inter-mediate. M. F.	Distances. Total. M. F.	Remarks.
G.O.C. Mandalay District and O.C. Bhamo.	Commissioner, Northern Division, and Deputy Commissioner, Bhamo.	**4. Kaoláng-pum (Frontier).**	**4 0**	27 4	The road runs east from the camp at Kumbaiti. It becomes a mere track through the jungle and very steep, an ascent of 2,200 feet being made in 4 miles. The jungle is thin, chiefly consisting of male bamboos. Several small streams have to be crossed; they are however of no importance. The top of the ridge is the frontier line, the road to Kayôn being down the reverse slope, and running due east. The town of Kayôn lies in the valley of the Wámáng Ka, about 5 miles distant. *Notes on road from Sadôn to Kaoláng-pum.* The road to Rukri is in very good order, after that the hill down to the Tumpaing Ka becomes very steep, the remainder of the road to Kaoláng-pum is up-hill and presents no difficulties to troops marching. The last 4 miles before the summit of Kaoláng-pum is reached is a very trying march, particularly for mountain guns and transport. *Streams.*—The streams are all fordable from the middle of November till the commencement of the rains. The crossing of the Tumpaing Ka is tedious; it can, however, be facilitated by throwing a temporary bridge over the stream suitable for pack animals. This can be easily done, as there are several big rocks convenient. *Camping grounds.*—Camping grounds were made for the troops at each spot where the column halted. Taungyas were generally chosen, as they present good sites and water is always at hand. *Trade.*—One of the principal trade routes runs from Kayôn beyond the frontier, across Kaoláng-pum, to Nawchôn over Lepai-pum, through Nawláng to Sadôn-pa, and then bifurcates, one road running to Sadôn and the other to Nawláng across Kaotu-pum to Ti-i.

No. 81.

From SADÔN to KUMPI-PUM viâ NAWCHÔN.

BY LIEUT. PEEBLES, 1ST NORFOLK REGIMENT, ATTACHÉ, INTELLIGENCE BRANCH, JANUARY 1892.

Military	Civil	Stages	Inter. M. F.	Total M. F.	Remarks
G.O.C. Mandalay District and O.C. Bhamo.	Commissioner, Northern Division, and Deputy Commissioner, Bhamo.	**1. Rukri**	**8 4**	8 4	*See* Route No. 80.
		2. Nawchôn ...	**6 0**	14 4	*See* Route No. 80.
		3. Waror-kyet ... Rutong, Katáng, Kônmai, and Anchi streams.	**9 0**	23 4	From Nawchôn the road runs due north to Waror-kyet. The first 2½ miles is down a sharp incline to the Rutong Ka. The road then leads over a small spur and across the Katáng Ka, then up a very steep hill called Pyawláng hill to Masa, 5 miles, passing the village of Kuntu on the right of the road. The road then leads over a small spur down to the Kônmai Ka, 6 miles, passing the small village of Yindam. About 1½ miles further on the road crosses the Anchi Ka and leads up a steep incline till the camp at Waror-kyet is reached. The road to Masa is good, after that gets very bad and rocky.

FROM SADÔN TO KUMPI-PUM *viâ* NAWCHÔN—*continued.*

Authorities. Military.	Authorities. Civil.	Number and Names of Stages, Rivers and Streams.	Distances. Intermediate.	Distances. Total.	Remarks.
G.O.C. Mandalay District and O.C. Bhamo.	Commissioner, Northern Division, and Deputy Commissioner, Bhamo.	**3. Waror-kyet**—*cont.*			The Rutong Ka is crossed by means of a bridge capable of supporting mules heavily laden, over a pool 15 feet deep. The Katáng Ka, Kônmai Ka and Anchi Ka are all small streams, the first running into the Rutong Ka and the two latter into the Tumpaing Ka. They are crossed by means of stepping stones, the animals crossing close by overfords, a few inches deep.
			M. F.	M. F.	
		4. Ningcham ... Nawku, Sum, and Kankôn streams.	9 4	33 0	Ningshan lies north-west of Waror-kyet. The road leads through the village of Waror soon after leaving camp, 2¼ miles further on, the village of Rutong (Marán) is passed and at 6 miles the Nawku Ka is reached. The road up to this point being down a steady incline. Fording the Nawku Ka the road leads over small spurs crossing the Sum Ka and the Kankôn Ka, after that it leads straight up a steep incline to the village of Ningshan. The road throughout is very good, the inclines being gradual and the road itself broad and in very good order. The Nawku Ka is a shallow stream 30 yards wide and 2 feet deep in the centre; current ordinary; bottom stony. The approach from the left bank is good, but that on the right bank is very steep and bad for pack animals. The Sum Ka and Kankôn Ka are two small streams easily forded by means of stepping stones.
		5. Camp on Shitugor Ka. Kanaw, Nankré and Shitugor streams.	8 4	41 4	General direction of road north. The road for the first 2 miles is up-hill till the crest is reached. It then runs down a sharp descent passing the village of Nankré. At 6 miles the road then passes over two small spurs across the Kanaw Ka and Nankré Ka and down to the Shitugor Ka. The road is good throughout, but steep in parts. The camp is on the right bank of Shitugor Ka. The Kanaw Ka and Nankré Ka are two small streams, both running into the Shitugor Ka and easily crossed. The Shitugor Ka is a big stream rising in Pángsen-pum and at the point of crossing is 30 yards wide and 4 feet deep. Current very rapid, the bottom being large boulders. Approaches very bad. Small bridge for foot-passengers; loads have to be rafted across.
		6. Kumpi	7 0	48 4	Kumpi lies north-east of Shitugor camp, the road is up-hill throughout and very good, sharp inclines being met with occasionally. At 2½ miles the village of Waga (Maru) is reached and at 4 miles Nawcha (Maru) is reached. Camp in village of Kumpi. The peak rising abruptly to the east about 2,000 feet in height.
					Notes on road between Nawchôn and Kumpi-pum viâ *Waror-kyet.*
					The road.—The road throughout is in very good order, but passes over several spurs, the ascents up them being very steep and very trying for mules.
					Rivers.—The Shitugor Ka is a big stream running into the 'Nmai Ka above 'Nsentaru and at the point of crossing runs very rapidly. Foot-passengers can cross by means of a bamboo bridge, but loads must be ferried across on rafts.

FROM SADÔN TO KUMPI-PUM *viâ* NAWCHÔN—*continued.*

Authorities. Military.	Authorities. Civil.	Number and Names of Stages, Rivers and Streams.	Distances. Intermediate.	Distances. Total.	Remarks.
G.O.C. Mandalay Dist. & O.C. Bhamo.	Commissioner, Northern Division, and Deputy Commissioner, Bhamo.	**6. Kumpi**—*cont.*			*Supplies.*—*Nil*, the Kachins only growing enough grain for their own immediate wants. A few pigs and fowls are found in each village, but the former are not fit for food, being very dirty feeders. *Camps.*—Camps have to be made at each place the column halts and are generally placed in taungyas, as the ground is ready cleared and water generally handy.

There is another road FROM SADÔN TO KUMPI-PUM *viâ* LAITÁNG AND SASSA-KYET. The distance is very much the same, but it is probably a better road on the whole than the above. The following is a description of it:—

ALTERNATIVE I.

FROM KUMPI-PUM TO SADÔN *viâ* LAITÁNG AND SASSA-KYET.

BY LIEUT. PEEBLES, 1ST NORFOLK REGIMENT, ATTACHÉ, INTELLIGENCE BRANCH, JANUARY 1892.

Military	Civil	Stages	Intermediate M.	Intermediate F.	Total M.	Total F.	Remarks
G.O.C. Mandalay District and O.C. Bhamo.	Commissioner, Northern Division, and Deputy Commissioner, Bhamo.	**1. Camp on Shitugor Ka.** Shitugor Ka.	9	0	9	0	The camp lies to south-west of Kumpi-pum. The road runs down a sharp descent, along a spur of Kumpi-pum, passing the village of Salaw (Maru), 40 houses, at 4¼ miles from Kumpi. This is a large straggling village, extending for ½ mile along the road. The road throughout is very good, being about 10 feet wide. The country on either side is thick jungle with occasional taungyas. The Shitugor Ka rises to the east of Kumpi, and at the point of crossing is 30 yards wide and 2 feet 6 inches deep; stony bottom; current rapid; approaches good. The camping ground is on the left bank of the river in a clearing in the jungle, about 3 miles lower down the stream than the camp, stage 5 of the route above.
		2. Camp on Tingcha ridge.	12	0	21	0	The camp on Tingcha ridge lies south-west of previous camping ground. The road for the first 2½ miles is up-hill till the village of Singma (Maru) is reached, after that the road runs along ridge past the village of Kumpáng (Maru), 4 miles distant. At 5½ miles the village of Mawun (Marán) is passed. The road then leads down-hill and bifurcates at 7 miles, the main road being to the right and leading to 'Nsentaru. At 7½ miles the village of Laitáng (Lashi) is passed, after leaving the village the road becomes a mere track, very steep and overgrown.* The camp is in a taungya near the village of Saré on the Tingcha ridge.
		3. Sassa-kyet ... Tumpaing Ka.	13	4	34	4	The road runs south-west, the first part running down-hill till the Tumpaing Ka is reached at 5½ miles. The road then makes a steady ascent to the camp, which lies 1 mile beyond the village of Sassa-kyet in a taungya. The villages of Laimakong (Maru), 7 miles, Kumpáng (Sadán), 8 miles, and Laika (Sadán), 10 miles are passed. The road to the village of Laika is good, after that it becomes much overgrown and evidently little used. The

* According to this route it is 18 miles from Laitáng to Sassa-kyet, 14¼ on thence to Sadôn—Total 32¼. Route No. 82, however, makes it 14 and 12½ respectively—Total 26½ or nearly 6 miles less.

FROM SADÔN TO KUMPI-PUM *viâ* NAWCHÔN—*continued.*

ALTERNATIVE I—*continued.*

Authorities. Military.	Authorities. Civil.	Number and Names of Stages, Rivers and Streams.	Distances. Intermediate. M.	F.	Distances. Total. M.	F.	Remarks.
G.O.C. Mandalay District and O.C. Bhamo.	Commissioner, Northern Division, and Deputy Commissioner, Bhamo.	**3. Sassa-kyet**—*cont.*					water-supply is limited. The Tumpaing Ka at the point of crossing is 50 yards wide, the ford running in an oblique direction up-stream from the right to the left bank and is about 2½ feet deep; current slow. The ford runs between two deep pools and would be impassable if the river rose to any degree.
		4. Sadôn	14	2	48	6	Sadôn lies due south of Sassa-kyet. At 1 mile the village of Ti-i is passed and at 9 miles it runs into the road from Kritu to Sadôn. The road runs up-hill throughout till the main road is struck at the top of Kaolang-pum, about ½ mile beyond the Tingri Ka. The road is very good throughout, but steep in parts. *Notes on road from Kumpi to Sadôn viâ Laitáng and Sassa-kyet.* *The road.*—The road from Kumpi to the village of Laitáng is in very good order, this being the main road to 'Nsentaru, after that it becomes a mere track. However, the main trade route is met with at Ti-i, the road from that place to Sadôn being very good. The road leads through jungle, the country near villages being generally cleared for cultivation. *Rivers.*—The Shitugor Ka is a big stream running into the 'Nmai Ka, north-east of 'Nsentaru the ford being where the river widens and becomes shallow. This stream drains all the country between Kumpi-pum and Tingsin-pum (previously called Pasángpum). The Tumpaing Ka rises near Sabu-pum and drains all the country between Kaoláng-pum and Sabu-pum on one side and Lepai-pum on the other, running into the 'Nmai Ka between Loingu and 'Nsentaru. It is very deep at the point where the road crosses, there being a narrow ford across the stream. *Camping ground.*—The camping grounds, as usual, in this part of the country, have to be made in convenient spots, taungyas being usually chosen if possible.

No. 82.

From SADÔN to SADÁNKONG viâ 'NSENTARU.

BY LIEUT. PEEBLES, 1ST NORFOLK REGIMENT, ATTACHÉ, INTELLIGENCE BRANCH, RANGOON, FEBRUARY 1892.

Military	Civil	Stages	Intermediate M.	F.	Total M.	F.	Remarks
* G.O.C. Mandalay District and O.C. Bhamo.	* Commissioner, Northern Division, and Deputy Commissioner, Bhamo.	**1. Sassa-kyet** ... Sadôn Ka.	12	4	12	4	General direction of road north-east. The road for the first mile leads down-hill till the Sadôn Ka is reached, it then leads up-hill through the village of Sana (Sadôn), now destroyed by fire, to the summit of the Kaotu range, which is reached 3½ miles from Sadôn. Here the road bifurcates, that to the left leading to Kritu and that to the right down the reverse slopes of the hill in the direction of Ti-i. At 8 miles from Sadôn the village of Manôn (Sadôn) is passed, situated some little distance to the left of the road. At 11½ miles Ti-i (Sadôn) is passed. The camp is situated in a big taungya about a mile beyond

* So far as any authority, Civil or Military, exists.

FROM SADÔN TO SADÁNKONG *viâ* 'NSENTARU—*continued.*

Authorities. Military.	Authorities. Civil.	Number and Names of Stages, Rivers and Streams.	Distances. Inter-mediate.	Distances. Total.	Remarks.
G.O.C. Mandalay District and O.C. Bhamo.	Commissioner, Northern Division, and Deputy Commissioner, Bhamo.	**1. Sassa-kyet**—*cont.*			Ti-i, water being obtained in a moderate quantity from a hill-side spring. The road throughout is good, the incline to Ti-i, from the top of the Kaotu ridge, is, however, very steep in parts. The Sadôn Ka at the point of crossing is bridged, the bridge being thrown over a deep pool where the stream narrows. The structure is of a permanent nature and strong enough to permit pack animals to cross over. The ford lies about 100 yards below the bridge.
		2. Laitáng ... Tumpaing Ka.	M. F. 14 0	M. F. *26 4	General direction north-east. The road leads up-hill for the first 3 miles till the village of Laika (Sadôn) is reached, the village of Sassa-kyet (Sadôn) is passed 1 mile from camp. Leaving Laika the road runs for 3 miles along the top of a ridge, passing the village of Kumpang (Sadôn) at 5½ miles and the village of Laimakong (Sadôn) at 6½ miles. The road from the village of Laimakong leads down-hill to the Tumpaing Ka which it crosses at 8 miles. The river is crossed by a ford and the road runs up a steep hill on the opposite side of the river for 1½ miles, it then runs along the top of the ridge for 1 mile, after that it leads up a slight incline to the village of Laitáng (Marán) 6 miles from the Tumpaing Ka. The camping ground is situated in a big taungya on the north side of the village, water being obtained from hill spring. The ford across the Tumpaing Ka runs in an oblique direction, down stream, from the left bank to the right; the river on both sides of the ford deepens considerably, the ford itself being 5 yards wide and 2 feet 6 inches deep; bottom stony, current slow; the approach from left bank bad, that from right bank good. The road throughout is in good order passing through thick jungle. The width of the roadway rises from 3 to 10 feet.
		3. 'Nsentaru Ferry. 'Nmai Ka.	8 4	35 0	General direction north-west. The road for the 1st mile is down-hill, running through the taungya on which the camping ground is situated; a small stream is then passed and the road leads up a steep hill for 1½ miles through dense jungle to the village of Laitáng (Lashi); ¼ mile further on the road bifurcates, that to the right leading to Kumpipum and that to the left to 'Nsentaru. From the village of Laitáng the road runs along the top of the ridge to the village of Laitáng (Sadôn), 3 miles from cross roads. This village owns the ferry at 'Nsentaru, and arrangements should here be made for any large parties crossing the 'Nmai Ka. The road then runs down-hill to the village 'Nsentaru, the slope being gentle. This village is on the banks of the 'Nmai Ka and consists of five houses in which the people who work the ferry live. The 'Nmai Ka at the ferry is 120 yards wide, of considerable depth, with a very swift current. The actual bed of the river is from 400 yards to 500 yards wide, and in the rainy season the river rises some 30 to 40 feet and becomes an impassable torrent, the river bed being covered with numerous large rocks and boulders. The river is crossed by means of a small ferry boat which is worked by two men and capable of carrying small loads only. In the event of troops crossing, light bamboo rafts should be made.

* *See* footnote in Route No. 81, Alternative I, referring to Laitáng, Stage 2. According to that route this distance should be 32½.

FROM SADÔN TO SADÁNKONG *viâ* 'NSENTARU—*continued.*

Authorities. Military.	Authorities. Civil.	Number and Names of Stages, Rivers and Streams.	Distances. Intermediate. M.	F.	Distances. Total. M.	F.	Remarks.
G.O.C. Mandalay District and O.C. Bhamo.	Commissioner, Northern Division, and Deputy Commissioner, Bhamo.	**4. Sampawng** ... Numshi Ka.	9	6	44	6	General direction of road north. A ½ mile after leaving the river, the Numshi Ka is reached and ½ mile further on the road runs through the village of Lakawng (Lepai), 15 houses. The Numshi Ka is again crossed 1¾ miles from the 'Nmai Ka. The road up to this point is fairly level, passing over several small boggy nullahs which cause considerable delay to transport animals. Leaving the Numshi Ka the road gradually ascends a gentle slope passing the village of Sum Ka (Lepai) at 4 miles and arriving at Sampawng (Lepai), 8½ miles from 'Nsentaru ferry. The camp is situated in a taungya about 1 mile further on, water being obtainable from two springs. The Numshi Ka is a small stream running into the 'Nmai Ka about ½ mile above the ferry; at the first crossing it is 5 yards wide and 12 inches deep, gravelly bottom with good approaches, and at the second crossing is 7 yards wide and 6 inches deep, gravelly bottom with boggy banks.
		5. Wabong ... Timli Ka and Namli Ka.	10	4	55	2	General direction north-west. The road for the 1st mile leads up-hill to the village of Wapya (Lepai), 12 houses, from there it runs along the top of a plateau to the wes for 1 mile to the village of Pumli (Maru), it then descends a gradual slope to the Timli Ka and ½ mile further on to the Namli Ka which is reached 4¾ miles from the last halting place. Ascending a hill on the opposite bank the village of Laikum (Maru) is passed 1 mile from the river. The road eads over a pass in the hills called Kumbakyet and down the opposite side to the village of Wabong (Maru) 10½ miles from last camping ground. The road throughout is good, the slopes of the hills being gentle and the river easily crossed. The Timli Ka and the Namli Ka are two small streams, the former running into the latter; they are both about 8 yards wide and 6 inches deep, bottom stony, and approaches good.
		6. Sadánkong ...	4	0	59	2	General direction north-west. The road for the first 2 miles is level and runs north to the village of Supma (Kunru Lepai). It then turns to the west and, ascending a gentle rise past the village of Singkong (Lepai) at 3 miles, Sadánkong is reached 4 miles from Wabong. The road throughout is in good order and can be easily marched in an hour and-a-half. The camp is in the village, large clear places being available. From the description of the route there seems little doubt that the last three stages could be easily done in two marches.

BRANCH I.

FROM SADÁNKONG (STAGE 6) TO LEKANNOI FERRY (*see* ROUTE No. 46).

BY LIEUT. PEEBLES, 1ST NORFOLK REGIMENT, ATTACHÉ, INTELLIGENCE BRANCH, RANGOON, FEBRUARY 1892.

Military	Civil	Stages	Inter. M.	F.	Total M.	F.	Remarks
G.O.C. Mandalay District and O.C. Bhamo.	Commr., Northern Dn., and Dy. Commr., Bhamo.	**1. Lapu** ... ... Nanséng Ka.	13	4	13	4	General direction of road south-west. The road for the first 3 miles runs west to the village of Saror (Marán) and then turns south to Marakaung

FROM SADÔN TO SADÁNKONG *viâ* 'NSENTARU—*continued.*

BRANCH I—*continued.*

Authorities. Military.	Authorities. Civil.	Number and Names of Stages, Rivers and Streams.	Distances. Intermediate.	Distances. Total.	Remarks.
G.O.C. Mandalay District and O.C. Bhamo.	Commissioner, Northern Division, and Deputy Commissioner, Bhamo.	**1. Lapu**—*cont.*			(Wawáng Lepai), 30 houses ; 5 miles. Up to this point the road runs along a level plateau, being broad and in very good order. The road then descends to the Nansáng Ka down a zigzag cut out of the hill side. Following the stream on its right bank for 2 miles, the road crosses it 9 miles from Sadánkong. The road then leads through a taungya and over a small hill past the village of Ningchum (Samka Lepai), 12 miles, and on to the village of Lapu (Samka Lepai), five houses. The camp is situated in a taungya beside the Namkong Ka about ¼ mile beyond the village. The Nansang Ka is a small stream, 5 yards wide and 12 inches deep, rising to the north of Lailon and running into the Mali Ka about 20 miles above the confluence.
		2. Lekannoi Ferry. Namkong Ka and 'Nmai Ka.	M. F. **13 0**	M. F. 26 4	General direction of road south. Crossing the Namkong Ka the road runs for 1 mile through paddy-fields, with several small bogs which cause great delay to the transport. The road then runs over a small hill, on the summit of which is the village of Lapu (Samka Lepai), 12 houses. At 4½ miles the village of Walor (Khunru Lepai) is passed. The road then ascends along incline, past the villages of Wakarât and Pousa (both of the Khunru-Lepai tribe) to the village of Seinma, 8½ miles (Malei Latawng), 12 houses, which is situated on the summit. About ½ mile beyond Seinma the village of Wallaw (Malei Latawng), 12 houses, is passed. The road then runs down a spur first at a slight incline gradually becoming steeper, till the 'Nmai Ka is reached, passing the villages of Wasat, Wagar, and Kaitwé (all Malei Latawng). The Namkong Ka is a small stream running into the Nansáng Ka and is about 20 yards wide and 12 inches deep with pebbly bottom. The 'Nmai Ka at the ferry is 200 yards wide with very little stream and (?) feet deep. The ferry is crossed by means of a big dug-out capable of holding 20 men. Baggage can be easily transported by means of bamboo rafts.

No. 83.

From SADÔN to SÁNSI FRONTIER.

BY LIEUT. PEEBLES, 1ST NORFOLK REGIMENT, ATTACHÉ, INTELLIGENCE BRANCH, RANGOON, FEBRUARY 1892.

Military	Civil	Stage	Intermediate	Total	Remarks
G.O.C. Mandalay District and O.C. Bhamo.	Commr., Northern Division, and Dy. Commr., Bhamo.	**1. Namliku** ... Saga Ka.	**5 2**	5 2	The road runs south and for the first 2 miles is down-hill, it then leads through the paddy plains surrounding the Shan Talôk village of Saga, which village is passed on the left. Crossing a small stream, which runs through the village, at 3 miles the road begins to ascend and almost immediately crosses the Saga Ka. The road then runs along the side of a hill for a short distance when it again leads up a gentle incline to the village of Namliku (Sadôn). This is a long straggling village extending along the road for about 1 mile. The camping ground is situated in a taungya on a spur lying to the west and below the village. The Saga Ka is a small mountain stream rising to

FROM SADÔN TO SÁNSI FRONTIER—*continued.*

Authorities. Military.	Authorities. Civil.	Number and Names of Stages, Rivers and Streams.	Distances. Intermediate.	Distances. Total.	Remarks.
G.O.C. Mandalay District and O.C. Bhamo.	Commissioner, Northern Division, and Deputy Commissioner, Bhamo.	**1. Namliku**—*cont.*			the north-west of Sabu-pum and running into the Namli west of Saga. It is crossed by a foot-bridge thrown across a rocky chasm 15 feet wide. Animals must cross by a ford 20 yards above the bridge. At the ford the stream is 20 yards wide, 2 feet deep; bottom stony; approaches steep.
		2. Camp on Shingôp Ka. Shingôp Ka.	M. F. 8 4	M. F. 13 6	Leaving the Namliku the road leads south, and up-hill for 1 mile. Here the Shingôp Ka is reached. The road follows the river on the right bank for 1½ miles up-stream when a ford is crossed. The road then leads up a steep incline to the village of Shingôp, a Chinese settlement with two Lishaw houses. The road then runs down a steep incline for ½ mile when it again crosses the Shingôp Ka. Fording the river the road leads up a gentle incline following the right bank of the river till it is again left at 6¼ miles from Namliku, the road crossing a small tributary when it runs into the main stream. The road then ascends a steep incline meeting the Shingôp Ka about 2 miles further on near its source. The camping ground is situated here, no other water being procurable within reasonable distance. The road for the first 1¼ miles is very good, after that it becomes rocky and very bad. The Shingôp Ka at the first ford is 15 yards wide and 2 feet deep; bottom composed of big boulders; approaches good. At the second crossing the river is bridged, a foot-bridge being thrown across two big boulders about 13 yards apart. The ford for animals is just above the bridge and is very bad, although not of any depth, the river bed being strewn with big boulders and the approaches being steep and very bad.
		3. Frontier on Sánsi road. Shingôp Ka.	6 0	19 6	Crossing the Shingôp Ka the road leads up a very steep incline through dense jungle consisting chiefly of oak trees with thick undergrowth. The hills to the east of the road are seen occasionally and are bare with a few small patches of cultivation. No water is met with till 4 miles from Shingôp Ka. At this point a small spring is met with. The two last miles of the road are very steep and rocky and almost impassable for transport. Above 8,000 feet the road passes through thick bamboo (male) jungle, and just below the summit the road passes through low jungle, chiefly rhododendrons. At the summit is a small spring of very good water. The crest of the ridge is the frontier line. The Shingôp Ka is easily forded, being only a few feet wide with good banks. The road throughout is steep and very rocky and very trying to pack animals. Beyond the frontier the road runs through a fine valley, the source of the Shap Ka, which can be followed for 1¼ miles. On either side of this valley are high hills covered with fine trees; the valley itself is grassy and open. No view can be obtained beyond 1½ miles south.

No. 84.

From SADÔN to TUNGAW.

BY LIEUT. E. C. PEEBLES, 1ST BATTALION, NORFOLK REGIMENT, ATTACHÉ, INTELLIGENCE BRANCH, MARCH 1892.

Authorities. Military.	Authorities. Civil.	Number and Names of Stages, Rivers and Streams.	Distances. Inter-mediate. M.	F.	Distances. Total. M.	F.	Remarks.
G.O.C. Mandalay District and O.C. Bhamo.	Commissioner, Northern Division, and Deputy Commissioner, Bhamo.	**1. Ti-i** ... ... Sadôn Ka.	**11**	**4**	11	4	General direction north-west. The road for the 1st mile leads down-hill till the Sadôn Ka is reached. It then leads up-hill through the village of Sana (Sadôn), now burnt, to the summit of the Kaotu Range which is reached 3½ miles from Sadôn; here the road bifurcates, that to the left leading to Kritu and that to the right down the north slope of the range in the direction of Ti-i. At 8 miles from Sadôn, the village of Manôn is passed (Sadôn), situated some way to the left of the road. At 11½ miles Ti-i (Sadôn) is passed. The camp is situated beside the road near village of Ti-i. The road throughout is good; the incline down to Ti-i from the crest of the range is very steep in parts. The Sadôn Ka is bridged at the point of crossing, the bridge being thrown over a deep pool where the stream narrows. The structure is of wood and is permanent, and capable of bearing pack animals. The ford lies about 100 yards to west of bridge.
		2. Manwing ... Namli Ka and Namlong Ka.	**8**	**4**	20	0	Leaving the village of Ti-i the road runs west down a steep incline till the Namli Ka is reached at 4 miles, it then runs along the right bank of the river for 200 yards, crossing by a ford running diagonally across the stream. The left bank of the river is then followed for ¾ of a mile to the village of Salaw (Shan Talôk); 12 houses. The track then runs through paddy plains, some deserted, others under cultivation, crossing the Namlong Ka at 5½ miles, and arriving at Manwing at 8¼ miles. The camp is situated in the paddy-fields about ¼ of a mile beyond the village. The ford across the Namli Ka is 60 yards wide and 2 feet deep; stony bottom; approaches good. The Namlong Ka is a small stream running into the Namli and is about 10 yards wide and 1 foot deep; bottom gravelly; banks low.
		3. Tungaw ... Manwing chaung.	**4**	**2**	24	4	The road runs north through village of Manwing (Shan Talôk); 20 houses; situated on the Manwing chaung. Crossing the stream the road leads along the level through paddy-fields and low jungle for 2 miles, it then leads up a slight ascent for 2¼ miles to village of Tungaw (Sadôn); 25 houses. This village is situated on the southern slopes of Loi Ngu. The road, which is a mere track, is very good, particularly so near the village of Tungaw where it becomes very broad. The Manwing chaung is a small stream running into the Namlong Ka and is about 5 yards wide and 1 foot deep; pebbly bottom; approaches good.

FROM SADÔN TO TUNGAW—*continued.*

BRANCH I.

FROM MANWING (STAGE 2) TO SAGONGYWA *viâ* CHAMCHA.

BY LIEUT. E. C. PEEBLES, 1ST BATTALION, NORFOLK REGIMENT, ATTACHÉ, INTELLIGENCE BRANCH, MARCH 1892.

Authorities. Military.	Authorities. Civil.	Number and Names of Stages, Rivers and Streams.	Distances. Intermediate. M.	Distances. Intermediate. F.	Distances. Total. M.	Distances. Total. F.	Remarks.
G.O.C. Mandalay District and O.C. Bhamo.	Commissioner, Northern Division, and Deputy Commissioner, Bhamo.	**1. Chamcha** ... Namlong Ka and Namlao Ka.	**9**	**4**	9	4	General direction of road west. Leaving the village of Manwing the road runs through paddy plains for about 2 miles, crossing the Namlong Ka about 1 mile from Manwing. The road then leads up a steep incline to the village of Chingwam (Sadun) 4 miles and then down a steep descent of ½ a mile across a small stream and up the opposite side for another ½ mile. The road then runs down a steep descent 2 miles to the Namlao Ka which is crossed near its head-waters and up a steep ascent to the village of Chamcha (Sadun); 10 houses. The camping ground is in the village; water is obtainable only in small quantities from a mountain spring. The Namlong Ka is 10 yards wide; 1 foot deep; gravelly bottom; good banks. The bed of the Namlao Ka is about 20 yards wide; the stream itself is, however, only 6 yards wide and 9 inches deep; rocky bottom; approaches very steep.
		2. Sagongywa * ...	**3**	**0**	12	4	General direction of road north. The road at the village of Chamcha bifurcates, that to left leading down to Kwitu and that to the right to Sagongywa (Sadun); 80 houses. The road leads up-hill at an easy gradient and is in good order; rocky in parts. The village of Sagongywa is divided into two parts, about ½ mile apart; the lower village consisting of 30 houses.

FROM SAGONGYWA there is an alternative route TO MANWING, passing through HPUMNATONG and NANKAI, the description of which is as follows:—

ALTERNATIVE BRANCH I.

FROM SAGONGYWA TO MANWING.

BY LIEUT. E. C. PEEBLES, 1ST BATTALION, NORFOLK REGIMENT, ATTACHÉ, INTELLIGENCE BRANCH, MARCH 1892.

Authorities. Military.	Authorities. Civil.	Number and Names of Stages, Rivers and Streams.	Distances. Intermediate. M.	Distances. Intermediate. F.	Distances. Total. M.	Distances. Total. F.	Remarks.
G.O.C. Mandalay District and O.C. Bhamo.	Commr., Northern Divn., and Dy. Commr., Bhamo.	**1. Hpumnatong**... Kanoi Ka and Kwitu chaung.	**10**	**6**	10	6	General direction of road north-east. Leaving Sagongywa the road runs north-west and down a sharp incline for 3 miles, crossing the Kanoi Ka at 3½ miles and again at 4 miles. From the foot of the hill the road runs through plains and changing direction leads eastward. The Kwitu chaung is crossed at 6 miles and again at 6½ miles from Sagongywa, and at 8 miles the road leaves the plains and ascends a very steep hill up which it zigzags. Hpumnatong (Sadun) is a small village ½ mile beyond the crest of the hill. The road throughout is

* There is apparently no reason why the village of Sagongywa should not be reached in one day's march from Manwing, though the "Irrawaddy column" of the cold season 1891-92 took two days over it.

FROM SADÔN TO TUNGAW—*continued.*

ALTERNATIVE BRANCH I—*continued.*

Authorities. Military.	Authorities. Civil.	Number and Names of Stages, Rivers and Streams.	Distances. Intermediate.		Distances. Total.		Remarks.
G.O.C. Mandalay District and O.C. Bhamo.	Commissioner, Northern Division, and Deputy Commissioner, Bhamo.	**1. Hpumnatong**—*cont.*					good, the ascents and descents, however, are very steep. Several small nullahs with mountain streams have to be crossed. The Kanoi Ka is about 6 yards wide and 1 foot deep; pebbly bottom; banks good: this stream rises to the north of Sagongywa and runs into Kwitu chaung. The Kwitu chaung is crossed near its source and is a small mountain stream 8 yards wide, 6 inches deep; bottom and banks good.
			M.	F.	M.	F.	
		2. Nankai ... Tungrán Ka and Kraokrán Ka.	**10**	**2**	21	0	General direction east. The road for the first 2 miles is down a steep incline across a small mountain stream and up a slight incline for ¼ mile to the village of Káchaing, situated on a small spur. Descending for ½ mile the Tungrán Ka is crossed, the road then ascends a gentle slope to the villages of Matáng (Sadun) and Kraokrán (Sadun) 3¾ miles and 4 miles respectively from Hpumnatong. Descending about 200 feet in height the road crosses the Kraokrán Ka, which is the main stream draining country north of Loi Lem and Loi Ngu. From here the road leads up a gentle incline to the village of (?), 8 miles. The remainder of the road to Nankai is along the level. The Tungrán Ka is a small mountain stream running into the Kraokrán Ka and is 5 yards wide, 6 inches deep; stony bottom; approaches good. The Kraokrán Ka is the main stream and runs into 'Nmai Ka rising to north of Loi Lem and Loi Ngu. At the ford the stream is 15 yards wide and 1 foot deep. The bottom is rocky, the banks steep, but good. The road throughout is good, but rocky where it passes over several small nullahs.
		3. Manwing ...	**10**	**4**	31	4	General direction of road south-west. The road for the first 1½ miles is along the level, after that for the next 5 miles it passes over several small spurs, varying from 100 to 150 feet in height. At 6½ miles the road begins to descend till the level of the Lakapyáng plain is reached at 8¼ miles; the rest of the route is level. The road throughout is very cramped and in parts very much overgrown with kaing grass and bamboos. This track appears to be little used.

No. 85.

From SENBO to KÁNTI (MÖNGYAKA) viâ MYITKYINA and PUMLUMPUM.

BY LIEUT. E. C. PEEBLES, 1ST NORFOLK REGIMENT, ATTACHÉ, INTELLIGENCE BRANCH, DECEMBER 1891, AND LIEUT. BLEWITT, KING'S ROYAL RIFLES, INTELLIGENCE DEPARTMENT, JANUARY 1891.

Military	Civil	Stages	Intermediate M.	F.	Total M.	F.	Remarks
G.O.C. Mandalay District and O.C. Bhamo.	Commr., Northern Divn., and Deputy Commissioner, Bhamo.	**1. Nansaing chaung camp.** Nankantel and Nansaing chaungs.	**15**	**0**	15	0	The road runs in a northerly direction and is level throughout; several small nullahs have to be crossed, but not of sufficient size to delay a column. The Nankantel chaung is passed 12 miles from Senbo; it is about 6 feet wide and 1 foot deep with steep

FROM SENBO TO KÁNTI (MÖNGYAKA) *viâ* MYITKYINA AND PUMLUMPUM—*continued.*

Authorities. Military.	Authorities. Civil.	Number and Names of Stages, Rivers and Streams.	Distances. Intermediate. M.	Distances. Intermediate. F.	Distances. Total. M.	Distances. Total. F.	Remarks.
G.O.C. Mandalay District and O.C. Bhamo.	Commissioner, Northern Division, and Deputy Commissioner, Bhamo.	**1. Nansaing chaung camp**—*cont.*					banks. Halt can be made here instead of at Nansaing chaung if desired. The Nansaing chaung, on the left bank of which the camping ground is situated at 15 miles, is 30 feet wide, 2 feet deep, gravelly bottom, and approaches good. Sufficient camping ground for 300 men and transport.
		2. Naungkán ... Môgaung chaung.	**12**	**0**	27	0	General direction north. The road throughout is good, passing through jungle; several nullahs, dry at this time of year, have to be crossed, causing considerable delay to a column. The small kachin village of Naungkán is situated on the left bank of the Môgaung chaung ½ mile below ford, the camp being situated on the left bank at the ford. Boats or rafts must be procured beforehand from village for the purpose of crossing. Only two dug-outs are kept there permanently.
		3. Hôkát ... ... Irrawaddy river.	**9**	**4**	36	4	General direction north. The road is same as before; several small nullahs having to be crossed. A small police post is built at the village of Hôkát. Camping ground for troops on bank of Irrawaddy in village. Hôkát (Wawáng Lepai) consists of 10 houses and is situated on the right bank of the Irrawaddy.
		4. Sinkaung ...	**7**	**6**	44	2	General direction north. Road good throughout the village of Laika (Wawáng Lepai), eight houses, is passed 4 miles from Hôkát, and Taiklôn (Wawáng Lepai), 12 houses at 5 miles. Camp in paddy-fields at new village of Sinkaung (Wawáng Lepai), eight houses on bank of Ángngōn chaung, a backwater of Irrawaddy, 50 yards wide (7¾ miles).
		5. Páraw	**9**	**0**	53	2	Direction north. The road good passing over several nullahs near Sinkaung. Passed the village of Ninglum (Wawáng Lepai), 10 houses, 5 miles; and Nawkhum (Wawáng Lepai), eight houses, at 6½ miles. Camp in village of Páraw (Latawng), eight houses, on right bank of Irrawaddy, which is 600 yards wide at this point; stream ordinary, gravelly bottom.
		6. Héchain ... Namkwi chaung.	**12**	**0**	65	2	Road leads north and is good throughout, passing through open spaces in jungle evidently once under cultivation. At 1 mile the village of Akyé (Lawkhum Latawng), 10 houses, is passed, and at 6 miles the Namkwi chaung is reached. The stream at the point of crossing is 50 yards wide, 2 feet deep, with gravelly bottom. Camp near village of Héchain (Maru) on right bank of Irrawaddy.

FROM SENBO TO KÁNTI (MÖNGYAKA) *viâ* MYITKYINA AND PUMLUMPUM—*continued.*

Authorities.		Number and Names of Stages, Rivers and Streams.	Distances.		Remarks.
Military.	Civil.		Intermediate.	Total.	
G.O.C. Mandalay District and O.C. Bhamo.	Commissioner, Northern Division, and Deputy Commissioner, Bhamo.	**7. Myitkyina** ...	M. F. 6 0	M. F. 71 2	General direction north-east. The road passes through open country covered with kaing grass, boggy in places. Tháyagôn (mixture of Shans and Shan Talôks) is passed at 5½ miles, being situated some way to the left of main road. * The road which can be marched in seven days is a mere track through the forest, any transport can move along it, elephants excepted, as they find the numerous nullahs to be crossed very trying.

Notes on the road from Senbo to Myitkyina.

The road.—The total distance is 71 miles and can very easily be marched in seven days. The road is little better than a narrow forest track, but it is perfectly level and presents no difficulties to troops with mule transport, provided a few picks and shovels are with the advance guard: Goorkha *kukris* or Kachin *dás* are also useful for cutting down boughs, &c.

Streams.—Water is plentiful everywhere. Streams are all fordable from November to the commencement of the rains, and the same remark applies to the Namkwi river.

Rivers.—Arrangements for crossing the Môgaung river have always to be made, as it is not fordable.

Camping grounds.—There are no regular camping grounds for troops, but spaces in the jungle can easily be cleared.

Supplies.—The country is very sparsely populated, and the small Kachin villages to be met with on the road cannot supply more than a very little paddy and poultry. From Senbo, Hôkát, Myitkyina, however, rather larger quantities can be obtained.

Boats.—Steamers do not ascend the Irrawaddy higher than Senbo, but could do so when the river is in flood during the rains and for a short time afterwards. Country boats such as *talés* and *laungs* take three days from Senbo to Hôkát, and three and-a-half days from Hôkát to Myitkyina.

Escorts.—British authority extends as far as Myitkyina, but a small escort is at present necessary, two to four sepoys being quite sufficient.

Lateral communications.—From Hôkát there is a road to Môgaung. It is 27 miles and can be easily marched in three days as follows :—

(1) Hôkát to Yinbát.
(2) Yinbát to Tápaw.
(3) Tápaw to Môgaung.

From Myitkyina there is also a road to Môgaung. The marches are rather longer and the Namkwi, Nanti and Môgaung rivers have to be crossed, but the distance is easily done in three days.

* I cannot understand this last remark unless *left* has been written in mistake for *right*, as Tháyagôn is certainly situated on the Irrawaddy (right bank) and the road does not cross the river. Even supposing this mistake to have been made, the village cannot have been far to the right, as it is only ½ a mile from Myitkyina down the river bank, and Myitkyina is reached according to the reporter within ½ a mile of passing Tháyagôn. As a matter of fact, the two villages are practically connected, and even though Lieut. Peebles may not have passed through Tháyagôn, he certainly *could* have done so.—A.F.

FROM SENBO TO KÁNTI (MÖNGYAKA) *viâ* MYITKYINA AND PUMLUMPUM—*continued.*

Authorities. Military.	Authorities. Civil.	Number and Names of Stages, Rivers and Streams.	Distances. Intermediate. M.	F.	Total. M.	F.	
G.O.C. Mandalay District and O.C. Bhamo.	Commissioner, Northern Division, and Deputy Commissioner, Bhamo.	**8. Wátu**	**8**	**6**	80	0	The road is along the right bank of the Irrawaddy through fairly open country and only crosses one or two nullahs. At 4½ miles Alet is reached, which is a small Kachin village of the Marán tribe. At Wátu there are a few Shan Talôks or Chinese Shans, and the Kachins are of the Nawkhum-Latawng tribe.
		9. Mawmé ...	**10**	**2**	90	2	The road was a bad one for the last half of the distance, crossing five large streams and two smaller ones. At the 5th mile the village of Sakáp is reached. It consists of about 20 houses, and the inhabitants are of the Nawkhum-Latawng tribe. Mawmé is a small Kachin village, Latawng, and about eight houses.
		10. Confluence of the Malí Ka and the 'Nmai Ka, latitude 25° 43′. Narong Ka, Sin Ka, Míkán Ka, Kyinkyun Ka, Konkhun Ka, Tongpu Ka, Kákun Ka, and Míma Ka.	**10**	**6**	101	0	The road or forest track becomes very much more difficult for mule transport. After crossing the large streams called Narong Ka, Sin Ka and Míkán Ka, Wátugyi is reached. It is a small village, six houses, and is inhabited by the Nawkhum-Latawng Kachins. The Sawbwa of Wátu and Wátugyi lives here. After leaving Wátugyi the following streams are crossed, the Kyinkyun Ka, the Konkhun Ka, the Tongpu Ka, the Kákun Ka, and the Míma Ka. They are all small streams, about 5 yards broad and 1 foot deep, with very steep banks on either side, stony bottom. The country, which every mile becomes more hilly, accounts for the deep nullahs through which these streams flow. Lapé Latawng Kachin, eight houses, is about 2 miles from Wátugyi. At the confluence there is no village, but a very fair camping ground on the river bank.
		11. Taláng ... Waisi Ka.	**11**	**0**	112	0	The road now enters the hills and no more level country is met with. The road on forest track becomes exceedingly bad and steep in places. After crossing the Waisi Ka, which is a small stream about 5 yards wide and 1 foot deep, the Pungin Ka is reached, which is 6 miles from the confluence. Pungin Ka is from 45 to 50 yards wide and the greatest depth not more than 3 feet 6 inches. The bottom was rocky. Village of Taláng belongs to the Salôn-Latawng tribe of Kachins and consists of about nine houses and is situated on a low hill 900 feet high and about 4 miles west of the Malí Ka.

FROM SENBO TO KÁNTI (MÖNGYAKA) *viâ* MYITKYINA AND PUMLUMPUM—*continued.*

Authorities. Military.	Authorities. Civil.	Number and Names of Stages, Rivers and Streams.	Distances. Intermediate. M. F.	Distances. Total. M. F.	Remarks.
G.O.C. Mandalay District and O.C. Bhamo.	Commissioner, Northern Division, and Deputy Commissioner, Bhamo.	**12. Paokaw** ... Insôp Ka.	**6 0**	118 0	Short march, but difficult. After leaving Taláng the road gradually descends into the valley of the Insôp Ka, which is reached 2 miles from Talang. The Insôp Ka was just fordable when we crossed, only a few of the loads getting wet. It was about 60 yards wide and 3 feet deep with a rocky bottom. Leaving Insôp Ka the road ascends a high range of hills, on which is Paokaw, a small village of five houses, Sana-Latawng tribe of Kachins. The height of the village is 2,300 feet.
		13. Pumwai ...	**10 2**	128 2	From Paokaw to Pumwai the road continues along the range. At 4½ miles the village of Shángyáng is reached, about 10 houses, of the Salon-Latawng tribe. From Shángyáng there is a good road to Môgaung *viâ* Pánláng. It leaves the road we were on about 1 mile from Shángyáng and, bearing south-west, passes through the big village of Nawkhun (Latawng tribe) and thence across the valley to Pánláng. Continuing along the range we reached Pumwai. It is a small village inhabited by Wawáng-Lepai Kachins; about six houses. From here there is a road to Sabaw and Kwitu ferries on the Malí Ka (*see* Route No. 46, Stages 5 to 8).
		14. Supka ... Tíyang Ka.	**8 0**	136 2	Leaving Pumwai the road for 4 miles is fairly good as far as the Kachin village Katnem (Sampaung-Lepai tribe); six houses. The next 2 miles to the Tiyáng Ka are very bad, in and out of deep nullahs and for some little distance along the bed of a stream. The Tiyáng Ka is about 20 yards wide, 1 foot to 18 inches deep, stony bottom, and steep banks. Leaving the bed of the stream the road ascends a steep hill and Supka is reached. Supka is a small village of eight houses (Malé-Latawng tribe). From Supka there is a road to Sawan on the Malí Ka 4 miles distant. It is important, as Sawan is the highest point that country boats, such as "laungs," can reach. Above Sawan the rapids prevent all navigation.
		15. Wara ... ... Tamáng Ka and Taru Ka.	**8 0**	144 2	Road bad, up and down a succession of steep hills. After travelling 3 miles the road descends into the valley through which the Tamáng and the Taru streams flow. The ford is at the confluence of the two streams, which was 40 yards wide and 3 feet deep at the most, with a good sound bottom. Leaving the river the road gradually ascends a steep hill, and the small village of Wara is reached (Wawáng-Lepai tribe); seven houses. Height of village 2,200 feet.
		16. Siyángkong.	**6 4**	150 6	A short march and a better road. Four miles from Wara, 'Nkánkong is reached (Lepai tribe, Kamlao); 12 to 15 houses. Continuing by the same good path Siyángkong, a small village ('Nkum tribe); six houses.

FROM SENBO TO KÁNTI (MÖNGYAKA) *viâ* MYITKYINA AND PUMLUMPUM—*continued.*

Authorities. Military.	Authorities. Civil.	Number and Names of Stages, Rivers and Streams.	Distances. Intermediate. M. F.	Distances. Total. M. F.	Remarks.
G.O.C. Mandalay District and O.C. Bhamo.	Commissioner, Northern Division, and Deputy Commissioner, Bhamo.	**17. Tingsa Pumlumpum.** Wasip Ka.	6 4	157 2	For 3 miles the road descends when the Wasip Ka is reached. It is a small stream, 18 feet wide and 1 foot deep with rocky bottom. Having crossed this the road ascends a high hill and skirting the village of Kaichaung Kong (Sana-Latawng tribe) reaches Tingsa Pumlumpum. Tingsa is a small village of about eight houses (Lepai tribe); the height of our camp 3,600 feet.
		18. Marao Satár.	4 0	161 2	Lieut. Blewitt, in his diary of the expedition that visited the Upper Irrawaddy in the cold season 1890-91, mentions Marao Satár as the next place they would have marched to beyond Tingsa Pumlumpum, had not they been compelled by the threatening attitude of the Sana Latawngs to turn back. This same place was mentioned in the account given to Major Fenton at Maingna in June 1890 of the route from Nawnaw (a rapid on the Malí Ka about 8 miles above the confluence) to Kánti *viâ* Sawan, which is appended for reference; stage 9 in it would become stage 19 of the through route from Senbo. *General Notes on the road from Myitkyina to Pumlumpum.* *State of the road.*—The road or forest track as far as the bifurcation, or rather the confluence of 'Nmai Ka and the Malí Ka, is a fairly easy one for mule transport. Its general direction is due north close to the right bank of the Irrawaddy. After leaving, however, the confluence the road continuing north enters the hills and becomes exceedingly bad. A succession of low hills is met with; there is no attempt made to make the gradients easy, and the descents into the deep valleys or gorges through which the Pungin Ka, Insôp Ka, Tiyáng Ka, Wasip Ka flow are barely passable for mules. The road is from 3 to 4 miles west of the Malí Ka and parallel to it. *Rivers.*—The rivers in January were all fordable and probably always are so from the middle of October until the beginning of the rains. *Supplies.*—The Kachins live principally on paddy, but they do not grow more than is sufficient for themselves. At every village one sees a little poultry and a few pigs. Troops marching along this road should not reckon on being able to get any supplies at all, as it was only with great difficulty we were able to get a little paddy for the mules. *The people.*—The Kachins do not yet recognize the authority of the British Government, and it is impossible to go through the country without an escort.

FROM NAWNAW TO KÁNTI (MÖNGYAKA) *viâ* SAWAN AND MARAO SATÁR.

BY MAJOR FENTON, DEPUTY ASSISTANT QUARTERMASTER-GENERAL, INTELLIGENCE BRANCH, FROM INFORMATION BY SÁN MAUNG PWA OF MAINGNA, JUNE 1890.

G.O.C. Mandalay District and O.C. Bhamo.	Comr., Northern Divn., and Deputy Comr., Bhamo.	**1. Wunnán** ...	...	...	There are no villages other than Kachin throughout this route until Kánti Shan country is reached. Möngyaka is apparently the chief place in the southern part of Kánti. Wunnán is a village on left bank of the Malí Ka.

FROM SENBO TO KÂNTI (MONGYAKA) *viâ* MYITKYINA AND PUMLUMPUM—*continued.*

Authorities.		Number and Names of Stages, Rivers and Streams.	Distances.		Remarks.
Military.	Civil.		Inter-mediate.	Total.	
			M. F.	M. F.	
G.O.C. Mandalay District and O.C. Bhamo.	Commissioner, Northern Division, and Deputy Commissioner, Bhamo.	**2. Álun**	...	...	At about one-third of the way past village of Nunglán, left bank, just south of which a small stream enters river by same bank. Álun is a village on left bank.
		3. Sawan	...	...	At about one-third of the way past village of Santá, left bank, just above which the Namsáng chaung, a good big stream (as large as the Natmyin below Ywadaw), enters by the same bank. At two-thirds pass village of Namsékataung at the mouth of a small stream that enters by the left bank. Sawan is a village on the right bank. "*Laungs*" (medium size [country boats) can get up so far, but no further, and apparently very few go up during the year even so far, the Shans trusting to the Kachins to come down themselves and fetch what they want. From Santá upwards there are numerous Kachin villages on the hills on either side of the river. Only "*peingaws*" (small "dug-outs") and bamboo rafts can be used on the river above Sawan.
		4. Tamáng Sakhán.	...	...	Halting place on left bank. No village near.
		5. Kasa Sakhán ...	...	...	Halting place on left bank. No village near.
		6. Tarátsup ...	...	...	At about two-thirds of the way village of Köngsungyáng, left bank. Tarátsup is just below the mouth of a stream that enters by the left bank. Doubtful whether this is a village or merely a halting place.
		7. Wulaw	...	...	Matkyikatawng village on left bank is passed midway. Wulaw is a village also on left bank.
		8. Lapaung and Pungleng.	...	...	Lapaung and Pungleng are villages on the river bank opposite each other, the former on the right bank, the latter on the left. No boats, however small, can get higher up than this, and travellers must take to the road which follows the right bank.
		9. 'Ntingnoi ...	...	...	A long day's march passing the villages of Marao* Satár (just beyond which a stream is crossed), Sanáyáng, and Lôpla, all on the right bank.

* See Stage 18 above.

FROM SENBO TO KÁNTI (MÖNGYAKA) *viâ* MYITKYINA AND PUMLUMPUM—*continued.*

Authorities. Military.	Authorities. Civil.	Number and Names of Stages, Rivers and Streams.	Distances. Intermediate. M. F.	Distances. Total. M. F.	Remarks.
G.O.C. Mandalay District and O.C. Bhamo.	Commissioner, Northern Division, and Deputy Commissioner, Bhamo.	**10. Káchaing** ...	...	...	Passing the villages of 'Nkán, Pomyáng, and Sakám, all right bank.
		11. Masi chaung.	...	...	Just north of Káchaing a large stream, called the Pungin Ka, enters by the right bank. It comes from the west and some little distance up it forks, the southern branch being called the Pungin and the northern the Pungsán Ka (Ka=river in Kachin). After crossing the Pungin pass the villages of Lashulatáp, Salékyet, Pási, Kátsu, and Taungmatsa and camp at halting place on Masi chaung, a short distance beyond the last-named village. This stream comes in from the north-west or west by the right bank.
		12. 'Ntaung ...	...	...	Village on right bank. Here the path apparently bears away to the west of the Malí Ka, and it is two days' march to Möngyaka.
		13. Möngyaka (or Möngyöka).	...	...	This is a large village or town in Kánti, probably situated in the valley of the Namyuk, which is shown in the 2nd edition of sheet No. 22 N. W. N. E. T. F. Series as joining the Namlung just above *its* junction with the Namkiu or Malí Ka in about latitude 27° 15′. From Lapaung upwards the country is thickly populated by Káku-Kachin tribes, who cultivate "taungya," wash for gold, and make *dás* which they sell in Assam and Mögaung. It is said to be eight days' journey from Káchaing into Assam, but they must be very long marches and even so would scarcely land one more than on the borders of that country. If, however, the high range forming the watershed between the Brahmaputra and the Irrawaddy be taken as bounding Assam on the east, then eight days' journey from Káchaing or thereabouts *viâ* the Chaukan pass would just about land one in Assam, and very likely this is what they mean. The first eight stages are by water, probably about 8 miles each, if so much, as there are numerous rapids and progress would be slow. The remaining stages are each a day's march. The distance from Nawnaw to Möngyaka, as the crow flies, must be about 80 miles, not more, and as travelled by water and road would not be as much as 120. Probably the land stages cannot, therefore, be long, and 14 days must be a very liberal estimate of the time required to perform the whole journey. Transport animals do not appear to be used, the Kachins carrying their loads on the back, with a band passing round the forehead and a yoke resting on the shoulders to steady the load just like the Manipur, Kuki, or Tonkul coolies carry theirs. A path runs northwards from Lapé below the bifurcation to Kwitao ferry, whence there must certainly be a path up the left bank to Sánta, and there is probably another path up the right bank, as there is another ferry at a place called 'Npáng about a day's journey above Nawnaw. The path crossing here may, however, go direct west to the Amber Mines district and not come down the river bank towards Lapé. A number of Kánti Shans come down every year to Mögaung *viâ* the Hnkong valley. They come down

FROM SENBO TO KÁNTI (MÖNGYAKA) *viâ* MYITKYINA AND PUMLUMPUM—*continued.*

Authorities. Military.	Authorities. Civil.	Number and Names of Stages, Rivers and Streams.	Distances. Intermediate.	Distances. Total.	Remarks.
G.O.C. Mandalay District and O.C. Bhamo.	Commr., Northern Divn., and Deputy Commr., Bhamo.	**13. Möngyaka (or Möngyöka)** —*cont.*			to make offerings at the pagodas at Bhamo, Shwégu, and even Mandalay and bring a certain amount of gold and musk-pods with them, apparently more with the idea of covering the expenses of their trip than with a view to trading. All their trade seems to go to Assam. From Nawnaw upwards the river is shut in on both sides by hills and numerous rapids are met with.

No. 86.

From SENBO to LWÉGYO (for Kaukkwé Valley).

BY LIEUT. W. H. MANNING, XII KHELAT-I-GHILZAI REGIMENT, APRIL 1890.

Military	Civil	Stages	Intermediate	Total	Remarks
G.O.C. Mandalay District and O.C. Bhamo.	Commissioner, Northern Division, and Deputy Commissioner, Bhamo.	**1. Lwégyo** ... Namkán chaung.	M. F. **13 6**	M. F. 13 6	This and the two following routes form the starting portions of three routes into the Kaukkwé valley, not yet fully explored. The road leaves Senbo in a north-westerly direction and follows the telegraph clearing for the 1st mile, then through thin tree jungle on to the paddy plains at 2½ miles. The road winds over the paddy plains, passing the village of Nanpapa at the 4th mile. From this village the road enters jungle and runs parallel to the course of the Namkán chaung, being in many places almost entirely overgrown with jungle. From the 7th mile the road runs up the centre of a narrow valley and beyond the 9th mile continually crosses and recrosses the Namkán chaung and passes into tall kaing grass at the 10th mile and on to a small paddy plain at the 11th mile. The valley is here about ½ mile in width. The road then runs in a northerly direction across the plain and commences the ascent of the hills at 11½ miles, through thick jungle for the first ¼ mile; ascent steep. The road then passes on to a paddy clearing, descends into a ravine, and ascends into the village of Malwé at 12¾ miles. This village consists of 12 houses and was unstockaded. The road runs north out of Malwé and ascends along the side of a spur through a large paddy clearing. At 13½ miles it passes from the paddy clearing into thick jungle and reaches the village of Lwégyo at 13¾ miles, the last ¼ mile being up and excessively steep ascent. The village consisted of 25 houses and was unstockaded. The road from the 5th mile of this march was extremely bad up to the 11th mile. It seemed to be a disused path. From the paddy plains below Malwé Makan village can be reached by a disused road. This road passes up a nullah on the opposite side of the plain to the Malwé road. It runs up this nullah for ½ mile, then ascends up a spur into a ridge through very thick jungle. Makan is reached at 4 miles, the road passing along the summit of the ridge the whole way.

No. 87.

From SENBO to MAKAN and PINZUN (for Kaukkwé Valley).

By Lieut. W. H. MANNING, XII Khelat-i-Ghilzai Regiment, April 1889.

Authorities. Military.	Authorities. Civil.	Number and Names of Stages, Rivers and Streams.	Distances. Intermediate. M. F.	Distances. Total. M. F.	Remarks.
G.O.C. Mandalay District and O.C. Bhamo.	Commissioner, Northern Division, and Deputy Commissioner, Bhamo.	**1. Camp in jungle below Makan.** Namkán and Thôkut chaungs.	7 2	...	The road turns south out of Senbo, passes through the village of Pinlong at 1¾ miles, then turns west out of Pinlong, and passes through thin jungle, crossing the Namkán chaung ¼ mile outside the village, then through thin tree jungle into a grassy plain at 3 miles, the road then winds across the plain in a north-westerly direction and enters bamboo jungle at 4 miles, it then commences slight ascent and crosses Thôkut chaung at 5 miles; rocky bed, excellent water. Road continues to ascend slightly, and at 6 miles passes through a small clearing, short kaing grass. The road at this point bifurcates, and the right-hand road must be taken (left-hand road leads up to the villages on Mansain hill). It continues to ascend and crosses over a small stream with rocky bed at 6¾ miles. Camp was reached at 7¼ miles on left bank of this stream. The camp was cleared in bamboo jungle and was very cramped. Road on this march was narrow, but good, and there were no swampy places.
		2. Pinzun ...	5 4	12 6	The road runs west out of camp and ascends very slightly for first 1,200 yards through thick bamboo jungle, it then passes through a paddy clearing for the next 200 yards and enters bamboo jungle at 1 mile, and passes on to the spur of a hill which it ascends for the next mile. Ascent gradual; road good through bamboo jungle. At 2 miles the ascent becomes steeper for 400 yards and further on passes into scrub jungle and enters the village of Makan, 2¾ miles. Makan consists of 16 houses, and the village was unstockaded. Water was found 300 yards below the village on the west side. South of Makan and overlooking it, about 800 yards distant, is the village of Léshwa consisting of 17 houses. The road to Pinzun runs south-west out of Makan and ascends for the 1st mile and is broad, it then passes over the summit of a hill through thick jungle and descends through grass and bamboo jungle to the village of Pinzun at 5¼ miles. Road good throughout this march. The village consists of nine houses and was enclosed by a bamboo stockade in bad repair. *Note.*—This is evidently the route leading to Máttát on the Kaukkwé chaung, *vide* Route No. 27.

No. 88.

From SENBO to MANSAIN HILL (for Kaukkwé Valley).

By Lieut. W. H. MANNING, XII Khelat-i-Ghilzai Regiment, April 1889.

G.O.C. Mandalay District and O.C. Bhamo.	Commr., Northern Divn., and Deputy Commr., Bhamo.	**1. Sompapaung (Mansain Hill).** Namkán and Thôkut chaungs.	9 0	9 0	Up to the 6th mile *vide* Route No. 87, Senbo to Makan and Pinzun. From the 6th mile the road is level through grass and scrub jungle for first ¾ mile running in a south-westerly direction and passing below a low hill on the right of the road, which then turns

FROM SENBO TO MANSAIN HILL (FOR KAUKKWÉ VALLEY)—*continued*.

Authorities. Military.	Authorities. Civil.	Number and Names of Stages, Rivers and Streams.	Distances. Intermediate.	Distances. Total.	Remarks.
G.O.C. Mandalay District and O.C. Bhamo.	Commissioner, Northern Division, and Deputy Commissioner, Bhamo.	**1. Sompapaung (Mansain Hill)** —*cont.*			south and ascends by a slight ascent into the village of Mansain at the 7th mile. This village consisted of eight houses and was unstockaded. The road out of the village runs west through bamboo jungle and passes a few small houses on the right just out of the village. It is level for the first 200 yards, then descends for next 200 yards, then ascends along the side of a hill path, having been cut out of hill side and passes over a nullah at 7¾ miles with a small stream in its bed; rocky bottom. The road rises out of the nullah and commences the ascent of the Mansain hill, which is exceedingly steep, through thick tree jungle and very rocky in some places, and reaches the village of Sampapaung at 9 miles. Sampapaung consisted of eight houses and was not stockaded. The village is situated on the summit of a spur from the hill some distance below the crest of the hill.

No. 89.

From SENBO to MÔGAUNG.

BY LIEUT. MOUL, 2ND CHESHIRE REGIMENT, COLD SEASON, 1887–88.

Military	Civil	Stages	Intermediate	Total	Remarks
G.O.C. Mandalay District and O.C. Bhamo.	Commissioner, Northern Division, and Deputy Commissioner, Bhamo.	**1. Nankán stream.** Nankán stream.	M. F. **11 2**	M. F. 11 2	The march from Senbo to Môgaung is fairly easy, the Môgaung river, however, has to be crossed twice, and this crossing occupies nearly a day with a large force. The first two marches are very easy over a good level road. The third march (camp on Môgaung river) to Yinbát is over a bad road which has not been cleared lately. The remaining two marches are easy. The Ghurka police unencumbered by baggage marched from Senbo to camp on Môgaung river in one day (26 miles), also from Yinbát to Môgaung (19 miles). There are no boats at the place where we crossed the first time, and arrangements should be made to get them from Tápaw or Môgaung. At Tápaw there are five or six boats (dug-outs). It took 9 hours to cross at the camp above Saungkán with six dug-outs; the transport animals can be easily swum across at both places. There are several marshy places on the road from Tápaw to Môgaung which are not practicable for transport animals unless unloaded, these should be bridged by a fatigue party starting early. The road runs north-west out of Senbo, leaving the river which here takes a bend to the east. First 2 miles through tree forest, one or two clearings for cultivation. At 2½ miles road turns north through forest. At 5 miles road comes down to the Irrawaddy (branch), crossing a little marshy stream which had to be bridged for transport. Tagôndein village on opposite bank. Next 2 miles north-east through forest. At 7½ miles road enters a big clearing and running north-east in a winding direction through paddy-fields becomes a mere track. At 8½ miles it turns north and at 9½ miles re-enters jungle. Next 2 miles north through forest. At 11½ miles cross the Nankán stream, 8 feet wide, 4 feet deep. A bridge had to be constructed across this for the transport and the banks had to be ramped. Good water. Camp on left bank of stream in forest very cramped for large force. Water from Nankán stream good and abundant.

FROM SENBO TO MÔGAUNG—*continued.*

Authorities. Military.	Authorities. Civil.	Number and Names of Stages, Rivers and Streams.	Distances. Inter-mediate.	Distances. Total.	Remarks.
G.O.C. Mandalay District and O.C. Bhamo.	Commissioner, Northern Division, and Deputy Commissioner, Bhamo.	**2. Môgaung river.** Namsen and Môgaung rivers.	M. F. 14 4	M. F. 25 6	First 3 miles north-west through forest with a few small clearings. At 3¼ miles cross the Namsen river about 30 feet wide, 2 feet deep, gravelly bottom, no difficulty to transport. Next mile north-east through forest, road then enters a large open clearing through which it runs in a north-east direction for 2 miles, then turns north through forest and clearing till at 9 miles it debouches on a large open plain through which it winds, general direction north-east, till at 11 miles it enters jungle. Three-quarter mile later cross a very marshy stream which has to be bridged for transport. Next mile north-east through forest. At 12¾ miles the road bifurcates—the right-hand road leading to Naungkán, a stockaded village of about 40 houses on the Môgaung river, the left runs north over a bad road through jungle down to the bed of the Môgaung river. Rear guard left 9-30 A.M., arrived 5-30 P.M. Camp in sand river bed, any space available. Water from Môgaung river. The river here is about 100 yards wide and shallow for some distance from the right bank; near the left bank, however, it is from 8 to 12 feet deep. No village here; current about 2 miles an hour. The left bank of the river is rather steep and should be ramped for transport. The above two marches are easy, the road being level and in good condition; it is about 6 feet wide in the forests; but through the clearings and paddy plains it becomes very indefinite; a guide should be taken. Camp on left bank of river cramped for large force; clearing difficult. Water from Môgaung river.
		3. Yinbát ... ... Pompiyé chaung.	10 2	36 0	Road leaves the river and runs north-east through grass jungle; at 400 yards a broad road comes in from the right and a little later one from the left; these are forest paths for timber cutting; proper path narrow. At ½ mile road turns north-west and runs through clearing and dense jungle till at 2¼ miles it comes down to the river, 400 yards later passing the village of Namyát, the greater part of which is burnt down. Next 3 miles north through forest and tree jungle, occasional clearings, path narrow and ill-defined. At 6 miles cross the Pompaha chaung, narrow marshy stream, which required bridging for the transport; good water. Next mile north-west, bad path, crossing the stream several times, then through dense bamboo jungle, till at 8¼ miles meet the stream again following the right bank for 600 yards. The road now becomes better and leads north-west through forest down to the Môgaung river which is reached at 10¼ miles. Camping ground on banks of Môgaung river; very little space for large force. Water good from river. The jungle in this march has overgrown the path, especially in latter part of the march, necessitating a great deal of clearing for the transport. From here there is good road to Hôkát, 9 miles.

FROM SENBO TO MÔGAUNG—*continued.*

Authorities. Military.	Authorities. Civil.	Number and Names of Stages, Rivers and Streams.	Distances. Intermediate. M. F.	Distances. Total. M. F.	Remarks.
G.O.C. Mandalay District and O.C. Bhamo.	Commissioner, Northern Division, and Deputy Commissioner, Bhamo.	**4. Tápaw** ... ... Tethé chaung.	8 6	44 6	First mile north through thick bamboo jungle; path narrow and ill-defined crossing one small stream. The road now becomes good and runs in a north-west direction through forest over a couple of nullahs. At 3½ miles road crosses the Tethé chaung, a stream about 8 yards wide, 2 feet deep, gravelly bottom, excellent water. Next mile north-west through grass. At 4 miles cross another small stream and then in a north-west direction through forest and small clearings. At 6½ miles road turns north and runs through bamboo jungle crossing two streams. Next 2 miles through jungle and clearings down to camp. Camping ground on bank of river, 20 feet above, cramped. Water from Môgaung river. Supplies at Tápaw, eggs, fowls, paddy, rice, &c. An easy march, path required clearing for 1st mile, remainder of march it was excellent though narrow. There are two or three nullahs and numerous small streams, but they present no obstacle to transport. The river is here about 200 yards wide; current 2 miles an hour. The banks are high and require ramping for transport. It is shallow near the left bank; near the right bank it is 12 feet deep. Camping ground in open clearing, about 300 yards from river, good. Water from river. Tápaw 30 houses, one pôngyi kyaung for 50 men; supplies paddy, rice, fowls, eggs, &c.
		5. Môgaung ...	10 4	55 2	Road leads north-west out of camp for 400 yards through tree jungle, it then emerges on a large open plain through which it runs in a winding direction for 3 miles crossing one or two small dykes between paddy-fields which have to be bridged for transport. At 4 miles there is a very marshy place, across which a causeway had to be built. Next mile through tree jungle over a hill, steep descent, at the bottom a marshy place, through grass. At 5 miles the road turns west and passes through grass and clearings in a winding direction. At 6½ miles pass over right spur of a conical hill with a pagoda on the summit, then in a south-west direction through paddy, marshy in places, coming down to Môgaung river at 6¾ miles. Next 2 miles south-west through tree jungle and paddy, passing small villages of Pinka, Lethma, Pinwé. At 8½ miles cross small stream, 8 feet wide, 1 foot deep, then north-west over grass plain to Môgaung, through which road runs to camp. Camp on sandy river bed; any room available. Môgaung bazaar is reached at 10 miles, ½ mile on through town to camp. Water from Môgaung river. *Note.*—During the rainy season (June to October inclusive roughly), small steamers of the Pathfinder class can run between Senbo and Môgaung, getting up in a day to a day and-a-half and returning easily in a day.

No. 90.

From SENBO to PAOLONG (Irrawaddy River) near mouth of MOSIT CHAUNG, or PÁTIN (for Bhamo).

BY LIEUT. W. H. MANNING, XII KHELAT-I-GHILZAI REGIMENT, MAY 1889.

Authorities. Military.	Authorities. Civil.	Number and Names of Stages, Rivers and Streams.	Distances. Intermediate. M. F.	Distances. Total. M. F.	Remarks.
G.O.C. Mandalay District and O.C. Bhamo.	Commissioner, Northern Division, and Deputy Commissioner, Bhamo.	**1. Camp on Thôkut chaung.** Nankán and Thôkut chaungs.	10 4	...	*Note.*—This route is only likely to be used in looking up the Kachin villages on the right bank of the Irrawaddy or possibly to get transport animals along when the defile is closed to steamers on account of floods. I expect, though that it would be easier in the latter case, now that the country is quieting down to take them *viâ* the Môlé chaung route to Ayaindama, from which there are sure to be branches to the Irrawaddy lower down at several points. Road turns south out of Senbo, passing through the villages of Pinlong and Mánlé, and at 2½ miles crossing Nankán chaung, the road then turns south-west and passes for next ½ mile through jungle, debouching on paddy plains at 3rd mile, and winds in a southerly direction across the paddy plains, passing two large villages on the right about 1 mile distant from the road. One swampy place at 4½ miles caused some delay. At 5¾ miles pass village of Mangin on left about ½ mile off the road. This village had a bamboo stockading round it At 6¼ miles cross the Thôkut chaung; bed rocky; depth about 3 feet; water good. Road now enters bamboo and tree jungle, crossing the Thôkut chaung three times up to the 8th mile. At the 8th mile the road leaves the stream and runs for ½ mile in an easterly direction, then turns south and strikes the stream again at 9th mile; from the 9th mile the road follows the course of the stream through bamboo and tree jungle, nowhere very thick, passing at 10 miles over a small hill with the remains of an old stockade on its summit. Camp is reached at 10½ miles, on the right bank of the Thôkut chaung site cramped; grass and bamboo leaves for transport animals. Water from the stream excellent and abundant.
		2. Camp below Kawan. Thôkut chaung.	6 4	17 0	The road runs up the bed of the Thôkut chaung, which varies from 6 inches to 3 feet in depth; bed rocky and full of large stones. In many places the stream passes between high precipitous banks. Camp at 6½ miles in a paddy clearing in the valley. Camp sufficient for a large force. This was a very trying march, as the bed of the stream was full of stones and very trying to the transport animals. Coarse grass for transport animals was obtainable, also water from stream.
		3. Asin ... ... Thôkut chaung.	4 4	12 4	The road for the 1st mile runs south up the valley and follows the course of the Thôkut chaung. At 1 mile the road turns west for 500 yards, crosses a small stream and then turns south again and ascends the spur of a hill, passing through thin jungle; path very steep and in many places rocky. The summit of the ridge is reached at 2 miles. At this point the road bifurcates, and the left-hand road must be taken, which descends along the side of the

FROM SENBO TO PAOLONG (IRRAWADDY RIVER) NEAR MOUTH OF MÔSIT CHAUNG, OR PÁTIN (FOR BHAMO)—*continued.*

Authorities. Military.	Authorities. Civil.	Number and Names of Stages, Rivers and Streams.	Distances. Intermediate. M.	Intermediate. F.	Total. M.	Total. F.	Remarks.
G.O.C. Mandalay District and O.C. Bhamo.	Commissioner, Northern Division, and Deputy Commissioner, Bhamo.	**3. Asin**—*cont.*					ridge for ¼ mile through paddy clearing, then ascends through thick jungle, and passes on to the summit of the ridge again at 2½ miles. The road from this point broadens and passes through scrub jungle and enters the village of Kawan at 3 miles. This village consisted of 14 houses and was not stockaded. Water found about 600 yards below the village on the west side. The road runs south out of the village and passes below the summit of the ridge for first ¼ mile through thick jungle, then ascends on to the summit of the ridge and passes through large paddy clearings as far as 4¼ miles, then enters tree jungle for last ¼ mile to the village of Asin at 4½ miles. Village consisted of six houses and was unstockaded. Camp was in a paddy clearing just before the entrance to Asin. Ample room for a small force. Water in very small quantities was found 800 yards below and to the east of the village of Asin. Bamboo leaves for transport animals.
		4. Camp on Môsit chaung. Môsit chaung.	2	2	23	6	The road passes south out of Asin and descends down a spur through thick jungle, fallen bamboos greatly obstructing the road in several places. Passing over several small muddy streams, Môsit chaung is reached at 1¾ miles; the road then follows the banks of the stream crossing it three times into camp at 2¼ miles. Camp on both banks of the Môsit chaung in a deep nullah; very cramped; a great deal of clearing required. Stream here about 6 inches deep; rocky bed; excellent water. Bamboo leaves and grass obtainable for transport animals.
		5. Paolong ... Môsit chaung.	13	2	37	0	The road ascends out of the nullah from the Môsit chaung through thick jungle up to the summit of a ridge at 1 mile and passes along the ridge through old paddy clearings now covered with bamboo and scrub jungle; it then runs along the summit of the ridge in a southerly direction for 3 miles. At the 3rd mile the road turns east and ascends through thin tree jungle to the village of Pônsi at 4 miles. This village consists of about 40 houses and is unstockaded. The road runs south out of Pônsi along the summit of a ridge through old clearings now overgrown with scrub jungle, and descends slightly. At 6½ miles the road passes through large paddy clearing in a hollow, ascends from this hollow passing over the end of a ridge at 7 miles; the road then descends slightly and passes round the face of hill with precipitous side and is cut out from the hill side, in some places being hardly 2 feet broad; exceedingly dangerous for transport animals; the path follows round the hill side for 1 mile, then passes on to a spur, and descends passing over a small stream at the foot of the spur to Môsit chaung at 9¼ miles, latter part of descent being very steep; bed of stream rocky; cross the stream and follow the left bank for next ½ mile through paddy clearing; then from 10th mile on

From SENBO to PAOLONG (Irrawaddy River) near mouth of MÔSIT CHAUNG, or PÁTIN (for Bhamo)—*continued.*

Authorities.		Number and Names of Stages, Rivers and Streams.	Distances.		Remarks.
Military.	Civil.		Inter-mediate.	Total.	
G.O.C. Mandalay District and O.C. Bhamo.	Commissioner, Northern Division, and Deputy Commissioner, Bhamo.	**5. Paolong**—*cont.*			follow the course of the stream crossing and recrossing it continually; from 12th mile pass up the bed of the stream, with precipitous bank on left side. At 13th mile, about 50 yards before the junction of the Môsit chaung with the Irrawaddy, the path leaves the stream and ascends the left bank; ascent precipitous up to a paddy clearing on the bank of the Irrawaddy, 13½ miles. Camp is in the paddy clearing about ¾ mile below the village of Paolong and is sufficient for a small force. Coarse grass for transport animals. Water from Irrawaddy. Hence to Bhamo by water. The Irrawaddy can also be reached at Pátin, a village on the right bank at the lower end of the defile, by branching off at Pônsi (*see* stage 5). Stages (1) Kaiguno (?), 10 miles; (2) Pátin, 7 miles. The first stage is not a very difficult one, though ascents and descents in parts are steep. Transport animals would take about 10 hours to do it. The villages of Kaniya and Tindaingsa are passed *en route*, both Kachin. The second stage is a very trying one for transport animals owing to the frequent steep ascents and descents. Plenty of water along the route, and course grass or bamboo for forage. No other supplies to be depended on.

No. 91.

From SHEINMAGA to SHWÉBO.

I. B. Compilation, March 1888.

Military	Civil	Stage	Intermediate	Total	Remarks
			M. F.	M. F.	
G.O.C. Mandalay District.	Commissioner, Northern Division, and Deputy Commissioner, Shwébo.	**1. Imbé**	8 0	8 0	Sheinmaga is a large village on the right bank of the Irrawaddy in the Shwébo district. Time of steaming from Mandalay in August 6½ hours. There is a good anchorage for steamers about ¼ mile south of the village. Steamers here take in salt, jaggery, cocoanuts, lime, and betel. Sheinmaga has a military police post, 50 strong, kyaungs available for troops passing through. There are six kyaungs in all, which would accommodate 300 men. Good water can be obtained from Nud stream. There are numerous tracks and foot-paths converging and diverging to avoid the water which lies across it in different places at different seasons of the year. The difficulty in finding the road without guides is to select that suited to the present season. Track is good for baggage animals and fair for carts in dry season. Much under water in places during rains, but always practicable for carts. Leaving Sheinmaga through water-worn defile road ascends to higher ground. Flat country, covered with low scrub jungle of prickly bushes, which could be ridden through almost anywhere. At 5 miles a track branches north-east to Sinain, leaving the small villages of Zanbinyaung and Bowenda. From this the most direct foot-path to Imbé leads across cultivation. Imbé is a small village of about 35 houses. Water good from tank 50 yards square.

FROM SHEINMAGA TO SHWÉBO—*continued.*

Authorities. Military.	Authorities. Civil.	Number and Names of Stages, Rivers and Streams.	Distances. Inter-mediate. M. F.	Distances. Total. M. F.	Remarks.
G.O.C. Mandalay District.	Commissioner, Northern Division, and Deputy Commissioner, Shwébo.	**1. Imbé**—*cont.*			There are also two wells, but these have brackish taste, accounted for by the amount of salt in the ground, which is extracted in the neighbourhood at numerous workings. Ground to west and south-west of villages marshy. One large and two small zayáts east; 60 men. One kyaung and two zayáts ½ mile north; would hold (kyaung) 50 men, (zayáts) 20 men. Cattle in abundance of good quality. Paddy, maize, and grass of fair quality procurable.
		2. Heléngyi ...	12 0	20 0	The road from Imbé to Thayain is north-north-west, for the most part through jungle which has been cleared to a breadth of 10 yards. First ½ mile through paddy when road enters open scrub jungle, passing the kyaung above mentioned enclosed by trees and thick fenced just east of the road. At 2 miles palm trees commence among the scrub jungle. At 4 miles thick jungle begins, which continues till ¼ mile from Thayain 5½ miles. At 3 miles the village of Thayain is passed, 500 yards west in the jungle. The road is very good over sandy soil and could be used by carts at all seasons. In the dry season Heléngyi can be reached at 5½ miles from Thayaing by a straight road across the paddy-fields, passing Nyaungbindwin just east of Heléngyi lake at 2 miles. In the rainy season carts follow the above road for 1 mile, then along a road north-east to Mathi at 3 miles, then north-west to Heléngyi *viâ* Sadaungyi. The latter road reaches Heléngyi at 6½ miles from Thayain, but is over high ground. Practicable for carts at all seasons. At Nyaungbindwin there is good water, and accommodation could be obtained for 40 men in kyaung north-east of village. Heléngyi is a straggling town of 250 houses. Salt abounds in the neighbourhood. There are three hot-springs of high temperature, the hand can scarcely be held in them. They emit a strong sulphurous smell. Good drinking water from one well north and from streams. Accommodation, 150 men, in two deserted kyaungs south of village; for 60 men in one south-east; 100 men in several scattered zayáts. Supplies as at Imbé with addition of rice.
		3. Shwébo ...	13 0	33 0	Road on. General direction north-west. Character as before. It crosses head of swampy ground north-west of town, and after gradual ascent reaches higher ground, from which an extensive view is obtained, and on which there is an old pagoda and zayát. At 1½ miles the road passes over open grass plain, sparsely covered with bushes and trees. At 3½ miles pass a small zayát and tank of fair water, although covered with green leaves. A track leaves south-west. Cross Múgalé stream running north to south at 6 miles. Here about 20 yards wide; current sluggish; bottom sandy; banks vary. The stream completely overflows its banks during rains; only a few inches water in April; said to join Múgalé river

FROM SHEINMAGA TO SHWÉBO—*continued.*

Authorities. Military.	Authorities. Civil.	Number and Names of Stages, Rivers and Streams.	Distances. Intermediate.	Distances. Total.	Remarks.
G.O.C. Mandalay District.	Commissioner, Northern Division, and Deputy Commissioner, Shwébo.	**3. Shwébo**—*cont.*			at Thayé, flowing through lake. Thitkynobin 7 miles, a small village of about 35 houses, situated on both banks of Múgalé stream. Water from stream good. Supplies as at Imoé, but less plentiful. Accommodation, one small zayát west bank, two east bank for 40 men. Road on, general direction north-north-west, along top of an embankment close to and parallel to which runs the Múgalé stream. Here little more than a ditch at this season. Bottom muddy, bank low with long grass. The embankment is said to date from the time of Alaungpaya, and to have been made to regulate the irrigation of the surrounding country. It is pierced in many places by well-built masonry sluices, evidently of ancient date, as they are unbridged. The track makes a detour at each. Tagondain, a village of about 30 houses. The Múgalé stream here has been practically diverted south for paddy cultivation. Two wooden bridges cross the Múgalé for foot-passengers or ponies in single file only. Of use during rains. The track leaves the embankment and goes west across open country. Flat; paddy; and a small stream of clear water with sandy bottom, about ½ mile to Shwébo. In the rainy season the direct road from Helėngyi to Shwébo is impracticable for carts. At that time the road used is north to Ôr.bok, 11 miles, and west to Shwébo 8½ miles—total 19½ miles. The ancient city of Shwébo, Môntsobo, or Yadana Thinga, by all of which names it is known, was formerly the capital of Burma in the time of Alaungpaya. It is surrounded by the remains of the old wall now much ruined and no great obstacle to an assault. In many places it is of great thickness. Its extent is about 1,700 by 1,500 yards. A small wooden erection near the remains of the site of the old palace, which latter is marked by some grass-grown ruins at the north-west extremity, is shown as the tomb of the celebrated king "Alaungpaya" (corrupted Alompra). The town, now consisting of 1,000 houses, occupies the north-east corner only of the space enclosed by the old city walls. There are three large and numerous small pagodas and several monasteries inside the walls, also an enclosure with several monasteries about ¼ mile outside the north-east gate, in which are three wells of good water. Supplies are plentiful (as before) with addition of rice and vegetables. Two hundred carts procurable in a day.

BRANCH I.

FROM HELÉNGYI (STAGE 2) TO YWATHIT (*see* ROUTE NO. 34).

BY LIEUT. T. W. B. MEADE, 3RD CAVALRY, HYDERABAD CONTINGENT, JANUARY 1887.

Military	Civil	Stages	Intermediate M.	Intermediate F.	Total M.	Total F.	Remarks
G.O.C. Mandalay District.	Commissioner, Northern Division, and Deputy Commissioner, Shwébo.	**1. Ywathit** ... Irrawaddy.	**12**	**4**	12	4	First 3½ miles through paddy cultivation, would be bad in wet weather, passing village of Matégyi at 3 miles. Thence over open down-like country, grass and small shrubs. Last 4 miles through low hills with thorn trees scattered about. Good fair weather cart road throughout, and except between Heléngyi and Matégyi, good going for cavalry. A little water in a nullah at 6½ miles.

No. 92.

From SHWÉBO to MALÉ.

By Lieut. HUGHES, 2nd Oxfordshire Light Infantry, April 1888.

Authorities. Military.	Authorities. Civil.	Number and Names of Stages, Rivers and Streams.	Distances. Intermediate. M. F.	Distances. Total. M. F.	Remarks.
G.O.C. Mandalay District.	Commissioner, Northern Division, and Deputy Commissioner, Shwébo.	**1. Yetha**	**11 4**	11 4	The road leaves Shwébo stockade by the north and follows the moat north till reaching the military police stockade, here it turns north-north-west leaving the police stockade on the left and keeps in that direction through thin scrub jungle to **Péktaw** at 5 miles. At 1¼ miles cross the **Múgalé** river dry in March, about 40 yards between banks which are 20 feet high. This place would probably be impassable during the rains when the Kyaukmyaung road would have to be followed till the bridge over the Múgalé river is passed, then turning northwards by a track meeting this one at 1½ miles. The road gradually rises till a zayát and tank (dry in March) are reached. From this point, which is about 40 feet higher than Shwébo, a good view of that town can be obtained, and the country for some distance all round. Road now descends slightly. At 3¼ miles one zayát for eight men. Here the road for 100 yards runs through paddy. Paddy again for 100 yards at 4 miles. At 4½ miles the road is slightly banked up, about 2 feet, with paddy on either side. Péktaw at 5 miles has 15 houses surrounded by paddy. Two kyaungs would hold 100 men, two zayáts 40 men. Good stabling for 30 ponies under one kyaung. Water clear, but of a muddy taste from two wells. One tank with muddy water in March. At Péktaw the inhabitants reported that road to Shwébo was impassable for carts during the worst of the rains. Road on due north to Nyaungôn at 9 miles, good for carts in dry season, very bad in rains, when carts use a longer route to the east of this, passing through Ngawmaw and Sudát to Kallalu. Road for ¾ mile through paddy, then thin jungle to the east and paddy west. At 6½ miles pass kyaung 200 yards east in a clearing in the jungle; would hold 50 men; one zayát for 20 men. Water in well from paddy-field west of road. At 8¼ miles cross a small nullah and enter paddy cultivation. The nullah has water standing in pools, and good camping ground could be found in the vicinity. From here there is a view of Nyaungôn and Wéaungôn, a mile to the east of it. Road through paddy to Wéaungôn at 9 miles. About 50 houses on slight rise of ground. Paddy south-east and west. Low ridge of hills covered with jungle to the north, running east and west. One kyaung east, 50 men, three zayáts 40 men, one kyaung in village 40 men, one zayát 15 men. Water good from one well, brackish from two. Road on north-north-east to Yetha at 11½ miles, good for carts at all seasons through open jungle and some dry cultivation, rising about 20 feet in the 1st mile. Yetha has 130 houses enclosed by thorn fence, 500 yards east to west; 200 yards north to south. Paddy cultivation south and west, jungle north and east. Good camping ground between the village and paddy-fields on the south side. Then jungle comes close up to the village at the north-east corner. Two kyaungs south for 60 men and one zayát for 20 men. One kyaung north-east corner 30 men and three zayáts for 40 men. Good water from five wells, and water for animals from chaung running ½ mile west of village. (Road east to Tama, road west to Kyúgán, for Kinu and Letpánhla on the Shwébo-Tántabin roads.)

FROM SHWÉBO TO MALÉ—*continued.*

Authorities. Military.	Authorities. Civil.	Number and Names of Stages, Rivers and Streams.	Distances. Intermediate. M.	Distances. Intermediate. F.	Distances. Total. M.	Distances. Total. F.	Remarks.
G.O.C. Mandalay District.	Commissioner, Northern Division, and Deputy Commissioner, Shwébo.	**2. Saingaung** ...	12	0	23	4	Road leaves by the north-west corner. General direction north, as far as Kallalu. First ½ mile through paddy. This might be avoided in the rains by taking a road by the jungle to the east road on through penetrable jungle and some dry cultivation to Yézin at 4 miles. At ¾ mile pass a kyaung west of the road, for 30 men, and four zayáts for 70 men. At 1⅛ miles cross a road, which is being cut through the jungle from Kinu on the Shwébo-Tántabin road to Kyibun and Kabwet on the Irrawaddy. Yézin at 4 miles has 100 houses, 600 yards from north to south, 100 yards east to west. Open paddy to south-east and west; jungle and dry cultivation close up to the village on the north. Cross a nullah bridged for carts in the centre of the village. One kyaung north with bamboo stockade for 50 men and two zayáts for 30 men. One zayát for eight men just outside on the road. Water very good from three wells. Water for animals from a chaung to the west of village. (From here there is a road east to Kungyi, whence roads branch to Mán and Kyibun on the Irrawaddy.) Road on 2¾ miles through young tree forest with no undergrowth to Sélwin at 6¾ miles. Traces of petrified wood continually on the road. From Sélwin the road turns north-west to Kallalu at 7½ miles. Through open jungle, 50 houses, paddy to the east, dense jungle on other sides. Police station south with bamboo stockade; strength 20 men. When the barracks are finished there will be accommodation for 20 more men. Water good from wells. (From here there was reported a road east to Yé-u *viâ* Nyaungán, Pindin, Sibautya. Pindin is about 3 miles east of the Shwébo-Tántabin road, also a road north-west to Tántabin *viâ* Aléshu.) From Kallalu there are two routes to Malé, one north-north-east to Yaukdain, 1 daing, then a path north to Kyátyé on the Tántabin-Malé road, 4 daings. Carts cannot go to Kyátyé, but could if the jungle was cleared. By this route Malé could be reached at 27½ miles from Kallalu, but the part from Kallalu to Kyátyé is from native information, and the distance appears under-estimated. The other road runs north-east to Saingaung at 12 miles, for ¼ mile through paddy, the remainder through forest and jungle for the most part bamboo. At 3 miles from Kallalu a road branches north to Yaukdain. Cross two nullahs. One at 9½ miles, one at 11½ miles, both would be impassable for cart some hours after heavy rains. They are dry in March. Saingaung, 12 miles, has 40 houses. Paddy to the east, jungle close up to the village on either sides. One kyaung, 300 yards north-east, for 30 men with one zayát for 10 men. Another kyaung 400 yards east for 20 men. Water good from three wells. This stage, Yetha to Saingaung, is very good for carts during the dry season and would be fair for carts during the rains. Another road to Saingaung was reported by the Thugyi of Yetha. It leaves the road reported above at Yézin and passes through Nadwingyi to the east. Yézin to Nadwingyi 2 daings, Nadwingyi to Saingaung, 1¼ daings—total 3¼. Taking this as 8 miles it would be the same distance as *viâ* Kallalu. If a direct road were cut from Yézin to Saingaung, it would be 6½ miles only.

FROM SHWÉBO TO MALÉ—*continued.*

Authorities. Military.	Authorities. Civil.	Number and Names of Stages, Rivers and Streams.	Distances. Intermediate. M. F.	Distances. Total. M. F.	Remarks.
G.O.C. Mandalay District.	Commissioner, Northern Division, and Deputy Commissioner, Shwébo.	**3. Mézataw** ... Mutha chaung.	**13 0**	36 4	In the next stage there is no road for carts further than Sabetchaung. Sabetchaung is reached at 4 miles by the path reported here, but carts go by a circuitous route to the south. General direction Saingaung to Mézataw north-east. Footpath ½ mile through paddy to Ôkmyingôn, a small village on the edge of the jungle. From Ôkmyingôn to within 1 mile of Mézataw the path is entirely through jungle and forests over the Myinwun range of hills bordering the Irrawaddy. The path winds a good deal to avoid the steep slopes. There would be a fair road for carts if the jungle were cleared. The path joins cart track at several places used by bamboo cutters, but there is at present no cart road the whole way to Mézataw. The forest trees vary a good deal, consisting of bamboo and different sorts of varnish trees, and other large trees not made use of by the Burmans. Traces of petrified wood throughout. At 2½ miles cross a nullah, sandy bottom, impassable for some hours after heavy rain. At 4 miles cross a stip of disused paddy. Sabetchaung village is ¼ mile south of this, deserted. Water scarce in dry season. Cross a large nullah at 4½ miles, sandy bottom, would be impassable after heavy rain. In the vicinity of this nullah the path was a good deal blocked by fallen bamboo, and baggage mules were slightly delayed. At 10 miles the path begins to descend gradually along a spur of hill, from which a view of the country east and south-east is occasionally obtained, apparently entirely covered with forest. At 12 miles a view of Mézataw is obtained about 1½ miles distant north-north-east of this point in the valley below, the Mútha chaung about 200 yards from the foot of the hill running in a south-east direction towards the Irrawaddy. There is some paddy cultivation to be seen near Mézataw and here and there along the course of the Mútha chaung, but the rest of the valley appears covered with forest and jungle to the Irrawaddy. The path descends the hill; at one place crossing a ridge of solid rock about 8 yards. Mules descended easily. This bit is very steep and would have to be considerably improved for carts, unless an easier descent could be found down one of the valleys north or south; 200 yards further cross the Mútha chaung, about 30 yards broad, with sandy bottom, dry in February. Water can be got by digging 1 foot deep, 1¼ miles on over level ground through open jungle to Mézataw. Twenty houses. Paddy south and east, jungle cleared north and west. Accommodation for 30 men in two small bamboo kyaungs and 10 men in one zayát. Water good from two wells. This last stage is not used by carts, but the civil authorities at Malé reported that a road was about to be cut from Mézataw to Saingaung through the jungle.
		4. Malé	**7 4**	44 0	**The next stage Mézataw to Malé is good for carts in the dry season, and practicable for carts at all times except at Chaungyi stream for some hours after heavy rain. Road north-north-east to Pasi through jungle over level ground, sometimes cleared for paddy. Pasi, 3 miles, is a village on the Malé-Tántabin**

FROM SHWÉBO TO MALÉ—*continued.*

Authorities. Military.	Authorities. Civil.	Number and Names of Stages, Rivers and Streams.	Distances. Intermediate.	Distances. Total.	Remarks.
G.O.C. Mandalay District.	Commissioner, Northern Division, and Deputy Commissioner, Shwébo.	**4. Malé**—*cont.*			road. It has 20 houses at South Pazi and 50 at North Pazi, $\frac{1}{4}$ mile north. One kyaung at South Pazi would hold 30 men, two zayáts at North Pazi 20 men. Water good from two wells and water from tank in rains. From Pazi the road runs nearly east to Malé at $7\frac{1}{2}$ miles, for $2\frac{1}{2}$ miles over flat ground through cleared jungle, remainder over hills. Cross nullahs at $3\frac{1}{2}$ and $4\frac{1}{2}$ miles. Cross Chaungu stream twice at the foot of the hills, the second time running north-east to the Irrawaddy. Water standing in places in March about 30 yards between high banks. A zayát on either side of second crossing about 12 men in each. Road winds on east over hills. There are three steep places on these hills where the slope is about $\frac{1}{10}$ for 40 yards, and the road much worn away by action of the water in rains. The country carts seem to make no difficulty of these places. *See* Route No. 49.

No. 93.

From SHWÉBO to WUNTHO.

I. B. COMPILATION, NOVEMBER 1888.

Military	Civil	Stages	Intermediate M.	Intermediate F.	Total M.	Total F.	Remarks
G.O.C. Mandalay District.	Commissioner, Northern Division, and Deputy Commissioner, Shwébo.	**1. Kinu** ... ... Múgalé or Mu bund.	**15**	**2**	15	2	Good cart road from Shwébo to Tántabin following generally the Mu bund (irrigation work). At 3 miles from Tántabin, it branches off north-east to that place. Leaving the Shwébo stockade the route lies through part of the city and emerges by the northern gate; then skirting the bund of the Mahánánda lake it strikes the great irrigation bund which runs in a south-south-east direction from near Myédu on the north to below Thitkyobin on the south. Passing small hamlets of Padukaw, Magyubaw, Mígyaumbé, the country alternating between low scrub jungle and rice cultivation. Sitha is reached at 6 miles; small village of some 20 houses; noticeable for a stone caravanserai built by King Thîbaw's father, pucka built and about 90 feet in length. The road continues along the side of the bund, which is, however, broken in several places. The country is flat with open scrub jungle, except where there is rice cultivation. A slight rise on to sandy soil some $5\frac{1}{8}$ miles on, where a shallow stream is crossed, when, after $1\frac{1}{8}$ miles of open country covered with rice cultivation, Lepánhla is reached, $11\frac{1}{8}$ miles. Here there is commodious kyaungs with accommodation for 150 men. Good water and supplies are procurable. Kinu, $3\frac{3}{4}$ miles further on through alternate scrub and paddy-fields, is the next village *en route*. It is a large and well-to-do place; good grass obtainable for animals; good well; fair amount of supplies of all kinds. Two hundred houses fenced in with thorns. Good kyaungs to the south-east of the village, and a capacious one on the north-east angle with a wall round it, which would make a good post and give shelter to a large convoy. Kinu has a military police post; strength 14; accommodation for 200 men in kyaungs. There is extensive rice cultivation round the village.

FROM SHWÉBO TO WUNTHO—*continued.*

Authorities.		Number and Names of Stages, Rivers and Streams.	Distances.				Remarks.
Military.	Civil.		Intermediate.		Total.		
			M.	F.	M.	F.	
G.O.C. Mandalay District.	Commissioner, Northern Division, and Deputy Commissioner, Shwébo.	**2. Wayaba Kyaung.**	**12**	**4**	27	6	Road still follows Mu bund at 4 miles, Thayetkán, small village with kyaung adjacent. Road crosses shallow sandy stream and through an open country to Pauktaw, 5 miles; small village; fine shady trees; good water. Madônhla, 6½ miles; fair-sized village of about 50 houses; fenced; good water; supplies limited; good kyaung north of village. Nedhwin at 8¾ miles. Road still follows the bund through alternate paddy and open scrub jungle, and cavalry could work anywhere over the country between here and Shwébo. From Nedhwin the road follows the line of the bund to Wayaba kyaung, 12½ miles. Good kyaungs here and plenty of water. Former site of village of Tada-u close by. The road to Tántabin leaves the line of the *bund* about ½ a mile beyond Nedhwin and strikes off north-east over cultivation to Tántabin, passing the hamlet of Letpángôn at ¾ mile on. Bidakôn at 10¼ miles. A creek with thick fringe of jungle at 11 miles (shallow water running south-west with steep banks 30 feet broad, good bottom), then past Einma hamlet at 11 miles, and over cultivation to Tántabin. Tántabin has 130 houses enclosed by a thorn fence surrounded on all sides by paddy cultivation, and cavalry can work freely to the north, south and west for some miles, and on the east some 3 miles where light jungle is met with. There are two stockades south of the village, the one further south having a ditch and parapet as well as bamboo stockade. The latter is occupied by military police, part of the other is taken up by the Myo-ôk of the township and civil offices. There is plenty of room for 200 more men in these stockades (1888), and good stabling for 100 horses and 50 ponies. Four kyaungs in the vicinity would accommodate 150 men, and one zayát at the kyaung east of the village would hold 30 men. Good water from one well between the two stockades and from three wells in the village. Water for animals from tanks throughout the year. Tántabin is the head-quarters of the northern sub-division of the Shwébo district. From here roads run to Malé and Yé-u, and a good cart track connects it with Wayaba kyaung, distance 3 miles, crossing the Múgalé at Tada-u, 2¾ miles.
		3. Tabayen ...	**13**	**0**	40	6	The road as far as Tabayen is good for carts in the dry season, but difficult in the rains, when a great part of it is under water. The same may be said of the road from Tabayen to Tôkoshát, though it is somewhat better than the first part. A metalled road will be made by the Public Works Department along the irrigation bund in a few years. From Wayaba road follows Mu *bund* northwards as far as Magaw, 6 miles, passing Kyinbigôn at 3¾ miles. There is one broad sandy nullah to cross about a mile south of Magaw, after crossing which the road runs through a patch of dense jungle to Magaw. Opposite Magaw it bears off north-west, passing close to the village of Nyaungzin, which lies to the left on an alternative route to Tántabin *viâ* Ngárané and Thabiyetha, joining this road at Wayaba. It is probably a little shorter, but more difficult in wet weather, as it is over paddy all the way. At 9½ miles cross wide sandy nullah and at 10 miles reach deserted village-site of Tabayen;

FROM SHWÉBO TO WUNTHO—*continued.*

Authorities.		Number and Names of Stages, Rivers and Streams.	Distances.		Remarks.
Military.	Civil.		Intermediate.	Total.	
G.O.C. Mandalay District.	Commissioner, Northern Division, and Deputy Commissioner, Shwébo.	**3. Tabayen**—*cont.*			ruined kyaung and zayát affording no accommodation. Well, but water probably unsafe, as the well is probably seldom if ever drawn from now.* Tabayen is about 3 miles south-west of Kawthandi, through which place a cart track runs from Myédu to Pyinzain and Yé-u (*q.v.*), also to Nwabeitgyi, crossing the Mu river about 2 miles above Kawthandi to the village on Kyunlé (or Kyundé). River fordable between November and June.† Cross a nullah at Kyinbigôn 3¾ miles further. Cross a wide stream, which is troublesome in the rains for carts. Road proceeds by the side of the bund in a northerly direction. Magaw at 9 miles. Leaving the bund at Magaw the road passes through paddy-fields and light jungle. Crosses another difficult nullah close to the halting place at Tabayen; at 13 miles there is one old kyaung and three dilapidated zayáts. Water from one well and the nullah. Accommodation for 100 men in kyaung, 30 men in zayáts.
		4. Tôkoshát ...	M. 11 F. 0	M. 51 F. 6	Road on through paddy-fields across two small nullahs to Ôkpo at 2 miles; a village of 30 houses with one kyaung. Road on in a north-west direction over open ground and paddy-fields crossing the Ngaka chaung at Môgyibyit; at Gyôgya, ½ mile to the west of the road, there is a kyaung and zayáts. From Gyôgya a good cart track runs to the Mu river meeting the Kawthandi-Myédu road about ½ a mile south of the village of Mogaung on the left bank of the Mu river, opposite to and slightly above Kyunlé. Reach Kywendaw at 5 miles. Reach Imbetaw at 6 miles. About ¼ mile beyond Imbetaw a broad nullah, impassable after a heavy shower of rain, has to be crossed; ½ mile of paddy-fields to bund. A mile to the west Pagándaw is seen in a grove of toddy palms. From the bund a newly cut straight road has been cleared through teak and bamboo jungle which extends up to the stockade. Tôkoshát stockade is situated on a ridge which has been cleared of jungle for 200 yards all round amidst groves of teak, tamarind and palms, bounded on the east and south by bamboo jungle, on the west by groves of palm and tamarind, on the north by rice fields, beyond which, at 250 yards distance on another ridge. The village of Tôkoshát is situated among magnificent tamarind and palm trees. To the east of the stockade is a tank, and to the east of the fields another large tank called the "Lotus tank." There are five wells, four of which have very little water in the dry weather, when an abundant supply can be procured by digging a couple of feet in the sandy bed of a creek ½ mile distant. The water, though generally good and wholesome, is during the hot weather so impregnated with minerals as to cause slow-healing ulcers. Petrified timber is found in abundance. There are 200 houses in the village. The

* At present (February 1890) Tôkoshát is given up as a post in favour of Myédu, and the villages on the Tabayen-Tôkoshát road having been moved under the Village Act, the route now followed in going to Tôkoshát is *viâ* Kawthandi and Myédu. From Tabayen to Kawthandi, 3 miles, police post and accommodation for 200 men in kyaungs; thence to Myédu, 10 miles; paddy all the way.

† The Mu Valley Railway passes close to Nyaungzin and Tabayen, crossing the road herein described between those places. It then runs *viâ* Ôkpo northwards, so that probably the villages along the Tabayen-Tôkoshát route will soon be re-occupied and the route from village to village re-opened.

FROM SHWEBO TO WUNTHO—*continued.*

Authorities. Military.	Authorities. Civil.	Number and Names of Stages, Rivers and Streams.	Distances. Inter-mediate. M.	F.	Distances. Total. M.	F.	Remarks.
G.O.C. Mandalay District.	Commissioner, Northern Division, and Deputy Commissioner, Shwébo.	**4. Tôkoshát**—*cont.*					military police post is ¼ mile south. Accommodation for 200 men besides in kyaungs on the south-east edge of the village.
		5. Létu	9	4	61	2	Good cart road through bamboo jungle. Reach Shédaung at 3½ miles surrounded by paddy-fields. Road on through country too thick for cavalry to work in, but not so thick for infantry that flankers could not be used. Reach Kambalu at 6 miles. Water from wells. Fair cart road, and the country is open, consisting of large and small teak and varnish trees. Reach Létu at 9½ miles. About 200 yards from the village there is a creek, but with no water in February. There is a kyaung near the creek which would hold 150 men. Water can be obtained by digging in the creek.
		6. Pégôn	9	0	70	2	Fair cart road and the country open with small teak trees. Ingyinzu at 2¼ miles. One good kyaung. Road on through fairly open country to the Gádandé creek, which is crossed at 5¼ miles. The crossing is easy, though there is a little water in February. In the vicinity of the creek the road passes through very thick jungle, reach Yethi at 6 miles. Fair cart road on through country open with paddy-fields, and not very thick jungle. One good kyaung at Tháyabin at 6¾ miles. Very good road on. The country is open with small teak trees. Reach Pégôn at 9 miles. One kyaung and two zayáts for about 150 men. There is a creek near Pégôn which goes round two sides of the village, about 200 yards from the kyaung. From Pégôn there is a branch track to Baw (*see* Route No. 3) about 30 miles, passing the villages of Tháyabin, Kyágôn and Sadwingyi.
		7. Thábiyedaw ...	11	4	81	6	Road good and jungle light as before. Bamboo occasionally thick, but no difficulty for moving flankers. The cart road crosses the Pégôn creek close to that place and is easy, about 1 foot of water, but the foot track crosses same creek immediately south of Magyigôn, 3½ miles, where the banks are 20 to 30 feet high and very steep, breadth of creek about 60 feet. Road on good through light jungle. At Pyaungdaw (9 miles) water is obtained in dry season by digging in creek. Has been a good deal of cultivation. Deserted in 1887. No kyaungs. Road on good through light jungle for 1 mile, thence through paddy-fields to Thábiyedaw at 11½ miles; deserted in 1887; three kyaungs and one zayát. Water from wells and tank. Good grass. Road on good through paddy cultivation for ½ mile with light jungle about 1 mile distant on each side. Pass a deserted village. From here to Taik at 2¼ miles the road is good through bamboo jungle.
	Commissioner, Northern Division, and Deputy Commissioner, Katha.	**8. Ukingyi** ...	7	0	88	6	Road on good to Ságyin at 3½ miles. From Ságyin there is a fair cart road through open forest and grass land with occasional bits of bamboo jungle to Thinauktu, 8¼ miles distant south-west. Road through waste land (*i. e.*, fallow paddy-fields); some light jungle. Over 100 cattle and plenty of

FROM SHWÉBO TO WUNTHO—*continued.*

Authorities. Military.	Authorities. Civil.	Number and Names of Stages, Rivers and Streams.	Distances. Intermediate. M. F.	Distances. Total. M. F.	Remarks.
G.O.C. Mandalay District.	Commissioner, Northern Division, and Deputy Commissioner, Katha.	**8. Ukingyi**—*cont.*			paddy and fowls. One small kyaung, one zayát, 70 or 80 houses, deserted; bad accommodation for 100 men. (At a point 1 mile south of Ságyin a cart road branches west to Hluttaik.) Road on good through bamboo jungle to Ukingyi at 7 miles. Bad accommodation for 100 men in kyaungs. Accommodation for 50 men in all at the stockade. One well with good water. Water is scarce in the dry season. The village of Maungbôn lies about 5 miles east by south from Ukingyi, a small village in dense jungle.
		9. Kyungôn ...	12 2	101 0	Good cart road on through paddy. Reach Pônnagyi at 1¼ miles; jungle 1 mile off; on either side tank, very good water. Cultivation going on; would get 300 or 400 baskets of paddy; 30 cattle, plenty of fowls, 25 houses, no kyaungs or zayáts. Road through paddy-fields uncultivated; jungle about ½ mile off; road easy for carts. Reach Kángyi at 3 miles; no kyaungs or zayáts. Good road through bamboo jungle and uncultivated paddy-fields. Cross the Zaw chaung at 5½ miles with 6 inches of water in February. This used to be the boundary between the Pyinzala and Kawlin districts. Thendaw at 6¾ miles. Water from wells. No kyaungs or zayáts. Road on good through uncultivated paddy-fields for 3½ miles, with jungle ½ mile off on either side. Pass Pazé at 9 miles, Yathit at 10 miles; no accommodation. Road on through open light jungle passing Maithelingôn at 10¾ miles. Reach Kyungôn at 12¼ miles. Can supply 300,000 or 400,000 baskets; large quantity of paddy up here. Good water in abundance from wells. One kyaung, two zayáts, 40 houses, accommodation for 150 men.
		10. Kawlin ...	8 4	109 4	From Kyungôn to Kawlin the road is good through light jungle till crossing Daungyu creek at 4 miles. From here a view of Kawlin can be obtained and the road runs for the remaining distance through paddy cultivation. Pass Kodumbaw at ½ mile. Pass Chikai at 3¼ miles. From this place there is a route to Kyaukpintha, 11 miles, general direction north-east, passing through the villages of Kathékôn (3 miles), Letpánkyo (3½), Sittaw (4½) and Chaungwé (9). Good cart track throughout, and kyaungs at all the above-named villages. No large streams to cross. No accommodation. Daungyu creek has a deep sandy bottom with light bamboo jungle on the banks. Boats use this creek in the rains. Pass Nyaungwun at 4½ miles. One good kyaung. Pass Zezôngôn at 5½ miles, Théyakôn at 6¼ miles, Nyaungbintha at 6¾ miles, Maingôn at 7¾ miles. Reach Kawlin at 8½ miles. Accommodation in seven kyaungs for 400 men. (From Ukingyi to Kawlin there is an alternative route about 7 miles longer than that described above along a line to the east, reported on by Colonel Atkins, 1st Bengal Infantry. The stages would be Singyidain 6½ miles, Kyaukpintha 10¾ miles, Kawlin 11½ miles. A good deal of thick jungle is traversed by this road, and the last stage from Kyaukpintha is very bad after rains.) The country to the south and west of the knoll, on which the stockade is built, is completely open; on the north-west, about 500 yards away, is a wooded hill which command it. On north front

FROM SHWÉBO TO WUNTHO—*continued.*

Authorities. Military.	Authorities. Civil.	Number and Names of Stages, Rivers and Streams.	Distances. Intermediate.	Distances. Total.	Remarks.
G.O.C. Mandalay District.	Commissioner, Northern Division, and Deputy Commissioner, Katha.	**10. Kawlin**—*cont.*			lies a large tank 200 by 500 yards with a bund on east and south sides. A ruined kyaung and several stone pagodas between tank and stockade partially obstruct fire on the north-east, and east. The open plain stretches away for miles. On the south-east is the village close to the stockade. Accommodation. Inside the stockade are six excellent buildings, capable of holding from 150 to 200 men at a pinch; stabling for four horses on the east side; within the walls 50 horses can be picketed, but have no shelter. Water: A pucka well stands 100 yards south of the place and has good water; another pucka well the same distance to the north rear edge of tank, and two others reported in village with good water. Animals can be supplied from the tank and a good watering place constructed there easily. A small muddy stream, the Mwélánseik, 350 yards to east, is fit for horses. The Daungyu river is some 3 miles distant to the east. From Kawlin there is a good cart track to Kyaukpaya (7 miles) *viâ* Saingôn (4 miles), Kaingôn (4½) and Maithelingôn (6). Kyaukpaya, which is at the mouth of a narrow gorge running westward into the hills, is on the road from Wuntho to Pinlebu *viâ* Wéhla. There are gold washings about here, and at Kudaung, 13 miles south by west of Kawlin, the villagers obtain copper and iron.
		11. Wuntho ... Daungyi chaung.	M. 9 F. 2	M. 118 F. 6	The general direction from Kawlin to Wuntho is north, slightly tending to east at times. The road is a cart track running through paddy-field and offers no difficulty to the passage of all arms except at the ford on the Daungyi chaung at Chaungzôn and on the track between Zibyubin and Chaungzôn, where only a narrow path runs through a light jungle. Fords: There are two fords in the Daungyi river and several other apparently practicable fords. The ford at Chaungzôn (meeting of the rivers) has a steep and narrow approach on the left bank and on entering the river a sharp turn down stream is necessary to avoid deep water. Impracticable for guns and carts and difficult for cavalry. The other ford near Gwégyi has easy approaches, 18 inches or 2 feet of water, and a stony bottom. Country: The route lies through a flat level valley, some 2 miles broad at Wuntho, narrower at Ôkpo, and an open plain many miles in extent between the hills at Kawlin. The whole valley is highly cultivated with paddy and round the villages with garden produce. There is much wood on the hills, but except between Gwégyi and Pégôn the country is free of it to any extent. In the valley there is but little jungle. Villages *en route.* (1) Kégégôn: A large village to the east of the direct road surrounded by thorn hedges. One well noticed at south end outside village; 30 houses. (2) Thita: Between this place and Yédwingôn runs a shallow muddy stream, a couple of feet broad (the Zayát chaung), which forms the boundary line between the Wuntho and Kawlin districts; unstockaded. (3) Pégôn and Yédwingôn: Some excellent zayáts here. Pégôn was attacked on the 15th or 16th January 1887 by dacoits and is deserted. Yédwingôn burnt and deserted. (4) Ôkpo: Unstockaded and deserted. (5) Zibyubin; seven houses; unstockaded, and Gwégyi, a larger village with good gardens round it. (6) Chaungzôn

FROM SHWÉBO TO WUNTHO—*continued.*

Authorities. Military.	Authorities. Civil.	Number and Names of Stages, Rivers and Streams.	Distances. Intermediate.	Distances. Total.	Remarks.
G.O.C. Mandalay District.	Commissioner, Northern Division, and Deputy Commissioner, Katha.	**11. Wuntho**—*cont.*			at the junction of the Daungyu and Nanlaing rivers; 14 houses; unstockaded and deserted. (7) Magyigôn and Zígôn: Two small villages of about 15 houses. Excellent water from the Daungyu at Magyigôn and a good ford; very slightly stockaded. Wuntho-Myoma contains about 300 houses, and more than 1,000 men were accommodated in the kyaungs during the occupation of the town. Wuntho could supply 200 carts with bullocks and 50 with buffaloes after a few days' notice. The town is strongly stockaded; teak stockade incompleted on west face; good water from Daungyu river.

BRANCH I.

FROM TÁNTABIN (*see* STAGE 2) TO TÔKTALÔK.

BY LIEUT. R. HUGHES, 2ND OXFORDSHIRE LIGHT INFANTRY, MARCH 1888.

Military	Civil	Stages	Intermediate M. F.	Total M. F.	Remarks
G.O.C. Mandalay District.	Commissioner, Northern Division, and Deputy Commissioner, Shwébo.	**1. Tôktalôk** ... Múgalé and Mu river.	**13 0**	13 0	General direction north-north-west. Road good for carts in dry season; difficult in rains; at first over paddy with trees and bushes on the bunds obstructing view for any great distance; after Miyénet through more open country. Pass Yédwingôn and Wayinzu, two small villages of about 10 houses each, at 1½ miles. Here there is a tank east of the road with water standing in March about 400 yards by 200 yards, about 4 feet deep at the bund. Pass Thádaw at 2½ miles with a kyaung and zayát east of the village. Here the irrigation bund is crossed just beyond the village. Stream dry in March except for water in pools in some places. Thabiyéba (3¾ miles); 40 houses. One kyaung south (20 men). Water from two wells and one tank north, with water in March. Gyimkakôn (4½ miles). Almost deserted. One kyaung for 40 men. Two zayáts for 20 men. Reach Miyénet at 6½ miles. One zayát for 15 men. The Miyénet chaung, which runs along the north side of the village, is crossed here (30 yards broad with sandy bottom); dry in March, but would be impassable for some hours after heavy rain. Water is obtained in the dry season by digging holes in the bed of the chaung. Three and-a-half miles further on the Kenyen chaung is reached with the villages of Kanyu and Kôkdaw on either bank (about 10 houses in each). The chaung is about 40 yards broad with sandy bottom, now dry except for pools in places. Water can be obtained by digging down a few feet. No accommodation. At 11 miles pass Eingutyi (40 houses). At 13 miles cross the Mu river (30 yards wide, 18 inches of water) which is the boundary between the Shwébo and the Yéu districts and between the Northern and Central divisions, and reach Tôktalôk, 80 houses. A station of the Bombay Burma Trading Corporation. There is good accommodation for 10 men at an empty bungalow at south-east corner of village. There is ample camping ground south of the village. Good water from wells and river Mu. The village is surrounded by a double bamboo stockade, well laid out and kept very clean. More accommodation could be found ¾ mile south-south-west of the village in one kyaung for 50 men; and six zayáts for 90 men, approached by a foot-bridge over the Sipadaung

FROM SHWÉBO TO WUNTHO—*continued.*

BRANCH I—*continued.*

Authorities. Military.	Authorities. Civil.	Number and Names of Stages, Rivers and Streams.	Distances. Intermediate.	Distances. Total.	Remarks.
G.O.C. Mandalay District.	Commr., Northern Divn., & Dy. Com., Shwébo.	**1. Tôktalôk**—*cont.*			chaung. These kyaungs are surrounded on the south and west by tall tree jungle and stand on the right bank of the Sipadaung chaung flowing south-east to the Mu. The place is much enclosed and looks unhealthy, the chaung here having about 2 feet of stagnant water in March.

No. 94.

From SINGU (NGA SINGU) (on Irrawaddy River) to BERNARDMYO viâ MALÉGALÉ and KINYWA.

BY H. C. HILL, ESQ., FOREST DEPARTMENT, MAY 1888.

Military	Civil	Stages	Intermediate M.	Intermediate F.	Total M.	Total F.	Remarks
G.O.C. Mandalay District.	Commissioner, Northern Division, and Deputy Commissioner, Mandalay.	**1. Kyunbingyi** ... Malégyi chaung. Broad gravelly bed, low banks up to Náttaung, but from there they gradually become higher. There is probably about 4 feet of water in the stream in flood, but in May just a trickle of water in it.	14	4	...		Road easy and good for pack animals. Passable also for carts. Covered by baggage elephants in 5½ hours. First 4½ miles or so through fallow land and paddy-fields with occasional patches of grass and forest. At 2½ miles pass village of Kyobin (25 houses); at 3½ Kyaukdaing, at 4 miles Wayôngán (the two last named have together about 25 to 30 houses). From a little beyond the last named village, the road passes through level forest-covered country up to Náttaung (small village on right bank of Malégyi chaung, 9½ miles), whence it follows the course of the Malégyi chaung up a narrow valley with parallel ranges, steep and densely wooded on either side. Mayingin (20 houses) on right bank of stream, which is crossed and recrossed, is reached at 10 miles. Letpadé at 10½ miles, Shan village of 15 houses, on left bank of stream which is crossed just after leaving Mayingin and Kyunbingyi at 14½ (20 houses) on right bank of stream, which is recrossed just before reaching it.
		2. Camp on Letpet chaung. Malégyi, Wabo, and Letpet chaungs, hill streams, perennial, gravelly beds.	10	0	24	4	For first 3 miles road still follows Malégyi chaung, crossing it now and again. Then steep ascent for about a mile, rising about 1,000 feet, to crest of main ridge between Irrawaddy and Maddaya rivers (4 miles). From the crest the road is easy for 1½ miles running through "indaing" forest over gentle slopes to the old village site of Nahat (deserted), 5½ miles. A small streamlet crosses the road here. From Nahat the road is a hill path with no serious rises or descents. At 7 miles cross the Wabo chaung, perennial stream, running water, 10 feet broad, 6 inches deep in May and at 10 miles the Letpet chaung. The descent to the latter is rather steep but short. Camp on chaung. No village. Water only in pools in the stream.

From SINGU (NGA SINGU) (on Irrawaddy River) to BERNARDMYO *viâ* MALÉGALÉ and KINYWA—*continued.*

Authorities. Military.	Authorities. Civil.	Number and Names of Stages, Rivers and Streams.	Distances. Inter-mediate.	Distances. Total.	Remarks.
			M. F.	M. F.	
G.O.C. Mandalay District.	Commissioner, Northern Division, and Deputy Commissioner, Ruby Mines.	**3. Malégalé** ... Letpet, Paya, Theinni, and Malégalé chaungs.	9 0	33 4	After crossing the Letpet chaung the road ascends past the old village site of Letpet and in 3 miles the water-shed of the Paya chaung is reached. From this the road descends the valley of the Paya chaung for 2 miles, then turning northward over a shoulder for a mile, strikes the main Theinni chaung at 6 miles. This stream higher up in its course flows past Kyauklebin on the main road from Thabeitkyin to Môgôk. The road thence follows the course of this chaung for 1¼ miles and then that of the Malégalé stream, an affluent of it, for 1¾ miles, reaching the village of Malégalé at 9 miles. The village is a prosperous one of 10 to 15 houses situated in an open space where there is a considerable quantity of paddy cultivation. The ascent for the first 3 miles and the descent to the Paya chaung are the only difficult bits. The elevation of Malégalé is probably about 1,600 feet. Forest mostly "indaing." Great quantities of bamboo ("Wábo") all about. The Paya chaung valley is one mass of *pônzôks* (*i.e.*, abandoned taungyas), and a herd of wild elephants was heard trumpeting and seen breaking down the bamboos ½ a mile from the road.
		4. Kinywa ... Nantôn, Nanpán, Thitsibin, Kyaukpyu chaungs, hill streams.	12 0	45 4	At about 2 miles reach Nantôn * (deserted), situated close to the junction of the Nantôn and Nanpán chaungs. Thence steep ascent difficult for laden elephants to Pinbaung (deserted) about 4 miles. Here there is a very little water in a ravine east of and 200 feet below the ridge. From Pinbaung the ascent to the Miginsindaung ridge is about the same in distance and height as that from the Nantôn chaung to Pinbaung, but the road is better and the ascent more uniform and easy. From the summit † (about 8 miles), there is a steep descent with bad road for about a mile to the valley of the Thitsibin chaung. Along this there is a good path past the village of Thitsibin (8¾ miles) and up the Kyaukpyu chaung valley to the cart road (9½ miles). There are some boggy places which, in the rains and early part of the cold weather, would be difficult to cross, but in May they present no difficulty.

* From here a track is said to run to Môgôk *viâ* Gwébin as follows. It runs east about 3 daings to a Palaung village called Kyauktôngyi containing about 50 houses and situated on a small stream. From here the road still good runs to the Shan village of Laingthin of about 15 houses on a large stream called the Kin chaung. From here the road runs 2 daings east to another Palaung village of about 20 houses called Pôyauk. Water from a small stream on the hill. From here Gwébin on the Bernardmyo road is distant about 1 daing.

† *N.B.*—From here a pack track to Kyátpyen (Native information) as follows:—

	DAINGS.
Pinzánzo	1
Namakán	1
Kin chaung	1
Nayôkywa	1
Gwébin	½
Kyátpyen	1½
Total ...	6 daings, about 15 miles.

FROM SINGU (NGA SINGU) (ON IRRAWADDY RIVER) TO BERNARDMYO *viâ* MALÉGALÉ AND KINYWA—*continued.*

Authorities.		Number and Names of Stages, Rivers and Streams.	Distances.				Remarks.
Military.	Civil.		Inter-mediate.		Total.		
			M.	F.	M.	F.	
G.O.C. Mandalay District.	Commr., Northern Divn., and Dy. Commr., Ruby Mines.	**5. Rest-house at upper end of Kabain valley.**	12	4	58	0	*Vide* Route No. 78, Thabeitkyin to Bernardmyo.
		6. Bernardmyo ...	14	4	72	4	

No. 95.

From SINGU (NGA SINGU) to MAINGLÔN (MAINLUNG) *viâ* MALÉGYI.

BY LIEUT. E. W. M. NORIE, INTELLIGENCE BRANCH, FROM NATIVE INFORMATION, JULY 1888.

Military	Civil	Stages	Inter. M.	Inter. F.	Total M.	Total F.	Remarks
G.O.C. Mandalay District.	Commissioner, Northern Division, and Deputy Commissioner, Mandalay.	**1. Malégyi** ...	8	0	8	0	*Vide* Route No. 96, Singu to Nungé.
		2. Ma-úbin ...	...		...		From Malégyi the track runs east to the deserted village of Ma-úbin about 3 daings. Water from a spring.
		3. Camp on Nga chaung. Nga chaung (left bank tributary of the Maddaya river).	...		...		The path now runs east apparently up the Nga chaung over the Papaw hills, and then cross the Ômun chaung at 5 daings.
	Superintendent, Northern Shan States.	**4. Chainyaung** ... Ômun chaung (?) left bank tributary of the Maddaya river.	...		...		From here it runs along the bank of the chaung to Kyainyaung village. This is a Shan village of about 20 houses. Water from the chaung, which is said to be a good large stream with water in it all the year round. It runs into the Subogyi creek (? Maddaya river). The Shans sleep one night on a chaung between Ma-úbin and Kyainyaung. This part of the road has been newly cleared and made.* It is only practicable for baggage animals.
		5. Namkao ...	...		...		From Kyainyaung the road runs east to Namkao, a Shan village of about 15 houses. This is one day's journey. Water is obtained from the Namkao stream, not very big, but good, and has got water in it all the year round.
		6. Tawza ...	...		...		From Namkao the road runs through jungle, one day's journey, to Tawza village. This is a Shan village of about 15 houses on a small stream.

* This requires confirmation.

FROM SINGU (NGA SINGU) TO MAINGLÔN (MAINLUNG) *viâ* MALÉGYI—*continued.*

Authorities. Military.	Authorities. Civil.	Number and Names of Stages, Rivers and Streams.	Distances. Intermediate.	Distances. Total.	Remarks.
			M. F.	M. F.	
G.O.C. Mandalay District.	Superintendent, Northern Shan States.	**7. Camp** ... **8. Mainglôn (Mainlung).**	...	...	From Tawza Mainglôn or Mainlung is reached on the second day. There are no more villages along the road, but there are halting places and water is plentiful. Marches probably 3 or 4 daings equals 7 to 10 miles.

No. 96.

From SINGU (NGA SINGU) to NUNG-É (on Maddaya River above Zagabin) viâ MALÉGYI.

BY LIEUT. E. W. M. NORIE, INTELLIGENCE BRANCH, JULY 1888.

Military	Civil	Stage	Intermediate	Total	Remarks
G.O.C. Mandalay District.	Commissioner, Northern Division, and Deputy Commissioner, Mandalay.	**1. Malégyi** ...	8 0	8 0	The road runs in an east-north-east direction and is a cart road the whole way. Leaving Singu on the east it runs across paddy land for about ½ a mile to the small village of Kyaungnaywa, containing about 10 houses and surrounded by a thorn hedge. Immediately beyond is a creek formed by the overflow of the Irrawaddy and crossed by a wooden foot-bridge. The cart road leads through the water which is at present too deep to be fordable. Beyond it the road again leads across paddy for about ¼ of a mile, when it is again interrupted by a second overflow, which inundates the country for a breadth of more than ½ a mile. Here there is at present about 4½ feet of water in the road. The natives get across by leaving the road and wading through the marsh and jungle at the side where the water is apparently less deep. There seems to be very little current. In the dry weather, when the river falls, the road is quite practicable for carts. On the eastern side of the overflow there are two small zayáts, and the road ascending slightly is firm and sandy and leads through tree and bamboo jungle. A short distance beyond pass the village of Téu, containing about 20 houses, surrounded by a thorn hedge. Water from a well in the middle of the village. From here the road running in the same direction, through jungle, passes the village of Kyauktát at about 3 miles; village of about 15 houses to the south of the road. Water from a well under a large peepul tree close to the road. At 3½ miles pass the village of Wayungôn on the road, containing about 15 houses. Kyaungs and zayáts to the south of the village capable of containing about 120 men. Water from a well in the enclosure. The road firm and dry as before. About ½ a mile beyond the village (4 miles), a road branches off to the north-east leading to Pyinlégyi. Further on the road, still good, takes a bend to the south-east and then again resumes its former direction east-north-east, running across open ground, at present uncultivated, and at about 5½ miles passes the village of Shwébandaw to the south of the road.

FROM SINGU (NGA SINGU) TO NUNG-É (ON MADDAYA RIVER ABOVE ZAGABIN) *viâ* MALÉGYI—*continued.*

Authorities. Military	Authorities. Civil.	Number and Names of Stages, Rivers and Streams.	Distances. Intermediate. M. F.	Distances. Total. M. F.	Remarks.
G.O.C. Mandalay District.	Commissioner, Northern Division, and Deputy Commissioner, Mandalay.	**1. Malégyi**—*cont.*			Kyaungs. Water from wells. Shwébandaw is situated on the right bank of the Malégyi chaung, at present (July) quite dry. Bed of stream sandy and about 80 yards broad. Banks steep, about 8 or 10 feet high. The road leads across the chaung and immediately beyond crosses a road running north and south from Pyinlégyi to Nyaungôn. This is a broad sandy cart road. From here the road runs on in the same direction through open bamboo jungle and cultivation, and afterwards through an open stretch of country, at present uncultivated, till it reaches Malégyi about 8 miles. Malégyi is situated close to the foot of the hills and is a village of about 50 houses. It contains a post of Burman police, surrounded by a breast work, pallisade and spiked ditch. Water from a well in the enclosure. To the south-east of the village is a pagoda on the top of a small steep hill, which forms the end of a long low spur running out from the higher range. The approach to the pagoda is paved and a good view is obtained from the platform.
		2. Ubiyégalé ...	15 0	23 0	From Malégyi the road runs east about ½ daing to the deserted village of Kôkôaing. Here it splits into two. One road leaving Kôkôaing runs south-east for about 3 daings to Ngwéobaw. Ngwéobaw comprises two villages, the lower village Ngwégalé is said to be situated on the Malégyi chaung. From here the road runs to the upper village of Ngwégyi, which is ½ a daing to the east on the hill. The inhabitants were mostly Shans. A pretty good road leads from here west to Nyaungôn. Ngwéobaw hill is locally reported to yield rubies of very superior quality From Ngwégyi the path runs east to the Shan village of Ubiyégalé, about 1½, total 5½, daings. The track is very steep up and down hill through thick bamboo and tree jungle, and so bad that baggage animals can scarcely get along it. Ubiyégalé is situated on the top of the ridge. At Ubiyégalé the road from Maddaya and Yenatha joins in (*see* Route No. 55).
		3. Nung-é	7 0	30 0	From Ubiyégalé the track runs downhill to the east and reaches the Shan village of Dandin at 4 miles. Water from a stream (*see* Route No. 55, Branch I). Here the track splits into three—one path leads north-east about 1½ daings to Nung-é, the second east about 1½ daings to Ledawywa, and the third south-east about 2 daings to Gwégyaung. All these three villages are situated on the Kaingyaung creek (Maddaya river), were inhabited by Shans, and are at present deserted (*see* Route No. 50, Branch I). The northern road runs east from Kôkôaing for about 2½ daings to the deserted Shan village of Ma-ubin on the hills, whence a jungle path runs south to Nung-é on the Kaingyaung creek (Maddaya river) about 6 daings from Ma-ubin. Very bad going, steep and rough. From Nung-é a path runs to Kaingyi on the Mandalay-Mainglôn-Môgôk road. (*See* Route No. 50, Branch I).

No. 97.

From SIPEIN to LWÉBYINÔK *viâ* NAMLAW and LWÉWAIN.

By Major GREENAWAY, 6th Madras Infantry, February 1890.

Authorities. Military.	Authorities. Civil.	Number and Names of Stages, Rivers and Streams.	Distances. Intermediate. M.	F.	Distances. Total. M.	F.	Remarks.
G.O.C. Mandalay District.	Commissioner, Northern Division, and Deputy Commissioner, Ruby Mines.	**1. Namlaw** ... One stream crossed several times.	14	0	14	0	Road level and good, running south-east through low grass jungle to 6½ miles. Then through bamboo jungle. A stream is crossed at 8 and again at 10 miles, and again four times just before reaching Namlaw through which it runs. At 10 miles pass Nawpa (deserted). Namlaw is a small Kachin village of five houses, situated in a ravine surrounded by hills except on the north-west.
		2. Mônhôn ...	6	4	20	4	Road runs south-east up a fairly steep spur to 2 miles. At this point a path branches off and runs along the crest of an undulating ridge in an east-north-east direction to Lwékin 2½ miles, consisting of two Kachin villages, one on the ridge, the other ¼ mile down the south slope. Water is scanty, but good. The main path for Lwéwain follows the hill crest. From here on it is only a track 1 foot broad cut in the precipitous hill side. At 4⅝ miles the road turns up steep hill side, and is very difficult for transport animals for ½ mile. Mônhôn is a Kachin village of 10 houses. Water scanty and indifferent from wells 300 yards down-hill.
		3. Lwéwain ...	8	4	29	0	The road continues along the ridge line running west. Taungya is crossed at 1 mile. Kônka, Kachin village of six houses, at 3½ miles. Water from wells indifferent. The road runs south-west along the crest line. It is good and easy for pack animals. At first for ½ mile it ascends steeply to Lônsa, a Kachin village of nine houses. Thence it descends to 1 mile, and at 3 miles pass Yému, a Kachin village of 15 houses. From here an indifferent road runs down-hill to the Shwéli, distant 2 miles.
		4. Lwébyinôk ...	7	0	36	0	General direction of the road south-west. Good and fairly level to ½ mile. Here is the Kachin village of Kawlaw. From this point a road runs south to Ekkyi on the Shwéli river, distant 2 miles. The road on is a jungle path to 5 miles and follows generally the crest of a ridge and is undulating. Here is the village of Kônmawan (Kachin), 14 houses. Water from two wells, muddy and indifferent. On to Lwébyinôk the road is fairly good. It descends 900 feet in the next 1¼ miles, and thence ascends 400 feet to the Kachin village of Lwébyinôk, crossing the road Sipein to Mômeik *viâ* Kyungyaung and Môlo (*vide* Route No. 98), between stages 1 and 2, just before reaching Lwébyinôk. Water from one well at some distance. Mátaw is 8 miles along the ridge in a westerly direction.

FROM SIPEIN TO LWÉBYINÔK *viâ* NAMLAW AND LWÉWAIN—*continued.*

BRANCH I.

FROM LWÉWAIN (STAGE 3) TO KYUNGYAUNG (*see* ROUTE NO. 98).

BY MAJOR GREENAWAY, 6TH MADRAS INFANTRY, FEBRUARY 1890.

Authorities.		Number and Names of Stages, Rivers and Streams.	Distances.				Remarks.
Military.	Civil.		Intermediate.		Total.		
			M.	F.	M.	F.	
G.O.C. Mandalay District.	Commissioner, Northern Division, and Deputy Commissioner, Ruby Mines.	**1. Kyungyaung** ...	**8**	**4**	8	4	The road runs south-west for ½ mile along the Kawlaw road, and then branches off north-west and descends steadily to 2 miles. Here the plain is reached. The road runs in the level through bamboo and tree jungle, and is a fair track to 6 miles, where it joins a cart track coming from the south, and follows this for the rest of the way. At 2½ miles a small stream is crossed twice and immediately after pass Sunpat, a small Shan-Burmese village stockaded. Kyungyaung is a stockaded village (Shan Burmese) of 30 houses on the banks of the Nampán chaung, from which the water-supply is plentiful.

No. 98.

From SIPEIN to MÔMEIK viâ KYUNGYAUNG and MÔLO.

BY MAJOR HOBDAY, SURVEY OF INDIA, FEBRUARY 1890.

Military	Civil	Stages	Int. M.	Int. F.	Total M.	Total F.	Remarks
G.O.C. Mandalay District.	Commissioner, Northern Division, and Deputy Commissioner, Ruby Mines.	**1. Kyungyaung** ... Nampán chaung.	**12**	**0**	12	0	Broad level road in good condition throughout. Road runs south-west for first 8½ miles to Simpégyi on the Nampaw chaung, the first 4 through grass jungle, remainder bamboo and tree. The direction of the route for the last 3½ miles is west. Kyungyaung is a stockaded Shan-Burmese village of 30 houses on the banks of the Nampán chaung, whence there is a plentiful water-supply. From Kyungyaung there is a road to Lwéwain, 8½ miles. *See* Route No. 97, Branch I.
		2. Wégyi ... ... Shwéli river.	**11**	**4**	23	4	Road runs south through tree jungle and is good. Pumwán, a small Kachin village at the foot of the Shwéli range, at 4 miles. The road now commences to ascend at once over the hills. It is somewhat steep, running along the beds of nullahs. The crest of the pass is 1,400 feet above the Shwéli, and this pass is much easier and lower than that between Ekkyi and Kawlaw. Naungpaung is the site of a deserted village on the right bank of the Shwéli at 11 miles. Crossing here is easy and banks roomy. After crossing the Shwéli the road runs along the left bank for ½ mile to Wégyi. A large Burman village stockaded with kyaung, 11½ miles.

FROM SIPEIN TO MÔMEIK *viâ* KYUNGYAUNG AND MÔLO—*continued.*

Authorities. Military.	Authorities. Civil.	Number and Names of Stages, Rivers and Streams.	Distances. Intermediate. M.	F.	Total. M.	F.	Remarks.
G.O.C. Mandalay District.	Commissioner, Northern Division, and Deputy Commissioner, Ruby Mines.	**3. Nayôk**	**6**	**4**	30	0	Road level and good in dry weather, running at first through paddy-fields and then through bamboo jungle. Nayôk is a Shan-Burmese village of 12 houses on the left bank of the Shwéli. There are no boats here.
		4. Paungadaw (camp).	**12**	**0**	42	0	Road good and level throughout, running through bamboo jungle. Water plentiful all along the road from hill streams. A forest clearing used as a camping ground.
		5. Mômeik ... Nameit chaung.	**13**	**4**	55	4	Road as before to 11½ miles and thence through open grass jungle. Two hill ridges, 600 feet and 700 feet high, are crossed at 2 and 8 miles respectively, the ascents and descents being easy. The Nameit chaung is crossed just before entering Mômeik. Fifty yards wide and 2½ feet deep. Mômeik, a large town, capital of the Mômeik State and residence of the Sawbwa.

No. 99.

From SI-U (Route No. 19) to TUKU (Route No. 17, Stage 6).

BY D. W. RAE, ESQ., BURMA POLICE, FEBRUARY 1892.

Military.	Civil.	Stages.	Intermediate. M.	F.	Total. M.	F.	Remarks.
G.O.C. Mandalay District and O.C. Bhamo.	Commissioner, Northern Division, and Deputy Commissioner, Bhamo.	**1. Kanni**	**13**	**4**	13	4	Si-u to Namkán, 3¾ miles, *see* Route No. 19, Branch IX, Namkán to Peswé, 6¼, and thence to Kanni, 3¼, *see* Route No. 19, Branch VIII.
		2. Makyaingkatawng. Lapé stream.	**10**	**2**	23	6	Kanni to Khagyin, 1½ miles, *see* Route No. 19, Branch VIII, Stage 1, thence Sakhángyi, 2¼, *see* Route No. 19, Stage 4. From Sakhángyi onwards, very good going all the way. General direction east-north-east, crossing Lapé stream twice, and passing village of Nanleik. Good camping ground, and plenty of water at Makyaingkatawng, 10¼ miles.
		3. Lwélôn	**5**	**0**	28	6	Cross Nanleik stream ¼ mile from camp and at ¾ mile pass through village of Hwésu. Road so far due east, but now turns north-east and ascends gradually to Ngapyuywa and Lwélôn. Camping ground and water sufficient only for a small column; about 3 hours' march.

FROM SI-U (ROUTE No. 19) TO TUKU (ROUTE No. 17, STAGE 6)—*continued.*

Authorities. Military.	Authorities. Civil.	Number and Names of Stages, Rivers and Streams.	Distances. Intermediate. M. F.	Distances. Total. M. F.	Remarks.
G.O.C. Mandalay District and O.C. Bhamo.	Commissioner, Northern Division, and Deputy Commissioner, Bhamo.	**4. Pángtán** ... Kanong and Katán streams, both very small with about 8 inches of water.	10 0	38 6	Road follows small ridge due north for about ½ mile, then turns south-east and passing Maleikatawng at 1 mile drops into the Kanong stream at 1¾ miles, ascending gradually thence to Kimbren. As far as this the road is rather rough, but greatly improves after leaving last-mentioned village, and changes its course to due east along a ridge, passes to the left or north of Lwékam and drops into the Katán Ka. Ascends another good ridge, continues along it for about 3 miles and passes through Pángtán. Camping ground fair and water sufficient at this time of year; about 4 hours' march.
		5. Namsa ... ... Mora, Yunman, Namkông, Miyong, Shi-yit and Namgaik streams; all of which streams flow into the Nanhu or Nahu chaung.	6 0	44 6	Road takes a due easterly course along barren undulating ground and through small paddy-fields in hollow formed by the innumerable hillocks, and at every mile crosses one of the streams mentioned in column 5. These are in the order they were crossed. Nos. 1. 3, and 6 are about from 6 to 10 yards wide and contain a considerable volume of water with a depth of between 1 and 2 feet; the other three streams are small and insignificant. Camping ground good and water sufficient; about 3 hours' march.
		6. Kasháng ... Namsa, Kapra, and Kamut streams.	7 0	51 6	Road north-east, crosses Namsa stream at ½ mile; ½ mile further passes through village of Walánkatawng, continues in same direction for ¾ mile and crosses the Kapra stream 1¼ miles; and at 2¼ miles the Kamut Ka, and at 3¼ miles passes through village of Kwéinkyeng-atawng, then goes in the same direction for about 2 miles, then turns west for ½ mile and arrives at camp Kasháng, 7 miles. Country for greater portion undulating and fairly open, patches of thick kaing jungle occurring at intervals. Camping ground good, and water sufficient.
		7. Wabawgát ... Katát and Kashán streams.	6 0	57 6	Left 7-30 A.M., arrived Wabawgát at about 10 A.M. Direction due north for 1st mile, crosses Katát stream at ½ mile, and passes village of Sinbwé-kakyan at 1 mile, then turns north-west, and at 2 miles crosses Kashán stream and at 3½ miles passes through village of Khashánku and here strikes the main caravan route from Bhamo to Nankán, follows it more or less due west for a mile, and reaches Wabawgát at 6 miles. Camping ground is just outside the village on north side of road and fairly good. Water is obtained from small stream south of road in a hollow.

FROM SI-U (ROUTE No. 19) TO TUKU (ROUTE No. 17, STAGE 6)—*continued.*

Authorities. Military.	Authorities. Civil.	Number and Names of Stages, Rivers and Streams.	Distances. Intermediate. M.	F.	Distances. Total. M.	F.	Remarks.
G.O.C. Mandalay District and O.C. Bhamo.	Commr., Northern Divn., and Deputy Commr., Bhamo.	**8. Tuku** ... ... Kapra and Kashán streams.	**8**	**0**	60	4	Caravan route is followed north-west for 3 miles along a very good ridge to Hôma; thence direction east-north-east. Road drops into Kapra stream, then ascends rather steeply to Tuku and descends again into the Kashán Ka. Water very good; likewise camping ground.

No. 100.

From TÁLAWGYI to KÁZU.

BY CAPT. G. H. H. COUCHMAN, D.S.O., SOMERSETSHIRE LIGHT INFANTRY, FEBRUARY 1892.

Authorities. Military.	Authorities. Civil.	Number and Names of Stages, Rivers and Streams.	Distances. Intermediate. M.	F.	Distances. Total. M.	F.	Remarks.
G.O.C. Mandalay District and O.C. Bhamo.	Commissioner, Northern Division, and Deputy Commissioner, Bhamo.	**1. Tungut** ... ... 'Nshut Ka and four smaller streams.	**11**	**0**	11	0	General direction north-east. The road at first goes along the Namsáng road (Route No. 21, Stage 12), but turns off a little north about 2 miles short of the hills. From here it enters dense tree, grass, bamboo and cane jungle, with occasional plantain trees, four small streams with very little water, and then over a larger stream called the 'Nshut Ka, which has a rocky bed, 10 yards broad, but has now only 3 feet width of water at the crossing. Water good. From here the road begins to ascend, at first gradually, then very steep, then again an easy ascent, and afterwards again a steep ascent to where it joins the big road from Kraokra. The ascent is about 1½ miles and up about 1,300 feet. The road now is good and broad, right up to the village of Tungut, distant about another ½ mile. Total 11 miles. All this road is good and has no obstacles, though two of the streams are a little muddy. At Tungut camp in village. Fodder and bamboos scarce. Water from a well just north of village, good, but not plentiful; also from a small stream, but not much.
		2. Nawbu ... ... Kamut and several smaller streams and Nam Mali.	**7**	**4**	18	4	From here the general direction of the road is east by a little north. The road descends from the village through tree jungle at first steeply and then very steeply over stones and loose soil. The road then descends into some taungyas, and then into some tree jungle where it crosses the Kamut Ka, 8 yards broad, 1 foot deep, rocky bed, good water, easy crossing. The road now goes along the valley of the Kamut through cane, bamboo, and tree jungle, and again crosses the Kamut, and in the next ½ mile three other small streams, each about 6 feet wide, with stony and muddy beds and about 6 inches of water. It now ascends very steeply, and is a little overgrown till at 3½ miles it comes to the junction with the Nawku (Kachin) road which branches off to the left, a small stream is crossed just before. It then ascends easily for ½ mile when it joins a large open and good road from Saré, which it follows. Jungle, bamboos, small tree, and good

FROM TÁLAWGYI TO KÁZU—*continued.*

Authorities. Military.	Authorities. Civil.	Number and Names of Stages, Rivers and Streams.	Distances. Intermediate.	Distances. Total.	Remarks.
G.O.C. Mandalay District and O.C. Bhamo.	Commissioner, Northern Division, and Deputy Commissioner, Bhamo.	**2. Nawbu**—*cont.*			fodder grass. A ¼ mile further on there is a road to the left to Nampowé, and the road now descends for a mile to a muddy stream, 9 feet broad, with little water, but mud, 1½ feet deep. Another rocky nullah 4 feet broad, with very little water, and that in pools, is crossed. From here the road enters into kaing grass, and crosses a deep dry nullah, with a little mud in it. The ascents and descents are steep, banks being 25 feet high. The actual bed is only 4 to 5 yards broad. After 2¼ miles the Mali Ka (Nam Mali) is reached. There is a descent of 25 feet, and then a level piece for about 50 yards into the stream, which is about 35 yards broad, 2½ feet deep, with sandy bottom, good water, current 1 mile an hour. The right bank is a little muddy. The village of Nawbu is about 200 yards up the right bank, stockaded, and has about 12 Shan houses. There is a large paddy-plain here, and excellent fodder grass, and a good camping ground for a large force.
		3. Kásu ... ... Mali, Tabak and several other smaller streams.	M. F. 11 0	M. F. 29 4	From here the road goes along paddy-fields for 1 mile and then through kaing grass and scattered trees for 2 miles to the village of Beinbin, which is at 3 miles on the right bank of the Nam Mali, the bank here being 25 feet high. Road to here good, but would be boggy in the rains. Half-a-mile further on the road crosses a dry nullah, and then goes over gently undulating ground into Manlin at 5¼ miles where there is good camping ground, water and fodder. Jungle, grass, and bamboos. Road good. From here the road passes for ½ mile through paddy-fields, and then crosses a muddy stream, 15 feet broad and 1 foot deep, which is no obstacle, and then ascends easily into bamboo jungle, and crosses another small muddy and stagnant stream 3 feet broad, with only a few inches of water. For ½ mile it now ascends, at first steeply and then more easily, and then descends with occasional ascents down to a small muddy and stagnant stream, 3 feet broad and ½ foot deep, ascending again steeply for 100 yards and then descending easily. At 8 miles it crosses a muddy and stagnant stream, 4 feet broad and a few inches of water, and then passes into kaing grass. Another similar stream is crossed at 8¼ miles, and shortly afterwards the road enters some taungyas along which it goes for ½ mile when it crosses a stream, 3 feet wide and 6 inches deep, ascending up a steep sandy bank into tree and bamboo jungle, and afterwards more taungyas. It then passes along the left bank of the Tabak Ka (Nántabet chaung) for ¼ mile, reaching the village of Kásu at 11 miles. Cross the river, which is here 5 feet deep with a bed of 100 yards (present width of water, 60 yards); water good; current 1 mile per hour, passable for big boats; has occasional rocks in the stream; sandy and gravelly bottom; sandy banks, 20 feet high, covered with bamboo, grass, and small tree jungle; high water mark 8 feet above present bund. Camp ½ mile down the right bank in an open clearing. Water from river. Grass and bamboos plentiful. This is an easy march with no obstacles. River is crossed by bamboo rafts. Kázu is an important place in that the routes from Tálawgyi, Waingmaw, Maingmaw, and Sadôn joining together, run on to the Maingla and Sanda districts *viâ* Laipong and Kao-i (*see* Route No. 29).

No. 101.

From TÁNTABIN to KAWLIN *viâ* BAW, UKINGYI and KYAUKPINTHA.

I. B. COMPILATION, 1887-88.

Authorities. Military.	Authorities. Civil.	Number and Names of Stages, Rivers and Streams.	Distances. Intermediate. M.	F.	Distances. Total. M.	F.	Remarks.
G.O.C. Mandalay District.	Commissioner, Northern Division, and Deputy Commissioner, Shwébo.	**1. Kángyi**	11	0	11	0	Road runs in north-east direction, and is for the first 6 miles very good through paddy-fields and open light scrub. After leaving the village of Sudát the jungle becomes very thick, but the road remains fair. Camp consists of one kyaung and one zayát capable of holding 50 and 20 men respectively. Water-supply bad, from a tank near camp, which is in thick jungle.
		2. Sabénetha ... Several nullahs.	15	0	26	0	The road is almost entirely through the densest bamboo jungle. The country is undulating and several nullahs have to be crossed. The road is exceedingly difficult for carts. No place to camp. Water-supply from nullah in rear of the village.
		3. Hlwéseik ... Several nullahs.	8	0	34	0	Cart track through dense jungle, bamboo, &c. *See* Route No. 48.
	Commissioner, Northern Division, and Deputy Commissioner, Katha.	**4. Baw**	9	0	43	0	For details *see* Route No. 48.
		5. Zin	7	4	50	4	
		6. Ukingyi ...	12	4	63	0	
		7. Singyidain ...	6	4	69	4	General direction north-east up to Kyaukpintha. Good cart road, except for a ¼ mile in one place. Tinmu, at 1¼ miles, a large inhabited village of about 50 or 60 houses, stockaded, but no kyaung. So far jungle light, but for a mile beyond Tinmu, road runs through close bamboo and teak (probably bastard) jungle, and is bad for carts. At 1 mile from Tinmu cross broad creek (or chaung), with steep banks and a few inches deep running water. It is passable by carts without ramping, though difficult. After crossing creek jungle becomes less thick. Pass two or three deserted villages, and at 6½ miles from Ukingyi reach Singyidain, a village of about 40 houses, now deserted. One small wooden kyaung in fair condition. Water fair.
		8. Kyaukpintha ...	10	6	87	2	Road good for carts through open teak jungle for first 5 miles passing two deserted villages, then across paddy-field to Zibyugôn 6¼ miles, which comprises two villages called East and West Zibyugôn, consisting of 15 houses each and situated on either side of the road. Immediately north of the village is a low hill with a kyaung built on the summit. No other kyaungs at Zibyugôn. Good drinking water. Good cart road passing through bamboo jungle in the 1st mile, thence through open paddy country with numerous villages on both sides of the road up to Kyaukpintha, crossing the Sinlin

FROM TÁNTABIN TO KAWLIN *viâ* BAW, UKINGYI AND KYAUKPINTHA—*continued.*

Authorities. Military.	Authorities. Civil.	Number and Names of Stages, Rivers and Streams.	Distances. Inter-mediate.	Distances. Total.	Remarks.
G.O.C. Mandalay District.	Commissioner, Northern Division, and Deputy Commissioner, Katha.	**8. Kyaukpintha—** *cont.*			creek, 1 foot deep, about 1½ miles south of the town. Kyaukpintha is a strongly stockaded village, about 180 yards long by 60 broad. Within this stockade there are some 50 houses, and close around it there are five or six smaller villages. To the east of the stockade is a large ruined wooden kyaung; about 200 yards west of the village is a low hill, whence Kyaukpintha is completely commanded. The headman is intelligent, and from the amount of cultivation and the fact that there are several good wood-built houses, the people appear to be most prosperous. On the hill to the west there is a small bamboo kyaung and several zayáts in bad repair. The water at Kyaukpintha is plentiful and of fair quality. Direction of road north-east. There are kyaungs and water at Thégán, Pégôn and Ywashé, all villages on or close to the road between Zibyugôn and Kyaukpintha.
			M. F.	M. F.	
		9. Kawlin	11 4	98 6	Road passable for carts in dry weather, but bad, and in wet weather impassable. For about 1 mile, that is, up to the village of Tubinthla, the road crosses paddy cultivation, then enters light teak jungle. At 3 miles pass village of Taungyi, and ½ mile further Endainbôn. For the next mile jungle is dense, and at 5 miles cross the Daungyu river, banks steep, bottom sound, water 2½ to 3 feet deep. After crossing the river pass through high kaing grass for ½ a mile or so, and thence to Kawlin over clayey, marshy ground, part cultivated, part swamp; distance 11 to 11½ miles. General direction west-north-west, passing the small villages of Myaungyi, Tát, and Saindu at 5¼, 7 and 8 miles respectively. This route from Ukingyi to Kawlin is not to be compared to Route No. 93 *viâ* Kyungôn. Under the most favourable circumstances it is more difficult and it is longer. Up to Kyaukpintha it is a fair fair-weather cart road, though between Ukingyi and Tinmu there are several swampy bits even in the dry season, which in wet weather would be impassable. From Kyaukpintha to Kawlin the road is at the best of times bad, and even a shower of rain renders it almost impassable. The jungle is generally free from undergrowth and consists chiefly of teak and bamboo. Population, except immediately around Kyaukpintha, sparse, and little to be had in the way of cattle or other supplies.

No. 102.

From TÁNTABIN to PÉGÔN (Route No. 93, Stage 6) viâ GÁDA.

BY LIEUT. MACSWINEY, 3rd CAVALRY, HYDERABAD CONTINGENT, JANUARY 1887.

Military	Civil	Stage	Inter. M.	Inter. F.	Total M.	Total F.	Remarks
G.O.C. Mandalay District.	Commissioner, Northern Division, and Deputy Commissioner, Shwébo.	**1. Chaungwa and Zindaw.** Water good and plentiful from stream.	7	0	7	0	Level sandy road through paddy-fields, tree jungle. Chaungwa, small village of about 15 huts at 2 miles. . 4 miles Yédwingôn, small village of about 20 huts. At 7 miles the villages of Chaungwa and Zindaw situated on

FROM TÁNTABIN TO PÉGÔN (ROUTE No. 93, STAGE 6) *viâ* GÁDA—*continued.*

Authorities. Military.	Authorities. Civil.	Number and Names of Stages, Rivers and Streams.	Distances. Intermediate. M. F.	Distances. Total. M. F.	Remarks.
G.O.C. Mandalay District.	Commissioner, Northern Division, and Deputy Commissioner, Shwébo.	**1. Chaungwa and Zindaw**—*cont.*			opposite banks of a large creek, running east and west. Each village contains from 15 to 25 huts, large, but dilapidated. Kyaung near latter village, which would accommodate 200 men.
		2. Malégyi ...	10 4	17 4	Road good. At 3 miles village of Meazi, about 25 huts, and at 5½ miles Thabiyetha. Road good through open tree jungle. Water from wells at both these villages. Road fair through open jungle. This and all other villages to the north, along this road as far as Wuntho, were burnt and deserted by dacoits in King Thibaw's time two or three years ago. Road good through tree jungle to site of Malégyi at 10½ miles. Small kyaung. Village burnt.
		3. Gáda ... ... Good water from creek and wells.	12 0	29 4	Road through thick bamboo jungle, which had to be cleared to enable carts to proceed. At 6 miles village site Shyadaw, a little water from wells. Road through same dense bamboo jungle and over a wide, deep creek. At 10½ miles Letpangôn, deserted. Thence road through bush and bamboo jungle and across a creek to Gáda at 12 miles. Large kyaung.
		4. Ingyinzu ...	12 0	41 4	*See* Route No. 47.
		5. Pégôn	7 0	48 4	

No. 103.

From THABEITKYIN to BERNARDMYO (or MÔGÔK).

BY LIEUT. HUGHES, 2ND OXFORDSHIRE LIGHT INFANTRY, AND OTHERS, MAY 1888.

Military	Civil	Stage	Intermediate	Total	Remarks
G.O.C. Mandalay District.	Commissioner, Northern Division, and Deputy Commissioner, Ruby Mines.	**1. Wápyudaung**...	11 0	11 0	Thabeitkyin is situated on the left bank of the Irrawaddy, about 60 miles north of Mandalay and about 10 miles south of Malé. There is a good anchorage for steamers throughout the year. The military post is situated about 500 yards north of the village, on rising ground overlooking the river. Accommodation for 90 men in the stockade, besides officers' quarters, &c.; hospital for 25 men; accommodation for 50 followers outside the stockade. There is no accommodation for troops marching through at the stockade, but good camping ground for 300 men in the vicinity. At the south end of the village there is a kyaung, which would hold 50 men. The new military police stockade has now been completed, 300 yards north of the military stockade, to accommodate 80 men. Supplies are obtained from Mandalay. Transport: Some carts are on the road now, employed

FROM THABEITKYIN TO BERNARDMYO (OR MÔGÔK)—*continued.*

Authorities. Military.	Authorities. Civil.	Number and Names of Stages, Rivers and Streams.	Distances. Inter-mediate.	Distances. Total.	Remarks.
G.O.C. Mandalay District.	Commissioner, Northern Division, and Deputy Commissioner, Ruby Mines.	**1. Wápyudaung**—*cont.*			by the Public Works Department, and go as far as Shwényaungbin, 34 miles. About 300 coolies, men and women, could be collected from Thabeitkyin and villages on the road if notice were given. There are about 30 boats, 15 ponies, and 15 bullocks at Thabeitkyin. The cart road is now open for carts as far as Shwényaungbin, but has not yet been metalled. It will shortly be completed to within 12 miles of Bernardmyo with the exception of the bridge over the Kin river, $5\frac{1}{2}$ miles beyond Shwényaungbin. This bridge has only been made for pack animals. For 12 miles from Bernardmyo the trace of the road only has been cut and will not be completed for some time on account of scarcity of coolies. From Shwényaungbin mules are still used as transport. They follow the cart road till after the Kin river and then the old mule road to Bernardmyo. The following are the distances and heights of the cart road:— Thabeitkyin, 600 feet; Wápyudaung, 11 miles, 1,700 feet; Kyauklébin, $6\frac{7}{8}$ miles, 2,300 feet; Shwényaungbin, 16 miles, 3,200 feet; Place where permanent rest-house will be built, $13\frac{3}{4}$ miles, 4,150 feet; Bernardmyo, $14\frac{1}{2}$ miles, 5,900 feet; Total $62\frac{1}{8}$ miles. Between Thabeitkyin and Wápyudaung the greatest slope is $\frac{1}{10}$. Country carts pass easily with ordinary loads. The road would have to be lined anew; this stage to obtain a maximum slope of $\frac{1}{20}$. From Wápyudaung to Bernardmyo the greatest slope is $\frac{1}{20}$. Metalling can be obtained in plenty throughout the route, and good water is met (30th April) with about every 2 miles, except from Thabeitkyin to Wápyudaung and Kyauklébin to Shwényaungbin. Direction east. Descend from the stockade $\frac{1}{4}$ mile, cross a valley to $\frac{1}{2}$ mile, and then begin to ascend gradually to $2\frac{1}{4}$ miles. Here the ascent becomes steep and winding till a plateau is reached at 3 miles, height 1,200 feet; this last $\frac{3}{4}$ mile has a maximum slope of $\frac{1}{10}$. Road from here is over nearly flat ground covered with "*In*" forest to Wápyudaung at 11 miles. At 5 miles there is some open ground at the side of the road. Space enough for a camp of 300 men. Water can be obtained from a stream crossing the road just beyond. The water is only to be found in pools in May, and the stream looks as if it only had water running after heavy rain. At Wápyudaung a good rest-house has been built inside the stockade, where there are temporary barracks (now slightly dilapidated) for 30 men and stabling for 20 animals. A well-built block-house at the corner of the stockade; would hold 10 men. One zayát in village, 10 men. One bamboo kyaung, 10 men. Water fair from stream in the rains and from pools dug in the bed of the stream in the dry season.
		2. Kyauklébin ...	M. 7 F. 0	M. 18 F. 0	General direction east. Rising most of the way through forest of bamboo and other trees. Pass the small villages of Nyaungbintha and Paza at $3\frac{1}{2}$ and 5 miles respectively. Kyauklébin at 7 miles has about 15 houses. A temporary rest-house has been built here, one end of which is at present occupied by military police. The whole building would accommodate 40 men. A dilapi-

FROM THABEITKYIN TO BERNARDMYO (OR MÔGÔK)—*continued.*

Authorities. Military.	Authorities. Civil.	Number and Names of Stages, Rivers and Streams.	Distances. Intermediate.	Distances. Total.	Remarks.
G.O.C. Mandalay District.	Commissioner, Northern Division, and Deputy Commissioner, Ruby Mines.	**2. Kyauklébin**—*cont.*			dated zayát, just outside the stockade, would hold 10 men. No other accommodation. There is good camping ground for 200 men on the banks of a stream in dry season on disused paddy-fields. Water good and plentiful from stream. The stream, 50 yards east of the village, runs south-wards; is about 8 yards broad with rocky bottom and would be always fordable for carts, except during very heavy rains. A wooden pile-bridge has been built across it, 25 yards long by 10 feet broad.
			M. F.	M. F.	
		3. Shwényaungbin. Stream running south to Madaya river.	**16 0**	34 0	Road continues over this bridge. General direction east. Country as last stage. At ½ mile the old mule road branches off to the right, the cart road taking a more northern line. The mule road proceeds by the deserted village of Nampán and crosses the cart road again about 5 miles short of Shwényaungbin. The mule road for this stage is about 2 miles shorter than the cart road, but has the disadvantage of a very steep rocky ascent about 2 miles beyond Nampán, which is said to be slippery and very difficult for mules during the rains. The cart road rises gradually to a height of 4,000 feet at 8 miles, where it crosses the watershed, draining south to the Madaya river and north to the Kin river. At this point Shwéútaung mountain becomes visible north-east; height 6,231 feet. The road now descends to Shwényaungbin, 8 miles on. The mule road crosses the cart road at about 11 miles and again at 12½. From 12½ miles the mule road is good and easy and preferable for any transport except carts, being about ¾ mile shorter from that point to Shwényaungbin. Shwényaungbin is a military police post and at present has also a military police detachment at the village. The stockade is on a narrow spur running north and south overlooking the valley 300 yards west. The ground round the stockade descends steeply on all sides except the north. A good rest-house has been built opposite the gate of stockade, 50 yards north, on the further side of the road. It has four rooms with a good verandah. It would accommodate 40 men. Accommodation for 70 men in stockade, besides officers' quarters; accommodation for 70 followers, and stabling for 100 animals. A kyaung in the village would accommodate 30 men in all. Good water is obtained from a small stream in the valley between the stockade and village, but not in large quantity.
		4. Rest-house near pagodas at upper end of Kabain valley. Kin running north to Sagadaung.	**13 6**	47 6	From Shwényaungbin the road descends gradually. General direction east to the Kin river. The village of Kin comes in sight at about 2 miles, lying in a flat, paddy plain 1½ miles by ¾ mile, through which the Kin stream winds. There are two villages (North and South Kinywa) about 1 mile apart; 25 houses in each; inhabited principally by Shans. The road descends along the south side of the valley. At 5½ miles the Kin stream is crossed by a wooden bridge suspended on wire ropes 1 inch in diameter. This is only a temporary bridge for mules. This bridge is about ½ mile up stream, from where the Kin enters the paddy plain. The stream runs about 2 miles per

FROM THABEITKYIN TO BERNARDMYO (OR MÔGÔK)—*continued.*

Authorities. Military.	Authorities. Civil.	Number and Names of Stages, Rivers and Streams.	Distances. Intermediate.	Distances. Total.	Remarks.
G.O.C. Mandalay District.	Commissioner, Northern Division, and Deputy Commissioner, Ruby Mines.	**4. Rest-house near pagodas at upper end of Kabain valley**—*cont.*			hour. The bed is composed of sand and big boulders. The water is about 10 yards broad in May; could be easily forded by mules. It would be difficult for carts, and probably impracticable, during the rains. The top of the banks here is about 15 feet above the water, and in most places the banks are steep. The bridge is 25 yards long. From the Kin stream the mule road takes a higher line than the cart road, which branches off to the left, winding round the spurs overlooking the Kin valley. The mule road crosses the cart road again at the saddle between the Kin and Kabain valleys. Here the cart road takes a north-westerly direction, leaving Kabain in the paddy plain below to the south-east. The mule road again takes a higher line and crosses the cart road at a saddle at the upper end of the Kabain valley. About 300 yards south of this point is a group of five small pagodas on the right of the mule road. A permanent rest-house will be built somewhere near here. Distance by cart road 13¾ miles.
		5. Bernardmyo ... Ingyauk stream running north-west to Sagadaung.	M. F. **14 4**	M. F. 62 2	The cart road continues rising gradually along the west of the spurs from Taungmé. It has been cut for about 3 miles, but from there to 12 miles, where it joins the mule road again, the trace has only been cut at present. The mule road takes a higher line, and about 3 miles on reaches Bôlung. This has for some time been used as a halting place. Barracks and rest-house have been built, but only temporary; they are now much dilapidated. Good water from stream. The country at Bôlung changes, the hills being covered with coarse grass, with clumps of trees here and there. Three miles beyond Bôlung the mule path enters the forest, which extends round Taungmé and the neighbouring hills from about 6,000 feet upwards. The path emerges from the forest again near which it is met by the trace of the cart road. From here, 12 miles, the cart road will probably be made by widening the present mule road, which reaches Bernardmyo 2½ miles further on, crossing the Ingyauk stream near the bottom of the valley by a wooden pile-bridge at 2 miles. The stream is here about 6 yards broad and 3 feet deep running about ¾ mile per hour; low banks with a soft bottom. It runs through rich soft soil throughout the valley, and the ground on the banks is marshy in places. The bridge has been made 80 yards long to avoid this soft ground. The Ingyauk valley runs from the foot of Taungmé in a north-westerly direction to the bridge mentioned above. Bernardmyo at present consists of the military station and a bazaar of about 20 huts. The barracks have accommodated one Native regiment, two companies, British Infantry, and half a battery. There is stabling for about 300 animals. Good camping ground for 600 men close to barracks and for an unlimited number if the bracken were cut from the hills in the vicinity. There is an ample supply of good water for men from a small stream on the hill side. Animals are watered at the Ingyauk stream, ½ mile distant.

No. 103.

FROM THABEITKYIN TO BERNARDMYO (OR MÔGÔK)—*continued.*

BRANCH I.

FROM KABAIN (*see* STAGE 4) TO MÔGÔK.

Authorities. Military.	Authorities. Civil.	Number and Names of Stages, Rivers and Streams.	Distances. Intermediate. M.	F.	Distances. Total. M.	F.	Remarks.
G.O.C. Mandalay District.	Commr., Northern Divn., and Deputy Commr., Ruby Mines.	**1. Môgôk**	**13**	**0**	13	0	The cart road is completed probably, but no detailed report at present. Môgôk is the chief civil station of the Ruby Mines District.

No. 104.

From TIGYAING to BHAMO viâ MÁBAIN and SI-U.

BY CAPT. C. POYNDER, OCTOBER 1887, AND CAPT. READ, 5TH BENGAL LIGHT INFANTRY, DECEMBER 1887.

Authorities. Military.	Authorities. Civil.	Number and Names of Stages, Rivers and Streams.	Distances. Intermediate. M.	F.	Distances. Total. M.	F.	Remarks.
G.O.C. Mandalay District.	Commissioner, Northern Division, and Deputy Commissioner, Katha.	**1. Thônbôn** ... Nullah 2 feet 6 inches deep, 30 yards wide, no banks. Nullah 100 yards wide, 4 feet deep, no banks, but approaches muddy and difficult.	**4**	**0**	4	0	By river to Kanni situated on left bank of Irrawaddy, 6 or 7 miles north of Tigyaing and Myadaung. High bank; sufficient water for steamers in a side channel of main stream from which it is divided by a large island. Long straggling village; 60 houses with good kyaung and zayát accommodation for 100 to 300 men, surrounded by kaing grass, through which road to Thônbôn passes for nearly a mile; one nullah. Muddy bad soil, several places deep; mud would dry if opened up to sun. Then ½ mile of jungle road very wet and muddy. Here a deep marshy piece of water is reached, to cross which boats required (brought from Kanni village). Animals can ford it; 50 yards to left water 3 feet 6 inches; thence road into Thônbôn 1½ miles, generally swampy and wet with deep mud. General direction of march east. Here a sandy ridge is reached covered with dense jungle, through which the road continues in a south-east direction. The village is in a clearing; 30 houses, no kyaung; accommodation for 100 sepoys in native houses; water from one good well. The road is a good cart road under large trees and shady, but at 3 miles it bifurcates, the left being the correct road, although that to the right which looks better only leads to the jungle.
		2. Kintha ...	**15**	**0**	19	0	Guide is necessary from Thônbôn. The road continues sound and good for the next 6 miles, when at the 9th mile a marsh about 500 yards is reached through dense elephant grass a difficult place, but if opened to sun and the water confined to one or two small channels would soon be made practicable for carts; at present they can only cross with difficulty. The road continues good to the 11th mile over a sandy rise of Eng jungle, but here another marsh of 200 yards, the same as before, has to be crossed. The road again continues good, but the jungle has in places overgrown the road. At 12½ miles the road turns due north to cross a marsh at a favourable point which is also about 200 yards wide. After

FROM TIGYAING TO BHAMO *viâ* MÁBAIN AND SI-U—*continued.*

Authorities. Military.	Authorities. Civil.	Number and Names of Stages, Rivers and Streams.	Distances. Intermediate.	Distances. Total.	Remarks.
G.O.C. Mandalay District.	Commr., Northern Divn., and Deputy Commr., Katha.	**2. Hintha**—*cont.*			some sound going another marsh at 14 miles is reached. It is 1,200 yards in extent. From here the road into Hintha is good, total distance being 15 miles. Village small; 15 houses; 60 men; stockaded; clearing in jungle. Water from a nullah near village, fair.
	Commissioner, Northern Division, and Deputy Commissioner, Ruby Mines.	**3. Nyaungbintha.** Shwéli river, breadth 300 yards, deep and swift, 4 miles per hour; 10 feet in the channel here, but generally 3 feet.	M. 15 F. 0	M. 34 F. 0	From here the road runs south through open jungle, then thick for about a mile and-a-quarter, when sandy nullah is reached. The road follows the bed; heavy sand in places and a few quicksands. A mountain stream, never very deep, inclosed in steep hills; general direction north. Road runs up stream. At 3 miles road suddenly leaves the bed of river and ascends a gentle gradient; rough cart road cut through bamboo jungle. The trees are very fine; at 4 miles the first summit is reached about 400 feet above Hintha. At 5 miles there is a steep descent to small nullah bed (no water), then a very sharp ascent for short distance. At 5¼ miles an open timber clearing with bamboo shed is reached, would make a halting ground, but no water. From here the road descends gradually ¾ mile, then sharp descent to a nullah bed, followed by a steep ascent over a very narrow saddle 10 feet broad. A descent at 9 miles leads down to a nullah bed about 9 miles, 30 feet wide; little water now, but more after rain, and the approach on further side between steep banks is 2 feet deep in thick black mud. At 10 miles the summit of next rise is reached where a circular clearing gives a good halting place for 150 men (no water near). From here road descends gradually for 2¼ miles. Bainbin is reached at 12¼ miles; small village on left bank of Shwéli river; 25 houses, no kyaung or zayáts; accommodation for 125 men. Some boats opposite to Máúgôn; numerous boats, rafts and kyaungs. Shwéli water good. Road generally is good through thick jungle of fine timber (teak) with bamboo undergrowth. Guides from Hintha are absolutely necessary. The road had cart tracks, but for large convoys it would be difficult unless improved. This would not be difficult. The road now follows the left bank of Shwéli river through the same jungle. A steep cutting through clay is reached at once which is impassable for carts about ½ mile long; at 15 miles, Nyaungbintha is reached, situated on river bank and stockaded; small accommodation.
		4. Mábain ... Shwéli river, breadth 300 yards, deep and swift, 4 miles per hour; 10 feet in the channel here, but generally 3 feet, and another unfordable stream.	16 0	50 0	From here road runs inland south-west for 6 miles, crossing two nullahs about 15 yards wide, 18 inches deep. The road follows second nullah for 200 yards, reaching crest of low hills inland, runs along a plateau of Eng jungle and descends in dense bamboo to a nullah at 9 miles. Here road enters thick teak forest behind (west of) Pinlaha (or Pinbla) and runs due east on to it; at 13½ miles the village is reached. Village small; about 15 houses; stockaded. The old trade route from Tagaung to Kachin hills passes through here and Kata opposite, *viâ* Si-u to head of Sinkán creek. Not now used, and from Maindaing probably very bad. The

FROM TIGYAING TO BHAMO *viâ* MÁBAIN AND SI-U—*continued.*

Authorities. Military.	Authorities. Civil.	Number and Names of Stages, Rivers and Streams.	Distances. Intermediate.	Distances. Total.	Remarks.
G.O.C. Mandalay District.	Commissioner, Northern Division, and Deputy Commissioner, Ruby Mines.	**4. Mábain**—*cont.*			road on to Wainlôu is a track following river bank. The village is a small stockaded one of 20 houses in good position on high ground above river bank; gravelly soil; double stockade all round, but surrounded, except on east side, with very dense jungle. Accommodation for 75 men. Cross river here 450 yards wide to Mábain 16 miles. Numerous boats; large rafts.
		5. Pingyaing ...	M. F. 17 6	M. F. 67 6	On leaving Mábain the road runs east across paddy-fields to Kônmábain, a small stockaded village 1½ miles from Mábain, with the Nampôn nullah on right hand. Here there is one small zayát and limited supply of good water from well. A foot-path also runs along bank of nullah. From Kônmábain the road turns north and passes through Eng and some teak forest, crossing two nullahs, the first about 3½ and the second about 4 miles from Mábain, both easily passable at present (middle of November), nearly dry, but would be fordable almost any time. At about 5 miles from Mábain the road turns north-east and then generally in an easterly direction through forest more or less open. At about 6 miles the cart road from Kata (on the Shwéli river) to Pingyaing joins the road from Mábain. Kata is about 5 miles distant from this point. The road still runs through forest, a good cart road for most of the way. The cart road and the foot-path followed by the troops often separate and rejoin again. At about 13¼ miles the road crosses a small range of hills and then runs through forest and finally along the bed of an almost dry nullah for about ½ a mile, when Pingyaing is reached. The first halt must be made at Pingyaing, between which place and Mábain there are no camping grounds.
		6. Sipein ...	6 2	74 0	From Pingyaing the road runs east crossing a small nullah and then for ¾ mile across an open plain, when a very swampy bit of ground is reached, which would be very bad in wet weather, and then through forest for 2 miles to Sinkán, crossing the Sinkán nullah, the village being on north bank. From Sinkán the road still runs east through forest to Sipein, 6¼ miles from Pingyaing, crossing a small nullah about 1 mile before reaching Sipein. Sipein is an open village, in two portions, about 200 yards apart, each containing eight houses. It is situated on the edge of a wide plain, backed by a chaung. Considerable amount of rice cultivation. Good camping ground and accommodation for 100 men in a kyaung and zayát. Water plentiful from well and chaung.
	Commissioner, Northern Division, and Deputy Commissioner, Bhamo.	**7. Thônkwa** ...	9 2	83 2	From Sipein the road runs east crossing an open grass plain for about 1¼ miles, and then through forest crossing a nullah at about 3 miles. Thence in a north-easterly direction crossing a nullah at about 6½ miles. Thence through forest for ¾ mile and for 1½ miles across an open grass plain, very heavy and swampy, and would be almost impassable in the rains. Then across a small paddy plain to Thônkwa, 9¼ miles. Thônkwa is a small open village of 10 houses. No kyaungs or zayáts. Camping ground on the paddy plain in the cold weather. Water good and plentiful from chaung.

FROM TIGYAING TO BHAMO *viâ* MÁBAIN AND SI-U—*continued.*

Authorities. Military.	Authorities. Civil.	Number and Names of Stages, Rivers and Streams.	Distances. Intermediate. M.	F.	Total. M.	F.	Remarks.
G.O.C. Mandalay District.	Commissioner, Northern Division, and Deputy Commissioner, Bhamo.	**8. Si-u**	**9**	**2**	92	4	From Thônkwa the road runs north-east through forest and across a few swampy bits of ground, crossing a small nullah at 2 miles, and others at about 4, 7, and 7$\frac{1}{2}$ miles respectively. At 9$\frac{1}{4}$ miles reach Si-u, a large open village of 120 houses, situated on a slight rise at the foot of hills. Considerable paddy cultivation. Accommodation for 300 men in one kyaung, one zayát, and two large houses in village. Water good and plentiful from chaung. The total distance from Mábain to Si-u is 42$\frac{3}{4}$ miles. The road when first traversed between 28th and 30th October was fairly passable for all transport but carts. All the nullahs crossed were only about knee-deep and would be fordable at almost any time except in the middle of the rainy season. From the beginning of November, by which time the rains are over, the road improves fast. It was again traversed between 11th and 14th November by cavalry and infantry and by carts. The cart road had been repaired (very slight repairs were needed) and laden carts carrying 500 lb. each did the journey in four days. Every day's sun improved the road, and on the final return of the column to Mábain, between 19th and 22nd November, the road was good for cavalry and infantry. All the marshy parts were fast drying, and the water only about ankle-deep in all the nullahs. The column halted at Pingyaing, Thônkwa, and Si-u, but the march between Pingyaing and Thônkwa could have been divided by halting at Sipein.
		9. Sikaw	**15**	**4**	108	0	*See* Route No. 19.
		10. Mankin ...	**16**	**0**	124	0	
		11. Sáwadi ...	**12**	**2**	136	2	
		12. Bhamo ...	**9**	**0**	145	2	

ALTERNATIVE I.

There is an alternative route BETWEEN HINTHA (STAGE 2) AND MÁÚGÔN (*see* STAGE 3).

Military	Civil	Stages	Intermediate M.	F.	Total M.	F.	Remarks
G.O.C. Mandalay District.	Commissioner, Northern Division, and Deputy Commissioner, Bhamo.	**1. Pwézamé** ... Shwéli river.	**7**	**0**	7	0	Road good through hills and open "Eng" forest. At 7 miles cross the Shwéli to Pwézamé, small village on right bank, one kyaung. River here 350 yards broad, strong current. Boats obtainable up to about 20 in number.
		2. Máúgôn and Taungôn. Shwéli river.	**10**	**0**	17	0	Good road through thick jungle; one small stream to be crossed at about 8$\frac{1}{2}$ miles. Máúgôn is a small village of 10 houses on the river bank, commanded by a hill 300 yards to the north, on which is situated the village of Taungôn, three pôngyi kyaungs and zayáts, sufficient for 170 men. Good water. Hill is surrounded by thick dense jungle and there is a large cane swamp to the south of it. Opposite Máúgôn, on the left bank of the Shwéli, is Bainbin, *see* Stage 3 above.

FROM TIGYAING TO BHAMO *viâ* MÁBAIN AND SI-U—*continued.*

There is also an alternative route BETWEEN MÁBAIN AND MYADAUNG OPPOSITE TIGYAING, the starting point of this route.

ALTERNATIVE II.

FROM MÁBAIN (STAGE 4) TO MYADAUNG (ON LEFT BANK OF IRRAWADDY RIVER OPPOSITE TIGYAING).

BY LIEUT. VESEY, 1ST BENGAL INFANTRY, NOVEMBER 1887.

Authorities. Military.	Authorities. Civil.	Number and Names of Stages, Rivers and Streams.	Distances. Intermediate. M. F.	Distances. Total. M. F.	Remarks.
G.O.C. Mandalay District.	Commissioner, Northern Division, and Deputy Commissioner, Ruby Mines.	**1. Camp**	14 0	14 0	Cross the Shwéli river to Pinlaha or Pinhla, a village of 19 houses. From Pinlaha the road runs through teak forest for the first 2 miles; the 3rd mile passes through a grass plain. From here the road gradually ascends for another mile, afterwards running along the top of a low range of hills for 3 miles, open forest on either side. It rises again gradually for another mile, and then descends for 5 miles to the first encamping ground. The road is uniformly good the whole way and fit for carts. The encamping place is situated in a hollow in the midst of the forest. There are two houses, the largest of which will accommodate 100 men, the smallest 12 men. Water from a nullah close by.
	Commissioner, Northern Division, and Deputy Commissioner, Katha.	**2. Maindaing** ...	15 0	29 0	From here the road is level for the 1st mile through open forest. It ascends for another mile and runs along the top of a low range of hills ending in a high hill for 4 miles. Descending into a nullah and ascending again it runs for 2 miles along some low hills. In the next mile it crosses the same nullah six times. The next 3 miles the road is level through bamboo and teak forest and crossing three nullahs. For the next 2 miles it passes through open forest, crossing one nullah, the last mile through an open grass plain to Maindaing. The road is good and fit for carts. There is a small amount of water in one of the nullahs. Maindaing is the remains of an old village. There are two houses partially surrounded by a bamboo paling; they are capable of holding the largest 100 men, the smallest 12 men. Good supply of water from nullah close by. From here track leads to Tagaungmyo *viâ* Kyauk-u, 25 to 30 miles distant nearly due west.
		3. Pôgôla	14 0	43 0	For the first 3 miles the road runs through bamboo and teak forest. In the next 2 miles it crosses two nullahs. In the next mile it crosses one nullah and then ascends a high hill. It descends for the next 2 miles into a nullah in which there is a fair supply of water. In the next 3 miles it is level crossing and running along the bed of the same nullah six times. Up to this point the road has run through bamboo forest. From here it runs through level, open forest for 3 miles to Pôgôla, a village of five houses, with good water-supply from well.

FROM TIGYAING TO BHAMO *viâ* MÁBAIN AND SI-U—*continued.*

ALTERNATIVE II—*continued.*

Authorities.		Number and Names of Stages, Rivers and Streams.	Distances.				Remarks.
Military.	Civil.		Inter-mediate.		Total.		
			M.	F.	M.	F.	
G.O.C. Mandalay District.	Commr., Northern Divn., and Deputy Commr., Katha.	**4. Myadaung** ...	**8**	**0**	51	0	From here to Myadaung there is a good broad road through open forest and paddy-fields, passing three villages, fair and fit for carts all the way. This route is the most direct, though not the best, from Mábain to Myadaung.

No. 105.

From TIGYAING to KINDÁT.

BY MAJOR H. A. SAWYER, ASSISTANT QUARTERMASTER-GENERAL, INTELLIGENCE BRANCH, FEBRUARY 1888.

Military.	Civil.	Stages.	M.	F.	M.	F.	Remarks.
G.O.C. Mandalay District.	Commissioner, Northern Division, and Deputy Commissioner, Katha.	**1. Tawma** ...	**9**	**0**	9	0	A well-known cart road crosses the Hmawgundaing pass and thence along low and heavy soil, impracticable for carts in wet weather. One furlong of the new road is visible at Kawlin; nowhere else.
		2. Singôn ...	**9**	**4**	18	4	
		3. Kyaukpyintha.	**8**	**0**	26	4	
		4. Kawlin	**11**	**0**	33	0	
		Short cut.					
		5. Gwédauktaw ...	**11**	**2**	49	2	Large village. Supplies procurable for 50 men. Road level and good. Cart track passes through a range of low hills between 3rd and 4th mile. Village and kyaung of Yádaung at 5½ miles; village of Kadaw at 9½ miles. Dense jungle on both sides after entering hills.
		6. Ôkán	**9**	**6**	59	0	On leaving Gwédauktaw rise to large plateau covered with large trees and no undergrowth. Good ground for station or camp; water close by; after 1 mile descends into low ground; dense undergrowth. At 4 miles pass village Kalôn; 10 houses; nullah 20 yards wide; sandy bottom; banks 12 feet deep. Path now leads along right bank of Daungyu river, which is 50 to 60 yards wide; still water 3 feet deep (in January); 20 feet banks; muddy bottom. Banks fringed with high kaing grass and jungle undergrowth. Large trees in plenty to form bridging material at any point. Ôkán, a large village, 53 houses, one large kyaung, on the left bank of the Láka chaung. Where this joins the Daungyu is a good place for permanent bridge crossing. From Ôkán hill (2,400 feet) the Mankintaung hill, near Kawlin, and the Wuntho peak can be seen.
		7. Gyobin	**8**	**0**	67	0	Cart track crosses the Láka chaung south of Ôkán village and is circuitous (11 miles). Short cut crosses chaung north of village, and winds through and over very broken undulating ground through dense jungle. At 6½ miles strike the Mu river, 80 to 100 yards wide; banks 10 feet to 20 feet; sandy bottom. Gyobin has 50 houses and one kyaung.

FROM TIGYAING TO KINDÁT—*continued.*

Authorities.		Number and Names of Stages, Rivers, and Streams.	Distances.				Remarks.
Military.	Civil.		Inter-mediate.		Total.		
			M.	F.	M.	F.	
G.O.C. Myingyán District.	Commissioner, Central Division, and Deputy Commissioner, Yé-u.	**8. Séywa ... ...**	**8**	**4**	75	4	Cross ford above village, enter jungle and undulating ground. At 4 miles touch the Nangyitha creek (flowing into Mu), keep on right bank, and cross at 8th mile. Nangyitha 30 yards wide; banks 10 feet; sandy bottom. Forest jungle all the way. Séywa, a small village; one kyaung.
		9. Payagôn ...	**13**	**4**	89	0	Cart track crosses Nangyitha creek at 2nd, 5th (twice), and 8th mile, and crosses Chaungna chaung at 11th mile; crossings easy in dry season; road through close jungle at Payagôn; much cultivation; several villages about; one large kyaung. Mettaung 1½ miles north-east of Payagôn; a large settlement with signs of resuscitation. Cart track ceases at Payagôn.
		10. Yézôn, East ...	**6**	**0**	95	0	Bridle-path crosses small creek above kyaung, and passes for 2 miles over low spurs and dense jungle, then entering the Nangyitha creek. The bed of this creek is followed for 4½ miles, offering no difficulties for laden mules at low water; a few inches deep in January. Camping ground in jungle suitable for half a battalion. Yézôn means "meeting of the waters."
		11. Yézôn, West.	**15**	**2**	110	2	From camp steep ascent for 400 feet; could be improved by small party in a few hours to much advantage. Track follows a remarkable and clearly defined hog's back, running straight east and west for 13 miles between the two Yézôns. At 2½ miles is a waterfall. Yetagôn; water not in large quantity in dry season. Camping ground for 100 men only. Half-a-mile farther on is a steep ascent of the small Sinkyát (elephant) hill for 50 yards; requires attention, but practicable for laden animals. A mile further is the highest bit of the range (2,650), being also the boundary of Wuntho territory. At 5 miles camp Kyunbingyi Sakhán (big teak tree camp). Water said to be abundant. Room for half battalion. At 9½ miles another optional camp called Wetlwaing (Pigmanspring). At 12½ miles pass over the Shwégántaung hill (2,280); no difficulties. Hence track descends rapidly to Kôdán stream. Camp at Yézôn, West. Forest the whole way; now and then glimpses of unknown peaks obtained: country north and south consists of wooded low ranges, spurs running east and west. Camp suitable for half battalion at a time. Water in Kôdán stream abundant.
	Commissioner, Central Division, and Deputy Commissioner, Upper Chindwin.	**12. Subet ... ...**	**3**	**2**	113	4	Cross Kôdán four times, and for some way in the water. The Kôdán stream is very winding with bank from 6 to 15 feet; is 30 yards wide at Yézôn, West and 150 yards at Lawtha; sandy

FROM TIGYAING TO KINDÁT—*continued.*

Authorities. Military.	Authorities. Civil.	Number and Names of Stages, Rivers and Streams.	Distances. Intermediate. M.	Distances. Intermediate. F.	Distances. Total. M.	Distances. Total. F.	Remarks.
G.O.C. Myingyán District.	Commissioner, Central Division, and Deputy Commissioner, Upper Chindwin.	**12. Subet**—*cont.*					bottom; signs of high and rapid water in flood time, making it impassable for days or weeks at a time. Subet is a small village; 18 houses; one kyaung. Reports of gold washings by villagers higher up stream and worthy of detailed investigation. *N.B.*—If local reports of water at Kyunbingyi Sakhán are good, these two marches are best divided by camping there instead of Yézôn, West.
		13. Gyôbin Sakhán	10	0	123	4	Track in and out of Kôdán, which is crossed 26 times with long stretches in knee-deep water (January). At 5 miles village Sayaing; seven houses. At 8 miles the Payinthataung (Amber hill), a steep pull of 1 in 3 for 300 yards; could be easily improved. Gyôbin Sakhán, a usual half-way camping place.
		14. Lawtha ...	6	4	130	0	Track in and out of Kôdán; stream crosses it 14 times. Lawtha 20 houses; one kyaung on the Nama chaung.
		15. Pántha ...	20	0	150	0	Track follows the Nama chaung to its commencement at 5½ miles (sandy bed), where it crosses low watershed for 200 yards and immediately drops into another nullah for 5 miles, where the Nanthinpin nullah with flowing small stream is met at a camping place (Yézôn). This stream is followed in and out to within 2 miles of Pántha. Forest and jungle on either side. Pántha, which is about 16 miles above Kindát, has some 50 houses; two kyaungs on left bank of Chindwin. Telegraph line to Tummu crosses 1 mile below. *Note.*—This track is open all the year round for cooly carriage and for five or six months for mule carriage. In its present state, however, it is only practicable for troops under grave necessity, as supplies are unobtainable between the Mu and the Chindwin, and the track itself is a rough one for beast and man. The run of the track is, however, well chosen, and there would be no difficulty in laying out a good pack or even a good cart road close to the present alignment, which is on the shortest line between the Irrawaddy and the Chindwin, running due west through Kawlin. From Payagôn to Lawtha the track passes through country composed of low-wooded ranges running east and west, with water-courses flowing south-east into the Mu and south-west into the Chindwin. The reports obtained at Subet about the gold washings are worthy of further enquiries being made.
		16. Kindát ...	16	0	166	0	

BRANCH I.

FROM SINGÔN (STAGE 2) TO WUNTHO.

BY LIEUT. T. F. B. RENNY-TAILYOUR, R.E., FEBRUARY 1887.

Military	Civil	Stage	Inter. M.	Inter. F.	Total M.	Total F.	Remarks
G.O.C. Mandalay District.	Commr., Northern Dn., and Deputy Commr., Katha.	**1. Taungmaw** ... Yeshi and Na chaungs.]	10	4	10	4	Cross Yeshi chaung and follow its course for about 1½ miles, then ½ a mile of low-lying country liable to inundation by above-named stream to the villages of Kanta and Kyeik-

FROM TIGYAING TO KINDÁT—*continued.*

BRANCH I—*continued.*

Authorities. Military.	Authorities. Civil.	Number and Names of Stages, Rivers and Streams.	Distances. Intermediate.	Distances. Total.	Remarks.
G.O.C. Mandalay District.	Commissioner, Northern Division, and Deputy Commissioner, Katha.	**1. Taungmaw**—*cont.*			thíta at 2 miles. Thence over open country for 2 miles and through 1 mile of thick jungle to Thitseingôn, 5 miles. Thence across paddy cultivation, and through a thick belt of bamboo jungle, over a low ridge, gradients easy to the Na chaung at 8½ miles. Cross this stream 3 times in the remainder of the march, and latterly following its bank westward, pass through the village Endaw and reach Taungmaw at 10½ miles. Large village, kyaung and zayáts. Water from wells. Road over vast plain (greater portion of which is under paddy cultivation), for about 2 miles, then through thick belt of bamboo, and cross Dôndôk chaung to village of same name 2½ miles. Thence through generally open country, a great deal of it under paddy cultivation, passing through the villages of Taukyándaw at 4 miles, Nyaungbintha at 4¾, Ôktaikgôn 6, Anga 6¾, Amakôn 7¾, Kyauktain 8¾, and reaching Wuntho at 10½ miles. General direction of this march north-east.

No. 106.

From TWINNGÉ (or KYÁNHNYÁT) to BERNARDMYO and MÔGÔK viâ SAGADAUNG.

BY CAPT. SEWELL, NORFOLK REGIMENT, INTELLIGENCE DEPARTMENT, JANUARY 1890.

Military	Civil	Stages	Intermediate M. F.	Total M. F.	Remarks
G.O.C. Mandalay District.	Commissioner, Northern Division, and Deputy Commissioner, Ruby Mines.	**1. Kyaukpyu** ... Two streams.	9 0	9 0	Twinngé is fenced village 1¼ miles from left bank of Irrawaddy; 200 houses; a police stockade 300 yards north of village. Accommodation for 400 men and 100 ponies in kyaung north of village and zayáts east of village. Water from three wells—one in kyaung, two in village; all good. One small well 200 yards west of village, bad; would do for washing. Water for animals from creek between village and river. Road from river rough, and crosses two creeks (full in rains). A good camp could be formed on a clearing west of village for 2,000 men. Bank of river wants improving and high grass near should be cleared, as landing stage is cramped. Telegraph line Thabeitkyin to Bhamo runs through village. Road an indifferent cart track through bamboo or teak jungle, except for 1 mile at village of Taungbôn and ½ mile before reaching Kyaukpyu, where it runs over paddy-fields. It is fairly level; several undulations, but nothing difficult. Runs north along telegraph line to ½ mile, then turns off north-east; bamboo jungle. At 3 miles runs across paddy-fields through Taungbôn village, 50 houses, fenced (or continues through jungle, bending south round the village clearing, rejoining the road ¼ mile beyond the village); 200 yards east of village cross a small stream. Next ¼ mile heavy. Direction then changes to the east. At 5½ miles road from Kyánhnyát joins from north-west. Road rises slightly over hard ground to 6¾ miles. At 7¾ miles cross a dry nullah, sharp descent. At 8¼ miles cross the Kyaukpyu stream, 30 yards bank to bank, 15 feet water

FROM TWINNGÉ (OR KYÁNHNYÁT) TO BERNARDMYO AND MÔGÔK *viâ* SAGADAUNG—*continued.*

Authorities. Military.	Authorities. Civil.	Number and Names of Stages, Rivers and Streams.	Distances. Intermediate. M. F.	Distances. Total. M. F.	Remarks.
G.O.C. Mandalay District.	Commissioner, Northern Division, and Deputy Commissioner, Ruby Mines.	**1. Kyaukpyu**—*cont.*			(December); steep ascent and exit. At 8½ miles cross rice fields to village, double fenced, 40 houses, 100 yards square. At south-east small kyaung to hold 50 men and two sayáts for 75 men. Water good from stream 100 yards south of village. Height 100 feet above Twinngé.
		2. Wébaung ... Three streams (nine crossings in all).	13 0	22 0	General direction east throughout through thick bamboo or teak jungle. Road as before, but more undulating. Runs north-north-east on leaving village for ¾ mile, cross nullah, and at 1 mile commence ascent, winding over hill spurs to 2½ miles, whence it descends gradually. The highest point reached is 350 feet above Twinngé and forms a column between a long spur from Bernardmyo range and another running in prolongation north-east and north for some 7 or 8 miles. The road is stony and bad, and some slopes as much as 6° or 1 in 10. The road runs through tree jungle under hill spurs 600 feet high and in a north-east direction for 2 miles further. Cross stream at 3½ miles. At 4½ miles bamboo jungle, which continues to end of march. Cross a stream, probably the Kôdán, at 4½ miles, and again at 4¾, 5, 6½, 8, 9, and 10 miles. From first crossing this stream the road practically level and follows the course of the stream, which runs between 10 feet banks with depth of water (December) 6 inches. At 12½ miles cross another chaung 40 feet wide, 6 inches deep; road runs now through a thick bit of jungle for 200 yards and then across rice fields to Wébaung; direction latterly south-east; village fenced, Shan and Burmese; 24 houses. One kyaung unoccupied and two sayáts on east for 140 men. Water from big stream 50 yards on east, 1 foot deep (December). Ground round village cleared 1 mile to west and ½ mile south-east to width of ½ mile. Height 200 feet above Twinngé.
		3. Sagadaung ... Seven nullahs dry (December).	9 6	31 6	General direction as the crow flies east-south-east. Road as before, not better and harder going. At starting to 1¼ miles runs north-east and rises over a rough track between low spurs, passing through bamboo and tree jungle. It then descends gradually running east to 2½ miles, then level and running south-east to 3 miles, then south to 3¾ miles. From this point it winds the rest of the way in a general south-easterly direction. At 7 miles is a slight rise, and the road runs along a low spur and descends at a slope of 1 in 15 for 300 yards. The jungle extends to within ½ mile of Sagadaung and is mostly young teak. At 8 miles the road runs parallel to a hill spur and at 9½ miles enter rice fields, on the opposite side of which is the village, fenced, 120 by 180 yards; 80 houses. Several shops supplying the road traders. A fenced post on east of village is occupied by the Thugyi. Big kyaung, in bad state of repair, and zayáts to hold 400 men. Two wells, one foul, and water from the river 350 yards south or east. Much ground cultivated all round, and on either side of the stream (Kinchang). There is an alternative route between Kyaukpyu (Stage 1) and Sagadaung (Stage 3) *viâ* Kanawé which has not, however, been reported upon as yet.

FROM TWINNGÉ (OR KYÁNHNYÁT) TO BERNARDMYO AND MÔGÓK *viâ* SAGADAUNG—*continued.*

Authorities. Military.	Authorities. Civil.	Number and Names of Stages, Rivers and Streams.	Distances. Intermediate. M. F.	Distances. Total. M. F.	Remarks.
G.O.C. Mandalay District.	Commissioner, Northern Division, and Deputy Commissioner, Ruby Mines.	**4. Bernardmyo (Pyaungaung).**	14 0	45 6	General direction south-south-east. Road leaves Sagadaung on the south side, crosses the Sagadaung river by a bridge and runs through bamboo jungle for 2¼ miles where there is a clearing and small camping ground. The ascent which is very steep now commences; for 2¼ miles road is rocky and runs through open tree jungle, the rest of the march being through low dense jungle, chiefly bamboo. At 7 miles Ywazo is reached; small plateau, some ruined zayáts and small camping ground with plenty of grass and water. From this place the road runs nearly due east to Lwékaw (3,290 feet); here there is a good camping ground on a spur to the left of the road with plenty of grass and fuel, but water-supply limited. The water is good and obtained from a stream crossed 200 yards below the post; village of Lwékaw on the same spur, but 250 feet lower. From here the road rises rapidly through thick jungle. At 9¼ miles a road runs north-east to Mômeik. At 10¼ miles Nampwot (4,560 feet) is reached, a prosperous stockaded village of about 25 good houses with a good kyaung (150 men). A road runs west from the village to Gyagyi. Leaving the village there is a steep ascent to a height of 6,300 feet with a small camping ground on a fresh clearance about half way up; good water, grass and fuel. At the top of the hill a road runs off south-west to Gyagyi. The road then drops rapidly through thick grass and undergrowth into the Myin valley, and running over rice fields and low hills reaches Bernardmyo (Pyaungaung) (6,020 feet) at 14 miles. Extensive camping ground, grass, water and fuel. The Myin stream rises under Taungmé and is the boundary between Mômeik and Kyátpyen, Ingyauk (*see* next stage) being in the latter and Pyaungaung in the former. There is a village of Lisaws near Pyaungaung camping ground. Military station, Telegraph office, &c., at Bernardmyo.
		5. Môgôk ...	13 4	59 2	At 2¼ miles Ingyauk (6,160 feet) extensive camping ground, grass, water, and fuel plentiful. From here the road runs south-east through fine tree jungle over the Taungmé Pass (6,720 feet), the summit being reached at 5¼ miles. At ½ a mile from Ingyauk a road branches south-west over the Kyaukkyántaung Pass to Kyátpyen. From the Taungmé Pass the road drops rapidly into the Yébu valley through tree jungle for the first 2 miles, then through long grass for 1 mile and for the remainder of the descent through jungle more or less dense. In the last 3 miles of descent the road is crossed and recrossed by streams and aqueducts built for mining purposes. At 11¼ miles the hamlet of Thipugaung is passed and ½ a mile lower the road crosses the Yébu stream in a rice-growing valley, crosses a low ridge covered with scrub jungle and drops down on the Môgôk valley. One mile from Môgôk a road runs west-south-west to Kyátpyen. Môgôk at 13½ miles lies in a valley running from north-east

FROM TWINNGÉ (OR KYÁNHNYÁT) TO BERNARDMYO AND MÔGÔK *viâ* SAGADAUNG—*continued.*

Authorities. Military.	Authorities. Civil.	Number and Names of Stages, Rivers and Streams.	Distances. Intermediate.	Distances. Total.	Remarks.
G.O.C. Mandalay District.	Commr., Northern Divn., and Deputy Commr., Ruby Mines.	5. **Môgôk**—*cont.*			to south-west and is a collection of thriving villages with good houses, six kyaungs (300 men each) from ¼ to ¾ mile apart. River water undrinkable; drinking water from wells and hill streams, good supply. Fuel and grass has to be brought in about a mile. Height of Môgôk 4,400 feet.

Kyánhnyát, situated rather higher up the river, is at present a more important place than Twinngé and Kyaukpyu, Stage 1 above, can also be reached from it. The following is the account of the road in 1886-87:—

FROM KYÁNHNYÁT TO KYAUKPYU (STAGE 1).

BY OFFICERS OF RUBY MINES COLUMN, 1886-87.

Military	Civil	Stage	Intermediate M. F.	Total M. F.	Remarks
G.O.C. Mandalay District.	Commissioner, Northern Division, and Deputy Commissioners, Katha and Ruby Mines.*	1. **Kyaukpyu** ...	14 4	14 4	Leaving Kyánhnyát to the south the road runs nearly south-east for 3⅝ miles to Kyathé, mostly through high grass with trees and some jungle before reaching village. The road is bad and difficult for carts, and there are three muddy nullahs to cross; a great part of this road is covered with from 5 to 15 feet of water in the floods. An alternative route, passable in the floods, exists to the north of this. This is a bad road through jungle nearly the whole way; it is about a mile longer; a fair path has now been made to the south, but this also will not be passable in the rains. Kyathé is a small village about 25 houses; no supplies; one well, always giving water. East of village are some kyaungs and zayáts for about 100 men. Cross a dry nullah and at 4 miles reach Thígôn. Good camping ground to the north of village; well water; no supplies. Road runs due south across nearly 1 mile of rice fields and would require an embankment in rains; then enter jungle, trees, and bushes, not very thick after ¼ mile; arrives at ruins of small village Yetha with two small zayáts. Here the new road joins, being about ⅝ mile shorter. Then through uncultivated fields and grass land to Pauktabin 5¾ miles; this part will require a low embankment. Pauktabin was formerly large village of about 200 houses; one large kyaung on east, which would hold about 150 men, if floor were repaired. Two zayáts in good repair hold 40 men and ruined kyaung on south; two small wells near zayáts, fair water. Burmans say water can be got anywhere by digging about 8 feet. Irrawaddy river only about 1 mile to west, but channel is on other side, of a mile or so of sand banks. Village very much overgrown with jungle and creepers. No good camp. Road runs due east through bamboo jungle, good at first, then indifferent, to Nansain creek; muddy bottom, 12 feet deep when full, now nearly dry, 20 to 30 yards wide, runs into Irrawaddy, then over slightly undulating ground through bamboo jungle; road hard and good; 1¾ miles small earth-tank (30 yards square) on right, dry in hot weather, but water can be got always by digging in it 5 or 6 feet deep. Road continues good through Tôngwé village at 11¼ miles on stream of the same name; bank to south of village steep, about 40

* Kyánhnyát is in the extreme south-west corner of the Myadaung Sub-Division of the Katha District, and the road soon after leaving that place enters the Môgôk Sub-Division of the Ruby Mines District.

FROM TWINNGÉ (OR KYÁNHNYÁT) TO BERNARDMYO AND MÓGÓK *viâ* SAGADAUNG—*continued.*

Authorities. Military.	Authorities. Civil.	Number and Names of Stages, Rivers and Streams.	Distances. Intermediate.	Distances. Total.	Remarks.
G.O.C. Mandalay District.	Commissioner, Northern Division, and Deputy Commissioners, Katha and Ruby Mines.	**1. Kyaukpyu**—*cont.*			feet high, slope more gradual at village. Good camping ground. Stream clear; sandy and gravelly bed. Burmans say always water in it; runs into the Nansain creek, about 2 miles below place where road crosses creek. Stream rises about 15 feet in flood. Left bank easy slope; road first through bamboo, then over gravel and rock through thin tree jungle over small low hills; then over hard sand; ground level; joins the road from Twinngé at 13 miles. Twingyi said to be 7 miles distant. Cross dry sandy nullah 20 feet deep and immediately after cross Tôngwé stream again. Both banks are here steep, about 18 feet high and 30 yards apart. There is good camping ground on both banks on the left for small force; on the right for large. Plenty of grass on right bank after going through jungle growing on bank. Road through open ground, formerly rice fields, to village of Kyaukpyu.

No. 107.

From TWINNGÉ to MÔMEIK.

BY CAPT. SEWELL, NORFOLK REGIMENT, INTELLIGENCE DEPARTMENT, JANUARY 1890.

Military	Civil	Stages	Intermediate M.	Intermediate F.	Total M.	Total F.	Remarks
G.O.C. Mandalay District.	Commissioner, Northern Division, and Deputy Commissioner, Ruby Mines.	**1. Kyaukpyu** ...	**9**	**0**	9	0	*See* Route No. 106.
		2. Wébaung ...	**13**	**0**	22	0	*See* Route No. 106.
		3. Sagadaung ...	**9**	**6**	31	6	*See* Route No. 106.
		4. Pathein ... Kin river and five streams.	**15**	**2**	47	0	Road runs east and crosses Kin chaung at 350 yards; right bank difficult for carts; river 2 feet deep and 30 yards broad (December). Follow the right bank of river to $2\frac{3}{4}$ miles; road as before, but level and fair. The general direction as far as where the road turns off to Pathein is east, but winds a good deal and is practically level. Teak and wood jungle all the way. Pass Siogwé at $3\frac{1}{8}$ miles, 12 houses, on south of road; zayát for 50 men. Cross streams at $1\frac{1}{4}$ miles, $3\frac{3}{4}$ miles, 7 miles, $11\frac{1}{8}$ miles, and $14\frac{1}{4}$ miles; first and last are 20 yards broad; deepest is 1 foot 6 inches, and banks of first, third and fifth are difficult for carts. At $14\frac{1}{8}$ miles road to Pathein turns off east from the direct road to Mômeik, bending to north $\frac{3}{4}$ mile. Village divided by a stream (the last one crossed); 60 houses on south and 20 on north bank. Stream here 30 yards broad and 1 foot deep (December); 2 miles an hour. Kyaung (good) and four zayáts for 160 men in all. Large rice fields to north and north-east. Outlying spurs from the Kachin hills run east and west about 3 miles to the north.
		5. Mômeik ... Nameit chaung and three streams.	**8**	**4**	55	4	Road runs through village and east-south-east for 1 mile, where it joins the direct road at a point 2,000 yards east of where it turned off to Pathein; 1,300 yards west of this junction a road from Bernardmyo runs in. Road east as a general direction and level, the parts between the 1st and 5th

FROM TWINNGÉ TO MÔMEIK—*continued.*

Authorities. Military.	Authorities. Civil.	Number and Names of Stages, Rivers and Streams.	Distances. Intermediate.	Distances. Total.	Remarks.
G.O.C. Mandalay District.	Commissioner, Northern Division, and Deputy Commissioner, Ruby Mines.	**5. Mômeik**—*cont.*			miles, being sandy and running alternately over rice fields and through thickish jungle. At 1¼ miles pass Magyibin, 100 houses; kyaung and zayáts for 120 men. At 2⅜ miles Mokungo on south of road; 20 houses; here is one zayát for 20 men. After 50 yards cross stream, banks difficult, 15 yards wide, 1 foot 6 inches deep; 2 miles an hour (January). At 4¾ miles Letkôkpin 100 yards north of road; 40 houses, one well, also water from chaung. Kyaung and zayáts for 200 men on the road. At 5 miles pass Atéywa; 30 houses; and at 5¼ miles road turns along the left bank of the Nameit and continues parallel to it, or to the branch which runs south of Mômeik. Here another road from Bernardmyo joins. At 5⅜ miles cross stream and at 6 miles a bad muddy creek; another is crossed at 7 miles. This part of the road is through high grass or over rice fields. Pass several small groups of houses. Cross at 8½ miles cross a tributary of Nameit, 70 yards broad, 6 inches deep (January), easy banks, to Mômeik, a large town of 500 houses, residence of Sawbwa of State of same name. The Nameit (Mômeik chaung) runs ½ mile to the north 40 yards of water, 2 feet deep in January; in rains about 120 yards broad; left bank steep. Good camping ground 200 yards south of tributary stream.

No. 108.

From WUMBAGÔN to THAYETA (up Kaukkwé Chaung).

I. B. COMPILATION, JUNE 1888.

Authorities. Military.	Authorities. Civil.	Number and Names of Stages, Rivers and Streams.	Intermediate. M.	Intermediate. F.	Total. M.	Total. F.	Remarks.
G.O.C. Mandalay District.	Commissioner, Northern Division, and Deputy Commissioner, Bhamo.	**1. Mátát** ... ... Kaukkwé chaung.	**10**	**0**	10	0	General direction north from Wumbagôn, which is situated on the right bank of the Kaukkwé chaung, where it joins the Irrawaddy, a little above Katha. Very good foot-path over high ground through light tree jungle with little undergrowth keeping to the left of the chaung. At 4 miles Ôkgyi; 12 houses; kyaung (roof in bad repair) to hold 30 or 40 men. At 5 miles Naungtaw, on opposite (right) bank of the chaung. From Ôkgyi the path traverses low ground through dense jungle, good in the dry season, but (mud) no doubt very bad in the rains. At 10 miles Mátát, small village of eight houses, on left bank of Kankkwé chaung. No accommodation for troops. No supplies.
		2. Thayeta ... Kaukkwé chaung.	**16**	**4**	26	4	There are two roads from Mátát to Mígé (4½ miles) and thence to Thayeta. One over high ground through light tree jungle with little undergrowth, good at all times; the other over low ground through dense jungle, good in dry weather and shorter than the other route, but muddy and bad in the rains. At 4½ miles Mígé, 30 houses, on left bank of Kaukkwé chaung and on the opposite banks of the chaung, here about 50 yards broad. Myohla, 20 houses and one kyaung. Both villages are very open, but there is little cultivation around them. At 16½ miles Thayeta, a small village of eight houses. No accommodation and no supplies. River here 20 yards broad. The inhabitants of all

FROM WUMBAGÔN TO THAYETA (UP KAUKKWÉ CHAUNG)—*continued.*

Authorities.		Number and Names of Stages, Rivers and Streams.	Distances.		Remarks.
Military.	Civil.		Inter-mediate.	Total.	
G.O.C. Mandalay District.	Commissioner, Northern Division, and Deputy Commissioner, Bhamo.	**2. Thayeta**—*cont.*			these villages are half-bred Shan-Burmese (speaking both languages) except at Thayeta where half are Kachin. They earn their livelihood chiefly by fishing and cutting timber. "Taungya" cultivation is carried on in the rainy season, and "mayin" or dry-weather crops in swampy hollows after the rains. The latter is a precarious crop. The Kaukkwé ("bent or twisting") is a bigger stream than the Môsit ("rain drain"), which enters the Irrawaddy further east; but a bar at its mouth stops big boats entering it from the Irrawaddy in the dry season, when only canoes can go up it, there is then very little current. It runs between high banks (at Mígé about 20 feet high), through soft alluvial soil, and in the rains overflows so much that the true course of the stream can with difficulty be traced, and boats of light draught could make a straight line from Wumbagôn to Thayeta instead of following the tortuous course of the stream, which much increases the distance to be traversed by river over that of the land route. The water is good for drinking purposes. From Mátát there is a dry-weather route to Senbo, over which the elephants of U Tu, forest contractor, were taken in November 1887. There are said to be no villages *en route*, and the hills to be crossed are said to be of no great height, probably under 2,000 feet. *See* Route No. 27. From Mígé there is a dry-weather route eastward to Senbo (*vide* Route No. 18). No villages on the road. There is also a road from Mígé westward to Môhnyin, about four marches. The teak forests along the chaungs tributary to the Irrawaddy in this district are worked by Karennis under the Government lessees. Maung Bauk works the Sinkán, Môlé, Kaukkwé and Môsit chaungs, U Tu the Senbo and Môgaung district. The Kachins do not, as a rule, molest the foresters or their employés. There are said to be no villages higher up the Môsit chaung than its mouth. There is probably a direct path leading on from Thayeta up the valley to Laungpu, whence there is a direct path to Môgaung *viâ* Mansin and Lwétôm.

No. 109.

From WUNTHO to MÁNSI (KAYINGÔN) viâ MANYU.

BY CAPT. M. A. TWITE, 23RD MADRAS LIGHT INFANTRY, APRIL 1892.

Military	Civil	Stages	Intermediate		Total		Remarks
			M.	F.	M.	F.	
G.O.C. Mandalay District.	Commissioner, Northern Division, and Deputy Commissioner, Katha.	**1. Kumbaung** ... Daungyu stream crossed seven or eight times; four times unbridged, 30 to 60 feet broad; fordable nearly throughout during dry season.	**13**	**0**	13	0	General direction of road to Satwégyin north, from Satwégyin to Kumbaung east. There is a cart track for the first 2 miles to Nimolé, and the road is fairly level as far as Môgyin, 4½ miles. Léu is passed at 3 miles. Soon after passing Môgyin the path passes round the base of a steep range of hills through thick bamboo jungle to Satwégyin, at 8 miles, a small village hemmed in by steep hills and thick jungle: from this place the path takes an easterly direction and leads over two steep ghâts, slopes from 20° to 30°. The path is rough and crosses stream seven

FROM WUNTHO TO MÁNSI (KAYINGÔN) *viâ* MANYU—*continued*.

Authorities. Military.	Authorities. Civil.	Number and Names of Stages, Rivers and Streams.	Distances. Intermediate. M.	F.	Total. M.	F.	Remarks.
G.O.C. Mandalay District.	Commissioner, Northern Division, and Deputy Commissioner, Katha.	**1. Kumbaung** —*cont.*					or eight times. From above Twédé (12 miles) the road commands an extensive view of the country around Wuntho. Myaukgalé and Nimolé and Léu are fair-sized villages possessing large herds of cattle and much land under cultivation, the remainder of the villages are small and unimportant, possessing scanty supplies and little or no cattle. There is not good lateral communication on this route. Water good and plentiful throughout. At 13 miles Kumbaung.
		2. Myogyin ... Kyaw chaung of no importance till near the gorge at Kyimakán. Here it runs deep and the banks are high.	15	4	28	4	Direction north. The road winds round the spurs of steep hills by the right bank of the river Kyaw chaung, which is here only a large stream flowing between two steep ranges of hills rising straight from the banks. At 4 miles the small villages of Aungbin is reached; here the space between the hills widens and the road (east) is good and level into Kyimakán at 6½ miles, a large village with considerable open cultivated ground around. From here the road again leads round the side of a range of hills, rough, and the gradient short and steep. At 9½ miles the road crosses the Kyaw chaung and recrosses four times before reaching Kyáûmaw at 13 miles. The river at these crossings is from 2 to 3 feet deep, about 40 yards across, and the bed contains immense boulders and projecting rocks rendering it difficult for the transport animals to keep their footing. Path now ascends and passes over saddle connecting high hills and winds down the side of a range into Myogyin, 15½ miles.
		3. Maingdauktaw	11	0	39	4	From Myogyin the road continues winding round the hills, keeping close to river, which it crosses several times. The unimportant villages of Ôkshitpen, Taungmôkin and Môkin are passed at 5, 6 and 6½ miles respectively. Water good and plentiful throughout the route. From Môkin the road again ascends the height and passes along the side of the hills at a considerable elevation, gradually descending to the village Maingdauktaw at the foot of the hills at 11 miles.
		4. Manyu ...	8	4	48	0	From Maingdauktaw it is about 8½ miles into Manyu passing Namôn at 2½ miles and Kyundawgyi at 7 miles. The path is good and level and at Kyundawgyi joins the cart track into Manyu. Maingdauktaw and the other villages between that and Manyu are larger than the villages passed in the jungle. They possess some heads of cattle and much land under cultivation. Kyundawgyi is a large village and an important one, there being roads leading from it in all directions and some large wooden buildings and kyaungs in it.
		5. Sagadaung ...	7	4	55	4	For full details *see* Route No. 59.
		6. Kya-in	13	0	68	4	
		7. Mánsi	8	0	76	4	

PART II.

ROUTES IN THE CENTRAL (CIVIL) DIVISION.

PART II.

ROUTES IN THE CENTRAL (CIVIL) DIVISION.

No. 1.

From ÁLÔN to PAUK (through Kyaw Valley).

I. B. COMPILATION, MAY 1888.

Authorities. Military.	Authorities. Civil.	Number and Names of Stages, Rivers and Streams.	Distances. Inter-mediate. M.	F.	Distances. Total. M.	F.	Remarks.
G.O.C. Myingyán District.	Commissioner, Central Division, and Deputy Commissioner, Lower Chindwin.	**1. Mônywa** ... Chindwin.	7	0	7	0	Álôn is an important town on the left bank of the Chindwin; 1,500 men could easily find accommodation in the numerous kyaungs and zayáts in and around the town. All steamers call. Many native boats also available for transport. Telegraph and post offices. Direction south. Road along river bank liable to be flooded in parts at high floods. Mônywa is an important commercial town on left bank of Chindwin and has a large bazaar. Head-quarters of Deputy Commissioner, Lower Chindwin, and Police Battalion. Barracks for 300 men. Kyaungs which can accommodate 1,200 men. Telegraph and post offices. Numerous native boats available for transport. All steamers call here. Has good road communication with Myinmu.
		2. Salingyi ...	12	0	19	0	Cross Chindwin by ferry and then along the bank in a south-south-west direction over level country, mostly under cultivation, to Salingyi, which is a large straggling village of about 300 houses with large kyaungs capable of containing 900 men. There is a police post built for 100 men. Water-supply from wells. Water from wells is brackish. Supplies scarce, except grass and cattle. Salt manufactures and potteries occupy the inhabitants.
		3. Kyádet ... ... South Yemma chaung.	14	0	33	0	Along a raised metalled and bridged road 12 feet wide, through gently undulating country, to Kyádet, passing Ywathit, where there are several kyaungs and zayáts, at 8½ miles. Kyaungs to accommodate 700 men. Grass, gram and paddy. Also many carts obtainable. The village of Sigyaing, ¼ mile south on the Yemma chaung, has also got many large kyaungs. Lingadaw is about 10 miles from Kyádet in a south-easterly direction.

FROM ÁLÔN TO PAUK (THROUGH KYAW VALLEY)—*continued.*

Authorities. Military.	Authorities. Civil.	Number and Names of Stages, Rivers and Streams.	Distances. Intermediate. M.	F.	Total. M.	F.	Remarks.
G.O.C. Myingyán District.	Commissioner, Southern Division, and Deputy Commissioner, Pakôkku.	**4. Chaungzôngyi.** South Yemma chaung.	7	0	40	0	A fair level road to Chaungzôngyi (or Kyauksôngyi), where there are kyaungs and zayáts capable of accommodating 150 men. Water from Yemma chaung.
		5. Kánlé	7	0	47	0	The road to Kánlé is at first along the bed of the creek, then crosses open country. Three or 4 miles from Kánlé the road passes over low rocky hills covered with jungle. Consist of two villages, big and little Kánlé divided by a creek. Accommodation for 250 men in kyaungs and zayáts. Forage plentiful.
		6. Léo	17	4	64	4	Indifferent road chiefly through thin jungle. Léo has one kyaung (100 men) and three zayáts, 20 houses. From Léo a road runs to Kyaukmasán, 13½ miles. The path is stony and undulating, but except the descent into, and ascent from, Kyaw creek there is nothing to effect the rate of marching for loaded animals. At the place noted the steep bits are very short. Kyaukmasán has 20 houses. Water is obtained from the Yéyu stream (in dry weather by digging the bed). There is one small kyaung in bad repair.
		7. Chaungu ...	15	0	79	4	Through Sathain at 13 miles and Chaungu at 15 miles, a cut road. Here the road from Pakôkku to Pauk, &c. (Route No. 30, Southern Division) is met.
		8. Pauk	7	4	87	0	*See* Route No. 30, Southern Division.

ALTERNATIVE I.

FROM ÁLÔN (STAGE 1) TO KÁNLÉ (STAGE 5) *viâ* KÁNTHA AND LÉMAUK.

BY OFFICER COMMANDING ÁLÔN, 1886-87.

Military.	Civil.	Stages.	Intermediate. M.	F.	Total. M.	F.	Remarks.
G.O.C. Myingyán District.	Commissioner, Central Division, and Dy. Commissioner, Lower Chindwin.	**1. Kántha**	11	0	11	0	Cross Chindwin river to Sethu; thence good cart road through cultivation, with occasionally light scrub jungle. Immediately before entering Kántha the Yemma creek (fordable in December) is crossed three times.
		2. Lémauk ...	12	4	23	4	A direct path exists 9 miles, but crosses very swampy ground. From Kántha to Myogyi, 4 miles, the road passes through thick jungle. One and-a-half miles south of Myogyi is the Ywadaung pagoda once held by dacoits. From here there is a road to Kyádet (15½ miles), passing through cultivated ground as far as Paléwa at 8 miles. Large village with kyaungs and good water-supply. From Paléwa onwards the road crosses broad open plains.

FROM ÁLÔN TO PAUK (THROUGH KYAW VALLEY)—*continued.*

ALTERNATIVE I—*continued.*

Authorities. Military.	Authorities. Civil.	Number and Names of Stages, Rivers and Streams.	Distances. Intermediate. M.	F.	Total. M.	F.	Remarks.
G.O.C. Myingyán District.	Commissioner, Central Dn., & Dy. Commr., Lower Chindwin.	**3. Nyaungôn** ...	11	0	34	4	Road good over open country. Kyauktaung, once occupied by the Myo-thugyi of Myogyi, lies 6 miles to the south-west.
	Commissioner, Southern Division, and Deputy Commissioner, Pakôkku.	**4. Chaungzôn** ...	8	0	42	4	Shinmadaung not visible from this place.
		5. Kánlé	8	0	50	4	Road runs nearly the whole way through dense jungle and over successive hilly ridges. Colonel Eyre says: "Had the road been contested, it "could hardly have been forced with-"out considerable loss." The country, on the whole, is open and flat, and well-cultivated; no difficulty in feeding the horses of the cavalry, the artillery mules, and the transport animals. *Note.*—There is another route to Nyaungôn from Sethu, 3 miles shorter than the above, passing through Myaukthayé and Miyéyé, but it passes through jungle and over ridges, and is harder marching, especially for wheeled transport, than the regular road above described.

BRANCH I.

FROM KÁNLÉ (STAGE 5) TO MYAING.

BY LIEUT. STANTON, ROYAL ARTILLERY, 1886-87.

Military	Civil	Stage	M.	F.	M.	F.	Remarks
G.O.C. Myingyán District.	Commissioner, Southern Division, and Deputy Commissioner, Pakôkku.	**1. Bunbin** ... Kánlé chaung.	13	0	13	0	General direction east-south-east throughout. Good going through a little bamboo and a great deal of scrub jungle. At 6 miles Seitchi, where there is accommodation for 200 men in kyaungs and zayáts. Good water and forage. At 13 miles Bunbin, where is accommodation for 250 men in kyaungs, &c.; two good tanks of water and a salt spring north-west of village; forage in plenty.
		2. Myaing ... Myaing chaung.	11	0	24	0	There is a direct road from Bunbin to Myaing passing no villages, distance 7 miles. Carts can go by it, but it is in bad order owing to disuse. It could easily be put in order by 20 men in a couple of days with picks and shovels. Soil all gravelly. No rock. The road generally used runs for 9 miles across country covered with scrub jungle and intersected by ravines. Last 2 miles down bed of Myaing chaung. The following villages we passed *en route*: Thánzôn, ½ mile; Bandôn, 1¼; Myoso, 3; Magyibinzu, 5; Sadônawé, 10. From Myoso there is a road to Kunlát 3 miles to the west.

No. 2.

From ÁLÔN to SHWÉBO viâ BAUNGYA.

By Capt. C. A. R. SAGE, 18th Bengal Infantry, 1887, and Capt. MORE-MOLYNEUX, 1st Bengal Infantry, March 1888.

Authorities. Military.	Authorities. Civil.	Number and Names of Stages, Rivers and Streams.	Distances. Intermediate. M. F.	Distances. Total. M. F.	Remarks.
G.O.C. Myingyán District.	Commissioner, Central Division, and Deputy Commissioner, Lower Chindwin.	1. **Thazi** ...	13 0	13 0	The road goes in a south-easterly direction through the villages of Sippin (¼ mile) and Kingyaung (½ mile), then turns to the north-east and passes the villages of Kándaw (1 mile), Naungkyidauk (2 miles), Kathán (5 miles), and Kánbin (6½ miles). At 3 miles the Ôkpôdaung creek is crossed; the bed is about 15 yards broad and is sandy; it is generally dry, but after heavy rain has 1½ feet of water. At 7½ miles another sandy bed of a stream is crossed; width 40 yards; always dry. The road is a mere cart track, and in the rainy season is very heavy. At 9 miles there is a pagoda and a well near the road; water good. Thazi is a very large village situated on the west slopes of a low range of hills. Kyaungs are numerous. Water from wells and from bed of stream, which runs south of the village.
		2. **Wadawma** ...	12 0	25 0	The road after leaving Thazi runs north-east over a rocky range of very low hills partly cultivated. Road bad. At 8 miles there is a tank called the Khátkyákán; this tank dries up about 15th March. At 9½ miles the small village of Hmawdaw is passed, ¼ of a mile to the north of the road. Wadawma is a large village; encampment in kyaung to the south and adjacent to the village. Water from well good and plentiful. From here there is a good road to Tántabin (next stage but one), distance 12½ miles (*see* Alt No. 1), by following which the journey to Shwébo would be reduced by one march.
		3. **Baungya** ...	12 0	37 0	A fairly good road through jungle; a small dry nullah crossed at 1 mile. The village of Magyigán is passed at 6 miles and Nainzin at 9 miles. Baungya is situated on the west bank of the river Mu. Water from river.
	Commissioner, Central Division, and Deputy Commissioner, Yé-u.	4. **Magyiôk and Tántabin.**	12 0	49 0	*See* Route No. 18, Stage 5.
		5. **Múgán** ... Mu river.	7 0	56 0	First mile and-a-half through paddy cultivation, thence through jungle to Nyaungain at 6 miles, general direction east. Midway cross Payampaga chaung which requires bridging, as it would probably be unfordable for 4 months of the year, remains of old bridge exist. Road fit for carts and clear of jungle, but in parts narrow. Nyaungain has 30 huts and accommodation for 50 men in kyaung and zayáts. Good water, open paddy ground to the east surrounded by jungle on all other sides. Cross deep nullah, close to kyaung, and over paddy-fields to Múgán, a group of

FROM ÁLÔN TO SHWÉBO *viâ* BAUNGYA—*continued.*

Authorities. Military.	Authorities. Civil.	Number and Names of Stages, Rivers and Streams.	Distances. Intermediate.	Distances. Total.	Remarks.
G.O.C. Mandalay District.	Commissioner, Northern Division, and Deputy Commissioner, Shwébo.	**5. Mugán**—*cont.* ...			three villages ½ a mile from right bank of Mu river amongst groves of palm and other trees in the midst of paddy-fields; 250 houses in all; accommodation in kyaungs, &c., for 500 men. Good and ample water-supply from wells.
			M. F.	M. F.	
		6. Setkaung ...	7 0	63 0	First mile over paddy and through jungle to the Mu river which is here crossed. Fordable except in the rainy season (June to November about). Water 50 yards broad and 2 feet deep in February. Road now east-north-east to Setkaung; road in parts much cut up and probably impassable in the rainy season. At 1½ miles Thayabin, long straggling village, surrounded by jungle on all sides except the east. At 4½ miles Saungdán, 20 huts, good well, but no accommodation. Setkaung is a large village of about 450 houses; accommodation for a large force (1,000 men at least) in zayáts belonging to the Setkaung pagoda. Cultivation around village, no good camping ground; market; good water.
		7. Shwébo ...	9 0	72 0	Road east, mostly over hard grounds through jungle, but in places over cultivation, to Kyíba 5¼ miles, passing small village of Ywathit at 1 mile. Kyíba is a large village of 150 houses; a good deal of silk-weaving is carried on here. Thence good going into Shwébo, crossing the old moat at 7½ miles and passing the village of Mingu at 8 miles. *Note.*—There should be a rather more direct route than this, running direct from Baungya (Stage 3) towards Shwébo or at any rate towards Mágán (Stage 5), it being an apparently unnecessary détour to go to Tántabin (Stage 4), but no such route appears to have been traversed, or at any rate recorded.

ALTERNATIVE I.

FROM WADAWMA (STAGE 2) TO TÁNTABIN *viâ* NYAUNGAIN.

BY CAPT. C. A. R. SAGE, 18TH BENGAL INFANTRY, 1886-87.

Military	Civil	Stages	Intermediate	Total	Remarks
G.O.C. Myingyán District.	Commissioner, Central Divn., and Dy. Commissioner, Lower Chindwin.	**1. Magyiôk and Tántabin.**	12 4	12 4	A good road. Direction due north, passing through open jungle after the village of Yé-o is passed at 2½ miles. Three small sandy nullahs are crossed, one at ½ mile, one at 2 miles, and one at 3 miles. At 5 miles there is a good tank and zayáts called Tédukán. Nyaungain is a large village on the northern border of the Álôn district. Water from wells good and plentiful. Six miles north of Nyaungain is the village of Tántabin.

No. 2.

From ÁLÔN to SHWÉBO *viâ* BAUNGYA—*continued*.

BRANCH I.

From THAZI (Stage 1) to MAGYIZAUK.

By Capt. C. A. R. SAGE, 18th Bengal Infantry, (? 1887).

Authorities. Military.	Authorities. Civil.	Number and Names of Stages, Rivers and Streams.	Distances. Intermediate. M.	F.	Total. M.	F.	Remarks.
G.O.C. Myingyán District.	Commissioner, Central Division, and Deputy Commissioner, Lower Chindwin.	**1. Kánbyu** ...	10	0	10	0	Leaving Thazi the road runs for ½ a mile along the bed of a sandy stream, then ascends a spur of the hills and runs in an easterly direction over a low range of hills, passing through cultivation till the village of Nyaungdu is passed at 5 miles, after which the road passes through jungle. The village of Nyaungdu consists of several clusters of huts scattered here and there. A small sandy bed of nullah is crossed at 4 miles, another at 6½ miles, and another at 9 miles. At 7½ miles a large tank called the Ségyikán is passed; this tank does not dry up till the middle of April. Kánbyu is a small poor village; no supplies procurable; water from tanks, except in April, when it is procured by digging wells in sandy bed of stream to north of village. Camping ground at kyaung to south-east of village.
		2. Magyizauk ...	14	0	24	0	The road passes through village of Ayadaw at 4 miles (a large but poor village; water from tanks) and through Minyuwet at 11 miles; road fairly good. Magyizauk is situated on the west bank of the river Mu. Country adjacent low, and in rainy season swampy.

No. 3.

From ÁLÔN to YÉ-U.

I. B. Compilation, 1887-88 (mostly Native information).

Military	Civil	Stages	Intermediate M.	F.	Total M.	F.	Remarks
G.O.C. Myingyán District.	Commr., Central Dn., and Dy. Commr., Lower Chindwin.	**1. Budalin** ...	15	0	15	0	Road mostly a cross country cart track, very heavy going in wet weather. Ôkpôdaung chaung is crossed about midway, nearly always dry. Budalin is a large village; daily market at which supplies are procurable; good water from wells. Lémiyé, police post on Chindwin river lies 10 miles to the west.
	Commr., Central Divn., and Dy. Commissioner, Yé-u.	**2. Sainbyin** ...	13	0	28	0	Road almost due north. Generally a good cross country track, but bad in parts in wet weather. Sainbyin, large village in Yé-u district, market, kyaungs and good wells.
		3. Tabayin ...	12	4	40	4	Formerly a large town. Road as before, direction generally north-east.
		4. Yé-u	11	2	51	6	Direction first half north-east, remainder east. Road bad in wet weather.

No. 4.

From ÁVA to WUNDWIN.

By Lieut. NICHOLSON, 1st Hampshire Regiment, February 1888.

Authorities.		Number and Names of Stages, Rivers and Streams.	Distances.		Remarks.
Military.	Civil.		Intermediate.	Total.	
G.O.C. Myingyán District.	Commissioner, Central Division, and Deputy Commissioner, Sagaing.				*General Report on route Áva to Wundwin.*
		1. Sagayin ... Pánláng river.	M. F. 7 0	M. F. 7 0	*Road.*—In most places a mere cart track, running through thin scrub jungle, or fairly open country. Very little used. Road very bad in some places, especially between Taungdwingyi and Yékán, and would be impassable for wheeled traffic during the rains. Road runs almost an exact straight line south-south-east from Sagayin to Wundwin and no detours are made. The route *viâ* Kyauksé is preferable. *Water.*—Very scarce in most places. Water scanty from a well obtainable from the Pánláng, 1½ miles distant. The wells, as a rule, are dug too shallow and only contain 1 foot 6 inches of water in some cases. A large force could not use this route on this account. *Supplies.*—No supplies can be obtained. There is no bazaar on the route between Tada-u and Wundwin (54½ miles), a little bhusa for bullocks can be obtained, but no chenna and very little grass for horses. *Accommodation.*—Zayáts at every stage; kyaungs more rare; there are some small villages along the route. Leaving Áva pagoda road runs east. Open and cultivated ground on the right. At 1 mile road turns south and continues south for 2 miles, where the Mandalay-Myingyán telegraph wire is met at the village of Yatán. Road good, newly made, and well shaded by trees on each side. The road now turns west for ¼ mile and then meets the old King's road, a brick causeway, in bad repair. Before reaching Tada-u the Myitha chaung is crossed by a wooden bridge in good repair and practicable for carts. At 3½ miles reach village of Tada-u. Good bazaar. All the surrounding villages get their supplies here. Leaving Tada-u the road runs south-south-east; brick causeway still continues alongside the road. At 6 miles pass the ruins of four very large pagodas on the right of the road. At 6½ miles Shwézigôn. At 7 miles Sagayin; small village, two pôngyi kyaungs, one on north and one on south side of village, two zayáts, and a good well at each kyaung. Pánláng river ⅓ mile north-east of village. No bazaar. From here there is a good cart road to Paleik 6 miles in a north-east direction crossing the Pánláng and Tôngyôngya chaungs which are unfordable in the rains, but the latter is bridged higher up, and in the rains carts cross there and are ferried over the Pánláng. The distance is thus increased by 2 miles.
		2. Ônghmin ... Samôn chaung.	8 4	15 0	Leaving Sagayin road runs due south. Half-a-mile from village road branches off at foot of large ruined pagoda south-south-west to Chaungwa. This road is impracticable during rains. At ¾ mile pass village of Kinywa, where two roads branch off west to Chaungwa. Country open, thin scrub jungle sloping gently to west. At 2½ miles two small zayáts. No water. Road runs along west slope of Sagayin hills and is level and practicable for carts at all times of the year. At 3 miles

FROM ÁVA TO WUNDWIN—*continued.*

Authorities. Military.	Authorities. Civil.	Number and Names of Stages, Rivers and Streams.	Distances. Intermediate. M. F.	Distances. Total. M. F.	Remarks.
G.O.C. Myingyân District.	Commissioner, Central Division, and Deputy Commissioner, Sagaing.	**2. Ônghmin**—*cont.*			two zayáts. Direction of road due south. No water. Large ruined pagoda visible for long distance 500 yards to left of road. Extensive view over country sloping to west. At 4½ miles begin to descend slightly. Small brick pagoda 6 feet high on right of road, direction due south. Another road crosses at right angles from Yéga on east to Shábyu on west. At 5½ miles pass two zayáts; water from well muddy unfit for drinking. Thin scrub jungle on each side of road. Road here changes direction to south-south-east and slightly up-hill. At 6¾ miles cross dry nullah, no bridge and bad in rains. At 8½ miles reach three zayáts. Well 100 yards west. Water scarce. Samôn river 1½ miles north-east from which water can be obtained. A road leads from zayáts to river. Very small village of Ônghmin, 300 yards west of zayáts. No bazaar or supplies of any sort. Accommodation for 120 men in zayáts. No kyaungs.
	Commissioner, Central Division, and Deputy Commissioner, Myingyân.	**3. Pyawbwé (Pwébwé).**	9 0	24 4	From Ônghmin zayáts road runs south through thin scrub jungle and at 1½ miles south-east by south. At 3 miles reach two small zayáts and village of (?). Leaving (?) road runs south-south-east. At 3¼ miles cross sandy nullah, 100 yards wide. After crossing nullah road runs up-hill and due south. Sandy ground and thin scrub jungle. At 4¾ miles four zayáts deserted. Kyaung and two pagodas on knoll on left of road. No water. Direction of road south-south-east. At 5¼ miles reach highest point of ridge and begin to descend. Direction of road due south. At 6½ miles reach two small zayáts with well, only 6 inches water in it. At 6¾ miles cross bed of river, 80 yards broad. Water undrinkable. At 7 miles reach villages of Ôngdaw (small) on left side of road and Piyébin (large) on right side. Good well at Ôngdaw. No zayáts or supplies at either. At 9 miles reach village of Pyawbwé (or Pwébwé). Two wells. No bazaar or supplies. Three zayáts. Village of Tagwa ½ mile north-east.
		4. Yékán	10 0	34 4	From Pyawbwé road runs south-south-east slightly up-hill through thin scrub jungle. At ½ mile pass ruined pagoda on top of hill to the left of road. Direction of road south. At 1¾ miles south-south-east extensive view over country sloping to west. High conspicuous hill 2 miles south-east with pagoda kyaung on top of it. Road runs south-south-east. A steep broken range of hills crowned with pagodas ½ mile to left of and parallel with road. At 5 miles reach Wégun. One zayát and small tank at foot of hills 300 yards east of zayát. At 7¼ miles reach Taungdwingyi. Two zayáts, two wells, no supplies, 10 houses. Leaving Taungdwingyi road runs up-hill south-south-east in bed of stream. Very bad road for carts. At 8¼ miles reach top of hill. Pagoda left of road. Road still very bad, descends south-south-west. At 10 miles reach small village of Yékán; 15 houses, two zayáts, room for 150 men. Good well at zayáts, 6 feet depth of water. No supplies of any sort. No bazaar. Dry bed of tank 150 yards by 40 on left of road.

FROM ÁVA TO WUNDWIN—*continued.*

Authorities. Military.	Authorities. Civil.	Number and Names of Stages, Rivers and Streams.	Distances. Intermediate. M. F.	Distances. Total. M. F.	Remarks.
G.O.C. Myingyán District.	Commissioner, Central Division, and Deputy Commissioner, Myingyán.	**5. Shwédaung** ... Taungbo chaung.	**9 4**	44 0	Leaving Yékán road runs south slightly up-hill. At 1½ miles two pagodas and one zayát, thin scrub jungle. Road here runs between banks 8 feet high for 200 yards. At 3½ miles country gets very open. Road good. Direction south-south-east. At 5 miles dry bed of tank on right of road; zayát and well on left. At 5½ miles enter Ywé; 100 houses, no bazaar, 25 carts, chenna or rice to be obtained. Four zayáts and one kyaung. Three good wells on west of village. Leaving Ywé road runs south through open country. At 7½ miles cross dry sandy bed of Taungbo chaung. At 8½ miles road runs along top of bank of Taungbo chaung. At 9 miles pass two ruined pagodas on right, and at 9½ miles enter Shwédaung. Three zayáts. Accommodation for 150 men. Three wells, one 200 yards south-west of zayáts, bad. Other, 300 yards north-west of zayáts, good. Sixty houses. No bazaar. A little rice and milk and a few chickens obtainable. No chenna. Fifty carts and 150 cattle.
G.O.C. Rangoon District.	Commissioner, Eastern Division, and Deputy Commissioner, Meiktila.	**6. Wundwin** ...	**14 0**	58 0	Leaving Shwédaung road runs south through village. At 3½ miles two zayáts. Country open and slightly wooded. At 3¾ miles deserted village of Ywashé. No water. Direction of road now south-south-east. At 4½ miles small village of Piyépyu. Kyaung and three zayáts, bad repair. Water from small tank. At 6 miles village of (?) Water from pond ½ mile north of village; 20 houses, 20 carts, one zayát. At 7½ miles pass large village of (?) on right of road. Two wells. At 8 miles kyaung and two zayáts. Direction of road south-south-east. At 11 miles well by right side of road. At 13 miles pass brick-field belonging to railway; and at 14 miles enter Wundwin. Accommodation for a regiment in kyaungs. Small bazaar at Wundwin, but large one every five days at Thédaw, 1½ miles south-west. Chenna difficult to obtain and grass for horses has to be brought in 8 miles from banks of Samôn river. Wundwin is the head-quarters of Assistant Commissioner and Assistant Superintendent of Police. Railway passes through Thédaw, 1½ miles south-east. Water supply plentiful from four wells.

No. 5.

From INDIN to FALÁM (TÁSHÔN YWAMA) viâ SIHAUNG.

By Capt. J. G. HUNTER, 10th Bengal Infantry, March 1890, and Lieut. E. W. M. NORIE, Middlesex Regiment, Intelligence Department, March 1890.

Authorities.		Number and Names of Stages, Rivers and Streams.	Distances.		Remarks.
Military.	Civil.		Intermediate.	Total.	
			M. F.	M. F.	
G.O.C. Myingyán District.	Commissioner, Central Division, and Deputy Commissioner, Upper Chindwin.	**1. Sihaung** ... Myittha and Nankathé rivers.	*16 4	16 4	From Indin (*see* Route No. 30, Southern Division), follow the Kalémyo-Kán road southwards for about 10 miles, the first 3 or 4 of which are through "kaing" grass, the remainder through jungle. At 10 miles the track to Sihaung branches west from the main road and in about ½ mile reaches the village of Taungpha (12 houses, including the villages from Pawnimé, removed to it from the opposite side of the river) situated on the right bank of the Myittha river, which is fordable in the dry season (1st December to 15th May) and crossed by a ferry in the wet. The river bed, however, is full of snags and fording must be carried out carefully. From Pawnimé (now removed to Taunghpa) the track runs nearly south through thorny jungle with "In" trees in considerable quantity, to Kado (19 houses), about 14½ miles. Here the track bends round more to the south-west reaching North Sihaung (45 houses) at 15 miles, South Sihaung (26 houses) at 15½ miles, and Sihaung post at 16½. The track has been cleared and widened by the Public Works Department, has no steep gradients, and in the dry season offers no difficulties, but in the rains the country is much inundated and what with crossing the Myittha and other nullahs in flood, and the track being unmetalled over heavy alluvial soil, troops would find it very difficult to march from Indin to Sihaung in one day, and arrangements should be made for providing shelter at Taunghpa or Pawnimé. At North Sihaung the present Public Works Department track from Kôko joins the path to Sihaung post. From Sihaung to its junction with the Myittha, the Nankathé (Manipur river) follows a very tortuous course with a succession of small but strong rapids. The river changes its channel considerably and when in flood overflows its branches inundating the country on either side, and forming numerous islands, some of considerable extent. The village of South Sihaung has been recently partly washed away, in one of these changes of course, and North Sihaung is also threatened. Throughout these jungles leeches are a great source of annoyance during the rains. Sihaung is now in telegraphic communication with the rest of Burma, and the post can accommodate 150 rifles. Boats can run from Sihaung to Indin in one day, thence to Kalémyozeik in one day and thence to Kaléwa in one day or if delayed at the rapids two days. The up-stream journey from Kaléwa to Sihaung when the river is not very low and not in flood takes seven or eight days. From Sihaung on to Kunchaung (*see* Branch I) they take three days, but can return in one day.

* Lieut. Kirby, R.E., reporting on this road in August 1892, gives the distance from Indin to Sihaung as 13 miles; he makes the distance to Taungpha within about 1½ miles of what Capt. Hunter makes it (10½), but the remainder of the route he makes only 4 miles as compared with Capt. Hunter's 6 miles. The Telegraph department however say they expended 17 miles of wire in constructing the line between Indin and Sihaung post and, as their line is probably more direct than that of the road, Capt. Hunter's distances even may be somewhat under-estimated, and Lieut. Kirby's still more so, rendering it desirable to divide this journey into two stages when there is no great hurry.—A. F.

FROM INDIN TO FALÁM (TÁSHÔN YWAMA) *viâ* SIHAUNG—*continued.*

Authorities.		Number and Names of Stages, Rivers and Streams.	Distances.				Remarks.
Military.	Civil.		Intermediate.		Total.		
			M.	F.	M.	F.	
G.O.C. Myingyán District.	Political Officer, Chin Hills.	**2. Tawyán** ... Myachaungyi, Myachaungalé, and two other streams.	15	0	31	4	From the Sihaung post the road to Falám runs nearly due west for 3 miles, beyond which the direction is north-west all the way to Tawyán. At ½ mile pass the village of Kyawywa of about 80 houses, surrounded by three stockades, and inhabited by tame Chins. So far the road runs through flat cultivated land and crosses two water channels, but beyond the village it enters the jungle and runs over very level ground for 2½ miles, when it crosses the dry bed of a nullah and, bending to the north-west, runs across dry undulating ground covered by "Eng" jungle and grass. Soil sandy and gravelly. At about 6¾ miles the path reaches the Myachaungyi which it crosses. The ford in the dry weather is about 20 yards broad and 1 foot deep, but higher up the chaung runs through a deep, narrow, and rocky valley. After crossing the chaung there are two roads for a short distance, one of which runs up the stream, crossing it again twice, and the other which runs up on to the high bank and so avoids crossing the stream. Beyond this the road crosses a small stream flowing in from the south-west and then runs over undulating ground as before, crossing several nullahs, all of which are dry except during the rains. At 8 miles reach the Myachaungalé, which joins the Myachaungyi from the south-west. Both banks of this stream are extremely steep and almost precipitous, steps having to be cut in the path to enable the ascent and descent to be made. The left bank is about 30 or 40 feet high and is crowned by log stockades which command the ascent. Beyond these stockades the road runs very steeply up the spur for about 800 yards. Beyond this the ascent becomes much more gradual with a few steep bits for short distances up to 10 miles, from which point it runs fairly level along the side of the hill to the first Minlédaung village of Talung at 11 miles. From Talung it runs to Haitwé at 11¾ miles and Kunleng at 12½ miles. Besides these three Minlédaung* villages there are also Hairôn and Lungpi, through which the road does not pass, but to which paths run from the other villages. Of these Lungpi seems to be the largest. It is about ½ mile south-west of Kunleng and contains about 100 houses. Haitwé contains about 50 houses, Kunleng about 30, and Talung about 15. Hairôn is to the south of Haitwé and out of sight of the path. Water is very plentiful from streams from the hill side. From Kunleng the path runs pretty steeply up to a saddle at 13 miles. There is another path which runs from about the 11th mile to this saddle and passes above the villages without entering any of them. From the saddle the path descends gradually, skirting along the side of the hill till it reaches the Tawyán stream just below the village of Tawyán at 15 miles. Tawyán is a village of about 80 houses. Passing to the west of village there is a good camping ground close by with a stream of good water flowing through it.

* These Minlédaung villages were supposed to be under the domination of, and tributary to, the Táshôns; this is not so. The Táshôns have nothing to do with them. They formerly paid triennial tribute to the Kalé Sawbwa.

FROM INDIN TO FALÁM (TÁSHÔN YWAMA) *viâ* SIHAUNG—*continued*.

Authorities. Military.	Authorities. Civil.	Number and Names of Stages, Rivers and Streams.	Distances. Intermediate. M. F.	Distances. Total. M. F.	Remarks.
G.O.C. Myingyán District.	Political Officer, Chin Hills.	**3. Liendri** ... Kumkyin Vár.	12 0	43 4	From Tawyán the road runs west for 7½ miles and then south-south-west for the rest of the stage. Leaving camp the path ascends to a saddle at 1½ miles, very steep at first and more gradual higher up, until the top is reached; from here it runs pretty level along the side of the ridge near the crest until it reaches the top of a spur at about 4 miles, down which it runs leaving the village of Thortáng to the south. This is a large village of over 100 houses in two parts. The large villages of Lumpté and Kumptsin, about a couple of miles to the north-west and west; these each contain about 80 houses. At 7½ miles the Kumkyin Vár is reached, the last ½ mile of descent being extremely steep. This stream is about 3 yards broad and flows south into the Nankathé. From the stream the path turns south-south-west and ascends very steeply at first and then more gradually for about a mile, after which it runs nearly level along the hill side to Liendri at 12 miles. Liendri contains about 100 houses and is surrounded by the usual village stockade. Water is plentiful from springs in the hill side, and a few supplies of fowls, &c., are procurable. The best place for a camp is above the village on the north-west. From above Liendri several villages can be seen to the south and south-west including Twinzé, Tuntwé, Sunhlán, Lenté, and Nanzaw.
		4. Falám (Táshôn Ywama). Nankathé or Manipur river.	8 0	51 4	From here the path runs south for about ½ mile and then bends to the west, gradually descending, till it strikes the Nankathé at about 3½ miles. In the dry weather, when the river is low, the ford at this point is only about 2 or 2½ feet deep and from 20 yards to 30 yards broad. The path now runs north-west along the right bank of the stream for a short distance and then, bending to the west, ascends rather steeply at first and then more gradually to 4½ miles. From here it runs level to the village of Kôtár at 6 miles. Kôtár contains about 60 houses. The most direct road from here to Falám, the Tashôn Ywama, runs nearly due north to the top of the ridge just above the village and thence down by a steep path to the village itself. This path is very steep all the way. The village of Sonté is passed at about 6¾ miles, about 500 yards to the east of the path, containing about 30 houses. Falám itself lies at the head of a small valley shut in by bold spurs on the east and west and by the high precipitous ridge of the Bilúma range to the south. At the foot of the valley to the north and some 2,000 feet below the village flows the Nankathé or Manipur river. Falám is commanded from the ridge and spurs and is surrounded by hedges, apparently of cactus. It contains from 450 to 500 houses. The chief village is called by Burmans the Táshôn Ywama, Falám by the Chins; there are several other large villages within a radius of 4 or 5 miles. Water is obtained from springs in the hill side above the village. Supplies of myithun and potatoes seem to be plentiful. The above route would be impracticable in its last stage after heavy rain, as the Nankathé river rises rapidly and the ford would become impracticable. In this case the present path from Liendri runs south as before for ½ mile and then level for 3 miles along the side of the hill to

FROM INDIN TO FALÁM (TÁSHÔN YWAMA) *vià* SIHAUNG—*continued.*

Authorities. Military.	Authorities. Civil.	Number and Names of Stages, Rivers and Streams.	Distances. Intermediate.	Distances. Total.	Remarks.
G.O.C. Myingyán District.	Political Officer, Chin Hills.	**6. Falám (Táshôn Ywama)**—*cont.*			the west. From here it drops by a very precipitous descent along the face of a tremendous khud to the river, which here rushes through a very narrow channel of rock over a fall of some 10 feet; over this a flimsy bridge of three bamboos with a slight trelliswork at the sides is thrown, advantage being taken of a rock in midstream to rest the bridge on. Having crossed the bridge, the path turns south-west and runs down the gorge for about a mile till it joins the other road beyond the ford. About 200 yards below the bridge the path runs along a ledge on the face of the rock, which is here nearly perpendicular for 400 yards or 500 yards at a height of from 100 feet to 200 feet above the river and is certainly dangerous. From the bridge another path runs straight up the precipitous side of the gorge and so into Falám at 2½ miles, but this is so steep as to be only practicable for bare-footed and unladen Chins, and troops certainly could not be taken up it. *Note.*—If a road was required to be made from Sihaung to Falám another track altogether should be looked for from the ridge to the east of Thawtáng to the village of Kôtár. This would probably run down the spur above Thortang in a south-west direction and thence along either bank of the Nankathé as might be found most practicable, crossing it at some convenient point by a bridge. Another road runs direct from Lieudri to Falám through Twetin to the north of the road described above, but it is said to be more difficult.

BRANCH I.

FROM SIHAUNG TO HANTA.

BY LIEUT. KIRBY, R.E., AUGUST 1892.

Military	Civil	Stage	Intermediate	Total	Remarks
			M. F.	M. F.	
G.O.C. Myingyán District.	Political Officer, Chin Hills.	**1. Kunchaung** ... Nankathé river.	17 0	17 0	General direction south and south-west. The route is a mere cooly path, there being no recognised road; the first 6 miles run along the valley of the Myittha. At 6th mile the route crosses the Nankathé and at the 7th mile enters the low hills on the edge of the plain. From 7th to the 17th mile the route runs along the right bank of the Nankathé. The following camping grounds are passed on this stage: Kabani 7 miles from Sihaung, and at miles 10½ and 13¼ respectively; there is also camping accommodation at Kunchaung. Boats take three days to ascend from Sihaung to Kunchaung, but can return in one day.
		2. Hanta	8 6	25 6	General direction north-west along Nankathé; then south-west. On leaving Kunchaung the route ascends right bank of the Nankathé for 1½ miles, gradient 1 in 7 or 1 in 8; steep khuds all the way and impracticable for mules to pass one another. From 1½ miles to mile 3 the route is nearly level; camping ground at mile 3. From mile 3 to mile 3¾ the route descends to the Netpyaw chaung, where there is plenty of water all the year round. From the Netpyaw chaung to Hanta is a steady rise at a gradient of 1 in 8, the

FROM INDIN TO FALÁM (TÁSHÔN YWAMA) *viâ* SIHAUNG—*continued.*

BRANCH I—*continued.*

Authorities.		Number and Names of Stages, Rivers and Streams.	Distances.		Remarks.
Military.	Civil.		Intermediate.	Total.	
G.O.C. Myingyán District.	Political Officer, Chin Hills.	**2. Hanta**—*cont.*			distance being 5 miles; 3 miles from Hanta there is a plentiful water-supply. Mules leaving Hanta unloaded at sunrise for Kunchaung, as a rule, return loaded at 2-30 P.M. The hill sides are more or less precipitous throughout, and a great deal of shale is met with, which is liable to slip at any time during the rains and thus block the road temporarily.

No. 6.

From KALÉMYOZEIK (on Myittha River) to FORT WHITE (Old).

BY MAJOR FENTON, DEPUTY ASSISTANT QUARTERMASTER-GENERAL, INTELLIGENCE BRANCH, MARCH 1890.

Military.	Civil.	Number and Names of Stages, Rivers and Streams.	Intermediate.	Total.	Remarks.
G.O.C. Myingyán District.	Commissioner, Central Division, and Deputy Commissioner, Upper Chindwin.	**1. Kalémyo** ... Small stream, perenniel.	M. F. 2 0	M. F. 2 0	Kalémyozeik is the landing place for troops and stores for the Fort White ine brought up by boat from Kaléwa n the Chindwin, or down by road or ver from Kán or Gángaw. The Kán road is on the right bank of the Myittha, which is crossed here by a ferry platform-raft capable of conveying ponies and boats. From Kalémyozeik the road runs over low ground overgrown by kaing grass where not cleared for paddy cultivation, which is evidently little better than a swamp from June to November, December, or even later if the October rains are heavy. The road is being raised and ditches dug on either side and, when metalled, will be a good cart road in all weather. Until, however, this is done elephants are the only transport suitable for employment from June to November. The direction of the road is almost due west throughout. For the first $1\frac{1}{4}$ miles runs at a short distance from the left bank of a small stream. At $1\frac{1}{4}$ miles this stream is crossed by a strong wooden bridge. At $1\frac{1}{2}$ miles enters the walled enclosure of Kalémyo. Wall in ruins and overgrown with jungle, but easily traceable. Kalémyo at present (1890) consists of about 100 wretched tumble-down looking huts, but signs of former prosperity are present in the shape of pagodas, and perhaps with increasing security from Chin raids it may revive again. The walled enclosure is about $\frac{1}{2}$ mile square. At $1\frac{3}{4}$ miles the Kalémyo Post bazaar commences and consists of a row of shops extending along the right of the road up to the post. English tinned stores of all sorts procurable at not very exorbitant prices. The post is on the left of the road and is surrounded by a thorn wire and post enclosure. Being on perfectly level ground the whole place must be under water in the rains, and there is no means of keeping the men out of the mud other than by raising the thatched barracks well off the ground and running raised paths from one building to another, which is already done. Accommodation for (200?) men and (fig.?) officers, besides hospital and Commissariat buildings for large quantity of stores and followers. The situation of the post, namely, on a dead level in a sea of kaing grass requiring to be cleared annually

FROM KALÉMYOZEIK (ON MYITTHA RIVER) TO FORT WHITE (OLD)—*continued.*

Authorities. Military.	Authorities. Civil.	Number and Names of Stages, Rivers and Streams.	Distances. Intermediate.	Distances. Total.	Remarks.
G.O.C. Myingyán District.	Commissioner, Central Division, and Deputy Commissioner, Upper Chindwin.	**1. Kalémyo**—*cont.*			is most objectionable from a sanitary point of view and cannot be other than most unhealthy at any time of year except perhaps from March to the end of May. Water from a small stream to the north of the post, the same as that crossed on the way from Kalémyozeik.
		2. No. 2 Post ... Good perennial stream, tributary of Nayinsaya river.	M. F. 7 0	M. F. 9 0	General direction of road in this stage west. First ¾ mile over level cleared ground, cart track but unmetalled and would be terrible going in wet weather; then cross small nullah, dry in March, but holding several feet of water and mud in wet weather no doubt. Here clearing ceases and track continues through light jungle with patches of kaing grass (for the next mile) and scrub undergrowth, so that, although there would be little difficulty in getting about through it, it is only possible to see for a very short distance and concealment is easy. Grass, &c., is cleared for about 50 feet on either side of the track, and a temporary telegraph line has been put up along it. At about 5 miles the track is rising very slightly, almost imperceptibly, and the undergrowth gets lighter and soon almost entirely ceases. At about 5½ miles cleared track branches off to the right, running near the base of the hills and joining the Kalémyo-Yázagyo route (Route No. 23) near Atéywa. A little beyond this track from Kambalé *vide* Route No. 30, Southern Division, joins in from left rear. Road now rises a little more perceptibly and turning slightly towards north-west crosses the end of a long spur running up west to the main range. The hill rises up steeply on the left of the road, but on the right falls gradually to good stream of running water, a tributary of the Nayinsaya river. At 7 miles No. 2 Post in a good clearing just at the entrance of a gorge running up westward into the hill, commanded from hill side south and north-west at distances from 200 yards upwards. All undergrowth had been removed and the soil is hard and drainage good. Ample water-supply at all seasons from stream running close to the north of the post which also contains quantities of fish (mahseer, ruhe, &c.) in the larger pools which occur here and there between the rapids; forage also plentiful. The post consists of a small log stockade at present fully occupied by thatched buildings to accommodate garrison of 80 rifles; the stockade is outside and to the west of another shed with raised floor, which would take about 40 men; two thatched mule sheds and two small huts for Commissariat and Transport subordinates; no other accommodation. This is an easy march and in the dry season, March (or perhaps, February) to June, there is no reason why troops should not march straight up from the river side at Kalémyozeik. In wet weather, however, the first 2 miles west of Kalémyo must be very bad until the road is raised, drained, and metalled. The rest of the way up to No. 2 is probably not very bad in any weather except during or immediately after heavy rain.

No. 6.

FROM KALÉMYOZEIK (ON MYITTHA RIVER) TO FORT WHITE (OLD)—*continued.*

Authorities.		Number and Names of Stages, Rivers and Streams.	Distances.		Remarks.
Military.	Civil.		Inter-mediate.	Total.	
			M. F.	M. F.	
G.O.C, Myingyân District.	Political Officer, Chin Hills.	**3. No. 3 Post** ...	7 4	16 4	From No. 2 Post the road is only practicable for mules or elephants, not carts. For the first 2½ miles it follows the course of the stream, whence No. 2 Post draws its water-supply ; steep jungle-clad hills on either side, undergrowth cleared away near the road ; track good but slippery in parts. At 2¼ miles steep descent to crossing of a stream, which a short distance lower down joins the No. 2 Post stream, only a little water running in it in March. Steep ascent from stream and at 2½ miles level open clearing between the two streams at the foot of steep spur dividing them up which the track zigzags. The spur rises in a series of steps,—steep ascent, then a short level ridge, steep khud on either side, then another ascent, and so on. After ascending a few hundred feet there is little or no undergrowth. At 6½ miles extensive taungya-clearing and No. 3 Post is in full view up above due west. From here the ascent is very steep, soil clayey, and very slippery after even a light shower. At 7½ miles reach No. 3 Post, aneroid showing a rise of 2,500 feet from No. 2. The general direction of the route is west and, with the exception of the 2½ miles which are steady but very gradual rise, the march is one practically continuous climb. In the valleys of the streams there are plenty of fine teak trees and bamboos, higher up you meet with the mountain oake, but no pines. No. 3 Post is well situated on a narrow jutting out, and comparatively level portion of the spur up which the path has ascended and continues to ascend towards No. 4 Post. The stockade itself on the highest and easternmost part of the ridge is small, but there are numerous outlying thatched sheds around below it, the whole surrounded by abattis, the whole of the trees on the site of the post having been cut down and thus utilized. In the stockade there is accommodation for five officers and about 150 rifles besides hospital and the usual subsidiary buildings. Outside there are store-sheds and sheds for commissariat and transport followers and about 150 transport animals. Ample water-supply from ravine about ½ a mile south-west of, and rather below, the post; good mule path leading down to it. Water runs freely in March and is collected in troughs for the animals and runs through bamboo spouts for convenience in filling water vessels. Forage for transport animals cut on the hill side above and brought in on the mules. There is a fine view from the highest part of the post in all directions,—Kalémyo in sight due east; No. 2 Post is just concealed by the point of a spur cutting in from the north close to it; and No. 5 Post on the Lítha ridge is also just out of sight, but by sending signalling parties a little to the north of No. 5 and to the south of No. 3 heliographic communication could be maintained with both those posts and with Kalémyo. There are no Chin villages in sight, but numerous taungya clearings. No. 3 is cold at night even in March. On the 13th and 14th (noon to noon) of that month the thermometer registered in the shade maximum 73°, minimum 60°.

FROM KALÉMYOZEIK (ON MYITTHA RIVER) TO FORT WHITE (OLD)—*continued.*

Authorities. Military.	Authorities. Civil.	Number and Names of Stages, Rivers and Streams.	Distances. Intermediate. M. F.	Distances. Total. M. F.	Remarks.
G.O.C. Myingyán District.	Political Officer, Chin Hills.	**4. No. 4 Post** ...	6 0	22 4	From No. 3 Post path ascends for about 2½ miles, zigzagging up the same spur as in the last stage, but gradient not so steep until just before this point; the path keeps generally to the northern side and ridge of the spur, but it then crosses a branch spur running down south from the main spur, and for the rest of the march keeps generally to the southern side, but never very far below the ridge and occasionally, where it dips, passing along it for a short distance. This point (2½ miles) is about 1,600 feet above No. 3 Post, and from here the path descends gently for about ½ mile to a small level open clearing on the ridge of the spur, whence there is a clear view north and south. The hill side is very steep indeed all along this stage, but the gradient of the path is less severe than in the last stage. The ascent on the northern side of the spur is clayey and slippery, but on the other side the soil is more friable and has a considerable admixture of stone and slate, and the path is very good indeed. From the clearing path rises to about 4 miles, where the highest point in this stage is reached, namely, 1,800 feet above No. 3 For the next ½ mile or so there are slight ascents and descents, but the general level of the path is about the same up to nearly 5 miles. The last mile is down-hill, not steep, and at about 6 miles reaches No. 4 Post situated on a narrow portion of the spur, very steep khud on the north, less so on the south; jungle well cleared and utilized as in No. 3 as abattis. The stockade itself (entrenchment is a more suitable term in this case and in that of No. 3) occupies a small underfeature rising in the centre of the cleared site, and is commanded from higher portions of the spur to the east and west; in the former case within 350 yards, but in the latter not within 500 yards or more. Within the entrenchment there is accommodation in very inferior thatched huts for a garrison of 100 rifles, besides hospital and minor buildings, and a large hut for officers or European soldiers passing through. There is also accommodation, if necessary, for 50 more rifles. To the west of the entrenchment are store-sheds and sheds for transport followers and 130 animals. Water-supply plentiful from springs and stream in ravine south of and about as far off from the post as in No. 3 (600 to 800 yards), but immediately below it is more troublesome to get at. A good mule path, however, has been constructed down to it. Arrangements for collecting the water similar to those in use at No. 3. Forage for transport animals has to be cut from the hill side above and brought in on the mules. The highest point of the entrenchment is 3,750 feet above No. 2, and affords a fine view in all directions except the west. None of the other posts, however, are visible from it, and no Chin villages though numerous taungyas. The general direction of the road in this stage is west, and the road is good throughout, though after rain the first ascent from No. 3 and the final descent to No. 4 become slippery and difficult. No. 4 is a cold and windy spot even in the middle of March, but is said to be much more healthy than No. 3 which has a bad name for fever.

From KALÉMYOZEIK (on Myittha River) to FORT WHITE (Old)—*continued.*

Authorities.		Number and Names of Stages, Rivers and Streams.	Distances.		Remarks.
Military.	Civil.		Intermediate.	Total.	
			M. F.	M. F.	
G.O.C. Myingyán District.	Political Officer, Chin Hills.	**5. No. 5 Post (New Fort White).**	**6 0**	28 4	Direction of route for first 3 miles west, then north-west to No. 5 Post. On leaving No. 4 Post the path ascends steadily, keeping always to the north side of the spur, thin oak forest with little undergrowth. At 2½ miles enter thick bamboo and tropical growth forest, undergrowth very dense, which continues for a mile, and in wet weather the path is sloppy and liable to give way, the soil being shaly. From here (3½ miles) path traverses oak forest with thick small bamboo, almost a kind of grass, undergrowth on both sides for a ¼ of a mile. At 3¾ miles (altitude above No. 2 Post 5,875 feet) rhododendrons above the path, with short grass and no undergrowth, but thick bamboo scrub below it. Here the spur, up which the path has ascended from within 2½ miles of No. 2 Post, joins the main ridge called the Lítha Range. The path turns north-west along, and somewhat below, the crest-line of the main ridge which direction it pursues with occasional slight ascents and descents to No. 5 Post (New Fort White). From 4 to 4½ miles the path runs over open down-like ground covered with short grass, then for ½ mile through a thick belt of jungle; path sloppy and bad after rain. At 4¾ miles path again enters open and follows the crest of the watershed (here 6,050 feet above No. 2) for a short distance and then runs along on the east of and below it. At 5 miles another thick belt of jungle oaks, and high grass, and scrub undergrowth, which continues for ¾ mile; thence to the post over open ground, short grass, path joining in from the right from the watering place shortly before reaching the post: total distance from No. 4 about 6 miles. Path generally good, but in parts likely to slip during the rains, at which time of year it would always be well for mule convoys to carry a few shovels with them to clear the path if required. The post is situated on the east of and about 100 feet below the crest of the ridge on perfectly bare ground fully exposed to the winds that seem to blow incessantly, occasionally with great violence. It is consequently very cold and bleak, notwithstanding which it appears to be healthy, and fever cases sent up from Fort White derive benefit generally from the change. There is accommodation for about six officers and 100 rifles, besides commissariat sheds, one of which is appropriated, when required, for European convalescents. All the huts are of a very poor description, turf walls which do not exclude the wind and thatch roofs which do not exclude the rain; in fact seen during rainy weather the post has a most miserable and uncomfortable appearance and is as bad as it looks. With good accommodation enabling the occupants to keep dry and warm the post would, notwithstanding its exposed position, be a good one, but the distance of the water-supply fully a mile down the khud to the south-east is a drawback. No transport animals are kept at this post, so no mule path has been made down to the water, but animals can, if required, get down the present foot-path. Signalling com-

FROM KALÉMYOZEIK (ON MYITTHA RIVER) TO FORT WHITE (OLD)—*continued.*

Authorities. Military.	Authorities. Civil.	Number and Names of Stages, Rivers and Streams.	Distances. Intermediate.	Distances. Total.	Remarks.
G.O.C. Myingyán District.	Political Officer, Chin Hills.	**5. No. 5 Post (New Fort White)**—*cont.*			munication can be maintained with Fort White (bearing about 262°), Kalémyo (about 110°), No. 3 Post (about 105°), Mwébingyi (about 256°), Sagyilain (about 240°), Yawlu signalling post on ridge north of that village (about 224°). There is plenty of grass obtainable, and quantities of rhododendron, which afford excellent fuel. On the east of the range there are not very many pine trees, but to the west of it there are numerous. From No. 5 Post the main range bears away northwards 350° and southwards 158°. *Note.*—Since this report was written old Fort White has been abandoned and a new Fort White erected close to No. 5, but in a more sheltered position.
		6. Fort White (Old).	M. F. * 7 4	M. F. 36 0	Leaving No. 5 Post path crosses the watershed and for about 3½ miles keeps a generally north-north-west direction, but gradually working round to west and eventually south-west before Fort White is reached. For the first ¾ mile road is pretty level, after the first short ascent from the post to the watershed, then it descends steadily, but gradient easy, with occasional short bits of level and two slight ascents, steep khud on the left. For the first 2 miles the hill side above the path is almost bare, and below not thick, the jungle consisting generally of rhododendron, oak, and pine with grass undergrowth not more than 18 inches or 2 feet high. As the path descends, trees grow thicker both above and below the path and, though nowhere for the first 4 miles, what could be called dense, yet sufficient for concealment. At about 3½ miles path quits the main ridge and follows down a spur running generally south-west. At this point there is a bit of level ground and a good view is obtained northwards across a deep valley to a long spur running parallel to the one the path now follows, covered with cultivation clearings belonging to the Kantôn Kanhow tribe of Chins, and there are traces of a path leading down the khud towards them, though from disuse of late it is not very apparent. From here easy, but constant descent to Fort White. The greater part of the spur has been cleared and cultivated at one time or another, though the clearings are much overgrown and consequently there is lots of cover on either side of the road. The upper side can, however, be secured by a flanking party following the Chin path which runs all down the top of the spur to within a mile or so of the post, after which the hill side is clear and there is little chance of ambushes. At 7½ miles reach Fort White (Old), head-quarters of Political Officer in Northern Chin Hills and large military post, with accommodation for 300 Europeans and 600 natives, besides commissariat stores and followers' huts, transport lines for followers and animals. Water from a large spring, whence it is carried in open wooden pipes raised on supports to the different parts of the post; there are also other sources of supply within easy reach.

* Another authority gives the distance as 9 miles, but it is certainly not as much as that unless the road now follows a different trace to what it did in 1890.—A.F. 5-11-93.

No. 7.

From KALÉWA to INDIN.

BY LIEUT. H. B. WRIGHT, R.E., "QUEEN'S OWN" SAPPERS AND MINERS, JUNE 1888.

Authorities.		Number and Names of Stages, Rivers and Streams.	Distances.				Remarks.
Military.	Civil.		Intermediate.		Total.		
			M.	F.	M.	F.	
G.O.C. Myingyán District.	Commissioner, Central Division, and Deputy Commissioner, Upper Chindwin.	**1. Minbwé and Kyaukka.** Myittha.	9	4	9	4	*N.B.*—The route between Kaléwa and Kyigôn has been much improved since this report was written and probably mules can get along it easily by this time (October 1892).

Kaléwa is a village on the right bank of the Chindwin and on the left or north bank of the Myittha, at the junction of these two rivers. It has about 40 houses, a strong police post in the zayáts, and pagoda buildings to the north-west of the village, also kyaungs and zayáts on south bank of the Myittha, sufficient to accommodate some 350 men in all. Steamers can land troops, horses, &c., here. For the first 2 miles, after leaving Kaléwa, the road is an easy path along the left bank of Myittha. Beyond this no loaded animals or doolies can be taken, as the path is merely a track over rocks which are difficult to cross even for men carrying rifles. At one place steps have been cut in a tree, at another two boats are tied to form a foot-bridge from one rock to another. Mules must swim across the river as soon as they reach the first rock and then back again about 300 yards further on, after which they have to swim round two other cliffs. The river is deep in the defile, but the current is not over 1½ miles an hour. Boats called lôndwins, about 30 feet long and 2½ feet wide, a few of which can be obtained at Kaléwa, are the only possible means of transport, These boats carry from 600 to 1,000 lbs. easily. Wayé is a small village of about 12 houses and an old kyaung; the whole village and kyaung can accommodate about 150 men, another small village about 300 yards down the river can accommodate about 100 men. Total 250. A party moving without baggage animals could easily push on and reach the second stage in one day. Owing to the present condition of the path, which necessitates the boats with the baggage being kept behind to assist the baggage animals in crossing and recrossing the stream, they could not reach the foot of the rapids in time to get over them the same day. For the first 1½ miles after leaving Wayé very rough and difficult road, one rock has to be crossed by steps cut in log, and at another point a foot-bridge formed of boats must be crossed. Mules must swim round two rocks and even when unloaded cannot get on unless the path over the rocks is improved. At 1½ miles the foot of the rapids, where there is a strong whirlpool, is reached. The road along the left bank to the head of the rapids (about ½ mile) is easy. Boats must cross the river and be unloaded and their contents carried ½ mile to the head of the rapids. The boats must be dragged through the rapids, and what with hauling the boats up the rapids and unloading and re-loading them after carrying the cargo across it will generally be found necessary to halt here. The sand bank between the foot and head of the rapids forms a good bivouac from December onwards until the rains commence. There is also a sand bank on the left bank, where a small bivouac can be formed. Road along the left bank of the river can with pioneering tools be made passable for loaded mules. Minbwé is a partially deserted village on the left bank of the river. Has a kyaung which can accommodate 50 men; 100 men can be accommodated in the village houses. Kyaukka on the right

FROM KALÉWA TO INDIN—*continued.*

Authorities.		Number and Names of Stages, Rivers and Streams.	Distances.		Remarks.
Military.	Civil.		Intermediate.	Total.	
G.O.C. Myingyán District.	Commissioner, Central Division, and Deputy Commissioner, Upper Chindwin.	**1. Minbwé and Kyaukka**—*cont.*			bank opposite is a village of about 30 to 40 houses with kyaungs which can accommodate 100 men. Total 250. A few boats can generally be obtained here. The river is about 4½ feet deep here and about 150 yards wide. *Note.*—Minbwé and Kyaukka afford good accommodation for troops, moreover Kyaukka is the starting point for troops using the short cut to Indin. Otherwise, the march being a very short and easy one both by road and along the river for the boats, troops had better march on to Yenatha, which is 3 miles further on, where there are 15 huts in which the troops might be sheltered, or to Nátkyigôn, 6 miles from Minbwé, the site of a deserted village with a fair camping ground on old paddy-fields. From Kyaukka there is a short cut to Indin (*see* Alternative I below).
		2. Kyigôn and Shwédaung. Myittha.	M. 13 F. 0	M. 22 F. 4	For the first 4 miles an easy road along the river bank, passing Yenatha and Nátkyigôn. Here the road leaves the river, striking into the jungle, and then over a succession of steep spurs and one long descent to Indaing (10 miles), which is a large village with a triple stockade with flanking platforms; inner stockade of teak. The village can easily accommodate 500 men. Water from wells. Road from Indaing to Kyigôn runs through kaing grass and small jungle. Road is passable for loaded pack animals throughout. Kyigôn consists of one sayát on the left bank of the river. The river is now crossed to Shwédaung, a small stockaded village of seven houses and one zayát. Good sand bank for bivouac in month of December under the village. The defiles end here and the valley opens out on both sides of the river.
		3. Taungu or Kalémyoseik. Myittha.	10 0	32 4	The road runs on the right bank of the river over some small spurs and through jungle for the first half of the way, then through kaing grass and over old paddy-fields crossing some deep nullahs. The river is touched once at a little more than half-way and forded opposite the village of Taungu; ford is about 4 feet deep in May. Taungu village is about ¼ mile from the river, is strongly stockaded, and has one kyaung (60 men and 30 houses). Good camping ground on sand bank in month of December close to Taungu; there is also other ground on the river bank. A few boats can be got here. Kalémyoseik is close to Taungu, a little lower down stream.
		4. Kinpwánkyun. Myittha.	8 0	40 4	After leaving Taungu the road passes the village of Kambalé, ½ mile, and Naungaung, 1 mile, then through long grass and until it reaches the river at Udu, 4½ miles. The river must be crossed here, fordable in May, but depth is about 4½ feet, and boats should be sent up from Taungu to assist. The road then passes through high grass for about 2 miles, then enters the jungle, crossing an insignificant spur to Kinpwánkyun, a double stockaded village of about 15 houses and one sayát on the right bank of the river. Good camping ground on south side of village.

FROM KALÉWA TO INDIN—*continued.*

Authorities. Military.	Authorities. Civil.	Number and Names of Stages, Rivers and Streams.	Distances. Inter-mediate.	Distances. Total.	Remarks.
			M. F.	M. F.	
G.O.C. Myingyán District.	Commissioner, Central Division, and Deputy Commissioner, Upper Chindwin.	**5. Indin** ... ... Myittha.	6 4	47 0	A level road through high grass on the top of the right bank of the river. Three deep nullahs are crossed in the first 4 miles. The village of Pauktaw, which has a good kyaung and 25 houses and is strongly stockaded, is passed at about half-way. Indin is a large village of about 150 houses with large kyaungs which can accommodate 350 men. The village is protected by a bamboo stockade and an inner stockade of teak logs, about 3 to 4 inches apart. Supplies very scarce. Boats in the dry weather come up to Indin in four days and go down to Kaléwa in two days, halting at Minbwé on the way down.

ALTERNATIVE I.

FROM MINBWÉ (OR KYAUKKA) TO INDIN *viâ* UYIN.

BY LIEUT. H. B. WRIGHT, R.E., "QUEEN'S OWN" SAPPERS AND MINERS, JUNE 1888.

Military	Civil	Stages	Intermediate	Total	Remarks
G.O.C. Myingyán District.	Commissioner, Central Division, and Deputy Commissioner, Upper Chindwin.	**1. Uyin**	10 0	...	An alternative and short route runs from Kyaukka (Stage 1) to Indin (Stage 5), which may be used with advantage in the dry season by parties destined for Indin or a further point on the same road as follow: Road leads from Kyaukka in a southerly direction. At 1 mile a deep nullah is crossed and a spur ascended, at first in a southerly direction, then following the spur up in a south-westerly direction, and finally in a northerly direction to the top of the ridge which is followed for some distance. The descent is made in a north-westerly direction until the bed of a large nullah is reached. The road then follows the turns of nullah with a general westerly direction for about 1½ miles, then runs for 2 miles through kaing grass in a south-westerly direction to Uyin. The ascents and descents are steep, but passable for loaded animals in fair weather. Uyin is a small village of 14 houses surrounded by a double bamboo stockade with a thorn hedge outside. In the centre of the village is a kyaung with a zayát surrounded by a teak stockade. The whole village could accommodate about 200 men. Water from a small jhil and from wells. Supplies scarce, but grass can be obtained.
		2. Indin	10 0	20 0	Through jungle in south-west by westerly direction for about a mile, then along the Myittha river bank through kaing grass to Kinpwánkyun and Indin.

No. 8.

From KINDÁT to TAMMU viâ MINTHAMI.

BY MAJOR HOWLETT, 2ND BURMA BATTALION, LIEUT. OXLEY, 4TH KING'S ROYAL RIFLES, AND C. E. HOUSDEN, ESQ., PUBLIC WORKS DEPARTMENT.

Authorities. Military.	Authorities. Civil.	Number and Names of Stages, Rivers and Streams.	Distances. Intermediate. M.	F.	Distances. Total. M.	F.	Remarks.
G.O.C. Myingyán District.	Commissioner, Central Division, and Deputy Commissioner, Upper Chindwin.	**1. Dathwégyauk.** Chindwin river, Payaswé, Hetpet, and Dathwégyauk chaungs.	18	0	18	0	Cross the Chindwin river here about 1,000 yards wide to Mígyaungdwin on the right bank directly opposite Kindát. The best route onwards is that known locally as the "Minthami" route. It is simply a track over the watersheds separating the Chindwin and Kubo valleys, but is passable for mules and elephants. During the winter months the first halt is usually made at the Payazwéchaung Sakhán, on a spur a short distance below the top of the first range of hills where there is a small stream. Distance about 11 miles from Kindát. During the months of March, April and May, however, the stream is probably dry and then the first halt has to be made at Dathwégyauk about 7 miles further on, where there is a large stream with a plentiful water-supply. A small quantity of water can also be obtained at the Nátgyigôn waterfall at 16 miles. General direction of road in first two stages is north-west. The first 4 miles from Mígyaungdwin to the foot of the hills is over fairly easy and level ground and water is obtainable in several places. The road now ascends, 1st mile steep and bad, the remainder to the top of the ridge (3,000 feet) which is reached at about 11 miles, fairly easy. Difficult descent from here to the Dathwégyauk stream, 18 miles. The stream is fordable and runs from south to north. On the right bank is a small stockade and a few huts. No supplies obtainable. There is also a temporary bungalow belonging to the Bombay Burma Company. This is a hard march for men and transport animals owing to the want of water from the 5th mile onwards.
		2. Tunté ... Nanpanlôn and small streams.	11	0	29	0	Steep ascent, after fording Dathwégyauk stream, to summit of ridge 3½ miles. Then about 3 miles descent to foot of hills, 1st mile steep and difficult, remainder easy. Thence over level ground to the Nanpánlôn chaung (branch of the Yu river) at 8 miles; stream about 70 yards broad, and fordable here on the dry season. Cross the stream to Minthami, a good-sized village situated on the left bank of the stream. Thence to Tunté (11 miles) over level cultivated ground, passing several small villages and two small streams. In this march there is no water to be obtained throughout the first 6½ miles, after that it is plentiful. Tunté is a fair-sized stockaded village, and supplies can be collected from it and the neighbouring villages, Minthami, &c. Water-supply good. At Tunté the road divides leading northwards to Tammu and southwards to Kalémyo (see Route No. 23), the latter passing through Auktaung, 1½ miles nearly west of Tunté, which is the halting place generally used in marching from Tammu to Kalémyo.
		3. Namunta river. Several good streams, tributaries of the Yu river.	12	0	41	0	Road due north, through well-watered and fairly open country, and track itself shows signs of attempts having been made at improvement. At 5 miles Wituk, formerly apparently a fairly large and prosperous village,

FROM KINDÁT TO TAMMU *viâ* MINTHAMI—*continued.*

Authorities. Military.	Authorities. Civil.	Number and Names of Stages, Rivers and Streams.	Distances. Intermediate. M. F.	Distances. Total. M. F.	Remarks.
G.O.C. Myingyán District.	Commissioner, Central Division, and Deputy Commissioner, Upper Chindwin.	**3. Namunta river**—*cont.*			but destroyed by fire in the early part of 1891. It is surrounded by cultivated land. Good camping ground outside the village 150 yards from water-supply which is good. (*Note.*—Wituk is probably rebuilt by now, October 1892.) From Wituk road continues due north, as before, through easy country to the Namunta river. Camp on the near (right) bank of the river at 12 miles.
		4. Tammu ... Several good streams.	**12 0**	53 0	General direction north. Road easy, passing the villages of Pántha, Mámaw, and Chaungnanaung at 4, 7¾, and 9 miles respectively. The latter village is strongly stockaded and seems fairly prosperous, with considerable cultivation around. From here on to Tammu the road is fit for carts, but would be heavy in parts during rainy weather. Water is plentiful throughout this march, eight perennial streams being crossed. There is accommodation at Tammu for 200 men and supplies are procurable. Water plentiful.

Lieut. H. Daly (now Capt. H. Daly, "C.I.E."), Political Assistant in the Upper Chindwin in 1886–87, gives the following accounts of two alternative routes between Tammu and Kindát, neither of which is likely to be used in preference to the Minthami route, and they are, therefore, reprinted in their original form. Pinthawa, the place where these routes terminate, is situated between the Auktaung-Kalémyo road and the Nanpánlôn river, about 4 miles to the south of Auktaung.

ALTERNATIVE I.

FROM KINDÁT TO TAMMU *viâ* MANKU, YÁTTAUNG AND PINTHAWA.

BY LIEUT. H. DALY, B.S.C., DECEMBER 1886.

Authorities. Military.	Authorities. Civil.	Names of Stages.	Time.	Distances. Intermediate. M. F.	Distances. Total. M. F.	Remarks.
G.O.C. Myingyán District.	Commissioner, Central Division, and Deputy Commissioner, Upper Chindwin.	**Manku** ...	20th Nov. 1886. 4 A.M.	...	...	
		Ywadaw ...	...	**1 0**	1 0	Leaving Manku village (which is just opposite Kindát and on the left bank of the Manku chaung) the track immediately crosses the chaung, which is here about 50 yards broad, bottom soft, not fordable in rains. After ½ mile over level paddy ground, the road crosses again to the left bank, passes through the little hamlet of Ywadaw, and then at once recrosses to the right. The stream is broad (40 to 50 yards) and not fordable in the rains; there are quicksands in the bed on the lower side of Ywadaw. From Ywadaw the road bears south-east, the first 2 miles or so across level ground and the rest up and down over low spurs running towards the creek; all this part is good going. I commenced surveying when we again struck Manku creek. This distance is perhaps under-estimated.

FROM KINDÁT TO TAMMU viâ MINTHAMI—*continued.*

ALTERNATIVE 1—*continued.*

Authorities. Military.	Authorities. Civil.	Names of Stages.	Time.	Distances. Intermediate. M.	F.	Distances. Total. M.	F.	Remarks.
G.O.C. Myingyán District.	Commissioner, Central Division, and Deputy Commissioner, Upper Chindwin.	**Manku creek.**	7-30 A.M.	5	0	6	0	From this point the road leads along the bed, only leaving it occasionally for short distances of about 100 yards; the stream has to be continually crossed and recrossed, and is even at this season 3 feet deep in places; the bed is full of large rocks, and loaded pack animals could not pass. The banks, as a rule, are not very high, but high ground, thickly wooded, runs right down to the edge of the stream.
		Yénán chaung	...	3	0	9	0	The Yénán chaung is almost dry at this season; at the meeting of the waters the bed is broad, and a camp might be made on the sand banks.
		Yézôn ...	12 noon.	1	2	10	2	Halted there for 2 hours to cook; after 4½ hours along the creek at a rate of under 1 mile an hour. There is some flat ground around here and troops might camp, but a good deal of clearing would have to be done.
		King's old picket.	...	1	2	11	2	Leaving Yézôn the road ascends a steepish hill, which is connected with Yáttaung by a saddle-back. A little way below the crest of this hill, on the west side, is the site of the old Burmese *thána*, where a picket used to be kept to protect travellers against Chins. The post was abandoned some ten years ago, but the site is plainly marked; there could only have been two or three small huts with a small enclosure round.
		Yáttaung ...	...	2	6	14	2	The road passes just under the summit; there is a very difficult little bit at the north-west corner, and the one pony, with me was only got up with great difficulty.
		Wébábin camp.	5-15 P.M.	0	2	14	4	Camped on a spur about 40 yards broad with steep sides and end; a good place, but not room for more than 100 men; plenty of good water at the bottom of the west slope of the spur; the first water reached is not very good, but beyond, at a distance of some 200 yards from the camp, is an excellent spring. Aneroid barometer 28·42 at 5-30 A.M. inside the bamboo hut where I slept; calculated height 1,480; crest of Yáttaung estimated at 1,800.
		Dathwégyauk chaung.	21st Nov. 8-15 A.M.	5	0	19	6	Marched 6 A.M. on 21st. The map makes this distance greater, but I believe I over-estimated it. Leaving Wébábin there is a sharp little piece of descent and little ascent on to another spur; thence to the creek the path is excellent along a gentle slope. Dathwégyauk chaung is about 20 yards broad here, banks high

FROM KINDÁT TO TAMMU *viâ* MINTHAMI—*continued.*

ALTERNATIVE I—*continued.*

Authorities.		Names of Stages.	Time.	Distances.				Remarks.
Military.	Civil.			Intermediate.		Total.		
				M.	F.	M.	F.	
G.O.C. Myingyán District.	Commissioner, Central Division, and Deputy Commissioner, Upper Chindwin.	**Dathwégyauk chaung**—*cont.*						and steep, bottom stony, said to be fordable at all seasons; excellent water. Kyátmátun creek meets Dathwégyauk chaung at this point, flowing from the north-north-west. Forward the path leads along Kyátmátun for about ½ mile. The ground on the left (east) bank is high and densely wooded, the creek about 15 to 20 yards broad, banks 8 to 12 feet and steep. On leaving the creek the path runs up a succession of spurs to the top of the Yômas.
		Crest of Yômas.	10-15 A.M.	1	2	21	0	The ascent is not difficult. The Yômas at the top are only 5 or 6 yards broad; estimated height not over 1,200 at this point. The descent on the west side is precipitous for 80 yards. A track used by Chins runs along the crest to the south-west from the point at which the Yáttaung road descends. After the first sharp descent it is easy going to Kanpát chaung, with the
		Kanpát chaung.	11-30 A.M.	1	6	22	6	exception of the last 300 or 400 yards, where the path runs through dense elephant grass and the ground would probably be a swamp in the rains. The bed of Kanpát chaung is certainly not less than 50 yards broad; there is a great deal of water, and the current is so swift that crossing was by no means easy even at the ford, where the depth did not exceed 2 feet. The bottom is very good, hard sand, with large pebbly stones.
		Tainkaya ...	...	0	2	23	0	The village is about ¼ mile below the ford on the left bank; it was burnt by Chins three years ago, and only a few charred logs mark the site.
		Pinthawa ...	2-45 P.M.	5	6	28	6	At this season the track is excellent and native carts could easily pass. The ground is flat and, with the exception of two clearings, there is continuous tree jungle all the way; the trees are small and poor and thickly grouped. The soil looks as if it would be very holding in wet weather. Pack animals could pass loaded from Pinthawa to Yézôn during the cold weather if the road were slightly improved at the west side of the summit of the Yômas. At the north-west of Yáttaung and at one or two other steepish bits on the east slope of Yáttaung a causeway, which would not be washed away by floods, could probably be made along the edge of the Manku creek, and very probably if the country were surveyed, it might be found possible and not difficult to make a road down the right bank of the creek, so as to strike the Chindwin at the point where the creek flows in without crossing it at all. This route, however, is always infested by Chins, and I cannot think it would be

FROM KINDÁT TO TAMMU *viâ* MINTHAMI—*continued.*

ALTERNATIVE I—*continued.*

Authorities. Military	Authorities. Civil.	Names of Stages.	Time.	Distances. Intermediate.	Distances. Total.	Remarks.
G.O.C. Myingyán District.	Commr., C. Divn., and Dy. Commr., U. Chindwin.	**Pinthawa**—*cont.*				worth spending money on. Colonel Johnstone used this route when he marched in 36 hours from Môré Thána to Kindát (which distance he estimated, I believe, at 65 miles) last December. *P.S.*—Coolie transport was used on this march.

ALTERNATIVE II.

FROM TAMMU TO KINDÁT *viâ* PINTHAWA, SITTAUNG AND MANKU.

BY LIEUT. H. DALY, POLITICAL ASSISTANT, KINDÁT, 17TH DECEMBER 1886.

Military	Civil	Names of Stages.	Time.	Intermediate M. F.	Total M. F.	Remarks.
G.O.C. Myingyán District.	Commissioner, Central Division, and Deputy Commissioner, Upper Chindwin.	**Pinthawa** ...	23rd Nov. 1886. 5 A.M.	...	...	*N.B.*—This route should, properly speaking, be reversed, but it seems scarcely worth the labour. The position was approximately fixed by two bearings from the Yômas, but the angle is a very bad one. The path of Kanpát chaung is fairly good at this season.
		Kanpát chaung.	5-30 A.M.	1 2	1 2	The stream is about 50 yards broad, current rapid, bottom hard at the ford. In the cold weather the path runs along the bed to the mouth of Wábo chaung, but there was too much water in the creek for us to go that way, and we had to make our way along the right bank through dense elephant grass.
		Wábo chaung.	...	0 2	1 4	Wábo chaung is only 15 to 20 yards broad, the bottom is stony and in places difficult; the banks are steep and high, and densely wooded, the bed very winding. The path finally leaves the bed at a distance of about 1¼ miles from Kanpát chaung. Pack animals could scarcely get up the bank as it is, but once up the road is excellent for about 1¾ miles, when it becomes very steep, and after about 300 yards of sharp ascent a small cliff is met with, after climbing up which the ascent continues very steep up to the crest.
		Crest of Yômas.	9-30 A.M.	3 4	5 0	Crest at this point about 20 yards broad; east slope easy. Aneroid barometer 28·47 at 9 A.M. on damp ground in the shade, estimated height about 1,400 feet. After reaching the crest the path runs along it for a short ¼ of a mile and then descends across a succession of spurs to Dathwégyauk chaung. Pack animals could descend loaded, but the road would have to be improved in places before they could ascend.
		Dathwégyauk chaung.	11-45 A.M.	2 6	7 6	Halted here for a couple of hours. There is an island in the bed at this point level, fairly open ground on the right bank, and a camp might be made here.
		Aukchin chaung.	...	3 2	8 4	Starting again the track leads over some easily sloping ground to Aukchin chaung, a tributary of Dathwégyauk chaung, and then for about 1¾ miles follows the bed of this stream. This part is very difficult going, as the bed is full of large rocks, and in places the path runs alongslabs of slippery stone sloping at a sharp angle

FROM KINDÂT TO TAMMU *viâ* MINTHAMI—*continued.*

ALTERNATIVE II—*continued.*

Authorities.		Names of Stages.	Time.	Distances.				Remarks.
Military.	Civil.			Intermediate.		Total.		
				M.	F.	M.	F.	
G.O.C. Myingyan District.	Commissioner, Central Division, and Deputy Commissioner, Upper Chindwin.	**Aukchin chaung**—*cont.*						to the centre of the bed. The banks, as a rule, are about 12 feet high; the ground on the right (east) bank is high and steep, that on the left lower; there is dense jungle all about this part. Fragments of coal are met with all along this stream and at two points, one of which is marked on the sketch, the ends of what look like broad seams of coal break out through the bank. After following the bed for 1¾ miles the path leads up over a sharpish knoll on the left (west) bank and then after ½ mile recrosses the stream on the other side of this high ground. After this crossing there is a sharp ascent and then fairly easy going (with the exception of one sharp steep hill) to the place where we camped. This is not a very good place for a camp, as there is very little water and the jungle round is dense.
		Camp ...	5-15 P.M.	**5**	**0**	13	4	
		Théda chaung	24th Nov. 6 A.M.	**2**	**0**	15	4	Two miles of a fairly good jungle path brings one to the source of Théda chaung, near which with a little clearing a good position for a camp might easily be found. For about 3 miles from this point the track follows the bed of the chaung, the banks of which are in some places very high, the jungle on sides is dense almost the whole way, and but little of the little neighbouring ground can be made out. On leaving the bed the path leads up the steep northern slope of Sittaung, the highest point of which is reached after about ½ mile; the path leads just under the crest on the west and then bends round the south side of it. The west side of the hill is almost precipitous and the path across it very difficult for animals. Having got round the crest an easy road down a gentle slope leads once more to Théda chaung; the undergrowth of brushwood is very dense about here. The path strikes Théda chaung at a point where the right bank is about 60 feet high; just opposite the left bank is low, flat, and fairly open. The stream is about 30 yards broad. Halt
		Sittaung ...	...	**3**	**4**	19	0	
		Théda chaung	11-30 A.M.	**1**	**6**	20	6	

FROM KINDÁT TO TAMMU *viâ* MINTHAMI—*continued.*

ALTERNATIVE II—*continued.*

Authorities.		Names of Stages.	Time.	Distances.				Remarks.
Military.	Civil.			Inter-mediate.		Total.		
				M.	F.	M.	F.	
G.O.C. Myingyán District.	Commissioner, Central Division, and Deputy Commissioner, Upper Chindwin.	**Théda chaung** —*cont.*	...					for 2 hours. For about 1 mile the onward track follows the stream bed, the going as before being difficult; after a mile the path strikes off south over some high ground and after 1¼ miles strikes Manku chaung; next 1¼ miles along which is quite impracticable for animals and *extremely* difficult for coolies. Théda chaung flows into Manku chaung at a point about 1½ miles from that at which the road enters the latter creek. At the junction the bed of Manku creek spreads out to a breadth of over 100 yards; thence to Ywadaw the going is fairly good at this season. Thence to Manku same as by Yáttaung route. This is by far the worst road of the three I have gone over and a very great deal would have to be done to it before animals could pass. It is much used by messengers and petty traders on account of its being comparatively safe as regards the Chins. Coal is found in Théda and Manku creeks, as well as in Aukchin. This is the route to which I have sometimes referred as the false Minthami. The Bombay Burma Corporation's employés, who guided me back from Pinthawa, declared they would take me by the Minthami and this was the result. When we reached our camp on the 23rd the guide said we had just passed a point from which the road to Migyaundwin might easily be reached.
		Manku chaung.	...	**2**	**2**	23	0	
		Ywadaw ...	...	**2**	**6**	25	6	
		Manku ...	5-45 P.M.	**1**	**0**	26	6	

No. 9.

From KINDÁT to TAMMU (by water, up the Chindwin and Yu Rivers).

BY LIEUT. F. H. S. THOMAS, COMMISSARIAT DEPARTMENT, NOVEMBER 1891.

Authorities.		Stages, Rivers and Streams.	Time.		Remarks.
Military.	Civil.		Inter-mediate.	Total.	
			Days.	Days.	
G.O.C. Myingyán District.	Commr., Central Divn., and Deputy Commr., Upper Chindwin.	**Yúwa**	**1**	1	All stores for Tammu and adjacent posts of Auktaung and Kampát are carried by boat from Kindát *viá* Yúwa up the Yu river. The distance is not known, but the time taken by loaded boats from Kindát to Yúwa (distance 23 miles) up stream is one day polling. Yúwa to Tammu (boats loaded up stream) is 6 to 7 days according to the state of the river.
		Chindwin river.			
		Tammu	**6 to 7**	7 to 8	
		Yu river.			

FROM KINDÁT TO TAMMU (BY WATER, UP THE CHINDWIN AND YU RIVERS)—*continued.*

Authorities. Military.	Authorities. Civil.	Stages, Rivers and Streams.	Time. Intermediate.	Time. Total.	Remarks.
G.O.C. Myingyán District.	Commissioner, Central Division, and Deputy Commissioner, Upper Chindwin.	**Tammu**—*cont.*			From Tammu to Yúwa (down stream) 3 days; Yówa to Kindát 1 day. This line was used for the transport of part of the troops on their return from the recent Manipur expedition. The boats obtainable are the same as those used in the Myittha river, namely (lôndwins) carrying 1,200 lbs. of stores. They are unloaded at a point on the river (Chaungzôn), 4 miles from Tammu, over which distance they are carted. Lieutenant Thomas writes: "The river is more difficult (there are many more rapids) than the Myittha, but is never, I believe, impassable for those boats." I learn, however, that for a few days at a time during heavy floods the water is too strong for boats. It is not, however, generally desirable to boat provisions up during the rains, since, as was found to be the case on the Myittha, damage to the rations results." Regarding the rationing of Auktaung and Kampát Lieutenant Thomas says: "Half-way between Yúwa and Tammu on the river bank is the small village of Maw, with a goodish kyaung. Maw is about 8 miles from Kampát. Stores for Auktaung and Kampát have this year been sent by boat to Maw and overland to the outpost. In the rains, however, boats can go up the Minthami creek right up to Kampát, at least so the natives told me." Maw is on the Yu just above the junction of the Minthami creek with it. The Minthami creek is only navigable for these small boats when swollen with rains.

The following more detailed account of the journey down stream is furnished by T. W. Macleane, Esq., of the Telegraph Department, dated March 1887:—

Authorities. Military.	Authorities. Civil.	Number and Names of Stages, Rivers and Streams.	Time. Intermediate.	Time. Total.	Remarks.
			H. M.	H. M.	
G.O.C. Myingyán District.	Commissioner, Central Division, and Deputy Commissioner, Upper Chindwin.	**1. Camp below large rapid, below the village of Suntha (? Tsôngatha of Map No. 1 S.-E. of South-east Frontier series, 3rd edition).**	9 0	...	Embark at Tammughât on the Yu (or Magláng) river. Boats available; about 14 on the whole course of the river from Tammu to the point where it joins the Chindwin. The boats are only small canoes and will not hold more than five men as passengers besides the boats crew (of three men). The current is at first slow (2 to 3 miles an hour). The following villages are passed:—Pántha, right bank; Áhlaw, left bank; Wélên, left bank; Kameik and Kameikpa, right bank; Kyawdaw, right bank; Maw, right bank. Maw lies 2 miles below Kyawdaw and 1 mile above the Kampát stream, which flows in from the south. About 2 miles below the Kampát creek the Thébin stream enters also from the south. There are seven small rapids between Thébin stream and the village of Suntha (? Tsôngatha of map), about 4 miles further down stream; but in the cold weather and up to April they are neither difficult nor dangerous. Below Suntha the largest rapid has to be passed. Even in March boats have to be unladen and passed round by a small channel. This rapid and the small size of the channel are the only obstacles to larger boats being used on this river. These boats, however, take a weight of nine maunds. The camping ground is about 1 mile below the foot of the large rapid.

FROM KINDÁT TO TAMMU (BY WATER, UP THE CHINDWIN AND YU RIVERS)—*continued.*

Authorities. Military.	Authorities. Civil.	Number and Names of Stages, Rivers and Streams.	Time. Intermediate.	Time. Total.	Remarks.
G.O.C. Myingyán District.	Commissioner, Central Division, and Deputy Commissioner, Upper Chindwin.	**2. Yúwa**	H. M. 9 0	H. M. ...	Yúwa is a village at the mouth of the Yu (*wa* meaning mouth). Below camp the Kyauktaung stream comes in from the south. The southern end of the inner (western) portion of the Angôkying range (which is double) is passed, and the Tilaung stream flows in from the north. The Tilaung stream splits the Angôkying range longitudinally. There is a village near the mouth, and a jungle path leads across from it over the spurs of the Angôkying to Pútba, a distance of about 13 miles. After Tilaung pass the Dathwégyauk or Tado-é stream coming in from the south. The outer (eastern) branch of the Angôkying (Lakatdaung) now approaches the river and some small rapids have to be descended. They are not dangerous in the cold weather, but some care has to be exercised to prevent an upset. Pass Yinna on the left bank and Pwéyazu on the right bank. After this the country becomes open and Yúwa is reached 2 miles below Pwéyazu.
		3. Kindát ...	2 hours or about 10 miles.		A road exists along the left bank of the Chindwin.
					Note.—In March 1887 the whole of the traffic on the Yu was carried on by 14 boats. The boats are simply dug-out canoes with the bamboos lashed along outside the gunwale to give them stability. There is a path along the right bank of the Yu, but it is little used. Tilaung is said to be 13 miles from Yúwa, and Mo 10 miles from Tilaung.

No. 10.

From KÔKO to MINGIN.

BY CAPT. F. S. SORELL, 2ND REGIMENT HYDERABAD CONTINGENT, JANUARY 1888.

Authorities. Military.	Authorities. Civil.	Number and Names of Stages, Rivers and Streams.	Distances. Intermediate.	Distances. Total.	Remarks.
G.O.C. Myingyán District.	Commissioner, Central Division, and Deputy Commissioner, Upper Chindwin.	**1. Tinkyulébyin.**	M. F. 13 0	M. F. ...	Kôko (*vide* Route No. 30, Southern Division) is a small village in Kalé Sawbwa's territory on the main road running from Pakôkku to Kalémyo *viâ* Kân and Gángaw. From Kôko the road runs through paddy-fields and jungle for about 3½ miles to foot of the hills, then the Kôko chaung is crossed seven times; track runs along bed and banks of chaung. At 5½ miles the Kyo-aung range of hills is crossed; very steep rocky path, impracticable for ponies or mules; no water between Kôko chaung and Tinkyulébyin. Tinkyulébyin is a small grass plateau surrounded with very fine fir (pine) trees and dwarf oaks. High altitude, very cold. Water-supply limited, no village. Troops had to bivouac.

FROM KÔKO TO MINGIN—*continued.*

Authorities. Military.	Authorities. Civil.	Number and Names of Stages, Rivers and Streams.	Distances. Intermediate. M.	F.	Total. M.	F.	Remarks.
G.O.C. Myingyán District.	Commissioner, Central Division, and Deputy Commissioner, Upper Chindwin.	**2. Satkyadu** ...	14	0	27	0	From Tinkyulébyin road gradually descends for about 1 mile, and then the Pôndaung range is crossed: 45 minutes very steep climbing in one part, like a ladder in others, and over sheet rock very slippery. No animals could go over this. After this road runs along crest of hill for ½ a mile, then some smaller hills are crossed. No village at Satkyadu. Small plateau; water-supply plentiful from chaung. Dense forest all round. Troops had to bivouac. Coal seam cropping out in chaung.
		3. Winwa	10	0	37	0	Steep hill to be crossed immediately on leaving Satkyadu; thick bamboo jungle, several chaungs crossed. For 5 miles, when the Winwa chaung is reached, there is no water. Last 2 miles to chaung over steep slippery sheet rock. Men only able to go very slowly; quite impracticable for laden ponies. Road runs for last 2 miles into Winwa along bed of chaung and opens out into the Taungdwin valley between very high cliffs. Police post in course of construction at Winwa. Small village.
		4. Mingin	20	0	57	0	For 2½ miles road runs along valley over paddy-fields, then ascent of the Shwémintaung range is commenced. Range about 1,800 feet high. Road being improved by Public Works Department, under the orders of the Assistant Commissioner, Mingin; track 8 feet wide finished for about 800 feet up, remainder of ascent very difficult; impracticable for ponies. Sayadaung pagoda on top; fine view of valley from here. Road now runs along crest for 4 miles to a small zayát; then gradual descent commences till Patôlôn creek is met; remainder of the road to Mingin runs through creek and heavy sand. Last 4 miles into Mingin over paddy-fields and jungle roads. This route, which is a short cut from the Kalé valley to the Chindwin river, would only be used on an emergency, and is then only suitable for cooly transport.

No. 11.

From KÔKO to SIHAUNG POST.

BY CAPT. J. G. HUNTER, 10TH BENGAL INFANTRY, MARCH 1890.

G.O.C. Myingyán District.	Commr., Central Divn., and Deputy Commr., Upper Chindwin.	**1. Sihaung Post.** Nankathé and Myittha rivers.	7	0	7	0	Kôko, *see* Route No. 30, Southern Division. Good fair weather track cleared and widened by Public Works Department crossing the Myittha river shortly after leaving Kôko by gabion pile bridge throughout dry season; ferry in the rains. The deserted village of Tintha: houses all removed and only the stockade remaining; is passed midway. From here tracks lead (1) east to Seiktha on the left bank of the Myittha; (2) west-south-west

FROM KÔKO TO SIHAUNG POST—*continued.*

Authorities. Military.	Authorities. Civil.	Number and Names of Stages, Rivers and Streams.	Distances. Intermediate.	Distances. Total.	Remarks.
G.O.C. Myingyán District.	Commissioner, Central Division, and Deputy Commissioner, Upper Chindwin.	**1. Sihaung Post** —*cont.*			to Hánta ; and (3) a little north by west to Kánhla on the left bank of the Nankathé, crossing that river opposite the village by ferry. From Tintha the track runs on passing East Sihaung (15 houses) at about 5½ miles. From here there is also a path to the Kánhla ferry. At about 6 miles cross Nankathé by bridge built by Burma Sappers and Miners, and join the path from Indin to Sihaung post, reaching the latter place at 7 miles. This path and bridge over the Nankathé were undertaken when the military post was at North Sihaung. Now that the post has been moved to its present site, the path from Tintha to Kánhla and thence to the post should be maintained, as the main line of communication with Kôko and the river should, if possible, be bridged at Kánhla instead of where it is now.

No. 12.

From KYUNHLA to KINDÁT and PAUNGBYIN.

BY MAJOR A. B. FENTON, DEPUTY ASSISTANT QUARTERMASTER-GENERAL, INTELLIGENCE BRANCH, FIRST FOUR STAGES; REMAINDER NATIVE INFORMATION, FEBRUARY 1890.

Military.	Civil.	Stages.	Intermediate.	Total.	Remarks.
G.O.C. Myingyán District.	Commissioner, Central Division, and Deputy Commissioner, Yé-u.	**1. Leseintaung** ... Pyaungthwé chaung.	M. F. **8 0**	M. F. 8 0	Leaving Kyunhla police post which is situated in the north-east of the Yé-u district on the right bank of the Mu river, a little above the place where the Pyaungthwé chaung joins the Mu river from the west, follow the main road to Aungzwa for about ½ mile passing kyaungs formerly used as military post. Here roads divide, that for Naungauk (or Indaing) branching off to the right. Carts would follow this road as far as Letpángyi, a small deserted village about 200 yards from left bank of Pyaungthwé chaung, but a bridle-path leaves this track after about ½ mile and, bearing off to the right through light jungle and patches of paddy cultivation, cuts off some distance and rejoins the cart track at site of old village of Sôndalin. From here the track is at present (February 1890) not used by carts, but capable of being so, though in wet weather it would be bad ; runs up the valley of the Pyaungthwé chaung, seldom actually touching it, but always within ½ mile of and generally nearer it. The sites of deserted villages of Ingôn, Pégôn, and Thayetpin are passed at about 4¼ miles, 5 miles, and 6 miles respectively. Of the villages passed so far Thayetpin is the only one likely to be re-occupied for a long time. Road thus far good in dry weather, but probably bad in wet, where it crosses paddy clearings. Between Letpángyi and Sôndalin there is a lot of garden cultivation, beans, tomatoes, &c., ripening in February and March. Thayetpin has one kyaung and good water from well. From this village road bad, over fallow paddy land for nearly 2 miles to Leseintaung. The clearing extends from the left bank of the Pyaungthwé up to a low jungle-covered ridge running parallel to the stream at a distance of ½ mile to 1 mile. This would be a very bad bit in wet weather and, if the cart road be improved, a trace should be sought for following the above-mentioned ridge. Leseintaung is a deserted village

From KYUNHLA to KINDÁT and PAUNGBYIN—*continued.*

Authorities. Military.	Authorities. Civil.	Number and Names of Stages, Rivers and Streams.	Distances. Intermediate.	Distances. Total.	Remarks.
G.O.C. Myingyan District.	Commissioner, Central Division, and Deputy Commissioner, Yé-u.	**1. Leseintaung**—*cont.*			surrounded by plantain groves on the left of the road and about 500 yards south of the Pyaungthwé. At present no accommodation here, but plenty of grass and water from the chaung, which in driest weather has clear water running in narrow sandy channels.
		2. Thekagyin ... Pyaungthwé and Maiwun chaungs.	M. 9 F. 0	M. 17 F. 0	Leaving Leseintaung road through thick jungles for ½ mile, when it crosses the Pyaungthwé; banks easy, but require a little ramping for carts; bed sandy, but firm; water running a few inches deep in several narrow channels in February. In the rains the stream would be 8 feet deep in flood and about 60 yards wide. It is, however, said never to be unfordable for more than 24 hours at a time and that only during or immediately after very heavy rain; thence for ½ mile through jungle, high trees, across a bend of the stream. After crossing the Pyaungthwé stream path up bed of Kabaungyôn chaung, which here joins the Pyaungthwé for a short distance; chaung quite dry in February; sandy bed, 30 yards wide, low banks. Road a sandy cart track through tree jungle passing at 1¼ miles Chaungsôn, deserted village, on the left. Track is good, and from this point soil more gravelly, ground undulating covered with *in*, *ingyin*, and in some places teak. At 4½ miles cross dry bed of Taungni chaung, thence for ½ mile across paddy cultivation to Taungni village, of about 40 houses on rising ground. Bamboo kyaung and zayáts to right of road just before reaching village; jungle close up on north and east. Good drinking water from holes in bed of small nullah south-east and about 200 yards from kyaung. Next 2 miles excellent, going over dry undulating ground covered with light tree jungle with a little bamboo in parts, then for 2½ miles across open ground, cleared for paddy from the left bank of the Pyaungthwé, here ½ mile off to the left and running parallel to the track. One steep banked nullah to cross at 7½ miles; thence no difficulty in dry weather and probably little in wet, as the soil seems sandy and pretty firm up to Thekagyin, 8½ miles; large village of 60 or 70 houses on left bank of Maiwun chaung, which here joins the Pyaungthwé. Cross Maiwun stream, about 50 yards wide, low banks, water a few inches deep in several narrow channels, sandy bottom, and up a rise to Ingôn kyaung, big kyaung, and three zayáts; ground clear all round for a few hundred yards. Drinking water from well about 100 yards in left rear of kyaung. Grass and paddy plentiful; quantities of jungle fowl about here. From here path runs westward to Mawké, distance about 5 miles, which is to be cleared to a width sufficient for carts to pass.
		3. Naungauk ... Maiwun chaung.	8 0	25 0	Leaving Ingôn kyaung road runs west for a short distance, but soon works round to north-west by north which is the general direction of the road in this stage, though it twists about a great deal. With the exception of between the 2nd and 3rd mile, where the road traverses thick kaing grass for about ¾ mile, it passes through thick jungle throughout, and the track has evidently not been much used by carts of late and is in many places quite impassable for carts until fallen trees have been removed, banks of Maiwun and other

FROM KYUNHLA TO KINDÁT AND PAUNGBYIN—*continued.*

Authorities. Military.	Authorities. Civil.	Number and Names of Stages, Rivers and Streams.	Distances. Intermediate.	Distances. Total.	Remarks.
G.O.C. Myingyán District.	Commissioner, Central Division, and Deputy Commissioner, Yé-u.	**3. Naungauk**—*cont.*			smaller nullahs ramped, and so on; but the villagers are now (February 1890) engaged in doing this, and by next rainy season the work will be finished and a fair cart road will be open. Leaving Ingôn track over dry ridges and through paddy cultivation for 2 miles, then down to the level of the Maiwun. Next mile through kaing grass, crossing the Maiwun midway; banks want a little ramping for carts; thence up to 4½ miles along left bank of Maiwun; good going. At 4½ miles drop down into bed of stream and follow up it (running water in narrow channels, banks 6 to 9 feet high, sandy bottom) to Wethaw, 5 miles. Small village on right bank of chaung with a little paddy clearing around. After passing this village road ascends right bank and strikes across a bend of the river, which is met again at 7½ miles; road mostly good through jungle, but a couple of paddy clearings crossed, which would be troublesome in wet weather unless the new track be cleared, as it easily might be, so as to avoid them. At 7½ miles cross Maiwun again, and on across paddy to Naungauk kyaung on rising ground surrounded by a narrow belt of plantain trees and thick bush jungle. Several wells close by. Village of Naungauk 150 yards to north, about 60 houses, strongly stockaded. A well-to-do village with a large area around cleared for paddy. The Maiwun chaung circles round two sides of the elevation on which the kyaung is built. On the south-east it is nearest, being there within 30 or 40 yards of it. Naungauk is at present the most northern village of the Yé-u district and about 6 miles from the Wuntho frontier south-west of Mettaung, up to which point a road is to be cleared. At present there seems to be little or no communication between the Maiwun-Pyaungthwé valley and the Mu valley, but tracks are said to exist (though for long in disuse, except by dacoits) between Naungauk and Thekagyin on the one side and Seitpu and Aingyi on the other.
		4. Camp on Chindwin-Mu watershed.	M. F. About **9 0**	M. F. ...	From Naungauk onwards there is at present only a foot-path, but it is to be made passable for ponies. This certainly can be done, but there will be many very steep bits. Leaving Naungauk cross paddy for ¾ mile, then enter hills and follow the general direction of the Maiwun stream, sometimes following the stream bed itself, water varying from a few inches to ankle-deep in February, clear and running fast; sandy or gravelly bottom generally, in places rocky; at others climbing over steep ridges in the bends of the stream; thick jungle throughout, and in parts very dense and large bamboos. At about 2¼ miles Thendôn chaung enters by left bank, and at 2¾ miles Tátnúwé stream same bank, both streams sandy bottom, 20 yards wide, dry in February. There is said to be a small village and some taungya cultivation about a mile up the Thendôn chaung. At about 3¼ miles a very steep climb of 500 or 600 yards, and precipitous descent the other side. Up to this point ponies could be led, but here they would be stopped until the descent is made practicable; no easy task. At about 3¾ miles reach bed of stream again. At 4½ miles Panyo chaung enters by right bank. A path runs up the bed of this stream and over the hills southwards to Mawké. Some taungya cultivation and small deserted village about 1½ miles up on left bank just above, where a smaller stream

FROM KYUNHLA TO KINDÁT AND PAUNGBYIN—*continued.*

Authorities. Military.	Authorities. Civil.	Number and Names of Stages, Rivers and Streams.	Distances. Intermediate.	Distances. Total.	Remarks.
G.O.C. Myingyán District.	Commissioner, Central Division, and Deputy Commissioner, Yé-u.	**4. Camp on Chindwin-Mu watershed**—*cont.*			runs in by left bank. Water to be got by digging in sandy bed of stream, 6 inches to 1 foot below surface in February. Stream is about 10 to 15 yards broad; dense jungle on either side. Continuing up the main chaung at 6 miles stream divides into two branches at the foot of a low waterfall, the northern branch again sub-dividing into two very shortly. From this point the name Maiwun ceases to be used and the southern branch, up which the path runs, is called the Cheik chaung, the northern one the Nyaungmyit chaung. About ½ mile further on (6½ miles) a waterfall of about 10 feet into a deep pool and two more smaller ones close by. On up bed of stream, steep hills on either side, and dense bamboo and tree jungle, crossing and recrossing stream, which is in many places full of petrified wood in big logs even, and at 7½ miles leave the stream, just above where a small chaung comes in by left bank, for good, climbing up the left bank and on up the hill side up a very steep spur. But for there being plenty of water all the way, and also that one is almost constantly in the shade, this march would be very trying even to soldiers with their arms, and coolies could only carry very light loads over it.*

The following description of the road on FROM NAUNGAUK TO KINDÁT was furnished by natives met on the road :—

Military.	Civil.	Stages, Rivers and Streams.	Intermediate M.	Intermediate F.	Total M.	Total F.	Remarks.
G.O.C. Myingyán District.	Commissioner, Central Division, and Deputy Commissioner, Upper Chindwin.	**5. Myaing** ... Maiwun and Cheik chaungs and Pôksaing chaung (2 feet deep in February, dry in April).	**10 to 12**		46	0	Burman coolies without loads left Myaing before 6 A.M. and reached Naungauk at 2-30 P.M., resting 20 minutes only on the way. Myaing is on the Pôksaing chaung, and water is obtained from a spring from a rock giving water enough for 70 men.
		6. Sagátpin Sakhán.	**5 or 6**		52	0	No water; merely a resting place.
		7. Mawtôngyi ... Wédaung chaung.	**12**	**0**	64	0	A deserted village. Water in stream all the year round.
		8. Indaw ... ... Kôdán chaung.	**7 to 9**		73	0	A deserted village. Water in stream all the year round.
		9. Gyobin Sakhán. Kyaukkwet chaung.	**10**	**0**	83	0	Gyobin Sakhán, a usual camping place. Water from stream all the year round. At some point in this stage the route from Tigyaing to Kindát *vid* Kánbin (*see* Route No. 105, Northern Division) joins in.
		10. Lawtha ... Kôdán and Nama chaungs.	**6**	**4**	89	4	Track in and out of Kôdán chaung crossing it fourteen times. Lawtha village consists of 15 to 20 houses and a police post (40 rifles in October 1890). Water from well by post and from the stream. Small supply of paddy procurable, and grass for forage also available. One kyaung on the Nama chaung.

* This was as far as the road was reconnoitred in February 1890. It was said to be 1½ miles on to the top of the watershed from this place, where the remains of a very large dacoit camp were found and burnt in February 1890.—A.F.

FROM KYUNHLA TO KINDÁT AND PAUNGBYIN—*continued.*

Authorities. Military.	Authorities. Civil.	Number and Names of Stages, Rivers and Streams.	Distances. Intermediate. M.	F.	Total. M.	F.	Remarks.
G.O.C. Myingyán District.	Commissioner, Central Division, and Deputy Commissioner, Upper Chindwin.	**11. Pántha** ... Kôdán and Pántha chaungs, Chindwin river.	**21**	**0**	110	4	General direction west. Track follows the Nama chaung to its commencement at 5½ miles (sandy bed), where it crosses low watershed for 200 yards and immediately drops into another nullah for 5 miles, where the Nanthinpin chaung, small flowing stream, is met at a camping place (Yézôn). This stream is followed in and out to within 2 miles of Pántha. Forest and jungle on either side. Pántha some 50 houses; accommodation for 150 men in two kyaungs on left bank of Chindwin. Paddy and grass procurable. Water from Chindwin. Telegraph line to Tammu crosses 1 mile below. The road is fair and is generally kept well cleared, the only difficult part being at the crossing of the watershed at 5½ miles.
		12. Kindát ... Chindwin river.	**14**	**0**	124	4	The easiest way of reaching Kindát from Pántha is by steamer or boat, but there is a road which presents no great difficulties to pack transport in the dry season, though in the wet it is practically impassable. The general direction of the route is south-southwest.

BRANCH I.

FROM LAWTHA (STAGE 10) TO PAUNGBYIN.

BY LIEUT. H. F. LOCH, COMMANDANT, MILITARY POLICE, UPPER CHINDWIN, OCTOBER 1890.

Military	Civil	Stage	Inter. M.	F.	Total M.	F.	Remarks
G.O.C. Myingyán District.	Commissioner, Central Division, and Deputy Commissioner, Upper Chindwin.	**2. Mainyaung** ... Kôdán and Mainyaung chaungs.	**32**	**0**	32	0	General direction north-east. Road fairly easy through bamboo and open jungle and along bed of creek. One saddle crossed. No water middle of March for 15 miles.* Mainyaung is a fairly large village unenclosed, with a good kyaung and a large stream flowing 100 yards to north; accommodation for 100 men. Paddy and fodder procurable. Water from creek.
		3. Ngámu ... Two streams.	**6**	**0**	38	0	General direction north. Road good; skirts the foot of thick jungle-covered spurs on one side and a paddy plain with kaing grass on the other; jungle chiefly bamboo. On leaving Mainyaung a large stream is crossed and a second creek is crossed before reaching Ngámu. Good kyaung; hold 100 men. Supplies, paddy and grass and fowls. Water from shallow wells.

* There seems no reason why this march should not be split up into two marches of 15 and 17 miles each, or even into three except during the height of the dry season.

No. 12.

FROM KYUNHLA TO KINDÁT AND PAUNGBYIN—*continued.*

BRANCH I—*continued.*

Authorities. Military.	Authorities. Civil.	Number and Names of Stages, Rivers and Streams.	Distances. Intermediate. M.	F.	Distances. Total. M.	F.	Remarks.
G.O.C. Myingyán District.	Commissioner, Central Division, and Deputy Commissioner, Upper Chindwin.	**4. Paungbyin** ... Chindwin.	20	0	58	0	General direction north. Road good; but ramps much too steep for any except cooly carriage. It skirts along the foot of the hills which bound the Paungbyin paddy plain, and then strikes through forest, for the most part dense bamboo jungle. Paungbyin is a village on the Chindwin, about 150 houses. Good kyaung, hold 150 men. Police post on hill hold about the same. Supplies, paddy and grass. Water from Chindwin river.

No. 13.

From MINGIN to TAUNGDWIN and PATÔLÔN VALLEY.

BY LIEUT. H. F. LOCH, COMMANDANT, MILITARY POLICE, UPPER CHINDWIN, OCTOBER 1890.

Military	Civil	Stages	Inter. M.	F.	Total M.	F.	Remarks
G.O.C. Myingyán District.	Commissioner, Central Division, and Deputy Commissioner, Upper Chindwin.	**1. Linlu** ... ... Patôlôn creek.	9	0	9	0	General direction. Road good and same as that to Seiktha till it reaches the village of Timbet, when it strikes off to left and, crossing a saddle, descends to the Patôlôn creek, which it follows upwards. Linlu is a small village of four or five houses with a good kyaung. No supplies.
		2. Tántabin ...	29	0	38	0	General direction south. Road shortly after leaving Linlu goes up a steep ascent and then runs along the crest of the hills between Linlu and Séywagyaung. Road pretty good. It then descends to a stream, where there is a small water hole; the first water met with since leaving the creek near Linlu. From here it runs along the side and down a spur to the Séywagyaung. Descent extremely bad, especially in one place where there is a drop of some 5 or 6 feet with a very steep slope below. Water in the valley. Road now passes the village of Kama and on to Tántabin. No accommodation here, as village burnt down. Indifferent kyaung at Bainbin village, ¾ of a mile to the north.
		3. Náttáya Sakhán. Thitkauk stream.	6	0	44	0	General direction south-west. Road good as far as Thitkauk and then bad to Náttáya up bed of nullah over boulders.
		4. Kaleikyé Sakhán.	9	0	53	0	From here it runs up a steep ascent along a ridge and then up and down along dividing watershed up the Pondaung range to Kaleikyé Saknán. No water along the road after leaving Náttáya. This is a very stiff march.

FROM MINGIN TO TAUNGDWIN AND PATÔLÔN VALLEY—*continued.*

Authorities. Military.	Authorities. Civil.	Number and Names of Stages, Rivers and Streams.	Distances. Intermediate. M. F.	Distances. Total. M. F.	Remarks.
G.O.C. Myingyán District.	Commissioner, Central Division, and Deputy Commissioner, Upper Chindwin.	**5. Kyémaôk Sakhán.** Stream.	**7 0**	60 0	General direction south-south-west. Road runs up to top of pass and is fairly easy. It then descends to Kya Sakhán, from which it ascends for a short distance and then runs along the ridge to Kyémaôk Sakhán. First water since leaving Kaleikyé.
		6. Chaungma ...	**11 0**	71 0	From here the path runs down a creek to the Thinmachaung and is very bad in parts over boulders and logs. It then crosses a hill and leads down by a very bad descent to the Chaungmachaung up which it runs to Chaungma.

ALTERNATIVE I.

FROM TÁNTABIN (STAGE 2) TO CHAUNGMA (STAGE 6) *viá* ZENAPÔK AND PAYA.

BY LIEUT. H. F. LOCH, COMMANDANT, MILITARY POLICE, UPPER CHINDWIN, OCTOBER 1890.

Authorities. Military.	Authorities. Civil.	Number and Names of Stages, Rivers and Streams.	Intermediate.	Total.	Remarks.
G.O.C. Myingyán District.	Commissioner, Central Division, and Deputy Commissioner, Upper Chindwin.	**1. Seiktha** ... Taungdwin chaung.	About **20 0**	About 20 0	A long day's march, easy road for all pack animals. *See* Mr. Bates' routes below, No. VII. Seiktha has 40 houses and accommodation in kyaung for 50 men. Paddy and grass. Water from chaung.
		2. Zenapôk ... Taungdwin creek.	**10 0**	30 0	General direction south-west. Road runs up chaung as far as Tôngyi and then bends off to right up another creek, up precipitous path and along the banks; very bad going. It then crosses the ridge and descends steeply for a long distance to Zenapôk. This road is impracticable for baggage animals, which have to go round by a longer road; Zenapôk contains 10 houses. Accommodation *nil.* Supplies *nil.* Grass and water in creek close by. There is an oil-well 1½ miles on Paya road.
		3. Paya ... ... Taungdwin creek.	**10 0**	40 0	General direction south. Road over hills and up creek is fairly good going except in creek. Paya is a very fair-sized village, containing about 60 houses. Accommodation zayát, about 20 men. Supplies, paddy and grass. Water in creek close by.
		4. Chaungma ... Chaungma stream.	**29 0**	69 0	General direction south. Road fairly good, crosses over three saddles and descends a creek and then leads up another to Chaungma. Accommodation *nil.* Fodder procurable. No other regular camping place on this march.* Water from creek.

* Although no other regular camping ground, there is probably no reason why the march should not be divided. It is much too long for any but Mounted infantry even on an emergency.

FROM MINGIN TO TAUNGDWIN AND PATÔLÔN VALLEY—*continued.*

BRANCH I.

FROM TÁNTABIN (STAGE 2) TO KALÉWA *viâ* SEIKTHA AND MYOMA.

BY LIEUT. H. F. LOCH, COMMANDANT, MILITARY POLICE, UPPER CHINDWIN, OCTOBER 1890.

Authorities.		Number and Names of Stages, Rivers and Streams.	Distances.				Remarks.
Military.	Civil.		Intermediate.		Total.		
			M.	F.	M.	F.	
G.O.C. Myingyán District.	Commissioner, Central Division, and Deputy Commissioner, Upper Chindwin.	**1. Seiktha** ... Taungdwin chaung.	**20**	**0**	20	0	As in Stage 1 of Alternative No. I above.
		2. Myoma ... Taungdwin chaung.	**14**	**0**	34	0	General direction north-north-west. Road chiefly through paddy plain, crossing Taungdwin stream about eight times, easily fordable in cold weather. Numerous villages of from 10 to 40 houses on or close to the road. Little accommodation at Myoma, but paddy procurable.
		3. Kaléwa ... Myittha and Chindwin rivers.	**22**	**0**	56	0	General direction north. First 4 miles through paddy cultivation, passing two or three small villages. Then crossing low saddle and quitting Taungdwin valley, through forest and somewhat broken country up to 17 miles. Thence chiefly along bed of Lébin chaung and over paddy cultivation to Kyawzin on the south (right) bank of the Myittha river opposite Kaléwa. One small village is passed at 17 miles. Road is fairly good and water obtainable most of the way. Paddy procurable.

The following note by S. B. Bates, Esq., of the Bombay Burma Company on routes FROM MINGIN, UPPER CHINDWIN INTO THE PATÔLÔN AND TAUNGDWIN VALLEYS and thence INTO THE MYITTHA AND YAW VALLEYS AND KANI, dated Mingin, the 11th March 1890, is added, as giving a good general account of the existing communications in this part of the country :—

FROM MINGIN INTO THE TAUNGDWIN VALLEY.

I.—Mingin to Kyawywa, 2 marches.

From Mingin *viâ* Kulé chaung to Kyawywa in Taungdwin.

Country.—Open ground as far as Kulé, rest of the way thin jungle.

Road.—Bridle path constructed by Government as far as the Taungdwin chaung.

Water.—(1) Kulé chaung, (2) below zayát at half distance, (3) Taungdwin chaung (perennial).
Accommodation en route.—Half-way zayát, 20 men.
Transport to be employed.—Elephants or any other pack animals, coolies.
Distance.—Two easy marches.

II.—Mingin to Myoma.

2. From Mingin *viâ* Kabyit, Mindin, and Nátkyun to Myoma in Taungdwin.

Country.—Fairly open to Kabyit ; thence to Mindin rough track through heavy forest ; thence to Myoma up bed of stream.

Water.—Plentiful throughout the year.
Accommodation.—Villages *en route.*
Transport.—Elephants and all pack animals, coolies. During the rains boats can run up the Taungdwin chaung as far as Nátkyun.

III.—Mingin to Kyauktán, 1 march.

3. From Mingin to Kyauktán in Taungdwin, *viâ* Pégán, very bad track.

Transport.—Coolies with very light loads.

FROM MINGIN TO TAUNGDWIN AND PATÔLÔN VALLEY—*continued.*

FROM MINGIN INTO THE TAUNGDWIN VALLEY—*continued.*

Tracks in Taungdwin Valley.

All the villages in the Taungdwin valley are connected by tracks through open country. Myoma is the chief place of the valley and from it several roads diverge into the Myittha valley, which were used chiefly by the Chins in their raids into the Taungdwin. Few, if any of these, with the exception of the route from Kôko, traversed by a detachment under Capt. Sorrell in 1887, are believed to be passable by transport animals. These are said to be Chin raiders' paths up the beds of the Tain, Taungbin, Paungdaung, Siyé, and Payathaung chaungs.

FROM THE TAUNGDWIN INTO THE MYITTHA VALLEY.

IV.—Seiktha to Gángaw.

The high road from the Taungdwin to Gángaw in the Myittha valley in the dry season starts from Saiktha, follows the bed of the Taungdwin stream to Paya and on to Chaungma (police post), thence over the hills (Pônyataung) and down the Kunzé chaung to Kunzé village on the right bank of the Myittha river, thence south along the river to Gángaw.

Country.—Very difficult travelling as far as Paya; bed of stream being very rough and rocky. Paya to Chaungma stream bed sandy; to Kunzé heavy forest.

Water.—Throughout.

Accommodation in Paya and Kunzé villages. Chaungma deserted and burnt.

Transport.—Elephants, coolies, and possibly mules. During the rainy season instead of going up the stream bed from Seiktha you proceed to Taungyi and cross the hills through heavy forest to Paya, thence to Chaungma, &c., as in the dry season.

V.—Seiktha, or Winwa, to Kôko, 2 or 3 marches.

From Seiktha, or Winwa, *viâ* the Nwa chaung to Kôko.

Country.—Forest; good route; water plentiful.

Distance.—Two or three marches.

Transport.—Elephants and other pack transport coolies.

VI.—Paya to Ngapôk, 1 or 2 marches.

From Paya over the hills to Ngapôk, south of Kyaukpyauk.

Country.—Forest; bad route; water.

Transport.—Elephants, &c.

The tracks down the Taungbin and other creeks mentioned before are impassable for troops with transport animals.

FROM THE TAUNGDWIN INTO THE PATÔLÔN VALLEY.

VII.—Seiktha to Tántabin, 1 long march.

From Seiktha *viâ* Taungyi and Tátywa to Tántabin in Patôlôn valley, one hard day's march.

Country.—Cross the watershed into the Dídôk chaung which is thence followed to Tántabin.

Transport.—Easy road for all pack animals.

VIII.—Seiktha to Mônbinywa.

Another route is from Seiktha over the Shwétha-Mintha range through forest coming out in the Patôlôn valley, a mile or 2 below Mônbinywa.

IX.—Tántabin to Chaungma (4 marches 33 miles) or Paya.

From Tántabin in Patôlôn to Chaungma in Taungdwin *viâ* the Thitkauk chaung, across the Pôndaung hills into the Kayán chaung, thence to Paya or Chaungma.

Country.—Difficult; steep ground and heavy forest.

Water.—In the dry season none obtainable after leaving Thitkauk chaung until the lower Kayán chaung is reached.

Transport.—Elephants, mules, &c.

X.—Mindôn to Chaungma, 2 long marches.

From Mindôn in Patôlôn to Chaungma in Taungdwin, across the Pôndaung range; water at Lédaung Sakhán on western slope; heavy forest and kaing grass; easy for elephants. Two long weary marches.

FROM MINGIN INTO THE PATÔLÔN VALLEY.

XI.—Mingin to Tántabin, 2 marches 38 miles (see above).

From Mingin to Tántabin in dry weather *viâ* Timbet and Tôngbán up the bed of the Patôlôn to Mônbin and in wet weather *viâ* Timbet and Linlu, 9 miles along the hills through forest to the Mingin chaung to Nama and down the Hati chaung to Yeinthwin.

Water.—Procurable half-way between Linlu and Nama.

Transport.—Easy road both ways for all kinds of pack animals.

From Linlu another road runs *viâ* Petôk, partly up the chaung, partly through heavy forest to Mahu, thence to Thingadôn and Kani, practicable for all pack animals.

Water.—Hard to get on the Upper Mahu plateau in the dry weather, but a forced march can always take you through.

From MINGIN to TAUNGDWIN and PATÔLÔN VALLEY—*continued.*

From MINGIN into the PATÔLÔN VALLEY—*continued.*

From Mahu across watershed to the south and you get into the Hati valley, follow the chaung down to Yeinthwin.

In fact there is hardly a single village in Patôlôn and Taungdwin that has not its direct track not only between the other villages in its vicinity, but to Thingadôn and Kani villages also.

Up the PATÔLÔN VALLEY.

From Tántabin to Alaungdaw-Kôthaba from Kôzeik in dry weather up the main chaung or over the hills to Mindôn Sakhán. Water everywhere and good road. From Mindôn track runs through heavy forest to Alaungdaw, where there are zayáts built by the Bombay Burma Trading Corporation sufficient to accommodate fully 100 men. Three good marches from Tántabin to Alaungdaw.

XII.—Tántabin to Alaungdaw-Kôthaba, 3 marches.

XIII.—Alaungdaw to Chaungma (Patôlôn). From Alaungdaw to Chaungma in Patôlôn along the Paya chaung to its mouth, there joining the road from Mindôn.

From the PATÔLÔN into the YAW DISTRICT.

XIV.—Mindôn to Yaw District, 3 marches. From Mindôn *viâ* Kaungdin chaung and along through heavy forest across the head-waters of the Patôlôn into Yaw. Easy for elephants and men; water plentiful; three marches.

XV.—Alaungdaw to Yaw. From Alaungdaw to Yaw up the Paya chaung.

From the PATÔLÔN into the KANI DISTRICT.

XVI.—Mindôn (in Patôlôn) to Kani. From Mindôn across Lema chaung down by the side of Lémataik up Pwédaung to Kyaungma (in Patôlôn), thence to Kani or Shitywagyaung, easy tracks, all traversed at one time or another by British troops since our occupation of Upper Burma.

XVII.—Patôlôn to Kani. The high road from Patôlôn to Kani is up the valley to Kôzeik, across the Kyaungnet and Sadán chaungs, over the Mahudaung to Thingadôn and *viâ* Yágyi.

Country.—Heavy forest and difficult track in some parts, but passable and generally easy for elephants and men.

Water.—Plentiful.

There are several other tracks from lower down the valley also, but most of them concentrate on Yágyi.

General remarks.—Accommodation in the forest, as far as any buildings are concerned, *nil* except for the zayáts at Alaungdaw.

Water gets very stagnant and putrid in most parts by April and May, except on the Taungdwin route to Gángaw, where the water is always fairly good.

Rice, fowls, &c., always to be got at the villages.

Yahaung is the last inhabited village up the Taungdwin, and Kôzeik up the Patlôn.

No. 14.

From MÔNYWA to GÁNGAW viâ SAGA.

By W. T. MORRISON, Esq., Deputy Commissioner, Lower Chindwin, January 1889.

Authorities: Military.	Authorities: Civil.	Number and Names of Stages, Rivers and Streams.	Intermediate. M.	Intermediate. F.	Total. M.	Total. F.	Remarks.
G.O.C. Myingyán District.	Commissioner, Central Division, and Deputy Commissioner, Lower Chindwin.	1. Salingyi ...	12	0	12	0	Cross Chindwin river at Mônywa. Police post at Salingyi.
		2. Léhnauk ...	15	0	27	0	Metalled road from Salingyi to Léhnauk in course of construction. Police post here.

FROM MÔNYWA TO GÁNGAW *viâ* SAGA—*continued.*

Authorities. Military.	Authorities. Civil.	Number and Names of Stages, Rivers and Streams.	Distances. Intermediate. M.	Distances. Intermediate. F.	Distances. Total. M.	Distances. Total. F.	Remarks.
G.O.C. Myingyán District.	Commissioner, Central Division, and Deputy Commissioner, Chindwin.	**3. Kyinbyit** ...	**17**	**0**	44	0	Good road during fair weather; during rains road is from Léhnauk to Mintainbin, 12 miles, and Mintainbin to Kyinbyit, 11 miles. Large police post at Kyinbyit.
		4. Thitkyidain ...	**18**	**0**	62	0	Road crosses north Yôma creek at Kyinbyit. This creek is generally passable, except during heavy floods in rains, which do not last more than three or four days at a time. Road gradual ascent almost whole way to Thitkyidain. Road recently improved and passable for lightly laden carts. At 12th mile from Kyinbyit pass Aingma, small village of eight or 10 houses. No kyaung accommodation at Thitkyidain. A better village to camp at is Zeittaung, 1 mile south.
	Commissioner, Southern Division, and Deputy Commissioner, Pakôkku.	**5. Saga**	**21**	**0**	83	0	First 3 miles easy road, then very steep ascent of 7 miles to top of Pôndaung range, about 3,500 feet. Pass Pápen Sakhán half-way up and Natak Sakhán at top. The ascent is very steep, unladen ponies can go with difficulty. From Natak Sakhán the descent to Gángaw is longer and more gradual. Good water procurable on road. Good kyaung accommodation at Saga for 150 men. Saga lies in valley between Pôndaung and Pônya range. From here there is a good pack track to Léo 50½ miles, *see* Route No. 36, Southern Division.
		6. Ké Sakhán ...	**15**	**0**	98	0	First 6 miles fairly easy ascent to top of Pônya range about 1,000 feet above Saga, then rapid descent to Chaungmazôn Sakhán. Here the Ké stream takes its rise, and the road from here lies alongside of, and in, its rocky bed, the whole to Gángaw. Jungle camp at Ké. No huts.
		7. Gángaw ...	**14**	**0**	112	0	Road lies whole way in bed of stream, crossing and recrossing repeatedly. Ponies can go from Thitkyidain to Gángaw, but road is very trying for them. Jungle uninhabited between Saga and Gángaw.

ALTERNATIVE I.

FROM MÔNYWA TO GÁNGAW *viâ* KYAW.

BY W. T. MORRISON, ESQ., DEPUTY COMMISSIONER, LOWER CHINDWIN, JANUARY 1889.

Military	Civil	Stages	Intermediate M.	Intermediate F.	Total M.	Total F.	Remarks
G.O.C. Myingyán District.	Commnr., Central Divn., and Deputy Commnr., Lower Chindwin.	**1 to 4. Thitkyidain.**	...		62	0	The same as in Route No. 14 above.

FROM MÔNYWA TO GÁNGAW *viâ* SAGA—*continued.*

ALTERNATIVE I—*continued.*

Authorities. Military.	Authorities. Civil.	Number and Names of Stages, Rivers and Streams.	Distances. Intermediate. M.	F.	Distances. Total. M.	F.	Remarks.
G.O.C. Myingyán District.	Commissioner, Central Division, and Deputy Commissioner, Pakôkku.	**5. Kyaw**	**23**	**0**	85	0	Road lies in the valley as far as Kyát village (5 miles), then turns west and crosses the Pôndaung range, 3,000 feet. A steep ascent, but not so difficult as Saga road. Lightly laden ponies could go. Good accommodation at Kyaw for 200 men.
		6. Yébôk	**10**	**0**	95	0	First 5 miles of road crosses Pônya range, steep but passable for ponies, then easier descent to Yébôk village. No accommodation for troops at Yébôk.
		7. Tawma	**10**	**0**	105	0	Fairly easy road through jungle, crossing and recrossing rocky beds of mountain streams. Kyaung accommodation for 100 men at Tawma.
		8. Gángaw ...	**23**	**0**	128	0	First 4 miles difficult jungle road, then joins Tilin-Gángaw road (*see* Route No. 30, Southern Division) at Kyauknet, thence *viâ* Minywa to Gángaw. *Note.*—This route, though longer, is much easier and preferable to the Saga one.

No. 15.

From MYINMU to ÁLÔN.

I. B. COMPILATION, NOVEMBER 1888.

Military	Civil	Stages	Inter. M.	F.	Total M.	F.	Remarks
G.O.C. Myingyán District.	Commissioner, Central Division, and Deputy Commissioner, Sagaing.	**1. Gwébindaw** ...	**12**	**0**	12	0	A road has been commenced by the Public Works Department as far as Mônywa, but has only been metalled for 6 miles from Myinmu, and bridges are not yet complete (February 1888). The road will eventually be continued as far as Álôn. The road for the first 7 miles is through cultivation, which will be difficult in rainy season until the road is completed. Alakapa at 7 miles has five kyaungs for 200 men. Water good from wells and a tank north of the village. This would make the best halting place until wells have been dug at Gwébindaw, where water is scarce and has to be brought from 2 miles distance during the dry season. From Alakapa the road is through scrub jungle to Gwébindaw. At 12 miles Gwébindaw has a police post, where a small party can be accommodated, not more than 20 men. There are no kyaungs, and water is scarce during the dry season as mentioned above. There is good camping ground near the fort.

FROM MYINMU TO ÁLÔN—*continued.*

Authorities.		Number and Names of Stages, Rivers and Streams.	Distances.				Remarks.
Military.	Civil.		Inter-mediate.		Total.		
			M.	F.	M.	F.	
G.O.C. Myingyán District.	Commissioner, Central Division, and Deputy Commissioner, Sagaing.	**2. Chaungu** ...	**10**	**0**	22	0	Road on through thick jungle, 2 miles, to Yabôsa, a small village surrounded by jungle. Good water from tank west of the village. Road on as before to Nátyégán at 5 miles. Accommodation for 25 men in a zayât on the bank of a tank east of the village. Water good from tank. Road on as before to Chaungu at 10 miles. Chaungu is about 1 mile long and nearly as big as Myinmu. It has a military police post and military post (February 1888). Besides the barracks it has accommodation for 500 men in kyaungs. Water good from wells.
	Commissioner, Cenl. Divn., and Deputy Commissioner, Lower Chindwin.	**3. Mônywa** ...	**15**	**4**	37	4	The road passes through much cultivated ground, but is raised very high, 10 to 15 feet, showing expected inundations. At 12 miles from Chaungu the river bank is met. There are great quantities of toddy-palm trees about this spot. From here Mônywa is 3½ miles. The ground is less cultivated. Mônywa is the head-quarters of the Lower Chindwin civil district. It has good accommodation and water.
		4. Álôn ...	**7**	**4**	45	0	*See* Route No. 1, Álôn to Pauk, Stage 1.

The following is the description of an alternative route FROM MYINMU *viâ* GÔNYINSEIK TO ÁLÔN :—

ALTERNATIVE I.

FROM MYINMU (STAGE 1) TO ÁLÔN (STAGE 4) *viâ* GÔNYINSEIK AND WADÁN.

I. B. COMPILATION, 1887-88.

Military.	Civil.	Number and Names of Stages, Rivers and Streams.	Inter. M.	Inter. F.	Total M.	Total F.	Remarks.
G.O.C. Myingyán District.	Commissioner, Central Division, and Deputy Commissioner, Sagaing.	**1. Gônyinseik** ...	**12**	**4**	12	2	*Viâ* Nyaungmyit and Nabé, *see* Route No. 17.
		2. Myinywa ...	**12**	**0**	24	2	Pass Einma at 2 miles. At 6 miles pass Ywatha. At 8 miles pass Naungkyidouk. Road for carts up to this stage very good. Soil reddish clay and gravel, not liable to inundation. Large masonry tank of good water. Trees plentiful. Village entirely burnt down and deserted (8th May 1886). Good camping ground.
		3. Wadán ...	**18**	**0**	42	2	Pass Ngakin at 2 miles, Malétha at 6, Gwéyin at 7. Road for carts very good up to Malétha. Soil same as above.

FROM MYINMU TO ÁLÔN—*continued.*

ALTERNATIVE I—*continued.*

Authorities. Military.	Authorities. Civil.	Number and Names of Stages, Rivers and Streams.	Distances. Intermediate. M. F.	Distances. Total. M. F.	Remarks.
G.O.C. Myingyán District.	Commissioner, Central Division, and Deputy Commissioner, Sagaing.	**3. Wadán**—*cont.*			Water scarce. The cart ruts have been cut into the stony soil of the low ridges to such an extent that the journey for carts is rendered difficult and toilsome. Wadán is a very large village with plenty of water, a well and a tank, large kyaungs with trees, and a good encamping ground.
		4. Kôthán ...	11 0	53 2	At 4 miles pass Indain; at 8 miles Kambya. Water and supplies plentiful. Numerous kyaungs. Good camping ground.
		5. Álôn	6 0	59 2	The road from Myinmu runs along high ground the whole way and is not liable to inundation; it is a better road than the Chaungu route, during wet weather. *Note.*—This is a good deal longer than the Chaungu route, and, as the latter has now, it is believed, been properly constructed by the Public Works Department, it is improbable that this route would ever have to be used in preference to it.

No. 16.

From MYINMU to SAGAING viâ YWATHITGYI.

BY LIEUT. FISCHER, 5TH BOMBAY LIGHT INFANTRY, 1888.

Authorities. Military.	Authorities. Civil.	Number and Names of Stages, Rivers and Streams.	Distances. Intermediate.	Distances. Total.	Remarks.
G.O.C. Myingyán District.	Commissioner, Central Division, and Deputy Commissioner, Sagaing.	**1. Ywathitgyi** ... Irrawaddy and Mu rivers.	7 0	7 0	Road along the river bank to Pabédán (Bombay Burma Trading Corporation village), where about 25 carts could be obtained. The Mu river must now be crossed in boats, of which there are plenty; neither bank steep; 100 yards broad; 20 feet deep; current $3\frac{1}{2}$ miles an hour. Reach Shwéhlé on the opposite bank. The road then continues on along the river bank to Myinzé at 4 miles (a foot-path straight across saves 1 mile). There is a nullah east of Myinzé, which runs from the north from Maungdaung. It can be crossed at Myinzé in the dry weather, but nowhere in the rains. Pass Letpadán and reach Kainbin at 5 miles. Then along good cart road to Ywathitgyi. The above is the dry-weather road. Another road runs as follows: 2 miles east to Nyaungyin, then 3 miles north to Máywazétaung. Two large kyaungs for 200 men. Plentiful supply of water. Rice and paddy in fair quantity. Fifty

FROM MYINMU TO SAGAING *viâ* YWATHITGYI—*continued.*

Authorities. Military.	Authorities. Civil.	Number and Names of Stages, Rivers and Streams.	Distances. Intermediate.	Distances. Total.	Remarks.
G.O.C. Myingyán District.	Commissioner, Central Division, and Deputy Commissioner, Sagaing.	**1. Ywathitgyi**—*cont.*			carts. Thus far the road is very bad in the rains. The Mu must now be crossed, fordable in the dry weather, depth 3 feet. Road then runs north-east by east reaching Múdaung at 7 miles. Thence road north-east to Ywathitgyi, total distance by this road 13 miles. Ywathitgyi is a very large village on the Irrawaddy nearly opposite Kyauktalôn. There is a police post on top of a large brick pagoda, about centre of village. Strength 25 rifles. Accommodation for 1,500 men in kyaungs and zayáts around the village. Water from river good to drink. Many cattle are raised for eating purposes, and rice, paddy, and vegetables can be obtained. From here there is a good cart road to Ôngdaw (Route No. 21, 3rd Road, Stage 1) 7 miles to the north. The road runs nearly straight chiefly over undulating sandy ground, but in three places paddy cultivation is met with, and here the road would be bad in wet weather.
		2. Sagaing ... Irrawaddy river.	M. F. **13 0**	M. F. 20 0	First mile and-a-half north-east, over sandy ground, about parallel to the Irrawaddy. At 1½ miles Nátyo village road bending away slightly from the river to the village. Leaving the village road approaches the river again and at 4 miles reach Sindát. Thence it runs due east along the right bank of channel from Kyaungmudaw lake which enters the Irrawaddy at Sindát. This channel is not fordable except in the dry weather and then only opposite Sindát and at Pégadaw 2 miles further up. Pass the villages of Biyédyaw (5 miles), Nyaungbinzin (5½ miles), and Pégadaw (6 miles). The last-named is on the edge of the Kyaungmudaw lake. Follow the edge of the lake for 2 miles and then strike into the Kyaungmudaw-Sagaing road at the village of Magyizin (8 miles). At 13 miles Sagaing. During the dry season a short cut can be used by foot-passengers (and probably by ponies too) from Pégadaw to Sagaing *viâ* Ma-úbin entering Sagaing by the Déwázé bazaar. This reduces the distance by 2 miles.

No. 17.

From MYINMU to SHWÉBO viâ MAGYIZAUK.

I. B. COMPILATION, NOVEMBER 1888.

Military	Civil	Stage	Intermediate	Total	Remarks
G.O.C. Myingyán District.	Commr., Central Divn., and Deputy Commr., Sagaing.	**1. Gônyinseik** ...	**12 4**	...	Myinmu is a village of 300 houses, about 5 miles below the mouth of the Mu river, on the right bank of the Irrawaddy. It is entirely surrounded by paddy-fields except where it faces the Irrawaddy. The fort is about 1 mile north-west of the landing place on slightly rising ground surrounded by a ditch, parapet, and bamboo stockades; could accommodate 150 men in all, and has good and ample water from well inside. Close to the landing place there are three kyaungs for 110 men and 13 zayáts for 75 men. There are two other kyaungs suitable for troops, one on the Chaungu and one on the Magyizauk road, about ½ mile from

No. 17.

From MYINMU to SHWÊBO *viâ* MAGYIZAUK—*continued.*

Authorities. Military.	Authorities. Civil.	Number and Names of Stages, Rivers and Streams.	Distances. Inter-mediate.	Distances. Total.	Remarks.
C.O.C. Myingyan District.	Commissioner, Central Division, and Deputy Commissioner, Sagaing.	**1. Gônyinseik**—*cont.*			the landing place. These kyaungs would hold 70 men, and 13 zayáts, 100 men. If all kyaungs and zayáts in the vicinity were used, accommodation could be found for 400 men in kyaungs and 450 in zayáts. Water is good and plentiful from wells at nearly all the kyaungs and from the midstream of the river. There is a military police post on the bank of the river at the landing place surrounded by parapet and stockade. Road north good for carts in dry season through cultivation 2½ miles, then ½ mile through scrub jungle to Htísaung. One kyaung south with two zayáts, 60 men. One kyaung east, 60 men. Good water from well at the latter and from three wells in the village. Road on north-east for the 1st mile through paddy almost impassable for carts in the rains, remainder good over sandstone through light jungle, except slight cultivation at 6½ miles to Gônyinseik at 12½ miles. Gônyinseik is on the right bank of the Mu river with a police fort on the east of the road close to the village. The fort has a block-house from which an extensive view can be obtained. The fort would hold 60 men in all. One well at kyaung at north-east with good water. Water good from river. There are six kyaungs which would accommodate 600 men in all. There is an alternative road from Htísaung *viâ* Kándaw running to the west of the one described above. It is through cultivation and more difficult in the rains. It is however sometimes used on account of better accommodation at Kándaw. Kándaw is 3½ miles from Htísaung and has accommodation for 200 men in three kyaungs and some zayáts. Water good from wells and tank. Kándaw to Gônyinseik 6 miles.
		2. Sintsalé ...	M. 10 F. 2	M. 22 F. 6	Road in general direction due north running on an average 1 mile from the bank of the Mu river. As fas as Mandalé road is bad for carts during the rains. The 1st mile through cultivation, then 2¼ miles through light jungle, and some cultivation to Tuma; at 3¼ miles 150 houses shaded by large trees. One kyaung south-east, 100 men. One kyaung north, 50 men. Water good from one well, nearly dry, and from the river. The road on as before except that the jungle on the right is sometimes very thick. Cross a nullah at 3 miles, impracticable for carts after heavy rain; an easier crossing could be found further west. Just south of the nullah on the right of the road is a good camping ground near a kyaung, one zayát for 10 men. Mandalé Mu is reached at 7 miles. The kyaung is about 600 yards north of the village on the road. Accommodation for 118 men and good water from the Mu river. The river is fordable to the east of the village from November to May. From Mandalé Mu there are roads east to Ôngdaw south-east to Ywathitgyi on the Irrawaddy west to Kaiba for Ayadaw. Road on north difficult for carts in rains to Sintsalé at 10¼ miles; crossing a nullah at 1 mile from Mandalé Mu, which would be difficult for a short time after heavy rain. Sintsalé has 50 houses, two kyaungs and zayáts for 200 men. Water good from river.
Commr., C.D., and Dy. Commr., Lower Chindwin.		**3. Magyizauk** ...	9 6	32 4	Road on north to Taléba, 3 miles, difficult for carts during the rains, 100 houses, good accommodation in large kyaungs. Water from Mu river.

FROM MYINMU TO SHWÉBO *viâ* MAGYIZAUK—*continued.*

Authorities. Military.	Authorities. Civil.	Number and Names of Stages, Rivers and Streams.	Distances. Intermediate.	Distances. Total.	Remarks.
G.O.C. Myingyán District.	Commissioner, Central Division, and Deputy Commr., Lower Chindwin.	**3. Magyizauk**—*cont.*			After this the road improves to Magyizauk, running for most of the way through jungle until within 2 miles of Magyizauk, where it enters paddy cultivation. Pass Seitkugyi at 6 miles (40 houses). Nayaho at 8¼ miles (50 houses). Magyizauk was a military post in February 1888. The fort is about 200 yards west of the river bank and 200 yards north of the village, it has a low parapet and thorn abattis 10 yards in front, 18 feet in breadth. It would accommodate 250 men, 140 followers, stabling for 100 horses and 100 mules. From Magyizauk there is a road 15 miles west to Kônbyu for Alôn 40 miles distant.
G.O.C. Mandalay District.	Commissioner, Northern Division, and Deputy Commissioner, Shwébo.	**4. Hládaw** ... Mu river. River Mu 300 yards from bank to bank fordable for carts in dry season only.	M. 13 F. 2	M. 45 F. 6	There are two roads to the first village of this stage, Thaníywa. The Mu river can be forded ¼ mile north of the fort; road on along the left bank. The Mu is fordable here from November to May. Two feet of water in February. A shorter road is due north keeping to the west of the Mu for 2½ miles through thick scrub jungle. At 2½ miles the road crosses the river to Thaníywa about ¼ mile east of the bank. Ford here 3 feet deep in January. Accommodation for 300 men in kyaungs. Road on north-east through cultivation and grass jungle to Shwébangán at 5¼ miles (100 houses, one kyaung). Road on north-east-east ¼ mile through paddy, then through scrub jungle to within 1 mile of Mégong, where it enters paddy again. Mégong (10 miles) has 40 houses and one small kyaung. Road on through cultivation north-east Kyígán at 11½ miles (100 houses). Road north through cultivation to Hládaw at 13¼ miles. Hládaw has 200 houses. Accommodation for 300 men in kyaungs south of village. From Magyizauk to Hládaw is a good cart road in dry season, but nearly impassable in the rains.
		5. Shwébo... ...	15 2	61 0	The same applies to the next stage, Hládaw to Shwébo, which is entirely through paddy cultivation. General direction due north. Pass Maukyo at 2½ miles: 40 houses, one small kyaung. Pass Tama at 3¾ miles: 80 houses. Pass Sinan-Taungywa at 6 miles: 100 houses, one kyaung, one zayát. Pass Sinan at 7½ miles: 50 houses, one small kyaung. Pass Baungywa at 9¾ miles: 70 houses, one large kyaung. Pass Zídaw at 11¼ miles: one good kyaung and several zayáts. Pass Tuganán at 13¾ miles: 30 houses. The ancient city of Shwébo is surrounded by the remains of an old wall, now much ruined and no great obstacle to an assault. In many places it is of great thickness, its extent is about 1,700 yards by 1,500 yards. The town now consists of only some 300 houses in the north-east corner of the space enclosed by the city wall.* There are three large and numerous small pagodas and several kyaungs inside the walls; also an enclosure with several kyaungs about ¼ mile outside the north-east gate, in which there are wells of good water. Supplies plentiful. Head-quarters of the Shwébo command. About 1,200 men and 250 houses can be accommodated in the post. Good water plentiful.

FROM MYINMU TO SHWÉBO *viâ* MAGYIZAUK—*continued.*

BRANCH I.

FROM MYINMU TO NGAKIN.

BY LIEUT. C. FARRANT, 2ND ROYAL MUNSTER FUSILIERS, FEBRUARY 1888.

Authorities.		Number and Names of Stages, Rivers and Streams.	Distances.				Remarks.
Military.	Civil.		Intermediate.		Total.		
			M.	F.	M.	F.	
G.O.C. Myingyán District.	Commissioner, Central Division, and Deputy Commissioner, Sagaing.	**1. Ngakin**	**15**	**0**	15	0	Road good; scrub jungle on each side of road; soil black; Kándaw at 7 miles. A tank about 2 miles from village on the west. One tank on west of village, one tank on north. Four kyaungs near village. Accommodation for about 150 men. A branch road running north-west to Sátwégyin. Nullah about 1 mile on road to Khwetkwin. Thick jungle near nullah. Road runs west to Khwetkwin at 11 miles. One kyaung, 60 men. Water good, two wells. Road east to Gônyinseik. North to Htingán good road. Thick jungle on each side. Red sandy soil. Road north-west to Ngakin good. Soil sandy. Cultivation on each side of road. Numerous palm trees on the west. Road north to Minywa; good soil; stony. Four kyaungs and numerous pagodas, accommodation for 150 men. Water good; one well, two tanks. One on north, the other on the south. Cultivation (paddy) on the east, thick jungle on the west.

BRANCH II.

FROM MANDALÉ MU (BETWEEN STAGES 1 AND 2) TO NAMATHIN *viâ* KAIBA.

BY CAPT. NICHOLETTS, 5TH BOMBAY LIGHT INFANTRY, FEBRUARY 1888.

Military.	Civil.	Stages.	M.	F.	M.	F.	Remarks.
G.O.C. Myingyán District.	Commissioner, Central Division, and Deputy Commissioner, Sagaing.	**1. Kaiba**	**4**	**0**	4	0	Road runs due north-west. The track for a short distance runs along the top of the high ground. At the foot of the high ground and about half-way there is a very difficult piece of country to get across in the rains, as the ground is a perfect swamp for about 1 mile. Also near Kaiba itself the road passes constantly through swamp in the rains. Low scrub and jungle are the main features.
		2. Namathin ... The nullahs referred to in the column of details are 4 feet deep and 10 feet wide. Every rains they get deeper, wider, and more formidable.	**6**	**0**	10	0	Cart track runs north-west to Namathin, crosses over a nullah 3½ miles from Kaiba, and again close to Namathin. Scrub jungle all the way.

FROM MYINMU TO SHWÉBO *viâ* MAGYIZAUK—*continued.*

BRANCH III.

FROM MANDALÉ MU (BETWEEN STAGES 1 AND 2) TO NAUNGKYIDAUK.

BY CAPT. NICHOLETTS, 5TH BOMBAY LIGHT INFANTRY, FEBRUARY 1888.

Authorities. Military.	Authorities. Civil.	Number and Names of Stages, Rivers and Streams.	Distances. Inter-mediate.	Distances. Total.	Remarks.
G.O.C. Myingyán District.	Commr., Central Divn., and Deputy Commr., Sagaing.	**1. Naungkyidauk.**	M. 8 F. 0	M. 8 F. 0	Road runs south-west to Naungkyidauk. Road at 2 miles passes through the burnt village of Yetha. Jungle all the way. Round Naungkyidauk the ground is a perfect swamp in the rains.

BRANCH IV.

FROM MANDALÉ MU (BETWEEN STAGES 1 AND 2) TO YWATHITGYI (ROUTE NO. 16, STAGE 3).

BY LIEUT. FISCHER, 5TH BOMBAY LIGHT INFANTRY, FEBRUARY 1888.

Military	Civil	Stages	Intermediate	Total	Remarks
G.O.C. Myingyán District.	Commissioner, Central Division, and Deputy Commissioner, Sagaing.	**1. Ywathitgyi** ... Mu river.	17 0	17 0	Road down bank of Mu river to Talsinkyun at 1 mile. Thence the road makes a detour to the left along the bund of a large nullah. This nullah cuts off a large island bounded by the the Mu. The nullah can be crossed at several places near Mutha (at 2 miles), but in the rains is extremely difficult. Then over low-lying grassy country (bad-going in the rains) to Tabiengwé at 4 miles. At Tabiengwé there is a police post, strength 20 rifles. Five kyaungs with accommodation for 300 to 400 men. Small quantity of paddy, plenty of kerbi, and good water. At Tabiengwé the river Mu makes a wide detour to west, and a road running along the chord of the curve reaches the river opposite Gônyinseik, 3 miles. Roads also run north-east to Taungya (a good cart road, distance 4 miles) and east, over the hills 6 miles, to Yinmagin. From Tabiengwé the road runs for the first ½ mile along the river bank. Reach Paukka at 8 miles on the river, with Pomada on the opposite bank. At 9 miles reach Kinywa (deserted). At 10½ miles pass ½ mile west of the White pagoda on Thánbôya, once a stronghold of dacoits. At 11 miles pass Môndwin. Road on due south, bad in rainy weather, but always practicable. At 12 miles reach Légyi, where there is a police post; strength about 20 rifles. Two kyaungs with accommodation for 100 men and stabling for 50 ponies. Good supply of water from a well south of the village. Small quantity of paddy and kerbi can be obtained. Hence for 1 mile through cultivation, then along a good cart road (direction south-east) over undulating sandy ground, with grass and stunted jungle to Ywathitgyi at 16 miles. *See* Stage 1 of Route No. 16.

BRANCH V.

FROM MAGYIZAUK (STAGE 3) TO NAMATHIN AND HLÉCHAUNGU.

BY CAPT. NICHOLETTS, 5TH BOMBAY LIGHT INFANTRY, FEBRUARY 1888.

Military	Civil	Stages	Intermediate	Total	Remarks
G.O.C. Myingyán District.	Commr., Central Dn., & Dy. Commr., Lower Chindwin.	**1. Ayadaw** ...	9 0	9 0	Road runs west, passes through Minet, 3½ miles from Magyizauk. Up to Minet scrub jungle and road very good, even in the rains. From Minet to Ayadaw fair road through thick

No. 17.

From MYINMU to SHWÉBO *viâ* MAGYIZAUK—*continued.*

BRANCH V—*continued.*

Authorities. Military.	Authorities. Civil.	Number and Names of Stages, Rivers and Streams.	Distances. Intermediate. M.	Distances. Intermediate. F.	Distances. Total. M.	Distances. Total. F.	Remarks.
G.O.C. Myingyán District.	Commissioner, Central Division, and Deputy Commissioner, Lower Chindwin.	**1. Ayadaw**—*cont.*					jungle. Ayadaw has been a very large village, but is now half in ruins. A police post is to be established there. Kyaukpyauk lies due south of Ayadaw. Road runs direct to Kyaukpyauk through thick jungle.
		2. Namathin ... The nullahs referred to in the column of details are 4 feet deep and 10 feet wide. Every rains they get deeper, wider, and more formidable.	8	4	17	4	Namathin is south-east of Kyaukpyauk. Road very bad. Crosses nullah 1 mile from Kyaukpyauk and again 1 mile from Namathin. Almost impassable for carts in the rains. In neighbourhood of Kyaukpyauk the jungle is very thick. Namathin village has been burnt down.
		3. Hléchaungu ... The nullahs referred to in the column of details are 4 feet deep and 10 feet wide. Increasing in size yearly.	6	0	19	4	Hléchaungu is due south of Kyaukpyauk. General direction of road south. At ½ mile road passes through nullah. At 2 miles road passes through Little Zíbinlé, 1½ miles further on Big Zíbinlé, is arrived at. A nullah runs between these two villages, ½ mile from Hléchaungu, and again at Hléchaungu road runs through nullah. Little Zíbinlé is at the top of a small hill and Big Zíbinlé at the foot. Road runs through jungle and scrub.

BRANCH VI.

From MAGYIZAUK (Stage 3) to NGAKIN.

By Capt. NICHOLETTS, 5th Bombay Light Infantry.

Military.	Civil.	Stages.	Inter. M.	Inter. F.	Total M.	Total F.	Remarks.
G.O.C. Myingyán District.	Commissioner, Central Division, and Deputy Commr., Lower Chindwin.	**1. Kaiba** ...	7	0	7	0	Ngakin is south-west of Magyizauk. Road passes through the village of Ngaho (or Mayaho), 1¼ miles south.
		2. Nyakin ...	8	0	15	0	Seitpugyi 3¼ miles south, Kaiba 7 miles south, then Naungkyidauk 2 miles south-west, and 6 miles further on is Ngakin. Jungle round Ngakin is very thick. Water-supply,—Ngaho (or Mayaho), from river and one well; Seitpugyi, from one tank and one well; Naungkyidauk, well; Kaiba, well and tank; Ngakin well.

BRANCH VII.

From MAGYIZAUK (Stage 3) to MINYWA.

By Capt. NICHOLETTS, 5th Bombay Light Infantry, February 1888.

Military.	Civil.	Stages.	Inter. M.	Inter. F.	Total M.	Total F.	Remarks.
G.O.C. Myingyan District.	Commr., Central Divn., and Dy. Commr., L. Chindwin.	**1. Minywa** ...	11	0	11	0	Road passes through scrub jungle and grass. At 1¼ miles south is Ngaho (or Mayaho). At 3¼ miles Seitpugyi. At 7 miles south Kaiba. On passing through Kaiba the road runs to the south-west.

FROM MYINMU TO SHWÉBO *viâ* MAGYIZAUK—*continued.*

BRANCH VII—*continued.*

Authorities. Military.	Authorities. Civil.	Number and Names of Stages, Rivers and Streams.	Distances. Inter-mediate.	Distances. Total.	Remarks.
G.O.C. Myingyân. District.	Commr., Central Dn., &c., L. Chindwin.	**1. Minywa**—*cont.*			The village has been burnt to the ground. The chief characteristic of Minywa is abundance of high grass. Minywa is south-west of Magyizauk.

BRANCH VIII.

FROM MAGYIZAUK (STAGE 3) TO SAMÔN.

BY LIEUT. ALEXANDER, 7TH BENGAL CAVALRY, JUNE 1887.

Authorities. Military.	Authorities. Civil.	Number and Names of Stages, Rivers and Streams.	Distances. Inter-mediate.	Distances. Total.	Remarks.
G.O.C. Mandalay District.	Commissioner, Northern Division, and Deputy Commissioner, Shwébo.	**1. Magyibyu** ...	M. F. **15 0**	M. F. 15 0	Samôn can be reached from Magyizauk by two routes, either *viâ* Magyibyu or *viâ* Sadaung. The latter is the shorter and preferable one. The Magyizauk post is situated on the right or west bank of the river Mu, which is 200 yards wide between banks (stream about 60 yards), and is crossed by a ford or by the ferry. The ford is situated ½ a mile up stream round the bend and is only 2½ feet deep ordinarily, except in the rains (June till October), when it becomes unfordable. The ferry is crossed by a raft made out of country boats capable of transporting horses. From the left or east bank the road, a mere jungle track, leads in a south-east direction to Hládwi. This track has been partially cleared to a width of about 100 feet and is very tortuous. The soil, "black cotton," cuts up and becomes very muddy and bad, heavy going with the slightest shower of rain, and will become almost impassable in the rains. The track leads through thick scrub interspersed with high trees for 3½ miles, when a nullah or depression crosses it at right angles; the head of this nullah is swampy and under rice cultivation. There is some cultivation round Hládwi, a fair-sized village fenced with thorn containing pôngyi kyaungs and zayáts enough to accommodate 150 men. Water-supply from wells, good and abundant. There are also tanks, but nearly or quite dry at this time of year (June). There is a Burman police post here with one Burman head constable and six men. Hládwi belongs to Shwébo district. In wet weather it might be necessary to halt here. From Hládwi the track leads south-east for 2½ miles and then turns almost due east to Magyibyu. It is only an ordinary Burman cart track through the jungle and apparently is seldom used: no clearing of the track has been attempted. For the first 4½ miles the track leads over low-lying "cotton" soil and is very heavy going after rain; from appearances large tracts seem to remain for a length of time under water. Then the ground rises gradually towards Magyibyu, and the soil is sandy and good going till within 1½ miles of that place, when the ground becomes swampy with dangerous bits of bog and quagmire. The track leads throughout through low, thick scrub jungle. Accommodation: Magyibyu is a small village with one kyaung sufficient to accommodate 60 or 70 men. Water-supply from wells and tanks sufficient, but not very good. Some rice and other cultivation round village, which has the usual slight thorn fence round it.

FROM MYINMU TO SHWÉBO *viâ* MAGYIZAUK—*continued.*

BRANCH VIII—*continued.*

Authorities. Military.	Authorities. Civil.	Number and Names of Stages, Rivers and Streams.	Distances. Intermediate.	Distances. Total.	Remarks.
G.O.C. Myingyán District.	Commissioner, Central Division, and Deputy Commissioner, Sagaing.	**2. Samôn**	M. F. **8 4**	M. F. 23 4	From Magyibyu there is a cleared track, 100 feet wide, cut in almost a direct line south-east to Ninnané. The jungle has been cut down, but no attempt has been made to dig out the stumps or roots, or to form a roadway. The clearing follows the old cart track mostly. From Magyibyu the ground rises gradually to the top of the low hills (about 200 feet above the surrounding country and covered throughout with scrub jungle) and then slopes down gradually to Ninnané, leaving the Shwémintha pagoda on the right. Accommodation: Ninnané is a small partly deserted village, with a kyaung capable of accommodating 60 men. Water-supply from wells and tanks fairly good and abundant usually, but tanks dry now (June). There is some cultivation round the village, rice, Indian corn, til, &c. Slight thorn fence round village. From Ninnané there is a cleared track, as above described, to Samôn. The soil is a red-coloured sandy one and good going at present, except where the track crosses rice fields now and then. The country is open and undulating with little jungle and appears to have been extensively cultivated at one time, and fine large trees are scattered about. At Samôn there was formerly a military post of Cavalry and Infantry situated on some rising ground overlooking the village. Around the village there is a considerable rice cultivation, the ground being low-lying. Also a little wheat, grain, &c., is cultivated. A cleared track leads south from here to Ôngdaw, 12 miles distant, on the way to Sagaing.

ALTERNATIVE ROUTE *viâ* SADAUNG.

Authorities. Military.	Authorities. Civil.	Number and Names of Stages, Rivers and Streams.	Distances. Intermediate.	Distances. Total.	Remarks.
G.O.C. Mandalay District. G.O.C. Myingyán District.	Commr., Northern Divn., and Deputy Commr., Shwébo. Commissioner, Central Division, and Deputy Commissioner, Sagaing.	**1. Sadaung** ...	**14 0**	14 0	For the first 8 miles the track is the same as in first stage in above route, when the track bifurcates, the right-hand one tending away south-east towards Paoma and Sadaung, and the left-hand leading to Magyibyu as already described. Paoma is distant 5½ miles from Hládwi. Between these two places the track is through thick scrub jungle and over "cotton" soil and is bad going. Paoma consists of two or three small hamlets and is partly deserted. There is considerable rice land around these hamlets along the edge of the swamp, which extends between Paoma and Thadawgôn (a small hamlet). The road bends south to Sadaung, 3 miles distant, passing through rice cultivation and low-lying "cotton" soil, bad going in wet weather. Sadaung is a large place consisting of a collection of five or more villages, but is mostly deserted and in ruins. Large quantities of salt are made here by washing the earth, which is impregnated with it. Water-supply is bad, all the wells being brackish except one situated east, 1 mile off the Samôn road; there are several tanks also, but the water is indifferent though drinkable, but nearly all are dry at this time of year (June). There is a little cultivation. Accommodation: There are several good large kyaungs and accommodation enough for a force of 500 or 600 men. Roads to

FROM MYINMU TO SHWÉBO *viâ* MAGYIZAUK—*continued.*

BRANCH VIII—*continued.*

ALTERNATIVE ROUTE *viâ* SADAUNG—*continued.*

Authorities. Military.	Authorities. Civil.	Number and Names of Stages, Rivers and Streams.	Distances. Intermediate.	Distances. Total.	Remarks.
G.O.C. Myingyán District.	Commissioner, Central Division, and Deputy Commissioner, Sagaing.	**1. Sadaung**—*cont.*			Magyibyu and Kyinaingyi: From Sadaung there is a cleared track north to Magyibyu, $4\frac{1}{2}$ miles, and one south to Kyinaingyi, 5 miles.
		2. Samôn ...	M. F. 7 0	M. F. 21 0	From Sadaung there is a cleared track over the low hills of the same character as described in first part of second stage in above route, but on nearing Samôn there is some low-lying ground with rice cultivation, now under water, to be crossed. *General remarks.*—The distances on the map appear less than noted, but allowance has to be made for the tortuous windings of the path or track, as even on the cleared portions the native path has to be adhered to on account of the stumps, &c., and general unevenness of the ground. Total distance, *viâ* Magyibyu and Ninnané, $23\frac{1}{2}$ miles, Sadaung 21 miles.

BRANCH IX.

FROM MAGYIZAUK (STAGE 3) TO SHWÉKUGYIPAYA.

BY LIEUT. A. DEWILTON, 1ST BATTALION, CONNAUGHT RANGERS, FEBRUARY 1887.

Military.	Civil.	Stages.	Intermediate.	Total.	Remarks.
G.O.C. Myingyán District.	Commissioner, Central Division, and Deputy Commissioner, Sagaing.	**1. Shwékugyipaya.** Mu river.	15 0	15 0	Mu river fordable in the dry season is crossed and a good cart track followed to Hládwi at 4 miles. Hládwi is a large prosperous village. Rice cultivation; 90 houses. Village about 1 mile round. Then along fair sandy cart road, with thin jungle on each side, to Payábyán at 11 miles. Payábyán is a large village overlooking a jheel. The road on is very bad across the bed of a jheel, clayey soil; very difficult in the rains to Singôt at 14 miles. A small village Salt manufacture and rice cultivation. Shwékugyi lies 1 mile further on along a bad cart track.

BRANCH X.

FROM KYÍGÁN (BETWEEN STAGES 3 AND 4) TO SHWÊKUGYIPAYA.

BY LIEUT. A. DEWILTON, 1ST BATTALION, CONNAUGHT RANGERS, FEBRUARY 1887.

Military.	Civil.	Stages.	Intermediate.	Total.	Remarks.
G.O.C. Myingyán District.	Commissioner, Central Division, and Deputy Commissioner, Sagaing.	**1. Shwékugyipaya.**	11 4	11 4	A good cart track passing through Mégong at 1 mile, a small village with two fine kyaungs near. Then over clayey soil to Ywatha at 4 miles. Good kyaungs. Water, &c., good. Thence good road to Katu at 5 miles, a small village of 25 huts. Thence a good sandy road to Pauktaw at 6 miles, a small village of 30 houses on high ground overlooking a jheel, and Payabyan at $7\frac{1}{2}$ miles, a large village similarly situated. Thence road is bad to Singôt, a small village of 50 houses. Salt manufacture and rice cultivation occupying the inhabitants. Then along cart track to Shwékugyipaya.

No. 18.

From MYINMU to WUNTHO viâ YÉ-U and HLUTTAIK.

I. B. Compilation, March 1888.

Authorities. Military.	Authorities. Civil.	Number and Names of Stages, Rivers and Streams.	Distances. Intermediate. M.	F.	Distances. Total. M.	F.	Remarks.
G.O.C. Myingyán District.	Commr., Central Divn., and Dy. Commr., Sagaing.	**1. Gônyinseik** ...	**12**	**4**	12	4	For description up to Magyizauk *see* Route No. 17, Stages 1 to 3.
		2. Sintsalé ...	**10**	**2**	22	6	
	Commissioner, Central Division, and Deputy Commissioner, Lower Chindwin.	**3. Magyizauk** ...	**9**	**6**	32	4	
		4. Baungya ...	**11**	**0**	43	4	The road from Magyizauk to Baungya follows the Mu, direction north-north-west about ½ mile from the right bank. One mile through scattered jungle over flat ground, then a mile over undulating ground. At 2 miles road runs through paddy cultivation to Dôndit, 3½ miles; 50 houses enclosed by dry thorn fence surrounded by fields and thorn hedges. One zayát east (10 men). One kyaung (50 men) and one zayát (30 men). Water from one well muddy. Road on through cultivation and hedges to Kyépagán at 4¾ miles, passing a kyaung to hold 30 and a zayát 15 men on the east of the road. Just before reaching Kyépagán the road runs down a cutting into a nullah running to the Mu, banks 12 feet high; following this 100 yards it emerges through similar cutting into the village. Kyépagán is situated on a spur between the nullah and one like it to the north on the Mu river, it has about 50 houses. Water from Mu river which can be forded in dry season by carts. About four boats available for ferrying. One kyaung, 100 yards north of nullah, north of village, would hold 40 men; two zayáts 40 men. These two nullahs would be impassable for carts after heavy rains; in the dry season the sand in the bottom is very heavy. Road on over sound ground to Wathé at 5½ miles, a prosperous village with 200 houses, 300 yards from the river Mu. One kyaung south would hold 70 men and one zayát 30 men; one kyaung north 30 men. Water from river. (The river is difficult to ford here, carts generally going to Kyépagán to do so.) Road on through scattered jungle. At ¼ mile beyond Wathé cross the bed of a broad stream; about 40 yards of deep sand; banks 3 feet high; impassable after heavy rains. One mile further paddy cultivation begins and continues to Aungtha with jungle here and there. Aungtha 8½ miles. A prosperous village, has 110 houses enclosed by dead thorn fence. Open paddy south-east and north-east to the river, scattered jungle to the west. South of the village one kyaung (100 men) and three zayáts (50 men). Water from well at kyaung and from the river. The river is fordable for carts in the dry season. Road on for 1½ miles through paddy, the remainder through thick high jungle, cleared 20 yards on either side to Baungya police fort at 11 miles. The police fort is ¼ mile south of Baungya and 400 yards west of the Mu, about 50 by 30 yards, with parapet 6 feet high and ditch, occupied by 25 police, would hold 35 altogether. One well with good water. The village has 80 houses on the bank of the Mu. There are three kyaungs for 100 men. One zayát dilapidated would shelter 10 men (carts cross the river here in the dry season and go to Shwébo, a distance of 7 daings. There is one big boat about 8 yards in length belonging to the pôngyis. There is a road from Baungya to Wadaw west-south-west 12 miles fairly good through jungle, passing Méwun at 3 miles, Magyigán at 6 miles. Wadaw is on the road from Yé-u to Álôn and

FROM MYINMU TO WUNTHO *viâ* YÉ-U AND HLUTTAIK—*continued.*

Authorities. Military.	Authorities. Civil.	Number and Names of Stages, Rivers and Streams.	Distances. Intermediate.	Distances. Total.	Remarks.
G.O.C. Myingyan District.	Commissioner, Central Division, and Deputy Commissioner, Lower Chindwin.	**4. Baungya**—*cont.*			25 miles from Álôn. The most direct route from Shwébo to Álôn would therefore be through Baungya, a total distance of about 55 miles). From Baungya a road has been cut north-north-west through the jungle direct to Mayagán running about 4 miles to the east of Magyiôk. It is not at present used by carts. It joins the Magyiôk-Mayagán road near Thayetkán.
	Commissioner, Central Division, and Deputy Commissioner, Yé-u.	**5. Magyiôk and Tántabin police post.**	M. 12 F. 0	M. 55 F. 4	The road from Baungya to Magyiôk is north-west, a good hard road through jungle for 8 miles, afterwards through paddy cultivation, which would be very difficult for carts in the rainy season, for 3 miles through dry cultivation and scattered jungle. At 3 miles pass through 100 yards of heavy sand in a piece of low-lying ground, just beyond past the partly deserted village of Shégôn, 800 yards west. At 4 miles pass tank on the left of the road with water in February. Reach Kyundaw at 4½ miles, village of 50 huts. There is a kyaung 200 yards south-east for 100 men and three zayáts to hold 30 men. Fair water is obtained from the tank passed ½ mile south of the village. Kyundaw is enclosed by a dead thorn fence surrounded on all sides by jungle which, however, is cleared 200 yards eastwards. Road continues for ½ mile through jungle with some sessamum cultivation till it crosses a large nullah 15 yards broad with deep sandy bottom, impassable for some time after heavy rain. Just beyond at 6½ miles reach two small villages called East and West Kuma. One zayát south would hold 20 men. One kyaung between the villages would hold 40 men. Road continues through paddy and scattered jungle to Néyékán at 8½ miles. Kyaung south would hold 20 men. One zayát 10 men. Water from two wells and tank. Road continues through paddy to Tántabin and Magyiôk passing Hlenla and Thetkyo, deserted villages, and Ôkshitgyi ½ mile from Tántabin. Ôkshitgyi is a prosperous village with good water from well to the west. At Tántabin there is a military police post stockaded with bamboo at the north-east corner of the village. In this stockade there is accommodation for 100 men besides the police now in occupation and stabling for 70 horses. Magyiôk is ¼ mile north-west. Between the two villages is a deserted kyaung which, with a little repair, would accommodate 30 men. There are two wells, one with good drinking water. It is a bad place for cavalry in the dry season. Cavalry had to be sent to Múgán 7 miles east on the Mu during February, March and April. Grass is very scarce in February. Water for horses in tank in the rainy season. (From Magyiôk there is a road east to Shwébo 23 miles *viâ* Múgán and Setkaung. *See* Route No. 2, Stages 5 to 7. A road west-north-west to Sainbyin 13 miles *viâ* Nagabo. At Sainbyin there is accommodation for 800 men in kyaungs, 20 in one zayát.)
		6. Mayagán ... Payampaga chaung.	10 0	65 4	From Magyiôk the road runs due north to Mayagán 10 miles. The first 6 miles is cut through thick jungle except near Magyiôk, where there is paddy cultivation. Cross the Payam-

FROM MYINMU TO WUNTHO *viâ* YÉ-U AND HLUTTAIK—*continued.*

Authorities. Military.	Authorities. Civil.	Number and Names of Stages, Rivers and Streams.	Distances. Inter-mediate.	Distances. Total.	Remarks.
G.O.C. Myingyán District.	Commissioner, Central Division, and Deputy Commissioner, Yé-u.	**6. Mayagán**—*cont.*			paga chaung at 3 miles bridged for carts. About 6 inches of water in the dry season. Pass Myinthugyi at 6 miles. From here the road continues north through open country and paddy cultivation passing Dina at 7½ miles. Water scarce and no accommodation till Mayagán is reached. There is another route to the east of the above but longer (total 15 miles), 5 miles east-north-east to Méyandain crossing the Payampaga chaung near Taikkán. At Méyandain good water and accommodation. Road north-east to Thayetkan 4 miles through thick jungle. Good water and accommodation in kyaung. Road 3 miles north to Tedaw, then 3 miles north-west to Mayagán. The only advantage of this latter route is the water and accommodation. The direct road from Baungya to Mayagán is met at Thayetkán. Mayagán has a police post of 28 men; 150 men can be accommodated in kyaungs and zayáts. Water brackish from wells and one tank which is dry in March. Good water is obtained from Kôndé 1½ miles distant. (There is a road from Mayagán to Shwébo about 20 miles crossing the river Mu at Wégyi.)
		7. Yé-u	M. 12 F. 0	M. 77 F. 4	From Mayagán to Yé-u the road has been made, but not metalled. It is, however, expected to be fairly good for carts during the rains. To 4 miles from Mayagán the road is only 12 feet broad, from there to Yé-u between 15 and 20 feet. General direction due north. To Nmawgaung 3½ miles through paddy. Road on through jungle and paddy mixed to Murúgôn at 8 miles. From Murúgôn to Yé-u the road is through jungle cleared to a breadth of 30 yards. Pass Magyidaw at 10 miles. For description of Yé-u *see* Route No. 33, Northern Division.
		8. Kabungyaing.	10 2	87 6	The road from Yé-u to Nwabeitgyi has been made, *i.e.*, the jungle has been cleared to a breadth of 30 to 40 yards, and the roadway has been slightly raised where it passes through paddy. It will eventually be metalled, but until then it will not be of much use in the rains, as it is not sufficiently raised in the wet country, and sufficient waterway is not given. It may be just passable for carts in the rains. It has been and will be most useful in cold and hot weather. General direction north-north-west. Where passing through paddy the roadway is 20 feet wide with ditches 1 foot wide by 2 feet deep. The road is principally through light jungle with paddy here and there to Kabungyaing at 10¼ miles. Pass Peinga at 3½ miles where track branches right to Tazé; at about 4 miles cart track to left to Kadúma 19 miles from Yé-u on the road to Kindát (*see* Route No. 25, Stage 2); Pégôn at 4¾ miles; Indaw at 5¾ miles; Pungezin at 8 miles; Sainya at 9¼ miles. Good water from wells, but no accommodation.

FROM MYINMU TO WUNTHO *viâ* YÉ-U AND HLUTTAIK—*continued.*

Authorities. Military.	Authorities. Civil.	Number and Names of Stages, Rivers and Streams.	Distances. Intermediate.	Distances. Total.	Remarks.
G.O.C. Myingyân District.	Commissioner, Central Division, and Deputy Commissioner, Yé-u.	**9. Nwabeitgyi (Nabekgyi).**	M. F. 7 4	M. F. 95 2	Kabungyaing has 70 houses. Three zayâts would hold 30 men; one kyaung 60 men. Water good from small tank. Road on through paddy-fields for 2 miles, then for ¾ mile through jungle, 100 feet clearing, remainder through paddy-fields as above to Saingé at 4¾ miles, passing Letpángôn at ½ mile, Tenné at 1 mile, and Kyanezwé at 2 miles. Road through paddy-fields as before, but without a ditch; one is going to be constructed to Ingoka at 6 miles. Road as before through open uncultivated ground to Nwabeitgyi (or Nabekgyi) at 7½ miles. Nwabeitgyi has a police post 42 strong. The stockade has held two companies of Native infantry. One kyaung would hold 70 men. Water good from wells. There is an alternative road *viâ* Tazé, a large village 3 or 4 miles east-north-east of Stage 8 of this route. The head-quarters of the sub-division and township of that name where reside Sub-Divisional Officer, Myo-ôk, and Assistant Superintendent, Police. It is a civil police post. Tazé has plenty of accommodation and good water. The total distance to Nwabeitgyi by this route would be 3 or 4 miles greater than *viâ* Kabungyaing, and the road is not so good as the main road, which would therefore always be followed in preference to it unless it is desired to visit Tazé on the way to Nwabeitgyi.
		10. Aungzwa ... Mu river and Paungdaung chaung.	11 0	106 2	Road as before level, fair weather cart track, bad in parts during rainy season, the streams having washed away almost all of the bridges owing to their insufficient waterway. For first 4 miles over open level country, all fit for paddy cultivation, but much till lying fallow (February 1890), clumps of palm trees scattered about thickly. General direction for first 2 miles about north-west, thence to Kyunhla north. At ¾ mile kyaung on right of road. At 1¼ miles cross Zibudôn chaung; sandy bed, channel extending in flood to about 500 yards, banks very low, and in full flood water would not exceed 3 feet in depth. Jungle to the west, distant about a mile; to the east clumps of trees gradually grow closer until they form rather close small tree jungle. At 2 miles road branches north towards Aungzwa, and north-west to Kabaungya At 4¼ miles cultivation ceases and from here the road ceases to be banked up or trenched on either side, though it has been cleared to a width of about 100 feet. Jungle on either side, light small tree jungle such as is usually met with on the higher and sandier parts of Upper Burma. *In*, *ingyin*, &c.; bamboo in parts, generally in the hollows between the undulations, and not very thick. At 4½ miles Pôt chaung; sandy bed, easy approaches, probably 5 or 6 feet of water in flood, and good pools in middle of February. At 5½, 5¾, 7¼, and about 8¾ miles good wooden bridges over narrow nullahs, 6 to 10 feet deep and with perpendicular banks; all dry in February. Although the roadway has been cleared in a direct line towards Aungzwa to a width of about 30 yards, the cart track does not as yet (February 1890) follow it, but winds about alongside and occasionally on it up to 8¾ miles. At

FROM MYINMU TO WUNTHO *viâ* YÉ-U AND HLUTTAIK—*continued.*

Authorities. Military.	Authorities. Civil.	Number and Names of Stages, Rivers and Streams.	Distances. Intermediate.	Distances. Total.	Remarks.
G.O.C. Myingyán District.	Commissioner, Central Division, and Deputy Commissioner, Yé-u.	**10. Aungzwa**—*cont.*			6½ miles kyaung to right of road, and paths and track to Yashé village about ¼ mile east of the cleared road; 85 houses. Drinking water from wells and for cattle from tanks. At 6¾ miles paddy clearing on east and north-east of road extending up to Yashé and a little on the west. The former extends along the road for nearly a mile and is ½ mile wide. At 6¾ miles track comes in from right rear from Yashé. Light jungle on west of road. At 8 miles paddy again on the right (east) of the road, then jungle on both sides. The usual In and other trees that like the hard, red soil. Up to this the road has been excellent for dry weather, and even in the rains there would be few difficulties and none severe. At 8¾ miles track bears off to the right of the cleared road and does not at present rejoin it until after passing Aungzwa, and clearing had been carried out up to only a short distance beyond that village in the middle of February 1890. The cart track now followed twists about a great deal through thick, but not at all impassable, jungle. It is said to be shorter to Aungzwa by this than by the cleared road, but it is impossible that this can be the case, as the latter passes within a short distance of that place and takes an almost bee line north from where the Aungzwa cart track now leaves it. At 10¼ miles enter cleared ground now much overgrown with thorny bushes and high grass. At 10½ miles Paungdaung chaung close on left (west) road, following parallel for ¼ mile and then crossing; bed sandy, dry in February, 60 yards wide, steep banks 15 feet high, but approaches not difficult. It joins the Mu river about ¾ mile further down, and is unfordable for some hours at least when in flood during or after heavy rain. At 11 miles Aungzwa kyaung on left village on right. Village only just given leave to return in February 1890, so few houses then, but will have over 30 houses at least. The village is on the right bank of the Mu and near the left bank of the Paungdaung. It overlooks the Mu from a height (50 feet or so) and precipitous bank. The river here 300 to 400 yards broad. In February the water occupied about one-third of the channel, which is sound sand, and coolies were fording it thigh-deep at the ford just below the village. It does not seem much used by carts, and the right bank approach is very steep, but the left bank of the river is low, big tree jungle down to the water's edge on that side. There is another kyaung a short distance to the north, and in the two kyaungs and their zayáts about 250 men could be accommodated. Water-supply of course ample and good at all seasons from the Mu. Grass plentiful, and paddy in large quantities after a good harvest.
		11. Padi ... ... Mu river and Yabin chaung.	M. F. **8 0**	M. F. 114 2	Road for first ¾ of a mile about north-west over undulating ground; soil red and hard, very good going in all weather; jungle light; In, &c., on both sides, with occasional small fields of paddy. At ¾ mile join cleared track and descend by easy gradient about 100 yards long to high flood-level of the Mu, where clearing ceases at present (February 1890); thence road generally northwards, level kaing grass on village clearing, with a little kaing grass on left about ½ mile broad, jungle beyond. This continues for about 1½ miles, then through a patch of big tree jungle, and at 2½ miles a small paddy clearing, then across a nullah with

FROM MYINMU TO WUNTHO *viâ* YÉ-U AND HLUTTAIK—*continued.*

Authorities. Military	Authorities. Civil.	Number and Names of Stages, Rivers and Streams.	Distances. Intermediate.	Distances. Total.	Remarks.
G.O.C. Myingyán District.	Commissioner, Central Division, and Deputy Commissioner, Yé-u.	**11. Padi**—*cont.*			easy banks, but deep sandy bed about 15 yards wide, dry in February, but water near surface. Mu is about ½ mile off to the east, kaing grass flats intervening and concealing it from view. Another small clearing at 3 miles; thence over undulating and broken ridges; generally easy gradient, and soil always hard and good going for next 4 miles. Jungle on either side, In, &c. This particular soil, which is met with all over the northern parts of the Shwébo and Yé-u districts, is very susceptible to the action of water, and the cart track and foot or pony track also, where they differ, wind about a great deal to avoid nullahs worn in the ridges traversed. At 7 miles enter paddy clearing 500 yards wide on either side of the track, and at 8 miles Padi village, stockaded (as all villages are now compelled by law to be), 38 houses in February 1890; kyaung and long zayát about ¼ mile north of village on the right of the Kyunhla cart track, but left of the shorter pony track. Accommodation for 200 men. Grass, paddy, and water from wells, and for cattle from Mu ¼ mile off east of village. There is a short cut from Aungzwa to Padi said to save 1½ miles. It crosses the Mu at Aungzwa and recrosses at Kabyu, whence there is a cart road to Padi about 3 miles. The first part of the road is a foot-path only, and in the rains the Mu is unfordable; even in February it was 2½ feet to 3 feet at the ford at Kabyu, from which place there is a much used cart track to Myédu about 3 miles south. Padi would make a very good halting place for troops, but the direct track that will inevitably be cleared from Nwabeitgyi to Kyunhla will probably so reduce the distance that it will be scarcely worth dividing the distance between Aungzwa and Padi into two marches.
		12. Kyunhla ... Mu river.	M. F. **8 0**	M. F. 122 2	Leaving Padi kyaung ½ mile through thick jungle to the Yabin chaung, sandy bed, 400 yards wide, making extreme flood level, deep and rather heavy going for carts. On north side the ordinary wet season channel, 60 yards wide, sandy bed, depth in flood about 8 feet. The cart track crosses about ½ mile higher up than the foot or pony track, which crosses at the junction of the stream with the Mu. In February 1890 the Yabin chaung was quite dry. Good place here for a large camp in the dry season. Grassy maidan, ¾ mile long, ½ mile broad, on left bank Yabin chaung, and more ground available close by; a whole brigade of all arms could concentrate here and find ample forage and water for their transport however numerous; the Mu is here about 200 yards wide and unfordable; jungle to the waterside opposite; thence through cleared and mostly cultivated flat ground to Nyaungaing, 4 miles, passing deserted village and kyaungs at 3½ miles. Nyaungaing village consists of about 60 houses; extensive paddy clearing round; small wooden "masjid," there being a small Muhammadan community here, an off-shoot from that at Myédu, three generations, if not four or even five, of which have been born in this district, their ancestors having come, so they say, from Dilli (Delhi). Amongst themselves they talk Burmese, but their "moola" could speak Hindustani. There is an alternative route from Padi *viâ* Sittaw, 2 miles, to Nyaungaing, 2½ miles more. Sittaw lies to the west of the direct

FROM MYINMU TO WUNTHO *viâ* YÉ-U AND HLUTTAIK—*continued.*

Authorities.		Number and Names of Stages, Rivers and Streams.	Distances.		Remarks.
Military.	Civil.		Inter-mediate.	Total.	
G.O.C. Myingyân District.	Commissioner, Central Division, and Deputy Commissioner, Yé-u.	**12. Kyunhla**—*cont.*			cart track from Padi to Nyaungaing and to the north of the Yabin chaung. From Nyaungaing good road, cleared and trenched where required, with paddy on right for a short distance; jungle left; then light. In jungle both sides; undulating ground; track very good going. At 6½ miles leave jungle and enter paddy clearing extending up to and all around Kyunhla. At 6¾ miles a bad bit of swampy road in wet weather, then kyaung on left and village of Kyigôn just behind it. At 7 miles big village of Satagôn adjoining Kyigôn on right bank of Pyaungthwé chaung, about 60 yards broad, rather steep descent to bed, but easy ascent; good sound sandy crossing and about 1 foot of clear running water in February. From Satagôn across paddy to Kyunhla post on rising ground north-east of village of same name, which is the official centre of the Indaing township; paddy all round; Mu about ½ mile to the east and north-east. The post can accommodate over 100 sepoys and about 50 ponies. Several wells. All this district has an evil reputation amongst Burmans for fever, and the police at the post have suffered severely from that disease. February to May seem the most healthy months. In the rains the post must be almost an island, with paddy swamp all round. From Kyunhla roads, or rather tracks (some cart, some not), to Indaing, 2 miles south-west, and other villages around, and also over the Chindwin watershed *viâ* Thekagyin and Naungauk to Lawtha and Kindât, *see* Route No. 12. Indaing was formerly the head-quarters of the township, and a broad track was cleared to it from Kyunhla, now becoming rather overgrown with bushes and low scrub.
		13. Hluttaik ... Mu river.	M. F. **11 4**	M. F. 133 4	Road north-east across paddy to Phyetsutwa (pronounced Pesowa) ½ mile on right bank of Mu. Deserted village of Tawbo opposite. Crosses chaung of same name as village which here joins the Mu river. About 1¼ miles pass Ônbingôn, ¼ mile to east, also on river bank. Country east of the road up to the river cultivated. West of the road jungle. At 2 miles the country to the east in the direction of the Mu is uncultivated, level, and mostly covered with long grass; on across open and partly cultivated ground generally parallel to the course of the Mu river. At 3½ miles deserted village of Mauktaung on river bank; small village of Kyaukin on opposite side of river. Water here very shallow in middle of February; on over rather broken ground, road winding in and out between knolls and ridges, 30 to 40 feet high, covered with thick clumps of bamboo. At 4½ miles cross Sadwin chaung, 30 yards wide, dry in February, right bank high. Follow left bank north-east by north for ½ mile, reaching deserted village of Sadwin situated on rising ground at 5 miles; thence north-east to Kyauksitgôn, 5½ miles, deserted village, on right bank of Mu river (here about 120 yards broad, banks 10 to 15 feet high), crossing Painyôma chaung, dry in February. At 6 miles Kinbinsaya chaung, dry in February, and at 6½ miles Kanja chaung, also dry in February. Road ever undulating hard ground, light jungle. At 7½ miles ground more sandy, bamboo thick on either side, and at 9 miles Nyaungin; thence to Hluttaik (11½ miles) in an easterly direction; light dry soil jungle; In, &c., and paddy as you approach Hluttaik. This route would be the one taken in travelling with carts at any season,

FROM MYINMU TO WUNTHO *viâ* YÉ-U AND HLUTTAIK—*continued.*

Authorities. Military.	Authorities. Civil.	Number and Names of Stages, Rivers and Streams.	Distances. Intermediate.	Distances. Total.	Remarks.
G.O.C. Myingyán District.	Commissioner, Central Division, and Deputy Commissioner, Yé-u.	**13. Hluttaik**—*cont.*			and compulsorily so in the rains even for pack transport, but there is a good deal shorter route for foot-passengers or riders crossing the Mu to Tawbo and again at Tindéyán which, cutting across a wide bend of the river, saves over 2 miles. Hluttaik, large village on right bank of Mu, formerly a military and police post strongly stockaded; very unhealthy in the rainy season and commencement of cold season. Paddy cultivation close round village on south and west; jungle north; river on the east. The general direction from Kyunhla is north-east, though the ground varies a good deal from this direction in following the course of the river. Except where the ground has been cleared for cultivation it is covered with In, &c., jungle, which is never very dense and is generally free from thick undergrowth. In parts bamboos grow very close and thick. This part of the Yé-u district is very sparsely populated; as it gets opened up the necessity of a good road will be felt and little difficulty will be found in running one in a very straight line from Nwabeitgyi to Hluttaik and on up the bank of the Mu. At present, too, there is little or no direct communication between the Upper Mu valley (Kyunhla and onwards) and the valley of the Pyaungthwé and Maiwun chaungs on the west, but tracks exist no doubt and only want re-opening. The country is jungle covered, In, ingyin, and bamboo predominating, and not what can be accurately described as hilly, nor can it be called flat irregular. Undulations perhaps explain what is meant. The tract is very dry, for, though there are numbers of nullahs, they are all dry before February. The quantity of petrified wood lying about is very remarkable, there being little stone about other than this, except a little laterite cropping out here and there. A dozen boats capable of carrying eight or 10 persons can be collected at Hluttaik and Phyetsutwa with notice, or at any of the villages on the river, but there are not more than two or three belonging to any one village.
		14. Gômbyu * ... Mu river.	M. F. **8** **2**	M. F. 141 6	On opposite bank small village of Thayetwa, 30 houses. There is a ford here in the dry season (2½ feet of water); in the rains there is a ferry, two boats. Both banks steep and 12 feet high. Road on north at 1 mile. From Hluttaik the road merely a sandy cart track, 7 feet wide, runs north-north-west through thin *in* forest. At 2 miles cross undu-

* "Although the shortest line from Hluttaik to Ôkkán would be *viâ* Gômbyu, &c., the country through which it passes is entirely uninhabited, except by dacoits, at present (February 1890), and it will be long before it recovers. On the other hand there are already several villages along the right bank of the Mu; it is therefore probable that the line selected for improvement would be that along the right bank passing through Saipu (10 miles), Naungu (14¼), Aingyi (15½), and Inyashé (17). From Inyashé, the Mu can be crossed to Ôkshitpin, whence tracks lead to Gyôbin, ? miles higher up the Mu, which is the border village of Wuntho, and to Ôkkán. The distances would be—

			MILES.	MILES.
14	...	Saipu ...	10	145½
15	...	Ôkkán ...	15¾	159¼

Capt. Appleton, R.E., who traversed this route in 1887, says a cart road (fair, in the Burmese sense) could be opened along this line with little work beyond jungle clearing and a few small bridges. The Mu, of course, requires to be ramped at the approaches to the ford at Inyashé and Ôkshitpin (18 miles, left bank of Mu)."

FROM MYINMU TO WUNTHO *viâ* YÉ-U AND HLUTTAIK—*continued.*

Authorities. Military.	Authorities. Civil.	Number and Names of Stages, Rivers and Streams.	Distances. Intermediate. M.	F.	Distances. Total. M.	F.	Remarks.
G.O.C. Myingyân District.	Commissioner, Central Division, and Deputy Commissioner, Yé-u.	**14. Gômbyu**—*cont.*					lating ground, soil gravelly. At 2½ miles the road descends a steep gradient and proceeds due north for ½ mile through dense forest of tall trees and undergrowth till it reaches the right bank of the Mu river, 200 yards broad at this point, banks 10 to 12 feet high. The road continues its direction north, skirting the right bank of the river through tall elephant grass, soil sandy, till it reaches the ruined village of Kabineng (3¼ miles). At ¾ mile from Kabineng the road bifurcates one branch going north-west to Kabyin and Saipu, the other continuing north till it reaches small village of Magyigôu (4½ miles) on the right bank of the Mu. Here there is a ford across the river to the village of Thayetaw. From the month of November to May the medium depth is 3 feet, in the rainy season 15 feet. There are two boats here. The road continues to skirt the Mu, passing the village Taungyaseik (4¾ miles), 10 houses, one small bamboo kyaung. From Taungyaseik a foot-path runs through thick tree forest to Taingpyauk (6 miles). Carts can go round by a cart road from Taungyaseik. Taingpyauk at 7 miles is a ruined village about ¼ mile from the right bank of the Mu. Quarter mile on north-west reach the Mu and cross by a ford to Gômbyu at 8¼ miles, descent and ascent gradual and easy; village deserted, February 1887. One ruined kyaung and one well.
G.O.C. Mandalay District.	Commissioner, Northern Division, and Deputy Commissioner, Katha.	**15. Ôkkán** ... ... Láka chaung and Daungyu river.	15	4	157	2	Road on through open tree jungle and bamboo to Taungya at 9¾ miles, 20 houses. One kyaung for 150 men and wells. Thence through bamboo jungle and bastard teak passing Thégôn at 10 miles to Sinywin at 11¾ miles surrounded by paddy; 20 houses; one kyaung for 150 men; wells and stream. Road on through paddy to Daungyu creek at 12¾ miles, 2 feet of water in February, sluggish, not fordable here in rainy season. Road on through jungle to Wunán at 14½ miles, 20 houses, surrounded by paddy. Water from wells and creek. Road on through paddy and bamboo jungle to Ôkkán at 15½ miles, crossing the Láka stream with 2 feet of clear running water in February at 15 miles. Ôkkán has 60 houses, one kyaung, and zayáts for 200 men. Water from wells and creek.
		16. Gwédauktaw.	9	2	166	4	Road on ¾ mile through paddy to Daungyu creek, thence through jungle along the right bank to 4 miles, where it strikes through tree jungle, bamboo and grass to Ôkkalôn 5½ miles, 20 houses with bamboo kyaung for 50 men. Water from wells and creek. Road on ¼ mile through paddy, thence through bastard teak bamboo to 8¼ miles, where it enters bamboo jungle and some paddy. Gwédauktaw at 9¼ miles, 15 houses, surrounded by paddy, one bamboo kyaung for 50 men. Water in wells and creek.

FROM MYINMU TO WUNTHO *viâ* YÉ-U AND HLUTTAIK—*continued.*

Authorities. Military.	Authorities. Civil.	Number and Names of Stages, Rivers and Streams.	Distances. Intermediate.	Distances. Total.	Remarks.
G.O.C. Mandalay District.	Commissioner, Northern Division, and Deputy Commissioner, Katha.	**17. Kawlin** ...	M. F. **10 2**	M. F. 176 6	Road on through dense jungle, at 1¼ miles pass Kado, 20 houses surrounded by paddy. One bamboo kyaung for 50 men. Water from wells and creek. Road on through thick jungle to Yâdaung at 5½ miles, 20 houses surrounded by paddy. One kyaung for 80 men. Good water from wells and creek. Thence through thick jungle, bamboo, bastard teak, and grass to Yégântha, 25 houses, and Thapángôn 30 houses, both at about 9¼ miles. One kyaung at Thapángôn for 100 men. Wells and paddy round villages. Road on through paddy to Kawlin passing Sandeha at 10 miles situated on a small hill, stockaded, 15 houses, surrounded by paddy. These distances from Hluttaik to Kawlin were measured by perambulator. The road is reported as good in February 1887. Kawlin has seven kyaungs for 400 men.
		18. Wuntho ... Daungyu river.	**9 2**	186 0	From Kawlin to Wuntho *see* Route No. 93, Northern Division, Shwébo to Wuntho, last stage.

BRANCH I.

FROM MAGYIÔK (STAGE 5) TO SAINBIN.

BY CAPT. P. W. A. A. MILTON, K.O.Y.L.I., FEBRUARY 1887.

Military	Civil	Stage	Intermediate	Total	Remarks
G.O.C. Myingyán District.	Commissioner, Central Division, and Deputy Commissioner, Yé-u.	**Nagabo** ... ... Water from wells.	**5 0**	5 0	Good road for carts. Direction west by south, mostly through thick jungle at 5 miles Nagabo. Last mile across paddy-fields. Good kyaung accommodation and water from wells; kyaungs also about half-way at village. From Nagabo good cart road. Direction west by north, mostly through jungle. At 8½ miles Yinyé, water from tanks and wells. Good kyaungs and zayâts. Road now crosses paddy-fields for 1½ miles to Ainya. Direction north. No kyaungs. From Ainya (10 miles) good road, mostly through scrub jungle to Sainbin 13½ miles, excellent kyaung accommodation north and south of village. Good water from tanks and wells.

BRANCH II.

FROM YÉ-U (STAGE 7) TO TÔKTALÔK (MU RIVER).

BY LIEUT. R. HUGHES, 2ND OXFORDSHIRE LIGHT INFANTRY, MARCH 1888.

Military	Civil	Stage	Intermediate	Total	Remarks
G.O.C. Myingyán District.	Commr., Central Divn., and Dy. Commr., Yé-u.	**1. Déyauk** ...	**9 6**	9 6	The road follows the Yé-u-Nwabeitgyi road, described in route for 5¾ miles to Indaw. The remainder of the road to Tôktalôk through paddy, except for 1½ miles before reaching

FROM MYINMU TO WUNTHO *viâ* YÉ-U AND HLUTTAIK—*continued.*

BRANCH II—*continued.*

Authorities.		Number and Names of Stages, Rivers and Streams.	Distances.		Remarks.
Military.	Civil.		Intermediate.	Total.	
G.O.C. Myingyân District.	Commissioner, Central Division, and Deputy Commissioner, Yé-u.	**1. Déyauk**—*cont.*			Sipadaung chaung, where it passes through jungle. General direction north. The whole distance is good for carts in dry season and is reported practicable in the rains. Sipadaung chaung would probably have to be crossed some miles further up in rainy season. Pass Pôntaga at 7¼ miles, 150 houses. Two kyaungs. Water from wells. Reach Déyauk at 9¾ miles, 57 houses. One kyaung, 50 men, and three zayáts, 30 men, on south edge of village. Water good from five wells. Plenty of camping ground could be found amongst scattered scrub jungle, ½ mile east.
		2. Tôktalôk ...	M. F. **9 2**	M. F. 19 0	Road on 1 mile to Aungtha, 30 houses. One kyaung for 30 men, two zayáts for 20 men. Three wells with good water. Pass Shwéthugyi at 2 miles, 50 houses, five zayáts for 50 men, and good camping ground on north side of village. Water good from wells. Reach Tazé at 4½ miles; 220 houses. Four kyaungs east of village for 160 men, with seven zayáts for 80 men. Besides these other kyaungs were reported, 500 men could easily be accommodated in all. Water good from eight wells. Gram was reported as being grown in some quantity. Road on north-west enters jungle at 7 miles, which continues to Sipadaung chaung. On the near bank of Sipadaung chaung is one kyaung for 50 men and six zayáts for 90 men. The water in the chaung is stagnant here, but there is one well. Better water could be got from the Mu river at ½ mile east. This kyaung is closely shut in by tall trees and jungle, and does not look a healthy place. At the kyaung there is a good foot-bridge, but carts cross further east. The water is about 2 feet deep in March. Road on through open ground, good for camping, to Tôktalôk at 9¼ miles. Tôktalôk is about 200 yards from the Mu. About 80 houses, well laid out, surrounded by double bamboo stockade. Accommodation for 10 men in empty bungalow just outside the stockade at south-east corner. Water good from wells and river.

BRANCH III.

FROM HLUTTAIK (STAGE 13) TO UKINGYI *viâ* MADÔN AND TÁKÔN.

BY LIEUT.-COL. SENIOR, 1ST BENGAL INFANTRY, JANUARY 1887.

Military.	Civil.	Number and Names of Stages, Rivers and Streams.	Intermediate.	Total.	Remarks.
G.O.C. Mandalay District.	Commissioner, Northern Division, and Deputy Commissioner, Katha.	**1. Nyaungôn** ...	**11 0**	11 0	Cross Mu river to Madôn (½ a mile). Road thence runs eastward through varnish and teak forest, free from undergrowth. The village of Swélwa at 5 miles was burnt to the ground in 1886. It was here that Prince Maung Hmát died in October 1886. His hut was still standing in 1887, and in front of it is his grave. At Swélwa another road crosses the one now under report, leading from Pamiyé on the north, distant about 2 miles, to Kôkôgôn, about 2 miles to the south. Road as before. At 8 miles another cart road crosses it, running north and south. It is said to come from Kyin, distant ? miles north, and to lead to Léla ? miles to the south. Nyaungôn is burnt and deserted in 1887. Water from creek close by, dirty.

FROM MYINMU TO WUNTHO *viâ* YÉ-U AND HLUTTAIK—*continued.*

BRANCH III—*continued.*

Authorities. Military.	Authorities. Civil.	Number and Names of Stages, Rivers and Streams.	Distances. Intermediate.	Distances. Total.	Remarks.
G.O.C. Mandalay District.	Commissioner, Northern Division, and Deputy Commissioner, Katha.	**2. Ingôntha** ...	M. F. **8 4**	M. F. 19 4	Cross creek and road through forest as before to Pelutha at 6 miles; only recognizable as the site of village by *zayát* and small space of cleared ground. Road as before for next 2 miles; it then enters open country. Half-a-mile to the north is the small village of Láha, and further away north the Tôngwé hills; to the east a small pagoda-crowned hill called Wédittaga. Ingôntha is situated on rising ground. It was deserted and burnt in 1887, but one dilapidated kyaung would afford some shelter on an emergency. Kangyi hill is visible from here as also some hills further north and said to be south of Wuntho.
		3. Ukingyi ...	**7 4**	27 0	Road through open country to Tákôn (3 miles). *See* Route No. 93, Northern Division, for description of remainder of this stage. This route is passable for carts throughout. Owing to disuse it is somewhat out of repair, but as there are no difficult places anywhere along it, it merely requires a little use to render it easy. It is important, as it connects Hluttaik and Ukingyi, both of which are points of military importance; and it is also said to be the only lateral communication between the river on the west and the Ukingyi-Kawlin road on the east.

No. 19.

From PAUNGBYIN (Upper Chindwin) to MAINGKAING (Uyu or Uru River).

BY LIEUT. H. F. LOCH, COMMANDANT, MILITARY POLICE, UPPER CHINDWIN, OCTOBER 1890.

Military	Civil	Stages	Intermediate	Total	Remarks
G.O.C. Myingyán District.	Commissioner, Central Division, and Deputy Commissioner, Upper Chindwin.	**1. Tawma** ... Cross a stream.	**12 0**	12 0	General direction north-north-east. Road good, path practicable for transport animals; leads along a ridge for the first 3 miles and then along base of small hills over plains covered with "kaing" grass; water met with at several places. The first village is passed an hour and 20 minutes after leaving Paungbyiu, and a jheel is reached in 2 hours. From here 40 minutes' march brings one to Ôngdôk village, where there is a good kyaung capable of holding 100 men. Three-quarters of an hour before reaching Tawma another jheel is passed. At Tawma there is a good kyaung and zayáts hold 150 men. Village, 50 houses. Supplies, paddy and grass. Water from stream.
		2. Wetkauk ... Cross a stream.	**12 0**	24 0	General direction east-north-east. Road good and had been lately repaired; runs mostly over high ground and through open jungle. Pass the village of Kámaing an hour and-a-quarter after leaving Tawma. Only one stream crossed on this march. Wetkauk contains a good kyaung which will accommodate 100 men. It is situated on the Kyinthé chaung. About 30 houses. Paddy and grass procurable.

No. 19.

From PAUNGBYIN (Upper Chindwin) to MAINGKAING (Uyu or Uru River)—*continued.*

Authorities. Military.	Authorities. Civil.	Number and Names of Stages, Rivers and Streams.	Distances. Intermediate. M.	Intermediate. F.	Total. M.	Total. F.	Remarks.
G.O.C. Myingyan District.	Commissioner, Central Division, and Deputy Commissioner, Upper Chindwin.	**3. Metkalet** ... Cross several streams.	**13**	**0**	37	0	General direction north. Road somewhat rough, but fairly good; runs for the most part along the ridges of hills. Reach the village of Nanan 3 hours after leaving Wetkauk. Large kyaung, hold 150; houses about 30. Paddy and grass procurable. Water good from stream.
		4. Hénu ... ... Cross several streams.	**16**	**0**	53	0	General direction north-east. The road is good except first after leaving the village of Leikthaw and again before reaching Hénu, when it runs across paddy cultivation. In other parts it runs over high ground. The village of Leikthaw is passed at 8 miles; it contains a good kyaung. At Hénu the kyaung is indifferent. Small kyaung, hold 50 men. Water from creek close by. Supplies, paddy and fodder.
		5. Maingkaing ...	**12**	**0**	65	0	General direction north-east. Good road and lately repaired. Runs somewhat up and down hill for first 7 miles, and then across plain to Uyu stream, turning sharp to east and along the bank to Maingkaing; about 15 houses. Old police post, hold 50 men. Supplies, paddy and grass. Water from Uyu stream.

Note.—The hills seen from Maingkaing about east-north-east are the Thônlôndaung (Taungthônlôn) in Wuntho territory; distant four marches, say 60 miles. The road from Maingkaing into the Wuntho territory is a bad one, and the stream which comes from it (Chaungmagyi?) is not practicable for boats except in the rains. There is a better road from Leikthaw or Hénu to Kyundaw. Transport is the great difficulty along these roads. Coolies want to change at each circle, and are of little use as they barely carry 20 lbs. apiece. If a column of 150 rifles was to go up to Wuntho from these parts, each circle would have to be called upon to furnish a certain number of coolies under a "gaung," who would be required to stay with and accompany the expedition until dismissed. The circles can furnish the following coolies:—

Paungbyin 60, or for longer period than one day ...	30
Ôngdôk Tawma 50, or for longer period than one day.	25
Wetkauk 40, or for longer period than one day ...	20
Nanan-Metkalet 50, or for longer period than one day.	25
Leikthaw 40, or for longer period than one day ...	20
Hénu 60, or for longer period than one day	30
Maingkaing 50, or for longer period than one day ...	25
Total ...	175

No animal transport procurable locally. The whole of this road is practical with very little work in the worst parts for pony and mule transport.

No. 20.

From PAUNGBYIN (Upper Chindwin) to WUNTHO.

By Lieut. W. H. DALY (from Native information).

FIRST ROAD.

Authorities.		Number and Names of Stages, Rivers and Streams.	Distances.		Remarks.
Military.	Civil.		Inter-mediate.	Total.	
G.O.C. Myingyán District. G.O.C. Mandalay District.	Commr., Central Divn., and Deputy Commr., Upper Chindwin. Commr., Northern Divn., and Deputy Commr., Katha.	1. **Kaketywa** ... Along Namenkwin chaung.	M. F. 17 4	M. F. ...	In the absence of any recorded routes between the Chindwin and Wuntho, the following two routes are given, though very old and only from native information.

Excellent dry weather road to Kaket. Namenkwin chaung crossed seven times, but in deepest place not above 18 inches at present (1st January 1887). Kaket lies on a small stream (which flows into Namenkwin from south-east) at about $\frac{1}{2}$ mile from the junction. Namenkwin stream flows almost due east to (?) the Setkadôn range from this point. The summit of the range is about 9 miles as the crow flies from the junction of the Kaket and Namenkwin streams. There are two roads from this point to Wuntho. The Thaungdut Kyámaing went to Wuntho by one, and returned by the other, during December. I met him at Paungbyin on his return, and he and his followers gave the following information as to their marches. From Kaketywa (or Kaget) there is said to be a good road branching southwards to Bahét (20 miles) on the Múwa chaung in Mainyaung district, whence the Chindwin can be reached at Múwá (about 10 miles above Sittaung), distant about 16 miles, passing through the villages of Manthé, Mathi, and Letpán at 5, 10 and 13 miles respectively—

	MILES.	
(*i*) *Going*—		
First day, Paungbyin to Kaket	$17\frac{1}{2}$	*The Setkadôn Route.* This road starts south-east from Kaket; it is the shortest route, but the Setkadôn range is very steep and mounted men cannot get over. Horses must be led.
Second day, Kaket to Mawlakainshé ...	30	
Third day, Mawlakainshé to Kaukthein ...	20	
Fourth day, Kaukthein to Pintha ...	$1\frac{1}{4}$	
Do. Pintha to Engwé (on Mu) ...	$\frac{3}{4}$	
Do. Engwé to Myelin	$17\frac{1}{2}$	
Fifth day, Myelin to Wuntho	20	
Total ...	107	
(*ii*) *Return*—		
First day, Wuntho to Myelin	20	This is called the Maw road; it is passable and easy for ponies and elephants. The two routes diverge from Mawlakainshé. Kakethánsaung is probably more than 17 miles from Paungbyin.
Second day, Myelin to Yeshin	$17\frac{1}{4}$	
Third day, Yeshin to Manlát (variously called Maw or Wayángôn)	$22\frac{1}{2}$	
Fourth day, camp in jungle at Kalawgyaung	20	
Fifth day (Kakethansaung), 3 *daings* from Kaket up Namenkwin valley) ...	20	
Sixth day, Paungbyin	$17\frac{1}{2}$	
Total ...	$117\frac{1}{4}$	

Maw (where salt is made) is $1\frac{1}{4}$ miles from Mawlakainshé.

Other routes from the Chindwin to Wuntho are—

(*iii*) Taungbyu road, through the pass opposite the end of Kauksa chaung. This joins the Maw road at Mawlakainshé. The Setkadôn range is very difficult where the road crosses.

(*iv*) Zíbin road through the pass, opposite the head of a small chaung, flowing from the north-east into Thayaung chaung, $12\frac{1}{2}$ miles from the big hills to Mandalet, and thence $42\frac{1}{2}$ miles to Wuntho. The Zíbin range is the northern continuation of the Setkadôn. The pass referred to is about 30 miles from Paungbyin.

FROM PAUNGBYIN (UPPER CHINDWIN) TO WUNTHO—*continued.*

FIRST ROAD—*continued.*

(*v*) Through pass opposite end of Kyinthé chaung south (which flows into Chindwin at Sanda) to Ganambwa (or Ganamwa) 12½ or 15 miles, thence south to Mandalet 10 miles, and so as by Route (*iv*).

(*vi*) Through the pass at the end of the Nankamu (about five days' journey from the big hills), distance 80 miles.

(*vii*) Through pass at head of Kôdán chaung 15 miles to Mettaung, thence 40 miles to Mawlakainshé.

SECOND ROAD.

BY LIEUT. HERBERT, 44TH GURKHA LIGHT INFANTRY (FROM NATIVE INFORMATION).

Authorities.		Stations.	Distances, Intermediate.		Distances, Total.		Remarks.
Military.	Civil.		Shan dines.	Approximate English miles.	Shan dines.	Approximate English miles.	
			M. F.	M. F.	M. F.	M. F.	
G.O.C. Myingyán District.	Commissioner, Central Division, and Deputy Commissioner, Upper Chindwin.	**Paungbyin** ...	...	...	...	...	Road from Paungbyin runs in an easterly direction to Thányit. It crosses the Kanshak, Tanet and Tháyaung streams each once. Water in these chaungs is good; in December about knee-deep, now (September) waist-deep; the banks are high and steep; bottom, sand; parts of the road pass through marshy ground.
		Thányit ...	**6 0**	**13 0**	6 0	13 0	This village contains one large pôngyi kyaung and 40 houses; rice is procurable and water-supply unlimited. The road from here crosses the Thayaung chaung four times; country level, no marshes.
		Thethla ...	**6 0**	**13 0**	12 0	26 0	Thethla village contains one small kyaung and eight houses; no supplies can be obtained here. Road from here to Kyundaungalé runs over undulating country, crosses the Môtai chaung four times; only a few inches of water in this chaung. No marshes on road.
		Kyundaungalé	**7 0**	**15 0**	19 0	41 0	This is a jungle camp in hilly country. Bamboos for building huts plentiful. Water obtained from a spring would require enlarging by digging reservoir for large number of men (in November there is only enough for 15 men). About four daings (8¾ miles) from here the road crosses the Zíbyu range and becomes very narrow in places, being shut in by high banks of sand-stone. Ponies could not pass unless road were prepared by pioneers. The road is bad here for three daings (6½ miles), but not impracticably steep. After this the road runs over flat and easy country to Kayáywa. No water is procurable while crossing the Zíbyu hills.

FROM PAUNGBYIN (UPPER CHINDWIN) TO WUNTHO—*continued.*

SECOND ROAD—*continued.*

Authorities. Military.	Authorities. Civil.	Stations.	Distances, Intermediate. Shan dines.	Distances, Intermediate. Approximate English miles.	Distances, Total. Shan dines.	Distances, Total. Approximate English miles.	Remarks.
			M. F.	M. F.	M. F.	M. F.	
G.O.C. Mandalay District.	Commissioner, Northern Division, and Deputy Commissioner, Katha.	**Kayáywa** ...	**8 0**	**17 4**	27 0	58 4	No kyaung; 15 houses; no supplies; belongs to Wuntho. From Kayáywa the road runs through the villages as shown and crosses the Wehara, Thayetkôn and Taw maw chaungs. Water in these streams only a few inches deep; banks, easy; bed, sand; no marshes; country, level; road good and fit for ponies, runs over Wumbé hills to Gyôbin Sakhán.
		Kauktaung.	**1 0**	**2 0**	28 0	60 4	Twenty houses; small kyaung; no supplies.
		Thayetkôn ...	**0 4**	**1 2**	28 4	61 6	Thirty houses; large kyaung.
		Kaket ...	**1 4**	**3 2**	30 0	65 0	Fifty houses; large kyaung.
		Maungkin ...	**3 4**	**7 4**	33 4	72 4	Two or three huts.
		Kénubauk ...	**1 0**	**2 0**	34 4	74 4	Eighteen houses; no kyaung.
		Gyôbin Sakhán.	**1 0**	**2 0**	35 4	76 4	Jungle camp. Road from here crosses Wunken chaung which is easy; also the Mu river on which the town of Pingyaing stands; breadth of Mu here 200 yards; depth in dry season 2 feet; now (September) waist-deep; bed, sand; banks, easy: no boats available.
		Pingyaing ...	**2 0**	**4 6**	37 4	81 2	Large town of 300 houses; supplies of rice procurable; 3 kyaungs; town not stockaded. Road from here runs over flat country, easy for ponies.
		Ngulai ...	**5 0**	**10 6**	42 4	92 4	Fifty houses, one kyaung. Road crosses Dathwégyauk stream; no difficulty; country flat and easy for ponies; no marshes.
		Hmangin (Mankin).	**7 0**	**15 0**	49 4	107 4	Eighteen houses and kyaung. Road runs over Hmangin hill about 1 daing (2 miles) from Hmangin; road easy. Wuntho town visible from Hmangin hills.
		Teinwa chaung.	**4 0**	**8 4**	53 4	116. 0	Eighty houses; one large kyaung; road into Wuntho easy.
		Wuntho-myo.	**0 4**	**1 0**	54 0	117 0	......

No. 21.

From SAGAING to SHWÉBO.

I. B. COMPILATION, NOVEMBER 1888.

There are three routes from Sagaing to Shwébo:—

First—

	MILES.
First stage, Sagaing to Sayé	10½
Second stage, Sayé to Samôn	15½
Third stage, Samôn to Kawdaw	14
Fourth stage, Kawdaw to Shwébo	14
Total ...	54

This route is the shortest, but from Samôn to Shwébo is from native information only, and distance seems to be under-estimated. From Samôn to Shwébo must be at least 30 miles. It would probably be impracticable in the rains between Samôn and Shwébo, and water is reported very brackish about Kawdaw.

Second—

	MILES.
First stage, Sagaing to Sayé	10½
Second stage, Sayé to Taungyin	9½
Third stage, Taungyin to Imbé	15
Fourth stage, Imbé to Heléngyi	12
Fifth stage, Heléngyi to Shwébo	13
Total ...	60

This road is practicable though difficult for carts in the rains as far as Helengyi. In the rains carts do the last stage *viâ* Ômbôk, which adds 6½ miles to the total, making 66½. Another stage in this case could be made at Ômbôk, a good halting place. By this road accommodation and water is good the whole way.

Third—

	MILES.
First stage, Sagaing to Ôngdaw (Kyaungmada could be made a halting place half-way)	15½
Second stage, Ôngdaw to Sadaung	11
Third stage, Sadaung to Hládwi	12
Fourth stage, Hládwi to Hládaw	12
Fifth stage, Hládaw to Shwébo	15¼
Total ...	65¾

This is the longest of the three roads in dry weather. Some places between Sadaung and Hládaw, the third and fourth stages, might be found impracticable for carts in the rains. Accommodation and water good the whole way.

FIRST ROAD.

Authorities. Military.	Authorities. Civil.	Number and Names of Stages, Rivers and Streams.	Distances. Inter-mediate. M.	Distances. Inter-mediate. F.	Distances. Total. M.	Distances. Total. F.	Remarks.
G.O.C. Myingyân District.	Commr., Central Divn., and Deputy Commr., Sagaing.	**1. Sayé**	**10**	**4**	10	4	Good cart road due north to Kaungmudaw (or Kyaungmadaw) at 5½ miles, passing many villages on each side of the road, amongst them Pabédán, Kyaukait and Magyitsen. At Kaungmudaw, on the west side of the pagoda of the same name, a land-mark for many miles, is accommodation for 500 men in zayáts, with a plentiful sup-

FROM SAGAING TO SHWÉBO—*continued.*

FIRST ROAD—*continued.*

Authorities. Military.	Authorities. Civil.	Number and Names of Stages, Rivers and Streams.	Distances. Intermediate.	Distances. Total.	Remarks.
G.O.C. Myingyán District.	Commissioner, Central Division, and Deputy Commissioner, Sagaing.	**1. Sayé**—*cont.*			ply of water from wells on the edge of the lake. South-west of Kaungmudaw is a large swamp, and on the east is the Yé-ka (*i.e.*, bitter water) swamp. Road on north over 2 miles of paddy-fields, difficult, but practicable in the rains, then over sandy, undulating ground covered with thorn jungle to Sayé ½ mile before reaching Sayé, which lies at the north-east base of a line of low-lying hills running west to Ôngdaw, in the midst of open fields. To the north and west lies the plain of Yémyitgyi, flooded in the rains. Sayé is a large village and has accommodation for 100 men in kyaungs and zayáts, with plenty of good water from wells.
			M. F.	M. F.	
		2. Samô ...	**15 4**	26 0	From Sayé this road runs north along the east side of Yémyitgyi plain. Pass Kyaukpanaw at 3 miles, Kángyi-gôn at 3½ miles. At 6½ miles reach Padhu, a large village with accommodation for 100 men in kyaungs and zayáts and plenty of water. From Padhu or Taungyi 3½ miles on. Samôn was a military post, February 1888. The fort is ½ a mile north of the village on high ground, and will hold 200 men and 50 horses, and has good water from two wells. Accommodation in the village for 100 men in kyaungs, 50 men in zayáts. Water good from wells. Road on north to Kawdaw at 14 miles.
G.O.C. Mandalay District.	Commr., Northern Divn., and Deputy Commr., Sagaing.	**3. Kawdaw** ...	**14 0**	40 0	At Kawdaw accommodation is reported for 200 men in kyaungs and zayáts. Water brackish but wholesome.
		4. Shwébo ...	**14 0**	54 0	From Kawdaw to Shwébo the road runs through paddy country, probably impassable in the rainy season. Pass the following villages, Magyibinsin, Kitkyigôn, Ponayendaw, Môksogôn, Shádaw. These villages are reported as on the road by natives. Probably a more direct road could be found.

SECOND ROAD.

Military.	Civil.	Stages.	Intermediate.	Total.	Remarks.
G.O.C. Myingyán District.	Commr., Central Divn., and Deputy Commr., Sagaing.	**1. Sayé** ...	**10 4**	10 4	*See* above.
		2. Taungyin ...	**9 4**	20 0	The second road is the same as the first as far as Padhu. From Padhu at 6½ miles the road continues north 3 miles over black soil to Taungyin. Very good in dry season, difficult in rains. Taungyin has accommodation for 150 men, with plenty of good water from tank and wells. From Taungyin the road runs for the most part through light jungle, and is good at all seasons, 4 miles to the former site of Thalain. Thalain has been brought into Taungyin by order of the civil authorities. There was plenty of accommodation in empty kyaungs in February 1888, but the water was bad. From Thalain there is a cart road to Singain on the Irrawaddy, 2½ miles over the hills. From Thanlain the road runs north-north-west for 4 miles, then north-west for 2 miles over hard sandy ground through thin jungle, which could be traversed anywhere by cavalry.
G.O.C. Mandalay District.	Commr., Northern Divn., &c., Shwébo.				

No. 21.

From SAGAING to SHWÉBO—*continued.*

SECOND ROAD—*continued.*

Authorities. Military.	Authorities. Civil.	Number and Names of Stages, Rivers and Streams.	Distances. Intermediate. M.	F.	Distances. Total. M.	F.	Remarks.
G.O.C. Mandalay District.	Commissioner, Northern Division, and Deputy Commissioner, Shwébo.	**2. Taungyin**—*cont.*					At 6 miles reach Budagôn, 20 houses; fenced and surrounded by paddy. One zayát east of the village, which would hold 10 men; one kyaung for 50 men. Water very good from three wells. The road on is north over undulating sandy soil. At ½ a mile Budagôn the road from Sheinmaga west to Shwékugyi is crossed.
			M.	F.	M.	F.	
		3. Imbé ...	15	0	35	0	For 2 miles from Budagôn the road passes through light jungle and some dry cultivation, mostly til seed, afterwards through scrub jungle and palm trees till within 1 mile of Imbé, where paddy cultivation begins. Reach Imbé at 15 miles. Remainder of road *see* Route No. 91, Northern Division.
		4. Helengyi ...	12	0	47	0	
		5. Shwébo ...	13	0	60 In rainy season 66	0 4	

THIRD ROAD.

Authorities. Military.	Authorities. Civil.	Number and Names of Stages, Rivers and Streams.	Distances. Intermediate. M.	F.	Distances. Total. M.	F.	Remarks.
G.O.C. Myingyán District.	Commissioner, Central Division, and Deputy Commissioner, Sagaing.	**1. Ôngdaw** ...	15	4	15	4	Good cart road. Old royal road under an avenue of fine trees the whole way to Kaungmudaw. At 5½ miles two nullahs are crossed, one near Sagaing and one near Kaungmudaw. Both have strong wooden bridges; one near Sagaing is passable by carts. At the first nullah carts have to be ferried across in the wet months. The other is almost always fordable. Bridge north of Kaungmudaw is not practicable; no ramp on to it. Villages border the road almost the whole way along, and there are numerous kyaungs and pagodas. There is accommodation in zayáts for 400 men at Kaungmudaw and for 100 more if two of the zayáts be put in repair. Grass and water-supply ample along the lake at the north-east corner of which the village is situated. The zayáts lie on the western side of the great pagoda for which the place is famous. Just north of the kyaungs roads branch off in many directions to Sayé and on to Shwébo, to Ţaingdé, and thence *viâ* Sadaung or Samôn to Shwébo, to Ôngdaw and other places to the west. The Ôngdaw road passes along the edge of the lake. Leaving the latter and the lake at Pégadaw village, pass through a stretch of paddy-fields and a nullah, which might be troublesome to carts in the rains (better road ¾ mile east in rains, and ascend on to some rising ground covered thickly with cactus). There are some zayáts and a kyaung in the middle of this cactus jungle which extends for 2 miles. Beyond the cactus jungle the country is laid out in wheat-fields, enclosed in fields of two or three acres with low thorn fence, then cross a very open bit of country and pass ½ mile east of Kônywa (6 miles). There are good wells to the west and south-east, both about 300 yards from the village road. Road now runs due north. Country still continues very flat. Road good for carts to Aungtha, which consists of several scattered hamlets. A well close to the village on the south is brackish, and water is obtained from another well 400 yards distant on the west, where there are some kyaungs. Road crosses a low spur along a lane, good for carts (ground cultivated with wheat) and winds along the western foot of low hills to Ôngdaw. Ôngdaw is at the western end of the low hills which run east and west across

FROM SAGAING TO SHWÉBO—*continued.*

THIRD ROAD—*continued.*

Authorities: Military.	Authorities: Civil.	Number and Names of Stages, Rivers and Streams.	Distances: Intermediate. M. F.	Distances: Total. M. F.	Remarks.
G.O.C. Myingyán District.	Commissioner, Central Division, and Deputy Commissioner, Sagaing.	**1. Ôngdaw**—*cont.*			the Sagaing district. There is a good camping ground under large trees for a regiment on the western side. There is a good well in a nullah at the north-east corner and outside the village. Roads go straight north to Shwébo and south to Ywathitgyi on the Irrawaddy. Two villages of Ôngdaw, north and south, ½ a mile apart. Accommodation in kyaungs of north village for 100 men and 20 ponies. There is a kyaung ¼ mile south of South Ôngdaw, with accommodation for 50 men and 20 ponies. Two good wells. Plentiful supply of water all the year round.
		2. Sadaung ...	11 0	26 4	The road is the main road to Magyízauk, and passing Yômingôn and Thitkyigôn at 5½ miles from Ôngdaw reaches a solitary tall tree, whence a cart road bends to the right off the main road, passing immediately Mindaw village and continues in a northerly direction. At 6½ miles pass Ngapyawdaw, a few houses under a group of trees to the right of the road; thence a foot track branches off to the left over paddy-fields, and at 2 miles from Ngapyawdaw reaches Tabudaw. From Ngapyawdaw the Sadaung road continues due north on a sandy track with paddy-fields on each side to Kyámingyi village at 8 miles, which lies on a hill. Pass to the right of the village and from the far side the road continues north over sandy undulating ground for 2 miles, whence paddy-fields commence and stretch for 1 mile reaching Sadaung at 11 miles. Sadaung consists of five villages grouped close together. The kyaungs lie on the south-east side, they are five in number, and contain accommodation for 500 men with a plentiful supply of water during the rainy season. Sadaung is very difficult to approach on account of the paddy-fields lying all round it. Water on the road at Kyámingyi, where there is a kyaung 200 yards west of the village, affording accommodation for 50 men. Paddy in small quantities.
G.O.C. Mandalay District.	Commissioner, Northern Division, and Deputy Commissioner, Shwébo.	**3. Hládwi** ...	12 0	38 4	Road north-west through paddy cultivation to Thazin, 3 miles. Thazin, has accommodation in kyaungs and zayáts for 100 men. Water wholesome, but dirty from tanks near the village. Good clear water can be obtained from a well ½ a mile north-west of the village. Road continues north-north-west to Hládwi at 12 miles. For the first 2 miles after Thazin the road skirts a marsh where it would be almost impracticable during the rains. Afterwards the road passes through light jungle over better ground to Hládwi. Paoma, a small village, is passed at about 6 miles. Hládwi has accommodation for 70 men in five zayáts and 50 men in a kyaung south of the village. Water good from wells.
		4. Hládaw ...	12 0	50 4	From Hládwi there are two roads to Hládaw, each about 12 miles, one *viâ* Yatha, the other *viâ* Shwébangán. Both are through jungle and difficult

FROM SAGAING TO SHWÉBO—*continued.*

THIRD ROAD—*continued.*

Authorities. Military.	Authorities. Civil.	Number and Names of Stages, Rivers and Streams.	Distances. Intermediate.	Distances. Total.	Remarks.
G.O.C. Mandalay District.	Commissioner, Northern Division, and Deputy Commissioner, Shwébo.	**4. Hládaw**—*cont.*	for carts in the rains; 6 miles north-east to Yatha. Yatha has a military police post. Ten men could be accommodated at the stockade besides the police. Water good from wells and tank. Road on north-north-west 6 miles to Hládaw. Shwébangán is north-west of Hládwi, a village on the Magyizauk-Shwébo road.		
		5. Shwébo ...	M. F. 15 2	M. F. 65 6	For remainder *see* Route No. 17, Stage 5.

BRANCH I.

FROM ÔNGDAW (STAGE 1 ON 3RD ALTERNATIVE ROAD) TO GÔNYINSEIK.

BY LIEUT. FISCHER, 5TH BOMBAY LIGHT INFANTRY, FEBRUARY 1888.

Military	Civil	Stage	Intermediate	Total	Remarks
G.O.C. Myingyán District.	Commissioner, Central Division, and Deputy Commissioner, Sagaing.	**1. Tabiengwé** ...	12 0	12 0	Leave the Mandalé Mu road (*see* Branch Route No. 3 at Yinmagin, 6 miles from Ôngdaw and bear north-west to the top of the first rise of hills, whence cart road winds west over hills to Tabiengwé, 12 miles. A track for infantry cuts across the windings of the cart road. Is a good mile shorter. A good guide should be taken at first, as many small tracks diverge into the jungle on each side. Tabiengwé is a very large, but poor village on bank of Mu river. Contains a police post, 20 rifles, and five kyaungs capable of accommodating 300 to 400 men, with plenty of water. Paddy in small quantities; many cattle.
		2. Gônyinseik ...	3 0	15 0	From Tabiengwé road goes west over low-lying land, many toddy trees, and comes out on left bank opposite Gônyinseik. River in rains 100 yards broad and 15 feet deep, current 4 miles an hour, and must be crossed in boats, of which there are many. In dry season two fords—one just above Gônyinseik and one just below, depth 2 to 3 feet—can be easily seen by cart tracks leading down to them. *See* Route No. 17, Stage 1.

ALTERNATIVE ROUTE.

Military	Civil	Stage	Intermediate	Total	Remarks
G.O.C. Myingyán District.	Commissioner, Central Division, and Deputy Commissioner, Sagaing.	**1. Taungya** ...	11 0	11 0	*See* Branch Route No. III (below).
		2. Gônyinseik ...	7 0	18 0	Road (good cart) leaves Taungya in south-west direction and reaches Tabiengwé at 4 miles, thence *viâ* Branch Route No. I to Gônyinseik. This road is much easier, if there is time to make two stages of it, and is good going all the way.

FROM SAGAING TO SHWÉBO—*continued.*

BRANCH II.

FROM ÔNGDAW (STAGE 1 ON 3RD ALTERNATIVE ROAD) TO LÉGYI.

BY LIEUT. FISCHER, 5TH BOMBAY LIGHT INFANTRY, FEBRUARY 1888.

Authorities. Military.	Authorities. Civil.	Number and Names of Stages, Rivers and Streams.	Distances. Intermediate.	Distances. Total.	Remarks.
G.O.C. Myingyán District.	Commissioner, Central Division, and Deputy Commissioner, Sagaing.	**1. Légyi**	M. F. **10 0**	M. F. 10 0	Pass along the north side of South Ôngdaw and bear to the left (260°) over paddy-fields for about ¾ of a mile, where the cart road appears and passes over a small nullah, and on winding through scrub jungle, intermixed with cultivation over sandy soil, and at 5 miles reach Nakhayin (or Makhayin) village. (This village is now being brought into Ôngdaw.) The road passes north of the village, good cart road over undulating thick jungle, gradually bearing slightly north of west and reaching Légyi at 10 miles. The road, as far as the first nullah, is very bad in the rains, but carts do get across. Légyi is a large village and there is a police post. Strength about 20 rifles in the kyaung due east of the village, with accommodation for 50 men and stables for 50 ponies. A kyaung on north side of village would put up 50 men. Plentiful supply of water from well south of village. A fair amount of paddy, rice, and kirbi to be obtained. The above is the best all round road in the dry season. An alternative road runs as follows:—Start along the Yinmagin road and at ½ mile turn west by cart road and pass over undulating cultivated ground for 4 miles when road passes across ½ mile of paddy-fields (difficult in the rains) and arrives just north of Kônywa village, 5 miles. Hence good cart road winds over the hills and reaches Kyidawya pagoda at 8½ miles. The road bears down to the left (at ½ mile road divides right to Tabyengwé and left to Légyi) and winding about to avoid numerous nullahs reaches Légyi at 12 miles. A foot-path practicable for baggage animals goes straight through the windings of the cart road to Légyi. Three miles from Kyidawya pagoda, east of Kyidawya (200 yards), is a large brick tank with good water all the year round. This is the best road in the rains. A third road runs as follows:—Pass north side of South Ôngdaw and follow road west for 2 miles; cross paddy-fields on "bunds" in rains in north-west direction to Shendát (4 miles), then west over bridle-path to Kyidawya pagoda (7 miles), then follows foot-path in second road. This path is only suited for men and ponies and not for baggage ponies in the rains. The jungle that stretches from Nakhayin *viâ* Kyidawya pagoda right up to Taungya is full of hiding places of dacoits, being full of deep nullahs.

BRANCH III.

FROM ÔNGDAW (STAGE 1, ALTERNATIVE ROUTE NO. III) TO MANDALÉ MU.

BY LIEUT. FISCHER, 5TH BOMBAY LIGHT INFANTRY, FEBRUARY 1888.

Military	Civil	Stage	Intermediate	Total	Remarks
G.O.C. Myingyán District.	Commr., Central Division, and Deputy Commr., Sagaing.	**1. Taungya** ...	**11 0**	11 0	From Ôngdaw road runs a little west of north and passing Yômingaung and Thitkyigôn at 6 miles reach Yinmagin. Half-a-mile before reaching Yinmagin road branches to right near a tall tree to Mindaw, Kyámingyi and Sadaung.

FROM SAGAING TO SHWÉBO—*continued.*

BRANCH III—*continued.*

Authorities. Military.	Authorities. Civil.	Number and Names of Stages, Rivers and Streams.	Distances. Inter-mediate.	Distances. Total.	Remarks.
G.O.C. Myingyán District.	Commissioner, Central Division, and Deputy Commissioner, Sagaing.	**1. Taungya**—*cont.*			From Yinmagin good cart road runs north and at 8 miles reach Lindalu, whence road bends west and running over sandy scrub jungle with numerous nullahs reaches Taungya at 11 miles. One kyaung to west of village has accommodation for 100 men and stables for 20 ponies. Water from well in this kyaung brackish; must be obtained from tank to west of the jungle. Kyaung ½ mile west of village has accommodation for 50 men. Water here scanty in dry season.
		2. Mandalé on the Mu. Mu river between Talaingyun and Mandalé.	M. F. 5 0	M. F. 16 0	From Taungya good cart road runs north-west by west. At 2 miles reach Ensa, whence road runs over low-lying ground, bad going in the rains, and at 4 miles reach Talaingyun on left bank of river. Hence the road runs up the bank in sight of Mandalé, and at 1 mile arrive opposite kyaung, which is on a small eminence on right bank, the village lying to the south. The river here during the rains is about 80 yards across and 10 to 15 feet deep. The left bank steep, but practicable for unloaded animals. The right bank low-lying. The current 3 to 4 miles an hour. The river must be crossed in boats, and animals can be swum. Large boats can be obtained from Gônyinseik, 6 miles south of Mandalé on the right bank. For Mandalé-Mu *see* Route No. 17, Stage 2.

BRANCH IV.

FROM ÔNGDAW (STAGE 1, 3RD ALTERNATIVE ROAD) TO SAMÔN (STAGE 2, FIRST ROAD).

BY LIEUT. FISCHER, 5TH BOMBAY LIGHT INFANTRY, FEBRUARY 1888.

Authorities. Military.	Authorities. Civil.	Number and Names of Stages, Rivers and Streams.	Distances. Inter-mediate.	Distances. Total.	Remarks.
G.O.C. Myingyán District.	Commissioner, Central Division, and Deputy Commissioner, Sagaing.	**1. Samôn** ...	12 0	12 0	The cart road branches in a north-north-west direction from the west side of North Ôngdaw. It runs over sandy undulating ground. At 2 miles reach Pagyi, passing to the north of and round the base of the hill on which Pagyi pagoda stands. From Ôngdaw fort a path, practicable for infantry and baggage animals, runs through the kyaung and branches over the hills from the village well, passing on the south side of Pagyi pagoda and joining the cart road in Pagyi village. From Pagyi the cart road runs over a few paddy-fields, difficult but practicable during wet weather, and on through a short stretch of lane to more open country. At 3 miles pass ¼ mile south of Môyingyaung and cross a large sandy nullah generally dry, always practicable. At 6 miles reach Yédwingaung passing to the north of the village, and at 6½ miles pass on south of Nyaungôn. From here the road runs over high-lying scrub jungle which extends to Kyákát village (10½ miles), whence Samôn fort can be seen built on the top of a slight gradual rise. At 12 miles reach Samôn fort. The village lies ¼ mile to the south. There are several wells and plentiful supply of water. Water on the road at any of these villages and paddy in small quantities and kirbi. *See* First Road, Stage 2.

FROM SAGAING TO SHWÉBO—*continued.*

BRANCH V.

FROM SADAUNG (STAGE 2 OF 3RD ROAD) TO KÔKO-CHAUNG-YWA (ON IRRAWADDY RIVER).

I. B. COMPILATION, 1887-88.

Authorities. Military.	Authorities. Civil.	Number and Names of Stages, Rivers and Streams.	Distances. Intermediate. M. F.	Distances. Total. M. F.	Remarks.
G.O.C. Mandalay District.	Commissioner, Central Division, and Deputy Commissioner, Sagaing.	**1. Kôko-chaung-ywa.**	**16 0**	16 0	There is an important road running from Sadaung to Kôko-chaung-ywa and Mézali-chaung-ywa on the right bank of the Irrawaddy near Mingún, which is, after the road leading from Sheinmaga (some miles north), the principal district thoroughfare from the Irrawaddy to the Mu river, and thence to Âlôn westwards or Myinmu southwards. The road is only a cart track, unmetalled throughout and is impassable in wet weather; it is unenclosed by fences. The country on either side of the road is interspersed with thorny bush jungle, but in some places is quite open. Cavalry could move over it easily, except in a few places where the thickness of the jungle would impede their action. There are numerous villages in the valley between the two low ranges of hills at Kôko-chaung-ywa and Sadaung; they are mostly enclosed by cactus hedges. Water is fairly plentiful all along the road, being obtained chiefly from wells in the villages. Supplies consisting of cattle, wheat, gram, bajree are plentiful, and at a few places paddy can be obtained in small quantities. The total distance is 16 miles and a halt can, if required, be made at Kekkathit 7½ miles, where there is accommodation for 150 men in kyaungs and zayáts, and a good water-supply from small tanks. The road crosses the Sagain-Shwébo road (Road No. 1 above) at Samôn, 5 miles from Sadôn. Mézali-chaung-ywa is on the river bank 1½ miles to the north of, and in sight of, Kôko-chaung-ywa. The village lies to the north and the kyaungs and zayáts (150 men) to the south of a road running inland. The right bank of the Irrawaddy is here steep and in most places good for landing. During the dry season when the river is low, a landing has to be effected at Phôdaw or Phôgwé, about 3 miles south of Kôko-chaung-ywa. There is a good cart track from this point to Kôko-chaung-ywa during low water season, but impassable in flood time.

BRANCH VI.

FROM SAYÉ (STAGE 1 OF 1ST ROAD) TO IMBÉ (ON ROUTE NO. 91, NORTHERN DIVISION).

BY COL. A. POOLE, 5TH BOMBAY LIGHT INFANTRY COMMANDING SAGAING.

Military	Civil	Stage	Intermediate M. F.	Total M. F.	Remarks
G.O.C. Myingyán District.	Commr., Central Division, and Deputy Commr., Sagaing.	**1. Kekathit** ...	**7 0**	7 0	Five miles to Budaywa pass villages of Kyaukpanán and Kángyigôn. Soil light and sandy; good cart road through fields interspersed with bushes. This is a large village situated on the east of Yémyitgyi lake; thence the road lies across a grassy plain at north of lake. Large village; water good; grass plentiful. General direction N. 20° W.

No. 21.

FROM SAGAING TO SHWÉBO—*continued.*

BRANCH VI—*continued.*

Authorities. Military.	Authorities. Civil.	Number and Names of Stages, Rivers and Streams.	Distances. Intermediate. M.	F.	Total. M.	F.	Remarks.
G.O.C. Mandalay District.	Commissioner, Northern Division, and Deputy Commissioner, Shwébo.	**2. Imbé**	**8**	**0**	15	0	Cart road runs 1$\frac{3}{4}$ miles north-east to Taungyi, thence north-west past Kamé. Road good, soil light and sandy. Imbé is a large rich village. Rice, paddy, and bullocks for slaughter plentiful. Grass procurable; wells are brackish; good water in a tank. Accommodation in one large and two small rest-houses. Here the road meets the route from Sheinmaga to Shwébo, No. 91, Northern Division.

No. 22.

From SITTAUNG to TAMMU.

BY LIEUT. C. J. W. GRANT,* 2ND BURMA INFANTRY, AND G. W. L. TOOZS, ESQ., PUBLIC WORKS DEPARTMENT, JANUARY 1891.

Authorities. Military.	Authorities. Civil.	Number and Names of Stages, Rivers and Streams.	Distances. Intermediate. M.	F.	Total. M.	F.	Remarks.
G.O.C. Myingyán District.	Commissioner, Central Division, and Deputy Commissioner, Upper Chindwin.	**1. Camp on Chaukhôn stream.** Wasélán, Kungaung, and Chaukhôn streams.	**12**	**0**	12	0	Sittaung is a small village situated on the right bank of the Chindwin river, about 50 miles north of Kindát and almost immediately opposite the large village of Kaya on the left bank. At Sittaung accommodation is available for 50 men and camping ground for 500. Water good. No supplies nor transport; they must be arranged for. Commanding ground on all sides, except east. General direction west. Road at first 8 feet wide, rises from 1° to 4°, average 3°, winding to top of first ridge which is reached in 25 minutes. The nullahs, which would be unfordable in the rains, are well bridged. Bridges 12 feet wide, will support elephants loaded. From the top the road winds down zigzag to west down the north side of a cliff till the bottom is reached in 45 minutes from Sittaung, distance 2$\frac{1}{2}$ miles, then west-south-west across open valley, $\frac{3}{4}$ mile wide running north and south, which is traversed by the Wasélán chaung, a sluggish stream which is bridged by a wooden trestle bridge 42 yards long, 10 feet wide; one of the trestle legs has sunk 2 feet. Elephant ford stream 1 foot deep below bridge. Valley extends south to Malu on Chindwin valley; contains jungly sort of cultivation, paddy and plantain. Road winds up the great range to north on the left side of a great nullah. Rise 2° to 8°, average 4°. Pass the 4th mile post in 1 hour 14 minutes from start. Crossing the Kungaung chaung in this mile by a timber bridge of two spans (10 and 8 feet long respectively). Road here only 4 feet wide, cut out of the side of cliff, and at 4$\frac{1}{2}$ miles only 3 feet wide. Five miles round head of nullah to west, then winds about to north zigzag along face of cliff. Ascent less steep. Average 2° up. All thick forest about 8 miles top of range; no view, trees very high; about 10 miles descent commences from 2° to 8°, average 4°, and path zigzags

* Now Brevet-Major C. J. W. Grant, V.C.

FROM SITTAUNG TO TAMMU—*continued.*

Authorities. Military.	Authorities. Civil.	Number and Names of Stages, Rivers and Streams.	Distances. Intermediate. M. F.	Distances. Total. M. F.	Remarks.
G.O.C. Myingyán District.	Commissioner, Central Division, and Deputy Commissioner, Upper Chindwin.	**1. Camp on Chaukhôn stream**—*cont.*			down to north-west to camp which is reached in 4 hours 15 minutes including 30 minutes' halt. Elephants arrive 1½ hours later. Camp consists of a bungalow 16 feet by 16 feet, with 6 feet verandah all round; stable, three ponies. Officers' quarters 8 feet by 24 feet, followers 10 feet by 12 feet. Good water in Chaukhôn stream 50 feet below. No village here or *en route.*
		2. Sagapin ... Chaukhôn stream and minor streams bridged, or else fordable at all seasons. Dry after January or February.	11 0	23 0	Road leads down 50 feet to stream probably unfordable in rains at times; bottom boulders 40 feet wide, then up slope; average 3°, steepest 8° round shoulder of hill to west; road very narrow in places, ledge having broken away. About 3 miles reaches a great saddle (after slight descent) which joins two great ranges which run north and south separating the Chindwin and Kubo valleys; saddle 8 miles long by road. Road runs west along south side of saddle. Near summit wonderful view down valley between ranges to south along Tilaung chaung (elevation 2,200 feet). From this saddle there is a descent, to where the old foot-path between Tammu and Auktaung is cut, and below which is a small spring known as Nátyádwin. Camp at junction of saddle and range which bounds the Kubo valley to the east; no village here or *en route.* Two barracks for 50 men each, and plenty of room for camping a large number of men; water in small brook good and plentiful up to the end of December, after that limited, and none at all after February until rains begin. Time of march 3 hours 35 minutes, including 30 minutes' halt. Elephants 4 hours 30 minutes. Country forest; no cultivation.
		3. Tammu ... Yu river. Lokchao stream.	17 0	40 0	Road runs north and west round north side of Phayatôn Peak to west, whence great view of Kubo valley and the Chin and Manipur hills. Tammu visible from here, *i.e.*, 1 mile from Sagapin. Two miles road turns to north-west down a great spur. The elephant road zigzags down the south side of it, while a foot-path, which shortens the way about 2 miles, runs along the crest of the spur, first north-west, then west, then west-south-west down the Kubo valley 10 miles: pace 4 miles an hour; here cross the Yunán chaung, a small sluggish stream, running southwards; muddy; bridge 21 yards by 10 feet. Eleven miles leave forest; open country, slightly cultivated. Twelve miles Yu river, ford waist-deep; about 4 boats, hold 10 men each; river now 30 yards wide. Sixty men took 23 minutes to cross in one boat 12 at a time. Current rapid, water clear. Road now greatly improved, 10 feet wide, level ground through forest to 13½ miles to Lokchao river; 15 yards wide, 1 foot deep, very rapid. Bamboo bridge 3 feet wide. Road runs west over level occasionally close to Lokchao river past Hasin, stockaded village at 15 miles, through forest to Tammu a long street 400 yards long, to barracks for 600 men. Boat ferry over Lokchao river in the rainy season. Temporary bridge during the dry. Good water for all purposes.

No. 23.

From TAMMU (Kubo Valley) to KALÉMYO.

BY MAJOR C. R. MACGREGOR, DECEMBER 1887 AND JANUARY 1888, AND MAJOR HOWLETT, 2ND BURMA BATTALION, 1891.

Authorities.		Number and Names of Stages, Rivers and Streams.	Distances.				Remarks.
Military.	Civil.		Intermediate.		Total.		
			M.	F.	M.	F.	
G.O.C. Myingyan District.	Commissioner, Central Division, and Deputy Commissioner, Upper Chindwin.	**1. Camp on Namunta river.** Lokchao and Yu rivers. Other smaller streams at frequent intervals throughout this route.	12	0	12	0	Tammu is a Shan village situated on the left bank of a stream which runs into the Lokchao river ¾ mile to north. Tammu is 66 miles (five days' journey for troops) to the south of Lángthôbál, and it is the frontier village between Burma and Manipur. Môré Thána, the frontier post of Manipur, is 3 miles to the north of Tammu. The military lines are at present situated close to the north of the village, but will probably be moved to a higher and decidedly better position on the left bank of the Tammu stream about 300 yards to north-east of present site. There is now (1891) accommodation for 200 men in the post. The path from Tammu, a fairly good and ridable one, sometimes through forest and sometimes through cultivation; several streams crossed, and two villages, Mámaw and Páutha, passed *en route*. Camp on high ground on right bank of the river, which is easily fordable in cold weather. Water and fuel abundant and good. Carts can now traverse the road as far as Chaungnenong 4 miles from Tammu.
		2. Auktaung ...	13	4	25	4	Path, as a rule, a bad one, principally through rice fields; the villages of Wituk 7 miles and Tunté 12 miles passed *en route*. The stockade is situated on the right bank of a stream; accommodation for 200 men. From Auktaung there are two routes to Kindát, one by land, the Minthami route, and the other by water *viâ* Maw and down the Yu and Chindwin rivers, the former branching off at Tunté, *see* Route No. 8.
		3. Kampát ...	13	0	38	4	After leaving Auktaung the path is for ⅜ mile through rice fields and then the usual jungle path for 3 miles; after crossing small streams Malu is reached at 3½ miles. At 6 miles reach Thinzin situated on the right bank of a stream over which there is a bridge; the village is on high ground, a good site for a stockade. The Chins used to annoy the villagers in the cold season, and some frontier police were located there. At 9¾ miles reach the Yéshin stream, a small stream fordable in the cold season, unfordable in the rains. On leaving the Yéshin stream the deserted village of Shwélé is passed, and at 12 miles the river Kampát, 3 feet deep, is crossed. One mile along the right bank of the Kampát reach the village of Kampát, where there is some accommodation. Kampát is a capital site for a stockade, situated as it is on high ground close to the river. Kampát is the most southern village of the Kubo valley. From Auktaung to Thinsin the path is a fairly good one, but between Thinzin and Kampát it is bad and swampy in places.

FROM TAMMU (KUBO VALLEY) TO KALÉMYO—*continued.*

Authorities. Military.	Authorities. Civil.	Number and Names of Stages, Rivers and Streams.	Distances. Intermediate. M. F.	Distances. Total. M. F.	Remarks.
G.O.C. Myingyán District.	Commissioner, Central Division, and Deputy Commissioner, Upper Chindwin.	**4. Camp on Pyaungbôk stream.** Lokchao and Yu rivers. Other smaller streams at frequent intervals throughout this route.	13 4	52 0	Path through jungle and over undulating forest country. The Nanpaulôn at 4 miles is a biggish stream, fordable except in rains, and the Nampanmun, rather a big stream, is crossed twice about half-way. The path from Kampát to Pyaungbôk is bad until the Pyaungbôk stream is reached. Way had to be cut through forest jungle overhead to allow laden elephants a free passage. Camp on the bank of a stream. On the left bank, which is the most elevated, there are a few old sheds which accommodate 50 men. This stream is said to be the boundary between the Kubo valley and the Sawbwa of Kalé's territory.
		5. Yázagyo (Shan village). Nayinsaya river (tributary of Myittha river).	13 0	65 0	From Pyaungbôk to Ingyizaung Bhil about 9 miles, the path is a fairly good one through heavy jungle. Six small streams *en route*. In 10th mile road begins to fall, the watershed between the Kubo and Kalé valleys being crossed. Camp on the right bank of the Nayinsaya river, 600 yards to south-west of village, which is situated on high ground. The village is surrounded by a good double stockade and has a very strong inner stockade which encloses the Sawbwa's house, a large wooden building capable of holding about 300 men. The Nayinsaya river is fordable at Yázagyo except in the rains. There are 10 villages (210 houses) in the Yázagyo district. Supplies plentiful.
		6. Kángyi (Shan village). Nayinsaya river (tributary of Myittha river).	8 0	73 0	Road more or less along the banks of Nayinsaya river, which is crossed five times between Yázagyo and Kángyi, none of the crossing deeper than 3 feet. A path to Kanhow Chin villages strikes off to the west near Kángyi. The villages of Kôntha, Paukkôn, Letpangôn, Kwémakôn, Intha, Hpyaukseik, Kyethpánet, Kôntha, and Sitha are passed in the order named. From Yázagyo to Indingyi 4 miles beyond Áhtéywa the road can be traversed by carts. Kángyi is a small village with stockade and water, but no supplies.
		7. Áhtéywa (Shan village). Nayinsaya river (tributary of Myittha river).	8 0	81 0	After leaving Kángyi the road is good and keeps along the left bank of the river and a little distance from it up the village of Imbaung situated near the junction of the Náttaga stream with the Nayinsaya river; ⅞ mile further on the river is crossed, and again at ⅞ mile. Camp on left bank of river. Three hundred yards from village a good open piece of dry ground; a guest-house outside the village. The path, as a rule, is a good one except for the difficult crossings. A path to the Siyin villages strikes off to the west near Áhtéywa. Áhtéywa is a large village and there is a stockade.

No. 23.

FROM TAMMU (KUBO VALLEY) TO KALÉMYO—*continued.*

Authorities.		Number and Names of Stages, Rivers and Streams.	Distances.		Remarks.
Military.	Civil.		Intermediate.	Total.	
			M. F.	M. F.	
G.O.C. Myingyán District.	Commissioner, Central Division, and Deputy Commissioner, Upper Chindwin.	**8. Kalémyo** ... Myittha river.	**11 0**	92 0	Leaving Áhtéywa the road continues to go south and strikes into the Kaléwa-Kalémyo mule track at the village of Indingyi, 4 miles from Áhtéywa. The distance from Indingyi to Kaléwa by road is 23 miles. Onwards to Kalémyo this road is a raised and bridged mule track. Kalémyo is the base for Fort White with supplies, buildings, &c., for 300 men. At Kalémyo, which is stockaded, the Sawbwa of Kalé has a residence. There are the ruins of a very large wall, perimeter 2,800 yards, 20 feet thick, 12 feet high, round the present village. At one time Kalémyo was the site of a large and flourishing town, but constant raiding of the hillmen have caused it to be almost deserted. The Siyins and the Sagyilains frequent Kalémyo in the cold season for purposes of trade. At present there is a cessation in the raiding.

No. 24.

From YAZÁGYO (Kalé Valley) to TUNZÁN (Chin Hills).

BY CAPT. H. B. VAUGHAN AND MR. P. E. DELA F. SHERMAN, MARCH 1892.

Authorities.		Number and Names of Stages, Rivers and Streams.	Distances.		Remarks.
Military.	Civil.		Intermediate.	Total.	
G.O.C. Myingyán District.	Commissioner, Central Division, and Deputy Commissioner, Upper Chindwin.	**1. Camp on Mônlôn river (1,500 feet).** Namin chaung and Mônlôn river.	**14 0**	14 0	Leave Yázagyo by one of the western entrances and proceed by a good track over level ground covered with forest trees. At 3¼ miles cross a small stream and cross two other small nullahs in the next ½ mile. At 9 miles the road enters between low hills and reaches the Mônlôn river, a fine mountain stream of clear water, with a rocky bed and quite impassable in the rains at 9½ miles. Full of mahseer fish. Banks steep and densely wooded, sometimes overhanging. The rest of the road is either in the bed of the stream or along its banks, whilst incessant crossings have to be made from side to side. Time 7½ hours. Camp in dense jungle on the left bank of the stream. Bamboos and wild plantains plentiful. Elevation 1,500 feet.
		2. Lôpa (2,000 feet).	**7 0**	21 0	Path up the bed of the river, stepping from rock to rock or wading in water knee-deep, often deeper. At 3 miles pass a waterfall about 60 feet high, where a stream empties itself from the right bank into the river. At 6 miles leave the river, crossing over to its right bank, and ascend up through some Chin clearing. Then up a steep ascent through jungle. Time 4½ hours. Lôpa is a village of about 20 houses, situated on a steep hill side below some high spurs of the Lítha range and 500 feet above the river bed. The inhabitants are leaving for a clearing called Paidin close to Haitsi. The village is stockaded and has a ditch outside. Elevation 2,000 feet.

FROM YÁZAGYO (KALÉ-VALLEY) TO TUNZÁN (CHIN HILLS)—*continued.*

Authorities. Military.	Authorities. Civil.	Number and Names of Stages, Rivers and Streams.	Distances. Intermediate. M.	F.	Total. M.	F.	Remarks.
G.O.C. Myingyán District.	Commr., Cenl. Divn., &c., Upper Chindwin.	**3. Camp on Karmzán stream.** Hwelhaum and Karmzán streams.	**10**	**0**	31	0	From here to Tunzán is said to be 21 miles. Water very scarce. Road ascends and crosses over the Lítha range. A Chin halting place. Water plentiful.
	Political Officer, Chin Hills.	**4. Tunzán (3,700 feet).**	**11**	**0**	42	0	Road passes through the village of Fie-tu at 7 miles; then up a steep ascent and along over an easy downward slope for 3 miles; then over a hill and down to Tunzán, the chief town of the Kanhao tribe; 116 houses. Elevation 3,700 feet. There is apparently an alternative route to the above in its first two stages. The road is said to be very bad, up and down over steep hills, and, as it makes the distance to Lopa 35 instead of 21 miles, there is apparently no object in using it except for the purpose of visiting Haitsi village which is 19 miles from Yázagyo. The stages are as follows:—

		MILES.	MILES.
1. Camp	... ...	9	9
2. Haitsi	... ...	10	19
3. Lôpa	... ...	16	35

The Namin chaung and Mônlôn river are touched in the third march; report does not say whether crossed or not. Captain Vaughan and Mr. Sherman are also the authority for this alternative.

No. 25.

From YÉ-U to KINDÁT.

BY LIEUT. T. F. B. RENNY-TAILYOUR, R.E., 24TH FEBRUARY TO 14TH MARCH 1888.

Military	Civil	Stages	Intermediate M.	F.	Total	Remarks
G.O.C. Myingyán District.	Commissioner, Central Division, and Deputy Commissioner, Yé-u.	**1. Ywathitgyi** ... Small nullah.	**13**	**4**	...	Direction north-west. The road from Yé-u passes through thin scrub jungle over cotton soil. At about 1 mile there is a small tank on the left of the road containing water all the year round. At 3 miles Bainga. This village has 35 houses; can supply about 20 carts; has two zayáts capable of putting up 30 men; drinking water from wells, and a tank for animals. Road from here, as before, with occasional paddy-fields. At ½ mile there is an inferior set of kyaungs for about 100 men (occupied at present by pôngyis). At 4¾ miles Phágôn; 40 houses; 30 carts, one set of kyaungs (occupied) for 150 men. Good water from three wells. Road as before, except that after here the soil is more or less sandy. At 6 miles Ywatha; seven houses. Water only from tanks. Road passes through paddy-fields. At 7¼ miles Htúmaung; 100 houses, 50 carts, one set of kyaungs (occupied) for 50 men. Water from two wells and three tanks, but only one of the latter contains water all the year round. Paddy plentiful, but grass scarce. Road as before. At ¼ mile a small nullah is crossed. At 9 miles Yatháywa; 75 houses (a group of four small villages); five sets of kyaungs (occupied) for about 400 men. Water from three wells and four tanks, but only two tanks contain water all the year round. This is the commencement of a palm-

FROM YÉ-U TO KINDÁT—*continued.*

Authorities. Military.	Authorities. Civil.	Number and Names of Stages, Rivers and Streams.	Distances. Intermediate.	Distances. Total.	Remarks.
G.O.C. Myingyán District.	Commissioner, Central Division, and Deputy Commissioner, Yé-u.	**1. Ywathitgyi**—*cont.*			tree district and there is a great jaggery trade. Road as before to Ywathitgyi at 13½ miles. This is the principal village of a group of 50, some of the smaller ones being passed 2 miles before the principal village is reached; 2,000 houses. Numerous sets of kyaungs (occupied) in the sites close round the principal village; 500 men could be put up. Water (from wells) and paddy are plentiful, but grass rather scarce. The principal trade is in jaggery.
		2. Môndaingyin. Small nullah.	M. F. **10 4**	M. F. 24 0	Direction north-west. Road as before across paddy-fields. At ¾ mile Indaw; 35 houses, 10 carts. Water from four wells. Road as before. Palm trees become scarcer. At 1 mile Einye; 20 houses, five carts. Water from two wells. Road as before. At 1¼ miles Inna; 10 houses, five carts. Water from five wells. One small set of kyaungs (occupied) for 50 men. Road as before. At 2½ miles Miyégu. This village is 300 yards to the left of the road; 20 houses, four carts. Water from six wells. The road here crosses a small nullah and runs for 1 mile as before, then through scrub jungle. At 4½ miles Miyégu kyaung, a good set of kyaungs (occupied) for 150 men. One well. Road as before. At 6 miles Kadúma; 40 houses, 25 carts. Three wells and one tank, which occasionally dries up. One set of kyaungs (occupied) for 150 men with one well. Road through alternate patches of paddy-fields and *in* and varnish tree jungle. At 7 miles Ainyayé; five houses, one well; grass more plentiful. Road as before. At 8½ miles Aingyéo; 35 houses, 10 carts, two wells. Half-a-mile beyond there is one set of kyaungs (occupied) for 150 men, with one tank. Road as before. At 9½ miles Putein, 20 houses, seven carts, and one well. Road as before. At ½ mile there is a tank for animals on right of road, apt to dry up during hot season. At 10½ miles reach Môndaingyin; 30 houses, 10 carts. One set of kyaungs (at present military police post) for 100 men. Water only from one tank, which is apt to dry up in an exceptionally hot season. Grass plentiful and paddy moderately so. Villagers make black gum and wash for gold in the nullahs after heavy rain. The cart road from Yé-u is very good, but after this it is only fairly good owing to there not being much traffic, and the beds of all the chaungs are heavy sand.
		3. Yamôntaung. Two small nullahs.	**16 2**	40 2	Road now runs through fairly open *in* and other tree jungle. The road is generally good for carts, with some difficult descents into dry nullahs. At 2 miles a deserted village is passed. Afterwards the jungle gets thicker until at 3 miles the right bank of the Sipadôn chaung is reached. This chaung is 300 to 400 yards wide here, flows into the Mu river, but only has water in it for a few hours after rain, when it is often impassable. Its banks are low, covered with fairly thick "*in*" and other tree jungle. The bed is heavy sand. The road runs up the right bank until 4¾ miles, where it crosses the chaung, but recrosses at 6½ miles to the right bank. At 8½ miles Paga, a deserted village, about 200 yards to the right of the road. One set of kyaungs (deserted by pôngyis) for 150 men, with one old well. Road as before. At 2¼ miles it crosses to the left bank of the chaung. At about 4 miles two small nullahs are crossed, and at 4¾ miles

FROM YÉ-U TO KINDÁT—*continued.*

Authorities. Military.	Authorities. Civil.	Number and Names of Stages, Rivers and Streams.	Distances. Intermediate. M.	Distances. Intermediate. F.	Distances. Total. M.	Distances. Total. F.	Remarks.
G.O.C. Myingyán District.	Commissioner, Central Division, and Deputy Commissioner, Yé-u.	**3. Yamôntaung** —*cont.*					the road returns to the right bank of the chaung. At 15⅜ miles Yamôntaung kyaung, a set of kyaungs (deserted) in very fair condition, accommodation for 150 men. About 200 yards from the right bank of the Sipadôn chaung, one old well; but plenty of good water can be obtained from streams which are here found all the year round in the bed of the chaung. The alternative road to Pyingyaing branches off here. The road now runs through paddy-fields and crosses the chaung. On the left bank of the Sipadôn chaung 100 houses, 30 carts. Water from the streams in the chaung. Plenty of grass and a fair supply of paddy. The villagers grow paddy in the hot weather by irrigating from the streams. They also make black gum and wash for gold in the bed of the chaungs after heavy rain. The country up to here is flat, but beyond this it is more or less hilly.
		4. Kankyi and Sénán. Satha, Laháthakyauk, and Labákataing chaungs. Two small nullahs. Aing and Sénán chaungs.	11	6	52	0	Immediately after Yamôntaung the road crosses the Satha chaung, which runs into the Sipadôn chaung just above Yamôndaung. The road now passes through fairly open "*in*" and other tree jungle, with patches of paddy-fields and clearings every here and there. At ¾ mile the Satha chaungis again crossed; five houses. Water from one tank. At 1 mile Twédi. Road as before, soon crosses the Laháthakyauk and the Lahákataing chaungs and gets on to slightly higher ground and runs along a ridge, crossing two small nullahs at 3 miles. At 4 miles the road descends into lower country and the jungle gets thicker with bamboo amongst it. The road at 4¾ miles strikes the right bank of the Aing chaung and runs down its valley, principally along the bed. At 6½ miles Aing, a deserted village on right bank, with one tank and a lake behind it. Road as before. At 8 miles Gádaké kyaung, a deserted set of kyaungs on right bank for 150 men; has one tank near, which is apt to dry up in the hot season. Road as before. At 9½ miles Gádaké, a group of three villages on the left bank of the chaung; 23 houses. Water from deep wells. Plenty of grass and a moderate supply of paddy. Road as before. At 11½ miles Yankintaung on right bank, 13 houses; three carts. Water from shallow wells in chaung. Road now leaves the Aing chaung and at ¼ mile crosses the Sénán chaung. The Aing chaung runs into the left bank of the Sénán chaung ¼ mile below and opposite Sénán village. The Sénán chaung runs into the Mu river. At 11¾ miles reaches Kánkyi, left bank of Sénán chaung; three houses, one very good set of kyaungs (occupied) for 250 men. Plenty of water from one deep well and from shallow wells in bed of chaung. Plenty of grass and a moderate supply of paddy. There is an alternative route from Yé-u to Kánkyi, *see* Alternative I below.
		5. Pyingyaing ... Kyaunnán, Ngaindôn, and Mawkadaw chaungs.	17	2	69	2	The road now runs up the valley of the Sénán chaung, which soon begins to have streams of water running along its bed. The banks are covered with fairly open bamboo and small tree jungle. There are paddy-fields every here and there; the road runs mostly along the bed of the chaung. At 2¾ miles the Kyaunnán chaung runs into the left bank of the Sénán. At 3½ miles Letpángaing, on the

FROM YÉ-U TO KINDÁT—*continued.*

Authorities. Military.	Authorities. Civil.	Number and Names of Stages, Rivers and Streams.	Distances. Intermediate.	Distances. Total.	Remarks.
G.O.C. Myingyán District.	Commr., Central Divn., and Deputy Commr., Yé-u.	**5. Pyingyaing**—*cont.*			right bank of the Sénán; two houses, one cart. Water from running stream in the chaung. Road as before. At 6½ miles Wain chaung, on the left bank; two houses, one cart. Water from running stream in chaung. Road as before. Just above Wain chaung the Ngaindôn chaung runs into the Sénán chaung. At 4½ miles the source of the Sénán chaung is reached and the road crosses over the Yéwédaung hill. The last 100 yards up is very steep, and loaded carts have to be assisted up. The road now runs through fairly thick bamboo and "*in*" jungle, and at 5 miles strikes the Mawkadaw chaung, down whose valley the road now runs occasionally along the bed. At 14 miles Thinwinbin, on the right bank; 25 houses, 10 carts. Water from one well only (in the bed of the chaung); one zayát on opposite bank of chaung for 10 men. Road as before. At 17¼ miles reach Pyingyaing on the left bank of chaung; 20 houses, 10 carts, two small sets of kyaungs (occupied) for 120 men. Water from two deep wells only (in the bed of the chaung), barely sufficient for a column with 100 animals. Paddy in moderate quantities and plenty of grass. The villagers grow paddy, make linseed-oil and black gum. The following is an alternative route traversed by Capt. Poynder from Yamôntaung kyaung to Pyingyaing; it is 11½ miles shorter. The road follows the Sipadôn chaung to its source, 11 miles, along a sandy bed, very heavy for men and animals. At the summit the six mules were unloaded and their loads carried for 1 mile by coolies taken out for the purpose; but this portion could soon be made passable by a working party of 50 men with entrenching tools and axes preceding the baggage column by some three or four hours. The water parting is here very narrow, and the route at once descends the Kulathé chaung ½ mile above Pyingyaing. This route throughout lies between rugged and steep hills, clothed with dense jungle, and, although it could be made practicable for animals at all seasons except after heavy rains, it is doubtful whether carts could ever travel by it. From Waingyo to Pyingyaing there is no water at this season for 16 miles. Total distance 17¼ miles.
	Commissioner, Central Division, and Deputy Commissioner, Upper Chindwin.	**6. Pékyundaw** ...	M. F. **10 6**	M. F. 80 0	Road as before to Zalôma at 4 miles. On left bank of the chaung 10 houses, three carts. Water from one deep well in chaung. One set of kyaungs (occupied) for 100 men. Road as before. At 6 miles Samyin on left bank of chaung; 25 houses, three carts. Water has to be obtained from Samyinywadaw. One set of kyaungs (occupied) for 75 men. Road as before. At 6½ miles Samyinywadaw on right bank of chaung; six houses, one cart. Water from one deep well in chaung. Road as before. At 10¾ miles reach Pékyundaw on left bank of chaung; 20 houses, four carts. One set of kyaungs (occupied) for 100 men. Water from a deep well in chaung and from a running stream on opposite bank, which, however, dries up for about two months each year. Plenty of grass, but little paddy.

FROM YÉ-U TO KINDÁT—*continued.*

Authorities. Military.	Authorities. Civil.	Number and Names of Stages, Rivers and Streams.	Distances. Intermediate. M. F.	Distances. Total. M. F.	Remarks.
G.O.C. Myingyán District.	Commissioner, Central Division, and Deputy Commissioner, Upper Chindwin.	**7. Paga** ... Taungnyi or Kôngyi, Niyánidet, and Myinbiyé chaung; one small stream; San chaung.	**15 0**	95 0	Road as before. At about 2 miles the Taungnyi or Kôngyi chaung runs into the right bank of the Mawkadaw chaung. At this spot there is water running down the Mawkadaw chaung all the year round. The road now runs up the valley of the Taungnyi or Kôngyi chaung, principally along the bed; the banks are covered with open "*in*" jungle. At $5\frac{1}{2}$ miles the road turns up the Niyánidet chaung, which runs into the right bank of the Taungnyi chaung. There has been no water in the chaung since its junction with the Mawkadaw chaung. At 6 miles the Myinbiyé chaung runs into the left bank of the Niyánidet chaung, but the road still runs up the latter. At $8\frac{1}{4}$ miles the source of the chaung and the crest of the hills are reached. The last 50 feet is very steep and only just passable for loaded carts with help. At $8\frac{1}{2}$ miles Kaunbyin, a deserted village. The road now runs on highish ground and through a very fine "*in*" jungle. At 1 mile a small stream is crossed, which has water in it all the year round. At $4\frac{1}{2}$ miles the road commences a gradual descent, at the bottom of which the San chaung is crossed. From Kaunbyin carts have not passed for two years, but with very slight labour the road could be made good for them. At 15 miles Paga, 30 houses, three carts, one zayát for 10 men. Water for drinking in shallow wells in the bed of the chaung, and for animals in pools in the paddy-fields near the village. The supply of water and grass is very fairly plentiful all the year round. Paddy can be obtained in moderate quantities.
		8. Kanyi ... Myinlán chaung; one small stream; Balet and Miyé chaungs.	**15 4**	110 4	After leaving Paga the road soon enters large tree jungle with fairly thick undergrowth and rises on to high ground, along which it runs until at $6\frac{1}{2}$ miles it descends into the Myinlán chaung, whose valley it then runs down. The descent into the chaung is rather steep and for about $\frac{1}{2}$ mile is bad going for loaded animals. There is no cart road from Paga to Tagôndain (Capt. Poynder). It would be an extremely difficult line for a cart road, but one could doubtless be made with some expense. At $13\frac{1}{2}$ miles Tagôndain, on the right bank of the chaung; seven houses. Water is obtained from a running stream in the chaung which commences to run opposite the village, and is always a fair-sized stream. The road is now fit for carts and continues down the valley of the Myinlán chaung, the bank being now principally covered with paddy-fields and small patches of bamboo jungle here and there. Just below Tagôndain a small stream runs into the right bank of the chaung. At 14 miles Ywadaw, on the left bank of the chaung; six houses. Water from running stream in the Myinlán chaung, which below here is called the Balet chaung. Road as before. At $1\frac{1}{2}$ miles reach Kanyi, about $\frac{1}{4}$ mile from right bank of the Balet chaung; 25 houses, one cart, two zayáts for 18 men. Water plentiful, obtained all the year round from streams in the Miyé chaung, which flows past Kanyi and into the Balet chaung a little below it. Paddy and grass fairly plentiful.

FROM YÉ-U TO KINDÁT—*continued.*

Authorities.		Number and Names of Stages, Rivers and Streams.	Distances.		Remarks.
Military.	Civil.		Intermediate.	Total.	
			M. F.	M. F.	
G.O.C. Myingyán District.	Commissioner, Central Division, and Deputy Commissioner, Upper Chindwin.	**9. Hédaung** ... Shwéta, Indain, Satha, Masein, and Hédaung chaungs.	13 4	124 0	Road as before on right bank of Balet chaung. At $1\frac{3}{4}$ miles Ywashé; six houses, one zayát for eight men. Road as before. At 3 miles Tangan on left bank; 19 houses. Road as before. At 4 miles Kwéda, on right bank, 30 houses. One good set of kyaungs (occupied) for 100 men. The road leaves the Balet chaung just above Kwéda and runs through paddy-fields, with here and there patches of bamboo jungle. At 1 mile it strikes, and for about $\frac{1}{2}$ mile runs down, the Shwéta chaung. At 6 miles Indain; 30 houses, 13 carts, one set of kyaungs (occupied) for 120 men. Water from Indain chaung, which is crossed by the road immediately beyond the village. Road as before. At $6\frac{1}{2}$ miles Nanbin; 25 houses, one set of thatched kyaungs (occupied) for 75 men. Water from Indain chaung. Road as before. At $1\frac{1}{2}$ miles it strikes and runs down the Satha chaung, a small chaung with running water. At 9 miles Lanyédaw, on left bank of Satha chaung, two houses. Water from stream in the chaung. At 200 yards below Lanyédaw the Satha flows into the Masein chaung, which is a fairly large one and always has plenty of water running in it. The road follows down the Masein valley, which passes between high banks at this part. At $9\frac{3}{4}$ miles Pyinlika, on the right bank of the chaung; 15 houses, three carts, one set of kyaungs (unoccupied) for 25 men. Road runs along right bank and then through a small gorge. At $10\frac{1}{4}$ miles Kanyinbin, on the right bank of the chaung; five houses. The road leaves the Masein chaung just above Kanyinbin and runs across paddy-fields. It strikes and runs up the Hédaung chaung; this chaung always has water running in it here. At $11\frac{3}{4}$ miles Nyaungbintha, on the right bank; seven houses. Road as before through paddy-fields and up the Hédaung chaung. At $12\frac{1}{4}$ miles Kythádaw (part of the village on each side of the chaung); 12 houses, six carts. Road as before. At $13\frac{1}{2}$ miles reach Hédaung (part of the village on each side of the chaung); 80 houses, 40 carts, two sets of kyaungs on the right bank (occupied) for 250 men. Plenty of grass and paddy. Water from wells and running streams. Road as before.
		10. Nanthi ... Yéwé, Kôko, Ma-o, Ôpo, and Pôndôn chaungs.	13 4	137 4	At $\frac{1}{2}$ mile Yakadaw, on left bank of chaung; 30 houses, 10 carts. Road as before. At 1 mile Bamwégôn, on both sides of Hédaung chaung, which above here is called Yéwé chaung; eight houses, one zayát for 15 men. There is a cart road from Kanyi to Bamwégôn, but none exists beyond. The road now runs up the bed of the chaung, which is rather stony, and the banks are covered with bamboo jungle. At $2\frac{1}{2}$ miles the top of the chaung is reached and the road crosses over the ridge and runs down the bed of the Kôko chaung. At $3\frac{1}{2}$ miles the Kôko chaung runs into the Ma-o chaung, which chaung the road then runs down. At $5\frac{1}{2}$ miles Thamadaw, on left bank of Ma-o chaung; three houses. Water from running stream in chaung. Road as before. At $7\frac{3}{4}$ miles Tántabin, on left bank of Ma-o; three houses. Just below Tántabin the Ôpo chaung runs into the Ma-o and the road then turns up the Ôpo. At $8\frac{1}{4}$ miles Ôpo, on right bank of Ôpo chaung; five houses, one zayát for 10 men. Water from running stream in Ôpo chaung. Road now up bed of Ôpo. At 1 mile it leaves the Ôpo and passes over

FROM YÉ-U TO KINDÁT—*continued.*

Authorities. Military.	Authorities. Civil.	Number and Names of Stages, Rivers and Streams.	Distances. Intermediate.	Distances. Total.	Remarks.
G.O.C. Myingyán District.	Commissioner, Central Division, and Deputy Commissioner, Upper Chindwin.	**10. Nanthi**—*cont.*			some difficult hilly ground and just passable for loaded animals. At 3¼ miles the road enters and runs down the valley of the Pôndôn chaung. After 4½ miles it goes across paddy-fields. At 13¼ miles reach Nanthi, a set of kyaungs (occupied) on a low hill, with an old military police post (unoccupied) close to it. Altogether enough for 250 men. Plenty of water all the year round from a tank and streams. Plentiful supply of paddy and grass can be obtained from the village of Nanthi (30 houses and five carts), about ¾ mile to the east of Tawya kyaung.
		11. Kindát ... Kôdaung, Myingwin, and Aw chaungs. Chindwin river.	M. F. **14 4**	M. F. 152 0	The road now runs alternately through patches of paddy and jungle. At 1 mile Nandaintha; seven houses. Water from the Kôdaung chaung, which is crossed by the road ¼ mile beyond. This is a large chaung with plenty of water running all the year round. The Pôngôn chaung flows into it about ½ mile above the crossing. Road now across paddy-fields. At 2¼ miles Hmábein; 20 houses, three carts, one set of kyaungs (occupied) for 150 men. Water from Kôdaung chaung. Road as before. At 3 miles Dôndôn; 25 houses, zayáts for 25 men. Water from small running stream in the Myingwin chaung, which is crossed just beyond the village. Road runs through a few paddy-fields and then through fairly open bamboo jungle. At 1¾ miles the road enters and runs up bed of Myingwin chaung, the top of which is reached at 2 miles. The road now passes over difficult and hilly ground, only just passable for loaded animals. At 7 miles the road descends rapidly and at 7½ crosses the Aw chaung. The road now passes over paddy-fields. At 10¾ miles Nwáko; seven houses. Water from a running stream in Aw chaung. Road as before until at 1 mile the Chindwin river is reached, when the road runs up the left bank through long grass. At 13¼ miles Mawlígalé; 30 houses. Water from Chindwin. Road runs up left bank. At 14½ miles reach Kindát, a military post. A column of about 75 men, two elephants, and 100 mules and ponies was taken from Yé-u and extra 30 followers and 80 mules picked up at Kindát and taken back to Mawkadaw. The road was very good for baggage animals except at the three places mentioned, and on no day did the baggage animals average less than 2½ miles an hour. Water plentiful throughout the route. After first stage grass was very plentiful, and in 2, 3 and 4 stages baskets of paddy could be supplied at each halt. Five or six carts were taken from Yé-u to Pékyundaw. Travelled very fairly well. The villagers declare that the road is open all the year round, except for a few days at a time, after very heavy rain.

ALTERNATIVE I.

FROM YÉ-U TO KÁNKYI (STAGE 4).

BY LIEUT. T. F. B. RENNY-TAILYOUR, R.E., 24TH FEBRUARY TO 14TH MARCH 1888.

G.O.C. Myingyán District.	Commr., C. Div., and Dy. Commr., Yé-u.	**1. Nwabeitgyi (Nabekgyi).**	**17 6**	17 6	Fairly good road. Soil at first cotton, afterwards sandy. A police post. Fairly good road. *See* Route No. 18.

FROM YÉ-U TO KINDÁT—*continued.*

ALTERNATIVE I—*continued.*

Authorities. Military.	Authorities. Civil.	Number and Names of Stages, Rivers and Streams.	Distances. Inter-mediate. M.	Distances. Inter-mediate. F.	Distances. Total. M.	Distances. Total. F.	Remarks.
G.O.C. Myingyán District.	Commissioner, Central Division, and Deputy Commissioner, Yé-u.	**2. Kabaungya** ... Sénán chaung.	**6**	**4**	24	0	Sixty-five houses, 10 to 12 carts, one set of kyaungs for 150 men. Paddy and grass plentiful. Water obtained all the year round from two tanks—one for men and one for animals.
		3. Chaungzôn ...	**11**	**0**	35	0	Fairly good road to Chaungzôn. On Sénán chaung 16 houses, two or three carts, two sets of kyaungs for 150 men. Water from the chaung (shallow wells). Plenty of paddy and grass.
		4. Kánkyi ...	**11**	**0**	46	0	Fairly good road, except for about 2 miles, which is hilly and rather bad for carts. At 10¾ miles Sénán on left bank of chaung ; 14 houses. Water from shallow wells in chaung. Road across paddy-fields. The road is said to be good for baggage animals and on the whole very fair for carts. It is open all the year round, except perhaps for a few days at a time after exceptionally heavy rain. From this report it will be seen that a cart road could be made from Yé-u to Kindát (total distance 152 miles, or if the route reported by the Shwéhmu of Sénán be correct, total distance 146 miles); also that pack animals can reach Kindát at 140¼ miles by using the direct path from Yamôntaung to Pyingyaing traversed by Capt. Poynder.

ALTERNATIVE II.

FROM PYINGYAING (STAGE 5) TO PAGA (STAGE 7).

BY LIEUT. T. F. B. RENNY-TAILYOUR, R.E., 24TH FEBRUARY TO 14TH MARCH 1888.

Authorities. Military.	Authorities. Civil.	Number and Names of Stages, Rivers and Streams.	Distances. Inter-mediate. M.	Distances. Inter-mediate. F.	Distances. Total. M.	Distances. Total. F.	Remarks.
G.O.C. Myingyán District.	Commissioner, Central Division, and Deputy Commissioner, Upper Chindwin.	**1. Kyundaw** ...	**14**	**0**	14	0	Road on to Kyundaw, 14 miles, principally along the Mawkadaw chaung, the bed being sandy and heavy. Pass Samyin at 7 miles. Water from one well at some distance and insufficient for a party of 40 men and 80 animals. Last 1½ miles through "*in*" tree jungle. Pass Pékyundaw at 10½ miles, passing through "*in*" jungle for 1½ miles before. Road on good for carts to Kyundaw, a prosperous village with good accommodation and plentiful supply of good water. (Mawkadaw lies 5¼ miles south of Kyundaw road along the valley of the chaung. Water is about 40 yards wide and 1 foot deep (February), and is crossed by road three times. It is nearly always passable for carts.) A route from Samyin to Kindát by the Dengwa chaung to Kôngyi, traversed by a native surveyor, was reported bad with very little water. At Pékyundaw a road was reported to Paga, the next stage, 13¾ miles, but accommodation and water-supply at Kyundaw is much better than at Pékyundaw and therefore more suitable for a column of more than 50 men and animals.

FROM YÉ-U TO KINDÁT—*continued.*

ALTERNATIVE II—*continued.*

Authorities. Military.	Authorities. Civil.	Number and Names of Stages, Rivers and Streams.	Distances. Intermediate.	Distances. Total.	Remarks.
G.O.C. Myingyán District.	Commissioner, Central Division, and Deputy Commr., Upper Chindwin.	**2. Paga**	M. F. **13 6**	M. F. 27 6	Road on from Kyundaw to Paga, 13¾ miles, following the Kôngyi chaung until its junction with the Niyánidet chaung, which it follows to its source. At 7 miles a steep ascent on to a ridge is reached, at present impracticable for carts for about 100 yards. It could be improved. On this ridge an excellent site for a camp exists in an open forest of "*in*" trees near the deserted village of Kaumbyo. There is a constant stream of water about 1 mile on. From this stream the road gradually ascends through fine open "*in*" tree jungle for some 3 miles, passing along a narrow ridge from which it gradually descends to Paga.

BRANCH I.

FROM PÉKYUNDAW (STAGE 6) TO MAWKADAW (CHINDWIN RIVER).

BY LIEUT. T. F. B. RENNY-TAILYOUR, R.E., MARCH 1888.

Military	Civil	Stages	Intermediate	Total	Remarks
G.O.C. Myingyán District.	Commissioner, Central Division, and Deputy Commissioner, Upper Chindwin.	**1. Mawkadaw** ...	**8 4**	8 4	Road down the Mawkadaw chaung valley. Tabawma at 2½ miles on the left bank of the chaung; 18 houses, five carts. Water plenty from running streams in chaung. From here to the Chindwin river the chaung has water running all the year round. Road on as before. Kyundaw at 3¼ miles on the left bank; 14 houses, three carts, one set of kyaungs (occupied) for 150 men. Water from two wells and from streams in chaung. The villagers cultivate cocoanut and plam trees, paddy, and also make black gum. Road on as before down the valley, which is covered with paddy-fields cultivated during the hot season with water from the chaung. There are numerous villages along the side of the valley. Reach Mawkadaw at 8½ miles on the left bank of the Chindwin just above where the Mawkadaw chaung runs in; 60 houses, 20 carts, four sets of kyaungs (occupied) for 500 men. Water from one well and from river. Small military police post. Plenty of paddy and grass. The road from Yé-u to Mawkadaw is very good for elephants and baggage animals; for carts very good up to Môndaingyin, and fairly good beyond. The road is always passable, except for a few days at a time after particularly heavy rain.

BRANCH II.

FROM PAGA (STAGE 7) TO THAMBAUK (ON THE CHINDWIN RIVER).

I. B. COMPILATION, NOVEMBER 1888.

Military	Civil	Stages	Intermediate	Total	Remarks
G.O.C. Myingyán District.	Commr., C. Divn., and Dy. Commr., Upper Chindwin.	**1. Kyundaw** ...	**13 6**	13 6	Road on to Kyundaw, 13¾ miles, at first ascends to a narrow gravel ridge, from which it descends for 3 miles through fine open "*in*" tree jungle, crosses a stream with water in February, then crosses a ridge with open forest of "*in*" trees very suitable for a

FROM YÉ-U TO KINDÁT—*continued.*

BRANCH II—*continued.*

Authorities. Military.	Authorities. Civil.	Number and Names of Stages, Rivers and Streams.	Distances. Intermediate. M.	F.	Total. M.	F.	Remarks.
G.O.C. Myingyán District.	Commissioner, Central Division, and Deputy Commissioner, Upper Chindwin.	**1. Kyundaw**—*cont.*					camp. At $6\frac{3}{4}$ miles the road descends a steep incline at present unfit for carts, but which could easily be improved, thence along the Niyánidet, and after the Kôngyi chaung very trying through deep sand to Kyundaw, at $13\frac{3}{4}$ miles, a prosperous village with plenty of good accommodation in kyaungs and good water. Mawkadaw lies $5\frac{1}{4}$ miles south of Kyundaw along the Mawkadaw chaung.
		2. Thambauk ...	**16**	**0**	29	6	Road on to Thambauk, 16 miles, very bad; a mere jungle track up nullahs and crossing five distinct ranges of hills by difficult and steep paths; loose gravel or sand-stone on these hills. A cart road would be very difficult over this track. Another track, also difficult, is reported to exist, but, as it had been blocked by the villagers to stop dacoits, it was not attempted. The distance would be about 12 miles and might afford greater facilities for a cart track, but it is impassable, as the same nullahs and hills would have to be crossed. The village of Thambauk is at present small and poor owing to dacoities. It has probably seen better days and would improve under protection of a police post.

BRANCH III.

FROM KANYINBIN (BETWEEN STAGES 8 AND 9) TO MASEIN (CHINDWIN RIVER).

BY LIEUT. T. F. B. RENNY-TAILYOUR, R.E., MARCH 1888.

Military.	Civil.	Stage	Int. M.	F.	Total M.	F.	Remarks
G.O.C. Myingyán District.	Commissioner, Central Division, and Deputy Commissioner, Upper Chindwin.	**1. Masein** ...	**3**	**0**	3	0	Road down the Masein chaung, $\frac{1}{4}$ mile to Sagyi, situated on both banks of the chaung; 15 houses, 10 carts, with one set of kyaungs (occupied) on left bank for 150 men. One well. Road on across paddy-fields to Taungyama, at $1\frac{1}{2}$ miles, on the left bank of the chaung; 14 houses, one set of kyaungs (occupied) for 200 men. Road as before down the chaung and through a small gorge to Kyaukséni, at $1\frac{3}{4}$ miles, on left bank of chaung; seven houses. Road as before. At $2\frac{1}{8}$ miles Painbin on left bank of chaung; four houses, two zayáts for 15 men, one well. Road on through paddy-fields to Masein, at 3 miles, on the left bank of the Chindwin river, just below where the Masein chaung flows in; 400 to 500 houses, 30 to 40 carts, four sets of kyaungs for over 500 men, five wells. Good supply of paddy and grass. Road is practicable for carts throughout the year.

BRANCH IV.

FROM KWÉDA (BETWEEN STAGES 8 AND 9) TO SINGAUNG (CHINDWIN RIVER) *viâ* BALETMYO.

BY LIEUT. T. F. B. RENNY-TAILYOUR, R.E., FROM NATIVE INFORMATION, MARCH 1888.

Military.	Civil.	Stage	Int. M.	F.	Total M.	F.	Remarks
G.O.C. Myingyán District.	Commr., Central Divn., and Dy. Commr., Upper Chindwin.	**1. Singaung** ...	**4**	**0**	4	0	Road $1\frac{1}{2}$ miles to Baletmyo on the left bank of the Chindwin; 30 houses, three carts. Road on $2\frac{1}{2}$ miles along the left bank of the Chindwin river to Singaung at 4 miles just above where the Balet chaung flows in; 50 houses. There is also a cart road from Kanyi to Singaung throughout the year down the Balet chaung.

PART III.

ROUTES IN THE CHIN HILLS DIVISION.

PART III.

ROUTES IN THE CHIN HILLS DIVISION.

No. 1.

From FORT WHITE (New) to HÁKA viâ FALÁM (TÁSHÔN YWAMA).

BY LIEUT. I. T. BROOKING, 21ST MADRAS PIONEERS, APRIL 1893.

Authorities. Military.	Authorities. Civil.	Number and Names of Stages, Rivers and Streams.	Distances. Intermediate. M. F.	Distances. Total. M. F.	Remarks.
G.O.C. Myingyân District.	Political Officer, Chin Hills.	**1. Táshôn camp, No. 1.**	9 6	9 6	From Fort White (New) the road runs for 1½ miles along the Fort White-Kalémyo road and at that point branches off in a south-east by east direction; to the point it leaves the Kalémyo road the road falls, but from there it rises again to about the level of Fort White. At about 2 miles the direction changes to almost due south; it is fairly level and, with the exception of one or two small bits of grass land, is principally through dense jungle till at 8 miles it runs through open grass land and fir trees for about a mile. At 9 miles it again enters thick jungle. At 9¾ miles No. 1 Táshôn camp is reached. Up to this point from Fort White no water is passed on the road. Just before reaching No. 1 camp you pass the cross-roads running east over the hill to Môntôk (Branch No. I below) and west along the ridge to Sagyilaing and Mwébingyi. There is a sign post here pointing out the various roads. No. 1 Táshôn camp is about 150 feet down the hill; some huts and leantos of leaves and grass were built here in March by the 21st Pioneers. The water-supply is sufficient in the hot weather for 200 men and could be improved by digging and opening up the spring; it is 100 feet further down the khud, and there is a rough path down to it.
		2. Táshôn camp, No. 2. Small mountain stream is crossed.	8 0	17 6	From No. 1 camp the road, principally through jungle, continues rising and falling in a southerly direction. At 1½ miles crosses a small mountain stream; there is plenty of water here all the year round. At 3¾ miles Bamboo camp is reached. Bamboo camp is situated in dense jungle on a piece of land between two nullahs with small streams in them. There are some grass and bamboo shelters here for about 150 men, built by the pioneers. There is plenty of fuel, and water enough for a regiment all the year round. From Bamboo camp the road rises and falls slightly and is through jungle. At 8 miles path passes below No. 2 Táshôn camp. The water is some little distance down the khud.

No. 1.

FROM FORT WHITE (NEW) TO HÁKA *viâ* FALÁM (TÁSHÔN YWAMA)—*continued.*

Authorities.		Number and Names of Stages, Rivers and Streams.	Distances.				Remarks.
Military.	Civil.		Intermediate.		Total.		
			M.	F.	M.	F.	
G.O.C. Myingyán District.	Political Officer, Chin Hills.	**3. Pine Tree camp.**	9	2	27	0	From here the road, running through jungle interspersed with open grass land, still continues its southerly course and at 2¾ miles reaches a triple sign post showing the way to Fort White, Falám and No. 3 Táshôn camp. The latter is situated on a grassy spot on the reverse slope of the hill. To get to it go up over the hill by a path close to the sign post and then down a rough zigzag path for 1,000 yards. Water can be got from three different places quite close and is sufficient for 200 men in the dry weather. There is no village quite close here, but fowls, eggs and beans are obtainable from the villages around. Grass sheds built here in March 1893 by 21st Pioneers. From here the road, which is still only about 500 feet below Fort White, begins to descend and runs through open grass land and fir trees. The soil is firm. The air all along here is strongly impregnated with the scent of pine trees. At 6¾ miles the road runs through No. 4 Táshôn camp, which is situated in the bend of a small valley. Shelters were built in March 1893 by the 21st Pioneers of grass and capable of accommodating 150 men. The water is lower down the khud and was sufficient for the above number of men, but the supply could be increased by a little excavating and opening up of springs there. The road still runs through sandy firm soil and open fir tree country. Up to the 26th mile from Fort White, the road was made by the 4th Pioneers in 1892 and repaired in 1893 by the 21st Pioneers; from this point to Longbán the road was traced by an officer of the Public Works Department and made by the 21st Pioneers. At 9¼ miles Pine Tree camp is reached. Here there are also grass sheds similar to those at the last camp, which would give shelter to the same number of men (150). Water sufficient for 200 men is obtainable close by. Between the last camp and here one or two small streams are passed.
		4. Longbán camp. Two mountain streams.	7	0	34	0	From Pine Tree camp the road, running through open jungle and cultivation, still descends and by a series of zigzags goes down into the Kholai valley, which is about [illegible]000 feet below Fort White. In this valley the road passes by another Pioneer camp called "Kholai camp," where there are shelters for 150 men and plenty of fuel and water; about ½ mile from this camp is the Táshôn village of Kholai, 35 houses. Fowls, eggs and beans are obtainable here; also a few sweet potatoes and yams. From Kholai camp the road again ascends for about 600 feet to the top of a spur above the village of Kholai and then descends gradually through sparse jungle to the head of a large valley, where a mountain stream is crossed, and ¼ mile further on another mountain stream is crossed; the road here is through loose shaly soil and has been well revetted with timber, but is apt to slip after and during heavy rains. From this second stream the road, running through good firm soil and cultivation, rises to the top of another spur, which it rounds and brings the village of Longbán in sight. At 6¼ miles the road passes above the village of Longbán consisting of 7[illegible] houses; a large quantity of fowls and eggs are obtainable

FROM FORT WHITE (NEW) TO HÁKA *vâ* FALÁM (TÁSHÔN YWAMA)—*continued.*

Authorities.		Number and Names of Stages, Rivers and Streams.	Distances.		Remarks.
Military.	Civil.		Intermediate.	Total.	
G.O.C. Myingyán District.	Political Officer, Chin Hills.	**4. Longbán camp** —*cont.*			here, and a limited supply of yams, sweet potatoes, broad beans and plantains. There are orange trees in this village; also a fair number of mythun and goats; ¾ mile from this village and off the road is the Longbán camp consisting of three long grass huts and three smaller ones; accommodation enough for 150 men. There is a track leading to the camp from the road and a sign post showing where the track commences. The camp can be seen from the road above the village. There is plenty of water and fuel. From about Longbán village the road for ½ mile is a 4-foot one.
		5. Falám ... ... Longbán stream, Nankathé river and small mountain streams.	M. F. **8 4**	M. F. 42 4	From above Longbán the road is 4 feet wide for ½ a mile, it then is merely an improved Chin path through cultivation. At about ½ mile it passes through the village of Páté, of 50 houses, where apparently the road from Old Fort White joins in (*see* Route No. 2, Stage 4). Here also fowls, eggs and vegetables as above can be procured. At ¼ mile from Páté the road passes under a small village of 10 houses called Bwelté. The road, still an improved Chin track, continues falling, and at ¾ mile from Bwelté crosses a stream in a small nullah. From here the road runs along a spur for about a mile and then leaves the Chin track and goes through open country down a series of very steep zigzags for about ½ a mile and then runs slightly dropping for about a mile and then by more steep zigzags right down to the river; the road in places is narrow, but the zigzags have all been widened. At 5 miles the Longbán stream, 15 feet wide and 8 inches deep, is crossed; between here and the stream at about 1¼ miles no water is passed. From the Longbán stream the road runs along the bed of the Nankathé river and at about 5 miles the ford is reached. There is a ford of 2 feet deep over half the river to an island and from there the remaining portion is crossed by a wooden single sling bridge capable of taking one loaded mule at a time. Last year at this point the river was fordable right across. From the bridge the road runs for ¼ mile along the bed of the river and then commences to rise by zigzags; it is a 3-foot road and good. At 6¼ miles a small stream is passed and at 8½ miles or 42½ miles from Fort White the present post of Falám is reached. If desired the journey can be performed in four marches, in which case the stages recommended are as follows:— MILES. 1. Fort White to Bamboo camp ... 13½ 2. Bamboo camp to No. 4 camp ... 10½ 3. No. 4 camp to Longbán camp ... 10 (stiff march). 4. Longbán camp to Falám ... 8½ (stiff march). After the 22nd April 1893 the heavy rains have washed away the sling bridge and river is unfordable, but a good track, fit for mules, has been made from about ¼ mile from the Longbán stream (on the way to Falám) up and along the hill on the left bank of the river to the site of the new bridge, to which it is 3½ miles from Longbán stream. Here a bridge

FROM FORT WHITE (NEW) TO HÁKA *viâ* FALÁM (TÁSHÔN YWAMA)—*continued.*

Authorities. Military.	Authorities. Civil.	Number and Names of Stages, Rivers and Streams.	Distances. Intermediate M.	F.	Distances. Total. M.	F.	Remarks.
G.O.C. Myingyán District.	Political Officer, Chin Hills.	**5. Falám**—*cont.*					is under construction and the river can now be crossed in a cradle.* From this point there are two Chin paths—one through Falám village and the other leads to the road which was being made by the pioneers to the new bridge. In coming this way the stages recommended are as follows :— MILES. 1. Fort White to Bamboo camp ... ... 13½ 2. Bamboo camp to Pine Tree camp ... 13½ 3. Pine Tree camp to Longbán stream † ... 12 4. Longbán stream to Falám ... ... 8 New Falám is about 2½ miles beyond the present post.
		6. Laiyaw	**6**	**4**	49	0	For details *see* Route No. 11.
		7. Hairon	**10**	**4**	59	4	
		8. Háka	**16**	**0**	75	4	

ALTERNATIVE I.

FROM FORT WHITE (NEW) TO FALÁM (TÁSHÔN YWAMA) *viâ* FORT WHITE (OLD) AND YAWLU.

BY LIEUT. CHAPMAN, R.E., MARCH 1890.

Military.	Civil.	Number and Names of Stages, Rivers and Streams.	Intermediate M.	F.	Total M.	F.	Remarks.
G.O.C. Myingyán District.	Political Officer, Chin Hills.	**1. Fort White (Old).**	**7**	**4**	7	4	*See* Route No. 6, Central Division, Stage 6.
		2. Yawlu post ... Kwenliu stream.	**11**	**0**	18	4	From old Fort White to stream, descent of 1,900 feet, made mule track, gradient 1 in 6, 2¾ miles. From the creek to top of Yawlu post road is also made, but is out of repair, and if mules are taken along this portion a working party of 10 men should accompany them. The road rises by zigzags up the north side of a spur, crosses it at a height of 4,400 feet (1,500 feet above stream), and rises along south side to height of 5,200, is level for about ¾ mile round the valley, and then rises by zigzags over another spur, runs level for a mile along the south side, and then crosses Lektaw ridge at a height of 6,200 feet. There is then a steep descent of 1,000 feet to the post. The road runs generally through low scattered jungle with occasional cultivation. Water is plentiful at several places all along the road. Good camping ground near old post. Water abundant. Road descends very steeply to a small creek (1,000 feet), then fairly level through Shinshé villages (1⅛ miles), turns at right angles, and descends steeply to Kwenliu stream. Ground fairly open and road commanded from above. The sides of the creek are very steep to a height of 600 feet, and crossing is commanded from both sides.

* This bridge was opened for traffic on the 1st of July. It was to be capable of taking mules by the 7th of July, though it was feared the roadway, which is composed of strong matting covered with earth, will not stand continuous traffic.

† There is no accommodation at this stream, so tents would be wanted or temporary shelters have to be made.

FROM FORT WHITE (NEW) TO HÁKA *viâ* FALÁM (TÁSHÔN YWAMA)—*continued.*

ALTERNATIVE I—*continued.*

Authorities. Military.	Authorities. Civil.	Number and Names of Stages, Rivers and Streams.	Distances. Intermediate. M. F.	Distances. Total. M. F.	Remarks.
G.O.C. Myingyán District.	Political Officer, Chin Hills.	**3. Camp 1½ to 2 miles beyond Balaw.**	8 4	27 0	The road rises very steep for 600 feet, then more gently to height of 400 feet to crest of spur, passing below the village of Lebwel at 3½ miles and above Tunmwel (4½ miles), each containing 60 houses. The Shinshé villages also lie a short distance to the right of the road to the west of Yawlu. The spur is covered with low scrub jungle, changing to small firs at top of crest. After the crest the road is very good and descends gradually over easy slopes, passing Balaw (50 houses); camping ground ½ mile before Balaw, but water-supply insufficient for more than 200 men. Good water-supply at Balaw, and good camping ground anywhere between 1½ miles to 2 miles beyond Balaw between two streams, both containing water. The road is commanded throughout by the slopes above, which are easy, except near the Kwenliu, and covered with low jungle.
		4. Camp 1 mile beyond Yati.	10 0	37 0	Road rises steeply for 600 feet, then more gradually for 500 feet through stunted jungle round spur at about 2 miles, then runs level along southern slope for 1 mile, and descends abruptly to village of Bwékwa, 3 miles (two villages of about 80 houses each). Good water-supply. From road above Bwékwa villages of Lati and Shinshaw are seen to the south on opposite spur. From Bwékwa precipitous descent to stream 2,100 feet. Camping ground on either side 300 or 400 feet above water. From stream long ascent of nearly 3 miles to crest through open cultivated country and occasional patches of low jungle. The road, as a rule, is easy, but there are short steep pieces. The slope of the spur is steep. Water found 2 miles up in a ravine. The village of Yati (50 houses, water-supply small) is passed at 9 miles immediately on rounding the corner of the spur. Falám, the Táshôn Ywama, can be seen from the heights above Yati. The road runs level for the next mile (8¾ miles), where there is camping ground and water.
		5. Camp on left bank, Nankathé river.	6 4	43 4	Road runs on fairly level for about 2½ miles along the face of the spur, descending over small saddle at south corner of the spur into village of Páté (2½ miles) consisting of one large and one small village, 70 and 15 houses respectively. Water good and plentiful. From Páté descends at an easy slope along steep sides of a minor spur for 2½ miles, then crosses it and makes a precipitous descent of nearly 2,000 feet to the river Nankathé, runs along the bed of the river for about a mile to the ford. Here there is space for camping in bed of river, banks precipitous for 700 or 800 feet.
		6. Falám (Táshôn Ywama).	5 0	48 4	From the ford, which is waist-deep in March, to the Táshôn Ywama is about 5 miles. *General remarks.*—The road is, as a rule, good and easy, but only fit for cooly transport after the first stage. The only steep portions are near the

FROM FORT WHITE (NEW) TO HÁKA *viâ* FALÁM (TÁSHÔN YWAMA)—*continued.*

ALTERNATIVE I—*continued.*

Authorities.		Number and Names of Stages, Rivers and Streams.	Distances.		Remarks.
Military.	Civil.		Inter-mediate.	Total.	
G.O.C. Myingyán District.	Political Officer, Chin Hills.	**6. Falám (Táshôn Ywama)**—*cont.*			streams. The slopes of the hills are fairly easy and, except where cultivated, covered with low scattered jungle. Streams passed would always be fordable except immediately after heavy rains. Water-supplies mentioned in report would always contain water. All along the road grass, branches, &c., for erecting rough shelters obtainable. Eggs and fowls can be bought from villages: no other supplies except perhaps mythun, but difficult to induce villagers to sell. The lengths of the marches in hours for the main body of a column of about 300 rifles that traversed this route in March 1890 were about as follows, including halts:— HOURS. Fort White to Yawlu ... ... 5-6 Yawlu to first camp (near Balaw) ... 8 First camp to second, 400 feet above stream below Bwékwa ... ... 4 Second camp to third, 1 mile beyond Yaté ... ... 3 Third camp to Páté ... ... 1 Páté to Nankathé ... ... 1½ On the return— Páté to Bwékwa ... ... 4½ Bwékwa to Yawlu post ... ... 8 The return was marched in cooler weather, much of it through steady rain.

BRANCH I.

FROM FORT WHITE (NEW) TO MÔNTÔK.

BY CAPT. BAKER, ROYAL ARTILLERY, AND LIEUT. H. T. BROOKING, 21ST MADRAS PIONEERS, DECEMBER 1892 AND APRIL 1893.

Military.	Civil.	Number and Names of Stages, Rivers and Streams.	Inter-mediate. M. F.	Total. M. F.	Remarks.
G.O.C. Myingyán District.	Political Officer, Chin Hills.	**1. Môntôk** ... Large stream.	14 0	14 0	At about 9 miles from Fort White, the Môntôk path leaves the Táshôn road and runs eastward and along the top of a ridge which forms an offshoot from the ridge along which the Táshôn road runs. For about a mile the path descends easily along the top of the ridge, the country on both sides covered with thin wood, but easily flanked. It then leaves the top of the ridge and runs along the north side of it in a north-east direction very steep indeed and the jungle in many places very thick and difficult to flank. About 1½ miles after leaving top of the ridge the path runs on to a flat underfeature which it soon leaves and runs right down into the ravine below through which runs a large stream. At the time these notes were taken (24-11-92), the stream was about 6 or 7 yards wide, and only a few inches deep, when we had not had rain for some time, but after heavy rain would probably be impassable. After crossing the stream, the path is very steep and difficult for about ½ a mile, running through cultivation, with thick jungle on the left, then it takes a turn to the north along the ridge, then to the east round end of spur, over a small re-entering angle, then over the ridge to the right and

FROM FORT WHITE (NEW) TO HÁKA *viâ* FALÁM (TÁSHÔN YWAMA)—*continued.*

BRANCH I—*continued.*

Authorities. Military.	Authorities. Civil.	Number and Names of Stages, Rivers and Streams.	Distances. Inter-mediate.	Distances. Total.	Remarks.
G.O.C. Myingyán District.	Political Officer, Chin Hills.	**1. Môntôk**—*cont.*			down into Môntôk. The distance from Fort White to the stream would be about 12½ miles, and then another mile or 1½ miles on into Môntôk. The path is only fit for cooly transport. Camp was established in Môntôk village. Water-supply good and close at hand. Môntôk (now burnt) was a fine village of 50 houses lying in a hollow, and surrounded by a good deal of cultivation. From here there is a path to Kalémyo, distant 18¼ miles almost due east. A halt can be made at Zí chaung (8 miles), where there is fairly good camping ground on a small plateau above the stream of that name. Water good and plentiful. Fine trees all round, but camp probably very unhealthy in wet weather. First 8 miles of this route in many places rough, steep and difficult, but from Zí chaung onwards, across low-lying flat country.

No. 2.

From FORT WHITE (New) to HTÁNWÉ.

FROM NOTES SUPPLIED BY LIEUT. BELLAMY, 1ST NORFOLK REGIMENT, 10TH NOVEMBER 1892.

Military	Civil	Stages	Inter-mediate M. F.	Total M. F.	Remarks
G.O.C. Myingyán District.	Political Officer, Chin Hills.	**1. Htánwé** ... One small stream.	7 0	7 0	Leaving new Fort White by the Tiddim road gate the route lies along the old Fort White road (Route No. 6, Central Division) for about 4 miles. Here the old Fort White road runs to the top of the ridge, and the route to Htánwé lies along a Chin path which branches off to the right, runs over a *col* turning about north-east down the north side of ridge, through very thick jungle, over the bottom and on to an underfeature along the ridge of which it runs down, direction north-west, to its base, then turns north over a small stream and up the opposite side; very steep for about 200 yards; country much enclosed. On completion of this ascent tne path turns west along fairly level, but enclosed ground and enters the village about ¼ mile after crossing the stream. Htánwé village is very straggling with groups of houses about every 50 yards. Total number about 16 (now burnt); water abundant from the stream crossed. This route is only fit for cooly transport.

No. 3.

From FORT WHITE (New) to MANIPUR.

BY CAPT. H. B. VAUGHAN, 7TH BENGAL INFANTRY, ATTACHÉ, INTELLIGENCE BRANCH, JANUARY 1892.

Military	Civil	Stages	Inter-mediate	Total	Remarks
G.O.C. Myingyán District.	Political Officer, Chin Hills.	**1. Camp (6,300 feet).**	11 4	11 4	General direction north. Leave Fort White and ascend to the crest of the Lítha ridge, and march along it by a good road, a mule track. Tho ground is destitute of trees. At 3¼ miles descend slightly and pass through forest for ½ mile. Lea[illegible] it and continue on over the open summit of the hills as before. At 4¼ miles enter a wood. At 4½ miles leave it.

FROM FORT WHITE (NEW) TO MANIPUR—*continued.*

Authorities.		Number and Names of Stages, Rivers and Streams.	Distances.				Remarks.
Military.	Civil.		Intermediate.		Total.		
			M.	F.	M.	F.	
G.O.C. Myingyán District.	Political Officer, Chin Hills.	**1. Camp (6,300 feet)**—*cont.*					At 5¼ miles up a very steep ascent till the 6th mile and then over fairly level ground. At 6½ miles pass underneath a small signalling station situated on false Kennedy Peak. There is a plentiful water-supply 1 mile off down a mule track to the left of the road and about 1,000 feet below it. Elevation 8,100 feet. On up a steep ascent and at 7 miles pass below Kennedy Peak and onwards descending slightly. At 7¼ miles enter forest and shortly after leave it. At 9¼ miles down a steep incline amongst trees. At 11 miles a road to Tiddim runs on to the left. We go down a steep hill side till camp is reached. Time 4 hours. A camping ground down below the main road and situated on a hill side facing north amidst jungle. Water scarce; is obtainable ¼ mile further on from a dry water-course, in which holes are dug, which fill slowly. It was insufficient for the 100 mules which were with the column. It is said to be 3 miles from here to Walawun village, through which a road runs to Tiddim,* *see* Alternative No. I below.
		2. Tiddim (5,100 feet).	12	6	24	2	Leaving camp we retrace yesterday's route for ½ mile and then turn to the right and go on through jungle over fairly level ground, continuing along the crest of a chain of hills, a spur thrown out from Kennedy Peak. At 3¾ miles and about 250 feet below the road is a good camping ground on a hill side and facing south; there is abundant space for a camp. There are trees dotted about and an abundance of long grass. There is a small supply of good water from a perennial spring close by a clump of banana trees. The place is in the old Dimlo cultivation. At 7½ miles over open ground. At 8¼ miles the road is cut in the hill side, and the soil, being shale, is liable to give. There is a stream of fresh water 200 yards below the road and to the right close by some cultivation; thence by a good road through long grass and amongst woods formed of small fir trees until Tiddim is reached. Time 4¾ hours. A small post garrisoned by 100 men. It is surrounded by a low stone wall and contains permanent stone buildings. There is a good camping ground outside and water is plentiful.
		3. Camp on Nankathé or Manipur river (2,000 feet). Manipur river.	14	4	38	6	Leaving the post the road ascends gently till 1¼ miles, when it runs along the crest of the hills, passing through forest. At 1¾ miles it rounds a knoll on its left and descends. At 4¾ miles the descent becomes very steep, and at 6¼ miles road crosses a stream which joins the Manipur river a few hundred yards down to the left. Bed gravel, 30 feet broad, contains 14 inches of water, current rapid. The right bank is high and commands the left. There is sufficient level ground on the left bank to form a camp. Elevation 2,000 feet. On up a very steep ascent over wooded hills. Track is cut in the hill side. It then descends, and at 7¾ miles passes through a well-situated pioneer camp on level ground on the left bank of the river. At 7¾ miles cross the river by a temporary bridge 58 yards in length and 5 feet broad.

* The distance from Fort White to Tiddim by this route, which was traversed by Lieut. Heycock, R.E., in January 1891, is 17½ miles, but between Walawun (11½ miles) and Tiddim there is a descent of 2,400 feet and an ascent of 2,200 feet; the path was made passable for mules and was a good path for coolies.

FROM FORT WHITE (NEW) TO MANIPUR—*continued.*

Authorities. Military.	Authorities. Civil.	Number and Names of Stages, Rivers and Streams.	Distances. Intermediate.	Distances. Total.	Remarks.
G.O.C. Myingyán District.	Political Officer, Chin Hills.	**3. Camp on Nankathé or Manipur river (2,000 feet)**—*cont.*			It is formed of timber supported on piles of stones sunk in the river bed; roadway 2 feet 6 inches above the water, which flows with a rapid current and is full of deep holes and rocks. On along the right bank of the river. At 8½ miles recross the Manipur river by another and similar bridge. Both bridges are below the flood level and therefore only temporary. Infantry could with difficulty find their way up the left bank and thus avoid the necessity of the double passage. On along the river's left bank close to its bed. At 10¾ miles the track ascends steeply and goes over the face of a shaly slip by a path cut in it 90 feet above the river bed, to which there is precipitous descent; then down and alongside of the river. At 12 miles cross a streamlet. At 14½ miles cross two dry stream beds in succession and reach camp. Time 5¾ hours. A camping ground on the left bank of the Manipur river situated on level ground a few hundred yards in length and overlooked on all sides by hills. Grass plentiful.
		4. Tunzán (3,700 feet). Small streams.	M. F. **6 4**	M. F. 45 2	Leave camp and go througr jungle. Cross a small fresh water stream flowing into the river on our left and climb up a spur in a north-north-east direction; gradient steep. At ½ mile the ascent is easier and at 1 mile it runs along the side of the hills in which it is cut. At 2 miles it enters some Chin clearings interspersed with cultivators' huts. Pass a spring of fresh water, and at 3 miles descend into a hollow and cross a streamlet of fresh water. A steep ascent out of its bed and on through more clearings. At 4½ miles round a spur of the hills and enter the Tunzán valley. The town and post are visible ahead. On through forest. Cross a small streamlet with steep and slippery approaches at 5 miles. At 5¼ miles pass through two stockaded gateways in succession, both of which are flanked by dense almost impenetrable jungle which clothes the steep hill side sloping north. At 5¾ miles cross a small streamlet; approaches steep and slippery. At 6 miles a track on the right leads to the town: we go straight on. The track after crossing one or two small streamlets reaches Tunzán post. Time 2½ hours. The march from the 3rd mile could be flanked by a party working over the hill-top on the right through the cultivation, who would reach the post by descending over a track into the town. A small post about ¼ mile from the town situated on a small clearing close by a streamlet, whence a plentiful supply of fresh water is obtainable. The post is protected by four block-houses, but is unavoidably commanded by high ground to the east. The town contains 116 houses.
		5. Camp (4,250 feet). Small streams.	**10 2**	55 4	Leave Tunzán by a good road, which, winding along the hill side, ascends steadily. At 2 miles it crosses a spur close by some Chin tombs and a track branches off on the left to a signalling station, whence Kennedy Peak is visible. On down a descent past the village of Twitum, which is close by on the left, but hidden by a hill. It contains about 30 houses. The road up to this point is flanked by a good pathway, which ascends the hills behind Tunzán post and here joins the route. At 3 miles the descent becomes steeper and at 4½ miles very steep, and then for a

FROM FORT WHITE (NEW) TO MANIPUR—*continued.*

Authorities.		Number and Names of Stages, Rivers and Streams.	Distances.				Remarks.
Military.	Civil.		Intermediate.		Total.		
			M.	F.	M.	F.	
G.O.C. Myingyán District.	Political Officer, Chin Hills.	**5. Camp (4,250 feet)**—*cont.*					distance of 100 yards excessively steep and difficult. It then runs over level ground for a few yards and at 4¾ miles, after a march of 1¾ hours, it crosses the Twisom stream about 30 feet broad, bed stony, which flows into the Manipur river close by on the left. This point is 1,600 feet below Tunzán. There is sufficient level ground for a camp. On over level ground, cross a low hillock, descend and cross another stream, the Twiyol, similar, but smaller at 5¼ miles, then on up a spur by a steep zigzag ascent for 800 feet. At 6½ miles the gradient is easier and the track runs along the side of the hills in which it is cut. At 7½ miles the road is good over hills covered with long grass and dotted with large fir trees. At 9½ miles there is a steep bit for a few yards followed by a descent. Time 4 hours. The camp is situated on a steep hill side facing west, amongst trees; wood and grass abundant. Water plentiful from two small streams.
		6. Camp on Shimol stream (2,250 feet). Shimol and other streams.	10	4	66	0	Road fair. At ½ mile a steep descent into a streamlet and out of it. At 1½ miles two streamlets are crossed. The track runs over shale and is cut in the hill side. Down a descent and at 1¾ miles cross a streamlet and ascend for a short distance. After a descent pass by a streamlet, where there is a good camping ground on the left of the road at 2¼ miles. At 2¾ miles over open grassy slopes covered with fine pine trees. At 3¼ miles cross a streamlet in a hollow. At 3½ miles an ascent commences, which lasts till 3¾ miles. At 4¼ miles cross a small stream; then on up a gradual ascent. At 5¾ miles leave the forest and pass over the open summit of a rounded ridge covered with thick long grass. At 6¼ miles pass the village of old Mwelpi Ngwité tribe, not Kanhow, now being deserted for another site to the south-east. Water from the ravine east of the village is sufficient for about 150 men. Tunzán signalling station is visible from here; elevation 4,750 feet. Road hence descends easily along a spur, ground fairly open and sparsely wooded till 9½ miles, when after a steepish descent and crossing a stream camp is reached. Time 4 hours. The camp is situated in a hollow on level ground between two streams and close to the Manipur river. Firewood and grass plentiful.
		7. Lénákôt post (Shielmong), (4,000 feet). Hévak and Twilom streams (fordable).	11	2	77	2	Cross a small stream and go up a spur by a steep ascent for ½ mile, when gradient becomes easier. At 1 mile on by a good road, still ascending. At 3¼ miles pass through a stockaded gateway backed by a trench and flanked to the right by a steep ascent covered with dense jungle and on the left by a very steep descent. At 4 miles pass through the village of Sinnum. It contained 30 houses (Yôté or Lôté tribe, tributary to Manipur), now in ashes, and was well situated. On by an easy descent. At 5¾ miles a steep descent into a nullah and out of it. At 6¾ miles a steep descent, very steep for a few yards. At 7 miles cross a couple of small streams (Hévak and Twilom) in succession. Elevation 2,600 feet. There is a good camping

FROM FORT WHITE (NEW) TO MANIPUR—*continued.*

Authorities. Military.	Authorities. Civil.	Number and Names of Stages, Rivers and Streams.	Distances. Intermediate.	Distances. Total.	Remarks.
G.O.C. Myingyán District.	Political Officer, Chin Hills.	**7. Lénákôt post (Shielmong), (4,000 feet)**—*cont.*			ground in a strong position at the extremity of a spur of the hills on the left. Then up a spur by a steep ascent, which at 7½ miles becomes easier, and on by a good and easy road with open ground on either side. At 10¼ miles a track branches off on the right to Shielmong (Tado tribe, neither Kanhow nor Manipuri, but paying a small tribute to the former) about ¾ mile off; our road goes on, being cut in the hill side, and is level till camp is reached. Time 4¾ hours. A post situated on a steep slope from a spur of the Lítha range and facing west. It is surrounded by a stout timber stockade strengthened by block-houses. Water plentiful from a small stream close by.*
		8. Camp on Kana stream. Several streams.	M. F. 18 0	M. F. 95 2	Road, leaving Lénákôt at ¾ mile, passes over a low spur connecting it with the hills right and left; a track branches off to the left and, ascending the hills on that side, reaches the remains of a stockade on their summit. Our road, running north, descends gently, and at 1½ miles commences a steep descent. Cross a small stream 1,250 feet below Lénákôt at 1¾ miles. Over a level track fringed by tall rushes. Cross a small stream at 2¼ miles and ascend. At 2¾ miles the gradient hitherto steep becomes gentle. At 6 miles the track curves round to the right and descends slightly and at 6¾ miles passes the village of Kwunum, 25 houses, stockaded, and on the right of the road. Water from a ravine close by. At 7¼ miles pass through a stockaded gateway. At 8¼ miles a road *viâ* Shimwel goes on to Manipur. We take the track to the left. At 8¾ miles two dry nullahs bridged. At 9¼ miles up a steep ascent and over the level summit of a chain of hills. At 11¼ miles leave the hill-tops and descend steeply into a hollow. At 12 miles pass a camping ground situated on a steep hill side in a hollow surrounded by jungle near the Shwenkwa stream. Water and grass plentiful. Elevation 3,750 feet. Road descends steeply and crosses the streamlet and ascends steeply till 12¾ miles. Then on by a level road till 13¾ miles, when a gentle descent commences. At about 15¼ miles the road inclines to the right. A track straight on goes to Bwankwa and thence to Tonglong. Road down a gentle incline into the valley hitherto on our right. Road crosses a dry ravine and ascends out of it at 16½ miles. At 18 miles it crosses two nullahs in succession. Time 7¾ hours. A camping ground situated on a level stretch of ground on the left bank of the Kana stream. Grass plentiful.
		9. Camp on Tapi stream. Kana, Tapi and other streams.	14 4	109 6	Road over an almost level plain between chains of hills. At 1½ miles crosses the Kana stream; passable, except after very heavy rain, and recrosses it again at 2½ miles. Both crossings are over a firm rocky bed. At 2¾ miles passes by a good camping ground in a strong position on the left bank of the stream.

* From Shielmong there is a path running eastwards to the Lítha range, and running south and then west through the villages of Tumbwel (10 houses), Hévak (10) and Sheiksán (25), all Tado tribe, rejoins the main road a little south of Shielmong.

From FORT WHITE (New) to MANIPUR—*continued.*

Authorities. Military.	Authorities. Civil.	Number and Names of Stages, Rivers and Streams.	Distances. Intermediate. M. F.	Distances. Total. M. F.	Remarks.
G.O.C. Myingyán District.	Political Officer, Chin Hills.	**9. Camp on [Tapi stream**—*cont.*			There is a good road from here to Bwankwa, 2½ miles off, up an ascent. It takes about 1½ hours to reach it. On over a level tract. Elevation 2,750 feet. At 4½ miles crosses the Kana stream, easily fordable, bed rocks and gravel. At 6¼ miles over some low hillocks, crosses the stream bed, and at 8¼ miles crosses a dry nullah. At 8¼ miles a track branches off on the right rear to Shimwei. At 12¼ miles down a hollow across a dry stream and over a low hill and on to a broad level stretch of ground, the southern extremity of the Manipur plain. Cross the stream; approaches steep. Bed 60 yards broad and very stony. Time 4¾ hours. There is a good camping ground here on the right bank of the stream. Grass and firewood plentiful.
G.O.C. Assam District.	Political Officer, Manipur.	**10. Shuganu or Shweklu (2,550 feet).** Manipur river.	5 4	115 2	Road over a level plain by a single foot track passes under groves of trees; the stream is on our left. After crossing over the foot of some low hills on the east of the plain, the track again runs over level ground and reaches camp. Time 2 hours. A Manipuri village containing about 100 houses and situated on the left bank of the Manipur river on an open grassy plain.
		11. Kaksing (2,750 feet). Singwai river.	14 6	130 0	Road over level ground. At 2½ miles passes over a chain of low hillocks. Several villages lie to the right and left. At 3 miles pass the Manipuri village of Tônchin away on the left. At 5½ miles still amongst low hills and pass a small stream. At 8½ miles through the village of Waikôn, 60 houses. At 8¾ miles pass the village of Tônchow and at 9¼ Lônbum, both on the left of the road. At 11 miles cross a small stream and pass a cluster of small villages; then up an ascent and over a chain of low hills by a pass and down on to a plain on the further side. Cross a river by a high-pitched wooden bridge 30 or 40 feet above the stream and halt at Kaksing 14¾ miles. Time 5¾ hours. A Manipuri village of about 150 houses. It contains a rest-house and a large square building, a durbar room, which sheltered the whole of the column during a shower of rain. Supplies procurable after due notice.
		12. Thôbál ... Thôbál river.	12 0	142 0	Road over level ground crosses several small streamlets by bridges made of beams and bamboo mats. At 2¼ miles the high road from Tammu to Manipur joins us and we proceed along it. At 4 miles the road is a causeway with swamp right and left. It is a raised and levelled. but unmetalled track, broad enough for carts in places. At 5½ miles the low hills on the right fall away and a track is visible running over the hill-top to the large village of Lambatel or Langatel. There is a good camping ground there and water. At 8 miles pass Wangching; the road then curves to the left. At 10¾ miles

FROM FORT WHITE (NEW) TO MANIPUR—*continued.*

Authorities. Military.	Civil.	Number and Names of Stages, Rivers and Streams.	Distances. Intermediate.		Total.		Remarks.
G.O.C. Assam District.	Political Officer, Manipur.	**12. Thôbál**—*cont.*					cross a river by a bridge of bamboos. At 12 miles cross the Thôbál river by a bridge of bamboos and halt. Time 4½ hours. A cluster of houses situated on both sides of the road amid gardens and cultivation. There are some low hills on the right of the track, which form a good position from which to hold the road against a force advancing on Manipur.
			M.	F.	M.	F.	
		13. Manipur (Imphál), (2,619 feet). River.	**13**	**0**	155	0	Road good over level ground. At 3½ miles passes the lake at the foot of the Phunan hill and, rounding it, runs northwards skirting the foot of the hill for a short distance. At 6½ miles crosses a river; on by a good road, which shortly enters amongst the outlying villages of Manipur, and at 13 miles reaches the old palace and fort. Time 4 hours.

ALTERNATIVE I.

FROM FORT WHITE (NEW) TO TIDDIM (STAGE 2).

BY LIEUT. HEYCOCK, R.E., JANUARY 1891.

Military	Civil	Stage	Inter. M.	F.	Total M.	F.	Remarks
G.O.C. Myingyán District.	Political Officer, Chin Hills.	**1. Tiddim**	**18**	**0**	18	0	Road runs to Kennedy Peak as above and continues along the same road till within 2 miles of Walawun, when, instead of turning down the spur to Walawun, it continues along the first spur for 4½ miles. Village of Dimlo can be seen below the road on the south, also villages of Shwimpi and Dimpi on opposite spurs to the south. Dimlo consists of two villages, each of 30 houses. Shwimpi has 20 houses and Dimpi 40 houses. There is no defence to any of them. The road after this turns to the north on a spur running at right angles to the first spur. It reaches Tiddim in 3 miles. Village of Losow can be seen on western slope of the spur. Number of houses 30. Across the Manipur river on the opposite range can be seen the village of Mwiyol. The road could easily be made passable for mules. Water is to be found about 400 feet below the road, 11 miles from No. 5 stockade on the northern slope of the spur.

BRANCH I.

FROM FORT WHITE (NEW) TO LAIBÔN.

BY CAPT. R. BAKER, 1ST NORFOLK REGIMENT, 10TH DECEMBER 1892.

Military	Civil	Stage	Inter. M.	F.	Total M.	F.	Remarks
G.O.C. Myingyán District.	Political Officer, Chin Hills.	**1. Laibôn** ... ... One stream, name unknown.	**8**	**4**	8	4	For the first portion the route runs along the Fort White-Tiddim road and at about 3½ miles it leaves this road and turns to the right direction about 60°. At this point there is another path to the left running to Thanwé. Almost at once it runs into the woods which clothe the eastern slope of the range, but only for a short way

FROM FORT WHITE (NEW) TO MANIPUR—*continued.*

BRANCH I—*continued.*

Authorities. Military.	Authorities. Civil.	Number and Names of Stages, Rivers and Streams.	Distances. Intermediate.	Distances. Total.	Remarks.
G.O.C. Myingyán District.	Political Officer, Chin Hills.	**1. Laibôn**—*cont.*			when it runs out again on a spur into grass land for 300 or 400 yards, at first fairly level, then very steep when it enters the wood again. The wood is at first fairly open, then gets thicker and thicker; trees and bamboo undergrowth. The path runs through this wood for about $1\frac{3}{4}$ miles; path very steep indeed in places and much overgrown. The wood now gets very thin with fairly long grass for about $\frac{3}{4}$ of a mile; the path very bad and steep in places when it runs into the cultivation on the north side of the spur through this cutivation for about $\frac{3}{4}$ mile, and down to a stream the path being about at its worst here. The path crosses the stream on fallen tree, turns to the right and runs on a fairly easy slope through thick jungle up the side of the ridge for about a mile when it reaches the top and crosses over it, after which it turns to the left and runs slightly down-hill along north side of ridge for about $\frac{1}{2}$ mile into the village, which cannot be seen until one is right on to it, as it is hidden by an underfeature. Laibôn (now burnt) consisted of about 20 houses; usual Chin pattern; good water-supply, but is not suitable to camp in, as it is commanded on three sides. The best camping ground is just above where the path rounds the top of the spur. It is fairly level amongst fir trees and the water-supply is about 600 or 700 yards down the Fort White path.

Laibôn can also be reached *viâ* Kennedy Peak as follows :—

Military	Civil	Stage	Intermediate M.	Intermediate F.	Total M.	Total F.	Remarks
G.O.C. Myingyán District.	Political Officer, Chin Hills.	**1. Kennedy Peak.**	**6**	**0**	6	0	Leaving Laibôn path turns to the right along the highest part of the ridge. It runs like most Chin paths along the top of this ridge almost up to Kennedy Peak point, and is a fair one, but exceedingly steep in places and quite unfitted for anything but cooly transport. The ground to its right is extremely precipitous and thinly wooded; to its left thickly wooded and not quite so steep. For about the last mile before reaching Kennedy Peak the country is open grass on south side of ridge thickly wooded on north side. Four or 500 yards before reaching Kennedy Peak it joins the Pimpi path at a large cairn or heap of stones, then inclining to the left runs under the peak very fairly level and joins the Fort White-Tiddim road. Camping ground at Kennedy Peak is on a steepish slope facing south-west, but level terraces here and there have been cut by troops camping here. The water-supply, moderate only, is in the wood at the foot of the camp.

BRANCH II.

FROM KENNEDY PEAK (*see* STAGE 1) TO PIMPI.

BY CAPT. R. BAKER, INTELLIGENCE OFFICER, CHIN HILLS.

Military	Civil	Stage	Intermediate M.	Intermediate F.	Total M.	Total F.	Remarks
G.O.C. Myingyán District.	Political Officer, Chin Hills.	**1. Camp**	**8**	**4**	8	4	Road strikes off east immediately under Kennedy Peak; here also another path runs south-east to Laibôn, *see* Branch No. I above. From Ken-

FROM FORT WHITE (NEW) TO MANIPUR—*continued.*

BRANCH II—*continued.*

Authorities. Military.	Authorities. Civil.	Number and Names of Stages, Rivers and Streams.	Distances. Inter-mediate.	Distances. Total.	Remarks.
G.O.C. Myingyán District.	Political Officer, Chin Hills.	**1. Camp**—*cont.*			nedy Peak path runs along ridge for 1½ miles through thick jungle, after which it becomes a little more open. Path an ordinary Chin one, but mules were got along it. There are some very bad bits in the 1st mile or two, but these were repaired by the pioneers. For the next 3½ miles the path is fairly good in most places, but still a few bad bits; passes through fairly open forest of fine pine trees. Here there is suitable ground for camping, but no water. For the next 2 miles path is very bad, most of it very steep and down-hill; it runs through very thick jungle, and flanking was found most difficult. At 8½ miles camping ground, bad, in thick jungle, commanded on the north side. No water.
		2. Pimpi	M. F. 4 0	M. F. 12 4	After leaving camp the path was fairly good and jungle not so thick for about 2 miles. At this point the path to Pimpi turns almost due north; another carries straight on; there was also another track turning off south. Path to Pimpi very steep and exceedingly difficult for the mules, the gun and its equipment having in one place to be carried down by hand. Path through very thick jungle and would be found awkward if held by a resolute enemy. As Pimpi is neared, the path gets worse, and is worst of all just above the village. Pimpi is built on a broad spur. A nullah of water on either side, commanded from three sides. Water good and ample.

BRANCH III.

FROM KENNEDY PEAK (*see* STAGE 1) TO UNGNO.

BY CAPT. R. BAKER, INTELLIGENCE OFFICER, 20TH MARCH 1893.

Military	Civil	Stage	Inter-mediate	Total	Remarks
G.O.C. Myingyán District.	Political Officer, Chin Hills.	**1. Camp near Vando Peak.**	7 2	7 2	Leaving the Fort White-Tiddim road just under Kennedy Peak the path runs in an easterly direction along the summit of the Pimpi ridge, and for about 4 miles is the same path that runs to Pimpi. At 600 yards a path to Laibôn branches off down a minor spur to the right. It descends gently for about 1¾ miles through thick jungle, though in places a bit steep, then up over a small peak from which point Kennedy Peak bears 255° and No. 3 stockade 133°. After crossing this peak the path undulates for about a mile, passing through a fine fir forest, then over another small peak and down-hill for about 450 yards after passing the half-way camping place to Pimpi. Now the ascent of the high peak in the Pimpi ridge commences, half-way up which the road divides, one going to the right to Pimpi, the other to the left to Ungno. This is about 4¼ miles from Kennedy Peak, and to this point the road is very fair, but now not so good. The path now runs through very thick jungle, turning gradually northward until at 5 miles it runs along the top of an important spur thrown out from the big peak on Pimpi ridge to the northward. Pimpi post is now seen in the

No. 3.

FROM FORT WHITE (NEW) TO MANIPUR—*continued.*

BRANCH III—*continued.*

Authorities. Military.	Authorities. Civil.	Number and Names of Stages, Rivers and Streams.	Distances. Intermediate.	Distances. Total.	Remarks.
G.O.C. Myingyán District.	Political Officer, Chin Hills.	**1. Camp near Vando Peak**—*cont.*			valley to the right. The path keeps this ridge for about 2 miles, then runs down from it north-west into the camping ground about $7\frac{1}{4}$ miles from Kennedy Peak. The ground is situated in thick jungle forest commanded on two sides. A fair supply of water close at hand. Aneroid showed 5,560 feet.
		2. Ungno	M. 7 F. 2	M. 14 F. 4	Leaving the camping ground on the northern side the path winds its way through thick jungle to the foot of the Vando Peak over which it rises, the summit of which is reached at about 2 miles. Aneroid at this point 6,000 feet. Crossing Vando the path runs down the eastern slope along top of a ridge running eastwards through thick jungle for another $3\frac{1}{2}$ miles, then turns down to the north running down a spur in that direction on the western slope of which lies Ungno, about $1\frac{1}{2}$ miles from the top of the ridge. Before reaching village way has to be made over a number of freshly felled trees for 300 yards, where the Chins had commenced to prepare cultivation grounds. Ungno contains about 100 houses and has a good water-supply, but is commanded to a more or less extent on three sides.

BRANCH IV.

FROM DIMLO POST (*see* STAGE 2) TO KAPTIÁL.

BY CAPT. R. BAKER, INTELLIGENCE OFFICER, NORTHERN CHIN HILLS, JANUARY 1893.

Authorities. Military.	Authorities. Civil.	Number and Names of Stages, Rivers and Streams.	Distances. Intermediate.	Distances. Total.	Remarks.
G.O.C. Myingyán District.	Political Officer, Chin Hills.	**1. Tsíyán**	7 0	7 0	Along the Tiddim road for $3\frac{1}{2}$ miles; here it turns almost due north, the path to Tsíyán continuing westward. About 200 or 300 yards after leaving Tiddim road the path, slightly descending, runs along southern side of ridge and is very narrow; ground to left-hand side very precipitous, but after this point it is fairly good, a little difficult in a few places, but easily put right in a few minutes. There is a nice-looking spot for a camp about a mile after leaving Tiddim road to the south of path about $\frac{1}{4}$ mile off; water was seen there. The path descends easily to 3 miles from Tiddim road, when it runs along north side of ridge; here it was found very steep and difficult; path very narrow and shaly. It was improved by the pioneers; but owing to the shaly nature of ground would not last long. This steep bit takes one down and lands one on the top of a flat and fairly open part of the ridge just above the village of Chínnwai about 500 yards to the right. Then along this flat piece and the path divides, the one to the right running down into Chínnwai, the one to the left running round a small spur when the village of Tsíyán is seen immediately below. The camping ground was selected just above the village. The ground is not a bad one, but commanded; room was found for about 800 men and coolies. Water was got from village below, but was deficient both in quantity and quality, having a decidedly unpleasant taste. The country after leaving Tiddim road

FROM FORT WHITE (NEW) TO MANIPUR—*continued.*

BRANCH IV—*continued.*

Authorities.		Number and Names of Stages, Rivers and Streams.	Distances.		Remarks.
Military.	Civil.		Intermediate.	Total.	
G.O.C. Myingyán District.	Political Officer, Chin Hills.	**1. Tsíyán**—*cont.*			is fairly open; grass and small trees thick in few places only; a good many fir trees about, but small ones only. In the neighbourhood of both Chínnwai and Tsíyán there is a good deal of cultivation. In the former about 32 houses and in the latter about 70 houses (counted). Aneroid at the camp showed 4,700 feet. Started from Dimlo 9-10 A.M., arrived Tsíyán 4-30 P.M.
		2. Camp on right bank (west) of Nankathé river.	M. F. 3 2	M. F. 10 2	Leaving camping ground path runs south-west by south to the top of the ridge, then fairly level. About 1 mile from Tsíyán path descends rapidly, in places very steep; ground fairly open and as it descends passes over patches of cultivation on top of ridge. At about 1¼ miles a path turns off sharp down side of ridge, nearly at right angles to path already traversed, into the valley below; path extremely steep; country jungle grass cut up by deep water-courses (without water). Path runs first south-west and then south-east to a point about 300 feet above and 500 yards from the river at 3 miles where there is camping ground. The path from the camp to river is extremely steep; in fact only a track made by men of column going down to get water. The camping ground was not a good one, being on such a steep slope, but nearest place we could get to river on account of water. There was also a minimum amount from two small drips found near camp in two water-courses south-east and north-west of camp. Distance from the top of the ridge where the path turns down, a little more than 1½ miles. Aneroid showed 1,600 feet. Aneroid at level of river 1,400 feet; river at this point varies from 25 yards to 40 and 50 yards wide. Current in rapids about 5½ miles an hour and in deep water 4 miles. The main path runs on down ridge for about ¾ of a mile and to camp on ridge just above the river, a portion of column going on and camping below by the side of the river. Camping ground on cultivation patches. Aneroid at camp showed 2,200 feet and about 80 feet above river. The shore bivouac, *i.e.*, the camping ground down in the river, is not large; it takes about 20 minutes to get down to it from the upper camp and 40 minutes to return; it is commanded from the other side, but to a certain degree protected by the picquets in the upper camp. The river varies from about 20 yards at the rapid just below the lower camp to 40 yards at deep water opposite camp. There was a rope and a cradle across here, but the Chins had cut it before we arrived. The gradient down to river extremely heavy and path not good; dangerous also on account of the loose stones on the side of the hill. Cross river by means of a raft swung on a wire hawser; raft carried about seven armed men each journey and took from 5 to 7 minutes for return journey. Then up the bank on the opposite side, very steep, old Chin path very much improved by pioneers for about 300 or 400 yards, then not so steep for the remainder of way into camp, a total distance from river of a little less than ¾ of a mile by the path. Camping ground in cultivation on an under-feature. Water-supply from a nullah west of camping ground; supply small. Aneroid at camp showed 2,250 feet.

No. 3.

FROM FORT WHITE (NEW) TO MANIPUR—*continued.*

BRANCH IV—*continued.*

Authorities. Military.	Authorities. Civil.	Number and Names of Stages, Rivers and Streams.	Distances. Intermediate. M.	F.	Total. M.	F.	Remarks.
G.O.C. Myingyán District.	Political Officer, Chin Hills.	**3. Kaptiál** ... Two small and one large stream.	3	4	13	6	For the first ¾ mile the path runs nearly north by north-west to top of the ridge, then runs along side (on the north side) of it for a little over ¼ of a mile. Path steep in places, but improved by the pioneers. Then due west, gradually turning north-west over two small streams. The path near these streams is bad, and rather dangerous for mules; the water-courses (several dry ones) are crossed by small logs and do not afford foot-hold for mules, so deviations had to be made in the path. At about 2 miles the path winds round a spur, path good, and when round it Kaptiál can be seen about 1 mile due north-west. From this spur the path is fairly good, but had to be improved in places. About 350 yards before reaching Kaptiál the path crosses a fair-sized stream, the descent to it being easy, but the ascent up to Kaptiál fairly steep. Country not much enclosed, but a thick bit of jungle near the two small streams. From the last stream up to Kaptiál also the jungle was thick. Kaptiál (now burnt) was a large place of about 300 or 400 houses, surrounded by a small ditch and a certain amount of stockading; water plentiful. Aneroid showed 4,300 feet. Bearing to Kennedy Peak 83°.

No. 4.

From FORT WHITE to NASHWIN.

BY CAPT. R. BAKER, 1ST NORFOLK REGIMENT, 5TH DECEMBER 1892.

Authorities. Military.	Authorities. Civil.	Number and Names of Stages, Rivers and Streams.	Distances. Intermediate. M.	F.	Total. M.	F.	Remarks.
G.O.C. Myingyán District.	Political Officer, Chin Hills.	**1. Nashwin** ...	4	4	4	4	Leaving Fort White by the upper or Tiddim gate, follow the path that leads to the top of the ridge, bearing slightly away to the left; near the top the path crosses the old Fort White road. The path now runs along the ridge of the Lítha range, going at first slightly up-hill through a thick bit of jungle, but very shortly afterwards runs out into the open, leaving the woods and jungle to the left. After about a ¼ of a mile along the ridge the path runs slightly down-hill and then fairly level along the western slope, till about 1½ miles from Fort White, when it commences to run down the spur along which it continues almost the whole way to the village of Nashwin, with the exception of the last ½ mile, when it turns off the main spur to the left. The country for the first 2 miles is very fairly open, grass with fir trees about, but as we get lower down the wood gets a bit thicker. About 2½ miles from Fort White there is the commencement of a clearing, and a good deal of timber is cut and lying on the ground. General direction of path is about south-west. At 3¾ or 4 miles from Fort White the path bends to the left and the village of Nashwin is seen

FROM FORT WHITE TO NASHWIN—*continued.*

Authorities.		Number and Names of Stages, Rivers and Streams.	Distances.		Remarks.
Military.	Civil.		Intermediate.	Total.	
G.O.C. Myingyán District.	Political Officer, Chin Hills.	**1. Nashwin**—*cont.*			lying in a hollow on the south side of the spur. The whole path is exceedingly steep and quite unfitted for anything but cooly transport. A mule was taken down with column, but could not be ridden, except in very few places. Nashwin contained about 40 houses surrounded by cultivation, mostly sweet potatoes. Water-supply close by and good. There is a good stream of water in the nullah below the village. It is commanded on almost every side. A column visiting Nashwin in December 1892 took 1 hour 40 minutes to get there, but 4½ to come back, so steep is the path.

No. 5.

From HÁKA to FORT TREGEAR.

BY LIEUT. C. R. BALLARD, ATTACHÉ, INTELLIGENCE BRANCH, BURMA, FEBRUARY 1892.

Military.	Civil.	Number and Names of Stages, Rivers and Streams.	Intermediate M.	Intermediate F.	Total M.	Total F.	Remarks.
G.O.C. Myingyán District.	Political Officer, Chin Hills.	**1. Camp on Sa Vár.** Boinu Vár, 1½ feet deep, 25 feet broad; Sa Vár, a tributary, 1 foot deep, 15 feet broad; several times.	**10**	**0**	10	0	Path leaves Háka nearly due west and is level and good. A short hill zigzagged leads down to the Boinu valley at 7 miles. From here the track is in the bed of a tributary of the Boinu, called the Sa Vár, sometimes very narrow, and the stream is crossed 22 times. At the last crossing there is a good camp with water and grass, but not much wood.
		2. Tlántláng Ywama, or Camp on La Vár.	**6**	**0**	16	0	A steep ascent for 1½ miles, but path is good; it then undulates along a ridge called Sarangputongkláng, whence the Tlántlang village of Tlánwra can be seen to the south-west for 2½ miles and descends again for 2 miles, the village of Tlántláng Ywama coming suddenly into view during the descent; a short ascent of ½ mile into the village. Here there is very little water and for troops and especially mules, it is better to go on for 2½ miles down the further valley, where there is an excellent camping ground with a good stream (the Lá Vár) wood, and grass. Tlántláng village consists of 150 houses on a spur facing south. It is commanded from the spurs above.
		3. Twalam ... Lá Vár and another stream.	**8**	**4**	24	4	From the camp this march would be only 6 miles. The path crosses one high range of hills, called the Wishipkláng, going up for 3 miles and then down for 3; fair camp at stream below Twalam village, which consists of about 50 houses on the top of a spur.

FROM HÁKA TO FORT TREGEAR—*continued.*

Authorities.		Number and Names of Stages, Rivers and Streams.	Distances.				Remarks.
Military.	Civil.		Intermediate.		Total.		
			M.	F.	M.	F.	
G.O.C. Myingyân District.	Political Officer, Chin Hills.	**4. Hmunlipi village or Hmunlipi post.** La-aw Vár, 6 inches deep, 15 feet broad. Another small stream called Shetsi Vár.	12 12	0 4	36 37	4 0	Path leaves camp going steeply up opposite spur, general direction west-north-west, and leaving Twalam on the left. After ½ mile level it descends again to a small stream. Crossing this there is a very long ascent for 3 miles and then a more easy descent for 3½ miles to La-aw Vár. An easy path for 3 miles more than the La-aw Vár is recrossed and a good path leads up to the village of Hmunlipi. A camp might be made at the second La-aw Vár or in the village. On the march the village of Hriankan (Tlántláng, 50 houses) can be seen on an opposite spur to the south-west across the La-aw Vár. Hmunlipi (Tlántláng) contains about 40 houses; grass and firewood plentiful. Chief's name Mangla. Half-a-mile before reaching Hmunlipi village a path leads off backwards in a southerly direction. This leads to Hmunlipi post. The La-aw Vár is below the post. Wood and grass obtainable here.
		5. Tao (5,000 feet). A few small streams.	13	0	50	0	Path leaves camp southwards, then bends gradually to the west, leaving Hriankan village on the left about ¾ mile off. At 6 miles the road crosses the "Tao gap." About this point the Northern route (*vide* Alternative I) from Háka joins in. There is water at 5½ miles. From the gap there is an easy descent for 5 miles, but the road requires mending. Here a stream is crossed, and there is 2½ miles very bad going up to the village. There is a large camping ground at this stream; water abundant. This last 2 miles is almost impassable for mules at present and will be very dangerous until a fresh path is traced. This is a hard march, and a halt at 11 miles at the stream is advisable. A camp was formed ¾ mile below the village, but it is small and inconvenient. Tao village belongs to the Tlántláng tribe and consists of about 80 houses built on top of a spur running north-west from the Taokláng, commanded by knolls on the spur above, covered with coarse grass. Head man's name Nga Poi. The Taokláng, a high bold peak seen from a long way off on all sides, was formerly known as the Sangalkláng, but Taokláng is the proper name. On the opposite side of the valley to the south of Tao is the Tiriankláng, another very prominent range.
		6. Camp in clearings above Shertôk river. Shertôk river.	7	0	57	0	After first 3 miles steep descent to the Shertôk river at a point where a large nullah joins it from the north of the path, 5 miles. Thence for 2 miles down bed of Shertôk, crossing and recrossing it frequently. Camp anywhere in the cultivation clearings along the valley of the Shertôk.
* G.O.C. Presidency District.	Political Officer, Southern Lushai.	**7. Sangao (4,680 feet).** Kolodyne river, Sesi and other streams.	11	0	68	0	Steep ascent of 500 feet from the bed of the Shertôk, thence westward along top of spur for a mile and then difficult descent to Sesi stream, down narrow water-course, in one part only 6

* The line of division does not appear to have been definitely fixed as yet.—A. F.

FROM HÁKA TO FORT TREGEAR—*continued.*

Authorities.		Number and Names of Stages, Rivers and Streams.	Distances.				Remarks.
Military.	Civil.		Intermediate.		Total.		
			M.	F.	M.	F.	
G.O.C. Presidency District.	Political Officer, Southern Lushai.	**7. Sangao (4,680 feet)**—*cont.*					feet wide with cliffs on both sides. Follow Sesi down to Kolodyne river; crossing at 5 miles, elevation 1,130 feet. Good ford just above some cliffs. After crossing path runs up bed of river for ¼ mile, then very steep ascent of a mile, from the river, most of the zigzags having been cut off; path still ascending improves and for the last 4 miles is in fair state of repair. Sangao consists of 40 houses; water-supply ¼ mile away in valley to east, not good; a still scantier supply west, close to village.
		8. Dopura	**9**	**0**	77	0	Along government cleared road in good repair and passable by mules throughout, except in one or two places where trees have fallen across the path. About a 3 hours' march. Dopura village is situated on a knoll, but is commanded on the east by another knoll about 300 yards off. Plenty of water in the valley below the village.
		9. Fort Tregear...	**7**	**0**	84	0	Along the government road, except the ascent from the valley of the Narchang to the Darjow spur, alterations have been made, all the zigzags having been cut out 2½ to 3 hours' march.

ALTERNATIVE I.

FROM HÁKA TO TAO (STAGE 5) *viâ* NORTHERN ROUTE.

BY LIEUT. E. W. M. NORIE, PAID ATTACHÉ, INTELLIGENCE BRANCH, FEBRUARY 1890.

Military.	Civil.	Number and Names of Stages, Rivers and Streams.	Intermediate M.	Intermediate F.	Total M.	Total F.	Remarks.
G.O.C. Myingyán District.	Political Officer, Chin Hills.	**1. Camp on Sa Vár.**	**10**	**0**	10	0	*Vide* above.
		2. Tlántláng ...	**16**	**0**	16	0	*Vide* above.
		3. Camp on Kying Vár. La Vár, Kying Vár.	**12**	**0**	28	0	The road from Tlántláng ran north-west along the side of the spur above the village and then began to descend, running gradually down by a long spur until it reached the La Vár at 5 miles, the last bit of the descent being pretty steep. The La Vár is a small stream here, about 10 feet broad. The path runs down the bed of the stream crossing it five times in ½ a mile and then begins to ascend skirting round the side of a hill. The ascent is pretty steep most of the way, and at 7½ miles the top of the ridge is reached. The La Vár can be seen flowing away to the north and it ultimately joins the Tipi. On a spur of a high precipitous range to the north-east can be seen the large independent village of Lônzat, about 3 miles off. It contains over 200 houses. The path now runs along the ridge through fir trees and at 8½ miles reaches Shopum, a village of about 40 houses, surrounded by a stockade and ditch. There is no place to halt on here owing to scarcity of water. Passing through the village the path runs down a long spur and at 11 miles reaches the Kying Vár, a stream of the same size as the La Vár. It then runs down

FROM HÁKA TO FORT TREGEAR—*continued.*

ALTERNATIVE I—*continued.*

Authorities. Military.	Authorities. Civil.	Number and Names of Stages, Rivers and Streams.	Distances. Intermediate.	Distances. Total.	Remarks.
G.O.C. Myingyán District.	Political Officer, Chin Hills.	**3. Camp on Kying Vár**—*cont.*			the valley of this, crossing and recrossing it several times, to camping ground. Camp might be made anywhere along the stream, grass, water, and firewood being plentiful.
			M. F.	M. F.	
		4. Camp on Bu Vár below Tángzáng. Bu Vár.	**11 0**	39 0	Leaving camp the road leads down the bed of the Kying Vár for about 3 miles and is very stony and rough. It then leads abruptly up to the top of the ridge to the south by a very steep ascent. Reaching the top it runs along for ½ a mile to the village of Shihmu. Shihmu is a Tlántláng village of about 20 houses. There is a camping ground beyond it about ½ a mile further on near a stream. The road leads through the village and continues pretty level with a pretty steep descent at about 5 miles. Skirting round the hill side it reaches the top of a long spur, at about 6½ miles, and leads down this with some steep descents in places. Soon afterwards the village of Tángzáng is seen straight in front on the side of a hill to the west and the road runs on as if going to the village. About a mile before reaching it, however, the path suddenly strikes off to the south, another path leading on to Tángzáng about 1 mile further and leads down pretty steeply to the Bu Vár. The last part of the descent is very steep. The Bu Vár flows west to the Tipi river. There is a good halting place on the left bank on the path. Water, grass, and firewood are plentiful. Tángzáng is a large village tributary to Tlántláng and contains about 100 houses. Fowls and eggs are procurable.
		5. Tao ... ... Small streams.	**12 0**	51 0	The path runs generally south. At first it ascends very steeply and then more gradually to the top of a spur and runs up this towards the main range for about 3 miles. Skirting round the hill side it strikes another spur, down which it runs to the saddle connecting this range with Taokláng. At about 6 miles it joins the main road described above.

ALTERNATIVE II.

FROM SANGAO (STAGE 7) TO FORT TREGEAR *viâ* DOKOLA.

BY CAPT. SHAKESPEAR, D.S.O., SUPERINTENDENT, S. LUSHAI HILLS, 1892.

Military	Civil	Stage	Intermediate	Total	Remarks
G.O.C. Presidency District.	Political Officer, Southern Lushai.	**1. Shemuna's village.**	**6 0**	6 0	The path from Sangao (Tingtua's village) to Shemuna's village branches off the Government road ¼ mile west of Sangao saddle and descends southwards for 200 feet into the bed of the Durjow; path very steep for the last ½ mile. It then ascends to Shemuna's at an easy gradient and enters the village from the south. Height of Shemuna's above sea-level 4,020 feet; number of houses 58. Water-supply scanty, ½ mile to westwards on road to Vantura. From Shemuna's the road ascends gradually for a mile to the west on to a

FROM HÁKA TO FORT TREGEAR—*continued.*

ALTERNATIVE II—*continued.*

Authorities. Military.	Authorities. Civil.	Number and Names of Stages, Rivers and Streams.	Distances. Intermediate. M.	F.	Distances. Total. M.	F.	Remarks.
G.O.C. Presidency District.	Political Officer, Southern Lushai.	**1. Shemuna's village**—*cont.*					saddle 250 feet above Shemuna's, from which it descends sharply 700 feet and then for 2 miles descends gradually another 150 feet into the bed of a nullah. The path then ascends at a very steep gradient through thick jungle into jhums, through which it runs to the top of the spur and then descends 100 feet into a small nullah which is the village water-supply and then ascends to Vantura. Height of Vantura above sea-level is 4,200 feet. Number of houses 119. The time taken from Sangao to Vantura was 7½ hours. Vantura's village is on the Lungtien hill.
		2. Vantura's village. Funka river.	5	0	11	0	To Dokola the path leaves Vantura's at the east entrance and descends through jhums and grass jungle for 1,600 feet into a small nullah, then runs along the main spur between Vantura and Dokola, running in and out of several small nullahs for 3 miles and then drops very abruptly through bamboo jungle 1,100 feet into the bed of the Funka. Leaving the Funka about 200 yards higher up the path runs straight up on to the Dokola spur, a ¼ mile north-west of the village, and then descends into Dokola on the Funka hill. The height of Dokola above sea-level, 3,600 feet; number of houses, 50. Time taken from Vantura is 3½ hours.
		3. Dokola	7	0	18	0	There is another path which leaves Vantura at the same entrance and descends into the valley of the Funka, along a spur which branches off from the main spur by the site of Howsata's old village, then runs off the bed of the Funka till the first-mentioned path is reached.
		4. Tregear (from Shemuna).	17	0	23	0	From Shemuna's to Tregear the path leaves the village at the north entrance and descends northwards along the crest of a spur which is covered with very dense bamboo and grass jungle into the bed of the Darjow. The drop from Shemuna is 2,200 feet. There is a good camping ground on the edge of the river. From the Darjow stream the path ascends very steeply for above 600 feet, then runs along the crest of a spur at a very easy gradient on to a saddle dividing the Dopura plain and the Darjow stream. Height of saddle above sea-level 4,100 feet. It then runs north-east across the plain till it joins the Government road about ½ a mile west of Dopura village, *i.e.*, 6½ miles from Fort Tregear. Time taken from Shemuna, 8½ hours.

FROM HÁKA TO FORT TREGEAR—*continued.*

BRANCH I.

FROM TLÁNTLÁNG YWAMA (STAGE 2) TO ZANHLUIN *viâ* DAWN.

BY LIEUT. E. W. M. NORIE, FROM NATIVE INFORMATION, APRIL 1890.

Authorities.		Number and Names of Stages, Rivers and Streams.	Distances.				Remarks.
Military.	Civil.		Intermediate.		Total.		
			M.	F.	M.	F.	
G.O.C. Myingyán District.	Political Officer, Chin Hills.	**1. Farôn** ... ... La Vár.	**13**	**4**	13	4	From Tlántláng the road runs to Shopum, 8½ miles. *See* Alternative Route No. I above. From Shopum it runs in a north-north-westerly direction to Farôn at 13½ miles. Farôn is a Tlántláng village of about 30 houses under a headman called Mingbur.
		2. Tlampi	**10**	**0**	23	4	From Farôn the road runs north-west for about 10 miles to the large Tlántláng village of Tlampi, containing over 100 houses.
		3. Dawn	***20**	**0**	43	4	From here it runs west to the large Tlántláng village of Dawn, containing over 100 houses under a headman called Lyankôn.
		4. Zanhluin ... Tipi river.	**25**	**0**	68	4	Road runs west and crossing the Tipi river reaches a village called Zanhluin at 25 miles.

BRANCH II.

FROM TWALAM (STAGE 3) TO VAMKWA.

BY LIEUT. E. W. M. NORIE, FROM NATIVE INFORMATION, APRIL 1890.

Military.	Civil.	Number and Names of Stages, Rivers and Streams.	M.	F.	M.	F.	Remarks.
G.O.C. Myingyán District.	Political Officer, Chin Hills.	**1. Shalen or Shangkal.** La-aw Vár and another stream.	**9**	**0**	9	0	General direction south-west. The path runs down-hill from Twalam for some distance to a stream which it crosses. The descent and ascent to and from this stream are steep. It then runs across a ridge and, descending again on the other side, reaches the La-aw Vár, which it crosses and ascends steeply to Shalen village on the opposite hill side. Shalen is a Tlántláng village of about 30 houses under a Chief called Lyankum. The village is also called Shangkal.
		2. Vamkwa or Tlángbwé. Stream.	**9**	**0**	18	0	General direction south-west. The road passing Shalen ascends to the top of the ridge behind it and then descends to a small stream. The name of this ridge is the Sanga (Sankali) kláng. Crossing the stream it ascends the opposite ridge, which is very steep and, reaching the top, descends to Vamkwa village on the other side.

* This must be a good deal over-estimated.

FROM HÁKA TO FORT TREGEAR—*continued.*

BRANCH III.

FROM HMUNLIPI POST (STAGE 4) TO WANTU *viâ* HRIAMKHAN AND VAMKWA.

BY LIEUT. C. AINSLIE, R.E., MARCH 1892.

Authorities. Military.	Authorities. Civil.	Number and Names of Stages, Rivers and Streams.	Distances. Intermediate. M. F.	Distances. Total. M. F.	Remarks.
G.O.C. Myingyán District.	Political Officer, Chin Hills.	**1. Camp on Lunliri Vár.** Tongshé and Lunliri streams.	8 0	8 0	First 1½ miles along Háka-Fort Tregear mule track, then southwards for about a mile to the village of Hriamkhan, road good and easy. Steep descent from Hriamkhan spur for a mile to the Tongshé stream, cross this stream and shortly after the Lunliri stream, in the valley of which there are many acres of flat grass land. Small uncomfortable camping ground on the left bank of the Lunliri stream at about 8 miles, commanded on all sides. Fair water-supply from stream.
		2. Vamkwa (4,150 feet). Vár Kaung and several small streams.	8 0	16 0	Path ascends through dense jungle for 800 feet to a gap in the range running east from the Tinangkláng at about 5,400 feet; thence long descent of about 2,000 feet along a long spur narrow and rocky towards the bottom, where great labour would be required to render it passable by mountain guns. The Vár Kaung is now reached and the path runs down its bed for a mile over large boulders, rising steeply from the bed of this stream for about 1,400 feet in a south-westerly direction, crossing several small streams, to Vamkwa 60 houses, mostly inferior. Water-supply very scanty 300 yards beyond the village on the path to Bwé (east). The village is built across a spur running south from the main Chirian range and is commanded from points higher up on the same spur and is within easy range of guns from the pass in the Chirian range on the road to Bwé (East), *see* Branch No. VI, Tao (Stage 5) to Wantu.
		3. Wantu ... ... Vár Kaung, La-aw Vár and Hnut Vár.	9 0	25 0	For description of this stage, *see* Branch No. VI below.

BRANCH IV.

FROM HMUNLIPI POST (STAGE 4) TO DAWN.

BY LIEUT. C. AINSLIE, R.E., MARCH 1892.

Military	Civil	Stage	Intermediate M. F.	Total M. F.	Remarks
G.O.C. Myingyán District.	Political Officer, Chin Hills.	**1. Tunzán** ... Bu Vár.	12 0	12 0	The road follows the Háka mule track for a short distance, nearly as far as Hmunlipi, after which it runs north fairly level and good round the west side of the range running north and south. About 2½ miles out you cross a little stream, where animals can water one by one. The highest point reached is 5,550 feet. After 8 miles of easy going the road curling round north-west runs down a steep spur to the Bu Vár. There is

FROM HÁKA TO FORT TREGEAR—*continued.*

BRANCH IV—*continued.*

Authorities. Military.	Authorities. Civil.	Number and Names of Stages, Rivers and Streams.	Distances. Inter-mediate.	Distances. Total.	Remarks.
G.O.C. Myingyán District.	Political Officer, Chin Hills.	**1. Tunzán**—*cont.*			plenty of camping ground here. Zigzags were cut out to enable the gun mules to descend safely. After crossing the Bu Vár there is ½ a mile of very steep road, up which the guns had to be carried by hand. A day's work with 50 pioneers would make this piece easy. Having reached the top of the spur, the road runs very level and easy for 1½ miles to the village. The road runs between small knolls, which offer great facilities for defence. There are at present no stockades. The village consists of about 70 wretched bamboo houses built on a saddle. The water-supply is some way below the village in nullahs. A path leads from the village down the hill side westwards, another north up the spur. The village is seen into from the road about 100 yards before reaching it across a small ravine.
		2. Lonler ...	M. F. 6 4	M. F. 18 4	The range runs north-west from Tunzán and the road skirts round the west of it. You can ride 5 miles; then there is rather a steep descent, but not impracticable for guns, to a low saddle below Bamkwa, a small village of 40 houses. Another small village, Funka, is passed about 4 miles from Tunzán, ½ mile to the left on a spur which runs towards the Tao Kláng. From Bamkwa to Lonler is a mile of easy going up and down. The village of Lonler is situated across a spur at about 5,000 feet elevation. It contains about 100 houses, mostly of poor construction. The country round it is open undulating grass land which affords no very good cover. A knoll, 100 yards south of the village, commands it, and guns could probably reach it at long range from the top of the spur 4 or 5 miles from Tunzán. Fort Tregear, Tengshai village, Rawkwa, a village of 40 houses, perched high up on the Tao Kláng bearing south, and Londin, 20 houses, bearing north-east, are visible from here and many high peaks.
		3. Dawn ...	10 0	28 4	General direction north-west. The road runs down to the saddle connecting the Lonler spur and Dawn Kláng, where water was found in a nullah on the right; height 3,700 feet; distance nearly 3 miles. From here commences a very steep ascent of 2,400 feet, the last 300 of which is impracticable for led ponies even, being a succession of steps over large rocks on a spur only a few feet wide with precipitous sides. The hill coolies had to pass their loads up from hand to hand. This is probably the worst bit of road in the Chin hills. The Chins call it "Oui soklat mat," or "The place where a dog falls down." Having reached the summit 6,100 feet, the road improves and runs along the crest of the range, rising to 6,300 at the 9th mile, when it drops steeply to Dawn, which is just 1,000 feet lower. There is reported to be another easier road; but, as it has not been used for five years, it is said to be so overgrown as to be practically useless. Dawn has about 70 very inferior bamboo houses crowded together. It is commanded from above and untenable if the Chins allow troops to ascend the Dawn Kláng, which ought to be impassable in the face of a determined resistance.

FROM HÁKA TO FORT TREGEAR—*continued.*

BRANCH V.

FROM HMUNLIPI POST (STAGE 4) TO RAWKWA.

BY LIEUT. C. T. SWAN, 4TH MADRAS PIONEERS, FEBRUARY 1892.

Authorities. Military.	Authorities. Civil.	Number and Names of Stages, Rivers and Streams.	Distances. Intermediate.	Distances. Total.	Remarks.
			M. F.	M. F.	
G.O.C. Myingyán District.	Political Officer, Chin Hills.	**1. Rawkwa** ... Several small streams.	**11 11**	11 0	The road is the same as that to Tunzan (*see* Branch No. IV) for 7½ miles, when it drops 1,500 feet to a stream flowing north (one of the sources of the Tipi or Bu Vár); 200 yards further on it crosses another stream, which joins the former a short way below; water plentiful. There is camping ground here. Animals cannot be taken further than this. The road runs north up a steep spur, then down west to a little water in a nullah, north again, and finally west into the village. There is a precipitous climb of 20 feet just below the village, about 2½ miles from the camping ground and about 3,000 feet above it. (The village is probably at 6,000 feet elevation or more.) The village is situated on a narrow spur running north-east from the Tao Kláng which is precipitous on both sides, a poor village of some 50 houses. Water is obtained from a well. It is bad in quality and small in quantity. There is said to be a difficult track running over the Tao Kláng to Tao village, but this requires confirmation.

BRANCH VI.

FROM TAO (STAGE 5) TO HMUNLIPI POST (STAGE 4) *viâ* BWÉ, VAMKWA AND WUNTU.

BY LIEUT. C. R. BALLARD, ATTACHÉ, INTELLIGENCE BRANCH, BURMA, FEBRUARY 1892, AND LIEUT. AINSLIE, R.E., MARCH 1892.

Authorities. Military.	Authorities. Civil.	Number and Names of Stages, Rivers and Streams.	Distances. Intermediate.	Distances. Total.	Remarks.
G.O.C. Myingyán District.	Political Officer, Chin Hills.	**1. Camp on small stream.** Stream 8 inches deep, 20 feet broad.	**10 0**	10 4	A very hard march; impassable for mules, path descends very steeply from Tao for at least 2,000 feet to the Shirtôk Vár at 3 miles, plenty of water. Crossing the stream there is one long steep ascent of about 2,000 feet, at first almost precipitous, and the whole path is extremely bad and much labour would be required to render it fit for guns, which could, however, be brought along the Háka-Tregear road which is crossed about one-third of the distance up the hill, after which the path is less steep; no water after this stream. From the top of the hill the path runs along the crest of the Bual Pin range and is fair. Camp at 10 miles, but water very scarce indeed even for drinking purposes; it is found in two small nullahs. Plenty of wood and grass. Direction of this march changes a good deal, but is generally south.

FROM HÁKA TO FORT TREGEAR—*continued.*

BRANCH VI—*continued.*

Authorities. Military.	Authorities. Civil.	Number and Names of Stages, Rivers and Streams.	Distances. Intermediate. M. F.	Distances. Total. M. F.	Remarks.
G.O.C. Myingyán District.	Political Officer, Chin Hills.	**2. Camp beyond Bwé (East).** Htampi Vár 1 foot deep, 30 feet broad.	12 0	22 4	Three miles very good going along the ridge which is narrow with steep sides in places to Bwé (West) village, called also Kwatsumkwa. This village together with Bwé (East) form Bwé; its individual name is Htúnfin. The village consists of about 100 bamboo houses, pleasantly situated amongst fir trees, commanded from the crest of the range on the east. Water-supply below the village, scanty. Very little supplies obtainable. Leaving village, path descends east for 1,500 feet down a steep hill to the Htampi or Puiaw Vár, crossing this an equally steep ascent of about 1,200 feet for 3 miles to Bwé (East), called also Vadunkwa or Kasún, which comes suddenly into view and has 70 houses mostly bamboo, and a good water-supply 100 yards south of the village. On the further side of this village there is a small stream, and a camp might be made here. After leaving the village the path goes up to the right and crossing the ridge keeps along the further side of it bending gradually to the left.* Four miles from the village is a stream with a camp on the further side. Water is also met with about 2 miles from Bwé (East) and frequently in next 2 miles.
		3. Vamkwa (4,150 feet). Several small streams.	8 0	30 4	The path goes up and down crossing several small spurs and nullahs, then turning eastwards it goes over a ridge and down a long descent for 3½ miles to another good stream. Elevation 4,150 feet. Soon after this the road runs south-east up a spur to 5,100 feet elevation, from whence Vamkwa is seen bearing 115°. To reach it the road descends a long spur rather easily to a stream at 4,000 feet, then running nearly east crosses the Chirian range at a pass about 4,200 feet elevation, descends very steeply for 900 feet to a small stream, and up again to the village which lies at 4,150 feet, passing the water-supply, which is very scanty, about 300 yards below the village. Vamkwa contains about 60 houses, mostly inferior. It is built across a spur running south from the main Chirian range; it is within easy reach of guns from the pass in the Chirian range and commanded from above on its own spur.
		4. Wantu ... ... Vár Kaung, Lá-aw Vár, Hnut Vár.	9 0	39 4	From Vamkwa the Chin track running through the village descends the spur easily except for the last few hundred feet to the Rumchi; elevation 2,000 feet; distance 2½ miles; direction southerly. The road then runs along down stream, soon meeting the Vár Kaung and following it down, crossing and recrossing it several times for a mile, when the valley opens out very level and the road runs more easterly to the Lá-aw Vár which is about 40

* About 3 miles from Bwé (East) on the way to Vamkwa there is a stretch of very bare ground at 5,000 feet elevation, free from jungle and covered with long grass. The crest of the hill is about 500 feet above on the west; on the east is a very deep precipice. It is well watered and suitable for a large camp *or a permanent post.*

FROM HÁKA TO FORT TREGEAR—*continued.*

BRANCH VI—*continued.*

Authorities. Military.	Authorities. Civil.	Number and Names of Stages, Rivers and Streams.	Distances. Intermediate. M.	F.	Distances. Total. M.	F.	Remarks.
G.O.C. Myingyán District.	Political Officer, Chin Hills.	**4. Wantu**—*cont.*					yards broad and a foot deep. After crossing this you climb 50 feet or more and arrive on an extensive flat island covered with grass, with bamboos at one corner. The island is bounded by the Lá-aw and Hnut Vár, and makes a capital camping ground in dry weather for a very large force. The road crosses the island and the Hnut Vár and ascends a spur covered with patches of dense small bamboo jungle, rising for the most part fairly easily for 4½ miles to Wantu; elevation 4,150 feet. The village is built on the hill side and is commanded from the spur above. The road runs level round the hill side for some distance before entering the village, and crosses a ditch dug for defence some distance outside the village. The actual entrance is protected by three lines of stockades, their ends resting on dense jungle, so a direct frontal attack by infantry would be difficult. Guns could be brought from Vamkwa without great difficulty, but to get them to Vamkwa would take several days' hard work from Hmunlipi post. Wantu contains about 70 houses, many of which are very fine with large compounds in front cut out from the hill side, as much as 20 feet in some cases. The Chief's house half-way down the village is the finest in the Chin hills, being 180 feet long and quite 40 feet wide. In the front room were planks 66 inches wide, and many over 3 feet wide of great length.
		5. Hmunlipi post. One stream 6 inches deep, 12 feet broad.	**9**	**0**	47	4	Path ascends slightly for 1½ miles, then descends to stream at 4 miles. Here there is plenty of open ground and a good camp might be formed. The path ascends very steeply for 2 miles to the village of Hriankan; passing through this there is an easy road for 3 miles into the post.

No. 6.

From HÁKA to HANTA.

BY LIEUT. F. CHURCHILL, 4TH MADRAS PIONEERS.

Military	Civil	Stages	Intermediate M.	F.	Total M.	F.	Remarks
G.O.C. Myingyán District.	**Political Officer, Chin Hills.**	**1. Camp (4,430 feet).**	**13**	**4**	13	4	From Háka the road goes south over hill, following the Háka-Kán road; from the top of this hill it descends gently to 6,700 feet (3¼ miles), where it leaves the road to Kán. From this point it keeps along the top of the hill to 4½ miles and then goes nearly east, several hundred feet below the top, until it crosses a saddle about 7 miles from Háka. At 7½ miles there is a camping ground with a good supply of water near. Half-a-mile further on the road crosses another saddle (6,016 feet) and from here, going round a reëntrant, gradually descends to 4,480 feet, at which point (13½ miles) there is a camping ground with water near. Between the 8th mile and this camp water is met at several places on the road.

Authorities.		Number and Names of Stages, Rivers and Streams.	Distances.		Remarks.
Military.	Civil.		Intermediate.	Total.	
			M. F.	M. F.	
G.O.C. Myingyán District.	Political Officer, Chin Hills.	**2. Camp (4,000 feet).**	**13 4**	27 0	From here, after ascending about 200 or 300 feet across a spur, the road descends by several zigzags to 3,280 feet, crossing a large nullah by a bridge. Here there is a large supply of water and a camping ground (3¾ miles), but there would probably be too much water during the rains for this to be a good halting place. The road now ascends over another spur, by several zigzags, the slope of the hill being in some places very steep and, descending the other side of the spur, crosses a large stream by means of a bridge, going round a reëntrant and over one small spur, a camping ground is reached at 6¾ miles. There is a large supply of water, but not much level ground for a camp. Immediately after leaving this camp the road goes up over another spur and there is a good camping ground, with a large supply of water near at 8¾ miles. Just before reaching this camp two large nullahs are crossed by bridges. From here the road keeps nearly along the level, slightly descending into and ascending from one small nullah. There is another camping ground at 13½ miles with a large supply of water near (altitude of camp 4,000 feet).
		3. Hanta ... ... Nanpathé river.	**12 0**	39 0	Half-a-mile beyond camp the top of the spur is reached, down which the road descends to the Nanpathé river. This spur, although very long, is in some places exceedingly steep, especially the final descent into the Nanpathé, and the road is taken down by a great many zigzags to the river, which is 1,600 feet above the level of the sea. The Nanpathé is nearly 32 miles from Háka. There is plenty of camping ground on either side of the river, the best being just above the bank on the Háka side. The hill, which the road now ascends, having crossed the river, is very steep and the road, crossing a saddle at an elevation of about 4,000 feet, keeps along the other side of the hill until Hanta post is reached at 12 miles. *General notes.*—For the first 8 miles from Háka there is open jungle of large trees on either side of the road. After the 8th mile the country through which the road passes is very open and shows signs of having been at some time or other under Chin cultivation. Water is met with in many places until the 27th mile is reached. Villages are very scarce and only two can be seen from the road, both these being 4 or 5 miles off. A few supplies, such as fowls, eggs, vegetables, are brought in by the Chins, but they are not to be depended upon. No shooting to be had on the road.

No. 7.

From HÁKA to HMUNLIPI POST viâ HRIPI and SHALEN.

BY LIEUT. EVATT, 39TH GARHWALI REGIMENT, MARCH 1892.

G.O.C. Myingyán District.	Political Officer, Chin Hills.	**1. Kusa**	**18 0**	18 0	Path steep in places, but passable with difficulty by laden animals.

FROM HÁKA TO HMUNLIPI POST *viâ* HRIPI AND SHALEN—*continued.*

Authorities.		Number and Names of Stages, Rivers and Streams.	Distances.		Remarks.
Military.	Civil.		Inter-mediate.	Total.	
			M. F.	M. F.	
G.O.C. Myingyán District.	Political Officer, Chin Hills.	**2. Tlángwra** ...	**6 0**	24 0	Road not at present passable for guns (mountain, of course), but could be rendered so without great labour. Camp close to village on Tlántláng side.
		3. Hripi ... ... Hripi Vár.	**10 0**	34 0	Descend to Hripi Vár and thence ascend to Hripi, steep all the way and impracticable for guns. Camping ground in village which contains about 100 houses.
		4. Shalen ... ... Shipi Vár, Lá-aw Vár.	**16 0**	50 0	Path descends spur northwards, good but commanded for ¾ of a mile from the slopes of the spur on which Hripi is built, which are covered with dense jungle. Reach the Shipi Vár at foot of spur and follow down it through bamboo jungle, very rough going, over boulders, to its junction with the Lá-aw Vár. Cross both and ascend steeply, mostly through bamboo jungle to Shalen. Camping ground near water ½ a mile before reaching the village. All this stage is quite impracticable for laden animals. Shalen has about 40 houses.
		5. Hmunlipi post. Tongshé river.	**9 0**	59 0	First 2 miles very steep, but could be made practicable for mules without much difficulty. Cross Tongshé river and thence easy ascent through Hriamkhan to Hmunlipi. *See* Route No. 5, Stage 4.

No. 8.

From HAKA to NARING viâ BWÔNLÔN and AIBUR.

BY LIEUT. E. W. M. NORIE, PAID ATTACHÉ, INTELLIGENCE BRANCH, APRIL 1890.

Military.	Civil.	Number and Names of Stages, Rivers and Streams.	Inter-mediate.	Total.	Remarks.
G.O.C. Myingyán District.	Political Officer, Chin Hills.	**1. Bwônlôn** ... Népár Vár, Uti Vár, Sorel Vár, Boinu river.	**16 0**	16 0	The road leaving the Háka post ran west along the road to Fort Tregear for 1¼ miles and then turned south-west and led along the lower slopes of the Rôngkláng gradually bending to the south. The road was a narrow path, with steep ascents and descents for short distances, where it crossed the numerous small nullahs flowing west. At 3½ miles it crossed a spur and began to descend steeply into the valley of the Népár Vár. This is a clear stream flowing west into the Boinu. From here it followed the course of the stream upwards for nearly 2 miles, crossing it about twenty times, and then ascended a spur, the top of which is reached at about 6½ miles. From this point another path leads off to the south-east to Thetta, about 15 miles from Háka. The road after running along the side of the spur for a short distance descends very steeply to the Uti Vár and ascends as steeply to the top of

No. 8.

FROM HÁKA TO NARING *viâ* BWÔNLÔN AND AIBUR—*continued.*

Authorities. Military.	Authorities. Civil.	Number and Names of Stages, Rivers and Streams.	Distances. Intermediate.	Distances. Total.	Remarks.
G.O.C. Myingyán District.	Political Officer, Chin Hills.	**1. Bwônlôn**—*cont.*			the opposite range, from which it immediately descends by a steep spur to the Sorel Vár at about 10 miles. This stream also flows west to the Boinu and, with the other two streams previously crossed, contains a plentiful supply of water all the year round. The road from here crosses another steep ridge and descends to the Boinu, at about 12 miles, so far the general direction is south-south-west, but for the next 4 miles it leads generally due south. On reaching the Boinu it at once crosses the river, which is here about 90 feet broad and 1½ feet deep in the dry weather, though it must be a large stream after rain and quite impassable in flood. It is a fine, clear stream, with deep pools flowing along the bottom of a deep valley. The bed is rocky, firm, and stony. After crossing it the path runs down the course of the stream along the right bank and in places the khud towards the river is dangerously steep and the path rather bad. Before reaching Bwônlôn another path runs off east to Thetta, which is said to be a little nearer than Háka. Bwônlôn is a village of about 70 houses, tributary to Háka. It is situated on the hill side, and is not defended except by the usual village fence. Camp was formed immediately south of the village beside a small stream. Very little level ground available.
		2. Dungvar ... Kuk Vár, Shurla Vár, Silashi Vár.	M. 9 F. 4	M. 25 F. 4	General direction nearly due south. Leaving the camp the road runs along above the river gradually descending and crossing numerous nullahs. At about 1¾ miles it descends very steeply to the Kuk Vár, which is crossed. The road then continues and, crossing two or three small but steep-sided spurs, reaches the Shurla Vár at about 4 miles. From here it leads up a very steep ascent to the top of the ridge at 5¼ miles, and from there descends gradually at first, but very steeply for the last ½ mile to the Silashi Vár at 8 miles. This is a clear stream in a deep rocky bed and is crossed like all these streams by a bridge consisting of a thick log. This, with a hand-rail attached, would be sufficient, but the rail is generally wanting. From the stream the road very steep at first, leads to the top of the ridge and then along the side, ascending slightly to the village. Dungvar village contains 110 houses and is tributary to Háka. It is undefended and can be easily commanded from the ridge above. The water-supply is very meagre and is brought to the village by pipes. Camp was formed immediately above the village. A few supplies of fowls, &c., are procurable. Boinu flows 1,300 feet below and to the east of the village, and its course can be seen far to the south by the deep valley along which it runs. No path leads down the right bank from Dungvar, though roads or tracks are said to exist along the left bank. It is reported to flow south, some 60 miles from this point before turning north.
		3. Aibur ... ... Three streams.	14 0	39 4	The path leads up a very steep slope for a few hundred yards on to the ridge behind the village and then rises steadily up a long spur to the top of the Yovailángkláng at 4 miles, the

FROM HÁKA TO NARING *viâ* BWÔNLÔN AND AIBUR—*continued.*

Authorities. Military.	Authorities. Civil.	Number and Names of Stages, Rivers and Streams.	Distances. Intermediate.	Distances. Total.	Remarks.
		3. Aibur—*cont.*			height of which is over 8,000 feet above sea-level. The Yovailángkláng is a great range running north and south up and down the great loop of the Boinu. The top of this range is generally thickly covered with forest, but at the place where the path crosses is more or less bare of trees. From the top the road after leading through a belt of forest jungle, through which runs a small stream of water, leads down by a long spur with several steep descents to the village of Laitet, containing some 100 houses. To a point about ½ mile beyond this village the direction from Dungvar has been nearly due west, but the path now runs nearly due south and for the last mile south-east to the village of Aibur. Flowing parallel to this part and along the bottom of a deep valley is the Tanghor Vár, a considerable stream coming from the north. The road running up and down over spurs crosses several nullahs and three considerable streams with water in them all the year round. From the last of these it ascends steadily up to the village Aibur of 110 houses. Camp was pitched to the south of the village, near a small stream of good water. Aibur is tributary to Háka and undefended. This is a long and tiring march.
G.O.C. Myingyán District.	Political Officer, Chin Hills.	**4. Naring** ... ... Tiarté Vár.	M. F. 16 0	M. F. 55 4	General direction south all the way. Pretty level for about 1 mile, when it descends steeply to a small stream, the ascent from which is also steep. After this it runs fairly level, but gradually rising, and at 4 miles passes the old deserted village Shurngan, while at 5 miles the large new village of the same name, containing about 200 houses, can be seen about 2 miles to the east on the opposite hill side. The road now descends steeply down a spur and at 6½ miles reaches the Tiarté stream, here about 20 feet broad. Crossing this the climb up the opposite hill is very steep and the ascent about 1,700 feet, but beyond this the path is fairly level and easy all the way to Naring. Naring is a large independent village of about 300 houses. Formerly tributary to Háka, it has ceased to pay any tribute for 12 years, and now claims to be independent and in fact to have some tributary villages of its own. They have no trade with outside and do not understand the use or value of money. To the west and round the south of the ridge, on which the village is situated, flows the Boinu river, here flowing north and three times as big as when seen last near Dungvar. Further on the Boinu is joined by the Tanghor and is then called the Tipi. The Boinu, Tipi, and Koladyne are undoubtedly one and the same river. This Tipi must be carefully distinguished from the other river of the same name, which flows into the Koladyne from the north to the west of the Taokláng. The name "Tipi" means "Big water." Water is scarce about Naring in the dry weather, but a place to camp in was found about ½ mile north-west of the village in a deep gully and here a sufficient supply was obtainable. *Note.*—This route throughout is impracticable for laden animals and can only be used by coolies.

No. 8.

From HÁKA to NARING *viâ* BWÔNLÔN and AIBUR—*continued.*

ALTERNATIVE I.

From HÁKA (Chin Hills) to NARING *viâ* HRIPI.

By Lieut. E. W. M. NORIE, Paid Attaché, Intelligence Branch, April 1890.

Authorities. Military.	Authorities. Civil.	Number and Names of Stages, Rivers and Streams.	Distances. Intermediate. M. F.	Distances. Total. M. F.	Remarks.
G.O.C. Myingyán District.	Political Officer, Chin Hills.	**1. Kusa** ... ... Boinu river, Népár Vár, Lawténa Vár, and other streams.	**16 4**	16 4	General direction south-west. Leaving the Háka post the road follows the Tlántláng road for about a mile and then turns off down the valley of the stream to the south-west of Háka. At about 3 miles it crosses this and runs steeply up a spur to the top of the ridge, beyond which it crosses and descends more gradually by another spur to the Népár Vár at about 6 miles. Crossing this it runs over another ridge and down to the Boinu river by a steep ascent and descent. It then runs down the left bank of the Boinu to a point where it crosses it at about 7½ miles. The stream is here about 20 feet broad and 1 foot deep. The path now ascends very steeply for about ¾ of a mile and reaches the top of a spur along which it runs, ascending much more gradually for about 1½ miles. It then ascends again steeply for about a ¼ of a mile to the top of the ridge at about 10 miles. From here the next ½ mile is level and then there is a very steep and almost precipitous descent into the valley beyond. Crossing the small stream at the bottom the path leads round the foot of the Pupikláng, a high conical peak, which can be seen from most points in the neighbourhood. At about 12½ miles reaches the Lawténa Vár and follows it upwards, still round the base of Pupikláng for about a mile, crossing it three or four times. The path then leaves it and runs up a spur, very steep where it leaves the stream, but more gradual higher up to the top of a high ridge, and from here it runs pretty steeply down the whole way to Kusa at 16½ miles. Kusa is a small poor village of about 30 houses, tributary to Háka. The camping ground is on a very small stream to the north of the village. The site is cramped and much overgrown. On the opposite hill to Kusa to the north-west, about 3 miles off, can be seen the large Tlántláng village of Tlánrwa.
		2. Hripi ... ... Several small streams.	**13 0**	29 4	General direction south-west. The path runs south along the side of the hill below the village till it reaches the top of a spur, when it runs down-hill pretty steeply to 1 mile, beyond which it is fairly level running along the hill sides and crossing two or three small streams. At 5 miles it reaches the village of Saungtia, through which it passes. Saungtia is a village of about 70 houses, tributary to Háka. Water from streams on both sides. From Saungtia a path runs south to Laitet, *see* Stage 3 above, distance about 14 miles. The path still continues fairly level to 7 miles, when it bends sharply round to the west along the watershed between the valleys of the Tanghor Vár and the Lá-aw Vár. At about 8 miles there is a pretty steep ascent to the top of a ridge. At about 9 miles from here there is a steep descent to a small stream and then the path runs up a long spur to the crest of the ridge above Hripi. From here

FROM HÁKA TO NARING *viâ* BWÔNLÔN AND AIBUR—*continued.*

ALTERNATIVE I—*continued.*

Authorities. Military.	Authorities. Civil.	Number and Names of Stages, Rivers and Streams.	Distances. Intermediate. M. F.	Distances. Total. M. F.	Remarks.
G.O.C. Myingyán District.	Political Officer, Chin Hills.	**2. Hripi**—*cont.*			it runs down a steep spur and crossing a small stream runs up into the village. Hripi is a very picturesquely situated village, situated on two parallel spurs, but commanded from the south. It contains about 80 houses and is claimed as tributary by the Hákas, but is virtually independent. Height above the sea is 5,700 feet. The camping ground is in a small valley 600 yards to the south of the village, where there is a small stream of good water. From Hripi the southern road from Háka to Fort Tregear and Lungleh branches off to the west.
		3. Wantu ... ... Paipi Vár, Nuit Vár, and several small streams.	9 4	39 0	General direction south-west. The road runs up from the village for about 300 yards and passes over a spur and begins to descend round the hill side by a good path, not very steep. At about 2 miles it leads out into a beautiful, flat, grassy valley of some 400 acres, beautifully situated among hills, which rise on the north side in perpendicular cliffs and watered by a fine clear stream called the Paipi Vár. The path runs down this valley for about a mile when it crosses the Paipi Vár by a foot-bridge and runs along the opposite hill side, fairly level and easy going, crossing several small streams and running west. At 6 miles the path bends to the south and commences to descend steeply for some 3,000 feet to the Nuit Vár, which is reached at 8½ miles. This is a fine clear stream flowing along the bottom of a very deep, narrow valley, the sides of which are in many places precipitous. The path crossing the stream leads steeply up the opposite hill side through jungle to the village of Wantu. It is a large independent village tributary to no tribe, but giving presents to the Háka Chiefs to ensure their friendship. There are about 100 houses in the village and some of them are large and well built; the head Chief's house being a particularly good one. There is no good site for camping on here and water is scarce. The best place for a halt appears to be on the Nuit Vár, a mile before the village is reached. Here water at least is plentiful, though the site is very cramped. Supplies of a few fowls, vegetables, &c., are procurable; also grass and firewood.
		4. Kabôn ... ... Hlampé and several small streams.	13 0	52 0	General direction south-south-east. The road runs up from the village on to the spur to the south and then leads steadily up this with some pretty steep ascents in places for about 4 miles, when it reaches the top of a high hill. From here the valley of the Boinu can be seen about 3 or 4 miles to the west. The river is flowing north up to this point and then bends away to the west to become what is known as the Koladyne. From the top of this hill the path leads down pretty steeply for about ¾ of a mile and then along a fairly level spur to the village of Yépai, at about 5½ miles, containing

FROM HÁKA TO NARING *viâ* BWÔNLÔN AND AIBUR—*continued.*

ALTERNATIVE I—*continued.*

Authorities. Military.	Authorities. Civil.	Number and Names of Stages, Rivers and Streams.	Distances. Intermediate.	Distances. Total.	Remarks.
G.O.C. Myingyán District.	Political Officer, Chin Hills.	**4. Kabôn**—*cont.*			about 60 houses and independent. From Yépai the path runs down pretty steeply for about 300 yards to a stream, which it crosses and runs down the valley fairly level, crossing the stream from time to time. At 7½ miles it enters a fine open grassy valley of 300 or 400 acres, watered by the head-waters of the Hlampé ("hlam" and "vár" both signify streams) and very beautifully situated. The path now runs down the valley for about 1½ miles, when the hills closing in, the level grassy plain is left, the road still running down the bank of the stream through jungle and across a great many small streams and nullahs. About ½ mile before Kabôn is reached the path leaves the Hlampé and ascends up a steep spur to the village. It contains about 100 houses and is undefended and commanded from the east and south. The best place for a camp is on the spur just below the village; water being procurable from a small stream close by on the south. A few supplies of fowls, eggs, vegetables, &c., are procurable.
		5. Camp on the Tanghor Vár. Hlampé and one small stream.	M. 7 F. 4	M. 59 F. 4	General direction south-east. The path runs through the village and up on to the top of the Kwépiklâng, which it crosses and descends the opposite side. The eastern slopes of the Kwépiklâng are in many places precipitous and the path is extremely steep for about a mile, when it reaches a minor spur, down the crest of which it runs, descending much more gradually to 5½ miles, when there is a final steep descent to the bank of the Hlampé. It continues down the bank, crossing a stream and two or three nullahs, and then runs along the face of a very steep khud descending again very steeply to the Hlampé at 7 miles. From here it follows the bed of the stream, crossing and recrossing it five times to its junction with the Tanghor Vár at 7½ miles. There is no village here and no supplies except water and firewood. Camp can be pitched on the right bank of the Tanghor Vár just below the junction.
		6. Naring . ... Tanghor Vár.	17 0	76 4	General direction south-south-east. The road runs down the bed of the Tanghor Vár for about 3½ miles, crossing and recrossing it thirteen times and running over stones and boulders and among rocks. It is a very tiring bit of road and would be impassable when the river is in flood. There is another path, which crosses the stream once and running over the hill beyond, joins this path further on. At 3½ miles the path leaves the stream and runs very steeply up to the crest of a spur to the point where the alternative path mentioned above joins it again at about 4½ miles. From here it runs gradually up along the top of the spur with a few steep ascents for short distances, till it strikes the road from Háka to Naring *viâ* Bwônlôn and Aibur at about 9 miles. For further description *see* above route. The Tanghor Vár flows into the Boinu river about 4½ miles north-west of Naring, and the river is locally called the Tipi below the junction, Tipi meaning "great water." At the point where it is joined by the Tanghor Vár, the Boinu again bends to

FROM HÁKA TO NARING *viâ* BWÔNLÔN AND AIBUR—*continued.*

ALTERNATIVE I—*continued.*

Authorities. Military.	Authorities. Civil.	Number and Names of Stages, Rivers and Streams.	Distances. Inter-mediate.	Distances. Total.	Remarks.
G.O.C. Myingyán District.	Political Officer, Chin Hills.	**6. Naring**—*cont.*			the south and flows round the base of a high mountain, the eastern slopes of which are in many places sheer precipices of great height. *Note.*—This route is impracticable for laden animals throughout and can only be used by coolies.

No. 9.

From HÁKA to SHURKWA viâ THETTA.

BY LIEUT. H. C. DUCAT, 2ND BATTALION, 4TH GOORKHAS, FEBRUARY 1891.

Military	Civil	Stages	Intermediate	Total	Remarks
G.O.C. Myingyán District.	Political Officer, Chin Hills.	**1. Saorel Vár Camp.** Nepár, Yao Vár and Saorel Vár.	M. F. **12 0**	M. F. 12 0	For the first 1¼ miles the path runs along the Háka-Fort Tregear mule track and then branches off in a south-west direction, crossing the lower spurs of the Rong-Tláng range in a series of short ascents and descents, gradually bending southwards till it reaches the Nepár stream about 3½ miles from Háka. The path then runs about 2 miles along the narrow winding valley of the Nepár, a tributary of the Boinu river, a clear gently flowing stream from 10 to 15 feet broad with firm stony bed, containing during the dry season only about 6 inches of water, but during the summer it becomes very swollen and is frequently impassable after heavy rain, which is crossed some twenty times. It then rises steeply in a south-south-east direction for about a mile, at which point is met the track leading to Bwônlôn village, some 9 miles further on, thence it continues fairly level, skirting along the southern slopes of the Arsong-Tláng range, and then gradually descends to the valley of the Yao Vár, a clear mountain stream, affording a plentiful supply of good drinking water, 9½ miles from Háka. Here there is a good camping ground, commanded to the north; water, grass, and firewood are abundant. Leaving the Yao Vár the path crosses several small nullahs containing water, and then ascends somewhat steeply to the top of a long gently sloping spur trending north and south which it traverses, and then descends steeply to the valley of the Saorel Vár, where there is a fairly good camping ground on a succession of short narrow terraces projecting from a spur on the right bank of the Saorel Vár, a mountain stream, similar to the Yao Vár. It is commanded on three sides, and more directly to the north. Water, fuel, and grass abundant.
		2. Thetta ... ... Ri Vár.	**6 0**	18 0	Leaving Saorel the path at once ascends south-south-east at an easy gradient, passing, about ¼ mile up, a spot where there was once a stockade, built by Thettas, facing north-west with trees felled across the path in front as obstacles. This position is

FROM HÁKA TO SHURKWA *viâ* THETTA—*continued.*

Authorities.		Number and Names of Stages, Rivers and Streams.	Distances.		Remarks.
Military.	Civil.		Intermediate.	Total.	
G.O.C. Myingyán District.	Political Officer, Chin Hills.	**2. Thetta**—*cont.*			bounded on the north-east by a wooded ravine and on the south-west by a knoll and a dense copse. It can, without difficulty, be turned on its left flank, and a front attack could also be made under cover of fire from the opposite spur, the range being about 600 yards. The stockade has been partially destroyed, but most of the felled trees in front remain. Leaving this position the path continues to ascend, at times steeply, for ¾ mile, where a path branches off south-south-west to Shurkwa, distant about 22 miles. A ½ mile further up the crest-line of the spur is reached and the path runs level for a short distance, and then descends rather steeply to a small stream, after crossing which it rises gradually to the top of a long ridge, trending south-east and north-west, along which it descends, with a very slight gradient, for about 1½ miles when the village of Thetta first comes into sight to the east-north-east, distant about 1¼ miles. From this point the path bends north-east descending a fairly steep spur and, crossing several small knolls, it gradually bends round east till it reaches the upper end of Thetta village. From here it branches off north-east and descends rather steeply to the Ri Vár stream (about ¼ mile from the north face of the village), on the opposite bank of which there is a fair camping ground, with a good supply of water, firewood and grass, on a rather steep and narrow spur, up which the path ascends towards Rawvan, distant about 12 miles. There is a level piece of ground alongside the stream suitable for picketing mules. The Ri Vár rises a few miles to the north of Thetta and flows past the east face of the village, at which point it is about 10 feet broad and quite shallow during the dry weather, but can only be crossed during the rains by a plank foot-bridge, as the current is then very rapid and the water about 4 feet deep. The country between Háka and Thetta is fairly open, especially during the dry weather, after the jungle grass has been burnt, though the ravines are always thickly wooden. Trees consist chiefly of oaks of various sizes, and occasionally pines. Water is good and plentiful along the road. The Chin path has been made practicable for laden mules, improvements being chiefly needed in crossing ravines and on steep slopes by making zigzags.
		3. Kapi ... ... Ri Vár and another stream.	M. F. 6 0	M. F. 24 0	Leaving the camping ground the path runs south-south-east following the course of the Ri Vár, which it crosses some ten times, at first through scrub jungle and long grass, and then through cultivation belonging to Thettas. At about 2½ miles the path leaves the stream, striking off south-west and ascending a long spur with cultivation on both sides for about a mile, and then descends along a spur, on the further side of the ridge through scrub jungle in places rather steeply for 1½ miles, when it reaches a shallow mountain stream of clear water. From this point up to the Kapi ridge, about a mile, the path ascends south-south-west and is steep in parts passing through thin jungle, though the spurs on either side are cultivated. On reaching the crest of this ridge the village of Kapi is seen on the further slope, the nearest house being about 50 yards from the summit. There is a good level camping ground on the top of the ridge, though water is more than ½ mile away and firewood is scarce.

FROM HÁKA TO SHURKWA *viâ* THETTA—*continued.*

Authorities. Military.	Authorities. Civil.	Number and Names of Stages, Rivers and Streams.	Distances. Intermediate. M. F.	Distances. Total. M. F.	Remarks.
G.O.C. Myingyán District.	Political Officer, Chin Hills.	**4. Paipa Camp** ... Boinu River.	7 0	31 0	The path runs west-south-west along the crest of the Kapi ridge, gradually ascending till a peak is reached about 4 miles from Kapi, from which it branches off south-west descending a long spur through scrub jungle for about 3 miles, till it reaches the Boinu river, on the opposite bank of which there is a suitable camping ground about a mile from the village of Paipa, which is situated on a long spur a considerable height above the river. This camping ground is commanded by spurs on the west. There is no water along the road till the Boinu is reached. At about the 3rd mile another path branches off south to Shurkwa, distant 9 miles. The Boinu river here runs south and averages about 40 feet in width with firm stony bed. There are numerous deep broad pools at the bends, but the shallows are fordable during the dry weather, being about 2 feet deep. The Paipa Chins have constructed a suspension bridge of about 100 feet span over the river for crossing when the fords are impassable. This bridge is made entirely of cane, which was probably obtained from Lushai land.
		5. Paizôn Camp ... Boinu river and several small rivulets.	6 0	37 0	The path runs south for about ½ mile along the right bank of the Boinu, and then branches off south-west ascending a spur for ¾ mile, till it reaches a point, about ½ mile to the north-west of which is the village of Paipa, whence it turns south running for about 5 miles along the eastern slopes of the Boipa-Tláng range, and crossing two deep re-entering angles between long spurs. At about the 3rd mile another path branches off south-east towards Shurkwa, crossing the Boinu a mile further on. The camping ground is a level piece of ground, about a mile above the river, and about the same distance to the north of Paizôn, water, forage, and fuel plentiful.
		6. Shurkwa ... Boinu River.	4 4	41 4	The path runs south for 1½ miles till it reaches the village of Paizôn, when it turns west and descends a spur for about a mile to the Boinu river. This descent is difficult and the last 300 yards almost precipitous. The Boinu river is the same size here as at Paipa, but is not bridged. The ford is about 2 feet deep in the dry season. After crossing the river the path ascends west-south-west up a long spur of the Dárkwong-hrianák-Tláng range, the first ½ mile being very steep, after which the gradient is easy. At about 2 miles from the river the path reaches a good level camping ground, a ½ mile from the crest-line of the Dárkwong-hrianák-Tláng, and ½ mile from the village of Shurkwa, which is on another spur about the same elevation; water is ½ mile away and fuel is limited. Accounts of two other routes between Háka and Shurkwa will be found under the head of Shurkwa, *see* Route No. 22.

No. 10.

From HÁKA to TAO (through Yahow country).

By D. ROSS, Esq., Political Officer, Chin Hills, 22nd October 1890.

Authorities. Military.	Authorities. Civil.	Number and Names of Stages, Rivers and Streams.	Distances. Intermediate. M.	F.	Distances. Total. M.	F.	Remarks.
G.O.C. Myingyán District.	Political Officer, Chin Hills.	**1. Hairôn**	**16**	**0**	16	0	*See* Route No. 11.
		2. Tlánrôn ...	**6**	**0**	22	0	Good pony road.
		3. Yatlír	**10**	**0**	32	0	Over a hill about as big as Rong. Ponies can be taken.
		4. Ser	**6**	**0**	38	0	Road level. Plenty of water. All cultivation. Good camping ground.
		5. Ngaithi ...	**20**	**0**	58	0	Over hill; good path. Water is found twice on the way. At half-way there is a big stream, but camping ground over the watershed between Rong and Tyao rivers.
		6. Dar Tati ...	**10**	**0**	68	0	Good easy road.
		7. Lamyoi	**16**	**0**	84	0	One hill; not difficult. Water plentiful.
		8. Tángzáng ...	**28**	**0**	112	0	Road not so good; crosses streams Tcing Vár and La Vár. Plenty of camping places.
		9. Tao	**13**	**0**	125	0	*See* Route No. 5, Alternative I, Stages 4 and 5.

No. 11.

From HÁKA to TÁSHÔN YWAMA (FALÁM).

By Lieut. E. W. M. NORIE, Paid Attaché, Intelligence Branch, Burma, and Major H. W. IND, Royal Artillery, March 1890.

Military	Civil	Stage	M.	F.	M.	F.	Remarks
G.O.C. Myingyán District.	Political Officer, Chin Hills.	**1. Hairôn (about 3,000 feet).** Hairôn Vár.	**16**	**0**	16	0	General direction north. Leaving camp the path at once descends very steeply for 700 feet to the village of Kôtár, through which it passes and leads along the hill side, gradually ascending through open park-like country, with oak trees and firs. At about 4 miles reaches the foot of a spur and ascends pretty steeply for a ½ of a mile on to a ridge of the Tinminlôn range about 7,000 feet. The mule path leads round by the saddle above Kôtár and joins at this point, being about a mile longer. The path now leads along the watershed, which separates the valley of the Boinu from that of the Nanpathi or Daung Vár, and is fairly easy going with some ascents and descents. At about 7 miles there is a pretty steep ascent to the highest point on the march and then the path begins to descend steadily, pretty gradual at first, but very steep further on till, at about 15 miles, it reaches the village of Hairôn, a Háka village of about 40 houses. The descent continues steep for another ½ mile to the Hairôn stream, which it crosses, and then leads along the hill side down the

From HÁKA to TÁSHÔN YWAMA (FALÁM)—*continued.*

Authorities.		Number and Names of Stages, Rivers and Streams.	Distances.				Remarks.
Military.	Civil.		Intermediate.		Total.		
			M.	F.	M.	F.	
G.O.C. Myingyán District.	Political Officer, Chin Hills.	**1. Hairôn (about 3,000 feet)**—*cont.*					valley to the halting place. The descent altogether is about 4,000 feet, and the march from Hairôn to Háka is, therefore, very severe. Camping ground fair ½ mile north-east of village on the Hairôn Vár on the Minkin road. Excellent water-supply. Road passable for transport animals throughout, time, actual marching about 6 hours. Fowls, &c., are procurable from the village. During the march the very large, independent village of Rumtlao is seen across the valley to the west, situated on the slopes of the Yinhmo-kláng. There is no water along the march after the first 4 miles until the Hairôn Vár is reached.
		2. Laiyaw ... Pao Vár, Tigna Vár.	**10**	**4**	26	4	Road from camp continues down the valley for about ¾ of a mile to the junction of the Hairôn Vár with the Pao Vár. At this point there is a good place for halting, suitable for transport animals. Crossing the Pao Vár the path leads up a very steep ascent of some 2,000 feet, till it reaches the top of the ridge at about 2½ miles, and then becomes fairly level running along the hill side through cultivation. At about 6 miles the large village of Minkin is reached, containing 250 to 300 houses, and tributary to Táshôn. The main road runs through the village; but there is another path which leads outside and above it. Beyond this the path leads up to the top of a ridge called the Laiyawkláng at about 7 miles, and then descends rather steeply into the valley of the Tigna Vár beyond. At 8 miles the path from Hanta (*see* Route No. 14) joins in. The main road passes through the village of Karôn at 8½ miles, descending to the stream and then ascending to Laiyaw; but there is another and more level road that passes round the head of the valley and avoids Karôn. There are several suitable places for halting on along the road, as water is plentiful from streams in the hill side, especially so at 9½ and 10 miles. Karôn is a Táshôn village of about 100 houses, and Laiyaw (1) is another Táshôn village of about 80 houses. Fowls, eggs, &c., are procurable.
		3. Táshôn Ywama (Falám).	**6**	**4**	33	0	The path leads through Laiyaw (1) and two other villages, all close together and known under the collective name Laiyaw, and then above a fourth and ascends the side of the ridge which is here very steep, until it reaches the top of a spur. From here it runs pretty level round the head of small valley and up to the top of the next spur at about 4 miles. It then runs round the head of another small valley and ascends rather steeply to the ridge above the Ywama, called the Bilúma-kláng. When visited, this ridge was defended by stone walls and stockades. Crossing the ridge the road runs steeply down to Táshôn, the old site of the Ywama, now only containing about a dozen houses. Camp was pitched on a flat piece of ground above this village, and the path could be seen running over the next spur into the present Ywama, called Falám, about a mile to the east. The Táshôns have, of course, got their name from the old site of their capital, but this was deserted some years ago for some reason, and the houses were transported to their present site. The spur over which the road runs is defended

FROM HÁKA TO TÁSHÔN YWAMA (FALÁM)—*continued.*

Authorities.		Number and Names of Stages, Rivers and Streams.	Distances.		Remarks.
Military.	Civil.		Inter-mediate.	Total.	
G.O.C. Myingyán District.	Political Officer, Chin Hills.	**3. Táshôn Ywama (Falám)**—*cont.*			also by walls and stockades and broad belts of stake entanglement. Falám contains 450 houses. There is fair camping ground and water-supply for 600 or 700 men on the slopes to the south of the old village. The position is incapable of defence when once the Bilúma ridge is gained and the spur between the old and the present village turned. Laden mules can be taken throughout this route with but little difficulty. Since the above report a good mule track has been constructed from Háka to the Páté Ford over the Nankathé river, 5 miles (by this road, 2 only by Chin path) beyond Falám. For the first 26½ miles is from 4½ to 4 feet wide, thence onwards it varies from 3 to 2½ feet. The work was completed in March 1892. The total distance to Falám by this route is 35 miles, so but little longer than the path above described. Camps can be formed at 12½, 19 (near Hairôn), 26 (Minkin), and, if required, at 30½ miles (Laiyaw), at all which places water is plentiful. The road crosses the Hairôn and Pao streams by fords. Both these streams are easily fordable in March, the former about 8 inches, the latter knee-deep. Bridges have not been made, not being necessary at ordinary times, and the sudden freshets that occur after heavy rain would carry away any thing but a very permanent structure. (Extract from report by Capt. G. B. Stevens, 4th Madras Pioneers).

ALTERNATIVE I.

FROM HÁKA TO TÁSHÔN YWAMA *viâ* TIPWÉ AND SIMPI.

BY LIEUT. E. W. M. NORIE, FROM NATIVE INFORMATION, APRIL 1890.

Military	Civil	Stages	Intermediate M.	Intermediate F.	Total M.	Total F.	Remarks
G.O.C. Myingyán District.	Political Officer, Chin Hills.	**1. Tipwé**	**14**	**0**	14	0	Leaving Háka the road runs along the Hairôn road for about 8 miles, and then turns off to the east and runs to the Tipwé village. Tipwé is a large Háka village of about 150 houses. Water and supplies procurable.
		2. Kônva ... ... Pao Vár.	**10**	**0**	24	0	From Tipwé the road runs steeply downhill for about 5 miles to the Pao Vár, which it crosses and ascends the opposite hill also very steep, till it reaches Kônva village, containing about 50 houses, and paying tribute to both Háka and Táshôn. Kônva is also called Lenhai.
		3. Rálaw	**13**	**0**	37	0	From Kônva the road again ascends steeply to the top of a ridge, which it crosses, and descends gradually to the village of Yômwé at about 5 miles on a small stream. From here it runs fairly level to Simpi at about 8 miles and on to Rálaw at 13 miles.
		4. Falám	...		...		From here a road runs to Falám, the Táshôn Ywama.

No. 12.

From HÁKA to TLÁNGKOI (TÁSHÔN).

BY LIEUT. E. W. M. NORIE, FROM NATIVE INFORMATION, APRIL 1890.

Authorities. Military.	Authorities. Civil.	Number and Names of Stages, Rivers and Streams.	Distances. Inter-mediate. M.	Distances. Inter-mediate. F.	Distances. Total. M.	Distances. Total. F.	Remarks.
G.O.C. Myingyán District.	Political Officer, Chin Hills.	**1. Camp on Boinu**	**6**	**0**	6	0	See Route No. 13.
		Boinu river.					
		2. Lônzát	**13**	**0**	19	0	
		Tipi Vár.					
		3. Lônsôn	**10**	**0**	34	0	The road continues to run in a northerly direction. Lônsôn contains about 30 houses and is not regularly tributary to any one, but gives presents to Háka.
		4. Hmwé Kai ...	**10**	**0**	44	0	Direction north. Contains about 30 houses and gives presents to Háka.
		5. Tlángkwa ...	**10**	**0**	54	0	Direction north. Contains about 80 houses and gives presents to Háka.
		6. Lushé ...	**20**	**0**	74	0	Direction north. Contains about 80 houses and pays tribute to Táshôn.
		7. Shinnai ...	**10**	**0**	84	0	Direction north. Contains about 40 houses and pays tribute to Táshôn.
		8. Tlángkoi ...	**8**	**0**	92	0	Direction north. Contains about 25 houses and pays tribute to Táshôn.

No. 13.

From HÁKA to TUNZÁN viâ SHÔPUM.

BY LIEUTS. S. MACNABB, I.S.C., AND ALLGOOD, K.R.R., MARCH 1892.

Military	Civil	Stages	Inter. M.	Inter. F.	Total M.	Total F.	Remarks
G.O.C. Myingyán District.	Political Officer, Chin Hills.	**1. Camp on Boinu river.**	**6**	**0**	6	0	First 4 miles along Háka-Tregear mule road, then 2 miles north-west to the Boinu river, here called the Mi-hti Vár. Easily passable by mules throughout. Excellent camp on river. The Háka-Tregear mule road crosses the Boinu about 3 miles further down stream.
		Boinu river (Mi-hti Vár).					
		2. Lônzát ...	**13**	**0**	19	0	Path rises up out of the Boinu valley and ascending a narrow spur reaches the summit of the lofty Twánhmunkláng, a peak nearly 7,000 feet high, whence Háka and Fort Tregear posts are both visible, the latter part of the ascent through dense jungle. Hence a path leads off south to the Sár Vár. Path now descends to the Tipi Vár which is reached at 8 miles. From here the path runs west to Lônzát (13 miles) passing the old site of Kwáfo village
		Tipi Vár.					

FROM HÁKA TO TUNZÁN *viâ* SHÔPUM—*continued.*

Authorities. Military.	Authorities. Civil.	Number and Names of Stages, Rivers and Streams.	Distances. Intermediate. M.	Distances. Intermediate. F.	Distances. Total. M.	Distances. Total. F.	Remarks.
G.O.C. Myingyán District.	Political Officer, Chin Hills.	**2. Lônzát**—*cont.*					*en route.* Mules could not traverse the first 8 miles of this stage, but thence onwards the road is fair and could be made passable for mules without much trouble. Lônzát has 104 houses. Water-supply very scanty, 300 yards to the west of the village.
		3. Shôpum … Pi Vár, Law Vár.	**7**	**0**	26	0	From Lônzát road descends for 1½ miles to the Pi Vár, where there is excellent camping ground. Thence ascends and, crossing two low ridges, reaches the Law Vár. Rising again cross a range, and running west along a saddle reach Shôpum at 7 miles. This village has about 30 houses and is built across a narrow spur with precipitous sides. It is strongly stockaded on the north-west by a double stockade with loop-holed gate; the sides are protected by strong bamboo and branch fence, but south end is weak.
		4. Shimu … Ting Vár.	**7**	**0**	33	0	Follow the spur for 1½ miles, then ½ a mile descent to the Ting Vár, which is followed for 5 miles to Shimu, crossing the stream several times. Good camping ground on the Ting Vár at 2 miles for a large force. There is a steep rise from the Ting Vár to Shimu, difficult for mules. Shimu is a small village of 13 houses under Yahaiwit; water very scanty.
		5. Tunzán …	**4**	**0**	37	0	First mile westward ascending spur from Shimu, thence at first north-west along ridge crossing streams with a little water in them, then westward along saddle between the Bu Vár and the Ting Vár up to about 3 miles. Last mile up the Tunzán spur. For Tunzán *see* Route No. 5, Branch IV.

No. 14.

From HANTA to TÁSHÔN YWAMA (FALÁM).

BY MR. TUCK, POLITICAL OFFICER AT FALÁM, 22ND AND 29TH MAY 1892.

Military	Civil	Stage	Intermediate M.	Intermediate F.	Total M.	Total F.	Remarks
G.O.C. Myingyán District.	Political Officer, Chin Hills.	**1. Nanpathi** …	**8**	**0**	8	0	Leaving Hanta post the road runs north-west over the range above and down nearly 3,000 feet to the river Nanpathi. Three miles from Hanta is a site for a camp with good water 40 yards north of the road. The mule track leads to junction of Nanpathi and Pao Vár. The Nanpathi river, 40 yards wide; fordable in dry weather, not in the rains; is crossed by a small temporary bridge built by the 4th Madras Pioneers. The Chin track, leading to

FROM HANTA TO TÁSHÔN YWAMA (FALÁM)—*continued.*

Authorities. Military.	Authorities. Civil.	Number and Names of Stages, Rivers and Streams.	Distances. Intermediate. M. F.	Distances. Total. M. F.	Remarks.
G.O.C. Myingyán District.	Political Officer, Chin Hills.	**1. Nanpathi**—*cont.*			the best dry weather ford, leaves the mule track at about $7\frac{1}{2}$ miles and crosses the Nanpathi below the bridge. The bridge crosses both Nanpathi and Pao Vár (has been damaged in the rains and is now (1st September 1892) being repaired).
		2. Trok	3 4	11 4	From the Nanpathi the road runs up to the top of the Minkin ridge passing Trok, a small Kwéshin village of 20 houses; there is no camp here. The road passes by two Kwéshin villages of 100 houses each called Ralong or Kwéshin, where coolies are procurable. There is a camp here with a small hut for 50 men above the village.
		3. Ralong	3 2	14 6	The road between the Nanpathi and Ralong is likely to become very bad during the rains. Water plentiful near camp.
		4. Karôn	11 6	26 4	From Ralong the road runs along the Minkin range and crossing it drops into the Laiyaw valley meeting the Háka mule track (*see* Route No. 11) at $11\frac{1}{4}$ miles. Half-a-mile beyond this is Karôn village. Between Ralong and Karôn there is only one spring of water, in dense jungle about 7 miles from Ralong.
		5. Laiyaw (Camp)	2 0	28 4	*See* Route No. 9. There is no apparent reason for not making one march only from Karôn to Falám instead of two. Water plentiful on road.
		6. Falám	4 6	33 2	

No. 15.

From KAPTYÁL to MWIÁL.

BY E. O. FOWLER, ESQ., ASSISTANT POLITICAL OFFICER, NORTHERN CHIN HILLS, 20TH MARCH 1893.

Military	Civil	Stages	Intermediate M. F.	Total M. F.	Remarks
G.O.C. Myingyán District.	Political Officer, Chin Hills.	**1. Litwi** ... ... Two streams.	5 0	5 0	Fort Kaptyál *see* Route No. 25. General direction north. The path leaves Kaptyál on the north side; crosses the Kaptyál stream and ascends and crosses ridge north of the village. The path winds slightly north-west and leaves Hírnawn to the west; the path then turning north descends direct into a deep nullah in which there is a large stream of water, after crossing which ascends direct into Litwi village. The ascent is steep, but the road fairly good. There is another road round by Shelpe: works west round the head of the big nullah, and then east into Litwi; it is longer, but does not necessitate so much climbing. Litwi is an undefended village, consisting of three settlements lying close together. About 90 houses; camping ground good, but water-supply very small and not good.

FROM KAPTYÁL TO MWIÁL—*continued.*

Authorities. Military.	Authorities. Civil.	Number and Names of Stages, Rivers and Streams.	Distances. Intermediate. M. F.	Distances. Total. M. F.	Remarks.
G.O.C. Myingyán District.	Political Officer, Chin Hills.	**2. Mwiál** ... ... One stream.	3 0	8 0	General direction north-east. Leaving Litwi on the north the road ascends to the top of a ridge; it then winds for a short distance to the west, after which it goes mainly north-east straight into Mwiál. After ascending the ridge to the north of Litwi the road descends gently for a short distance and then for ¼ mile it is fairly flat; it then descends abruptly into a nullah, in which there is a good supply of water. This water is about ¼ mile outside Mwiál to the south of it. The road during the descent is bad and not passable for mules. It then ascends direct into Mwiál village. Mwiál village is an unstockaded village of 75 houses: camping ground to the north; it is a good one, but the water-supply is small and not good. This village is almost north of Litwi; if anything, slightly north-east.

No. 16.

From KAPTYÁL to SHELPE (New).

BY CAPT. CAULFIELD, 1ST BURMA RIFLES, AND CAPT. BAKER, ROYAL ARTILLERY, 1893.

Military	Civil	Stages	Intermediate M. F.	Total M. F.	Remarks
G.O.C. Myingyán District.	Political Officer, Chin Hills.	**1. Hírnawn** ... Three streams.	...	2 0	Keeping the path that runs along western edge of village and above it crossing the two nullahs that run through the village the path descends into the main nullah beyond, crossing the stream at the bottom, then up the other side almost due north to the top of opposite ridge, then descending easily alongside of an under-feature from this ridge until Hírnawn (burnt) is reached at about 2 miles. No good camping ground. There is another settlement of Hírnawn a little beyond on another under-feature. Country: high grass and trees; cultivation here and there; several springs of water about.
		2. Old Shelpe ... One stream.	1 4	3 4	Path runs through the second settlement of Hírnawn about at ½ mile west, then winds round over several small nullahs and under-features, then down into a big nullah just under old Shelpe up the khud in opposite side into village (now burnt). Old Shelpe consisted of about 30 houses originally, but when burnt by column there were only about seven houses standing.
		3. New Shelpe ...	2 0	5 4	Path runs up from old Shelpe over the crest of the ridge, then turns in a westwardly direction descending easily along the side of the ridge into new Shelpe. This is a village that consisted of about 60 houses (now burnt); no good camping ground, the village itself would probably be the best; plenty of water. Path fair all the way except between Hírnawn and old Shelpe, but not fit for mule transport.

No. 17.

From KAPTYÁL to SHWEMPE.

By Lieut. NORTHCOTT, 1st Norfolk Regiment, January 1893.

Authorities. Military.	Authorities. Civil.	Number and Names of Stages, Rivers and Streams.	Distances. Intermediate. M. F.	Distances. Total. M. F.	Remarks.
G.O.C. Myingyán District.	Political Officer, Chin Hills.	**1. Shwunzán** ... Three streams.	...	4 0	General direction of the road is due south. The first ½ mile is flat, the path then descends gradually for 200 yards and then rises abruptly, but continues to be good for mule transport until a small river running at the bottom of a deep nullah is reached, about 1¼ miles from Kaptyál. Mules can cross the stream without difficulty, but the opposite side is very steep and loads must be carried for about 250 yards, then the path runs along the flat for a short way, then again commences to rise, but still passable for mules. At a little over 2 miles the path runs along the top of the ridge, 5,500 feet, with a steep khud on both sides for 200 yards, then falls gradually into the village of Shwunzán. Just before entering this village there is a small river to cross with steep banks. There is a very good bridge across for ordinary foot traffic; the mules can cross a little above the bridge. There were about 70 houses in it; aneroid showed 4,200 feet; very fair camp on spur over village; good water-supply; about 90 houses in village.
		2. Hélé ... ... One stream 2 yards wide, 6 inches deep.	3 4	7 4	General direction of path is south-west. For the first 150 yards the path rises steadily when a nullah is crossed, the path on the Hélé side of which is very steep and bad for mules, but after reaching the top the rise is even and the path good. Surrounding country open; extensive grass slopes with trees here and there. A mile from Shwunzán another nullah is easily crossed and the path continues to rise for another ½ mile and then descends with the same even slope, then along the flat for ¾ mile when it begins to fall again easily for another ¾ mile, then steeply for 100 yards, here is a bad bit for the mules, the remainder of the way into Hélé is level, country open the whole way. Hélé consisted of 50 houses; camp above and north of village; very good supply of water. There are two small suburbs of Hélé west.
		3. Shwempe ... Three small streams.	2 0	9 4	Path runs eastwardly along side of ridge. Path good and available for mules; crosses three small streams with very little water in them. Shwempe (about 50 houses) was burnt by column.

BRANCH I.

From HÉLÉ (Stage 2) to TWITIL (WENHO).

By E. O. FOWLER, Esq., Assistant Political Officer, Northern Chin Hills, March 1893.

G.O.C. Myingyán District.	Political Officer, Chin Hills.	**1. Twitil**	6 4	6 4	General direction of road north-west. Road leads out of Hélé north-west. Water is met with ¼ mile outside Hélé. The road winds up-hill and works round a spur north-west of Hélé for ½ mile; the road then runs fairly level for about 2 miles; it then ascends abruptly to the top of the Imbuk-kláng, the distance here from Hélé being about 3½ miles. The road then descends into a mountain pass which is about 1½ miles long, with steep precipitous sides, thickly wooded. A good stream

FROM KAPTYÁL TO SHWEMPE—*continued.*

BRANCH I—*continued.*

Authorities. Military.	Authorities. Civil.	Number and Names of Stages, Rivers and Streams.	Distances. Intermediate.	Distances. Total.	Remarks.
G.O.C. Myingyán District.	Political Officer, Chin Hills.	**1. Twitil**—*cont.*	of water runs through the pass. The road through the pass is very bad, passing over large boulders and rocks. After leaving the pass the road becomes good again and descends gradually into Twitil village. The road up to the pass is passable for mules, but impassable through the pass owing to immense rocks and boulders. The village contains 30 houses. Water on north and west sides; good camping ground. The village is commanded on all sides and has no defence of any kind.		

No. 18.

From KAPTYÁL to WALLIÁL.

BY CAPT. R. BAKER, ROYAL ARTILLERY, INTELLIGENCE OFFICER, NORTHERN CHIN HILLS, 20TH JANUARY 1893.

Military	Civil	Stages	Intermediate M. F.	Total M. F.	Remarks
G.O.C. Myingyán District.	Political Officer, Chin Hills.	**1. Walliál** ... ... Two small streams.	**3 0**	3 0	Leaving the camp at the west end of Kaptyál move down through village to the north-east gate, cross the two small streams outside gate and move up the path which leads to the *col* on opposite ridge. On arrival at the *col* the path divides into three. Taking the right one, which runs nearly north-east after crossing the *col*, the path runs along the west side of a ridge at an easy gradient downwards. At about a mile the path rounds an under-feature and skirts a reëntrant, then continues in the same direction, namely north-east, until Walliál is reached, about 1½ miles further. Path only fit for infantry, but with a few repairs could be made available for mules. The only camping ground available would be just above village, but it is very sloping ground. Water-supply comes into village by water-leads from about ¼ mile south; supply small. The path passes through kaing grass, jungle and patches of cultivation; at Walliál fairly open pine woods. Walliál contained about 30 houses; now burnt.

No. 19.

From KÔTÍR (Saipuya's Village) to LINGRÁNG.

BY CAPT. J. SHAKESPEAR, D.S.O., SUPERINTENDENT, SOUTHERN LUSHAI HILLS, 1892.

Military	Civil	Stages	Intermediate	Total	Remarks
G.O.C. Presidency District.	Superintendent, Southern Lushai Hills.	**1. Lalthangbunga's village (Howlong Peak).** Chi-ti-lúi. Bed of small shingle with a few larger stones. In dry season only a few inches of water.	**12 0**	12 0	*Note.*—This Saipuya's village is apparently that marked on the ⅛ inch scale map, about 4 miles north-east of Lungleh Fort, not the peak marked Kôtír, about 17 miles nearly due north of Demagiri. The summit of the Kôtír is on a plateau 900 yards long with an average width of 500 yards. It is clear of jungle and covered with short grass. The village occupies the eastern half of it. The plateau breaks up into several grassy spurs between

FROM KÔTÍR (SAIPUYA'S VILLAGE) TO LINGRÂNG—*continued.*

Authorities. Military.	Authorities. Civil.	Number and Names of Stages, Rivers and Streams.	Distances. Intermediate.	Distances. Total.	Remarks.
G.O.C. Presidency District.	Superintendent, Southern Lushai Hills.	**1. Lalthangbunga's village (Howlong Peak)**—*cont.*			which are shallow wooded nullahs, all containing springs of good water. The ground falls away abruptly on all sides. This is one of the most pleasant sites I have seen in these hills. There are 140 houses. The road ascends northwards very abruptly to a saddle. This part of the road is very difficult for mules. From the saddle the road ascends steadily by an easy gradient in a north-east direction to Valcheng, an old village site of Saipuya's, on the summit of the ridge. There is a good supply of water to the north of the ridge at no distance, north-east of the grave of one of Saipuya's children. The road continues eastward along the ridge, which descends suddenly about 300 feet. Here the path bifurcates, one continuing to the east to Sangliena's village, the other turning to the north to Lalthangbunga's. The path descends by an easy gradient, save for about 400 yards, through bamboo jungle, till immediately above the Chi-ti-lúi stream when the last 200 yards are very steep. The road strikes the stream at the confluence of another small stream. There is a level space on the right bank of the stream suitable for an encampment, but it is an unhealthy, feverish place, save in the middle of the cold weather. The path for the next mile runs up the bed of the Chi-ti-lúi. Turning out of the stream the path follows the right bank and ascends by an easy gradient to a saddle which is the watershed between the 12 to 18 inches and the Mat river. Thence it runs along the face of the hill for a mile to Lalthangbunga's village. The village is situated on a saddle between two peaks, the northern one being the Howlong hill. The village consists of 130 houses. There are two good supplies of water, both on the western slope. The distance is about 12 miles.
			M. F.	M. F.	
		2. Lallowa (Bualpin). Van Vár.	**10 0**	22 0	The path runs down a spur through jhums and is very good till the Van Vár is reached, a distance of 5 miles. The path crossing the stream, which is 40 feet wide, sluggish at point of passage in May, after rains nearly waist-deep, ascends northwards up to the eastern face of a spur to a saddle, whence it runs almost level to the village. The village is in portions; the old village on the summit of the Bualpin hill and the new village on a ridge. Below there is a plentiful supply of water in the nullah on each side of the ridge. There are 150 houses, but numbers are fast increasing.
		3. Vansanga (Shippier).	**6 0**	28 0	The path from the village ascends to the summit of the spur just below the old village, whence it ascends in an easterly direction by an easy gradient to a small crossing, which it ascends very gently to the north to a saddle, whence it descends slightly to a ridge along which it runs to the village of Vansanga which has been burnt. It was situated on the summit and eastern slopes of a detached ridge running north and south. The water-supply is from two nullahs on the eastern slope and gets very scanty in the dry season. The village has been rebuilt near the old site.

FROM KÔTÍR (SAIPUYA'S VILLAGE) TO LINGRÁNG—*continued.*

Authorities. Military.	Authorities. Civil.	Number and Names of Stages, Rivers and Streams.	Distances. Inter-mediate. M. F.	Distances. Total. M. F.	Remarks.
G.O.C. Presidency District.	Superintendent, Southern Lushai Hills.	**4. Zanté**	5 0	33 0	The road to Zanté branches off from the Bualpin-Vansanga road about 300 yards from the village and continues north along the main ridge. There are two small ascents, but the road is good all the way. The distance is about 5 miles. Half-a-mile from Shippier there is a good supply of water near to the road on the east face of the ridge. Zanté is a steep hill rising some 200 feet above the main ridge. Extending some 200 yards to the west of it, Lalthôna's mother's village of 100 houses, which stood there, has been burnt. The position is a strong one. There is water in two nullahs on the west face of the main range, one to the north and one to the south of Zanté. The latter is the best supply.
		5. Lingráng ...	8 0	41 0	The road continues along the main ridge and is very good except for two short lengths of 200 yards each, where it goes along the face of a precipice. These could easily be improved. I do not know of any water on the road. The road takes a sudden bend to the west about ½ a mile from the Lingráng, which is a plateau some 200 feet above the general level of the range. The ascent to this plateau is up an extremely steep spur flanked by precipices. The plateau slopes gently to the west and is covered with short grass. There is a good supply of water. In the centre Lalthôna's village of 100 houses, which stood upon this site, is burnt. The total distance from Zanté is 8 miles. There is a road from here leading to Tenzjol (?) and another leading to Lalrhima, both said to be good. The former crosses the Van Vár and the latter the Mat.

BRANCH I.

FROM SHIPPIER (STAGE 3) TO CHONGTHLENG.

BY CAPT. J. SHAKESPEAR, D.S.O., SUPERINTENDENT, SOUTHERN LUSHAI HILLS, 1892.

Military.	Civil.	Number and Names of Stages, Rivers and Streams.	Inter-mediate. M. F.	Total. M. F.	Remarks.
G.O.C. Presidency District.	Superintendent, Southern Lushai Hills.	**1. Chongthleng** ... Van Vár Té, 10 feet wide, a few inches deep. Mat river.	16 0	16 0	From Shippier to Chongthleng the road descends to the eastward from the northern end of the late village and runs along a spur and descends by an easy gradient for about 1,500 feet to the Van Vár Té. From the stream the path descends fairly easily in a northerly direction to Maorop, an old village site of Vansanga's. Maorop consists of two large bare knolls. On the summit of the ridge between them to the east there is a good supply of water. From Maorop is an old and unused road to Zanté, which runs along the ridge all the way and is said to be very good; the distance must be about 2 miles. The path to Chongthleng leads down a spur which starts from northern knoll and runs due east, descending rather abruptly for the first ¼ of a mile, then ascending slightly along the northern slope, then down the spur to the Mat river, the last ½ mile being exceedingly steep. The distance to the Mat is 9 miles. After crossing the Mat, which is in May knee-deep, bed shingle, 30 yards wide, almost impassable after heavy rains, the path is most difficult to find. It runs through a dense plantain grove north-east for some

FROM KÔTÍR (SAIPUYA'S VILLAGE) TO LINGRÂNG—*continued.*

BRANCH I—*continued.*

Authorities. Military.	Authorities. Civil.	Number and Names of Stages, Rivers and Streams.	Distances. Intermediate.	Distances. Total.	Remarks.
G.O.C. Presidency District.	Superintendent, Southern Lushai Hills.	**1. Chongthleng**—*cont.*			100 yards into a muddy stream bed, up which it goes for 300 yards when it turns out on the right bank and shortly after recrosses the same stream and strikes east along the bottom of a valley, down which runs a good stream of water. At about 3 miles from the Mat the path recrosses the stream and commences to ascend sharply. The road is fair, but for 4 miles the ascent is continual. For the last 2 miles the spur is very narrow and the sides most precipitous. If stockades were constructed and held, they could only be carried with great loss of life. The total distance is about 16 miles. It is a very trying march for coolies, but quite a practicable one.* Chongthleng, the site of Daokhoma's village, is extremely strong. It consists of two knolls, the southern one rising 200 feet above the northern and ending in a bluff which commands the approach from Shippier. These two knolls are connected by a saddle. The ground on all sides falls away sharply. There is a good water-supply on the Shippier road about ½ a mile from the village.

BRANCH II.

FROM SHIPPIER (STAGE 3) TO HRIÂNTLÂNG.

BY CAPT. J. SHAKESPEAR, D.S.O., SUPERINTENDENT, SOUTHERN LUSHAI HILLS, 1892.

Military	Civil	Stages	Intermediate M. F.	Total M. F.	Remarks
G.O.C. Presidency District.	Superintendent, Southern Lushai Hills.	**1. Shership (Lalrhima's).** Mat river.	**16 0**	16 0	The path from Shippier to Shership is the same as that to Chongthleng to about 1½ miles beyond Maorop, when the Chongthleng road turns down the southern face of the spur, the Shership road continuing along the top of the spur for about 2 miles, when it begins to descend in a northerly direction into the Mat valley, the last ½ mile being very steep. Crossing a small stream it runs quite level through ground quite clear, from recent cultivation, for about a mile, it then crosses a stream called the Mat-té and runs up it for 2 miles, much of the path being in the water; the bed of the stream is very muddy. It then crosses over a low saddle and descends to the Mat at 11 miles which is here about 15 yards wide and was about 2 feet deep in May. It would probably never be unfordable here. The path now runs through a dense plantain jungle for ½ a mile and then ascends the spurs through jhums. The ascent continues right up to Shership. The path is very fair and the gradient fairly easy. Shership is the site of Lalrhima's village which has been burnt. It is one of the best sites as yet seen in these hills and consists of a series of knolls and spurs clear of jungle and covered with short grass. The general direction of the ridge is north and south. The triangulation point, Benkhoya, is the summit of a ridge about a mile to the north-east. From the northern and southern ends of the ridge on the eastern side run two level ridges in a semi-circle, each ending abruptly in the space enclosed between them. On the main ridge is a plentiful supply of water which escapes through the gorge between the two ridges.

* There, however, appears no reason why it should not be divided into two marches, halting on the Mat river about 9 miles.

FROM KÔTÍR (SAIPUYA'S VILLAGE) TO LINGRÁNG—*continued.*

BRANCH II—*continued.*

Authorities. Military.	Authorities. Civil.	Number and Names of Stages, Rivers and Streams.	Distances. Intermediate. M.	Distances. Intermediate. F.	Distances. Total. M.	Distances. Total. F.	Remarks.
G.O.C. Presidency District.	Superintendent, Southern Lushai Hills.	**2. Bomchom** ...	6	0	22	0	From Shership the path runs through the above-mentioned gorge down a steep spur to a saddle, a descent of about 800 feet, it then ascends by a very easy gradient about the same height, and passing round the northern shoulder of the Túiphim hills, it descends to the site of Rochaungnunga's late village. The total distance is about 6 miles. The road is good. Rochaungnunga's village stood on the eastern slope of the Túiphim and Bomchom hills, which are only two summits of the same hill. Below the village was an open grassy space. There are several abundant springs below the village.
		3. Hriántláng ... Túikum, 30 yards broad, 3 feet deep; bed bouldery.	9	0	31	0	The road from Bomchom to Hriántláng (on which hill Lalkanglova's village stood and was burnt) descends north-east for 2,000 feet into the bed of the Túikum. Descent easy. It then ascends up the spur through bamboo jungle eastwards for 2 miles, then runs almost level northwards for 1 mile, then ascends on to the village site from the north. The road is fair; passable for mules. Distance about 9 miles; time about 4 hours.

BRANCH III.

FROM CHONGTHLENG (*see* BRANCH I) TO BOMCHOM (*see* BRANCH II).

BY CAPT. J. SHAKESPEAR, D.S.O., SUPERINTENDENT, SOUTHERN LUSHAI HILLS, 1892.

Authorities. Military.	Authorities. Civil.	Number and Names of Stages, Rivers and Streams.	Distances. Intermediate. M.	Distances. Intermediate. F.	Distances. Total. M.	Distances. Total. F.	Remarks.
G.O.C. Presidency District.	Superintendent, Southern Lushai Hills.	**1. Bomchom** ... Lungtúi.	9	0	9	0	There are two paths from Chongthleng to Bomchom, one leaves Chongthleng or Baokhoma hill at the northern end and descends along a spur into the bed of the Lungtúi and from there ascends very steeply up on to the saddle and then runs practically level into Bomchom. The path, which leaves the southern end of Chongthleng, runs along a spur eastward for ½ a mile and then runs northwards across a saddle on to the Bomchom ridge and joins the former. This one is very good and fairly level. There is a little water 5 miles from Chongthleng, and plenty on approaching Bomchom. Distance is about 9 miles; time 4½ hours.

No. 20.

From LÉNÁKÔT (SHIELMONG, Route No. 3, Stage 7) to TONGLONG YWAMA and MANIPUR.

BY CAPT. H. B. VAUGHAN, 7TH BENGAL INFANTRY, ATTACHÉ, INTELLIGENCE BRANCH, JANUARY 1892.

Authorities. Military.	Authorities. Civil.	Number and Names of Stages, Rivers and Streams.	Distances. Intermediate. M.	Distances. Intermediate. F.	Distances. Total. M.	Distances. Total. F.	Remarks.
G.O.C. Myingyán District.	Political Officer, Chin Hills.	**1. Camp on Shwenkwa stream (3,750 feet).** Several small streams.	12	0	12	0	Road fair; is a track cut in the hill side. At ¾ mile it passes over a low spur connecting the hills right and left. A track branches off to the left and ascends the hills on that side, on whose summit are the remains of a Chin

FROM LÉNÁKÔT (SHIELMONG, ROUTE NO. 3, STAGE 7) TO TONGLONG YWAMA AND MANIPUR—*continued.*

Authorities. Military.	Authorities. Civil.	Number and Names of Stages, Rivers and Streams.	Distances. Intermediate.	Distances. Total.	Remarks.
G.O.C. Myingyán District.	Political Officer, Chin Hills.	**1. Camp on Shwenkwa stream (3,750 feet)**—*cont.*			stockade. Road runs north descending gently. At 1½ miles a steep descent commences. At 1¾ miles cross a small stream 1,250 feet below Shielmong. On by a level track fringed by high rushes. At 2¼ miles cross a small stream and commence an ascent. At 2¾ miles the gradient, which was steep, becomes more gentle. At 6 miles the road curves round to the right and descends slightly, passing the village of Kwunum, 25 houses, stockaded, and on the right of the road at 6¾ miles. Water from a ravine close by. At 7¼ miles pass through a stockaded gateway. At 8¼ miles a road goes straight on to Manipur. Follow the track to the left. At 9¼ miles up a slight ascent and on over the level summit of a chain of hills. At 11¼ miles leave the hill tops and descend steeply to a camping ground situated in a hollow; surrounded by jungle; slope very steep. Water and grass plentiful. Time taken on march 5 hours.
		2. Camp on Manipur river (2,350 feet). Manipur river.	M. F. **12 0**	M. F. 24 0	Road descends steeply and, after crossing the small Shwenkwa streamlet which names the place, ascends steeply till ¾ mile; then on by a level road till 1¾ miles, when a gentle descent commences. At about 3¼ miles a track branches off on the right down-hill towards Manipur. Tonglong road keeps straight on. At 3½ miles up an ascent and at 4 miles down again. At 4¼ miles a very steep ascent commences. At 5 miles along a narrow ridge. Road more level. At 9¼ miles up a steepish ascent. At 9½ miles pass by Bwankwa village, which is a little above the road and contains 30 houses, each within a stout fence of its own. It is completely commanded by high ground to the north, and the water-supply is said to be insufficient for the column. Elevation 4,100 feet. At 10¾ miles down a steep descent towards the Manipur river till the camp is reached at 12 miles. Time 5 hours. Camping ground amidst dense bamboo jungle on the left bank of the Manipur river. There is a better situation for a camp on the right bank. Grass abundant.
		3. Twidam (4,500 feet). Manipur river (fordable).	**10 4**	34 4	Cross the river just above its junction with the Lepai stream. The river is 60 yards broad from bank to bank. The water is about 35 yards broad and 2 feet deep with a rapid current; banks steep; impassable after heavy rain. On over open level ground up a valley till 4 miles, crossing a small stream occasionally; then on up the rocky bed of a mountain torrent amidst dense jungle with high hills on either side. At 7 miles leave the stream and go up a very steep ascent for ¼ mile. Then on, still ascending, though more easily, along a spur of Howbi peak. At 9¾ miles along a road cut in the hill side. Cross a small streamlet in a hollow. The camp, which is above the village of Twidam, is situated on the west slope of Howbi peak at 10½ miles. Water and grass plentiful. Road bad. Required blasting and cutting in places. Time 4½ hours.

FROM LÉNÁKÔT (SHIELMONG, ROUTE NO. 3, STAGE 7) TO TONGLONG YWAMA AND MANIPUR—*continued.*

Authorities. Military.	Authorities. Civil.	Number and Names of Stages, Rivers and Streams.	Distances. Intermediate. M. F.	Distances. Total. M. F.	Remarks.
G.O.C. Myingyán District.	Political Officer, Chin Hills.	**4. Camp on Twitár stream (2,750 feet).** Twitár and other smaller streams.	**8 6**	43 2	Leave camp and at ½ mile pass the village of Twidam, 25 houses, below the road and to its left. It then crosses two small streamlets in succession, then on by a fairly level track cut in the steep hill side. At 2¼ miles cross over the summit of the hills and commence a descent down into a valley. At 3½ miles pass the village of Chenglam and then cross a dry stream bed, whence water is obtained a few yards higher up in the hills above the road. At 3¾ miles pass through the second village of Chenglam; both settlements aggregate about 50 houses. A track branches off on the left from this village to Mulam, 60 houses and about 4 miles off. Lunkôt, 25 houses, is visible away on the hills to our right. On by an easy road till 6 miles and down a steep descent across a narrow but deep and dry nullah. At 6¼ miles cross a small stream which comes from near Mulam. There is a fairly good camping ground here on the hill side and on the right of the stream. On through jungle ascending slightly, then down an easy descent towards a plain. At 8¾ miles cross a stream, bed gravel, banks steep, and about 30 feet broad; impassable after heavy rain. It now contains but a few inches of water. Camp on the left bank of the stream on a level plain; a few trees and an abundance of long grass about. The plain extends north as far as one can see. Time of march 3½ hours.
		5. Camp on Twilár stream (2,300 feet).	**14 2**	57 4	Leave camp and cross the plain. At 1¼ miles enter low hills; and at 1¾ miles cross the Zézaw streamlet, which is small and fordable, unless after very heavy rain. At 2¾ miles pass some huts and diggings, where Chins extract salt from the soil. Then on, ascending gradually and along the crest of a ridge to the village of Tundkár (Tungkwa), 30 houses. The village is situated on a rounded hill and surrounded by a stockade, in addition to which each house is surrounded by a stout fence. Distance 4 miles. On across a valley towards the village of Tunzán, which is visible from here on the crest of the hills to the west. At 5 miles cross a small stream of fresh water running north and ascend steeply. At 6 miles pass through a stockaded gateway; a road to the left rear runs along the summit of the ridge just reached. Descend, cross a little streamlet in a hollow, and ascend again. At 7 miles reach the village of Tunzán, which lies on the right of the road. It is strongly placed, well stockaded, and full of interior timber fences, all new; about 70 houses in all. The houses in the western extremity of the village are situated on a rounded eminence commanding the rest of the village. From here Tanvum is visible to the south. On over level ground. At 7¾ and at 8 miles tracks branch off to the left in a southerly direction. At 9½ miles pass through a small undefended settlement belonging to Tanvum. At 9¾ miles there is water down in the hollow to the left of the road and 100 yards off. At 10 miles pass by the village of Tanvum, 60 houses, which lies about 150 yards off and to the left of the road; on, ascending slightly, at 10½ miles round the summit of the hills (elevation 3,300 feet), go down a steep and very difficult descent. At 11

FROM LÉNÁKÔT (SHIELMONG, ROUTE No. 3, STAGE 7) TO TONGLONG YWAMA AND MANIPUR—*continued.*

Authorities. Military.	Authorities. Civil.	Number and Names of Stages, Rivers and Streams.	Distances. Intermediate.	Distances. Total.	Remarks.
G.O.C. Myingyán District.	Political Officer, Chin Hills.	**5. Camp on Twilár stream (2,300 feet)**—*cont.*			miles reach the Lower Tanvum village, six houses. Water plentiful from two streams, one north and one south of the village and close by. A good camping ground just below and another one to the north of the village. The road turns a little to the left and still descends, but slightly, along a spur projecting into the valley ahead. At 14 miles a steep descent down into a valley through dense jungle. Cross the stream, approaches steep; about 40 feet broad and containing 8 inches of water. Bed rocks and gravel; probably impassable after heavy rain. Up the further bank and camp in a Chin clearing. The camp is on a steep hill side. Grass and water plentiful and thick bamboo jungle close by. Time taken 5 hours.
		6. Tonglong Ywama (Súnkumkwár) (3,750 feet). Orlu and smaller streams.	M. F. **10 0**	M. F. 67 4	The track ascends steeply up a spur and over portions of level ground. At $2\frac{3}{4}$ miles it passes through a stockaded gateway, then down and across a dry stream bed with a little fresh water and proceed up an ascent. At 3 miles pass through the village of Tornvum, 20 houses, and continue ascending steeply. At $3\frac{1}{4}$ miles along a steep hill side by a track cut in it. At $4\frac{1}{2}$ miles over the summit of the hills. Elevation 3,500 feet. Down a very steep descent on the further side. Enter the nearly dry bed of a mountain torrent 1,300 feet below and, after going up its stony bed a short distance, turn sharp to the left and proceed up a steep ascent and pass through some clearings. At $7\frac{1}{4}$ miles the ascent is easy and a track branches off on the left to the south along the ridge we are on. Just beyond this is a steep climb for about 150 feet. The hill sides to the left and right are precipitous. Were resistance to be offered, this is the most probable place in which to expect it. Road then through clearings on the steep hill side, which slopes down to the right and is encumbered with fallen trees till camp is reached on a slope to the south of and commanding the village, whose Chin name is Súnkumkwár, also known as Tonglong-ywama. It is the village where the Chief resides, but contains only 50 houses. It is commanded from the north and south. Water is procurable from a small hollow down below and to the east of the village. Supply just sufficient for the column. Time taken for the march $4\frac{1}{2}$ hours.

FROM TONGLONG it is said to be four days' march TO MANIPUR (IMPHÁL), and the following account of the route has been obtained from natives on the spot :—

Military	Civil	Stages	Intermediate	Total	Remarks
G.O.C. Myingyán District.	Political Officer, Chin Hills.	**1. Howkip** ...	**15 0**	15 0	Road leaving Tonglong runs over hilly country, being a series of steep ascents and descents to Howkip, a village containing 50 houses and belonging to the Thadow Chins. Water plentiful.
		2. Moirang ...	**15 0**	30 0	Down a hill side on to the Manipur plain and on over level ground till Moirang is reached. The Chin name for this place is Mailam and the lake is called the Twikhan.

No. 20.

FROM LÉNÁKÔT (SHIELMONG, ROUTE No. 3, STAGE 7) TO TONGLONG YWAMA AND MANIPUR—*continued.*

Authorities. Military.	Authorities. Civil.	Number and Names of Stages, Rivers and Streams.	Distances. Intermediate.	Distances. Total.	Remarks.
G.O.C. Assam District.	Political Officer, Manipur.		M. F.	M. F.	
		3. Lumnumtwung.	...	...	Road over level plain to Lumnumtwung village.
		4. Manipur ...	...	58 0	Road over level plain. *Note.*—This journey occupies the Chins four days, but the first march would probably be a very long one for troops.

No. 21.

From LÉNÁKÔT (SHIELMONG) to YÁZAGYO.

BY CAPT. H. B. VAUGHAN, 7TH BENGAL INFANTRY, ATTACHÉ, INTELLIGENCE BRANCH, MARCH 1892.

Authorities. Military.	Authorities. Civil.	Number and Names of Stages, Rivers and Streams.	Distances. Intermediate.	Distances. Total.	Remarks.
G.O.C. Myingyán District.	Political Officer, Chin Hills.	**1. Camp (4,000 feet).** Twipu and smaller streams.	10 2	10 2	Along the road to Fort White (*see* Route No. 3) in a southerly direction for ½ mile, then sharp off to the left through trees, ascending a spur. At 3 miles the track becomes bad owing to the heavy rain and the small foot-hold obtainable on the precipitous mountain side. At 4 miles the summit of Lítha range about 6,100 feet in height is crossed and 2,100 feet above Shielmong; then on skirting the bare hill-tops of the Lítha range. At 4½ miles enter a fine forest of immense trees overhung with moss. Road slippery; descends gently. At 6¾ miles pass Chin camping ground of Katumtwi, where there is a scanty supply of water near and to the right below the road. On down along a spur; dense forest in the valleys to the right and left. At 7¼ miles a steep descent into the valley commences and the village of Hínzán is visible on the hill ahead. At 9½ miles cross the rocky bed of the Twipu stream, a mountain torrent 3,650 feet below the summit of the Lítha range. Up a steep ascent and down to a hollow. Camping ground on a steepish hill side amongst jungle. Water plentiful from a stream close by. Elevation 2,600 feet. Time 5 hours.
		2. Hínzán ...	2 4	12 6	Descend and cross a small mountain torrent and then on up a steep ascent until the village of Hínzán is reached at 2½ miles. It contains 20 houses situated on a spur 1,400 feet above the Twipu stream. A strong position commanded only from the north. Camping ground good. Water plentiful close by.
		3. Camp beyond Balbil (3,150 feet). Twipu, Twiyárl, and other streams.	10 0	22 6	Road runs along the south foot of a spur of the Lítha, which runs towards Kampat in the Kubo valley. At 1 mile cross a streamlet. Then on down a steep descent for 1,300 feet and cross the rocky bed of a swift mountain torrent amidst dense jungle at 1¾ miles. On up an easy ascent for 300

FROM LÉNÁKÔT (SHIELMONG) TO YÁZAGYO—*continued.*

Authorities. Military.	Authorities. Civil.	Number and Names of Stages, Rivers and Streams.	Distances. Intermediate.	Distances. Total.	Remarks.
G.O.C. Myingyán District.	Political Officer, Chin Hills.	**3. Camp beyond Balbil (3,150 feet)**—*cont.*			feet and along a hill side the Twipu stream below on the right. Road ascends gradually at 3¼ miles, then down a steep descent for 1,500 feet and cross the rocky bed of a mountain torrent at 4½ miles; impassable after heavy rain. Elevation 2,550 feet. Then on along the hill side for a short distance and down through a tropical jungle amongst dense bamboo thickets and wild plantain trees. The Twipu close by on the right, and at 6¼ miles cross it. Bed gravel and rocks; now fordable, but impassable after heavy rain. Elevation 1,550 feet or 2,450 feet below Hínzán. Up a steep ascent on the further bank. At 7¾ miles the village of Balbil is visible high up on a hill ahead. The track runs through some Chin clearings amongst tall grass and, descending, crosses a broad and rocky tributary of the Twipu called the Twiyárl by a single tree bridge at 8¾ miles, stream fordable. On up a very steep ascent for 1,300 feet until it passes the village of Balbil, 20 houses. Then over a low hill-top and down on to a level camping ground under immense trees and surrounded on three sides by low hill-tops. A small stream of water runs through the camp. Time 5¾ hours.
		4. Camp on Naulzál stream (1,100 feet). Several streams.	M. F. **8 0**	M. F. 30 6	Leaving camp the track descends gently and, after going ⅛ mile, passes through Chin clearings and entering the jungle crosses two small streams of fresh water in succession. It then runs over a low hill. At 3¾ miles it passes some Chin clearings, then descends and crosses a large torrent, usually passable by fording. Elevation 1,600 feet. Then on up a very steep ascent till 1,900 feet above the stream and 5½ miles from Balbil and down again through dense jungle. Reach the banks of the Naulzál stream and camp. A good camping ground in dry weather amid dense bamboo jungle on the left bank of the stream. Time 4¼ hours.
		5. Camp above Haitsi (2,600 feet).	**8 2**	39 0	Leave camp, recross the stream, and go up a very steep ascent through dense bamboo jungle. At 1 mile, after ascending 1,800 feet, the track runs along the crest of some low hills, an off-shoot of the Lítha range, through forest consisting of bamboo, canes, and some fine forest trees. At 7 miles a descent commences for 900 feet until camp is reached. A camping ground on a spur above the village of Haitsi. Water and bamboos plentiful. Time 4 hours.
		6. Camp (1,450 feet). Several streams.	**10 0**	49 0	Road descends along a spur towards the village of Haitsi, 20 houses. Leaves the road to the village and goes off sharp to the left along the hill side at ½ a mile. At ¾ of a mile cross a stream at the bottom of a deep nullah with steep approaches. A small stream of fresh water. On along the hill side and up a steep ascent amongst Chin clearings. At 2½ miles cross over the summit of a hill and down a very steep descent through dense bamboo jungle. At 3½ miles cross a small stream of fresh water and go up a steep ascent through bamboo jungle. The road thence descends easily along a wooded spur. Camp at 10 miles on the spur, close by a stream, which is down in the valley to the right. Water-supply fair. Level space for a camp limited. Time 4½ hours.

FROM LÉNÁKÔT (SHIELMONG) TO YÁZAGYO—*continued.*

Authorities. Military.	Authorities. Civil.	Number and Names of Stages, Rivers and Streams.	Distances. Intermediate.	Distances. Total.	Remarks.
G.O.C. Myingyán District.	Commissioner, Central Division, and Deputy Commissioner, Upper Chindwin.	**7. Yázagyo (650 feet).** Nyinzyin chaung.	M. F. 9 0	M. F. 58 0	Road good; runs on descending the spur traversed in yesterday's march. At 4½ miles the track descends into the Yázagyo valley and runs over level ground under fair-sized trees. At 7½ miles the track crosses the Nyinzyín stream (Chin name Twime), about 30 yards broad; bed gravel; approaches easy; fordable, except after very heavy rain. A clear stream full of fine mahseer. On over level ground in the vicinity of the river. Enters the stockaded village of Yázagyo. Time 3 hours. One hundred houses, containing the half ruined palace of the Sawbwa, the head-quarters of a sub-division, containing one Civil and one Police Officer and a military post of 50 sepoys. Water plentiful. Camping ground good and supplies procurable after due notice.

No. 22.

From SHURKWA to HÁKA.

BY LIEUT. C. R. BALLARD, ATTACHÉ, NORFOLK REGIMENT, JANUARY 1892.

There are three alternative routes between Shurkwa and Háka. One has already been described, *vide* Route No. 9, the other two are as follows :—

FIRST ROUTE.

Military.	Civil.	Stages.	Intermediate.	Total.	Remarks.
G.O.C. Myingyán District.	Political Officer, Chin Hills.	**1. Kapi**	13 0	13 0	Path leaves camp in north-east direction and for first 4 miles is rather bad, along some narrow ridges and steep hill sides. After this it is level and easy, a very good track indeed. At 10½ miles the path divides: on the left is the direct road to Háka (*see* below) leading due north, on the right the road to Kapi leading north-east. This road leads down a spur with slight descent for 1½ miles, then turns north for 1 mile steeply down to camp. A fair camp in cultivation; water from stream 400 yards lower down. Supplies may be got from the village which is on the opposite spur ½ a mile away. The first 4 miles of this road should be improved before mules are sent along it again. There is no water on the road.
		2. Second camp ... A small stream, 1 foot deep, 6 feet wide.	11 0	24 0	The stream is first crossed, then there is a stiff pull up through the village which lies on the south side of the spur. On reaching the top of the spur the path turns west and along the top of it till it rejoins the Háka main road (*see* below) at 3 miles. From here there is 6 miles very good easy going on the level. At 9 miles the track again descends rather steeply to a small stream; keeping along this for ¾ mile a good camp is found on the right bank. Plenty of water, wood, &c.

FROM SHURKWA TO HÁKA—*continued.*

FIRST ROUTE—*continued.*

Authorities. Military.	Authorities. Civil.	Number and Names of Stages, Rivers and Streams.	Distances. Inter-mediate. M. F.	Distances. Total. M. F.	Remarks.
G.O.C. Myingyán District.	Political Officer, Chin Hills.	**3. Third camp** ...	11 0	35 0	An easy march, but no water on the way. Mostly level going on a very good road. At first slight ascent for 1 mile, then level and undulating for 9 miles, then 1 mile descent into camp. Very good camp; plenty of room; a good stream, wood and grass.
		4. Háka Post ... A small stream, 6 inches deep, 10 feet wide, several times.	13 0	48 0	Another easy march. Still keeping due north the path undulates for 6 miles, then goes down to the bed of a small stream which it crosses continually in the next 3 miles. At 9 miles, leaving the stream, it goes up a short hill and bend eastwards down to Háka. This is all easy for mules, and except for the first 4 miles out of Shurkwa would be an excellent road throughout.

SECOND ROUTE.

FROM SHURKWA TO HÁKA.

BY LIEUT. H. C. DUCAT, 2ND BATTALION, 4TH GURKHAS, 25TH FEBRUARY 1891.

Military	Civil	Stages	Inter-mediate	Total	Remarks
G.O.C. Myingyán District.	Political Officer, Chin Hills.	**1. Dinlaopa camp.**	13 0	13 0	Leaving the camping ground near Shurkwa the path ascends north-east for ½ mile to the crest line of the Dár-kwong-Hrianák Tláng, along which it runs in a general northern direction, at times following the crest-line, which is narrow in places, at others skirting round the peaks. In the first 4 miles three stockades are met with at intervals of about a mile. They are erected some 50 yards in rear of places where the crest-line is very narrow, with a precipitous slope on either side, so that turning movements would be most difficult. The stockades themselves are about 20 yards long and constructed of pine logs 8 feet high, with loopholes cut at the base; on the inside are banquettes of stone with trenches about 2 feet deep. They are visible from some distance in front. At about 9 miles the path joins the Kapi-Paipa track (Route No. 9) and then continues along the ridge, still in a general northerly direction, for 4 miles, when it descends a short spur to the camping ground a level piece of ground in a hollow, called Dinlaopa, where water is good though limited; grass and fuel abundant. Water is not met with throughout this march.
		2. Saorel Vár camp.	11 0	24 0	The path ascends to the ridge again and running along the crest-line for 2 miles in a northern direction, descends ½ mile a spur to the Vao Vár, whose course it follows for a mile, and reaches the junction of the Vao Vár with the Namtlak Vár. At this point the path turns off north-east up a spur, which it ascends for ½ mile to the crest of a ridge, along which it runs almost perfectly level north-north-west for 4 miles, when it gradually bends

FROM SHURKWA TO HÁKA—*continued.*

SECOND ROUTE—*continued.*

Authorities. Military.	Authorities. Civil.	Number and Names of Stages, Rivers and Streams.	Distances. Intermediate.	Distances. Total.	Remarks.
G.O.C. Myingyán District.	Political Officer, Chin Hills.	**2. Saorel Vár camp**—*cont.*			round eastwards for 2 miles, still along the crest-line, till it joins the Saorel Thetta path (Route No. 9) and then turns north, descending a spur for a mile to the camping ground on the Saorel Vár.
		3. Háka	M. F. **12 0**	M. F. 36 0	*Vide* Ronte No. 9, Stage 1. This last appears to be the most direct route.

No. 23.

From SHURKWA to LUNGO viâ LÔTAW.

BY LIEUT. C. R. BALLARD, UNPAID ATTACHÉ, NORFOLK REGIMENT, AND LIEUT. SACKEVILLE WEST, K.R.R., JANUARY 1892.

Military	Civil	Stages	Intermediate M.	Intermediate F.	Total M.	Total F.	Remarks
G.O.C. Myingyán District.	Political Officer, Chin Hills.	**1. South camp** ... Boinn Vár (crossed four times), 2½ feet deep, 20 yards broad.	**8**	**4**	8	4	eaving camp the path goes through he village southwards and then turns to the right and goes down a long steep descent to the Boinu Vár which it reaches at 4 miles. Path bad in places. It then goes down bed of the river for 1 mile crossing four times. This would be impassable after rain. Leaving the river path ascends very steeply up to the left round a shoulder and down into camp at a stream. Fair ground, plenty of water and wood. This is a hard march, especially for mules.
		2. Aika ... ... Small stream at the camp.	**3**	**4**	12	0	A steep ascent for 2 miles, then 1 mile level into the village. Camp ½ mile south of village; good large ground with plenty of water, &c. A very easy march. Aika village is strongly stockaded and has 250 houses which are well built. Plenty of supplies may be had here. The villages of Lunráng and Lunkying can be seen on the opposite side of the Boinu, looking westwards.
		3. Hti Hti Vár camp. Streams at the camp and at 3½ miles.	**7**	**0**	19	0	Path ascends for first ½ mile, then continues level and good for 3 miles where there is a stream, then there is a very long steep hill for 2 miles; difficult for men and mules. After this a capital path with slight descent from top of hill to near camp. Last mile into camp very steep and dangerous for mules. An excellent camp with plenty of wood, water, and grass. *N.B.*—These two stages might be doubled up.

FROM SHURKWA TO LUNGO *viâ* LÔTAW—*continued.*

Authorities. Military.	Authorities. Civil.	Number and Names of Stages, Rivers and Streams.	Distances. Intermediate. M.	F.	Total. M.	F.	Remarks.
G.O.C. Myingyán District.	Political Officer, Chin Hills.	**4. Lôtaw** ... ... Hti Hti Vár seventeen times; 2 feet deep, 15 yards broad.	2	4	21	4	This march is entirely up the bed of the Hti Hti Vár which it crosses continually. Direction nearly due south. A post has been built on the left bank of the river about 300 feet up and opposite the village of Lôtaw. There is a good supply of water, but not much wood. The village is on the right bank about 500 feet up. Supplies may be got here. This is a good base for operations to the south and south-west, as runners can reach Minywa in two days and coolies can be got from the village to bring up supplies.
		5. First camp on Hti Hti Vár. Hti Hti Vár; many times; 2 feet deep, 15 yards broad.	3	4	25	0	The track leaves camp and runs along the bed of the Hti Hti Vár which it crosses frequently. Camp on the left bank; fair ground, plenty of grass and wood. *Note.*—There is an alternative path over the hills which the Chins use: it avoids the river.
		6. Second camp on Hti Hti Vár. Hti Hti Vár; many times.	3	4	28	4	Path still in bed of the stream and often actually in the water. At 3½ miles a slight opening in the valley and by ascending the right bank a camp is found for 200 men; by the stream more ground is available by clearing grass, &c. *N.B.*—These two marches may be doubled, especially if marching back down stream.
		7. Lungo ... ... Hti Hti Vár; many times.	11	4	40	0	Path keeps along stream occasionally rising over spurs; mule track along bed of stream. At 4 miles, the track ascends a steep spur up to ridge and thence by good road to the camp which is opposite Lungo. Good camp; water from a small stream just below. This route is difficult for mules. *Note.*—It will be observed that this journey can be performed in five marches and perhaps even in four by combining the 4th, 5th and 6th stages, which would even then only make a 9½ miles march.

ALTERNATIVE I.

FROM LÔTAW TO LUNGO *viâ* ROWYVA.

BY LIEUT. BALLARD, NORFOLK REGIMENT, JANUARY 1892.

Military	Civil	Stage	Intermediate M.	F.	Total M.	F.	Remarks
G.O.C. Myingyán District.	Political Officer, Chin Hills.	**1. Shirklai** ... Hti Hti Vár.	5	0	5	0	Long ascent up water-course from Hti Hti Vár, then slight descent to camp near Shirklai village; good camping ground; easy march.

FROM SHURKWA TO LUNGO *viâ* LÔTAW—*continued.*

ALTERNATIVE I—*continued.*

Authorities. Military.	Authorities. Civil.	Number and Names of Stages, Rivers and Streams.	Distances. Intermediate. M.	Distances. Intermediate. F.	Distances. Total. M.	Distances. Total. F.	Remarks.
G.O.C. Myingyán District.	Political Officer, Chin Hills.	**2. Sawtaw (5,200 feet).** Small streams.	12	0	17	0	Pass through village of Shirklai; at 1½ miles cross stream. Ascend to 4 miles (7,800 feet) and thence steep, and in places difficult descent for 3 miles to stream with camping ground on both banks. Ascend from stream to village of Sáshé, thence along hill and across the valley to Sawtaw. Camp on hill side by small stream.
		3. Rowyva ... Small streams.	14	0	31	0	A long march, but not hard except for animals. Water at 5, 7½ and 8½ miles. Excellent camp just short of the village.
		4. Camp	13	0	44	0	Track ascends from village to ridge, which it follows for about 9 miles. Elevation then 9,500 feet. Thence descend bare hill sides for nearly 4 miles where there is a bad camp on the hill side with a limited water-supply.
		5. Kilung ... ... Stream.	4	4	48	4	Steep, and for first 3½ miles in parts precipitous, descent, passing through the village of Kilung shortly before reaching camp on stream; good ground.
		6. Lungo (or Lungu).	10	6	59	2	Ascend from camp and cross hill; pass village of Belai, and cross another hill to Lungo. The path would require mending before it would be fit for mules to traverse it.
							Note.—All this route would be passable for mules except for short distances, which would require improvement with tools. It is not, of course, the direct route between Lôtaw and Lungo, but may be used to visit the villages situated along or near it.

No. 24.

From TLÁNTLÁNG to HRIPI.

BY CAPT. BAKER, 1ST NORFOLK REGIMENT, INTELLIGENCE BRANCH, APRIL 1893.

Military	Civil	Stages	Int. M.	Int. F.	Total M.	Total F.	Remarks
G.O.C. Myingyán District.	Political Officer, Chin Hills.	**1. Klángwra** ... One large stream called the Rachiar Vár and several small streams.	6	4	6	4	General direction south-south-west. Leaving the camp, which is north of and above Tlántláng, the direct road runs straight through the village. This is, however, not passable for laden mules, the lanes being so narrow. The best way for them is to return along the Tlántláng-Háka road (Route

FROM TLÁNTLÁNG TO HRIPI—*continued.*

Authorities. Military.	Authorities. Civil.	Number and Names of Stages, Rivers and Streams.	Distances. Inter-mediate.	Distances. Total.	Remarks.
G.O.C. Myingyán District.	Political Officer, Chin Hills.	**1. Klángwra**—*cont.*			No. 5) for about 450 yards, then turn off along a path running south down-hill over the water-supply; then for a short way along left bank of this stream, which is then crossed, and strike into the path running south from the village. Then down this path into the nullah southward and across the stream running westwards south of the village at 1½ miles from camp. By going through the village about ¾ mile is saved. After crossing stream the path rises to top of small ridge beyond, then over this and down into the valley of the Rachiár Vár, a large stream running south-east and north-west at 2¼ miles. The path then crosses this stream and runs up a spur at an easy gradient, and winds along in a southerly direction for another 2½ miles, crossing two or three small streams, at which point it passes over a neck from whence Klángwra is seen bearing 199°. From here the road winds southwards for 2 miles into Klángwra. About 200 yards before reaching the village there is a good camping ground with excellent water-supply close at hand. Path mostly good but steep in places, but available for mules. Klángwra, which contains about 100 houses, is built on a spur jutting out eastwards from the main range. It is not stockaded. It has a good water-supply in a stream north of and just outside village. Aneroid showed 5,200 feet.
			M. F.	M. F.	
		2. Camp on Láwár Vár. Láwár Vár.	**2 4**	9 0	The path runs right through village and continues along eastern slope of range for about 2,300 yards, when it inclines more to the west. Here there is a very bad place where the road passes along the face of a precipitous rock (a diversion was made above it for the mules). Leaving the rock, the road runs along a blunt spur to the valley of the Láwár Vár below. Good camping ground alongside of river, but of necessity much commanded, 3,000 feet.
		3. Hripi ... ... Láwár Vár and Bankluán Vár and three small streams.	**6 0**	15 0	The path runs out of camp for about 100 yards along right bank of river, which it then crosses and runs up the hill in the opposite side, direction west-south-west, and then winds over a couple of spurs and down into a deep nullah beyond, in which runs the Bankluán Vár about 1¾ miles from camp. Road bad. A few mules were taken with the column, but before reaching this stream their loads had to be taken off and carried down by hand. The path now crosses the river and runs up the opposite hill side, direction south-west, to the top, which is reached at 3½ miles. From near this point the village of Hripi is seen bearing 204°. The path now runs along ridge south-east for some little way, then leaves the top and runs along south side winding gradually south round the head of the big nullah over three or four small streams into Hripi village. The village is approached through a narrow gorge with dense bramble jungle on either side, defended by three stockaded gateways. The water-supply is crossed before entering this gorge. Camp in the village; no suitable ground outside. Hripi contains about 100 excellent houses, and is situated at the head of a large nullah, built on a spur running into the nullah. The road is very steep most of the way, and, although a few mules were brought with the column, it is certainly not fitted for mule transport. Aneroid showed 6,100 feet.

No. 25.

From TWITIL to KAPTYÁL viâ TEINSAN.

By E. O. FOWLER, Esq., Assistant Political Officer, Northern Chin Hills, 1892-93.

Authorities. Military.	Authorities. Civil.	Number and Names of Stages, Rivers and Streams.	Distances. Intermediate.		Distances. Total.		Remarks.
			M.	F.	M.	F.	
G.O.C. Myingyán District.	Political Officer, Chin Hills.	**1. Teinsán** ... Two streams.	**3**	**4**	3	4	General direction of road north-west. Leaving Twitil village (Wenho) on the western side the road ascends to a distance of ½ a mile. It then descends for ¾ mile into a nullah, in which there is a good stream of water. It then ascends for ¼ mile at a steep ascent. The road then winds along the top of a ridge which is level for ½ a mile and then descends at a gentle incline for ¾ mile into a nullah, in which there is a small supply of water. This water is not good. It then ascends direct into Teinsán village. The road on the whole is good and passable for mules. Teinsán is a stockaded village containing 14 houses (Wenho). Water in five wells in the south-west side; supply small; camping ground good, but owing to small supply of water not suitable for large bodies of troops.
		2. Tawti ... ... One stream.	**2**	**0**	5	4	General direction of road north-east. Leaving Teinsán village on the north side the road ascends slightly for ¼ mile and then descends for another ¼ mile. It then winds north-east for another ¾ mile, then descends abruptly into a nullah, in which there is a good stream of water. It then ascends in a north-easterly direction for ¾ mile and passes Tawti village on the west side. The village lies east of road and is on a slope. Road on the whole fairly good and passable for mules. Tawtí contains 20 houses. There is a good supply of water from a stream to the north-east of the village.
		3. Kaptyál ... Several small streams.	**10**	**4**	16	0	Up-hill for 5 miles, then over a nullah along which path runs for 500 yards, then steep up-hill. At 6 miles the Imbuk Kláng range is crossed; from here it is down-hill the remainder of the way to Kaptyál (Nwengál). At 7½ miles a small stream is passed, which runs into the big nullah under new Shelpó.

No. 26.

From UNGNO to KÁNGYI.

By Lieut. JONES, Inniskilling Fusiliers, March 1893.

G.O.C. Myingyán District.	Commissioner, Central Division, and Deputy Commissioner, Upper Chindwin.	**1. Kángyi** ... Five streams.	**17**	**4**	17	4	Ungno is 7 miles due north of Pimpi Post. Leaving Ungno the path rises to the top of the ridge south (5,000 feet); here it divides, one running west to Fort White and one east to Kángyi. The latter runs along down ridge to its termination at an easy gradient; path good except at 3¼ miles,

FROM UNGNO TO KÁNGYI—*continued.*

Authorities. Military.	Authorities. Civil.	Number and Names of Stages, Rivers and Streams.	Distances. Intermediate.	Distances. Total.	Remarks.
G.O.C. Myingyán District.	Commissioner, Central Division, and Deputy Commissioner, Upper Chindwin.	1. **Kángyi**—*cont.*			where it is steep, but only for a short distance. At 6¾ miles the spur ends and the path crosses stream at bottom (1,200 feet) about 8 yards wide and ankle-deep. From this out the path is level right into Kángyi. It now runs for about 2½ miles along left bank of the stream and at 9¾ miles crosses another stream 4 yards wide and ankle-deep; at 12½ it crosses a large stream 20 yards wide and knee-deep, then two more within the last mile of Kángyi about 35 yards wide with water above the knee. Kángyi is on the bank of the last of these streams. Path is available for mules the whole way from Kángyi. Country through which it runs is mostly forest land with bamboo undergrowth, but in some parts through high kaing grass. Kángyi is a strongly stockaded village of about 100 houses about 19½ miles north of Kalémyo, to which place a good cart road runs. Good camping ground on bank of river.

No. 27.

From UNGNO to No. 3 STOCKADE on KALÉMYO-FORT WHITE ROAD (Route No. 6, Central Division) viâ PIMPI POST.

BY CAPT. BAKER, INTELLIGENCE OFFICER, NORTHERN CHIN HILLS, 1893.

Authorities. Military.	Authorities. Civil.	Number and Names of Stages, Rivers and Streams.	Distances. Intermediate.	Distances. Total.	Remarks.
			M. F.	M. F.	
G.O.C. Myingyán District.	Political Officer, Chin Hills.	1. **Pimpi Post** ... Four streams.	7 0	7 0	The route follows the path to Fort White, which runs up to the top of the ridge (5,000 feet) and for another 700 yards after turning west along ridge. At this point it branches off sharp to the left in a southerly direction down a short spur, and runs into the nullah beneath, where hidden away under a cliff, is a deserted settlement of 12 houses, probably made by Pimpi people after their village was burnt. This nullah 100 yards further on joins a larger one, in which is a good stream of water and whose course the path follows for about 500 yards. The path then turns off sharp to the right up the khud on the other side and runs along the side of the spur for about 1,500 yards through dense jungle (path exceedingly bad), when it rises to the top of the spur and passes to the left of another deserted settlement, and 700 yards further on a third one. From this settlement Pimpi Post is seen on the opposite side of the valley and bears 216°. The path leaves this settlement at its south-west corner and runs steeply down to the nullah below, in which there is a good stream of water about 700 yards from the last settlement. The path here crosses the stream and rounds the head of the spur on the opposite side. At 1,300 yards further on it crosses a very small stream, and 300 yards further runs down into the nullah in which the Pimpi river runs. The path follows the bed of the stream upwards for a short way, then crosses it and ascends the opposite side and follows side parallel to it up stream, some distance above it, for about 400 yards, when it enters some cultivated fields; then crosses another small stream and runs up the head of the spur into Pimpi Post. The path throughout is bad and not suitable for mule transport. (Aneroid 3,600 feet.)

From UNGNO to No. 3 STOCKADE on KALÉMYO-FORT WHITE ROAD (Route No. 6, Central Division) *viâ* PIMPI POST—*continued.*

Authorities. Military.	Authorities. Civil.	Number and Names of Stages, Rivers and Streams.	Distances. Intermediate.	Distances. Total.	Remarks.
G.O.C. Myingyán District.	Political Officer, Chin Hills.	**2. No. 3 Stockade.** Three streams.	M. F. **8 6**	M. F. 15 6	The path leaves the post, south-east, crossing the water-supply at that side, and 300 yards further on crosses a second stream and rises gradually until at ¾ of a mile it rises to the ridge of a spur running almost due with from the Pimpi range. It follows up this spur (almost due south) for about ½ a mile and soon after rounds the top of the ridge (elevation 4,750 feet). The path now follows to the top of the ridge, from which No. 3 and No. 4 Stockades are seen for about 3 or 3½ miles, when it reaches a small spur which bears 28° from No. 3 Stockade. Here the path divides, one portion continuing along ridge, probably to No. 2, the other to No. 3, down the khud, to the right, in a south-west direction, and runs down a spur to the nullah below, in which flows a third stream. The descent to the stream for the last 100 yards is most precipitous. The path runs up stream on left bank for about 100 yards, then crosses and rises the khud on opposite side. The stream at present is about 8 yards wide and knee-deep. There are plenty of fish in it. The path at first is very steep, rising 1,150 feet in 800 yards, but soon runs along ridge of a spur which juts out from No. 3, along which it ascends easily, until, just outside the post, it joins the Fort White-Kalémyo road (Route No. 6, Central Division). Path very fair except in neighbourhood of the third stream, where it is bad. No. 3 Stockade is one march from Kalémyo, two (or perhaps one long one) from Fort White.

PART IV.

ROUTES IN THE EASTERN (CIVIL) DIVISION.

PART IV.

ROUTES IN THE EASTERN (CIVIL) DIVISION.

No. 1.

From KYAUKSÉ to ÁVA viâ CHAUNGWA.

I. B. COMPILATION, 1888.

Authorities. Military.	Authorities. Civil.	Number and Names of Stages, Rivers and Streams.	Distances. Intermediate. M. F.	Distances. Total. M. F.	Remarks.
G.O.C. Myingyán District.	Commissioner, Eastern Division, and Dy. Commissioner, Kyauksé.	**1. Chaungwa** ... Pánláng river.	**15 0**	15 0	The route to Chaungwa, distance from Kyauksé 15 miles, is by Názu village, which is about half-way. The road leaves Kyauksé on the west and after crossing the Zídaw canal by a wooden bridge, much out of the perpendicular and scarcely passable for carts, it runs due north along the canal bank for about a mile; thence to Názu the road takes a westerly direction, and is a good, hard cart track, passable at all seasons. At Názu the road crosses the Pánláng river. Názu village is on the right of the road and contains accommodation for about 50 men in kyaungs. Water plentiful from the Pánláng, which runs nearly north and south. From here the road runs west and is a good, hard track through low scrub jungle. At 15 miles reach Chaungwa, large village of over 100 houses. Water rather scarce in dry season.
G.O.C. Myingyán District.	Commissioner, Central Division, and Deputy Commissioner, Sagaing.	**2. Áva** ... ... Irrawaddy.	**14 0**	29 0	Direction north-north-east, first 7 miles through low jungle and then low-lying cultivated ground; road difficult and impassable for wheeled transport in wet weather. At 4½ miles small village of Nazinyain and at 7 miles Sagayin where the Áva-Wundwin route joins in (*see* Route No. 4, Central Division) and is followed to Áva 14 miles. For wet weather the route followed between Chaungwa and Áva runs east-north-east through Yégyi to Kinywa ¾ of a mile south of Sagayin on the Wundwin road. This makes the distance 2 miles longer, a total of 16 miles.

No. 2.

From KYAUKSÉ to PWÉHLA viâ NATTIK PASS.*

BY LIEUT. J. A. S. TULLOCH, R.E., 1888.

Military	Civil	Stage	Intermediate	Total	Remarks
G.O.C. Myingyán District.	Commr.,* Eastern Divn., &c., Kyauksé.	**1. Yéwun** ...	**14 0**	...	*See* Route No. 6, Lower Burma Division.

* The nearest point on the railway to the Nattik Pass is Myittha station, whence there is a good, level, bridged cart road to Yekaingyi, 10 miles south-east, passing several villages.—A. F.

FROM KYAUKSÉ TO PWÉHLA *viâ* NATTIK PASS—*continued.*

Authorities. Military.	Authorities. Civil.	Number and Names of Stages, Rivers and Streams.	Distances. Intermediate. M. F.	Distances. Total. M. F.	Remarks.
G.O.C. Myingyán District.	Commissioner, Eastern Division, and Deputy Commissioner, Kyauksé.	**2. Yekaingyi** ...	**9 0**	23 0	Leaving Yéwun road runs south-east. At ½ mile pass village of Yáza, where large number of cattle and carts are procurable. A little further on a difficult bit for carts, just beyond which a zayát (20 men). At 1 mile village of Ywashé on the left bank of the Myaung Madaw canal on opposite bank is Ywabu. From Ywashé there are two roads to Yekaingyi, the eastern and the western roads. The western road runs most of the way through paddy cultivation, and crosses two shallow streams. This route is apparently used by the villagers in preference to the eastern route. The eastern road crosses the canal immediately after leaving Ywashé by a ford nowhere more than 18 inches deep. At 1¼ miles (from Yéwun) pass kyaung on opposite bank of canal (50 men); cross small stream flowing into the canal; country open with a few bushes scattered about and occasional palm topes. About 2 miles pass deserted kyaung and small zayát (20 men) close to the road. The flooring of this kyaung is in bad repair, but the roof is good and 100 men could find shelter in it; there is a well near. About 5 miles the country becomes more jungly; road good; soil sandy clay. Further on pass through a lot of long grass jungle. At 7 miles recross Myaung Madaw canal by ford, 2 feet deep; banks about 6 feet high and 35 yards apart. At 8 miles pass pagoda and 12 zayáts (100 men). There are two wells here and it would make a good camping ground. At 9 miles reach Yekaingyi (200 houses). Yekaingyi consists of two villages lying north and south of each other. The southern village is the more important; it is situated on the right bank of the Pánláng river. It is surrounded by a strong thorn hedge, with a deep ditch inside. The houses are good and would afford good accommodation for a large number of troops. The Bombay Burma Company have an agency here at present (January), but it will probably be removed to some station on the line of rail, possibly Myittha. The northern village is 2 or 300 yards from the other. It is surrounded by a thorn hedge; this village is small at present, but is apparently increasing, new houses being built. There is accommodation in kyaungs and zayáts here for at least 350 men. Good water from wells near kyaungs and from canals close by. There was formerly a military post here. A range of hills approaches Yekaingyi somewhat closely on the east. It is detached from the main range which lies further east and is known as the Tilaing Taungdaw. From Yekaingyi roads run east to Lungyaw (police post) and Pedaw, small village of 19 houses.
		3. Nagu or Ingôn.	**8 0**	31 0	Road south-east. At 1 mile cross some low ground dry in the cold weather, but probably all under water in the rains. A wooden causeway bridge crosses about 100 yards of it, and is strong enough at present to allow transport animals to cross over it, but it is falling into decay. At 1½ miles the Pánláng river is close on the right, here about 60 yards wide. Road leaves the river now and passes to the left of a hill, on which there is a large pagoda and several zayáts. From the summit of the hill Kyauksé is clearly visible, and

FROM KYAUKSÉ TO PWÉHLA *viâ* NATTIK PASS—*continued.*

Authorities.		Number and Names of Stages, Rivers and Streams.	Distances.		Remarks.
Military.	Civil.		Intermediate.	Total.	
G.O.C. Myingyán District.	Commissioner, Eastern Division, and Deputy Commissioner, Kyauksé.	**3. Nagu or Ingôn** *—cont.*			also the entrance to the Nattik pass. Cross a deep chaung running into the Pánláng by good strong bridge, able to bear elephants. At 3 miles road again nears Pánláng, following a bend of the river which brings it to the Nátlwé dam from which a canal takes off, supplying water to the Thabiyédaung district. In August 1887 this dam gave way and caused a great scarcity of water throughout the Thabiyédaung district for some time. The Pánláng at this point is about 60 yards wide; current swift, but not deep, fordable in January. At 4 miles pass village of Daing (12 houses), where there is a kyagun and five zayáts which would shelter 150 men. The country now becomes jungly, bamboo and cactus chiefly. At 8 miles Nagu is reached, a little village of 30 houses, and a small bazaar, situated in an open space. Immediately on leaving the village cross a canal, formerly the bed of the Pánláng river. It is fordable in January, but there is also a good bridge over it. Ingôn lies ¼ mile or so further on across paddy-fields. Betwee.. it and Nagu there is a p(ngyi kyaung (in rather bad repair) situated on a small knoll · it would accommodate 60 men, and was formerly used as a post, but was abandoned chiefly owing to its extreme unhealthiness. The Pánláng river runs ½ mile to the south, and is bunded near here, the Kindaw dam. Grass plentiful here. The road between Yéwun and Ingôn is said to be very heavy throughout in the rains, and would certainly be very bad in the low-lying portions. Captain Davies, who traversed this route in April 1893, makes the distance of this stage 8¾ miles, and thence to Nabagyi (Nabángyi, *see* in Stage 5) 11¼ as compared with the 9¼ of this route.
G.O.C. Rangoon District.	Superintendent, Southern Shan States.	**4. Thayetyé** ...	M. 4 F. 4	M. 35 F. 4	Road south-east and soon enters jungle at the foot of the hills, level and good as far as Kinlé on right of road at 1 mile, then becoming very rocky and rough. The ascent of the Nattik Pass then begins, very rocky and rough, steepest slope 18°, but the whole ascent is about the same. At the summit there is an open space called Kinlé Sakhán where there is room to pitch 20 to 30 tents (mountain service); there is also a zayát (20 men). Water obtainable close by a little higher up the hill near a ruined pagoda, and a small stream runs in the valley below. Formerly there was a village here, but it is now deserted. Soon after passing Kinlé Sakhán the road turns almost due south skirting the base of a very high hill called the Hngetgyitaung. It is round topped, very steep and in places precipitous, and is a very prominent object when looking towards the pass from Ingôn. The path now crosses a valley, down which a small mountain stream flows, bed rocky, water excellent, but supply limited, unless it be collected by a dam, which could easily be done. Shortly after this the entrance to the pass is reached, 3 miles from Nagu. The general direction of the pass is east by south, initial slope 24°, but slightly steeper than this a little higher up. Huge boulders lie scattered about at the bottom of the pass. It is very much enclosed throughout, but especially in its lower portion, the hill side on either hand being almost precipitous. The general breadth of the track is about 10 yards, but the passage of animals is limited to a small portion of this. It lies over rock all the way up to Ywangánkin,

FROM KYAUKSÉ TO PWÉHLA *viâ* NATTIK PASS—*continued.*

Authorities.		Number and Names of Stages, Rivers and Streams.	Distances.		Remarks.
Military.	Civil.		Intermediate.	Total.	
G.O.C. Rangoon District.	Superintendent, Southern Shan States.	**4. Thayetyé**—*cont.*			and is much worn by the passage of Shan bullock caravans. These animals go up very lightly laden and even then frequently require to have their loads taken off and carried up. In addition to the steepness of the slope, rocks 2 feet high or so are frequently met with, over which the animals have to scramble as best they can; many falls are naturally the consequence. Cooly transport is no doubt the most convenient for a party traversing this pass, but when animals have to be taken, their loads should be light and compact. A bulky though light load would greatly hinder the animal carrying it, owing to its knocking against the rocks which encroach upon the path in many places. At 3½ miles a little water may be obtained from a rivulet, probably a continuation of the Thayetyé spring higher up the pass. A couple of animals could drink at a time. Very little view can be obtained on either side, the sides of the hill near the path, that is to say, just above the valleys, being covered with thick jungle and high trees. At 4¼ miles there is good open space for a camp at a place called Taungdet Sakhán, and a little further on but at the top of a very steep bit of ascent, is Thayetyé. Here there are three zayáts (100 men) and a little water from a spring rising from under the roots of a mango tree, from which fact the name of the place (Mango-water) is derived. This may be taken as the top of the first half of the ascent, and the full march from Nagu to Nabángyi at the top of the pass (9¼ miles) and still more on to Ywangán (11½ miles) is so trying to animals that it should not, unless absolutely necessary, be attempted. It will be found much better and probably in the long run shorter to halt at Thayetyé. This has been proved practically in January 1888. Out of 125 mules and ponies carrying the baggage of a small column that marched up this pass, only 21 got up the first day, all mules. Of the remainder none got beyond Thayetyé, and some not so far, and it was 5 P.M., the second day before the last animal got into Ywangán. All were much fatigued and several went over the khud, though fortunately these got off with a few scratches and bruises only.
		5. Ywangán ...	M. F. 7 4	M. F. 43 0	Leaving Thayetyé the path turns north-east for a mile, crossing and in some places following the now dry bed of a mountain stream. No view what-ever on either side. It then reverts to its original direction (south-east) and soon after climbs the steepest portion of the pass by a zigzag up a slope of 28°. From here a path, said to be much used by dacoits, runs north into Yé-u territory some miles south of Sakhángyi. On surmounting this a very fine view back down the pass is obtained. A little further on is an open space called Ywangán-kin. Here a "*kin*" or guard is placed by the Ywangán State to keep the pass open and to collect toll from passing caravans. Here there is a very deep valley on the north of the road, which now runs up and down at fairly easy gradients round the lower spurs of hills on the right. The last ascent to the plateau, which is reached at 4½ miles, is steep. At 4¾ miles reach Nabángyi, a scattered village of about 50 houses. A kyaung (150 men) lies ½ a mile to the south of the village. Water-supply bad and scanty from small tank and well. Considerable number of cattle here, for which there is good grazing ground. Quantities of

FROM KYAUKSÉ TO PWÉHLA *viâ* NATTIK PASS—*continued.*

Authorities. Military.	Authorities. Civil.	Number and Names of Stages, Rivers and Streams.	Distances. Intermediate.	Distances. Total.	Remarks.
G.O.C. Rangoon District.	Superintendent, Southern Shan States.	**5. Ywangán**—*cont.*			mustard grown in the fields here. Here a route branches to Yátsauk, *see* Branch I below. From Nabángyi to Ywangán the track is excellent, sloping gradually down to that place. Between 6¾ and 7 miles pass two lakes, both on the left of the road. Water in these is excellent and comes from springs. At 7¼ miles pass the old fort of Ywangán on the right, beyond which is the village. Ywangán is the capital of the Shan State of the same name. It has about 200 houses, and a bazaar is held every fifth day. Trade here is good and increasing. Large caravans from the more eastern Shan States and from Yunnán (China) pass through. The people are engaged in manufacturing clothes, baskets, das, jaggery, &c. There are plenty of cattle which, however, their owners are very unwilling to sell, as they think it more profitable to use them as beasts of burden earning Rs. 30 a month. The average price when animals *are* sold is about Rs. 25 apiece. Although in many individual places on this plateau there may be plenty of cattle, there is no doubt that, speaking generally, they are scarce owing to the troublous times the country has lately passed through. There are three kyaungs with zayáts attached and no difficulty would be found in accommodating 500 or 600 men. All three kyaungs could easily be put into a state of defence. The water-supply is drawn entirely from a small lake or jheel about ½ a mile long by 100 yards broad, which lies to the north-west of the town. It is 6 or 7 feet deep in places. The water is excellent and comes entirely from springs, the supply is therefore constant all the year round. The jheel is crossed from east to west near its southern end by a strong wooden bridge consisting of 36 eight-feet spans; roadway 10 yards in the clear, fit for the passage of loaded carts. The soil of the district is a reddish clay, very fertile. Besides numerous fruits the people grow leeks, beams, mustard, tobacco, and several other kinds of vegetables. In January there are no crops on the ground, but the fields are being got ready for paddy, which is grown in the rains.
		6. Alégyaung (or Alé chaung).	M. F. **13 0**	M. F. 56 0	Road south-east (142°) over open country with a little scrub jungle fit for carts. A range of hills runs parallel to the road about a mile off on the right. At 1 mile descend into a valley, gradient 3° at first, but steeper and rougher as it nears the bottom. The valley is probably a continuation of the one running north and south-east of Ywangán. There is a shallow stream in the valley (dry in January) crossed by a bridge now in bad repair. Direction of road now 120°. It now ascends opposite side of valley and then reverts to its original direction. Country very open, with good view to the hills on either side. Here pass Sissingbin, about a mile off to the left. It has a kyaung and water is obtainable from springs. Soon afterwards a track branches off to the right to Letpánbin (¼ mile), where there is a good kyaung. Cross another valley with well-bridged stream at the bottom (no water in the stream in January) and ascend to village of Sôpôgôn (30 houses), lying a little off the road to the right. Here Bo Lán, formerly a dacoit leader, now one of the regents of Ywangán, has his head-quarters. There are two zayáts at this village, which would accommodate 40 men, but water is scarce all round here. At 4 miles pass village of Thôndaung, near

No. 2.

From KYAUKSÉ to PWÉHLA *viâ* NATTIK PASS—*continued.*

Authorities. Military.	Authorities. Civil.	Number and Names of Stages, Rivers and Streams.	Distances. Intermediate.	Distances. Total.	Remarks.
G.O.C. Rangoon District.	Superintendent, Southern Shan States.	**6. Alégyaung (or Alé chaung)**—*cont.*			which there is a spring. At 5 miles the range of hills on the right, here about 2 miles off, ceases abruptly. At 8 miles pass Nyaungôn, a large scattered village with a kyaung (100 men). The country which has hitherto, in this stage, been very open, now becomes the reverse. Road turning east descends a deep valley by steep path too narrow and rocky to allow of the passage of carts. In the bottom of the valley is a stream of excellent water, flowing south, which the road crosses by a strong bridge. Ascend the opposite side of the valley by ascent as steep as the descent into it. Over the watershed and down into another valley, but at a less steep gradient, a stream at the bottom. Both these valleys are thickly wooded, and a lot of bamboo jungle is passed soon after. Road now turns south-east again at an easy gradient and soon after bears still more to the south and runs parallel to the Yátsauk range of hills which lie about 2 miles to the east. This range looks steep from here and is thickly wooded. At about 10 miles reach the village of Myaing, kyaung and zayáts to accommodate 100 men; ⅛ mile north-west of village ½ mile to the north-east is the village of Inywa with small tank. A bazaar is held periodically at Myaing and cattle, paddy, &c., would be procurable. Myaing is the last village in Ywangán, and Léywa territory is entered about ⅛ mile further on. There are two roads from here to Alégyaung, both of which are good. Distance by the shortest 3 miles, a total of 13 miles, from Ywangán; that through Léywa is 2 miles longer than the other; it is a good road, but one or two rocky places render it unfit for carts. The steepest gradient met with is 10°, but most of the road is only 3° or 4° and presents no difficulties to laden animals. At (?) miles reach Léywa, about 50 houses, two zayáts (50 men); water from stream close by, which is crossed by strong wooden bridge. From here a road runs south direct to Pwéhla, distant about (?) miles. The road to Alégyaung runs east crossing a valley, with rocky and difficult ascent and descent, unfit for carts. At the bottom of this valley there is a rocky unbridged stream, dry in January, but probably a torrent in the rains. At 15 miles reach Alégyaung (50 houses) lying close under the hills. Accommodation in kyaung (floor in bad repair) and two zayáts for 80 men. The houses in the village are good and further accommodation could be obtained in them if required at 15 men per house comfortably. Small supply of paddy and vegetables obtainable here. No cattle. Water from stream ¼ mile to east of the village.
		7. Pindaya (about 3,600 feet).	M. 10 F. 0	M. 66 F. 0	Road runs slightly north of east along the north side of a valley running up into the hills with a stream flowing down it. The road is fair for about 1 mile, when the head of the valley is reached; it then ascends for 200 yards at a very steep gradient (20°), the remainder of the ascent is not so steep, and none of it is rocky. At (?) miles reach the top and drop down by steep descent into another valley in which there is a stream running to the right and joining the Alégyaung stream lower down. At the head of this valley is the small hamlet of Wábôgyi

FROM KYAUKSÉ TO PWÉHLA *viâ* NATTIK PASS—*continued.*

Authorities.		Number and Names of Stages, Rivers and Streams.	Distances.		Remarks.
Military.	Civil.		Inter-mediate.	Total.	
G.O.C. Rangoon District.	Superintendent, Southern Shan States.	**7. Pindaya (about 3,600 feet)**—*cont.*			(four houses). From this valley ascend again, gradient very steep, but otherwise no difficulty. Direction of road 10° south of east. The hill tops around are rocky and bare, the lower portions wooded and the valleys full of bamboo jungle. Road keeps ascending the northern spurs of a hill on the right. A deep valley on the left. At about 5 miles there is an open space about ¼ mile square. An excellent camping ground. (Just before reaching this place Pindaya territory is entered.) Kyaung and zayáts here sufficient to accommodate 100 men. Water from stream and tank in valley close by. Cross the valley and pass through village of Bingyi-é ((?) miles). Cross two streams well bridged. This valley is all cultivated, nothing but leeks in January, but of these there are fields and fields. Climb steep and difficult ascent winding along above a deep valley to the right. Turning south-east it then descends towards Pindaya. From here a magnificent view of the Yátsauk plateau is obtained. It appears bare, soil red, and crossed by numerous tracks. Three distinct ranges of hills are visible to the east; ¼ mile down the descent ((?) miles) pass the village of Paseinbin (eight houses) to the left, and ½ mile further on west Taungbôywa to the right (20 houses, zayát, and pagoda). A little further on is east Taungbôywa in a low valley to the left, bearing of road now 160° and Pindaya can be seen at the foot of the hills. A mile further on pass large kyaung and zayáts (150 men) belonging to village of Meshudôn, which lies ½ a mile or so to the south and appears a scattered place. Water not very good, obtainable from tank near kyaung. Half-a-mile further and about half-way down the hill pass a large tank about 60 yards by 30 yards and a zayát (30 men) with very good camping ground near.* At 10 miles close to the foot of the hill reach Pindaya, a large town extending for about a mile on the lower slopes of the hill just above the valley. It has four kyaungs affording accommodation for a considerable number of troops. Water-supply obtained from a lake about 1 mile long and ½ mile wide, formed artificially by a strong "bund" at its northern extremity, below which there is wet cultivation. Close to the north-east corner of the lake there is a group of kyaungs, which would alone accommodate 300 to 350 men easily. A large bazaar is held every fifth day. Vegetables, sugar, charcoal, silver (both ore and ornaments), silks and other articles produced locally or brought up from the plains through Pyinmana, Toungoo, &c. Grass rather scarce in January and has to be brought in from a distance. There are good ponies in this district, but the owners ask exorbitant prices. The Pindaya district is ruled by a Ngwégunhmu and appears prosperous. It is bounded on the east by the small district of Bawzaing also a Ngwégunhmuship. Its chief village is called Siser, and the district is believed to be very rich in minerals.
		8. Pwéhla ...	M. F. 6 4	M. F. 72 4	*See* Route No. 52, Shan Division.

* No streams or even rivulets were met with on the eastern slope of the hills throughout the route traversed. The villagers depend entirely for their water-supply on tanks formed by cup-shaped hollows in the hill side. These hollows are filled in the rains and contain plenty of water in January. The supply appears to last through the hot weather, and may possibly not entirely depend upon surface drainage.

From KYAUKSÉ to PWÉHLA *viâ* NATTIK PASS—*continued.*

BRANCH I.

From YWANGÁN (Stage 5) to YÁTSAUK.

By Lieut. T. A. TANCRED, Royal Artillery, Intelligence Department, Burma, April 1890.

Authorities.		Number and Names of Stages, Rivers and Streams.	Distances.		Remarks.
Military.	Civil.		Intermediate.	Total.	
			M. F.	M. F.	
G.O.C. Rangoon District.	Superintendent, Southern Shan States.	**1. Alégyaungywa.**	**18 4**	18 4	From Ywangán the direct route is *viâ* Kyauknet and Alégyaungywa (Shwépángwet). Kyauknet is reached at $6\frac{1}{2}$ miles. It is a large village, situated on a stream. After this the road bends northward and crosses the Darani (10 miles) by a bridge after a steep winding descent. Paths from all the villages on the plateau join in before reaching the Darani chaung. The bridge is a good wooden bridge. Then the track follows a nullah, very bad in parts, for $2\frac{3}{4}$ miles, and then up the spur of a hill which it follows for a long time, and then descends to Alégyaungywa (Shwépángwet), 12 miles further on. For 12 miles there is no water.
		2. Yátsauk ...	?	?	One day's march.

BRANCH II.

From NABÁNGYI (in Stage 5) to YÁTSAUK.

By Capt. H. R. DAVIES, April 1893.

Military.	Civil.	Stages.	Intermediate.	Total.	Remarks.
G.O.C. Rangoon District.	Superintendent, Southern Shan States.	**1. Kyauknyit (Kyauknet).**	**9 6**	9 6	General direction east. Good mule road. Level road over the Baw plateau for $6\frac{1}{4}$ miles; then cross small range of hills. At $4\frac{1}{2}$ miles Kátseyet, Danu (25). Camping ground here and water from a stagnant nullah, $\frac{1}{2}$ mile west. At Kyauknyit large camping grounds, good water, and fair grass.
		2. Shwébingwet (Shwépángwet). Kalani.	**15 2**	26 0	General direction east-north-east. Fair mule road; very steep in places. Along a spur to $3\frac{1}{2}$ miles; then downhill, very steep for $\frac{1}{4}$ mile, and cross the Kalani chaung (6 yards by 1 foot). Here a small camp (30 by 40 yards). Up a small dry nullah, very rocky and bad to $5\frac{3}{4}$ miles, where there are two or three stagnant pools of water in the nullah and room to camp. Thence very steep and rocky ascent to the top of the range, which is reached at $7\frac{1}{4}$ miles. Along the ridge, more or less up and down to $11\frac{1}{2}$ miles (6,700 feet above sea). Thence steep and difficult descent to $14\frac{3}{4}$ miles and $\frac{1}{2}$ mile of level ground to Shwébingwet. Plenty of room to camp; fair grass; water from two streams each 1 yard by 2 inches, and a pond at the kyaung for animals.

FROM KYAUKSÉ TO PWÉHLA *viâ* NATTIK PASS—*continued.*

BRANCH II—*continued.*

Authorities.		Number and Names of Stages, Rivers and Streams.	Distances.				Remarks.
Military.	Civil.		Intermediate.		Total.		
			M.	F.	M.	F.	
G.O.C. Rangoon District.	Superintendent, Southern Shan States.	**3. Yátsauk (Lawksawk).**	**12**	**0**	38	0	General direction east-north-east. Good level mule road over gently undulating country, through thin jungle for 5 miles, then very bare. Pass several Danu villages. At 7½ miles Magyigôn chaung, from the left (5 yards by 8 inches). Yátsauk contains 110 houses—Shan, Danu, and Burmese. Good camping ground under trees (250 by 100 yards) just outside the east gate to the left. Good water from Zawgyi chaung and small stream. Good grass. Zayáts in the town for 150 men.

No. 3.

From KYAUKSÉ to YAMÁN viâ YÉ.

BY G. B. SCOTT, ESQ., SURVEY OF INDIA, AUGUST 1890.

Military	Civil	Number and Names of Stages, Rivers and Streams	Intermediate M.	F.	Total M.	F.	Remarks
G.O.C. Myingyán District.	Commissioner, Eastern Division, and Deputy Commissioner, Kyauksé.	**1. Pyaukseitpyin.** Canals in Kyauksé itself, bridged; leaving bridge at 3 miles the Thingdwé canal; bridged.	**10**	**0**	10	0	A made road runs along the southern base of a low range of hills, which runs due east from Kyauksé pagoda for 3 miles; the range then breaks into hillocks and a canal has been cut through for irrigating the country to the east, not far from the villages of Ywanán and Kalékyaung, which lie 2 miles to the south of the road. It continues over undulating country with jungle on each side and passes the hill at the distance of about a mile to the south, the ground between being covered with heavy jungle. About 2 miles from the village of Pyaukseitpyin the road passes between dry fields. The village contains some 50 huts and a good zayát. Water can be procured from the Kyaungzaung chaung, about ½ mile from the village, between November and March, but for the rest of the year water is only procurable in the bed of the same watercourse, about a mile higher up, near village of Taunghla or Ywathit.
		2. Kyaungzaung.	**6**	**0**	16	0	On leaving the village the road continues due east between fields for nearly a mile, when on nearing a small hill it descends to and crosses the Kyaungzaung chaung. The banks, as a rule, are high and steep, but the ascent and descent are easy and constantly traversed by carts carrying bamboos, &c. After crossing the chaung, which is generally dry and has a stony bed, a gradual ascent is made through heavy jungle. Beyond the road is good and level to Taunghla. This is a village of about a dozen huts at present, but is increasing, as near it is a large supply of running water in the bed of the chaung to the south of and close to the village. Here the road enters the hills and is now only a rough cart track over broken, but not difficult, country between the hills. At 4½ miles from the start the small village of Yethayauk, 20 huts, is passed. Here there

FROM KYAUKSÉ TO YAMÁN *viâ* YÉ—*continued.*

Authorities. Military.	Authorities. Civil.	Number and Names of Stages, Rivers and Streams.	Distances. Intermediate.	Distances. Total.	Remarks.
G.O.C. Myingyán District.	Commissioner, Eastern Division, and Deputy Commissioner, Kyauksé.	**2. Kyaungzaung** —*cont.*			is a fine spring of water, an unfailing supply, under precipitous cliffs, which hem in the village on the left like a wall (from Taunghla, a path practicable for mules and ponies, winds up the hills to the crest of the Pyittaw plateau—*See* Alternative Route I:—Paths, only practicable for men, also go up between clefts in the clip to the same plateau from Yethayauk and Kyaungzaung). On the right the hills are a succession of easy spurs covered with "*sál*" forest rising to the crest of the Walu range. Kyaungzaung is a mile further up stream, consists of 35 huts in a few acres of cultivation. There is room for an encampment. Water must be procured from the spring near Yethayauk. Grass and wood are obtainable, but no supplies. Jungle fowls abound in the forests. Laden carts can go on up the valley past Kyaungzaung, a couple of miles.
		3. Yé	M. F. **8 0**	M. F. 24 0	A cart track for 2 miles; then comes 2 miles of an ascent practicable for laden mules and ponies to the crest of a pass about 1,200 feet in elevation above sea, or about 400 from the base to the top. From the crest a rather steep descent of a mile into the Yéchaung is made, then the route follows the dry bed of this water-course to Yé on the Myitngé. The village consists of 35 huts and a kyaung. A few acres are cultivated. There is good camping ground near. The river is crossed in dug-outs and rafts to Gwébin, a few huts on the Mandalay (right) bank, whence there is a route to Kywetnapa down the bank of the river and another up it to Kaingyi *vide* Route No. 35, Northern Division. The Myo-ôk of Yamán resides here with a small police guard.
		4. Yamán ...	**6 0**	30 0	A pathway along the bank of the Myitngé, at present only practicable for ponies, but could be easily widened into a cart road. There are no difficult ascents or descents. The hamlet of Kyaung, about 10 huts, is passed a mile this side of Yamán. Yamán consists of 20 huts in a few acres of cultivation. The hills round are covered with *sál* and the valleys with bamboos.

ALTERNATIVE I.

FROM KYAUKSÉ TO YÉ (STAGE 3).

BY G. B. SCOTT, ESQ., SURVEY OF INDIA, AUGUST 1890.

Military	Civil	Stages	Intermediate	Total	Remarks
G.O.C. Myingyán District.	Commissioner, Eastern Division, and Deputy Commissioner, Kyauksé.	**1. Yébo** ... Irrigation—some canals and at times irrigated fields.	6 0	6 0	A cart track runs directly to Yébo, which is in constant use during the dry months, though at times it is rendered difficult owing to the water for irrigation running over it. Yébo contains 60 or 60 huts surrounded by a strong fence. Heavy jungle is passed on the way and covers much of the country all round, but there is a fairly large piece of cultivation round the village. Theg reat difficulty here is the water-supply, which, for greater part of the year, is only obtainable from a large pucka well near the smaller village of the name.

FROM KYAUKSÉ TO YAMÁN *viâ* YÉ—*continued.*

ALTERNATIVE I—*continued.*

Authorities. Military.	Authorities. Civil.	Number and Names of Stages, Rivers and Streams.	Distances. Intermediate.	Distances. Total.	Remarks.
			M. F.	M. F.	
G.O.C. Myingyán District.	Commissioner, Eastern Division, and Deputy Commissioner, Kyauksé.	**2. Hngetgyitaik.**	**9 0**	15 0	There is a rough path, though carts can go along it for about 4 miles as far as the part known as Sôdaung. Here there are two or three fair supplies of water in the bed of the Yédaw water-course. From this point the path enters the hills and a sharp ascent is made a mile or so from the "camp." It continues among low hills with easy gradients till it falls to Hngetgyitaik, a deserted site on the Myitngé.
		3. Yé	**7 0**	22 0	From Hngetgyitaik it follows the river bank to Yé.

ALTERNATIVE II.

FROM PYAUKSEITPYIN (STAGE 1) TO YÉ (STAGE 3).

BY G. B. SCOTT, ESQ., SURVEY OF INDIA, AUGUST 1890.

Authorities. Military.	Authorities. Civil.	Number and Names of Stages, Rivers and Streams.	Distances. Intermediate.	Distances. Total.	Remarks.
G.O.C. Myingyán District.	Commissioner, Eastern Division, and Deputy Commissioner, Kyauksé.	**1. Pyettaw** ...	**10 0**	10 0	Continue from Pyaukseitpyin to Taunghla as before; thence a path, practicable only for mules and ponies, winds up the rather steep sides of the hill to the north for a mile, when it reaches the crest of a plateau. The plateau is about 30 square miles in area, is broken here and there by hillocks and ravines, but, as a rule, is practicable for carts all over. It is covered with bamboo forest and there are a few small springs of water, to which elephants resort in rather large numbers. The path to Pyettaw runs across the plateau, about 6 miles. The village is now deserted, but was a steady resort of dacoits till lately. There is a fairly large supply of water in the rocky bed of a small water-course under a low hill, about ¼ mile north-west of the village site, sufficient for a company or two.
		2. Yé	**8 0**	18 0	After leaving Pyettaw the rest of the plateau to the north, about a mile across, is traversed; then the route enters a succession of low hills and descends through them to Thayetpyin, a few huts, on the Myitngé (4 miles); thence it follows the river bank under steep hills to Yé.

BRANCH I.

FROM KYAUNGZAUNG (STAGE 2) TO MYOGYI (OR MAYAGYI).

BY G. B. SCOTT, ESQ., SURVEY OF INDIA, AUGUST 1890.

Authorities. Military.	Authorities. Civil.	Number and Names of Stages, Rivers and Streams.	Distances. Intermediate.	Distances. Total.	Remarks.
G.O.C. Myingyán District.	Commissioner, Eastern Division, and Dy. Commr., Kyauksé.	**1. Myogyi or Mayagyi.**	**10 0**	10 0	A pathway turns southward from Chaungzaung and Yethayauk and winds along the base and slopes of a small spur, easy of ascent to the crest of the Walu range, a distance of 2 miles; it then crosses the pass, elevation about 400 feet above the valley, and descends easily the further slope into the Ngámúwé chaung; continues at an easy gradient down the bed of the chaung to Séywa, a fair-sized village

FROM KYAUKSÉ TO YAMÁN *viâ* YÉ—*continued.*

BRANCH I—*continued.*

Authorities. Military.	Authorities. Civil.	Number and Names of Stages, Rivers and Streams.	Distances. Inter-mediate.	Distances. Total	Remarks.
G.O.C. Myingyán District.	Commr., Eastern Dn., &c., Kyauksé.	**1. Myogyi or Mayagyi**—*cont.*			on the banks of the Zawgyi river, which is forded by the path which continues between fields to Myogyi. The path is practicable for mules and ponies laden.

BRANCH II.

FROM YAMÁN (STAGE 4) TO YÁTSAUK.

BY G. B. SCOTT, ESQ., SURVEY OF INDIA, FROM NATIVE INFORMATION, AUGUST 1890.

Military.	Civil.	Stages.	Intermediate.	Total	Remarks.
G.O.C. Myingyán District.	Commissioner, Eastern Division, and Deputy Commissioner, Kyauksé.	**1. Uyama**	6 0	6 0	The first 4 miles along the bank on Myitngé easy and level to the deserted site of Yégyán, where a dry water-course joins the river. The next 2 miles ascend the water-course to a few huts known as Uyama; easy and rideable.
		2. Zeitkhé or Malika.	8 0	14 0	First continues up the bed of water-course, then ascends the slopes of hills by a winding pathway used by Shans with their bullocks. Zeitkhé consists of 15 huts on a small plateau near crest occupied by Dhanus (half Shan, half Burman) and has a good water-supply from a spring. Elevation about 5,000 feet above sea-level; 4,600 feet above Myitngé.
		3. Ôngyo	8 0	22 0	A Shan village of 40 huts at the farther end of a plateau on the crest of the same range as Zeitkhé. Water-supply good; people Shans; cultivation about 100 acres of maize, &c.
		4. Thándaung ...	10 0	32 0	Down the eastern slopes of the mountains by an easy descent; rideable and used by pack bullocks to the village on the banks of the Zawgyi in the State of Yátsauk.
		5. Yátsauk ...	10 0	42 0	A pathway for laden animals along the banks of the Zawgyi, but occasionally making detours across spurs where high banks and scarps close in on the river.

No. 4.

From KYAUKSÉ to YATZAUK viâ MYOGYI (or MAYAGYI).

BY LIEUT. T. A. TANCRED, ROYAL ARTILLERY, APRIL 1890.

Military.	Civil.	Stages.	Intermediate.	Total	Remarks.
G.O.C. Myingyán District.	Commr., Eastern Divn., and Dy. Commr., Kyauksé.	**1. Singaung** ...	17 0	17 0	Direction south to Imembu, then east to Singaung. The road follows the main cart road from Kyauksé to Yéwun and Myittha as far as Imembu, a distance of 9 miles; cart road

FROM KYAUKSÉ TO YÁTZAUK *viâ* MYOGYI (OR MAYAGYI)—*continued.*

Authorities. Military.	Authorities. Civil.	Number and Names of Stages, Rivers and Streams.	Distances. Intermediate.	Distances. Total.	Remarks.
G.O.C. Myingyán District.	Commissioner, Eastern Division, and Deputy Commissioner, Kyauksé.	**1. Singaung**—*cont.*			then branches off to the east over flat ground, once under cultivation, crossing several small irrigation channels, and reaches Singaung at 17 miles. Singaung is a village of 100 houses, several zayáts (150 men), and good water.
			M. F.	M. F.	
		2. Myogyi ... Canal from Zawgyi.	**10 4**	27 4	Direction east. The cart road to Myogyi branches off to the left ¼ mile before reaching Singaung, and at 1 mile the track widens out for ½ mile to from 50 yards to 100 yards broad. At 2 miles a canal is reached, 50 yards broad, very rapid and 3 feet deep, in the rains the depth is 5 feet. The track then passes through thick jungle. At 3 miles Thábiyébinsakhán, two zayáts (20 men). Well water. Good camping ground. There is a village on the top of the hill to the southward. For 3½ miles the road goes through a succession of clearings on both sides of road and reaches Kin at 6½ miles, situated in a narrow pass. The Zawgyi is here 150 yards wide, very rapid, but shallow, and is within 50 yards of Kin to the northward. The road becomes rather rocky and steep in places and reaches Myogyi at 10½ miles. There is another cart road in the valley, which can only be used in the dry weather, as it crosses the Zawgyi several times. The valley of the Zawgyi is very broad and fertile between Kin and Myogyi. Many small villages are passed between Singaung and Kin. Myogyi is a large village of 150 houses with pôngyi kyaungs and zayáts (200 men), and is the capital of the Northern Baw State ruled over by the Shwéda Bo.
		3. Myitzôn ... Zawgyi and Darani rivers.	**9 0**	36 4	A path runs up the Zawgyi valley, crossing several irrigation channels and crossing the Zawgyi three times, also passing through two or three small villages in the valley. At 4 miles a bad rocky path on the right bank and several awkward places. The path continues on right bank for 3 miles. The Zawgyi is crossed three times more and Myitzôn is reached at 9 miles. Myitzôn is a small village of 10 houses at the junction of the Zawgyi and Darani. The Zawgyi is very rapid and 3 feet 6 inches deep in the dry season. From Myitzôn a path goes up the Zawgyi valley, which becomes very narrow. The river is crossed several times (very deep and rapid). This path is a very bad one. From Myitzôn a path goes up the Darani and reaches Chaungtha at 5 miles; the Darani is crossed eight times quite shallow, but the path is very awkward in places. Chaungtha is a village of three houses on the left bank; a small zayát on right bank.
		4. Ywé-Ywa ...	**7 0**	43 4	The path continues up the Darani, crossing it six times. For 1¾ miles good track. Here the river bends to the southwards and a path, reported to be a very bad one, follows the river on to the Ywangán plateau. Another path goes up the spur of a hill, direction east, and the path is one continuous ascent for 7 miles, where a small deserted village is reached called

FROM KYAUKSÉ TO YÁTSAUK *viâ* MYOGYI (OR MAYAGYI)—*continued.*

Authorities. Military.	Authorities. Civil.	Number and Names of Stages, Rivers and Streams.	Distances. Intermediate.	Distances. Total.	Remarks.
G.O.C. Myingyán District.	Commr., Eastern Div., and Dy. Commr., Kyauksé.	**4. Ywé-Ywa**—*cont.*			Ywé-Ywa. Water very scarce. A party of 50 men without animals would exhaust it. The inhabitants report that there is no more for 12 miles. This path continues through Nan Lua to Yátsauk.
G.O.C. Rangoon District.	Supt., Southern Shan States.	**5 & 6. Yátsauk** ...	M. F. 20 0	M. F. 36 0	From Myogyi there is a route to Zéywa and Ywangán keeping up the Taungbo valley and skirting the east side of the range of hills (*see* Route No. 5). The inhabitants report it is not as good a route as that *viâ* Sakhángyi.

No. 5.

From KYAUKSÉ to YWANGÁN viâ MYOGYI.

BY LIEUT. T. A. TANCRED, ROYAL ARTILLERY, APRIL 1890.

Military	Civil	Stage	Intermediate M.	Intermediate F.	Total M.	Total F.	Remarks
G.O.C. Myingyán District.	Commissioner, Eastern Division, and Deputy Commissioner, Kyauksé.	**1. Singaung** ...	17	0	17	0	*See* Route No. 4.
		2. Myogyi ...	10	4	27	4	*See* Route No. 4.
		3. Sakhángyi ...	9	0	36	4	Direction south. A cart road runs up the Taungbo valley, passing the village of Taungmi. At 2½ miles the path branches up a dry broad nullah, which it follows for 2 miles, with thick jungle on each side. The path then goes up a spur of a hill, very steep and rocky, and then winds along the top of the hills for 3 miles, where there are some signs of cultivation. There is a bad rocky piece of ground here. The path then descends a rocky path and reaches Sakhángyi at 9 miles. Sakhángyi is a village of 30 houses; three zayáts (50 men). Water scarce (from spring). Pine-apple cultivation. This march would be a very bad one for transport ponies, as many falls would be likely to occur. No water obtainable for last 7 miles. A road from here goes to Nagu down the Tihlaing pass. The inhabitants say the distance is 12 miles, but the road is bad.
		4. Duktôywa ...	11	0	47	4	Direction south. After going ¾ mile path ascends and descends rocky place. At 1½ miles a little village with cultivation. The path then ascends up a steep hill for 1 mile. Direction so far south-west; then path turns south-east and still ascends; very bad in places. At 4 miles the Tihlaing pass is 3 miles off to the west. At 6 miles the path descends into a valley; no water; it then follows up this well-wooded valley and then bends to the eastward through grass land to Duktôywa at 11 miles. Duktôywa is a village of 30 houses, height 5,200 feet. Water very scarce, from hole in valley, 1 mile away. One zayát (10 men).

FROM KYAUKSÉ TO YWANGÁN *viâ* MYOGYI—*continued.*

Authorities. Military.	Authorities. Civil.	Number and Names of Stages, Rivers and Streams.	Distances. Intermediate.	Distances. Total.	Remarks.
G.O.C. Myingyán District.	Commissioner, Eastern Division, and Deputy Commissioner, Kyauksé.	**5. Zéywa** ... Kazet chaung.	M. F. 8 0	M. F. 55 4	Direction south-east. The road is comparatively good. At 1¼ miles road turns to the right southwards and descends gradually finishing up with a steep rocky descent at 5 miles. The path then crosses flat plain, height 4,600 feet, and, passing several small villages, reaches Zéywa at 8 miles. The villages past on the plain are Kyaukubyin (50 houses), water from stream 1 mile away; Kyaukinyaung (20 houses) near chaung; Tâtlwin (five houses). Zéywa is a village of 40 houses with a bazaar every fifth day. Two zayâts (30 men), water plentiful from Kazet chaung.
G.O.C. Rangoon District.	Superintendent, Southern Shan States.	**6. Ywangán** ...	4 0	59 4	The road passes over open undulating grass plains and reaches Ywangán at 4 miles. Ywangán is a big village of 200 houses. Water from pond with stream running through it. Zayât (50 men); large kyaungs (400 men). Bazaar every fifth day.

No. 6.

From MEIKTILA to FORT STEDMAN (MAINGSAUK).

BY CAPT. H. R. DAVIES, OXFORDSHIRE LIGHT INFANTRY, INTELLIGENCE DEPARTMENT, NOVEMBER 1892.

Military	Civil	Stages	Intermediate	Total	Remarks
G.O.C. Rangoon District.	Commissioner, Eastern Division, and Deputy Commissioner, Meiktila.	**1. Meiktila road.**	13 0	13 0	General direction south-east. Road bridged and metalled throughout and in excellent order. Good inspection bungalow at Meiktila road. Railway station. Good water-supply.
		2. Camp on road-side. All streams crossed by bridges in good repair.	15 4	28 4	General direction south-east. Good level cart road. At 8¾ miles pass Hlaingdet, bungalow and large camp-ing ground; room for 500 men in kyaungs and zayâts; a tank for watering animals, but very bad drinking water. At 15¼ miles a well 50 yards to the left of road, with camping ground (50 by 80 yards); more room could be got by clearing jungle. Water from well; the stream near it is dry now.
		3. Yébôksôn ...	10 2	38 6	General direction north-east. Good mule road. Up-hill by very easy slopes for 5¼ miles. At 3¾ miles pass Yemébin; bungalow and rest-house for 30 men; cleared camp-ing ground (30 by 70 yards); no village: water from stream, now in stagnant pools. At 5¼ miles begins to go down-hill gently; at Yébôksôn (10¼ miles) * rest-house for 30 men; small camp-ing ground. Water from Thelôn chaung (10 yards by 1 foot).

* In a subsequently received route by Havildar Juggut Singh, 19th P.I. (Military Surveyor), the distance from Hlaingdet to Yébôksôn is given as 14½ miles, as compared with the 17 of this route.—A. F.

FROM MEIKTILA TO FORT STEDMAN (MAINGSAUK)—*continued.*

Authorities.		Number and Names of Stages, Rivers and Streams.	Distances.				Remarks.
Military.	Civil.		Intermediate.		Total.		
			M.	F.	M.	F.	
G.O.C. Rangoon District.	Commissioner, Eastern Division, and Deputy Commissioner, Meiktila.	**4. Nampándet** ... Thelôn and Kwémasa chaungs.	**15**	**0**	53	6	General direction north-east to Pyinyaung, thence south-east; good cart road though only partly metalled. Down-hill to beyond Pyinyaung, thence up-hill; very easy slopes. At 4½ miles pass Pyinyaung; bungalow and rest-houses for 60 men; water from Thelôn chaung. At 9 miles * Kyát Sakhán, rest-house for 20 men; water from Kwémasa chaung. Here the road *viâ* Singu branches off, *see* Alternative I below. At Nampándet bungalow and rest-house for 20 men; water from Kwémasa chaung.
	Superintendent, Southern Shan States.	**5. Wetpuyé (Wetpuyet).** Stream.	**8**	**4**	62	2	General direction south-east. Cart road completely bridged, but only partly metalled and therefore very bad in wet weather owing to deep mud, making it difficult even for mules; steadily up-hill all the way; mules started at 7, arrived at 12; at Wetpuyé (Wetpuyet) bungalow and rest-house for 40 men; not much room to camp; good water-supply from stream.
		6. Kalaw ...	**10**	**4**	72	6	General direction south-east. Cart road as in last stage, bad and muddy for 5 miles, thence good; steadily up-hill all the way; at Kalaw, bungalow and large camping ground; good water; five-day bazaar.
		7. Thamakán (Hsámöngkán). ...	**11**	**4**	84	2	General direction north-east. Good cart road over open undulating country, passing several villages; road passes to the south of the village; the bungalow is on the road and there is a good camping ground here with water from stream, but firewood very scarce. *Note.*—From here there is a route to Yaméthin said to be eight marches distant south-west. It has not yet been fully reported on.
		8. Hého ... ... Stream.	**12**	**4**	96	6	General direction east. Good cart road over easy country, crossing the B[illegible]wnin plain. At Hého a bungalow and good camping ground and water; five-day bazaar.
		9. Bawyétát ... Balu chaung.	**7**	**4**	104	2	General direction east to Bawyétát, thence south. Good cart road down-hill for 5 miles, thence perfectly level. At 7½ miles Bawyétát; bungalow and room to camp; water from Balu chaung very thick and bad. From here a road goes on to the east to Taungyi and Mòné, *see* Route No. 7, Stages 9 and 10.

* Havildar Juggut Singh makes it only 7½ miles.

FROM MEIKTILA TO FORT STEDMAN (MAINGSAUK)—*continued.*

Authorities. Military.	Authorities. Civil.	Number and Names of Stages, Rivers and Streams.	Distances. Intermediate. M.	F.	Distances. Total. M.	F.	Remarks.
G.O.C. Rangoon District.	Superintendent, Southern Shan States.	**10. Fort Stedman (Maingsauk).**	**11**	**0**	115	2	The route to Fort Stedman goes south through Nyaungywé at 4 miles; large camping grounds at Fort Stedman and plenty of grass and water. Large bungalow. Five-day bazaar. Head-quarters of Superintendent, Shan States; post and telegraph offices and civil treasury. There is a more direct road from Hého to Fort Stedman through Nyaungywé without going to Bawyétát; carts cannot go by it, as the only cart bridge across the Balu chaung is at Bawyétát. *Note.*—The road is metalled only properly as far as Hlaingdet. Grass or bamboo leaves are obtainable everywhere in November. Small quantities of rice and paddy can be got. Vegetables are difficult to get except on bazaar days. There are many short cuts practicable for mules, but they are not kept in repair, and are sometimes difficult and muddy. Firewood plentiful everywhere except at Thamakán.

ALTERNATIVE I.

FROM YÉBÔKSÔN (STAGE 3) TO HÉHO (STAGE 8).

BY LIEUT. E. W. M. NORIE, MIDDLESEX REGIMENT, INTELLIGENCE DEPARTMENT, 1888.

Military	Civil	Stage	Inter. M.	F.	Total M.	F.	Remarks
G.O.C. Rangoon District.	Superintendent, Southern Shan States.	**1. Singu** ... One large chaung.	*16	4	16	4	Same as above described as far as Kyat Sakhán (9 miles); thence general direction of road north-east. Path a good mule track, follows the course of the Gwékauk chaung for 2 miles. Bed of stream 20 to 30 yards broad. Steep hills covered with bamboo jungle on both sides. At 2½ miles reach a camping ground where bamboo forage and water are plentiful, the road up to this point being nearly level. Road now ascends for about 1 mile to north and 1½ miles to east, passing under a precipitous red sand-stone cliff of the Pyindet hill. There is a spring of good water and a large patch of fine green grass about one-third of the way up. From the pass the path is steep running south-east down to the Tôklek chaung, which is bridged. Cross the bridge and Singu, which consists of 45 houses, is 300 yards beyond. At Singu there is a bamboo stockaded police post north of village. Accommodation in post for 20 ponies and 100 men besides garrison. Encamping ground ¼ mile beyond the village, where there is one zayát and a patch of green grass 100 yards square. No water here. Water obtainable from chaung to west of village, where it is good and plentiful. Supplies obtainable.
		2. Nankôn ...	*9	4	26	0	Road crosses three low ranges and comes on to a plateau 7½ miles from Singu. Then across slightly undulating downs, partly cultivated. No water along the road. Nankôn is a large village of 45 houses in two parts, one-half being on a high spur immediately above the other. There is a ruined kyaung and accommodation in two zayáts for 35 men. All the

* Havildar Juggut Singh makes this distance only 13 miles, and hence to Nankôn only 8¼. Total 21¼ as compared with 26 of this route. From Nankôn to Pwe la he makes 7 miles instead of 5¼.—A.F.

FROM MEIKTILA TO FORT STEDMAN (MAINGSAUK)—*continued.*

ALTERNATIVE I—*continued.*

Authorities. Military.	Authorities. Civil.	Number and Names of Stages, Rivers and Streams.	Distances. Inter-mediate.	Distances. Total.	Remarks.
G.O.C. Rangoon District.	Superintendent, Southern Shan States.	**2. Nankôn**—*cont.*			ground round about suitable for camping on. Water good and sufficient from a stream close to kyaung, and excellent drinking water from wells. Supplies and pack bullocks are procurable.
			M. F.	M. F.	
		3. Pwéhla ... One nullah.	5 4	31 4	Road east through slightly undulating open grass country, with patches of cultivation in parts, follows the telegraph line. No water along the road. Pwéhla is a large village with a stockaded post for 50 rifles. There are four officers' quarters and accommodation in post for 25 men. Telegraph office and post office are about to be opened. There is accommodation on a hill about a ¼ of a mile to north-east in kyaungs and zayáts for 150 men. Ground round is all suitable for encamping on. Water for drinking from a spring about 800 yards to east of post, also from well in fort which is not so good as the spring. Water for animals from a tank below the above spring. There is a large bazaar every fifth day. Supplies and grass fodder plentiful. Firewood scarce. Several hundred pack bullocks procurable from headman of village at short notice.
		4. Hého	14 0	45 4	Road runs south-east, good, passing one village at 6½ miles. Water also obtainable from a tank on left of road at 8 miles. For particulars of Hého *see* Stage 8 above.

BRANCH I.

FROM HÉHO (STAGE 8) TO YÁTSAUK (LAWK SAWK).

BY CAPT. H. R. DAVIES, OXFORDSHIRE LIGHT INFANTRY, INTELLIGENCE DEPARTMENT, BURMA, NOVEMBER AND DECEMBER 1892.

Military	Civil	Stages	Inter-mediate	Total	Remarks
G.O.C. Rangoon District.	Superintendent, Southern Shan States.	**1. Kyauktát** ... Several small streams crossed by easy bridges or fords. Most of them dry at this time of year.	12 0	12 0	General direction north-north-west. Good mule road over bare undulating country, with no hills to speak of. At 1 mile a cart road goes to the left to Pwéhla, meeting the present route again at Maining. The road follows the foot of the hills which border the Bawnin plain on the east for 5 miles, where it goes through a gap in low hills at Taungpát, thence between low hills, with a slight ascent at the end to Kyauktát, a Danu village of 100 houses. One small zayát and room for 150 men in bazaar sheds. Water from wells. A pond for mules.
		2. Taungya ... Small streams crossed by easy bridges or fords. Most of them dry.	11 0	23 0	General direction north. Good mule road. Over bare undulating country. No steep up or down hill. Large camping ground. Water from wells. A kyaung. Two zayáts just above the village. There is a five-day bazaar here. The village is inhabited by Danus, Taungyos, and Taungthus.

FROM MEIKTILA TO FORT STEDMAN (MAINGSAUK)—*continued.*

BRANCH I—*continued.*

Authorities. Military.	Authorities. Civil.	Number and Names of Stages, Rivers and Streams.	Distances. Intermediate. M.	F.	Total. M.	F.	Remarks.
G.O.C. Rangoon District.	Superintendent, Southern Shan States.	**3. Sankhawnhto camp.** At 5½ miles two muddy streams from the right. Difficult for mules in wet weather. At 6¾ miles Zawgyi chaung. From the left (15 yards by 3 or 4 feet) good wooden mule bridge. Other streams by easy bridges or fords.	**14**	**4**	37	4	General direction north. Good mule road. Through bare undulating country for 6 miles. Thence through tree jungle. Cross the Zawgyi chaung at 6¾ miles, and thence follow its course more or less closely all the way to Yátsauk. At 11½ miles there is a camp (150 by 50 yards) on the Paw-i chaung, and more room could easily be found for pitching tents, but the stream is said to dry up in the hot season. At Sankhawnhto a small zayát on the left of the road, and camping ground (¼ mile square). Water from the Zawgyi chaung. From Maining at 7 miles the road is passable for carts.
		4. Yátsauk ...	**10**	**4**	48	0	General direction north-east. Good mule road, passable for carts. Through tree jungle as far as Letpeit (Lepaik). Thence over bare, undulating country. From Letpeit there are two roads, the cart road and the bullock road, the latter to the west of the former. The cart road is said to be very muddy. The bullock road, though slightly longer, is the best. It passes through Magyigôn. Yátsauk contains about 110 houses, Burmans, Shan and Danu. Room for 150 men in zayáts, 200 in bazaar sheds, and 60 more in kyaung. Large camping grounds. Water from Zawgyi chaung and another stream at the east edge of the town.

BRANCH II.

FROM PWÉHLA (ALTERNATIVE I, STAGE 3) TO NATIT (ROUTE NO. 76, SHAN DIVISION, STAGE 3).

BY HAVILDAR JUGGUT SINGH, 19TH PUNJAUB INFANTRY, MILITARY SURVEYOR, APRIL 1893.

Military	Civil	Stages	Inter. M.	F.	Total M.	F.	Remarks
G.O.C. Rangoon District.	Superintendent, Southern Shan States.	**1. Kyaungkôn** ... Small streams, most of them dry.	**13**	**4**	13	4	General direction east. Level cart road as far as Kyauktát at 6 miles, a town of 100 houses. Water not very good. Thence gentle descent for a mile; then level till 10½ miles where there is a slight descent for a mile: thence level. Beyond Kyauktát it is a good mule road, but not passable for carts. At Kyaungkôn good camp, water, and grass. The village contains six houses.
		2. Páng Nam Kat. Namkát and small dry nullahs.	**8**	**4**	22	0	General direction north-east. Good mule road, nearly level the whole way. At the camp there is no village, grass scarce; bamboo leaves can be got. Fair water from the Nam Kát; only 20 yards broad and 3 inches deep in April; steep banks 12 feet high, bridge broken, ford a little way off on the right of the road.

FROM MEIKTILA TO FORT STEDMAN (MAINGSAUK)—*continued.*

BRANCH II—*continued.*

Authorities. Military.	Authorities. Civil.	Number and Names of Stages, Rivers and Streams.	Distances. Intermediate. M.	Distances. Intermediate. F.	Distances. Total. M.	Distances. Total. F.	Remarks.
G.O.C. Rangoon District.	Superintendent, Southern Shan States.	**3. Serai** ... ... Nam Kát, Nam Lit and Thiyé chaung.	9	4	31	4	General direction east-north-east. Good mule road; level for 7 miles; afterwards up and down over slight undulations to Serai, 50 houses, Taungthu. Good camp, grass scarce; water from a tank ½ mile off. At 5¾ miles Nam Lit, from the left (20 yards by 3 inches); mule bridge. At 6 miles and at 8½ miles, Thiyé chaung (15 yards by 3 inches); easy fords.
		4. Laisak or Lethet.	9	4	41	0	General direction north-east. Cart road level all the way. At 5½ miles Nam Pángku, from the right (5 yards by 1½ feet). At Laisak good camping ground round the kyaung. Water from Nam Et, ¼ mile off; fair grass.
		5. Na Nyu ... Nam Et.	5	6	46	6	General direction north-east. Good mule road, nearly level all the way. At ½ mile Nam Et, from the right (15 yards by 1½ feet). At Na Nyu, seven houses, good camping ground, water and grass.
		6. Natit ... ... Several small streams.	10	6	57	4	General direction north-east. Good mule road, nearly level all the way, crossing one small hill near Na Nyu. At 2½ miles is Páng Hong Htum. Room to camp and good water, but grass scarce. At Natit large camping ground, good water, and fair grass. Village contains 50 houses; five-day bazaar on the Nam Pawn. Natit is on the direct road from Yátsauk to Légya and Ta Kaw, *see* Route No. 76, Shan Division.

No. 7.

From MEIKTILA to MÔNÉ.

BY LIEUT. H. E. STANTON, ROYAL ARTILLERY, 1887–88, LIEUT.-COL. CLARK, OXFORDSHIRE LIGHT INFANTRY, APRIL 1890, CAPT. H. R. DAVIES, OXFORDSHIRE LIGHT INFANTRY, NOVEMBER 1892, AND OTHERS.

Military	Civil	Stage	Int. M.	Int. F.	Total M.	Total F.	Remarks
G.O.C. Rangoon District.	Commissioner, Eastern Division, and Dy. Commr., Meiktila.	**1. Meiktila road.**	13	0	13	0	*See* Route No. 6.
		2. Camp	15	4	28	4	
		3. Yébôksôn ...	10	2	38	6	
		4. Nampándet ...	15	0	53	6	

FROM MEIKTILA TO MÔNÉ—*continued.*

Authorities.		Number and Names of Stages, Rivers and Streams.	Distances.				Remarks.
Military.	Civil.		Intermediate.		Total.		
			M.	F.	M.	F.	
G.O.C. Rangoon District.	Superintendent, Southern Shan States.	**5. Wetpuyé (Wetpuyet).**	8	4	62	2	*See* Route No. 6.
		6. Kalaw ...	10	4	72	6	
		7. Thamakán ...	11	4	84	2	
		8. Hého ...	12	4	96	6	
		9. Bawyétát ...	8	0	104	6	Road good. At Bawyétát, there is accommodation in a good barrack for 80 men. Formerly a bazaar here, but huts now in ruins.
		10. Taungyi ... Three bridged streams; all flow north and then west into Nyaungywe valley.	10	0	114	6	General direction east-north-east. Pack track. One-and-a-half miles due east across the Nyaungywe valley. Most of the way along a bund overgrown with jungle and pampas, road swampy and much cut up by cattle passing over it, then turn north 1½ miles along another bund along the east edge of the valley. From this point the road is good all the rest of the way to Taungyi. For 5 miles the track is over undulating country covered with scrub jungle for 5 miles to a sakhán and sayát at the foot of a steep pass. Cross one well-bridged stream 2 miles from zayát. Bullocks from Nyaungywe usually halt here. Forage plentiful. The pass is 1½ miles very rough, stony, and steep; it zigzags up the face of a hill clad with bamboo and tree jungle. The track ascends gently through open hills for another ½ mile, and then leads down two short steep descents to an open valley at the foot of limestone crag called Taungyi. Crosses one bridged perennial stream in west of valley and one unbridged stream which is dry from February to May. Grass good and plentiful. Water good and plentiful from east brook except when dry and then from west brook. Small village. Good camping ground round a kyaung. Police barracks. Very cool and site expected to be extremely healthy.
		11. Hôpôn ... Six bridged brooks, all flowing south in Hôpôn valley.	9	4	124	2	General direction east. Pack track. For 2 miles gradually descending. It leads through a gorge between rounded hills covered with pampas and scrub jungle. It continues gradually descending into the Hôpôn valley for 2½ miles down an open slope crossing three or four small streams of water all bridged. The last 2½ miles lead across the open pampas grown valley, passing through a gorge in a row of limestone rocks which crop up from the soil of the valley; the track is over loam soil and good throughout. Hôpôn is a large village with rest-house, and plenty of accommodation in kyaungs and zayáts. Forage plentiful. Water from Tabet chaung, plentiful. Accommodation for 60 men in zayáts. Camping ground 1 mile west of village swampy and uneven, unsuited for troops. But there is good open camping ground near bazaar. Residence of Myo-ôk. Big five-day bazaar. From here there is a short cut to Fort Stedman, *vide* Branch No. I below.

FROM MEIKTILA TO MÔNÉ—*continued.*

Authorities. Military.	Authorities. Civil.	Number and Names of Stages, Rivers and Streams.	Distances. Inter-mediate. M.	F.	Distances. Total. M.	F.	Remarks.
G.O.C. Rangoon District.	Superintendent, Southern Shan States.	**12. Sáôn** ... ... One fordable brook; three or four streams flowing south in Hôpôn valley; two bridged brooks flowing north in hills to east.	12	0	136	2	General direction east. Pack track. First 2 miles across a swampy plain by a bund, crossing several streams all bridged. Thence over undulating ground for 4 miles when it passes through a defile. Thence runs level for a couple of miles and then crossing a stream rises gradually from the Hôpôn valley. About the 9th mile there is a short descent. The road then crosses a narrow cultivated valley with a stream flowing down the centre. Cross small ridge and then cross steep hill 600 feet in height into Sáôn. This last bit of road is very bad and impassable for transport in wet weather. Sáôn is situated on the west side of a narrow valley. A good-sized village. Accommodation in kyaung for 60 men. Small five-day bazaar. Also a rest-house. Good water from stream. Forage scarce in April. Good shady camping ground and a number of caves which can be used for shelter.
		13. Möngpwán (Maingpun). Nampwán or Pôn chaung, fordable.	12	0	148	2	Cross a stream running north, indifferently bridged, immediately on leaving Sáôn. Ascend and descend two high ranges. A stream between the two ranges bridged. Road continues up and down, but not over high hills. One mile short of the stage cross the Nampwán or Pôn chaung, 40 yards wide, fordable except after heavy rain; depth 2 to 3½ feet; thence follow down stream to Möngpwán. A large village with carriage. Supplies and accommodation for 200 men in zayáts and rest-houses. Big five-day bazaar. The first 7 miles the road is rough, last 5 very good. Forage scarce in April and May. Good camping ground.
		14. Man-pyen (Bampein). Three streams bridged.	11	0	159	2	Cross three streams shortly after leaving Maingpun. At 1 mile begin to ascend 4 miles of steep ascent. A small village with water from stream at the top (5,200 feet). Then 4 miles descent, clay soil, the first two extremely steep and impassable for bullocks if the ground be very wet. Then 1½ miles level, crossing bridged river just before arriving. A large village with carriage and supplies, but no accommodation. Big five-day bazaar. Water and forage plentiful. Good camping ground.
		15. Hépék (Hépét). Nampwán and Namlet bridged; seven small streams bridged.	18	0	177	2	Cross the Nampwán river by good bridge immediately on leaving Bampein, then over open level country to small village of Namein (4 miles) and here is the southern boundary between Môné and Maingseik territory. At 6 miles cross the Syethôn chaung, a little water in pools in April. At 9 miles Nasaweit is passed, here there is a large tank, but water bad. A mile further good, water close to the road from a well, marked by a pagoda. Up to this point the road is through swampy country. Lawat at 13½ miles, a moderate-sized village. This would make an easier stage. Road from here onwards nearly all good, over loam soil all the way. The country is undulating downs bare of trees. One or two slightly broken bits on the

FROM MEIKTILA TO MÔNÉ—*continued.*

Authorities. Military.	Authorities. Civil.	Number and Names of Stages, Rivers and Streams.	Distances. Inter-mediate.		Distances. Total.		Remarks.
			M.	F.	M.	F.	
G.O.C. Rangoon District.	Superintendent, Southern Shan States.	**15. Hépék (Hé-pét)**—*cont.*					fringe of the hills, along which the road passes between the 7th and 16th miles. Good camping ground at Hépék near the bazaar, plenty of room but no shade. Accommodation for 100 men in large bamboo house in the village. Forage plentiful, but water scarce in April. Big five-day bazaar. From Hépék a pack track runs east and joins the route from Möngnai (Mônê) to Ta Kaw. *Note.*—This route is difficult in parts during the rainy season, particularly in Stages 4, 6 and 7; but in the dry season is only bad on the clayey descent to Bampein. The actual village of Bampein is 1 mile north of the road. All the villages here have been lately burned, but are now springing up again. Water and forage good and plentiful at all stages.
		16. Mônê (Möng-nai). Namtwán (or Mônê) chaung and several smaller streams.	**17**	**0**	194	2	General direction south. First 8 miles road generally along a causeway through paddy cultivation. Then cross the Namtwán, narrow and shallow, and shortly beyond reach village of Máhlin. Following left bank of Namtwán, at about 9 miles, Linlôn, small village of 20 houses, one zayát. At 12 miles cross Namtwán by ford (18 yards wide, 2 feet deep, stony bottom); remains of broken bridge exist. Half-a-mile further pass the police post. At 17 miles Mônê. Large town. Residence of Sawbwa. The road is generally very good, traversing undulating downs covered with thin bushes and large banian trees; numerous small water-courses mostly dry in April. Many of them bridged.

BRANCH I.

FROM HÔPÔN (STAGE 11) TO FORT STEDMAN.

BY MAJOR J. G. COLLINS, "THE QUEEN'S," 1ST MAY 1887.

Authorities. Military.	Authorities. Civil.	Number and Names of Stages, Rivers and Streams.	Distances. Inter-mediate.		Distances. Total.		Remarks.
G.O.C. Rangoon District.	Superintendent, Southern Shan States.	**1. Tawpaya** ... Tabet.	**14**	**0**	14	0	The road has been used as a cart road for first 6 miles, good throughout; 2 miles from Hopôn crosses some old cultivation, which would be difficult in the rains; 2½ miles crosses Tabet stream (bridge, wood, in bad repair); river 30 feet wide, bank steep, fordable, but very difficult in rains. Timber procurable from pôngyi kyaung on Tawpaya side for repairs. Country open. Gradual ascent to Tawpaya. There is no village here, but several close round, could accommodate about 25 men in each.
		2. Fort Stedman (Maingsauk).	**11**	**0**	25	0	First 4½ miles easy, gradual ascent. Country open at first, afterwards road commanded in several places. Ascent to pass steep and difficult for mules for ½ mile. Descent difficult for first 200 yards over rocks and stones. Gradual descent to

FROM MEIKTILA TO MÔNÉ—*continued.*

BRANCH I—*continued.*

Authorities. Military.	Authorities. Civil.	Number and Names of Stages, Rivers and Streams.	Distances. Intermediate.	Distances. Total.	Remarks.
G.O.C. Rangoon District.	Supt., Southern Shan States.	**2. Fort Stedman (Maingsauk)**—*cont.*			Maingsauk except at 5¼ miles. Several small collections of houses, accommodate 10 men each. At 6½ miles a kyaung, which would accommodate 70 men; plenty of water on road. At 11 miles Fort Stedman or Maingsauk.

No. 8.

From MEIKTILA to PYINMANA viâ HLAWBÔN, TAUNGNYO, &c.

BY LIEUT. E. W. M. NORIE, 2ND MIDDLESEX REGIMENT, MARCH 1888.

Military	Civil	Stage	Intermediate	Total	Remarks
G.O.C. Rangoon District.	Commissioner, Eastern Division, and Deputy Commissioner, Meiktila.	**1. Subégyin** ... Two small nullahs.	M. F. **16 0**	M. F. 16 0	Leave Meiktila by west, cross the bridge and keep down west side of the south lake till Mézlébin is reached at 3 miles. It is a fair-sized village with some kyaungs on east side and good water from wells east of kyaungs. Road (a good cart track) leads from here over paddy land to the small village of Pyaukseitgôn, where there is a good well to north of village. The wet weather road runs more to the west and skirts the paddy. A dry chaung is crossed just after leaving Mézlébin. Beyond the paddy the road runs over high ground covered with scrub jungle and is good and hard. Three miles on reach the village of Thibigôn, small village. Accommodation in kyaungs for 30 men on south-east of village. Good water from a well about 350 yards to south-east. There is a well of fairly good water on the path, about ½ mile before reaching the village. From here the road dips to a strip of paddy, which is always passable, and about a mile on passes the village of Noyaungôn and from there runs across a broad belt of paddy land to Thidakán. This paddy would be very heavy in wet weather. Thidakán is a fair-sized village. Kyaungs for 50 men on west of village. Good water from wells on north-west. The road runs through the same sort of country, namely, sandy, jungle covered ridges with strips of paddy in the hollows to Aléywa, 10¼ miles from Meiktila. Kyaungs for 300 men on south of village. Good water from a large well outside village close to kyaungs. Plenty of good shade from large trees. North part of the village, which is a large one, has just been burnt by dacoits. All supplies and a number of carts available. From here the road runs through the same sort of country for about 2 miles to Thapánbinywa, a fair-sized village with a large tank on east side. Kyaungs for 50 men on east, and water from three wells on different sides of village. Leaving this the road crosses a strip of paddy and enters open forest jungle, running along a high and dry ridge to Subégyin, a small village, on high ground. Kyaungs for 30 men ¼ mile to west of village on bank of chaung. Good water from well in kyaung enclosure. No supplies, but "*kerbi*" procurable for fodder. About 2 miles to west is the Didôt hill with a pagoda on the top and a brick stair-case all the way up the hill. A road runs from Subégyin south-west to Kyégôn across the same description of country. Kyégôn is on the route from Shánmangé to Kyundôn.

FROM MEIKTILA TO PYINMANA *viâ* HLAWBÔN, TAUNGNYO, &c.—*continued.*

Authorities.		Number and Names of Stages, Rivers and Streams.	Distances.				Remarks.
Military.	Civil.		Intermediate.		Total.		
			M.	F.	M.	F.	
G.O.C. Rangoon District.	Commissioner, Eastern Division, and Deputy Commissioner, Yaméthin.	**2. Kyundôn (Séywa).** Several nullahs.	**18**	**0**	34	0	Road now runs across the chaungs through the same forest jungle to the top of the ridge. From here it descends to the Chaungyauk along the bed of which it runs for a short distance to the village of Nyaungbintha. Kyaungs for 50 men on north-east of village where there is a good well. Water also from surface wells in chaung. Road now crosses the chaung and runs over the same sort of country to Telébin, crossing a nullah about half-way. Telébin is a large double-hedged village. Good water from well on south and kyaungs to accommodate 30 men to east. From here the road same as before. Crosses two or three small nullahs and reaches Nátsônwa about 8 miles from Subyégyin. Here the track crosses the nullah and ascends the opposite bank, which is steep and passes through the same description of country to Ngakhaintát, a small village. Good water from wells on north. About 2½ miles beyond this reach Hlainpán, a small village. Water from a chaung on east. Three miles further pass the large village of Noyaungôn and 3 miles beyond reach Kyundôn (*see* Route No. 14, Southern Division, Stage 7). All the above road is really a very good track for baggage animals. There is also a very good road, which more or less follows the track and is good going for carts, but it winds about a great deal in order to avoid rough pieces of ground, paddy, steep gradients, &c., and so is much larger. If used by carts, a better distribution of stages would be— MILES. 1. Aléywa ... ... 10½ 2. Nátsônwa ... ... 13½ 3. Kyundôn 10
		3. Hlawzin ... Thitsôn chaung and several small nullahs.	**14**	**4**	48	4	For road from Kyundôn as far as Gaigyi (3½ miles), *vide* Route No. 14, Southern Division, Stage 8. From Gaigyi it branches off to the south-east and passes through the same country as before, namely, forest jungle, and reaches the village of Kyaukpaya on the further side off a chaung at 6 miles from Kyundôn. Two miles beyond it reaches the Thitsôn chaung which is easily crossed and passes several small villages to Hlawzin, which is a small post for 50 men. Village rapidly increasing in size. Supplies procurable: *kerbi*, paddy, fowls, &c., also a few carts. Water from wells is very scarce in dry weather. There is another more direct road which runs pretty straight from Kyundôn to Hlawzin, but it is very rough and said to be bad going.
		4. Hlawbôn ... Maungya chaung twice and smaller nullahs.	**17**	**0**	65	4	Road same as before over hilly ground covered with forest jungle. On the whole, a good, dry cart track. Passes no villages for the first 13 miles when it reaches the Maungya chaung, along the bed of which it runs to the deserted village of Satôgyi. Road runs on and a mile beyond again crosses the chaung and passes through the deserted village of Ywagyo to Gwébin on the Hlawbôn chaung and thence to Hlawbôn, *vide* Route No. 20, Stage 2.

No. 8.

FROM MEIKTILA TO PYINMANA *viâ* HLAWBÔN, TAUNGNYO, &c.—*continued.*

Authorities. Military.	Authorities. Civil.	Number and Names of Stages, Rivers and Streams.	Distances. Intermediate. M.	Distances. Intermediate. F.	Distances. Total. M.	Distances. Total. F.	Remarks.
G.O.C. Rangoon District.	Commissioner, Eastern Division, and Deputy Commissioner, Pyinmana.	**5. Bôtaung** ... Hlawbôn chaung twice and Sinthé chaung.	9	0	74	4	Cross the Hlawbôn chaung and pass the village of Thayetpin. At 3 miles cross the chaung again and at 4½ miles pass village of Kéyin on the Sinthé chaung. Crossing this chaung pass villages of Tapaungyaung, Nesigôn, and Toyin; all recently deserted and in good order, and can accommodate a large body of troops. Water plentiful along the road. For Bôtaung, *see* Route No. 17, Stage 2.
		6. Taungnyo ...	17	0	91	4	*See* Route No. 17.
		7. Mengôn ...	7	4	99	0	*See* Route No. 15, Alternative I.
		8. Chaungmagyi...	6	0	105	0	
		9. Pyinmana ...	10	0	115	0	

No. 9.

From PYINMANA to ETHNATAUNG.

I. B. COMPILATION, 1888.

Authorities. Military.	Authorities. Civil.	Number and Names of Stages, Rivers and Streams.	Intermediate. M.	Intermediate. F.	Total. M.	Total. F.	Remarks.
G.O.C. Rangoon District.	Commissioner, Eastern Division, and Deputy Commissioner, Pyinmana.	**1. Zibyubin** ...	9	0	9	0	*See* Route No. 13, Stages 1 and 2.
		2. Seikpudaung ...	11	0	20	0	
		3. Camp (in jungle).	11	0	31	0	Road good in dry weather, but probably first 6 miles of march would have to be traversed in rains. Road track crosses the river Yé Bu several times.
		4. Kôdi	4	0	35	0	Small village. Path very steep and difficult. Jungle dense. Colonel Sartorius's column had to make places passable for baggage animals in 1887.
		5. Ethnataung ...	11	0	46	0	Path same as above, very difficult. Jungle dense. Small village. Supplies meagre. *General remarks.*—During the rains cooly carriage alone passable. From Seikpudaung there is an easier but longer route to the north reported; but, to avoid misunderstanding with the Karens, it was not traversed, *vide* Route No. 22, Shan Division.

No. 10.

From PYINMANA to KYAUKPYAZAN (Northern Route).

BY CAPT. A. C. YATE, 1ST BELUCH LIGHT INFANTRY, NOVEMBER 1887.

Authorities. Military.	Authorities. Civil.	Number and Names of Stages, Rivers and Streams.	Intermediate. M.	Intermediate. F.	Total. M.	Total. F.	Remarks.
G.O.C. Rangoon District.	Commr., Eastern Divn., and Dy. Commr., Pyinmana.	**1. Kain**	12	0	12	0	*See* Route No. 15, Stage 1.
		2. Madawbin ...	7	0	19	0	This route is practicable for pack transport.

FROM PYINMANA TO KYAUKPYAZÁN (NORTHERN ROUTE)—*continued.*

Authorities. Military.	Authorities. Civil.	Number and Names of Stages, Rivers and Streams.	Distances. Intermediate. M. F.		Distances. Total. M. F.		Remarks.
G.O.C. Rangoon District.	Commissioner, Eastern Division, and Deputy Commissioner, Pyinmana.	**3. Thayet*** ...	**14**	**0**	33	0	There is believed to be no village except (Sakhángyi) capable of sheltering troops between Madawbin and Thayet. At $3\frac{1}{2}$ miles pass village of Sakhángyi. At $4\frac{1}{2}$ miles enter Chaungmangé chaung and follow its course or parallel to it to Thayet. *Note.*—About $1\frac{1}{4}$ miles before reaching Thayet the Thabúmyaung creek falls into the Chaungmangé from the south. Up the Thabúmyaung is a difficult path leading over the hills to the village of Shaukmyaung, where there is good water and housing for 150 men, distance about 9 miles. From Shaukmyaung there is a difficult road north-west over the Yômas to Kyaukpyazán, a good cart road to Singyidain $4\frac{1}{8}$ miles, a road to Dalangyun on the Minbin chaung 6 miles (*see* Route No. 12, Stage 5), and a road eastward down the Shaukmyaung-ngé creek to its junction with the Chaungmangé chaung near the old village of Kyauktalôn, distance about 12 miles. At Thayet there is a good kyaung and several houses capable of housiug 75 to 100 men. Good water.
G.O.C. Myingyán District.	Commissioner, Southern Division, and Deputy Commissioner, Magwé.	**4. Thôngwa** ... or **Kyaukpyazán** ...	**12** **13**	**0** **0**	45 46	0 0	Up Chaungmangé stream. At $1\frac{1}{8}$ miles pass deserted village of Mebyadaung, and at $4\frac{1}{4}$ miles reach junction of Pwégôn and Lébinkwin creek. (From this point, there are two roads across the Yômas to Taungdwingyi. That to the right *viâ* Lébinkwin and Pangámyaung used to be considered the best, but there is now no accommodation for troops on that road between Mebyadaung and Pangámyaung, a distance of about 20 miles. From Pangámyaung to Taungdwingyi, there is a good road, and no difficulty about water, supplies, or accommodation.) At $6\frac{1}{2}$ miles, proceeding up Pwégôn creek, pass village of Pwégôn.† At 8 miles leave Pwégôn creek, and cross Yôma hills. At $8\frac{1}{2}$ miles cart road branches off to left to Kyaukpyazán village west of Yômas, distance $6\frac{1}{2}$ miles from Pwégôn. At $10\frac{3}{4}$ miles road descends from Yômas into Thôngwa chaung; then down Thôngwa chaung for $1\frac{1}{4}$ miles to Thôngwa village. Housing for 100 men; good water, some supplies. It is two marches from Thôngwa to Taungdwingyi; good road. *Note.*—There is an alternative road from Madawbin to Myinbin *viâ* Thegu, distance about 16 miles. It is a jungle path practicable for pack transport. For route to the Yômas from Myinbin *see* Route No. 12.

ALTERNATIVE I.

FROM PYINMANA TO MADAWBIN (STAGE 2) *viâ* LÉWÉ.

BY LIEUT. A. C. YATE, 1ST BELUCH LIGHT INFANTRY, NOVEMBER 1887.

Military	Civil	Stage	Intermediate M.	F.	Total M.	F.	Remarks
G.O.C. Rangoon District.	Commr., Eastern Divn., &c., Pyinmana.	**1. Léwé**	**12**	**0**	12	0	Road across level country, mostly rice fields, very heavy in rains. Raised road is now (June 1887) being

* From Kain (1st stage) to Thayet there are more direct routes practicable for pack transport, as for instance, *viâ* Tétha Thitkaungdé and Thôgalé, or *viâ* Pedankôn, Kyinbit and Thayetkyin.

† From Pwégôn to Taungdwingyi distance is given as 25 miles, passing villages of Sinkyun (5), Nyaungma (9), Gôninta (14), and Thúgán (18 miles). The Pwégôn creek is now quite impassable for carts.

FROM PYINMANA TO KYAUKPYAZÁN (NORTHERN ROUTE)—*continued.*

ALTERNATIVE I—*continued.*

Authorities. Military.	Authorities. Civil.	Number and Names of Stages, Rivers and Streams.	Distances. Intermediate. M.	F.	Total. M.	F.	Remarks.
G.O.C. Rangoon District.	Commissioner, Eastern Division, and Deputy Commissioner, Pyinmana.	**1. Léwé**—*cont.*					constructed, but will be of no use till 1888. At 2¼ miles pass village of Gyinlo. Good accommodation for half battalion. Good water. Supplies procurable. Between Gyinlo and Léwé many villages. Whole country under cultivation. At Léwé stockaded fort held by police. Accommodation for a battalion. Water good. Supplies procurable: paddy, rice, bullocks, chickens, vegetables, fruits, &c. From here there is a route to Payagôn, *see* Route No. 8, Lower Burma Division, generally bad or indifferent; two stages, Kôntha 19 miles, Payagôn 12, total 31 miles, passing the villages of Ugyinsu, Sétágyi, Tambingôn, Kôntha, Kyiaung and Kyauktainbyu.
		2. Madawbin ... Palwé chaung.	9	4	21	4	To Shánzu 2¾ miles. Shánzu large village. Good water. Supplies as at Léwé. Accommodation for half battalion. From Shánzu to Madawbin 6 miles up Palwé chaung, passing at 3 miles village of Padônmyaung and at 5¼ miles Zéyain. Madawbin stockade (held by police) and village lie ¾ mile west of the chaung. Accommodation at Madawbin for 50 to 100 men. Water good. The above is dry weather road. The wet weather road crosses the Palwé chaung just opposite Shánzu, and then crosses rice fields and low hills *viâ* Thalopin, Padônmyaung, Kônywa, and Mémin to Madawbin. Total distance from Léwé 9½ miles. At Thalôpin accommodation for 100 men. Water from wells. From Madawbin there are two roads to Tyésaw, one a foot-path 2½ miles long, the other a cart track *viâ* Zéyain, 3 miles.

BRANCH I.

FROM MADAWBIN (STAGE 2) TO GWÉGYO.

BY LIEUT. A. C. YATE, 1ST BELUCH LIGHT INFANTRY, NOVEMBER 1887.

Authorities. Military.	Authorities. Civil.	Number and Names of Stages, Rivers and Streams.	Distances. Intermediate. M.	F.	Total. M.	F.	Remarks.
G.O.C. Rangoon District.	Commissioner, Eastern Division, and Deputy Commissioner, Pyinmana.	**1. Chaungmangé.** Palwé chaung.	8	4	8	4	Road up Palwé chaung good in dry weather. In rainy season quicksands and floods to be contended with. At ¾ mile pass Madawbin-Kyaingywa (deserted). Here foot-path to right through jungle for ¾ mile, then recrossing chaung over hills straight to Kyimbyit, deserted village, 3¾ miles by the chaung from Madawbin, but by foot-path only 3 miles. Foot-path is practicable for pack transport. From Kyimbyit to Ôkshithlaing by hill path 1½ miles, by chaung 2 miles. Accommodation for 150 men at Ôkshithlaing. Water from chaung. Ôkshithlaing to Chaungmangé, 3 miles, village lies on both banks of the Palwé-Chaungmangé creek; 200 yards above and west of its junction with the Palwé chaung. On the opposite (left) bank of Palwé chaung is the village of Gyándaukwin, whence road to Kyauko, Kain, Mílaungôn, &c. Chaungmangé village can, although most houses are roofless, accommodate 100 men. Good water.
		2. Gwégyo ...	21	0	29	4	Road up Palwé chaung to Wetpôk. Village on left bank, 2½ miles. Thence path through jungle and rice fields to west of Lédágalé and Lédágyi, rejoining Palwé chaung about a mile

FROM PYINMANA TO KYAUKPYAZÁN (NORTHERN ROUTE)—*continued.*

BRANCH I—*continued.*

Authorities.		Number and Names of Stages, Rivers and Streams.	Distances.		Remarks.
Military.	Civil.		Intermediate.	Total.	
G.O.C. Rangoon District.	Commissioner, Eastern Division, and Deputy Commissioner, Pyinmana.	**2. Gwégyo**—*cont.*			above the latter village. This path is shorter by a mile than the road by the chaung. For road onward to Gwégyo, *see* Route No. 15. *Note.*—From Chaungmangé village up the Chaungmangé creek to Chakainmaung village is $8\frac{1}{2}$ miles. At $1\frac{1}{2}$ miles Zanônmyaung creek joins Chaungmangé. Road up Zanônmyaung creek to Zanônmyaung and Twégyaung villages, both deserted and respectively $\frac{3}{4}$ and $1\frac{1}{2}$ miles from Chaungmangé creek. Good accommodation and water for 100 or 150 men at Twégyaung. The best road from Chaungmangé to Twégyaung is by cart road through rice fields and jungle on the left or north bank of creek. Returning to Chaungmangé creek, at 2 and $2\frac{1}{2}$ miles from Chaungmangé village of Lugwin and Punzunyaung. At 5 miles track up small creek to left over hills to Tho chaung (3 or 4 miles distant,—*see* Branch Route No. II). At $8\frac{1}{2}$ miles village of Chakainmaung. Accommodation for 50 to 75 men. Water from well and chaung. From Chakainmaung to Thôgyi, 3 miles south-east by difficult hill track across Yômas to Taungdwingyi.

BRANCH II.

FROM MADAWBIN (STAGE 2) TO THÔGYI *viâ* ÔKSHITHLAING.

BY LIEUT. A. C. YATE, 1ST BELUCH LIGHT INFANTRY.

Military	Civil	Stages	Intermediate M.	Intermediate F.	Total M.	Total F.	Remarks
G.O.C. Rangoon District.	Commissioner, Eastern Division, and Deputy Commissioner, Pyinmana.	**1. Ôkshithlaing** ...	5	6	5	6	*See* Branch I, Stage 1.
		2. Thôgalé ...	5	0	10	6	Road practicable for pack transport across hills to Tho chaung, 4 miles, and then for 1 mile up Tho chaung to the village of Thôgalé. Accommodation for 100 men. Good water. *Note.*—Opposite Thôgalé village is junction of Tho and Chaungyauk chaungs. There is a road up the latter to the village of Chaungyauk (2 miles) and to another village ($5\frac{1}{2}$ miles). From the latter village there are hill tracks across to Dônwé and Shaukmyaung on the Tho chaung and to Mebyadaung, or Leibinkwin, on the Chaungmangé chaung.
		3. Thôgyi	7	4	18	2	Road up chaung. At 4 miles village of Dônwé. At $5\frac{1}{2}$ miles village of Shaukmyaung, $\frac{1}{2}$ mile above junction of Shaukmyaung and Tho chaungs. At $7\frac{1}{2}$ miles village Thôgyi. All these three villages can accommodate each about 75 men; water plentiful; carts can get up to Thôgyi. From Thôgyi path across Yômas to Taungdwingyi side, said to be 11 miles, without water. Also path to Lébinkwin, 5 miles, and Chakainmyaung, 3 miles. *Note.*—There is another route from Madawbin to Thôgalé, which follows the courses of the Chaungmangé and Tho chaungs. The distance is 10 or 11 miles, and the road is reported to be a fairly good cart road.

No. 11.

From PYINMANA to KYAUKPYAZÁN (Central Route).

By Capt. A. C. YATE, 1st Beluch Light Infantry, November 1887.

Authorities. Military.	Authorities. Civil.	Number and Names of Stages, Rivers and Streams.	Distances. Intermediate. M.	F.	Total. M.	F.	Remarks.
G.O.C. Rangoon District.	Commissioner, Eastern Division, and Deputy Commissioner, Pyinmana.	**1. Kain**	**12**	**0**	12	0	*See* Route No. 15, Stage 1.
		2. Madawbin ...	**7**	**0**	19	0	This route is practicable for pack transport.
		3. Shaukmyaung.	**17**	**0**	36	0	Road *viâ* Sakhángyi (3½ miles) and Kyauktalôn (about 5 miles) and then up chaung (name unknown) for 12 miles to village of Shaukmyaung. Good accommodation for 100 men. Good water. For roads radiating from Shaukmyaung *see* Route No. 10, Stage 3.
G.O.C. Myingyán District.	Commr., Southern Division, and Deputy Commr., Magwé.	**4. Kyaukpyazán**...	**5**	**0**	41	0	Road very difficult up Shaukmyaung nullah for 1½ miles, hardly practicable for pack mules and ponies: very difficult for elephants; steep ascent out of nullah. Then across Yômas for 3½ miles, cross Kyaukpyazán chaung twice. Kyaukpyazán can accommodate 50 men. Good water; a few supplies.

No. 12.

From PYINMANA to KYAUKPYAZÁN (Southern Route).

By Capt. A. C. YATE, 1st Beluch Light Infantry, November 1887.

Military	Civil	Stages	Int. M.	F.	Total M.	F.	Remarks
G.O.C. Rangoon District.	Commissioner, Eastern Division, and Deputy Commissioner, Pyinmana.	**1. Léwé**	**12**	**0**	12	0	*See* Route No. 10, Alternative I, Stage 1.
		2. Kathaung-daung.	**9**	**4**	21	4	At 2½ miles from Léwé cross Palwé chaung at Sibaing. Then 3 miles first through rice fields and then jungle to the Chaungmangé, crossing that stream about half-way between Kani and Gyôgya-in. Thence 4 miles through level jungle to Madán chaung, on the left bank of which is Kathaungdaung. (There are two alternative routes *viâ* Gyôgya-in and Kani, distance about 10½ miles.) This road and both the others only fit throughout for pack transport, and in occasional short sections for carts. At Kathaungdaung housing for 75 men in kyaung and village. Good water; no supplies.
		3. Myinbin ...	**10**	**0**	31	4	Road mostly through thick jungle; level country crossing Madán chaung several times and in places following the bed of the chaung. The villages of Kiláng-u and Pindámyaung lie to

FROM PYINMANA TO KYAUKPYAZÁN (SOUTHERN ROUTE)—*continued.*

Authorities. Military.	Authorities. Civil.	Number and Names of Stages, Rivers and Streams.	Distances. Intermediate. M.	F.	Distances. Total. M.	F.	Remarks.
G.O.C. Rangoon District.	Commissioner, Eastern Division, and Deputy Commissioner, Pyinmana.	**3. Myinbin**—*cont.*					the left or south of the road. One and-a-quarter miles before reaching Myinbin the village of Tambagôn is passed. There are two villages and a police post at Myinbin. There is a road from Myinbin direct to Madawbin *viâ* Thegu, distance 16 miles. *See* note at the end of Route 10, Stage 4. Good water; housing for 100 men; some supplies.
		4. Kyawbôn ...	**8**	**0**	39	4	Road up chaung all the way. Bad going in rains. Huge logs block the chaung in several places. Road is practicable for pack transport. Where the chaung is blocked by timber pack animals can be taken round through the jungle. There are two inhabited villages near Kyawbôn, Chaungnapa, 1¼ miles south, and Kônmyaung, 2 miles north. Kyawbôn can house 100 men.
		5. Dalángyun ...	**6**	**0**	45	4	Road up chaung or parallel to it. At 3 miles junction of Kyauktaya and Dalángyun chaungs. At 6 miles reach Dalángyun. The village is burnt. Good water. From here there are at least three roads across the Yômas—one to Kyauklôn, 4 miles, one south-west to Hmunza, 5½ miles, and one north-west to Singyidaing, 4 miles. From Singyidaing to Kyaukpyazán is 3 miles, and to Shaukmyaung (*see* Route No. 11, Stage 3), 4¼ miles. From Dalángyun to Shaukmyaung by foot-path straight over the hills is 3½ miles. From Kyaukpyazán to Thôngwa is 5 miles. At Kyaukpyazán there is accommodation for 50 men; good water. Kyaukpyazán and Thôngwa are both on the Taungdwingyi side of the Yômas. It is said to be 10 miles from Singyidaing to Kywéda by a fair cart road. Good accommodation in Kywéda (village and kyaung) for 100 men. Water fair from well; supplies scarce.
G.O.C. Myingyán District.	Commissioner, Southern Division, and Deputy Commissioner, Magwé.	or **Kyaukpyazán** ...	**13**	**0**	52	4	

No. 13.

From PYINMANA to LEPETAUNG viâ ZIBYUBIN.

BY CAPT. A. C. YATE, FROM REPORTS BY CAPT. W. A. BROOME (APRIL 1887), CAPT. SINCLAIR (MAY 1887), AND LIEUT. PINK (FEBRUARY 1887).

Military	Civil	Stages	Inter. M.	F.	Total M.	F.	Remarks
G.O.C. Rangoon District.	Commr., Eastern Divn., and Deputy Commr., Pyinmana.	**1. Zibyubin** ... Sittang river. In the cold season a temporary trestle bridge spans it.	**9**	**0**	9	0	General direction south-east. Along a raised metal road, bridged recently, constructed by Public Works Department. At 4 miles Thanetpin, on left of road remains of earth work of old stockade. At 6 miles village and stockade of Sinthéwa on Sittang river. At 9 miles village of Zibyubin and

FROM PYINMANA TO LEPETAUNG *viâ* ZIBYUBIN—*continued.*

Authorities. Military.	Authorities. Civil.	Number and Names of Stages, Rivers and Streams.	Distances. Intermediate.	Distances. Total.	Remarks.
G.O.C. Rangoon District.	Commissioner, Eastern Division, and Deputy Commissioner, Pyinmana.	**1. Zibyubin**—*cont.*			opposite, on left bank of Sittang, is the stockade garrisoned by the military police. No supplies at village. Water good from river. No accommodation for troops. The river has to be crossed here. In fine weather, *i.e.*, from February to June, there is a temporary bridge here; at other times the crossing has to be done in boats.
			M. F.	M. F.	
		2. Seikpudaung ... Small stream constantly occurring, but forming no obstacle.	11 0	20 0	General direction south-east. At 1 mile road goes off to right to Légathain, 3 miles. At 2 miles cross range of hills, impassable for wheeled transport. At 3 miles through *in* jungle, where path from Sinthéwa joins. At 6 miles ascend: 1,500 yards brings you to top of very steep hill. Elevation here 1,000 feet higher than Sinthéwa. Road now descends all the way. At ½ mile from stockade road runs along stream. Stockade garrisoned by military police on a hill about 150 feet high commanded on all sides by hills; no supplies; water from stream throughout the year. Road runs through *in* jungle the whole way except the first 2 miles, which is through bamboo and kaing grass. In April the road was cleared of jungle throughout 100 yards wide. No camping ground between stages.
		3. Lepetaung ...	5 0	25 0	Good road along 1st mile to village Bamupa, burnt. Then 3 miles along defile with precipitous hills on each side, up a very steep hill 1,000 feet high and about ½ mile along the ridge through thick jungle about 10 or 12 feet high. Village on the summit of several hills, forming a circle about a mile in diameter with a deep valley in the centre. About 30 or 40 houses at considerable distances apart. Large clearing on the sides of the hills. Substantial houses, well stocked; some four or five were burnt.

ALTERNATIVE I.

FROM PYINMANA TO SEIKPUDAUNG (STAGE 2) *viâ* KYIDAUNG (OR KIDAUNG).

BY COL. YATE, FROM REPORTS BY COL. SARTORIUS, AND CAPT. SINCLAIR, 1ST BELOOCHEES, AND LIEUT. WHIFFIN, 2ND QUEEN'S, NOVEMBER 1887.

Military	Civil	Stages	Intermediate	Total	Remarks
G.O.C. Rangoon District.	Commr., Eastern Divn., and Deputy Commr., Pyinmana.	**1. Kyidaung (or Kidaung).** Ngálaik; Sinthé.*	9 0	9 0	Road good in dry season through bamboo jungle, kaing grass and paddy-fields. Cross Ngálaik and Sinthé chaungs. In rains whole road very bad. At 3½ miles Kyaukkyet, small village on the left bank of the Sinthé river, which is 90 yards wide here at this season of the year (March). The river flows at about 1½ miles an hour and is now fordable, but in the rains it is unfordable. One or two

* Unfordable in the rains.

FROM PYINMANA TO LEPETAUNG *viâ* ZIBYUBIN—*continued.*

ALTERNATIVE I—*continued.*

Authorities. Military.	Authorities. Civil.	Number and Names of Stages, Rivers and Streams.	Distances. Intermediate.	Distances. Total.	Remarks.
G.O.C. Rangoon District.	Commissioner, Eastern Division, and Deputy Commissioner, Pyinmana.	**1. Kyidaung (or Kídaung)**—*cont.*			native boats available. The stockade, 60 yards square, is occupied by the police. No supplies or accommodation. Water from river. The road is fairly good generally, but in some places might be much improved by cutting down stumps of trees; chiefly through thick jungle, in places cut and burnt on both sides. There is a wooden bridge across the pond, which is charred at the far end; height above water 10 feet, raised in the middle 1 foot; is not broad enough for carts, which have to go round. At 4¼ miles village of Ainzauk. The road for the next ½ mile is bad, but afterwards gets much better. Road very bad, parts impassable in rains; at 6 miles Môndagwin and just after leaving the village cross the Chaung Magyi, which is 10 feet broad and 1 foot deep. Quarter of a mile further on is the other village of Môndagwin eight huts, only two inhabited; also a pôngyi kyaung and a zayát. Road fairly good, in parts through paddy-fields, where there is only a foot-path; but carts can go over the fields except in rains perhaps. At 7½ miles Wetôn, whence remainder of road is good, in parts very good and hard. Kyidaung village is right under the stockade, which is 50 yards square. The road leads direct to the west gate.
			M. F.	M. F.	
		2. Temyaung ...	**10 0**	19 0	Cross Sittang river, fordable except in the rainy season; current very swift; boats can only cross with difficulty. For first 5 miles road good, through teak jungle. Three dry nullahs; last 5 miles through defile, crossing and recrossing torrent. Hills on each side precipitous, about 600 feet high, quite impassable for animals. Village about 30 houses (deserted) in basin of hills completely closed in. No cultivation. Good water. There are three villages of Temyaung, the other two occupied.
		Sittang.			
		3. Mayándaung. *	**9 0**	28 0	Two roads, one straight over the hills, other round by the chaung. Hilly road over four steep hills. Jungle open at the top, thick with marshy ground in the valleys. Pyinmana visible through opening in forest on the second hill (295°). Village about five houses (deserted). Bad water. Very insignificant cultivation; 1,500 feet above Sinthéwa. Two other villages called Mayándaung, distant ½ and 2 miles respectively, over the same sort of hilly difficult road. Second village much the same as the first, but third on the summit of what is evidently highest point of range. Beautiful site, but water down a very steep descent; take bhisties 25 minutes. Time taken by coolies from Temyaung to Mayándaung 10 hours.

* **Captain Sinclair estimates distance from Seikpudaung to Mayándaung at 6 miles, and says path is passable only for coolies and elephants. Only a few Karens live in Mayándaung. Large Karen village in valley to north of Mayándaung. Distance from Sinthéwa to Mayándaung same as that from Seikpudaung, namely, 6 to 7 miles. Distance from Temyaung to Kyidaung 7 miles. Sittang forded breast high in May; current gentle, easy ford.**

FROM PYINMANA TO LEPETAUNG *viâ* ZIBYUBIN—*continued.*

ALTERNATIVE I—*continued.*

Authorities. Military.	Authorities. Civil.	Number and Names of Stages, Rivers and Streams.	Distances. Intermediate. M.	F.	Total. M.	F.	Remarks.
G.O.C. Rangoon District.	Commissioner, Eastern Division, and Deputy Commissioner, Pyinmana.	**4. Sittaung** ...	**8**	**0**	36	0	Same as previous march. On some hill sides large clearings called cultivation. One or two huts near these clearings. Passed through three villages called Sittaung at intervals of 1 or 2 miles, all on the banks of nullah and where the hills recede slightly from it. Ten or 12 houses in each.
		5. Seikpudaung ...	**5**	**0**	41	0	From nullah about 3 miles to a fourth village called Sittaung. This village is shut in on three sides by hills; thick jungle all round. Hills too steep to allow of taking coolies. From this fourth Sittaung to Seikpudaung road good, flat, through thick undergrowth of jungle. Seikpudaung about 20 houses, all falling to pieces. Good site and good water; 500 feet above Sinthéwa.

BRANCH I.

FROM KYIDAUNG (STAGE 1 OF ALT. NO. I) TO SHWÉMYO (ON THE TAUNGU-MANDALAY RAILWAY).

BY CAPT. SINCLAIR, 1ST BELOOCHEES.

Military.	Civil.	Stages.	M.	F.	M.	F.	Remarks.
G.O.C. Rangoon District.	Commissioner, Eastern Division, and Deputy Commissioner, Pyinmana.	**1. Yézin**	**8**	**0**	8	0	Good road. Old and rotten kyaungs, &c.; better accommodation at Zibyagôn, a mile to the south.
		2. Talaing village	**10**	**0**	18	0	Cart track along left bank of Yézin chaung, and then up to steep ascent into hills, distance 10 miles. Height of top of Talaingtaung above Sinthéwa 2,400 feet. Several villages near inhabited by Karens.
		3. Pôgôn	**8**	**0**	26	0	Well defined, but very steep road.
		4. Shwémyo ... Sinthé chaung.	**8**	**0**	34	0	Pass the villages of Yégyi and Kyaukwet, and ford Sinthé chaung (3 feet to 4 feet of water when in flood).

No. 14.

From PYINMANA to PÉKÔN (or PAYAKÔN, in Môbyé) viâ GWÉGÔN.

BY LIEUT. WHIFFIN, "THE QUEEN'S," AND LIEUT. SEAGRIM, ROYAL ARTILLERY, 1887–88.

Military.	Civil.	Stages.	M.	F.	M.	F.	Remarks.
G.O.C. Rangoon District.	Commr., Eastern Divn., and Dy. Commr., Pyinmana.	**1. Gwégôn** ...	**7**	**4**	7	4	Pyinmana to Ainzauk 4¼ miles, *vide* Route No. 13, Alternative I, Stage 1. Thence to Thittat 6¾ miles, road more or less bad the whole way, with thin jungle on both sides. In parts much

FROM PYINMANA TO PÉKÔN (OR PAYAKÔN) IN MÔBYÉ *viâ* GWÉGÔN—*continued.*

Authorities.		Number and Names of Stages, Rivers and Streams.	Distances.				Remarks.
Military.	Civil.		Inter-mediate.		Tótal.		
			M.	F.	M.	F.	
G.O.C. Rangoon District.	Commissioner, Eastern Division, and Deputy Commissioner, Pyinmana.	**1. Gwégôn**—*cont.*					cut up and is quite impassable in the rains. This village is deserted; but there is another village of the same name, 1,000 yards to the north-east by a winding path, which is inhabited. The road continues bad and the jungle becomes thicker at 7½ miles Gwégôn. Three hundred yards from the village there is a rotten wooden bridge, 40 feet long, raised 5 or 6 feet, which shows that the country is inundated in the rains. At Gwégôn there is a large kyaung and four zayáts, which would hold 200 men easily. Forage for horses and elephants abundant. Water excellent from the Yézin chaung, which is here joined by the Nébán chaung.
		2. Kyunbin Sakhán.	7	4	15	0	The road crosses Yézin chaung immediately after starting, then crosses paddy-fields for 1 mile when it crosses the Nébán chaung and joins the cart track from Yézin to Gwégôn in the *aeng* woods. It follows this track northwards for ¼ mile and then turns up a hill in a north-east direction through *aeng* woods. After a slight ascent for 1¼ miles the summit of a ridge is reached and the path follows this along the top almost north for over 2 miles. It then turns north-east again and at 7 miles reaches the jungle halting place of Zibyubin Sakhán. This is merely a cleared camping ground, and water is obtained from a chaung about 150 yards east of the road; ½ mile further on is the halting place of **Kyunbin Sakhán**, the path having been good for pack carriage all the way.
		3. Yébyaungbya..	8	0	23	0	Kyunbin Sakhán (the teak tree halting place) is a jungle halting place on the west bank of the Nébán chaung. The jungle is fairly open and free from undergrowth; the water of the chaung abundant and bamboo forage obtainable from its banks. The track after leaving the halting place of Kyunbin Sakhán crosses the Nébán chaung and turns north along the river for 1 mile, passing many small Shan camping places, none of which would hold a large party. At 1 mile a larger halting place is at the foot of the Zéditaung hill, and this is strongly recommended for parties going east. The path so far is fairly good, but here the ascent of Zéditaung begins and the path is very steep and very rough up to the top of the hill, which is (by barometer) 2,050 feet above Gwégôn. From the top of the hill the rest of the way to Yébyaungbya is up and down a good path without any very serious ascent until Yébyaungbya chaung, a very small stream, is reached. The camping ground is good on a low hill about 400 yards beyond the chaung and overlooking a cleared glade. Abundant forage for pack animals. Elephants took 6 hours. After leaving Yébyaungbya the road is steep, but good for 1½ miles, when top of Haintaung

From PYINMANA to PÉKÔN (or PAYAKÔN) in Môbyé *viâ* GWÉGÔN—*continued*.

Authorities.		Number and Names of Stages, Rivers and Streams.	Distances.		Remarks.
Military.	Civil.		Inter-mediate.	Total.	
G.O.C. Rangoon District.	Commissioner, Eastern Division, and Deputy Commissioner, Pyinmana.	**3. Yébyaungbya** —*cont.*			hill is reached. A magnificent view is obtainable by ascending some hills to the right of the road. The following bearings were taken from here:— Ningyán (Pyinmana), Biluch Mess ... ... 236° Kyídaung ... ... 220° Sinthawa ... ... 217° Léda (near Kyídaungán) ... ... 265° Sinyindôn ... ... 242° Tha Hmán's camp on Pôsendaung top ... 276° Mayindaung (?) ... ... 195° Kwédu and Nachia chaung ... ... 160° Talaintaung ... ... 315° Big mountain opposite Gyôbin ... ... 168° West peak of two-peaked hill opposite Gwébin and visible from Yaméthin, Kundôn, and Pyinmana ... ... 11°
	Superintendent, Southern Shan States.	**4. Hlwégyi chaung.**	M. 8 F. 4	M. 31 F. 4	From here there was an almost continuous and in parts very steep descent to the Hlwégyi chaung camping ground. The path was, however, good under foot. Elephants took 9 hours; the halting place is a "*kwin*" or glade on the bank of the river, which is clear and rapid with a rocky bed, and with about 2 feet of water in the ford now that the river is low. Bamboo forage plentiful and some grass is obtainable from sand pits in the bed of the river which averages 30 yards wide. The road after crossing the river ascends a small but steep hill and it then descends at 1 mile to the banks of the Kaukwé chaung, a fair-sized stream, which flows into the Hlwégyi chaung. The track now follows this stream going almost due north and east along a good level path and after crossing the Kaukwé seven times Taungbyin is reached. This is a village of 10 houses on a cleared hill on the north bank of the Kaukwé chaung. Very few supplies obtainable. Bamboo forage plentiful. Camping ground on south bank of Kaukwé suitable for any force. Water good. From Taungbyin there is a path leading to some hot-water springs about 4 miles distant. Water 188°. The road on leaving Taungbyin runs east crossing the Kaukwé chaung thirteen times. This chaung receives three other streams which flow north and south.
		5. Seikpudaung hill (foot).	11 0	42 4	Clearing the jungle was necessary for 4 miles about, when the foot of Seikpudaung was reached. This would be the next stage from Hlwégyi chaung. A good camping ground watered by a small running stream of good water. Bamboo fodder, besides other trees suitable for elephants. There is a jungle all the way from Taungbyin, which would require to be cut previous to the march in order not to delay elephants who could do the march in 6½ to 7 hours. The road from the foot of Seikpudaung ascends

FROM PYINMANA TO PÉKÔN (OR PAYAKÔN) IN MÔBYÉ *viâ* GWÉGÔN—*continued.*

Authorities. Military.	Authorities. Civil.	Number and Names of Stages, Rivers and Streams.	Distances. Intermediate. M.	Distances. Intermediate. F.	Distances. Total. M.	Distances. Total. F.	Remarks.
G.O.C. Rangoon District.	Superintendent, Southern Shan States.	**5. Seikpudaung hill (foot)**—*cont.*					north-east for 3 miles when the top is reached, from which the following bearings were taken:— West peak of two-peaked hill ... ... 309° Two peak ... ... 307° Pyinmana (?) ... ... 255° about. Kazôndaung ... ... 93° Gaungyidaung ... ... 50° Taungbyin ... ... 270°
		6. Pada-u In ...	**9**	**0**	51	4	From a point 2,100 feet up the hill from the foot, bearing of Toungoo hill 212°. Top height by barometer 2,750 feet above Gwégôn. Road then descends due east for 4½ miles and then south for 1½ miles to halting place near village of Pada-u In. Elephants took 6¼ hours to do the march owing to the descent in parts being very steep indeed. Good halting place amongst bamboo jungle; chaungs on north and south of it. Good water; bamboo forage plentiful; space unlimited. Close by there is a village of Padauns, consisting of about 10 families. Supplies, such as vegetables, obtainable therefrom. Cattle plentiful 5 miles or so further on at Kazor and easily obtained if warned beforehand. There are two roads from here to Kazor, it being necessary in one case to cross a chaung several times and in the other not at all. They both are of about the same distance.
		7. Kazor	**5**	**0**	56	4	The road from Pada-u. In camp to Kazor is flat through bamboo jungle, which requires constant cutting to enable elephants to go. A small chaung running into the river Panlaung is crossed six times. It is waist-deep, but much deeper after the rains; soft bottom; 10 yards broad. The road goes south-east for 1 mile, east for 1½ miles, and north-east for 2 miles, when the ford across the Panlaung (Sittang) chaung is reached. The river is about (?) yards wide and 4 feet deep, running at miles the hour. Numerous bamboo rafts obtainable which are quite safe; firm bottom; west bank 3 feet high. Numerous villages all along this river, the valley being most fertile. Rice cultivation plentiful. After crossing the road goes due north through several houses and across a paddy-field to a large open field on the west side of Kazor village. Water plentiful and good from Kazor chaung which runs into Panlaung chaung here. Elephant fodder plentiful and good pony and cattle grazing. The road was firm under foot up to here all the way from Gwégôn. Kazor is really composed of two villages of Yepagôn and Zégôn, but they adjoin each other. Vegetables and cattle obtainable, also paddy and rice. From here there are paths to all the various villages on the banks of the Panlaung. There is a sudden fall (or rather a series of steep rapids) of 150 feet above Kídaung, about 4 miles distant: thus the river is impassable to boats. Pingaung, a village about 1¾ miles south from Kazor, was the largest one seen. It consisted of about 80 houses; buffaloes being the only cattle. Lwégyi 6½ miles, Yuathit 6 miles, Padingaung 5½ miles, Gwégôn 4 miles, Kôngta 2½ miles are villages all on west bank of Panlaung and south of Kazor. Tangugôn on east bank 2¾ miles south of Kazor. From the top of Kazordaung the course of the

FROM PYINMANA TO PÉKÔN (OR PAYAKÖN) IN MÔBYÉ *viâ* GWÉGÔN—*continued.*

Authorities. Military.	Authorities. Civil.	Number and Names of Stages, Rivers and Streams.	Distances. Intermediate.	Distances. Total.	Remarks.
G.O.C. Rangoon District.	Superintendent, Southern Shan States.	7. **Kazor**—*cont.*			Panlaung (Sittang), south of Kazor, is visible for many miles. The following bearings were taken from there :— Kyídaung hill ... ... 241° Seikpudaung ... ... 287° No. 1 peak of two-peaked hill ... ... 291° No. 2 peak ... ... 292° Maunghlátaung ... ... 45° Pinlaung hill (?) ... ... 34° Pinga waterfall ... ... 78° Laudataung ... ... 86° Nampö ... ... 321° Pangyigôn ... ... 296° Namaungtaung ... ... 341°
		8. **Camp (½ mile beyond Pinga).**	M. F. 8 6	M. F. 65 2	From this last mentioned place a road goes to Nampö across hills. The road from Kazor to Pinga goes east. It crosses Kasor chaung almost immediately and after going level along its north bank for 2,000 yards it crosses it again. Here there are bad rocks which delay elephants a little. The stream is about 35 yards wide, shallow, firm bottom, and rapid. The road continues along the stream about 25 yards from it. Landslips occur often, and hence warning should be sent on to prepare a road for elephants. There is thick jungle on one side. After crossing the river thrice again (and about 5 miles from Kazor) the road goes up, ascending at 45°, leaving river which is joined again later on, it having taken a bend to the north. The road a steep ascent of 2½ miles reaches some paddy-fields where the famous waterfall lies to the east. The road then turns east and level after crossing the Kazor chaung again (which is here about 3 feet deep), and in another ¼ mile the village of Pinga is reached. Good camping ground in paddy-field suitable for small force. Good water. Forage for elephants and ponies plentiful. Vegetables obtainable from village which has about 10 houses. Five miles from Kazor a few houses are passed, as also at 6 miles respectively, named Pinga and Pingun. A more favourable encampment is reached ¾ mile further on, the road leading to it going level chiefly, and in a direction of about 100° through slight jungle. Large camping ground on both sides of Kazor chaung. Good fodder for pack animals, and quite close is the Yébán (hot water) chaung flowing into Kazor chaung. Large rice cultivation. By halting here only a small march is made of the next one, which is a very bad road for elephants, who should arrive here from Kazor in 6 hours.
		9. **Yé-é**	5 2	70 4	The road then ascends up Yébán chaung in a general direction of 40°. The ascent is steep and 1½ miles long, when the rocky portion is reached. The road after this goes up and down alternately over a very bad bit of ground, the rocks, sharp limestone, being injurious to the elephants' feet. Before the ascent begins the Yébán chaung is crossed three times. The water is very hot; stream shallow and small. Then going in a general direction of 70° the halting place of Yé-é is reached. Small open space at foot of a small hill. Water very scarce and only obtained from a small stream flowing out under the rocks. The main chaung was dry in Decem-

FROM PYINMANA TO PÉKÔN (OR PAYAKÔN) IN MÔBYÉ *viâ* GWÉGÔN—*continued.*

Authorities. Military.	Authorities. Civil.	Number and Names of Stages, Rivers and Streams.	Distances. Intermediate.	Distances. Total.	Remarks.
G.O.C. Rangoon District.	Superintendent, Southern Shan States.	**9. Yé-é**—*cont.*			ber. (This water will also dry up completely by the end of January and the camp would have to be moved close to Yé-é.) Good elephant and pony fodder. Bamboo jungle plentiful. There is a small Karen village of Yé-é about 3 miles away. Few fowls obtainable; few vegetables. There is a small running stream near this village which lies north-west of the halting place. A good path through jungle leading there. The road from Yé-é halting place ascends in a northerly direction and somewhat steeply up a clear path. After 1 mile the top is reached and then the road goes level and descending alternately in a southerly and then northerly direction for several miles. Slight jungle and good hard road.
		10. Nanta ...	M. F. 8 2	M. F. 78 6	Then the road becomes open and excellent all the way to Nanta, passing two small streams in a valley 2,000 yards from there. Nanta is composed of two villages, 1,500 yards apart, each of about 40 houses. Good camping ground and one zayát and bazaar houses. Long open valley, no jungle being visible. Cattle very numerous, chiefly bullocks. The water-supply is small, but sufficient for a small body of troops and good, about 200 yards away. Elephant fodder scarce and far away. Good pony and cattle grazing. No fowls; vegetables scarce. Supplies may be obtained in small quantities from one of the many neighbouring towns on their respective bazaar days. Elephants take 4 hours to do the march. Various roads branching off over the district. Pinlaung is about 10 miles distant from here (native information). Rice cultivation only sufficient for the wants of the people. In the western village there is a large kyaung and accommodation for a very large force. There is also a blacksmith's shop if required for repairs.
		11. Kyaungyi ...	15 2	94 0	The road from Nanta to Kyaungyi went in a general southerly direction for about 10 miles when it went east for 5 miles nearly. The road was good and firm all the way, chiefly level along a valley and free of all jungle, thus suitable for elephants who would do the march in 7 to 7½ hours easily. Three small chaungs are crossed at 9½, 10, and 12 miles respectively. Villages of Laingli (3 miles), Kôntha (4 miles), Kyaungbyiaung (6 miles), Lé-né Shein (8 miles), and Kyatôn (10 miles). All passed on the road from Nanta from whence the distances are stated approximately. They all are small villages of no particular importance. Kyaungyi is a large village of about 100 houses. Rice cultivation plentiful. Cattle (bullocks) and vegetables numerous. Good water-supply. Elephant fodder scarce.
		12. Pékôn or Payakôn.	6 2	100 2	Good road all the way on to Pékôn or Payakôn. Accommodation for a small force in a big kyaung and zayáts in the village. Grazing for cattle and ponies some distance away, 1½ miles. There is a small hill close by from which following bearings were taken:—Naungwé village and hill 355°, Lwélôntaung 260° to 201°, Saga pagoda 359° 30′. This peak is not Lwékaw (?), but is a very remarkable one on the east of the Mépôn

FROM PYINMANA TO PÉKÔN (OR PAYAKÔN) IN MÔBYÉ *viâ* GWÉGÔN—*continued.*

Authorities. Military.	Authorities. Civil.	Number and Names of Stages, Rivers and Streams.	Distances. Inter-mediate.	Distances. Total.	Remarks.
G.O.C. Rangoon District.	Superintendent, Southern Shan States.	**12. Pékôn or Payakôn**—*cont.*			and called Hsintaung. Lwékaw is a small hill between Kunzôn 57°, Sanka 44°, Meinkôn 47°, Pali and Palaik 56°, Payakôn 73°, Kyaungyi 230°. The road to Payakôn from Kyaungyi is a good broad one going in a north-east direction for 6½ miles, crossing between 1 and 2 miles from Payakôn, the main road from various towns to Môbyé and Toungoo. There is no jungle and nothing to impede marching. Payakôn village lies on the north and south bank of the Saga river, but chiefly on the south. Very little accommodation for any force in the stockade, but good camping ground in the open. Several kyaungs and zayáts on the south bank. Villages numerous and close. The town of Payakôn consists of about 120 to 140 houses. Plentiful rice cultivation and good supplies of vegetables on market days. Snipes abound in this district. Forage for elephants good and plentiful on southern bank, about 1 mile from village. Cattle obtainable in small numbers for which there is good grazing. The Saga river is deep and impassable to a loaded elephant. Even in January numerous boats, "dug-outs," varying from 200 to 3,000 pounds burden are available at short notice. The bridge only wants the flooring firmly fixed and would then do excellently for ponies and cattle, but not elephants. Saga river is 25 yards to 30 yards broad, firm bottom, 9 feet deep, not rapid, and scarcely any banks. Current 2½ miles an hour. *N.B.*—(1) All heights taken by barometer.

No. 15.

From PYINMANA to TAUNGDWINGYI viâ GWÉGYO.

BY CAPT. A. C. YATE, 1ST BELUCH LIGHT INFANTRY, NOVEMBER 1887.

Military	Civil	Stages	Inter. M.	Inter. F.	Total M.	Total F.	Remarks
G.O.C. Rangoon District.	Commissioner, Eastern Division, and Deputy Commissioner, Pyinmana.	**1. Kain** ... ... Ngálaik chaung twice, Seséyo stream.	**12**	**0**	12	0	At ¼ mile cross Ngalaik chaung and then by cart road past Mílaungôn (2 miles) to Sinyándôn (4 miles), keeping to east of Ngálaik chaung between Mílaungôn and Sinyándôn, cross Seséyo stream. Sinyandôn, large village, police post. Good supplies and water. Accommodation for several hundred men. At 7 miles cross Ngálaik chaung. At 8 miles reach Kyetpyé, where there are several zayáts accommodating 100 men. Water from chaung. At 10½ miles reach Kain. Ngálaik chaung full of quicksands. At Kain indifferent housing for 100 to 200 men in village. Water from wells or stream.
		2. Lédágalé ... Palwé chaung.	**11**	**4**	23	4	At ¾ mile pass old Kain. At 2¼ miles foot-path to left to Taungdi and thence to Pyinmana. At 3 miles road to left to Tetha (4 miles), and thence to Gyándaukwin and Thikaungdé

FROM PYINMANA TO TAUNGDWINGYI *viâ* GWÉGYO—*continued.*

Authorities. Military.	Authorities. Civil.	Number and Names of Stages, Rivers and Streams.	Distances. Intermediate. M.	F.	Distances. Total. M.	F.	Remarks.
G.O.C. Rangoon District.	Commissioner, Eastern Division, and Deputy Commissioner, Pyinmana.	**2. Lédágalé**—*cont.*					At 7 miles road to right (north-east) to Mílaungôn, distance 5½ miles. At 8 miles foot-path to left to village of Kyauko or Kayin (1½ miles). At 9½ miles reach zayát. So far good cart road across undulating country. No water between old Kain and Palwé chaung. From the zayát the cart road goes to Wetpo (1½ miles) and Gyándaukwin (3 miles), both deserted villages on the Palwé chaung. A foot-path, practicable for pack transport, leads direct from the zayát west by north to the Palwé chaung (11 miles), thence up chaung for ½ mile to Lédágalé.
		3. Gwégyo ... Palwé chaung.	18	0	41	4	Road follows Palwé chaung all the way. Quicksands, very bad in rains, so bad as to be impassable at times even for elephants. Following villages (not one habitable) passed *en route*: Lédágyi (1¼ miles), Shwétawmyaung (3 miles), Nyaungbu (4 miles), Kyanklôngyi (5 miles), Panyobauk (6 miles), Magyinyaung (10 miles), Thetkégyin (14 miles). Quarter mile north of last village the Tipo chaung falls into the Palwé chaung from west road up Tipo chaung and over Yômas to Taungdwingyi. At Gwégyo accommodation for 75 men, and at Chaungyo (¾ mile up Palwé chaung) for 100 men.
		4. Kyainmyaung. Palwé and Alémyaung chaungs.	8	4	50	0	For 2 miles up Palwé chaung passing at ¾ mile Chaungyo. Then 2½ miles up Alémyaung chaung. Then over hills for 3¼ miles, very steep gradients, back into Palwé chaung. Then ⅜ mile up Palwé chaung to Kyainmyaung. This road is practicable though difficult for pack transport. The distance *viâ* the Palwé chaung all the way to Kyainmyaung is not more than 9½ miles, but that route is quite impracticable for pack-transport, being blocked by boulders and trunks of trees. At Kyainmyaung there is accommodation for 75 men. Houses required roofing. Water from chaung.
G.O.C. Myingyán District.	Commissioner, Southern Division, and Deputy Commissioner, Taungdwingyi.	**5. Thabiyéaing.**	8	0	58	0	Road crosses steep hills. Path is very bad. In many places animals have to be led singly. Thabiyéaing is burnt and is badly situated for camping. The water is very indifferent. From Kyainmyaung there is a track across the Yômas to Bawma and Thabyéyaing; but it cannot be called practicable for pack transport. The gradients in places are almost precipitous, and so slippery in the rains as to afford no grip. In the dry weather pack mules and ponies and elephants could, with great difficulty, get over it. At 3½ miles a track to right (north-north-east) leads to source of Palwé chaung, distance 3 miles, whence there is a difficult route down the same chaung back to Kyainmyaung, another 3 miles. From Kyainmyaung to Bawma and Thabiyéaing (whence Taungdwingyi can be reached *viâ* Ngámin in two marches) is about 8 miles of very difficult road.

FROM PYINMANA TO TAUNGDWINGYI *viâ* GWÉGYO—*continued.*

Authorities. Military.	Authorities. Civil.	Number and Names of Stages, Rivers and Streams.	Distances. Intermediate. M.	F.	Total. M.	F.	Remarks.
G.O.C. Myingyán District.	Commissioner, Southern Division, and Deputy Commissioner, Taungdwingyi.	**6. Ngámin** .. Ngámin chaung.	**10**	**0**	68	0	Road more or less follows Ngámin creek. In places where it crosses the hills it is good for pack transport, except in one very steep place. There is no cart road. The jungle is mostly bamboo. Ngámin is a large village of about 125 houses and with a population of 500. It is hedged and has strong gate defences. There is a very large kyaung with two zayáts and a well of good water. There are other wells in the village and water can also be got from pits in the creek.
		7. Taungdwingyi.	**8**	**0**	76	0	Good cart road gently descending. Half-way is a tank, but water brackish. Taungdwingyi large town, head-quarters of a district, military and police station, telegraph office. *See* Route No. 20, Southern Division.

ALTERNATIVE I.

FROM PYINMANA TO GWÉGYO (STAGE 3).

BY CAPT. A. C. YATE, 1ST BELUCH LIGHT INFANTRY, NOVEMBER 1887.

Military.	Civil.	Number and Names of Stages, Rivers and Streams.	Intermediate. M.	F.	Total. M.	F.	Remarks.
G.O.C. Rangoon District.	Commissioner, Eastern Division, and Deputy Commissioner, Pyinmana.	**1. Chaungmagyi.** Ngálaik and Seséyo chaungs.	**10**	**0**	10	0	At ½ mile Ngálaik chaung crossed by ford, thence 2 miles to old village of Yébiya. To left of road villages and cultivation; to right jungle. Several cart roads traverse this jungle to Niyambeya and Tawdégyaung on the Toungoo-Mandalay road. At 4 miles reach Kánhla. Village burnt. Accommodation in zayáts for 30 men. Good well and large tank. (From Kánhla there is a cart road north-east to Théagôn on the Toungoo-Mandalay road, distance about 4 miles; also a cart road north to Tetéyn, 3 miles, and thence to Thinkwindaing, 7 miles.) At 6 miles cross Seséyo stream, which is bridged. Here cart road to right to Tetéyn 1½ miles. Road from here to Chaungmagyi hilly, with steep gradients. At 9 miles pass two zayáts holding 50 men. Small spring of water 150 yards south-west of zayáts. At 10 miles reach Chaungmagyi, last ½ mile steep descent. Village of Chaungmagyi in ruins. One zayát holding 25 men. Water good and abundant from two streams that meet there. There is a foot-path direct from Tetéyn to Chaungmagyi, distance 3½ miles. There is a foot-path from Chaungmagyi to Thinkwindaing, distant 4 miles east, and thence on to Pyokôn and Thityagôn on the Toungoo-Mandalay road. *Note.*—The shortest route (cart road) from Chaungmagyi to Taungnyo is over the hills east of the Ngálaik chaung *viâ* Batyo, Sinthékwin, and Nanánmyaung, distance 13 miles, with no halting place between. Road very bad in rains; very steep gradients. In last 3 miles crosses Taungnyo chaung twice.

From PYINMANA to TAUNGDWINGYI *viâ* GWÉGYO—*continued.*

ALTERNATIVE I—*continued.*

Authorities. Military.	Authorities. Civil.	Number and Names of Stages, Rivers and Streams.	Distances. Inter-mediate. M.	F.	Distances. Total. M.	F.	Remarks.
G.O.C. Rangoon District.	Commissioner, Eastern Division, and Deputy Commissioner, Pyinmana.	**2. Mengôn** ... Chaungmagyi and Ngálaik chaungs.	**6**	**0**	16	0	Foot-path practicable for elephants and other pack animals. Bad in rains. At 5½ miles crosses Ngálaik chaung by easy ford. Kyaung and three zayáts at Mengôn holding 150 men; also several villages. Water good and abundant. The cart road from Chaungmagyi to Mengôn passes through Maungyán, distance 7 miles. From Mengôn there is a foot-path to Nanánmyaung (above mentioned), distance 1⅛ miles. Supplies at Mengôn paddy, rice, cattle, and chickens.
		3. Taungnyo ... Ngálaik and Taungnyo chaungs.	**7**	**4**	23	4	Passing deserted hamlets of Nanda and Aungôn to Léma, 1½ miles. Road crosses rice fields. At Léma cross Ngálaik chaung, thence 5 miles through rice fields and jungle past old villages of Manlébin and Méángôn, keeping to west of the Taungnyo chaung. This is the cart road. The foot-path is shorter and follows the course of the Taungnyo chaung. At Taungnyo good and plentiful water from wells and chaung. Stockaded fort with garrison of 150 police. Supplies as to Mengôn, but more plentiful. Accommodation for 200 or 300 men. From Léma following the course of the Ngálaik chaung for 3 or 4 miles further the old village of Palégyi is reached. Near Palégyi the Myawmya chaung joins the Ngálaik from the north. There is a road up the Myawmya chaung to Payataung (8 miles), Kayinywa (12 miles), and Lébinma (16 miles), also *viâ* Bôdet and Gyoyu to Tetshain (12 miles), *see* route Taungnyo to Gwébin *viâ* Ombôk. The descent from the hills into the Wanámyaung nullah is very steep. Road descends Wanámyaung nullah (rough and difficult going) for ½ mile, then enters Gwégyo village in angle formed by junction of Gwégyo and Salwé chaung.
		4. Gwégyo ... Taungnyo and Ngálaik chaungs.	**16**	**0**	39	4	General direction of road nearly due west. Leaving Taungnyo road at once crosses Taungnyo chaung and then ascends low range of hills; gradient steep. At 2⅛ miles path left (south-west) to Kyaungôn, an old village on bank of Ngálaik chaung 7 miles from Taungnyo. At 4½ miles path to left to Thetmwé, another old village on Ngálaik chaung, 6 miles from Taungnyo. At 5 miles road descends (steep gradient) to rice cultivation. At 5⅛ miles crosses Môswé chaung and passes ruined village of Môswé. At 6½ miles enters Ngálaik chaung, ascends chaung for 4 miles. At 7½ miles old Léwun village on right bank. At 7¾ miles hill path to left leads due west to new Léwun, distant 2⅛ miles. At 10 miles Léwun chaung joins Ngálaik chaung from the south. Road up Léwun chaung to new Léwun, distance 1½ miles. At 10⅛ miles road leaves Ngálaik chaung and strikes west across hill for 4½ miles to the Wanámyaung nullah for Gwégyo.

FROM PYINMANA TO TAUNGDWINGYI *viâ* GWÉGYO—*continued.*

ALTERNATIVE II.

FROM MENGÔN (STAGE 2 OF ALTERNATIVE I) TO GWÉGYO (STAGE 3) *viâ* KYWÉYIN AND THABIYÉMYAUNG.

BY CAPT. A. C. YATE, 1ST BELUCH LIGHT INFANTRY, FROM NATIVE INFORMATION.

Authorities. Military.	Authorities. Civil.	Number and Names of Stages, Rivers and Streams.	Distances. Intermediate. M.	F.	Distances. Total. M.	F.	Remarks.
G.O.C. Rangoon District.	Commissioner, Eastern Division, and Deputy Commissioner, Pyinmana.	**1. Kyaungôn** ...	5	4	5	4	Past Manda and Aungôn to Kywéyin, 1½ miles. At Kywéyin large kyaung and two sayâts holding 100 men. Good water. Village deserted, but capable of sheltering 200 men (from Kywéyin to Lédágalé *viâ* Mônit, 7 miles, *see* Branch Route No. I below). From Ngâlaik chaung for 4 miles to old village of Kyaungôn, probably now in ruins. Water from chaung.
		2. Magyimyaung.	9	0	14	4	Pathway over hills, said to be impracticable for any animals. It is probable, however, that lightly laden mules, ponies, and elephants can get over it. Natives say there is another similar pathway from Taingma or Kyaungôn to the village of Thabiyémyaung and then on to Panyobauk on the Palwé chaung, distance about 8 miles. No houses at Magyimyaung; water plentiful.
		3. Gwégyo ...	8	0	22	4	Up Palwé chaung. *See* Route No. 10, Branch I.

BRANCH I.

FROM MENGÔN (STAGE 2, ALTERNATIVE I) TO LÉDÁGALÉ (STAGE 2).

BY CAPT. A. C. YATE, 1ST BELUCH LIGHT INFANTRY.

Military	Civil	Stage	M.	F.	M.	F.	Remarks
G.O.C. Rangoon District.	Commissioner, Eastern Division, and Deputy Commissioner, Pyinmana.	**1. Lédágalé** ...	8	4	8	4	Cart road. First mile across rice fields, passing villages of Mandaw (½ mile) and Aungôn (1 mile), direction north-west; then west through jungle for ½ mile, passing to south of Kywéyin (*see* Alternative Route No. II above); then across hills for 2½ miles. At 3 miles (from Mengôn) road to right to village of Taungma on Ngâlaik chaung. At 4 miles reach narrow valley with small stream of water. Descent into and ascent out of valley very steep. At 4½ miles nullah and village of Mônit. Thence 3 miles across hills. At 7½ miles reach Lédágalé rice fields. At 8¼ miles enter bed of Palwé chaung and ascend it for ¼ mile to Lédágalé village, on right bank, now almost in ruins.

FROM PYINMANA TO TAUNGDWINGYI *viâ* GWÉGYO—*continued.*

BRANCH II.

FROM MENGÔN (STAGE 2, ALTERNATIVE I) TO TAWPYU *viâ* NANÁNMYAUNG.

BY CAPT. A. C. YATE, 1ST BELUCH LIGHT INFANTRY.

Authorities. Military.	Authorities. Civil.	Number and Names of Stages, Rivers and Streams.	Distances. Intermediate. M.	F.	Distances. Total. M.	F.	Remarks.
G.O.C. Rangoon District.	Commissioner, Eastern Division, and Deputy Commissioner, Pyinmana.	**1. Tawpyu and Pindi.**	**8**	**0**	8	0	Foot-path through jungle practicable for pack transport, but has fallen into disuse. General direction north. At ½ mile crosses Ngálaik chaung. At 1¼ miles deserted village of Sízôngôn. At 1½ miles crosses cart road from Chaungmagyi to Taungnyo. At 2¾ miles village (ruined) of Nanánmyaung. At 3¼ and 3¾ miles villages (ruined) of Ságyingyi and Saginbya. Thence about miles to Tawpyu and Pindi (*see* Route No. 17, Alternative I).

No. 16.

From PYAWBWÉ to HLAWZIN viâ YENAUNG.

BY LIEUTS. E. W. M. NORIE, MIDDLESEX REGIMENT, INTELLIGENCE BRANCH, AND F. PINK, "THE QUEEN'S," MARCH 1888.

Military	Civil	Stages	Inter. M.	F.	Total M.	F.	Remarks
G.O.C. Rangoon District.	Commissioner, Eastern Division, and Deputy Commissioner, Yaméthin.	**1. Yenaung** ... Two or three small chaungs.	**10**	**0**	10	0	Road leaves Pyawbwé or Pwábwé near the railway station and runs west across paddy land. At about 1⅝ miles it crosses a nullah, which lower down is deep and muddy and impassable for carts. From here the road runs south-west still over paddy ground and along bank of a small chaung. At about 3 miles pass the small village of Pattaw on the left of the road. No accommodation. Good water from a well on the road. Lwinbyin village lies about ¼ of a mile to west and contains some kyaungs. The road same as before reaches Yôngôn at about 5 miles. This is a small village in the jungle. Water from wells in a small chaung ½ mile to north. From here the road enters jungle and begins to ascend. The jungle has been cleared for 30 yards on each side of the road and it is good going. Reaching the top of a ridge the road runs over high ground and then descends on Yenaung. About a mile before reaching Yenaung it crosses a pretty deep chaung with pools of water in it. Yenaung is a large village with a military police post to south. Accommodation for 400 to 500 men in a large number of kyaungs on south and east of village. Good water from wells on west of village. All the ordinary supplies obtainable from the Myo-ôk. Village of Yenru lies to south of police post.
		2. Hlawzin ... Thitsôn chaung.	**15**	**4**	25	4	Good cart road mostly on high ground and dry. Passing the villages of Sametkyin (4¼ miles), Kángyi (5¾ miles), Kyánpaung (7 miles), Thitsôngyi (7½ miles), and Zigatgôn (10½ miles). All large villages except Kyánpaung. Good water and considerable supplies of paddy at each. Kyaungs and sayáts affording accommodation for 150 men at Thitsôngyi. Thitsôn chaung about 4 yards wide, good crossing, seldom if ever dry.

No. 17.

From TAUNGNYO to GWÉBIN *viâ* OMBÔK.

BY CAPT. A. C. YATE, 1ST BELUCH LIGHT INFANTRY, 1887-88.

Authorities.		Number and Names of Stages, Rivers and Streams.	Distances.		Remarks.
Military.	Civil.		Intermediate.	Total.	
			M. F.	M. F.	
G.O.C. Rangoon District.	Commissioner, Eastern Division, and Deputy Commissioner, Pyinmana.	**1. Ombôk**	14 4	...	Taungnyo, *see* Route No. 15, Alternative I, Stage 3. Cart road level for first 10 miles, heavy in rains; runs through jungle and rice fields, crosses various nullahs five times. At 5½ miles passes village of Pôzataw (ruins). Road to left here up Gyobintha nullah to village of Gyobintha (1 mile) and Pabingôn (2 miles). At 7 miles pass village (deserted) and zayáts of Kazonin. At 7½ miles road to left to Gyoyu (1 mile), Badet (3 miles), and Palégi on the Ngálaik chaung (12 miles). Road to right to Tetshain (1 mile), kyaung and zayát for 100 men; good water. Mézalingé (1½ miles) and Thamaw (2½ miles). From these villages several foot-paths lead to, and across, the Pazaung hills, probably to Kanhla and Pyokôn. The main road reaches at 9 miles Lébinma, a large village on a hill. Accommodation for 200 men; water from wells; some supplies. From Lebinma road west to Chaungwa, Kayinywa, and Tántabin, each 4 to 5 miles distant, and to Pelyataung (8 miles) and thence on *viâ* Gwégyi to Yôuss and Taungdwingyi. At 10½ miles steep gradient, ascending. Road crosses hills for 2½ miles, and then for 3 miles past old villages of Miyéyé and Twinni across rice fields to Ombôk. Villages of Miyéyé, Twinni, and Ombôk burnt. Ombôk kyaung holds 50 men. Water from wells limited. Animals can be watered from Pingyaung chaung, distant about ⅓ mile.
		2. Gwébin ...	17 0	31 4	From Ombôk to Bôtaung, crossing Pingyaung chaung twice, through jungle and rice fields 2½ miles. Bôtaung is on left bank of chaung, Aingyi opposite on right bank. Accommodation for 200 or 250 men. Water good from chaung. Road from Bôtaung follows Pingyaung chaung for 1 mile, then strikes east for 5 miles, across Pazaungtaung. Gradients steep, but road practicable for pack transport. At 8½ miles (from Ombôk), descent into plain ½ mile south of Sinthé chaung. At 9 miles ruined village of Kyuyin; good water. At 10½ deserted village of Gwégyi, then for 3 miles through dense jungle, so far keeping to right bank of Sinthé chaung. Bad quicksands in places in the Sinthé chaung. At 14 miles pass Kayánza (two villages), at 14¼ miles recross Sinthé, and at 14½ reach large village of *Yé-é*. Good accommodation, water, and supplies for 200 or 300 men. At 15 miles village of Shádaw, thence to Gwébin (*see* Route No. 6, Lower Burma Division) 2 miles, road mostly along bed of Sinthé chaung. Stockaded post at Gwébin. Sinthé chaung impassable in floods. From Gwébin two stages to Yaméthin (namely, Nyaunglun 13 miles, Yaméthin 15 miles—total 28 miles) and 2 to Pyinmana (namely, Pyokôn 13 miles, and Pyinmana 17 miles—total 30 miles). In the rains, however, the roads are so bad that stages of 6 or 7 miles can, with difficulty, be accomplished. There is another route from Ombôk to junction of Pingyaung with Sinthé and then all along bed of Sinthé passing Lézán, Kayánza, &c., to Gwébin. Distance about 18 or 19 miles.

FROM TAUNGNYO TO GWÉBIN *viâ* OMBÔK—*continued.*

ALTERNATIVE I.

FROM TAUNGNYO TO GWÉBIN *viâ* PINDI AND TAWPYU.

BY CAPT. A. C. YATE, 1ST BELUCH LIGHT INFANTRY, 1887-88.

Authorities. Military.	Authorities. Civil.	Number and Names of Stages, Rivers and Streams.	Distances. Intermediate. M.	Intermediate. F.	Total. M.	Total. F.	Remarks.
G.O.C. Rangoon District.	Commissioner, Eastern Division, and Deputy Commissioner, Pyinmana.	**1. Tawpyu** ...	3	4	3	4	Road east for 1 mile through rice fields and jungle to Pindi chaung, then for ½ mile up (½ mile further up chaung, Pindi village and kyaung), then for 1½ over low hills to Tawpyu chaung. At 3½ miles villages of old and new Tawpyu. Water and housing for 50 men. This road throughout is with difficulty practicable for pack transport.
		2. Nyaungôn ...	19	4	23	0	From Tawpyu track runs east over hills. Steep gradient. At 2 miles descends into Kyundawgyi nullah and follows that for 4 miles to its junction with the Chaungmagyi chaung. (From here road down Chaungmagyi chaung to Chaungmagyi village, distance about 7 miles.) Road then runs north up Chaungmagyi chaung for about 5 miles, and then east by north for about 7 miles across Puzaungtaung to Nyaungôn. Water is procurable at Nyaungôn, but no water between it and the Chaungmagyi chaung. If Nyaungôn cannot accommodate troops, Yé-é is only about 1½ miles off.
		3. Gwébin ...	4	4	27	4	Road through fairly open and cultivated country past Yé-é (1½ miles) and Shádaw (2 miles) to bed of Sinthé chaung, then down Sinthé chaung for 2½ miles.

No. 18.

From TAUNGNYO to LÉWÉ viâ MENGÔN and KAIN.

BY CAPT. A. C. YATE, 1ST BELUCH LIGHT INFANTRY, NOVEMBER 1887.

Military	Civil	Stage	Int. M.	Int. F.	Total M.	Total F.	Remarks
G.O.C. Rangoon District.	Commr., Eastern Divn., and Deputy Commissioner, Pyinmana.	**1. Mengôn** ...	7	4	7	4	*See* Route No. 15, Alternative I. Another road is to Mîlaungôn *viâ* Léma, Aungôn and Mandaw, distance 8½ miles, and thence *viâ* Zalaung and Nanzat to Kain, *see* Route No. 15, Stage 1.
		2. Kain	9	0	16	4	Cart road *viâ* Yessing (1 mile), Zalaung (3 miles), and Nanzat (6 miles), through rice fields and jungle; level all the way. Very heavy in rains.

FROM TAUNGNYO TO LÉWÉ *viâ* MENGÔN AND KAIN—*continued.*

Authorities. Military.	Authorities. Civil.	Number and Names of Stages, Rivers and Streams.	Distances. Intermediate. M. F.	Distances. Total. M. F.	Remarks.
G.O.C. Rangoon District.	Commissioner, Eastern Division, and Deputy Commissioner, Pyinmana.	**3. Léwé**	11 4	28 0	Cart road to Pedaukkôn, 4 miles. At 4½ miles village of Magyigôn. Both these villages deserted and probably in ruins. Water procurable at both. (From Pedaukkôn there is a road direct to Madawbin 3 miles, and another to Tyésa-u, 1¼ miles.) At 8 miles pass ruined village of Yédi. Between Pedaukkôn and Yédi the Yéaung chaung is probably crossed twice. The Palwé chaung is ¼ mile west of Yédi. From Yédi to Léwé, 3½ miles; good cart road. Yédi to Shánzu direct 1½ miles. For Léwé *see* Route No. 10, Alternative I.

ALTERNATIVE I.

FROM TAUNGNYO TO LÉWÉ *viâ* MÍLAUNGÔN, KYAUK-O, AND TYÉSA-U.

BY CAPT. A. C. YATE, 1ST BELUCH LIGHT INFANTRY.

Authorities. Military.	Authorities. Civil.	Number and Names of Stages, Rivers and Streams.	Intermediate. M. F.	Total. M. F.	Remarks.
G.O.C. Rangoon District.	Commissioner, Eastern Division, and Deputy Commissioner, Pyinmana.	**1. Mílaungôn** ...	8 4	8 4	Taungnyo to Léma, 6 miles (*see* Route No. 15, Alternative I, Stage 3). Cart road through rice fields and jungle, heavy in rains, distance 2½ miles. Two villages of Mílaungôn ¼ mile apart, also kyaung; housing for 200 men; water abundant; some supplies procurable.
		2. Kyauk-o ...	9 0	17 4	Cart road. At ½ mile pass hamlet of Môn-u and cross small nullah. Then for 5 miles across low hills and through thick jungle till the cart road from Kain to Lédágalé (*see* Route No. 15, Stage 2) is joined. (One mile from Mílaungôn a foot-path branches off to right to the Kywéyin-Monit road. *See* Route No. 15, Branch I.) From 5½ to 7½ miles road follows the Kain-Lédágalé cart road. Thence foot-path practicable for pack transport turns off to the left (south by west) to Kyauk-o, distant 1½ miles. Kyauk-o, large village, 60 to 70 houses; good water, paddy, rice, chickens, eggs procurable, also a few cattle.
		3. Tyésa-u ...	10 0	27 4	Road practicable for pack transport, rather difficult foot-path as far as old Kayin, distant 1½ miles. Thence onward cart road ¼ mile beyond old Kayin cart road to right leading to Thitkaungdé and Kyándaukwin on the Palwé chaung, and at ½ mile cart road to left to Tetha and Kain. At 5½ miles reach Kyaukkyin. About 1 mile south-west of Kyaukkyin is the Aingyaung lake, 1 mile long by ½ mile broad. Accommodation in kyaung at Kyaukmyin 30 men. Water very bad and scarce. At 6¾ miles descend from hilly tract into plains. Thence 3¼ miles across level ground, jungle and rice fields, parallel more or less to the course of the Yé-aung chaung to Tyésa-u. The villages of Pedaukkôn and Magyigôn are passed to the left, being respectively 1¼ and ¾ miles north of Tyésa-u. One mile before reaching Tyésa-u a path branches off to right to Madawbin. From Pedaukkôn there is a good road to Kain. Tyésa-u can house 100 men; good water. From Tyésa-u road to Madawbin 3 miles.

FROM TAUNGNYO TO LÉWÉ *viâ* MENGÔN AND KAIN—*continued.*

ALTERNATIVE I—*continued.*

Authorities. Military.	Authorities. Civil.	Number and Names of Stages, Rivers and Streams.	Distances. Intermediate. M.	F.	Distances. Total. M.	F.	Remarks.
G.O.C. Rangoon District.	Commissioner, Eastern Division, and Deputy Commissioner. Pyinmana.	**4. Léwé**	7	0	34	4	Cart road all the way. At 2⅛ miles enter Palwé chaung, for ¾ mile follow bed of chaung, then turn to left out of chaung to Yédi, ¼ mile (Shánzu is 1½ miles further down the Palwé chaung than Yédi). For road from Yédi to Léwé *see* Stage 3 above, and for Léwé *see* Route No. 10, Alternative I.

No. 19.

From YAMÉTHIN to HLAWZIN.

BY LIEUT. PINK, THE "QUEEN'S," 1886-87.

Military	Civil	Stages	Inter. M.	F.	Total M.	F.	Remarks
G.O.C. Rangoon District.	Commissioner, Eastern Division, and Deputy Commr., Yaméthin.	**1. Yédaw** ...	10	0	10	0	*See* Route No. 14, Southern Division, Stage 9.
		2. Thitsôngyi ...	8	6	18	6	Good road passing Napasé, small village at 3½ miles, good water and Gwégôn, large village, good water and supplies, at 5¾.
		3. Hlawzin ...	7	4	26	2	*See* Route No. 16, Stage 2.

No. 20.

From YAMÉTHIN to THAZI viâ TAUNGDWINGYI.

I. B. COMPILATION, NOVEMBER 1888.

Military	Civil	Stages	Inter. M.	F.	Total M.	F.	Remarks
G.O.C. Rangoon District.	Commissioner, Eastern Division, and Deputy Commissioner, Yaméthin.	**1. Myohla** ... One small nullah.	7	4	7	4	Road is a good cart track and runs south-west across paddy for 4 miles, which is very bad going in wet weather. It then rises and runs over a small ridge, the descent from which is rather steep, and across a small chaung at 5 miles. From here it runs over low hills to Myohla. Water procurable along the first part of the road. Myohla is a large village, with a police post to the east. Accommodation for 150 men in kyaungs to south of post. Ground suitable for camping all round. Water good from wells in the village. Ordinary supplies and about 35 carts procurable.
		2. Hlawbôn ... Small chaung crosses three times Hlawbôn chaung.	16	0	23	4	Road runs along the bed of a chaung for 1 mile, then follows the course of the chaung, crossing it twice and reaches Imbaung at 4 miles, where there is a large tank. It then runs west over a small hill and drops down to the Hlawbôn chaung at 6½ miles The road now

FROM YAMÉTHIN TO THAZI *viâ* TAUNGDWINGYI—*continued.*

Authorities.		Number and Names of Stages, Rivers and Streams.	Distances.				Remarks.
Military.	Civil.		Intermediate.		Total.		
			M.	F.	M.	F.	
G.O.C. Rangoon District.	Commissioner, Eastern Division, and Deputy Commissioner, Yaméthin.	**2. Hlawbôn**—*cont.*					runs south along the bottom of the chaung for about 6 miles, past two small villages and reaches Gwébin at about 13 miles from Myohla. From here it runs through scrub jungle to Hlawbôn. This road is quite impracticable in wet weather when the chaung is flooded. There is a fresh road under construction across the hills from Imbaung, which cuts the chaung about 3 miles above Hlawbôn. The country is covered with eng and bamboo jungle and is hilly and broken, unhealthy after rains. Hlawbôn is a large village with a police post on south-east. Accommodation for 50 men in the post. Encamping ground all round. Water from the chaung to east of post and from wells. Supplies scarce. Fodder, bamboo leaves. Twenty carts probably procurable.
		3. Thitchaung ... Sattabôk chaung twice; Thitchaung.	11	0	24	4	Road runs south-west for 4 miles to deserted village of Sattabôk; crosses the Sattabôk chaung on both sides of the village. It then crosses west along a ridge for about 5 miles, then turns south and then south-east along the precipitous bank of a chaung to the deserted village of Thitchaung. Country the same as before, hilly and covered with eng jungle and bamboo jungle along the chaungs. Encamping ground on old site of village. Water always from the chaung. Bamboo fodder. No accommodation or supplies.
G.O.C. Myingyán District.	Commissioner, Southern Division, and Deputy Commissioner, Magwé.	**4. Pebingôn** ... Two chaungs.	8	4	33	0	The road runs south-west and is only practicable for pack animal transport, as the hills are very steep. Rising from the chaung a good road runs up a steep slope and along a ridge for about 4 miles when it descends suddenly and crosses a chaung; then up again and along the ridge, descending again and crossing the Ayaung chaung, on the far side of which is the deserted village of Pebingôn. The country is the same as before. Encamping ground on old site of village. Water from the chaung. Fodder, bamboo. No accommodation or supplies.
		5. Baw ... ... Five nullahs.	11	4	44	4	General direction west-south-west over the same description of country. Road crosses chaungs at 1½, 3, 4, 7, and 9 miles and passes the deserted villages of Shwébaw 3 miles, and Kyánkya 4 miles, both on the Tsatôn chaung. Road, rough and hilly, through eng jungle, only practicable for mule and elephant transport. Baw is a deserted village. Accommodation for about 50 men in sayáts. Water from a well on old site of village and from a stream to west. No supplies.

FROM YAMÉTHIN TO THAZI *viâ* TAUNGDWINGYI—*continued.*

Authorities. Military.	Authorities. Civil.	Number and Names of Stages, Rivers and Streams.	Distances. Intermediate. M.	F.	Distances. Total. M.	F.	Remarks.
G.O.C. Myingyán District.	Commissioner, Southern Division, and Deputy Commissioner, Magwé.	**6. Nyébintha** ... One small nullah and Zun chaung.	9	0	53	4	Road runs west-north-west, crosses the stream to west of Baw, and descends gradually from the chain of the Yômas to Nyébintha on the Zun chaung. No water along the road. Country covered with scrub jungle. Nyébintha is a large village of about 70 houses. Accommodation for about 70 men in kyaungs to south-east of village. Encamping ground all round. Water from the chaung. All ordinary supplies and about 20 carts procurable.
		7. Taungdwingyi. Lun and Tsatôn chaungs.	14	4	68	0	The road runs south and is a good level cart road crossing the Tsatôn chaung at 9 miles. For Taungdwingyi *see* Route No. 20, Southern Division, Stage 11.
		8. Kôkôywa ...	13	0	81	0	Road runs west through paddy-fields, which decrease as Taungdwingyi is left further behind, and near Kôkôywa there is a good deal of scrub jungle interspersed. Pass some small villages, among them Kanyi and Wéchanga, at both of which there are good kyaungs and water. Kôkôywa—There are three or four large villages dotted about and several kyaungs. Several places suitable for a camp, and good and plentiful water from the river. Paddy and bullocks obtainable.
		9. Thityagauk ... Yebain chaung.	9	0	90	0	Near Kôkôywa the road runs over paddy, and carts would have great difficulty in getting along after rain. Two branches of the Yebain river come in here, the water being only 6 inches deep and 5 yards wide in February, but liable to flood in the rains. From here the road runs through fairly thick jungle till within a mile or two of Thityagauk where the ground is partially cleared. Thityagauk is a good-sized, thorn-fenced village with a stockade. Military post for 30 men on north side and a very good camping ground under mango trees for a regiment on south side. Very limited supply of fair water from two or three surface wells and a tank to water animals at. No supplies except bullocks and a small amount of paddy.
		10. Thazi ...	16	0	106	0	Road, good and easy for carts, runs the whole way over sandy undulating ground, covered with thin jungle and here and there patches of cultivation, sandy and heavy in places. Water along the road not good as chiefly from small muddy tanks. There is a small well at Mézali, 8 miles. For Thazi *see* Route No. 19, Southern Division, Stage 13. It is exactly opposite Minhla.

PART V.

ROUTES IN THE SOUTHERN (CIVIL) DIVISION.

PART V.

ROUTES IN THE SOUTHERN (CIVIL) DIVISION.

No. 1.

From CHAUNGU (YAWDWIN) to HNAW CHAUNG (Chinbôk Hills).

BY CAPT. J. WILLCOCKS, D.S.O., 1ST BATTALION, LEINSTER REGIMENT, INTELLIGENCE BRANCH, AND NATIVE SOURCES, JANUARY 1890.

Authorities.		Number and Names of Stages, Rivers and Streams.	Distances.				Remarks.
Military.	Civil.		Intermediate.		Total.		
			M.	F.	M.	F.	
G.O.C. Myingyán District.	Commissioner, Southern Division, and Deputy Commissioner, Pakôkku.	**1. Hnaw-ywa** ... Ché and Yaw.	10	0	10	0	You can go by Kyauktu on Ché chaung Tékyin, Lônbaung, and Ywama direct to Hnaw-ywa. However, so many paths are available till you reach Hnaw-ywa, that this line is only given as a sample. Fit for all laden transport. Village of Hnaw. Water and fodder plentiful. Camp in fields.
		2. Camp	14	0	24	0	From Hnaw-ywa you turn up to the north-west, ascend the Kinu or ridge on south bank of the Hnaw stream and continue along that for about 14 miles. Road through forests of teak, &c. Can easily be made good for baggage animals. You can now drop down on to villages in the valley.

No. 2.

From CHAUNGU (YAWDWIN) to KYÉ CHAUNG.

BY CAPT. J. WILLCOCKS, D.S.O., 1ST BATTALION, LEINSTER REGIMENT, FEBRUARY 1890.

Military	Civil	Stages	M.	F.	M.	F.	Remarks
G.O.C. Myingyán District.	Commissioner, Southern Division, and Deputy Commr., Pakôkku.	**1. Mindát (camp)**	11	0	11	0	For full details *see* Route No. 4, Chaungu (Yaw) to Maung and Ché chaungs.
		2. Sonaing ...	9	0	20	0	Leaving Mindát Sakhán the path runs due west along the Ché-Maung ridge for 7 miles. Road is easy and broad; ridge covered with fir, oak, and rhododendrons. Good grass grows all

No. 2.

FROM CHAUNGU (YAWDWIN) TO KYÉ CHAUNG—*continued.*

Authorities.		Number and Names of Stages, Rivers and Streams.	Distances.		Remarks.
Military.	Civil.		Intermediate.	Total.	
G.O.C. Myingyân District.	Commissioner, Southern Division, and Deputy Commissioner, Pakôkku.	**2. Sonaing**—*cont.*			along the track. Splendid view on both hands. Valleys of Ché and Maung appear very clearly in a panorama. All the large villages in Maung, which were destroyed by the column, can be pointed out as you proceed up the ridge. Path rises from 4,100 to about 5,000 feet and at the 7th mile descends to the right down a very steep slope for 2 miles to Sonaing, which is placed on a very steep hill side on right bank of the Kyé chaung, a tributary of the Maung. Camp space enough for 300 men in the fields. Water good by an artificial channel from a spring. Grass and wood sufficient. This is the best spot in the Kyé valley for a camp. From here by crossing the Kyé valley and ascending opposite fields you can get direct to the "Panchaung Ywamas" or any of the villages in the Western Maung to its source. *Important villages.* On your right hand, in Maung and Kyé valleys— Aikan, 10 houses, left bank Maung. Two Pôkhaungs, 16 houses, left bank Maung. Kyi Dut, 10 houses, left bank Maung. Myauk Tailân, 3 houses, right bank Maung (Burmese name is "Kh[illegible]kai"). Kolaung, 22 houses, right bank Maung. Sonaing, seven houses, right bank Kyé. Myin, 40 houses, right bank Maung (Burmese name is "Wetkyauk"). On your left, in Ché chaung— Pôn Laing, 20 houses, left bank Ché. Mélaung, 21 houses, right bank Ché. The remaining villages of note in Ché are— Op Chaung Yapé. | Ké Daw. Ché Duk. | Kyauk Kwet.

No. 3.

From CHAUNGU (YAWDWIN) to KYI CHAUNG (Chinbôk Hills).

BY CAPT. J. WILLCOCKS, D.S.O., 1ST BATTALION, LEINSTER REGIMENT, INTELLIGENCE BRANCH, JANUARY 1890.

Military	Civil	Stages	Intermediate	Total	Remarks
G.O.C. Myingyân District.	Commissioner, Southern Division, and Deputy Commissioner, Pakôkku.	**1. Natho** ... ... Ché and Kyi chaungs.	M. F. 6 0	M. F. 6 0	Leaving Chaungu road runs down the Ché river by either bank. Pass village of Tékyin and along river to Natho. Road through cultivation and grass lands. You cross Kyi chaung near Natho. This village has about 20 houses and is stockaded like all these border villages. Camp in paddy-fields. Water plentiful.

FROM CHAUNGU (YAWDWIN) TO KYI CHAUNG (CHINBÔK HILLS)—*continued.*

Authorities. Military.	Authorities. Civil.	Number and Names of Stages, Rivers and Streams.	Distances. Intermediate. M.	F.	Distances. Total. M.	F.	Remarks.
G.O.C. Myingyán District.	Commissioner, Southern Division, and Deputy Commissioner, Pakôkku.	**2. Kyi** ... ... Cross small streams.	6	0	12	0	Road leads along stream; villages on right bank. First pass through cultivation and then cross a stream frequently till road reaches Kyi. Road fit for all laden animals. Village of Kyi has 50 houses, one kyaung, one zayát, stockaded. Camp in paddy-fields. Water and fodder plentiful. Road good.
		3. Camp ...	9	0	21	0	From Kyi village road turns west and ascends the Kinu (or ridge running east and west). This is kept to for 5 daings or 9 miles. You can then drop down on to any village in the valley. Transport from Kyi should be coolies.

No. 4.

From CHAUNGU (YAWDWIN) to MAUNG and CHÉ CHAUNGS.

BY CAPT. J. WILLCOCKS, D.S.O., 1ST BATTALION, LEINSTER REGIMENT, JANUARY AND FEBRUARY 1890.

Military	Civil	Stage	Int. M.	F.	Total M.	F.	Remarks
G.O.C. Myingyán District.	Commissioner, Southern Division, and Deputy Commissioner, Pakôkku.	**1. Mindát (camp), 4,100 feet.*** River Ché; by good ford.	11	0	11	0	Leaving Chaungu path leads up the right bank of the Ché river for a mile and crosses by a ford; only 18 inches of water in dry weather. Here it turns west and crosses over paddy-fields for 2 or 3 miles, passing three villages. Jungle now begins, bamboos, &c., and large forest trees. Half-a-mile of this brings the road to a small tributary of the Ché and, turning to the north-west, it ascends a steep hill and gets on to the ridge. For 4 miles it continues to climb and then leads up a precipitous bit for ½ mile and on to a fairly level good broad ridge, which, rising gradually by easy ascents, runs to within ¼ mile of camp. Here the path turns due west along the ridge and is broad. Camp is reached comfortably in 5 hours' walking. Ridge all the way up beautifully wooded. Firs, hill oak, *in*, rhododendrons. Grass in parts of road 5 feet high, generally from 1 to 2 feet. Camp extensive on ridge; commanding position and view. Wood and grass abundant. Water 300 yards below camp on north-west side with a good path leading down to it. Road so far improved by column, which took all kinds of laden transport. *Important villages on either hand.* On right, in Maung chaung— Chaungzôn, 12 houses, left bank. Môgaung, 20 houses, left bank. On left hand in Ché chaung, *nil* so far.

* Lieutenant Harvest, reporting on this route in February 1893, says :—From Yawdwin (*see* Route No. 35) to Yésin at 4 miles the path, though fit only for cooly or pack transport, is good going, passing several small villages and crossing several streams. Thence steady climb of 8 miles to Mindát Sakhán, very steep in parts. Small stockaded post with accommodation for 100 to 150 men. Water difficult to procure, but two good springs about ½ a mile off.—A. F.

FROM CHAUNGU (YAWDWIN) TO MAUNG AND CHÉ CHAUNGS—*continued.*

Authorities. Military.	Authorities. Civil.	Number and Names of Stages, Rivers and Streams.	Distances. Intermediate.	Distances. Total.	Remarks.
			M. F.	M. F.	
G.O.C. Myingyán District.	Commissioner, Southern Division, and Deputy Commissioner, Pakôkku.	**2. Camp on ridge.**	**12 0**	23 0	From Mindát the road leads west along the ridge, which is broad. Good track. Fir, oak, &c. Camp can be formed in any part by looking down the valleys for water. Water is found at the 7th mile near descent to Kyé and is reported at 12th mile on summit of hill, but we had not time to look for it, only making a reconnaissance. Ridge westwards is all ups and downs, gradually ascending to over 5,000 feet, from which point two peaks of Yômas are seen. This ridge dominates both Ché and Maung valleys, any village of which can be reached. *Important villages on either side of ridge as you go up it.* On your right, in Maung and Kyé chaungs— Aikan, 10 houses, left bank, Maung. Pôkhaung, 16 houses, left bank, Maung. Kyi Dut, 10 houses, left bank, Maung. Myauktailán, 13 houses, right bank, Maung. Kolaung, 22 houses, right bank, Maung. Sonaing, seven houses, right bank, Kyé. Myin, 40 houses, right bank, Maung. On your left hand in Ché chaung— Pôn Lain, 20 houses, left bank, Ché. Mélaung, 21 houses, right bank, Ché. Others, but importance not known. This route is important, as the Ché and Maung are the strongest valleys in these hills.

No. 5.

From CHAUNGU (YAWDWIN) to NÉ CHAUNG.

BY CAPT. J. WILLCOCKS, D.S.O., 1ST LEINSTER REGIMENT, INTELLIGENCE BRANCH (NATIVE INFORMATION), FEBRUARY 1890.

Military	Civil	Stages	Intermediate	Total	Remarks
G.O.C. Myingyán District.	Commissioner, Southern Division, and Deputy Commissioner, Pakôkku.	**1. Té village** ... Ché twice, Yaw twice, Té twice.	**6 0**	6 0	Road lies through cultivation on low flat jungles as far as Té village. You pass villages of Kyauktu (on Ché) and Gumbaw on Yaw and ascend the Yaw for a mile up its bed. Té village has 35 houses; stockaded; one kyaung and one zayát; camp ground; water and fodder all plentiful.
		2. Camp ... Té and Né chaungs.	**10 0**	16 0	After leaving Té village you go up the Yaw to its junction with Té, then ascend Té stream till you come to junction of Té and Né. Valley narrow, high hills on both sides. Trees—teak, bamboos, and others. Bits of high grass and jungle. From this point you may ascend the ridge on either bank with cooly transport and drop down to village on the Né.

No. 6.

From CHAUNGU (YAWDWIN) to TÉ CHAUNG (Chinbôk Hills).

By Capt. J. WILLCOCKS, D.S.O., 1st Leinster Regiment, Intelligence Branch (Native sources), January 1890.

Authorities. Military.	Authorities. Civil.	Number and Names of Stages, Rivers and Streams.	Distances. Intermediate. M. F.	Distances. Total. M. F.	Remarks.
G.O.C. Myingyân District.	Commissioner, Southern Division, and Deputy Commissioner, Pakôkku.	**1. Té** ... ... Yaw and Ché.	**6 0**	6 0	Road lies through cultivation on open maidan as far as Té. You pass village of Chauktu on Ché and Gumbaw on Yaw, and then for a mile up bed of Yaw stream. Té village has 35 houses, one sayát, on Chinbôk border, at foot of hills. Camp; water and grass plentiful.
		2. Téchaungywa. Té chaung.	**10 0**	16 0	Leaving Té you go up stream for 1 mile to junction of Yaw and Té rivers. Then you can go along bed of Té to villages or up to Chaukbin. Camp on ridge. Good track for laden beasts. From this point you can drop down to Téchaungywa; but would have to improve path for baggage animals. Only a small village, the first on this side in the Chinbôk hills.

No. 7.

From CHAUNGU (YAWDWIN) to UPPER YAW CHAUNG.

By Capt. J. WILLCOCKS, D.S.O., 1st Battalion, Leinster Regiment, January 1890.

Authorities. Military.	Authorities. Civil.	Number and Names of Stages, Rivers and Streams.	Distances. Intermediate. M. F.	Distances. Total. M. F.	Remarks.
G.O.C. Myingyân District.	Commissioner, Southern Division, and Deputy Commissioner, Pakôkku.	**1. Té village** ... River Ché, shallow, and River Yaw, shallow.	**6 0**	6 0	Leaving Chaungu you go down Ché valley, cross stream at 1 mile, pass two villages over easy, flat country, and cross Yaw near Panjan village and up its left bank to Té, or go up right bank and cross at Té according to channel cut out by river. Camp. Water, supplies, &c., plentiful.
		2. Kyaukbin (camp). River Té, shallow (several times).	**8 0**	14 0	The path runs up Té stream for a mile through jungle and crossing stream several times, then turns up bed of Knaw stream along bouldery bed for another mile; from this point it runs up a steep ridge and between Knaw and Té streams; along this you climb a steepish path for 6 miles to Kyaukbin Sakhán (or camp). View down valleys on each side. Road improved by troops and is now a good track for all laden transport. Bamboo, teak, and fir abound; grass good. Water 400 yards from camp on south side, reached by a good path. Camping space extensive and a good strong position, 4,000 feet high.

FROM CHAUNGU (YAWDWIN) TO UPPER YAW CHAUNG—*continued.*

Authorities. Military.	Authorities. Civil.	Number and Names of Stages, Rivers and Streams.	Distances. Intermediate. M.	F.	Distances. Total. M.	F.	Remarks.
G.O.C. Myingyan District.	Commissioner, Southern Division, and Deputy Commissioner, Pakôkku.	**3. Chaungzôn (camp).** River Yaw, shallow.	7	0	21	0	Leaving Kyaukbin Sakhán you move along top of a ridge south-west; view extensive on both sides. After going for a mile you begin to descend and after another mile you palpably go down until you reach top of a steep descent to Yaw; this is good, but very slippery after rain; another few hundred yards you cross the Yaw, much swollen in rains. A very steep ascent now begins going north-west. After a mile you come on open fields and, passing these, still ascending for 2 miles, you come to the open fields of Chaungzôn village, which lies a mile on your left-hand side down in a deep valley, difficult to get to. The country to top of ridge near Chaungzôn fields is densely wooded, first 2 miles with firs, oaks, and bamboos, last 4 miles on either side of Yaw with fine teak, hill oak, firs, and other magnificent straight, tall forest trees. From the last fields of Chaungzôn you descend south-west down a steep path to the camp, ¾ mile above Chaungzôn and Môgaung villages, which are on the Maung chaung. Camp is on sloping ground, but can camp 400 men. Fodder plentiful ¼ mile from camp. Water is dammed up in a small stream, and rather scarce. Wood and grass plentiful near camp. Large stores of grain in field huts. Important villages on the Yaw chaung to the right between Kyaukbin and Chaungzôn: Kagyin, 10 houses, on right bank. Magyi, 10 houses, on right bank. Maung chaung, 15 houses, on left bank. On the Maung chaung to the left are— Môgaung, 20 houses, on left bank. Chaungzôn, 15 houses, on left bank. Aikan, 10 houses, on left bank.
		4. Camp (on Yaw-Maung ridge).	10	0	31	0	This camp is on the Maung side of the ridge and a mile below the top of the hills. Leaving Chaungzôn road ascends for ½ mile north-west up a steep path till it reaches top of ridge dividing Yaw and Maung valleys, then the ridge runs west almost level for a mile; road broad and easy. For 5 miles it ascends gradually and then up and down to within 1 mile above camp, which is in the field huts of Chaunglôn (?) village. The ridge is covered with grass from 1 to 5 feet high, lovely rhododendrons, fine firs, and hill oak; orchids abound. Many Chinbôk grave-yards are passed. Road fit for all laden beasts till it descends to camp. The last mile is rather a steep descent and slippery. Camp is on a sloping field with five or six huts in it. Water from spring good and plentiful. Grass and wood good and plentiful. A few pigs and fowls found.
		5. Camp (towards Yômas), 5,000 feet.	12	0	43	0	To proceed on towards the Yômas (mountains) the road would continue along top of this ridge for, say, another 8 or 9 miles. It then dips down and again ascends; only 5 miles of this bit has been explored, but country beyond was visible. It appears as if this ridge joined the ridge running north and south and which probably forms the east side of the Maw valley. If so, it would be a

FROM CHAUNGU (YAWDWIN) TO UPPER YAW CHAUNG—*continued.*

Authorities.		Number and Names of Stages, Rivers and Streams.	Distances.		Remarks.
Military.	Civil.		Intermediate.	Total.	
G.O.C. Myingyán District.	Commissioner, Southern Division, and Deputy Commissioner, Pakôkku.	**5. Camp (towards Yômas), 5,000 feet**—*cont.*			good way of reaching the source of the Maw. Water was reported as being near camp at 12 miles from Chaunglôn (?), the last camp. Important villages on either hand as you pass along ridge— On right hand in Yaw chaung— Pyamin, 15 houses, right bank. Tabyin, 12 houses, right bank. Lôkshé, 10 houses, right bank. Pé, 20 houses, left bank. On left hand in Maung chaung— Two Pôkhaungs, 16 houses, left bank. Kolaung, 22 houses, right bank. Wetkyauk or Myin, 40 houses, right bank. *Note.*—In giving a route to any valley in the Chinbôk hills it is difficult to fix the exact line to be followed. If a position is required dominating two valleys, as can always be obtained, then a camp on a ridge, such as the above described, is certainly the best as from it you can pounce down on any village in either valley. If a track to the Yaw valley only had been required, it would have been better— (i) if to north bank of Yaw to turn half right at Kyaukbin camp and go along the ridge till the path got above the village you wished to reach; (ii) if to south bank it would have been preferable to turn to the right above Chaungzôn camp and, before descending the path down to it from the fields, to go at right angles to the right and get down to Kagyin, Magyi, and Pimin villages if you wished to reach those, or to have gone on by ridge described in route and then dropped down to any village required. The ridges are the highways to all valleys.

No. 8.

From GANGAW to HÁKA viâ THETTA.

BY LIEUT. L. A. FORBES, 39TH GARHWAHLIS, FEBRUARY 1891.

Military	Civil	Stage	Intermediate	Total	Remarks
G.O.C. Myingyán District.	Commissioner, Southern Division, and Deputy Commissioner, Pakôkku.	**1. Taré** ... ... Myittha river, Zahaw chaung.	M. F. **12 0**	M. F. 12 0	The road to Taré leaves the Gángaw main road about ½ mile from Gángaw and turns to the left passing through fields down to the river Myittha. The ford is just above the junction of the Zahaw creek with the Myittha. The depth of the water in the dry season is from 2 to 2½ feet and the current is easy. The path ascends the bank directly and runs quite level. Bamboo jungle on each side. About 2 miles from Gángaw the village of Zahaw is

FROM GÁNGAW TO HÁKA *viâ* THETTA—*continued.*

Authorities. Military.	Authorities. Civil.	Number and Names of Stages, Rivers and Streams.	Distances. Intermediate. M. F.	Distances. Total. M. F.	Remarks.
G.O.C. Myingyán District.	Commissioner, Southern Division, and Deputy Commissioner, Pakôkku.	**1. Taré**—*cont.*			passed on the right. It contains about 50 houses and is stockaded with bamboos. A short distance from Zahaw the road passes through paddy-fields and then through a short, low defile which opens into the valley of the Zahaw chaung which is well cultivated. The village of Dunhnaw is situated on the left bank of the creek and is stockaded. It contains 40 houses. The road keeps level for about a mile after leaving Dunhnaw when nullahs are met with and low hilly country commences. Four nullahs are crossed, between which the road is very level and good. Taré is the first ravine containing water. The camping ground is on the spur above the ravine. Water is good and plentiful. There are plenty of bamboos for making shelters. Laden mules can travel as far as Taré only.
	Political Officer, Chin Hills.	**2. Bong-yong** ...	9 0	21 0	The path descends straight into Taré chaung, after which there is no path practically. The bed of the chaung forms the road. It contains large rocks and boulders. The bed of the Taré stream is followed up for about 600 yards when the path is met with again and ascends the hill side, immediately after which it is good and proceeds along a ridge. A couple of dry ravines are crossed, after which it ascends the hill of Ramfi. It then contours the hill and traverses a deep ravine, after which it ascends the hill Nuassu about 3,000 feet high. Gángaw visible from this hill. The road then descends with intervals of level until the Zahaw chaung is reached. The camping ground is on the further side. The Zahaw chaung here makes a very sharp bend so that a peninsula is formed and the camping ground is thereon. It is situated on high ground and the stream on either side of it is about 30 feet broad and running fast but shallow. There is accommodation for a large number of men and the bamboo jungle is thick. There is no village in the neighbourhood.
		3. Su-i-vár ...	9 0	30 0	After leaving Bong-yong the road follows the course of the Zahaw chaung in the bed for about 300 yards when the river is crossed into a thick bamboo jungle. A short ascent is made out of a dry nullah. The road has no difficulties and the jungle becomes thinner. Water is found in one or two nullahs on the way. A steep ascent is made with a corresponding descent until the Su-i-vár is reached, which flows into the Zahaw chaung about 20 yards below the road. The camp is about 400 yards beyond the Su-i-vár and a dry stony nullah has to be traversed, at the further end of which the Zahaw chaung appears. On crossing the latter the camping ground is reached. There is plenty of room for a large number of men. Bamboo and teak jungle. The river is at the foot of the camping ground.
		4. Beta ... ... Ri-vár.	8 0	38 0	The road after leaving this camp is very difficult to trace for about 1 mile. It then gradually ascends to a broad, open, undulating jungle, and then the hill of Beta is ascended, which is a long steep climb. Then the path contours the higher path of the ridge and then descends abruptly for 1½

FROM GÁNGAW TO HÁKA *viâ* THETTA—*continued.*

Authorities.		Number and Names of Stages, Rivers and Streams.	Distances.		Remarks.
Military.	Civil.		Inter-mediate.	Total.	
G.O.C. Myingyán District.	Political Officer, Chin Hills.	**4. Beta**—*cont.*			miles to the Ri-vár. There is no water to be obtained on the way till this stream is reached. The Ri-vár is from 25 to 30 feet broad; shallow in the dry season, but flows rapidly. The road now crosses and recrosses the river 16 times before camp is reached. After the second crossing the Panauk stream is seen flowing into the Ri-vár by the right bank. After the fourth crossing the Panauk hill is ascended. The gradient is very steep but short. The descent on the other side is immediately made down to the Ri-vár again. About 3 miles from the foot of the Panauk hill the stream called Si-vár enters the Ri-vár on the right bank. The camping ground is on the right bank of the Ri-vár and has a high ridge of hills on the opposite flank to the river. Ground is level, but jungle very dense.
			M. F.	M. F.	
		5. Lunhaw ...	**11 0**	49 0	The road leaves the camping ground of Beta on the hilly side and immediately ascends with great abruptness some 600 feet: such an ascent is impossible for laden mules unless the path was reconstructed and made to zigzag more than the Chin road does. The road then follows the crest-line, continually rising until another high hill has to be ascended, which is exceedingly fatiguing and trying, no water being obtainable anywhere along this march. At the summit of this hill there is a short pass on debouching from which the village of Lunhaw is visible to the left front, and to the right front Bondwa hill is seen, behind which lies the village of that name. The road then continues at a high level contouring the hills for about 5 miles when a "*col*" is reached called Manwarina, which is said to be the camping ground, but there is no water within a mile and-a-half. From this "*col*" the road to Bondwa turns off to the right. About 1½ miles beyond the "*col*" the village of Lunhaw is reached. Camping ground is on spur between the village and a stream in which there is plenty of water. It contains about 32 houses and a few supplies can be obtained, such as eggs, fowls, and some vegetables.
		6. Bondwa ... Ri-vár.	**8 0**	57 0	It is necessary to return to Manwarina "*col*" to pick up the road to Bondwa. From the "*col*" the road descends very abruptly through very long grass to a water-course, the bed of which then becomes the road for some 500 yards. It is covered with large rocks and boulders. The road then dives into the jungle, ascends a ridge, and abruptly falls into the river Ri-vár. After crossing the river the road uninterruptedly ascends till the summit of the Bondwa ridge is attained. Immediately on the further side is the village containing about 25 houses. The camping ground is on the ridge. There is water on both sides, but at some distance. The best supply is on the village side. There is little cultivation to speak of and only a few fowls and eggs are to be obtained.
		7. Retu	**8 0**	**65 0**	**After leaving the camp at Bondwa the road follows the crest-line of the ridge and contours the hill alternately. About 2 miles out water is to be found in a ravine, after which no**

FROM GÁNGAW TO HÁKA *viâ* THETTA—*continued.*

Authorities. Military.	Authorities. Civil.	Number and Names of Stages, Rivers and Streams.	Distances. Inter-mediate. M. F.	Distances. Total. M. F.	Remarks.
G.O.C. Myingyán District.	Political Officer, Chin Hills.	**7. Retu**—*cont.*			more water can be obtained. About 4 miles from Bondwa a short but steep ascent is made. In some places the path is only the breadth of a man's hand and very slippery in the early morning owing to the dew. About 1 mile beyond the top of this ascent the village of Lungtauk is visible to the left rear and contains about 15 houses. About 6 miles from Bondwa a very high hill is met with and is a very trying climb towards the end of a march. The road then follows the crest-line of the ridge and very shortly the village of Thetta comes in view on the opposite side of the valley. The camp lies off the road to Thetta and is half-way down a big spur. The water is about 300 yards from the camp down an abrupt slope. This spur is called Retu.
		8. Thetta ... Ri-vár.	6 0	71 0	The road to Thetta is picked up again on the top of the ridge and turns to the left from the road up the spur. The road continues to contour the upper part of the ridge for about 1 mile and then it bifurcates, one road (to the left) being the shortest, but most difficult owing to having to traverse rocks, the other (to the right) is the longest but best. It then ascends to the summit of a hill fairly easily and then opens out into a plateau on which water is to be found. The road crosses this plateau and then descends uninterruptedly and in some places very abruptly to the Ri-vár which is at the foot of the hill upon which the village of Thetta is situated. The camping ground is quite close to the stream and is level in some places. The village of Thetta is distant from the Ri-vár about 600 yards.
		9. Saorel-vár camp.	6 0	77 0	*See* Route No. 7, Chin Hills Division.
		10. Háka ...	12 0	89 0	

No. 9.

From GÁNGAW to HÁKA viâ YÔKWA (direct).

BY LIEUT. E. W. M. NORIE, PAID ATTACHÉ, INTELLIGENCE BRANCH, JANUARY 1890.

Military.	Civil.	Number and Names of Stages, Rivers and Streams.	Inter-mediate. M. F.	Total. M. F.	Remarks.
G.O.C. Myingyán District.	Political Officer, Chin Hills.	**1. Bongzôn camp.** Zahaw river, Rai-vár, and nullahs.	16 0	16 0	General direction north-west. The road, leaving Gángaw, crosses the Myittha river at once by the bridge below the post and then strikes straight across to Lônhow village at 4 miles on the left bank of the Zahaw chaung. The road is good and level, running through the usual terai jungle. The Zahaw chaung is here about 80 feet broad and 1½ feet deep in the dry weather. Lônhow is a small tame Chin village of about 30 houses, surrounded by double stockades. If the march of 16 miles is considered too far, this is the best place to make the first halt, as, though there are some streams and nullahs further on, it is

FROM GÁNGAW TO HÁKA *viâ* YÔKWA (DIRECT)—*continued.*

Authorities. Military.	Authorities. Civil.	Number and Names of Stages, Rivers and Streams.	Distances. Inter-mediate. M. F.	Distances. Total. M. F.	Remarks.
G.O.C. Myingyán District.	Political Officer, Chin Hills.	**1. Bongzôn camp** —*cont.*			uncertain in the dry weather whether they will contain water. The path runs on through *in* jungle and is very good, except where it crosses dry nullahs, which are generally stony and rough. It is necessary to take a guide, or the path will certainly be lost, as other paths join it and cross it from all directions. At about 13½ miles the road begins to ascend and crosses a low range of hills, descending at once on the other side; from here the path again is level for a mile to the camp. The camp is on high ground on the left bank of the Rai-vár and is level and large enough to accommodate any number of troops. No village in the neighbourhood.
		2. Tui-vár camp. Rai-vár, Tui-vár, and two nullahs.	11 0	27 0	The path, leaving camp, at once crosses the Rai-vár, a fine clear stream 40 feet broad and 1½ deep. About ½ mile further on it crosses it again and then runs up a dry nullah for a short distance and strikes across through level *in* jungle, very good going, and at about 2 miles comes to a dry nullah with pools of stagnant water in it. Beyond this it again runs through forest by an easy path till it reaches another nullah at about 4 miles. This nullah also contains pools of water. The road runs up the bed for some distance and then again strikes into the jungle and is good going all the way to the Tui-vár at 8 miles, which it strikes at a point called the Thayetpin Sakhán from an immense mango tree which stands here. If preferred, a halt can be made here, as there is suitable ground for camping on and abundance of water. Crossing the stream the path ascends the other bank and leads upwards, being rather steep in places to the top of a low spur. The Rai-vár is again seen close by to the south. At about 11 miles the path again descends pretty steeply to the Tui-vár, which it crosses and reaches a good site for halting on a level piece of ground with bamboos round about. Water plentiful from the stream.
		3. Rudein camp. Tui-vár.	7 0	34 0	Leaving the camp the road leads up the bed of the stream, crossing and recrossing it several times. This part would not be practicable for mules or other baggage animals, as a good deal of smooth shelving rock has to be crossed. At 2 miles the Tui-vár is left and the road begins to ascend, very steep in places, and continues to rise all the way to the camp, which is about 2,000 feet above the Tui-vár. The jungle passed through is open *in* with a few teak trees here and there. At Rudein the water-supply is from a small stream to the south of the camp and is very scanty in January and probably dry by the middle of February. The camping ground is good and extensive. Grass and firewood are plentiful. There is no village in the neighbourhood.
		4. Rawván ...	17 0	51 0	The path from camp runs along the top of a high ridge covered with fir trees and gradually ascends, with a few short descents in places, some of which are rather steep. At 7 miles it reaches a place called Kyi-vár Sakhán, where a little water is obtainable down the hill side to the south-west; but this dries up at the beginning of the year, and one must go

FROM GÁNGAW TO HÁKA *viâ* YÔKWA (DIRECT)—*continued.*

Authorities. Military.	Authorities. Civil.	Number and Names of Stages, Rivers and Streams.	Distances. Intermediate. M.	F.	Distances. Total. M.	F.	Remarks.
G.O.C. Myingyán District.	Political Officer, Chin Hills.	**4. Rawván**—*cont.*					down about 300 or 400 feet. The hill side is also very steep and rocky. At about 12½ miles there is another place where water can be obtained from a stream on the north side of the ridge. Beyond this the path passes round the side of the Lamtôk hill and runs up the spur, connecting it with the main ridge. Descending from the ridge it strikes into the road from Rawván to Tinam and follows this along the hill side, pretty level, and crossing two small streams, till it joins the road from Káu to Yôkwa and Háka.
		5. Yôkwa ...	**9**	**0**	60	0	For rest of route *see* Route No. 11.
		6. Bwétet ...	**9**	**0**	69	0	
		7. Háka ...	**10**	**0**	79	0	

No. 10.

From GÁNGAW to KYAUNGZÔN (CHAUNGZÔN).

BY LIEUT. S. WILLCOCK, 2ND BATTALION, GLOUCESTERSHIRE REGIMENT, JANUARY 1888.

Authorities. Military.	Authorities. Civil.	Number and Names of Stages, Rivers and Streams.	Distances. Intermediate. M.	F.	Distances. Total. M.	F.	Remarks.
G.O.C. Myingyán District.	Commissioner, Southern Division, and Deputy Commissioner, Pakôkku.	**1. Kwenzé** ...	**8**	**0**	8	0	For description of Gángaw *see* Route No. 30, Stage 13. The general direction of the valley and river is north. The trade routes are south *viâ* Minywa to Pauk and Pokôkku; north to the Chindwin; east to Saga, Kyaw, Thitkyidain, Pagyi and Pakhángyi districts. Boats descend the river Myittha to the Chindwin in a few days during and immediately after the rains with paddy and Indian corn leaves (for cheroots). They return loaded with gnapi, salt and pickled tea. The return journey occupies a month at this season—January. It is said to be twenty marches across the Arakan hills to the Bay of Bengal; the roads are very bad and water scarce. There are two kyaungs in the village capable of accommodating 300 to 400 men. The inhabitants say that strangers or Burmans from other districts suffer much from fever during their first year's residence in Gángaw. The general direction of the road is north-east. Myakôn is passed at 1,000 yards (30 houses and one large kyaung). Yébôk (about 20 houses) at 2 miles, Po-u at 4 miles. Up to this point the road is level and good; between Po-u and Kwenzé a high spur is crossed; both ascent and descent are steep, but the path is good. Kwenzé is reached at 8 miles. It is situated in a valley running north and south, and is surrounded by paddy. It has a treble stockade and contains 40 houses, but no kyaung. The principal crop is paddy; a little Indian corn is grown. The water is good, but very scarce in the hot weather and is obtained from the Kwenzé creek.
		2. Kyaungzôn (Chaungzôn).	**15**	**0**	**23**	**0**	**The road is almost due north throughout and runs along the bottom of a valley except crossing a hill which forms the watershed between Kwenzé and Maw creeks. The path repeatedly**

FROM GÁNGAW TO KYAUNGZÔN (CHAUNGZÔN)—*continued.*

Authorities. Military.	Authorities. Civil.	Number and Names of Stages, Rivers and Streams.	Distances. Intermediate.	Distances. Total.	Remarks.
G.O.C. Myingyán District.	Commissioner, Southern Division, and Deputy Commissioner, Pakôkku.	**2. Kyaungzôn (Chaungzôn)**—*cont.*			crosses the creeks as shown in the sketch, and the crossings are much encumbered by boulders, otherwise the path is good. At the 9th mile Maukchaungywa is passed. It is a new village with a treble bamboo stockade, but only three houses have yet been built. Water is scarce in the hot weather. There is very little ground cleared. At 11½ miles junction of Kyaungzôn and Mauk chaungs whence a route runs to Letpán on the Kán-Gángaw road (*vide* Route No. 35) about midway between Myinza (Stage 11), and Kán (Stage 12), for description of which *see* below. Kyaungzôn is reached at the 15th mile. The village has 15 houses and a treble stockade, the inner one of teak logs. It is situated in a valley and the ground for ½ a mile south is under paddy cultivation. On the north-east and west there is thin jungle. A little Indian corn and tobacco is grown. Water is obtained from the Kyaungzôn creeks and is good, but during the hot weather little can be obtained and that only by digging in the bed of the creeks. There is a path to Mingin 75 miles *viâ* Paya 25 miles, and Alaungdaw Pagoda 50 miles. It is said to be impassable for animals.

BRANCH I.

FROM JUNCTION OF KYAUNGZÔN AND MAUK CHAUNGS (STAGE 2) TO LETPÁN (ROUTE NO. 35, STAGE 12).

BY LIEUT. S. WILLCOCK, 2ND BATTALION, GLOUCESTERSHIRE REGIMENT, JANUARY 1888.

Military	Civil	Stage	Intermediate	Total	Remarks
G.O.C. Myingyán District.	Commissioner, Southern Division, and Deputy Commissioner, Pakôkku.	**1. Letpán**	M. F. **6 0**	M. F. 6 0	From the junction of the Kyaungzôn and Mauk, the path turns west for 1,000 yards, a detour is then made to south across a steep spur to avoid the creek in which there is deep water (January). On reaching the level the direction is south-west as far as Tawzelé, a small village of five or six houses, 4½ miles. South of Tawzelé there is a deep nullah with steep banks. Letpán to which Taunglé is adjacent is reached at 6 miles. These villages (within the same stockade) contain 20 houses and are situated on the right bank of the Myittha river. Water is plentiful and good. The principal crop is paddy, a little tobacco and indigo are grown. There are no kyaungs or zayáts.

No. 11.

From KÁN to HÁKA.

BY LIEUT. E. W. M. NORIE, MIDDLESEX REGIMENT, PAID ATTACHÉ, INTELLIGENCE BRANCH, APRIL 1890.

Military	Civil	Stage	Intermediate	Total	Remarks
G.O.C. Myingyán District.	Commr., Southern Division, and Dy. Commr., Pakôkku.	**1. Laungkat camp** Myittha river, Kabé and Laungkat streams.	**12 4**	12 4	The road leaving Kán close to the post crosses the Myittha river at present by a temporary bridge of logs on stone piles which, however, will not stand a rise of 2 feet in the river. The Burmans use a ford, along which the bridge is built and which is not

FROM KÁN TO HÁKA—*continued.*

Authorities.		Number and Names of Stages, Rivers and Streams.	Distances.		Remarks.
Military.	Civil.		Inter-mediate.	Total.	
G.O.C. Myingyán District.	Commissioner, Southern Division, and Deputy Commissioner, Pakôkku. Political Officer, Chin Hills.	**1. Laungkat camp** —*cont.*			more than 2 or 2½ feet deep in the dry weather. During the rains, when the river is more or less flooded, it must be crossed by boat or ferry just below the bridge. Beyond the bridge the path runs up-stream along the left bank for about ½ mile and then turns west over dry undulating ground covered with open *in* jungle and grass with bamboo clumps here and there in the hollows. It runs generally along a low spur and is excellent going. At 6 miles the Kabé Sakhán is reached, and beyond this the path runs down to a small stream, dry in January, which it crosses at 6½ miles and, running gradually upwards, crosses a spur of the Kabé hill at about 7½ miles and descends towards the Kabé stream at 8 miles. This stream has good water in it in the end of the year, but by February it is dried up. The path follows the course of the stream, which it crosses several times. At 9 miles the Kyaukpyo-daung Sakhán is passed, and just beyond this the road is steep and rocky for some 400 yards or 500 yards. Descending again to the bed of the stream it runs up it to 10 miles, when the foot of the Kabé hill is reached. The ascent of the Kabé hill is very steep, but it has been zigzagged so as to allow loaded mules to ascend it, the general gradient being 1 in 7. At about 11½ miles the summit is reached at an altitude of about 2,000 feet above the sea. The path, after running along the ridge for a short distance, descends very steeply to the Laungkat stream (12½ miles), but is zigzagged for baggage animals. The Laungkat post can be seen from the path as it descends the hill side. In the dry weather the Laungkat chaung is a clear stream about 50 feet broad and 1½ feet deep. It the rains its greatest rise is probably from 8 to 10 feet. It runs along a narrow channel with high banks covered with jungle and precipitous in many places, besides being much cut up by side streams and nullahs. The path follows the bed of the stream, which is covered with loose shingle and boulders, with here and there rock and sand; marching along it is in consequence very tiring to transport animals. The Laungkat post is situated on a high ridge of rock with very steep khuds on both sides. It has accommodation in four huts or sheds for about 100 men, and there is also an officer's shed. It is garrisoned (May 1890) by 30 sepoys of a Madras regiment. The transport lines are below the post on the edge of the stream.
		2. Chaungkwa ... Méshaung stream and Lantôk stream.	M. F. 8 4	M. F. 21 0	From the Laungkat camp the path runs up the bed of the stream, continually crossing and recrossing it till Chaungkwa is reached; the exact number of crossings is 40, of which only one is bridged, and it then crosses the Lantôk chaung, also bridged. In one or two places the path leaves the chaung and runs through jungle or across some spur for a short distance. At 1½ miles reach Taungwadet Sakhán on the left bank of the stream, and at 3½ miles Indwin Sakhán, also on the left bank. At 4½ miles reach Thayetpin Sakhán on the right bank of the stream. This camp was found to be unhealthy and feverish when occupied by troops between December and March. Chaungkwa is situated at the foot of the Taopi hill, at the junction of the Méshaung and Lantôk streams, which

FROM KÁN TO HÁKA—*continued.*

Authorities. Military.	Authorities. Civil.	Number and Names of Stages, Rivers and Streams.	Distances. Intermediate.	Distances. Total.	Remarks.
G.O.C. Myingyán District.	Political Officer, Chin Hills.	**2. Chaungkwa—** *cont.*			together form the Laungkat stream. In the camp there is accommodation for 200 men in barracks, including the garrison of 50 sepoys. There are also Commissariat sheds, hospital, mule lines, and cooly camp. The officers' quarters are on a high spur above the camp, and there are also other quarters in the post higher up the same spur. There is no village, and only grass and firewood can be obtained locally. Water is good and plentiful from the chaungs.
		3. Taungtek camp.	M. F. 7 0	M. F. 28 0	From the Chaungkwa camp the road runs very steeply up the spur of the Taopi hill and passes through the post. The ascent continues pretty general all the way up to the point at which the path reaches its highest about 300 feet below the summit of the hill and some 4,200 feet above sea-level. A path for mules has been with great difficulty and labour constructed up this spur, sometimes by zigzags and sometimes along the face of tremendous khuds. From the steepness of the hill side landslips must be looked for in the rainy season, and the road will need constant repair. Already two or three mules have been killed from falling down the khud. On ascending the hill the open is jungle is first met with, but at about 2,000 feet firs begin to appear, and at 3,000 feet rhododendrons become plentiful. These are in full bloom about February. At about 5½ miles a saddle is reached, and down the khud on the south side, 300 feet below the ridge, water is procurable. From the top of the hill a fine view of the Myittha valley is obtained, and signalling with Kán can be carried on. The road skirting the side of the hill for a short distance descends to the Taungtek camp by another spur equally steep and zigzagged like the ascent. The camp is about 900 feet below the summit. Here there is accommodation for about 100 men in huts above the post. Officers' quarters are also built here. Water is obtained for drinking from a small stream below the post, but mules have to be watered at a different stream beyond their lines, which are on a spur some 400 yards to the south. Grass and bamboos are plentiful here.
		4. Rawván ...	7 4	35 4	From the camp the road is easy all the way to Rawván and gradually ascends up a long spur, skirting round the sides of the small hills and nowhere steep. At 2 miles it passes over a long saddle, where there is a halting place called Bômbôk. Water is plentiful from a small stream about 250 yards down the hill side on the north. At the western end of this saddle, about 2½ miles from camp, the road to the old site of Néshaung turns off to the north-west. At about 5½ miles the road ascends to a saddle of the main ridge to the north of a peak called Torsongklang (about 5,700 feet). From this point a path runs south-east to Lamtôk village. From the saddle Rawván is in sight and the road descends along the hill side all the way to it. The village of Farong can also be seen to the west and Hrongwin to the north-north-west. At about 6½ miles the path to Tinam turns off to the east, and at about 7 miles two well-defined paths are seen, the

FROM KÁN TO HÁKA—*continued.*

Authorities.		Number and Names of Stages, Rivers and Streams.	Distances.		Remarks.
Military.	Civil.		Intermediate.	Total.	
G.O.C. Myingyán District.	Political Officer, Chin Hills.	**4. Rawván**—*cont.*			first of which leads to the Rawván village, "*taungyas,*" while the other goes to Bôndwa. Rawván is a Chinmé village of about 50 houses and is under Yôkwa. There are also Baungshé families living in the village. Water is plentiful from streams from the hill above, and a few fowls, &c., are procurable. The post is on a spur to the north-west of the village; accommodation for 100 men. Water is obtained from a stream between it and the village. Grass and firewood are plentiful.
		5. Yôkwa ... ... Lai-vár and three other streams.	M. F. 9 0	M. F. 44 4	General direction west-north-west. On leaving camp the road at first runs north and is level along the hill side. It then descends a spur to Farong village, also called Sorva, a Yôkwa village, containing about a dozen houses. From here it runs west along the hill side and gradually descends to two small streams in the bottom of the valley, which it crosses and ascends pretty steeply to the top of the next spur. From here it is again level along the side of the hill and then gradually descends through taungya, crossing another spur to a small stream at about 6 miles. From here it crosses another low spur and descends at about 7 miles to the Lai vár stream, about 12 feet broad and bridged. From here it ascends a very steep spur by zigzags and, crossing this, keeps along the hill side, gradually ascending to the spur above the post, whence it runs down at an easy gradient into the post. The path to the village leads along the hill side above the post. The post is situated on a spur and is garrisoned (May 1890) by a force of 100 2-4th Gurkhas under a British Officer. Water is obtained from streams on both sides. The village is about a mile to the west of the post. It contains about 150 houses. Supplies of fowls and vegetables are procurable.
		6. Bwétet ... Ein-vár and Bwétet-vár streams.	9 0	53 4	Direction north-north-west. The road from the post runs gradually down to the Ein-vár at about 2 miles, which is bridged; beyond this the ascent is very steep and zigzagged up to the top of a spur at about 4½ miles. From here it descends again gradually, working along the hill side and round spurs until at 8½ miles it reaches the Bwétet stream about 10 feet broad and bridged. From the stream there is a pretty steep ascent, which is zigzagged up to the village. The road, however, does not pass through the village, but passing below it gradually rises to the post, which is on a level piece of ground on the hill side. The site is good and well sheltered. Water is obtained from a small stream 200 yards to the west. The village of Bwétet is independent and contains about 46 houses. The Chief, Shulut, is brother to two of the head Chiefs in the Háka Ywama. A few fowls and vegetables are procurable. Grass and firewood are plentiful.
		7. Háka ... ... Mingnu-vár stream.	10 0	63 4	General direction north-north-west. Leaving the Bwétet post the road crosses the stream, from which water is obtained, and runs over a spur, descending gradually till it reaches the

FROM KÁN TO HÁKA—*continued.*

Authorities. Military.	Authorities. Civil.	Number and Names of Stages, Rivers and Streams.	Distances. Intermediate.	Distances. Total.	Remarks.
G.O.C. Myingyán District.	Political Officer, Chin Hills.	**7. Háka**—*cont.*			Mingnu stream at about 2 miles. This stream is about 12 feet broad and is bridged. From here the ascent is steep and the road, zigzagged at first, leads gradually up the side of a spur till Mingnu village is seen at 4 miles. The road passes round the back of the village and continues to ascend steadily to the top of the range, which is reached at about 7½ miles. Mingnu village contains 46 houses. Water is brought by leads from the hill side above. Some fowls, &c., are procurable. The road, after reaching the top of the ridge, runs along it for some distance and then begins to descend about 1½ miles from Háka post. The altitude of the ridge, where the road leaves it, is about 7,100 feet above sea-level, and Rongkláug, the highest peak above Háka, is about 7,500. From the top of the ridge the path runs through dense tree jungle until on nearing the post it suddenly emerges on open grassy spurs and runs down to the post. The post is square in shape and is surrounded by a thick hedge of abattis. There are no earthwork defences along the faces, but the corners are guarded with block-houses. There are seven large barracks, one of which contains officers' quarters and mess and another Commissariat stores and hospital. It is garrisoned by a wing of a regiment. There are also the Commanding Officer's quarters and the house of the Civil Officer, besides servant and followers' quarters, cook-houses, magazine, and mule lines. The post is commanded by the hills to the south-east. Háka Ywama is built just below the post and contains about 250 houses, while the new village called Kôtár is about ¼ a mile to the west and contains about 200 houses. Water is plentiful from streams rising in the hill side, and two of these flow down, one on each side of the post. Supplies of all sorts are obtainable, but paddy is scarce.

ALTERNATIVE I.

FROM KÁN TO CHAUNGKWA (STAGE 2).

BY H. GROVES, ESQ., PUBLIC WORKS DEPARTMENT, APRIL 1890.

Military.	Civil.	Stages	Intermediate M.	Intermediate F.	Total M.	Total F.	Remarks.
G.O.C. Myingyán District.	Political Officer, Chin Hills.	**1. Thayetpin camp.** Myittha river, Lukh, Kabé, Panné, Likh, Kôntung, and Laungkat chaungs.	**15**	**4**	15	4	General direction west. Leaving Kán the road crosses the Myittha river and then runs down the left bank to the mouth of the Panné chaung at about 1 mile. Before reaching it it crosses first a small nullah called the Lukh chaung and then the Kabé chaung and is impassable in the wet weather, when another line has to be taken down the right bank of the Myittha to the village of Yanyéshin at about 3 miles. Here the river is crossed and the wet weather road runs along the top of a spur and joins the dry weather road at about 6 miles. The dry weather road runs up the Panné chaung, keeping pretty close to the stream until it reaches the Panné Tandan Sakhán at 9 miles. Here, in the dry weather, the only water is from pools in the bed of the stream; continuing up the chaung the road reaches the Yeshin Sakáhn at 12½ miles, where there is a

No. 11.

FROM KÁN TO HÁKA—*continued.*

ALTERNATIVE I—*continued.*

Authorities.		Number and Names of Stages, Rivers and Streams.	Distances.		Remarks.
Military.	Civil.		Intermediate.	Total.	
G.O.C. Myingyán District.	Political Officer, Chin Hills.	**1. Thayetpin camp**—*cont.*			perennial spring of good water. From here the road crosses a small spur and descends to the Likh chaung, beyond which it again crosses a small spur and descends to the Kôntung chaung. This is a stream of some length and, though dry in the dry weather, it comes down in flood during the rains and will have to be bridged where the road crosses it. The path runs up the left bank of the nullah for some distance and then, crossing it, ascends another small spur, from which it descends to the Thayetpin Sakhán. All the gradients on this march are easy. Thayetpin camp is well situated on high ground on the left bank of the Laungkat chaung.
		2. Chaungkwa ... Wuntu, Shimpi, and Méshaung chaungs.	M. F. 4 0	M. F. 19 4	From camp the road runs up the left bank of the Laungkat chaung and has been cut out of the hill side. In most places it runs about 50 or 100 feet above the stream. It crosses the Wuntu chaung at about 1½ miles and then the Shimpi chaung at 2½ miles. This stream is also liable to flood in the wet season, though dry in the hot weather. Arriving opposite Chaungkwa the road crosses the Méshaung var by a bridge and so avoids the 40 crossings necessary by the old road *viâ* Kabé hill, the steep ascent and descent of the Kabé hill being also avoided. The wet weather road by Yanyéshin village is about 3 miles longer than the dry weather road described above, and the distance can be better divided by a stage at the Panné Tandan camp; but in the hot weather, when the dry weather road would naturally be used, a good supply of water for watering transport animals cannot be obtained till the Laungkat chaung is reached. The wet weather stages would therefore be (1) Panné Tandan camp, 12 miles; (2) Chaungkwa, 10½ miles—total 22½ miles.

BRANCH I.

FROM RAWVÁN (STAGE 4) TO THETTA *viâ* POMLÁN.

BY CAPT. J. H. JONES, 2ND MADRAS INFANTRY, MAY 1890.

Military.	Civil.	Number and Names of Stages, Rivers and Streams.	Intermediate.	Total.	Remarks.
G.O.C. Myingyán District.	Political Officer, Chin Hills.	**1. Thetta** ... ... Two or three small streams and the Rai-vár.	(?)10 0	(?)10 0	From the Rawván post the road ascends the spur behind to the top of the ridge, along which it runs and then descends to Pomlán village at about 3 miles. Pomlán is a small independent village of about 30 houses. It is undefended and commanded from the north. Water from two small streams, not very plentiful. The path now crosses a small stream and ascends the spur, beyond which is steep and difficult. Crossing this it descends to another stream, the ascent from which is also rough and steep. The path now runs along a wooded plateau, and then runs down gradually over a cultivated hill side to the Rai-vár, from which it ascends to Thetta village. For description of Thetta *see* Branch Route No. II below.

FROM KÁN TO HÁKA—*continued.*

BRANCH II.

FROM YÔKWA (STAGE 5) TO THETTA.

BY LIEUT. E. W. M. NORIE, PAID ATTACHÉ, INTELLIGENCE BRANCH, APRIL 1890.

Authorities. Military.	Authorities. Civil.	Number and Names of Stages, Rivers and Streams.	Distances. Intermediate.	Distances. Total.	Remarks.
			M. F.	M. F.	
G.O.C. Myingyán District.	Political Officer, Chin Hills.	**1. Thetta** ... ... Rai-vár and a small stream.	**9 0**	9 0	General direction south-south-west. From the Yôkwa post the road runs up on to the ridge at the back of the Ywama, and it is pretty steep. From here it runs along the ridge pretty level for a short distance and then ascends again steeply. At about 2 miles a broad ditch has been cut right across the crest, which is here very narrow. The ditch is about 10 feet wide and 10 feet deep and the ascent from the Yôkwa side is very steep. The path continues steep up to 2¼ miles, after which it runs along very fairly level and is good. At about 4½ miles it crosses another ditch similar to the last, but rather smaller. Both these ditches are crossed by foot-bridges, consisting of a couple of logs laid side by side. The path continues level to 6 miles, when the main ridge is reached, and Thetta can be seen lying in the bottom of the broad open valley beyond. From here it leads down a very steep spur, which becomes almost precipitous lower down and reaches the Rai-vár at about 7½ miles. From here the path into Thetta is level and easy. Thetta is an independent village of about 200 houses and pays tribute to none of the neighbouring tribes. It is situated on a spur above the Rai-vár and is undefended. It could be best attacked from the spur on the north-west. The Rai-vár ("vár" means a stream) is the main tributary of the Zahaw stream. It flows in a south-easterly direction and joins the Zahaw about 10 miles above its mouth. There is no water along the road till the Rai-vár is reached.

No. 12.

From KÁN to HANTA.

BY D. ROSS, ESQ., FROM INFORMATION SUPPLIED BY THA PÉ, AUGUST 1889.

Military	Civil	Stages	Intermediate	Total	Remarks
G.O.C. Myingyán District.	Political Officer, Chin Hills.	**1. Hnanka creek.**	**11 0**	...	Small creek with plenty of water now, but it goes dry in the cold weather, say, about the beginning of January. Plenty of coarse grass. Ponies will eat it readily at present.
		2. Taungwun creek.	**9 0**	20 0	Called Pépa by Chins. Large creek with plenty of water at all seasons. Road passes through the same kind of jungle as from Kán to Hnanka. No ascents or descents. There is room for a very large camp here. Plenty of *eng-daing*, grass, and *kaing*.

FROM KÁN TO HANTA—*continued.*

Authorities. Military.	Authorities. Civil.	Number and Names of Stages, Rivers and Streams.	Distances. Intermediate. M. F.		Distances. Total. M. F.		Remarks.
G.O.C. Myingyén District.	Political Officer, Chin Hills.	**3. Gwébin Sakhángyi (on the Taungwun creek).**	**8**	**0**	28	0	At the last camp the creek divides into two branches. The path follows the north one and runs up the bed, crossing here and there to avoid bends. No hills to cross. There is room for a large camp at this place also. There is running water here at all seasons. Bamboo jungle about this camp.
		4. Tinshubin Sakhán.	**10**	**0**	38	0	Leaving the camp, road begins going up-hill after a few 100 yards, and it continues to ascend the whole way, but it is not steep in any place and could easily be made fit for transport animals. There are no narrow or difficult places. About half-way fir trees are first met. There is room at this place for over 1,000 men on some flat ground. In the north side, about 50 yards from the camp, there is a small ravine with a perennial spring of good water. In the dry weather this supply becomes less, but if it were carefully collected in cisterns would probably supply enough for a 100 men (from the description I think that the water-sup[p]ly of this place will be capable of great improvement). Th[e] Myintha road comes in about midway between Gwébin an[d] Tinshubin Sakháns.
		5. Langwé ...	**7**	**0**	45	0	This is the parting of the roads—one leads to Wünhla, the other to Hanta. This camp is on the top of the range. To the west you look into the Nanpathé valley and you can see the taungyas of Wünhla, Háka, Hanta, and Kwéshin. To the east a large hill obstructs the view into the Myittha valley. Water is very scarce here at all seasons. It is obtained from the bottom of a ravine (called Napyaw-Uyin chaung), about a mile distant to the east. There is plenty of water there at all seasons. The way down is very steep. There is plenty of level ground here. The jungle is fir and sé, with short grass. No jungle undergrowth. The road all the way is along the top of a ridge.
		6. Hanta	**10**	**0**	55	0	Capital road along an open ridge to within 1 mile of Hanta, when the village can be seen. The road then goes rather steeply down the side of the hill through taungyas and, crossing a little nullah with some water in it, ascends for a few yards and enters the the village from the south side. Hanta Ywama contains 80 houses and has 50 or 60 guns. The headmen are Neykat, his brother, Yauntaba Asseyin and Bizanpa. The villages under Hanta are— Haipa (25 houses, 15 guns), about 7 miles to the west. Kaipan (15 houses, 10 guns), about 4 miles to the north. *Note.*—From Langwé Sakhán to Wunhla is 4 daings (10 miles)—6 miles down to the Nanpathé and 4 up to Wunhla. This part has already been described. Transport animals could go at present to Gwébin Sakhán and, with little work on road, they could go on to Hanta and Wunhla. From Hanta Lieutenant Norie gives a route from native information (April 1890) to Kwéshin, a large Táshôn village of over 50 houses, distant about 20 miles. Passing another smaller Táshôn village called Hrinte about midway before reaching

FROM KÁN TO HANTA—*continued.*

Authorities.		Number and Names of Stages, Rivers and Streams.	Distances.		Remarks.
Military.	Civil.		Inter-mediate.	Total.	
G.O.C. Myingyán District.	Political Officer, Chin Hills.	**6. Hanta**—*cont.*			which the Nanpathé river has to be crossed. The road appears to be the usual Chin road, full of steep ascents and descents, especially at the crossing of the Nanpathé which is very difficult. From Kwéshin roads run to Minkin (*vide* Route No. 9, Chin Hills Division) *viâ* Simpi, about 15 miles and thence to Táshôn Ywama (Falám) and to the Minlédaung villages (*vide* Route No. 5, Central Division).

No. 13.

From MAGWÉ to TAUNGDWINGYI.

BY LIEUT.-COL. M. CARY, COMMANDING DETACHMENT RIFLE BRIGADE AND AT TAUNGDWINGYI, 1886.

Military	Civil	Number and Names of Stages, Rivers and Streams	Intermediate M.	Intermediate F.	Total M.	Total F.	Remarks
G.O.C. Myingyán District.	Commissioner, Southern Division, and Deputy Commissioner, Magwé.	**1. Thamandalaing.**	12	0	...		Accommodation for 150 men. Water not plentiful, but good. Paddy plentiful. Road from Magwé at first very bad, afterwards firmer and more open, finally very loose sand.
		2. Tamo	5	0	17	0	Good accommodation for 200 men. Kyaung well situated on high ground overlooking Yen river. Paddy reported scarce. Water good and plentiful. Road from Thamandalaing very bad; country open for 2 miles, then hilly and very thick jungle. Half-way passed Shabinhla village.
		3. Gwégaung ...	12	0	29	0	Small kyaung close to river. Poor accommodation; water plentiful. Road from Tamo very bad indeed, narrow lanes with loose sand. Forded Yen river at Ondwé 100 yards wide, 2 feet deep; afterwards road very bad. Had to cross fields of high standing Indian corn. Afterwards road on higher ground; but rains had washed the wheel ruts out to such a depth that the ridge in the centre was higher than the axle trees. This had to be cut off for a distance of 2 or 3 miles. Many carts were broken.
		4. Wagyin ...	5	0	34	0	Very large kyaungs on high ground above river. Good accommodation for 300 or 400 men. Good water and plentiful; not much paddy or grass. Ford river beyond Gwégaung, 100 yards wide and 2 feet deep. Very sandy lanes through dense jungle. In places the track was entirely concealed by grass 5 feet high.
		5. Kani	5	0	39	0	Small kyaung. Accommodation for 150 men close to river. Good water and plenty of paddy. Road very bad. River impassable after heavy rain.

FROM MAGWÉ TO TAUNGDWINGYI—*continued.*

Authorities. Military.	Authorities. Civil.	Number and Names of Stages, Rivers and Streams.	Distances. Intermediate.		Distances. Total.		Remarks.
			M.	F.	M.	F.	
G.O.C. Myingyán District.	Commissioner, Southern Division, and Deputy Commissioner, Magwé.	**6. Shwéyándaw pagoda.**	9	0	48	0	This is a large pagoda in thick jungle. No water. On leaving Kani crossed the Yen river, above men's waists and very rapid, 100 yards wide. Afterwards crossed Sidôn river four times; this was not in flood, but about 2 to 3 feet deep and the banks high and very difficult for carts. Reached Shwéyándaw pagoda and rest-huts at 4 P.M.; but there is no water near. The column therefore proceeded to Kyésadaw 2 miles north-east, where there is a kyaung. Crossed river again; deep muddy banks, into which the oxen sank to their shoulders and had to be unyoked and the carts dragged up by the troops. Halted at Kyésadaw, Thursday, 21st October.
		7. Taungdwingyi.	6	0	54	0	Marched from Kyésadaw at 12-30 A.M., 22nd; recrossed river and repassed Shwéyándaw pagoda; thence the pathway lies through dense jungle in which the guide frequently lost the track, until about 5 miles from Taungdwingyi, about the village of Changain, the country becomes more open and the road after crossing some paddy-fields becomes much better until Taungdwingyi is reached. The country here is much more open and well fitted for cavalry. The column consisted of— 1st Rifle Brigade, two companies; 1st Madras Lancers, one troop; Punjabi Police, 55 men. Left Magwé 15th October 1886 and made seven marches to Taungdwingyi, having halted one day, the 21st, at Kyésadaw and reached Taungdwingyi 22nd October.

No. 14.

From MAGWÉ to YAMÉTHIN *viâ* NATMAUK.

I. B. COMPILATION, MARCH 1888.

Military	Civil	Stages	M.	F.	M.	F.	Remarks
G.O.C. Myingyán District.	Commissioner, Southern Division, and Deputy Commissioner, Magwé.	**1. Kántha** ...	10	0	10	0	Magwé on left bank Irrawaddy. Direction east. The road rises very gradually from the Irrawaddy; it is good for traffic of all sorts, except that the sandy nature of the soil makes it very heavy and tiring in the dry season. Almost the whole length of this first stage is cultivated with dry crops, principally oil-seeds and jowari. Villages are numerous, the principal one being Kántha, 7½ miles, where there is accommodation in kyaungs for 200 men. Water from ponds; scarce in the dry weather. Kántha is a group of three villages. There is one kyaung with accommodation for 40 men (30 square feet a man). Water from surface wells; very scarce after March. Supplies procurable.
		2. Gyokôn ... Wet chaung.	7	4	17	4	Direction east-north-east. The road remains the same in character for 4 miles, then it falls suddenly to the valley of the Wet chaung, but rises

From MAGWÉ to YAMÉTHIN *viâ* NATMAUK—*continued.*

Authorities. Military.	Authorities. Civil.	Number and Names of Stages, Rivers and Streams.	Distances. Intermediate. M. F.	Distances. Total. M. F.	Remarks.
G.O.C. Myingyán District.	Commissioner, Southern Division, and Deputy Commissioner, Magwé.	**2. Gyokôn**—*cont.*			again immediately to the high ground which borders that stream. Cultivation is not so general as in the first stage and is confined to a radius of a mile or so round each village. The Wet stream flows close to Gyokôn on the north; it is very sandy with high banks, and is here 400 yards wide. No running water except in rains. Gyokôn, a large strongly-fenced village on the edge of the left bank of the Wet stream. Kyaungs with room for 270 men. Water from surface wells in the water-course.
		3. Téhôn ... Yé-aung chaung.	**10 0**	27 4	Direction north-north-east. Road as in the latter part of last stage for 2 miles to Thánbôk, a small village on the left bank of the Yé-aung stream, about a mile above its junction with the Wet river. Water here is very scarce as early in the dry weather as February. Thence cross the nullah and over undulating country to Téhôn, the last mile being very heavy going. Yé-aung stream course crossed north of Thánbôk. Téhôn is a group of several villages; the largest has a market place and weekly bazaar. Kyaungs with room for 80 men. Water very poor and scarce.
		4. Natmauk ...	**12 4**	40 0	Direction east. Road very heavy with sand at first, then becomes firmer and rises gradually to the ridge of the Magula hills, the watershed between the Wet and Yen rivers and the boundary line between the Magwé and Taungdwingyi townships. The country here is very open; cultivated round villages, and covered elsewhere with thin scrub jungle and coarse grass. After crossing the hills the scarcity of water becomes greater even than before. Palambin, 5½ miles, is deserted for six months of the year on this account. Thwingyi, 8 miles, a small village with one kyaung. Water poor. This road now passes through woods of small *in* and teak trees until close to Kángyi, which is the western of the four villages which form the parish of Natmauk. For description *see* Route No. 21, Stage 9.
		5. Thamôngôn ... Yen river.	**16 0**	56 0	Direction east-north-east. A winding sandy road from Natmauk to the Yen river, crossed 1 mile from Natmauk, is here 300 yards broad. Ford easy, except in floods. Right bank low; left bank 25 feet high ascended by a steep cutting. For 2 miles over undulating ground and through very thin jungle, thence the jungle gets thicker and the country more hilly. At 8 miles reach the deserted village of Kalashin. The road runs north-north-east through thick jungle for 8 miles and over low stony hills to Thamôngôn, a village of about 50 houses, approached by a steep road from the Pin chaung, 50 yards broad. Water from surface wells in dry weather. A fair accommodation in kyaungs and zayáts for 65 men.
		6. Uyin	**15 0**	71 0	Good cart track for a mile or so past the village through cultivated land, fairly level. Then turns suddenly and passes over west spur of the Nyindgyi hills through thin jungle to Thigyaung. Thigyaung is a village of about 40 houses. Accommodation in kyaungs and zayáts for about 40 men. Water fair and plentiful from

FROM MAGWÉ TO YAMÉTHIN *viâ* NATMAUK—*continued.*

Authorities. Military.	Authorities. Civil.	Number and Names of Stages, Rivers and Streams.	Distances. Intermediate.	Distances. Total.	Remarks.
G.O.C. Myingyán District.	Commissioner, Southern Division, and Deputy Commissioner, Magwé.	**6. Uyin**—*cont.*			well and chaung to east. Road now runs east across three chaungs to Myinthagyi, a very large and rich village with a police post. Accommodation for a large force in kyaungs in the village. Ground for encamping all round. Water good and plentiful from the chaung to north of village and from wells. Supplies, cattle, and carts plentiful. From here a good road runs north-east over undulating country covered with *in* jungle and crosses three chaungs. Uyin is a large village, with accommodation for 200 men in kyaungs and zayáts in the village. Ground for camping all round. Water good and plentiful from a chaung to north of village. Supplies plentiful. Cattle and carts procurable. From Thigyaung in this stage there is a branch road to Pinzi, Stage 8 of Route No. 24, for details of which *see* that route. The distance is 18 miles, and the road is practicable for carts.
G.O.C. Rangoon District.	Commissioner, Eastern Division, and Deputy Commissioner, Yaméthin.	**7. Kyundôn-Séywa.** One chaung.	M. 6 F. 0	M. 77 F. 0	Road runs north-east and is a good cart road. Country the same as before. No water along the road which follows the crest of a ridge. Kyaundôn Séywa was in February 1888 a military post capable of accommodating 150 men. There are no kyaungs, but a large number of men could be put up in the houses of the village. There is plenty of good water from a well in the fort and a tank where animals could be watered on the north. There is a signal station here, and ordinary supplies and about 40 carts procurable.
		8. Yenaung ...	18 0	95 0	General direction east. At 2½ miles Nyaungôn; at 3½ miles Gaigyi. Hence to Pébingalé, a small village with no accommodation. Water from a chaung ½ mile to south. Then descend for some time and then passing through jungle cross two chaungs, the first of which has water in it in February. The road here passes over low ground and is probably difficult in wet weather. Reach Thanatgôn, a small village with no accommodation. Water from one well in the village. About 1 mile further on reach Thapángyaung, a fair-sized village with kyaungs for 100 men on the south side. Water from wells on north side. Ordinary supplies obtainable. Thaphangyaung is about 8 miles from Yenaung. Then cross a chaung and ascend, passing a small tank on the right of the road. At 9 miles pass to south of steep hill with pagodas on it, sides covered with forest jungle. Then along high ground crossing two chaungs to a well on the road side. Hence the village of Saitchu is seen about ½ mile to the north with kyaungs on the west and wells in a chaung on east and west sides. From the well on the road continue for ½ mile and reach Kantsún at 15½ miles. Then along a road cleared of jungle over hard soil through forest jungle with one or two belts of paddy land, which are probably bad in the wet weather, to Yégyán at 16½ miles. Water from well to south of the village. Pass over some paddy before reaching Yenaung. A large village with a military police post to the south. Accommodation for a large force in numerous kyaungs on south and east of the village. Good water from wells to the west of the village. All ordinary supplies obtainable from the Myo-ôk. Village of Yenzu to south of police post.

FROM MAGWÉ TO YAMÉTHIN *viâ* NATMAUK—*continued.*

Authorities. Military.	Authorities. Civil.	Number and Names of Stages, Rivers and Streams.	Distances. Intermediate. M. F.	Distances. Total. M. F.	Remarks.
G.O.C. Rangoon District.	Commr., Eastern Divn., and Deputy Commr., Yaméthin.	**9. Yaméthin** ...	17 0	112 0	Road from here runs south-east and is good though sandy for the first 6 miles. It runs along the foot of a ridge of hills covered with thin scrub jungle and crosses some small nullahs. About 1 mile from Yédaw it enters paddy and runs across paddy almost the whole way to Yaméthin, and in the wet weather is almost impassable as the ground is very heavy. Yédaw, at 7 miles, is a large village on the Thitsôn chaung and contains a police post. Accommodation for a considerable number of men in kyaungs, &c. Water from a chaung to east of village. Supplies and a considerable number of carts obtainable. For description of Yaméthin, *see* Route No. 6, Lower Burma Division.

ALTERNATIVE I.

FROM NATMAUK (STAGE 4) TO THAMÔNGÔN (STAGE 5).

I. B. COMPILATION, MARCH 1888.

Military	Civil	Stages	Intermediate	Total	Remarks
G.O.C. Myingyán District.	Commissioner, Southern Division, and Deputy Commissioner, Magwé.	**1. Lébu** ... ... Yen river, 1½ miles from Natmauk. Pyin chaung, 20 yards broad.	16 0	16 0	General direction east by north. A winding and sandy road from Natmauk to the Yen river. Ford easy except in floods. Right bank low, left bank 25 feet high. Road ascends by a steep cutting. Sadaw village south of the road on the left bank of the river. From the Yen for 2 miles through very thin jungle, thence to Lébu. The jungle is thicker, but nowhere very dense. At 8 miles cross small chaung with a little stagnant water, and pass the site of the village of Kalashin (deserted and burnt). The main road between Taungdwingyi and Yaméthin crosses here. At 11 miles pass small village of Kabaungán on the top of a low hill. (Fair water from well south-west of village.) A good mule track, but bad for carts. Lébu, 40 houses. A moderately plentiful supply of bad water from pools in the Pin chaung. Well-built pôngyi kyaung with accommodation for 65 men (at 30 square feet per man). Supplies for rationing men and transport animals procurable.
		2. Thamôngôn ... Pin chaung.	6 4	22 4	General direction north-west to 1 mile beyond Thamôngôn; thence north-east over low hill through thin jungle of small *in*, &c., to Thamôngôn, 6½ miles.

No. 15.

From MIMBU to NAPÉ.

I. B. COMPILATION, 1887.

Military	Civil	Stages	Intermediate	Total	Remarks
G.O.C. Myingyán District.	Commr., Southern Divn., and Deputy Commr., Mimbu.	**1. Segu** ... ... Maw chaung.	12 0	12 0	There are several routes from Mimbu to Napé, the best of which *in the dry season* appears to be as follows,* but in the rainy season the routes described in Alternatives II and III must be used. Direction west-north-west. Cart track over low hills through undulating jungly country, good in dry season, difficult

* From a report by Lieut. H. B. Walker, D.C.L.I., dated March 1891, it appears that the route now used is as follows: Mimbu to Singaing (10), thence to Pyawbwé (15), Padeng (11), and Napé (7)—total 43, though he commences by stating the distance to be 45 miles. He gives no details of the road.

FROM MIMBU TO NAPÉ—*continued.*

Authorities.		Number and Names of Stages, Rivers and Streams.	Distances.		Remarks.
Military.	Civil.		Intermediate.	Total.	
G.O.C. Myingyán District.	Commissioner, Southern Division, and Deputy Commissioner, Mimbu.	**1. Segu**—*cont.*			in the rains and impassable after heavy rain for one to three days. Segu is a large village of upwards of 500 houses on the right bank of the Maw river. Accommodation in kyaungs for 1,000 men. Good water from river and wells. Large bazaar; cattle and carts plentiful. Road to the north leads to Legain and Salin.
		2. Paung ... ... Maw chaung.	M. F. 10 0	M. F. 22 0	Direction south-west. Cart track following right bank Maw river. It traverses fairly open and level country partly cultivated and passes several villages. Paung village of 40 houses on Maw river. Accommodation for 50 men in kyaung. Good water.
		3. Shwézetdaw ... Maw chaung.	14 0	36 0	Direction west. Cart road; cross the Maw at starting and follow left bank passing Kôntha, and recrossing the river before entering Sedaw at 6 miles. Country so far jungly, but fairly level. From Sedaw cart road through undulating and fairly open jungle country, impassable for carts in rains, but good in dry season. Cross Maw river three times. At 14 miles Shwézetdaw, about 60 houses, inhabited by pagoda slaves, descendants of people given as slaves by the king to the pagoda which is a very sacred one. Accommodation in zayáts for 200 men. Good water. Strong position amongst the pagodas here, frequently held by dacoits in 1886-88.
		4. Napé ... ... Maw chaung.	9 0	44 0	Direction west-south-west. The distance by the cart road, which follows the bed of the Maw river, and is only passable in the dry season, is 9 miles. There are besides two foot-paths through the hills, one north, the other south of the Maw river, by which the distance is about 6 miles; these paths are hilly, stony and difficult. Napé is a place of 200 houses, and the entrenched position there is very strongly situated on high ground above the Maw river. The surrounding country is thick jungle, and the place is very unhealthy in the rainy season, and up to the beginning or middle of December. It is an important position, being situated at the junction of several roads, which lead from here to Myothit and Tainda, to Mimbu, to Salin, to the Yaw district, and to Arakan *viâ* the Aeng pass. There is accommodation for 150 men in three kyaungs, also for 250 men and two guns in the post. Good water and cattle can be obtained, also fowls and paddy in small quantities. About 50 carts for transport could be procured in and about Napé.

ALTERNATIVE I.

FROM SEGU (STAGE 1) TO SEDAW (*see* STAGE 3).

I. B. COMPILATION, 1887.

Military	Civil	Stage	Intermediate	Total	Remarks
G.O.C. Myingyán District.	Commr., Southern Divn., and Deputy Commr., Mimbu.	**1. Sedaw** ... ... Maw river.	15 0	15 0	Direction south-west. Cart track through undulating, fairly open jungle, impassable in the rains, but good at other seasons. Cross the Maw river, fordable, on leaving Segu, and follow left bank, recrossing the river before entering Sedaw which consists of two small villages, Sedawgôn and Tetetywa, aggregating about 35 houses; no kyaungs; good water.

FROM MIMBU TO NAPÉ—*continued.*

ALTERNATIVE II.

FROM PAUNG (STAGE 2) TO NAPÉ (STAGE 4) *viâ* PYAWBWÉ AND PADENG.

I. B. COMPILATION, 1887.

Authorities. Military.	Authorities. Civil.	Number and Names of Stages, Rivers and Streams.	Distances. Inter-mediate. M. F.	Distances. Total. M. F.	Remarks.
G.O.C. Myingyán District.	Commissioner, Southern Division, and Deputy Commissioner, Mimbu.	**1. Pyawbwé** ...	**13 0**	13 0	Direction south-south-west. For 8 miles the road, which is sandy and gravelly, passes through low hills in a jungly country, and about a dozen water-channels are crossed, which are dry except for an hour or so during and after heavy rain. For the remaining 5 miles the road is hilly, steep, jungly, and difficult for carts during the rains. For the first 8 miles no water can be obtained except for a day or so after heavy rain, and during the dry season none can be obtained the whole way. Two small villages are passed, Khôtgyi or Manmani at mile 10 and Mezalibu at mile 12. Pyawbwé is a wretched village of about 15 houses, has no kyaungs, but has good water.
		2. Padeng ... Man chaung.	**11 0**	24 0	Direction west. This road, though used by carts, is difficult as it crosses hills with steep gradients the greater part of the way. The ascents and descents are difficult from the rockiness of the ground. The whole route is jungly; thin *in* and cutch, till within 1 mile of Singyidain, after that thick bamboo. There are no villages on the road till Singyidain on the opposite bank of the Man river to Padeng is reached. The river has good clear water with a sandy bed and is about 1½ feet deep in the dry season. Padeng has about 150 houses with some large kyaungs suitable for 250 men. Supplies as at Napé. Like Napé the place is said to be very unhealthy.
		3. Napé ... ... Man chaung.	**7 0**	31 0	Direction north-west. There are two roads, an upper and a lower. The latter is somewhat shorter than the former and leads along the left bank of the Man river, through level and open ground cultivated with paddy, but is impassable for carts in the rains; at that season even the upper road is heavy and difficult.

ALTERNATIVE III.

FROM MIMBU TO PYAWBWÉ (STAGE 1 OF ALTERNATIVE II) *viâ* SINGAING.

I. B. COMPILATION, 1887.

Military	Civil	Stage	Inter-mediate	Total	Remarks
G.O.C. Myingyán District.	Commr., Southern Divn., and Deputy Commr., Mimbu.	**1. Singaing** ...	**12 0**	12 0	Direction south-west. For the first 2 miles, the road leads through jungle, is heavy and difficult; for the remainder of the way it is good, the soil being sandy and the country fairly open. Kôntha, a small village, is passed at mile 7. Singaing has 250 houses, and kyaungs for 100 men. Good water is obtained from wells, which are mostly dug in the bed of a water-course, which is dry except in the rains.

FROM MIMBU TO NAPÉ—*continued*

ALTERNATIVE III—*continued.*

Authorities. Military.	Authorities. Civil.	Number and Names of Stages, Rivers and Streams.	Distances. Intermediate. M. F.	Distances. Total. M. F.	Remarks.
G.O.C. Myingyán District.	Commr., Southern Divn., and Deputy Commr., Mimbu.	**2. Pyawbwé** ...	**15 0**	27 0	Direction south-west. For 10 miles the road is good and fairly level, with a gravelly and sandy soil. Then for 3 miles low hills are crossed. The last 2 miles are steep and difficult, and one large creek, which is however dry except after storms, is crossed. The route leads the whole way through thin *eng* jungle, and no villages are passed.

BRANCH I.

FROM PAUNG (STAGE 2) TO SEGU (ROUTE NO. 17, STAGE 3).

BY LIEUT. SANDBACH, R.E.

Military	Civil	Stages	Intermediate	Total	Remarks
G.O.C. Myingyán District.	Commr., S. Div., and Deputy Commr., Mimbu.	**1. Segu** ... ... Pyaungdalin and Segu chaungs, both sandy beds 20 to 25 yards wide, dry in March.	**8 4**	8 4	First 5½ miles through open jungle, nearly level, no villages and no water from February onwards until the rains. At 5½ miles Pégôn. Thence straight road over cultivated land to Segu.

BRANCH II.

FROM KÔNTHA (*see* STAGE 3) TO PYÍLÔNGYAW (ROUTE NO. 17, STAGE 5).

I. B. COMPILATION, 1887.

Military	Civil	Stages	Intermediate	Total	Remarks
G.O.C. Myingyán District.	Commr., Southern Divn., and Deputy Commr., Mimbu.	**1. Pyílôngyaw** ... Môn chaung.	**17 0**	17 0	First 2 miles through jungle, following left bank of an irrigation canal, dry in March, to Kadingôn. Thence mostly over paddy cultivation for next 3 miles, passing the villages of Kyígôn, Sedaw and Shwégyaung at 3½, 4½ and 5 miles respectively. Thence mostly through open ground, light jungle and some paddy, passing Taingdaw (6½), Sainmalé (8), Padaw (9), and Kolohaung (14). At 16½ miles descend into valley of Môn river, and pass through paddy cultivation to Pyílôngyaw.

BRANCH III.

FROM PYAWBWÉ (STAGE 1 OF ALTERNATIVE II) TO KYAUKPÉ.

BY LIEUT. CARDEW, 2ND BENGAL LIGHT INFANTRY, JANUARY 1887.

Military	Civil	Stages	Intermediate	Total	Remarks
G.O.C. Myingyán District.	Commr., S. Divn., and Dy. Commr., Mimbu.	**1. Kyaukpé** ...	**3 2**	3 2	Direction south. Road fair, undulating, stony soil, thin small tree jungle. At 1¼ miles small village of Minlagyin west of road (? deserted).

FROM MIMBU TO NAPÉ—*continued.*

BRANCH IV.

FROM PADENG (STAGE 2 OF ALTERNATIVE II) TO KYAUKPÉ *viâ* DAKÔN AND MYOGÔN.

BY LIEUT. CARDEW, 2ND BENGAL LIGHT INFANTRY, JANUARY 1887.

Authorities. Military.	Authorities. Civil.	Number and Names of Stages, Rivers and Streams.	Distances. Intermediate. M.	F.	Total. M.	F.	Remarks.
G.O.C. Myingyán District.	Commissioner, Southern Division, and Deputy Commissioner, Mimbu.	**1. Dakôn** ... Môn river. Small stream from east 2¾ miles from Padeng. Maipya river from west opposite that village.	5	2	5	2	General direction south by west. The whole distance of the road follows the bed of the Môn river which is crossed seven times in this stage through high grass and scrub jungle. The fords are all from 6 to 18 inches deep; they would be quite impassable in the rains. Villages passed: Yaungbindôk, west of road, 1 mile from Padeng; Kyittaw 1¾ miles from Padeng, west of road (deserted); Kyauktalôn and Sedatku on opposite banks of river, 2¾ miles; Maipya, west of road, 4 miles. All the above are small villages except Maipya, where there are some kyaungs. Dakôn is on the right bank; about 40 houses, kyaungs and zayáts for 150 men.
		2. Myogôn ... Ki chaung ¼ mile from Dakôn. A very deep water-course, but little water in dry weather. Padeng chaung 5 miles, 200 yards, deep course; dry deep nullah, 6¼ miles; nullah with pond 60 by 80 yards, north of Myogôn.	8	0	13	2	General direction east by north for 5 miles, then south-east. A good cart track through jungle; 6 miles fairly open, 2 miles bamboos. Soil stony; no steep slopes except at nullahs. Ki chaung would be impassable in rains. Villages: Taungôn, two divisions, 500 yards apart (first about 800 yards from Dakôn), Sedatku (1,600 yards) north of road; all, including Myogôn, are small villages; about 15 houses. Good well at Myogôn; no kyaungs; cattle and a few fowls obtainable.
		3. Kyaukpé ... Padeng chaung recrossed (½ mile west of Myebyu); deep nullah in hills, 1½ miles from the ridge and 2 miles west of Kyaukpé; none of the above have running water. Standing pools in Padeng chaung at Yenshé and Kyaukpé.	11	2	24	4	No. 2 stage retraversed for nearly 3 miles. Thence general direction north for 2 miles and north-east or east, remainder of road. Road good, undulating through thin jungle for 6 miles to foot of high range of hills; then over ridge to Chaukpé; very stony and rough, with steep gradients, but fairly easy for mule carriage, except where blocked by fallen trees. The chaungs noted would be impassable in rains. Villages: Myébyu, Yinshé (5½ miles), a large village, about 40 houses, two small kyaungs and two zayáts; accommodation for 60 men; water scarce in nullah. Kyaukpé (about 35 houses), one kyaung and four zayáts, room for 100 men; water fair from nullah.

FROM MIMBU TO NAPÉ—*continued.*

BRANCH V.

FROM SINGAING (STAGE 1 OF ALTERNATIVE III) TO YAUNGYÁNDAUNG (ON THE RIGHT BANK OF THE IRRAWADDY, ABOUT 30 MILES NORTH OF THAYETMYO).

BY LIEUT. MARTER, 1ST BATTALION, RIFLE BRIGADE, 17TH NOVEMBER 1886.

Authorities. Military.	Authorities. Civil.	Number and Names of Stages, Rivers and Streams.	Distances. Intermediate. M.	F.	Distances. Total. M.	F.	Remarks.
G.O.C. Myingyán District.	Commissioner, Southern Division, and Deputy Commissioner, Mimbu.	**1. Chaungpyu** ...	8	0	8	0	No description is given of this stage.
		2. Thígôn ...	5	6	13	6	From Chaungpyu general direction of road south and south-west. Road fair and level, thick jungle on both sides. About 1 mile from Chaungpyu crosses nullah with high banks on both sides. Three miles from Chaungpyu village of Maungdaung, which has been deserted for a long time and is quite overgrown. From here there is a road leading to Yébaw. After leaving Maungdaung the road crosses the nullah before mentioned twice and the village of Thígôn is reached (deserted). There is no camping ground here. Water (obtained from nullah) is running and good, and at this time of year apparently plentiful.
		3. Dahatkôn ...	4	4	18	2	From Thígôn general direction south and south-west. After leaving the village road crosses the nullah at once. Road fair and level, dense jungle on both sides. One mile from Thígôn cross the nullah again, after which it runs along the left of the road. At 2½ miles village of Zigubin, very old and deserted and of no importance. After Zigubin the road crosses the big nullah once, and also a branch of the same. Four-and-a-half miles Dahatkôn, a fairly large village, but deserted. No camping ground or water, so the force moved on ½ mile and camped on rising ground to right of road. Water from nullah on the right, plentiful and good, but too far from camping ground.
		4. Kadé	4	6	23	0	From Dahatkôn general direction south-east and south. One mile after leaving camping ground is the village of Chaungpyu, deserted. From this village there are roads leading to Pagángán and Muthet. After Chaungpyu the country becomes hilly, but the jungle on either side not so dense and allowing of flanking parties to be thrown out. At 3½ miles the road crosses another road running from Minhla to Muthet. Road over hills very rough in places and difficult for carts; 4¾ miles camp Kadé. There is no village here, but it is the usual halting place for carts. As a camping ground very bad indeed, very small and enclosed by thick jungle. Water near from a small stream on the left of the road, good but not plentiful. Big nullah on the right with water, but no means of getting at it, owing to very high and steep banks.
		5. Dwébumyaung.	8	4	31	4	From Kadé general direction south-south-east. Road very rough and apparently long unused. Jungle on each side very dense. One-and-a-quarter miles from Kadé is a road branching off to Yébaw; road fairly level with

FROM MIMBU TO NAPÈ—*continued.*

BRANCH V—*continued.*

Authorities.		Number and Names of Stages, Rivers and Streams.	Distances.				Remarks.
Military.	Civil.		Intermediate.		Total.		
			M.	F.	M.	F.	
G.O.C. Myingyán District.	Commissioner, Southern Division, and Deputy Commissioner, Mimbu.	**5. Dwébumyaung** —*cont.*					low hills on either side of it. After crossing a small stream, 3 miles from Kadé, Kyuaktwin is reached, deserted some time ago. From here there are three roads, one on the right to Dônda 4 or 5 miles off, and two to Dwébumyaung. Half mile beyond the village the road crosses a small nullah, fair level road to Dwébumyaung, 4 miles. The column apparently took the wrong road and the longer one, here making the distance 4 miles, whereas it is supposed to be far shorter. Dwébumyaung, a small village, deserted, no camping ground here. Water obtainable from nullah close to village, but very scanty and not good.
		6. Léhla	12	4	44	0	From Dwébumyaung general direction south-east. Immediately on leaving the village a small stream has to be crossed and the road, which is here very bad indeed, goes down and up two verp steep inclines, nearly impassable for carts, 3 miles to the village of Manbin, deserted. After leaving Manbin the right road was apparently lost and the column followed a winding track leading through very hilly country covered with jungle; soil stony and very rough. Five-and-a-half miles from Manbin the track ran into the dry bed of a nullah and continued along its course for 1½ miles. After leaving the nullah the road at once ran over high ground and a few huts, called Léhla-galé, were reached, quite deserted. A mile further on is Léhla proper, also deserted and overgrown with weed, &c. There is a good camping ground here, large and level. Water from nullah close by and good, and the camping ground is not commanded by any other ground. The ground would accommodate a battalion of infantry for a short time, but the water is not very plentiful.
		7. Kanengyi ...	10	4	5[illegible]	4	From Léhla general direction south-east. Road crosses a small stream at once, and a mile further on it runs along the bed of the same stream for 300 or 400 yards. Road bad and very difficult for carts. At about 4 miles from Léhla the road again runs into the bed of a stream and continues along it for ½ mile. Country very hilly, covered with jungle. Six miles om Léhla is the village of Mindé, where the villagers were found and information gained about the road. After leaving Mindé the road continues over hills, which appear to form part of several low ranges running nearly north and south. At 10½ miles the village of Kanengyi is reached, a fair-sized village, but deserted. Small camping ground on a knoll around a pôngyi kyaung, which was not occupied. Ground small and enclosed by a fence, suitable for a small force. The kyaung will accommodate about 30 men. Water obtainable from a nullah, also a tank, but too far from the camp, being about ½ mile distant, good in quality and fairly plentiful.

FROM MIMBU TO NAPÉ—*continued.*

BRANCH V—*continued.*

Authorities. Military.	Authorities. Civil.	Number and Names of Stages, Rivers and Streams.	Distances. Intermediate. M. F.	Distances. Total. M. F.	Remarks.
G.O.C. Myingyán District.	Commissioner, Southern Division, and Deputy Commissioner, Mimbu.	**8. Bigaing** ...	9 0	63 4	From Kanengyi general direction south-east and east. Road very bad indeed and impassable for carts, leading over hills covered with jungle as before. Three and-a-half miles from Kanengyi is a very old deserted village, now only a few posts, no name. Six and-a-quarter miles village of Thapángaing, deserted. Immediately on leaving Thapángaing the road crosses a *nullah*, which again crosses the road three times before reaching the village of Bigaing. Two and three-quarter miles from Thapángaing a small village, deserted. No camping ground near. Water from a big nullah close by; running water, good and plentiful.
		9. Swégyu ...	7 4	71 0	From Bigaing general direction south-east and east. Immediately on leaving the village the road descends into a hollow and crosses the big nullah, which was on the right of the village of Bigaing. At first the road is good and level, high hills ½ mile to left of road. Large nullah called "Tanyaung chaung," short distance on right of road. Two and-a-half miles village of Chaungwa, deserted. Road continues fair as far as Htainin, 1½ miles further on, deserted. Shortly after leaving Htainin the road crosses the Tanyaung chaung once or twice and runs along the bed of it entirely. Road very bad indeed, large boulders on the road and pools 3 or 4 feet deep, which make it impassable for carts. On both sides high hills covered with dense jungle making it a defile. After 3¾ miles Swegyu is reached, an old deserted village. No ground even for a small force. One kyaung and one zayát in village capable of accommodating about 80 men.
		10. Segu	7 0	78 0	From Swégyu general direction south-east. The cart road after leaving the village continues along the bed of the nullah until it comes out at Yaungyán chaung, but this was found impracticable, so another road running south was found and followed up. After leaving Swégyu the Tanyaung chaung was at once crossed and the road taken turned from the nullah in a southerly direction, very rough and stony. After first leaving the Tanyaung chaung the road follows the bed of a small stream, which is very rough and almost impassable for carts. It follows this for 1 mile and then leaving it commences an extremely steep and difficult ascent on to high ground. From here the road lies entirely among hills, apparently crossing another range running roughly north-north-west and south-south-east. At 4 miles is the village of Kalaghat, once a large village, but long deserted and of no value as regards accommodation. Leaving Kalaghat the road runs in a southerly direction constantly crossing and recrossing a small stream, which at this time of year makes it difficult for carts. Three miles from Kalaghat is Segu, which was inhabited. There is no camping ground, but one kyaung accommodating about 40 men with a small space around it. Water near from stream good, but scarce.

FROM MIMBU TO NAPÉ—*continued.*

BRANCH V—*continued.*

Authorities. Military.	Authorities. Civil.	Number and Names of Stages, Rivers and Streams.	Distances. Intermediate.	Distances. Total.	Remarks.
G.O.C. Myingyán District.	Commissioner, Southern Division, and Deputy Commissioner, Mimbu.	**11. Yaungyándaung.**	M. F. **11 2**	M. F. 89 2	From Segu general direction north-east. Road after leaving the village is very bad indeed and rough. It runs near the river, that is from 1 to 1½ miles from it. At 4 miles from Segu is the village of Shábingyaung, the first village on the river and not deserted. From here road runs in a northerly direction and improves in condition. Two and-a-quarter miles from Shábingyaung is Aléywa, a very small village of no importance, not deserted. Hills on left of road ½ mile from it. After Aléywa the road leaves the river and runs inland at the foot of the hills. Three and-a-half miles from Aléywa is Einma, a large inhabited village on the river, with several kyaungs and zayáts. Accommodation for 150 or 200 men. Space around the kyaungs for a battalion to camp. Water from river. To Yaungyándaung, 1½ miles. Road makes a detour in order to cross the mouth of the Tanyaung chaung, which here joins the Irrawaddy; crossing difficult, owing to the deep mud forming the bed of the chaung. There are no means of temporarily bridging this creek, and getting carts across is a matter of great difficulty. Yaungyándaung has been entirely burnt down and is not a good place to camp at. There is no open ground, it is shut in by low hills. One kyaung and two zayáts would accommodate about 100 men, but there is no open space around them. River quite close, whence all water is obtained.

No. 16.

From MINHLA to PAUK.

I. B. COMPILATION, NOVEMBER 1888.

G.O.C. Myingyán District.	Commissioner, Southern Division, and Deputy Commissioner, Mimbu.	**1. Yethaya** ...	**12 2**	12 2	General direction of road north-west. On leaving Minhla the road takes a westerly direction, but changes after about 1 mile to north and north-west going close to the river. Road level and good with low hills running parallel to it on the left. At 4 miles the road passes through the village of Nyaungbintha, after which it passes several small villages of no importance. Half-a-mile from Nyaungbintha a small stream is crossed, after which the small village of Yépalé is reached. There is nothing of importance to note, as the villages of Magyibin, Shánzu, Môlé, and Kyunpogôn are passed on the right-hand side of the road; these villages being about ¾ mile from each other. The road is enclosed on either side by a hedge, and the adjoining country is more cultivated, chiefly with jowari (millet) and Indian corn than any hitherto passed. Quarter mile after leaving Kyunpogôn another small nullah has to be crossed. One and three-quarter miles from Kyunpogôn is the village of

FROM MINHLA TO PAUK—*continued.*

Authorities.		Number and Names of Stages, Rivers and Streams.	Distances.				Remarks.
Military.	Civil.		Intermediate.		Total.		
			M.	F.	M.	F.	
G.O.C. Myingyán District.	Commissioner, Southern Division, and Deputy Commissioner, Mimbu.	**1. Yethaya**—*cont.*					Taindán, and from here the road takes a northerly direction to Tabayin 2½ miles further on, passing the small village of Tátkôn situated on the river bank about 1 mile to the right of the road. From Tabayin there is a foot-path along the river bank to Yethaya, distant about ½ mile. This path is suitable for mules and ponies, but carts have to follow the road, which makes a detour of about 1 mile. Yethaya is a large village on the river. There is a camping ground under the trees on the river bank and several kyaungs and zayáts affording accommodation for about 200 men. Water from the river.
		2. Mimbu	8	2	20	4	General direction north-west. Immediately on leaving Yethaya a road is passed leading to Yébaw. The road continues along the bank of the river and is a good one for carts and level. At 2 miles the village of Sánshin is passed some little distance on the right. At 3 miles reach Nandagôn. At 4 miles Palángôn, situated on a broad nullah with running water. The country here becomes hilly. From Palángôn a foot-path suited for loaded animals leads along the river bank to Mimbu, which is a large military station and head-quarters of a Commissioner.
		3. Segu ... ... Maw river.	12	0	32	4	Direction north-west. A good made and metalled road through undulating country, covered with scrub jungle. Segu is a village of about 500 houses on the right bank of the Maw river. There are a large number of kyaungs which could accommodate 300 men. Water from the Maw river and from wells. There is a large bazaar; cattle and carts plentiful.
		4. Leghain ...	6	0	38	4	Direction north. The Maw river is crossed at starting, fordable by carts except during or after heavy rain. Made road to Leghain, which has 250 houses in a walled town; kyaungs which can accommodate 150 men. Cattle, rice, vegetables, and about 100 carts obtainable. Water good.
		5. Pyilôngyaw ... Môn river.	10	4	49	0	Direction west-north-west. A cart road throughout, except in the rains, principally through cultivation and thin jungle. Directly after leaving Leghain a deep swamp is crossed, 130 yards broad. Carts avoid it by making a detour. Beyond the road has been cleared of jungle, width of 200 feet. Pyilôngyaw on the south bank of the Môn river has 35 houses and accommodation for 300 men in the principal and surrounding villages. The military post accommodates 200 men, 120 animals. Water good. The country round is liable to inundation by the Irrawaddy, but only about once in three years, on the occasions of exceptionally high floods. The post is ½ mile from the village and stands in very open ground. The surrounding country is very level, cultivated with dry crops.

FROM MINHLA TO PAUK—*continued.*

Authorities. Military.	Authorities. Civil.	Number and Names of Stages, Rivers and Streams.	Distances. Intermediate.	Distances. Total.	Remarks.
G.O.C. Myingyan District.	Commissioner, Southern Division, and Deputy Commissioner, Mimbu.	**6. Kyutwun** ...	M. F. **10 4**	M. F. 59 4	Direction west. Road over level country for ½ mile to the Môn river, which is a river of some size and even in the dry season is at times not fordable, so that enquiries should be made beforehand. The bottom is shingle. Two fords exist about 300 yards east and west of the ferry. Môndélé lies about 400 yards north of the Môn; has 80 houses, good water from six wells; two kyaungs; 3 zayáts, 40 carts; bullocks, paddy, gram, tobacco and plantains. From Môndélé the road is bad, enclosed by elephant grass to Yônbinzu (at 3½ miles), which has 45 houses, 2 wells, 30 carts. Cattle, tobacco, plantains, Indian corn and some til seed. There are several kyaungs and a plentiful supply of good water. Thence the road passes through dense crops over alluvial soil, which is very liable to be cut up and is badly drained, but yields very rich crops, to Kyaungôn at 4½ miles. Kyaungôn consists of two villages on both sides of a chaung, with precipitous banks about 50 feet deep. The chaung, which is about 50 yards wide, is liable to sudden and heavy floods, during which it is unfordable; shingly bottom. Kyaungôn has 50 houses, 45 carts, 2 wells of good water, and some cattle. There are two small kyaungs and three large zayáts on the south side of the chaung. Plantains and fruit garden cultivation; soil sandy; village surrounded by thorn fence. The road on is very good, running over sandy shingle. Cultivation in patches all along it. The jungle is not too thick for infantry to work in. Reach Kaligôn at 8½ miles. Kaligôn is a small village of 18 houses with some cattle. Water obtained by digging in the sandy bed of a nullah situated about 80 yards north. Village fenced. Thence road runs through a jungle cutting 100 yards wide over sandy gravel through thin scrub jungle which is easy for all arms. Road good to Kyutwun, which is a large village in four parts, about a mile long, running east and west; two wells, one at each end of the village. At the west end is also a large sheet of water. The zayáts are about 250 yards from the well; camping ground is unlimited in the south shore of the lake. One kyaung at the east end of the village; 120 houses, 80 carts, 200 bullocks, 2 zayáts; paddy plentiful; also some til seed; village stockaded and fenced.
		7. Salin	**8 0**	67 4	Road good for 1 mile over sandy gravel and thence indifferent as far as Watheyé. At 4½ miles cultivation in large patches along the road, interspersed in places by jungle; the jungle, whenever it appears, averaging about 8½ feet high and would prove no obstacle for Infantry movements in skirmishing order. All round Wathéyé the country is well cultivated. Hence the road is bad, running for the last mile through numerous kyaungs, pagodas, and zayáts in the outskirts of the town, which it enters by the west gate. Salin is an old walled town, whose walls are partly ruined, but still form a strong defence. There are five gates: two on the north face and one on each of the other faces. The town is surrounded on the south and west sides by paddy-fields and the other two sides by its suburbs and outskirts. It is the head-quarters of an Assistant Commis-

FROM MINHLA TO PAUK—*continued.*

Authorities: Military.	Authorities: Civil.	Number and Names of Stages, Rivers and Streams.	Distances: Intermediate. M.	F.	Distances: Total. M.	F.	Remarks.
G.O.C. Myingyan District.	Commissioner, Southern Division, and Deputy Commissioner, Minbu.	**7. Salin**—*cont.*					sioner, and has a garrison of three companies of Infantry and some police. There is a commissariat store and some pack transport animals. The town and district could supply 500 carts. Almost unlimited accommodation for troops in the numerous kyaungs outside the town on the east side. Water is obtained partly from wells and partly from irrigation canals. Supplies of rice, grass, and vegetables can always be obtained. The Salin river is about 1 mile distant to the north.
		8. Zibyubin ... Salin river dry in hot season; 2 feet deep in the rains, when in flood for two or three days at a time.	17	0	84	4	Direction north-east. Along the made road towards Sinbyugyun for 4½ miles, then strike off and cross the Salin river to Nwédamé at 6 miles, which is a large village. Hence the road is good and level, passing through dry cultivation until about 1 mile from Zibyubin, where a small nullah bed is followed. Zibyubin is close to the Irrawaddy; is a Burmese police post; has 150 houses and good kyaungs, which would accommodate 300 men. Good water. Carts obtainable.
		9. Myénu	9	0	93	4	Level road to Tángyaung at 4 miles, which has kyaungs which could accommodate 2,000 men, and very good water from wells. Hence there is a road to Zigat (*see* Route No. 43) on the Irrawaddy at 5 miles. At 9 miles road Myénu with one kyaung and several zayáts. Water from a well. Supplies plentiful.
	Commissioner, Southern Division, and Deputy Commissioner, Pakôkku.	**10. Letsé** ... ... Kyé chaung. Letsé chaung, which has water at all seasons.	14	0	107	4	Through low hills to Thézu at 4 miles, whence there is a road to Zigat 7 miles, Myinkándaw at 5 miles, a small village with one small kyaung and good water from wells. Hence there is a road to Seikpyu on the Irrawaddy, distance 7 miles, then over level ground to Letsé, crossing the Kyé chaung near Kyadé at 10 miles. Letsé is a military police post with a garrison of 50 sepoys; also two kyaungs which would accommodate 150 men. Supplies plentiful. Good water from the Letsé chaung.
		11. Kinmandaung. Right bank of Yaw river.	13	0	120	4	Direction north by west through Zibingyi at 3½ miles, Wéma at 5½, and Ingôn on the Yaw river, with one kyaung and zayáts at 11 miles. Kinmandaung is a large village with one kyaung and zayáts. Water from Yaw river. Supplies plentiful.
		12. Nyaungwun. Yaw river.	13	0	133	4	Level road along right bank of Yaw river to Nyaungwun, which is 1½ miles south-east of Pyinchaung. *See* Route No. 30. Nyaungwun contains one large kyaung and good zayáts. Water from wells. Supplies plentiful.

FROM MINHLA TO PAUK—*continued.*

Authorities. Military.	Authorities. Civil.	Number and Names of Stages, Rivers and Streams.	Distances. Intermediate. M. F.	Distances. Total. M. F.	Remarks.
G.O.C. Myingyán District.	Commr., Southern Div., and Dy. Commr., Pakôkku.	**11. Pauk**	13 0	147 4	The road joins the Pyinchaung-Pauk road at about 3½ miles. *See* Route No. 30.

BRANCH I.

FROM YETHAYA (STAGE 1) TO SINGAING.

I. B. COMPILATION.

Military.	Civil.	Stages.	Intermediate.	Total.	Remarks.
G.O.C. Myingyán District.	Commissioner, Southern Division, and Deputy Commissioner, Mimbu.	**1. Singaing** ...	17 4	17 4	Yethaya to Palángôn 4 miles. *See* commencement of Stage 2 above. From Palángôn a road branches west to Singaung. For 3 miles it follows the bed of the nullah mentioned before, crossing and recrossing the nullah, with high hills on either side. Road bad and very heavy for carts. Three miles from Palángôn the road leaves the nullah bed, the village of Pagânsit being left ½ mile to the left of the road. After this it continues among hilly country in a north-west direction. At 9½ miles it crosses a road leading from Yébaw to Mimbu at right angles. The country here is hilly, covered with fairly open jungle. At 12 miles a big nullah, the Sabwet chaung, has to be crossed immediately on the other bank, being the village of Yémyit. There is no good camping ground here, but a small space around a kyaung in which are two zayáts. Accommodation for about 80 or 100 men. Water from the nullah, which is good and plentiful; also from a good well near the kyaung. On leaving Yémyit the road continues nearly the whole way in a westerly direction. The road is good and level, easy for carts. Country on either side fairly open jungle with cultivation and clearings at intervals. No village is passed until Singaing is reached at 17½ miles. *See* Route No. 15, Alternative III.

No. 17.

From MYINGYÁN to MEIKTILA ROAD.

BY LIEUT. E. W. M. NORIE, 2ND MIDDLESEX REGIMENT, FEBRUARY 1888.

Military.	Civil.	Stages.	Intermediate.	Total.	Remarks.
G.O.C. Myingyán District.	Commissioner, Southern Division, and Deputy Commissioner, Myingyán.	**1. Taungtha.** Four large nullahs and several small ones.	15 0	15 0	General direction south-west. After leaving the military post cross a nullah running through the town by a strong wooden bridge and passing a large number of kyaungs.* Cross a second broad nullah on the south of Myingyán also by a good wooden bridge. The road is a good, hard, sandy road the whole way and is partially metalled for the first 4½ miles. All the nullahs are bridged except one at about 9½ miles, over which a bridge is apparently to be made and a broad, shallow, sandy nullah 1 mile before reaching Taungtha. Water can be got at the above two nullahs and a very limited supply at the village passed at 7½ miles, as it has to be brought from some distance, though plentiful

* These kyaungs have since been all burnt down in the great fire at Myingyán in the hot weather of 1888.

FROM MYINGYÁN TO MEIKTILA ROAD—*continued.*

Authorities.		Number and Names of Stages, Rivers and Streams.	Distances.				Remarks.
Military.	Civil.		Intermediate.		Total.		
			M.	F.	M.	F.	
G.O.C. Myingyán District.	Commissioner, Southern Division, and Deputy Commissioner, Myingyán.	**1. Taungtha**—*cont.*					earlier in the season. The country is generally under dry cultivation, bounded by irregular hedges, and is quite practicable for cavalry. From the bed of the nullah passed at 9½ miles the road rises pretty sharply to the summit of a gap in the short range of hills to the north-east of Taungtha, at about 11 miles. It then descends abruptly to the plain which it reaches at 12 miles. These hills are covered with thin scrub jungle. The names of the village seem to vary and there is only the one mentioned above passed at 7½ miles from Myingyán, which is actually on the road. Taungtha is a cluster of villages, the road passing to the east of the main village. There is accommodation for 300 men in kyaungs to the south-east of this village and for 150 men in the police post close by. Round here the ground is suitable for encampment of a large force. The police post is surrounded by a brick breastwork, a small ditch, and a thorn hedge. Water is procurable close by from wells and is good and plentiful. After the rains there is also water in a tank close to the police post. There is a signal station on the top of a high peak in the range of hills to the north-east, about 3 miles off. There is a Myo-ôk of the village and ordinary supplies can be got in large quantities. Probably 200 carts are also available. A large trade passes through here to Myingyán. A road runs south from here to Wélaung.
		2. Yônzin ... Several small nullahs.	12	0	27	0	Road, the same as before, crosses a nullah about 1 mile from Taungtha by a wooden bridge, then passes a small village and rises to the crest of a low range of hills at 17 miles from Myingyán. Telegraph line from that place to Meiktila crosses the road. At 3 miles pass the small village of Kyawkyán, surrounded with thorn hedge. There are some small kyaungs on left of road. Plenty of good water in a well about ¼ of a mile down the the road and 300 yards off to the right under some cocoanut palms. At 5 miles pass the village of Aungtha. Some kyaungs and zayáts on right of road. Water from a well ½ mile to south of village. At 12 miles reach Yônzin, a large village. The road before reaching the village runs across the bund of a small tank. Plenty of accommodation in kyaungs for 300 or 400 men to north-east of village. Good camping ground on road just above the tank. Water from tank and good drinking water from five or six wells in village. Supplies obtainable from the thugyi.
G.O.C. Rangoon District.	Commissioner, Eastern Division, and Deputy Commissioner, Meiktila.	**3. Máhlaing** ...	8	0	35	0	At 1 mile the telegraph line touches the road and at 2 miles joins it again and runs along it. At Panaing it again leaves the road. At 5 miles reach Panaing, which is a very large village with plenty of accommodation to east of village in kyaungs and zayáts. There is abundance of excellent drinking water from numerous wells. Good encamping ground on north-west of village with wells close by. All supplies and a number of carts obtainable from thugyi. Máhlaing, at 8 miles, is a large village under a Myo-ôk. There is a small police post surrounded with a breastwork and ditch south-east of village, commanded by a police officer. Head-quarters of an Assistant Commissioner and contains a court-house, jail, post office and telegraph office. There is plenty of accommodation in kyaungs for a large force north of the post, with a

FROM MYINGYÁN TO MEIKTILA ROAD—*continued.*

Authorities. Military.	Authorities. Civil.	Number and Names of Stages, Rivers and Streams.	Distances. Inter-mediate.	Distances. Total.	Remarks.
G.O.C. Rangoon District.	Commissioner, Eastern Division, and Deputy Commissioner, Meiktila.	**3. Máhlaing**—*cont.*			plentiful supply of good water from wells. Good ground for encampment round police post. A large bazaar every fifth day. All supplies obtainable. Grass for horses. Water in well close to police post not good. A large number of carts obtainable from Máhlaing, Panaing, and surrounding villages. Cultivation chiefly cotton. A large number of toddy trees in the district round. A considerable trade passes through the place.
			M. F.	M. F.	
		4. Yégyi	**14 0**	49 0	Road still continues good and passes through the same description of country for the first 4 miles till it reaches the village of Thengôn, beyond which there are two wells of good water on the side of the road under a large peepul tree. From about a mile beyond here a broad clearing is made through the jungle to within about 2 miles of Meiktila, and along this strip the road is at present being constructed. The old road follows generally the same line. There is a dry weather road which branches from the road at about 4 miles from Meiktila and crosses the bridge between the lakes to the west of the village, but the proper road runs round the north end of the north lake and down the east side to the cantonment. At 10 miles from Máhlaing pass Yégamo, and before reaching Yégyi cross a nullah about 100 yards broad, over which a bridge is being made. At Yégyi, about 14 miles from Máhlaing, there are two good wells on the right of the road to north-west of village. There is a kyaung much out of repair here, but there is plenty of ground suitable for encampment and the ordinary supplies are obtainable. The country is generally covered with scrub jungle, but for the first 8 miles there is a good deal of cotton cultivation to the south of the road.
		5. Meiktila ...	**10 0**	59 0	Road as described above. Meiktila is a large village with numerous kyaungs, at present occupied by troops, on the east of a narrow arm which joins two lakes of considerable size. About 600 yards to the east of the village the military cantonment is at present being built, on high ground, overlooking the south lake. There is a telegraph office, post office, and signal station, and it is the head-quarters of a brigade. There is also a Deputy Commissioner, Inspector of Police, and a Myo-ôk. There is a large bazaar every fifth day and supplies are plentiful. Water good and plentiful.
		6. Meiktila Road.	**13 0**	72 0	Good metalled and bridged road. *See* Route No. 6, Eastern Division.

BRANCH I.

FROM MÁHLAING (STAGE 3) TO NYÔK.

BY LIEUT. C. BENSON, ROYAL MUNSTER FUSILIERS, FEBRUARY 1886-87.

Military	Civil	Stage	Intermediate	Total	Remarks
G.O.C. Rangoon District.	Commr., Eastern Div., and Dy. Commr., Meiktila.	**1. Nyôk**	**15 4**	15 4	**Road good, but sandy soil; high hedges on each side. At 4 miles Lôndwin, a large village through which the road passes for over ½ a mile. Accommodation in kyaungs for about 120 men.**

From MYINGYÁN to MEIKTILA ROAD—*continued*.

BRANCH I—*continued*.

Authorities. Military.	Authorities. Civil.	Number and Names of Stages, Rivers and Streams.	Distances. Intermediate.	Distances. Total.	Remarks.
G.O.C. Rangoon District.	Commissioner, Eastern Division, and Deputy Commissioner, Meiktila.	**1. Nyôk**—*cont.*			Water good. Road after Lôndwin passes through cultivation for about a mile, and then for about a mile and-a-half through barren ground with low bushes thinly scattered about, intersected by one dry nullah, otherwise good. At 7 miles Dhatein, a small village west side of road, with high thorn hedge round it. Water good. Road for about 1⅛ miles out of Dhatein passes through cultivation, next 3½ miles through a thick scrub jungle, where it winds a great deal. Soil in parts sandy, but road good. At 13 miles Bôkywadaw, a large village through which road passes for about ¼ of a mile and is very muddy. Accommodation for about 100 men in kyaungs, not in good repair. Water good. Road after leaving the village rather heavy; crosses two streams; cultivation on both sides. At 15⅛ miles reach Nyôk, a large village divided into three parts by stream, principal part on north bank and intersected by four roads; surrounded by high thorn hedge. Accommodation for 250 men; kyaungs in good repair and surrounded by a cactus hedge with two zayáts on north and east sides. Water close to kyaungs and good. Village able to supply 12 carts. *Note.*—This is apparently the Nyaungôk of the ⅛″ scale map on the road between Myingyán and Pindalé though it is not mentioned in the description of that route (No. 18)—A. F.

BRANCH II.

From MÁHLAING (Stage 3) to PINDALÉ (Route No. 18, Stage 5).

By Lieut. E. W. M. NORIE, 2nd Middlesex Regiment, February 1888.

Military.	Civil.	Stages.	Intermediate. M. F.	Total. M. F.	Remarks.
G.O.C. Rangoon District.	Commissioner, Eastern Division, and Deputy Commissioner, Meiktila.	**1. Yôndaw** ... One stream.	7 4	7 4	General direction of road north-east through open country. Good cart track over undulating country, cultivated with paddy, grain and cotton. Pass two small villages at 2⅛ and 3¼ miles. Water good and plentiful from wells in villages and from a creek at second village. Yôndaw is a large village. Accommodation for 200 men in one large kyaung and six zayáts south-east of village and good camping ground just outside the kyaung enclosure. Plenty of good water from well in the kyaung enclosure. Ordinary supplies and about 30 carts procurable. The village is in the Mindwindain.
		2. Pindalé .. One stream.	12 4	20 0	Road crosses a broad creek about ⅛ mile from Yôndaw. Water very brackish. Always passable for carts. Beyond this the road is very rough and stony. At 9 miles from Yôndaw pass the small village of Thayetpin, where there is a good well. Between here and Pindalé pass three small tanks. The country is rough, rocky, uncultivated, and covered with thick scrub jungle. Pindalé is a large village of 184 houses with a large tank. Accommodation in four kyaungs and 20 zayáts on north-east of village for a large force. Good water-supply from well in kyaung enclosure which is close to the tank. There is a Burman police post. Supplies procurable from the Myo-ôk. Pindalé is the rice-growing place of the district (Meiktila). Said to be feverish in early part of the year when the lake is drying up. Roads from here to Myingyán *viâ* Natôgyi and to Meiktila, *see* Route No. 18, and also to Wundwin, *see* Route No. 22.

No. 18.

From MYINGYÁN to MEIKTILA viâ NATÔGYI and PINDALÉ.

By Deputy Assistant Adjutant and Quartermaster-General, 4th Brigade, U.B.F.F., 1887-88.

Authorities. Military.	Authorities. Civil.	Number and Names of Stages, Rivers and Streams.	Distances. Intermediate. M.	Distances. Intermediate. F.	Distances. Total. M.	Distances. Total. F.	Remarks.
G.O.C. Myingyán District.	Commissioner, Southern Division, and Deputy Commissioner, Myingyán.	**1. Ywagyi** ...	**11**	**0**	11	0	*See* Route No. 22, Stages 1 and 2.
		2. Natôgyi ...	**10**	**0**	21	0	
		3. Tabair ...	**11**	**0**	32	0	At 2½ miles from Natôgyi pass Pébin, small village, 15 houses, accommodation none; water from well and tank, fair. At 6½ miles pass Payagyi, 50 houses; water from wells and tank, good; camping ground excellent, two large kyaungs and many zayáts. At 8 miles pass Taungbu, 50 houses; water from tanks and well, three large kyaungs and many zayáts; camping ground fair. Tabair at 11 miles is a village of 80 houses, large kyaungs; water-supply from wells, indifferent; camping ground good and open.
		4. Tinghán ...	**9**	**0**	41	0	At 2¼ miles from Tabair pass Thôndu, 40 houses; no accommodation; water from tank. At 4 miles pass Kyenya, small village, water-supply from river, good; one kyaung (small) off the road. At 7 miles pass Minthi, 10 houses; water, one well; no accommodation. At 8 miles pass Tazu, small hamlet; cross rocky bed of small river; water good; no accommodation. At 9 miles Tinghán, a small village on high ground, one kyaung (in good order) and zayáts, accommodation for 75 men; water good, from well.
G.O.C. Rangoon District.	Commissioner, Eastern Division, and Deputy Commissioner, Meiktila.	**5. Pindalé** ...	**7**	**0**	48	0	At 3 miles pass Gwégôn, 50 houses; small broken-down kyaung. At 7 miles Pindalé, a large important place; 400 houses, kyaungs and zayáts; ample accommodation for 200 troops; water good, from wells.
		6. Ômadwé ...	**11**	**0**	59	0	At 1¾ miles pass Tazu, no accommodation and at 7 miles Ségwa, 50 houses; cross river; low banks north side; broken-down kyaung; water from well, good. At 9½ miles pass Kyaungôn; small village, no accommodation. At 11 miles Ômadwé, large village, two kyaungs, good water from wells.
		7. Meiktila ...	**12**	**0**	71	0	At 2 miles pass Thapán; kyaungs; water good, from wells; open on north; paddy cultivation; south jungle. At 4½ miles pass Kánywa village, 60 houses; kyaungs ¼ mile off the road; water good, from river and wells; jungle around. At 6½ miles pass Kanné, small village in middle of paddy cultivation; accommodation in kyaungs; water from wells, good. At 8½ miles pass Shwépyukán, large village; no accommodation; water good, from wells. At 12 miles Meiktila.

No. 19.

From MYINGYÁN to THAYETMYO viâ PAGÁN, YÉNÁNGYAUNG and ALLANMYO, along the river bank.

By Lieut. E. W. M. Norie, 2nd Middlesex Regiment, February 1888.

Authorities. Military.	Authorities. Civil.	Number and Names of Stages, Rivers and Streams.	Distances. Intermediate. M. F.	Distances. Total. M. F.	Remarks.
G.O.C. Myingyán District.	Commissioner, Southern Division, and Deputy Commissioner, Myingyán.	**1. Dhattaw** ... Three nullahs; two bridged and the other sandy, but passable for carts except after heavy rain.	16 0	16 0	Road runs south through town of Myingyán. The first nullah, close to the barracks, is crossed by a new strong wooden bridge. Beyond the town there is a second large nullah bounding the town to the south. Banks steep. Bed of nullah dry except immediately after rain. Crossed by a strong wooden bridge. Passing the village of Kyingré the road turns to the west and runs south-west by west. Road in fair condition, passes Kyedaw and Thapain. At the latter the road to Wélaung branches off to the left running south-west and then south-east. At about 6 miles the road bends to the south running parallel to the river in a south-west by south direction. A good road all the way to Dhattaw and water plentiful. Dhattaw is a large village containing a police post and stockade and ample accommodation for troops in kyaungs, with good water-supply from a tank. All ordinary supplies can be got here and fodder for horses. There is also good encamping ground.
		2. Letpángyibwa. One nullah.	11 4	27 4	From Dhattaw the road runs west-south-west, still parallel to the river, crosses one large nullah and some small ones, but is a good cart road. Water obtainable along the road. The country is open and cultivated. Letpángyibwa is a small village containing a police post. It is on the bank of the Irrawaddy, and there is good accommodation for troops in kyaungs and ground suitable for encamping on. Water is plentiful and good, and a limited amount of common supplies are obtainable.
		3. Nyaung-u (Pagán). One nullah.	10 0	37 4	From Letpángyibwa the road runs south-west to Nyaung-u, which is the military post of Pagán. The road is still good though a little more broken, but carts can go along it easily. There is one sandy nullah and a few small ravines. Water is easily procurable along the road and the nature of the country remains the same. Pagán is a large and flourishing town on the left bank of the Irrawaddy, and a great deal of trade passes through it. The landing place for steamers is close to Nyaung-u. It is the head-quarters of a civil district. There is a large bazaar and all supplies can be obtained in the town. A large number of transport animals and carts are also obtainable. It has a court-house, treasury, post office, telegraph office, and jail. There is ample accommodation for troops at the military post at Nyaung-u and good ground for encamping on. The chief exports are *jowári*, cotton, lacquer work and *jágari*. A large number of native boats are always procurable.

FROM MYINGYÁN TO THAYETMYO *viâ* PAGÁN, YÉNÁNGYAUNG AND ALLANMYO, ALONG THE RIVER BANK—*continued.*

Authorities. Military.	Authorities. Civil.	Number and Names of Stages, Rivers and Streams.	Distances. Intermediate. M.	Distances. Intermediate. F.	Distances. Total. M.	Distances. Total. F.	Remarks.
G.O.C. Myingyán District.	Commissioner, Southern Division, and Deputy Commissioner, Myingyán.	**4. Gángaw** ... Several small nullahs.	9	0	46	4	Road bad, bank of the river low, and the country flat. Pass several small villages. Water is obtainable all along the road, which runs parallel to the river and due south. Gángaw is a small village and the encamping ground is just outside the village. Supplies not plentiful. Water from the river.
		5. Singu ... ... Several small nullahs.	9	0	55	4	Road bad, heavy and rough, over several nullahs. Water from the river, which is close by. This place stands on a small creek close to the Irrawaddy. Some kyaungs and zayáts are on a strip of high ground, which stretches along the river to the south of village; will accommodate 300 men; and there is good camping ground round them. Supplies of all sorts procurable. Military police post stockaded is to south of village. Anchorage in the river here is not good, owing to the rocks and the strength of the stream. A road runs from here east to Kyaukpadaung (30 miles). There is a large trade in grains, paddy, and other produce, and a large number of native boats are procurable.
		6. Silé ... ... One nullah.	9	0	64	4	The road is a sandy cart track over undulating country and through scrub jungle, direction south-west still following generally the river bank. Rather heavy for carts. A broad sandy water-course is crossed just after leaving Singu. Water from the river. Silé is a flourishing town, with bazaar, police post, and considerable trade. The anchorage for steamers is good, opposite to Zigat, the outlet of a good deal of traffic with the Yaw country (*see* Route No. 43).
		7. Pakhán-ngé ...	10	0	74	4	Sandy cart road, the same as before. Pakhán-ngé is a large village situated on high ground opposite the mouth of the Salin river. There are several kyaungs and zayáts. Water good. Supplies procurable.
		8. Kyaukyé ... Several small sandy nullahs.	11	0	85	4	The road, same as before, is in some places very sandy. Follows the bank of the Irrawaddy. Most of the country cultivated with dry crops. Elsewhere there is low scrub jungle. Kyaukyé is a large village with accommodation in several kyaungs and zayáts for 200 men. Supplies are procurable and water from the river. Steamers sometimes stop here for cargo, and there is a large number of boats.

From MYINGYÁN to THAYETMYO *viâ* PAGÁN, YÉNÁNGYAUNG and ALLANMYO, along the river bank—*continued*.

Authorities. Military.	Authorities. Civil.	Number and Names of Stages, Rivers and Streams.	Distances. Intermediate. M.	F.	Total. M.	F.	Remarks.
G.O.C. Myingyán District.	Commissioner, Southern Division, and Deputy Commissioner, Magwé.	**9. Yénángyaung.** Pin river.	**10**	**0**	95	4	Road runs over low hills to Thôngyetkán (6 miles); here it crosses the Pin river which, at this point, is 400 yards broad; bottom sandy with precipitous banks. Very little running water except in the rains. From here the road, rough and stony, passes Thwingôn and runs over the hills behind Yénángyaung and down to that town on the Irrawaddy. Yénángyaung, a flourishing place with considerable trade in earth-oil from the springs at Thwingôn, 3 miles distant. A police post, telegraph station, and large bazaar.
		10. Wetmasut ... One broad nullah close to Wetmasut and several small nullahs.	**11**	**0**	106	4	Road fair, but in a few places very steep, sandy. Crosses several small nullahs and one large one at Wetmasut. All dry except after rain. Road follows generally the course of the river. Wetmasut is a large village with several fine kyaungs and many zayáts. Water good and plentiful. Supplies procurable.
		11. Magwé ... Two nullahs.	**14**	**0**	120	4	Fair cart road with heavy sand in hollows and very steep in a few places. Follows generally the course of the Irrawaddy, of which the banks are high and precipitous. Country undulating, covered with cultivation and thin jungle. Pass a sandy nullah at 2½ miles and the village of Magyikyidauk at 5½ miles; here cross the Wet chaung, very broad, with sandy bottom. No water except in rains. Bank low here, but high in other places. A mile further on pass Kayen and a mile beyond that Padígôn. Magwé is a place of considerable size and importance and a great centre of trade. There is a police post here and telegraph station. Mimbu is 3 miles higher up the river on the opposite bank.
		12. Théyalébin ... Yen river.	**13**	**0**	133	4	Road hard, gravelly, and good; rises gradually. At 3 miles passes Sayingáu and at 5 miles Magyigán. About a mile beyond this the road rises to the edge of a plateau about 2 miles broad and then descends by a steep slope to Kaundu and Shábinhla, about 9 and 12 miles from Magwé respectively. Road very sandy and heavy. The road now crosses the Yen river about 500 yards broad. Bottom sandy, banks high and steep. Water all the year round except about two months in the hot weather. Impassable after rains, as the river is then swift and deep. Country generally under dry crop cultivation. Théyalébin, a village of about 40 houses. Good water from the Yen, on the left bank of which it stands. Supplies procurable. Two large kyaungs.

From MYINGYÁN to THAYETMYO *viâ* PAGÁN, YÉNÁNGYAUNG and ALLANMYO, along the river bank—*continued.*

Authorities. Military.	Authorities. Civil.	Number and Names of Stages, Rivers and Streams.	Distances. Intermediate. M. F.	Distances. Total. M. F.	Remarks.
G.O.C. Myingyán District.	Commissioner, Southern Division, and Deputy Commissioner, Magwé.	**13. Thazi** ...	10 0	143 4	Road rises from the valley of the Yen by a steep ascent, after which it is almost level and good though very sandy. Passes some small villages. Country generally covered with low scrub jungle. Cultivation only round the villages. Thazi is a large village, with telegraph station opposite to Minhla. The main road to Taungdwingyi and the interior formerly started from here, but a new road is in progress starting from Mingyaungwé. There is a stockade for a guard of 20 men round the telegraph office and accommodation for over 100 men in an old pôngyi kyaung and zayáts on river with shady trees all round. Telegraph line to Taungdwingyi starts from here and runs along the road to that place.
		14. Taungwin ...	13 0	156 4	Road runs past the village of Gwégyaung to Kulikun, 3 miles, where it leaves the river and runs over low hills covered with jungle to Mingyaungwé, 10 miles. This is a good-sized village with several zayáts and kyaungs. Here the river is again reached and the road runs parallel to it for the rest of the distance. Mingyaungwé is a place of some importance and from here the main road runs to Taungdwingyi. It has a considerable trade. Taungwin is a small village of about 30 houses. Water from the river. One small kyaung on hill above the village. Camping ground on fields. Supplies of all sorts procurable.
G.O.C. Rangoon District.	Lower Burma.	**15. Sinbaungwé**... Several small creeks.	12 0	168 4	Road follows generally the bank of the Irrawaddy over low hills and through small scrub jungle with patches of cultivation near the villages. Sinbaungwé is a place of some importance. There is a police post and telegraph station here.
		16. Ingya ...	8 0	176 4	Lower Burma.
		17. Nyaungbintha	8 0	184 4	Lower Burma.
		18. Tagônmaw ...	8 0	192 4	Lower Burma.
		19. Allanmyo ...	8 0	200 4	Lower Burma nearly opposite Thayetmyo.

BRANCH I.

From SILÉ (Stage 6) to GWÉGYO (Route No. 41, Stage 2).

Military	Civil	Stage	Intermediate M. F.	Total M. F.	Remarks
G.O.C. Myingyán District.	Commr., Southern Division, and Deputy Commr., Myingyán.	**1. Twemlut** ... A defile about ¾ of a mile in length and from 15 to 25 feet deep is reached at about 8 miles from Silé and one nullah at 10 miles from Silé.	12 0	12 0	Road very heavy and sandy, passing the village of Kyaungdat at 4 miles.

FROM MYINGYÁN TO THAYETMYO *viâ* PAGÁN, YÉNÁNGYAUNG AND ALLANMYO, ALONG THE RIVER BANK—*continued.*

BRANCH I—*continued.*

Authorities. Military.	Authorities. Civil.	Number and Names of Stages, Rivers and Streams.	Distances. Intermediate. M.	F.	Distances. Total. M.	F.	Remarks.
G.O.C. Myingyán District.	Commr., Southern Divn., and Deputy Commr., Myingyán.	**2. Gwégyo** ... Two nullahs between Twemlut and Gwégyo at 4½ and 5 miles from Twemlut.	8	0	20	0	Road heavy and sandy in parts. A zayát on road side at half-way. There is a large tamarind tree on the south of the road, at about 3 miles from Twemlut, which affords a good landmark. Water at Gwégyo very good. *See* Route No. 41, Stage 2.

No. 20.

From MYINGYÁN to THAYETMYO viâ NATÔGYI, TAUNGDWINGYI and ALLANMYO.

BY LIEUT. E. W. M. NORIE, 2ND MIDDLESEX REGIMENT, FEBRUARY 1888.

Military	Civil	Stages	Inter. M.	F.	Total M.	F.	Remarks
G.O.C. Myingyán District.	Commissioner, Southern Division, and Deputy Commissioner, Myingyán.	**1. Ywagyi** ...	11	0	11	0	*Vide* Route No. 22, Stages 1 and 2.
		2. Natôgyi ...	10	0	21	0	
		3. Thekagyin ...	12	0	33	0	General direction of road south. A hard sandy cart track. First 2 miles passes through low cultivated country, afterwards through thin scrub jungle perfectly practicable for cavalry. One place about 6 miles from Natôgyi, where the road crosses a deep dip, is probably very bad in the rains. Pass small villages at 3, 5, and 7 miles from Natôgyi. Good water from wells at all the villages. Country generally sandy and undulating with narrow strips of paddy in the villages. Cultivation cotton, *jowári* and paddy. Thekagyin is a large village. Accommodation for 100 men in kyaungs on west of village. Large tank close to kyaungs and very good water from numerous wells (in kyaung enclosure). Supplies procurable from thugyi.
G.O.C. Rangoon District.	Commissioner, Eastern Division, and Deputy Commissioner, Meiktila.	**4. Máhlaing** ...	14	0	47	0	Road the same as before. Cotton more plentiful and a good number of toddy trees about. At 3½ miles pass the large village of Kwégyán, which appears to have a flourishing trade in cotton carried on by a Chinaman. Several kyaungs on south side of village. Plenty of excellent water from several wells. Supplies plentiful. At 6 miles pass a small village on left of road. Water from a well ¼ mile to right of road. No accommodation. About ½ mile on the road passes over some paddy and is very bad in rains. Two miles further on pass a village on right of road. Kyaungs. Before reaching the village, a large tank ½ mile to east of road. Plenty of good water from wells. About 1 mile further on the road passes over some paddy probably very bad in the rains. At 11 miles reach Panaing and join main road from Myingyán, *vide* Route No. 17, Stage 3.

FROM MYINGYÂN TO THAYETMYO *viâ* NATÔGYI, TAUNGDWINGYI AND ALLANMYO—*continued.*

Authorities. Military.	Authorities. Civil.	Number and Names of Stages, Rivers and Streams.	Distances. Intermediate. M. F.	Distances. Total. M. F.	Remarks.
G.O.C. Rangoon District.	Commissioner, Eastern Division, and Deputy Commissioner, Meiktila.	**5. Sídaw** ... One nullah.	13 0	60 0	A hard sandy cart track through thin scrub jungle. At 8 miles from Máhlaing pass big village of Sukingyi, where there is plenty of good water from wells. At 12 miles cross a nullah 60 yards wide with very steep banks. This nullah is impassable after heavy rains, but in hot weather is dry with sandy bed. Sídaw is a large village under a Myo-ôk. There is a police post here. Accommodation for a large force in kyaungs south of village. Small tank in kyaung enclosure. Plenty of good water from wells. Usual supplies can be obtained. Cotton is grown about here in large quantities.
		6. Shánmangé ...	9 0	69 0	Broad hard sandy road through thin jungle. Very little cultivation and no water along the road. Shánmangé is a large village. There is a military police post with accommodation for 200 men in post and for 200 more in kyaungs, about 500 yards to north of post. Water good and plentiful from a well in kyaung enclosure and for animals in nullah close by. There is an Assistant Superintendent of Police and a telegraph office. The headman is the thugyi and there is a bazaar every five days. Ordinary supplies plentiful and about 100 carts procurable from surrounding villages. There is a road from here to Meiktila, *see* Route No. 25.
		7. Kyetpyet ...	9 0	78 0	A good cart road through scrub jungle. At 2 miles pass the village of Inga and at 7 miles the village of the Sintán on a hill about 1 mile of road. Kyetpyet is a village of about 40 houses. Accommodation for about 150 men in kyaungs and zayáts. Camping ground all round. Water from a large pond 150 yards south-east good. Supplies plentiful and probably a few carts could be obtained.
G.O.C. Myingyán District.	Commissioner, Southern Division, and Deputy Commissioner, Myingyán.	**8. Sulégôn** ... One rocky chaung.	8 0	86 0	Road, same as before, at about 2 miles passes a kyaung about 300 yards to west of road. At 4½ miles it crosses the Myinmana hills which are a steep rocky range about 500 feet above surrounding country. At about 6 miles pass Ségyi, a good-sized village with a large kyaung ½ mile west. Myinmana hills run ½ mile east of road. Sulégôn is a small village. Accommodation for about 130 men in kyaungs and zayáts which are rather out of repair. Water from a well about ½ mile from the kyaung good. Supplies obtainable in small quantities.

FROM MYINGYÁN TO THAYETMYO *viâ* NATÔGYI, TAUNGDWINGYI AND ALLANMYO—*continued*.

Authorities. Military.	Authorities. Civil.	Number and Names of Stages, Rivers and Streams.	Distances. Intermediate. M.	F.	Total. M.	F.	Remarks.
G.O.C. Myingyán District.	Commissioner, Southern Division, and Deputy Commissioner, Magwé.	**9. Shwébandaw**... Myu chaung.	**12**	**4**	98	4	At 3½ miles road passes Kyauktaga, a small village with one small kyaung. At 7½ miles pass Kyaukwet, a village of about 40 houses with accommodation for 150 men in kyaungs and zayáts. Water from a large tank and supplies plentiful. The country is undulating, sandy and rocky covered with grass and thin scrub. Cultivation dry crop and only in small spaces round the villages. About 1 mile from Shwébandaw road descends and runs through paddy land.
		10. Ywamôn ...	**8**	**0**	106	4	*See* Route No. 21.
		11. Natmauk ...	**14**	**0**	120	4	
		12. Myothit ...	**12**	**0**	132	4	
		13. Taungdwingyi.	**17**	**0**	149	4	
		14. Zibinwaing ...	**10**	**0**	159	4	
G.O.C. Rangoon District.	Lower Burma.	**15. Kadinmatha.**	**18**	**0**	177	4	
		16. Hlándaing ...	**11**	**0**	188	4	Accommodation at al stages in kyaungs zayáts or bungalow for at least 100 men.
		17. Thánbôhla ...	**11**	**0**	199	4	
		18. Kyaukpadaung.	**10**	**0**	209	4	
		19. Yedaung ...	**13**	**0**	222	4	
		20. Thayetmyo ... or	**3**	**0**	225	4	Crossing Irrawaddy.
		16. Letpánsun ...	**13**	**0**	190	4	
		17. Myothit ...	**9**	**0**	199	4	
		18. Talôkgyaung.	**4**	**0**	203	4	
		19. Allanmyo ...	**14**	**0**	217	4	
		20. Thayetmyo ...	**5**	**0**	222	4	Crossing Irrawaddy.

BRANCH I.

FROM SHÁNMANGÉ (STAGE 6) TO KYWÉGÁN.

BY LIEUT. E. W. M. NORIE, 2ND MIDDLESEX REGIMENT, FEBRUARY 1888.

Military	Civil	Stage	Int. M.	F.	Total M.	F.	Remarks
G.O.C. Rangoon District.	Comr., Eastern Divn., and Deputy Comr., Meiktila.	**1. Kywégán** ... Three nullahs.	**14**	**0**	14	0	Road crosses chaung just outside Shán mangé and runs in a southerly direc tion. Road a good sandy cart track At 2 miles reach Yéma, a large villag with kyaungs and good water. Fro

FROM MYINGYÁN TO THAYETMYO *viâ* NATÔGYI, TAUNGDWINGYI AND ALLANMYO—*continued.*

BRANCH I—*continued.*

Authorities. Military.	Authorities. Civil.	Number and Names of Stages, Rivers and Streams.	Distances. Intermediate.	Distances. Total.	Remarks.
G.O.C. Rangoon District.	Commissioner, Eastern Division, and Deputy Commissioner, Meiktila.	**1. Kywégán**—*cont.*			here the road runs through thin jungle and crosses the chaung again, at 6 miles, beyond which it passes village of Myokè. Good water. Road from here runs through open country and paddy cultivation, and passes five small villages about 1 mile apart. At 11 miles pass a chaung and the village of Lusai. Kywégán is a big village with accommodation in kyaungs and zayáts to north of village for 200 men. Plenty of good water from wells. No good camping ground. Usual supplies and about 30 carts procurable.

BRANCH II.

FROM SHÁNMANGÉ (STAGE 6) TO NABÉGÔN.

BY CAPT. TINLEY, 1ST BOMBAY LANCERS, FEBRUARY 1888.

Military.	Civil.	Stages, Rivers and Streams.	Intermediate. M. F.	Total. M. F.	Remarks.
G.O.C. Rangoon District.	Commissioner, Eastern Division, and Deputy Commissioner, Meiktila.	**1. Nabégôn** ... Several small streams with steep banks and between the villages of Yengán and Tawbu the Shánmangé chaung is crossed.	8 0	8 0	On leaving Shánmangé fort the road runs north-west and passes for 1½ miles along a sandy lane, bordered by thick hedges, thence through scrub jungle to village Yengán 2½ miles. Patches of cultivation on both sides of road and around village. At 5½ miles on the road which has been through small chaungs, passes Tawbu village and thence on over good hard gravel and fairly high to Nabégôn post, which is a small earthwork 180 feet square to accommodate 25 native and 25 Burman police. The road has been cleared, and in places made by the military police; it is one of the best in the neighbourhood. There is good water all along the road. Yengán and Tawbu have no accommodation, but ½ mile north of Nabégôn is the large village of Chaungôn with good kyaungs and accommodation for 100 men. Good water. General direction north-west.

BRANCH III.

FROM SHÁNMANGÉ (STAGE 6) TO SUGYIETÁN.

BY CAPT. TINLEY, 1ST BOMBAY LANCERS, FEBRUARY 1888.

Military.	Civil.	Stages, Rivers and Streams.	Intermediate. M. F.	Total. M. F.	Remarks.
G.O.C. Rangoon District.	Commissioner, Eastern Division, and Deputy Commissioner, Meiktila.	**1. Sugyietán** ... Near Athetmyit the Shánmangé chaung is crossed and further on 1½ miles before Sugyiétan village is reached, another large steep-banked stream.	6 0	6 0	The road runs from Shánmangé Fort generally west-south-west, and is an ordinary jungle track at present, but will very shortly be improved by the military police. One mile village Athetmyit, small, with small kyaung. Then on through jungle crossing one or two large nullahs, but generally on fairly rising ground, hard and capable of improvement; to Sugyietán police post 6 miles. This is an earthwork 180 feet square with accommodation for 25 native and 25 Burman police. Fair water. Sugyietán village is 5½ miles on road. Small and no accommodation.

No. 20.

FROM MYINGYÁN TO THAYETMYO *viâ* NATÔGYI, TAUNGDWINGYI AND ALLANMYO—*continued.*

BRANCH IV.

FROM SHÁNMANGÉ (STAGE 6) TO WAMATAW (FOOT OF PÔPA HILL).

BY LIEUT. STAVELEY, 1ST BOMBAY LANCERS, AND CAPT. TINLEY, 1ST BOMBAY LANCERS.

Authorities. Military.	Authorities. Civil.	Number and Names of Stages, Rivers and Streams.	Distances. Intermediate. M.	F.	Total. M.	F.	Remarks.
G.O.C. Rangoon District.	Commissioner, Eastern Division, and Deputy Commissioner, Meiktila.	**1. Taungu** ... Several small nullahs. Shánmangé nullah to be crossed close to the post impassable in flood. Small streams and nullahs.	12	4	12	4	Kyetpeta, 8½ miles, cart road over hard, sand and gravel passing along ridges. Jungle and patches of cultivation. Good kyaungs and water good. At 12½ miles reach Taungu cart road as above. Good village. Accommodation: kyaungs to north of village will accommodate 60 men. Water good.
		2. Wamataw ... Several small nullahs. One very bad nullah just before village.	13	0	25	4	At 3½ miles Watkyukôn village lately changed from old site. Water good. No kyaungs. Very good position to hold. At 7 miles reach Letpábya. One small kyaung. Cultivation all round village. Water fair. Police post occupied by 30 men. At 11 miles Watakyin village. Good water and good kyaungs. At 13 miles reach Wamataw. Good position. No kyaungs. Water excellent. Always a stream running from Pôpa. Wamataw is situated on a wedge of land between two nullahs. Village destroyed.

No. 21.

From MYINGYÁN to THAYETMYO viâ PAGÁN, KYAUKPADAUNG, TAUNGDWINGYI, and ALLANMYO.

BY LIEUT. E. W. M. NORIE, 2ND MIDDLESEX REGIMENT, FEBRUARY 1888.

Military.	Civil.	Stages.	Intermediate. M.	F.	Total. M.	F.	Remarks.
G.O.C. Myingyán District.	Commissioner, Southern Division, and Deputy Commissioner, Myingyán.	**1. Dhattaw** ...	16	0	16	0	*Vide* Route No. 19.
		2. Letpángyibwa.	11	4	27	4	
		3. Nyaung-u (Pagán).	10	0	37	4	
		4. Taungzin ... Three nullahs.	13	4	51	0	Good road all the way through small jungle, with patches of cultivation (dry crops) enclosed with hedges. Cavalry can manœuvre over all this ground. No water along the road.

FROM MYINGYÁN TO THAYETMYO *viâ* PAGÁN, KYAUKPADAUNG, TAUNGDWINGYI, AND ALLANMYO—*continued.*

Authorities. Military.	Authorities. Civil.	Number and Names of Stages, Rivers and Streams.	Distances. Intermediate.	Distances. Total.	Remarks.
G.O.C. Myingyán District.	Commissioner, Southern Division, and Deputy Commissioner, Myingyán.	**4. Taungzin**—*cont.*			Crosses two nullahs about half-way and a third broad sandy one just before Taungzin. About 5 miles from Pagán reach the end of a range of hills, which runs parallel to the road about ½ mile to the south as far as Taungzin. Hills from 300 to 500 feet high and covered with scrub jungle. Taungzin is a small village, about 50 houses, surrounded by a thorn hedge. It is a police post. There is accommodation for about 50 men in a kyaung about ¼ mile south of a tank, and plenty of good ground for encampment. Water from tank good and plentiful. Grain, grass, and probably 30 carts procurable from the thugyi.
			M. F.	M. F.	
		5. Kyaukpadaung. Two dry nullahs.	**17 0**	68 0	Road good through the same description of country for 10 or 12 miles. Water to be got at the different villages. Kyaukpadaung is a large village with a thorn fence round it. It contains many kyaungs and zayáts, which afford a certain amount of accommodation. There are two large tanks, but the water is very indifferent and muddy in dry weather. There is a police post and stockade here and good encamping ground close to a tank. There is a good bazaar, and bullocks, fowls, paddy, *jowári*, and other supplies are obtainable. A limited quantity of transport is also procurable, say, 100 carts. The first 12 miles of the road lead through thick jungle, which has been cleared for the first 5 miles. Road fair, but rocky and rough, crosses several deep, broad, sandy nullahs with no water in them; all quite passable for carts. View very limited and country not practicable for cavalry. The last 2 miles are under dry crop cultivation. There is another road from Pagán to Kyaukpadaung, through Sé (16½ miles), Pôpa (20 miles), and Kyaukpadaung (11 miles)—total 47½ miles, *see* Branch I below. It is much longer; and the road is rough, hilly, and much cut up with nullahs. Water is also not to be got along a great part of this route. There is a road from here to Silé 28 miles, very heavy and sandy. There is also a road to Singu, *see* Route No. 41.
		6. Magyigôn ...	**14 0**	82 0	Good road, no nullahs, hard and firm, mile-stones along the road. Low hills about 1 mile to south of road for first 4 miles. At about 7 miles there is a large hill with a pagoda on it, close to the road on the north side, covered with thin scrub jungle. Water is scarce for first 8 miles. The country for the last 6 miles is under paddy. Pass two small villages. A river runs to the south of Magyigôn, which is a large village. It contains a police post and a court-house, head-quarters of an Assistant Commissioner. All supplies, &c., are procurable. Accommodation in kyaungs for 200 men. Water good and plentiful. Fifty carts probably procurable.

FROM MYINGYÁN TO THAYETMYO *viâ* PAGÁN, KYAUKPADAUNG, TAUNGDWINGYI, AND ALLANMYO—*continued.*

Authorities. Military.	Authorities. Civil.	Number and Names of Stages, Rivers and Streams.	Distances. Intermediate. M.	F.	Total. M.	F.	Remarks.
G.O.C. Myingyán District.	Commissioner, Southern Division, and Deputy Commissioner, Magwé.	**7. Shwébandaw**... Pin river.	**14**	**0**	96	0	On leaving Magyigôn the road crosses the Pin river, about 200 yards wide, but nearly dry in hot weather. In the rainy season it is impassable after rain. Half-way to Shwébandaw it crosses a low range of hills. Highest point 1,500 feet above sea-level. Country undulating and covered with scrub jungle, except near the villages. Water good, obtainable at the villages. Shwébandaw is a large village and situated on high ground. There is a stockaded post for 50 men 400 yards to east of village and accommodation for about 100 men in two kyaungs and zayáts. Water from wells good and plentiful. There is a Myo-ôk and the country to the east is well cultivated, and supplies of *jowári*, paddy, and *kerbi* are procurable. A large number of carts and cattle can be got from this and the neighbouring villages.
		8. Ywamôn ... Myo river twice and small stream.	**8**	**0**	104	0	Road a good cart track cleared of jungle, fairly open for last few miles. Country same as before. Pass the village of Pin with a high thorn hedge. It is the head town of the district and contains a post. All supplies obtainable and a large number of carts. Ywamôn is a fair-sized village. Accommodation is good in kyaungs. Water good Ordinary supplies obtainable and probably about 30 carts.
		9. Natmauk ... One small stream.	**14**	**0**	118	0	Road and country are the same as before. At 4 miles pass the village of Zalôkgyi, where the water is bad. At 8 and 10 miles pass Lé-aing and Naungyaung, at both of which places there is good water; at the latter accommodation for 50 men in two kyaungs. The road here crosses a dry sandy chaung. Natmauk is a strong, large thorn-fenced village and is really composed of four villages. It stands on the high bank of the Yen river. Accommodation for 50 men in police post and for 100 more in two kyaungs and zayáts. Good camping ground to north-west and south. Supplies of all sorts procurable from the Myo-ôk. Water good and plentiful from wells and chaung. About 50 carts can be obtained.
		10. Myothit ... Yen river.	**12**	**0**	130	0	The dry weather road runs along the bed of the Yen for about a mile. That used in the wet weather follows the river bank as far as Nakhángyi, where it crosses and thence runs along the lower bank to Myothit. The Yen river is here about 500 yards broad and is dry in the hot weather, though impassable after rain. Water from the chaung. Road passes several fair-sized villages. Myothit is a large village with a military police post for 50 men. Accommodation

FROM MYINGYÁN TO THAYETMYO *viâ* PAGÁN, KYAUKPADAUNG, TAUNGDWINGYI, AND ALLANMYO—*continued.*

Authorities. Military.	Authorities. Civil.	Number and Names of Stages, Rivers and Streams.	Distances. Intermediate. M.	Distances. Intermediate. F.	Distances. Total. M.	Distances. Total. F.	Remarks.
G.O.C. Myingyán District.	Commissioner, Southern Division, and Deputy Commissioner, Magwé.	**10. Myothit**—*cont.*					for 150 more in kyaungs. Camping ground to east. Water good, though not very clear, from two or three wells and from chaung. It is the centre of a sub-division; and all supplies and a good many carts are obtainable from the thugyi.
		11. Taungdwingyi. Three chaungs.	**17**	**0**	147	0	As far as Myolin the road is good, running through thin jungle and crossing the Sûn and Palin chaungs, both of which are always fordable. From here it runs through paddy interspersed with patches of jungle the whole way to Taungdwingyi and is in dry weather very good, but in the rains is impassable for carts, which go by a road further to the west. There are a great many cart tracks and it is hard to say which is the regular road. Cross the Sidôn chaung at 12 miles, which is dry most of the year. Taungdwingyi is a large walled town with a stockaded military post for 400 men. There is also a large bazaar and supplies are plentiful. There is a Deputy Commissioner's court-house and treasury.
		12. Zibinwaing ...	**10**	**0**	157	0	The road throughout from Taungdwingyi to the Kadinmatha is a fair one over undulating country, covered for the most part with jungle. Villages passed are Nyaungbinhla (1 mile), Kalégán (5 miles), Thaingôn (7¼ miles). At all of these villages there are kyaungs and good water. At Zíbinwaing there are five kyaungs and zayáts and good water.
G.O.C. Rangoon District.	Lower Burma.	**13. Kadinmatha.**	**18**	**0**	175	0	Six villages passed. The principal ones are Pyogyaung, good water, two kyaungs and two zayâts; Pelé (16 miles), good water, three kyaungs. Kadinmatha is a village of about 40 houses with three kyaungs. The water is good. From Kadinmatha to Allanmyo is a distance of about 40 miles south-west and west. The route is said to be a good cart road, but has not yet been reported on, beyond merely giving the stages as follows.
		14. Letpánsun ...	**13**	**0**	188	0	*Vide* Route No. 20, crossing the Irrawaddy at Allanmyo.
		15. Myothit ...	**9**	**0**	197	0	
		16. Talôkgyaung.	**4**	**0**	201	0	
		17. Allanmyo ...	**14**	**0**	215	0	
		18. Thayetmyo ...	**5**	**0**	220	0	

No. 21.

FROM MYINGYÁN TO THAYETMYO *viâ* PAGÁN, KYAUKPADAUNG, TAUNGDWINGYI, AND ALLANMYO—*continued.*

BRANCH I.

FROM KYAUKPADAUNG (STAGE 5) TO SÉ.

I. B. COMPILATION, MARCH 1888.

Authorities. Military.	Authorities. Civil.	Number and Names of Stages, Rivers and Streams.	Distances. Intermediate. M. F.	Distances. Total. M. F.	Remarks.
G.O.C. Myingyán District.	Commissioner, Southern Division, and Deputy Commissioner, Myingyán.	**1. Pôpa**	**11 0**	11 0	The road, a sandy cart track, partially cleared, over undulating ground as far as village of Sakyin, 8½ miles. Leaving this on the right it rises after crossing a sandy nullah to the deserted military post of Sakyin. From this point it is a good bridle road winding up the hill to west and north till it reaches the fine open plateau 2,000 feet above the sea on which Pôpa is situated. The plateau is about 1 mile each way, and is well cultivated and there are many fruit trees. The military post is 400 yards east of the village, a strong and nicely-shaded post with stream of good water running close by it and accommodation for 100 men. From here a bridle road leads to the top of Pôpa hill, distant 4 miles, the height of the top 5,150 feet above the sea. There is a signal post here with accommodation for 20 men, but the water has to be brought up from near Pôpa post. There are several plateaux suitable for camps on the west slope of the hill at heights of 2,800, 3,000 and 4,500 feet.
		2. Sé	**20 0**	31 0	The road runs for a mile over the plateau and then descends by a very steep cart road to the plain below. The country is covered with thick thorn jungle, broken and undulating, the general height being 1,000 feet above sea-level. Four dry nullahs are crossed. There is no water on the road except one muddy tank at Kudán, 12 miles. The road is sandy and heavy. Sé is a fair-sized village, with military post for 50 men, and good water from surface wells in nullahs. There is also a kyaung and zayát in which 50 men more could find shelter. The country about Sé is much broken by ravines and covered with thick thorn jungle. From here there is a road to Pagán 16½ miles.

BRANCH II.

FROM SHWÉBANDAW (STAGE 7) TO YÉGALÉ.

BY LIEUT. F. G. CARDEW, 2ND "Q.O." B.L.I., MARCH 1887.

Authorities. Military.	Authorities. Civil.	Number and Names of Stages, Rivers and Streams.	Intermediate. M. F.	Total. M. F.	Remarks.
G.O.C. Myingyán District.	Commissioner, Southern Division, and Deputy Commissioner, Magwé.	**1. Singaung** ... One large stream.	**10 0**	10 0	General direction north. A good cart road. At 2½ miles pass the village of Didôkôn, at 4 miles Danditôn, at 5 miles Pethánthawgôn, at 6½ miles Pethánthaw, at 7 miles Kyaungwet, and at 9 miles Thangyin. At 8½ miles the road crosses a large chaung about 30 yards broad, bed very sandy, banks steep and 20 feet high, approached by cuttings. Water in pools. The country is generally very flat, especially near Shwébandaw. Villages are numerous and the amount of

From MYINGYÁN to THAYETMYO *viâ* PAGÁN, KYAUKPADAUNG, TAUNGDWINGYI, and ALLANMYO—*continued.*

BRANCH II—*continued.*

Authorities. Military.	Authorities. Civil.	Number and Names of Stages, Rivers and Streams.	Distances. Intermediate. M.	F.	Distances. Total. M.	F.	Remarks.
G.O.C. Myingyán District.	Commnr., Southern Divn., and Dy. Commissioner, Magwé.	**1. Singaung**—*cont.*					cultivation considerable. Dry crops with a large quantity of paddy along the first 4 miles of road. Singaung is a small village with accommodation in kyaungs and zayáts for over 200 men. Water fairly good and plentiful from a surface well and large pond.
	Commissioner, Southern Division, and Deputy Commr., Myingyán.	**2. Letpábya** ...	7	6	17	6	Good road over open undulating country. General direction north. At 1 mile pass Thagôndain and at $7\frac{3}{4}$ miles reach Letpábya. Nature of country becomes more hilly about 1 mile from the town. Letpábya is a village of about 80 houses. Supplies and water plentiful. Accommodation in kyaungs for 60 men. (For this village *see* also in Stage 2 of Branch IV, Route No. 20.)
G.O.C. Rangoon District.	Commissioner, Eastern Division, and Deputy Commissioner, Meiktila.	**3. Yégalé** ... ... Byégyi chaung.	12	6	30	4	The nature of the road changes and it becomes a very winding and rough mountain road only practicable for pack animals. Beyond Letpábya cross the Byégyi chaung 10 yards wide, rocky bed and running water till end of February. Slopes begin, at first gentle, but increasing in steepness as the road goes further north. At 4 miles pass Pettaw, a good-sized village standing on an open spot of very high ground. Water procurable, good. Accommodation in kyaungs and zayáts for about 100 men. From here road fairly level for about $2\frac{1}{2}$ miles and then leads to the range of hills to the north of which Yégalé is situated. The highest point is reached at about 8 miles and the descent on the north side is much steeper than the ascent from the south. The hills are of hard sandstone, covered everywhere with small trees.

BRANCH III.

From PIN (*see* in Stage 8) to UYIN (Stage 6 on Route No. 14).

I. B. Compilation, November 1888.

Military.	Civil.	Number and Names of Stages, Rivers and Streams.	Intermediate. M.	F.	Total. M.	F.	Remarks.
G.O.C. Myingyán District.	Commissioner, Southern Division, and Deputy Commissioner, Magwé.	**1. Tanaunghla** ... Yen river and small rocky stream near Tanaunghla.	12	0	12	0	Go down the road towards Natmauk for $1\frac{1}{4}$ miles. Road then branches off to south-east over level cultivated country and is a cart road. Pass village of Kángyigôn. Water from a pond not very good. At $4\frac{1}{4}$ miles reach Bôaing on the right bank of the Yen river. Accommodation in kyaungs for 45 men. Supplies plentiful. Water from stream good. From here descent to river is steep. The stream is 70 yards broad and sandy. Impassable when in flood. From here the road gradually rises for about $4\frac{1}{2}$ miles to the top of a ridge whence there is an extensive view. Country low. Hills covered with scrub jungle. Tanaunghla is a small village with accommodation in kyaungs for 35 men. Water good from stream to north of village. Supplies obtainable.

FROM MYINGYÁN TO THAYETMYO *viâ* PAGÁN, KYAUKPADAUNG, TAUNGDWINGYI, AND ALLANMYO—*continued*.

BRANCH III—*continued*.

Authorities. Military.	Authorities. Civil.	Number and Names of Stages, Rivers and Streams.	Intermediate. M.	Intermediate. F.	Total. M.	Total. F.	Remarks.
G.O.C. Myingyán District.	Commr., Southern Divn., and Dy. Commr., Magwé.	**2. Uyin** ... ... Pyen chaung crossed twice and five small nullahs.	**15**	**0**	27	0	Fair cart road over low hills. Country very open and covered with long coarse grass. Cross a small chaung at 2¼ miles. At 6 miles reach Thigyaung. Thence to Uyin, *see* Route No. 14, Stage 6.

BRANCH IV.

FROM MYOTHIT (STAGE 10) TO THAMÔNGÔN (ROUTE NO. 14, STAGE 5).

I. B. COMPILATION, 1887-88.

Military	Civil	Stage	Int. M.	Int. F.	Total M.	Total F.	Remarks
[G.O.C. Myingyán District.	Commissioner, Southern Division, and Deputy Commissioner, Magwé.	**1. Magyigôngalé.**	**10**	**0**	10	0	Road runs along the bank of the Yen river. At 5¼ miles cross a stream (a tributary of the Yen). At 6 miles pass Talopan village. The road still runs north parallel to the Yen river. At 8 miles it changes direction and runs east. At Magyigôngalé there are some kyaungs close to the bank of the stream before mentioned.
		2. Kalashin ...	**9**	**0**	19	0	Road runs in a south-east direction, but is very circuitous and passes over a hilly country covered with jungle. On leaving Magyigôngalé the stream above mentioned has to be crossed. At Kalashin the road joins Route No. 14.
		3. Thamôngôn ...	**8**	**0**	27	0	*See* Route No. 14, Stage 5.

No. 22.

From MYINGYÁN to WUNDWIN viâ PYINZI.

I. B. COMPILATION, NOVEMBER 1888.

Military	Civil	Stage	Int. M.	Int. F.	Total M.	Total F.	Remarks
G.O.C. Myingyán District.	Commissioner, Southern Division, and Deputy Commissioner, Myingyán.	**1. Ywagyi** ...	**11**	**0**	11	0	General direction east. Road passes through cultivation. Pass Kyaungdaung at 1 mile, Thitpinshé at 3 miles, Kyetnaga at 7 miles, Nyaunginwé at 9 miles. Road good and fit for carts. At Ywagyi roads branch off to Kánswé (5 miles) and Nanwindawbo (5 miles).
		2. Natôgyi ...	**10**	**0**	21	0	Road good and fit for carts. Pass Kánywa at 1 mile, Pôngtha at 3 miles, Shábu at 6 miles. From Shábu there is a branch road to Tebi and Myotha, passing through Minywa at 2 miles,

FROM MYINGYÁN TO WUNDWIN *viâ* PYINZI—*continued.*

Authorities. Military.	Authorities. Civil.	Number and Names of Stages, Rivers and Streams.	Distances. Intermediate.	Distances. Total.	Remarks.
G.O.C. Myingyán District.	Commissioner, Southern Division, and Deputy Commissioner, Myingyán.	**2. Natôgyi**—*cont.*			Bôgain at 4 miles, Lethugalégôn at 1½ miles, and branch from the latter to Kánsokôn 2 miles, and to the Sekyadaung hill. Natôgyi contains a small police post, surrounded by a breastwork and ditch on the west of the town. There is an Assistant Superintendent of Police. Natôgyi is a large village with a Myo-ôk. Good accommodation in kyaungs about 600 yards north of village. There is a large tank about 200 yards south of police post and plenty of good drinking water from a well just outside the fort. There is also a well of good water in the kyaung enclosure. Ground for camp all round the post. The supplies are *kerbi* and paddy; and there is also a large quantity of cotton and *jowári* cultivated in this district. A large number of carts are procurable.
		3. Pyinzi	M. F. 14 4	M. F. 35 4	At 2¼ miles from Natôgyi pass the village of Tsin, 20 houses. Water from tank and two wells. One small kyaung and zayáts. Camping ground small. At 5¼ miles pass village of Ôtwin, 30 houses. Water from well good. A few zayáts only. Camping ground bad. At 7¼ miles pass village of Pakku, 23 houses. Water-supply one tank, one well. One zayát only. Camping ground none. At 11¾ miles pass the village of Ywadaw, 15 houses. Water from one well; no accommodation; camping ground none. The road throughout from Natôgyi is good and travelled by carts. Thick jungle between Pakku and Ywadaw. For description of Pyinzi *see* Route No. 56, Northern Division.
		4. Taungbo ... Two nullahs.	12 2	47 6	Direction of road south-east through cultivation and jungle; fairly open and road in good condition and level. At 5 miles pass Paungtha village (60 houses) and cross sandy bed of nullah. Water good. At 7½ miles pass Yôgán road through cultivation. Beyond Yôgán a good road has been cleared through thick jungle. Immediately before reaching Taungbo cross the sandy bed of a nullah. Village of 100 houses. Accommodation in kyaungs and zayáts bad. Well water good and plentiful. A large number of cattle here. Big pagoda ½ mile before Taungbo. Good camping ground for 300 men with a built reservoir and tank of good water.
G.O.C. Rangoon District.	Commissioner, Eastern Division, and Deputy Commissioner, Meiktila.	**5. Wundwin** ... Two nullahs and several small ravines.	12 0	59 6	From Taungbo the road, bad in wet weather, runs through cultivation to Kángyi, a small village of 40 houses with a few cattle and good water. Passing Kángyi the road crosses a dry nullah and passes the village of Kánzwé, about ¼ mile to the left of the road. From here the road has been cleared through jungle and at 6 miles from Taungbo passes the small deserted village of Nabagôn, situated on rising ground surrounded by jungle. From here the road is level to Payázu and crosses a dry sandy nullah just before reaching that village. From here a good level road runs to Wundwin.

FROM MYINGYÁN TO WUNDWIN *viâ* PYINZI—*continued.*

ALTERNATIVE I.

FROM MYINGYÁN TO WUNDWIN *viâ* DAUNGBU.

Authorities.		Number and Names of Stages, Rivers and Streams.	Distances.				Remarks.
Military.	Civil.		Intermediate.		Total.		
			M.	F.	M.	F.	
G.O.C. Myingyán District.	Commissioner, Southern Division, and Deputy Commissioner, Myingyán.	**1. Ywagyi** ...	11	0	...		As above.
		2. Natôgyi ...	10	0	21	0	As above.
		3. Daungbu ...	7	2	28	2	Natôgyi to Pébin, 2¼ miles, south-east direction. Road fairly good and open cultivation on both sides. Tank 1½ miles on left of road, probably dry in hot weather. Just here is thin jungle on either side down to Pébin, when country all fairly under cultivation, principally paddy and a little maize. To Payagyi 3¼ miles; 50 houses. Kyaungs on either side of road capable of holding 250 men, also pagodas on right or village side, surrounded by 3 feet walls. Quarter of a mile further on small kyaungs on left; ¼ mile further Aunga. Kyaungs on right side capable of holding 250 men. The small village of Aunga, about 300 yards, to left of road. Troops are recommended to halt at Aunga, where there is plenty of water and good kyaungs, as at Daungbu water is bad. Road between Payagyi and Daungbu is bad after rains. Ordinary supplies procurable. A large number of cattle and some 20 carts.
		4. Kôkôgyi ... One nullah 1 mile below Sôngôn; good water.	11	0	39	2	Daungbu to Sôngôn 5 miles, on a very good road rising from Daungbu and running along a ridge. Thick jungle to within 1 mile of Sôngôn, when country open and fairly cultivated. A few pagodas on left side of road, about 300 yards distant down slope of ridge. Sôngôn 40 houses. Little water. No accommodation. Little cultivation round village. To south about ¾ mile is Thadígôn village, possessing one big kyaung and lots of water. One mile to west of this is another village of 80 houses and two big kyaungs, a small lake being between these villages. Sôngôn pagodas, about ½ mile to east. No kyaungs. Sôngôn to Kôkôgyi 6½ miles. Road up and down gravel soil, and would be good in dry weather, with exception of part entering Kôkôgyi itself, across a swamp (which took 300 men three hours to carry 200 carts over 150 yards). Thickish jungle about nullah, especially to within 1 mile of Kôkôgyi, where country is cultivated principally with paddy and maize. A few small villages seen in jungle and one large one 4 miles to north of Kôkôgyi. Kôkôgyi 100 houses. Kyaungs and zayáts on north side. Accommodation for 300 men. Good water in wells. Several tanks, but water bad. Running stream to south of village.
		5. Taungbo ...	12	6	52	0	Kôkôgyi to Hlédutaung 3 miles. Road fairly good, but muddy in parts. Usual supplies and fodder obtainable, also a number of cattle and some carts. Hlédutaung 100 houses. One large kyaung and encampment for 300 men. Water unlimited from built reservoir and stream. Encamping ground for one regiment. To Paungtha proper 2½ miles. Road good except where stream to be crossed in one or two places. Thence to Taungbo 7½ miles, as above.

FROM MYINGYÁN TO WUNDWIN *viâ* PYINZI—*continued.*

ALTERNATIVE I—*continued.*

Authorities. Military.	Authorities. Civil.	Number and Names of Stages, Rivers and Streams.	Distances. Intermediate. M. F.	Distances. Total. M. F.	Remarks.
G.O.C. Rangoon District.	Commr., Eastern Div., and Dy. Commr., Meiktila.	**6. Wundwin** ...	**12 0**	64 0	Thence to Wundwin as above.

ALTERNATIVE II.

FROM MYINGYÁN TO WUNDWIN *viâ* TAZU AND NYAUNGÔK.

Authorities. Military.	Authorities. Civil.	Number and Names of Stages, Rivers and Streams.	Distances. Intermediate. M. F.	Distances. Total. M. F.	Remarks.
G.O.C. Myingyán District.	Commissioner, Southern Division, and Deputy Commissioner, Myingyán.	**1. Tazu** ... ... Three nullahs.	**12 0**	12 0	Leaving the barracks by the south the road crosses the nullah which runs through the town of Myingyán by the bridge and then bends away to the south-east. At about 2½ miles it crosses a second nullah running along its bed for a short distance. At 4 miles the village of Phaunga is reached. Phaunga, a large village, 80 houses. Kyaungs and zayáts sufficient for 150 men. Water from wells and chaung good. So far the road is bad, being almost entirely through heavy sand. Country mostly scrub jungle. Beyond Phaunga a third nullah is crossed and from here the road to Tazu is good, passing through high undulating country, mostly cultivated. At 7½ miles pass small village of Kánzin and 2 miles further on Thanakándaw, a village of about 50 houses and two kyaungs, sufficient for 100 men. Two and-a-half miles from here reach Tazu, a large village. Kyaungs on south of village and camping ground in kyaung enclosure. Accommodation for 300 men. Good water from wells. Usual supplies obtainable. Cultivation, cotton and *jowári*. Roads to north-west and south.
		2. Ingyaung ...	**6 0**	18 0	The road still continues good and runs through cultivation, passing small village of Malé. At 1½ miles it runs to Ingyaung. A prosperous village, 80 houses. Large kyaung on west, separated by river 120 to 200 yards wide. Banks steep on left side. Good water from wells and river. Usual supplies procurable.
		3. Palángôn ... One nullah.	**7 0**	25 0	At 2½ miles from Ingyaung the road ascends and runs along a high ridge of land for 4½ miles, when it reaches a poor village called Palángôn, with no accommodation, but ground for camping and plenty of water from wells.
		4. Nyaungôk ...	**10 0**	35 0	**The road from here to Nyaungôk is good, running through well cultivated country past Ywathi, 3 miles, a small village, and Thayetkaungain, 6 miles; 80 houses and kyaungs capable of holding 150 men; to Nyaungôk, a large village, said by the thugyi to have 400 houses, but really about 200. Excellent kyaungs, hold 100 men, on east, separated from village by chaung about 40 yards wide, low banks. Water good and plentiful from wells. Usual supplies procurable. Position of Nyaungôk very strong, as it is bounded on three sides with streams and creeks covered with vegetation up to the banks. From where there is a route to Máhlaing, 15½ miles, *see* Route No. 17, Branch I.**

FROM MYINGYÁN TO WUNDWIN *viâ* PYINZI—*continued.*

ALTERNATIVE II—*continued.*

Authorities. Military.	Authorities. Civil.	Number and Names of Stages, Rivers and Streams.	Distances. Intermediate. M.	F.	Distances. Total. M.	F.	Remarks.
G.O.C. Rangoon District.	Commissioner, Eastern Division, and Deputy Commissioner, Meiktila.	**5. Pindalé** ... Stream in two places.	10	6	45	6	Road bad, alternating from sand to stone and stone to cotton soil, the last, however, predominating. Passed the villages of Myinthé, Mônbain, and Yénán: the second is in a very strong position. Cross stream near Nyaungôk. Little water. No bridge. Sandy bottom. Cross again at Mônbain, rocky bottom. Pwégán is a good-sized village, with accommodation for some 70 men in kyaungs. Water good from wells. Ordinary supplies obtainable and probably 50 carts. Road good, but soft in places. For Pindalé *see* routes Nos. 17, Branch II, and 18.
		6. Aintha ... One nullah.	11	0	56	6	Road by no means good in the wet weather. For the first 5 miles the road has been cleared and runs through low cactus jungle. Cross the Thimbôn chaung and pass Thôndaungaing. About 50 houses. No accommodation. Road crosses a good deal of paddy for 6 miles to Aintha, village of about 100 houses. Accommodation in kyaungs for about 300 men. Water good from wells. Ordinary supplies obtainable and probably some 20 carts.
		7. Wundwin ... One stream close to Wundwin; sandy bottom.	7	0	63	6	Road by no means good in wet weather, as it passes over a good deal of paddy. At 3 miles pass village of Nwanán, at 6 miles Tanaungôn and at 7 miles Wundwin.

No. 23.

From NAPÉ to AKYAB viâ AENG PASS and MYOHAUNG.

BY LIEUT. H. B. WALKER, 1ST DUKE OF CORNWALL'S LIGHT INFANTRY, ATTACHÉ, INTELLIGENCE DEPARTMENT, 1891.

Military	Civil	Stage	Inter. M.	F.	Total M.	F.	Remarks
G.O.C. Myingyán District.	Commissioner, Southern Division, and Deputy Commissioner, Minbu.	**1. Minlwin** ... Three dry nullahs and the Doé chaung beyond village of Minlwin, the stream running to the right of the village and across its front almost north and south. The Doé chaung is about 1½ feet deep and 10 to 15 yards wide, except in dry weather when it is about 5 yards wide.	4	4	4	4	Direction of road west-south-west. The road runs almost entirely along the top of a low ridge ascending and descending, with short gradients and ordinary windings through a jungle of "*in*" easily removable either by fire or axe. Easily engineered. Soil sandy and rocky. Passable for carts, but requiring improvement. Average width of road 3 to 4½ or 5 feet. The dry nullahs which cross the road appear to act as drains to the roadway, and run parallel with it. Minlwin is a small village of 30 houses, with an excellent halting place or zayát outside. Village on left hand and 50 yards from river Doé or Du. Supplies, *nil.* Cooly labour difficult

FROM NAPÊ TO AKYAB *viâ* AENG PASS AND MYOHAUNG—*continued.*

Authorities. Military.	Authorities. Civil.	Number and Names of Stages, Rivers and Streams.	Distances. Intermediate.	Distances. Total.	Remarks.
G.O.C. Myingyán District.	Commissioner, Southern Division, and Deputy Commissioner, Minbu.	**1. Minlwin**—*cont.*			to obtain and only in small numbers. Said to be very unhealthy during the rains. Inhabitants: Burmans and Chins. There is no military pos ition near and all is dense jungle. Half-a-mile to the south is a small village, Pagaung, 12 houses, stockaded. Inhabitants are Chins.
		2. Chauchin ... Man chaung is crossed 55 or 56 times by the road. Depth 1½ feet to 4½ feet. Direction of river west, ordinary rate per hour. Fords easily crossed. Bottom of river gravelly and stony, the stones being unstratified.	M. F. 12 0	M. F. 16 4	Direction of road west-south-west. Leaving Minlwin, it is level through paddy-fields for ⅛ a mile and then through "*in*" and bamboo jungle. Easily cleared and the road easily workable. Soil more or less sandy, and little material available for repairs, unless brought from the river, whence small gravel is easily obtained. Average width of road 2½ to 4 feet. It works along the river bed upwards towards its source. This route therefore during the rains lies principally under water, and the natives who pass along the road work from hill side to hill side crossing the river when obliged in small bamboo rafts. (*N.B.*—It is to be observed that where the present route lies along the river bed it would be very easy to engineer a road along the hill side clearing away the jungle and cutting into the slope; by doing so also several crossings could be avoided. The soil of the hill sides is of firm composition and would stand working into a road, though the gradients running towards the river are very steep. In many places the road has been cut in the hill side. The river is crossed twice in the last 200 yards, while on the left bank is a new village called Padaung, the old village of Sinwangaung being deserted. Chauchin itself lies on the right bank; seven or eight houses on the hill side. It is a bad camping ground, though camping grounds on the dry river bed are all along the route. The river bed being often 300 yards wide, thus giving the river a great width during the rainy season. All the fords, as shown in the column "Rivers," are easy of crossing except the last two which are rough and stony.
		3. Thát Sakhán or Thaya Sakhán. The Man river is crossed and recrossed ten times up to the junction of the Man and Kin rivers, the current running 8 miles an hour.	6 4	23 0	Leaving Chauchin the road runs west-south-west for 4½ miles, as far as the junction of the Kin and Man chaungs; the road is level, but rough at river crossings. Though running along the river bed chiefly, it could be easily taken through the jungle which merely requires clearing. From the junction of the Kin and Man chaungs, the road rises precipitously up to Thát Sakhán. It is one long rise, the path running along the ridge. The jungle is dense and path stony and much broken. Thát Sakhán is a plateau formed by the flatening out of the ridge into a

FROM NAPÉ TO AKYAB *viâ* AENG PASS AND MYOHAUNG—*continued.*

Authorities. Military.	Authorities. Civil.	Number and Names of Stages, Rivers and Streams.	Distances. Inter-mediate. M. F.	Distances. Total. M. F.	Remarks.
G.O.C. Myingyán District.	Commissioner, Southern Division, and Deputy Commissioner, Mimbu.	**3. Thát Sakhán or Thaya Sakhán** —*cont.*			broad glade which rises to the west, slopes to the south or valley of the Kin chaung and rises to the north-east. It is a fine camping ground, and as a position would be impregnable to an attack from the Napé side. Water in any quantity is obtained ½ of a mile down the southern slope; it is of excellent quality. Eight hundred men could be accommodated on this plateau.
G.O.C. Rangoon District.	Lower Burma.	**4. Top of An Pass or Nayékan-taung.**	5 0	28 0	From Thát Sakhán the road runs south-west sometimes easy, sometimes difficult. The average width of the roadway being from 1 to 5 feet. At 1½ miles Padí Sakhán is passed, a small plateau, where there is water to the left of the road, 200 yards down the slope, and camping ground for 200 men and ½ a mile further, Thémyu, where there is a little water, is passed. The top of the pass is a plateau capable of camping 1,000 men, with a small knoll rising on right, on which are the two large tanks taken up by the 1854 column. Water is said to be obtained down the hill to the right, but the jungle is now so overgrown that it is impossible to get at it. It is the same stream which supplies Yugé with water 1½ miles down towards Arakan.
		5. Wadát ...	5 0	33 0	From top of pass the road runs down the hill. Precipitous and narrow; thick jungle; little bamboo. Yugé consists of three plateaux, one below the other, each capable of camping 200 men. These plateaux lie to the right of the road, and water is obtained 200 yards beyond the lower plateau from a small stream capable of supplying, say, 300 men. Yugé is an old police guard station, removed to Wadát on account of its being a bad military position. Leaving Yugé, Naudaung, a caravan halting place, is passed at 1 mile, but water has to be sunk for. Road still runs west-south-west. Wadát is reached at mile 3¾ from Yugé, a clean, well kept police guard. It is commanded by a plateau immediately above it, but the two places in conjunction, would make a powerful position. From here a road runs back below the An and Chauchin route to Payé near Sidôtia. Wadát is one of a chain of guards running south to the An river.
		6. Chauché ...	4 0	37 0	From Wadát the road runs along a fairly level spur straight to the Chin village of Chauché. Bamboo jungle all the way, the Ché chaung running on the right at the foot of the hill, and ¾ of a mile from the road and village. Chauché:—The camping ground is ¼ of a mile before

FROM NAPÉ TO AKYAB *viâ* AENG PASS AND MYOHAUNG—*continued.*

Authorities. Military.	Authorities. Civil.	Number and Names of Stages, Rivers and Streams.	Distances. Inter-mediate.	Distances. Total.	Remarks.
G.O.C. Rangoon District.	Lower Burma.	**6. Chauché**—*cont.*			the village. Accommodation for 200 or 300 men, and there is accommodation for half a company upon the roadway by the village. Supplies practically *nil* except pig. Water has to be carried from the Ché chaung $\frac{3}{4}$ of a mile away. There are eight houses in the village. The adjoining jungle is all bamboo and there is a little cultivation on the hill side.
		7. Théwát ... An chaung rises above Théwát. Navigable for small boats and rafts from this point to An. Width from 10 to 40 yards; depth $1\frac{1}{2}$ to 5 feet. Above Théwát it is unnavigable.	M. F. **8 0**	M. F. 45 0	Direction of road south-west. First 3 miles on the descent are fairly good, though stony under foot and narrow. At 2 miles is passed the Chin village of Ngassa, to the right of the road, down a steep path. Ngassa stands on a jutting out spur facing north-east and has six houses, plenty of water, and a camping ground just above it for 50 men. Magai at 4 miles to the right has eight houses and plenty of water. The road steadily descends, the jungle being bamboo with patches of cultivation visible. Napégu Sakhán, a halting place, and water a long way off is passed at 6 miles. At 8 miles Théwát is reached, a village of 10 houses (Chins), situated on the An river which, rising in the interior, flows within 10 miles of Wadát, though inapproachable from that place on account of the thick jungle, and too stony and shallow for traffic. The camping ground at Théwát is small and bad on the river bed, and very feverish. The water is good. Théwát has no supplies.
		8. An or Aeng ... An river is crossed and recrossed by the lower route; the upper route runs parallel.	**13 0**	58 0	From Théwát to An there are two routes, one over the hills and most generally preferred. The other, though more level, runs along the river bed and crosses and recrosses it, some of the fords being breast high. It crosses the river twelve times as far as Sédaung, a small village on both banks, where the two routes join and become one. The upper route, for the 1st mile, runs down a very steep descent, crosses a nullah at the bottom, then along the level for a short stretch again descends. Then it alternately rises and descends through a thick jungle, the path being broken and bad, till it touches the river at 2 miles, runs along the river bed for a short stretch and then up again over the hills. Baintnabin, a small village, is passed just before descending to the river. At $3\frac{1}{2}$ miles a view of the hill above An, a general land mark to the country can be obtained. The road now commences to be good, fairly wide, and soft underfoot; jungle, bamboo. At 2 and 3 miles there are positions facing towards Théwát, either of which is capable of being converted into a strong position

FROM NAPÉ TO AKYAB *viâ* AENG PASS AND MYOHAUNG—*continued.*

Authorities. Military.	Authorities. Civil.	Number and Names of Stages, Rivers and Streams.	Distances. Intermediate.	Distances. Total.	Remarks.
G.O.C. Rangoon District.	Lower Burma.	**8. An or Aeng**—*cont.*			The hill Taungmyo is visible to the east at 5 miles, and at 6 miles the village of Paungma is passed on the river with a few paddy-fields. The next 4 miles to Sédaung zayát the road alternately ascends and descends and is very good. Sédaung consists of two villages, one where the river road leaves the bank and joins the hill road, the other a little lower down towards An. The zayát, or resting place, is a small camping ground with a fine zayát capable of holding 50 men. At 9¾ miles the above village of Sédaung is reached and from here into An the road gradually descends. Several dry nullahs, as shown by the sketches, are crossed. Bônchaung, once occupied by the British, is passed 3 miles from An. Bônchaung proper and lower Bônchaung, both within 300 yards of each other, are merely insignificant villages. From Bônchaung the river into An itself is crossed three times by bamboo bridges, being 100 yards wide and 3 feet deep; rate 2½ miles an hour; gravelly bottom. Throughout the whole way the soil of the road is good, and an excellent road for carts could be made with but little cost. The last 3 miles into An the road is wider and allows two or three people walking abreast. A Burman guard of 12 men at the entrance into An is the key of the Aeng pass itself from this side.
		9. Maungubin ... Kôn chaung, after leaving the An chaung at Bônchaung, 2 feet to 2½ feet deep. Rate 1 mile an hour. Crossed and recrossed eight times.	M. F. 8 0	M. F. 66 0	Direction north-west. The road traverses for 2 miles (through Bônchaung), the route by which An is entered from the An or Aeng Pass. It then strikes off from the river An and almost immediately crosses the Kônchaung river twice and passes the village Kônchaung. Four or five houses of no importance. The road here is bad, being precipitous on each side of the nullahs or bed of the river. This, however, could be easily avoided by carrying the road to the right of the river, *i.e.*, to its left bank; an easy matter as the jungle is light and the soil good and firm. Eight or nine small nullahs are crossed during the 8 miles to Maungubin, but they are easily spanned and would only need to be converted merely into drains. A few houses in the midst of a clearing are passed at 5½ miles, but they are not permanent and are no guide. A fair quantity of the country is under cultivation. Maungubin is a Chin village of half-a-dozen houses of no importance. Supplies trifling. There is no water to be obtained on this route, the last 4 miles before Maungubin.
		10. Chauché ... The Kôn chaung is crossed and recrossed eight times on route; shallow and easy; scarcely passable in the rains.	3 0	69 0	Leaving Maungubin, the road still runs north-west and though the Kôn chaung is crossed eight times, these crossings could be avoided entirely, the slopes on either bank being gradual and the jungle only light bamboo. Maungbônwéywa, Chéywa, and Noétáng, insignificant villages, being passed on the way. There is only a very small camping ground for, say, 50 men on the river at Chauché, a larger one for 200 men being obtainable ¼ of a mile further on,

FROM NAPÉ TO AKYAB *viâ* AENG PASS AND MYOHAUNG—*continued.*

Authorities.		Number and Names of Stages, Rivers and Streams.	Distances.		Remarks.
Military.	Civil.		Intermediate.	Total.	
G.O.C. Rangoon District.	Lower Burma.	**10. Chauché**—*cont.*			though there is no water nearer than the river. Maungbônwéywa was formerly an old police guard, but is now done away with. The road on the whole is very good and could easily be made a good cart road with very little cost. The water is excellent.
			M. F.	M. F.	
		11. Kônwa ... Kôn chaung and a tributary of the Dalet river unites with the Kôn chaung at Kônwa. Three to 15 yards wide; 1 to 4 feet deep; navigable for small boats all way to Dalet, and hence in communication by water with the sea. Runs into big river at Dalet.	**8 4**	77 4	Almost immediately after leaving Chauché the road descends into the river bed, and follows its course for 7 miles, only leaving it to cross the Nga Ya Taung, a steep hill with precipitous ascent and descent of half an hour at 2¼ miles after leaving Chauché. This hill could be avoided by carrying the road round either to the right or left. The road is practically in the river is wet, stony, and difficult, and completely impassable in wet weather and rains. The jungle is heavy in parts, but a road could always be carried above the level of the river and many of the crossings avoided. This is the case with nearly all the paths which are taken along the river bed. At 7th mile the road gradually deserts the river bed and runs along its banks 30 or 40 feet above it and is excellent travelling, only descending at about 6½ miles to cross the Kôn chaung and again a mile and-a-half further on at the junction of the Kôn chaung and a tributary of the Dalet river, just beyond which at 8½ miles is situated Kônwa, a small Chin village of 15 houses, while Taungbwiyé, another village of the same sort, is situated in the bend of the junction of the two rivers. A small camping ground is on the river bed below the village, but there is a fine camping ground just opposite the village on the road, the river being, however, nearly ½ a mile off and the water-supply thus difficult.
		12. Dalet ...	**6 0**	83 4	Leaving Kônwa halting place up to the plateau on which the village of Kônwa stands, the road runs almost perpendicularly; too steep for horses, but passable for infantry. This could be obviated by simply producing the slant through a cutting making the slope longer and less difficult. The road then is excellent and running north-west still through large glades passes the following Chin villages: Pailôn, Singu, Tao, Alaiyutaung and finally at 6 miles Myauktaung where the police guard is, and opposite which, on the other side of the river, is Dalet, a small village of no importance except in name. At 3 miles the road crosses a wet nullah and runs for the distance of 300 yards through a narrow cutting just wide enough for a man on horse-back. At 4 miles, the road leaves the wide plain of jungles, runs round the side of a hill for about 300 or 400 yards at a height of 80 feet above the big Dalet river, which is here seen for the first time. The road in this place is dangerous and requires additional width, obtained as usual by cutting away the hill-slope above the road. It then debouches into the plain passing through immense paddy-fields and the well-to-do villages of

FROM NAPÉ TO AKYAB *viâ* AENG PASS AND MYOHAUNG—*continued.*

Authorities. Military.	Authorities. Civil.	Number and Names of Stages, Rivers and Streams.	Distances. Intermediate. M.	F.	Distances. Total. M.	F.	Remarks.
G.O.C. Rangoon District.	Lower Burma.	**12. Dalet**—*cont.*					Alaiyutaung and Myauktaung, the situation of the police guard, this 6 miles being all fertile and capable of being largely cultivated. Alaiyutaung and Myauktaung form one long place with only a few tobacco fields dividing each. They are all under the same Taungmin or Thugyi and have identical interests.
		13. Swetzaw ... Dalet river, 600 yards wide ; fordable at low tide only between the two villages of Myauk and Dalet proper.	**11**	**0**	94	4	The river Dalet is crossed to *Dalet proper* ; direction north-west ; fordable at low tide. Small boats are obtainable as ferry-boats. The route then leads for nearly a mile through a loose jungle over firm soil, when the river which has taken a sharp bend is reached again. Here it is very deep and unfordable ; at low tide it is 300 yards wide with shingly bottom. Leaving the river, the ascent is very steep and at low tide almost impassable the first 300 yards on account of the mud. Impassable for animals except at high tide. The route, scarcely perceptible, then leads along a mile and-a-half of excessively bad road merely a dry nullah bed about 3 feet wide and covered with huge stones and with almost perpendicular banks on either side ; at intervals a swamp knee-deep is crossed. The open plain is then reached and the road, a good one, crosses several paddy-fields to the Chin village of Chinywa, at 3 miles a small collection of houses in *a good position*, being on a slight eminence between two large plains, the neighbouring heights being low and covered with jungle. From Chinywa the general direction is at first north, then north-west. Crossing a mile of paddy-fields, the road leads into the jungle through ½ a mile of what would be swampy ground in wet weather, then through dense uncleared jungle to the river again ; ferry-boats are obtainable. Animals have to swim across. The river being chiefly used, this route is much overgrown, otherwise it would be good and easy marching. The Chin (Shendu) village of Pindaung or Paideng is on the opposite or right bank at 6 miles ; four houses and no supplies. From here the route runs through the jungle still north-west, crossing in succession the Simbutaung, the Swetzawtaung, two rather steep though insignificant hills ; the road here is broken and stony. The plain is then reached and the last mile is good level marching. The village of Swetzaw Chins (Shandu) is ½ a mile to the west of the road at 11 miles. There are also a few Laidu Chins living in the village. It stands on the Dalet river ; has 15 houses and a few scanty supplies, chiefly paddy. Water is scarce ; only obtainable from small wells, the river being salt.
		14. Sakyin ...	**10**	**0**	104	4	The road towards Sakyin runs north-west over an immense plain capable of cultivation, then up the bed of a dry nullah for 2 miles with perpendicular hills on either side, then round the hill side and over a small hill, the Chauchétaung, by a bad bit of road, when the telegraph line from Ru is reached and followed for 3 miles, the road on the whole being good, except for occasional swamps. The wretched village of Taiya is then reached, where water is obtainable, the first since Swetzaw, and then 4 miles of good roads into

FROM NAPÉ TO AKYAB *viâ* AENG PASS AND MYOHAUNG—*continued.*

Authorities. Military.	Authorities. Civil.	Number and Names of Stages, Rivers and Streams.	Distances. Intermediate.	Distances. Total.	Remarks.
G.O.C. Rangoon District.	Lower Burma.	**14. Sakyin**—*cont.*			Sakyin, winding to and from telegraph line to avoid an occasional hill or swamp. Sakyin is the first Arakanese village met with; consists of about 30 houses; clean and well-kept; has its headman or thugyi. Supplies considerable: paddy, fowls, and large numbers of buffaloes are in the possession of the villagers. Water is plentiful, obtainable from wells, and abundant grass for horses, &c. There is camping ground for any number of troops. Said to be healthy during the rains, the hills widening out and forming the valley. A good position can be obtained on the opposite side of the valley.
			M. F.	M. F.	
		15. Tôkh ... ... Injâm chaung, 20 yards wide; tidal; fordable at low tide; suspension bridge or ferry-boats for crossing at high tide.	**8 0**	112 4	Direction of road north-west crossing the large plain on which Sakyin is situated. The road branches through the jungle over indifferent ground, probably marshy in wet weather, and over an insignificant hill called Púdawdautaung, when the village of Injâm is reached at 3 miles a Chin village (Laidu); a few houses. Water obtainable from wells. Crossing the Injâm chaung, fordable at low tide only, the road runs across a large level plain 4 miles, when the foot of the Injâmtaung is reached. The telegraph and road here run together all the way, the hill being crossed almost in a direct line and is an hour's climbing to the top. The descent passes through alternate clearings when touching the telegraph lines and jungle, when branching away from the telegraph line (zigzagging all the way) the lower ground is reached; then 2 miles of good road along the telegraph line clearing, needing but little labour to convert it into a good road, lead to the Chin village of Tôkh on a small plain, ½ a mile off the road to the south-west; 20 houses, neatly built, and fair supplies with tobacco plantations.
		16. Pinlwin ... Pinchaung on entering the village, 15 yards wide; tidal; fordable at all times.	**8 0**	120 4	Leaving Tôkh and regaining the main road, which is good travelling and soft under foot, the direction is west-north-west. A small hill, the Pintaung, is crossed, the road the first 2 miles being good, afterwards broken, and then along the stony bed of a dry water-course, 5 feet wide, with the usual precipitous slopes on either side, then 3 miles of good road, 4 to 5 feet wide, through bamboo jungle, or over short plains, which are cultivated with paddy, running with the telegraph line all the way, and the small Chin village (Laidu) of Pin chaung is reached at 5 miles; four or five houses; no supplies; but water is obtainable from wells. Leaving Pinchaung the road runs through bamboo jungle and chiefly along the side of the low hills which bound the valley on the right, the telegraph line having struck *more east*. On leaving Pin chaung the road is good and soft, but completely unmade except by traffic. Pinlwin at 8 miles is a wretched Chin village on the right bank of the Yu river; has a fair camping ground for 500 men and water of indifferent quality from wells. The village consists of six or eight houses. No supplies; two or three ferry-boats for crossing the Yu chaung.

FROM NAPÉ TO AKYAB *viâ* AENG PASS AND MYOHAUNG—*continued.*

Authorities. Military.	Authorities. Civil.	Number and Names of Stages, Rivers and Streams.	Distances. Intermediate. M.	F.	Distances. Total. M.	F.	Remarks.
G.O.C. Rangoon District.	Lower Burma.	**17. Yé** ... Yu chaung, 150 yards wide; deep at low tide, with dangerous landing on the Yôsinan side through swamp and bog; unfordable.	14	0	134	4	Direction north-west. The road, leaving Pinlwin accompanied by the telegraph lines, crosses the Yu chaung and, after nearly ½ a mile of mangrove swamp, dangerous to animals at low tide, emerges into a level clearing through the jungle, perhaps 50 yards wide, with firm soil, when an excellent road without interruption leads to Ôkhán, a Chin village of nine houses at 4 miles, where excellent water can be obtained from a large well. A little paddy, 20 to 30 buffaloes and a few pigs obtainable. Good camping ground. Leaving Ôkhán the road strikes through a loose jungle, the road being excellent, requiring only a little clearing here and there to enable troops to march in fours. Yôsinán at 6 miles has 15 houses, capital drinking water, and very good camping ground. Supplies as at Ôkhán. Direction still north-west. The road runs for 6 miles over vast plains, dead level, and, though rough in places from buffalo tracks in wet weather, the road is excellent. At 12 miles the jungle is re-entered; two dry water-courses are crossed, at the second of which the road turns west into the Chin village of Yé, 15 houses at 14 miles. Good water in plenty can be obtained. Plenty of pigs and a few fowls. Good camping ground, but no shade except in the jungles.
		18. Pingat guard. Zamiyé chaung; tidal, with bad landing both sides; 20 yards wide.	6	0	140	4	From Yé the road, leading north-west, strikes through swampy ground for nearly ¼ a mile, subject to tidal influence from the Yé chaung which flows near; then along the side of a low hill; then through dense jungle, the road being scarcely perceptible though level and easily made into a good one, the hills also opening out a little on either side, the level ground between them being quite 5 miles in width. At 5¼ miles an insignificant Chin village called Gángaw is passed, and another ¾ mile of good plain road leads to Pingat guard with water in plenty.
		19. Mailông ... Pingat river, 10 yards wide, 1½ feet to 4 feet deep; tidal and navigable for small boats and used to go to Myohaung. Chon chaung, 50 to 80 yards wide; tidal, with muddy banks on either side. Ferry boats obtainable. Kanniyé river, 40 yards wide; tidal, deep and bad crossing. Ferry boats obtainable. Commuication with Akyab.	8	0	148	4	Pingat guard is a temporary civil guard, the first since Dalet in the Myohaung district. The village consists of about 30 houses (Arakanese). Supplies fair; paddy, fowls, &c., and good grass for ponies. From Dalet there is a plentiful supply of grass for animals all along the route. Direction north-west over the Pingat river at once through some swampy ground (easily drained) and then over three large plains in succession; dead level to the village of Sônchaung (Arakanese) 1½ miles. Between this village and Pingat in the jungle and off the road there is a cluster of five Chin villages (all Laidu) within a radius of 3 miles. Sônchaung has 50 houses, good camping ground, and

FROM NAPÉ TO AKYAB *viâ* AENG PASS AND MYOHAUNG—*continued.*

Authorities. Military.	Authorities. Civil.	Number and Names of Stages, Rivers and Streams.	Distances. Intermediate.		Distances. Total.		Remarks.
		19. Mailông—*cont.*					and two large zayáts. Large country boats can come up here by the Chôn chaung from Akyab, Dalet, An, &c. One and-a-half days to Akyab. Supplies inconsiderable. Ten to 15 boats obtainable (small). Direction of road north-west. The river is crossed near the village. A swampy jungle for ¼ of a mile is succeeded by a series of large paddy-fields and plains as far as Kanniyé 5 miles. At 3 miles a jungle path, which strikes the Lemru river opposite Minbya, commences and is said to be a good one, though there is no water on the route. Kanniyé consists of two villages, one on either side of a paddy plain, three or four houses in each; good camping ground. Supplies *nil.* The telegraph line runs here between the two villages. Leaving Kanniyé the road runs north-west, accompanied by the telegraph line, over a succession of paddy-fields and plains and crossing an occasional creek, the road being good going and soft approaching Mailông, the hills which bound the plains on the right, the Môné chaung being on the left. The hills widen out to a distance of nearly 2 miles from the river, forming a large plain, which is cultivated entirely with paddy. A good position could be taken up on these hills, which are low and covered with jungle and cover the whole plain. Mailông is a large village of 60 or 70 houses (Arakanese) at 8 miles. Supplies considerable. Paddy in large quantities, fowls, &c. Buffaloes in large numbers also along this tract of country are obtainable.
			M.	F.	M.	F.	
G.O.C. Rangoon District.	Lower Burma.	**20. Ngapaya** ... Zôn chaung 50 yards wide, tidal and deep, with excessively difficult landings on both sides; almost inaccessible for animals, except at high tide. Ferry boat obtainable. Pabru river, 50 to 60 yards wide; tidal, deep; swarming with alligators; dangerous landing on the Mailông side; swampy approach.	**5**	**0**	153	4	Direction of road north-west across paddy-fields, then a large plain, then more paddy-fields; dead level and good going for a mile as far as the Zôn river, where there is a small ferry boat. The village of Zôn chaung (Arakanese) lies on the other side of the river of that name, a small dirty place of six houses (Arakanese). Good water for drinking from wells for 100 men. The road then continues for 2½ miles or so over paddy-field and plain as far as the Pabru river. Here a ferry boat has to be obtained from Zôn chaung, the Pabru and the Zôn chaung joining each other below Zôn chaung; the road then runs over large plains, crossing two small creeks for another 1½ miles, when the village of Ngápaya is reached (Arakanese) on the bank of the Môné chaung at 5 miles, 60 houses. Local supplies fair, chiefly paddy. Water from a large reservoir for 500 men. Good camping ground.
		21. Minbya ... Chéyé river, 20 yards wide; tidal and deep; a mere creek. Thimbaung and Kwoizun creeks.	**11**	**0**	164	4	Leaving Ngápaya the road runs north-west over plains and, except at the crossings of creeks, &c., is excellent and needs no making. At 1½ miles the small village of Chéyé is reached and a creek is crossed. From here the road runs from the telegraph line (which is continued in a perfectly

From NAPÉ to AKYAB *viâ* AENG PASS and MYOHAUNG—*continued.*

Authorities.		Number and Names of Stages, Rivers and Streams.	Distances.				Remarks.
Military.	Civil.		Intermediate.		Total.		
			M.	F.	M.	F.	
G.O.C. Rangoon District.	Lower Burma.	**21. Minbya**—*cont.*					straight line) and inclines to the right through the lower part of the jungle to avoid in succession the Thimbaung, Kwoizun, and Chéyé creeks, the latter running at the foot of the hill, whence it winds back again and is lost (all these creeks are mere tributaries to the big river to the Môné chaung). From here the road runs straight into the large Arakanese village of Minuya, at 8 miles 100 houses, facing Minbya on the opposite side of the river, which is 3 miles wide. The village is intersected by creeks and is very unnealthy. The large island of Sampala lies more to the north, where there is a telegraph station with European Telegraph Master. Crossing the river (Môué chaung) a distance of 3 miles, the large well-built Arakanese town of Minbya is reached; has 200 houses or more, an Assistant Commissioner being the Myo-ôk. There is a large supply of boats, both big and little, at Minuya and Minbya, and the mail steamer plies once a week from Akyab. Water-supply from tanks for any number of troops. Supplies considerable, there being a Government bazaar.
		22. Maungbwé ... Lemru on the right of road and crossed into Maungbwé; innumerable creeks all bridged with solid bridges capable of bearing troops and light guns.	9	4	174	0	Direction north. A Government road built like a bund and passable in the rains, 12 feet wide, in good order though requiring repairs in one or two places; dead level, and passing many small Arakanese villages on the way. (Arakan under the supervision of Government officials. Cadastral survey, &c., begins properly at Minbya.) Maungbwé is a large straggling Arakanese town of some importance; a steamer plying once a week from Akyab and traffic being considerable with the interior. There is no place particularly suitable from military position. The immediately surrounding country is very level. Supplies considerable; paddy, &c. Boats in large quantities can be obtained, the larger sort capable of containing 8 men and their baggage.
		23. Myohaung ... An arm of the Lemru is crossed at about mile 5.	9	0	183	0	From Maungbwé the road runs north and north-west and is a similar route to that from Minbya. Government construction; in good repair. Many villages are passed on the way and water is obtainable all along the route. The telegraph line also runs along here as also from Minbya to Maungbwé.
		Akyab ... ... Lemru river all the way, there being no land route.	44	0	227	0	From Myohaung to Akyab the route is by river, the land route being impracticable on account of the numerous crossings and creeks; steamers plying twice a week.

From PA-ENG to PYILÔNGYAW (Route No. 16, Stage 5).

By Lieuts. BROOKE-MURRAY, 2nd Bengal Infantry, and SANDBACH, R.E., February 1887.

Authorities. Military.	Authorities. Civil.	Number and Names of Stages, Rivers and Streams.	Distances. Intermediate. M. F.	Distances. Total. M. F.	Remarks.
G.O.C. Myingyán District.	Commissioner, Southern Division, and Deputy Commissioner, Mimbu.	**1. Kán**	9 0	9 0	Pa-eng *vide* Route No. 9, Lower Burma Division. The road runs along the valley skirting the hamlet of east Pa-eng on the west and south, it then turns abruptly to the north-east after the 1st mile and runs along the foot of the hills for another ½ mile, here turning east and making a rapid and very steep ascent to the crest of the Yamadaw hills, about 3½ miles from Pa-eng (time taken by a small party with seven mules, 1 hour 15 minutes); the last 500 yards is very steep and difficult for both pedestrians and animals. After reaching the crest the road runs level for 200 or 300 yards, then by a sudden dip enters a horse-shoe shaped gully, running immediately above and parallel to the bed of a mountain torrent, which is crossed about ½ mile down. Here a small spring of water bubbles up on the path, only very little water descending into the narrow valley overgrown with bamboo jungle. The road immediately ascends its eastern slope by an easy ascent, height about 250 feet, running along a spur and then across the hill side. A fine view is obtained of the Yônbin valley from just above Kán, the road into which is in places very steep and difficult. Road generally passable for mules, but not so for carts without considerable improvement. Kán is a ruined village in midst of dense jungle of thorn and bamboo. Water is obtainable here from a tank about 100 by 50 yards, depth about 2 feet, bottom muddy, water slightly brackish, believed to be supplied from small springs as the tank is free from weeds, though filled with decayed vegetable matter. Natives report that by the middle of March no quantity of water is obtainable.
		2. Yaungbin ...	6 0	15 0	The road from Kán runs in a north-easterly direction, three times cutting into the bed of the nullah flowing north. Water is here and there obtainable from pools in this nullah, though generally speaking it is but a stagnant puddle; banks of nullah steep and precipitous, about 20 feet. General route over slightly undulating country, covered with thin thorn and bamboo jungle, good for mules, but could be made so for carts without much difficulty as the ground is hard; an excellent road for marching. Yaungbin, on south bank of river Môn, is a village of about 30 houses, fenced round with a thorn hedge. Kyaung and zayát to accommodate 150 men standing in an enclosure on south-east side of village with nullah; steep bank on south and east sides, distant about 100 and 300 yards respectively. River Môn, distant about 500 yards on north side. Water good and abundant. Kyaung and village commanded by small hill, with pagoda on it from the south, distant 350 yards. Cart transport, rice, &c., easily obtained. River ford immediately in front of village, 27 inches deep, current very rapid. Ground in vicinity of village open. Bamboo basket and mat manufacture extensively carried on. The village of Yônbin is situated on high ground and commands all approaches to it.

FROM PA-ENG TO PYILÔNGYAW (ROUTE No. 16, STAGE 5)—*continued.*

Authorities. Military.	Authorities. Civil.	Number and Names of Stages, Rivers and Streams.	Distances. Inter-mediate. M.	F.	Distances. Total. M.	F.	Remarks.
G.O.C. Myingyán District.	Commissioner, Southern Division, and Deputy Commissioner, Mimbu.	**3. Pyilôngyaw** ...	**17**	**0**	32	0	From Yônbin the road runs across the nullah on the south, passing close under some small hills for about 1½ miles till it reaches Kyotaka, where cutch-boiling is extensively carried on. Crossing fairly open cultivation, it then proceeds almost east past Sadaw (burnt) (2½ miles), keeping close along the Môn river till it reaches Kyutwun (burnt). Between Kyutwun and Magyizu are 10 large kyaungs enclosed by plantain gardens. Magyizu (4 miles) is a large village of about 40 houses situated on level ground; hilly ground rising in rear, distant about ¼ mile; distance from river about 600 yards. The road from hence runs due east past Léyinzu (5 miles) (Zígôn opposite on north bank of river), which is on high ground with plantain garden on north side and a few detached houses on east side, distant from river about 700 yards, fenced in with thick thorn hedge, surrounded by *jowári* and cotton fields on east, north and west sides, jungle on south. Two wells, water good. From Léyinzu the road skirts the river almost into Kyinidaung (6½ miles). Half this village situated on side of rising ground, stands about 40 feet above road; consists of two villages, each containing about 30 houses. Eastern village on low, flat ground, hedged in with thorn hedge. Five entrances, two on north side, one on each south, east and west. The road passes through rich cultivation, which throughout the route extends to the foot of the rising ground from the river, averages 1½ miles in width. After leaving Kyinidaung the road passes Palángyé (7 miles), and Ôkpho on the left, a large village of about 50 houses, extending to the river at 8½ miles; several enclosed zayáts to south-east side; two large kyaungs, distant from Kyinidaung 1½ miles. The road continuing through rich cultivation passes Kyikain on the right (12 miles), approached from plantain cultivation, clear all round, with good encamping ground on river side. One large well on north-west front of village, near a large peepul tree. At 13 miles Mônglebin and at 15 miles Yagyibin. Good water from wells at all these villages. Pyilôngyaw on south bank of Môn river, about 30 houses at 17 miles; cart transport readily obtained from neighbouring villages. Military post. Road clear and open throughout and good for carts. Follows right bank of Môn river throughout the march and country on either side well cultivated.

No. 25.

From PAGAN to MEIKTILA viâ WÉLAUNG and SHÁNMANGÉ.

I. B. COMPILATION, DECEMBER 1888.

G.O.C. Myingyán District.	Comr., Southern Division, and Deputy Comr., Myingyán.						
		1. Yôngyi ...	**7**	**0**	7	0	*See* Route No. 21, Branch I.
		2. Sé	**12**	**4**	19	4	*See* Route No. 21, Branch I.
		3. Ungyin ...	**13**	**0**	32	4	*Reference cannot be traced.*

FROM PAGÁN TO MEIKTILA *viâ* WÉLAUNG AND SHÁNMANGE—*continued.*

Authorities. Military.	Authorities. Civil.	Number and Names of Stages, Rivers and Streams.	Distances. Intermediate. M.	F.	Total. M.	F.	Remarks.
G.O.C. Myingyán District.	Commissioner, Southern Division, and Deputy Commissioner, Myingyán.	**4. Wélaung** ...	**10**	**0**	43	0	From Ywatha the road runs on the same as before and crosses two nullahs and reaches Wélaung. Wélaung is a large village and contains a police post and accommodation for 50 men. There is also plenty of accommodation for 150 men in kyaungs and zayáts in the village. Water good and plentiful from wells. Ordinary supplies obtainable and about 40 carts procurable.
G.O.C. Rangoon District.	Commissioner, Eastern Division, and Deputy Commissioner, Meiktila.	**5. Sunlun** ... ... Sunlun chaung five times; called by different names and different places.	**18**	**0**	61	0	Road fairly good running between parallel ranges of hills for a long way. Except near Wélaung there is not much cultivation. Pass several villages. Crops cotton, *jowári*, rice, and vegetable. Water plentiful. Country more or less under cultivation, but the hills on either side are covered with scrub jungle and very stony. Sunlun is a police post and a fair-sized village. Accommodation for 70 men in kyaungs and plenty of ground suitable for encamping on all round. Water good and plentiful, and supplies and fodder procurable. Also a certain number of carts.
		6. Shánmangé ... Sunlun chaung three times and several small nullahs.	**18**	**0**	79	0	Road fairly good. Country the same as before. Pass Shôgán (or Shawgôn) at 6 miles. Here there are good kyaungs and water, and supplies plentiful. The road from Sunlun is in parts very good, but in others it follows the bed of the chaung and would probably be difficult in wet weather. At 13 miles pass Tambu, the road running along ridges. From here there is a very fair road south-east into Shanmangé. *See* Route No. 20, Stage 6.
		7. Meiktila ...	**20**	**0**	101	0	*See* Route No. 17, Stage 5.

No. 26.

From PAKHAN-NGÉ to GANGÁW viâ PAKHANGYI, MYAING and SAGA.

BY LIEUTS. STANTON, ROYAL ARTILLERY, WILLCOCK, GLOSTER REGIMENT, AND OTHERS, 1888.

Military	Civil	Stage	Int. M.	F.	Total M.	F.	Remarks
G.O.C. Myingyán District.	Comr., Southern Divn., and Dy. Comr., Pakôkku.	**1. Shéhnet** ... Two sandy beds of nullahs, with a little water, called Thayetpyin and Myainggán chaungs.	**12**	**0**	12	0	Pakhán-ngé to Pakhángyi 3 miles, *vide* Route No. 27; thence to Shéhnet. General direction west and road for 4 miles through open scrub jungle. Here there is a muddy tank. After this the road is a little up and down,

FROM PAKHÁN-NGÉ TO GÁNGAW *viâ* PAKHÁNGYI, MYAING AND SAGA—*continued.*

Authorities. Military.	Authorities. Civil.	Number and Names of Stages, Rivers and Streams.	Distances. Intermediate. M.	F.	Distances. Total. M.	F.	Remarks.
G.O.C. Myingyán District.	Commissioner, Southern Division, and Deputy Commissioner, Pakôkku.	**1. Shéhnet**—*cont.*					still through scrub jungle, and passes between Shinmataung (Shemadaung) on north, Kyauktataung and Shintaung on the south. Accommodation for 50 men in an old kyaung, ¼ mile east of village, on banks of sandy bed of nullah; 200 men could bivouac under tamarind trees round the kyaung. Good water from two tanks; forage plentiful. Good cart road all the way except between 7th and 9th miles.
		2. Kyauksauk ... One dry chaung, the Wagán and the Shwé chaungs.	9	0	18	0	General direction west-north-west. The first 4 miles is through low jungle on gravelly ravines, then the road lies through scrub jungle and *jowári* cultivation, passing two tanks and the villages of Wagán and Bôgadawsu. Good cart road the whole way.
		3. Myaing ... Myaing chaung.	9	0	27	0	General direction north-west good, road through scrub jungle and cultivation, practicable for carts. Myaing at 9 miles contains 100 houses and accommodation in kyaungs for 500 men. Water from bed of stream, slightly brackish.
		4. Baungbin ... Myaing creek.	9	0	36	0	Road runs for about 1 mile in sandy bed of Myaing creek: a little running water. Two small creeks, dry, are crossed near Baungbin. The road crosses over undulating ground after leaving the creek and passes through scrub jungle fairly open. The road is good for carts. There is a large pôngyi kyaung and several zayáts capable of accommodating 400 men; there is a tank with plenty of good drinking water in the kyaung enclosure. Animals can be watered on west side of village about ½ mile away. Water is good, but not plentiful. There are 10 houses in the village, and a little *jowári* is cultivated.
		5. Saitkyi ... ... Saitkyi creek.	7	0	43	0	The road runs through thin jungle over undulating ground and is a good cart road. About ½ mile from the village Saitkyi creek is crossed; during the rains it is liable to floods and is some time impassable during the dry weather. There is no running water; but by digging, water is always procurable. There are two large kyaungs inhabited, and one small one deserted. There is a good deal of *kerbi* cultivation round the village. Between Baungbin and Saitkyi the road has been cleared in most places to a breadth of about 15 yards.

FROM PAKHAN-NGÉ TO GÁNGÁW *viâ* PAKHÁNGYI, MYAING AND SAGA—*continued.*

Authorities. Military.	Authorities. Civil.	Number and Names of Stages, Rivers and Streams.	Distances. Intermediate. M. F.	Distances. Total. M. F.	Remarks.
G.O.C. Myingyán District.	Commissioner, Southern Division, and Deputy Commissioner, Pakôkku.	**6. Wédaung (South village).**	**7 0**	50 0	Leaving Saitkyi the road runs over slightly undulating ground, highly cultivated, to Thelayin about 1¼ miles. About ¼ mile east of the village the road crosses the Thelayin creek. There is running water at present (December), but in the dry weather it is necessary to dig for water. About 1 mile from Thelayin the road passes the village of Minyán and a ¾ of a mile further on Bahin. It has been proposed to establish a post in this village. Between Bahin and South Wédaung the ground undulates more and there are some bad nullahs: the road is cleared to about 15 yards and there is cultivation nearly throughout, mostly *jowári*.
		7. Seinzwé ...	**6 0**	56 0	The road after leaving South Wédaung passes through paddy and *kerbi* cultivation for about 1½ miles: crossing some small nullahs. The ground then becomes more undulating and is covered with jungle. North Wédaung, a village of about 25 houses and a large kyaung, is passed at 2½ miles. It is surrounded by *jowári* fields and thin jungle; there is a good well on south-east side of village. Between North Wédaung and Seinzwé, 3½ miles, the ground undulates and is covered with thick jungle. The cart road is practicable. Seinzwé is deserted, but the houses (about 25) and the kyaung (accommodates 200 men) are in good repair. Crops have been planted, but are neglected (December).
		8. Letpán	**9 4**	65 4	Leaving Seinzwé the road runs through cultivation and thin jungle for about 2 miles to Kyawywa. The Seinzwé and a branch of Kyawywa creek are crossed on the way. The ground is undulating. Just before reaching Kyawywa, a valley about ½ mile wide and 2 miles long is crossed. About ½ mile west of Kyawywa the deserted village of Kyundaik is seen: there is a deserted kyaung, but apparently much dilapidated as are the houses in the village (about 10 houses). Leaving Kyawywa the road ascends rapidly for rather more than 2 miles, the track is a very stony and narrow foot-path. At this point the existing path was entirely impracticable for animals even unloaded, and a fresh path had to be cleared and cut for about 300 yards. Thence to Letpán the road runs for the most part along narrow crests, but frequently descends into deep valleys between. The character of the path is, as before, rugged and stony. Letpán is reached at about 5 miles. This village, of about eight houses, is on high ground overlooking the creek and a few paddy-fields. There is always water in the Letpán creek. Except the clearing below the village there is dense jungle all round. The ruins of a former village are seen on the bank of the creek.

From PAKHÁN-NGÉ to GᶜNGAW *viâ* PAKHÁNGYI, MYAING and SAGA—*continued.*

Authorities. Military.	Authorities. Civil.	Number and Names of Stages, Rivers and Streams.	Distances. Intermediate. M.	Distances. Intermediate. F.	Distances. Total. M.	Distances. Total. F.	Remarks.
G.O.C. Myingyân District.	Commissioner, Southern Division, and Deputy Commissioner, Pakôkku.	**9. Sého**	**9**	**4**	75	0	The road is very hilly and stony, passing through thick jungle (mostly bamboo) the whole way. Several creeks are crossed. The rate of marching was hardly a mile an hour; but the road has been made much easier for future passage. A considerable quantity of paddy near the village which is situated in a narrow deep valley and is deserted.
		10. Kyaukmasin.	**5**	**0**	80	0	The road is very hilly and stony. East and West Kyaukmasin, deserted villages, about ½ a mile apart in a deep narrow valley. The houses in West Kyaukmasin, seven or eight, are in very bad repair, as is also the kyaung; but there are two good zayáts. In East Kyaukmasin there are about 15 houses in fair condition. The village is commanded by high ground on east and west, but a small guard on the high bank on east side of the creek protects it amply. The valley is full of paddy and the crops are very heavy.
		11. Kyawtha ...	**11**	**0**	91	0	Direction east. A good road. At about 3 miles Kaungbaung village of 10 houses, deserted. There is said to be a good road on north side of the Kyaukmasin creek. From here road fairly good for most part in bed of Taung and Yényu creeks. At 7½ miles Kabin, whence to Kyawtha (11 miles) road is very good all the way: first through paddy cultivation now dry (December) for 1,000 yards, then over a small hill, 600 yards. The path then descends into sandy bed of Yésama creek; till reaching Kyawtha the path continually crosses the creek, now dry.
		12. Wetbin ...	**13**	**0**	104	0	Leaving Kyawtha the road runs through cultivation and thin jungle continually crossing the Kyaw creek which turns due west just opposite the village. From this point the general direction of the road and Kyaw creek (up stream) are the same. The bed of the creek is in most parts encumbered with large boulders and the banks generally steep: it is said to be impassable during the rains. Immediately after passing Thadawkyauk the road makes a rapid ascent and the path is very stony and difficult. The direction continues westerly as far as Bambyin, where there are the remains of a burnt village much overgrown by jungle. About 3 miles north-west of Bambyin the road, hitherto very bad on account of heavy gradients and stones, improves and descends gently to Wetbin (13 miles).

FROM PAKHÁN-NGÉ TO GANGAW *viâ* PAKHÁNGYI, MYAING AND SAGA—*continued.*

Authorities. Military.	Authorities. Civil.	Number and Names of Stages, Rivers and Streams.	Distances. Intermediate. M.	Distances. Intermediate. F.	Distances. Total. M.	Distances. Total. F.	Remarks.
G.O.C. Myingyán District.	Commissioner, Southern Division, and Deputy Commissioner, Pakôkku.	**13. Kyaw**	6	4	110	4	The general direction is almost north. The road runs through cultivation and thin jungle or in the bed of Kyaw creek the whole way, and is good throughout. The Kyaw creek has a sandy bed in this part of its course.
G.O.C. Myingyán District.	Commissioner, Southern Division, and Deputy Commissioner, Pakôkku.	**14. Saga**	6	0	116	4	Road runs in a northerly direction and crosses Kyaw creek several times; is a good road throughout, slightly undulating and jungle generally thin. Several small clearings for cultivation, both taungya and by irrigation. Gángaw is said to be 30 miles north-west and a good road all the way, but no villages on or near the road.
G.O.C. Myingyán District.	Commissioner, Southern Division, and Deputy Commissioner, Pakôkku.	**15. Camp on Laungtaung chaung.**	12	0	128	4	The road runs north for about 1 mile and crosses the Kyaw creek. It then turns west and crosses the Naw creek several times in the 2nd and 3rd miles. The road then ascends rather rapidly till the 7th mile, when the highest point is reached. The general direction is north-west. Thence the road descends for about 4 miles (11th mile) when the Laungtaung chaung is reached. The descents are frequently steep, but there is nothing to stop the passage of pack animals. About a mile (13th mile) down the Laungtaung chaung a few pools of water are reached and the bamboo jungle is fairly open (January).
G.O.C. Myingyán District.	Commissioner, Southern Division, and Deputy Commissioner, Pakôkku.	**16. Gángaw** ...	18	0	146	4	The road is level and good throughout: crosses the Laungtaung creek repeatedly. There is abundant water in the Laungtaung stream in January. For Gángaw *see* Route No. 30, Stage 13.

No. 27.

From PAKHÁN-NGÉ to PAUK.

BY LIEUT. BIGGS, R.E., AND NATIVE INFORMATION, 1886–87.

Authorities. Military.	Authorities. Civil.	Number and Names of Stages, Rivers and Streams.	Distances. Intermediate. M.	Distances. Intermediate. F.	Distances. Total. M.	Distances. Total. F.	Remarks.
G.O.C. Myingyán District.	Commissioner, Southern Division, and Deputy Commissioner, Pakôkku.	**1. Pakhángyi** ...	3	0	3	0	Direction west. Pakhán-ngé is on the right bank of the Chindwin river, and is the landing place for Pakhángyi, which is approached by a level road only passable in the dry season, as at other times the ground is flooded by the Chindwin. Pakhángyi is the capital of the district of that name, has about 200 houses, and was a walled city with walls 40 feet high and very thick, but it is now in ruins and accessible on three sides, the east side being quite open. There is an excellent camping ground in kyaungs ½ a mile to the south-south-west with good shade, but in the rainy season this ground would probably be flooded. Water is obtained from wells, is fairly good and plentiful, but a little salt.

No. 27.

FROM PAKHÁN-NGÉ TO PAUK—*continued*.

Authorities. Military.	Authorities. Civil.	Number and Names of Stages, Rivers and Streams.	Distances. Intermediate. M. F.	Distances. Total. M. F.	Remarks.
G.O.C. Myingyán District.	Commissioner, Southern Division, and Deputy Commissioner, Pakôkku.	**2. Shábyindaw or Kyensain.**	9 0	12 0	Direction west. For 1 mile a good road, then rough, rocky, and bad for carts. Carts can travel, but they should be lightly laden. The road winds about very much to avoid ravines. Country undulating, cut up with ravines, and covered with scrub jungle, in some places very thick. At 3½ miles the foot of the Shinmadaung range is reached, then for a mile the road, which is very rough and rocky, winds along the foot of the hill. After this it improves, passing into open ground, and towards the end is a good road. Kyensain is a village of 20 houses, and the kyaungs, which would hold 100 men, are dilapidated and leaky. Water is good but scanty, and has to be obtained from the bed of a water-course ¾ of a mile to the east of the village, at the foot of a small hill to the south of the road.
		3. Myotha... ...	15 0	27 0	Direction west. The road, which is good, level, and suitable for carts, passes through open ground and twice crosses a dry water-course. Scrub jungle, thick at places, is soon entered and continues to Wagán, a village of 30 houses at mile 3. Water here is scarce, and has to be carried some distance. The road, which is good and level, now passes through cultivated ground, with some light scrub jungle the rest of the way. Paikthin, a village of 100 houses, with two kyaungs and good water, is passed at mile 8. Myotha has some 300 houses and kyaungs for 200 to 300 men. Cattle as well as 40 or 50 carts can be procured, and the water-supply is good.
		4. Kyauktaung ...	14 0	41 0	Direction west. The road, which is good and level, traverses cultivated land with some scrub jungle the whole way. Kyauktaung is a village of about 200 houses, and has kyaungs for 300 to 400 men. Water good.
		5. Thaingôtpyin.	9 0	50 0	Direction south-south-west. The road, which is somewhat rough, but passable for carts, ascends from Kyauktaung to the low hills forming the watershed between the Chindwin and Yaw basins. The camping ground of Winwa is reached in 4 miles, and the bed of the small Winwa creek is then followed the remainder of the way. This creek has about 1 foot of water in wet weather, but is at other times dry; the banks are jungly; with cultivation near the villages. Thanutpyin with 50 houses is passed at mile 7. Thaingôtpyin is a village with about 100 houses and one indifferent kyaung. Cattle, some carts, maize, and good water are obtainable.

FROM PAKHÁN-NGÉ TO PAUK—*continued.*

Authorities. Military.	Authorities. Civil.	Number and Names of Stages, Rivers and Streams.	Distances. Intermediate. M.	F.	Total. M.	F.	Remarks.
G.O.C. Myingyán District.	Commissioner, Southern Division and Deputy Commissioner, Pakôkku.	**6. Thambya-aing.**	**10**	**0**	60	0	Direction south-south-west. The Win-wa creek is again followed for 1 mile past Nyaungzwédé 30 houses, to Magyízin, 100 houses at mile 5. The creek is then left and Saphé, on the bank of the Yaw river, is reached, 2 miles further on. The Pakôkku road is now joined and followed the rest of the way. *See* Route No. 30, Stage 4.
		7. Pauk	**9**	**0**	69	0	*See* Route No. 30, Stage 4. There is said to be another road from the high ground to Magyízin. It lies further to the west, passing through Kabyu-Môndaw and Sulégôn, and as it does not follow the bed of a creek it may be a better route. *Note.*—As far as Wagán this information is authentic. After that it is from Native information and cannot be implicitly relied on.

No. 28.

From PAKÔKKU to ÁLÔN viâ LINGADAW.

UNKNOWN, PROBABLY I. B. COMPILATION, 1887-88.

Authorities. Military.	Authorities. Civil.	Number and Names of Stages, Rivers and Streams.	Intermediate. M.	F.	Total. M.	F.	Remarks.
G.O.C. Myingyán District.	Commissioner, Southern Division, and Deputy Commissioner, Pakôkku.	**1. Pákhángyi** ...	**18**	**0**	18	0	Road across sandy cultivated plain for 6 miles, passing the village of Kô-dwin at 2½ miles and Paunglaungán at 3 miles; then for 5 miles over more broken ground. Road passable for carts, but rough. At 9 miles Kyauk-hléga, where there is a small tank and two zayáts by the road side, is passed. About 60 men could be sheltered in the zayáts, which form a half-way halting place to Pakhángyi. The water in the tank is, however, dirty in the dry weather. The road 2 miles beyond Kyauk-hléga descends into level country with many toddy palms, passing many deserted villages. Pakhángyi is an old walled town. At present there are only about 200 houses, most of which are on the south side outside the town. There is a good position for a post among some pagodas and temple buildings on the south side; accommodation in kyaungs for 400 men. Supplies paddy, gram, grass, and cattle plentiful. About 20 carts. Good water from wells. From Pakhángyi there is a good dry weather road over a paddy plain to Yetagyo on the Chindwin, distance 7 miles. Pakhán-ngé on the Chindwin is about 3 miles distant. In the rains can be reached in boats.

FROM PAKÔKKU TO ÁLÔN *viâ* LINGADAW—*continued.*

Authorities. Military.	Authorities. Civil.	Number and Names of Stages, Rivers and Streams.	Distances. Intermediate. M.	F.	Distances. Total. M.	F.	Remarks.
G.O.C. Myingyân District.	Commissioner, Southern Division, and Deputy Commissioner, Pakôkku.	**2. Mongín** ...	**10**	**0**	28	0	Road fair for carts through low level ground round Pakhangyi to more broken ground. Through Thetywa at 2 miles, Tatein 3½ miles, Kyégán 4 miles, Kánsit 6 miles, to Mongin, a large village of 300 houses and several large kyaungs and zayâts. Accommodation for 300 men. Water from wells. The Yetagyo-Kánlé road passes through Mongin. Distance from Yetagyo 6 miles.
		3. Lingadaw ...	**13**	**0**	41	0	Through low hills and several villages. Fair cart road to Lingadaw, a village of about 100 houses with a police post of 50 military police. Kyaungs can accommodate 250 men. Water good from a running stream. The staple of the place is toddy cultivation and jaggery manufacture.
	Commr., Cenl. Divn., and Dy. Commr., Lower Chindwin.	**4. Salingyi** ...	**17**	**0**	58	0	Road fair for carts through in Uyinzayât at 2 miles, Kainlé at 4½, Gwézôn at 7 miles, Linziyet at 9½. *See* Route No. 1, Central Division.
		5. Mônywa ...	**12**	**0**	70	0	*See* Route No. 1, Central Division, Stages 1 and 2.
		6. Álôn	**7**	**0**	77	0	

No. 29.

From PAKÔKKU to GÁNGAW viâ WÉDAUNG and SAGA.

BY LIEUT. R. B. SCALLON, 23RD BOMBAY LIGHT INFANTRY, JANUARY 1887.

Military.	Civil.	Stage	Inter. M.	F.	Total M.	F.	Remarks
G.O.C. Myingyân District.	Commissioner, Southern Division, and Deputy Commissioner, Pakôkku.	**1. Paungan** ...	**12**	**0**	12	0	*See* Route No. 33.
		2. Nyaungywa ...	**13**	**0**	25	0	Direction north-west. Road good; first 3 miles through scrub jungle, thence country open and cultivated. At 4½ miles Yaingaung; village has been destroyed. Two kyaungs. Water from well ½ mile and tanks 1½ miles. Thence good road, 1st mile through jungle, thence cultivation up to Nyaungdwin (6 miles); good accommodation in kyaung; water good, from wells; number of houses 30. Road still good, through open scrub jungle for 3 miles, thence cultivation up to Padengdaw (12 miles). No kyaungs. Water from wells. Number of houses 25. Road good as before through cultivation. At 13 miles Nyaungywa. Good accommodation in numerous kyaungs. Water from wells and from tank 1½ miles. Forty houses. Supplies procurable.

FROM PAKÔKKU TO GÁNGAW *viâ* WÉDAUNG AND SAGA—*continued.*

Authorities. Military.	Authorities. Civil.	Number and Names of Stages, Rivers and Streams.	Distances. Intermediate. M.	F.	Distances. Total. M.	F.	Remarks.
G.O.C. Myingyán District.	Commissioner, Southern Division, and Deputy Commissioner, Pakôkku.	**3. Wetpôk**	**8**	**4**	33	4	Good road through cultivation for 1 mile and then scrub jungle and toddy topes. At 3 miles Kyauktaung. One hundred houses. Water scarce. One kyaung, one zayát. At Sidaingán (4½ miles) water from tank; one kyaung, one zayát; six houses. At 5½ miles Ywathit. Water from well; no kyaungs; 10 houses. At 8½ miles Wetpôk. Water by digging holes in nullah; two kyaungs four zayáts; 40 houses.
		4. Taungzôn ...	**8**	**4**	42	0	Good road passing Kunlát at 3 miles. At 8½ miles Taungzôn; water plentiful from wells and running streams. Very good accommodation. Road passes through scrub jungle, but fairly open.
		5. Wédaung ...	**13**	**4**	55	4	Road good through Wetpôk, 5 miles. Cultivation near villages; otherwise scrub jungle. Good water-supply at Wetpôk (25 houses, one large kyaung, three zayáts). At 11 miles Bahim; water from stream and wells. Houses 55, kyaung one, zayáts three. Supplies obtainable. Thence to Wédaung (2½ miles, total 13½ miles). Good road through jungle (cultivation near village). Water from well and tank. Houses 40, kyaungs two, zayáts four. Supplies obtainable.
		15. Gángaw ...	**96**	**4**	152	0	From Wédaung to Gángaw 10 marches, *see* Route No. 26, Stages 7 to 16.

No. 30.

From PAKÔKKU to KALÉMYO viâ PAUK, KÁN and GÁNGAW.

BY LIEUT. E. W. M. NORIE, MIDDLESEX REGIMENT, INTELLIGENCE DEPARTMENT; CORRECTED BY LIEUT. M. R. E. RAY, 7TH (D.C.O.) REGIMENT, BENGAL INFANTRY, UP TO NOVEMBER 1891; AND FIRST FOUR STAGES UP TO JANUARY 1893 BY CAPT. HARVEY, ROYAL ARTILLERY, THENCE TO STAGE 15 UP TO OCTOBER 1893 BY LIEUT. B. TRYDELL, 1ST BURMA RIFLES.

G.O.C. Myingyán District.	Commr., Southern Divn., and Deputy Commr., Pakôkku.	**1. Kánhla**	**6**	**0**	6	0	The road starts from between the Burman police guard and the Myo-ôk's court-house, and goes out almost due west through a portion of the village of Pakôkku consisting chiefly of kyaungs and pagodas, and then on mostly between cactus hedges. The telegraph wire runs along it for the first 2½ miles, and then branches off to the left, rejoining the road at the foot

FROM PAKÔKKU TO KALÉMYO *viâ* PAUK, KÁN AND GÁNGAW—*continued.*

Authorities.		Number and Names of Stages, Rivers and Streams.	Distances.		Remarks.
Military.	Civil.		Inter-mediate.	Total.	
G.O.C. Myingyán District.	Commissioner, Southern Division, and Deputy Commissioner, Pakôkku.	**1. Kánhla**—*cont.*			of a low range of hills, beyond the village of Léya, and keeping to it thence up to Kánhla. At 3½ miles the village of Sinlán is reached, consisting of about 30 houses surrounded by a thorn hedge. There is a kyaung to the north of the village with a well near it, but the water from this well is not good; good water can be obtained in the village. The road up to this is good, but sandy in places. Beyond Sinlán it passes over broken ground with short ascents and descents, some of them very steep, till it reaches the village of Léya, a mile further on, consisting of about 40 houses. Thence it runs level to Kánhla. The portion of the road from Léya onwards is impassable when the Irrawaddy is in high flood (July to August), as the river washes right up to the foot of the hills. At such times a detour inland has to be made from about the 4th mile-stone. Cultivation on both sides as far as Léya and high ground on the north and cultivation on the south thence to Kánhla. Sinlán and Léya, as well as a third village called Séwa, all lie about ½ a mile to the left of the road from which they are concealed by intervening high ground. Troops marching can, if preferred, follow the telegraph wire as far as Léya, which runs to the north of, and parallel to the road. There is no actual road along here, but the clearing is as good and one or two nullahs met with are no obstacle. About ½ a mile is saved by this means, as this curve in the road is avoided. Kánhla consists of three villages (east and west) containing about 200 houses in all. The ground to the north is broken and covered with scrub jungle, but to the south there is a cultivated plain. There are hardly any large trees anywhere in sight. The rest-camp is situated between the two villages, and there is a pôngyi kyaung to the south and some zayáts in an enclosure to the east. There is accommodation for 300 troops in open sheds, and an officer's bungalow. In case of necessity the kyaung and zayáts could be utilized and would provide accommodation for about 100 men more. Water in plenty from two wells near the kyaung, but is likely to prove insufficient for a large number of animals during the dry season. Green fodder is plentiful in the rains, and dry fodder can be obtained at all seasons. There are some Burman police stationed in the village, but no regular guard.
		2. Tibia ... ... Some dry nullahs.	M. F. **15 0**	M. F. 21 0	From Kánhla the road runs westwards and after crossing a nullah rises gradually for about 2 miles to the top of a ridge which is crossed. At about 4 miles there is a tank, which is however dry in the hot weather, and close by on the left is the small village of Ngapaungán. The next 4 miles over still barer country. At 8 miles Kándaw, 80 houses, one kyaung and zayáts affording accommodation for 100 men at a pinch. Water-supply scanty except in the rains, when there is plenty in two large tanks west of the kyaung. The road up to this has been fair, but heavy in parts and broken in others; from here onwards it becomes very sandy and heavy and passes over level ground. For the next 4 miles the road passes over a sandy tract covered with scrub jungle, but with scarcely a single

FROM PAKÔKKU TO KALÉMYO *viâ* PAUK, KÁN AND GÁNGAW—*continued*.

Authorities. Military.	Authorities. Civil.	Number and Names of Stages, Rivers and Streams.	Distances. Intermediate.	Distances. Total.	Remarks.
G.O.C. Myingyán District.	Commissioner, Southern Division, and Deputy Commissioner, Pakôkku.	**2. Tibia**—*cont.*			shade-giving tree visible. The telegraph wire follows the line of road. At 12 miles the road ends abruptly at a wide dry nullah, on the other side of which it enters an extensive belt of palmyra trees, which continues for miles north and south. There are numerous small villages scattered about in this, but none are of any importance. The road here becomes most puzzling, winding in and out amongst the palm trees, and intersected frequently by paths running between the numerous villages situated in the palm belt. A guide should be taken for this last portion of the march. At about 14 miles is the village of Ingyinbin with a small kyaung and some zayáts. The kyaung is good and zayáts bad; 30 men might be accommodated here. Onward from here the road crosses a stream two or three times, and at 15 miles is the village of Tibia which consists of about 30 houses with a civil police post. There is a well in the enclosure, but the quality of the water is doubtful. There is a rest-camp here with sheds in fair order, enough accommodation for 300 men, also a good Public Works bungalow on the east side of the camp surrounded by a bamboo single stockade. Water can be got by digging holes in the chaung about 100 yards from the camp, and small supplies of chickens and eggs in the village, also grass and paddy for animals, though for any large number notice must be given to admit of its collection from the surrounding villages. This march is a very trying one for troops and is more so in the winter and dry weather than in the rains, as the ground, which is in some places undulating and others flat, is very sandy, and water on the way is scarce, at any rate until the 12th mile. The Burmans make wells in the numerous stream beds passed between the 12th and 15th miles, but the positions of these are changed. For carts this is a very long march and barely 1 mile per hour can be depended on, as the bullocks get very tired in the heavy sand, and for a party with cart transport it may be reckoned as an 11 hours' march including necessary halts.
			M. F.	M. F.	
		3. Pyinchaung ... Yaw river and several nullahs.	**12 0**	33 0	The direction of this march is west. For the first 2 miles the road passes through the palmyra belt entered in the last march, it then emerges into undulating country with scrub jungle. Within the first 2 or 3 miles several nullahs are passed having a little water in the rains, but dry at other seasons. At 2 and 2½ miles, respectively, the villages of Wetké, Gyobyán are passed, of about 30 houses each, and neither actually on the road. At 3½ and 5 miles are two tanks on the north of the road. In this march a range of low hills called the Tángyidaung is crossed, the ascent to which is gradual and is accomplished in about the first 6 miles, after that there are occasional ascents and descents for about 2½ miles, from which point the road descends rapidly. From the 5th to the 9th mile the road consists alternately of deep hollow ways through defiles, or of cuttings round the sides of hills. It then emerges from the hills and crossing the Pyinchaung nullah gets on to high, but fairly level ground to which it keeps up to Pyinchaung at 12 miles. The telegraph wire follows the road throughout this stage. Pyinchaung is on the left of the nullah and is situated on a spur. Beyond the village on the brow of

FROM PAKÔKKU TO KALÉMYO *viâ* PAUK, KÁN AND GÁNGAW—*continued.*

Authorities. Military.	Authorities. Civil.	Number and Names of Stages, Rivers and Streams.	Distances. Intermediate.	Distances. Total.	Remarks.
G.O.C. Myingyân District.	Commissioner, Southern Division, and Deputy Commissioner, Pakôkku.	**3. Pyinchaung** —*cont.*			the spur is the rest-camp consisting of about three sheds, two old kyaungs and some small zayâts. There is also a Public Works Department bungalow. Accommodation in all for about 300 men. There are some Burman police constables stationed here, but they have no regular post and occupy the rest-camp. The village contains about 70 houses, and a small quantity of fowls, &c., can be got. Water plentiful from stream and from a well some way off. Fodder also plentiful, and green fodder obtainable all the year round with a little notice. This march is at present a bad one for troops and very bad for carts, as the part of the road lying over the hills is most difficult to get over, especially in the defiles where the rush of water in the rain washes away the road and leaves the cart ruts deep and uneven and large boulders sticking up all along. When they get to the foot of the hills there is the sandy part of the road for the already tired bullocks to take them over; troops will do the march in about 8½ hours including necessary halts, but only about a mile an hour can be reckoned on for carts. From here there is a good cart track to Myaing *viâ* Thitputwé and Nyaungywa, 26 miles, for details of which *see* Route No. 34.
		4. Pauk ... ... Some dry nullahs and river Yaw.	M. F. *20 0	M. F. 53 0	There are several ways of going from Pyinchaung to Pauk. The following is considered the best. It is known as the Sapé-Anigain (or Aingaing) route. Leaving the rest-camp you strike the road to Pauk, which is lined on each side with the remains of a thorn hedge. To reach this road the nullah passed over in yesterday's march is crossed, and the Public Works Department bungalow is left on the right. After about a mile there is a small clearing with a village on the right. This is easily recognized by a grove of palm trees being in the village. There are low hills on the right. At about 3 miles the road turns off a little to the left over very sandy ground. It then crosses a broad, dry nullah, very heavy going, and enters the village of Thamadaw, 4 miles from Pyinchaung. This village contains zayâts and a kyaung with accommodation for 200 men. From Thamadaw the road goes north-west with sandy hills to the right. Leaving the road by a track almost due west, a dry heavy nullah with very steep banks is reached. This is very bad for carts. The road then leads past small village of Yébyataw through a short defile to low-lying land on which is a grove of palm trees. The Yaw is now reached and crossed not far from the village of Sapé † (8 miles) which consists of about 60 houses. The rest-camp has fallen out of repair. The river here is at this time of the year quite shallow, but the current is very strong. After crossing the road leads through a steep woody defile, and near its entrance is the village of Thambya-aing, 80 houses, kyaung and zayâts for 50 men a little beyond the 40th mile-stone from Pakôkku. This would be a good place to break the march. From here, after going round several spurs, the road runs west for about 3 miles and Yaw is again crossed, and the road

* This march is not necessarily 20 miles. The guides know a great many short cuts, and therefore cannot be depended upon to always lead the same way.—H. DEV. H.

† Apparently the Yaw river may on this route be equally well crossed at Hlángédaw (*see* Alternative No. II) about 6½ miles, apparently, from Pyinchaung.

FROM PAKÔKKU TO KALÉMYO *viâ* PAUK, KÁN AND GÁNGAW—*continued.*

Authorities.		Number and Names of Stages, Rivers and Streams.	Distances.		Remarks.
Military.	Civil.		Inter-mediate.	Total.	
G.O.C. Myingyán District.	Commissioner, Southern Division, and Deputy Commissioner, Pakôkku.	**4. Pauk**—*cont.*			leads up a steep hill, over high cultivated ground to Anigaing at 15 miles. This is a large village and contains from 80 to 100 houses, many of them quite new, and there is a kyaung and three zayáts; here the river is again crossed. It is slightly deeper, but not so broad. From Anigaing the road passes south Ôndaw on the left and north Indaw on the right, small villages, and after passing over a couple of bridges, the village of south Indaw is reached, which is passed also on the right. The road then lies at the foot of a low range of hills on the left. After about a mile and-a-half a turn is taken to the right and Pauk is about a mile off along a more or less straight road. Pauk is a large town containing over 250 houses, with a military police post of 50 rifles, and post and telegraph offices. There is a rest-camp which can accommodate 200 men and a bungalow which can be made use of by officers. Water can be easily obtained, and supplies of all sorts are procurable in the town and from the Commissariat. Pauk is the head-quarters of a sub-divisional office. *Note.*—Capt. Harvey, R.A., reporting on the route from Pakôkku to Pauk in January 1893, says the road is generally a good unmetalled country road throughout, easy gradients, and nothing to delay troops or transport except the sandiness of the soil.
		5. Chaungu Pauk chaung; several bridged nullahs and the Sindaung creek.	M. F. **7 4**	M. F. 60 4	General direction north-north-west. The road on leaving Pauk at once crosses the Pauk chaung, which has ramps leading down to it on both sides and is about 100 yards wide. This is generally dry, but is liable to floods lasting about 6 hours at most. After this has been crossed the road runs along the right bank of the Kyaw river, keeping along the foot of some low hills. The road is level and good in dry weather, but after rain it becomes very heavy. At $3\frac{1}{2}$ miles out the village of Thayetdaw, 40 houses, is passed on the right; soon after the Sindaung stream is crossed (which generally has a few inches of water in it in the early part of the dry season); it is ramped on both sides and is liable to floods which may interrupt traffic for as much as 24 hours. The Yawdwin road (*see* Route No. 35) turns off here, the Gángaw road running in a rather more northerly direction. At $6\frac{1}{2}$ miles the road passes to the west of the village of Pyinma, containing about 50 houses, and $\frac{1}{2}$ a mile farther on a track turns off on the right to Chaungu, which is distant about $\frac{3}{4}$ a mile from the cart road. Chaungu contains about 110 houses and stands on the bank of the Kyaw river. The rest-camp contains accommodation for 300 men, and water is obtainable either from the river or from three wells in the enclosure of a small kyaung. Grass, &c., is obtainable.
		6. Yébyu ... ... Some nullahs and Yébyu chaung.	**10 4**	70 4	General direction north-west. The main cart road must first be regained and the route then runs along it. For the first 5 miles the road though taken through the hills is fairly level. It then descends abruptly to the Ôknesu stream, banks ramped; this stream is liable to floods after rain which,

FROM PAKÔKKU TO KALÉMYO *viâ* PAUK, KÁN AND GÁNGAW—*continued.*

Authorities.		Number and Names of Stages, Rivers and Streams.	Distances.		Remarks.
Military.	Civil.		Intermediate. (M. F.)	Total. (M. F.)	
G.O.C. Myingyan District.	Commissioner, Southern Division, and Deputy Commissioner, Pakôkku.	**6. Yébyu**—*cont.*			however, only last for a few hours. The road shortly after makes a sharp turn to the west and runs over some small hills into Yébyu. Here there is a small village of 13 houses, also a rest-camp accommodating 300 men and a Public Works Department bungalow. There is no well here and water must be got by digging in the bed of a stream. Towards the approach of the hot season, as the water subsides, these holes may have to be made pretty deep. The excavation of a well here is advisable. Grass, &c., can be got up till about February, after which it is advisable to bring fodder for animals.
		7. Yédu ... ... Some nullahs and Yébyu stream.	7 4	78 0	General direction north-west. Leaving Yébyu the cart road runs north-west, crosses the Yébyu stream, and then begins the ascent of the Pôndaung (or Pindaung) hills. The road is zigzagged up and is fairly level, but becomes very much cut up after rain by the traffic and is then very bad indeed and almost impassable to carts. The total ascent is 1,150 feet and is accomplished in about 4 miles. The descent from here to Yédu in the next valley is only 550 feet and the distance is about 2½ miles, a foot-path, passable for ponies and mules, makes a short cut down from the top. Yédu is a small stockaded village of 20 houses and there is a rest-camp on the south side for 300 men. There is a good well in the camp enclosure, and water can also be obtained from the Pôndaung chaung ¼ mile south of the village, and from a well near the village. Fodder, if required, must be ordered beforehand, as the villages around are all small.
		8. Buyaban ... or **Anyaban.** Some bridged nullahs.	12 0	90 0	From Yédu the road runs north through a jungle-covered valley and reaches the village of Chin (or Kyin) 1½ miles from Yédu, crossing a chaung which is bridged just before. Chin is a large stockaded village of 50 houses and has a kyaung big enough to accommodate 50 or 60 men. From this point there is a foot track which runs north over the hills to Gángaw, reducing the journey to three days. After Chin the ascent of the Inbinhla range is commenced; the total ascent is 1,130 feet and the top of the pass is reached 5½ or 6 miles from Chin. The descent is 920 feet on the other side to Buyaban and is accomplished in 4½ miles. There is a short cut down from the top of the hill practicable to ponies and mules. There is also another foot-path all the way from Yédu to Buyaban which keeps to the south of the cart road up to Chin and then to the north side with the exception of about 1½ miles on Buyaban side of the ridge, when the road makes a bend northward. The same remarks apply to the road over the hills as in the previous march. Buyaban contains 20 houses and there is a rest-camp with accommodation for over 300 men and a Public Works Department bungalow on the right of the road. Water is got from a well on the main road about ½ a mile west of the camp and also from the bed of the Ban chaung, also on the west of the camp. Fodder in small quantities always available and in large quantities with notice.

FROM PAKÔKKU TO KALÉMYO *viâ* PAUK, KÁN AND GÁNGAW—*continued.*

Authorities. Military.	Authorities. Civil.	Number and Names of Stages, Rivers and Streams.	Distances. Intermediate. M. F.	Distances. Total. M. F.	Remarks.
G.O.C. Myingyán District.	Commissioner, Southern Division, and Deputy Commissioner, Pakôkku.	**9. Tilin** ... ... Ban chaung and several bridged nullahs.	**13 4**	103 0	The road runs along the valley of the Ban chaung over undulating and jungle-covered country, passing the two stockaded villages of Alêban (20 houses) and Akyiban (50 houses) at 2 and 3½ miles respectively. The latter contains a kyaung with accommodation for about 100 men. Beyond Akyiban a strip of paddy land has to be crossed about ½ to ¾ of a mile wide, the cart road being along a bund; this bit after rain and in the wet season is very bad; after it the ground rises again and the road is good and level, over laterite hills to Tilin. Tilin is a large Burman village of about 100 houses or more, the head-quarters of a Myo-ôk, has a telegraph office and a police guard, and letters can be posted here, though there is no post office. There is a Public Works Department bungalow and rest-camp for 200 men and accommodation for another 100 in a kyaung. There is also another kyaung in the centre of the village opposite the telegraph office. There is a Burman police guard here and a telegraph office and head-quarters of a Myo-ôk. A path runs south from here to Yawdwin, which can be used by troops with animal transport, but not carts, during the dry season. During the rains it is passable, but scarcely to troops. Yawdwin is 26 miles distant by this route. It is four short marches—(i) to Tachaung, 6 miles; (ii) to Kyi, 8 miles; (iii) to Nathu, 6 miles; (iv) into Yawdwin, 6 miles. In the last march the Yaw and Chê rivers have to be crossed. Water is plentiful at all seasons from the Maw stream. Supplies are obtainable here in small quantities, and fodder is plentiful. Tilin stands on the right bank of the Maw, a tributary of the Myittha. Though the distance to Tilin from Anyaban is 13 miles, it is nearly 14 to the rest-camp.
		10. Shwégôndaing. Tanti and Laungbo chaungs.	**14 0**	117 0	The road now turns due north and leaving the valley of the Maw on the left runs over undulating and forest-covered laterite hills, good going throughout this march. At 3 miles the village of Pônna with 40 houses is passed, and just beyond the Tanti stream is crossed, banks ramped. It is about 20 yards wide and though not deep (ordinarily there is a little water in it in the early part of the dry season, and about 2 feet in the rains) is liable to heavy floods which may interrupt traffic as much as two days. From this point the road keeps to the watershed ridge and no water can be got till Shwégôndaing is reached. Some small villages exist on both sides of the ridge ½ a mile or more from the road. Shwégôndaing is a Taungtha village, a race distinct from the Burmans, speaking a different language and the women wearing a totally distinct costume; as they all speak Burmese however no difficulty in communication exists. The rest-camp here is 1½ miles beyond the village, some distance to the right of the road. There is a Public Works Department bungalow exactly at the 63rd mile-post; the village is about ½ a mile north of the bungalow. The road to the camp turns off at a nullah just after the 64th mile-post. If this is missed, there is another cart track after the 64½ mile-post, whence the camp can be seen. It is hidden by trees until nearly abreast of it, consequently

FROM PAKÔKKU TO KALÉMYO *viâ* PAUK, KÂN AND GÂNGAW—*continued.*

Authorities. Military.	Authorities. Civil.	Number and Names of Stages, Rivers and Streams.	Distances. Inter-mediate.	Distances. Total.	Remarks.
G.O.C. Myingyân District.	Commissioner, Southern Division, and Deputy Commissioner, Pakôkku.	**10. Shwégôndaing**—*cont.*			it is better to get a guide at the village. There are four huts and water is obtainable from the stream close by. On this march the Tanti stream is crossed just 4 miles out of Tilin, generally low, but subject to floods in the rains; after that no more water is obtainable till Shwégôndaing is reached. Water can be obtained in plenty by digging in the bed of the stream, but grass and firewood is scarce. The village contains about 20 houses.
		11. Mawlé ... Setni chaung.	M. F. 13 0	M. F. 130 0	The road continues north over the same country as in the last march, and passes the Taungtha village of Semindaw about 7 miles out. From here a track runs to Tawma, the old rest-camp, but the cart road runs northward direct to Mawlé. The Setni chaung is crossed about ½ a mile before Mawlé; it is not deep, but is perennial and liable to flood. A small ferry boat is kept on this stream, but is not generally required to be used except in the rains, and not always then. Mawlé is a village of 20 houses in the angle formed by the junction of the Maw and Setni streams; water is plentiful from the stream; fodder scarce. The rest-camp which contains four huts is between the Setni chaung and Mawlé village. There is a small Public Works Department bungalow close by.
		12. Minywa or Mingwa. Maw river.	6 0	136 0	The Maw river is crossed immediately after leaving the rest-camp; it is about 60 yards wide and barely knee-deep in the dry season. There is a ferry boat here capable of taking over 15 men at a time and a raft to convey 30. The road to Minywa is good and level; it passes through jungle with patches of cultivation here and there. Minywa or Mingwa (6 miles) is a large village of about 300 houses with an independent thugyi. There are some shops here and supplies of all sorts can be got. The dâk bungalow is on a hill overlooking the village. The rest-camp is about 1½ miles beyond the village and accommodates about 300 men. The Myittha has to be crossed to get to the camp, but the river is shallow at this point, not having been yet joined by the Maw; bridge does not exist, but there are boats ready at hand, and the river is fordable in the dry season, but even then it is waist-deep.
		13. Gângaw ... Myittha river, the Pawlé and Laungdaung chaungs.	14 0	150 0	On leaving Minywa the Myittha river is crossed, the road then runs north over undulating jungle-covered country, good, though in parts liable to get heavy after rain past the village of Péwun and crosses the Pawlé stream 2½ miles after starting. This is sometimes passable, at others it is deep, but there is a ferry of two boats over it. After November this stream should be fordable. At 5 miles the village of Kyauki (or Kyauksé) is passed, and at 11½ miles the Myittha has to be crossed at the village of Shaukpin. There is a Government ferry here in the rains consisting of two boats capable of carrying about 12 men; during the dry season the river is fordable. Opposite is the village of Paya. The

FROM PAKÔKKU TO KALÉMYO *viâ* PAUK, KÀN AND GÁNGAW—*continued.*

Authorities. Military.	Authorities. Civil.	Number and Names of Stages, Rivers and Streams.	Distances. Intermediate. M.	F.	Distances. Total. M.	F.	Remarks.
G.O.C. Myingyán District.	Commissioner, Southern Division, and Deputy Commissioner, Pakôkku.	**13. Gángaw**—*cont.*					road beyond is good, being above the flood level. About ½ a mile out of Gángaw it crosses the Laungdaung stream, which varies from 2 to 3 feet deep and has a ferry. From there into Gángaw the road runs through paddy-fields. Gángaw is a large town of over 300 houses and is the head-quarters of a Sub-divisional Officer, has a post and telegraph office and several shops. It is divided into two villages, "Old" and "New" Gángaw, the former being the larger, both situated on the right bank of the Myittha river. Paddy cultivation all around. There are shops here, and supplies of all sorts are procurable in small quantities. The military stockade is about a mile to the north of Gángaw near a small village called Myaukkôn. There is accommodation for about 200 men at the camp, and a Public Works Department bungalow close by. There is also a kyaung in the village. Water from the river.
		14. Myinza ... Kônsaing chaung, another stream, and some bridged nullahs.	**12**	**0**	162	0	Leaving the camp the road runs north along the right bank of the Myittha river and passes the village of Yébôk, 10 houses, at 2 miles. For the next 2 miles the country is partly undulating through forest and partly level through cultivation till the Kôngaing chaung is crossed at 4 miles with the village of Ywazé, of about 30 houses, and a kyaung beyond it. The Kônsaing chaung is about 30 yards broad with quick sandy bottom, and is shallow except just after rains. From Ywazé there is a branch route to Kyaungzôn, *vide* Route No. 10. After Ywazé there is a long stretch of flat road between paddy-fields which becomes heavy in wet weather, and then again the country is undulating with forest on both sides and the road is less likely to be affected by the weather. At about 8½ miles a small stream with rather high banks has to be crossed and a little further on the village of Kyawywa is seen on the opposite side (left bank) of the Myittha, and at 10 miles Myinza is reached. This is a small village of 30 houses with a double stockade and lies on the right of the road. Water plentiful, fodder as in Stage 8. Opposite to it on the left there is a rest-camp with two rather large sheds capable of holding nearly 200 men, and beyond it a Public Works Department house. There are numerous small nullahs on the road bridged with wooden bridges, of which the roadway is formed of untrimmed logs. Most of these are at this time in very bad repair. They are not passable for elephants, which have to go round by jungle paths.
		15. Kán ... ... Tawzalé chaung and some bridged nullahs.	**12**	**0**	174	0	From Myinza into Kán the road still running north passes over undulating and jungle-covered ground nearly the whole way, here and there are paths of flat ground with cultivation. The road is good and owing to the nature of the ground not much likely to be affected by the weather except in one place where a stretch of about ½ a mile of flat between fields would probably be bad in the rains. At 8 miles from Myinza the Tawzalé or Mauk chaung has to be crossed.

FROM PAKÔKKU TO KALÉMYO *viâ* PAUK, KÁN AND GÁNGAW—*continued.*

Authorities. Military.	Authorities. Civil.	Number and Names of Stages, Rivers and Streams.	Distances. Inter-mediate.	Distances. Total.	Remarks.
G.O.C. Myingyán District.	Commissioner, Southern Division, and Deputy Commissioner, Pakôkku.	**15. Kán**—*cont.*			This is only a very shallow stream in the dry season, but gets flooded and difficult to cross in the rains. There are also numerous small nullahs to cross with bridges of similar construction and in a similar condition to those in the previous march. There is only one small village passed actually on the road; it contains 15 houses and is just 4 miles from Myinza.* The last part of the road runs over some spurs and is very good, after which it passes over a paddy plain into Kán at 12½ miles from Myinza. Kán is a large village of 150 houses, a third of which are occupied by Chins. It is not far from, and on the right bank of, the Myittha. On the north, south and east it is surrounded by an extensive paddy plain. The military post is to the west of the village on the bank of the river. It is stockaded and can hold 100 men. On the north of it is a rest-camp meant for 400 men. On the east of the post there is a kyaung for officers and also a Public Works Department bungalow. Both post and telegraph offices exist. There is a large Commissariat store here and rations can be obtained. Water is got from the river. The road to Háka *viâ* Chaungkwa, &c., *vide* Route No. 11, starts from here, crossing the Myittha a little lower down.
		16. Myintha ... Myittha river, To, Sanséyé, Chauna and Umi chaungs, and other dry water-courses.	M. F. 15 4	M. F. 189 4	From Kán the general direction of the road is north. Leaving Kán the road runs across the paddy plain to the north, but in the wet weather this is not practicable, and the road keeps through the jungle to the west of the cultivation. At about 1½ miles the village of Kántha is reached on the right bank of the Myittha, a small village of about 15 houses. Here the river is crossed and the path leads along the other bank for about a mile, when the river is again crossed. It is easily fordable in both places when the river is low during the dry weather, but when the river is fuller the path along the right bank must be taken, which is much longer, as it makes a wide detour to avoid a loop of the river, which the above path cuts off. Leaving the stream, after crossing it the second time, the path leads through jungle and soon joins the other path and continues good and dry, running over undulating ground and crossing several dry water-courses. At about 8 miles the village of Mozo is reached containing some 30 houses and situated on the bank of the river. There is an extensive stretch of paddy land here. The kyaungs in the village, which were formerly good, have fallen into disrepair. Leaving Mozo the path continues as before, and at about 11 miles reaches the deserted village of Yésháng on the left bank of the To chaung. At about 13 miles it crosses the Sanséyé chaung, and at 14 miles the Chauna chaung and the Umi chaung. At about 15 miles it passes the village of Ywama, stockaded and containing about 20 houses, and about 15½ miles the village of Aléywa, also of about 20 houses. Immediately afterwards Myintha is reached. The various chaungs crossed on the road are all liable to flood after heavy rain, but they subside very rapidly and are seldom impassable. Myintha is also called Wadet. It is a large village of about 80 houses and is really made up of several

* This is probably Letpán, *vide* Route No. 10, Branch I.

FROM PAKÔKKU TO KALÉMYO *viâ* PAUK, KÁN AND GÁNGAW—*continued.*

Authorities.		Number and Names of Stages, Rivers and Streams.	Distances.		Remarks.
Military.	Civil.		Inter-mediate.	Total.	
G.O.C. Myingyán District.	Commissioner, Southern Division, and Deputy Commissioner, Pakôkku.	**16. Myintha**—*cont.*			smaller villages collected into one for safety. It is under a hereditary *thugyi*. There is accommodation in kyaungs in the village for 100 men and also in sheds on the bank of the river for about 300. Supplies of grass, &c., are procurable. A road runs west from Myintha through Wunhla to Háka in the Chin Hills.
		17. Kyaukpyauk. Tanthé and Nabôk chaungs and others.	M. F. 7 4	M. F. 197 0	General direction north. Leaving Myintha the road runs across some paddy-fields, which have to be avoided in wet weather, to the village of Kônywa at about 400 yards. It contains about 40 houses, and the road runs through the middle of it. Beyond this the road enters the jungle and is good going, though very muddy in places after rain. At about 1½ miles the deserted village of Kyinywa is passed on the right and immediately afterwards the Tanthé chaung is crossed. This stream is seldom impassable and only so after heavy rains. There is a well of good water on the right bank just above the road. Beyond this, at about 2½ miles, the deserted village of Nyaungda is passed, and a mile further on the village of Nabôk is reached after crossing a stream of the same name. Nabôk is a village of about 30 houses on the right bank of Myittha river. Beyond this the road runs through paddy cultivation almost the whole way to Kyaukpyauk. At about 4½ miles a stream is crossed and at 5½ miles the village of Légyi is passed about ½ mile to the west of the road on the Myittha. Légyi contains about 30 houses. At 6½ miles the village of Winwa is reached containing about 40 houses, and a mile further on Kyaukpyauk. The descents to and ascents from all the streams are ramped, but the streams need to be bridged. This bit of the road is said to be very bad in the wet season, from June to October. Kyaukpyauk is a stockaded village of about 40 houses. There is accommodation in some kyaungs and zayáts to east of the village for about 40 men, also in temporary sheds, and another zayát for 100 more. The village is near the river, and on the bank there are more sheds, which would hold 200 men. A few supplies of fowls, vegetables, grass, firewood, &c., procurable. Water from the Myittha and from a well in the village.
	Commissioner, Central Division, and Deputy Commissioner, Upper Chindwin.	**18. Natin** ... ... Nwa chaung and several other nullahs.	13 4	210 4	General direction north. The road runs across cultivation for about ¼ mile, when it crosses a nullah, the descent to and ascent from which are ramped. Immediately beyond it passes the village of Kyauksé of about 20 houses and enters jungle. At about 1 mile it crosses another nullah, and at 1½ miles passes the village of Manta, about 300 yards to west of road among palmyra trees, containing about 20 houses. Crossing another nullah it reaches the village of Yéshin at 3½ miles, 20 houses, and, crossing a nullah reaches Sigôn at 4½ miles, a stockaded village of 30 houses. Immediately beyond this the road crosses the Nwa chaung, in which there is always water; but it is always fordable, except immediately after heavy rain. From here the road runs chiefly through cultivated land to Kôko, the village of Hmánbé being seen about ½ a mile to west of road on the bank of the Myittha. Kôko is reached at 6½

FROM PAKÔKKU TO KALÉMYO *viâ* PAUK, KÁN AND GÁNGAW—*continued.*

Authorities.		Number and Names of Stages, Rivers and Streams.	Distances.		Remarks.
Military.	Civil.		Intermediate.	Total.	
G.O.C. Myingyán District.	Commissioner, Central Division, and Deputy Commissioner, Upper Chindwin.	**18. Natin**—*cont.*			miles and is a stockaded village of about 40 houses. The road to Sihaung branches off here and crosses the Myittha by a temporary bridge. There is very little accommodation at Kôl-o in one zayát for about 30 men. From here the road continues to run near the river.bank till Shádaw is reached at about 7½ miles. This is a small village of about 15 houses. There are sheds here which would hold 150 men. Beyond Shádaw a very deep narrow nullah, with steep sides, is crossed, and ponies have to have their loads carried across; but by ramping it it could be made easily passable. The small village of Nwa is reached at about 9 miles, containing about 15 houses, and at about 11 miles another bad nullah is crossed. Nyaungbin is reached at about 12 miles, containing about 20 houses, and at 13½ miles Natin, a village of 30 houses. Here there is accommodation in a good zayát for about 30 men to south of village. A few fowls, &c., grass, and firewood procurable. Water from the Myittha river close by and from a well in the village. The whole of this stage is said to be very bad going and nearly impracticable in the wet weather. The road has not yet been made, but will probably be looked to shortly.
		19. Indin ... ... Several nullahs.	M. F. **12 0**	M. F. 222 4	Leaving Natin the general direction of the road is still north. At first it runs along the bank of the river, and about a mile below Natin the mouth of the Nankathé river can be seen flowing into the Myittha from the west. Beyond the road runs through high reeds on the foreshore of the river, which is doubtless under water when the river is in flood. There appears at present to be no trace of a path above high flood level. The path now runs along the foot of some low hills and is very stony and rough, crossing several rocky nullahs, but this could easily be put all right with little labour. At about 4 miles the path from Sihaung through Taungpa (*see* Route No. 5, Central Division) joins the road from the west, and ½ mile beyond the road passes the village of Sinywa, containing about 20 houses. From here the road runs along without any difficulties until Indin is reached. There are a few nullahs to cross, which are probably impassable when in flood. The present path is probably impassable during the wet weather, from June to October. The curious peak of Kyésagôk is passed during this march. It is a jaggy rock with precipitous sides, which rears itself out of a low ridge of hills, and is a very prominent object from most points in the Kalé valley to the north. Indin is the largest and most prosperous village in the Kalé State. It contains more than 200 houses, and there is accommodation for a large force in kyaungs in the village. The Kalé Sawbwa has a palace here, or at least a house. There are sheds in the old post of Indin, but they are much dilapidated. All ordinary supplies are obtainable here. Water from the Myittha river close by.

FROM PAKÔKKU TO KALÉMYO *viâ* PAUK, KÁN AND GÁNGAW—*continued.*

Authorities. Military.	Authorities. Civil.	Number and Names of Stages, Rivers and Streams.	Distances. Inter-mediate. M.	F.	Distances. Total. M.	F.	Remarks.
G.O.C. Myingyán District.	Commissioner, Central Division, and Deputy Commissioner, Upper Chindwin.	**20. Kalémyo** ... Several nullahs and the Myittha river.	**13**	**0**	235	4	General direction north. The road runs along above the river, and at 2 miles reaches the village of Paukdaw, containing about 40 houses. The path must be bad in wet weather. From here it runs to the village of Bugyi at 4 miles containing about 20 houses, crossing a deep nullah just before reaching the village. At 5 miles reach Kinbôngyôn, a village of about 35 houses, and just beyond cross another nullah. At about 6½ miles pass the small village of Udu, and 2 miles beyond the village Uyin, 800 yards to the east of the road, containing 40 houses. At 9½ miles pass the old village site of Ywazo, and at about 11 miles reach the ferry over the Myittha called Pyinthazet. Here there are always boats and a ferry, the river being unfordable. The village is on the left bank and, though at present there are only two or three houses, it is expected that there will be a large village shortly. This is also the landing place for boats from Kaléwa. From here the road runs along an embankment above flood level, but is at present unmetalled and unbridged and is probably very soft after rain. The old city of Kalémyo is reached about ½ mile east of the post, and the shape of the outer walls, when it was once the thriving capital of the State, can be seen. Now, however, there is only a very small village of about 30 houses, though it is expected that it will greatly increase in size before long. It is situated in the midst of an extensive paddy plain and has the reputation of being extremely feverish. The post is also in the plain and there is accommodation for about 600 men inside. There are also a telegraph office, post office, and Civil Officer's bungalow. The main road to Fort White in the Chin Hills (*see* Route No. 6, Central Division) starts from here, and there also roads to Kaléwa (*see* Route No. 7, Central Division) and to Tummu (*see* Route No. 23, Central Division). There is a bazaar outside the post, and all supplies are obtainable. Water is brought from irrigation channels and wells.

ALTERNATIVE I.

FROM PYINCHAUNG (STAGE 3) TO PAUK (STAGE 4) *viâ* PAYADAUNG AND YÉYIN.

BY LIEUT. RAY, 7TH BENGAL INFANTRY, NOVEMBER 1891.

Military	Civil	Stage	Inter. M.	F.	Total M.	F.	Remarks
G.O.C. Myingyán District.	Commissioner, Southern Division, and Deputy Commissioner, Pakôkku.	**1. Pauk** ... ... Yaw and Kyaw rivers.	**15**	**0**	15	0	The direction of this march lies west-north-west. The road crosses the Yaw river the first time about ¼ of a mile from Pyinchaung. This ford is only practicable in the dry season, at which time the river is about 100 yards wide and 2 feet deep. The current is strong and the bed of the river firm. After the crossing the road follows the course of the river for about 1½ miles and then turns gradually to the left and passes the village of Payadaung at 3½ miles from

FROM PAKÔKKU TO KALÉMYO *viâ* PAUK, KÁN AND GÁNGAW—*continued.*

ALTERNATIVE I—*continued.*

Authorities: Military.	Authorities: Civil.	Number and Names of Stages, Rivers and Streams.	Distances: Intermediate.	Distances: Total.	Remarks.
G.O.C. Myingyán District.	Commissioner, Southern Division, and Deputy Commissioner, Pakôkku.	**1. Pauk**—*cont.*			the commencement of the march. Payadaung is a small village, but there is accommodation for about 50 men in a kyaung and some zayáts. From there the road runs on to Yéyin at 11 miles, which is near the second crossing of the Yaw. Yéyin contains about 40 houses and some dilapidated zayáts. From Payadaung to Yéyin the road runs over undulating and jungle-covered ground. The ford at Yéyin is practicable in the dry season and is then about 2½ feet deep. After a heavy fall of rain in the hills at any season these rivers are liable to be much deeper and wider, but are not calculated to be impassable except during the rains. The last 4 miles into Pauk are good going in dry weather, and one small village of about 40 houses, Tawtha, is passed about half-way. A long march, but good dry weather road. The above route is the shortest between Stages 3 and 4, but is impracticable during the rains, as the Yaw river near Pyinchaung is unfordable.

ALTERNATIVE II.

FROM PYINCHAUNG (STAGE 3) TO PAUK (STAGE 4).

BY LIEUT. TRYDELL, BURMA RIFLES, 1893.

Military.	Civil.	Number and Names of Stages, Rivers and Streams.	Intermediate. M. F.	Total. M. F.	Remarks.
G.O.C. Myingyán District.	Commissioner, Southern Division, and Deputy Commissioner, Pakôkku.	**1. Sapé** ... ... Yaw.	8 0	8 0	In the dry weather the Yaw has about 3 feet of water in it, but in the rains it is unfordable, and, as the only ferry boats in use are little dug-outs, the route across the Yaw is impracticable for large bodies of troops or transport. The following route must then be taken:—After reaching Hla-ngé daw (*see* Stage 4 above) instead of crossing the Yaw, the march must be continued north-west for 1½ miles until Sapé is reached and here a halt must be made if carts are being used, as the next day's march is a trying one for carts. Sapé has no rest-camp, but the kyaung and zayáts could accommodate perhaps 100 men. Water is plentiful, but notice must be given if fodder is required. In the dry weather only dry fodder can be obtained.
		2. Pauk ... ... Kyaw.	15 0	23 0	The road goes on north-west; about 1½ miles out a bridle-path branches off to the west, by which the distance from Sapé to Nyaungwunbauk, where the Kyaw river has to be crossed, is only about 6 miles. The cart road continues to the west, and by it the distance to Nyaungwunbauk is about 10 miles. There is no water in the Kyaw in the dry weather, but in the rains it has about 2 to 3 feet of water; occasionally, when in full flood, it is impassable and causes a delay of 24 hours before it runs down. After crossing the Kyaw river the only road there is crosses paddy-fields and swampy ground and strikes the main road to Pauk near the village of South Indaw (*see* Stage 4).

FROM PAKÔKKU TO KALÉMYO *viâ* PAUK, KÁN AND GÁNGAW—*continued.*

ALTERNATIVE III.

FROM PAUK (STAGE 4) TO YÉDU (STAGE 7).

BY CAPT. J. WILLCOCKS, D.S.O., 1ST BATTALION, LEINSTER REGIMENT, AND INFORMATION COLLECTED, 1889–90.

Authorities. Military.	Authorities. Civil.	Number and Names of Stages, Rivers and Streams.	Distances. Intermediate. M.	F.	Distances. Total. M.	F.	Remarks.
G.O.C. Myingyán District.	Commissioner, Southern Division, and Deputy Commissioner, Pakôkku.	**1. Minbôn (camp).** Cross Minbôn and Salaung chaungs and go up bed for some distance.	**6**	**0**	6	0	Whole road fit for laden animals. The road follows the Gángaw cart road for $3\frac{1}{2}$ miles and then turns up the Salaung chaung and thence into the Minbôn chaung to westward for 1 mile; from this point up the left bank of the chaung to Minbôn, an old site of a deserted village. Camp in paddy-fields. Water plentiful; fodder ditto.
		2. Wabin ...	**14**	**0**	20	0	Road crosses and recrosses the Minbôn chaung (which has some water in it for 4 miles above Minbôn) until it gets on the top of the Pandaung hills, 8 miles. The path descends then steeply into the Pindaung valley and goes on to within a mile south of Wabin on the chaung. Jungle, *in*, teak and bamboo. Ground for several miles is rocky and broken with rather steep bits here and there. Wabin has 30 houses, but no kyaungs or sayáts. Camp in large fields. Water plentiful. Fodder good.
		3. Yédu	**7**	**0**	27	0	The road follows the Pandaung chaung through paddy and other cultivation. Fairly level going. Yédu is on the Pakôkku-Gángaw road and well known.

BRANCH I.

FROM MINYWA (STAGE 12) TO SHURKWA (*see* ROUTE No. 9, CHIN HILLS DIVISION).

BY LIEUT. C. R. BALLARD, NORFOLK REGIMENT, INTELLIGENCE DEPARTMENT, JANUARY 1892.

Military.	Civil.	Stages.	Intermediate. M.	F.	Total. M.	F.	Remarks.
G.O.C. Myingyán District.	Commissioner, Southern Division, and Deputy Commissioner, Pakôkku.	**1. First camp** ... Two small streams at $3\frac{1}{2}$ and $8\frac{1}{2}$ miles.	**11**	**0**	11	0	The path is at first rather difficult to hit off and a guide should be taken for the 1st mile; after this it cannot be mistaken. It immediately enters the jungle and continues in it throughout fairly level and easy. At $2\frac{1}{4}$ miles and 3 miles are broad nullahs or valleys (300 yards broad by 150 feet deep) with steep sides. A small stream of water in the second nullah. Another stream at $8\frac{1}{2}$ miles. Camp at third stream in bamboo jungle.

FROM PAKÔKKU TO KALÊMYO *viâ* PAUK, KÁN AND GÁNGAW—*continued.*

BRANCH I—*continued.*

Authorities. Military.	Authorities. Civil.	Number and Names of Stages, Rivers and Streams.	Distances. Intermediate. M.	F.	Distances. Total. M.	F.	Remarks.
G.O.C. Myingyân District.	Political Officer, Chin Hills.	**2. Pawlôn camp...** A small stream at $1\frac{1}{2}$ miles.	**9**	**0**	20	0	Path begins to ascend at 2 miles and top of ridge is reached at 4 miles; goes up and down with steep gradients for 1 mile and then descends very steeply to the valley. Water may be got at $5\frac{3}{4}$ miles by digging in a small nullah. Path level the rest of the way to the stream. Camp on left bank of stream 500 yards below first crossing. Bad camping ground in undulating bamboo jungle, plenty of water.
		3. First camp on Zahaw stream. Zahaw chaung.	**5**	**0**	25	0	An easy march over another range of hills; gradients on each side sometimes rather steep for mules. Total ascent about 1,200 feet. A good camping ground with plenty of water, wood and grass, but it is feverish.
		4. Tônwa ...	**10**	**0**	35	0	A very hard march for men and mules and no water all the way. Path first ascends steeply for 2 miles and in places is very bad, then it undulates along the ridge for 2 miles and then descends for $1\frac{1}{2}$ miles. At 7 miles it rises to the top of another ridge and continues along the ridge into the village of Tônwa (or Domvar). Camp about $\frac{1}{2}$ mile on the further side of the village; plenty of ground, but not good being on the hill side. Water from two small streams on each side of camp, but it is not good. Small quantities of good water may be had from a well in the village. The streams are difficult for mules to cross. The village contains 220 houses and supplies of goats, fowls, eggs and vegetables are obtainable.
		5. Second camp on Zahaw stream. Zahaw chaung.	**5**	**0**	40	0	An easy march all down-hill after the 1st mile; descent for the last mile very steep and mules require to be assisted. Camping ground in bamboo jungle by side of stream (stream 2 feet deep and 20 feet wide; rocky bed). The ground is very small and confined and our column (250 men, 1 Sec. Art. and 500 coolies) could scarcely find room. Hills rise precipitously on all sides. This place is very feverish indeed, but cannot be avoided.
		6. Camp on Shurkwa stream. Two small rivulets at 8 and $8\frac{1}{2}$ miles.	**12**	**0**	52	0	A very hard march, first along steep ascent for 4 miles; the first part of this is very steep indeed and mules had to be hauled up. At 7 miles the path crosses a big watershed leaving the valley of the Myittha and entering the valley of the Boinu. There are two watering places at 8 miles and a few hundred yards further on. From $7\frac{1}{2}$ miles path descends, but not steeply. Road here is very broken and requires mending. A good camp, plenty of room and water, but not much wood.

FROM PAKÔKKU TO KALÉMYO *viâ* PAUK, KÁN AND GÁNGAW—*continued.*

BRANCH I—*continued.*

Authorities. Military.	Authorities. Civil.	Number and Names of Stages, Rivers and Streams.	Distances. Intermediate. M. F.	Distances. Total. M. F.	Remarks.
G.O.C. Myingyán District.	Political Officer, Chin Hills.	**7. Shurkwa** ... Small stream at the camp.	3 4	55 4	Path crosses the stream at once and ascends steeply for 2½ miles into the village. In places road is very bad. A camp was formed 1 mile north of the village: plenty of good ground here, but little wood. Water in very small quantities from nullah 200 yards from camp and another nullah 400 yards from camp. Mules must be taken down to nullah about 1½ miles north of camp. The village is strongly stockaded and consists of 250 houses. Supplies of goats, fowls, &c., obtainable. The post does not seem to be healthy, and is not recommended as a base. A small stockade was partially built, but afterwards adandoned.

BRANCH II.

FROM MYINTHA (STAGE 16) TO HÁKA (*vide* ROUTE NO. 11) *viâ* WUNHLA.

BY CAPT. G. VERNER, KING'S OWN SCOTTISH BORDERERS, APRIL 1890.

Military	Civil	Stages	Intermediate M. F.	Total M. F.	Remarks
G.O.C. Myingyán District.	Commissioner, Southern Division, and Deputy Commissioner, Pakôkku.	**1. Sunka chaung.** Myittha river.	8 2	8 2	General direction west. Crossing the Myittha river by a ford the path is level and easy, running through forest of small teak (I ?) trees. Camping ground good, and water from the Sunka chaung plentiful from large pools in the bed, 20 feet deep, with small stream flowing through them, which in the dry weather loses itself in the ground after 200 yards.
	Political Officer, Chin Hills.	**2. Runlong chaung.**	11 2	19 4	General direction north-west. Path good, ascending very fairly gradually all the way, following the tops of ridges and spurs. Country thickly wooded; trees, *in* and fir. No water along the road. Camping ground good, but unsuitable on account of scarcity of water, which is only sufficient for a small force; supply would probably become exhausted in two or three days, being derived from small pools at the bottom of a narrow, rocky gully, about 200 yards below the camp.
		3. Kôtár Vár ... Nanpathi river.	11 0	30 4	General direction west. Gradual ascent to the top of the Nanpathi hill; then steep descent to the Nanpathi, here from 20 yards to 40 yards wide and 2 feet deep. No camping ground at the ford, as hills on either side descend very steeply straight down to the water, leaving no room for a camp. The ascent from the Nanpathi is also very steep. The village of Wunhla is passed about a mile before camp is reached, containing 150 houses. No other village. The camp is bad and cramped at the bottom of a narrow valley. Water plentiful. Site for a camp for a small party exists close to

FROM PAKÔKKU TO KALÉMYO *viâ* PAUK, KÁN AND GÁNGAW—*continued.*

BRANCH II—*continued.*

Authorities. Military.	Authorities. Civil.	Number and Names of Stages, Rivers and Streams.	Distances. Intermediate. M. F.	Distances. Total. M. F.	Remarks.
G.O.C. Myingyán District.	Political Officer, Chin Hills.	**3. Kôtár Vár**—*cont.*			Wunhla village beside a small stream. Path throughout well defined, but hilly and steep. Country thickly wooded. East of Nanpathi trees, chiefly firs. Water only procurable near Wunhla and in the Nanpathi.
		4. Fyer-thi or Shai-thi. Kôtár Vár, Twombi Vár, Arfilaung Vár, Dawchim Vár, and Ban Vár.	11 4	42 0	General direction west-north-west. Path as a whole not good, being comparatively new and not worn or well defined. Some very steep ascents and descents. Country thickly wooded as far as the Twombi Vár, beyond which it is fairly open up to the highest part of the hill. From here to the Dawchim Vár it is again thickly wooded; beyond the Dawchim it is thinly wooded. There is a considerable amount of cultivation in the Twombi valley. Water fairly plentiful except between the Twombi Vár and the Arfilaung Vár. No villages on road. All the streams from 2 to 4 yards wide, except the Arfilaung, which is very small. Camping ground well situated on a spur commanding the village, but small, only suitable for a small force without transport animals. Good camping ground could be formed at the end of the spur below the camp and just above the Ban Vár, from which an unlimited supply of water could be had. Fyer-thi contains about 80 houses and is Háka.
		5. Háka ... ... Tidar Vár, Tipi Vár, Hé-hwé Vár, Tisom Vár, Rawnu Vár, and Rawtôn Vár.	11 0	53 0	General direction west-south-west. Path throughout very good, slight ascent from the hill above Kôbé village to Háka; also steep descent to and ascent from the Hé-hwé Vár. Country open and only slightly wooded. Ground near villages cultivated. The following villages are passed. Farôn, containing about 150 houses, is a Háka village as are all the others on this stage. A small part of the village is detached from the main part, which is surrounded by a high-banked fence. Byao-té contains about 60 houses and Kôbé about 24 houses. For description of Háka *see* Route No. 11.

No. 31.

From PAKÔKKU to LAUNGSHÉ viâ MYITKYI and LETSÉ.

BY CAPT. J. WILLCOCKS, D.S.O., 1ST LEINSTER REGIMENT 1890; FROM INFORMATION COLLECTED FROM LIEUT. RAINEY AND FOREST OFFICERS.

Military	Civil	Stage	Intermediate M.	F.	Total M.	F.	Remarks
G.O.C. Myingyán District.	Commr., Southern Divn., and Dy. Commr., Pakôkku.	**1. Kánhla** ...	6	0	6	0	Road heavy sand, but fit for laden carts. This stage is the first on the Gángaw cart road, *vide* Route No. 30. Water scarce, from wells.

FROM PAKÔKKU TO LAUNGSHÉ *viâ* MYITKYI AND LETSÉ—*continued.*

Authorities. Military.	Authorities. Civil.	Number and Names of Stages, Rivers and Streams.	Distances. Intermediate. M. F.	Distances. Total. M. F.	Remarks.
G.O.C. Myingyân District.	Commissioner, Southern Division, and Deputy Commissioner, Pakôkku.	**2. Myitkyi** ...	**16 0**	22 0	A road used by laden carts passes through cultivation and scraps of jungle and topes of toddy palms. A few villages are met with. The camping ground is wide. Fodder and water plentiful in rains and winter, but grass and water scarce in hot weather; latter from wells. Kyaungs in village.
		3. Dibya ...	**20 0**	42 0	The road leads in a south-west direction to the village of Pauksu at about 6 miles and passes through dry cultivation. Here it enters hilly country and goes over this for 14 miles to camp. The camping space is on the west bank of the river Yaw, which is impassable during the rains, except at intervals. Water and fodder plentiful; grass scarce, kyaungs.
		4. Letsé	**6 0**	48 0	First 2 miles road leads along the Yaw river till it gets to a village, then turning west it passes through low hills and cultivation to Letsé. Road all fit for carts. Water in camp is plentiful from streams and well. Grass is scarce; *kerbi* any quantity. Kyaungs. Letsé is on the road from Minbu to Pauk, *see* Route No. 16, Stage 10. From here there is a cart track eastward to Seikpen (or Seikpyu) 17 miles off, on the right bank of the Irrawaddy opposite Salé. There are many villages on the road and much cultivation. Zigat (*see* Route No. 43), a police post on the Irrawaddy, can also be reached from here *viâ* Kyidôk.
		5. Néaungi ...	**16 0**	64 0	The first 2 miles are through low hills and cultivation. From this road runs along north bank of Kyaik chaung (which divides the Minbu and Pakôkku districts) through villages and patches of jungle. Cart road. Camp anywhere near village. Kyaungs. Water plentiful, but occasionally runs dry during hot weather.
		6. Kawtôn ...	**10 0**	74 0	The road passes through scrub jungle and small hills. There is very little cultivation. Cart road. Kawtôn is on the left bank of a stream which joins the Salin chaung. Kawtôn is a town possessing large kyaungs and many zayáts. Site for camp is limited, but any amount of room in kyaungs. Water-supply good from stream near camp. Paddy and grass plentiful, as also all ordinary supplies. There is a good cart track from here to Zigat (*vide* Stage 4) along the south bank of the Kyaik chaung.

No. 31.

FROM PAKÔKKU TO LAUNGSHÉ *viâ* MYITKYI AND LETSÉ | *continued.*

Authorities. Military.	Authorities. Civil.	Number and Names of Stages, Rivers and Streams.	Distances. Intermediate. M.	F.	Total. M.	F.	Remarks.
G.O.C. Myingyân District.	Commissioner, Southern Division, and Deputy Commissioner, Pakôkku.	**7. Yébôk**	**17**	**0**	91	0	Cart road ceases and there is only a track fit for all laden beasts. You pass through jungle trees and bamboo forests. The road is broken and uneven and country hilly throughout. At 8 miles you cross the Dedaw range, steep and zigzaggy. There is another nasty bit near Yébôk. Camp is on the right bank of the Salin chaung near village in fields. Water plentiful from stream. Grass is scarce. Village has about 10 houses, two zayáts.
		8. Laungshé ...	**9**	**0**	100	0	Road passes through jungle and bamboos. Ordinary forest trees abound. The country is very hilly and the track all ups and downs. Only one village met till you get into valley of Laungshé, then you have open fields and streams. A few villages. For description of Laungshé *see* Route No. 42.

No. 32.

From PAKÔKKU to MYAING viâ KAING.

BY LIEUT. STANTON, ROYAL ARTILLERY, 1887.

Authorities. Military.	Authorities. Civil.	Number and Names of Stages, Rivers and Streams.	Distances. Intermediate. M.	F.	Total. M.	F.	Remarks.
G.O.C. Myingyân District.	Commissioner, Southern Division, and Deputy Commissioner, Pakôkku.	**1. Kaing** ... ... Two sandy nullah beds, 80 yards wide between Inbin and Kaing, both dry in December.	**11**	**0**	11	0	General direction north-west. For 5 miles to Kyaukkán pass one muddy tank at 2½ miles; surrounding country open, covered with scanty scrub jungle and a few *jowári* fields; the latter extend for ½ mile round the village of Kyaukkán. Half-way a road runs south to Myitkain. Kyaukkán has 40 houses and a shallow muddy tank near a small zayát. From Kyaukkán roads lead south to Myitkyin, north-east to Magyigolin, north-west to Kin, and north 6 miles to Kaing. Pass village of Inbin at 2½ miles, surrounding country flat, sandy, and covered with scrub jungle rather thick in places; *jowári* cultivation near villages. No accommodation or good water on road. At Kaing there are two tanks of good water, one kyaung, seven zayáts; forage plentiful. Road throughout is sandy, rather deep in places.
		2. Kyauksauk ... One sandy nullah, 50 yards wide, 3 miles from Kaing. Shwé chaung, sandy bed, 100 yards wide, passes Kyauksauk. The stream is lost in the sand at the village.	**12**	**0**	23	0	General direction north-west. For 9 miles to the hamlet of Yédwet (three houses) and thence west for 2½ miles. Pass villages of Wetkya at 3½ miles, Sékán at 5½, Magyizu at 7, Balôndaw at 8½, Yédwét at 9½; four tanks are passed on the road, the only good water being at Balôndaw. The villages are small, poor, and afford no supplies or accommodation; *jowári* grows round each village; the rest of

FROM PAKÔKKU TO MYAING *viâ* KAING—*continued.*

Authorities. Military.	Authorities. Civil.	Number and Names of Stages, Rivers and Streams.	Distances. Intermediate. M. F.		Distances. Total. M. F.		Remarks.
G.O.C. Myingyán District.	Commissioner, Southern Division, and Deputy Commissioner, Pakôkku.	**2. Kyauksauk**—*cont.*					the country is flat and sandy, covered with open scrub jungle. At Chauksauk there is accommodation for 500 men in kyaungs and zayáts; water good, forage plentiful. Road good and sandy throughout.
		3. Myaing ... One dry sandy nullah bed 50 yards wide. U chaung runs by Myaing; water is lost in sand at the village.	**11**	**0**	34	0	General direction north-west. Surrounding country open scrub jungle, with groves of toddy palms in places and near the nullah. Pass three muddy tanks and villages of Thanetdaw, Tawwé, South Myaing. Road level, good, and sandy. Pass through much *jowári* on approaching Myaing. At Myaing accommodation for 300 men in kyaungs and zayáts; water good, forage plentiful. *Note.*—Another route, the authority for which is not stated, gives the same stages as above, but distances 10, 9 and 9 miles respectively, making the total distance 28 instead of 34 miles.—A.F.

No. 33.

From PAKÔKKU to MYAING viâ LETPAGAN.

BY LIEUT. R. B. SCALLON, 23RD BOMBAY LIGHT INFANTRY, JANUARY 1887.

Military	Civil	Stages	Int. M.	Int. F.	Total M.	Total F.	Remarks
G.O.C. Myingyán District.	Commissioner, Southern Division, and Deputy Commissioner, Pakôkku.	**1. Letpagán** ...	**6**	**0**	6	0	Road good, open ground, and cultivation. Village divided into two portions. Water scarce, from tanks. About 40 houses; no kyaungs; carts and bullocks procurable.
		2. Camp near Kanyát. Kyaungmagaing.	**6**	**0**	12	0	Road, good through scrub jungle, rises to within 1½ miles of Paungán and then falls gradually. Village has been destroyed. No kyaungs, but good camping ground under tamarind trees. Good water, from tanks, scarce in hot weather. Supplies obtainable from Kanyát ¼ mile north-west.
		3. Myodin ... Myodin creek close to kyaungs.	**8**	**4**	20	4	Road good chiefly through scrub jungle. Water at Paungwé 5½ miles; several kyaungs; water obtained by digging holes in nullah; 150 houses.
		4. Myotha ...	**3**	**0**	23	4	Country for first 1½ miles through open scrub jungle, thence open and through toddy groves. Fair accommodation in kyaungs. Water from well and nullah; 15 houses.
		5. Myaing ...	**11**	**0**	34	4	Road good, chiefly through scrub jungle and toddy topes.

No. 34.

From PAUK to ÁLÔN viâ MYAING, LINGADAW and MÔNYWA.

By Lieut. HENEGAN, 27th Madras Infantry, and Lieut. SCALLON, 23rd Bombay Light Infantry, 1887-89.

Authorities.		Number and Names of Stages, Rivers and Streams.	Distances.				Remarks.
Military.	Civil.		Intermediate.		Total.		
			M.	F.	M.	F.	
G.O.C. Myingyán District.	Commissioner, Southern Division, and Deputy Commissioner, Pakôkku.	**1. Pyinchaung** ...	**15**	**0**	15	0	*See* Route No. 30, Stage 4.
		2. Thingapyin ... Broad nullah runs at foot of kyaung. There is water in it only during rains.	**10**	**0**	25	0	Road along bottom of nullah for about ½ mile before reaching village. Bad during rains. Good kyaungs. Could accommodate 150 to 200 men in the kyaungs; good shelter also from trees in compound. Water-supply: One good well in compound, other wells sunk in the nullah by villagers during dry weather; generally water in nullah during rains.
		3. Kyauktaung (West).	**12**	**0**	37	0	Road along nullah for short distance, then for about 1 mile over open country. After that along deep nullah with fairly thick jungle on banks for ½ mile. Then rough bridle-path over bare hills for 2 or 3 miles, after that good road to Kyauktaung (East), fit for carts, 4 miles. Two miles from Kyauktaung (East) good camping ground, but no water. Two miles good road, open country, Kyauktaung (West). Two good kyaungs and zayáts to accommodate 50 men easily; good camping ground. Good well about 600 yards from kyaung.
		4. Myaing ...	**10**	**0**	47	0	Good cart road through cultivated land and scrub jungle to Myaing, 10 miles. There is another good cart road between Stages 1 and 4, by which the journey can be performed in two marches, the midway halt being at Nyaungywa, 15 miles, where there is accommodation and good water at all seasons for 300 to 400 men. Thence to Myaing, 11 miles. The villages of Nanzigán (11 miles), Pebingán (13 miles), Nyaungywa (15), Kainyágôn (19), Thayetkwa (21½), Salingôn (22), and Kyibingán (25) are passed *en route*. The road appears to be good and is the shorter of the two.
		5. Taungu ...	**18**	**0**	65	0	Good road through cultivation; at 5 miles Alégán; accommodation two kyaungs and four zayáts; water from tank and well; supplies obtainable. At 18 miles Taungu 110 houses; water plentiful from tanks (brackish) and wells; several kyaungs and zayáts; supplies obtainable.
		6. Lingadaw ...	**5**	**0**	70	0	Road good through cultivation for first 3 miles, then through jungle; accommodation for 250 men in several kyaungs; water good, from nullah and wells; supplies obtainable. Much toddy and "jaggery" is manufactured here. There is another route *viâ* Kyigán. Road (chiefly through scrub jungle) good. Water at Kandaw from wells (5 miles); water at Kyigán (10 miles) from tanks, good and plentiful; one kyaung and three zayáts. Good ground for bivouac under

FROM PAUK TO ÁLÔN *viâ* MYAING, LINGADAW AND MÔNYWA—*continued.*

Authorities. Military.	Authorities. Civil.	Number and Names of Stages, Rivers and Streams.	Distances. Intermediate. M.	F.	Total. M.	F.	Remarks.
G.O.C. Myingyân District.	Commr., S. Divn., and Dy. Commr., Pakôkku.	6. **Lingadaw**—*cont.*					tamarind trees; number of houses 40. Thence to Lingadaw 5 miles, good road through scrub jungle.
	Commr., Central Divn., and Dy. Commr., Upper Chindwin.	7. **Salingyi** ...	17	0	87	0	Fair cart road through Uyinzwat (2 miles), Kainlé (4½), Gwézôn (7) and Linziyet (9½). Thence to Álôn, *see* Route No. 1, Central Division.
		8. **Mônywa** ...	12	0	99	0	
		9. **Álôn** ..	7	0	106	0	

ALTERNATIVE I.

FROM MYAING (STAGE 4) TO SALINGYI (STAGE 7) *viâ* LÉYINMA AND KYÁDET.

BY LIEUT. STANTON, ROYAL ARTILLERY, 1887.

Military.	Civil.	Number and Names of Stages, Rivers and Streams.	Intermediate. M.	F.	Total. M.	F.	Remarks.
G.O.C. Myingyân District.	Commissioner, Southern Division, and Deputy Commissioner, Pakôkku.	1. **Shwébinzwé** ... River is crossed at Myaing and passed 4 miles off near village of Gwébinlé.	11	0	58	0	General direction north-east; for 5 miles to Kyaungôn road leads through *jowári* cultivation under toddy palms, passing the villages of Engyaung, Sulabôn, Gwébinlé, Thégyun. This part of the district is populous and there are two or three good kyaungs. From Kyaungôn to Shwébinzwé is 6 miles through open uncultivated scrub jungle, till within ½ mile of village, where *jowári* plantations are cultivated. In Shwébinzwé there is accommodation for 150 men in kyaungs and zayáts; water and forage plentiful. Road good and sandy.
		2. **Léyinma** ...	6	0	64	0	General direction north. Good road through open country, cultivated with *jowári*, paddy, sessamum, and tomatoes. Pass village of Gaungwé, with a good kyaung, at 3 miles. Half-a-mile from Leyinma pass village of Kyauksauk in a tamarind grove; from this ½ mile road lies under tamarind trees; surrounding country open scrub jungle; water and forage plentiful; 100 houses in village. Cattle plentiful; kyaungs and zayáts; accommodation for 150 men.
	Commr., Centl. Divn., and Dy. Commr., L. Chindwin.	3. **Kyádet** ...	...		...		No description of this stage available, but evidently from the map a route exists.
		4. **Salingyi** ...	12	0	...		*See* Route No. 1, Central Division.

No. 35.

From PAUK to CHAUNGU (YAWDWIN) viâ YAW RIVER.

BY CAPT. J. WILLCOCKS, D.S.O., 1ST BATTALION, LEINSTER REGIMENT, DECEMBER 1889, CAPT. HARVEY, ROYAL ARTILLERY, AND LIEUT. H. deV. HARVEST, 9TH MADRAS INFANTRY, JANUARY AND FEBRUARY 1893.

<table>
<tr><th colspan="2">Authorities.</th><th rowspan="2">Number and Names of Stages, Rivers and Streams.</th><th colspan="2">Distances.</th><th rowspan="2">Remarks.</th></tr>
<tr><th>Military.</th><th>Civil.</th><th>Inter-mediate.
M. F.</th><th>Total.
M. F.</th></tr>
<tr><td rowspan="2">G.O.C. Myingyân District.</td><td rowspan="2">Commissioner, Southern Division, and Deputy Commissioner, Pakôkku.</td><td>1. Kyaukka ...
Yaw river.</td><td>10 0</td><td>10 0</td><td>Leaving Pauk the road, an unmetalled cart track, passes through broken hills as far as Tabôsu, 3 miles. Thence goes south along foot of low hills as far as Miyégya 4 miles; cultivation along left of road. At Lélán, 5½ miles, are large numbers of cattle and carts; road keeps to foot of hills till you cross the Yaw river at 9 miles by a shallow ford; bottom hard, banks sandy. From this ford to where you recross the Yaw again is a mile over muddy ground. Ford at Kyaukka is 2½ feet; hard bottom. Left bank steep for carts. Kyaukka is a large village. Supplies plentiful. Cattle, fowls, &c., cheap. Water from river. Fodder plentiful. Camping ground near village large. The following places were passed on the road from Pauk :—
<table>
<tr><th></th><th>HOUSES.</th><th>KYAUNGS.</th><th>DISTANCES.</th></tr>
<tr><td>Tabôsu village ...</td><td>32</td><td>1</td><td>3 miles.</td></tr>
<tr><td>Miyégya village ...</td><td>20</td><td>...</td><td>4 "</td></tr>
<tr><td>Lélán village ...</td><td>100</td><td>1</td><td>5½ "</td></tr>
<tr><td>Kalapi village ...</td><td>30</td><td>1</td><td>6½ "</td></tr>
<tr><td>Tizaung village ...</td><td>5</td><td>...</td><td>7¾ "</td></tr>
<tr><td>Akyiba Kyaukka village ...</td><td>50</td><td>Many</td><td>10 "</td></tr>
<tr><td>Kyaukka village ...</td><td>50</td><td>7</td><td>10½ "</td></tr>
</table>
The road is in parts broken and difficult, and a detachment marching in February 1893, with cart transport, took 8½ hours over this march owing to numerous "break-downs" due to the roughness of the track.</td></tr>
<tr><td>2. Tézu ... ...
Yaw river.</td><td>8 0</td><td>18 0</td><td>Carts can be taken through to Yawdwin by this route, but with difficulty, and the Yaw river has to be crossed repeatedly. Wun chaung at 2½ miles is prettily situated on high cliffs above river banks. After crossing the ford here the path runs up a steep hill and for 3 miles goes over high lands broken by ravines and through high trees and bamboos. A steep descent to village of Maluka at 7 miles and cross the river twice. Bad ford; bank rather steep, but solid bottom. A little labour would make a good tract along banks. At Tézu, 8 miles, cross Yaw by a temporary bamboo bridge. River along this route runs through deep gorges and has one bank very steep at all its turns, water about knee-deep in most places in February. Tézu is a small village of 17 houses. Cattle, fowls, pigs, &c., are plentiful and cheap. Fodder good. Water in river. The road all along fit for baggage animals. Jungle fowl all along road and tracks of deer. Fair space for camp 300 yards from village. The following places are passed on the road from Kyaukka :—
Wuchaung village, 17 houses.
Maluka village, four houses.
River Yaw; ford 3 feet, shingle.
River Yaw; ford 2½ feet.
Tézu village, 50 houses, one kyaung.
The detachment above referred to took 5 hours to do the first 6 miles of this march, and about 7 hours more to complete</td></tr>
</table>

FROM PAUK TO CHAUNGU (YAWDWIN) *viâ* YAW RIVER—*continued.*

Authorities. Military.	Authorities. Civil.	Number and Names of Stages, Rivers and Streams.	Distances. Intermediate.	Distances. Total.	Remarks.
G.O.C. Myingyán District.	Commissioner, Southern Division, and Deputy Commissioner, Pakôkku.	**2. Tézu**—*cont.*			it; which they did by night after a long halt of 8 hours to rest the cart bullocks.
			M. F.	M. F.	
		3. Kyawlé ... Yaw river.	4 4	22 4	A halt is necessary at Kyawlé when moving with cooly transport, as coolies have to be changed, but with pack transport you would march on to Hngetchaung. Road over undulations and grass jungle; easy going for all pack transport, but dangerously steep in many places, and throughout difficult for carts. The river has to be crossed twice. Rice, Indian corn, fowls, cattle and pigs plentiful in Kyawlé which consists of about 25 houses. Fodder good. Water from a spring stream 150 yards from village. Good bird shooting, snipe and jungle fowl. Camp room plenty.
		4. Hngetchaung. Yaw river.	5 4	28 0	After leaving Kyawlé road ascends on to a sort of plateau and goes over this in ups and downs for 1½ miles, and again ascending goes over broken ground till within a mile of Hngetchaung. From here is seen the village of Myaungyaung, 25 houses, near a palm grove on right bank of Yaw, as well as junction of Saw and Yaw rivers. Road descends on to a "doob" grass plain and crosses river Yaw by ford. Shallow and good bottom ¼ mile from Hngetchaung at junction of Yaw and Kyauksitchaung. Country so far wooded. Hngetchaung is a strongly-stockaded village. Supplies plentiful. Fodder good. Water from river. Twenty houses, one kyaung, one zayát. Plenty of room for camp. Good shooting.
		5. Pasôk ... ... Yaw river.	6 4	34 4	Path runs along river bed whole way to Kánbo at 5½ miles, village of 20 houses. Easy going for all animals; bed sandy. Hills on both sides close to river banks. Fish plentiful. Pass Kánbo at 5½ miles villages of North and South Letpán, 25 and 15 houses, on opposite bank of river. From Kánbo to Pasôk the road follows the right bank of the Yaw. Pasôk is a large village, 25 houses, on right bank. River runs below a very high bank. Supplies of all sorts. Sawing station for teak. Fodder and corn plentiful. Camping room sufficient for small bodies of troops. The detachment above referred to attempted to march through from Tézu to Pasôk in one day apparently, but it took from 9-30 P.M., on the first day until 4 P.M. on the 3rd day before the last cart was in, owing to the great difficulty in getting the carts along.
		6. Chaungu (Yawdwin).	8 0	42 4	The path goes over a plain of shrubs and trees for 2 miles. Tobacco and grain grown freely. Then over a plateau of ups and downs. Several streams of good water. Above Léywa, 4½ miles, descends into the plain of the Ché. The valley is very fertile. All villages stockaded with watch towers, &c. From Léywa you go up valley, which is flat, to Chaungu, passing many villages within ¼ to ½ a mile on either hand. Chaungu is the head-quarters of

FROM PAUK TO CHAUNGU (YAWDWIN) *viâ* YAW RIVER—*continued*.

Authorities. Military.	Authorities. Civil.	Number and Names of Stages, Rivers and Streams.	Distances. Intermediate.	Distances. Total.	Remarks.
G.O.C. Myingyán District.	Commissioner, Southern Division, and Deputy Commr., Pakôkku.	**6. Chaungu (Yawdwin)**—*cont.*			the Sub-Divisional Officer and of a Myo-ôk or Civil Subordinate Officer. Supplies, fodder, water, camping ground, all plentiful and good. Healthy site in dry season. A ½ mile further on is the small village of Yaw. Yawdwin is really the name of the police post a little further on. It is stockaded and has accommodation for 100 men. The following places are passed on the road :— HOUSES. Kwinhla ... ... 12 Léywa ... ... 20 Myagyi ... ... 20 Pôkhaung ... ... 15 Chaungu ... ... 60 Yaw ... ... Small village.

ALTERNATIVE I.

FROM PAUK TO CHAUNGU (YAWDWIN) *viâ* MAN.

BY CAPT. J. WILLCOCKS, D.S.O., 1ST BATTALION, LEINSTER REGIMENT, AND INFORMATION COLLECTED, 1890.

Military	Civil	Stages	Intermediate M. F.	Total M. F.	Remarks
G.O.C. Myingyán District.	Commissioner, Southern Division, and Deputy Commissioner, Pakôkku.	**1. Kyaukka** ...	**10 0**	10 0	*See* Stage 1 above.
		2. Man	**16 0**	26 0	From Kyaukka path turns half right and, leaving the Yaw on the left, goes over plateau and broken land gradually ascending till it reaches the foot of Pandaung hills. Ascent a bit steep, but road fit for all laden animals. This is a bullock route to the Pasôk valley. Crossing the hills you descend to the village of Man, 20 houses, one zayât. Water is scarce here in the dry season (December, January, &c.) and obtained from wells. Camping space plenty.
		3. Pasôk ... ... Yaw river.	**9 0**	35 0	Leaving Man path gradually descends through forests of bamboo, *in* and large common trees. Road is fit for all laden animals. The Yaw is crossed near Pasôk, which is a large village of 25 houses. Supplies, &c., plentiful. Water close to village from river. Grass, &c., abundant. Contains two kyaungs and three zayâts.
		4. Chaungu (Yawdwin).	**8 0**	43 0	*See* Stage 6 above.

ALTERNATIVE II.

FROM PAUK TO CHAUNGU (YAWDWIN) *viâ* PANDAUNG HILLS.

BY CAPT. J. WILLCOCKS, D.S.O., 1ST BATTALION, LEINSTER REGIMENT, JANUARY 1890.

Military	Civil	Stages	Intermediate M. F.	Total M. F.	Remarks
G.O.C. Myingyán District.	Commr., Southern Divn., and Deputy Commr., Pakôkku.	**1. Pindaung** ... River Pauk (dry, 200 yards wide), Palaung and Pindaung chaungs.	**18 0**	18 0	After leaving Pauk the road leads along the Gángaw cart road for 3½ miles and then turns west up the Palaung creek or ch ung for 5 miles till it comes to the junction of the stream with the Bômagyi chaung. Bed sandy with water in pools at intervals. Impassable during rains, but another path reported over north

FROM PAUK TO CHAUNGU (YAWDWIN) *viâ* YAW RIVER—*continued.*

ALTERNATIVE II—*continued.*

Authorities.		Number and Names of Stages, Rivers and Streams.	Distances.		Remarks.
Military.	Civil.		Intermediate.	Total.	
G.O.C. Myingyán District.	Commissioner, Southern Division, and Deputy Commissioner, Pakôkku.	**1. Pindaung**—*cont.*			hills to junction of the two chaungs. From this point to the Pandaung hills and within 4 miles of Pindaung the road runs up gradually, crossing a few small streams. Teak, bamboo, &c., abound near the hills and *in* in the ascent. Road is good, but stony and steepish in bits. On top of hills a small plateau is crossed, then descend a steep $\frac{1}{2}$ mile into the plain again to Pindaung village, through bamboos and thick forest vegotation; fit for all laden animals, only a few bits are nasty going with loads. Pindaung is a small village of 15 houses, one zayát; $\frac{1}{2}$ mile off are some famous salt springs. Water from stream. Grass scarce, but plenty of paddy, straw, and rice. Good camp space.
		2. Chaungu (Yawdwin).	M. F. **13 4**	M. F. 81 4	The first $\frac{1}{2}$ mile to the salt springs is over the flat through rice fields, then through broken hills to Yadi, 2 miles, which is on the Pindaung chaung and parallel to the chaung as far as village of Léhna, 5 miles; then through fields to Aning at $5\frac{3}{4}$ miles and up on to a plateau till it crosses the river Yaw by a good ford, 2 feet deep, 2 miles beyond this village. From here the road runs up on to a broken plateau, with a good many ascents and descents till you reach Léywa in the Kyé valley and move up that valley to Chaungu. The country is studded with bamboos and forest trees, and the scenery in parts is very pretty. Road good for all laden transport. Jungle fowls and deer abound. The following places are passed on the road:— Salt springs, always at work— Yadi village, 10 houses. Léhna village, 15 houses, one zayát. Aning village, 15 houses, one zayát. River Yaw; ford— Léywa village, 20 houses, two zayáts. Myagyi village, 20 houses, one zayát. Pôkhaung village, 15 houses, one zayát. Chaungu, head-quarters of Sub-Divisional Officer. Yaw, small village.

ALTERNATIVE III.

FROM PAUK TO YAWDWIN *viâ* TIBYIN.

BY LIEUT. M. R. E. RAY, 7TH REGIMENT (D.C.O.), BENGAL INFANTRY, AND NATIVE INFORMATION, NOVEMBER 1891.

Military.	Civil.	Number and Names of Stages, Rivers and Streams.	Intermediate.	Total.	Remarks.
G.O.C. Myingyán District.	Commissioner, Southern Division, and Deputy Commissioner, Pakôkku.	**1. Nadet Sakhán.** Lindaung chaung and some nullahs.	**8 0**	8 0	Leaving Pauk at the west gate the road crosses the Pauk chaung, which is generally dry, but subject to floods, and follows the Gángaw-Kán cart road along the foot of some low hills on the right bank of the Kyaw river. At 3 miles the village of Thayetdaw is passed on the right, and at $3\frac{1}{2}$ the road turns off to the left and, crossing the Linding stream, continues as a foot-path only in a south-west direction. Several dry nullahs have to be crossed, and in places the path follows the beds of nullahs. The country is under cultivation in parts and covered with grass and jungle in others. At 8 miles the rest-camp at Nadet is reached. There is no village here, and the camp,

FROM PAUK TO CHAUNGU (YAWDWIN) *viâ* YAW RIVER—*continued.*

ALTERNATIVE III—*continued.*

Authorities. Military.	Authorities. Civil.	Number and Names of Stages, Rivers and Streams.	Distances. Intermediate.	Distances. Total.	Remarks.
G.O.C. Myingyán District.	Commissioner, Southern Division, and Deputy Commissioner, Pakôkku.	**1. Nadet Sakhán** —*cont.*			which consists of one shed, capable of accommodating about 50 men, and a bungalow with two rooms, stands on the high bank of a nullah. Water can be got from the bed of the streams.
		2. Tibyin ... ... Several nullahs.	M. 12 F. 0	M. 20 F. 0	On starting from Nadet the ascent of the Pandaung hills is at once commenced. The road ascends and descends, crossing several nullahs between the spurs and gradually gaining a greater elevation for about 4 miles; then the ascent gets steeper and at last runs up in a stiff climb of about a mile to the top of the ridge, which is reached at 6 or 6½ miles. From there the descent is begun and is continuous for about 4 miles, when the village (? Pandaung) is reached. Soon after entering the valley a stream is crossed, dry in the dry season and about knee-deep in the rains, and the road runs on for 2 miles through paddy-fields to the village of Tibyin. There is a rest-camp here, on the east of the village, consisting of a shed which will hold about 75 men, two zayáts, and there is a kyaung capable of putting up 50 more men. The village has about 40 houses, and small supplies can be got. During the rains this march is a hard one as there is a good deal of mire in parts, and the ascents and descents get very slippery; also the road gets blocked with fallen bamboos. In the dry season the only difficulty is the stiff climbing.
		3. Chaungu (Yawdwin). Yaw and Kyé rivers and some streams.	16 0	36 0	From Tibyin the ascent of another range of hills is begun at once. The road crosses the hills in a direction about west-south-west and at first runs principally over spurs, which cause both ascents and descents. The road is much the same as that over the hills in the previous march, but perhaps a bit worse. The ascent is accomplished in about 3½ or 4 miles, and the descent on the other side in about 1½. After reaching the valley the road turns south-west and runs along over some jungle-covered spurs, during which portion it is mostly very good and wide and runs into the open valley of the Yaw at 7 miles. At 8 miles the Kyé stream is crossed, about 15 yards wide, waist-deep in the rains, but nearly dry at other seasons, and on the other bank the village of Pampelôn is found. This is a Taungtha village of about 20 houses, and there is a good pôngyi kyaung and a zayát which will hold 100 men easily. This place is frequently used as one of the halting places by troops going to or from Yawdwin, and in the rains it is best to break the march here, making four marches into Yaw altogether. From Pampelôn the path is level and good in the dry season, but miry in the rains, and follows the valley of the Yaw, which river is touched about 1½ miles on, from which point the path runs along its bank, and there is a ford at about 3½ miles from Pampelôn. In the dry season the river is passable almost anywhere and is not more than knee-deep, but in the rains it is never less than waist-deep, very rapid, and frequently impassable for as much as a fortnight. A guide should always be taken in the rains to

FROM PAUK TO CHAUNGU (YAWDWIN) *viâ* YAW RIVER—*continued.*

ALTERNATIVE III—*continued.*

Authorities. Military.	Authorities. Civil.	Number and Names of Stages, Rivers and Streams.	Distances. Intermediate.	Distances. Total.	Remarks.
G.O.C. Myingyán District.	Commissioner, Southern Division, and Deputy Commissioner, Pakôkku.	**3. Chaungu (Yawdwin)**—*cont.*			show the fords, as they change. After crossing the Yaw the road runs over a spur with jungle, and very soon after passes a village with a deserted kyaung. The Kyé, a tributary of the Yaw and resembling it in every way as regards size, &c., is met soon after and the path follows the left bank. It is good dry going in the dry season, but very wet and miry in the rains. The best ford is just about 7 miles from Pampelôn and is exactly similar to the ford of the Yaw. After crossing the Kyé the path runs on through paddy-fields, crosses an irrigation stream, and into the village of Chaungu, which has about 60 houses and a police post about ¾ of a mile from the ford; ¼ of a mile further on the village of Yaw with about 40 houses is reached, and the road running both through and round it enters the military post of Yawdwin just beyond the village. This is a strongly built stockade with accommodation for 100 men and is built on the edge of a spur. Yaw is the head-quarters of a Sub-divisional Officer and a Myo-ôk, and supplies of paddy, grass, &c., are obtainable. It is more generally known to the Natives by the name of Chaungu.

BRANCH I.

FROM HNGETCHAUNG (STAGE 4) TO SAW *viâ* YAW AND SAW RIVERS.

BY CAPT. J. WILLCOCKS, D.S.O., 1ST BATTALION, LEINSTER REGIMENT, FEBRUARY 1889-90.

Military	Civil	Stage	Intermediate M.	Intermediate F.	Total M.	Total F.	Remarks
G.O.C. Myingyán District.	Commissioner, Southern Division, and Deputy Commissioner, Pakôkku.	**1. Saw**	**17**	**0**	17	0	After leaving Hngetchaung cross the Kyauksit stream, which comes direct from the Chinbôk hills. Following the Yaw you come at 1 mile to village of Nyaungaung of 25 houses situated near lovely groves of palms. Still following the Yaw the path comes to its junction with the Saw, after which the latter river is followed to Saw itself. Above this junction at 3 miles is the village of Kyinlaing of 30 houses frequently raided by Chinbôks in former years. From the junction the road can follow either bank of the Saw, but the left bank is probably the best. Path fit for all laden beasts, and bullocks frequent it a good deal. Continuing up stream at 8 miles the village of Kyauktu is reached. The hills come down close to both banks of stream. From Kyauktu keep in river bed or cross over to right bank and at 5 miles further you come to junction of Saw and Kadin chaungs; shallow ford. One mile more through cultivation brings you into Saw. Stream has to be crossed, but it is only a detail in dry weather. Saw is a very large town, containing 130 houses, and any number of kyaungs and zayâts. Supplies of all kinds are plentiful. Camp anywhere in dry weather; near town in wet on high ground. Large shady trees and water abound. Fodder to any extent; shooting all round the country. A capital spot for a small cantonment. Saw is on the main route between Tilin and Laungshé, *see* Route No. 42.

No. 36.

From PAUK to GÁNGAW viâ CHAUNGU, LÉO, KYAUKMASIN, &c.

By Lieut. S. WILLCOCK, Gloucestershire Regiment, December 1887–January 1888.

Authorities.		Number and Names of Stages, Rivers and Streams.	Distances.				Remarks.
Military.	Civil.		Intermediate.		Total.		
			M.	F.	M.	F.	
G.O.C. Myingyan District.	Commissioner, Southern Division, and Deputy Commissioner, Pakôkku.	**1. Chaungu** ...	7	4	7	4	Pauk to Chaungu 7½ miles, *see* Route No. 30, Stage 5.
		Kyaw river.					
		2. Zibya	7	0	14	4	The road is a cart road and good throughout. During the rains it is necessary to make a detour to avoid the stream. The country is open or cultivated the whole way; several villages are passed. Zibya has 30 houses, one large kyaung and five zayáts (200 men). Well in kyaung enclosure.
		3. Léo	9	6	24	2	The road is a fairly good foot-path road throughout, but rather stony in the nullahs. The bed of the stream is sandy. Mezalibin, a village of four houses, is passed at ¼ a mile. Mingyain, deserted, at one mile and-a-quarter. Crossing the stream beyond Mingyain the road runs through a defile for 500 yards, the sides of the defile can be turned by flanking parties. On re-entering the Kyaw stream the left bank continues high for 700 yards, the road then runs along the bed of the Kyetnu stream for ¾ mile. On leaving the Kyetnu stream there is rather a steep and stony ascent for 500 yards. After this the road runs along the crest of a line of hills only occasionally crossing a stony nullah. Léo has one kyaung (100 men) and three zayáts, 20 houses.
		4. Kyaukmasin ...	13	4	37	6	The path is stony and undulating, but except the descent into, and ascent from, Kyaw stream there is nothing to effect the rate of marching for loaded transport animals. At the place noted the steep bits are very short. Kyaukmasin has 20 houses. Water is obtained from the Yéyu stream (in dry weather by digging in the bed). There is one small kyaung in bad repair.
		5. Kyawtha ...	11	0	48	6	For detailed description, *see* Route No. 26, Stages 11 to 16.
		6. Wetbin ...	13	0	61	6	
		7. Kyaw	6	4	68	2	
		8. Saga	6	0	74	2	
		9. Camp on Laungtaung chaung.	12	0	86	2	
		10. Gángaw ...	18	0	104	2	

FROM PAUK TO GÁNGAW *viâ* CHAUNGU, LÉO, KYAUKMASIN, &c.—*continued.*

ALTERNATIVE I.

FROM CHAUNGU (STAGE 1) TO KYAUKMASIN (STAGE 4).

BY LIEUT. S. WILLCOCK, GLOUCESTERSHIRE REGIMENT, DECEMBER 1887–JANUARY 1888.

Authorities. Military.	Authorities. Civil.	Number and Names of Stages, Rivers and Streams.	Distances. Intermediate. M.	F.	Total. M.	F.	Remarks.
G.O.C. Myingyán District.	Comr., S. Div., and Dy. Comr., Pokôkku.	**1. Kyaukmasin** ...	**18**	**2**	18	2	First 6¼ miles cart track as in Stage 2 above, thence to Kyaukmasin rough and stony bridle path keeping to the west of the Kyaw river.

ALTERNATIVE II.

FROM LÉO (STAGE 3) TO KYAW (STAGE 7).

BY LIEUT. S. WILLCOCK, 2ND BATTALION, GLOUCESTERSHIRE REGIMENT, INTELLIGENCE OFFICER, MYAING COLUMN, JANUARY 1888.

Military	Civil	Stage	M.	F.	M.	F.	Remarks
G.O.C. Myingyán District.	Commissioner, Southern Division, and Deputy Commissioner, Pakôkku.	**1. Letpán**	**13**	**4**	13	4	A good bridle-path all the way passing a good deal of old cultivation. At 3½ miles Léma village, which has been burnt some time and of which nothing remains but a few posts. The village of Letpan has been deserted a long time and is much overgrown with jungle, it is better to camp on the hill commanding the ruins of the village.
		2. Kyetyin ...	**6**	**4**	20	0	Road for 1 mile in bed of Kyetyin creek, then makes a short steep ascent, after which it continues along crest of hills, undulating but good throughout.
		3. Ekené	**11**	**4**	31	4	The road is fair throughout. There is a foot-path impracticable for pack animals, and exceedingly difficult for led animals, about 2 miles shorter.
		4. Kyaw	**13**	**0**	44	4	The road ascends rapidly for about 5 miles, at which point the ridge of Pôndaung hills is reached. (Bearings Kyaw 314°, Wetbin 235°.) The road up to this point is very bad, both on account of steep gradients and its rugged stony nature. The descent is more gradual, but as far as Lédama (10 miles) is stony and rough; thence to Kyaw is good.

No. 37.

From SALIN to LAUNGSHÉ.

BY CAPT. CHANNER, 2ND Q. O., BENGAL LIGHT INFANTRY, MAJOR FORBES AND CAPT. NOEL, RIFLE BRIGADE, AND OTHERS, 1886–88.

Authorities.		Number and Names of Stages, Rivers and Streams.	Distances.				Remarks.
Military.	Civil.		Intermediate.		Total.		
			M.	F.	M.	F.	
G.O.C. Myingyán District.	Commissioner, Southern Division, and Deputy Commissioner, Mimbu.	**1. Paukma** ...	**12**	**0**	12	0	Direction west. A good cart track following the Salin river and passing through Peinabin, Shwébu, Banbyin, Öthéywa, and Kyumyin. The first 4 miles through level cultivated ground, and past several villages to the Salin river, which is crossed between Peinabin and Shwébu. In the dry season there is about 2 feet of water in the Salin river, which is then fordable, but in the rains it can only be crossed in boats. There is cultivation around the villages and a little scrub jungle here and there. At Paukma, a village of 50 houses, there is accommodation for 200 men in kyaungs and zayáts. Water-supply good. Carts can be procured at most of the villages on this route, also bullocks and paddy.
		2. Pédauk ...	**10**	**2**	22	2	Direction north-west. Cart track as above through cultivation and passing Kyauksit and Shwédé. Between Kyauksit and Shwédé, the road passes through low hills and bamboo jungle. After leaving Shwédé at mile 5 the cart road becomes heavy as it follows the river bed. It is impassable in the rains, but there is a foot-path along the banks which now become jungly. There are kyaungs at Shwédé for about 200 men. At Pédauk and Kangyauk which faces it on the opposite bank, there is accommodation for 200 men. There is cultivation around the villages and beyond at a distance of from a ½ to 1 mile the country, which is hilly, is covered with tree jungle. Supplies as before. Jungle path from Kwémalôn joins here (*see* Route No. 9, Lower Burma Division, Stage 15).
		3. Minlin	**15**	**0**	37	2	Direction north-west. Cart road as from Shwédé to Pédauk heavy going, as it follows the river bed. Foot-path on the banks. Léma, a village of 30 houses and having kyaungs for 150 men, is passed at 5 miles, and Thair, large village with accommodation for 200 men, 3 miles further on. Country hilly and jungly with cultivation near the villages up to Thair. Captain Noel, reporting on this route in june 1888, makes the distance from Paukma to Thair 16 miles as compared to the 18½ miles of the description. After Thair a good road leads through some rice cultivation to Minlin (or Minyán). Supplies as before. Minlin has shelter for 150 men and good water, and is close to the border of the Yaw district.

FROM SALIN TO LAUNGSHÉ—*continued.*

Authorities. Military.	Authorities. Civil.	Number and Names of Stages, Rivers and Streams.	Distances. Intermediate. M.	F.	Distances. Total. M.	F.	Remarks.
G.O.C. Myingyân District.	Comr., Southern Division, and Deputy Comr., Mimbu.	**4. Tendu**	15	0	62	4	Direction north-west. This road, which is merely a foot-path through jungle and forest, crosses high, projecting hills between the bends of the Salin river. Some water channels running to the river are crossed. Tendu is in the Yaw district, has 30 houses, good water and kyaungs for 50 men.
	Comr., S. Div., and Dy. Comr. Pakôkku.	**5. Laungshé** ...	13	0	65	4	Direction north-west. Road similar to the last march till within 3 miles of Laungshé, when the valley of that place is entered and open cultivated ground is traversed the rest of the way. Laungshé (*see* Route No. 42).

ALTERNATIVE I.

FROM MINLIN (STAGE 3) TO LAUNGSHÉ (STAGE 5).

BY CAPT. CHANNER, 2ND Q. O., BENGAL LIGHT INFANTRY, MAJOR FORBES AND CAPT. NOEL, RIFLE BRIGADE, AND OTHERS, 1886-88.

Military	Civil	Stage	M.	F.	M.	F.	Remarks
G.O.C. Myingyân District.	Commissioner, Southern Division, and Deputy Commissioner, Pakôkku.	**1. Ngakwé** ...	8	0	8	0	Direction north-north-east. A cart road following the bed and banks of the Namwé chaung, is crossed several times. Road somewhat heavy. On both sides of the route the ground is hilly and covered with thick jungle trees and bushes. There are high hills, distant from 1 to 2 miles on each bank. Cultivation scanty and only found close to the villages. The small village of Tawlalin is passed about half-way. Ngakwé has about 70 houses and large kyaungs suitable for 300 men. Water good. A few carts available. Supplies: Paddy in small quantities and bullocks.
		2. Yébôk	18	0	26	0	Direction west-north-west. Road level for 1 mile and thence a foot-path through jungle and forest across the Dudaung range of hills. There are many ascents and descents, and some of the hills are high. Streams running to the Salin river are crossed in the valleys. Yébôk has 40 houses and can shelter about 20 men in zayáts. Water good and plentiful.
		3. Laungshé ...	12	0	38	0	Direction west-north-west. The road up to Mandu, a small village at the 6th mile, is a very hilly foot-path, as in last march, but the jungle is less thick. The bank of the Salin river is then followed by a fairly level and open road for 3 miles to Thégyin, after which the route lies through rice cultivation in the Laungshé valley. Captain Willcocks gives this stage as 9 miles, but he did not traverse the route himself. It is believed that Burmans prefer the longer route, which is therefore probably somewhat easier than the other.

No. 38.

From SALIN to PAUK viâ NGAKWÉ.

By Capt. NOEL, R.B., June 1888.

Authorities. Military.	Authorities. Civil.	Number and Names of Stages, Rivers and Streams.	Distances. Intermediate. M.	F.	Total. M.	F.	Remarks.
G.O.C. Myingyán District.	Comr., S. Div., and Dy. Comr., Pakôkku.	**1. Paukma** ...	12	0	12	0	*Vide* Route No. 37.
		Salen river, Pauk chaung.					
		2. Pédauk ...	10	2	22	2	*Vide* Route No. 37.
	Commissioner, Southern Division, and Deputy Commissioner, Pakôkku.	**3. Minlin** ...	15	0	37	2	*Vide* Route No. 37.
		4. Ngakwé ...	8	0	45	2	*Vide* Route No. 37.
		Namwé chaung.					
		5. Pein	17	0	62	2	Follow up the Mo chaung to Kawtôn, 2½ miles (*see* Route No. 43, Stage 6). Two large kyaungs and several zayáts. Wells. Supplies plentiful. Hence there is a cart road east to Letsé (*see* Route No. 16, Stage 10), about 20 miles. Also a road to Zigat on the Irrawaddy (*see* Route No. 43). From Kawtôn road follows the Mo chaung to Pibingyi, a village on the left bank (no kyaung) 5½ miles from Ngakwé. Thence through jungle and over low hills, which form the watershed between the Salin and Yaw rivers. At 9½ miles pool of water in nullah bed in February, dry in June. At 13 miles cross the ridge, thence down the hill to Pein on the right bank of the Kin chaung. Here there is a small kyaung and zayát. Village fenced. Supplies scanty.
		Kin chaung.					
		6. Kyaukka ...	14	0	74	0	At 3 miles Shéhla with a kyaung and zayát on the right bank (alternative camp with Pein). Bridle-path hence west over hills to Saw, distance 20 miles, passing at 15 miles Kyauktu on Saw river, a fenced village with a large kyaung through a defile, thence to Saw. At 8 miles reach Kinsôk on right bank of Kin haung. Here the wet-weather road leaves the valley and runs over a low spur difficult for carts and crosses Yaw river opposite Kyaukka 14½ or 15 miles. The dry-weather road follows the valley. The Kin chaung flows into the Yaw river, which latter is crossed five times before reaching Kyaukka, 14 miles, where there are several large kyaungs and zayáts. Supplies are plentiful in the cold weather, but scarce in June.
		Yaw river 1 to 2 feet deep in dry weather, 3 feet in June; when in flood unfordable for many days together.					
		7. Pauk	9	0	83	0	Dry-weather road crosses the Yaw river twice, wet-weather road leads over cliffs on left bank and, although steep in places, is practicable for pack transport. At 4½ miles Lélán, a large village with kyaung. At 6 miles leave the Yaw valley. Bridle road goes over low hills direct to Pauk. Cart road leads to the right and joins the Pakôkku road about 2 miles from Pauk. *See* Route No. 30. Captain Harvey, R.A., reporting in January 1893, makes the last stage 10½ miles. *Note.*—This road lies much along sandy nullahs and river beds and would be impassable for loaded carts in the rainy season and very heavy marching at any time.

No. 39.

From SAW to LWINBÔN.

BY CAPT. J. WILLCOCKS, D.S.O., 1ST BATTALION, LEINSTER REGIMENT, AND NATIVE INFORMATION, FEBRUARY 1890.

Authorities. Military.	Authorities. Civil.	Number and Names of Stages, Rivers and Streams.	Distances. Intermediate. M. F.	Distances. Total. M. F.	Remarks.
G.O.C. Myingyân District.	Commissioner, Southern Division, and Deputy Commissioner, Pakôkku.	**1. Lauktu** ... ... Saw stream.	7 0	7 0	Road runs south-west for a mile till it reaches the village of Lwaingyaung. It then turns west and moves up the bed of the Saw stream, crossing it several times. The path so far is fit for laden animals. Trees, grass, and water abundant.
		2. Sawmaungyaung Sakhân.	10 0	17 0	From Lauktu the path turns north and ascends the ridge north of the stream. The road is fairly level and easy going. Trees: firs, oak, &c., at the Sawmaungyaung Sakhân camping ground sufficient. Water ¼ mile from camp but plentiful, though near summit of ridge. Wood, grass, &c., plentiful. From Lauktu you can ascend a ridge south of the valley and go along that, but this is an inferior route altogether.
		3. Lwinbôn ...	10 0	27 0	Leaving camp at Sawmaungyaung Sakhân path continues along the ridge; country same as before and road good till within a few miles of Lwinbôn, when it becomes very steep. Camp, wood, and water sufficient. There is excellent shikar along this route. *Mithun* (Assam *gaur*), black cattle, deer, and a few elephants are found between Sawmaungyaung Sakhân and Lwinbôn. *Note.*—This village is *not on* the Sawchaung, but is given here, as this is a short cut to the Lwinbôn villages from Chaungu (Yawdwin).

No. 40.

From SAW to SINGAUNG.

BY CAPT. J. WILLCOCKS, D.S.O., 1ST BATTALION, LEINSTER REGIMENT, AND NATIVE INFORMATION, FEBRUARY 1890.

Military	Civil	Stages	Intermediate	Total	Remarks
G.O.C. Myingyân District.	Commissioner, Southern Division, and Deputy Commissioner, Pakôkku.	**1. Camp Myauk Kangyu (i.e., North Kangyu).** River Saw shallow, river Kadin up the bed for 5 miles or more.	8 4	8 4	Leaving Saw road leads in a northerly direction. Cross the river by a shallow ford and move along the Chaungu-Saw road as far as the village of Anauk Kadin (or Kateng) *i.e.*, West Kadin at 3½ miles. From here path turns up to the west and goes along bed of the Kadin stream for about 5 miles, when you reach Myauk Kangyu, a Chinbôk-Kadin village of 10 houses. The path so far is easy for laden animals. Camp can be formed anywhere along here, water and fodder being plentiful. Wood and trees abundant; also bamboos.

FROM SAW TO SINGAUNG—*continued.*

Authorities. Military.	Authorities. Civil.	Number and Names of Stages, Rivers and Streams.	Distances. Intermediate. M.	F.	Distances. Total. M.	F.	Remarks.
G.O.C. Myingyán District.	Commissioner, Southern Division, and Deputy Commissioner, Pakôkku.	**2. Môndaw** ... River Mu, branch of Kyausit chaung.	6	0	14	4	From Kangyu path ascends the Kinu village dividing the Kadin and Kyauksit chaungs by a steep but good path. Transport should be coolies. Descending rapidly road leads on Môndaw, which is on the Mu chaung, a branch of the Kyauksit. From the Kinu village (or ridges running east and west) other Kyauksit villages can also be reached. Camp good. Water, wood, &c., plentiful. Ridge has oak, firs, &c. Môndaw has only four or five houses.
G.O.C. Myingyán District.	Commissioner, Southern Division, and Deputy Commissioner, Pakôkku.	**3. Singaung** ... Kyauksit.	12	0	26	4	From Môndaw road may either move along the Kadin stream by a fair track or before descending the ridge may turn to the left and go along it till above Singaung and then drop down to it. Path good and fairly level. At Singaung wood, water, &c., plentiful. *N.B.*—Kyauksit chaung may also be reached *viâ* Kyauksit village near Kabaung on Chinbôk border, from either Saw or Chaungu.

No. 41.

From SINGU to KYAUKPADAUNG.

BY LIEUT. F. G. CARDEW, INTELLIGENCE OFFICER, 4TH BRIGADE, UPPER BURMA, F.F., 1886-87.

Authorities. Military.	Authorities. Civil.	Number and Names of Stages, Rivers and Streams.	Distances. Intermediate. M.	F.	Distances. Total. M.	F.	Remarks.
G.O.C. Myingyán District.	Commissioner, Southern Division, and Deputy Commissioner, Myingyán.	**1. Ômbindwin** ... A large sandy nullah, 300 yards broad, but with no water in it, is crossed 2 miles from Singu. Several small nullahs in the last 4 miles of the march.	12	0	12	0	At Singu there is good camping ground among some kyaungs near river and alongside of post, capable of holding 500 men. Water obtained from wells, good. Direction south-south-east. A cart road which would be good but for the sand, which makes marching very heavy. It passes generally along narrow hedged lanes, with fields on either side. The country is open and undulating, rising gradually from the Irrawaddy. At 6½ miles the village of Kyeni is reached, where there are some good-sized kyaungs and water. Ômbindwin is a village of about 40 houses; zayáts and kyaungs with room for 80 men. Water fair, but muddy from a pond (in August), is probably scarce in the dry weather. Here the road from Salé joins.
G.O.C. Myingyán District.	Commissioner, Southern Division, and Deputy Commissioner, Myingyán.	**2. Gwégyo** ...	8	0	20	0	Direction east-south-east. A good firm road over high undulating ground through thin jungle. The last 3 miles descend into the Gwégyo valley, and the road becomes sandy and

FROM SINGU TO KYAUKPADAUNG—*continued.*

Authorities. Military.	Authorities. Civil.	Number and Names of Stages, Rivers and Streams.	Distances. Intermediate.	Distances. Total.	Remarks.
G.O.C. Myingyán District.	Commissioner, Southern Division, and Deputy Commissioner, Myingyán.	**2. Gwégyo**—*cont.*			heavy. Gwégyo, a large village with a police post, is situated at the head of a broad, well watered, and very fertile valley, which opens to the Irrawaddy between Salé and Pakhán-ngé. Water here is very good. There is a large number of kyaungs and zayáts.
		3. Kyaukpadaung.	M. F. 8 0	M. F. 28 0	Direction east. A winding sandy road between fields of dry crops over an almost level plain. Marching is very heavy and tiring. Kyaukpadaung is a large village with a military post, but the water is bad and in the dry weather the supply fails entirely. *Note.*—Alternative No. I is a more direct route than the above, but, although 3 miles or so longer, the Ômbindwin road is preferable, especially in the rainy season, as shelter can be obtained in kyaungs at every stage, whereas at Shingán there is only a very small village and hardly any shelter available.

ALTERNATIVE I.

FROM SINGU TO KYAUKPADAUNG *viâ* SHINGÁN.

BY LIEUT. G. ANGELO, 23RD W.L.I., 1886.

Authorities. Military.	Authorities. Civil.	Number and Names of Stages, Rivers and Streams.	Distances. Intermediate.	Distances. Total.	Remarks.
G.O.C. Myingyán District.	Commissioner, Southern Division, and Deputy Commissioner, Myingyán.	**1. Shingán (or Singan).**	11 0	11 0	Distance 11 miles; no accommodation for troops; officers and Europeans put up in some small sheds north-east of village which is a small one; natives bivouacked alongside tank about ½ mile from Europeans; water obtained from tank, indifferent. Road from Singu to Shingán good over sandy soil, the first part over hills.
		2. Kyaukpadaung.	14 0	25 0	Distance 14 miles. Road passes through a gorge about a mile from tank, good over red soil and over hills. The last 4 miles of road very heavy over thick sand. Village, a very large one, of about 1,000 houses fortified, but commanded by a small hill on the west side. Two large tanks, one for drinking purposes and one for watering animals, on east side of village. Accommodation for 100 men in zayáts in open ground on east side. Kyaungs for 200 more on east side of village. No village between Shingán and Kyaukpadaung, and no means of obtaining water on the road. On return journey we encamped at Sindagôn, where there was plenty of accommodation and water fairly good; water at Taungu not good and not very easy to get.

NO. 42.

From TILIN to LAUNGSHÉ viâ CHAUNGU (YAWDWIN).

BY CAPT. J. WILLCOCKS, D.S.O., 1ST BATTALION, LEINSTER REGIMENT, AND LIEUT. WILLCOCK, GLOUCESTERSHIRE REGIMENT, DECEMBER 1889. LAST 3 STAGES CORRECTED UP TO APRIL 1893, BY CAPT. J. HARVEY, ROYAL ARTILLERY, INTELLIGENCE DEPARTMENT, BURMA.

Authorities.		Number and Names of Stages, Rivers and Streams.	Time.				Remarks.
Military.	Civil.		Intermediate.		Total.		
			M.	F.	M.	F.	
G.O.C. Myingyán District.	Commissioner, Southern Division and Deputy Commissioner, Pakôkku.	**1. Tenchaung** ...	6	0	6	0	General direction south-east. After leaving Tilin the road skirts the Maw river for ¼ mile and then runs over a low hill; the remainder of the road runs over undulating country, fit for all laden animals. Forests of teak, *in* and other trees; also in places grass lands. Road only fit for dry weather movements near camp. Camp in paddy-fields. Water on west close to camp and plentiful in a nullah for animals. Tenchaung is a village of 20 houses. Ordinary supplies plentiful. Village stockaded.
		2. Kyiywa ... Two small streams.	8	0	14	0	General direction south in next three stages. The road passes through teak and *in* forests and small hills forming watershed of Maw and Yaw rivers; good and fit for laden animals. Kyiywa is in the valley of the Kyi-chaung. Camp ground is in paddy-fields. Water plentiful from stream 100 yards south of village; stockaded. Contains 50 houses, one kyaung, and one zayát.
		3. Nati or Nathu. Kyi chaung.	6	0	20	0	Track leads along bed of river which is crossed several times; gravelly bottom. Road fit for all laden animals. At 1 mile from Nati you get into the fields. Both banks generally are cultivated. Many villages on right bank. Nati has about 20 houses. Camp in paddy-fields. Water plentiful 200 yards from village; stockaded.
		4. Chaungu or Yawdwin. Yaw river, Kyi and Kyé chaungs.	6	0	26	0	Near Nati cross the Kyi chaung. Road goes over grass land and through rice fields. Cross Yaw river near Thayetkyin, 1½ miles, and again beyond Kyauktu, 3 miles. The fords are easy, but there is an alternative road by Togolôn, avoiding the river once. Choice of a road on either bank of Kyé. Valley wide till you reach Chaungu. Head-quarters of a Sub-Divisional Officer, &c., *see* Route No. 35. The village is situated about 300 yards from the right bank of the Kyi * chaung. From the north and west the approaches are over paddy-fields, from south and east through jungle. Yaw, also called Kyikát, is about 300 yards south-west of Chaungu, on a small hill. Thick jungle to the east of it, paddy-fields on the other three sides. The Kyi chaung has, even in the hottest season (April and May), 3 to 4 inches of running water in it. *Note.*—Lieutenant Willcock, Gloucestershire Regiment, reporting on this route in February 1888, mentions no less

* Lieutenant Willcock calls this the Kyé chaung.

FROM TILIN TO LAUNGSHÉ *viâ* CHAUNGU (YAWDWIN)—*continued.*

Authorities. Military.	Authorities. Civil.	Number and Names of Stages, Rivers and Streams.	Distances. Intermediate.	Distances. Total.	Remarks.
G.O.C. Myingyân District.	Commissioner, Southern Division, and Deputy Commissioner, Pakôkku.	**4. Chaungu or Yawdwin**—*cont.*			than 20 other villages on or near the route. He says the valley in which the road runs varies in width from 100 yards to a mile, appears to be very fertile and the whole of the level ground is under paddy cultivation.
		5. Kachaung ...	M. F. 10 0	M. F. 36 0	Leaving Chaungu the path (at present [April 1893] only fit for pack transport, but the construction of a cart road is under consideration) follows the banks of the Kyé stream for about 2 miles, going south-west and turning due south at the village of Kyándaw which is on rising and high ground. From here a broad and good track, fit for all laden animals (throughout to Laungshé), runs for 8 miles through dense forest, teak, bamboos, and other tall straight trees. The road is up and down and crosses many minor under-features, &c. From the 5th mile it runs along the Pinchaung chaung, crossing it many times. Hills come down in parts close to the track. A mile from Kachaung a large suspension aqueduct crosses the Pinchaung stream. Kyauksit village stands a little off the path, on the right hand, on a hillock. At Kachaung you can get fodder and paddy, fowls, &c. Camp is in paddy-fields (or a hill in rains). Water close by in stream. Jungle fowl and deer in valleys. Kachaung contains 20 houses, one kyaung, and a sayát.
		6. Saw ... ... Kyauksit chaung; shallow ford. Kadin chaung, shallow. Saw, river shallow.	10 4	46 4	General direction south-south-east. A cart road is under construction from Saw to Kachaung, but has at present (April 1893) only got as far as Anyákateng. Path only a pack track, crosses the Kyauksit near camp, and again a bit further on, for a mile, it passes through cultivation and paddy-fields, and then for 5 miles through jungle and trees growing gradually smaller than the previous day, till there are only large shrubs. Road descends from its uneven plateau to Anyákateng village, at 8 miles, a stockaded Taungtha village of 25 houses, where catechu is manufactured in large quantities. Plenty of room and water here for a camp if required. Crossing Kateng stream road goes through paddy-fields in a pretty valley to Akyikateng 15 houses, at 9¼ miles, built on rising ground. To Saw from this is 1 mile, mostly through cultivation. Saw is a town of 130 houses. Dâk Bungalow and two large kyaungs. Water, fodder, paddy, camp grounds and supplies all to any quantity.
		7. Laungshé ... Saw river shallow. Yéyin stream.	12 0	58 4	General direction south. Leaving Saw cross the river (always fordable except after heavy rains) by a temporary bamboo and stone pillared-bridge, through paddy and cultivation for a mile to Minlé village. Thence another mile and ¾ brings you to Thigôn village. Road so far level, easy, and fit for carts. For 2 miles more it crosses and recrosses a stream several times, going still south and ascends a hill and keeps over low hills and valleys, with occasional steep bit for 3 miles. Jungle low, straight trees. Jungle fowl and deer abound along the ridges. Going down a descent it crosses small streams

FROM TILIN TO LAUNGSHÉ *viâ* CHAUNGU (YAWDWIN)—*continued.*

Authorities. Military.	Authorities. Civil.	Number and Names of Stages, Rivers and Streams.	Distances. Intermediate.	Distances. Total.	Remarks.
G.O.C. Myingyán District.	Commissioner, Southern Division, and Deputy Commissioner, Pakôkku.	**7. Laungshé**—*cont.*			till it reaches the Yéyin (or Yengé) stream, which comes direct from the Chinbôk hills. Keeping to the stream road passes villages of Môngyin (7½ miles) and Taungbôgyi (10¼ miles) and reaches junction of Salin (on which Laungshé stands) and Yéyin chaungs. Valley rich and cultivated; road broad and good. ¾ of a mile from Laungshé you cross the Salin by a temporary bridge (the river is generally easily fordable) and enter the town. Laungshé is a large town divided into three portions. Head-quarters of a Myo-ôk and a British Police Officer and guard. Dâk Bungalow, Court House and many fine kyaungs and zayáts. Streets paved with brick and many pagodas. Chinaman's shop with stores (Europe). Accommodation for 400 troops or more. Water ¼ mile from camp, which is on a hillock. The town is strongly stockaded; valley is rich and all supplies are plentiful. The Chins come down here to trade, exchanging maize for paddy.

No. 43.

From YAWDWIN (CHAUNGU) to ZIGAT viâ LAUNGSHÉ, &c.

BY CAPT. HARVEY, ROYAL ARTILLERY, INTELLIGENCE DEPARTMENT, BURMA, APRIL 1893.

Military.	Civil.	Number and Names of Stages, Rivers and Streams.	Intermediate M.	Intermediate F.	Total M.	Total F.	Remarks.
G.O.C. Myingyán District.	Commissioner, Southern Division, and Deputy Commissioner, Pakôkku.	**1. Kachaung** ...	**10**	**0**	10	0	*See* Route No. 42, Stages 5 to 7.
		2. Saw	**10**	**4**	20	4	
		3. Laungshé ...	**12**	**0**	32	4	
		4. Lébyu ... Salin chaung and Pin chaung.	**7**	**0**	39	4	Road runs through rice-fields; easy going and good country cart track. Cross Salin chaung at ¼ of a mile, ford always practicable, except in very exceptionally heavy rain. At 1½ miles pass Thagyin village. Up to 2½ miles road runs parallel to Salin chaung, but here leaves it and turns to north. At 4 miles Pôpagain. This village, formerly of 40 houses, was burnt in March last, but is now rebuilding. Road runs through rice-fields and jungle; same quality as before. Lébyu at 7 miles is a Chinbôn village. 30 houses. Very little grass in hot weather, but water plentiful in pools. The Pin chaung is not a perennial stream, though a big one in the rains.
		5. Shwélagwé Sakhán. Sanwin chaung.	**13**	**0**	52	4	At 7 miles Thônlánbyi, a small Chinbôn village of 10 houses, under Kyundaw village 6 miles to south. Water very scarce in hot season and no forage. A bad halting place. At Shwélagwé Sakhán (13 miles) a bamboo hut has been recently constructed. Shelters under banks of chaung. Water plentiful, but does not run on surface in hot weather. Grass and forage plentiful, but coarse. Sanwin chaung has broad rocky bed, but is not perennial. 'Dug-out' for crossing when in flood.

FROM YAWDWIN (CHAUNGU) TO ZIGAT *viâ* LAUNGSHÉ, &c.—*continued.*

Authorities. Military.	Authorities. Civil.	Number and Names of Stages, Rivers and Streams.	Distances. Intermediate. M. F.	Distances. Total. M. F.	Remarks.
G.O.C. Myingyán District.	Commissioner, Southern Division, and Deputy Commissioner, Pakôkku.	**6. Kawtôn** ... Wun chaung.	12 2	64 6	Road crosses Dudawdaung range at 3 miles from Shwélagwé Sakhân. The steep part of the rise in the road over these hills is small, being about 650 feet on each side. It is steep and zigzags on both sides, but the alignment is good and quite fit for carts. From Lébyu thus far the road is nearly finished and is carefully aligned and made easy in gradient. It is unmetalled, and will probably require a year or two before it settles down into a useful cart road. It runs from Lébyu to Shwélagwé through a broken intersected country, but where the rainfall is not heavy, nor would the road or bridging suffer much in the monsoon. The ford at Shwélagwé might be troublesome in heavy rain. From the top of the Dudawdaung, down to Wun Chaung Sakhân, the road is now being made and requires a good deal of cutting and earthwork, but is well aligned and likely to be permanent. There is plenty of water in many pools near Wun Chaung Sakhân, the water percolating down the bed of the stream in the hot weather. Grass is also plentiful. At Wun Chaung Sakhân there are good bamboo huts for 100 men. The track is as yet unfinished and how it will stand or how far it will be practicable in monsoon weather I cannot for certain say, but expect it would be almost always practicable. Last 3½ miles between Wun Chaung Sakhân and Kawtôn are a now used cart tracks, sometimes in bed of chaung and sometimes along its banks, but the stream has now emerged from the low hills and runs through a flat country. Its banks are, however, steep in places. Kawtôn (*see* also Route No. 31, Stage 6) is a large village of 116 houses with some 70 carts and 200 good bullocks and many more in neighbouring villages. It is a good centre to collect carts or pack bullocks at. A road runs from here direct to Sinbyugyun, a port of call for steamers on the Irrawaddy; distance 50 miles.
		7. Yema ... ... Maw and Zíbin chaungs.	14 0	78 6	At ½ mile road crosses from right to left bank of Maw chaung, but this stream is no obstacle, having a broad, sandy bed, and being generally dry; bottom is fairly firm sand. At 2½ miles Nabíbin Sakhân, camping ground and a small water hole in bed of chaung; no more water from here until Yema is reached. Water good; more procurable by digging. At 6 miles cross the watershed between Salin and Yaw rivers. At 13 miles half mile to south of road across the chaung is Zíbin 18 houses. Very little and indifferent water there. At 14 miles Yema, 18 houses water always plentiful from small stream running even in hot weather. Cart track always in use. This march is at present a troublesome one and is generally done by the Burman carters in two stages in the hot season, carrying water with them at night. Better arrangements could easily be made by digging for water in the sandy nullah bed, and thus watering bullocks on the road in all seasons.
		8. Zigat ... ... Zíbin chaung and Irrawaddy.	2 6	91 4	Road is cart track, always in use. At 1½ miles pass Shwégángyi small village, and at 2 miles Tanabin, ¼ mile to south of road. At 2¾ miles Kyaungnadet and Ywathit two im-

FROM YAWDWIN (CHAUNGU) TO ZIGAT *viâ* LAUNGSHÉ, &c.—*continued.*

Authorities. Military.	Authorities. Civil.	Number and Names of Stages, Rivers and Streams.	Distances. Intermediate.	Distances. Total.	Remarks.
G.O.C. Myingyân District.	Commr., Southern Divn., and Dy. Commr. Pakôkku.	**8. Zigat**—*cont.*			portant villages. At 4½ miles Kôngyi, and at 7½ miles Myénu big village. At 12 miles Ausé, 170 houses; headquarters of Myo-ôk, police guard of mounted infantry, and a company of Pakôkku police battalion infantry. At 12¾ miles the river port of Zigat, 107 houses; ferry across Irrawaddy to Salé; boats, carts, &c., easily procurable. Agent of Bombay Burma Company lives here. Both Ausé and Zigat under one Myothugyi.

No. 44.

From YÉNÁNGYAUNG to MEIKTILA.

I. B. COMPILATION, MARCH 1888.

Authorities. Military.	Authorities. Civil.	Number and Names of Stages, Rivers and Streams.	Intermediate. M.	Intermediate. F.	Total. M.	Total. F.	Remarks.
G.O.C. Myingyân District.	Commissioner, Southern Division, and Deputy Commissioner, Magwé.	**1. Ôkshitgôn** ... Pyin and Paungwé chaungs and several small nullahs.	**9**	**0**	9	0	Road runs in an east-north-east direction and is rough and hilly and much cut up by the traffic of oil carts. At 3 miles reach Thwingôn, a large straggling village with large trade in earth-oil. From here the road is rough and steep and descends to Naka-u (or Nakánu) at 6 miles. This is a large village at junction of Paungwé and Pyin chaungs and has a considerable trade in jaggery. Accommodation for 200 men in kyaungs and good water from chaungs. The Pyin chaung is almost dry and sandy with high precipitous bank. It is about 500 yards broad and is deep and flooded in the wet weather. From Naka-u the road crosses the Paungwé chaung; about 300 yards broad; dry sandy bed; no water except in rains; then leads up a steep ascent and over a high ridge for 2½ miles; then along a good gravel cart track to Ôkshitgôn, a large village on south side of ridge which slopes down to Paungwé water-course. Accommodation for 150 men in kyaungs and zayáts. Good camping ground all round. Two large ponds, but best drinking water from holes dug in the chaung. All ordinary supplies and 30 carts. The country between the Pin valley and Yénángyaung is almost exactly the same in character as that between Magwé and Natmauk; the soil is for the most part sandy, but here and there, especially on the top of the high ground, are patches of flinty gravel. Where the sub-soil is seen, it is generally sandstone. In some places, however, for instance near Tergyi (*sic ?* Thagyi), there are a few yards of black igneous rock. The cultivation, especially east of the Irrawaddy, is confined to a radius of a mile or so round each village. The country is overgrown with bushes of the ber tree, and often in cultivating their fields the villagers do not even take the trouble to remove those in order to leave the ground clear for the crops. The only place of any importance is Naka-u, which is dependent on its jaggery trade.

FROM YÉNÁNGYAUNG TO MEIKTILA—*continued.*

Authorities. Military.	Authorities. Civil.	Number and Names of Stages, Rivers and Streams.	Distances. Intermediate. M. F.	Distances. Total. M. F.	Remarks.
G.O.C. Myingyán District.	Commissioner, Southern Division, and Deputy Commissioner, Magwé.	**2. Magyigán** ... Magyigán chaungu three times and several small nullahs.	9 0	18 0	From here the road runs east along high ground to village in Pindé where it crosses the Magyigán chaung, about 300 yards broad with sandy bottom and little water. From here the road runs over undulating ground cut up by nullahs past Sindékyaung and again crosses the chaung at 6 miles and runs over another ridge past Alégôn and down a steep cutting and over the chaung a third time to Magyigán village. The chaung is here about 100 yards broad, sandy and dry. The right bank is about 80 feet high and descent by cutting mentioned above. The road on the whole is very winding and rough for carts, but fairly good for marching, being firm and gravelly except in the hollows. There is another path which follows the bed of the chaung all the way, but it is very heavy going. Magyigán is a fair-sized village. Accommodation for 50 men in kyaungs. Encamping ground all round. Water good but not very plentiful in dry weather. Ordinary supplies and about 30 carts procurable.
		3. Thébin Sakhán.	7 0	25 0	Road fair, runs east-north-east through undulating country gradually rising from Irrawaddy. The latter part of the road is sandy. At 2½ miles pass Wethawgán and at 6¼ miles Légyimyo, both small villages. Thébin Sakhán is the first village in the Pin township. About 30 houses. Accommodation in kyaungs and zayáts for about 50 men. Water indifferent and scarce as early as March. The whole of this country is very dry and sandy and the villages depend for their water on stagnant ponds here and there. Few supplies.
		4. Tergyi ... ... (*Sic ?* Thagyi) Wábo chaung.	8 4	33 4	Road runs north-east ; very sandy. Country low and undulating, covered with scrub jungle and very dry. Cultivation only round the villages (dry crop). Road very heavy and winding. At 4¾ miles cross the Wábo chaung, about 40 yards wide, dry sandy bottom, steep and high banks. At 5 miles pass Ôkshitgôn, a small village of some 30 houses. The thugyi of the district lives here. Tergyi is small and a poor village. Accommodation in kyaung and zayáts for about 40 men. Encamping ground all round. Water, from a surface well close to kyaung, poor and very scarce in dry weather. No supplies.
		5. Taungu ...	10 4	44 0	Direction of road east-north-east. Fair cart road, very sandy and heavy in places and very winding. Country same as before. Pass Nyaungyabin at 5¼ miles and Maitpin at 6¼ miles, both large stockaded villages, but very badly off for water Taungu is a poor village of about 30 houses. Water very poor from a surface well below a stagnant pond. Accommodation for about 40 men in a kyaung and zayáts. Encamping ground all round. Supplies scarce.

FROM YÉNANGYAUNG TO MEIKTILA—*continued*.

Authorities. Military.	Authorities. Civil.	Number and Names of Stages, Rivers and Streams.	Distances. Intermediate. M.	Distances. Intermediate. F.	Distances. Total. M.	Distances. Total. F.	Remarks.
G.O.C. Myingyân District.	Commissioner, Southern Division, and Deputy Commissioner, Magwé.	**6. Shwébandaw** ...	8	0	52	0	Road runs north-east. A fair cart track but rather rough and stony in places; rises rapidly to a high ridge, which runs south-west from Pingadaw hill. From this ridge it slopes gradually down to the valley beyond. At 3½ miles crosses a small nullah flowing south-east towards the Yen chaung, dry bed. The road then passes Kángyigôn, and the last 2 miles runs along the road from Kyaukpadaung. For Shwébandaw, *see* Route No. 20, Stage 9.
G.O.C. Rangoon District.	Commissioner, Eastern Division, and Deputy Commissioner, Meiktila.	**7. Sulégôn** ...	12	4	64	2	*See* Route No. 20, Stages 6 to 9.
		8. Kyetpyet ...	8	0	72	4	
		9. Shanmangé ...	9	0	81	4	
		10. Môndain ... Three nullahs.	12	0	93	4	Road is a very fair cart track and runs east through thin jungle. Country undulating, covered with thin jungle and cultivation in patches. Cross the chaung and pass Thabiyéwa at 5½ miles. It is a fair-sized village on high bank of chaung and contains several kyaungs. Water good. From here the road runs over paddy for some distance and is bad in wet weather. At 10 miles pass a small tank. Road now runs south-east and descends a slightly stony slope to the Môndain chaung, which it crosses. Môndain is a large village. Accommodation in kyaungs and zayáts to east of village for 500 men. Good camping ground to west of kyaungs. Water good and plentiful from wells and nullah. All ordinary supplies and probably about 30 carts obtainable from thugyi. There is a large bazaar every fifth day.
		11. Meiktila ... Two nullahs.	10	0	103	4	Good sandy road, runs east past some small villages where good water can be got from wells. Country undulating and covered with scrub jungle, with a good deal of cultivation. Paddy and jowári in places. For Meiktila, *see* Route No. 17.

ROUTES IN UPPER BURMA

ROUTES

IN

UPPER BURMA

INCLUDING

THE CHIN HILLS AND SHAN STATES,

TO WHICH ARB ADDED

A NUMBER OF ROUTES LEADING FROM LOWER BURMA AND SIAM INTO THOSE DISTRICTS.

COMPILED FOR

THE QUARTERMASTER·GENERAL OF THE MADRAS ARMY

BY

MAJOR A. B. FENTON,

COMMA NDANT, 2 ND MADRAS LANCERS (LATE DEPUTY ASSISTA.NT QUARTERMASTER-GENERAL FOB INTELLIGENCE) BURMA).

(IN TWO VOLUMES)

VOLUME II

GYAN

ISBN : 978-81-212-1474-2(Set)

ISBN : 978-81-212-1476-6

Published, 2018

Published by

Gyan Publishing House
5, Ansari Road
Daryaganj, New Delhi-110002
Phone: 011-47034999, 9811692060
www.gyanbooks.com
E-mail: books@gyanbooks.com

Printed at: G. Print Process, Delhi.

PREFACE.

Eight years having elapsed since the occupation of Upper Burma, it has been considered desirable to collate the large mass of route material that has been collecting in the Burma Intelligence Office during that period into book form, both to prevent the loss of material already collected and to ensure its proper correction up to date, from time to time, as opportunity offers.

In the compilation of this work every available source of information has been taken advantage of up to the date each section has gone to press, and further information received subsequently has been added up to the latest possible date in the appendices.

Owing to the fact that for a long time there was no very special form adhered to in the transliteration of Burmese, and especially of Shan, names, so much so that even now the same name, though apparently a simple one, is found spelt in several different ways in the same route, even by the most practised officers of the Intelligence Department, it is evident that there must be many instances of incorrect spelling and accentuation in this work, but every endeavour has been made to adopt a uniform and, as nearly as possible, the Hunterian method of spelling. This issue of the work must, however, necessarily be considered merely a preliminary one, and it is hoped that its publication even in this imperfect form is the surest way to the production of a reliable and useful book of reference.

Communications are therefore invited from all officers and others in a position to point out mistakes or to supply additional information.

Quartermaster-General's Office,
Ootacamund, 1st *June* 1894.

CONTENTS.

VOLUME-I

PART I.

ROUTES IN THE NORTHERN (CIVIL) DIVISION.

PART II.

ROUTES IN THE CENTRAL (CIVIL) DIVISION.

PART III.

ROUTES IN THE CHIN HILLS DIVISION.

PART IV.

ROUTES IN THE EASTERN (CIVIL) DIVISION.

PART V.

ROUTES IN THE SOUTHERN (CIVIL) DIVISION.

VOLUME–II

PART VI.

ROUTES IN THE SHAN HILLS DIVISION.

PART VII.

ROUTES IN THE LOWER BURMA DIVISION.

APPENDIX I.

ADDITIONAL ROUTES IN NORTHERN DIVISION.

APPENDIX II.

ADDITIONAL ROUTES IN THE SHAN HILLS DIVISION.

APPENDIX III.

ROUTES IN SIAM.

APPENDIX IV.

ADDITIONAL ROUTES IN SOUTHERN (CIVIL) DIVISION.

APPENDIX V.

ADDITIONAL ROUTES IN CENTRAL (CIVIL) DIVISION.

FROM FORT STEDMAN (MAING-AUK) TO MÔBYÉ—*continued.*

WATER ROUTE—*continued.*

The average breadth of the river I should put at about 60 yards, but it varies and is broader in places. The banks on either side are of clayey soil, for the most part above the water level, but there is low-lying swampy ground after leaving Nampôn, at the southern end of the lake.

Temporary encamping ground for the night can be found on either bank; but well water is not met with except near or in the villages.

Halts were made at the following places on the way down:—

First day—Nampôn. Second day—Saga. Third day—Nantôk. *Up journey*— First day—Minu. Second day—Saga. Third day—Tauntu.	Ordinary river side villages with the usual weekly market day. Saga is a village of some size with a stockaded enclosure.

the men disembarking and pitching camp. A short halt was also made at Sagwé. The town of Payakôn, which apparently would be the place selected for troops to remain at, is on the right bank of the river and distant from Môbyé about 15 to 17½ miles.

I would recommend awnings of bamboo matting being provided for the boats as protection from the sun and glare, which is very trying.

No. 2.

From FORT STEDMAN (MAINGSAUK) to MÔNÉ *viâ* MÖNGSIT and BAMPÔN (MÔNÉ POST).

BY LIEUT. A. WALLACE, 27TH PUNJAUB-INFANTRY, MAY 1887.

Authorities. Military.	Authorities. Civil.	Number and Names of Stages, Rivers and Streams.	Distances. Intermediate. M. F.	Distances. Total. M. F.	Remarks.
G.O.C. Rangoon District.	Superintendent, Southern Shan States.	**1. Nampi (Naungpé).**	**11 0**	11 0	The best route from Fort Stedman to Môné is *viâ* Bawyétát, Hôpôn, &c., *see* Route No. 7, Eastern Division. Leave the Nyaungywé road at 1 mile, ascend a gradual slope 2 miles, road then steep for 1 mile, a village here, then over the crest of the range; a very rocky bad road, but passable in all weathers for 1 mile; descend 4 miles on east side of hill and for 2 miles along undulating level road; open country to Nampi, a good-sized Taungthu village, with supplies and accommodation for 50 men.
		2. Pôko (Hôko) ... Tabet chaung; boats.	**8 0**	19 0	A gently undulating road in an open country; pass small villages of Nati and Wankin about half-way. At about 6 miles there are old spikes on the ground right and left of the path; accommodation for 100 men in zayáts just before arriving at the river. The Tabet is about 60 feet broad and 10 feet in May. There are the remains of a bridge, which will probably be repaired. No village to speak of at Pôko (Hôko on survey map); a kyaung gives accommodation for 50 men.

FROM FORT STEDMAN (MAINGSAUK) TO MÔNÉ *viâ* MÖNGSIT AND BAMPÔN (MÔNÉ POST)—*continued.*

Authorities. Military.	Authorities. Civil.	Number and Names of Stages, Rivers and Streams.	Distances. Intermediate. M.	Distances. Intermediate. F.	Distances. Total. M.	Distances. Total. F.	Remarks.
G.O.C. Rangoon District.	Superintendent, Southern Shan States.	**3. Náthán (Násán).**	**10**	**0**	29	0	Good road over level open country for 2 miles, then along causeway over paddy-fields for 2 miles to the large village of Banyin, the seat of a Myoza. Supplies, carriage, and accommodation available. One mile beyond Banyin the road begins to ascend to Náthán, in no part very bad. Náthán (or Násán) would furnish supplies and has accommodation in zayáts for 50 men.
		4. Banpen (Ban Pyin).	**11**	**0**	40	0	For the first 1½ miles the path is level over paddy-fields. It then rises for 3 miles in thin jungle, road generally steep, in parts very steep; water at 3½ miles; drop down for 2 miles of steep path on the other side, then through some paddy-fields on the banks of the Pôn stream, path then passes over a rather high spur of a hill for 2 miles, the descent being very rocky and bad, and then runs along 2 miles of the bank of the Pôn stream, in many places narrow, rocky and steep. This a trying march.
		5. Möngsit (Maingseik). Nam Pwán or Pôn chaung, fordable.	**14**	**0**	54	0	Cross the Pôn immediately on leaving Banpen, ford in May about 3 feet, then 3 miles along level road through paddy-fields to small village of Nampôk; road then ascends, in no place very steep, for 4 miles, drop down on the other side by a bad and very steep road for 1½ miles. At the foot there is water and Shan bullock-drivers' camp here. It is called Namlin, but there is no village. On for 3 miles of very rocky and narrow up-and-down road, emerge into the Namlát valley, cross it by 2 miles of paddy-fields to Maingseik (or Möngsit), a large village, the seat of a Myoza, with carriage and supplies available. A shorter road leaves Maingseik on the north and passes to Kampôk *viâ* Bamôn.
		6. Kampôk ... A branch of the Namlát, fordable.	**15**	**0**	69	0	Ford over the stream 1 foot 6 inches. Road passes through a fair-sized village at 2 miles, open level country for 5 miles to two villages, turn to the east and ascend for 2 miles of steep road and on for 6 miles over undulating hills covered with jungle; camping ground; no supplies or accommodation.
		7. Môné (Möngnai).	**12**	**0**	81	0	Undulating hills with jungle as before. A small village and water at 6 miles, no other on the road; jungle becomes thicker towards Môné, but road on the whole good. Camp on the south-west of town, supplies and carriage ample. Many zayáts and kyaungs; the seat of a Sawbwa.

FROM FORT STEDMAN (MAINGSAUK) TO MÔNÉ *viâ* MÖNGSIT AND BAMPÔN (MÔNÉ POST)—*continued*.

Authorities.		Number and Names of Stages, Rivers and Streams.	Distances.				Remarks.
Military.	Civil.		Intermediate.		Total.		
G.O.C. Rangoon District.	Superintendent, Southern Shan States.	**7. Mône (Möngnai)**—*cont.*					*Note.*—This route must, in Stage 7, pass through Bampôn which has been selected as the Môné Military post since this route was written. There is another and shorter route between Möngsit (Stage 5) and Môné Military post (Bampôn), *see* Alternative No. I below.—A. F.

ALTERNATIVE I.

FROM MÖNGSIT (MAINGSEIK), (STAGE 5) TO BAMPÔN (MÔNÉ POST), (*see* STAGE 7).

BY CAPT. H. R. DAVIES, DECEMBER 1892.

Military	Civil	Stages	M.	F.	M.	F.	Remarks
G.O.C. Rangoon District.	Superintendent, Southern Shan States.	**1. Camp on the Nam Sit.** Nam Sit.	**9**	**6**	9	6	This is an alternative route to the regular road. It is about 2 miles shorter, and is the best for walking, but as some of the streams are not bridged, the main road would probably be the best for transport. Very little labour would make it into a good road, as it is nearly level the whole way. General direction south-east. Follow the course of the Nam Sit the whole way (crossing it three times; 4 to 7 yards by 1 to 1½ feet) along a nearly level road with hills on each side of it. Good camping ground near the source of the Nam Sit.
		2. Bampôn (Mônè Post). Nam Yum (Nam Yôn).	**10**	**4**	20	2	Cross the Nam Sit-Nam Yum watershed, 400 feet above Möngsit, thence follow the course of the Nam Yum (Nam Yôn) (crossing it twice; 3 yards by 6 inches) down to Kungpôk, where the main road joins in from the right. Thence over undulating ground to Bampôn; large camping ground; water below, a little way off.

No. 3.

From FORT STEDMAN (MAINGSAUK) to THÍBAW (MÖNG SIPAW) viâ YÁTSAUK (LOKSOK).

BY CAPT. V. C. TONNOCHY, JANUARY 1890.

Military	Civil	Stages	M.	F.	M.	F.	Remarks
G.O.C. Rangoon District.	Superintendent, Southern Shan States.	**1. Bawyétat** ...	**12**	**0**	12	0	Good cart road. (In middle of rains route to Yátsauk by Hého and Pwéhla would be used, *see* Routes Nos. 52 and 54 and No. 6, Eastern Division.)
		2. Camp beyond Pôngwa. One large stream unbridged at 1 mile beyond Pôngwa.	**15**	**0**	27	0	Route north-east along paddy-fields to foot of hills and along them to Kunthun village (7 miles). Then past Weksauk village another 7 miles north over much same ground to Pôngwa

FROM FORT STEDMAN (MAINGSAUK) TO THÍBAW (MÖNG SIPAW) *viâ* YÁTSAUK (LOKSOK)—*continued.*

Authorities. Military.	Authorities. Civil.	Number and Names of Stages, Rivers and Streams.	Distances. Intermediate.		Distances. Total.		Remarks.
G.O.C. Rangoon District.	Superintendent, Southern Shan States.	**2. Camp beyond Pôngwa**—*cont.*	village which is on a rising ground. This piece of road would be almost impassable in the rains from lowness of the ground; at present an easy track. One mile beyond Pôngwa on the north side of a large stream (excellent water; 30 yards broad), there is a good place to camp.				
			M.	F.	M.	F.	
		3. Kônlôn ...	**7**	**0**	34	0	From this to Kônlôn 7 miles a fair village, the road leading over fairly high ground, easy, undulating. No kyaungs or zayáts.
		4. Pángun ... Stream 1 mile beyond Pháphylet, 20 yards broad, bridged; very little water at this season.	**20**	**0**	54	0	Thence road goes 13 miles over much the same country to Pháphylet, a small village; one or two villages of a house or two are passed on the road; of these Tikán was once a fair village and is growing again, 7 miles further to Pángun. Road whole way easy. Water at Pángun not very good, being in the middle of marsh land. Camping ground has to be cleared near village and pagodas. No kyaungs or zayáts.
		5. Yátsauk (Loksok). One or two small streams at Yátsauk, Zawgyi, bridged.	**7**	**0**	61	0	Easy road. The streams crossed would have to be ramped if large numbers were travelling. Yátsauk has large stream or river rather, the Zawgyi, on east and south. A good camping place on its west bank before entering the town among large trees. There is water also in south-west of town more or less marshy in character. Zayáts, bazaars, kyaungs.
		6. Myinni ... Stream at Myinni.	**7**	**0**	68	0	An easy road. Cart road for most part over rolling uplands to Myinni, small village with kyaung and two zayáts in middle of small hills. Good water-supply close by.
		7. Camp on stream. Frequent streams mostly bridged; Zawgyi river also bridged with good bridge.	**12**	**0**	80	0	This march is the worst. The path is narrow, hilly; frequent streams are crossed, in some of which the bridges are broken; the road is in places too narrow for paths and requires widening. The road is through forest and much obstructed with fallen trees and bamboo. At 12 miles is a stream with a piece of level ground, where a small camp could be made.
		8. Thôndán ... Zawgyi river.	**11**	**0**	91	0	About 2½ miles from camp the road reaches the bank of the Zawgyi and continues more or less along it. Here a hot stream flows into the Zawgyi from south. After this the country opens a little, some fields are passed, and the small villages of Kyauki and Ungkoi. At the 6th mile Indaw, a fair-sized village, where a halt might

FROM FORT STEDMAN (MAINGSAUK) TO THÍBAW (MÖNG SIPAW) *viâ* YÁTSAUK (LOKSOK)—*continued.*

Authorities.		Number and Names of Stages, Rivers and Streams.	Distances.		Remarks.
Military.	Civil.		Inter-mediate.	Total.	
G.O.C. Rangoon District.	Superintendent, Southern Shan States.	**8. Thôndán**—*cont.*			be made. Here before entering Indaw the Zawgyi is crossed. Thence along level grounds and paddy-fields to Thôndán (11 miles); a sayát. Water close to village.
			M. F.	M. F.	
		9. Kyauku ... Two or three streams.	**18 0**	109 0	Road up and down gentle slopes, easy and good, through open teak forest. A stream at 3 miles unbridged, but not difficult. At about 14th or 15th mile is the small village of Ywathit, Kyauku, a fair-sized village; no good zayát. A mile beyond it is an open plain used for camping by bullock caravans near good stream. Large camp could be had here. This road would present difficulties in middle of rains; easy now.
		10. Wánchaung ... Largish stream (Nankam) at 7th mile or so; bridged.	**16 0**	125 0	Road same as march before, slightly more hilly, and thicker forest. About half-way an extended view is had across valley to hills about Mainkaing, all intervening country thickly wooded. This road would also be bad here and there in middle of rains. Camp in paddy-fields near stream just this side (½ mile) of Wánchaung, which is a fair village. No zayáts or kyaungs.
		11. Loimut ... No water between Nánchaung and Loimut.	**12 0**	137 0	A steep banked stream just the other side of Nánchaung bridged with two planks; is dangerous crossing for animals. This stream would have to be ramped if any considerable force were travelling. Thence hilly, but not difficult road through forest about 12 miles to Loimut, a deserted village, where the first water is reached.
		12. Pánghai ...	**10 0**	147 0	From Loimut, the shortest road is direct to Pánghai, a small village at 10 miles, passing small village of Séhen at 3 miles and 7 miles further Pánghai; road easy. Pánghai, small village, no zayáts; supplies not obtainable. Camp can be cleared near village. Water ½ mile off. Another road is north-west to Nawlong, a large village at 5 miles where supplies could be had. This road is same as before, but crosses the stream Nam Myelaing at the 6th mile and the Bamu at the 10th. Camping ground near pagodas with water about ½ mile off. From this to Pánghai is 6 miles.
G.O.C. Mandalay District.	Superintendent, Northern Shan States.	**13. Camp on Namtu or Myitngé river.** Myelaing stream (bridge broken) at 2 miles or so and Myitngé river at 10 miles. Small streams near Kunhen (boats can go up Myitngé 20 or 30 miles it is said, but not down).	**10 0**	157 0	Road chiefly down-hill and jungly, but not otherwise difficult. At 2 or 3 miles the Myelaing is crossed, unbridged. In rains it would probably be impassable. At 4 or 5 miles the road comes in sight of the Namlán, a stream about the same size as Zawgyi at Indaw, but with a number of rapids which falls into Myitngé (or Namtu) just above ferry. At 10 miles the Myitngé is reached. It is here deep, not rapid, about 150 to 200 yards broad, north bank is precipitous; two dug-outs to cross by. Ponies, &c., have to be swum across. A mile above the ferry are the falls of the Namlán, which

No. 3.

From FORT STEDMAN (MAINGSAUK) to THÍBAW (MONG SIPAW) viâ YÁTSAUK (LOKSOK)—*continued*.

Authorities. Military.	Authorities. Civil.	Number and Names of Stages, Rivers and Streams.	Distances. Intermediate.		Distances. Total.		Remarks.
G.O.C. Mandalay District.	Superintendent, Northern Shan States.	**13. Camp on Nam-tu or Myitngé river**—*cont.*					are about 20 feet high, falling in a continuous sheet of water about 150 yards broad. Hills appear to diminish eastward, but are considerable just here. Thick forest on both sides.
			M.	F.	M.	F.	
		14. Kunhen ... A large hot stream, bridged, at 3 miles from Kunhen (Nampuk).	11	0	168	0	Crossing the river the road ascends for 2 miles to the village of Táhom. A camp could be had here or on north bank of Myitngé at this season. Táhom, small village with stream. At 4 or 5 miles further small village Namsongkbo. At 11 miles from the Myitngé Kunhen. The country from Thôndán to this is almost all forest, there being very few villages and small population. Kunhen is a fair-sized village with a largish stream on the further side. Kyaung and two zayâts.
		15. Kunyu ... Small streams, all bridged.	22	0	190	0	Road is easy and leads through well cultivated and populous country up to Naungkwáng, passing villages of Pángwo (large), Mankhai, Nangong, and Konglâng. Naungkwáng, good village where halt might be made at about half-way. Thence Möngnwai and Namthán (two houses). Here good stream and camp might be had. Thence over a jungly road, but easy to Namôn (small village) at 20 miles. Kunyu is a small village and near it is another small village, Nawund, with a hot stream near it. Camp can be had in paddy-fields near Kunyu, with good stream (bridged) near. No zayát, &c.
		16. Namsim ... Namsim stream.	10	0	200	0	A jungle road, but easy, to Kyinthi or Namsim. Here the Mandalay road is joined (*see* Route No. 53, Northern Division). At all the above-mentioned villages, except the very small ones, paddy and rice for a small party can be obtained; fowls at Indaw.
		17. Thíbaw ... Namtu.	8	0	208	0	*See* Route No. 53, Northern Division, Stage 13.

No. 4.

From FORT STEDMAN (MAINGSAUK) to YWATHIT viâ SAWLÔN.

I. B. Compilation, 1889.

G.O.C. Rangoon District.	Supt., Southern Shan States.	**1. Manku (2,800 feet).**	10	0	10	0	*See* Route No. 1, Stage 1.

FROM FORT STEDMAN (MAINGSAUK) TO YWATHIT *viâ* SAWLÔN—*continued.*

Authorities. Military.	Authorities. Civil.	Number and Names of Stages, Rivers and Streams.	Distances. Intermediate. M.	F.	Total. M.	F.	Remarks.
G.O.C. Rangoon District.	Superintendent, Southern Shan States.	**2. Kyundaung (Kyauk Taing), 2,750 feet.**	**10**	**0**	20	0	*See* Route No. 1, Stages 2 to 5.
		3. Mawpi (2,750 feet).	**7**	**0**	27	0	
		4. Saga (Samka), 2,700 feet.	**11**	**0**	38	0	
		5. Nammawkala (2,650 feet).	**13**	**0**	51	0	
		Several small streams.					
		6. Léya (2,750 feet).	**10**	**0**	61	0	Road excellent; *in* jungle. At 3, 4½ and 5 miles road passes through three Karen villages and at the last distance the Mimpôn gorge opens out on to the plains from the hills on the east, about 1 mile distant, and the road passes for 1 mile through paddy. The road is undulating and easy for all arms. Mounted infantry can act as flankers the whole way. The jungle gets more dense (chiefly high grass) before reaching Léya, which is a small village of 20 houses; and immediately to the south of it runs the Léya chaung, which is the boundary of Sawlapaw's territory. Camp was cleared on the south side (left bank) of the river. Water about 3 inches deep on 31st December.
		7. Ngakyaing (2,700 feet).	**7**	**4**	68	4	Grass plentiful, road excellent, through fair open jungle, but with high grass, about 6 feet long. Camping ground on open paddy plain, about ¾ mile west of village and immediately north of three small knolls. Water good from a small stream. The hills on east side of road end about a mile beyond the village.
		8. Lwékaw (Loikaw), 2,630 feet.	**9**	**0**	77	4	Road runs over open paddy plains past several rich villages; would be very difficult in the rains. The whole country to Môbyé on the west to Lwékaw to the south of the hills on the east is one large open plain intersected by deep irrigation channels. Lwékaw (60 houses) is on the Balu (Môbyé) river, which is about 130 yards broad and unfordable. About six large "dug-outs" available to hold 10 men each, and there is accommodation in a kyaung and zayát close to the river for 250 men. Supplies: rice and fowls, pigs, &c., plentiful. The village is commanded at about 200 yards by the long ridge which runs from east to west to the north of it. The river is navigable to Fort Stedman at all seasons. Signallers can communicate by heliograph with Môbyé from "One Tree" hill on right bank of river.
		Balu river.					
		9. Lawpita (Loi-pi-dha), 2,450 feet.	**12**	**0**	89	4	Best route is to cross to the right bank of the Balu river. The road then runs through open downs on which are several villages for the first 4 miles, after which there is scrub

FROM FORT STEDMAN (MAINGSAUK) TO YWATHIT *viâ* SAWLÔN—*continued.*

Authorities.		Number and Names of Stages, Rivers and Streams.	Distances.		Remarks.
Military.	Civil.		Intermediate.	Total.	
G.O.C. Rangoon District.	Superintendent, Southern Shan States.	**9. Lawpita (Loi-pi-dha), 2,450 feet**—*cont.*			jungle and low hills on left side, through which mounted infantry can work; onwards the jungle is thicker and much cut up by ravines. Though the road is excellent of red clay, yet mounted men had difficulty in scouting. At 11 miles is a small Karen village. Camping ground to north-west of village of Lawpita (which was burnt by the troops), about 400 yards from Balu river. The river disappears into the ground about 4 miles further down the valley. Fowls and pigs can be got from neighbouring villages. Lawpita consisted of about 60 houses.
			M. F.	M. F.	
		10. Tilanga Ferry (500 feet). Nam Pwán or Pôn river.	11 0	100 4	The village of Chésolé is passed at 2 miles. This is the last place where water can be procured till Tilanga is reached. Road for first 5 miles is good, slightly falling towards the Pôn river; the next 3 miles are rocky and steep in places with bamboo jungle, the next 3 miles are down hill but good. The Pôn river is 150 yards broad, with deep channels on either side and shoals in the middle. It runs here at about 3 miles an hour; there are small rapids just above the ferry. Five dug-outs can be collected taking five men each besides boatmen; the river banks are shelving at the ferry. Elephants can ford river (5th December). Camping grounds either on river bank or in open jungle. Village on left bank burnt by troops.
		11. Nanko or Nankyi Sakhán (450 feet).	6 4	107 0	Road runs along the bank of Pôn river at 2½ miles; the hills come down upon the road, making a very narrow defile. The hills are from 200 to 500 feet above the road covered mostly with bamboo jungle; the hills on the right bank command the road. The river is unfordable even for elephants. The path 3 miles is rocky and difficult for baggage animals. The defile extends to within 2 miles of Sawlôn and the path is commanded by rifle fire from the hills on both sides of the river and for the greater part within even smooth-bore musket range. The camp is in the jungle a mile beyond a spring. Water from the Pôn river. Only infantry can operate.
		12. Sawlôn (400 feet).	10 0	117 0	Road as above. The Ngwédaung ferry is reached at 7½ miles. Here the hills open out and at 9 miles end. The road then turns eastward round the foot of the hills and passes through high hedges up to Sawlôn village. Sawlôn has about 150 houses laid out in streets with water channels on either side, and is commanded at a range of from 600 to 700 yards by a plateau running along the east of it. This plateau can be reached by a steep detour from Ngwédaung ferry, but it would take at least 2 hours to do so. Through the plateau runs a fine stream of water which supplies Sawlôn and falls in cascades over the almost sheer rock to the level of the village. A steep path from the village is the only regular approach to the plateau. There is a "haw" * on the

* That is, a large house in a strongly-fenced enclosure such as is generally occupied by a Sawbwa or headman.

FROM FORT STEDMAN (MAINGSAUK) TO YWATHIT *viâ* SAWLÔN—*continued.*

Authorities. Military.	Authorities. Civil.	Number and Names of Stages, Rivers and Streams.	Distances. Intermediate.		Distances. Total.		Remarks.
			M.	F.	M.	F.	
G.O.C. Rangoon District.	Superintendent, Southern Shan States.	**12. Sawlôn (400 feet)**—*cont.*					plateau in which 150 men could be accommodated. Three hundred men could be accommodated in the kyaung and audience hall, and another 250 men in the old "haw" about a mile to the south of village. Supplies plentiful, except rice, which is imported. Camping ground ¾ mile to west of village on the banks of Pôn river. Forage scarce.
		13. Hôta (970 feet).	12	0	129	0	At 3 miles the road leaves the valley and the ascent to the Pôn-Salween watershed commences. The ascent is very stiff at first. At 5 miles and at about 2,250 feet above sea, there is a small plateau with a fine large teak zayát, but no water; at 7 miles and at 3,750 feet above sea reach the watershed, from which a glimpse of the Salween may be had. The descent is very bad in places, about half-way down pass close to the Karen village of Kaungtwa, below which there are one or two clearings. The road throughout runs through jungle; camp in the paddy-fields west of Hôta. Firewood abundant, splendid water from stream. This march is a very severe one, and would take a column at least 10 hours. It may with advantage be shortened by marching over night to the foot of the hill, *i.e.*, 3 miles from the Sawlôn camp.
		14. Ywathit (? 700 feet).	4	0	133	0	A very easy march of 4 miles, passing Hôta village and crossing two or three deep ravines. Camp in paddy-field west of town. Excellent water from stream. Supplies of all sorts plentiful. Ta Hsáng Lé the ferry across the Salween in distant about 3 or 3½ miles from Ywathit. The road to it is very good, descending slightly. The last few hundred yards is very steep. At the ferry there is a splendid teak zayát.

ALTERNATIVE I.

FROM NAMMAWKALA (STAGE 5) TO LAWPITA (STAGE 9) *viâ* MÔBYÉ.

I. B. COMPILATION, 1889.

Military.	Civil.	Stages.	Int. M.	Int. F.	Total M.	Total F.	Remarks.
G.O.C. Rangoon District.	Superintendent, Southern Shan States.	**1. Pékôn (Payakôn).** Balu river.	11	0	11	0	Road follows the main road for 5 miles, then, after crossing bridged stream, it turns away south-west and becomes a foot-path running through paddy-fields. At 10 miles reach the Balu river at the village of Pékôn (Payakôn). River fordable only for elephants. Banks steep and 20 to 30 feet high. Troops and baggage animals can cross by a wooden bridge about 60 yards long and 8 feet broad. There are kyaungs and zayáts in the village capable of accommodating 300 to 400 men. Usual supplies. Camping ground 800 yards south-west of village at a spring where there is good shade. *Note.*—This road would be impracticable for troops before January.
		2. Môbyé ...	10	0	21	0	Road excellent, running south over downs for the 1st mile and then along high ground through low and in jungle alternately. Camp on high ground north-west of village.

FROM FORT STEDMAN (MAINGSAUK) TO YWATHIT *viâ* SAWLÔN—*continued.*

ALTERNATIVE I—*continued.*

Authorities. Military.	Authorities. Civil.	Number and Names of Stages, Rivers and Streams.	Distances. Intermediate. M.	F.	Distances. Total. M.	F.	Remarks.
G.O.C. Rangoon District.	Superintendent, Southern Shan States.	**3. Nammékôn** ... Nampé river.	**5**	**0**	26	0	Road at ½ mile crosses the Nampé; banks steep, but only 6 inches of water in the stream in February; but during the rains it is a swift and deep torrent. There is a foot-bridge a mile below the ford. The road from here runs across dry marsh land and crosses a stream before reaching camp; no difficulty. Nammékôn consists of two villages divided by a fine stream of water mentioned above. There is one kyaung capable of accommodating 150 men. Camp to south of stream on high ground amongst bamboo clumps.
		4. Ngwédaung (? Kyetpogyi). *	**9**	**0**	35	0	Direction of road south-east. Several rivulets cross the road, and it would be impracticable for troops before January at the earliest. At 1¾ miles reach Pôbya, a large village. At 3¾ miles road crosses a deep nullah with, however, little water in it at this time of year. Road runs across a huge swamp land, at present (February) mostly dry, but impassable earlier in the season. At 7¼ miles cross another large stream, 30 yards broad; good bottom, but steep banks, about 10 feet high; 2½ feet of water, current rapid and deep, and would be unfordable by laden animals earlier in the season. There is a foot-bridge for men and one boat. Camp on a small stream 1 mile north-west of village. Ngwédaung is a large stockaded village celebrated for silver work.
		5. Lawpita ...	**11**	**0**	46	0	Direction of road east. At 1 mile cross a nullah, muddy bottom and about 1 foot of water in it; would be difficult for transport animals after rains. From here the road is excellent, over red clay soil, through clump jungle and grass. At 2 miles pass a low double-crested hill; beyond pass two or three Karen villages; at about 10 miles strike the main route from Fort Stedman again and at 11 miles reach Lawpita.

BRANCH I.

FROM SAGA (STAGE 4) TO SISAING (STAGE 6, ROUTE NO. 17).

I. B. COMPILATION, MARCH 1889.

Military	Civil	Stage	Int. M.	F.	Total M.	F.	Remarks
G.O.C. Rangoon District.	Superintendent, Southern Shan States.	**1. Banpu**	**6**	**4**	6	4	*Note.*—This route is only practicable for transport animals. The road runs north-east and ascends the ridge to the east of Saga. There is a very steep and difficult bit at 1

* *See* Route No. 5, Lower Burma Division.

FROM FORT STEDMAN (MAINGSAUK) TO YWATHIT *viâ* SAWLÔN—*continued*.

BRANCH I—*continued*.

Authorities. Military.	Authorities. Civil.	Number and Names of Stages, Rivers and Streams.	Distances. Intermediate. (M. F.)	Distances. Total. (M. F.)	Remarks.
G.O.C. Rangoon District.	Superintendent, Southern Shan States.	**1. Banpu**—*cont.*			mile. The road is cut out of the hill side in places especially near the top of the ridge, which is reached at 1¼ miles. From here the road turns south-east and winds down the opposite side of the ridge and is good. The descent continues for 2 miles, after which the road is fairly level through jungle with patches of cultivation in places. At 6½ miles reach Banpu, a small village among jungle-covered hills. Camping ground extensive and water plentiful. There is a shorter road, only practicable for passengers, straight across the hills. By this path the distance is only about 4 miles.
		2. Nansawmyet...	**9 0**	15 4	For the first 3½ miles the road is level and runs through jungle, passing the small villages of Banphán at 1½ miles, on a small hill to south, and Lawacho at 2½ miles, 300 yards south of road. At 3½ miles the road begins to ascend gradually to the top of a ridge, which is reached at 5¼ miles, the last ¼ mile being steep and rough. The ridge forms the boundary between Saga and Thatôn districts. The road now runs east and descends to Nansawmyet village. For the first ½ mile the descent is steep and rough and after that gradual, running as before through jungle. Nansawmyet is a village of about 20 houses, lying at the foot of the ridge, and situated on a stream of good water. Camping ground fair. No supplies.
		3. Sisaing... ... Tabet river.	**7 4**	23 0	Road now runs north-east and descends slightly through jungle, passing the small village of Mushaung at 1 mile and reaching the Tabet river at 2½ miles at the small village of Khônyát. The river is here about 30 or 40 yards broad and 5 or 6 feet deep with a fairly rapid current. It is crossed by a wooden trestle bridge. From here the road still running north-east passes the small villages of Banno at 3 miles and Kǒnni at 4 miles, where there is good water from a stream, and at 7¼ miles reaches Sisaing, a village of about 40 houses (*see* Route No. 21, Stage 5).

No. 5.

From HÉHO to PYAWBWÉ viâ TAUNGLEBIN and SHWÉNYAUNGBU.

BY LIEUT. A. H. BATTYE, 3RD GURKHAS, 22ND MARCH 1887.

G.O.C. Rangoon District.	Supt., Southern Shan States.	**1. Bawnin** ... nmi chaung and small streams.	**6 0**	6 0	Ηého, *see* Route No. 6, Eastern Division, Stage 8. Left Hého kyaung at 9 A.M., passing the bazaar on the left. The track went south-west, passing the village of Hého (quite defenceless), then skirting the base of an isolated hill (with pagoda on summit) crossed a valley (1½ miles wide). The country is here destitute of trees, but under cultivation. The path is good for ponies or bullocks. Cross the Inmi

FROM HÉHO TO PYAWBWÉ *viâ* TAUNGLEBIN AND SHWÉNYAUNGBU—*continued.*

Authorities.		Number and Names of Stages, Rivers and Streams.	Distances.				Remarks.
Military.	Civil.		Intermediate.		Total.		
			M.	F.	M.	F.	
G.O.C. Rangoon District.	Superintendent, Southern Shan States.	**1. Bawnin**—*cont.*					chaung, good bridge, just opposite the small village of Inmi. The path now runs westward along the foot of the Inmi range. The black clayey soil of the plain has changed to a reddish colour. Passed village of Yônkôn on the left; the country is perfectly open and flat on the right. The Inmi range is low and only wooded in parts. About a mile beyond Yônkôn lies the village of Payabin, surrounded by bamboo clumps. Water plentiful all the way, as the Inmi chaung flows northward, almost parallel with the path. Crossed two or three small wooden bridges over dry water-courses coming down from the hills, which now recede from the path (direction 220°). Passed small village of Ywathit, 1 mile beyond Payabin. The soil is clayey and easily workable, but is only cultivated near the villages. Cross the Inmi chaung by good wooden bridge just before reaching Bawnin, where we arrived at 12 (noon). The village is stockaded and has a ditch (recently dug) all round. Forage and water good. Large kyaung in an enclosure about ½ mile away. Good camping ground.
		2. Thamakán ... Stream.	7	0	13	0	Left at 9 A.M. Path ran north-west past the kyaung on the right, then across a bare plain along a small bund (5 feet broad) for about 1½ miles to village of Myakyit, then along north side of the village (which is fortified) and up a gradual ascent over a low range of hills, which bounds the Hého plain on the west. Crossed a deep nullah (dry in March) about ¾ mile from Myakyit. The country is now hilly and undulating, but still bare of trees; the soil clayey and easily workable. The country has been under cultivation at one time, but now seems neglected except in the immediate vicinity of the villages. About 3½ miles beyond Myakyit the ground becomes rocky, but the track is still good. From here it descends gradually into a valley, passing small village of Thayetpin, which lies about ¼ mile off the path. It is quite defenceless. Here good drinking water can be obtained. The path now crosses valley and ascends gradually for about a mile to Thamakán, which is a strongly stockaded village situated on summit of a bare grassy hill. The bazaar lies on north-west slope of hill, just outside the village. Arrived at 12-30 P.M. Thamakán is the residence of a Ngwégunhmu. Grass is rather scarce, but bamboo forage plentiful. Good water obtainable from stream at foot of hill.
		3. Kalaw ... ... Small stream.	10	0	23	0	The path crosses a valley going due west and over a bridged stream, then up and over a small ridge and down again into another valley up a rather steep hill side, where there is a small spring of good water (1½ miles from Thamakán). The path now goes over bare undulating downs for 3 miles past the small village of Kyégôn and Nyaungbingôn, then up a hill and down into a valley by a rather rough and steep descent. The sides of the valley are thinly sprinkled with bushes (direction 240°). Across the valley and over a dry water-course by small wooden bridge, ascend for ½ mile over a ridge bounding south-west end of valley to village of Kyauktán, consisting of a few wretched huts quite defenceless; a large pagoda on the right. Then

FROM HÉHO TO PYAWBWÉ *viâ* TAUNGLEBIN AND SHWÉNYAUNGBU—*continued.*

Authorities. Military.	Authorities. Civil.	Number and Names of Stages, Rivers and Streams.	Distances. Intermediate.	Distances. Total.	Remarks.
G.O.C. Rangoon District.	Supt., Southern Shan States.	**3. Kalaw**—*cont.*			up over a *col* between two hills and down into a valley thickly wooded with pines by rough path, crossing small stream at the bottom and over a clearing to the foot of a conical-shaped hill surmounted by a white pagoda. Here it turns off to the left and continues on up a thickly-wooded valley for 2 miles to Kalaw pagoda, which lies in open ground near a stream and at the foot of a hill, on the top of which is the village of Kalaw. Forage and water good and plentiful.
	Commissioner, Eastern Division, and Deputy Commissioner, Meiktila.	**4. Pyinmôn Sakhán.**	M. F. **9 0**	M. F. 32 0	The path crosses some marshy ground by a small bund (3 feet wide), then leads round the side of a hill and up a narrow-wooded valley to a strong stockade on top of a hill on the left. Just beyond this the path turns off to the left and passes the village of Magwé (1 mile) on the right. The ground here is quite open. It now goes up a valley for ½ mile and reaches the head of the Taunglebin pass. It now descends suddenly into a narrow valley, thickly wooded, and goes along it till it reaches the foot of the Sapeiktaung. The ascent is very steep and rocky for about ½ mile, then along the top of the ridge, path good. It now goes along the north side of the ridge; then along a fairly level path for a short distance (direction 230°), passes a small camping ground (sakhán) used by traders, then up a short ascent. Here there is a spring of good water (4 miles from Kalaw) on side of hill just below the path. We are now on the highest point of the pass and the path continues along the ridge for ½ mile, then commences to descend to Pyinmôn Sakhán. The hill side is covered with pine trees and clumps of bamboos, very little undergrowth. Descent easy for 1½ miles, when it reaches Sinbyintin, where it becomes very rocky and bad for pack animals, but only for about 100 yards. It now goes north-west for a short distance, then turns due west, fairly level-going, but path very much worn by Shan bullocks. It now goes down a narrow valley with a small stream running down it until it reaches Pyinmôn Sakhán lying at the foot of the Pyinmôn range. Here there is a good camping ground (200 by 25 yards); bamboo forage plentiful. Water good, but not sufficient for a large force.
		5. Taunglebin ... Myittha and Máhti streams.	**7 4**	39 4	Left camp at 7 A.M. Path runs down the valley in north-west direction; thick jungle and undergrowth on either side. The path was very good at first, then rocky, but quite practicable for ponies or bullocks. Two miles away from Pyinmôn Sakhán the path follows the course of the dry bed of a stream and works along the foot of the lofty Pyinmôn range for 1½ miles. Ground fairly level and not so confined, but much broken by small nullahs. Reddish-colored soil. Path now turns to 320°, passing two or three small clearings in the jungle and follows up a valley formed between two rocky and conical-shaped hills (5 miles from Pyinmôn Sakhán). Here a path turns off to the left and is a short cut to Taunglebin, but is impracticable for bullocks. The track continues on in a northerly direction for another mile, then turns round a hill to the left and gradually works down a valley and through paddy-fields to the village of

FROM HÉHO TO PYAWBWÉ *viâ* TAUNGLEBIN AND SHWÉNYAUNGBU—*continued.*

Authorities.		Number and Names of Stages, Rivers and Streams.	Distances.		Remarks.
Military.	Civil.		Intermediate.	Total.	
G.O.C. Rangoon District.	Commissioner, Eastern Division, and Deputy Commissioner, Meiktila.	**5. Taunglebin**—*cont.*			Taunglebin, which lies on the banks of the Myittha stream. Reached camping ground at 10-15 A.M., situated in open fields on the banks of the Máhti stream. Grass scarce, bamboo forage plentiful. We are now only about 12 miles to the south of Pyinyaung. *N.B.*—The Máhti stream, on which lies Taunglebin, must not be confused with the Myittha stream, which flows into the first-named river a few miles to the north of Taunglebin.
		6. Ma-u-gyi Sakhán. Myittha stream.	M. F. 9 4	M. F. 49 · 0	Started at 6-45 A.M. Path goes in a westerly direction at first across open fields (formerly cultivated), then through thick jungle past a pagoda and three old zayáts, standing in small clearing (¼ mile). Direction 240°. Path now becomes rough and stony in places, going down a narrow valley and across a stream (the Myittha), the water being only a few inches deep. It now ascends a valley, rocky ground and thick jungle on either side, in some places quite steep and difficult even for Shan bullocks. Crosses a small ridge (3½ miles from Lebyin) and drops down by a steep and much worn path with a ravine on the right to the dry bed of the Myittha. From this point the path follows the course of the stream (now merely a trickling rill), winding in and out among low hills covered with jungle (mostly bamboos). The general direction is south-west. The path is rocky and bad for pack animals. There is a steady ascent the whole way to Ma-u-gyi Sakhán. There are two or three small clearings on the banks of the stream; no scarcity of water. After going up the course of the stream for 6 miles or so we reached Ma-u-gyi (12-30 P.M.). Here thare are two small camping grounds (each 50 by 50 yards), situated on the banks of the Myittha chaung, surrounded by dense bamboo jungle. A small village quite close by, but it has been deserted some time. Water good and plentiful, also bamboo forage.
		7. Thabiyetaung-gyi Sakhán. Small stream.	5 4	54 4	Path led across the dry bed of the Myittha and continued the ascent, going due south-west. Thick bamboo jungle on both sides up the ravine formed by the stream; pools of water here and there along the rocky bed; ascent much steeper than last march. About 1 mile from Ma-u-gyi the path leaves the bed of the stream on the right and ascends steep hill side in zigzags for a short distance. It now gets on to more level and better ground (reddish-colored soil), passes a clearing 2 miles from Ma-u-gyi (direction 240°); reaches the top of a ridge; ground quite open. From this point the descent begins along a very stony and difficult path with a deep "khud" on the left, path going down the ridge of a spur most of the way. Direction 215°. Passed Shábindet Sakhán (good camping ground, but no water) and from this the path becomes much better and comparatively level. Quarter mile further on reach the camping ground of Thabiyetaunggyi (100 by 50 yards) surrounded by thick bamboo jungle. Water obtainable from small stream (almost dried up in March) about ½ mile away to the north-west, so the supply is very limited. Forage scarce, as the bamboo jungle about here has been recently burnt.

FROM HÉHO TO PYAWBWÉ *viâ* TAUNGLEBIN AND SHWÉNYAUNGBU—*continued.*

Authorities. Military.	Authorities. Civil.	Number and Names of Stages, Rivers and Streams.	Distances. Intermediate. M. F.	Distances. Total. M. F.	Remarks.
G.O.C. Rangoon District.	Commissioner, Eastern Division, and Deputy Commissioner, Meiktila.	**8. Shwényaungbu.**	**8 4**	63 0	Left camping ground at 6-20 A.M. Path good, leading in a south-west direction through bamboo jungle (recently burnt) for about 3 miles; reached the foot of a hill and skirting the northern end descended for a short distance over rocky ground. The country is now more cultivated (plantain groves), but not for long, as turning southwards the road passes through scrub jungle and over sandy ground. At this season of the year (March) everything looks parched and dried up, owing to the great scarcity of water in this district. The path (now a very good cart track) turns to the south-west for another 3 miles, still continuing through open scrub jungle until it reaches Shwényaungbu, a large village surrounded by a good fence. We encamped near a large kyaung just outside the village. Time of arrival 10-15 A.M. Good water obtainable from a well, but at this time of year the supply is limited. Grass plentiful. The country in the last stage is quite flat and a good cart road could easily be made.
		9. Pyawbwé ...	**8 6**	71 6	Road level and wide the whole way. Last half of the way mostly over paddy cultivation so bad in wet weather. Several villages *en route*, at most of which there is accommodation in kyaungs for from 50 to 100 men, with sufficient water-supply. For Pyawbwé *see* Route No. 6, Lower Burma Division, Stage 16.

No. 6.

From KUNLÔN to MÖNGKYET *viâ* KANGMÖNG.

BY CAPT. A. C. YATE, 1ST BELOOCHEES, FEBRUARY 1888.

Military	Civil	Stages	Intermediate	Total	Remarks
G.O.C. Mandalay District.	Superintendent, Northern Shan States.	**1. Pángwo** ...	**9 2**	9 2	*See* Route No. 67, Stages 5 to 7.
		2. Kángmöng ...	**7 4**	16 6	
		3. Namsa ... Namkwé and Namsa streams.	**12 4**	29 2	From Kángmöng the road to Náti branches to the north, *see* Route No. 67. At ¼ mile path to right to village of Wengkáng, distant ½ mile. At ¾ mile path to right to Kachin village of Kôngkaw (five houses), 1 mile distant, and at 1 mile another to the same. At 1½ miles village of Manmaw (Kachins, 10 long houses). Opium and rice cultivated. Pigs, fowls, buffaloes, eggs procurable. From here path to left to Kachin Kángmöng. The road to Möngkyet then keeps to the right, that straight on leading to Supkyet, (*see* Route No. 67, Branch I). Road hilly, but fairly good for pack transport. Only low hills are crossed, the gradients are not very steep, and there are no swamps. The road mostly traverses tree jungle and thick high grass, but there are large tracts under cultivation near

FROM KUNLÔN TO MONGKYET *viâ* KÁNGMONG—*continued.*

Authorities.		Number and Names of Stages, Rivers and Streams.	Distances.				Remarks.
Military.	Civil.		Intermediate.		Total.		
G.O.C. Mandalay District.	Superintendent, Northern Shan States.	**3. Namsa**—*cont.*	the villages. At 3¼ miles path to left to Kachin village of Lwépyé. At 4½ and 5 miles two Kachin villages, both called Maukwé. At 6¼ miles cross Namtwé stream. From there to Namsa is 6¼ miles. Namsa is a Kachin village of 10 houses. There is a good camping ground in the rice fields ½ a mile west of the village on the east bank of the Namsa stream.				
			M.	F.	M.	F.	
		4. Möngkyet ...	5	6	35	0	Hilly road, but fairly good for pack transport. Road crosses low hills. Gradients moderate. No swamps. At 1¼ miles pass village of Konghong. At 1¾ miles cross Namli stream. At 2 miles village of Hônai ½ a mile to left. From this point follow course of Namli stream to its junction with the Namkyet river, near the Shan village of Kongho, 2 miles further on (*i.e.*, at 4 miles). From there to Möngkyet (1¾ miles) follow course of Namkyet river. There is a good camping ground on the bank of the river near the Möngkyet bazaar which is situated in the valley. The village is on the higher ground to the south of the bazaar. The valley of the Namkyet is naturally very fertile. Möngkyet is on the main road between Pánglông and Láshio, *see* Route No. 30, and from it there are also roads north to Náti (*see* Route No. 67), southwards to Manmák, and the Lantao (or Lantu) District (*see* Route No. 39, Stages 2 and 3).

No. 7.

From KUNLÔN to MÖNGSI.

BY CAPT. A. C. YATE, 1ST BELOOCHEES, FROM NATIVE INFORMATION, 1888.

Military.	Civil.	Stages, Rivers and Streams.	M.	F.	M.	F.	Remarks.
G.O.C. Mandalay District.	Superintendent, Northern Shan States.	**1. Sômati** ... Namnim.	10	0	...		General direction north-west. Hilly road. Cross Namnim 2 miles from Kunlôn by a ford just above its junction with the Salween. Somati. Kachin village. Fifteen long houses. Water from spring.
		2. Pöngpáng ... Unknown.	10	0	20	0	Road hilly. Pass villages of Kongit and Wákyong. All three Kachin villages. Water from spring or stream.
		3. Möngpaw (Möngtám). Unknown.	6	0	26	0	Road hilly, mostly descent. Large village population mixed Shan and Kachin. Kyaungs, zayáts, and bazaar. Kachin Myoza. Water from stream.
		4. Nongphai ... Unknown.	8	0	34	0	Road level. Pass largish Kachin village called Nongsáng. Nongphai also Kachin village. Water and some supplies at both as at most Kachin villages.

FROM KUNLÔN TO MÖNGSI—*continued.*

Authorities. Military.	Authorities. Civil.	Number and Names of Stages, Rivers and Streams.	Distances. Intermediate. M.	F.	Distances. Total. M.	F.	Remarks.
G.O.C. Mandalay District.	Superintendent, Northern Shan States.	**5. Möngsi** ... Unknown.	10	0	44	0	Road level. Pass at 3 miles Hô-it, Kachin village, and at 7 miles Hôkáng, a Zawti-Shan village. Thirty houses and bazaar. Stream. • Möngsi, large village. Shan and Kachin population. Kachin Myoza. Kyaungs, zayáts, and bazaar. Water from stream and wells (pits). *See* Route No. 68, Stage 4.

No. 8.

From KUNLÔN to TAWNIO (KÔKÁNG) *viâ* NAMHU.

BY LIEUT. H. B. WALKER, PAID ATTACHÉ, INTELLIGENCE BRANCH, BURMA, 1891-92.

Military	Civil	Stages	Int. M.	F.	Total M.	F.	Remarks
G.O.C. Mandalay District.	Superintendent, Northern Shan States.	**1. Namhu** ... Nampôn, Namting, and Namlwé.	6	4	6	4	General direction east-north-east. Leaving Kunlôn the route runs by a well-beaten path and within a short distance of the left bank of the Salween river, from which, at a little less than a mile, the path parts company and small Shan village of Möngkho is passed to right hand. The route then runs along the side of a spur as far as mile 2, where the Nampôn stream, bridged and with steep approaches, is crossed. The Nampôn stream is 6 or 7 yards wide, 2 feet deep, sluggish and muddy. It joins the Namting river a little to south-east. The Namting river runs south of path, 60 yards broad here and flowing from the east through Möngting 2 miles an hour. Fordable in places. Leaving the Nampôn the route rises a little passing the small Kachin village of Nampôn at mile 2¼. The route then descends slightly into the Namting valley. The path continues along the northern side of the valley over the lower edges of the hills, the continuation of Loikwoilin. At mile 4 the Namlwé, a small stream, 6 or 7 yards wide, practically no water in dry season, bridged with stone and capable of bearing heavy traffic, is passed. The Namting river here makes a wide bend and is lost to view for a while. The path still follows the valley; thick jungle to the left; kaing grass to the right or south. At 5 miles the small village of Kônkán is passed to the right hand or south, three or four houses. Just before 6 miles Lower Namhu is passed to the north, three houses, Kachins; and ½ a mile further on Upper Namhu, eight or nine houses, a kyaung and camping ground for 300 men is reached. Just before entering village a path leads away south-east to Hôpáng and south to Pánglông, the Panthay settlement. *See* Route No. 30, Stage 10. Water plentiful and grass good; a few supplies obtainable. The path all the way from Kunlôn is good and easy marching; the ascents and descents are short and none are difficult.
		2. Ho Tao ...	6	0	12	4	} *See* Route No. 58, Stages 20 and 21.
		3. Tawnio (Kôkáng).	16	0	28	4	

No. 9.

From KYENG HUNG (KENG HUNG, KYAINGYUNGYI) to MÖNGMA (MÖNG LEM) via TA LAW FERRY.

By Capt. G. V. BURROWS, Attaché, Intelligence Branch, March 1891.

Authorities.		Number and Names of Stages, Rivers and Streams.	Distances.		Remarks.
Military.	Civil.		Intermediate.	Total.	
			M. F.	M. F.	
G.O.C. Mandalay District.	Superintendent, Northern Shan States.	**1. Man Pit** ... Nam Ôt, Nam Hsin.	8 0	8 0	Leaving Kyeng Hung in a south-easterly direction, the road runs through jungle for a mile and-a-half, when it passes the small village of Man Hawng and turning slightly south runs on into open country passing several small hamlets; those on the right being Man Na, Man Náng, Kaung Wat, and Man Tsáng Tsai, on the left Man Mawng, nearly 3 miles from Kyeng Hung. Half-a-mile further on it crosses the Nam Ôt, a considerable stream, 30 feet broad and 18 inches deep, with low, sloping, open banks, moderate current, firm gravel bottom. On the right bank stands the small village of Man Ôt. The country is quite open and level for the next 3 miles, and going south-west the road crosses here the Nam Ôt, again passing through the village of Man Ôt on the right bank. Half-a-mile further on it passes through a large bazaar and about 300 yards to the south of the village of Hatsai, a considerable place, consisting of about 40 houses. At the western end of the bazaar there is a substantially built kyaung, surrounded by a wall of brick, 18 inches thick and 4 feet 6 inches high. Rice and paddy are plentiful here. Leaving the kyaung on the left, the road passes a large pond and running across the open cultivated plain another mile touches the village of Man Pit, where the Nam Hsin (25 feet broad, 1 foot deep; right bank 6 feet high; left bank low; gravel bottom; good water) flows close to the road, and there is a good camping ground close to the right of the road and just beyond the village.
		2. Man Sen Camp.	14 0	22 0	The road runs on in a south-west by west direction up the valley. After 1 mile it passes through the little village of Nam Ta lying in a hollow. Half-a-mile further on it crosses the Nam Hsin (crossing as above, but banks wooded by low jungle) and the road commences to rise through thick jungle. In another quarter of a mile the village of Kyeng Hung is passed through. It is a very small, insignificant place, but commanded from the wooded hill on the south. The road now rises steadily for the next 8 miles through dense jungle and high grass and is in some places very narrow and rocky. The country is quite closed on both sides and at the 9th mile, after passing through a very deep narrow ravine, the road rises suddenly on to a broken spur. There is a small stream of good water, always running down this ravine in a rocky bed, and there is space enough to camp on the west side if the high grass is cleared. There would be room for 100 men on the small plateau. Elevation 4,300 feet. The road now turns slightly in a more southerly direction and passes for miles over a very rugged piece of wooded country, and it is in some places difficult for loaded animals. At the 14th mile it runs into a small cultivated valley, on the western side of which under oak trees, there is ample camping ground for a large force with good water in the valley 100 yards below the site. The total rise in the first 10 miles is 2,600 feet.

FROM KYENG HUNG (KENG HUNG, KYAINGYUNGYI) TO MÖNGMA (MÖNG LEM) *viâ* TA LAW FERRY—*continued.*

Authorities. Military.	Authorities. Civil.	Number and Names of Stages, Rivers and Streams.	Distances. Intermediate. M. F.	Distances. Total. M. F.	Remarks.
G.O.C. Mandalay District.	Superintendent, Northern Shan States.	**3. Hôna** ... ... Stream at Naung Lam and Nam Hu.	**11 0**	33 0	For the first mile and-a-half the road goes on south-west by south over very low and undulating open hills. Fields appear on the right through which a very small stream flows south-west. Crossing the fields at right angles the road turns again south-west through scrub jungle. Hills continue to the right and left a mile on either side. About 1 mile from the road on the left is the small Kaw village of Man Hwé. Three-quarters of a mile further on it runs through some paddy-fields, an open space of about 400 yards square. Two hundred yards further on and 300 yards to the right of the road there is a large village, Naung Lam, with a tank below it, 50 houses, with a large brick-built kyaung walled in at the south end of the village. Rice and paddy are plentiful here. Four hundred yards further on the road crosses some more fields and a small stream. The country is open to the left. Half-a-mile further on it crosses another small stream (12 feet broad, 9 inches deep; gravel bottom; low banks; good water). The road now runs on skirting the jungle on the right and 1 mile farther on it crosses a considerable stream called the Nam Hu (18 feet broad, $1\frac{1}{2}$ feet deep; clear water; gravel bottom; low banks; both wooded; flows down from a large village high up on the hills to the left called Pa Sha). Rising gradually for about 1 furlong the road runs on to a long low spur which continues for the next 5 miles; there are several places along this spur where troops could camp with water in the valleys on either side. In some places the crossings over very small streams are muddy, but could not very easily be repaired. In another mile the road runs rapidly off the spur down a rocky slope and crossing a small stream with high banks, 12 feet broad and 6 inches deep, it runs into the Möng Hung valley. A quarter of a mile from the stream and out in the open in paddy-fields, with the Nam Hu running below it, stands the village of Hôna, consisting of 30 houses. Just beyond the village, on the edge of the wood, is a good, large camping ground.
		4. Camp on Nam Hak. Nam Hak.	**10 0**	43 0	Leaving the village of Man Hôna to the right the road runs on along the edge of the jungle, and $\frac{1}{2}$ a mile from the last camping ground it passes through another village of the same name. Half-a-mile more and you come to another small village, Man Myen, with a large swamp lying just below it in the valley. Going on through open country the road comes to another village called Man Yáng and in another $\frac{1}{2}$ mile it runs past another large village called Man Páng. There is a large kyaung here standing on a knoll overlooking the village and nearly surrounded by water, the ground due west of it being a swamp. The road now runs on through low scrub jungle, at the end of which and $\frac{1}{2}$ a mile from Man Páng, 400 yards to the left stands the village of Man Hai. One mile farther on, across open ground with another long swamp on the right and left, the road enters the village of Man To Hao, where there is a large kyaung surrounded by a brick wall 4 feet high. The building is of brick and overlooking the village. Opposite this place and a mile away to the right, at the edge of the plain, there is a large

FROM KYENG HUNG (KENG HUNG, KYAINGYUNGYI) TO MÖNGMA (MÖNG LEM) *vid* TA LAW FERRY—*continued.*

Authorities.		Number and Names of Stages, Rivers and Streams.	Distances.		Remarks.
Military.	Civil.		Intermediate.	Total.	
G.O.C. Mandalay District.	Superintendent, Northern Shan States.	**4. Camp on Nam Hak**—*cont.*			village and to the left and ½ a mile distant is a village called Man Nawng. Going on across the plain through paddy-fields in ¾ of a mile the road was past the village of Man Kông, consisting of about 20 houses. About ½ mile to the left stands Man Na, 600 yards further on and on the road stands another small village known as Man Kawng, where it crosses a small stream, about 8 feet wide. Here the valley ends and the road rises 500 feet in the next mile through dense jungle, running along a ridge for the next 5 miles when it drops suddenly falling 600 feet to a small stream known as the Nam Hak, running down a rocky bed, between high banks along a deep ravine, on the opposite bank of which is a small camping ground sufficiently large to hold 100 men only. It is surrounded, however, by dense jungle.
		5. Möng Law ferry (Ta Law). Nam Pit, Nam Ta, Nam Páng, and Nam Lam.	M. F. **12 4**	M. F. 55 4	In the first ¼ of a mile the road rises 100 feet, then runs a fairly level course rising only another 100 feet in the next 800 yards, when it suddenly descends. The descent continues in a zigzag form for nearly 2 miles, when it crosses a smaller stream of no consequence. Total descent from this point 900 feet. It runs along level for the next 400 yards when it again descends 300 feet to a considerable stream called the Nam Pyit flowing over boulders of rock 30 feet broad and 1 foot deep; is rapid and both banks are high, but sloping and covered with jungle. For the next 2½ miles the road runs on through jungle: it is broken and rocky and crosses three very small streams. Between the 5th and 6th miles there is an open space about 150 by 50 yards, where a small force could encamp. The road now again descends into the valley of the Nam Ta (15 feet broad, 8 inches deep; gravel bottom; rapid; good water), falling nearly 200 feet. After mounting a small rugged spur it crosses this stream which flows along here between very high banks, at least 60 feet high and precipitous. The right or southern bank commands the left by a few feet and the ford would be difficult to pass if either bank were held. From this point for the next 4½ miles the road winds along through thick jungle. It is fairly level, the descent being very gradual. Total descent 400 feet. It then runs into the large open valley, which is cultivated, and ⅝ a mile further on on the road stands the village of Möng Páng, consisting of 35 houses and a brick-walled kyaung. Just beyond the village is a large camping ground with excellent water flowing along the foot of it. The road runs through thick jungle in a south-westerly direction, and after 1 mile has been covered passes some open ground to the right covered with very high grass. Here, crossing a very small, insignificant stream, the road runs on through dense jungle for another 2 miles, when it drops into a narrow valley and recrosses a considerable stream, probably the Nam Páng, flowing west (40 feet broad, 1 to 2 feet deep; low banks; sandy soil; pebbly bottom; rapid; both banks covered with thick jungle. Total descent to stream from Möng Páng 300 feet). The stream winds through the valley round these large spurs which the road goes over, thus crossing the stream four times within a mile. Each crossing is easy and the stream at these points is easily forded.

FROM KYENG HUNG (KENG HUNG, KYAINGYUNGYI) TO MÖNGMA (MÖNG LEM) *viâ* TA LAW FERRY—*continued.*

Authorities. Military.	Authorities. Civil.	Number and Names of Stages, Rivers and Streams.	Distances. Intermediate.	Distances. Total.	Remarks.
G.O.C. Mandalay District.	Superintendent, Northern Shan States.	**5. Möng Law ferry (Ta Law)** —*cont.*			The road now runs over a low spur and drops about 60 feet into the valley of the Nam Lam. Turning here in a north-west direction it follows the left bank for about 1 mile, when it turns still more north and passes through the small village of Man Pwon, beyond which it skirts some fields on the right and rises gradually over a rugged, but low spur thickly wooded; it is here somewhat broken, but it is easy going for pack mules. After another mile and-a-quarter it runs into a broad open cultivated valley which it crosses in a south-west direction, passing about 400 yards to the left a small village called Man Hpa. Standing in the middle of the plains, ½ a mile further, it passes to the left of a small village called Möng Law on the left bank of the Nam Lam, which is flowing due east (low banks at the ford; left bank wooded; right bank level and slightly wooded; stream rapid; velocity 3 miles). The greatest portion of the village is on the right bank about 300 yards above the ford. There is a very good large camping ground about 100 yards south-west of the village on the left bank of another stream called the Nam Lam. Möng Law, the village at the ford, consists in all of about 40 houses. Rice and paddy are procurable in considerable quantities. The country to the south of the village is open for the distance of about a mile and closed on the west side. The camping ground is sufficiently large to hold a force of 4,000 men, and across the Nam Lam there is ample room for a large number of transport animals, affording also facilities for grazing, the ground being covered with thick, short green grass. There is a high ground just west of the camp and within 900 yards of the ford and its approaches.
		6. Möng Ma (2,200 feet). Nam Lam and Nam Mi.	M. 12 F. 4	M. 68 F. 0	The road leaves the village of Keng Law in a south-westerly direction, running up the open level valley of the Nam Lam, which it crosses about 1 mile from the village, open banks; low gravel bottom; 16 yards broad and 18 inches deep; rapid. Running on along the right bank it crosses a small very low spur covered with thin jungle, and about ½ mile further on again crosses the stream here, 22 yards broad and 1 foot deep; low banks; open to east and west. North-east and south-east by the bend of the stream, two wooded hills run down to banks commanding the ford at a short range, 250 yards, that on the north-west bank commands the hill on the south-east by about 25 feet. The road runs on up the valley and turning a few points to the south keeps along the left bank again till 100 yards from the ford, at the edge of the jungle, on the right of the valley it runs through the small village of Möng La Tao. It is just beyond this that the boundary of Kyeng Tung runs. Five hundred yards further on due south-west on a small knoll stands a brick-walled kyaung overlooking the small village of Kyeng Hpa. The kyaung is only 200 yards to the left of the road. The country is closed to the right and open to the left. For the next 5 miles the road runs along this side of the valley. The Nam Lam winds along below to the left in open country, while the slopes to the right of the road are wooded. At the 5th mile from Kyeng Hpa it crosses a small stream flowing south, called Nam Mi, 14 feet broad, 6 inches deep, flowing along between narrow dip

FROM KYENG HUNG (KENG HUNG, KYAINGYUNGYI) TO MÖNGMA (MÖNG LEM) *viâ* TA LAW FERRY—*continued.*

Authorities. Military.	Authorities. Civil.	Number and Names of Stages, Rivers and Streams.	Distances. Intermediate. M.	Distances. Intermediate. F.	Distances. Total. M.	Distances. Total. F.	Remarks.
G.O.C. Mandalay District.	Superintendent, Northern Shan States.	**6. Möng Ma (2,200 feet)**—*cont.*					in the road. Easy crossing; pebble bottom. The valley from this point is cultivated and is about $\frac{3}{4}$ mile broad. About $2\frac{1}{2}$ miles further on and close to the right of the road stands the small village of Man Paw. About 400 yards further on, and on the left stands a strongly built and brick-walled kyaung, on a knoll, about 40 feet above the road, which it completely commands. Two miles further on, and about 800 yards to the left in the valley and hidden among trees lies the small village of Man Kôk. The road now again runs along the left bank of the Nam Lam and a mile more brings you to a village, and $\frac{1}{4}$ mile further to Möng Ma, a village consisting of some 30 houses with a capital camping ground below the village and sheltered by trees about 500 yards from the Nam Lam. At the southern end of this camp there is a small rounded hill covered with jungle which appears to have been fortified at some distant period. There is a small moat all round it. From its position it commands the valley in both directions, north and south.
		7. Nam Yi ... Stream.	8	0	76	0	The road leaves Möng Ma in a westerly direction and after $\frac{1}{4}$ mile passes the small village of Man Lem on the left of the road and close to it. It then runs along in thick jungle, branching off to the right about 200 yards beyond the village and leaving the main road to Kyeng Tung, which runs along south-west up the right side of the valley. A $\frac{1}{4}$ of a mile after leaving the Kyeng Tung road, it commences to rise rapidly. The ascent continues for about $\frac{3}{4}$ mile (900 feet) when it turns in a north-west direction and is level for nearly a $\frac{1}{4}$ mile, then it rises 350 feet again very rapidly in about $\frac{1}{2}$ mile, when it passes just above a small village called Nam Khai lying in a fork-shaped ravine. Rising a few feet over the neck above the village, it runs level along the side of the hill, with a long steep-wooded slope on the left for a mile, when it rises rapidly some 400 feet over another neck, and from here it turns in a west-south-west direction, gradually descending to the head of a very deep and precipitous ravine, which has been cleared for cultivation. Ascending the opposite side it rises about 300 feet in a $\frac{1}{2}$ mile, and then runs along a ridge for about $3\frac{1}{2}$ miles quite level, a broad open valley appearing on the right. At the end of this ridge and about 200 yards below a brick-walled kyaung standing on the right of the road, lies the village of Nam Yi, the head-quarters of a Tamôn. There is a good but small camping ground 400 yards beyond the village, which consists of about 40 houses to the left of and close to the road. Water is, however, some distance below, about 350 yards down in the valley to the left of the camping ground. There is a good path running down to the stream, but the country is closed by a thick jungle.
		8. Man Pön ... Nam Lwi Hsa.	12	0	88	0	Leaving Nam Yi in a west-north-west direction, this road runs along a level ridge for about 900 yards, when it commences a long and steep ascent, rising 800 feet in the next mile. Then it is nearly level for about $\frac{1}{2}$ mile, when it ascends again 750 feet in the next 1,100 yards. It then runs level for about 400 yards, the country up to the top of the first rise is open, but

FROM KYENG HUNG (KENG HUNG, KYAINGYUNGYI) TO MÖNGMA (MÖNG LEM) *viâ* TA LAW FERRY—*continued.*

Authorities.		Number and Names of Stages, Rivers and Streams.	Distances.		Remarks.
Military.	Civil.		Intermediate.	Total.	
G.O.C. Mandalay District.	Superintendent, Northern Shan States.	**8. Man Pön**—*cont.*			the slopes on the left of the road are very long and very steep. The ground has all been cleared and burnt for cultivation; it is closed for the rest of the way until within a mile and-a-half of Man Hôk. It then drops very rapidly falling 1,200 feet in the next mile and-a-half, when it reaches and crosses a small stream, the Nam Lwi Hsa, flowing south by south-east, and on the opposite bank of this stream there is a good but small camping ground 150 yards by45 yards. Just after passing this open space in a north-westerly direction the road divides into two paths at an acute angle. The right-hand path is the one to Man Hôk. It rises immediately over a saddle, the rise being 750 feet in ¾ mile, and from this point the village of Man Hôk can be seen lying in a north-westerly direction across the valley. The road winds the hill side, with open ground to the left and about 1 mile further on, descends rapidly into a sharply cut valley below the village, where it crosses a small insignificant stream called the Nam Ki flowing south-west. Rising over a very low-wooded spur, it crosses another very small stream flowing in the same direction and at once rises 200 feet up to the village of Man Hôk, which has recently been burnt, but consisted of 40 houses. Above the village to the left and overlooking the road stands a brick-walled kyaung with walls 3 feet 6 inches and covering 26 yards square. From this point the road turns in a more northerly direction and is 10 feet broad and very good, being cut out of the side of the hill through open grass land with a deep valley on the left. Quarter mile past Man Hôk, the road divides: that to the right leads to Möng Yáng, the other to Möng Loi. A mile after leaving Nam Hôk it falls about 350 feet and falling slightly for another 2 miles rises again over a wooded spur, and ½ mile further on runs down into the cultivated valley of Man Pön, which stands on the opposite side of the valley, and about 200 yards above the stream which flows down the centre of the valley. There is a good camping ground just to the right of the road, half-way across the valley, on a strip of rising ground. There is no ground for a camp at Man Hôk. Man Pön is a small hamlet consisting of about 20 houses. The total ascents on the march are nearly 3,500 feet, while the descent is 4,000 feet.
			M. F.	M. F.	
		9. Möng Yáng (Man Yáng Lan). Nam Yáng.	**9 4**	97 4	Crossing the valley and passing close under Man Pön the road runs on in a north-westerly direction for 2 miles over a succession of very low-wooded broken hills, when it passes through an open space for about 200 yards long by 80 yards broad, a good camping ground. It drops gradually for another 150 yards into a small open cultivated valley, about a mile long and 400 yards broad, crossing a stream 150 yards beyond the stream. On the edge of the jungle stands the small village of Kum Phi, consisting of 16 houses surrounded by bamboo and jungle. About 600 yards up the valley to the right is the village of Naung Laung, 80 houses, each village with a small masonry monastery, surrounded by a low brick wall. Passing close to the left on Kum Phi the road is broader

From KYENG HUNG (KENG HUNG, KYAINGYUNGYI) to MÖNGMA (MÖNG LEM) *viâ* TA LAW FERRY—*continued.*

Authorities.		Number and Names of Stages, Rivers and Streams.	Distances.		Remarks.
Military.	Civil.		Inter-mediate.	Total.	
G.O.C. Mandalay District.	Superintendent, Northern Shan States.	**9. Möng Yáng (Man Yáng Lan)** *—cont.*			and level for about a mile. It turns due west about 300 yards after passing the village, and by a very gradual descent enters a long open valley with sugar-cane breaks along both sides. This valley, along which the road runs, is 3½ miles long and about 300 miles broad. It is marshy ground, but quite level. The hills on either side are low and covered with thin jungle. At the end of this valley the road turns off in a north-west direction and by a gradual descent of 140 feet runs past a small village called Pa Phun (10 houses) into a long valley about 2 miles in length and 900 yards broad opposite the village. About 200 yards from the village it crosses the branch of the stream called Nam Yáng, which divides at Mong Yáng, about 1,400 yards to right of Pa Phun, and hidden from view by a wooded point jutting out into the valley. About 200 yards beyond the ford under a tope of large trees, on slightly elevated ground, there is a site for a small camp about 120 yards square. The water of the Nam Yáng is sluggish, but appeared to be good. Crossing the valley in a north direction the path runs over a bad bit of swampy ground, about 25 feet broad in all, which could very easily be improved with brushwood and leads close up to the left bank of the main stream flowing west. Turning with the stream it runs along through a few fields for about 5[illegible]0 yards, when it turns to the left turning the stream by a substantial foot-bridge with a roadway of 8 feet and 40 feet long, sufficiently strong to bear loaded pack animals and enters the village of Möng Yáng or Yáng Lau. There is a good camping ground just beyond the village to the right of the road on an open gradual slope. On the opposite side of the village stands the village of Naung Kam. Möng Yáng is the principal village in the circle and is the head-quarters of a "Paya," which corresponds to a Burman Myoza, who lives there. The place consists of about 80 houses.
		10. Möng Noi ... Nam Lwi and Nam Ho Na.	M. F. 12 0	M. F. 109 4	Running along the valley north-north-west for ½ a mile the road passes just below the village of Ma Kao Khom, of 20 houses, and 1 mile further on Pong Hik and running below the village turns north-north-west and enters the jungle. Half-a-mile further the road again enters the valley, turning west-north-west. For 1,000 yards to the hills it is open ground. In the centre of the valley, 300 yards to the right of the road, is a small village of Möng Lwi, standing on the left bank of the Nam Lwi, flowing south, 40 yards broad (water line), 2 feet deep; rapid, clear water; pebbly bottom; steep banks 15 feet high, both open; distance from bank to bank 50 yards, the ford is commanded from both sides. From right to front at 1,000 yards range is a bare rocky hill, 600 feet high. To the left front are low-wooded hills with precipitous sites composed of white rock. Range 800 yards. There is a good artillery position ¾ mile behind on a small hill 600 feet high. The ferry is ½ a mile above the ford directly under first-mentioned hill, where there is one boat. Half-a-mile above the ferry the river flows down between thickly-wooded low hills is a narrow gorge; 300 yards beyond the edge the road rises 150 feet by a rocky path on a small plateau and descends gradually into a narrow ravine. There are rocky

FROM KYENG HUNG (KENG HUNG, KYAINGYUNGYI) TO MÖNGMA (MÖNG LEM) *viâ* TA LAW FERRY—*continued.*

Authorities. Military.	Authorities. Civil.	Number and Names of Stages, Rivers and Streams.	Distances. Intermediate.	Distances. Total.	Remarks.
G.O.C. Mandalay District.	Superintendent, Northern Shan States.	**10. Möng Noi**—*cont.*			hills on the right, the slopes of which are very steep for a distance of 600 yards. This small valley is closed on the left and in front by two huge jungle-covered masses of perpendicular rock, both about 700 feet high. The road passes along the right of the valley and rises over a neck joining the precipitous rock closing the west ends of the valley and the long rocky hill on the right. This position for covering the ford is an exceedingly strong one, the height being assailable. The road rises over the neck about 200 feet and runs level along the right side of a narrow ravine, the slopes of which are steep and covered with thin jungle. Six hundred yards further the road gradually drops into a narrow valley about $\frac{1}{2}$ mile broad; 300 yards to the right there is a perpendicular cliff of rock 600 feet high. The hills on the left are low and wooded slopes, accessible. The Nam Lwi flows along through this ravine north-west and is very deep and sluggish, 30 yards broad. There are several large caves in the rock on the right, where saltpetre is found in considerable quantities. For $\frac{1}{2}$ mile the road runs along the right bank of the Nam Lwi. The river then turns to the left, flowing south-west and the road goes on west-north-west a $\frac{1}{4}$ of a mile further on. On the slope of the right stands the small village of a Man Nam Mo, 10 houses, with a stream of clear water, 14 feet broad, 16 feet deep, flowing south-east between low banks. The ground opposite the village is cultivated and open for about 400 yards $\frac{1}{2}$ a mile beyond the village on the right of the valley which is here only 300 yards broad. There is a camping ground on a gentle slope with stream flowing at the foot of it. It is sufficiently large to hold one regiment with the transport. The village of Ho Na, surrounded by low-wooded hills on the right, is just beyond the camping ground, 15 houses. The road turns to the right just before entering the village and runs along another narrow ravine. Just below is a brick-walled kyaung standing on a small knoll at the northern end of the village. It is commanded by a hill on the right of the road, range 300 yards. Running round the small spur on which the kyaung stands the road drops again 50 feet and crosses the Nam Ho Na stream (flowing west between low banks, both open, rocky bottom, easy crossing). It then rises about 150 feet, running round a low bare hill and keeping over the stream gradually descends into a narrow ravine, close by a succession of low-rounded hills, with scrub jungle. The road runs along the bottom of the ravine for about 1 mile, when it again crosses the stream and runs along the left bank for 200 yards, rising gradually for another mile and-a-half, the total rise being about 300 feet. It then turns slightly to the right, passing just below the village of Man Hwé Mi (18 houses), with a few small paddy-fields lying below it and crosses the stream. The road runs on in a north-westerly direction along a narrow winding defile, almost following the bed of the stream, which it crosses no less than fourteen times in the next $3\frac{1}{2}$ miles. These fords are all easy, the banks being everywhere low and the bottom firm gravel and pebbles, and at the third, sixth, and eighth crossings rocky. Half-a-mile after the last crossing, the road runs into a small open cultivated valley, half-way up which is the village of Mŏng Noi (20 houses). There is ample ground for camping anywhere on the side of this valley and a stream of good water flows down the centre of it.

No. 9.

FROM KYENG HUNG (KENG HUNG, KYAINGYUNGYI) TO MÖNGMA (MÖNG LEM) *vid* TA LAW FERRY—*continued.*

Authorities.		Number and Names of Stages, Rivers and Streams.	Distances.		Remarks.
Military.	Civil.		Inter-mediate.	Total.	
			M. F.	M. F.	
G.O.C. Mandalay District.	Superintendent, Northern Shan States.	**11. Tong Khek (3,800 feet).** Nam Ku.	**13 0**	122 4	The road runs up the right of the valley for ½ a mile, when it commences a long ascent through thick jungle. The ascent for the 1st mile is 350 feet. It then runs nearly level for about 600 yards round two spurs and again rises 150 feet in the next 800 yards running nearly level again round the sides of two more spurs, thickly wooded and covered with pine trees. In the next mile and-a-half it again rises 250 feet and crossing a small sharply defined ravine rises 150 feet in another 600 yards when it descends 600 feet by a very steep gradient into a narrow cultivated valley and crosses a stream called Nam Ku, 20 feet broad, 18 inches deep; good water; low, open banks, gravel bottom, flowing south-west. It then rises over a small neck on the other side of which and 400 yards from the fort stands the village of Tôn Nin, 20 houses, elevation 3,850 feet, the stream running below it with fields beyond. The road passes close to the right of the village, and 100 yards further on again crosses the stream, the opposite bank of which is about 25 feet high and wooded and, crossing the fields, runs along the right of a narrow valley, rises 200 feet immediately above the stream, and leaving it on the left runs along under low hills for a mile through pine trees. Troops could camp here in several places near the stream. For the next 6 miles the road runs along a narrow ravine, following the Nam Ku, which it crosses frequently. The crossings are all easy for men and transport and the road is tolerably good, but runs through thick jungle the whole of this distance, till it enters an open valley, surrounded by high-wooded hills. At the northern end of the valley stands the small village of Tong Khek. There is a good camping ground about 500 yards east of the village and just off the main road on the right, with a stream of good water flowing immediately below it.
		12. Möng Ma (3,100 feet). Nam Ku, Nam Ma, and several small streams.	**16 0**	138 4	Road runs along the valley for 2 miles crossing the stream four times: it then rises over a low hill at the northern end of the valley, the rise in the first 800 yards is 420 feet. It is then level for another 150 yards, when it again rises 200 feet in ¼ of a mile and then gradually descends 250 feet in about 500 yards into a deep ravine. The Nam Ku flows along the bottom turning south-west. Passing close to the west of the stream the road rises immediately by a steep gradient of 420 feet on to a sharp ridge. It crosses a very steep ravine falling and rising about 100 feet and then runs level along the side of the hill for 150 yards and again drops into a small valley. The high hills on the left of the valley, the crest-line of which is about 1½ miles distant, are bare; crossing three muddy spots in this valley, the road winds up the opposite side by a steep gradient to a low neck rising 150 feet. Falling the other side about 80 feet and crossing a sharp ravine it ascends a steep slope for 600 yards on to a saddle, the elevation of which is 5,000 feet. It then descends gradually on to an

FROM KYENG HUNG (KENG HUNG, KYAINGYUNGYI) TO MÖNGMA (MÖNG LEM) *viâ* TA LAW FERRY—*continued.*

Authorities.		Number and Names of Stages, Rivers and Streams.	Distances.		Remarks.
Military.	Civil.		Inter-mediate.	Total.	
G.O.C. Mandalay District."	Superintendent, Northern Shan States.	**12. Möng Ma (3,100 feet)**—*cont.*			open valley about ¾ of a mile broad. The high steep hills on the left are bare except along the crest-line. It then crosses a small stream flowing down the centre of the valley in a south-westerly direction. This apparently forms the parting of the watershed between the Cambodia and the Salween. The road then runs along the right of the valley, passing over a cluster of low-wooded hills into another narrow valley. It is across the foot of this valley that the boundary line between the Kyeng Tung and Möng Lem runs. The small Mu Hsö village of La Phuk stands on the left side of the valley over a considerable stretch of paddy-fields, ½ a mile broad. The village consists of about 20 huts. Leaving the village the road enters low thick jungle, keeping along the left of the valley, and ¾ of a mile further on it passes the village of Pu Seng, standing on a bare-wooded slope, 600 yards to the left, consisting of 30 huts. Gradually descending into the open valley and crossing a stream 100 yards further on (20 feet broad, 2 feet 6 inches deep; very muddy bottom; bridged by a substantial foot-bridge), it again crosses the same stream with a muddy bottom, but here only 6 feet wide. It then runs along an open undulating plain for nearly a mile. The whole of this ground would form an excellent site for a camp. The valley is well watered, is open and the elevation approximately 4,800 feet, with a good road running through the centre of it. At the head of the valley the road crosses a small stream, 1 foot deep, 4 feet broad; firm gravel bottom, and then rises 180 feet gradually in ¾ of a mile round a wooded spur. It then crosses narrow-wooded ravine and descending up the opposite slope passes over a low-wooded neck between two conical hills. From this point the road drops by an easy gradient about 200 feet and then running along level for about ½ a mile rapidly descends for another ½ a mile to a stream flowing along the bottom of the valley in a westerly direction. The total descent in the last mile and-a-half is 900 feet. Rising 50 feet over a low-wooded spur, the road gradually descends into a narrow valley, terraced with paddy-fields, and crosses the stream here 15 feet wide, 1 foot deep, low banks, 80 feet lower than the above-mentioned spur, rising again gradually along the slopes on the right of the valley, when it crosses the stream and dropping down into another similar valley runs along the right bank of the stream for a distance of 400 yards where it is broken and rocky. It then rises over another low open spur and runs level for 500 yards through thin jungle. It then gradually passes along to the right side of a deep narrow gorge, through which the stream flows 200 feet below the road. Turning to the right it falls about 60 feet in 300 yards, crosses a very small ravine and rises 300 feet again over a long slope for a distance of 500 yards, then keeping fairly level for a mile, it descends through a thickly-wooded ravine on to another road and, turning due west, descends rapidly by a rocky path down a thickly-wooded ravine for a distance of 1,400 yards, the total descent being 500 feet when it crosses the Nam Ma flowing between low-wooded banks in a rocky bed, 16 yards broads, 18 inches deep, into the valley of Möng Ma. Keeping about 500 yards from the left bank of it the road runs through open fields for ¾ of a mile when it again crosses the Nam Ma and passes just below a slightly elevated piece of ground about 150 yards square, above the left bank. This forms an excellent camping ground.

No. 10.

From KYENGTUNG (KENG TUNG or KYAINGTÔN) to KYENGMAI (ZIMMÉ).

By W. J. ARCHER, Esq., British Vice-Consul, Zimmé, May 1888.

Authorities.		Number and Names of Stages, Rivers and Streams.	Distances.				Remarks.
Military.	Civil.		Intermediate.		Total.		
			M.	F.	M.	F.	
G.O.C. Rangoon District.	Superintendent, Southern Shan States.	**1. Müang Chém...**	**7**	**0**	7	0	See below.
		2. Ban Pon Luang (Müang Pak).	**15**	**0**	22	0	
		3. Pangtin Doi (Müang Pak).	**9**	**0**	31	0	
		4. Mé Hét ...	**14**	**0**	45	0	
		5. Sop Yum ...	**13**	**0**	58	0	
		6. Müang Hai (Tai).	**17**	**0**	75	0	
		7. Pang Sut ...	**16**	**0**	91	0	
	Siam.	**8. Mé Sai ...**	**14**	**0**	105	0	
		9. Mé Kham ...	**18**	**0**	123	0	
		10. Mé Katom ...	**12**	**0**	135	0	
		11. Chienghai (Kyenghai).	**12**	**0**	147	0	
		12. Huei San (or Hnei San).	**21**	**0**	168	0	
		13. Sala Mé Sui (or S. M. Sin).	**13**	**0**	181	0	
		14. Tha Ko ...	**18**	**0**	199	0	
		15. Ban Pa Rin...	**16**	**0**	215	0	
		16. Mé Phong ...	**20**	**0**	235	0	
		17. Mé Lai ...	**15**	**0**	250	0	
		18. Ban Müang Luang.	**10**	**0**	260	0	
		19. Chiengmai (Zimmé).	**12**	**0**	272	0	

Note.—These are the stages of the main route between Kyengtung and Kyengmai or Zimmé, but no details whatever are forthcoming.* Communication by water exists between Bangkok and Chiengmai, but is tedious owing to the strong current in the upper part of the river. Telegraphic communication also exists along this route. This is the line of communication in Siamese territory between the presidency and the most important northerly town in Siam.

From British Burma there are three routes to Chiengmai from Moulmein—

First.—By the Salween and Yunzalín rivers as far as Páphun, taking by boats about eight days from Páphun, over high hills to the Salween two days, with either bullocks or elephants. On crossing the Salween river the route lies almost east for two days to Mainglungyi town, and from there the route lies east-north-east for five or six days over high hills and mountains till reaching the Maipáng river and thence by the banks of this river to Chiengmai for three or four days.

Second.—From Moulmein by the Salween and Gain rivers two days to Kôkarit, from there almost east-north-east to Myawadı; thence crossing the Thaungyin river and entering Siamese territory due east to Raheng; thence the route lies for four days almost due north by the banks of the Maipáng river. All along this route is at present telegraphic communication.

Third.—From Moulmein by the Salween river for three or four days as far as Yinbin, from there north-east overland a short distance to the Thaungyin river, and having crossed this river the route lies almost due north to Mainglungyi and from Mainglungyi to Chiengmai as in No. 1 route. This route is good in the dry season, but in the wet season too many chaungs have to be crossed. Chiengmai or Zimmé is the most important town in the north of Siam, and from it there is a good military road for about eight or nine days to the frontier of Siam. Crossing the frontier this road remains the same for another six or seven days and

*** Since the above was written, a copy of Lieut. Younghusband's account of this route dated 1887, between Stages 1 and 11 inclusive, has been received and is included in Appendix III as Route No. I-A.—A.F.**

FROM KYENGTUNG (KENG TUNG OR KYAINGTÔN) TO KYENGMAI (ZIMMÉ)—*continued*.

Authorities. Military.	Authorities. Civil.	Number and Names of Stages, Rivers and Streams.	Distances. Intermediate.	Distances. Total.	Remarks.
Siam.					then by crossing some low hills you enter the town of Kyengtung. Kyengtung is the most extensive Shan district in the states, which on the north extends to Yunnan, west to the Salween river, south Siam, and east it extends for many miles across the Cambodia river or into Anam. Here they will have in the course of time the French as their neighbours. No. 2 route from Moulmein to Chiengmai and into Kyaingtôn is that of the railway to Yunnan proposed by Messrs. Hallett and Colquhoun. No. 1 route goes up the Yunzalín as far as Páphun, because the Salween river is unnavigable owing to rapids.

ALTERNATIVE I.

FROM KYENGTUNG (KENG TUNG OR KYAINGTÔN) TO KYENGMAI (ZIMMÉ).

BY W. J. ARCHER, ESQ., BRITISH VICE-CONSUL, ZIMMÉ, MAY AND JUNE 1888.

Military	Civil	Stages	M.	F.	M.	F.	Remarks
G.O.C. Rangoon District.	Superintendent, Southern Shan States.	**1. Pung Mao** ... No considerable stream. Mé Pung Mao stream.	21	0	...		Slightly undulating open fields as far as Müang Chém, then about 3 miles up the valley of the Mé Chém, then leaving the road to Müang Pak on the left, gradual ascent, but not very high or steep, and the road fairly good and not blocked. It goes along the side of the valley nearly all the way and there is good fodder. No good encampment before Pung Mao (3,200 feet), but water all the way.
		2. Tha Chio ... Streams.	15	0	36	0	Ascents and descents, then steep ascent to top (4,200 feet), descent of stream, steep ascent top (3,800 feet), steep descent along ridge, with no water, and down to Tha Chio and large stream with good encampment. Road rather bad and blocked (for elephants) in some places.
		3. Hnei Po ... Streams.	20	0	56	0	Short ascent and descent to encampment; stream; very steep and bad ascent, then better; top (3,450 feet) along ridge and steep descent to Hnei Po (2,800 feet) along valleys (road blocked); steep descent to 2,500 feet. Road latterly fairly good and level with occasional steep descents. A very fatiguing day's march.
		4. Mé Kong, Müang Phayák. Mé Kong (large shallow stream).	11	0	67	0	Along narrow valley, then Ban Phayák Noi, first village since Müang Chém; short ascent and descent, then level; large stream. Road open valley, undulating ground, along plain, close to the several poor villages of Müang Phayák; camp near Mé Kong market at Müang Phayák, but provisions not abundant.

FROM KYENGTUNG (KENG TUNG OR KYAINGTÔN) TO KYENGMAI (ZIMMÉ)—*continued.*

ALTERNATIVE I—*continued.*

Authorities. Military.	Authorities. Civil.	Number and Names of Stages, Rivers and Streams.	Distances. Intermediate. M.	F.	Distances. Total. M.	F.	Remarks.
G.O.C. Rangoon District.	Superintendent, Southern Shan States.	**5. Pangkhaluang.** Stream.	**15**	**0**	82	0	After crossing a range several hundred feet high, with gradual ascent and descent, came to the Nam Lin (1,150 feet), a river flowing between narrow banks. Hence the road goes along its left bank all the way to Müang Lin, either close to the river or up and down the steep sides. Path shady and rather good; several small encampments.
		6. Müang Lin ...	**17**	**0**	99	0	Along the valley of the Nam Lin (few encampments) close to Müang Lin, when we come out on to the plain studded with numerous villages and extensive rice fields: provisions rather abundant.
		7. Ban Pang Pahat (Müang Kho). Man Len (river).	**18**	**0**	117	0	A long stretch of level bamboo jungle and rice fields, then over a low range and down to the plain of Hnapông. Bamboo rather thick, but road fairly good. Good camps.
Siam.		**8. Ban Tham** ... Mé Hnok (river), Mé Khao (stream), Mé Sai (large stream), Mé Chong (stream).	**19**	**0**	136	0	Villages and rice fields all the way to Honglük, a large village, then forest; cross Mé Khao and Mé Sai, the latter a little below the Siamese fort (frontier). A mile further on we come out on the main road from Chiengtung to Chiengmai, then good road all the way to Ban Than; road level.
		9. Mé Chan ...	**15**	**0**	151	0	No details recorded.
		10. Chienghai ...	**18**	**0**	169	0	
		11. Hnei San (or Huei Sán).	**21**	**0**	190	0	
		12. Sala Mé Sin (or Sui).	**13**	**0**	203	0	
		13. Near Mé Lao	**21**	**0**	224	0	
		14. Mé Chedé ...	**19**	**0**	243	0	
		15. Mé Küang west, foot of pass.	**18**	**0**	261	0	
		16. Ban Müang Lüang.	**21**	**0**	282	0	
		17. Chiengmai (Zimmé).	**12**	**0**	294	0	

No. 11.

From KYENG TUNG to MÔNÉ (MÖNGNAI) viâ MÖNG SÁT and MÖNG PU.

By Capt. F. G. PINK, "The Queen's," 1890.

Authorities. Military.	Authorities. Civil.	Number and Names of Stages, Rivers and Streams.	Distances. Intermediate. M. F.	Distances. Total. M. F.	Remarks.
G.O.C. Rangoon District.	Superintendent, Southern Shan States.	**1. Möng Kwon** ... Nam Kwon.	7 4	7 4	Leaving Kyeng Tung by the southernmost of the east gates, the cart road goes almost due south over undulating grass country dotted with villages. At 3 miles crosses a small stream. At 4 miles a hot sulphur spring; here track leaves road and turns south-west over low range of hills. Two steep but short ascents of 300 and 450 feet respectively. Track descends into large paddy plain, crosses Nam Kwon river, and reaches the village of Möng Kwon, river from bank to bank 40 feet, water 20 feet by 1 foot deep, good bottom, village 20 houses: paddy, rice, fowls and pigs, also cattle. Height 3,275 feet above sea. Ample camping ground.
		2. Camp on Nam Na Mok. Nam Na Mok.	5 0	12 4	Track proceeds for 1 mile almost due south, crossing three small streams, then turns south-west up a long spur ascent, constant though fairly easy for 3½ miles when top of range is reached (5,400 feet). Then short and rather steep descent of ½ mile to Nam Na Mok stream 15 feet broad, 1 foot water, rapid good bottom. Ample camping ground on right bank. All hills are covered with fine trees, and little undergrowth. Height of camp 5,050 feet.
		3. Camp on Nam Ing. Nam Won, Nam Lu, and Nam Ing.	11 6	24 2	General direction south-west by south. Ascent begins almost at once on leaving camp and lasts for 5 miles when 7,025 feet is reached. Steep only near the summit. Soil soft and could be easily worked. Fine timber on upper slopes and pines on the lower ones. Descent generally easy and continues till the Nam Won stream is crossed, 11 miles within a few hundred yards the Nam Lu and Nam Ing rivers join and together flow towards the Nam Sim. Camped on the Nam Ing. This stream as also the Nam Lu has about 15 feet of water by 1 foot deep; shows signs of heavy flood; bottom good; best camping ground is on the Nam Won stream; ample space and good grazing. Height of Nam Ing 3,775 feet.
		4. Camp Na Niu. Small streams.	9 4	33 6	Track turns south and makes sharp ascent immediately on leaving Nam Ing and two or three similar ones later on, but as a whole it is flat and good going over pine clad ridges. Pass two good-sized tanks of water at 7½ miles; ford the southernmost; fairly hard bottom. Na Niu Camp is watered by two small streams meeting at the foot of the spur down which the track goes; each about 3 to 4 feet broad and 6 inches water. Most of surrounding ground marsh, but enough dry to encamp 400 men; excellent grazing. Height of camp 3,525 feet.

FROM KYENG TUNG TO MÔNÉ (MÖNGNAI) *viâ* MÖNG SÁT AND MÖNG PU—*continued.*

Authorities.		Number and Names of Stages, Rivers and Streams.	Distances.				Remarks.
Military.	Civil.		Intermediate.		Total.		
			M.	F.	M.	F.	
G.O.C. Rangoon District.	Superintendent, Southern Shan States.	**5. Camp on Nam Kok.** Nam Kok.	7	0	40	6	Track continues south along a stream bed and for 1st mile is swampy and bad going, then circling south-east, makes a succession of rather steep ascents till highest point 4,300 feet is reached. At 3¾ miles the last ½ mile of descent is steep. Camp on Nam Kok river about 20 yards from bank to bank (half dry), 1 foot to 1½ feet water, swift good bottom subject to flood; shut in by steep hills on both sides. There are two ruined zayáts and ground to encamp 100 men. Ample room could be made by clearing small underwood. Height of camp 3,025 feet.
		6. Möng Kok ... Nam Na Wong, Nam Kok, Nam Ho Kut, Mé Tung, and Nam Kung Noi.	10	0	50	6	First ½ mile stiff climb of 600 feet and an equal amount of ascent (after a short descent) in the next mile, onwards track is excellent following along tops of ridges. At 5 miles is a small village. At 7½ miles begin descent into Möng Kok paddy plain. At foot of hills cross the Nam Na Wong stream 15 yards broad, 1 foot water, good bottom. Passing through a small village, track makes a slight ascent and passes between two hillocks and then crosses the Nam Kok river here 30 yards broad and 2 feet deep, rocky bottom; immediately afterwards it crosses the Nam-Ho-Kut river 30 feet broad, 1 foot water; following this stream up it crosses the Mé Tung and Nam Kung Noi streams, each 15 feet broad by 1 foot deep, camp on latter. These rivers and streams water a considerable paddy plains; there are several villages. Inhabitants chiefly Shans, but there are some Kaw villages also. Supplies of paddy, fowls, &c., plentiful. Height of camp 2,800 feet.
		7. Na Mak ... Nam Kung Noi, Nam Tin To, Nam Kok, and Nam Na Mak.	9	6	60	4	For 1st mile and quarter track follows the Nam Kung Noi stream due west, then turning south ascends a steep spur. After short descent ascends the Loi Hsáng hill, very steep in places and difficult, 4,450 feet, first part of descent easy, but it becomes very steep just before the Nam Tin To stream is reached (2,500 feet); here is a small camping ground and ruined zayát. This stream is the boundary between Kyeng Tung and Möng Sát, leaving this stream ascent is very steep through dense bamboo and grass jungle till 3,250 feet is reached, then fairly easy descent, steep towards face, and track enters paddy cultivation, watered by Nam Kok river and Nam Na Mak stream. Cross stream and encamp near Na Mak village 10 houses, fowls, paddy, &c.
		8. Páng Hatsai ... Nam Kok, Nam Pung, Nam Pa Ing, and Nám Hsapu.	8	0	68	4	Track turning little south of west follows the right bank Nam Kok river: here 30 yards broad and unfordable; road mostly level or slightly undulating, but here and there short sharp ascents and descents caused by crossing streams and rivulets. At 1¾ miles a very hot stream is crossed (too hot to keep one's hand in it) called the Nam Pung. There is no trace of sulphur in it. At 4½ miles cross the Nam-Pa-Ing 25 feet broad, 1 foot water; good bottom, and at 6 miles the Nam Hsapu stream, path in places very narrow along hill sides and through strips of

FROM KYENG TUNG TO MÔNÉ (MÖNGNAI) *viâ* MÖNG SÁT AND MÖNG PU—*continued.*

Authorities.		Number and Names of Stages, Rivers and Streams.	Distances.		Remarks.
Military.	Civil.		Intermediate.	Total.	
G.O.C. Rangoon District.	Superintendent, Southern Shan States.	**8. Páng Hátsai**—*cont.*			dense jungle. Camp in bamboo jungle: some miles of which is called by the one name Páng Hátsai, water from Nam Kok river.
			M. F.	M. F.	
		9. Möng Sát ... Nam Kok, Mé Nga Kham, and Mé Mok.	8 4	77 0	On leaving camp cross a fair-sized rivulet three times and then continue along bank of Nam Kok river for 3 miles, then ascend a hill 350 feet, rather steep; descent easy: and again meet Nam Kok and turning west for a short distance leave river and go a level marshy gorge and over undulating ground. At 6¼ miles cross Mé Nga Kham stream 20 feet broad, steep banks 1 foot water, pass through village of Náhsán and then cross the Mé Mok stream. The country onwards is a large level plain, for the most part wooded, crossing a rivulet path enters the old defensive wall of Möng Sát enclosing about a square mile. There are only about 60 houses and supplies, except paddy, are very limited. Camp on paddy-field south of town on Mé Kok. Height of camp 2,150 feet.
		10. Páng Ngá Khan (2,500 feet). Mé Nga Kham and Mé Long.	9 0	86 0	General direction north-west by north. For first 2¼ miles back over last stage as far as Náhsán, where the Kyeng Tung road branches off to the east. At 3 miles pass through village of Hôna (12 houses). The track here is very narrow and passes through dense scrub jungle for nearly 2 miles and then enters bamboo forest. The ground becomes slightly undulating between low hills and the track cuts into and follows up the Mé Nga Kham stream. At 8¾ miles this stream is joined by the Mé Long on which is camp ground and a zayát (= 20 men). At the back of this zayát there is a fair grazing and suitable ground for 400 men.
		11. Pang-Taw-Maw (2,700 feet). Mé Na Noi and Mé Nam Lông.	10 2	96 2	General direction north-west by north. On leaving camp track ascends a long spur. Generally easy but steep for short bits, then running almost level for long stretches, good going. At 5 miles the top of Loi Mé Na Noi hill is reached (4,275 feet), steep towards summit. Descent abrupt and in parts steep. At 7 miles the Mé Na Noi stream is reached. Here there is a camping place. Water ample for any force; 100 men could encamp without clearing. Crosses stream twice and makes steep ascent over a bare hill; descent steep and bad going; small stream at bottom. Then short steep ascent and follows the undulations of a ridge. Final descent to Mé Nam Lông is rather steep; ample camping ground on both banks. River about 20 feet broad, 1 to 1½ feet water, good bottom; subject to flood. Bamboo forage plentiful. This is a hard march for transport.
		12. Htam Lông (2,120 feet). Mé Nam Lông.	7 0	103 2	Track follows course of Mé Nam Lông a little north of west. At 2½ miles pass village of Wan-Nating. At 3 miles enter a very narrow gorge, precipitous rocks on both sides, very bad for baggage animals. At 4½ miles gorge opens out. At 4¾ miles pass

FROM KYENG TUNG TO MÔNÉ (MÖNGNAI) *viâ* MÖNG SÁT AND MÖNG PU—*continued.*

Authorities. Military.	Authorities. Civil.	Number and Names of Stages, Rivers and Streams.	Distances. Intermediate. M. F.	Distances. Total. M. F.	Remarks.
G.O.C. Rangoon District.	Superintendent, Southern Shan States.	**12. Htam Lông (2,120 feet)**—*cont.*			village of Wan Kyulôn. At 6 miles village of Htam Lông; camped a mile further down stream in bamboo jungle. During this march track crosses river twenty-four times, and there are several short but steep ascents and descents. All the villages *en route* are small, but keep fowls and pigs.
		13. Wan Noi, 1,850 feet (ford on Nam Sim). Mé Nam Lông, Nam Na Ken, and Nam Sim.	**9 2**	112 4	Track still follows river Mé Nam Lông westward through a gorge. At 4 miles the Nam Na Ken flows in from the south, and the track crossing it ascends to 3,100 feet (from 2,050 feet). Descent in places very steep and difficult. At 7 miles pass south village of Páng Mát, which is on the Nam Sim river. On the opposite bank is village of Wan Káng. There are two or three "dug-outs" track turns north up left bank and makes steep ascent of 400 feet over a spur and descends into and crosses the Mé Nam Lông at its junction with the Nam Sim and almost opposite the Nam Lông comes in from west. A little further on is the ford. Over 200 yards long and requires careful marking, near the right bank it is up to a man's middle. Camping ground small and uneven near village of Wan Noi. The Nam Sim is about 150 yards in breadth and current swift.
		14. Páng Ná Möng (3,275 feet). Small stream.	**6 0**	118 4	Track continues west and first 5 miles a continual ascent till 3,450 feet is reached, then a descent and second rise to 3,750 feet. All through pine forest; descent is steep into the marshy valley through which the Na Möng rivulet runs. Ample camping ground, but uneven.
		15. Möng Noi (1,780 feet). Nam Pu.	**8 0**	126 4	General direction little north of west. First 3 miles steady ascent till 4,450 feet is reached, all through pine forest. Then rapid and steep descent of 1,150 feet. Track becomes very narrow and winds along steep hill sides and along ridges, but is fairly level. At 6½ miles there is another very steep descent to the Nam Pu river, here a mere stream, camp in open ground near small village of Möng Noi.
		16. Möng Pu (1,500 feet). Nam Nu, Nam Noi Su, Nam Hsup Hsaikao, and Nam Tin.	**11 0**	137 4	Track following river Nam Pu goes almost north-west. In first 7¼ miles perpetually crosses the river which at 1 mile is joined by the Nam Noi Su from the north and at 5¼ miles by the Nam Hsup Hsaikao or from the south. At this place the water is from 1 foot to 2 feet deep, the current is very swift and large boulders greatly impede baggage animals. The track above the river bed is not practicable: there being only small foot holes in slippery rock, onwards the hills open out and the track is level and good, and only crossing the river twice more, debouches on to a level plain covered with open jungle which further on opens into paddy plain, 2 miles broad with villages dotted over it and along the bottom of the spurs. Möng Pu is the capital of the State of that name. There are but some 30 houses in the village itself, but the plain is well populated, and the people appear rich and well-to-do. Cattle, pigs, fowls and rice can be procured. The last named in large quantities. A small stream, the Nam Tin, flows along the south side of the village and joins the Nam Pu. There are nine villages in the plain.

FROM KYENG TUNG TO MONÉ (MÖNGNAI) *viâ* MÖNG SÁT AND MÖNG PU—*continued.*

Authorities. Military.	Authorities. Civil.	Number and Names of Stages, Rivers and Streams.	Distances. Intermediate. M. F.	Distances. Total. M. F.	Remarks.
G.O.C. Rangoon District.	Superintendent, Southern Shan States.	**17. Náng Kwun**... Nam Tin and Nam Náng Kwun.	**14 0**	151 4	Track follows up the Nam Tin stream due west for the first 2 miles and crosses it several times, easy going; then steep ascent south-west by west up a spur and along a ridge till the 7th mile when 4,250 feet is reached, then 2 miles of easy descent and again ascent of about 500 feet in next 2 miles, onwards track is fairly easy. At 13¾ miles the Nam Náng Kwun is crossed about 10 feet broad and 1 foot water, good bottom. Camp at 14 miles in paddy-fields on a rivulet. There are 2 bullock camping grounds at 10 and 11½ miles, respectively, but the water in the stream bed had dried up, the cleared ground too was very limited. This is a trying march for transport.
		18. Káng Kham... Salween.	**11 6**	163 2	Pass through Náng Kwun village, about a dozen houses, and crossing some old cultivation, make a slight ascent (200 feet) and steep descent of nearly a thousand feet to a small stream, where bullocks encamp (3¼ miles), next 2 miles almost level and good going, then easy ascent of about 150 feet over bare hills and again level till at 6½ miles and ascent to the top of a ridge (about 2,200 feet), circling round the western face of which track turns south and rises to 2,525 feet onwards to the Ta Pyen (Ta-U-Pyen) ferry over the Salween. The descent is constant and the latter part very steep and rocky, the Salween is about 250 yards broad and very swift. The approach to the ferry from the east is steep. There are no boats kept at the ferry. They have to be collected from villages up and down stream. Eight were collected, three of which came from the village of Tálong about 5 miles distant. Four boats were made into two rafts. Each carrying four ponies (or mules) or 15 men. A return trip, including putting animals on board, occupied on an average 12 minutes. The ferry is about 400 yards broad. This road from Möng Pu was a much frequented route, but owing to feuds has been closed for over three years and has fallen into bad order.
		19. Tôn Hông ... Nam Môt.	**13 0**	176 2	From the Salween into Mônê Post the general direction south-west by west is maintained throughout. On leaving the ferry there is a steep sharp rise of 900 feet. The track then turns south for 1¾ miles, and passes through the village of Kang Kham about 20 houses situated on a plateau of about 1 square mile in extent. Camping ground ample on paddy-fields; water from spring and rivulet south of village. There is no camping ground on the right bank of the Salween, and any force coming from the east should encamp here after crossing the ferry. In 1st mile rise 1,000 feet, then easy but somewhat rocky, descent of about 300 feet; the track then crosses a small stream, and winds about between low hills in places, crossing patches of old paddy cultivation spanned by mostly decayed bridges, but ground at this season is dry (April). After about 3 miles the track becomes almost level all the way. At 8 miles cross the Nam Môt stream well bridged, about 15 feet broad, steep banks and rapid, about 1½ feet water. At 10 miles pass village of Pôn Yun about 15 houses. This

FROM KYENG TUNG TO MÔNÉ (MÖNGNAI) *viâ* MÖNG SÂT AND MÖNG PU—*continued.*

Authorities.		Number and Names of Stages, Rivers and Streams.	Distances.				Remarks.
Military.	Civil.		Intermediate.		Total.		
			M.	F.	M.	F.	
G.O.C. Rangoon District.	Superintendent, Southern Shan States.	**19. Tôn Hông**—*cont.*					would make a good halting place, but water is very scarce from wells. Tôn Hông is a well-built village of about 30 houses, but several others are being built. It has a large kyaung with zayáts, which although in bad repairs could accommodate 200 men. It is on the Nam Môt stream and is surrounded by fine paddy ground, fowls and rice procurable.
		20. Camp at Nam Teng ferry. Nam Môt, Nam Tum and Nam Teng.	2	6	179	0	At ¾ mile track crosses the Nam Môt stream by a good bridge and then passes over paddy-fields. At 2 miles the Nam Tum stream is forded. About 20 feet broad rather steep banks, good bottom; about 10 inches of water and very rapid. At 2¾ miles reach the Nam Teng. Camping ground on both banks. The river is from 100 to 120 yards broad, current very slow, but unfordable for elephants. There are only two small "dug-outs," each capable of carrying eight men. A raft made on these takes three ponies or 16 men. Ponies and mules swim, but the landing place on the right bank is rather abrupt. The river is full of rocks. There is a zayát on either bank capable of accommodating 20 men each. The old ruined city of Kyaingtaung is about 1 mile distant on the left bank.
		21. Náng Môn ... Small stream.	17	2	196	2	Track passes over undulating wooded country, soil red clay. At this season there is no water and no halt can be made short of Náng Môn, a small village of four huts. Camping ground 500 yards to north of track in paddy-field on a small rivulet.
		22. Camp on Nam Pong. Nam Pong.	9	0	205	4	First 1½ miles steady, but easy rise to foot of hills which rise abruptly; ascent 550 feet steep and rocky. Track thus passes in between the higher hills making however several ascents till 4,450 feet is reached, several villages passed. At 8½ miles there is a well and spring, then sharp descent for a short distance and a easier one till the Nam Pong stream is reached at 8½ miles. This stream becomes dry a little further down, although there is 4 feet of water at the crossing. The ground on both banks is sloping, but it is the best place to break the march.
		23. Mônê Police Post. Stream.	7	0	212	4	Easy going the whole way over undulating country. At 4 miles track cuts into the Mônê-Ta Kaw Ferry route. At 6 miles crosses the Mônê stream (bridged) and ascend to police post. In the last 3 miles there are some swampy bits, mostly roughly bridged, but it would be bad going when the fields were under water.

No. 12.

From KYITHI BANSAM (KISI MANSÁM) to TA KAW FERRY viâ MÖNGNONG.

By Lieut. H. E. STANTON, Royal Artillery, 1888.

Authorities.		Number and Names of Stages, Rivers and Streams.	Distances.				Remarks.
Military.	Civil.		Intermediate.		Total.		
			M.	F.	M.	F.	
G.O.C. Rangoon District.	Superintendent, Southern Shan States.	**1. Camp on Nongkao stream.** Nam Nongkao.	11	0	11	0	General direction south-south-east. Good pack track over open rolling downs for 6½ miles; it then crosses a small dip cultivated with paddy and enters some low hills between the ranges of Loi Sötao (Lwé Sötao) on the north and Loi Löm (Lwé Lüm) on the south. At 3 miles cross the Bansám-Möngnong boundary near two trees. At 6½ miles a track leads off to the south-east through a grove of trees: this is an alternative road for the next 6 or 7 miles. It is about 1 mile longer than the direct road, but is shady and level, passing the big village Naungswun. Here is a good shady camping ground. Water and forage plentiful. The direct road leads up and down some low open round hills, passing the site of a strong entrenched position which commanded the entrance to the pass beyond. Pass a tank of water at 7 miles. The village of Wanpáng at 9½ miles and reach the banks of the Nam Nongkao (a good brook running south). At 11 miles good open camping ground on low hills (at present the bridge is broken and the best ford some 200 yards north of it is hard to find. February 1888). Grass is scarce. Bamboo leaves plentiful from neighbouring plantations. The track is over loam soil and easy going throughout. Except two tanks passed on leaving Bansám and a tank at 7 miles, there is no other water *en route* except a well 300 yards along the branch road at 6½ miles.
		2. Mantát or Mansát. Streams.	7	4	18	4	General direction east. Pack track. Start south. Road level and good for 1½ miles, then turning east pass through a short rough stony gorge and descend to Songplong kyaung (also called Mönghen kyaung). Water is good and plentiful in a stone well 200 yards south of the kyaung. For the next 2¼ miles the track leads over low hills passing through a gorge and by the site of a village. At 4¼ miles cross a small stream running into a valley lying east and west, continue along north side of the valley. At 5¾ miles pass a good open camping ground near the village of Köngniö. Cross over a low spur and ford the main stream of the valley at a good ford with steep ramps. Pack bridge is broken. Continue along the level valley. Pass the village of Mantát or Mansát at the mouth of the pass, under a peak of the same name. Camp ½ mile further on in the open, shelter from banyan trees and some large mangoes. Water from the stream. Bamboo forage plentiful. Village is residence of a Tamôn. Small eight-day bazaar. The road is good throughout, except at the two gorges, where for 100 yards or so it is rough and rocky.
		3. Möngnong (Maingnaung).	8	0	26	4	General direction south-west. Pack track. Continue 1 mile in an easterly direction passing the bazaar and then turn south-west diagonally across a tract of open rolling country between two ranges of hills. The road is nearly level and very good over loam soil the whole way. At 2 miles pass an old entrenched position commanding the road near two good tanks of fresh water.

From KYITHI BANSÁM (KISI MANSÁM) to TA KAW FERRY *viâ* MÖNGNONG—*continued.*

Authorities. Military.	Authorities. Civil.	Number and Names of Stages, Rivers and Streams.	Distances. Intermediate.	Distances. Total.	Remarks.
G.O.C. Rangoon District.	Superintendent, Southern Shan States.	**3. Möngnong (Maingnaung)** —*cont.*			At 4 and 5 miles respectively cross and recross a stream by two good fords. Water is 2 yards wide by 6 inches deep. At the second crossing there is a rickety foot-bridge and the ramps to the ford are deep and steep. At 7¾ miles cross a bridged stream some 200 yards from where it springs out of the rocks. It is 3 yards wide, 1 foot deep and rapid. Open camping ground near the stream. Shelter under a fine tope of three banyan trees. Bamboo forage plentiful. Möngnong is 1 mile further on and is well watered by two springs dammed up to form lakes; but the above mentioned is the best camping ground. The main route from Thibaw to Tákaw Ferry leaves the route followed by Lieut. Stanton (described below) and continues south to Mansein, 24 miles from Möngnong, on the road between Légya (Laika) and Tákaw, *see* Route No. 23, Branch II, Stage 5. The road is said to be easy and level, and bullock caravans do the 24 miles in two or three marches, and forage and water is always plentiful. In 1888 the whole country between Möngnong and Mansein was depopulated owing to raiding between the different states, but it will probably recover, as peace is established.
		4. Nongé ... ... Stream.	M. 11 F. 0	M. 37 F. 4	General direction south. Pack track. One mile from camp pass Möngnong, situated at the north end of a range of limestone hills running north and south. The road leads across the bund of each of the lakes (above mentioned) and through the bazaar on a knoll between them. It continues east round the shoulder of the range along a rough old paved road and at 2½ miles turns south down a strip of rolling country between two ranges of hills about 2 miles apart. At 4½ miles cross a stream 3 yards wide spanned by a single plank. There is a ford 50 yards to the east, about 1 foot deep with a little mud. At 6 miles pass the Mankun five-day bazaar; and crossing a stream past camping ground in an open piece of ground near Mankun on a bend of the stream. The ford is rather rocky and awkward for pack animals. Water and forage good and plentiful. From Mankun general direction south-east. Road, as before, good and level throughout. Starting south it passes between the two prominent peaks of Loi (Lwé) Nacháug and Loi (Lwé) Nongé, and turns east to the village of Nongé at the foot of the latter. Cross *en route* a deep dry nullah, to which traffic has worn steep ramps. Water from a stream 200 or 300 yards south. Shelter under banyan trees. Forage plentiful. *Note.*—The road for 4½ miles further on was reconnoitred. Its general direction is east-north-east through a gorge in the hills. It is level for 3½ miles, crossing the bed of a torrent with water in pools. It then descends some 300 feet down a rough rocky pass; crossing *en route* the Namkong-long, a right bank tributary of the Ben Chaung, in the valley below. It is a considerable body of water. A succession of falls and deep pools in a rocky limestone bed.
					From this point the account of the route is from Native information.
		5. Naungtaw ... Streams.	9 0	46 4	Pack track. Cross one slight ascent and descent, then over undulating country to top of steep and rocky

FROM KYITHI BANSÁM (KISI MANSÁM) TO TA KAW FERRY *viâ* MÖNGNONG—*continued.*

Authorities. Military.	Authorities. Civil.	Number and Names of Stages, Rivers and Streams.	Distances. Intermediate. M.	F.	Distances. Total. M.	F.	Remarks.
G.O.C. Rangoon District.	Superintendent, Southern Shan States.	**5. Naungtaw**—*cont.*					descent to stream, 3¼ miles from Nongé. Good ford over this stream and over another smaller stream passed at 2 miles. Beds of both rocky, with no mud and foot-bridges over second stream. Small zayát at Naungtaw village. Water and grass plentiful.
		6. Maingshaung (Maing Chaing). Nam Páng or Ben Chaung.	**5**	**0**	51	4	Pack track. Over undulating country to Nam Páng or Ben Chaung, on bank of which Maingshaung (or Maing Chaing) village is situated with ferry across river of two or three boats. Accommodation in two zayáts.
		7. Namyim ... Stream.	**10**	**0**	61	4	Cross Ben Chaung by ferry. Good road through jungle, fairly level. Cross two small streams which become muddy in the rains. Accommodation in one kyaung at Namyim village. Water from stream. Grass plentiful.
		8. Loitám ... ... Stream.	**7**	**0**	68	4	Road rough and stony and steep in places, ascending to village which is burned down. One kyaung standing. Water from stream. Forage scarce. A few bamboo clumps.
		9. Nongkamgyi ... Stream.	**11**	**0**	79	4	Level road all the way. Pass Wansáp village at 7 miles. Stream at Nongkamgyi bridged.
		10. Kali	**7**	**0**	86	4	Pack track. Level all the way. Water and grass good and plentiful. Kali is Stage 1 on Route No. 23, Branch II.
		11. Kenglom ...	**9**	**4**	96	0	*Vide* Route No. 23, Branch II, Stage 1.
		12. Ta Kaw ferry. Salween.	**15**	**0**	111	0	*Vide* Route No. 23, Alternative II, Stages 3 and 4.

No. 13.

From LÁSHIO to MANTÔN viâ MÖNGYIN and MÖNGTÁT.

BY CAPT. R. B. SHAWE, FEBRUARY 1890.

Military	Civil	Stage	Intermediate M.	F.	Total M.	F.	Remarks
G.O.C. Mandalay District.	Superintendent, Northern Shan States.	**1. Möngtôn** ... Nam Yaw river and several small streams.	**14**	**0**	14	0	Starting from Láshio bazaar the track, a broad fairly level one, runs in the direction of a large bazaar village called Inai, before reaching which, however, it bears to the right and runs by some hill cultivation to the river Nam Yaw, 7 miles. The ford is deep and not straight; bottom good, approaches difficult, unfordable during the rains. After fording the river some paddy-fields and small hamlet of Inailông (formerly the head village of the Inai circle) is passed, and the road, crossing a small rivulet,

FROM LÁSHIO TO MANTÔN *viâ* MÖNGYIN AND MÖNGTÁT—*continued.*

Authorities.		Number and Names of Stages, Rivers and Streams.	Distances.				Remarks.
Military.	Civil.		Intermediate.		Total.		
			M.	F.	M.	F.	
G.O.C. Mandalay District.	Superintendent, Northern Shan States.	**1. Möngtôn**—*cont.*					ascends some low-lying hills, along a spur of which it runs for some distance. Two fair-sized ravines are crossed, dry during dry season, and the road again winds over low hills to the village of Möngtôn. Large paddy-fields extend on the left of the road with a stream flowing through them. Good camping ground is found in these fields from the end of October to the end of May. Several small villages lie round the edges of the cultivated ground hidden by jungle. Paddy and a little rice only is procurable.
		2. Möngyin ... Namtu, Nami, and several small streams.	**14**	**0**	28	0	The road from Möngtôn to Möngyin is good, but for the first 7 or 8 miles hilly. There are no difficult bits, and the streams to cross are small. For the last 4 miles it runs through forest land. A deep drainage cut runs for some distance along the right-hand side of the track. The road would not require much work to be made practicable for country carts from Láshio to this. Möngyin is really a collection of large hamlets situated some little distance apart on both sides of the Namtu (Myitngé). There are two bazaars, one at a village on either bank. A very large extent of ground is under paddy cultivation. The Namtu is not fordable here, and the supply of dug-outs limited to three small ones. Animals have to swim over. Country products are plentiful here. In the dry season there is plenty of camping ground. In the wet it would be very difficult to accommodate any number of troops on this (south) side; but across the river, about a mile farther on, more elevated ground could be found. From here roads also lead east to Theinni, *see* Route No. 70, and north to Möngwi, *see* Route No. 14.
		3. Möngtát ... Namsa, Nampaw, Namta, Namyi, and Namtát.	**13**	**0**	41	0	General direction west. Road leads north for 1st mile; thence turns west along right bank of Namtu river, which it follows for ½ a mile; thence through paddy-fields to Hôna village. From there it leads through jungle over undulations, descending steeply to Namtu river; fords the Namyi river, leading through jungle to Náti village; thence fording the Namtát river to Möngtát village, 13 miles. Good road throughout, with exception of steep and rocky descent to Namtu river at 9½ miles. Swampy crossings at 8 miles, 200 yards, 8¼ miles, and 8¾ miles. Bridges: At ¾ mile wooden bridge; longitudinal planks, 10 feet long, 4 feet broad; passable. At 2¼ miles wooden bridge; longitudinal planks, 20 feet long, 4 feet broad; passable. At 3¾ miles wooden bridge; transverse planks, over Namsa stream; 50 feet long, 6 feet broad; passable. At 4¾ miles wooden bridge; longitudinal planks, 40 feet long, 4 feet broad; passable at present, but needs repair; timber obtainable close at hand. At 7 miles wooden bridge; longitudinal planks, 50 feet long, 3 feet broad; passable; but also needs repair by under-propping. At 12½ miles bamboo foot-bridge over the Namtát. Villages passed:— MILES. HOUSES. Nammawkum ... ... ⅛ 20 Manhai ... ... 1⅛ 20 Nalin 3 25

FROM LÁSHIO TO MANTÔN *viâ* MÖNGYIN AND MÖNGTÁT—*continued.*

Authorities.		Number and Names of Stages, Rivers and Streams.	Distances.		Remarks.
Military.	Civil.		Intermediate.	Total.	
G.O.C. Mandalay District.	Superintendent, Northern Shan States.	**3. Möngtát**—*cont.*			MILES. HOUSES. Hôna ... ... 4¼ 30 Pánghai ... ... 5¾ 20 Náti ... ... 12¼ 15 Möngtát ... ... 13 ... Möngtát is situated on the left bank of the Namtát river. Camping ground for a battalion or still larger force in paddy-field on east and west of village. Streams crossed: Namsa bridged at 3¾ miles; average breadth 25 feet, depth 2½ feet; high jungle banks; current 2 miles per hour. Nampaw bridged at 7 miles; breadth 30 feet, depth 3 feet; sandy bottom; low banks, covered with jungle; current 1½ miles per hour. Namta at 8 miles; breadth 20 feet, depth 2 feet; rocky bottom. Namyi at 11 miles; breadth 50 feet; depth 6 feet; pebble bottom; low banks with overhanging trees, the stream flowing between wooded hills; water clear and good; current 2½ miles per hour. Namtát at 12½ miles; breadth 30 feet, depth 2 feet; pebble bottom; sloping banks covered with bamboo jungle, with paddy-fields on Möngtát side; current 2½ miles per hour; water clear and good.
		4. Katlwi ... ... One large stream and two small streams.	M. F. 12 0	M. F. 53 0	Road runs nearly west from Möngtát along hill with river Namtát on left hand. About 3rd mile cross a large stream; the road now crosses hills and ravines and is very bad. Two streams are crossed, having rocky bottoms, the second about 9½ miles from Möngtát. The track now passes over a steep hill and through a straggling Kachin village of Katlwi, then down again into paddy-fields through which a brawling stream flows. Paddy procurable in small quantities. The road for Bawdwingyi, where there are said to be silver mines, branches here. Distance two easy marches. These mines are now worked for lead. Elevation 2,000 feet. The boundaries of Mômeik, Theinni, and Taungbaing meet in this camping ground. The Mômeik border is crossed immediately after leaving camp.
		5. Manpát ... Two streams.	8 0	61 0	Two roads lead from Katlwi to Manpát. With a little labour the lower could be rendered the easiest. The upper road leads by a steady ascent to Kachin village of Mankôp, then by a steep descent across a small stream up a very steep ascent and along spur to Manpát, a Palaung village with Kachin neighbours. The water here is not very abundant. Paddy is plentiful. Elevation 5,300 feet. The lower road is less used at present and goes by the villages of Pángsáng and Kyopán; the first quarter only is bad.
		6. Mantôn ... Three small streams, one large stream.	9 0	70 0	The road rapidly descends from Manpát, then crosses a stream through paddy-fields and marshy ground across another stream and again enters the hills. About the 5th mile a large stream is crossed; the road then ascends and runs along a wooded hill to Mantôn valley. One small Kachin village, Mantôngôn (small Mantôn), is passed on this road. Mantôn is on the opposite slope of the valley and the Namsim has to be forded. This valley has many paddy-fields, and many Kachin and Palaung villages dot its slopes. These

FROM LÁSHIO TO MANTÔN *viâ* MÖNGYIN AND MÖNGTÁT—*continued.*

Authorities. Military.	Authorities. Civil.	Number and Names of Stages, Rivers and Streams.	Distances. Inter-mediate.	Distances. Total.	Remarks.
G.O.C. Mandalay District.	Superintendent, Northern Shan States.	**6. Mantôn**—*cont.*			were the refuge for the Mintha,* and the Mômeik Sawbwa, their nominal ruler, has obtained no revenue from them for some time. Elevation 4,200 feet. Paddy abundant. Mantôn is almost due west of Möngtát. *Note.*—All streams mentioned above are liable to flood in the rains, when many of the larger ones are occasionally unfordable. They quickly subside when breaks in the rains occur. All the roads are bullock tracks and more or less broken and bad going.

No. 14.

From LÁSHIO to MÖNGWI viâ MÖNGYIN.

BY CAPT. R. B. SHAWE, BURMA MILITARY POLICE, FEBRUARY 1890.

Military	Civil	Stages, Rivers and Streams	Inter. M.	Inter. F.	Total M.	Total F.	Remarks
G.O.C. Mandalay District.	Superintendent, Northern Shan States.	**1. Möngtôn** ... Nam Yaw river and several small streams.	**14**	**0**	14	0	*See* Route No. 13, Stages 1 and 2.
		2. Möngyin ... The Namtu, Nami, and several small streams.	**14**	**0**	28	0	
		3. Pánghai ... Namtu ferry and two small streams.	**13**	**0**	41	0	After crossing the river, which it is advisable to do the day before if possible, the road bears to the left and passes through the bazaar for the villages situated on the right bank of the river; after this it leaves the paddy-fields, and the ascent of the range running along the right bank of the Namtu commences. This ascent is steep (1,800 feet), being surmounted in the first 5 miles. Two Kachin villages, of which Hsampu is the larger, are passed through. Pánghai is a Palaung village with much dry cultivation round it. A fair-sized mountain stream flows across the road just before the village is reached. It is advisable to camp in paddy-fields near the stream, the ground being so much cleaner than in or near the village. Paddy is the only commodity for sale.
		4. Namhu ... Several small streams.	**7**	**0**	48	0	The road to Namhu is very fair, and but for the bad bottoms of the small streams would be good. These rotten bottoms are very trying for baggage animals. Namhu is a small Shan hamlet of seven houses. No kyaung. Several other villages lie close round it hidden amongst the wooded hills. The stream here is a fine clear one in the dry season. Good camping ground can be

* One of the Chaungwa princes who has hitherto evaded capture and has been the cause from time to time of hostile gatherings in the Mômeik and South-east portion of the Bhamo District. —A. F. Jan. 1894.

FROM LÁSHIO TO MÖNGWI *viâ* MÖNGYIN—*continued.*

Authorities. Military.	Authorities. Civil.	Number and Names of Stages, Rivers and Streams.	Distances. Intermediate.	Distances. Total.	Remarks.
G.O.C. Mandalay District.	Superintendent, Northern Shan States.	**4. Namhu**—*cont.*			found all through the year, as the slopes on the right of the road admit of tents being pitched. Elevation 3,200 feet. The bazaar village of Hsaikhao is passed through on this march.
			M. F.	M. F.	
		5. Pángkutlông ... Namyi and two small streams.	**10 0**	58 0	At starting the road is hilly, especially after crossing the Namyi, when several very steep bits are met with. The hill sides are well wooded. About half-way a large village (Kôngpaw) is passed and the road bends to the right. It now runs over fairly level good ground to Pángkutlông (or Paungkutôn), a new Palaung village with open ground round it. Good camping ground can be found near the Nampun for a 100 or 150 men in paddy-fields. During wet weather the camp would have to be pitched nearer the village, which at a pinch could furnish shelter for 50 men. Paddy procurable. This place is only 12 miles, as the crow flies south-south-west of Möngyu (Stage 2 of Route No. 42). The intervening country appears easy and the distance could probably be done in one march.
		6. Namta (or Namtán). Nampun and two small streams.	**7 0**	65 0	The first half of the march runs up a grassy valley and is fairly level, and here and there patches of dry cultivation are met with. The old Palaung village of Pángkutlông, centre village of the circle, is passed on the right of the road. Little and bad water only is procurable here. The track now runs along the foot of the hills and, after crossing the shallow muddy ditch and a little farther on a small stream of clearer water, the ascent commences. This soon becomes a very steep zigzag with a deep khud on the right hand. A muddy water-hole is crossed and the narrow saddle back on which Namta is situated is reached. The camping ground is bad and the water-supply so scarce that in the dry weather baggage animals have to go without, and it is necessary to curtail the allowance of the men. Namta is a small new Kachin village and has small supplies of paddy only.
		7. Möngwi ... Three small streams.	**15 0**	80 0	The road after leaving Namta is very little used and is consequently overgrown with grass jungle and blocked by fallen trees. After 2 miles a steep ascent is met with, very severe for infantry and baggage. About 6 miles from Namta a small stream is crossed and the track runs along a ravine blocked by fallen trees; after emerging from this the track again ascends till the top of the range separating the Shwéli from the Myitngé valleys is crossed. On the last 7 miles of this road five good-sized villages are passed, occupied by Kachins and Palaungs. They appear prosperous. The extreme height reached on this march would be about 7,500 feet. Möngwi is 2,700 feet and is situated on the right bank of the Namwi, a tributary of the Shwéli. The inhabitants are Shan. The whole valley, as far as the eye can reach, is under wet cultivation Paddy abundant. Many Kachin and Palaung villages are concealed in the hills round this valley. Roads to Namkham, (No. 45), Theinni *viâ* Möngyu (Nos. 69 and 42), and Mantôn *viâ* Möngtât (No. 35), meet here. It has a bazaar.

No. 15.

From LÁSHIO to MÖNGYAI (MAINGYÉ) viâ MANSÉ.

By Capt. A. C. YATE, 1st Beloochees, from Native information, January 1888.

Authorities. Military.	Authorities. Civil.	Number and Names of Stages, Rivers and Streams.	Distances. Intermediate. M.	F.	Distances. Total. M.	F.	Remarks.
G.O.C. Mandalay District.	Superintendent, Northern Shan States.	**1. Mantuleng or Hôlwé.** Namshio, Nammé, and other small streams.	**12**	**0**	12	0	*N.B.*—There is no published report of the first two stages of this route, but by comparing Captain Yate's native information report with the map and taking his "daing" at 2½ miles, a fair estimate of the distances is obtained. The total length of each stage is certainly not more than the estimates herein given. General direction south-east. Road fairly good for pack transport. The approaches to the streams, where they are not bridged, are difficult and require to be ramped. The streams should be bridged, the beds of some being from 1 to 2 feet deep in mire. At 1 mile from Láshio bazaar pass Mansu village, ½ mile to right (20 houses, kyaung), and Humôn, ½ mile to left (10 houses). At 3 miles enter hills. Then easy ascent for 4 miles to Nonglem Sakhán where camping ground and water for small force. Then cross watershed between the Namyaw and Nampôn rivers. The Namshio flows into the Namyaw and the Nammé into the Nampôn. From Nonglem to Mantuleng is about 5 miles. Level road. Rice cultivation. Camping ground. Water from stream. The Nammé, which is crossed just before reaching camp, is about 30 feet broad by 1½ feet deep, and the road follows the valley of this stream from Nonglem.
		2. Mansé ... ... Nampôn.	**10**	**0**	22	0	At 4 miles reach Shan village of Naleng (road hilly and descending), 10 houses, one kyaung. Rice cultivation. Water from stream. At 6 miles reach Kôpát (road hilly and descending). Shan village of 10 houses. Rice cultivation. From Kôpát to Mansé road hilly and descending. Shan village of 40 houses. Bazaar. Kyaung. Rice cultivation. Mansé is on the north bank of the Nampôn, a river some 50 yards broad, fordable in the dry weather and crossed by ferry in the wet. On south bank, opposite Mansé, is Shan village of Wingleng; 10 houses, kyaung, &c. The Nampôn flows into the Namma.
		3. Hpáseng ... Namma river fordable; moderate current; 50 feet broad, 2 feet deep; rough stony bottom.	**14**	**4**	36	4	Road good and level throughout. Direction south by west. Country mostly jungle, intersected by patches of cultivation. At 2½ miles pass village of Kyusôngnáng to left. At 4 miles past Katpu, village and bazaar. At 7½ miles cross Namma. At 8 miles village of Páklön to right. At 9½ miles village of Saileng to left. Here good camping ground and water. At 10½ miles road to left to Hôya. At 11¼ miles path to left to Kalö and to right to Makmun and Haikö, and thence on to Naungmwon (*see* Route No. 36). At 12¾ miles Namhu and Papök villages. Good camping ground and water. At 14½ miles Hpáseng, large village with kyaung, pagodas and bazaar. Camping room. Water, fuel, and fodder for a large force. From here direct roads to Hôya and Thîbaw.
		4. Namtông ...	**9**	**6**	46	2	*See* Route No. 36, Stages 1 to 3.
		5. Möngyai ...	**12**	**2**	58	4	

FROM LÁSHIO TO MÖNGYAI (MAINGYÉ) *viâ* MANSÉ—*continued.*

ALTERNATIVE I.

FROM HPÁSENG (STAGE 3) TO MÖNGYAI *viâ* MANSANG.

BY CAPT. A. C. YATE, FEBRUARY 1888.

Authorities. Military.	Authorities. Civil.	Number and Names of Stages, Rivers and Streams.	Distances. Intermediate. M. F.	Distances. Total. M. F.	Remarks.
G.O.C. Mandalay District.	Superintendent, Northern Shan States.	**1. Mansáng** ... Small streams.	**15 0**	15 0	Direction south-east. Good road all the way for pack transport. Streams mostly bridged for pack transport. Road crosses one low range of hills, dividing the Möngsit from the Mansáng valley. Gradients rather steep in places, but only for very short distances. The country traversed is undulating and covered with jungle. A great part of it is cleared for cultivation. Both the Möngsit and Mansáng districts are comparatively populous and productive. Shan population. At 1 mile, village of Kônsa (whence road to Naungmwon and Thíbaw, distance from Kônsa to Naungmwon about 14 miles). At 2¼ miles, village of Namhulongsán to right and to left path to the village of Namtông on the direct Mansé-Möngyai road. At 3 miles path to left (east) to Loi Ngön, a village on the same road. At 4¾ miles Pánghai Mansawpak (or butchers' village). Near it good camping ground and ample water for a brigade. At 5½ miles Möngsit (residence of Myoza of district, 31 houses, kyaung and bazaar). Good camping ground on high or low ground and abundant water here for a large force. From here roads to Naungmwon (about 15 miles) and to Hôya (about 8 miles). At 6¾ miles road to right (west) to Hôtu (Utu) about 6 miles and Thíbaw. At 7½ miles villages of Mankaulôn to right and Kongmöng and Konglön to left. At 9¼ miles pass Mannong village to left. At 10 to 11 miles cross the Loi Kyu-hôtong, a low range of hills running south-east and north-west. At 12 miles pass Mansôngai village. At 12½ miles two other small villages, and at 13¾ miles Mannamsu and cross Namsu stream. At 15 miles reach Mansáng (two kyaungs, bazaar and many villages grouped around). Here there is water and camping ground for any force, both on high and low ground. Fuel and fodder procurable, also some supplies. The country south-east and west from here for some 15 miles is an undulating plain. The position is a fairly good one for a post or cantonment, for which a good site can be found on high ground. Water, fodder and fuel are plentiful. Supplies should be plentiful as soon as the country recovers from the late disturbances. From Mansáng there are good roads in every direction by which any place of importance in Theinni and the other adjacent States can be reached. The roads from Mansáng to Láshio are (1) *viâ* Möngsit and Naungmwon or (2) *viâ* Möngsit and Mansé. The Namsáng stream flows to the east and the Namnongthing to the west of Mansáng village. The Namsáng flowing south by east falls into the Namlaung which (still further south or south-east) joins the Namhen and falls into the Nampáng or Ben chaung, which joins the Salween south of Tákaw ferry.

FROM LÁSHIO TO MÖNGYAI (MAINGYÉ) *viâ* MANSÉ—*continued.*

ALTERNATIVE I—*continued.*

Authorities. Military.	Authorities. Civil.	Number and Names of Stages, Rivers and Streams.	Distances. Intermediate. M. F.	Distances. Total. M. F.	Remarks.
G.O.C. Mandalay District.	Superintendent, Northern Shan States.	**2. Möngyai (Maingyé).** Namsáng and Namlaung streams, both bridged.	9 4	24 4	Road good throughout over open undulating country. Streams mostly bridged for pack transport. Soil good, but water-supply seems insufficient for the proper irrigation of rice crops. Villages are dotted all over the country on either side of the road. At $1\frac{1}{2}$ miles cross Namsáng stream. At $4\frac{1}{4}$ miles pass large village (bazaar, kyaung) of Hongleng (or Hengling). Good camping ground here for any force. The water of this district is very inferior to that usually seen in the Northern Shan States. At $5\frac{1}{2}$ miles cross small streamlet. At $7\frac{1}{2}$ miles cross Namlaung stream. At 9 miles pass kyaung and bazaar, grouped around which are numerous villages. Good camping ground and water here. Supplies at present *nil*, rice being Rs. 12 a basket. From here there are roads leading in every direction.

No. 16.

From LÁSHIO to TÁKÖT viâ NAWNGHPA and NALAO.

BY CAPT. G. V. BURROWS, PAID ATTACHÉ, INTELLIGENCE DEPARTMENT, BURMA, JANUARY 1891.

Military	Civil	Stage	Intermediate	Total	Remarks
G.O.C. Mandalay District.	Superintendent, Northern Shan States.	**1. Man Ping** ... Nam Yaw.	14 0	14 0	The path runs down a gentle slope in a north-easterly direction for about 1 mile, where it meets the old cart road. It passes the only pagoda in this part of the country, which stands on the left on a small mound. At the 2nd mile a small stream is crossed by a broad wooden bridge capable of bearing all arms. On the opposite bank there are a few huts where a bazaar is held every fifth day. The road runs on in an easterly direction crossing some paddy-fields, very heavy in the rainy season, about 600 yards in extent, rises over a low spur passing a few huts on the right and drops down into the valley of the Nam Yaw. The banks are steep, the bottom firm gravel, and the current strong, but only about 2 feet deep and 18 yards broad. The path now runs due east and on the rising ground at 6 miles is the Government farm. The road runs past the farm on the left and about 600 yards further on crosses a swamp which is passable in winter, but would be extremely difficult in wet weather. About 800 yards further on it crosses a small stream, gravel bottom, with the eastern or right bank very steep, and rises on to a magnificent camping ground capable of holding 10,000 men. The path runs on in an easterly direction along the plateau and turning round the eastern end drops into a small water-course, very difficult to cross, being a quagmire. There is high grass close at hand and with it thrown into the stream animals can cross one at a time slowly. Moving on in a south-east direction the road turns, passes some pagodas in a north-

FROM LÁSHIO TO TÁKÖT *viâ* NAWNGHPA AND NALAO—*continued.*

Authorities. Military.	Authorities. Civil.	Number and Names of Stages, Rivers and Streams.	Distances. Intermediate.	Distances. Total.	Remarks.
G.O.C. Mandalay District.	Superintendent, Northern Shan States.	**1. Man Ping**— *cont.*			easterly direction, and runs through some heavy jungle till it comes to a small village. The road then rises very rapidly and runs along a ridge, after crossing several small insignificant streams, till at 14 miles on the northern side of the valley it comes to the village of Man Ping.
		2. Mŏng Yaw ... Nam Yaw.	M. F. **15 4**	M. F. 29 4	The path crosses a small stream immediately after leaving Man Ping camping ground and runs due east for a mile and-a-quarter, where it rises over a long low spur, winds round to the north-east, and immediately drops into the valley. Half-a-mile further on there is a large bazaar on the left of the path and on the right a large tank. The path goes round the northern side of the tank and turns south-east again. About ½ mile in front is a large pôngyi kyaung on a low hill. The path turns here again round to east and about 200 yards further on due north and, after passing over a high spur, suddenly falls into a cultivated valley passing through the village of Möng Yen. It then turns east, crossing some paddy-fields and then the Nam Yaw stream again. The banks are very steep, about 10 feet high, the current strong, about 2 feet deep, and the bed is of gravel. The ford is crossed immediately under a high sharp spur, up which the path goes, and it is commanded completely from three sides. The path is very steep and runs in an easterly direction over a spur, then along a ridge, sometimes on one side and sometimes the other. The drop varies in height, being as much as 500 feet in some places; all along precipitous. After running along the ridge for about 2½ miles it suddenly drops down very steeply into the Möng Yaw valley. Looking due east you see from this ridge the hill at the eastern end known as Loi Sák, which is 6,400 feet high. Immediately below there appears a long line of dark green trees, in which is situated the village of Möng Yaw, and it is 4 miles distant from this spur. The road runs along an undulating valley through quite open grass land.
		3. Loi Ngŏn ... Small streams.	**11 0**	40 4	Leaving Möng Yaw the path runs in an easterly direction across an undulating grass land for about 2 miles. It then rises suddenly, passing a small village, and continues to wind along the slopes and spurs of Loi Sák till it has risen to a height of 5,500 feet, where it passes within ½ a mile of the peak. It very suddenly drops now in an easterly direction and runs along the eastern spur for some 2 miles, then rises suddenly and, after crossing an insignificant stream, comes to a Chinese village called Loi Ngön. It then runs along the valley, ascends another short spur, and after falling some 200 or 250 feet runs out of a gorge on to an elevated plateau, on the eastern edge of which is a Kachin village called also Loi Ngön or Möng Loi Ngön.
		4. Man Mák ... Small streams.	**9 0**	49 4	Leaving the plateau the path gradually descends into the valley and, running slightly south-east after the 3rd mile has been reached, it enters the village of Páng Law inhabited by

FROM LÁSHIO TO TÁKÖT *viâ* NAWNGHPA AND NALAO—*continued.*

Authorities.		Number and Names of Stages, Rivers and Streams.	Distances.		Remarks.
Military.	Civil.		Intermediate.	Total.	
G.O.C. Mandalay District.	Superintendent, Northern Shan States.	**4. Man Mák**—*cont.*			Palaungs. It then turns south-east and about 600 yards from the village, crossing a small stream which has a muddy bottom and would be difficult to cross in rainy season. Plenty of timber is, however, at hand. The path then turns suddenly due east. Avoiding another path which runs south-east it takes its way along a long succession of small spurs and runs a fairly level course, finally at the 8th mile dropping into the valley of Man Mák, where it runs along the western side, crosses a stream over which there is a bridge of wooden planks very strong and durable. There is no village here, but it is the old site of Man Mák. The country here is open and mostly cultivated by Kachins, who inhabit all the villages round these hills.
		5. Weng Káng ... Small streams.	M. F. 14 0	M. F. 63 4	There are two large villages on the low hills lying north-west of the valley, about 1 mile distant, called Páng Káng and Loi Kham. Small quantities of rice and paddy can be obtained up to fifteen baskets. Leaving Man Mak the path runs due south over a long spur, crosses a stream at the end of the 1st mile, which would be difficult in wet weather, the bottom being clayish mud. It is only about 10 feet broad. The path now rises about 60 feet round a spur through dense jungle and enters a fine level valley lying between this and the spurs of the great range, of which Loi Maw is the highest peak, due east. After running through the valley for about 1 mile the path turns in an easterly direction and passes between two knolls and so out into the continuous slopes and spurs of the great range. It runs generally in a south-east direction and at the 6th mile goes through North Ping Káng, a small, insignificant village. Nearly the whole of the jungle here, which is fairly dense, is of oak. The trees are, however, small, being on an average of 7 or 8 inches in diameter. The path now turns in a southerly direction and runs down into a deep valley, at the head of which is the village of South Ping Káng, also a very insignificant place. It now rises rapidly after crossing a small stream, gravel bottom and very shallow, about 6 feet broad, easy approach, and turns nearly south-east, passing on the left a good camping ground capable of holding some 800 men,* and running off the spur, 600 yards further down it crosses the Nam Ma stream. The stream is easy to approach from both banks, is about 30 feet broad, 1 foot deep, and has an excellent gravel bottom. It now rises very rapidly up an almost precipitous spur, and at the top to the right of the path is the little village of Weng Káng.
		6. Nawngleng (7,300 feet). Small streams.	11 0	74 4	After leaving Weng Káng it runs due east along a high ridge for nearly a mile, then drops down a long steep spur. The descent is in some places very steep and covers about 1,900 yards. Leaving the camping ground in the valley the path runs up a succession of sharp spurs for nearly 3 miles. The rise in this distance is 1,300 feet approximately. At the top of this long, sharp spur there is a very small piece of cultivation, level enough to camp on with

* Apparently the halt should be made here and not at the village.—A. F.

FROM LÁSHIO TO TÁKÖT *viâ* NAWNGHPA AND NALAO—*continued.*

Authorities. Military.	Authorities. Civil.	Number and Names of Stages, Rivers and Streams.	Distances. Intermediate.	Distances. Total.	Remarks.
G.O.C. Mandalay District.	Superintendent, Northern Shan States.	**6. Nawngleng (7,300 feet)**—*cont.*			water close at hand, a running stream supplying any quantity of water. From this point the road runs on in a southerly direction, crossing many insignificant small streams running between hills rising perhaps another 700 or 800 feet and, passing about 1¼ miles west of the mountain of Loi Lan, runs on to a plateau, where the chief village is known as Nawng Leng. There are several small villages all round it.
		7. Páng Wa ... Small streams.	M. 13 F. 0	M. 87 F. 4	The road leaves the village in a south-easterly direction for nearly ½ mile, then turning due south and after 1¼ miles crosses a stream (foot-bridge 20 feet by 2 feet; easy crossing; bed gravel; 9 inches deep) which is running south-west below a village close by to the left of the road. Nearly a mile further on the road turns in a south-east direction running over a spur, and at 3½ miles passes through a small village. About 600 yards further on it crosses a stream (foot-bridge about 20 feet by 2 feet; water clear and 6 inches deep), and runs along the side of a very deep ravine and at the 5th mile runs along a similar spur on the other side of an equally steep ravine and rises rapidly on to a small plateau, descending rapidly at the 6th mile, and about 700 yards further on crosses a stream, which is unbridged. Very thick, muddy bottom, about 18 feet wide and 2 feet deep. The opposite or southern bank is steep and very slippery, but capable of improvement in a very short time. There is plenty of timber and long grass at hand. For the next mile and-a-half the path wind along a spur and at 7½ miles it drops suddenly into a partially-cultivated valley and crossing two small streams, which are insignificant, runs in a south-east direction across the valley and up the other side, there it rises gradually over the neck and running for another ½ mile in a fairly level but southerly course, commences to descend very rapidly between a long spur on the left and the mountain of Loi Kahan on the right. In 1½ miles the fall is nearly 1,800 feet and the path is very steep, difficult and rocky in some places. It then runs along the valley for nearly 3 miles quite level and at about the 13th mile enters the village of Páng Wa, where supplies, such as paddy and rice, are not easily procured. A stream runs along the valley about 200 yards due east of the village
		8. Nawng Hpa ... Small streams.	10 0	97 4	The path runs on in a south-easterly direction and goes over a low spur, crossing a stream at the foot of it. (Muddy crossing about 18 feet wide, 2 feet deep. Would be difficult in wet weather, but timber at hand.) There is a large clump of bamboo trees on the ridge in the otherwise perfectly open country which marks the lie of the road. It winds along the valley, turning east, and at the end of the 2nd mile runs up a very sharp spur with a small muddy stream at the bottom of it. The whole of this spur is covered with fir trees of considerable girth, generally about 30 or 40 inches. The road then winds down to a neck, crosses it, going nearly south, then turns and runs along and of a sharp, steep spur into a valley which is cultivated. Rising

FROM LÁSHIO TO TÁKÖT *viâ* NAWNGHPA AND NALAO—*continued.*

Authorities.		Number and Names of Stages, Rivers and Streams.	Distances.		Remarks.
Military.	Civil.		Intermediate.	Total.	
G.O.C. Mandalay District.	Superintendent, Northern Shan States.	**8. Nawang Hpa**—*cont.*			on the southern side it runs through the little village of Páng Seng. From this point the road gradually descends, but is generally level; the country becomes more open. It runs almost due east for above 1¼ miles, then turning south-east it runs down the centre of a long wide valley, where the country is perfectly open, representing a huge plain. It runs thus for nearly 2½ miles past a clump of bamboo trees on the right over a small rapid stream in the valley, which is easy to cross at all seasons of the year and is only about 6 feet wide and 8 inches or 10 inches deep with a hard gravel bottom. About 800 yards to the east-south-east of this spot lies the village of Nawng Hpa which is on the borders of the two states of South Theinni and West Möng Lön. There is good camping ground on a small flat-topped knoll about 400 yards across the stream. *Note.*—The whole of the country, except in those places mentioned as open, is densely wooded; where grass, however, exists, it should be remembered that between the months of February and May it would be more open, as nearly the whole country is burnt by the people. The grass fires are now commencing. The rapidity with which they travel becomes a source of danger to a force encamped on a ridge with long stretches of grass slopes on either sides, should the wind set towards the camp when a fire is burning anywhere in its vicinity.
			M. F.	M. F.	
		9. Tun Hông ... Streams.	10 0	107 4	The road leaves Nawng Hpa in a south-easterly direction and runs along the valley, passing the small hamlet of Nam Ka on the left at the 1st mile. At the 3rd mile the village of Nam Hpa Kum is passed and about ½ mile further on the village of Pan Gya, both insignificant. The road falls into the Tun Hông valley about 3 miles after this and, running between two long spurs, turns slightly in a southerly direction into a very well-watered valley, in the middle of which is the large and prosperous village of Tun Hông. There is an excellent camping ground just before you reach the village. Water is close at hand. Rice and paddy to any extent available. Tángyán (*see* Routes Nos. 17 and 38) lies about 15 miles to the west of Tun Hông.
		10. Nalao ... Nam Löm.	7 0	114 4	Leaving Tun Hông the road passes at once over the Nam Löm stream 10 feet by 2 feet; easy banks; foot-bridge, but indications of flood rise of 6 feet. A rapid stream here about 18 feet wide and 2 feet deep. Banks sloping and easy. There is a good foot-bridge and the ford is immediately below it. The bottom is of mud, but easy to cross. The road then rises over a sharp rocky spur. The rise is gradual from this to the gorge below the hill known as Loi Pán Táng, where the ascent is very steep. From this point the road falls at a steep gradient about 1 in 14 the whole way down to the village of Hsai Kôn, which is 4⅛ miles from Tun Hông. It is an insignificant village. From this the road again falls rapidly, rounding the spur and running in an easterly direction. At the foot of this hill and on a knoll

FROM LÁSHIO TO TÁKŎT *viâ* NAWNGHPA AND NALAO—*continued.*

Authorities.		Number and Names of Stages, Rivers and Streams.	Distances.		Remarks.
Military.	Civil.		Intermediate.	Total.	
G.O.C. Mandalay District.	Superintendent, Northern Shan States.	**10. Nalao**—*cont.*			in the centre of the valley is Nalao, the capital of West Möng Lön. Rice and paddy are procurable in moderate quantities and water is close at hand. There is a good camping ground about 600 yards south of the town on high ground between paddy-fields. The Sawbwa lives here.
			M. F.	M. F.	
		11. Ta Supkyet (or Supket) Ferry. The Salween; 85 yards broad, 52 feet deep; average from seven soundings; rapid current. Deepest sounding showed 58 feet. Velocity of current tested and found to be 3½–4 miles an hour.	7 0	121 4	The road leads down in a south-easterly direction and crosses a small insignificant stream below the village of Kôn Kaw, at ½ a mile's distance. After the 2nd mile the road runs down off the high sloping tableland, passing two small villages. The descent is gradual but steep in places. There is plenty of water near the road all the way. At the foot of the hill the road turns to the south and runs along the bank of the Salween, till nearly opposite Supkyet, where the ferry is. The river is 100 feet lower here than at Man Yö or Man Yi, where it is crossed by the route Nawng Hpa to Môt Hai (or Môthai). It is more rapid, and about 400 yards below the ferry, there are rapids, very dangerous to boats, as the stream races from some 200 yards above, when the water is low, as it is at this time of the year (January). Troops could camp on the sand on the eastern bank, otherwise there is no camping ground. The general degree of slope of both banks is 33° and there are indications of a flood rise of 32 feet.
		12. Mankát .. Namkyet.	5 0	126 4	Leaving the camping ground just north of Supkyet, the road crosses the Nam Kyet stream about 200 yards from the point where it flows into the Salween and passes over the rise on which the village stands. From this it turns in an easterly direction which it maintains for a little more than 2 miles, but following, as it does, the bed of the stream it crosses the stream over and over again. From this point it runs generally in a south-easterly direction for nearly 3 miles till the village of Man Kyet is reached on its right bank. It is a small village of about 15 houses and the camping ground is just beyond it on the road, in some neglected fields. It is 130 yards long by about 50 broad, but is entirely surrounded by thick jungle. The stream runs past the southern side within 20 yards. The road crosses the stream no less than twenty times between the Salween and Man Kyet village, and is impassable in wet weather. The Nam Kyet is generally from 30 to 40 feet broad and from 1 to 2 feet deep. Is rapid and lies between very steep banks. Indicates a flood rise of from 6 to 8 feet and runs through country which is very thickly wooded close up to both banks. Bottom firm gravel.
		13. Kawng Hsáng. Nam Sáng.	11 0	137 4	Moving on the same path and crossing the same stream nine times in the first 2 miles the road turns off in a south-easterly direction up the hill opposite a village and leaves the Nam Kyet stream which runs down from the hill known as Loi

FROM LÁSHIO TO TÁKÖT *viâ* NAWNGHPA AND NALAO—*continued.*

Authorities. Military.	Authorities. Civil.	Number and Names of Stages, Rivers and Streams.	Distances. Inter-mediate.	Distances. Total.	Remarks.
G.O.C. Mandalay District.	Superintendent, Northern Shan States.	**13. Kawng Hsáng** —*cont.*			Lao. The gradient is steep and the rise is about 300 feet. The road runs along the top of this hill for about a mile, then falls suddenly into a small deep valley, rises over the next spur about 100 feet, turns slightly south-east and drops into the valley passing the village of Nam Náng (5 miles) on the left, down in a hollow, a small insignificant place consisting of some 16 houses. It takes its name from the stream flowing through the valley. This stream is in every respect similar to the Nam Kyet; has everywhere a firm gravel bottom; is rapid but only 1 foot deep and easy to cross. The path runs out of the valley in a southerly direction, crosses the Nam Sáng about 100 yards from the camping ground which is the only one available, and is in the midst of paddy-fields in a hollow commanded from the east, north and south with thick jungle on the right or west side. It is sufficiently large to encamp 600 men without horses or 200 men with horses. Water is plentiful and good. The road from the crossing turns in a southerly direction and ascends the hill, which is very steep and in some places only just practicable for loaded mules. The ascent continues for about one mile and-a-quarter, with bits of level ground as the path winds along the actual crest-line of the hill passing the little village of Kông Káng on the top of the hill. From here the path runs a fairly level course, but ½ a mile further on it runs over another spur and skirts another hill rising some 200 feet more over a sharply-defined ridge, when it falls gradually for ½ a mile, runs round the sides of the hill, a fairly level course for the rest of the distance to the village of Kawng Hsáng. The camping ground is on the path just before you reach the village, a clearing in the jungle on the side of the hill, on a gentle slope, at the bottom of which and about 100 yards off is a good stream of clear water. Total ascent during the march 950 feet.
			M. F.	M. F.	
		14. Man Put ... Nam Put.	5 0	142 4	Leaving Kawng Hsáng the path runs round the slope of the hill which is here naturally terraced. Pine woods appear on the slopes and the path winding down the hill in a south-easterly direction for nearly 2 miles. Crossing a small insignificant stream in the valley and rises at a very steep gradient for 500 yards over a spur turning slightly in a southerly direction, then crossing below the Nam Put stream and following it along the valley for nearly 1 mile more the path runs into some paddy-fields which, in dry weather, could be used for camping. A better camping ground could, however, be made on the last spur alluded to above, the top of which is fairly level, with space enough to hold from 280 to 300 men comfortably. It overlooks the valley and water is at the foot of it not more than 100 yards distant, and the camp would command all the approaches to it save one due east, which is high ground covered with very thick jungle. The village, a very small insignificant place called Man Put, is just off the road to the left coming off the spur.
		15. Na Lông ... Streams.	7 0	149 4	The road turns back from the camping ground and runs up the very steep spur of the hill which is due south of Man Put. It continues to rise for

FROM LÁSHIO TO TÁKÖT *viâ* NAWNGHPA AND NALAO—*continued.*

Authorities.		Number and Names of Stages, Rivers and Streams.	Distances.				Remarks.
Military.	Civil.		Intermediate.		Total.		
			M.	F.	M.	F.	
G.O.C. Mandalay District.	Superintendent, Northern Shan States.	**15. Na Lông**—*cont.*					more than a mile. The total rise is nearly 1,700 feet. It winds along the crest-line passing the little Wa village of Man Méán and runs down into the valley of Na Lông, where there is any amount of good camping ground with a good broad stream flowing through it. The Shan village of Na Lông is at the south-western end of the valley, but is an insignificant place. The lower road to the Man Sawm ferry runs into this road at the south-west end of this valley, the two villages between this and Man Sawm being Kwon Yé and Loi Lông.
		16. Páng Yáng ... Streams.	6	4	155	4	From this point the road runs over a long, gradual spur in a south-easterly direction and continues to rise gradually for nearly 2 miles. It then runs in an easterly direction, is fairly level and runs round the side of the hill on which the village of Páng Yáng stands. It rises very rapidly another 200 feet quite close to the village, crossing a small stream, in the ravine, which flows over small rocks and furnishes the drinking water for the camp. The camping ground is on the summit of the hill at the elevation of 4,600 feet. It is well cleared and would hold 800 men and overlooks the village which consists of some 60 houses and is the head-quarters of the Sawbwa Awn, who lives in a newly built haw overlooking the village from the western side of the small plateau. From Páng Yáng there is a route to Weng Kyeng Tung, the stages of which are said to be as follows:—(1) Ho Mwán, (2) Yong An, (3) Nam Kha, (4) Páng Hôn, (5) Nam Twan Tai, (6) Nam Twan Naé, (7) Si Kyauk, (8) Möng Nyin, (9) Hôk Khun, (10) Na Séang Hai, (11) Nam Náng, (12) Páng Tum Lum, (13) Man Htai, (14) Weng Kyeng Tung.
		17. Kát Maw ...	7	4	162	4	The road runs along the side of the hill in an easterly direction, is well cut and about 10 feet broad, and, though following the shape of the hill, is fairly level. It runs off the eastern spur of the long hill at the end of the 4th mile passing the village of Nawk Wa down on the right on the slope about 600 feet below the road. Another mile on it passes the village of Kông Hsa and ½ a mile further the village of Peng Mak Man. The road now runs over a neck and takes a north-easterly direction and after another mile runs on the south-west spur of the long hill, at the foot of which is Kát Maw, a very small insignificant village. Water would be scarce during the hot weather months along this bit of the road. The only space for a camp at Kát Maw is just below the village and immediately to the east of it and would hold 200 men. There are lead mines here close to the road to the right of the village.
		18. Táköt ...	8	0	170	4	From this point the road rises rapidly up the long spur rising 1,000 feet in the first 2 miles and then runs along the ridge passing a village and continues to run along the same ridge for 6 miles, and after another mile rising slightly it runs over the ridge and off the hill and crosses a small deep valley

FROM LÁSHIO TO TÁKÖT *viâ* NAWNGHPA AND NALAO—*continued.*

Authorities. Military.	Authorities. Civil.	Number and Names of Stages, Rivers and Streams.	Distances. Intermediate.	Distances. Total.	Remarks.
G.O.C. Mandalay District.	Superintendent, Northern Shan States.	**18. Táköt**—*cont.*			and runs on to the small hill on the top of which Táköt stands. Táköt is completely commanded from the point where the road runs off the ridge at a range of about 1,100 yards. Táköt is the capital of East Möng Lön State, contains about 50 houses including the Sawbwa's palace, a miserable shed. There is no ground for camping at Táköt, but a fairly level camping ground is that on the ridge above mentioned overlooking Táköt. Water is, however, scarce the whole way from Páng Yáng to this place, and a force of anything over 50 men with, say, more than 30 or 40 animals, would find itself much hampered through want of water, except at Kát Maw. The road at the end of the ridge, at the point where it overlooks the village of Táköt, is 6,100 feet above the sea, and there is no water save in the valley below, which is certainly 1,200 feet lower and the gradient almost precipitous. From Táköt roads lead to Möng Nga (*see* Branch V); Na Hpán (*see* Branch VI); and to Páng Seng (*see* Branch VII).

ALTERNATIVE I.

FROM MÖNGYAW (STAGE 2) TO WENG KÁNG (STAGE 5).

BY LIEUT. C. AINSLIE, R.E., ATTACHÉ, INTELLIGENCE DEPARTMENT, BURMA, DECEMBER 1892.

Military	Civil	Stages	Intermediate M. F.	Total M. F.	Remarks
G.O.C. Mandalay District.	Superintendent, Northern Shan States.	**1. Hpa Leng** ... Nam Hpai 10 feet wide, 1 foot deep. Numerous small streams.	10 4	10 4	The path runs out east towards the high peaks known as Loi Sák. At ½ mile a stream is crossed on a strong bridge 15 feet by 5 feet. The path runs over flat grass land and crosses the Nam Hpai. At the foot of the hills a little to the left is the village, Na Hpai. The climb up is very steep at first and in a few places afterwards, but loaded mules went up. At about 4 miles the Palaung village of Páng Hsa Pé is reached and the road runs towards the right hand, one of the peaks of Loi Sák passing a Palaung village, Man Loi Sák, it skirts round the left of the peak passing a small Chinese village on the right Hké Loi Sák. The greatest height is reached here, about 5,000 feet and a steep descent begins. The Palaung village of Hpa Leng is reached soon after 10 miles and a small camp can be made in a few paddy-fields below close to a stream.
		2. Weng Káng ... Nam Hpán Kyen, about 10 feet wide, 1 foot deep. A few streams.	8 4	19 0	The path crosses the stream and running south-east skirts round the foot of the spurs from the range which divides north from south Theinni, it soon enters a flat grassy valley which has two small streams in it and gives plenty of ground for camping. Crossing the valley it enters the jungle again and there are some nasty places on the path for mules. Passing round the right of a conical peak a camping ground is found in paddy-fields at 5 miles with a small Kachin village on either side, Kong Hsáng and Möng Hawm. The path thence crosses the valley and runs up and down among low wooded ranges following the valley of the Nam Ma more or less. A village, Wai Leng, lies on the right at ½ mile, after which the road turns left along the spur and soon commences to descend very rapidly. About 3 miles it turns to the right and soon ascends a few hundred feet passing near small Kachin village, Weng Káng.

FROM LÁSHIO TO TÁKÖT *viâ* NAWNGHPA AND NALAO—*continued.*

ALTERNATIVE II.

FROM NALAO (WEST MÖNGLÖN), (STAGE 10) TO PÁNGYÁNG (STAGE 16).

BY LIEUT. AINSLIE, R.E., ATTACHÉ, INTELLIGENCE DEPARTMENT, BURMA, DECEMBER 1892 AND JANUARY 1893.

Authorities. Military.	Authorities. Civil.	Number and Names of Stages, Rivers and Streams.	Distances. Intermediate. M. F.	Distances. Total. M. F.	Remarks.
G.O.C. Mandalay District.	Superintendent, Northern Shan States.	**1. Pánghka** ... Numerous small streams and Nam Pông.	9 4	9 4	Nalao, the former capital of West Mönglön, is a village of some size standing on a knoll about 100 feet above the paddy-fields which lie west and south of it; a strong stream runs west of it from north and south, which is crossed by a good plank bridge. The Salween here is only 3 or 4 miles away in a direct line east. A road runs south-west to Ta Supkyet. The road to Pánghka runs west from the village, across a narrow strip of paddy-fields to Man Hsaikhao (four or five houses), then ascends for a mile, rising 500 feet, crossing several streams; path steep and slippery in places; it crosses a spur, descends slightly and then runs south along a level plateau on the side of the range passing through Man Nampông, 2½ miles, across the Nampông to Man Mák Soi on the left (both from 10 to 20 houses), at 4th mile, then through some swampy grounds covered with long, coarse grass, over a small stream, no water on road after this, on a good bridge, then curls to the left round the foot of a spur and running south again ascends a short, steep defile which could be easily blocked, and is commanded from both sides. The road crosses a range, then traverses a flat, grassy valley passing the kyaung of Man Pát (deserted) on the left and soon crosses another range; rise 1,000 feet; path narrow and steep; old stockades commanding it; then descends about 300 feet on a spur gently to a saddle on which the camp was pitched. Pánghka is a small village on the hill side above to the east, and ½ mile west, and below is another small Palaung village, Manpöt; small quantities of rice and paddy. Water from a stream below Manpöt a long way away and a trickle in a nullah on the road 300 yards ahead (south) below the road. Not a good place to stop at, it would be better to push on to Namkao.
		2. Manping ... Namkao, 20 feet wide, 18 inches deep; rapid current; crossed by a good wooden bridge, and another stream 20 feet wide, 1 foot deep; bridged; easily forded if necessary.	6 0	15 4	Leaving Pánghka camp the road descends very soon down a spur which runs down west; steep at first and more gently lower down where it turns south. The drop to the Namkao valley is 1,600 feet; distance 2 miles or more. The valley is flat and covered with paddy-fields which were very wet when we crossed them. The Namkao is crossed on a bridge just below the junction of three streams and a path runs along the right bank down stream to Man Nam Kao. The road rises a little over a small spur on which there are several open spaces for camps and drops again to a narrow strip of paddy-field, which it crosses passing a pôngyi kyaung on the left; here is another stream like the Namkao, which is crossed on a good plank bridge; the road rises from this valley and passing near a small village on the right crosses some very swampy ground and a muddy rapid stream, 10 feet wide, and nearly knee-deep; there is a short, very steep ascent after this, and another small shallow stream is crossed, after which the

FROM LÁSHIO TO TÁKÖT *viâ* NAWNGHPA AND NALAO—*continued.*

ALTERNATIVE II—*continued.*

Authorities.		Number and Names of Stages, Rivers and Streams.	Distances.		Remarks.
Military.	Civil.		Inter-mediate.	Total.	
G.O.C. Mandalay District.	Superintendent, Northern Shan States.	**2. Manping**—*cont.*			rise is very gradual. The road soon runs nearly level, passing Manmaw (10 houses) on the right at the 5th mile and turns west along the foot of the hills through thick jungle to Manping. A road at 5½ miles leads to the right through a gap in the hills to Namkao about 7 miles off; a ¼ mile before Manping the road crosses several streams where it is bad, going over muddy and rocky places. Manping is the present capital of West Mönglön; has about 60 houses, a dilapidated palace and several kyaungs; there is good camping ground for a large force. Water and supplies are plentiful.
		3. Ta Man Hsöm Ferry. A river, 30 feet wide, 1 foot deep; rapid; firm bottom; banks steep, but ramped 1½ miles east of Manping; several small streams and the Salween or Nam-kông, 119 yards wide, about 60 feet deep; current nearly 4½ miles an hour; good ferry; sandy bottom with large rocks.	M. F. 10 4	M. F. 26 0	Four roads leave Manping: north to Nalao, west to Mankao, south to Náhka and east to Ta Man Hsöm on the Salween. The latter road runs through the village and soon descends, crosses a small stream and drops several hundred feet to a narrow strip of paddy-fields through which a small river runs from south to north which has to be forded, easy crossing at this time of year; just below a foot-bridge of two or three trees thrown across the river; the road ascends and runs across a fairly level spur covered with fir trees, then a steep descent to a strip of paddy-fields at 4 miles where a small stream is crossed, followed by a steep slippery rise of 700 feet over a spur of Loi Lán covered with large clumps of bamboo; the descent beyond is more gradual though steep and rocky at first. A small stream is crossed at 7 miles; at 8¼ miles a turning to the right will take you up to the top of Loi Lán, a very steep climb of over 4,500 feet. At 9½ miles there is another good stream. A small stockade has been built over the road and there is flat ground for a small camp, but no room for animals on the spot. This place is called Peng Hpi; just beyond a path runs straight into Umhai (two houses); the road to the Salween runs down to the left; a fairly steep descent of a mile. The banks are covered with dense jungle down to the level of flood rise, about 30 feet above present water level. They are steep, about 30°, and rocky on both sides, but there are occasional small sandy beaches at the ferry on both sides; at flood level there is a narrow stretch of flat ground; that on the right bank is rocky, that on the left is grassy; loads can be taken off on these flat places and carried down to the boats, but it is a rough scramble down, and it is easier to unload a few animals at a time at the water's edge or on the right bank to unload on a sandy beach below the ferrying place, and let the loaded boats pole up stream till they are high enough to cross over. The usual complement of boats here is two dug-outs which hold about 12 mule loads together. If made into a raft with a bamboo platform it is difficult to put on more than 10 mule loads. They would take eight or nine men each; more boats can be got from Ta Supkyet above and Ta Lwawu below by giving notice. Mules should be driven into the water at least 100 yards above the ferry as they drift down stream a great deal, though they can scramble up the banks anywhere on the left bank for some distance

FROM LÁSHIO TO TÁKÖT *viâ* NAWNGHPA AND NALAO—*continued.*

ALTERNATIVE II—*continued.*

Authorities. Military.	Authorities. Civil.	Number and Names of Stages, Rivers and Streams.	Distances. Intermediate.	Distances. Total.	Remarks.
G.O.C. Mandalay District.	Superintendent, Northern Shan States.	**3. Ta Man Hsöm Ferry**—*cont.*			below the ferry. A raft of two boats makes about four trips an hour; single boats cross quicker. Man Hsöm is a village of seven houses at the ferry on the left bank and can supply plenty of men to work boats. The banks above flood rise on the left is flat for nearly ¼ mile below the village, and by clearing the jungle a long narrow camp for several hundred men with their transport can be made. Three clear streams run down from the hill side for drinking water. The village can supply some rice and paddy. The passage of this river under fire from either bank could be made extremely difficult and dangerous. The jungle on both sides consists of trees up to 40 feet in length and 12 inches in diameter, and large bamboos and thick undergrowth.
		4. Hkônyé ... Namné (?).	M. F. 9 4	M. F. 35 4	There are two roads from Man Hsöm, one goes up-hill north and curls round south-east to Pángyáng, but this is said to be very rough. The other runs down stream along the left bank of the Salween for a mile. Part of the road had just been revetted when a bad landslip occurred. It runs up the valley of the Namné which it very soon crosses. The river is 50 feet wide; knee-deep on 3rd January 1893; rough crossing, very rapid; impassable when in flood; the approach on the left bank is steep and very slippery and should be ramped. After this no water till Hkônyé except stagnating pools where pack bullocks water. There is then a steep climb of 1,500 feet, after which the rise along the hill side is gradual for the most part till the top of the spur is reached at 2¼ miles. The path runs along the spur passing two entrances to Manleng north (a village down hill to the left at 3rd mile) and continues rising by steep ascents with level intervals another 1,500 to about 4,300 feet at 7 miles. At 5½ miles, a path down hill on the right leads to Ta Mansôk on the Salween, said to be only a ferry for men, not animals. A little further the road falls, the right path leading to Manleng south, the main road passing over the old site of the village. Higher up there are clearings for cultivation on the right of the path. At 6½ miles another path to Ta Mansôk leads down to the right and a steep ascent beyond is commanded by an old stockade which might be heard to turn as the hill runs down on both sides of it. After this there are short ups and downs to the camp just beyond Hkônyé at 9½ miles. Height about 4,000 feet; plenty of open ground. Two springs, each about a gallon a minute below the village 100 feet, one north, one east, and water obtainable on the western slope of the spur above the village except in the hot weather. Two separate villages, the upper one eight houses, Was; the lower, six houses, Shans, and a kyaung near latter. Highland and lowland cultivation; supplies obtainable.
		5. Camp in Namlông valley. Namlông.	**6 0**	41 4	**The path leaves the lower village of Hkônyé and runs down rather steep north by east; at 1¼ miles path to the left leads to cultivation and villages. The main road, which is a broad one, runs down to the right, descending at**

FROM LÁSHIO TO TÁKÖT *viâ* NAWNGHPA AND NALAO—*continued.*

ALTERNATIVE II—*continued.*

Authorities. Military.	Authorities. Civil.	Number and Names of Stages, Rivers and Streams.	Distances. Intermediate.		Distances. Total.		Remarks.
			M.	F.	M.	F.	
G.O.C. Mandalay District.	Superintendent, Northern Shan States.	**5. Camp in Namlông valley**—*cont.*					2 miles rather steeply to a small stream at 2½ miles where there is flat ground for a small, dry weather camp; beyond is a steep slippery rise of about 300 feet, after which the road runs along the top of the spur for 1 mile, where a path leads up hill to the left to Mankao; ½ a mile further on the road from Ta Supkyet joins in on the left at a "Nát" house, just above the road. On the left is Mankao upper village, about 10 houses with water-supply in a nullah below; rather scarce in hot weather; a little further on the road passes lower Mankao (eight houses and a kyaung) on the left, with its water-supply in a nullah on the right of the road; also slight in hot weather. There is plenty of open ground between these two villages to camp on. The road descends past Mankông (two houses on a knoll) to the valley of the Namlông where there is a strip of paddy-field about 60 yards wide extending some distance down the valley; suitable for a large camp when dry. Several small villages near; supplies obtainable.
		6. Pángyáng ... Namlông and several small streams.	5	4	47	0	The road crosses the Namlông (12 feet wide; shallow; easy crossing) at once at the eastern end of the paddy-fields and runs up a spur for 1½ miles nearly south, then turns east, descends through open cultivation to a saddle from which there is a general rise in the last 2 miles to Pángyáng. The camp is on an open grassy spur south of and commanding the village, and there is more open ground above and west of the village. Plenty of room for a large force. Water-supply on the road before the short steep rise to camp plentiful. Village said to have had 60 houses; about half burnt down in recent attacks by the Sawmaha. The Amátchôk, or Prime Minister of the Tákôt Sawbwa, lives here.

BRANCH I.

FROM NAWNGHPA (STAGE 8) TO MAN HPÁNG (MÔT HAI).

BY CAPT. G. V. BURROWS, PAID ATTACHÉ, INTELLIGENCE DEPARTMENT, BURMA, JANUARY 1891.

Military.	Civil.	Stages.	Inter. M.	Inter. F.	Total M.	Total F.	Remarks.
G.O.C. Mandalay District.	Superintendent, Northern Shan States.	**1. Salween river.** Salween.	6	4	6	4	The road passes through the village and runs between the hills, going south-east. After the 1st mile it begins to descend very rapidly and the path is very steep and rocky, twisting and turning in all directions it runs finally down the next long spur in a north-easterly direction and passes through the little village of Man Ping about 600 yards from the foot of the hill. It continues to run along the hill in a generally north-easterly direction for about 1½ miles, when it rapidly falls again some 300 feet in 800 yards and, running along a level ridge, it turns abruptly down the western bank of Salween.* The river Salween is here about 100 yards broad. From two measurements taken in different places I found it to be—in breadth: (i) at the ferry 138 yards, and (ii) 60 yards below the ferry, 100 yards.

* This is apparently Capt. Yate's Hatseng ferry.—A.F.

FROM LÁSHIO TO TÁKÖT *viâ* NAWNGHPA AND NALAO—*continued.*

BRANCH I—*continued.*

Authorities. Military.	Authorities. Civil.	Number and Names of Stages, Rivers and Streams.	Distances. Inter-mediate.	Distances. Total.	Remarks.
G.O.C. Mandalay District.	Superintendent, Northern Shan States.	**1. Salween river** —*cont.*			I sounded the river in three places and found it to be— (i) 20 yards from west bank, 44 feet. (ii) Mid-stream, 48 feet, (iii) 20 yards from east bank, 14 feet. The banks are precipitous and very rocky, except where the ferry is worked, where there is an approach to the water's edge on sand. The banks are some 40 feet high and show signs of the river having risen some 30 feet when in flood. The bed of the stream appeared to be of sand. The western bank is commanded by the eastern bank and both are thickly wooded. There is no village at the crossing, but due east, ¾ of a mile from the ferry, is the little village of Páng Hé and about 500 yards further on the village of Man Yi (or Man Yö). The current at this time of the year (January) was running nearly 3½ miles an hour. The only means of conveying men and baggage consists of two small boats known by the Burmese as "peingaw." They carry (when lashed together) 12 men or six loads from mules and occupy on an average quarter of an hour on each trip, *i.e.*, time of leaving the west bank and the time of returning to it.
			M. F.	M. F.	
		2. Man Hpáng ...	**6 0**	12 4	The road then runs in a south-east direction through the village of Páng Hé about ¾ mile from the river, turns north-east through the village of Man Yi (or Man Yö) and commences a long steep rise along spur. At 2½ miles it passes to the left of the little village of Nam Kum Hpa. Rising again the road runs up to very nearly the summit of the hill, turns off to the east and, running along the side of the hill, a fairly level course for nearly ¾ mile, it rises over neck, passes the village of Kôn, Kha and, rising over the next small spur, turns to the left to the village of Man Hpáng, capital of Môt Hai (or Môthai), which is, however, only a small village of 30 houses. The Sawbwa resides here. Paddy and rice are procurable.

BRANCH II.

FROM PÁNG YÁNG (STAGE 16) TO MAN HPÁNG (MÔT HAI).

NATIVE INFORMATION, JANUARY 1893.

Military.	Civil.	Number and Names of Stages, Rivers and Streams.	Intermediate. M. F.	Total. M. F.	Remarks.
G.O.C. Mandalay District.	Superintendent, Northern Shan States.	**1. Nam Ya Yung**	**5 0**	5 0	Jungle camp.
		2. Nam Hka Káng.	**12 0**	17 0	A road branches to west here which goes direct to Nalao; stages, Na Kao and Ta Loi Sáng.
		3. Nam Hsai Kam.	...	...	
		4. Páng Mwé ...	...	25 0	
		5. Yawng U ...	...	30 0	A rough road, but passable for pack animals.
		6. Man Seng ...	...	...	
		7. Man Hka ...	...	...	
		8. Man Hpáng ... Nam Náng.	...	55 0	

FROM LÁSHIO TO TÁKÖT *viâ* NAWNGHPA AND NALAO—*continued.*

BRANCH III.

FROM MAN HPÁNG (BRANCH I, STAGE 2) TO MÔT LÉ.

NATIVE INFORMATION, JANUARY 1893.

Authorities.		Number and Names of Stages, Rivers and Streams.	Distances.		Remarks.
Military.	Civil.		Intermediate.	Total.	
			M. F.	M. F.	
G.O.C. Mandalay District.	Superintendent, Northern Shan States.	**1. Man Kun (?)**...	...	...	*Note.*—The stages in this route are bullock stages of about 7 miles each.
		Nam Hsum.			
		2. Kawng Hsen Wi.	...	...	Wa.
		Nam Ngoi.			
		3. Erg Mu ...	...	...	The Nam Pa marks the boundary between Môt Hai and Môt Lé.
		Nam Pa. Waist-deep in cold weather.			
		4. Tatáng Yawng Palim.	...	...	Wa.
		5. Yawng Nông...	...	...	Wa.
		6. Páng Lai ...	...	...	
		7. Môt Lé ...	...	...	Very short march.

BRANCH IV.

FROM KAT MAW (STAGE 17) TO KENG TUNG (KYENG TUNG).

NATIVE INFORMATION, JANUARY 1893.

Authorities.		Number and Names of Stages, Rivers and Streams.	Distances.		Remarks.
Military.	Civil.		Intermediate.	Total.	
G.O.C. Mandalay District.	Superintendent, Northern Shan States.	**1. Man Nam Tao (Wa village).**	...	...	*Note.*—The stages given in this route are bullock stages of about 7 miles each. Traders go to sell opium, Burmese silk, and Shan cotton cloths and buy *ngapi*; straw hats: ponies Rs. 40 to Rs. 50, cows Rs. 30 to Rs. 40, buffaloes Rs. 30 to Rs. 35.
		Nam Mong.			
		2. Man Nawk (Shan).	...	...	
		Nam Yawng Nam Ya.			
		3. Hsup Ya (Shan).	...	...	
		Nam Ya, Nam Hka at Ta Hsup Ya, which is here the boundary of Mang Lön.			

FROM LÁSHIO TO TÁKÖT *viâ* NAWNGHPA AND NALAO—*continued.*

BRANCH IV—*continued.*

Authorities.		Number and Names of Stages, Rivers and Streams.	Distances.		Remarks.
Military.	Civil.		Intermediate.	Total.	
			M. F.	M. F.	
G.O.C. Mandalay District.	Superintendent, Northern Shan States.	**4. Man Kat Ka (Wa).**	...	...	
		Nam Kyawng.			
		5. Páng Hung (deserted site).	...	...	
		6. Man Nam Tön Tao (Kun).	...	...	
		Cross frequently the Nam Tön, breast-deep; not fordable in rains.			
		7. Tön Nö (jungle camp).	...	...	
		8. Man Seng ...	...	...	
		Nam Nung; not passable in rains.			
		9. Nga Muhsö ...	...	...	
		Nam Nung.			
		10. Man Ang (Kun).	...	...	
		Nam Lwi at Ta Mun Kak.			
		11. Nawng Mu (Shan).	...	...	
		12. Hsup Háng (jungle camp).	...	...	Long march.
		13. Na Tai (jungle camp).	...	...	
		Nam Lwi at Ta Lông.			
		14. Loi Pyit (jungle camp).	...	...	
		15. Neo Hsúm ...	...	...	Short march.
		16. Kat Tau ...	...	...	
		17. Keng Tung (or Kyengtung).	...	...	
		Nam Kön.			

FROM LÁSHIO TO TÁKÖT *viâ* NAWNGHPA AND NALAO—*continued.*

BRANCH V.

FROM TÁKÖT (STAGE 18) TO MÖNG NGA.

NATIVE INFORMATION, JANUARY 1893.

Authorities. Military.	Authorities. Civil.	Number and Names of Stages, Rivers and Streams.	Distances. Intermediate. M. F.	Distances. Total. M. F.	Remarks.
G.O.C. Mandalay District.	Superintendent, Northern Shan States.	**1. Tu La** ...	...	...	*Note.*—The stages in this route were given as bullock stages. The road is said to be good.
		Cross the Nam Ma.			
		2. Wing Kao ...	...	...	
		3. Yawng Kawng	...	...	
		Cross the Nam Köng and Nam Páng by a ford.			
		4. Hsup Wo ...	...	...	
		5. Hkawng Hka...	...	...	
		Cross Nam Hka at Ta Man Pyen.			
		6. Möng Nga ...	...	...	

Another account gives stages as follows :—

Military.	Civil.	Stages.	Intermediate.	Total.	Remarks.
G.O.C. Mandalay District.	Superintendent, Northern Shan States.	**1. Lai Yuk** ...	...	...	*Note.*—The stages in this route are bullock stages.
		Cross Nam Páng, only fordable in hot weather; not now.			
		2. Nam Ling ...	...	...	No village; a jungle camp.
		3. Man Lien ...	...	...	Wa village.
		4. Hkawn Hka ...	...	...	Shan village.
		Cross Nam Hka at Ta Mán Pien.			
		5. Möng Nga ...	...	...	

And a third account as follows :—

Military.	Civil.	Stages.	Intermediate.	Total.	Remarks.
G.O.C. Mandalay District.	Superintendent, Northern Shan States.	**1. Wa Kák** ...	...	...	*Note.*—The stages in this route are evidently double stages; said to be a good road.
		Cross Nam Mawn.			
		2. Páng Kyé ...	...	...	
		Cross Nam Páng at Ta Hsup Man.			
		3. Möng Nga ...	...	...	
		Cross Nam Hka at Ta Man Pyen.			

FROM LÁSHIO TO TÁKÖT *viâ* NAWNGHPA AND NALAO—*continued.*

BRANCH VI.

FROM TÁKÖT TO NA HPÁN.

NATIVE INFORMATION, JANUARY 1893.

Authorities. Military.	Authorities. Civil.	Number and Names of Stages, Rivers and Streams.	Distances. Intermediate. M. F.	Distances. Total. M. F.	Remarks.
G.O.C. Mandalay District.	Superintendent, Northern Shan States.	**1. Wing Kao** ...	...	...	*Note.*—The stages in this route were given as bullock stages. Approximate distance is 40 miles.
		Cross the Namma.			
		2. Kông Yông ...	...	...	
		3. Tu Kalông ...	...	...	
		4. Páng Luk ...	...	...	
		5. Nam Lông ...	...	...	
		Small stream.			
		6. Nam Kung ...	...	...	
		Small stream.			
		7. Na Hpán ...	...	40 0	From Na Hpán it is one march north to Môt Ting, which is in the Wa State Ngek Let, 1½ days' journey from the capital.
		Cross the Nam Páng.			

BRANCH VII.

FROM TÁKÖT TO PÁNG SENG.

NATIVE INFORMATION, FEBRUARY 1893.

Authorities. Military.	Authorities. Civil.	Number and Names of Stages, Rivers and Streams.	Distances. Intermediate. M. F.	Distances. Total. M. F.	Remarks.
G.O.C. Mandalay District.	Superintendent, Northern Shan States.	**1. Man Hsúm** ...	...	...	*Note.*—Probably these are all the villages on the road. The distance cannot be much over 20 miles.
		2. Môt O ...	...	...	
		3. Nam Hsai Kam.	...	...	
		4. Môt Köt ...	...	...	
		5. Um Lông ...	...	...	
		6. Lak Möng ...	...	...	
		7. Nam Tu ...	...	...	
		8. Páng Seng ...	...	20 0	

Another account gives stages as follows:—

Authorities. Military.	Authorities. Civil.	Number and Names of Stages, Rivers and Streams.	Distances. Intermediate. M. F.	Distances. Total. M. F.	Remarks.
G.O.C. Mandalay District.	Superintendent, Northern Shan States.	**1. Tula**	...	...	*Note.*—Distance probably 20 miles these are the villages on the road.
		Cross the Nam Ma.			
		2. Wing Kao ...	...	...	

No. 16.

FROM LÁSHIO TO TÁKÖT *viâ* NAWNGHPA AND NALAO—*continued.*

BRANCH VII—*continued.*

Authorities. Military.	Authorities. Civil.	Number and Names of Stages, Rivers and Streams.	Distances. Intermediate.	Distances. Total.	Remarks.
			M. F.	M. F.	
G.O.C. Mandalay District.	Superintendent, Northern Shan States.	**3. Kwáng Hông** ...	...	...	
		4. Maw Wet ...	...	...	
		5. Maw Pieng ...	...	...	
		6. Môt Si Ung ...	...	...	
		7. Páng Seng ...	...	20 0	

No. 17.

From LÁSHIO to YAWNG U (Ngek Hting State).

INFORMATION OBTAINED BY INTELLIGENCE DEPARTMENT, BURMA, IN FEBRUARY 1893.

Military	Civil	Stages	Intermediate M.	F.	Total M.	F.	Remarks
G.O.C. Mandalay District.	Superintendent, Northern Shan States.	**1. Nawng Hio** ...	9	0	9	0	*Note.*—These stages were made by a convoy of Panthay mules. The Salween is crossed at Man Ang ferry. The road is good throughout, except near Yawng Li. There is a steep rise from the Salween to Páng Hôk and a gradual rise from Páng Hôk to Páng Sáng. Undulating between Páng Sáng and Yawng U. There are two boats at the Salween ferry. Man Ang is about 1,000 feet above the rivet on eastern side. On western side are two Shan villages—Na Táp and Kôn Koi—nearly 1 mile from the river. A small camp on paddy-fields 100 feet above the river on western bank. No camp on eastern bank nearer than Man Ang. An easy ferry to which boats can be brought up from Ta Loi Sáng close to Nalao. Up to the Salween the villages are all Shan, but after crossing the river they are all Wa.
		2. Ho Pai ...	10	0	19	0	
		3. Nam Hsum ...	12	0	31	0	
		4. Möng Tôm ...	10	0	41	0	
		5. Möng Kát ...	9	0	50	0	
		6. Táng Yán ...	11	0	61	0	
		7. Tun Hông ...	*11	0	72	0	*See* Route No. 16, Stage 9.
		8. Ta Man Ang.	...		...		
		9. Páng Hôk ...	13	0	85	0	
		10. Páng Sáng ...	11	0	96	0	Capital of a Wa State and seat of a Sawbwa.
		11. Man Mai ...	9	0	105	0	
		12. Môt Nga ...	9	0	114	0	

* Distance seems from the map to be underestimated. It is more than this as the crow flies.—A.F.

FROM LÁSHIO TO YAWNG U (NGEK HTING STATE)—*continued.*

Authorities. Military.	Authorities. Civil.	Number and Names of Stages, Rivers and Streams.	Distances. Intermediate. M.	Distances. Intermediate. F.	Distances. Total. M.	Distances. Total. F.	Remarks.
G.O.C. Mandalay District.	Supt., Northern Shan States.	**13. Yawng Li** ...	**7**	**0**	121	0	
		14. Yawng U ...	**6**	**0**	127	0	

No. 18.

From LOIKAW (LWÉKAW) to MÔNÉ POST (BAMPÔN) viâ SEKYAWPIN and THATÔN.

BY SECOND LIEUT. M. R. W. NIGHTINGALE, 1ST CHESHIRE REGIMENT, JULY 1892.

Authorities. Military.	Authorities. Civil.	Number and Names of Stages, Rivers and Streams.	Distances. Intermediate. M.	Distances. Intermediate. F.	Distances. Total. M.	Distances. Total. F.	Remarks.
G.O.C. Rangoon District.	Superintendent, Southern Shan States.	**1. Tolong** ... ... Nam Tam-Hpák or Tabet chaung.	**18**	**0**	18	0	Loikaw (Lwékaw) *see* Route No. 4, Stage 8. There are three routes from here to Thatôn (Stage 7): (1) The first crosses the Nam Tam-Hpák or Tabet chaung near Pinkyit and joins Thatôn road at Sisaing. This road is suitable for animal traffic; is the best and most direct. The Tabet chaung is unfordable, but has a ferry of one dug-out. Three days' march. (2) The second road crosses the Tabet chaung at Vinkhun and is suitable for animal traffic; three days' march. (3) The third road is described in detail and is as follows:— General direction north-east and north. Road for first 1½ miles through open plain, then gradually ascends to 8th mile, open jungle with thick undergrowth. Crosses small range at right angles and descends into open undulating grass country; no water. After 12th mile runs along a spur with deep nullahs both sides and thick jungle. Up to 15th mile road suitable for wheeled traffic, it then turns along a narrow path, thick jungle (bamboo and teak), and reaches Tolong, a Shan village, nine houses, 36 people. Bad camping ground on side of Tabet chaung and is a swamp in rains. The river is 80 yards wide, 30 feet deep; mud bottom, rapids above and below; precipitous banks; thickly wooded. Runs in south-east direction into Pônchaung 80 miles off. It is crossed by a ferry of two dug-outs.
		2. Talaungtaung. Talaungtaung chaung, 12 feet broad, 6 inches to 1 foot deep; sandy bottom; precipitous banks; difficult of access.	**6**	**0**	24	0	General direction north-east. Bad jungle track continues up and down; thick bamboo and teak jungle. After 1½ miles road rises and runs along top of several small hills. After 6 miles reach Talaungtaung, a Shan village, 12 houses, 40 people, on side of sloping hill. Bad camping ground. Water from river ¼ mile north.
		3. Taungkaw ...	**6**	**0**	30	0	General direction north. Path lies through thick jungle and over paddy-fields. Taungkaw, three houses, no inhabitants; remainder of village burnt. Good camping ground, and water from small stream. (Possibly this and the next stage could be combined.)

No. 18.

FROM LOIKAW (LWÉKAW) TO MÔNÉ POST (BAMPÔN) *viâ* SEKYAWPIN AND THATÔN—*continued.*

Authorities.		Number and Names of Stages, Rivers and Streams.	Distances.				Remarks.
Military.	Civil.		Intermediate.		Total.		
			M.	F.	M.	F.	
G.O.C. Rangoon District.	Superintendent, Southern Shan States.	**4. Sekyawpin** ...	**6**	**0**	36	0	General direction north. After ½ mile path joins a road suitable for wheeled traffic. Runs over undulating jungle to Sekyaupin, a Shan village, seven houses, 30 inhabitants, on summit of small hill. Good camping ground, but very little water to the west of village 1 mile away.
		5. Kongwáng (Kawnweng).	**6**	**0**	42	0	General direction north-east. Cart road passes through open jungle. At 6th mile a Shan village, Kongwáng, on top of undulation, 20 houses, 80 people. Camping ground. (This and the next stage could probably be combined.)
		6. Sisaing (Hsiksang).	**4**	**0**	46	0	General direction north. Cart road passes over open undulating grass country. At 4th mile Sisaing, a Shan village, 30 houses, 100 inhabitants; many other small villages in immediate neighbourhood. A bazaar is held here once in five days. Good camping ground and water. From here roads lead to Saga (Samka) (*see* Route No. 4, Branch I), to Payákôn and Môbyé (*see* Route No. 21) and to Mokmai (Maukmé, *see idem*).
		7. Thatôn (Satôn) or Loiput (Loipôk).	**8**	**0**	54	0	General direction north-north-east. Good cart road. First mile open undulating country, then through fairly thick jungle; last mile through open country. Thatôn, a Shan town, capital of the state of same name, 100 houses, 300 inhabitants; many small villages in neighbourhood. Bazaar once in five days. Good camping ground, zayáts, and plenty of water.
		8. Pônywa ...	**12**	**0**	66	0	General direction east. Open undulating grass country. At 4th mile crosses at right angles range of hills and descends 1,200 feet by steep rocky road to Pôn chaung. Camping ground 200 feet above river. Pônywa, a Shan village, 15 houses, 40 people.
		Nam Pawn or Pôn chaung, 80 yards wide, 20 feet deep; rocky bottom; rapid current; fordable in dry season; one dug-out for ferry boat. Flows 100 miles south into Salween river.					
		9. Namping ...	**12**	**0**	78	0	General direction east. Steep rocky path, ascending 900 feet through thick swampy jungle on to open undulating grass plateau with many scattered villages. Namping, a Shan village, 20 houses, 50 inhabitants; bazaar once in five days; zayáts; camping ground; plenty of water.

FROM LOIKAW (LWÉKAW) TO MÔNÉ POST (BAMPÔN) *viâ* SEKYAWPIN AND THATÔN—*continued.*

Authorities. Military.	Authorities. Civil.	Number and Names of Stages, Rivers and Streams.	Distances. Intermediate.	Distances. Total.	Remarks.
			M. F.	M. F.	
G.O.C. Rangoon District.	Superintendent, Southern Shan States.	**10. Nákyem** ... River (name unknown), 20 feet broad, 1 foot deep; sandy bottom; rapid current; precipitous banks; 10 feet high; difficult of access.	**11 0**	89 0	General direction east and north-east. Path continually up and down; thick jungle; small river at 8th mile. Nákyem, a Shan village, 12 houses, 30 inhabitants; many villages in neighbourhood; camping ground; water; zayáts.
		11. Bampôn (Môné Post), 4,000 feet.	**9 0**	98 0	General direction north-east. Path continually up and down, passing through paddy-fields and swampy jungle; several small villages in neighbouring valleys. Bampôn, a small Shan village; 10 houses; 30 inhabitants; camping grounds; water. A military station here for the protection of Môné, with accommodation for 100 sepoys.

No. 19.

From MAINGLÔN (MAINLUNG) to MANPUN.

BY H. F. HERTZ, ESQ., BURMA POLICE, JANUARY 1890.

Military	Civil	Stages	Intermediate	Total	Remarks
G.O.C. Mandalay District.	Superintendent, Northern Shan States.	**1. Mankung** ... One stream.	**10 0**	10 0	Road good. Cross small stream at 8 miles. Direction of road east.
		2. Nampyit (camp). One stream.	**10 0**	20 0	Road good, running through light bamboo and tree jungle. It rises steadily for 5 miles, and the remainder of the road is a steep descent. Cross a small stream just before reaching camp. There is good ground for camp in light bamboo jungle. The village lies 2 miles north and consists of 25 houses and a small kyaung. Practically no accommodation.
		3. Möngngaw ... One stream and chaung (three times).	**12 0**	32 0	General direction east by north. A steady ascent for 5 miles along the ridge of a range. The road then descends to 7 miles and here crosses a stream. After this it rises rather steeply, and again descends to 10 miles. A chaung is crossed three times between 10 and 12 miles. It is 15 yards wide, 3 feet deep. The road runs throughout jungle and is fair. The Palaung village of Hkön is passed at 6 miles. It contains 20 houses. Möngngaw affords good accommodation in kyaung and zayáts.

FROM MAINGLÔN (MAINLUNG) TO MANPUN—*continued.*

Authorities. Military.	Authorities. Civil.	Number and Names of Stages, Rivers and Streams.	Distances. Intermediate. M.	F.	Total. M.	F.	Remarks.
G.O.C. Mandalay District.	Superintendent, Northern Shan States.	**4. Lungloi (Longlwi).** One chaung.	8	0	40	0	Direction north-east. A good road, 6 feet wide and well kept. It ascends a small hill to 1 mile and then descends into paddy-fields, and crosses the same chaung as in the last march. The remainder of the road is a steady ascent. Pass Loipeng at 4 miles, 10 houses, no kyaung. At Lungloi is accommodation for 150 men in kyaung and zayáts.
		5. Pángsali ...	8	0	48	0	General direction north-east. A good wide well kept road. It ascends to 1 mile and then runs over undulating hill crests. The country is open. Pass Wengmun at 5 miles, a large village with kyaung and zayáts. At Pángsali is accommodation for 150 men in kyaung and zayáts. Water close by. From here there is a road to Namsán, which lies 15 miles east-south-east.
		6. Manpát (Raosi, Palaung). One stream (bridged).	8	0	56	0	The road runs north and is good and wide. It descends at first to a stream crossed by a good wooden bridge. This stream is fordable at all times. From the stream the road ascends the whole way to Manpát steep through the jungle. Room for 150 men in kyaung and zayáts. Pass Yanghen (Shan) or Yanghai (Palaung) *en route.*
		7. Pánglun (Penglong).	8	0	64	0	The road runs north-east and is fairly good. It runs up a very steep ascent to 5⅛ miles and then descends in a similar manner to the village. Small kyaung and zayáts.
		8. Humöng ...	8	0	72	0	The road runs north by west along a ridge. It is level, but is narrow. Humöng is a large village with ample accommodation in kyaung and zayáts.
		9. Manpun (4,784 feet).	12	0	84	0	The road is indifferent, and in the latter part difficult. It descends steep spurs to stream at 8 miles and then runs up a steep ascent to Manpun. General direction is north by east.

No. 20.

From MANGMAW (Route No. 62, Stage 9) to NAMKHAM viâ MANPÁN FERRY and SÉLÁN,

BY CAPT. H. B. WALKER, ATTACHÉ, INTELLIGENCE BRANCH, MARCH 1892.

G.O.C. Mandalay District.	Supdt., Northern Shan States.	**1. Tákyo Kyi or West H'Senshán.**	8	0	8	0	Mangmaw, *see* Route No. 62, Stage 9. General direction first 4 miles south, then west. Leaving the camp at Mangmaw the route runs through the village in a southerly direction along

FROM MANGMAW (ROUTE No. 62, STAGE 9) TO NAMKHAM *viâ* MANPÂN FERRY AND SÉLÂN—*continued.*

Authorities. Military.	Authorities. Civil.	Number and Names of Stages, Rivers and Streams.	Distances. Intermediate.	Distances. Total.	Remarks.
G.O.C. Mandalay District.	Superintendent, Northern Shan States.	**1. Tákyo Kyi or West H'Senshán** —*cont.*			the route to Kya Sa Yo and Si Tôn Phyin for 4 miles when it reaches the long spur Pálián S'Shán. Instead then of following the route to Kya Sa Yo, it turns west along the spur by a good sound path passing at 4¼ miles to left hand, or south, Kyin Kyi village; at mile 5½ La Phán Kyi and at mile 7 Tonánza; each five or six houses. The stream Ma Tai Haw (or Kwinpwé Haw) flows parallel to the ridge all the way. On an opposite or southern ridge are seen the villages of Mantinshán and Yawyaio, while on its western summit is the village of Kwin Pwé or Kem Pwé. At Tákyo Kyi, five or six houses (Kôkáng); few supplies and camp for 50 men on southern side. The route continues along the spur for ½ mile and descending reaches camp on route for 100 men, then follows path to north for 300 yards to village of H'Senshán; three or four houses; no supplies; where there is camping ground for 50 men on a small knoll on southern side of and immediately above the village. The water-supply for both these two camps lies in a hollow between them at equal distance from both; plentiful supply, but of inferior quality. *N.B.*—Both these camps are much exposed to the high winds that blow during the months of March and April.
		2. Kwin Pwé (Kem Pwé), 5,050 feet. Kwin Pwé Haw or Ma Tai Haw.	M. F. 4 6	M. F. 12 6	General direction south-west. Leaving the camp at H'Senshán village, the route runs for 1¾ miles, winding round first the northern, then the western slopes of the range of Pálián S'Shán down to the Kwin Pwé or Ma Tai Haw, the Salween being visible for the first ½ mile below to the right hand or north. The Kwin Pwé Haw (15 to 20 yards from bank to bank; 1 to 3 feet deep; very rocky bed; rapid current), which discharges itself into the Salween, is crossed by a covered bridge 3 feet wide built of stout timbers 10 inches thick, and capable of sustaining heavy traffic. The route then runs northward along and rather above the left bank of the river for ¼ of a mile, then strikes up a steep ascent of nearly 2 miles to the village of Yaio; 12 houses; usual supplies, paddy, &c., obtainable; water in centre of village. Small camping ground for 50 men possible to be made just beyond the village on road side. No grass; bamboo leaves obtainable. To the south of spur thus ascended runs a parallel spur on which is situated the double village of Mantin Shán, a stream dividing the two spurs. Passing the village of Yaio the route runs north-west along the top of the spur for nearly a mile up to the large well-to-do Lawa village of Kwin Pwé; 30 houses; good supplies; situated on the ridge, which continues to run northwards, eventually sloping to the Salween. The usual camping ground is 300 yards below the village to the south where there is accommodation for 100 men, there being accommodation for as many more along either side of the road with difficulty between the village and camp. There is, moreover, accommodation for another 500 or 600 men in the village itself and along the spur running westwards before it begins to descend, though it would have to be cleared of jungle and the water-supply is rather distant, being obtained (1) from a hill-side stream 50 yards south of

FROM MANGMAW (ROUTE NO. 62, STAGE 9) TO NAMKHAM *viâ* MANPÁN FERRY AND SÉLÁN—*continued*.

Authorities.		Number and Names of Stages, Rivers and Streams.	Distances.		Remarks.
Military.	Civil.		Intermediate.	Total.	
G.O.C. Mandalay District.	Superintendent, Northern Shan States.	**2. Kwin Pwé (Kem Pwé), 5,050 feet**—*cont.*			usual camp, and (2) from a reservoir east of village which is supplied from the first-mentioned stream, being carried across the intervening space by means of a bamboo aqueduct. The march, on account of the long climb up from the Ma Tai Haw, though short, is a fair stage for laden animals. From Kwin Pwé a route runs out southwards to Mantôn, the first onward stage being Kwinpáng, situated on the western slope of the next spur but one to the south. The next Tamachán, the next Nan Kong Haw, then Mantôn, *see* Route No. 64. The route is said to be a good one, each march being judged for laden mules.
		3. Manpán ferry. Salween river.	M. F. **3 0**	M. F. 15 6	Leaving Kwin Pwé for the Manpán ferry the route goes out of the village west and runs along the spur on which it is situated, and so descends for 3 miles by a good path and tolerable gradient. There is camping ground for 70 or 80 men on a small level spot by the river, here 80 yards wide, 40 feet deep in centre, and with a current of 4 miles an hour. The ferry consists of only one raft and one small dug-out. The fer y house being on the western side or right bank of the r. ver and half-way up the steep ascent. *Note.*—From the account of the route there would apparently be no difficulty in marching from West H'Senshán to Manpán ferry if more convenient, but the camping ground at Kwin Pwé is mor extensive than at Manpán ferry.
		4. Powáng (4,650 feet).	**5 6**	21 4	General direction west. After crossing to the right bank of the Salween the route strikes up a steep spur for nearly 2 miles by a zigzagging but sound path through open jungle, the direction being north-westerly. Another route branches off south-west to Möng-hawm two marches distant. At the top of a spur stands the Kachin village of Hi To Shán, 20 houses, in two parts, one immediately opposite where the route debouches from the spur on to the ridge, the other a mile along the route, which now runs in a more westerly direction on the top of the ridge. Water is here obtained down the northern side of the ridge $\frac{1}{4}$ of a mile, and there is an excellent camping ground, capable of being formed along the ridge between the two portions of Hi To Shán by clearing away the kaing grass on either side of the road, capable of accommodating 300 or 400 men. The route to Manhin runs along the ridge eastwards. The onward route now, after crossing a slight ascent by an excellent broad path, follows the ridge westerly for 2 miles. After passing larger Hi To Shán the route winds along the northern slopes of the ridge, with the valley of the Nampun (or Namyo) or Manpán stream below and to the right hand or north. The prominent hill of Myin S'Shan is also visible to that side. At mile $4\frac{1}{2}$ the large Kachin village of Takyin (18 houses) is passed through, while clusters of villages of the same name lie to southern side of ridge. The Palaung village (Palaungkyi) is passed to right hand on a small hill at mile 5, the clusters of villages which form Powáng circle being reached at mile $5\frac{3}{4}$; Upper Powáng (40 houses) is most suitable for a camp, there being accommodation for 100 men on the ridge to the north after passing through the village. Supplies

FROM MANGMAW (ROUTE No. 62, STAGE 9) TO NAMKHAM *viâ* MANPÁN FERRY AND SÉLÁN—*continued.*

Authorities. Military.	Authorities. Civil.	Number and Names of Stages, Rivers and Streams.	Distances. Intermediate.	Distances. Total.	Remarks.
G.O.C. Mandalay District.	Superintendent, Northern Shan States.	**4. Powáng (4,650 feet)**—*cont.*			obtainable, though with difficulty and delay paddy Rs. 1-8-0 a basket, rice Rs. 2-10-0 a basket. Water is obtainable 600 yards to south from a small stream, sufficient, if carefully husbanded, for 150 men. Animals must be watered a mile to north of camp in a small stream. No grass; bamboo leaves in abundance.
		5. Pônseng or Nônkyáng.	M. F. **8 0** **9 6**	M. F. 29 4 31 2	General direction a little north of west. The route leaves the village of Powáng on the south-westerly side, descending from the spur on which Powáng stands for a short distance into a narrow ravine, a route striking off to the left hand or south to Möngya, broad and apparently much used. [At about 700 yards a route strikes off to the right or north to Manhin (one short march) or H'Senshán (two marches) along a narrow valley running in front of the spur Powáng stands on.] Route then ascends a short spur for a mile, the Palaung village of Manka on spur sloping to left or south being passed at mile 1 from Powáng. A few yards further on a route to left or south runs to Möngya, another to right, opposite, leading towards Manhin or H'Senshán, both roads apparently well used. At mile 1½ the route runs level for a little, passing to left or south village of Shiokupai. Another route broad and well used striking off along a valley (which apparently runs into the Manpán valley) to Manhin (or H'Senshán). The route then rises a little, commencing to ascend a long ridge running along a narrow valley on its summit, which is chaotic, minor ridges and spurs traversing it. The valley is cultivated with opium. At mile 3 route crosses the western slopes of a minor ridge and, passing through a gap, descends to the small Kachin village of Lunyintán (four houses), which it leaves on left hand, a fourth route striking off to north or right hand to Manhin, which descends the northern slopes of main ridge into valley of the Manpán stream, a mile distant. Water in small quantities may be obtained at this village, being obtained along a minor valley, west of the village. The route now rises a little and runs along the northern slopes of main ridge. The Manpán valley, apparently 300 or 400 yards wide, and cultivated, intersected by stream of same name flowing into the Salween, lying below to right hand or north. On the opposite side of the Manpán valley the ridge or hill called Hôpáng dotted with villages is visible. At mile 5¼ route rises to cross a spur branching from ridge south-west, runs level a short distance through jungle, having taken a more southerly turning, and then descends at mile 6½ on to ridge (turning west again, which here broadens out and is cultivated) by a zigzagging route. Pônseng, standing on a rise in the ridge, is visible ahead. The distinctive hill Loi Seng in valley to left or south-west, a route to Manhin between route and Manpán stream, the hill Hôpáng, the hill Kongmo, more westerly, and between these two, further north, a ridge known as Manyôpa hill, along the crest of which the frontier runs, being all visible. On Manyôpa are situated the extreme frontier villages of Ta Phyinsa and Hôsipa. [*N.B.*—Manyôpa is a day's march from Pônseng, and Chéfán (Séfán) town in a north-westerly direction is two days'

FROM MANGMAW (ROUTE No. 62, STAGE 9) TO NAMKHAM *viâ* MANPÁN FERRY AND SÈLAN—*continued.*

Authorities. Military.	Authorities. Civil.	Number and Names of Stages, Rivers and Streams.	Distances. Intermediate.	Distances. Total.	Remarks.
G.O.C. Mandalay District.	Superintendent, Northern Shan States.	**5. Pônseng or Nônkyáng**—*cont.*			march further on *viâ* Sinkyi (400 houses), Chinese-Shans, the road being good and down-hill to Chéfán.] The last mile into Pônseng rises a little, the route to right hand to Manhin striking along the lower northern slopes of ridge at 7½ miles and another to Ma htáng village to left or south. The path, though broken and narrow in places, is good, the last ⅛ mile into Pônseng being broad and well used. Pônseng consists of three villages, one Palaung (also called Nônseng), and two Kachin villages, in all containing about 40 houses. There is only camping ground in the Palaung portion (1) at entrance to village near kyaung for 60 men; (2) along the spur ½ mile through village to west for same number; (3) to north of kyaung along Möngko road, about 300 yards for 100 men. (There is a large stagnant tank which can be utilized for watering horses here.) Water-supply for 300 men in village. Other supplies, paddy, and rice can be obtained from neighbouring villages in fair quantities (paddy 12 annas a big basket). To Nônkyáng, 1¾ miles along Möngko road. The route strikes down a spur to north-west of village rising at ¾ of a mile, then descending to Nônkyáng passing on spur to left hand or south-west one of the several villages named Manyáng, which are situated on this spur, and along the spur running to left hand of route from Nônkyáng to Möngya, *see* Route No. 68. Nônkyáng is a Kachin village, 10 houses; limited paddy and rice, no other supplies; water is obtained down slope to north from small stream in plenty. Möngko is 9½ miles further west; good road (*see* Route No. 68).
		6. Camp or Namko Haw. Namko Haw.	M. 5 F. 0	M. 36 F. 2	General direction a little west of south. Leaving Nônkyáng route strikes southward along a continuous spur, passing to left hand or east of Upper Nônkyáng (in ruins) and another Manyáng (Kachin villages). The route then winds along the ridge for 2 miles, then descends for ⅛ mile, runs level along the dip of the spur for 200 or 300 yards, rises for ¼ of a mile, and on level to the large village of Pansita (Palaungs) at mile 3. *N.B.*—Here supplies must be obtained and carried on to camp on the Namko Haw (paddy, &c.). Pansita, 20 or 30 houses, is situated on eastern side of ridge below path. From Pansita a broad well used track leads northwards for Möngko, skirting the western slope of ridge; from Pansita route follows spur descending a little and winding across it from its western to eastern slopes, the valley of the Namko Haw being beneath to right hand. The route then zigzags down into the valley by a very steep path across cultivation for a mile, the last ⅛ mile following ridge of a minor spur. With the exception of where route leaves Nônkyáng and passes Pansita, it runs through open jungle ½ a mile before Pansita, the hill sides being completely bare. Except at this village, no water can be obtained on the route till the valley of the Namko Haw is reached. Namko Haw flowing from Möngko flows onward to Salween some 2 or 3 miles distant and there discharges itself. There is camping ground in the valley, which is semi-circular, for 300 men; good grass obtainable, also bamboo leaves. Stream is 25 yards broad, 1 foot to 3 feet deep, and rapid and stony; easy crossings.

FROM MANGMAW (ROUTE No. 62, STAGE 9) TO NAMKHAM *viâ* MANPÁN FERRY AND SELÁN—*continued.*

Authorities.		Number and Names of Stages, Rivers and Streams.	Distances.				Remarks.
Military.	Civil.		Intermediate.		Total.		
			M.	F.	M.	F.	
G.O.C. Mandalay District.	Superintendent, Northern Shan States.	**7. Camp below Hupong.** Nammoi or Namwé river and two small streams.	8	0	44	2	General direction south. Leaving the camp on the left bank of the Namko Haw the route crosses the stream and commences to ascend the opposite side of the valley, first working up between two spurs across half-an-acre of paddy cultivation, where there is camping ground for 40 men, then striking up the left hand or eastern spur crossing a narrow stream (2 yards wide, good drinking water) and following the spur to the top of the ridge where the small Kachin village of Loiyin is situated (four houses and scarcely any supplies); at mile 1½ the route then crosses and descends south side of ridge by a steep winding broken path for ½ mile and at bottom crosses a stream 3 yards wide, 9 inches deep, stony bottom, good drinking water. The route then commences to ascend by a zigzag path 6 feet broad and good under foot, and after crossing from one minor spur to another reaches the Kachin village of Akákyi at mile 4 (six or seven houses), until recently belonging to Möngko circle, now handed over to Möngya, standing on top of ridge to left hand or east of route and 70 yards along ridge. The route then descends in a southerly direction down the southern slopes of the ridge, crossing a hill-side stream at mile 4½, when it strikes the long spur, which running south-eastward is terminated by the hill Pánghai Shán, which slopes abruptly into the Nammwé or Nammoi valley. The route runs along the northern side of the spur to mile 5¾, passing the large Palaung village of Pángtáp situated on a parallel spur to left hand or north-east. At mile 6 the route strikes across to southern side of spur and commences to descend by a subsidiary spur into the Nammwé or Nammoi valley, crossing on to the lower slopes of another spur at mile 7, reaching the valley at 7¾ miles; here the desolate village of Nahet or, as it is sometimes called, Náshi (Kachins and Shans, three houses) is passed through. At mile 8 the camping ground is reached in paddy-fields, beneath the village of Hupong (seven houses, Kachins) situated on a hill of the same name. The valley of the Nammoi or Nammwé, which here widens out a little, is about 500 yards across from stream to foot of the Hupong hill; the hills on opposite side of stream, the termination of the range in which the hill Loi Saw is situated, run precipitously down to stream, which flows on eastward into Salween. The Nammoi or Nammwé stream is 1 foot to 4 feet deep, with rapid current, and stony bottom, 40 feet to 60 feet wide. Supplies difficult to obtain from Hupong, though there is paddy in the village; other supplies *nil*. With the exception of the climb up to Akákyi, from the valley between that village and Loiyin, the path is broken, narrow, and rocky; the last 2½ miles, descending into the Nammoi or Nammwé valley being specially bad, while the march, if made, from Nahet or Náshi to Namko Haw camp would be a very rough one and trying to pack animals.

FROM MANGMAW (ROUTE No. 62, STAGE 9) TO NAMKHAM *viâ* MANPÁN FERRY AND SÉLÁN—*continued.*

Authorities. Military.	Authorities. Civil.	Number and Names of Stages, Rivers and Streams.	Distances. Intermediate. M. F.	Distances. Total. M. F.	Remarks.
G.O.C. Mandalay District.	Superintendent, Northern Shan States.	**8. Möngya** ... Nammoi, Möngya Haw, and small streams.	5 6	50 0	General direction south-west. Leaving the camp route follows the left bank of Nammwé or Nammoi, passing through jungle and crossing the lower slope of a spur, which runs from the Hupong hill; at mile 1 a route strikes back from right hand northwards to Hupong, a small stream running into the Nammoi being crossed 200 yards further on; the Nammoi at this point is 150 yards from route, while to the right hand or west the hills run back, forming a valley down which a small stream flows. At mile 2 the valley narrows, the hills on either side of the Nammwé running down closely and ending precipitously over the stream. The path rising to get on the slopes of the ridge on left bank. At mile 3 the valley commences to widen again, the hills to west or on left bank (along which route lies) running back. Up to this point the path is broken and very narrow and requires much repair where rising and descending. At mile 3½ route debouches on large paddy-fields capable of affording camping ground for a brigade or more, passing the small villages of Namao on opposite bank of the stream, 300 yards along the paddy-fields, one small stream is crossed, flowing into Nammwé, and 100 yards further on the Möngya Haw (5 yards wide, 1 foot deep; rocky; easy crossings) which flows down a valley from the west, up which valley also a route to Möngko is said to run. Just before mile 4 the paddy-fields are left and the route continues along the left bank of Nammwé and close to it, passing the well-to-do Shan village of Mannimaw or Mannaw, eight or 10 houses, and half-a-dozen mills for husking paddy worked by water. The route then becomes broad and excellent and runs almost straight to mile 5, passing a large tiled pôngyi kyaung to left hand or bank of the stream, 500 yards past the village of Manhaw. At mile 5¼ the large Shan village of Manmaw is passed (20 houses), and at mile 5½ the small village of Mankôn (good supplies of paddy can be obtained at the price of 6 annas a big basket from either village, but nothing else). Möngya is reached ¼ of a mile further, six or eight houses, and plentiful paddy supply at 6 annas a basket. Möngya lies 700 yards from the Nammwé, the intervening space being large paddy-fields, where an excellent camp is obtained. Accommodation for a brigade. Across the stream on the right bank are hot springs strongly impregnated with sulphur; these discharge themselves into the Nammwé which is here 90 feet across, 2 feet deep, and flows 2½ miles an hour; gravelly bottom. From here roads lead south to Mönghawm and Möngsi (*see* Route No. 68), and north to Möngko (*see* same route).
		9. Mukhwon (5,880 feet). Nammoi.	9 2	59 2	General direction west. The route follows the valley of the Nammoi or Nammwé for rather more than ¼ mile after leaving the camp, when it crosses from the left to right bank by a very solid bridge for foot-passengers, 3 feet wide, 11 inches thick. The route then, after rising a little, runs along right bank by a level, though narrow, and rather stony path,

FROM MANGMAW (ROUTE No. 62, STAGE 9) TO NAMKHAM *viâ* MANPÁN FERRY AND SÉLÁN—*continued.*

Authorities.		Number and Names of Stages, Rivers and Streams.	Distances.		Remarks.
Military.	Civil.		Intermediate.	Total.	
G.O.C. Mandalay District.	Superintendent, Northern Shan States.	**9. Mukhwon (5,880 feet)**—*cont.*			through jungle, to mile 1. The route to Mönghawm strikes off to left or south immediately after crossing the bridge. At mile 1¾ route descends a little and recrosses the stream to left bank, traversing a large paddy-field after doing so, capable of camping 1,500 men. There the ridge Loi Wámao on northern side of valley bends away, while the head of another ridge commencing and continuing as the northern side enclosure of Nammwé valley, another valley is formed, which runs parallel with the Nammwé valley and to north of it. After crossing the paddy-field the route enters the jungle again by a level path and runs close to the Nammwé as far as mile 2½, when it bears away a little and commences to ascend the ridge. At mile 3 the path takes a northern turn and then ascent becomes very steep until top of ridge is reached at mile 3¾. The Nammwé valley is here left, and the valley of a smaller stream flowing into Nammwé is traversed. At mile 4¼ a small village down slopes to right hand or north is passed, bearing the name of Mukhwon, probably an off-shoot of the larger village at end of stage. The first range here also winds round again (Loi Wamao) the large Kachin village whence the range derives its name lying on summit. The route follows the ridge by an excellent and almost level path through light jungle to mile 6¾, when the ridge terminates in Loi Mukhwon along the northern slopes of which, by a subsidiary spur, the route ascends by an excessively steep zigzagging path to mile 8, when it follows another ridge for ½ a mile, then striking northward along a spur to mile 9, when it reaches the Kachin village of Mukhwon (15 houses) belonging to the Möngpa circle. Supplies: paddy (Re. 1 a big basket), rice, and opium. The camping ground is very limited, for 40 men, in centre of village (soiled and dirty), and 50 more ¼ mile north-east of village on small knoll on spur. The water-supply is very scanty; for 100 men and animals in limited quantities can be obtained (1) from ½ mile down hill to north-east, (2) ½ mile down spur to south-east; obtained in both cases from springs, troughs having to be formed of mud to collect the water temporarily for animals. The route for the last ½ mile before village, crosses extensive opium cultivation on sides of slopes. The path after once leaving the Nammwé valley is bad wherever it ascends, and no water is obtainable after leaving the Nammwé stream.
		10. Möngpaw (3,350 feet). Nampaw.	M. F. 7 6	M. F. 67 0	General direction north-west. The route, leaving Mukhwon, follows the route back towards Möngya for 400 yards, when it takes a westerly turn and runs along the southern slopes of the main spur as far as 1¼ miles, when it descends slightly, rising again to the large Kachin village of Vimkôk (30 houses) at 1½ miles, situated on small knoll running southward from spur. A long ridge to southward runs parallel to route, thickly wooded and separated by a narrow valley; a third ridge still further to the south being visible and parallel to the first two. As far as Vimkôk the spur sides are bare, or only lightly clad with thin scanty jungle. After passing through Vimkôk the route descends again and winds as far as mile 2½ amongst

From MANGMAW (Route No. 62, Stage 9) to NAMKHAM *viâ* MANPÂN FERRY and SÉLÂN—*continued*.

Authorities. Military.	Authorities. Civil.	Number and Names of Stages, Rivers and Streams.	Distances. Intermediate.	Distances. Total.	Remarks.
G.O.C. Mandalay District.	Superintendent, Northern Shan States.	**10. Möngpaw (3,350 feet)**—*cont.*			the lower eminences of the southern slopes of the spur; thick jungle on either side of route; the path though narrow is good and sound and capable of sustaining heavy traffic. At mile 2 there is a wet nullah containing drinking water in scanty quantities. At mile 2⅛ path rises on to top of ridge or spur, once more at mile 3 the parallel ridge south of Vimkôk joins with other ridge and route passes on to it, and runs along its southern slopes to mile 3½, when it passes below the highest point of the ridge Loi Namkyet to right hand or north. The route then descends for ¼ mile into the first part of the wide spreading village (Kachin) of Namkyet, said to contain over 200 houses, and to be the residence of the Myoza of the Möngpaw circle. Large supplies can be obtained here. A further descent of 400 yards reaches the centre of the village, which runs all the way along the slopes on both sides of the route. From this point a fine view is obtained to the west of the Möngpaw valley beneath, the main ridge just crossed forming the watershed between the Salween and the Irrawaddy, towards which river the Shwéli drains all minor streams. Numerous spurs dotted with light jungle run down westward into the Möngpaw valley more or less parallel with each other. The route now descends by an excellent path, averaging 6 feet wide, to mile 6¼, along an easy spur clad with light jungle and abounding in orchids, when the Möngpaw valley is reached, passing on a parallel spur to south the Kachin village of Namkhwon at mile 5¾. The Möngpaw valley, which here runs south-west and north-east and is intersected by the Nampaw stream, is entirely under cultivation and is ½ a mile wide, the route crosses it (Nampaw stream here 3 yards wide, 1 foot deep; gravelly bottom, grassy, sound bank; requires bridging for traffic) in a westerly direction to the village of Möngpaw (40 houses, Shan) which is situated on a knoll or slope from the hills on western side of valley. Here there is good camping ground for 300 men, water being obtained from the valley from any of the numerous rivulets flowing through it. There is also accommodation in the paddy-fields for any number of men. Supplies: paddy 6 annas a basket, rice, vegetable, &c., excellent grass for animals obtainable in valley. The village is stockaded by a fence of prickly growth and entered under an archway guarded by a wooden gate. It is under the usual subordinate official, who takes orders from the Namkyet Myoza. The route from Mukhwon is good marching throughout, but with the exception of one wet nullah, and at Vimkôk and Namkyet, no water is obtainable *en route*. From here there is a road direct to Möngko (*see* Alternative I below) and another to Sélán *viâ* Hôké, &c. (*see* same Alternative route). Other villages in the Möngpaw circle are said to be Hupong, Loisa, Nongheng, Pankham, Pupak, Loilak, Pankyôn, Hukyé, Taliak, Loilem, Namkyet, Namhông, Hawwa, Pyinhoi, Manphyin, Mansé, Hôkáng, Manmông.
		11. Wanteng or Manlim. Namyáng and several small streams.	M. F. 8 0	M. F. 75 0	General direction a little west of north. Leaving Möngpaw the route runs along the western side of the Nampaw valley for ⅛ mile and then enters the hills which, running down from the western side, here narrow the

FROM MANGMAW (ROUTE No. 62, STAGE 9) TO NAMKHAM *viâ* MANPÁN FERRY AND SÈLÁN—*continued.*

Authorities. Military.	Authorities. Civil.	Number and Names of Stages, Rivers and Streams.	Distances. Intermediate.	Distances. Total.	Remarks.
G.O.C. Mandalay District.	Superintendent, Northern Shan States.	**11. Wanteng or Manlim**—*cont.*			Nampaw valley. Light jungle on both sides. The route ascends an easy spur by a good path 4 feet broad to mile 1½, where the Kachin village of Loilem (eight houses) is reached, the route passing through the village. From Loilem a route strikes off east to the Kachin village of Hupong in the Möngpaw circle. The route now descends for ¼ of a mile into a narrow and bare valley, on the western or left-hand side of which the sugarloaf-shaped hill Loilem stands prominently in notice. The path along this valley is narrow, but capable of being widened with little trouble. At 3 miles the Kachin village of Tángdet is passed to right hand or east, situated on the crest of the eastern ridges of the valley. At 4¾ miles the valley ends and the route commences to rise, crossing three small spurs and reaching the Kachin village of Tungaw (30 houses) to right hand or east of road at 5¾ miles. The Kachin village of Páliak is said to be a little lower down on the slopes to same side. Close jungle of bamboo and larger timber on both sides of path which, after leaving the valley, is good and sound, though narrow, not exceeding 3 feet anywhere. The route now passes on to another spur and rising a very little reaches a gap in the summit of the ridge which forms the southern enclosure of the Wanteng valley at 6 miles. Here a path to right hand runs up to top of ridge to the Kachin village of Kanna, ½ a mile distant and the residence of the Kachin Sawbwa of the Wanteng circle. The route now commences to descend a long, winding, easy spur into the Wanteng valley, assuming a rather westerly direction. The path here is excellent, being 8 feet broad in some places. Thin jungle on either side. The Wanteng valley spread out beneath, green and fertile, affords a fine view. At 7½ miles the small Shan village of Mankáng (five houses) is reached situated on a knoll formed by the extremity of one of the spurs running from the main ridge into the valley, the last 300 yards into the village of Mankáng being perfectly level and affording camping ground for 300 men, though there is no water nearer than the Namyáng intersecting the valley at a distance of 400 or 500 yards. There is plenty of accommodation for camping any number of men in the valley itself, the best places being (1) along the southern and most remote side from the frontier line, (2) along the foot of the slopes of north side of valley about the village of Wanteng or Manlim itself, (3) a little to eastward along the Möngko road, (4) at the foot of the knoll on which the village Mankáng is situated. This last is the best situation for small camps. The village of Wanteng lies on the opposite side of the valley and almost opposite Mankáng. It is known also as Manlim. It is situated on the lower southern slopes of the range of hills bounding the northern side of the valley and along the crest of which the frontier line runs, the Chinese dependency Chéfán (Séfán) lying on the northern side. Wanteng has 16 houses; average supplies. Mankáng the same. A little to the eastward of Wanteng or Manlim is the village of Manpáng, 12 houses, while the valley westward is studded with villages belonging to the Wanteng circle. The Namyáng stream, which intersects the valley (which is nearly a mile wide), flows westward along the valley and eventually discharges itself into the Nammao or Shwéli river. It is here 16 feet wide, 1 foot to 3 feet deep; current about 1½ miles an hour; grassy banks 3 feet high. A direct route to Möngko continues along

FROM MANGMAW (ROUTE No. 62, STAGE 9) TO NAMKHAM *viâ* MANPÁN FERRY AND SELÂN—*continued.*

Authorities. Military.	Authorities. Civil.	Number and Names of Stages, Rivers and Streams.	Distances. Intermediate.	Distances. Total.	Remarks.
G.O.C. Mandalay District.	Superintendent, Northern Shan States.	**11. Wanteng or Manlim**—*cont.*			the valley eastward by a good and well-defined path parallel with and close to a stream for nearly 3 miles, when it leaves the latter and bears along the northern side of the valley, a parallel ridge running between and separating the route and the Namyáng. The village of Yingla is passed at 3½ miles on the frontier ridge, the village of Mainlung being reached at 8 miles, and Möngko at 16 miles, the distance being usually done in two stages, though the route is said to be good going and possible to be traversed in one day. A direct route also leads from Wanteng to Chéfán (Séfán) town by a good sound path; two days' march. Is said to contain 800 to 1,000 houses; is surrounded by wall and moat; and is provided with interior and secondary defences. It is situated in a circular valley. Is bounded on the west by the small stream Wonko Haw, on the east by the Möngka Haw. It is, moreover, said to be commanded on the western side by a hill Hukyán Sháu, 600 yards from the town and west of the Wonko Haw. The water-supply is said to be drawn from the two streams on its east and west, but the town is provided with a large tank usually filled with water and affording a supply in cases of emergency. Villages in Wanteng circle are Kanna, Tungaw, Mankáng, Manpáng, and Wanteng already mentioned; others are Loimôn, Namhu, and Kônyin lying westward along valley.
		12. Kinyáng ... Namyáng and small streams.	M. 6 F. 2	M. 81 F. 2	General direction a little south of west. The route strikes down the valley along its southern side passing rather above the cultivated and wetter portion of the valley, by running along the extremities of the northern slopes of the low ridge which forms the immediate boundary of the valley to the south. At mile 1 the small Shan village of Namhu (six houses) is passed close to path on left hand or south. The Namyáng stream running parallel, and at a distance varying from 20 to 100 yards; from path at 1¼ miles the Shan village of Kônyin on a knoll to right hand or north and close to path is passed, and the Namyáng is crossed and recrossed within 400 yards. Crossings easy, low banks, water about 1 foot deep. Here on northern side of valley the ridge Loi-Ngapak ends and Loi Kaihtao begins, their western and eastern extremities respectively running slightly south, thereby narrowing the valley. Immediately behind the eastern extremity of Loi Kaihtao within Chéfán territory stands Loi Páliön. At 1½ miles route crosses low spur which runs out south across the valley from the ridge Loi Kaihtao, the country being quite bare here except for scanty jungle. On this low spur to right hand or north of path is situated the new village of Loimôn (Chinese-Shan) in the Wanteng circle and the last village belonging to the Northern Shan States on northern side or right bank of the Namyáng stream. After crossing this spur the route runs close to and along the right bank of the Namyáng stream to 3 miles, when it crosses over to left bank. The river is here 20 feet wide by 1½ feet deep; gravelly bottom; banks 4 feet high on right bank, 3 feet on left; slippery crossing for laden animals. The route now inclines to the ridge on southern side of valley again, and at 4 miles passes a route to right hand which, running northwards, crosses the valley and eastwards of the small village of Pápaw ¼ of a mile from path (on right bank of

FROM MANGMAW (ROUTE No. 62, STAGE 9) TO NAMKHAM *viâ* MANPÂN FERRY AND SÉLÂN—*continued.*

Authorities. Military.	Authorities. Civil.	Number and Names of Stages, Rivers and Streams.	Distances. Intermediate.	Distances. Total.	Remarks.
G.O.C. Mandalay District.	Superintendent, Northern Shan States,	**12. Kinyáng**—*cont.*			stream) strikes across Loi Kaihtao to the town of Chéfán. Where this route strikes the Namyáng stands a banyan tree. The frontier line descending abruptly from Loi Kaihtao touches this banyan tree and then follows the Namyáng westward. Here also on the northern side of the frontier Chéfán ends and Möngmao commences. Pápaw, the first Möngmao village, is situated picturesquely in a clump of bamboos and is inhabited by Chinese Shans. The route now inclines a little more to the south hugging the foot of ridge on that side of the valley. At $5\frac{1}{2}$ miles is passed the Möngmao village of Hoyo, apparently 15 or 16 houses and similarly situated to Pápaw amongst bamboos. At 6 miles the larger village of Kônpáng (Möngmao) is passed. Here there is a very large fifth-day bazaar, people from both sides the frontier flocking to it; all these Möngmao villages are connected by a main caravan route from Möngmao town to Chéfán. The first part of Kinyáng is reached a few yards further lying almost opposite Kônpáng (10 houses, Chinese-Shan) and situated at entrance to the short semi-circular valley, in which stands the larger portion of Kinyáng (28 houses) and camping ground in paddy-fields for 600 men. Crossing a small stream, which discharges itself into the Namyáng, the village is reached at $6\frac{1}{2}$ miles, picturesquely situated like the Möngmao villages on opposite side of the valley within clumps of bamboos. Supplies: paddy 6 annas a basket, rice of a superior kind, and vegetables. The valley of the Namyáng is here more than $\frac{1}{2}$ a mile wide, fertile, and cultivated, and a great deal under water. It abounds in duck, geese, &c., while on the drier portions excellent grass can be obtained. Villages in the Kinyáng circle: Hután, the seat of the Myôsa of the circle (Kachins), Namtao, Namkát, Phápheik, Shipuk, Kônka, Loimalaw, Myintán, Pônkán, Kaungsôn.
		13. Musé ... Nammao (Shwéli), Namyáng, and small stream.	M. F. 7 0	M. F. 88 2	General direction a little south of west. Leaving larger Kinyáng the route runs along the extremities of the northern slopes of the southern ridge, the Namyáng lying to the right hand or north, some 300 or 400 yards distant. At 1 mile route crosses small stream, which discharges itself into the Namyáng and rises on to a low ridge or spur, the Namyáng flowing just below and to right hand of route which crosses the northern extremity of spur. Along this spur, southwards 400 yards, is the large Chinese-Shan village of Kônkhwon, whence *viâ* Téma there runs back a direct route to Theinni, eight ordinary stages; may be accomplished on foot in six and riding in three or four stages. Immediately on the other side of the Namyáng (in Möngmao territory) runs the main caravan route connecting Möngmao town and Chéfán, while on a small knoll 500 yards from and north of the Namyáng stands the Möngmao village of Sobiyáng, apparently containing about half-a-dozen houses, bare and unsurrounded by bamboos. Further to the east can be seen the village of Manmôn, $1\frac{1}{4}$ miles distant. Here the Nammao or Shwéli river is seen flowing from the north-east from between Loi Kaihtao and Loi Hôma, the range on its northern or right bank. At $2\frac{1}{4}$ miles the route still running

No. 20.

From MANGMAW (Route No. 62, Stage 9) to NAMKHAM *viâ* MANPÂN FERRY and SÊLÂN—*continued.*

Authorities.		Number and Names of Stages, Rivers and Streams.	Distances.		Remarks.
Military.	Civil.		Intermediate.	Total.	
G.O.C. Mandalay District.	Superintendent, Northern Shan States.	**13. Musé**—*cont.*			close to the left bank of the Namyáng passes the Chinese-Shan village of Namswáng to immediate right hand of path and in Theinni territory. Here the Namyáng flows into the Shwéli, which runs 150 yards below and to the north of route; on its other bank on a small ridge stands the Möngmao village of Yenkim (12 houses) with ferry boats. Well within Möngmao on the crest of Loi Hôma can be seen several Kachin villages, among which Loi Hôma, Hôlán, and Loivieng are the most noticeable. On the low ground of the Shwéli valley beneath (the river flowing from between Loi Hôma and Loi Kaihtao in an almost southerly direction as far as Yenkim, when it takes a more decidedly western turn) can be seen the villages of Manka, Lower Hôlán (Chinese-Shans), and Loivieng. The route now crosses a low spur or ridge, which terminates the Wanteng valley, and runs above and parallel to the Shwéli to 3 miles, when it crosses a small stream and rising round the lower slopes of a small eminence lying between it and the stream continues to follow the course of the Shwéli to 4 miles, when it passes to the left hand or south of the Shan village of Nampáng (eight or 10 houses), the path being good and sound throughout. Here the route takes a southern bend bearing away from the Shwéli and follows an undulating valley, a low ridge intervening between it and the Shwéli, the country being bare and devoid of foliage, while the soil is of red colour overlying sand-stone. At 5 miles on the hills to left or south of valley and below the hill called Loitama is the Kachin village of Mankáng, Manta and Namkôn being also passed in the distance to the south. At 6 miles a route branches off along the ridge to right hand to Musé and another at $6\frac{1}{3}$ up the ridge, Musé being situated at 7 miles on the crest of the ridge overlooking the Shwéli river. A mile distant to north there is camping ground on the level of the ridge round and about Musé for a brigade or more, while in the valley below the ridge south and along which the route runs there is accommodation by the small stream, whence water is obtained for 300 men, this being a more convenient camp for passing parties since Musé is $\frac{1}{3}$ mile distant from stream. Immediately above this camp and 600 yards west of Musé is the village of Hômôn (Shans, 16 houses), another village of the same name facing it on opposite side of the stream. Camping ground for 100 to 150 men can be obtained on the ridge the latter stands on. Musé is a stockaded village of some 40 houses and, standing on a level ridge uncommanded by any other high ground, is admirably adapted for a position. It commands the route on to Sélán and Namkham and overlooks the Shwéli and the wide level tract of country northward in Möngmao territory. In this strip of level country, 3 or 4 miles wide, may be seen the following Möngmao villages:—Panpôn, Hômôn, Tônhôn, Mansa, Naungkhán, Hôphi, Yanpa, Kyiengkhán, Sénu, Namôn, Ywinkyán, Ywinkhan, Naungôn, Kônna, Naungin and further west and behind those, at the foot of the slopes of Loi Hôma, Möngmao town, containing over 1,000 houses, surrounded by parapet and ditch, the former broken down, and garrisoned by 100 regular Chinese troops. On the Theinni side of the Shwéli below Musé are the two villages of Hôsôn and Phóhôn, ferry villages. Supplies plentiful: paddy 6 annas a big basket. Grass in the valley traversed by route and northward of the ridge Musé stands on towards the Shwéli.

FROM MANGMAW (ROUTE No. 62, STAGE 9) TO NAMKHAM *viâ* MANPÁN FERRY AND SÉLÁN—*continued.*

Authorities.		Number and Names of Stages, Rivers and Streams.	Distances.				Remarks.
Military.	Civil.		Intermediate.		Total.		
			M.	F.	M.	F.	
G.O.C. Mandalay District.	Superintendent, Northern Shan States.	**14. Sélán** ... Shwéli, Nampaw and two small streams.	4	4	92	6	General direction south-west. From Musé, dropping into the valley south of the ridge Musé stands on, the route takes a south-south-westerly direction for a little over ½ a mile and then turns decidedly west to 2 miles, running parallel with the Shwéli and about 350 yards from its left bank and passing the villages of Manwing,* Tönkyo, and Kángko, crossing the Nampaw just before it flows into the Shwéli and passing through the large fortified village of Pankham (40 houses), Chinese-Shans. The Nampaw at 1½ miles is 25 yards broad, current 2 miles an hour; from 3 to 7 feet deep; ford at crossing 1½ feet deep, sandy bottom; easy approaches. From Pankham there is a road to Manhung (*see* Branch I below). From 2 miles to 3 miles the route bears a little more to the south, the route all the way from Musé being perfectly level, sound under foot, and easy going. Numerous villages are passed on both sides of route and at distances from it varying from 300 yards to 2 miles. (The village of Tanaikhu lying 2 miles inland to left of route.) The chief villages thus passed are Nongyeng, Tönglong, Hôsai, Wengkhong, Töngkho, and Lingkho, while on the opposite side of the Shwéli and in Möngmao territory can be seen the villages of Namkham, Tama, &c. At 3 miles route crosses the northern points of a low spur (shown on survey sheets as a fixed point) and taking a rather southern turn crosses two small streams and runs up on to the small plateau on which Sélán stands at 4½ miles. Sélán consists from 200 to 250 houses. It measures about 700 by 500 yards, is defended by a parapet, 10 feet thick, 15 feet high, surmounted by a hedge, and ditch 15 feet broad and 9 feet to 15 feet deep, in good repair, standing clear of the valley and yet uncommanded from the south or inland; is in a capital defensive position. Supplies plentiful: sheep and goats brought from China being obtainable. Large camping ground on grass plain. Firewood has to be brought from the hills 2 miles off. From Sélán two routes run back to Theinni, both said to be direct and to be good roads; passable for laden animals and troops: *Number* 1 *route.*—Sélán, Teingkyán, Nalôn, Tanni, Manmwôn, Kônpyet, Namhu, Theinni. *Number* 2 *route.*—Sélán, Teingkyán, Naphi, Nampakka (on the direct Namkhán-Theinni route), Pángnim, Namkhí, Namhu, Theinni, or from Nampakka the Namkham-Theinni route may be followed *viâ* Möngyu and Pinghoi. The stages given in the two above routes are easy ones, and in each case the distance can be shortened by at least one march if necessary; there are camping grounds at each stage and supplies are obtainable.
		15. Namkham ... Nam Sélán, Nam Saw Haw, Nam Saung, Nam Sao, Nam Siri, and Shwéli.	13	0	105	6	From Sélán to Namkham is 13 miles in a south-westerly direction along the Shwéli valley by an excellent road, broad, much used, and well known. It is in good repair. All bridging is in masonry of a circular one arch pattern. The following villages are passed on or near the route,—

* Here the route from Pônseng *viâ* Möngko, Möngpaw and Hôké joins in *see* Alternative I below.

FROM MANGMAW (ROUTE No. 62, STAGE 9) TO NAMKHAM *viâ* MANPÁN FERRY AND SÉLÁN—*continued.*

Authorities. Military.	Authorities. Civil.	Number and Names of Stages, Rivers and Streams.	Distances. Inter-mediate.	Distances. Total.	Remarks.
G.O.C. Mandalay District.	Superintendent, Northern Shan States.	**15. Namkham**—*cont.*	Naungsen, Manhai, Namsáng ($5\frac{1}{4}$ miles), Naungkháng (8 miles), Kongreng, Mankáng, Kungsa, Senai, Mankham, and Naungsán. The boundary between Namkham and Sélán runs between Naungkháng and Namsáng, nearer the former than the latter. There are kyaungs at all the above mentioned Namkham villages.		

ALTERNATIVE I.

FROM PÔNSENG (STAGE 5) TO SÉLÁN (STAGE 14) *viâ* MÖNGKO.

BY LIEUT. G. W. T. PROWSE, 1ST DUKE OF CORNWALL'S LIGHT INFANTRY, ATTACHÉ, INTELLIGENCE BRANCH, JANUARY 1891.

Military	Civil	Stages	Intermediate M.	Intermediate F.	Total M.	Total F.	Remarks
G.O.C. Mandalay District.	Superintendent, Northern Shan States.	**1. Möngko** ... Namko.	9	2	9	2	Path throughout good and passable for transport except in one part between 5th and 6th mile where it is narrow, stony and steep. At $1\frac{1}{2}$ miles Nongsung, Kachin village of six houses. Last $3\frac{1}{2}$ miles across paddy-fields, crossing Namko just before reaching camp, 30 feet broad, $2\frac{1}{2}$ feet deep (in January), rock and pebbly bottom, low banks. For Möngko *see* Route No. 68, Stage 9.
		2. Camp near Nongheng. Small streams easily forded at $2\frac{1}{2}$ and $10\frac{1}{2}$ miles.	12	0	21	2	General direction south-west. Leaving camp at Pánglôm village the path skirts southern edge of valley through short grass for 2 miles, runs between wooded hills across small stream $2\frac{1}{2}$ miles, then ascends steeply to Mankáng village $4\frac{1}{2}$ miles. Up to this point the path is very good; average width 5 feet. From Mankáng village the path narrows to 3 feet, leading round the side of steep, grassy hills. Narrow and sharp turn at $6\frac{1}{2}$ miles the path being bad and getting gradually worse, covered with loose soil and stones. Descends very steeply at $8\frac{15}{16}$ miles, ascending again steeply leads to the right of Hongsé village. From here to Nongheng the path is narrow and winding, descending to camp in narrow sloping valley $\frac{1}{2}$ mile beyond village. The path from Mankáng to Nongheng would be quite impassable for pack transport in its present state, but could be improved at the cost of slight labour in most places. Villages: Kongsung at $2\frac{1}{2}$ miles, situated on wooded spur south of path; Sengpáng at $2\frac{1}{2}$ miles on wooded spur north of path; Mankáng at $4\frac{1}{2}$ miles, 10 houses, is a Kachin village; Hongsé at 9 miles, 18 houses (Kachin), Nongheng, $11\frac{1}{2}$ miles, 12 houses (Kachin). Small and sloping camp for 100 men about $\frac{1}{2}$ mile beyond Nongheng village. Water from small spring led through a bamboo shoot. The ground here contains saltpetre in large quantities with which the water is impregnated. Supplies from Nongheng village. Paddy at 4 annas per small basket. There is a better camping ground for 100 men by the side of the path $\frac{1}{4}$ mile nearer the village.

FROM MANGMAW (ROUTE NO. 62, STAGE 9) TO NAMKHAM *viâ* MANPÂN FERRY AND SÊLÂN—*continued.*

ALTERNATIVE I—*continued.*

Authorities. Military.	Authorities. Civil.	Number and Names of Stages, Rivers and Streams.	Distances. Intermediate. M.	F.	Distances. Total. M.	F.	Remarks.
G.O.C. Mandalay District.	Superintendent, Northern Shan States.	**3. Möngpaw** ... Nampaw.	8	4	29	6	Path averaging 3 feet wide and good leads down valley to Loisa village. There it widens to 12 feet forming an excellent road as far as ford over Nampaw stream (breadth 12 feet, depth 1 foot; rocky bottom; current 3 miles per hour; banks of mud 4 feet covered with grass) at 3¼ miles; thence it leads along the northern edge of valley over several swampy unbridged nullahs to Möngpaw village at 8¼ miles. Bad swampy crossings at 4, 6, 7½ and 7¾ miles which would render the path impassable for transport in wet weather, none of them being bridged. *Bridges.*—At 9 miles 300 yards, and 9 miles 400 yards, wooden plank bridges 12 feet long by 3 feet wide and passable for transport. *Villages passed.*—Pânglôm, north-west of path and close above it at ½ mile from camp. Loisa at 1¼ to 1¾ miles, 25 houses (Kachin). Möngpaw, 30 houses, is a Shan village. Unlimited camping ground in paddy-fields in Nampaw valley, also for half battalion on grassy spur overlooking valley and just outside the village. Paddy 4 annas per small basket. Water good and plentiful. Small bamboo kyaung, 40 men; vegetables are the only supplies obtainable in the village.
		4. Hôké ... ... Nampaw.	11	0	40	6	General direction south-west. Path crosses over to left bank of Nampaw stream, recrosses it at 3½ miles and leaving the valley ascends steeply to Pinhoi village; breadth of path 10 feet; thence it narrows to 3 feet, descends at 8 miles and again ascends through grass jungle to Kôngpawen village at 9½ miles; thence it winds round the hedge of a rocky hill and descends to the village of Hôké. Unmetalled path throughout, with the exception of rough stone paved causeway at 2¼ miles; good path as far as Pinhoi, but afterwards it is narrow, steep and much cut up by bullocks. The Nampaw forded at 1¼ and 3½ miles; breadth 35 to 40 feet, depth 2 feet; flows through paddy-fields; low banks 3 feet high; pebble bottom; current 3 miles per hour; water clear and good. *Bridges.*—At 2½ miles, wooden longitudinal planks 30 feet long, 3 feet wide; unfit for transport owing to being too roughly made. At 3¾ miles, wooden foot-bridge 10 feet long, 1 foot wide. At 6¾ miles, wooden planks, 20 feet long, 2 feet wide, passable for transport. At 8¼ miles plank bridge 8 feet long, 2 feet wide, in bad repair. *Villages passed.*—Mansé 1½ miles; Manmao 2½ miles (Shan); Manpin 3 miles, 40 houses (Shan); Pinhoi 6 miles, 50 houses (Kachin); Manong 7 miles, six houses; Kôngpawen 9½ miles, eight houses. Hôké, eight houses, is a Shan village situated in an undulating valley. Low grassy hills to the north-west and south-west. Camping ground for 200 men in paddy-fields by stream 200 yards east of village. Water from stream 12 feet by 3 feet; clear and good. Only a few vegetables obtainable from village, which is almost deserted owing to depredations of Kachins from the neighbouring hills.

FROM MANGMAW (ROUTE NO. 62, STAGE 9) TO NAMKHAM *viâ* MANPÁN FERRY AND SÉLÁN—*continued*.

ALTERNATIVE I—*continued*.

Authorities. Military.	Authorities. Civil.	Number and Names of Stages, Rivers and Streams.	Distances. Intermediate. M. F.	Distances. Total. M. F.	Remarks.
G.O.C. Mandalay District.	Superintendent, Northern Shan States.	**5. Pánglôm** ...	**11 4**	52 2	General direction west. Path unmetalled and good throughout. Leads over grassy undulating country to Kongwet village, passes to the right of Tingsang village and turns north-west ascending narrow-wooded valley to crest of hills which form the southern boundary of the Shwéli river valley. Thence there is a good path to Namláng village, after passing which the path descends long spur into the valley to Pánglôn village. *Bridge* over dry nullah at 5 miles, 10 feet long, 2 feet broad, and passable for transport. *Villages passed.*—Kongwet 3 miles, 11 houses and small pôngyi kyaung which would hold 30 men; is a Palaung village. Tingsang at 4½ miles, ½ mile on left of road, 12 houses, Palaung village. Manhung (or Manháng) 1 mile west of road at 5 miles, large Sawbwa's palace said to be the finest in the Northern Shan States, Palaung village. Namláng at 7 miles, seven houses, Kachin village. Kongloi, 8¾ miles, seven houses, Kachin village. Konglung, 9 miles, Kachinvillage. Pánglôm, 11½ miles, six houses, is a Shan village. Good camping ground for 300 to 400 men in paddy-fields 100 yards east of Pánglôm village. Water from stream 6 feetbroad, 1 foot deep.
		6. Sélán ... ... Nampaw.	**6 2**	58 4	General direction south-west. The road is good but unmetalled throughout, could easily be made passable for carts; present average breadth 5 feet. From Pánglôm village the road leads over undulating country through patches of pine-apple cultivation to Manwing village where the route previously described joins in, and Sélán is reached at 6¼ miles.

BRANCH I.

FROM PÔNSENG (STAGE 5) TO MÖNGKA.

BY LIEUT. G. W. PROWSE, DUKE OF CORNWALL'S LIGHT INFANTRY, JANUARY 1891.

Military.	Civil.	Number and Names of Stages, Rivers and Streams.	Intermediate.	Total.	Remarks.
G.O.C. Mandalay District.	Superintendent, Northern Shan States.	**1. Möngka** ... Namyo and small streams.	**14 0**	14 0	General direction east. The road, 10 to 12 feet in width, leads down to Mankáng village (four houses) at ¼ mile; thence follows the north side of ridge narrowing to 3 feet; gradually descends to 3 miles, where there is a steep descent by zigzags to valley of Namyo at 3½ miles. Namyo stream forded at 5th mile (breadth 35 to 40 feet, depth 2½ feet; long grass 10 feet high on both banks, very thick, low stony banks and rocky bottom; current 4 miles per hour; water clear and good); path then follows the left bank in places at an elevation of 40 to 50 feet above with steep drop into the stream; this portion is narrow and would be dangerous in wet weather; continues along the left bank of stream to camp in paddy-fields at Mannin (or Manhin) village, 9½ miles, passing Manpa (six houses) at 7¼ miles.

FROM MANGMAW (ROUTE No. 62, STAGE 9) TO NAMKHAM *viâ* MANPĂN FERRY AND SÉLĂN—*continued.*

BRANCH I—*continued.*

Authorities.		Number and Names of Stages, Rivers and Streams.	Distances.		Remarks.
Military.	Civil.		Intermediate.	Total.	
G.O.C. Mandalay District.	Superintendent, Northern Shan States.	**1. Möngka**—*cont.*			*Bridges.*—New wooden bridge at 5¾ miles, 20 feet long, 3 feet wide, longitudinal planks, passable for transport. Camp at 9½ miles for a battalion; water from Namyo stream plentiful and good. Paddy 4 annas per small basket; supplies scanty from Möngka village, 4 to 5 miles off on the hill side to the east. Fowls and eggs can be obtained from the Kachin villages on the neighbouring hills; but the Kachins are not under control, and supplies, with the exception of paddy, are not to be depended upon. A path leads from the valley at Mannin (or Manhin, *see* in Stage 4 above) across the Namyo stream and over the hills in a south-east direction to the Kachin village of Pinhung; thence there is a good path to Powung (or Powáng) (also Kachin) on the Kôkáng-Namkham road (*see* Stage 4 above).

BRANCH II.

FROM PANKHAM (*see* STAGE 14) TO MANHUNG.

BY COL. COLVILLE, GRENADIER GUARDS, MARCH 1893.

Military.	Civil.	Number and Names of Stages, Rivers and Streams.	Intermediate.	Total.	Remarks.
			M. F.	M. F.	
G.O.C. Mandalay District.	Superintendent, Northern Shan States.	**1. Manhung (Manháng).** Nampaw and another small stream.	**11 0**	*11 0	After crossing the Nampaw chaung, the road follows the main track towards Musé for ½ a mile, then turns in a south-east direction across flat open ground for ¾ mile; a stream is then crossed and a steep ascent commenced, winding round the spurs of hills and over a series of saddles. Below and to the right the valley of the Nampaw is always in view. After 1 mile the gradient becomes less severe, the southern slope of the ridge being followed. At mile 3 from the foot, the Kachin village of Tu Mu Yi (15 houses) is reached: ¼ mile further on the road, following the shape of the ground, turns abruptly to the south. Up to this point the road has been over ground which has been cleared, now, however, thick tree jungle begins and continues for the rest of the way. One and three-quarter mile from Tu Mu Yi a rounded hill is passed on the left of the road, from which a magnificent view of the surrounding country is obtained. From this point a steep descent and ascent over a saddle of a ¼ mile leads on to the first of the series of hills and saddles on which Manhung is situated. Good water is obtainable from a small stream.

* The distance is not given, but, by reference to Alternative No. I, Stages 5 and 6 above, it would appear to be about 11 miles, viz., from Pankham to Pánglôm 3¼, thence to Manhung 7½—total 10¾ miles.

No. 21.

From MÔBYÉ to MÖNGPWÁN (MAINGPÁN) viâ PAYAKÔN and MAUKMÉ.

BY LIEUT. H. E. STANTON, ROYAL ARTILLERY, JANUARY AND FEBRUARY 1888, AND LIEUT. L. C. COLOMB, 42ND GURKHA LIGHT INFANTRY, MARCH 1890.

Authorities.		Number and Names of Stages, Rivers and Streams.	Distances.				Remarks.
Military.	Civil.		Intermediate.		Total.		
			M.	F.	M.	F.	
G.O.C. Rangoon District.	Superintendent, Southern Shan States.	**1. Payakôn (Pékôn).** Balu Chaung.	9	4	9	4	*See* Route No. 1, Stage 7.
		2. Namhlut ... Small streams.	13	4	23	0	Pack track. At 3 miles pass Sagwé. One short swampy place about 4½ miles from Payakôn, where track crosses small stream, otherwise good. Camp in forest not cleared. Good water from stream running west of camp.
		3. Letmaing ... Tabet river.	14	4	37	4	Pack track good. Camping ground about 1½ miles beyond village, large and good. Water indifferent from small stream north of camp. One small well on same side of fairly good water, but quickly runs dry. The Tabet river is crossed by bridge close to village of Letmaing.
		4. Camp	5	4	43	0	Track for first ½ mile crosses marshy ground near small stream above mentioned, after that it is good. Camping ground about 2 miles east of village (name not given) on rising ground. Good water and plentiful from stream north of it.
		5. Sisaing	6	0	49	0	Road good. Good camping ground on rising ground north-west of village. Water good from stream. Country open and fairly cultivated.
		6. Thatôn (Satôn), Loiput (Loipôk).	8	0	57	0	Road good. Camping ground on high ground south of village. Water good from spring. (Description of this stage is also given in Route No. 18, Stage 7).
		7. Camp on Nampwán. Nampwán (Pun river).	11	0	68	0	Pack track. Long and fairly steep descent into valley of Pun river. The river is crossed by ferry at this time (February) about 4 feet deep and fordable, 30 yards wide; current fairly swift. Camping ground on right bank good, on left bank rather confined. Water good.
		8. Hnitséngáywa.	7	6	75	6	Road good. Pass small pieces of water about 5 miles from Pun river. Country open and well cultivated. Villages well populated. Camping ground good and large.

FROM MÔBYÉ TO MÖNGPWÀN (MAINGPÁN) *viâ* PAYAKÔN AND MAUKMÉ—*continued.*

Authorities. Military.	Authorities. Civil.	Number and Names of Stages, Rivers and Streams.	Distances. Intermediate. M.	F.	Distances. Total. M.	F.	Remarks.
G.O.C. Rangoon District.	Superintendent, Southern Shan States.	**9. Yédwingyi** ...	4	0	79	6	Pack track. Fairly good camping ground confined and jungly near site of old village. Water scarce in small well.
		10. Maukmé (Mokmai). Nam Twán.	12	0	91	6	Pack track. From 5th to 9th mile not good, through rocky gorge, down fairly steep descent. At 9 miles there is good camping ground near site of old burying ground 2 miles south of Maukmé town. Water good. Hence to Maukmé good track across dry paddy-fields. Camping ground on east of town large and open. Water good and plentiful from the Nam Twán running between town and camp, crossed by good bridge.
		11. Wanhát (Banhát). Nam Teng or Tein river.	12	0	103	6	Pack track. First 5 miles through rocky gorge, bad in places. Remainder of road good, through fairly open country. At 7¾ miles Namsé where there is camping ground on bank of stream, dry at this time of year, 400 yards on left of road; good water from spring. At about 12 miles Wanhát. *Note.*—Of this place there is at present (June 1893) no recorded description.
		12. Ta Möng Ké (1,300 feet). Tein, Phâleng, and Namtwán rivers.	15	4	119	2	Road leaves Wanhát (or Banhát) (spelt Wanhat on survey maps) from east and leads down to the Tein river, then turns north-east up right bank of stream through scrub jungle. At 1½ miles pass Wanyôn and at 1¾ Wanteng. At 2¼ miles hills on the west close down on to river bank. Path here is narrow with a drop of 10 feet to the river. At 2¾ cross a deep nullah, bridged. At 3¼ another road from Maukmé joins from west. At 3¾ cross the Phâleng chaung, a small stream and fordable; banks ramped. At 4 miles the road is rocky and narrow with a steep hill side to left. Between the 4th and 6th miles cross three bridged nullahs and one ramped. At 6½ miles is a short stiff rocky ascent with a precipitous fall of 150 feet into the river. Getting transport animals over this piece of ground is a matter of great difficulty and danger. As the dangerous part is only about 150 yards long, it is advisable to unload transport animals and carry the baggage over. At 7½ miles cross the Namtwán or Môné river; fordable; banks low; channel 30 yards broad; knee-deep in March; bottom stony. Bank of river still followed up to 9 miles when, river taking a bend east, road leaves it. Up to 11½ miles road level through scrub and bamboo jungle. At 11½ miles emerge on cultivated valley. At 11¾ pass Tanka, and at 12½ Linkhé (or Linkéö), a large village, whence a road branches north-west to Môné, 16½ miles. At 13 miles Pyimpaung, and at 13¾ Pyintanaung. Reach Ta Möng Ké at 15½ miles; last 2 miles through thorn jungle. Ta Möng Ké is a small village scattered along the right bank of

FROM MÔBYÉ TO MÖNGPWÁN (MAINGPÁN) *viâ* PAYAKÔN AND MAUKMÉ—*continued.*

Authorities. Military.	Authorities. Civil.	Number and Names of Stages, Rivers and Streams.	Distances. Intermediate.	Distances. Total.	Remarks.
G.O.C. Rangoon District.	Superintendent, Southern Shan States.	**12. Ta Möng Ké (1,300 feet)**—*cont.*			the Tein river. There is a bazaar every fifth day at Linkhé and supplies, the produce of the country, are available there. Camping ground at Ta Möng Ké on either side of the Tein river. *Note.*—This march may be broken into two, the halt being made a mile to the north of the Namtwán or Môné river. The ground here is flat and shady. Water from the Tein river.
			M. F.	M. F.	
		13. Sawa (2,500 feet). Tein river.	**9 4**	128 6	The Tein river at Ta Möng Ké is about 80 yards broad with a sluggish current; it is not fordable. The ferry ordinarily consists of one small dug-out, but boats can be collected on due notice being given. The banks on either side of the river are ramped. On crossing river road starts in a south-easterly direction, rounding to east and north-east. At 1½ miles pass Myittha village, six houses. At 2 miles reach foot of hills. Up to this point road is level through thin bush and tree jungle. Ascent commences winding up a rocky hill side; road rough and broken, but gradient easy. At 3 miles turn south continuing a gentle ascent over rocky ground through thin bamboo jungle. At 4 miles rocks give place to red earth. At 5 miles, having ascended about 1,[illegible]0 feet, cross a saddle and descend gently into a valley. At [illegible] road is along bed of a dry nullah which is followed either in the bed or along the banks up to 7½ miles. Water in small quantities may be obtained in nullah by digging. At 7¾ emerge on open cultivated valley and cross to its southern side, passing a small village at 8½. From here road along low spur with cultivated valley to north. Reach Sawa at 9½ and camp to east of village in paddy-fields. Water from the Namtwán stream good.
		14. Pingsalán (2,400 feet). Namlwán and Nampán.	**9 0**	137 6	Cross the Namlwán stream four times in the 1st mile; road level with hills to north and south. At 1 mile pass Wankán, a small village, and between this and 2 miles cross four nullahs, all bridged. Cross the Nampán river twice at 2 miles and then proceed up its right bank; narrow in places; hill sides sloping directly into river bed. At 3 miles hill recedes and road emerges on to undulating valley in process of clearing. At 6 miles flat grassy valley cultivated in places; pass village of Nalao. Beyond Nalao road crosses marshy ground, bad bits bridged. Hills close in again at 8 miles and at 9 miles reach camp. Pingsalán is a collection of about half-a-dozen huts on the left bank of the Nampán river. The most suitable ground for camping is across the stream on a tract of grass land between the stream and the village.
		15. Maingpán (Möngpwán), 2,100 feet. Namtun and Nampán.	**7 4**	145 2	Road south-east through scrub jungle with low hills to left. At 3 miles hills become rocky and overhang the road here; there are numerous springs; the ground is covered with dense jungle and is marshy. The road here is embanked and the worst portion of the marsh is bridged. At 3½ miles pass Meikthôm, a small village of eight houses. At 4 miles a spring of good water, over which is built a pagoda. At 4½ miles cross roads, the right-hand one being followed. At 5½ cross the Namtun river by a wooden bridge, 40 yards long, in bad

FROM MÔBYÉ TO MÖNGPWÁN (MAINGPÁN) *viâ* PAYAKÔN AND MAUKMÉ—*continued.*

Authorities. Military.	Authorities. Civil.	Number and Names of Stages, Rivers and Streams.	Distances. Intermediate.	Distances. Total.	Remarks.
G.O.C. Rangoon District.	Superintendent, Southern Shan States.	**15. Maingpán (Möngpwán), 2,100 feet**—*cont.*			repair. Pass Taunglé village after crossing river and emerge on paddy plain. Just beyond the village is a bad marshy bit of ground, where road requires making. Round a low hill and follow artificial water-course through paddy-fields and occasional patches of grass jungle to Maingpán or Möngpwán. The greater portion of the road through the paddy-fields is embanked and bridged. In the cold weather months the more direct route across the paddy-fields is generally followed. Cross the Nampán river by a ford on reaching Maingpán and, passing through the village, camp on bank of stream. Maingpán stands at the eastern end of an extensive cultivated valley, surrounded on all sides by low hills, and dotted with numerous smaller hamlets. The present site of the village is new and the houses are very poor. It is built on the usual plan round a square enclosure, the residence of the Maingpán Sawbwa. The village numbers about 80 houses in all. A bazaar is held every fifth day, and supplies in small quantities are then procurable.

BRANCH I.

FROM LINKHÉ (*see* STAGE 12) TO MÔNÉ (MÖNGNAI).

BY LIEUT. F. C. COLOMB, 42ND GURKHA LIGHT INFANTRY, MARCH 1890.

Military.	Civil.	Stages.	Intermediate M.	Intermediate F.	Total M.	Total F.	Remarks.
G.O.C. Rangoon District.	Superintendent, Southern Shan States.	**1. Tadágyi (3,000 feet).** Namtwán (bridged).	**11**	**0**	11	0	Road, after leaving Linkhé north-west (leaving the Tein river, up which runs the road to Maingpán), flat for 1 mile to foot of hills through thin scrub jungle. Enter hills by stony nullah. At 1½ miles leave nullah and ascend easy spur, stony, but not difficult. At 3 miles road more level through bamboo jungle. At 3½ miles cross a saddle and descend into shallow valley. Commencement of ascent from valley is gentle, latterly rocky and very steep. At 5 miles cross a second saddle and descend slightly into a level valley enclosed by steep jungle-clad hills. At 6½ miles a short rocky ascent followed by an easy descent north to valley. Road north-west and undulates easily over two low ridges, after crossing the second of which road descends to Kyauktaung village at 10 miles. Carts ply between this village and Mônê. At 11 miles, after crossing a low spur, road drops down to the valley of the Namtwán. The river is bridged, but it is also fordable. Stream is 20 yards broad, current slow, banks steep, ramped at ford. Camp on either side of the stream, ground unlimited. Water from the river fair.
		2. Môné (2,900 feet).	**5**	**4**	16	4	Cart road over undulating ground. At 2 miles strike road from Wanhát *viâ* Phâleng. From here it is 3½ miles to Môné town; police post is 4 miles further. If it is necessary to camp at Môné town, the best ground is to the west of the Sawbwa's enclosure. Ground is undulating and requires clearing. Water from a spring sufficient for a large force and transport.

No. 22.

From MÔBYÉ to PYINMANA viâ PÔBYA and SEIKPUDAUNG.

By Capt. W. A. BROOME, 1st Beluch Light Infantry, 1887.

Authorities.		Number and Names of Stages, Rivers and Streams.	Distances.				Remarks.
Military.	Civil.		Inter-mediate.		Total.		
			M.	F.	M.	F.	
G.O.C. Rangoon District.	Karenni.	**1. Pôbya ... ...**	**7**	**0**	7	0	Good pack track. First 5 miles over high wooded ground, remainder level, old paddy-fields. Good camping ground at Pôbya village. Cattle obtainable. No bazaar. Water rather warm, but drinkable.
		2. Kyala ...	**15**	**0**	22	0	At ½ mile beyond Pôbya is a deep cutting formed by a mountain torrent running from west to east, delimitating Lusan's and Pôbya's territories. Road runs now through the former Chief's territory through a valley, arable and quite flat, for 4 miles. This valley was formerly cultivated, but had to be abandoned as it is inundated yearly by a torrent overflowing its banks. (There was a bund, but when it broke down there was no money to repair it, the inhabitants having left during the last two years' disturbances.) The valley is 3 miles across. At 9 miles pass village of Wathako (Karen) on left. Water scarce and none in dry season. From village, ascend slightly, ⅛ mile from camping ground a plain. Wild raspberries and pear trees passed on route. Arrive Kyala ⅛ mile from village. Water scarce.
		3. Kapu	**11**	**0**	33	0	For first 2 miles over rocky mountains, fir trees here and there, path stony in places. After next ⅛ mile flat plain thickly covered with kaing grass. Next ⅛ mile pass over flat cultivated ground. At 4⅛ miles a large tank; road to Kôngyi (Kaungi) branches off to right from here. At 5 miles reach cutting down side of a hill about 6 feet wide. Stream at bottom. Road goes now between and over base of big hills. Camping ground in paddy-fields. Running stream of good water.
		4. Káklu river ...	**10**	**0**	43	0	Start over very steep hill for ½ mile (men took 30 minutes to get up), elephants one hour. General direction south-west. Proceed up and down hills. At 8 miles a stream. At 10 miles Káklu river. All along this march there is much jungle. About half-way on right is a Padaung village.
		5. Camp on hill-top.	**6**	**4**	49	4	Road good for 2⅛ miles; then a steep ascent for ⅛ mile, at the top of which on right is the Gekko Karen village of Pressaung. Elephants took 3¼ hours to reach this. For ⅛ mile descend and cross a streamlet. For 2 miles ascent is very steep and difficult, when summit of hill is reached. Water ¾ mile below hill-top on west. Elephants took 6 hours in all.

FROM MÔBYÈ TO PYINMANA *viâ* PÔBYA AND SEIKPUDAUNG—*continued.*

Authorities. Military.	Authorities. Civil.	Number and Names of Stages, Rivers and Streams.	Distances. Intermediate. M.	F.	Distances. Total. M.	F.	Remarks.
G.O.C. Rangoon District.	Karenni.	**6. Camp on stream.**	**7**	**0**	56	4	Descend 1 mile; ascend for $\frac{1}{2}$ mile; road very steep and rocky; ascend $\frac{1}{2}$ mile; descend $\frac{1}{2}$ mile; rest of road descends to water through thick jungle, when water, a stream, is reached at 7 miles; here we encamped. Elephants took 7 hours.
		7. River Kresaung.	**5**	**0**	61	4	Road ascends and descends the whole way and is difficult and runs through thick jungle. At 5 miles Kresaung river is reached. This river marked the old British border. Here is a zayát, but camping ground is very filthy. We encamped $\frac{1}{2}$ mile further on up a hill.
		8. Maung Kyaw.	**7**	**0**	68	4	Track ascends steep hill for $\frac{1}{2}$ mile. Pass through gully with running water for $\frac{3}{4}$ mile; ascend a similar gully for $\frac{1}{2}$ mile, descend for $\frac{1}{2}$ mile, when river is reached; ascend for 1 mile level for $\frac{1}{4}$ mile, ascend very steep hill for 1 mile, when police post of Maung Kyaw is reached. Elephants took $8\frac{1}{2}$ hours.
		9. Camp in river bed.	**8**	**0**	76	4	Towards Athataung. At 2 miles is village of Athataung, 2 miles further to streamlet. In next mile cross and recross stream sixteen times; 2 miles steep ascent, 1 mile steep descent, when stream is reached. Road goes through dense bamboo jungle. Elephants took 9 hours.
		10. Athataung village.	**5**	**0**	81	4	First mile ascend; $\frac{1}{2}$ mile descend to stream; road fairly level for 2 miles; last portion very steep ascent for 1 mile; difficult descent along side of hill for $\frac{1}{2}$ mile to village of Athataung on hill. Elephants took 5 hours.
		11. Kôdi, No. 1 ...	**4**	**0**	85	4	Descend for 4 miles through dense jungle grass; last $\frac{1}{4}$ mile of descent very steep. Village on stream. Elephants took $3\frac{1}{2}$ hours.
		12. Kôdi, No. 2 ... Nanchaw river.	**5**	**0**	90	4	Ascend very steep hill for $1\frac{1}{4}$ miles; descend for $1\frac{1}{2}$ miles to Nanchaw river. Water good and plentiful; $\frac{1}{2}$ mile ascend when the ascent becomes exceedingly steep and difficult for $1\frac{1}{2}$ miles. At top is village (Gekko Karen). Elephants took 7 hours.

FROM MÔBYÉ TO PYINMANA *viâ* PÔBYA AND SEIKPUDAUNG—*continued.*

Authorities. Military.	Authorities. Civil.	Number and Names of Stages, Rivers and Streams.	Distances. Intermediate. M.	Distances. Intermediate. F.	Distances. Total. M.	Distances. Total. F.	Remarks.
G.O.C. Rangoon District.	Karenni.	**13. Camp on hill-top.**	9	0	99	4	Descend for 2 miles, when the Kôdi river is reached; road along side of chaung for about 5 miles and level, but through thick jungle; ascend for 2 miles over two hills. Camping ground on top; river water ½ mile distant on onward road. Elephants took 8 hours.
		14. Camp No. 1 on Yépu chaung.	5	4	105	0	Sharp descent along hill side for ½ mile, when water is reached; ½ mile along stream bed. Ascend for ¾ mile, when top of hill is reached; descend ¼ mile to Kôdi village, No. 3, a stream below village; ascend and descend hill side through thick jungle for 2 miles; 1 mile descends very steep, when the Yépu is reached; descends river bed for ½ mile, when camping ground on left bank is reached. Water good and plentiful. There is a hot spring above the camping ground. Elephants took 8½ hours.
		15. Camp No. 2 on Yépu chaung.	10	0	115	0	Road goes for 8 miles along or along side of river; road not difficult; camp on right bank. Elephants took 7 hours.
	Commissioner, Eastern Division, and Deputy Commissioner, Pyinmana.	**16. Seikpudaung.**	8	0	123	0	Road here leaves the Yépu chaung and is level and good for 2 miles through thin jungle country, when the Méhaw chaung is reached; road follows this chaung for 6 miles; road good; at ½ mile from Seikpudaung road branches to left to Zibyubin. Elephants took 4½ hours.
		17. Zibyubin ...	11	0	134	0	*See* Route No. 13, Eastern Division, Stages 1 and 2.
		18. Pyinmana ...	9	0	143	0	*Note.*—In Stages 8 and 9 the name of the district is evidently used instead of that of each village.

No. 23.

From MÔNÉ (MÔNGNAI) to KYENGTUNG (KENGTUNG) viâ TA KAW FERRY.

BY CAPT. PINK, "THE QUEEN'S," 1890.

Military	Civil	Stage	Int. M.	Int. F.	Total M.	Total F.	Remarks
G.O.C. Rangoon District.	Supdt., Southern Shan States.	**1. Naung-Wop** ... **Mônê river and streams.**	12	2	12	2	Môné police post is 4 miles north of the town. Leaving post road descends to the Môné river about 100 feet, easy slope. River about 40 feet broad, high banks, good bottom, bridged,

FROM MÔNÉ (MÖNGNAI) TO KYENGTUNG (KENGTUNG) *viâ* TA KAW FERRY—*continued.*

Authorities. Military.	Authorities. Civil.	Number and Names of Stages, Rivers and Streams.	Distances. Intermediate.	Distances. Total.	Remarks.
G.O.C. Rangoon District.	Superintendent, Southern Shan States.	**1. Naung-Wop** —*cont.*			about 1 foot water, current moderate. Keeping north-north-east road rises to Pángkyeng village and crosses undulating down country, here and there cleared of grass and cultivated. The valley through which the road passes is flanked on either side by hills about 6 miles apart. Those on the left appear to have several passes. At 4 miles a small stream is crossed, at 7 miles the little village of Makôn. From the Mônè river to 9½ miles the ascent is constant though slight and from there into Naung-Wop there is a gradual descent of 100 feet. Naung-Wop, 30 houses; supplies, fowls and rice. Camp near bazaar; water from good stream to east near camp; road excellent.
		2. Pátong Small stream.	M. 14 F. 0	M. 26 F. 2	There are two roads on, one crossing stream by bridge and passing over marsh ground (now dry) going north-east and the other avoiding marsh strikes nearly north over high open country. This road runs almost due north for first 5 miles passing villages of Táko, Táklek and Hak-Kom. At the second of these track turns a little south of east for 2 miles, then north-north-east (at this bend the eastern track cuts in), continuing north-north-east, reach Pátong Kyaung, passing *en route* Hoi-Ai and Wán Kán villages. Ample camping ground on paddy-fields. Water from small stream; village 30 houses; supplies: paddy and fowls. The Loi U hill some 4,000 feet almost overshadows the camp; road excellent.
		3. Ko-ut (Camp). Nam Téng or Tein chaung.	4 0	30 2	Road circle round Loi U hill to the east and descending crosses a small stream, and at 3 miles reaches the village of Tulôn on the right bank of the Nam Téng. The river is 100 yards across, unfordable even for elephants; current moderate; bottom sound and rocky; bank about 15 feet above water level. River was spanned by an excellent bamboo trestle bridge: made in 10 days by the villages over which laden mules passed, there was also a raft constructed on two "dug-outs" capable of carrying 15 men or four ponies a trip. There were also several (some five) "dug-outs" of moderate size; a camp could be pitched on either bank, 1 mile on is Ko-ut camp. Ample space, large peepul trees. Water from the Nam Sara river about 500 yards west of camp. Banks very steep, about 50 feet broad, 1½ feet water; current rapid; road excellent.
		4. Makláng ... Pak-kyé and smaller streams.	14 4	44 6	General direction a little north of east; road passes over gentle undulating country through low detached hills. At 10 miles there is a gorge about 100 yards long and a little further on a rather steep and rocky descent (a few pioneers could do all that is required). The track then crossed a level valley with high grass, and at 12½ miles crossed the Pak-kyé stream (the small hamlet of the same name is being re-built). The stream is about 10 feet broad, good bottom and bridged; water 1½ feet, swift, onward the ground is marshy but now dry, excepting where small streams cross it. This would be bad going in the rains; cross stream. Camp on knoll, site of burnt kyaung, water from two streams east and west about 300 yards distant. Ample camping ground on west side of knoll in paddy-fields; road excellent.

FROM MÔNE (MÖNGNAI) TO KYENGTUNG (KENGTUNG) *viâ* TA KAW FERRY—*continued.*

Authorities. Military.	Authorities. Civil.	Number and Names of Stages, Rivers and Streams.	Distances. Intermediate. M. F.	Distances. Total. M. F.	Remarks.
G.O.C. Rangoon District.	Superintendent, Southern Shan States.	**5. Saikhao** ... Nam Ku and numerous other streams.	8 2	53 0	Descending knoll cross Nam Ku stream about 10 feet broad, good bottom, 1 foot water. General direction north-east; track excellent, except last mile over which constant rivulets are crossed; high grass and jungle on both sides; pass small villages of Kun-Sha and Nam Maw-Kyeng. Entire route is flanked by detached hills. Saikhao is a straggling village of 60 houses; fowls and paddy plentiful; ample camping space on level grass ¼ mile beyond first village. This a regular table-land with many villages running north and south ending north apparently in the rugged and lofty Nam Kuk hill; the east edge of this plateau is just beyond the village and camping ground, and the descent in the valley of the Nam Kung is almost precipitous. Water from two streams; bottom good, and 1½ feet water. Here the route from Yátsauk *viâ* Légya joins in (*see* Route No. 76).
		6. Kyaingkán (Kengkham), 1,250 feet. Nam Kung, Nam Loi, and Nam Pán.	9 4	62 4	General direction east. Track descending 500 feet into valley by a fairly laid out and good mule road 6 feet broad cut in the hill side. At 2 miles cross a stream with rather steep banks and then the Nam Kung 40 yards broad high banks; 1 foot water; paddy-fields on both sides. The track onwards is undulating along the foot of low hills with thick jungle and would be impossible in the rains, it being red clay, but now good enough. At 7 miles the track debouches from the low hills and enters a paddy plain, and shortly afterwards crossed the Nam-Loi by a good wooden bridge, rising high above the river. The river is 40 yards in breadth and 5 feet deep with rocky bottom. There is a deep ford 50 yards below the bridge crossing a small stretch of paddy, the track goes along hillocks and paddy alternately, and at 8½ miles skirts the Nam-Loi again (a track running south crosses it by a good bridge). At 9½ miles Kyaingkán is reached on the Nam Pán or Ben chaung. The village is very straggling occupying both banks and the islands in the river; there are about 60 houses; supplies: paddy (large quantities) and fowls, cattle, &c.; ample space for a large camp could be found near the ferry amongst ruined pagodas. The river at the ferry is nearly 400 yards broad unfordable for elephants which swim it ½ mile up; the current is slow, although there is a rapid ½ mile up stream. There are two islands just north of ferry. The bottom is full of large rocks, ponies and mules consequently have to be ferried across. The banks are about 10 feet above the water. There is a raft capable of taking 30 men or five mules and 10 men, and a boat taking eight men a trip, at the ferry, but there are five or six more "dug-outs" available and more rafts could be made at short notice. Ferry men live on both sides of the river. A return trip takes 15 minutes with ponies. There is ample camping ground on paddy-field just north-east of the ferry on the far (left) bank on the river.
		7. Hónlin (2,400 feet). Nam Pán and several streams.	14 0	76 4	Track takes northern direction along foot of low hills gradually rising at 2 miles, the track again cuts into the Nam Pán (a succession of broad rapids) and follows its course for about a mile.

FROM MÔNE (MÖNGNA) TO KYENGTUNG (KENGTUNG) *via* TA KAW FERRY—*continued.*

Authorities. Military.	Authorities. Civil.	Number and Names of Stages, Rivers and Streams.	Distances. Intermediate.	Distances. Total.	Remarks.
G.O.C. Rangoon District	Superintendent, Southern Shan States.	**7. Hônlin (2,400 feet)**—*cont.*			then turning north-east, crossing two small streams at 5½ miles, makes a short and rather steep ascent (a few picks and shovels would much improve it in an hour), at the top of which is a small cultivated plateau and village (ample camping ground and good water from stream). At 9 miles cross a stream and turn northwards. At 12 miles there is a short steep descent and ascent (quite practicable), then slight descent into Hônlin village, cross stream and passing through village camp 1 mile east of it on paddy-fields near shrine; water from stream; ample and good large camping ground. Hônlin has some 30 houses; supplies: bullocks, paddy and fowls. Track good. For alternative route between Stages 6 and 9, *see* Alternative II below.
			M. F.	M. F.	
		8. Nanö (1,700 feet). Nam Aw and small streams.	9 0	85 4	General direction little north of east; road undulating and badly cut up by bullock traffic in places. At 5 miles there is a steep ascent straight up a spur with another through shorter one, a little further on about 1 mile from bottom to top. There has been no attempt to zigzag the path though the soil is soft. The descent for the same reason is steep in places, and is 2 miles in length when a level paddy clearing is entered after crossing a stream, at the east end of which is the small village of Nanö surrounded by orange trees; paddy and fowls can be procured. Camping ground for a large force on paddy-fields; water good and plentiful from Nam Aw. The alternative route referred to in the last stage joins in here. It would be better for any large force moving along this route to make the halt here rather than on the river at Ta Kaw.
		9. Ta Kaw Ferry. Salween river (Nam Khong and Hwé Lôn).	3 0	88 4	Track goes due east following a spur with one or two rather steep little descents. At 2¼ miles is Ta Kaw (or Tákaw) village, some 15 houses, ½ mile on following a stream in the Salween and ¼ mile up stream is the ferry. The river here runs under the right bank and the stream is some 200 yards broad. The right bank commands the left at about 400 yards distance, the river bed is sand and shingle. The stream is very deep and rocky; ponies are always rafted across. The current too is rapid, elephants being carried nearly ½ mile down when swimming. There is a raft capable of taking 20 men or six ponies a trip and two good-sized "dug-outs" which could each take six men besides boatmen or could be made into another raft. A return trip takes about 8 minutes. Ferrymen live on both banks. There is ground near Tá Kaw village, on which a considerable body of men, say 400 could manage to encamping on the right bank, but on the left bank troops would have to march 1 mile along the Kyengtung road to a clearing, when by cutting brushwood and grass, 400 men could find accommodation on the Hwé Lôn river.
		10. Páng-Paw (1,525 feet).	9 0	97 4	Passing through the small village of East Tá Kaw on the left bank of the Salween, the track strikes east undulating over some small spurs—at 1 mile is a clearing suitable for camp, within a 100 yards of which flows the Hwé Lôn river to its junction with the Salween. Hwé Lôn here 50 yards broad, rocky

FROM MÔNE (MÖNGNAI) TO KYENGTUNG (KENGTUNG) *viâ* TA KAW FERRY—*continued.*

Authorities.		Number and Names of Stages, Rivers and Streams.	Distances.		Remarks.
Military.	Civil.		Intermediate.	Total.	
G.O.C. Rangoon District.	Superintendent, Southern Shan States.	**10. Pang-Paw (1,525 feet)**—*cont.*			bottom, and low banks, 1½ feet water (in March); continuing east track makes a short steep ascent, then becomes very narrow (just breadth for one laden mule) and skirts the Hwé Lôn, at times just above its bed, at other 300 feet above it. The ravine through which the Hwé Lôn passes is very precipitous. From the track into the river is often almost sheer drop and for 2½ to 3 miles it would be impossible for caravans to pass each other. The summits of the hills on either side of the ravine are some 1,000 to 1,300 feet above the river. Their lower slopes covered with bamboo, the upper one with good-sized timber. This is the worst bit of the whole route for laden baggage animals owing purely to the narrowness of the path. At 5 miles the gorge opens out, there are clearings and the path is good going. At 6 miles is the small village of Hwé Háng. Here the Hwé Lôn comes in at a sharp bend from the north. Passing through the village path turns north still following course of Hwé Lôn, cross the Nam Pán flowing in from east (40 feet broad, 1½ feet water, good bottom, banks 10 feet above water) just above its junction with the Hwé Lôn. Keeping along left of that river at 8 miles cross a small tributary, ½ mile on cross to right bank of Hwé Lôn, ½ mile further jungle camp of Páng-Paw amongst bamboo jungle on Hwé Lôn. Old site of a village which adjoins camp only requires grass to be cut to enable 500 men to encamp. Good going from village.
		11. Longsalé camp (2,900 feet). Hwé Lôn and Nam Mawng.	M. F. **10 0**	M. F. 107 4	Track continues in northerly direction, make steep but short ascent on leaving camp descending almost at once to level of Hwé Lôn again. Following its course crosses small tributary and the river itself; here is short boggy piece about 30 feet long. Track leaves Hwé-Lôn turning east, ascends a hill first 200 yards steep, onwards gradients are fairly easy to top. Turning north make another short ascent (2,559 feet), then easy descent of 2 miles in north-east direction, cross Nam Mawng river (20 feet broad, 1 foot water, hard bottom) and enter Nataung paddy plain averaging 400 yards broad and 2 miles long, running east and west, pass Nataung villages, some 40 houses (north of Nataung on the far side of low hills is Hsen Mawng village, through which northern route to Kyengtung passes, *see* Alt. III), continue up valley across paddy-fields crossing Nam Mawng three times. (There is another wet weather track to the north running along foot of low hills avoiding paddy plain.) Enter low hills continuing up bed of Nam Mawng, and crossing it about twenty times, river is however narrower. At 10 miles, reach Longsalé jungle camp. Space for 400 to 500 men with little clearing. Infantry took 3 hours 40 minutes marching, Panthay mules ¾ hour longer, elephants 7 hours 4 minutes.
		12. Jungle camp (4,000 feet). Nam Mawng, Nakhán stream and Nam Paw.	**9 6**	117 2	Direction south-east. First 2 miles fair going, but still along bed of Nam Mawng. Then leaving river almost at its head waters ascend the Tangmán hill, slope easy top 4,300 feet, descent very easy. At foot cross Nakhán stream and follow its course till it joins Nam Paw at ruined village of Pankhán. Nam Paw 15 feet broad, 1 foot water, following up this river track

FROM MÔNE (MŎNGNAI) TO KYENGTUNG (KENGTUNG) *viâ* TA KAW FERRY—*continued.*

Authorities. Military.	Authorities. Civil.	Number and Names of Stages, Rivers and Streams.	Distances. Intermediate. M.	F.	Distances. Total. M.	F.	Remarks.
G.O.C. Rangoon District.	Superintendent, Southern Shan States.	**12. Jungle camp (4,000 feet)**—*cont.*					turns little north of east and were it not for the constant crossing of stream is very good. At 6½ miles pass ruined village of Wan Maw. At 8 miles the river and road turns south-east and the gorge opens out into a small level valley about 500 yards broad. At 9¾ miles camp on small tributary of Nam Paw about 4 feet broad, 3 inches water. Camp space here cramped; but there is ample ground for 500 men ½ mile back on Nam Paw.
		13. Möng Puon (2,300 feet). Several streams, small except when in flood.	11	6	129	0	On leaving camp track makes a slight ascent over a spur, hill sides cleared. Then easy descent cross Nam Paw and begin ascent of Loi Pán Mong hills; gradients for most part easy, road good, top of hill 5,200 feet; hill covered with pines and other timbers of fine growth. Going south for 2 miles along ridge, the descent is very easy. Track then turns east, just beyond this bend on the south side close to the road is a spring of water used by bullock caravans; descent continues easy through pine trees, and at 8½ miles ends. Cross Nam-Na-Aw stream and pass through Wan-Na-Aw village. From this to Möng Puon there are two roads. The direct one turning south across a low spur enters the paddy plain and crosses the Nam Wong. The other continuing east down a short valley crosses the Nam Pying and turning south crosses the Nam Pu and cuts into the other track. The river formed by the junction of the Nam Wong and Nam Pu is called the Nam Pying. These rivers are each about 40 feet broad, 1 foot water, gravel bottoms, banks 4 feet above waters and apparently overflow these banks. Track continues south over paddy plain, which is about 1 mile broad, and ascends low rising ground, on which is the large straggling village of Möng Puon (about 80 houses), flanked on either side by the Nam Wong to the north, and Nam Pu to the east. Camp on paddy plain east of village on Nam Pu. Supplies: rice, paddy, fowls, cattle, pigs are plentiful. The rice is red, and sepoys consider it unwholesome. Elevation 2,300 feet.
		14. Páng Páklôn (5,125 feet). Streams.	9	4	138	4	General direction east. On leaving camp sharp ascent in first 1½ miles, rise 775 feet, then undulating along spurs. At 4½ miles slight descent, cross small stream and ascend the Táklet hill (easy going) onwards, the ascent is constant though easy till the Palaung village of Pámin is reached 5,150 feet (8 miles). Pámin consists of about 40 houses, and the Palaungs cultivate the poppy and manufacture opium extensively. It is situated on a hilly plateau ranging from 5,000 to 6,000 feet. Fowls, pigs and cattle are plentiful. Passing through the village the road runs along a hill side, crosses several rivulets, camp at Páng Páklôn in a narrow valley watered by three small streams which flow across the road. Five hundred men could find camping room at Pámin itself, there is better ground on grass knolls, but water has to be brought for some distance.

FROM MÔNÉ (MÖNGNAI) TO KYENGTUNG (KÉNGTUNG) *viâ* TA KAW FERRY—*continued.*

Authorities.		Number and Names of Stages, Rivers and Streams.	Distances.				Remarks.
Military.	Civil.		Intermediate.		Total.		
			M.	F.	M.	F.	
G.O.C. Rangoon District.	Superintendent, Southern Shan States.	**15. Möng Sen (4,000 feet).** Nam Sen.	**10**	**0**	148	4	On leaving camp road makes a steep ascent in first ¾ mile rising to 5,725 feet. The hills on either side of this *col* about 1 mile distant are probably over 6,500 or even 7,000 feet; onwards direction south-east, the track is good, but with constant rise and fall. At 3 miles pass the Palaung village of Möng Nung about 30 houses (fowls, pigs, &c.). The poppy is also cultivated here. After a slight descent the Nam Sen is reached (4,400 feet). The stream is only about 15 feet broad, 1 foot bridge, and 1 foot water. In the next 2 miles the road again rises to 5,025 feet, and following along the tops of hills for some distance gradually descends to Möng Sen. The road is excellent, the only at all steep descent is just before Möng Sen is reached. This is a village of about 40 houses on the west side of a paddy plain, about 500 yards broad, watered by two small streams. Camp on east side on paddy-fields on stream which rises out of the paddy-fields close to camp.
		16. Hsup Mut (2,650 feet). Nam Sim and Nam Mut.	**8**	**4**	157	0	Road ascends rugged hills to east of camp, rather steep in places and with two short bad rocky bits at the top and at the descent (total rise from plain 475 feet), onwards the track is very good descending east till at 3rd mile, turns north under a precipitous rock. Passing through magnificent bamboos at 6 miles reaches the Nam Sim (2,300 feet), the river is from 60 to 70 yards broad, but divided by a sand bank. At the ford the main channel is under the left bank and is about 40 yards broad and from 2 to 2¼ feet deep. Just below the ford the water is deep, from 6 to 10 feet probably. On the far side of the sand bank there is about 1 foot of water. The banks are 15 feet above present water level, but there are signs of flood. The bottom is gravel and rock. The ford is just where the river flowing in from the north-east turns sharp southwards. During the rains rafts are kept as a ferry. The path following along the left bank passes through a narrow ravine with high precipitous rocks on either side about 500 feet above river. The road here is rough in parts and requires a little blasting to make it wider. After about 1 mile the ravine opens out where the Nam Sim flowing from the north is joined by the Nam Mut coming from the east. The Nam Mut is about 40 feet broad, but with only about 1½ feet of water and good gravel bottom, following along the left bank of the Nam Mut, the paddy-fields and village of Hsup Mut are reached. Camp on fields or just beyond village on river; supplies: paddy, fowls, pigs, cattle, about 30 houses.
		17. Tong Wa (3,875 feet). Nam Mut.	**12**	**0**	169	0	Cross Nam Mut 250 yards beyond village, track going north-east ascends nearly 700 feet in first 2 miles, then a mile of easy descent to the Nam Mut (2,750 feet) crosses it, and passing village of Yánpong on the right ascend a spur which separates two stretches of paddy ground (would make excellent camp), and bending to east rises about 750 feet in 2 miles, then following along the ridge of a minor range of hills south-east pass village of Pápun (7 miles) off the road to

FROM MÔNÉ (MÖNGNAI) TO KYENGTUNG (KENGTUNG) *viâ* TA KAW FERRY—*continued.*

Authorities. Military.	Authorities. Civil.	Number and Names of Stages, Rivers and Streams.	Distances. Intermediate.	Distances. Total.	Remarks.
G.O.C. Rangoon District.	Superintendent, Southern Shan States.	**17. Tong Wa (3,875 feet)**—*cont.*			the right. Turning north-east at 8¼ miles rise to 4,075 feet. Then descent to Nam Mut river, last part rather steep. River only 10 feet broad here with high banks, on far side in Kôken camping ground, room for 500 men, a *zayát* (20 men) beyond this camp, track is wet for a short distance. Cross a small stream and ascend spurs and descend into Tong Wa camp on Nam Mut, small camping ground.
		18. Camp Mong Maw. Nam Mut and Nam Kun.	M. 12 F. 0	M. 181 F. 0	Crossing Nam Mut (here a mere stream) track goes north-east along its course crossing its twice, for 2¼ miles; road wet and rocky in places; ascent constant. At 3 miles leave Nam Mut almost at its head waters and ascend spurs of the Loi Pé-möng range, steep in places, but with several fairly level pieces; summit 6,000 feet. This is the water parting of the Salween and Mé Khong rivers, the descent is very easy following down a long spur right into Möng Maw camp. The camp is at junction of the Nam Kun and a tributary, 500 men could encamp.
		19. Kyengtung (Kengtung).	5 0	186 0	Road crosses Nam Kun's tributary and rising over a low spur crosses the Nam Aw just above its junction with the Nam Kun. Following the Nam Kun, the road passes through a gorge, the hills on either side gradually opening out into the Kyengtung plain. At 3 miles crosses Nam Kun and passing through village of Káng Pong, crosses a small stream about 15 feet broad, 1 foot water, and follows along a raised cart road through paddy-fields. Kyengtung is situated under a low range of hillocks, 800 to 1,000 yards distant to the south, on the last of these there is a kyaung which commands town at 700 yards distance; height of paddy plain about 2,600 feet. Kyengtung is surrounded by a deep ditch and high earthwork surmounted by a brick wall 4¾ miles in circumference. Barely half the enclosed space is inhabited. The houses occupy the northern half, there are several villages on the east, west and north sides close under the walls. The wall follows the contours of the hillocks on which the town is built. To the north east are two large tanks, through which a man can walk. The houses are some brick, some wooden, others bamboos. Some brick-tiled, others the greater portion thatched. The population numbers from 5,000 to 6,000, mostly Shans, but with a sprinkling of Burmans, and in the cold season about 200 Chinamen, the greater portion of whom return to China before the rains. It is the capital of the state and the residence of the Sawbwa. Supplies are plentiful, including rice, *goor*, fresh milk, cattle, goats, pigs, fowls, ducks, salt, sulphur, camphor, earthenware, and rough cutlery. The Burman shopkeepers sell English calico, silk, &c., there are a considerable number of flint and matchlock guns made, ponies of a good stamp seem plentiful, and there are always caravans of Panthays with their mules. There are several kinds of vegetables including green peas and yams or sweet potatoes. Fresh fish can always be caught, rice sells at 4 annas for 38 lbs. The people are very rich; water is obtained from wells and tanks, but a force would either encamp to the north-west on the Nam Lamoi or to the north-east on the Nam Lap. Large mule caravans yearly pass through Kyengtung, coming from and returning to China.

FROM MÔNÉ (MÖNGNAI) TO KYENGTUNG (KENGTUNG) *viâ* TA KAW FERRY—*continued.*

General remarks on the road from Môné to Ta Kaw Ferry.

Môné to Saikhao, 53 miles.

(*a*) For the first 53 miles, *i.e.*, to Saikhao village, carts could now run during the dry season where the track but broader and the Téng river and smaller streams bridged, and the short and rather sharp descent, 2¼ miles west of Makláng, eased by the gradients being properly laid out, a very easy matter.

Saikhao to Kyaingkán on Nam Pán river, 9½ miles.

(*b*) Onwards to Kyaingkán the present track would be followed. The work required being more easing of present gradients by lengthening the zigzags, making the road broader, here and there a little embanking across "paddy" cultivation and the bridging of streams.

Nam Pán river.

(*c*) The bridging of the Nam Pán river would be a large work and only an engineer could give a useful opinion about it; the river is very deep, but the bed is hard and rocky. It is as shown in the report divided into two channels just above the present ferry by islands, these are well wooded, and about 100 to 150 yards broad: as they are inhabited it seems importable that they are subject to flood. If these islands were utilized, there would be about 150 yards of bridging to be done on either side of them. The current is so gentle that, at any rate during the cold weather, a pontoon or boat bridge would certainly carry cart traffic across.

From Kyaingkán to Nanö, 23 miles.

From foot of hills to Nanö village, 4 miles.

(*d*) The road onwards to 5 miles beyond Hônlin would present no difficulties, only in two short pieces would the gradients have to be altered, but at this point the only at all formidable difficulty presents itself in the form of a steep ascent of about 600 feet and descent of 1,500 feet to Nanö village. The present track goes almost straight up and down this double-topped hill. Here therefore a road would have to be laid out and made. The soil is red clay and therefore easy to work.

From Nanö to Ta Kaw ferry, 3 miles.

(*e*) From Nanö to Ta Kaw Ferry 3 miles, the present track could be followed almost the whole way as it descends a long spur.

Timber for bridging.

(*f*) Timber from Pácang right down to Ta Kaw is plentiful, and it is in this section of the road that all bridging of any size would have to be done, as between Môné and the Téng river only mere streams are crossed.

The Nam Téng.

(*g*) The Téng river would, I think, present no difficulty to bridging. The bamboo bridge, which now spans it, is 100 paces in length, and remains quite steady whilst laden mules pass over it. It was made in 10 days by the villages. The banks are 15 to 20 feet above the present water level. The bottom is gravel and rock.

Soil.

(*h*) The soil along the route is for the most part the red clay, common to the Shan plateaux. Very little rock is encountered and what there is, is usually in the form of large detached boulders, very little blasting would have to be done.

Taungyi to Kyaingkán probable line of a road.

(*i*) As it is intended by Government to make Taungyi the head-quarters of the Superintendent of the Shan States, and as this place is on the direct road from the railway at Meiktila road to Ta Kaw, any future road would not touch Môné, but go almost direct to Kyaingkán, about 10 marches from Taungyi and the road reported to be as good as that from Môné.

Road in rains.

(*k*) Good as the road is at this season of the year, in or after the rains, it would be very difficult, owing to want of bridges and short stretches of marshy ground.

Notes for a force of 500 men marching.

Ample camping space and water can be found at all the halting places named on the route for a force of 500 men, including followers and transport animals. Such a force would take ten days from Môné Post to Ta Kaw Ferry granting that the Nam Téng be bridged as it now is, and allowing a whole day for crossing the Nam Pán on rafts.

General remarks on the road from Ta Kaw Ferry to Kyengtung.

(*l*) The present track is fairly good, merely broadening the present path along the hill sides would make it easily practicable. Panthay mules carrying an average load of 140 lbs. took only from ½ to ¾ of an hour longer over a stage than sepoys marching. The following notes may be of use, should it ever be intended to make a good mule track to Kyengtung.

FROM MÔNÉ (MÖNGNAI) TO KYENGTUNG (KENGTUNG) *viâ* TA KAW FERRY—*continued.*

The first 4 miles after leaving the Salween is one of the worst bits in the whole route, the path about 2 to 2½ feet broad following up the course of the Hwé Lôn river along the side of a very steep, in places precipitous, hill, falling sometimes to almost the level of the river bed, at others rising to over 300 feet above it. All this could be obviated by letting the path follow one general contour and bridging the gullies. A considerable amount of blasting would have to be done here in places, but generally the soil is soft and the rocks detached fragments.

Onwards right into Kyengtung there is no difficulty about making a capital mule road. The steep ascent and descent on leaving Páng Paw camp (9½ miles) can be altogether avoided by merely cutting the road along the hill side along the banks of the Hwé Lôn. This would shorten the road by perhaps 400 yards. A considerable amount of bridging would have to be done (I attach a list of the large streams). The present track takes a bee line straight up the course of all streams when there is no reason why the path should not skirt them following their banks which are nearly all very small. There is not a single ascent or descent which could not be made quite easy for laden mules with a little lengthening of present zizags and making them when necessary. The Shans apparently go straight up a slope as far as they can, before they begin to make the gradients easy, the same thing is often found near the top of a hill. Again they take their paths along the crest of a ridge straight over all rises when by keeping an almost level track you can pass round them. I am inclined to think that the slopes to the west are steeper than those to the east, the soil is all soft and could be easily and rapidly worked.

Embanking would be necessary across the paddy-fields, especially at Möng Puon and Möng Sen. At Kyengtung there is a road across the paddy plain 2 miles in length, which only requires repair.

Some blasting would have to be done in the gorge through which the Nam Sim flows, and again a little at the foot of the Loi Pémöng hills.

(*m*) Fine timber is abundant all along the road by the streams. All the beds are round gravel and rock. No timber is floated down them.

(*n*) The following is a list of all rivers and streams of importance which would have to be bridged, taking them in order from the Salween :—

Name of river or stream.	Breadth.	Depth (march).
Nam Paw (once) ... ... } Hwé Lôn (twice) ... ... }	30 yards	1½ feet.
Nam Mawng (thrice) *	10 yards	1 foot.
Nam Paw (twice) *...	15 feet	1 "
Nam Wong (once)	30 "	1 "
Nam Pu (once)	30 "	1 "
Nam Sen (once)	20 "	1 "
Nam Sim (once)	60 yards	2½ ft. at ford.
Nam Mut (four times) ...	50 feet	1½ feet.
	40 "	1½ "
	15 "	1 foot.
	10 "	1 "
Nam Kun (twice)	10 yards	1 "
Nam Aw (once)	10 "	1½ feet.

* This is if the track be made to follow their courses and not take a bee line.

A force of 500 men including followers and baggage animals could find camping space and water at all stages.

FROM MÔNÉ (MÖNGNAI) TO KYENGTUNG (KENGTUNG) *viâ* TA KAW FERRY—*continued.*

ALTERNATIVE I.

FROM MÔNÉ (MÖNGNAI) TO KYAINGKÂN (KENGKHAM), (STAGE 6) *viâ* KYAINGTAUNG.

BY LIEUT. H. E. STANTON, ROYAL ARTILLERY, JANUARY 1888.

Authorities. Military.	Authorities. Civil.	Number and Names of Stages, Rivers and Streams.	Distances. Intermediate. M.	Distances. Intermediate. F.	Distances. Total. M.	Distances. Total. F.	Remarks.
G.O.C. Rangoon District.	Superintendent, Southern Shan States.	**1. Wantom and Nannong villages (4,200 feet).** Three bridged streams, one dry nullah bridged.	12	0	12	0	Pack track. General direction north-east. Start east across the Môné valley through tall grass; cross two well-bridged streams and at 4 miles cross another stream; bridge out of repair; bad ford for animals; steep ramps down to and up from water; some mud. Commence a gentle ascent through open scrub jungle and spear grass. Gradually turning north-north-east pass behind hill called Loi (Lwé) Nampu. Descend a dry nullah, cross a good bridge and ascend gradually. Enter a gorge at 10 miles and continue in a valley between two ranges of hills, some 1 mile apart. The highest point on the road is 5,000 feet above the sea. The track is a little rough in one or two place , otherwise it is good. Pass two small villages in Môné v lley and one just after crossing the dry nullah. No accommodation. Open camp. Six houses in village. Bamboo leaves plentiful. Water scarce, about ½ mile north in a stream. (Water plentiful May to October.)
		2. Naungkukam (2,700 feet).	6	0	18	0	Pack track. General direction east-north-east. Leave Wantom due east; for 2 miles continue to descend through rough gorges, the hills on either side covered with dense jungle. Thus far the track is rough and rocky, then issue on the south side of a valley running east. The north side of the valley is formed of high limestone crags; continue along the south side of the valley crossing some undulations and two small streams, big enough for men to drink at. The stream in the valley is lost in the limestone rocks. At 3 miles reach Naunglem; the village is small and is situated some 1 mile from the road. There is one kyaung and perpetual water in well (water plentiful from May to October). Grass and bamboo leaves obtainable. Leaving Naunglem track turn south through open jungle along the sides of some hills, and at 4½ miles descend a steep rocky path into a valley. The descent is about 200 feet; turn Nalong, a good path through thick jungle, and cross a swamp some 50 yards wide. It is muddy and bad from May to December. In January water is obtained by digging 1 foot below the surface. Grass plentiful. Village completely burned and deserted.
		3. Naungsiôm Sakhân.	7	0	25	0	Pack track. General direction north-east. Track good and level. Cross 20 yards of swamp at starting; 2½ miles further on the Namnong (Mön chaung) runs within 300 yards of the road to the north-west. It is under some big trees, visible from the road. Continue past a burned and deserted village over some undulations through open tree jungle of pine and *in.* Shelter in one zayát and under a banyan tree. Water is obtained by digging in the bed of a stream ¼ mile south of camp. Grass plentiful.

FROM MÔNÉ (MÖNGNAI) TO KYENGTUNG (KENGTUNG) *viâ* TA KAW FERRY—*continued.*

ALTERNATIVE I—*continued.*

Authorities. Military.	Authorities. Civil.	Number and Names of Stages, Rivers and Streams.	Distances. Intermediate. M.	F.	Distances. Total. M.	F.	Remarks.
G.O.C. Rangoon District.	Superintendent, Southern Shan States.	**4. Pongsáng Sakhan (2,030 feet).**	11	4	36	4	Pack track. General direction east-north-east. Through forest of pine, *in*, and teak, no undergrowth, up and down over slight undulations. Between the 7th and 8th miles the track is rough and stony; all the rest is good. Cross four bridged nullahs, all dry in January except one at the 3rd mile, in which there are one or two small pools. Shelter under banyan trees. Good water from a well 30 yards north of camp. The water is 2 feet from surface; the well is deep and quickly re-fills as the water is drawn.
		5. Mönghai (Mainghé), 2,150 feet. Nam Téng (or Tein chaung), 60 yards wide and deep, and one stream bridged in two places.	8	4	45	0	Pack track. General direction north-east. At 2 miles cross three swamps, 30 yards to 40 yards, each bridged. The swamps are open, the rest of the road is through thick jungle. There is a zayát on either side of the Nam Téng at Ta Long ferry; the ramps to and from the river are easy and sandy. At Ta Long ferry, charge 1 anna for four persons or two bullock loads; one boat available takes four loads per trip. The remains of two large kyaungs are on the left bank of the river; all the rest of the town of Kyaingtaung is completely burned and jungle grown. Cross a big stream by a substantial bridge and keep along the banks of the stream for 2 miles through an open plain formerly cultivated with paddy. Recross the stream by a good bridge and reach Tôn Hôn (elevation 1,850 feet) hidden in the trees. It is a fort 40 yards square, surrounded by a breast-work and two roads of open bamboo hurdles and bamboo spikes. It has an east and west entrance defended by bastions. At present the fort is garrisoned by 140 Môné men with 50 guns under an Amát. Accommodation in one kyaung and five or six zayáts outside fort. Grass and water good and plentiful. Road continues north along rising ground on the east edge of the Kyaingtaung plain. Jungle dense on either side of the road, which is good and easy throughout. Pass a fine mango tope. Grass and water good and plentiful. Accommodation for 500 men in a ky-aung and zayáts. The kyaung is on top of a knoll some 250 yards by 150 yards, the ascent to which is steep from all sides but the south. A stream with high steep banks runs round north and west sides. This was held and fortified by Twet Nga Lu in the recent fighting.
		6. Namsáng (1,600 feet). Kôhák and Pakhi chaungs and Nam-ting.	15	4	60	0	Pack track. General direction north. Leave Mainghé kyaung by the path on the west leading to the stream. Cross the stream down and up steep ramps; ½ mile on recross the stream by a good pack bridge and join the path which leaves the kyaung to the north. This path is impracticable for laden animals, owing to steep banks of stream and the bridge being broken. Continue north over undulating country through *in* forests. Good road. At 5 miles pass Pángpaw kyaung. At 6 miles cross the Kôhák stream by a bridge. This is the Kyaingkán-

FROM MÔNÉ (MÕNGNAI) TO KYENGTUNG (KENGTUNG) *viâ* TA KAW FERRY—*continued.*

ALTERNATIVE I—*continued.*

Authorities.		Number and Names of Stages, Rivers and Streams.	Distances.				Remarks.
Military.	Civil.		Intermediate.		Total.		
			M.	F.	M.	F.	
G.O.C. Rangoon District.	Superintendent, Southern Shan States.	**6. Namsáng (1,600 feet)** —*cont.*					Kyaingtaung boundary. At 7 miles turn south through a narrow gorge in the Takam hills; then continue north on the other side of the range. From 9 to 13½ miles the track leads up and down over knolls along the valley of the Pakhi chaung which is crossed once by a good bridge and five times by ford. Water about 1 foot 6 inches deep; gravelly bed; no mud. At 12 miles pass Pakhi kyaung. A good camping ground. Water and grass good and plentiful. At 13½ miles leave the Pakhi valley and cross a knoll to the west into the valley of its tributary the Namting chaung, well bridged near the village. Camp in paddy-fields. Accommodation in one good zayát near the road and one kyaung off the road some ½ mile east of village. Water and grass good and plentiful. The Kyaingkán-Môné boundary is crossed in this march.
		7. Kyaingkán (Kengkham) ferry, 750 feet. Nampán river (Ben chaung).	**8**	**0**	68	0	Pack track. General direction north-east. Cross some paddy-fields and down a steep descent some ½ mile to the Namting; cross by a ford and commence at once the steep ascent of the Mawték range; 1 mile up a steep ascent to 2,000 feet and 1 mile down a very steep, slippery, clayey descent into the rocky bed of a hill stream. At 2½ miles continue a series of small ascents and descents over small knolls. Cross three or four small alluvial valleys about 100 yards broad. At 3½ miles ford the Nampong, 2 yards wide, 6 inches deep in January. Good ford with steep ramps. At 4 miles pass Nongkaw, a burned village, then issue into the Ben chaung (Nam Pán) valley. Paddy cultivation. At 5 miles reach the village of Wanhao on the right bank of the Ben chaung. Big five-day bazaar. Opposite Wanhao is the new town of Kyaingkán (or Kengkham). The river here is 60 yards broad and deep. One ferry boat which carries 10 men at a trip. The main ferry with platform for animals is 2 miles further up the river at the old town of Kyaingkán. This ferry crossed 100 yards to an island and 40 yards further to the left bank. Animals can swim at the new town ferry, but cannot do so at the old town ferry, as the river passes over a bed of limestone rocks which are some 2 feet below the surface in January. At the new town ferry the current is strong, some 30 yards per minute; at the old town ferry it is slow, about 20 yards per minute. There are some zayáts and kyaungs and a good camping ground on the right bank at the old town ferry, and open camping ground on the left bank on paddy land. Between the two ferries the river is a series of rapids, and below the new town ferry it splits up into five or six channels, each of which falls some 30 feet over a rocky barrier, straight across the river. Grass plentiful. Residence of a Myoza. (The old town is now burned and nearly deserted; the new town is springing up. January 1888.—H. E. S.)

FROM MÔNÉ (MÖNGNAI) TO KYENGTUNG (KENGTUNG) *viâ* TA KAW FERRY—*continued.*

ALTERNATIVE II.

FROM KYAINGKÁN (STAGE 6) TO TA KAW FERRY (STAGE 9).

BY LIEUT. H. E. STANTON, ROYAL ARTILLERY, JANUARY 1888.

Authorities. Military.	Authorities. Civil.	Number and Names of Stages, Rivers and Streams.	Distances. Intermediate. M. F.	Distances. Total. M. F.	Remarks.
G.O.C. Rangoon District.	Superintendent, Southern Shan States.	**1. Nakak (1,900 feet).** Nam Pán, Nam Nakak and two other streams.	7 0	7 0	General direction north-north-east. Pack track. At 2 miles strike the Ben chaung near Wantung village (one small boat ferry). This river is a series of falls and rapids where passed. These 2 miles up and down over low undulations, crossing two small stream beds, through jungle; 1 mile along the open left bank of Ben chaung to the burned village of Wanpa, turn east through thick jungle and continue for 1 mile over undulating country, then 2 miles north along the course of a big stream which is crossed by two good fords with 1 foot of water in January. At 6½ miles commence a steep ascent of 300 yards and issue on a level open valley; cross a stream 2 yards wide and 3 feet deep with steep banks and no bridges; continue along the edge of the valley into Nakak; the road throughout is over loam soil; the ascent is very steep and difficult. Camp near a kyaung on a low knoll. Water from the stream. Grass plentiful. Village of 10 houses in sugar-cane and paddy cultivation.
		2. Keng Lom* (Kyaing Lôm), 2,050 feet. Nam Wantong and Nam Phawm.	7 4	14 4	General direction north-north-east. Pack track. Cross the stream again just after starting; there is a foot-bridge; ford for animals; steep ramps; some mud; the road continues gradually rising over undulations covered with bamboo and teak forests. Pass within 2 miles of the high pointed peak of Loitáng (Lwétáng). Cross a good ford and enter the valley of the Kwángtôn stream which here forms the Kyaingkán Môné boundary. Pass the village of Tôn under the Sabáng peak at 2½ miles. At 4 miles cross two fords of a stream 2 yards wide, 1 foot deep; ¾ mile further on cross big stream by a substantial pack bridge. From this stream the track runs straight up a steep hill for 400 yards (named Mawték) and down a similar descent to a small stream; up another smaller ascent and descent gradually to Kyainglôm. The track is through jungle throughout, very dense for the last mile); the soil is loam and is nowhere rough or stony. Kyainglôm is in an upland valley watered by several channels of the Namhuseng. One kyaung and two or three zayáts. Three or four villages scattered about. A five-day bazaar. Residence of a Hein under the Môné Sawbwa. Plenty of good camping ground. Water and grass good and plentiful.

* Capt. H. R. Davies, traversing this route in April 1893, did these two stages in one march. His description of the stage is as follows:—

1. Keng Lom, 13 miles. General direction north-north-east. Good mule road, nearly level all the way, passing among rocky hills. Cross the Nam Pán at Keng Kham. At 6¼ miles pass Mak Kyeng: good camping ground, water, and grass. At 9 miles Wan Tong, a village with a five-day bazaar. Most of the road is through jungle, not very thick. At Keng Lom camping ground in paddy (700 by 400 yards), good water and grass. Keng Lom belongs to Môné and contains about 30 houses.

FROM MÔNÉ (MÖNGNAI) TO KYENGTUNG (KENGTUNG) *viâ* TA KAW FERRY—*continued.*

ALTERNATIVE II—*continued.*

Authorities. Military.	Authorities. Civil.	Number and Names of Stages, Rivers and Streams.	Distances. Intermediate. M.	F.	Distances. Total. M.	F.	Remarks.
G.O.C. Rangoon District.	Superintendent, Southern Shan States.	**3. Camp under Loi Pángpé hill (Salween-Ben chaung watershed), 2,350 feet.** Nam Pung and Hwé Hok.	7	4	22	0	General direction east-north-east. Pack track. Leave Kyainglôm bazaar to the east over some undulations, crossing over four small channels of the Namhusáng stream. At a mile after the fourth crossing ascend a steep 100 feet, pass through a gorge, and descend 50 feet over jagged limestone rocks into the valley of the Hwé Hôk; the valley is level, cultivated with paddy in places, elsewhere covered with dense jungle. It is shut in on all sides by hills, mostly limestone crags. The valley is some 5 miles long by 3 to 4 broad, and is divided in two by the Nampamôn range. The track passes round the south and along the south-east side of the range, running for 2⅛ miles along the banks of the main stream, and leaving Nampamôn village to the north. Throughout the valley the track is nearly level, it crosses one dry nullah bed by a bridge, and one small stream by a ford. At 6 miles it leaves this valley, and after crossing one or two undulations it descends a gorge over sticky clay to the valley of the Nam Pung, a tributary of the Namhusáng (of Kyainglôm); it crosses this stream four times by fords, the first of which is muddy, the rest good and sandy. Camp in a clearing at the last crossing. Grass scarce. Bamboo leaves plentiful. No accommodation. The rocky gorge 1⅛ miles from Kyainglôm is the only stony bit in the road.
		4. Ta Kaw Ferry * (Salween river ferry), 1,700 feet. Nam Kyé, Nam Aw, and Salween.	7	4	29	4	General direction east. Pack track. Rise straight up a steep spur of the Loi Pángpé range and cross the crest at 3,250 feet, ⅛ mile from camp and 600 feet above it. The crest of the range is the highest point passed between the Ben chaung and the Salween; it forms the watershed and is the Môné-Thinyut (Hseniwot) boundary. The track descends a spur of the range 1,100 feet in 1 mile into the rocky bed of a stream; 400 yards further down leave this stream bed, ford a small stream, and after two or three short steep ascents, and longer easier descents, enter a small alluvial valley ⅝ mile long at an elevation of 1,700 feet; cross tributary of the Nam Aw (the main stream of the valley) by a muddy ford, pass the village of Namö in an orange grove at the edge of the valley; cross a muddy ford of the Nam Aw after a short steep descent, and

* Capt. Davies also did these two stages in one march. Description as follows:—

2. Ta Kaw, 13 miles. General direction east-north-east. Good mule road. For the first 8 miles the road is nearly level, passing among rocky hills, the only difficulty being at 1⅛ miles where there is a steep rocky descent for 100 yards. At 7 miles cross the Hwé Pung and at 8 miles the Hwé Hok: both these streams run into the hill to the north. At 8 miles ascend steeply for 600 yards to a height of 3,520 feet: thence steep descent for a mile and more gentle descent for another mile and-a-half: level for ½ a mile to the Nam Kyé at 11¼ miles. Pass the village of Nanö: good camping ground and water. Then ascend for 200 yards and descend gently to Ta Kaw. Small camping ground. For a large column it would be best to camp at Nanö.

FROM MÔNÉ (MÖNGNAI) TO KYENGTUNG (KENGTUNG) *viâ* TA KAW FERRY—*continued.*

ALTERNATIVE II—*continued.*

Authorities.		Number and Names of Stages, Rivers and Streams.	Distances.		Remarks.
Military.	Civil.		Inter-mediate.	Total.	
G.O.C. Rangoon District.	Superintendent, Southern Shan States.	**4. Ta Kaw Ferry (Salween river ferry), 1,700 feet**—*cont.*			continue for 2½ miles along the crest of a spur which forms the right bank of a stream, then ford the stream twice at 1,150 feet and reach Ta Kaw 150 feet above the low water level of the Salween on the right bank. There are 10 houses in the village, one zayát, and there is plenty of camping ground by the river. The situation is said to be healthy Grass and bamboo leaves obtainable at low water.

ALTERNATIVE III.

FROM HSENMAWNG (*see* STAGE 11) TO KYENGTUNG (KENGTUNG) *viâ* MÖNG PYING.

BY CAPT. H. R. DAVIES, OXFORDSHIRE LIGHT INFANTRY, APRIL 1893.

Military.	Civil.	Number and Names of Stages, Rivers and Streams.	Inter-mediate. M. F.	Total. M. F.	Remarks.
G.O.C. Rangoon District.	Superintendent, Southern Shan States.	**1. Pángnam Lai Pin.** Nam Löng.	13 0	13 0	General direction east-north-east. Fair mule road. Up the Nam Mawng valley for a mile passing Namunao and Hsenmawng (Seumong). Thence over low hills to the Nam Löng at 2 miles: up the Nam Löng crossing it five times to 4 miles (20 yards wide by 2 feet deep). Thence steep ascent to 7 miles; here a road goes off to the left to Peitkáng, and the route turns to the right and goes up, but less steeply to 10 miles; thence up and down over the undulations of the spur to the camp which is on the Nam Löng-Nam Pying watershed. The camp measures 400 by 20 yards; good grass. Water from a small stream (1 yard by 4 inches) 300 yards below.
		2. Möng Pying ... Nam Löng, Nam Yuk, Nam Ang, and Nam Pying.	9 0	22 0	General direction east. Fair mule road. Steadily down-hill to the Nam Löng at 1¼ miles: here there is a small camp. Up and down over small spurs and streams to 2¼ miles; thence descent to the Nam Yuk at 3¼ miles; ascent for 200 yards, then steep descent to the Nam Ang at 5½ miles. Down the Nam Ang for ¾ of a mile, then cross a small hill, descend to the Nam Ang, again at 8¾ miles, and just beyond cross the Nam Pying and enter Möng Pying, 25 houses, under a phaya. Good small camp at the kyaung and large camp in paddy. Good water and grass. All the streams crossed are shallow and easily fordable, except the Nam Pying which is deeper than the rest, about 2½ feet.
		3. Páng Ping ... Nam Lap and Nam Löm.	12 4	34 4	General direction east. Good mule road. Level along the Nam Pying valley to 1⅓ miles where the Nam Lap (1 foot deep, 12 yards broad) is crossed at its junction with the Nam Pying. Thence up-hill, not very steep, to 2¾ miles, where the top of Loi Khawkwo is reached. From here steep descent to the Nam Löm valley at 4¼ miles. Follow up its right bank, crossing small spurs, the road being narrow in places, till the Nam Löm is crossed at 7½ miles (2 feet deep, 15 yards broad). Thence up the left bank of the Nam Löm and its tributary, the Nam Htum, keeping

FROM MÔNÉ (MÖNGNAI) TO KYENGTUNG (KENGTUNG) *viâ* TA KAW FERRY—*continued.*

ALTERNATIVE III—*continued.*

Authorities.		Number and Names of Stages, Rivers and Streams.	Distances.		Remarks.
Military.	Civil.		Inter-mediate.	Total.	
G.O.C. Rangoon District.	Superintendent, Southern Shan States.	**3. Páng Ping**—*cont.*			some way above the streams and crossing a lot of small spurs and nullahs to Páng Ping. Large camp; good grass; water from the Nam Htum (10 yards by 1 foot).
			M. F.	M. F.	
		4. Nawngbong ... Nam Htum and Nam Leng, both easily fordable.	**9 0**	43 4	General direction north-east. Good mule road. Up the Nam Htum valley across paddy for a mile, when the Nam Htum is crossed; thence very gradual rise to the Nam Pying-Nam Hsim watershed at 4 miles; thence very gradual descent to the Nam Leng at 6¼ miles. Pass the village of Nawngcho, where a camp could be cleared. Thence ascent to 8 miles and steep descent of a mile to Nawngbong. Large camp on grass; good water and grass.
		5. Möngphö ... Nam Hsim and Nam Paw.	**10 6**	54 2	General direction south-east. Good mule road. Level road down a small stream for 2 miles, and then down the Nam Leng to its junction with the Nam Hsim at Tôngta at 4 miles; cross the Nam Hsim (50 yards by 2½ feet; rapid current. Has to be crossed by boat in the rains: there is only one boat), follow up its valley to Möngka at 5¾ miles, then very gradual ascent to the Nam Hsim-Nam Phö watershed at 7½ miles; thence slight descent of 600 yards to Pángpaw. Down the valley of the Nam Paw till 9 miles, then ascent of a mile and descent of ¾ of a mile to the Nam Phö. Here there is room to camp, and good water and grass. The village of Möngphö is a mile away on the right and is not passed through.
		6. Páng Hsáng ... Nam Phö, Nam Kwong, and Nam Khai or Nam Aw.	**14 0**	68 2	General direction east. Good mule road, but steep. Cross the Nam Phö (12 yards by 1½ feet), level ground for 1 mile, where the Nam Kwong is crossed (3 yards by 4 inches); thence very steep up-hill to Páng Salalong, a small zayát at 2½ miles; thence still steep, but less so than before to 4 miles; from here easy ascent with occasional bits of down-hill to the Salween-Mékong watershed at 7½ miles. Here is a camp, but the water from the Nam Lön is not fit to drink in April. Hence steady descent by a good broad road to the Nam Khai (Nam Aw) which is crossed at 13 miles (12 yards by 1½ feet). From here level road to the camp; large camping ground; good water and grass.
		7. Kyengtung (Keng Tung). Nam Khai and Nam Khün (30 yards by 1 foot).	**8 4**	76 6	General direction east. Good mule road. Down the Nam Khai valley for ½ mile, then ascent of a ½ mile and steep rocky descent to the Nam Khai at 1¼ miles. Down the Nam Khai valley, crossing some small spurs, and re-crossing the Nam Khai at 4½ miles at the village of Wing Kawng. Thence over level cultivated plain to Kyengtung. Good camp inside town near the north-east corner, and large camping ground outside; water from wells; good grass.

FROM MÔNÉ (MÖNGNAI) TO KYENGTUNG (KENGTUNG) *viâ* TA KAW FERRY—*continued.*

BRANCH I.

FROM KYAINGKÂN (STAGE 6) TO TA SEK FERRY (AT JUNCTION OF BEN CHAUNG AND SALWEEN).

Authorities. Military.	Authorities. Civil.	Number and Names of Stages, Rivers and Streams.	Distances. Intermediate. M.	F.	Distances. Total. M.	F.	Remarks.
G.O.C. Rangoon District.	Superintendent, Southern Shan States.	**1. Ta Sek ferry (600 feet).** Salween.	**6**	**0**	6	0	Pack track. General direction south-south-east. Leave old Kyaingkán east through dense jungle following the left bank of the Ben chaung down a rough descent of 40 feet narrow path between limestone rocks. At 1 mile enter open paddy-fields; 1½ miles turn south following a bend in the river; follow the bank for 2½ miles passing the villages of Namkán and Mônaing-tángkwa, opposite the first of which the river falls in six or seven channels over a barrier some 20 feet to 40 feet high. For the next mile the path is a steep ascent and descent on the face of a limestone cliff overhanging the river, the last mile is level east-south-east to the village. Here the Ben chaung falls some 20 feet into the Salween. One boat at the ferry carries 10 men at a trip. The river is 200 yards wide, very deep and sluggish, in a rocky channel 800 feet above the sea-level. Between Kyaingkán and the Salween the Ben chaung falls 300 feet in six or seven falls and rapids; between the rapids the river is deep with slight current; the rapids are impassable for canoes or timber. The Salween is here the boundary between Möngpu and Kyaingkán.

BRANCH II.

FROM KENGLOM (ALTERNATIVE II, STAGE 2) TO LÉGYA (LAIKA).

BY LIEUT. H. E. STANTON, ROYAL ARTILLERY, RECONNAISSANCE, JANUARY 1888.

Authorities. Military.	Authorities. Civil.	Number and Names of Stages, Rivers and Streams.	Distances. Intermediate. M.	F.	Distances. Total. M.	F.	Remarks.
G.O.C. Rangoon District.	Superintendent, Southern Shan States.	**1. Káli (Kálwoi), 2,450 feet.** Stream.	**9**	**4**	9	4	General direction north-north-west. Pack track. Leave Kenglom bazaar to the north and cross the stream by a bridge; continue north in the Kenglom valley through thick jungle; pass the two peaks of Loi Nga and Loi Illa, crossing one small ford of a stream and two or three slight undulations. At 3 miles turn west down a short rough descent between Loi Illa and the next peak to its north Loi Pyémöng, and enter a valley 2 to 3 miles broad, of undulating ground shut in by hills; the road is nearly level, very good, and leads through pampas grass and a little scrub jungle. The old village of Káli is burnt and covered with dense jungle; the present village consists of three houses. No accommodation. Good camping ground. Water and grass plentiful.
		2. Kunhin (1,400 feet). Ferry of Nam Pán (Ben chaung).	**8**	**0**	17	4	General direction west. Pack track. On leaving Káli pass by a stream with water in it; road then descends for 150 yards, rather steep over stones. At 4 miles after passing along a good track over jungle clad undulations cross a bridged stream. At 6½ miles the road issues into open cultivation on the left bank of the Nam Pán or Ben chaung. Good open camp.

From MÔNÉ (MÖNGNAI) to KYENGTUNG (KENGTUNG) *viâ* TA KAW FERRY—*continued*.

BRANCH II—*continued*.

Authorities. Military.	Authorities. Civil.	Number and Names of Stages, Rivers and Streams.	Distances. Intermediate.	Distances. Total.	Remarks.
G.O.C. Rangoon District.	Superintendent, Southern Shan States.	**2. Kunhin (1,400 feet)**—*cont.*			No accommodation. Shelter under two or three banyan trees. Road good throughout, rough only at the descent from Káli. At the foot of the pass below Káli is the Môné-Möngnong boundary. Good open camp on the banks of the river under a tope of trees. Residence of a Tamôn under the Möngnong Myoza. At Kunhin the Ben chaung is 400 yards wide, where the ferry crosses. Most of the inhabitants live on an island in the middle. There is one ferry raft of two dug-outs with a bamboo platform kept ready; it takes three ponies at a trip; with notice four or five dug-outs could be collected and two more small rafts made. Above and below Kunhiu are falls and rapids; the bed of the river is composed of rough rocks at right angles to the stream.
			M. F.	M. F.	
		3. Laikam (1,700 feet). Three fords of Namhéhai, the Namkôlong bridged.	8 0	25 4	General direction north-north-west. Pack track. The track is good and easy throughout over undulations through tall jungle. At 1½ miles cross three fords of the Namhéhai stream, the first two are level crossings, 10 yards broad, 1 foot 6 inches deep with sandy beds; the third has steep ramps is 3 yards wide, 1 foot deep; no mud. At 2½ miles pass Mamoi village where there is a good camp and four zayáts. Water and grass plentiful. At 6 miles cross the Namhôlong; there is a substantial bridge slightly out of repair. The ford is good, but 2 feet 6 inches to 3 feet deep; stream is 10 yards wide. Camp on the edge of a paddy valley on banks of a stream 3 yards wide. There is one kyaung, no zayáts. A five-day bazaar. Residence of a Tamôn. Grass and water good and plentiful.
		4. Kwáng Loi Sakhán (2,840 feet). The Laikam stream by a ford, the Taimôn stream by a brdge.	12 4	38 0	General direction west. Pack track. Cross the stream at starting by a good ford; the bridge is broken down. A stone causeway runs straight across the valley. Cross two dry nullah beds and over some undulations. At 4 miles reach Tamawkam Sakhán, which at present consists of three houses; then ascend 100 feet over some rough rocks and enter the Taimôn valley. At 7 miles cross the main stream of the valley by a bridge and continue for 2½ miles over undulations in scrub jungle and pampas along the north side of the valley. At 9½ miles rise gradually round the foot of a pointed peak (Loi Lom), and enter another open valley at a higher level and running north and south at right angles to the one just left. Camp at the further side of this valley under some banyan trees opposite to and 300 yards from a small gorge through which a good stream runs into the valley. No village. Grass and water good and plentiful.

FROM MÔNÉ (MÖNGNAI) TO KYENGTUNG (KENGTUNG) *viâ* TA KAW FERRY—*continued.*

BRANCH II—*continued.*

Authorities.		Number and Names of Stages, Rivers and Streams.	Distances.				Remarks.
Military.	Civil.		Intermediate.		Total.		
			M.	F.	M.	F.	
G.O.C. Rangoon District.	Superintendent, Southern Shan States.	**5. Mansain (Bansaing), 2,950 feet.** The Kwángloi stream three times and the Nam Mansain twice.	8	0	46	0	General direction north-north-west. Pack track. Start through the gorge and issue at ½ mile on the other side of the hills in open rolling country. The track up the gorge is easy and good going; ford the stream twice and cross it by a bridge once. At 4½ miles pass the deserted village of Pángtong amongst a few trees. Cross a small valley of paddy cultivation and turning north-north-west ascend some 200 feet crossing a gorge in a range of low round hills; issue again on open rolling downs. At 5½ miles cross two fords just outside camp, little or no mud and about 1 foot of water. Camp on open rising ground. Grass and water good and plentiful. Accommodation one kyaung, one zayát. Residence of a Tamôn. This was a big village, but has recently been burned and now consists of 14 houses. From Mansain the main pack track to Möngnong and Möngsipaw (Thíbaw) runs to the north (*see* Route No. 12) and another road leads to Môné (Müngnai) to the south.
		6. Kunat (3,400 feet). Seven streams from 2 yards to 4 yards wide and 6 inches to 2 feet 6 inches deep, all bridges broken except the first one out of Mansain.	10	0	56	0	Pack track. Has been formerly used for carts. General direction west through open undulating country the whole way. Pass through no jungle. Cross seven streams varying from 2 yards to 4 yards wide and 6 inches to 2 feet 6 inches deep. All were formerly bridged, but only one bridge is now serviceable, that being over a big stream just after leaving Mansain. The fords are all good though few of them would stand much traffic, as they are rather muddy; other fords could be easily made by cutting ramps to the streams. Pass three deserted villages and two deserted kyaungs. Camp on rising ground in a large pine grove. Accommodation in two large kyaungs and two or three zayáts. Grass and water good and plentiful.
		7. Salailoi (3,400 feet).	4	0	60	0	Pack track. Country same as last stage. Pass over some rather larger knolls at the foot of a limestone crag where there is a tank of water. Pass a large kyaung in a pine grove on the top of a knoll, and cross ¼ mile of old paddy land to a stream 3 yards wide and 6 inches to 2 feet 6 inches deep; all the bridges are broken; the banks of the stream are high and abrupt, but by ramping them fords could be made in several places. One ford exists in a bend of the river under the village. It has been worn by cattle and the bed of the stream being muddy requires digging out to admit of baggage animals passing. Camp on a knoll directly above the stream in a grove of bamboo and jack fruit trees on the side of a deserted village and kyaung. Grass and water good and plentiful. *Note.*—No apparent reason why this and the next stage should not be combined—A. F.

FROM MÔNÉ (MÖNGNAI) TO KYENGTUNG (KENGTUNG) *viâ* TA KAW FERRY—*continued.*

BRANCH II—*continued.*

Authorities.		Number and Names of Stages, Rivers and Streams.	Distances.				Remarks.
Military.	Civil.		Intermediate.		Total.		
			M.	F.	M.	F.	
G.O.C. Rangoon District.	Superintendent, Southern Shan States.	**8. Salaikun (3,100 feet).** One stream by ford, Namtôn by bridge or good sandy ford.	4	0	64	0	General direction west. Pack track. Over open undulating country on loam soil. Cross a similar stream 1 mile from camp; bridges all broken, one ford exists off the track, hidden in the jungle, others could be made. Cross 200 yards of paddy land and a small stream. Cross the Namtôn by a good bridge and sandy ford just outside camp. Camp on rising ground in a bamboo and fir grove round a big kyaung and several zayáts. Accommodation for 500 men. Grass and water good and plentiful. Three or four houses are occupied in the remains of a large village.
		9. Wôlong (3,150 feet). One bridged stream, one small muddy streamlet.	12	0	76	0	General direction south-south-west. Pack track. Over open undulations. Along the west side of the Hángkáng ridge, on the top of which is the Légya-Möngnong boundary. Cross one small stream by a muddy ford some 10 yards in length. At 4 miles pass Wanti bazaar near two or three inhabited villages, crossing Namkát 3 yards wide and 2 feet deep by a good pack bridge. Here is a good site for a camp. Water and grass good and plentiful. No accommodation. Leaving Wanti turn west across a low range of round hills, and then south-west to Wôlong village deserted. Plenty of room for camp on rising ground under pine and bamboo grove. Water from a deep-bricked well, 7 feet square, to the west of a large kyaung. Water and grass good and plentiful.
		10. Légya (Laika), 2,950 feet. (3,200 feet) ferry and ford of Namting (Tein chaung).	4	4	80	4	General direction west-south-west. Pack track. Two miles level through a plantation of pollard ash. An easy smooth descent of 50 feet to the Tein chaung, Tá Moláng ferry. Two small dug-outs available. A ford exists about 2 feet 6 inches deep; should be carefully staked out, as it is hard to find; the river is 50 yards wide with a strongish current. Remainder of distance along bunds across a low-lying valley to Légya. Accommodation in two or three kyaungs. The town is burned. About 15 houses have been recently built. Residence of a Sawbwa. A good camping ground exists in a walled pagoda enclosure 200 yards square, ½ mile to the north of the old town on rising ground. Water and grass good and plentiful. *Note.*—Watson and Fedden's route, Salween survey, 1864-65, page 27, makes distance Ta Kaw to Kunhin only 22 miles. This route is at present closed. Instead of going west to Kenglom and then north-north-west to Káli (Kálwoi), it runs almost direct north-west from the 9th mile from Ta Kaw. Watson's distance, 14 miles Ta Kaw to Káli, must, however, be under-estimated, it being 15 miles as the crow flies (*vide* Fedden's map compiled from observations on the spot). I should estimate the distance from Ta Kaw to Káli by the direct route at 20 miles, saving 4½ on the route given here.—H. E. S. *Note.*—Route Ta Kaw to Légya. The route *viâ* Kenglom to Káli is very roundabout. It is suggested that in compiling

FROM MÔNÉ (MÖNGNAI) TO KYENGTUNG (KENGTUNG) *viâ* TA KAW FERRY—*continued.*

BRANCH II—*continued.*

Authorities. Military.	Authorities. Civil.	Number and Names of Stages, Rivers and Streams.	Distances. Inter-mediate.	Distances. Total.	Remarks.
G.O.C. Rangoon District.	Superintendent, Southern Shan States.	**10. Légya (Laika), 2,950 feet**—*cont.*			this route Kenglom should be omitted and the route carried direct from Ta Kaw to Káli, 20 miles * The track from Kenglom to Káli is important, as it connects the two approaches from Môné and Légya and by being continued north approaches Nongkamgyi on the direct track from Möngnong to Ta Kaw. All these three routes converge on the site of an old village under the Nampamôn hill 3 miles east of Kenglom.—H.E.S.

No. 24.

From MÔNÉ (MÖNGNAI) to MÖNGYAI (MAINGYÉ) *viâ* LÉGYA (LAIKA).

BY MAJOR ROSE, D.S.O., 27TH PUNJAB INFANTRY, AND LIEUT. H. E. STANTON, ROYAL ARTILLERY, JANUARY AND FEBRUARY 1888.

Military	Civil	Stages, Rivers and Streams	Inter. M.	Inter. F.	Total M.	Total F.	Remarks
G.O.C. Rangoon District.	Superintendent, Southern Shan States.	**1. Pennébyin** ... One stream bridged.	**10**	**4**	10	4	Cart road part of the way, then pack track. Good over undulating country. Camp in bamboo grove. Water from stream good and plentiful. Good grass.
		2. Naungpa ... Namsáng or Namlak.	**19**	**0**	29	4	Pack track over undulating and open country good. At 4 miles pass Hepet (Haipak). A road from here goes to Fort Stedman (Mainsauk) *viâ* Maingpôn (Möng Pawn). At 12 miles pass Namkaing (? Nongmakyeng). Encamping ground here good, but no drinking water. Several stagnant tanks. Small quantities of drinking water obtainable from filter wells at side of tanks. Encamped on bank of Namsáng stream. Water good and plentiful. Plenty of grass. Stream fordable.
		3. Malangek ... Streams.	**5**	**4**	35	0	Pack track in good order. Cross one stream before reaching camp; fordable. Encamping ground jungly and confined. Water good and plentiful. Cross Môné-Légya boundary on the watershed between the Namlak and the Amhôn rivers.
		4. Nannin ... Nam Teng or Tein chaung.	**9**	**4**	44	4	Pack track over undulating ground. Encamped ground on good open ground on left bank of Tein chaung. Grass and water good and plentiful. Coal found at this camp, but apparently not of very good quality.

*** Capt. Davies, Oxfordshire Light Infantry, traversed a somewhat different route between Légya and Ta Kaw in April 1893 (*see* Route No. 76), and as he passed through Keng Lom and makes no mention of any other shorter route to Ta Kaw than this, it is to be presumed that this is after all the best route for troops.—A. F.**

FROM MÔNÉ (MÖNGNAI) TO MÖNGYAI (MAINGYÉ) *viâ* LÉGYA (LAIKA)—*continued.*

Authorities. Military.	Authorities. Civil.	Number and Names of Stages, Rivers and Streams.	Distances. Intermediate. M.	Distances. Intermediate. F.	Distances. Total. M.	Distances. Total. F.	Remarks.
G.O.C. Rangoon District.	Superintendent, Southern Shan States.	**5. Wansán** ... Nam Teng or Tein chaung.	**10**	**4**	55	0	Encamped on bank of stream (bridged) near bamboo grove. Grass and water plentiful. Road from last camp good.
		6. Légya (Laika), 2,950 feet. Nam Teng or Tein chaung.	**5**	**6**	60	6	Road from Wansán fairly good through low-lying country. Cross several irrigation channels, mostly bridged. Encamp in pagoda enclosure north of town. Water for animals from stream, for men from two or three wells. Drinking water good, but said to contain iron. Grass plentiful. Distances given were from surveyed maps.
		7. Wankan (or Mankan), 3,125 feet. Streams.	**8**	**4**	69	2	General direction north-north-west. Good pack track (old cart road) over loam soil throughout; 4 miles through open level country; then a steep descent of 25 feet to a stream 2 yards wide, 6 inches deep, with a gravelly bed. Ford the stream and enter low undulating hills at the foot of the range, which bounds the Tein chaung valley on the west. At 6½ miles cross another similar stream by a bridge, and at 8 miles gentle descent through some big trees to a valley of paddy cultivation, some 300 yards wide. At the further edge of the paddy cross a good stream, 2 yards wide, 6 inches deep, by a substantial bridge, and camp on rising ground above the stream. Good open camp, with good well-bridged stream on either side of the old village, ½ mile off to the south-west (deserted), water and forage good and plentiful.
		8. Kinseiksuywa (Kángseiksu), 3,625 feet. Several streams.	**8**	**0**	77	2	General direction north-west. Pack track. At 4 miles over pine clad undulations on loam soil to Myésin Sakhán; cross the bridged stream out of camp; one deep banked muddy nullah at 2 miles, and a good level ford in some open paddy-fields just short of the sakhán; then turn west along the north side of the valley of hill stream flowing east continuing over spurs of hills up to the watershed 2½ miles. There are three short steep rises and small streams to cross; total rise of 750 feet. Pass the Légya-Maingkaing boundary at 5½ miles from camp; cross the watershed at a low neck, and after short steep descent, descend gradually to camp 500 feet below the neck; cross four streams by easy fords (one rather muddy). Camp on rising ground round the old village on the north side of the valley. Village deserted. Shelter under bamboo jungle. The load leads through open tree jungle, thick in places. Water and forage good and plentiful.
		9. Maingkaing (Möngköng), 3,325 feet. Streams.	**11**	**0**	88	2	General direction north. Pack track. The first 7 miles are over low undulations covered with open pine forest; cross two small valleys cultivated with paddy at 1 and 3 miles respectively. In each valley is a stream some 3 yards wide and 1 foot deep with good fords (no mud). In the second valley is the big village of Yangnáng with a good camping ground. The last 3 miles are through paddy land on a bund. Cross

FROM MÔNÉ (MÖNGNAI) TO MÖNGYAI (MAINGYÉ) *viâ* LÉGYA (LAIKA)—*continued.*

Authorities. Military.	Authorities. Civil.	Number and Names of Stages, Rivers and Streams.	Distances. Intermediate. M. F.	Distances. Total. M. F.	Remarks.
G.O.C. Rangoon District.	Superintendent, Southern Shan States.	**9. Maingkaing (Möngköng), 3,325 feet**—*cont.*			two bridges one over the Tein chaung 20 yards wide, 6 inches deep; good ford. The road throughout is very good on loam soil, nowhere steep. Where it passes through jungle it is clear 20 feet wide. There is at present (January 1888) some mud in two little unbridged streams *en route.* Residence of Myoza. Big village. Five-day bazaar. Plenty of good camping ground. Water and forage good and plentiful.
		10. Nati (3,125 feet). Nam Ko, Nam Hong, and Nam Hwénoi.	8 0	96 2	General direction north. Pack track. At 1 mile cross Namko, at 3½ Namnong, both 5 yards wide, 1 foot to 2 feet 6 inches deep; both fordable and bridged with temporary bamboo bridges. The road is over open undulations on west of Tein chaung valley; cross two or three small muddy streams. Road nearly level. Hôna is a big village and pottery manufactory. No kyaungs or zayáts. Good camping ground under trees. Grass and water good and plentiful. Between Maingkaing and Hôna the remains of two old towns of Maingkaing are passed. Road continues nearly level and very good over low undulations on the west of Tein chaung valley. Two kyaungs. Two or three zayáts. Good open camp. Water and forage good and plentiful. At Nati there are two other villages under the same headman, Hwénoi and Namôk.
		11. Nápôn (3,325 feet). Small streams.	6 0	102 2	General direction north-north-east. Good pack track over low pine clad undulations; no undergrowth. Cross three small streams in muddy beds, one of which is temporarily bridged; cross a big stream 4 feet wide, 1 foot deep; steep banks; gravelly bed. Good drinking water and camp on rising ground. North of valley cultivated with paddy through which the stream flows. Grass plentiful. No accommodation.
		12. Haing-Ngé (Ham-Ngaing), 3,225 feet. Small streams.	6 0	108 2	General direction north-north-east. Good pack track over low pine clad undulations; no undergrowth. Cross two small muddy streams; cross a big stream, 4 yards wide, 1 foot to 1 foot 6 inches deep; steep banks; two good gravelly fords. Plenty of good open dry camping ground. No accommodation. Shelter under banyan trees. Water and grass good and plentiful.
		13. Kyithi Bansám (Kisi-Mansám), 3,075 feet. Nam Hen.	11 0	119 2	General direction east. Pack track nearly level, winding about among low pine clad undulations. Soon after leaving camp cross a small stream with muddy bed. At 2½ miles pass the Maingkaing-Bansám boundary; then down a gentle descent cross a substantial bridge over a dry nullah and go for 1½ miles along a narrow path cut into the side of a hill. At 5 miles near small village of Nábôn there is camping ground in a valley cultivated with paddy.

FROM MÔNÉ (MÖNGNAI) TO MÖNGYAI (MAINGYÉ) *viâ* LÉGYA (LAIKA)—*continued.*

Authorities.		Number and Names of Stages, Rivers and Streams.	Distances.				Remarks.
Military.	Civil.		Intermediate.		Total.		
			M.	F.	M.	F.	
G.O.C. Rangoon District.	Superintendent, Southern Shan States.	**13. Kyithi Bansám (Kisi-Mansám), 3,075 feet**—*cont.*					Good stream of water and forage is plentiful, but the valley is narrow and shut in by jungle-clad hills on both sides. Another small village, Kunsák, is close by, but neither it nor Nábôn can afford accommodation. There are some hot springs near the camping ground. Leaving Nábôn cross a stream by a good bridge; continue 2½ miles through paddy cultivation; crossing two fords of a tributary of the Nam Hen; in both places the banks are high and paddy ramped, but the bottom of the stream is firm and sound; the first ford is 2 yards wide, 6 inches deep, the second is 5 yards wide, 1 foot deep, the rest of the road is over a low undulation covered with scrub jungle into the main valley of the Nam Hen. The river is 10 yards wide, rapid and full of deep pools; the bed consists of jagged limestone rocks; it is crossed by a rickety bridge. Just after crossing the main river another stream is crossed, also by a rickety bridge. A good ford to this stream exists ¼ mile east. The fords near the road are deep and muddy, impassable for pack animals. Residence of a Myoza. Big five-day bazaar. Fish are plentiful from the river. Iron from the neighbouring hills is worked in Bansám. Plenty of open camping ground. Shelter under a large tope of banyan trees. Water and forage good and plentiful.
		14. Banwáp (Manwap), 2,550 feet. Streams.	**15**	**4**	134	6	General direction north-east. Pack track across open rolling downs and undulating country, passing several villages inhabited principally by Yins. Cross three streams, one at ½ mile from Bansám, with gravelly bottom, bad bridge; one at 1½ miles, muddy, fairly good bridge; one at 2¾ miles, muddy, small bamboo bridge. At 10 miles pass tank on east of road. Camp close to bazaar. Ground open and level.
		15. Wánpiet (2,920 feet). Nam Kong.	**8**	**2**	143	0	General direction north. Pack track through open jungle to river Nam Kong at 2¾ miles good ford with hard gravel bottom; steep ramps, about 50 feet broad; current rapid; then through tree jungle to Wánpiet. Pass village of Nongmaw ¾ mile from river and village of Saikhao at 6 miles from Banwáp; latter village deserted, but kyaung and bazaar still standing on west of road. Cross small stream bridged at 5 miles. Good open camping ground with stream running through it 6 inches deep and 3 yards wide at ford with hard bottom.
		16. Bampôn ... Nam Pwán.	**9**	**0**	152	0	General direction north. Good level pack track generally gently rising. At 4½ miles pass a well in a grass-grown swamp at Hônán. Bampôn is a big village with a large five-day bazaar. Residence of a Tamôn. Plenty of good open camping ground. Grass plentiful. Water from the Nampwán stream. At the south end of the bazaar a direct road starts to Maingnaung.

FROM MÔNÉ (MÖNGNAI) TO MÖNGYAI (MAINGYÉ) *viâ* LÉGYA (LAIKA)—*continued.*

Authorities. Military.	Authorities. Civil.	Number and Names of Stages, Rivers and Streams.	Distances. Intermediate.	Distances. Total.	Remarks.
G.O.C. Mandalay District.	Superintendent, Northern Shan States.	**17. Möngyai (Maingyé).** Nam Laung and Nam Yé.	M. F. 3 4	M. F. 160 4	General direction north. A road runs direct, but is not much used, as it is rough where it crosses a low range of hills half-way. The usual route, a pack track is round the west end of these hills. Cross the Nampwán at starting by a good level gravelly ford 4 yards wide, 6 inches deep, and continue across open undulating country. At Ta Pauk (4 miles) ford the Namlaung; 30 yards wide, good gravelly bottom; the banks are 10 feet high and easily ramped; this crossing is 1 mile west of where the river issues through a gorge in the above-mentioned hills. At 3 miles ford the Namlaung, again ½ mile, above its junction with the Namyé, good gravelly bed, 1 foot of water, banks, some 10 feet high, require ramping; continue east-north-east across the open to Maingyé. Plenty of open camping ground. Grass plentiful. Water from the Namyé stream. Big five-day bazaar.

ALTERNATIVE I.

FROM LÉGYA (STAGE 6) TO KYITHI BANSÂM (STAGE 13).

BY LIEUT. H. E. STANTON, ROYAL ARTILLERY, FROM NATIVE INFORMATION, JANUARY 1888.

Military	Civil	Stages	Intermediate	Total	Remarks
G.O.C. Rangoon District.	Superintendent, Southern Shan States.	**1. Banwán (Manwán).** Two bridged streams and Nam Teng or Tein chaung.	9 0	9 0	This route, though described by Lieut. Stanton as the "direct route up Tein chaung valley," is longer by 8¼ miles than the route above described (also by Lieut. Stanton), which is presumably a less direct one.—A. F. General direction north. Cart road up the west of the Tein chaung valley over low undulations in pampas. Cross one pack bridge over stream. At 6 miles pass Bambôn village and bridge over stream. The road passes through some paddy land about Bambôn. At 8 miles reach the Tein chaung after passing through undulating country. Ford 1 foot 6 inches to 2 feet deep, about 50 yards wide; level banks; sandy crossing; no mud. Camp on rising ground. Two or three zayáts. Water and grass plentiful.
		2. Nasán Manlögh. Nam Tôn.	9 0	18 0	Pack track, north, up the valley of Tein chaung over undulations to the Namtôn. Stream deep and unfordable, crossed by a bridge. At 8½ miles rest of road runs east. Three zayáts. Water from stream. Grass plentiful.
		3. Manlôn ... Nam Teng.	11 0	29 0	Pack track, north. At first turn west following up the right bank of Namtôn, then north at one point passing close to left bank of Tein chaung. Pass villages of Nán Sampwin and Tamok. At 7 miles pass the Légya Maingkaing boundary at village of Nyaungbin. Road level and good throughout. Cross no streams. Big village under Hein. Grass and water good and plentiful.

FROM MÔNÉ (MÖNGNAI) TO MÖNGYAI (MAINGYÉ) *viâ* LÉGYA (LAIKA)—*continued.*

ALTERNATIVE I—*continued.*

Authorities. Military	Authorities. Civil	Number and Names of Stages, Rivers and Streams.	Distances. Intermediate. M.	F.	Distances. Total. M.	F.	Remarks.
G.O.C. Rangoon District.	Superintendent, Southern Shan States.	**4. Maingkun** ... Stream.	9	0	38	0	Pack track, north. Three miles level and good to foot of hills bounding Tein chaung valley. Cross a bridged stream at Pánguim, then for 3 miles road is rough and stony over some hills. Issue from hills at Kôngláng village and continue along open undulating country to camp. In the march the level country is open, the hills are jungle clad. Four or five zayáts. Big five-day bazaar. Water from stream. Grass plentiful. *N.B.*—There is no water on road between Maingkun and Bankuon except at Kamput.
		5. Kamput ...	7	0	45	0	Pack track, north, rough and hilly for 2 or 3 miles and then level. Jungle on the hills is thick; the rest is open loam soil. The road passes close to a stream at Kamput. One zayát. Water and grass good and plentiful.
		6. Bankuon ... Nam Koling.	10	0	55	0	Direction north. Pack track rough and difficult over a considerable range of hills. At 9 miles pass near Pahi village, which draws its water from a well some 2 miles off the road. Cross the Nam Koling by a bridge into camp. Four zayáts on rising ground. Grass and water good and plentiful.
		7. Bansám ... Nam Hen bridged.	12	0	67	0	Pack track, north. Good road over open undulating country covered with short grass. At 3 miles cross the Mainkaing-Bansám boundary. Cross the Nam Hen by a bridge. Village of Möngnem is passed *en route.* Camp on rising ground 1 mile from village. A few zayáts. Shelter under big trees. Grass and water good and plentiful. Residence of a Myoza. Five-day bazaar.

No. 25.

From MÔNÉ to ZIMMÉ (CHIENG MAI) *viâ* MÖNG PWÁN and MÖNG HÁNG.

By MAJOR E. G. BARROW, 7TH BENGAL INFANTRY, 1890.

Military	Civil	Stage	Int. M.	F.	Total M.	F.	Remarks	
G.O.C. Rangoon District.	Superintendent, Southern Shan States.	**1. Thit Náng or Tadágyi.**	8	0	8	0	Good level road.	*Vide* Route No. 21, Stages 13 to 15, and Branch No. I. *Note.*—Major Barrow makes the total of the first five stages of this route 2½ miles more than Lieut. Colomb.
		2. Ta Möng Ké ...	15	0	23	0	Cross hilly country.	
		3. Sawa	8	4	31	4	Cross Nam Téng.	
		4. Páng Saláu ...	8	4	40	0	Road good.	

FROM MÔNÉ TO ZIMMÉ (CHIENG MAI) *viâ* MÖNG PWÁN AND MÖNG HÁNG—*continued.*

Authorities.		Number and Names of Stages, Rivers and Streams.	Distances.				Remarks.	
Military.	Civil.		Intermediate.		Total.			
			M.	F.	M.	F.		
G.O.C. Rangoon District.	Superintendent, Southern Shan States.	**5. Möng Pwán** ...	**8**	**0**	48	0	Town, Sawbwa's residence.	
		6. Páng Hwé Wai.	**9**	**0**	57	0		
		7. Tin Loi Hsáng.	**10**	**0**	67	0	Cross Loi Hsáng.	
		8. Wán Mé Sili.	**7**	**4**	74	4	Down bed of stream.	
		9. Mé Sala (camp).	**5**	**4**	80	0	Cross Salween.	*Vide* Route No. 28.
		10. Páng Tôk Sôk.	**10**	**4**	90	4	Cross Loi Vieng Náng.	
		11. Möng Tuen ...	**10**	**4**	101	0	Large village.	
		12. Wán Mé Ken.	**10**	**4**	111	4	Village.	
		13. Möng Háng...	**10**	**0**	121	4	Village.	
		14. Mé Nayôn ...	**15**	**4**	137	0	Jungle camps.	
		15. Páng Nam ...	**14**	**0**	151	0		
Siam.		**16. Möng Ngai** ...	**9**	**0**	160	0	Large village.	
		17. Chieng Dao ...	**8**	**0**	168	0	Large village.	
		14. Ban Mé Wák.	**6**	**0**	174	0		*Vide* Route No. 29.
		15. Mé Teng ...	**15**	**0**	189	0		
		16. Mé Lim ...	**18**	**0**	207	0		
		17. Zimmé or Chieng Mai.	**13**	**0**	220	0	Large town, British Vice Consulate.	

No. 26.

From MÖNG HÁNG to MÖNG FÁNG (SIAM).

BY CAPT. H. R. DAVIES, INTELLIGENCE DEPARTMENT, BURMA, JANUARY 1893.

Military	Civil	Stage	Inter. M.	Inter. F.	Total M.	Total F.	Remarks
G.O.C. Rangoon District.	Superintendent, Southern Shan States.	**1. Mé Háng Heng.** Mé Háng Heng.	**9**	**0**	9	0	General direction south-east. Fair mule road through tree jungle, not very thick; nearly level for 4 miles, then gently up-hill for 2 miles, then steep and rocky ascent for 1 mile, thence descent of 2 miles to the camp on the Mé Háng Heng (6 yards by 1 foot). There are several small camps here measuring 50 by 40 yards, 60 by 50 yards, 50 by 40 yards, 50 by 50 yards, and one on the left bank of the stream 100 by 50 yards. It is difficult to find level ground for tents. Plenty of grass.

FROM MÖNG HÁNG TO MÖNG FÁNG (SIAM)—*continued.*

Authorities. Military.	Authorities. Civil.	Number and Names of Stages, Rivers and Streams.	Distances. Intermediate. M.	F.	Total. M.	F.	Remarks.
Siam.		**2. Mak Möng Sum.** Hwé San and smaller streams.	10	0	19	0	General direction south-east. Fair mule road through tree jungle. Up hill rather steeply for 2½ miles to the boundary mark 7-3-90 cut on a tree; thence descent steep for 1½ miles, afterwards gentler. At 1 mile Nam Hu camp (150 by 70 yards), and more room could be cleared; water from stream (1 yard by 2 inches). At 5 miles Páng Tin Tum camp (400 by 80 yards); water from stream (2 yards by 3 inches), but a larger stream ¼ mile to the left. At 7 miles camps 100 by 50 yards and 50 by 40 yards on stream (6 yards by 9 inches); more room could be cleared. At Mak Möng Sum (S and L) 15 houses; cross the Hwé San) 8 yards by 1 foot); camp the other side of the village (600 by 300 yards). Good water; plenty of grass.
		3. Möng Fáng ... Mé Mao, Mé Phö, Mé Sai, and smaller streams, all fordable.	8	0	27	0	General direction south-east. Good mule road. Slight descent all the way, but nearly level; all through jungle. At 1 mile village of Mé Mao south, 30 houses. At 5½ miles Ban Mawn Pyin (L) 20 houses. At 6½ miles another village called Mé Mao (L), 40 houses. Möng Fáng is a walled town 1,800 yards long by 1,000 yards broad. Camping ground in the paddy (½ by ¼ mile) on west of town and in another paddy-field (½ by ¼ mile) to the east of the town; also room in grass (500 by 300 yards) to the north of the Mé Sai close to Ban Mé Sai. In wet weather the best ground would be inside the city wall to the north of the town on grass (400 by 100 yards); water from Mé Sai. Here there is accommodation for 200 men in kyaungs and 200 more in the bazaar sheds which is on the bridge crossing the Mé Sai. This camp inside the city wall is on rising ground and commands the town. Supplies of rice, beef, paddy and vegetables can be got, but not in very large quantities. From here there is a road to Chieng Hai *viâ* Ban Méchan, eight stages, 79 miles, *see* Appendix III, Route No. 5.

No. 27.

From MÖNG HÁNG to MÖNG HENG (SIAM).

BY CAPT. H. B. WALKER, PAID ATTACHÉ, INTELLIGENCE BRANCH, JANUARY 1893.

Military	Civil	Stage	Int. M.	F.	Total M.	F.	Remarks
G.O.C. Rangoon District.	Supt., Southern Shan States.	**1. Pöngpakem** ... Mé Háng.	12	0	12	0	General direction south. The route leaves the camping ground south of Möng Háng, and crossing the Mé Háng at once runs first through kaing grass and then through open jungle, the path being excellent and level all the way to the west of, and almost parallel to, the Mé Háng. Open spaces, cultivated for paddy, are passed at intervals, and the three

FROM MÖNG HÁNG TO MÖNG HENG (SIAM)—*continued.*

Authorities.		Number and Names of Stages, Rivers and Streams.	Distances.		Remarks.
Military.	Civil.		Intermediate.	Total.	
G.O.C. Rangoon District.	Superintendent, Southern Shan States.	**1. Pöngpakem**—*cont.*			villages of Naliu, Nakawngmu, and Hwéaw at 3, 5 and 7 miles. Small plantations of young teak intersperse the jungle at intervals, which consists, in addition to teak, of miscellaneous species. The camping ground at Pöngpakem is situated on the left bank of a small stream. Accommodation for 250 men with a dilapidated zayát. Grass abundant.
		2. Namyom ... Several small streams and the Namyom.	M. F. 7 4	M. F. 19 4	General direction south. The route leaves the camping ground and immediately crosses the small stream which flows into the Mé Háng, and runs through open jungle for nearly ½ a mile where the main road to Zimmé branches off to left hand or east, running in a south-east direction, and gradually converging from the Namyom route; the path then enters dense jungle, which, in the month of January, is greatly choked up with undergrowth, and running nearly level all the way reaches the village of Namyom at mile 7½, a village of 16 houses (Shans). There is camping ground about Namyom for 200 men in the taungya. A little paddy obtainable. Grass plentiful and of good quality. This village should be very prosperous, the taungyas being said to be very good. The Namyom is from 10 to 15 yards broad, 1 foot deep to right hand at mile 5, where it runs parallel with route, afterwards running south of Namyin.
Siam.		**3. Möng Na** ... Several half-dry nullahs on the northern side of the frontier and the Mé Ping.	6 0	25 4	Leaving the village of Namyom the route ascends rather steeply; crosses the lower extremity of one of the Loi Htwé spurs descending and ascending again to cross another spur, a valley being here formed by a ridge to the left hand or east, into which the terminations of the spur crossed run. At mile 1½ the route becomes perfectly level and runs through an open, almost park-like, jungle of teak and *in*, and other miscellaneous species of timber. The ranges east and west, or the spurs therefrom, also recede, and at mile 3 the route rises gradually and easily on to a spur, running direct from Loi Htwé. Down this the frontier runs south-eastward. The frontier is therefore here crossed and Siam entered; the descent on the opposite side into the valley of Möng Na is easy and gradual; the Mé Ping is crossed at mile 4½. At mile 6 some open disused paddy-fields are crossed, and the Mé Ping again at mile 6¼ immediately south of the village. Möng Na is a Shan village of 20 houses. Supplies fair; vegetables, fowls, and paddy. Grass in abundance and of good quality. The camping ground lies south of the village in some disused paddy-fields and within the village, where additional accommodation could be found for 2,000 men or more. From Möng Na a route runs south-east by a good path some 6 miles and strikes the Zimmé road, running from Möng Háng at a spot called Linlôn, at one time recognized as the frontier, now within Siamese territory. The Mé Ping is crossed twice within the last mile and-a-half into Möng Na camp, 10 or 15 feet wide, 1 to 1½ feet deep; good drinking water, flowing to the crossings having easy approaches.

FROM MÖNG HÁNG TO MÖNG HENG (SIAM)—*continued.*

Authorities. Military.	Authorities. Civil.	Number and Names of Stages, Rivers and Streams.	Distances. Intermediate. M. F.	Distances. Total. M. F.	Remarks.
	Siam.	**4. Kénoi** ... ... Mé King, Mé Ting, and several small streams.	**11 0**	36 4	General direction south-south-west. Leaving the village of Möng Na the route enters the camping ground which it crosses and winds by a level path through thick jungle round the small hill or knoll at back of camp, and slightly descending crosses a small stream, the Mé King, a hill stream flowing into the Mé Ting at mile 1. Here the route begins to rise, and after ½ a mile begins to ascend the steeper slopes of a long spur, up which the route winds at a steep gradient to mile 6, when the summit is reached and a fine view is obtained northwards of Loi Htwé and its long spurs running south-south-eastward into the Mé Ting valley. The route then descends to mile 7½ by a steep incline, where a small level spot, capable of camping 50 men, is reached. Here water is obtained from a small hill stream for the first time during the march; hitherto a thirsty one for troops. The route then ascends abruptly a small steep hill, which it crosses and descends to the junction of the small stream flowing past camping ground and a parallel one flowing on the southern side of the spur descended, the junction being reached at mile 9½. From this point the route rises easily for ½ a mile and descends for a mile into the village of Kénoi (11 houses; Shans; few supplies) in the valley of the Mé Ting (4 or 5 yards wide, 1 foot deep, easy crossings with firm banks) which flows close to the village in a south-westerly direction. Ample camping ground, though overgrown with kaing grass.
		5. Camp on the Mé Yangkum stream. Mé Ting, Mé Wé Wai, Mé Yangkum and three small streams.	**12 0**	48 4	General direction south-south-west. Leaving the village of Kénoi the route runs contiguous with the Mé Ting until mile 1, crossing the lower slope of a spur, when it crosses a small stream flowing from the east into the Mé Ting; the route then ascends a spur on to the top of a ridge, which it reaches at 2½ miles. It then descends until mile 6 into the valley of the Mé Wé Wai (flowing Mé Ting-wards), the crossing being marshy and overgrown with kaing grass is difficult. A short climb is succeeded by a long descent down a spur for over a mile into the valley of a small stream which flows into the Mé Wé Wai and is also joined by another small stream, along which the route runs by a bad narrow path, stony under foot, and steeply enclosed for nearly a mile; then a steep ascent on to a ridge and down the slope towards the Mé Yangkum stream, on the banks of which and some 100 feet above it, there is accommodation for 300 men, but the jungle would require clearing. The Mé Yangkum here flowing from north-east to south-west runs into the Mé Ting, some 2 miles above Möng Heng. Grass and bamboo leaves in plenty on the banks of the stream for fodder.
		6. Möng Heng ... Mé Yangkum, Mé Haungsu, Mé Wé Wai, and Mé Ting.	**12 4**	61 0	General direction south-south-west. Leaving camp at Mé Yangkum the route descends to the stream of that name; runs for 100 yards or so along its bed, and then strikes up a steep spur of the opposite ridge, which it crosses at mile 1 and descends by a

FROM MÖNG HÁNG TO MÖNG HENG (SIAM)—*continued.*

Authorities.		Number and Names of Stages, Rivers and Streams.	Distances.		Remarks.
Military.	Civil.		Intermediate.	Total.	
Siam.		**6. Möng Heng** — *cont.*			long gradual spur of 7 miles into the valley of the Mé Haungsu stream, which commencing near the summit of the ridge runs parallel with the route the whole way, the Mé Wé Wai running on the western side of the spur. At mile 8 the route reaches the valley of the Mé Haungsu, some ½ mile wide and overgrown heavily with kaing grass; the route then assumes a still further southerly direction, running parallel with the Mé Haungsu, along the lower ridges of the western spurs of the valley and through loose jungle. At mile 12 open outlying houses of Möng Heng are reached, the village being an intensely scattered one of 102 houses, and inhabited by Shans, Karens, and Siamese, the former in preponderance. Supplies good; paddy, rice, vegetables, and occasionally meat. At mile 12½ the Mé Ting is crossed by a rough wooden bridge for foot-passengers and easy ford for animals, 10 yards broad, 2 feet deep; gravelly bottom, the camp being now reached. There is accommodation for some 2,000 or 3,000 men in and about Möng Heng. The valley of the Mé Ting is here wide and is thickly overgrown with kaing grass, as all the streams in the valley appear to be. Wild game is said at one time to have been plentiful, and tigers still render their existence known by their depredations. The hill Loi Métao, some 10 miles distant, is visible at the end of and beyond the valley, bearing 327° from Möng Heng. From here there is a road to Méhawngsawn *viâ* Möng Noi and Möng Pai, 11 marches, 77¼ miles (*see* Appendix III, Route No. 6), and another to Möng Ta *viâ* Kiu Kaw 14½ miles, where the Siamese and Möng Ta boundary is crossed, whence to Möng Ta is about 16 miles (*see* Appendix III, Route No. 7).

No. 28.

From MÖNG HÁNG to MÖNG PWÁN.

BY MAJOR E. G. BARROW, 7TH BENGAL INFANTRY, 1890.

Military	Civil	Stage	Intermediate M. F.	Total M. F.	Remarks
G.O.C. Rangoon District.	Superintendent, Southern Shan States.	**1. Wan' Mé Ken (1,600 feet).** Nam Hu, Mé Háng, and Mé Ken.	**10 0**	10 0	General direction north. Pass through the village of Möng Háng and ford the Nam Hu 15 yards broad. Then for 5 miles through jungle over undulating ground rising and falling about 200 feet. At 6 miles strike the Mé Háng and follow its left bank for 2 miles or so. At 9 miles drop down to the broad paddy plain of the Mé Ken valley. At 9½ miles pass through the flourishing village of Mé Ken and camp on the right bank of the river, which is about 15 yards broad and shallow. Forage and firewood plentiful.
		2. Möng Tuen (1,750 feet). Mé Loi Heng, Mé Tuen, and Mé Na Niu.	**10 4**	20 4	An easy march through jungle. At 3½ miles descend to and cross the dry bed of the Mé Loi Heng. At 10 miles reach Möng Tuen, a large village of about a hundred houses. Ford the Mé Tuen, 20 yards broad and camp on the left bank of the Mé Na Niu its tributary. Supplies procurable as well as forage and firewood.

FROM MÖNG HÁNG TO MÖNG PWÁN—*continued.*

Authorities.		Number and Names of Stages, Rivers and Streams.	Distances.				Remarks.
Military.	Civil.		Intermediate.		Total.		
			M.	F.	M.	F.	
G.O.C. Rangoon District.	Superintendent, Southern Shan States.	**3. Páng Tôk Sôk (4,300 feet).** Mé Na Niu.	10	4	31	0	Cross the Mé Na Niu. The road then ascends a spur rising gradually about 400 feet. At 1½ miles pass village of Ho Ha ½ a mile to right. At 3½ miles there is a short steep rocky descent to the valley of the Mé Na Niu. Up the valley of the Na Niu. At 4½ miles, hamlet of Kanka (eight houses). The road ascends a hundred feet or so, and at 6 miles descends in like manner to the village of Na Niu (20 houses). From here the road goes up the bed of the Mé Na Niu crossing it over twenty times. At 8½ miles Páng Tin Doi (camping ground at foot of the hill), altitude about 3,200 feet. A very good camping ground, but it is better to ease the next march by ascending the hill to Páng Tôk Sôk 2 miles further on. The ascent is very steep in places, the road going up about 1,500 feet in the 2 miles. The camping ground is indifferent, forage scarce, but wood plentiful. Water from stream.
		4. Mé Sala (1,200 feet). Mé Mok and Mé Sala.	10	4	41	4	General direction north-east. Ascent gradual, at ¾ mile reach the crest of the watershed (4,800 feet). The road now runs along a spur for 6 or 7 miles. At 1¼ miles Loi Vieng Náng, the site of an ancient fort. From here the descent may be said to commence. It is at first easy, but the last 2 miles are very steep. At 7½ miles reach the foot of the spur at 1,600 feet. Here is the junction of the Mé Mok and Mé Sala, both clear rapid shallow streams 5 to 10 yards broad and full of rocks and boulders. Down the bed of the stream for 3 miles, crossing repeatedly. Excellent camping grounds.
		5. Wan Mé Sili (850 feet). Salween river and Mé Sili.	5	4	47	0	Two miles down stream to Wan Mé Sala (20 houses). The descent is very rapid as at the Salween, the altitude is not more than 800 feet. At 2½ miles reach the Salween, here more than 200 yards broad. Follow its left bank over stretches of sand and rock, cross the river at the Ta Hsang or elephant ferry (3 miles). Here half-a-dozen boats can be collected, if necessary, each boat carrying from 5 to 10 men or 2 to 5 mule loads at a trip. The road now goes for 1½ miles down the right bank of the Salween to its junction with the Mé Sili, a shallow stream 10 yards broad, up which the road goes. Pass through the hamlet of Wan Sili and camp ½ mile beyond.
		6. Tin Loi Hsáng (1,800 feet). Mé Sili and Mé Su Tong.	7	4	54	4	General direction west. Up the Mé Sili. At 3 miles reach the junction with the Mé Su Tong up which the road now turns. The stream is an insignificant one, frequently disappearing in its bed. Road rather bad in places; camp confined and bad.
		7. Páng Hwé Wai (2,500 feet). Hwé Wai.	10	0	64	4	General direction west. Ascend the Loi Hsáng. The path is very steep going up 1,400 feet in 1¼ miles (crest 3,200 feet). The descent on the west is very easy, and after about 500 feet of descent the Hwé Wai is reached

FROM MÖNG HÁNG TO MÁNG PWÁN—*continued.*

Authorities. Military.	Authorities. Civil.	Number and Names of Stages, Rivers and Streams.	Distances. Intermediate.	Distances. Total.	Remarks.
G.O.C. Rangoon District.	Superintendent, Southern Shan States.	**7. Páng Hwé Wai (2,500 feet)**-*cont.*			(2½ miles). Follow its course crossing repeatedly. At 5½ miles Wan Tham (five houses). At 10 miles camp on the right bank of the Hwé Wai. Forage and firewood plentiful. The road lies through jungle the whole way, except about Wan Tham, where there are a few fields. Except the ascent of the Loi Hsáng it presents no difficulties.
		8. Möng Pwán (2,100 feet). Hwé Wai and Nam Pán.	M. 9 F. 0	M. 73 F. 4	Down the course of the Hwé Wai, which is left at 1 mile, the road bending north-east. At 3 miles village of Wan Wua Lai (six houses) through paddy-fields. At 3¾ miles Wan Ma Khua Ché. Half-a-mile beyond, a stream with steep banks has to be crossed and requires ramping for mules. Road now runs over a low ridge and through jungle into the Möng Pwán valley, which is entered at 8½ miles through paddy-fields and across the Nam Pán by a solid timber bridge. Camp near the bridge at the east end of the town and on the left bank of the Nam Pán. Möng Pwán contains about 400 houses, has two large kyaungs and is the residence of the Sawbwa. The valley is about 3½ miles long and from 1 to 2 miles broad. Supplies plentiful.

BRANCH I.

FROM MÖNG TUEN (STAGE 2) TO MÖNG SAT (ROUTE NO. 11, STAGE 9).

BY CAPT. H. M. JACKSON, R.E., SURVEY OF INDIA, 1890.

Military.	Civil.	Number and Names of Stages, Rivers and Streams.	Intermediate.	Total.	Remarks.
G.O.C. Rangoon District.	Superintendent, Southern Shan States.	**1. Na-Ho-Un** ... Mé Tuen, Hwé Páng-Ka-Tong, and Hwé Un.	13 0	13 0	Through Nongpayin village, a suburb of Möng Tuen. Up Mé Tuen crossing and recrossing about 1 mile. Then along hill side, left bank Mé Tuen, passing Tang-Na-Man and Namhu villages; down on to Hwé Páng-Ka-Tong and Páng-Tam-Yaú which is a very good camping ground for a fairly large force, about 5½ miles from Möng Tuen. From this up the Hwé Páng-Ka-Tong crossing and recrossing, passing little Páng-Ka-Tong and through big Páng-Ka-Tong village, about ½ a mile apart, the latter about 8 miles from Möng Tuen. Rice and paddy obtainable here in small quantities. On up Páng-Ka-Tong as before until it is joined by a large stream from the west, after which it is known

FROM MÖNG HÁNG TO MÁNG PWÁN—*continued.*

BRANCH I—*continued.*

Authorities. Military.	Authorities. Civil.	Number and Names of Stages, Rivers and Streams.	Distances. Intermediate. M.	F.	Distances. Total. M.	F.	Remarks.
G.O.C. Rangoon District.	Superintendent, Southern Shan States.	**1. Na-Ho-Un**—*cont.*					as the Hwé Un. Pass Tun Tong, small village, and at 10½ miles Mōng Tun. About ½ a mile beyond the village there is fair camping ground for a small force. Road on up the Hwé Un taking the eastern feeder at the junction. About a mile beyond this is a large old field clearing. Camping room and grass for a large force. This is called Na-Ho-Un (*i.e.*, "the field at the head of the Un"). A small party could camp almost anywhere along this part of road. Small bullock camps about every 2 miles.
		2. Na-Si-Lik ... Hwé Un and Mé Son.	9	0	22	0	Leaving camp ascent begins. Crossing minor spurs and the head-waters of the Hwé Un at the foot of the ridge; up the ridge (ascent and descent easy about 1,000 feet up and down) and along east-south-east, then down to the head of the Mé Son and down this to an open clearing (old fields) called Na-Sa-Lik. Camping ground and grass for a large force. There are three camping grounds for a *small* party between Na-Ho-Un and Na-Sa-Lik, one half-way up each side of the range and one on the ridge.
		3. Mōng Sat ... Mé Son and Mé Kok.	15	0	37	0	From Na-Sa-Lik the road goes down the Mé Son, crossing and recrossing to Páng Sang, small village, after which it is mostly off the river, passing Páng Sak, large village, and two smaller villages. At 12 miles reach Mé Son village in the valley of the Mé Kok. From this leave the course of the Mé Son and cross the fields north (mostly dry in March, and probably never very heavy going) 3 miles to Mōng Sat on the Mé Kok. Two straggling villages, bridge (very shaky bamboo one) over Mé Kok connecting them; five-day bazaar. Supplies, *i.e.*, rice, paddy, goor and tobacco plentiful. Best camping ground just to south of town in field on small stream from west running into Mé Kok. *N.B.*—No difficulties on any part of this road in dry weather; would be very bad though in rains. Mōng Sat is on the road from Kyeng Tung to Mōné, *see* Route No. 11, Stage 9, and this Branch Route is an important one in that with Routes Nos. 29, 28 (first two stages only) and No. 11 (first nine stages) it forms the shortest route between Zimmé and Kyeng Tung—a total of 22 marches in all.

No. 29.

From MÖNG HÁNG to ZIMMÉ (CHIENGMAI) (Siam).

BY W. J. ARCHER, ESQ., VICE-CONSUL, ZIMMÉ, 1888.

Authorities.		Number and Names of Stages, Rivers and Streams.	Distances.				Remarks.
Military.	Civil.		Intermediate.		Total.		
			M.	F.	M.	F.	
G.O.C. Rangoon District.	Superintendent, Southern Shan States.	**1. Camp on Mé Nayôn.** Mé Háng, Mé Nayôn.	**15**	**4**	15	4	Good road (except for about 1⅓ miles) with slight descent, mostly through fine teak forest. Mé Háng, clear river 2½ feet deep, is forded close to Möng Háng. Villages of Ban Kong Mu, Vieng O (deserted town) and Páng Pakhem passed *en route.* Camp on Mé Nayôn, a largish clear stream.
		2. Páng Nam ...	**14**	**0**	29	4	Good road ascending gradually for 9 miles to the watershed of the Mé Háng and Mé Ping (2,400 feet). Forest all the way. This is the frontier of Möng Háng and Siam. Gradual descent to camp, in one place road is bad for ½ a mile passing through narrow gorge with overhanging rocks.
Siam.		**3. Möng Ngai** ...	**9**	**0**	38	4	In Siam. Fair road generally. Supplies plentiful, much rice cultivation. In Stage 6 the Mé Ping river is crossed frequently and some of the fords are difficult, the stream being deep and banks high.
		4. Chieng Dao ...	**8**	**0**	46	4	
		5. Ban Mé Wak.	**6**	**0**	52	4	
		6. Mé Teng ...	**15**	**0**	67	4	
		7. Mé Lim ...	**18**	**0**	85	4	
		8. Zimmé (or Chiengmai).	**13**	**0**	98	4	

No. 30.

From MÖNG KA to LÁSHIO viâ PÁNG LÔNG and TA SUPKYET.

BY LIEUT. C. AINSLIE, R.E., INTELLIGENCE OFFICER, NORTHERN SHAN STATES COLUMN, FEBRUARY–MARCH 1893.

Military.	Civil.	Number and Names of Stages, Rivers and Streams.	Int. M.	Int. F.	Total M.	Total F.	Remarks.
G.O.C. Mandalay District.	Superintendent, Northern Shan States.	**1. Yawng Hsung.** A few streamlets in first 1⅓ miles only.	**6**	**4**	6	4	The general direction from Möng Ka is west. The road crosses the range south-west of the main village, where there is a plentiful spring on the top of the hill, and runs down a spur, west, for ⅓ mile, after which it turns to the left a little and runs down along the side of the hill for 2 miles, crossing water in several small nullahs on the way. This hill side is all under poppy cultivation. At 2⅓ miles the road crosses a spur and runs on to the south slope of another which it follows with a general descent to Yawng Hsung. The total drop is about 2,500 feet, and the road is fairly easy throughout. Half-way

FROM MÖNG KA TO LĀSHIO *viâ* PĀNG LÔNG AND TA SUPKYET—*continued.*

Authorities. Military.	Authorities. Civil.	Number and Names of Stages, Rivers and Streams.	Distances. Intermediate.	Distances. Total.	Remarks.
G.O.C. Mandalay District.	Superintendent, Northern Shan States.	**1. Yawng Hsung** —*cont.*			a Wa village, Mak Hin, is passed, below the road on the left, which is the limit of Möng Ka territory in this direction. Yawng Hsung is a Wa village of at least 150 houses in two parts, separated by a nullah which is their water-supply. The road runs through it, but could be diverted through bamboo jungle along the top edge of the village. It is built on the slope of the hill and is stockaded on the lower side. The camp is west of village on a flattish spur covered with long grass, with a fair spring of water close by. Supplies of paddy and firewood in the village, but the Was do not care to sell, and were sending their paddy away as we entered the village. There are also plenty of fowls and village pigs, equally unobtainable by purchase.
		2. Hsung Ra Mang. Nam Sé.	M. F. 8 0	M. F. 14 4	From Yawng Hsung there are two roads to Hsung Ra Mang. The lower road is shortest and best : (i) *Lower road.*—The road leads out of Yawng Hsung village running south-west, and descends fairly easily for nearly a mile, when it crosses a small but difficult rocky nullah with water in it, and turning north-west runs fairly level to another nullah with water in it also; a difficult crossing. It turns west then and descends to the Nam Sé; fairly steep latterly, passing near a Wa village Yawng Law at 2 miles. The Nam Sé is here about 30 yards wide, easy ford; nearly 2 feet 6 inches deep near the right bank. Left bank rocky, but fairly easy. Right bank a steep, rocky slope, very difficult for loaded animals. River impassable in the rains. Bamboo foot-bridge all the year round, at a high level. There is a single bamboo slung across the stream for a foot-bridge. The ford is a little below this. From the river there is a rise of 2,000 feet in 5 miles to Hsung Ra Mang passing through a Wa village, Hsi Na, after the 1st mile. The ascent is not very steep anywhere, and crosses numerous little streams in cultivation patches about half-way up, but side slopes are steep here, and there are only small scattered level sites for pitching tents. The road runs through Hsung Ra Mang village which is nearly ½ a mile long and there are the usual deep ditches and stockaded entrances to be avoided. The village is a very

FROM MÖNG KA TO LÁSHIO *viâ* PÁNG LÔNG AND TA SUPKYET—*continued.*

Authorities.		Number and Names of Stages, Rivers and Streams.	Distances.		Remarks.
Military.	Civil.		Inter-mediate.	Total.	
G.O.C. Mandalay District.	Superintendent, Northern Shan States.	**2. Hsung Ra Mang**—*cont.*			large one commanded by a knoll north of it. It could be easily attacked from the upper side. The main entrance south-east is strongly defended by a ditch and narrow lane leading to the gate. South-west there appear to be no defences at present. In any case the position is an untenable one. There are said to be 300 houses and a Wa Chief, who rules over 25 to 30 large villages round and lives here. (ii) *Upper road.*—This path leads out of the top of the village, and running north-west soon strikes a spur down which it descends to stream similar to the Nam Sé with rather bad approaches. It then ran up for a mile, passed through a village and descended for a mile to the Nam Sé which was crossed without difficulty. Then ascended and ran long a spur to another village, from which the main road ran south. A foot-track led east to Hsung Ra Mang, down a very steep spur to a nullah with a bad crossing for pack animals, after which there was an ascent of nearly 2 miles to camp. This road is not used, the other being shorter and much easier.
			M. F.	M. F.	
		3. Hsán Htung ... Three small streams.	9 0	23 4	The path runs south-west from Hsung Ra Mang along a narrow saddle covered with trees and then ascends steeply about 1,000 feet in a mile. This path is apparently not used, as it was very much overgrown. Paths to the left lead to another Wa village, Ai Kyeng. At the top of the range the road turns sharp to the right and runs along the top of the spur, rising at first and then falling to a saddle at the 3rd mile, where paths to the left lead down to a Wa village, Köng Mang, ½ mile away. Rising from the saddle the road turns north and runs for a mile along the hill side, passing three villages, Yawng Té (all Wa) below on the right. There is water running across the road here and ground suitable for camping and little further on the road runs on to the top of the range, again, follows it for a mile, then descends and rises, turning west to another spur running north-west up which it climbs steadily for 2 miles, then bends round left along the hill side, crossing water at 8½ miles, where there is some fairly good ground for camping on above the road. Hsán Htung village is ½ a mile west of this at 5,500 feet elevation. It is built on a saddle commanded by peaks east and west, and extends mostly down the northern side of the hill. It could be approached better from the top of the range than from the road below, which runs up to the main entrance, defended in the usual way. There is a very small spring just outside the gate on the road. The village contains about 150 houses and is the head of an independent circle of Was. Probably no supplies obtainable.
		4. Lak Lai ... Small streams.	7 4	31 0	The road to Lak Lai branches off 1 mile before Hsán Htung coming up from Hsung Ra Mang. It runs along through groves of trees, passing Yawng O, off the road below to the right at 1½ miles, then follows the spur which curls round to the left and rises to a village hidden from view. We avoided this village by going down and up, very steep round

FROM MÖNG KA TO LÁSHIO *viâ* PÁNG LÖNG AND TA SUPKYET—*continued.*

Authorities. Military.	Authorities. Civil.	Number and Names of Stages, Rivers and Streams.	Distances. Intermediate. M. F.	Distances. Total. M. F.	Remarks.
G.O.C. Mandalay District.	Superintendent, Northern Shan States.	**4. Lak Lai**—*cont.*			the right (north), over cultivated ground, and struck the main road beyond. There was then visible a village, Ka Lu, ¼ mile away on the left below the road on a narrow spur. Our path ran level along the main range north-west, passed Yaung Ló off the road on the right, and then fell and rose to the range again, which it crossed at 4 miles. It then ran very easily along the side of the hill for 1½ miles, rising to a small village, Hkum Paw, with a very long narrow lane to the gates and impenetrable belt of jungle on both sides. The detour to the left on a cattle track was easy, and led down a little to poppy cultivation and up again, rather steep, to join the main road running through the village. There was water in a nullah here. At 7 miles the road ran up to the ridge again and descended easily to Lak Lai, which is built across a saddle, with four ditches across dividing it into two parts. The camp was on fairly level ground to the right just beyond a nullah with three small springs in it and commanded part of the village from the east. Supplies as at Hsán Htung.
		5. Camp on the Nam Ma. Nam Ma and four small streams.	8 4	39 4	The road runs through Lak Lai, which was avoided by going down round the village on the north side. There are four ditches which require bridging or ramping. Beyond the road runs west, descending a little to a good site for a camp with plenty of water, then rising gently it crosses a spur at 1½ miles and runs easily along the side of the hill for 1½ miles crossing water once. It then turns to the left and descends rather steeply for ½ mile to a stockaded village, which can be avoided by going round to the right. From here the path turns west on a spur and very soon striking another spur running nearly south, descends to Té Pala (Wa) which it passes through. From here there is a fairly steep descent of a mile to a small stream, followed very soon by another which presents no difficulty. There is then a steep climb south-west for ½ mile, after which the road curls round to the right, running level, and passes through a Wa village, Yawng To, from which it falls on a rough path to the junction of the Nam Ma and the stream last crossed. This is a dry weather camp only. There is a little flat ground on left hand of this stream, and troops can camp in the bed of the Nam Ma on sand, 200 yards below the junction. Height of river, 2,000 feet.
		6. Möng Maö ... Nam Ma and one small stream.	13 0	52 4	From our camp the stream is crossed at the junction and mules follow the left bank of the Nam Ma, but must have a path cut, as they cannot pass a tree below the bamboo bridge. The Nam Ma at the crossing is 120 feet wide at the ford, 50 feet above the bridge. Two feet deep. Easy crossing. Right bank rather difficult. Bamboo foot-bridge for one or two men at a time. Unfordable in rains. Numerous small streams across the road after the 2nd mile. From the bridge head on the right bank, the path is to the right (north) and ascends rather steep for 1½ miles, then runs undulating along the side of the hill into a large cultivated valley well watered. There is a nice site for a large

FROM MÖNG KA TO LÁSHIO *viâ* PÁNG LÔNG AND TA SUPKYET—*continued.*

Authorities. Military.	Authorities. Civil.	Number and Names of Stages, Rivers and Streams.	Distances. Intermediate.	Distances. Total.	Remarks.
G.O.C. Mandalay District.	Superintendent, Northern Shan States.	**6. Möng Maö**—*cont.*			camp below to the left, and another good site on the right at the second stream crossed. From here the road runs up through the first Kawng Hsáng village, which has a deep ditch across the lower side and rises to narrow spur or saddle running west, which it follows, passing through three more villages of Kawng Hsáng, where the road could easily be blocked. After leaving the fourth village it turns to the right, crosses a nullah with water in it and rises over open cultivated spurs to a fifth Kawng Hsáng village on a knoll of a spur which runs north-east from the main big hill Loi Mu. It avoids this village, running up a muddy water-course on the left, and skirts round the north-east of Loi Mu, rising and falling over small spurs with water in the valleys for nearly 2 miles. The largest of these valleys was a very marshy crossing after a steep descent through cultivation. The road continues skirting round Loi Mu turning gradually west and crosses several small swamps before reaching To Tat, a La village on the right at 11 miles, beyond which there is a small stream from which the road rises for ½ mile to a saddle which it crosses. There is a Shan-Chinese village, Wan Nawng on the left, and Möng Maö is nearly a mile further on. The whole valley below is terraced into paddy-fields and rice and paddy can be brought here in large quantities, but the price is high. The people are Chinese-Shans, possess pack mules and bullocks, and seem very thriving. There is a stream running through the paddy-field and room for a large force. Height, 4,800 feet.
		7. Man Kin ... One stream.	M. F. 6 4	M. F. 59 0	From Möng Maö the path runs down across the paddy-field, crosses a stream at once, and ascends to a ridge which it follows for the next 6 miles. At 2¼ miles there is a descent of ½ mile to the La village Wan Nawng, which has gates wide enough to let loaded mules pass. At 6 miles it crosses the spur and runs down the western slope easily to Man Kin. The road is very good throughout. There are paddy-fields in terraces on a narrow saddle, just before Man Kin, with a good water-supply for a camp. Height, 4,100 feet. Small supplies.
		8. Páng Kwawng. One small stream.	7 0	66 0	The road descends from Man Kin to a narrow saddle from which it rises to a small village, Man Awt, then descends and rises fairly easily to a large La village, Man Hkúm, which it just touches. A little beyond it drops to a narrow ravine, with water running in it, and re-ascending rather steep at first, passes through Yawng Let and skirts level round the side of the hill. At 5½ miles it curls round to the left, rises to a spur at 6 miles, which it crosses and then descends fairly steeply for a mile to Páng Kwawng. The first village contains some 15 houses and a large walled-in kyaung which would be quite untenable. The main village of 25 houses is ¼ of a mile further on down the spur. The camping ground to the left just before the first village is a small one, and there is not very much water. Páng Kwawng is the capital of the Sumu (Sômö) State and the Sawbwa lives here, but it is a wretched village. There is another walled-in kyaung on the right of the entrance to the larger village.

FROM MÖNG KA TO LÁSHIO *viâ* PÁNG LÔNG AND TA SUPKYET—*continued*.

Authorities.		Number and Names of Stages, Rivers and Streams.	Distances.				Remarks.
Military.	Civil.		Intermediate.		Total.		
			M.	F.	M.	F.	
G.O.C. Mandalay District.	Superintendent, Northern Shan States.	**9. Páng Yao** ... Nam Kûn.	**10**	**0**	76	0	The road from the upper village of Páng Kwawng runs at once down the side of the hill and descends a spur running north-west for 3½ miles to a small Shan village, Möng Hit, on the right, below which it turns to the right and runs level on paddy-fields on the left bank of the Nam Kûn for a mile, then rises to a rocky path, crosses a spur, and descends for ½ a mile through cultivation to the Nam Kûn, which it crosses just below a Shan village, Na Káng, on the right bank. The Nam Kûn is here 60 yards wide, 2 feet to 3 feet deep; low banks; easy crossing; one small boat for a ferry in the rains. A very large force could camp below Möng Hit or beyond Na Káng in dry weather. Passing Na Káng on the left, it runs for nearly a mile over fields, rising gently, then turning left, strikes up hill. The ascent is steep and rocky at first, then gradual, and, lastly, rather steep for a mile. Total rise about 2,000 feet. At the top there is a large cultivated plateau surrounded by rocky peaks which the road traverses, and then descend by a rocky path to Páng Yao (20 houses), ½ a mile beyond, where there is a site for a camp and water for a small force, say, 200 men. There is more water in a nullah about ¼ of a mile further on. Small supplies from Páng Yao.
		10. Páng Lông ... No water on the road.	**8**	**4**	84	4	Leaving camp the path runs over a small spur and down to a small stream at once, then rises and runs along, rising and falling on a rather rough road for 2 miles, when it crosses some cultivation and again rising over rough ground at 5 miles, enters a flat, narrow valley between rocky peaks, along which it runs very easily to Páng Lông. This is a Panthay village of about 300 houses, where supplies are obtainable, but prices rule rather high. The water-supply rises and disappears in the village. The best camping ground is just beyond the village, ½ mile before the road passes through a small Chinese village, with a very small water-supply. Páng Lông is a place of much importance, as it contains nearly 1,000 pack mules with which the Panthays trade in all directions. Good roads connect it with Ta Sup Kyet and Ta Kunlôn, important ferries on the Salween river.
		11. Man Nam Pöng. Nam Pöng.	**4**	**4**	89	0	The road leaves Páng Lông at the south end, passes through the small Chinese village and runs along the valley for 1½ miles to forked roads, the left one leading to Möng Maö. The other very soon enters tree jungle and descends, rather steep and rough at first, but latterly easily, dropping 1,600 feet in 3 miles to the Nam Pöng, which is a small stream (about 15 feet; wide and shallow; easy crossing), flowing through some four or five acres of paddy-fields. The village is beyond on a small knoll, seven houses, Las. A little paddy perhaps obtainable. Elevation here 3,000 feet.

FROM MŎNG KA TO LÁSHIO *viâ* PÁNG LÔNG AND TA SUPKYET—*continued*

Authorities. Military.	Authorities. Civil.	Number and Names of Stages, Rivers and Streams.	Distances. Intermediate.	Distances. Total.	Remarks.
G.O.C. Mandalay District.	Superintendent, Northern Shan States.	**12. Kawng Sa** ... Nam It and two small streams.	M. F. 10 4	M. F. 99 4	The road passes below the left of the village and entering jungle rises steadily about 800 feet, trending from west to south. At 2 miles it strikes the top of the ridge which it follows for 1½ miles to Man Wa, a Kachin village of about 20 houses. From here the road runs south by west, easily at first, but soon descending a narrow spur with very steep sides, which leads down to the Nam It (25 feet wide, 1 foot deep, easy crossing). This spur could be easily held against troops ascending from the Nam It, as the slopes on both sides are very steep and difficult. On the left bank of the Nam It is a small clearing, and this could be extended to make a camp for at least 100 men with animals. This would make a good first stage from Páng Lông—distance 10 miles. From here the road ascends, steep in places, for 1 mile, where it crosses over the spur to river, rising and falling along the southern slope, with a gradual rise to Mung Yun. This is a Kachin village in two parts, about 30 houses in all. Sites for camps above the upper or below the lower. Water for the first across the road 300 yards back; for the second a little down the hill east of the village. One hundred men with animals could camp at either place. From Mung Yun it is a short 2 miles to the Kawng Sa camping ground. The road is excellent. Kawng Sa is a scattered Kachin village of some 40 houses. Rice, paddy and fowls obtainable. Water from a well in the village. An "Adu" or petty Sawbwa lives here. The camp is in paddy-fields south-east of the village on the high road to Ta Saileng or Ta Mŏng Nong (*see* Route No. 31). Just beyond is Kawng Sum, a Shan village of four houses. A good stream here and about 4 acres of flat ground.
		13. Páng Ka ...	7 4	107 0	From the last camp you must go back a short ½ mile to Kawng Sa, and striking left through the lower part of the village, reach the road to Supkyet which descends a little at first, then rises gently to a long stretch of level grass land at mile 1, after which there is an ascent to a Kachin village Páng Hpi, which the road traverses. It runs on with slight ups and downs, rising gradually to Wing Kao (or Kaw), a Kachin village in three parts. There is room for 100 men to camp at either Páng Hpi or Wing Kao. Passing the latter on the right, the road passes through a small gap in the hills and runs very level at first, and then with small rises and falls through a Kachin village of four houses past the lower Páng Ka on the left, down to a small saddle on which opium is grown and then round the hill to the right to the Upper Páng Ka, ½ a mile on. One hundred men could camp just before the first Páng Ka, where there is plenty of room, but little water. Three hundred yards before the second Páng Ka, there is a small clearing above the road, and a little water in the nullah below, and there is room for 100 men below the second village with a small water-supply about 100 feet below the road. The first village contains about 12 houses; the second 20, including the residence of an "Adu." Small supplies of rice, paddy, and fowls.

FROM MÖNG KA TO LÁSHIO *viâ* PÁNG LÔNG AND TA SUPKYET—*continued.*

Authorities. Military.	Authorities. Civil.	Number and Names of Stages, Rivers and Streams.	Distances. Intermediate.	Distances. Total.	Remarks.
			M. F.	M. F.	
G.O.C. Mandalay District.	Superintendent, Northern Shan States.	**14. Ta Supkyet (or Supket).** Salween river.	**10 0**	117 0	From Páng Ka the road follows a ridge running east, descending gradually for $2\frac{1}{2}$ miles to two La villages, called Wing Ngön. The upper has a few houses of Kachins and contains 15 houses, the lower 34, and a kyaung at the lower end; both are well stocked with pigs and fowls, and I saw about 20 head of cattle. One hundred men could camp just above the upper or below the lower village, the water-supply at which is down hill on the left. Below the lower village there is a small saddle from which a road runs to the left to a ferry on the Salween called Ta Man Ôn and on to Manmák. The right-hand path ascends, rising about 600 feet, then runs along the side of the hill over ground which must be very marshy in wet weather. It descends gradually and passes through a La village, Man U, which has about seven houses on the right of the ridge and 30 clustered together in a hollow on the left. Height 3,200 feet. From here the descent to the Salween is very gradual and easy the whole way. The ferry village on the left bank is a Shan village of about 10 houses, called Supkyet. On the opposite bank is a Shan village of seven houses Ting Tán (or Tao) on the left bank of the Nam Kyet, close to its junction with the Salween. This ferry is an excellent one, served by four dug-outs, which can make four trips an hour, when worked in pairs. The larger pair should carry 10 saddles, the smaller about seven. Both banks have a gentle slope, so that loads can be put down at the water's edge. On both sides there is a large stretch of fairly level sand, and plenty of level ground above flood-level which could be cleared for camping on. Ferry charges for 50 men with animals from 20 to 30 rupees. No fixed scale is at present demanded. The Salween at the ferry is about 200 yards in width. Estimated depth, 30 feet. Surface current $2\frac{1}{4}$ miles an hour. Low banks; the left commanding the right. Very good approaches and easy crossing by ferry of four dug-outs. River said to be practicable down to Ta Saileng, so that more boats could be brought up.
		15. Möng Kyet ... Nam Kyet.	**7 0**	124 0	From the ferry the road runs along the right bank of the Salween to the Nam Kyet which can be easily forded at its junction with the Salween, where widens out to about 30 yards and is knee-deep. A little higher up it is narrower nd waist-deep. From here the path runs up above flood-level and along the left of a strip of paddy-field for about 300 yards. This would make a good camping ground for a large column. At $\frac{1}{2}$ a mile it passes near a small Shan village, Na Pying, on the right, and runs along over broken ground for nearly 2 miles, rising to flat ground which continues for 3 miles, running south-west. Here the path turns west and descends for a mile fairly easily to the Nam Kyet, crossing water on the road once. All villages near were burnt out. The site of Möng Kyet is on the left bank of the river, where there is a very large extent of flat ground for camping. The valley here is 2 or 3 miles wide, and nearly all under paddy cultivation. From here there is a road to Kunlôn, *see* Route No. 6.

FROM MÖNG KA TO LÂSHIO *viâ* PÁNG LÔNG AND TA SUPKYET—*continued.*

Authorities. Military.	Authorities. Civil.	Number and Names of Stages, Rivers and Streams.	Distances. Intermediate.		Distances. Total.		Remarks.
			M.	F.	M.	F.	
G.O.C. Mandalay District.	Superintendent, Northern Shan States.	**16. Camp on Nam Léng.** Nam Kyet (or Nam Léng) and several small streams.	12	4	136	4	From Möng Kyet the path strikes south-west, running level for a mile to the Nam Kyet again, which it crosses (river as above, but a little deeper and higher banks). It touches the right bank of the river ½ a mile further on near the site of a Shan village, Hôko. This would be the best place to camp when marching from Ta Supkyet to Nam Léng to equalise the two marches. The road then rises gently and runs for 2 miles over undulating country, passing a small Shan village, Páng Hai, on the left, and soon crosses a stream (30 feet wide) on a strong plank bridge, ½ a mile beyond which is another small Shan village on the left of the road. Plenty of camping ground between the stream and this village. From here there is an easy descent of 1½ miles to the Nam Kyet again, the road passing through a Shan village Hôkai (40 to 50 houses) and turning down to the right to the bazaar which is near the river. On the left bank of the river there is a strip of paddy cultivation ½ a mile wide which extends for several miles up the valley. The road runs across this, then turning round to the left runs along the side of the hill over small spurs rising 800 feet in about 3 miles to a small stream, beyond which is a large extent of level grass land, which would make an excellent camp, when dry, but is probably marshy in rainy weather. The road traverses this plateau, crosses some marshy ground and runs past a small Shan village, Man Káng, on the left, after which it trends down-hill to the left and descends fairly steeply to a small stream, bridged, beyond which is a strip of paddy-field, 100 yards wide, which it crosses, then runs through long grass for about 300 yards to the Nam Léng. Camp can be pitched in the paddy-fields or beyond the river. There is plenty of flat ground and water. Height here, 2,250 feet. The Nam Léng is the upper water of the Nam Kyet and is also called the Nan Lin Löng here.
		17. Möng Yaw ... Nam Léng, Nam Yaw, and several other small streams.	9	0	145	4	The road crosses the Nam Léng (about 15 yards wide, 2 to 3 feet deep). The best ford for animals is about 100 yards below the foot-bridge; it is a bad ford with deep holes and rapid current on a ridge of rocks, below which is deep water. It then runs along the side of a valley, crossing water once and some marshy ground at 1 mile, and again crossing a small stream at 2 miles, after which it rises on to a watershed which it crosses at 3½ miles. From here there is a slight descent—part paddy-fields—and a small stream on the right to the Möng Yaw valley. At 4½ miles there is a stream across the road and a Shan village, Man Wai (about 30 houses) above the road on the left. It then traverses paddy-fields and runs over undulating ground for a mile, passing a Shan village (about 15 houses) off the road to the right, to a stream which it crosses. From here it is nearly level going to Möng Yaw, which is a large Shan village surrounded by clumps of bamboos. There is a large bazaar here held every five days. Rice and paddy plentiful, but grass rather scarce. Troops can camp anywhere in the last 6 miles. Water from Nam Yaw about 25 yards wide, crossed on a substantial wooden

FROM MÖNG KA TO LÁSHIO *viâ* PÁNG LÔNG AND TA SUPKYET—*continued.*

Authorities. Military.	Authorities. Civil.	Number and Names of Stages, Rivers and Streams.	Distances. Intermediate. M.	F.	Distances. Total. M.	F.	Remarks.
G.O.C. Mandalay District.	Superintendent, Northern Shan States.	**17. Möng Yaw**—*cont.*					bridge, fordable, but the banks are high and steep. From here there is said to be a hilly road to Theinni *viâ* Mönglen (12 miles), Lunglé (10) and Sé-u (8), thence to Theinni 6 miles—total 36 miles. There is also a road connecting this route with the direct route from Láshio to Möngyai (No. 15), *see* Branch III below. There are also roads to Möng Ma and Möng Kyeng (*see* Route No. 39), and to Mansé, Naungmwon and Thíbaw (*see* Route No. 40).
		18. Möng Yáng ... Nam Yaw and several small streams.	8	4	154	0	After crossing the Nam Yaw the path runs west between small outlying villages of Möng Yaw, crosses a small stream in the first ½ mile, then enters a level grassy plain which it traverses at 3 miles. It passes between two Shan villages, Lông Mun and descends to a small stream, crosses this and runs over undulating ground for a mile, passing close to a Shan village, Sup Kin, above on the left, from which it descends to a stream about 10 feet wide. Beyond this there is plenty of ground for camping on, which the path traverses, rising gently for ½ a mile to the foot of the hills. There is then a fairly steep ascent, 300 feet, after which the path strikes a spur, running west, which it follows for over 2 miles down to the Nam Yaw again here about [illegible] yards wide, knee-deep, easy crossing, but the river banks are steep. The road is rough, but not very steep, and quite good enough. On the right bank of the river there is a very large extent of paddy-fields which the path crosses. A large force could encamp here; a small one a little further on near a small village. The main village of Möng Yáng is on a knoll 100 feet above surrounded by bamboos. Its water-supply is in a flat and generally marshy nullah north-east. Rice and paddy obtainable in moderate quantities.
		19. Wing Tán ... Several small streams.	9	0	163	0	From Möng Yáng the road runs south-west along paddy-fields on the left for ½ a mile, crosses a stream and passes between the two Shan villages of Kông Lum (both very small), crosses another small stream and rises on to undulating ground. At 2½ miles it runs over cultivated ground, past Ta Yán, on the left, and then crosses a deep nullah, beyond which is a large stretch of paddy-fields intersected by a canal about 10 feet wide, temporarily bridged. At 4½ miles the road leaves the paddy-fields and rises a little, passing Man Káng on the right and between the two villages of Man Ping; then rising slightly and dropping to a muddy stream with steep banks which are ramped, but the crossing is liable to be swampy and difficult, though easy in favourable weather. The road rises again, then drops 200 feet to a very marshy nullah, which is bridged, then rises again about 200 feet and runs for a mile with a gradual descent to the Nam Poi, a small stream in a flat sandy bed; crossing this it runs over a spur, passes two Shan villages off the road to the left and descends easily to Wing Tán, running between the village and a large deep jheel on the right, north-east of the village are bazaar sheds, and here is excellent camping ground for several 100 men. All these villages on the road can supply rice and paddy. Troops could camp from 3rd to 5th mile, and at the Nam Poi, and between Wing Tán and the Nam Yaw to the south-east if required.

FROM MÖNG KA TO LÁSHIO *viâ* PÁNG LÔNG AND TA SUPKYET—*continued.*

Authorities. Military.	Authorities. Civil.	Number and Names of Stages, Rivers and Streams.	Distances. Intermediate. M. F.	Distances. Total. M. F.	Remarks.
G.O.C. Mandalay District.	Superintendent, Northern Shan States.	**20. Láshio Post.** Nam Yaw and two deep nullahs.	9 0	172 0	It is 3 miles from Wing Tán to the Government farm at Na Hpa over undulating grass land. There is a small marshy nullah at mile 1, and a deep, very marshy one at mile 2, and just before the farm a broad swamp is crossed on an embankment. Half-a-mile beyond the farm, a path to the right leads to the Shan bridge over the Nam Yaw, which is usually very unsafe. The Nam Yaw is here about 30 yards wide, 2 to 3 feet deep in dry weather. Fairly good. Ramped approaches. The left-hand road leads down to the river to a dry weather ford. It is 5 miles from here to the post. The road is good throughout and passes through old Láshio bazaar. Troops can camp almost anywhere along the road on this march.

BRANCH I.

FROM PÁNG LÔNG (STAGE 10) TO MÖNG KAW.

NATIVE INFORMATION, MARCH 1893.

Military	Civil	Stages	Intermediate	Total	Remarks
G.O.C. Mandalay District.	Superintendent, Northern Shan States.	**1. Nam Hsai** ...	...	...	
		2. Ya Kö Ché ...	...	...	Was.
		3. Páng Hung ...	...	...	The seat of the Sawbwa of Ho Nö.
		4. Hsing Nga ...	...	...	The boundary. Was.
		Cross the Nam Hsing Nga.			
		5. Möng Kaw ...	...	...	Shan-Chinese. These were given by a Panthay as mule marches, say, 15 to 20 miles each.

BRANCH II.

FROM PÁNG LÔNG (STAGE 10) TO MÖNG YUNG.

NATIVE INFORMATION, MARCH 1893.

Military	Civil	Stages	Intermediate	Total	Remarks
G.O.C. Mandalay District.	Superintendent, Northern Shan States.	**1. Ho Pán**	...	...	
		Cross Nam Hôpán.			
		2. Man Ka ...	...	...	
		3. Möng Ting ...	...	...	Hot springs. } These were given as mule stages 15 to 20 miles.
		Cross Nam Ting.			
		4. Sufáng Ching.	...	...	Shan-Chinese.
		5. Möng Cheng ...	...	...	Shan-Chinese.

FROM MÖNG KA TO LÁSHIO *viâ* PÁNG LÖNG AND TA SUPKYET—*continued.*

BRANCH II—*continued.*

Authorities. Military.	Authorities. Civil.	Number and Names of Stages, Rivers and Streams.	Distances. Intermediate. M. F.	Distances. Total. M. F.	Remarks.
China.	China.	**6. Ta Ché** ...	...	...	Chinese. } These were given as mule stages 15 to 20 miles.
		7. Sate Sa Ti ...	...	...	Chinese.
		8. Möng Sa ...	...	...	Chinese, Shan-Chinese, and Pantheys.
		9. Tai Ya Ko ...	...	...	Shan-Chinese.
		10. Möng Yung.	...	...	

Beyond Mong Yung the following route was given:—

Military	Civil	Stages	Intermediate	Total	Remarks
China.	China.	**Sé Tôn Ling** ...	...	...	
		Shiang Tu Ling.	...	...	
		Ta Sha Pa ...	...	...	

The Nam Kong is now crossed by the Ta Mat Hai ferry, and from the opposite bank of the river there are two roads. The left goes to Sung Ling in 13 mule marches and to Ying Kiu, three mule marches beyond. Both have large bazaars, the latter the largest. The right-hand road goes as follows in mule marches:—

Military	Civil	Stages	Intermediate	Total	Remarks
China.	China.	**Táng Song Ling.**	...	...	
		Ma Tai Hsing ...	...	...	
		Hé Tao Ché ...	...	...	Walnuts grown here.
		Sai Ying Hsing ...	...	...	White salt here.
		Shak Haw ...	...	...	
		Pa Chaw Ling ...	...	...	Red salt here.
		Pöng Môt Ling ...	...	...	

BRANCH III.

FROM MÖNGYAW (STAGE 17) TO MANTULENG (ROUTE NO. 15).

BY LIEUT. ORMISTON, ROYAL ARTILLERY, FEBRUARY 1888.

Military	Civil	Stages	Intermediate M. F.	Total M. F.	Remarks
G.O.C. Mandalay District.	Superintendent, Northern Shan States.	**1. Hônaw (Hôné).** Four streams.	8 4	8 4	Course west-south-west. Road branches south-west from Hantao road at 1 mile. At 3¾ miles Nongbun. At 6⅛ miles Mönghet, ¼ mile left of road. (From Mönghet there is a bullock road southward *viâ* Pánghun to Nánáng, the head village of the Lantao district. From Nánáng there are roads to Mansé, Möngma, Mankát, Kunka, Sarán, Hôya, &c.) At 7½ miles Mankonglun. The first 2½ miles on level plain—grass, open; the remainder undulating with thin tree jungle. Very good road for troops with pack transport. Good camping ground at Mankonglun on paddy-fields with good water-supply. Camp at Hônaw limited. Water not very plentiful.

FROM MÖNG KA TO LÁSHIO *viâ* PÁNG LÔNG AND TA SUPKYET—*continued.*

BRANCH III—*continued.*

Authorities. Military.	Authorities. Civil.	Number and Names of Stages, Rivers and Streams.	Distances. Inter-mediate.	Distances. Total.	Remarks.
			M. F.	M. F.	
G.O.C. Mandalay District.	Superintendent, Northern Shan States.	**2. Mantuleng** ... Three streams.	**10 6**	19 2	Course west-south-west. Undulating thin tree jungle. Good road for pack transport. At $1\frac{3}{4}$ miles Manpalun, $\frac{1}{4}$ mile right of road. At 5 miles Mankwékun. At $9\frac{3}{4}$ miles Lwépángkun. Mantuleng at $10\frac{3}{4}$ miles where ground for camp is large and good. Water from stream through camp. Mantuleng is on the main road from Láshio to Möngyai, *see* Route No. 15, Stage 1.

No. 31.

From MÖNGKYENG to PÁNG LÔNG viâ TA SAILENG FERRY.

BY CAPT. A. C. YATE, 1ST BELOOCHEES, FEBRUARY 1888.

Military	Civil	Stages	Intermediate	Total	Remarks
G.O.C. Mandalay District.	Superintendent, Northern Shan States.	**1. Nam-Usé** ... Several streamlets.	**11 4**	11 4	Direction north by east. Road fairly good for pack transport. In the passes over the Loi Kôhao (or Kôhaw) and Loi Pápun hills the pathway is in some paces rough and rocky and the gradients very steep. Leaving Möngkyeng the road traverses open undulating country, till at $5\frac{1}{2}$ miles the Loi Kôhao hills are reached. The following villages lie to the left of the road :—Hôten, Hômyeng, Nongpakyeng, Tongkun, and Nanyu. The cross road from Nanyu to Pángkyeng crosses the main road 4 miles from Möngkyeng. On nearing the Loi Kôhao hills the following villages lie to the right of the road in the Namsutai valley :—Pángwa, Pángkyeng, Tongpyet, Kongpao, and Pánghung. The last named village lies about 2 miles south-east and towards the direct road from Möngkyeng to the Hatseng ferry in the Lawa State of Môkhai. Sugar-cane largely grown in Namsutai valley. At 6 miles path southward to village of Pengkyé (1 mile off) and eastward to Vyengtong (3 miles off). Country now hilly and overgrown with tree jungle. At $6\frac{3}{4}$ miles reach Paung Vyengkáng. Camping room here for 200 men by clearing jungle. Water, fodder, and fuel plentiful. From here continuous and often steep and rocky ascent to village of Pánghowo (Palaungs and Shans). Ten houses. Good kyaung. Good water and camping ground. Opium largely cultivated here. Pánghowo is 9 miles from Möngkyeng. From here continuous descent to village of Nam-Usé. From Pánghowo and Nam-Usé there is a road practicable for pack transport, direct over the Loi Koi hills to Möngma, distance said to be 8 daings, passing at 2 daings Palaung village of Nam Papáng. Nam-Usé, Shan village, 10 houses, good camp. Water, fodder, and fuel plentiful.
		2. Papáng ... Nam Saikhao, Nam Kosán, and Nam Kyeng.	**8 4**	20 0	Direction north-east. Fairly good road for pack transport. At $\frac{1}{4}$ mile pass Kaiten (old village). Camping ground there and water from stream. At $\frac{1}{2}$ mile cross Nam Saikhao stream by

FROM MÖNGKYENG TO PÁNG LÔNG *viâ* TA SAILENG FERRY—*continued.*

Authorities. Military.	Authorities. Civil.	Number and Names of Stages, Rivers and Streams.	Distances. Intermediate.	Distances. Total.	Remarks.
G.O.C. Mandalay istrict.	Superintendent, Northern Shan States.	**2. Papáng**—*cont.*			wooden bridge. (Stream 30 feet broad and 2 feet deep.) This stream is said to be the boundary line between the Möngkyeng and Möngma districts. At $2\frac{1}{2}$ miles cross Nam Kosán stream by wooden bridge. Good water. Camping ground limited. (The Nam Saikhao and Nam Kosán unite their waters a short distance north-east from here and take the name of Nam Kyeng. The Nam Kyeng flows south-east past the villages of Namíkyeng and Vyengtong and falls into the Salween just north of the village of Mankyu, at which point the boundaries of Möngma, Möngkyeng, and Môthai (Lawas) are said to meet. Möngkyeng fits in like a wedge between the other two.) At $3\frac{1}{4}$ miles road to left to Líshaw (Shan-Tayôk) village of Manping, 3 miles distant. At $4\frac{1}{2}$ miles Palaung village of Nongtao. From here road across hills direct to Möngma, distance said to be 8 to 10 daings. From Nongtao to Manping is about 2 miles. Much opium is cultivated around Nongtao and Manping (even to the higher slopes of the Lwémaw range) and at most of the villages hereabouts. (From Nongtao there is a road east down the valley of the Namlo stream to Ta-Namôn, a small local ferry over the Salween. Distance about 7 miles. The Namôn village (Shans probably) is on the east bank in Kángsö territory. From Namôn there is said to be a foot path over the hills to Möng-Kángsö, the chief town of Kángsö, distance 40 to 50 miles. There is a bullock road from Namôn to Wieng Lwélom, the chief town of the Lawa State of Môthai on the east bank of the Salween, distance 30 to 40 miles.) At Nongtao good camp, water, fuel, and fodder. At $8\frac{1}{2}$ miles reach Palaung village of Papáng, 15 houses. Good camp, water, fuel, and fodder. The country from Pánghôwo to Papáng lies high, probably 5,000 feet above sea-level. The cold at night in the winter is considerable. Snow lies in winter on the surrounding hill-tops. The road from Nongtao to Papáng traverses a level sort of plateau overgrown with thin tree jungle, where not cleared for cultivation. To the left is the Lwé Maw and to the right the Loi Sáng range of hills. The Namlôn flows east to the Salween, south of the Loi Sáng, and north of the Lwé Möng range. From Papáng there is a road over the hills to Möngma, but it is very difficult for pack transport. That from Nongtao is preferable.
		3. Pánglao or Pánglaw. Nam Ngam, and several other streams.	M. F. **5 4**	M. F. 25 4	Direction north-east. This road is very trying and difficult for pack transport. Pánglao is the name of a sub-division of the Möngma district. There are four villages in it within a radius of 2 miles of each other. Their names are Mankong, Kongsun, Mansauhaw, and Namtawmaw. The distance of 4 miles is taken to a central point between them near the bazaar, where water and room for camping are available. A few supplies, rice, paddy, bullocks, buffaloes, fowls, &c., may be drawn from these villages, such as rice, fowls, paddy, vegetables, salt, &c. At 1 mile path to Loi Sáng, Palaung village 2 to 3 miles to the east on the Loi Sáng hills. From Loi Sáng bullock road to Panglao and Namôn. The bullock road from the Ta Saileng (otherwise called Ta-Möngnong) ferry to the Ta Kongpun ferry passes through Pánglao and Loi Sáng. From Patáng the road is a continuous and very steep descent of 4 miles to the Namngam stream (20 feet broad and

FROM MÖNGKYENG TO PÁNG LÔNG *viâ* TA SAILENG FERRY—*continued.*

Authorities.		Number and Names of Stages, Rivers and Streams.	Distances.		Remarks.
Military.	Civil.		Inter-mediate.	Total.	
G.O.C. Mandalay District.	Superintendent, Northern Shan States.	**3. Pánglao or Pánglaw**—*cont.*			2 feet deep). Several streams are crossed *en route*, and several small camping grounds passed. The road traverses dense luxuriant jungle. From the Namngam very steep ascent to Pánglao bazaar, distance $1\frac{1}{2}$ miles. At 5 miles road to right to Kongpun. At $5\frac{3}{4}$ miles cross two shallow streams. At $5\frac{1}{2}$ miles another road to right to Kongpun. Here good camp and water for 300 or 400 men. Numerous other places in the vicinity where troops can camp.
			M. F.	M. F.	
		4. Ta Saileng otherwise called Ta Möngnong. Nam Ma and Salween river.	7 6	33 2	The road to Ta Saileng is level and easy for the first 3 miles. It passes at short intervals in the 1st mile the four Shan villages of Mankong, Kongsung, Mankun, and Konghyao. At $2\frac{1}{2}$ miles the direct road from Panlao to Manmak branches off to the left near the hamlet of Manlaklun. This road has a very steep descent for $\frac{3}{4}$ mile to the valley of the Namma. (This part is difficult, but practicable for pack animals.) It then follows the right bank of that river for $\frac{3}{4}$ mile and crosses it by an easy ford at the village of Pángmôn. Good water, fuel, and fodder, but camping ground only for a battalion. There is a good level road from Pángmôn to Saileng, distance about $3\frac{1}{2}$ miles. From Manlaklun to Ta-Saileng the road is steep and difficult. Caravan mules not unfrequently fall over the cliffs above the Salween. About half-way the road crosses the Namma river by a ford. Just opposite Saileng is the western extremity of the Loi Pyémöng which bounds on the north the other Namma river which flows into the Salween from the north-east a little south of Ta-Möngnong. The people on the right bank of the Salween call this ferry Ta-Saileng, and those on the left bank Ta-Möngnong. To the north of Pángmôn is the range called Loi Kaw and north-east of that the Loi Nongkyo to the west of the Salween. The former lies in the Möngma and the latter in the Manmak district. The Western Namma flows from Manmak and falls into the Salween 1 mile south of Saileng village. There is camping room for a battalion at Saileng. Only two or three boats at this ferry, which is used chiefly by the Panthays from Pánglông.
		5. Nawi	15 0	48 2	Capt. Yate ascertained from native information (1888) that a hilly road runs from this ferry to Páng Lông. The distance is about 30 miles and the road appears suitable for pack transport.
		6. Páng Lông ...	15 0	63 2	

BRANCH I.

FROM PÁNGLAO (OR PÁNGLAW), (STAGE 3) TO TA KONGPUN.

BY CAPT. A. C. YATE, 1ST BELOOCHEES, FEBRUARY 1888.

Military	Civil	Stage	Inter-mediate	Total	Remarks
G.O.C. Mandalay District.	Supdt., Shan States.	**1. Ta Kongpun** ... Salween and small streams.	3 4	3 4	From Pánglao there are two roads to the Salween, not to mention the road south-east *viâ* to Ta Namôn. The road to Ta Kongpun is a steep descent almost the whole of the way.

FROM MÖNGKYENG TO PÁNG LÔNG *viâ* TA SAILENG FERRY—*continued.*

BRANCH I—*continued.*

Authorities. Military.	Authorities. Civil.	Number and Names of Stages, Rivers and Streams.	Distances. Intermediate.	Distances. Total.	Remarks.
G.O.C. Mandalay District.	Superintendent, Northern Shan States.	**1. Ta Kongpun**—*cont.*			It is trying and in places difficult for pack animals. At ¼ mile cross the Nam Pángho stream and again at ⅜ mile. (This stream flows into the Nam Ngam, which is said to fall into the Salween just south of Ta Saileng.) At ½ mile pass village of Mansuhaw (Shans, eight houses) to right. At ¾ mile pass through the Pánglao district bazaar. (This place has been a refuge lately for all the unfortunates from Möngkyeng and Möngma districts.) Just beyond bazaar path to right to Shan village of Namtawmaw (20 houses) which lies some 300 yards to the right of the road. At 1½ miles steep descent commences. (From here distant view obtained of the Namma valley bending north-east from the Salween towards Vyeng Pángkhwon, the chief town of Sômö. The broad valley of the Namma is in Kángsö territory, but the range that bounds it on the north called Loi Pyémung is in Sômö. To the north-east are seen two peaks of the Loi Samngam range said to be near Vyeng Pángkwon. Beyond the Loi Samngam is said to lie the Möngting state.) At 2¾ miles reach village of Man Pawat (Shans and Las, 10 houses). At 3 miles new village of Kongpun on high ground ½ mile to right. At 3½ miles reach right bank of Salween. Natural hot springs near here. Old Kongpun village is on left bank (two or three houses only). The road to Kángsö mounts direct over the hills east of the village. The road to Kángsö is not a good one for bullocks, and there is said to be no bullock road from Kongpun to Pángkhwon in Sômö. All the trade from Pánglông and Pángkwon comes to Ta Möngnong. The Salween is very rapid just below Kongpun ferry. Boats come down here from Möngnong and some say also from Supkyet; but boats cannot go, on account of the rapids, to Ta Namôn and Ta Hatseng. There is camping ground for a battalion on the banks of the Salween, which here runs through a narrow gorge, as indeed it seems to do everywhere.

Capt. A. C. Yate gives the following account from native information of a route FROM TA KONGPUN TO WINGKÁNGSÖ:—

Military	Civil	Stages	Intermediate M.	Intermediate F.	Total M.	Total F.	Remarks
G.O.C. Mandalay District.	Superintendent, Northern Shan States.	**1. Manmyeng** ... Unknown.	6	0	6	0	General direction east-south-east. The roads from Ta Möngnong and Ta Kongpun meet at Manmyeng, which is a La village perched on high ground and visible from the west bank of the Salween. The road is hilly. There is a kyaung and sayát at Manmyeng.
		2. Mantông ...	6	0	12	0	Hilly road. La village of 10 to 15 houses.
		3. Yonglö ...	9	0	21	0	Hilly road. Half-way pass Longkáng, small La village. Yonglö La village of 50 houses, with kyaungs and zayáts.
		4. Wingkángsö ...	10	0	31	0	Hilly road. Pass village of Nalem at 7 miles. Wingkángsö large village, bazaar, kyaungs, and sayáts. Population Shans and Las. Chief lives there. Water and camping ground.

No. 32.

From MÖNG MAÖ to MÉHAWNGSAWN.

By H. G. A. LEVESON, Esq., Assistant Superintendent, Southern Shan States, February 1893.

Authorities.		Number and Names of Stages, Rivers and Streams.	Distances.		Remarks.
Military.	Civil.		Intermediate.	Total.	
			M. F.	M. F.	
G.O.C. Rangoon District.	Superintendent, Southern Shan States.	**1. Namun (3,050 feet).** Mé Lé and Hwé Namun.	8 0	8 0	General direction south-east, 2 miles up the Mé Lé valley, crossing the stream several times (10 to 15 feet broad, 2 to 3 feet deep; rocky bed; current fairly swift; said to be fordable for pack bullocks throughout the rains); at mile 1 road to left (east) leads *viâ* Hwékahan to Nápúpawn. At mile 2 road turns south up the hill, steady ascent for about a mile, then runs up and down spurs, and at mile 4½ reaches watershed, then descends to narrow ravine of Hwé Namun, up this stream mostly in its bed for 3 miles. Camp in clearing in the site of the old village of Namun; accommodation for 500 men. The Namun, a tributary of the Mé Lé, is here 6 feet broad; shallow, rocky, fairly swift.
Siam.		**2. Pánghpöng** ... Mé Pángma, Hwé Pángkaw, and Mé Hsanyi.	8 0	16 0	General direction south. At ½ mile reach watershed of Namun and Mé Hsanyi (Mé Si Ngé of Capt. Barrow), *i.e.*, of Mé Sé on the north and Mé Pai on the south. At this point is the boundary pillar erected in February 1893 marking the frontier between Siamese and British Shan States, namely, Méhawnghsawn and Möng Maö. The road now descends rapidly by a narrow ravine crossing one or two spurs on the way. At mile 2½ reach the Mé Pángma and at 3½ the Hwé Pángkaw; narrow, shallow, tributaries of the Mé Hsanyi. Ascend a spur known as the Mikyitaung and go along its crest, gradually descending. At mile 6 reach the old boundary mark between the kingdoms of Burma and Siam. From here is a very steep descent to the Mé Hsanyi at mile 6¾, on the south of which lies the village of Mikyitaung (seven houses). The river is here 10 to 15 feet broad, 2 to 3 feet deep; rocky bed, rapid current. Camping ground for 200 men on right bank at mile 7. Descend the stream crossing three times to Pánghpöng village (four houses) at mile 8. Camping ground good, but confined in the vicinity of the village.
		3. Hwéhpa ... Hwé Hai and Napa Hsát.	11 0	27 0	General direction south. Road follows course of Mé Hsanyi and is good throughout; crosses stream eight times. At mile 3 crosses Hwé Hai, 6 feet broad, shallow, rocky, and swift, near which is a village of same name (three houses). At mile 4 crosses the Napáhsát, a stream similar to the Hwé Hai, with two villages of five and 17 houses, and several small patches of paddy land.
		4. Méhawngsawn.	8 0	35 0	Capt. Barrow gives the distance from Mé Hsanyi (Mé Si Ngé) to Méhawngsawn 20 miles; deducting the distances above from the former place to Hwéhpa (12 miles), this leaves the distance remaining to Méhawngsawn 8 miles. Capt. Barrow says the route traverses dense tropical forest and passes a halting place called Pin Mu. The other halting place he mentions, Na Pa sayát, is evidently the same place as Stage 3 above.

No. 32-A.

From MÔNG MAÖ to MÔNG HÁNG viâ MÔNG TA.

BY MAJOR E. G. BARROW, 7TH BENGAL INFANTRY, 1890.

Authorities. Military.	Authorities. Civil.	Number and Names of Stages, Rivers and Streams.	Distances. Intermediate. M.	F.	Distances. Total. M.	F.	Remarks.
G.O.C. Rangoon District.	Superintendent, Southern Shan States.	**1. Camp near Lukcháng (3,250 feet).** Hwé Khán Môn and Hwé On.	8	4	8	4	General direction north for 2½ miles, then east to Lukcháng, the road first goes towards Kung Long for 2½ miles (*see* Route No. 82, Branch III). It then turns sharp to the east and crosses a spur about 300 feet high. At 3 miles cross the Hwé Khán Môn, a narrow stream. Then a steep ascent, ultimately reaching 4,600 feet. The road now runs along a narrow pine-clad ridge. At 4 miles pass the turning for Kung Long. At 7¾ miles descend to Lukcháng, a Taungthu village of 40 or 50 houses. Camping ground nearly a mile further on and 400 feet below. Water from Hwé On stream.
		2. Mé Yin (2,900 feet). Mé Yin.	7	0	15	4	General direction north-east. The road descends nearly 1,000 feet in the 1st mile. It then crosses a stream, and ascends a spur rising about 400 feet above the stream. Descend to Kham Ta (2,500 feet), a small hamlet on a plateau. Descend again to a stream 300 feet below and 2 miles from camp. From here very steep ascent of 500 feet. The road then rises gradually along the crest of the hill. At 3 miles Kham Ta Noi (3,150 feet), a hamlet of three or four houses. The road continues rising gradually up to 3,700 feet at 3½ miles. Then comes a steep descent to stream which cross at 4½ miles (elevation 2,850 feet), another short steep ascent and then a gradual rise to 3,700 feet. Road now runs along crest and for ½ a mile is fairly level. Grand view to south of Nam Khong, a tributary of the Mé Pai. Descend to Mé Yin, a village of 25 houses. Water from Mé Yin stream 200 feet below. Camping ground confined. General direction north-east.
		3. Nam Hu (2,800 feet). Mé Sakun and Nam Hu.	8	0	23	4	Descend 1,200 feet in nearly 2 miles, cross a stream, then ascend 300 feet and descend 500 feet crossing a spur at the foot of the descent (3 miles). Strike the Mé Sakun, a rapid river, knee-deep and 20 yards broad. The road goes down the river for nearly a mile crossing several times. At 3¼ miles pass through Mé Sakun (five houses). At 4 miles turn northwards up the valley of the Mé Wing. Road good and level. At 6 miles steep ascent of at least 1,000 feet, then gradual rise till at 7½ miles crest (3,300 feet) is reached drop down 500 feet to camp. Space very limited. Water from Nam Hu stream. Mules average rate of march 1½ miles an hour.
		4. Hwé Paw (2,100 feet). Hwé Paw.	7	0	30	4	General direction east. Cross the marshy bed of the Hwé Paw stream and ascend the hill opposite, steep ascent for about 600 feet. At 1 mile cross a level bay in the hills the site of a deserted village (Long Paha) road now over the hills, which are here gently undulating, never rising above 3,800 feet. The jungle is mostly oak and pine and is fairly open. At 3 miles Naung Aw where there is a little water. At 4 miles commence descending to the Hwé Paw which drains south to the Mé Sakun. Descent easy and gradual. At 7

FROM MÖNG MAÖ TO MÖNG HÁNG *viâ* MÖNG TA—*continued.*

Authorities. Military.	Authorities. Civil.	Number and Names of Stages, Rivers and Streams.	Distances. Intermediate.	Distances. Total.	Remarks.
G.O.C. Rangoon District.	Superintendent, Southern Shan States.	**4. Hwé Paw (2,100 feet)**—*cont.*			miles village of Hwé Paw (30 houses). Here gunpowder is made. Camp in fields. Water from stream. Fuel and forage obtainable.
		5. Ná Niu (2,300 feet). Mé Nak.	M. 7 F. 0	M. 37 F. 4	General direction north-east. Commence by an ascent of about 600 feet reaching the crest of the spur at 1 mile, dip down into an old clearing and at 2 miles reach the crest of the watershed at 2,900 feet, descend to the valley of the Hwé Long Wai. Path here very narrow through thick jungle. At 4½ miles Naung Palam, a village of 20 houses in an open valley. From here onwards the road follows the bed of the Mé Nak. Camp in paddy-fields, Na Niu is a village of 12 houses. A road runs north from here to Ta Sányi, a ferry on the Salween, 2 bullock marches distant. Ta Sányi is the ferry to Möng Pán.
		6. Nam Ok Hu (3,700 feet).	12 4	50 0	General direction east. Cross the stream and passing through the village ascend a steep hill rising 800 feet in the 1st mile. Here a path turns off to the left to the village of Kúnka (20 houses) less than a mile distant. At 2½ miles a path turns off to the right to Mé Lu (30 houses). The main road runs right along the crest of the watershed amongst pine and oak, the general elevation being over 3,600 feet. At 6 miles pass over the main watershed, just 4,700 feet high between the Mé Sakun and Maing Tha drainage. The road now descends to Tam Wo (4,000 feet). This is usually considered a bullock stage, but the water-supply is very deficient. From Tam Wo there are two roads to Möng Ta. The direct one is two marches, but very difficult for animals. The one followed, though scarcely ever used, is easier. This road follows a crest in the most absurd fashion going up to the tops of peaks merely to come down again. In this manner peaks 5,200 feet and 5,500 feet, respectively, are ascended at 9¼ and 10 miles. Descend from here to Nam Ok Hu (3,700 feet), the last few hundred feet being very steep. Nam Ok Hu is a very good little camping ground with an excellent supply of water.
		7. Möng Ta (1,300 feet). Mé Nen.	11 2	61 2	General direction east-south-east. A short steep bad bit on leaving, but only for about 100 yards, then an easy gradual ascent to 4,300 feet. At ½ mile path joins in on left from Hwé Pú. At 3½ miles reach the Mé Nen after a steep and stony descent of 2,500 feet. The Mé Nen is a lovely stream about 1 foot deep and 15 feet wide. From this point there is a direct path to Tam Wo, but it is very bad. The road now goes down the Mé Nen crossing it repeatedly. No difficulties. At 8 miles leave the river, altitude at this point 1,200 feet. Up a dry ravine for ½ a mile, then over some low hills rising some 200 feet or 300 feet to the Möng Ta valley. At 9½ miles a path goes off to the Ta Palaung ferry on the Salween, distant 2 marches (*vide* Branch I below). Camping grounds everywhere. From here there is a road to Möng Heng *viâ* Kiukaw, *see* Route No. 4 of Appendix II and No. 7 of Appendix III.

FROM MÖNG MAÖ TO MÖNG HÁNG *viâ* MÖNG TA—*continued.*

Authorities. Military.	Authorities. Civil.	Number and Names of Stages, Rivers and Streams.	Distances. Intermediate. M.	F.	Total. M.	F.	Remarks.
G.O.C. Rangoon District.	Superintendent, Southern Shan States.	**8. Chaung Zo (junction of Mé Ta and Mé Chuat), 1,100 feet.** Mé Ta and Mé Nen.	7	2	68	4	General direction north-north-west. Through jungle and over low hills for 2 miles. The road then goes down a dry ravine. At 3½ miles enter the bed of the Mé Ta river 1 foot deep, 15 yards broad. This the road continually crosses. At 4½ miles the Mé Nen joins in from the west. The road still follows the river, and is practically a defile, with steep hills and open jungle on each side. The camping ground is a good one. The road to Möng Pán runs north down the valley.
		9. Camp in jungle (1,300 feet). Mé Chuat.	13	4	82	0	General direction east. Road goes up the Mé Chuat, which is, generally speaking, about 15 or 20 yards broad and 2 feet deep. The river has to be forded about fifty times. At 12 miles leave the river and cross a low spur. Camp on the banks of a tiny rill. Water not very plentiful.
		10. Möng Chuat (1,900 feet). Mé Tuen.	8	4	90	4	General direction east. Road ascends gradually for 3 miles to 3,400 feet. Jungle fairly open, being mostly oak and pine. On the east side of the watershed the jungle is mostly bamboo. At 7½ miles strike the Mé Tuen, a stream 2 or 3 yards broad. Möng Chuat consists (1890) of half a dozen houses, but it has till lately been a large village, and there is a considerable extent of paddy ground.
		11. Hwé Pa Kut (2,600 feet). Pa Kut.	8	2	98	6	General direction north-east. For 1½ miles the road goes through paddy-fields. Then it ascends very easily and gradually through oak and pine jungle to about 2,700 feet. At 5½ miles the road drops down to the Pa Kut stream up which it goes. At 7 miles pass the site of a deserted village. Good camping ground 1¼ miles further on.
		12. Möng Háng (1,700 feet). Hwé Pa Kut and Mé Háng.	11	4	110	2	General direction east-north-east. Up the Hwé Pa Kut here but a brook. At 3 miles reach the crest (3,400 feet). The descent is very gradual. At 5 miles reach some hot sulphur springs. Follow the stream therefrom for about a mile through some very fine teak forest. The road now practically enters the valley and is fairly level the rest of the way. At 10 miles a forester's village Na Niu. At 11¼ miles cross the Mé Háng 20 yards broad, 2 feet deep. The village, 30 houses, is ¼ of a mile further on.

FROM MÖNG MAÖ TO MÖNG HÁNG *viâ* MÖNG TA—*continued.*

BRANCH I.

FROM MÖNG TA (STAGE 7) TO MÖNG PWÁN (MAING PÁN, ROUTE No. 21, SHAN HILLS DIVISION) *viâ* TA PHALEING.

BY MR. OGLE, SURVEY OF INDIA, 1890.

Authorities. Military.	Authorities. Civil.	Number and Names of Stages, Rivers and Streams.	Distances. Intermediate. M.	F.	Distances. Total. M.	F.	Remarks.
G. O. C. Rangoon District.	Superintendent, Southern Shan States.	**1. Chaung-Zo** ... Mé Ta, Mé Chuat, and Mé Nen.	7	0	7	0	First mile over a flat, then over low hills and down into the dry bed of a sandy stream, which for about ½ mile before its junction with the Mé Ta becomes rocky. Three miles from the village the Mé Ta is reached, stony bed, water ankle and knee deep. The road crosses and recrosses it several times to its junction with the Mé Chuat. Road good and a good large camping ground below junction of rivers. At 3½ miles pass mouth of Mé Nen stream.
		2. Páng Sak ... Mé Chuat.	10	0	17	0	Road follows bed of Mé Chuat, which is stony and crosses and recrosses it several times. In the beginning of March it is in many places 2½ feet deep at the crossings, otherwise the road is good and there is no hill climbing, camping ground good.
		3. Ta Phaleing ... Mé Chuat and Salween.	4	4	21	4	Road continues along bed of Mé Chuat to near its junction with the Salween 2¾ miles, then goes over low spurs for 1¾ miles up stream to the Ta Phaleing ferry, which is about 200 yards wide. Road fairly good, but it frequently crosses and recrosses the Mé Chuat, which is in many places 2½ feet deep. Bad camping ground.
		4. Nam Tong ... Salween.	9	0	30	4	Cross the Salween by the ferry. The path goes straight up a hill for 800 feet without a break and then for a short distance pretty level, round a ridge and over a saddle back, then another steep ascent of 1,000 feet, and lastly a long rise of 1,000 feet, in parts steep and in others gradual. Then a descent of 900 feet to the village of Namkhai. For a short distance from Namkhai there is a slight rise and then a level bit for 1½ miles, another slight rise and lastly a fall of 300 feet to the village of Namtong. Road good. Good camping ground and water plentiful.
		5. Möng Pwán ... Patep, Pangyong, and Tonkai chaungs, and Naloi river.	14	6	45	2	Road level throughout, except for the first 4 miles out from Namtong when it went over little low hills. Then there was an easy descent into the Patep Chaung dry and sandy in places and water in others. Then the Pangyong Chaung was crossed 6 miles from Nam Tong. It was crossed and re-crossed in all four times, and the path led along the right bank of the stream through thick bamboo jungle, and then the Tonkai Chaung was crossed near the village of that name. Here the path went through paddy-fields for a short distance and entered forest again when at 2 miles from Möng Pwán the Naloi was first crossed, and a short distance further again crossed, the road emerging into paddy-fields. Camping ground good and road good.

No. 33.

From MÖNG MAÖ to MÖNG HENG (SIAM).

By H. G. A. LEVESON, Esq., Assistant Superintendent, Southern Shan States, February 1893.

Authorities. Military.	Authorities. Civil.	Number and Names of Stages, Rivers and Streams.	Distances. Intermediate. M. F.	Distances. Total. M. F.	Remarks.
G.O.C. Rangoon District.	Superintendent, Southern Shan States.	**1. Nápúpawn** ... Hwé Mámônawn, Mawkhatnawng, Mé Nawn, and Mé Hkawng.	12 0	12 0	General direction east-south-east. First mile lies up the Mé Lé valley crossing the stream three times. (This is part of the Möng Maö-Méhawngsawn road, *see* Route No. 32.) Road then ascends the Hwé Mámônawn (6 to 8 feet broad; shallow, rocky, swift) to mile 2½ and its tributary, the Nam Mawkhaimang, a narrow rocky brook, to mile 3½, where the village of the same name is passed on the right (five houses). After an ascent of ½ a mile the watershed of the Mé Sé and Mé Hkawng (a tributary of the Mé Pai) is reached. Here is the boundary pillar erected in February 1893 between Siamese and British Shan States (Méhawnghsawn and Möng Maö). A steep descent of 1 mile and the Mé Nawn is reached and descended to mile 10. The river is 10 feet broad; shallow, rocky, swift. Camping grounds at several places for 100 to 200 men. The road then winds over a low spur, passing the village of Nampamöng on the right at mile 11½; crosses the stream of that name and reaches Nápúpawn village (70 houses) at mile 12. Village lies on the right bank of the Mé Hkawng; ample camping ground either above or below the village. The Mé Hkawng is 12 to 15 yards broad, 2 to 3 feet deep; bed rocky, current swift. Camping ground anywhere along the right bank; said to be impassable at times in the rains.
Siam.		**2. Hwéhkan** ... Mé Hkawng, Pahteng, and Hwé Hkan.	9 0	21 0	General direction south-east. Descend the valley of the Mé Hkawng on its right bank to the village of Tonghsaté (18 houses) at mile 2; then cross stream and ascend a small spur to mile 2½; here a road on the right leads south to Méhawngsawn. Descend to the Páhteng, narrow, shallow, swift; feeder of the Mé Hkawng. Then ascend on the other side of the stream for ½ a mile. Five hundred yards north of the road lies a small village of eight houses of the same name. Road then winds along an undulating ridge to mile ½ and descends a steep spur meeting the Hwé Hkan at its junction with the Puhsánpik at mile 9. The Hwé Hkan is a tributary of the Mé Hkawng, 5 to 6 yards broad, 2 to 2½ feet deep; rocky, swift. Small camping grounds along the bank, but grass for animals scarce. Between the streams is the site of a deserted village; camping ground good, but confined, on the bank of the stream.
		3. Mélana ... Puhsánpik and Mélana.	8 0	29 0	General direction east. Ascend the Hwé Hkan for 1¼ miles, crossing stream seven times; then a very steep ascent to mile 3, when a small spring, the Nam Hôwo, is passed with a village of five houses (partially deserted). Road again winds along an undulating ridge to mile 7, when a steep descent of 1 mile leads to the village of Mélana. Village consists of two hamlets, ½ a mile apart, of 10 and 20 houses respectively. Ample camping ground in or near paddy-fields near stream of same name, which sinks into the ground south of the village; current slow and bed muddy; higher up 3 to 4 yards broad; shallow.

FROM MÖNG MAÖ TO MÖNG HENG (SIAM)—*continued.*

Authorities. Military.	Authorities. Civil.	Number and Names of Stages, Rivers and Streams.	Distances. Intermediate. M. F.	Distances. Total. M. F.	Remarks.
	Siam.	**4. Möng Pem** ... Mé Lang and Mé Pem.	11 0	40 0	General direction east. Steep ascent of ¼ a mile, then along a level ridge to mile 3, after which a series of low hills are crossed descending gradually to the Mé Lang at mile 7, a tributary of the Mé Pai, 5 yards broad, 2 feet deep; stony bottom. Ascend this stream for ½ a mile, crossing three times to the village of Wántang (16 houses); here the Mé Pem joins the Mé Lang; camping ground for 500 men near junction of the Mé Pem or in paddy-clearing near Wantang village. Mé Pem, 8 to 10 feet broad, shallow, recky bed; swift current. Ascend the former to mile 11 when the village of Möng Pem is reached, a fairly well-to-do village of 15 houses. Road crosses the stream eighteen times. Ample camping ground in paddy-field south of the village or by clearing jungle on the bank of the stream.
		5. Nampamöng ... Nam Hkawngtong, Nam Hkawngnoi, and Nampamöng.	11 0	51 0	General direction east. Easy ascent of ½ a mile, and then the road lies on the top of an elevated ridge to mile 5½, then after a steep descent of ½ a mile the Nam Hkawngtong is reached (feeder of Mé Pai, 4 to 5 yards wide, 2 feet deep; swift; bed rocky), just below its junction with the Nam Hkawngnoi a similar stream; the latter stream is ascended to mile 8, the road lying partly in and partly alongside of the bed of the river. Cross over a fairly easy spur for 3 miles, and at mile 11 reach the Nampamong stream (3 yards broad; shallow, swift, rocky) with village of same name on its right bank. Small camp on left bank of stream or north of village in jungle clearing.
		6. Möng Noi ... Hwé Ken, Hwé Hkit, Hwé Kan, Hwé Lam, Hwé Hok, and Mé Pai (15 yards wide, 1½ feet deep, rapid current and rocky bed).	10 0	61 0	General direction east-south-east; steep ascent for ½ a mile, then follow the ridge for 1½ miles, and gradually descend to the Hwé Ken at mile 2½; follow down this stream for ¾ mile, then cross a series of low spurs between which lie the Hwé Hkit at mile 4 and Hwé Kan at mile 4½, reaching the Hwé Lam at 5½. This stream is descended to its junction with the Hwé Hok at mile 6½, which is descended to mile 7½, passing the village of that name at mile 7 and crossing the stream several times. A series of low hills are then crossed and Möng Noi village reached at mile 10. All the above streams are narrow, rocky, shallow; very little water except in the rains. The Hwé Hok is 8 to 10 feet broad, 1 to 2 feet deep; bed rocky; current swift. Ample camp on left bank in paddy-field above village, or by clearing jungle below. Möng Noi consists of 17 houses (Shans) and a kyaung, there being accommodation for 600 men in the *taungyas* and on the left bank of the Mé Pai, Möng Noi itself being on the right bank of that river.

No. 33.

FROM MÖNG MAÖ TO MÖNG HENG (SIAM)—*continued.*

Authorities. Military.	Authorities. Civil.	Number and Names of Stages, Rivers and Streams.	Distances. Intermediate. M.	Distances. Intermediate. F.	Distances. Total. M.	Distances. Total. F.	Remarks.
Siam.		**7. Möng Heng** ... Mé Pai, Hwé Maw, and Hwé Méli.	13	0	74	0	The path throughout is good though narrow. Grass, bamboo leaves and water abundant, but no other supplies. For description of Möng Heng see Route No. 27. *N.B.*—A considerable part of this route lies in the beds of streams where the path is rocky and the jungle thick; on the ridges the jungle is open (chiefly pine and "*in*"), but the path is in many places steep and rocky. It is, however, passable throughout for all kinds of pack animals.

No. 34.

From MÖNGNGAW to MANTÔN viâ MANMÔK (MAMAUK).

BY LIEUT. G. W. T. PROWSE, 1ST DUKE OF CORNWALL'S LIGHT INFANTRY, ATTACHÉ, INTELLIGENCE BRANCH, MARCH AND APRIL 1891.

Authorities. Military.	Authorities. Civil.	Number and Names of Stages, Rivers and Streams.	Distances. Intermediate. M.	Distances. Intermediate. F.	Distances. Total. M.	Distances. Total. F.	Remarks.
G.O.C. Mandalay District.	Superintendent, Northern Shan States.	**1. Namtwé** ...	6	6	6	6	General direction north-west. Path leads back towards Kwégon (stage 5 on Route No. 48) for 1,100 yards, then strikes off north-west. Gradual ascent all the way, very steep for the last ½ mile, the path leading along the crest of a wooded spur. Good path 2 feet for the first 2 miles gradually widening to 4 feet and afterwards to 6 feet. Total ascent 2,500 feet. *Bridges.*—Five and three-quarter miles, longitudinal planks, 2 feet 6 inches by 10 feet; passable, but need not be used in dry weather, as there is a path 4 feet wide at the side. *Villages.*—Taumôn ⅜ mile east of path, 1 mile from camp; eight houses. Shan village and few Palaungs. Namtwé 6 miles; 27 houses; three zayáts equal 70 men. Kyaung being built. Small grassy camping ground for 100 men on hill side at edge of tea plantation at 6¾ miles, ¼ mile north-west of village. Water from small spring on side of hill. This is a Palé village. Highland paddy Rs. 1-4-0 per basket and a few tea plantations.
		2. Longlwoi ... Nampin and one small stream.	8	6	15	4	General direction north. Good path 10 feet wide, leads round side of wooded hill turning north, gradually descending at 1½ miles. At 2¼ miles passes deserted hamlet of Loitôk on west of path, thence round side of high wooded range to Longlom 5¼ miles, descending to camp below road on north side of village 5¾ miles. The last 3 miles of road average 4 feet wide. There is a good grassy camping ground passed at 2 miles, but water scarce. *Villages.*—Máhmo at ½ mile 1¼ miles south of road; 11 houses. Loitôk at 2¼ miles; deserted. Longlom at 5¼ miles; 21 houses and a small bamboo kyaung. This is a Palaung village. Small camping ground for 800 men, ⅜ mile north of village below the road. Water from small spring 100 yards below the camp through bamboo pipe. Supplies: tea and highland paddy. From Longlom the path leads east up the valley of Nampai stream gradually descending through alternate patches of tea plantations and jungle. Breadth average 6 feet. Crosses Nampai stream at 7¼

FROM MÖNGNGAW TO MANTÔN *viâ* MANMÔK (MAMAUK)—*continued.*

Authorities. Military.	Authorities. Civil.	Number and Names of Stages, Rivers and Streams.	Distances. Intermediate.	Distances. Total.	Remarks.
G.O.C. Mandalay District.	Superintendent, Northern Shan States.	**2. Longlwoi**—*cont.*			miles (flowing through paddy cultivation; steep stony banks 3 feet; breadth 20 feet and 1 foot deep; stony bottom; current flowing 3 miles per hour; water clear and good) and then ascends steeply by series of zigzags through occasional tea plantations to Longlwoi on wooded ridge $8\frac{3}{4}$ miles. Good road though steep ascent. *Bridges.*—At 600 yards wooden longitudinal planks, 4 feet by 20 feet, over small nullah; passable; need not be used in dry weather, as road by the side of it is sufficiently good. Broken wooden bridge 40 feet by 6 feet, over Nampai stream at $7\frac{1}{4}$ miles. Bamboo foot-bridge, 40 feet by 3 feet, at $8\frac{1}{2}$ miles. *Villages.*—Longlwoi at $8\frac{3}{4}$ miles; 13 houses. This is a Palé village. Bamboo kyaung and a zayát equal 70 men. Small and level camping ground at west end of the village for 150 men. Water from small spring 100 yards below. Paddy obtainable at Rs. 1-4-0 per basket.
		3. Pángsari ... Nam Pai.	M. F. **10 6**	M. F. 26 2	General direction north-east. Good road, averaging 10 feet in width, ascending all the way. This is the main road by which tea is sent down to Thíbaw State and to Mandalay. The trade road after passing Wengmul and Longlwoi turns south to Loiping, thence to Meungngaw, whence it debouches on the Thíbaw-Maymyo road at Kyaukmé. The road from Longlwoi to Wengmul passes through tea gardens and scrub jungle leading up the ridge on the east side of Nampai stream. *Bridges.*—At 1 mile 600 yards, longitudinal planks, 30 feet by 6 feet; two planks have given way, but the bridge is still passable for transport. *Villages.*—Loikwáng on west side of valley opposite Longlwoi; eight houses. This is a Palaung village. Wengmul 4 miles; 62 houses. Palaungs and a few Shans. Good road side camping ground at south end of the village for 200 men. Water from a small spring $\frac{1}{4}$ mile below camp. Paddy Rs. 2 per larger basket. This is a large and apparently prosperous village. Large wooden kyaung and zayát to accommodate 100 men; also three tea store-houses outside kyaung for 100 men. The people are Wuntôk Palaungs. Though the village stands on a high ridge the inhabitants state that they can obtain water all the year round from the springs on the hill side. A little highland paddy grown, but more tea than anything else. From here the general direction is north-north-east. Good road all the way. Leads round hill above village to group of pagodas, then turns north descending steeply on to a *col* which terminates the valley of the Nampai stream. Average breadth of road 10 feet. At 2 miles ascends wooded hill, the Mômeik road branching off to the north-west; follows along the wooded ridge to $4\frac{3}{4}$ miles when it begins to descend, still keeping along the ridge, ascending to Pángsari village at $10\frac{3}{4}$ miles. *Villages.*—Pankalao 1 mile north of the road at 8th mile. Pángsari $10\frac{3}{4}$ miles; 27 houses. Palé village. Good wooden kyaung and zayát for 70 men; also shed outside kyaung enclosure for 30 men. This village is also on the main tea route to Namsán; distant three very short bullock marches, two ordinary ones. A road also runs from here to Mômeik. Good camp for 100 men north of the village at foot of small hill on which the kyaung is built. Water from a well below the camp on north side.

FROM MÖNGNGAW TO MANTÔN *viâ* MANMÔK (MAMAUK)—*continued.*

Authorities. Military.	Authorities. Civil.	Number and Names of Stages, Rivers and Streams.	Distances. Intermediate.	Distances. Total.	Remarks.
			M. F.	M. F.	
G.O.C. Mandalay District.	Superintendent, Northern Shan States.	**4. Ngôksarit** ... Numerous small streams.	**11 0**	37 2	General direction north-west. This is a long and difficult march. The path leads back towards Wengmul to 3¼ miles, then turns north-west and descends the hill. The path is very steep, bad and narrow; 2 feet in breadth. At 3 miles the path becomes broader and descends again, passing beneath Pankalao village to stream at 4¾ miles. Ascends again steeply to Ngôkreo village 6¼ miles, thence descends again to stream at 7¼ miles, ascending from there to 9¼ miles by bad, narrow, and rocky path. From 9¼ miles easy descent into Ngôksarit at 11 miles. Road side camp ¼ mile north-west of village, small and narrow, for 50 to 70 men; good kyaung and zayáts for 100 men. Water from a stream 6 feet wide, 6 inches deep, ¼ mile south of the camp. *Bridges.*—Passed at 4¾ miles, wooden longitudinal planks, 18 feet by 6 feet; passable. *Villages.*—Pankalao 4 miles; 27 houses. Wooden kyaung and zayáts. Ngôkreo 6¼ miles; 12 houses. Very small bamboo kyaung. Ngôksarit 11 miles; 48 houses. These two latter are Palé villages. Ten or 11 short bullock marches from here to Mômeik town, three more to Môgôk.
		5. Manpát ... Nam Ôm and Nam Long.	**9 2**	46 4	General direction east. Path leads back through the village for ½ mile, then turns east and ascends; rocky and steep; average 18 inches. Begins to descend steeply 1½ miles to Nam Om stream at 4¼ miles, which it crosses by a wooden bridge. This stream is 25 feet wide, 2 feet deep, rocky bottom, with large boulders, current 3 miles an hour. Ascends steeply and then more gradually up the valley of Namlong stream by good path to camp at 7¼ miles. Good camping ground on grassy clearing for 100 men and another for 200 men 200 yards east of it. There is a wooden zayát for 15 men in good repair at both camping grounds. Water good and plentiful from Namlong stream and another which joins it here. *Bridges.*—At 4¼ miles over Namôm stream, 40 feet by 6 feet, wooden covered bridge; longitudinal planks; passable. At 7¼ miles, 35 feet by 6 feet, wooden covered bridge; longitudinal planks; passable. *Villages.*—At 6½ miles, temporary village of six to eight houses on hill side, above road on south side, used when the highland paddy is being harvested. Kángwuntôk 1½ miles from camp; 50 houses. Good wooden kyaung and zayáts equal 100 men; also rest-house equals 30 men; latter at the foot of the hill on which the kyaung is built. From here the path crosses Namlong stream by wooden bridge and ascends wooded hill in north direction; width 5 feet. Manpát, a Palaung village of 28 houses at 9¼ miles. *Bridges.*—Over Namlong stream at camp, wooden longitudinal planks, 60 feet by 6 feet, 15 feet above the stream. In good repair and passable for transport. From Manpát there is a good path north-west along crest of ridge to village of Hôkai 3½ miles. This is a Palé village. Small but good camping ground 100 yards south of the village for 100 men; also another for the same number ¼ mile south of the village lower down the hill. Paddy Rs. 1-8-0 per basket. Small bamboo kyaung and zayát for 40 men.

FROM MÖNGNGAW TO MANTÔN *viâ* MANMÔK (MAMAUK)—*continued.*

Authorities. Military.	Authorities. Civil.	Number and Names of Stages, Rivers and Streams.	Distances. Intermediate. M.	F.	Distances. Total. M.	F.	Remarks.
G.O.C. Mandalay District.	Superintendent, Northern Shan States.	**6. Pinglom** ...	6	4	53	0	General direction north-east. Steep ascent by good path to 2 miles where the path again descends through wood. Thence good road 6 feet wide over undulations to a Kachin village 5 miles, descending to Pinglom 6¾ miles. Camp for 50 men on road side at ¼ mile north of village. *Villages.*—Manklánglwi at 4 miles; 12 houses. Kachin village 5 miles; three houses. Pinglom at 6½ miles; 21 houses. The first and the last are Palaung villages. There is no camping ground available close to the village with the exception of the one above mentioned which is small and uneven. Water from springs on hill side at camp. Wooden kyaung and zayâts in village for 100 men. This village is within 3 to 4 hours' march of Namsán; good road; steep ascent and descent over the ridge of Loi Tángkyaw. No villages passed *en route*. Distance to Serám about 12 miles. There is a good road-side camping ground on the road to Serám and Namsán. Distance from Pinglom 1½ miles, but water scarce.
		7. Hôkun ... ... Namchong and small streams.	7	6	60	6	General direction north-east. Path descends steeply after leaving camp leading through the jungle to 2 miles where it ascends. The path, 1 foot to 18 inches in width, winding round side of hill with steep descent on right hand descends to Namchong stream at 3¼ miles, crossing by bridge (also fordable; 25 feet by 2 feet; large boulders; sandy bottom. Drop of 18 inches to bed of stream on Pinglom side; current flowing 3 miles per hour; steep, jungly banks 6 feet on the left bank; high hill on right), then ascends steep and difficult path to Tungpán village on ridge at 5¼ miles; 10 houses, Palaungs; small bamboo kyaung; thence descends steeply to a stream at 6½ miles, another steep and difficult ascent to Hôkun camp on south side of village, 7¾ miles. This route is very steep in many places, the path narrow, uneven, and impassable in wet weather. *Bridges.*—At 3¼ miles wooden bridge, rough transverse sticks, 5 feet by 30 feet, but passable for transport. Hôkun, 10 houses, Palaung; good camping for 150 men at Hôkun. The village was deserted a short time ago and has only lately been occupied by Palaungs from Namsán.
		8. Humung ... Namkao and one smaller stream.	6	4	67	2	General direction north. Path descends steeply to Namkao stream (6 feet wide, 1½ feet deep), crosses small stream by stone bridge at 1⅛ miles, ascends steeply at 1½ miles; path narrow; averaging 2 feet, thence good path gradually rising to 5 miles crossing the watershed of Namkao stream. Ascends steeply at 5 miles; path narrow and slippery in places to camp by road side at 6½ miles, ½ mile north of Humung village. The path would be difficult for transport in wet weather, but not impassable. At 1¾ miles the road to Namsán *viâ* Mámul strikes off to the south, distance about 12 miles. *Bridges.*—At ⅛ mile stone slab bridge 9 feet by 4 feet; passable. At 1⅛ miles stone slab bridge, 6 feet by 4 feet; passable. At 5½ miles wooden pole bridge; at present broken down; sufficient room at the side.

FROM MÖNGNGAW TO MANTÔN *viâ* MANMÔK (MAMAUK)—*continued.*

Authorities. Military.	Authorities. Civil.	Number and Names of Stages, Rivers and Streams.	Distances. Intermediate. M.	Distances. Intermediate. F.	Distances. Total. M.	Distances. Total. F.	Remarks.
G.O.C. Mandalay District.	Superintendent, Northern Shan States.	**8. Humung**—*cont.*					*Villages.*—Humung is a Palaung village of 12 houses. Good road-side camp at Humung for 150 men; water from spring 200 yards below. Paddy Rs. 1-8-0 per large basket. Small bamboo kyaurg and zayáts equal 70 men.
		9. Manmôk ... Namkong.	7	4	74	6	General direction north. Path descends to Kachin village of Manmaru (or Lower Humung) at ½ mile, three houses, thence along crest of ridge to Umlôk (or Manlök) at 1¾ miles, 14 houses, Kachin, through undulating jungle still following crest to 5 miles at which point it descends to 6¼ miles, thence turns east and descends to Manmôk on spur at 7 miles; camp on old pagoda platform. Path good all the way, varying from 10 feet to 2 feet in breadth. Road continues north along covered crest of hill to Mômeik, said by Kachins to be 3 days' march distant. Bridge below camp at Humcng over small spring, wooden longitudinal planks, 15 feet by 5 feet; passable. Upper Maumôk at 7 miles has 16 houses (Kachin), Lower Manmôk at 7½ miles has 31, also Kachin. Camping ground on old pagoda platform, the village having originally been Palaung. Room for 100 to 150 men. Water from hill-side springs at the village. Paddy Rs. 1-8-0 per large basket. The river Namkong, which flows below the village, is the boundary at this point, the hills opposite being Mômeik territory.
		10. Mantôn ...	10	0	84	6	About 10 miles in a due northerly direction by survey map, no report of this stage is forthcoming.

BRANCH I.

FROM HUMUNG (STAGE 8) TO NA-AW (MA-O).

BY LIEUT. G. W. T. PROWSE, 1ST DUKE OF CORNWALL'S LIGHT INFANTRY, ATTACHÉ, INTELLIGENCE BRANCH, MARCH AND APRIL 1891.

Authorities. Military.	Authorities. Civil.	Number and Names of Stages, Rivers and Streams.	Distances. Intermediate. M.	Distances. Intermediate. F.	Distances. Total. M.	Distances. Total. F.	Remarks.
G.O.C. Mandalay District.	Superintendent, Northern Shan States.	**1. Na-aw** ... ... Namkong.	6	2	87	0	General direction east. From Lower Humung, Kachin village, ½ mile north of Humung camp, the path runs east through the village and descends the hill to the Namkong valley. Good path all the way, average 2 feet broad with the exception of the last ½ mile which is very steep and slippery. Camp at the foot of the hill in paddy-fields on right bank of Namkong river. Ground for 500 to 600 men; good and level; water from river. *Villages.*—Lower Humung, Kachin village. At ½ mile Pángkhem, Kachin village, 3 miles; 14 houses. Na-aw 6½ miles; 12 houses; Palaung and Kachin on left bank of Namkong river. There are three Kachin houses in this village, the remainder being Palaung, but only one Kachin house is inhabited. Narrow path from this village to opposite side of valley leading to Hinpôk village and thence to Bawdwingyi. The Namkong river at camp is 40 feet wide, 18 inches deep; clear and good; stony bottom; current flowing 4 miles an hour; jungly hills on the left bank above Na-aw village, paddy-fields on right bank. Sometimes impassable owing to floods during the rainy season.

No. 35.

From MÖNGWI to MANTÔN viâ MÔNG-TÁT.

By Capt. R. B. SHAWE, December 1889 and January 1890.

Authorities. Military.	Authorities. Civil.	Number and Names of Stages, Rivers and Streams.	Distances. Intermediate. M.	F.	Distances. Total. M.	F.	Remarks.
G.O.C. Mandalay District.	Superintendent, Northern Shan States.	**1. Makwao** ... Namwi and several small streams.	11	0	11	0	The road traverses paddy-fields for the first 3 miles. At 1st mile the Namwi is forded; ford fair, bottom soft. At $2\frac{1}{2}$ miles village of Hôpáng is passed and shortly afterwards the hills are entered. At about the 8th mile Lawnaw is passed and Makwao is reached after about 11 miles' march. The track ascends considerably the last 7 miles. Makwao is a large Palaung village, well-to-do. Paddy and rice plentiful: houses large and in good repair to the number of about 40. Elevation 4,700 feet. The Mômeik-Theinni boundary runs through the middle of the village of Makwao.
		2. Nongpát ... Nammin and two small streams.	10	0	21	0	At the 4th mile the road passes through the village of Pángnim on the left bank of the Nammin. The road for Möngtát branches here, one going *viâ* Awlaw, Tinlwoi, and Na-un, the other as given further on. Nongpát is a Palaung village on a high hill, from whence a good view of the surrounding country is obtained. The camping ground is in some paddy-fields lower down. Paddy and grass procurable here. Just before reaching the camping ground, which is in the Thakkôk paddy-fields, the small Palaung village of Makkôk is passed through. Silver pheasants are common in the jungle here. The Mômeik border is crossed just before reaching Pángnim.
		3. Mani ... ... One small stream.	9	0	30	0	Road difficult for baggage animals. In places this road forms the boundary between Mômeik and the Theinni State. The track runs along hills, for the most part covered with forest. Mani is a small Kachin village. The camping ground is a little beyond the village and the supply of water scarce. The only staple procurable is, as usual, paddy.
		4. Manna ... ... Namyôk and two small streams.	8	0	38	0	The first 3 miles the descent is steep, then the track crosses a small stream and shortly afterwards passes through a Kachin village, after which the Shan village of Möngyôk on a small stream called the Namyôk is reached. The track leads through the Namyôk and across paddy-fields on its right bank. The last 3 miles are along a jungle track, which leaves the main bullock track on its left. Seven houses.

FROM MÖNGWI TO MANTÔN *viâ* MÖNG-TÁT—*continued.*

Authorities. Military.	Authorities. Civil.	Number and Names of Stages, Rivers and Streams.	Distances. Intermediate. M.	F.	Total. M.	F.	Remarks.
G.O.C. Mandalay District.	Superintendent, Northern Shan States.	**5. Möngtát** ... Namna, Nami, several boggy ravines, and two small streams.	7	0	45	0	Shortly after leaving Manna the track crosses the Namna. The ford slants considerably and should be marked before being crossed by troops unacquainted with the road. The track now traverses several marshy bits drained by two small streams. The road descends rapidly and the Nami is reached. The ford is fair, but the landing on Möngtát side is steep. Möngtát is some little distance from the right bank of the river on the Namtát, left bank. It has good paddy land and the usual Shan bazaar. Paddy procurable in any quantity. Here the road from Láshio *viâ* Möngyin joins in, *see* Route No. 13.
		6. Katlwi	12	0	57	0	*Vide* Route No. 13, Stages 4 to 6 inclusive.
		7. Manpát ...	8	0	65	0	
		8. Mantôn ...	9	0	74	0	

No. 36.

From MÖNGYAI (MAINGYÉ) to NAUNGMWON (Route No. 53, Northern Division) viâ HÔYA and HPÁSENG.

BY CAPT. A. C. YATE, 1ST BELOOCHEES, MARCH 1888.

Military	Civil	Stages	M.	F.	M.	F.	Remarks
G.O.C. Mandalay District.	Superintendent, Northern Shan States.	**1. Hôya** ... ... Namlong and Namkyushim by wooden bridges; also several other small streams and nullahs.	7	0	7	0	Direction north-west. The road is good. Some of the streams are bridged for pack animals and some of the narrower valleys are crossed on raised causeways. To make the road good and passable in all weathers all streams should be bridged and raised, roadways constructed across all the valleys. The country traversed is a succession of undulations, intersected by cultivated valleys, varying in breadth from $\frac{1}{8}$th mile to $\frac{1}{2}$ mile or more. There is very little jungle except on the distant ranges of hills. The following villages (all inhabited by Shans) are passed *en route*. At $1\frac{1}{2}$ miles Nákyem, $\frac{1}{2}$ mile to right and Kônkaw to left. At 2 miles Hôna-pyem to right. (Here the Namlong valley opens up to left, and that of the Namkyushim to right.) At $2\frac{3}{4}$ miles Kunim and at $3\frac{1}{4}$ Tai-aw, both to right. At 4 miles cross Namkyushim stream, which is the boundary between Möngyai and Hôya. At $4\frac{1}{4}$ miles Naláng, $\frac{1}{4}$ mile to left and Pyengnim, $\frac{3}{4}$ mile to right. At $4\frac{3}{4}$ miles Namkyushim, $\frac{1}{2}$ mile to right. At 5 miles Pôpa to right and Kônkaw to left. At $5\frac{1}{4}$ miles Nongwyen, $\frac{1}{4}$ mile to left,

FROM MÖNGYAI (MAINGYÉ) TO NAUNGMWON (ROUTE No. 53, NORTHERN DIVISION) *viâ* HÔYA AND HPÁSENG—*continued.*

Authorities.		Number and Names of Stages, Rivers and Streams.	Distances.		Remarks.
Military.	Civil.		Intermediate.	Total.	
G.O.C. Mandalay District.	Superintendent, Northern Shan States.	**1. Hôya**—*cont.*			and Nonglom, 1 mile to right. At $5\frac{1}{2}$ miles Nongmoleng, $\frac{3}{4}$ mile to left. At $5\frac{3}{4}$ miles cross Namlong stream (flows south and falls into Nampang *alias* Ben chaung). At 6 miles villages of Nonglom, Nongweng, and Mamwai, $\frac{1}{3}$ mile to right. At $6\frac{1}{2}$ miles Hôya kyaung to right. Here large tank, but water of indifferent quality. At 7 miles Hôya bazaar, 600 yards south-east of village of the same name, but also apparently called Nongtaw. South of Nongtaw is the best camping ground. Water good and plentiful from running stream. From the bazaar there is a road north to village of Manpong, 1 mile distant. There are several other villages grouped round the bazaar. The road to Mansang runs south-west from Nongtaw, distance about 7 miles (*see* Route No. 38, Branch I). The road to Möngsit diverges from that to Mansang just before reaching Kowa ($2\frac{1}{2}$ miles from Nongtaw), passes village of Namaklâng and near Mannong joins the Mansáng-Möngsit road, distance about 10 miles. This is the most direct road from Hôya to Möngsit. Between Hôya and the districts of Mansáng and Möngsit intervene the ranges of hills called Lwé Hánghung, Lwé-Sinu and Lwé-Palum. In the dry weather there is unlimited choice of camping ground between Möngyai and Hôya, in fact, wherever there is water. Fodder and fuel fairly plentiful, and supplies of rice and bullocks procurable.
			M. F.	M. F.	
		2. Namtong ... Namtongsen and Namtong streams.	**5 2**	12 2	Direction north-west. Road fairly good for pack transport. Crossing the streams is difficult. The streams all want bridging. Country traversed undulating and in places hilly, covered with spare tree jungle. Starting from Hôya bazaar, at $1\frac{1}{2}$ miles village of Kongkam 1 mile to right. At 2 miles foot-path to right (north) to Sarán. At $2\frac{1}{4}$ miles stream and small camping ground, called Pángtaw. At 3 miles the bullock road to Sarán diverges to right (north).* At $3\frac{1}{2}$ miles cross Namtongsen (flows north and falls into Namma near village of Hôpung, about a mile west or south-west of Tengun, on the Sarán road). Village of Mantongsen, $\frac{1}{2}$ mile up stream to left. At 4 miles village of Manlwésong, $\frac{1}{2}$ mile to left (south-west). At $4\frac{3}{4}$ miles cross Namtong stream. Valley all under rice cultivation. Descend valley along left bank of stream. Good camping ground hereabouts for a brigade. Water good and plentiful. Fodder and fuel abundant. (The Namtong flows north and falls into the Namma south of the Loi Yôt hill.) From Namtong there is a direct road to Sarán, meeting the Hôya-Sarán road at Kongnya bazaar. The direct roads from Namtong to Möngsit and Mansé diverge at points on the Namtong-Hpáseng road, *see* the next stage.

* *Note.*—From here to Sarán 9 to 10 miles. Road hilly but fairly good, passing villages of Kongnya at 3 miles and Tengun at $4\frac{1}{2}$ miles. Beyond Tengun the road crosses the Namma river six or seven times. From Sarán to Mansé is about 7 miles, passing village of Pángmöngneng at 2 miles. From Sarán to Kunka 7 miles. Road hilly but fairly good for pack transport. Sarán to Müngyaw three easy stages—(1) Nánáng about 11 miles, crossing Nampong river about 1 mile south of Nánáng; (2) cross Loi Patan to Mönghet; (3) to Möngyaw.

FROM MÖNGYAI (MAINGYÉ) TO NAUNGMWON (ROUTE NO. 53, NORTHERN DIVISION) *viâ* HÔYA AND HPÁSENG—*continued.*

Authorities. Military.	Authorities. Civil.	Number and Names of Stages, Rivers and Streams.	Distances. Intermediate. M. F.	Distances. Total. M. F.	Remarks.
G.O.C. Mandalay District.	Superintendent, Northern Shan States.	**3. Hpáseng** ... Several small streams.	9 6	22 0	Direction west-north-west. Road fairly good for pack transport. Country hilly and overgrown with tree jungle. Numerous clearings for cultivation. Streams and nullahs require bridging. At 1⅛ miles pass village of Mannatit, ⅛ mile to right. Inhabitants employed in iron-working and charcoal-burning. The iron is obtained from the surface soil and is of very inferior quality. At 2 miles Hinláp nullah (dry), the boundary between Hôya and Möngsit districts. At 2¼ miles small stream and camp called Pángsápiyé. Water and space for 500 men or more by clearing away jungle. From 3rd to 5th mile pass three or four villages (Kongsáng, Kongsám, Nahi, &c.), all lying to the left of the road at a distance of ½ to 1 mile. At 3½ miles cross bullock road leading direct from Möngsit *viâ* Tengun to Sarán. Just beyond this cross Namkoyôk stream. Good water and camp for 500 men. At 4¾ miles road to right (east) to Sarán, being the direct road from Hpáseng *viâ* Tengun (it does not go to Kongnya) to Sarán. At 5 miles cross Namkotung stream (which flows north-east and falls into Namma river). Camp here for a battalion. Water, fodder and fuel plentiful. At 6¾ miles road to right to Loi Ngum (½ mile) and then on to Mantawmaw. At 9¾ miles reach Hpáseng (*see* Route No. 15). Good camp and water.
		4. Nalwé ... ... Namhukyo stream and Namma river.	10 4	32 4	Direction north-west. Road fairly good for pack transport. Country traversed, undulating and rather hilly, covered with tree jungle. The road to Naungmwon branches off just to the north of the Hpáseng kyaung. At 1 mile cross Namhukyo stream by bridges. This stream at this point is the boundary between Thîbaw and the Möngsit district of Theinni. From this point to the Namma the boundary is a low range of hills stretching north and south between the Hpáseng-Násaileng and the Hpáseng-Namma roads. Thîbaw territory is confined to the left bank of the Namma river. At 2½ miles cross small nullah. At 4 miles path to right to Násaileng and to left to Kôngka (1 mile distant). At 5 miles cross small stream. Here good water and camp for 300 to 400 men. At 5½ miles path to left to Nakum (distant about 1½ miles and 2 to 3 miles south of Namma river). At 6 miles pass village of Nalôt to left. Good water from stream and camp in rice fields. At 7 miles path to left (south-west) to Nammaw, some 2 to 3 miles distant. At 7½ miles road to right to Kunpaw (½ mile). At 9 miles pass village and kyaung of Namma. Here resides a Hein, appointed from Thîbaw. The Nampong and Namma meet just north of the village at a place called Ta Tingtám. Here the Namma valley is broad, open and well cultivated. The crest of the low hills, some 2 to 3 miles east of Namma village, form the boundary between Thîbaw and Theinni.

FROM MÖNGYAI (MAINGYÉ) TO NAUNGMWON (ROUTE NO. 53, NORTHERN DIVISION) *viâ* HÔYA AND HPÁSENG—*continued.*

Authorities. Military.	Authorities. Civil.	Number and Names of Stages, Rivers and Streams.	Distances. Intermediate.	Distances. Total.	Remarks.
G.O.C. Mandalay District.	Superintendent, Northern Shan States.	**4. Nalwé**—*cont.*			Till only lately this neighbourhood has been quite deserted, all the villages seem new, and even the Hein and the inhabitants seem to be all strangers. From Namma kyaung the surrounding country as far as Loi Ling (east), Loi Patan (north-north-east), up the valley of the Nampong river to the hills towards Láshio (north) and Naungmwon (north-west), and for some miles down the valley of the Namma (south-west) is commanded. At 9¾ miles pass hamlets of Kunpán and Namák, and at 10¼ miles reach and ford Namma river. The village of Nalwé is on the right bank. Excellent camping ground of unlimited extent can be obtained anywhere hereabouts. Water, fuel and fodder abundant. From here there are roads to Manpyen (4 or 5 miles) and thence on to Mansé, Mönghet, and Láshio; also roads *viâ* Kennim and Pánghai to Pángkyem, Inai, Mansám, &c. There are a number of villages grouped round Namma and Nalwé, namely, Möngtôn, Nasaw, Kunpán, Nammák, Kônsa, Páuglé, &c., situated on the banks of the Namma and Nampong. In ordinary times supplies should be procurable here, such as bullocks, buffaloes, paddy, rice, vegetables, &c.
		5. Naungmwon ...	M. F. 12 2	M. F. 44 6	General direction north by west, namely, for 6 miles north-west till the Loi Wo range is crossed, then west for(?) miles and then south for(?) miles. Country traversed undulating and covered with tree and bamboo jungle. From Nokkut to Naungmwon (8¼ miles) there is no water on the road, though it can be obtained at one or two villages lying some distance off the road. Jungle in many places cleared for taungya cultivation. The district of Naungmwon, in point of impoverishment, is at present on a par with the rest of Theinni. In time of peace supplies of beef, rice, paddy, &c., can be obtained in fair quantities. At 1¼ miles cross road leading from Kônsa to Manpyen. At 1¾ miles Kônsa, ¼ mile to left. (There is an alternative road *viâ* Kônsa, Pánglé and Nongkwon to Naungmwon, but it presents no advantages.) At 2½ miles road to left to Nampuhong village, 2 miles distant. At 4 miles Nokkut (village) kyaung. Fair camping ground. Water enough for 300 or 400 men and for a similar number of animals. (At 3¾ miles cross path leading from Nokkut to Nampuhong.) From Nokkut there is a road direct to Manpyen, Mansé, &c. At 5¾ miles cross low neck of Loi Wo range. Ascent and descent steep; but short bamboo jungle here. At 7 and 8 miles paths left, foot-paths leading southward across Loi Wo. At 8½ miles village of Manlwékaw (or Pángkaw), about 1 mile to right of road. Here water procurable. At 10 miles village of Mannampok to right. At 10½ miles cross a road leading from Naungmwon village northward, probably to Kunim, Inai, Pángkyem, Láshio, &c. At 12¼ miles reach Naungmwon kyaung and bazaar. Good camp and water here. Village and Myoza's stockaded residence on high ground ¼ mile to the east.

No. 37.

From MÖNGYAI (MAINGYÉ) to NAWA.

By Capt. H. R. B. DONNE, Norfolk Regiment, January 1889.

Authorities.		Number and Names of Stages, Rivers and Streams.	Distances.				Remarks.
Military.	Civil.		Intermediate.		Total.		
			M.	F.	M.	F.	
G.O.C. Mandalay District.	Superintendent, Northern Shan States.	**1. Nawa**	9	4	...		General direction east. The path for this march, after leaving the level, is rough in several places; after crossing the disused paddy-fields it lies through jungle over a succession of short ascents and descents, the track gradually rising until the highest ridge is crossed at $8\frac{1}{8}$ miles, 4,000 feet above sea level, after which it descends for the rest of the march. Fifty ponies occupied $5\frac{1}{2}$ hours in going. It would be advisable if animals are taken to provide the advance party with some tools in order to make the route easier in places. At 500 yards path crosses small stream; water good. At $\frac{1}{8}$ mile another small stream is crossed; left bank rather slippery for animals. At $\frac{1}{4}$ mile path crosses small stream. At $1\frac{1}{4}$ miles the path descends at a gradient of 1 in 3 for 80 yards, where it is rough for animals, and then crosses stream. At 2 miles the path, after traversing short defile, descends to small stream. The ground is very soft and the opposite bank steep and difficult. At $2\frac{3}{8}$ miles the track is rough for 80 yards of descent. At $3\frac{1}{2}$ miles path crosses stream near bank, steep, 18 feet wide, 8 inches deep, $2\frac{1}{2}$ miles per hour; disused paddy-fields on left bank, sufficient to encamp 400 men in dry weather. The path now runs along the level for 120 yards, after which is a stiff ascent. At 5 miles there is a steep and rough ascent for 150 yards. At $6\frac{1}{4}$ miles path crosses small stream; water good; further, banks steep and slippery. At $6\frac{3}{4}$ miles ruined shed on left and burnt remains of three huts on right. At 7 miles well on left; water good; ground sufficient to camp 200. Shortly after commencing its final descent the track follows the course of a small stream, which it crosses and recrosses six times. At 9 miles paddy-fields on right, sufficient to camp 500 men. At $9\frac{1}{2}$ miles halting place is 200 yards to the left; just above some paddy-fields good camping ground, sufficient for 500 men, not including paddy-fields. Water close by from stream and good. The village of Nawa, lately burnt, lay 400 yards further east on the right side of the Nam Ha valley.

No. 38.

From MÖNGYAI (MAINGYÉ) to TÁNGYÁN (Route No. 17) viâ HÔYA and MÖNGPÁT.

By Capt. H. R. B. DONNE, Norfolk Regiment, January 1889.

G.O.C. Mandalay District.	Superintendent, Northern Shan States.	**1. Hôya** ...	7	0	7	0	*See* Route No. 36, Stage 1.
		2. Möngpát ...	8	2	15	2	General direction east. Path at first runs through open ground and disused paddy-fields until at $1\frac{1}{2}$ miles it gradually enters jungle and at $3\frac{1}{2}$ miles ascends rapidly until the highest

FROM MÖNGYAI (MAINGYÉ) TO TÁNGYÁN (ROUTE No. 17) *viâ* HÔYA AND MÖNGPÁT—*continued.*

Authorities. Military.	Authorities. Civil.	Number and Names of Stages, Rivers and Streams.	Distances. Intermediate.	Distances. Total.	Remarks.
G.O.C. Mandalay District.	Superintendent, Northern Shan States.	**2. Möngpát**—*cont.*			point is reached at $4\frac{3}{8}$ miles; the path then descends until it touches a stream at 7 miles, the rest of the way being fairly level over open ground. At $\frac{3}{8}$ mile path crosses small stream, ruins of bridge on left, single plank for foot-passengers, animals cross to right where the ascent up opposite bank is easy. At $\frac{7}{8}$ mile small wooden bridge over soft bit of ground at present awkward for animals, who have to make a detour to the left, leaving the direct route when at 200 yards from the bridge and striking it again $\frac{1}{4}$ mile on the other side. At $1\frac{3}{8}$ miles path crosses paddy-fields sufficient to encamp 800 men in dry weather. At $2\frac{1}{8}$ miles path traverses defile and swampy ground for 60 yards, a little rough for animals. At $2\frac{1}{4}$ miles path crosses small stream; water good; paddy-fields on left. The track follows the course of this stream, crossing and recrossing it several times as it winds among the hills. At $3\frac{5}{8}$ miles the path commences an abrupt ascent at a gradient of 1 in 3 and is rough and difficult for animals for 160 yards. At $4\frac{1}{4}$ miles another steep bit of ascent for 50 yards. At $6\frac{1}{8}$ miles path crosses small stream, water good. From 7 miles the route lies along the right bank of a stream, which it crosses at $7\frac{1}{4}$ miles. At $7\frac{3}{8}$ miles another stream is crossed by ford 8 yards wide, 1 foot 3 inches deep, $2\frac{1}{2}$ miles per hour, bottom hard, water good. At $7\frac{1}{2}$ miles path crosses another stream similar to the above. At $7\frac{3}{4}$ miles track strikes small stream. At $8\frac{1}{4}$ miles camping ground at cluster of small pagodas sufficient to encamp 400 men. A kyaung lies 200 yards south-east of pagodas, 36 by 36 yards; no zayáts. Water good from small stream close by. The village of Möngpát, said to have contained 35 houses, has been burnt.
		3. Náhuk (6,100 feet). Nampán.	M. F. **10 2**	M. F. ...	General direction east. The path is fairly level and good the whole way and lies through open ground. At 190 yards from camping ground at pagodas the path crosses a covered wooden pile bridge, 48 yards long, 5 feet wide, over small stream, passable for animals. At $\frac{1}{8}$ mile bit of swampy ground is crossed by single planks as foot-bridge; animals cross to the right. At $1\frac{1}{8}$ miles the remains of village of Man Lwoi (lately burnt) on the left. At $1\frac{1}{2}$ miles small stream, water good. At $1\frac{3}{4}$ miles jungle on left for $\frac{1}{4}$ mile. At $2\frac{3}{8}$ miles path crosses stream by ford 10 yards wide, 1 foot deep, 2 miles per hour, and then lies through long grass. At $3\frac{3}{8}$ miles small deserted village consisting of seven huts at 100 yards on the right. At $3\frac{5}{8}$ miles small stream crossed by wooden bridge, passable for animals. At $4\frac{1}{4}$, $4\frac{3}{8}$ and $4\frac{7}{8}$ miles track crosses small streams; water good. At 5 miles, small kyaung, 17 by 6 yards, uninhabited, on the left deserted village, name not known, containing eight houses, $\frac{1}{4}$ mile west-north-west of kyaung. At $5\frac{3}{4}$ miles track crosses small stream; water good. At $6\frac{3}{4}$ miles two small springs immediately on left; water good, but limited supply. At 7 miles site of the village of Khön recently burnt, formerly consisting of 16 huts, surrounded by bamboos. At $7\frac{1}{8}$ miles path crosses stream by ford 15 yards wide, 1 foot 6 inches deep, $1\frac{1}{2}$ miles per hour. This stream flows into the Nampán 100 yards further, where the path crosses it by

No. 38.

From MÖNGYAI (MAINGYÉ) to TÁNGYÁN (Route No. 17) *viâ* HÔYA and MÖNGPÂT—*continued*.

Authorities. Military.	Authorities. Civil.	Number and Names of Stages, Rivers and Streams.	Distances. Intermediate.	Distances. Total.	Remarks.
G.O.C. Mandalay District.	Superintendent, Northern Shan States.	**3. Náhuk (6,100 feet)**—*cont.*			fort 40 yards wide, 2 feet 3 inches deep, $2\frac{1}{2}$ miles per hour. There are one or two small dug-outs used by native fishermen about 12 feet long, 18 inches wide. At $7\frac{1}{8}$ miles path commences to ascend, leading over grass covered undulations (steepest gradient 1 in 6) and gradually rising to the end of march. At $9\frac{3}{8}$ miles pass crosses small stream. At $9\frac{1}{2}$ miles site of bazaar recently burnt on the right. At $10\frac{1}{4}$ miles camping ground at kyaung (30 by 30 yards) and cluster of pagodas in bamboo clump. Space to camp 600 men in kyaung enclosure and 2,000 outside. Water good from stream close by. The sight of the burnt village of Náhuk is $\frac{1}{4}$ mile to south-west of kyaung and the Nampán flows at 800 yards to the south. From Náhuk there is a good road to Möngkyeng through open undulating country, rice and cotton cultivation, the distance is said to be about 15 miles, and the villages of Nongsaw, Loisáng and Námka are on or close to the road.
		4. Tángyán ... Nam Hong.	M. F. **10 2**	M. F. 20 4	Direction east. Path generally level and good throughout; the only part of this march at all difficult for transport animals was at 3 miles in crossing a small stream, but this was rendered easy by digging away some of the near bank. After descending for 300 yards path crosses small stream; water good; 50 yards further is a spring of good water on the left. The track then ascends through short jungle for 1,000 yards, during which the steepest gradient in the march is met with 1 in 6. At 1 mile the country is open. At 3 miles track strikes above-mentioned stream; animals cross to the left of foot-bridge. At $4\frac{1}{2}$ miles path crosses; small stream; water good. Animals cross to the right, where it opens out into a small sheet of water 10 yards across, 1 foot deep. At $5\frac{3}{4}$ miles track descends through jungle for 300 yards, after which it lies across undulating country covered with burnt grass with occasionally a few trees until the halting place is reached. At $6\frac{1}{4}$ and $7\frac{1}{2}$ miles small streams crossed by wooden bridges; available for animals. At $10\frac{1}{2}$ miles large banyan tree, good camping ground for 1,000 men. Water good from *jheel* close by. Three-quarters of a mile beyond camping ground the path crosses the Nam Hông by bamboo foot-bridge; transport animals cross by ford on left 10 yards wide, 1 foot 8 inches deep, $2\frac{1}{2}$ miles per hour. Water good, bottom hard, banks high. The site of Tangyan village, which has recently been burnt, is $\frac{1}{4}$ mile further east of stream. The kyaung, 60 by 34 yards, is situated $\frac{3}{4}$ mile south-east of this ford; there is one zayát, accommodation for 20 men. Small group of pagodas surrounded by a 3-feet brick wall close to kyaung. This enclosure is about 60 yards across in an irregular form; good camping ground here for 600 men. Duck and teal on above-mentioned *jheel*. For route hence to Tun-hông, *see* No. 17, and to Möngma, *see* No. 60.

FROM MÖNGYAI (MAINGYÉ) TO TÁNGYÁN (ROUTE NO. 18) *viâ* HÔYA AND MÖNGPÁT—*continued.*

BRANCH I.

FROM HÔYA (STAGE 1) TO MANSÁNG (ROUTE NO. 15, ALTERNATIVE I).

BY CAPT. H. R. B. DONNE, NORFOLK REGIMENT, JANUARY 1889.

Authorities.		Number and Names of Stages, Rivers and Streams.	Distances.		Remarks.
Military.	Civil.		Intermediate.	Total.	
G.O.C. Mandalay District.	Superintendent, Northern Shan States.	**1. Mansáng** ...	M. F. **7 6**	M. F. 7 6	General direction south-west. The path is generally level and good throughout, commencing with a very gradual ascent for the first 3½ miles, after which it descends at a similar gradient for the rest of the way. The steepest part is 12°, but this only lasts for 100 yards just before highest point is reached. The track passes to the right of the conspicuous conical shaped hill situate in almost a direct line between Hôya and Mansáng. For the first 1½ miles the route lies over grass covered ground and then enters thin low jungle, which gradually increases in density, the country becoming more open for the last 1½ miles. At ⅛ mile duck jheel on right, 300 by 150 yards, fed by small stream. At ½ mile pass Hôya bazaar on left and two zayáts (accommodation 30 men) on right, 100 yards further wooden bridge in bad repair over dry nullah. At 1 mile village of Hôya is 150 yards on right. At 1⅛ miles path crosses small stream by wooden bridge 40 by 5 feet, passable for animals, some planks are loose At 1⅞ miles small village at 100 yards on left, five huts. At 2⅜ miles two huts among bamboos on left. At 2¾ miles cross small stream by single plank; animals go round to right. At 3⅜ miles small stream crossed by plank, animals to left. Paddy-fields to right and left. Encampment for 500 men in dry weather. Another small stream 50 yards further. Water in both good. At 3¾ miles cross swampy bit of ground by single planks; animals to left. At 4⅝ miles a village of 10 huts at 600 yards on hill to right. At 6 miles village of Kônké, 18 huts. At 6¾ miles kyaung with pagodas at ½ mile on right, and village of Nankán at ¾ mile on left containing 23 houses. At 6⅞ miles path left rear of above village. Track at this point crosses stream (high banks) by wooden bridge; animals cross to right. Good camping ground for 2,000 men. At 7⅜ miles three ruined pagodas on right. At 7⅝ miles Mansáng bazaar on left. At 7¾ miles Mansáng kyaung.

No. 39.

From MÖNGYAW to MÖNGKYENG *viâ* MÖNGMA.

BY CAPT. A. C. YATE, 1ST BELOOCHEES, FEBRUARY 1888.

Military	Civil	Stages	Intermediate	Total	Remarks
G.O.C. Mandalay District.	Superintendent, Northern Shan States.	**1. Pángnáng (about 5,000 feet).** Namyán and Nammanmák.	**7 0**	7 0	Road fairly good for pack transport Level for first 1½ miles, then a steady and often steep ascent for 4 miles. Last 1½ miles level. The surrounding country is open and free from jungle, much of it being under cultivation. Rice, opium and sugar-cane. The approaches to the streams that are crossed *en route* are, as usual, bad, and require ramping. Bridges can easily be laid across any of

FROM MÖNGYAW TO MÖNGKYENG *viâ* MÖNGMA—*continued.*

Authorities.		Number and Names of Stages, Rivers and Streams.	Distances.		Remarks.
Military.	Civil.		Inter-mediate.	Total.	
G.O.C. Mandalay District.	Superintendent, Northern Shan States.	**1. Pángnáng (about 5,000 feet)**—*cont.*			these streams. The road issuing from Möngyaw village leaves the Namyán stream to the left. At $1\frac{1}{2}$ miles pass the two villages and kyaung of Nanwat on the right, to the south of which lie the villages of Nyaungswé and Kyushim. All these villages lie in the midst of groves of bamboos. At $1\frac{7}{8}$ miles road to left to Manmák (about 15 miles). The road then ascends the Lwésák* range (the hills to the right or south-west are known as Lwéwenglek). At $2\frac{1}{2}$ miles road to right to Nyaungswé (1 mile). At 4 miles path to right to Pánsápyé (Palaung village), $\frac{1}{2}$ mile distant. To the left or east, at the foot of the Lwésák peak, lies a village called Mankyé (Chinese-Shan village), the inhabitants being Shan-Tayôks. The Palaung and Shan-Tayôk villages here all cultivate opium, which sells in Möngyaw at Rs. 8 to Rs. 10 for a viss=$3\frac{1}{2}$ lb. At 5 miles Palaung village of Mansák (30 houses), $\frac{1}{2}$ mile to left of road. There are several cross-roads from Mansák to Pánsápyé. At $5\frac{1}{2}$ miles cross a swampy bit of ground by stone causeway and wooden bridge. Good camping ground and water here. At $6\frac{1}{4}$ miles cross Nammanmák, small Shan-Tayôk settlement to left of road. At 7 miles again cross Nammanmák. Good camping ground on left bank. Water good and abundant. Fuel and grass not very plentiful. This would probably be a healthy site for a cantonment. Shan-Tayôk settlement of Pángkyeng, five houses, $\frac{1}{3}$ mile to west of Pánguáng camping ground.
		2. Pángung .. Nampôn river and Namsin stream.	M. F. **15 0**	M. F. 22 0	*Note.*—This stage is too long for any but a small party with a short baggage. To march from Möngyaw to Nángyun on the banks of the Nampôn is $15\frac{1}{2}$ miles; also too long a march for a large column. Between Pángnáng and Nángyun there is no place suitable for a camp and next to no water. The best stages to make from Möngyaw to Möngma seem to be (1) Pángnáng, (2) Phásö on the Namsin stream, (3) Möngma. The road throughout compared with some other roads in the Shan States is a good one; but there are swampy bits on it and very steep ascents and descents that cause both delay and discomfiture to pack transport. The road runs for first 4 miles south, then for $4\frac{1}{2}$ miles south-west, then for $6\frac{1}{2}$ miles south-east. This circuitous route is adopted evidently to avoid the valley of the Nampôn and the Loi Wan range, both of which intervene in the direct line from Pángnáng to Möngma. The route mostly traverses an undulating or hilly country covered with trees and grass jungle, with here and there narrow and rough defiles. The descent from the crest of the Loi Wenglek to the valley of the Nampôn is long (7 miles) and in places difficult. The valley of the Nampôn (9th and 10th miles), which is about $\frac{1}{4}$ mile broad and in or near which the villages of Nátong, Nángyun, and Phásö are situated, is all cultivated with rice, tobacco and vegetables. From Pángnáng ascent for $1\frac{1}{2}$ miles to crest of Loi Wenglek, height about 5,500 feet. Thence descend for $1\frac{1}{2}$ miles into Péngwéhin valley (formerly village there). Camping ground and spring of water $\frac{1}{2}$ mile or more to left of road. At $3\frac{1}{2}$ miles road to left (east), across Pángwéhim valley, leading to Manmák (distant 10 or 12 miles). At 4 miles enter thick jungle and rocky gorge. Road difficult. At 5 miles emerge into cultivated clearing between the hills.

* Lwé is the Burmanized form of the Shan word Loi = hill.

FROM MÖNGYAW TO MÖNGKYENG *viâ* MÖNGMA—*continued.*

Authorities.		Number and Names of Stages, Rivers and Streams.	Distances.		Remarks.
Military.	Civil.		Intermediate.	Total.	
G.O.C. Mandalay District.	Superintendent, Northern Shan States.	**2. Pángung**—*cont.*			Water here from tiny spring, enough for 50 men. Camp in fields good. This place is called Namsángsôk. At $5\frac{1}{8}$ miles path to left to Pángngwé, Palaung village (six houses), 1 mile distant. At $6\frac{3}{4}$ miles another path to left (north) to the same village, which is situated on a spur of the Loi Wenglek range. At $7\frac{1}{4}$ miles good stream of water (called Nampángngwé), but no place for a camp unless the jungle is cleared. At $8\frac{1}{4}$ miles path to right to first village of Nátong (distant about 1 mile, five houses, Shans), and thence on over the crest of the low hills to the south-west to Nánúng (Lantu) and Mansé. At $8\frac{1}{8}$ miles cross the Nampôn river (40 feet broad, $1\frac{1}{2}$ feet deep) by easy ford and reach village of Nángyun (Shans, 10 houses; good camp in fields; water, fuel and grass abundant). Up to this point the road has been rocky, steep and through jungle. For the next 2 miles, $8\frac{1}{2}$ to $10\frac{1}{2}$, it follows the foot of the Loi Waw range, which bounds the Nampôn valley on the north. At 1 mile south of Nángyun and south of the Nampôn is the second village of Nátong (seven or eight houses). At $10\frac{1}{4}$ miles pass Shan village of Phásö (20 houses; good camp; water, fodder and fuel). At $10\frac{1}{2}$ miles the road turns eastward leaving the valley of the Nampôn (which river here turns south and subsequently flows westward to Mansé, and thence south or south-west to the Namma river). From here to Pángung, the road is throughout through tree and grass jungle. Here and there steep gradients and swampy bits of ground hinder transport. At $12\frac{1}{3}$ miles cross Namsin stream (15 feet broad, 1 foot deep). (The Namsin is probably the boundary between the Lantu and Möngma districts.) From 13th to 14th mile several roads to right (south) to Limpôk (Shan village, distant about $\frac{1}{2}$ mile), and thence on to Mankát and Möngpát. Half-a-mile along road to Möngpát the road to Nanang (Lantu) and Mansé branches off to the east, *see* Route No. 59. The hamlet of Pángung is reached at 15 miles, where there is a small camping ground in fields. Good water, fodder and fuel.
		3. Möngma ... Namhai and several other small streams.	M. F. **7 0**	M. F. 29 0	Road very good throughout. Traverses at first undulating country overgrown with thin tree jungle, and as Möngma is approached, open undulating downs. The beds of the streams crossed are firm and the approaches to them fairly easy. No swampy ground. Near the village the jungle is cleared for cultivation (rice, opium, cotton, tobacco, mustard, &c.). At 1 mile pass spring of water. At $1\frac{1}{2}$ miles Shan village of Pátáng (30 houses), $\frac{1}{4}$ mile to right of road. There too, path branches off north-west to the Kachin villages of Hôhai and Loi Waw, both situated on the lower spurs of the Loi Waw range, and $1\frac{1}{2}$ to 2 miles north of the village of Makmu. To the left at the southern foot of the Loi Waw range the Namtwé stream flows east into the Nampôn. At $4\frac{1}{4}$ miles Shan village of West Makmu to left of road. From here road north to Hôhai and Manlwéwaw, north-west to Manmák, over the lower spurs of the Loi Waw (distance about 15 miles), south by west to Kônkut ($3\frac{1}{2}$ daings), where it joins the Limpôk-Möngpát road. At $4\frac{5}{8}$ miles cross small stream flowing south into Nampáng, which falls into Salween (the watershed between the Salween and Irrawaddy is crossed near Pátáng), just beyond this path to left to village of East Makmu. At $5\frac{7}{8}$ miles cross Namhai (comes down from Hôhai) stream also flowing into Nampáng. At

FROM MÖNGYAW TO MÖNGKYENG *viâ* MÖNGMA—*continued.*

Authorities.		Number and Names of Stages, Rivers and Streams.	Distances.		Remarks.
Military.	Civil.		Intermediate.	Total.	
G.O.C. Mandalay District.	Superintendent, Northern Shan States.	**3. Möngma**—*cont.*			7 miles reach Möngma, village of 40 or 50 houses. Kyaung, pagoda, &c. Myoza of district lives here. Bazaar. Rice, tobacco, opium, mustard, vegetables, fruits, &c., cultivated here. The soil of this neighbourhood does not seem to be very productive, any how not good for rice cultivation. There is also a great lack of water from springs and streams. Cultivation depends mainly on the rainfall. Dry crops should do best here. The range east of Möngma is Lwékyo, the Lwémaw lying east by south near the Salween, and the Lwéling south-west. There is very little forest growth near Möngma, and the grass is of poor quality. The Nampáng river flows on the east and south sides of the village; width about 20 feet and 1½ feet deep. From Möngma there are roads north *viâ* Manmák to Möngkyet; three stages, viz., Pánglôn 12 miles, Manmák 10, and Möngkyet 8 miles—total 30 miles. Hilly road all the way, crossing Nam Páng river and Lwéwaw range of hills in the first stage; east to Ta Möngnong ferry on the Salween (meeting the road from Möngkyeng to the Salween at Pápáng); south-south-east to Möngkyeng; south-south-west to Mankát and Möngpat (also to Tángyán, Hôya, Möngyai, &c.), and west to Lantu and Mansé. The road to Möngkyet follows the Nampáng valley for 3 miles to the foot of the Lwéwan hills. This valley is fertile, well irrigated, and highly cultivated. There are four villages in it, Kongkyông, Tôngkyi, Namho, and Manpáng.
		4. Nalu * ... Nampáng and Namsôk, large streams, and other smaller streams.	M. F. **9 6**	M. F. 38 6	Direction south. Road good. The bullock road goes along the right bank of the Nampáng from the village of Mannamsôk to Nalu. There is also a nearer road on the left bank, but it is apt to be impassable for pack animals. The country traversed is bare and undulating, well watered by numerous streams and intersected by fertile valleys. The Lwékyo range to the east is inhabited by Palaungs. At 2 miles pass villages of East and West Namôn, both burnt. The Kunka pagoda east from here is a good landmark; it is situated on a spur of the Lwéling just above the village of Kunka on the road from Mankát to Mansé. At 2¼ miles cross Namnamôn stream and its cultivated valley. At 3½ miles Nakai to left. At 3¾ miles cross Namnakák stream. At 4 miles village of Nakák, ½ mile to left, and beyond it in the hills a Palaung village. At 4¼ miles path to right to Sômwôn village, 1 mile distant, on right bank of Nampáng. At 4¾ miles another path to right to Sômwôn and one to left to Hôna. At 4⅞ miles cross Nam Hôna stream. At 5 miles Nampaklun village and path to right (west) to villages of Namkham (2 miles) and Savé (4 miles). At 7½ miles ford Namsôk stream (50 feet broad by 2 feet deep). The village is situated on both banks. From here the country traversed is hilly and overgrown with jungle. The Namsôk falls into the Nampáng just below the village of Namsôk. Nalu has been a large village but, like all the other villages of the Möngma and Möngkyeng districts, has been recently attacked and burnt. The Wélán pagoda stands on a hill 2 miles south of Nalu. Good camping ground and abundant water. Grass and fuel for a large force. **From** here there is a road to Tángyán, *see* Route No. 60.

* Capt. Donne, in Route No. 60, makes the distance 11½ miles.

FROM MÖNGYAW TO MÖNGKYENG *via* MÖNGMA—*continued.*

<table>
<tr><th colspan="2">Authorities.</th><th rowspan="2">Number and Names of Stages, Rivers and Streams.</th><th colspan="2">Distances.</th><th rowspan="2">Remarks.</th></tr>
<tr><th>Military.</th><th>Civil.</th><th>Intermediate.</th><th>Total.</th></tr>
<tr><td>G.O.C. Mandalay District.</td><td>Superintendent, Northern Shan States.</td><td>5. Möngkyeng ...
Nammyeng and several small streams.</td><td>M. F.
10 4</td><td>M. F.
49 2</td><td>Road good for any pack transport. Direction east. For first 4 miles crosses Loi Miyin (height above sea level 4,000 to 5,000 feet) overgrown with pine, fir and oak. The kyaungs in this neighbourhood are built of this wood. From the summit of the pass over the Loi Miyin, the surrounding country is commanded west to the Loi Ling, north-west to the Loi Patan and Loi Vyenglek, north to the Loi Waw, north-east to the Loi Kyo and Loi Maw, east to the hill ranges near the Salween, south to the Loi Kyé in the independent State of Mönglön, and south or south-west to the Loi Páng range, to the south or south-west of which is the Müngyai district. South of the Loi Páng is seen the hill called Loi Nalôn or Loi Namlok. South of the Loi Páng is the Tángyán, and north of it the Möngkyeng district. The Nampáng flows north of the Loi Páng and then turning south or south-east falls into the Salween below Möngshu. Crossing the Loi Miyin range the road descends into the Möngkyeng valley. Gradient steep in some places. At 4 miles cross Namsamwán stream. At 4¼ miles path to left to old Palaung village of Kôhin, and thence on over the Loi Kyo to Nakat and Möngma. At 4⅓ miles pass village of Mantáklet or Kôkmu. Here path to right to Shan village of Kôtaung, 2 miles off. At 5¾ miles Shan village, or collection of hamlets called Nahung, and from there path southwards to Kôtaung. At 6¼ miles path to right to village of Lwésáng. The country here is open and undulating, overgrown with thin tree jungle. Numerous streams. Valleys cultivated. At 7½ miles village of Tingtam. At 8½ miles cross Nammyeng river (which flows into the Nampáng) by wooden bridge. From here path to left to Shan village of Mansángnu, and to right to Nongsaw (both 1 mile distant). At 9 miles another path to right to Nongsaw and left to Mansalek. At 9¼ miles pass Möngkyeng bazaar. At 10½ miles reach Möngkyeng, formerly large place, but now entirely destroyed except the kyaung. North-east of Möngkyeng, on the banks of the Nammyeng, the following villages lie :—Hôten, Hômyeng, Nongpakyeng, Tongkun, Nanyu. To the east and north-east, in the valley of the Namsutai stream, are the villages of Pánghung, Kôngpaw, Tôngpyet, Pángkyeng and Pángwa, all within a radius of 3½ miles from Möngkyeng village. Camping ground and water for force of any size at Möngkyeng. Grass and fuel not very plentiful. From here roads to the Möngnong, Kongpun, Namôn, and Hátseng ferries over the Salween, to Mönglön, Nalao, Tángyán, Möngpát, Mankát, Hôya, Möngyai, &c.</td></tr>
</table>

BRANCH I.

FROM MÖNGMA (STAGE 3) TO MÖNGPÂT.

BY CAPT. DONNE, JANUARY 1889, LIEUT. DALY, MARCH 1889.

<table>
<tr><td>G.O.C. Mandalay District.</td><td>Superintendent, Northern Shan States.</td><td>1. Makhám ...
Nam Ti, Nam Yauk, and Nam Hön.</td><td>17 0</td><td>17 0</td><td>General direction south-south-west. The path throughout this march is easy. For the first 13⅞ miles the route is generally level and open, leading over gentle undulations covered with grass. At 11 miles the track passes through scattered trees, which gradually becomes denser, and</td></tr>
</table>

From MÖNGYAW to MÖNGKYENG *viâ* MÖNGMA—*continued.*

BRANCH I—*continued.*

Authorities. Military.	Authorities. Civil.	Number and Names of Stages, Rivers and Streams.	Distances. Intermediate.	Distances. Total.	Remarks.
G.O.C. Mandalay District.	Superintendent, Northern Shan States.	**1. Makhám**—*cont.*			continues thus through jungle to the end. At 13⅝ miles the first rise of any importance begins and the path ascends until the highest point, 400 feet above the Nam Hön, is passed at 14⅛; from this ridge there is a gradual descent to the village of Makhám. Sites for camps in dry weather close to the banks of most of the streams. At ½ mile path crosses small stream; steep rise on further side for 10 yards, but not difficult. At 1⅛ miles small stream; water good. At 2⅛ miles about 5 acres of paddy on the right. At 3⅛ miles path crosses small stream. At 4 miles the Nam Ti is crossed by bamboo foot-bridge; animals cross to the right; deepest part 1 foot 5 inches. At 7⅜ miles small stream; water good; ground soft near it. At 3¼ miles another small stream is crossed; 100 yards further small pagoda on left at 150 yards, and *nát* house under trees 100 yards on right. At 8⅜ miles the Namyauk is crossed by ford (small stream). At 9⅛ miles path crosses a stream three times in 200 yards. At 10⅜ miles the village of Mannông is about 1,200 yards on the left, containing about 14 huts, and the village Hôna to the right front about ½ mile up the valley. At 11⅝ miles small stream. At 11½ miles a path leads off to the right front to village of Kôngkut, 7 miles distant. At 12¾ miles the Nam Hön is crossed by single plank; animals cross to the right by ford 8 yards wide, 1 foot 8 inches deep, 2¾ miles per hour, bottom hard. At 12⅝, 13⅜ and 13 miles small streams are crossed. At the last point two small streams are crossed close together; ground soft and would be difficult in wet weather. At 13⅝, 14¾, 15¼, and 15⅝ miles small streams. At 17 miles deserted village of Makhám; 13 houses, one kyaung (20 by 20 yards), uninhabited. Good ground for camp for 1,000 men close to kyaung. Two small streams at 200 and 400 yards to south-west flowing through paddy-fields; water good.
		2. Möngpát ...	M. 8 F. 1	M. 25 F. 1	General direction south-west. The path is good and easy throughout, running across some of the lower spurs of Lwé Ling (Loi Lin). At 3 miles the path strikes the main track from Mankát to Möngpát. At 3⅝ miles the village of Naheng is passed, containing 12 houses, one pôngyi kyaung, and zayát (Mankát circle). At 4½ miles the villages of Kunwôn and Namkát are visible about a mile distant to the west under Lwé Ling. At 5 miles pass through the village of Kinka (Mankát circle) containing about half-a-dozen huts. At 5¾ miles path crosses the Nampôn, which forms the boundary between the Möngpát and Mankát circles; ford 15 yards across, low banks, 1 foot deep. At 6 miles Mansai village; six houses, one ruinous kyaung built of pine wood. Just at the foot of the hill on which Mansai is situated is a branch of the Nampôn, 10 yards wide, 2 feet deep at ford. There is a large single plank across this stream and, if a similar plank were laid, it would be passable for animals: both streams unfordable when in flood. The valley of the Nampôn is ½ mile in width and under paddy cultivation; this part of the road might be difficult in rainy weather. After Mansai the path leads along high ground to Möngpát. At 7 miles the village of Mankáng is ¼ mile to south of road.

No. 40.

From MÖNGYAW to THÍBAW viâ MANSÉ and NAUNGMWON.

By Capt. STEWART, Royal Munster Fusiliers, March 1888.

Authorities. Military.	Authorities. Civil.	Number and Names of Stages, Rivers and Streams.	Distances. Intermediate. M.	Distances. Intermediate. F.	Distances. Total. M.	Distances. Total. F.	Remarks.
G.O.C. Mandalay District.	Superintendent, Northern Shan States.	**1. Hônaw (Hôné).**	**8**	**4**	8	4	*See* Route No. 30, Branch III.
		2. Mantuleng ...	**10**	**6**	19	2	*See* Route No. 30, Branch III.
		3. Mansé	**10**	**0**	29	2	*See* Route No. 15, Stage 2.
		4. Manpyin ... Nampôn, Nammé and Nammôn rivers, and five small streams.	**7**	**4**	36	6	Course west-south-west. For 1st mile road runs through extensive rice fields, then country becomes more undulating and covered with thin tree jungle, till at 5½ miles much former rice cultivation which continues till Manpyin is reached. At start ford small stream. At ¼ mile, ford Nampôn, 30 yards broad, 1½ feet deep; medium current; stony bottom; low banks. At 1 mile village Sanya (six houses), 200 yards to left of road. At 2 miles village of Kônkaw (10 houses) both sides of road. Ford Nammé stream 10 yards broad, 1 foot deep, slow current, stony bottom, high and rather difficult banks (flows into Nammôn), immediately after passing village. At 3 miles village of Nátong (nine houses) both sides of road. At 3½ miles village of Lulwai to right. At 4¾ miles road runs along side of Nammôn river for a short distance. At 5¼ miles cross bridge (good for pack transport) over stream. At 7½ miles cross Nammôn river (20 yards broad, 1 foot deep. Slow current, flows into Nampôn) bridged, passable for pack animals. Camp in paddy fields on right bank. Ground ample and water good.
		5. Naungmwon ... Three small streams.	**9**	**4**	46	2	Course west. The road runs through hilly country covered with thin jungle, good throughout, offering no impediment to pack transport. Three small streams are passed at 1 mile, 5½ miles, and 6½ miles. At 6½ miles village of Pánghai (eight houses), round which ground is cleared and preparations for new cultivation are being made. Good camping ground near old pagodas. At 9½ miles village of Naungmwon is reached. Large kyaung in large open space. Excellent camping ground. Water in stream near at hand. A bazaar is held here every fifth day. Small supplies of rice procurable.
		6. Ta Sé-án ... Three small streams, Namma river.	**9**	**0**	55	2	Course west by south. Country generally fairly level, through thin jungle. Gradual descent to the Namma river. Road good throughout. At 2¼ miles village of Nongkwai, 20 houses, 50 yards to left of road. At 3¼ miles Pánghai, five houses. At 4¾ miles Nongkwai, 11 houses. At 8¾ miles Sé-án, 37 houses, on right bank of Namma river. Good camping ground in paddy-fields near village. Ford the Namma here (50 yards broad, 2½ to 3 feet deep. Stony bottom, swift current) rather difficult, being a winding one and should be staked out beforehand. (The Namma is only fordable late in the dry season at Sé-án. It is not fordable at Táti some 3 or 4 miles higher up stream. Crossing by boat and raft is a very tedious process.) No camping

FROM MÖNGYAW TO THÍBAW *viâ* MANSÉ AND NAUNGMWON—*continued.*

Authorities. Military.	Authorities. Civil.	Number and Names of Stages, Rivers and Streams.	Distances. Intermediate. M.	F.	Total. M.	F.	Remarks.
G.O.C. Mandalay District.	Superintendent, Northern Shan States.	**6. Ta Sé-án**—*cont.*					ground on left bank, but room found here and there in the jungle. No supplies procurable. The Namma is the boundary here between Thíbaw and Theinni.
		7. Hônong ... One small stream.	**9**	**0**	64	0	Course west-south-west. Country undulating and covered with tree jungle, amongst which are a few teak trees. Road easy and good throughout. At 3 miles village of Pálán to right. At 6 miles village of Pángkáug, seven houses. At 9 miles camping ground is reached in rice fields, near the small village of Hônong. Space ample, and water in small stream near camp.
		8. Thíbaw (Möng-sipaw). Namtu or Myitngé.	**6**	**0**	70	0	Course west. Country undulating and covered with thin jungle. At 1 mile village of Pánglwai, 20 houses. At 3 miles and onwards road runs along left bank of river Namtu or Myitngé 160 yards broad, 10 to 15 feet deep, low banks; ferry; three large dug-outs (canoes). At 5½ miles village of Sánkun, four houses. At 6 miles ferry over river is reached opposite Thibawmyo. The following are two alternative routes from Mansé to Thíbaw:— (*a*) (1) Nakun, crossing Namma river at Namma village; (2) Pánghyo; (3) Kônsa; (4) Thíbaw. (*b*) (1) Násaw (on right bank of Nampôn); (2) Nongkwai, 2 miles south of Naungmwon; (3) Pánghyo, crossing Namma by the Kotamöng ferry; (4) *viâ* Kônsa to Thíbaw. Near Kônsa the road to Möngyai is met. *Note.*—For the last four stages of this route, *see* also No. 53, Northern Division.

No. 41.

From MÖNGYIN (see Route No. 13) to NAMSÁN viâ BAWDWINGYI.

BY LIEUT. G. W. T. PROWSE, 1ST DUKE OF CORNWALL'S LIGHT INFANTRY, FEBRUARY 1891.

Military	Civil	Stages	Inter. M.	F.	Total M.	F.	Remarks
G.O.C. Mandalay District.	Superintendent, Northern Shan States.	**1. Möngtát** ...	**13**	**0**	13	0	*See* Route No. 13, Stage 3.
		2. Camp near Katlwi. Namtát, Namlwi, Nampwi, and several smaller streams.	**12**	**6**	25	6	General direction west. Path leads up to head of Namtát valley; ascends thence through thick jungle to Namtát river, forded at 3¼ miles (40 feet broad, 2 feet deep; pebble bottom; water clear and good; low grassy banks). Ascends and then descends again to Namlwi stream which is forded at 7¾ miles; breadth 30 feet, depth 3 feet; sand and rocky bottom; grassy banks 6 feet high; current 3 miles per hour. Very steep ascent from here by zigzag to top of hill at 9¼ miles, descending to camp by Nampwi stream at 12¾ miles. Bad, narrow and rocky path in many places.

FROM MÖNGYIN TO NAMSÁN *viâ* BAWDWINGYI—*continued.*

Authorities. Military.	Authorities. Civil.	Number and Names of Stages, Rivers and Streams.	Distances. Intermediate.	Distances. Total.	Remarks.
G.O.C. Mandalay District.	Superintenden t, Northern Shan States.	**2. Camp near Katlwi**—*cont.*			*Bridges.*—None with exception of few bamboo foot-bridges. *Villages passed.*—Naungmôn at 2 miles; 12 houses; Katlwi at 9¼ miles; 10 houses (Kachin village); Hôlem at 10 miles, 1 mile north of road. Camp on Nampwi stream in small paddy-fields for 150 men. Supplies in small quantities from Katlwi village.
		3. Bawdwingyi ... Nampwi.	M. F. 8 0	M. F. 33 6	General direction south and south-east. Path crosses valley and ascends hills on south side. The Nampwi is forded on leaving camp; 30 feet broad, 2 feet deep; water clear and good; stony bottom; banks 6 feet high, covered with grass and jungle; current 2 to 3 miles an hour. Steep ascent to 1 mile, thence more gradual; path averaging 2 feet in width, passes over crest of grassy hills. At 2 miles path is rotten and covered with loose stones, continuing over undulations to 5 miles, where it is much broken away and very narrow. At 5 miles it turns south-east and enters narrow defile between high, bare hills, descending to Bawdwingyi at 8 miles. The path down this defile averages 18 inches in width and leads over slippery rock in many places, with several bad swampy crossings. Average width of defile 150 yards, the path along the bottom of it being commanded the whole way to camp from the hills on both sides, which are covered with short grass and rocks. No villages are passed *en route*. Bad and rocky camping ground at Bawdwingyi for 150 men. Water from small stream at bottom of defile, 6 feet broad; 1 foot deep, muddy, but drinkable. No supplies and grass scanty. Two stone huts inhabited by Chinamen, which would accommodate 15 to 20 men apiece; a third hut about 3 miles down valley beyond old workings and also inhabited by a Chinaman. A path averaging 3 feet in width leads from camp to the workings, which commence about 1½ miles further down the valley. This path is carried across the small stream which flows down the valley at three points by three hewn stone segmental arches built by Chinese labour. The first bridge is situated between camp and workings and is flattened at the top, the second is at the commencement of the workings and is built in steps, the third rather further down the valley, and also built in steps. Dimensions of all three 15 to 20 feet span, 6 feet broad. The path continues about 4 miles along the valley, when it ascends the hills on the south side and strikes off to Pángyaung village about 5 miles distant.
		4. Haitong ... Namkhong.	12 0	45 6	General direction south-south-east. Path re-ascends to head of valley, then strikes over grassy hills to south. Steep descent to the Namkhong valley at 4 miles. River forded at 7½ miles (breadth 30 yards, 2 feet deep; rocky bottom; low grassy banks 3 feet high; current 3 miles per hour; water clear and good. Good and ample camping ground in paddy-fields on the right bank), after which gradual ascent to Haitong, 12 miles; the path from the valley good, averaging 2 feet wide. The descent to the Namkhong river on the Bawdwingyi side would be impracticable for transport in wet weather. Haitong (4,400 feet), 12 miles, 15 houses, is a Palaung and Kachin village. Small

No. 41.

From MÖNGYIN to NAMSÁN *viâ* BAWDWINGYI—*continued.*

Authorities. Military.	Authorities. Civil.	Number and Names of Stages, Rivers and Streams.	Distances. Intermediate.	Distances. Total.	Remarks
G.O.C. Mandalay District.	Superintendent, Northern Shan States.	**4. Haitong**—*cont.*			camping ground for 100 men on ridge in centre of village itself which is situated on the summit of a wooded hill with higher wooded hills behind it. Paddy Rs. 2 per basket, very limited water-supply from small spring on south of village, ¼ of a mile from camp.
		5. Manlwoi (5,200 feet).	M. F. 11 4	M. F. 57 2	General direction south. Path ascends hill at back of village. Several tracks gradually converging and all steep, rough and broken. Ascent to 5 miles, where the shoulder of Loi Pángyôk is crossed; thence gradual descent along grassy ridge, path averaging 2 feet. Passes through thick wood at 8¼ miles on the side of Loi Namlin, descending steeply at 9 miles to Upper Manlwoi; thence through Lower Manlwoi to camp. *Villages.*—Manlwoi (Upper), 9½ miles; 16 houses; Palaung village: Manlwoi (Lower), 10½ miles; 29 houses; Palaung village. Excellent level camping ground for a battalion on grassy ridge at 11¼ miles near site of old Sawbwa's residence. Water from small spring. Paddy Rs. 2 per basket.
		6. Namsán (5,500 feet). Namkwai.	8 4	65 6	General direction west. Steep descent from camp to Namkwai stream (30 feet broad, 2 feet deep; rocky bottom; water clear and good; banks 3 to 6 feet high with small paddy-fields on either side; current 2 to 3 miles per hour. There is a wooden log foot-bridge at this point) by good road, 10 feet wide; thence steep ascent to Sélôn village by good path, averaging 6 feet wide. From Sélôn to Namsán there is an excellent road, nowhere less than 8 feet in width, with short and steep ascent from Sélôn, after which it continues along ridge passing Mankai village and descends abruptly into Namsán, 8½ miles. *Villages.*—Sélôn 5½ miles; 15 houses. Mankhai 7 miles; 14 houses. Small and dirty camp at Namsán, 100 yards west of kyaung for 150 men. The ground is apparently in constant use by Chinese traders passing through or temporarily living at Namsán. There is a small spring of water on the southern slope immediately below the camp. If desirable to have the camp near Namsán, it would be best to camp at Sérám, which is closer than Sélôn (mentioned as best place in Lieut. Willcock's report), besides there being room for a larger number of men at Sérám. At Namsán resides the Sawbwa of Taungbaing.

ALTERNATIVE I.

From KATLWI (Stage 2) to NAMSÁN (Stage 6).

By Lieut. G. W. T. PROWSE, 1st Duke of Cornwall's Light Infantry, February 1891.

Military	Civil	Stages	Intermediate	Total	Remarks
G.O.C. Mandalay District.	Supt., Northern Shan States.	**1. Hinpôk** ...	12 0	12 0	*Note.*—No direct path is mentioned in any reports, as existing between Katlwi and Hinpôk which are 4 miles apart as the crow flies, but there is almost sure to be one,* at any rate, suitable for foot-passengers. In any case, however, there is a path to Manpát (*see* Route No. 13, Stage 5), 8 miles, and thence to Hinpôk about 4 miles further, which is on the east side of the Namkong valley opposite Na-aw (Ma-o), *see* Route No. 34, Branch I.

* Lieut. Prowse, in the Route Map of Taungbaing attached to his "Report on north-east portionof Theinni State, Mines at Bawdwingyi and the Taungbaing State, 1890-91," shows this path as actuay traversed, but he gives no description of it.—A. F.

FROM MÖNGYIN TO NAMSÁN *viâ* BAWDWINGYI—*continued.*

ALTERNATIVE I—*continued.*

Authorities. Military.	Authorities. Civil.	Number and Names of Stages, Rivers and Streams.	Distances. Intermediate.	Distances. Total.	Remarks.
			M. F.	M. F.	
G.O.C. Mandalay District.	Superintendent, Northern Shan States.	**2. Camp on Nam On.** Namkong and Nam On.	**9 4**	21 4	General direction south. Descend to Namkong and thence down valley of that stream crossing it several times. At about 3½ miles ascend steeply by good path to Hônwé (Kachin, 24 houses) at about 6 miles. Camping ground on road side ¼ mile south of village for 100 men. Water 500 yards south of camp from small hill side spring. The Namkong, which is crossed three times in this stage, is from 60 to 70 feet broad and 2 to 3 feet deep; stony bottom; banks jungle, grass or paddy; 4 to 6 feet; current 2 to 4 miles per hour. From Hônwé the path ascends ridge behind village continues to ascend to 3 miles, the path being from 2 to 3 feet wide; rocky and steep in places; descent at 3 miles to camp on Nam On stream, 3½ miles. No villages are passed on the road itself, but there are two Palaung villages at 5 and 7 miles on west of road, and two Kachin villages at 2 and 3½ miles, east of road. Good small camping ground (jungle) on Nam On stream; water from stream. No supplies; grass fairly plentiful. The Nam On is 8 to 10 feet wide, 2 feet deep; current flowing 2 miles per hour; water clear and good.
		3. Sérám ... or **Namsán** ... Nam Kwai.	**14 0** **15 0**	35 4 36 4	General direction south. Ascends steeply to the shoulder of Loi Táng-kyaw, 4 miles; thence there is a long descent to the valley of Namkwai stream (18 inches deep, 15 feet wide; stony bottom; clear and good; low, grassy banks, 2 feet high) crossed at 11 miles by bridge; steep ascent through tea gardens to camp on ridge ½ mile north of pagodas and ¾ mile from Sérám village. Road narrow in places, but good with exception of abrupt descent to Namkwai stream where it is much cut up and very steep. *Bridges.*—At 11 miles over Namkwai stream, 20 feet by 6 feet; longitudinal planks; passable. *Villages.*—Two Líshaw villages on east of road at 7 miles; three to four houses each. Good camp at junction of road with the one to Penglom, but water scarce. Room on pagoda hill for 150 men, but road-side camps better ¼ mile and ½ mile north, at both of which places there is room for 100 men. Water either from town of Sérám or from stream ½ mile down hill on west of camp, which latter is sufficiently large for watering purposes; there is also a very small spring 100 yards west of camp, but liable to dry up. Sérám, which is only a mile from Namsán, is the great tea trading centre, on which all the trade routes converge. From here the tea traders march to Mandalay by the following route to Pángsari (two marches), Wengmul (half a march), Longlwoi (half a march), Loiping Möngngaw, and Kyaukmé (each one march), thence to Mandalay *viâ* Kywégôn and Pyaungaung, 11 marches.

No. 42.

From NAMKHAM to LÁSHIO viâ MÖNG YU and THEINNI.

By Lieuts. WALKER and PROWSE, Duke of Cornwall's Light Infantry, Attachés, Intelligence Branch, April 1892.

Authorities.		Number and Names of Stages, Rivers and Streams.	Distances.				Remarks.
Military.	Civil.		Intermediate.		Total.		
			M.	F.	M.	F.	
G.O.C. Mandalay District.	Superintendent, Northern Shan States.	**1. Maosao (? Mawsôn).** Namkhampông and small streams.	**13**	**6**	13	6	General direction south-east. Leaving Namkham the route continues across the valley of the Shwéli, in which Namkham is situated, southward reaching the foot of the hills which terminate the valley on this side at 500 yards; a route striking off to right hand or west at 300 yards to Möngwi, another at foot of hills leading to the village of Manna ½ mile distant to right hand or west. The route enters the hills by a gradual ascent by a central spur the path being here 10 yards wide. At mile 1 a path strikes off to right hand or west to Kachin village of Manka on a ridge to that side. At 1½ miles path narrows to 4 yards becoming broken and needing repair. Light jungle on both sides. At mile 2 path narrows to 4 feet and winds along the sides of the slopes of ridge to south-west ascending very steeply for a short distance, then running along the level. To the left hand or east the Namkhampông stream is visible in valley flowing towards the Shwéli, due north. A path also strikes to right hand or west to the Kachin villages of Manka and Loilom, the Palaung village of Manmao, and two Chinese-Shan hamlets, Namshiri or Manshi, all situated on crest of parallel ridge to west. From here the path continues to rise by a gradual ascent to mile 3 when the ridge flattens out and the path becomes level, the Palaung village of Loiyin (8 or 10 houses) being passed to left hand or east at 3¼ miles and another portion of the same 150 yards further on. At mile 4 the Kachin village of Kônka, to left hand or west on parallel ridge, and the Kachin village of Mankôn Loilom (four houses) to immediate right hand are passed. The path then rises again becoming rocky and broken for the next 400 yards when it improves once more. Thick jungle on both sides. At mile 5 the villages on the parallel spur to the west again become visible, the path rising by a steady ascent. At mile 5¾ path crosses the Namkhampông easily fordable a path to left or east leading to the distant Kachin village of Manvao. Another to right hand or west to the villages Namshiri or Manshi, Loilom, &c. After crossing stream the path continues to ascend passing at mile 7 a small, level halting place with *no* water, and at mile 7½ another for 50 men, with scanty supply of water 200 yards down steep slope to right hand or west. Here the spur joins the main ridge of the range, a further ascent up to mile 8 reaching the summit. The path then commences to descend through thick jungle at 8½ miles, passing the Kachin village of Hoiluk to left hand or east on parallel spur and rather more than 2 miles distant. At mile 9 path passes a small halting place; accommodation for 20 men only, water being obtained in small quantities from a spring to right hand of path. The path then rises a little, roughish and very much worn away by bullock traffic, and runs along the eastern or left-hand slope of ridge to mile 10 when it recommences to descend gradually, in places much cut up by traffic; inclined to be stony. At mile 11 the Kachin villages of Manvao and Hoiluk come in view to left hand or east. From the 11th to the 13th mile the path is excellent, running along a gradually descending spur; open jungle on both sides; at mile 12 passing remains of old Kachin village, the cultivation still remaining under work. At mile 12¼ path

FROM NAMKHAM TO LÁSHIO *viâ* MÖNG YU AND THEINNI—*continued*.

Authorities.		Number and Names of Stages, Rivers and Streams.	Distances.		Remarks.
Military.	Civil.		Inter-mediate.	Total.	
G.O.C. Mandalay District.	Superintendent, Northern Shan States.	**1. Maosao (? Mawsôn)**—*cont.*			leads to Manvao to left hand or east and 1½ miles distant. At mile 13 the descent becomes rough and stony to mile 13¾ when the ridge rises into a knoll on which is situated the Palaung village of Maosao; 15 houses and a kyaung. Supplies moderate: vegetables and paddy; the latter 12 annas a basket. There is camping accommodation for 40 men on road to south of village, water being obtained from stream to left hand or east of, and immediately below the ridge; camping accommodation for 300 men may also be obtained to right hand or west of route before entering village down a steep descent of 600 yards into paddy-fields situated on a small stream flowing southwards; camping ground for 1,000 men or more can be obtained 2 miles further south past the village in the Nammaw valley where there is excellent grass, &c. Should this latter camp be chosen grain for ponies will have to be brought or sent for. For any number of men over 40, the latter camp makes the best stage from Namkham although 2 miles further to march. The route, though broken in places and worn, is a good one, passable for all troops and laden traffic. It would be the better for repair which could be easily given by the villages in its vicinity.
		2. Möng Yu ... Namkaw, Nammaw, and NamYu.	M. F. 10 4	M. F. 24 2	General direction south. With the exception of the first 2 miles the path is in first-rate order throughout this stage. After leaving Maosao village the path, which averages 6 feet in width, descends a wooded spur gradually and then more steeply to the valley of the Nammaw stream (1 foot deep; 30 feet wide; pebbly bottom; current about 2 miles per hour; good approach from both banks which are low, cultivated with paddy), which is crossed by a ford at 2¼ miles. This first portion of the route is much cut up by bullock tracks. After the Nammaw is crossed the path, which averages 3 feet wide and is in very good order, leads through thinly-wooded undulating country. A marshy valley is crossed at 3 miles; timber at hand for bridging, &c. At 3¼ miles Nampaka bazaar is reached, the village of that name lying about ¼ mile to the west of the path. At this point there is a path from the east leading from Saopun (Kachin) village; also another leading south which strikes into the route from Möng Yu to Theinni about 1 mile south of the former village. After passing Nampaka bazaar the path now turns westwards and leads through thinly-wooded level country to Nampalam village, leaving it on the left hand and within 200 yards of the path. At 9½ miles the path strikes into the Möng Yu valley, following down the west side of it fording the Nam Yu twice to Hôko village, after which the Nammaw stream has to be forded to Möng Yu village ¼ mile further on. As mentioned in the first stage there is ample camping ground available during the dry season in the valley of the Nammaw stream, passed at 2 miles. Paddy would have to be procured from Maosao village. *Bridges.*—All the bridges on this stage are merely single plank ones. *Villages passed.*—Mangwán (Kachin) on spur to the west of path at 1 mile. Kongchung (Kachin) at ¼ mile to the west of path at ¾ mile. Loi Káng and Hôsi (Kachin villages) at 1 mile

FROM NAMKHAM TO LÁSHIO *viâ* MÖNG YU AND THEINNI—*continued.*

Authorities.		Number and Names of Stages, Rivers and Streams.	Distances.				Remarks.
Military.	Civil.		Intermediate.		Total.		
			M.	F.	M.	F.	
		2. Möng Yu—*cont.*					to west of path at 6½ miles. Namkom (Palaung) to east of path at 6¼ miles. Nampalám (Palaung) about six houses and small bamboo kyaung passed at 9 miles. Hôko (Shan) at 9¾ miles; about 20 houses. Möng Yu (Shan) at 10½ miles; has about 30 houses and bamboo kyaung; situated on the right bank of the Nammaw stream. The main route to Theinni does not cross to Möng Yu, but keeps along the left bank. Ample camping ground for a brigade if necessary in paddy-fields by the Nammaw stream; good grass, paddy and water. Fifth-day bazaar held here attended by about 300 Shans, Palaungs, and Kachins from the neighbouring hills. The Palaung village of Loi Poi situated on a wooded ridge 1 mile to the south-west is the head of the circle. There is a small bamboo zayát near the kyaung in which about 15 men could be accommodated in wet weather. From Möng Yu a path leads in a north-west direction to the Kachin villages of Tônkaw and Hômaw, and another to Möngwi, *see* Route No. 69.
G.O.C. Mandalay District.	Superintendent, Northern Shan States.	**3. Pinghoi** ... Nammaw, Nam Yu, Nam Khai, Nam Nim, and Nam Ngwán.	12	4	36	6	General direction south-east. Leaving Möng Yu the route crosses the Nammaw stream (60 feet wide, 1 to 3 feet deep; 1½ miles an hour; rather steep banks on either side of usual ford leading to village) into the paddy-fields, usually the camping accommodation, and leaving Hôko on the left hand runs down a narrow valley at right angles and at first eastward to the Nammaw valley. At ½ mile a path follows the Nammaw valley and leads to Kônka. At 1¼ miles a path strikes off to the left or north-east leading to Pamakán village at some distance off. The valley along which the route runs is grassy and clothed on either side of path with light jungle. At 1½ miles a path to left or north-east leads to the Kachin village of Loisao (Maru Kachins), and said to be 2 miles distant. A small stream flows to left hand of path down centre of valley which averages about 300 yards in width. At mile 2 the Namkhai stream is crossed by a difficult ford 3 feet deep. The Namkhai stream is 35 to 40 yards across, 2½ feet to 5 feet deep; current 4½ miles an hour; rocky bed; steep approaches to ford; dangerous crossing. *Note.*—Should the ford be put into requisition for the crossing of much military traffic, a rough bamboo rail on both sides of ford would be of advantage, while the rocky, irregular bottom could be levelled with advantage. As it is now, the ford is a dangerous one without a guide, the current being strong and animals being very liable to be swept off their legs. After crossing the Namkhai the path continues along a grassy valley for ¼ of a mile when it strikes up a rocky pass rising a little, and as far as mile 2¾, when it becomes good again and the undulating valley, which the route traverses, opens

Authorities. Military.	Authorities. Civil.	Number and Names of Stages, Rivers and Streams.	Distances. Intermediate.	Distances. Total.	Remarks.
G.O.C. Mandalay District.	Superintendent, Northern Shan States.	**3. Pinghoi**—*cont.*			out. At mile 3 the Shan village of Pángnim is passed (seven houses), situated on a low spur to right hand of route, while at intervals to left hand two or three paths lead to Loisao. At mile 3½ path crosses the Namnim (3½ yards wide, 6 inches deep; water almost stagnant), still traversing the undulating valley, and runs level as far as mile 4 when it crosses one low spur, and after descending passes the Shan village of Kônka to right hand or south (8 or 10 houses), to which a broad well-made path strikes off from main route at mile 4¼. The path then begins to ascend by an easy gradient, but rather rough, leaving now what can be styled the Namkhai valley, the ridge thus ascended being called Loipángwam. At mile 5¼ the Kachin village of Pángwam (Hpángom) (8 or 10 houses) is passed to left hand of route, the path the last ¼ mile being much cut up by bullock traffic. Thick jungle on both sides. Two hundred yards further on a path to right hand or south-west leads to the distant village of Kônping (Kachins); 150 yards further on a path to right hand or south-west leads to upper village of Pángwam said to be 2 miles distant. The path now runs along the side of eastern hills through a narrow gorge, very narrow and dangerous owing to precipitous descent to the bottom of the gorge to right hand of the path. At mile 6 route descends into a small valley where there is camping ground for 150 to 200 men with water obtainable from stream to right hand or south-west of valley. At 6¼ miles after rising a little a path to left leads to the Kachin village of Manlong (Konlong or Manlong tribe) 3 miles to north-east of route. The path then descends a little, crosses a small stream with patch of cultivation capable of affording accommodation for 200 men; thence along steep ascent up side of spur for ¾ mile, the range called Loi Namnwáng lying to right hand of route. At mile 9 route descends into the valley of the Namnwáng stream (8 yards wide, 3 feet deep; 1½ miles an hour; steep banks and bad crossing), where there is accommodation in paddy-fields for 800 or 1,000 men, and up a spur; light jungle on either side to the Palaung village of Emngo; 11 houses at mile 10½. The route then runs along the eastern side of the ridge after first descending on leaving Emngo, and beginning to descend from the main ridge at mile 11½ the large plateau lying between Pinghoi and Theinni is visible below and southwards. At mile 12 the route passes the Palaung village of Mankán on knoll below and to right hand of path. At mile 12½ Pinghoi (Palaungs), 12 houses, is reached situated on a small knoll or spur, after crossing which the route enters the large level plateau. There is accommodation and water for 200 men north of village. Supplies: paddy, 8 annas a basket; a few vegetables and rice; grass and bamboo leaves abundant. The whole of this stage, with the exception of the crossings, is good going, the path averaging from 1½ to 5 or 6 feet. It is much worn by bullocks and could be improved by repairs. This route is the most direct one from Namkham to Theinni, being only four ordinary stages, while it is under 30 miles from Theinni to Láshio. The second and fourth stages are the best, the first out from Namkham being the worst. If necessity arose the two middle stages could be done in one march; with mounted men the distance could be marched easily in two days. This is the main caravan route as is attested by the much worse condition of the track. Should it be necessary to move any large number of men by this route, it could be easily repaired by the villages along the line.

FROM NAMKHAM TO LÁSHIO *viâ* MÖNG YU AND THEINNI—*continued.*

Authorities. Military.	Authorities. Civil.	Number and Names of Stages, Rivers and Streams.	Distances. Intermediate.	Distances. Total.	Remarks.
G.O.C. Mandalay District.	Superintendent, Northern Shan States.	**4. Theinni** ... Pengwán and Nampakyi.	M. F. **13 0**	M. F. 49 6	General direction south. After leaving Pinghoi village the path leads over a level, open plain with patches of dry paddy cultivation here and there. The path is an excellent order. At 2½ miles the hamlet of Loi Weng (Palaung) is passed ¼ mile to the west of the path. Kôtkoi bazaar is reached at 3¾ miles and here there is an excellent camping ground for 200 men by the side of the Peng Wán stream, grass and water-supply plentiful; paddy obtainable from neighbouring villages. The Theinni route crosses the stream (20 feet broad; 12 inches deep; water clear and good; gravel by and sandy bottom. Good approach from both banks which are 4 to 5 feet high with short grass) by a ford, a path leading east from here to Loi Om village (Palaung), and another also in the same direction to Möngwin and Möngnyé, two Chinese villages. After a slight rise through thinly-wooded country a path strikes off to the south-east at 3¾ miles leading to the village of Sé-u in the Theinni valley on the road to Kunlôn. At 4½ miles the Palaung village of Imöng is reached, thence the path continues good and level to just before reaching Namhu village at 6¾ miles where two bad swampy crossings have to be made. The average width of each is from 25 to 30 yards, no attempt at bridging having been made. There is, however, plenty of small timber available close at hand. From Namhu there is a path leading westwards to Namwai, a Kachin village. After leaving Namhu the country is wooded, the path still continuing good and level. At 8¼ miles a path leads west to Pakyi (Kachin) village and another east to Nantauk (Palaung and Shan). At 9¼ miles the path descends rather steeply on to a lower plateau. After this the Nampakyi stream is forded three times (gravelly bottom; low, marshy banks; width at first crossing about 12 feet, 1 foot deep; timber for bridging available close at hand. The same stream forded at 9¾ miles. Width at ford 30 feet; hard, gravelly bottom; 18 inches deep; low jungly banks. Two hundred yards further on the same stream is crossed again; the banks 3 to 4 feet in height and swampy in wet weather), the path continuing level to 11¾ miles where the descent to the Theinni valley commences. The path down the hill, though steep and rocky in places, is quite practicable for mule or bullock transport in dry weather, though it would be slippery and difficult in the rains. Half-way down the hill a small stream is forded, and the path after leading round the base of a small wooded knoll enters the town of Theinni, 13 miles. There are no bridges along the route with the exception of a single plank over the boggy places. *Villages passed.*—Loi Weng ¼ mile west of path at 2½ miles, Palaung village. Loi Om ½ mile east of path at 2¾ miles, Palaung. Nambulong 1¼ miles east of path at 3 miles, Palaung. Imöng 4½ miles, Palaung village of about 10 houses and a small bamboo kyaung. Namhu at 6¾ miles is a Palaung village of 16 houses; small bamboo kyaung in bad repair; a small bamboo zayát which would accommodate 12 to 15 men. In dry weather any number of men could be camped in the paddy-fields round the village of Theinni. In wet weather the only available accommodation is two or three small bamboo zayáts built on rising ground between the Sawbwa's house and the bazaar; there is only a small bamboo kyaung, at present in bad repair.

FROM NAMKHAM TO LÂSHIO *viâ* MÖNG YU AND THEINNI—*continued.*

Authorities. Military.	Authorities. Civil.	Number and Names of Stages, Rivers and Streams.	Distances. Intermediate. M.	F.	Distances. Total. M.	F.	Remarks.
G.O.C. Mandalay District.	Superintendent, Northern Shan States.	**5. Pángtonmông.**	**14**	**4**	64	2	*See* Route No. 53, Northern Division.
		6. Láshio ...	**13**	**6**	78	0	

No. 43.

From NAMKHAM to MÔMIEN (China) viâ HÔTHA.

BY CAPT. H. B. WALKER, DUKE OF CORNWALL'S LIGHT INFANTRY, AND LIEUT. H. R. DAVIES, OXFORDSHIRE LIGHT INFANTRY, INTELLIGENCE BRANCH (FROM NATIVE INFORMATION), 1892–93.

Authorities. Military.	Authorities. Civil.	Number and Names of Stages, Rivers and Streams.	Intermediate.	Total.	Remarks.
China.		**1. Möngmao** ... Shwéli river crossed.	...	...	Direction north-west. Route, which is a good one, crosses the Shwéli at Kyetkhun ferry. Two dug-outs always kept here for plying passengers across. A day's journey.
		2. Sánhao ...	...	...	Direction north-west. The road crosses the Kônka or Kônyo by an up-hill route from spur to spur. A day's march. Sánhao has about 200 houses and a fifth-day bazaar.
		3. Möngwán (Mowáng).	...	...	Direction north-west. A day's march. Road said to be level and good. Möngwán is the residence of a Sawbwa and contains 1,000 houses.
		4. Yinkha	...	...	Direction. A day's march. Road hilly and difficult. Yinkha is a Kachin village of about 30 houses.
		5. Maingtha ...	...	...	Direction north-west. A day's march. Road down and easy travelling. Maingtha is the seat of a Sawbwa and has about 150 houses.
		6. Hôtha (or Hôsa).	...	...	Direction west. Half-a-day's march. Road level and good. Hôtha or Hôsa is the seat of a Sawbwa and has 150 houses. From here there is a road to Mainla and Sánda, direction east-south-east, half a day's march to the former place. The route crosses the Loi Ma Hé range of hills by a good path. Mainla is the seat of an influential Sawbwa and contains nearly 2,000 houses. Sánda is distant half-a-day's march north-north-east of Mainla. Route crosses the Namwan stream at Pin-In. Route level and good all the way. Pin-In contains 40 houses. Sánda is the seat of Sawbwa, contains 1,000 houses.
		7. Hanaungsán ...	...	...	A village in the Möngla district. Road over hills and down into the plain again.
		8. Séyinkhwán ...	...	...	A Chinese town on a hill. Road up-hill. A Chinese Civil Officer and a few soldiers here.

FROM NAMKHAM TO MÔMIEN (CHINA) *viâ* HÔTHA—*continued.*

Authorities. Military.	Authorities. Civil.	Number and Names of Stages, Rivers and Streams.	Distances. Intermediate. M. F.	Distances. Total. M. F.	Remarks.
China.		**9. A Chinese village.**	...	...	
		10. Mômien ...	...	...	A large Chinese town surrounded by a high stone wall. A Chinese Commissioner here and a number of troops and artillery.

ALTERNATIVE I.

FROM NAMKHAM TO MÔMIEN.

BY LIEUT. E. W. M. NORIE, OFFICIATING DEPUTY ASSISTANT QUARTERMASTER-GENERAL, INTELLIGENCE BRANCH (FROM NATIVE INFORMATION), OCTOBER 1890.

Military.	Civil.	Stages	Intermediate.	Total.	Remarks.
China.		**1. Lônghu** ... Shwéli river.	...	...	The road leaves Namkham and crosses the Shwéli river and is easy and level the whole way. Lônghu is a Chinese village of about 100 houses on the right bank of the river.
		2. Möngmao (Maingmao).	...	...	The road is level and easy in dry weather, but as it runs chiefly through cultivation it gets very much cut up in wet weather, when temporary footbridges are constructed across the streams, which, however, will not bear animals. Möngmao is a large fortified Chinese town and the residence of a Sawbwa. All supplies procurable. Water from wells and a stream. The town is about 2 miles distant from the river.
		3. Kyángfôm ...	...	...	The road runs across the plain for about a mile after leaving Möngmao and then entering the hills leads up to the Kachin village of Mönghyo at about 6 miles, containing about 10 houses. From here the road leads down to Kyángfôm, a large Chinese-Shan town of about 200 houses, situated on a stream. The road is fairly good throughout; but blackmail is levied on travellers by the Kachins of Mönghyo village.
		4. Lôngkyawn ...	...	...	The road is across a plain and is level and easy, and though this is a long march it can be easily done in a day. Lôngkyawn is a large Chinese-Shan town of about 300 or 400 houses, under a Sawbwa. All supplies, &c., are obtainable.
		5. Shamalôn ...	...	...	At about 2 miles from Lôngkyawn the path enters the hills and becomes very steep and rough and just practicable for laden animals. Shamalôn is a Chinese village of over 100 houses. Water from springs in the hills and small streams.

FROM NAMKHAM TO MÔMIEN (CHINA) *viâ* HÔTHA—*continued.*

ALTERNATIVE I—*continued.*

Authorities. Military.	Authorities. Civil.	Number and Names of Stages, Rivers and Streams.	Distances. Intermediate. M.	F.	Distances. Total. M.	F.	Remarks.
China.		**6. Sholôngkyawn.**	...		...		Road down hill all the way rough and steep till just before entering the town, when it runs across a plain for about a mile and is level and easy. The town is Chinese-Shan and contains about 100 houses. Water from a stream. There is a small bazaar here, and supplies are obtainable.
		7. Nantin	...		...		Road runs over a level plain nearly all the way and is level and easy. This is the frontier town of China proper, and there are two large fortified villages, one under a Chinese-Shan Sawbwa of over 200 houses and the other a Chinese town of 300 houses with a garrison of 500 men. There are bazaars in both towns and supplies are procurable. Water from a stream and wells.
		8. Mômien ...	...		...		Road runs for the most part over low hills and is good going and fairly easy. At about 6 miles pass the Chinese village of Nansônkwáng of about 50 houses. Mômien is a large fortified Chinese town of 2,000 or 3,000 houses, with a garrison of about 3,000 men. All supplies, &c., procurable.

No. 44.

From NAMKHAN to MÖNGSI.

BY LIEUT. S. WILLCOCK, 2ND GLOUCESTERSHIRE REGIMENT, MAY 1889.

Military	Civil	Stages	Int. M.	F.	Total M.	F.	Remarks
G.O.C. Mandalay District.	Superintendent, Northern Shan States.	**1. Sélán** ... ... Nam Siri, Nam Sao and many small streams, all easily fordable, the larger ones all bridged with stone bridges of very solid make.	14	2	14	2	General direction north-east. Nature of path very good throughout in all weathers. Runs over the lower slopes of small spurs and skirts paddy throughout. Fit for pack transport throughout. Hills on south for most part bare red earth or short grass. Broad valley, 2 to 3 miles, watered by Shwéli river (Nammaw) and Nampaw; very fertile and all under paddy; full of large villages. Roughly speaking the Shwéli divides the Chinese from the Burmese Shan States, but there are several Namkham villages on right bank and some Chinese on left bank.

FROM NAMKHAN TO MÖNGSI—*continued.*

Authorities. Military.	Authorities. Civil.	Number and Names of Stages, Rivers and Streams.	Distances. Intermediate.	Distances. Total.	Remarks.
G.O.C. Mandalay District.	Superintendent, Northern Shan States.	**1. Sélán**—*cont.*			Villages passed:— At ¾ mile Longsáng (or Naungsán), about 25 houses and kyaung. 1¾ miles Mankham, about 21 houses and kyaung. 2¾ miles Séhai, about 60 houses and kyaung. About 3½ miles Kônsa, 24 houses and a kyaung. 4¾ miles Mankongweng, 19 houses and kyaung. 5¾ miles Longkáng (or Naungkháng), 30 houses and a kyaung. This is the last Namkhan village, those beyond belonging to Sélán. 8½ miles Manlim, about eight houses. About 9 miles Namsáng ¼ mile to left. 11¼ miles Manhai, about 15 houses. 12½ miles Nongseng, about 24 houses. 13¾ miles Sélán, about 200 houses. Sélán is a walled town, about 700 yards long by 500 broad, situated on a ridge running north and south. It is surrounded by a deep, dry ditch, 15 feet broad and 9 feet to 15 feet deep and parapet 10 feet thick, 15 feet high. There are numerous small earthworks on top of the inner wall to hold three or four men each. There are six gates. The cuttings in the wall are filled with sun-dried brick curtains, loopholed for musketry, and small earthworks (for musketry) are thrown up on the flanks of the cuttings on the wall. The slope, a few yards west of the north gate, is less steep than elsewhere and is not obstructed at present by jungle or bamboo entanglement. The south-west portion of the town contains most houses and is cut off from the remainder by an interior wall and gates, which are, however, out of repair. This quarter is slightly higher than the rest of the town. It contains the *tamon's* house, surrounded by loopholed wall of sun-dried brick, about 4 feet 6 inches high. The town would be very hard to take for ill-armed men; but it is commanded by a spur at about 1,200 yards on south-west side and another on south-east at about 1,600 yards. There is a small spring on the east side within the walls, and plenty of water close to the walls on all the other sides. There are two bamboo kyaungs, that near the north gate would accommodate 150 men, the one near the south gate 250. The best camping ground is on a ridge ½ mile east of the town. There is a good well and a stream between this place and the town. There is a fifth-day bazaar held inside the walls. Paddy, rice, poultry, and vegetables can be procured in large quantities. Sélán is the principal town of the Pankham circle (3 miles east). Pankham was burnt about three years ago and has only been partially rebuilt (about 20 houses). About 4 miles north of the right bank of the Shwéli is Möngmao, the principal town of the Chinese-Shans in this neighbourhood. It is surrounded by a high brick wall visible from Sélán, and is said to contain about 150 brick houses and a large bazaar. *Note.*—Lieut. Davies paced the distance of this march in January 1892 and made it 13 miles.
		2. Tingsáng ... Nampaw.	M. 14 F. 4	M. 28 F. 6	General direction north-east for 5½ miles, south-east for 9 miles. Nature of path good, except about ½ mile, descending into Tingsáng valley which is steep and rocky. Till 6th mile the road is level, thence running up one long spur rises continually for 7 miles. Slopes easy for the most part, 13 to

FROM NAMKHAN TO MÖNGSI—*continued.*

Authorities. Military.	Authorities. Civil.	Number and Names of Stages, Rivers and Streams.	Distances. Intermediate. M.	Distances. Intermediate. F.	Distances. Total. M.	Distances. Total. F.	Remarks.
G.O.C. Mandalay District.	Superintendent, Northern Shan States.	**2. Tingsang**—*cont.*					13½ miles steep descent; 13½ to 14½ miles gradual descent. The country is open throughout. The hills altogether bare or covered with short grass. The Nampaw is a tributary of Shwéli (or Nammaw), 40 yards broad, 18 inches deep. Good, sandy bottom; probably impassable after heavy rains. Villages passed :— Pangkham at 3½ miles, about 10 houses. Manmaw at 8½ miles, about 14 houses. Namlong at 10½ miles, about 14 houses. Tingsáng at 14 miles, about 20 houses; small bazaar. Manháng on the hill above Tingsáng appears to have about 20 houses and a large kyaung. The ruins of Mutsyé, a large village, are passed at 4½ miles. Camp on a small stream about 1,200 yards beyond Tingsáng. The water is not good and there is little at this season (May), but in the village there is only one small well.
		3. Manhai (Manhé). Namtaw, Namti, and several small streams	**12**	**4**	41	2	General direction south-east. Nature of path excellent throughout. Passes through a succession of small valleys connected by easy passes; tends continually downwards. Villages passed :— At 5⅛ miles Pôngka, about 30 houses and one small bamboo kyaung, would accommodate 70 men. 8¼ miles Saikhao, about 15 houses. 12½ miles Manhai, about 20 houses and small bazaar. Near Manhai are Nalôn, 30 houses, and Kônsa, 25 houses. Camp near bazaar. Water from the Namti good and plentiful. The Namtaw is about 30 yards wide and 8 inches deep; pebbly bottom; steep bank; probably impassable after heavy rains. The Namti is about 35 yards wide and 6 inches deep; pebbly bottom; low banks.
		4. Hôna ... Namti.	**9**	**0**	50	2	General direction south-east. Nature of path fair throughout; gradients for about a ¼ of a mile on each side of Namti steep. Villages passed on road :— At 3½ miles Senghawmtal, eight houses. 4¾ miles Senghawmnö, 21 houses. 7½ miles Saikhao, about 20 houses, small bazaar. 9¼ miles Hôna, 15 houses and large bamboo pôngyi kyaung, would accommodate 150 men. Camp ¼ mile before reaching village. Water from Namti and small streams good and plentiful.
		5. Möngwön ... Small streams.	**9**	**0**	59	2	General direction south-east. Nature of path fair, but gradients are steep in places for short distances. From 5 miles to 5 miles 3 furlongs road is very rocky and bad. No villages on the road. Camp ¾ mile south-south-west of Möngwön (20 houses) in paddy-fields. Water good and plentiful. No streams of any size are met with in this march, but some of the small ones and irrigation canals are very boggy, but there is grass at hand to improve the crossing. Watershed between Salween and Nam Tu (Myitngé) is crossed at 2¼ miles.

FROM NAMKHAN TO MÖNGSI—*continued.*

Authorities.		Number and Names of Stages, Rivers and Streams.	Distances.				Remarks.
Military.	Civil.		Intermediate.		Total.		
			M.	F.	M.	F.	
G.O.C. Mandalay District.	Superintendent, Northern Shan States.	**6. Campon Nammaw.** Nammaw, steep banks, but very little water at crossing. No other streams of importance.	**11**	**2**	70	4	General direction south-east. Nature of path good; hilly, but no very steep gradients. Villages passed on road:- At 1½ miles Kônkaw, five houses and one kyaung (10 men). 4½ miles Manpyin, 12 houses. 6 miles Kongnim, 30 houses and one kyaung (150 men). Six hundred yards from Kongnim is Loilemtal, a village of 20 houses.
		7. Möngsi ... Namsi and Namkán.	**8**	**2**	78	6	General direction north-east. Nature of path very good throughout. Villages passed:— At 3¼ miles Namwan, 20 houses. 4¼ miles Mansawman, 15 houses. 5¾ miles Maupun, 20 houses. 6¼ miles Manpun (part of), five houses. 7½ miles { Hôkán, four houses / Kônlôn, six houses } ¾ mile off road. 7¾ miles Manpaw, 18 houses. Möngsi contains about 50 houses and a small bazaar. There is a large kyaung on north-west of town, about ¼ mile off, which would accommodate 250 men. It is on rising ground commanding the town, and is surrounded by a brick wall about 3 feet high. Möngsi is a Shan village, but most of the villages on the hills in the neighbourhood are Kachin. Paddy, eggs, and fowls can be obtained at low prices. Camping ground about 500 yards north of village in paddy-fields. Water from several small streams plentiful and good. The Namsi is crossed four times in this march; depth not more than 6 inches; hard bottom; easy banks. The Namkán, a small stream with steep banks, has a good stone bridge about 4 feet wide.

No. 45.

From NAMKHAM to MÖNGYIN.

BY LIEUT. G. W. T. PROWSE, 1ST DUKE OF CORNWALL'S LIGHT INFANTRY, ATTACHÉ, INTELLIGENCE BRANCH, 1892.

Military	Civil	Stage	Int. M.	Int. F.	Total M.	Total F.	Remarks
G.O.C. Mandalay District.	Superintendent, Northern Shan States.	**1. Mansák** ... Namma and Nampwon.	**9**	**6**	...		General direction south-west. The path, which is unmetalled and good throughout, after leaving the town of Namkham, leads through paddy-fields on the south side of the valley. For the 1st mile the path is carried along a raised causeway crossing several small bridges of hurdle work. This portion could be easily made passable for carts. Half-a-mile from Namkham the direct route to Theinni *viâ* Möngyu (Route

FROM NAMKHAM TO MÖNGYIN—*continued.*

Authorities. Military.	Authorities. Civil.	Number and Names of Stages, Rivers and Streams.	Distances. Intermediate.	Distances. Total.	Remarks.
G.O.C. Mandalay District.	Superintendent, Northern Shan States.	**1. Mansák**—*cont.*			No. 42) branches off, ascending the hills to the south. After following the valley of the Shwéli for about 1½ miles the path turns southwards, averaging 2 feet in breadth and gradually ascending. The Namma forded at 3¾ miles; 30 feet wide and 2 feet deep; rocky bottom; low gravel banks on both sides; current from 2 to 3 miles per hour. At 7½ miles the Nampwon stream is crossed by a wooden bridge 40 feet in length. Breadth of stream 25 feet, depth 2 feet; pebble bottom; bank of earth 6 feet high on the south side. During the last portion of the stage the path runs through thick jungle and is hollow in many places. With the exception of the bridge over the Nampwon at 7½ miles, the remaining bridges are small and passable for pack transport. The Nampwon bridge is 40 feet long by 3 feet broad, wooden pier, and passable for pack transport. Villages passed *en route* are:— HOUSES. Manna ... ... at ¾ mile, about 40 Manhong ... ... at 1¼ miles „ 30 Manhôpôm .. ... at 1½ „ „ 20 Manti ... ... at 2¼ „ „ 40 Longyin or Nongyin ... at 2½ „ „ 20 Manti ... ... at 2¾ „ „ 20 Kengmán ... ... at 3 „ „ 40 Namma ... ... at 3¼ „ „ 60 Manma ... ... at 3¾ „ „ 30 There is camping ground for about 250 men in paddy-fields ½ mile before reaching Mansák village which lies on the hills to the south-east; water from stream 3 to 4 feet broad and 6 inches deep. *N.B.*—This camp could not be occupied in wet weather.
		2. Pángyôk ... Nampaw.	M. F. **9 4**	M. F. 19 2	General direction south by west. On leaving camp a bad swamp has to be crossed (timber at hand for bridging, &c.), thence through thick jungle to the Nampaw stream which has to be forded. Breadth about 40 feet, depth 3 to 4 feet; rocky bottom; full of holes. Six feet banks covered with jungle on each side; current 3 miles an hour. The ford, such as it is, is a little to the right of the point where the path from Mansák camp strikes the stream. From this point the path ascends a steep hill, the top of which is reached at 4 miles. Thence it descends again to swampy crossing at 5 miles, the jungle on both sides of the path being very thick. From 5 miles there is a steep ascent through jungle to 6½ miles, the path being only 2 feet wide. At 7 miles the path begins to descend to camp, it is steep and rocky in places, but passable for pack transport. Good camping ground for a battalion in paddy-fields at 9½ miles; water plentiful and close at hand. Supplies from village of Pángyôk. There are no bridges on this stage with the exception of a single tree trunk laid across the Nampaw stream at 2½ miles. Villages passed *en route*: Manpo (Palaung) at 4½ miles. Pángyôk (Palaung) at 9½ miles is a scattered village of about 50 houses. *N.B.*—This stage would be very difficult, if not impassable, in rainy weather owing to steepness of path in many places and the bad crossing over the Nampaw stream.

FROM NAMKHAM TO MÖNGYIN—*continued.*

Authorities. Military.	Authorities. Civil.	Number and Names of Stages, Rivers and Streams.	Distances. Intermediate. M.	F.	Distances. Total. M.	F.	Remarks.
G.O.C. Mandalay District.	Superintendent, Northern Shan States.	**3. Hôpáng** ... ... Namhongya, Namma, Namting, Namsi, and Namwi.	**8**	**0**	27	6	General direction south. The path after leaving camp fords the Namhongya stream at ½ mile (breadth 25 feet, depth 3 feet; rock and gravel bottom; current 3 miles per hour), after which it is rocky and slippery for a little distance, gradually improving until the same stream is crossed at 1¾ miles. After this the path continues good and leads down the eastern side of the Möngwi valley through thin jungle and paddy-fields alternately. The Namma is forded at 2¾ miles; bridged but much out of repair. Width of stream 40 feet, depth 3 feet; clear and good water; rocky bottom; good approach from both banks. The Namting (breadth 30 feet, depth 1 foot; clear; pebble bottom; current about 3 miles per hour) is forded at 4 miles, after which Möngwi village is passed, standing on a slight rise on the eastern side of the valley. From here the route fords the Namsi and the Namwi streams, leading to Hôpáng village at the southern end of the valley at 8⅛ miles. Villages passed *en route:* Tungcháng at 4 miles, 2 miles to west of path. Möngwi at 5 miles; 35 houses. Nongpát, at 7⅛ miles, 1 mile to east of path; about 20 houses. Hôpáng at 8½ miles; 15 houses; Shan and Palaung; also a small kyaung. There is good camping ground in the paddy-fields to the north of the village for a battalion. Water from a stream close at hand, 4 feet wide and 6 inches deep. Paddy 6 annas per large basket.
		4. Pángnim ... ... Namsasa, Namlwi, and Namwi.	**11**	**4**	39	2	General direction south. The path ascends a steep and rocky hill on leaving camp, then fords the Namsasa (breadth 10 feet, depth 2 feet; current 3 to 4 miles an hour; rocky bottom), after which it is in good condition averaging 3 feet wide. After fording another small stream (the Namlwi, breadth 30 feet, depth 2 feet; rocky bottom; current 3 to 4 miles per hour), it winds up a steep and wooded hill reaching the crest of the hills which bound the Möngwi valley on the south, at which point the village of Lawnaw is situated. From here to the village of Makwao reached at 7½ miles, the path is in good order and averages 4 feet wide leading over undulating ground. From village the path descends gradually at first and then more steeply to Pángnim village at 11⅛ miles. This latter portion is in good condition and 3 feet wide. Bridges on this stage are:—No. 1, at 1¼ miles: wooden planks laid longitudinally; 14 feet long by 4 feet wide; passable for pack transport. No. 2, at 1⅛ miles: a stone slab, 3 feet long by 4 feet wide. No. 3, at 1¾ miles; single plank. No. 4, wooden bridge over stream at Pángnim village; 40 feet long by 12 feet wide; passable for pack transport. Villages passed *en route:* Lawnaw at 5½ miles; 40 houses; a single bamboo palisade across path leading to village. A Palaung village. Makwao at 7⅛ miles; 50 houses and wooden kyaung to hold 60 men. There is a double bamboo palisade across the path leading into this village. Pángnim, 15 to 20 houses, is a Palaung and Shan village. There is a large wooden kyaung with bamboo zayáts on hill to north of village which would hold 200 men. There is a fifth-day bazaar held here. Camping ground for a battalion on either side of the Namwi, a clear stream, 30 feet to 40 feet wide, 3 feet deep, pebbly bottom, at Pángnim, which is the boundary at this point between Mômeik State and North Theinni; Pángnim village itself being in Mômeik territory.

FROM NAMKHAM TO MÖNGYIN—*continued.*

Authorities.		Number and Names of Stages, Rivers and Streams.	Distances.		Remarks.
Military.	Civil.		Intermediate.	Total.	
			M. F.	M. F.	
G.O.C. Mandalay District.	Superintendent, Northern Shan States.	**5. Namhai** ... Namraw and several other small streams.	**15 4**	54 6	General direction south. The path at first ascends steeply, then descends to a small stream crossing it by a bridge. Thence it leads into a large paddy valley, follows it down to its southern end and then again ascends steeply through very thick and overhanging jungle. The jungle continues very thick and the path is much obstructed by fallen trees until the summit is reached. Thence the path runs over wooded summits, pine trees being plentiful on this portion of the route. Malu village is reached at $11\frac{3}{4}$ miles after a steep descent. From here the path descends again to Hôlaw; it is in good condition at this point; average width 4 feet. After another descent the valley is reached, in which lies the village of Namhai. Bridge at $1\frac{3}{4}$ miles of longitudinal planks, 15 feet long by 3 feet wide, and passable for pack transport. Villages passed *en route:* Malu at $11\frac{3}{4}$ miles; four houses; a Kachin village. Hôlaw at $12\frac{3}{4}$ miles; 40 houses; also Kachin. Namhai at $15\frac{1}{2}$ miles; 25 houses; Palaung. There is a small kyaung here, and a fifth-day bazaar is held. Camping ground for a battalion $\frac{1}{4}$ mile south of village in paddy-fields.
		6. Möngyin ... Namyi and three other small streams.	**17 0**	71 6	General direction south. The path leads down the valley for 2 miles over grassy undulations. The Namyi stream has then to be forded (breadth 30 yards, depth 2 feet; pebble bottom; grassy banks on both sides; about 10 feet high; current 3 miles per hour), after which the path leads up a steep hill to Taungyi village. It afterwards descends leading past Manpu village, whence there is another long descent through thick jungle to the valley of the Namtu (Myitngé) river, the path being passable for pack bullocks or mules. The path across the Namtu valley is level and in good order and averages 4 feet in width. At 17 miles the river is reached, the village of Möngyin lying on the left or further bank. There is a good dry weather camping ground for a battalion in paddy-fields on the right bank of the river opposite Möngyin (Shan) village, which consists of about 40 houses. There is a ferry at the village consisting of two dug-outs; the river at this point being about 100 yards in width; very deep with a sluggish current of about 1 mile per hour. There is a ford which can be used in the dry season about 1 mile above the ferry. Bridges on this stage:—No. 1, at $7\frac{3}{4}$ miles; 15 feet long by 4 feet wide; longitudinal planks; passable for pack transport. No. 2, at $9\frac{3}{4}$ miles; wooden plank bridge; 35 feet long and 3 feet wide; passable. No. 3, at $16\frac{3}{4}$ miles, wooden plank bridge 10 feet long by 4 feet wide; passable. Villages passed *en route:* Môta at $\frac{1}{2}$ mile; 10 houses. Tánglet at $2\frac{1}{4}$ miles; nine houses; Shan village. Taungyi at $6\frac{3}{4}$ miles; 25 houses. Manpu at $9\frac{3}{4}$ miles; 50 houses; Shan and Palaung. Manhai at $15\frac{3}{4}$ miles; 20 houses. Mankángmöng at $16\frac{1}{2}$ miles; 30 houses. Manmaw at $16\frac{3}{4}$ miles; 20 houses. From Möngyin to Láshio is 28 miles. *See* Route No. 13. *Note.*—This route, although affording an alternative route to Namkham, is far more circuitous, in much worse condition, and considerably longer than the route *viâ* Theinni and Möngyu (No. 42).

No. 46.

From NAMKHAM to YUNGCHÁNGFU (China).

BY LIEUT. E. W. M. NORIE, OFFICIATING DEPUTY ASSISTANT QUARTERMASTER-GENERAL, INTELLIGENCE BRANCH, FROM NATIVE INFORMATION, OCTOBER 1890.

Authorities. Military.	Authorities. Civil.	Number and Names of Stages, Rivers and Streams.	Distances. Intermediate. M. F.	Distances. Total. M. F.	Remarks.
China.		**1. Lônghu** ...	...	...	*See* Route No. 43, Alternative I.
		2. Mŏngmao ... Shwéli river.	...	...	*See* Route No. 43, Alternative I.
		3. Séfán (Kyé-fán).	...	...	The road runs over low hills and is fairly good going all the way. At about half-way the Kachin village of Awkhwé is passed, containing about 10 houses. Kyéfán (or Séfán) is a Chinese-Shan village, burnt down some three or four years ago and only lately re-built; there are only about 100 houses, though formerly it contained 500 or 600 houses. There is a good bazaar. The Shwéli river is about 2 miles distant to the south-east, and this place can also be reached by boat from Namkham.
		4. Mangshu ... Shwéli river.	...	...	The road passes over a small range about 4 miles from Kyéfán, but after that is level and good going. Mangshu is a large Chinese-Shan town of 300 or 400 houses and is under a Sawbwa. The country all round is very rich, and there are many smaller villages scattered about. Water from a small stream, said to be the head-waters of the Myitngé * river. There is a good bazaar. The Shwéli river is crossed at the beginning of the march.
		5. Lukyáng ...	...	...	Road is good all the way, running over plains and low hills. Lukyáng † is a Chinese-Shan village of about 40 or 50 houses under the Mangshu Sawbwa. It is situated on or close to the Salween river.
		6. Pupiáng ... Lukyáng (Salween).	...	...	On leaving Lukyáng the river is crossed by a bridge and China Proper is entered. The road is all good over plain and hills and is a made Chinese road. Pupiáng is a Chinese village of about 40 houses. Supplies procurable. Water from a stream and wells.
		7. Lônlin	...	...	Road good, the same as last stage. Lônlin is a large Chinese town of 500 or 600 houses and a garrison of 1,000 men, but not fortified. Water from wells. Supplies, &c., procurable. ‡

* Perhaps of *a* Myitngé, but certainly not the Myitngé best known to us, which joins the Irrawaddy at Ava and is called in Shan the Namtu.—A. F.

† Lukyáng is the Chinese name for the Salween river and is probably not really the name of this village, but of the stage.—A. F.

‡ Some mistake here evidently, as Lônlin is on the right or west bank of the Salween.—A. F.

FROM NAMKHAM TO YUNGCHÁNGFU (CHINA)—*continued.*

Authorities. Military.	Authorities. Civil.	Number and Names of Stages, Rivers and Streams.	Distances. Intermediate.	Distances. Total.	Remarks.
			M. F.	M. F.	
China.		**8. Famakyáng** ...	...	...	Good road, same as last stage. Famakyáng is a Chinese village of about 50 houses with a bazaar. Supplies obtainable and water from a stream and wells.
		9. Yungchángfu.	...	...	Good road, same as last stage. Yungchángfu is a very large, fortified Chinese town with a garrison of about 6,000 men under a General (Chintai), and a Commissioner (Fugwan) also resides here. All supplies, &c., procurable.
			Captain E. W. Dun, "D.S.O.," Deputy Assistant Quartermaster-General, Intelligence Branch, 1886-87, gives the following stages for the same route up to the Salween, and is probably more correct as regards the portion of the route beyond Séfán :— 1. Bawligokaung. 2. Kyélakha. 3. Séfán. 4. Mangshu. 5. Lônlin. 6. Kyinganaaw. 7. Lukiáng Kyaing. 8. Cross the Salween river (Lukiáng) to Famakyáng.		

No. 47.

From NAMSAN to LASHIO viâ PÁNGLÔN and MANSAM.

BY CAPT. A. C. YATE, 1ST BELUCH LIGHT INFANTRY, JANUARY 1888.

Military	Civil	Stages	Intermediate M.	Intermediate F.	Total M.	Total F.	Remarks
G.O.C. Mandalay District.	Superintendent, Northern Shan States.	**1. Taungma (5,500 feet).** *Nil.*	7	4	7	4	*See* Route No. 72, Stage 4.
		2. Lilu (1,700 feet). Namkwai and Namtu (Myitngé).	11	0	18	4	Road for ½ mile south-east as far as hamlet of Taungmé. Here road to left to Lilu and straight on to Lwéseng pagoda. About 1 mile village of Mankáng lies about 2 miles to left or north; road to it from Taungmé. At 1½ miles pass small village of Mansáng. At 3 miles road bifurcates—that to the left being the longer and easier road (about 6 miles to Pánghu from point of bifurcation on lower road which winds round the ridge and passes the village of Haitom) and that to the right over the ridge the shorter and more difficult (about 3½ miles to Pánghu). These two roads meet again at Pánghu Sakháu 7½ miles where there is camping room (but crowded and very inconvenient) for mixed force of about 300 men with the

No. 47.

From NAMSÁN to LÁSHIO *viá* PÁNGLÔN and MANSÁM—*continued.*

Authorities. Military.	Authorities. Civil.	Number and Names of Stages, Rivers and Streams.	Distances. Intermediate.	Distances. Total.	Remarks.
G.O.C. Mandalay District.	Superintendent, Northern Shan States.	**2. Lilu (1,700 feet)**—*cont.*			usual transport. Elevation of Pánghu about 4,450 feet. Water very limited and ⅓ mile from camp. In April or May probably little or no water. Animals at any time may have to go without water, unless tank be constructed beforehand. Fuel and grass plentiful. The road from the point where it bifurcates (as mentioned above) to Lilu is very difficult, the ascents and descents being very steep, and path narrow and overhanging precipices. Pack mules and ponies are liable to fall over. From Pánghu to Lilu continuous and precipitous descent, giving a fall of from 2,000 to 2,500 feet in 4 miles. Lilu is a village of about 15 houses. Owing to the rapids in the Myitngé it is impossible to communicate by water either with Tápök (5 or 6 miles north) or with Táti, 12 or 15 miles below or south-east. There is a road from Lilu north-west (leaving the Myitngé to the east) to the village of Manpeng (about 6 miles), and thence to Lontôk, Manlwoi and Namsán. At Lilu the Namkwai stream flows into the Myitngé. The Namkwai is easily fordable. Myitngé is about 100 yards broad, 15 or 20 feet deep, and with very slow current at ford. Only one boat available capable of carrying 20 men or 40 or 50 maunds of kit at each trip. A small bamboo raft can be put together in two or three hours from material procurable in the village or from the surrounding jungle. There is foot-path straight up the wooded heights overhanging the left bank of the Myitngé to Tápu and Pánglôn. It is only used by men. It took the Northern Shan Column (about 600 men, 500 mules and ponies, and 1,500 maunds of luggage, ammunition, stores, &c.) over 48 hours to cross this ferry, the water carriage available being one boat and one raft, as mentioned above. The raft had to be built and the boat strengthened. The animals were all swum across. The ford is well commanded from the left bank and would be difficult to cross in the face of determined resistance. Rice, fruit, vegetables and tobacco cultivated at Lilu. Fairly good camping ground for small force on either bank of river. Kyaung. From Lilu a foot-path runs due north up the Namkwai valley and then north-west through the village of Mankáng and Taungma to Namlin (or Mannamlin), *see* Route No. 49, Stage 2, distance 2 marches. This route is practicable for men only. Tea grows wild on the hills around Lilu; also bamboos in abundance. Supplies procurable at Lilu; buffaloes, a few bullocks, and some rice, paddy and vegetables.
		3. Pánglôn (2,900 feet). A stream bridged for pack transport.	M. F. **8 0**	M. F. 26 4	After crossing the Namtu (the Northern Shan Column took from 12 A.M. on 11th to 2 P.M. on 13th to cross it, actual working hours about 27), the road runs for 1¾ miles along the left bank of the river. Road so far level and good for pack transport. At 1¾ miles it begins to ascend and continues to ascend till Pángtápu is reached at 3¾ miles. Here camp and water sufficient for a brigade. Water from spring and for animals from several small pools. At about 2½ miles pass camping ground called Napángsán for small force of 200 men; water good and abundant. Part of Pángtápu is swampy, and the locality generally is chilly and probably malarious. From Pángtápu road ascends very gently for 2 miles and then descends by easy gradients for 2 miles more passing through a wide area

FROM NAMSÁN TO LÁSHIO *viâ* PÁNGLÔN AND MANSÁM—*continued.*

Authorities.		Number and Names of Stages, Rivers and Streams.	Distances.		Remarks.
Military.	Civil.		Intermediate.	Total.	
G.O.C. Mandalay District.	Superintendent, Northern Shan States.	**3. Pánglôn (2,900 feet)**—*cont.*			of taungyas to Pánglôn. At $\frac{1}{2}$ mile from Pángtápu pass small hamlet of Tápu. Here path to left to join foot-path from Lilu to Pánglôn, and to right to hamlet of Chongsa, distant from 1 to 2 miles. The foot-path from Lilu meets the bullock road close to the village of Pánglôn. Pánglôn large village; good water; one kyaung. Bazaar once or twice a week. Supplies rice, bullocks, buffaloes, vegetables, &c. Fair camping ground round the village for a brigade. In the spring and summer, however, the water-supply is much reduced, and is probably barely sufficient for 500 men. The water-supply at Napángsán will then be much better than that of Pángtápu. It is about 9 miles from Pánglôn to Táti, where is ferry over the Namtu, and about 5 miles thence Thíbaw. Road fairly good. There are four boats at Táti which can be lashed together so as to make two rafts. Each raft can carry 13 or 14 bullock loads. It would, therefore, take about 76 trips to cross over the 990 bullocks of rations that met the Northern Shan Column at Pánglôn on 14th January. The bullocks are trained to swim across. From here, too, there are roads east to Naungmwon (*see* Route No. 53, Northern Division, distance about 20 miles, and to Tápök ferry about 8 miles).
		4. Mansám (2,600 feet). Cross many streamlets, all bridged for bullocks.	M. F. **9 6**	M. F. 36 2	The direction of the road from Pánglôn to Mansám is north-north-east. The road is throughout good and level and could be easily made into a cart road; all the little streams crossed are bridged for bullock transport. The country traversed is jungly with clearings at intervals for *taungyas*. Several small hamlets and villages are passed at distances varying from $\frac{1}{4}$ mile to 1 mile from road. At 2$\frac{1}{4}$ miles pass village of Pánghát (10 houses), $\frac{1}{8}$ mile to left of road. At 2$\frac{3}{4}$ miles path to left to hamlet of Mansám (three houses), distant 1 mile. At 3 miles passing Naungyai, camping ground for small force. Water for animals from pond. At 4 miles road to right to Nángön ($\frac{1}{2}$ mile, 12 houses) and to Nahôk (1 mile, 30 houses). At 5$\frac{3}{4}$ miles path to right to Bankom (1 mile, 12 houses), and at 6 miles hamlet of Samka (three houses) to right of road. At 7$\frac{1}{4}$ miles Longmök to left ($\frac{1}{4}$ mile, 10 houses), and Nongkök to right (1 mile, 10 houses). At 8$\frac{1}{4}$ miles north and south Möngmö, 30 houses. At 9$\frac{1}{4}$ miles Hotáng, eight houses. At 4$\frac{1}{2}$, 8$\frac{1}{4}$, and 8$\frac{3}{4}$ miles there are roads to the left to the village of Pángshaw, a Palaung village, which lies on the road to Tápök and west of the range of hills which runs 1 or 1$\frac{1}{2}$ miles west of and parallel to the Pánglôn-Mansám road. At 9$\frac{1}{4}$ miles there is a road to the left to the village of Mönghwé (4 miles), and then on to the Pángtông ferry over the Namtu. Pángtông is one bullock march west of Mansám. Mansám is a large village of some 50 houses with a bazaar and kyaung. It can accommodate or furnish camping ground for a battalion. Plenty of water. In ordinary times supplies, such as rice, bullocks, vegetables, fruits, &c., procurable. Paddy for transport cattle can be procured at almost any village. The numerous villages and *taungyas* between Pánglôn and Mansám prove that rice is usually plentiful in the neighbourhood. At Mansám four roads at least meet, namely, from Thíbaw *viâ* Pánglôn, from Namsán

FROM NAMSÁN TO LÁSHIO *viâ* PÁNGLÔN AND MANSÁM—*continued.*

Authorities.		Number and Names of Stages, Rivers and Streams.	Distances.		Remarks.
Military.	Civil.		Inter-mediate.	Total.	
G.O.C. Mandalay District.	Superintendent, Northern Shan States.	**4. Mansám (2,600 feet)**—*cont.*			*viâ* Pángtông, from Namkham and Möngyin, and from Theinni and Láshio. The frontier of Theinni and Taungbaing is the river Nammi, which flows about 2 miles north of Mansám and then turning south forms the eastern boundary of Taungbain at a distance of about 2 or 3 miles west of the Pánglôn-Mansám road. At the village of Hathai, about 3 miles west of Pánglôn, the Nammi stream is the boundary between Taungbaing and Thíbaw territory.
			M. F.	M. F.	
		5. Pángkyem (2,200 feet). Nammi river and many small streams.	8 6	45 0	Bad road crossing several small streams deep in mud and mire. Steep gradients. Track deeply cut up by pack bullocks. Banks of streams unramped. Some of the streams are bridged. Road crosses a succession of low hill ranges and ravines. The Nammi stream is crossed at $2\frac{1}{8}$ miles from Mansám. The approaches to it are difficult and should be ramped. It is an easy ford. There is a foot-bridge over it just above the ford. The path to the foot-bridge leads straight from the village of Ngakyé, which is about $\frac{3}{8}$ of a mile north-west of the ford. Road passes through jungle the whole way. Few signs of cultivation. At $\frac{1}{8}$ mile pass hamlet of Namutwé (five houses, rice cultivation), close to the road on the right. At $2\frac{3}{8}$ miles pass village of Ngakyé (15 houses, rice cultivation). Just beyond, *i.e.*, on the east bank of the Nammi river, is a bullock camping ground called Pángsaw. Pángkyem is a scattered village of 30 houses on high ground. It is fully $\frac{1}{4}$ mile from the stream which supplies it with water. It is a dirty straggling village, and was half destroyed in December 1887 by raiders from Taungbaing. The bullock halting place is about $\frac{1}{2}$ mile east of the village and forms a better camping ground for a small force than any ground near the village. No supplies at present owing to impoverished state of village.
		6. Pángyáng ... Several small streams and the Namyaw river ford; three deep streams; current moderate.	7 7	52 7	Road hilly and rather difficult. Gradients steep in places, but not for long distances. The bullock bridges over the small streams are in need of repair. The road traverses jungle all the way and crosses a succession of ranges, the highest some 3,000 to 3,500 above sea-level. On the summits of the highest ridges the fir tree, but of small size, re-appeared. A good deal of sâl grows about here. Quarter of a mile from Pángkyem road to right to Kachin village of Katáng (16 houses), distance 1 mile, and 1 mile further Kachin village of Lwéngnm (10 houses); 1 mile from Pángkyem, Pángsáng, whence road to right (south-east) to Naungmwon. Palaung village of Pángleng, 1 mile distant along the road. Distance to Naungmwon about 12 miles. At 2 miles road to right (south) to Pángleng. At 4 miles road to left to Kachin villages of Húkong (2 miles, five long houses) and Pángtôn ($2\frac{1}{4}$ miles, six long houses). At $5\frac{1}{8}$ miles Kachin village of Pánghön (eight long houses). At $5\frac{3}{4}$ miles Lwékaw (four long houses). At both pigs, chickens, &c., procurable. At 7 miles reach Namhwai stream and at $7\frac{1}{8}$ cross Namyaw river, ford 3 feet deep, but not difficult. Good, sound, but rather stony bottom.

FROM NAMSÁN TO LÁSHIO *viâ* PÁNGLÔN AND MANSÁM—*continued.*

Authorities. Military.	Authorities. Civil.	Number and Names of Stages, Rivers and Streams.	Distances. Intermediate. M.	F.	Distances. Total. M.	F.	Remarks.
G.O.C. Mandalay District.	Superintendent, Northern Shan States.	**7. Láshio** ... Several small streams, some bridged.	**10**	**6**	63	5	Road fairly good for pack transport. Level as a rule, easy gradients. Streams and swampy ground require bridging. Pass numerous villages and much land under rice cultivation. After passing Inai jungle becomes very sparse. Little or no jungle in the Láshio valley. At 2 miles cross Namyai stream. At $2\frac{3}{4}$ miles village of Pángkwaitai (Palaungs, five long houses), $\frac{1}{4}$ mile right of road. At 3 miles Namyai river to left of road. At $3\frac{1}{4}$ miles road to right (110°) to Kônsong, and thence south-west to Naungmwon, distance two bullock marches (equal about 12 miles). At $4\frac{1}{4}$ miles village of Kaunyim to right and left of road (15 houses, five hamlets, one kyaung). At $4\frac{1}{2}$ miles bazaar and road to left to Inai, distant 1 mile. Inai has 20 houses, but has been recently burnt. At 5 miles cross small streams. At $5\frac{1}{8}$ miles road to left to Kônsa (1 mile), eight houses, one kyaung, and some zayáts. In next 2 miles several roads to left to Kônsa. At $5\frac{1}{4}$ miles road to right to Hpálong (1 mile, Palaung village, four houses). At 7 miles pass through gorge among low hills. At $7\frac{1}{4}$ miles path to left to Könim (2 miles, Shan village). At $8\frac{1}{2}$ miles high rock to right, full of caves, and close to it village of Bantám, "the village of the caves." At $8\frac{3}{4}$ miles path to Shan village of Kônkaw, distant 1 mile. At $9\frac{1}{4}$ miles Palaung village of Myowan on hill, $\frac{1}{3}$ mile to right of road. At $10\frac{1}{4}$ miles pass house of Hein of Láshio and large kyaungs. At $10\frac{3}{4}$ miles reach Láshio bazaar. It is said there were 1,000 houses hereabouts formerly. Now all have been burnt. Very large area of rice cultivation here. Stream called Namshio flows within $\frac{1}{3}$ mile of the bazaar and falls into Namyaw, $1\frac{1}{2}$ miles further north-east. Good camping ground on the high land in the rains and on the paddy-fields in the dry season. No supplies at present, but usually rice, bullocks, chickens, fruits, vegetables, coarse sugar, &c., procurable. From Láshio roads diverge to all parts of the Northern Shan States.

BRANCH I.

FROM MANSÁM (STAGE 4) TO MÖNGYIN.

BY CAPT. A. C. YATE, FROM NATIVE INFORMATION, JANUARY 1888.

Military	Civil	Stages	Int. M.	F.	Total M.	F.	Remarks
G.O.C. Mandalay District.	Superintendent, Northern Shan States.	**1. Kumlom** ... Unknown.	**5**	**0**	5	0	Hilly road. Palaung village of 30 houses. Kyaung. Water from wells.
		2. Hatu ... ... Unknown.	**2**	**0**	7	0	Hilly road. This is the frontier village of Taungbaing. It is a mere hamlet, inhabited by Palaungs.
		3. Mákamwán ... Unknown.	**6**	**0**	13	0	Level road. Palaung village of 10 houses. Water from stream.
		4. Möngyin ... Unknown.	**6**	**0**	19	0	Hilly road.

From NAMSÁM to LÁSHIO *viâ* PÁNGLÔN and MANSÁM—*continued*.

BRANCH II.

From MANSÁM (Stage 4) to NAMLIN (Route No. 49, in Stage 2).

By Lieut. S. WILLCOCK, Gloucestershire Regiment, April 1889.

Authorities. Military.	Authorities. Civil.	Number and Names of Stages, Rivers and Streams.	Distances. Intermediate. M.	F.	Distances. Total. M.	F.	Remarks.
G.O.C. Mandalay District.	Superintendent, Northern Shan States.	**1. Pángtôn ferry.** Myitngé river.	**4**	**6**	4	6	General direction west. Nature of path for $3\frac{1}{2}$ miles excellent open jungle, perfectly level. Last $1\frac{1}{4}$ miles leaving the plateau makes a very sharp descent. Near the top the path is narrow, rocky, and very rough; the last mile is steep, but a fair path. The hills come down to the river's edge almost precipitous on both sides. Pángtôn at $4\frac{3}{4}$ miles on right bank of Myitngé river (or Namtu), about 10 houses. Ferry about 60 yards. Only two dug-outs available. Very deep, current sluggish; rapid a little below ferry.
		2. Mannai ...	**4**	**4**	9	2	General direction west by north. Nature of path good except first $\frac{1}{2}$ mile, but for 3 miles the road is very steep, rising about 1,800 feet in that distance. Path runs through bamboo jungle; many fir forests seen on hills near. At Mannai there are about 20 houses and a bamboo pôngyi kyaung (100 men). Water is scarce. A small spring at $\frac{1}{2}$ mile on south and another $1\frac{1}{2}$ miles north. Small open space on west of town very cramped for camping, and a small space beyond the pôngyi kyaung. *Villages.*—Natao, 10 houses, at $1\frac{3}{4}$ miles. Mannai at $4\frac{1}{2}$ miles, 20 houses and one pôngyi kyaung. From the top of the hill Mannaital, a village of eight houses is seen on a hill-top about 2 miles north.
		3. Camp near Namlin (Mannamlin).	**9**	**0**	18	2	General direction north-west. Nature of path good except two or three very short rocky bits. Gradients in almost all places steep. Path lies for the most part along ridges and spurs and is continually ascending and descending. Manláng at $5\frac{1}{2}$ miles, about 40 houses and a small bamboo kyaung (50 men). At 9 miles Namlin camping ground about 1 mile south-east of village of that name which has 50 houses and a kyaung (200 men). Namlin is on the main trade route between Namsán and Namkham *viâ* Möngtât, Namhai, &c., *see* Routes Nos. 45 and 49.

No. 48.

From NAMSAN to MÖNGNGAW.

By Lieut. G. W. T. PROWSE, 1st Battalion, Duke of Cornwall's Light Infantry, Attaché, Intelligence Branch, March 1891.

Military	Civil	Stages	Inter. M.	F.	Total M.	F.	Remarks
G.O.C. Mandalay District.	Superintendent, Northern Shan States.	**1. Kwonhai** ... Namch n.	**8**	**0**	8	0	General direction south by west. Road runs through Mankai to Sélôn; steep descent into Sélôn village; thence gradual descent along ridge to Sétônhôn; path leads down-hill to

FROM NAMSÁN TO MÖNGNGAW—*continued.*

Authorities. Military.	Authorities. Civil.	Number and Names of Stages, Rivers and Streams.	Distances. Inter-mediate.	Distances. Total.	Remarks.
G.O.C. Mandalay District.	Superintendent, Northern Shan States.	**1. Kwonhai**—*cont.*			south-west, narrowing from 8 feet to 4 feet; descends steeply to Namchôn stream which is forded at 5½ miles (25 feet broad, 2 feet deep; gravel bottom; low grassy banks, 3 feet high; current 3 to 4 miles per hour. Stream forded 100 yards further on; breadth 20 feet, depth 2 feet; rocky bottom; current 3 to 4 miles per hour), thence ascend again steeply and then more gradually to Kwonhai. Road good; ascent and descent to Namchôn steep in places. Double plank foot-bridge over Namchôn at 5½ miles. *Villages.*—Pángkôk 1½ miles east of Sélôn, Palaung village. Sétônhôn, 2 miles; 24 houses; wooden kyaung and zayáts for 150 men; Palaung village. Kwonhai, 8 miles; 35 houses; Palaung village. Camping ground at north end of village on pagoda platform for 50 to 70 men. Water from small pipe 300 yards east of camp. Paddy Rs. 2 per large basket. Small bamboo kyaung and zayáts for 50 men. No supplies obtainable, except vegetables. *Note.*—There appear to be paths direct from here to Ommatát and Ommasôm (Stages 3 and 4 below).
		2. North Kunhot (or Kunwot). Kwonhai and smaller streams.	M. 9 F. 0	M. 17 F. 0	General direction south. Path descends ridge on which village is built to Kwonhai stream at 2¼ miles (15 feet broad, 1 foot deep; pebble bottom; high and steep jungly banks; current 2 miles per hour); thence ascends steeply by good path 6 feet wide over undulations, descending at 5½ and 7½ miles, whence there is very steep ascent by bad and narrow path, 1 foot wide, to North Kunhot. This last ascent would be impracticable for transport in wet weather. *Bridges.*—At 2¼ miles foot-bridge of unsquared poles (over Kwonhai stream), 25 feet by 4 feet. *Villages.*—Suneng, above path at 2½ miles (Palaung). Kungpong, 1 mile east of path at 7 miles; eight houses (Palaung). North Kunhot, 9 miles; 45 houses; is a Palaung village. Small camping ground at south end of village for 50 to 70 men; also 150 men at north end near pagodas. Water from springs on side of hill on which village is built. Paddy Rs. 2 per basket. Wooden kyaung and zayáts (in bad repair) for 150 men. A new kyaung is being built by Chinese labour. Tea is the staple crop here. The road leads on from here to South Kunhot; thence through Pánsapyé (boundary village of Taungbaing State) to Thíbaw (*see* Route No. 72).
		3. Ommatát ... Namlo and another small stream.	5 6	22 6	General direction north-west. Path leads back to north end of village, where it descends very steeply through tea plantation; steep ascent on opposite side of valley; path at first bad and rocky, afterwards good and undulating to 4½ miles, where it descends to Namlo stream (15 feet broad, 1 foot deep; stony bottom; current 2 to 3 miles per hour); thence steep ascent by good path to Ommatát, which has 10 houses; Palaung. Bamboo kyaung and zayáts for 40 men. Excellent grassy camping ground for 200 men on road side ½ mile beyond village. Water from spring at camp.

FROM NAMSÁN TO MÖNGNGAW—*continued.*

Authorities: Military.	Authorities: Civil.	Number and Names of Stages, Rivers and Streams.	Distances: Intermediate. M.	Distances: Intermediate. F.	Distances: Total. M.	Distances: Total. F.	Remarks.
G.O.C. Mandalay District.	Superintendent, Northern Shan States.	**4. Ommasôm** ...	**5**	**6**	28	4	General direction west. Path leads up ridge at back of camp; gradual ascent to $1\frac{1}{2}$ miles; path good and 6 feet wide. At 2 miles descends steeply down wooded spur to 3 miles, where it turns sharply to the left and runs to along the valley to camp $\frac{3}{4}$ mile east of Ommasôm (Ommasông) village, which has 10 houses; Palaung. Good, but rather marshy camping ground for 150 men. Water from stream at camp 10 feet wide, 1 foot deep. Paddy Rs. 2 per basket.
		5. Kwégôn ... Namsim and small fordable streams.	**8**	**0**	36	4	General direction west. Road good and 10 feet broad; ascends hill to Ommasôm village; top of hill reached at 1 mile; thence runs along crest, descending at 5 miles to Namsim valley; crosses river at 6 miles by ford (breadth 40 yards, depth 2 feet; pebble and sandy bottom; banks 4 feet high, covered with grass and jungle; current 2 to 3 miles per hour; clear and good water) and runs along river bank over roughly paved road; at 7 miles Kwégôn; after 6th mile the path is narrow and very stony in places. *Villages passed.*—Haikum, $5\frac{3}{4}$ miles; five houses; Shan village. Kwégôn has six houses; Shan and Palaung. Excellent camp for battalion in paddy-fields round village. Water from the river. Paddy Rs. 1-8-0 per basket. This village has only been built a few months and supplies are limited to a few vegetables.
		6. Möngngaw ... Namsim and Nammaw.	**6**	**4**	43	0	General direction south-west. River Namsim forded just beyond village and again ... $\frac{3}{4}$ mile; thence steep ascent and descent into valley at 2 miles, running parallel to river, which is forded at 3 miles and again at $4\frac{1}{4}$ miles; thence Nammaw stream (breadth 25 feet; depth 1 foot; stony bottom; low grass banks, with paddy-fields on either side; current 2 to 3 miles per hour) and valley is crossed, after which the path ascends, slightly descending again to Möngngaw on right bank of Namsim river. Good path all the way, except short and steep ascent at $1\frac{1}{4}$ miles. *Bridges.*—At $5\frac{1}{8}$ miles wooden covered bridge; longitudinal plank; length 40 feet, 4 feet broad; out of repair and unused. Stream at the side easily forded. *Villages.*—Tungpán, $2\frac{1}{2}$ miles; four houses; Shan village. North and South Loikeo, 4 miles; 16 and 8 houses; Shan village. Manhai, $5\frac{1}{2}$ miles, $\frac{1}{4}$ of mile north of road; 23 houses; Shan village. Tawmôn $5\frac{3}{4}$ miles, $\frac{1}{2}$ a mile west of road; eight houses; Shan and Palaung village. Möngngaw 53 houses; Shan village. This is a large and prosperous village. It is the residence of a "Haing" and head of a circle. Excellent and practically unlimited camping ground in paddy-fields along right bank of river. Paddy Rs. 1-8-0 per basket. Wooden kyaung and zayáts for 150 men. The river was originally spanned at this point by a large wooden bridge, only the frame of which is left standing. There is a ford at the same spot, the depth 2 feet and bottom hard

FROM NAMSÁN TO MÖNGNGAW—*continued.*

Authorities. Military.	Authorities. Civil.	Number and Names of Stages, Rivers and Streams.	Distances. Intermediate.	Distances. Total.	Remarks.
G.O.C. Mandalay District.	Superintendent, Northern Shan States.	**6. Möngngaw**—*cont.*			and pebbly; no large timber available for repairs; but smaller trees are plentiful for temporary bridging, &c. Throughout the whole of Taungbaing vegetables are the only articles of supply to be depended on. Fowls and eggs and generally pork can be bought from Kachin or Lishaw villages; but these lie mostly on the borders of the state. From here roads lead west to Mainglôn, south to the Mandalay-Láshio road which is struck at Loikaw (*see* Route No. 53, Northern Division, Stage 11) and north to Mantôn (*see* Route No. 34).

No. 49.

From NAMSÁN to NAMHAI (for NAMKHAM) viâ MÖNGTAT.

BY LIEUT. S. WILLCOCK, 2ND GLOUCESTERSHIRE REGIMENT, APRIL 1889.

Military	Civil	Stages	Inter. M.	Inter. F.	Total M.	Total F.	Remarks
G.O.C. Mandalay District.	Superintendent, Northern Shan States.	**1. Namkwai (creek).** Namkwai.	6	0	6	0	General direction east. Gradual descent almost all the way. Mankhai, 10 houses, is passed about half-way. Camp on Namkwai stream about 20 feet wide in April and about 1 foot deep.
		2. Camp near Kökön. Stream.	9	6	15	6	General direction north-east. Nature of path good. Ascent from Namkwai creek and descent to creek from Kökön are very steep. *Villages.*—Manloi (or Manlwé)* at 3¼ miles, 30 houses; kyaung for 200 men. Manloital at 4 miles, 25 houses; kyaung (150 men). Namlin or Mannamlin at 7½ miles, 50 houses; kyaung for 200 men. Here road joins in from south-east from Lilu (*see* Route No. 47, Stage 2). Kökön at 8¾ miles, 25 houses; kyaung for 100 men. One stream is forded 1¼ miles north of Kökön village, unbridged, width 7 to 10 feet, depth 4 to 6 inches at this season. Water good.
		3. Pángkôk ...	6	2	22	0	General direction north-east half-way, north-west half-way. Nature of path good, except one or two short rocky bits, rising gradually most of the way. *Villages.*—Manloi at 2¼ miles, about 20 houses; small pôngyi kyaung to hold 50 men. Pángkôk at 6¼ miles, 18 houses; small pôngyi kyaung for 50 men.
		4. Shöpkôn ... Myitngé or Namtu and Namkôn.	7	4	29	4	General direction east by south. Nature of path good in most places, but a few short rocky pieces; gradients easy, except last ¼ mile leading down to

* Loi and Lwé are the Shan and Burmese rendering respectively of the same word.—A. F.

FROM NAMSÁN TO NAMHAI (FOR NAMKHAM) *viâ* MÖNGTÁT—*continued.*

Authorities. Military.	Authorities. Civil.	Number and Names of Stages, Rivers and Streams.	Distances. Intermediate. M.	Distances. Intermediate. F.	Distances. Total. M.	Distances. Total. F.	Remarks.
G.O.C. Mandalay District.	Superintendent, Northern Shan States.	**4. Shöpkôn**—*cont.*					Namkôn creek (about 10 yards wide, 8 inches deep; pebbly and rocky bed). No village. Camp in clearing on bank of Namtu, where it is joined by Namkôn. The Namto is here about 20 yards wide, and there is neither ford nor ferry across it here.
		5. Camp on Yómu stream. Namhángmaw Namlak, Yéháng and Yómu, insignificant streams except when in flood after heavy rain.	8	6	38	2	General direction north-north-east. Nature of path for 3 miles along the river bank is rough and rocky, remainder good. The path follows the bank of the Myitngé for 5¼ miles, at which point the Namlak, dividing Taungbaing from North Theinni, joins the river. From this point the path runs over small hills and undulating ground with thin jungle. Camp on Yómu stream in a large clearing. Water good and sufficient for a large party. *Villages.*—Yéháng at 5¼ miles, 12 houses. Loikáng at 8 miles, five houses (long Kachin houses), ½ mile west of road.
		6. Möngtát ... Pongmu, Namtát, and several smaller streams.	6	0	43	6	General direction north. Nature of path excellent throughout. Camp in old paddy-fields near junction of Namtát and Namyi. Former has 8 inches water and is about 20 yards wide in April. Road passes through thin jungle and old and present cultivation all the way. *Villages.*—Pongmu (or Yómu) at ¼ mile, eight houses. Möngtin at 2¼ miles, 18 houses. Möngtát at 5½ miles, about 40 houses and a small kyaung (50 men). Small five-day bazaar here. From here route east to Möngyin, &c., and west to Mantôn (*see* Route No. 13).
		7. Mannaôn ... Namyi and several small streams and nullahs; two bad mud nullahs.	10	0	53	6	General direction north-east. Nature of path good throughout, except two mud nullahs. Small hills and thin jungle all the way. The Namyi is crossed on leaving camp, just above its junction with Namtat. Pebbly bed. Width 20 yards, depth 10 inches. *Villages.*—Pángwa (Kachins) at 6 miles, five houses, small. Old Pangwát at 6¾ miles, one house, deserted. Camp ¼ mile east of village of Náun (or Mannáôn) in paddy-fields. Good and plentiful water.
		8. Namhai ... Namyi.	4	6	58	4	General direction north. Nature of path excellent throughout, over open ground slightly undulating. *Villages.*—Mannáôn at ¼ mile, 10 houses. Mannáôn at 2 miles, six houses. Taklet at 2½ miles, seven houses. The Namyi is forded again at 3 miles, 10 yards wide, 6 inches deep. Namhai at 4¾ miles, about 25 houses, a small kyaung and a small bazaar. Here the road from Möngyin to Namkham joins in, *see* Route No. 45, Stage 5.

No. 50.

From PÁNG YANG to MAN PÁN (WING MAW HPA).

By Lieut. C. AINSLIE, R.E., Attaché, Intelligence Branch, January 1893.

Authorities. Military.	Authorities. Civil.	Number and Names of Stages, Rivers and Streams.	Distances. Intermediate. M. F.	Distances. Total. M. F.	Remarks.
G.O.C. Mandalay District.	Superintendent, Northern Shan States.	**1. Camp on Nam Ngé Lam.** Nam Ngé, Pök and Nam Ngé Lam.	**7 0**	7 0	Páng Yáng in East Mang Lön. Lat. 22° 7′ 45″ N., Long. 98° 50′ 10″ E. From Páng Yáng the road descends south-east; steep and stony at first for 3½ miles to the Nam Ngé Hpök passing Mo wet (Wás) at 1 mile and Kawng Pé (Shans) at 2¼ miles. A path strikes off to the left up the valley. There is a narrow strip of cultivated land by the stream where a small force could camp. The path runs south-west down the stream which is here about 15 feet wide, 1 foot deep; low banks and easily crossed; crosses it three times and then rises steeply 700 feet, after which there is a stretch of nearly level road; easy except at one rocky stream containing water in January. At 6 miles a path to the right leads off to Kawk Mu, not visible from the road, after which there is a steep descent of 1,200 feet to the river Ngé Lam. Camping ground for at least 100 men on the right bank by clearing the jungle and room for a few tents on the left bank. No supplies at hand. Difficult march in wet weather, there being a drop of 2,500 feet, then a rise of 700 feet, then a drop of 1,200 feet. The camp is 1,650 feet above sea-level.
G.O.C. Mandalay District.	Superintendent, Northern Shan States.	**2. Man Kát or Man Nöng or Ta Mawn.** Nam Ngé Lam, Nam Wat, and Nam Wa.	**9 4**	16 4	The path crosses the Nam Ngé Lam 30 feet wide, knee-deep, rapid, low banks, and ascends steeply through some narrow cuttings in zigzags for ½ mile, when a path down a spur to the right leads to Páng Hai. After this road ascends more easily. At 3 miles there is a slight descent and a broad road to the left runs up to Lông Lawk (or Nawk, from which there is an excellent bullock road to Kéng Thúng (Kyengtung *)). The road runs down to the right, crosses three rocky nullahs in which there is water and then ascends steeply for a short distance; Páng Mak Láng (Wás) at 3½ miles. Total rise 1,800 feet. Sites for small camps in clearings near the last nullah or at the village if necessary. The path runs through the village and down at once past some large rocks which block the road (mules can go round to the right) and descends gradually at first and latterly very steeply to the Nam Wat about 25 feet wide and 1 foot deep; rapid and likely to rise quickly after rain. The road is down the stream itself for several hundred yards, then along the banks with frequent crossings, to an ascent of 400 feet of the left bank which is steep and slippery; the path then descends to the Salween, which makes a right angle bend above Ta Mawn. At 9 miles there are four cross-roads to the left up to Kawng Ling, straight on to Man Nam Wa, and following the river bank to Ta Mawn crossing the Nam Wa on the way a small rapid stream; easy to cross in dry weather; below the flood level of the Salween, but the right bank 20 feet high and very steep; of sand. There is camping ground near Man Nam Wa or on the sand below Man Kát and near the bazaar above. A ferry called Ta Mawn crosses the Salween here, which is about 150 yards wide, running from 4 to 5 miles an hour; probably about 30 feet deep with gently sloping, sandy banks on both sides. On the right bank

* This appears to be the latest way of spelling the name of this place.—A. F. (Jan. 1894).

FROM PÁNG YÁNG TO MAN PÁN (WING MAW HPA)—*continued.*

Authorities. Military.	Authorities. Civil.	Number and Names of Stages, Rivers and Streams.	Distances. Intermediate.	Distances. Total.	Remarks.
G.O.C. Mandalay District.	Superintendent, Northern Shan States.	**2. Man Kát or Man Nöng or Ta Mawn**—*cont.*			there is a small ferry village, Supsa. The road beyond is said to be not a bullock track, but though bad, it is not impassable for pack animals. It branches off as above to Möng Kán, Möng Awt, and Möng Su. This march would be very difficult in wet weather.
			M. F.	M. F.	
		3. Law Kiu ... Nam Náng, Nam Pán, Nam Sem, and Salween.	**9 0**	25 4	Leaving Man Kát the road runs up hill south-west for $\frac{3}{4}$ mile and drops $\frac{3}{4}$ mile to the Nam Náng (about 40 feet wide, 2 feet deep; rocky bed; high steep banks which require ramping; very rapid and impassable when in flood), leaving a path to Wan Ngum on the left just before reaching the river, where ground could be cleared for camping if required. The path rises over the spur where the Nam Náng joins the Salween and follows the left bank of the latter high up for over 2 miles to the Nam Um, passing through Man Sŭp Pán (Shans) and across a small stream with low banks, called the Nam Pán. At the Nam Um the Salween turns off west and the road runs up the stream for nearly a mile, crosses it finally below Kawng Hu and runs up a stream 6 feet wide, shallow, but full of rocks, and overgrown with dense jungle for 500 yards, and then ascends 900 feet to a ridge on Loi Ngek Nôk, a very steep and slippery climb. From here there is an easy descent along a spur of nearly 3 miles to the Nam Sem (30 feet wide, 1 foot deep; easy crossing and fairly good approaches), passing two springs near the ridge on the road and avoiding a path to the left about a mile down. A cross-road near the bottom comes from Punkán on the left to Um Köt on the right. After crossing the Nam Sem there is a short ascent to a large clearing, where a regiment might camp. The village of Law Kiu is a mile further on—a Kyemmöng (minor civil official) lives there, who can get in supplies if warned beforehand. The Nam Náng divides East Mang Lön from Maw Hpa.
		4. Ta Pông ... Nam Ka, Nam Nga, Nam Pwawn, and numerous other smaller streams, also several deep nullahs with steep and slippery approaches.	**12 0**	37 4	The road now follows the left bank of the Salween. General direction west by south. At 1 mile it passes through Law Kiu, at 2 miles Kat Wun Nawng, where there is a small bazaar and $\frac{3}{4}$ mile beyond crosses the Nam Sáng below the flood level of the Salween. It then runs along on the sand for over a mile passing Man Mat Lông half-way. Camps can be pitched on the sand in dry weather or near the village in wet weather. Pack animals should keep low down after crossing the Nam Sem to avoid the rocks. After leaving the river bed the path runs over small spurs, crossing several nullahs with steep sides. At 5 miles it runs up a steep spur and avoiding a path to the left descends to the Nam Ka about 30 feet wide, knee-deep; very steep approach on left bank. Two miles further on it crosses the Nam Nga about 20 feet wide; easy crossing and approaches, and about 2 miles beyond this the Nam Pwawn about 20 feet wide; rocky bed; fairly good approaches. The camp is $1\frac{1}{2}$ miles further on in a small cultivated valley on the left with water in it. There was formerly a ferry here, and a village on the river bank, but it no longer exists.

FROM PÁNG YÁNG TO MAN PÁN (WING MAW HPA)—*continued.*

Authorities. Military.	Authorities. Civil.	Number and Names of Stages, Rivers and Streams.	Distances. Intermediate.	Distances. Total.	Remarks.
G.O.C. Mandalay District.	Superintendent, Northern Shan States.	**4. Ta Pông**—*cont.*			*N.B.*—Instead of marching to Ta Pong it is better to stop a mile beyond the Nam Nga, ½ mile beyond a small village Páng-ön above the road on the left, with water in nullahs each side about 600 yards distant. There is flat ground in a clearing here and room for 200 men.
		5. Man Pán or Wing Maw Hpa. Several small streams, Nam Aw.	M. 4 F. 4	M. 42 F. 0	The road ascends from Ta Pong camp for a short distance and then descends for 4 miles to the Nam Aw (about 20 feet wide; low banks; good approaches), passing a path at 1 mile on the left up to Páng Tawng. Beyond the Nam Aw a cross-road comes from Man Pán on the left to the ferry Ta Sup Aw on the right. The road straight on leads to extensive paddy-fields below Man Pán on the right bank of the Nam Nga, close to its junction with the Salween. A very large force could camp here in dry weather. A path from the paddy-fields leads up to the village. In wet weather troops can camp on a level grassy spur below the kyaung in the village. Man Pán situated in Lat. 21° 48′ 30″ N. and Long. 98° 37′ 40″ E., is the capital of the Maw Hpa State and contains the Sawbwa's palace, a large kyaung and about 50 houses, built on small knolls on a spur with gentle slopes covered with small jungle. Its water-supply is from nullahs below and some little distance from the village. Most of the houses are close to the kyaung. A road enters the village from above and another from below from the paddy-fields. The inhabitants are Shans. Supplies are plentiful. There is a bazaar in the paddy-fields.
					General remarks.—This road is said to be impassable in the rains. There is another *viâ* Löng Lawk, which runs high up among the hills and is said to be a very bad road even for loaded men. There are boats on the Salween at Ta Mawn 2, Kat Wun Nawng 1, Ta Mat Lông 2, Páng Ön 1, and Ta Sup Aw 2, and a ferry below the Nam Nga, Ta Hwé Lu; 1 boat. Bullock tracks lead from the South Shan States and West Mang Lön to Ta Wun Nawng, Ta Mat Lông and Ta Sup Aw, and possibly to Ta Mawn. A good road runs east from Kat Wun Nawng to Keng Thung (otherwise spelt Chiengtung, Kyeng-tung, Kyangtung, Kĕng Thûng, Kĕng Tûng, &c.), stages as follows:—1. Páng Ön, 2. Mat Lông, 3. Páng Wo, 4. Nam Háng Nu, 5. Sup Wo, 6. Yawng Kát, 7. Kát Hpök, 8. Na Lông or Hông, 9. Yáng Hai, 10. Nam Töng, 11. Ho Tum, 12. Páng Yo, 13. Nam Hpök, 14. Páng Mak Hin, 15. Páng Kwai, 16. Sáng Hai, 17. Nam Nöng, 18. Neo Loi, 19. Man Ku, 20. Kĕng Tûng. All bullock stages, about 7 miles. Road said to be very good. The Nam Ka is crossed at Ta Man Kán in Stage 8. There is said to be another road from Man Pán to Yawng Kát (Stage 6). It is, however, said to be bad for animals owing to scarcity of water. The stages are:—1. Man Gyaung, 2. Ho Nam Nga, 3. Maw Gyi, 4. Yawng Kát. From Man Pán there is also a road to Môné, stages as follows:—1. Ho Seng (in the Hôklap), 2. Na Kaw, 3. Hông Luk, 4. Nam Kút, 5. Nawng Kham, 6. Ta Kawng Hing, 7. Man Law, 8. Nawng Kham Ôn, 9. Kát Sai Kao, 10. Páng Paw, 11. Kát Tôn Hôn, 12. Ho Nga, 13. Môné. These were given as bullock stages. By another account it is 16 bullock marches. The Salween is crossed at Ta Sup Aw in Stage 1; the Nam Páng in Stage 6, and the Nam Sing at Ta Man Sát

FROM PÁNG YÁNG TO MAN PÁN (WING MAW HPA)—*continued.*

Authorities. Military.	Authorities. Civil.	Number and Names of Stages, Rivers and Streams.	Distances. Intermediate.	Distances. Total.	Remarks.
G.O.C. Mandalay District.	Superintendent, Northern Shan States.	**5. Man Pán or Wing Maw Hpa** —*cont.*			in Stage 11. From Ta Sup Aw roads branch to—(1) Kawng Ya, Na Ka; not a bullock road; pakôndán stages. (2) Nam Ka, Nam Un, Sông Lông, Man Loi; bullock stages. (3) Ho Seng, Na Kaw, Möng Sáng; not a bullock road beyond Na Kaw.

ALTERNATIVE I.

FROM TA MAT LÔNG (*see* STAGE 4) TO NAM NGÉ LAM (STAGE 2).

BY LIEUT. C. AINSLIE, R.E., ATTACHÉ, INTELLIGENCE BRANCH, JANUARY 1893.

Military.	Civil.	Number and Names of Stages, Rivers and Streams.	Intermediate. M. F.	Total. M. F.	Remarks.
G.O.C. Mandalay District.	Superintendent, Northern Shan States.	**1. Páng Wo** ... Nam Sáng.	**8 2**	8 2	From Mat Lông the path runs for ¾ mile on the sand along the left bank of the Salween, crosses the Nam Sáng (easy crossing in dry weather below the flood level of the Salween. No road when the Salween rises) and leaving the road along the river which runs to Man Kát strikes up a spur, which runs all the way to Páng Wo. The ascent is about 2,800 feet and is an easy one. The road passes by large cultivation clearings, but there are no villages on the road nor water. Páng Wo is a Wa village of 15 houses, which can supply a lot of hill rice. There is good camping ground round the left of the village for 200 men or more. The water is got from a nullah about 300 feet below, a steep path running down north-east from the village. The main road skirts round the village and on along the spur descending a little to a bullock camp ¾ mile beyond the village, with very little water in a nullah 300 yards to the right and plenty 350 feet below on the left.
		2. Pák Lông ...	**8 2**	16 4	The general direction of the road is east for 4 miles. There is a descent of 500 feet or more to a mixed Shan and Wa village of 10 houses, Páng Ku, at 1¾ miles and about the same gradual rise to Páng Hông or Man Nam Háng Nu, a Shan village of nine houses 100 yards off the road. The Nam Háng Nu is a trickle of water which supplies the village and is part of the boundary between Maw Hpa and East Manglön, this village belonging to the Páng Yáng circle in the latter state. There is a small bazaar here. The road through the village is the main road to Kéng Túng and is said to be a good bullock track, and there is a track along the hills and down to Man Pán from the east which is said to be very bad near Man Pán. From here the general direction of the road runs nearly north. There is a descent of 1½ miles, rather steep in places to the Nam Hsö and followed by a rise of 500 feet to the camp at Pák Lông. The camp is on the spur before reaching the village, with water from two small streams in nullahs below to the right. There is room for camping on the spur beyond the village, but only this one water-supply. There is a good deal of paddy stored in Pák Lông in five small huts. It is a Wa village of 12 houses under Maw Hpa.
		3. Nam Wa ... Nam Náng.	**6 4**	23 0	From Pák Lông there is a path running down a spur north to the lower village of Pák Lông probably 1½ miles distant, passing a Shan village, Man Kwoi (two houses) at ⅜ of a mile. The main

FROM PÁNG YÁNG TO MAN PÁN (WING MAW HPA)—*continued.*

ALTERNATIVE I—*continued.*

Authorities. Military.	Authorities. Civil.	Number and Names of Stages, Rivers and Streams.	Distances. Intermediate.	Distances. Total.	Remarks.
G.O.C. Mandalay District.	Superintendent, Northern Shan States.	**3. Nam Wa**—*cont.*			road branches to the left (east) a little above the village and descends 1,150 feet in 3 miles to the Nam Náng, passing a Shan village (five houses) called Na Lö 250 feet above the stream at 2¾ miles. The Nam Náng is here about 35 feet wide, knee-deep, low banks, easy crossing. From here there is an ascent of 800 feet to a Wa village, Môt No (six houses) on the right of the road at 5 miles, from which one path runs down west to the Ta Mawn ferry on the Salween, the other running down north and descending rather steeply 1,100 feet in 1½ miles to the Nam Wa. There is flat ground on the left bank of the stream for 100 men or more to camp. On the left bank of the Nam Náng there is room for a large camp if required. Villagers from Môt No go to the bazaar at Ta Mawn and back in a day.
		4. Nam Ngé Lam (or Páng Tawng). Nam Wa and Nam Ngé Lam.	M. F. **9 0**	M. F. 32 0	Leaving camp the path crosses the Nam Wa, about 30 feet wide and knee-deep, easy crossing, and ascends at once, very steep at first, for 1,500 feet running north to the top of the ridge, then westerly along the top, at 2½ miles the road turns north-west and descends a path along the ridge south leading to Páng Song. The road crosses water a little further on and runs with small ups and downs along a saddle to a Wa village of 13 houses with grain stores, called Löng Nawk (or Lawk), passing right and left turnings to villages at about 5 miles. The road descends north-west from Löng Nawk about 2,000 feet in 3½ miles to the Nam Ngé Lam, passing turnings on the left to Páng Mak Láng (on the lower road to Man Pán already described, *see* Stage 2).

No. 51.

From PÁNG YÁNG to MÖNG KA viâ WING LÖN LÔNG.

BY LIEUT. C. AINSLIE, R.E., ATTACHÉ, INTELLIGENCE BRANCH, JANUARY 1893.

G.O.C. Mandalay District.	Superintendent, Northern Shan States.	**1. Camp at Nam Ya Yung.** *Nil.*	**5 4**	5 4	Leaving Páng Yáng the path runs up at once north-west on to the Pé Möng range and along the top of it; direction north, rising generally, with a few reverse slopes, to a Kachin village (Páng Pák Mung), at 4½ miles from which there is a fairly steep rise of 800 feet to the camp. Water is fairly plentiful a little way down the hill to the left at a small saddle. There is a little flat ground here and plenty on the hills either side 100 feet to 200 feet above. No supplies.

FROM PÁNG YÁNG TO MÖNG KA *viâ* WING LÖN LÔNG—*continued.*

Authorities.		Number and Names of Stages, Rivers and Streams.	Distances.				Remarks.
Military.	Civil.		Intermediate.		Total.		
			M.	F.	M.	F.	
G.O.C. Mandalay District.	Superintendent, Northern Shan States.	**2. Camp at the cross-road to Man Hsum.** *Nil.*	7	4	13	0	The path continues to follow the range with rises and falls up to 500 feet, sometimes following the crest-line, sometimes skirting round the peaks, through alternate stretches of open grass land and thick tree jungle. There is a site for a camp at the 4th mile, where the ground has been cleared for poppy cultivation. Water is some way down on the eastern slopes, sufficient for 100 men with animals. The camp is on the eastern slope just below the crest of the hill, where a path strikes down half right to a village (Man Hsum), about ½ mile away. The water-supply is 300 yards away in a nullah 150 feet below, where there is barely enough for 100 men with animals. A path strikes diagonally through the camp to Möt O, from which supplies in small quantities only can be obtained.
		3. Páng Seng ... *Nil.*	11	0	24	0	The road continues along the crest of the hill in a series of rises and drops, some of which are very steep and rough; ¼ mile from camp a broad road from Táköt joins in on the right (east). At nearly 2 miles a path runs down a spur west to Ta Hsup Ket (Supkyet) on the Salween. There is a village (Man Hka Káng) not far from the road, where there is said to be camping ground. The junction of these roads is commanded by old stockades. In several places in the next 6 miles the crest is very narrow with precipitous sides, where resistance could very easily be offered. About 1 mile from Páng Seng the road crosses a spur which commands the village and then descends several hundred feet to a saddle, from which it rises fairly easily to Páng Seng. The village is on an isolated knoll only commanded from the south-west at 1,500 yards or more. It is not stockaded at present. The northern slope is covered with thorny jungle; the other sides are more or less open. There are five roads from the village. The water-supply is low down south of the pôngyi kyaung, near which there is room for camping, and by clearing the jungle both sides of the road leading up to it a large camp could be made. Páng Seng is a Wa village of about 20 houses, and there are two or three houses of Shans. A petty Sawbwa, tributary to Táköt, lives here. Rice and paddy obtainable. There is no water throughout this stage.
		4. Yawng U ... Nam Ma and a few smaller streams.	5	6	29	6	General direction north by west. First a fairly steep descent of 2½ miles to the Nam Ma, passing a Wa village of 23 houses (Páng Myvé) on the right at 1 mile. After crossing the Nam Ma (12 feet wide and shallow) there is flat ground by the river enough for a large camp. The path rises over a small spur and then descends to a long stretch of paddy-fields, crossing several small streams. At 4 miles it rises gently 200 feet to a gap in the range in front and descends a little to a large flat valley with water in the north-west corner. Yawng U village is on a peak of the range, which bounds the valley to the north. Another peak on the range north-west of the village commands it at about 200 yards' range, and a spur separated from it by a steep ravine commands it from the south-east at about 1,000 yards. Roads lead out of the village east and

FROM PÁNG YÁNG TO MÖNG KA *viâ* WING LÖN LÔNG—*continued.*

Authorities. Military.	Authorities. Civil.	Number and Names of Stages, Rivers and Streams.	Distances. Intermediate.	Distances. Total.	Remarks.
G.O.C. Mandalay District.	Superintendent, Northern Shan States.	**4. Yawng U**—*cont.*			west. The village was burnt out; it probably contained about 20 houses. Water fairly near from ravines on both sides. The northern slope of the range is steep. The village is surrounded by a belt of thick thorny jungle. The entrance is a lane about 2 feet wide cut through this and fenced in on both sides and above. The Nam Ma, or the next stream the Nam Miyé (or Mei), divides Mang Lön from Ngek Hting. Yawng U is in the latter state. From here there is a route to Láshio *viâ* Ta Man Ang ferry, Tun Hông, and Tángyán, *see* Route No. 17.
		5. Môt Hso Mo ... Two streams.	M. F. 9 0	M. F. 38 6	The road runs east out of Yawng U, descends to a saddle, and then trending north rises along the hill side to the spur on which Páng Kaw stands, about 3 miles away. Páng Kaw was burnt out; it probably contained at least 20 houses. A camp might be formed on the spur before reaching the village. Water is down below to the east. The village is situated on a small knoll on the spur, which is narrow, with steep, wooded slopes east and west. The road runs on through the village and down the spur north for 1 mile, when it divides the left-hand path leading to Môt Waw. The path to the right turns east and descends rather steeply for 1 mile to a stream about 40 feet broad. From here there is a steep rise for 1½ miles, then a little level going followed by a steep descent of 1½ miles to a small stream. Water in a small nullah, about ¼ mile before reaching the stream, but very little flat ground, and all covered with long grass and jungle. From here there is a steep climb up to Môt Hso Mo of nearly a mile. Quarter mile below the village is a very small spring. A path to the left along the hill side leads to a fair water-supply some 200 yards away. There is a kyaung on the left of the road 200 yards before the village. There is excellent camping ground on the spur some 400 yards north of the village on the road to Môt Waw. Water as noted above, and also ½ a mile along the road to Môt Waw down the eastern slope. Môt Hso Mo is the capital of the Ngek Hting State. It contains 25 houses built on the highest point of the range and cannot be commanded by rifle fire except at extreme ranges from the hills east and west. The spur it is built on is very narrow, and the eastern and western slopes are very steep and covered with jungle. The village is fenced in and surrounded by a belt of thick thorny jungle about 30 feet broad, through which are entrances north-west and south-east.
		6. Môt Hsana ... Nam Sarong.	3 2	42 0	Leaving the village south-east, the path runs down the spur for ¼ mile and then branches down to the left, descending steeply to the Nam Sarong about 750 feet; rising from this stream there is nearly level going for ½ a mile, passing a temporary village on the left, where a camp could be made. The road then crosses some rocky nullahs and rises by zigzags up a cultivated spur for more than a mile to Môt Hsana. The camp is below the village on the spur with water on the northern slope fairly near and plentiful. There is room for 200 men. The village is on the spur, with a jungle covered slope above it, but there appears to

FROM PÁNG YÁNG TO MÖNG KA *viâ* WING LÖN LÔNG—*continued.*

Authorities.		Number and Names of Stages, Rivers and Streams.	Distances.				Remarks.
Military.	Civil.		Intermediate.		Total.		
			M.	F.	M.	F.	
G.O.C. Mandalay District.	Superintendent, Northern Shan States.	**6. Môt Hsana**—*cont.*					be no path through this. The main road strikes in at the south side of the village and leaves at the east end. It is a Wa village of 35 houses with a number of stores for grain, &c. The bottom (east) of the village is fenced in with a belt of prickly jungle with the usual narrow lane through it.
		7. Yawng Kawng.	6	4	48	4	Leaving Môt Hsana the road runs east by north to the top of the range for 2 miles, then turns east by south along the crest for a while and then descending. At about 4 miles the road from Tákŏt to Na Phán crosses and forms the boundary between the states of Ngek Hting and Lön Lông. Half-a-mile down the right hand (south) turning there is a small stream and camping ground called Páng Lut. The main road to Lön Lông runs on east, up for a little, along the crest of a hill and then down rather steep to Yawng Kawng. The first village is on the right of the main road and contains seven houses. The main village is ½ a mile on. It is a Wa village of 20 houses on a knoll at the end of a spur, and is visible from the road above about ½ a mile away, after which it is hidden by large trees. The slopes on three sides are very steep and wooded. There is room for a small camp on the left a little below the road, 200 yards from the village with a small water-supply. Mules can camp down in the ravine below, where there is a stream. No water on road.
		8. Ngek Hté ... Nam Páng.	7	0	55	4	The road runs on east by south descending about 2,000 feet to the Nam Páng and rising a little more to Ngek Hté. The last ½ mile on the west bank is very steep and rough, and the first 1,000 feet up the east bank not much better. The Nam Páng is about 40 yards wide, 2½ to 3 feet deep at the ford; fairly slow current; very steep ascent at left bank; a small stony beach on the right; not fordable after much rain. The village is not visible owing to the usual encircling belt of thorny jungle. The camping ground is on the spur just before the village. Water is a long way down the north slope and not plentiful. Ngek Hté is a Wa village of 35 houses; rice and paddy obtainable. There is another of the same name about 1 mile north-east. The only hill which commands Ngek Hté is east of it at some distance.
		9. Páng Lát ...	6	4	62	0	The road leads through the village, or you can make a detour round the left (north) side. At about ½ mile there are three houses, where the road divides, running to the left to lower Ngek Hté and thence to Lön Lông by a road which is said to be steep at the Nam Pawng. To the right the road descends to a saddle, along which it runs, rising later fairly easily to Páng Lát. This is a Wa village of 76 houses, where iron work is carried on largely. It is built on two spurs, one running south, the other east. The ground falls all round it and the jungle is thick. A path runs out south-east to Möng Nga and water is drawn from

FROM PÁNG YÁNG TO MÖNG KA *viâ* WING LÖN LÔNG—*continued.*

Authorities. Military.	Authorities. Civil.	Number and Names of Stages, Rivers and Streams.	Distances. Intermediate.	Distances. Total.	Remarks.
G.O.C. Mandalay District.	Superintendent, Northern Shan States.	**9. Páng Lát**—*cont.*			the valley to the left going down; sufficient, but at some distance. The only good camping ground is on a level open spot in the middle of the village. There is a bad camp ½ mile down the Möng Nga road and another can be made about ¼ mile down the Lön Lông road, but the nearest water-supply is little better than a buffalo wallow down on the left. No water on road.
		10. Wing Lön Lông (Lat. 22° 28′ 40″ N., Long. 99° 13′ 50″ E.).	M. 4 F. 2	M. 66 F. 4	The road leaves Páng Lát at the east end and runs along the spur to a saddle 650 feet below, which connects with the Lön Lông range, and which it crosses ½ mile south of the Wing. There is a small Muhsö village on a spur to the left, where there is plenty of camping ground with a small water-supply on the road up. There is excellent camping ground south-east of the Wing Lön Lông about 100 feet below it, with plenty of water near, but it is commanded by it. Wing Lön Lông is the capital of this state. It contains 40 houses crowded together on a peak with the palace in the centre. It is looked into from a knoll about 250 yards south-west and commanded by a wooded peak about 800 yards north-west. It is surrounded as usual and has two or three covered-in entrances. The slopes all round are very steep and open except on the east. Roads run from here to Na Phán, to Möng Ka (north-east), and to Möng Lem. There are several villages close by, occupied chiefly by Was, but there are a few Kachins and some Shans, who keep the bazaars. Rice and paddy obtainable. No water along this stage.
		11. Pa Núng (Muhsö village). A trickle of water across the road in first 1½ miles.	6 6	73 2	The road runs along the spur east from Wing Lön Lông, passing a Wa village, Kyé Prai, on the left at once and, crossing the spur, runs down along the hill side, dropping 800 feet to a saddle. It crosses a little water about 1 mile from Kyé Prai and there is some nearly flat camping ground below the road; it then rises fairly steep to a range over 5,000 feet elevation, along the top of which it runs, turning sharply to the left at 2½ miles, just below Páng Lông, the Kyemmöng's village, which is not visible from the road here. From here onwards the path undulates along the crest, passing many acres of hill rice and poppy cultivation. There is a short, steep, rocky rise at 5 miles over a peak, shortly after which the Wa village of Pa Núng is passed on the right, off the road, which, turning north again, descends rather steeply for ½ mile and then rises gently to the Muhsö village of Pa Núng (29 houses, unfenced). **Fairly flat ground above the village for camp (about 200 men with transport). Water from both sides of the hill. Sufficient grass and firewood obtainable, but only a little rice and paddy.**

FROM PÁNG YÁNG TO MÖNG KA *viâ* WING LÖN LÔNG—*continued.*

Authorities. Military.	Authorities. Civil.	Number and Names of Stages, Rivers and Streams.	Distances. Intermediate.	Distances. Total.	Remarks.
G.O.C. Mandalay District.	Superintendent, Northern Shan States.	**12. Camp** ... ... Two or three small streams.	M. F. 7 6	M. F. 81 0	The road follows the main ridge, rising and falling along the crest. It runs north-east for 2 miles, skirts round the left of a peak, and turns north-west for 2 miles, passing Hsa Awt off the road on the right at 2½ miles. At 4 miles it rises round the right of another peak and turns north again for 2 miles, passing a small Wa village near and below the road on the left at 5 miles. At 6 miles it descends sharply, turning north-west and runs through Hto Nawng (six houses; Was) to a saddle, from which it rises again, passing Hto Tung (about 80 houses; Was), ½ mile to the left and below. At 7 miles (up to which point no water is met with) the road turns north-east for a short distance, then north along the side of the main range, crossing several small streams. There are several places fit for camps in the last mile, but firewood is scarce here and no supplies are obtainable. The road along the crest from Pa Núng is not well defined for the first few miles, the side tracks to cultivation patches being much more used than the main road.
		13. Camp 1 mile short of Yawng Seng. Several nullahs.	7 2	88 2	From the last camp the road runs through paddy-fields past a Wa village of three houses Ka Si, crossing water in a nullah here and rising to the top of the ridge in the 1st mile, then skirted round the left of a peak and, striking the ridge again, followed it to the 6th mile, when the road from Na Hpán (? Na Phán) cuts in on the left. It then rose over the ridge and ran rather steeply down a spur to the Muhsö village of Yawng Seng (15 houses), where it turned sharp to the right and ran with short steep rises and falls along the hill side, crossing several small streams. The best site for a camp is about 1 mile from the Muhsö village, where grass and water are plentiful, but firewood is scarce. The Wa village of Yawng Seng is a short mile further on; but you cannot depend on it for supplies, though the Was generally store paddy. They are wild Was and do not care to sell, but would probably barter readily for salt, beads, &c.
		14. Pa Soi [Lower (Shan) village]. Namsé.	5 0	93 2	The road runs level for ½ a mile, then crosses the spur, and descends passing above the Wa village of Yawng Seng (40 houses), from which descends about 2,500 feet in 3 miles to the Namsé (about 35 yards broad, knee-deep, easy crossing, but probably not fordable in the rains. The main road runs through one or two villages on the spur called Ôk Lawng, which have probably narrow stockaded passages through them, impassable for pack animals. We were taken down-hill to the left through cultivation to avoid them and joined the main road about 1 mile from the river. The cultivation we passed through was well watered lower down and suitable for camping on if required. The last mile of descent to the Namsé is not very steep. There is a very small strip of flat ground on the right bank of the Namsé and a small pebbly beach on the left, where the river is low,

FROM PÍNG YÁNG TO MÖNG KA *viâ* WING LÖN LÔNG—*continued.*

Authorities.		Number and Names of Stages, Rivers and Streams.	Distances.				Remarks.
Military.	Civil.		Intermediate.		Total.		
			M.	F.	M.	F.	
G.O.C. Mandalay District.	Superintendent, Northern Shan States.	**14. Pa Soi [Lower (Shan) village]** —*cont.*					but practically no camping ground. The ascent to Pa Soi is about 1,000 feet. There are three short steep ascents and the rest is easy going. There is plenty of camping ground just before and also below Pa Soi, with a good stream in a nullah close to the village. This is Shan village of 14 houses subordinate to a larger Wa village of the same name on the ridge above. No supplies.
		15. Möng Ka (22° 44′ 30″ N., 99° 29′ E.). Nam Sak Ké (nearly dry) and several small streams between 3rd and 6th miles.	**9**	**0**	102	2	The road runs up through Shan Pa Soi and ascends nearly 1,000 feet, gradually passing (Wa) Pa Soi on the left at 1 mile, and after 2 miles there is a rather steep descent of 1,800 feet to a small stream in a large rocky bed which drains the valley, which is open, cultivated, and well watered. There are fairly flat places for camping almost anywhere in the 2 miles beyond the Muhsö village of Nam Sak Ké, the best at 1 mile on flat cultivated ground just before the ascent begins. The ascent is 3,300 feet, fairly easy throughout. There are several small Muhsö villages on this hill side and much poppy cultivation. After crossing the range the road runs easily along the eastern slope for nearly 3 miles to Möng Ka, passing water and camping ground after 1 mile and again at 2 miles near a Chinese village of some 20 houses. Möng Ka itself is a collection of small Muhsö villages about 100 feet below the top of the range. Elevation 6,600 feet. Water springs on the top of the hill; plentiful supply; grass is rather scarce. There is a great deal of fairly flat ground up here for camping on or for a post if required, with a good view all round. The villages round here are mostly Muhsö and the Sawbwa of Möng Ka is a Muhsö. It is said to be only two marches from here eastwards to the Chinese frontier and two long marches northwards to Nawng Kheo, where there is a lake from which the Nam Ka and three other rivers are said to start. The wildest of the Was live round Nawng Kheo, near which the rivers are said to contain gold washings of considerable value. There are silver mines near here, which are at present being worked. Very small supplies of rice and paddy at Möng Ka. From here there is said to be a road to Möng Lán (or Möng La) in China, the stages being as follows:—1. Tanáng, 2. Möng Saw, 3. Palông, 4. Náng Lé, 5. Mông Lán, each march 8 to 10 miles. The Nam Ka is crossed in Stage 2 and Chinese territory entered just before reaching Náng Lé. There is also a route to Möng Lem as follows:—1. Nam Ka (or Hka), 2. Pa Ha, 3. Nawng Lung, 4. Ho Yáng, 5. Ho Ai, 6. Wing Sáng, 7. Möng Lem. The boundary of Möng Ka is crossed in Stage 1. Stages 2 to 5 inclusive belong to the Ho Ai circle. At Wing Sáng is the boundary of Möng Lem. Marches of 8 to 10 miles.

No. 52.

From PINDAYA to PWÉHLA.

By Lieut. J. A. S. TULLOCH, R.E., 1888.

Authorities.		Number and Names of Stages, Rivers and Streams.	Distances.				Remarks.
Military.	Civil.		Intermediate.		Total.		
			M.	F.	M.	F.	
G.O.C. Rangoon District.	Superintendent, Southern Shan States.	**1. Pwéhla** * ...	**6**	**4**	6	4	The road leaves Pindaya in a southerly direction, bordered for the first 500 yards on the west by the Pindaya lake and on the east by a small plantation of "*tillai*." At about 1,000 yards from the village there are kyaungs to the east of the road, but in very bad condition, the flooring being almost entirely stripped. The accommodation of these kyaungs if repaired would be for 80 men. Water is obtainable near from the Pindaya lake. On leaving the lake the country opens out and is easily accessible from the road. To the west there is a range of hills about 900 feet high and about 1 mile distant from the road, the country between being perfectly open and undulating. To the east the country has a slight general slope of about $\frac{1}{9}$ to $\frac{1}{12}$ from the road, the country on both sides being open and affording no cover. At $1\frac{1}{4}$ miles from Pindaya there are to the west of the road at a distance of $\frac{3}{4}$ mile large caves with an open kyaung which could afford shelter for about 100 men. The flooring is plastered and not raised from the ground. The caves are of considerable extent. To the east of the road there are some small pagodas. At 2 miles the road commences a slight ascent of about $\frac{1}{8}$. There is a nullah about 12 feet deep and 15 feet wide crossing the road, the banks of which are steep, except where the road crosses. This nullah on the west of the road turns southwards and runs parallel with the road for about $\frac{1}{4}$ mile. About 30 yards distant at this point there are paddy-fields on both sides of the road. At $2\frac{1}{4}$ miles village of Tharaiko, a small village about 500 yards to the west of the road; about 20 bamboo huts raised 1 foot to 2 feet from the ground. The village is built on a hill and surrounded by a hedge. There has been no attempt to make any stockade and the hedge is thin and easily passable for men on foot. There are kyaungs in good order 300 yards to the north of the village capable of accommodating 150 men. In the village there are about 20 head of cattle, but no ponies. No water to be found in the immediate vicinity, and the inhabitants state they get their water-supply from the Pindaya lake 2 miles distant. From Tharaiko onwards for about 1 mile the country on both sides of the road is hilly, but the hills are not steep and the road is fit for all arms and for wheeled transport. The hills through which the road passes are under features of those lying to the west of Pindaya, the general slope being from north-west to south-east. The general direction of the road is southerly passing through hills about 50 to 100 yards distant on either side, their general height above the road being from 100 to 150 feet. The average slope of these hills is from $\frac{1}{6}$ to $\frac{1}{4}$. On nearing Pwéhla the hills are more rocky and steeper. About $6\frac{1}{2}$ miles from Pindaya is a large village of about 150 houses and 1,000 inhabitants. The bazaar is nearly as extensive as that of Pindaya, and supplies of meat and vegetables are plentiful. Grass is scarce, and for any large number of animals bamboo leaves would have to be substituted. The village is scattered and much enclosed, hence it is difficult to estimate its size. There are kyaungs to the east of the village capable of accommodating 100 men. Water is procured from a small lake. The supply is plentiful and good.

* In the latest Survey Map, sheet No. 5, S.W., sixth edition, this place is spelt Pawela.—A. F.

No. 53.

From PINDAYA to TWINTAYA.

BY LIEUT. H. E. STANTON, ROYAL ARTILLERY, JANUARY 1888.

Authorities. Military.	Authorities. Civil.	Number and Names of Stages, Rivers and Streams.	Distances. Intermediate.	Distances. Total.	Remarks.
			M. F.	M. F.	
G.O.C. Rangoon District.	Superintendent, Southern Shan States.	**1. Twintaya** ...	8 0	8 0	Immediately on leaving Pindaya, the ground rises gradually, road due east all the way. At ⅛ mile cross a deep (30 feet) nullah by a strong bridge fit for laden animals. These nullahs are quite a feature about here. They are great rents in the ground and generally follow the direction of the valleys, the sides are perpendicular and of a bright red clay. The beds have too steep a fall to allow water to stand in them. These nullahs carry off all the rainfall from these hills and drain into the low ground near the sources of the Zawgyi river. They can only be crossed and near their head where they are shallow, where there are bridges. They would effectually stop animals anywhere but at the above places, but infantry would not find them insuperable except perhaps in the rains and then only till the water ran off. Four of these nullahs were passed on the road. Of these the only two difficult ones are strongly bridged. The other two were crossed near their heads where they were shallow. Two miles out a road was crossed leading to Kyauksé (to the north) 2 miles off and to Saingyébwin (to the south). At 3 miles cross second deep nullah by a bridge. At 4 miles the village of Tamwet is seen some distance to the right at 6 miles. Mwédwin village, a large tank of water here, about 20 houses; ¼ mile further is a large kyaung (150 men). Just beyond is the small hamlet of Payani, a collection of some half-a-dozen huts, inhabited by miners. From here the path runs up a valley east for ½ mile, climbs a hill on right and then turns sharply to the south of the silver mines. These are called by name of Twintaya. They are about 1½ miles from Payani. They lie high up on the south-west corner of a deep valley in the hills. This valley seems to be a real *cul de sac*, as no outlet could be seen. The miners all live in small sheds over the mines, of which several are sunk. They number about 100 at this mine, that is, about 8 per shaft. The shafts are sunk at an angle of 45° into the hill. They do not go very deep, they are stepped on one side, the miner sits on these facing up the hill. The earth is put into small hand-baskets and passed up the shaft to the top. The shaft is started by the ordinary long excavator, but as it gets deeper a small hand-pick is used. The miners state that they work entirely for themselves and do not pay any percentage to the Ngwégunhmu, but this is highly improbable. These mines lie in Bawzaing territory.

No. 54.

From PINDAYA to YÁTSAUK (LOKSOK).

BY LIEUT. J. A. S. TULLOCH, R.E., FEBRUARY 1888.

Military	Civil	Stage	Intermediate	Total	Remarks
G.O.C. Rangoon District.	Superintendent, Southern Shan States.	**1. Mainghin** ...	9 0	9 0	The direct road runs north-east. The route described below is by the sources of the Zawgyi river which

No. 54.

From PINDAYA to YÁTSAUK (LOKSOK)—*continued.*

Authorities. Military.	Authorities. Civil.	Number and Names of Stages, Rivers and Streams.	Distances. Intermediate.	Distances. Total.	Remarks.
G.O.C. Rangoon District.	Superintendent, Southern Shan States.	**1. Mainghin**—*cont.*			strikes the direct road about 1 mile or so south of Mainghin. On leaving Pindaya the latter route runs north bearing slightly away from the range of hills on the left. Cross a nullah by bridge. Pass kyaung (100 men). Cross a second and deep nullah by a bridge. This is probably a continuation of the one met with on the road to the silver mines. The road is fairly elevated. The valley (all paddy land) lies to the right (east). At 1 mile the village of Kyauknao is seen the left situated on a low spur of the range. There is said to to be extensive pine-apple cultivation at this place. Several nullahs are seen on the left, but none of them cross the road. At (?) miles pass between two villages ¼ mile apart, both of which go by the name of Yébyu. A kyaung. Water from the Zawgyi. There are extensive pine-apple and plantain gardens here. Away to the right Kyauksu can be seen. Soon after this the road descends to a valley, at the head of which the Zawgyi river rises. The sources are two in number and consist of big springs close together under the foot of the hills. These springs supply enormous quantity of water, as the river close to sources is 12 yards wide and is deep. At (?) miles, ½ mile from the sources, the river is crossed by a bridge fit for laden animals. The stream runs fast here. Half-a-mile to the left the village of Takí-ywa can be seen on some rising ground. At (?) miles pass the Shwébadaw pagoda and zayâts. Good camping ground. Accommodation for 50 men. This pagoda is on a low hill. Soon after cross the Zawgyi twice(flowing first to left, then to right) by bridges. At (?) miles ascend a low hill on which there is a bazaar belonging to the village of Nangyithaw. The latter is a big place. Large kyaung. On the right at (?) miles is the village of Shwéingôn. One mile on pass through a lot of sugar-cane gardens, beyond which is the village of Taungshi (?) miles; some streams are crossed before this, none of any size now (February), but they might make the ground difficult in the rains. At (?) miles, cross the Zawgyi by a stout new bridge. At (?) miles pass village of Phabyigôn on left. Then through more sugar-cane. Road now ascends slightly and soon after at (?) miles strikes the direct road mentioned above. The latter up to this point is easy and fit for carts. It passes between the villages of Kyauksu and Kolôn, about 2 miles out from Pindaya, and at 4 miles it passes Patawgaung on the right, soon after which it goes through Pinyôn. After the junction of the two above routes the road passes village of Saingeik on left ((?) miles). This place marks the boundary between Yátsauk and Pindaya districts. Half-a-mile to the right lies the village of Tanaunggôn. At (?) miles cross the Zawgyi, flowing to the right, by a good bridge, and at 9 miles reach village of Mainghin. This is considered rather an important place. There is a large bazaar. The village itself is not very large. Kyaung. Water from river. The place is noted for its extensive orange orchards.
		2. Lépeik ...	M. F. 11 0	M. F. 20 0	At 4 miles ford the Yamôn creek. At 6 miles pass through a lot of paddy land. The country before being covered with open tree jungle. At (?) miles reach small village of Wuntso. The country now becomes wild and close, the road passing between low hills. At 10 miles pass Upho on the right. At 11 miles Lépeik, small place with kyaung (50 men).

FROM PINDAYA TO YÁTSAUK (LOKSOK)—*continued.*

Authorities. Military.	Authorities. Civil.	Number and Names of Stages, Rivers and Streams.	Distances. Intermediate. M. F.	Distances. Total. M. F.	Remarks.
G.O.C. Rangoon District.	Superintendent, Southern Shan States.	**3. Yátsauk** ...	7 0	27 0	At 2 miles reach Magyigôn. This is a fair-sized place consisting of two villages about ½ mile apart. A kyaung and four zayáts (120 men). Water from the Kandia stream close by. A plentiful and excellent supply. No cattle could be obtained here. From here to Yátsauk is 5 miles of excellent road over undulating country. Yátsauk is a scattered place built chiefly on a saddle between two hills which lie north and south of each other. The old fort, some remains of which are still extant, was on the southern hill. The Sawbwa lives on this hill. It is skirted on the east by the Zawgyi river, and on the south and west by a broad and in places deep lake or jheel. The latter is said to get all its water from springs. It is quite 100 yards wide all along and about ½ mile in length. It is crossed in the centre by a rickety bridge, not fit for animals and only fit for infantry in single file. The water from this lake flows into the river. The bazaar is in the centre of the village. The latter is not so large a place as Pindaya and is said to contain 1,200 houses. There are only 3,000 houses in the Yátsauk district by native report, but it is highly improbable that the number is as small as this. Supplies of rice, flour, salt. Cattle can be bought. The price of a bullock is Rs. 15, or Rs. 10 cheaper than in Ywangán. Oranges in large quantities and several other fruits and vegetables can be obtained. The Zawgyi river here is crossed by two bridges, only one of which is fit for laden or unladen animals. The people here are extensively employed in paper-making. They also manufacture pottery and *dhás*. Resin and ebony were to be had at the bazaar. The latter is larger than at Pindaya. There is plenty of accommodation in several kyaungs and zayáts on the north hill. One thousand men could easily be put up; most of these kyaungs are some distance from water. Grass has to be got from a distance. The Sawbwa's chief minister bears the title of Atwinwun. He is also assisted by his "amátgyis" or councillors.

No. 55.

From PÔNSENG (Route No. 20, Stage 5) to MÔMIEN viâ LÔNLIN.

BY CAPT. H. B. WALKER, DUKE OF CORNWALL'S LIGHT INFANTRY, PAID ATTACHÉ, INTELLIGENCE BRANCH (NATIVE INFORMATION), 1892.

Military	Civil	Stage	Inter. M.	Inter. F.	Total M.	Total F.	Remarks
G.O.C. Mandalay District.	Superintendent, Northern Shan States.	**1. Möngko** ...	*7	4	7	4	General direction west. Good road all the way. *See* Route No. 68, Stage 9.
		2. Nan Pyi Pyi ...	15	0	22	4	General direction north-east up hill by a good road *viâ* the Theinni village of Pángmát on frontier ridge.
China.		**3. Sán Kyo I** ...	15	0	37	4	General direction north-east; 200 houses and a fifth-day bazaar; road level.

* Lieut. Prowse makes it 9½ miles, *see* Route No. 20, alterative I, Stage 1.

FROM PÔNSENG (ROUTE NO. 20, STAGE 5) TO MÔMIEN *viâ* LÔNLIN—*continued.*

Authorities.		Number and Names of Stages, Rivers and Streams.	Distances.				Remarks.
Military.	Civil.		Intermediate.		Total.		
			M.	F.	M.	F.	
China.		**4. Möngka** ... The Möng Ka haw, 15 yards broad, 2 feet deep, crossed just before reaching village.	12	0	49	4	General direction north-east; road good and level; about 1,000 houses and an every-day bazaar.
		5. Möngwin ...	15	0	64	4	General direction north; road level; 200 houses.
		6. Man Nyo ...	10	0	74	4	North; 100 houses; road good and level.
		7. Manshi (or Möngkhwôn). Manli haw, 20 yards broad, Péshwé haw 10 yards broad.	15	0	89	4	General direction north; road good and level; a fifth-day bazaar here. Manthi is one of the dependencies of Lônlin and contains 1,000 houses. Good supplies.
		8. Lônlin (Lungling).	...		...		Direction north. A day's march. Lônlin is the capital of the province, which includes Manshi or Möngkhwôn. Is said to have a garrison and some four or five guns. Another native account makes it two stages from Manshi to Lônlin, the intermediate halting place being Tawmakhan, a village of 30 or 40 houses.
		9. Hawto Swin ...	...		...		Direction north-west. A day's journey. Road hilly and rough; camping ground near the village for 200 or 300 men; water and supplies, &c.
		10. Liánsikai ...	...		...		Direction north-west. A day's march. Road descends and winds a good deal, presumably from spur to spur. There is a bazaar here near to which is the camping ground. Accommodation for 200 or 300 men; water.
		11. Situ ferry on the Lônkyáng or Shwéli.	...		...		Direction north-west. A day's march. Road is said to be good and level. Camping ground near the village for 500 men; water, &c.
		12. Pasônkwán ...	...		...		Direction north-west. A day's march.
		13. Mômien ...	...		...		Direction north-west. A day's march. Road is said to be good and level. Mômien, the residence of the "Wun," is said to be fortified with a wall or ditch. The number of houses have been variously computed at from 1,000 to 10,000 houses. Contains a garrison and several guns.

FROM PÔNSENG (ROUTE No. 20, STAGE 5) TO MÔMIEN *viâ* LÔNLIN—*continued.*

BRANCH I.

FROM MANSHI (STAGE 7) TO SÉFÁN (CHÉFÁN).

BY CAPT. H. B. WALKER, DUKE OF CORNWALL'S LIGHT INFANTRY, PAID ATTACHÉ, INTELLIGENCE BRANCH (NATIVE INFORMATION), 1892.

Authorities. Military.	Authorities. Civil.	Number and Names of Stages, Rivers and Streams.	Distances. Intermediate.	Distances. Total.	Remarks.
			M. F.	M. F.	
China.		**1. Sinkyaikyi** ...	...	...	Direction south. A day's march. Good level road across paddy-fields. Sinkyaikyi is said to contain over 1,000 houses. Camping ground on paddy-fields for 1,000 men or more; water and supplies obtainable.
		2. Santi Shán ...	...	...	Direction south. A day's march. Road crosses a range of hills. Camping ground in paddy-fields for 1,000 men. village contains only six houses. Supplies and water obtainable.
		3. Séfán	...	...	Direction south. A day's march. Road good and level along foot of Santi Shán range and across paddy-fields. Séfán is a large Chinese town.

No. 56.

From SAGA (SAMKA) to YAMÉTHIN viâ TAUNGKAMAUK and KINYWA ZÉDIGÔN.

BY LIEUT. D. E. SEAGRIM, ROYAL ARTILLERY, 1887-88.

Military	Civil	Stages	Intermediate	Total	Remarks
G.O.C. Rangoon District.	Superintendent, Southern Shan States.	**1. Banpien** ... Saga river.	6 4	6 4	Saga (*see* Route No. 4, Stage 4) lies on the Saga river, which here divides itself into two portions, which join lower down again, there being a large marsh between. Good accommodation for a large force in zayáts and kyaungs. The river here is too deep to be crossed by loaded elephants. Supplies of vegetables and rice. Elephant-grazing about 1 mile distant. Good grass for ponies. The road to Payakôn is good and level, distance about 23 to 25 miles. Silver mines are found in this district. The road to Séyo, where the river is crossed, is good but marshy in parts, and goes in a north-east direction. The road to Inlé, distance said to be about 12 miles, is passed about 1 mile from Saga. Séyo, at about 3 miles is a small village on both sides of the river. Fair accommodation in the zayáts on the east bank. Boats obtainable easily from Saga. Bottom of river was firm and about 30 feet broad and 9 feet deep; slow current. The land on the east bank would be a swamp in and shortly after the rains. Grazing for elephants and ponies. The ground on the west bank was ploughed. The road to Banpien goes in north-west direction, ascending and descending alternately through small hills. At $5\frac{1}{2}$ miles the village of Limpôk is passed. It consists of about 20 houses and forms the boundary between the Saga and Lwélôn districts, belonging to the

FROM SAGA (SAMKA) TO YAMÉTHIN *viâ* TAUNGKAMAUK AND KINYWA ZÉDIGÔN—*continued.*

Authorities. Military.	Authorities. Civil.	Number and Names of Stages, Rivers and Streams.	Distances. Intermediate. M.	Distances. Intermediate. F.	Distances. Total. M.	Distances. Total. F.	Remarks.
G.O.C. Rangoon District.	Superintendent, Southern Shan States.	**1. Banpien**—*cont.*					former. Good rice cultivation. A short mile further reach Banpien, the first halting place, 1,000 feet above Saga. Good open ground suitable for a large force. Water obtained from rocks near village, but not very plentiful. Good grazing for ponies, and elephants could get forage in the neighbouring hills. The village consists of about 20 houses. Vegetables and rice, the only supplies, obtainable. There are two routes from Banpien to Namké (Stage 3); both are of similar character.
		2. Pinmun ...	7	0	13	4	The road from Banpien to Pinmum is good and runs north-west; generally level as far as Naunghpé, about 3 miles on. This is a large village of about 100 houses in all. Vegetables and rice plentiful. Large running stream close by on the west. Good open camping ground at the foot of some rocky hillocks. Height of Naunghpé is 3,400 feet above Pyinmana. The road to Pinlaung goes up a valley from here at 166° and is apparently good. This could not be reached in one day by a column owing to the delay necessitated by crossing the Saga chaung at Séyo. Good elephant and pony grazing. After leaving Naunghpé the road curves in and out along the side of a hill up a valley and after about a mile goes up sharply ascending up to 4,400 feet above Gwégôn. It continues along this ridge and then the Pinmun valley comes in sight. Here after a sharp descent and crossing a small stream is a good halting place in paddy-fields at the bottom of a village which stands on a hill. There is a good fast-flowing stream and good grazing for pack animals. The village called Pinmun (also) is small and with no supplies. There are in all some five or six villages fairly close together, all called Pinmun. The elephants so far have no difficulty from Saga. Rice is most plentiful in all these plains and valleys.
		3. Namké (Namkhai). Namké chaung.	7	6	21	2	The road from Pinmun to Namké is good and fairly level; the general direction is north-west. After about ¾ mile the village of Pong is passed. Rice cultivation most plentiful. There are numerous villages to be seen all round. Red chillies are greatly grown. Then the road gradually descends to the Namké chaung which is about 1 mile in front of the first village of that name. The river was full of duck, and other game would doubtless be found in the neighbouring swamps. From here onwards the land became gradually less fertile until the neighbourhood of No. 2 Namké is reached. There is a good broad cart road crossed at the first village of Namké; it leads to Pinlaung. The road from there begins to ascend and descend and finally goes between two hills to Namké No. 2. This is a large village on the river Belu and a tributary to it. There are about 45 to 60 houses, and good rice cultivation. Good accommodation for troops in the bazaar huts. Vegetables, rice, and cattle plentiful. There is a road going south to Pinlaung. Road from Pinmun is good all the way.

FROM SAGA (SAMKA) TO YAMÉTHIN *viâ* TAUNGKAMAUK AND KINYWA ZÉDIGÔN—*continued.*

Authorities. Military.	Authorities. Civil.	Number and Names of Stages, Rivers and Streams.	Distances. Intermediate. M. F.	Distances. Total. M. F.	Remarks.
G.O.C. Rangoon District.	Superintendent, Southern Shan States.	**4. Lônpu** ... ... Lôupu and Belu chaungs.	9 0	30 2	Road to Lônpu, good, in a northerly direction, following the course of the Belu chaung for half the way. Numerous villages are passed on the way, the most important of which are Payabyu 2 miles, To-6 3½ miles and Tina. The following bearings were taken from Pintôntaung near Namké: Pinlaung 155°, Myinmidu village 20°, Myinmidu hill 1°, Tônghla 334°, the Thénigôn and Yaméthin Pokintaung 30° and 45°. The Belu is a rapid stream of about 15 yards broad, shallow, firm bottom and low banks. A tributary to it, the Lônpu chaung, is crossed on the road. Then Lônpu is reached. This is a large village with numerous small ones in its neighbourhood. Ponies, cattle, rice, vegetables plentiful, and there is a large bazaar here once a week. The ground to the east is one broad extent of rice fields intersected by various small streams. There are routes from here to Kinywa Zédigôn and Yaméthin (six marches), and to Fort Stedman (three marches).
		5. Taungkamauk.	11 0	41 2	The road from Lônpu to Taungkamauk runs north-west, being considerably hilly, but good under foot all the way. After about 2 miles a small chaung and swamp are reached, there being a village on the north and south of the road, the former 1 mile distant, the southern ¼ mile. Lwé-6 pagoda and the Belu chaung are reached shortly afterwards. From Lwé-6 there is a road going to Taungthada and Yaméthin. After passing the village of In-ni and another one on the top of a hill, Taungkamauk is reached, being a total distance of 11 miles. There are three villages all close together of this name. Height by barometer 4,600 feet above Gwégôn. Good camping ground on a long *col.* Fowls, rice, and vegetables obtainable from the village which consists of about 20 houses. Water good and plentiful. Good forage for cattle and elephants; numerous wild plantain trees. A good view of the Yaméthin range is obtainable here.
		6. Thekagyin ...	9 0	50 2	The road from Taungkamauk to Thekagyin is also hilly and good under foot, following a north-west direction for 9 miles. There is no water on the road. After 2 miles village of Namin is visible, about 3 miles distant, consisting of about 50 houses. The jungle requires constant cutting and hence the rate of marching for elephants is slow, chiefly owing to the hilliness. The halting place is actually only about 8 miles, but owing to the scarcity of water for the animals it is necessary to go in a southerly direction for 2 miles to a small running stream. If a well could be sunk here permanently, the only obstacle of the whole route would be removed. This is said to be about 3 daings from the source of the river Panlaung, which rises in a mountain called "Sintaung," by barometer 2,400 feet above Gwégôn. Good forage for elephants. Long plantain groves. There is a village to the south about 3 miles away. There is a stream close by to the north 1 mile, but inaccessible owing to the steepness of the banks. The road to Bwet goes off here in a northerly direction.

FROM SAGA (SAMKA) TO YAMÉTHIN *viâ* TAUNGKAMAUK AND KINYWA ZÉDIGÔN—*continued.*

Authorities. Military.	Authorities. Civil.	Number and Names of Stages, Rivers and Streams.	Distances. Inter-mediate. M.	F.	Total. M.	F.	Remarks.
G.O.C. Rangoon District.	Commissioner, Eastern Division, and Deputy Commissioner, Yaméthin.	**7. Panlaung (or Paunglaung) river.**	**6**	**0**	56	2	The road from Thekagyin to the river Panlaung goes in a westerly direction for 6 miles ascending and descending through thick jungle which would require to be cut. The Panlaung river is here (at an elevation of 1,650 feet) about 20 yards broad, rocky bottom, rapid, crossed by a small bamboo bridge, 1 foot deep. There is a good open halting place on the west bank, a large zayát being available for about 50 men. Water and animal forage plentiful.
		8. Wayôngyi ...	**10**	**0**	66	2	The road from here to Wayôngyi goes in a south-west direction for 10 miles. Hilly. Water only met at the beginning and none afterwards till Wayôngyi. Elephant marching very slow from want of water and thickness of jungle and hilliness. Road good under foot. A small village is passed about 5 miles on, but it lies 1½ miles away. There is a good halting place at Wayôngyi. Large supply of good water and good forage for all animals.
		9. Kinywa Zédigôn.	**9**	**2**	75	4	The road on to Kinywa Zédigôn goes south-west for about 9 miles; good under foot, thick jungle, slightly hilly, but there is nothing to delay a column except perhaps the jungle. Kinywa Zédigôn is a police post 13 miles from Yaméthin. If the difficulty of water at Thekagyin could be overcome, the only obstacle to any column moving from Yaméthin to Lônpu would be removed. This is said to be the best of the three roads from Lônpu and is the one usually followed by traders. The road from Yaméthin to Zédigôn has already been surveyed and is being made by the Public Works Department. Several villages near and connected by cart tracks; the usual supplies procurable.
		10. Yaméthin ... Samôn river and other streams.	**13**	**0**	88	4	Road, country road, fit for carts all the way. First 6 or 7 miles along the base of the hills, last portion across paddy cultivation along raised embankment and bridged; Samôn river is crossed close to Yaméthin, narrow and easily fordable; it starts from the Yaméthin lake. The small village of Shwémindin is passed at 6½ miles and the large village of Theingôn at 10 miles, about 200 houses, large kyaung and zayáts. Water and supplies plentiful.

No. 57.

From TÁKÖT to KYENGHUNG viâ MÖNG LEM, KYENG MAI and MÖNG SÉ.

By Capt. G. V. BURROWS, Attaché, Intelligence Branch, February 1891.

Authorities. Military.	Authorities. Civil.	Number and Names of Stages, Rivers and Streams.	Distances. Intermediate. M.	F.	Distances. Total. M.	F.	Remarks.
G.O.C. Mandalay District.	Superintendent, Northern Shan States.	**1. Kát Maw (4,500 feet).**	**8**	**0**	8	0	*See* Route No. 16, Stage 18.
		2. Nam Awn valley. Nam Awn and Nam Páng.	**6**	**0**	14	0	The road leaves the village in a north-easterly direction and skirts the long slopes. The descent is gradual, but continual, and at the 5th mile it drops into Nam Awn valley and runs due east. The village of Nam Awn is situated on a small rounded hill not visible from the point at which the stream is crossed (8 to 12 feet broad; unbridged; gravel bottom; easy crossing liable to flood, but the depth would not much increase; is very rapid, but only from 8 inches to 1 foot deep), but round the small spur running down into the valley from the south-east. The road crosses the stream four times in the valley, which is cultivated, and it runs through the paddy-fields, crosses to the opposite side, passes the lower village, which is also called Nam Awn, and again crossing the stream runs on to a small bit of paddy land, a little higher than the rest, and which is the only ground suitable for camping and that only in dry weather. The whole of this part of the road, *i.e.*, down the valley, would be exceedingly difficult if, indeed, practicable in wet weather. It is, moreover, entirely commanded from both flanks for a distance of 2 miles, being flanked by thickly-wooded hills which are almost precipitous, and on an average from 800 to 500 yards apart from slope to slope. Just beyond the lower village and on the western side of the valley stands a large well-built kyaung which would afford shelter to 80 men. Total descent 2,250 feet.
		3. Nam Páng, Hsup Mawng.	**9**	**0**	23	0	The road runs on down the centre of the ravine, taking the course of the stream as its direction and continually crossing and recrossing it for about 2 miles, when it runs out into a valley and on to some paddy-fields below the little village of Na Nin, a small hamlet perched on the spur jutting out from the southern slopes. The path now takes a more northerly direction and running generally north-east by east passes down the valley for another 2 miles, when it suddenly rises on to a small plateau on which, unseen from below, stands the village of Nam Páng, containing some 25 houses and a large and dilapidated kyaung. There is camping ground between the kyaung and the village, sufficiently large to hold 200 men and 40 ponies close to the bazaar sheds. Not more than 100 yards to the left of the village along a deep valley flows the Nam Páng river rapid, *i.e.*, from 3 to 3½ miles an hour. In the dry season from 3 feet to 3 feet and 6 inches deep at the ferry. Its banks are low, and it is fordable by men and mules; bottom of large shingle and sandy. Indications of flood rise of 9 feet. It is 42 yards broad at the ford which is just below the ferry. It joins Nam Kha about 6 miles further south-east. Passing through the village the path runs down a small but deep ravine; from this point it rises about 400 feet in ½ a mile and winds along the crest-line of a small

From TÁKÖT to KYENGHUNG *viâ* MÖNG LEM, KYENG MAI and MÖNG SÉ—*continued.*

Authorities. Military.	Authorities. Civil.	Number and Names of Stages, Rivers and Streams.	Distances. Intermediate.	Distances. Total.	Remarks.
G.O.C. Mandalay District.	Superintendent, Northern Shan States.	**3. Nam Páng, Hsup Mawng**—*cont.*			spur, then taking a north-easterly direction falls into a deep valley running up the other side; again winds along the side of a spur and in another $\frac{1}{2}$ mile suddenly falls into the Nam Páng valley and runs along the right bank for about a mile, crossing two insignificant streams, till it reaches the ferry known at Hsup Mawng. There is barely sufficient camping ground on the opposite bank for 150 men, and that only actually along the bank of the river, both banks being thickly wooded.
			M. F.	M. F.	
		4. Na Tôk ... Nam Ma, banks low and quite easy; gravel bottom, liable to flood; and Nam Kha.	**7 0**	30 0	Leaving the Nam Páng the path ascends rapidly in a north-easterly direction. The gradient is steep and continual for $\frac{3}{4}$ of a mile. At $1\frac{3}{4}$ miles, the path runs below the village of South Páng Háng, and about a mile further on passes North Páng Háng, both on the left. The road now turns in an easterly direction and passes the village of Mai Kha, a small hamlet of only some six small huts. It then descends rapidly for nearly 2 miles passing the village of Hôtai and a stream about 10 feet wide and 4 inches deep, with firm gravel bottom running along the valley which is cultivated, and on the left slope of which stands the little village of Na Tôk; there is space enough for a small force of 150 men and baggage animals to encamp on the high ground in the centre of fields. Water is close at hand and there is plenty of it throughout the year. Na Tôk is a small insignificant village, but grain (paddy) is plentiful. Peas are cultivated to some extent. There is a large kyaung near the village and the ground in its immediate vicinity is sufficient to hold a camp of 100 men. The kyaung would accommodate 60 men.
		5. Möng Nga ... Nam Ma.	**4 0**	34 0	The path runs on in a north-easterly direction, passes two small insignificant villages $\frac{1}{2}$ a mile further on and, falling into a cultivated valley, passes the large village of Páng Sáng, and 300 yards further on runs into the Nam Kha. There are in all three boats here capable of carrying from four to five men each, or three loads from mules; but there is a better place for crossing, where in the dry season the people construct a small bamboo foot-bridge about 800 yards above and round the bend. The Nam Ma stream, which runs down from Möng Lem way, and the Nam Páng both fall into the Nam Kha just below this spot, and the latter then becomes a very considerable stream. It is here 35 yards broad and at the foot-bridge 3 feet 6 inches in depth. Both banks are here open. The eastern bank commands the western bank and is about 6 feet high, while the eastern or right bank is approached by a long beach of shingle and sand. The foot-bridge is only an erection of bamboos and is exceedingly frail. The velocity is about $3\frac{1}{2}$ miles an hour, and the bottom is firm; gravel shows indication of flood rise of 10 feet at the ford. The Nam Kha marks the boundary between Möng Lön East and Möng Lem. The path runs on through paddy-fields in a north-easterly direction for about a mile till it comes to another considerable stream called the Nam Ma (about 18 yards broad, 18 inches to 2 feet deep; rapid; gravel bottom; both banks low and open. Easy to cross anywhere), which flows beneath the village of Möng

FROM TÁKÖT TO KYENGHUNG *viâ* MÖNG LEM, KYENG MAI AND MÖNG SÉ—*continued.*

Authorities. Military.	Authorities. Civil.	Number and Names of Stages, Rivers and Streams.	Distances. Inter-mediate.	Distances. Total.	Remarks.
G.O.C. Mandalay District.	Superintendent, Northern Shan States.	**5. Möng Nga**—*cont.*			Nga here. Möng Nga is a fairly large village consisting of some 30 houses and overlooked by strongly built brick-work kyaung, which commands the valley for some $\frac{3}{4}$ of a mile in every direction, save the south, from which point it could be approached, but would even then perhaps be difficult to take with infantry alone. The brick walls are about 18 feet thick and 8 to 10 feet high. The floor inside is of brick, thus affording supply for use when more material is required. The slopes and approaches to this building from the west and north-west are abrupt and at all times would be difficult for infantry.
		6. Möng Ma ...	M. F. 14 4	M. F. 48 4	Leaving Möng Nga, for the next mile the road runs along the right bank of the river **Nam Ma**, which flows between low open banks over a rocky bed, and is here 35 yards broad and 2 feet deep, and then at the end of the mile the road crosses the river; 200 yards from the river is a small hill where, 300 yards above the road on the right, is the small village of Ho Yáng. The road then passes through a valley, when turning to the right it passes over rising ground 150 feet above the Nam Ma, which flows 100 yards distant with open ground on the opposite bank. It then crosses a considerable stream, 20 yards broad and 1 foot deep with pebbly bottom, and then through thick jungle close to the village of Anma, and 800 yards further on it turns to the left entering a valley about a mile long and $\frac{1}{2}$ a mile broad, in the centre of which is the village of Man Káng, about 20 houses on slightly rising ground. Running about 100 yards from the left bank of the stream until passing along the edge of the jungle above the stream, on the other side of which there is open ground for $\frac{1}{2}$ a mile, it crosses a low flat spur covered with jungle on which stands the village of Man Lán, consisting of 40 houses and a brick-built pôngyi kyaung 40 feet square, through which the road passes, and leaving the jungle crosses a small stream 30 feet broad, 5 inches deep in a rocky bed and flowing between low rocky banks. It then passes between open paddy-fields about 300 yards wide for about another mile. It then crosses a stream and 100 yards further on crosses another still smaller stream and touches the banks of a larger one and 200 yards further on enters an open cultivated spot, 300 yards square, from which it makes a steep ascent of 350 feet and then winds, ascending very gradually for $\frac{3}{4}$ of a mile along the base of the hill. It then crosses a very small stream in a ravine and passes over a low-wooded spur with open ground on the left and keeping 200 yards from a stream on the left for 800 yards passes through open fields, then under a hill and rising over a thickly-wooded spur by a steep and rocky path to the height of 100 feet. It goes down the other side and crosses a very small stream flowing down to the river in a rocky bed 20 feet broad and 6 feet deep and enters a flat cultivated piece of ground about 150 yards square, at the foot of which the river flows. This would form a good camping ground for a small force. The road then rises suddenly 100 feet by a rocky path, and continuing for 400 yards over rocky ground ascends gradually for another $\frac{3}{4}$ mile. It then crosses a deep ravine 200 yards broad with a stream flowing down the centre in a rocky bed. The slopes of the ravine are very steep and rocky, about 60 feet high,

FROM TÁKÖT TO KYENGHUNG *viâ* MÖNG LEM, KYENG MAI AND MÖNG SÉ—*continued.*

Authorities. Military.	Authorities. Civil.	Number and Names of Stages, Rivers and Streams.	Distances. Intermediate.	Distances. Total.	Remarks.
G.O.C. Mandalay District.	Superintendent, Northern Shan States.	**6. Möng Ma**—*cont.*			passing through jungle. The road then emerges into open fields in a broad valley and after 500 yards crosses a small stream, 8 feet broad and 6 inches deep, with rocky bed, and running between high-wooded rocky banks down the centre of the valley. Leaving the valley there is a steep ascent for ½ mile and 300 yards of level ground afterwards. After which the road crosses a small stream with low banks and rocky bottom leaving a little open cultivated ground on the left. A ¼ of a mile further on, on the left of the road and overhanging the right bank of the river, is a long hill 3,000 feet in height and thickly wooded. The road then crosses another small stream and passes through 300 yards of thick jungle. It then gradually rises and crosses a small stream, with a pebbly bottom, the left bank of which is steep and rocky, which flows down a thickly-wooded ravine, out of which the ascent by a steep, rocky, and difficult path is 100 feet. After this it runs level for 300 yards and then crosses a stream flowing north in a low rocky bed 20 feet broad and 6 inches deep and passes over a low, rocky wooded spur. It then crosses a stream with low open banks and gravel bottom, 16 yards wide, 1 foot deep and rapid, and recrosses it 300 yards further on at a similar ford. With the exception of the left bank being wooded, both fords are commanded by a wooded hill, 800 to 1,000 feet high. Then for 1¾ miles the path ascends very gradually 150 feet, passing through open paddy-fields until, leading due west, it reaches Möng Ma, which is situated in a clump of bamboo trees. It is a large village consisting of some 70 houses and is the head-quarters of a Tamôn. Paddy and rice are plentiful, and there is ample ground for camping on the southern side of the village, marked by a huge banyan tree. Water plentiful and within 20 yards of site. Möng Ma is 1,300 feet higher than Möng Na.
		7. Ho Khai ...	M. 3 F. 0	M. 51 F. 4	Leaving Mong Ma the path runs along the valley following the course of the river for about 800 yards, when it crosses it and the valley on to a small spur on which the village of Manlé stands, consisting of some 35 houses; the village is divided into two portions, known as Upper and Lower Manlé, but they are only 500 yards apart. Passing Upper Manlé on the left the path runs off the spur into another small valley about 600 yards broad, at the opposite side of which at the edge of the cultivation is the little village of Ho Khai. The stream, an insignificant one, running down this valley, is crossed three times in the next mile. Half-a-mile further on the valley ends. There is a camping ground at the head of the valley sufficiently large to hold 150 men, with plenty of water at hand. Water should be drawn for drinking from the top of the valley. It is not so pure below, as it oozes through a quagmire and contains a certain amount of sulphurous matter and is not considered good for drinking even by natives. It is advisable to halt here, as the next stage is some 15 miles to Möng Lem and there is a scarcity of water for the first 8 miles.

FROM TÁKÖT TO KYENGHUNG *viâ* MÖNG LEM, KYENG MAI AND MÖNG SÉ—*continued.*

Authorities.		Number and Names of Stages, Rivers and Streams.	Distances.				Remarks.
Military.	Civil.		Intermediate.		Total.		
			M.	F.	M.	F.	
G.O.C. Mandalay District.	Superintendent, Northern Shan States.	**8. Möng Lem (3,200 feet).** Nam Sa, Nam Kyeng, and Nam Lwi.	15	0	66	4	The road moves up the long low hills in a north-easterly direction rising 1,100 feet in the 1st mile. It then runs on to a small plateau about a mile square and skirts the hill at the northern end of it passing down its eastern slopes. Here the road falls gradually and the gradient, though continuous, is nowhere steep for nearly 3 miles till the upper valley is reached; from which point it takes a more easterly direction, is steep and runs down the side of the hill with a steep khud on the northern side the whole way down into the valley, on entering which it crosses the Nam Sa (low banks; eastern bank commands western, being close to hill which is thickly wooded; 22 feet broad; rapid; gravel and stony bottom, 2 feet deep; but easy crossing shows indications of flood rise, 8 feet). Crossing the open valley, which is only $\frac{1}{4}$ mile broad and $\frac{3}{4}$ mile long, and well adapted for camping in dry weather the road recrosses the stream twice and then rises a little, passing between two hills thickly wooded. In this valley and to the right of it, about 60 yards from the road, lies the village of Tung Sa. There is a fine pôngyi kyaung here capable of holding 60 men. Immediately below the village the road again crosses the Nam Sa. This crossing is well commanded from the opposite bank, being immediately below a craggy hill, the crest of which is only some 200 yards from the ford. The hill is very steep and clothed with thick, low jungle and is rocky. The road now runs down into a narrow cultivated valley with the stream on the right, and about $\frac{3}{4}$ of mile further on runs into the broad open cultivated valley of Möng Lem. Crossing the Nam Kyeng (18 feet broad, 1 foot deep; easy crossing, but liable to flood in very wet weather), the town is hidden for a while from view on entering the valley and lies on the southern slopes of a low-rounded hill about half-way down the valley to the left, where the river Nam Lwi flows into the valley through a gorge in the hill opposite Möng Lem. The Nam Lwi is 30 yards broad, 2 feet deep; gravel and stony bottom. Velocity 2 miles an hour; banks low and open indications of flood rise 4 feet. Spanned by a strong wooden foot-bridge of 9 piers, planks on roadway easily removeable; roadway 5 feet broad. The bridge head on the town or western side is well adapted for defence, being directly covered by a masonry wall of bricks, 7 feet high and 18 inches thick. A gate leads into the town from the bridge about 15 yards above the bridge-head. In the valley there are three distinct villages besides Möng Lem, one on the eastern bank of the river opposite Möng Lem and under the next hill looking east about 800 yards from the stream. Another, where the majority of the Chinese live, is in the centre of the valley and is the head-quarters of the Kyeng Möng or heir-apparent. The best site for a camp is the ground on the open slope of the spur running out into the valley, on the left as you enter it and about 800 yards from the town. This is only 300 yards from Nam Kyeng stream, where it joins the Nam Sa. Ducks, pigs, poultry, eggs, and beef in small quantities are available. Capt. Burrows gives the following routes leading from Möng Lem, derived from native information collected on the spot:— (1) To Kyeng Tung (Keng Tung), distance roughly 140 miles. Bullock caravans perform the journey in 17 days, but men

FROM TÁKÖT TO KYENGHUNG *viâ* MÖNG LEM, KYENG MAI AND MÖNG SÉ—*continued.*

Authorities. Military.	Authorities. Civil.	Number and Names of Stages, Rivers and Streams.	Distances. Intermediate.	Distances. Total.	Remarks.
G.O.C. Mandalay District.	Superintendent, Northern Shan States.	**8. Möng Lem (3,200 feet)**—*cont.*			travelling without animals do it in nine stages, viz., 1. Man Hin, 2. Ho Tao, 3. Möng Yáng, 4. Möng Lwé, 5. Möng Khak, 6. Möng Hang, 7. Ta Long, 8. Hang Möng, 9. Kyeng Tung. The road follows the course of the Nam Lwi in Stages 1, 2, 6 and 7, the river being crossed by ferry at the last named. (2) To the Cambodia river by Ta Song Kyeng ferry, distance about 170 miles, bullock stages about 20, men travelling fast 10, viz., 1. Keng Hin, 2. Möng Yen, 3. Páng Tong, 4. Maw Ngun, 5. Táng Pen, 6. Hu Láng, 7. Hó Yong, 8. Möng Nyim, 9. Páng Pen, 10. Ferry at junction of river Nam Song and Cambodia river. (3) To Yen Ten in Chinese territory, about 14 days' journey, viz., eight stages as follows: 1. Möng Láng, 2. Möng Peng, 3. Möng Lam, 4. Sán Phang, 5. La Mai, 6. Pen Tán Sen, 7. Tai Khen, 8. Nam Khong (Cambodia), thence six stages (names not known) to Yen Ten, where there are salt mines.
		9. Ho Sit (Nam Sit). Nam Nyin and Nam Sit.	M. 10 F. 0	M. 76 F. 4	Crossing the Nam Lwi by the foot-bridge opposite the town the road runs through paddy-fields in an easterly direction and passes the Chinese village of Wengkian at the first ½ mile. Half-a-mile further on it crosses the Nam Nyin (a small stream running across the valley from the eastern end joins the Nam Lwi in the valley. At the ford just below the village of Man Kaw it is 10 feet broad, 9 inches deep; rapid; firm gravel bottom; banks 6 feet high; indication of flood rises 8 feet) just below the little village of Man Kao and moving over open ground with scrub jungle on the right it enters the village of Kyeng Möng standing on a knoll. The heir-apparent of Möng Lem lives here. There are about 50 houses, paddy and grain plentiful, ducks and poultry with some pigs procurable. A mile further on the path runs into a belt of bamboo jungle, passes the little village of Mai Kwi and runs up the hill in an easterly direction. It is here that the road enters country occupied by the Muhsös. Rising over the hills in an easterly direction the road runs up on to a ridge 1,200 feet above the valley and 1½ miles from it. The road here turns in a south-easterly direction, and after another 2 miles it begins to fall very rapidly, the descent being 900 feet in ¾ of a mile. In the valley and just to the right of the road lies the small Wa village of Ho Sit. The road winds over a small low neck and falls rapidly again for another ¾ mile, running into the valley of the Nam Sit, flowing west (20 feet broad, 1 foot deep; stony gravel bottom; rapid, low easy banks; indications of flood rise 6 feet; timber handy. Right bank wooded). There is a good camping ground on the opposite bank within 50 yards of the ford. There is no water to be had from Man Kwi to this stream near the road.
		10. Nawng Káng. Small stream.	10 0	86 4	The road runs up the hill in an easterly direction, taking the shape of the hill, and rising over a small spur turns again in a north-easterly direction passing round the head of a sharply defined valley. It then moves again eastwards, passes over the small spurs and falling each time very nearly as much as it rises. In another 2 miles it runs down into a small valley where there is a small stream

FROM TÁKÖT TO KYENGHUNG *viâ* MÖNG LEM, KYENG MAI AND MÖNG SÉ—*continued.*

Authorities. Military.	Authorities. Civil.	Number and Names of Stages, Rivers and Streams.	Distances. Intermediate.	Distances. Total.	Remarks.
G.O.C. Mandalay District.	Superintendent, Northern Shan States.	**10. Nawng Káng** —*cont.*			capable of supplying a small force of 200 men and 200 animals. The latter would have to be watered by means of buckets. The stream is sluggish 2 feet broad, 6 inches deep, banks low and boggy, and runs through soil which much resembles peat. There is no village here and no supplies are obtainable. Water could not be had during the hot months, *i.e.*, after the end of April, unless rain had fallen. There is no water to be had near the road between the Nam Sit and this valley. The elevation of the valley is about 4,500 feet. There is a small fairly level spot of ground about 400 yards square, beyond the point where the stream is crossed and quite close to the water. There is no other site for a camp. Plenty of pine timber close at hand.
		11. Tun Möng Song.	M. 7 F. 0	M. 93 F. 4	Moving on up the valley for ½ a mile due east, the path turns off to the right passing over a low neck and descends about 100 feet, running along a sharply defined ridge turning south. It then winds along a small valley and rises over another ridge, rising in all 250 feet. From this point a good view of the surrounding country can be obtained. It is thickly wooded, but as the predominating tree is the fir, there is no undergrowth in the jungle. Winding along the sides of small valleys and crossing small spurs, the road suddenly runs down into a small valley known as Tun Möng Song. There is a small Mu Hsö village about a mile to the left of the camping ground, which faces you as you descend the valley. Water runs down on two sides of it. The road immediately ascends the hills due east of the camping ground and rises very rapidly for the first ½ mile, the total rise being 600 feet. It now winds along crest-lines of hills. Commanding both slopes for some 3 miles where it runs round the side of a large hill moving north-east. At the eastern end of this hill there is sufficient level ground to encamp 100 men and animals, and water sufficient in the cold weather and rains only, runs down the side of the hill close by.
		12. Páng Kwai (3,500 feet). Nam Mök.	11 0	104 4	From this point the road turns in an easterly direction and descends again on to another continuous ridge for about 2 miles. It again descends some 200 feet in the next mile and finally running along the crest-line of a long low spur, drops into the valley of the Nam Mök flowing south. The only camping ground is in the paddy-fields along the opposite bank of the stream. The village of Páng Kwai lies in the valley at the north end of it. The Nam Mök is here 25 feet broad, 8 inches deep; low banks; indications of flood rises 10 feet; bed of fine gravel. Plenty of pine timber at hand for bridging.
		13. Keng Mai (or Kyeng Mai), 4,700 feet. Small stream.	6 0	110 4	Leaving the Nam Mök valley the road winds up the spurs in an east-north-east direction. The gradient is steep and continual, the total rise to the ridge being 1,600 feet in 2 miles. From this point the road falls about 300 feet into a small valley, thickly covered with large trees, and ¾ of a mile below the ridge lies the village of Nawng Káng, consisting of some 25 houses.

FROM TÁKÖT TO KYENGHUNG *viâ* MÖNG LEM, KYENG MAI AND MÖNG SÉ—*continued.*

Authorities.		Number and Names of Stages, Rivers and Streams.	Distances.		Remarks.
Military.	Civil.		Intermediate.	Total.	
G.O.C. Mandalay District.	Superintendent, Northern Shan States.	**13. Keng Mai (or Kyeng Mai), 4,700 feet**—*cont.*			A small insignificant stream of good water flows north-east through the village. Leaving the village the road rises rapidly over a spur running due east. In ½ a mile it turns in a north-easterly direction and the descent into the valley of Nam Lam commences, winding down the hill in an easterly direction; the descent is very gradual and after another mile the large village of Keng Mai is reached. Keng Mai is in Keng Hung (or Kyeng Hung) territory. It consists of 50 houses. Rice and paddy not plentiful. Tea plantations cover the hill sides between the two villages. The road is good and broader than the ordinary hill tracks and shows signs of regular and considerable traffic. The elevation of Keng Mai is about 4,700 feet. From here Captain Burrows gives the following routes from information collected on the spot:— (1) To the Cambodia river at Ta Song Tsáng, about 100 miles, 12 bullock stages, viz., 1. Möng Maung, 2. Kyu Hao, 3. Láng Nö, 4. Hsen Yao, 5. Ho Möng, 6. Pán Sikaw, 7. Tawyit Sen, 8. Nam Seng, 9. Kam T'sé-u, 10. Ta Ké-u, 11. Pun Paw, 12. Ta Song Tsáng. (2) To the Cambodia river at Ta Ya Ké-u, about 70 miles, four foot stages for travellers without pack animals, vis., 1. Möng Maung, 2. Láng Nö, 3. Ho Möng, 4. Ta Ya Ké-u. *Note.*—The above routes are given separately by Captain Burrows though they are apparently the same route.
		14. Möng Máng. Nam Lam and Nam Máng.	M. 7 F. 0	M. 117 F. 4	The road passing through the village runs along a fairly level spur due east for nearly a mile and-a-half passing the small Chinese village of Man Khwi in the valley below to the right and about ¾ of a mile distant. At 1½ miles from Kyeng Mai the road passes through the village of Man Pung containing some 30 houses and situated on a small spur. Half-a-mile further due east it passes a similar smaller village called Man Keng; from this point the road runs very rapidly to the Nam Lam flowing down the deep valley in a west-south-westerly direction and joining the Nam Lwé below Kyeng Hung. Here it is 50 feet broad; very rapid; from 3 feet 6 inches to 4 feet deep; flowing between precipitous banks; both heavily wooded and high with a rocky bottom. It is fordable at this season at a point just 120 yards above the foot-bridge which spans it, and just above where the Nam Máng enters it from the eastern side. The total descent from Kyeng Mai in the 4 miles to the river is approximately 2,000 feet. From here crossing the Nam Lam by foot-bridge the road runs along the left bank of the Nam Máng, which joins the Nam Lam about 100 yards north of the foot-bridge. The Nam Máng is of precisely the same nature as the Nam Lam, but narrower and not so rapid, its velocity being only 2 miles an hour. It flows down from the hills in a south-easterly direction and is at Möng Máng flowing through a flat alluvial valley with low banks and is liable in rainy season to flood. The bottom is of gravel and it is only from 18 inches to 2 feet deep anywhere in the valley. The path is difficult for about ¾ of a mile for pack animals, being narrow and in some places overhanging the stream and about 15 to 20 feet above it. Running along the ravine due east the path crosses the stream about ½ mile from the ravine and ford. Möng Máng lies about a mile up the valley south-east and on the right edge of the jungle. It is a large village

FROM TÁKÖT TO KYENGHUNG *viâ* MÖNG LEM, KYENG MAI AND MÖNG SÉ—*continued.*

Authorities. Military.	Authorities. Civil.	Number and Names of Stages, Rivers and Streams.	Distances. Intermediate.	Distances. Total.	Remarks.
G.O.C. Mandalay District.	Superintendent, Northern Shan States.	**14. Möng Máng** —*cont.*			containing 100 houses. Two of the buildings are of brick and surrounded by brick walls roughly loopholed, but only about 4 feet high. The kyaung stands on ground higher than the rest of the village and is built of brick. It is a spacious building capable of holding 100 men. Rice and paddy are plentiful. There is a good camping ground on some rising ground covered with large trees about 800 yards north-west of the village and separated from it by marshy ground. Keng Tung can be reached from here, distance about 20 bullock stages. There is also a route to Möng Nyin in Möng Lem, distance about 112 miles, 13 bullock stages as follows: 1. Pauk Kyaung, 2. Len Long, 3. Hath Pa, 4. Na Mu, 5. Nam Kaw, 6. Möng Lem, 7. Lôk Me, 8. Htin Hpa, 9. Táng Pen, 10. Nam Láng, 11. Kyaw Haw, 12. Man Ping, 13. Möng Nyin. Foot-travellers do the journey in seven stages making their halts at Stages 2, 4, 6, 8, 9 and 11 above.
		15. Man Kaw ... Nam Ha.	M. 12 F. 0	M. 129 F. 4	Passing through the village the road runs on south-east by south for a mile following the Nam Máng. It crosses the stream at the village of Man Pyen, a considerable place consisting of some 60 houses and possessing a fine kyaung made of bricks enclosed by a brick wall 2 feet 6 inches high and overlooking the ford. Here the road enters the jungle and keeping close to the stream the ascent commences. The gradient is steep in some places and the road is rocky and bad. The total rise up to the 10th mile is approximately 2,600 feet. By moving off the path here a little to the right a good view of the plain of Möng Sé can be obtained. The descent commences after the 11th mile and passing over the Nam Ha, a very small trickling stream, here it runs past an open spot in the jungle where there is a good camping ground for a force of 250 men. Running down the hill for about another mile brings you to the village of Man Kaw on the right, a large straggling village of 70 houses.
		16. Möng Sé ... Nam Ha.	6 0	135 4	The road crosses the Nam Ha again by a small but well-built stone bridge with a roadway 8 feet broad and a single span of 12 feet, and enters the valley. The path runs up the broad open valley following the Nam Ha which is now on the left of the road flowing along between perpendicular sand banks, 6 feet high and about 18 feet broad. Möng Sé is on the low-rounded hill 6 miles up the valley almost due south-east from Man Kaw. Möng Sé is a large town consisting of some 400 houses and scattered over the hills for the greater part on the eastern, southern and northern slopes. There are two wells on the southern side where there is a good site for a camp at the foot of the hill 300 yards from the well. From here Captain Burrows gives the following routes from native information:— (1) To Keng Tung, eight bullock stages, three days' journey for a traveller without pack animals. Stages: 1. Man Kán, 2. Möng Hai, 3. Möng Söng. 4. Nam Pöng, 5. Hwé Sing, 6. Páng Sán, 7. Páng Möng, 8. Keng Tung. (2) To Ta Káng ferry on Cambodia river, a good road, eight bullock stages as follows:—1. Nam Mu, 2. Möng Ti, 3. Möng Káng, 4. Nam Sön, 5. Kát Káng, 6. Mong Wáng, 7. Páng Hpa, 8. Ta Káng. Travellers without pack animals do the journey in four days.

FROM TÁKÖT TO KYENGHUNG *viâ* MÖNG LEM, KYENG MAI AND MÖNG SÉ—*continued.*

Authorities.		Number and Names of Stages, Rivers and Streams.	Distances.		Remarks.
Military.	Civil.		Inter-mediate.	Total.	
			M. F.	M. F.	
G.O.C. Mandalay District.	Superintendent, Northern Shan States.	**17. Möng Hai** ... Namha and Nam Hung.	12 0	147 4	Leaving Möng Sé the road runs across the open valley, east-south-east, reaching the low-wooded hills on the reverse slopes of which lies the little village of Keng Tsung. There is a brick-built monastery here standing on a small knoll east of the village. It is surrounded by a brick wall 4 or 5 feet high. The Nam Ha, which is crossed about 300 yards below Möng Sé, flows along here almost under the walls of this building, 2½ miles from Möng Sé. It is here 12 feet broad; shallow, 1 foot deep, sandy bottom, steep banks, open sluggish stream; indications of flood rise to 7 feet; water is always muddy. There is a large swamp on the other or northern side of the village. The road runs along the centre of the valley, with open ground on either side, for about 2 miles more with the Nam Ha close to it on the right. It passes the villages of Man Ké, Man Na, and Man Lwi at the 6th mile and a mile further on, to the right of the valley, which is here only 2 miles broad, it passes the village of Nam Káng, past which, flowing down from the south, comes the Nam Hung, a considerable stream of precisely the same nature as the Nam Ha, which it here joins. The road now enters thin jungle, passes over and round a succession of very low, rounded wooded hills and 3 miles further on it runs into the cultivated valley of Möng Hai. The Nam Ha flows north through the centre of this valley and is spanned by a long, well built, wooden foot-bridge. The roadway is capable of bearing loaded cattle, is 8 feet broad and 40 yards long and the bridge is roofed over with tiles. The Nam Ha is here 3 feet deep; sluggish sandy bottom; low banks; bed of stream 4 yards broad. Actual water-line 38 feet broad; flood rise up the roadway of bridge, which floods the valley. The road from this bridge across the valley is raised about 2 feet 6 inches and is 6 feet broad. Möng Hai stands on the low hills due east of the valley. On the right on entering the valley and 800 yards from the bridge stands the village of Man Söng. Overlooking the valley and below the town of Möng Hai stands a well-built brick monastery, capable of holding 100 men. It consists of four blocks, and is surrounded by a brick wall loopholed, 5½ feet high. There is a good camping ground 300 yards south of the town, close to but not under the trees, as further on there is a burial ground. In the dry season troops could camp anywhere in the plain. About 1,200 yards further, south, in a strip of jungle jutting out into the plain, lies the village of Man Ho. From Möng Hai to Keng Tung is about 90 miles; travellers without pack animals do the journey in 6 days. For bullock caravans it is 14 stages, viz., 1. Möng Hön, 2. Nam Hak, 3. Möng Pun, 4. Möng Kawn, 4. Ta Law, 6. Möng La. 7. Nam Mi, 8. Möng Ma, 9. Páng Phai, 10. Ta Peng, 11. Möng Wák, 12. Na Tráng, 13. Pakhun, 14. Keng Tung.
		18. Möng Sung Taw. Nam Ha and Nam Pöng or Nam Kyaung.	13 0	160 4	The road leaves Möng Hai in a northerly direction running through low hills, covered with jungle, passing every 300 or 400 yards strips of cultivated ground lying between the low spurs. At the 3rd mile it passes the village of Peng Kham and a mile further it crosses the Nam Ha by a well-built

From TÁKÖT to KYENGHUNG *viâ* MÖNG LEM, KYENG MAI and MÖNG SÉ—*continued.*

Authorities.		Number and Names of Stages, Rivers and Streams.	Distances.		Remarks.
Military.	Civil.		Inter-mediate.	Total.	
G.O.C. Mandalay District.	Superintendent, Northern Shan States.	**18. Möng Sung Taw**—*cont.*			wooden bridge, 38 yards in length, with a roadway of substantial plank 8 feet broad. Camping ground on the right bank. The stream here is from 2½ to 4 feet deep, the banks are about 8 feet high and perpendicular, the current rapid. Two hundred yards from the bridge-head on the opposite bank lies the village of Man Long. The road here rises over a low thickly-wooded spur for about 260 yards and ½ a mile fnrther on passes through the village of Man Wan. It now turns nearly due east and runs along the southern slopes of a round low hill, and a mile further passes through Man Laung, a village of 40 houses with small stream of good water flowing along the western side of the village. The country to the right is open for about 600 yards, being under cultivation. Running along through open cultivated ground for another mile and-a-half it crosses the Nam Pöng stream (10 feet broad; very rapid; bridged by means of a couple of large trunks of trees thrown across, safe for mounted men and pack animals; bank steep; 6 feet high; muddy bottom; any amount of timber close at hand) after falling nearly 80 feet from a low spur. Three-quarters of a mile further east the village of Man Pöng is reached. After crossing another small stream flowing across the road south and which joins the Nam Pöng in the open valley, ½ a mile to the right, running along the foot a long wooded spur past tea gardens, the road going almost due east, reaches the village of Möng Sung Nŏ. Two miles from Man Pöng and turning slightly to the south it comes to another large village ½ a mile further on called Möng Peng. There is a large kyaung, situated on rising ground, about 200 yards north of the village. It is built of brick and would form a strong point for defence of the village if the small knoll, situated in the centre of the paddy-fields and immediately overlooking the road, were also held, as it is commanded from this point. Paddy and rice are plentiful. The valley is nearly a mile broad, watered by the Nam Kyaung, so called after the confluence of the above-mentioned streams. There is good ground for a camp at the side of the road, half-way between Man Pöng and Man Möng Sung Nŏ, where the stream Nam Kyaung flows along only 100 yards south of the road (12 feet broad, 1 foot deep; gravel bottom; rapid; very low banks, flowing through paddy-fields which could be easily flooded).
			M. F.	M. F.	
		19. Kát Tông ...	**16 0**	176 4	Passing through the village the road runs round a steep wooded spur for a mile and-a-half, passing the small village of Man Wan, down in the valley, ½ a mile to the right and through which the Nam Kyaung flows. Another ¼ mile further on the road runs along by the side of the stream for about 200 yards and suddenly leaves it, turning to the left and crosses a narrow neck with a rise of 120 feet, from which it drops rapidly, with a steep descent of 300 feet, at the foot of which the Nam Pöng Noi (25 feet broad; sloping low banks; right bank commands left; gravel and rocky bottom; slow stream; 18 inches deep) flows in a south-easterly direction. On the opposite bank and on the western spur of the hill, known as Loi Maung Sôn, there are paddy-fields terraced and would give ample room for camping in dry weather. Half-a-mile to the left up in the valley lies a village called Man Hpa, and ½ a mile due north-east of the ford is the small village of Man Pwi
		Nam Pöng Noi and Nam Ha.			

FROM TÁKÖT TO KYENGHUNG *viâ* MÖNG LEM, KYENG MAI AND MÖNG SÉ—*continued.*

Authorities. Military.	Authorities. Civil.	Number and Names of Stages, Rivers and Streams.	Distances. Intermediate.	Distances. Total.	Remarks.
G.O.C. Mandalay District.	Superintendent, Northern Shan States.	**19. Kát Tông**—*cont.*			on the hill. The road now rises very rapidly in a south-easterly direction, for ¾ of a mile, the total ascent being 850 feet. From the top of the hill it runs along a fairly level course, is broad and good. It runs round spur after spur, dropping about 100 feet in every ½ mile for the next 3 miles, when it runs along a low narrow ridge for a mile. It then descends very rapidly for 400 yards only falling 800 feet into the valley of the Nam Ha, which here is a roaring torrent 25 yards broad, flowing between rocks and small islands at a great rate, through a gorge, 150 yards broad, quite impassable at all seasons. The road runs down close to the side of the torrent and, when the river is in flood, would be impassable. From this point it follows the Nam Ha, running along the left bank for nearly 6 miles through dense jungle and in some places barely passable for pack animals, being very narrow and lying between cuttings of rocky gravel. (Animals should be well loaded so that their loads should be as much as possible high up on the saddle and not hanging on the sides, as such animals could not pass through.) At the 6th mile, from the point where the road touches the Nam Ha, lies the large village of Kát Tông, the greater portion of it lying on the right bank where there is ample ground for camping in dry weather as it is quite open. In wet weather the best site for a camp would be opposite the ford, where the bazaar stands on the left bank. The river is fordable in the dry season at this point, being only 2 feet 6 inches deep with a firm gravelly bottom.
		20. Kyeng Hung (Keng Hung). Nam Ôt, Nam Ha, and Mé Kong (Cambodia river).	M. 8 F. 0	M. 184 F. 4	The road passes through Kát Tông and runs through fields and open level country passing the villages of Keng Tai, Man Na, and Man Kawng, all of which are small and insignificant. Camping ground is abundant all the way. Four miles from Kát Tông, the road crosses the Nam Ôt (low open banks; 18 inches deep; gravel bottom; 30 feet broad), which joins the Nam Ha ½ a mile to the left. On the right bank and within 100 yards of the ford across the Nam Ôt is a small village of the same name. The road now turns slightly south-east and passing close to the village of Sawn Hé runs through a small belt or elephant grass for 2 miles, when it runs into the bazaar of Kyeng Hung, a large open flat space 200 yards long by 60 yards broad. This ground would do for a small force to camp on, but it is some distance from water, and a large force, say over 60 men with pack animals, should camp on the sand banks between the Nam Ha and the Cambodia. There is a path from the bazaar to a ford over the Nam Ha which is due south-west 1,000 yards distant (30 yards broad; near east or right bank it is 3 feet deep and the bottom is soft; half-way across and to the opposite bank it is only 18 inches deep; current 2½ miles an hour; pack animals can cross in the dry season). The banks are steep, but could easily be improved being of clay. The Nam Ha flows down and joins the Cambodia below Kyeng Hung town, which stands much scattered on the slopes of the spurs jutting out into the bed of the river, which here turns round the hill and flows down in an easterly direction between low hills. Opposite Kyeng Hung, which is much scattered and consists of some 200 houses

FROM TÁKÖT TO KYENGHUNG *viâ* MÖNG LEM, KYENG MAI AND MÖNG SÉ—*continued.*

Authorities.		Number and Names of Stages, Rivers and Streams.	Distances.		Remarks.
Military.	Civil.		Intermediate.	Total.	
G.O.C. Mandalay District.	Superintendent, Northern Shan States.	**20. Kyeng Hung (Keng Hung)**—*cont.*			only, the river bed is about 1 mile broad. The water however being at present only 350 yards wide. There are four boats; which when lashed together, 8 feet apart in pairs and fitted with platforms, are capable of carrying 30 men on each pair. The current is rapid, being very nearly 4 miles an hour. The principal ferry is at Ta Kaw, a village 3½ miles up the Cambodia from the ford over the Nam Ha (last mentioned above), where there are eight boats generally used, as mentioned, in pairs. The Cambodia at Kyeng Hung is at this season only 18 feet deep and opposite Ta Kaw 24 feet deep and 280 yards broad. When in flood, however, it rises every year 32 feet. Once every three years it is said to rise much higher, the bazaar buildings being submerged. The only camping ground in that case would be where the haw or palace is built. It is a piece of level ground overlooking the river and nearly 200 feet above it, ½ a mile due north of the bazaar, and is 8 yards square. From here there are four roads to Ta Ya Ké-u ferry, but the following is the only one used by traders and is considered the shortest and best. The distance by it is about 50 miles, and bullock caravans do it in seven stages, viz., 1. Mong Sung, 2. Möng Awn, 3. Möng Ngat, 4. Hu Láng, 5. Man Hum, 6. Name not known, 7. Ta Ya Kéu. In the first, second and fifth stages, low hills are crossed; the third and fourth stages are level. In the sixth stage a high range is crossed and a halt is necessary at the top of the pass. Descent therefrom is very steep. Foot-passengers can do the journey in four stages.

No. 58.

From TÁKÖT to TAWNIO (KÔKÁNG) viâ PÁNG SÁNG, &c.

BY CAPT. G. V. BURROWS, ATTACHÉ, INTELLIGENCE BRANCH, 1891.

Military.	Civil.	Stages	Intermediate M.	Intermediate F.	Total M.	Total F.	Remarks
G.O.C. Mandalay District.	Superintendent, Northern Shan States.	**1. Kát Maw** ...	**8**	**0**	8	0	*See* Route No. 57, Stages 1 to 5.
		2. Nam Páng ...	**15**	**0**	23	0	
		3. Páng Sáng ...	**9**	**4**	32	4	
		4. Nam Tông ... Nam Nga, Nam Lin and another stream.	**9**	**4**	42	0	Leaving Páng Sáng in a north-western direction the road rises quickly for the first ½ mile and passes close to the right of a large bamboo-built pôngyi kyaung, surrounded by a small mud wall, 3 feet high, and 300 yards further on, passing through the village of King Tsong, lying in a small hollow, it continues to descend another 200 yards when it crosses the Nam Nga stream, 20 feet broad; 6 inches deep; low wooded banks; gravel bottom; rapid. The road at once rises about 300 feet on to a long wooded spur, running almost due north. It continues to run along the spur, rising 370 feet in the next mile; when it reaches the village of Kawng Hsáng, and running over a low neck, 100 yards to the right of the village, it drops 100 feet into a narrow ravine just beyond it. The stream running down this ravine, called Nam Lin, forms the boundary

FROM TÁKÖT TO TAWNIO (KÔKÁNG) *viâ* PÁNG SÁNG, &c.—*continued.*

Authorities. Military.	Authorities. Civil.	Number and Names of Stages, Rivers and Streams.	Distances. Intermediate.	Distances. Total.	Remarks.
G.O.C. Mandalay District.	Superintendent, Northern Shan States.	**4. Nam Tông**—*cont.*			between Eastern Möng Lön and the Wa State of Nga (? Ngek) Ting. The road continues to rise by a steep gradient for the next ½ mile where it crosses another little stream and passing round the head of the ravine, continues to rise round another spur passing a small collection of bazaar huts. It continues to rise rapidly round successive spurs for the next 2 miles through thick jungle. The next ¼ of a mile it runs nearly level, then rises continually for another mile and-a-half when it gets on to an undulating piece of open plateau, the height of which is 5,190 feet, and crossing a small open valley turns to the right, ascends a steep hill for 400 yards and enters a wood, the edge of which is fenced with a light stockade. To the right of the road, which here again turns to the left, stands the village of Nam Mak Kho. It then turns down a long ridge and by an easy gradient falls 180 feet on to a level spur, from which it passes over a low saddle into a more open and undulating valley and passes close to the left of a small village called Nam Tông (20 houses). There is a very small low-lying camping ground just below the village, sufficiently large to hold 200 men, and water, though good, is not plentiful, but sufficient for the above strength.
		5. Loi Núng ...	M. F. **9 4**	M. F. 51 4	Passing the village on the north the road turns immediately due east, running level for ½ a mile when it drops 200 feet by a steep gradient into a narrow open valley. Rising on the other side in a north-easterly direction, the road ascends for 600 yards where the elevation is 5,300 feet and runs along a sharp spur. In the next mile the road gradually descends 200 feet, being level for the next 400 yards. It again rises 250 feet in about ¼ mile and passes a small Wa village, Yong Páng, about 100 yards to the left. It then runs level about 600 yards and passes over a low saddle, 100 yards from which, turning to the right, it descends by a very steep gradient in a north-easterly direction into a small cultivated valley, falling 400 feet in 500 yards; 200 yards further on it rises 240 feet over a spur, on the left of a conical hill by a steep gradient, and then runs level for about 600 yards, when it commences along and steep descent for ¾ mile, through cultivation and is open on both sides, with steep slopes on the right. It now passes close to the left of the village of Páng Hai, elevation 5,730 feet. Just above the village is a good camping ground, and good water is obtainable just beyond it in a narrow ravine. It then runs on for 200 yards over a low neck and descends in a northerly direction, passing at once, through a few houses, on to a long steep spur, the slopes of which are all cultivated with poppy. In little more than ½ a mile it has fallen 350 feet, where it again commences to rise and passes over two low rounded spurs with steep open slopes on the right, and turning to the left over a low saddle it undulates along the left side of a broken but open range for a mile and three-quarters, with bare steep slopes on left chiefly cultivated with poppy. It then suddenly drops into a valley descending 230 feet in about 400 yards and rises up the hill called Loi Núng. There is a small camping ground just below the road to the right in this small valley, where water is good and plentiful. The ground is large enough to hold a force of about 200 men.

FROM TÁKÖT TO TAWNIO (KÔKÁNG) *viâ* PÁNG SÁNG, &c.—*continued.*

Authorities.		Number and Names of Stages, Rivers and Streams.	Distances.		Remarks.
Military.	Civil.		Intermediate.	Total.	
			M. F.	M. F.	
G.O.C. Mandalay District.	Superintendent, Northern Shan States.	**6. Lön**	5 0	56 4	The road rises 450 feet by a steep gradient and passes over a spur to the right of hill called Loi Núng within ½ a mile of the camping ground and runs on in a north-north-west direction, dropping about 60 feet and winding across the head of a ravine for 800 yards when it passes over another low spur. The slopes on the right are open. Turning slightly to the left the road passes a small flat open space about 150 by 60 yards with water just below it. This ground, however, is commanded from the village which is 250 yards beyond it, lying in a hollow under the wooded crest-line of the highest point of the hill. Just past the village it crosses a sharply defined ridge, the valley below which is open. It winds round the head of the valley and in ¾ of a mile passes close to the left of a small Mu Su (or Muhsö) village, So Saw (15 huts) standing on a small bare ridge. It then passes over a sharp bare ridge dropping 100 feet the other side and turns due west. Running round the head of the steep valley for 700 yards it rises 200 feet on to a wooded ridge by a very steep gradient and runs north-west and falls 700 through thick jungle by a very steep path and crosses a narrow saddle. It then rises the other side of the valley. In 300 yards it rises on to a narrow ridge, covered with jungle with precipitous slopes on the left, along which it runs for ¾ mile, when it rises about 100 feet and then winds along the sides of hills through open grass country for 3 miles, when it rises about 160 feet over a sharp spur by a steep ascent and runs along level in thick jungle. There is a little water here on either side of the road in the ravines. Rising by a steep gradient 450 feet over broken ground it passes through the village of Páng Lát (30 houses; elevation 5,350 feet). Then turning north-east by east it runs off this ridge, dropping 120 feet on to another, along which it runs level in a north-eastern direction. The slopes and ravines surrounding Páng Lát are on all sides thickly covered with jungle. Turning north-east by east, 500 yards further on, it continues level for about a ¼ of a mile when it rises nearly 120 feet, and again runs level for ½ mile descending then nearly 300 feet in 600 yards and runs along a narrow ridge with a very deep broad wooded valley on either side for nearly 1 mile. The village of Lön, where the petty Chief Naw Kham U lives, is visible from this point looking due north. The road passes through some open fields on the south-east slopes of the hill, and ascends over undulating ground, nearly 200 feet to the village, which stands on the very top of the flat hill and consists of a collection of about 20 huts. There is ample space for camping here on the undulating ground below the village, and water is procurable in small quantities from a small stream below the kyaung, on the eastern slope of the hill. There is also a very small stream trickling down the hill on the side of the hill due north of the village. The town of Táköt is visible from this point on a clear day looking north-west by west.
		7. Man Pru ... Nam Pru.	7 0	63 4	Passing down the hill by a very steep, but good, broad path on the north-west slopes, the road descends very rapidly for ½ a mile where it passes through a small open clearing which

FROM TÁKÖT TO TAWNIO (KÔKÁNG) *viâ* PÁNG SÁNG, &c.—*continued.*

Authorities. Military.	Authorities. Civil.	Number and Names of Stages, Rivers and Streams.	Distances. Intermediate. M. F.	Distances. Total. M. F.	Remarks.
G.O.C. Mandalay District.	Superintendent, Northern Shan States.	**7. Man Pru**—*cont.*			is level enough to camp on for a small force of about 100 men and transport. There is a good but very small stream of water flowing across the road here. It rises by a long gradual ascent nearly 200 feet and continues to run along the side of the hill, fairly level, through thick jungle for nearly 3 miles, when it passes across a flat spur cutting out to the left on which there is a small Wa village, Man Mug, consisting of about 10 houses. The road drops about 60 feet and runs then along level for the next 3¼ miles, when it suddenly drops into a small cultivated valley about 200 yards broad, and in the centre of which, at the foot of a steep spur, jutting out from the hills opposite, stands the little village of Man Pru, consisting of about 20 houses, the inhabitants of which are Shans. The Nam Pru (8 feet broad; 6 inches deep; gravel bottom; good water; rapid) flows through the valley at the foot of the valley. Troops must camp here in the dry and hot season.
		8. Na Pháng (or Mankong). Nam Pháng and Nam Hôk.	7 0	70 4	The road rises 600 feet from the village very rapidly through thick jungle, for nearly a mile, when it falls 140 feet into a narrow densely-wooded ravine and crosses four times in the next 400 yards a small stream flowing north-west to join the Nam Pháng which is about 1 mile further at the end of this ravine. Crossing the stream (18 yards broad; 18 inches deep; rapid, round pebbly bottom; low easy banks; both densely wooded) the road keeps along its right bank running in a more westerly direction by the side of a small stream called the Nam Hôk 3 feet broad; 6 inches deep; low banks; gravel bottom for nearly a mile through dense jungle, rising about 125 feet in that distance. It then enters a more open, but very narrow valley up which it runs in a northerly direction for nearly a mile, when it rises at a steep gradient, just 600 feet in a little less than ½ a mile. Running round a spur north-west level for about 300 yards, it again turns north and descends slightly into a small cultivated valley, crosses it and runs over a low wooded saddle into another open valley, on the opposite side of which on elevated ground in thick jungle stands the village of Man Kong (20 houses). There are three villages here, the largest is about 1½ miles due west of the one seen on entering the valley and consequently to the left. It consists of about 40 houses. Guns and dhás are manufactured here. The population are Shans and Was. The three villages together are known by the name of Na Pháng. There is a very good and large camping ground just below the village of Man Kong about 140 by 60 yards, with a good stream called the Nam Pháng flowing at the foot of it.
		9. Yôk La ... ... Nam Wat.	7 4	78 0	The road leaves the village due north, runs for 400 yards over a low spur into a narrow cultivated valley, and crosses the fields and a small stream called the Nam Wat (6 feet broad, 6 inches deep; rapid; low banks; gravel bottom; good water) below the village of Paung Wo (15 houses). It then rises through the village and crosses the stream twice again after leaving the village, namely, at the foot and the head of another cultivated valley, which is ¼ mile long and terraced, it then ascends a long spur. The rise is 700 feet in about 1,000 yards and

FROM TÁKÖT TO TAWNIO (KÔKÁNG) *viâ* PÁNG SÁNG, &c.—*continued.*

Authorities. Military.	Authorities. Civil.	Number and Names of Stages, Rivers and streams.	Distances. Intermediate.	Distances. Total.	Remarks.
G.O.C. Mandalay District.	Superintendent, Northern Shan States.	**9. Yôk La**—*cont.*			in some places very steep indeed, in dense jungle. The road then continues to descend very gradually for about 400 yards, when the ascent is more marked, and in the next 600 yards it rises another 300 feet and passes through the small village of Páng Lun or Pen Len (12 houses; elevation 4,224 feet). It descends 150 feet at once by a steep gradient running north-north-west by north on to a level spur through dense jungle for about 500 yards, when it turns north-north-west down the slopes of a long, broad, and broken hill, which has been cleared for cultivation. To the right of the road, about ⅛ mile distant, stands the village of Wa Prôm. The road continues to descend, passing round the head of a deep ravine in a west-north-west direction for nearly ½ mile, the total descent from Páng Lun being 300 feet. It then rises 250 feet over open ground on to a wooded hill, along which it runs level, almost due north-west, opposite to two villages standing in ridges 1 and 2 miles respectively to the right of the road. Between these villages and the road there are two deep broad, wooded valleys. From this point, for about 500 yards, the road descends slightly, crossing a low neck and winding round a spur, where it is very narrow and broken with a precipitous slope on the left. It runs along a flat ridge for about ¼ mile, when it again passes along the side of the hill through long grass and dense jungle for about 600 yards. It then crosses a low saddle and turning in a north-east direction, gradually descends about 100 feet in the next 450 yards, when it rises 150 feet on to a long sharp spur, when it is level for the next ¼ mile; a ¼ mile further on it passes another Wa village standing on a low spur about a mile to the right of the road. It runs on nearly level for about ¾ mile, where there is a sharp steep rise of about 150 feet on to a flat spur, open on the left, and from which is visible, about 3 miles distant, due south-west a village perched on the very top of a peak considerably higher than the road. The road then rises gradually for the next 200 yards with a deep open valley on the left. It then rises 400 feet by a sharp ascent in about 400 yards on to a flat-topped wooded hill, on which stands Yôk La, a Wa village about 80 yards to the left of which it passes. It runs down the other side through thick jungle, falling about 130 feet in 350 yards, and runs on to a small open knoll above a few huts. There is space enough here for a small force of 100 men and transport to camp with a small stream of a water close by on either side of the camping ground, from which good water can be obtained at the rate of one bucket in 2½ minutes.
		10. Nam Ma ...	M. F. 7 0	M. F. 85 0	Leaving the camping ground in a north-west direction, 500 yards further on it passes the small village on a conical hill, up the left slope of which the road rises about 120 feet. For the next ¾ mile the road gradually descends 320 feet through thick jungle. It then runs level for about 500 yards, when it emerges on to a bare hill and, descending slightly, passes along a saddle dividing two deep valleys. Again, entering the jungle, it begins to rise, where there is a very steep ascent running west-north-west over the left or west slopes of a conical hill. The rise, which is 330 feet in about 500 yards, brings you to a flat-

FROM TÁKÖT TO TAWNIO (KÔKÁNG) *viâ* PÁNG SÁNG, &c.—*continued.*

Authorities.		Number and Names of Stages, Rivers and Streams.	Distances.				Remarks.
Military.	Civil.		Intermediate.		Total.		
			M.	F.	M.	F.	
G.O.C. Mandalay District.	Superintendent, Northern Shan States.	**10. Nam Ma**—*cont.*					topped hill on which the small village of Páng Win stands (10 houses). For the next mile the road winds round the open slopes of the hill and reaches the small village of Yong Páng (six houses). Half-a-mile further on descending 60 feet gradually through thick jungle, it runs into the village of Yang Lút (10 houses). Leaving the village in a south-west direction it rises over a low wooded neck within 100 yards of the village and runs along level over open ground on the side of the hill with a deep broad valley on the right; 400 yards further on it turns due west and rises about 150 feet up a level slope on to a ridge on the left of a deep valley on the opposite side of the valley, and a mile and-a-half from the road stands another large Wa village. It runs level along this ridge for nearly a mile. The valleys on both sides are open. It then gradually descends nearly 300 feet through thick jungle for about $\frac{3}{4}$ mile, running due west and $\frac{1}{2}$ mile further on running level it passes the small village of Páng Lông; elevation 3,100 feet. From this point the road descends gradually for $2\frac{1}{2}$ miles through dense jungle of very high elephant grass. The path in some places is very narrow and the slope in some places almost precipitous. The gradient then becomes very much steeper and continues winding down the hill side, passing in $\frac{1}{2}$ mile over ground which has been cleared for cultivation. After this it is not quite so steep, but continues to descend rapidly for another 900 yards, where it runs on to the left bank of the Nam Ma, along the bank to the right of where the road touches the river there is a long flat strip of sand, about 20 yards broad and 150 yards long. This is the only spot on which troops could camp. The opposite side is steep and the whole hill side is covered with jungle. No village here.
		11. Kawng Kwa. Nam Ma. This stream is not to be confounded with another of the same name which flows into the Salween opposite (or nearly so) to the point at which this stream enters that river.	4	4	89	4	Crossing the Nam Ma (30 yards broad, rapid; 2 feet deep; stony and sandy bottom; left bank low and open, right high and wooded), the road runs due west along the right bank through a strip of jungle and a little clearing for about 500 yards, where it crosses a small rapid stream, 6 feet broad and 6 inches deep, stony bottom, flowing through thick jungle between banks 6 feet high. The ascent commences about 100 yards after leaving the stream in a north-west direction, the rise in the first 500 yards is 400 feet on to a flat spur for 160 yards, when it ascends very rapidly again, rising 500 feet by a very steep gradient in about 600 yards. The road there runs level for about 300 yards and again commences to rise gradually for the next $\frac{1}{4}$ of a mile, where it passes on the opposite side of a deep ravine and 500 yards from the road a small village. From this point the road continues to rise very rapidly passing open cultivated slopes on the left. The rise continues for about $\frac{3}{4}$ of a mile, when it reaches the top of the hill and winds along a few feet below the crest-line level for about 200 yards. The total ascent from the river to this point is 2,060 feet. It then crosses a depressed saddle and descends a bare spur, rising 150 feet, when it passes about 20 yards to the right of the village of Páng Tsông, 20 houses. The village is divided into two groups of huts.

FROM TĀKÖT TO TAWNIO (KÔKÁNG) *viâ* PÁNG SÁNG, &c.—*continued.*

Authorities. Military.	Authorities. Civil.	Number and Names of Stages, Rivers and Streams.	Distances. Intermediate.	Distances. Total.	Remarks.
G.O.C. Mandalay District.	Superintendent, Northern Shan States.	**11. Kawng Kwa**—*cont.*			The second portion lying about 60 yards to the left of the road on a wooded spur. The road running level now turns east-north-east and runs round the head of a deep broad wooded valley on the opposite side of which, on a ridge, stands another village called **Kawng Kwa**. At the head of this valley the road turns gradually due north-west and rises over a spur separating a ravine from a low neck along which the road runs. From Páng Tsông to Kawng Kwa, 1 mile and 350 yards, it rises in all 430 feet. Kawng Kwa is divided into two distinct villages, separated by narrow ridges on the east and west of which they stand about 700 yards apart. In the east village the inhabitants are Chinese-Shans, in the west Was. There is good camping ground 150 by 20 yards along the ridge with water just below it.
		12. Na Nit ... Nam Na.	M. 5 F. 4	M. 95 F. 0	Leaving the camp north-east the road rises 150 feet through the village on to a level spur, where it turns north and then gradually north-west; 300 yards further on it crosses a narrow ravine, on the right of which there is a very deep, broad wooded valley and on the left slopes of which, about 3 miles from the road, and about 1,000 feet below it, there is a large scattered village called Mo Paw. It then rises 300 feet up a steep thinly-wooded spur in 350 yards, runs level along the top of it for about 200 yards, and turns north-west by west up a wooded conical hill rising 450 feet in 500 yards. On a low spur, about a mile and-a-half to the left of the road stand two villages called Upper and Lower Man Páng. Reaching the top of the hill the road turns due north-west and runs along a ridge rising very gradually for the next 300 yards. The slopes on both sides are covered with jungle and are precipitous. The ridge then becomes much broader and the jungle thicker. The road runs level along the centre of it for another 300 yards, where it descends another 150 feet on to another flat ridge in a north-west direction; 200 yards further on it descends 420 feet by a steep path between open slopes, cleared for cultivation to the large Wa village, Loi Lông, 30 houses. Leaving the village in a westerly direction it winds down the side of a hill with a broad open valley on the right. Half-way down the hill it turns due north-west and passes close to the left of a small village called Man Maung, and 400 yards further on it runs through Yáng Hong (six houses). From this point it descends rapidly through jungle into a narrow cultivated valley, through the centre of which it runs, following a small stream called Nam Na (3 feet broad, 6 inches deep; gravel bottom and very rapid), which flows down from Loi Lông. At the north end of the valley on the ridge to the left and about 250 feet higher than the stream stands a small village called Man Na Nit. On this ridge and about ½ mile west of Na Nit there is another village called Man Phai, not visible from the valley. The only site for a camp is that on the raised field, which are terraced just below Na Nit.
		13. Maung (? Mông) Maw. Nam Lông and another stream.	8 4	103 4	Leaving the camp north-west the road crosses a stream called Nam Lông (10 feet broad, 1 foot deep; rapid), 100 yards from the end of the valley in thick jungle, flowing between large boulders of rocks, spanned by a good foot-bridge, roadway of 6 feet. The road then rises up a long gentle slope through scrub jungle and thick long grass

FROM TÁKÖT TO TAWNIO (KÔKÁNG) *viâ* PÁNG SÂNG, &c.—*continued.*

Authorities.		Number and Names of Stages, Rivers and Streams.	Distances.		Remarks.
Military.	Civil.		Inter-mediate.	Total.	
G.O.C. Mandalay District.	Superintendent, Northern Shan States.	**13. Maung (? Möng) Maw** —*cont.*			for a mile, rising 560 feet. Half-a-mile further on it runs level round the side of a hill passing the village of Kon Lai (20 houses) standing on the opposite slope of a small deep ravine, 700 yards from the road. It runs level for the next ½ mile and winding round a sharp wooded spur, it drops 200 feet by a steep gradient running round the head of a broad valley, rises over another low spur and drops by a steep rugged narrow path into a deep ravine, which is thickly wooded with a small stream flowing down it, in a rocky bed, between steep banks. The stream is bridged, the bridge is substantial and constructed of heavy logs, with a roadway of 5 feet, from which the road rises 300 feet by an equally steep path on to an open slope along which it runs level for 600 yards, passing the small Wa villages Ho Mung and Loi Páng. The former standing on a ridge 400 yards to the left of the road, the latter on a neck with a broad flat bit of ground between it and the road for the distance of 160 yards. This would form a good camping ground ; water is good and an ample supply is obtainable from a stream about 260 feet below the latter village. The road winds round the hill running level for the next ½ mile, when it again descends 370 feet, rapidly crossing a deep ravine and small stream (2 feet broad, 6 inches deep; rocky bed ; between banks 25 feet high and precipitous) running round the head of another broad open valley and passing a small Wa village called Yáng Krong (10 houses) standing on a knoll 50 yards to the left of the road and about 100 feet above it. About 1½ miles further down this valley stands another village called Kawng Pai, about 20 houses. The road now crosses a small but deep ravine, with precipitous slopes and a small stream flowing down the centre of it. The rise on the opposite side would be exceedingly difficult in wet weather, as the ground is fine red earth, and there are flat standing rocks protruding on the path. The ascent is 140 feet in about 120 yards. From this point the road again drops a little, crossing another but much less steep ravine and another very small stream, and then rises up a long steep spur through cultivated ground. Half-way up it crosses a small ridge and ascends by a still steeper gradient another portion of the spur. The total rise is 920 feet in not more than 1,000 yards. From here the path runs along a level bit of ground which is quite open on both sides, and there is space enough for several small camps on the right, on the gentle slopes of the mountain known as Loi Mu, 8,000 feet, the top of which is only about 2 miles above and to the right of the path here. The road winds along under the hill, and in the next 400 yards crosses another sharp ravine and a small stream of good water flowing down in a rocky bed. It is bridged with substantial logs 20 feet long with a roadway of 5 feet. From here the road runs level for the next ¾ mile to Maung (? Möng) Maw. The country on the left is quite open and an extensive view is obtained from here. Several large villages appear on the tops of the hills some 3 and 4 miles distant. Maung Maw is a large, compact, prosperous village. The inhabitants are Chinese-Shans. It consists of about 40 houses, and lies at the foot of a deep ravine between two large hills which stand on either side of the huge crater-like formation of this side of Loi Mu. There is ample and good ground for a camp opposite, or north-west of the village on a thinly-wooded knoll, skirting the terraced fields, with a good supply of water running close by on the left.

FROM TÁKÖT TO TAWNIO (KÔKÂNG) *viâ* PÁNG, SÂNG, &c.—*continued.*

Authorities. Military.	Authorities. Civil.	Number and Names of Stages, Rivers and Streams.	Distances. Intermediate. M. F.	Distances. Total. M. F.	Remarks.
G.O.C. Mandalay District.	Superintendent, Northern Shan States.	**14. Man Méán** ...	7 0	110 4	Leaving the camp north-west by west the road runs across undulating open country for ¾ mile when it runs up a spur on to a low narrow neck, separating the narrow wooded valleys. There is a village, Um Lé, to the left 2 miles from the road. It then rises 200 feet by a steep gradient and runs along the side of a hill nearly level for ½ mile, when it descends gradually for 600 yards, where it enters the villages of Man Naung (15 houses). The country on the left of the village is open, but very hilly. Running over a low wooded hill it passes two villages close together, Ma Kôk and Yáng Kyit, a mile to the right of the road. The road now rises 200 feet by an easy gradient and runs along through thin jungle, and passes over a succession of low spurs for a mile, when it commences to descend gradually for the next 1,000 yards on to a low neck separating two broad valleys. From this point it again rises 120 feet by an easy gradient and passing over a narrow saddle winds along the hill side almost due north with a narrow valley on the left. The hills on the left are generally bare and cleared for cultivation. It continues to descend very gradually for about ½ mile, when it runs over another low saddle and keeping nearly level it runs round the head of a broad ravine for ¾ mile on to a small cultivated neck on which the fields are terraced. There is a good, small rapid stream of water at the south end of the fields which are about 250 by 50 yards in area and just beyond them on to the top of the hill, and about 200 yards' distant stands the small Wa village of Man Méán (20 houses).
		15. Möng Hit ...	7 0	117 4	Leaving the village north-west the road descends 150 feet gradually down the side of a spur and crosses a narrow neck between two deep valleys. About ½ mile to the right of the road, on the opposite ridge, stands the village of Man Nawk and about ½ mile further on the same ridge Tak Tin. At the end of the neck the road turns off to the left and ascends very gradually passing on to a ridge along which it runs level for 200 yards and passes through the village of Nan Mi (eight houses). It continues to run level along this ridge for the next 300 yards when it descends 180 feet gradually on to a low saddle, and rises 450 feet by an easy gradient on to the opposite ridge and passes about 200 yards to the left of the large Wa village of Páng Kôm. To the right of the road, on this ridge, about 1 mile distant, stands another village called Yáng Sáng, and just beyond it another called Yáng Mai, and just beyond that again a small village called Môt Ku, all Was. Altitude of Páng Kong 4,330 feet. The road then immediately descends 230 feet, crossing a narrow ravine with a very small stream flowing down it and rises 260 feet up the opposite slope by a very steep gradient through dense jungle turning due north it passes through the large Wa village of Nong Máng (30 houses). It then gradually rises 160 feet running along the side of a densely-wooded hill, with a deep valley on the right and turning round the point it runs down by an almost continual and in some places steep gradient for nearly a mile, where it enters the village of Páng Kawng (30 houses). Páng Kawng is the capital of the State of Su Mu (Sômö) and the

FROM TÁKÖT TO TAWNIO (KÔKÁNG) *viâ* PÁNG SÁNG, &c.—*continued.*

Authorities. Military.	Authorities. Civil.	Number and Names of Stages, Rivers and Streams.	Distances. Intermediate.	Distances. Total.	Remarks.
G.O.C. Mandalay District.	Superintendent, Northern Shan States.	**15. Möng Hit**—*cont.*			Sawbwa resides here. In the centre of the village and overlooking the jungle on both sides stands a walled enclosure surrounding a brick building 25 yards square. The walls are 5 feet high. Leaving the village the road, turning to the right, descends by a steep gradient through dense jungle. It turns again to the left about 300 yards after leaving the village and runs due west from here through dense jungle for another mile and-a-half when it passes close to the left of the small Shan village of Mong Hit (eight houses) and runs on to some level field on the left bank of the stream called Nam Kôn where there is room to camp.
		16. Nam Maw ... Nam Kôm.	M. F. 7 4	M. F. 125 0	Leaving the camping ground the road runs north-north-east through dense jungle and small open plots of ground alternately rising 300 feet very gradually for a mile on to and crossing a thickly-wooded neck between a conical hill and a high ridge. Running down due north for about ½ mile it crosses the stream Nam Kôm (60 yards broad, 2 feet deep; low banks; both wooded; indication of flood rise 8 feet; firm, stony bottom) exactly opposite the large Shan village of Na Káng (30 houses), head-quarters of a Tamôn. Where the road enters the river there are some hot springs and the water issuing from them warms the surrounding river water very considerably. The road turns due north again passing through the village and enters a stretch of fields which are level for about 300 yards and are 400 yards broad. It then rises nearly 400 feet by a gradual ascent up a long stretch of open cultivated ground for nearly 700 yards and turns to the left into jungle (1,980 feet). The ascent is now very steep and continual for about 1,200 yards, but as the road winds up in a zigzag manner it traverses nearly a mile and-a-half. The total ascent from the village is 2,220 feet. The road then runs on to a slightly undulating plateau, the whole of which is cleared for cultivation. It is about 1,100 yards broad and about a mile long and nearly surrounded by low wooded hills. *There is no water here.* Running down the centre of this open plateau, the road falls suddenly into a small circular basin, in which lies the small village of Páng Tawn (20 houses). Passing through the village the road falls slightly, winding along the sides of rough spurs in thick jungle and about ¾ mile past the village comes to a small ravine at the head of which there is water. The place is known as Nam Maw. About 400 yards above this place on the hill stands the small village of Páng Yaw (eight houses); water is good at Nam Maw, but not plentiful. It was sufficient for our party consisting of 100 men and 120 animals. The ground for camping is sufficiently large to accommodate a force of 150 men and is on the road.
		17. Páng Lông ...	12 4	137 4	Leaving Nam Maw in a north-north-east direction, the road at once drops into and crosses a narrow deep wooded ravine, and rising up the opposite slope winds through a long narrow wooded valley over rocky ground for nearly 2 miles. The path runs along a fairly level course through densely-wooded country for the next 11 miles. There is no water along the road. For the last 2½ miles it runs through broad cultivated valleys and enters Páng Lông by a narrow gorge. Páng Lông contains some 300 houses.

FROM TÁKÖT TO TAWNIO (KÔKÁNG) *vià* PÁNG SÁNG, &c.—*continued.*

Authorities. Military.	Authorities. Civil.	Number and Names of Stages, Rivers and Streams.	Distances. Intermediate. M. F.	Distances. Total. M. F.	Remarks.
G.O.C. Mandalay District.	Superintendent, Northern Shan States.	**18. Möng Kun** ... Nam Kun.	5 0	142 4	Leaving Páng Lông in an almost due northerly direction the road passes through a narrow ravine about 150 yards long and enters another open narrow cultivated valley, down the centre of which it runs about ¾ of a mile. It then descends rapidly through thick jungle for nearly ½ mile, when it runs along the right side of a densely-wooded valley passing about 200 yards to the right of a small Chinese village called Kông Hwa Kyaung. It continues to descend again very rapidly. The path is good. It descends for about ¾ of a mile when it enters another valley more open; and the hill sides are cleared for cultivation. At the foot of the hill stands the small hamlet of Nam Pa Chi (eight houses). Passing on down the valley and descending now very gradually for the next mile and-a-half it crosses the Nam Kun, a small stream (15 feet broad, 1 foot deep; banks low but covered with jungle; banks are high and precipitous just below the ford. The stream is very rapid. Irrigation channel leads water past village) and enters the village of Mong Kun (16 houses). Rice and paddy are scarce. A good camping ground just beyond the village under trees and close to the kyaung. There are a few fields stretching down the valley. They are well terraced and would afford ample ground for camping on for a considerable force up to a brigade with transport.
		19. Nam Hu ... Nam Leng and Nam Ting.	10 4	153 0	The road runs on north-west by north keeping a level for about ¼ a mile when it crosses at a small stream flowing between low wooded banks in a rocky bed, 6 feet broad and 6 inches deep. It then ascends gradually up a narrow wooded ravine keeping in the centre for nearly a mile when it rises suddenly on to the hills on the right and running along the side of the valley, which is here more open, continues to rise for about ¼ of a mile, when it passes over a rugged rocky neck and runs along through a succession of low rounded hills for about ½ a mile (altitude 3,300 feet). It then descends very rapidly, running down into a deep thickly-wooded ravine and turning slightly to the west it again falls by a steep and rugged path through dense jungle for another mile and-a-half; when it runs past the left of the village ot Möng Leng (15 houses). Just after Möng Leng it crosses a stream called the Nam Leng, 8 feet broad, 6 inches deep; gravel bottom; rapid, clear stream; low open banks; rapid gravel bottom; good water. It then runs over low undulating ground partially cleared for cultivation for nearly a mile and-a-half where it passes the large village of Ho Páng (25 houses). About ¼ of a mile further on it crosses another small stream called the Nam Hu with a village standing on the left bank of the river Nam Ting. This village is called Nam Hu and contains some 20 houses. The Nam Ting is a rapid river, 5 feet 6 inches deep in the centre; 80 yards broad at the ferry; gravel and sandy bottom; both banks of sand; swelling 14 feet high; joins the Salween 7 miles west of this about ¾ mile below Kunlôn. The ferry over the Nam Ting is about 200 yards above and north-east of the village. There

FROM TÁKÖT TO TAWNIO (KÔKÁNG) *viâ* PÁNG SÁNG, &c.—*continued.*

Authorities. Military.	Authorities. Civil.	Number and Names of Stages, Rivers and Streams.	Distances. Intermediate.	Distances. Total.	Remarks.
G.O.C. Mandalay District.	Superintendent, Northern Shan States.	**19. Nam Hu**—*cont.*			are four boats capable of carrying eight men at a time each. Opposite this ferry and about ½ a mile from the river stands the village of Weng Môk (30 houses). Head-quarters of a Hein. The village belongs to Su Mu State.
		20. Ho Tao ... Nam Tao.	M. F. **6 0**	M. F. 159 0	The road leaving Nam Hu due east crosses the Nam Ting and runs through high grass and scrub jungle within 200 yards of the right bank of that river for about 3½ miles, when it passes through the small village of Páng Hai and ½ a mile further on another village of the same name consisting of 6 and 10 houses, respectively. Half-a-mile further on it turns gradually to the left (north-east by north) and passes over low undulating wooded ground up the Nam Tao valley. A mile and-a-half up the valley it runs through the village of Ho Tao (10 houses). The hill in front of the village marks the boundary of the Shan States. The Nam Tao (30 feet wide, 11 feet deep) flows past the village in a thickly-wooded ravine in a rocky bed.
		21. Tawnio (or Kôkáng). Small stream.	**16 0**	175 0	The road then runs into the thickly-wooded hills in a north-north-west direction and runs continually for the first 3 miles. It is a bad rocky path in dense jungle. It then passes the small hamlet known as Nam Aung perched on the side of a steep slope, which is just to the left of the road, and cleared for cultivation. Descending slightly for the next ½ mile, it then again rises gradually for about 600 yards reaching an altitude of 3,350 feet, making the total ascent from Ho Tao 1,850 feet approximately. For the next 11 miles the road runs along the centre of a broad undulating valley, much of which is cleared for cultivation. At the 12th mile it passes a few huts standing about 300 yards to the left of the path. From here it winds along nearly due west for nearly 2 miles when it runs up a gentle rise on which stands the village of Tawnio called also Kôkáng. It is the head-quarters of a Hein. The circle is a large one and pays tribute to the North Theinni Sawbwa. The inhabitants are all Chinese. There are 20 houses and two brick buildings, temples, standing in open ground, close to the village. A small rapid stream (8 feet broad, 6 feet deep; gravel bottom; high but gently shelving banks; both open) flows past the village down a narrow open ravine, on the opposite side of which there is any amount of continuous open level grass land suitable for a large camp. *No water is to be had throughout this march.* Altitude of Kôkáng 3,000 feet.

No. 59.

From TA MÖNGNONG (or TA SAILENG) FERRY to MANSÉ.

By Capt. A. C. YATE, February 1888.

Authorities. Military.	Authorities. Civil.	Number and Names of Stages, Rivers and Streams.	Distances. Intermediate. M. F.	Distances. Total. M. F.	Remarks.
G.O.C. Mandalay District.	Superintendent, Northern Shan States.	**1. Páng Sé Möng.** Nam Náti and some small streams.	13 0	13 0	Direction west. The road is practicable for pack transport, but not an easy one. The long steep ascent from the bed of the Nam Náti stream to the village Páng Sé Möng is very trying, otherwise the road presents no difficulties in the dry weather. For the first 5 miles from Saileng the road follows the valley of the Namma, keeping more or less closely to the right bank. At 3½ miles pass Shan village of Pángmôn (10 houses). Here good water, fuel, and fodder. Camping ground small. At 5 miles pass Shan village of Namngam (eight houses. The present inhabitants are refugees from Láshio). Here the road diverges from the right bank of the Namma river. From here to Páng Sé Möng the road traverses dense jungle. The Loi Maw range (grows the finest opium in the Shan States) lies to the south and the Loi Kaw to the north. At 8 miles path to left to Little Manmák, a village situated south of the Namma on the lower spurs of the Loi Maw range. At 9 miles cross Nam Náti. No camping room here. From here continuous steep ascent to Kachin village. Pigs and fowls bred as usual. At 11 miles path to left to Palaung village of Loi Law situated on the Loi Maw range of hills. Camp for 500 men. Fuel and fodder procurable, but water-supply rather limited (15 houses). From Páng Sé Möng the direct road to Manmák is *viâ* Kyé-káng, a Kachin village 5 miles off. Distance to Manmák about 10 miles.
		2. Mönghom ...	10 4	23 4	General direction south-west. Road fairly good for pack transport. Descent for 1½ miles to valley of Nam Pángwong stream. Here good camping ground with abundance of good water, grass, and fuel. This place should be used as a camping ground in preference to Páng Sé Möng. Thence steep ascent for 1¼ miles to Kachin village of East Kongkyé (six houses). From here road fairly level as far as Nongwo. At 1¾ miles west Kongkyé (five houses, Kachins) and ½ mile to left of road Loikam (five houses). Opium, rice, tobacco, and mustard cultivated, and cattle, pigs, and fowls bred in all these villages. At 4½ miles Vyengkáng group of Kachin villages, 20 to 30 houses. Vyengkáng is in Möngma district. From here roads radiate north to Manmák (about 5 miles) west to Möngmaw (about 10 miles), south-west to Nanang; south to Möngma (about 16 miles); and east to Saileng and Pánglaw. The direction of the road from Páng Sé Möng to Vyengkáng is west-north-west. From here the road turns south-west and then due south. At 5½ miles road to right (west by north) to Möngyaw, crossing the Loi Sák range. At 6¾ miles road to right to Kachin village of Manna (seven houses). At 7½ miles pass through Nongwo (15 houses, Kachins). Good camping ground here, and fuel and fodder procurable, but water not good and limited in quantity. From Nongwo ascent for 1 mile, thence descent for 1½ to north village of Mönghom (Kachins, six houses). South Mönghom (six houses) ½ mile further south. Good camp in fields ½ mile west of Mönghom villages. Water good and abundant from stream. Fuel and grass plentiful. The road to Möngma runs south from

FROM TA MÖNGNONG (OR TA SAILENG) FERRY TO MANSÉ—*continued.*

Authorities. Military.	Authorities. Civil.	Number and Names of Stages, Rivers and Streams.	Distances. Intermediate.	Distances. Total.	Remarks.
G.O.C. Mandalay District.	Superintendent, Northern Shan States.	**2. Mönghom**—*cont.*			Mönghom, distance about 12 miles, crossing Loi Law and Loi Waw ranges. There is also a road north to Möngyaw, distance about 10 miles. There is also a road to Hôkai and Makmu, and so to Limpôk, Kônkut, and Möngma (*see* Route No. 39, Stages 2, 3, &c.).
		3. Makham (Nakham). Nampôn river and Namtôn and other small streams.	M. 13 F. 0	M. 36 F. 4	Direction south-west. The road is tolerably good for pack transport. The steep descents into the valley of the Nampôn and the crossing of the numerous small streams which flow into the Nampôn just opposite the village of Nampa Küm present difficulties for transport. From the village of Manpakum (Nampaklum) to that of Nángyun (*see* Route No. 39), there are two roads, the hill and the valley road. The latter is preferable in the dry season and is quite practicable for pack animals. The hill path can also be used in the rains. Between Mönghom and Nángyun the road has of late been little used. As a matter of fact this route from Saileng to Mansé is, as Shan roads go, a very fair one, and it might, with advantage, be improved. At 1¼ miles path to left (south) to Kôngsáng (¼ mile off, five houses, Kachins). At 1¾ miles path from left Kôngsáng. At 2 miles path to left (south-south-west) to Kachin village of Loi Waw, which is situated on the northern slopes of the Loi Waw range. For 3½ miles the descent is very gentle; after that there is a steep descent for about 1 mile towards the Nampôn river. At 4½ miles Shan village of Manpakum on opposite side (left bank) of Nampôn. Left bank of Nampôn well cultivated. Right bank too steep for cultivation except in one or two places. The road then runs above and parallel to the right bank of the Nampôn, crossing in rapid succession a number of small streams, so numerous indeed as almost to flood the hill slopes. The soil has fortunately no tendency to become swampy, otherwise the place would be impassable without a causeway and bridges. At 5½ miles path to left to Manpakum. Beyond that descent to and at 6 miles reach right of Nampôn (60 feet broad, 2 feet deep). At 6½ miles ford it. At 6¾ miles pass village of Manpakum (Shans; 10 houses). The valley of the Nampôn here and for a mile below is all cultivated. The rice crops are irrigated from the river. At 7½ miles the road bifurcates, the left branch going over the hill and the right branch along the banks of the river to Nángyun. The hill road passes through the Shan village of Pángmôn Loi Sáng. The road by the river wants clearing and repairing in places, otherwise it is easy enough for pack animals. At 9¾ miles reach Nángyun (Shans; 10 houses) (*see* Route No. 39, Stage 2). At 10 miles cross Nampôn river and pass to right (west) of Shan village of Napayin (eight houses). At 10½ miles Shan village of Natong, 15 houses and kyaung. At 11 miles cross valley and stream of Namtôn. Valley extensive and well cultivated. At 11½ miles Shan village of Namkungpa to right, 30 houses and kyaung. Anywhere about here there is room to camp an army corps in the dry weather. Water, wood, and fodder abundant. In time of peace supplies of rice, paddy, cattle, &c., should be obtainable from the numerous villages round about. Passing Namkungpa enter narrow but well cultivated valley of the Nampôngalé flowing south-south-west to the Nampôn river, which from Nángyun flows south for a

FROM TA MÖNGNONG (OR TA SAILENG) FERRY TO MANSÉ—*continued.*

Authorities.		Number and Names of Stages, Rivers and Streams.	Distances.		Remarks.
Military.	Civil.		Intermediate.	Total.	
G.O.C. Mandalay District.	Superintendent, Northern Shan States.	**3. Makham (Nakham)**—*cont.*			mile and then turns westward towards Mansé. Road follows the Nampôngalé for a mile and then diverges west to the village of Makham (spelt Nakham on Survey Map) (Shans; 10 houses), where is camping room, water, fodder, and fuel for a force of moderate size. The country hereabouts is a succession of small well-watered and cultivated valleys separated by low hills, overgrown with bamboo and tree jungle. A mile before reaching Makham the village of Makpai is found, and $\frac{3}{4}$ mile from Makham the road from Möngma joins in from the left (south-east, *see* Route No. 39).
		4. Mansé ... ... Many small streams and the Nampôn river.	M. F. **19 0**	M. F. 55 4	General direction west-south-west. Road good for pack transport, crosses a succession of cultivated valleys intersected by higher ground (low spurs of the Loi Pátan) overgrown with jungle. The cultivated valleys being often swampy and cut up by deep irrigation channels are difficult for transport to cross. The streams, nullahs, &c., are in many places bridged for pack transport, and the swampy places are crossed on wooden causeways. The whole of the Nampôn valley from Nángyun to Mansé (23 miles) is highly cultivated, fertile, and, for the Shan States, thickly populated. The inhabitants are all Shans. Road for 2 miles across low hills covered with jungle. At 2 miles road comes in from south-east from Makpai and Könka (the latter on left bank of Nampôn). At 3 miles road to right to Kônhyo, $\frac{1}{4}$ mile distant. At 3$\frac{1}{8}$ miles cross valley of Namtôn stream, cultivated, $\frac{1}{4}$ mile broad. (The valley of Nampôn here tends east-north-east and west-south-west, and is bordered on the north by the Loi Pátan and on the south by the Loi Ling range. The road from Nángyun to Mansé traverses the low spurs of the Loi Pátan at a distance of from 1 to 2 miles north of the Nampôn river.) At 3$\frac{1}{8}$ miles pass Sépong (20 houses, kyaungs). At 4 miles Mankhaisim to right. At 4$\frac{1}{4}$ miles cross cultivated valley by wooden causeway, 100 yards long. At 4$\frac{1}{2}$ miles Namyong village, $\frac{1}{4}$ mile to right. At 5$\frac{1}{4}$ miles cross a stream. Here good water and camping ground. At 5$\frac{1}{2}$ miles village of Tingtáwon, $\frac{1}{8}$ mile to left. At 6$\frac{1}{2}$ miles cross Namnáng stream and valley $\frac{1}{2}$ mile broad and cultivated. At 7 miles pass bazaar of Nanang, the chief village of the Lantao district. Village $\frac{1}{8}$ mile to right and Mansanö (butcher's village) $\frac{1}{4}$ mile to left. There is a road north from here to Möngyaw, distance about 15 miles. At 7$\frac{3}{4}$ miles road to right to Náka Myauk (North Náka). At 8$\frac{1}{2}$ miles cross valley of Namká, $\frac{1}{2}$ mile broad and cultivated. At 8$\frac{3}{4}$ miles village of Náka Taung (South Náka) to left. At 9 miles path to left to Kugyum 1 mile off. Then cross valley and stream of Namsa, valley $\frac{1}{2}$ mile broad and cultivated. At 9$\frac{1}{2}$ miles Tawni village of 20 houses and kyaungs to left. At 10 miles pass through village of Lôkpán (good camp and water in any of these villages in the dry season, in the wet season must camp on high ground). At 11 miles direct road from Tawni comes in from right. At 11$\frac{3}{4}$ miles path to left to Namleng 1 mile off and just beyond Namleng stream

FROM TA MÖNGNONG (OR TA SAILENG) FERRY TO MANSÉ—*continued.*

Authorities.		Number and Names of Stages, Rivers and Streams.	Distances.		Remarks.
Military.	Civil.		Intermediate.	Total.	
G.O.C. Mandalay District.	Superintendent, Northern Shan States.	**4. Mansé**—*cont.*			and valley (all these streams flow south into Nampôn). At $13\frac{1}{2}$ miles reach Hôkai, large Shan village with good kyaung. Good camp and water either on the high ground or in the valley of the Namkhai stream. Valley $\frac{1}{4}$ to $\frac{3}{4}$ mile broad and all under cultivation. (These numerous streams furnish ample water for irrigation, each stream irrigating its own valley. Two crops of rice at least might be raised here in the year.) At 15 miles village of Kôngpán, 1 mile to left, and Kalong, $\frac{1}{2}$ mile to right of road. At $15\frac{1}{2}$ miles road comes in from the south-east, being the direct road from Möng Kát, Möng Ma, Kônkut, &c., to Mansé. It is optional, however, for troops marching from Könkut to Mansé to pass through, or rather a little south of, Makmai and Nanang and thence follow the route now under report. At 18 miles pass Namhyit stream and valley. At 19 miles reach the pagoda and bazaar of Mansé, close to the south of which flows the Nampôn. Easy ford here, $1\frac{1}{2}$ feet deep, moderate current, firm pebbly bottom. Villages grouped all round. Choice of camping ground anywhere on either bank of river. In time of peace supplies of rice, paddy, beef, &c., should be available, the district being fertile and populous. Grass and fuel plentiful.

No. 60.

From TÁNGYÁN to MÖNGMA.

BY CAPT. H. R. B. DONNE, NORFOLK REGIMENT, 11TH AND 12TH JANUARY 1889.

Military.	Civil.	Number and Names of Stages, Rivers and Streams.	Intermediate. M. F.	Total. M. F.	Remarks.
G.O.C. Mandalay District.	Superintendent, Northern Shan States.	**1. Nalu** ... ... Namyeng and Nampán.	**13 4**	13 4	Tángyán, *see* Route No. 38, Stage 4. General direction north-west. Starting from the large banyan tree the track lies across open ground alternating with thin jungle (for the most part pine trees) the whole way. For the first 5 furlongs it ascends at an easy gradient and then runs along fairly level, gradually descending past the kyaung of Hôtông until the river Namyeng is reached at $7\frac{3}{4}$ miles. After this it ascends the opposite range, attaining its greatest elevation at 10 miles, from which point it descends to the village of Nalu. The path is easy throughout, with the exception of two places at $7\frac{3}{4}$ and $8\frac{3}{4}$ miles in crossing streams, where there is slight difficulty. Steepest gradient 1 in 5. At $3\frac{5}{8}$ miles the path runs between the two small villages of Pángyen, lately burnt. At $4\frac{3}{4}$ miles spring on right; water good. At $6\frac{1}{2}$ miles a path leads to village of Hôtông visible at 500 yards on the left, consisting of 21 houses, deserted. At 7 miles passes close to kyaung of this village, 16 by 2 yards, also deserted. At $7\frac{3}{4}$ miles path crosses the Namyeng by a rough bamboo foot-bridge; animals cross by ford to the left, 16 yards wide, 2 feet 2 inches deep, bottom hard, $2\frac{1}{2}$ miles per hour. Camping ground for 2,000 men on left bank. Water good. Right bank a little steep and slippery. At $8\frac{3}{8}$ miles path crosses small stream; water good. At $8\frac{3}{4}$ miles path crosses stream by bough as foot-bridges, animals cross 50

FROM TÁNGYÁN TO MÖNGMA—*continued.*

Authorities.		Number and Names of Stages, Rivers and Streams.	Distances.		Remarks.
Military.	Civil.		Inter-mediate.	Total.	
G.O.C. Mandalay District.	Superintendent, Northern Shan States.	**1. Nalu**—*cont.*			yards higher up. The banks are soft; it was necessary to lay down grass for footing. The village of Saikôn is about 500 yards further up stream; contains a kyaung. At 13¼ miles path crosses small stream, and 200 yards further two others. Water good. At 13½ miles camping ground close to and west of a clump of bamboos and kyaung (17 by 20 yards). The village of Nalu (*see* also No. 39, Stage 4, and foot-note) contains 17 houses; no zayáts. It was in a semi-deserted state when we passed through. The Nampán flows at 300 yards to the west of camping ground, which would accommodate 1,000 men.
			M. F.	M. F.	
		2. Möngma ... Nampán.	**11 4**	25 0	General direction north-north-west. Country open all the way with occasionally a few scattered trees. The path is fairly level throughout, with the exception of one marked ascent commencing at 9⅛ miles, the path attaining an altitude of about 600 feet above the general level at 10 miles (steepest gradient 14°), from which it gradually descends over undulating ground to Möngma. At two places the ground was a little difficult for animals, namely, at ⅜ mile and at 11⅜ miles (two streams). At ⅜ mile path crosses the Nampán by ford 27 yards across, 4 feet 6 inches deepest part, rate 2 miles per hour, bottom hard, the opposite or right bank being very steep and slippery for 15 yards. At 1½ miles a path leads off to right front. At 1 mile path crosses stream by ford 9 yards wide, 1 foot 2 inches deep, rate 1½ miles an hour, bottom hard. At 4⅜ miles two deserted huts at 200 yards to the left. At 4½ miles small bit of swamp with stream; water good. At 6⅝ miles stream is crossed by ford 18 yards wide, 1 foot 4 inches deep, 2 miles per hour, bottom hard. Good camping ground, sufficient for 1,500 men. At 7⅝ miles deserted village of Nôka on right containing 20 houses; bazaar held every 5 days in quiet times on the left. The track then lies across paddy-fields, crossing a small stream at 8 miles. Water good; might encamp 1,000 men here in dry weather. At 8¾ miles a track leads to village of Suplông situated at 1,000 yards on the left and containing about 15 huts. At 8⅜ miles the route traverses thin jungle for 300 yards. At 9½ miles stream crossed by single plank; animals cross to the right. One hundred yards beyond the deserted village of Namôn lies at 200 yards to the right, consisting of 15 huts; a cluster of seven huts belonging to this village is situated at 500 yards to the left on opposite slope. At 11⅜ miles path crosses stream by a very rough bamboo foot-bridge; transport animals cross by ford 100 yards to the right. The left bank had to be cut away to facilitate descent into stream, which flows in a deep nullah. Ford is 7 yards across, 1 foot 6 inches deep, bottom hard, water good. By making a detour ¼ mile to the right the transport animals could cross by wooden bridge close to kyaung. The camping ground is 250 yards further on, good and sufficient for 1,500 men. The village of Möngma, at present deserted, consists of 21 houses. A kyaung on left bank of stream, 500 yards east of camping ground, measures 33 by 35 yards; no zayáts (large numbers of imperial pigeons here). For another description of this stage, *see* Route No. 39, Stage 4, in which Captain A. C. Yate makes the distance only 9¾ miles.

No. 61.

From TAWNIO to HINSHÁN (on Köngma border).

BY LIEUT. H. B. WALKER, PAID ATTACHÉ, INTELLIGENCE BRANCH, BURMA, FEBRUARY 1892.

Authorities.		Number and Names of Stages, Rivers and Streams.	Distances.				Remarks.
Military.	Civil.		Intermediate.		Total.		
			M.	F.	M.	F.	
[G.O.C. Mandalay District.	Superintendent, Northern Shan States.	**1. Hinshán** ... Small stream.	**5**	**4**	5	4	General direction east-south-east. Leaving Tawnio by the south-east end of village and by a path parallel to and east of the main road to Namhung and Kunlôn the route runs across cultivation along a spur to the north of which runs the stream on which Tawnio stands (6 inches deep, 10 yards wide ; sound crossings and excellent drinking water). At $\frac{3}{4}$ mile the path drops a little and crosses this stream rising then over a small knoll and crossing a half dry muddy stream, at $1\frac{1}{4}$ miles descending slightly to do so the route then runs up a valley south-east, the valley running almost due east and west and $1\frac{1}{2}$ miles wide. The hill of Namhatán land mark to all south-east and southern routes out of Tawnio is passed $\frac{1}{2}$ a mile distant to right hand or south-west at commencement of valley, while the hill of Lahangai is plainly visible to the left hand or north in the range which runs south-west and north-east, separating the Kyásáshö (Satisu) plateau from the Tawnio valley. At mile 2 a path strikes off to the left or due east leading into Köngma territory and crossing the frontier south of Shio Nanku. At mile 3 on a knoll to north of path is passed the small Kôkáng village of Chinchi, $1\frac{1}{2}$ miles distant. From here the route rises and winds slightly by a good path along the under-features of an irregular series of small hills on either side which thus enclose the path. At $3\frac{3}{4}$ miles to right hand or south is passed the small village of Pákyunshwé, with scanty water-supply. From here the route rises and winds slightly by a good path along a spur rising by an easy ascent passing between two rocks, where the path becomes stony and is covered with large slabs of slippery rocks. Hinshán is reached at mile $5\frac{1}{2}$, a dirty Kôkáng village of 10 or 12 houses. Few supplies and water very scarce, being obtained from a dirty tank. The frontier runs just in front of or to the east of the village crossing a narrow cultivated valley running from the south and half-way up the hill parallel with the village and on which stand the Köngma villages of Tawmôn and Múka Shwé and then passing north round the eastern shoulder of a small knoll to left or north-east of village. From Tawmôn a route is said to run south-east to Köngma town passing (1) Pánglôn Sán 15 miles, Maintha 15 miles, Nayôn 12 miles, Nawan 18 miles, Loi Pyé 18 miles, Manang 12 miles, and Köngma 12 miles. It is little used by caravans and is said to be a rough road. A path also runs along the hills south and drops down to the village of Kôtáng in Kôkáng, which commands the Möngting-Tawnio route (*see* Route No. 63, Alternative I).

No. 62.

From TAWNIO (KÔKÁNG) to HONGHAI (KÔKÁNG).

By Lieut. H. B. Walker, Paid Attaché, Intelligence Branch, February 1892.

Authorities. Military.	Authorities. Civil.	Number and Names of Stages, Rivers and Streams.	Distances. Intermediate. M.	Distances. Intermediate. F.	Distances. Total. M.	Distances. Total. F.	Remarks.
G.O.C. Mandalay District.	Superintendent, Northern Shan States.	**1. Kyásáshŏ** ...	**10**	**0**	10	0	*See* Route No. 64.
		2. Nampanaw ...	**5**	**6**	15	6	*See* Route No. 64.
		3. Manlaw ...	**5**	**4**	21	2	*See* Route No. 64.
		4. Shiokai ...	**5**	**4**	26	6	*See* Route No. 64.
		5. Shyinkyi ... Sipa (or Sima) Haw and two small streams.	**8**	**0**	34	6	General direction north. Leaving Shiokai, the route runs by a rough path along the right bank of the Sipa (or Sima) Haw (65 feet wide, 1 foot to 2½ feet deep; very stony bottom; rapid current), which it crosses in the first 600 yards at a bend, crossing also a small stream flowing into the river Sipa Haw, easy crossings. At mile 1 some paddy-fields are crossed affording camping for 300 men. The route then begins to ascend and runs up a spur for a mile as far as the village of Páfáng to right hand or east at mile 2¼, then crossing a couple of spurs, ascending and descending into two narrow valleys. It then continues to ascend and descend crossing a series of spurs, winding along from one to another and crossing two small streams running down into the Sipa Haw (6 inches deep, 1 foot to 2 feet wide; good drinking water). At mile 5 the route passes the prominent village of Shio Táng standing on the top of a hill (15 to 20 houses, Palaungs). The route then, after crossing a low spur from the east, runs through a short cultivated valley and winds by a long gradual ascent up to the Palaung village of Shyinkyi, a small, neat, well-built Palaung village fenced in with a bamboo fence. A few supplies and water from wells. There is a camping ground just below and to the west of the village for 60 men, the village being built on the only level part of the spur. A larger one for 150 men is found ½ mile from and to the north-east of village, water being obtained from a hill stream to north and north-east. Bamboo leaves, but little grass obtainable. *Note.*—From the hill above the second camp on the southern side of the spur a good view is obtained west towards Mantôn, east towards the frontier and northwards towards Mawhtai. The first 5 miles of the route also run parallel with the spur, along which is the route leading to Mantôn ferry *viâ* Kônkyáng, on western side of Sipa Haw, the prominent hill (with village) Sankaw Kywan Shán, being visible also in that direction; villages east of Shyinkyi towards frontier and within easy radius (Pánkayun, Panyôn, Pankyôn, and Shiotáng) passed *en route*. Height of Shyinkyi 3,768 feet.
		6. Phyin Haw ... Kyankung, Shiokai, and several small streams.	**6**	**0**	40	6	General direction north-north east. Leaving the camp at Shyinkyi, which is ¼ a mile north of village, the route winds through the valley of a small stream for a mile running along the eastern slopes of the hills on western side and passing at ½ mile to left hand

FROM TAWNIO (KÔKÁNG) TO HONGHAI (KÔKÁNG)—*continued.*

Authorities.		Number and Names of Stages, Rivers and Streams.	Distances.		Remarks.
Military.	Civil.		Intermediate.	Total.	
G.O.C. Mandalay District.	Superintendent, Northern Shan States.	**6. Phyin Haw**—*cont.*			or west the small Palaung village of Manmin (four or five houses) at mile 1; the route, leaving the valley, passes to western side of slopes and winds on to a long descending spur, passing the Palaung village of Kyinkáng situated on top of spur (Kyinkáng; six houses; no supplies). The route then runs down the spur (half-way down passing a path to left leading to Homalin) for a mile into a narrow valley, crosses a small stream, and runs up another valley threaded by a narrow stream, follows it to mile 3½, when it strikes across a spur by a steep ascent and descent into another valley, crossing the Kyángkung Haw (3 or 4 yards wide, 6 inches to 1 foot deep; stony bottom; rapid) at mile 4¼. The route then follows the valley of another small stream running along the eastern slopes of the western hills, passes through a gap in the left-hand or western ridge at mile 5½, and descends into valley of the Shiokai Haw, on the bank of which in paddy or old cultivated fields is the camping ground. The Shiokai Haw, as the Sipa Haw is called at Shiokai, is crossed by onward route to Sitôn Phyin and runs behind the western ridge of route from Shyinkyi and down into Shiokai valley. It is here 3 to 4 yards wide, 1 foot to 1½ feet deep; low crossings; gravelly bottom. The camping ground is reached at mile 6, situated on the stream and capable of affording accommodation for 800 or 1,000 men; grass of a coarse kind obtainable. The entire absence of timber, even the smallest shrub on the march, is to be noted, and firewood, even the most limited quantity, is unobtainable and must be brought from Shyinkyi or notice given to the village of Phyin Haw, which is 1 mile further on north-east, two days' notice being required for any number of men over 50. From the village of Ta Shwé Shán, 1½ miles distant to the east, a good view is obtained and the Möngkyeng village of Kyinkáng is visible beyond the frontier: distant here from 5 to 6 miles. Phyin Haw (eight houses) has few supplies in the shape of grain, but has approximately 15 to 20 head of cattle for each house.
		7. Sitôn Phyin (6,230 feet). Shiokai or Sipa Haw.	M. F. 6 4	M. F. 47 2	General direction north. The route leaves the camping ground at Phyin Haw in an easterly direction and follows the valley of the Shiokai Haw running along the slopes of the left hand or northern hills, which are destitute of foliage, passing the Kôkáng village of Phyin Haw at 1 mile (eight houses; few supplies) to right hand or east. (There is camping ground for perhaps 800 men along the Shiokai valley as far as the village of Phyin Haw, where it becomes very narrow.) The route then takes a more northerly direction, descends into another and narrow valley, then crosses a small stream which intersects it, and ascends north very steeply a route to right hand or east leading to Shwéko, said to be a frontier village, 2 miles distant. From top of ascent the route winds by a good path through a broken mass of low hills, the ridge along which the frontier runs covered with trees and jungle (the first seen since Shyinkyi) being visible to right hand or east; distance about a mile. At mile 4½ the route ascends on to the spur on which (running almost north and south) stands the village of Sitôn Phyin, the route running along the slopes of the ridge which ¾ of a mile before reaching the village are covered with loose, thin jungle. Just before

FROM TAWNIO (KÔKÁNG) TO HONGHAI (KÔKÁNG)—*continued.*

Authorities. Military.	Authorities. Civil.	Number and Names of Stages, Rivers and Streams.	Distances. Intermediate. M. F.	Distances. Total. M. F.	Remarks.
G.O.C. Mandalay District.	Superintendent, Northern Shan States.	**7. Sitôn Phyin (6,230 feet)**—*cont.*			entering Sitôn Phyin the route crosses a streamlet, which, together with a similar one at the south end of valley, form the water-supply in good quantities. Sitôn Phyin is a wretched Kôkáng village of four or five houses; few supplies; a little paddy, &c., but possesses 30 or 40 head of cattle per house. The camping ground is very limited, being situated on the level spot on the ridge on which village stands; capable of accommodating 200 men, but would require cleaning first. Grass of a very coarse kind and a few bamboo leaves obtainable. From Sitôn Phyin a direct and excellent track runs to the Manpán ferry, one day's march, a gradual descent all the way passing *en route* the villages of Pánglônkyi at 2 miles, Phungshwépaw at 4 miles, Pawpawkyi at 6½ miles.
		8. Kyásáyeo ... Taung and Paiwé Haw.	**5 4**	52 6	General direction a little east of north. Striking up a steep ascent for about 200 yards the route attains top of ridge, then passes through a cleft on to a spur, along which it runs for nearly 2 miles by an irregular and broken path, ascending and descending; jungle on both sides. Stream to right hand at foot of spur, the Taung Haw, 1½ yards wide; shallow and stony. At mile 1½ a view along a valley to the east is obtained of the ridge of hills along which the frontier runs, distant about 3 miles. At mile 2 the route winds through a gap in the spur and so runs by a bad, stony path for ½ a mile, when it ascends steeply on to the main ridge of hills which are called the Kywinpwyé hills. From the top of this ridge which runs north-east and south-west a view northwards across a narrow valley is obtained of a parallel ridge, the Ahwakyin hills, on which is situated, half-way up the slopes, on a level spot, the village of Kyásáyeo, which is also visible. The route then descends steeply for 600 yards into the valley and, crossing the Paiwé Haw stream (6 yards wide, 1 foot deep; stony and rapid; flows from east to north-west towards Salween; stony and difficult crossings; steep approaches), ascends the Ahwákyin slopes for about ½ of a mile, and then runs along the slopes about half-way mid the valley and summit of ridge, reaching the Kôkáng village of Kyásáyeo (10 houses) at mile 5¼. The camping ground is reached ½ of a mile beyond village to the north-west in a stony clearing capable of accommodating 80 men. Grass of a coarse kind and bamboo leaves obtainable. Good water-supply from hill stream between camp and village. The range Ahwakyin is clothed with jungle, bamboo predominating, while the white-flowering tree "Tôkshio" dots the hill sides with pleasing effect. The route is a very rough one, being much broken and stony, while the ascents and descents are very steep. Laden animals can, however, traverse it. Villages in view to north and west,—Sinkyi, Lônhángkyi, Tákyo Kyi (*see* Route No. 20, Stage 1), and Kwin Pwé (*see* same route, Stage 2).

FROM TAWNIO (KÔKÁNG) TO HONGHAI (KÔKÁNG)—*continued.*

Authorities. Military.	Authorities. Civil.	Number and Names of Stages, Rivers and Streams.	Distances. Intermediate.	Distances. Total.	Remarks.
G.O.C. Mandalay District.	Superintendent, Northern Shan States.	**9. Mangmaw** ... Paiwé, Pyinyé, and Hánshwé streams.	M. F. 6 6	M. F. 59 4	Direction a little east of north. Leaving the camp the route continues to run along the southern slopes of the range Ahwákyin within the valley of Paiwé Haw Shwé, which, flowing westward, lies below and to left hand of route. The end of the ridge is reached at mile $1\frac{1}{2}$, and the route then crosses its lower slope and turns eastward into the valley of the Pyinyé Haw ($5\frac{1}{2}$ yards wide; rapid current; stony bottom; difficult crossings), which, joining the Paiwé Haw Shwé and forming one stream, flows with it into the Salween. After $\frac{1}{8}$ mile along this valley, running over the northern slopes of the Ahwákyin, the route descends precipitously by a broken path to the stream, crosses it and ascends along steep spur up to the top of another lofty ridge of hills, the hill Kyinlong, from which this portion of the range derives its name to right hand or east, the well-defined elevation Laphankyi terminating the ridge to the west. Less than $\frac{1}{2}$ mile up the ascent a small village (Kôkáng) Máhsyi is passed to right hand, a path branching along the centre of the elevation westward to the Kôkáng village of Kyinkyi, 1 mile distant and situated 300 yards below the summit of the ridge, which is reached at mile $2\frac{1}{2}$. The route then runs westward along the top of the ridge from a short distance until it arises above the village of Kyinkyi, down to which a route runs; it then turns north and descends the ridge, a route continuing along the top of the ridge to Tákyo Kyi and Kwin Pwé *en route* for Manpán ferry (*see* Route No. 20). A small village Sônkán (Kôkáng) is passed to left hand or west just below summit of ridge on northern side; right ahead is seen the village of Mangmaw situated on a lofty ridge. The route then winds along the western slopes of a ridge perpendicular to that just crossed by a rough and irregular path and descending to the Hánshwé Haw (5 or 6 yards broad; stony and rapid; $1\frac{1}{2}$ feet deep) at mile 4, which, running down into the valley to left and or west, flows into the Salween. From here the route ascends steeply for $\frac{3}{4}$ of a mile to the Kôkáng village of Longláng (six houses), whence it continues to wind descending and ascending steeply to the Kôkáng village of Mangmaw at $6\frac{3}{4}$ miles. The Salween is visible from several points along the route between Longláng and Mangmaw distant about 3 miles to the west and flowing from north-east to south-west along a deep ravine; beyond it is visible the hill on which the village of H'sen Shán is situated and from which the ferry below it derives its name, while beyond it again a lofty elevation some 9,000 feet, the Myin S'shán, is seen, still further to the north-west. Mangmaw is a Kôkáng village of about eight houses; few supplies; paddy, &c., and possesses a few head of cattle. There is no camping ground here, accommodation for 100 men at a pinch being obtained a mile beyond to the north and on the Mawhtai road on a narrow ridge. Water is obtained from a narrow stream on northern side of the ridge; grass and bamboo leaves obtainable. From the camp the Salween is seen lying below to the west and H'sen S'shán village on the hill, the route westward towards Möngka and Möngko (No. 20) being also visible. There are several villages within easy radius and view of Mangmaw camp, Ahwákyi, a Kôkáng village, lying between the camp

FROM TAWNIO (KÔKÁNG) TO HONGHAI (KÔKÁNG)—*continued.*

Authorities. Military.	Authorities. Civil.	Number and Names of Stages, Rivers and Streams.	Distances. Intermediate.	Distances. Total.	Remarks.
G.O.C. Mandalay District.	Superintendent, Northern Shan States.	**9. Mangmaw**—*cont.*			and the river on the slope. The onward route to Mawhtai winding round the spurs and slopes is visible for about 3 miles until it reaches the village of Kyukoyin due north of camp.
		10. Myinkwalin (camp for Mawhtai). Kyukoyin Haw and a small mountain stream.	M. F. 6 0	M. F. 65 4	General direction east. Leaving the camp the route runs along the northern slopes of the spur in an easterly direction for about ¼ of a mile when it begins to assume a more northerly direction, winding along the slopes and descending to the Kyukoyin Haw, which the route crosses at mile 1½ (5 yards broad, stony bottom, steep approaches) and ascends by a stiff climb the hill of the same name for ½ a mile. Kyukoyin village situated on summit of the hill and lying to the left hand or north-west of a path contains four or five houses and is in the Mawhtai district. After a few yards of very rough path the route then descends for a little to rise again along another slope, the path being broken and very rough and in places stony and incapable of sustaining much traffic without repair, which could be easily given. At mile 4 a small stream is crossed, whence the route runs fairly level and round to the village of Myinkwalin (Kôkáng); six houses, Mawhtai being about 2,000 yards further on and lower down the slope towards the river. There is camping ground for 60 men on level spot on the path and above the village. Few supplies; very little rice; paddy; and Indian corn. Water from springs sufficient for the camp. Grass and bamboo leaves obtainable. Villages passed *en route* to the left hand (or north) towards the Salween— (1) Linkawkyi, (2) Howamyo, (3) Kyukoying, top of hill of that name, (4) Myapháng, (5) Táng S'shán, (6) Kyinkyi, from which villages with a day's notice supplies can be obtained. The lower slopes of the spurs towards the river are cultivated in small patches for paddy, the upper slopes with opium.
		11. Honghai (5,374 feet). Shánsitán, Mawhtai, Mawhtaw, and other small hill streams.	4 6	70 2	General direction east (a little south of). Leaving the camp at Myinkwalin, which is just above and to the south of the village, the route runs by a slightly descending path along northern slopes to the three villages of Mawhtai at 1 mile and in an easterly direction, thence after a few 100 yards of level ground down a steep ascent to a narrow stream. It then, by a steep broken path for a short distance, runs level along the side of slope and again descends to the Shánsitán stream (5 or 6 yards wide, stony; hill-side stream; 1 foot deep; excellent drinking water; steep approaches) crossing one or two small hill-side rivulets, the village whence the stream derives its name lying a mile and-a-half among the hills to south-east of the path. From the Shánsitán stream the route crosses the slopes of another spur by a steep ascent, a short, level stretch and a long, steep descent, passing a Palaung village; six or eight houses; few supplies, but possessing buffaloes and cattle, in all about 30 head with good water-supply from

FROM TAWNIO (KÔKÁNG) TO HONGHAI (KÔKÁNG)—*continued.*

Authorities. Military.	Authorities. Civil.	Number and Names of Stages, Rivers and Streams.	Distances. Intermediate.	Distances. Total.	Remarks.
G.O.C. Mandalay District.	Superintendent, Northern Shan States.	**11. Honghai (5,374 feet)—** *cont.*			small stream south of path and camp for 30 men situated on level portion of slope. At bottom of descent the route crosses (at mile 3) the Mawhtai Haw (a mountain stream 6 or 7 yards broad; stony; rapid; 1 to 1½ feet deep; excellent drinking water), and then ascends by a continual steep and winding ascent for 1¾ miles in an easterly direction to the camping ground of Honghai below and to the north of village. In the last of ¾ a mile the route runs for ¼ a mile along the valley of the Mawhtaw Haw (a mountain stream flowing westward) and 200 or 300 feet above and to the south of the stream. It then leaves the valley and almost due south up the slopes for ½ mile when it reaches Honghai. Honghai is a wretched Kôkáng village of about 10 or 12 houses, ½ a mile as the crow flies from the low, jungle-covered range of hills which form the frontier line. It has few supplies, though they may be obtained from the villages which lie north and east within a radius of 2 miles, namely, Kyushwé, Chinmolin, &c. The camping ground at Honghai (old paddy-fields in steppes on the side of slope) is capable of affording accommodation for 200 or 300 men under tents and double that number in addition bivouacking on the narrower shelves where the ordinary sepoy tent could not be pitched. Water obtained from two small mountain rivulets between camp and village, and troughs would have to be dug to accumulate the water in any quantity. Facing the camp and on the other side of Mawhtaw Haw valley is the prominent hill Kyushwé Shán with village of same name. Along the Mawhtaw Haw valley in a south-easterly direction runs the route to Möngpôn (or Möngphôn) a large, well-to-do Chinese village of Möngkyeng; 60 houses; fifth-day bazaar, and distant from Honghai rather less than 10 miles. This stage, though only 4¾ miles, is a very stiff one and quite a sufficient day's work for troops moving ordinarily. At a pinch the whole distance from Mangmaw could be accomplished in the day by active men and in good marching condition. The hill Lien S'shán immediately on the right bank of Salween and in Lônlin territory is visible to the left hand or north and west of route nearly all the way. It is studded with villages and bears the appearance of being freely cultivated, while numerous routes leading to Lônlin town stripe the hill side in every direction. From Honghai to the eastward lies the lofty hill Kyushwé S'shán with village of same name; six houses (Kôkáng); 1½ miles distant. From Kyushwé S'shán, still looking east, can be seen the boundary hill Páhu Shan; 2 miles still further east, on its western slopes, are the Kôkáng villages of Chinmolin, a Palaung village, and on its northern slopes Mangyem. Honghai being enclosed north-east and south by frontier is a weak and isolated position and liable to be overrun from Möngpôn.

Capt. Walker gives the following routes from Honghai from Native information collected on the spot:—

(1) TO LÔNLIN.

	China.		M.	F.	M.	F.	
		1. Möngpôn (or Möngphôn).	...		...		General direction south-east. A day's march. Möngpôn has a large fifth-day bazaar, and is a proposed post for a Chinese garrison. (The position of the village can be made out from the hills within Kôkáng, east of the Honghai.)

FROM TAWNIO (KÔKÁNG) TO HONGHAI (KÔKÀNG)—*continued.*

(1) TO LÔNLIN—*continued.*

Authorities. Military.	Authorities. Civil.	Number and Names of Stages, Rivers and Streams.	Distances. Intermediate. M. F.	Distances. Total. M. F.	Remarks.
China.		**2. Nan Saw Pa** ...	...	...	General direction north; a day's march by a difficult road uphill; village has 30 houses.
		3. Sancha Ko ferry. Salween river 80 yards wide.	...	...	General direction north. Route crosses Salween by ferry (one dug-out only). Day's march. Village contains 25 or 30 houses.
		4. Möngnao ...	...	...	General direction west. A day's march; road good, but hilly; climbs northern extremity of Lien S'shán; 200 houses; fifth-day bazaar.
		5. Phyinka ...	...	...	North-west; a day's march; village contains 300 horses and has fifth-day bazaar.
		6. Shanta	...	...	North-west; road good and level; a day's march. Village has 500 houses; fifth-day bazaar; and 50 regular soldiers as garrison.
		7. Lônlin ...	...	...	North-west; a day's march. From Lônlin to Manshi (or Maingkhwon*) is said to be two days' march, a little east of south, *viâ* Taw Ma Khan, a village of 30 or 40 houses. The road is said to be good though hilly.

The following is an alternative route to the same place:—

Authorities. Military.	Authorities. Civil.	Number and Names of Stages, Rivers and Streams.	Intermediate.	Total.	Remarks.
China.		**1. Malíshu** ...	...	...	One long day's march.
		2. Kyánlôn ...	...	...	
		3. Sitán Haw ... Salween.	...	...	One long day's march; ferry over the Salween.
		4. Yako Tin ...	...	...	One long day's march.
		5. Phyinka ...	...	...	One long day's march. A fifth-day bazaar here.
		6. Húkyákyi ...	...	...	One long day's march.
		7. Wunyin Haw.	...	...	
		8. Shanta ...	...	...	One long day's march. Bazaar and garrison of 50 men.
		9. Whatan Lin ...	...	...	One long day's march.

* Not to be confused with the town of that name in the Húkong valley near the Amber Mines.—A.F.

FROM TAWNIO (KÔKÁNG) TO HONGHAI (KÔKÁNG)—*continued.*

(1) To LÔNLIN—*continued.*

Authorities. Military.	Authorities. Civil.	Number and Names of Stages, Rivers and Streams.	Distances. Inter-mediate. M. F.	Distances. Total. M. F.	Remarks.
China.		**10. Lônlin** ...	...	...	One long day's march. Bazaar; 500 to 1,000 houses; garrison of 800 men.

(2) To MÖNGKYENG.

Authorities. Military.	Authorities. Civil.	Number and Names of Stages, Rivers and Streams.	Distances. Inter-mediate. M. F.	Distances. Total. M. F.	Remarks.
China.		**1. Möngpôn** ...	...	...	Direction east. A day's journey. Large village with big fifth-day bazaar. Proposed post for Chinese troops.
		2. Pyékutin ...	...	...	Direction north-east. A day's march. Climbs hill of same name.
		3. Liengkôshwé.	...	...	North-east.
		4. Pi I	...	...	North-east.
		5. Lôn Kyu Lôn.	...	...	North-east.
		6. Samônfôn ...	...	...	North-east.
		7. Shán Sunba ...	...	...	North-east.
		8. Möngkyeng ...	...	...	North-east. Formerly the residence of the Möngkyeng Sawbwa, who now lives at Môn Hôn Takyi (*see* in Route No. 63).

(3) To YUNGCHÁNGFU.

Authorities. Military.	Authorities. Civil.	Number and Names of Stages, Rivers and Streams.	Distances. Inter-mediate. M. F.	Distances. Total. M. F.	Remarks.
China.		**1. Möngpôn** ...	...	...	All these stages are convenient marches for men and transport animals. Water-supply and camping ground said to be obtainable at each place.
		2. Sán Kyôn Shwé.	...	...	
		3. Yéyatán ...	...	...	
		4. Mansôn ...	...	...	
		5. Mônsataw Haw.	...	...	
		6. Kwin To Shwé.	...	...	
		7. Yaukwán ...	...	...	
		8. Shédin ...	...	...	
		9. Pôncháng ...	...	...	
		10. Kwánsawlin.	...	...	
		11. Sinku ...	...	...	
		12. Yungchángfu	...	...	Garrison of Yungchángfu is said to be 1,000 strong.

No. 63.

From TAWNIO to MÖNGTING viâ KYWANYINPA.

By Lieut. H. B. WALKER, Paid Attaché, Intelligence Branch, January 1892.

Authorities. Military.	Authorities. Civil.	Number and Names of Stages, Rivers and Streams.	Distances. Intermediate. M. F.	Distances. Total. M. F.	Remarks.
G.O.C. Mandalay District.	Superintendent, Northern Shan States.	**1. Kywanyinpa** ...	11 0	11 0	General direction north-east. Leaving Tawnio, the route runs south along the main road between Namhung and Tawnio for 4½ miles, passing the hill Namhutan at 2½ miles. At mile 4½, the Namhung road continues south-west along the main valley and to the west of the short range of hills, with Kyé-kyuhsán at its northern extremity, and directly facing. Namhutan hill shuts off the Namhung road. At this point three valleys as it were meet: (1) the Namhung-Kunlôn route valley; (2) a parallel valley; and (3) a valley striking east, along which the Möngting route runs. The rising ground at the foot of Kyékyuhsán and a number of small flat topped circular knolls at entrance of this valley afford a good position for commanding the junction of the three valleys and the routes along them. The valley of the Möngting route almost immediately after entrance narrows, a path striking to the right hand south-east, to the village of Píshánshwé (*see* Route No. 66) lying on the frontier between the Möngting route and Namhung. The width of the Möngting route valley averages from 300 to 500 yards. It is practically level to mile 7, cultivated in patches with opium. At mile 7 the route rises a little and passes to right hand or south, the large well-defined hill (in the ridge which forms the valley's southern boundary) called Kyinkyulin. Average width of path from 1½ to 5 feet. If necessary by clearing, the whole valley could be utilized as a road. At mile 8 the frontier is reached, at this point running north and south and crossing the eastern shoulder of the hill Kunlônpho (on right hand of path). On left hand of route a path runs up the hills on that side to the Kôkáng village of Kôtáng (*see* Alt. Route No. I below), a well-to-do village commanding the Möngting route from its eastern portion. From this point the path runs south-east along the lower slopes of the hills on northern or left-hand side of valley, which meet the slopes of the hills on right hand or southern side and form a dry water-course. The route now ascends slightly for 1½ miles, a second path leading from Kôtáng into Möngting territory running in here. The valley then widens out, the path gradually descending into it. The valley here is a mile long and nearly a mile wide, nearly level and cultivated in patches. It would accommodate 5,000 to 6,000 men in camp. At the south-east end, 11th mile, is the Chinese-Shán village of Kywanyinpa, 10 or 12 houses, and just underneath a peak called Shánkyékyulin.
China.		**2. Möngting** ... Namting.	9 0	20 0	The route runs through the village to right hand or south of peak, and passing through a break in the hills reaches the small village of Kwépein, at mile 5, standing on the Kwépein stream which flows into the Namting close to the town of Möngting at mile 9. Möngting town, capital of Möngting province, is a fortified town of 400 or 500 houses. The wall surrounding it being now broken down; it is garrisoned (on paper) by 200 men (60 men in reality) and four or five useless guns. This route is a principal caravan route and chiefly used. *Note.*—After leaving Tawnio to the north, or Namhung to the

FROM TAWNIO TO MÖNGTING *viâ* KYWANYINPA—*continued.*

Authorities. Military.	Authorities. Civil.	Number and Names of Stages, Rivers and Streams.	Distances. Intermediate.	Distances. Total.	Remarks.
China.		**2. Möngting**—*cont.*			south, there is no water (except a very small quantity of inferior quality in a small muddy pool up Möngting valley, 2¼ miles from Kyékyushán hill) until Kywanyinpa is reached.

ALTERNATIVE I.

FROM TAWNIO TO MÖNGTING *viâ* KÔNTÁNG.

BY LIEUT. H. B. WALKER, DUKE OF CORNWALL'S LIGHT INFANTRY, PAID ATTACHÉ, INTELLIGENCE BRANCH, 31ST JANUARY 1892.

Military	Civil	Stages	Intermediate	Total	Remarks
			M. F.	M. F.	
G.O.C. Mandalay District.	Superintendent, Northern Shan States.	**1. Kôtáng**	**5 2**	5 2	General direction south-east. From Tawnio Mongting can be reached (1) either by a route running as far as Namhutan hill by the main route to Namhung and Kunlôn southwards and then turning east across main valley to village of Namhutan at 3½ miles; or (2) by a route parallel to and east of (1) route, which it joins ¼ of a mile before reaching Namhutan. This is a small Kôkáng village, six or eight houses fenced in with prickly growth and entered through archway of same material, about 15 or 20 yards through. Supplies: paddy and a few fowls and pigs. Passing through the village of Namhutan the route runs south for a short distance along the ridge of a spur, turning eastward along a narrow valley which runs almost parallel to and north of the valley along which runs the Möngting route. The village of Khaika being passed at 4 miles, 1 mile distant to the left or north the route now begins to ascend and runs up by a steep, rocky path passable though difficult for animals to a short stretch of hills lying north and south across the valley, and through a cleft in which the route runs to other side into southern end of a narrow valley or ravine which, here running almost parallel with the frontier and beneath the village of Kôtáng, carries a route north-eastward towards Hinshán, a frontier village further north (*see* Route No. 61). Kôtáng, village is divided into four parts, two of which, the northern and eastern parts, are nearly *impregnable* positions; the latter portion commands the Mongting route into which it looks down opposite the hill Kunlôn Pho. The frontier line here also crosses the Möngting route from Kunlôn Pho on southern side and passes just in front of or to east of Kôtáng. The Möngting village of Kywanyinpa is just concealed from view by the narrowing of the Möngting route valley eastward. From Kôtáng village the hill Kôtáng Shán, a distinctive hill, is visible 1¾ miles northward. Within the Chinese-Shan province of Köngma, whose western extremity here runs up to the frontier and whose southern boundary is Möngting, is seen the village of Tátôn; the Köngma hill of Sekwai Shán is viewed north-east. Kôtáng has fair supplies and is a well-to-do village; water and grass in moderate supplies.
China.		**2. Möngting** ...	**?10 0**	? 15 2	No details are given, but apparently you can drop down into the route described above at about Kywanyinpa (Stage 1) so that the distance from Kôtáng to Mongting does not in all probability exceed 10 miles.

FROM TAWNIO TO MÖNGTING *viâ* KYWANYINPA—*continued.*

ALTERNATIVE I—*continued.*

From Möngting routes lead to (1) Köngma town and (2) Möngkyeng, of which Captain Walker obtained the following particulars from natives on the spot:—

(1) FROM MÖNGTING TO KÖNGMA.

Authorities. Military.	Authorities. Civil.	Number and Names of Stages, Rivers and Streams.	Distances. Intermediate. M. F.	Distances. Total. M. F.	Remarks.
	China.	**1. Kyé Ha** ... Ti-ki-haw.	...	...	Direction east. The road, which is said to be level and good, runs for the most part through paddy-fields. At 6 miles the Ti-ki-haw is crossed (20 yards broad; knee-deep in dry weather; stony bed; rapid current). Kyé Ha has about 100 houses, and a fifth-day bazaar. Large camping ground on the paddy-fields near the Namting river; 5,000 or 6,000 being able to be accommodated, the camp being distant about a mile from the river. There is also camping accommodation within the village for 500 or 600 men; supplies very plentiful.
		2. Si Fan Sin ... One small stream.	...	...	Direction north-east. Route continues along paddy-fields all the way. The village contains 40 houses. Supplies good. Camping ground in the paddy-fields; ample water-supply either from wells or stream.
		3. Kulôn	...	...	Direction north. The route is good though undulating, crossing low spurs, running down to the Namting, along whose left bank the route runs. Kulôn is a small village of 15 houses. Camping ground near the village in paddy-fields for 500 men. Good supplies, for size of village, obtainable.
		4. Shio Kyin Si ...	...	...	Direction north. Road said to be good, winding over the lower slopes of spurs, running towards the Namting stream, along the left bank of which the route runs. Camping ground in the paddy-fields near the village for 500 men. Village contains some 30 or 40 houses. Good supplies.
		5. Mainkyin ...	...	...	Direction north. Route crosses a spur running towards the Namting by a good path, descending again into the Namting valley. Mainkyin contains some 70 or 80 houses; supplies moderate; accommodation for 1,000 men outside village; water-supply from Namting.
		6. Takyi	...	...	Direction north-east. Route now leaves the Namting valley and strikes up into the hills, crossing a range called the Sini Shân on which the village stands, a Lawa village of 1,000 houses. Camping ground for 1,000 men in the heart of the village; water obtainable from hill streams. Supplies plentiful.

FROM TAWNIO TO MÖNGTING *viâ* KYWANYINPA—*continued.*

ALTERNATIVE I—*continued.*

(1) FROM MÖNGTING TO KÖNGMA—*continued.*

Authorities. Military.	Authorities. Civil.	Number and Names of Stages, Rivers and Streams.	Distances. Intermediate. M.	F.	Distances. Total. M.	F.	Remarks.
China.		**7. Tashéchan** ...	...		...		Direction north-east. Road good though hilly. Tashéchan is a village of four or five houses. Camping ground about á mile from the village on a spur of the hill on which the village stands. Accommodation for 500 men. Supplies very little or nothing.
		8. Möngsa ...	...		...		Direction north. Road descends into valley in which Möngsa is situated; a village of about 100 houses surrounded by a wall. There is a good standing bazaar here outside the walls, there being a straggling suburb. Camping accommodation in the paddy-fields outside for 1,000 men. Water from a stream near the bazaar. Möngsá is the head-quarters of the Köngma Sawbwa.
		9. Köngma ...	...		...		Direction north-east. The road is said to be good and level all the way. Köngma is no longer the seat of the Sawbwa, who removed to Möngsa some 12 years back. Köngma was formerly surrounded by a wall, but it is now broken down and out of repair, nor is a garrison maintained. The supplies at both Köngma and Möngsa are said to be very plentiful. All the above stages have been given as being ordinary marches for troops and transport animals, and all the marches are said to be easy ones.
		(2) FROM MÖNGTING TO MÖNGKYENG.					
China.		**1. Kyán Pyé ferry.** Namting.	7	4	7	4	Direction north-north-east. The route runs across level ground as far as the Namting river when it follows the right bank of that stream to Kyán Pyé when it crosses by a ferry (three or four dug-outs) to the left bank. The village stands on both sides of the river and contains about 20 houses. Camping accommodation for about 300 men. Water, supplies, &c., obtainable.
		2. Shamain Kan.	8	0	15	4	Direction north. Road ascends and descends alternately. The village only contains two houses. Camping ground for 40 or 50 men. Water is rather scarce and has to be obtained from hill-side streams.
		3. Hé Haw ...	7	0	22	4	Direction north. Road a little uphill. Camping ground in the village for 60 men. The village contains only six houses. Water from the Hé Haw stream. Supplies : a few only.

FROM TAWNIO TO MÖNGTING *viâ* KYWANYINPA—*continued.*

ALTERNATIVE I—*continued.*

(2) FROM MÖNGTING TO MÖNGKYENG—*continued.*

Authorities. Military.	Authorities. Civil.	Number and Names of Stages, Rivers and Streams.	Distances. Intermediate. M.	F.	Distances. Total. M.	F.	Remarks.
China.		**4. Táshio**	**8**	**0**	30	4	Direction north. Road good and downhill. Camping ground in the paddy-fields near the village where there is accommodation for over 1,000 men. Water obtained from the Ta Pa Haw. There are 20 houses in the village. A few supplies obtainable.
		5. Ta Wé	**9**	**0**	39	4	Direction north. Route follows the Ta Shi Haw valley and is good, level going. Camping for 500 men near the village which contains 40 or 50 houses. Supplies obtainable.
		6. Môn Hôn Ta Kyi.	**10**	**0**	49	4	Direction north. Road good and level all the way. Môn Hôn Ta Kyi is a town of some 400 or 500 houses and has a garrison of 1,000 soldiers (?). The village is situated in a valley well cultivated for paddy, where camping ground can be obtained for any number of men. A route from Hôn Sitôn Haw * leading to Möngkyeng runs in here. There are hot springs round and about Môn Hôn Ta Kyi, which is now the seat of the Möngkyeng Sawbwa or acting Sawbwa.
		7. Kan Kyi Yin ...	**11**	**0**	60	4	Direction north. Road good and level through paddy-fields. Camping ground for any number of men in the paddy-fields near the village which contains 40 or 50 houses; water and supplies obtainable.
		8. Möngkyeng ...	**12**	**0**	72	4	Direction north. Road good and level all the way through paddy-fields. Möngkyeng, once a strongly fortified place, has fallen into disrepair and the walls are broken down.

No. 64.

From TAWNIO (KÔKÁNG) to NAMKHAM viâ MANTÔN FERRY.

G.O.C. Mandalay District.	Superintendent, Northern Shan States.	**1. Kya Sa Shö (Sa Tis Su).** Tawnio stream, Cha Haw, and several smaller streams.	**10**	**0**	10	0	General direction first 5½ miles north-west, last 4½ miles south-west. Leaving Tawnio the route runs along the high ground and to the west of the small stream which supplies Tawnio valley (5 yards wide, 1 foot deep, stony

* Hôn Sitôn Haw is situated on the Kôkáng-Möngkyeng frontier about 10 miles east of Kya Sa Shö (*see* Route No. 64, Stage 1). Captain Walker in his other Kôkáng routes frequently refers to a route from Kya Sa Shö to this place, but it must have been lost as it is nowhere recorded—A.F.

FROM TAWNIO (KÔKÁNG) TO NAMKHAM *viâ* MANTÔN FERRY—*continued.*

Authorities.		Number and Names of Stages, Rivers and Streams.	Distances.		Remarks.
Military.	Civil.		Inter-mediate.	Total.	
G.O.C. Mandalay District.	Superintendent, Northern Shan States.	**1. Kya Sa Shö (Sa Tis Su)**—*cont.*			bottom, to right hand or north-east of path, flowing south-east). The route is a good sound path, through jungle following the long, narrow valley with stream lying to right hand or east. This valley is cultivated entirely for paddy and is the usual camping ground. At mile $1\frac{1}{4}$ the well-to-do Palaung village of Thimpha is passed to the right hand or north-east, overlooking the cultivated valley, the route descending slightly. Here a path to left hand or south is said to lead to the village of Nalé some distance off. At mile 3 the route crosses a narrow valley which would be a marsh in wet weather and then commences to ascend, and so ascends by a steep zigzagging path to mile 4 when it slightly descends by a spur for $\frac{1}{2}$ a mile. It then rises again up to mile $5\frac{1}{2}$ when the top of the range, Namchaupha, is reached. There is a small rivulet at roadside $\frac{1}{4}$ mile below top of Namchaupha with wooden trough to collect water, which, when full, would allow a scanty supply to 100 men. This range separates the Tawnio valley from the Kya Sa Shö plateau, runs from west-south-west to north-east and crosses the frontier close to the stone bridge near Nansang (*see* Route No. 65) and Hônsitôn Haw (*see* at end of this stage). The route now commences to descend and runs down a steep gradient for a few hundred yards, passing the small village of Chin Kyan Chao to the left hand or south. The gradient then becomes very steep and continues so for $\frac{1}{2}$ mile to the small stream Cha Haw, 5 or 6 yards wide, 2 feet deep, with 4 feet banks, bridged by stone bridge; flows from north to south. The path then ascends for a couple of hundred yards north-east and commences to run through a narrow valley along the lower slopes of the southern side elevations bounding the valley on that side. The small village of I-la is passed to the north. At mile 7 a path to north-north-east side of route leads to Ta Shwé Tan and *viâ* Ta Shwé Tan to Kywé Kywé Pa and Hôn Sitôn Haw. (At Ta Shwé Tan there is a fifth-day bazaar.) The route now again inclines south-west and after running along the valley by a well-defined path for another $\frac{3}{4}$ mile, passing three half-dry streams roughly bridged springing from wells (on the left hand there is camping ground in opium cultivation at foot of southern hills for 150 men), it commences to descend and continues to do so until the valley in which stands the hill on which the village of Kya Sa Shö, the chief village of Kôkáng and residence of the Höng, is situated, is reached, at mile 10. At foot of hill on which village stands is a pool for watering animals. There is camping ground at foot of hill in valley for 600 men. Grass abundant, but of bad quality bamboo leaves obtainable. Kya Sa Shö, though situated on a hill, is commanded (for fire-arms) on all sides except south, in which direction the valley runs. For attacks against it by a savage enemy, Kachins, &c., it is well situated and the ascents up the hill on which it stands are very steep. The village consists of about 50 houses inside a stockade and fence of prickly growth through which the road passes under a porch or archway propped up by wooden pillars. The only building inside that is properly built and clean is the Höng's house. Supplies very inconsiderable, except opium. Rice, paddy, &c., has to be sent for west and south from the Palaung villages. Height of camp at Kya Sa Shö 4,978 feet above sea-level. *Note.*—Hôn Sitôn Haw, a place situated at the junction of the boundaries of Köngma and Möngkyeng (on the east) and Kôkáng (on the west) lies about 10 miles to the east of Kya Sa Shö.—*A.F.*

FROM TAWNIO (KÔKÁNG) TO NAMKHAM *viâ* MANTÔN FERRY—*continued.*

Authorities. Military.	Authorities. Civil.	Number and Names of Stages, Rivers and Streams.	Distances. Intermediate. M. F.	Distances. Total. M. F.	Remarks.
G.O.C. Mandalay District.	Superintendent, Northern Shan States.	**2. Nampahaw (or Nampanaw).** Three small streams.	5 6	15 6	General direction north. Leaving Kya Sa Shö the route runs back along the main road to Tawnio, for $2\frac{1}{2}$ miles easterly when it bears to the north or left hand up a narrow valley towards the bazaar place of Ta Shwé Tan; a collection of sheds as stalls and four or five houses. The path rising a little though sound and good. At mile $3\frac{1}{2}$ the wretched little village of Kyákháywa is reached, crossing the little stream (6 inches deep, 1 yard wide, boggy approaches) deriving its name from the village. At mile 3 Kyákháywa; 15 houses; few supplies. From Kyákháywa the route continues northward by a good sound path, through an open valley for $1\frac{1}{4}$ miles when the valley narrows for another mile, and so runs for $\frac{1}{2}$ a mile when a route to right hand well defined leads to Tawnio. At $5\frac{1}{2}$ miles a path to left hand or west leads to the villages of Tapinshán and Tawantáng distant about $1\frac{1}{2}$ miles, from the former of which the ascent of the hill Linshán is made, whence a commanding view is obtained and the village of Kya Sa Shö; south visible. The route then runs down a steep ascent for $\frac{1}{4}$ of a mile into the camping ground of Nampahaw, the village of Lushuwa (two or three houses) being on the hills to north-east and a mile distant, there being no village of the name of Nampahaw. The camp is situated in paddy-fields; accommodation for 400 or 500 men; plentiful water-supply; grass and bamboo leaves available. An alternative route runs *viâ* Kywékywépa as follows: Following the route direct, as far as Kyákháywa through which it passes, thence bearing in a more easterly direction than the direct route, and passing at mile 6 through the village of Ta Shwé Tan; seven or eight houses and a few supplies. (Its bazaar place attended every fifth day, where vegetables, rice, salt, and pigs can be obtained, being close to Kyákháywa as mentioned above.) From Tá Shwé Tan the route runs through an open valley winding along the slopes of the left-hand spurs. Kywékywépa is reached at mile $7\frac{1}{2}$. Leaving lower Kywékywépa the route turns west and ascends $\frac{1}{2}$ a mile to the upper village of Kywékywépa (four houses), then descending and winding south-west across a valley cultivated with paddy and affording camping ground for 400 men. It then winds at a slight ascent along the southern slopes of the hills on the northern side of a valley, here very narrow, and running from cultivated valley. Reaching the large well-to-do village of Nankha or Nankaw at mile $3\frac{1}{2}$. Nankha consists of 30 houses and is situated on a ridge which terminates the western end of the valley; good supplies; water is plentiful in quantities from stream to left hand on south. There is no camping ground at Nankha, but passing through the village the route descends western side of ridge and enters another valley $\frac{1}{4}$ of a mile long through which by a very low ridge route runs, and on either side of which ridge there is indifferent camping ground, there being plenty of room length ways, but no depth. From this point a route runs south to Ta Shwé Tan and Kya Sa Shö. The route then crosses a low range of hills

FROM TAWNIO (KÔKÁNG) TO NAMKHAM *viâ* MANTÔN FERRY—*continued.*

Authorities. Military.	Authorities. Civil.	Number and Names of Stages, Rivers and Streams.	Distances. Intermediate.	Distances. Total.	Remarks.
G.O.C. Mandalay District.	Superintendent, Northern Shan States.	**2. Nampahaw (or Nampanaw)**—*cont.*			winding through a gap (formed by the Talinshán hill and a low hill facing it) and descends by a long steep descent into the camping ground of Nampahaw (or Nampanaw) at mile 3½ from Kywékywépa (lower) or 11 miles from Kya Sa Shö. This is a much longer route than the direct one, but it is only 2½ miles from the frontier at Kywékywépa.
			M. F.	M. F.	
		3. Manlaw ...	5 4	21 2	General direction north-west. Leaving the camp in the paddy-fields at Nampahaw the route runs up a steep ascent on to the upper slopes of a minor ridge of hills, running north and south through which the route winds running on to the western slopes of the same ridge at 1½ miles and obtaining fine view of the western country. At this point along a valley running westward Loipánglom is seen in the distance across the Salween, while the hill Linshán (*see* Nampahaw) above the village of Tapinshán lies to left hand or south of valley, the route after winding along the south-western slopes then turns north passing through a gap in the hills back again on to the western slopes ascending and descending by short ascents and descents, the path being good and the gradients more or less studied. At mile 3 the route passes through a second gap in the hills down a short steep ascent and up the corresponding rise on the other side on to the southern slopes of the spurs which run in that direction. At 3½ miles the hill Shwéminkan to the left hand or west is passed, the route running on to and crossing the short ridge of which Shwéminkan is the western terminus. The route then winds on to a long, gradual spur which stretches into the main western valley of the Sipanaw stream and along which spur the route runs descending by a steep gradient, to the village of Manlaw at 5½ miles. The camping ground lies to the west of road, above the large village of Manlaw, and on a small level spot cultivated for paddy, forming a knoll on the side of the general slope. Here 200 men could be accommodated; water in abundance between road and camp. A smaller portion of Manlaw, five or six houses, occupies the upper portion of knoll on which camp stands. Bamboo leaves plentiful, but no grass. Manlaw consists of three parts, the two main parts below, the smaller part just above camp. In all it contains 35 houses; good supplies. It is the residence of a Pawmaing, who administrates for Kôkáng from this point to Honghai at extremity of province, and who will give every assistance in his power. A fine view north and north-west is obtained from Manlaw camp. The hill of Sunkawshán, passed near to Konkyáng (Stage 5) is visible with its village. The route from Nampanaw is good under foot, but would be a stiff climb southwards towards Kya Sa Shö.
		4. Shiokai	5 4	26 6	General direction just 4 miles north-north-west, the due north. Leaving the western portion of main Manlaw (which must be distinguished from the eastern portion whence the circuitous route to the frontier village
		Lamushwé Haw and Sipa Haw.			

FROM TAWNIO (KÔKÁNG) TO NAMKHAM *viâ* MANTÔN FERRY—*continued*.

Authorities.		Number and Names of Stages, Rivers and Streams.	Distances.		Remarks.
Military.	Civil.		Intermediate.	Total.	
G.O.C. Mandalay District.	Superintendent, Northern Shan States.	**4. Shiokai**—*cont.*			of Kyinmalin or Chinmalin runs) the route descends along spur as far as a well-to-do Palaung village (20 houses, kyaung and good supplies) at mile 1. From here, looking east, the village of Nampukyin, through which runs the Chinmalin route, is visible on an opposite spur. There is a camping ground below the spur in some paddy-fields for 80 men; water plentiful near camp; bamboo leaves and a little grass. Leaving the Palaung village, which also bears the name of Manlaw, the spur is followed by a steep and rather broken path to the valley of the Sipa Haw at 4 miles. Here the small stream Lamushwéhaw flowing from the south and running into the Sipa Haw is crossed (5 yards wide, 6 inches deep; stony and rapid). After a short rough ascent the route runs along the left bank of the Sipa Haw over the western slopes of hills, and at a distance varying from 300 yards to 100 yards from the Sipa Haw for 1½ miles. Paddy-fields affording camping ground 600 men lie between route and the river which is here from 40 to 60 feet wide, 2½ to 3 feet deep; stony bottom; rapid; low banks. On opposite or right bank are said to exist some gold washings. The last 1½ miles very rough and stony; camp close to village in paddy-fields where there is accommodation for 400 men. Shiokai is a small Palaung village; six or eight houses. There is fifth-day bazaar here when only supplies can be obtained. Height of camp 2,550 feet above sea-level.
		5. Kônkyáng ... Sipa Haw and another small stream.	M. F. 8 4	M. F. 35 2	General direction north-west. Leaving Shiokai the road runs back for ½ a mile on the Manlaw road and crosses the Sipa Haw (50 feet wide, 1 foot to 3 feet deep; stony botttom; rapid current). From the Sipa Haw the route strikes up a steep long spur passing close to its foot; camping ground in paddy-fields for 800 men. The route follows the spur by a good path, though dusty in the dry season, to mile 4 where stands the Palaung village of Kônlong; 10 houses; few supplies; camp for 60 men on level space immediately to west of village which lies to east of route short open jungle all the way up spur. From Kônlong the route continues to ascend to mile 4½, where it passes through a wood of large timber 300 yards in extent. On either side of the spur thus ascended run parallel spurs on which are visible, to the east, the villages of Kingai and Shioláng (the latter being on the forward route to Mawhtai). To the west the double village of Kyônláng and at the summit of same spur the eminence and village of Sankawshán. After passing through the wood at mile 5 the path levels a little and turning northwards runs through a cleft in the hills into a semi-circle formed by hills to the north and east and the hill on which Kônkyáng is situated to the south, being open towards the west, and looking across a narrow valley cultivated with opium. Kônkyáng is a Palaung village; contains 20 or 30 houses with moderate supplies; water-supply scanty; obtained from small stream north-east of village; camping ground for 30 men only, but with difficulty.

FROM TAWNIO (KÔKÁNG) TO NAMKHAM *viâ* MANTÔN FERRY—*continued.*

Authorities.		Number and Names of Stages, Rivers and Streams.	Distances.				Remarks.
Military.	Civil.		Intermediate.		Total.		
			M.	F.	M.	F.	
G.O.C. Mandalay District.	Superintendent, Northern Shan States.	**6. Mantôn ferry.**	**12**	**0**	47	2	General direction north-west. Leaving Kônkyáng, the route runs out through a cleft in the hills from north side of village and reaches by a short steep ascent the top of a ridge, the crest of which it follows by a good though narrow path as far as mile 2, when it descends a little and crosses a small level spot to left hand or south-west of which is a small marsh whence water might be obtained, while on other side of path is a small post containing supply for 20 or 30 men. From here the route rises again to run along the eastern slope south of a series of s small bare hills. The land marks, Loi Pánglôm, Loi Chaima, and Loi Saw are practically visible all the way. At mile 4 the village of Manshwéla (Kôkáng) is passed to right hand or east; eight or 10 houses. At mile 4½ the route crosses a low ridge and then commences to descend by a long winding spur into the Salween valley rising for short distance at mile 7 before reaching the large well-to-do Kôkáng village of Swankawlin, passing on parallel spur to south the village of Shyántáng; eight or 10 houses. A good water-supply in a tank with a spring lies 200 or 300 yards down the southern slopes below Swankawlin. Descending along the spur for 1½ miles the village of Mantôn (upper) is reached; 20 or 30 houses standing on a point of the spur to the north-west. Facing it are the hills Loi Chaima to the south and Loi Sa to the north; supplies paddy; rice of an inferior sort in small quantities; the camping ground is on the spur just before reaching the village and accommodates 1,000 men; water is obtained (1) ½ mile to the north in small quantities, (2) 1 mile down the spur below lower Mantôn to left hand or south. From Mantôn village to the ferry the route follows the spur south-west for 3¼ miles by a steep descent of about one in twelve passing lower Mantôn at ½ a mile (eight or 10 houses). The spur running level here affords camping ground for 300 men. The route then recommences its descent to the Salween jungle on both sides of path which is good though dusty. The Salween here runs through a narrow ravine, is about 120 yards wide, 50 feet deep in centre, and flows 3½ miles an hour. The ferry consists of one large dug-out, usually retained on the western or right bank. The route throughout, though good and passable for laden animals, involves a great deal of climbing, and the stages given will be found sufficient for dismounted troops and heavily laden pack animals. Between each stage water-supply is scanty except where crossing the Sipa Haw at Shiokai and where the route touches at villages. At the Mantôn ferry itself there is very little standing room for troops, 200 men at most could be accommodated, and there is no room to camp except for small parties. Mantôn together with Swankawlin form an important position commanding the route to the ferry. The former standing 4,900 feet above the sea-level. From Mantôn a route runs direct to Mawhtai within close proximity to the river bank. The stages are (1) Namkonnaw, (2) Famakyán, (3) Kwinpáng, (4) Kwyinpé or Kwinpé, (5) Mangmaw (*see* Route No. 62, Stage 9), (6) Mawhtai or Myinkwalin (*see* Route No. 62, Stage 10). Since there is no camp at Mawhtai and but little room at Myinkwalin two

FROM TAWNIO (KÔKÁNG) TO NAMKHAM *viâ* MANTÔN FERRY—*continued.*

Authorities. Military.	Authorities. Civil.	Number and Names of Stages, Rivers and Streams.	Distances. Intermediate.	Distances. Total.	Remarks.
G.O.C. Mandalay District.	Superintendent, Northern Shan States.	**6. Mantôn ferry** —*cont.*			more stages to Honghai at extremity of Kôkáng, and one more to the Möngkyeng village of Möngpôn or Möngphôn, a large well-to-do village with bazaar and proposed garrison of Chinese troops, *see* after Stage 11 of Route No. 62. Three routes run onward after crossing Salweeń, one to Möngsi said to be four days' march; two to Namkham *viâ* Mönghawm each said to be two days' march, the southern one *viâ* Taiyaku; the northern one *viâ* Lawsitán (or Loisitán).

Capt. Walker gives the following description of the route to Namkham from Native information:—

FROM MANTÔN FERRY TO NAMKHAM.

Military	Civil	Stages	Intermediate M.	Intermediate F.	Total M.	Total F.	Remarks
G.O.C. Mandalay District.	Superintendent, Northern Shan States.	**1. Lawsitán** ... Cross the Salween at the Mantôn ferry.	**12**	**0**	12	0	Direction a little north of west. After crossing the Salween the route strikes up a steep spur to the top of the ridge or range of hills which lie on the western bank of the Salween, and which contains the fixed points Loi Saw, Loi Chaima the route passing between them. The route crosses the ridge and descends the other side into the village Lawsitán situated in paddy-fields. Village contains 30 houses, while there is camping accommodation in the paddy-fields for 200 men. Water rather scarce from small stream; other supplies in small quantities.
		2. Mönghawm (Mönghom).	**12**	**0**	24	0	Road said to be good and downhill the first part of the journey. Mönghawm is a Shan and Palaung village of 50 or 60 houses, and is on the direct route from Theinni to Möngsi and Möngko (*see* Route No. 68, Stage 6). Good supplies obtainable from Kachin villages round about Mönghawm.
		3. Pukwán ... Nammoi or Namwé.	**16**	**0**	40	0	Direction west at first, then turns north and crosses the Nammoi or Namwé stream at mile 8. The route ascends to the village, which is Kachin and contains 20 houses. The road is said to be good travelling. Camping ground in the village for about 100 men. Water-supply rather scarce; supplies obtainable; eggs, &c.
		4. Mansé ...	**12**	**0**	52	0	General direction a little north of west. The road is said to be good all the way. Mansé is a Shan village of 30 houses (*see* in Stage 4 of Route No. 20, Alternative I). Camping ground in paddy-fields; accommodation for 1,000 men. Water and supplies obtainable.

FROM TAWNIO (KÔKÁNG) TO NAMKHAM *viâ* MANTÔN FERRY—*continued.*

Authorities. Military.	Authorities. Civil.	Number and Names of Stages, Rivers and Streams.	Distances. Intermediate. M.	Distances. Intermediate. F.	Distances. Total. M.	Distances. Total. F.	Remarks.
G.O.C. Mandalay District.	Superintendent, Northern Shan States.	4. **Mansé**—*cont.*					*Note.*—The remainder of this route is the same as No. 20, Alternative I, the distances in this route being overestimated, and the total from Mansé to Namkham being brought up to 48 miles instead of 40¼.—A.F.
		5. **Manpin**	11	0	63	0	Direction north-west. Road good and level. Manpin is a Shan village of some 40 houses. Camping ground in paddy-fields near village for 500 men. Water and supplies obtainable.
		6. **Khútché** ...	12	0	75	0	Direction at first west, then north. Road good and level all the way; village contains six houses; Shans. Camping ground on the paddy-fields for 500 men. Water and supplies.
		7. **Pankham** ...	12	0	87	0	Direction north-west. Road level along paddy-fields for a couple of miles when it ascends and then descends again into paddy-fields where Pankham stands; a Shan village of 40 houses. There is a large fifth-day bazaar here attended by Kachins, Palaungs and Shans. There is camping accommodation in the fields for 200 men.
		8. **Namkham** ...	13	0	100	0	Direction north-west. Road good and level after descending into the Shwéli valley. The above route is a direct route from the Salween river to Namkham. It avoids the tract of country inhabited by Kachins, which lies northward, and is the route usually taken by small and unprotected caravans or travellers.

BRANCH I.

FROM HÔN SITÔN HAW (KÔKÁNG), (*see* STAGE 1) TO HONGHAI (KÔKÁNG) *viâ* MÖNGKYENG TERRITORY.

BY CAPT. H. B. WALKER, DUKE OF CORNWALL'S LIGHT INFANTRY, PAID ATTACHÉ, INTELLIGENCE BRANCH (NATIVE INFORMATION), 1892.

Authorities. Military.	Authorities. Civil.	Number and Names of Stages, Rivers and Streams.	Intermediate.	Total.	Remarks.
China.		1. **Namchinli** ...	...	...	Möngkyeng village, visible from Hôn Sitôn Haw to north-east.
		2. **Malileng** ...	...	...	Möngkyeng village.
		3. **Möngpôn** (or **Möngphôn**).	...	...	Möngkyeng village, with large bazaar (*see* Route No. 62, after Stage 11).
G.O.C. Mandalay District.	Supt., Northern Shan States.	4. **Honghai** ...	...	...	Kôkáng village at east extremity of that province (*see* Route No. 62).

FROM TAWNIO (KÔKÁNG) TO NAMKHAM *viâ* MANTÔN FERRY—*continued.*

BRANCH II.

FROM HÔN SITÔN HAW (KÔKÁNG FRONTIER), (*see* STAGE 1) TO MÔN HÔN TA KYI (MÖNGKYENG).

BY CAPT. H. B. WALKER, DUKE OF CORNWALL'S LIGHT INFANTRY, PAID ATTACHÉ, INTELLIGENCE BRANCH (FROM NATIVE INFORMATION), 1892.

Authorities. Military.	Authorities. Civil.	Number and Names of Stages, Rivers and Streams.	Distances. Intermediate. M. F.	Distances. Total. M. F.	Remarks.
China.		**1. Tansán Shwé.**	...	...	Direction north-east. A day's march; road good and level; camping ground for about 200 men; water near the village and supplies.
		2. Môn Twé ... Môn Twé Haw.	...	...	Twenty houses in village Môn Twé; direction north-east, a day's march. Road good, crosses Môn Twé Haw (15 yards broad, 1½ feet deep; stony bed; rapid current). Camping ground in the paddy-fields for about 1,000 men; 10 houses in village; water and supplies obtainable.
		3. Tansán Shwé (2).	...	...	Direction north. A day's march; road uphill and rough. Camping ground near the village for 50 or 60 men only; water from a hill stream; a few supplies; 10 houses in village.
		4. Môn Ta Pa ...	...	...	Direction north. A day's march; road downhill. Camping ground in the paddy-fields for about 1,000 men; water in good supplies; paddy, &c., obtainable. Village contains 50 houses.
		5. Môn Hôn Ta Kyi.	...	...	Direction north. A day's march; road uphill (for description of Môn Hôn Ta Kyi *see* in Route No. 63, Alternative I (2), Stage 6). All the above marches are average marches from 12 to 15 miles, and possible for both troops and transport animals. The route is said to be a good one and in regular use.

BRANCH III.

FROM MANLAW (STAGE 3) TO KYINMALIN (NEAR NORTH-EAST CONFINES OF KÔKÁNG).

BY CAPT. H. B. WALKER, DUKE OF CORNWALL'S LIGHT INFANTRY, PAID ATTACHÉ, INTELLIGENCE BRANCH (NATIVE INFORMATION), JUNE 1892.

Military	Civil	Stages	Intermediate M. F.	Total M. F.	Remarks
G.O.C. Mandalay District.	Superintendent, Northern Shan States.	**1. Kyinmalin** ... Manlaw Haw, 5 yards wide, 6 feet 3 inches deep; mountain stream; rapid; rocky bottom; steep approaches; very difficult though passable for laden animals.	12 0	12 0	Direction east-north-east. Leaving lower and bigger Manlaw the route runs northwards down an excessively steep spur for over 2 miles into the valley of the Manlaw Haw which it crosses twice. The onward route from Manlaw to Honghai *viâ* Shiokai running down a parallel spur to the west (*see* Route No. 62), the route then assumes a more easterly direction and commencing to ascend winds up a

From TAWNIO (KÔKÁNG) to NAMKHAM *viâ* MANTÔN FERRY—*continued.*

BRANCH III—*continued.*

Authorities. Military.	Authorities. Civil.	Number and Names of Stages, Rivers and Streams.	Distances. Intermediate.	Distances. Total.	Remarks.
G.O.C. Mandalay District.	Superintendent, Northern Shan States.	**1. Kyinmalin**—*cont.*			very steep spur for a mile and-a-quarter to the small Kôkáng village of Namushwéyin; six houses; camping ground north of village for 60 men; water from small stream running through village. Few supplies: a little paddy, &c. The path up to this point is narrow, but, except where dips into the valley, good and sound. The ascent and descent bare and open on either side of route, the valley of the Manlaw Haw, which is a mere ravine, being filled with jungle. From Namushwéyin the route continues to ascend by a very steep, though sound, path along ridge or spur. To the village of Hôshishán to left hand or north and below the path a couple of hundred yards Kôkáng; eight houses; scanty supplies; water can here be obtained beyond the village to the north. From this point also a good view is obtained of the Kôkáng villages, Kwanyinkyi, Pangtôn, and Pankwyitung, all of them lying between the main route to Mawhtai (No. 62) and the eastern boundary of Kôkáng. From Hôshishán the route continues to ascend by a good sound path; jungle on both sides; following a lengthy ridge until the top is reached at mile 8, when the route follows the east for 2 miles, then descending and ascending for a mile and finally dropping down again into the village of Kyinmalin, a wretched Kôkáng village of three or four houses; practically no supplies, except opium, which is cultivated here on the hill sides in large quantities. Kyinmalin is a frontier village, the boundary running in front of it, following a south-east ridge (which runs from east to west), then striking north from the western end of the ridge, and, consequently, bearing away from the route as it approaches Hôshishán, Namushwéyin and Manlaw being at least 6 miles distant from the latter place. Kyinmalin is a link of communication between the Mantôn ferry and Hônsitôn Haw (*see* Stage 1 above) a hill route, little used, rough and difficult, leading from Kyinmalin to the latter place in an easterly direction. From the hill of the same name above Kyinmalin, if cleared of the jungle with which it is clothed, a fine view of this angle of Möngkyeng including the Möngkyeng village of Namchienli could be obtained.

No. 65.

From TAWNIO to NANSÁNG viâ SHIOCHANKU.

By Lieut. H. B. WALKER, Paid Attaché, Intelligence Branch, Burma, January 1892.

Military	Civil	Stage	Intermediate	Total	Remarks
G.O.C. Mandalay District.	Superintendent, Northern Shan States.	**1. Shiochanku** ... Mankha Ka.	M. F. **5 0**	M. F. 5 0	General direction east. Leaving Tawnio the route follows a well-defined path, which bears at first north-east, across undulating ground running along a continuation of the long Tawnio valley, being bounded on the left hand or north by the long range of hills containing Loi Sihpaw and Loi Nangai; on the right hand or south by the hills through which the Namting valley route winds. The route runs within a mile of left hand or north range. At mile $1\frac{1}{2}$ the Shan village of Mankha is reached, with

FROM TAWNIO TO NANSÁNG *viâ* SHIOCHANKU—*continued.*

Authorities.		Number and Names of Stages, Rivers and Streams.	Distances.		Remarks.
Military.	Civil.		Inter-mediate.	Total.	
G.O.C. Mandalay District.	Superintendent, Northern Shan States.	**1. Shiochanku** *—cont.*			plentiful water-supply from a stream 2 yards wide, 1 foot deep (diverted from its course to irrigate paddy-field and thence turned down natural well or hollow in ground) and excellent camping ground for a brigade or more. Paddy obtainable. One mile to the south is the Kôkáng village of Monga Shwé or Mongadaing since it is called by both names, where there is also camping ground and water-supply. The valley between the two villages is under cultivation (paddy). Passing Mankha the route runs through the jungle, crossing a stone bridge over a dry nullah from which the water has been diverted to the cultivation. The path alternately ascends and descends short distances to mile 4, where the jungle is left and the valley becomes open again and cultivated ; from this point a path branches to left or north-east to Nansáng, a large village in Köngma 1 mile on other side of frontier and 2 miles distant. The route to Shiochanku continues east reaching that village at mile 5. Shiochanku is a Shán village of 8 or 10 houses, situated in a cleft of a low spur, the frontier running ½ mile in front of or to the east of it. A secondary part of the same village stands on other side of frontier and belongs to Köngma, the boundary or frontier line being marked by the small hill Shiochanku Shán, which lies between the two parts of the village. Supplies few : fowls, pigs, and paddy. The village also possesses a dozen buffaloes, several ponies and half-a-dozen cows. Water from a small stream on frontier line north of village. The route which branches off to Nansáng crosses the frontier by a stone bridge over a stream, Nansáng, lying 1 mile further on within Köngma. This place possesses a bad reputation for harbouring professional robbers who are said to have come from the neighbouring province of Möngkyeng. It has 40 houses, a large camping ground and good water-supply from tanks and wells.

Capt. Walker ascertained that a route leads from here (Nansáng) to Möngpôn (or Möngphôn) in Möngkyeng a day's march from Honghai (*see* Route No. 62, Stage 11). The stages were given to him as follows:—

Military.	Civil.	Number and Names of Stages.	Inter-mediate.	Total.	Remarks.
China.		**1. Huya**	...	...	Direction north-west. Route runs uphill all the way to Huya, a Chinese village of some 60 houses. Camping ground for 100 men near the village and water-supply from hill streams ; paddy and rice obtainable.
		2. Kwanko ...	...	...	Direction north-west. The route follows the crest of a ridge most of the way. Camping ground for about 200 men near the village. Water from hill-side stream. Supplies : paddy and rice obtainable. The village has 15 houses.
		3. Isitôn	...	...	Direction north-west. Road follows the crest of the hills. Camping ground for 100 men ; water, &c. The village has 16 to 20 houses.
		4. Môntwé ...	...	...	Direction north. Route runs downhill into the Môntwé valley.

FROM TAWNIO TO NANSÁNG *viâ* SHIOCHANKU—*continued.*

Authorities. Military.	Authorities. Civil.	Number and Names of Stages, Rivers and Streams.	Distances. Inter-mediate.	Distances. Total.	Remarks.
China.		**5. Chayélin** ...	...	...	Direction north-east. Road ascends again to village which contains about 10 houses. Camping ground near the village for about 100 men.
		6. Möngpôn (or Möngphôn).	...	...	Direction north. Route runs down into the Möngpôn valley. Möngpôn is a large well-to-do village with a fine fifth-day bazaar. Camping ground and water-supply for a large number of men in the paddy-fields round and near the village. All the above stages are those ordinarily in use. The route is said to be a good one and is regularly used.

No. 66.

From TAWNIO to PISHÁNSHWÉ (on Möngting-Kôkáng Border).

BY LIEUT. H. B. WALKER, PAID ATTACHÉ, INTELLIGENCE BRANCH, JANUARY 1892.

Military	Civil	Stage	Inter. M.	Inter. F.	Total M.	Total F.	Remarks
G.O.C. Mandalay District.	Superintendent, Northern Shan States.	**1. Pishánshwé** ...	**1**	**0**	10	0	General direction south-east. The route leaves Tawnio and follows the Namhung-Kunlôn route, branching up the Möngting route valley (*see* Route No. 63), which it follows for ¼ mile, thence striking by a good path south-east, skirting the lower slopes of a series of hills forming magnificent ranges on either side of path which rises as it proceeds. After a mile and-a-quarter and after passing behind the southern slope of Kyin Kyu Lin Shán, a small valley running from north-east, south-west is crossed, the route then running eastward up a steep rise by a broken path for ¾ of a mile when it drops down into a small circular valley in which stands the Kôkáng village of Kyu Shin; 10 houses; few supplies; water being obtainable only from a small tank of filthy dirty water. From here along a steep climb of over a mile the path ascends south through a cultivated strip (entirely opium), the hills on all sides sloping steeply towards the path which thus runs up through an indentation. Half-way up the path makes a western bend as far as the top when running between two low hills it passes the Kôkáng village of Takantan; six or seven houses: a few supplies; a filthy tank the only water-supply. The route then bears eastward crossing a narrow valley up a steep ascent and after winding along the western side of a low hill drops down into Píshánshwé at mile 10; 15 houses; purely Kôkáng. No supplies except pig and no water except that contained in two filthy tanks which is all the inhabitants have to drink. Several other villages, each as badly supplied with water, lie south of Píshánshwé and close to the frontier which runs ½ mile east of and below the hill beneath which the village stands.

No. 67.

From THEINNI (SENWI) MYOMA to KUNLÔN FERRY.

BY CAPT. A. C. YATE, 2ND BELOOCHEES, 1888, AND LIEUTS. WALKER AND PROWSE, ATTACHÉS, INTELLIGENCE BRANCH, BURMA, JANUARY 1892.

Authorities. Military.	Authorities. Civil.	Number and Names of Stages, Rivers and Streams.	Distances. Intermediate. M.	Distances. Intermediate. F.	Distances. Total. M.	Distances. Total. F.	Remarks.
G.O.C. Mandalay District.	Superintendent, Northern Shan States.	**1. Tánkaw** ...	**10**	**4**	10	4	*See* Route No. 68, Stages 1 and 2.
		2. Namsarap ...	**8**	**0**	18	4	
		3. Náti ... ... Namtu, Namyé, Namnim, and other smaller streams.	**12**	**0**	30	4	General direction east. Road very difficult for transport animals, not so much on account of the steepness of the gradients as on account of the swampy places, which are due to the fact that the hills crossed (which here form the watershed between the Irrawaddy and the Salween) are saturated with water to the very surface. Here and there this water collects and forms a bog into which animals sink to their girths. Leaving the camp in the paddy-fields below the village of Namsarap the track runs through high kaing grass for ¼ of a mile crossing a nullah just after entering jungle with slippery banks and requiring bridging for much traffic. At ½ a mile a path leads to the left or north to the Shan village of Manpôk, ⅓ of a mile distant; five or six houses. The same village is approached by another path a little further on, and here also the road to Möngsi branches off (*see* Route No. 68). At 1 mile path descends about 50 yards to a nullah with swampy approaches, then along level for a short distance and up steep ascent on to firm ground passing at 1⅛ miles a path to left or north leading to the Kachin village of Kônlông, 3 miles distant, containing five or six houses. At 2 miles the Namkát stream, good water, is crossed with bad approaches. A swamp extends on the far side for 20 yards, across which path runs up slight ascent on to level ground; thick jungle and kaing grass on both sides of the path all the way. Here path to left or north leads to Paliáng, a small Shan village, ½ mile distant; five or six houses. The path also crosses a nullah here. At this point a large peak to the left front, Loi Paliáng, comes into view, beneath which a valley runs and into which a path descends just past village (off the route). The route crossing the valley, which is about 300 yards wide here, very swampy and difficult for pack animals, then crosses the Namtu or Myitngé stream (7 yards wide, 1½ feet deep and flowing 2 miles to 2½ miles an hour; stony bottom; slippery crossing) and a bad nullah immediately beyond at 2¼ miles. Just beyond this a broad clearing cultivated with rice called Nahôtu and belonging to a Kachin village 1 or 2 miles off in the hills to the south. Camping ground for a large force. Water, fuel and fodder abundant. Up to this point the road runs through thick tree and grass jungle, except where there are rice clearings. The route then runs along the east (or south) side of the valley on rather higher ground and firm under foot crossing a succession of low spurs and passing Loi Paliáng at 3¼ miles where there is a bad swamp 30 or 40 yards wide and only passable by a small number of troops at a time. At 3¼ miles the Nam Kônlông (1 foot deep; stony and rapid; 3 yards wide) is crossed. A path to right hand or south running up ascent to Kachin village Loikáng 3 or 3½ miles off. At mile 5 the path again crosses the Namtu (or Myitngé, here a mere stream) and a very bad

FROM THEINNI (SENWI) MYOMA TO KUNLÔN FERRY—*continued*.

Authorities. Military.	Authorities. Civil.	Number and Names of Stages, Rivers and Streams.	Distances. Inter-mediate.	Distances. Total.	Remarks.
G.O.C. Mandalay District.	Superintendent, Northern Shan States.	**3. Náti**—*cont.*			swamp beyond. From here path begins to ascend crest of an easy spur rising between the hills on either side of valley which here close in, the Loi Lu Tu being passed to the left hand or north. The path now crosses the watershed between the Namtu (Myitngé) and the Salween rivers. After ascending for some considerable distance the path drops down by a steep and difficult ascent, being intersected by a bad bog almost impassable for lightly-laden pack animals. Another swamp occurs 200 or 300 yards further, after which the path winds along the spur still descending. At 7 miles a path crosses the road and runs to a Kachin village on the right called Loisaung. At 9 miles Loi Náti at head of valley above Náti is seen, the path descending for 2¾ miles crossing four nullahs, unbridged, and one roughly bridged, into the valley of the Namyé stream, ¼ of a mile across old paddy and grass fields and Upper Náti is reached; a Shan village of 20 houses. It is situated on rising ground, while a short spur runs east to a knoll on which a kyaung is situated. The Namyé is 15 yards wide; stony; 1 foot deep and rapid and runs into the Namnim to the north. There is camping ground to north of village in large paddy-fields for a brigade. Water to north of camp in Namyé and Namnim streams. The knoll on which kyaung stands affords good defensive position for 400 men, the hills commanding it being too far distant to be dangerous. Grass for animals abundant. Supplies in village: few eggs and vegetables. From Náti there is said to be a difficult foot-path straight over the hills to the north-east to Möngtám, to which place the proper road branches off at Sôptáng, 5½ miles further on towards Kunlôn (*see* Alternative No. I below).
			M. F.	M. F.	
		4. Namlôk ... Namnim and Namti.	**8 0**	38 4	General direction east. Leaving the camp in paddy-fields which lie to the left hand or north of the village the route runs along paddy and grass fields which lie on right bank of Namnim river (here 40 yards wide, 2 miles to 2½ miles an hour and unfordable except at a point about a mile from Upper Náti and close to Lower Náti) for about a mile, passing Lower Náti (whence an alternative route to Kunlôn branches off to the left following the valley of the Namnim, *see* Alternative No. I below), the path then crosses the Namti stream (7 yards wide; 1 foot deep; rapid current; stony bottom, with short steep ascent towards east side) and runs by a well-defined mule and bullock track for more than ½ a mile along eastern side of valley and then ascends by a steep ascent a spur from Loi Pángwa. Here the Loi Nongchu to the south or right hand, and the Loi Pansák to the north-east or left, are visible on either side. Half-way up spur the slope becomes more gradual and the path runs along below the ridge of the spur to 2½ miles where a path to left hand or north leads towards Taung chaung. The route following the spur now winds along its north-east side ascending and descending for short distances, but rising generally. At mile 3 the Loi Pengyé comes in view to the left hand or north and Loi Pyé or Loi Nung to right hand or south, the path in places becomes very narrow and difficult, and in wet weather would be impassable to mounted men. Numerous tracks of wild elephants are visible; many quite fresh. After the 3rd mile a path to right or south leads to

FROM THEINNI (SENWI) MYOMA TO KUNLÔN FERRY—*continued.*

Authorities. Military.	Authorities. Civil.	Number and Names of Stages, Rivers and Streams.	Distances. Intermediate.	Distances. Total.	Remarks.
G.O.C. Mandalay District.	Superintendent, Northern Shan States.	**4. Namlôk**—*cont.*			Hôti, a small Kachin village, and at mile 4½ another path strikes off to the left or north-east to smaller Pôngwa; said to be difficult and not much used by other than foot traffic. At 5⅜ miles another path to left or north-east runs to this village; an offshoot of the larger village and only containing three houses. This descent ½ a mile difficult and steep. Scanty water-supply here. Direction now south-east. At 6¼ miles the bigger village of Pôngwa is reached; six or seven houses; Kachins; from here a path to the right hand or south leads to Möngkyet. From Pôngwa the route turning north-east again runs down a steep descent to a nullah with slippery crossing up a steep ascent and down again, three nullahs and three spurs being crossed in succession. Each passable with difficulty to laden animals and possessing slippery approaches. The last ¾ of a mile run along the spur leading to the village of Namlôk and the path here is good; the camping ground lies to the right hand or east of path, about 70 feet below it and 200 yards before reaching the village. It is a small plateau circular in shape and rather uneven on surface; capable of affording accommodation for 250 men, while a similar number could find room on the path above just before reaching the camp where the spur flattens out, though with difficulty. Grass abundant and plenty of water for 500 men in stream below or further to east of the camp. Namlôk is a Kachin village of eight houses under the Sawbwaship of Kángmöng. Supplies: paddy in small quantities for perhaps 50 horses or ponies and obtained from taungya cultivation on eastern side of camp; pigs and fowls.
		5. Kángmöng ...	M. 7 F. 4	M. 46 F. 0	General direction first 3 miles east-north-east, last 4½ miles east-south-east. Leaving the village of Namlôk the route runs along a well-defined spur by a good path, descending gradually for 3½ miles. At ¼ mile from Namlôk a path to right hand or south leads to the Kachin village of Loi Ning about 1 mile distant (10 houses). For the first 1½ miles the road bears towards the prominent hill Loi Pengyé in the range to the north passing Loi Namsam to the left or north at about 1¼ miles. Half-a-mile further a path leads to the left to Kônsa, another path from the same place striking in again a little further on. The path here is very narrow running along the southern side of a knoll for a short distance passing on to the ridge of the spur again and descending by short stretches. At 3 miles a view is obtained towards the south of the onwards path running below in a southerly direction along valley covered with high kaing grass. At 3¼ miles, just before reaching the turn south into the valley, a path to the left and running eastward leads to the Kachin village of Namleng (five houses at the foot of the hill Loi Pha Pheik). The route now follows the valley in a southerly direction for ½ a mile by a good sound path, a track crossing the road at this point leading from Namleng. A little further on a path to the right leads to the remains of a deserted Chinese village, Loi Kyáng; all its inhabitants having died from fever in 1889. At 4th mile the jungle is again entered and the path which now inclines south-east descends slightly over rough and stony ground, then across a small oval valley intersected by the stream Mônlông Hpa at 4½ miles. At mile 4¾ passing through young jungle a path crosses route

FROM THEINNI (SENWI) MYOMA TO KUNLÔN FERRY—*continued.*

Authorities. Military.	Authorities. Civil.	Number and Names of Stages, Rivers and Streams.	Distances. Intermediate.	Distances. Total.	Remarks.
G.O.C. Mandalay District.	Superintendent, Northern Shan States.	**5. Kángmöng**—*cont.*			leading from Loi Nim into cultivation. At mile $5\frac{1}{2}$ paths to left lead to villages of Nonglông and Ho Káng, two Kachin villages lying to the north and about $1\frac{1}{8}$ miles distant. At mile 6 the Namtauk is crossed (a small stream 3 or 4 yards wide, 4 feet deep with slippery banks, $2\frac{1}{2}$ feet to 3 feet high). An excellent path then leads through large park-like jungle for more than $\frac{3}{4}$ of a mile; fine trees capable of supplying large quantities of building timber predominating. The route then crosses the Namkángmöng (5 yards wide; 6 inches to 1 foot deep; level crossings and always easily passable), on the opposite bank of which there is accommodation for 300 men, though the surface is uneven. The route crosses this camping ground and after $\frac{1}{4}$ of a mile reaches the lower village of Kángmöng; four houses; Shan and Kachins. Here there is accommodation on a small camping ground below, and on a space capable of being cleared above the village for 200 men. Water supplied by a streamlet close to camping ground, but not of very good quality. A path from Möngkyet from the south, on another route to Kunlôn (*see* Route No. 6) passes through the upper village of Kángmöng, a little over $\frac{1}{2}$ a mile distant from the lower village. It consists of 22 houses, Kachin, and is the residence of the Sawbwa, whose power extends back to Namlôk and eastward to Pángwo. Grass is plentiful though of a coarse kind. Supplies of the two villages combined: paddy in some quantity, rice, fowls, pigs, and a very few vegetables. Here the route from Möngkyet joins in from the south-west (*see* Route No. 6), forming an important connecting route between the Supkyet and Kunlôn ferries.
		6. Pángwo ... Kangmöng and Möngleng streams.	M. F. 7 4	M. F. 53 4	General direction east-north-east. Good path throughout, but steep descents and ascents. On leaving Kángmöng the path, which averages 4 feet in width, runs over undulating wooded country in an easterly direction for $\frac{1}{8}$ mile, it then turns into a small valley overgrown with kaing grass crossing a small rivulet. At 1 mile the path averaging 2 feet in width runs out of the valley over the Kángmöng stream which it crosses by a ford. The stream is 15 feet broad, 18 inches deep, except when in flood; gravelly bottom; current from $1\frac{1}{2}$ to 2 miles per hour. Firm banks on either side. During the rainy season it is waist-deep, but bullocks can cross it all the year round. Thence it leads through kaing grass ascending a small spur and descending to the Möng-Leng stream at 1 mile, 600 yards. One hundred yards further on another branch of the same small stream is crossed. At $1\frac{1}{2}$ miles a path strikes off to the right leading to the village of Nam-syékha beyond the Salween river. At $1\frac{3}{4}$ miles a path to the left leads to Namleng village and another to the right to deserted village of Patu. At 2 miles the path, which here turns to the north, begins to ascend a spur of Loi Pyé through taungya clearing. For the next mile the ascent is steep until at $3\frac{1}{8}$ miles the range of Loi Pengyé to the north of the Namnim river comes in sight, the ground falling steeply away on the left hand to the valley of the Nam Leng stream. After another steep ascent the Kachin village of Lower

FROM THEINNI (SENWI) MYOMA TO KUNLÔN FERRY—*continued.*

Authorities. Military.	Authorities. Civil.	Number and Names of Stages, Rivers and Streams.	Distances. Intermediate.	Distances. Total.	Remarks.
G.O.C. Mandalay District.	Superintendent, Northern Shan States.	**6. Pángwo**—*cont.*			Loipyé (two houses) is reached at 4¼ miles. Thence the path again ascends through wooded jungle to Upper Loipyé (Kachin 12 houses) 5 miles. A path strikes off here to the north to the village of Mankwé. From here the path runs east along the crest for another ¼ mile where the descent to Pángwo commences. A view is obtained at this point over the valley of the Salween river to the north-east. The path, which continues to descend, passes through Upper Pángwo Kachin village, seven houses at 7 miles, whence Lower Pángwo is reached ½ mile further down the hill. This also is a Kachin village. Good but small camping ground in the village itself for about 100 men. Water ¼ mile downhill to the north-east and also 500 yards downhill to the north. A few pigs and poultry obtainable.
		7. Kunlôn ferry. Salween, Namsa (or Namnim), and other streams.	M. 9 F. 2	M. 62 F. 6	General direction first 5 miles north, then east. On leaving the village of Lower Pángwo the path descends along a spur at about ¼ mile, the first view of the Salween ahead is obtained while the Loi Pyé range is visible above the same valley. At mile 2½ the spur flattens and the path becomes level, while a route joins in from the right hand or south-east from upper village of Pángma, the lower village being passed at 2¾ miles; six houses; Kachin. The path is good under foot though narrow. At ¾ mile the path runs down a steep descent above and to the east of a circular valley along which the Nam Hubôn flows. At mile 4 a path to left or north leads to Namsa river, while a further descent by a rather broken path leads to the junction of the Namna stream (or Namugé as Capt. Yate calls it) with the Namsa, (or as Capt. Yate calls it the Namnim) river. The latter river is fordable here, the ford being indicated by a path on opposite bank. The Namna river is 20 yards wide; 1 foot deep, rapid; stony bottom. The Namsa or Namnim river is 40 yards broad; generally deep though fordable opposite junction with Namna; 2½ miles an hour. One-fourth of a mile past junction there is a good camping ground, on the right bank of the Namsa (or Namnim) for 300 men, and another place on the higher ground in a kaing grass clearing for as many more. Here the alternative route from Náti *viâ* Sôptáng joins in (*see* Alternative I below). The route now runs along the valley of the Namsa (or Namnim). At 5½ miles a path to the right or east leads to the village of Pansák. At mile 6¼ just before junction of the Namsa (or Namnim) and Salween a bamboo bridge over former stream leads to village on opposite bank, Pônkyet. About mile 6½ the Namsán flows into the Salween which here, flowing from the north, takes an eastward bend as far as Kunlôn. The route then runs along the right bank of the Salween at an elevation of 30 or 40 feet above the stream. At mile 7¼ the Namsa (or Namnim) stream is crossed. At mile 7¾ the path descends into the river bed,

FROM THEINNI (SENWI) MYOMA TO KUNLÔN FERRY—*continued.*

Authorities. Military.	Authorities. Civil.	Number and Names of Stages, Rivers and Streams.	Distances. Inter-mediate.	Distances. Total.	Remarks.
G.O.C. Mandalay District.	Superintendent, Northern Shan States.	**7. Kunlôn ferry**—*cont.*			which, sometimes sandy and sometimes rocky, and intersected by strips of wet ground rising from springs, is followed as far as Kunlôn. The bank above is steep and covered with kaing grass. There is an upper path through the jungle, but it is at present broken down and out of repair. In flood season however this upper route would have to be used, the lower route being in many places much below flood level, and a good permanent road could be made there if the jungle were cleared. West Kunlôn is reached at mile 9¼. It is a Shan village of 15 or 20 houses, and the residence of a Sawbwa or Amát under the Theinni Sawbwa. The village has a good bazaar every fifth day, where food supplies in small quantities may be obtained. The wild Wás occasionally visit this bazaar trading paddy for salt, &c. The main village which is on the east (left) bank of the river has about 30 houses. There is excellent camping ground in paddy-fields about ¼ of a mile before reaching West Kunlôn, but only available in the dry season of course. Wood, grass and water abundant. The Salween is here 226 yards wide, 18 feet deep, and it flows 2½ miles an hour. Half-a-dozen ferry boats at most obtainable. A short distance above and below the ferry rapids render navigation, even in light boats, dangerous. It is said to be possible, though very dangerous to travel by boat from Kunlôn to Möngnong ferry (*see* Route No. 5.).

ALTERNATIVE I.

FROM NÁTI (STAGE 3) TO KUNLÔN (STAGE 7).

BY CAPT. A. C. YATE, 2ND BELOOCHEES, 1888.

Military.	Civil.	Number and Names of Stages, Rivers and Streams.	Inter-mediate.	Total.	Remarks.
			M. F.	M. F.	
G.O.C. Mandalay District.	Superintendent, Northern Shan States.	**1. Sôptáng** ... Namnim river and one or two small streams.	5 4	5 4	Road very bad. The best proof of its difficulty is the fact that the rear guard of a small column, whose advance guard left Náti at 8 A.M. did not reach Sôptáng till 4-15 P.M. The Namnim river is only once forded. This is about half-way and the ford is easy, water 2 feet deep, moderate current, bottom stony. The road at first keeps to right bank of the Namnim river. At ⅜ mile cross Namhinleng stream, flowing north into the Namnim, and at ¾ mile pass Lower Náti village; seven or eight houses. From here the road *viâ* Kángmöng branches off as described above. At 3 miles cross Nammin by ford. At 4 miles cross small stream. Here path to left to Kachin village. At 5¼ miles path to left leading over hills to Möngtám. Bullocks are sometimes brought by this path, so it must be practicable for pack transport. At 5½ miles reach Namtáng flowing from the north into the Namnim. The level ground lying at the foot of the hills in the angle formed by the Namnim and Namtáng is called Sôptáng. If the jungle was cleared, this would form an excellent camping ground for a largish force. Troops can also be encamped on the left bank of the Namtáng. At this point a foot path from Möngtám to Kángmöng crosses the road. The Namnim is here crossed on a bamboo raft which is kept moored here for the use of travellers to and fro. The Namtáng stream is the western boundary of the Kunlôn district.

FROM THEINNI (SENWI) MYOMA TO KUNLÔN FERRY—*continued.*

ALTERNATIVE I—*continued.*

Authorities. Military.	Authorities. Civil.	Number and Names of Stages, Rivers and Streams.	Distances. Intermediate.	Distances. Total.	Remarks.
G.O.C. Mandalay District.	Superintendent, Northern Shan States.	**2. Pángpyet** ... Namnim and several small streams.	M. 5 F. 1	M. 10 F. 5	Very difficult road and, having been but little used for one or two years, had in places to be made and cleared. The baggage of a small column took 10 hours to do this stage and lost several mules and ponies that slipped and fell down steep inclines. Gradients in places very steep and in others the soil is so saturated with water as to form a bog in which mules and ponies flounder up to their girths. There is very little doubt that any force marching between Theinni and Kunlôn should use the route *viâ* Kángmöng unless its transport consists solely of coolies. The road follows the left bank of the Namnim all the way. At 2½ miles is the halting place of Pángtám. Not more than 100 men with their transport, &c., can camp there. At Pángpyet (5⅛ miles) from 200 to 300 Infantry with their transport can find room to camp. Water, grass, and fuel abundant.
		3. Kunlôn ... Namnim river by ford, Sôptám and other streams.	11 6	22 3	Road is difficult for pack transport for the first 5 miles. There are swampy bits to cross, and here and there steep gradients. The road, however, throughout is much better than that of the two previous stages. For the remaining 6¾ miles the path, though often very narrow and steep, is good. The jungle and the bamboos overhead require cutting and clearing away. The path from the point where the Namnim flows into the Salween (Namkong) to Kunlôn is in many places much below flood level. Presumably in the flood season the path is carried through the jungle above. A very good permanent road could be made at the higher level, if the jungle were cleared away. At ¾ mile Pángön camping ground, room for 100 men. At 1½ miles Namleng stream comes in from south. This stream flows from Kángmöng and is crossed on the road from Kunlôn to Kángmöng. At 2 miles path to left to Kachin village of Man-wyeng-yé, said to be 2½ daings distant up in the hills. At 2¼ miles Pángyi camping ground, room for 100 men. At 5½ miles Pángsán camping ground, room for 100 men. At 6 miles hills on left bank recede. Here Phásán camping ground, room for two or three battalions, but jungle requires clearing. Fuel and grass abundant. At 7¾ miles Sôpngé, the place where the Namngé called by Lieuts. Walker and Prowse the Namma, flows into the Namnim, called by the officers just mentioned the Namsa, from the south. Just above the junction is a weir. Two other weirs are passed higher up. They are made by the Kachins, of whom there are many living in the hills north and south of the Namnim valley for fishing purposes. The Namnim is forded just below the Sôpngé weir. There is no good camping ground here on the left bank of the Namnim, but from 200 to 300 men can be encamped in several divisions on the right bank in the angle between the Namnim and Namngé. Here the road from Kángmöng joins in from the south-west. The high hills to the north of Sôpngé are called Loi Pengyé.

From THEINNI (SENWI) MYOMA to KUNLÔN FERRY—*continued.*

BRANCH I.

From KÁNGMÖNG (see Stage 2) to TA SUPKYET FERRY (see Route No. 30, Stage 14).

By Capt. A. C. YATE, 2nd Beloochees, 1888.

Authorities. Military.	Authorities. Civil.	Number and Names of Stages, Rivers and Streams.	Distances. Intermediate.	Distances. Total.	Remarks.
			M. F.	M. F.	
G.O.C. Mandalay District.	Superintendent, Northern Shan States.	**1. Mansák** ...	**6 0**	5 0	This route branches off from the direct route from Kángmöng to Möngkyet at the village of Maumaw 1½ miles south of Kángmöng. The general direction from Kángmöng to Supkyet is south-south-west. The road as far as the large village of Mansák is a good one for any pack transport. From Mansák to Suptaw, where the Namtaw falls into the Salween, the road is somewhat difficult, steadily and rapidly descending and traversing thickish jungle. For 6 miles from Manmaw the road traverses an open undulating and comparatively populous and fertile country. The people are all Kachins. Every village abounds with pigs, fowls and eggs, also some oxen and buffaloes. Opium, mustard, and rice are largely cultivated. Seven-eighths of a mile beyond Manmaw path to left to Kachin Kángmöng. At 1⅜ miles two Kachin villages (close together) called Lwékám (about 20 houses). At 2 miles the descent to the Salween commences, but only becomes steep a mile or two beyond Mansák. At 2¾ miles village of Nongkám (eight houses). Here path to left to village of Pákum, a mile off. At 3½ miles village of Nongmôn. Ten houses. Water from wells. From here road west by south to Möngkyet (said to be 4 daings distance). At 6 miles large Kachin village of Mansák, 40 to 50 houses.
		2. Supkyet ferry (Ta Supkyet).	**10 4**	16 4	Beyond Mansák the road becomes less marked, being evidently less used. It continues good for 2 miles beyond Mansák, after which the gradients are often steep and the path narrow, rocky, and winding along the almost precipitous slopes of the valley of the Namtaw. At 4 miles reach Shan village of Wengsôn. Ten houses. Thence steep descent for 1½ miles to the ford over the Namtaw. Here there is room for 50 men to camp; 50 can camp on the opposite bank just at the mouth of the Namtaw which falls into the Salween 200 yards below the ford. The Salween is here as at Kunlôn 200 yards broad, the current being more rapid. The Namtaw is 20 yards broad by 1½ feet deep. Ford itself is easy, but banks very steep and require ramping. The right bank is especially steep and slippery. The village of Pánglôn is 1 mile distant up the same bank of Salween (right). Cross Namtaw at once. Banks steep and slippery. Then for 3½ miles through jungle by narrow paths mostly along precipitous slopes above Salween. Then descend to Tingtán. (Formerly village there, whence ferry also known as Ta Tingtán.) Thence along sands to opposite Supkyet ½ mile, Shan village of 10 houses. Pays revenue to Lawa chief of Suma. Only two small dug-outs at ferry. No caravan trade now worth speaking of. Four marches hence to Pánglôn and one to Möngkyet, *see* Route No. 30.

No. 68.

From THEINNI-MYOMA to MÖNGKO (Route No. 20) viâ MÖNGSI.

By Lieut. S. WILLCOCK, Gloucestershire Regiment, Intelligence Department, June 1889, and Lieut. G. W. T. PROWSE, 1st Duke of Cornwall's Light Infantry, Attaché, Intelligence Branch, January 1891.

Authorities. Military.	Authorities. Civil.	Number and Names of Stages, Rivers and Streams.	Distances. Intermediate. M.	F.	Distances. Total. M.	F.	Remarks.
G.O.C. Mandalay District.	Superintendent, Northern Shan States.	**1. Tánkaw** ... Nammyin, Namsiri, and several swampy nullahs.	**10**	**4**	10	4	General direction east. Road on the whole fairly good. The path crosses several swampy nullahs, keeping along the northern edge of the valley. At 1½ miles the village of Pánglaw is passed. At 2¼ miles the path descends into paddy-fields and at 3½ miles crosses the Nammyin river (30 yards broad, 2 feet deep (in May only 20 yards broad and 8 inches deep), pebbly bottom; mud banks; 3 to 4 feet high; current from 4 to 5 miles per hour) to the village of Naku; thence it runs south-east and east to Séung, after which the country is covered with grass and scrub jungle until the camp is reached at Tánkaw, the site of a deserted village. The Namsiri (12 yards broad, 6 inches deep, good ford), is crossed at 5¾ miles. The path is unmetalled throughout; breadth from 3 to 6 feet. Very bad swamp at 9½ miles. Owing to the numerous swampy, unbridged nullahs this route would not be passable for pack transport during the rains. *Villages passed.*—Ving-náng, 1 mile, 30 houses. Pánglaw, 1½ miles; 24 houses. Manháko (or Manmaket) 2¾ miles; 12 houses. Ngakö, 3¾ miles. Séung, 5½ miles; 30 houses. There is camping ground on the site of Tánkaw village for 100 men, also a zayát, in bad repair, to hold 20 men. Water from stream at camp, 5 inches deep and 3 feet wide. Supplies in small quantities obtainable from Tansaw village 2½ miles off. Paddy at 4 annas per basket. It might be preferable to make Séung or the Namsiri stream the first halting place and march thence to Namsaráp on the second day. There is good camping ground on the west of Séung village. Supplies and paddy easily obtainable with due notice. At Namsiri there is also camping ground in a jungle clearing by the stream, whence good and plentiful water-supply is available.
		2. Namsarap ... Namtu, Namsán, Namkö, and Namsarap.	**8**	**0**	18	4	General direction east. The path follows the north side of the valley for the first 2 miles, then along the centre, following the right bank of the Namtu river. At 6¾ miles the path leaves the river bank and ascends to Kônkaw seven houses; thence it descends steeply through thick jungle to the Namsarap stream, which is crossed by a ford, to camp at 8 miles. Camping ground for a large force in paddy-fields between Namsarap village and the stream of that name. There is a bad swampy crossing ½ mile after leaving Tánkaw. With this exception the road is good throughout. Breadth 3 to 4 feet. Namsarap is a Shan village of 16 houses. The road throughout this stage is hardly ever more than a mile from the Namtu, so that water and space for camping could be found at almost any required length of march.

FROM THEINNI-MYOMA TO MÖNGKO (ROUTE No. 20) *viâ* MÖNGSI—*continued.*

Authorities.		Number and Names of Stages, Rivers and Streams.	Distances.				Remarks.
Military.	Civil.		Intermediate.		Total.		
			M.	F.	M.	F.	
G.O.C. Mandalay District.	Superintendent, Northern Shan States.	**3. Ômli (deserted).** One stream.	**5**	**4**	24	0	General direction north. The path runs through jungle for the 1st mile; bad, marshy crossing at ¾ mile from camp. At 1 mile pass Manpôk, eight houses, very little water. At the end of the 1st mile the path turns north and begins to ascend the hills on the south side of the Namtu valley. The path becomes gradually steeper ascending by zigzags, then winding along the side of a wooded ridge to Konglung (or Kungsum) 4½ miles (12 houses, Kachin) very little water. From there it descends into a grassy valley to camping ground on the edge of a stream at the site of the deserted village of Ômli. The path from Namsarap to Ômli has been recently remade by order of the North Theinni Sawbwa, and, though very steep, is good throughout and 4 to 6 feet in width. The only bridges are small single plank ones, but transport can easily cross by the side cuts. Small camping ground at Ômli for 100 men. Water-supply limited from stream 4 feet wide, 1 foot deep. Supplies obtainable from Konglung village. Paddy Re. 1 per basket.
		4. Yungmaw ... Namnim.	**13**	**0**	37	0	General direction north. The path ascends through jungle; very steep hill at 1½ miles overlooking Konglung village, thence it passes over high and jungly ground to the 5th mile, where it skirts the side of Loi Lôngwai, crossing several swampy places at 6½ miles. At 7½ miles pass Lôngwai, eight houses, and road begins to descend to the valley of the Namnim river, which is crossed by a ford at 10 miles (depth 3½ feet, breadth 40 to 50 yards; water clear and good; low wooded banks; pebble bottom; alternate rapids and pools; current from 2 to 6 miles per hour. The bank on the Yungmau side requires clearing to enable a fresh landing place to be made, as at present there is a deep and muddy pool close under the bank; 4 feet deep). From the river the path leads through grassy jungle rising slightly until Yungmaw village is reached. Path unmetalled throughout. *Bridges.*—At 11½ miles wooden plank bridge, 12 feet long, 4 feet wide; passable for transport. There are also a few single plank foot-bridges. Yungmaw, 31 houses, is a Shan village. Camping ground for about 100 men on the north side of kyaung and for a large force in the paddy-fields on the south of the village. The kyaung is of bamboo and would accommodate about 70 men. Water and supplies plentiful, but one day's notice should be given if possible. Paddy 12 annas per basket.
		5. Möngsi ... Namtam (or Namtin).	**14**	**0**	51	0	General direction north-east. After leaving Yungmaw the path leads over undulating country open or thin jungle, for 1½ miles, after which it drops into paddy-fields crossing three small nullahs, all of which are bridged. From here to 4 miles the path lies through grass and wooded country alternately. At 4 miles the path turns east and follows the gorge of the Namtam (or Namtin) stream (shingly bottom; current 3 miles per hour; breadth 30 feet, depth 2½ feet; muddy banks 6 feet high; paddy-fields on either side), which

FROM THEINNI-MYOMA TO MÖNGKO (ROUTE NO. 20) *viâ* MÖNGSI—*continued.*

Authorities.		Number and Names of Stages, Rivers and Streams.	Distances.		Remarks.
Military.	Civil.		Intermediate.	Total.	
G.O.C. Mandalay District.	Superintendent, Northern Shan States.	**5. Möngsi**—*cont.*			it crosses by a ford at 5½ miles, after which it again turns north-east and north; passes village of Sanking at 12th mile where the Möngsi valley begins to open out. The path skirts the southern edge of the valley to the 13th mile and then crosses paddy-fields to Möngsi village situated on the north side of the valley. The path is unmetalled, but very good throughout, breadth 3 to 4 feet, with the exception of a rough, stone-paved causeway, 3 feet wide for the last mile before reaching Möngsi. *Bridges.*—Stone bridge at 13th mile at the edge of the Möngsi valley consisting of one segmental arch of hewn stone. Span 10 feet, breadth of roadway 4 feet. Height of key-stone above water level about 6 feet in dry weather. Built by Chinese-Shan masons. *Villages passed.*—At 1¾ miles Nangu, 15 houses; at 2 miles Loi Pwi, 10 houses. Man Namting, 5¾ miles, 20 houses. Man Sanking, 12 miles, eight houses. Manpun and Pángnai, 13 miles, six houses each. Möngsi is a Shan village containing 50 houses and the residence of the headman of the circle. There is unlimited camping ground in the paddy-fields outside the village. A small kyaung with large bamboo *zayáts* is built on the hill at the back of the village. The *zayáts* would accommodate 50 to 70 men. Water and supplies plentiful; five-day bazaar held here which is well attended. Paddy 6 annas per basket. *Note.*—When marching with pack-bullock transport it will be found preferable to make three stages from Ômli to Möngsi, thus— (1) Ômli to Namnim river. One day's supply of paddy to be taken; camp by river side. Supplies from Lôngwai village. (2) Namnim river to Namping village; camp in paddy-fields. Supplies and paddy from village. Notice required. (3) Namping to Möngsi.
		6. Mönghawm ... Namnim.	M. F. **16 0**	M. F. 67 0	General direction north. Road leads in a westerly direction through village over rough stone-paved causeway 4 to 5 feet wide. On western edge of village it crosses small stream, 10 feet wide, 18 inches deep by a ford, the stone bridge at this point being broken down; thence it skirts north edge of Möngsi valley for 1½ miles over open and undulating country. At 1½ miles meets Namnim river; leads through short pass between wooded hills and then follows left bank of river to the north-west; leads through paddy-fields following the course of the river which it crosses by ford at 4½ miles (depth 3 to 4 feet, breadth 30 feet; current 3 to 4 miles per hour; banks 6 feet high, steep and muddy; rocky bottom); thence in a northerly direction passing Pinkhán village at 6¼ miles, built on a narrow neck of cultivated land; thence the path ascends steeply through narrow, hollow road thickly wooded on both sides, from there over grassy undulations to Longhoi village 8¾ miles (30 houses, Kachin). From here the path runs north-west and north through grassy valley to Mankong village 10½ miles (20 houses, Kachin); ascends slightly through grassy jungle to stream at 14½ miles; wooden bridge at this point unsound; thence through wooded valley descending sharply to Mönghawm village at

FROM THEINNI-MYOMA TO MÖNGKO (ROUTE NO. 20) *viâ* MÖNGSI—*continued.*

Authorities. Military	Authorities. Civil.	Number and Names of Stages, Rivers and Streams.	Distances. Intermediate.	Distances. Total.	Remarks.
G.O.C. Mandalay District.	Superintendent, Northern Shan States.	**6. Mönghawm**—*cont.*			16 miles. Road unmetalled throughout, with exception of rough paved causeway in Möngsi village, which carts could not traverse. Average breadth of path 3 feet; passable for pack transport, but difficult in wet weather owing to sharp ascents and descents; bad swampy crossing; 10 miles. *Bridges.*—All passable for transport (pack). At 1¼ miles wooden bridge, 20 feet long, 4 feet wide; at 9¾ miles wooden bridge, 20 feet long, 4 feet wide; at 10 miles two wooden bridges, 12 feet long, 3 feet wide; broken wooden bridge at 14½ miles: timber for repairs procurable close at hand. *Positions.*—Strong position on wooded hill on bank of Namnim river at 1½ miles, commanding road east to Möngsi and north to Mönghawm. Mönghawm 50 to 60 houses, Shan and Palaung villages. Eggs and fowls procurable from Kachins in the neighbourhood, but notice must be given. Paddy at 4 annas per basket. Ample supply of water from two streams, the larger 10 feet wide, 18 inches deep. Unlimited camping ground in paddy-fields outside village. From here there is a road to Tawnio (Kôkáng) *viâ* Mantôn ferry (*see* at end of Route No. 64), and another to Namkham (*see* same route). When proceeding with a small force it will be best to break this march at Longboi, 8¾ miles; camping ground for 100 men on ridge on which village is built. Water, grass, fowls, and eggs procurable; one day's paddy should be taken.
		7. Möngya ... Nammoi.	M. F. **7 0**	M. F. 74 0	General direction north. Follows east side of Mönghawm valley skirting paddy-fields; thence north-west to head of narrow valley leading to Nammoi river. Follows down east side of valley along side of steep grass-covered hills, crossing several narrow but deep streams which are bridged and passable for pack transport with exception of one or two easily forded. At 5⅛ miles pass Manpa, 10 houses (Shan). Descends to Nammoi river by steep zigzags; ford at 6⅝ miles (breadth 40 yards, depth 3½ feet; bad crossing owing to swift current and large boulders. Low muddy banks, 3 feet; current 4 to 5 miles per hour; water clear and good). This ford would not be passable after a slight flood rise, and the wooden bridge at 6¼ miles would be the only means of crossing. Camp in paddy-fields east of Möngya village for large force. Möngya, 7 miles, 17 houses, situated on the left bank of the Nammoi at the foot of high wooded hills which here enclose the river on either side. Water from river clear and good; supplies obtainable from Kachin villages in neighbourhood; paddy 6 annas per basket. Path good, but owing to narrowness and steepness would be dangerous in wet weather. Bad swampy crossings at 4¼ miles; small ones 5 miles; also on leaving Manpa village. *Bridges.*—At Mönghawm wooden bridge; longitudinal planks, 15 feet long, 5 feet broad; passable. At 1 mile covered wooden bridge, 15 feet long, 5 feet broad; passable. Small plank bridges at 5 miles; average breadth 3 feet. At 6¼ miles and 200 yards west of the path a wooden pile bridge over the Nammoi river, 100 feet long, 4 feet broad, longitudinal planks: gradually falling out of repair, but at present passable.

FROM THEINNI-MYOMA TO MÖNGKO (ROUTE NO. 20) *viâ* MÖNGSI—*continued.*

Authorities.		Number and Names of Stages, Rivers and Streams.	Distances.				Remarks.
Military.	Civil.		Intermediate.		Total.		
			M.	F.	M.	F.	
G.O.C. Mandalay District.	Superintendent, Northern Shan States.	**8. Camp near Pángsák.** Nammoi and Möngya stream.	**7**	**0**	81	0	General direction north. Path runs along the left bank of Nammoi river for 2 miles, then turns into paddy-fields fording Möngya stream (breadth 30 feet, depth 3 feet; rocky bottom; low stony banks, 3 feet high; current 3 miles per hour) to Nasa village (eight houses) at 3 miles, passing Mankong (10 houses) ½ mile north of the road at ½ a mile, and Manhaw (20 houses and tiled wooden kyaung) at 2 miles. Thence very steep and trying ascent for 2 miles up wooded hill. The crest is reached at 5 miles, the path continuing along it descending slightly and again ascending to Pángsák village; thence through grassy jungle to roadside camp 7 miles. Short march, but very trying owing to great steepness of the ascent from Nasa village. Camping ground at 7 miles for 200 men; supplies in small quantities from Pángsák which is passed at 6¼ miles (12 houses Kachin); water from small stream at camp 4 to 5 feet wide and 1 foot deep. Paddy 6 annas per small basket.
		9. Möngko ... Namling and Namko.	**12**	**0**	93	0	General direction north. Path descends through grass jungle to Namling stream which is forded at ⅛ mile; breadth 30 feet, depth 2½ feet; flows through a jungle gorge; banks steep and rocky; current 3 miles per hour; rocky bottom; thence very steep ascent to Loikong village (eight houses) 1¾ miles, ascending again to 2½ miles where crest is reached, the path running along it to Pánglom, 4 miles (eight houses); at 5 miles the path begins to descend to the Möngko valley; passes through Pasông village at 7 miles (25 to 30 houses), where the path broadens to 10 feet; thence steep descent down spur of the hill to 10 miles where the path turns to the west and continues along the edge of paddy-fields to camp outside Pánglom village opposite Möngko. The path is narrow and very steep in places to Pasông, averaging 2 feet in width; from Pasông it averages 8 feet and is good though steep. There is a bad swampy crossing at 10¾ miles. Möngko is a Shan village of 20 houses situated on a slight eminence ¼ mile from the left bank of the Namko stream on the road from Mangmaw (Kôkáng) *viâ* Manpán ferry to Namkham (*see* Route No. 20, Stage 5, and Alternative I, Stage 1). The defences consist of a wall of sun-dried brick forming a rectangle ¼ mile by ⅛ mile; two principal gates closed by wooden doors 7 feet by 7 feet. The wall averages 4½ feet in height, 18 inches thick, and is loopholed on each side of the two principal gates. Except at the gates this wall is in bad repair and broken down in many places. An abattis formed of thorn trees and 20 yards thick surrounds the wall, passages being cut to the entrance gates. The village could easily be made impregnable against men without fire-arms. It is commanded by hills on the north-east side at 800 yards distance. The inhabitants show a considerable admixture of Chinese blood, and live in wattle and daub straw-thatched houses on the ground level, the floor being made of hardened mud. A fifth-day bazaar held here; the buildings being 1½ miles south-west of the village. Paddy 4 annas per small basket. The kyaung was burnt by the Sawbwa of Séfán

FROM THEINNI-MYOMA TO MÖNGKO (ROUTE No. 20) *viâ* MÖNGSI—*continued*

Authorities. Military.	Authorities. Civil.	Number and Names of Stages, Rivers and Streams.	Distances. Intermediate.	Distances. Total.	Remarks.
G.O.C. Mandalay District.	Superintendent, Northern Shan States.	**9. Möngko**—*cont.*			about nine months ago and has not been rebuilt. Pánglom, ½ mile from Möngko village and on south side of valley; consists of about 12 houses. *Bridges.*—At 9½ miles covered wooden bridge, longitudinal planks; 30 feet long by 3 feet wide; only available for foot traffic owing to lowness of roof; easy ford at side over small stream 3 to 4 feet wide.

No. 69.

From THEINNI-MYOMA to MÖNGWI viâ MÖNGYU.

BY CAPT. R. B. SHAWE AND LIEUT. H. DALY, SUPERINTENDENT, NORTHERN SHAN STATES, DECEMBER 1889 AND JANUARY 1890.

Military	Civil	Stages	Intermediate M.	Intermediate F.	Total M.	Total F.	Remarks
G.O.C. Mandalay District.	Superintendent, Northern Shan States.	**1. Namhuon (or Namhu).** Several small streams with rocky bottoms much broken up.	**6**	**0**	6	0	The first ¾ mile the track, a fairly broad one, leads over level ground through a small hamlet to the foot of the pass; the track then becomes very steep and in places narrow. This track is here very trying both for men and baggage. As the track ascends several streams, shallow but with trappy bottoms, cross it and a perpendicular fall of water for some hundreds of feet is passed on the right hand. Several boggy places bad for transport animals. After about 2 miles the pass ends and undulating grassy country is met with; in places the trees, mostly the Shan oak, become fairly thick. About the 4th mile a Kachin village on the left hand (Nampakhyi) is passed and a little further on another on the right hand. Namhuon (or Namhu) is situated in a hollow with cultivated low hills on its east and south, and jungle-covered hills rise to the north of it, at thefoot of which a marshy stream flows. This is a Palaung village of about 12 large houses and can supply a fair amount of paddy, but little else. Grass can be procured in abundance. Many good camping grounds can be found and the village could afford shelter to some 250 men.
		2. Pángngom (Hpángom, or Pángwam), 4,050 feet. Two small streams, Namkhai, and two other small streams.	**10**	**0**	16	0	For the first 4 miles track is good, remainder rough and uneven. Path over low hills difficult only in wet weather. Leaving Namhuon the track crosses a stream flowing through marshy ground and then traverses some undulating country more or less under dry cultivation. About 1½ miles a marshy bit is crossed, then the village of Imöng is passed. At the 4th mile a large village of Pinghoi or (Pengwoi) on a clear shallow stream is passed and after going through tall grassand marshy land for about a mile the Namkhai is crossed bya difficult ford; bottom rocky, but the depth considerable in places; care is necessary in taking across baggage animals; the landing is bad. The track then leads over hills, passing

FROM THEINNI-MYOMA TO MÖNGWI *viâ* MÖNGYU—*continued.*

Authorities. Military.	Authorities. Civil.	Number and Names of Stages, Rivers and Streams.	Distances. Intermediate.	Distances. Total.	Remarks.
G.O.C. Mandalay District.	Superintendent, Northern Shan States.	**2. Pángngom (Hpángom, or Pángwam), 4,050 feet**—*cont.*			one village with kyaung, then gradually descends till the paddy-fields of Pángngom are reached. It is advisable to camp here and not visit the Kachin village of Pángngom, which is off the direct route and is a small one. A stream of good water, called Nampángngom, flows through these fields. Paddy is difficult to procure; grass plentiful.
			M. F.	M. F.	
		3. Möngyu (3,350 feet). Namkhai, Namkyai, and Nammaw rivers.	**6 0**	22 0	The track leads over hills 1st mile rather rough, remainder easy and although the distance is short, the baggage animals have plenty to do. The Namkhai is forded midway, deep and difficult, better place for doing so about a mile further up stream. The Nammaw has a good ford. Möngyu is on the right bank of the Nammaw in a valley with plenty of good wet cultivation on the north and east sides. Several fair-sized villages are situated in the hills round it. The usual Shan bazaar every fifth day is held here. Paddy and rice procurable, and fowls and pigs occasionally are brought in by the neighbouring Kachins. For another description of these three stages *see* Route No. 42, Stages 3 and 4. From Möngyu three important roads branch—(1) to Kunlôn (no details yet recorded), (2) to Namkham (*see* Route No. 42), (3) *viâ* Möngtát to Taungbain for tea (no details yet recorded).
		4. Hôpông (3,300 feet). One small stream.	**6 0**	28 0	The track leads over a steep hill called Lwoi Pao by a narrow difficult path; both the ascent and descent are steep and difficult, particularly the latter. After completing the descent a small stream is crossed and the paddy-fields of Hôpông are entered. It is advisable to camp here. There are two villages in the neighbourhood, but both off the direct road. Paddy and grass are procurable here.
		5. Mankaokyé (6,400 feet). Two small streams.	**8 0**	36 0	The Mankaokyé, so called by the Shans because it is a deserted village of the Líshaws, considered by the Shans to be Chinese. The track is very difficult in places, running along the side of steep hills and the last 3 miles very narrow, steep and treacherous. The camping ground at Mankaokyé is small and hilly and the water-supply scanty. This is a hard march. The mountain is called Lwoi Löng.
		6. Tunhông (5,050 feet).	**10 0**	46 0	The track after leaving Mankaokyé is very hilly and bad over very little used jungle paths continually ascending and descending. Last 3 miles easy descent; afterwards it runs up and down spurs of the hills and is easier. When nearer Tunhông considerable hill cultivation is met with and many hamlets dot the hill sides. The steamers of their kyaungs are visible for some distance. At Tunhông itself there are two

FROM THEINNI-MYOMA TO MÖNGWI *viâ* MÖNGYU—*continued.*

Authorities. Military.	Authorities. Civil.	Number and Names of Stages, Rivers and Streams.	Distances. Intermediate.	Distances. Total.	Remarks.
G.O.C. Mandalay District.	Superintendent, Northern Shan States.	**6. Tunhông (5,050 feet)**—*cont.*			kyaungs. The village consists of about 20 large sized houses. Water has to be brought some distance. Plenty of paddy procurable here and vegetables in season. In the winter the English broad bean and peas are cultivated. Camping grounds are hilly, but 250 men might be billetted on the villagers at a pinch. Elevation 5,000 feet.
			M. F.	M. F.	
		7. Möngwi (2,700 feet). Namwi and one small stream.	**6 0**	52 0	Fairly easy track in dry weather, almost continuous descent. Möngwi is on the right bank of the Namwi, a tributary of the Shwéli. The valley of the Namwi is almost entirely under paddy. Many villages, Shan, Kachin, and Palaung, nestle in the neighbouring hills. At Möngwi there is a bazaar every five days. Namkham is two marches to the north-east, *see* Route No. 45. Crops, sugar-cane, cotton, maize, tobacco, sweet potatoes, yams, mustard, fruit, cucumber and pumpkins. Eggs also procurable.

No. 70.

From THEINNI-MYOMA to MÖNGYIN.

BY CAPT. A. C. YATE, FROM NATIVE INFORMATION, JANUARY 1888.

Military	Civil	Stages	Intermediate	Total	Remarks
G.O.C. Mandalay District.	Superintendent, Northern Shan States.	**1. Möngpa** ... Namtu.	**8 4**	8 4	General direction west-south-west. Road at start runs along causeway through swamp. At ¼ mile river Namtu is crossed by ford, gravelly bottom, current moderate, easy approaches. At 1⅜ miles village of Myohaung, 20 houses. At 2⅛ miles road branches off left to Manmaw (or Manmao). At 2⅜ miles village of Tunkaw (four houses) on the right. At 3¼ miles village of Namsángsök to right. From 4 to 8 miles pass through grass and tree jungle. At 8 miles village of Nongpyali (20 houses) to left, good camping ground. At 8⅜ miles Möngpa (15 houses) to right of road. Camping ground for small force. Fuel, grass, and water procurable. Water from wells according to Native information. Kyaung and several zayáts. Road so far level and good; probably deep in mud in rains.
		2. Manhyu .. *Nil.*	**5 0**	13 4	Good, level road. At 1 mile village of Thaikôn (Kônkut) to left, 30 houses. Good camping ground. Between that and Manhyu thick jungle. Manhyu has 10 houses. Small camping ground. Fuel, grass, and water procurable. Namtu river is 300 yards north-north-west of village, 150 yards broad, and about 6 feet deep; crossed by ferry. From this point there are two

FROM THEINNI-MYOMA TO MÖNGYIN—*continued.*

Authorities.		Number and Names of Stages, Rivers and Streams.	Distances.		Remarks.
Military.	Civil.		Intermediate.	Total.	
G.O.C. Mandalay District.	Superintendent, Northern Shan States.	**2. Manhyu**—*cont.*			roads to Möngyin. The longer one does not cross the river here, but follows its left bank. The road is in places hilly and bad. One and-a-half miles from Manhyu village of Tákhai, 10 houses, and another small village ½ mile further. Four and-a-half miles from Manhyu reach the right bank of the Namtôn river. The village of Möngtôn, a stage on the road from Láshio to Mongwi (*see* Route No. 14), lies from here about 1½ miles to left. The road then follows the right bank of the Namtôn for some 2 or 3 miles; hilly and bad, steep ascents and descents, and then crosses it by a ford. The Namtôn falls into the Namtu. From the ford over the Namtôn to Möngyin is about 12 miles, passing the village of Namhong half-way. By this road the Namtu is crossed only once between Theinni and Möngyin. The other route crosses it three times, once close to Theinni, again at Manhyu (Native information states that the Namtu at Manhyu can be forded in the dry weather), and a third time at Möngyin. As the passage of even a few hundered men and animals across one of these ferries takes from 24 to 48 hours, it is obviously easier to take the longer route and avoid the ferries. It is probable, however, that there is a road from Theinni keeping to the right bank of the Namtu to Nakaw (*alias* Banmakaw) and Tákhai. Under any circumstances, however, the Namtu must be crossed once. The road by the ferries is the best of the two and is as follows :—
			M. F.	M. F.	
		3. Tákhai ... ... Namtu and Namkhai.	9 0	22 4	Road good and level. Pass three Kachin villages called Pánglut, Lôkpáng, and Nakaw (*alias* Banmakaw). A direct road from Láshio to Möngyu crosses here, passing from Möngtôn by the villages of Nákaw and Nákyem to Kaleng and Möngyu. Roads from Láshio and from Theinni to Möngyu meet some 5 miles north or north-east of Kaleng. Road crosses Namkhai river by ford just east of the village of Tákhai. In rains Namkhai is crossed by a ferry. Tákhai, 15 houses, one kyaung.
		4. Möngyin ... Namtu.	8 0	30 4	Good level road. Pass at 4 miles Nálôklôn (Shans, six houses). At 5 miles Násán (Shans, kyaung, five houses). At 6 miles Bansáon (Shans, 10 houses, kyaung). At 6½ miles Bansalôn (Shans, 25 houses, kyaung). Cross Namtu just east of Möngyin, a village of 50 to 100 houses, seat of Myoza, kyaung and zayáts. Supplies procurable, such as bullocks, rice, fish, salt, vegetables, fruits, fuel, grass, &c. From Möngyin there are roads south-east to Láshio or west to Mantôn (*see* Route No. 13), to Namsán and Thíbaw, south-west (*see* Route No. 49) and to Möngwi and Namkham, north (*see* Routes Nos. 45 and 49).

No. 71.

From THÍBAW (MÖNGSIPAW) to MÖNGYAI (MAINGYÉ) viâ SAUNKYE.

By Capt. H. R. B. DONNE, Norfolk Regiment, 25th December 1888.

Authorities.		Number and Names of Stages, Rivers and Streams.	Distances.				Remarks.
Military.	Civil.		Intermediate.		Total.		
			M.	F.	M.	F.	
G.O.C. Mandalay District.	Superintendent, Northern Shan States.	**1. Namun (Nammôn), 2,000 feet.** Namtu (Myitngé) and Namláng.	**12**	**4**	12	4	General direction south-east. For the first $3\frac{1}{2}$ miles the path is perfectly level, running east close to left bank of Myitngé, after which it continues south-east to end of march. It is easy throughout except at $5\frac{1}{8}$ miles, where the ascent at 20° is a little rough for 70 yards. The track is through jungle, and after the first 5 miles of level ascends abruptly for $\frac{1}{2}$ mile and then runs along fairly level ground gradually ascending to Namun. At $1\frac{1}{8}$ miles the small hamlet of Sinkwot is reached; it consists of two houses with a small guard of the Sawbwa's men. At $3\frac{1}{2}$ a path leads off to the small village of Supláng on the left, situate on the right bank of the Nam Láng, 200 yards off; consists of seven huts; no accommodatiou or supplies. The track follows the left bank of this stream for $1\frac{1}{2}$ miles; breadth of stream 4 yards, depth 1 foot, rate $2\frac{1}{2}$ miles per hour. At $4\frac{1}{2}$ open spot sufficient to encamp 200 men. At $4\frac{3}{8}$ path crosses small stream; water good. At $6\frac{1}{4}$ and again $6\frac{1}{2}$ sites for encampments for 400 men in each. At 9 path crosses small stream; water good; 4 yards wide, 6 inches deep; 2 miles per hour. At $9\frac{1}{4}$ track crosses another small stream. At $10\frac{1}{8}$ Nákaw is on the right, consisting of three huts and a bazaar held once every five days. At $10\frac{3}{8}$ path on left leads to village of Manlôn. At 11 miles ground available to camp 500 men; 100 yards further crosses small stream; water good. At $11\frac{1}{4}$ small well on left, wants cleaning; at this point there is a strip of open ground on the left sufficient to encamp 800 men. At $11\frac{3}{4}$ path crosses stream; paddy-fields on right. For the rest of the march the path is raised 18 inches above the ordinary level. There are 19 wooden bridges in this march by which the streams and dry nullahs are crossed, 4 feet wide, and ranging between 13 and 60 feet long, all passable for transport animals; the camping ground, sufficient for 500 men, lies 600 yards to the south-west of Namun village. Good water from stream close by. Paddy pentiful. Namun consists of 17 houses with a bazaar held every five days.
		2. Saunkyé (2,600 feet). Small streams.	**13**	**2**	25	6	General direction east-south-east. The path which lies through long grass and jungle is good and generally level with the exception of a few gentle undulations gradually ascending to Saunkyé. At $1\frac{1}{8}$ paddy-fields on right sufficient to encamp 1,000 men in dry weather; water close. At $1\frac{1}{4}$ small village of Kátkao at 300 yards on the right, which consists of five huts; no accommodation; a little paddy. At $2\frac{5}{8}$ village of Kwaláng at 100 yards on left, consisting of seven huts. At $3\frac{1}{8}$ village of Husôn on right; four huts; small supply of paddy. At $3\frac{1}{2}$ and $3\frac{3}{4}$ open places sufficient for small encampments. At $5\frac{7}{8}$ steepest part of path is reached, gradients of one-fourth for 40 yards. At $7\frac{3}{4}$ the village of Hôna is 100 yards on the left, consisting of eight huts, one kyaung on the right, one zayát; accommodation 30 men; 200 yards further the track leaves the main route to the left and does not join it again until the Lekha (Likka) bazaar. Of these two routes the main track is the shorter by $\frac{5}{8}$ mile.

FROM THÎBAW (MÖNGSIPAW) TO MÖNGYAI (MAINGYÉ) *viâ* SAUNKYÉ—*continued.*

Authorities.		Number and Names of Stages, Rivers and Streams.	Distances.		Remarks.
Military.	Civil.		Intermediate.	Total.	
G.O.C. Mandalay District.	Superintendent, Northern Shan States.	**2. Saunkyé (2,600 feet)**—*cont.*			It is a level and easy path throughout, passing through jungle with occasional partial clearings. One or two small streams have to be crossed, but there is generally no difficulty. About midway between Hôna and Lekha, a path to the left front leads to Sailé (or Sili) 200 yards distant; it consists of 16 houses and a small bamboo kyaung with two zayáts attached; camping ground on paddy-fields close by for 1,000 men. Water close by and good. At 8¼ small stream flows at 20 yards on right. From 9⅛ to 12¾ there is a succession of small strips of paddy cultivation on the right, affording excellent camping ground for a large number of men in dry weather. Water close. At 11 miles path runs across taungya cultivation and is fenced on both sides for 200 yards. At 12⅞ track crosses small stream by wooden bridge, passable for animals. At 13⅛ village of Saunkyé, consisting of 13 houses. A stockade, 50 yards square, 9 feet high, surrounds the Hein's quarters; one kyaung at ⅛ mile to north-east, 24 by 20 yards; one zayát, accommodating 18 men. At 13¾ path crosses small stream by wooden bridge passable for animals; camping ground on paddy-fields on the right of path and left bank of stream sufficient for 600 men. Saunkyé belongs to Thîbaw; has a bazaar every five days.
		3. Senkyao (3,100 feet). Small streams.	M. F. **13 6**	M. F. 39 4	General direction east-north-east. The path lies through thin jungle and long grass, occasionally traversing patches of taungya cultivation. It is good and easy throughout. At 600 yards the Saunkyé kyaung lies on the right; 160 yards further small stream is crossed by wooden bridge, passable for animals; water good. At 1¼ good open camping ground 250 by 100 yards. At 2 miles the path commences to ascend. At 4¾ spring on right; water good. At 4⅛ the small village of Wanság is 300 yards on the left and consists of 14 huts; no accommodation. At 5⅛ pond on right and good site for camp for 1,000 men on left, but water is ½ mile away. At 5⅛ a path leads to a village ⅓ mile distant on the left. At 7¾ Lehka bazaar. At this point the track joins the main route (which after leaving Hôna lies through the village of Sailé). The village of Lekha is situated ¼ mile to the south; the bazaar is held every five days. At 8½ and at 10⅜ the route strikes two small streams crossed by wooden bridges, passable for animals. At 12¾ path crosses small stream by foot-bridge; water fair. Just beyond this point is the steepest gradient in the march, being one-fifth for 50 yards. At 13⅛ small village on left, 13 huts; name not known. At 13⅜ spring on right; water good; 70 yards further small stream is passed by wooden bridge, practicable for animals; paddy-fields on right and left sufficient to encamp 600 men in dry weather. At 13¾ camping ground on the left sufficient to accommodate 600 men; on the right of path cluster of pagodas enclosed by a 3-foot brick wall, 45 yards square. The village of Senkyao is situated 400 yards north-east of halting place and contains 19 houses, one kyaung, and two zayáts; accommodation 20 men. The bazaar lies 300 yards north-north-west of camp and is held every five days. Principal articles for sale—paddy, rice, tobacco, sweet potatoes, salt, vegetables and clothing, &c.

FROM THÍBAW (MÖNGSIPAW) TO MÖNGYAI (MAINGYÉ) *viâ* SAUNKYÉ—*continued.*

Authorities.		Number and Names of Stages, Rivers and Streams.	Distances.				Remarks.
Military.	Civil.		Intermediate.		Total.		
			M.	F.	M.	F.	
G.O.C. Mandalay District.	Superintendent, Northern Shan States.	**4. Mansáng (3,000 feet).** Small streams.	**12**	**4**	52	0	General direction north-east. At first the path lies through thin jungle and long grass, but the country is open for the latter half of march. It is easy throughout except at $\frac{7}{8}$ mile, where the bed of a small stream is very soft, and also at 4 miles, where the track runs through a swamp for 170 yards, which would be very awkward in the rains. The path is generally level leading over gentle undulations. At $\frac{1}{8}$ stream crossed by foot-bridge; animals must cross 80 yards to the left. At $3\frac{1}{4}$ path crosses bit of soft ground for 20 yards. About here is the boundary between Thíbaw and Theinni. In the above-mentioned swamp at 4 miles the water is not more than 1 foot deep, and a small stream runs through it. At $7\frac{1}{4}$ path crosses stream in deep nullah by wooden bridge, passable for animals, but in bad repair. The stream is 14 feet wide, 3 feet deep; 2 miles per hour. There is in some places 6 feet of water; 150 yards further on another small stream is crossed; water good in both; and between these two there is a capital site for a camp sufficient for 1,000 men. At $7\frac{1}{2}$, 15 yards of soft ground. At $8\frac{1}{8}$ small stream; further bank a little steep. At $11\frac{1}{8}$ small villages of Kungyôn half burnt and altogether deserted. At $12\frac{1}{8}$ small stream; water good. At $12\frac{1}{2}$ camping ground close to dilapidated kyaung, one zayát; accommodation 20 men. The deserted village of Mansáng lies 300 yards to the east, consists of 21 huts, and belongs to Southern Theinni. Bazaar held every five days in quiet times. Is situate $\frac{1}{3}$ mile north-east (Snipe *jheel* close by). Here the road from Láshio *viâ* Mansé joins in (*see* Route No. 15).
		5. Möngyai (Maingyé). Small streams.	**10**	**1**	62	1	General direction east. Path good the whole way, except at $7\frac{1}{2}$ miles where the right bank of stream descends at an angle of 25° for 20 yards. It is fairly level. As in the previous march travelling over undulating grass covered ground and occasionally thin jungle. At $1\frac{1}{2}$ path crosses stream by covered wooden bridge, passable for animals, 30 feet by 5 feet. At 2 miles a deserted village on right containing 13 huts in good repair. At $2\frac{1}{2}$ small stream is crossed; bamboo foot-bridge. At $4\frac{1}{2}$ track strikes another small stream; water good; 200 yards further dilapidated bazaar sheds. At $4\frac{3}{4}$ the village of Hunkwin on left, deserted. It contains 15 huts, one kyaung; on the right, 30 yards by 15 yards, no accommodation. At $5\frac{3}{8}$ and again at $6\frac{1}{2}$ miles the path crosses small streams by wooden bridge, the last being a covered one passable for animals. At $7\frac{1}{2}$ path crosses stream 9 yards wide, 8 inches deep; $2\frac{1}{2}$ miles per hour. There is a rough bamboo foot-bridge, below crossing, but is not safe. At $8\frac{3}{8}$ pôngyi kyaung, 24 by 24 yards, with five small pagodas on the left and three deserted houses. At $9\frac{1}{2}$ three pagodas on the right. Between this and the camping ground are the blackened remains of several houses on both sides of the path, which once formed the village of Möngyai. At $9\frac{7}{8}$ a rough stockade, 50 yards square, newly erected, lies on the right and constitutes at present the head-quarters of the Nanmaing. The camping ground is situated on a small hill, good ground and sufficient for 600 men. Water close by. The whole of the Möngyai valley was once covered with paddy

FROM THÍBAW (MÖNGSIPAW) TO MÖNGYAI (MAINGYÉ) *viâ* SAUNKYÉ—*continued.*

Authorities. Military.	Authorities. Civil.	Number and Names of Stages, Rivers and Streams.	Distances. Intermediate.	Distances. Total.	Remarks.
G.O.C. Mandalay District.	Superintendent, Northern Shan States.	**5. Möngyai (Maingyé)**—*cont.*			cultivation, but at present only small patches here and there are kept up. A portion of the Shan columns of 1887-88 followed this road generally, halting as follows:—1. Sôpláng, 4 miles; 2. Kátkao, 9½; 3. Namlaktong, 11¾; 4. Namsáng, 8½; 5. Kunkaw, 11; and 6. Möngyai, 10½—total 55½ miles. Grass and water plentiful at all of these stages, and ample room for camping at each, though clearing and cleaning required at some if the force marching is a large one.

No. 72.

From THÍBAW to NAMSAN (TAUNGBAIN).

BY CAPT. A. C. YATE, 1ST BELUCH LIGHT INFANTRY, DECEMBER 1887.

Military	Civil	Stage	Intermediate	Total	Remarks
G.O.C. Mandalay District.	Superintendent, Northern Shan States.	**1. Nam-ngum or Namwum.** One or two streams near Thíbaw town, all bridged for pack transport.	M. F. **7 0**	M. F. 7 0	General direction 322°. Starting from the north-west corner of the Sawbwa's residence the road runs for ½ mile westward through the western part of the town. It then turns north-west crossing two bridged streams to the Kôdaung kyaung, a distance of ¼ mile. Here a road branches off west or west by north, said to lead to Kôdaung, distant some 20 miles from Thíbaw. This road passes the villages of Manpyet (5 miles), Ummu (10 miles), and Pángnim (17 miles). Kôdaung is 1 or 2 miles beyond Pángnim. Round Kôdaung are the Thíbaw Sawbwa's tea plantations. Kôdaung is a big village with one or more kyaungs and zayáts. From Manpyet there is a path passable, but very difficult for pack transport, to Nam-ngum. Consequently this may also be used as an alternative route to Taungbain. There is said to be a foot-path direct from Kôdaung to Namsán. From Kôdaung kyaung the road runs nearly due north, and at 1½ miles the steep ascent commences. The road henceforward is steep, often exceedingly steep, stony and trying to pack animals. The jungle on either side is small and not very thick. As Nam-ngum is approached the fir trees grow more and more numerous. At 2½ miles there is a path to the left (245°) to the village of Punkaw, distance 3 or 3 miles. From here the general direction of the road as far as Nam-ngum is north-west or north-west by west. At 3¼ miles cross two nullahs bridged. Here there is a halting place (*sakhán*) and water. (There is a scarcity of water on this route.) At 4½ miles road to Taungbain *viâ* Paungmaláng, Namlu, and Taungma branches off to right (360°). This latter route is said to be more difficult than the one now reported on. From here to Paungmaláng is said to be one bullock march (viz., 5 or 6 miles). At 4¾ miles path to left (185°) to Manpyet (on Thíbaw-Kôdaung road), distant 2 to 3 miles. From here onwards the road is very steep indeed. At 6¾ miles path to left (200°) to Manpyet, distant 2 or 3 miles. At 7 miles reach Nam-ngum, village of 10 houses on confined level space on a spur, great difficulty to camp even a small force

FROM THÍBAW TO NAMSÁN (TAUNGBAIN)—*continued.*

Authorities. Military.	Authorities. Civil.	Number and Names of Stages, Rivers and Streams.	Distances. Inter-mediate.	Distances. Total.	Remarks.
G.O.C. Mandalay District.	Superintendent, Northern Shan States.	**1. Nam-ngum or Namwum**—*cont.*			of 200 men. Must scatter here and there wherever ground is fairly open and not too steep. The halting place for caravans is about $\frac{3}{4}$ mile beyond, *i.e.*, north-west of village on the banks of a small stream which forms the boundary between Thíbaw and Taungbain. A small force of 50 to 100 men with transport could camp there. Great difficulty about water at Nam-ngum.
		2. Pángwonsai ...	M. F. 8 6	M. F. 15 6	The road is an alternation of steep ascents with shorter and somewhat easier descents. The height of Nam-ngum above sea-level is estimated at 3,500 feet, and of Pángwonsai 5,500 feet. The hills are covered with firs (*Pinus longifolia*), a species of oak (*ilex*) among other vegetation. Bullock *sakháns* are passed every 2 miles on confined open level spaces on tops of spurs or ridges. There is no water near the road, except at Pángsápyé village, but it can be obtained by descending several hundred feet into the neighbouring ravines. About $\frac{3}{4}$ mile beyond the village of Nam-ngum is camping ground for a small force of 200 or 300 men. There is a fair supply of water there. The ranges of hills crossed on this route have no names, being designated either from the village near them (as Loi Nam-ngum) or from their nature (as Loi Pek—fir tree range—or Loi Lôn—Big range). At 2 miles pass *sakhán*. Thence ascent up ridge westward. Fine valleys north and south. The road generally is carried from one range to another along a *col.* At $2\frac{3}{4}$ miles come in sight of Pángsápyé. At $3\frac{1}{2}$ miles (descent steep) reach Pángsápyé, 20 houses. Fair water-supply. No good camping ground. From Pángsápyé there is a bullock road east-north-east to Paungmaláng, distant 3 or 4 miles, the first stage on the easterly route to Taungbain. One mile beyond Pángsápyé largish *sakhán*, but no water near. At $5\frac{1}{2}$ miles another small *sakhán*. Here long and steep ascent. At $7\frac{1}{2}$ miles reach top of ascent some 6,000 feet above sea-level. Thence descend for $1\frac{1}{4}$ miles to Pángwonsai Sakhán. Village (deserted) $\frac{3}{4}$ mile south of Sakhán, very difficult to camp troops here. Level ground very limited; have to camp anywhere on level and slopes. Spring in ravine below to west. If dam made, ample water could be stored for 1,000 animals. Water good and sufficient for any force that could encamp near it, on a knoll just to left of road near remains of some formerly fortified position. Caravans send their bullocks to graze near old village of Pángwonsai; grass scarce here as also at Nam-ngum. Fuel abundant, climate invigorating. The site of Pángwonsai lies $\frac{1}{2}$ mile south-west of the *sakhán*, and there both fair grazing and picketing ground for 500 animals can be obtained. It is, however, very damp down in the hollows. There is a spring below the old village, and by damming it up a tank could be formed. In the event of a force of more than 250 men marching by this route, this additional camping room would be necessary. It is, moreover, nearer to water.

FROM THÍBAW TO NAMSÁN (TAUNGBAIN)—*continued.*

Authorities. Military.	Authorities. Civil.	Number and Names of Stages, Rivers and Streams.	Distances. Intermediate. M. F.	Distances. Total. M. F.	Remarks.
G.O.C. Mandalay District.	Superintendent, Northern Shan States.	**3. Namlu Sakhán.** Several little streams.	7 6	23 4	Road as before hilly with steep ascents and descents; jungle very thick; vegetation luxuriant. Water more plentiful near the road, but camping grounds few and very limited in extent. At ¾ mile is a *sakhán* where 150 men would be encamped. At 1 mile road to left (215°). At 4½ miles reach village of South Kunwot (or Kunhot), 10 or 12 houses, the main street used as a caravan halting place. Water plentiful, no accommodation or supplies, and no camping ground. At 6 miles reach North Kunwot (kyaung, pagodas and 30 houses). Here troops can camp, water sufficient for a force of 500 men. From here steep descent to Namlu Sakhán, where water good and plentiful, but camping ground very bad. Some miles lower down on this stream is the Namlu Sakhán on the eastern road from Thíbaw to Namsán. For another description of the road hence to Namsán *see* Route No. 48, Stages 1 and 2.
		4. Taungma ... Numlu and Namchôn streams, both fordable, water 1 foot deep.	5 6	29 2	This is the most difficult portion of the road from Thíbaw to Namsán. Crossing Namlu stream, steep ascent for ⅛ mile, then continues steep descent for 3¼ miles. At 3½ miles cross Namchôn stream by easy ford (a road here branches off up the near or right bank of the stream to Kwanhai, through which village the roads to Namsán from Nammaw, Kyaukmé, and perhaps Thônzé pass). Small Sakhán on bank of Namchôn stream; crossing it very steep ascent. At 4½ miles road to left direct to Sétônhôn and Namsán. I went along this road for 2 miles, and though evidently regularly used by pack bullocks, it was from its narrow and precipitous nature decidedly dangerous for mule or pony transport. It avoids, however, the very steep ascent to Taungma and descent thence to Sétônhôn. Between Namlu and Taungma noticed very little tea, but much rice cultivation. At 5¼ miles pass to west of and below Loiseng pagodas (road to right leads up to them), and at 5¾ miles reach Taungma. In last mile passed two hamlets perched on spurs below the road. Taungma has 15 to 20 houses; one kyaung; a zayát; good camping ground. Water sufficient, but has to be brought from springs below village. Here road from Lilu joins in (*see* Route No. 47).
		5. Namsán ...	7 4	36 6	Road comparatively level throughout; steep ascents and descents in one or two places. (At 2½ miles the direct road from the Namchôn ford to Sétônhôn comes in. There are several hamlets along this road.) At 2 miles a spring of water by road side. At 4 miles Sétônhôn, good kyaung; 25 houses. Accommodation for a small body of troops and some supplies available there. At 5 miles village of Sentauk, 10 houses. At 5½ miles road to right diverges to a village, road to left goes to Namsán which is built in straggling fashion on several eminences. The Sawbwa's residence, a stockaded tumble-down old barrack, is on the highest point. The houses are on the slopes all round. Here paddy, rice, tea, bullocks, and vegetables can be obtained. There is a fine kyaung. Camping room for a small force obtainable.

FROM THÍBAW TO NAMSÁN (TAUNGBAIN)—*continued.*

Authorities. Military.	Authorities. Civil.	Number and Names of Stages, Rivers and Streams.	Distances. Intermediate.	Distances. Total.	Remarks.
G.O.C. Mandalay District.	Superintendent, Northern Shan States.	**5. Namsán**—*cont.*			Convenient site for a cantonment in the immediate vicinity on a commanding site and yet near water difficult to find if to be found at all. From here roads diverge to Láshio (*see* Route No. 47), to Mômeik (Mongmyit), and Môgôk *viâ* Mantôn (*see* Routes Nos. 49 and 13), and to Namkham (*see* Route No. 49).

No. 73.

From YÁTSAUK (LAWK SAWK) to HÔPÔN viâ MÖNGPYING (MAINGPYIN.)

BY CAPT. DAVIES, OXFORDSHIRE LIGHT INFANTRY, DECEMBER 1892.

Military	Civil	Stages, Rivers and Streams	Intermediate M.	Intermediate F.	Total M.	Total F.	Remarks
G.O.C. Rangoon District.	Superintendent, Southern Shan States.	**1. Nampamôn camp.** Zawgyi and small streams.	**12**	**0**	12	0	General direction south-east by east. Good mule road. The Zawgyi chaung is crossed at ½ mile, from the right, 20 or 30 yards wide. Good cart bridge. For 2 miles through scrub jungle in a plain, thence through tree jungle among hills, but not very steep up and down. No villages passed. At Nampamôn no villages but zayát for 15 men; camping ground 150 by 100 yards, and more room could be cleared. Water from stream (2 yards by 8 inches). No village. The stream is said not to dry up in the hot weather.
		2. Möngpying (Maingpyin). Namet and small streams.	**11**	**4**	23	4	General direction east. Good mule road among hills for 2¼ miles, thence descent to the Namet valley, but not very steep. For the last 6 miles across a level plain, through jungle the whole way. At 11 miles the Namet from the right (15 yards by 4 feet). Good cart bridge. At Möngpying (30 houses) room in zayáts for 80 men, in kyaung for 70 and in bazaar sheds for 80 more. Good water from Namet and plenty of room to camp.
		3. Saikhao ... Namet and Nam Saikhao.	**16**	**4**	40	0	General direction south. Good mule road through tree jungle nearly the whole way. Level as far as Naungyôn bazaar at 14 miles, thence uphill, but not very steep. At 6 miles cross two branches of the Namet, from the left. The first (a backwater) 10 yards by 2 feet, the second 15 yards by 4 feet; both crossed by wooden cart bridges. At 7¼ miles Laisák (Lethet), 30 houses; zayáts for 40 men and room in kyaung for 100, and in bazaar sheds for 80; plenty of room to camp Water from the Namet. Between this and Saikhao there is no good water on the road. At Saikhao, a Taungthu village, a camping ground (100 yards square), and more room in taungyas to right of road. Water from Nam Saikhao which crosses the road just this side of the camp. It measures 1 yard by 3 inches.

FROM YÁTSAUK (LAWK SAWK) TO HÔPÔN *viâ* MÖNGPYING (MAINGPYIN)—*continued.*

Authorities.		Number and Names of Stages, Rivers and Streams.	Distances.				Remarks.
Military.	Civil.		Intermediate.		Total.		
			M.	F.	M.	F.	
G.O.C. Rangoon District.	Superintendent, Southern Shan States.	**4. Hôpôn** ... ... Nam Kyeng (Tabet chaung) and several small streams with easy crossings.	**9**	**4**	49	4	Ascent for ¼ mile, thence gradual descent. General direction south. Good mule road. Pass several Taungthu villages. Through jungle for 1 mile, thence open ground. At 8 miles Nam Kyeng (Tabet chaung) from right (10 yards by 3 feet); good cart bridge. At Hôpôn (*see* Route No. 7, Eastern Division, Stage 11) room for 250 men in zayáts, 250 in kyaungs and 350 in bazaar sheds. Large camping ground. Water from Nam Kyeng. As the stream at Saikhao is very small, it would be better for a large column to clear a camp at Lángso, 12 miles from Möngpying and get water from the Namet which is not far off. Three marches may be made of it by halting at Lethet, and again at Saikhao, and if there was not enough water at Saikhao, part of the column might camp on another stream (1 yard by 3 inches) ¾ mile further on, and on the Nam Tawng (1 yard by 3 inches) 1¼ miles further on. Lieut. Wallace, 27th Punjaub Infantry, reporting on the same route in April 1887, makes the distance from Yátsauk to Möngpying only 20 miles, thence to Hôpôn 27 miles, the total distance thus 47 instead of 49½. His third halting place is called Metlinso (?Lángso, *vide* above) 15 miles from Möngpying. This is a market place (no village) at the foot of the hills. This road connects the routes from Fort Stedman to Thíbaw (No. 3) and from Meiktila to Môné (No. 7, Eastern Division).

No. 74.

From YÁTSAUK to KYWETNAPA viâ YÉ-U and MYOGYI.

BY LIEUT. J. A. S. TULLOCH, R.E., FEBRUARY 1888.

Military	Civil	Stage	Intermediate M.	Intermediate F.	Total M.	Total F.	Remarks
G.O.C. Rangoon District.	Superintendent, Southern Shan States.	**1. Shwépángwet.**	**15**	**0**	15	0	Road starts west, but soon changes to south-west. At ¾ mile pass a small village on the left. At 2 miles cross a stream in a deep nullah, by a bridge, in bad repair, then over some paddy-fields and marshy ground. Ford a small irrigation stream. The village of Myénígôn is seen 1 mile off on the right. This looks a large place, and is said to possess a big kyaung. Pass Magyigôn ¼ mile to left, and ford the Kandia creek. Road now turns west and is fit for carts. Pass some high ground on left; village of Kanaingyi is seen ¼ mile to right. Half mile on pass Nyaungbu village 200 yards to left. Road turns south-west. Pass village of Naungthakaw on hill, ½ mile to left. Road slopes down at a very easy gradient. About 10 miles out a small stream of good water is passed in hollow. Country thickly wooded. From this to the hills cross another small stream. At 12½ miles road turns north-east to Alégyaung, a place of 12 houses. Then east to Shwépángwet, another 2½ miles. A kyaung (in bad repair) and three zayáts (100 men). Water a few yards off. Lots of bamboo jungle here. Village of 20 houses. A herd of buffaloes, but no other cattle.

FROM YÁTSAUK TO KYWETNAPA *viâ* YÉ-U AND MYOGYI—*continued.*

Authorities. Military.	Authorities. Civil.	Number and Names of Stages, Rivers and Streams.	Distances. Intermediate. M.	F.	Distances. Total. M.	F.	Remarks.
G.O.C. Rangoon District.	Superintendent, Southern Shan States.	**2. Kyauknet** ...	**14**	**0**	29	0	The road winds about a good deal owing to the hilly character of the country passed through, but the general direction may be taken as east to west. Almost immediately after leaving Shwépángwet the ascent commences and is very steep, being 20° in places, but the general slope is 15°. About 1 mile out the slope becomes easier and the path follows the back of a narrow ridge with valleys on either side. At 2 miles an open place for camp, but no water to be had. At 3 miles there is a very difficult bit for a short distance of 50 yards or so. Laden animals would probably require to have their loads taken off for this portion. From here the path runs at an easy slope along the side of the hill. The slope of the hill side is very steep. At 4 miles a magnificent view of both the Yátsauk and Ywangán plateaux can be seen. Here the road takes a bend, goes south-west for 1½ miles, then north-west. About 5 miles out a difficult rocky bit leads to the highest point of the ascent. The path then runs up and down for about a mile, and then the real descent begins. This lasts for about 2 miles and is very steep. It is 20° nearly the whole way, and is very trying to man and beast. At the bottom is the head of a valley in which a little water from a stream is to be got. This stream is lost sight of soon after and disappears somewhere into the ground. From this point the path for 2 miles follows the valley, crossing and in many places following the bed of a mountain torrent. Up to about 1 mile this bed is now dry, but at that point a lot of water comes down from the sides of the hills. A little further on the stream drops down a fall of some 30 feet, and at 2 miles it has to be forded. It is here a rushing stream, about 12 yards wide and 1 foot deep. The valley is very narrow, being more a gorge than anything else, the hills on either side being very steep. On crossing the stream the path leaves the valley and commences a second ascent (gradient 12°). The stream turns north a mile or so below the ford. The second ascent is soon surmounted and then the path runs with easy gradients uphill. A mile from Kyauknet a very steep (25°) ascent for 150 yards is surmounted. The slope then is downwards to Kyauknet. Laden animals could come all the way along this road with help at one or two places. They would require to be lightly laden and would have to halt frequently. There are plenty of open places for halting, but no water except from the streams in the valley mentioned above. Kyauknet is a straggling village of some 50 to 100 houses. Kyaung and two zayáts (100 men). Water from valley below (stream). A valley lies to north and south, the latter is closed and has no outlet. The hills on east of this place are much higher than those on west. From here there is a route to Ywangán (*see* Route No. 78).
		3. Yé-u	**6**	**0**	35	0	There are two routes, one through the silver mines and Theingôn (*see* Route No. 79). The other runs west, following the Ywangán road for 2 miles (*see* Route No. 78) and is difficult and rocky in places. The most difficult bit occurs just before the plateau is reached. It is, however, practicable for animals. From this point the road branches north-west and is level and easy. Pass

FROM YÁTSAUK TO KYWETNAPA *viâ* YÉ-U AND MYOGYI—*continued.*

Authorities. Military.	Authorities. Civil.	Number and Names of Stages, Rivers and Streams.	Distances. Inter-mediate.	Distances. Total.	Remarks.
G.O.C. Rangoon District.	Superintendent, Southern Shan States.	**3. Yé-u**—*cont.*			between two villages which go by the name of Kábyen at ½ mile. At 2 miles Kaséywa. Kyaung (100 men and animals). Water from stream.
		4. Sakhángyi (1,800 feet above Mandalay).	M. F. **15 0**	M. F. 50 0	Road west. At ¾ mile village of Taungôngbaw. Kyaung and zayát. At 2½ miles cross a spur on which is a kyaung and four zayáts (100 men). The country to north of road is all high hills, to the south lie the Yé-u and Ywangán plateaux. A good view can be obtained to the summit of the Náteik pass. Pass through two villages both called Kyaukubyin. Bad water-supply. These are the biggest villages in Yé-u. At 5 miles the road turns north, descends a valley, and then ascends a steep, rough, and rocky road. It then turns north-west, which is the general direction to Sakhángyi. It now follows course of a valley to north-west for some way. Descent to valley very steep and difficult. It then ascends hill on right after which the gradient is easy. At 7 miles is the camping ground of Sekubyin. Two zayáts (30 men), but no water. The road now follows course of a valley; gradient easy. In places it overhangs a nullah (stream in rains). Here it would probably be difficult in the rains. After this the road is cut up into deep ruts by the passage of oxen and is very trying to ponies. There is very little rock here. Road leaves valley and ascends hill to left at a steep gradient. This is the highest point of road. From this to Sakhángyi is a descent of 4 or 5 miles. The road follows course of stream (now dry) which brings it to the valley. Sakhángyi village, 40 houses, lies 1 mile or so from the foot of the descent. Kyaung and two zayáts (100 men). Very little water and that bad and a distance of ½ mile. This is a very trying march, as no water is to be had the whole way. Sixty baggage animals took nine hours to do the distance. Sakhángyi valley is almost entirely given up to the cultivation of pine-apples, of which there are several acres. From here there is a route to Ywangán *viâ* Myogyi (*see* Route No. 5, Eastern Division).
		5. Myogyi (1,000 feet above Mandalay).	**8 0**	58 0	Road good for ½ mile, then there is a steep, rocky ascent and descent. For 4 miles the road is difficult and rough for laden animals. Here the Myogyi valley is reached and the road runs through level paddy-fields. The valley is ¼ mile wide with hills, about 400 feet high on either side. The paddy lasts for 1½ miles, and then it is a flat road to Myogyi. Large village. Head-quarters of Baw. Stores of paddy, &c., available. Excellent grass and water. The place is said to be very unhealthy in rains. There is plenty of accommodation. The houses in village are of a good class and could be utilized for troops. Zayát in middle of village (50 men); also a pôngyi kyaung with two zayáts (100 men). There are three kyaungs about 1 mile to west of village (200 men). The latter lies somewhat off the main road to Yéwun. Zawgyi river ½ mile to north. A tank in the village of excellent water. This place is the residence of the Ngwégunhmu and Shwéda Bo of Baw. There are routes from Myogyi to Yéwun and Kyauksé through the Daunghmé pass. The Kyauksé route is not much frequented (*see* Routes Nos. 4

FROM YÁTSAUK TO KYWETNAPA *viâ* YÉ-U AND MYOGYI—*continued.*

Authorities.		Number and Names of Stages, Rivers and Streams.	Distances.		Remarks.
Military.	Civil.		Inter-mediate.	Total.	
G.O.C. Rangoon District,	Superintendent, Southern Shan States.	**5. Myogyi (1,000 feet above Mandalay)**—*cont.*			and 5, Eastern Division). There appears to be a much shorter route between this and Yátsauk (*see* Route No. 4, Eastern Division), the distance by it being 36 miles instead of 58.
			M. F.	M. F.	
		6. Yethéyauk (500 feet above Mandalay). Zawgyi river.	11 0	69 0	Road north. Cross the Zawgyi river, which here splits up into four branches. In the rains it is one river and the whole space between the banks is under water. It is then quite unfordable and very difficult to cross owing to the swiftness of the current. At present (February) none of the above branches are more than 2 feet deep and so are easily fordable. They are each about 20 yards wide. On opposite bank is the village of Séywa (50 houses). Kyaung on river (100 men). Road good, of sandy clay, for 1½ miles. It then becomes somewhat rocky, but carts could go along easily. At 5 miles road follows what appears to be the dry bed of a water-course. Country bamboo jungle, long grass, and scrub. View restricted, as ranges of hills lie not far off on either side. Road descends gradually. Carts could go along for 7½ miles. At this point cross a steep, low hill, then ascend a high hill. The descent of this is long and tedious. It is very steep, difficult, and rocky (20° in many places). In the valley there is a deep nullah or water-course, along which the road runs. The rock on these hills is of a slaty character, with veins of very good white marble showing through. Road turns north-west and continues bending round until it becomes west, ½ a mile or so from Yethéyauk. Here there is a large kyaung and two zayáts, both in bad repair; fairly good roof covering, but the side walls are gone in many places. Accommodation for 40 men. The village lies ¼ mile further on. There is accommodation here for 100 men. Thorn stockade, 30 houses. The valley is fairly big, surrounded by high hills. Excellent grass and plenty of it. Water-supply from springs, but limited.
		7. Yé ... ... Myitngé river.	9 0	78 0	Road north-east ascends steep hill, part of range which runs east and west and lies north of the village. This is a steep and rocky, but short ascent. The road then runs level on a plateau for 4½ miles. Very little view, as the country is all bamboo jungle. Some hills skirt the plateau on the right to the east. These lie generally ¼ mile off, but at places approach close to the road. The latter runs north on the plateau, but it then turns north-east and descends a steep hill (20° in places). A difficult rocky descent with a deep valley on either side. On reaching the latter the road runs along a water-course, crossing and following it alternately. It then bends round north-west to Yé (*see* in Stage 1 of Route No. 35, Northern Division). The latter is a village of 50 houses. Kyaung and three zayáts (120 men). Water from the Myitngé river 200 yards off. The river now (February) is about 70 yards wide. The main channel hugs the right bank and is about 7 feet deep. The river, however, covers a much greater area in the rains, the banks here being 200 yards apart. Bamboo rafts can be easily made here. On the opposite bank is Gwébin or Magyidaw, a place with seven houses. Yé is head-quarters or capital of Yéyamán. The latter is under the Baw Chief,

FROM YÁTSAUK TO KYWETNAPA *viâ* YÉ-U AND MYOGYI—*continued.*

Authorities. Military.	Authorities. Civil.	Number and Names of Stages, Rivers and Streams.	Distances. Intermediate.	Distances. Total.	Remarks.
G.O.C. Rangoon District.	Superintendent, Southern Shan States.	**7. Yé**—*cont.*			who receives a monthly salary of Rs. 250 for administering it. At Yé there is a great scarcity of grass, in fact none was obtainable (February). The bamboos also were all burnt, and the animals had to fall back on plantain leaves, of which there were plenty. No supplies to be got here. A road runs east to Yátsauk territory, two marches off. Yéyaman district lies between the Zawgyi river and Myitngé, south and north, and Yátsauk and Kyauksé, east and west. It is a wild and very poor place. Hardly any water to be had except at the above rivers. Along the route taken no water was met with between the above rivers, except the scanty supply at Yethéyauk.
G.O.C. Mandalay District.	Commissioner, Northern Division, and Deputy Commissioner, Mandalay.	**8. Kywetnapa** ... Myitngé river.	M. 15 F. 0	M. 93 F. 0	Road runs north-east (290°). Range of hills close to river all the way. A steep range on right bank about 500 feet high. Easy gradient, but road is rough and rocky. Bamboo jungle. At 3 miles a rocky and difficult bit is passed. River here is about 100 yards wide. Road about 30 feet above the present level of river. At 5 miles a good open space for camp. Direction now 300°. Reach village of Thayetpin, 50 houses. River, 120 yards, can be crossed on rafts. A road on the opposite bank, which runs to Kywetnapa, said to be a difficult path. One-and-a-half miles from here is the village of Kyuywa or Kyöwa, 15 houses. A mile further on is the village of Hngetgyiteik on the right or opposite bank of the river. There are some Burman police here. A road runs from here to Kyauksé. Very little to note about road from here to Kwetnapa (*see* Route No. 53, Northern Division, Stage 2). It lies through bamboo jungle all the way, which wants clearing in many places. The road makes a great bend from the river just before coming to Kywetnapa which is on opposite bank of the Myitngé river, unfordable.

No. 75.

From YÁTSAUK to MÖNGNONG (MAINGNAUNG) viâ MÖNGKÖNG (MAINGKAING).

BY LIEUT. H. E. STANTON, ROYAL ARTILLERY, FROM NATIVE INFORMATION, 6TH FEBRUARY 1888.

Military	Civil	Stages	Intermediate	Total	Remarks
G.O.C. Rangoon District.	Superintendent, Southern Shan States.	**1. Hékwi** ... ... Zawgyi.			*Note.*—This road is practicable for laden bullocks, but is not much utilized and is very difficult. The length of Stages 1 to 5 varies from 7 to 10 miles, the whole distance is three marches on foot and will be about 45 miles. Pack track. General direction east. Cross the river Zawgyi Myaung by a substantial bridge. On leaving the town cross level open country, crossing some small streams. Camp in a small open valley cultivated with paddy round the village. Water and forage good and plentiful.
		2. Paingnam ...			Pack track. General direction east-north-east. Over low forest clad undulations to the foot of the range, which bounds the Zawgyi valley on the east. Road good over

FROM YÁTSAUK TO MÖNGNONG (MAINGNAUNG) *viâ* MÖNGKÖNG (MAINGKAING)—*continued.*

Authorities. Military.	Authorities. Civil.	Number and Names of Stages, Rivers and Streams.	Distances. Intermediate. M.	F.	Distances. Total. M.	F.	Remarks.
G.O.C. Rangoon District.	Superintendent, Southern Shan States.	**2. Paingnam**—*cont.*					loam soil. Accommodation in a kyaung. Water from a brook. Grass plentiful. Village is on rising ground. It is situated on the main road from Möngsipaw (Thibaw) to Hôpôn. This road is the Möngköng Yátsauk boundary.
		3. Möngláng (Maingling). Cross Möngbyen (Maingbyin) stream.	...		...		Pack track. General direction east-north-east. Over some small hills. Road rather rough in places. Pass through jungle. Camp in a valley near the village. Water from a stream. Accommodation in a kyaung with zayáts. Grass plentiful.
		4. Kômông Sakhán.	...		...		Pack track. General direction east. Cross the Loi Anpa hill, the watershed between Irrawaddy and Salween; steep ascent and descent. Camp at the foot of the hill in a jungle sakhán. Grass and water good and plentiful. The peak of Loi Anpa is the highest in the range. From it the whole surrounding country can be seen as far as the eye can reach.
		5. Möngköng (Maingkaing).	...		45	0	Pack track. General direction east-north-east. Over low undulations divided by two or three rather muddy valleys of from 20 feet to 80 feet wide. Camping ground and zayát. Accommodation plentiful, as also water and forage. Residence of a Myoza. Five-day bazaar. On the main road from Légya to Möngyai (*see* Route No. 24, Stage 9).
		6. Naunglialön ... Namting.	12	0	57	0	Cross Namting ferry. Good camp. Water and forage plentiful.
		7. Manna	14	0	71	0	Road over undulating country. Good camp. Water and forage plentiful.
		8. Möngnong (Maingnaung).	14	0	85	0	Cross rough difficult pass of Loi (Lwé) Nakat. Residence of Myoza. Good camp. Water and forage plentiful (*see* Route No. 12, Stage 3).

No. 76.

From YÁTSAUK to TA KAW FERRY.

BY CAPT. H. R. DAVIES, OXFORDSHIRE LIGHT INFANTRY, APRIL 1893.

Military	Civil	Stage	Inter. M.	F.	Total M.	F.	Remarks
G.O.C. Rangoon District.	Superintendent, Southern Shan States.	**1. Nampamong** ... Zawgyi.	12	0	12	0	General direction south-east by east. Good mule road. At ¼ mile cross Zawgyi chaung, from the right (25 yards by 2 feet) by good cart bridge. For 2 miles through scrub jungle in a plain.

FROM YÁTSAUK TO TA KAW FERRY—*continued.*

Authorities. Military.	Authorities. Civil.	Number and Names of Stages, Rivers and Streams.	Distances. Intermediate. M. F.	Distances. Total. M. F.	Remarks.
G.O.C. Rangoon District.	Superintendent, Southern Shan States.	**1. Nampamong**—*cont.*			Thence through tree jungle among hills, but not very steep up and down. At 8 miles Nammawlong on the right. At Nampamong no village; zayát for 10 men; camping ground (150 by 100 yards), and more room could be cleared. Water from stream (2 yards by 8 inches), which does not dry up in the hot weather.
		2. Maingpyin or Möngpying. Nam Et.	11 0	23 0	General direction east. Good mule road; nearly level on top of range for 2¼ miles; thence descent to the Nam Et valley, but not very steep. The last 6 miles across a level plain. The whole road through tree and bamboo jungle. At 8½ miles village of Namkön. At 10¼ miles cross Nam Et, from the right (20 yards by 4 feet) by cart bridge. At Maingpyin large camping ground; room in zayáts for 80 men; good grass; water from well ¼ mile north of the kyaung and from the Nam Et 600 yards off. The village contains 30 houses.
		3. Natit ... ... Nam Khuklao.	13 0	36 0	General direction east-north-east. Good mule road; level for 4 miles through jungle. Thence very gentle ascent for 2 miles; cross two small spurs and descend slightly to the Namkhuklao (5 yards by 1 foot) at 8¼ miles; follow it up for a mile, then ascend slightly to the Nam Et; Nam Pawn watershed at 10¼ miles. Thence easy descent to the Nam Pawn valley. The following villages are passed:—At ¾ mile, Nalôn; at 1¾ miles, Kungwon; at 4 miles, Kungyawng; at 9½ miles, Khuklaw, ½ a mile away on the right. At Natit large camping ground; good water and grass; five-day bazaar. There is a Hein here under the Légya Sawbwa.
		4. Namsim ... Nam Pawn, Hwé Heo, and Nam Sai.	13 0	49 0	General direction east-north-east. Good mule road, up the Nam Pawn valley and cross the Nam Pawn at 1½ miles (50 yards by 2 feet, easy ford). At 2 miles cross the Nam Nama: thence uphill to Sampán at 4¼ miles. Cross a spur and descend to the Hwé Heo at 6 miles (2 yards by 6 inches); camping ground, but grass scarce. At 7½ miles good camping ground on the Nam Sai (1 yard by 6 inches); more grass than on the Hwé Heo. Cross some small spurs and ascend slightly to 5,800 feet at 8¼ miles; thence easy descent to the Nam Pawn valley. At 12¾ miles cross Nam Pawn again from the right, 30 yards by 2 feet, easy ford; ½ mile further reach Namsim kyaung. No village of Namsim, but three or four other villages close by. Large camping ground; good water and grass.

FROM YÁTSAUK TO TA KAW FERRY—*continued.*

Authorities. Military.	Authorities. Civil.	Number and Names of Stages, Rivers and Streams.	Distances. Intermediate. M.	F.	Total. M.	F.	Remarks.
G.O.C. Rangoon District.	Superintendent, Southern Shan States.	**5. Légya (Lai-kha).** At $2\frac{3}{4}$ miles Hwé Kom and small streams by easy fords.	11	4	60	4	General direction east-north-east. Good mule road, up the valley of Nam Pawn for $1\frac{1}{4}$ miles, then gentle ascent to 4,750 feet at $2\frac{1}{4}$ miles. Easy descent to the Hwé Kom at $2\frac{3}{4}$ miles (3 yards by 8 inches). Then cross some small spurs and streams, and at 5 miles descend rather steeply for a mile. Thence a nearly level road through scrub jungle to Légya (100 houses), under a Sawbwa. The best camping ground is to the north-west of the town, 600 yards off across the Nam Pwi (15 yards by 2 feet) on some rising ground, where there is a large pôngyi kyaung. Good grass; water from the Nam Pwi.
		6. Namkát ... Nam Teng and Nam Kát.	9	4	70	0	General direction east. Good mule road. Across flat ground to the Hôta ferry across the Nam Teng at $2\frac{1}{2}$ miles. The Nam Teng is 80 yards by 6 feet; sandy bottom, gentle current, steep banks; but the approaches to the ferry are good. Crossed by one raft, taking three mules or 15 men, but mules are easily swum across. Besides the raft there are three small dug-outs, out of which another raft could be made. Ferry men live in Hôta on the left bank. Large camping grounds on either bank. Thence over bare undulating country. At Namkát large camping ground and good water from the Nam Kát (5 yards by 1 foot) and good grass, but firewood rather scarce.
		7. Nampángsuk. Nam Kángwun and Nam Pángsuk.	8	2	78	2	General direction east. Good mule road. Over a bare undulating country. At $2\frac{1}{4}$ miles Namkángwun from the left (8 yards by $1\frac{1}{2}$ feet); good mule bridge. At $2\frac{1}{2}$ miles Kángwun: good camping. At $6\frac{1}{2}$ miles deserted village of Nawngkaw. At $8\frac{1}{4}$ miles Nam Pángsuk from the left (10 yards by $1\frac{1}{2}$ feet); ford rather muddy, but passable. At Nampángsuk no village. Good camping ground, water and grass.
		8. Nam Mawng ... Nam Makai and Nam Mawng.	15	6	94	0	General direction east. Good mule road. Over a nearly level country, with rocky isolated hills in places. At $1\frac{1}{4}$ miles Nawng Ché, a lake (500 by 200 yards) on right of road. At $7\frac{3}{4}$ miles, villages of Htaolai and Loi-sao: from here the best road makes a detour to the left to avoid a bad ford over the Nam Makai, rejoining the regular road again at Kungtáp at $13\frac{3}{4}$ miles. At $9\frac{1}{2}$ miles Nam Makai from the left (4 yards by 8 inches). At $15\frac{3}{4}$ miles Nam Mawng from the left (50 yards by 5 feet). There is marshy ground for 50 yards on each side of the river crossed only by a foot-bridge, mules have to be swum across and their loads carried across the foot-bridge, which is 150 yards long. At the Nam Mawng no village. Good camp, grass and water.

FROM YÁTSAUK TO TA KAW FERRY—*continued.*

Authorities. Military.	Authorities. Civil.	Number and Names of Stages, Rivers and Streams.	Distances. Intermediate. M. F.	Distances. Total. M. F.	Remarks.
G.O.C. Rangoon District.	Superintendent, Southern Shan States.	**9. Tasai (Hônawng).**	**10 0**	104 0	General direction south-east by east. Good mule road except for some unbridged streams. Over undulating country at first bare, then covered with scrub jungle. At 1¾ miles Nam Nö, from the left (8 yards by 1½ feet). At 2¾ miles Hwé Maklup, from the left (5 yards by 1 foot): muddy and difficult; wants bridging. At 7 miles Nam Nakha, from the left (4 yards by 1 foot): muddy and difficult ford. Tasai is on the Meng Kyaw lake. Camping ground round pôngyi kyaung: good grass: water from pools dug on the shore of the lake. This halting place is sometimes called Hônawng from a deserted village of that name.
		10. Saikhao ... Nam Makpai.	**14 4**	118 4	General direction south-east. Good mule road; level through thin scrub jungle for 3 miles. Then slight descent to the Nam Makpai (2 yards by 4 inches) at 3½ miles: here is the village of Kángtilap. Level again and at 6 miles cross Nam Kung, from the left (5 yards by 1 foot), and passing among some low hills, ascend Loi Pángkhan for ¼ mile, the top being reached at 10½ miles. Thence descent of 800 feet to Hôti at 12 miles. Room can be found to camp here, but the water is from a very small stream. At 12½ miles Pángsáng, a large village in three bits. Then cross a low hill and descend slightly to Saikhao, 30 houses and large bazaar; large camping ground and good water and grass. Here the Môné-Kyengtung road joins the route (*see* Route No. 23).
		11. Kyaingkán (Keng Kham).	**9 4**	128 0	General direction east. Good mule road. Across a flat grassy plateau for ¾ mile Nam Saikhao, from the left (4 yards by 1 foot) at ¾ mile; then steep descent for ½ a mile to the valley of the Nam Keng (40 yards by 2 feet), which is crossed at 2 miles. Pass through some low hills and at 4½ miles cross the Nam Páng (a small stream, not the big Nam Páng), from the right (7 yards by 1 foot). Thence up and down by easy slopes over low hills and descend to the Nam Loi at 7 miles (from the left 40 yards by 5 feet; good mule bridge). From here over level plain, partly cultivated, passing several villages, to Keng Kham, 60 houses, under a Sawbwa. Camping ground on the bank of the Nam Páng (Ben chaung): good grass and water. At Keng Kham, Nam Páng or Ben chaung flowing from the left, 450 yards wide, bottom sandy with occasional rocks sticking up: current moderate, though there is a rapid ¼ mile higher up. At the ferry are one raft taking 30 men, or five mules and 10 men, and one boat taking eight men. There are also five or six more boats which could be made into rafts. Camping ground on either side of the river. Ferrymen live on both sides.
		12. Keng Lom ...	**13 0**	141 0	General direction north-north-east. Good mule road, nearly level all the way, passing among rocky hills. Cross the Nam Páng at Keng Kham. At 6¼ miles pass Mak Kyeng: good camping ground, water and grass. At 9 miles Weng Tong, a village with a five-day bazaar. Most

FROM YÁTSAUK TO TA KAW FERRY—*continued.*

Authorities. Military.	Authorities. Civil.	Number and Names of Stages, Rivers and Streams.	Distances. Intermediate.	Distances. Total.	Remarks.
G.O.C. Rangoon District.	Superintendent, Southern Shan States.	**12. Keng Lom** —*cont.*			of the road is through jungle, not very thick. At Keng Lom camping ground in paddy (700 by 400 yards), good water and grass. Keng Lom belongs to Môné and contains about 30 houses. The Nam Nakak is crossed three times in this stage, viz., at 4½, 5½, and 6½ miles (10 yards by 2 feet). At 9 miles cross Nam Wantong, from the right (7 yards by 1 foot), and the Nam Phawm is crossed twice, viz., at 12 and at 13 miles (10 yards by 1½ feet).
			M. F.	M. F.	
		13. Ta Kaw ferry. Hwé Pung, Hwé Hôk, and Nam Kyé.	**13 0**	154 0	General direction east-north-east. Good mule road. For the first 8 miles the road is nearly level, passing among rocky hills, the only difficulty being at 1½ miles where there is a steep rocky descent for 100 yards. At 7 miles cross the Hwé Pung (from the right, 5 yards by 10 inches) and at 8 miles the Hwé Hôk (from the right, 5 yards by 8 inches), both these streams run into the hill to the north. At 8 miles ascend steeply for 600 yards to a height of 3,520 feet; thence steep descent for a mile and more gentle descent for another mile and-a-half; level for ½ a mile to the Nam Kyé at 11¼ miles (from the right, 7 yards by 8 inches). Pass the village of Nanö; good camping ground and water. At 12¾ and at 13 miles, Nam Aw (10 yards by 1 foot). Then ascend for 200 yards and descend gently to Ta Kaw. Small camping ground. For a large column it would be best to camp at Nanö. The Salween or Nam Khong, here flowing from the left, channel 400 yards wide, water 180 yards wide: bottom sandy with rocks sticking up; rapid current: good approaches to the ferry. Crossed by one raft taking six mules or 20 men; there are two boats besides, out of which another raft might be made. Camping ground on the left bank. Ferrymen on both banks. Lieut. H. E. Stanton, Royal Artillery, followed an apparently somewhat different route to the above between Légya and Ta Kaw with the Southern Shan column of 1887-88. His account of the route is contained in Route No. 23, Alternative II, and Branch II.

No. 77.

From YWANGÁN to HMAW-AING viâ NÉYAUNGA.

BY LIEUT. J. A. S. TULLOCH, R.E., JANUARY AND FEBRUARY 1888.

Authorities. Military.	Authorities. Civil.	Number and Names of Stages, Rivers and Streams.	Distances. Intermediate.	Distances. Total.	Remarks.
G.O.C. Rangoon District.	Superintendent, Southern Shan States.	**1. Néyaunga** ...	**11 0**	11 0	From Ywangán there is a second pass leading down to the Pánláng valley. It is said that Shans prefer this pass to the Nattik at certain seasons of the year, but have been afraid to use it on account of dacoits. It comes out at Néyaunga and the back of Hmaw-aing. On leaving Ywangán there are two routes to the head of the pass: *Route No.* 1.—Road starts in south-west direction (210°). At ½ mile pass village of Kángyi, a dozen huts. At 1 mile there is some difficult rocky ground. Then cross a valley running north and south in which paddy is largely cultivated in the rains. Excellent water to be got here from a

FROM YWANGÁN TO HMAW-AING *viâ* NÉYAUNGA—*continued.*

Authorities. Military.	Authorities. Civil.	Number and Names of Stages, Rivers and Streams.	Distances. Intermediate.	Distances. Total.	Remarks.
G.O.C. Rangoon District.	Superintendent, Southern Shan States.	**1. Néyaunga** —*cont.*			mountain rivulet. The path which has been bearing more and more to the west now turns north-west along the lower spurs of the range of hills which lie south-west of Ywangán. The head of the pass is about 4 miles out from Ywangán. Practicable for laden animals. *Route No.* 2.—Direction west. At ½ mile pass village of Shisébôgyin. A narrow gap which occurs about a mile from Ywangán could be avoided by a detour. At 2 miles hamlet of Lézaing (15 houses). Animals could go to the head of the pass without much difficulty, the road being at about the same level throughout, though here and there rough and somewhat difficult bits are met with, but on account of several narrow places with rocky sides and the steepness of the road the descent of the pass itself to the Pánláng valley is impracticable for laden animals. From the head of the pass the descent to the Pánláng valley is rapid and the path is exceedingly bad, worse than the Nattik pass. The descent is 4 miles in length. On reaching the valley the path turns southwards and continues along the right bank of the Pánláng river for 3 miles. It then crosses the river by a ford and reaches Néyaunga on the left bank at 11 miles. The valley of the river is only about 300 yards wide. In February there was about 3 feet of water in river. Néyaunga has 12 houses and a ruined pôngyi kyaung. At the village itself the valley is somewhat broader than usual, being about 500 yards across. A path leads from this village through the Hmaw-aing gorge, and there is no doubt that the dacoits when driven out of the latter place from the Thábiyédaung side retreated on Néyaunga. The latter place was burnt by our troops (April 1887), but was formerly a large village. A path is said to lead up the valley to Minpalaung, but this requires confirmation. *Note.*—From some high ground near the head (top) of the pass the bearings to the Pyetkawé west was 292°. This high ground lies a little to the south. The general bearing of the pass itself was taken as 250°. The Hmaw-aing gorge was distinctly visible from this point. The hills on the opposite side of the Pánláng valley looked bare and rocky.

No. 78.

From YWANGÁN to KYAUKNET (Route No. 74, Stage 2).

BY LIEUT. J. A. S. TULLOCH, R.E., JANUARY AND FEBRUARY 1888.

Military	Civil	Stage	Intermediate M.	Intermediate F.	Total M.	Total F.	Remarks
G.O.C. Rangoon District.	Superintendent, Southern Shan States.	**1. Kyauknet** ...	**8**	**0**	8	0	The road runs through undulating but uninteresting country. General direction west. At present (January) it is covered with long grass which is being burnt down. The valleys are being prepared for cultivation. The hill-tops are covered with a few trees and some scrub jungle. After leaving Ywangán road descends to a valley, at the bottom of which is a small stream. A sharp ascent up the opposite side and then the road descends gradually down a valley running to east. At 2 miles pass village of Myélezôn, a few huts ¼ mile to the south. This village is not seen until

FROM YWANGÁN TO KYAUKNET (ROUTE NO. 74, STAGE 2)—*continued.*

Authorities. Military.	Authorities. Civil.	Number and Names of Stages, Rivers and Streams.	Distances. Inter-mediate.	Distances. Total.	Remarks.
G.O.C. Rangoon District.	Superintendent, Southern Shan States.	**1. Kyauknet**—*cont.*			some time after it is passed, as it lies in a hollow. Several cross paths are met with, those on the left all lead to Yé-u. Just ½ mile before reaching the foot of the hills the village of Öktwit is passed ¼ mile to the north. From here Kyauknet is reached by a narrow winding and rocky path through the hills about 2 miles long. This path is steep in places and would be difficult though practicable for laden animals. For description of Kyauknet (*see* Route No. 74, Stage 2).

No. 79.

From YWANGÁN to YÉ-U (BAW), (Route No. 74, Stage 3).

BY LIEUT. J. A. S. TULLOCH, R.E., JANUARY AND FEBRUARY 1888.

Military	Civil	Stage	Intermediate	Total	Remarks
G.O.C. Rangoon District.	Superintendent, Southern Shan States.	**1. Yé-u**	M. F. ...	M. F. ...	On leaving Ywangán bazaar the road turns northwards, bearing 10°. About a mile out it bears off more to the eastward (40°) and its general direction to Yé-u may be taken at north-east. The road or track is excellent and fit for transport of any kind up to the top of the descent to Yé-u. Here it is in one or two places too narrow for wheeled transport. A very little labour, however, would remove these obstructions which only extend over ¼ mile of the road. No cultivation was passed along the road, but the valleys all grow paddy in the rains. About half-way the boundary between Baw (Yé-u) and Ywangán is crossed. It is marked by a big tree. Soon after a sort of plateau is reached, from which the road gradually descends to Yé-u. Quarter mile from head of what is called the Yé-u pass a road branches to the village of Taung Kombaw. The village of Kaséywa can be seen about 2 miles to right (*see* Route No. 74, Stage 3). The descent to Yé-u is down the side of a hill and is not through a pass. It is short and not steep. Yé-u itself is a small place as a village, but is important as possessing the district bazaar. There are two zayáts in the latter with accommodation for 30 men, but more could be put up under cover in houses and in the bazaar sheds. There is a stout wooden palisade stockade round the bazaar. An excellent and ample water-supply is obtained from stream close by. The latter is a foot deep and 4 or 5 yards wide. The Yé-u valley here is narrow (½ mile); is enclosed by steep hills; it runs generally north and south, the slope being to the south. It is used for paddy cultivation. The village lies a ½ of a mile higher up the valley than the bazaar. There are about 30 houses. Some of a good class. The road from Ywangán lies through very open country. Grass land with a very few trees. A very good view can therefore be obtained on either side of the hills. The latter appear to be thickly wooded. From Yé-u a road runs north-east to Theingôn, 1 mile away, 40 houses, a large kyaung with zayáts. Accommodation for 150 men and stabling for 100 animals under kyaung. Water-supply good, but limited from springs. From here a road runs south-east through the hills to Kyauknet passing the old silver mines (not being worked now) about 4 miles out.

No. 80.

From YWATHIT to KUNYUOM (HKUNYOM, SIAM).

By Capt. Walker, Intelligence Branch, Native information, March 1893.

Authorities. Military.	Authorities. Civil.	Number and Names of Stages, Rivers and Streams.	Distances. Intermediate. M.	F.	Total. M.	F.	Remarks.
G.O.C. Rangoon District.	Superintendent, Southern Shan States.	**1. Mé Saya** ... The Salween and the Mé Saya.	**9**	**0**	9	0	The route runs down to the Salween at Ta Saug Lé along an easy spur for 2 miles, last 1½ miles steeper, the road being broad enough for men to march in "fours." On the right bank of the river where the village stands, there is a fine zayát capable of accommodating two companies. The ferry consists of the usual "dug-out," the river here being about 270 yards across and very deep and swift. After crossing, the route runs along the left bank of the Saiween southwards, the going being sandy and rocky under foot. At 5½ miles from the ferry a small stream, the Mé Saya, about 10 feet across, 1 to 1½ feet deep, and a steep crossing on the left bank. Here there is the Karen and Shan village of Mé Saya (nine houses). Camping ground in paddy-fields for 1,000 men or more.
		2. Me Sipaw ...	**8**	**0**	17	0	Leaving Mé Saya the route continues along the banks of the Salween southward through big tree jungle for about 3 miles to where the Mé Sipaw stream flows into the Salween, the route now runs up the valley of the Mé Sipaw eastward, crossing and recrossing for about 5 miles. A shady camp with room for 500 men on the river bank. For another description of these two stages *see* Route No. 83.
		3. Nam Pé Kyauk. Nam Pé Kyauk.	**13**	**4**	30	4	*See* Route No. 83, Stage 2.
		4. Mé Sé or Mé Ché. Mé Sé.	**13**	**0**	43	4	*See* Route No. 83, Stage 3. Mé Sé (southern) situated on the left bank of the stream of that name contains 30 houses, with a large kyaung and a large camping ground in the fields to the east of the village. Accommodation in and about the villages for 800 to 1,000 men. Supplies plentiful. Grass, fruit, &c.
		5. Camp on Nam Pông. Nam Pông.	**8**	**0**	51	4	General direction north-east. Path follows Mé Ché stream for first 3 miles and is good. At 3 miles village of Nampông (18 houses. Shan). Accommodation for about 500 men in and about the village which is a point for concentration of troops of some importance. Remainder of stage up Nam Pông valley, path good; crossing and recrossing the stream which flows from north to south frequently. Camping ground (elevation 2,000 feet) at 8 miles on the stream room for about 300 men. Grass and bamboo available for fodder, no other supplies. The valley is here steeply enclosed. Heavy open jungle on both sides; mostly teak.

FROM YWATHIT TO KUNYUOM (HKUNYOM SIAM)—*continued.*

Authorities. Military.	Authorities. Civil.	Number and Names of Stages, Rivers and Streams.	Distances. Intermediate. M.	F.	Distances. Total. M.	F.	Remarks.
Siam.		**6. Mé Ngau** Tunun, Hwé Pông, Mokpai, and Mé Ngaw streams.	10	4	62	0	The path now ascends the Loi Tunun which is the watershed between the Hwé Pông on the Siam side and the Nam Pông on the Burmese. It crosses the frontier ridge at an elevation of 3,500 feet at 1½ miles, the ascent being steep but good under foot, descending in the valley of the Tunun, which stream is followed until absorbed by the Hwé Pông, when a steep spur is crossed into the valley of the Mok Pai, which flows into the Mé Ngau (Nam Méngau) stream near the eastern portion of the double village of the same name. There is accommodation in the taungya above this portion of the village for 100 men; below the western portion in fields for 300 men.
		7. Kunyuom (Hkunyom). Mé Ngau and Mé Kunyuom streams.	8	0	70	0	General direction first 5¼ miles east-south-east, then east-north-east. For the 1st mile and a-half the route runs down the Mé Ngau valley, when it crosses a low ridge and descends into the valley of the Mé Hkunyom, which it follows, crossing and recrossing it eight or nine times to mile 4, where the village of Tawhpé (20 houses, Shans) is passed to the right hand and situated on a small stream flowing into the Mé Hkunyom. The route then rises slightly and crosses the lower slopes of a low ridge lying to the right hand or south-east and enters Hkunyom at its south end. (For description of Hkunyom, *see* Appendix III, Route 2.)

ALTERNATIVE I.

FROM MÉ SIPAW (STAGE 2) TO MÉ NGAU (STAGE 6) *viâ* PONG PING LONG.

BY CAPT. WALKER, INTELLIGENCE BRANCH, NATIVE INFORMATION, 1893.

Military	Civil	Stage	M.	F.	M.	F.	Remarks
C.O.C. Rangoon District.	Superintendent, Southern Shan States.	**1. Pong Ping Long.** Mé Sipau and Mé Ngau streams.	9	0	9	0	General direction east-south-east. The route follows the course of the Mé Sipaw to its source, crossing and re-crossing by a path overgrown and needing clearing; otherwise it is said to be a good one. Since 1890 it has only been used to convey rations to the Siamese post at Mé Sipaw. At mile 8½ the route crosses the frontier ridge by an easy ascent, the boundary mark lying to the left hand or north of the route. The path now almost immediately strikes the course of the Mé Ngau, narrow and containing but little water, its valley being about 50 to 100 yards wide and the route almost level as far as the camp at mile 9. Here there is accommodation for 200 to 300 men on the left bank of the stream, the water-supply of which is very scanty and requires husbanding. Grass in abundance and wild plantains for roofing "machans" or sheds.

FROM YWATHIT TO KUNYUOM (HKUNYOM SIAM)—*continued.*

ALTERNATIVE I—*continued.*

Authorities.		Number and Names of Stages, Rivers and Streams.	Distances.				Remarks.
Military.	Civil.		Intermediate.		Total.		
			M.	F.	M.	F.	
G.O.C. Rangoon District.	Superintendent, Southern Shan States.	**2. Pong Wong Long.** The Mé Ngau rising below the frontier flowing south-eastwards, 5 or 6 yards broad, 6 inches to 2 feet deep; gravelly bottom; muddy crossings and apt to become difficult with much traffic.	**9**	**0**	18	0	General direction east-south-east. Leaving the small camp at Pong Ping Long the route follows the course of the Mé Ngau. The valley of this stream is enclosed on either side by two minor ridges clothed with jungle, the valley itself varying in width from ¼ to 1 mile and containing dense jungle. Large teak, bamboo, and tropical undergrowth. The route, which is only faintly defined, having been but little used during the years of 1890-92, is narrow and in the month of March 1893 choked by fallen timber and bamboos, though easily clearable. The stream, which maintains an average width, is crossed and recrossed many times. The route is passable for laden animals, but requires widening and repairing in places. There are several places *en route* which could be utilized as camps for small parties, but there is no regular encampment until Pong Wong Long is reached at the 9th mile. Here there is accommodation on the left bank of the stream for 250 men. Grass of good quality and bamboo leaves.
Siam.		**3. Mé Ngau** .. Mé Ngau and Mok Pai.	**12**	**0**	...		General direction east-south-east. The route continues along the Mé Ngau, crossing and recrossing, narrow in places, put passable for laden animals; thick jungle on either side; the path being now better defined. At mile 11 lower or western portion of the village Mé Ngau is reached (six houses, Shans; a few supplies only). Here to left hand of the route there is accommodation in old paddy-fields for 300 men and grass for animals, while between this and the eastern portion of the same village 1 mile further on there are taungya clearings affording accommodation for 300 more, though the ground slopes unevenly. The eastern portion of the village contains 12 houses and tolerable supplies. Just below and to the south of the village the Mok Pai stream joins the Mé Ngau flowing west-south-west, along the course of which runs the route to Ywathit *viâ* Nampông and Mésé described above.

No. 81.

From YWATHIT to MÉHAWNGSAWN (Siam Water Route viâ Mépai River).

BY CAPT. WALKER, INTELLIGENCE BRANCH, NATIVE INFORMATION, MARCH 1893.

From Ywathit to Méhawngsawn is said to take four days by boat; from Méhawngsawn to Ywathit one day. The Mépai is navigable all the year round by small boats. The valley sides are steep and only small encampments can be obtained. At the junction of the Mé Hsulin the latter stream can be followed until the frontier at Paktumöng, and thence to Hkunyom. There is a bullock track along the Mépai, but it is out of repair and in 1893 said to be impassable.

No. 82.

From YWATHIT to MÔNÉ viâ SATAW (SADAW) and MAUKMÉ.

By Major E. G. BARROW, 7th Bengal Infantry, 1890.

Authorities. Military.	Authorities. Civil.	Number and Names of Stages, Rivers and Streams.	Distances. Intermediate. M. F.	Distances. Total. M. F.	Remarks.
G.O.C. Rangoon District.	Superintendent, Southern Shan States.	**1. Paw Kōta or Wan Nakún (1,600 feet).** Small stream.	9 4	...	The first 4 miles easy and level between hills. The next two still level, but the ground more or less broken along the banks of a shallow stream which it crosses several times. At 6 miles a wall-like cliff bars the way, this is ascended by a zigzag which in places is very rocky and bad for mules. The total ascent is about 200 feet, at the top one reaches a small plateau, whence after a slight descent one follows the rocky bed of a dry ravine between high banks overhung by trees. At 7½ miles there is a steep ascent nearly ¾ of a mile in length (altitude about 2,200 feet). Follow the crest for ½ a mile or more, after which the path descends rapidly to camp on the left bank of a stream flowing towards Paw Kōta. The camping ground is a paddy-field between steep jungle clad hills. Water, firewood and bamboo forage abundant.
		2. Na Môn (1,800 feet). Small stream.	8 0	17 4	The first ½ mile easy and level, then a stiff ascent of a mile, to a point about 2,500 feet above sea. At the crest the Salween comes into view rather a stiff descent to the paddy-fields known as Na On. Cross streams both on entering and leaving Na On (altitude about 1,600 feet). At 3 miles a stiff ascent of about 400 feet, the path then becomes fairly level for a bit, and then another ascent brings one up to 2,500 feet at 4½ miles. At 5 miles a Karen village, near which one gets a good view of the Salween (here a mile or so distant and flowing from north-north-east). At 6 miles cross a narrow brook. At 7 miles gain the valley and cross a clear sparkling stream. At 8 miles cross another stream and camp in the paddy-fields known as Na Môn. Forage, firewood and water plentiful. One mile to the westward there is a gap in the hills, through which runs a path to Sawlôn, said to be practicable for bullocks.
		3. Na Makwán (1,800 feet). Small stream.	8 0	25 4	For 5 miles along the lower slopes of the western watershed. There are one or two rocky bits, especially 1 mile out of camp, and some of the ascents are troublesome, but on the whole the road is not bad. At 5 miles ascend to and pass through a sort of natural gateway between some peculiar limestone crags. At 5¼ miles Karen village on knoll to right of road (no water). At 6 miles a path goes off to left towards Tilanga, *see* Branch II below. From this point there is a long winding descent of a couple of miles to camp on the banks of a shallow stream, 40 feet wide. The best place probably for camping is a paddy clearing ¼ of a mile to north of stream. Forage and firewood abundant. This march is not, on the whole, a very bad one, except for the want of water *en route*.
		4. Na Môn (2,350 feet).	8 0	33 4	Stiff ascent of a mile or more to about 2,800 feet. From the top a gentle descent to a Karen village at 2½ miles. At 3½ miles another village. From here the road goes up and down along the hill slopes crossing spur after spur and hamlet after hamlet, the path generally a very narrow one through tall

FROM YWATHIT TO MÔNÉ *viâ* SÁTAW (SADAW) AND MAUKMÉ—*continued.*

Authorities. Military.	Authorities. Civil.	Number and Names of Stages, Rivers and Streams.	Distances. Intermediate.	Distances. Total.	Remarks.
G.O.C. Rangoon District.	Superintendent, Southern Shan States.	**4. Na Môn (2,350 feet)**—*cont.*			grass or low jungle. At 7½ miles a path from Tilanga joins in and at 8 miles reach some paddy-fields where there is space for a camp.
		5. Sataw (900 feet). Sataw stream.	M. 7 F. 0	M. 40 F. 4	Cross the southern watershed of the Sataw chaung by a low and easy *kôtal* not more than 300 feet above camp. The descent is long and gradual. At 4 miles strike the Sataw chaung and follow the stream, crossing it repeatedly, to the south gate of Sataw. The best camping ground is perhaps the paddy-fields to the north of the town. There is no shade, but the water is unpolluted. Sataw lies at the junction of the trade routes from the Shan States and Karenni to Méhawngsawn. It has a population of nearly 2,000, mostly Shans, and supplies are procurable in considerable quantities, especially paddy and rice. From here there is a branch road to Tilanga, *see* Branch II below.
		6. Camp on the Hwé Lôn (900 feet). Hwé Lôn and small streams.	8 4	49 0	General direction north-east by north. Road excellent. Cross Sataw chaung (12 feet broad) on leaving camp and again at 2 miles. Here there is a short rather steep rise. Near the top of which are springs. At 3¾ miles road crosses a stream twice. At 4½ miles a slight rise and descent, and at 5 miles reach Nga Kyaing village and stream. Village about dozen houses with good camping ground in paddy-fields. Stream about 20 feet broad; good bottom about 1 foot of water; swift and running south-east. Road then crosses between two low hills for ¾ mile, cuts into a dry nullah with very steep banks and proceeds up it for 1½ miles, direction north-west by north, then leaving nullah by short steep ascent turns north-east and north along the hill top and down an easy descent to the Hwé Lôn river running south-east, where there is excellent camping ground. Hwé Lôn 40 yards broad, rapid, good bottom, low banks, and 1 to 1½ feet water.
		7. Camp Na-On (1,450 feet). Hwé Lôn, Nam Pakpai, Pankôn, and another stream.	9 0	58 0	Road onwards follows bed of the Hwé Lôn and along its banks. Fairly high hills on both sides; several open places in jungle, where camps could be formed. At about 3 miles, the river bed is strewn with large boulders which delayed baggage mules considerably for nearly a mile, when the track leaves the river bed at a narrow gorge and passes above it on right bank. The remainder of the track is good across low undulating hills and river bed till Na-On village is reached. Ample camping ground on paddy-fields on left bank of stream. Na-On about 15 houses, considerable amount of teak logs in river bed. Close to the village the Hwé Lôn is joined by the Nam Pakpai from the north-west and the Pan Kôn and another stream from the north and north-east respectively.
		8. Katulon (or Kadawgyi), 1,900 feet. HwéLon, Pankôn, Nam Sangan or Mé Ngaim.	11 0	69 0	Cross Nam Pakpai, a small stream with about 9 inches of water. Proceed north along Hwé Lôn for 1 mile, it is there crossed and left; road continues up the Pankôn river (stream rocky bed) for 2½ miles where river is left. Next 3 miles good going

FROM YWATHIT TO MÔNÉ *viâ* SÁTAW (SADAW) AND MAUKMÉ—*continued.*

Authorities. Military.	Authorities. Civil.	Number and Names of Stages, Rivers and Streams.	Distances. Intermediate. M. F.	Distances. Total. M. F.	Remarks.
G.O.C. Rangoon District.	Superintendent, Southern Shan States.	**8. Katulôn (or Kadawgyi), 1,900 feet**—*cont.*			over undulating hills north-east by north when the track becomes broad and beaten amongst groups of pine trees. Then turning a little west of north continues over undulating low hills crossing a couple of dry nullahs. Two and-a-half miles further on there is a sharp but easy descent near the bottom, of which a road goes east to Taung Ku under La-Kao-Wen Taung. At the foot flows the Nam Sangan or Mé Ngam river about 10 yards broad, swift with steep banks about 1 foot water, on the far side of which is a small village. Continuing north-west the country becomes cultivated and fairly open, and two streams flowing east are crossed, then after a slight ascent to the top of a plateau Katulôn is reached. Camped on east side. Katulôn is really a group of village. The largest near the camp has a double row of bamboo stockading round it and about 30 houses. Supplies paddy and fowls. Camping ground very extensive on large paddy plain and dub grass plentiful. *General remarks.*—Along all the river beds the jungle is almost entirely bamboo and on the higher and undulating hills also interspersed with large trees. After leaving the Pankôn there is no water along the route till the Nam Sangan is reached. The road in the dry season is practicable for all arms (not wheeled), but in the rains it would be absolutely impassable, for most of the streams carry timber and run many feet deep.
		9. Salaung (700 feet). Mé Ngam and Nam Yum.	13 4	82 4	There are two routes from Katulôn to Maukmé, one is as described below *viâ* Salaung, the other practicable for pack transport is *viâ* Hwé Hlwet 14 miles (passing Pánglu, 20 houses at 5 miles), where there is bad camping ground on a stream surrounded by hills and very feverish looking; thence to Maukmé 11 miles. Road difficult. Direction north. Leaving Katulôn track proceeds east-south-east for 2 miles passing small village on left and the Mé Ngam stream (bridge broken), then north-east with a gradual rise over undulating hills through *in* and bamboo jungle. At 8½ miles the highest point is reached some 500 feet above Katulôn. The descent is steep and rocky, working down a spur in an easterly direction for 3 miles (100 laden mules took 1 hour 50 minutes to cover these 3 miles). Half-a-mile from the foot of the hill strike the Nam Yum and cross it a little lower down opposite some huge irrigation wheels. The river is about 40 yards broad and 2 feet deep, good bottom, low banks. Road follows left bank to Salaung, a Shan village of 40 houses. (There is a very good camping ground 1 mile east of Salaung near some tamarind trees, but it is of course off the Maukmé road.)
		10. Nam Pôk ... Nam Nu Gyo.	11 0	93 4	Leaving the village of Salaung the road turns north, crossing the Nam Nu Gyo stream thrice, it continues up a constant ascent, partly over rocky ground, till Nam Nu Gyo camping ground is reached. There is a zayát (= 30 men). The water at this season is somewhat scarce confined in pools in the stream bed on the north side of the camp. Ground open. Three miles further on over a fair track is Páng Kyeng zayát and camping ground (zayát = 50 men), large clear space. Water from the bed of a stream about 300 to 400 yards from camp,

FROM YWATHIT TO MÔNÉ *viâ* SATAW (SADAW) AND MAUKMÉ—*continued.*

Authorities.		Number and Names of Stages, Rivers and Streams.	Distances.		Remarks.
Military.	Civil.		Intermediate.	Total.	
G.O.C. Rangoon District.	Superintendent, Southern Shan States.	**10. Nam Pôk**—*cont.*			obtained at this season by digging holes. One and-a-half miles on there is a zayát, but no water. Here a road branches off north-east to Banhát, *see* Branch No. IV below. The track here turns north-west, and at 2½ miles on passes Nampôk camp, ground open, and water obtained by digging in stream bed (200 bullocks obtained water by this means on 8th February).
			M. F.	M. F.	
		11. Maukmé (Mokmai). Nam Yum.	**10 4**	104 0	Two miles on (the track from Nampôk turns north-east) is Nyaung Su camp. Water obtained by digging. There is a little cultivation. The track now ascends over boulders, but is quite practicable for laden mules, and then taking a sharp turn west ascends for 3 miles to the top (2,600 feet) of the range of hills which run north and south. The last mile and-a-half is very steep and stony, but presents no insuperable difficulty to laden transport. Turning north for a few hundred yards on level ground it turns north-west and after a steep descent for a mile reaches the level again. Here there is a stream with ample water for, say, 300 animals. Continuing in a north-west direction across undulating ground and paddy plain, it reaches the bridge over the Nam Yum and Maukmé. Camped on banks of river, which is here about 60 yards in breadth, but barely fordable for men. Maukmé is rapidly regaining its old importance and has some 400 houses; bullocks, fowls, paddy, rice, tinned-milk, &c., can be purchased. Paddy and rice are very plentiful, and the grazing is excellent, but climate has proved unhealthy; bullock carts are used.(for local purposes only). *General remarks.*—Bamboo can be got in small quantities as forage at all halting places between Salaung and Maukmé, and the camping grounds are good but water is scarce, and "hard" at this season, and probably by the end of April unobtainable. Most of the timber along the route is *in.* From Pángkyeng to Maukmé is a six hours' march for mules.
		12. Camp on Mélôn stream or Myelwán Sakhán. Nam Yum, and Méln stream.	**12 0**	116 0	Road proceeds north through paddy-fields and crosses two streams, tributaries of the Nam Yum river. At 3 miles reaches the foot of a steep ascent, up which a zigzag road runs (carts used to traverse the entire road between Maukmé and Mône, but the road has fallen into bad repair, and requires bridges at various points), from the top of this rise the road passes over a plateau (700 feet above Maukmé) and through the village of Mõng Law at about 5 miles crosses the Nam Yum by a bridge about 20 yards in breadth, and bending north-east. At 9½ miles branches off north and north-east. The former is the direct Môné road, but the latter is used in the dry season. Following it Mélôn village is reached at 11 miles, and a mile further on there is a good camping ground on paddy-fields on the Mélôn stream. This stream, like so many others, after flowing above ground for some distance, suddenly becomes a dry bed. The water was good and ample.

FROM YWATHIT TO MÔNÉ *viâ* SATAW (SADAW) AND MAUKMÉ—*continued*.

Authorities. Military.	Authorities. Civil.	Number and Names of Stages, Rivers and Streams.	Distances. Intermediate.		Distances. Total.		Remarks.
			M.	F.	M.	F.	
G.O.C. Rangoon District.	Superintendent, Southern Shan States.	**13. Mône (Möngnai).**	11	4	127	4	Three-quarter mile after leaving camp the track strikes into the main road again at a camping ground on the same stream. Here water was unexpectedly found. The road continues a constant though easy rise for the next 5 miles north-east when the ascent becomes steeper and the highest point is reached (about 3,700 feet) and the gradual descent begins. Four miles on there is a zayát and well, in which there is always water through "hard" and another mile on there is a bridge over a deep ravine, from which water could probably be got by digging. Two miles further on Môné town is reached. It like Maukmé is recovering rapidly and has some 400 houses, with notice 200 to 300 pack bullocks can be collected and rice and paddy in almost any quantities.
		14. Môné Police Post. Môné river.	4	4	132	0	Leaving the town to the east and proceeding north by the Fort Stedman road the new post is reached, after crossing the Môné river a mile to the south of it by a long wooden bridge which, though safe, requires repairs. The road from the town to the post is flanked by a brick wall for the last 2 miles. The police post consists of 75 rifles Shan Levy and a small earthwork has been built near the barracks. The barracks are supplied by water from springs and a well. *General remarks.*—This road from Maukmé is in the dry season very good, but in the rains bad, especially the first 3 miles from Maukmé which becomes a quagmire, raising this and a little blasting on the zigzag path, and also 2 miles from Môné, would make the road quite practicable for carts and would greatly open up the country.

BRANCH I.

FROM SATAW (STAGE 5) TO MÉHAWNGSAWN (ROUTE NO. 32) *viâ* TA TA MAW.

BY MAJOR E. G. BARROW, 7TH B.I., J. G. SCOTT, ESQ., 1890, AND H. G. A. LEVESON, ESQ., FEBRUARY 1893.

Military.	Civil.	Stages.	Intermediate M.	Intermediate F.	Total M.	Total F.	Remarks.
G.O.C. Rangoon District.	Superintendent, Southern Shan States.	**1. Ta Ta Maw ...** Sataw chaung, Salween river.	7	4	7	4	Leave the town by the east gate and go through the paddy-fields on the left bank of the Sataw chaung. At 1 mile pass a hot sulphur spring in the river, at 2 miles the road may be said to enter the bed of the river, that is to say, in the next 3½ miles it crosses it ten times. It is nowhere more than a foot or so deep and about 30 feet wide. At 4½ miles pass the Shan village of Salaung (three houses). At 5½ miles leave the river which flows south-east to the Salween. At 7½ miles Ta Ta Maw (50 houses). This is the ferry for Sataw. Boats are always procurable. It is probably best to encamp on the right bank of the Salween, though room may also be found on the left bank.
		2. Mé Hsaté ... Mé Sisap, Mé Hsaté.	8	0	15	4	The road runs south-east over a low spur to the Mé Sisap, and so far is very good. Ford the Mé Sisap, which, in the dry season, is only a few inches deep. A spur from the Loi Lán 2,500

FROM YWATHIT TO MÔNÉ *viâ* SATAW (SADAW) AND MAUKMÉ—*continued.*

BRANCH I—*continued.*

Authorities. Military.	Authorities. Civil.	Number and Names of Stages, Rivers and Streams.	Distances. Intermediate. M.	F.	Distances. Total. M.	F.	Remarks.
G.O.C. Rangoon District.	Superintendent, Southern Shan States.	**2. Mé Hsaté**—*cont.*					feet high has now to be crossed, the ascent is somewhat steep, but the gradient on the southern side is better and the road fairly good. Mé Hsaté is a Shan village of about 40 houses, paddy procurable.
		3. Tin Loi ... Mé Hsaté, Mé Layu.	9	0	24	4	Ford the Mé Hsaté. The road which is fairly good and level goes up the Mé Hsaté On, it then crosses the watershed between the Mé Hsaté and Mé Layu 3,450 feet high, but neither ascent nor descent are very difficult. Camp at the foot of the hill. Ground confined but otherwise good.
		4. Hwé Káhán ... Mé Layu, Hwé Káhán.	7	0	31	4	Cross the Mé Layu three times, then up the Hwé Káhán crossing it repeatedly. The last 3 miles are rocky and bad. Camping ground limited.
Chins.		**5. Méhsoi** ... Hwé Pángsalán, Mé Hsoi.	6	4	38	0	General direction south-east up to Méhawngsawn. Cross the Loi Lán, which is here only 2,500 feet, by the Pángsalán pass which is very gradual and easy. The crest which is about 500 feet above camp is reached in ½ a mile and here is the boundary pillar erected in February 1893 to mark the boundary between Siam and Eastern Karenni. At 1 mile reach the Hwé Pángsalán stream and follow its course to its junction with the Mé Hsoi at 5 miles. It then follows the course of that stream to Mé Hsoi, Siamese village of eight houses. Road generally good and passable for pack animals. Camp near village; the Mé Hsoi is a tributary of the Mé Pai.
		6. Méhawngsawn. Mé Hsoi, Mé Pai.	8	0	46	0	Down the Mé Hsoi to its junction with the Mé Pai at 6 miles, which is crossed at the village of Hsuppawng lying on both banks, 45 houses in all, thence over undulating country to Méhawngsawn, a Siamese town of 2,000 inhabitants in a large paddy plain; road good throughout; supplies procurable, *see* Route No. 32.

BRANCH II.

FROM SATAW (STAGE 5) TO TILANGA (ROUTE NO. 4, STAGE 10).

I. B. COMPILATION, 1888.

Authorities. Military.	Authorities. Civil.	Number and Names of Stages, Rivers and Streams.	Distances. Intermediate. M.	F.	Distances. Total. M.	F.	Remarks.
G.O.C. Rangoon District.	Superintendent, Southern Shan States.	**1. Lokoru** ... Streams.	13	0	13	0	General direction of road south-west. The road running through the large rice plain, in the centre of which Sataw is situated, leads along a winding stream from 1 to 2 feet deep, which it crosses several times. At 3 miles the plain is left and the road begins to ascend. At 5 miles cross a shallow stream of good running water springing from a high rock on the right. Here there is a good shady space for a camp. At 7 miles the road crosses a bad bit of slippery shelving rock for 50 yards. A mile further

FROM YWATHIT TO MÔNÉ *viâ* SATAW (SADAW) AND MAUKMÉ—*continued.*

BRANCH II—*continued.*

Authorities. Military.	Authorities. Civil.	Number and Names of Stages, Rivers and Streams.	Distances. Intermediate. M.	F.	Total. M.	F.	Remarks.
G.O.C. Rangoon District.	Superintendent, Southern Shan States.	**1. Lokoru**—*cont.*					on reach a shallow stream of good water with sandy bed. From here the road rises steadily to the top of a ridge, which it crosses at the height to 3,500 feet and descends to the Karenni village of Lokoru, with extensive paddy cultivation in the valley. Supplies of pigs, fowls, and paddy plentiful. Water good and plentiful. Camp to west of village.
		2. Dorda ... ... Small streams.	6	0	19	0	Path continues good and rises through jungle for first 4 miles, passing villages in jungle on both sides. Two very small streams on road. For the last 2 miles the path turns south and descends steadily to the small Karenni village of Dorda, supplies as before, camp small, ona spur 1,000 yards beyond the village, near a small stream. Water scarce and requires banking and damming up to water animals.
		3. Tilanga Ferry. Pôn river.	7	0	26	0	Road still good; ascends for the 1st mile to the top of the ridge at 2,550 feet and then, after running up and down hill, descends at 5 miles to the valley of the Pôn river. Rough stony bit for 100 yards, difficult for transport animals, three-fourths of the way down. At 5 miles a little water, though scarce. The last 2 miles runs over fairly open wooded level ground to Tilanga ferry (*see* Route No. 4, Stage 10).

BRANCH III.

FROM KATULÔN (STAGE 8) TO MÖNG MAÖ (ROUTE No. 32) *viâ* TA HSUP TENG.

BY HAVILDAR SEWAMBAR SING, 7TH BENGAL INFANTRY, 1890.

Authorities. Military.	Authorities. Civil.	Number and Names of Stages, Rivers and Streams.	Distances. Intermediate. M.	F.	Total. M.	F.	Remarks.
G.O.C. Rangoon District.	Superintendent, Southern Shan States.	**1. Ta Hsup Teng.** Hwé Pásu, Salween, Nam Teng.	16	4	16	4	For 7 miles road good over slightly undulating ground. Here the track cuts into the Hwé Pásu river and for a short distance there are large boulders along the track. Onwards follow the river bed or its banks. The river when first encountered is dry, but at 8½ miles, there are pools of water, another stream joins it from the south. The road which hitherto ran south-east by east, turns more southwards, and at 19 miles almost due south, from 2 miles onwards south-east. At 12¼ miles there are some hot springs, from this spot to where the river flows into the Salween there is water all along the river bed. The entire track is at this season of the year practicable for laden mules. The Salween is reached at 15¾ miles, and then following Salween to north-east for ¼ mile, the ferry is reached close to mouth of the Nam Teng (or Tein river). Ta Hsup Teng village consists of three houses, but a small quantity of rice and paddy is stored there for use of traders; excellent camping grounds on both banks. There are 6 (six) ferry boats which could carry 60 to 70 men across in one trip.

FROM YWATHIT TO MÔNÉ *viâ* SATAW (SADAW) AND MAUKMÉ—*continued.*

BRANCH III—*continued.*

Authorities. Military.	Authorities. Civil.	Number and Names of Stages, Rivers and Streams.	Distances. Intermediate. M. F.	Distances. Total. M. F.	Remarks.
G.O.C. Rangoon District.	Superintendent, Southern Shan States.	**2. Hsup Hwé Lông Wai.** Mé Sé, Hwé Lông Wai.	8 4	25 0	Fairly good path, an old bullock track spoilt by disuse. The Mé Sé is so rapid that at any time except in the dry weather it would be difficult to cross. At 5 miles Hsup Hwé Paw, camping ground on the sands. From there road is mostly over the sands with here and there rather troublesome places over the rocks and boulders. At 8¼ miles Hsup Hwé Lông Wai, good camping ground. The Ong Mu ferry is a short mile further up the river.
		3. Hwé Yúp Yáp (2,900 feet). Hwé Lông Wai, Hwé Yup Yáp.	10 2	35 2	General direction east-south-east. The path goes for 2¼ miles up the rocky bed of the Lông Wai or along its banks. It then turns sharp to the south-west and zigzags up the hill for 1½ miles to the crest of the spur (3,350 feet). From the top the Salween is visible below almost due west. The path now turns sharp to the left, and runs along the crest or the higher slopes for 5 miles, the highest altitude reached being about 3,700 feet above sea. It then descends pretty steadily to camp which may be made on the left bank of the Yúp, Yáp, a trickling stream of indifferent water sufficient, however, for the needs of a small camp. Fuel and forage plentiful.
		4. Kong Long (2,950 feet). Streams.	3 6	39 0	An easy downhill march, the last mile and-a-half in the flat. At 2 miles road to Ta Hwé Pôn goes off to the left. It is said to be an easy one. The village of Kong Long contains 12 or 15 houses and two or three shops. Rice and paddy procurable. Camp ½ a mile beyond, fuel and forage plentiful, water from streams.
		5. Möng Maö (2,300 feet). Hwé Möng Maö, Mé Lé.	9 0	48 0	General direction east-south-east. The road ascends for nearly 2 miles to a point about 3,100 feet above sea. Then descends slightly and again ascends to 3,400 feet at 2½ miles after winding for a couple of miles among spurs, the road descends at 4½ miles to the valley of the Hwé Möng Maö, which it follows mostly on the left bank all the way to Möng Maö, the stream is a mere brook and the valley a ravine till about the 6th mile near the hamlet of Ho Möng, where paddy-fields are reached. From here onwards the valley is from 100 to 200 yards broad and mostly cultivated. Pass two other hamlets Káng Möng and Háng Möng 6½ and 7 miles respectively, each of these hamlets has about 12 houses. At 8½ miles the Hwé Möng Maö turns off south-west to join the Mé Lé which stream is about 10 yards wide and 1½ feet deep. Ford it and enter Möng Maö 60 houses. There is a good camping ground just west of the village. Forage, fuel and water plentiful. Supplies of rice, &c., procurable.

FROM YWATHIT TO MÔNÉ *viâ* SATAW (SADAW) AND MAUKMÉ—*continued.*

BRANCH IV.

FROM SALAUNG (STAGE 9) TO BANHÁT (ROUTE No. 21, STAGE 11).

BY LIEUT. F. C. COLOMB, 42ND GURKHA INFANTRY, 1890.

Authorities. Military.	Authorities. Civil.	Number and Names of Stages, Rivers and Streams.	Distances. Intermediate.	Distances. Total.	Remarks.
			M. F.	M. F.	
G.O.C. Rangoon District.	Superintendent, Southern Shan States.	**1. Na Kun** ... Nam Teng.	16 0	16 0	For the first 9 miles the road is the same as Stage 10, Route No. 80, after which cross numerous dry nullahs. At 12 miles descend slightly to broad flat valley; track is then level, through bamboo jungle to within 1 mile of camp when cultivation commences. Camp on the right bank of the Nam Teng requires clearing. In dry season camp may be formed in paddy-fields on the bank of the river where space is unlimited. The want of water *en route* is a serious drawback to this route.
		2. Banhát (or Wanhát). NamTeng.	4 0	20 0	Good path across open paddy-fields leaving the Nam Teng about 1½ miles to east. Banhát is a large village with a bazaar every fifth day. Supplies available for a small force. There are two good camps, one in grounds of a ruined kyaung to north of village, water from wells, which are numerous in the village, the other ¾ mile to the east on the right bank of the Nam Teng, ground here available for a large force if scattered.

BRANCH V.

FROM SALAUNG (STAGE 9) TO TA UNG MU (SALWEEN).

BY CAPT. F. G. PINK, "THE QUEEN'S," 1890.

Authorities. Military.	Authorities. Civil.	Number and Names of Stages, Rivers and Streams.	Distances. Intermediate.	Distances. Total.	Remarks.
G.O.C. Rangoon District.	Superintendent, Southern Shan States.	**1. Ta Pon Ku Ferry.** Nam Teng.	2 4	2 4	Leaving Salaung village the road goes south-east for 1 mile to a tamarind grove which is a favorite camping ground. Here it turns almost east for 1¼ miles to the Nam Teng. The river is here about 90 yards broad, but a shoal 20 yards from the right bank lessens the distance for swimming or ferrying. The ferry boats maintained here are only two in number, capable between them of carrying 28 bullock loads a trip, or 15 to 20 men. Stream swift and deep. Elephants (unladen) can ford it. Excellent camping ground for 1,000 men or more on left bank. About ½ mile down stream the Nam Yun flows in. Salaung supplies, paddy and vegetables.
		2. Ta Ung Mu ... Pengleng stream, Ung Mu, and Salween river.	12 0	14 4	Track takes general south-west course to the Salween. Steep rise ¼ mile from camp and continues to rise for the first 6 miles passing at 4 miles Penleng village on the stream of that name (only a few pools of water in the bed). This stream flows into the Hwé Pen Yán up the dry bed of which the road passes for over a mile. After leaving Penleng village which consists of only about 10 houses, the ascent becomes a series of steep short ascents and fairly level resting places like a succession of large steps. At 6 miles the highest point which is 2,000 feet above the ferry. The descent is 2 miles long and like the ascent, steep in places and easy in

FROM YWATHIT TO MÔNÉ *viâ* SATAW (SADAW) AND MAUKMÉ—*continued.*

BRANCH V—*continued.*

Authorities. Military.	Authorities. Civil.	Number and Names of Stages, Rivers and Streams.	Distances. Intermediate.	Distances. Total.	Remarks.
G.O.C. Rangoon District.	Superintendent, Southern Shan States.	**2. Ta Ung Mu**—*cont.*			others. Near the bottom it is very steep and zigzagged, and cuts into the Ung Mu river continuing along its bed till its junction with the Salween 2 miles further on. The Ung Mu is shut in by steep high hills on either side; water lay along its course in pools only. Following down the banks of the Salween for 1½ miles Ta Ung Mu ferry is reached. The Salween is about 130 yards broad here, but the stream being swift, the boats have to go some 300 yards, two boats capable of taking about 10 men each. On the left bank the track goes south for a mile and the turning up the Hwé Lông Wai river goes on to Möng Maö (*see* Branch III).

BRANCH VI.

FROM MAUKMÉ (OR MOKMAI), (STAGE 11) TO TA MÉ SAKUN (SALWEEN).

BY HAVILDAR JAGAT SING, 19TH PUNJAB INFANTRY, 1890.

Military	Civil	Stages	Intermediate M. F.	Total M. F.	Remarks
G.O.C. Rangoon District.	Superintendent, Southern Shan States.	**1. Na Kun** ... Nam Yum, Nam Peng.	12 0	12 0	From Maukmé the shortest route to the Salween is that leading through Salaung to Ta Ung Mu, but as a route to Möng Maö and Méhawngsawn, this is a very bad one. The best would appear to be *viâ* Ta Hwé Pôn. The Havildar unfortunately did not take this route, but still it is all given below except the last stage. General direction east. Cross the Nam Yum by a good bridge, after crossing a little paddy ground the road goes through jungle. At 3 miles the ascent to the watershed of the Nam Yum and Nam Teng commences. At 5 miles again the crest. At 7½ miles reach the foot of the hills and cross a level plain mostly jungle, but with cultivation near villages. Pass a hamlet of six houses at 9 miles and another of 10 houses at 10 miles. Just beyond this enter a fine paddy plain stretching to the Nam Teng. At 12 miles reach Na Kun, a village of 50 houses close to the Nam Teng. Carts are used here and large supplies of grain are obtainable. From Na Kun roads go to Banhát (4 miles) and Salaung (16 miles), *vide* Branch No. IV below.
		2. Camp on Hwé Pin. Nam Teng, Hwé Pin.	7 4	19 4	General direction east-south-east for 2 miles, then south. Over level cultivated ground through Té Kan village (15 houses) to the Ta Ung ferry (2 miles). The Nam Teng is here a deep unfordable river nearly a hundred yards wide. At the ferry there are two small boats. The village of Ta Ung is on the left bank and consists of 15 houses. From Ta Ung the road goes south along the left bank of the Teng and is very good indeed. At 7 miles reach the Pin stream. At 7½ miles cross to its left bank and camp.
		3. Kua ... ... Streams.	10 0	29 4	General direction south for 4 miles, then east-south-east. Commence ascending at once on leaving camp. Up a spur for about 3 miles, then along crest. At 7 miles commence descending. At 9 miles reach a stream. Road goes up its bed for a mile or so to Kua. There is a good camping ground here on the right bank of the stream just above the village.

FROM YWATHIT TO MÔNÉ *viâ* SATAW (SADAW) AND MAUKMÉ—*continued.*

BRANCH VI—*continued.*

Authorities. Military.	Authorities. Civil.	Number and Names of Stages, Rivers and Streams.	Distances. Intermediate. M. F.	Distances. Total. M. F.	Remarks.
G.O.C. Rangoon District.	Superintendent, Southern Shan States.	**4. Camp on Bat Ung.** Hwé Pôn, Bat Ung stream.	**9 0**	38 0	General direction east-south-east. For 1½ miles up stream. The road then ascends to the crest of a ridge along which the road now runs. At 3 miles hamlet of Ku Mung, eight houses. At about 5 miles a path turns off south down the hill side to the Hwé Pôn ferry, which is about 8 miles further on. This is the best road to Möng Maö and Méhawngsawn. To continue: the Mé Sakun road still runs along the crest of the hills. At 6½ miles Bat Ung (nine houses); water from spring 700 yards west of village. At 7 miles the road descends by a long spur to the Bat Ung stream. Half-a-mile down stream there is a fair camping ground.
		5. Ta Mé Sakun. Salween.	**6 4**	45 0	General direction south. Road down stream for 5½ miles, mostly in the bed and rather bad for pack animals. Then up the right bank of the Salween for 1 mile to the ferry, one small boat. The route up the Mé Sakun valley is very bad.

No. 83.

From YWATHIT to MÖNG CHÉ (or MÖNG SÉ), for KYAUKHNYÁT and PÁPHUN, viâ TA HSANG LÉ.

BY CAPT. F. G. PINK, "THE QUEEN'S," 1890.

Military	Civil	Stages	Intermediate M. F.	Total M. F.	Remarks
G.O.C. Rangoon District.	Superintendent, Southern Shan States.	**1. Mé Sipaw (Camp).** Salween, Mé Saya, Mé Sipaw.	**15 0**	15 0	From Ywathit to Ta Hsang Lé, 3½ miles, good road. For description of which place *see* Route No. 4, Lower Burma Division, Stage 15. From the ferry a foot-path turns south along the left bank of the Salween. (There is a wet season, road running almost parallel a short way to the east.) Track sandy and in parts rocky. At 5½ miles reach the Mé Saya which cross, width 10 feet, depth 1 foot left bank, very steep and about 30 feet high; 3½ miles further on the road makes a sharp turn east up the Mé Sipaw crossing and recrossing the stream many times. The whole way from Mé Saya the road passes through fine forest.
		2. Nam Pé Kyauk (Camp). Mé Sipaw, Nam Pé Kyauk.	**13 4**	28 4	Path continues along the bed of the Mé Sipaw * for close on 5 miles. It then leaves it, crossing a hill some 400 feet above the river, ascent and descent both steep. The road runs in a south-west direction for 4 miles, then south-east. At 12 miles first cross the Nam Pé Kyauk. Water a few inches deep. River bed 40 yards broad; banks steep. The ground between the two streams is undulating forest land. Chiefly *in* and bamboo.

* The road up the Mé Sipaw goes to Kunyuom (or Hkunyom) 3 days' march from the Salween (*see* Route No. 80, and Appendix III, Route No. 2).

From YWATHIT to MŌNG CHÉ (or MŌNG SÉ) for KYAUKHNYÁT and PÁPHUN, *viâ* TA HSANG LÉ—*continued*.

Authorities. Military.	Authorities. Civil.	Number and Names of Stages, Rivers and Streams.	Distances. Intermediate. M. F.	Distances. Total. M. F.	Remarks.
G.O.C. Rangoon District.	Superintendent, Southern Shan States.	**3. Mé Sé or Mé Ché camp.** Nam Pé Kyauk, Nam Pé So, Hwé Tum Kai, Mé Sé river.	13 0	41 4	Route goes almost due south whole way. At 2½ miles arrive at the junction of the Nam Pé Kyauk and Nam Pé So, which united turn west. The next 2 miles follow the Nam Pé So, leaving it (where it flows in for the west) the road begins to ascend a somewhat steep *in*-covered hill and making an equally steep descent continues along dry nullahs, and through bamboo jungle till the Hwé Tum Kai river is reached at 10½ miles; following down its course for a short distance it again passes through "*in*" forest and at 1½ miles crosses the Mé Sé river; banks rather steep; river about 30 to 40 yards broad. Water 1 foot deep and rapid. Cross Mé Sé twice more and then camped.
		4. Mōng Ché or Mōng Sé. Mé Sé, Nam Man or Nam Pông.	13 0	51 0	At ½ mile cross Mé Lé river, then 3½ miles over high ground; direction little south of east. Again cut into Mé Sé and for 4 miles follow up river course to where it is joined by the Nam Man or Nam Pông from the east. The Mé Sé here turns due south. The road crossing it four or five times in the next 1½ miles, runs parallel to it on its left bank. At 11 miles old Mé Sé is passed (15 houses and a small kyaung), 2 miles on new Mé Sé is reached, 20 to 30 houses, one kyaung. Inhabitants Shan, Burmese, White and Red Karens, few Laos. For another description of the first two stages of this route *see* Route No. 80, Stages 1 and 2.

General Notes on Route.—(*a*) This road was followed up for another 6 miles south, it crossed the Mé Sé twice, but the river here is not far from its source and is a small though rapid stream. This road is said to be the main route from Ywathit to Páphun or rather to the Kyaukhnyát ferry opposite on the Salween. At 6 miles, on a pine-covered water-parting it enters undoubted Siamese territory at a spot called Kyaukdain, where there is a large natural pillar in a ravine just off the road. This is said to be a boundary mark between Karenni and Siam. The road so far is excellent and the onward road to Kyaukhnyát is reported equally good. An account of it, from Native information, is contained in Route No. 2 of Appendix III.

(*b*) Elephants or mules lightly loaded find no difficulty, except in a few places where logs of timber have got wedged in between rocks and blocked the roadway somewhat. The entire road at this season is quite practicable. A Mountain Battery could march along it. A few charges of dynamite would do all that is required.

(*c*) The jungle (undergrowth) is suitable at all the halting places for the construction of shelters for men, tents need not be carried.

(*d*) All the rivers are rapid and utilized for floating "teak logs" into the Salween. Till the rains are over the route is not practicable and the jungles are poisonous with malaria till December at earliest.

No. 84.

From YWATHIT to TA HSUP TENG viâ TA HSANG LE and TA TA MAW.

BY J. G. SCOTT, Esq., BURMA COMMISSION, 1890.

Authorities. Military.	Authorities. Civil.	Number and Names of Stages, Rivers and Streams.	Distances. Intermediate. M.	Distances. Intermediate. F.	Distances. Total. M.	Distances. Total. F.	Remarks.
G.O.C. Rangoon District.	Superintendent, Southern Shan States.						*Note.*—This route along the left bank of the Salween was taken by a detached party of the Anglo-Siamese Commission in 1890. The party was accompanied by elephants and mules, but the route cannot be considered fit for laden animals, and as a matter of fact is never used by local carriers. It was only used under special circumstances.
		1. Kyok Ting ... Salween, Mé Pai.	11	4	11	4	Very good road from Ywathit to Ta Hsang Ló (*see* Route No. 4, Lower Burma Division, Stage 5) 3½ miles. Cross the river at Ta Hsang Ló by ferry boat. Thence fair road for 2½ miles over sand and boulders to Ta Hsup Pai. The Mé Pai very rapid and unfordable by laden mules; boats have to cross in the Salween, Mé Pai being too rapid. Above Ta Hsup Pai heavy going over sand for 2 miles. Then rough road along steep bank, good deal incumbered with jungle and fallen bamboos. Camping ground on sands.
		2. Tá Hsai Cheong. Salween.	6	0	17	4	Narrow path on slope of the bank, very bad going in some places. Much blocked with fallen trees. Good camping ground on sand bank. There is a foot track from here to Méhawngsawn, impassable for animals; very mountainous.
		3. Kyok Peit On. Salween.	9	0	26	4	Six miles on the sands to Tong Ni passing the Paw Kuta ferry about half-way. Then over huge boulders under precipitous cliff, impassable when the river is high. Very bad going for animals. Camp good on high bank.
		4. Camp "Narrows of the Salween." Salween.	11	0	37	4	Fairly good path for 3 miles. Then along face of very steep bank rising to 500 feet above the Salween. Very dangerous road, but would be improved very easily. About a mile of this, then alternate heavy sand and steep bank.
		5. Mé Hsaté ... Salween.	7	0	44	4	Rocky just at the start for ½ a mile. Then path over loose sand. At 2 miles Mé Layu. From here the road is rocky in places, but, on the whole, good over the sand.
		6. Ta Ta Maw ... Salween.	6	0	50	4	One or two difficult places, otherwise heavy work over the sand.
		7. Hwé Lôn ... Salween.	4	4	55	0	Road up the river bank very bad for animals in a good many places, but nowhere dangerous and capable of easy improvement. The Hwé Na Cheng and the Hwé Lôn are crossed, neither offering any difficulty at this time of year. Camp on the sands.

FROM YWATHIT TO TA HSUP TENG *viâ* TA HSANG LÉ AND TA TA MAW—*continued.*

Authorities. Military.	Authorities. Civil.	Number and Names of Stages, Rivers and Streams.	Distances. Intermediate. M. F.	Distances. Total. M. F.	Remarks.
[.]O.C. Rangoon District.	Superintendent, Southern Shan States.	**8. Hsup Hwé Kwai.** Salween.	**5 4**	60 4	Fairly good path all the way, except near the Hwé Tam, where the track climbs high up the side of the hill and is rather bad going for a mile-and-a-half. The Hwé Tam is a little beyond the half distance. Good camping ground.
		9. Hsup Teng ... Salween.	**10 4**	71 0	Path, on the whole, good for the greater part of the way, crossing the Hwé Lai and the Hwé Kha, which offer no difficulties except in the rains. Close to the Nam Teng the banks become very steep; the path rises along the side of a precipitous bank and is very troublesome for animals. Good camping ground on the spit between the Nam Teng and Salween (*see* also Route No. 82, Branch III, Stage 1).

PART VII.

ROUTES IN THE LOWER BURMA DIVISION.

PART VII.

ROUTES IN THE LOWER BURMA DIVISION.

No. 1.

From AKYAB to LAUNGSHÉ viâ MYOHAUNG and "The Sawbwa's Route."

By Lieut. H. B. Walker, Duke of Cornwall's Light Infantry, Intelligence Department, April 1891.

Authorities. Military.	Authorities. Civil.	Number and Names of Stages, Rivers and Streams.	Distances. Inter-mediate. M.	Distances. Inter-mediate. F.	Distances. Total. M.	Distances. Total. F.	Remarks.
G.O.C. Rangoon District.	Lower Burma.	**1. Myohaung** ... Lemru river all the way.	44	0	44	0	River steamers ply twice a week each way. Land route impracticable, owing to the numerous backwaters rivers and streams to be crossed. For Myohaung *see* Route No. 23, Southern Division, Stage 23.
		2. Léyingdôn ... Two small nullahs. Lemru navigable for steam launches at low tide, and in dry season up to but not beyond Sino. Tide scarcely felt here; depth from 2 to 7 feet; good supply of boats always plying on river.	12	0	56	0	Direction east-north-east. Road level and good; evidently remains of old Government road. Thick jungle on both side. Two large tidal tanks are passed at miles 2 and 3. Sino at 4½ miles is half Arakanese, half Chin; has 15 houses. Stands on the right bank of the Lemru. Supplies large quantities of jack fruit. Direction north-east. At first the road is dead level and good for 2 miles, then it runs over the lower edge of steep hill covered with jungle for nearly 3 miles, and then along a good level path into Léyingdôn along river all the way, Léyingdôn is an Arakanese village; has 30 houses. Clean and well kept. Supplies small. *N.B.*—The headman of Léyingdôn has traversed the Sawbwa's route and is the best informant on the Arakan side.
		3. Kyépaung ...	8	0	64	0	Direction north-north-west. The road runs within a short distance of the Lemru, separated from it only by a low, long hill. It ascends and descends short gradients till within ¼ mile of Kyaktala (2 miles) when ascent is long and steep up to village, which has a most commanding position of the Lemru and opposite bank. Path good under foot, but overgrown being little used. Supplies *nil*. The village is Chin; stockaded; 25 houses.

FROM AKYAB TO LAUNGSHÉ *viâ* MYOHAUNG AND "THE SAWBWA'S ROUTE"—*continued.*

Authorities. Military.	Authorities. Civil.	Number and Names of Stages, Rivers and Streams.	Distances. Intermediate. M.	Distances. Intermediate. F.	Distances. Total. M.	Distances. Total. F.	Remarks.
G.O.C. Rangoon District.	Lower Burma.	**3. Kyépaung**—*cont.*					*N.B.*—Simbawgaing, a large Burmese village with good bazaar, is on the opposite bank, and from it there runs, first, the supposed Sawbwa's route as far as Hetwai over the hills now overgrown and not easy to be discovered; and, secondly, the alternative route along the river on the other bank as far as Kônchaung, and the better route of the two. Here it may also be said that the plains are left and the hills entered. From Kyaktala direction north, through jungle; path good and open, though in places washed away by the rains. At 4 miles Nakún or Payágyi. Five houses. Supplies *nil.* Thence direction north-west. The road striking from the river runs for 1½ miles along a bund, 6 feet wide and the remains of a good road, the level plain is then entered, the path being good though probably marshy in wet weather. Two villages unseen from the road are passed here lying between the road and the river. Kyébaung is reached at 8 miles a large Chin village on a small eminence. Supplies: a few pigs and fowls. Inhabitants are Saidoos.
		4. Kônchaung ... Wet nullah bed along which route runs for nearly 9 miles. Lemru. The river here narrows and is only 300 yards (or less) wide; fordable (except for 100 yards) between the two villages; stony bottom.	11	0	75	0	Direction north, along a stony nullah, wet and slippery with precipitous hills on either side. Very difficult marching and impassable for horses. In places the nullah is left for a short distance for the jungle though there is practically no road, the nullah bed being the only marked route. At about 7 miles the path turns east towards the river (Lemru) which is struck at 9 miles and thence the path runs down the right bank of the river to Kônchaung (11 miles), and is easy going. Kônchaung is a Chin village (Laidu); 20 houses on each bank of the river. Supplies: pigs, fowls, and paddy, rice, &c., and an abundance of grass. There is fair supply of boats to be obtained, small and cranky, the usual dug-out, but available for ferry boats. *N.B.*—This bad stretch of road can be avoided by crossing the river at either Kyaktala or Léyingdôn and proceeding by the opposite or left bank. The road on that side is better by far, and more frequented, the two routes joining at Kônchaung.
		5. Hmet ... ... The Lemru crossing the Kyi chaung and Pein chaung; both dry except in the rainy season, rising in the interior and flowing into the Lemru between Kôn chaung and Hmet.	12	0	87	0	Crossing from the right to the left bank the route runs the bed of the Kyi chaung for 4 miles; rough and stony, but passable for laden animals; then into the jungle by an easy but little used path striking the Pein chaung at the 8th mile. The route then runs along the bed of the Pein chaung striking the Lemru again 1 mile to the north of Hmet. Hmet is a Chin village (Laidu); 20 houses. Supplies few. By the river to this point, the easiest and most used route, the following villages are passed situated on the river banks:— *Right bank.*—Aletsingyi, Pyilôngyi, and Lower Lemru Guard. The latter being a well constructed and situated guard

FROM AKYAB TO LAUNGSHÉ *viâ* MYOHAUNG AND "THE SAWBWA'S ROUTE"—*continued.*

Authorities.		Number and Names of Stages, Rivers and Streams.	Distances.		Remarks.
Military.	Civil.		Intermediate.	Total.	
G.O.C. Rangoon District.	Lower Burma.	**5. Hmet**—*cont.*			garrisoned by Gurkas belonging to the Palawak district on the Koladyne. From this guard a patrol road runs across the hills to the Yan chaung and from thence on to the Koladyne river. *Left bank.*—Auksingyi and Ngalôn all are Chin villages (Laidu) averaging 15 to 20 houses each. Small supplies. Boats obtainable in small numbers.
			M. F.	M. F.	
		6. Kwépéshé ... The Lemru all the way, the route running along its bed. The last mile along the Thán chaung, the Lemru flowing from the west.	12 0	99 0	Direction east as far as the junction of the Thán chaung with the Lemru, then north-east. The road runs along the bed of the river, crossing and recrossing the stream; always fordable except once; stony but good marching. Small boats can pass up, but at every crossing there is a shallow rapid up which the boat must be pulled or pushed. At junction of Thán chaung the Lemru is left, and the Thán chaung rapidly narrowing and becoming more shallow is followed, its average depth being 9 inches to 2 feet; banks on either side precipitous. Only lightly laden boats can go up here and that with difficulty. In the rains this route must be impassable at this point. Kwépéshé and Kwépégyi are two Chin villages (Laidu), each of 50 houses; unstockaded. Considerable supplies of paddy, fowls, and pig. Said to be very unhealthy.
		7. Lemru guard patrol hut below Alangtingé. The Thán chaung bed to its junction with the Maw chaung at the 6th mile.	6 0	105 0	Direction north-east still along the Thán chaung river bed crossing and recrossing, always fordable for 6 miles, when the patrol hut is reached on the junction of the Thán chaung and Maw chaung. Alangtingé is ½ a mile higher up on the left bank of the Maw chaung. It has 25 houses, few supplies, and is the first point on the Man chaung of the Lower Yanan route, which here follows the bed of the Thán chaung, east Yanan being three days' journey distant. Good camping ground is all along as far as Alangtingé.
		8. Kôkh ... ... The Maw chaung along which the route runs. At Kôkh the Met chaung joins the Maw chaung.	6 0	111 0	Direction north, along Maw chaung bed, crossing and recrossing; very rough marching and impassable for heavily laden animals, the ground being covered with large boulders, slippery and firmly bedded. Thick jungle on either side on the hills which are very precipitous. Small camping ground at junction of streams, water being scarce in the village and of inferior quality. The village which is 1½ miles up the road towards (Hetwai) is small and untidy: Chins, Laidu inhabitants; 12 houses. Supplies *nil.*

Authorities. Military.	Authorities. Civil.	Number and Names of Stages, Rivers and Streams.	Distances. Intermediate. M.	Distances. Intermediate. F.	Distances. Total. M.	Distances. Total. F.	Remarks.
G.O.C. Rangoon District.	Lower Burma.	**9. Kyauksein-Yé-Sanán.**	**10**	**4**	121	4	Leaving junction of the Maw and Met chaungs the road runs north-west for ½ a mile through a thick jungle, then up a steep ascent by a much overgrown path, north, for nearly 3 miles passing the village on the right hand in a clearing ½ a mile off the path at a mile and-a-half from the junction of the river, the spur then flattens out for nearly 2 miles, the jungle still being very thick, and then the road ascends again as far as mile 10 sometimes gradual, sometimes steep, the whole road running along a series of spurs which abut from the Yômas at right angles. At the 10th mile there is a descent into a valley, the road rising again to run along the side of a hill north-east, the path being narrow and broken, from which the old village of Hetwai, now deserted, can be seen on the parallel spur to the west. Half-a-mile further on at Kyauksein-Yé-Sanán the first water on the route can be obtained down a steep descent to the left of the road; its whereabouts being indicated by the circular bend the path makes, leaving a small, flat space to its left immediately over the descent to the water. This space is generally covered with traces of fire, bamboos shaped for drinking, &c., while the jungle below is green and fresh looking. With this exception there is no water the whole way from Kôkh to Hetwai.
		10. Hetwai ...	**11**	**4**	133	0	Leaving Kauksein-Yé-Sanán the path runs along the side of a spur for a mile and then rising to the top, Hetwai is seen on the same level on a parallel spur to the north-west and from here into Hetwai the road is open and good, only light bamboo jungle on either side, and the ground soft. The whole route is passable for laden animals and merely requires to have the jungle cleared away a little on either side. The slopes along which the path runs are, on the whole, gradual and comparatively easy; the soil all the way is good and firm and a good hard road could be easily made. Traffic by the route is comparatively small and it soon gets overgrown. Hetwai is a large Laidu Chin village of 40 houses, well stockaded, situated in a good position at the extremity of the spur before it begins to descend to the Set chaung; its inhabitants are not paying revenue to Government at the present date. Supplies considerable: paddy, fowls, pig, &c. No grass obtainable for horses, but bamboo leaves are plentiful. Water is obtained from the Set chaung some little way off. Kantôkh is a small village on the side of the spur to the right hand of Hetwai, under the authority of the same Taungmin, and yielding the same supplies.
		11. Tôgyi (1st route; that taken by the Sawbwa). Set and Kyi chaungs.	**9**	**0**	142	0	From Hetwai to Tôgyi there are two routes: the first, the original Sawbwa's route, being by far the better of the two; the second route is only useful as being as far as Shâli the same as the Upper Yanán route. It is necessary to bear in mind the fact that there are two routes, since the Chins of Hetwai being extremely averse to disclose the better road will, if it is possible, direct the traveller on to the second or

FROM AKYAB TO LAUNGSHÉ *viâ* MYOHAUNG AND "THE SAWBWA'S ROUTE"—*continued.*

Authorities.		Number and Names of Stages, Rivers and Streams.	Distances.		Remarks.
Military.	Civil.		Inter-mediate.	Total.	
G.O.C. Rangoon District.	Lower Burma.	**11. Tôgyi (1st route; that taken by the Sawbwa** —*cont.*			Yanán route, and endeavour to persuade him to proceed so far towards Yanán that he will not care to return and find out the direct route to Tôgyi which is an easy day's journey, the other being two days' severe marching and climbing. Direction north-west down a steep spur to the Set chaung, then north-east up a long, gradual easy spur passing Tonu at mile 4, a village of no importance. A short descent leads down to the Kyichaung and up a gradual rise by a long, easy spur into Tôgyi, the (upper) village which lies on the flattened out summit of the spur. The road all the way is soft, good marching, and open; passable for laden animals. Tôgyi consists of two villages, upper and lower. Both well stockaded, each containing about 55 houses. Inhabitants are Chins and Yindus. Supplies considerable as in Hetwai. Water is obtained from (1) the Klôn and Hpa chaungs at the foot of the hill, and (2) from small springs on the hill side, the water being brought within the stockades by means of bamboos. Lower Tôgyi is situated in a circular valley, lower down the same spur on which Upper Tôgyi stands. It is ¼ of a mile up the hill from the bottom, and is immediately above the junctions of the Klôn and Hpa chaungs which are crossed in the Shâli or second route from Hetwai, *vide* Alternative I.
		12. Yánlaung Toë. Bulaung and Yánlaung chaungs.	M. F. 16 0	M. F. 158 0	From the lower village, past the Upper Tôgyi, the path runs directly north up to the top of the spur ½ of a mile distant, then it turns east running along the top of the spur which juts out at right angles from the Yômas, while Hetwai is distinctly visible almost due west. The whole hill side is largely cultivated with rice; the road gradually ascends, being soft and good marching, till the higher ground running perpendicular to the spur is reached at 2nd mile, where it becomes broken and stony and running along the side of a hill is narrow and impassable for laden animals. Jungle bamboo for first 4 miles, when the thick and larger jungle is entered and the path becomes good, again and hard, and after a further mile and-a-half debouches on a small camping ground for 150 men, with plenty of shade and water for about 100 men with care, in a small hollow to the left of the path beneath a tree. From here the road runs up a steep ascent north-east, afterwards turning north to river along the side of a hill covered with bamboo jungle, descending slightly, the path being broken away, the originally broad, carefully engineered road being overgrown with jungle, though still distinguishable. The route runs alternately along the side of the spur where it is narrow and bad, or along the summit where it flattens out and is good, for 6 miles, when a long steep descent runs into the Bulaung chaung. At the top of the descent a large Chin village (Yindu), called Satu, is visible north-west about 5 miles distant. Crossing the chaung the road runs due north up a short spur and then down a long gradual spur covered with bamboo jungle, when the Yindu village of Yánlaung Toë is reached at the 16th mile from Tôgyi. The Chin villages of Maungdu, Bawsa, Hmuntu, Dikma, Kinsaw, and Kinéywa all lie within a radius of 4 miles north-west. Yánlaung Toë is a well-stockaded village of 44 houses. Supplies considerable: paddy, fowls, pigs, and a few plantains. Water from the river ⅓ a mile distant.

From AKYAB to LAUNGSHÉ *viâ* MYOHAUNG and "The Sawbwa's Route"—*continued.*

Authorities. Military.	Authorities. Civil.	Number and Names of Stages, Rivers and Streams.	Distances. Intermediate. M.	Distances. Intermediate. F.	Distances. Total. M.	Distances. Total. F.	Remarks.
G.O.C. Rangoon District.	Lower Burma.	**12. Yánlaung Toë**—*cont.*					The whole of the Yánlaung valley is largely cultivated, while grass can be obtained; game abounds along this valley both large and small.
G.O.C. Rangoon District.	* Commissioner, Southern Division, and Deputy Commissioner, Pakôkku.	**13. Camp on Yômas.**	10	0	168	0	*N.B.*—From Yánlaung Toë to Kindwé there are two routes : the first, namely, that taken by the Sawbwa and, by far the best, does not touch at any village until Kindwé is reached 26 miles from the Yánlaung chaung. The other, a longer and more difficult route, passes through the villages that lie between the Yánlaung chaung and Kindwé, *see* Alternative II. It is necessary as at Hetwai to be aware of these alternative routes, since the Chins are strongly averse to disclosing the shorter and better route, and invariably endeavour to persuade the traveller to advance by the longer and more difficult one. Leaving Yánlaung Toë the route runs down a steep slope south-north-east to the Yánlaung chaung, a distance of about 1 mile, leaving the second route more to the left hand, crosses the Yánlaung chaung and ascends a moderately steep spur east-north-east. For nearly 6 miles the first-half through bamboo jungle, the rest of the path as far as the top of the Yômas being bare of trees, though towards the north side the jungle is thick and dense; the route then runs along the top of the Yômas slightly descending for 3 miles to a small camping ground on the ridge of the spur, the water being obtained from a small spring 300 yards off the road. There is water for 400 or 500 men with care. For large bodies of troops a further advance would have to be made of 3 miles down towards junction of Ai and Pu chaungs, and the stream gained by leaving the road and striking down the valley 1½ miles.
G.O.C. Rangoon District.	* Commissioner, Southern Division, and Deputy Commissioner, Pakôkku.	**14. Junction of Ai and Pu chaungs.**	11	0	179	0	From this camp the path runs down to the junction of the Ai and Pu chaungs, ascending and descending the small knolls which are crossed *en route*, descending nearly 3,000 feet in the 11 miles; the road is soft and good and marching easy. From Yánlaung Toë laden animals can march with ease.
G.O.C. Rangoon District.	* Commissioner, Southern Division, and Deputy Commissioner, Pakôkku.	**15. Kindwé** ...	6	0	185	0	Leaving the junction of the Ai and Pu chaungs the route runs up bed of Ai chaung for 2 miles, when it reaches the Môn chaung and runs up its course for 4 miles north when the Chinbôk village of Kindwé is reached. The road is rough along the river bed, but passable for laden animals except at flood time. Grass and bamboo leaves are obtainable for horses or ponies. Kindwé is a well-to-do village. Supplies as usual—rice, paddy, kyaung, fowls, &c. *N.B.*—The Taungmin of this village is the only man who is thoroughly acquainted with the Sawbwa's route all through, and who can be depended on to show it to any one connected with Government.

* ***Note.—Probably*;** the crest of the Yômas being probably the dividing line between Lower Burma (Arracan) and the Southern Division, but it appears to be as yet uncertain how far south the Chin Hills District extends.—*A. F.*

FROM AKYAB TO LAUNGSHÉ *viâ* MYOHAUNG AND "THE SAWBWA'S ROUTE"—*continued.*

Authorities. Military.	Authorities. Civil.	Number and Names of Stages, Rivers and Streams.	Distances. Intermediate. M. F.	Distances. Total. M. F.	Remarks.
G.O.C. Rangoon District.	Commissioner, Southern Division, and Deputy Commissioner, Pakôkku.	**16. Paukaing** ... Môn chaung.	**12 0**	197 0	Leaving the camping ground on the left bank of the Môn chaung (direction south-east), the route follows the left bank of the river for ½ a mile, when it strikes up a long, steep spur (east) for 4½ miles. Bamboo jungle on both sides of the path which is well worn, and though requiring repair is in fair order on the whole. Reaching the top of the spur the route then runs along a valley, open, covered with grass and with a good supply of water off the path to the right down the face of the hill. The valley is 1½ miles long, slightly rising the last ½ mile where the top of the Yômas, east of the Môn valley, is reached and a magnificent view of the surrounding country is obtained. From this point a gradual descent commences through dense forest of the finest timber largely interspersed with fir or pine trees. (The *valley* at the top of the Yômas (*sic ? plateau*) is capable of being rendered a powerful defensive position, and but for its inaccessibility from the Irrawaddy would make a capital sanitarium for troops.) The descent is gradual for the next 6½ miles as far as the camping ground of Paukaing, which is reached at 12 miles. It is a small, hollow plateau, capable of camping 300 men, water-supply being obtained from a well or spring down the hill to the north for about 250 men with care.
		17. Laungshé ... Nanaing, Manin, and Salin chaungs.	**16 0**	213 0	Leaving Paukaing the route runs in an easterly direction, descending towards the valley by a capital path (though narrow in places) and easy gradients for 4½ miles. Here two roads meet, one to the left hand leading towards Laungshé, the other to the right, and the better path, to the Chin village of Zingé, the last Chin village along the route and 6 miles off. Following the Laungshé path the descent is very steep and broken under foot, though passable for laden animals as far as the valley of the junctions of the Nanaing and Manin chaungs. The route then follows the latter for about 6 miles, constantly crossing and recrossing from one bank to the other. Direction south-east. The junction with the Salin chaung is then reached, and the route runs along its bed into Laungshé, which is reached at the 16th mile from Paukaing, this latter part of the distance being through paddy-fields, and passing several small villages the pathway being good though rough along the river bed. Laungshé is a large dilapidated but picturesque town, purely Burman. It is on the right bank of the Salin chaung. It has a new, well-built civil guard, has a Myo-ôk, and is in the Pakôkku district. The Salin chaung only has water in it in the month of May, the others being dry. The Salin chaung has plenty of water though shallow and impassable for boats. Native information reports another route from Kindwé which, leaving the Môn valley more to the north, strikes the Nanaing chaung above its junction with the Manin chaung and runs through the jungle parallel with the Manin chaung junction when Salin chaung is reached, but it is an inferior route to that along the river bed though the latter is rough going, and from Paukaing till the Salin chaung is reached there is no water except a very small supply in the Nanaing chaung at the foot of the hill where it joins with the Manin chaung. Capt. Harvey, R.A., traversed yet another route between Laungshé and Kindwé in April 1893, *see* Alternative No. III, below.

FROM AKYAB TO LAUNGSHÉ *viâ* MYOHAUNG AND "THE SAWBWA'S ROUTE"—*continued.*

ALTERNATIVE I.

FROM HETWAI (STAGE 10) TO TÔGYI (STAGE 11).

BY LIEUT. H. B. WALKER, DUKE OF CORNWALL'S LIGHT INFANTRY, INTELLIGENCE DEPARTMENT, APRIL 1891.

Authorities. Military.	Authorities. Civil.	Number and Names of Stages, Rivers and Streams.	Distances. Intermediate. M.	F.	Distances. Total. M.	F.	Remarks.
G.O.C. Rangoon District.	Lower Burma.	**1. Shâli** ... ... Set chaung. Maw chaung stony and rapid; shallow; fordable; 20 to 25 yards wide. Kyi chaung, along the bed of which for 3½ miles the route runs.	**6**	**4**	6	4	Direction north-west down spur to Set chaung, then north-east over difficult and stony crossing (impassable on landing side for laden animals) across a small taung or hill down to the Maw chaung, then across a strip of jungle down to the Kyi chaung; distance about 3 miles. From here the route runs along the bed of the Kyi chaung; direction east-north-east for 3½ miles as far as Old Shâli, the point at which the two roads branch off, namely, to Yanân eastward and Tôgyi north-east. The route is bad, stony, and wet, impassable for animals, and excessively difficult marching. The river bed has precipitous sides covered with jungle through which a pathway could not run and hence the river bed has to be followed.
		2. Tôgyi ... Klôn chaung and Hpa chaung junction; two small mountain streams, shallow and rocky.	**12**	**0**	18	4	Leving Old Shâli the road crosses the Kyi chaung and strikes at once into the jungle north-north-east up a long, steep spur for about 2 miles when the top is reached, water being found off the road to the right down a steep descent of ¼ of a mile, and is the only water until the junction of the Klôn and Hpa chaungs are reached on the route. The route then runs north-west up a further ascent for a mile when it begins to descend though loose jungle, the pathway being good under foot and soft. Where it runs along the side of any hill it is dangerous for animals on account of the recent fires which have loosened the soil. From mile 8 without interruption the path runs down an easy spur to the junction of the Klôn and Hpa chaungs, crosses the former and runs along its banks for a few hundred yards, then along its bed for nearly ¼ of a mile and up a steep ascent of ¼ of a mile into the lower village of Tôgyi. (*N.B.*—This being a route little used, it is very indistinct and difficult to trace.)

ALTERNATIVE II.

FROM YÁNLAUNG TOË (STAGE 12) TO KINDWÉ (STAGE 15) *viâ* SETWAI AND PUZAW.

BY LIEUT. H. B. WALKER, DUKE OF CORNWALL'S LIGHT INFANTRY, INTELLIGENCE BRANCH, MAY 1891.

Military	Civil	Stages	M.	F.	M.	F.	Remarks
G.O.C. Rangoon District.	Commr., Southern Divn., and Deputy Commr., Pakôkku.	**1. Lesser Setwai.** Yánlaung chaung; narrow, shallow, and rocky.	**4**	**0**	4	0	From the village the road runs down a steep descent for ½ a mile to the Yánlaung chaung, striking it nearly 2 miles north of the first or Sawbwa's route. Crossing the river at right angles the route runs up a long steep ascent for

FROM AKYAB TO LAUNGSHÉ *viâ* MYOHAUNG AND "THE SAWBWA'S ROUTE"—*continued.*

ALTERNATIVE II—*continued.*

Authorities. Military.	Authorities. Civil.	Number and Names of Stages, Rivers and Streams.	Distances. Intermediate.	Distances. Total.	Remarks.
G.O.C. Rangoon District.	Commissioner, Southern Division, and Deputy Commissioner, Pakôkku.	**1. Lesser Setwai** —*cont.*			3 miles, through bamboo jungle, the path being scarcely discernible. At the summit of the spur the path runs north into a valley which runs up at right angles from the Yánlaung chaung. Here the small Chin village of Lesser Setwai lies on a half dry nullah or stream.
		2. Greater Setwai. Yánlaung and Lulong chaungs.	M. F. **12 0**	M. F. 16 0	From Greater Setwai the bed of the nullah is followed east for a short distance when it strikes north across a bamboo covered hill, the ascent being steep and the path scarcely discernible. It then turns east again and runs for several miles up a half-dry chaung; rough, stony and impassable for horses; it then leaves the chaung and runs for ¼ of a mile across a strip of jungle to the Lulong chaung. From here the route rises for ½ a mile up a spur and runs along the top and then down along gradual descent into the valley of the Yánlaung chaung again, the river being considerably narrower and stony than when crossed at Yánlaung Toe village. Crossing east a winding ascent leads to the large stockaded Chin village (Yindu) of Setwai; 50 houses. Supplies: plenty of rice and paddy, pigs, and a few fowls. Water-supply from the chaung below village. There is a small camping ground on the river, but none other.
		3. Yinywa ... Kyi chaung; narrow, rocky, with little water. Pí chaung 20 yards wide; rapid and shallow; stony crossing.	**10 0**	26 0	Leaving Greater Setwai the road ascends east a narrow, rocky path and crossing the spur runs down to the Kyi chaung; distance 2 miles. Crossing north-east the path ascends through bamboo jungle, a rocky, precipitous ascent for ½ a mile descending again on the other side of the hill to the Pí chaung. From here a good path east ascends a long spur till near the top when it turns south and winds along the side of the hill; narrow and precipitous, rising gradually until the Yindu village of Yinywa is reached; 15 or 20 houses; unstockaded. Supplies *nil.* Water from a spring just outside the village supplies about 200 men with care.
		4. Puzaw or Buruya. Pá chaung; narrow, stony and rapid. Pu chaung; narrow and sandy.	**10 0**	36 0	Leaving Yinywa a long steep descent with a general direction of north-east leads to the Pá chaung at the 1st mile. Crossing the Pá chaung a wearisome ascent for nearly 3 miles still north-east, eventually debouches on the summit of the spur, which, gradually widening with the route, becomes a thick forest of fine timber, while the road becomes 6 feet broad and capital marching; dead level and soft under foot. The road runs thus for 4 miles when water in a hollow to the left is passed; a scanty supply for 50 men only. The spur then runs down into the valley of the Pu chaung at mile 8. The Pu chaung is then followed for another mile when the Chinbôk village of Nataingzin, stockaded and new, is passed on the left bank; 15 to 20 houses. Supplies *nil.* A mile further on the village of Puzaw or Buruya is reached (Chinbôk). No supplies.
		5. Kindwé ...	**(?)**	(?)	Route incomplete.

FROM AKYAB TO LAUNGSHÉ *viâ* MYOHAUNG AND "THE SAWBWA'S ROUTE"—*continued.*

ALTERNATIVE III.

FROM LAUNGSHÉ TO KINDWÉ (OR KYINDWÉ).

BY CAPT. J. HARVEY, ROYAL ARTILLERY, ATTACHÉ, INTELLIGENCE BRANCH, APRIL 1893.

Authorities. Military.	Authorities. Civil.	Number and Names of Stages, Rivers and Streams.	Distances. Intermediate. M.	F.	Total. M.	F.	Remarks.
G.O.C. Rangoon District.	Commissioner, Southern Division, and Deputy Commissioner, Pakôkku.	**1. Bôzain Sakhán.** Salin and Nganaung chaungs.	**15**	**0**	15	0	Road runs through rice fields along right bank of stream. At 1½ miles Embu, two villages—57 houses. One is Burmese, the other Chinbôn population. Road crosses the Salin chaung at about 2¼ miles and is somewhat stony in places; when rice is growing there are many small streams, diversions from the river, to cross. At 3 miles Ayainké, large Burman village, surrounded by rice fields and pagodas. Opposite Ayainké is Sitaw village on right bank, in twoparts; has 58 houses. Road now turns to south and runs up the bed of the Nganaung chaung, which is dry in hot weather, leaving Pyingé or Swélwégyin to its north. At 7 miles Thessédaung, Chéyin Sakhán. This sakhán is principally used by bullock-drivers before commencing the steep ascent in front of them. There is a little water here in the stream. Road ascends steeply through bamboo jungle up a spur of Thessédaung for 1,500 feet, then it becomes gradually easier and finishes by a gentle up and down rise along the watershed between the Môn and Salin chaungs, through oak forest. A few fir trees. At Bôzain is a small stream 150 yards to the north and 60 feet below ridge, giving (on 7th April 1893) 1¼ gallons per minute at its source and more lower down. This is in a very dry season.
		2. Kindwé (Kyindwé). Môn chaung.	**13**	**0**	28	0	Road runs along ridge up and down, easy gradients, gradually ascending under the highest point on the Samboyu hills; then gradually descending about 2½ miles. Kampillé Sakhán is reached at 7 miles on the borders of a small lake (dry in hot season), passing over about 2 miles of fine grassy downs. Water flows perennially from a stream rising 500 yards to westward of the lake, which gave 2 gallons per minute at source on 10th April 1893. There is water also obtainable in some quantity about 30 yards from and 30 feet below the path at about half-way, to the north of the biggest saddle a good stream rises from under a big rock. Path now runs straight down a steep spur through oak and bamboo jungle to the banks of the Môn river. Fall is about 4,500 feet. The river here is 100 yards wide and 1 to 2 feet deep in dry season, with a current of 2 to 3 miles per hour. In flood it is an unfordable torrent. It abounds in mahseer. In the rains a foot-bridge of cane ropes is made of similar pattern to the Himalayan rope bridges for crossing the river. Kindwé has about 20 good houses and no stockade. About ½ mile down the left river bank from the village are excellent bamboo huts for about 300 men.

FROM AKYAB TO LAUNGSHÉ *viâ* MYOHAUNG AND "THE SAWBWA'S ROUTE"—*continued.*

BRANCH I.

FROM LAUNGSHÉ (STAGE 17) TO KINDWÉ (STAGE 15).

BY CAPT. J. WILLCOCKS, D.S.O., 1ST BATTALION, LEINSTER REGIMENT, AND LIEUTS. RAINEY AND DALY, 2ND BURMA BATTALION, MARCH 1890.

Authorities. Military.	Authorities. Civil.	Number and Names of Stages, Rivers and Streams.	Distances. Intermediate. M.	Distances. Intermediate. F.	Distances. Total. M.	Distances. Total. F.	Remarks.
G.O.C. Rangoon District.	Commissioner, Southern Division, and Deputy Commissioner, Pakôkku.	**1. Chaungzôn Sakhán.** River Salín, Nanaing and Twé chaungs.	**8**	**0**	8	0	*N.B.*—This is really an *alternative* route, but is so round about that it could never be followed in preference to the main route; so it seems best to show it as a branch route, by means of which the centre of the Yindu country can be reached either from Laungshé or Kindwé. General direction north-west. Road level throughout and along bed of stony stream. First 4 miles through cultivation, then through steep and precipitous hills on both banks of stream; fit for all laden beasts. Camp in dry bed of stream. Water good and fodder of all kinds abundant. Camp not well situated and limited, but good enough for a day's halt. In rains this road would be impassable.
		2. Pinda Sakhán (4,150 feet). Salin chaung.	**8**	**0**	16	0	The road is over boulders of Salin bed for ½ mile, then turns north and up a steep bit for ¼ mile; after that it ascends gradually up the spur or range between the Salin and Twé chaungs till it reaches camp. Road fit for all laden transport. Water 200 yards from camp on south side of ridge plenty. Fodder for all animals (except elephants) plentiful. Road passes through oak, bamboo, firs, &c.
		3. Zaiti Sakhán (7,150 feet).	**8**	**0**	24	0	Road ascends by an easy slope along the ridge for 3 miles through open pine forests for a mile, it then runs through grass over a steep ascent; after this for 4 miles road goes up and down through dense forest to camp at Zaiti. Firs cease on beginning steep ascent, and evergreen and oak prevail. Camp fairly level ground between two springs. Water plentiful. Fodder of sorts, but no grass. Road fit for laden transport.
		4. Kachaungzôn Sakhán.	**8**	**0**	32	0	For first 4 miles the road runs by ups and downs over small spurs to a bare stony patch covered with short grass; height by barometer 7,400 feet; the next 4 miles is down a steep ridge for 4 miles to camp. First 4 miles of today's road is through dense forest. After leaving the bare peak it again goes through forest for a mile, when it becomes more open and jungle is succeeded by grass. The last 2½ miles are very stony. The camp is situated between the Ka and Hnaw chaungs at their junction, and is commanded by hills, but is an important position, being in the middle of the Yindu country. Water plentiful. Space limited. Fodder and grass abundant.
		5. Sainbôn Sakhán (1,600 feet). Ká stream, Twédu stream, Aukz n Pauktu stream, and Môn.	**11**	**0**	43	0	General direction south. First ½ mile the road is over rough ground. Crossing the stream it ascends a very steep bit for ½ mile; then 1½ miles up good easy slope to 4,000 feet; for 2 miles more it rounds the hill by easy gradients and then descends very steeply by a spur to village of Aukzôn Pauktu; rising for a bit it again goes down

FROM AKYAB TO LAUNGSHÉ *viâ* MYOHAUNG AND "THE SAWBWA'S ROUTE"—*continued.*

BRANCH I—*continued.*

Authorities. Military.	Authorities. Civil.	Number and Names of Stages, Rivers and Streams.	Distances. Intermediate. M.	F.	Distances. Total. M.	F.	Remarks.
G.O.C. Rangoon District.	Commissioner, Southern Division, and Deputy Commissioner, Pakôkku.	**5. Sainbôn Sakhán (1,600 feet)**—*cont.*					a steep path to the river Môn; up bed for 2 miles to camp. This is on level ground on left bank. Fodder and water plentiful. Road only fit for cooly transport. Local supplies *nil.*
		6. Tainkwé Sakhán (1,250 feet). Môn chaung.	7	0	50	0	Road runs along bed of stream the whole way, crossing several times from bank to bank. Bamboos and grass, &c., plentiful. Large and good camp. Road only fit for cooly transport.
		7. Kindwé (Chindwé). Môn chaung.	11	0	61	0	For 7 miles the path runs along left bank of Môn over spurs; here it joins the stream and keeps in its bed for 2 miles. At this point it meets the old Tilin Sawbwa's road from Laungshé to Arakan and, still keeping to the bed of the stream, reaches camp over a fairly level gravelly path. The first 3 miles from Tainkwé Sakhán are very bad and slippery. Kindwé is a Chinbôn village of 15 houses built on poles about 40 feet high. Water, grass, &c., all plentiful. A few pigs and fowls can be obtained here.

No. 2.

From KÔKARIT (KÔKAYIT) to SAWLÔN viâ PÁPHUN, PAZAUNG and BAWLAKÉ.

BY LIEUT. E. W. M. NORIE, INTELLIGENCE BRANCH, APRIL 1888, AND LIEUT. W. HUSSEY WALSH, CHESHIRE REGIMENT, JANUARY 1889.

Military.	Civil.	Stages, Rivers and Streams.	Intermediate. M.	F.	Total. M.	F.	Remarks.
G.O.C. Rangoon District.	Lower Burma.	**1. Camp** ... ... Salween and Yunzalín rivers.	12	0	12	0	From Kôkayit, at the mouth of the Yunzalín river, a good government road for pack animals and foot-passengers runs all the way to Páphun. It follows generally the course of the river, running along the right bank as far as Kusaik, where it crosses the stream and then continues up the left bank to Páphun. The entire distance by road is 67 miles. Water is plentiful along the road, as it seldom goes far from the river. The larger streams are bridged, but the bridges are out of repair. The first night it would be necessary to camp unless a long march were attempted. The road is quite level, and places suitable for camping on are frequent. Provisions are not procurable on the road and there is no accommodation.
		2. Kadinti ...	16	0	28	0	The road continues the same as before, running through forest jungle and crosses the Karendaung creek half-way by a bridge at present out of repair. Beyond reach the village of Kadinti. This is a large village of 150 to 200 houses, stretching across a strip of land in a bend of the river. The northern part of the village is inhabited by Shans, whose chief occupation seems to be cultivating fruit and tobacco. There is here a detachment of police from Páphun and a court-house.

FROM KÔKARIT (KÔKAYIT) TO SAWLÔN *viâ* PÁPHUN, PAZAUNG AND BAWLAKÉ—*continued.*

Authorities. Military.	Authorities. Civil.	Number and Names of Stages, Rivers and Streams.	Distances. Intermediate.	Distances. Total.	Remarks.
G.O.C. [illegible]angoon District.	Lower Burma.		M. F.	M. F.	
		3. Camp	**15 0**	43 0	The road runs on the same as before through the same sort of forest jungle and near the river. Pass Palaung, a small Karen village of about 15 houses, between the road and the river. From here a road runs to the lead mines, 6½ miles to the west. Beyond this pass the village of Kúchaung, a good-sized village of about 30 houses. Camp in the forest.
		4. Kúseik (crossing place).	**14 0**	57 0	The road goes on as before and passes no villages. The going is good and easy. At 14 miles reach Kúseik, where the road crosses the Yunzalín. Kúseik is a good-sized village of about 30 houses on the right bank of the river. The river is easily fordable in the dry weather when there is about 2½ feet of water at the crossing. If too deep there are usually boats to be had, and, if necessary, a ferry raft can be easily constructed by lashing a flooring of bamboos across a couple of boats.
		5. Páphun ...	**10 0**	67 0	After crossing the river the road goes on the same as before up the left bank of the river; crosses some open ground and passes the Shan village of Thégundain at about 6 miles. Páphun is a large village on both banks of the Yunzalín. It contains numerous shops and is the terminus for trade by boat up the Yunzalín. It is the head-quarters of a Superintendent of Police, who also acts as Deputy Commissioner of the district. There is a police post (stockaded), court-house, dâk bungalow, and post office. Accommodation for 150 men in kyaungs in the village. Supplies fodder, &c. Rice, Rs. 6 a basket.
		6. Takota camp... Yunzalín river and many nullahs.	**8 0**	75 0	General direction first three marches north-east by north. Shortly after leaving Páphun the road becomes very narrow, intersected by numerous channels, so narrow as to seriously impede the progress of baggage mules. The river Yunzalín, which varies from 80 yards to 130 yards in width, flows in a southerly direction to the left of the road: current about 4 miles an hour; shallow and fordable in numerous places. The road crosses many nullahs, which lead to the Yunzalín. The track was very steep both when ascending and descending those places.
		7. Taungbain Sakhán, Stream, fordable; several nullahs.	**5 4**	80 4	After Takota camp more nullahs. About 3 miles from Takota the track leads through sharp rocks, which impede the progress of the transport very seriously owing to the depth of their fall in many places. Road fairly good for a short way after this, but on crossing a stream a little further on it leads over a hill about 400 feet high, very precipitous in places; in fact the march up and down this hill is about as difficult for troops and transport elephants as any one could conceive in any very mountainous country. Camped at Taungbain Sakhán at the foot of this hill.
		8. Kalothuta camp.	**4 6**	85 2	The track on leaving this camp is good for several miles, passing through fairly open country. Jungle cleared for cultivation in many places. Some bad bits of road on approaching Kalothuta camp.

FROM KÔKARIT (KÔKAYIT) TO SAWLÔN *viâ* PÁPHUN, PAZAUNG AND BAWLAKÉ—*continued.*

Authorities. Military.	Authorities. Civil.	Number and Names of Stages, Rivers and Streams.	Distances. Intermediate. M. F.	Distances. Total. M. F.	Remarks.
G.O.C. Rangoon District.	Lower Burma.	**9. Peinmabun Sakhán.** Yunzalín stream, name unknown.	8 4	93 6	On leaving camp the road changes direction and goes due north, leaving the river Yunzalín, which turns off to the north-west towards its source as far as could be seen from a considerable height. The road now ascends steadily for 4 or 5 miles till it reaches the top of a mountain, which is said to be 3,300 feet high, when it suddenly descends a steep hill, leading to the bed of a stream, along the course of which the descent continues till Peinmabun Sakhán is reached. Half-way down this hill come across the road from Kyaukhnyát.
		10. Koludo ... Stream, name unknown.	7 6	101 4	On leaving camp the track continues along the bed of the same stream for about 5 miles, thence a short and easy ascent to Koludo. Police station, stockaded, situated on a small hill closely surrounded by higher hills on all sides.
		11. Mémulo ... Puddi and Mémulo streams.	10 6	112 2	On leaving Koludo the track crosses a high hill by a steep and narrow pathway leading up the side of the hill, precipitous above and below in the ascent, but descent not so difficult, then reach the Puddi stream about 20 to 30 feet in width; water at all seasons. Two miles beyond this reach Mémulo camp on the stream of the same name.
	Superintendent, Southern Shan States.	**12. Pákchaung** ... Mémulo and Tuklulo streams and Pa river (fordable).	6 2	118 4	Track follows the bed of this stream for some distance until a hill, the ascent of which is very steep, is reached. This hill is covered with "*in*" forest. At the foot of it a difficult track leads along the bed of the Tuklulo stream. The mountain on both sides covered with bamboo jungle. Pákchaung, the camp on the river Pa, which marks the frontier between Lower Burma and Karenni, has been slightly cleared of jungle.
		13. Tuchaung ... Nga river (fordable).	7 0	125 4	Cross the Pa on leaving camp, and the road leads up and down hills covered with "*in*" forest. The Nga river is reached about 4½ miles from camp. The track leads along the bank of this stream for some distance through thick bamboo jungle, then along some ravines bordered by hills, on descending which Tuchaung camp is reached.
		14. Pazaung ... Nga river and Kemapyu stream (fordable).	9 4	135 0	The track follows bed of same stream for some distance, then up a hill, but to no great height, when the Salween river comes in view, varying from 300 to 400 yards in width, apparently very deep; current about 6 miles an hour; "*in*" forest on all sides. About 1½ miles further on enter cultivation (millet and tobacco) and pass Karen village of Kemapyu (well provisioned); about 30 houses; inhabitants shy but friendly; then cross stream of the same name 60 yards wide and shallow. Three miles beyond reach foot of very steep hill covered with bamboo on all sides but one; the ascent very steep. The stockade of Pazaung crowns this hill. Road good.

FROM KÔKARIT (KÔKAYIT) TO SAWLÔN *viâ* PÁPHUN, PAZAUNG AND BAWLAKÉ—*continued.*

Authorities. Military.	Authorities. Civil.	Number and Names of Stages, Rivers and Streams.	Distances. Inter-mediate. M. F.	Distances. Total. M. F.	Remarks.
G.O.C. Rangoon District.	Superintendent, Southern Shan States.	**15. Bawlaké** ...	**16 0**	151 0	The remainder of this route is from native information. The road from Pazaung runs north and is good. The distance is from 16 to 20 miles being described as one long march. Bawlaké is a village of about 50 houses and is the head town of a Sawbwaship. The Sawbwa is very weak and his rule only extends over about five or six villages. The village is situated near the right bank of the Pun chaung.
		16. Sawlôn ...	**5 10**	156 0	On the other side of the Pun river, 4 or 5 miles due east of Bawlaké, is Sawlôn, Sawlapaw's capital, situated high up on the range of hills on a sort of plateau below the crest. The approach to Sawlôn is by a steep path running straight up the face of the hill. A route runs from Bawlaké north-west to Kyetpogyi about 20 miles across a limestone range, said by one account to be a good road, but by another it is said that where the road crosses this ridge it is very rough and bad, as the ridge is covered with very sharp loose stones, over which a pony can hardly be led.

BRANCH I.

FROM BAWLAKÉ (STAGE 15) TO NAUNGPALÉ.

BY LIEUT. E. W. M. NORIE, INTELLIGENCE DEPARTMENT, FROM NATIVE INFORMATION, MAY 1888.

Military	Civil	Stages	Inter. M.	F.	Total M.	F.	Remarks
G.O.C. Rangoon District.	Superintendent, Southern Shan States.	**1. Camp on Pun river.**	**10**	**0**	10	0	From Bawlaké the route runs up the Pun river and is good going. For the first two marches it is close to the river, and then striking north-west leads round the end of a limestone ridge, which runs between Kyetpogyi and the Pun river and reaches Naungpalé.
		2. Camp on Pun river.	**10**	**0**	20	0	
		3. Naungpalé ...	**16**	**0**	36	0	

No. 3.

From MOULMEIN to RAHAING (RAHENG).

NATIVE INFORMATION, DECEMBER 1892.

Military	Civil	Stages	Inter. M.	F.	Total M.	F.	Remarks
G.O.C. Rangoon District.	Lower Burma.	**1. Gyaing** ... ... Haungdara and Gyaing rivers.	**18**	**0**	18	0	Direction east. One day by ferry boats which run every tide. These boats carry 30 passengers usually. They are of the ordinary native rowing boat. Gyaing is a Burmese-Shan village of about 50 houses. Supplies not easily procurable, but fowls can be obtained at a cheap rate. Roads run along the bank from village to village, but these are mere paths and very little used, the general traffic being by boat.
		2. Kokhrait ... Several small streams bridged.	**18**	**0**	36	0	Direction east. Excellent government road, level, and no hills to be crossed. Kokhrait is a Karen-Burmese and Shan town of 200 houses, with good bazaar, Telegraph and Post offices. The Forest department has also a representative there.

FROM MOULMEIN TO RAHAING (RAHENG)—*continued.*

Authorities.		Number and Names of Stages, Rivers and Streams.	Distances.				Remarks.
Military.	Civil.		Intermediate.		Total.		
			M.	F.	M.	F.	
G.O.C. Rangoon District.	Lower Burma.	**3. Myawaddi** ...	**26**	**0**	62	0	Direction east. By road (mule or elephant track) hilly, and indifferent marching. Myawaddi is a Karen and Burmese village of 30 or 40 houses; usual supplies, though dear. A halt must be made end of first day at one of the small chaungs which are crossed at intervals. A good camping ground is met with 11 miles after leaving Kokhrait.
		4. Rahaing ... Several streams are said to be crossed.	**45**	**0**	107	0	Direction east. Roughly speaking it is three days' march, and three days' rations should be carried. Water is said to be plentiful *en route.* Much information could be obtained from the Forest Department at Myawaddi concerning the onward route to Bangkok. Large numbers of traders pass through Rahaing, and their caravans would afford guidance and companionship to a traveller. They could also be utilized to obtain information from.

No. 4.

From MOULMEIN to SAWLÔN viâ PÁPHUN (Water Route).

BY LIEUT. E. W. M. NORIE, INTELLIGENCE BRANCH, JUNE 1888.

G.O.C. Rangoon District.	Lower Burma.	**1. Méong**	**20**	**0**	20	0	Starting up the Salween river from Moulmein in a dinghy boat with an average cargo the course is up the left bank, on which Moulmein is itself situated. A little above Moulmein is passed an island in mid-stream, covered with pagodas, and higher up the mouth of the Gyaing river, which joins the Salween from the east and receives the waters of the Attaran river, flowing from the south-east just above its mouth. Here the Salween is very broad and the current is not rapid. When the Gyaing is full the boats have to ascend it for some distance and then cross, thus going considerably out of their way. Opposite the mouth of the Gyaing on the right bank of the Salween is the site of the old town of Martaban, now only occupied by a few huts. Continuing up the Salween the boat runs along the flat banks of numerous islands covered with elephant grass, very similar to those in the Irrawaddy. Where the true bank of the river is met with, it is covered with high grass and trees and numerous gardens of plantains are seen. The hills to the west, which descend close to the river bank at Martaban, retire further back as you ascend. Straight in front on the left bank of the river is a high ridge of rock with precipitous sides; it rises to the height of over 2,000 feet and on the highest point is the Zwagabin

FROM MOULMEIN TO SAWLÔN *viâ* PÁPHUN (WATER ROUTE)—*continued.*

Authorities. Military.	Authorities. Civil.	Number and Names of Stages, Rivers and Streams.	Distances. Intermediate.	Distances. Total.	Remarks.
G.O.C. Rangoon District.	Lower Burma.	**1. Méong**—*cont.*			pagoda visible from the boat. Before getting opposite this hill pass the village of Méong on the left bank. This is about as far as the boat (dinghy) will get on the first day. It is a village of about 50 houses with kyaungs, and all the usual supplies would probably be obtainable.
			M. F.	M. F.	
		2. Méngtsán ...	20 0	40 0	The boat travels all day and halts at whatever point it reaches at dark for the night. A suitable place for encamping can be found almost anywhere on the bank of the river. Continuing up stream the islands disappear and the river runs between its true banks. Pass the village of Turpula on the left bank lying a little back from the stream and little higher up Pagat on the opposite bank also lying back from the stream. This is a pretty large village. There is a landing stage here. The river now runs past the base of several small hills of limestone rock, rising abruptly out of the plain to the height of 300 to 500 feet, with precipitous sides. Pa-án is on the left bank. Here there is a small guard of police, six men under a naick. Water deep right up to the bank, which is sand. A little below on the right bank is Maungalé hidden among groves of mango, palmyra, and plantain. There is also more wood about the banks, and fine jungle trees and bamboos are plentiful. Above Pa-án at the south end of a steep rocky ridge is the small village of Méngtsán on the left bank. This is as far as the boat will probably get on the second day.
		3. Shwégun ...	20 0	60 0	Higher up on the right bank is Mogadi. The river above this runs along the base of two high limestone ridges on the right bank, the rock rising up from the water's edge like a wall to the height of 400 or 500 feet. Between these ridges is the small village of Miging. The village of Méngtsai on the left bank is much higher up than shown on the map and lies back from the river. Above this on the right bank is Wugyi, a large village, with pôngyi kyaungs and pagodas, and opposite it is Udaung higher up than shown on the map and lying back from the river. At a bend of the river is Mibo on the right bank where there are a number of huts built on rafts floating in the river. From here can be seen Shwégun a little higher up on the left bank. At Shwégun there is a landing stage, court-house, and police post. It is a good large village of about 100 houses under a Myo-ôk. A dinghy conveying a passenger with only 1 or 1½ maunds of baggage, a very light load, that is to say, as compared with a full cargo, will come up so far in two days, and this is as high as the steam launches generally run though they *can* get up further.
		4. Kôkarit (Kôkayit).	20 0	80 0	Immediately above Shwégun the river is split up into four or five channels by large islands, but there is plenty of water in the two larger ones. It is here that the dinghies which so far have been poling up the left bank cross over to the right bank. Further up the river becomes shallow and the water runs among limestone rocks. In the

FROM MOULMEIN TO SAWLÔN *viâ* PÁPHUN (WATER ROUTE)—*continued.*

Authorities. Military.	Authorities. Civil.	Number and Names of Stages, Rivers and Streams.	Distances. Intermediate.	Distances. Total.	Remarks.
G.O.C. Rangoon District.	Lower Burma.	**4. Kôkarit (Kôkayit)**—*cont.*			dry weather anything larger than a dinghy would probably be unable to ascend, but launches and cargo boats would also get up from July to March. Pass the village of Kôsing on the right bank and higher up Khôlu on the left. About ½ a mile above the latter there is a small pagoda on the same bank. The banks are now higher and well wooded. Higher up on the right bank is Kumamu. Above this the shallow Meng creek joins the Salween from the west. Here the Salween is very broad and immediately above very deep and narrow where it bends to the east with limestone rocks on both banks, through which it has apparently worn its way. At this point there is a timber trap formed of two large booms or cables of logs and bamboos lashed together and stretching right across the river. The timber floating down is caught on the first of these booms and guided inside the trap; here it is formed into rafts, which are then passed through the second boom and sent off down the river. Above this the Salween is split into two by a large island covered with grass and jungle. On the right bank of the western branch is the village of Kôkarit also very generally called Kôkayit at the mouth of the Yunzalín river. Here there is police post of Gurkhas and Karens from Páphun, to which place a good road for baggage animals runs (*see* Route No. 2). To the north and west are high mountain peaks covered with forest. It is just above Kôkarit that the first serious rapids on the Salween are met with and navigation becomes impossible.
		5. Camp on the Yunzalín.	M. F. **20 0**	M. F. 100 0	The Yunzalín flows into the Salween from the west, though till immediately above its mouth its course is south-south-east. Its breadth near the mouth is 120 yards and in the dry weather near Páphun it is not more than 20 yards broad in places. It is a clear rapid stream flowing along the bottom of a narrow valley. The bed of the river is narrow and deep, between high banks covered with forests and jungle, and winds about a good deal. In the dry weather small rapids, where the water runs pretty strong over shallows and among rocks, are of constant occurrence. The rocks are almost all limestone and in some places have been blasted to form a channel. Only dinghies ply on the Yunzalín and only the smallest size of these can get up the river in the dry season, from March to June. Even they are constantly sticking, though they are at once got off again, but if they are heavily laden the progress is very slow, as in the rapids and shallow parts the men have to get out and drag and push them through. The valley of the Yunzalín is formed by high ranges of hills. Those on the western side are at some distance from the river at the mouth, but approach rapidly as you ascend. Higher up the lower slopes begin in most places from the very banks of the stream. The hills on either side are covered with fine forest, with large patches of bamboo in many places. Cultivation there is none to speak of and hardly any villages are visible from the stream. The villages passed as you ascend are as follows:—Mégula on the right bank and Mépli and Myataung on the left. They cannot be seen from the boat as they lie back in the jungle and are small, poor Karen villages, from which no supplies

FROM MOULMEIN TO SAWLÔN *viâ* PÁPHUN (WATER ROUTE)—*continued.*

Authorities. Military.	Authorities. Civil.	Number and Names of Stages, Rivers and Streams.	Distances. Intermediate. M. F.	Distances. Total. M. F.	Remarks.
G.O.C. Rangoon District.	Lower Burma.	**5. Camp on the Yunzalín**—*cont.*			can be obtained. The first night a halt must be made at some convenient place on the bank. Ground fit for encamping on with fodder, and firewood can be found almost anywhere.
		6. Palaung ...	20 0	120 0	Going on Shwébelagya village is passed, but it lies about 2 miles back in the jungle. Next pass the mouth of the Karendaung creek, which joins the Yunzalín from the west, and above this the first village seen since leaving Kôkarit is reached. This village is called Kadeinti, and is situated at a bend of the river on the right bank. Directly facing the boat as it ascends is the police post and court-house. The police are a detachment of Gurkhas and Karens from Páphun. Kadeinti is a large village of about 200 houses, but no supplies beyond perhaps some fowls could be depended on. The river now makes a large circular bend and again passes Kadeinti about a mile from the former place. Here the village is on both banks of the river and is inhabited by Shans, who cultivate gardens of tobacco and fruit. The next village passed is Thawkélaw on the left bank a ¼ of a mile back from the river and not seen from the boat. Next is the village of Palaung on the right bank. A small, poor Karen village close to the river. Just below this the channel is full of rocks. From Palaung a road runs 6½ miles to the west to the lead mines.
		7. Mindabi ...	16 0	136 0	The next village is Domwé, not seen from the boat, on the left bank, and then Kun chaung on the right bank. This is a pretty big village of about 50 houses and a forest ranger lives here. The river is now getting shallower and progress is not quite so fast as before. Mindabi is a Shan village on the left bank about 100 yards from the river. It contains about 50 houses. There is an old Government zayát here on the side of the river, but it has fallen to pieces.
		8. Camp on the Yunzalín.	16 0	152 0	Going on the river is the same as last stage. Pass the two small villages of Minulaw and Shentumaw, both on the left bank lying back in the jungle. Towards evening reach Kúseik (crossing place) where the road from Kôkarit to Páphun crosses the Yunzalín by a ford when the river is low (*see* Route No. 2, Stage 4). Kúseik is a village of about 30 houses on the right bank of the river. The boat will probably not get more than 3 or 4 miles beyond this before dark.
		9. Páphun... ...	8 0	160 0	The valley above this opens out and is free from trees for some distance and there is some cultivation on the left bank, on which is situated the Shân village of Thégundain about 3 miles below Páphun. Thégundain contains about 50 houses. At Páphun the valley again closes in. Páphun is the furthest point to which dinghies can ascend (for description *see* Route No. 2, Stage 5).

FROM MOULMEIN TO SAWLÔN *viâ* PÁPHUN (WATER ROUTE)—*continued.*

Authorities.		Number and Names of Stages, Rivers and Streams.	Distances.		Remarks.
Military.	Civil.		Intermediate.	Total.	
G.O.C. Rangoon District.	Lower Burma.	**9. Páphun**—*cont.*			*Note.*—Steam launches of about 20 tons and cargo boats to carry from 35 tons to 50 tons would most probably be able to ascend the Salween as far as Kôkarit from August till January. The former would do the distance in one day, but the latter would probably take six or seven days. They could, however, be towed up in strings of two or three by the launches. Dinghies only can ascend the Yunzalín. For particulars of capacity, numbers, hire, &c., *see* separate note "Boat transport on the Salween and Yunzalín rivers" at end of this route.
			M. F.	M. F.	
		10. Camp	**12 0**	172 0	The next two stages are by land. The road leaving Páphun runs east and immediately enters the hills by a small water-course. Here there is a short steep ascent, after which the road runs along comparatively level for some distance. The road is a track constantly used by bullocks and elephants and runs through bamboo and tree forest. At about 3 miles the real climbing begins and the road runs right up the face of the high steep ridge to the top. The soil is red clay, and very slippery in wet weather. Passing over the top of the ridge the road descends as abruptly on the other side. There is a halting place at about 12 miles with water, where the Shans usually break the journey. There is no village and the road lies through forest the whole way.
		11. Kyaungyát ...	**9 0**	181 0	Leaving the valley it again ascends and crosses over a smaller ridge and then leads on to Kyaungyát through tolerably level forest. At Kyaungyát there is a police post of Gurkhas and Karens. It is situated on the Salween above the rapids. From here the traders carry their supplies up the river in Shan boats.
		12 to 14. Camps on river bank.	**(?)**	(?)	From Kyaungyát the traders carry their stores up the Salween to Luwut by boat. Three or four days' journey from sunrise to sunset with occasional rests. Kyaungyát is situated on the right bank of the Salween river and above the rapids. There is a police guard here of Gurkhas and Karens. The navigation of the river is easy, and the boats are Shan boats, each carrying about 60 baskets (about lbs. 2,800) or 20 men. Probably 100 boats could be collected at Kyaungyát in a fortnight. The Shans usually sleep on board their boats, but they say, if necessary, that there are plenty of places where troops could land and encamp. There are some villages along the Salween, but apparently they are not numerous. Troops proceeding up stream by boat could be landed at any point considered desirable on either bank of the river. "Luwut, better known as Ta Hsang Lé, is on the right bank
		15. Luwut or Ta Hsang Lé.	**(?)**	(?)	

FROM MOULMEIN TO SAWLÔN *viâ* PÁPHUN (WATER ROUTE)—*continued.*

Authorities.		Number and Names of Stages, Rivers and Streams.	Distances.		Remarks.
Military.	Civil.		Inter-mediate.	Total.	
G.O.C. Rangoon District.	Lower Burma.	**15. Luwut or Ta Hsang Lé**—*cont.*			of the, Salween south-east of Sawlôn, Lat. 19° 8′ and Long. 97° 34′; altitude 550 feet. Here there is a ferry across the Salween, 3½ miles south-east of Ywathit (Wan Mau). It is the starting point for the Ywathit boat traffic with Moulmein *viâ* Kyaukhnyat and with Sataw *viâ* Ta Ta Maw, as well as with Méhawngsawn *viâ* the Mé Pai. Travellers going from Ywathit to Kun Yuom and Chieng Mai cross the Salween at this point. The Salween in the dry season is here about 250 yards broad. There are usually half-a-dozen boats of various sizes available at the ferry, but many more can be collected at a week's notice. The boatmen dwell at the village on the right bank of the river where there are 12 or 16 houses of Shans and Karens. There is also a very fine zayát of the best teak. Interior area 75 feet by 24 feet. It is capable of housing a company of infantry. There is space for encamping on the river bank, and here and there in the woods behind. Forage and firewood plentiful. Water from the Salween. In 1890 there was a Siamese post on the left bank of the Salween guarding the ferry. The right bank commands the left".—(*Barrow*).*
			M. F.	M. F.	
		16. Hôta	7 4	7 4	The road runs north-west to Ywathit at 3½ miles. The first ½ mile is steep, the next 3 miles gradual ascent. Road very good, through jungle most of the way, with a few paddy clearings. At 1½ miles cross shallow, narrow stream. From Ywathit on to Hôta at 7¼ miles, *see* Route No. 4, Shan Division.
		17. Sawlôn ...	12 0	19 4	*See* Route No. 4, Shan Division.

Boat Transport on the Salween and Yunzalin Rivers.

BY LIEUT. E. W. M. NORIE, ATTACHÉ, INTELLIGENCE BRANCH, SEPTEMBER 1888.

There are no regular routes from the north to Moulmein, almost all the trade being brought down the Salween and Yunzalin rivers by boat.

These boats are classed as follows :

Dinghies.

1. Dinghies, or passenger boats, of which there are about 400 available. These boats are of different sizes. The small size is 45 feet in length and about 5 feet broad, manned by three men, one of whom steers, and carrying about 50

* Captain Barrow also writes as follows with reference to this place : " Tá Hsang Lé is the 'port' of Ywathit or Wan Mau from which it is 3½ miles distant (*vide* article Tá Hsang Lé). It is apparently the same as the Luwnt of the old maps and Lieutenant Norie's report, but locally the place is always spoken of as Tá Hsang Lé. I never heard the name Luwut though living at the place a fortnight."

Lieutenant Norie says : "Probably 100 boats would be collected at Kyaukhnyát in a fortnight. These boats belong to various owners, 40 or 50 to traders at Páphun and Kyaukhnyát of which 20 or 30 could most likely be got together at Kyaukhnyát for Government use at any time." He says too that the boats each carry about 60 baskets (say 2,800 lbs.), or 20 men, I think myself that the majority of the boats procurable would not take more than 10 or 12 men at the outside.

He reckons the distance at " three or four days journey from sunrise to sunset with occasional rests," and he also says the navigation is easy. My information differs; some Ywathit traders told me that the down journey took one day to Pahzaung and three to Kyaukhnyát, that the river was very difficult and even dangerous on account of rocks, snags and rapids. However from what boatmen told me I believe the down journey can be done in two days, and judging from my experience of the river between Ta Hsang Lé and Ta Ta Mau, I should say the average up journey would be at least 6 or 7 days. There are but few villages on the river, but plenty of places where troops could land and encamp on either bank.

baskets, or 2,800 lbs. They are not very suitable for carrying troops, as about 20 feet of the front part is used as a walk for the men poling and would only be available for stowing a small amount of kit, &c., which would have to be made up in small lots, say 60 lbs. or 80 lbs., to facilitate packing. The next 17 or 18 feet is decked in and covered by a mat roof, and this is the passengers' part of the boat. A trader hiring the boat will fill all this part up with his stores, only leaving room enough for himself to sit in. To make it suitable for the carriage of troops the deck would have to be removed and seats substituted; also the roofing would be taken off and an awning with open sides substituted to procure air, light, and greater accommodation. As the boats are narrow, not more than two men can sit abreast, and there would be probably six benches or sitting room for 12 men. Their kit would be packed small and stowed under the seats. A flooring would be necessary to keep kits and stores off the bottom of the boat and so enable them to be kept dry. There is no accommodation for sleeping at night on board. The last 6 or 7 feet of the boat are very narrow and occupied by the man steering. This size of boat will ply the whole way from Moulmein to Páphun all the year round. The largest size of dinghies are about 60 feet in length and about 9 feet broad, usually manned by five men including the steersman. They will carry about 120 baskets or about 6,500 lbs. In construction they are exactly the same in plan as the small size described before and could no doubt be fitted with eight seats instead of six, and would accommodate from 24 to 30 men with sitting room. They cannot ascend the Yunzalín when the river is at its lowest, which is from February or March till June, but they can always get up as far as Kôkarit at the mouth of the river. The dinghies all belong to and are manned by Chittagonians, and the steersman is usually the owner of the boat. The labour of poling is very great and the wages high. The pay of an ordinary boatman is Rs. 15 a month. The hire of a small sized dinghy from Moulmein to Páphun is from Rs. 35 to Rs. 40, according to the season of the year. The hire of a large dinghy is Rs. 65 to Rs. 70. Journey up takes eight or nine days, and if heavily laden, 11 or 12 days. The journey down takes three days. The boats are all registered in the office of the Port officer of Moulmein. They are divided into different batches, each under a tindal or foreman, who makes arrangements as to the supply of boats and terms of hire. Only dinghies ply on the Yunzalín river.

Cargo boats.

2. The next class of boats are those known as cargo boats, of which there are about 175 registered in the office of the Port Officer. The smallest will carry about 20 tons and the largest over 100 tons, but the majority carry from 35 to 50 tons. They can only ascend to Kôkarit at the mouth of the Yunzalín during the four rainy months of the year, namely, from June to September, and then only the smaller sized boats of from 30 to 35 tons register, partly laden and carrying 10 to 15 tons cargo, can proceed up. The draft of these boats when empty is 4 feet and when partly laden 5 and 6 feet. These boats will carry about 50 men per boat. Awnings would be necessary to protect the men from the sun and also to keep their kits dry in the event of rain. The best way of getting the boats up would be by towing. Only a single boat can be towed by a launch at a time. Time occupied would be six to seven days. (?) Boats sailing or poling would take about 15 days.(?) The number of crew per boat is six men. Terms of hire per boat, if sailing or poling themselves, Rs. 150; if towed, Rs. 100. These boats are chiefly used about Moulmein harbour and along the coast.

Launches.

3. Besides the dinghies and cargo boats there are about 12 private and two Government launches. They could carry about 15 to 25 tons of cargo, but are chiefly used for passengers, of whom they can carry 40 or 50. They never ascend beyond Shwégun or a little above it, doing the distance up stream from Moulmein in eight or nine hours, counting stoppages and running so far all the year round. A launch with a small draft ought certainly to be able to ascend to Kôkarit any time between June and February and should do the distance in a day. The hire of a launch is Rs. 75 a day inclusive of fuel.

No. 5.

From TAUNGU (TOUNGOO) to KYETPOGYI (KARENNI) viâ BUKO.

BY LIEUT. E. W. M. NORIE, INTELLIGENCE BRANCH (FROM LOCAL INFORMATION), JUNE 1888.

<table>
<tr><th colspan="2">Authorities.</th><th rowspan="2">Number and Names of Stages, Rivers and Streams.</th><th colspan="4">Distances.</th><th rowspan="2">Remarks.</th></tr>
<tr><th>Military.</th><th>Civil.</th><th colspan="2">Intermediate.</th><th colspan="2">Total.</th></tr>
<tr><td></td><td></td><td></td><td>M.</td><td>F.</td><td>M.</td><td>F.</td><td></td></tr>
<tr><td rowspan="5">G.O.C. Rangoon District.</td><td rowspan="5">Lower Burma.</td><td>1. Seven Pagodas
Sittang river.</td><td>5</td><td>0</td><td>5</td><td>0</td><td>The road leaving Toungoo cantonment crosses the Sittang by ferry below the transport lines and leads along a made road, or causeway, to the south-east; passing through the village of Paunglaungdain on the left bank of the river, it reaches the Shwétada (golden bridge) at about 2 miles. Here there is a bridge, capable of bearing elephants, over a deep creek. From here the road runs to the Seven Pagodas, where there is a Government rest-house. Ground for encamping and good water from a stream.</td></tr>
<tr><td>2. Thekréklat ...</td><td>10</td><td>0</td><td>15</td><td>0</td><td>The road is level and good, running through jungle. Thekréklat is a small Karen village lying back from the road. On the road there is good ground for encamping and good water.</td></tr>
<tr><td>3. Péléwata ...
Délao stream.</td><td>10</td><td>0</td><td>25</td><td>0</td><td>The road, the same as before, reaches Péléwata on the east bank of the Délao stream at 10 miles. Here there is a good halting place and water from the stream.</td></tr>
<tr><td>4. Bawgalé ...</td><td>9</td><td>0</td><td>34</td><td>0</td><td>From Péléwata the road leads up a long hill to Bawgalé. This is a large village of Christian Karens, and supplies can be obtained here in limited quantities. It is just inside the boundary of Lower Burma. Good ground for encamping and good water. There is a Mission house here where travellers can put up. The Myo-ôk of the district used to live at Bawgalé, but has lately been moved to Ômbingyaung, another Karen village about 20 miles off. He speaks English well, but does not appear to have much influence or information.</td></tr>
<tr><td>5. Klélo stream ...</td><td>10</td><td>0</td><td>44</td><td>0</td><td>The road runs over hills and finally descends to the Klélo stream. There is a camping ground on either side of the stream, which is unfordable during the rains, when it can only be crossed by a bamboo foot-bridge made by the Karens in the neighbourhood. These bridges are constructed out of four or five bamboos laid together and another generally placed as a hand-rail. They are not practicable for animals.</td></tr>
</table>

FROM TAUNGU (TOUNGOO) TO KYETPOGYI (KARENNI) *viâ* BUKO—*continued.*

Authorities. Military.	Authorities. Civil.	Number and Names of Stages, Rivers and Streams.	Distances. Intermediate. M.	F.	Total. M.	F.	Remarks.
G.O.C. Rangoon District.	Lower Burma.	**6. Berkerléko** ... Klélo stream.	**9**	**0**	53	0	From the stream, the road runs uphill again and finally reaches the Karen village of Berkerléko. This is a large village of Christian Karens, and a limited quantity of food can always be obtained here. There is a good camping ground, and travellers can always put up in the Mission house. There is plenty of good water. Bullocks can be used so far, but beyond this only elephants and coolies can get along as the hills are very steep.
		7. Kwaké	**15**	**0**	68	0	From here the road leads up to the top of the main ridge of the "Gamong" range by a very steep ascent. The ridge is here very high (probably over 6,000 feet) and the path is difficult, but though steep, is fairly good. Down the other side the descent is also very steep, and for the first 10 miles of this stage there is no water. Kwaké is a Karen village, and here a little food can be procured. There is good water and ground for encamping.
		8. Buko	**4**	**0**	72	0	Four miles further on is the large Karen village of Buko, where there is a Karen pastor and Mission house, in which travellers can put up. In this village a certain quantity of rice and fowls can be obtained. There is plenty of good water from a stream and ground suitable for encamping on.
		9. Kerpé ... ... Holo stream.	**8**	**0**	80	0	From Buko the path descends into a deep valley, at the bottom of which is the Holo stream, a large stream unfordable during the rains. Beyond is the village of Kerpé, a friendly Brék (wild Karen) village, where a small quantity of rice and fowls can be obtained. Ground for encamping.
		10. Nampolo stream.	**20**	**0**	100	0	The road now runs down the bank of the Holo stream nearly to the point where it joins the Nampolo stream. The camping ground is on the bank of the latter stream, which is a large one and unfordable in the rain.
		11. Terko ... ... Nampolo.	**9**	**0**	109	0	From the Nampolo the road runs up a long hill to the Red Karen village of Terko, a friendly village, where a few fowls might be obtained. There is no water in this stage after the Nampolo is left.
		12. Plélo stream. Plélo stream.	**9**	**0**	118	0	The road, the same as before, leads over steep hills and then descends to the Plélo stream. Here there are two villages, only one of which, Plélo, is on the road, the other being a little to the east. Some food supplies could be obtained at these villages.

FROM TAUNGU (TOUNGOO) TO KYETPOGYI (KARENNI) *viâ* BUKO—*continued.*

Authorities. Military.	Authorities. Civil.	Number and Names of Stages, Rivers and Streams.	Distances. Intermediate. M. F.		Distances. Total. M. F.		Remarks.
G.O.C. Rangoon District.	Lower Burma.	**13. Talépéta** ...	**12**	**0**	130	0	Along this stage the road is good, but there is no water. Talépéta is a small village and about 3 miles beyond it is Kyetpogyi, or, as the Karennis call it, Kelea, which is, I believe, the proper name.
		14. Kyetpogyi (Kelea).	**3**	**0**	133	0	For description of Kyetpogyi, *see* Route No. 4, Shan Hills Division, Alternative I. *Note.*—This is the most direct road from Toungoo into Karenni, but it is very steep and hilly.

The country passed through consists almost entirely of ranges of mountains covered with forest, and, like all other roads in Karenni, no attempt has been made to avoid the steep ascents and descents, the road running straight up the one side of each range of hills and straight down the other. For a small party, it would perhaps be the best road; but for a large party, probably one of the other routes would be more suitable. This route is at present unfit after the 6th stage for troops moving with mule or bullock transport, and even small parties would have to carry their own supplies with them.

ALTERNATIVE I.

FROM TAUNGU (TOUNGOO) TO KYETPOGYI (WEST KARENNI) *viâ* UBO AND POKHAI.

BY LIEUT. E. W. M. NORIE, 2ND MIDDLESEX REGIMENT, JUNE 1888 (FROM NATIVE INFORMATION).

Military	Civil	Stages	M.	F.	M.	F.	Remarks
G.O.C. Rangoon District.	Lower Burma.	**1. Seven Pagodas** Sittang river.	**5**	**0**	5	0	*See* Route No. 5, Stages 1 to 4.
		2. Thekréklat ...	**10**	**0**	15	0	
		3. Péléwata ... Délso stream.	**10**	**0**	25	0	
		4. Bawgalé ...	**9**	**0**	34	0	
		5. Nauthéder ...	**9**	**0**	43	0	From Bawgalé the road runs across the hills to Mawkôder about 7 miles. This is a small friendly Karan village, where there is a good stream of water, and here a halt might be made. Two miles beyond is the village of Nauthéder, about 20 houses and good halting place and water.
		6. Ubo	**10**	**0**	53	0	From Nauthéder the road runs down by a steep descent to the Kyé chaung. The Karens call it Klélo. This stream is not fordable in the rains until November; the Karens make a bridge of bamboo over it for foot-passengers. From the stream the road

From TAUNGU (TOUNGOO) to KYETPOGYI (KARENNI) *viâ* BUKO—*continued.*

ALTERNATIVE I—*continued.*

Authorities. Military.	Authorities. Civil.	Number and Names of Stages, Rivers and Streams.	Distances. Intermediate. M.	F.	Distances. Total. M.	F.	Remarks.
G.O.C. Rangoon District.	Lower Burma.	**6. Ubo**—*cont.*					leads up a steep high hill and then along the ridge, with some short steep slopes, to the village of Ubo. Water here good and plentiful from a stream, and good halting place. In the village there are about 25 houses. From Ubo to Berkeléko (*see* Route No. 5, Stage 6) is about 4 miles by a rough road.
		7. Halting place...	**11**	**0**	64	0	From Ubo the road runs east and ascends the main ridge of the "Gamong." The ascent is very steep, and the top of the ridge is probably about 6,000 feet above the sea. Thus the loads of bullocks and elephants are very light. On reaching the top, which is about 10 miles from Ubo, the path descends for about a mile to the halting place on the banks of a small stream.
		8. Homulo stream	**16**	**0**	80	0	The road continues to descend passing over some lower hills and at last reaches the Homulo stream, where there is a halting place. This stream is not fordable in the rains from June to October, when it is crossed by a bamboo foot-bridge. Between the last halting place and here there is no water along the road. There is no village here.
		9. Hosalo stream	**30**	**0**	110	0	From the Homulo stream the road runs across two or three high ridges to the Hosalo stream: distance said to be about 30 miles. There is no water along this part of the road, travellers having to carry it for themselves and their animals. It is said to be a very bad bit of road. There is a place to halt, but no villages.
		10. Molo stream.	**20**	**0**	130	0	From the Hosalo stream the road runs across a high hill. There is a place about half-way where there is a little good water from a spring. There is a halting place on the Molo stream, but no village. This is a good big stream and not fordable for about six months in the rains. It is bridged for foot-passengers.
		11. Kautuder ...	**10**	**0**	140	0	From Molo stream the road runs across hills to the village of Kautuder. Water from streams along the road. Kautuder is a friendly White Karen village of about 10 houses. There is a good open space for camping and plenty of water from a stream.

FROM TAUNGU (TOUNGOO) TO KYETPOGYI (KARENNI) *viâ* BUKO—*continued.*

ALTERNATIVE I—*continued.*

Authorities. Military.	Authorities. Civil.	Number and Names of Stages, Rivers and Streams.	Distances. Intermediate. M.	F.	Distances. Total. M.	F.	Remarks.
G.O.C. Rangoon District.	Lower Burma.	**12. Sauthwéko** ...	**10**	**0**	150	0	The road, the same as before, runs across hills to Sauthwéko, a village of about 40 houses of White Karens. There is no water here; it has all to be brought from a distance.
		13. Hawtiper ...	**10**	**0**	160	0	From here a good road goes to Hawtiper, a village of about 100 houses with a mixed population of Red and White Karens. Sawlapaw used to have a guard here. Plenty of good water and a place for camping.
		14. Sélawlo stream.	**6**	**0**	166	0	From Hawtiper fair road runs to the Sélawlo stream, where there is a halting place and good water.
		15. Pokhai ...	**10**	**0**	176	0	From Sélawlo stream the road, the same as before, passes the village of Dermu of about 30 houses. Water good from a stream, and 4 miles beyond reaches the village of Pokhai on the Htu chaung, on the road from Páphun to Kyetpogyi. Pokhai is a small village, but from here two roads run to the north, one to the east towards Zimmé and one south to Páphun. From here the road follows that from Páphun to Kyetpogyi.
		16. Camp on Nampé stream.	**16**	**0**	192	0	*Vide* Route No. 4, Shan Hills Division.
		17. Kyetpogyi ...	**14**	**0**	206	0	*Note.*—The distances in this route are almost certainly less than here stated. This is a route practicable for bullocks and is used by Shans and Karennis. All the streams are of course fordable for elephants immediately after the rain stops. This route was taken by Major Lloyd, Deputy Commissioner of Toungoo, in 1874, when he went to see Kunti, who was then the nominal chief of Western Karenni.

No. 6.

From TAUNGU (TOUNGOO) to MANDALAY.

BY CAPT. YATE, FROM VARIOUS SOURCES, 1887-88.

Military	Civil	Stage	Inter. M.	F.	Total M.	F.	Remarks
G.O.C. Rangoon District.	Lower Burma.	**1. Lédaungaung**... Small streams bridged.	**9**	**0**	9	0	The Toungoo-Mandalay Railway, which has been open since 1889, follows the line taken by this route and most of the stages are either railway stations or midway between stations.

FROM TAUNGU (TOUNGOO) TO MANDALAY—*continued.*

Authorities. Military.	Authorities. Civil.	Number and Names of Stages, Rivers and Streams.	Distances. Intermediate.	Distances. Total.	Remarks.
G.O.C. Rangoon District.	Lower Burma.	**1. Lédaungaung** —*cont.*			Road good and metalled for first 5 miles; for remaining 4 miles unmetalled, but in fair order. The following small villages are passed: at 2 miles Kango, 5 miles Talôkgôn, 6 miles Bôntagôn, 7 miles Letpaeng. Accommodation for ½ a battalion in rest-house and zayáts. In dry weather camping ground in paddy-fields. Water from wells good, but quantity unknown. No information about supplies, probably rice, paddy, and bullocks obtainable.
		2. Yédashé ... Small streams bridged.	M. F. **8 0**	M. F. 17 0	Good unmetalled road. Two or three clearings met with, otherwise through jungle. Following villages passed: at 4 miles Náuchôn, at 6 miles Nagádwin. Rest-house, court-house, and police station at Yédashé. Accommodation for half a battalion in kyaung, zayáts and large village. Water plentiful from wells. Paddy, rice, fowls, &c., procurable. Camping ground in paddy-fields in dry season. Myo-ôk resides here. Railway station.
		3. Swa ... ... Swa river.	**7 0**	24 0	Good unmetalled road, bridged, passing villages as follows: at 1 mile Myaungbin, at 3 miles Thabyadán, and at 4 miles Pesut. The rest-house and zayáts of Swa appear to be on the north side of the river. There are several villages in the vicinity of the ferry. The ferry is only needed in the rains; in the dry season the water at the ford is quite shallow, and the bed of the stream is sandy and firm. Carts can then cross it at the rate of from 200 to 250 in an hour. In the rains for purposes of crossing there is a ferry boat capable of taking eight men or one horse at a time. Additional boats can be collected from the neighbouring villages on the banks of the river, and bamboo rafts can easily be constructed. When the river is in high flood (these floods last from 12 to 15 hours as a rule), boats and rafts cannot be used, nor can even elephants cross the river. Water plentiful from river Swa and wells. Ordinary supplies probably procurable. The Swa is sometimes in flood as late as the end of November. Railway station.
		4. Thágaya ... Several nullahs bridged.	**6 0**	30 0	Easy, sandy cart track. From the Swa river as far as Myohla (*see* next stage) the road traverses thick bamboo and *in* jungle. Rest-house at Thágaya. Water plentiful from wells. Three zayáts capable of holding about 100 men. Good camping ground in dry weather. Ordinary supplies probably procurable. Railway station.

FROM TAUNGU (TOUNGOO) TO MANDALAY—*continued.*

Authorities. Military.	Authorities. Civil.	Number and Names of Stages, Rivers and Streams.	Distances. Intermediate. M. F.	Distances. Total. M. F.	Remarks.
G.O.C. Rangoon District.	Lower Burma.	**5. Gyobin**	**12 0**	42 0	Road as far as Myohla indifferent, and from Myohla to Gyobin difficult. It is unmetalled. It crosses a succession of low hills of laterite. Myohla is a small village with a police post on the right bank of the Sittang. It is also a Railway station. At Gyobin is the old frontier outpost, now a stockaded police post. Well in the stockade. Post and telegraph offices. Accommodation for troops in zayáts, extent unknown. Good camping ground in dry season. Water plentiful, and ordinary supplies (paddy, rice, bullocks, fowls, &c.) procurable.
	Commissioner Eastern Division, and Deputy Commissioner, Pyinmana.	**6. Kábain** ... ... Canal and Thawati stream.	**10 0**	52 0	For 6 miles a good cart track; the road then bifurcates, one branch going to Éhla, often sandy and heavy. The Kábain road is to be preferred, as that to Éhla lies through paddy-fields. Éhla itself lies low, and is not suitable as a camping ground. Water from three wells at Éhla. To revert, however, to the Gyobin-Kábain road, it is in parts difficult for carts; at 2 miles it crosses a canal, at 3 miles the Thawati stream and passes Thawati village. Railway station. The village of Míbyagôn is just on the other side of this stream opposite to Thawati. At Míbyagôn is a zayát and police guard. At 7 miles village of Taveng passed and between that and Kábain road is swampy. At Kábain are two small zayáts, one well. Clearing round zayáts insufficient.
		7. Pyinmana (Ningyán). Yônbin creek.	**13 0**	65 0	Good road. Two feet of water in Yônbin creek in December. Several large villages passed, including Thawmagôn, Pyinmana at 9 miles and Gyinlo at 12 miles. The road from Éhla to Thawmagôn is also good. At Thawmagôn there is a fairly good camping ground for a battalion in the dry season with good water from the Yônbin stream close by. Pyinmana is a largish town, and with the suburb of Ywagauk on the north or left bank of the Ngáleik chaung (which flows between the two and falls into the Sinthé near the junction of the Sinthé and Sittang rivers) has a population of 3,000 or 4,000. Very extensive rice cultivation for miles round. Large bazaar. Supplies of all kinds procurable, prices high. Water and accommodation for troops in abundance. Railway station. During the rains steam launches of the Bombay-Burma Trading Corporation, Limited, drawing about 2 feet of water run from Taungu to Sinthéwa in from two to three days (anchoring from sunset to sunrise) and from Sinthéwa to Taungu in from 12 to 14 hours. Sinthéwa is a small village and military post on the right bank of the Sittang, 6 miles east-south-east of Pyinmana and connected

FROM TAUNGU (TOUNGOO) TO MANDALAY—*continued.*

Authorities. Military.	Authorities. Civil.	Number and Names of Stages, Rivers and Streams.	Distances. Intermediate.	Distances. Total.	Remarks.
G.O.C. Rangoon District.	Commissioner, Eastern Division, and Deputy Commissioner, Pyinmana.	**7. Pyinmana (Ningyán)**—*cont.*			with it by a good metalled road. These launches ply, as a rule, from the middle of June to the end of October, or even somewhat later; but it all depends on the duration of the rainfall. During the rains the cart road from Taungu to Pyinmana is at present very heavy, but it will be raised and metalled at an early date. * Possibly the railway may be open to Pyinmana by April 1888, if the bridges can be completed in time. From Pyinmana several routes lead into the Shan States, to Môbyé, Payakôn, Lwélôn, Saga, Nyaungywe, Fort Stedman, Thamakán, &c. All are said to be practicable, and that with difficulty, for pack transport only, namely, elephants, mules, ponies, and Shan pack bullocks. Of the last the Shans own very large numbers, and almost all their trade is carried on by their means. The loads are slung in baskets, being balanced on the bullocks' backs. Light loads of from 60 to 100 lbs. are usually carried. Westward there are several roads from Pyinmana to Taungdwingyi. From Pyinmana to Yaméthin there are two routes, the western and the eastern. The western one is preferable for troops marching.
			M. F.	M. F.	
		8. Thityakôn ... Ngáleik chaung.	**7 0**	72 0	Excellent bridge for carts and any traffic over Ngáleik chaung. Most of the small chaungs between Pyinmana and Yaméthin are also bridged. Road fairly good, sandy or gravelly; bad in only one or two places. At 2 miles pass railway police post at Nyaungbinywa. Small village, bazaar, and police post at Thityakôn. Position of police stockade high and open. Water from well limited. No supplies for certain.
		9. Pyokôn ... Small chaungs, mostly bridged.	**9 0**	81 0	Road muddy in places and difficult for carts. At 4 miles Kyidaungán police post. Accommodation for troops very limited. Good camping ground in dry weather, but water-supply limited, mostly from wells in the bed of a dry stream. Railway station. From here there are two routes to Yaméthin (Stage 15), the western road runs mostly through bamboo and *in* jungle. Here and there paddy-field. Several villages passed. Road difficult for carts in rains. Small village at Pyokôn and some old zayáts. Stockaded police post able to accommodate 100 men. Good camping ground on high ground near police post. Water limited. No supplies. Site of post good. For description of Eastern road *see* Alternative I below.
		10. Kánhla ... Small chaungs.	**8 0**	89 0	Road very bad in places through thick tree jungle. Some stiffish gradients and deep nullahs, bad in rains. Small village at Kánhla. Stockaded police post on an eminence in the centre of a clearing of 15 or 20 acres. Good water. Some supplies. Accommodation in the stockade for 50 men. Good camping ground in dry season.

* Probably done long since.—A. F.

FROM TAUNGU (TOUNGOO) TO MANDALAY—*continued.*

Authorities. Military.	Authorities. Civil.	Number and Names of Stages, Rivers and Streams.	Distances. Intermediate. M. F.	Distances. Total. M. F.	Remarks.
G.O.C. Rangoon District.	Commissioner, Eastern Division, and Deputy Commissioner, Pyinmana.	**11. Gwébin** ... Small nullahs.	**6 0**	95 0	Road bad in places through the jungle. Some old villages and paddy clearings passed. Stockaded police post at Gwébin on right or south bank of Sinthé. Gwébin village was lately deserted, but large villages of Shádaw, Yé-6, and Kayánza lie 2 to 3 miles to the west on banks of Sinthé chaung. Water abundant, and supplies good from Yé-6 and Shádaw. Very little accommodation for troops at Gwébin, but ample in Shádaw or Yé-6. Good camping ground at Gwébin. From Gwébin there are roads to Ombôk and Mézalígyin on the road from Taungnyo to Hlawbôn.
		12. Imbetgôn ... Sinthé river impassable when in flood. Dry from December to May.	**5 0**	100 0	Road fairly good, sandy over undulating country through tree jungle. Sinthé difficult to cross for carts and pack ponies in rains. Elephants often necessary. Ascending Sinthé chaung to Lézan, quicksands very troublesome. Imbetgôn is a large village. Good water and some supplies. One kyaung well situated in open ground. There is a cross-road from Imbetgôn to Mézalígyin on the Taungnyo-Hlawbôn road as follows: (1) Imbetgôn to Alégyán, 8 miles. Road very heavy in places. Accommodation for troops in Alégyán indifferent. Good water. Three-fourths mile east-south-east of Alégyán is village of Inkyun, in which is good accommodation for 300 men. (2) Alégyán to Mézalígyin, 6 miles. Road along the bed of the Sinthé chaung very heavy and in the rains full of quicksands. Good accommodation in Mézalígyin and several other villages on right or south bank of Sinthé. Good water. The area under cultivation here is very large, about 10 square miles. There is also a cart track to Kyinzu 16½ miles, passing Naungaing at 6 miles, Ságyinkôn at 13¾, and numerous other villages, probably difficult in wet weather. Here there was formerly a military post. There is a direct track on to Yaméthin from Kyinzu mostly across paddy-fields, distance 16 miles.
	Commissioner, Eastern Division, and Deputy Commissioner, Yaméthin.	**13. Nyaunglun** ...	**7 0**	107 0	Road good throughout over undulating country passing by several villages. At Nyaunglun is a collection of several largish villages. Water and supplies abundant. Accommodation for troops ample, either in post or in kyaungs, zayáts, and village. Good camping ground in dry weather. Railway station.
		14. Tauk-kyángyin. Some nullahs.	**9 0**	116 0	Road good. Formerly the road through Hngettaik used to be taken, the distances being Hngettaik 7 (which is a station on the line of rail) and Yaméthin 15 miles. Now a stockaded post has been established at Tauk-kyángyin, the point of junction of the eastern and western routes. There is a village at Tauk-kyángyin, and good water and some supplies. Just south of the village the road crosses a nullah, very difficult if not bridged.

FROM TAUNGU (TOUNGOO) TO MANDALAY—*continued.*

Authorities. Military.	Authorities. Civil.	Number and Names of Stages, Rivers and Streams.	Distances. Intermediate. M.	F.	Distances. Total. M.	F.	Remarks.
G.O.C. Rangoon District.	Commissioner, Eastern Division, and Deputy Commissioner, Yaméthin.	**15. Yaméthin** ...	6	0	122	0	The road is heavy with mud and water in and after rains, as it runs mostly through paddy-fields. In the dry season it is good enough. Yaméthin is a large town, but situated in a low, swampy, unhealthy position. South of it is a lake several miles square which is never dry. There is ample accommodation for troops and abundant supplies, but the water is of indifferent quality. From some of the wells water is good enough, but that of most wells is of impure quality, and that of the tanks become foul at the end of the dry season. It is the centre of a very extensive and populous rice district, and also commands two or three of the principal trade routes with the Shan States, routes leading from Yaméthin itself direct and from Shwényaungbu *viâ* Ngakwé or Taunglebin to Nyaungywé. A brigade (say one cavalry and three infantry regiments and a battery) could, as a rule, be quartered in Yaméthin and in the villages in its vicinity. In the dry season, however, fodder suitable for elephants is procurable with difficulty. Railway station. Yaméthin is of importance, because it commands the best routes to Pyinmana, Hlaingdet, Meiktila, as well as the Shan States and Taungdwingyi roads. The short stages given between Pyinmana and Yaméthin are quite as long as carts can manage in the rains. In the dry season and with good pack transport, double stages can be done.
		16. Pyawbwé ... Shwéda, Pyawbwé, and some small chaungs now probably all bridged.	14	0	136	0	Road fairly good. At 8 miles the Shwéda chaung is crossed (bridged). Both it and the Pyawbwé stream are shallow. The Pyawbwé chaung is 150 yards broad, but the bottom is sandy and firm, and the water shallow. The ground around Pyawbwé is high and undulating, and affords a healthy site for barracks. The water is good and plentiful, and supplies abundant. If accommodation for troops is necessary, half a brigade could be housed in the kyaungs, zayáts and village. Railway station. From here a cart track runs to Hlaingdet, distance 11¼ miles, fairly smooth, over grass fields covered with scattered bushes.
	Commissioner, Eastern Division, and Deputy Commissioner, Meiktila.	**17. Nyaungyán**... Some small streams.	14	0	150	0	Good cart track, but probably heavy in rains. There are good kyaungs situated on high ground at Nyaungyán. Railway station. Nyaungyán is a large village giving the appearance of three villages clubbed together and each separated with an enclosure. A large white pagoda on a mound just in front of the village strikes the eye from a distance. Plenty of accommodation for troops in kyaungs and zayáts. Water good and plentiful. Extensive cultivation, especially betel-nut and *pán*. From here a road runs to Hlaingdet, 10 miles, and another to Meiktila about 12 miles.

FROM TAUNGU (TOUNGOO) TO MANDALAY—*continued.*

Authorities: Military	Authorities: Civil	Number and Names of Stages, Rivers and Streams.	Distances: Intermediate (M. F.)	Distances: Total (M. F.)	Remarks.
G.O.C. Rangoon District.	Commissioner, Eastern Divn., and Dy. Commissioner, Meiktila.	**18. Magyizén** ... Some small streams.	13 0	163 0	Cart track generally good in dry season. There is difficulty hereabouts in finding a halting place or camping ground. At Magyizén there is fairly good water, but no accommodation. Troops must bivouac under the trees; that can be done in the cold and dry seasons, but not in the rains. The water at some of the villages hereabouts is very brackish. At Magyigôn, which is about 4 miles beyond Magyizén, there is a kyaung, while 1½ miles beyond Magyizén are two zayáts and two wells.
		19. Wundwin ... Some small streams.	13 0	176 0	Cart track generally easy in dry season. At 4 miles pass village of Magyigôn with pôngyi kyaung. Good water from wells and bed of stream and supplies. But water from well among kyaungs at south-east corner of village. Large village, kyaungs, zayáts, &c., enough to house a battalion. Good camping ground. Roads from here eastward to Hlaingdet and westward to Natôgyi and Myingyán and south-westward to Meiktila.
	Commissioner, Eastern Division, and Deputy Commissioner, Kyauksé.	**20. Thabyédaung.** Samôn river. Two chaungs.	13 4	189 4	There are two roads as far as Kaingyi, 3½ miles, one direct running chiefly over paddy-fields, the other over level country through scrub jungle to Thédaw at 1 mile, where there is a bazaar and railway station and thence to Kaingyi. Kaingyi is a large village of 120 houses with zayáts. Water from a pool which never dries. From Kaingyi through jungle to Ingán, where the Samôn river is crossed at 8½ miles. Ingán is a village of 70 houses and Samôn railway station is close by. Supplied with water from pools in the bed of the Samôn. In the dry season water has to be brought 1½ miles. After passing Ingán two chaungs have to be crossed. The chaung nearest Ingán has a very strong current and is impassable when the Samôn is in flood except by rafts. The road from Kaingyi to Thabyédaung runs through jungle. Camping ground at Thabyédaung for a regiment east of the railway close to the police post, which is 60 yards square; earthen breastwork; bamboo stockade. The ground outside the ditch is spiked with bamboo spikes for a width of 12 feet. Signalling can be carried on with Kyauksé and Wundwin. Pôpa hill can also be seen. Railway station 200 yards south-east of post. A good well has been constructed east of post.
		21. Yéwun ... Samôn river.	14 0	203 4	At 4 miles Thanietdaw; road through jungle which has been cleared for a width of 100 feet; at 7½ miles Kúmé, a series of small villages, increasing daily. Large bazaar every five days. Large kyaungs. Railway station Kúmé Road. Made road very heavy in the rains. Cultivation extends for miles

FROM TAUNGU (TOUNGOO) TO MANDALAY—*continued.*

Authorities. Military.	Authorities. Civil.	Number and Names of Stages, Rivers and Streams.	Distances. Intermediate. M.	F.	Distances. Total. M.	F.	Remarks.
G.O.C. Rangoon District.	Commissioner, Eastern Division, and Deputy Commissioner, Kyauksé.	**21. Yéwun**—*cont.*					on both sides of the road at 98½ miles. Myitzôn close to large bridge over the Myittha. At 11 miles Taungdaw, a small, miserably poor village. At 12½ miles small deserted village of Katiyula. From Myitzôn to Yéwun a fair cart track, except for ¼ mile north of Myittha bridge. In the rains only elephant transport can be used, as the Pánlàng, Myittha and Samôn rivers flood the country. All nullahs are now bridged. The village of Yéwun is built on both banks of the Tôngyi canal at an angle of the canal when it turns from a southern to a western direction.
		22. Kyauksé ... Dunyaung and Zídaw canals.	14	0	217	4	At 1 mile reach the Dunyaung canal, which is very deep and very rapid when in flood. Cross Dunyaung canal by a bridge and reach Ingyinbu at 3 miles. A large village with plenty of supplies and good water, crossing numerous irrigation canals which are all bridged. At 4 miles reach Talé, road passing through low, but thick, jungle. Crossing one small stream at 5 miles reach some zayáts, kyaungs, and a good well, then over flat cultivated ground to Kyauksé, passing numerous villages during the last 4 miles. The cart road is during rains very muddy and bad, and occasionally impassable streams are all roughly bridged. The road has always been a great trade route to Shan States. Kyauksé is a large town, the head-quarters of a Deputy Commissioner and a police battalion. Good bazaar, railway station, post and telegraph offices. A canal called the Zídaw-myaung connects Kyauksé with Paleik. Boats take about eight hours going down to Paleik and about double the time coming up against the stream. No accommodation for troops in the town. Some kyaungs to the east would shelter troops.
		23. Talukso ... Zídaw canal.	10	0	227	4	Road along the canal almost impassable during the rains. Boats can be used for transport of troops or baggage. At 8½ miles Singaing and at 10 miles Talukso, a small village with a police post. Accommodation for 200 men in kyaungs. Water from the canal. Paddy cultivation all round. From here there is an alternative route to Mandalay, *see* Alternative IV below.
		24. Paleik ... Zídaw canal, Myitngé river.	8	0	235	4	Road along the bank of the Zídaw canal almost impassable in rains. Boats can be used for transport of baggage or troops. Paleik is a large village on the left bank of the Myitngé river, which at this place varies in breadth from 80 yards in the dry season to 350 in the floods, and is unfordable at all times. There is a fortified post, 100 yards by 40 yards without a ditch, on the river bank held by a detachment of military police. The railway runs 1 mile east of Paleik crossing the Myitngé at Myobingyi by an iron bridge, and there is a station called Myitngé, a short distance from the northern (Mandalay) end of the bridge and another south of the bridge called Paleik Road. Steamers ply three times a week betweenPaleik and Mandalay.

FROM TAUNGU (TOUNGOO) TO MANDALAY—*continued.*

Authorities. Military.	Authorities. Civil.	Number and Names of Stages, Rivers and Streams.	Distances. Intermediate. M. F.	Distances. Total. M. F.	Remarks.
G.O.C. Mandalay District.	Commissioner, Northern Division, and Deputy Commissioner, Mandalay.	**25. Mandalay** ...	15 0	250 4	The Myitngé may be crossed by boats or by the raft ferry which can carry two carts or about six horses and a dozen or 20 people. The Myitngé might also be crossed by the railway bridge mentioned above, as it is provided with a path 6 feet wide for the use of ordinary traffic. Opposite Paleik, on the northern side of the river, is the village of Lessaingôn chiefly populated by Manipúri silk-weavers. The road leads through Sinywa, and Tungyidaw to Letpánzin, where there are kyaungs which could accommodate 150 men. Beyond Letpánzin reach a deep nullah spanned by a bridge fit for baggage animals, but not for carts. The nullah has in the rainy season a depth of about 8 to 12 feet of water. Thence through country chiefly covered with kaing grass and scrub jungle to the Thugyin chaung, which is fordable in the dry season, but not in the rains, along causeway and bridge almost 1 mile long in bad repair spans the chaung, but is only passable for foot-passengers. Guides must be procured to show the way over the fords. Thence to Amarapura and along a paved causeway to the Arakan pagoda, 3 miles south of the city of Mandalay (Fort Dufferin) where the suburbs commence.

ALTERNATIVE I.

FROM PYINMANA (STAGE 7) TO YAMÉTHIN (STAGE 15).

I. B. COMPILATION, NOVEMBER 1888.

The following is a description of the eastern route from Pyinmana to Yaméthin :—

Military	Civil	Stages	Intermediate	Total	Remarks
G.O.C. Rangoon District.	Commissioner, Eastern Division, and Deputy Commissioner, Pyinmana.	**1. Kyidaungán** ...	11 0	11 0	*See* Stage 9 above; the two roads separate here.
		Ngáleik chaung, small nullahs unbridged.			
		2. Shwémyo ...	13 0	24 0	Road often difficult for carts. At 8 miles Otneida is passed. At Kyaukkwet (11½ miles) are paddy clearings and two small zayáts. The road to the post at Shwémyo keeps about 1 mile to the west of the village. At the post is a large clearing, stockade, and a zayát, also several huts. Water from wells and the Sinthé river, 400 yards distant. Railway station. From Shwémyo there is a road eastward (crossing the Sinthé) *viâ* Ywathit to Kángyi, a village lying close at the foot of the Shan hills. Distance 7 or 8 miles. *Note.*—The eastern route at Shwémyo is connected with the western at Kánhla and Gwébin by the two routes mentioned below :— *Kánhla to Shwémyo*, 2½ *miles.*—Good cart road through bamboo jungle. A branch road 1 mile on leading to Pyinmana; ¾ mile further on road crosses a nullah by wooden bridge 18 yards long; ¼ mile on cross road leading from Pyinmana to Gwébin. A few yards further on the road meets the new railway embankment. Average width of road 20 feet. *Gwébin to Shwémyo*, 5 *miles.*—A village of 100 houses separated by paddy-fields from the road. Water good. The

FROM TAUNGU (TOUNGOO) TO MANDALAY—*continued.*

ALTERNATIVE I.

Authorities. Military.	Authorities. Civil.	Number and Names of Stages, Rivers and Streams.	Distances. Intermediate. M.	F.	Total. M.	F.	Remarks.
G.O.C. Rangoon District.	Commissioner, Eastern Division, and Deputy Commissioner, Pyinmana.	**2. Shwémyo**—*cont.*					Sinthé chaung about ¼ mile north, direction west to east. Bamboo stockade on the road held by 25 rifles of Railway levies. Several small villages in neighbourhood. Road the whole way a track through thick jungle of teak and bamboo, running parallel to the Sinthé river.
		3. Bawhlaing ... Sinthé chaung, shallow and fordable except when in flood.	**8**	**0**	32	0	Road from Othneida to Bawhlaing runs entirely through bamboo and tree jungle, with here and there a paddy clearing. Cart road, but muddy and heavy in and just after rains. At Bawhlaing small clearing for camp and zayát. Kyaung on hill. Water from chaung quite close. The river Sinthé is crossed about half-way between Shwémyo and Bawhlaing. Crossing easy, sandy bottom, shallow bed. There is a cart road from Bawhlaing to Imbetgôn (Stage 12 above), distance about 5 miles.
	Commissioner, Eastern Division, and Deputy Commissioner, Yaméthin.	**4. Thayetpin** ... Ngawin and two or three other small chaungs.	**10**	**2**	42	2	Good track for carts. Tree jungle alternates with paddy-fields. Several villages passed situated as camping grounds. Accommodation, water, and supplies at Thayetpin for a small body of troops, say 200 to 300 men.
		5. Yaméthin ...	**13**	**6**	56	0	Road, as usual, heavy in rains, good in dry season. At 7¾ miles Tauk-kyán-gyin kyaung and good-sized village, police post, &c. Hence to Yaméthin 6 miles, *vide* Stage 14 above.

ALTERNATIVE II.

FROM PYAWBWÉ (STAGE 16) TO WUNDWIN (STAGE 19) *viâ* MEIKTILA.

I. B. COMPILATION, NOVEMBER 1888.

Authorities. Military.	Authorities. Civil.	Number and Names of Stages, Rivers and Streams.	Intermediate. M.	F.	Total. M.	F.	Remarks.
G.O.C. Rangoon District.	Commr., Eastern Division, and Dy. Commissioner, Yaméthin.	**1. Yindaw** ...	**13**	**4**	13	4	Direction north-west. Road runs over sandy soil through scrub jungle to Walet at 4½ miles, passing close to a cluster of three pagodas on high ground, visible from some distance, 1½ miles, before reaching Walet and crosses a muddy chaung, which is nearly impassable in the rains, at 1½ miles from Walet. Walet has accommodation for 120 men in kyaungs west of the village, and a good well 100 yards west of the kyaung fence. Between Walet and Yindaw there are two or three cart tracks, all practicable in dry weather, but probably almost impassable in the rains. From Walet the road runs to Yatha, a small village with a good well on the north side, then over paddy-fields to Thamakôn at 8½ miles, where there is accommodation for 150 men in kyaungs on the north side of the village. But the best wells are ½ mile

FROM TAUNGU (TOUNGOO) TO MANDALAY—*continued.*

ALTERNATIVE II—*continued.*

Authorities. Military.	Authorities. Civil.	Number and Names of Stages, Rivers and Streams.	Distances. Intermediate.	Distances. Total.	Remarks.
G.O.C. Rangoon District.	Commissioner, Eastern Division, and Deputy Commissioner, Yaméthin.	**1. Yindaw**—*cont.*			south-east of the village. There are also two kyaungs which could hold 70 men to the south, about 200 yards from the well. Water good, but slightly muddy. Continuing along the road Sadaung is seen about 1 mile to right, and three pagodas on the west of a ridge will be at once recognized. There are some kyaungs south of Sadaung; but the water is said not to be good. From Thamakôn road over level cultivation for 1⅛ miles; then reach a deep nullah with sandy bed and precipitous sides, dry in February, but impassable in the floods. The road descends and follows the bed of the nullah for some time and then ascends, runs through scrub jungle over sandy soil for 1⅛ miles; then for 2 miles through a large tract of paddy land which would probably be quite impassable in wet weather to Yindaw. Yindaw is a large village under a Myo-ôk. There is a large tank to the west which is dry in February. On the south is a military police post with a post office and signal station. Close to the post are kyaungs which would accommodate 400 men. Water from a well in the kyaung enclosure good. There is a very good bazaar here and all supplies procurable. A large number of carts and several ponies would be obtained. From here there is a cart road, excellent most of the way, to Yenaung (*see* Route No. 14, Southern Division, Stage 8), passing through Pyinyin at 4¾ miles, Shánzu at 6¼, and crossing the Nátsôngwa chaung at 8 miles.
	Commissioner, Eastern Division, and Deputy Commissioner, Meiktila.	**2. Meiktila** ...	M. F. 13 4	M. F. 27 0	Across a broad belt of paddy land in north-west direction, along a banked and made road. Then for about 2 miles over sandy soil covered with patches of dry cultivation and scrub jungle to the Kwégán chaung, which is 100 yards broad, but in February nearly dry and covered with deep sand banks, easy. In wet weather said to be quicksandy. Reach Kyauka at 3 miles. Accommodation for 300 men in kyaungs. Situated to west of the village. Water from wells and from the chaung. Through level cultivation, and reach Mya on the left of the road at 5 miles. Accommodation for 150 men in kyaungs and good water from a well in the kyaung enclosure. Thence over country covered with cotton cultivation and jungle with strips of paddy cultivation in the valleys. At 6½ miles pass a cluster of ruined pagodas on the right of the road with a well of good water. Thence to the village of Kándaung on the right of the road, where there is accommodation for 50 men in kyaungs and zayáts. Water from a well in the kyaung enclosure and in the rains from a tank to the west of the village. A bazaar is held here every five days. Thence a good cart track over hard, sandy soil, through country covered with thin scrub jungle and uncultivated to the cantonment at Meiktila, and then along the bund of the south lake.
		3. Thabiyéywa.	10 0	37 0	The road from here runs over paddy and through jungle alternately all the way and would be impracticable in wet weather. There is another longer road to the west which is practicable in wet weather, but not at all good.

FROM TAUNGU (TOUNGOO) TO MANDALAY—*continued.*

ALTERNATIVE II—*continued.*

Authorities. Military.	Authorities. Civil.	Number and Names of Stages, Rivers and Streams.	Distances. Intermediate. M.	F.	Distances. Total. M.	F.	Remarks.
G.O.C. Rangoon District.	Commissioner, Eastern Division, and Deputy Commissioner, Meiktila.	**3. Thabiyéywa**—*cont.*					Pass several villages, all fair-sized and prosperous, and numerous kyaungs and zayáts standing in groves of palmyra and cocoanut. The valley is watered by the overflow of the Meiktila lake and is a rich stretch of paddy. Thabiyéywa is a large village with accommodation in kyaungs on the east side for 300 men. Water from a large tank to the east and from wells. All the ordinary supplies obtainable and probably 100 carts.
		4. Wundwin ... One stream three times.	11	0	48	0	Across a belt of paddy land and then over sandy soil through scrub jungle for 6 miles; then pass fair-sized village with a large number of kyaungs. Water for animals from a stream slightly brackish. Good water from wells Then for 5 miles along a valley covered with coarse grass, in which nothing else seems to grow on account of the sand, to Wundwin.

ALTERNATIVE III.

FROM WUNDWIN (STAGE 19) TO KYAUKSÉ (STAGE 22) *viâ* PAYÁPYU.

BY CAPT. A. C. YATE, 1888.

Military	Civil	Stage	Intermediate M.	F.	Total M.	F.	Remarks
G.O.C. Rangoon District.	Commissioner, Eastern Division, and Deputy Commissioner, Meiktila.	**1. Payápyu** ...	10	0	10	0	Cart track fairly good, except after heavy rain, passing through alternate jungle and cultivation. At 5 miles pass village named Payazu with zayáts and kyaungs. At the second Payápyu there is a kyaung and three zayáts. Water from village requires filtration. No information about supplies, but probably usual supplies procurable. Payápyu is on the main road from Wundwin to Pyinzi and Chaungwa (*see* Route No. 4, Central Division).
G.O.C. Mandalay District.	Commissioner, Eastern Division, and Deputy Commissioner, Kyauksé.	**2. Yaungyi** ... Unknown.	12	0	22	0	Fair cart track, same apparently for some distance as that to Chaungwa, then leaves Chaungwa road and runs north-west to the bank of the Samôn river. Muddy in places even in December. Road winds and zigzags very much. At 4 miles pass village of Shwédaung with kyaungs and pagodas. At Yaungyi kyaung and well beyond the village, on the banks of the Samôn river. No information about supplies.
		3. Ywamôn ... Samôn river in December not passable by carts, but later believed to be fordable.	12	0	34	0	The road to Dalaingôn (8 miles) traverses a flat country, always inundated by the Samôn during the rains. Dalaingôn is a village seemingly on the right or east bank of the Samôn. No information about supplies and accommodation there. At Dalaingôn,

FROM TAUNGU (TOUNGOO) TO MANDALAY—*continued.*

ALTERNATIVE III—*continued.*

Authorities. Military.	Authorities. Civil.	Number and Names of Stages, Rivers and Streams.	Distances. Intermediate.	Distances. Total.	Remarks.
G.O.C. Mandalay District.	Commissioner, Eastern Division, and Deputy Commissioner, Kyauksé.	**3. Ywamôn**—*cont.*			in December 1886, carts had to be unloaded and the baggage passed over in boats. Sandy bed. Water 3 feet deep. Current slight. A foot-bridge fit for pack animals (not elephants) spans the river; thence easy road (in December) to Ywamôn. There is accommodation for troops at Ywamôn in zayáts to the west of the village, and in other zayáts on the east or right bank of the Pánláng river. That river can be forded at Ywamôn. Water only 2 feet deep.
			M. F.	M. F.	
		4. Kyauksé ... Pánláng river.	7 0	41 0	Road crosses Pánláng at once by ford. Road then fairly good within 2 miles of Kyauksé, when it becomes muddy and heavy.

ALTERNATIVE IV.

FROM TALUKSO (STAGE 23) TO MANDALAY (STAGE 25) *viâ* MÍGYAUNGDET.

I. B. COMPILATION, NOVEMBER 1888.

Authorities. Military.	Authorities. Civil.	Number and Names of Stages, Rivers and Streams.	Distances. Intermediate.	Distances. Total.	Remarks.
G.O.C. Mandalay District.	Commissioner, Eastern Division, and Deputy Commissioner, Kyauksé.	**1. Mígyaungdet.** Zídawmyaung.	5 4	5 4	The road runs along the east bank of the Zídawmyaung. At 3½ miles village of Hmaungwa-Ngetpyadaw, where the road to Mandalay *viâ* Paleik branches off to the north-west. At this village the Zídawmyaung divides into two branches. The road is on the bund of the Zídawmyaung all this stage. In places it is narrow and very uneven and only fit for men to march along in single file. Transport animals have often to leave the road and go through paddy-fields for short distances, as the bund is cut in places to allow water to flow into the fields. From Hmaungwa-Ngetpyawdaw to within a mile of Kinlát is through wide stretch of paddy cultivation. Last mile into Kinlát through cactus and scrub jungle. At Kinlát ample accommodation in kyaungs clear of the village. Cross Myitngé by ferry to Mígyaungdet. There are six or seven native boats for ferry purposes. The river is from 200 to 250 yards broad with a current of 2½ miles an hour and 9 to 10 feet deep in the deepest parts. Water clear. Banks sloping on both sides. Elephants even cannot ford it. Horses and ponies have to be swum across, and several cases of their being drowned have occurred. Police post at Mígyaungdet. Very little accommodation for troops.
	Commissioner, Northern Division, and Deputy Commissioner, Mandalay.	**2. Néyagán** ... Myitngé.	7 0	12 4	Between Mígyaungdet and Néyagán the land is only partially cultivated, and there is a good deal of jungle. From Mígyaungdet to Mandalay the road is practicable for wheeled traffic, though in the rains it is very swampy and at all seasons much cut up. Just after leaving Mígyaungdet road traverses forest of large trees almost clear of undergrowth. At 1½ miles village of Sinywa. Bend of Myitngé 100 yards to left or west. Just beyond village cross nullah by bridge. At 2½ miles three good zayáts holding 200 men. Water from stream. Mandalay hill signal station visible from here. At 3 miles village of Thitkyobin to left. Between

From TAUNGU (TOUNGOO) to MANDALAY—*continued.*

ALTERNATIVE IV—*continued.*

Authorities. Military.	Authorities. Civil.	Number and Names of Stages, Rivers and Streams.	Distances. Intermediate.	Distances. Total.	Remarks.
G.O.C. Mandalay District.	Commissioner, Northern Division, and Deputy Commissioner, Mandalay.	**2. Néyagán**—*cont.*			Thitkyobin-Néyagán ground is in places very swampy in the rains. The road at first runs through cactus and other jungle, and as it nears Néyagán along a bund to the west of a large tank. At Néyagán three kyaungs and a fair camping ground to south-east of village.
			M. F.	M. F.	
		3. Mandalay ... Swamp and nullah.	8 0	20 4	The road is perfectly level throughout. It is unmetalled. At Amarapura there is a brick causeway a mile long. Country for 1st mile undulating and sparsely covered with trees and thorn jungle. Then cross a swamp by a causeway 150 yards long, with two bridges, under which the water flows. Water good. At $1\frac{1}{2}$ miles pass Tagôndaing village to left of road. Thence road runs parallel to east ditch of Amarapura along a brick causeway to the Mandalay bund, 5 miles south of Mandalay. At $4\frac{1}{2}$ miles pass the Arakan Pagoda. Thence road runs straight to south-west corner of Mandalay city (Fort Dufferin).

BRANCH I.

From YAMÉTHIN (Stage 15) to HLAINGDET.

I. B. Compilation, November 1888.

Authorities. Military.	Authorities. Civil.	Number and Names of Stages, Rivers and Streams.	Distances. Intermediate.	Distances. Total.	Remarks.
G.O.C. Rangoon District.	Commissioner, Eastern Division, and Deputy Commissioner, Yaméthin.	**1. Shwényaungbu**	10 4	10 4	Road a mere cart track leading over rice fields, good in dry weather, very bad in rains. After a fall of rain country is almost entirely under water. About 2 miles from Yaméthin road crosses a wet nullah over which is a two-plank bridge (about 2 feet 6 inches to 3 feet wide); it has a railing on either side. Ponies or unloaded mules can be led across. Width about 8 yards. Water about 2 feet deep. At $2\frac{1}{4}$ miles pass Thengôn, and at 5 miles Nagu. Nagu is about $\frac{1}{4}$ mile to east of road, is a small village, can supply small quantities of rice straw and rice. A kyaung, with two zayáts in a high bamboo enclosure on east side of village. On north side of kyaung is a square tank. Water fair. Water too from Sawmé chaung, which is here crossed by foot-bridge. At 6 miles Panángôn. Road over paddy-fields. Patches of jungle. Then pass several small villages from 10 to 30 houses. At Dakôn is a kyaung holding 60 men. From Panángôn to Wágôn road is along very low ground, over paddy-fields and very heavy. From Wágôn the soil is more sandy, patches of jungle, the intervals being under cultivation. The west side of road is much more open than the east which is towards the Shan hills. Strong stockaded post in open clearing. Large village, about 100 houses. Kyaungs on north side of village. Well about $\frac{1}{2}$ mile to north-west of village. Two large kyaungs and a few zayáts just inside village enclosure. Water, supplies, and accommodation for half a battalion at least.
		2. Dwinywa ...	7 0	17 4	Road mere track across rice fields for about 1 mile; it then gradually rises and soil becomes more sandy. Pass villages of Kundôn, Pintaga, and Myaukmégôn. Small patches of

FROM TAUNGU (TOUNGOO) TO MANDALAY—*continued.*

BRANCH I—*continued.*

Authorities. Military.	Authorities. Civil.	Number and Names of Stages, Rivers and Streams.	Distances. Intermediate.	Distances. Total.	Remarks.
G.O.C. Rangoon District.	Commr., Eastern Divn., and Dy. Commr., Yaméthin.	**2. Dwinywa**—*cont.*			jungle (low thorny scrub). This continues as far as Dwinywa. A spur of the Shan hills runs down to Dwinywa on east side of village. There is a pagoda on the peak of the hill. The kyaungs and zayáts (four) are on east side of village. Water from well to south ¼ mile. Usual supplies procurable. Village small, about 40 houses.
	Commissioner, Eastern Division, and Deputy Commissioner, Meiktila.	**3. Hlaingdet** ...	M. F. **10 0**	M. F. 27 4	Road fair, country more open, largely cultivated to west. Good deal of forest clearing going on. At 2 miles pass Tányaungôn, where are two kyaungs and some zayáts. Water from wells. At 3 miles pass Kôkôgôn (kyaungs and zayáts), at 5 Winmakmau, and at 7 reach Tawgin. Middling-sized village. Water from wells. Road passes through it. Country open. Passed a large tank to east of road. Road crosses paddy-fields about ½ mile north of Tawgin. About 2 miles from Hlaingdet patches of jungle became more dense, and this continues up to within 200 yards of the fort. Hlaingdet is a large village. Three tanks. Several kyaungs dotted round village. Large well to north. Supplies of *kerbi* and rice plentiful. Bamboo and teak logs procurable in large quantities. There is a tank about 40 yards to the north-east with a large kyaung close by it. This will be shortly included within the post. Very dense jungle close to the village on the north side. At Hlaingdet the route from Meiktila to Fort Stedman, &c., in the Southern Shan States is met (*see* Routes Nos. 6 and 7, Eastern Division).

BRANCH II.

FROM PYAWBWÉ (STAGE 16) TO YENAUNG.

BY LIEUT. E. W. M. NORIE, INTELLIGENCE BRANCH, MARCH 1888.

Authorities. Military.	Authorities. Civil.	Number and Names of Stages, Rivers and Streams.	Distances. Intermediate.	Distances. Total.	Remarks.
G.O.C. Rangoon District.	Commissioner, Eastern Division, and Deputy Commissioner, Yaméthin.	**1. Yenaung** ... Two or three small chaungs.	**10 0**	10 0	Road leaves Pyawbwé near the railway station and runs west across paddy land. At about 1½ miles it crosses a nullah, which lower down is deep and muddy and impassable for carts. From here the road runs south-west still over paddy ground and along bank of a small chaung. At about 3 miles pass the small village of Pattaw on the left of the road. No accommodation. Good water from a well on the road. Lwinbyin village lies about ¾ of a mile to west and contains some kyaungs. The road same as before reaches Yôngôn at about 5 miles. This is a small village in the jungle. Water from wells in a small chaung ¼ mile to north. From here the road enters jungle and begins to ascend. The jungle has been cleared for 30 yards on each side of the road and it is good going. Reaching the top of a ridge the road runs over high ground and then descends on Yenaung. About a mile before reaching Yenaung it crosses a pretty deep chaung with pools of water in it. Yenaung is a large village. Accommodation for a large force in a large number of kyaungs on south and east of village. Good water from wells on west of village. All the ordinary supplies obtainable from the Myo-ôk. Village of Yeuru lies to south of police post.

FROM TAUNGU (TOUNGOO) TO MANDALAY—*continued.*

BRANCH III.

FROM THABYÉDAUNG (STAGE 20) TO PYINZI (ROUTE No. 56, NORTHERN DIVISION).

I. B. COMPILATION, NOVEMBER 1888.

Authorities. Military.	Authorities. Civil.	Number and Names of Stages, Rivers and Streams.	Distances. Intermediate. M.	F.	Distances. Total. M.	F.	Remarks.
G.O.C. Mandalay District.	Commissioner, Southern Division, and Deputy Commissioner, Myingyán.	**1. Paungmyaing.** Samôn river.	**14**	**0**	14	0	At 6 miles pass village of North Kain on Samôn river, 15 houses. At 6¼ miles Didoyua, six houses. At 10 miles South Sadaung, about 100 houses. On Samôn river there are sites of three villages between Thídawywa and Sadaung, 1 mile apart. At North Sadaung there is a bridge across Samôn to Lángdaw. Zayáts at both villages. At 14 miles Paungmyaing, a large prosperous fenced village. Three gates on north side, two on south, one on river bank. Thirty guns. Water from Samôn river. Kyaungs and zayáts.
		2. Yôgán	**8**	**0**	22	0	At 3 miles Watti; 30 houses surrounded by paddy-fields. Well. At 5 miles burnt village of Thaingyi. At 7 miles Taungwin, 20 houses; well, two zayáts. Quite close is another small village Mézalíyaung. From here a road leads to Chaungwa along foot of Sagâyin hills, also one to Yékán and another to Déyégaung. At 8 miles Yôgán. Two villages close to hills. Well, kyaungs, and zayát.
		3. Pyinzi	**11**	**0**	33	0	At 4 miles Padaung, about 70 houses. Well, kyaung, and zayáts. At 11 miles Pyinzi, large village (*see* Route No. 56, Northern Division). The road as far as Kain runs through jungle on left bank of Samôn river, and from there to Paungmyaing through open fields. From Paungmyaing to Pyinzi road runs through thin jungle. From Paungmyaing a road leads to Gwé and one to Déyégaung, at which place is a bridge across the Samôn.

BRANCH IV.

FROM THABYÉDAUNG (STAGE 20) TO YÉKAINGYI (ROUTE No. 2, EASTERN DIVISION, STAGE 2).

BY CAPT. PRESGRAVE, 15TH MADRAS INFANTRY, FEBRUARY 1888.

Military	Civil	Stages	Int. M.	F.	Total M.	F.	Remarks
G.O.C. Mandalay District.	Commissioner, Eastern Division, and Deputy Commissioner, Kyauksé.	**1. Yékaingyi** ... Pánláng river.	**15**	**0**	15	0	From Thabyédaung to Kúmé 7½ miles, *see* in Stage 21 above. Thence *viâ* Myitzôn at 8½ miles; Ôdindaungôn pagoda, well and zayáts at 9½ miles; Bawdígôn, kyaungs, at 12½ miles. At 15 miles Yékaingyi on Pánláng river. About 200 houses, divided into two villages. Kyaungs and zayáts. This was formerly a depôt of the Bombay-Burma Company and residence of their agent.

FROM TAUNGU (TOUNGOO) TO MANDALAY—*continued.*

BRANCH V.

FROM YINDAW (ALTERNATIVE NO. II, STAGE 1) TO PASÔBYA HILL AND NÁTSÔNWA.

BY LIEUT. E. W. M. NORIE, 2ND MIDDLESEX REGIMENT, MARCH 1888.

Authorities. Military.	Authorities. Civil.	Number and Names of Stages, Rivers and Streams.	Distances. Intermediate. M. F.	Distances. Total. M. F.	Remarks.
G.O.C. Rangoon District.	Commissioner, Eastern Division, and Deputy Commissioner, Yaméthin.	**1. Nátsônwa** ... Four nullahs; all easily passed.	**11 0**	11 0	The road runs south-west round the end of the tank and for the first 5 miles passes over paddy cultivation and is very bad in the wet weather, almost impassable for carts. Pass Kômbya at about 1½ miles, Yégyángôn at 2 miles, Naungyaung at 2½ miles, at all of which there is good water from wells. At 4½ miles reach Kaungyôngaung, a large village with accommodation in kyaung and zayáts for 70 men. Water good from wells. From here the road begins to rise and improves as it passes from the cultivated country into jungle. Here the road to Pasôbya hills leaves the Nátsônwa road and runs up a steep incline to the top of the hill. This would make an excellent signal station for communication with Meiktila, Yindaw, Pyawbwé, Kundôn, and Pôpa hill. Water in dry weather has to be brought ½ mile from a tank. The road to Nátsônwa still running south-west is at first rather rough and stony, but the rest of the way very good running through scrub jungle. No water along this part of the road. Nátsônwa is a fair-sized village. Accommodation in kyaungs and zayáts for 100 men. Water from bed of a nullah good. Supplies procurable.

No. 7.

From TAUNGU (TOUNGOO) to NAUNGPALÉ (WEST KARENNI) viâ LEPETENG.

I. B. COMPILATION, JUNE 1888.

Military	Civil	Stage	Intermediate M. F.	Total M. F.	Remarks
G.O.C. Rangoon District.	Lower Burma.	**1. Padé** ... ... Sittang river.	**12 0**	12 0	The road lies along the river bank and is level, passing through scrub and tree jungle. Half-way pass the village of Banaung. The river can be crossed either here or at Padé by fords in the dry season. In the rains there is too much water, and the crossing must be made in boats. The river can also be crossed at Toungoo, where there is a ferry. Padé is on the left bank of the Sittang.
		2. Ngamwézayát.	**10 0**	22 0	Road follows left bank of river for a short distance and then turns off to the east. First part level through tree jungle and thick undergrowth; afterwards ground undulating, soil sandy and stony, and jungle open. Trees, *eng*, teak, and bamboo. Cross several small streams with rocky beds

FROM TAUNGU (TOUNGOO) TO NAUNGPALÉ (WEST KARENNI) *vid* LEPETENG—*continued.*

Authorities. Military.	Authorities. Civil.	Number and Names of Stages, Rivers and Streams.	Distances. Intermediate. M.	F.	Distances. Total. M.	F.	Remarks.
G.O C. Rangoon District.	Lower Burma.	**2. Ngamwézayát** —*cont.*					and steep banks, and small hills with steep ascents for short distances. Ngamwézayát is on the banks of a clear mountain stream with a stony bed. Water good in dry weather. It is 1,200 feet above the sea.
		3. Lepeteng ... Ké-eng stream.	6	0	28	0	The road is a steady ascent up the side of the narrow valley of the Ké-eng stream. The path is very steep and crosses several small streams, passing through open jungle and bamboo. The top of the hill is reached at 3,500 feet. From here the road descends to Lepeteng and is a good path. Lepeteng is the head-quarters of the Toungoo hill tracts, and there is a police post here. It is situated in a small valley. Good water from a stream. A little rice is grown in the valley.
		4. Ngapyawdaw stream. Small streams.	8	4	36	4	Road runs across ranges of hills running north and south with valleys between. There are small streams in almost all the valleys, which are deep and narrow. The road leads straight up the face of the hills and, on reaching the top, runs straight down into the valleys beyond, so that the slopes both up and down are very steep. The halting place is at the bottom of the narrow valley through which the Ngapyawdaw stream flows.
		5. Thaukyégat stream. Small streams and Thaukyégat stream.	8	0	44	4	Road same as before, descending gradually to the Thaukyégat stream, which is the main stream into which all the others flow. It is a fast-running stream with pebbly bottom, some 2 or 3 feet deep and about 40 feet wide. Running south and then east it joins the Sittang river about 8 miles south of Toungoo. Beyond is the Thaukyégat post.
		6. Kawzaw stream. Kai stream.	8	4	53	0	The road ascends again and crosses a small hill and then descends to the Kai stream, a small stream which flows into the Thaukyégat stream. Along the bed of the Kai stream the road now runs and is very stony and rough. Leaving the stream it runs up the side of the valley on the south side, and then crosses the stream again higher up and reaches the top of the ridge at 3,600 feet. Crossing the ridge the road descends into the Kawzaw valley, inhabited by the Brés, or Breks, a tribe of wild Karens. The valley is cultivated and the road runs up it a short distance to the halting place on the side of the stream. The Kawzaw is a sluggish stream, about 5 yards wide.

FROM TAUNGU (TOUNGOO) TO NAUNGPALÉ (WEST KARENNI) *viâ* LEPETENG—*continued.*

Authorities. Military.	Authorities. Civil.	Number and Names of Stages, Rivers and Streams.	Distances. Intermediate.	Distances. Total.	Remarks.
G.O.C. Rangoon District.	Lower Burma.		M. F.	M. F.	
		7. Htu stream ... Kawzaw stream.	6 4	59 4	The path lies over the hills to the east of the valley, rising to a height of 4,500 feet. This ridge divides the valleys of the Sittang and the Salween rivers. The slopes are very steep as usual. From the top of the ridge the road descends a little to a saddle connecting the ranges of hills and then rises again to 4.550 feet. From here it descends by zigzags into a narrow valley, the bottom of which is 2,800 feet above the sea and about 20 yards wide. The road runs south down the valley in which there is a little cultivation and through which a small stream flows. From the end of the valley a steep descent leads to the Htu stream (called by some the Hoto). The Htu stream is here about 10 yards wide and about a foot deep with a stony bed. This country is inhabited by the Hashwé tribe of Karens.
		8. Tsamaung range. Htu and Pulo streams.	3 4	63 0	Road lies up the Pulo stream, which flows into the Htu stream close to the camp. It then leads up the spur of a hill by a steep ascent for about 1,200 feet. From here the path is level for a bit and then rises to 4,200 feet. From here it descends, slanting down the hills, to a stream at 3,500 feet and, crossing this, ascends to the camping ground at 4,200 feet. The jungle during this march is very thick and the water-supply at the halting place is not good; so, if possible, a halt should not be made here.
		9. Sari	8 0	71 0	From here a gradual ascent is made to 4,750 feet, at first through jungle and afterwards through bush and grass. The high jungle now ceases and it becomes apparent that the hill up which the path has been going is a spur of a range running north and south and higher than any crossed as yet. The tops of the hills are rounded and covered with grass. The soil is white and chalky in appearance, and grey limestone appears through it in places. The top of the hill is reached at 5,650 feet, and from here the road descends and crosses a saddle at 5,450 feet and, running over a spur and along the side of a hill overlooking a richly wooded valley to the south, ascends a peak to the height of 6,100 feet. The top of this peak, "Prösoko," is 6,500 feet above the sea. Descending it on the eastern side, the path reaches the Thidawlut stream and from here runs through a wood and over gently undulating country, cleared in places for cultivation; then down a spur into a narrow valley 4,900 feet, and crossing a small steep hill, descends the other side into another valley 4,500 feet. Here the aspect of the country changes and becomes bare, and the hills smaller and more rocky. The halting place is in a narrow cultivated valley with the village of Sari a little to the north and Gisho to the south. The valley is about 100 yards wide. Water from a stream.
		10. Milaung stream.	8 0	79 0	The path runs east over hills which are rocky and steep. The country beyond is composed of small steep hills and valleys, the level of the country varying from 4,200 to

From TAUNGU (TOUNGOO) to NAUNGPALÉ (WEST KARENNI) *viâ* LEPETENG *continued.*

Authorities. Military.	Authorities. Civil.	Number and Names of Stages, Rivers and Streams.	Distances. Intermediate. M.	F.	Distances. Total. M.	F.	Remarks.
G.O.C. Rangoon District.	Lower Burma.	**10. Milaung stream**—*cont.*					5,000 feet. It is covered with grass and grey rocks and sometimes low trees. The path then descends into Karenni down a narrow valley, bordered on either side by rocky hills. The country below is a highly cultivated plain, with small grey rocky ridges running over it from north to south. The soil is red and the land is divided into small fields by hedges and mud and stone walls and ditches. It is well watered, but little or no timber is grown. The stream on which is the halting place is sluggish and muddy and about 20 feet wide.
		11. Naungpalé ...	**7**	**0**	86	0	Road runs through this level, cultivated, and enclosed country to Naungpalé which is close to Ngwédaung, *see* Route No. 4, Shan Division, Alternative I. *Note.*—The ascents and descents on this road, which beyond the first stage is only passable for pack animals and foot-passengers, are very steep, so that baggage animals must be loaded very light. Many of the Shan caravans use this route. The distances are probably a good deal understated. Troops passing along this road, in however small parties, would have to carry their own supplies as little or nothing, beyond fodder for animals (grass or bamboo leaves), can be depended upon.

No. 8.

From THAGAYA (Route No. 6, Stage 4) to PAYAGÔN (Route No. 10, Stage 6).

By Capt. A. C. YATE, 1st Beluch Light Infantry, 1885-86.

Authorities. Military.	Authorities. Civil.	Number and Names of Stages, Rivers and Streams.	Distances. Intermediate. M.	F.	Distances. Total. M.	F.	Remarks.
G.O.C. Rangoon District.	Lower Burma.	**1. Kayenlégyin** ...	**14**	**0**	44	0	Thagaya is the fourth station north of Taungu on the railway line to Mandalay. Here there is a Public Works Department bungalow. There are also three zayáts capable of accommodating 60 men. There is a good well near the zayáts. In dry season after harvest there is a good camping ground. Beyond Thágaya there is no accommodation for encamping troops at any of the halting places. From Thágaya to Kayenlégyin, 14 miles, the first 6 miles good laterite road. The remaining distance path through jungle very steep hilly path, impracticable for any pack animals except elephants in the rains. Kayenlégyin is a very small village with a stockaded police post, but no accommodation except for the 20 men now there. If troops have to encamp here huts would have to be built. There would be considerable difficulty in constructing huts, and at this season impossible to make them water proof.
		2. Minhé	**10**	**0**	54	0	Kayenlégyin to Minhé 10 miles. This is the worst bit of the road through dense jungle and over very steep hills. I have always found it difficult to march with pack ponies on this part of the road even in the dry season, at the present time it is impossible. The only accommodation at Minhé is a small Forest bungalow.

FROM THÁGAYA (ROUTE No. 6, STAGE 4) TO PAYAGÔN (ROUTE No. 10, STAGE 6)—*continued.*

Authorities. Military.	Authorities. Civil.	Number and Names of Stages, Rivers and Streams.	Distances. Intermediate. M.	F.	Distances. Total. M.	F.	Remarks.
G.O.C. Rangoon District.	Lower Burma.	**3. Bámbwébin Sein.**	**10**	**0**	64	0	There is no village from Minhé to Bámbwébin Sein. Much the same kind of road as the last. Hills not quite so steep. Distance 10 miles. Very thick jungle. At Bámbwébin there is a small village and a stockaded police post, with accommodation only for the present garrison.
		4. Pôlôngyi ...	**9**	**0**	73	0	Bámbwébin Sein to Pôlôngyi 9 miles. Road not so steep as last, but jungle very thick and deep mud. At Pôlôngyi there is a small village.
		5. Payagôn ...	**8**	**0**	81	0	Pôlôngyi to Payagôn 8 miles. Road steep till villages of Thitkopin and Ôshitgôn are passed; then very muddy and frequently along Swa river knee-deep in water. At Payagôn there is a small village and a stockaded police post. There is also a Public Works Department bungalow on hill above stockade, capable of accommodating 20 to 30 men. For the last three stages *see* also Route No. 10, Stages 6 to 8 inclusive.

No. 9.

From THAYETMYO to LAUNGSHÉ.

BY CAPT. SHONE, R.E., 1886–87.

Military	Civil	Stage	Intermediate M.	F.	Total M.	F.	Remarks
G.O.C. Rangoon District.	Lower Burma.	**1. Yémyit** ...	**15**	**0**	15	0	Direction west. Metalled road over hills, with steep ascents and descents at places, which are however easily passable for carts. The road follows the crest of a ridge for a considerable portion of the way. The surrounding country is all hilly and is covered with thick jungle. At 8th mile village of Padaukbin is reached. Very little cultivation. Water bad. Public Works Department bungalow, but no other accommodation. Mile 10, Nwathé, a small village with good water, but no accommodation for troops. At Yémyit there is a Public Works Department bungalow and a small zayát capable of accommodating 30 men. Good water from two wells. Supplies must all be brought from Thayetmyo. A little cultivation of paddy and Indian corn.
		2. Gainyé ...	**16**	**0**	31	0	Direction west. Beyond Yémyit the road is unmetalled, the soil in places being of clay, which renders those parts indifferent in the dry season, and impassable for carts in the rains. The entire route is hilly, and the surrounding ground is covered with jungle. At 6½ miles the village of Kauki, on the bank of the Panni creek, is reached. Water good and plentiful. No supplies. Public Works Department bungalow, but no zayáts. At Thapángain,

FROM THAYETMYO TO LAUNGSHÉ—*continued.*

Authorities.		Number and Names of Stages, Rivers and Streams.	Distances.		Remarks.
Military.	Civil.		Intermediate.	Total.	
G.O.C. Rangoon District.	Lower Burma.	**2. Gainyé**—*cont.*			9 miles, the Panni river is crossed. It is impassable immediately after heavy rain, and during the wet season can only be crossed by elephants, as there is but one very small boat available. After a few days dry weather the creek is fordable, and in the dry season of the year it is but a small stream. There is a kyaung capable of accommodating about 100 men on the left bank, and a police thana on the right. Léchaung, a small village, is passed at 11 miles, and at 13 miles the crossing of the Wa creek is reached. In floods this creek is difficult to pass, but is dry after the wet season is over. The best road for carts from Léchaung to the Wa creek crossing in the dry season is through the bed of the Panni creek. Gainyé is situated on high ground and the pull up to it is heavy. Water is scarce and has to be brought a ¼ of a mile up a steep hill. No supplies obtainable. Public Works Department bungalow, but no other accommodation. There is a direct foot-path from Thapángain to Hmuwa; distance about 25 miles.
			M. F.	M. F.	
		3. Mindún ...	**13 0**	44 0	Direction west. The road is hilly, and similar to that in the slat march: the surrounding country is all hills covered with jungle. Police thana at Régántseng, 2 miles. There is also a small zayát and a little water of indifferent quality. This point is the summit of the road between Thayetmyo and Mindún, and an alternative and somewhat shorter route to Teinda turns off from here to the north. At 5 miles the small village of Detché is reached, and the crossing of the Aima creek; the banks are steep and the creek is impassable during rain, but the water runs off in a couple of hours after the rain has ceased and it is then fordable. This creek is crossed and recrossed about twenty times in the next 2 miles. There are high hills on each side, which are inaccessible and covered with dense jungle. After mile 7 the road leaves the creek and traverses level ground for a mile; then there is an ascent, and the top of a range is followed for about another mile to Nyaungkyát. From this point to Mindún an open and level cultivated plain is traversed. This plain is only passable for elephants from May to November. The Matún river is crossed just before reaching Mindún; it is fordable in the dry season, but at other times must be crossed in boats. Mindún is a cluster of villages comprising a considerable community. There is a Court, Public Works Department bungalow, a police thana, and a number of zayáts: 700 to 1,000 men could be accommodated. There is a small bazaar; and paddy, vegetables, &c., can be obtained in small quantities. The Matún river, which joins the Irrawaddy near Kamé, is navigable to Mindún in the rains. The place is feverish, and should not be occupied by troops longer than is absolutely necessary.
		4. Hmuwa ...	**14 0**	58 0	Direction north-north-west. About 1 mile after leaving Mindún the Matún river is crossed close to a small earthen redoubt. The road then for 2 or 3 miles traverses a sparsely cultivated and level tract, where there are some small villages. Ranges of hills covered with jungle are next crossed and followed, the road at places being steep and difficult for carts in the dry season.

FROM THAYETMYO TO LAUNGSHÉ—*continued.*

Authorities. Military.	Authorities. Civil.	Number and Names of Stages, Rivers and Streams.	Distances. Intermediate. M.	F.	Total. M.	F.	Remarks.
G.O.C. Rangoon District.	Lower Burma.	**4. Hmuwa**—*cont.*					From May to November elephants only can be used. About 1 mile before reaching Hmuwa the road strikes a creek and follows its bank the rest of the way. At Hmuwa there is accommodation for about 100 men in kyaungs and some zayáts, plenty of good water, and supplies as before.
		5. Teinda	6	0	64	0	Direction north-north-west. There are two roads; the distance by the shorter one over the hills is 6 miles. For two-thirds of the way the route lies through fairly open jungle, when the old frontier line is passed at a small village and a creek is followed the remainder of the way. Though this road is a cart track, carts generally go by a more circuitous route which follows the creek the whole way. Both routes are indifferent, and are impassable for carts from May to November. Teinda is a village of about 100 houses; there is a police station and good water, but the kyaungs are in an insanitary state, and no supplies are obtainable. There is a shorter route to Teinda turning off the Mindún road at Régántseng, and crossing the hills through Sángyi and Pwédu. Sángyi is about 11 miles from Régántseng, has good water, and cover for 200 men in kyaungs. Pwédu on the old frontier is about 2 miles further on and has a police thana, but the water-supply is scanty. Pwédu to Teinda is 8 miles. This route is one march shorter than the other and it must be followed during the rains, but it is impassable for carts. In the dry season the longer route is believed to be better.
		6. Bumyaung ...	13	0	77	0	Direction north-north-west. The road, which passes through very thick jungle, is rough and not suitable for cart traffic. Bumyaung has 40 houses and a kyaung for 100 men, water being obtained from a stream.
		7. Myothit ...	9	0	86	0	Direction 7 miles north, then east. Road same as last march. The Panni river is crossed before entering Thábyabin; it has about a foot of water in the dry season, and can be crossed by elephants in floods. The left bank of the Panni is followed to Myothit, which is also situated on that river. Thábyabin has 40 houses, but no kyaungs, and is unhealthy in the rains. Myothit was a place of some importance, with over 100 houses and good kyaungs, but the whole place has been burnt. There is another road from Teinda to Myothit which, being level, is suitable for cart traffic in the dry season, but no water is obtained near the centre of this route, which is 21 miles in length. The road lies through very thick jungle the first half of the way, after that fairly open ground with patches of bamboo jungle is traversed, the last 5 miles being along the Panni river, which is crossed five times. At 5 miles from Teinda was Kadin; 7 miles, Yépauk; 10 miles, Sintelin; and 15 miles, Zígwé, but these villages are now burnt, and there is no water from the 5th to the 15th mile.

No. 9.

FROM THAYETMYO TO LAUNGSHÉ—*continued.*

Authorities. Military.	Authorities. Civil.	Number and Names of Stages, Rivers and Streams.	Distances. Intermediate. M.	F.	Total. M.	F.	Remarks.
G.O.C. Mandalay District.	Commissioner, Southern Division, and Deputy Commissioner, Mimbu.	**8. Kambauk** ...	13	0	99	0	Direction north-west. Cart road over level ground through a fairly open jungle. About mile 10 cart track to Minhla turns off to east. At Kambauk the water-supply, which is from a tank, is bad and limited. The village consists of about 40 houses, the only other accommodation being a small kyaung and two zayáts suitable for about 100 men.
		9. Padeng ...	12	0	111	0	Direction north-west. Dákôn is about half-way; it is a small village with good water from the Mán river, which is on the north side. A good kyaung and some zayáts suitable for 150 men. Troops should, if possible, march from Myothit to Dákôn without halting at Kambauk. Road level and good, jungle fairly open up to Dákôn; after that open. Cultivation near villages only. Mán river crossed several times between Dákôn and Padeng. Padeng 150 houses, kyaungs for 200 men. Clear, good water from Mán river, which has a sandy bed and runs about 1½ feet deep in the dry season.
		10. Napé	7	0	118	0	Direction north-west. There are two roads, an upper and a lower. The latter is somewhat shorter than the former and leads along the left bank of the Mán river, through level and open ground cultivated with paddy, but is impassable for carts in the rains; at that season even the upper road is heavy and difficult. For description of Napé *see* Route No. 15, Southern Division.
		11. Páeng ...	21	0	139	0	Direction north. To Magyigôn 12 miles. For 4 miles open, after that hilly and jungly. The road crosses a stream near Napé and another at Magyigôn. The bank of this stream is then followed through jungle, over fairly level ground, for 6 miles to Dhônchôn. To Páeng 3 miles further; road through open ground following the stream, with hills 2 to 3 miles distant on each side. The Ki creek, with 2 feet of water in the dry season, is crossed just before reaching Páeng. The whole road from Napé is passable for carts in the dry season. Magyigôn is a small village with no kyaungs. Dhônchôn has about 50 houses and zayáts for 50 men. Páeng, which is on rising ground above the Ki river, is a strong position, has about 70 houses and kyaungs for 250 men. Supplies: cattle, a little paddy, and about 20 carts. Steatite quarries near here. There is another and somewhat shorter way of reaching Sidôtia from Páeng *viâ* Awkwa and Sôngôn, the distance by this route being 16¾ miles instead of 23, but it is in parts very bad going even for pack animals.

FROM THAYETMYO TO LAUNGSHÉ—*continued.*

Authorities. Military.	Authorities. Civil.	Number and Names of Stages, Rivers and Streams.	Distances. Intermediate. M. F.	Distances. Total. M. F.	Remarks.
G.O.C. Mandalay District.	Commissioner, Southern Division, and Deputy Commissioner, Mimbu.	**12. Kyiwa (Kíwa)**	13 0	152 0	Direction north. About 2 miles from Páeng the road crosses a high hill, which is stony and somewhat difficult for carts. Low hills and the Ki creek are then crossed alternately several times. Country on both sides of the road hilly and jungly, the road itself being fairly open and passable for carts except after heavy rain, when the Ki would not be fordable. The spurs of the Yôma range are 3 or 4 miles distant on the west. Kyiwa is passed at mile 11, and both it and Kíwa, which is situated on both banks of the Môn river, are small places with no kyaungs or zayáts. Water from the river good.
		13. Sidôtia ...	10 0	162 0	Direction north-west. The Môn, which is a fine river, 300 feet wide, with excellent water, is crossed at Kíwa, and again before reaching Sidôtia. When the river is high it must be crossed in boats; when low, carts can go to Sidôtia. The road is very stony and crosses some low hills, but is passable for carts in the dry season. Country jungly, but jungle not very dense. At about 3 miles Thawzé, a large village whence supplies and transport (carts and coolies) can be obtained. There is a small bazaar in Sidôtia, which is a place of some 200 houses, and there are good zayáts suitable for 200 men. Carts cannot go beyond Sidôtia. Supplies of paddy and millet in large quantities. Also up to 150 carts in two or three days. From here there is a stony foot-path up the Môn river to Tabwin which alternately crosses the stream and ascends and descends the hills on its banks. The valley of the Môn lies between the Arakan Yôma on the west and the Namadaung hills on the east. This path through thick jungle passes several villages, reaching Kôndala (30 houses) in 12 and Tabwin and Légyin in 23 miles. These two villages, which are close together, are situated near the Arakan Yôma range, and there are also high hills to the north; they are either in, or on, the border of the Yaw district. The country to the north is inhabited by wild Chins. There is said to be a kyaung for 50 men. Water from the Môn river. Supplies scanty.
		14. Paukchaung.	6 0	168 0	Direction north. A foot-path for single file through undulating and thick jungle, and following a small stream. From reports there is reason to suppose that the road could be made passable for carts by clearing the jungle. Paukchaung is a small village of some 40 houses with a kyaung for 40 men. Water from a stream. From Sidôtia to Laungshé ponies, coolies, or elephants must be used for transport, and elephants are said to be the most suitable. From here there is an alternative route to Laungshé *viâ* Dabwin and the upper Môn valley, *see* Alternative I below.
		15. Kwémalôn ...	9 0	177 0	Direction north-north-west. Road similar to the last march. High hills all round. About 50 houses in Kwémalôn and kyaungs for 50 men. Water from a small stream. A difficult and stony foot-path leads from here in a west-north-west direction through dense jungle and over high hills, which form part of the Namadaung range, to Dabwin 10 miles. Another rough track leads to Pídauk (*see* Route No. 37, Southern Division) as follows: to Handauk, 8 miles by a bad road which is

FROM THAYETMYO TO LAUNGSHÉ—*continued*.

Authorities. Military.	Authorities. Civil.	Number and Names of Stages, Rivers and Streams.	Distances. Intermediate.	Distances. Total.	Remarks.
G.O.C. Mandalay District.	Commissioner, Southern Division and Deputy Commissioner, Mimbu.	**15. Kwémalôn**—*cont.*			merely a foot-path through dense jungle and across high hills. Handauk has 20 houses and a kyaung suitable for 30 men, but water is very scarce. From here to Wônyur, 15 miles, the foot-path becomes very stony and difficult, the ascents and descents over the high hills being so steep that ponies have to be dismounted at places. Dense jungle and trees the whole way. Wônyur is a village of 50 houses, and has cover in kyaungs for 80 men. Water from a stream. Seven miles further on Pidauk is reached. This part of the route there is a cart track leading through jungle over low hills, and crossing and recrossing a stream by fords. The direction from Kwémalôn to Wônyur is about east-south-east, and from Wônyur to Pídauk north. For description of Pídauk *see* Route No. 37, Southern Division.
			M. F.	M. F.	
		16. Kwédu or Chinsain.	10 0	187 0	Direction north-north-west. A stony foot-path for single file through hills covered with jungle. The dry beds of some small water-channels are crossed. The only water obtainable at Kwédu, which is a village of 30 houses, is by excavation in the dry bed of a water-course.
		17. Taungsu ...	8 0	195 0	Direction north-north-west. Road similar to the last march. Taungsu has 20 houses and no kyaungs. Water from a small stream.
G.C. Chin Hills.	Commissioner, Southern Division, and Deputy Commissioner, Pakôkku.	**18. Laungshé** ...	9 0	204 0	Direction north. Road similar to the last march until within ½ a mile of Laungshé, when cultivated ground is reached. Laungshé, which is one of the chief towns of the Yaw district, has about 300 houses in the town itself, but there are several villages or hamlets in the valley on the Salin river, in which the town is situated. The valley, which is cultivated chiefly with paddy, extends from 1 to 3 miles on the north, south and east sides of the town, and is surrounded by hills which are covered with jungle and forest. There are kyaungs and zayáts capable of accommodating 350 men. The water-supply, which is from the Salin river, is good. There is a very small bazaar, and the principal products of the place are teakwood, paddy, onions, Indian corn, lac, hides and buffalo horns. The inhabitants are both Burmans and Chins. There are few or no carts, and pack bullocks are the only kind of transport procurable. A road to the north leads to Saw, Yaw and Tilin (*see* Route No. 42, Southern Division).

ALTERNATIVE I.

FROM PAUKCHAUNG (STAGE 14) TO LAUNGSHÉ (STAGE 18) *viâ* DABWIN AND LÔNGYI.

BY LIEUT. H. BROOK-MURRAY, 2ND QUEEN'S OWN BENGAL LIGHT INFANTRY, 1886–87.

Military	Civil	Stage	Intermediate	Total	Remarks
G.O.C. Mandalay District.	Commr., Southern Division, and Dy. Commr., Mimbu.	**1. Magyi** ...	14 2	14 2	The road runs through Paukchaung, level going, used by carts, running for a mile along the bed of the stream it crosses the stream three times; banks steep and precipitous, evidently liable to sudden and heavy floods, and then passing through rich paddy cultivation reaches Thinchaung, a stockaded Chin village of 16 houses. Population 60, carts four, cutch-boiling, and millet crops. Passing through a very narrow

FROM THAYETMYO TO LAUNGSHÉ—*continued.*

ALTERNATIVE I—*continued.*

Authorities.		Number and Names of Stages, Rivers and Streams.	Distances.		Remarks.
Military.	Civil.		Intermediate.	Total.	
G.O.C. Mandalay District.	Commissioner, Southern Division, and Deputy Commissioner, Minbu.	**1. Magyi**—*cont.*			and steep cutting in the precipitous bank, the road running north crosses the stream and reaches Kyauktheik at 3½ miles. This is a large Chin village with double stockade all round it. One zayât on north side holds 15 men under knoll, on which is a small pagoda; 35 houses, men 50, population 150, bullocks 50, carts 3; paddy, millet, and cutch-boiling. Hills on west side distant about 1,200 yards, 250 feet high, valley about 2½ miles broad. Houses fair, people friendly, but lazy; grass obtainable in small quantities; straw abundant; water good and abundant, from creek. The road continues north for about ¼ mile, then crosses the river and bending westerly reaches Pángyet on the right. Double stockaded village on low ground, under the rise of the saddle between two hills; about 16 houses, all raised about 10 feet from the ground. The Hti run continues in a due northerly direction, the road branches west-north-west, running through thick bamboo jungle, making a steep ascent 2 miles out from Pángyet and a steep descent a mile further on into a nullah, the ascent on the far side being gradual except for a short distance; then level going with thin scrub jungle into Kyi (10½ miles), which is divided into two parts, the larger portion recently burnt to the ground; only 12 houses remain on the left of the road. A good space in a grove of jack fruit trees could be used as a camping ground for a large force. Population 100, bullocks 60, goats 30; road good and easy going. Carts are north of this little used, sleighs made out of the fork of a tree taking their place. From Kyi the jungle on the hill sides has been cleared and in places broken for cultivation. The road passes through this and is good going for man and beast, running due north from Kyi for 1½ miles, when it enters the hills, making two sudden and steep ascents. It now runs level for a few hundred yards, then descends into the bed of the Payani river along which it runs, commanded on both sides by jungle-covered spurs until it reaches the Môn river, when it runs across the stony bed of the stream. Caution must be used in moving transport animals across the smaller waste channels owing to quicksands which occur in several places. The road then runs in a north-north-west direction up the bed of the river through thin low scrub jungle till it reaches a small spur over which it ascends, reaching Magyi on the north slope about ½ mile further on, at 14¼ miles. Large village, 34 houses, population 160, bullocks 80; paddy, grass, straw in large quantities; houses inferior; entrances to the village three, north, south and west. Two kyaungs on north side, one large (new), one old: two zayáts; water from creek, distant ½ mile. Village situated on hill overlooking the valley northerly; hill side from the river precipitous.
		2. Lôngyi ...	M. F. 14 6	M. F. 29 0	Road runs down a sudden and steep incline into paddy-fields beneath in north-west direction; road steep for animals, once on the level easy going, leaving Bu on the right at 1½ miles, a large stockaded village in two rows of houses; 30 houses, population 120, bullocks 70. The road after running north for ½ mile turns due east under the foot of the hills and bordering on the paddy-fields in rear of the village, suddenly turning north-north-west through a gap in the saddle between two hills; road fair but trying for animals; two steep ascents of about 150 yards each, difficult for animals, about ¼ mile apart, then level going with one descent into a small nullah, along

FROM THAYETMYO TO LAUNGSHÉ—*continued.*

ALTERNATIVE I—*continued.*

Authorities. Military.	Authorities. Civil.	Number and Names of Stages, Rivers and Streams.	Distances. Intermediate.	Distances. Total.	Remarks.
G.O.C. Mandalay District.	Commissioner, Southern Division, and Deputy Commissioner, Minbu.	**2. Lôngyi**—*cont.*			which it passes into the bed of the Môn river, continuing in the same close under the banks till it reaches Dabwinmyo at 6 miles, a large village of 250 houses, under a Myo-ôk of Taungtha origin, as are most of his townspeople. He is an illiterate old man, and in the hands of his Burman clerk. The village is prettily situated ½ a mile from the left bank of the Môn river, towards which the ground slopes, in a large grove of palm trees. Extensive paddy cultivation to the west. One large kyaung holds 100 men and eight zayáts holding 200. Dwé lies behind a small spur on the west (right) bank of the Môn, a couple of miles to the west of Dabwin and is situated on the Dwé river; 24 houses and two kyaungs. From Dabwinmyo road runs through rice fields along left bank of Môn river, inclining towards the river and reaching it at Zídaw (6¾ miles) here the river is crossed by two foot-bridges, and at 7¼ miles Akyéywa is reached. This is a flourishing Chinbôn village of 46 houses sandwiched between the two flourishing Burmese villages of Tanlagyin (88 houses) and Nabidôn (39 houses). It is on a slight eminence of about 75 feet and has several Burmese pagodas, &c., just outside it. From Akyéywa road runs up right bank for ½ a mile, then crosses by ford to left bank, and 1½ miles further up recrosses the river by foot-bridge, ½ a mile below the village of Auk-kyin (9¾ miles). This is also called Burmese-Tauksôk and is a flourishing village of 46 houses. Thence the road runs up right bank through paddy-fields to Tauksôk (also called Chin-Tauksôk), a Chinbôn village of 56 houses at 11¼ miles. The river is then crossed just below a *bund* opposite Tauksôk, and the road continues up the valley to Lôngyi, 14¾ miles, crossing innumerable irrigation channels. Lôngyi is a flourishing double village of 79 houses, part Burmese, part Chinbôn. It is surrounded by paddy-fields, amply irrigated from the Môn river.
O.C. Chin Hills.	Commissioner, Southern Division, and Deputy Commissioner, Pakôkku.	**3. Kyaukka** ... Môn river, Pônzaing, Sin, and Kyaukka chaungs.	M. 12 F. 6	M. 41 F. 6	General direction north. Road, now merely a cooly or bullock path, runs up the Pônzaing chaung which enters the Môn river at Lôngyi for about 3 miles. It then crosses a low pass into the valley of the Sin chaung, also a left bank feeder of the Môn river, which it joins at Apaw (*see* at end of this stage); descent for first 100 feet on other side steep. At 4½ miles Ngatawzôk, a poor Chinbôn village of 27 houses on the Sin chaung. A little rice cultivation round village, but water-supply insufficient to irrigate much. Path now runs up bed of Sin chaung, stony but practicable at all seasons. Cutch tree jungle on both sides. At 6¾ miles Sinchaungywa, Chinbôn village of 21 houses on Sin chaung. Cultivation as at Ngatawzôk. The Sin chaung is in the rains a broad torrent, stony bottom. In the dry season no water above ground, but can always be found by digging in the stream bed. At 7¼ miles Daingywa, Chinbôn village of 28 houses on Sin chaung. Here there are huts for 100 police, at present (March 1893) rather out of repair. The villagers are good guides and shikáris for the Samboyu hills to the west and north-west. Path after ½ a mile leaves Sin chaung and turning north-east ascends rather steeply to Mahawtaung (3,000 feet) on the watershed between the Môn and Salin rivers at 9¾ miles. Passing slightly to the west of the highest point of this hill, path, easily practicable

FROM THAYETMYO TO LAUNGSHÉ—*continued.*

ALTERNATIVE I—*continued.*

Authorities.		Number and Names of Stages, Rivers and Streams.	Distances.		Remarks.
Military.	Civil.		Intermediate.	Total.	
O.C. Chin Hills.	Commissioner, Southern Division, and Deputy Commissioner, Pakôkku.	**3. Kyaukka**—*cont.*			for transport animals, descends gradually for 500 feet to Kyaukka at 12¾ miles, through numerous *taungyas.* This is a Chinbôn village of 43 houses, under Yan (*see* next stage). Some police huts available for shelter. Water scanty and bad, from Kyaukka chaung, a tributary of the Pôndo chaung. There is an alternative route between Lôngyi and Daingywa. It is a good path and easy all the way, but is 6¼ miles longer than that just described. It runs as follows. First 1½ miles from Lôngyi, up Pônzaing chaung, then cross Shwékyauktaung, diagonally, north-westward back into the Môn valley, reaching the bank (left) of that river a little north of Yethungyin, and following the river bank thence northward, crossing Maw chaung, to Apaw (6½ miles), a small dilapidated village of six houses on a low hill on right bank of Maw chaung at its junction with the Môn river. On the opposite bank of the Môn is the flourishing Chinbôn village of Mintaingyin, 26 houses. The Môn is bridged ½ a mile below the villages by bamboo foot-bridge on gabions. It is here from 60 to 100 yards wide, varying in depth. In the dry season it is fordable (1½ feet deep) between Apaw and Mintaingyin. Its general character is that of a not very impetuous Salmon river. The Maw chaung is similar in character to the Sin chaung. Dense cutch forest around and much cutch-boiling carried on in these villages. Path now quits Môn river and runs up Maw chaung for about 2½ miles, it then turns north-eastward away from the stream and ascends a steep hill, through *taungyas* to just below Daing-kyauki (11 miles; 2,600 feet), the remains of an old Chinbôn village on top of a precipitous limestone rock, a former place of refuge in times of raids, got at only by means of ladders up the rock Excellent spring at foot of rock. There is a small cutch-boiling village and *taungya* a little to the north. The path now descends rapidly to Daingywa (1,600 feet) which is reached at 13½ miles.
		4. Laungshé ... Pôndo or Pein, Pa, and Salin chaungs.	M. 9 F. 2	M. 51 F. 0	General direction a little east of north. Road is an ordinary cart track through rice fields and scrub jungle, following the course of the Pôndo chaung, tributary of the Salin chaung, more or less closely all the way. This stream is dry in the dry season. The following villages are passed *en route* :— HOUSES. POPULATION. At 2¾ miles Yan ... ... 25 Chinbôn. At 3½ miles Ngahaung ... 5 Do. At 4 miles Pa chaung ... 6 Do. At 4¾ miles Kinbauk ... 33 Do. At 6 miles Kyeingyi ... 51 Half Chinbôn, half Burmese. At 7 miles Tôndin ... 23 Do. At 7½ miles Pein chaung ... 37 Do. At 9 miles Ywathit ... An offshoot of Laungshé. Laungshé at 9½ miles on right bank Salin chaung has 361 houses, court-house and travellers' bungalow ; bamboo sheds to accommodate 400 men. Rice and pack bullocks plentiful and a few carts. Population mixed Burmese and Chinbôn.

FROM THAYETMYO TO LAUNGSHÉ—*continued.*

BRANCH I.

FROM DABWINMYO (*see* ALTERNATIVE I, STAGE 2) TO YANÁN.

BY CAPT. J. HARVEY, ROYAL ARTILLERY, ATTACHÉ, INTELLIGENCE BRANCH, W. A. HERTZ, ESQ., EXTRA ASSISTANT COMMISSIONER, AND NATIVE INFORMATION, MARCH 1893.

Authorities. Military.	Authorities. Civil.	Number and Names of Stages, Rivers and Streams.	Distances. Intermediate. M.	F.	Total. M.	F.	Remarks.
O.C. Chin Hills.	Commissioner, Southern Division, and Deputy Commissioner, Pakôkku.	**1. Ma Awé** ... Môn river.	12	0	12	0	Road is a Chin path up a long spur of Ma Awé hill and then along the top. Will always require some clearing of bamboos, through thick jungle of which it runs. An alternative route runs *viâ* Tauksôk and Tauk chaung up the northern spur is a little longer and through similar jungle. The upper part is clear of bamboos. At 12 miles Ma Awé, Chinbôn village on top of hill; 30 houses; water scarce; got from three very small wells, but villagers always keep a reserve in gourds also; even in hot weather more can easily be got by digging in suitable beds of nullahs.
		2. Thaung chaung Sakhán. Thaung chaung.	8	0	20	0	Road runs along spur down from Ma Awé, across saddle, and up a short spur of Yengwétaung; then it runs down into the Thaung chaung, which stream rises from the northern slopes of Yengwétaung or Tuditaung, which is about 7,000 feet high. Here there is only a halting place, no village.
		3. Pyawbwé Sakhán.	17	0	37	0	Road runs through fir and oak forest over a high spur of Yengwétaung and down another to the eastward, ascending and descending many times. Water to south-east of camp. The distance is only approximate.
		4. Yanángyi ... Daung chaung.	8	0	45	0	The Yôma watershed is crossed; an easy road gradually descending to the Daung chaung. There is also a route from Dabwinmyo up the Dwé chaung and over the watershed of the Yômas, leaving Yengwétaung to the north, but it is longer and much worse going.

No. 10.

From THAYETMYO to TAUNGU (TOUNGOO).

BY CAPT. A. D. ANDERSON, ROYAL ARTILLERY, FEBRUARY 1880.

Military	Civil	Stage	Intermediate M.	F.	Total M.	F.	Remarks
G.O.C. Rangoon District.	Lower Burma.	**1. Camp** ... ... Irrawaddy and numerous small streams.	12	4	12	4	A road runs more or less along the old frontier line from opposite Thayetmyo to Taungu, but it would seldom be used for the movement of troops, as the central stages traverse very

FROM THAYETMYO TO TAUNGU (TOUNGOO)—*continued.*

Authorities. Military.	Authorities. Civil.	Number and Names of Stages, Rivers and Streams.	Distances. Intermediate. M.	F.	Distances. Total. M.	F.	Remarks.
G.O.C. Rangoon District.	Lower Burma.	**2. Thambuhla** ...	11	0	23	4	difficult country in crossing the Yôma range which divides the watersheds of the Irrawaddy and Salween rivers, and it would be easier and probably also cheaper in the long run to move them by river to Prome and thence by rail *viâ* Rangoon. The first two stages are good and easy going, the third stage also fairly good in dry weather. The fourth and fifth stages, between which the Yôma watershed is crossed, are very difficult indeed, the road being the worst possible description of cart track. From the sixth stage to the beginning of the 5th mile of the twelfth stage, the road is a good cart track, thence to Toungoo metalled road. Small camping grounds at all the stages and supplies of rice, fowls, &c., can be provided with due notice at all stages, except the fourth and fifth. At most of the stages there are police posts, and at the tenth and eleventh (also at Tabaing between eleventh and twelfth) stages there are good rest-houses. Grass and bamboo leaves for forage throughout the route, and water may be said to be plentiful upto the end of February certainly. The small double bullock carts of the country are procurable for transport, as are ponies and, on the Toungoo side of the Yômas, bullocks for pack transport. From Bámbwébin, Stage 8, there is a direct road to Thágaya on the railway, four stations north of Toungoo, distance 34 miles, *see* Route No. 8, Stages 1 to 3 inclusive.
		Small streams.					
		3. Thetngabaing.	15	0	38	4	
		Kyoting chaungyi.					
		4. Mingyi Sakhán	12	0	50	4	
		Kyoting chaungyi and Baing-haung chaung.					
		5. Magu Sakhán...	20	0	70	4	
		Kyetyetmyaung and Magu chaungs.					
		6. Payagôn ...	9	0	79	4	
		Kyaukmasein and Theing chaungs.					
		7. Pôlôngyi ...	8	0	87	4	
		Theing chaung.					
		8. Bámbwébin ...	8	0	95	4	
		Theing chaung.					
		9. Zibyubin ...	18	0	113	4	
		Theing chaung.					
		10. Shwégýityit...	16	0	129	4	
		Theing chaung and Swa river.					
		11. Lédaungán ...	9	0	138	4	
		Small streams.					
		12. Toungoo ...	9	0	147	4	
		Salween river.					

No. 11.

From YAUNGYÁNDAUNG to MINHLA.

BY LIEUT. MARTER, 1ST BATTALION, RIFLE BRIGADE, 1886–87.

Military	Civil	Stage	Intermediate M.	F.	Total M.	F.	Remarks
G.O.C. Rangoon District.	Lower Burma.	**1. Munatkôn (Monakôn).**	12	4	12	4	Yaungyándaung is situated on the right bank of the Irrawaddy about 30 miles above Thayetmyo. General direction north-west and north; leaving Yaungyándaung the road is fair and level. Range of hills running north-north-west on the left of the road. Two and-a-half miles inlet, a very small village on river. Five miles Htúbauk, a small village of only eight houses some little distance from the river. The road continues in a northerly direction and is a fair one for carts. One and-a-half miles from Htúbauk is Nabeya, a fair-sized village not on the river, but getting water from a well. One kyaung and one sayát giving accommodation for about

FROM YAUNGYÁNDAUNG TO MINHLA—*continued.*

Authorities.		Number and Names of Stages, Rivers and Streams.	Distances.				Remarks.
Military.	Civil.		Intermediate.		Total.		
			M.	F.	M.	F.	
G.O.C. Rangoon District.	Lower Burma.	**1. Munatkôn (Monakôn)**—*cont.*					60 men. Six miles from Nabeya is the village of Munatkôn, about a mile from the river. No good camping ground here, but a mall open space would accommodate a force of about 100 men. Water plentiful and very good from a well, which supplies the village all the year round.
		2. Thabyadaw ...	**9**	**2**	21	6	General direction north-west. After leaving Munatkôn the road, which is a fair one for carts and good for mules and pony transport, runs slightly inland leaving low hills, between it and the river, 3¼ miles, is the village of Padaukkán, a small "Chin" village of about 10 houses. The road continues inland to avoid several small creeks running into the Irrawaddy. After leaving Padaukkán one stream is crossed and then the small village of Sanaing is reached, off the road, 1 mile from Padaukkán. Three-quarters of a mile after leaving Sanaing the road crosses the Pedi creek, and about 3 miles beyond this it crosses another stream, continuing along its bed for a short distance. Five miles from Sanaing the road runs in a north-easterly direction reaching Thabyadaw, a small village on the river. There is a certain amount of open space here for a camping ground, but it is not good from a military point of view, being commanded by some high cliffs overlooking the ground, and being far from the water, which is drawn from the river.
		3. Kada	**9**	**0**	30	6	General direction north and north-west. In this march the road, which is fair, makes several detours between the villages which are on the river to avoid small streams and creeks running into the river. Leaving Thabyadaw the road continues on the river bank for 2½ miles to Paidaw, a village of no importance. After Paidaw the road runs inland and about 2 miles from Paidaw crosses two small streams, after which it takes a north-easterly direction towards the river passing Kainywa, but not entering it. Kainywa is about 3½ miles from Paidaw and is a fairly-sized village of about 30 houses. Leaving Kainywa the road again runs inland about 2 miles from Kainywa crossing two streams. Hills on the left of the road and low hills between it and the river. Three miles from Kainywa the small village of Kada is reached, of no importance. There is no camping ground here whatever, nor does the village afford any accommodation, but the force camped on the river bank.
G.O.C. Myingyán District.	Commissioner, Southern Division, and Deputy Commissioner, Mimbu.	**4. Minhla**	**6**	**0**	36	6	General direction north-west. The road on first leaving Kada runs due west for a short distance and then north, reaching Malun 2¼ miles, now burnt down and affording no accommodation. Malun to Ywathit, a small village ½ mile further on and of no importance. After running north-west for 1¼ miles the road crosses a fairly-sized nullah called the Kywénaban chaung, on which is situated the village of Wyin, of no importance. One mile from Uyin is another very small village, Latlán, and from Latlán the road runs due north passing through Inywa, a suburb of Minhla and finally reaching Minhla, 1 mile from Latlán. The latter part of the road was good and easy for the carts. At Minhla there is a large camping ground perfectly open, with several kyaungs and zayáts on rising ground capable of accommodating a fairly large force. Water for the camping ground drawn from wells in the village, about ¼ mile distant.

APPENDIX I.

ADDITIONAL ROUTES IN NORTHERN DIVISION.

APPENDIX I.

ADDITIONAL ROUTES IN NORTHERN DIVISION.

No. 1.

List of Roads made or taken in hand by the Public Works Department in the Bhamo District up to end of the cold season 1892-93.

BY H. O. WALLING, ESQ., PUBLIC WORKS DEPARTMENT, AUGUST 1893.

Name of road.	Class of road.	Rest-house.	Remarks.
(1) Bhamo past Siyán to Hantôn (Hángtôn).	Raised, bridged, and unmetalled.	None ...	This road is in two sections—in plains and in hills. The section in the plain is wide enough for cart traffic, the hill section is only a mule track. *See* Route No. 10, Northern Division.
(2) Bhamo to Mánsi...	Ditto ...	Do. ...	This is a fair weather cart road; some of the gradients into nullahs, however, are rather steep. It crosses two large swamps, which practically close the road in the rains; ferries have been established across these during the present rains and it can be used only by ponies and foot-passengers. *See* Route No. 12, Northern Division.
(3) Bhamo, Môping, Myothit to Nampaung.	Ditto ...	Do ...	The first section of this road to Myothit can be used by carts in the fair weather. From Myothit to Nampaung is in the hills and this portion is only a mule track. *See* Route No. 11, Northern Division.
(4) Senbo to Môgaung *viâ* Tápaw.	Village road ...	Do. * ...	This is a fair weather mule track. *See* Route No. 89, Northern Division.
(5) Môgaung to Myitkyina *viâ* Tápaw and Akyé.	Ditto. ...	Do. * ...	This is a fair weather mule track. It is proposed to abandon this route, and this will be done as soon as the new direct road from Myitkyina to Môgaung has been made.
(6) Waingmaw to Sadôn.	Raised, bridged, and unmetalled.	Do. * ...	This is a mule track. It is not yet complete, although opened to traffic since last March. *See* Route No. 79, Northern Division.
(7) Môgaung to Kámaing.	Village roads ...	Do. ...	This is a fair weather mule track. *See* Route No. 66, Northern Division.
(8) Thamaingyi to 4 miles (just begun).	Raised, bridged, and unmetalled.	Do. ...	Only 4 miles of this mule track was made last year. It will be completed during the present cold weather.

* It is proposed to build rest-houses during the present year on roads (4), (5) and (6).

LIST OF ROADS MADE OR TAKEN IN HAND BY THE PUBLIC WORKS DEPARTMENT IN THE BHAMO DISTRICT UP TO END OF THE COLD SEASON 1892-93—*continued.*

Name of road.	Class of road.	Rest-house.	Remarks.
(9) Tálawgyi to Sima (Fort Morton), (Kachin road).	Raised, bridged, and unmetalled.	None * ...	This is a Kachin road, which it is proposed to improve and bridge this cold weather. It was the route taken by the troops proceeding to Sima during the late disturbances. *See* Route No. 100, Northern Division, and Appendix I, Route No. 8.

* It is proposed to build a rest-house during the present year on this road.

No. 1-A.

From BHAMO to MÁTIN *viâ* KADAW.

BY LIEUT. CARLETON, 3RD BURMA INFANTRY, OCTOBER 1893.

Authorities. Military.	Authorities. Civil.	Number and Names of Stages, Rivers and Streams.	Distances. Intermediate. M.	F.	Total. M.	F.	Remarks.
G.O.C. Mandalay District and O.C. Bhamo.	Commissioner, Northern Division, and Deputy Commissioner, Bhamo.	**1. Pomprai** ...	(?)15	0	15	0	General direction east. Follow the Hángtōn road (*see* Route No. 10, Northern Division) for 9 miles, then turn off north-east, and at 12 miles enter hills and go steep up to Kampan, then through Loncha and Kyetyin to Pomprai. Very good water-supply, but bad camp. At Kampan, Loncha, and Kyetyin water-supply is not good. Time on march 10 hours.
		2. Pakwan ... Nantabet chaung.	14	0	29	0	The direct road to Pakwan being impassable for animals in October, went by circuitous route. Downhill in a northerly direction for about [illegible] miles to the Nantabet chaung (50 yards by 3 feet; fairly strong current), reached in 1½ hours. Before reaching river are cross-roads, left-hand road going to Bhamo-Nampaung road (*see.* Route No. 11, Northern Division) and right-hand road to Pakwan which was followed. Cross the river and go down the bank for 500 yards, then turn sharp to the right up a long steep hill to Pakwan at 14 miles; 4¼ hours. Water-supply small and camping ground indifferent.
		3. Kadaw ...	7	0	36	0	Road to Mátin *viâ* Karomkong being impassable, took the road to Kadaw. From Pakwan descend and cross paddy-fields, then uphill through taungyas past small village of Manto at 5 miles to Kadaw. Fair water-supply. Time on march from Pakwan to Kadaw 2¾ hours.
		4. Mátin	9	0	45	0	From Kadaw to Mátin is said to be 9 miles by a good road.

FROM BHAMO TO MÁTIN *viâ* KADAW—*continued.*

ALTERNATIVE I.

FROM BHAMO TO PAKWAN.

BY LIEUT. CARLETON, 3RD BURMA INFANTRY, OCTOBER 1893.

Authorities. Military.	Authorities. Civil.	Number and Names of Stages, Rivers and Streams.	Distances. Intermediate. M.	F.	Total. M.	F.	Remarks.
G.O.C. Mandalay District and O.C. Bhamo.	Commissioner, Northern Division, and Deputy Commissioner, Bhamo.	**1. Môping** ...	**8**	**0**	8	0	This route is better than the more southerly route *viâ* Pomprai, as it is over level ground to the foot of the hill on which Pakwan stands. General direction north-east. Level road along the Nampaung road (*see* Route No. 11, Northern Division).
		2. Pakwan ... Nantabet chaung.	**21**	**0**	29	0	General direction east. Level road to the Nantabet chaung at 13 miles (50 yards by 3 feet, fairly strong current), cross it, and then uphill to Pakwan. Water-supply very small and camping ground indifferent.

No. 2.

From BHAMO to NAMKHAM viâ SÁWADI, MANSÔK and SÔPKAM.

BY CAPT. ATKINSON, BURMA MILITARY POLICE, NOVEMBER 1892, AND OTHERS.

The Government road to Namkham through Punkaw and Mansi is just passable in the rains, but is not so good as the Pita Warabôn road (*see* Route No. 12, Northern Division). The road on from Mansi to Tuku (*see* Branch No. I below) is impassable even for men on foot owing to deep water in the neighbourhood of the Nam Yu or Moyu chaung. A full description of the route does not appear to have been compiled, but the stages are as noted below, and such information as is available is recorded.

Military	Civil	Stages	Int. M.	F.	Total M.	F.	Remarks
G.O.C. Mandalay District and O.C. Bhamo.	Commissioner, Northern Division, and Dy. Commr., Bhamo.	**1. Sáwadi** ...	**9**	**0**	9	0	*See* Route No. 19, Northern Division.
		2. Mankin ...	**12**	**2**	21	2	
		3. Namlôn chaung.	(?)		(?)		No details recorded.
		4. Mansôk ...	(?)		(?)		
		5. Mawsi ... Mawsi chaung.	(?)		(?)		Mansôk to Punkaw (?) miles, thence to Mawsi 7¼ miles. Leave Punkaw following the ordinary trade route running east. Cross the Mawsi

FROM BHAMO TO NAMKHAM *viâ* SÍWADI, MANSÔK AND SÔPKAM—*continued.*

Authorities. Military.	Authorities. Civil.	Number and Names of Stages, Rivers and Streams.	Distances. Inter-mediate.	Distances. Total.	Remarks.
G.O.C. Mandalay District and O.C. Bhamo.	Commissioner, Northern Division, and Deputy Commissioner, Bhamo.	**5. Mawsi**—*cont.*			chaung at ½ a mile and on the far side of the chaung leave the trade route and go nearly due south, for the first 2¼ miles from Punkaw over a small hill covered with small very thick high jungle mostly kaing grass; through which a road had to be forced. At 2¾ miles cross some paddy-fields about ½ mile broad, and at 3¼ miles recross the Mawsi chaung, and then by a small path up and down hill through big jungle along a fair path to Mawsi, a large village of 50 houses in Mômeik territory situated at the head of the valley of the Nammak chaung and 7½ miles from Punkaw.
			M. F.	M. F.	
		6. Sôpkam ... Shwéli river and Nammak chaung.	6 6	...	From Mawsi the road descends in an easterly direction for 2¼ miles, crossing a small hill *en route*, and then into the Nammak valley on the right or Mômeik side, then along the valley for about 1½ miles, and then due south up a very steep hill to the village of 'Yangun at 4¼ miles from which the road goes in an easterly direction through the Mômeik hills to Sôpkam at 6¾ miles, where it strikes the Shwéli river at the mouth of the Nammak chaung. Road as good as the trade route from Mawsi throughout.
	Supt., N. Shan States.	**7. Namkham** ...	4 2	...	*See* Route No. 14, Northern Division, Stage 7.

BRANCH I.

FROM MANSÔK (STAGE 4) TO MANSI.

BY LIEUT. J. H. WHITEHEAD, 3RD BURMA INFANTRY, INTELLIGENCE BRANCH, MARCH 1893.

Authorities. Military.	Authorities. Civil.	Number and Names of Stages, Rivers and Streams.	Distances. Inter-mediate.	Distances. Total.	Remarks.
G.O.C. Mandalay District and O.C. Bhamo.	Commissioner, Northern Division, and Deputy Commissioner, Bhamo.	**1. Camp Makha.** Pásang Ka, Kapya and Makha chaungs.	13 0	13 0	General direction north-westerly. At 1 mile, after crossing a small hill, good camping ground in dry paddy-fields; water from two streams. (*N.B.*—This is a better camping place than Mansôk village which is on a ridge and ¼ mile from water.) At 3 miles descent to Irrawaddy valley begins (Bhamo visible through glasses). At 4 miles present road joins trade route, coming in from the south-east. At 5 miles Kunswai (Kachin, 10 houses). Here another trade route joins on from south-east. At 6 miles Samá (Kachin, 25 houses) extends about ½ mile along road. At 6½ miles Tuku (1) (Kachin,) about ½ mile off; road to right front. At 7 miles fair camping ground in dry paddy-fields. At 7½ miles Pásang Ka (1 yard by 6 inches, rocky bottom) crosses road from left. At 8¼ miles Tuku (2) (Kachin, 30 to 40 houses). From Tuku steep descent in south-westerly direction to Kapya chaung (2 yards by 6 inches, rocky bottom), which crosses road from left at 10 miles. Here there is a good camping ground in dry paddy-fields. Having crossed paddy-fields road turns north-west again uphill and along a long ridge, then descends by a short and steep descent to Makha chaung (2 yards by 6 inches, rocky bottom), which crosses from left. Camp of dry paddy-fields on left bank of chaung, a fair camping ground also on right bank. The road throughout this stage is a good mule track. There are several bullock camps and small streams.

FROM BHAMO TO NAMKHAM *viâ* SÁWADI, MANSÔK AND SÔPKAM—*continued.*

BRANCH I—*continued.*

Authorities.		Number and Names of Stages, Rivers and Streams.	Distances.		Remarks.
Military.	Civil.		Inter-mediate.	Total.	
			M. F.	M. F.	
G.C.C. Mandalay District and O.C. Bhamo.	Commissioner, Northern Division, and Deputy Commissioner, Bhamo.	**2. Mansi** ... ... Namyu chaung.	**11 6**	24 6	At $\frac{1}{4}$ mile path to left to Namlé (six houses) about $\frac{1}{4}$ mile from road; old site of Namlé on right by road side. Up to 4 miles road is crossed and re-crossed by Makha chaung. At 4 miles Namyu chaung (at ford, 20 yards by 1 foot 3 inches, rocky bottom) crosses road from right front. Makha chaung flows into it near here. This stream rises in hills, flows through Saopung, near Kunswai, then on through Punkán (Káráu) and Mansi, where it is 20 yards by 1 foot 6 inches, sandy bottom. At 5 miles Madángya (Kachin, three houses). At 9$\frac{1}{2}$ miles Chaungdauk (Kachin, 13 houses, built in Shan manner, but with Kachin thatching). At 10 miles road from Kyawgaung joins present road from right front. At 10$\frac{3}{4}$ miles road passes through old British fort (parapet and ditch remain much overgrown). At 11$\frac{3}{4}$ miles Mansi (Shan). The road for first 4 miles descends gently; very rocky in many places. After 4 miles follows right bank of Namyu chaung, but not close to river; nearly flat and good mule track. From Chaungdauk to Mansi mostly through "kaing" grass; this part is still boggy in places and would probably not be practicable for at least six weeks after rains. Throughout this stage the road is crossed by many small streams and there are several bullock camps. Mansi is 14 miles from Bhamo, *see* Route No. 12, Northern Division.

No. 3.

From BHAMO to SIMA (FORT MORTON*).

BY CAPT. G. H. H. COUCHMAN, D.S.O., 1892-93, LIEUT. HUSSEY WALSH, 1890-91, LIEUT. DENT, 1892-93.

Military	Civil	Stages	Intermediate	Total	Remarks
G.O.C. Mandalay District and O.C. Bhamo.	Commissioner, Northern Division, and Deputy Commissioner, Bhamo.	**1. Malula** ... ... Tapin river and small streams.	**11 0**	11 0	General direction north-east. After leaving Fort A, Bhamo, the road takes a north-east direction and passes the police fort and jail on its left. As far as here the road is metalled. A mile or so from Fort A the road crosses over two bridges, both strong enough for cavalry or mountain battery, about 30 yards long each. The track is a broad road in most places (varying from 8 to 15 feet) and runs through tree jungle to near the village of Nampa Chaungwa, 15 houses, at 5 miles, which is on a small stream about 10 yards wide. From here the road runs on to the village of Môping, 26 houses, at 7 miles, which is about 400 yards to the west (left) of the road and rather hidden away and difficult to see: here the river is crossed, if the Theinlôn route is taken. Then on for about 1 mile and across a stream unfordable and 12 yards wide with a bridge over it: this stream has banks about 1 yard deep and perpendicular and runs through dense jungle. Sima

* So called after Capt. Morton, Commandant, Magwé Battalion, Military Police, who was killed in action there in January 1893.—A.F.

FROM BHAMO TO SIMA (FORT MORTON)—*continued.*

Authorities. Military.	Authorities. Civil.	Number and Names of Stages, Rivers and Streams.	Distances. Inter-mediate. M. F.	Distances. Total. M. F.	Remarks.
G.O.C. Mandalay District and O.C. Bhamo.	Commissioner, Northern Division, and Deputy Commissioner, Bhamo.	**1. Malula**—*cont.*			column camped near Môping on the banks of the Tapin. From here the road runs through jungle to Malula, 15 houses, at 11 miles, which is just off the road on the right. On either side of this village is good camping ground and plenty of forage.
		2. Myothit ... Tapin river and one small stream.	8 0	19 0	The track after leaving Malula runs along a paddy plain up to the village of Kywégyo, 23 houses, at $1\frac{1}{4}$ miles, and then on along the river bank up to the village of Ma-ubin at 2 miles. Before reaching this village there is a small stream of little importance. From Kywégyo the road is not so good, being soft and sandy. Next we come to Mainyé, about 400 yards from Ma-ubin: this is a small village of a few houses. From here on to the village of Naungpaung, 26 houses, at 3 miles, and in $\frac{3}{4}$ of a mile more Kanni, 26 houses, is reached. There is scarcely any jungle from Malula to Kanni; the track leads through fine paddy and beautiful fields with rich grass. From here the road runs through tall kaing grass; it is sandy and indifferent and about 7 feet wide, till the bridge over the Tapin river is reached at $7\frac{3}{4}$ miles. The bridge over the Tapin is made of bamboo and is only temporary, but in May 1893 strong enough to take over mounted troops and mountain batteries. The river is here 10 feet deep, 180 yards wide. Myothit, 40 houses, at 8 miles, is on the right bank of the river, a little from it, and has a civil police station in the village. Chinese caravans camp here and the ground is rather dirty in consequence, but the ground available for camping on is very large. There are two or three shops here, in which are sold milk and a few other necessaries. With the exception of Kanni, which is a Chinese-Shan village, all the villages passed so far are Burmese-Shan. For these two first stages, *see* also Route No. 11, Northern Division, Stages 1 and 2, in which the distances are given at $13\frac{1}{2}$ and $10\frac{1}{2}$ miles respectively.
		3. Lower Karwun (or Karwan). Namsong Ka and Liya Ka.	7 6	26 6	General direction north. The road passes down the right bank of the Tapin and after $\frac{1}{4}$ mile turns to the north. It crosses two swamps $2\frac{1}{2}$ feet deep (muddy bottom), which are offshoots of the Namsong Ka. Up to here is through kaing grass. It then passes along paddy-fields and again crosses an offshoot of the Namsong Ka, and thence into Sihet at $2\frac{3}{4}$ miles. The road now goes north passing the small village of Thágôn; no supplies; 15 houses. From here it crosses the plain through alternate kaing grass and cultivation in a north-east direction. At 4 miles it crosses a small chaung, 10 yards broad, knee-deep; course from south-east to north-west; water good; rapid current; sand and gravel bottom, kaing grass banks. At $4\frac{1}{2}$ miles the village of Namyaw (three houses, mixed Shan-Burman and Kachin village; no supplies) is passed. It is about $\frac{1}{4}$ mile to the left of the road. The route now ascends a steep, tortuous, rough road to Lapáng at $5\frac{3}{4}$ miles (1,000 feet above Sihet). From here there is a path to Peto. The road now ascends gradually by several small ascents to Karwun $7\frac{3}{4}$ miles. From Namyaw to Lapáng the path is mostly through tree jungle, but beyond this it is through kaing grass. It is overgrown and not used

FROM BHAMO TO SIMA (FORT MORTON)—*continued.*

Authorities.		Number and Names of Stages, Rivers and Streams.	Distances.		Remarks.
Military.	Civil.		Inter-mediate.	Total.	
G.O.C. Mandalay District and O.C. Bhamo.	Commissioner, Northern Division, and Deputy Commissioner, Bhamo.	**3. Lower Karwun (or Karwan)**—*cont.*			all the way from Myothit, especially the latter part. There is a track to Pônlein from Lower Karwun. Good grass and bamboo for forage. Water good, but not very plentiful; no supplies. Height above sea 1,570 feet. For another description of this stage and of the next as far as Tálí Uma, *see* Route No. 11, Northern Division, Alternative V.
		4. Wédu Uma ... Tumpi, Nakut and two other small streams.	M. F. **12 6**	M. F. 39 4	From Lower Karwun the road ascends steeply for 200 feet to Upper Karwun. From here there is a road north-west to Tálí. The road descends to Tiya ¾ of a mile. From here the road is fair and up an easy ascent to Jawmaw (Tátlôn) village at 3 miles. There is good grass along this part of the route. Just before Jawmaw (Tátlôn) there is a good road to Tálí Kabar (big) and Numkaw. From here the road . very good and smooth, but steep up to Jawmaw (Tátlôn), passing through kaing grass and tree jungle. Just before Jawmaw (Tátlôn) there is a magnificent view to the north, and the Shwédaungyi range near Môgaung is distinctly visible. Beyond Jawmaw (Tátlôn), after descending to a spring, the road ascends steeply to Saré (4 miles), passing several taungyas on the left. The road is still excellent. It runs along the ridges till the village of Tálí (Uma) is reached at 6¼ miles. For another description of the remainder of this stage, *see* Route No. 7, Northern Division, Branch I. General direction north-east. From Tálí (Uma) the road descends into some taungyas and crosses a small stream 3 feet wide, muddy and bad crossing, but very easily bridged. From here the road ascends into Taláng (7¼ miles). Road much overgrown with grass. Branch road to Marawkatawng from Taláng. From here the road descends into some taungyas and then ascends into Lawpum (8½ miles). Road as before. From Lawpum road passes through taungyas and descends steeply to the Tumpi Ka, 4 yards broad, stony bottom, 1 foot deep; and ascends steeply to Wédu Lagatán along the right bank of the stream and high above it (10½ miles). Road now ascends steeply and over good smooth ground into Kukam (11¼ miles). From Kukam road descends steeply and crosses the Nakut Ka, 3 yards broad, 1 foot deep, muddy bottom, and passes along some paddy-fields. It then ascends steeply into the straggling village of Wédu (Uma) at 12¾ miles, crossing one other small stream. All this route is good and there is plenty of good fodder all along the route.
		5. Teingár ... Karong, Byup, Tálí, 10 yards wide, 2 to 3 feet deep, and one other small stream.	**8 4**	48 0	General direction is north. The road from Wédu (Uma) runs downhill very steeply and then turns a little to the right and runs round the Wédu hill; very thick tree jungle and a very steep khud on the left. After this it gradually descends to the Karong Ka, which is a small tributary of the Tálí Ka, and from here runs up to Machong-Katawng. Karán at 1½ miles, a small village which is subservient to Machong. Here the road is not good, being narrow and rough. From this village the road descends to the Byup Ka, 6 yards wide and 2 feet deep. From here the road runs uphill to Macháng, eight houses, at 2¼ miles; here the road turns west, from Wédu, it has been running nearly due

FROM BHAMO TO SIMA (FORT MORTON)—*continued.*

Authorities. Military.	Authorities. Civil.	Number and Names of Stages, Rivers and Streams.	Distances. Intermediate.	Distances. Total.	Remarks.
G.O.C. Mandalay District and O.C. Bhamo.	Commissioner, Northern Division, and Deputy Commissioner, Bhamo.	**5. Teingár**—*cont.*			north, and runs downhill through open country, but it is very steep and is zigzagged. The road drops down very suddenly to the Tálí Ka, which is a small mountain stream, at 4 miles. The stream is here 10 yards wide and 2 to 3 feet deep with a fairly strong stream; bottom sandy with a few large rocks. Above the crossing there is a Kachin bridge made of bamboos for foot-passengers: this being high above the stream, will probably last through the rains. From here the road goes up a very steep incline to the village of Kukam (5 miles); the road from Macháng is bad on account of the descent to the Tálí Ka. Nearing Kukam the road runs through thick tree jungle. The road now runs north-north-east along top of range and is fairly level, with a few easy ascents and descents to the village of Lana (7 miles). Here the water is scarce and has to be collected by a dam for animals. Camp in the village. Fodder plentiful; no supplies. From here road runs on to Laryáng (shortly after leaving Lana, there is a road to the east leading to Teingrám) and descending to a small stream the village is reached at 7½ miles. From here the road passes through taungyas and at the top enters some fine large tree forest. On nearing the village of Teingár the road gets rather stony. Good camp here (8¼ miles) for small force, but it is possible to encamp 300 men and transport if required. For another description of this stage *see* Route No. 7, Northern Division, Branch II, Stages 2 and 3.
		6. Ngetpyadaw ... Ula, Kalai, Lagun, Môlé, and three smaller streams.	M. 12 F. 2	M. 60 F. 2	From Teingár the road runs down a very steep hill in a north-westerly direction through thick jungle and then through taungya clearings. The road here is very good and keeps on descending till the Ula Ka, a small tributary of the Kalai Ka, is reached at 2 miles: this stream has a stony bottom and is 7 yards wide and about 1 foot deep. Crossing the stream the road runs along level ground through tree jungle up to a small village called Waloung: this has only two houses and probably are put here for cultivation, but they have been regularly inhabited of late. Passing the village there is a road to the west which leads to Laimôk and here the road is not so good being rather soft. The route now takes a north-north-easterly direction and arrives at a stream called the Kalai Ka at 3 miles. This is about 8 yards wide and 1 foot deep and would be much larger and presents a nasty obstacle during the rains: the bottom is muddy. From here the road is good and quite level, but rather low lying, and on account of the several streams in the vicinity would probably be rather wet during the rains. After crossing two small streams, tributaries of the Kalai Ka, the road runs through small teakwood jungle and then through some paddy-fields up to the Lagun Ka, at 5 miles, 4 yards wide and 6 inches deep. Then the road runs through this year's taungya clearings uphill and after about ½ mile the road gets into bamboo jungle and so on till the village of Unkaw is passed at 7 miles. This village is off the road about 200 yards to the east. From Unkaw the road descends over stony ground for ½ mile and then passes along the side of a hill along grass and bamboo jungle; gradually ascends at first, and then very steeply over stony ground and in zigzags through first kaing grass and then tree jungle into Pumpein at 3½ miles. One small nullah,

FROM BHAMO TO SIMA (FORT MORTON)—*continued.*

Authorities. Military.	Authorities. Civil.	Number and Names of Stages, Rivers and Streams.	Distances. Intermediate.	Distances. Total.	Remarks.
G.O.C. Mandalay District and O.C. Bhamo.	Commissioner, Northern Division, and Deputy Commissioner, Bhamo.	**6. Ngetpyadaw**—*cont.*			3 feet wide, is crossed. The road from Pumpeiu to the plain is very steep, but good. It varies from 6 feet to 15 feet broad, is very smooth and good, and descends in zigzags through tree jungle and taungyas to the plains below. From here it passes through alternate paddy-fields and kaing grass to Ngetpyadaw, a small village on the Môlé chaung at 12¼ miles. Good fodder and camping ground. A little paddy to be got here. For another description of the road between Unkaw and Ngetpyadaw *see* in Route No. 7, Stage 7.
		7. Kaichi camp ... Môlé, Pakha, and another small stream.	M. F. **8 0**	M. F. 68 2	From Ngetpyadaw the road runs down to the Môlé chaung: here as well as on the other side is excellent camping ground for a large force, abundance of fodder, and the Môlé chaung for water: best camping ground is on the right bank of river. The ford is good over the river at this time of year, though the bottom is stony; in other places the river is unfordable. There is a fishing dam quite close to the ford, river about 40 yards wide and average depth at crossing about 1¼ feet. River unfordable in floods, but boats come up here from Manmögh and Bhamo. The road now runs to the Shan-Talôk village of Nalôn at ½ mile through beautiful pasture land and on to Möngsain, Shan-Talôk at 1½ miles. The road now is running in a northerly direction till it meets the Manmögh and Namsángyáng route. From the river road is open and good. At 1¾ miles a road goes to the north-west to Ningtap. At 3¼ miles crosses a stream which has now three beds, each respectively 1 foot, 4 feet, and 8 feet broad and which is no obstacle. At 3½ miles is a shorter and smaller road to Kaichi. At 3½ miles cross the Pakha Ka, 18 feet wide, with stony bottom and which has an easy crossing. From here the road ascends steeply for about 2,000 feet to Khaiya, passing through old taungyas and bamboo and kaing grass jungle with small trees, till at the top it passes into some taungyas now under cultivation. Here it is joined by the road mentioned above, and after 200 yards reaches Khaiya. There is a branch road to Ningtáp from Khaiya. From here the road ascends and descends gently and finally passes through tree jungle into some taungyas which form a good camp. One stream is crossed close to camp. Water, wood, and bamboo plentiful. This road is very good, but rather steep, and there are occasional stony pieces in the ascent. Camp ½ a mile below Kaichi.
		8. Namsángyáng. Several small streams.	**7 4**	75 6	The road now ascends easily into Kaichi, crossing a small stream. It then passes the village of Pumnoikhet (1½ miles) and then descends, being very steep in parts and slippery on account of the red clay the path is cut in. Jungle trees on the plain. Two streams, 2½ feet deep, are crossed, the stream nearest Namsángyáng being the chaung of that name. Camp on some extensive paddy plains north-east of village. Namsángyáng at 7½ miles is a Chinese-Shan village and consists of six houses; supplies, paddy, and good fodder; water good from chaung. Would be very damp in rains, but in cold season excellent camping ground. Villagers are

FROM BHAMO TO SIMA (FORT MORTON)—*continued.*

Authorities. Military.	Authorities. Civil.	Number and Names of Stages, Rivers and Streams.	Distances. Intermediate.	Distances. Total.	Remarks.
G.O.C. Mandalay District and O.C. Bhamo.	Commissioner, Northern Division, and Deputy Commissioner, Bhamo.	**8. Namsángyáng** —*cont.*			unenterprizing and move very little among the Kachins. Time of march 3 hours for the north-eastern column from Kaichi camp to Namsángyáng.
		9. Ningrong-Majángkatawng. Four small streams.	M. 10 F. 6	M. 86 F. 4	From Namsángyáng camp the road runs in an easterly direction. After leaving the open paddy-fields it enters long grass and bamboo jungle, crossing two small streams about 1 mile from the village; then through tree jungle. As soon as the hill is reached up a spur of which the road runs, road is good, but the ascent is very long and tedious as far as the village of Nambáng ($3\frac{1}{4}$ miles). This is a fairly large village and has fowls, rice, paddy, &c. Camp could be made here if necessary. From here through thick tree jungle and undergrowth, ascending and descending, the village of Sara ($4\frac{3}{4}$ miles) is reached. Near this village the roads are good and well kept; small village and partly burnt, on the top of the ridge along which the road is running; dense undergrowth adjoins the track. Sara could be made a camp if necessary, but would be very small. Then the road still keeping along the ridge, though also going up and down, runs into the village of Ningpwot, which is on the top of a high hill at $5\frac{3}{4}$ miles. Before reaching the village, there is a level space of about 400 yards. Just outside Ningpwot there is a road to the left to Hpáneng. The road leaves this and ascends steeply for about 60 yards into some tree jungle, and is level for about 300 yards, when it begins to descend first through grass jungle, where it is rather overgrown, then through taungyas and finally through tree jungle again. There are one or two fairly steep descents, but not too great for transport. Road good throughout to Ningrong-Warúkatawng through which it passes at $7\frac{3}{4}$ miles. Just before reaching the village there is a road east to Kumsai. From here the road is very good, gradually descending the whole way through tree jungle with occasional small ascents along a spur. At 4 miles a road goes east to Wuláng village which is only a $\frac{1}{4}$ mile off. Two streams, one crossed just after leaving Ningrong-Warúkatawng, namely, a small one 3 feet broad and good water, and the Pási Ka 9 feet broad, stony bottom and good water; the latter having rather steep approaches, but no obstacle. The village of Ningrong-Majángkatawng is situated on a spur at $10\frac{3}{4}$ miles; most of the houses down on either side. Camp either in village or along the road above it, rather confined. Water scarce, from a small spring 200 feet below on east side; fodder plentiful. Wild plantains in neighbourhood and a very large number of fruit trees—plum and apple.
		10. Sima (Fort Morton). Mali Ka and three small streams.	15 4	102 0	From here the road runs in a north-westerly direction, at first uphill through tree jungle and then down through short jungle to $1\frac{1}{2}$ miles where a road to the left is passed leading to Kantaoyáng. Road here turns north and goes through thick grass jungle, matted overhead about 5 feet high. The road is very narrow and low, but otherwise good. Up to the cross-road to Kantaoyáng road is broad and very good. It now runs downhill a little at first and then along a spur which is level, going till

FROM BHAMO TO SIMA (FORT MORTON)—*continued.*

Authorities.		Number and Names of Stages, Rivers and Streams.	Distances.		Remarks.
Military.	Civil.		Intermediate.	Total.	
G.O.C. Mandalay District and O.C. Bhamo.	Commissioner, Northern Division, and Deputy Commissioner, Bhamo.	**10. Sima (Fort Morton)**—*cont.*			it runs to a small hillock about 1 mile from the last cross-road; here is tree jungle. Past the hill the road descends very steeply through thick grass jungle and is still very narrow, otherwise good. Another cross-road to Kantao-yáng is passed about 1 mile further on. Here the road turns to the east and drops down to the Mali Ka at 4¼ miles, after going through some soft ground near the river. Round here jungle becomes tree and thick undergrowth. The stream at crossing is 30 yards wide and 2 to 3 feet deep; the bottom is gravel and good, there being only a few rocks; current slow; bed of the river about 60 yards wide in full water and in floods must overflow the banks, the ground being level on either side. Crossing is very good, but would be unfordable; the current, too, would be very rapid. Direction of the stream is north-west. About 200 yards below the crossing is a bamboo foot-bridge. Here the river decreases in size, flowing between some large rocks: this crossing is known as Pumpi Rai. From here the road goes up a little and then down to a small stream and then rises, through grass jungle, but fairly open. At about 5 miles there is a branch road to Kukam, *see* Route No. 27 of this Appendix, Stage 4. The path ascending the Mali hill drops down again to a small stream and then up again to one of the villages of Mali (7¼ miles): this is now burnt. Jungle, thick trees. From Mali the road runs through bamboo jungle. It is fairly good here though rocky in parts, gradually going down to a small stream and then uphill through bamboo and small tree jungle. In parts the ascent is very steep and road bad. As Paláp (at 11¼ miles) is reached the road runs through thick jungle (tree). Here the road turns north and travels along the ridge to North Paláp (burnt) (11½ miles); from here it runs slightly downhill through thick tree jungle and along the ridge with small ascents and descents through taungya clearing and tree jungle till Sima is reached from the south at 15½ miles.

ALTERNATIVE I.

FROM BHAMO TO SIMA (FORT MORTON) *viâ* THEINLÔN AND MANMÖGH

BY CAPT. COUCHMAN, D.S.O., 1891-92, LIEUT. HUSSEY WALSH, 1890-91, AND LIEUT. DENT, 1892-93.

An alternative route to Sima from Bhamo runs as follows:—

Military	Civil	Stage	M.	F.	M.	F.
G.O.C. Mandalay District and O.C. Bhamo.	Commr., Northern Divn., and Deputy Commr., Bhamo.	**1. Mannaung** ...	**18**	**0**	18	0
		2. Pinthet ...	**8**	**0**	26	0
		3. Theinlôn ...	**14**	**4**	40	4
		4. Manmögh ...	**12**	**0**	52	4

This route joins that described above about 2 miles beyond Manmögh.* Thus the distance from Bhamo to Sima *viâ* Manmögh is nearly 97 miles. This is the best road, as up to Manmögh it runs along the plains, but they are hot and oppressive, and the Sima military column of 1893 returned by the hills in preference to marching in the heat of the plains. Manmögh can also be reached by large boats up the Môlé chaung. It takes six to seven days from Bhamo to Manmögh and 4 to 5 to return.

* It is not exactly stated in the route referred to where Manmögh is, but apparently it is near Ngetpyadaw, Stage 6. For description of this alternative route as far as Theinlôn *see* Route No. 6, Northern Division, Stages 1 to 3.—A. F.

No. 4.

From KANNI (see Route No. 19, Northern Division, Alternative IV, Stage 5) to TAUNGMI.

By D. W. RAE, Esq., Civil Officer, Sinkán Column, January 1893.

Authorities.		Number and Names of Stages, Rivers and Streams.	Distances.				Remarks.
Military.	Civil.		Intermediate.		Total.		
			M.	F.	M.	F.	
G.O.C. Mandalay District and C.C. Bhamo.	Commissioner, Northern Division, and Deputy Commissioner, Bhamo.	**1. Kwilán camp** ... Kwilán stream.	**12**	**0**	12	0	General direction west-south-west; road passes through deserted villages of Píswé and Maingnaung. About 3 miles from last-named place a path leading to Taungmi *viâ* Sônkaung branches to left of present route. The whole way, except 1½ miles before reaching camp, is through open grass plains. Camping ground on left bank of stream. Water-supply and fodder for animals ample.
		2. Maingheing ... Nama stream, Maingheing.	**7**	**0**	19	0	Direction west-south-west. Road for first 4 miles is through open country and dense jungle alternately and then enters the bed of the Nama stream and continues along it till camp is reached. About the 5th mile from last camp a bog some 500 yards long and blocked by dense cane brake and other thorny undergrowth has to be crossed, and it was owing to this portion of the road that the column took 7½ hours to do a distance of 7 miles only. Camping ground on deserted site of village and very close to water; grass scarce, and no bamboo leaves to be had within 4 miles.
		3. Maingtha camp. Naungmo, Kwe, Thaibyu, and Ngulin streams.	**7**	**0**	26	0	Left camp 8 A.M. and arrived at Maingtha stream camp at noon. Direction west-south-west. Road passes through fairly open forest country for about 5 miles, then ascends Letkataung (also deserted village of same name) and drops into the Ngulin stream just before it empties itself into the Maingtha stream. Water and fodder for animals abundant.
		4. Kawdaw ... Maingtha stream.	**9**	**0**	35	0	Left camp 7 A.M. and arrived at camp Kawdaw at 11 A.M. Direction west. Road at ½ mile crosses stream and passes through small Kachin village of two houses called Thé-Kégôn; thence along bed and banks of the same stream and at 3 miles passes Tônkyauk, Shan-Burman village of about 16 houses. After leaving Tônkyauk crosses and recrosses the same stream for about 2 miles and then goes along left bank till Kawdaw is reached. Supplies for both man and beast ample. The Maingtha stream enters the Shwéli river 2 or 3 miles above Ma-u-gôn, *see* in Stage 3 of Route No. 104, Northern Division.
		5. Taungmi ... Sôkkyin stream.	**6**	**0**	41	0	Left Kawdaw 3 A.M., and arrived at Taungmi at 7 A.M. Direction east-south-east. Road for first 2 miles through fairly open country, then enters Sôkkyin stream, continues along its bed for 2 miles, and then ascends to Taungmi. No water to be had on hill. About 2½ miles south-east of village a good camping ground with abundant water and fodder for animals is available.

From KATHA to MÔHNYIN viâ MAWLU and KAUNGRA.

By Lieut. E. F. COOKE HURLE, Somersetshire Light Infantry, December 1892

Authorities. Military.	Authorities. Civil.	Number and Names of Stages, Rivers and Streams.	Distances. Intermediate. M.	F.	Distances. Total. M.	F.	Remarks.
G.O.C. Mandalay District and O.C. Bhamo.	Commissioner, Northern Division, and Deputy Commissioner, Katha.	**1. Petsut** ... ... Chaungwa.	**10**	**0**	10	0	General direction north-west, a fair road for carts passing through thick forest and gradually rising to the pass. At 5½ miles the village of Langwa, nine houses; at 6 miles, Pinmalut, 16 houses; at 10 miles, Petsut, which is composed merely of cooly lines for the men constructing the railway and is situated at the head of the pass. The Chaungwa is crossed several times, crossings easy in the dry weather, but would be impassable for a short time after very heavy rains. A railway line is being constructed, which is likely to be open in a year's time. Time of march for column with mule transport 3½ hours.
		2. Pinwé ... ... Petsut chaung.	*11	0	21	0	General direction for 3½ miles west, remainder of stage north. A fair cart road now although boggy in places, it would be very deep in wet weather. At 3 miles the village of Kanni, nine houses; at 8 miles, Pintin, 10 houses; at 11 miles, Pinwé, four houses. The Petsut chaung is crossed in this stage, easy crossing, 18 inches deep. Time of march for column with mule transport 4 hours.
		3. Mawlu ... Mawlu chaung.	*11	0	32	0	General direction north, a cart road. Time of march for column with mule transport 4½ hours. At 3 miles Sônlôn (or Tônlôn) 47 houses and small kyaung; at 10 miles Nyaungbintha, 18 houses; at 10½ miles Simaw, eight houses; at 11 miles Mawlu, large village with kyaung houses. The Mawlu chaung is crossed by a strong bridge not wide enough for carts which can ford the stream, depth 2 feet, width 20 feet. A railway station is being built at Mawlu. There is a military police post also, strength 42 sepoys under a jemadar.
		4. Sáhmaw ... Nankyi and Laidán chaungs.	8	4	40	4	General direction for 3 miles north; for remainder of stage north-west. For 5 miles along the Môhnyin road a bad cart track; remainder of stage jungle path. At 1 mile Hénu village, 22 houses, small pôngyi kyaung; at 4 miles Manhé (or Mahai), 15 houses; at 5 miles Haungtôn, nine houses. The Nankyi chaung is crossed at Hénu; easy crossing, depth 2½ feet, breadth 20 yards. At Manhé the Laidán chaung is crossed, depth 2 feet, width 10 yards. Both chaungs impassable after heavy rains, but soon run down. One mile before reaching Manhé the road is very boggy and must be very deep in the rainy weather. † Time of march for column with mule transport 4½ hours.

*Previously recorded information has set these distances down at 9½ and 10 miles respectively, Route No. 26, Stages 2 and 3.—A. F.

† For another description of this route from Katha up to Manhé see Route No. 26, Stages 1 to 4.

FROM KATHA TO MÔHNYIN *viâ* MAWLU AND KAUNGRA—*continued.*

Authorities. Military.	Authorities. Civil.	Number and Names of Stages, Rivers and Streams.	Distances. Intermediate. M.	Distances. Intermediate. F.	Distances. Total. M.	Distances. Total. F.	Remarks.
G.O.C. Mandalay District and O.C. Bhamo.	Commissioner, Northern Division, and Deputy Commissioner, Katha.	**5. Kaungtônzi** ... Wábo and Nammi chaungs.	12	0	52	4	General direction north-west. A jungle path lately cleared through low undulating forest with steep nullahs to cross at frequent intervals. At 7 miles Nammakyaing, 20 houses; at 12 miles Kaungtônzi, 17 houses. The Wábo chaung is crossed at 5 miles, depth 2 feet, easy crossing; at Nammakyaing the Nammi chaung is reached and is crossed three times, depth 2 feet to 2½ feet, width 30 yards, current swift; impassable after rain, when it is crossed by means of rafts. Time of march for column with mule transport 5¼ hours.
		6. Tinba ... ... Nankhán chaung.	11	0	63	4	General direction for 8 miles north-west, 3 miles east, jungle path, steadily ascending to Latawng, 8 miles, seven houses, height 2,000 feet; from there path falls to Tinba, seven houses, height 1,630 feet with some very steep ascents and descents. The Nankhán chaung is crossed at ⅛ mile and 1⅛ miles, easy crossing.
		7. Kaungra ... Wara chaung.	13	0	76	4	General direction of route north. For the first 5 miles the path ascends until the top of the main ridge of hills is reached; height 3,140 feet, thence gradually descending to Wara chaung at 9½ miles through some very steep, rugged, and in places rocky ground; from Wara chaung path ascends to Kaungra, 13 miles, 14 houses, with several short steep ascents. A hard march. Time for column with mule transport 6 hours, if path has been thoroughly cleared beforehand. Actually time taken 8 hours.
		8. Kumsi ... ... Nammi chaung.	14	4	91	0	General direction of route south-east. A jungle path which descends to a boggy stream at 1 mile, thence ascends to high ground, when path is easy until Nammi chaung is reached at 5½ miles. Path then follows bed of stream, stony bottom for 1 mile, when by a steep ascent it rises to high ground and remains easy until it descends through kaing grass to a boggy stream at 11 miles, out of which there is an almost precipitous ascent for ½ mile; remainder of route easy Kumsi (10 houses) being reached at 14½ miles. A very hard march, but no other available halting place befor Kumsi is reached. Time of march for column with mul transport if road has been cleared 8 hours; actual tim taken 10 hours.
		9. Makaukli ... Laidán chaung.	9	4	100	4	General direction of route east. jungle path passing through taungy for ½ mile, thence descending by slippery descent through thick jung to a small stream at 1 mile, out which there is a very steep ascent to high ground. Pa then is easy for 1 mile, when it descends to small stre with very steep banks reached at 2½ miles; from ther ascends to Natmauk, 15 houses, at 3 miles. Leavi Natmauk path descends to Laidán chaung at 4¾ mi easy banks, stony bottom, thence ascends 500 feet

FROM KATHA TO MÔHNYIN *viâ* MAWLU AND KAUNGRA—*continued.*

Authorities. Military.	Authorities. Civil.	Number and Names of Stages, Rivers and Streams.	Distances. Intermediate.	Distances. Total.	Remarks.
G.O.C. Mandalay District and O.C. Bhamo.	Commissioner, Northern Division, and Deputy Commissioner, Katha.	**9. Makaukli**—*cont.*			immediately descends to small stream. At 7 miles easy crossing, from which it steadily ascends for 1,800 feet to Makaukli, seven houses, at 9¼ miles. A hard march; time for column with mule transport 8½ hours. A halt may be made at Natmauk if necessary. Jungle path must be cleared beforehand.
		10. Môhnyin ... Nampallauk, Nampauk, and Namyin chaungs.	M. F. 13 4	M. F. 114 0	General direction of route east. Leaving Makaukli path commences to descend at once through thick jungle to Káhtu, four houses, at 3 miles; then continues to descend for 2 miles through thick bamboo jungle to the foot of the hills, when it passes through teak forest and kaing grass until the clearing for the proposed railway line is reached at 6¼ miles, when the railway clearing is followed till Môhnyin is reached at 13½ miles. A large Shan Burman village (109 houses) with military police post, strength 100 men under a subadar. At 7 miles Nampallauk chaung is crossed, boggy approaches. At 11¼ miles Nampauk chaung is reached; depth 1 foot, boggy approaches. At Môhnyin is the Namyin chaung, which passes through the centre of the village, stony bottom, depth 2 feet, fordable in dry weather, is bridged by strong wooden bridge capable of bearing carts. Time of march for column with mule transport 5¼ hours. A halt might be made at Káhtu if proceeding from Môhnyin to the hills.

No. 6.

From KAUNGTÔN CHAUNG (HLWÉMAO) to LÔNTÔN.

COMMISSIONER'S OFFICE, MANDALAY, 1893.

Military	Civil	Stage	Intermediate	Total	Remarks
G.O.C. Mandalay District.	Commissioner, Northern Division, and Deputy Commissioner, Katha.	**1. Lôntôn** ... At 7 miles Nam Yankán. Flows from Khatôk hill into small bay southwest of Indaw lake.	9 0	9 0	Half-a-mile from camp, at base of Hlwémao or Noimaw hill (on road Namsai-Hlwémao) along bed of Kaungtôn chaung; then 5¼ miles through fairly level tree jungle coming out in view of Indaw lake. Hence road joins that from Lépôn near a muddy well and follows the shore through tree jungle and kaing to Lôntôn.
		2. Hlwémao ... Kaungtôn. Rises in Hlwémao and spreading disappears south of Indaw.	8 0	17 0	General direction east by south. Start from Madáng through hilly forest passing two stockades and old taungya and reaching Mansi or Namsai, lesser village (five houses) in 2nd mile. In 3rd mile pass Kasi chaung; then up steep hill reaching Namsai at the 5th mile (eight

FROM KAUNGTÔN CHAUNG (HLWÉMAO) TO LÔNTÔN—*continued.*

Authorities. Military.	Authorities. Civil.	Number and Names of Stages, Rivers and Streams.	Distances. Inter-mediate.	Distances. Total.	Remarks.
G.O.C. Mandalay District.	Commr., Northern Divn., and Deputy Commr., Katha.	**2. Hlwémao**—*cont.*			houses). Change here for Nampu. After crossing two small streams (nearly dry) reach good camp with fodder and water at Kaungtôn chaung (8 miles), at foot of Hlwémao hills; hence 1 mile rising ground to Lasakat chaung. Water plentiful. Hence 3 miles very steep; climb to Hlwémao (15 houses), passing site of burnt village half-way whence good view of Indaw and country north and east. The journey up (3 hours without transport) and back can be done from the Kaungtôn camp. *Note.*—This route is printed including title, exactly as received from the Burma Intelligence Branch Office, but is very hard to understand. It seems two routes—A. F.

No. 7.

From KÁZU to PALONG viâ MANLIN.

BY H. F. HERTZ, ESQ., POLITICAL OFFICER, NORTH-EASTERN COLUMN, DECEMBER 1892 AND JANUARY 1893.

Military	Civil	Stages	Inter. M.	Inter. F.	Total M.	Total F.	Remarks
G.O.C. Mandalay District.	Commissioner, Northern Division, and Deputy Commissioner, Bhamo.	**1. Manlin** ...	5	6	5	6	*See* Route No. 100, Northern Division, Stage 3.
		2. Kantaoyáng ... Mali Ka, Shillop Ka, and several small streams.	12	6	18	4	General direction of route is south-south-west. Level road through long kaing grass and bamboo and tree jungle and one shallow stream about 5 yards broad to cross. At 2½ miles Bainbin. Road leads across the Mali Ka, which is about 75 yards broad and fordable at this place during the present time of year (2½ feet to 3 feet deep at ford; crossing does not go straight across river; a guide is necessary to show the way); then through plantain gardens and long grass jungle, leaving some paddy-fields on the right; then it passes through thick bamboo jungle interspersed with small trees. Five small streams are crossed between the Mali Ka and where the road commences to rise at 4¼ miles, still through bamboo and tree jungle till Kumka is reached at 4¾ miles. Except for the first ½ mile, which is boggy, the road at this time of year is good and slightly undulating. It continues along the ridge, crossing three small streams before Kázu (2) is reached at 7¾ miles. This is a small village of five houses. Half-a-mile further on Ninglaw is reached, which is an insignificant and small village. Road then descends gradually for about 1 mile and ascends again for the rest of the way to Khama; about 1 mile from Khama there is a branch road to the left leading to Shila (Sadan); Khama at 11¼ miles is a fairly large village of about 25 houses. From here the road descends steeply, crossing two unimportant streams and then just before reaching Kantaoyáng (12¾ miles) the Shillop Ka is crossed; this is a tributary of the Mali Ka and about 2 yards broad with a muddy bottom. Camped here for the night.
		3. Palong ... Several small streams.	16	2	34	6	Level road for 1st mile, then gradual ascent for the second. Very dense jungle, chiefly bamboo; several boggy streams to cross and very difficult for mule

FROM KÁZU TO PALONG *viâ* MANLIN—*continued.*

Authorities. Military.	Civil.	Number and Names of Stages, Rivers and Streams.	Distances. Inter-mediate.	Total.	Remarks.
G.O.C. Mandalay District.	Commissioner, Northern Division, and Deputy Commissioner, Bhamo.	**3. Palong**—*cont.*			transport; thence to Shinglumkong at 2 miles. From here road descends slightly and crosses the Shillop Ka, ascending to Shillop village at 4 miles, four houses. From here road good through thick tree jungle; ascent gradual to first group of Ningpwon houses and then level to the main village of Ningpwon at 5 miles where the chief of the tribe lives. Road along the ridge of the hill, very thick jungle on either side, and has appearance of seldom being used. Crossing several small streams the road reaches Tumpéng at 10 miles; then ascends through open jungle and old cultivation for the 1st mile and afterwards through a thick tree and bamboo jungle, crossing several little streams. The road is good, but owing to the thick-matted jungle, which has overgrown, there was considerable delay, as the transport found difficulty in advancing, and riding is impossible. The dung of wild elephants was frequently seen; at 14 miles Punkrong; about ½ a mile before reaching which village the road ascends steeply. From there to Tingsa the road is broad and open. It descends gradually for a short distance and then descends again to level ground on which Tingsa is situated at 15½ miles. Thence to Palong at 16½ miles road is good, broad, and fairly level. Distance—pacing.

No. 8.

From KÁZU to SIMA (FORT MORTON).

BY LIEUT. W. H. DENT, YORKSHIRE REGIMENT, DECEMBER 1892.

Military	Civil	Stages	Inter. M.	F.	Total M.	F.	Remarks
G.O.C. Mandalay District.	Commissioner, Northern Division, and Deputy Commissioner, Bhamo.	**1. 'Nkráng** ... Several small streams.	**11**	**2**	11	2	General direction south-east. Road through thick jungle. Five small streams of no consequence; about 6 inches deep and 1 to 2 yards wide. Probably all flow into Nantabet chaung and would be rather bigger in wet weather. Over the first are two logs of wood placed for a foot-bridge. Road is level up to turning off for Tálawgyi about 3 miles from start, then rises up to Maikôn fairly steep. Maikôn at 5 miles is a small Wadu Kachin village. Leaving Maikôn on turning back you get an excellent view of the country. Road now fairly level; jungle kaing grass. After going up and down about a mile road runs down big hill with tree jungle on either sides. Road goes across a small stream about 4 yards wide and a few inches deep, and then goes uphill to Kásu(2) 9½ miles. Latawng Kachins. Road then goes downhill to Halyea Ka. Small camping ground, but good water; untenable for many men and jungle will have to be cut down each year. Road goes up a steep hill to 'Nkráng at 11¼ miles, Latawng Kachins. Good road, but very steep. Some big houses would make a strong post if necessary. Road goes downhill; fairly open near road; very good for transport. Good camp here for 2,000 men; good water.
		2. Sima (Fort Morton). Several small streams.	**10**	**2**	21	4	Branch of road crossed Kadaung Ka just at foot of camp, then uphill through jungle, and then downhill to Kadaung Ka about ½ mile, then uphill for

FROM KÁZU TO SIMA (FORT MORTON)—*continued.*

Authorities.		Number and Names of Stages, Rivers and Streams.	Distances.		Remarks.
Military.	Civil.		Inter-mediate.	Total.	
G.O.C. Mandalay District.	Commissioner, Northern Division, and Deputy Commissioner, Bhamo.	**2. Sima (Fort Morton)**—*cont.*			about 2 miles to second stream. Road and jungle very thick and very steep though fairly good for transport. Samja at 7¼ miles is a good camping ground, holding about 2,000 men. Village burnt this year. Road goes steep uphill to Sima through thick jungle and is good. Sima post (or Fort Morton) at 10¼ miles being now made. Plenty of water. Road from Kázu, though only comparatively short, is towards Sima rather hard going on account of the height of the hills.

No. 9.

From KÁZU to TABÔN.

BY LIEUT. W. H. DENT, YORKSHIRE REGIMENT, DECEMBER 1892.

Military	Civil	Stages	Intermediate	Total	Remarks
G.O.C. Mandalay District.	Commissioner, Northern Division, and Deputy Commissioner, Bhamo.	**1. Tabôn** ... ... Wasik Ka and five small streams.	M. F. **4 2**	M. F. 4 2	General direction west-south-west. Road runs through thick jungle for about 500 yards up to a small, swampy stream, then for another 400 yards to a stream called the Wasik Ka about 12 yards wide and about 2½ feet deep. Road runs on level ground to Tabôn and is at present very bad going; streams are small and of little consequence except that when wet would be boggy. The village of Tabôn, which is half Kachin and half Shan-Talôk, has 13 houses in it. Road would be good, if properly opened, and troops could camp anywhere if necessary.

No. 10.

From KÁZU to TÁLAWGYI viâ KUNTÔN.

BY LIEUT. W. H. DENT, INTELLIGENCE OFFICER, NORTH-EASTERN COLUMN, MARCH 1893.

Military	Civil	Stages	Intermediate	Total	Remarks
G.O.C. Mandalay District.	Commissioner, Northern Division, and Deputy Commissioner, Bhamo.	**1. Nawku (Nawbu).** Nam Mali and three small streams.	**6 0**	6 0	To Mali Ka general direction is south-west. The road leaves Kázu from the north-west end of it and crosses a stream which runs in a deep nullah; this would be impassable if not crossed over by a bridge during the rains. The road then runs through open tree jungle and plantain jungle, is 3 yards broad and very good up to the village of Kuntôn at 2½ miles. Before the village is reached two small streams are crossed of no importance as rivers, but would be impassable in rains on account of the very thick and adhesive mud. Here the road makes a sharp turn and runs in a southerly direction through tree jungle which becomes denser and thicker than before till an open maidan of thatching grass is reached (this in the rains would be swampy), then through paddy cultivation to the village of Nawku which is situated on the left ¼ of a mile from the road; here the other route from Tálawgyi comes in, *see* Route No. 100, Northern Division. In this paddy-field the grass is very plentiful and excellent fodder for animals. Nawku (or Nawbu) is Shan Talôk (about 12 houses), and near this village on the paddy ground is an excellent camp for a large body of men.

FROM KÁZU TO TÁLAWGYI *viâ* KUNTÔN—*continued*.

Authorities. Military.	Authorities. Civil.	Number and Names of Stages, Rivers and Streams.	Distances. Inter-mediate. M. F.	Distances. Total. M. F.	Remarks.
G.O.C. Mandalay District.	Commissioner, Northern Division, and Deputy Commissioner, Bhamo.	**2. Tungut** ...	**7 4**	13 4	Crossing the Nam Mali, 35 yards broad, is a bamboo bridge made in December for the column when it crossed before; is still in very good condition; is 1½ yards wide with bamboo bottom covered over with earth; will probably be destroyed in the floods. On the left bank of the Nam Mali is good camping ground immediately adjoining the river, but only a small one; could, however, be increased by clearing jungle. Thence to Tálawgyi, *see* Route No. 100, Northern Division, Stages 1 and 2.
		3. Tálawgyi ...	**11 0**	24 4	Distance by pacing. Road very good for mules except at the nullahs; there are several of these between Kuntôn and Nawku and are very muddy.

No. 11.

From LÉPÔN to TAGWAN CHAUNG.

BY W. H. C. MINNS, ESQ., SUB-DIVISIONAL OFFICER, MÔGAUNG, 1893.

Authorities. Military.	Authorities. Civil.	Number and Names of Stages, Rivers and Streams.	Distances. Inter-mediate. M. F.	Distances. Total. M. F.	Remarks.
G.O.C. Mandalay District.	Commissioner, Northern Division, and Deputy Commissioner, Bhamo.	**1. Kánsun** ... Lépôn chaung.	**7 0**	7 0	General direction south-east. Start over *kaing* plain passing Lépôn. Ywathit on the right. Muddy in parts. At 1 mile cross Lépôn chaung at foot of hills; hence steady ascent, steep in parts and roads almost impassable, liable to be rendered slippery by showers. Steps had to be cut for mules when traversed. An alternative but steeper road to Wapaw forks to the left. Kánsun, four houses; no paddy procurable; very little water. This is the Lépôn-Taungni road, but the first stage should be Wapaw, the next Lashu.
		2. Tagwan chaung. Kasi and Kadôn and Tagwan chaungs.	**9 0**	16 0	Along high ridge passing stockade in 1st mile. Good road west. Gradual ascent to Wapaw, five houses, at 2 miles. After 3rd mile steep descent down Loi Ein hill begins with good view of Taungni plain. In 5th mile pass site of Old Wapaw and at 6th mile cross Kasi chaung close to its junction with Kadwan chaung, whose bed (slippery boulders; water plentiful) is followed down stream at intervals over ½ mile. The Lépôn-Taungni road splits off here, ascending the right bank; 20 yards further on route also leaves the stream on the same side; a small tributary falls in just before the Taungni road separates. The road from this point to the camp is about 1 mile. It passes through Lébôk and old taungyas. The camp is just below the junction of the Kadôn with the Tagwan chaung and situate in a clump of fine teak. Water is plentiful.

No. 12

From LÔNTÔN (INDAWGYI) to KHATÔK and MATÁNG.

By W. H. C. MINNS, Esq., Sub-Divisional Officer, Môgaung, April 1893.

Authorities. Military.	Authorities. Civil.	Number and Names of Stages, Rivers and Streams.	Distances. Intermediate. M.	Distances. Intermediate. F.	Distances. Total. M.	Distances. Total. F.	Remarks.
G.O.C. Mandalay District.	Commissioner, Northern Division, and Deputy Commissioner, Bhamo.	**1. Camp on Namtônmet chaung.** Several streams.	9	0	9	0	General direction north-west, along the Mansain road, *see* Route No. 36, Northern Division. Two miles through paddy and low kaing northwards between the lake and the low hills west of Lôntôn; then bending inland over two small chaungs to the Hépán range. Deep mud in the bed of one chaung. Pass Hépán, Shan-Burman village, close on the right at 2 miles. Next 5 miles gradual ascent through low bamboo jungle. Some cutting necessary, but track well defined. The old Môgaung-Môhnyin boundary and seven streamlets crossed. Last 2 miles fairly level; not so thick. Camp good; little water in chaung; 5 hours' march.
		2. Camp on Namsáng chaung.	12	0	21	0	General direction south-west. Ten minutes' march over kaing plateau, then across the Monpôk hills, passing sites of deserted villages at 2 miles, where the road re-enters plateau, and, inclining southwards, makes across very boggy kaing between prominent Ngwédaungyi peak at the north extremity of the Lwélun range and the small Paklákatawng which is surmounted by a ruined pagoda. The road skirts and then crosses the two rows of hills which diverge southwards from Ngwédaungyi, coming out through level tree jungle at the 8th mile. A bald row of low hills called the Ngwékaungkyein range is then ascended and followed. A good view is obtained of Taungthônlôn, south-west, and towards the Uru in the far distance of Nansinku mountain, north, and Nwékánkyet mountain north by east; also of the course of the Namsáng chaung, which can be traced through the tree jungle which stretches west and south-west. The road is not shaded, but bar a little bamboo jungle, and the marshy bit is good travelling throughout. The Namsáng chaung, which runs through at the base of the Ngwékaungkyein hills is here a fine broad stream; pebbly bottom; 1 foot deep. Good camp on site of former village of Kwékông, often confounded with Mansöng which is higher up stream. The Mansain road split off at the 5th mile near Lwélun chaung: 5 hours' march.
		3. Camp on Namsaungtaung chaung. Namsáng chaung.	11	0	32	0	General direction south-west. Two miles through tree jungle to Namput chaung, now nearly dry; crossing near site of a former Shan-Burmese village of that name. In the 4th mile the Mattain and Pinlébu road spilts off west. Shortly afterwards cross Namhwé chaung, also nearly dry. Road good so far. From here onward considerable cutting needed. At 5 miles, and again at 6 miles, meet the Namsáng (broad stream; between high banks; bottom of pebbles and boulders; 1 to 2 feet in depth; swarms with fish) and follow it to this camp in bamboo jungle east of river, which is crossed three times; the first time in the 7th mile. The proper camp is at the junction of the Namsaungtaung, a western tributary of the Namsáng which falls in just above. Road hilly, but shady. March took 6½ hours.

FROM LÔNTÔN (INDAWGYI) TO KHATÔK AND MATÁNG—*continued.*

Authorities. Military.	Authorities. Civil.	Number and Names of Stages, Rivers and Streams.	Distances. Intermediate.		Distances. Total.		Remarks.
			M.	F.	M.	F.	
G.O.C. Mandalay District.	Commissioner, Northern Division, and Deputy Commissioner, Bhamo.	**4. Camp on Eila chaung; 7 miles from mouth.** Namsáng and Eila chaungs.	**10**	**0**	42	0	Three and-a-half miles to the mouth of Eila chaung, crossing a small salt stream, the Pông (Shan) or Chi I (Kachin) chaung, then up the bed of the Eila of which the stream fills, but half. It is shallow and runs over pebbles and boulders. Road shady throughout and level, but needs considerable clearing. Five and-a-half hours' march.
		5. Khatôk	**4**	**0**	46	0	Steep climb up central peak of the Khatôk hills. Water is scarce in the village itself, but passing through one of the two hamlets on the north-east slope, a good camp is reached just beyond an old village site and near the Kasáng chaung; 1 mile from main village; 2½ hours' march. Steep descent from Khatôk hill, then at 3rd mile up the Matáng hill from which a good view of hills both sides, and Indaw lake.
		6. Matáng ... Kasáng.	**8**	**0**	54	0	On descending, the village (? of Matáng) (12 houses) is reached, and a camp 10 minutes' march further by a small streamlet. No grass; water scanty. Road through bamboo jungle; shady, but steep in parts, and needs much cutting.

No. 13.

From MÁTIN to MANWEIN (MANWAING).

BY E. H. PARKER, ESQ., OFFICIATING CHINESE ADVISER IN BURMA, 1892.

Authorities		Stages	Intermediate M.	F.	Total M.	F.	Remarks
Doubtful.		**1. Pengsi or Pônsi.** Chéhai stream.	**9**	**0**	9	0	Mátin (*see* Route No. 10, Northern Division) contains 60 houses, Kachin. In former days, 100 years ago, 300 Chinese are said to have lived there, who have since merged into Kachin manners and customs.* General direction from Mátin to Pônsi east, route mountainous. Pass village of Chéhai at 1¼ miles.
		2. Maichuk ...	**15**	**0**	24	0	Direction east; route mountainous. Maichuk contains 50 or 60 houses, Kachin.
		3. Látha (Lása).	**21**	**0**	45	0	Direction east; route as before through a district subject to the jurisdiction of the Mátin Sawbwa. Látha has a population of 5,000 to 6,000, one-third of whom are Chinese. The town is surrounded by a mud wall, now in ruins. It is ruled by a Shan Sawbwa, who has complete authority except over Chinese subjects in capital cases. A five-day bazaar is held 3 miles outside Látha at a place called Láthakai where supplies are procurable in good quantities.

* The Mátin Circle contains 12 villages, amongst them the following:—1. Chéhai (60 houses) 2. Hulung (100 houses), 3. Mantao (40), 4. Méngsung (30), 5. Loilung, 6. Linying (20), 7. Léhmaipáng

FROM MÂTIN TO MANWEIN (MANWAING)—*continued.*

Authorities. Military.	Authorities. Civil.	Number and Names of Stages, Rivers and Streams.	Distances. Intermediate. M.	F.	Distances. Total. M.	F.	Remarks.
Doubtful.		**4. Manwein (Manwaing).**	**27**	**0**	72	0	General direction north-west. Road rises into the hills, then drops again to Manwaing, which lies low, situated in a valley. At 18 miles a village is passed.

No. 14.

From MÔGAUNG to LÔNTÔN (INDAWGYI).

BY SUB-DIVISIONAL OFFICER, MÔGAUNG, APRIL 1893.

Authorities. Military.	Authorities. Civil.	Number and Names of Stages, Rivers and Streams.	Intermediate. M.	F.	Total. M.	F.	Remarks.
G.O.C. Mandalay District.	Commissioner, Northern Division, and Deputy Commissioner, Bhamo.	**1. Taungni** ... Nanyin, Nampaung, Sadwin, and Nampadaung chaungs.	**17**	**0**	17	0	For other descriptions of what appears to be practically the same route as this, *see* Route No. 65, Northern Division. Direction south-west. Good cart road starting from Môgaung along Nanyin 1 mile. It then bends slightly south leaving Ywathit 200 yards off on the right, passes Kyaingyi-Zédi and Taungpaw, some way off on the left and meets the Nanyin at Lwélaw (3 miles) crossing by a ford, knee-deep, 300 yards above the village. Sadwin chaung is near the site of old salt works at 11½ miles. At 14 miles reach Nampadaung chaung, here there is good camping ground; just beyond it a path crosses leading right and left to the Kachin and Shan-Burmese (300 yards) villages of Nampadaung respectively. Road is through kaing grass and excellent throughout; streams offer no difficulty.
		2. Camp on Namsankyen or Sanken chaung. Ngôglé, Namtinkauk, and Namsankyen chaungs.	**8**	**0**	25	0	Half mile by path across paddy, then, rejoining cart track, through tree jungle to Lébyin, a Shan-Burmese hamlet of Taungni, left of the road 2 miles out. Left of the road are the Lébyin paddy-fields and on the right those of Waranaung, who lives in the western range, while the Taungrong Sawbwa, on the eastern, is under him. Road is through kaing grass on the level throughout, and is marshy in parts, but neither this nor the chaungs give any trouble. Tinkauk chaung at 6 miles is stagnant, but the Ngôlé chaung at 4 miles and the Namsankyen at 8 miles offer excellent camps.
		3. Camp on Hkwésankán chaung. Namkwán chaung.	**12**	**0**	37	0	Road still through kaing-grass plain, good throughout. Excellent camps on both streams. Telegraph crosses about half-way and then runs parallel ½ mile north. Just beyond this camp Môhnyin cart road parts to the left from the Indaw track.
		4. Camp on hill stream near source of Nam Sakwan. Sakwan chaung.	**9**	**0**	46	0	Mule track makes towards western hills and crossing wire 1 mile from camp skirts tree jungle. It crosses the Namsakwan 3 miles out, and passing over small wooded hills meets it again at 5 miles, following up the stream bed ½ mile. At 7 miles it again meets

FROM MÔGAUNG TO LÔNTÔN (INDAWGYI)—*continued.*

Authorities. Military.	Authorities. Civil.	Number and Names of Stages, Rivers and Streams.	Distances. Inter-mediate. M.	Distances. Inter-mediate. F.	Distances. Total. M.	Distances. Total. F.	Remarks.
G.O.C. Mandalay District.	Commissioner, Northern Division, and Deputy Commissioner, Bhamo.	**4. Camp on hill stream near source of Nam Sakwan**—*cont.*					and follows the same stream emerging on the right bank as before, whereas the road to Lépôn, east of the lake, goes further up stream here and emerging on the left bank crosses over the pass to the Sankai chaung near Lépôn. Two miles through thick hill jungle to camp. The track is difficult to follow owing to diverging paths made by elephants.
		5. Namun chaung. Kyusanlaik chaung.	**10**	**0**	56	0	Two miles hilly road through tree jungle mainly teak, then a steep ascent and descent over the Kyusanlaik taung to the Kyusanlaik chaung. The jungle is thick and the road bad up and down the steep, stony beds of dry mountain torrents. Last 3 miles fairly level through forest. Namun Kachin village, ½ mile from camp, deserted. This march took 5 hours.
		6. Lôntôn ... Three hill streams.	**12**	**0**	68	0	Road crosses Namun chaung, then through kaing skirting north side of a small range which (running east-south-east to west-north-west) branches from the high Wapaw range crossed in Stages 4 and 5, which divides the Taungni and Indaw plains. The track goes up the beds of the first two streams which contain but little water, the third is larger and provides an excellent camp. A few marshy bits, but on from here the road skirts through tree jungle round the south of lake Indaw and is excellent throughout. At 4 miles first view of lake. Several small streams are crossed and one is followed ¼ mile; on the 6th mile the road follows along the bank of one and comes down to the water's edge. A very little rain would make a swamp of the whole land south of Indaw through which to-day's march passes.

No. 15.

From MÔHNYIN to NAMLAW (for Môgaung) viâ LAIKHÉ HILLS.

BY LIEUT. E. F. COOKE HURLE, SOMERSETSHIRE LIGHT INFANTRY, JANUARY 1893.

Military	Civil	Stage	Inter. M.	Inter. F.	Total M.	Total F.	Remarks
G.O.C. Mandalay District.	Commissioner, Northern Division, and Deputy Commissioner, Katha.	**1. Sailing** ... ... Shama chaung.	**9**	**4**	9	4	General direction of route for 4½ miles east, remainder east-south-east. Road on leaving Môhnyin proceeds through teak forest and is a good, level cart road. At 1¾ miles a small stream is crossed. At 2⅓ miles route leaves main road, which proceeds in a north-east direction to the village of Mainaung, distant 4½ miles, and thence to Hôpin, Nyaungbintha and Môgaung, *see* Route No. 67, Northern Division. A jungle path is then followed, which is good and level, crossing Shama chaung three times between 4½ and 5 miles; easy banks; strong, stony bottom; depth 1½ feet, width 12 feet; it then commences to ascend the hills and at 6 miles proceeds through old, disused taungya, a path branching to Mainaung at 6½ miles and at 7½ miles to

FROM MÔHNYIN TO NAMLAW (FOR MÔGAUNG) *viâ* LAIKHÉ HILLS—*continued.*

Authorities. Military.	Authorities. Civil.	Number and Names of Stages, Rivers and Streams.	Distances. Intermediate. M.	F.	Distances. Total. M.	F.	Remarks.
G.O.C. Mandalay District.	Commr., Northern Divn., and Deputy Commr., Katha.	**1. Sailing**—*cont.*					Taman, distant about 6 miles, in a south-easterly direction. Path still continues to ascend until Sailing (1) is reached at 8¾ miles, when it descends to a small stream and then rises to Sailing (2) reached at 9½ miles; large village; 24 houses. Time of march for column with mule transport 4 hours.
G.O.C. Mandalay District and O.C. Bhamo.	Commissioner, Northern Division, and Deputy Commissioner, Bhamo.	**2. Peinsain** ...	**12**	**4**	22	0	General direction north-north-east. On leaving Sailing path passes through tree jungle and descends for ¾ mile to a small stream from which it ascends to the main ridge, along which it passes, gradually descending; at 3½ miles there is a branch path to Shiyáng (2), distant ¼ mile, and a small stream is passed just before Tamaw (eight houses) is reached at 3¾ miles. Path now ascends, passing along a very narrow ridge and Khuttu (three houses) is reached at 5 miles, whence it continues to ascend till at 6 miles it passes over a peak and descends to 7 miles. It now again ascends, passing a second peak at 7½ miles and then descends to Maw (six houses) at 8½ miles. From Maw route is fairly level to 10 miles, when it descends for ½ mile and again rises till 4 miles is reached, when it passes along a very narrow ridge to 4¾ miles and then descends to Peinsain (14 houses) at 12½ miles. Good jungle road throughout. Time of march for column with mule transport, 5 hours.
		3. Kumba	**5**	**4**	27	4	Path ascends a steep hill for ½ mile through tree jungle to top of main ridge along which it continues very easy to Katpra (13 houses) reached at 3 miles, where there is very good camping ground; it then gradually ascends till at 5 miles a peak is passed over and a gradual descent is made to Kumba (20 houses) at 5½ miles.
		4. Kángong ... Áhsôn and Námtun chaungs.	**9**	**4**	37	0	General direction of route east. Half mile after leaving Kumba the Kángong road branches off in an easterly direction (the Lachinpum road continuing straight on, *see* Branch I below), passing through taungya for ½ mile and making a steep descent till 1½ miles is reached, when there is a slight ascent through tree jungle for ½ mile and then a steep descent to Áhsôn chaung, reached at 2⅛ miles; 10 feet wide, 1 foot deep; stony bottom; flowing in a southerly direction, eventually joining the Námtun chaung. Path then rises through tree jungle to Lámai (11 houses) at 3¼ miles, where there is a branch road to Makyain 3½ miles due east. On leaving Lámai route ascends for 1 mile and then follows the side of the hill till at 5 miles there is steep descent to Námtun chaung, reached at 6½ miles; easy approaches; stony bottom; depth 2 feet; width 20 feet; impássable in the rains; flowing south and eventually joining Kaukkwé chaung. Path now ascends till at 7½ miles it passes over a narrow ridge and descends to Kángong (seven houses) at 9½ miles, leaving 'Ngakyet (four houses) on the left hand at 8 miles, the descent from which is very steep. Time of march for column with mule transport, 5 hours.

FROM MÔHNYIN TO NAMLAW (FOR MÔGAUNG) *viâ* LAIKHÉ HILLS—*continued.*

Authorities. Military.	Authorities. Civil.	Number and Names of Stages, Rivers and Streams.	Distances. Intermediate.	Distances. Total.	Remarks.
G.O.C. Mandalay District and O.C. Bhamo.	Commissioner, Northern Division, and Deputy Commissioner, Bhamo.	**5. Lepai** ... ... Pansán, Punkaw, and Namyin chaungs.	M. F. **13 0**	M. F. 50 0	General direction of route for 9 miles east-north-east; remainder north. Path descends for ¾ mile through small tree jungle to small stream with easy crossing, where there is a branch path running north-north-east to Pángwa, distant about 4 miles. Route now ascends a large spur, which it tops at 1½ miles and gradually descends to Kaukkwé valley at 2¾ miles; it then becomes level and crosses a small stream at 3¼ miles and the Pansán chaung; depth 1 foot, width 10 yards; stony bottom; swift current; impassable in rains at 3½ miles. Path continues level and passes through tree jungle, crossing small streams at 4½, 6, and 7 miles, and when 7½ miles is reached Punkaw chaung is crossed; depth 1 foot, width 15 feet; current swift. At 8¾ miles there is a branch path to Lwémaw, 3 miles west among low hills. Path continuing at foot of hills and crossing Namyin chaung at 10¾ miles; depth 1½ feet, width 25 yards; stony bottom; level banks which overflow in the rains, rendering it impassable; flowing in a west direction to Kaukkwé chaung. From there path remains level and good, passing through kaing grass and small tree jungle and crossing a small stream at 11½ miles, whence it ascends to Lepai, reached at 13 miles; good camping ground. Time of march for column with mule transport, 6 hours.
		6. Pumkin ... Nampáng chaung.	**13 0**	63 0	General direction of route north. On leaving Lepai, path descends for ½ mile to valley, when it remains level to 1¾ miles, crossing small streams at ¾ and 1½ miles. It then rises over small hill and descends to small stream, reached at 2¼ miles. Thence it passes along the side of a low hill and descends to valley at 2½ miles, when two small streams are crossed before 3 miles is reached, and from 3¼ to 3¾ miles, another small stream is crossed three times, path continuing level, passing through tree jungle and kaing grass. Route remains level till at 5¼ miles small spur is crossed and a fall made to valley at 6¼ miles, and at 7 miles small streams are crossed, when path makes a slight ascent, keeping along the side of a small hill, and descends to valley again at 7½ miles crossing a small stream. It now is level till at 8 miles it crosses a stream and passing between two small hills descends to Nampáng chaung at 9 miles, which it crosses five times before 10 miles is reached; depth 1 foot, breadth 15 yards; rocky bottom; swift current, impassable in rains. There is a branch path to Tingrám at 9¼ miles distant about 4 miles in north-eastern direction. After crossing Nampáng chaung the fifth time path makes a steep ascent to Tunbaugong, reached at 11 miles, when it continues along a spur, slightly descending to Pumkin at 13 miles. Path good throughout route; jungle dense. Time of march for column with mule transport, 6 hours 20 minutes.
		7. Namlaw ... Pumkin chaung.	**7 4**	44 0	General direction of route north-east. On leaving Pumkin route descends through small tree jungle for ¾ mile to Pumkin chaung by a zigzag path, the stream being 1 foot deep, 10 yards wide; with steep banks and

FROM MÔHNYIN TO NAMLAW (FOR MÔGAUNG) *viâ* LAIKHÉ HILLS—*continued.*

Authorities. Military.	Authorities. Civil.	Number and Names of Stages, Rivers and Streams.	Distances. Intermediate.	Distances. Total.	Remarks.
G.O.C. Mandalay District and O.C. Bhamo.	Commissioner, Northern Division, and Deputy Commissioner, Bhamo.	**7. Namlaw**—*cont.*			impassable in the rains. From there path commences to ascend, being very steep for ¼ mile, and passing through thick bamboo jungle; it is then fairly level till 1½ miles is reached when a steady ascent on a spur is made to Wesaw village which is reached at 4¼ miles, the jungle being very thick throughout. Path now makes a steep ascent to a peak ¼ mile above the village, when it descends to 5¼ miles and then again ascends through kaing grass till the top of the main ridge is passed at 6¾ miles. Route is now level for ¼ mile and then makes an easy descent to Namlaw, reached at 7¼ miles. There is a branch path to Kalangai, distant 2 miles north-east at 7 miles. Saumong village lies 1¼ miles north-north-east and Lámai village 1½ miles south-south-east of Namlaw. A rise of 2,500 feet is made in this stage. Time of march for column with mule transport, 5 hours.

BRANCH I.

FROM KUMBA TO LÔNKÁT.

BY LIEUT. E. F. COOKE HURLE, SOMERSETSHIRE LIGHT INFANTRY, JANUARY 1893.

Military	Civil	Stages	Intermediate M. F.	Total M. F.	Remarks
G.O.C. Mandalay District and O.C. Bhamo.	Commissioner, Northern Division, and Deputy Commissioner, Bhamo.	**1. Lachinpom** ...	**4 0**	4 0	From Kumba the road commences to descend, passing through taungya, and at 1 mile there is a very steep descent for ½ mile. Path now becomes rough and rocky, keeping on the side of the hill with steep descents and short, steep ascents till at 4 miles Lachinpom is reached (17 houses). The 1st mile of this stage is very good, but remainder is difficult.
		2. Lônkát ... ... Mawpát, Teinlôm, and Teinkum chaungs.	**7 0**	11 0	General direction for 2½ miles north-west, remainder north-east. Path passes through tree jungle and ascends for ¼ mile when it gradually descends to Welup (six houses) at 2½ miles, passing through taungya ½ mile before reaching the village. Route now descends, and is very steep and difficult for transport until Pawlaw (three houses) is reached at 3½ miles, passing through taungya just before entering the village. Path then continues to descend gradually through *kaing* grass till Mawpát chaung is reached. At 4¾ miles a small hill stream, when it remains level till 6 miles, is reached, passing through teak forest and *kaing* grass. At 5 miles Teinlôm chaung is reached; stony bottom; depth 6 inches to 1 foot; current swift; approaches easy and path follows bed of stream for ¼ mile after crossing it three times. Teinkum chaung is crossed at 5½ miles, a small stream, and from 6 miles path gradually ascends to Lônkát (12 houses) at 7 miles. Time of march for column with mule transport, 3 hours.

No. 16.

From MYITKYINA to SANA.

BY CAPT. H. R. DAVIES, OXFORDSHIRE LIGHT INFANTRY, FROM NATIVE INFORMATION, SEPTEMBER 1893.

First Road (Eastern) viâ Lapé.

Myitkyina to Mansen	Six hours.
Mansen to Naunglán	
Naunglán to Chakat	

FROM MYITKYINA TO SANA—*continued.*

First Road (Eastern) viâ Lapé—cont.

Chakat to Mawmiyé ...	Six hours.
Mawmiyé to Wátugyi ...	
Wátugyi to Lapé ...	
Lapé to Sadônkáng ...	One day.
Sadônkáng to Penin Ka ...	Six hours.
Penin Ka to Kaori ...	
Kaori to Saraw ...	One day.
Saraw to Karán ...	
Karán to Maiktum ...	Six miles.
Karán to Wakásaku ...	
Karán to Hônakong ...	

Second Road (Western) viâ Pánláng.

Myitkyina to Naora ...	One very long day.
Naora to Tônta Ka ...	
Tonta Ka to Peli Ka ...	One day.
Peli Ka to Pônrông ...	
Pônrông to Senneinwa ...	One day (short).
Senneinwa to Pánláng ...	Six hours.
Pánláng to Kaya ...	Four miles.
Kaya to Katu ...	
Katu to Laken ...	
Laken to Katampon ...	One long day.
Katampon to Karán ...	Six hours.
Pônrông to Chimu ...	Six hours.
Chimu to Saraw ...	Four miles.
Saraw to Pônrang ...	Five miles.
Pônrang to Katun ...	Six hours.

The first road (Eastern *viâ* Lapé) is very good till it enters the hills in the neighbourhood of Sadôn Káng.

The second road (Western *viâ* Pánláng) is difficult owing to swamps, but is much less hilly than the first road.

At the end of December the second road has still a lot of water on it, especially near the Naora lake, but it becomes passable for animals by December.

No. 16-A.

From NAMKHAI (see Route No. 29 of this Appendix, Alternative I) to PÁNGHTÁN viâ HSAULÁM.

BY LIEUT. H. R. DAVIES, OXFORDSHIRE LIGHT INFANTRY, MARCH 1892.

Authorities. Military.	Authorities. Civil.	Number and Names of Stages, Rivers and Streams.	Distances. Intermediate. M. F.	Distances. Total. M. F.	Remarks.
G.O.C. Mandalay District and O.C. Bhamo.	Commissioner, Northern Division, and Deputy Commissioner, Bhamo.	**1. Pankaw** ... Nammak, and Mawsi chaung.	**8 6**	8 6	General direction south-south-west. Fair mule road. Steep downhill to the Nammak at $1\frac{1}{2}$ miles (from the right, 7 yards by $1\frac{1}{2}$ feet; banks rather steep and muddy at ford, but passable for mules), thence uphill. At $2\frac{1}{4}$ miles a road to the left to Manna and Nálôn. At $2\frac{3}{4}$ miles a road to the right to Kaihtik. At $3\frac{1}{4}$ miles a road to the right to Saupôn, thence along top of a ridge to Mansám at 5 miles; 52 houses; 'Ssi tribe. At $6\frac{1}{2}$ miles

No. 16-A.

FROM NAMKHAI (*see* ROUTE No. 29 OF THIS APPENDIX, ALTERNATIVE I) TO PÁNGHTÁN *viâ* HSAULÁM—*continued.*

Authorities. Military.	Authorities. Civil.	Number and Names of Stages, Rivers and Streams.	Distances. Intermediate.	Distances. Total.	Remarks.
G.O.C. Mandalay District and O.C. Bhamo.	Commissioner, Northern Division, and Deputy Commissioner, Bhamo.	**1. Pankaw**—*cont.*			road to the right to Mowun, a mile off the road, thence downhill to Manlep at 8 miles, 10 houses; Páhtum-Phunkán. At 8½ miles cross the Mawsi chaung (from the right, 8 yards by 6 inches; easy ford), thence uphill to Pankaw; 29 houses; Páhtum-Phunkán. Water from Mawsi chaung.
			M. F.	M. F.	
		2. Loiyai .. Mawsi, Simma, Nachin, Nampán, and Walai chaungs.	**10 2**	19 6	General direction south-south-east. Fair mule road, but steep in places. Along the Namkha road to the Mawsi chaung at ¾ mile (from the left at ¾ mile and from the right at 2¼ miles; 10 yards by 1 foot), thence turn to the right along a spur for ½ a mile, then steep down for ¼ mile, hence along paddy-fields and cross the Mawsi chaung again at 2¼ miles. From here roads to the left to Nahong and to the right to Saga Tingsa, thence uphill for ¾ of a mile, from here a road to the right to Wara and Saga Tingsa, thence downhill to the Simma chaung (from the right, 5 yards by 6 inches) at 3 miles, thence very steep uphill to Mawsi at 4¼ miles; 50 houses; 'Szi tribe. This is on the Namkham-Sikaw road. At 5 miles cross the Nachin chaung (from the right, 3 yards by 6 inches), hence steep uphill for 2½ miles up the Loi Chow range, thence steep downhill to the Nampán chaung (from the right, 2 feet by 4 inches), at 8¾ miles. At 9¼ miles cross the Walai chaung (from the right, 2 feet by 3 inches), thence uphill to Loiyai; 30 houses; Lahtaw tribe.
		3. Hsaulám ... Tinbôk and Nammen chaungs.	**6 0**	25 0	General direction south-south-west. Good mule road. Very steep downhill to the Tinbôk chaung (from the right, 7 yards by 1 foot) at 1½ miles, thence uphill to the deserted Kachin village of Saga Tinbôk, hence along top of ridge to Palaung village of Tinbôk or Manphai; 15 houses. From here a road to the left to Namkham downhill to the Nammen chaung (from the right, 7 yards by 1 foot) at 3½ miles, thence uphill to Pakmôn or Nawpu; six Lena-Kachin houses; three Palaung houses. From here a road to the right to Loipháng. At 5 and 5¼ miles roads to the left to Loikyep. At 5¾ miles a road to the left to Mantát (Palaung). Hsaulám is a Palaung village of 12 houses and kyaung. Camping ground 200 by 150 yards above village. Water from small stream.
		4. Loipháng ... Tinbôk chaung.	**8 2**	33 2	General direction north-west. Good mule road. Uphill at first for 2 miles. At 1½ miles a road to the right to Pakmôn. At 4 miles cross the Tinbôk chaung (from the left, 4 yards by 6 inches), thence uphill, but not very steep, over the Loichaw range. The top is reached at 5 miles, thence steep descent for 1¾ miles. At 7¼ miles village of Tinkrong; 11 houses; Lahtaw tribe, under Loipháng; thence an easy road to Loipháng; seven Lahtaw-Kachin houses; eight Palaung houses. This is on the Namkham-Sikaw road. Room to camp in the village. Water from a small stream, the Sinya chaung, close to the village, and from the Namkhat (7 yards by 8 inches), ¾ mile along the Sikaw road.

FROM NAMKHAI (*see* ROUTE NO. 29 OF THIS APPENDIX, ALTERNATIVE I) TO PÁNGHTÁN *viâ* HSAULÁM—*continued.*

Authorities. Military.	Authorities. Civil.	Number and Names of Stages, Rivers and Streams.	Distances. Intermediate.	Distances. Total.	Remarks.
G.O.C. Mandalay District and O.C. Bhamo.	Commissioner, Northern Division, and Deputy Commissioner, Bhamo.	**5. Pánghtán** ... Namkhat, Kyálim chaung; from the left, 4 yards by 6 inches.	M. F. **7 2**	M. F. 40 4	General direction west. Good mule road along a ridge. At ¾ mile cross the Namkhat and immediately afterwards the Kyálim chaung. At 2 miles Pángkyem; 30 houses; Páhtum-Phunkán. At 2½ miles a road to the left to Makauk and Loi Sáng, said to be passable for bullocks only as far as Makauk. At 3½ miles Tinkhon or Tônhôn; nine houses; Phunkán. At 5¾ miles Sama; 10 houses; Phunkán. At 6½ miles Krimmu; six houses; Phunkán. At 7 miles Pánglôn; six houses; Phunkán. Pánghtán, which is on the Tuku-Möngkák road (*see* Route No. 28 of this Appendix, Stage 2), contains 15 houses; Phunkán tribe. Water from small stream; rather scarce.

BRANCH I.

FROM PANKAW (STAGE 1) TO KHASHÁNG.

BY LIEUT. H. R. DAVIES, OXFORDSHIRE LIGHT INFANTRY, FEBRUARY 1892.

Military	Civil	Stages	Intermediate	Total	Remarks
G.O.C. Mandalay District and O.C. Bhamo.	Commissioner, Northern Division, and Deputy Commissioner, Bhamo.	**1. Khasháng** ... Khapra and Inkhrut chaungs.	**4 6**	4 6	General direction west. Fair mule road downhill to the Khapra chaung (from the right, 6 yards by 8 inches) at ½ mile. At 1 mile a road to the left to Mankáng, 600 or 700 yards off the road; 10 houses; Páhtum-Phunkán; under Pankaw. At 1½ miles village of Saikhao; three houses; Páhtum-Phunkán; under Pankaw. At 2 miles cross the Inkhrut chaung (from the right, 4 yards by 6 inches); here there is a bullock camp 100 yards square. Thence uphill for a mile. At 3½ miles a road to the left to Lakhumkatawng. At 4 miles a road to the right to Sittan, Warrapum, and Mansôk. Thence downhill to Khasháng; 31 houses; Páhtum-Phunkán tribe. Small stream; near village; Khahtat chaung (4 yards by 6 inches) ½ mile north.

BRANCH II.

FROM PANKAW (STAGE 1) TO WARA.

BY LIEUT. H. R. DAVIES, OXFORDSHIRE LIGHT INFANTRY, MARCH 1892.

Military	Civil	Stages	Intermediate	Total	Remarks
G.O.C. Mandalay District and O.C. Bhamo.	Commissioner, Northern Division, and Deputy Commissioner. Bhamo.	**1. Wara** ... Khapra and Inkhrut chaungs, and four small streams (from the right, each 2 feet by 3 inches).	**3 0**	3 0	General direction south. Good mule road. At ¼ mile a road to the right to Saikhao. At ½ mile cross the Khapra chaung (from the right, 12 yards by 1 foot). Just beyond this a road to the right to Pumkatawng. At 1 mile cross the Inkhrut chaung (from the right, 4 yards by 8 inches), thence a steady ascent to Saga Tingsa at 2¼ miles, 30 houses, Lakhum tribe; thence across a taungya crossing four small streams to Wara; 15 houses; Phunkán tribe. From Wara there is a road which joins the main road (*see* in Stage 2 above) 1¾ miles from Wara.

No. 17.

From PALÁP (Route No. 3 of this Appendix, Stage 10) to SIMA (FORT MORTON) viâ MAITONG and PONTU.

BY LIEUT. W. H. DENT, INTELLIGENCE OFFICER, NORTH-EASTERN COLUMN, FEBRUARY 1893.

Authorities.		Number and Names of Stages, Rivers and Streams.	Distances.				Remarks.
Military.	Civil.		Intermediate.		Total.		
			M.	F.	M.	F.	
G.O.C. Mandalay District and O.C. Bhamo.	Commissioner, Northern Division, and Deputy Commissioner, Bhamo.	**1. Maitong** ... Paknoi Ka, 'Npu Ka, Kaona Ka, and several small streams.	9	6	9	6	*Note.*—This and No. 27 of this Appendix are routes running more or less in a circle round Sima visiting the Kachin villages in the vicinity. General direction east-north-east. The road to Waraw leaves the main China route about half-way between the two villages of Paláp taking at first an easterly direction. It passes through thick tree jungle and is rather a steep descent to the Paknoi Ka, on nearing which the land in the vicinity of the road is terraced for paddy cultivation. One small stream is crossed before the Paknoi is reached. At the crossing the river is 20 yards broad and $2\frac{1}{2}$ feet at deepest. The bottom is rocky and stream swift. Would be impassable on foot during the monsoons. The river flows in a northerly direction, and is very clear and good for drinking. Country on its banks fertile and paddy sown yearly. From Paláp side the river is difficult to cross under fire, because hill ascends directly from river and is covered with thick jungle, which would give excellent cover to enemy. From the stream to Waraw the road ascends through thick tree jungle which commences at the river. Road from Paláp is good, and the crossing at present safe for mules. Ours crossed satisfactorily, with very few loads getting wet, but during monsoons road would be bad on account of ascent and descent and crossing impassable. One small stream is crossed shortly after the Paknoi Ka. Waraw at $3\frac{3}{4}$ miles is a straggling village (Kumlao-Sedán); 21 houses, 3,850 feet altitude. Camping ground here fair. It is large enough for 1,000 men, but large numbers of piquets necessary. Water good. Large number of fowls, pigs, &c., but only saw one basket paddy, all inhabitants having fled. We left Paláp at 10-30 A.M. and arrived Waraw 12-30 P.M. From here the road still takes an easterly direction to the village of Shirawkong. Good road and broad. Passes at first through thick tree jungle and then through old taungya clearings, ascending till the top of the hill is reached from which a good view is obtained. It then proceeds downhill to the village through jungle, crossing a small stream, which flows into the Namlu Ka, a tributary of Kaona Ka. This stream is about 6 yards wide, and has a large quantity of water for small stream. Supplies wants of village. By clearing jungle a good camping ground could be got on top of hill over which road passes. It would be, however, about $\frac{1}{2}$ a mile from water. Shirawkong at $6\frac{1}{4}$ miles (40 houses, 4,200 feet altitude) is a fine village on slope of hill, facing east. At present paddy scarce, but village has a wealthy appearance—one of the most important of Kamlao-Sedán tribe. Fair camping ground in village; small; good water, but commanded by high ground to rear (*i.e.*, west). From Shirawkong road leads down spur of hill and through last year's taungya clearings and till 'Npu, or Nampu Ka, a tributary of Kaona, is reached at $7\frac{1}{4}$ miles. This stream flows in a north-easterly direction. The ground on either bank is terraced for paddy cultivation and would afford a splendid camping ground for any number of troops. Water very clear and good. The stream is 12 yards wide, about 1 foot to 6 inches deep; bottom rocky and pebbly. The road now proceeds to take a north-easterly

FROM PALÁP (ROUTE NO. 3 OF THIS APPENDIX, STAGE 10) TO SIMA (FORT MORTON) *viâ* MAITONG AND PONTU—*continued.*

Authorities. Military.	Authorities. Civil.	Number and Names of Stages, Rivers and Streams.	Distances. Intermediate. M.	F.	Distances. Total. M.	F.	Remarks.
G.O.C. Mandalay District and O.C. Bhamo.	Commissioner, Northern Division, and Deputy Commissioner, Bhamo.	**1. Maitong**—*cont.*					direction till the Kaona Ka is reached at 8⅛ miles. On either side of road terraced paddy-fields. Looks very rich soil. Land all round fairly open and very little jungle. The river at crossing is 30 yards wide, and from 2⅓ to 3 feet deep. The bottom is rocky and banks are steep. The high water mark is 6 feet above present level. Trees on both banks. Just below the crossing which offers no difficulties river gets into rapid water. About 300 yards away from the right bank is rising ground which commands the crossing. Water good, but no fish in river. From here to Maitong the road ascends, but has open ground round it, till nearing the village, when the jungle becomes very thick and trees large. Maitong at 9¾ miles (13 houses, Kamlao-Sedán) is commanded by rising ground on north and east side. Camping ground bad in village. Best camping ground would be near the Kaona Ka. Village looks poor. Houses in bad condition. Village very much scattered and hidden away in valley. Cannot be seen on approach. Bad place to hold and to attack unless thoroughly well flanked to north and east. Left Shirawkong at 8 A.M. and arrived at 10-15 A.M., mules following closely.
		2. Pontu ... ... Small streams, tributaries of Kaona Ka.	4	0	13	6	General direction north-north-west. The road to Pontu is very good, and for the m t part runs along level ground on the valley of the Kaona Ka. At first downhill through clearings. Saw violets and wild lime trees; then down to Kaona Ka, where it joins road to Upra to Pontu (*see* Route No. 29, Northern Division, Branch IV). Distance by pacing.
		3. Sima (Fort Morton). Paknoi Ka and two small streams.	6	4	20	2	General direction west-south-west. Road passes through thick tree jungle and jungly undergrowth the 1st mile, and then goes downhill through old taungya clearings; it is very steep indeed, goi g straight down to Paknoi Ka and winding about a great deal; two small streams are crossed, one of which is crossed by a large tree fallen over it; before this the road passes through bamboo and reedy jungle, and then opens out on to level, terraced paddy-fields at 3½ miles where the Paknoi Ka is crossed, now 15 yards broad and very deep, owing to there being large rocks through which river flows. Unfordable. Bamboo bridge is thrown over it; not safe for more than six men; better to be crossed singly. Mules cannot cross by it and only broad enough for one man at a time. Water is very clear and good and stream very rapid, having been joined by the Kaona Ka waterfalls about 400 yards up stream. Mules can cross about 200 yards up stream. At present this crossing is about 30 yards wide and the mules passed over with their loads on them. During the rains river would be impassable. High water mark 7 feet higher than present height; in floods would be 45 yards wide. Height at crossing 1,900 feet. From here road goes uphill to village of Sima, at first through last year's taungya clearings; the ascent is very steep, too much so for tired

FROM PALÁP (ROUTE NO. 3 OF THIS APPENDIX, STAGE 10) TO SIMA (FORT MORTON) *viâ* MAITONG AND PONTU—*continued.*

Authorities. Military.	Authorities. Civil.	Number and Names of Stages, Rivers and Streams.	Distances. Intermediate.	Distances. Total.	Remarks.
G.O.C. Mandalay District and O.C. Bhamo.	Commissioner, Northern Division, and Deputy Commissioner, Bhamo.	**3. Sima (Fort Morton)**—*cont.*			mules, though fresh ones can do the march all right. For about 2 miles before the village is reached the road passes through thick tree jungle. Road very good throughout and broad. Started at 8-10 A.M., reached Paknoi Ka in one hour, took one hour to cross it, and did not arrive camp till 12 noon. Baggage and mules not getting in till 2 P.M. Distance estimated by pacing. Sima is a Kumlao Sedán village, partially burnt; about 15 houses remaining in February 1893.

BRANCH I.

FROM MAITONG (STAGE 1) TO PUMPRI PUM.

BY LIEUT. W. H. DENT, INTELLIGENCE OFFICER, NORTH-EASTERN COLUMN, FEBRUARY 1893.

Military.	Civil.	Stages.	Intermediate.	Total.	Remarks.
G.O.C. Mandalay District and O.C. Bhamo.	Commissioner, Northern Division, and Deputy Commissioner, Bhamo.	**Pumpri Pum** ... Small streams.	M. 2 F. 4	M. 2 F. 4	The road runs through thick tree jungle which surrounds the village of Maitong. Several small streams are crossed which supply water for the village. The road is very steep and is only a village track to taungya clearings. After about 1 mile the road clears the jungle and comes into taungya clearings and passes near a little poppy cultivation. After this it passes through grass and reedy jungle, and is here impassable for mules till the Pumpri Pum is reached, which is a large rock of conical shape, and the side facing west drops perpendicularly into a valley 1,000 feet below. Distance pacing.

No. 18.

From PALONG to NKÁNGKONG.

BY H. F. HERTZ, ESQ., CIVIL OFFICER, NORTH-EASTERN COLUMN, 2ND TO 4TH JANUARY 1893.

Military.	Civil.	Stages.	Intermediate.	Total.	Remarks.
G.O.C. Mandalay District and O.C. Bhamo.	Commissioner, Northern Division, and Deputy Commissioner, Bhamo.	**1. Kacháng (Yibu).** Two small streams.	14 0	14 0	General direction north. A very good road, fairly level from Palong to Namien at 1 mile, which is left on the right about ½ mile off the route. It then proceeds steeply through dense bamboo tree jungle. This part of the road is very bad, and has not apparently been used for some time, being quite overgrown with jungle, which in some places had to be cut away for our mule transport. Two small streams are crossed at 6 miles, which have good water; the crossings are easy and shallow. After this the jungle is thinner and consists of small trees; a good camping ground can be made here, if necessary, using the water from the streams for drinking water. After this the jungle gets more dense and the road gradually ascends and the jungle gets thick and matted. At 10 miles a road branches off to the left to Lama about 1 mile away. After this the road descends slightly about 200 or 300 feet till Kacháng or Yibu is reached at 14 miles.

FROM PALONG TO NKÁNGKONG—*continued.*

Authorities. Military.	Authorities. Civil.	Number and Names of Stages, Rivers and Streams.	Distances. Intermediate. M. F.	Distances. Total. M. F.	Remarks.
G.O.C. Mandalay District and O.C. Bhamo.	Commissioner, Northern Division, and Deputy Commissioner, Bhamo.	**2. Nkángkong** ... One small stream and the Lamoi Ka.	**15 0**	29 0	From Kacháng the road is good and broad along the Namcháng range up to Namcháng village at 2½ miles. This is the chief village of the Appao Chingma tribe of Kachins (Sawbwa La Kong). The road then goes in an easterly direction for about 1½ miles till Wâmya is reached at 4 miles; there is another village to the right about ½ mile off with same name. Then after descending slightly Shiyang is reached at about 7 miles. The road then descends very steeply to a large stream, 3 feet deep and 12 yards broad, called the Lamoi Ka, at 9 miles. The crossing for mules is very difficult, the banks being muddy and slippery. The road then ascends through taungya and small tree jungle to Nkángkong, a small dilapidated village at 15 miles and seemingly very poor.

No. 19.

From SADÔN to CHINNA PA VILLAGES.

BY LIEUT. W. H. DENT, YORKSHIRE REGIMENT, INTELLIGENCE OFFICER, NORTH-EASTERN COLUMN, NATIVE INFORMATION, MARCH 1893.

Authorities.	Number and Names of Stages, Rivers and Streams.	Intermediate.	Total.	Remarks.
China.	**1. Shinghôp (Chinese).** Small streams.	...	...	General direction south-east. This route runs for the first part of the way along the Sánsi route *viâ* Saga, Namliku, and Shinghôp and still following the same road till the Sánsi gorge is reached; here it takes a slightly more easterly course and, leaving the Sánsi road on the right, runs downhill. On the right hand is the Shángpé Ka, a tributary of the Takhaw; a little further on the road crosses a small stream which flows into the Shángpé Ka. This stream rises in Saba Pum, while the Shángpé Ka rises near the Sánsi gorge. After crossing the stream Shángpé Pum is reached; this is of lower altitude than Santipan. From here the road runs down to Limaukao; the inhabitants of this village are Szis, and there are about 32 houses in it. Limaukao is situated on the plains. From here the road runs along to what is known as the Chinna Pa group of villages, the inhabitants of which are Shan-Talôk. The following are their names:—Luchu, Tingka, Pasán (this is the largest village in the group), Mônbauk, Mankán, and Mankhai. These villages have about 30 houses in each and are situated quite close to each other. There is near here a Chinese village called Kaushin-chai consisting of 30 houses.
	2. Chinna Pa group (Shan-Talôk).	...	...	The Chinna Pa villages are on the plain; to the east of these villages there is a hill called Makai Pum on the far side of which flows the Tákaw. This river is about 4 or 5 miles from the Chinna Pa villages. The first stage of this march from Sadôn is Shinghôp, and the second Chinna Pa villages. This is rather a long two days' march.

No. 20.

From SADÔN to MÖNGTIEN.

By Lieut. W. H. DENT, Yorkshire Regiment, Intelligence Officer, North-Eastern Column, Native information, March 1893.

Authorities.		Number and Names of Stages, Rivers and Streams.	Distances.		Remarks.
Military.	Civil.		Inter-mediate.	Total.	
			M. F.	M. F.	
China.		**1. Shinghôp (Chinese).** Pángpé Ka. **2. Möngka (Chinese).**	... ...	... ...	General direction south-south-east. Following the same route as from Sadôn to Sánsi through Saga, Namliku, Shinghôp, over the Sánsi gorge as far as Möngka. Here the road turns to the south and runs somewhere near the right bank of the Möngka. After some distance the road crosses a small stream called Pángpé Ka, flowing into the Möngka, which eventually joins the Tabôk Ka, a tributary of the Nántabet chaung. This route does not pass through the village of Pángpé, but the villages situated some little distance to the east of it.
		3. Möngtien (Chinese).	...	...	Still running south-south-east the road passes through the village of Seden. Tho inhabitants of Seden are Yawyins, and there are about 80 houses in it. Pángpé has about 50 houses, and the inhabitants are also Yawyins. From Seden the road leads on to Möngtien, which is situated in the hills. Seden and Pángpé are both in the plains. From Seden to Möngtien the road runs over small hills through tree jungle and a large quantity of poppy cultivation. Möngtien is a Chinese village of about 400 or 500 houses. From Sadôn to Möngtien is three days' easy marching. There is a road from Pángpé to Sansi.

No. 21.

From SADÔN to SÁNTA viâ SÁNSI.

By Lieut. W. H. DENT, Yorkshire Regiment, Intelligence Officer, North-Eastern Column, Native information, March 1893.

Military	Stages	Intermediate	Total	Remarks
China.	**1. Shinghôp (Chinese).**	...	...	General direction south-east. This route runs from the fort downhill to Saga, which is a small Shan-Talôk village, then on to Namliku, the inhabitants of which are Szis, and from there on to Shinghôp. This village is situated well within the boundary, but the inhabitants are Chinese. From Sadôn this is the first stage, one day's march. After passing the village the Shinghôp Ka is crossed. This is a tributary of the Namli Ka and is spanned by a bamboo bridge, which is strong enough to carry mules, but which will probably not last through the rains. After crossing this stream the road runs uphill near a hill called Santifán.*

* This hill is to the left of the road, while the road runs through a dip known as Sánsi gorge, also called Möngka kiet or Kanlaw kiet.

FROM SADÔN TO SÁNTA *viâ* SÁNSI—*continued.*

Authorities. Military.	Authorities. Civil.	Number and Names of Stages, Rivers and Streams.	Distances. Intermediate.	Distances. Total.	Remarks.
			M. F.	M. F.	
China.		**2. Möngka villages.** Shinghôp Ka.	...	...	From Santifán the road takes a more southerly direction till the Möngka villages are reached. I was told that Möngka was the collective name for the following villages, which are all close together, namely, Lantaw, Yáng-kia-shia, Yáng-nia-pum, in all about 100 houses with Chinese as inhabitants. From Shinghôp to Möngka is the second day's march; this is a short march.
		3. Sánsi ... ... Tákaw or Táho Ka.	...	...	The road now runs up and down hill till the Chinese gate called Law-kwan-shen is reached. This is probably what is marked on the map as Shenhui-kwan; if so, it is placed incorrectly. This gate is made out of the natural rock which joins overhead. From here the road runs downhill to Punkaw, which is about 6 or 7 miles away from Möngka. Punkaw is inhabited by Szis, who are an offshoot of the Kachins; this village consists of 30 houses. From here the road drops down to the Tákaw or Táho Ka. This river here is about as wide as the Namli Ka at the suspension bridge, *i.e.*, about 60 yards wide. There is no bridge over the river, but it is crossed by rafts. In the fine weather, however, the stream is not too rapid to swim. Sánsi is situated on the left bank on this river; it is a Chinese town of about 2,000 houses and is not fortified.* The Táho or Tákaw is a tributary of the Tapin. To the east of Sánsi, about 4 miles distant, are some hills called Seichi-Shán. I was told that silver is found in these hills. This is a long three days' march. There is a road from here that runs on to Mômien, which takes two more days.
		4. Lamien ... Tákaw or Táho Ka.	...	...	General direction south-south-west. Sánsi and Sánta are both on the same river, namely, the Tákaw or Táho Ka, a tributary of the Tapin river. It takes two days to march from Sánsi to Sánta. The road runs through the Chinese villages of Santantia, Lamien, and Taukaw.
		5. Sánta ... ... Tákaw or Táho Ka.	...	...	Opposite Sánta is the Chinese village of Khangnai on the other side of the river.

No. 22.

From SIMA (FORT MORTON) to MÖNGTIEN.

BY LIEUT. W. H. DENT, YORKSHIRE REGIMENT, INTELLIGENCE OFFICER, NORTH-EASTERN COLUMN, NATIVE INFORMATION, MARCH 1893.

G.O.C. Mandalay Dist. and O.C. Bhamo.	Commissioner, Northern Division, and Dy. Comr., Bhamo.	Stage	Inter. M.	Inter. F.	Total M.	Total F.	Remarks
		Paláp	4	2	4	2	*See* Route No. 3 of this Appendix, Stage 10.
		Warawkrán ...	3	6	8	0	*See* Route No. 17 of this Appendix, Stage 1.

* I am uncertain if Sánsi is situated on the Tákaw Ka, or if it is on a small tributary of it called the Sánsi Ka.—W. H. D.

FROM SIMA (FORT MORTON) TO MÖNGTIEN—*continued.*

Authorities. Military.	Authorities. Civil.	Number and Names of Stages, Rivers and Streams.	Distances. Intermediate. M.	F.	Distances. Total. M.	F.	Remarks.
G.O.C. Mandalay District and O.C. Bhamo.	Commissioner, Northern Division, and Dy. Commr., Bhamo.	**Shirawkong** ...	**2**	**4**	10	4	*See* Route No. 17 of this Appendix, Stage 1.
		Maitong	**3**	**4**	14	0	
		Khunru	**2**	**4**	16	4	*Note.*—This route runs through Paláp, Warawkrán, Shirawkong, Maitong, Khunru, Maimai, Shalaokrán, all Kachin villages, and then up to Möngtien. After passing the Kachin village of Shalaokrán the road crosses a small stream, which is a tributary of the Kaona Ka, and then runs uphill. Here is situated Möngtien, which is a Chinese village of about 200 or 300 houses. In front of Möngtien is the Chinese gate called Wanjen kwan; this is made of limestone and was called by some Kachins near Sadôn "Chiwao." Distance from Shalaokrán to Möngtien is doubtful.
		Maimai	**2**	**0**	18	4	
		Shalaokrán ...	**3**	**0**	21	4	
China.		**Möngtien** ...	**(?)6**	**0**	27	4	

No. 23.

From SIMA (FORT MORTON) to SAMA PA.

BY LIEUT. W. H. DENT, YORKSHIRE REGIMENT, INTELLIGENCE OFFICER, NORTH-EASTERN COLUMN, NATIVE INFORMATION, MARCH 1893.

Authorities. Military.	Authorities. Civil.	Number and Names of Stages, Rivers and Streams.	Intermediate. M.	F.	Total. M.	F.	Remarks.
G.O.C. Mandalay District and O.C. Bhamo.	Commissioner, Northern Division, and Deputy Commissioner, Bhamo.	**1. Pajao**	**14**	**0**	14	0	General direction south. From Sima this route runs along the ridge due south, passing through the villages of Paláp, Naru, Pajao at 4¼, 7 and 14 miles respectively; two former are Kachin, while the latter is Yawyin. This route runs quite close to Ngatong (Kachin), but passes to the east of it and then, running along the left bank of the Pajao Ka, through taungyas and a little tree jungle, the village of Pajao is reached.
China.		**2. Sama Pa** ... Pajao Ka and Mönglai Ka.	**12**	**0**	26	0	From Pajao the road still running south goes parallel with the Pajao Ka along its left bank up and down spurs, the gradients of which are rather steep.

About 2 miles from Pajao this stream is crossed. It is pretty well at the headwaters and the stream is quite small, about 6 yards wide. There are several small streams which run down from the various khuds and swell the Pajao Ka very quickly. From here the road runs up and down spurs, each spur in succession increasing in altitude till the high range which stops the view into China is reached. The altitude of these hills is about 7,900 feet. There is little or no cultivation up here and no trees. On reaching the highest point the road runs over fairly level ground for about ½ mile till the hill called by the Kachins Sama Mata Pum and by the Chinese Sama Mata is reached at 6 miles. This in itself is no feature, but from here the

FROM SIMA (FORT MORTON) TO SAMA PA—*continued.*

Authorities.		Number and Names of Stages, Rivers and Streams.	Distances.		Remarks.
Military.	Civil.		Inter-mediate.	Total.	
	China.	**2. Sama Pa**—*cont.*			first view of China is obtained; the ground drops immediately in long spurs to the Khwikaw Ka and in the distance Sama Pa is visible in the plains, with the Sama Ka, also called Mönglai or Môlé Ka, running and twisting about in the plains. The large hill Hpunra Shikong is about 1 mile to the west of Sama Mata Pum. From Sama Mata Pum the road runs downhill along a spur till the Khwikaw Ka is reached at 7 miles; it is here quite a small stream as its source is close, being about 1 mile to the east. The road from here runs uphill to the Pincháng Pum and through the site of the deserted village of the same name at 8 miles. The village of Laoba is to the east of the road and about 1 mile distant. This village is Chinese and has about 20 houses in it. From Pincháng Pum the road drops down to the Môlé, Mönglai, or Sama Ka at 11 miles. This stream has a stony bottom and is about 12 to 15 yards wide and fordable. As soon as the river is crossed there is a branch road to the left which leads to the village called Marán-katawng; this is about ½ mile distant from the crossing. The river turns and twists about a great deal, the road runs along its left bank till the Chinese village of Sama Pa is reached at 12 miles; this is not stockaded and has between 200 and 300 houses in it. It is situated in a large plain through which the Sama Ka flows. The river divides into two parts and forms a large island in the plain.

No. 24.

From SIMA (FORT MORTON) to SANTA.

BY LIEUT. W. H. DENT, YORKSHIRE REGIMENT, INTELLIGENCE OFFICER, NORTH-EASTERN COLUMN, NATIVE INFORMATION, MARCH 1893.

Military	Civil	Stages	Inter. M.	Inter. F.	Total M.	Total F.	Remarks
G.O.C. Mandalay District and O.C. Bhamo.	Commissioner, Northern Division, and Deputy Commissioner, Bhamo.	**1. Shirawkong (Kachin).** Paknoi Ka and a stream.	**10**	**4**	10	4	Sima to Paláp 4¼ miles, *see* Route No. 3 of this Appendix, Stage 10. Thence to Shirawkong 6¼, *see* Route No. 17 of this Appendix, Stage 1.
		2. Kacháng ... Paisha Ka.	**10**	**2**	20	6	From Shirawkong the road still runs east until near the Khaona Ka, where it branches to the south and runs along the left bank of the Ka till nearing Upra, when the road ascends to that village, which is reached at 5 miles. From here the road runs through the Kachin villages of Kalyen 7½ miles, Tungfut 9 miles, to Kacháng at 10¼ miles.
China.		**3. Pincháng** ...	**8**	**0**	28	6	From here it runs through some paddy-fields, in which is a small ka which flows to the right called the Paisha Ka; this is a small tributary of the Kunlong Ka. Beyond this stream there is a branch road to the right which leads to the villages of Sinyen and Sinchai, both of which are

FROM SIMA (FORT MORTON) TO SANTA—*continued.*

Authorities. Military.	Authorities. Civil.	Number and Names of Stages, Rivers and Streams.	Distances. Intermediate. M.	F.	Total. M.	F.	Remarks.
China.		**3. Pincháng**—*cont.*					Chinese; they are about 2 miles away from the Kachin villages of Kacháng. This branch road, which leads to Sinyen and Sinchai, crosses the main road and goes off to Möngtien. Our route then goes up and down hill to a village called Pincháng (Chinese), which has 10 houses in it.
		4. Santa (Chinese).	8	0	36	4	From here the road goes to 'Nacháng, a Kachin village of about seven houses. From 'Nacháng there is a branch road to the left which leads to Möngtien. About here the road is fairly level with small tree jungle on either side; from 'Nacháng it runs more or less downhill to Santa. This is often called Tanta; it is a large Chinese village of about 2,000 houses. Here a Sawbwa lives, who is in a kind of way in charge of all the surrounding Chinese villages and is responsible for a deal of trouble in the Kachin hills. This distance of 36½ miles cannot be called accurate, as a large part of this route has never been traversed and is only estimated. This is the best route into China; it runs through the centre of the fertile Khaona Ka valley tract and is regularly used by the Chinese who come into the Kachin hills with mule convoys for trading purposes.

ALTERNATIVE I.

FROM SIMA TO SANTA *viâ* KAUNLA.

[BY LIEUT. W. H. DENT, YORKSHIRE REGIMENT, INTELLIGENCE OFFICER, NORTH-EASTERN COLUMN, NATIVE INFORMATION, MARCH 1893.

Military	Civil	Stages	Inter. M.	F.	Total M.	F.	Remarks
G.O.C. Mandalay District and O.C. Bhamo.	Commissioner, Northern Division, and Deputy Commissioner, Bhamo.	**(1) Viâ Wurákrán (Warawkrán)—**					
		Paláp (S) ...	4	0	4	0	General direction south-south-east. There are three routes to be taken either (1) through Paláp, Wurákrán (Warawkrán, *see* Route No. 22 of this appendix,) Shirawkong and on to Longprawyáng; or through (2) Paláp, Naru, and across the Paknoi to Longprawyáng (Kachin); or through (3) Paláp, Naru, near Ngatông, and Pajao to Paknoi Prán (Yawyin). The first is the best, but the last is also a good road, because the Paknoi Ka is much smaller where it is crossed. By (1) to Paknoi Prán, 20¾, by (2) 17¼, by (3) to Paknoi Prán is 19. If transport is used, I think (1) route is best, (2) is shortest, but the crossing of the Paknoi Ka is difficult. (3) From Pajao Ka to Paknoi Prán this route has not been traversed, but it has the advantage of having no deep river to cross; on the other hand, as the road runs across in the upper waters of the Pajao Ka and the Paknoi Ka, the inclines are very steep and in many places the road is muddy and difficult to cross where there are small streams.
		Wurákrán ...	3	6	7	6	
		Shirawkong ...	2	4	10	2	
		Longprawyáng.	4	4	14	6	
		or					
		(2) Viâ Naru—					
		Paláp (N) ...	4	2	4	2	
		Naru ...	2	6	7	0	
		Longprawyáng.	4	2	11	2	
		or					
		(3) Viâ Paknoi Prán—					
		Paláp ...	4	2	4	2	
		Naru ...	2	6	7	0	
		Paknoi Prán.	12	0	19	0	

FROM SIMA (FORT MORTON) TO SANTA—*continued.*

ALTERNATIVE I—*continued.*

Authorities. Military.	Authorities. Civil.	Number and Names of Stages, Rivers and Streams.	Distances. Intermediate. M.	Distances. Intermediate. F.	Distances. Total. M. F.	Remarks.
G.O.C. Mandalay District, O.C. Bhamo.	Commissioner, Northern Division, and Deputy Commissioner, Bhamo.	**Longprawyáng (Yawyin).** Small stream.	1	0	(1st route) 15 6 or (2nd route) 12 2	From the first Longprawyáng, which is a Kachin village, the road runs downhill through paddy-fields, which make an excellent camping ground, across a small ka and then through jungle, and then ascends till the Yawyin village of Longprawyáng is reached. The road now runs through jungle and taungya clearings to the village of Paknoi Prán, which is of two parts, the first and northerly is Maru and the second is Yawyin.
G.O.C. Mandalay District, O.C. Bhamo.	Commissioner, Northern Division, and Deputy Commissioner, Bhamo.	**Paknoi Prán (Kachin and Yawyin).** Mönglai, Môlé or Sama Ka, Sambaw Ka, and Malai Ka.	5	0	(1st route) 20 6 or (2nd route) 17 2 or (3rd route) 19 0	The Paknoi Ka flows to the right of the road. A small stream, which is a tributary of the Paknoi Ka, flows between the two villages. Paknoi Prán has six houses. The road now runs uphill between two peaks called Untaláng, which means two pointed rocks; then over undulating ground till a small stream, which flows to the right, but is of no consequence, is crossed; after which the road descends to the Mönglai, Môlé, or Sama Ka, which is here about 10 yards wide with a pebbly bottom and flows to the right. Here there is a branch road to the left which leads to Sinyen and Sinchai. This route now leads uphill to the Mönglai hills; these possibly are called the Sambaw hills, but are of no great height; then descending again the road crosses the Sambaw Ka, a tributary of the Mönglai Ka,—here quite a small stream. The road then goes uphill to the Pumnoi hills, which are very large and are visible from Longpraw Pum and Sama Mata Pum. I was told the road went between two large peaks on the Pumnoi hills. Now the route descends to the Malai Ka, a small stream with stony bottom about 10 yards wide: this stream is a tributary of the Tapin. From the Malai Ka the road ascends steadily to the Kaunla range of hills on the opposite (southern) slopes of which is the village of Kaunla, partly Kachin and partly Chinese. Kaunla is a large village and does a good deal of trade with cotton in the Kachin hills. From here the road runs on to Santa. This is a good route, but not so frequently used as the one *viâ* Upra. However, traders often come from Kaunla to Sima and 'Nkráng.
China.		**Kaunla (Kachin and Chinese).**	14	0	(1st route) 34 6 or (2nd route) 31 2 or (3rd route) 33 0	
China.		**Santa (Chinese).**	4	0	(1st route) 38 6 or (2nd route) 35 2 or (3rd route) 37 0	

FROM SIMA (FORT MORTON) TO SANTA—*continued.*

BRANCH I.

FROM MÖNGLAI KA (*see* ALTERNATIVE I) TO MÖNGTIEN.

BY LIEUT. W. H. DENT, YORKSHIRE REGIMENT, INTELLIGENCE OFFICER, NORTH-EASTERN COLUMN, NATIVE INFORMATION, MARCH 1893.

Authorities. Military.	Authorities. Civil.	Number and Names of Stages, Rivers and Streams.	Distances. Intermediate. M.	Distances. Intermediate. F.	Distances. Total. M.	Distances. Total. F.	Remarks.
China.		**Sinyen and Sinchai (Chinese).**	...		...		General direction east. This route connects the Longprawyáng, Kaunla, Santa, and the Shirawkong, Upra and Santa routes with the Chinese towns of Möngtien, Sinyen, and Sinchai. Leaving the main Kaunla route at the crossing of the Mönglai Ka the road runs near the river, which ascends slowly till the Chinese villages of Sinyen and Sinchai are reached. There are about 40 houses in the two villages and they are separate about 1 mile. They are situated on the lower slopes of the Pumnoi hills and are near the source of the Mönglai or Môlé Ka. There appears to be a watershed here between the Mönglai and the Kunláng Ka; this last is a tributary of the Khaona Ka. I was told that the Mönglai Ka rose from the Untaláng hill, which is near Loibép Pum. From here the road runs to the south of the Kunláng Ka, crosses the Shirawkong, Upra and Santa route and so on up to Möngtien. I was unable to fix any approximate distances. Road is fairly good.

No. 25.

From SIMA (FORT MORTON) to SEDEN.

BY LIEUT. W. H. DENT, YORKSHIRE REGIMENT, INTELLIGENCE OFFICER, NORTH-EASTERN COLUMN, NATIVE INFORMATION, MARCH 1893.

Military	Civil	Stages	Int. M.	Int. F.	Total M.	Total F.	Remarks
G.O.C. Mandalay District and O.C. Bhamo.	Commissioner, Northern Divn., and Deputy Commissioner, Bhamo.	**1. Shirawkong (Kachin).**	**10**	**4**	10	4	General direction north-east. For description of this route as far as Pumpri Pum, *see* Route No. 17 of this Appendix and its Branch I. From Pumpri it runs into Waraw, which is inhabited by Szis, Yawyins, and Chinese. Here the road descends, and inclining to the right and crosses the Möngka Ka; ascends to Pajao, small Chinese village of eight or nine houses, and from there on to the village of Seden, which is composed of 80 houses, and it is in the plains. The inhabitants are mixed, but are chiefly Yawyins.
		Paknoi Ka.					
		2. Pumpri (Kachin).	**6**	**4**	17	0	
		Khaona Ka.					
		3. Seden (Yawyin).	**14**	**0**	31	0	
		Möngka Ka.					

No. 26.

From SI-U to PANGKHA (see Route No. 28 of this Appendix, Stage 3).

By Lieut. H. R. DAVIES, Oxfordshire Light Infantry, March 1892.

Authorities. Military.	Authorities. Civil.	Number and Names of Stages, Rivers and Streams.	Distances. Intermediate. M. F.	Distances. Total. M. F.	Remarks.
G.O.C. Mandalay District and O.C. Bhamo.	Commissioner, Northern Division, and Deputy Commissioner, Bhamo.	**1. Loisaing (Lwésain).** Si-u or Pángkhwan and Loilem chaungs.	7 6	7 6	General direction east. Difficult mule road; steep and narrow in places. Nearly level for the first 4 miles. Cross the Sin chaung at Si-u. This stream is crossed five times, first from the left at Si-u; 6 yards by 8 inches, afterwards 5 yards by 6 inches. At $\frac{3}{4}$ mile a road to the left to Tátmanán. At $1\frac{1}{4}$ miles a road to the right to Khamôt and Pánglum. At $3\frac{1}{4}$ miles a road to the right to Tingprong. At $3\frac{3}{4}$ miles cross the Si-u or Pángkhwan chaung. It is crossed again three times in the next mile. At $4\frac{1}{4}$ miles very steep ascent for a mile and-a-quarter. At $6\frac{1}{2}$ miles cross the Loilem chaung (from the right, 1 yard by 2 inches). Just beyond this the Tinkánkyet camp, 40 by 30 yards. From here a road to the right to Pánglun and to the right front to Tônhôn. Route turns to the left and ascends steadily for a mile and-a-quarter to Loisaing, 25 houses; Lakhum tribe. Water from small streams; rather scarce.
		2. Pangkha ... Namla, Inkhrut or Hinlap, Nam Hu, and Papri chaungs.	10 2	18 0	General direction east. Good mule road downhill for the first $4\frac{1}{2}$ miles. At $1\frac{1}{2}$ miles Sarikatawng; 14 houses; Lakhum tribe. From here a road to the left to Kindáng, Tinkhát, and Loi Veng. At $3\frac{1}{2}$ miles Supla; five Palaung houses; five Lakhum-Kachin houses. At $4\frac{1}{2}$ miles cross the Namla (from the left, 10 yards by 1 foot). At 6 miles cross the Inkhrut or Hinlap chaung (from the left, 2 feet by 1 inch). At $6\frac{1}{4}$ miles Makawk or Tángpyen, a Palaung village of 12 houses. From here a road to the left to Loi Veng and to the right to the ferry over the Shwéli near Phyipaw. At $7\frac{1}{2}$ miles cross the Nam Hu (from the left, 5 yards by 1 foot) and the Papri chaung (from the left, 3 yards by 6 inches). The Nam Hu and Papri chaungs join 50 yards below where the road crosses them. At $8\frac{3}{4}$ and $9\frac{1}{4}$ miles roads to the right to Loi Mun, a small Palaung village a mile off the road. At $9\frac{1}{2}$ miles a road to the right to the Pangkha ferry and Möngkák. The route turns to the left. Pangkha is a Palaung village of 20 houses and kyaung (*see* Route No. 28 of this Appendix, Stage 3). Good camping ground, but water rather scarce.

No. 27.

From THAYETTA to SARAWKONG and ATÁN.

By E. P. CLONEY, Esq., Civil Officer with Kaukkwé Column, 1892-93.

Military	Civil	Stages	Intermediate M. F.	Total M. F.	Remarks
G.O.C. Mandalay District and O.C. Bhamo.	Commissioner, Northern Division, and Deputy Commissioner, Bhamo.	**1. Myohla or Migé.**	6 4	6 4	*See* Route No. 2, Northern Division. Road, leaving village of Thayetta, runs through grass and bamboo jungle for about $\frac{1}{4}$ mile and, continuing in a southerly direction, generally over high ground covered with teak,

FROM THAYETTA TO SARAWKONG AND ATÁN—*continued.*

Authorities. Military.	Authorities. Civil.	Number and Names of Stages, Rivers and Streams.	Distances. Intermediate. M.	Distances. Intermediate. F.	Distances. Total. M.	Distances. Total. F.	Remarks.
G.O.C. Mandalay District and O.C. Bhamo.	Commissioner, Northern Division, and Deputy Commissioner, Bhamo.	**1. Myohla or Mígé**—*cont.*					"*in*" and other large tree jungle, for about 4 miles, comes out on a large *jheel*. Skirting *jheel* for about $\frac{3}{4}$ mile crosses the dry bed of a chaung and gets into high ground again; jungle, bamboo, and a large tree with *thetké* (coarse grass) undergrowth; goes on for about $\frac{1}{2}$ mile over same ground, crosses the dry bed of a chaung (crossing muddy), and at 6 miles Myohla is reached. The path descends from the high ground to Myohla which is on the bank of the chaung; Mígé across the chaung on the opposite bank. Both Mígé and Myohla are good camps. Myohla has a kyaung and zayáts. Mígé has a rest-house built by the villagers for Government officials and one house that belonged to Maung Bauk's workmen formerly. Road good all the way.
		2. Ségyi ...	4	4	11	0	Leaving Mígé, direction southerly along edge of *jheel* $\frac{1}{2}$ mile, then on high ground, skirting *jheel* into big tree jungle with undergrowth for 1 mile; another 1 mile in same big tree jungle with dense undergrowth, meets the metal road and goes in an easterly direction on high ground for about 1 mile. Descends into low ground near Ségyi *jheel* continuing in an easterly direction, then on high ground skirting *jheel* for $\frac{3}{4}$ mile and $\frac{1}{4}$ mile through open jungle and Ségyi is reached ($4\frac{1}{2}$ miles). Ségyi is on high ground. Camping ground confined but good. Road good all the way.
		3. Camp on Namhsongtán or Nantán chaung. Nabu, Nansalin or Namsatáng, Nampateng, Namhsongtán, or Nantán chaungs.	7	6	18	6	Road runs from Ségyi for $\frac{1}{4}$ mile in a northerly direction through big tree jungle with short undergrowth (principally *thetké*). Turns east and runs for about 2 miles through same sort of jungle, coming out on a small plain goes through this for $\frac{1}{4}$ mile; runs through the Ségyi paddy-fields (dry now, but would be bad going in the rains), doubtless a bit of jungle for $\frac{1}{4}$ mile, and goes on again generally in an easterly direction. After about 2 miles passes right bank of Nabu chaung (an old Sakhán with one tumble-down hut here); plenty of good drinking water; comes out on another small plain, goes through it in the same easterly direction for $\frac{1}{2}$ mile and re-enters jungle, big tree with short undergrowth, and after $1\frac{1}{2}$ miles cross the Namsatáng (Nansalin) chaung, 6 inches deep; clear, good running water; goes on for $\frac{1}{4}$ mile, crosses the Nampateng (crossing very bad; has since been bridged; would require bridging every year). Another plain for $\frac{3}{4}$ mile and re-enters bamboo jungle and goes on for $\frac{1}{4}$ mile and crosses a stream with plenty of clear water; depth about $1\frac{1}{2}$ feet. A smaller stream about 200 yards off encircles the camp; hence the name Namhsongtán, "*between two waters.*" Camp in open bamboo jungle; kaing grass plentiful towards north of camp.
		4. Sarawkong ... **or** **Atán** ... ... Nampahôk and Namhsai or Nanthi chaungs.	6 7	4 6	25 26	2 4	Leaving camp, road runs in an easterly direction through bamboo jungle (open for $\frac{1}{2}$ mile); crosses the Nampahôk stream, shallow with clear running water (very likely quite dry later on); comes out on a small plain, goes through it for $\frac{1}{2}$ mile in south-east direction, enters jungle of large "*in*" trees with a few teak trees interspersed, and runs through this jungle with occasional cleared patches for

FROM THAYETTA TO SARAWKONG AND ATÁN—*continued.*

Authorities. Military.	Authorities. Civil.	Number and Names of Stages, Rivers and Streams.	Distances. Inter-mediate.	Distances. Total.	Remarks
G.O.C. Mandalay District and O.C. Bhamo.	Commissioner, Northern Division, and Deputy Commissioner, Bhamo.	**4. Sarawkong or Atán**—*cont.*			about 3 miles and, turning to the right instead of following the straight path which leads to Maisákyán, crosses the Nambsai or Nanthi chaung. Up to here it is 4 miles easy going. From hence the ascent commences stiff for a bit, then rising gradually for ½ mile; then road runs along a broad ridge; splendid road (with deep ravines on both sides) for about 1 mile, turning around the base of a hillock. The road for ¼ mile is narrow, but good until it runs over the spreading roots of a very large tree. Here mules and ponies are apt to trip and if not careful will possibly roll down the khud. Still ascending gradually for ¼ mile road runs along ridge covered with *thetké*, which the Kachins have cleared off the path by simply laying heavy bamboos to keep the grass down and off the path; cutting simply makes the jungle grow more luxuriantly. Another level ridge for about ¾ mile, along which the usual Kachin graves with deep trenches are seen on both sides. This is a sure sign a village is not very far off. Road ascends for about 100 yards and meets a long road. To the right is Kinlukong village, ¼ mile off. Turning to the left north-east road descends about 100 yards, then runs along level cleared hill side. Path broad; jungle, small bush and large tree, but bush is thick. About ¼ mile from path is a large pagoda-like structure made of grass with a weather-cock-looking wooden steeple. This is the grave of a wife of the late Saoseng (Maitongwa). Turning east the road gradually ascends for a little more than ¼ mile; jungle on both sides, thick, and the stockade of the village is reached. About 100 yards further on rising ground is Sarawkong village of 12 houses (6½ miles). Water-supply small and down the khud to the west of village. Leaving Sarawkong in a north-easterly direction path descends and runs along a level, but for about half-way road very good; jungle thick on both sides. For another ¼ mile level, then ascends. Road to the right leads to the taungyas. Road straight ahead ascends and leads into the village of Atán. Water-supply not large. Turning to the south a path leads to the Atán Sawbwa's taungya. The camp is a good one. Down at the bottom of the hill is a small stream called the Kwai Kon Ka. Plenty of water. Camp is a good one, but next year this camping ground will be of no use, as the site will be overgrown and the taungya cultivation will be removed elsewhere.

No. 28.

From TUKU (see Route No. 99, Northern Division) to MÖNGKÁK (MAINGKÁT), (see Route No. 77, Northern Division, Stage 11, and No. 78 of same division, Stage 8).

BY LIEUT. H. R. DAVIES, OXFORDSHIRE LIGHT INFANTRY, MARCH 1892.

Military	Civil	Stages	Inter. M.	Inter. F.	Total M.	Total F.	Remarks
G.O.C. Mandalay District and O.C. Bhamo.	Commr., Northern Divn., and Deputy Commr., Bhamo.	**1. Khasháng** ... Wayok, Mawsi, Páng-ché, Khapra, and Khawan chaungs, and two other streams.	**11**	**0**	11	0	General direction south. Fair mule road. From camping ground on Katsan chaung uphill for ¾ mile. At 1¼ miles village of Soma; 15 houses; Lena-Marán tribe. At 2¼ miles Kúm-shoi, 10 houses; Lakhum tribe. From

FROM TUKU (*see* ROUTE NO. 99, NORTHERN DIVISION) TO MÖNGKÁK (MAINGKÁT), (*see* ROUTE NO. 77, NORTHERN DIVISION, STAGE 11, AND NO. 78 OF SAME DIVISION, STAGE 8)—*continued.*

Authorities. Military.	Authorities. Civil.	Number and Names of Stages, Rivers and Streams.	Distances. Intermediate. M.	Distances. Intermediate. F.	Distances. Total. M.	Distances. Total. F.	Remarks.
G.O.C. Mandalay District and O.C. Bhamo.	Commissioner, Northern Division, and Deputy Commissioner, Bhamo.	**1. Khasháng**—*cont.*					here roads go off to the left (1) to Namyu and Kaih tik, (2) to Saupon and Nálôn or Tagaung Naswé. At 2¾ miles cross the Wayôk chaung (from the right, 1 yard by 3 inches) and just beyond it a muddy ditch, 5 yards wide, which would be difficult for animals in wet weather. At 3¼ miles a road goes straight on to Saupon, the route turns sharp to the right for ¼ mile, then sharp to the left again, a road going straight on from this point to Kailé. At 5¾ miles cross the Mawsi chaung (from the right, 8 yards by 6 inches; easy ford), and just beyond it the Pongché chaung (from the right, 4 yards by 6 inches; easy crossing). At 6¼ miles Mansôk; 50 houses; Phunkán. At 7½ miles cross the Khapra chaung (from the right, 4 yards by 6 inches; easy crossing). At 7¾ miles cross the Khawan chaung (from the right, 1½ yards by 6 inches) and two other streams close to it, here there is a lot of mud for 50 yards; difficult for mules, but passable. At 9¼ miles Warapum Sittan; seven houses; Páhtum-Phunkán; thence steep downhill to Khasháng; 30 houses; Páhtum-Phunkán. Good camping ground in village; water for animals from Khahtat chaung, ¾ mile off; 4 yards wide by 6 inches deep.
		2. Pánghtán ... Wubamyang, Khapra, Namsa, Namkhat, Shiyit, and Mankhong chaungs.	**10**	**4**	21	4	General direction south-south-west. Good mule road. Steep downhill to Lakhum Katawng at ¾ mile; two houses; Páhtum-Phunkán. From here a road to the left to Saikhao and Pankaw. At 1¼ miles a road to the left to Mankáng. At 1½ miles cross the Wubamyáng chaung (2 yards by 6 inches; easy). From here a road to the right to Khapra. At 2¾ miles cross the Khapra chaung (from the left, 5 yards by 8 inches; easy). At 3¼ miles Wotang Katawng; four houses; Páhtum-Phunkán. From here a road to the left to Santing and Pángkyem. At 3¾ miles cross the Namsa chaung (from the left, 8 yards by 1 foot; easy), thence uphill to Namsa. At 4 miles road to the left to Loi Pháng. At 4¼ miles Namsa, ¼ mile to right of the road; three houses; Páhtum-Phunkán; thence downhill for ½ mile, thence over undulating open country with very little jungle for 2½ miles. At 5 miles cross the Nam Khat (from the left, 6 yards by 8 inches easy). At 5¼ miles cross the Shiyit chaung (from the left, 3 yards by 8 inches). At 6¼ miles road to the left to Pángkyem and to the right to Timmaw; just beyond this cross the Mankhong chaung (from the left, 5 yards by 8 inches). At 7 miles begin a steady ascent up to Sama. At 9 miles, 10 houses; Phunkán. The Namkham-Sikaw road is here reached. Along this road to the right to Pánghtán; 20 houses; Phunkán. Camping ground on the road or in the village. Water rather scarce; small stream.
		3. Pángkha ... Kahtan, Mankong, Kaihtan, and Namlwi chaungs.	**10**	**0**	31	4	General direction south-west by west for 4 miles to beyond Loikham, thence south-east to Pángkha. Good mule road. At 2 miles cross the Kahtan chaung twice (from the right and left within 100 yards; 1 yard by 2 inches). At 2½ miles a road to the left to Manmao and

FROM TUKU (*see* ROUTE No. 99, NORTHERN DIVISION) TO MÖNGKÁK (MAINGKÁT), (*see* ROUTE No. 77, NORTHERN DIVISION, STAGE 11, AND No. 78 OF SAME DIVISION, STAGE 8)—*continued.*

Authorities. Military.	Authorities. Civil.	Number and Names of Stages, Rivers and Streams.	Distances. Intermediate.	Distances. Total.	Remarks.
G.O.C. Mandalay District and O.C. Bhamo.	Commissioner, Northern Division, and Deputy Commissioner, Bhamo.	**3. Pángkha**—*cont.*			Mikhu; small villages under Loikham, a mile off the road. At 3 miles a road to the right to Kumbren, Loilôn, Khamôt, and Sikaw; thence uphill to Loikham at 3½ miles; 40 houses; Lakhum. At 3¾ miles roads to the left to Mikhu and to the right to Mankao. At 4¼ miles a road to the right to Yama, from which roads branch off to Sikaw and Lwésaing. From here downhill crossing the Mankong chaung and Kaihtan chaung (from the right, each about 2 yards by 3 inches) at 5½ miles, and the Namlwi at 6½ miles (from the right, 3 yards by 4 inches); thence uphill for a mile. At 7½ miles roads to the left to Kumsaw and to the right to Khôchik and Loiveng, thence downhill. At 8¼ miles a road to the right to Maiteng, a Palaung village 1½ miles off. At 9¼ miles roads to the left to Kumsaw and to the right to Maiteng, thence uphill to Pángkha, a Palaung village of 20 houses. Good camping ground. Water from small stream; rather scarce.
		4. Möngkák ... Shwéli or Nammao, Nam Ma, and Nam Möngkák.	M. F. 4 6	M. F. 36 2	General direction south. Good mule road downhill for 2¼ miles to the Shwéli, thence level. At ¾ mile a road to the right to Lwésaing and Tônhôn. At 2¼ miles cross the Shwéli or Nammao from the left, 100 yards by 8 feet deep, the deepest part being near the right bank. Hills come close down to the right bank and are a mile away from the left. Room for camp on both banks; easy, sandy approaches; bottom sandy and rocky; strong current. Crossed by one boat with bamboos fastened to it; will hold 10 men besides the boatmen. Animals swam across. Boatmen live in a village of three houses 300 yards from river on left bank. At 2½ miles cross the Namma (from the left, 10 yards by 1 foot; easy). Just beyond this the small village of Möngkák; eight houses; Shan. At 3¾ miles and again at 4 miles cross the Nammöngkák (from the left and right, 5 yards by 6 inches; easy fords, foot-bridge at second crossing). Between these two crossings a road to the right to Tônhôn, the road traversed by the column in 1889, thence skirting paddy-fields to the big village of Möngkák; 30 houses; Shan and Palaung. Bazaar every five days. It is the chief place in Humai. Camping grounds on paddy-fields 1¼ by ½ mile.

BRANCH I.

FROM MANSÔK (*see* IN STAGE 1) TO MANSÁM.

BY LIEUT. H. R. DAVIES, OXFORDSHIRE LIGHT INFANTRY, FEBRUARY 1892.

Military	Civil	Stage	Intermediate	Total	Remarks
G.O.C. Mandalay District and O.C. Bhamo.	Commr., Northern Division, and Deputy Commissioner, Bhamo.	**1. Mansám** ... Mawsi and Tubong chaungs.	6 0	6 0	General direction east. Fair mule road. Along the Namkha road to Hômakatawng, at 1½ miles; five houses; Páhtum-Phunkán tribe; under Pankaw; thence downhill to the Mawsi chaung (from the left, 7 yards by 8 inches) at 2¼ miles. Just beyond this cross the Tubong chaung (from the left, 4 yards by 8 inches). At 3 miles ascent for ½ a mile. At 3½

FROM TUKU (*see* ROUTE NO. 99, NORTHERN DIVISION) TO MÖNGKÁK (MAINGKÁT), (*see* ROUTE NO. 77, NORTHERN DIVISION, STAGE 11, AND NO. 78 OF SAME DIVISION, STAGE 8)—*continued.*

BRANCH I—*continued.*

Authorities. Military.	Authorities. Civil.	Number and Names of Stages, Rivers and Streams.	Distances. Intermediate.	Distances. Total.	Remarks.
G.O.C. Mandalay District and O.C. Bhamo.	Commissioner, Northern Division, and Dy. Commissioner, Bhamo.	1. **Mansám**—*cont.*			miles just short of the village of Mowun route turns to the right. Mowun contains 10 houses; Loika-Marán tribe. At $4\frac{1}{2}$ miles road from the right from Manlep and Pankaw, route turns to the left. Mansám contains 52 houses; 'Szi, Issi or Assi tribe. Water rather scarce from small stream. There is said to be a more direct route from Mowun to Mansám passable for transport, but I have not been along it.

BRANCH II.

FROM MANSÔK (*see* IN STAGE 1) TO NAWKHAM.

BY LIEUT. H. R. DAVIES, OXFORDSHIRE LIGHT INFANTRY FEBRUARY 1892.

Military	Civil	Stages	Intermediate M.	Intermediate F.	Total M.	Total F.	Remarks
G.O.C. Mandalay District and O.C. Bhamo.	Commissioner, Northern Division, and Deputy Commissioner, Bhamo.	1. **Nawkham** ... Mawsi, Nammak, and Tuku chaungs.	**9**	**4**	9	4	General direction north-north-east. Fair mule road; difficult in places. Starting from camp above village at $\frac{1}{2}$ mile village of Mansôk. Thence very steep downhill to the Mawsi chaung (from the left, 8 yards by 8 inches) at 1 mile. At 2 miles Kahtankawng; 23 houses; Phunkán tribe; under Mansôk. At $3\frac{1}{4}$ miles a road to the left to Kumshoi. At 4 miles village of Saupôn, Warrapôn; 21 houses; Lakhum tribe. From here a road to the right to Mowun. At $4\frac{1}{4}$ miles a road straight on to Namkhai and Nálôn. The route turns to the left. At $5\frac{1}{4}$ miles village of Saupôn Maitôn, five houses, Lakhum tribe. At $5\frac{1}{2}$ miles strike into the Tuku-Saupôn-Tingsa road, 600 yards from Saupôn Tingsa. Follow the Tuku road for 200 yards, then turn to the right along a narrow, difficult road, not much used for bullocks to Kaihtik, at $8\frac{1}{2}$ miles, seven houses, Lena-Marán tribe. At $8\frac{3}{4}$ miles cross the Nammak (from the left, 2 yards by 3 inches). From the Nammak very steep uphill for 600 yards. At $9\frac{1}{4}$ miles cross the Tuku chaung (from the left, 2 yards by 3 inches). Nawkham is on the Lena route from Namkham to Bhamo. It contains seven houses; Lena-Marán tribe; under Kaihtik; water from Tuku chaung. To avoid the difficult road between Saupôn and Kaihtik there is another route *viâ* Kumshoi and Namyu (*see* Route No. 29). This is only $\frac{1}{4}$ mile longer.

No. 29.

From TUKU (see Route No. 99, Northern Division) to NÁLÔN (TAGAUNG NASWÉ).

BY LIEUT. H. R. DAVIES, OXFORDSHIRE LIGHT INFANTRY, FEBRUARY 1892.

Military	Civil	Stages	Intermediate M.	Intermediate F.	Total M.	Total F.	Remarks
G.O.C. Mandalay District and O.C. Bhamo.	Commissioner, Northern Divn., and Deputy Commissioner, Bhamo.	1. **Nálôn or Tagaung Naswé.** Namyu or Lowang, Khawn, and Nammak chaungs.	**12**	**0**	12	0	General direction east. Good mule road, but steep in places. From camp on Kátsan chaung uphill for $\frac{3}{4}$ mile. At $1\frac{1}{4}$ miles Soma; 15 houses; Lena-Marán. At $2\frac{1}{4}$ miles Kúmshoi; 10 houses; Lakhum. From here road

FROM TUKU (*see* ROUTE NO. 99, NORTHERN DIVISION) TO NÁLÔN (TAGAUNG NASWÉ)—*continued.*

Authorities. Military.	Authorities. Civil.	Number and Names of Stages, Rivers and Streams.	Distances. Intermediate.	Distances. Total.	Remarks.
G.O.C. Mandalay District and O.C. Bhamo.	Commissioner, Northern Division, and Deputy Commissioner, Bhamo.	**1. Nálôn or Tagaung Naswé**—*cont.*			to the right to Mansôk. At 3 miles steep down for a ¼ of a mile to the Lowang chaung (from the right, 3 yards by 6 inches; easy crossing), thence steep ascent to Namyu at 3¾ miles, 10 houses, Lena-Marán. From here road to left to Waraw and Letsai. At 4¾ miles paddy-fields 300 by 100 yards, with stream, 1 yard by 2 inches, running through them. At 5¼ miles road to the left to Kaihtik. At 5¾ miles Saupôn Tingsa; 26 houses; Lakhum. At 6 miles cross a small stream. At 7¾ miles after steep descent of a ¼ of a mile, cross the Khawan chaung (from the right, 3 yards by 8 inches), thence steep uphill for a ¼ of a mile. From here a road to the right to Mansám. At 8¾ miles a road to the left to Kaihtik. At 9 miles a road to the left to Namkhai, thence downhill to the Nammak (from the left, 8 yards by 1½ feet). At 9¾ miles, thence steep uphill to Manna at 10¼ miles; 14 houses; Lakhum. From here a road to the right to Ponglin; route goes to the left along the top of a ridge to Nálôn, called Tagaung Naswé or Ngasul by the Shans; seven houses; Lakhum.

ALTERNATIVE I.

FROM TUKU TO NÁLÔN *viâ* NAMKHAI OR PAUNOI.

BY LIEUT. H. R. DAVIES, OXFORDSHIRE LIGHT INFANTRY, FEBRUARY 1892.

Military	Civil	Stages	Intermediate M.	Intermediate F.	Total M.	Total F.	Remarks
G.O.C. Mandalay District and O.C. Bhamo.	Commissioner, Northern Division, and Deputy Commissioner, Bhamo.	**1. Namkhai or Paunoi.** Nam Yu or Moyu chaung. From the right, 8 yards by 8 inches; easy ford. Nammak and Tuku chaungs.	**10**	**0**	10	0	General direction east. Fair mule road. First 5¼ miles as in Route No. 29, here road to Saupôn Tingsa and Nálôn direct, keeps to right that to Namkhai keeping to left. At 6 miles Kaihtik, seven houses; Lena-Marán. (This place is marked Palaungtu in the survey map. Palaungtu is the Sawbwa's name, not the name of the village.) At 6¾ miles cross the Nammak (from the left, 2 yards by 4 inches), and just beyond it the Tuku chaung (from the left, 2 yards by 4 inches). At 7¼ miles Mankao, four houses; Lena-Marán. At 7¾ miles Khalum or Nampôn, eight houses; Lena-Marán. From here a road to the left rear to Nawkham (1 mile off), Waraw, Warapom, Mansi, and Bhamo. At 8¼ miles another bit of the village of Khalum. At 9¼ miles a road to the right to Mansám, thence uphill to Namkhai or Paunoi, 20 houses; Lena-Marán; under the Kaihtik Sawbwa.
		2. Nálôn	**2**	**2**	12	2	General direction south-east. Fair mule road, but steep. Along the Namkhai ridge for ½ mile, whence a road to the left to Tingka, thence downhill for a mile, thence very steep uphill to Nálôn; 14 houses; Lakhum. Just before reaching the village a road to the left front to Kongai (½ mile off); Manawan and Namkham.

No. 30.

From WARÁKRÁN (or WARAW), (Appendix I, Route No. 17, Stage 1) to SIMA (FORT MORTON) viâ NARU, PUMKATAWNG and KUKAM.

BY LIEUT. W. H. DENT, INTELLIGENCE OFFICER, NORTH-EASTERN COLUMN, 1893.

Authorities. Military.	Authorities. Civil.	Number and Names of Stages, Rivers and Streams.	Distances. Intermediate. M.	F.	Total. M.	F.	Remarks.
G.O.C. Mandalay District and O.C. Bhamo.	Commissioner, Northern Division, and Deputy Commissioner, Bhamo.	**1. Naru** ... ... Longpraw Ka, Pabnoi Ka, and Naru Ka.	**11**	**4**	11	4	Warákrán (or Waraw) *see* Route No. 17 of this Appendix, Stage 1. From Warákrán general direction south-south-west as far as Shirawkong, 2½ miles (*see* Route No. 17 of this Appendix). The road here turns south and goes uphill with taungya clearings on either side. The road is good, but rather steep at first, with deep valleys to the west running down to Khaona Ka. Here (5 miles) a road branches off straight to Warákrán, but this is not so good for mules; it is, however, much shorter and good enough for foot-soldiers. Before reaching Longprawyáng the road goes uphill to a great height and then down to the first village. This village is half-way down the hill at 6½ miles, and is composed of four or five houses and is only an offshoot of the larger village of Longprawyáng, which is lower down and about ¼ mile further on. This village has about 15 houses in it and runs north and south; the houses are scattered about and there is thick jungle all round it. There is an excellent camping ground at 7½ miles, about ¼ mile lower down, on terraced paddy-fields, capable of camping 3,000 men. Good water from a stream that runs just below it. Camping ground good during present season of year, but would be unsuitable later on as it is tilled yearly and irrigated. There is some commanding ground to the north-east, about 400 yards off, from which signalling can be carried on with Sima. There is a road from here which runs through the paddy-fields, crossing two small streams, both tributaries of the Longpraw Ka, to the Yawyin village of the same name. The houses are much smaller than the Kachin village; looks cleaner and has a wealthy appearance. Large quantity of fruit trees in neighbourhood. Longprawyáng has 21 head of cattle, and is well off. From here a road leads on to Paknoi Prán and Kaunla for Santa. The road leaves the central Longprawyáng village in a north-easterly direction, and travels down a spur towards the river on either side of the road, at first thick jungle and then old taungya clearings, with long wavy grass. The road is very broad and very good, though rather steep. At 8¾ miles the Pabnoi Ka, 20 yards broad, 3 to 5 feet deep, is reached. The river here has steep banks, the bottom is rocky, and there are large boulders up and down stream. The current is very rapid and unfordable because of the large rocks. High water mark 10 feet above present level. River drops in series of small waterfalls. Crossed by a bamboo Kachin bridge, and Goorkhas had to make a bamboo and log bridge, with grass and leaves put on it to allow the mules to cross. Both bridges only temporary, and will be washed away in floods. There is an excellent place for throwing over a permanent bridge from two big tall rocks, and a platform has already been made on one of them as a commencement. Left bank slightly commands the right. From here the road runs for some way parallel with the stream round a steep spur; jungle on either side at first, and then long grass till the Naru Ka is reached at 10¼ miles before this, however, the road descends steeply. This is a small stream, a tributary of the Paknoi, 5 yards broad. From here road runs uphill through tree jungle, which is rather open; on the summit of

FROM WARÂKRÂN (OR WARAW), (APPENDIX I, ROUTE No. 17, STAGE 1) TO SIMA (FORT MORTON) *viâ* NARU, PUMKATAWNG AND KUKAM—*continued.*

Authorities. Military.	Authorities. Civil.	Number and Names of Stages, Rivers and Streams.	Distances. Intermediate.	Distances. Total.	Remarks.
G.O.C. Mandalay District and O.C. Bhamo.	Commissioner, Northern Division, and Deputy Commissioner, Bhamo.	**1. Naru**—*cont.*			this spur at 11½ miles is the village of Naru. Road good throughout and very broad; bad crossing for mules, otherwise very good. Distance by pacing.
		2. Pumkatawng... Kaiya Ka, Kaprawn Ka, and Mali Ka.	M. F. **9 0**	M. F. 20 4	General direction south-south-west. The road to Pumkatawng leaves Naru village just to the north of it and drops down very steeply for about a mile; road here is bad and stony. Thick jungle and underwood on either side, then inclines get gentler and jungle is trees with grass meeting over head, and as the Kaiya stream (8 yards wide, 1 foot deep; tributary of Mali Ka, 2,500 feet by aneroid) is neared bamboos are noticed. This stream is left on the right at 3 miles, the road running near its left bank for few hundred yards; the stream is rocky and has a strong current, about 8 yards wide and 1 foot deep. The road forks here to Pumkatawng and to Kaiya (latter bearing 264°). Terraced paddy-fields here and little thatching straw. From here the former road gets bad through thick grass and difficult to move along; several small streams are crossed, tributaries of the Kaiya Ka; road is wet now and would be very difficult to move along in the rains. About 2 miles further on the road gets better and goes round several spurs till a cross-road to Sumlong is passed at 5½ miles, and a ¼ of a mile further the Kaprawn Ka, a tributary of the Kaiya, is crossed. This is quite a small stream, 4 yards wide and 1 foot deep, with small, rocky bottom, but in rains will be rather difficult to cross. From here road runs through some rather difficult grass jungle till the Mali Ka is met at 6½ miles. This stream is 12 yards wide and 2½ feet deep now, but in floods will be 40 to 50 yards wide and unfordable. The bottom is rocky and the stream now fairly rapid, and flows at crossing in north-westerly direction. The water is very clear and good to drink. Banks on either side covered with thick grass jungle, and 8 to 10 feet high, but easy for mules as road is made. From here the road runs a little uphill till some terraced paddy-fields are reached at 7½ miles; surrounding country is covered with thick jungle, but this makes a very good camp. No commanding ground within 400 yards. Good water to north-west of camp; road not good. About a 5 hours' march with mules. From here the road runs uphill fairly gently as first, afterwards very steeply and with very precipitous sides, but road is good. Pumkatawng is on the top of a spur at 9 miles, the houses are rather nearer together than usual; good camping ground in village on spur. Water 200 yards down the khud to the west. Number of fowls, pigs, &c. Poppy cultivation.
		3. Ningrong Majángkatawng (2,096 feet). Kumsai Ka and another small stream.	**5 2**	25 6	General direction north-north-west. The road runs downhill from Pumkatawng fairly steeply at first through tree jungle and under growth. A small stream is crossed at ½ a mile just at its source, this flows towards the Mali Ka. Near here the jungle is tall grass, the road then runs up and down hill till Kumsai (16 houses) is reached at 2 miles. This village is about ¼ mile from the road on the right-hand

FROM WARÁKRÁN (OR WARAW), (APPENDIX I, ROUTE NO. 17, STAGE 1) TO SIMA (FORT MORTON) *viâ* NARU, PUMKATAWNG AND KUKAM—*continued*

Authorities.		Number and Names of Stages, Rivers and Streams.	Distances.		Remarks.
Military.	Civil.		Intermediate.	Total.	
G.O.C. Mandalay District and O.C. Bhamo.	Commissioner, Northern Division, and Deputy Commissioner, Bhamo.	**3. Ningrong Majángkatawng (2,096 feet)**—*cont.*			side and is surrounded by tree jungle, and is on a spur parallel to the Pumkatawng spur. There is a good camping ground in this village, if necessary, and water quite close. From here the road runs downhill with occasional rises till the Kumsai Ka is reached, the jungle on either side was cleared last year and is now open. The river is a small stream here, 12 yards wide, 1 foot deep, with a gravelly bottom and few rocks; the ground is level on either side for about 30 yards. Tree jungle on immediate proximity to the ka. In the rains the crossing would be unfordable (but animals could easily swim it) and would be 30 yards wide. It flows in a north-easterly direction. The river is visible from the road and it appears to run parallel with it from Kumsai. From the stream the road goes uphill at first; jungle is cleared, but afterwards it becomes large tree jungle with little undergrowth. The trees are very fine; a large number of fruit trees. Just outside the village of Ningrong Tingnukatawng (Lepai Seden; 16 houses) at 4½ miles, there is an excellent place for an encampment. This village is one of three (all Lepai Seden) that are called Ningrong. There is a large quantity of bamboo cut outside the village for building purposes. About ¾ mile further on there is a road which branches to the left to Kantaoyáng, and on the right the Marukatawng village (three houses, Maru), which is about a mile down in the khud on the stream called the Ninpong Ka. The road runs for another ½ mile through jungle till Ningrong Majángkatawng is reached at 5½ miles. This village consists of 28 houses and is situated on a spur; most houses down on either side. Camped in middle of village: not a good camp. Wild plantains in this neighbourhood, and a large number of fruit trees. Took 3 hours; mules arriving soon after advanced guard. Good road throughout. Here road from Bhamo (No. 3 of this Appendix) joins in.
		4. Kukam ... Mali Ka and Lasa Ka.	M. F. **9 6**	M. F. 35 4	From here the road runs in a north-westerly direction at first uphill through tree jungle, and then down through short jungle up to 1½ miles when a road to the left is passed leading to Kantaoyáng. One road here turns due north and goes through very thick grass jungle matted over head about 5 feet. The road here is very narrow and low, but otherwise good, up the cross-road to Kantaoyáng the road is broad and very good. The road runs downhill a little at first and then along a spur, is very level-going till it rises in a small hill about 1 mile from the turning. This is covered with tree jungle. After passing the hill the road descends very steeply through thick grass jungle and is still very narrow, otherwise good. Another cross-road to Kantaoyáng is passed at 3½ miles. Then the road turns to the east and falls down to the Mali Ka at 4¼ miles. After going through some soft ground near the stream, jungle becomes tree and thick underwood. The stream at crossing is 30 yards wide and 2 feet deep, the bottom is gravel and is good, there being few rocks, current slow, the bed is about 60 yards in full water, and in floods must overflow the banks, which are level on either side. The crossing now is very good, but would be unfordable and current rapid in floods, here the river flows in a north-westerly direction. About 200 yards below the

FROM WARÁKRÁN (OR WARAW), (APPENDIX I, ROUTE NO. 17, STAGE 1) TO SIMA (FORT MORTON) *viâ* NARU, PUMKATAWNG AND KUKAM—*continued.*

Authorities. Military.	Authorities. Civil.	Number and Names of Stages, Rivers and Streams.	Distances. Intermediate.	Distances. Total.	Remarks.
G.O.C. Mandalay District and O.C. Bhamo.	Commissioner, Northern Division, and Deputy Commissioner, Bhamo.	**4. Kukam**—*cont.*			crossing there is a bamboo bridge for foot-passengers. Here the river gets small and runs between some large rocks crossing known as Pumpi Rai. From here the road goes up a little and then down to a small stream, and it then rises along grass jungle, but this is fairly open. About $\frac{3}{4}$ mile from the Mali Ka (about 5 miles) road goes to the north leaving the Mali road on the right, and drops very suddenly down to the Lasa Ka at $5\frac{1}{4}$ miles, a tributary of the Mali. This stream has a much faster current than the Mali Ka, the banks to it are very steep and covered with thick jungle. After crossing the river road runs north through undulating ground; this has all been cleared for paddy cultivation and is quite open. The village of Kukam at $9\frac{3}{4}$ miles is on the top of a spur of the Kukam Pum. Before reaching this village a road branches off to the right which leads to Mali, and from here the jungle is thick tree. Road good throughout. Time of marching from Ningrong, 5 hours and 50 minutes; mules did not arrive till 40 minutes later. Distance, pacing. Kukam is a Kamlao village of 67 houses, 3,260 feet.
		5. Sima (Fort Morton). Manlin Ka and Tama Ka.	M. F. **5 0**	M. F. 40 4	General direction east. From here the road runs downhill through tree jungle very steeply at first till some taungya clearings are reached, then uphill and down again to the Manlin Ka (3 yards, 6 inches deep), a tributary of the Lasa Ka, at 1 mile. This is quite a small stream and of no importance. Half-a-mile further on the road crosses the Tama Ka (2 yards wide) which is now only swampy ground; this would be a bad place in rains. From here the road runs up at first through grass jungle and then through large tree and thick underwood till Kamja is reached on the top of the hill at $3\frac{3}{4}$ miles; village burnt. Road good for transport. Time from Kukam to Kamja, $2\frac{1}{4}$ hours. From Kamja the road passes over the site of the burned village, leaving the destroyed Kachin fort on the left, and ascends through jungle to Sima (Fort Morton) at 5 miles. Road very good and ascent not very great.

BRANCH I.

FROM KUKAM (STAGE 4) TO 'NKRÁNG (APPENDIX I, ROUTE NO. 8, STAGE 1).

BY LIEUT. W. H. DENT, 2ND P.W.O. YORKSHIRE REGIMENT, INTELLIGENCE OFFICER, SIMA COLUMN, 27TH APRIL 1893.

Military.	Civil.	Number and Names of Stages, Rivers and Streams.	Intermediate.	Total.	Remarks.
G.O.C. Mandalay District and O.C. Bhamo.	Commissioner, Northern Division, and Deputy Commissioner, Bhamo.	**1. 'Nkráng** ... Lahra Ka and five small streams.	**5 2**	5 2	This road runs from the north end of the village of Kukam and runs towards Kukam Pum; $\frac{3}{4}$ of a mile out of the village there is a branch road to the left, which leads to the village of Maitong on the west of Kukam Pum; the road runs to this point slightly uphill and through tree jungle; from here it runs along the side of the Kukam and 'Nkráng hills. It is fairly level keeping nearly to the same contour the whole way. Five small streams are crossed; these, though quite small, being practically at the source, make the road very boggy and would cause much difficulty for transport during the rains; the road runs through long grass jungle and a little bamboo. At 3 miles the road crosses a larger stream called the

FROM WARÁKÁN (OR WARAW), (APPENDIX I, ROUTE NO. 17, STAGE 1) TO SIMA (FORT MORTON) *viâ* NARU, PUMPAKATAWNG AND KUKAM—*continued*.

BRANCH I—*continued*.

Authorities. Military.	Authorities. Civil.	Number and Names of Stages, Rivers and Streams.	Distances. Intermediate.	Distances. Total.	Remarks.
G.O.C. Mandalay District and O.C. Bhamo.	Commr., Northern Division, and Deputy Commissioner, Bhamo.	**1. 'Nkráng**—*cont.*			Lahra Ka; this is 2 yards wide and 6 inches deep and has a rock and stony bottom: at $3\frac{3}{4}$ miles the road joins the Sima-'Nkráng route and $1\frac{1}{2}$ miles further on (total $5\frac{1}{4}$ miles) 'Nkráng is reached. The road is good throughout and, except for the boggy places, may be called a very good road. This is the shortest road to take to go to Mali from 'Nkráng. Distance by pacing time 2 hours and 10 minutes, mules arriving with party. For 'Nkráng *see* Route No. 8 of this Appendix, Stage 1.

No. 31.

ROUTES IN THE EXTREME NORTH OF UPPER BURMA.

I.—ITINERARY OF ROAD NORTHWARD FROM LEKANNOI FERRY ON THE 'NMAI KA TO SUPSIRAN FERRY ON THE MALI KA.

BY CAPT. F. H. ELLIOTT (NATIVE INFORMATION).

		Intermediate M.	F.	Total M.	F.	Remarks
Doubtful.	**1. Patwe**	**3**	**0**	3	0	Straight uphill.
	2. Singman ...	**3**	**0**	6	0	Tree jungle; flat country.
	3. Walor	**4**	**0**	10	0	Fairly level; streams small.
	4. Sanmikong ...	**1**	**0**	11	0	Paddy-fields, then ascent.
	5. Marakong ...	**5**	**0**	16	0	Descent to Namsang Ka (4 yards wide), then ascent.
	6. Sadankong ...	**3**	**0**	19	0	Descent and ascent; good road.
	7. Ningpien ...	**1**	**0**	20	0	Road level.
	8. Ningtong ...	**1**	**0**	21	0	Road level; fairly open country.
	9. Kachang ...	**3**	**0**	24	0	Easy descent to ka and then ascent.
	10. Tupauyan ...	**3**	**0**	27	0	Good, level road.
	11. Pauri	**1**	**0**	28	0	Road fairly level; one small stream.
	12. Pungyuamningsa.	**1**	**0**	29	0	Good road.
	13. Punka	**4**	**0**	33	0	Good road. Fairly level. No big streams.
	14. Lakong ...	**4**	**0**	37	0	Fairly level and good.
	15. Manran ...	**10**	**0**	47	0	Descent to Singma Ka; then ascent.
	16. Khikhripum ...	**5**	**0**	52	0	Steady ascent; road good.

ROUTES IN THE EXTREME NORTH OF UPPER BURMA—*continued.*

I.—ITINERARY OF ROAD NORTHWARD FROM LEKANNOI FERRY ON THE 'NMAI KA TO SUPSIRAN FERRY ON THE MALI KA—*continued.*

Authorities. Military.	Authorities. Civil.	Number and Names of Stages, Rivers and Streams.	Distances. Intermediate. M.	F.	Distances. Total. M.	F.	Remarks.
Doubtful.		**17. Rapum** ...	**3**	**0**	55	0	Ascent; good road.
		18. Lachowka-tong.	**9**	**0**	64	0	Descent to Tura Ka, then ascent. Tura Ka unfordable; crossed in rafts.
		19. Washa ...	**3**	**0**	67	0	Steady ascent.
		20. Ningkomla ...	**3**	**0**	70	0	Fairly level; small streams.
		21. Wakalon ...	**3**	**0**	73	0	Fairly level; good road.
		22. Ningron-kong.	**5**	**0**	78	0	Fairly level; good road.
		23. Kasitu ...	**5**	**0**	83	0	Fairly lev. l.
		24. Lautka ...	**9**	**0**	92	0	South-west, easy descent.
		25. Khumkhao ...	**3**	**0**	95	0	Easy descent.
		26. Supsiran Camp.	**3**	**0**	98	0	No village; a ferry here over the Mali Ka.

II.—ITINERARY FROM TALANG (LAT. 25° 51′, LONG. 97° 29′) NORTHWARDS TO MANZE IN THE KHAMTI COUNTRY.

BY CAPT. F. H. ELLIOTT (NATIVE INFORMATION), 1893.

Authorities. Military.	Authorities. Civil.	Number and Names of Stages, Rivers and Streams.	Intermediate. M.	F.	Total. M.	F.	Remarks.
Doubtful.		**1. Paukkaw** ...	**8**	**0**	8	0	Hilly road; cross Insop Ka, 12 yards wide.
		2. Changyang ...	**4**	**0**	12	0	Level road.
		3. Kanetka (Kanem ?).	**5**	**0**	17	0	Cross Tupum hill.
		4. Supkha ...	**4**	**0**	21	0	Level road; cross Tayang Ka, 7 yards wide and always fordable.
		5. Seinsiyao ...	**4**	**0**	25	0	Tree and bamboo jungle; good level road.
		6. Tumsanang ...	**4**	**0**	29	0	Descent to Taru Ka (14 yards wide and never fordable), then ascent.
		7. Wara	**4**	**0**	33	0	Hilly road.
		8. Wawun	**4**	**0**	37	0	Hilly road, but good.
		9. Siyankong ...	**3**	**0**	40	0	Good, level road.
		10. 'Nsein	**10**	**0**	50	0	Descent to Wasip Ka (14 yards wide and fordable in cold weather), then ascent.
		11. Pumlumbum.	**1**	**0**	51	0	Road good and level.
		12. Saraukatong (Sarongkang ?).	**1**	**0**	52	0	Hilly road.

ROUTES IN THE EXTREME NORTH OF UPPER BURMA—*continued.*

II.—ITINERARY FROM TALANG (LAT. 25° 51', LONG. 97° 29') NORTHWARDS TO MANZÉ IN THE KHAMTI COUNTRY—*continued.*

Authorities.		Number and Names of Stages, Rivers and Streams.	Distances.				Remarks.
Military.	Civil.		Intermediate.		Total.		
			M.	F.	M.	F.	
Doubtful.		**13. Pumrong** ...	**1**	**0**	53	0	Good, level road.
		14. Impaokatong	**1**	**0**	54	0	Good, level road.
		15. Maraoka, camp.	**1**	**0**	55	0	No village; camp in jungle.
		16. Lutlaka ...	**4**	**0**	59	0	Road fairly level.
		17. Kumsang-neing (Teinloi).	**4**	**0**	63	0	Road hilly.
		18. Marunka ...	**4**	**0**	67	0	Road hilly. Cross Sinan Ka, 17 yards wide and never fordable.
		19. Walaupum ...	**4**	**0**	71	0	Hilly road. Cross Pumwi Ka, 7 yards wide and always fordable.
		20. Lachunnong.	**6**	**0**	77	0	Cross Sailong hill; said to be good going.
		21. Tangku ...	**2**	**0**	79	0	Hilly road.
		22. Lanannong ...	**2**	**0**	81	0	Good level road.
		23. Kwontap-katong.	**4**	**0**	85	0	Good level road.
		24. Tawauka ...	**4**	**0**	89	0	Hilly road, but good.
		25. Wabyit ...	**4**	**0**	93	0	Hilly road, but good. Cross Pining Ka, 14 yards wide; fordable in winter.
		26. Kareinka ...	**1**	**0**	94	0	Road up and down, but good.
		27. Kazuka ...	**4**	**0**	98	0	Road up and down, but good.
		28. Lawunka ...	**10**	**0**	108	0	Level road. Cross Pinsi Ka, 14 yards wide and fordable in winter.
		29. Pasika... ...	**5**	**0**	113	0	Good, level road. Tree and bamboo jungle.
		30. Ningtong ...	**5**	**0**	118	0	Cross Mineya Ka (10 yards wide, fordable in winter), then ascent of Kaopum hill and descent by good road to Lumsha Ka (17 yards wide and fordable in winter); thence level to Ningtong.
		31. Kadautu ...	**3**	**0**	121	0	Good level road.
		32. 'Nkhum Pasi.	**1**	**0**	122	0	Level road through bamboo and tree jungle.

ROUTES IN THE EXTREME NORTH OF UPPER BURMA—*continued.*

II.—ITINERARY FROM TALANG (LAT. 25° 51′, LONG. 97° 29′) NORTHWARDS TO MANZE IN THE KHAMTI COUNTRY—*continued.*

Authorities. Military.	Authorities. Civil.	Number and Names of Stages, Rivers and Streams.	Distances. Intermediate. M.	F.	Total. M.	F.	Remarks.
Doubtful.		**33. Meinglang** ...	**3**	**0**	125	0	Open plain. Cross Meinglang river, 27 yards wide; crossed by ferry. This is the first Khamti village.
		34. Lakhun ...	**8**	**0**	133	0	Open plain.
		35. Manze... ...	**5**	**0**	138	0	Open plain; small streams.

III.—ITINERARY FROM PUMYUAMNINGSA (ABOUT LAT. 25° 56′, LONG. 97° 56′), (NO. 12 OF ITINERARY NO. I), NORTHWARDS TO LAWKHUM.

BY CAPT. F. H. ELLIOTT (NATIVE INFORMATION), 1893.

Authorities. Military.	Authorities. Civil.	Number and Names of Stages, Rivers and Streams.	Intermediate. M.	F.	Total. M.	F.	Remarks.
Doubtful.		**1. Pumpu**	**6**	**0**	6	0	Good level road.
		2. Kwiwan ...	**6**	**0**	12	0	Hilly road. Cross Singma Ka, 18 yards wide, fordable in winter.
		3. Lipong	**4**	**0**	16	0	Level road.
		4. Sumpaungmata	**14**	**0**	30	0	Hilly road. Cross Sakyi Ka, 14 yards wide and fordable.
		5. Milom	**4**	**0**	34	0	Hilly road.
		6. Patwa	**2**	**0**	36	0	Good level road.
		7. Lachun ...	**4**	**0**	40	0	Hilly road.
		8. Lawkhum ...	**4**	**0**	44	0	Hilly road.

IV.—ITINERARY FROM LAPÉ JUST BELOW THE CONFLUENCE NORTHWARDS TO LAMONGMAREIN ABOUT LAT. 6° 30′. (THIS ROAD IS TO THE WEST OF ITINERARY NO. II.)

BY CAPT. F. H. ELLIOTT (NATIVE INFORMATION), 1893.

Authorities. Military.	Authorities. Civil.	Number and Names of Stages, Rivers and Streams.	Intermediate. M.	F.	Total. M.	F.	Remarks.
Doubtful.		**1. Tanbyé**	**4**	**0**	4	0	Only camp; no village.
		2. Kadonkong ...	**(?)3**	**0**	7	0	
		3. Miteing ...	**(?)6**	**0**	13	0	Road good.
		4. Kwonsana ...	**6**	**0**	19	0	Road good and fairly level.
		5. Kamika	**12**	**0**	31	0	Hilly road.
		6. Tuka	**5**	**0**	36	0	Fairly level road. Cross Sinlong Ka, 14 yards wide, fordable in winter.
		7. Kadaunong ...	**2**	**0**	38	0	Hilly road.
		8. Kayuntu ...	**12**	**0**	50	0	Hilly road.
		9. Ningkanpataw.	**6**	**0**	56	0	Hilly road through tree and bamboo jungle.

ROUTES IN THE EXTREME NORTH OF UPPER BURMA—*continued.*

IV.—ITINERARY FROM LAPÉ JUST BELOW THE CONFLUENCE NORTHWARDS TO LAMONGMAREIN ABOUT LAT. 6° 30′. (THIS ROAD IS TO THE WEST OF ITINERARY NO. II)—*continued.*

Authorities. Military.	Authorities. Civil.	Number and Names of Stages, Rivers and Streams.	Distances. Intermediate. M.	Distances. Intermediate. F.	Distances. Total. M.	Distances. Total. F.	Remarks.
Doubtful.		**10. Lakakong** ...	**6**	**0**	62	0	Hilly road. Cross the Su Ka, 14 yards wide, fordable in winter.
		11. Walaka ...	**12**	**0**	74	0	Cross Taru Ka, 14 yards wide, always fordable.
		12. Kaotu	**2**	**0**	76	0	Good road.
		13. Kanluka ...	**4**	**0**	80	0	Good road.
		14. Ningranka ...	**4**	**0**	84	0	Good road.
		15. Sapyinkakatong.	**4**	**0**	88	0	Hilly road.
		16. Wagaka ...	**4**	**0**	92	0	Hilly road.
		17. Lamongmarein.	**12**	**0**	104	0	Hilly road. Cross Sinan Ka, 14 yards wide, fordable in winter.

V.—ITINERARY FROM NAWPUM NEAR SADÁNKONG BETWEEN THE MALI KA AND 'NMAI KA, NORTH-EAST TO SINKRON (LAT. 25° 53′, LONG. 97° 55′).

BY CAPT. F. H. ELLIOTT (NATIVE INFORMATION), 1893.

Authorities. Military.	Authorities. Civil.	Number and Names of Stages, Rivers and Streams.	Distances. Intermediate. M.	Distances. Intermediate. F.	Distances. Total. M.	Distances. Total. F.	Remarks.
Doubtful.		**1. Ningpwon** ...	**3**	**0**	3	0	Cross Singma Ka, 20 yards wide, always fordable.
		2. Sinkong... ...	**2**	**0**	5	0	Good road: no obstacles.
		3. Kunzu	**2**	**0**	7	0	Hilly road.
		4. Lawpum ...	**1**	**0**	8	0	Good road.
		5. Shinkwon ...	**2**	**0**	10	0	Good road.
		6. Sinkron or Sinkong.	**4**	**0**	14	0	Good road.

VI.—ITINERARY FROM SINKRON (LAT. 25° 53′, LONG. 97° 55′) SOUTHWARDS TO TAMJA.

BY CAPT. F. H. ELLIOTT (NATIVE INFORMATION), 1893.

Authorities. Military.	Authorities. Civil.	Number and Names of Stages, Rivers and Streams.	Distances. Intermediate. M.	Distances. Intermediate. F.	Distances. Total. M.	Distances. Total. F.	Remarks.
Doubtful.		**1. Tiya (Tiyon?).**	**1**	**0**	1	0	Good road.
		2. Katuyan ...	**8**	**0**	9	0	Good level road.
		3. Punwa Lidan (Hpungwa).	**4**	**0**	13	0	Good level road.
		4. Tamayan (Matangyan).	**6**	**0**	19	0	Hilly road.
		5. Tausun Ferry.	**5**	**0**	24	0	Descent, road hilly, but good; no village; ferry over 'Nmai Ka; one boat worked by the Adan (Atang) villagers.

ROUTES IN THE EXTREME NORTH OF UPPER BURMA—*continued.*

VI.—ITINERARY FROM SINKRON (LAT. 25° 53′, LONG. 97° 55′) SOUTHWARDS TO TAMJA—*continued.*

Authorities. Military.	Authorities. Civil.	Number and Names of Stages, Rivers and Streams.	Distances. Intermediate. M.	Distances. Intermediate. F.	Distances. Total. M.	Distances. Total. F.	Remarks.
Doubtful.		**6. Adan (Atang).**	1	0	25	0	
		7. Lanmipum ...	2	0	27	0	Road hilly, but good.
		8. Kunzu	3	0	30	0	Hilly road.
		9. Latté	4	0	34	0	Fairly level road. Cross Latté Ka, 14 yards wide, fordable in winter.
		10. Sikum	8	0	42	0	Hilly road.
		11. Sikli	2	0	44	0	Good level road.
		12. Chonmaw ...	1	0	45	0	Good level road.
		13. Lowsam ...	1	0	46	0	Good road. Cross Chonmaw Ka, 10 yards wide, fordable.
		14. Longkya ...	4	0	50	0	Good level road.
		15. Mikukatong...	4	0	54	0	Cross Sinmaw Ka, 17 yards wide, fordable in winter only.
		16. Tamja	4	0	58	0	Cross Kowlan Taung and Panseingkatong. About 2 miles from Kowlan is Tapaw Ka. Tamja is a Chinese village.

VII.—ITINERARY FROM SADÁNKONG, SOUTH-EAST TO PANTU OR PINDU, ABOUT 6 MILES NORTH-EAST OF SADÔN.

BY CAPT. F. H. ELLIOTT (NATIVE INFORMATION), 1893.

Authorities. Military.	Authorities. Civil.	Number and Names of Stages, Rivers and Streams.	Intermediate. M.	Intermediate. F.	Total. M.	Total. F.	Remarks.
Doubtful.		**1. Supma**	2	0	2	0	Hilly road.
		2. Wapong... ...	1	0	3	0	Level road.
		3. Likhum	8	0	11	0	Cross Pumpa Pum.
		4. Terong	4	0	15	0	Good road.
		5. Wapya	4	0	19	0	Hilly road. Cross Namli Ka, 3 yards wide.
		6. Pinle	1	0	20	0	Hilly road.
		7. Pumli	2	0	22	0	Hilly road.
		8. Sampawng ...	2	0	24	0	Good level road.
		9. Sumkha	1	0	25	0	Good road.
		10. Sumkhalakong.	3	0	28	0	Cross Sumgi Ka, 3 yards wide.
		11. Leitang ...	3	0	31	0	Cross 'Nmai Ka.
		12. Lashi Leitang	4	0	35	0	Hilly road.

ROUTES IN THE EXTREME NORTH OF UPPER BURMA—*continued.*

VII.—ITINERARY FROM SADÁNKONG, SOUTH-EAST TO PANTU OR PINDU, ABOUT 6 MILES NORTH-EAST OF SADÔN—*continued.*

Authorities. Military.	Authorities. Civil.	Number and Names of Stages, Rivers and Streams.	Distances. Intermediate. M.	F.	Distances. Total. M.	F.	Remarks.
Doubtful.		**13. Kalaokong ...**	**4**	**0**	39	0	Hilly road.
		14. Paléy	**2**	**0**	41	0	Good road.
		15. Ningc.'am ...	**2**	**0**	43	0	Good road.
		16. Pasang ...	**2**	**0**	45	0	Good road.
		17. Pukpienning-ta.	**(?)3**	**0**	48	0	
		18. Pindu or Pantu.	**10**	**0**	58	0	Hilly road. Cross Kangon Ka, 3 yards wide, and Nawku Ka, 17 yards wide; fordable.

VIII.—ITINERARY FROM SADÁNKONG SOUTH-WEST TO KWITAO FERRY.

Authorities. Military.	Authorities. Civil.	Number and Names of Stages, Rivers and Streams.	Distances. Intermediate. M.	F.	Distances. Total. M.	F.	Remarks.
Doubtful.		**1. Marakong ...**	**2**	**0**	2	0	Hilly road.
		2. Kinruwaru ...	**6**	**0**	8	0	Good road.
		3. Seintong ...	**2**	**0**	10	0	Good road.
		4. Laitong... ...	**3**	**0**	13	0	Good road.
		5. Kalik	**10**	**0**	23	0	Hilly road.
		6. Pinlan	**5**	**0**	28	0	Hilly road.
		7. Kwitao	**6**	**0**	34	0	Hilly road.

APPENDIX II.

ADDITIONAL ROUTES IN THE SHAN HILLS DIVISION.

APPENDIX II.

ADDITIONAL ROUTES IN THE SHAN HILLS DIVISION.

No. 1.

From KYAUKHNYÁT to MÉHAWNGSAWN (Siam) viâ MÉCHÉ and HKUNYUOM.

BY CAPT. H. B. WALKER, DUKE OF CORNWALL'S LIGHT INFANTRY, INTELLIGENCE BRANCH, BURMA 1893.

Authorities. Military.	Authorities. Civil.	Number and Names of Stages, Rivers and Streams.	Distances. Intermediate. M.	Distances. Intermediate. F.	Distances. Total. M.	Distances. Total. F.	Remarks.
G.O.C. Rangoon District.	Superintendent, Southern Shan States.	**1. Karé ... ...**	**10**	**0**	10	0	See Appendix III, Route No. 2.
		2. Umpauk ...	**6**	**4**	16	4	
		3. Camp on branch of Mépa river.	**11**	**4**	28	0	
		4. Nam Mépa ...	**8**	**0**	36	0	
		5. Camp on Hwé Páng Ting.	**12**	**0**	48	0	
		6. Méché (Mésé).	**6**	**4**	54	4	
Siam.		**7. Camp on Nam Pông.**	**8**	**0**	62	4	
		8. Méngau ...	**10**	**4**	73	0	
		9. Hkunyuom ...	**8**	**0**	81	0	
		10. Méhsulín ...	**6**	**4**	87	4	
		11. Mé Sakyi ...	**8**	**0**	95	4	
		12. Palán	**9**	**0**	104	4	
		13. Pông Sakhán.	**6**	**6**	111	2	
		14. Hpahpawng...	**6**	**0**	117	2	
		15. Méhawng-sawn.	**6**	**6**	124	0	

No. 2.

From KYENGTUNG (KENG TUNG) to MÖNG LWI.

By Capt. H. R. DAVIES, Oxfordshire Light Infantry, Intelligence Branch, Burma, March 1893.

Authorities. Military.	Authorities. Civil.	Number and Names of Stages, Rivers and Streams.	Distances. Intermediate. M.	F.	Total. M.	F.	Remarks.
G.O.C. Rangoon District.	Superintendent, Southern Shan States.	**1. Ban Sai** ...	11	6	11	6	See Appendix III, Route No. 9.
		2. Tálö	11	0	22	6	
		3. Möng Ngawm.	15	2	38	0	See Appendix III, Route No. 9.
		4. Möng Kai ...	11	0	49	0	
		5. Hwé Kut ...	9	2	58	2	
		6. Páng Waw ...	8	2	66	4	
		7. Möng Yawn ...	11	0	77	4	
		8. Ban Namhkuk.	13	0	90	4	
		9. Möng Lwi ...	10	0	100	4	

No. 3.

From KYENGTUNG (KENG TUNG) to MÖNG HSING (SING) viâ KENGLAP.

By Havildar JAGAT SINGH, 19th Punjaub Infantry, Intelligence Branch, Burma, March 1893.

Authorities. Military.	Authorities. Civil.	Number and Names of Stages, Rivers and Streams.	Distances. Intermediate. M.	F.	Total. M.	F.	Remarks.
G.O.C. Rangoon District.	Superintendent, Southern Shan States.	**1. Möng Chum** ...	7	2	7	2	See Appendix III, Route No. 9, Alternative I.
		2. Möng Phak ...	13	4	20	6	
		3 Páng Namhet.	14	4	35	2	
		4. Möngphayak ...	10	2	45	4	
		5. Páng Khalong.	12	0	57	4	
		6. Mönglin ...	12	0	69	4	
		7. Namkhum ...	7	4	77	0	
		8. Páleo	10	0	87	0	
		9. Kenglap ...	14	0	101	0	
		10. Camp on Nam Un.	8	4	109	4	
		11. Möng Long ...	11	0	120	4	
		12. Möng Náng.	15	4	136	0	
		13. Pánghai ...	8	4	144	4	
		14. Möng Hsing.	8	4	153	0	

FROM KYENGTUNG (KENG TUNG) TO MÖNG HSING (SING) *viâ* KENGLAP—*continued.*

BRANCH I.

FROM PÁLEO (STAGE 8) TO MÖNG YAWN (YÔN), (APPENDIX III, ROUTE NO. 9, STAGE 6).

INFORMATION FURNISHED BY NO. 11 PARTY (TOPOGRAPHICAL), SURVEY OF INDIA, MARCH 1893.

Authorities. Military.	Authorities. Civil.	Number and Names of Stages, Rivers and Streams.	Distances. Intermediate. M.	F.	Total. M.	F.	Remarks.
G.O.C. Rangoon District.	Superintendent, Southern Shan States.	**1. Jangal Sakhán** Nam Won river.	9	0	9	0	Leave the Paleo-Kenglap road at 1¼ miles from Paleo, bearing north-west at wooden post* through open flat ground (old fields) to foot of hills ½ mile, up gradual slope of winding spur 2 miles to top (old site of Meshur village), along range trending north and passes 80 feet below highest point of range (height 4,300 feet) 6¼ miles from the Paleo-Kenglap road, steeply down for 200 yards, crossing stream at 7th mile, descending gradually to Jangal Sakhán on the Nam Won river 3,800 feet except 200 yards above river, which is steep.
		2. Banwanháng ...	10	4	19	4	The road runs for 3 miles through a curious bit of undulating tableland nearly flat. It ascends gradually from camp for ¾ mile. Crossing hill stream at 1 mile and again at 1¼ miles near its source and another hill stream with steep banks at 1¾ miles which courses from north, along the right of road for another mile, the hill-top being broad from the second stream to its source. At 3 miles the road runs round the shoulder of a somewhat precipitous peak and descends rather rapidly at first, after which it lies down a long, undulating, gradually descending grassy spur, crossing main stream from the right at 8 miles. Road continues along hill range gradually descending to within ¼ mile of village of Banwanháng, 1,960 feet in the valley; the stream hard by the village is crossed and recrossed ¼ mile south before reaching the village: a large block of the village is hidden away among low hills ½ mile east.
		3. Möng Yawn (Möngyôn).	9	4	29	0	Traverses flat country in jungle crossing village stream at 200 yards and main stream 20 yards in width at ¾ mile, meeting road from Möng Phayak Stage 4 above) at 1¼ miles, alongside left bank of above main stream for 1 mile through cultivated land, stream 200 yards off, over stream bridged at 2¾ miles, by hamlet and stream at 3 miles, through river Namyôn, 22 yards wide with high banks, passing large kyaung on the right and by Wanphai at 4 miles, crossing shallow stream at 5 miles, Möngyôn village 5¼ miles, Mönglun at 6½ miles, large stream 7 miles 5 furlongs, smaller stream at 8 miles 1 furlong, Nam Khap river at 9¼ miles in two rivulets at crossing. The road skirts low hills from Wan Phai to Möng Yawn.

* Wooden posts mark the resting places of the Sawbwa of Kyaingtôn (? Kengtung) when he made a pilgrimage to Möng Yawn. There is one at the latter place.

No. 4.

From MÖNG TA (HTA) to MÖNG HENG (Siam) *viâ* KIUKAW.

THE SURVEY OF INDIA, JANUARY 1893.

Authorities. Military.	Authorities. Civil.	Number and Names of Stages, Rivers and Streams.	Distances. Intermediate. M.	F.	Total. M.	F.	Remarks.
G.O.C. Rangoon District.	Superintendent, Southern Shan States.	**1. Camp on Pángwon stream.** Nam Mé Ta and Hwé Möng Sáng.	11	4	11	4	The general run of the road from the village of Möng Ta is south. There are two sites, one on either side of the stream, Nam Mé Ta; the camping ground is near the western side. There is a fairly large plain, and good and shady camp can be secured. From the western side the road runs for about a mile along the left bank of the Nam Mé Ta stream and then enters the dry bed of a stream. It goes along this for about 1 mile and reaches the top of the spur almost at its source. Thence the road runs for about 2¼ miles over low hilly ground difficult for laden animals till it reaches the point where the Hwé Möng Sáng meets the Nam Mé Ta. From this junction the road runs along the Hwé Möng Sáng, crossing and recrossing it several times till it reaches the watershed, whence the stream takes its rise, and where the boundary pillar Kiukaw is situated. The portion of the route along the Hwé Möng Sáng is fairly good, but is very difficult during the rains. Camping ground for 200 men in the jungle, if cleared, on the bank of the Pángwon stream.
Siam.		**2. Möng Heng** ... Mé Ting, &c.	14	0	25	4	*See* Appendix III, Route No. 7. This is the direct route from Möng Ta to Zimmé *viâ* Möng Heng (*see* Appendix III, Route No. 8).

No. 5.

From NAWNG PALÁN to MÉLANA (Route No. 33, Shan Hills Division, Stage 3).

THE SURVEY OF INDIA, FEBRUARY 1893.

Authorities. Military.	Authorities. Civil.	Number and Names of Stages, Rivers and Streams.	Intermediate. M.	F.	Total. M.	F.	Remarks.
G.O.C. Rangoon District.	Superintendent, Southern Shan States.	**1. Kahán** ... Mé Mak, Mé Sakun, and Mé Pyet.	12	0	12	0	Nawng Palán is a fairly large village situated on the Mé Mak; there is a good camping ground, and small quantities of rice and vegetables can be obtained. Leaving Nawng Palán the stream Mé Mak is crossed at the village and the road keeps along the stream, crossing and recrossing it several times till it reaches the Má Sakun stream at the 7th mile. Here there is good camping ground and a sufficient supply of good water from the Mé Sakun. There is a gentle ascent for about 1 mile and then the road branches into two: one descends into the valley of the Mé Pyet, and then goes along that stream until Kahán is reached; the other goes to the village of Payak about 2 miles further, and thence round to Kahán. The descent from Payak to Kahán is somewhat difficult; at Kahán a small camp can be obtained by clearing the jungle.
Siam.		**2. Mélana** ... The Mélana stream.	14	4	26	4	From Kahán the road keeps along the Mé Pyet stream till the village of Taklet is reached. A small camping ground, but no shade good water, but no supplies. Hence this once large

FROM NAWNG PALÂN TO MÉLANA—*continued.*

Authorities. Military.	Authorities. Civil.	Number and Names of Stages, Rivers and Streams	Distances. Inter-mediate.	Distances. Total.	Remarks.
Siam.		**2. Mélana**—*cont.*			village is now deserted and the only inhabitants are an old man and his son (in February 1893). From Taklet there are two roads to Mélana; the eastern road crosses the boundary watershed about 1½ miles to the east of the boundary pillar. Thence it runs along a gradual slope, keeping to one spur all the way till it reaches the Mélana stream and meets the other road. The other road keeps along the Mé Pyet till it reaches the source of the stream, at which place the boundary pillar Nam Hsa Möng is situated. From here it runs along the main spur, till it reaches the Mélana stream and is met by the eastern road at a little to the north of the village of Wan Inyak. From Wan Inyak the village of Mélana is reached after a run of about 2 miles. The camping ground here is a very poor one, very little and bad water, and no shade. This place is on the main road between Möng Maö and Möng Heng (*see* Route No. 33, Shan Hills Division).

No. 6.

From NGÁPÚPÔN to CAMP on the Hwé Hsán (Siam).

THE SURVEY OF INDIA, FEBRUARY 1893.

Authorities. Military.	Authorities. Civil.	Number and Names of Stages, Rivers and Streams	Intermediate M.	Intermediate F.	Total M.	Total F.	Remarks.
Siam.		**1. Hwé Hsán Camp.** Namkhawng (tributary of the Mépai), Hwé Hsán, a small stream of 10 or 15 feet wide, 1 foot to 1½ feet deep, flowing into the Namkhawng.	**9**	**0**	9	0	At Ngápúpôn (*see* Route No. 32, Shan Division, Stage 1), there is a fine camping ground with good water. The route from Ngápúpôn village runs south, keeping along the right bank of a small stream called the Nam-Khang. At 2 miles the hamlet of Wan Thong Salé is reached. From here the route simply follows the Namkhawng, crossing and recrossing it several times till the Hwé Hsán camp situated on the junction of the Hwé Hsán stream with the Namkhawng is reached (*see* Route No. 6, Stage 9, Appendix III). The route is good the whole way, and though the stream has to be crossed several times, no difficulties present themselves for transport.

APPENDIX III.

ROUTES IN SIAM.

APPENDIX III.

ROUTES IN SIAM.

No. 1.

From CHIENG HAI (CHIENG RAI) to MÖNG LONG viâ CHIENG KONG (CHIENG KHAWNG).

BY CAPT. H. R. DAVIES, OXFORDSHIRE LIGHT INFANTRY, INTELLIGENCE BRANCH, BURMA, FEBRUARY 1893.

Authorities.		Number and Names of Stages, Rivers and Streams.	Distances.				Remarks.
Military.	Civil.		Intermediate.		Total.		
			M.	F.	M.	F.	
Siam.		**1. Camp on the Mé Khwa.** Mé Kawn.	**8**	**4**	8	4	General direction east; good, level mule road; through paddy for a mile, afterwards through jungle and high grass. Follow the course of the Mé Khok more or less closely for 7 miles. At 1¼ miles Mé Kawn from the right (15 yards by 1½ feet). At 1½ miles Sôpkawn, 17 houses. At 3¾ miles Pabong on the right and road to left to ferry across the Mé Khok, ¼ mile off; two boats and a waist-deep ford; the ferrymen live in Pabong and the road the other side leads to Ban Du. At 8½ miles the Mé Khwa (30 yards by 4 feet) runs along the edge of the road on the right; water muddy. Camp in thin bamboo jungle; good grass.
		2. Tong Yáng ... Mé Lao, Hwé Silik, and Hwé Tak Noi.	**10**	**0**	18	4	General direction east. Good level mule road: easy, except for the first 2½ miles, which is overgrown with grass 10 feet high. At 2 miles cross the Mé Lao from the right (20 yards by 2 feet); moderate current; easy ford; room for a very small camp about 20 yards square on each bank: no room here for a column to camp; all round is grass 10 feet high which would be difficult to clear. At 2½ miles a marsh 20 yards wide, easy in February. At 5 miles the road passes among hills, but the road itself is practically level. At 6 and at 7 miles Hwé Silik, in stagnant pools. At 9 miles enter paddy plain at Tong Yáng; large camping ground in paddy and jungle: one sayát holding 20 men. Water from Hwé Tak Noi (3 yards by 6 inches): good grass.

FROM CHIENG HAI (CHIENG RAI) TO MÖNG LONG *viâ* CHIENG KONG (CHIENG KHAWNG)—*continued.*

Authorities.		Number and Names of Stages, Rivers and Streams.	Distances.				Remarks.
Military.	Civil.		Intermediate.		Total.		
			M.	F.	M.	F.	
Siam.		**3. Ban Hta** ... Mé Tak and Mé In.	**13**	**6**	32	2	General direction south-east by east. Good level mule road, chiefly through jungle with occasional open spaces: the last mile and-a-half through paddy. The following villages are passed:—At $2\frac{3}{4}$ miles Mé Pao, four houses; at $3\frac{1}{2}$ miles Ban Métak, 10 houses; at 6 miles Hai Tai, six houses; at $1\frac{1}{2}$ and at 3 miles Mé Tak (5 to 10 yards by 6 inches). At $11\frac{1}{4}$ miles the Mé In is crossed (from the right, 60 yards by $1\frac{1}{2}$ feet; gentle current, sandy bottom, steep banks 25 feet high); room to camp on either bank. At Ban Hta large camping ground: good grass and water. Village contains 100 houses; large supplies of cattle, rice, and paddy.
		4. Pukyeng ... Numerous streams.	**16**	**4**	48	6	General direction north. Good level mule road. Just beyond Ban Hta the route joins the main road from Chieng Kong to Möng Nan. Through tree jungle all the way along the foot of a high range of hills on the right with the Mé In some distance off on the left. The following villages are passed:—At $3\frac{1}{2}$ miles Páhtán (100); at $4\frac{1}{4}$ miles Sidi (15); at $8\frac{3}{4}$ miles Yánghawm (10); at $10\frac{1}{4}$ miles Chunpu (10); at $10\frac{3}{4}$ miles Ban Long (15); at 12 miles Pabong (10), $\frac{1}{2}$ mile away on the left; at 13 miles Ban Namphé (20); at $14\frac{1}{4}$ miles Denmong (10); at 15 miles Tônpawng (20). In Pukyeng there are 60 houses, and zayáts and camping ground in the middle of the village; good water and grass. This march, though a long one, is along an easy, level road. Camps could be pitched on any of the streams crossed, as the jungle is everywhere thin and easily cleared. The following streams are met with in this stage:—At $3\frac{1}{2}$ miles Hwé Páhtán (6 yards by 6 inches); at $4\frac{1}{4}$ miles Hwé Sidi (5 yards by 6 inches); at 6 miles Hwé Hawm (5 yards by 6 inches); at $6\frac{1}{2}$ miles Hwé Pasap (6 yards by 9 inches); at $9\frac{1}{2}$ miles Hwé Yánghawm (5 yards by 6 inches); at $9\frac{3}{4}$ miles Hwé Luk, 5 yards wide, in stagnant pools; at $10\frac{1}{4}$ miles Hwé Chunpu (5 yards by 8 inches); at $10\frac{3}{4}$ miles Hwé Long (5 yards by 6 inches); at 11 miles Hwé Meleng (6 yards by 8 inches); at 13 miles Hwé Namphé (2 yards by 6 inches); at 14 miles Hwé Denmöng (5 yards by 4 inches); at 15 miles Hwé Tônpawng (4 yards by 4 inches); at $16\frac{1}{2}$ miles Hwé Pukyeng (5 yards by 6 inches).
		5. Ban Lung ... Numerous streams.	**13**	**6**	62	4	General direction north. Good level mule road through the same sort of country as the last stage. The following villages are passed through:—At $\frac{1}{4}$ mile Sama (6); at $3\frac{1}{2}$ miles Ban Sán, a Lu village (6); at $4\frac{1}{2}$ miles Ban Khöng (50); at $5\frac{3}{4}$ miles Ban Long (20); at $7\frac{3}{4}$ miles Kyilek (6); at $8\frac{1}{4}$ miles Paokhut (12); at 12 miles Ban Tawng (10). In Ban Lung there are 12 houses. Best camping ground on the left bank of the Mé In, where the road crosses the river; good grass. The following streams are met with in this stage:—At $\frac{3}{4}$ mile Hwé Hôk (6 yards by 6 inches); at $2\frac{1}{2}$ miles Hwé Nampôk (4 yards by 6 inches); bad water; at $3\frac{1}{2}$ miles Hwé Sán (3 yards by 6 inches); at $4\frac{1}{2}$ miles Hwé Khöng (6 yards by 6 inches); at $5\frac{3}{4}$ miles Hwé Long (3 yards by 4

FROM CHIENG HAI (CHIENG RAI) TO MÖNG LONG *viâ* CHIENG KONG (CHIENG KHAWNG)—*continued.*

Authorities. Military.	Authorities. Civil.	Number and Names of Stages, Rivers and Streams.	Distances. Intermediate. M. F.	Distances. Total. M. F.	Remarks.
		5. Ban Lung—*cont.*			inches); at 7¾ miles Hwé Kyilek (3 yards by 4 inches); at 8¼ miles Hwé Paokhut (6 yards wide, stagnant); at 10¾ miles Hwé Musum (3 yards by 4 inches); bad water; at 12¼ miles Hwé Tawng (10 yards by stagnant pools); at 13¾ miles Mé In from the left (80 yards by 2 feet); banks steep and 30 feet high; easy fords; two small boats here.
		6. Chieng Kong ... Several streams.	9 4	72 0	General direction north. Good level mule road. First through very thin jungle and open grass. At 5½ miles through paddy for a mile, thence through tree jungle. The following villages are passed:—At 5½ miles Tongniu (16); at 5¾ miles Namsáng (8); at 6 miles Sakhán (40); at Chieng Kong (150 to 200 houses) zayáts for 150 men; camping grounds inside town very dirty. The best place to camp would be in jungle just before entering the town. Supplies in moderate quantities; vegetables very scarce. The following streams are met with in this stage:—At 5 miles Nam Ma from the left (5 yards by 1 foot); at 5¾ miles Hwé Sáng from the left (5 yards by 8 inches); at 6½ miles Hwé Wong from the left (2 yards by 6 inches); at 9 miles Hwé Luk from the left (6 yards by 1 foot).
	Siam.	**7. Camp on the Nam Haw.** Mé Kong and several small streams by easy fords.	6 0	78 0	General direction east. Good mule road; a short march, but the Mé Kong has to be crossed (from the left, 300 yards wide; sandy bottom, with rocks sticking up; rapid current; mules cannot be swum across; crossed by one raft, which will take 30 men, 6 mules, or 15 mule-loads. There are 70 or 80 boats in Chieng Kong and more rafts could easily be made): up the right bank of the river for 1¼ miles to the ferry, cross the Mé Kong and follow its left bank down to the village of Ban Wan at 2 miles; then turn eastward, crossing several spurs and streams to the Nam Haw, where there is a small camp; more room can be got by clearing jungle. Good water from the Nam Haw (8 yards by 1 foot).
		8. Katang ... Several streams.	11 2	89 2	General direction north-east. Good mule road. The Nam Haw is crossed on leaving camp, 8 yards wide, 1 foot deep, from the left. Cross small spurs and streams for 5¼ miles, when the Nam Yung is crossed. At 2½ miles Hwé Salalong from the left (5 yards by 10 inches). At 5¼ miles, Nam Yung from the left (8 yards by 6 inches); thence steep ascent to the top of a ridge at 6 miles; along the top of the ridge to 7 miles; thence descent of ¼ mile to the Hwé Tintôk. From here cross several more streams, the spurs between them being less steep than those crossed before. At Katang zayáts for 60 men and small camping ground; more room could be cleared; water from Hwé Makkeao (5 yards by 8 inches). The village of Katang (Khamu) is ¼ mile away on the left of the road. Grass is scarce here, but bamboo leaves can be cut. The whole road is through bamboo jungle.

FROM CHIENG HAI (CHIENG RAI) TO MÖNG LONG *viâ* CHIENG KONG (CHIENG KHAWNG)—*continued.*

Authorities. Military.	Authorities. Civil.	Number and Names of Stages, Rivers and Streams.	Distances. Intermediate. M.	F.	Distances. Total. M.	F.	Remarks.
Siam.		**9. Páng Long** ... Several streams.	14	0	103	2	General direction north-east. Fair mule road; a lot of climbing up and down little spurs; all through bamboo jungle. At 3 miles cross the Nam Nga and follow up its course for the rest of the way—sometimes in the bed of the river, sometimes crossing small spurs and streams just above it. Good camp at Páng Long and good water. Pass two villages on the way—at 2 miles Ban Pong (Khamu), 15 houses; at 5 miles Ban Mawn (Khamu) 10 houses, on the left, out of sight. The following streams are met with *en route*:—At the camp, Hwé Makkeao from the right (5 yards by 8 inches); at 2 miles Nam Pong from the right (6 yards by 1 foot); at 3 miles Hwé Haw from the right (5 yards by 4 inches); at 5¼ miles Nam Ngao from the right (30 yards by 1 foot); stony bottom; moderate current; at 8 miles Nam Nga, crossed seven times; 30 to 40 yards wide, 2 feet deep, rocky bottom, strong current.
		10. Páng Niu ... Hwé Long and Nam Kan.	8	0	111	2	General direction east-north-east. Fair mule road, all through bamboo jungle. Follow the course of the Nam Nga, crossing several spurs as far as Páng Tama at 3 miles. At 5 miles cross the Nam Kan, a tributary of the Nam Nga, and follow up its course to Páng Niu. Zayáts for 60 men: camp 150 yards square: more room could be cleared. Good water. The following streams are met with *en route*:—At the camp Hwé Long from the left (6 yards by 1 foot); at 2½ miles Nam Nga, crossed three times (30 yards by 1½ feet); at 5 miles Nam Kan, crossed five times (20 yards by 1½ feet).
		11. Páng Pabong Nam Kan.	10	4	121	6	General direction east-north-east. Follow up the general course of the Nam Kan (10 to 20 yards by 1 to 1½ feet) the whole way, crossing it twenty times. Fair mule road, through bamboo jungle the whole way. Small spurs (some of them steep) and small streams are constantly being crossed. At 5¼ miles Páng Möng; good camp. At 7½ miles Páng Maidö, where a good camp could be cleared. From here there is a steep ascent of ½ mile; thence along a ridge for a mile and downhill steep for ½ mile to Páng Tintôk, bad camp, at 9 miles. At Páng Pabong zayáts for 80 men and room for a camp could be cleared.
		12. Camp on Hwé Mop. Nam Kan, Hwé Mi, and Nam Ma.	11	4	133	2	General direction east-north-east. Fair mule road. At ½ mile cross the Nam Kan; thence steady ascent to the Nam Kan-Nam Pha watershed at 2 miles: along the ridge for 2½ miles, then downhill to the Hwé Mi at 7 miles; follow the bed of the Hwé Mi (crossing it constantly in the next mile, 3 yards by 6 inches) to its junction with the Nam Ma at Páng Hôk at 8 miles; here are zayáts for 50 men and a small camping ground; thence down the Nam Ma (crossing it constantly 8 yards by 1 foot) to an open space, 300 yards square, just beyond which is the Hwé Mop (6 yards by 1 foot). Grass and bamboo leaves. No village. Khamu village of Panya a little way off.

FROM CHIENG HAI (CHIENG RAI) TO MÖNG LONG *vid* CHIENG KONG (CHIENG KHAWNG)—*continued*.

Authorities. Military.	Authorities. Civil.	Number and Names of Stages, Rivers and Streams.	Distances. Intermediate. M.	Distances. Intermediate. F.	Distances. Total. M.	Distances. Total. F.	Remarks.
Siam.		**13. Phukha** ... Nam Pha and other smaller streams, easily fordable.	9	4	142	6	General direction north-north-east. Good mule road. At 3½ miles cross the Nam Pha (from the right, 20 yards by 2 feet) and just beyond is Takat; zayáts for 120 men; camping ground 350 by 150 yards. After this cross several spurs and streams, tributaries of the Nam Pha. At Phukha large camping ground in grass; zayáts for 100 men: good water and grass. Only two houses in the village: no supplies obtainable: it was formerly a large town, but has been deserted for many years and is now being repopulated from Möng Nan.
		14. Páng Ta Aw. Nam Kyuk or Nam Suk, Nam Eng, and Nam Pawn.	11	0	153	6	General direction north-east. Good mule road, through bamboo and tree jungle; follow up the course of the Nam Kyuk and its tributary the Nam Eng, crossing both streams, which are easily fordable, several times, by a nearly level road to the Nam Pha-Nam Hta watershed at 8 miles; thence down the Nam Pawn, crossing it four times (8 yards by 1 foot), to the camp at Páng Ta Aw. No village here, the village of Sama a mile or two away on the right. At Ta Aw are zayáts for 30 men, and room can be cleared for a camp. Good water and grass.
		15. Páng Namsôn. Nam Pawn, Nam Ha, and Nam Som.	9	2	163	0	General direction north-east. Good mule road, through bamboo and tree jungle; follow the Nam Pawn crossing it several times (7 to 12 yards by 1 to 1½ feet) to its junction with the Nam Ha at Páng Samsôp at 4½ miles. Here is a camp 100 yards square; hence follow the Nam Ha down to 7½ miles crossing it several times (18 yards by 1½ feet); then follow up its tributary, the Nam Som crossing it several times (3 to 7 yards wide, 6 inches to 1 foot deep) to Páng Namsôn. No village. Zayáts for 30 men; camping ground along the stream beyond the zayáts. Good water and grass.
		16. Möng Löng ... Nam Som, Nam Lö and two other streams, the Nam Hoi and the Nam Myen, both fordable.	13	0	176	0	General direction north-east. Good mule road through jungle. Follow up the Nam Som for 1½ miles crossing it several times; then ascend for ½ mile to the Nam Ha Nam-Hta watershed; then downhill to the Nam Lö at 2½ miles and follow its course crossing it constantly (3 to 10 yards by 6 to 12 inches) downto 10½ miles, when the Möng Long plain is entered; thence over level ground through alternate bamboo jungle and open grass to Möng Long, 30 houses: formerly a large town: deserted for some years and repopulated in 1892 from Mong Nam. Good camping ground, water, and grass. No supplies now, as the people have only just settled there, but there will be supplies of rice obtainable in fair quantities in another year.

No. 1-A.

From CHIENG HAI to KYENGTUNG (KENG TUNG or KYAINGTÔN).

By Lieut. G. H. YOUNGHUSBAND, "Queen's Own Corps of Guides," 1887.

Authorities. Military.	Authorities. Civil.	Number and Names of Stages, Rivers and Streams.	Distances. Intermediate. M.	Distances. Intermediate. F.	Distances. Total. M.	Distances. Total. F.	Remarks.
Siam.		**1. Camp beyond Yunglé.** Mé Kok.	**10**	**6**	10	6	Direction north-east. Cross the Mé Kok river by a ford, $\frac{3}{4}$ mile below the town of Kyeng Hai. The river is here 300 feet broad and $2\frac{1}{2}$ feet deep at the ford; current strong. The near bank is perpendicular, 10 feet high, but easily ramped. Opposite bank easy and sloping. Then enter thin, level forest, with high dry grass. At $3\frac{1}{2}$ miles reach the village of Dúng, with extensive paddy-fields. Continue through open paddy-fields to Yunglé at $6\frac{3}{4}$ miles. Water, fuel and grass. Supplies: cows, pigs, poultry and rice to a moderate extent. Four miles further, through paddy-fields and level forest, is an extensive camping ground, covered with high dry grass, on the banks of a good stream, with very steep high banks.
		2. Mé Khé ... Mé Khé and many small streams.	**10**	**0**	20	6	Direction north to north-west. Continue through level thin forest, overgrown with high dry grass, and with occasional bamboo clumps and thick forest. Cross many small streams and several swampy bits. After 6 miles, the path enters thick high forest, and skirting the low spurs from the western range, takes a very winding course in a generally north-west direction. Much swampy ground in the low lying land. Bounding the last spur and continuing through open forest and dry grass, reach the Mé Khé river at 10 miles; here 60 feet broad, $2\frac{1}{2}$ feet deep, bottom firm and good; current fast. The village of the same name is on the opposite bank, and beyond it very extensive camping ground. Water, fuel, grass abundant. Supplies: cows, rice, pigs, and poultry to a moderate extent. Just before reaching Mé Khé the road to Kyeng Sen branches off to the eastward.
		3. Thom ... ... Mé Kham, Mé Liu, and Mé Thom.	**16**	**0**	36	6	Direction north-west. Continue through paddy-fields, and passing through another portion of Mé Khé village enter open level forest. At $4\frac{1}{2}$ miles pass a few huts, and a small clearing and cross a stream. At 6 miles ford the Mé Kham river; here 90 feet broad, 2 feet deep; strong full current; sandy bottom. On the opposite bank pass small village of Mé Kham with camping ground, 200 yards square. No supplies to speak of. Continue through undulating forest. At $9\frac{3}{4}$ miles passing to left of small village of Mé Liu, on a stream of the same name. On through bamboo forest, reaching the Mé Thom river at 16 miles; here 50 feet broad, 2 feet deep; current moderate; bottom sandy. On the opposite bank is the fair-sized village of Thom, with extensive camping grounds. Water, grass, and fuel abundant. Supplies: cows and rice to a moderate extent.

FROM CHIENG HAI TO KYENGTUNG (KENG TUNG OR KYAINGTÔN)—*continued.*

Authorities. Military.	Authorities. Civil.	Number and Names of Stages, Rivers and Streams.	Distances. Inter-mediate. M. F.	Distances. Total. M. F.	Remarks.
Siam.		**4. Mé Sai** ... Mé Sai.	9 0	45 6	Direction north-east through high thick forest and bamboo jungle with occasional openings, skirting some rugged precipitous hills to the west and an open grassy plain to the east. At 3 miles the small village of Chong on a good stream; extensive camping ground. After the 6th mile the forest is alternately very thick and very thin; country nearly level; path broad and good. At 9 miles reach Mé Sai village; extensive camping grounds. Water, fuel, and grass abundant; supplies scarce. This village is situated on the Mé Sai river, which is now claimed by Siam as the boundary.
G.O.C. Rangoon District.	Superintendent, Southern Shan States.	**5. Camp in hills.** Má Thao.	12 0	57 6	Direction north. Crossing the Mé Sai river, here 100 feet broad, 2 feet deep; very strong current: pebbly bottom: enter thick high forest. At 2 miles cross the Mé Thao river, here 30 feet broad, 1 foot deep, and follow its course up stream. Path narrow and difficult, through dense forest, crossing and recrossing the river constantly, sometimes up its bed and sometimes over small steep spurs to avoid bends. At 12 miles is a small camping ground, 300 yards by 50 yards. No supplies. Water, fuel, and little grass.
		6. Camp near Kung. Mé Thao.	4 4	62 2	Direction north-west. Ascend gradually up stream as before, narrow and difficult in parts. At 3¼ miles reaching the source of the Mé Thao river and crossing the watershed, descend by a steep, narrow path through high, thick forest, reaching a small camping ground with room for one regiment, in a basin surrounded by hills at 4½ miles. Supplies *nil*. Water, fuel, and grass; the latter very scarce. Close by, but out of sight amongst the hills to the east, is the Karen village of Kung: further off the south is Tawchalí, another Karen village. These two villages supply small quantities of paddy and rice to passing caravans.
		7. Camp at foot of hills. Mé Gham and Mé On.	13 0	75 2	Direction north. Continue the descent, following the course of the same stream as at the last camp. Constantly crossing and recrossing it, and passing over small steep spurs to avoid bends. At 4½ miles cross the Mé Gham river; here 60 feet broad, 2 feet deep; bottom gravelly; current fast. Crossing a very steep rocky hill, the Mé On river is reached at 6½ miles. Here is camping ground for one regiment. Fuel and water plentiful: grass scarce. The river is here 120 feet broad, 2 feet deep; current very fast; bottom pebbly and full of boulders. Then pass through gently undulating forest, reaching a small camping ground, 300 yards by 100 yards at 13 miles. Water, grass, and fuel. No supplies.

FROM CHIENG HAI TO KYENGTUNG (KENG TUNG OR KYAINGTÔN)—*continued.*

Authorities.		Number and Names of Stages, Rivers and Streams.	Distances.				Remarks.
Military.	Civil.		Intermediate.		Total.		
			M.	F.	M.	F.	
G.O.C. Rangoon District.	Superintendent, Southern Shan States.	**8. Hai Tuk** ... Mé Hok.	**3**	**0**	78	2	Direction north-north-west. Through level thick forest, swampy in parts, down a broadening valley, with occasional open spaces. At 3 miles reach Möng Hai or Hai Tuk, a considerable village on the Mé Hok river. Supplies: cows, pigs, poultry, rice, and sugar to a moderate extent. Extensive camping ground. Water, fuel, and grass. The first purely Shan village reached. The Mé Hok is 100 feet broad by 3 feet deep. Strong current.
		9. Pabaung ... Mé Hok.	**8**	**4**	86	6	Direction north-west. The path leads up the Mé Hok river valley, which is 10 miles long and never more than 2 miles broad. At ¼ mile pass the small village of Namoi, and cross a small tributary of the Mé Hok river, 40 feet broad, 1 foot deep. At ½ mile cross the Mé Hok river; here 120 feet broad, 2 feet deep; current very strong; bottom pebbly. Continue through low thick forest, mostly bamboo, following the river up stream. At 4 miles recross the river; ford as before, but bottom sandy. Passing through a small strip of forest, enter a large camping ground, 800 yards by 100 yards, and reach another part of Hai Tuk village at 5¼ miles. Pass it, and continuing through paddy-fields, cross the Mé Hok for the last time and encamp beyond the village of Pabaung at 8½ miles. Extensive camping ground. Water, fuel, and grass.
		10. Camp in hills. Nam Hsup Nium.	**9**	**0**	95	6	Direction north-east. Leaving the paddy-fields and passing through a belt of thick bush. At ¾ mile cross a good stream, 30 feet broad, 1 foot deep; ascend the opposite hill through high forest and follow its crest to 3 miles. Then descend abruptly to a small stream bed, very narrow, rocky, and difficult, and follow it till it joins the Hsup Nium river at 6 miles. The Nam Hsup Nium is here 120 feet broad, 2 feet deep; current strong; bottom pebbly. Crossing it, meet a small tributary, 20 feet broad, 1 foot deep, and follow its valley up stream, rising gently through dense forest to a small camping ground for a brigade at 9 miles. Water and fuel plentiful; grass not abundant.
		11. Camp on the Mé Hai river. Mé Hai.	**12**	**0**	107	6	Direction north-north-west. Continue up the same stream, up a narrow valley passing a string of small camping grounds, and reach the crest of the watershed at 5½ miles. Following the crest at 6¼ miles a path branches off to Paung Chak. At 6⅝ miles drop obliquely down a steep descent, and at 8½ miles reach the Mé Hai river, a rapid bouldery stream. Here 40 feet broad and 2½ feet deep. Current very strong, and crossing difficult for baggage animals. Recrossing a little further, reach a small camping ground, 50 yards square at 8⅝ miles.

FROM CHIENG HAI TO KYENGTUNG (KENG TUNG OR KYAINGTÔN)—*continued.*

Authorities. Military.	Authorities. Civil.	Number and Names of Stages, Rivers and Streams.	Distances. Intermediate. M.	F.	Distances. Total. M.	F.	Remarks.
G.O.C. Rongoon District.	Superintendent, Southern Shan States.	**11. Camp on the Mé Hai river**—*cont.*					Water, fuel, and a little grass. Continue up the narrow-wooded valley of the Mé Hai stream, passing several small camping grounds, 100 yards square, and halt at one of them on the banks of the river at 12 miles. Water, fuel, and a little grass.
		12. Camp in the Mé Pak Valley. Mé Pak and small stream.	13	4	121	2	Direction north-north-west. Leaving the Mé Hai river ascend the Loi Chang mountain up a very steep grassy spur, reaching the crest after two hours' climb. Then follow the crest, reaching the highest point at 11 miles, height 5 000 feet. The summit is thinly wooded and covered with dry rank grass. Descent very steep, reaching a small stream at 12 miles. Then crossing another small steep hill, descend gradually into the Mé Pak valley. Camping ground for a large force on undulating downs, covered with high reed grass. Water, fuel, and coarse grass.
		13. Möng Pak ... Mé Pak.	6	0	127	2	Direction north-north-west. The path leads over gently undulating hillocks, covered with high reed grass, with here and there clumps of trees. At 2 miles pass along paddy-fields, reaching at 4½ miles a few houses belonging to Möng Pak. Here cross the Mé Pak river, 20 feet broad, 2 feet deep; current moderate, banks steep and high, and reach the main village of Möng Pak at 6 miles. Extensive camping grounds, though rather damp and low-lying. Water, fuel, and grass plentiful. Supplies: cows, rice, sugar, and tobacco to a moderate extent. Hence two roads lead to Kyeng Tung—(1) leading over the Loi Luang (Löng) mountain, which is here described; (2) leading up the Mé Pak valley and crossing a pass at the head of it, into the Kyeng Tung valley.
		14. Camp	12	4	139	6	Direction north. Ascend very gradually the Loi Luang mountain, the path leading through high reed grasses and occasional thin clumps of trees for 6 miles; then descend abruptly by a very steep path through thick forest to a small camping ground, 100 yards square, on a stream, at 12½ miles. Water, fuel, and grass plentiful.
		15. Kyeng Tung. Mé Chím (or Chem).	11	4	151	2	Direction north. Continue down the stream, crossing one or two swampy places down the gradually broadening valley of the Mé Chím river to Mé Chím village at 5 miles. Supplies: cows, pigs, poultry, and rice to a

FROM CHIENG HAI TO KYENGTUNG (KENG TUNG OR KYAINGTÔN)—*continued.*

Authorities. Military.	Authorities. Civil.	Number and Names of Stages, Rivers and Streams.	Distances. Intermediate.	Distances. Total.	Remarks.
G.O.C. Rangoon District.	Supt., Southern Shan States.	**15. Kyeng Tung**—*cont.*			moderate extent. Hence onwards is a cart track to Kyeng Tung, over gently undulating open downs. At 7 miles pass Mong Laung, a large village, in three parts. Supplies as at Mé Chím. After 7 miles cross the Mé Chím river twice, 30 feet broad by $2\frac{1}{2}$ feet deep; current slow; bottom sandy; high steep banks. At $11\frac{1}{2}$ miles reach Kyeng Tung and enter by south gate. *N.B.*—There is no large camping ground between Mé Sai and Hai Tuk; a large force therefore would have to cross the hills, a distance of $32\frac{1}{4}$ miles in detachments. The same remark applies to the next range of hills crossed from Pabaung to Möng Pak.

No. 2.

From MÉHAWNGSAWN to KYAUKHNYÁT viâ KUNYÙOM (HKUNYOM) and MÉCHÉ.

BY CAPT. H. B. WALKER, PAID ATTACHÉ, INTELLIGENCE BRANCH, MARCH 1893.

Military	Civil	Stages	Intermediate	Total	Remarks
Siam.		**1. Hpáhpawng** ... Méhawngsawn and Méhkit streams.	M. F. **6 6**	M. F. 6 6	General direction south. The route leaves Méhawngsawn by the Mé Pai ferry route; descends into the paddy-fields crossing and recrossing the Méhawngsawn stream easy banks, gravelly bottom, 9 inches to 18 inches deep, and 3 feet to 4 feet (? yards) wide; crosses them, and at mile $1\frac{1}{4}$ leaves the route to the ferry on the right hand, the ferry being 1 mile distant from the junction of the roads. From the junction the route lies between two low ridges, the one on the left or east being the termination of the main range, dividing Méhawngsawn from Zimmé. Light jungle; teak and *in* on both sides. The path is broad, but stony under foot; nearly level. All the drainage flows Mé Pai-wards. At mile $4\frac{1}{4}$ the route strikes the Méhkit stream (6 inches deep, 3 yards wide), which it crosses, (crossing stony and difficult for pack animals), and then runs along its left bank by a rather narrow path, passing through the two villages of Papu at the entrance into the Mé Hsumat valley, and at mile 6. The Mé Sumat valley is here a mile in width, and cultivated from east to west, Hpáhpawng lying on the eastern side of the valley. It consists of a long, narrow village of 70 houses, a fine large kyaung situated at the north end, affording accommodation for 150 men. There is camping ground at the south end of the village on the Mé Hsumat for another 150 men, and for the same number immediately after crossing the stream. Supplies good and cheap, paddy being exceedingly plentiful. From Hpáhpawng to the Mé Pai river, along the course or valley of the Mé Hsumat is some 7 miles, a mere path and impassable for mules. This path strikes the Mé Pai 3 miles below the ferry.

FROM MÉHAWNGSAWN TO KYAUKHNYÁT *viâ* KUNYUOM (HKUNYOM) AND MÉCHÉ—*continued.*

Authorities: Military.	Authorities: Civil.	Number and Names of Stages, Rivers and Streams.	Distances: Intermediate.	Distances: Total.	Remarks.
			M. F.	M. F.	
Siam.		**2. Pôn Sakhán (1,000 feet).** Mé Hsumat and Mé Sa streams.	**6 0**	12 6	General direction a little west of south. The route leaves the southern end of the village, and running along the dry ground above the cultivation (wet during the months of February, March, and April) it crosses the Mé Hsumat (crossing easy, stream 20 yards broad, 1½ feet deep, rapid current); passes through light jungle between two ridges enclosing the valley of the Mé Hsumat, and crosses that stream twice more by 1¼ miles. At the second crossing the Méhawngsawn side is steep and bad, and the route runs along the wet stream, itself knee-deep in February and March, for 150 yards, when it strikes across a strip of cultivation for a ¼ mile (path level), and arrives at the junction of the Mé Hsumat with the Mé Sa, which flows from the south, the Mé Hsumat coming from the south-east and separated southward before its junction by a steep range of hills, the Loi Hpo Hsan Khan from the Mé Sa, three intermediate minor streams and ridges also lying between the two main streams. The route now follows the course of the Mé Sá to Pôn Sakhán. The Mé Sa, at first 15 yards broad, afterwards 5 yards broad; 1 to 1½ feet deep is crossed and recrossed by easy crossings. Pôn Sakhán is a jungle camp marked by a deserted zayát, there being accommodation for 300 or 400 men; open jungle; teak and other marketable timber, and a little bamboo. Grass obtainable in small quantities along the banks of the stream, and bamboo leaves.
		3. Palán ... ... Mé Sa stream.	**6 6**	19 4	General direction a little west of south. The route continues up the course of the Mé Sa, crossing and recrossing stream which is narrowing rapidly all the way, the path being broken and very stony, and in places barely passable for laden animals, though level. At mile 4 it improves and gradually improves to mile 6¼, when it debouches on the large paddy plain at the southern extremity of which Palán stands on the right bank of the Mé Sa, on a slightly elevated knoll and commanding the plain. Palán is a Shan village, containing 30 houses, a kyaung, and two or three substantial buildings belonging to Moulmein timber traders. Supplies good. Paddy and rice; fruit, fowls, vegetables; grass for animals in abundance on the banks of the Mé Sa.
		4. Mé Sa Kyi (1,400 feet). Mé Sa and numerous dry or insignificant side streams.	**9 0**	28 4	General direction south-east. Leaving the village of Palán the route crosses a deep nullah, dry in the cold season, and bridged with a narrow bridge for foot-passengers, and after crossing the lower extremities of a low ridge, descends again to the Mé Sa and runs by a tortuous path along its valley crossing the stream which is from 5 to 6 yards wide, frequently, easy crossings; thick heavy jungle on both sides, the route being narrow, and in places very ill-defined. At mile 3¼ the northern village of Hlôngyán (five houses) is passed, and at mile 4½ the southern portion (four houses, Shans). The inhabitants employed in timber felling. No supplies. At mile 6½ a route strikes off to left hand or east to Hwépôn *viâ* which

From MÉHAWNGSAWN to KYAUKHNYÁT *viâ* KUNYUOM (HKUNYOM) and MÉCHÉ—*continued.*

Authorities.		Number and Names of Stages, Rivers and Streams.	Distances.				Remarks.
Military.	Civil.		Inter-mediate.		Total.		
			M.	F.	M.	F.	
		4. Mé Sa Kyi (1,400 feet)—*cont.*					there is another route from Méhawngsawn to Hkunyuom, the two routes becoming one at Mé Sá Kyi. The easterly, or Hwépôn, route is said to be good and practicable for all laden animals, but is more hilly than the westerly route. There is accommodation at Mé Sá Kyi on the right and left banks of the Mé Sá, for 250 men, and small camps can be obtained at intervals along the valley which is from 1½ to ½ a mile wide. Of the jungle timber, teak and bamboo predominate. Grass and bamboo leaves for animals obtainable all the way along the route.
Siam.		**5. Méhsulín** ... Mé Sa, Hwé Ho, and Méhsulín streams.	8	0	36	4	General direction almost due south. The route still continues up the valley of the Mé Sa, crossing and recrossing, the path being good through narrow. At mile 4½ the route begins to rise, and Mé Sa source is reached; and at mile 5 the watershed between it and the Méhsulín is crossed at an elevation of about 1,800 feet. On commencing to descend the route becomes narrow and broken and requires repair. Once the Hwé Ho valley (50 yards wide) is reached, the route, as in all these stream valley routes, crosses and recrosses the stream (6 inches deep at first, 4 or 5 yards broad, stony bottom, and crossings easy), and it is impossible to remain dry if marching on foot. At mile 7 the stream broadens a little, and at mile 8 it joins the Méhsulín flowing from the east towards the west. The village of Méhsulín is situated on the right bank of the Méhsulín stream, in the triangle formed by the junction of the Hwé Ho. Contains 23 houses, and a fine pôngyi kyaung. Supplies good, the Méhsulín valley in the proximity of the village being well cultivated for paddy. Here the route from the frontier at Paktumong (*see* Route No. 81, Shan Hills Division) joins in.
		6. Kunyuom (Hkunyom). Méhsulín and Tauknyin or Kunyuom streams.	6	4	43	0	General direction south. At first on leaving Méhsulín the route is bad and marshy, traversing the Méhsulín itself for 50 or 100 yards at a depth of 1½ feet. At mile 3 the route becomes broad and well defined, and ascending crosses the watershed between the Méhsulín and the Tauknyin or Kunyuom stream, and thence runs by an easy, almost level, route to Kunyuom at mile 6½, this latter portion of the road being excellent. Loose teak jungle on either side. Kunyuom is situated on eastern slopes of the ridge which lies to the right hand of the route, and a little above the valley of the Mé Kunyuom stream, and consists of one long broad street, descending towards the south, with a fine pôngyi kyaung at each end of the town, and contains 400 houses, several shops, and a standing bazaar. Supplies plentiful and cheap. The Kunyuom (Tauknyin) valley is ½ a mile wide and cultivated, the stream flowing from the east and here turning southward to Mainglungyi.
		7. Méngau * ...	8	0	51	0	*See* Route No. 80, Shan Hills Division, Stage 7 for this stage.

* This is the spelling adopted in the Survey map.—A. F.

FROM MÉHAWNGSAWN TO KYAUKHNYÀT *viâ* KUNYUOM (HKUNYOM) AND MÉCHÉ—*continued.*

Authorities: Military.	Authorities: Civil.	Number and Names of Stages, Rivers and Streams.	Distances: Intermediate.	Distances: Total.	Remarks.
Siam.		**8. Camp Nampông on western side of boundary.** The Môk Pai, a tributary of the Nam-Méngau, Hwépông, Tunun, a tributary of the Hwépông, and Nampông streams.	M. F. 10 4	M. F. 61 4	General direction first 4½ miles a little west of south, then due west. Leaving Méngau the route runs along a narrow valley traversing the course of the Môk Pai (2½ yards wide, and 1 foot deep) crossing and recrossing to mile 2, when the village of Môk Pai (four houses), Shans; no supplies; is passed to the left hand. At mile 3 the route commences to ascend the watershed between the two streams, Nam-Méngau and Hwépông, and crosses it at mile 4 (3 yards wide, 1 foot deep; gravelly bottom); it then runs down a gradually descending spur for ½ a mile, the Hwépông rising in the high ridge which separates the two main valleys of the Nam-Méngau and the Tunun stream, now flowing eastward. At mile 5 the route descends abruptly to the Hwépông which it crosses and follows for ½ a mile, when it absorbs the Tunun stream, both vanishing under the ground, leaving the superficial course quite dry, rising again a day's march further eastward in a body of water of considerable volume. The route now turns due west and traverses the Tunun stream valley to mile 7, the route in several places being so broken and stony when passing up the stream bed (2 yards wide, 6 inches deep) as to be almost impassable for animals. At mile 7 the stream divides into two, both of them being near the source quite dry in the cold season. Here there is accommodation for 25 men, while, if the jungle were cleared, accommodation for as many more could be found further back. A spur running between the two branches of the Tunun is now ascended, the summit thereof at mile 9, Loi Tunun, being the watershed between the Hwépông on the Siam side (or the Tunun) and the Nampông on the Burma side. This point is the boundary which runs as shown in the survey sheet nearly north and south. Elevation 3,500 feet. The route now descends into the valley of the Nampông, at first dry, water appearing in its bed at mile 1½ from frontier where there is accommodation for 300 men—grass and bamboo leaves. The valley here is steeply enclosed. Heavy open jungle on both sides, teak predominating. Height of camp 2,000 feet approximately.
G.O.C. Rangoon District.	Superintendent, Southern Shan States.	**9. Méché or Mésé.** Nampông, Mannam, and Méché or Mésé streams.	8 0	69 4	General direction south-west. The route continues down the valley of the Nampông to mile 4 by a good path crossing and recrossing the Nampông (6 or 8 yards broad, 1½ feet deep) flowing from the north-south-ward and on the other side of the right-hand ridge to the Nampông valley. At mile 5 the village of Nampông is reached (18 houses, Shans). At mile 5½ the Méché stream flowing from the south absorbs the Mannam (6 or 8 yards wide, 1½ feet deep) and takes a westerly turn, eventually flowing into the Salween and carrying with it the Ywathit route, which takes, at mile 7, from Nampông a northerly turn and leaves the Méché or Mésé. The path now, except for the repeated though easy crossings, is good; the valley widens, and accommodation for troops could be found to the number of 400 or 500 in and about

FROM MÉHAWNGSAWN TO KYAUKHNYÁT *viâ* KUNYUOM (HKUNYOM) AND MÉCHÉ—*continued*.

Authorities. Military.	Authorities. Civil.	Number and Names of Stages, Rivers and Streams.	Distances. Intermediate. M.	Distances. Intermediate. F.	Distances. Total. M.	Distances. Total. F.	Remarks.
G.O.C. Rangoon District.	Superintendent, Southern Shan States.	**9. Méché or Mésé**—*cont.*					Nampông village, which must be looked upon as a point for concentration of troops of some importance. The valley is almost clear of jungle, and is cultivated near the river side for paddy. Teak abounds all along this valley, though the heavier timber has been felled. Grass in good quantities and of excellent quality obtainable along the valley. Méché or Mésé is reached at 8th mile, and is situated on the left bank of the stream. Thirty houses, with a large kyaung. Accommodation in and about the village for 800 or 1,000 men. Supplies plentiful. Grass, fruits, plantains, &c. The remainder of this route is from native information collected by Captain Walker.
		10. Camp on the Hwé Páng Ting. Méché or Mésé and Hwé Hkopi.	6	4	76	0	The route passes out of the western side of Méché or Mésé and strikes through thick jungle along the narrow course of the Hwé Hkopi, flowing into the Méché or Mésé near the village, crossing and recrossing it. The route along this stream is stony and rough and difficult in places. At mile 4 the source of the Hwé Hkopi is reached and the route crosses the watershed between the Méché or Mésé and the Mépa, the jungle as the route leaves the source of the Hwé Hkopi behind becoming dry, open, and a complete contrast to the dank luxuriance just passed through; across the crest of the watershed the route runs through a widish pass or gap by a good sound route, the crest itself offering a defensive position towards either side, though there is no water here, the ground being arid and stony. The descent into the Mépa valley is good though stony through loose, dry jungle with (in the spring of 1893) numerous teak logs scattered about, felled by Siamese and unremoved owing to the embargo on the logs by the British. There is no water until 2½ miles is reached, where the Hwé Pángting first supplies a sufficiency of water for 200 men, and there is camping accommodation for double the number; no grass, and few bamboo leaves.
		11. Nam Mépa ... The Mépa.	12	0	88	0	Leaving the camp at Hwé Páng Ting the route runs through dead jungle down a gradually descending spur and along its south-east edge to the Mépai at mile 6, whence the route strikes through greener jungle, and along the course of the Mépa towards its source. At mile 5 a route leads to right bank or north-west, down to the Mépa (20 to 50 yards broad, partially dry in the cold season ; steep banks clothed with jungle, stony course) ; further south-westerly course which route follows the Mépa to its confluence with the Salween. Along this route until November 1892 the Siamese used to communicate with their post situated on the Salween, at the mouth of the Mépa. Nam Mépa is reached at mile 12, an insignificant hamlet (Karenni) lying in a small kaing-grass grown plain, which has been partially cultivated and which afford accommodation for 2,000 men. Grass good and plentiful and water from the Mépa.
		12. Camp on branch of the Mépa. Mépa.	8	0	96	0	General direction a little east of south. The route leaves Nam Mépa and strikes up the course of the Mépa through a broad valley 1½ miles wide and cultivated here and there by the

FROM MÉHAWNGSAWN TO KYAUKHNYÁT *viâ* KUNYUOM (HKUNYOM) AND MÉCHÉ—*continued.*

Authorities. Military.	Authorities. Civil.	Number and Names of Stages, Rivers and Streams.	Distances. Intermediate. M. F.	Distances. Total. M. F.	Remarks.
G.O.C. Rangoon District.	Superintendent, Southern Shan States.	**12. Camp on branch of the Mépa**—*cont.*			Karennis, who sparsely and invisibly populate the country; at mile 1 the route to Hpa chaung frontier mark, opposite to which, on the right bank, the Hpa chaung flows into the Salween, turns off to right bank or west. At miles 3 and 5 there are two very bad crossings, rocky and slippery, over the Mépa. The remaining crossings are easy. At mile 8 the extreme southernmost point on the Karenni side of the frontier is reached, where there is any water, the intervening space along the route between the camp and the frontier being destitute of water. There is accommodation in the small camping ground for 200 men on both banks of the stream, while the water-supply would not allow of a halt exceeding 24 hours for that force. Grass and bamboo leaves abundant.
		13. Umpauk ... Umpauk stream.	**11 4**	107 4	General direction south. The route leaves the camping ground and strikes across a steep ridge up one of the small branches of the Mépa, and then turns up along a gradual spur leading to the watershed of the Mépa-Mété. The frontier is reached at 4½ miles, the route crossing it by an easy gradient at an elevation of 1,975 feet. As far as this the route, though little used, is a good one and passable for laden animals and all arms. There are said to be a few Karenni villages in the neighbourhood, but they are difficult to find and hidden in the jungle, and are a long way from their taungyas, which are on the upper waters of the Mépa proper. After crossing the frontier native information states that the route runs down a spur for 3 miles to the valley of the Umpauk stream (flowing into the Mété, a mere hill-side drainage), which it follows to its junction with the Mété at 11½ miles. Here there is accommodation and water for 200 or 300 men and animals at a pinch.
		14. Karé ... ... Mét stream.	**6 4**	114 0	General direction west of south. From the camp at the junction of the Umpauk with the Mété the route ascends a long spur on to the crest of a ridge to the small Karen or Shan village of Karé, 10 houses, where there is a spring and stream of water and a small camping ground.
		15. The Salween (Kyaukhnyát). Kôko stream and the Salween.	**10 0**	124 0	From Karé the route runs down a spur on opposite side of ridge to the Kôko stream (an insignificant drainage towards the Salween) which it follows, crossing and recrossing until the Salween is reached, opposite Kyaukhnyát, the Salween being crossed and the main Páphun route being gained. Native information gives this route from the frontier southwards as being only practicable for elephants. From Méché or Mésé to the frontier it is passable for all arms and laden animals, and judging from the appearance of the onward country from the frontier, it is more than probable that the southern side of the frontier is equally passable.

No. 3.

From MÉHAWNGSAWN to LAGON (LAKON) viâ LABON (LAPÚN).

BY CAPT. WALKER, PAID ATTACHÉ, INTELLIGENCE BRANCH (NATIVE INFORMATION), JANUARY 1893.

Authorities. Military.	Authorities. Civil.	Number and Names of Stages, Rivers and Streams.	Distances. Intermediate. M.	F.	Distances. Total. M.	F.	Remarks.
Siam.		**1. Hwépong** ... Méhawngsawn stream.	10	0	10	0	The route leaves Méhawngsawn by the north-easterly exit; crosses the paddy-fields in the valley and enters the hills in an easterly direction, turning southward along a spur to Hwépong, whence routes to Zimmé and Kunyuom or Hkunyom also run. Route passable for elephants and perhaps mules. Water at camp plentiful.
		2. Nawngcho ... The Mé Sa Mat crossed *en route* eleven times.	12	0	22	0	General direction south-south-east. The route is good but hilly. Nawngcho is merely a jungle camp, with good accommodation for caravans or small bodies of troops.
		3. Mé Sa Mat ... The Mé Sa Mat crossed *en route* eleven times.	5	0	27	0	General direction east of south. Route continues to cross and recross the Mé Sa Mat, near the source of which is the camp. Accommodation for 300 men and animals.
		4. Jungle camp ...	5	0	32	0	The route now crosses the watershed from the source of the Mé Sa Mat to the source of the Méwun, a small stream running towards the Mékhunyom (?)
		5. Mé Wun ... Mé Wun, a hill-side stream.	7	0	39	0	The route descends and follows the course of the Mé Wun, crossing and recrossing the stream being a small narrow one. From Mé Wun camp route strikes off and joins the Zimmé road, one day's march distant.
		6. Mé Hta Shwé.	7	0	46	0	General direction south-east. Route hilly and rough. There is a branch route to Maung Haut and also from Mainglungyi from Mé Hta Shwé. Camp accommodation and water-supply supposed to be good. Mé Hta Shwé is a Siamese village containing 50 houses.
		7. Kyon Taung ...	6	0	52	0	General direction south of east. Kyon Taung is a Laos town (?), possessing 200 houses and 100 elephants.
		8. Labon or Lapún. The Méping crossed.	10	0	62	0	General direction east. Route good. Several small villages passed through.
		9. Ban Mé Ta ... Mé Sao and Mé Sun streams.	12	0	74	0	General direction east. Along the Mé Sao up its course, crossing several spurs and then on to the Mé Sun valley.
		10. Camp near the Mé Sun. Mé Sun.	10	0	84	0	General direction east. Through jungle and approaching Mé Sun across paddy plains.

FROM MÉHAWNGSAWN TO LAGON (LAKON) *viâ* LABON (LAPÚN)—*continued.*

Authorities. Military.	Authorities. Civil.	Number and Names of Stages, Rivers and Streams.	Distances. Intermediate. M.	Distances. Intermediate. F.	Distances. Total. M.	Distances. Total. F.	Remarks.
		11. Hang Sat ...	**9**	**0**	93	0	General direction east. Across large plains; several villages passed through.
		Mé Hao, a small stream.					
		12. Lakon ...	**10**	**0**	103	0	General direction east. Across plains dotted with villages. Route good. Lakon is a fortified place; 600 or 700 houses. Ample accommodation for camping ground and supplies.

No. 4.

From MÉHAWNGSAWN to ZIMMÉ (KENGMAI).

BY CAPT. WALKER, PAID ATTACHÉ, INTELLIGENCE BRANCH (NATIVE INFORMATION), FEBRUARY 1893.

Authorities. Military.	Authorities. Civil.	Number and Names of Stages, Rivers and Streams.	Intermediate M.	Intermediate F.	Total M.	Total F.	Remarks.
Siam.		**1. Hpápawng** ...	**6**	**6**	6	6	*See* Route No. 2 of this appendix.
		2. Jungle camp ...	**8**	**0**	14	6	
		3. Hwépong ...	**8**	**0**	22	6	Route hilly through jungle; passable for elephants.
		Hwépong stream.					
		4. Camp foot of Hwépong hills.	**9**	**0**	31	6	Route through jungle narrow; passable for elephants.
		Hwépong stream.					
		5. Top of Hwépong hills.	**7**	**0**	38	6	Steep ascent. Water to be had on route and good supply in camping ground.
		6. Camp on the Mé Sa Mat.	**5**	**0**	43	6	Ample water-supply. Route rough and broken.
		7. Jungle camp ...	**9**	**0**	52	6	Through jungle.
		8. } 9. } Jungle camp.	**9**	**0**	59	6	Through jungle.
		10. Jungle camp.	**6**	**0**	65	6	Crosses hills, route being bad and rocky.
		11. Jungle camp.	**5**	**0**	70	6	
		Mé Lim (source of).					
		12. Möng Nwé village.	**8**	**0**	78	6	Village of three houses, Shans. Small camping ground. Water-supply good.
		13. Myát Min ...	**7**	**0**	85	6	A village of 100 houses (Siamese (?)).
		14. Möng Ha ...	**9**	**0**	94	6	Twenty houses.
		15. Man Pong ...	**10**	**0**	104	6	Twenty-two houses.
		16. Zimmé ...	**10**	**0**	104	6	

No. 5.

From MÖNG FÁNG to CHIENG HAI viâ BAN MÉCHAN.

By Capt. H. R. DAVIES, Oxfordshire Light Infantry, Intelligence Branch, Burma, January and February 1893.

Authorities. Military.	Authorities. Civil.	Number and Names of Stages, Rivers and Streams.	Distances. Intermediate. M.	F.	Total. M.	F.	Remarks.
		1. Meleng ... Nam Kawila, Nam Méháng, Nam Mésao, and Nam Meleng.	8	4	8	4	General direction north-north-east. Level mule road, but swampy in places. All along the Mé Fáng valley, chiefly through jungle, with paddy near the villages. The following villages are passed:—At 4 miles Ban Tabong (Laos), 11 houses; at 5 miles Ban Mehang (Laos), 10 houses; at 6¼ miles one bit of Ban Mesao; and at 7½ miles another bit of the same village (Laos), 10 houses. Meleng (Siam) contains 30 houses. Camp in village (200 by 100 yards), or in paddy (¾ square mile) to the right. The following streams are crossed or met with *en route*:—At 3½ miles Nam Kawila, from the left (10 yards by 2 feet); at 5 miles Nam Méháng, from the left (7 yards by 1½ feet); at 7½ miles Nam Mesao, from the left (8 yards by 2 feet); at Meleng the Nam Meleng, from the left (6 yards by 1½ feet).
		2. Tatôn ... ... Nam Mé Ai and Mé Khok.	8	0	16	4	General direction north-east by east. Level mule road, but swampy in places; all through jungle. At 2½ miles Ban Mé Ai (Siam), three houses, on the right, out of sight. Tatôn (Siam) contains 20 houses, on the right bank of the Mé Khok. Best camp on the left bank on site of old village. Jungle has to be cleared; no regular camping ground. Plenty of grass. The following streams are crossed or met with *en route*:—At 2½ miles Nam Mé Ai, from the left (7 yards by 1½ feet); at 8 miles Mé Khok, from the left (100 yards wide); waist-deep, strong current, rocky bottom, fordable; two boats one holding eight men, the other six men.
	Siam.	**3. Möng Ngam** ... Nam Möng Ngam.	11	4	28	0	General direction east. Good level mule road; all through jungle. At 3½ miles Wiengkhé ferry across the Mé Khok, ¼ mile on the right. This road leads back to Möng Fáng (*see* Route No. 9). At 5 miles Hinlaw (Siam), four houses, ¼ mile away out of sight. Möng Ngam (Siam) contains 10 houses. Best camp about ½ a mile beyond the village on the Nam Möng Ngam. At 11½ miles Nam Möng Ngam, from the left (6 yards by 1 foot), several small streams, 2 or 3 yards wide.
		4. Páng Mé Chan Sawng Sôp. Nam Möng Ngam and Mé Chan.	11	6	39	6	General direction east. Difficult road; a good deal of steep up-and-down and some very narrow places. Follows up the general course of the Nam Möng Ngam (3 to 6 yards by 6 inches to 1 foot) for 7 miles. Then uphill over the Kiusitai pass, and down the Mé Chan (5 to 10 yards by 1 foot) constantly crossing it to the camp where another stream joins the Mé Chan. Large camp. The Kiusitai pass is the Möng Fáng-Chieng Hsen boundary.
		5. Páng Tong Tang. Mé Chan.	9	0	48	6	General direction east. Fair mule road, but one bad muddy place, 8 yards long, at 7 miles. Down the Mé Chan (10 to 20 yards by 1 to 2 feet); rocky bottom the whole way, constantly crossing it in the first 5 miles, but afterwards less frequently. At the camp the jungle is thin and plenty of room can easily be cleared. Water from Mé Chan. Good grass.

FROM MÖNG FÄNG TO CHIENG HAI *viâ* BAN MÉCHAN—*continued.*

Authorities. Military.	Authorities. Civil.	Number and Names of Stages, Rivers and Streams.	Distances. Intermediate. M.	F.	Total. M.	F.	Remarks.
Siam.		**6. Ban Méchan** ... Mé Chan.	11	0	59	6	General direction east. Fair mule road; some muddy places, but not very difficult. At 5 miles a large hot sulphur spring. At 8 miles Ban Patung (Laos), 30 houses. Hence through paddy up to Ban Méchan (Laos), 130 houses. Camped in thin jungle on the right bank of the Mé Chan. The paddy ground too wet. Supplies of beef, rice, and paddy obtainable. From here roads branch off to Keng Tung and Chieng Hsen.
		7. Tongpao ... Hwé Luk and Mé Khao Tom.	10	0	69	6	General direction south. Good level mule road. One muddy place at $2\frac{1}{8}$ miles, rather difficult. Through bamboo jungle, with occasional stretches of open grass 4 or 5 feet high. No villages passed through. At 5 miles Hwé Luk, from the right (4 yards by 6 inches). At $6\frac{1}{8}$ miles Mé Khao Tom from the right (6 yards by 1 foot). At $6\frac{1}{2}$ miles camp (200 by 150 yards) on the Mé Khao Tom; more room could be cleared here. At Tongpao (seven houses) camp in paddy ($\frac{1}{3}$ by $\frac{1}{4}$ mile); water from Mé Khao Tom. The Chieng Hsen-Chieng Hai boundary is crossed at 4 miles.
		8. Chieng Hai ... Several small streams, and the Mé Khok.	9	2	79	0	General direction south. Good level mule road, partly through jungle, partly through paddy-fields. The following villages are passed:—At $\frac{5}{8}$ mile Pabung, three houses; at 2 miles Méyanglé Ai, 50 houses, in three bits; at 4 miles Ban Du or Ban Lu, 20 houses. At Chieng Hai camping ground (150 by 40 yards) just inside north gate; also ground (300 by 50 yards) along river bank outside north gate. Large camping grounds on paddy to the east, west and south. Town is surrounded by high parapet and wall, and contains with its suburbs 600 houses. Large supplies of beef, paddy, and rice. At 9 miles the Mé Khok, from the right (120 yards by 4 feet); sandy bottom. Crossed by ferry. No raft kept ready, and the ferrymen are liable to be absent. There are about 10 boats in the place. To carry mule loads across two boats have to be tied together. Rather rapid current, but mules can swim easily.

ALTERNATIVE I.

FROM MÖNG FÁNG TO WIENGKHÉ (SOUTHERN ROUTE).

BY CAPT. H. R. DAVIES, OXFORDSHIRE LIGHT INFANTRY, JANUARY 1893.

Military	Civil	Stage	Inter. M.	F.	Total M.	F.	Remarks
Siam.		**1. Hwé Möng** ... Nam Fáng, Hwé Pasarak, Hwé Ménawang, and Hwé Möng.	9	0	9	0	This route is an alternative to Stages 1 and 2 above. It is about a mile shorter, but the road is much overgrown with jungle and would be very swampy in wet weather. General direction north-east. Fair mule road, level throughout; much overgrown with long

No. 5.

From MÖNG FÁNG to CHIENG HAI *viâ* BAN MÉCHAN—*continued.*

ALTERNATIVE I—*continued.*

Authorities. Military.	Authorities. Civil.	Number and Names of Stages, Rivers and Streams.	Distances. Intermediate. M.	F.	Distances. Total. M.	F.	Remarks.
Siam.		**1. Hwé Möng**—*cont.*					grass and said to be impassable for anything but elephants in the rains. Through paddy for ½ mile; thence through tree jungle and long grass. At 1¼ miles cross the Nam Fáng, from the right (25 yards by 2½ feet); moderate current; has to be crossed by boat in the rains. At 3½ miles Nam Pasarak, from the right (1½ yards by 8 inches). At 5 miles village of Ménawang (Laos); five houses and the stream Hwé Ménawang, from the right (4 yards by 1 foot); but at the ford it is 2½ feet deep with steep banks; banks should be ramped just above or below the ford. At 9 miles cross the Hwé Möng (2 yards by 6 inches deep). Camp on old paddy ground, 300 by 200 yards, just beyond the stream. Water rather muddy. Fair grass and bamboo leaves can be cut. The village of Hwé Möng is ½ mile away on the left.
		2. Wiengkhé ... Hwé Kyikyu and Mé Khok.	9	4	18	4	General direction north-east. Fair mule road, much overgrown with jungle and grass; level nearly the whole way. At 4 miles Hwé Kyikyu, from the right (4 yards by 8 inches). At 4½ miles pass village of Nayao (Siam); five houses. At 8 miles cross a small spur for a mile. Wiengkhé is a new village on the right bank of the Mé Khok. Room can be cleared for a camp here. Best camp on the left bank of the river, a ½ of a mile from it where the road joins Route No. 8. At 9½ miles, Mé Khok, from the left, 120 yards wide, with an island in the middle. Between the right bank and the island 5 feet deep; between the left bank and the island 2½ feet deep. Two boats at the ferry, one holding 10, the other six men; the two fastened together will take five mule-loads; mules are swum across.

No. 5-A.

From MÖNG FÁNG to KAING SEN.

By W. J. ARCHER, Esq., Vice-Consul, Zimmé, 1888.

Military	Civil	Stages	Int. M.	F.	Total M.	F.	Remarks
Siam.		**1. Ban Mé Si-Tin.** Mé Fáng and Na Wang.	12	0	12	0	Down to the Mé Fáng 1½ miles distant, river waist-deep with high banks. After crossing through forest pass one or two small villages. At 7½ miles village and stream of Na Wang.
		2. Wiengkhé ... Mé Kok.	5	0	17	0	Through bamboo forest. On approaching the Mé Kok road goes through a gorge; cross the Mé Kok here 6 feet deep with strong current; camp near Wiengkhé, a small village of Kyeng Tung people on the left bank. From here there is route to Kyeng Tung.
		3. Mé Möng Ngam. Mé Ngam.	10	0	27	0	Through forest. Good camp on the Mé Ngam stream.

FROM MŎNG FÁNG TO KAING SEN—*continued.*

Authorities: Military.	Authorities: Civil.	Number and Names of Stages, Rivers and Streams.	Distances: Intermediate. M.	F.	Distances: Total. M.	F.	Remarks.
Siam.		**4. Mé Chan** ... Mé Ngam, Mé Lu, and Mé Chan.	14	0	41	0	Up the left bank of Mé Ngam road rather bad, cross the watershed (2,700 feet). Steep ascent and descent. At 9 miles reach Mé Lu, a small stream, road now rough with many ups and downs, steep descent to Mé Chan, a large stream.
		5. Camp on Mé Chan. Mé Chan.	14	0	55	0	Down the Mé Chan, frequently crossing it, good camping ground.
		6. Ban Mé Khi (or Mé Khé). Mé Khi.	12	0	67	0	A good fairly level road through jungle. At 6 miles leave Mé Chan to the right, at 7 miles some hot springs, at 9 miles Ban Patung, a Lao village. Valley there opens out and there are extensive rice fields. At 11 miles strike Chieng Hai road to Kyeng Tung, respectively, 2 and 13 marches distant (*vide* Route No. 1-A, Appendix III, Stage 2). At 12 miles Ban Mé Khi, a large straggling Lao village. Water from Mé Khi.
		7. Ban Pasak ... Mé Khi.	7	0	74	0	Cross Mé Khi road level, through bare open plain. Pass Ban Phui Pao, a long straggling village, then across rice fields, pass Wieng Manôla, the site of an old city. Pasak is a village of 30 houses.
		8. Kaing Sen (1,150 feet). Mé Chan.	14	0	88	0	Road level, cross the Mé Chan, then between the river and low hills to right at 10 miles recross to left bank. Through paddy-fields to city of Kaing Sen, a large walled town on the Mé Khong. Population and supplies scanty.
Mr. Gould gives the following itinerary from Mé Khi:—							
Siam.		**7. Kin Pao** ... Mé Chan.	8	0	75	0	Direction north-east. Road level through grassy plain, covered with scattered trees. No difficulties. Ban Kin Pao is a small straggling village, with a few paddy-fields, situated on the Mé Chan river. Extensive camping ground. Water, fuel, and dry grass.
		8. Kaing Sen (1,150 feet). Mé Chan and Mé Kham.	15	4	90	4	Direction north of east. Road good and level through open grassy forest, passing at 2½ miles, Wieng Manôla village, surrounded by earth ramparts, much overgrown with jungle, but capable of being turned into a strong position. Continue through level forest with open glades and patches of cultivation. At 7 miles a small village and wells of water. At 8 miles reach

FROM MÖNG FÁNG TO KAING SEN—*continued.*

Authorities. Military.	Authorities. Civil.	Number and Names of Stages, Rivers and Streams.	Distances. Intermediate.	Distances. Total.	Remarks.
	Siam.	**8. Kaing Sen (1,150 feet)**—*cont.*			the north corner of a small wooded range of hills, running north and south. The Mé Chan river rounds the same corner and the road and river run together due east. The path now becomes hilly, skirting and crossing low spurs from the hills mentioned above. At 10 miles leave the Mé Chan river, flowing north-east, and taking an easterly direction follow an irrigation canal, crossing and recrossing it constantly. The canal is 3 feet deep and 12 feet broad. Continue thus, still hugging the hills to the right up to 14 miles. Here turn north and cross the Mé Kham river (*N.B.*—Not the Mé Chan) and reach Kaing Sen at 15⅝ miles.

BRANCH I.

FROM KAING SEN (STAGE 8) TO MÉ SAI (ROUTE NO. 1-A, APPENDIX III, STAGE 4).

BY LIEUT. G. H. YOUNGHUSBAND, "QUEEN'S OWN" CORPS OF GUIDES, 1887.

Military	Civil	Stages	Intermediate M.	Intermediate F.	Total M.	Total F.	Remarks
	Siam.	**1. Camp on Mé Ma.** Mé Kham and Mé Ma.	13	0	13	0	Leaving Kaing Sen head up the Mé Kham river. The road is undulating and passes through thick forest, being skirted on one hand by hills, and having an extensive plain to the west. At 6 miles leave the Mé Kham river, and, striking across an open grassy plain with scattered groves of trees, reach the Mé Ma river at 13 miles. Extensive camping ground.
		2. Mé Sai ... ... Mé Ma.	8	0	21	0	Crossing the Mé Ma river by an easy ford, 2½ feet deep, continue through the same open grassy plain in a north-west direction to Mé Sai, Stage 4 of Route No. 1-A of Appendix III.

No. 6.

From MÖNG HENG to MÉHAWNGSAWN viâ MÖNG NOI and MÖNG PAI.

BY CAPT. H. B. WALKER, PAID ATTACHÉ, INTELLIGENCE BRANCH, FEBRUARY 1893.

Military	Civil	Stages	Intermediate M.	Intermediate F.	Total M.	Total F.	Remarks
	Siam.	**1. Camp in jungle above junction of the Hwé Maw (or Mao) and a hill-side stream.** Hwé Méli and Hwé Maw.	7	0	7	0	General direction a little south of west. The route leaves Möng Heng from the west; crosses the Mé Ting into the camping ground, and strikes up by a gradual ascent and good path into the low range of hills lying on the western side of the Mé Ting valley, crossing an unimportant stream, flowing Mé Ting-wards at mile 1, rising to 1½ miles, and crossing the Hwé Méli, an insignificant stream, at 2 miles flowing to the Mé Ting; and running away on the south-eastern side of the spur ascended. The route winds along west of the spur almost level with the summits of a succession of knolls lying to left hand of the path till mile 4. It descends to mile 5 when it drops

FROM MÖNG HENG TO MÉHAWNGSAWN *viâ* MÖNG NOI AND MÖNG PAI—*continued.*

Authorities. Military.	Authorities. Civil.	Number and Names of Stages, Rivers and Streams.	Distances. Intermediate.	Distances. Total.	Remarks.
Siam.		**1. Camp in jungle above junction of the Hwé Maw (or Mao) and a hill-side stream** —*cont.*			into the bed of the Hwé Maw (or Mao) whose bed, stony and winding, it follows till mile $6\frac{1}{2}$, when a small stream flowing into the Hwé Maw (2 yards wide, 6 inches deep; stony) from the left hand or southern side forms a spur, $\frac{1}{2}$ a mile up which by an easy gradient lies the camping ground which delineates the half-way to Möng Noi. Accommodation can be found for 100 men, though the ground is sloping and uneven. The whole route is through jungle. Bamboos and pine trees and thick undergrowth; the path good, but narrow, and would require widening if a large force were intended to pass along. Grass and bamboo leaves abundant. Water from either streams.
		2. Möng Noi ... Mé Pai and one or two insignificant streams *en route.*	M. F. **6 0**	M. F. 13 0	Leaving the camp the route rises to the summit of the spur which lies between a range of hills to right hand, or north, and left hand, or south, and crosses the watershed between the Mé Ting and the Salween, returning to the latter; the route then is one long continuous ascent into the valley of the Mé Pai, which flowing from beneath Loi Métaw is crossed at mile $11\frac{3}{4}$ for the first time (15 yards wide, $1\frac{1}{2}$ feet deep; rapid and rocky bottom; easy crossing). Möng Noi is reached at mile 13, situated in the Mé Pai valley, or, as it should here be more correctly termed, Mé Pai gorge, which is separated from the first few miles of the onward route to Möng Pai town (two days' march westward) by a short low ridge of hills, round which the Mé Pai winds on the northern side, the route lying on the western side. Möng Noi consists of 17 houses (Shans) and a pôngyi kyaung, there being accommodation for 600 men in the taungyas, and on the left bank of the Mé Pai, Möng Noi itself lying on the right bank. The whole neighbouring country is thick jungle, teak, pines. The chief industry of Möng Noi is timber-cutting, logs of teak choking up the stream during the dry season waiting for the rains to carry them down to Moulmein. Grass abundant. The above two marches can be done in one day. Supplies few and scanty.
		3. Wansilan (jungle camp). Hwé Pöng Noi and Mé Pai.	**6 0**	19 0	General direction south-west. Leaving Möng Noi the route passes through the kyaung compound, crosses the Mé Pai, and after $\frac{1}{4}$ a mile of jungle, leaving a short ridge lying between it and the Mé Pai, it strikes the bed of the Hwé Pong Noi, an insignificant stream, flowing into the Mé Pai, and follows it till mile $2\frac{1}{4}$ (crossing it several times, easy crossings) where it leaves it, crosses the termination of a low spur, and drops down to the Mé Pai, which it also crosses. It then crosses the termination of two or three small spurs and rises steeply across a third, dropping down to the Mé Pai and crossing it again at mile $4\frac{1}{2}$. From this point to Wansilan the route follows the course of the Mé Pai, crossing and recrossing it six times, all crossings easy, the stream 20 yards broad and $1\frac{1}{2}$ feet deep, gravel bottom and very clear. There is accommodation at Wansilan for 300 men. Grass and bamboo leaves on right bank of stream.

FROM MÖNG HENG TO MÉHAWNGSAWN *viâ* MÖNG NOI AND MÖNG PAI—*continued.*

Authorities. Military.	Authorities. Civil.	Number and Names of Stages, Rivers and Streams.	Distances. Intermediate. M.	Distances. Intermediate. F.	Distances. Total. M.	Distances. Total. F.	Remarks.
Siam.		**4. Möng Pai** ... Mé Pai and hill-side streams flowing into it.	**8**	**0**	27	0	General direction south. Leaving Wansilan the route follows the course of the Mé Pai by an excellent and level route (except at the crossings) through jungle, the Mé Pai being crossed and recrossed twenty-four times. At mile 2 a small stream flowing into the Mé Pai is crossed, and hot sulphur springs named Pôn Pat; at mile 5 the route debouches on to the wide paddy plains, some 2 miles in width from hill range to hill range, and passes the small Shan village of Téngkétawn just below, or west of which the Mé Pôn stream joins the Mé Pai, flowing from the western range of hills or Loi Mena. At mile 6 the route crosses a stream flowing from the eastern range into the Mé Pai. At mile 6½ the route passes through a ruined stockade and enters the Siamese portion of Möng Pai, a wretched village, the only good building being a new Wut house. The stockade is in ruins, but was formerly some 600 square yards. At mile 7 the route passes through the upper part of the Shan portion of the town, and crossing the Mé Pai at mile 7½ enters the lower Shan town at mile 8. The Siamese portion contains 122 houses, the Shan portion 250. Population employed in timber-felling. Supplies good and cheap. There is a bazaar here every eighth day. The valley of the Mé Pai towards Möng Peng is fruitful and better populated than the rest of the country frontierwards. There is accommodation for a division or more. Ample grass and of good quality. A kyaung and a large new building belonging to the Sawbwa would afford house accommodation for a battalion.
		5. Tin Loi Mena. Namköng and several small streams.	**10**	**6**	37	6	General direction north-west. The route leaves the largest and southern portion of the Shan end of the town and strikes by a good path across paddy-fields, leaving the centre portion of the Shan village to right hand where the Mé Pai makes a westerly bend. Here crosses a small water-course, with good drinking water, flowing into the Mé Pai. The route then gently rises and runs through thin jungle across the final extremity of the spurs from Loi Mena range and crosses a stream flowing Mé Pai-wards at mile 2; the route then crosses the lower extremities of another spur and crosses another stream at mile 3, reaching the Shan village of Ménateng (30 houses), and then crosses fresh paddy-fields, bending slightly towards the north for ¾ mile, when a stream is crossed, and the route enters the hills following the course of the Mena stream (6 or 7 yards broad, 6 inches to 1 foot deep; clear and rapid, gravelly bottom, here and there stony, crossing and recrossing), which runs, between a ridge, separating it from the Mé Pai, into which it ultimately flows a little north of Ménateng village, and a long spur together with its minor spurs running south-eastwards from the Loi Mena range. The route is level and good travelling; passable for all arms, and passes at mile 5¾ the small camping ground of Pamélaung. Accommodation for 100 men and animals, though more room could be made by clearing the jungle. Leaving Pamélaung the route follows the bed (against stream) of the Mena until mile 7, when the Namköng flows into it from the north. The route having assumed

FROM MÖNG HENG TO MÉHAWNGSAWN *viâ* MÖNG NOI AND MÖNG PAI—*continued.*

Authorities. Military.	Authorities. Civil.	Number and Names of Stages, Rivers and Streams.	Distances. Intermediate.	Distances. Total.	Remarks.
Siam.		**5. Tin Loi Mena** —*cont.*			a more westerly direction, and still following the left bank of the Mena continues level to the next mile, when it is joined by another stream from the right, enclosing a spur up which the route runs on along its south-west slopes until mile 9¾, when it crosses to the right bank of the Mena by a steep ascent and descent, the path here being stony, narrow, and bad, and continuing so for a ¼ of a mile, when it broadens and again crosses the Mena to the camping ground whose name signifies the camp at the foot of the hills, after which the onward route leaves the course of the Mena to cross the range of the same name. There is accommodation on both sides of the stream for 100 men with difficulty. Grass scanty, but bamboo leaves in plenty. The whole route from Ménateng rises very slightly, working into the range, this camp being at the foot of the steeper portions. Thick jungle, teak, bamboo and pine trees all the way, and the route is shaded from the sun, enabling men to march in the heat of the day without difficulty.
			M. F.	M. F.	
		6. U Möng ... Several mountain or hill-side water-courses; mostly dry, and the Mé U Möng.	**9 0**	45 6	General direction north-west. Leaving the camp the route strikes upwards by a good path along a steeply ascending spur, the Ména, rising among the spurs to the left or south, being left behind; the route continues to rise, working slightly towards Loi Mena, crosses the main ridge at 4½ miles, half-way between Loi Ména and Loi Ména Teng, the last mile and-a-half assuming a more northerly direction. From the summit of the ridge, which is some 4,500 feet high where crossed, a fine view is obtained of the Mé Pai valley, the village of that name, being visible, and onward to the west the valleys of the Mé U Möng; and thereafter when joined by that stream, the Mé Láng; this latter also taking the water of the Mé Mao: all these three streams flowing nearly parallel with one another till the lower ground is reached, the Mé U Möng occupying the centre position. The crest of the ridge is covered with fir or pine trees, with teak and another miscellaneous jungle interspersed; the crest of the ridge is narrow where crossed, and the route, on descending, follows the direction of a minor spur, a larger and longer one lying to the south and dividing the courses of the Mé U Möng and Mé Mao. The downward path is good, though broken in places and stony at first. At mile 7½ a route to the left or south leads to the village of the Mé Mao, some 9 miles distant, and *en route* to Möng Peng *viâ* Namayan, &c.; the U Möng is here crossed 5 yards wide, 1 foot deep, stony but easy crossing. At mile 9 the Mé U Möng is crossed again. The village lies up a small stream to left hand or south, ¾ of a mile distant (15 houses; Shans; employed in timber-cutting). The camping ground on the left bank of the stream would accommodate 300 men amongst teak and bastard teak trees.

FROM MÖNG HENG TO MÉHAWNGSAWN *viâ* MÖNG NOI AND MÖNG PAI—*continued.*

Authorities. Military.	Authorities. Civil.	Number and Names of Stages, Rivers and Streams.	Distances. Intermediate. M.	F.	Total. M.	F.	Remarks.
		7. Páng Mak Hpa Mé U Möng and Mé Láng streams.	**9**	**4**	55	2	General direction north-west. Leaving U Möng the route follows the course of the Mé U Möng, crossing and recrossing it, all the crossings being easy, as far as mile 4½, where a route strikes off to the right to Mé Mao village, and the onward route takes a more westerly direction and passes on left hand, or south, the new Shan village of Mé Láng; seven houses; few supplies; inhabited by timber-fellers. Here the Mé Láng stream (6 yards wide, shallow and stony) debouches from the right, or north, and absorbs the Mé U Möng. The route now follows the course of the Mé Láng, passing the deserted village of Mé Láng at mile 7, the route now being excellent. At mile 7½ the route crossing the Mé Láng for the second time, runs along its left bank through a kaing grass valley. At mile 9 it turns south-west and crossing the Mé Láng, reaches Páng Mak Hpa, a Shan village of 25 houses and kyaung, situated on the right bank of the stream. Supplies few, being in the month of February 1893, nearly deserted on account of small-pox being prevalent. It is the centre of timber-felling in this district, a depôt for the logs being kept here during the felling season. From Páng Mak Hpa the Mé Láng continues its course in a westerly direction, eventually joining the Mé Pai. There is also from here a branch route to Möng Peng *viâ* Namayan, but it is little used beyond Namayan and is blocked up usually with timber. Méhawngsawn can also be reached by this route, branching off from Namayan.
	Siam.	**8. Pöng Hsán Pik** Hwékán and Pu Hsán Pik.	**10**	**0**	65	2	General direction the first 6 miles north-west, the last 4 miles south-west. Leaving Páng Mak Hpa the route strikes across a low ridge which encloses on the eastern side a sort of basin formed by it and a ridge of rugged rocks on the western side, whence the water does not appear to escape, these "devil's cauldrons" being common in this part of Siam. It then dips and runs along the northern confines of the basin; rises and crosses a low ridge; descends again on the opposite side and winding through a dank rock-enclosed valley, whence it emerges at mile 2. Here a route to right hand, or north, leads to Mé Mao; the route then descends into another basin, the water of which presumably sinks to re-appear some distance further on in the shape of the stream Hwékán, issuing in a considerable body from the base of a rock. The route now makes its way out of the basin by a narrow defile and descending a little reaches the crest of a long ridge overlooking the valley of the Hwékán and Pu Hsán Pik streams, the latter flowing from the north absorbing the former. On the ridge, on the opposite side of the valley, is visible the village of Kawng Pawng, one of the few villages in thin sparsely populated district. The route then descends precipitously into the valley of the Hwékán, which rises abruptly from the heart of a rock to the right hand, or north, of the route, which now commences to take a slightly southern turn and reaches small camping ground of Hwékán at mile 5. At mile 5½ a small stream flows into the Hwékán, and at mile 6 the latter joins the Pu Hsán Pik (10 or 15 yards wide, 1 foot deep; gravelly bottom; all crossings easy) flowing from the north. Here a route strikes

FROM MÖNG HENG TO MÉHAWNGSAWN *viâ* MÖNG NOI AND MÖNG PAI—*continued.*

Authorities. Military.	Authorities. Civil.	Number and Names of Stages, Rivers and Streams.	Distances. Intermediate.	Distances. Total.	Remarks.
Siam.		**8. Pöng Hsán Pik** —*cont.*			up the valley of a hill-side stream to Kawng Pawng; the route now assumes a decided south-westerly direction and crossing and recrossing the Pu Hsán Pik stream reaches the camping ground at mile 10, passing a hot water sulphur spring at 9½ on left bank of the stream, the camping ground lying on the right of the stream, which is crossed immediately before entering it. The route is good all the way, the last 4 miles being excellent; jungle thick on the slopes on either side. The crossings of the Pöng Hsán Pik are usually knee-deep. There is accommodation for 200 men on both banks. Grass and bamboo leaves abundant. A route from here strikes back northward along a lengthy ridge, which forms the eastern boundary of the valley of the Namkhawng which flows from north-west to south-east at its base, and along which the main route from Mélana and Möng Maö runs (*see* Route No. 32, Shan Hills Division).
		9. Pánghom ... Nam Khawng, Hwé Sán, Nam Kha, Mé Kha, Pánghom, Heiyok, and Pônchuk.	M. F. **10 0**	M. F. 75 2	General direction south-west. Leaving the camp on the banks of the Pöng Hsán Pik the route strikes across the lower extremities of the long spur mentioned in previous stage as being the eastern boundary of the Nam Khawng valley and reaches the Nam Khawng at mile 2, which it crosses eight times as far as Hwésán, 3¼ miles, all crossings being easy, the route being perfectly level, sound and good. Hwésán is the junction of the Hwésán stream with the Nam Khawng and the main road from Mélana (three days) to Méhawngsawn. There is a small camping ground for 100 men on the right bank of the Hwésán. Grass and bamboo leaves obtainable. The route now runs up the course of the Hwésán for 2 miles, a route to right hand, a mile leading to Hwésán village, said to be some 5 or 6 miles distant; the route then strikes across the lower extremities of a spur running from the north-west to south-east and towards the Nam Khawng and descends to the junction of Nam Kha and Mé Kha (two small streams) at mile 5 by a rocky but broad path, on the right bank of which stream is situated the small village of Méhsomnya (six houses; Shans). Here after crossing the Nam Kha there is accommodation for 600 men under large shady trees. From here the route runs level along the valley which is enclosed by low hills, with steep precipitous sides, of rocky nature, to mile 8 when it reaches the small village of Hoiyôk, situated on stream of the same name, which flows into the Pánghom stream; along up narrow stony bed the route runs to Pánghom, the village being reached at mile 9½ (20 houses; Shans); and the camping ground on the right bank of the Pánghom stream at mile 10. Accommodation for 200 men with difficulty, the village being capable of holding 150 men. Grass and bamboo leaves obtainable. The route is good under foot, though stony; from mile 6½ is level and passable for all arms throughout. The following streams are met with or crossed *en route*:— The Nam Khawng. At mile 2·25 to 30 yards broad, 1 foot deep; gravelly bottom; easy current; crossed eight times; low banks. The Hwésán flowing north-east into the Nam Khawng, 10 yards wide, 6 inches deep; stony and rapid.

FROM MÖNG HENG TO MÉHAWNGSAWN *viâ* MÖNG NOI AND MÖNG PAI—*continued.*

Authorities. Military.	Authorities. Civil.	Number and Names of Stages, Rivers and Streams.	Distances. Intermediate. M.	Distances. Intermediate. F.	Distances. Total. M.	Distances. Total. F.	Remarks.
		9. Pánghom—*cont.*					The Nam Kha and Mé Kha, junction of two small streams, the former flowing from south-west to north-east, the latter from west to east. At mile 5 the Pánghom, Hoiyôk, and Pônchuk streams, converging into the first and flowing to the Nam Kha.
	Siam.	**10. Hwéhpa** ... Hwéhsalawp and Mé Hsángé.	10	0	85	2	General direction south-west. Leaving the Pánghom camping ground the route crosses the small stream and ascends a steep ridge for a mile by a broad track; crosses it and descends by one continuous descent into the valley of the Mé Hsángé (Mé Hsanyi or Mé Si Ngé) occasional glimpses of the valley being obtainable, lying right hand or west; the route is excellent and broad; light jungle for some portions of the way, the rest being teak. At mile 5½ the Shan village of Hwésalawp (14 houses) is passed on the left hand or east; the stream Hwéhpa or Hwéhsalawp (6 yards wide, 1 foot deep) being crossed, the route then ascends slightly and runs along a ridge lying between the valleys of the Hwéhpa (?) and Mé Hsángé. At mile 8½ a short cut runs down a spur into the valley of the Mé Hsángé and into the village of Hwéhpa, the main route continues down the termination of the ridge, the short cut being impassable for animals. Hwéhpa, containing 30 houses, is situated on the eastern edge of the paddy-fields, lying in the valley formed by the junction of the Mé Hsángé with the Hwéhpa, and towards the south, some 1½ miles along the valley, with the Mé Hsánga. There is accommodation for a brigade. Grass and bamboo leaves, and good supplies. Paddy, rice, and vegetables. The main road from Möng Maö (*see* Route No. 32, Shan Hills Division) runs in here with the Mé Hsángé and a route to Möng Heng leaves the valley eastward, for which also *see* Route No. 32, Shan Hills Division.
		11. Méhawngsawn. Mé Hsángé, Mé Hsánga, Mé Pai, and two or three small streams.	10	0	95	2	General direction first 2 miles west, then south. Leaving Hwéhpa and crossing the paddy-fields the route runs along the valley of the Mé Hsángé (15 to 20 yards broad; 1 foot deep; gravelly bottom; easily fordable) as far as mile 2½ by a good path, keeping to the left bank of that stream. Light jungle on either side, perfectly level, except at mile 1¼, where the route crosses the end of a low ridge, descending again, on the other side, at mile 1¾ into the valley of the Mé Hsángé, where there is camping ground in paddy-fields for 1,500 or 2,000 men. The route then commences to bear southward and reaches the double village of Mauksánpé (Shans; 50 houses in paddy-fields), situated at the junction of the Mé Hsángé with the Mé Hsánga, which here flowing from the north-north-west absorbs the Mé Hsángé. The route now follows the Mé Hsánga valley, crossing to the right bank of the stream (25 to 30 yards wide, 1½ feet deep; avarage current; easily fordable everywhere; gravelly bottom) at mile 3. The valley here is ⅛ a mile to ¼ broad and well watered or irrigated for cultivation. At mile 3½ the village of Mé Hsánga is reached; a large village of 200 houses. Good supplies and a few European stores from Méhawngsawn. Paddy-fields on the southern side afford accommodation for a large number of men—a brigade or more. The

FROM MÖNG HENG TO MÉHAWNGSAWN *viâ* MÖNG NOI AND MÖNG PAI—*continued.*

Authorities. Military.	Authorities. Civil.	Number and Names of Stages, Rivers and Streams.	Distances. Intermediate.	Distances. Total.	Remarks.
Siam.		**11. Méhawngsawn**—*cont.*	route passes through Mé Hsánga across the paddy-fields and follows the valley of the Mé Hsánga (the right bank of stream running along the lower extremities of the western spurs, thus avoiding the moist valley) so far as mile 4¼ where the village of Namun is reached and passed through (20 houses; Shans). At mile 4¾ passes the village of Kongpahsak (20 houses; Shans). At mile 5¾ the stream Mé Hsánga is crossed by an easy ford. A branch route from Hwéhpa here chimes in on the left hand; the route runs through light jungle for a short distance, the open valley lying to the right hand. At mile 6 the village of Pángmu (60 houses; Shans) is passed. A straggling and dirty place with one kyaung; then the Mépai flowing from the east chimes in; is crossed (30 yards wide, 2 feet deep; easy crossing; gravelly bottom and easy current) and absorbs the Mé Hsánga. The route now follows the valley of the Mé Pai left bank of stream as far as mile 7, passing through the two southern portions of Pángmu (40 houses; Shans). At mile 7 the route leaves the Mépai valley and crosses behind a low hill, a continuation of the eastern spurs, and winds behind the ridge it forms, slightly descending, the path being broad and capable of admitting carts. At mile 8½ a well is passed to the left of the road; at 8¾ a large fine kyaung supplied with wells; and the hill, crowned with a large kyaung to the west of and commanding Méhawngsawn, comes in sight; the route then turning a little more to the south descends slightly, crosses the Nam Hpo, a small stream, by a very fine bridge capable of sustaining all traffic and artillery; and Méhawngsawn is entered at mile 10.		

BRANCH I.

FROM MÖNG PAI (STAGE 4) TO ZIMMÉ.

BY CAPT. H. B. WALKER, INTELLIGENCE BRANCH, FROM NATIVE INFORMATION, FEBRUARY 1893.

Military	Civil	Stages	Intermediate M.	Intermediate F.	Total M.	Total F.	Remarks
Siam.		**1 Mo Peng** ... Crosses the Méyin; Mé Né Na Pong.	**11**	**0**	11	0	General direction south-east. Road good. Mo Peng contains 12 houses. Eggs and fowls plentiful; also passes through three villages, namely, Méyin at 2 miles, Mi Né at 4 miles, Sopeng at 9½ miles.
		2. Mé Palán ... Crosses the Mé Pong Sát at 3 miles; the Mé Palak at 5 miles.	**11**	**0**	22	0	General direction south-east. Mé Palán is a jungle camp situated on stream of the same name. The route is hilly and rough.
		3. Paleng ... ... Crosses the Mé Hong Paleng at the camp.	**12**	**0**	34	0	General direction south-east. Route crosses a kaing grass grown plain, Paleng being a mere jungle camp.
		4. Sôpong .. ... Crosses the Hong Sôpong.	**11**	**0**	45	0	Sôpong is a village of 16 houses; the route passes through several villages, all Siamese.

FROM MÖNG HENG TO MÉHAWNGSAWN *viâ* MÖNG NOI AND MÖNG PAI—*continued.*

BRANCH I—*continued.*

Authorities. Military.	Civil.	Number and Names of Stages, Rivers and Streams.	Distances. Intermediate. M.	F.	Total. M.	F.	Remarks.
Siam.		**5. Zimmé** ... ... Mé Ping.	10	0	55	0	Route debouches into the Mé Ping valley and passes through many Siamese villages before reaching Zimmé.

No. 7.

From MÖNG HENG to MÖNG TA viâ KIUKAW.

BY CAPT. H. B. WALKER, PAID ATTACHÉ, INTELLIGENCE BRANCH, FEBRUARY 1893.

Military	Civil	Stages	M.	F.	M.	F.	Remarks
Siam.		**1. Camp on Páng-won stream.** Méhawnghkam, Mé Ting, Mé Wan Lông, and Pángwon streams.	14	0	14	0	General direction north. The route leaves Möng Heng by its easterly exit, passing through a gap in a mound or parapet (remains of old fortification) overgrown with jungle, and then turning north, skirts some disused paddy-fields on the western side of which lies the small village of Kongsitán, an off-shoot of Möng Heng. The route then rises slightly through jungle, crossing a small stream, the Méhawnghkam, flowing into the Mé Ting, at mile 1. It then runs level for nearly ¾ of a mile through jungle, with a kaing grass grown valley lying to left hand, or west, which receives the stream just crossed, while another small stream permeates its centre. The route then descends, turns westward, crossing this kaing grass valley and its small stream. At mile 2 turns north-west and runs through jungle, skirting a low ridge to the eastward to mile 3, when it rises over a low spur and enters the Mé Ting valley, which stream it crosses at mile 4¼ (25 to 30 feet wide; 1½ feet deep; easy current; gravelly and sandy bottom; banks 5 feet high on each side and apt to become slippery with much traffic). The same stream is crossed at mile 4½, the route now running along the Mé Ting valley through jungle and kaing grass. A low spur is crossed at mile 4¾, and the Mé Ting for the third time at mile 5. The route now runs very close to the Mé Ting and is perfectly level (kaing grass and jungle on both sides) and continues so till mile 8¾, when it reaches the Shan village of Wantiong (8 or 10 houses, and a kyaung), crossing the Mé Ting at mile 5¾, 7 and 8½, near its junction with the Mé Wan Lông, flowing from the north-west, stream here 20 feet wide, 1¼ feet deep, bottom sound, banks rather steep at all crossings. There is ample accommodation for 2,000 or 3,000 men in the disused paddy-fields intersected by the Mé Wan Lông (6 feet wide; 6 inches deep), west of Wantiong and below it. Supplies few. *N.B.*—Wantiong would probably be the base of operations on the frontier on the Siam side along this route, being the last place where open and ample accommodation could be obtained without clearing jungle). The valley of the Mé Ting now continues to the right hand or east of Wantiong which is situated on a small knoll, at end of a low ridge, and which could be made defensible though partially commanded by similar ridges on western side of the paddy-

FROM MÖNG HENG TO MÖNG TA *viâ* KIUKAW—*continued.*

Authorities. Military.	Authorities. Civil.	Number and Names of Stages, Rivers and Streams.	Distances. Intermediate. M.	F.	Total. M.	F.	Remarks.
Siam.		**1. Camp on Pángwon stream**—*cont.*					fields recommended for encamping troops. Leaving Wantiong the route now follows the valley of the Mé Wan Lông to mile 9¼, which crosses again at 9½. From mile 9½ until mile 11, the route runs along a gradually ascending spur, clad with it, by an excellent path, the valley of the Pángwon stream lying to the right hand or east. At mile 11¼ the route descends slightly to mile 12½, when it crosses a small stream (flowing eastward to Pángwon, where there is a little lime to be procured by washing) and rising up a short steep knoll, passes through the deserted village of Kampyet. The route then descends into the valley of the Pángwon and runs through jungle and thick overgrowth until mile 14, where it crosses the Pángwon, turning eastward at this spot, there being camping ground in the jungle, if cleared, for 200 men.
G.O.C. Rangoon District.	Superintendent, Southern Shan States.	**2. Möng Ta** ...	11	4	25	4	From here the route winds round the lower slopes of the extremities of the spurs from the main ridge, and reaches the frontier at ½ a mile here running through a steeply enclosed and jungle-clad pass, the track being very narrow, though sound under foot, the frontier coming from Loi Htwé and crossing here strikes up again to Loi Mé Taw—a wooden pillar and a cross on a tree demarcating the boundary at this place which is known as Kiukaw. After crossing the frontier the onward route continues to Möng Ta town, within the state of Möng Ta, and about 11 miles distant (*see* Appendix II, Route No. 4).

No. 8.

From MÖNG HENG to ZIMMÉ (KENGMAI).

BY CAPT. H. B. WALKER, INTELLIGENCE BRANCH, FROM NATIVE INFORMATION, JANUARY 1893.

Military	Civil	Stages	Intermediate M.	F.	Total M.	F.	Remarks
Siam.		**1. Möng Khong.** Hwé Pakka, Mé Pa Sat, Mé Won San, and Hwé Ta Maw draining to Mé Ting.	**14**	**0**	14	0	General direction south along valley of the Mé Ting. Route good and level. Möng Khong is a Shan village containing 60 houses; fair supplies; ample camp accommodation.
		2. Möng Kit ... Mé Mong, Mé On, and Mé Kit.	**8**	**0**	22	0	General direction south. Route still follows valley of Mé Ting. Möng Kit contains 40 houses (Shans). The route is good and level.
		3. Kônpasat ...	**10**	**0**	32	0	General direction south. Route hilly, the Mé Ting being now left and the right bank of the Mé Ping being followed. No villages and water *en route*. Kônpasat is a Shan village of 70 houses.

FROM MÖNG HENG TO ZIMMÉ (KENGMAI)—*continued.*

Authorities. Military.	Authorities. Civil.	Number and Names of Stages, Rivers and Streams.	Distances. Intermediate. M.	F.	Total. M.	F.	Remarks.
	Siam.	**4. Mé Wan Sán.** Mé Wan Sán.	**10**	**0**	42	0	General direction south. Route hilly, crossing low ridge of hills. Mé Wan Sán contains 50 houses.
		5. Zimmé ... ... Mé Tasan.	**14**	**0**	56	0	General direction south. The route descends into paddy plains and, crossing them, passes through the villages of Tyilak, Namlyin, Nam-ap-sán, Wan Maw, Möng Hpa, Mé Lyin, and Mé Sa (Siamese and Shans).

No. 9.

From MÖNG LONG to KYENGTUNG (KENGTUNG) viâ MÖNG HSING and MÖNG LWI.

BY CAPT. H. R. DAVIES, OXFORDSHIRE LIGHT INFANTRY, FEBRUARY 1893.

Authorities. Military.	Authorities. Civil.	Number and Names of Stages, Rivers and Streams.	Intermediate. M.	F.	Total. M.	F.	Remarks.
	Siam.	**1. Mouth of Nam La.** Numerous streams.	**12**	**4**	12	4	General direction north. Good mule road along the Möng Long plain for 3¼ miles; thence difficult road over hills; all through jungle. At 3½ miles, after crossing the Hwé Bawn, begin crossing a succession of small spurs and streams, tributaries of the Nam Hta; some very steep bits of up and down, and the road is narrow and overgrown with jungle in places. At 1¼ miles road to the right to Mong La, where there are salt mines. At 7¼ miles Ban Li, Lanten (three houses). At 9 miles Ban Hok, Lanten (20 houses). At 10½ miles Ban Phong, Lanten (25 houses). At 12½ miles the Nam La joins the Nam Hta; here a camp, 300 by 100 yards, can be cleared on the right bank of the Nam Hta. Good water, but grass is scarce, and there is no bamboo. The following streams are crossed or met with *en route*:—At ¼ mile Nam Hta from the left (40 yards by 2 feet); crossed again at 12½ miles (20 yards by 1¼ feet); at 1 mile Nam Htong from the right (10 yards by 1 foot); at 3¼ miles Hwé Bawn from the right (2 yards by 6 inches); at 7 miles Nam Li from the right (10 yards by 1 foot); at 9 miles Hwé Hok from the right (3 yards by 4 inches). At 10½ miles Hwé Phong from the right (3 yards by 4 inches); at 12½ miles, Nam La from the right (10 yards by 1 foot).
		2. Páng Tintôk ... Numerous streams.	**14**	**0**	26	4	General direction north-west. Fair mule road, but the Nam Hta and its tributary, the Nam Long, are crossed 105 times, which makes marching slow. The whole way through jungle up the Nam Hta valley for 11 miles, thence up the Nam Löng. Good camps could be cleared at 7 and 8 miles, but there is scarcely any grass till Páng Tintôk is reached, and no bamboo. At Páng Tintôk two small streams, the Hwé Li and Hwé Khai, join and form the Nam Löng; here is a camp 150 yards square. Good water and fair grass. The following streams are crossed or met with *en route*:—Nam Hta crossed seventy-one times (15 to 20 yards by 1 to 1½ feet);

FROM MÖNG LONG TO KYENGTUNG (KENGTUNG) *viâ* MÖNG HSING AND MÖNG LWI—*continued.*

Authorities. Military.	Authorities. Civil.	Number and Names of Stages, Rivers and Streams.	Distances. Intermediate. M.	F.	Distances. Total. M.	F.	Remarks.
		2. Pang Tintôk—*cont.*					at 11 miles, Nam Long crossed thirty-four times (10 to 15 yards by 1 to $1\frac{1}{2}$ feet); at $5\frac{1}{2}$ miles Nam Wa from the left (10 yards by 1 foot); at 8 miles Hwé Möng from the left (6 yards by 6 inches); at $8\frac{1}{2}$ miles Hwé Khwi from the right (5 yards by 6 inches).
	Siam.	**3. Ban Sai** ... Hwé Sai.	6	6	33	2	General direction north-west. Fair mule road, but very steep. Steep ascent from the camp for $\frac{3}{4}$ mile, then nearly level along a spur to $2\frac{1}{4}$ miles; thence steep ascent to the Nam Hta-Nam Hsing watershed at 3 miles, 5,120 feet high; thence down a spur, sometimes very steep, sometimes less so, to the Hwé Sai (5 yards by 6 inches), which is crossed at $6\frac{1}{4}$ miles; here is a camping ground, but there is more room $\frac{1}{2}$ a mile further on at Ban Sai, a Lanten village (eight houses). Good water and fair grass.
		4. Möng Hsing ... Hwé Sai and other small streams and Nam Hsing.	7	2	40	4	General direction west. Good mule road. Cross the Hwé Sai and some low spurs and small streams till $2\frac{1}{2}$ miles where the Möng Hsing plain is entered; thence level road through grass and scrub jungle, passing three villages. Möng Hsing is surrounded by a low parapet and small ditch. Large camping grounds anywhere, but in the town water from wells only. The Nam Hsing (15 yards by $1\frac{1}{4}$ feet) is 1,000 yards off to the north of the town; good camping ground on its banks. Supplies of rice, paddy, and cattle obtainable. Goats can be got from Khakui villages in the hills. This road has not been much used lately, as Mong Long has been deserted till recently. Now that Möng Long is repopulated the road will probably improve.
		5. Ban Wa ... Nam Hsing and other streams.	12	0	52	4	General direction north. Good mule road, level most of the way. At 4 miles cross some low hills for 3 miles. Most of the road through thin jungle; at 10 miles through paddy for a mile. The following villages are passed:—At $2\frac{1}{2}$ miles Kangna (Lö), five houses; at 4 miles Pangbawn (Lo), two houses; at 10 miles Mong Wom (Lö), 15 houses, $\frac{1}{2}$ mile off on the right. Here is a large camping ground in paddy. At Ban Wa large camping ground in paddy. Good grass and water. From here a road goes off to the right to Möng Yôn. The following streams are crossed or met with *en route*:—At $\frac{3}{4}$ mile Nam Hsing from the right (20 yards by 1 foot); at $5\frac{1}{4}$ miles Nam Lawng from the right (8 yards by 8 inches); at $8\frac{3}{4}$ miles Hwé Saikhao from the right (4 yards by 6 inches); at $9\frac{1}{4}$ miles Nam Yôn from the left (30 yards by 2 feet); stony bottom; at 10 miles Hwé Hin from the left (6 yards by 8 inches).
		6. Ban Law ... Hwé Hin, Nam Htun, and Mé Kong.	14	0	66	4	General direction north-west. Fair mule road, but steep. Level road for $1\frac{1}{4}$ miles; then cross the Hwé Hin and commence ascent which continues steadily to the top of the ridge at 6 miles, with one short piece of downhill

FROM MÖNG LONG TO KYENGTUNG (KENGTUNG) *viâ* MÖNG HSING AND MÖNG LWI—*continued.*

Authorities. Military.	Authorities. Civil.	Number and Names of Stages, Rivers and Streams.	Distances. Intermediate. M.	F.	Distances. Total. M.	F.	Remarks.
		6. Ban Law—*cont.*					and up again on to another spur just before reaching the top. Here is the Kaw village of Wokhet, ½ mile on the left. Here there is a small camping ground, but water has to be brought up from a long way down below. From here along the ridge to 8 miles ascending and descending occasionally; thence along a spur, but only slightly downhill, passing Phayalokö (Kaw), 25 houses at 10 miles, and Senpitsai (Kaw), 15 houses at 10½ miles. From here a road to the left to Pakha ferry. Hence downhill to the Nam Htun at 11¾ miles; down the course of the Nam Htun to 12¾ miles; thence across small spurs and streams, tributaries of the Mé Kong, to Ban San (Lö), 15 houses. Here is the ferry across the Mé Kong to Ban Law which is on the right bank. There is more room to camp in Ban San than in Ban Law. Ban Law is a Lö village; eight houses. The following streams are crossed or met with *en route*:—At 1¼ miles Hwé Hin from the right (6 yards by 8 inches); at 11¾ miles Nam Htun, crossed several times (5 yards by 9 inches); at 14 miles Mé Kong from the right; channel 250 yards wide; water 120 yards wide; strong current; bottom sandy with rocks sticking up. One raft taking 25 men, or four mules and 10 men. Mules cannot be swum as the current is too strong. Ferrymen live on both sides of the river.
Siam.		**7. Phayakham** ... Mé Kong and small streams.	11	6	78	2	General direction south to Pakha; thence west-north-west to Phayakham. Fair mule road. Down the right bank of the Mé Kong by a nearly level road to Pakha at 4½ miles (Lö), 18 houses. Here is a ferry with three boats, but the current is so strong that a raft cannot be managed, so animals cannot cross here Thence along the side of a spur, fairly level, till the Hwé Kayan is crossed at 6 miles; thence steady ascent to Phayakham which is on top of a ridge, and contains 15 houses (Kaw). Room to camp in the village, but the best place is ¾ mile further on, where a stream is crossed and there is open grass (300 by 100 yards) just beyond. Good water here and fair grass: camp not very level. The following streams are crossed or met with *en route*:—At 6 miles Hwé Kayan from the right (8 yards by 1 foot); at 10 miles stream from right (1 yard by 2 inches); at 11¾ miles stream from the right (3 yards by 6 inches).
		8. Ban Phek ... Small streams.	12	0	90	2	General direction south-west by west. Fair mule road. Cross a spur and descend very steeply for ½ mile to a tributary of the Nam Khan; thence up steep for 1,000 yards on to another spur; along the spur, and gradually down again to the same stream which is crossed again at 4½ miles. Thence uphill for ½ mile on to a spur and gradually down to Möng Khan at 6½ miles. Large camping grounds and good water and grass here. Supplies in small quantities. The town contains 25 houses and is under a Phaya; it is in a plain about 2 miles by 1 mile, containing five other villages. Cross the Nam Khan, and at 7 miles pass Ban Haw; 26 houses. At 7½ miles cross the Nam Haw and follow up it and its tributary, the Hwé Heao, to 10 miles; thence steep ascent to Ban Phek (Kaw) 12 houses, a little way off the road to the left. Room for a camp in the village, but the water is some way

FROM MÖNG LONG TO KYENGTUNG (KENGTUNG) *viâ* MÖNG HSING AND MÖNG LWI—*continued.*

Authorities.		Number and Names of Stages, Rivers and Streams.	Distances.		Remarks.
Military.	Civil.		Intermediate.	Total.	
	Siam.	**8. Ban Phek**—*cont.*			off below. The following streams are crossed or met with *en route*:—At 1 mile stream from right (6 yards by 6 inches); at 4¼ miles the same stream; at 6½ miles Nam Khan from the right (20 yards by 1½ feet); at 7½ miles Nam Haw from right crossed several times (10 yards by 1 foot); at 8¼ miles Hwé Heao crossed several times (7 yards by 6 inches).
			M. F.	M. F.	
		9. Sôpnam ... Nam Hé.	**12 4**	102 6	General direction north-west. Fair mule road. Along the top of the ridge, but with a good deal of steep ascent and descent, for 7½ miles, passing the Kaw village of Ban Salé at 5 miles, a little way off on the right. At 7½ miles the descent begins and continues, very steeply in places, down to the Nam Hé (20 yards by 1½ feet) which is crossed at Sôpnam. Small camping ground in village; large camping ground in paddy south of the village. Good grass and water. Sôpnam is a Lö village containing 25 houses.
		10. Möng Lwi ... Nam Lwi and several small streams.	**13 0**	115 6	General direction south-west. Good mule road, nearly level the whole way. Down the Nam Hé for a mile to its junction with the Nam Lwi, then up the left bank of the Nam Lwi, crossing numerous small streams. At 4½ miles road to the right to Möng Long and Keng Hung. Opposite Möng Lwi cross the Nam Lwi, the town being on the right bank. Room to camp along the river bank at the ferry; also large camping ground just above the town; good water and grass. The town contains 30 houses and is under a Phaya. The Nam Lwi valley is here about 1½ miles wide The following streams are crossed or met with *en route*:—At 3 miles Nam Phôn from the right (5 yards by 8 inches); at 4½ miles Hwé Ngan from the right (8 yards by 8 inches); several small streams; at 13 miles Nam Lwi from the right, 150 yards broad, fairly strong current: crossed by a raft holding 35 men, or six mules and 16 men.
		11. Ban Namkhuk. Several streams.	**10 0**	125 6	General direction south-west. Good, level mule road. Up the right bank of the Nam Lwi through paddy and thin jungle till the Nam Phawn is crossed at its junction with the Nam Lwi at 4½ miles. From here a road goes straight on to Möng Yu, ¾ of a mile off, a walled town of 80 houses. The route turns sharp to the left and follows up the Nam Phawn valley through open ground, passing the villages of Ban Pawt and Tasan, and crossing to the right bank of the Nam Phawn at Hôkho; thence through jungle over the end of a spur, passing the village of Seling to Ban Namkhuk. Good camp; water and grass. The following streams are crossed or met with *en route*:—At 4½ miles Nam Phawn from the left (25 yards by 2 feet); crossed again at 7½ miles; at 6¾ miles Nam Pyen from the right (8 yards by 8 inches); at 9 miles Nam Seling from the left (7 yards by 8 inches); at 10 miles Nam Khuk from the left (6 yards by 6 inches).

FROM MÖNG LONG TO KYENGTUNG (KENGTUNG) *viâ* MÖNG HSING AND MÖNG LWI—*continued.*

Authorities. Military.	Authorities. Civil.	Number and Names of Stages, Rivers and Streams.	Distances. Intermediate. M.	F.	Distances. Total. M.	F.	Remarks.
G.O.C. Rangoon District.	Superintendent, Southern Shan States.	**12. Möng Yawn.** Several streams.	**13**	**0**	138	6	General direction south-west. Good mule road, nearly level all the way. Through jungle up to the Nam Phawn-Nam Wong watershed which forms the boundary here between Möng Yu and Möng Yawn. The ascent to and descent from this watershed are very easy and gradual. At 6 miles pass Ban Tap; thence nearly all the way over paddy and grass plain, passing several villages. At Möng Yawn camp (200 yards by 50 yards) just inside the gate by which the town is entered; large camping grounds in paddy outside: good grass: water from Nam Khap (15 yards by 1 foot). The town contains 70 houses and is fortified. Large supplies of beef, rice and paddy. The following streams are crossed or met with *en route*:—At 7½ miles Nam Wong from the right (10 yards by 1 foot); at 10½ miles Hwé Eng from the right (5 yards by 8 inches); several small streams.
		13. Páng Waw ... Several streams.	**11**	**0**	149	6	General direction south-west. Fair mule road. Along the Möng Yawn plain for 4½ miles where the Nam Poi is crossed: thence ascent of ½ a mile: along a spur slightly uphill to 6½ miles, where there is a steep ascent to 7 miles; at 8 miles a steep bit of down and up hill from one spur to another, crossing a small stream. Thence up the bed of a small stony stream and down another, but keeping well above it, to the Nam Samang and Nam Pung, which are crossed close together at 10½ miles. At the camp a cleared space of 100 by 50 yards; more room can be cleared: good grass and water. The following streams are crossed or met with *en route*:—At ¼ mile Nam Khap from the right (15 yards by 1 foot); at 2 miles Nam Kawn from the right (5 yards by 8 inches); at 4¼ miles Nam Poi from the right (10 yards by 1 foot); at 10½ miles Nam Samang from the right (15 yards by 1½ feet); at 10¾ miles Nam Pung from the right (20 yards by 1 foot).
		14. Hwé Kut ... Nam Pung and several of its tributaries.	**8**	**2**	158	0	General direction west-north-west. Good mule road; up the narrow valley of the Nam Pung (10 to 20 yards by 1 to 1½ feet) constantly crossing the river. At 2¾ miles the road leaves the river for a time, crossing Loi Sôpsun and descending to the Nam Pung again at 4½ miles. At 5½ miles and at 6¼ miles are small camps, where jungle could be cleared for large camps. At Hwé Kut, a Lö village of five houses, camp in paddy (150 by 100 yards), or a camp could be cleared in jungle. Good water and grass.
		15. Möng Kai ... Nam Pung and Nam Kai.	**9**	**2**	167	2	General direction north-west. Good mule road; up the Nam Pung for 5¼ miles; then ascent to the Nam Pung-Nam Kai watershed at 6 miles. Thence descent of ½ mile to a small stream which is followed down till it joins the Nam Kai at 8¼ miles; thence over open ground, crossing the Nam Kai (10 yards by 8 inches) at 9 miles to some bits of jungle on high ground among the paddy-fields; this is the best place to camp: good water and grass. The town of Möng Kai

FROM MÖNG LONG TO KYENGTUNG (KENGTUNG) *viâ* MÖNG HSING AND MÖNG LWI—*continued.*

Authorities.		Number and Names of Stages, Rivers and Streams.	Distances.				Remarks.
Military.	Civil.		Intermediate.		Total.		
			M.	F.	M.	F.	
G.O.C. Rangoon District.	Superintendent, Southern Shan States.	**15. Möng Kai** —*cont.*					is $\frac{3}{4}$ mile further on: it contains 60 houses. Large supplies of beef, paddy and rice.
		16. Möng Ngawm. Nam Htum, Nam Ngawm, and Nam Ngawm Noi.	**11**	**0**	178	2	General direction west. Good mule road; level for 2 miles, then cross a spur and the Nam Htum, and ascend slightly on to the low ridge which forms the watershed between the Nam Kai and Nam Lwi; no steep ascent. Along the ridge, passing Tongkyit, four houses at 4 miles, and an Akkö village on the left of the road at 6 miles; at $7\frac{3}{4}$ miles descent to 9 miles where the Nam Ngawm is crossed; thence level road to Mong Ngawm. Good camp just before the village at $10\frac{1}{2}$ miles, and beyond the village at 11 miles. Village contains 18 houses. Water from Nam Ngawm Noi in first camp and Nam Lwi in second: good grass. The following streams are crossed or met with *en route*:—At 3 miles Nam Htum from the right (8 yards by 1 foot); at 9 miles Nam Ngawm from the left (25 yards by $1\frac{1}{2}$ feet); at 10 miles Nam Ngawm Noi from the left (15 yards by 1 foot).
		17. Talö ... ... Several streams.	**15**	**2**	193	4	General direction north-west. Good mule road over low spurs from the range to the south of the Nam Lwi, but no steep up and down hill. The following villages are passed:—At $1\frac{1}{4}$ miles Wan Tai, 12 houses; at 7 miles Möng Lai; room to camp here; six houses: at 8 miles Lai Long, five houses; at 10 miles Lai Khang, five houses: at 12 miles Pakha (Akkö), six houses: at $13\frac{1}{2}$ miles Wan Pying, 10 houses; good camping ground. At Talö large camping ground; good water and fair grass. The village contains 15 houses: there is a ferry across the Nam Lwi here; two boats. The road the other side leads to Samtao, one march off, where guns are made. The following streams are crossed or met with *en route*:—At 1 mile Nam Ngat from the left (15 yards by $1\frac{1}{2}$ feet); at $7\frac{1}{2}$ miles Nam Hti from the left (15 yards by $1\frac{1}{2}$ feet); at $10\frac{1}{2}$ miles Hwé San from the left (3 yards by 4 inches); at $13\frac{3}{4}$ miles Nam Sung from the left (12 yards by 1 foot).
		18. Ban Sai ... Stream.	**11**	**0**	204	4	General direction west. Good mule road; nearly level for a mile; at $1\frac{1}{4}$ miles Nam Pai from the left (4 yards by 8 inches); then steady ascent up a spur to the top of the range at $7\frac{1}{2}$ miles, 5,800 feet. Thence more level, but up and down a little to $10\frac{1}{4}$ miles, where there is a steep descent of $\frac{1}{2}$ mile and a short ascent to Ban 'Sai, a Kon Loi village of 17 houses. Two camps (100 by 30 yards and 100 by 60 yards) just beyond the village, and more room can be found in and round the village. Water from stream 600 yards beyond the village. Grass very scarce; has to be brought from a mile off.

FROM MÖNG LONG TO KYENGTUNG (KENGTUNG) *viâ* MÖNG HSING AND MÖNG LWI—*continued.*

Authorities. Military.	Authorities. Civil.	Number and Names of Stages, Rivers and Streams.	Distances. Intermediate. M.	Intermediate. F.	Total. M.	Total. F.	Remarks.
G.O.C. Rangoon District.	Superintendent, Southern Shan States.	**19. Kengtung (Kyengtung).** Nam Phok, Nam Lang, and Nam Lap.	**11**	**6**	216	2	General direction south-west. Good mule road; steep downhill for 4 miles; thence level ground in the Kengtung plain, passing several villages. At $5\frac{1}{4}$ miles is Pakham good camping ground, grass and water. Kengtung contains about 1,900 houses; supplies in large quantities. Good camp on grass inside the town near the north-east corner; and large camping grounds outside town; water from wells; good grass. The following streams are crossed or met with *en route*:—At 4 miles Nam Phok from the right (3 yards by 6 inches); crossed again at 6 miles; at $9\frac{1}{4}$ miles Nam Lang from the left (10 yards by 8 inches); at $10\frac{1}{8}$ miles Nam Lap from the left (20 yards by 1 foot).

ALTERNATIVE I.

FROM MÖNG HSING (STAGE 4) TO KENGTUNG (STAGE 20) *viâ* KENGLÂP.

BY HAVILDAR JAGAT SING, 19TH PUNJAUB INFANTRY, MARCH 1893.

Military.	Civil.	Number and Names of Stages, Rivers and Streams.	Intermediate. M.	Intermediate. F.	Total. M.	Total. F.	Remarks.
	Siam.	**1. Páng Hai** ... Several streams.	**8**	**4**	8	4	General direction south-west. Good mule road. Nearly level the whole way. At the Hwé Sán-Hwé Mésán watershed there is scarcely any hill. At Páng Hai a camp (150 yards square), and more room could be cleared. Water from Hwé Mésán. The following villages are passed:—At $\frac{1}{2}$ mile Namkyu, 20 houses; at $2\frac{1}{2}$ miles Tongmai, 15 houses; at $3\frac{1}{3}$ miles Ban Namlai, 10 houses; at 4 miles Ban Khwang, 10 houses; at 6 miles is Páng Bung (200 yards square). Plenty of grass. The following streams are crossed or met with *en route*:—Nam Lai at $1\frac{3}{4}$ and at $3\frac{1}{2}$ miles, first from left, then from right (8 yards by 1 foot); at 4 miles Nam Ho from the right (8 yards by 9 inches); at $5\frac{1}{2}$ miles Hwé Sán (5 yards by 1 foot); at Páng Hai, Hwé Mésán (10 yards by 10 inches).
		2. Möng Náng ... Several streams.	**8**	**4**	17	0	General direction west-south-west. Good mule road. Level throughout. No villages passed. At 1 mile Páng Maktalu (400 by 100 yards) on grass. Good grass and water. At Möng Náng (15 houses) large camping ground in paddy. Water from Nam Wak. Plenty of grass. The following streams are crossed or met with *en route*:—Hwé Mésán (10 yards by 10 inches); at $\frac{3}{4}$ mile Nam Ma (30 to 50 yards by 2 feet), rocky bottom; at $2\frac{1}{4}$ miles Hwé Tung (10 yards by 9 inches); at $5\frac{1}{3}$ miles Hwé Pabung (10 yards by 8 inches); at $8\frac{1}{3}$ miles Nam Wak (20 yards by $1\frac{1}{2}$ feet).

FROM MÖNG LONG TO KYENGTUNG (KENGTUNG) *viâ* MÖNG HSING AND MÖNG LWI—*continued.*

ALTERNATIVE I—*continued.*

Authorities. Military.	Authorities. Civil.	Number and Names of Stages, Rivers and Streams.	Distances. Intermediate. M.	Distances. Intermediate. F.	Distances. Total. M.	Distances. Total. F.	Remarks.
Siam.		**3. Möng Long** ... Several streams.	**15**	**4**	32	4	General direction south-west. Good, level mule road. At 5½ miles Bankáng, 12 houses; at 9 miles Páng Yulong camp (200 by 100 yards), good water: at Möng Long good camping ground in paddy (½ mile by ⅓ mile). Water from Nam Ma (70 yards by 2½ feet). The following streams are crossed or met with *en route*:—At 3¼ miles Hwé Mu (10 yards by 6 inches); at 5½ miles Hwé Pakam (10 yards by 6 inches); at 8¼ miles Hwé Long (20 yards by 6 inches); at 10½ miles Hwé Pasáng (15 yards by 6 inches); at 12¼ miles Nam Long (40 yards by 2 feet).
		4. Camp on Nam Un. Nam In and Nam Un.	**11**	**0**	43	4	General direction south-west by west. Good mule road. Nearly level, but crossing some small spurs. Camp on Nam Un on old paddy ground (300 by 200 yards). Plenty of grass. Water from Nam Un. The following streams are crossed or met with *en route*:—At 3 miles Nam In (7 yards by 9 inches); at 6¾ miles Nam Un (4 to 10 yards by 9 inches).
		5. Kengláp ... Nam Un, Nam Ma, and Mé Kong.	**8**	**4**	52	0	General direction south-west by west. Good mule road, except for three muddy nullahs between the 5th and 27th miles. Good camping ground in paddy; water from Nam Phun. In Kengláp 30 houses. The town is on the right bank of the Mékong. The following streams are crossed or met with *en route*:—Nam Un (10 yards by 1 foot); at 2¼ miles Nam Ma (30 yards by 3 feet); at 8¼ miles Mé Kong (180 yards wide; deep, unfordable; crossed by ferry).
G.O.C. Rangoon District.	Superintendent, Southern Shan States.	**6. Páleo** ... ... Several streams.	**14**	**0**	66	0	General direction south-west by west. Good level mule road. At 1 mile Ban Nat, 45 houses; at 1½ miles Ban Long, 80 houses; at 11¾ miles Ban Nampheng, 15 houses; in Páleo 15 houses. Good camping ground in paddy. Water from Nam Lo and Nam Dan. From here a road leads to Möng Yawn, 29 miles distant, *see* Appendix II, Route No. 3, Branch I. The following streams are crossed or met with *en route*:—At 1½ miles Nam Phun (20 yards by 9 inches); at 4½ miles Hwé Hikon (10 yards by 4 inches); at 6¾ miles Nam Si (20 yards by 6 inches); at 10½ miles Nam Wun (30 yards by 1½ feet); at 11¾ miles Nam Pheng (30 yards by 9 inches); at 13¾ miles Nam Lo (7 yards by 9 inches).

FROM MÖNG LONG TO KYENGTUNG (KENGTÜNG) *viâ* MÖNG HSING AND MÖNG LWI—*continued.*

ALTERNATIVE I—*continued.*

Authorities. Military.	Authorities. Civil.	Number and Names of Stages, Rivers and Streams.	Distances. Intermediate. M.	F.	Distances. Total. M.	F.	Remarks.
G.O.C. Rangoon District.	Superintendent, Southern Shan States.	**7. Namkhum** ... Several streams.	**10**	**0**	76	0	General direction south-west by west. Good level mule road. At $1\frac{1}{2}$ miles Ban Namkyu, 16 houses; at $2\frac{1}{4}$ miles Ban Kôko, 40 houses; in Ban Namkhum 10 houses. Camping ground in paddy-fields (800 by 300 yards). Water from Nam Khum. The following streams are crossed or met with *en route* :—At $1\frac{1}{2}$ miles Nam Kyu (20 yards by 1 foot); at $3\frac{1}{2}$ miles Nam Kai (20 yards by $1\frac{1}{4}$ feet); at $3\frac{3}{4}$ miles Nam Phyidong (15 yards by 6 inches); at $9\frac{1}{4}$ miles Nam Khum (20 yards by 1 foot).
G.O.C. Rangoon District.	Superintendent, Southern Shan States.	**8. Mönglin** .. Hwé Sán and Nam Mai.	**7**	**4**	83	4	General direction south-west. Good level mule road. At $\frac{1}{4}$ mile Ban Hai, eight houses; at $\frac{3}{4}$ mile Ban Mai, eight houses; at $3\frac{1}{2}$ miles Pakla, eight houses; at $4\frac{1}{4}$ miles Namké, 40 houses; at $4\frac{3}{4}$ miles Hamtung, 10 houses; at $4\frac{3}{4}$ miles Mangbaw, six houses; at $5\frac{3}{4}$ miles Venglâng, 35 houses; at $6\frac{1}{2}$ miles Ban Ké, 15 houses; at 7 miles Ban Long, 15 houses; in Möng Lin, 40 houses. Camping ground in paddy. Water from small stream. Large kyaung, room for 400 men; water in the kyaung. The following streams are crossed or met with *en route* :—At 1 mile Hwé Sán (7 yards by 9 inches). At $4\frac{1}{2}$ miles Nam Mai (50 yards by $1\frac{1}{2}$ feet).
G.O.C. Rangoon District.	Superintendent, Southern Shan States.	**9. Páng Khalong.** Several streams.	**12**	**0**	95	4	General direction west. Good road, but crosses a number of small nullahs, some of which have steep sides and are difficult. At $\frac{1}{2}$ mile Phéhai, 15 houses; at 1 mile Tángkháng, eight houses; at $1\frac{1}{4}$ miles Namlintôk, 15 houses; at $1\frac{1}{2}$ miles Ban Pai, 12 houses; at $3\frac{1}{4}$ miles Méliuhtao, five houses; at Páng Khalong camp in jungle (100 yards square), and more room can be cleared. Water from Nam Khalong. No grass, only bamboo leaves. The following streams are crossed or met with *en route* :—At 3 miles Nam Maktan (10 yards by 6 inches); at $5\frac{1}{2}$ miles Hwé Khum (7 yards by 9 inches); at $5\frac{1}{2}$ miles Nam Len, not crossed, runs alongside of road (50 yards by 3 feet); at $9\frac{3}{4}$ miles Nam Mahankhao (8 yards by 6 inches); at 12 miles Nam Khalong (7 yards by 6 inches).
G.O.C. Rangoon District.	Superintendent, Southern Shan States.	**10. Möngphayak.** Several streams.	**12**	**0**	107	4	General direction north-west. Good level mule road. At $10\frac{3}{4}$ miles Yángkhun, eight houses. In Möng Phayak 36 houses. Good camp in paddy-fields. Water from stream (5 yards by 6 inches). The following streams are crossed or met with *en route* :—At $1\frac{1}{4}$ miles Hwé Víng (30 yards by 9 inches); at $3\frac{3}{4}$ miles Hwé Saikhao (7 yards by 9 inches); at $7\frac{1}{4}$ miles Nam Khung (20 yards by $1\frac{1}{2}$ feet); at 10 miles Nam Kawng (30 yards by $1\frac{3}{4}$ feet).

From MÖNG LONG **to** KYENGTUNG (KENGTUNG), *viâ* MÖNG HSING **and** MÖNG LWI—*continued.*

ALTERNATIVE I—*continued.*

Authorities.		Number and Names of Stages, Rivers and Streams.	Distances.				Remarks.
Military.	Civil.		Intermediate.		Total.		
			M.	F.	M.	F.	
G.O.C. Rangoon District.	Superintendent, Southern Shan States.	**11. Páng Nam-het.** Nam Len and Nam Het	**10**	**2**	117	6	General direction west. Good mule road, level up to $1\frac{1}{2}$ miles, where the Nam Len (80 yards by 2 feet) is crossed, then ascent of big range of hills to the top at 6 miles; thence descent to the camp. Camp (100 by 50 yards). Water from Nam Het (20 yards by 1 foot). Grass can be got $\frac{1}{2}$ mile beyond. The following villages are passed:—At $\frac{3}{4}$ mile Ban Mu, eight houses; at $1\frac{1}{2}$ miles Ban Yung, 17 houses.
		12. Möng Phak ... Several streams.	**14**	**4**	132	2	General direction north-west. Good mule road, but a good deal of up and down hill. Möng Phak, 20 houses. Camp in paddy ground (500 yards square). Water from Nam Peng. The following streams are crossed or met with *en route*:—At the camp Nam Het (20 yards by 1 foot); at $8\frac{1}{2}$ miles Hwé Wulong (7 yards by 6 inches); at $13\frac{1}{4}$ miles Nam Yôk (3 yards by 6 inches); at $14\frac{1}{2}$ miles Nam Peng (7 yards by 10 inches).
		13. Möng Chum. Several streams.	**13**	**4**	145	6	General direction north-north-west. Good mule road, level most of the way, but crossing some small hills. At $1\frac{1}{4}$ miles Khôkyin, 16 houses; at $1\frac{1}{2}$ miles Tonglong on the left, 15 houses. In Möng Chum 50 houses. Large camp in paddy-fields. Water from Nam Hun. The following streams are crossed or met with *en route*:—At $\frac{1}{4}$ mile Nam Phak (7 yards by $1\frac{1}{2}$ feet); at $9\frac{1}{4}$ miles Nam Huu (7 yards by 4 inches to 1 foot); at $10\frac{1}{4}$ miles Nam Ka (7 yards by 6 inches).
		14. Kengtung (Kyengtung). Nam Hun.	**7**	**2**	153	0	General direction north-north-west. Good level cart road along the Kengtung plain. At $\frac{3}{4}$ mile Ban Tai, 12 houses; at $1\frac{5}{8}$ miles Ban Lum, 17 houses; at $2\frac{3}{4}$ miles Ban Cham, 11 houses; at $2\frac{3}{4}$ miles Hôkho, nine houses; at $3\frac{1}{4}$ miles Bengsai, 12 houses; at $4\frac{1}{4}$ miles Ban Hung, 50 houses; at $4\frac{1}{4}$ miles Tinta, 30 houses; at $5\frac{1}{4}$ miles Pángsán, 20 houses. At Kengtung good camp inside town near the north-east corner, and large camping grounds outside. Water from wells; good grass. At $2\frac{1}{4}$ miles Nam Hun (20 yards by $1\frac{1}{2}$ feet).

No. 10.

From MÖNG NGAI (Route No. 29, Shan Hills Division, Stage 3) to MÖNG FÁNG.

BY W. J. ARCHER, ESQ., VICE-CONSUL, ZIMMÉ, 1888.

Authorities.		Number and Names of Stages, Rivers and Streams.	Distances.				Remarks.
Military.	Civil.		Intermediate.		Total.		
			M.	F.	M.	F.	
Siam.		**1. Mé Pam Noi (1,900 feet).** Mé Ping, Mé Na Oi, and Mé Pam Noi.	**7**	**0**	7	0	A rough path over a rocky hill. At 1 mile cross the Mé Ping here 50 feet wide shallow, for a short distance up the Mé Na Oi, then through open teak forest, road good and gradual ascent and to a rocky pass (2,180 feet), then steep descent to Mé Pam Noi.
		2. Mé Fáng (1,700 feet). Mé Fáng.	**12**	**0**	19	0	The road crosses three ranges in the first 7 miles, the second one at 5 miles is very rocky and is the true watershed (2,740 feet). Then up and down through bamboo forest, across a grassy plateau (altitude 1,800 feet) cross the upper Mé Fáng stream and then a small brook near Ban Mé Fáng (12 miles).
		3. Mé Khi ... Mé Khi.	**6**	**0**	25	0	Good almost level road through forest to the Mé Khi. A stream with high banks. Pass Ban Mé Khi, a hamlet at 3 miles, good encampment on bank of stream.
		4. Möng Fáng ... Mé Khi.	**13**	**0**	38	0	Cross Mé Khi. Good level road; passing villages of Mé Ngon and Mé San at 4 and 5 miles. Möng Fáng is a town of about 600 inhabitants surrounded by a rampart. *See* Route No. 26, Shan Hills Division.

APPENDIX IV.

ADDITIONAL ROUTES IN SOUTHERN (CIVIL) DIVISION.

APPENDIX IV.

ADDITIONAL ROUTES IN SOUTHERN (CIVIL) DIVISION.

No. 1.

From SAWMYO (or SAW, Route No. 42, Southern Division, Stage 6) to MÔNDAW (or MAUNGDAW, see Route No. 40, Southern Division) viâ WENUBIN.

BY CAPT. J. HARVEY, ROYAL ARTILLERY, ATTACHÉ, INTELLIGENCE BRANCH, FEBRUARY 1893.

Authorities. Military.	Authorities. Civil.	Number and Names of Stages, Rivers and Streams.	Distances. Inter-mediate. M.	F.	Distances. Total. M.	F.	Remarks.
O.C. Chin Hills.	Commissioner, Southern Division, and Deputy Commissioner, Pakôkku.	**1. Wenubin** ...	**7**	**0**	7	0	*Vide* Route No. 2 of this Appendix, Stage 1.
		2. Auk-Kangu ... Kadin chaung.	**3**	**0**	10	0	Path from Wenubin runs north diagonally downhill partly through the village taungyas; is very steep, but not quite so bad as that to Saw Chaungbya (*see* Branch I below). This march, though only 3 miles, took the Panthay mules 4½ hours and nearly produced a strike amongst them. Auk-Kangu is a small Chinbok village on right bank of Kadin chaung. Seemed similar in size to Saw Chaungbya, but a little better off. Abundant excellent water in stream. Vegetation and immense forest trees here, very magnificent. Inhabitants Chinbôks; Lenadaung steatite quarry is close by.
		3. Maungdaw (Môndaw). Kadin and Mu chaungs.	**6**	**0**	16	0	The ascent from the Kadin stream is very steep and was accomplished with difficulty by the Panthay mules. Atet-Kangu at 1 mile is on left bank of Kadin stream, but 500 feet above it and 1 mile from it in a northerly direction from Auk-Kangu, about 15 houses. Path from Atet-Kangu runs first uphill north-west for about 2 miles, then west along crest for 1 mile, then north by east for 2 miles downhill. Between Atet-Kangu and Maungdawywa the path is not difficult, but was at the time much encumbered by a new big taungya not yet burnt clear near the latter village. Maungdaw is apparently a growing, though at present small Chinbôk village of about

FROM SAWMYO (OR SAW, ROUTE NO. 42, SOUTHERN DIVISION, STAGE 6) TO MÔNDAW (OR MAUNGDAW, *see* ROUTE NO. 40, SOUTHERN DIVISION) *viâ* WENUBIN—*continued.*

Authorities. Military.	Authorities. Civil.	Number and Names of Stages, Rivers and Streams.	Distances. Intermediate.	Distances. Total.	Remarks.
O.C. Chin Hills.	Commissioner, Southern Division, and Deputy Commissioner, Pakôkku.	**3. Maungdaw (Môndaw)**—*cont.*			12 or more houses, very picturesquely situated near head of Mu chaung with Maungdaw-Namadaw hills to east-north-east and east by south respectively. Here there is the merest drain of water, but after a hunt a good stream was found out of sight over a rise to the west. The Panthay mules took 3½ hours from Atet-Kangu to Maungdaw, 6 miles. Saw can be reached from Maungdaw by going back uphill to the watershed towards Atet-Kangu, and then keeping steadily south along and down it by a good and easy path towards the main valley of the Saw for 2 miles, then turning south-east through splendid teak forests after 4 miles reach Anya-Kadin village in the Kadin chaung, and from there the regular route Yawdwin to Sawmyo is met with, *see* Route No. 40, Southern Division.
		4. Maungdaw hill top.	M. F. **4 0**	M. F. 20 0	A circuitous path up a steep slope in north-north-west direction from Maungdaw village for 1 mile to the watershed, then a rough and very seldom used path of 3 miles along watershed due south takes us to Maungdaw summit, whence a splendid view is obtained. Maungdaw hill is green stone, very sparsely forested, and of totally distinct geological formation to the neighbouring hills. It makes an excellent signal station to north and south towards Yawdwin and beyond Laungshé.

BRANCH I.

FROM WENUBIN (STAGE 1) TO SAW CHAUNGBYA.

BY CAPT. J. HARVEY, ROYAL ARTILLERY, ATTACHÉ, INTELLIGENCE BRANCH, FEBRUARY 1893.

Military.	Civil.	Number and Names of Stages, Rivers and Streams.	Intermediate.	Total.	Remarks.
O.C. Chin Hills.	Commr., Southern Division, and Deputy Commr., Pakôkku.	**1. Saw Chaungbya village.** Saw chaung.	**3 0**	3 0	Path from Wenubin runs direct west-south-west to it; is very steep in a diagonal direction to the general slope of the ground, only practicable for Mountain Battery Transport mules, not for Commissariat, and that with difficulty. Saw Chaungbya is a very small poor and scattered Chinbôk village on a steep hill side about 1,000 feet and ¾ mile above the Saw chaung. Some five houses.

No. 2.

From SAWMYO (SAW) to MOUNT VICTORIA.

BY CAPT. J. HARVEY, ROYAL ARTILLERY, ATTACHÉ, INTELLIGENCE BRANCH, MARCH 1893.

Military.	Civil.	Number and Names of Stages, Rivers and Streams.	Intermediate.	Total.	Remarks.
O.C. Chin Hills.	Commr., Southern Divn., and Dy. Commr., Pakôkku.	**1. Kyetthwin-Tainshu.** Saw chaung.	**12 0**	12 0	Path runs west through rice fields, or along their edge skirting the hills. Sawmyo at 2 miles is a small Burman village of about 150 houses; height above sea-level 1,400 feet. Thence Chin path up the lower spurs of

FROM SAWMYO (SAW) TO MOUNT VICTORIA—*continued.*

Authorities. Military.	Authorities. Civil.	Number and Names of Stages, Rivers and Streams.	Distances. Intermediate.	Distances. Total.	Remarks.
O.C. Chin Hills.	Commissioner, Southern Division, and Deputy Commissioner, Pakôkku.	**1. Kyetthwin-Tainshu**—*cont.*			Wumbutaung hill. Gradient on an average about 1 in 10; some parts are 1 in 6, but others nearly level. Two small knolls are passed. At Wenubin (7 miles) a Chin path diverges to the south to Saw Chaungbya village, distant 3 miles, and to the north to Auk-Kangu village at the same distance (*see* Route No. 1 of this Appendix and its Branch). At the cross-paths the height above sea-level is 3,400 feet. Time of ascent, average marching, from Sawmyo 2¼ hours. Path through thick bamboo jungle and forest trees always running west. No obstacles occur to easy road-making. Close to the cross-roads a small clear perennial spring rises, which gave 4 gallons per minute on the path to Auk-Kangu on 18th February 1893, and is estimated to never in any season yield less than 2 gallons per minute. A suitable place for watering animals or changing dâk ponies, &c. Building sites on a small scale available. Path runs along a spur of average slope 10° to 15°, but quite easy for road-making; the spur is fairly broad and gets broader as Kyetthwin-Tainchu (12 miles) is approached. Here is a small stream, about 100 yards distant, and 100 to 150 feet below the path to the north. This stream has a little water in March, and never quite dries. Height above sea-level 5,150 feet. Time of ascent from Sawmyo, average marching, 5⅜ hours; of descent about 3⅓ hours. This place is used by Chins as a sakhán occasionally. The forest from Wenubin thus far is Turkish (?) oak and pine trees, and has much good timber in it. Road-making would require no bridging, little drainage, and little engineering.
			M. F.	M. F.	
		2. Kyachedaung Sakhán.	**8 0**	20 0	The ascent from Kyetthwin-Tainchu to the top of Wumbutaung (4 miles about), is steep for some distance, but the spur is very broad and uniform and a road of uniform gradient could be zigzagged up this part without any difficulty. This is the steepest bit of the path, but does not exceed 20° anywhere in the steepest bits, and such bits could be easily avoided. The top of Wumbutaung is rounded and undefined, so this distance is only approximate. The steeper parts are roughly from the 1st to 3rd mile, after which the road gets on to open grass downs and would be perfectly easy. The path from Wumbutaung runs up and down over three small hills, but the rise and fall are not great. It is mostly through dense forest. The spur is narrow, but gradients are not great. The small hill-tops could be skirted round. Its general direction is still west up to 7 miles when it turns north. The path is for the most part over open grass land, very easy, and runs nearly due north for ¾ of a mile, then turns west, again descending into a big saddle, which is broken up by several small hillocks.
		3. Mount Victoria.	**8 0**	28 0	From Kyachedaung Sakhán the path runs straight up the watershed and is steep in places, but nearly the whole of the western face of this hill near the top is a rounded open grass down, and the road could be made anywhere required. It is not anticipated that beyond this hill a road would be necessary, as the elevation being over 9,000 feet houses would not probably be built any further in the hills. The remainder of the way is a very little used and barely traceable Chin path. By escorts and their mules going

FROM SAWMYO (SAW) TO MOUNT VICTORIA—*continued.*

Authorities.		Number and Names of Stages, Rivers and Streams.	Distances.		Remarks.
Military.	Civil.		Inter-mediate.	Total.	
O.C. Chin Hills.	Commissioner, Southern Division, and Deputy Commissioner, Pakôkku.	**3. Mount Victoria**—*cont.*			backwards and forwards on it, it is now worn into a plain bridle path and will probably so remain for some years to come. The path runs straight west along the ridge, crossing two big hill-tops, namely, Wepyudaung, and an unnamed one, which is near to but distinct from the last and highest hill. The heights of these hills are about as follows :— FEET. Kyachedaung ... ... 9,300 Wepyudaung ... ... 10,000 Victoria, 1st peak ... ... 10,300 Victoria, 2nd peak ... ... 10,400 In between each the path runs down into a saddle, but nowhere are gradients very steep, and one or two smaller hillocks occur in between the more marked features. On the saddle between the first Victoria Peak and a smaller hill is a tank, about 50 yards by 20 yards, which contains a remnant of water throughout the year. Beyond this small hill and the last peak is a sheltered gully down the hills, and in it, near the watershed, water and a very sheltered camp or bivouac is always to be found. It is due south, distant about 300 yards downhill from a cairn of stones about 5 feet high erected by my party by the path. The water is the very small source of a stream, which afterwards runs under ground down towards the Môn valley, not into the Saw chaung. *Note.*—It appeared to Capt. Harvey that making a road from Sawmyo to Mount Victoria would present no engineering difficulties at all.

BRANCH I.

FROM MOUNT VICTORIA TO PAUKADU-PIÉDAW.

BY CAPT. J. HARVEY, ROYAL ARTILLERY, ATTACHÉ, INTELLIGENCE BRANCH, MARCH 1893.

Military.	Civil.	Number and Names of Stages, Rivers and Streams.	Intermediate.	Total.	Remarks.
O.C. Chin Hills.	Commissioner, Southern Division, and Deputy Commissioner, Pakôkku.	**1. Paukadu-Piédaw group of villages.**	M. F. **5 0**	M. F. 5 0	From the extreme peak the ground is more or less open and descends rapidly down towards the Môn valley in a south-westerly direction ; the path runs down a long spur in the same direction and parallel to the Kalaung or Ka river, till the first of the group of villages named is met with. These villages are scattered over a large extent of ground in the Kalaung and the Môn valley, but do not in all contain very many inhabitants. The people are Yendus. To the west a spur runs down to a smaller hill and then turns north joining the hills in the Chinmé country, but gradients are very steep, and beyond Victoria there are no hills above 7,000 feet or less. To the north all is dense forest, and no path down towards the Dap Yôma villages and Kyangyi, could be found, as Capt. Harvey had been led to expect. There were only some wild animals' paths through the forest.

APPENDIX V.

ADDITIONAL ROUTES IN CENTRAL (CIVIL) DIVISION.

APPENDIX V.

ADDITIONAL ROUTES IN CENTRAL (CIVIL) DIVISION.

No. 1.

From KINDÁT to PAUNGBYIN (by river).

By Lieut. W. PARRY, Wiltshire Regiment, Intelligence Branch, December 1893.

Authorities.		Number and Names of Stages, Rivers and Streams.	Distances.				Remarks.
Military.	Civil.		Inter-mediate.		Total.		
			M.	F.	M.	F.	
O.C. Chin Hills.	Commissioner, Central Division, and Deputy Commissioner, Upper Chindwin.	**1. Paungbyin** ... Chindwin and tributaries.	**75**	**0**	75	0	General direction north-north-east. By Government steamer. Time of journey two days in cold weather, owing to heavy mists which do not clear until 10 A.M. and later; done in 1½ days when seasonable. Visited Inbauk and Sittaung *en route;* the former contains about 20 houses, the latter a few more. Room to camp almost anywhere between Kindát and Paungbyin. Sittaung contains a furnished Public Works Department bungalow; a letter box at Sittaung. Road from here is being built to Tamu due east. Paungbyin, head-quarters of sub-division of Upper Chindwin district; Assistant Commissioner here. A large place; about 200 houses and 700 people. Large supplies of rice. Small supplies obtainable at many places between Kindát and Paungbyin.

No. 2.

From KINDÁT to TINSIN.

By Lieut. W. PARRY, Wiltshire Regiment, January 1894.

Military	Civil	Stages	Inter. M.	Inter. F.	Total M.	Total F.	Remarks
O.C. Chin Hills.	Commissioner, Central Division, and Deputy Commissioner, Upper Chindwin.	**1. Camp by Yézôn chaung.** Chindwin river and Yézôn chaung.	**11**	**4**	11	4	*Note.*—This is the same route as No. 8, Central Division, Alternative I, and having been received too late to correct that route up to date, is reprinted in full.—A.F. General direction north-west. A good mule road, but in places the

FROM KINDÁT TO TINSIN—*continued.*

Authorities.		Number and Names of Stages, Rivers and Streams.	Distances.		Remarks.
Military.	Civil.		Intermediate.	Total.	
O.C. Chin Hills.	Commissioner, Central Division, and Deputy Commissioner, Upper Chindwin.	**1. Camp by Yézôn chaung**--*cont.*			gradients are severe. Leaving Kindát the Chindwin is crossed to the village of Manku; from there the track crossing a small stream, passes through paddy-fields and elephant grass up to 1¼ miles; thence through thick tree and bamboo jungle, following the right bank of the Yézôn chaung (20 yards by 1 foot, fordable everywhere) from 7¾ miles to camp. Good water all along the road and close to camp from chaung. Yézôn is a large clearing where 500 or 600 troops could be camped comfortably. Three bamboo sheds and a stable have been built here, and they are to be kept in repair. Stream by camp measures 20 yards by 1 foot. Most of the jungle round camp is bamboo, so any amount of bamboo leaves could be got for fodder.
		2. Tinsin ... ... Dathwégyauk, Kanpát, and Tinsin chaungs.	M. F. **16 0**	M. F. 27 4	General direction north-west. A very steep ascent from Yézôn, along the top of a ridge, and then a gradual descent to Dathwégyauk chaung (8 yards by 6 inches) at 6 miles; from there a gradual ascent is made to the top of a ridge from which a bird's eye view of the Kubo valley is obtained on the right; the track gradually descends leaving the jungle and hills at 9½ miles and passes through elephant grass up to 10 miles where the Kanpát chaung (30 yards by 3 feet 6 inches) is met. Crossing the river a large open space is passed where the village of Tainkaya, now deserted, once stood. The tract now goes through moderately dense tree jungle along a perfectly level road to Tinsin at 16 miles, the chaung being crossed just before arriving at the village. Large space for camping just outside the village. Water good from Tinsin chaung (25 yards by 1 foot); all streams fordable; nullahs bridged or passable. Tinsin, or Tinzin, is a strongly stockaded village of 102 houses, the population being 128 men and 367 women and children. The inhabitants very pluckily hold their own with only 20 guns against any possible attack by the Chins. The village lies in the Kubo valley with the Chin hills rising up about 3 miles to the west, the valley extending for 6 miles to the east as far as Tainkaya on the Kanpát chaung. The Tinsin chaung flows on the west side of the village. There is a double stockade, weak in one or two parts, notably on the north side, but a *cheveux de frise*, of bamboo, temporarily covers the weak parts. The majority of the buffaloes, which number 250, are kept between the outer and inner stockades at night. The kyaung which lies in the very centre of the village is strongly stockaded, and would form a sort of keep which would be held in case of the outer stockades being hopelessly breached. There are over 1,500 fields of paddy belonging to the village, and as the fields, I saw, seemed to be about an Indian bigah each, the inhabitants must be looked upon as well-to-do.

No. 3.

From PAUNGBYIN to WAYÔNGÔN.

BY LIEUT. W. PARRY, 2ND BATTALION, WILTSHIRE REGIMENT, INTELLIGENCE BRANCH, JANUARY 1894.

Authorities. Military.	Authorities. Civil.	Number and Names of Stages, Rivers and Streams.	Distances. Intermediate. M.	F.	Distances. Total. M.	F.	Remarks.
O.C. Chin Hills.	Commissioner, Central Division, and Deputy Commissioner, Upper Chindwin.	**1. Kauksa** ... ... Kauksa chaung, fordable everywhere; nullahs bridged or passable for pack animals.	**13**	**0**	13	0	General direction south-east by east. After a sharp climb from Paungbyin the path goes through more or less dense tree and bamboo jungle along a good broad track to Pintha, which is reached at 4 miles. Road would be suitable for carts where the tracks leaving Paungbyin and arriving at Pintha built at an easier gradient. This could be easily done. Just before reaching Pintha the path crosses a stream called the Kauksa chaung. On leaving Pintha the path crosses the same stream several times (good approaches), and so to Kauksa at 13 miles. At Kauksa 13 houses, which would hold 200 men. Room for another 500 men to camp in and around village. Water good from Kauksa chaung (15 feet by 6 inches). Small store of rice; no other supplies.
		2. Kagat (Kaget or Kaket). Tawet chaung, Nunbingaung chaung, fordable everywhere; all nullahs bridged.	**8**	**0**	21	0	General direction south. From Kauksa the path ascends through thick bamboo jungle, then winds up and down, finishing by following the bed of a stream, practically dry, and thus arrives on to a plain, on which there is a collection of five villages, namely, Mumbin, Numbin, Bahauk, Pawsai and Kagat or Kaket, all known by the last name (*see* Route No. 20, Central Division). The Nunbingaung chaung flows between the villages from east to west (60 yards by 1 foot); good approaches, sandy bottom. Room for a very large camp in and around the five villages. Large store of rice, 50 buffaloes; no other supplies. Water good from stream.
		3. Nun-nain ... Nunbingaung chaung; fordable everywhere, but approaches bad in places; nullahs not bridged from Hawzaing to Nun-nain.	**8**	**0**	29	0	General direction east. A good road all the way to Nun-nain, but not suitable for pack animals from Hawzaing to Nun-nain. After leaving Kagat a path goes north-east to Chindö (deserted); track crosses Numbingaung chaung, at 1¼, 1¾ and at 2 miles just before reaching Hawzaing. Small camping ground here. Good water from stream and a fairly good supply of rice; no other stores. Path crosses same stream again at 3, 3½ and 3¾ miles round the side of a hill for about 3 miles up to 7 miles. Very easy going, but nullahs not bridged. At 7 miles Pinwai, a village of one house. Camp at Nun-nain at 8 miles. Small camping ground in village. Small store of rice; no other supplies. Good water from stream.
		4. Padi chaung camp. Nunbingaung chaung and Padi chaung, both fordable everywhere; nullahs unbridged.	**18**	**0**	47	0	General direction north-east. Track crosses stream four times, then goes along bed of river for 2 miles, depth of water averaging 1 foot; sandy bottom; fairly easy going. Leave stream at 4 miles; bad up and down hill climbing for 12 more miles to

FROM PAUNGBYIN TO WAYÔNGÔN—*continued.*

Authorities. Military.	Authorities. Civil.	Number and Names of Stages, Rivers and Streams.	Distances. Intermediate.		Distances. Total.		Remarks.
			M.	F.	M.	F.	
O.C. Chin Hills.	Commissioner, Central Division, and Deputy Commissioner, Upper Chindwin.	**4. Padi chaung camp**—*cont.*					camp. Path unsuitable for pack animals. No water between 4th and 18th mile. Camp at Padi chaung; only room for very small camp. Water good from stream. Road is broken away in many places and the gradients are very steep.
		5. Ulén chaung camp. Taman chaung.	**9**	**0**	56	0	General direction south-east. A steep climb for 2 miles, then a sharp descent, part of track going straight down hill side by a ladder. Very bad road. Path crosses Taman chaung (3 yards by 6 inches) at 3½ miles. Small camping ground by stream. Path then ascends a hill for about 1 mile along the brow down a nullah; ascends another hill and down the other side to camp at 9 miles. Camp very small. Water good from stream.
		6. Wayôngôn ... Several small chaungs, all fordable.	**18**	**0**	74	0	General direction south. Downhill nearly all the way to Kyauktán at 4 miles; then along a level road to Tôeman at 6 miles. This is a large village with room in and around to camp a large body of men. Good water from stream. Large store of rice; 70 head of cattle; no other supplies. Track then goes south along a stream which it crosses; road good and suitable for pack animals from Kyauktán to Wayôngôn; nullahs bridged or passable. Kaya is reached at 9 miles, level road all the way; thence to Tawbyu at 12 miles, but very bad from here to Wayôngôn at 18 miles. Good water in all the villages from streams or well. Small camping ground. There is an alternative route to Wayôngôn from Tôeman with a better but slightly longer road.

No. 4.

From WAYÔNGÔN to KINDÁT viâ THÁNGA.

BY LIEUT. W. PARRY, WILTSHIRE REGIMENT, INTELLIGENCE BRANCH, JANUARY 1894.

Military	Civil	Stages	M.	F.	M.	F.	Remarks
O.C. Chin Hills.	Commissioner, Central Division, and Deputy Commissioner, Upper Chindwin.	**1. Magyíbin** ... Gyobin chaung and Mu river, both 10 yards by 1 foot; fordable everywhere.	**7**	**4**	7	4	General direction south-west. A very good road along the Gyobin chaung nearly the whole way. Taungbotha; a small village at 2 miles; Nyungôn at 4 miles, and camp at Magyíbin, at 7½ miles. Good water from Mu river (¼ mile from village). Small camping ground in village, but room for a large camp between village and river. Small store of rice; no other supplies.
		2. Camp on river bank. Mu river, 50 to 80 yards by 1 foot to 6 feet; fordable nearly everywhere.	**9**	**0**	16	4	General direction west. Track crosses river three times, then ascends and descends a very steep hill, ultimately going along the bed of the Mu river to camp. Small camping grounds at many places on river bank, but advisable to halt at fairly large ground at 9 miles at junction of Mu river with Kanki chaung.

FROM WAYÔNGÔN TO KINDÁT *viâ* THÁNGA—*continued.*

Authorities. Military.	Authorities. Civil.	Number and Names of Stages, Rivers and Streams.	Distances. Intermediate. M.	F.	Total. M.	F.	Remarks.
O.C. Chin Hills.	Commissioner, Central Division, and Deputy Commissioner, Upper Chindwin.	**3. Camp on river bank.** Mu river, 80 to 100 yards by 1 foot to 6 feet.	**12**	**0**	28	4	General direction west. Road goes along the bed of river the whole way, but there is a path straight to Nu Naung across high ground, crossing the river several times, but a guide is required. Small camping grounds at many places on bank.
		4. Tunain ... Mu river, 80 to 150 yards by 1 foot to 6 feet.	**16**	**0**	44	4	General direction west. Along the bed of the river to 6 miles, then across rising ground, crossing the river three times to Thayetpin at 9 miles. Across the river again to Nunyaung at 10 miles. A small village with small camping ground. Water good from river. The track then follows the right bank of the river which it crosses at 12 miles and again at 12¼, 12½ and at 14 miles, following the right bank of the river to Tunain at 16 miles. The village of Tunain is divided into three parts, and there is room for a very large camp. Water good from river.
		5. Maingaung ... Mu river, 150 yards by 1 foot to 6 feet; Nundhi chaung, 50 yards by 1 foot; fordable; approaches good.	**8**	**0**	52	4	General direction west. A very good road the whole way, at 3½ miles joining a wide unmetalled road, suitable for carts, which comes from the north from Naubôn. This latter road averages about 7 feet in width and the gradients are easy. It is, however, in bad repair in parts and would have to be mended before carts could travel on it with any safety. Bahai (Bahé) is reached at 1 mile, Thabyadaw at 2 miles and Mainkain at 7 miles. Tamkwain and Nyaunghla (both being known as Maingaung) are reached at 8 miles, just after crossing the Nundhi chaung, which flows northward.
		6. Thánga ... Chindwin.	**14**	**0**	66	4	Road from Maingaung on to Thánga good and fit for carts as in last stage. Water at two places between Maingaung and Thánga. At Thánga room for a large camp. Water good, from Chindwin river. Thánga is about midway between Paungbyin and Kindát.